Encyclopedia of Hinduism

Encyclopedia of Hinduism

Edited by
Denise Cush
Catherine Robinson
Michael York

Routledge
Taylor & Francis Group
LONDON AND NEW YORK

First published 2008
by Routledge
2 Park Square, Milton Park, Abingdon, OX14 4RN
www.routledge.co.uk

Simultaneously published in the USA and Canada
by Routledge
270 Madison Avenue, New York, NY 10016
www.routledge.com

Routledge is an imprint of the Taylor and Francis Group, an informa business

Typeset in Times New Roman and Optima by
Taylor & Francis Books
Printed and bound in Great Britain by
TJ International Ltd, Padstow, Cornwall

British Library Cataloguing in Publication Data
A catalogue record for this book is available from the British Library

Library of Congress Cataloging-in-Publication Data
A catalog record for this book has been requested

ISBN13: 978-0-7007-1267-0

To all scholars and students of Hinduism, past, present and future

Contents

Advisory board

John Brockington
University of Edinburgh

Wendy Doniger
University of Chicago

Dermot Killingley
University of Newcastle

Kim Knott
University of Leeds

Arvind Sharma
McGill University

Preface

The Ninth Edition of *The Encyclopaedia Britannica* of 1878 has no entry for 'Hinduism' *per se* but rather one for 'Brahmanism' presented as the 'term commonly used to denote a system of religious institutions originated and elaborated by the *Brahmans*, the sacerdotal and, from an early period, the dominant caste of the Hindu community'. In our day and age, Richard Gombrich has complained that the term 'Hinduism' is an artificial superimposition instituted by Western scholars onto the multifarious and divergent traditions of the Indian subcontinent. Hindus themselves often refer to their tradition as the sanātana-dharma or the 'eternal law'. It was, however, the Persians who first coined the term 'Hindu' to designate the inhabitants of northern India in and beyond the Sindhu (Indus) river basin. In time, the term was adopted by the people of the subcontinent who identified with its dominant religious tradition.

For better or for worse, Hinduism has come to be the accepted term designating the religion that traces its origins to the Veda dating from the second millennium B.C.E. The present *Encyclopedia of Hinduism*, edited by Denise Cush and Catherine Robinson of the Study of Religions Department, Bath Spa University, with Lynn Foulston at University of Wales, Newport, represents a considerable accomplishment that encompasses the diverse and endlessly fascinating multitude of traditions, sects and practices that are today approached – both within India and beyond – as Hinduism. With its overwhelming complexity of both practice and textual tradition, Hinduism is certainly one of the more interesting of the world's religions. In many respects, it is as much a behavioural activity as it is a definable religion. It both tantalises through inconsistency and fascinates with its confident reach toward the ineffable.

Contributors to this volume include both leading authorities and emerging scholars in this field. Their expertise enables the reader to gain insights into the rich heritage and contemporary vitality of Hinduism which has so much to offer academically but also in terms of inspiring answers to fundamental questions about the meaning and purpose of life.

Michael York

Introduction

There is a challenge in producing an encyclopedia of Hinduism when the editors, many of the contributors, and scholarly debate in general are not sure that such a thing as Hinduism really exists or that an encyclopedia can do justice to the fluidity, diversity, and complexity of the beliefs and practices so designated. The issues surrounding Hinduism both as a term and as a concept are legion. Scholars have devoted a great deal of time and energy to critical examination of the meaning and implications of Hinduism as well as to its origins and provenance. Debate has focused on whether Hinduism is a helpful category of analysis or whether it lends itself to a reified view of a bounded entity. Similarly, opinions differ as to the status of Hinduism in terms of its genesis either from within the subcontinent as an organic development or alternatively from the West as an exogenous construct imposed upon indigenous beliefs and practices. Another controversy centres on the unity and multiplicity of Hinduism with arguments ranging from those advocating an essence to Hinduism (though, of course, disagreeing as to what that essence might be) to those who argue that Hinduism is best used as an umbrella term covering a wide variety of traditions or even discrete religions. For some Hinduism is timeless, for others it is ancient, but there are many others for whom Hinduism is a product of encounter with Islam or later colonial rule. Such a short summary does not convey the strength and subtlety of the numerous books and articles that have been written on this subject. It does, however, give some insight into the contested nature of Hinduism and the challenge inherent in any attempt to represent it fully and fairly.

Inevitably, there are sensitivities when scholars trespass upon sacred ground. That said, among the contributors to this work are not only leading researchers but practising Hindus. Of course, Hindus themselves adopt a variety of positions on the role of academic study of their traditions, especially where such study calls into question certain cherished truths. The editors have attempted to ensure that the *Encyclopedia of Hinduism* offers a balanced treatment that enables the reader to encounter a range of views and decide for him/herself on their merits. If, in spite of their efforts, members of the faith community find some of the opinions expressed unacceptable, the editors apologise for any offence taken though they remain committed to academic values and their application to the study of such a rich and enriching religion.

The last few years have seen some valuable new reference works for the study of Hinduism, often containing series of substantial essays on key topics and themes and incorporating the insights of an impressive array of scholars. This encyclopedia differs in terms of its structure and design from the format of these reference works because it can easily be consulted to discover basic facts as well as providing extended discussions of major subjects. The reader will find in this encyclopedia a comprehensive coverage of many different aspects of Hinduism and related areas. These provide the reader with an introductory overview. Where appropriate, entries focus on contemporary relevance and, especially in longer entries, indicate points of scholarly disagreement and debate. Both Hinduism and its study continue to change and readers are encouraged to use this work as a foundation for and guide to ongoing exploration of the subject.

Scope and purpose

This encyclopedia combines an accessible style suited to a primarily undergraduate readership with a depth of scholarship that encompasses recent debates and discoveries. Without conceding some of the more standard material that any encyclopedia aimed at this audience needs to contain, the *Encyclopedia of Hinduism* emphasises certain themes and trends, one of which is the history of scholarship itself.

Its entries stress the popular and vernacular dimension of Hindu observance revealed by ethnography to complement the elite and classical picture gained from textual study. Related to this is the imperative to include non-orthodox groups and New Religious Movements. In so doing, the editors recognise a North Indian bias to many existing works that they sought to correct though in this respect they had less success than desired. However, in terms of diversity, entries highlight the worldwide presence of the Hindu tradition and community and its interaction with other cultures. When supplementing the ancient and historic with modern and contemporary material, entries devote particular attention to the role and impact of print, visual, and electronic media in the lives of Hindus today. Similarly, they demonstrate the relevance of Hindu beliefs and values for ethical judgement and political and social issues. Given the power of feminist critiques of past models of religion and research, the editors also aimed to reflect the significance of women as religious agents in their own right and as innovative researchers in the field. However, because one of the agreed criteria for a biographic entry on a scholar was that sufficient time had passed to facilitate an accurate assessment of their enduring influence, women are underrepresented in these biographies. Nevertheless, the composition of the editorial team and the International Editorial Advisory Board go some way towards redressing this imbalance as does the proportion of women contributors to this volume.

Editors and contributors

The project was first conceived in 1999 as a result of conversations with Jonathan Price of Curzon Press. Little did the editors know at the outset just how fascinating, demanding, and, of course, educational the project would be. During its progress, not only has the editorial team changed, but also the development editors with whom the editors have worked and even the publisher of the work.

The original team comprised Denise Cush, Catherine Robinson, and Michael York based at Bath Spa University. Crucial to the success of the project was the formation of an International Editorial Advisory Board consisting of leading scholars, John Brockington, Wendy Doniger, Dermot Killingley, Kim Knott, and Arvind Sharma, who undertook an advisory role as well as contributing articles in their specialist fields.

Over the years, with Michael York's retirement, Lynn Foulston of the University of Wales, Newport joined the editorial team. Throughout, Jan Sumner played a vital part in managing the project and liaising with editors, contributors, and publishers.

Among them, the editors were able to offer expertise in teaching and learning in the subject at undergraduate level, ancient history, modern developments, and vernacular traditions. Members of the International Editorial Advisory Board provided invaluable ethnographic, philosophical, textual and linguistic scholarship. In all this, the editors were dependent upon the rich and varied knowledge of the academic community across a range of disciplines such as anthropology, history and philosophy in addition to Religious Studies (the last multidisciplinary in any case). Over a hundred scholars, mainly from the English-speaking world, have written entries for this encyclopedia. These scholars include both internationally acknowledged experts and emerging voices that will no doubt become more widely heard in years to come.

How to use this encyclopedia

The *Encyclopedia of Hinduism* is composed of nearly 900 separate entries, ranging in length from about 150 to 5,000 words. Major articles deal with surveys, overviews, central concepts, and important themes, such as Hinduism in the modern and contemporary Period, the Status of Women in Hinduism, Popular and vernacular traditions, Diaspora and nationalism. Other shorter entries address more specific topics such as individual figures, deities, festivals, philosophies, texts and sites. The list of entries was generated both by identifying areas commonly found in reference works and introductory texts on Hinduism and by noting what seemed to be some lacunae whether in terms of past omissions or recent developments.

The encyclopedia is organised in an easy to use A–Z format. Cross-references alert the reader to related entries. Entries contain selected references including those used by the author and sources for further reading on the topic. Dummy entries are employed where there are several ways of referring to the same topic, for example, Liṅgāyats – see Vīraśāivas, or where the entry may be listed under the Sanskrit name, but the reader is looking under a more familiar English term, for example, Funeral – see Antyeṣṭi. An index provides an additional way for the reader to find the most useful entries. The thematic lists of entries assist those who are researching within a particular area to locate related material. Survey or overview articles are listed with other relevant entries given under appropriate headings.

Readers will notice that most entries are listed in a Sanskrit form with diacritics rather than in other Indian languages or in English. This is because such Sanskritised vocabulary is commonly employed even in introductory texts on Hinduism and because there is often no clear agreed English translation for Sanskrit terms. Despite the obvious disadvantages of reinforcing a Sanskritic bias that downplays both other classical languages such as Tamil and the vernaculars, Sanskritised terms remain the shared parlance of the academic community. Moreover, in an effort to mitigate any negative consequences of this decision, an entry on languages has been included that problematises the role and impact of Sanskrit and, where there is an obvious English equivalent, this has been included as a dummy entry for ease of reference.

It will also be noticed that some entries use diacritics and others do not. The decision was taken to use diacritics for ancient and classical material, and not to use them when dealing with modern and contemporary material. Obviously the divide between the two is somewhat arbitrary, but at least to some extent it reflects different practices associated with different academic disciplines – for example, the linguistic expertise of textual scholars and the ethnographic work of contemporary anthropologists. The system of transliteration adopted is one in frequent use which avoids the complications in spelling linked with varying degrees of Anglicisation. For instance, Śiva, not Siva or Shiva, and Kṛṣṇa, not Krsna or Krishna.

Acknowledgements

The editors express their sincere thanks to the members of the International Editorial Board who provided help and guidance throughout the project. They are also grateful to the many publishing staff with whom they have had the pleasure of working including Jonathan Price who encouraged them to embark upon this project, Kate Aker who spurred them on to its completion, and Beth Renner who discharged the difficult task of day-to-day management with unfailing equanimity. None of this would have been possible without the generosity and expertise of the authors who contributed entries and were so courteous and patient in dealing with editorial queries and requests.

On a more personal note, the editors wish to acknowledge the role of Professor Michael York in the initial stages as well as thank him for his preface to the Encyclopedia, the practical support and personal encouragement of Dr Fiona Montgomery of Bath Spa University and, last but by no means least, the extraordinary forbearance, dedication and efficiency of Mrs Jan Sumner, project manager, who has kept the editors in line.

Contributors

Nick Allen
University of Oxford

Kelly D. Alley
Auburn University

Lawrence A. Babb
Amherst College

Greg Bailey
La Trobe University

Michael Baltutis
University of Iowa

Martin Baumann
Universität Bielefeld

Vivienne Baumfield
Institute of Education, University of London

Gwilym Beckerlegge
Open University

Johannes Beltz
Museum Rietberg Zurich

Brian Black
School of Oriental and African Studies

Cynthia Bradley
Independent Scholar

Marcus Braybrooke
World Congress of Faiths

Horst Brinkhaus
Universität Kiel

John L. Brockington
University of Edinburgh

Mary Brockington
University of Edinburgh

Simon Brodbeck
University of Edinburgh

Johannes Bronkhorst
Université de Lausanne

Nick Campion
Bath Spa University

Christopher Chapple
Loyola Marymount University

George Chryssides
University of Wolverhampton

Tracy Coleman
Colorado College

Alice Collett
Cardiff University

Peter Connolly
Turning Point Consulting

Denise Cush
Bath Spa University

Anna L. Dallapiccola
Edinburgh University

Michael S. Dodson
Indiana University

Wendy Doniger
University of Chicago

Rachel Dwyer
School of Oriental and African Studies

Fabrizio M. Ferrari
School of Oriental and African Studies

Harald Fischer-Tine
Humboldt-Universitat zu Berlin

Lynn Foulston
University of Wales, Newport

Jessica Frazer
The Oxford Centre for Hindu Studies

Surendra Gambhir
University of Pennsylvania

Theodore Gabriel
University of Gloucestershire

Ron Geaves
University of Chester

Abhishek Ghosh
Oxford Centre for Hindu Studies

Anthony Good
University of Edinburgh

Robert Goodding
Southwestern University

William Gould
University of Leeds

Ann Grodzins Gold
Syracuse University

Ravi M. Gupta
Centre College

Sanjukta Gupta
Oxford University

Rishi Handa
School of Oriental and African Studies

Adam Hardy
Cardiff University

Edeltraud Harzer
University of Texas

Perwaiz Hayat
Dalhousie University

Christopher Helland
Dalhousie University

Philip Hughes
Edith Cowan University

Manfred Hutter
Universitäat Bonn

Stephen Jacobs
University of Wolverhampton

Ian Jamieson
Independent Scholar

Klaus Karttunen
University of Helsinki

Dermot Killingley
University of Newcastle upon Tyne

Anna S. King
University of Winchester

Richard King
Vanderbilt University

Klaus K. Klostermaier
University of Manitoba

Kim Knott
University of Leeds

Jeff Kripal
Rice University

Ethan Kroll
University of Chicago

Pratap Kumar
University of KwaZulu Natal

Julius Lipner
Cambridge University

J.E. Llewellyn
Southwest Missouri State University

David N. Lorenzen
El Colegio de Mexico

Daniel Mariau
University of Hull

Sanjoy Mazumdar
University of California, Irvine

Shampa Mazumdar
University of California, Irvine

June McDaniel
College of Charleston

Allyn Miner
University of Pennsylvania

Lance E. Nelson
University of San Diego

Eleanor Nesbitt
University of Warwick

Geoffrey A. Oddie
University of Sydney

Martin Ovens
Wolfson College, Oxford

Deven M. Patel
Seton Hall University

S. Patmanathan
University of Peradeniya

Andrea Marion Pinkney
Columbia University

Tracy Pintchman
Loyola University

Elizabeth Puttick
Elizabeth Puttick Literary Agency

Angela Quartermaine
Oxford University

Kokila Ravi
Atlanta Metropolitan College

Paul Reid-Bowen
Bath Spa University

Catherine Robinson
Bath Spa University

Sandra Robinson
Sarah Lawrence College

Claire Robison
Oxford University

Valerie J. Roebuck
University of Manchester

Emma Salter
Open University

Deepak Sarma
Yale University

William S. Sax
Südasien Institut

Peter M. Scharf
Brown University

Annette Schmiedchen
Humboldt-Universität zu Berlin

Christina Schwabenland
London Metropolitan University

Mary Searle-Chatterjee
Manchester University

Karabi Sen
California Institute of Integral Studies

Arvind Sharma
McGill University

Sarah Shaw
University of Reading

Bahman A.K. Shirazi
California Institute of Integral Studies

Jameela Siddiqi
Independent Scholar

Mark Singleton
University of Cambridge

Frederick M. Smith
University of Iowa

Travis L. Smith
Columbia University

Davesh Soneji
McGill University

Sharada Sugirtharajah
University of Birmingham

Barry William Hay Sweetman
University of Otago

Kathleen Taylor
School of Oriental and African Studies

Lynn Thomas
University of Southampton

Shrinivas Tilak
Independent Scholar

Kevin Tingay
Independent Scholar

Archana Venkatesan
St Lawrence University

David Gordon White
University of California, Santa Barbara

Raymond B. Williams
Wabash College

Martin Wood
Independent Scholar

Michael York
Bath Spa University

Katherine K. Young
McGill University

John Zavos
University of Manchester

Xenia Zeiler
Humboldt-Universität zu Berlin

Thematic list of entries

Caste and lifestyles

Ambedkar, Bhimrao Ram
Artha
Arthaśāstra
Āśramas (stages of life)
Brahmacarya
Caste
Dalits
Dharma
Dharmaśāstras
Dharmasūtras
Dvija
Gārhasthya
Gotra
Gṛhyasūtras
Jāti
Kāma
Kāmasūtra
Kauṭilya
Kula
Manu
Narayana Guru
Purity and pollution, ritual
Puruṣārthas
Saṃnyāsa
Śreṇi
Vānaprasthya
Varṇa
Vātsyāyana, Mallanāga

Central concepts

Ātman
Bhagavān
Brahman
Íśvara
Jīva
Jīvanmukta
Karma (law of action)
Māyā
Mokṣa
Saṃsāra

Contemporary media

Books, comics, newspapers and magazines
Film
Iconography, modern
Internet
Sound recordings
Television and radio

Cosmology

Bhūtas (elements)
Brahmā, Day of
Calendar
Cosmogony
Cosmology
Dikpālas
Kalpa
Manvantara
Navagrahas (planets)
Pitṛloka
Pralaya
Saṃsāra
Stars
Svarga
Time
Yuga

Deities

Aditi
Agni
Alakṣmī
Aṅkālaīśvarī
Annapūrṇā
Ardhanārīśvara
Aryaman
Asunīti
Aśvins
Avatāra
Ayyapaṉ
Balarāma
Bhagavān
Bhagavatī
Bhārat Mātā
Brahmā
Bṛhaspati
Cāmuṇḍā
Cappāṇi
Cellattammaṉ
Deities
Deities, domestic and family
Deities, folk and popular
Deities, village and local
Durgā
Dyaus Pitṛ
Gaṇeśa
Grāmadevatās
Gṛhadevī
Hanumān
Hiraṇyagarbha
Indra
Iṣṭadevatā
Īśvara
Jagannātha
Jyeṣṭhā
Kālī and Caṇḍī
Kāma
Kāṇṇaki
Kanyākumārī
Kṛṣṇa
Kṣetrapāla, Kṣetrasya Pati, Kṣetrasya Patnī
Kubera
Kubjikā
Kuladevatā
Kumbhamātā
Lakṣmaṇa
Lakṣmī, Śrī
Lakṣmī-Nārāyaṇa
Mahādeví
Mahāvidyās
Māl
Manasā
Maṅgaḷā
Māriammā
Maruts
Mātṛkās
Mīnākṣī
Mitra
Mohinī
Murukaṉ
Muttapaṉ
Nirṛtis
Pārvatī
Pēcciyammā
Prajāpati
Pṛthivī
Rādhā
Rāma
Rati
Rohiṇī
Rudra
Rukmiṇī
Śakti
Saṇtoṣī Mātā
Saptamātṛkās
Sarasvatī
Satī (Goddess)
Sītā
Śītalā
Śiva
Skanda
Soma
Subramanya
Sundarēśvarar
Sūrya
Tārā
Trimūrti, The
Tulāsī
Tvaṣṭṛ
Umā
Uṣas
Vaiṣṇo Devī
Varuṇa
Vāstoṣpati

Diaspora

Ethics and contemporary issues

Inter-faith and inter-religious dialogue

Major movements and figures

Modern and contemporary period

Myth and mythical characters

Garuḍa
Gopī(s)
Hariścandra
Hiḍimbā
Hiraṇyakaśipu
Janaka
Jaṭāyu
Kabandha
Kāmadhenu
Kaṃsa
Kaṇva
Karṇa
Kauravas
Kinnaras
Kuntī
Lopāmudrā
Mādrī
Mahiṣa
Maitreyī
Manu
Mārkaṇḍeya
Medhātithi
Myth
Naciketas
Nāgas
Nakula
Nala
Nandi
Nārada
Nirṛtis
Pāṇḍavas
Pāṇḍu
Parāśara
Parikṣit
Piśācas
Pitṛs
Prahlād(a)
Pretas
Pūtanā
Rāhu
Rākṣasas
Raktabīja
Rāvaṇa
Sahadeva
Śatrughna
Satyabhāmā
Sāvitrī
Śeṣa
Subhadrā
Sugrīva
Uddālaka Āruṇi
Vāhanas
Vālmīki
Vasiṣṭha
Vāsuki
Viśvamitra
Vṛtra
Vyāsa
Yājñavalkya
Yakṣas
Yaśodā
Yudhiṣṭhira

Philosophy and theology

Advaita
Ahaṃkāra
Antaḥkaraṇa
Arthavāda
Aṣṭāṅga Yoga
Bādarāyaṇa
Bhedābheda
Brahman-Ātman
Brahmasūtras
Citta
Dvaita
Gaṅgeśa Upādhyāya
Gauḍapāda
Guṇas
Īśvarakṛṣṇa
Jaimini
Kaivalya
Kaṇāḍa
Kapila
Kośa
Kṣetra
Kṣetrajña
Līlā
Liṅgaśarīra
Lokāyata
Madhva
Mahat
Manas
Māyā
Mīmāṃsāsūtras
Moha, dveṣa, rāga
Nimbārka
Nyāya

Politics and nationalism

Sacred geography

Rāmeśvara
Sacred animals
Sacred geography
Saptapurī (seven sacred cities)
Sarasvatī
Tīrthayātrā (Pilgrimage)
Ujjayinī
Vaiśālī
Vārāṇasī
Vṛndāvana
Yamunā (river)

Sacred texts and languages

Āraṇyakas
Āstika and Ṉāstika
Āśvalāyana
Bhagavadgītā
Brāhmaṇas
Brahmasūtras
Chandas
Devī Māhātmya
Dharmaśāstras
Dharmasūtras
Gāyatrī Mantra
Gītagovinda
Gṛhyasūtras
Harivaṃśa
Itihāsa
Jayadeva
Kalpasūtras
Languages
Mahābhārata
Manu
Mīmāṃsāsūtras
Nirukta
Nītiśāstras
Nyāyalīlāvatī
Nyāyasūtras
Padārthadharmasaṃgraha
Pañcatantra
Purāṇas
Rāmāyaṇa
Sacred Texts
Saṃhitā
Sāṃkhyakārikās
Śikṣā
Śilpaśāstras
Somadevabhaṭṭa
Śrautasūtras
Śulvasūtras
Sūtra
Tamil Veda
Tantras
Tulsīdās(a)
Upaniṣads
Vaiśeṣikasūtras
Vālmīki
Veda
Vyākaraṇa
Vyāsa
Yogasūtras
Yogavāsiṣṭha

Scholars and writers

Anquetil-Duperron, Abraham-Hyacinthe
Arnold, Sir Edwin
Asiatic Societies
Asiatick Researches
Basham, Arthur Llewellyn
Bharati, Swami Agehananda
Bühler, Georg
Buitenen, Johannes Adrianus Bernardus van
Burnouf, Eugène
Chaudhuri, Nirad C.
Coeurdoux, Gaston-Laurent
Colebrooke, Henry Thomas
Coomaraswamy, Ananda Kentish
Dasgupta, Surendranath
Deussen, Paul Jakob
Dow, Alexander
Dubois, Jean-Antoine
Dumont, Louis
Edgerton, Franklin
Eidlitz, Walther
Eliade, Mircea
Emerson, Ralph Waldo
Farquhar, John Nicol
Filliozat, Jean
Frauwallner, Erich
Glasenapp, (Otto Max) Helmuth von
Gonda, Jan
Griffith, Ralph Thomas Hotchkin
Guénon, René-Jean-Marie-Joseph
Hacker, Paul

Traditional arts and sciences

Women and gender

Worship and practice

Ramakrishna Utsava
Rāmanavamī
Ratha Yātrā
Religious specialists
Ṛṣi
Śabda
Sādhu
Samāvartana
Saṃpradāya
Saṃskāras
Śaṅkarācāryas
Sant
Sarasvatī Pūjā
Satsaṅg
Seva
Shrines, Wayside
Siddha
Śilpaśāstras
Sīmantonnayana
Śiṣya
Śivarātri
Skanda Ṣaṣṭi
Snānā Yātrā
Śrāddhā (faith)
Śrāddhā (rites to deceased ancestors)
Śramaṇa
Svāmi
Svāstika
Tai Pusan
Tapas
Tarpaṇa
Temple worship
Tīj
Tīrthayātrā
Tulāsī-vivāha
Upanayana
Utsava
Vaiśākhi
Vedārambha
Vedi
Vibhūti
Vidyārambha
Vivāha
Vrata
Yajña
Yantra
Yogi

List of entries

N

A

ABHAYANANDA, SWAMI

Little is known about the early life of Madame Marie Louise/Swami Abhayananda, one of the first two Western-born disciples initiated into saṃnyāsa in 1895 by Swami Vivekananda in the United States. French by birth, she had been associated with radical causes in New York where she had lived as a naturalised American citizen. Complaining about a lack of support when leader of the New York Vedanta Society during Vivekananda's absence in England, she threatened in 1897 to transfer her allegiance to Theosophy. Soon after, she established the Advaita Society in Chicago. After lecturing independently in India in 1899, Abhayananda broke with the Ramakrishna movement, reportedly because Vivekananda had taught that Ramakrishna was an avatāra, although Vivekananda's followers have attributed her behaviour to personal ambition. She subsequently founded the School of Mind and Soul Culture in New York.

See also: **Avatāra; Ramakrishna Math and Mission; Ramakrishna, Sri; Saṃnyāsa; Theosophy and the Theosophical Society; Vivekananda, Swami**

GWILYM BECKERLEGGE

Further reading

French, H.W. 1974. *The Swan's Wide Waters.* New York: Kennikat Press.

ABHIMANTRAṆA

See: **Dīkṣā**

ABHINAV BHARAT SOCIETY

An organisation founded in 1902 by Vinayak Damodar Savarkar (1883–1996), more popularly known as Veer Savarkar, with the aim of achieving absolute independence for India from the British. This was to be achieved by all means, including armed struggle and violence. The organisation was started whilst the young Savarkar was at Ferguson College in Pune and soon became the cradle of young revolutionaries from the region. In 1906 he came to Britain to study law at Grays Inn and whilst here he opened a branch of the organisation in London, founding India House as a meeting place for Indian students.

The Abhinav Bharat Society represented the views of its founder and was at odds with the non-violence of Gandhi. The fiery rhetoric advocating violence heard at the organisation's meetings attracted many young Indians, and many notable members of the first Congress government were once members. The organisation came to notoriety after the murder of Curzon Wylic in London by Madan Lal Dhingra, a committed supporter of the movement.

Many of the core members of the organisation were sentenced to death by the British or passed many years in exile on the Andaman Islands. Savarkar himself was kept away from the Indian masses for twenty-seven years in either exile or prison.

See also: **Gandhi, Mohandas Karamchand; Nationalism; Savarkar, Vinayak Damodar**

RON GEAVES

ABHINAVAGUPTA (late tenth century)

Major thinker in Kashmiri Śaivism, son of the scholar Narasiṃhagupta, who was his first tutor, Abhinavagupta produced some forty-one works exploring, in both commentaries and independent treatises, the three main branches of Kashmiri Śaivism: Krama, Pratyabhijñā and Trika as well as aesthetics, poetics and the theory of language, becoming in all fields the most prominent and influential teacher.

It was Abhinavagupta who systematised the doctrine of the Trika on the basis of a number of older and often obscure texts, particularly in his masterpiece, the *Tantrāloka* (*Light on the Tantras*), an immense work in thirty-seven āhnika ('day-times', i.e. chapters) which, with Jayaratha's commentary, occupies no fewer than twelve volumes in the Kashmir Series of Texts and Studies (1918–38). The *Tantrāloka* was summarised by its author in the *Tantrasāra* (*Essence of the Tantras*), a widely read treatise where yoga, devotion to the Lord and non-dualism (advaita) are blended in such a way as to become relevant to many different systems. The *Patrātrimśikā Vivarana* is a long commentary on the thirty-six pithy stanzas of the Tantra *Parātrimśikā*, which elaborates speculations on all aspects of Word/speech, be they ritual, cosmogonic, psychological, epistemological or metaphysical. Two other commentaries of note are the *Mālinīvijaya Varttika* and the *Īśvarapratyabhijñā Vimarśinī* on Utpaladeva's *Pratyabhijñā Kārikā*, central texts of the tradition. All these works are momentous and Abhinavagupta's influence was not restricted to his own school but extended as far as Tamil Nadu where he even came to be seen as an incarnation of Śiva. His works on aesthetics were to be equally authoritative and of lasting relevance, not only in the field of poetics, with his emphasis on the centrality of suggestion, but also to all performing arts, notably theatre, dance and music.

See also: **Advaita; Dance; Drama; Kashmiri Śaivism; Music; Poetry; Śiva; Tantras; Tantrism; Yoga**

DANIEL MARIAU

ABHIṢEKA

Abhiṣeka or consecration, during which the image or mūrti of a deity is ritually bathed, is one of the most common practices carried out in temples and shrines on a daily basis. This fundamental ceremony ranges from the simple bathing of a deity with water or milk to the ritual consecration of a whole temple. This temple abhiṣeka or kumbhābhiṣeka is undertaken every twelve years by those temples that can afford to renew or repair the temple structure. The abhiṣeka is then considered to renew the power of the deities within.

In the more complex abhiṣeka ceremonies, performed in the larger temples, the deity might be ritually bathed with a variety of different substances ranging from turmeric water, considered to be cooling and purifying, to honey, fruit and curds. It is difficult to find written sources that explain why various substances are used but in one particular temple in Tamil Nadu a small booklet indicated that the juice of sugar cane is offered for health, sandalwood oil might bring happiness and rice-flour powder might be offered for the removal of debt (Foulston 2002: 125–26). The quantity of ingredients used at an abhiṣeka ceremony is dependent on what is offered by the devotees or the funds of the temple. In Tamil Nadu, where flowers, turmeric and sandal-paste appear to be more readily available and more economical, the abhiṣeka ceremonies seem more elaborate in the larger temples. However, the simple act of showering flowers, water or milk on a deity also represents a very personal act that reinforces the relationship between deity and devotee. The abhiṣeka ritual is generally followed by ārtī and by the decoration of the deity. In South India this generally includes the plain black stone image being transformed with deep yellow sandal-paste, flowers and richly decorated silk clothing into a feast for the eyes and the nose.

See also: **Ārtī; Deities; Image worship; Mandir; Temple worship**

LYNN FOULSTON

Further reading

Foulston, Lynn. 2002. *At the Feet of the Goddess: The Divine Feminine in Local Hindu Religion*. Brighton and Portland, OR: Sussex Academic Press.

ABORTION

The practice of abortion is clearly on the increase in India and is due to the country's own social and cultural problems. Indeed, traditional perspectives view this practice with deep contempt, although, as with all things when seen through the eye of dharma, there are circumstances where it may be argued as justified, such as when the mother's life is a risk. The principal hegemonic precept underlying the condemnation is that all life is sacred, with the notions of compassion, karma and ahiṃsā (non-violence) following a close second. Life is believed to begin at conception and any prevention of the development of the foetus, a potential child, is seen as no less than killing. The ancient texts, composed in a culture which encouraged large family units, speak vehemently against abortion, describing punishments and afterlife consequences for women terminating their unborn. Karmically, the jīva (soul) has lessons to learn and to teach others. It is inappropriate therefore, for a child's karmic progress to be hindered, even if the child is disabled. Once life, at conception, has been given, humans have no right to take someone else's away for their own convenience. If a couple do engage in sexual activity, the primary purpose of which is reproduction, with fertilisation as the result, it is their moral duty to take responsibility for their actions and for the life that they have now conceived. Thus, in this regard at least, it would be argued that only sexual activity between husband and wife is dharmic.

The control of population increases in India requires abstinence (unless children are intended), abortion or contraception. Although too idealistic, the first is the solution proposed by some. Abortion simply for unwanted pregnancies would not be found acceptable by many. Thus, contraception, even if disapproved of by some, would be the practical answer, at least by using a barrier or the rhythm method rather than emergency contraception as a form of abortion.

The introduction of medical technology has enabled many Indians to find out the sex of their unborn, and to opt to keep it if a boy and terminate it if a girl. Those in poverty, unable to do this, kill the baby girl at birth. While all this may seem unacceptable to Westerners, the parents often face 'dharma dilemmas' in that they argue that the death of their daughter is better than giving her a life of misery in a society where dowry demands exist, and in addition where boys are often seen as the breadwinners, not the girls. Thus, daughters are seen by some families as a financial liability offering problems to all, including themselves.

See also: **Ahiṃsā; Celibacy; Contraception; Dharma; Dowry; Foeticide; Infanticide; Jīva; Karma; Saṃskāras**

RISHI HANDA

Further reading

Coward, Harold G., Julius J. Lipner and Katherine K. Young. 1991. *Hindu Ethics.* Delhi: Sri Satguru Publications.

Crawford, S. Cromwell. 2003. *Hindu Bioethics for the Twenty-First Century.* Albany, NY: State University of New York Press.

Jackson, Robert and Dermot Killingly. 1991. *Moral Issues in the Hindu Tradition.* Stoke on Trent: Trentham Books Limited.

Menski, Werner. 2001. 'Hinduism'. In Peggy Morgan and Clive Lawton, eds, *Ethical Issues in Six Religious Traditions.* Edinburgh: Edinburgh University Press, 1–54.

ĀCĀRYA

Ācārya is one of several Sanskrit words for a teacher. *Nirukta* 1.4 derives it from ācāra, 'conduct', but Kātyāyana and perhaps also Pāṇini understood it as 'the one to be approached' (Scharfe 2002: 90f.). In the Veda, the upanayana establishes a relationship between the ācārya and the brahmacārin, who lives in the teacher's household (ācārya-kula, later called guru-kula). Typically an ācārya had only a few students, but some accounts mention large numbers, with assistant teachers (Scharfe 2002: 220). Ācārya can also refer to a master craftsman who teaches an apprentice (Scharfe 2002: 265). The words guru and ācārya often refer to the same person, but ācārya connotes his authority in his subject, while guru connotes the respect and affection due to him (Hara 1980).

Ācārya may be added to names, e.g. Droṇācārya (Droṇa), Śaṅkarācārya (Śaṅkara). The Buddhist logician Dignāga is referred to by his followers simply as Ācārya. Brahmo Samaj preachers are called ācārya, or in English 'minister'.

See also: **Brahmo Samaj; Droṇa; Guru; Kātyāyana; Nirukta; Pāṇini; Śaṅkara; Upanayana; Veda**

DERMOT KILLINGLEY

Further reading

Hara, Minoru. 1980. 'Hindu Concepts of Teacher: Sanskrit *guru* and *ācārya*'. In M. Nagaromi, B.K. Matilal, J.M. Masson and E. Dimock, eds, *Sanskrit and Buddhist Studies: Essays in Honour of Daniel H.H. Ingalls.* Dordrecht: Reidel, 93–118.

Scharfe, Hartmut. 2002. *Education in Ancient India.* (Handbuch der Orientalistik, Section 2, vol. 16.) Leiden: Brill.

ADITI

'Not-falling, firm'; 'unrestrained'. A celestial mother-goddess; mother of the Ādityas (Varuṇa, Mitra, Aryaman, Bhaga, Dakṣa, Aṃśa and possibly Tvaṣṭṛ). Aditi represents the sky as spatial expanse rather than luminous shining. She constitutes an early personification of primordial night but survives essentially as an abstraction of infinity. While occasionally confused with Uṣas or even Pṛthivī (*Ṛgveda* 1.72.9), Aditi is actually an instance of the cosmic anti-mother who rejects her eighth son, Mārtāṇḍa/ Vivasvat the sun (10.72.8f), in favour of the Ādityas, the asuras *par excellence.* Unlike the devas, who are expressions of nature, Aditi and her offspring are preoccupied with sin and retribution. With the emergence of the devas, however, Aditi is limited and becomes Diti, the mother of the post-ṛgvedic demons, the Daityas.

See also: **Aryaman; Asuras; Deities; Mitra; Pṛthivī; Saṃhitā; Tvaṣṭṛ; Uṣas; Varuṇa; Vedic pantheon**

MICHAEL YORK

ADVAITA

Literally 'not two-ness' or non-duality. Advaita is the philosophical position advocated by one of the main schools of Vedānta. It is the idea that in the final analysis plurality is in fact the manifestation of a non-dual reality. This philosophical stance is sometimes described in the West as monism (the belief that reality is one), but the meaning of 'non-duality' in a Hindu context is more subtle than this, since, strictly speaking, it does not involve the postulation of even a single entity, since 'Being' (sat) is said to be beyond all signification, including postulation of a One. The non-dual principle of reality underlies the universe, but is not an entity like the various objects and entities within that universe. It is the ground of their being. Moreover, describing such philosophies as monistic is also problematic because such schools often maintain a multi-levelled conception of truth that does not necessarily involve denying the reality of the multiplicity. The point is rather that the ontological substrate that allows such entities to manifest is, in its essence, a non-dual principle of being.

The earliest clear expression of non-dualist ideas can be found in the *Upaniṣads*, where the underlying substrate of existence is called Brahman and is that out of which the universe is said to emerge. According to early *Upaniṣads* such as the *Chāndogya*, the relationship between Brahman and the essential self of each individual being (Ātman) is like the commingling of salt and water in salty water. Just as Brahman cannot normally be seen yet pervades the entire universe, the water tastes of salt that cannot be seen and the difference between the two is imperceptible. Finally, the sage declares 'You are That' (*tat-tvam-asi*, *Chāndogya Upaniṣad* 6.10.3). With the development of various attempts to create a systematic philosophical interpretation of such phrases in the *Upaniṣads* (veda-anta or 'end of the vedas'), a number of different schools arose with regard to the central question of the relationship between the individual self and Brahman, the essence of the universe. These included the difference-non-difference school, the dualists (who posited a distinct ontological separation of the two), the qualified non-dualists and the non-dualist interpretation. The philosophy of Advaita finds its first clear exposition in the form of the *Māṇḍūkyakārikā* (otherwise known as the *Āgamaśāstra* or the *Gauḍapādakārikā*), probably composed around the sixth century of the Common Era. The most famous exponent of the Advaita position however is Śaṅkara (eighth century CE).

According to the followers of the Śaṅkarite interpretation the world of plurality is in the final analysis nothing more than a magical illusion (māyā). The precise nature of this illusion was subject to considerable discussion (and disputation from rival schools) but the position that became generally accepted was that māyā is inexplicable, being neither fully existent nor non-existent. The key to understanding this idea is to appreciate that for Śaṅkara there are two levels of truth – the ultimate truth (where the non-dual Brahman is the sole reality) and everyday, practical truth, where there exists a multitude of different entities. Māyā is a kind of cosmic illusion but is not thereby a delusion of an individual mind (such as in a hallucination or a dream), not least because even the notion of an individual self (jīvātman) is ultimately illusory from the perspective of ultimate truth. Śaṅkara rejected the idea that the world of waking experience was a subjective delusion – it exists and functions on an everyday level of practical truth. This world is unreal *as such*, that is, as the world, but is real insofar as it is identical with Brahman, the ground of all existence. According to Śaṅkara, the cause of the *apparent* manifestation of the universe is avidyā – metaphysical ignorance – fundamentally our ignorance of the truth that everything is Brahman. At the individual level this involves projection (adhyāsa) of categories or 'adjuncts' deriving from previously acquired experiences (including those from previous incarnations) onto the non-dual reality, making it appear as something that it is not. To illustrate this Śaṅkara uses the famous analogy of the rope and the snake. In poor light a rope may appear as a snake. What we 'see' is a snake but in fact there is only a rope. In daylight (that is, with the benefit of wisdom), we can see the mistake that was made and no longer project the idea of a snake onto the rope. Similarly, Brahman is the ground of all things, but is misconstrued as separate objects by our failure to overcome our ignorance of the true nature of reality.

Śaṅkara's version of Advaita, however, is by no means the only form of non-dualism to be found within the Hindu traditions. The *Bhagāvatā Purāṇa* (*c.* tenth century CE) combines non-dualistic ideas with Vaiṣṇava devotionalism (bhakti) and is centred upon the playful figure of Kṛṣṇa. We also find non-dualistic philosophies amongst the various Śaivite movements. Notable here is the Pratyabhijñā or Recognition School, often associated with the region of Kashmir but also existing further afield, for its explicit rejection of Śaṅkara's understanding of māyā as illusion. According to this school, the world is real, being a vibration (spanda) of the dynamic and creative consciousness that is Śiva. We also find later works such as the highly poetic *Yoga Teachings of Vāsiṣṭha* (*Yogavāsiṣṭha*) which synthesises themes and concepts from a number of different non-dualist schools (including Buddhist ones), but with a clear orientation towards Vedāntic intepretations.

Interest in Śaṅkara's philosophy by various Western Orientalists and Hindu reformers in the late nineteenth and early twentieth centuries helped to establish non-dualist ideas as important sources for the intellectual renewal and interpretation of Hindu theology in the twentieth century. Many of the key intellectual figures and gurus of Hinduism in the modern period – such as Ramakrishna, his disciple Swami Vivekananda, Sarvepalli Radhakrishnan, Ramana Maharshi, Nisargadatta Raj, Sri Aurobindo and to some extent even Mahatma Gandhi, espouse some form of non-dualism as central aspects of their teaching. Perhaps more than anyone, however, it was Swami Vivekananda who succeeded in capturing the imagination of Hindus and Westerners alike with his advocacy of non-dualism as the central theology of Hinduism and 'spirituality' as the defining feature of Hindu religiosity.

See also: **Ātman; Bhakti; Brahman; Buddhism, relationship with Hinduism; Gandhi, Mohandas Karamchand; Ghose, Aurobindo; Hinduism, modern and contemporary; Kashmiri Śaivism; Kṛṣṇa; Māyā; Purāṇas; Radhakrishnan, Sir Sarvepalli; Ramakrishna, Sri; Ramana Maharshi; Śaivism; Śaṅkara; Śiva; Upaniṣads; Vaiṣṇavism; Vedānta; Vivekananda, Swami; Yogavāsiṣṭha**

RICHARD KING

Further reading

King, Richard. 1999. *Indian Philosophy: An Introduction to Hindu and Buddhist Thought*. Edinburgh: Edinburgh University Press.

Ram-Prasad, C. 1991. *An Outline of Indian Non-realism: Some Central Arguments of Advaita Metaphysics*. Oxford: Oxford University Press.
Sharma, A. 1993. *The Experimental Dimension of Advaita Vedanta*. Delhi: Motilal Banarsidass.

AESTHETICS

Referred to as alaṃkāra (ornamentation/beauty), Sanskrit aesthetic theory (alaṃkāra śāstra) in India develops as a means to explain the purpose of drama as well as that of poetry. For early theoreticians, alaṃkāra implied both beauty as well as beauty produced through ornamentation. In the first sense, alaṃkāra is inherent like the guṇas (virtues/qualities), while in the latter it is produced through the manipulation of language or dramatic gesture to produce a specific effect. However, a philosophical shift occurred in this understanding of the relationship of alaṃkāra to the guṇas with the theoretical writings of Ānandavardhana (*c.* ninth century). Without denying the significance of alaṃkāra and guṇa to aesthetic experience, he suggested that even someone with little training in technical matters, but with a perhaps intuitive sensibility, could be moved to an aesthetic experience (Krishnamoorthy 1979: 123–25). This of course suggests that there is something inherent in the work of art which transcends its mechanics, be it poetry, drama or painting.

Rasa theory

Arguably, the most pervasive and influential Indian aesthetic theory is that of rasa, which makes its first appearance in the sixth chapter of the second-century Sanskrit dramaturgical manual *Nāṭyaśāstra*. The word rasa literally means flavour or relish. In aesthetic terms, rasa is the result of the judicious conjunction of stimulus (vibhāva), involuntary reaction (anubhāva) and voluntary reaction (vyabhicaribhāva). Rasa is compared to the cooking process, where the ingredients, distinctive in their own way, combine to produce an altogether unique flavour. The flavour is the aesthetic experience known as rasa, the ingredients are the various bhāvas (emotions), while one capable of experiencing rasa is referred to as a rasika. The *Nāṭyaśāstra* tabulates eight fundamental rasas, with their corresponding bhāvas (emotions). That is, if bhāva is the emotion, rasa can be understood as the aesthetic experience of that emotion. The eight rasas and their corresponding sthāyi bhāvas (permanent/stable emotions) are as follows (Rangacharya 1986: 38–39).

Rasa	Bhāva
Śṛṅgāra (erotic)	Rati (desire)
Hāsya (comic)	Hāsa (laughter)
Karuṇa (compassion)	Śoka (grief)
Raudra (fearsome)	Krodha (anger)
Vīra (heroic)	Utsāha (energy)
Bhayānaka (fearsome)	Bhaya (fear)
Bībhatsa (loathsome)	Jugupsā (disgust)
Adbhuta (wonder)	Vismaya (astonishment)

When rasa theory is incorporated into an Advaitic philosophical system an important ninth rasa, Śānta (tranquillity) is added. It is interpolated into the *Nāṭyaśāstra* text quite late and the philosopher Udbhaṭa (eighth century) is usually credited with its inclusion. However, Śānta is not just another rasa, but rather the foundational state of mind, and all other rasas are but its variation (Krishnamoorthy 1979: 206–10).

Another equally important concept is that of sādhāraṇikaraṇa (universalising emotion) introduced by Bhaṭṭa Nāyaka (ninth century) and further developed by the later Kashmiri Śaiva theologian, Abhinavagupta (tenth century) in his *Abhinavabhārati*, a commentary on the *Nāṭyaśāstra*. Abhinavagupta, in commenting on Bhaṭṭa Nāyaka's idea of sādhāraṇikaraṇa, is primarily speaking in the context of Nāṭya (drama). Nāṭya here refers to both the actual text and the actual acting that renders meaning to the text. Within this framework, the emotions that arise as a response to art (or art-like experiences) cause readers/audience to transcend their subjectivity and their individuality, unlike emotions that one experiences in life, which bind one to the world. For Abhinavagupta, then, without sādhāraṇikaraṇa rasa experience is impossible (Krishnamoorthy 1979: 214–15) and therefore aesthetic experience corresponds to that of the yogin's mystical enjoyment.

Bhakti rasa

With the emergence of bhakti as both a major literary and religious phenomenon, it too comes to be understood as a rasa. Especially within the philosophical circles of Vallabha, Caitanya and the Gosvāmis, bhakti rasa became the predominant and pre-eminent metaphor of divine experience. Bhakti was conceived initially as a bhāva rather than a rasa. However, Vopadeva and Hemādri, two thirteenth-century commentators on the *Bhāgavata Purāṇa* not only promulgated the idea of bhakti as a rasa, but displaced Śānta to argue for its place as the rasa *par excellence*. The other nine rasas are now variations of bhakti, rather than Śānta. A simple definition of bhakti rasa would be the experience of bliss engendered through hearing, reading and participating in some way in the exploits of God and his devotees. There is a crucial differentiation in the formulation of bhakti rasa in other Vaiṣṇava schools, namely that of Caitanya, Vallabha and the Gosvāmis, who have differences among themselves as well. For them, śṛṅgāra or mādhurya (sweetness) was the chief rasa, the most efficacious vehicle to approximate the bliss of mystical union (Krishnamoorthy 1979: 198–201).

Tamil aesthetic theory

Tamil aesthetic theory hinges on the complementary principles of interior/exterior, public and private worlds that were termed akam (inner) and puṟam (outer). It developed alongside the poetry of what is referred to as the Caṅkam period (first to third centuries). While akam poetry concerned itself with matters of love, desire and longing, puṟam poetry depicted kings, war and ethics. The akam world was governed by dividing the world and emotions into five landscapes (tiṇai), each of which represented a stage in the development of love. The characters of the akam world were anonymous and archetypal – the hero, the heroine, her friend, his friend and so on. The puṟam poem, on the other hand, was peopled with named kings, with 'real' events, and with bards who toured the countryside in search of a generous patron.

The aesthetic conventions of Caṅkam poetry greatly influenced emergent Tamil bhakti poetics (sixth to ninth centuries). The wandering poets of this period appropriated the forms and genres of the past literary age to express a new religious sensibility. In a sense, bhakti religiosity also ushered in its own new literary genre. The bhakti poem utilised the form of the anonymous hero and heroine of the akam poems, though by naming the hero (god) and the heroine (the poet in his/her persona) it violated a cardinal aesthetic principle. In addition, the poets valorised the god as king in their newly imagined puṟam poems, translating the relationship of mutual dependence of bard and king into that of the devotee and his chosen deity. Perhaps the most significant aesthetic shift of these new poems was in breaking the invisible and impenetrable barrier between the poet and the imagined poetic situation. The new bhakti poems, through identifying their characters and personalising their poetic narratives, invited the audience into the poem in a way that was impossible for the antecedent akam and puṟam poems (Selby 2000: 26–35).

See also: **Abhinavagupta; Advaita; Bhakti; Caitanya; Drama; Guṇas; Kashmiri Śaivism; Languages; Poetry; Purāṇas; Sanskrit; Vaiṣṇavism; Vallabha; Yogī**

ARCHANA VENKATESAN

Further reading

Krishnamoorthy, K. 1979. *Studies in Indian Aesthetics and Criticism*. Mysore: Mysore Printing and Publishing House.

Rangacharya, Adya. 1986. *Natyasastra (English Translation with Critical Notes)*. Bangalore: IBH Prakashana.

Selby, Martha Ann. 2000. *Grow Long Blessed Night: Love Poems from Classical India*. New York: Oxford University Press.

Tapasyananda, Swami. 1990. *Bhakti Schools of Vedānta: Lives and Philosophies of Rāmānuja, Nimbārka, Mādhava, Vallabha and Caitanya*. Madras: Sri Ramakrishna Math.

AFRICA, HINDUS IN

South African Hindus

By 1833, slavery was abolished in the colonies. However, by the mid-nineteenth century the British Empire had grown enormously, thus requiring a labour force to work on the plantations in the colonies. In view of the abolition of slavery, the colonies had to use a different system of labour, which came to be known as the 'indenture system'.

After many discussions, both in Natal and India as well as in England, and after passing many laws, the first group of indentured Indian workers arrived in Natal on 11 October 1860. This group came from the Madras province. Between 1860 and 1866, about 6,445 indentured labourers were brought to Natal. The emigration was stopped between 1866 and 1874 due to the ill treatment of labourers hired under the new system in Natal.

When it was resumed in 1874, the immigration department in Natal placed advertisements in India to attract labourers. Among other things, they guaranteed that 'Your religion will in no way be interfered with, and both Hindoos and Mahomedans [*sic*] are alike protected'. The advertisement also stated that there were already more than 5,000 Indians in Natal, thus pointing to the fact that a community of Indians had begun to develop in South Africa.

In order to protect the interests of the indentured labourers, the powers of the Protector of Indian Immigrants were strengthened under Law 19 of 1874. Law 20 of 1874 further provided for the protection of future immigrants. Despite all these laws, there were many irregularities, and promises made to the indentured labourers were not adequately fulfilled.

As indentured labourers became free, some of them were rehired into the indenture system but others were not. Of the latter some moved into rural areas to grow and sell fruit and vegetables, while others pursued a variety of occupations

Between 1874 and 1911, nearly 146,000 new immigrants came to Natal in 364 ships. It was during this period that many 'free passenger' Indians also arrived. They were mostly traders holding British passports and entered Natal at their own expense. Most of them came from Gujarat and a significant number of them had a Muslim religious background. Thus by this time, i.e. between 1874 and 1911, there were three distinct categories of Indians within South Africa: those who were still under the indenture system, those who had previously been indentured labourers, and those who came as free passengers or what Maureen Swan (1985) calls 'the merchant class'. The Indian merchants began trading and supplying groceries and other items to the Indian and African communities.

Once the freed indentured labourers and the merchant class began to enter small trading enterprises, their economic interests clashed directly with those of the European merchants. The anti-Indian feeling among the European settlers was conspicuous by 1890. The general increase in the Indian population coupled with the arrival of a new merchant class raised alarm among the European colonists. By this time the Indian community had already spread to the other colonies, such as Transvaal, Cape and Free State.

Many Indians, especially the merchant class, protested against the harsh treatment and discrimination meted out to them by the European colonists. At the same time, from 1890 onwards, there was a clash of interests between the planters in Natal and the colonists. The planters wanted the indenture system to continue, but the colonists saw the Indian community as a threat to their economic interests. In 1893 Natal was given the status of Representative Government. This intensified the anti-Indian feeling among the Europeans. Act 17 of 1895 required, *inter alia*, that the indentured labourers be repatriated upon completion of their contract. But if they stayed they must pay a £3 penalty annually and £1 poll tax per person annually.

By this time Gandhi had already arrived in South Africa and become involved in merchant politics. The year 1895 saw the formation of the Natal Indian Congress, which spearheaded the Indian struggle against oppressive laws in Natal. Many protests were launched by the Indians. Swan (1985) highlights that most of the struggle centred around merchant interests, and the concerns of the indentured labourers were taken as a pretext to lobby for the merchant class. By 1908 the English merchants in Natal were demanding the repatriation of Indians by introducing the Asiatic Trading Bill. But in 1909 the British government intervened to allow the Indians to appeal to the Supreme Court.

The discovery of diamonds in 1867 attracted many Indian traders to move to Cape Colony. Here the laws pertaining to Indian traders were fewer. So by 1910 there were about 10,000 Indians in the Cape Colony.

The Orange Free State was independent of the British Empire by 1854. During the 1880s, some 'Arab' merchants tried to set up businesses in the Free State but they were soon prevented by severe restrictions.

In the Transvaal, the 1899 Anglo-Boer war created a great deal of confusion in the sense that during the war thousands of British subjects, including Indians, left Transvaal. After the war many Indians returned as refugees. But when the refugees began to return, the government officials were unable to determine who had the right to enter the colony. That was the context in which fingerprinting was made compulsory for Indians. Gandhi and his associates protested against it. By the time Transvaal received its status of Representative Government in 1907, there was already a significant number of Indian traders living there. The period between 1907 and 1910 witnessed a barrage of protests by Indians in Transvaal, and the role that Gandhi played during that period was significant.

The decade 1900 to 1910 is crucial for understanding the Hindu presence in South Africa. In 1903 the first Indian newspaper, *Indian Opinion*, was started by Gandhi in both Gujarati and English. In 1904 a branch of the Arya Samaj was formed, and in 1905 Professor Bhai Paramanand of the Arya Samaj visited South Africa. In the same year the Pretoria Tamil League was established; in subsequent years other Indian organisations were founded: the Surat Hindu Association (1907), the Young Men's Hindu Association (1909), the Pretoria Hindu Seva Samaj and the New Castle Tamil Association (1910).

The year 1911 heralded a new phase of experience for Indians when all the colonies joined to create the Union of South

Africa. This put an end to Indian immigration to South Africa. From now on the question was not so much about the immigration of Indians but their repatriation. While the South African government viewed it as repatriation, the Indians took it as expatriation. In light of this situation, many new organisations and lobbies supporting the Indian cause came into existence. In 1911 the Colonial Born Indian Association and the South African Indian Committee were formed. Meanwhile, in India, in 1910, Professor G. Gokhale of the Indian National Congress introduced a resolution in the Imperial Legislative Council which sought the prohibition of future indentured immigration into Natal. In 1912, Professor Gokhale visited South Africa at the invitation of Gandhi. In 1913 Indian immigration was finally ended. On 29 October 1913, Gandhi led what was called the Great March to oppose the £3 tax. After a great deal of political involvement, Gandhi finally left for India on 18 July 1914.

There were two major ports in India from which indentured Indians were shipped – the Madras port, which sent mainly Tamil- and Telegu-speaking people, and the Calcutta port, which sent mainly Hindi-speaking people. The passenger Indians or traders largely came from Gujarat and Bombay. The ship lists from the Madras port for the initial period between 1860 and 1877 do not give us any details regarding the castes of Indians. Up to 1877 all Hindus coming from Madras were listed under the generic term 'Gentoo'. Only from 1878 onwards did the ship lists from Madras contain details of castes. Therefore, it is not easy to find out exactly which caste groups came from South India during the early part of immigration. However, most of the last names of the South Indian groups do indicate caste background. On the other hand, the ship lists from the Calcutta port do give details of caste. In the case of both North Indian groups and South Indian groups, there seems to have been some mobility in terms of caste background. Often the documents of individuals reflect caste names that do not match with family names. For instance, in one of the documents a person is listed as belonging to the Vanniya caste, which is a non-brahmanical caste. But the same person has a last name 'Iyer' which is a specific brahmanical caste name from South India. Such anomalies, however, need to be carefully investigated and studied by social scientists to see whether some individuals had claimed higher caste status by changing their last names, and for what reasons. Such investigation would offer new insights into how social mobility might have occurred among the South African Indians.

In general, the Madras group constituted 12 per cent Muslims, 5 per cent Christians, 5 per cent Rājputs, some Pillais (Traders) and the remaining were labourers of low social rank. The Calcutta group constituted 5.5 per cent Rājputs; others were either from the Lohar caste (Blacksmith) or Koris (Weavers) or some other low rank. The first group, i.e. the Madras group, comprised not so much agricultural labourers as mechanics, household servants, gardeners, traders, carpenters, barbers, accountants and grooms. Thus, the Indian community which eventually settled in South Africa may be divided along cultural lines into North Indians and South Indians.

When the Indian labourers arrived in South Africa they were allocated to different employers, some in the sugarcane industry, some in the railways and so on. The employers then took them away to their respective locations of work. Although there seems to be no documentation on which linguistic group went to which area, some indirect evidence could be proffered to show that a significant number of families coming from the same language group may have gone to the same area. For instance, one could take a look at some areas, such as Verulam and Tongaat, where mostly Tamil- and Telegu-speaking people seem to have settled, and also survey the background of the early temples in those areas, which might give some indication of which language group might have been present there in the early days. So by taking a careful inventory of the older settlements, it would be possible, perhaps, to find out the settlements of various linguistic groups. However, more careful field study is required to discover the exact situation in terms of linguistic background in each settlement of Indians in the early periods.

In terms of religious background, the Indian community may be divided mostly into Hindus and Muslims, and a small group of Christians and Parsees. The Christian group was the result of nineteenth-century mass conversion in India. However, subsequent conversions did occur in South Africa. Although linguistically speaking there are several groups (e.g. Hindi- and Gujarati-speaking people in the North Indian group; Tamil- and Telegu-speaking people in the South Indian group), in general all North Indians share a similar cultural milieu and, likewise, all South Indians share a similar cultural milieu. This trend may be identified in the observance of festivals. Distinct South Indian and North Indian architectural styles are noticeable in temple building. Mikula *et al.* (1982) note these distinct architectural backgrounds.

The present Hindu community in South Africa may be treated largely as belonging to four language groups. These are, as identified earlier: (1) Tamils, (2) Telegus, (3) Hindis and (4) Gujaratis. There seems to be a greater awareness of their respective languages and traditions at the present time than during their initial period of settlement. And, therefore, the linguistic group identities seem to be becoming reified. Nowbath *et al.* (1960: 18) points out that at one time the North Indian groups were unaware of the fact that the Telegus and the Tamils were distinct groups in terms of their language and culture. However, it must be noted that over the years there has been a great deal of assimilation between the Tamils and the Telegus, more from the side of the Telegus. In other words, a great many Telegus appropriated the Tamil culture and tended to identify themselves with Tamil society. This trend may be clearly noticed among both the Reddy community and the Naidoo community, who seem to have come largely from the Tamil-speaking regions in India. But those who came from the interior regions of Andhra seem to have a greater awareness of their being Telegu-speaking and it is these groups that are more actively involved in the Andhra Maha Sabhas.

Much of the information which follows on geographical backgrounds of Hindus is gathered from oral interviews with people corroborated by immigration documents. The Tamil group came from places such as Chittoor, Tanjore, north and south Arcott Districts, Tiruvannamalai, Madurai and the greater suburbs of the then Madras port. The Telegus came from Tirupati, Chittoor (both bordering Andhra and Tamil Nadu states), Guntar, present Rayalaseema (Cuddapa) area, the Godavari delta area of Andhra Pradesh, and along the east coast of Andhra Pradesh up to the Orissa border. The Hindi group seems to have come largely from Uttar Pradesh – 61 per cent (Allahabad, Varanasi/Benares, Gorakhpur, Lucknow, Barielly, Kanpur, Agra); Bihar – 31 per cent (Patna, Gaya, Arrah, Monghyr). There were about 6 per cent from Bengal and 2 per cent from central India (Madhya Pradesh). The Gujarati people came largely from two main areas in Gujarat, namely Sarat and Kathiawad in Gujarat on the western coast of India.

Hindus built a wide variety of temples, mainly in the Natal region to begin with. Some of the earliest temples go back to the later part of the nineteenth century. The initial temple activity was mainly among the indentured labourers in Natal and they were predominantly of South Indian background. Two types of temples were built – South Indian style and North Indian style. They are distinguished by the shrine, the tower and the flagpole. The North Indian temples are relatively simple and plain in design, whereas the South Indian ones are elaborately decorated.

There are three types of temples – Śāiva, Vaiṣṇava and Goddess temples. However, often deities belonging to different branches of Hinduism and their devotees are found in the same temple complex. This reflects the inclusive tendency of the early Indian settlers, who attempted to create a unified understanding of Hinduism in the diaspora. One finds that the worship or ritual patters reflect a mixture of brahmanical and non-brahmanical elements. The earlier ritual patterns were mostly non-brahmanical, whereas in the last few decades brahmanical elements have become more pronounced with the arrival of priests from Sri Lanka. Generally, when the term 'brahmin' is used there is no caste reference to it in South Africa. It simply refers to someone who is a priest and may have belonged to any caste or language. Over the years of adaptations, many changes in ritual procedures and rules have occurred. Either due to lack of expertise or due to other social considerations, most rituals have been simplified. The prohibitions against lighting camphor inside the temple, breaking the coconut outside the temple, etc., reflect the adjustments that people had to make in their worship patterns. Religious ceremonies and festival celebrations have even been moved to weekends and the religious calendar has been adjusted accordingly. Observance of Parattasi (fasting during the months of September and October), performance of the Kāvadi (a procession in which devotees carry a yoke when they circumambulate the temple) and firewalking (walking across a fire pit in commemoration of Draupadī's demonstration of her purity) are among the most important rituals for South Indian Hindus. Dīvālī is much more popular among the North Indian Hindus, although it has now been declared a pan-Hindu festival. Among the North Indian Hindus the recitation of praise to Hanumān during the festival of Rāmanavamī is very common.

In the face of the existence of the Arya Samaj, the distinction between the Sanātana Hindus and the Arya Samajists is very important. The Arya Samaj had arrived in South Africa in the early twentieth century. Following Bhai Paramanand in 1905, other Arya Samaj leaders came to South Africa: Swami Shankaranand in 1908 and Pandit Bhavani Dayal Sanyasi in 1912. The Arya Samaj also played a vital role in politics under the leadership of Bhavani Dayal Sanyasi. By this time, Gandhi's Satyagraha movement in South Africa was gaining momentum and the Arya Samaj leaders quite eagerly participated in the Satyagraha struggle along with Gandhi.

In subsequent decades, many other Hindu groups emerged among the South African Hindus. Prominent among them were the Shaiva Siddhanta Sangam, the Ramakrishna Centre, the Divine Life Society, the International Society for Krishna Consciousness (ISKCON), popularly known as the Hare Krishnas, the Sathya Sai group, among many other smaller groups. With the re-establishment of ties with India since 1994, many religious leaders and intellectuals have brought different Hindu influences to South Africa in recent years. For further details of Hindus in South Africa, see Kumar (2000).

East African Hindus

The trade relations between India and East Africa go back a very long way (ninth to tenth centuries). For instance, iron-working in East Africa came through the Indian trade orbit. The trading kingdoms included the Cholas in South East India, Sri Vijaya of Sumatra, Gujaratis of Cambay and Bahmanis of the Deccan from the ninth to the fourteenth centuries. The slave trade also flourished during this period when East African slaves were taken to India and China. Marco Polo refers to ships sailing from the Malabar coast to Madagascar and Zanzibar. During this period, Mombasa was also an important port.

The first colony of Indians in East Africa appeared in Aden and Muscat by the eighteenth century. In 1811 Captain Suree mentions that Hindu traders held the best part of the trade. Kenneth Ingham notes that Sayyid Said of Zanzibar allowed both Hindus and Muslim Banians to trade in East Africa (Ingham 1965: 58). When Sultan Said moved his capital from Muscat to Zanzibar, many Hindu traders followed him. The key post of customs master was in fact held by a Hindu. It was indeed the customs master who was the real power. Hindus were also key advisors to the sultan. The Commercial Treaty between the sultan and the British in 1839 gave Hindu traders greater security and a trading advantage. By the mid-nineteenth century 6,000 Indians were counted in East Africa. With the British gradually gaining the upper hand in trading, the Indians felt better protected under the British consul in Zanzibar. The Indians looked upon the British as their protectors and friends (Beachey 1996: 365). However, in East Africa many Indian traders openly held slaves and often gave up British protection in the interest of slave holding (Beachey 1996: 367).

The arrival of the Punjabis in East Africa was due to their recruitment in 1895 into the East Africa Rifles as part of East African Defence, i.e. the Zanzibar sultans under the protection of the British used the Punjabi regiments to protect their territories. In 1901 the railways brought 2,000 Indians to East Africa. Most of the clerical posts on the railways were provided by Parsees, maintenance services were held by Punjabis, while the ex-indentured Indians took up shopkeeping. From the 1870s onwards there was a large flow of Free Indian immigration to East Africa. By 1911 there were nearly 2,000 Indians in Uganda, 11,000 in the East African Protectorate, and between 4,000 and 10,000 in Zanzibar. Indians in East Africa were mainly involved in commercial activities and did not go into agriculture (Beachey 1996: 370–71). However, Ingham points out that when the commercial-class Indians tried to acquire agricultural lands the government prevented them from doing so, especially in the cooler parts of the Protectorate (Ingham 1965: 211–12). Harlow *et al.* (1965: 214) notes that Indian farming was only on a small scale and not suitable from a commercial point of view.

Under British control of East Africa many Indian associations emerged and played a key role in politics. Two examples were the role played by the Indian Association of Dar es Salaam in the debate on the Unification of East African Territories and the role of the Kampala Indian Association in recognising the British administration in Uganda. By 1912–13 the Indian population surpassed the white community in aggregate wealth and this led to discrimination against Indians by the government. In 1903 Sir Charles Eliot, the new commissioner of East Africa, gave an order to the Land Office not to issue land grants to Indians except small plots (Harlow *et al.* 1965: 271). Low and Smith (1976: 468) point out that, whereas Indians did very well in trading during Omani rule in Zanzibar due to the enlightened policy of Sultan Sayyid Said, under imperial rule Indian trading was controlled. Nevertheless, by the 1920s Asian/Indian business capital and enterprise represented an important factor in the economy of East Africa. There was a steady flow of Indians into East Africa until 1944, when immigration began to be restricted. By 1948 there were 87,000 in Kenya, 35,000 in Uganda, 46,000 in Tanganyika and 16,000 in Zanzibar. By the end of the colonial period the Asian population in East Africa was in the region of 350,000, against a total population of 25 million (Low and Smith 1976: 484).

Through education and economic status, Indians gradually became more and more urbanised. Changes in dress code, food habits and language (fluency in English and Swahili) are very obvious. However, as Indians settled down in their adopted land a greater consciousness of the country of origin began to emerge. This has gradually led to their isolation as a distinct racial and cultural group in East Africa. Low and Smith attribute this to Indians' religious and communal traditions, which have tended to emphasise close-knit communities and not entering into partnerships with other communities in the development of society (Low and Smith 1976: 485). Although in the aftermath of World War II Africans and Asians collaborated in politics with the government of India adopting a pro-African policy, growing African nationalism in the 1950s overshadowed African and Asian collaboration and the future prospects of Asians in East Africa became uncertain. Under the subsequent dictatorial regimes in East Africa, many Indians left and settled in various Western countries. The only country in East Africa that still has a reasonably sized Indian population is Kenya (about 65,000 of whom are Hindus).

In Kenya, the bulk of the Hindu population belongs to the Sanatana Hindu Temple in Nairobi. The other significant groups are Arya Samajists, Brahma Kumaris and the followers of the Swami Narayana sect. There are two Swami Narayana temples in Nairobi; one is older but the other was built recently.

The majority of Hindus are Hindi- or Gujarati-speakers or generally North Indians. They tend to follow Sanskrit-based rituals. There is a Śri Veṅkaṭeśvara temple which caters for the South Indian Hindus. The Hindus in Kenya have strong links with India and its culture. The presence of Hindutva/Rashtriya Swayamsevak Sangh (RSS) in Kenya is quite visible. Some temples are often visited by Hindutva leaders from India. Many Kenyan Hindus have business links with not only India but also Mauritius, South Africa and other diasporas elsewhere. The Hindu Council of Kenya is very well organised and structured, and is a part of the Hindu Council of Africa. The Hindu Council of Kenya has endowed a chair in Hindu studies at the University of Nairobi. The Hindu Council participates in various interfaith conversations with other religious groups and many prominent Hindus are involved in the political life of Kenya.

See also: **Arya Samaj; Brahma Kumaris; Caste; Diaspora; Dīvālī; Divine Life Society; Draupadī; Gandhi, Mohandas Karamchand; Gokhale, Gopal Krishna; Hanumān; Hindutva; International Society for Krishna Consciousness; Madurai; Mandir; Nationalism; Ramakrishna Math and Mission; Rāmanavamī; Rashtriya Swayamsevak Sangh; Sai Baba (as movement); Śaivism; Śaktism; Sanātana Dharma; Sthāpatyaveda; Sri Lanka, Hindus in; Swami Narayana Sampradaya; Utsava; Vaiṣṇavism; Vārāṇasī**

PRATAP KUMAR

Further reading

Beachey, R.W. 1996. *History of East Africa 1592–1902*. London: Tauris Academic Studies, I.B. Tauris Publishers.

Brain, Joy B. n.d. 'Movement of Indians in South Africa: 1860–1911' (unpublished manuscript). Durban: University of Durban-Westville.

Harlow, Vincent, E.M. Chilver and Alison Smith (eds). 1965. *History of East Africa*, vol. 2. Oxford: Clarendon Press.

Henning, C.G. 1993. *The Indentured Indian in Natal 1860–1917*. New Delhi: Promila & Co.

Hofmeyr, J.H. and G.C. Oosthuizen. 1981. *Religion in a South African Indian Community*. (Report No. 2, October 1981.) Durban: Institute for Social and Economic Research, University of Durban-Westville.

Ingham, Kenneth. 1965. [1962] *A History of East Africa*. London: Longmans.

Kumar, P. Pratap. 2000. *Hindus in South Africa: Their Traditions and Beliefs*. Durban: University of Durban-Westville.

Low, D.A. and Alison Smith (eds). 1976. *History of East Africa*, vol. 3. Oxford: Clarendon Press.

Meer, Y.S. 1980. *Documents of Indentured Labour: Natal 1851–1917*. Durban: Institute of Black Research.

Mikula, Paul, Brian Kearney and Rodney Harber. 1982. *Traditional Hindu Temples in South Africa*. Durban: Hindu Temple Publications.

Morris, H.S. 1968. *The Indians in Uganda*. London: Weidenfeld and Nicolson.

Naidoo, T. 1992. *The Arya Samaj Movement in South Africa*. Delhi: Motilal Banarsidass.

Nowbath, R.S. *et al.* (eds). 1960. *The Hindu Heritage in South Africa*. Durban: The South African Hindu Mahasabha.

Oliver, Roland and Gervase Mathew (eds). 1963. *History of East Africa*, vol. 1. Oxford: Clarendon Press.

Pillay, Govindamma. 1991. 'An Investigation into the Caste Attitudes that Prevail amongst Hindus in Durban Metropolitan Area' (unpublished MA thesis). Durban: University of Durban-Westville.

Rocher, H.J.W. 1965. 'A Study of the Theory and Practice of the Hindu Religious Tradition among a Selected Group of Tamil Speaking Hindus in South Africa: A Sociological Approach' (unpublished MA thesis). Pretoria: University of Pretoria.

Swan, M. 1985. *Gandhi: The South African experience*. Johannesburg: Ravan Press.

ĀGAMAS

See: **Sacred Texts**

AGASTYA

A famous sage, associated with southern India, where he migrated from the north. He is credited with the introduction of the Vedic tradition there, and played a crucial role in the formation of Tamil language and culture. Agastya was born, along with Vasiṣṭha, from a pot when the gods Mitra and Varuṇa spilled their seed at the sight of the nymph Urvaśi. He appears in Vedic mythology and a number of ṛgvedic hymns are attributed to him. He plays a great part in the purāṇic and epic traditions, which narrate many legends about him. One of the most famous is his curbing the pride of the Vindhya mountains, an exploit which is reflected in the name Agastya, 'mover of the mountain'. In the *Rāmāyaṇa*, Agastya is described as a friend, advisor and protector of Rāma, who visited him during his exile. He is identified with the star Canopus.

See also: **Itihāsa; Mahābhārata; Mitra; Purāṇas; Rāma; Rāmāyaṇa; Saṃhitā; Varuṇa; Vasiṣṭha; Veda**

A.L. DALLAPICCOLA

Further reading

The myth of the Vindhya Mountains is narrated in the 10th Skanda, ch. 7, of the *Śrīmad Devī Bhāgavata*.

Swami Vijnanananda (trans.). 1986. *The Srimad Devi Bhagawatam*, 3rd edn. New Delhi: Munshiram Manoharlal.

AGNI

'Fire'. The popular Vedic fire-god, son of Dyaus Pitṛ and Pṛthivī, (twin) brother of Indra. Agni represents not only domestic fire but, more importantly, the sacrificial fire of religious ritual. Along with Indra, Agni is revered as an asura-slayer (*Ṛgveda* 6.22.4, 7.13.1). Beside Indra, the deity reveals strong links with Rudra – both figures being known as Kṣetrapati ('lord of the field'). Another figure with whom Agni is identified is Bṛhaspati, the priest of the devas. Both Bṛhaspati and Agni are equated with Mātariśvan ('growing in the mother'), an aquatic lightning figure, who is otherwise understood as the discoverer of Agni. Agni's own watery origins are to be seen in his epithet or alternative name, Apām Napāt ('child of the waters'). An obscure ṛgvedic myth relates how he fled from the gods and hid in the waters until his discovery by Yama-Mātariśvan. With Soma, Agni shares the epithet Tanūnapāt ('son of himself'). In post-Vedic or Epic times, Agni often emerges as the Lokapāla or protector/ruler of the southeast.

See also: **Asuras; Bṛhaspati; Deities; Dyaus Pitṛ; Indra; Pṛthivī; Rudra; Soma; Vedic pantheon; Yama**

MICHAEL YORK

AGNI PURĀṆA

See: **Purāṇas**

AGNIHOTRA

The Agnihotra is one of the main Śrauta rituals described in the Veda, along with other 'yajñas' such as the Agniṣṭoma, Somayajña, Vājapeya, Rājasūya and Aśvamedha. Today, it is perhaps the Vedic ritual with the most pervasive place in everyday Hindu religious life.

It is a daily rite in which oblations to the gods are offered in the ritually established household fires, at dawn and dusk of each day. Into these fires libations largely consisting of milk and water are offered, and these are accompanied by acts of homage to various figures, including deities, the fathers (Pitṛs), the seven seers, Agni, the cow from which the offering was taken, and the son of the sacrificer. The Agnihotra could also be combined with other rites, such as the Agnyupasthāna ceremony of homage to the fires themselves.

The ritual itself is short but complex, and the many phases originally described may signal the integration of a wide range of smaller rites into a single daily act (Heesterman 1985; Minkowski 1991; Staal 1990). Like other Śrauta rituals, it has propitiatory elements, seeking blessings from the gods: rains, cattle, sons, social status, a long life and a future in heaven. Thus the gods are invoked both as the recipients of offerings conveyed to them by Agni and as a divine presence at the sacrifice itself.

In addition to its propitiatory features, the Agnihotra also performs the 'mesocosmic' function of maintaining the social and natural order. Hence certain symbolic aspects of the ritual are seen to ensure the successful passing of the sun through night into each succeeding day (Bodewitz 1976; Witzel 1992, 2003). Other symbolic actions support the flow of fluids essential to the continuance of life, e.g. the heavenly course of the Milky Way, the flow of milk in women and of semen in men. Generally the rites are also seen as integral to the maintenance of the household and all that it signifies in Vedic thought (Keith 1989). The meanings of some actions in the Agnihotra clearly derive from related hymns and stories, but others retain their efficacy where the meaning remains obscure, thus lending the ritual a characteristically multi-vocal character.

As a Śrauta ritual, the Agnihotra is required of all pious householders (Gārhasthya) belonging to the 'twice-born' (dvija) castes. However, the sacrifice as described in the Vedic literature has also been modified into other 'Agnihotras' which vary according to culture and period, accruing new applications, interpretations and spheres of practice. Thus, like the rituals which mark marriage and death, it is a vital modern continuation of Vedic Hinduism.

See also: **Agni; Antyeṣṭi; Caste; Deities; Dvija; Gārhasthya; Pitṛs; Sacred animals; Śrautasūtras; Veda; Vedism; Vivāha; Yajña**

JESSICA FRAZIER

Further reading

Bodewitz, H.W. 1976. *The Daily Morning and Evening Offering (Agnihotra) According to the Brāhmaṇas.* Leiden: Brill.

Heesterman, J.C. 1985. *The Inner Conflict of Tradition: Essays in Indian Ritual, Kingship, and Society.* Chicago, IL: University of Chicago Press.

Keith, A.B. 1989. *The Religion and Philosophy of the Vedas and Upanishads.* New Delhi: Motilal Banarsidass.

Minkowski, Christopher Z. 1991. *Priesthood in Ancient India: A Study of the Maitravaruna Priest.* Vienna: Sammlung De Nobili, Institut für Indologie der Universität Wien.

Staal, F. 1983. *Agni: The Vedic Ritual of the Fire Altar.* Berkeley, CA: University of California Press.

Staal, F. 1990. *Rules without Meaning: Ritual, Mantras, and the Human Sciences.* New York: P. Lang.

Witzel, M. 1992. 'Meaningful Ritual: Structure, Development and Interpretation of the Tantric Agnihotra Ritual of Nepal'. In A.W. van de Hoek, D.H.A. Kolff and M.S. Oort, eds, *Ritual, State and History in South Asia: Essays in Honour of J.C. Heesterman.* Leiden: Brill.

Witzel, M. 2003. *Das alte Indien [Old India].* Munich: C.H. Beck.

AHALYĀ

Ahalyā, a princess of the Puru dynasty, was the wife of the ascetic Gautama. Indra, disguised as Gautama, seduced her while her husband was performing his morning rituals. Gautama cursed both of them: Ahalyā was turned into a stone, and Indra was affected by a skin disease which left marks resembling female genitalia on his body. The later tradition describes these marks as eyes, hence Indra's epithet Sahasrāksa, or 'thousand-eyed'. The story of Ahalyā is narrated in detail in the *Rāmāyaṇa*. During his wanderings, Rāma touched the stone imprisoning Ahalyā with his foot, restored her human form and then reconciled her to Gautama. The unswerving loyalty to her husband makes Ahalyā one of the five exemplary chaste women invoked by Hindu wives in their daily prayers. Her story, illustrating the plight of the chaste wife unjustly accused of adultery by her husband, has been a constant inspiration for writers.

See also: **Indra; Rāma; Rāmāyaṇa; Strīdharma; Tapas**

A.L. DALLAPICCOLA

Further reading

Goldman, Robert P. (trans.). 1984. *The Ramayana of Valmiki*, vol. I, Balakanda. Princeton, NJ: Princeton University Press, 214–16.

AHAṂKĀRA

The term ahaṃkāra, 'individuality', derives from ahaṃ, the nominative singular first-person pronoun 'I', and kāra, 'doing, making' (from the root *kṛ*, 'do, make'). It refers to one's sense of one's own individual identity devoid of any of the content of personality and experience, and hence is often translated as 'ego'. In Sāṃkhya, Ahaṃkāra is the second evolute of unmanifest Prakṛti after Mahat/Buddhi 'intellect'. Both are manifestations of insentient nature, not aspects of a conscious self, yet appear to be conscious due to conjunction with pure consciousness (Puruṣa). According to *Sāṃkhyakārikās* 25, with purity (sattva) dominant, the Ahaṃkāra evolves into mind (Manas), the five senses, and the five organs of action. With dullness (tamas) dominant, it evolves into the five essential elements (tanmātra). In Advaita Vedānta, Ahaṃkāra is the identification of the unbounded self with particular entities through the superimposition of one's body and its characteristics on Brahman and vice versa.

See also: **Advaita; Ātman; Brahman; Brahmaṇ-Ātman; Mahat; Manas; Prakṛti; Puruṣa; Sāṃkhya; Sāṃkhyakārikās**

PETER M. SCHARF

Further reading

Podgorski, Frank R. 1976. *Ahamkara (Self-awareness): Its Dimensions in the Samkhya-Karika and Its Role in Spiritual Liberation.* PhD Diss. Fordham University.

AHIṂSĀ

Ahiṃsā (non-violence) means not killing or injuring, not even wanting to do so. But the word has positive implications as well: benevolence, protection and compassion. This concept became central to the worldview of ascetics (śramaṇas) in approximately the sixth century BCE – perhaps as a rejection of both the endemic warfare of the time, as kingdoms were being established by force in the Gangetic plain, and the brahmanic ritual of animal sacrifice. It was interpreted in various ways by Jains, Buddhists and brāhmaṇa ascetics (the latter's views being elaborated in the *Saṃnyāsa Upaniṣads* and the *Dharmasūtras*).

You can find female forest-dwellers/ascetics in the *Ṛgveda* (Lopāmudrā), the *Upaniṣads* (possibly Gārgī and Maitreyī), the epics (Sāvitrī, Kuntī, Gāndhārī, Sītā and Anasūyā), the *Arthaśāstra* (which mentions brāhmaṇa widows who are ascetics), and Kālidāsa's dramas (the characters of Śakuntalā and Kauśikī). Nonetheless, female asceticism was gradually curtailed. Manu, for instance, says that husbands may choose to bring their wives to the forest in the stage of the life-cycle called vānaprasthya. Eventually, however, total renunciation (saṃnyāsa) was prohibited altogether for Hindu women in most sects (saṃpradāyas).

Because of competition between non-Vedic religions (Jainism and Buddhism) and Vedic ones (brahmanical sects), as well as a perception that asceticism was endangering both the householder orientation and the military, Hindu authorities carefully structured the practice of asceticism as the final two stages of life and therefore after all duties were fulfilled. They did not want asceticism to compete with the legitimate goals (puruṣārthas) of householders such as reproduction and an occupation that upheld society. The virtues of ascetics were extended, however, as ideals to all people under the category sāmānya. As a result, Hindu ethics (dharma) came by the classical period to consist of two types: sāmanya and viśeṣa. Sāmānya, the general or common moral virtues, is also known as sādhāraṇa dharma (the dharma resting on the same support) or sānātana dharma (the eternal dharma, which is universal and unconditional). There are minor variations in ordering the items from one source to another in the list of sāmānya dharmas. According to the *Yogasūtras* 2.20–31, for instance, it includes non-violence, truthfulness, non-stealing, celibacy, renunciation of possessions and self-control.

Kṣatriyas were not allowed to be ascetics because this would have provided an opportunity for them to avoid war and justify doing so by claiming superior spirituality. Other groups of householders (non-ascetics) based their identity on the principle of ahiṃsā (the brāhmaṇa class, for example, and some sectarian groups such as the Vaiṣṇavas). The practice of ahiṃsā by elite castes and sects encouraged its imitation by other upwardly mobile groups. The principle of non-violence thus expanded in Hindu society (although warfare as a kṣatriya enterprise was prevalent).

Ahiṃsā promoted the sanctity of life in Hinduism. This had ethical implications for abortion (which was categorically rejected in the pre-modern period). There were a few exceptions to this protection of life (aside from the role of warriors to protect society). One was self-defence (including abortion to defend mothers whose lives were endangered by their foetuses). Another was capital punishment, whether imposed by the state or by the individual (as a kind of expiation), although that was eventually prohibited after the tenth century. Yet another was self-willed death of various types (to avoid death by the enemy in battle, say, or debilitating illness and old age, or the socially imposed inauspiciousness of widowhood).

In the modern age, Mahatma Gandhi took up the ethical principle of non-violence. He connected ahiṃsā with self-purification, fasting and abstinence (from drugs, drink, tobacco), which correspond to purity (śauca) in some sāmānya lists as well as with non-stealing (asteya), non-possession (aparigraha), and sexual abstinence (brahmacarya) – also sāmānya virtues. But Gandhi also politicised these virtues – especially non-violence as the just means to fight for the just cause of Indian independence.

See also: **Abortion; Arthaśāstra; Blood sacrifice; Brahmacarya; Buddhism, relationship with Hinduism; Dharma; Dharmaśāstras; Dharmasūtras; Gandhi, Mohandas Karamchand; Gārgī; Itihāsa; Jainism, relationship with Hinduism; Kālidāsa; Lopāmudrā; Mahābhārata; Maitreyī; Puruṣārthas; Rāmāyaṇa; Saṃnyāsa; Saṃpradāyas; Sānātana Dharma; Sītā; Śramaṇa Culture; Upaniṣads; Vaiṣṇavism; Vānaprasthya; Widowhood; Yogasūtras**

KATHERINE K. YOUNG

Further reading

Chapple, C.K. 1993. *Nonviolence to Animals, Earth, and Self in Asian Tradition.* Albany, NY: State University of New York Press.

Crawford, S.C. 2003. *Hindu Bioethics for the Twenty-first Century.* Albany, NY: State University of New York Press.

Gandhi, Mahatma. 1978. *Collected Works of Mahatma Gandhi*, vol. 73. Delhi: Government of India: Ministry of Information and Broadcasting.

Iyer, R. (ed.). 1986. *The Moral and Political Writings of Mahatma Gandhi*, vol. 2: *Truth and Non-violence.* Oxford: Clarendon Press.

Janaki, S.S. 1998. *Freedom Fighters and Sanskrit Literature: With Special Reference to Mahatma Gandhi and Subrahmanya Bharati.* New Delhi: Rashtriya Sanskrit Sansthan.

Kotturan, G. 1973. *Ahimsa: Gautama to Gandhi.* New Delhi: Sterling Publishers.

Olivelle, P. 1998. *The Early Upaniṣads.* New York: Oxford University Press.

Tahtinen, U. 1976. *Ahiṃsā: Non-violence in Indian Tradition.* London: Rider.

AIRĀVATA

'Produced from the Ocean'. Airāvata, the four-tusked white elephant, is one of the fourteen jewels which emerged from the churning of the Ocean and Indra's mount (vāhana). He is the king of elephants (*Viṣṇu Purāṇa* 1.22) and the guardian of Svarga (Indra's abode). According to Hindu cosmogony, Brahmā created eight pairs of elephants out of a cosmic egg and Airāvata was the prototype. Male elephants arose from the right part of the eggshell while females arose from the left. The eight couples hold the main and middle cardinal points. Airāvata, mounted by Indra, with his female companion Airavatī, protects the eastern quarter and is alternatively called 'brother of the sun' and 'elephant of the clouds'. His flight is believed to bring clouds and rains and thus fertility. Airāvata is also the name of a demon descended from a mythological serpent (nāga) (*Atharvaveda* 8.10.29).

See also: **Brahmā; Indra; Nāgas; Purāṇas; Sacred animals; Saṃhitā; Vāhanas**

FABRIZIO M. FERRARI

Further reading

Doniger, W. (ed.). 1975. *Hindu Myths: A Sourcebook Translated from the Sanskrit.* Harmondsworth: Penguin.

AITAREYA UPANIṢAD

See: **Upaniṣads**

ALAKṢMĪ

Alakṣmī, also called Jyeṣṭhā, 'The Elder', is Lakṣmī's ugly elder sister. The qualities that Alakṣmī embodies, such as ill fortune, hunger and poverty, are the antithesis of auspiciousness, which Lakṣmī embodies. The *Padma Purāṇa* claims that Alakṣmī, like Lakṣmī, emerged from the ocean of milk when it was churned by the gods and demons, and the gods instructed Alakṣmī to go forth and dwell in the homes of quarrelsome and pernicious persons and to bring such individuals grief and poverty. Alakṣmī is more feared than revered, and Hindu wives are enjoined to propitiate Alakṣmī to ward off in their homes and families the bad fortune she embodies. In North India at the time of Dīvālī women perform a ritual to pave the way for Lakṣmī to enter their homes by driving Alakṣmī away with loud noises, including loud drumming and banging of pots and pans.

See also: **Dīvālī; Lakṣmī, Śrī; Purāṇas**

TRACY PINTCHMAN

Further reading

Leslie, Julia. 1992. 'Śrī and Jyeṣṭhā: Ambivalent Role Models for Women'. In Julia Leslie, ed., *Roles and Rituals for Hindu Women*. Delhi: Motilal Banarsidass.

ALMSGIVING

See: **Dāna**

ALTARS, DOMESTIC

Domestic altars are the focus of daily worship for the majority of Hindus. In each Hindu household there is a space set aside for the family shrine. In smaller houses, a corner of the kitchen (the purest room in the house) is made into a shrine containing small images of one or more gods and goddesses. Most home shrines would include at least one popular pan-Indian deity, such as Śiva, Viṣṇu or a goddess, and perhaps some regional or family deities. A small statue or picture of Gaṇeśa, the elephant-headed deity who is considered the 'Remover of Obstacles', would almost certainly be present at the domestic altar. If space is at a premium the home shrine may simply consist of a picture of the family's chosen deity. In larger, richer houses there may be a separate shrine room containing an elaborate altar decorated with many statues and pictures of a plethora of Hindu deities and even a separate kitchen in which their food is prepared. Many households would see no contradiction in including icons from other religions at the home shrine. As well as the deities, the domestic altar may contain religious artefacts such as sacred coins or pictures of the deities of particular pilgrimage sites that have been collected by the family. These religious souvenirs, especially those that have been blessed, remind the family of their sacred pilgrimage (which might have been a once in a lifetime trip) and are thought to bring continued prosperity. One prized possession on the domestic altar is perhaps a small metal pot containing sacred Gaṅgā (River Ganges) water. A small lamp, either electric or an oil lamp of clay or brass, would be lit every day and the shrine itself would be kept spotless. Incense would also be burnt every day to honour the deities and to keep their environment fragrant.

Worship in the home is an important part of most people's daily religious life. While many people do not visit the temple on a daily basis, some only on special occasions, they would almost certainly offer a brief prayer at their domestic altar. Officially, it is only the twice-born males who are sanctioned to perform pūjā at home. After waking, the senior male in a brāhmaṇa household would take a ritual bath and recite the *Gayatrī mantra*. He would then make an offering of water to the sun before performing pūjā for the household deities. Alongside the offerings of water, flowers, rice, incense and prayer, he might also recite Vedic hymns and enumerate the 1,008 names of the most important chosen deity. Only after the household deities have been honoured would the family take their breakfast, before carrying on with their respective duties.

See also: **Gaṇeśa; Gaṅgā; Gayatrī Mantra; Pūjā; Śiva; Saṃhita; Viṣṇu**

LYNN FOULSTON

ĀḺVĀRS

The religion of the Bhāgavatas or Vaiṣṇavism, after it ceased to be a force in the north after the fall of the Gupta dynasty, spread in the Tamil region through the work of the poet-singers known as Āḻvārs. They were basically devotees of Viṣṇu who went from temple to temple in the then Tamil country and sang the praise of Viṣṇu and spread his worship. They are said to have composed, all together, 4,000 hymns in praise of Viṣṇu. These hymns were later collected and compiled as a single compendium called the *Nālāyira Divya Prabandham*. Yāmuna and, after him, Rāmāṉuja developed the simple teachings of the Āḻvārs by integrating them into the Sanskritic philosophical texts, such as the *Brahmasūtras* (*Vedāntasūtras*), the *Upaniṣads* and the *Bhagavadgītā*. One of the unique things about the south Indian Vaiṣṇavism is its ability to combine the Tamil hymns of the Āḻvārs and the philosophical texts of the Sanskritic tradition. For this reason, the Āḻvārs occupy a significant place in south Indian Vaiṣṇavism. Śrī Vaiṣṇavism, which is the more dominant form of south Indian Vaiṣṇavism, in fact speaks of dual Vedānta (Ubhaya Vedānta), meaning that both the Āḻvār hymns and the Sanskritic Vedānta tradition together form the philosophy of Vaiṣṇavism. The Āḻvārs' hymns are also known as the Tamil Veda (Nammāḻvār).

See also: **Bhagavadgītā; Bhāgavatas; Brahmasūtras; Nammāḻvār; Rāmānuja; Tamil Veda; Upaniṣads; Vaiṣṇavas, Śrī; Vaiṣṇavism; Viṣṇu; Yāmuna**

PRATAP KUMAR

AMARĀVATĪ

The capital city (literally, 'home of the immortals') of the heaven realm presided over by Lord Indra, king of the gods (devas). According to the *Devī Bhāgavata Purāṇa*, it is one of the nine cities (representing the eight ordinal directions, in addition to their central axis) located on the top of the mythical mountain Meru, east of the central city of Manovatī (Lord Brahmā's city). The other cities of the eight lords of the directions (aṣṭadikpālakas) include the southeastern city of Tejovatī (Lord Agni's city), the southern Saṃyamani (Lord Yama's city), the southwestern Kṛṣṇāñjanā (Lord Nirṛti's city), western Śraddhāvatī (Lord Varuṇa's city), northwestern Gandhavatī (Lord Vāyu's city), northern Mahodaya (Lord Kubera's city), and the northeastern Yaśovatī (Lord Śiva's city). Also located in Amarāvatī is the famed 'garden of the gods' known as Nandanavana.

See also: **Agni; Brahmā; Indra; Kubera; Mount Meru; Purāṇas; Śiva; Varuṇa; Vāyu; Yama**

DEVEN M. PATEL

Further reading

Mani, Vettam. 2002. *Purāṇic Encyclopaedia*. Delhi: Motilal Banarsidass.

AMBĀ

See: **Durgā**

AMBEDKAR, BHIMRAO RAM (1891–1956)

Dr Ambedkar, a key figure in the Dalit movement, was born on 14 April 1891 into an 'untouchable' Mahar family in a military camp in central India where his father was working as a teacher. A brilliant student, he continued his studies in Bombay and at Columbia State University, New York. Later he became professor of law, advocate and president of a textile union in Bombay. In 1927 the governor of Bombay nominated him to the Bombay Legislative Council.

The first major protests during which Ambedkar emerged as the leader of the untouchables were organised with the aim of obtaining free access to water resources as well as temples. In the Mahad Satyagraha, a conference of the Depressed Classes held in 1927, Ambedkar demanded the abolition of untouchability and caste. As a result all participants went to the local water tank and drank water in public. When the Mahad Civil Court prohibited them from doing so, the *Manusmṛti*, one of the major Hindu codices that legitimises untouchability, was publicly burnt.

According to Ambedkar, the problem of untouchability could not be resolved through the grace and willingness of the higher Hindu castes. In 1928 he demanded from the colonial Simon Commission political representation for the Depressed Classes. In the Round Table Conference in London, he repeated his demands for separate political representation and became a political adversary of Mohandas Karamchand Gandhi, who considered the four varṇas as the ideal social order. Gandhi was also against the idea of political representation separate from the Hindu community. Finally, Ambedkar and Gandhi accepted the solution of separate seats for the untouchables within the Hindu electorate.

After this forced compromise, the rupture with Hinduism became inevitable. On 13 October 1935, during the Yeola Conference, Ambedkar announced that he would not die a Hindu. He affirmed that social equality could not be attained if the untouchables remained Hindus.

In 1947 Ambedkar was appointed Minister of Law and became president of the Drafting Committee which was in charge of the Constitution. His interest in Buddhism influenced him to such a degree that he proposed the Buddhist wheel as a symbol of the Indian flag and the Aśoka pillar at Sarnath as the national emblem.

The conversion ceremony finally took place on 14 October 1956 at Nagpur. Ambedkar reinterpreted Buddhist tradition in order to preach a modern and rationalist Buddhism based on progressive values such as fraternity, equality and liberty. He considered conversion indispensable to the progress of Indian society and an ideal basis for a civil society. Ambedkar called the converts to follow his example and to administer dīkṣā to others. He died six weeks later, on 6 December 1956. Ambedkar is considered a bodhisattva by some of his followers.

See also: **Buddhism, relationship with Hinduism; Caste; Conversion; Dalits; Dharmaśāstras; Dīkṣā; Gandhi, Mohandas Karamchand; Varṇa**

JOHANNES BELTZ

Further reading

Ambedkar, Bhimrao Ramji. 1970ff. *Dr. Babasaheb Ambedkar Writings and Speeches*, ed. Vasant Moon, Education Department, Government of Maharashtra. Bombay: Government of Maharashtra Press.

Beltz, Johannes. 2005. *Mahar, Buddhist and Dalit. Religious Conversion and Socio-Political Emancipation*. New Delhi: Manohar.

Zelliot, Eleanor. 1992. *From Untouchable to Dalit, Essays on the Ambedkar Movement*. New Delhi: Manohar Publications.

AMERICAS, HINDUS IN

Hinduism in America has been the focus of extensive scholarly research (Coward 2000; Eck 2000, 2001; Fenton 1998; Khandelwal 2002; Kurien 1998, 2005; Mann *et al.* 2001; Mazumdar and Mazumdar 2003, 2005, 2006; Min 2003; Rayaprol 1997; Williams 1998). Here we will describe the religious experience of

Hindus in the United States of America (on which the literature is extensive) and Canada (on which the literature is limited, but will be included wherever possible), focusing on three interrelated facets: domestic practice, temple building and maintaining Hindu identity in the second generation. Through our analysis we hope to understand the transplantation of Hinduism, the use of adaptive strategies to contextualise and make religion relevant in the new setting, to document continuity and change, and finally to describe the difficulties encountered in practising Hinduism in these diasporic settings.

Domestic practice: the importance of home

For Hindus, home is an important site for the practice of religion. Although temples are many and important, Hinduism is not a congregational religion and does not require regular temple visits. In India homes are viewed as sacred after consecration. For Hindus in America, domestic practice of religion has become even more important. Home is considered sacred, its sanctity affirmed and maintained through the creation of ritual spaces, performance of daily and periodic rituals, incorporation of religious art and artefacts into the home, landscaping, and through the maintenance of ritual purity.

Religious spaces

Sacredness is evident in the creation within the home of special religious spaces that facilitate the enactment of religious ritual. Hindu immigrant families take special care to create and maintain these spaces. Primary among them is the pūjā (prayer and worship) area. As in India, so also in the United States and Canada, this is the most sacred space in the Hindu home (Coward 2000; Mazumdar and Mazumdar 1994, 2003). Several considerations are important for selecting the most appropriate space in the immigrant home for this function. Foremost among these are privacy, secluded location and the ability to maintain ritual purity and prevent pollution. Accordingly, care is taken not to locate the pūjā area in close proximity to the entrance or near the major passages of the house. It is usually a location not open to public view and contact. Neither should the pūjā area be located near 'unclean' spaces such as bathrooms, kitchen trash and the kitchen sink (where dirty dishes could be stacked up) (Mazumdar and Mazumdar 2003). Seclusion and privacy facilitate the creation of a quiet contemplative ambiance conducive for pūjā and meditation.

A number of spatial strategies are used to maintain the sacrality of this space. First is strict separation. In some Hindu homes a spare bedroom or study is transformed into a pūjā room (see also Coward 2000). For families who lack a spare room, a common practice is to convert a walk-in closet into a pūjā space. Although small, this allows for the same degree of seclusion, walled enclosure and visual privacy. Others add space, in some instances a room or more, to their existing homes for pūjā. Second, in homes lacking space for expansion, an extra room, a walk-in closet or where space is limited, the pūjā area is located in other sacred spaces, such as the kitchen. A third strategy used is symbolic partitioning. A ritually neutral area such as a study, family room or bedroom is compartmentalised into sacred and neutral domains with the pūjā area in the symbolically defined sacred zone (Mazumdar and Mazumdar 2003). Fourth, when no better space is available, although located in more public spaces in the home, linen or coat closets are sometimes used. Some families make use of symbolic markers, such as coloured lights, a string of mango leaves or the ॐ (Oṃ) sign to indicate that this is not an ordinary closet but a sacred area.

The risk of ritual pollution is minimised if entry to the pūjā area is limited to members of the family and close Hindu friends familiar with Hindu rules, traditions and principles of purity and pollution. This becomes particularly significant in immigrant homes, where visitors may be non-Hindus unaware of polluting influences. An attempt is made not to locate the altar under stairways, as this could be disrespectful because people could be walking above or over deities.

Religious artefacts

Home is also the repository of several sacred artefacts. Foremost among them is the family religious altar (Coward 2000; Mann *et al.* 2001; Mazumdar and Mazumdar 2003; Richardson 1985). It is usually located in the pūjā area, but additional ones can be located outside it. The floor of the home altar is usually covered with beautiful fabric (silk, satin, velvet or cotton) and on it are placed the kuladeva (family deity) and pictures, paintings, mūrtis (figures) of Hindu gods, goddesses, saints, gurus and other divine beings. Altars may also contain books, representations considered sacred, and objects. These include brass and silver lamps, incense stick holders, incense, stone for making fresh sandalwood paste, and brass, stainless steel and silver utensils for offering fruit and water to the deities. A few families go to considerable expense to outfit the altar with beautifully framed pictures, exquisitely carved mūrtis of deities made out of gold, silver or marble, intricate miniature jewellery and clothing for the deities. Some immigrant home shrines are elaborate and ornate, with custom designed and built miniature replica of a temple with a maṇḍapa (platform) and conical roof.

Immigrant families also incorporate religious art into home aesthetics and décor. They thus visually create and articulate a Hindu identity. In some homes, paintings of Hindu avatāras such as Rāma and Kṛṣṇa adorn the walls of living rooms, family rooms, hallways and bedrooms, and in others stone sculpture and bronze statues of Hindu deities such as Śrī-Lakṣmī, Śiva, Gaṇeśa, Sarasvatī, Durgā, Kālī (among others) both decorate and sacralise the home. These could be expensive ornate antique art pieces, treasured family heirlooms handed down from generation to generation, a collection of religious souvenirs and artefacts acquired during pilgrimage to sacred sites in India, or unpretentious yet lively folk art. Sacred symbols, such as the ॐ (Oṃ) sign, are also placed on the front door, and on special days in the Hindu calendar the threshold of the front entrance is ritually sanctified with temporary, decorative rangoli or ālpanā art executed by women of the household.

Religious rituals

Sacredness of the home is established and maintained through the enactment of rituals, which also plays a pivotal role in the transplantation of religion. Rituals in the immigrant household are of two kinds: daily individual rituals and periodic congregational rituals. Daily individual rituals play a significant role in domestic Hinduism. Immigrant families take time every day for bhakti or 'honor, love and devotion' (Eck 1981: 37; see also Buchignani *et al.* 1985: 189). Daily bhakti rituals in the pūjā area involve cleaning the altar, decorating it with fresh flowers, offering prasāda (consecrated food), such as fruits, lighting incense, singing or listening to devotional music (bhajans), praying and meditating (Mazumdar and Mazumdar 2003; Ramaswamy and Ramaswamy 1993).

Although daily rituals continue to be important, immigrant families have made adjustments. First is the contraction of daily rituals. Weekend rituals continue to be lengthy, detailed and more complete, but weekday rituals are shortened. Second is the combination of rituals. In some families, morning and evening rituals are combined into one. Third is temporary suspension of ritual activity during the week and resumption on weekends. This happens most commonly when a family member is travelling or away from home for short periods. Fourth is delegation of ritual responsibility. Elder family members who have disengaged from paid employment and have time are given the task of conducting daily rituals on behalf of the entire family (Mazumdar and Mazumdar 2003). Fifth, the simplification of ritual is evident, in, for example, the reduction of Hindu observance to chanting a guru mantra, also reflecting the vital role of the guru in diaspora (Coward 2000: 163).

The Hindu immigrant home is also the setting for congregational prayers (Buchignani *et al.* 1985: 189). Some families host congregational bhajan sessions (religious music and singing), where devotional songs in praise of Hindu gods and goddesses are sung accompanied by traditional Indian musical instruments, such as harmonium, tabla (drums) and cymbals. Other families sponsor kathā (narrations of religious stories). Through such narrations the history, context and symbolic meaning of myths are clarified and made explicit (Moore and Myerhoff 1977). Collective rituals are held on auspicious occasions, regularly or irregularly as convenient or possible, and for a variety of reasons. Some families host a kathā on a regular basis, such as on every pūrṇimā (full moon), while others hold them when a goal has been accomplished or achieved. They are also held to celebrate significant events, such as before marriage and after the birth of a child. Some congregational meetings are held to mark religious holidays such as Dīvālī and Makara Saṃkrānti, among others. These events express collective sentiments and are important for group solidarity.

A few congregational rituals are hosted for women only. One such event, Karvā Chauth, is an expression of a married woman's loyalty and devotion to her husband. On this day she fasts for the well-being and longevity of her husband. In the evening she invites other Hindu families to her home to celebrate the end of the fast and to participate in a ritual meal together. Families also invite women friends (particularly married ones) periodically to their home to worship female deities and perform rituals that involve only women.

Immigrant families have had to make modifications to the content and nature of collective rituals. Postponement of Hindu ritual celebrations and holidays to weekends or holidays is one form of adjustment. In India, Hindu festivals would be marked by a holiday from work and school, allowing families to celebrate at the auspicious time. However, in the United States this is not the case and therefore the concept of sacred/auspicious time is compromised. Substitution is a second mechanism used. Some items are substituted: for example, instead of clay lamps, candles are used; instead of 'temporary' clay images, 'permanent' silver images are substituted. Instead of narration in Sanskrit or a regional language, kathā is narrated in English, thus making it more understandable and relevant to the immigrant audience. Instead of priests conducting such rituals, knowledgeable non-priests stand in. Rotation is a third technique. Whereas in India every family would try to celebrate major Hindu festivals, abroad families use their friendship networks to celebrate festivals on a rotating basis, thus sharing the work. Mixing is a fourth strategy. The diversity of Hindu practices makes it highly likely that people who hold different beliefs and have variant practices will be invited to attend these congregational events. An attempt is made to accommodate their beliefs and practices, thus leading to mixed services.

Selectivity is a fifth technique. In the United States, Hindu families selectively choose to celebrate a few festivals only.

Ritual purity

Ritual cleanliness, purity and sacredness of the home are maintained through regular sweeping, vacuuming, mopping and dusting. Immigrant families often express dissatisfaction with carpets as floor coverings. Accustomed in India to bare terrazzo or tiled floors which are swept and mopped twice daily, they feel that carpets trap dirt and cannot give the feeling of being thoroughly clean and fresh. Stone and wood are preferred materials because they are easier to clean. Some families have chosen to buy homes with stone or wood floors. Others install new carpets before occupancy. One way of keeping the carpet clean is not allowing footwear, such as shoes that have travelled outside, onto the carpet. Shoes are not worn in the home; family members walk barefoot or wear rubber sandals. These rubber sandals, however, are specifically and exclusively for internal use and are not taken outside. Not allowing shoes onto the carpet serves a dual purpose. Leather is considered to be a 'ritually unclean' material. So keeping footwear off the carpets keeps them clean and restricts the entry of 'polluting' items into the home.

Purity of the home is maintained also through food taboos and non-entry of profane food items into the kitchen. There are three categories of food taboos. First, there are strict vegetarians, for whom all non-vegetarian items are taboo at all times. There are no exceptions to this rule and no compromises are made. No meat, chicken, fish, eggs or items made with any of these are allowed into the kitchen or the home. Children are taught very early to be vegetarians, avoiding school lunches for fear of pollution due to unknowingly consuming taboo ingredients. Second are the no-beef-eaters. These families practise a strict taboo and do not eat, cook or allow beef and beef products into the kitchen. Other non-vegetarian items such as chicken and fish are allowed into the kitchen, though vegetarianism is preferred but not insisted on. Although some kinds of meat are eaten, an attempt is made to observe some meat-free days, by designating certain days of the week as vegetarian only or certain days of the week as meat days and the rest of the week as meatless. In a few of these households food taboos and orthodoxy are increased with the visit of relatives. Third are the non-vegetarians; these are families who eat meat and sometimes even beef outside the home (for example in school, offices, parties, etc.). In many of these cases, the woman maintains a vegetarian diet but allows meat into the kitchen, cooks the non-vegetarian food product, whether it is meat, chicken or seafood, but does not eat it herself.

Landscaping

Landscaping and gardens are also influenced (wherever climatically possible) by Hindu ideals through the careful selection, planting and nurturance of particular plants, trees and flowers. In Hinduism, certain flowers and plants are considered śubha (auspicious) and offered in daily pūjā (prayer); examples of such flowers found in immigrant home gardens are roses, gardenias, marigolds, hibiscus and different varieties of the jasmine family. The plant given the most sacred status in the Hindu home and garden is the tulāsī (holy basil) plant. It is usually located in a pot in the backyard, though some families keep it in the kitchen. Immigrant families go through considerable effort to acquire this plant, either through their network of friends and family or through visits to the local Hindu temple (importing live plants is severely restricted in the USA). Surrounded by familiar trees, plants and flowers, with their fragrance, colour and ambiance, Hindu families are able to recreate and reconnect with landscapes of the past, which in turn facilitates their practice of religion in the present.

Temple building: continuity and change

Hindu temples in Canada and the US are of three kinds: first are the 'authentic' centres (Bhardwaj and Rao 1998; Mazumdar and Mazumdar 2006; Narayanan 1992). These monumental temple projects are begun from scratch using traditional Hindu architectural design, including the maṇḍala plan, the location of the garbhagṛha (the most sacred centre of the temple), gateways and spires. Careful attention is paid to the location. Important in this process is the selection of a ritually auspicious or at least appropriate site, which involves location in close proximity to natural elements such as a mountain, river, lake or ocean (Eck 2000, 2001). Also significant is the performance of rituals at key stages during the temple building process such as at groundbreaking and installation of deities. For this, knowledgeable experts are brought from India, including sthāpatis (temple architects), śilpis (artisans and craftsmen) and purohits (priests), in order to create an authentic centre. The design and building of such places present major challenges because they require collaboration between traditional and local (American or Indo-American) architects, traditional craftsmen and local building construction workers. They also require interpretation and modified application of traditional design principles in the context of local building codes and regulations (Mazumdar and Mazumdar 2006).

The Hindu temples in Malibu, California, Ashland, Massachusetts, and Pittsburgh, Pennsylvania, to name a few, as well as the Ganesh Temple in Toronto, Canada, are examples of 'authentic' centres. In terms of religious tourism they have become pilgrimage sites for the Hindu-American community as well as for visiting relatives from India (Mann *et al.* 2001).

Second are temples that are converted or modified structures using pre-existing buildings (Buchignani *et al.* 1985: 189; Coward 2000; Weightman 1993), such as libraries, retail spaces, office buildings, banks and former churches, among others. In their location, layout, architecture, design and décor, 'authenticity' is neither completely possible nor fully accomplished. In a few cases, the existing structure has been drastically modified to look like a Hindu temple through the incorporation of Hindu architectural elements. In other cases, such temples may not resemble a Hindu temple at all but an attempt is nevertheless made to operate like one through the installation of deities (usually carved in India), the availability of priests (imported from India), the performance of temple rituals (such as daily prayers at auspicious times), the celebration of significant holidays in the Hindu calendar and the provision of services related to life-cycle rites such as birth, marriage and death.

Third, buildings or spaces within are rented and used as temple space. Mostly, these are temporary, until another more suitable location or building can be found or constructed.

In the United States and Canada, temples are important places for performing, continuing and sustaining Hindu religious practices, traditions and rituals. And yet, in predominantly Judeo-Christian America and Canada these are undergoing significant changes, which include the following. First is the increased focus on the congregation, congregational rituals and congregational events (Coward 2000; Ebaugh and Chafetz 2000; Mazumdar and Mazumdar 2006; Yang and Ebaugh 2001). Internet, websites, newsletters, newspapers and brochures are used in attempts to reach the Hindu-American community. Second is the active involvement of the community in temple affairs through participation in temple committees, volunteering, fundraising and outreach programmes (Mazumdar and Mazumdar 2006). Third is the incorporation of religious education through formal classes (such as bāl vihār), lectures on the *Bhagavadgītā* and philosophical discourses either by local gurus or by local or visiting scholars from India (Mazumdar and Mazumdar 2006). Fourth is the introduction of new facilities such as classrooms (for teaching religion, dance, music), libraries, auditoriums (for cultural performances, religious rituals, weddings), kitchens and dining areas (Coward 2000). Fifth is the inclusion of new activities and services, such as the celebration of secular holidays (Mother's Day, Father's Day, Graduation Day), classes on yoga, meditation, music, dance and the sponsoring of health clinics (Bhardwaj and Rao 1998; Mazumdar and Mazumdar 2006; Narayanan 2003).

Religious socialisation: maintaining Hindu identity

Religion is transplanted through socialisation and the teaching and transmission of Hindu beliefs and values to children. Since Hinduism is fundamentally non-congregational, formal religious schools, the equivalent of Christian Sunday schools or Islamic madrassas were not a significant part of religious education. In India, Hindu children learn through interaction with family, extended kin, neighbours and friends who are primarily Hindus. Grandmothers, real and surrogate, narrate stories from Hindu myths; literary writings elaborate on them; plays, musicals, movies and television programmes reinforce religious values and ideas. Hindu immigrant children living in a Judeo-Christian society do not have these facilities and opportunities. Families are nucleated, often living in isolation from other relatives. Friends, peers and neighbours are mostly non-Hindus. Lack of formal knowledge of their own religion leaves children defenceless and vulnerable to curiosity, criticism and even ridicule from peers in schools and colleges.

Insufficient understanding of their faith also leads to boredom with and a lack of interest in their own religion. When participating in religious ritual they do not understand the meaning and context of the ślokas (prayers) or bhajans (devotional music) conducted in Sanskrit. Teaching and keeping the faithful within the fold and not losing the second generation to the proselytising religions dominant in the American religious milieu are seen as important challenges for the Hindu-American community.

Maintaining identity: music and dance

One popular means of teaching Hindu children their religion and culture is classical Indian dance. Religion and dance are intimately connected. Lord Śiva is the King of all dancers (Naṭarāja). Every dance begins with an invocation to Naṭarāja. Several different dance styles and traditions are taught, such as Bharatnātyam, Kucipudi, Kathakali and Odissi, among others. Classes are held in local Hindu temples, community/cultural centres or in dance academies and schools. Through dance lessons, children at times also learn Indian languages. Furthermore, classical Hindu dance is a powerful medium of storytelling, incorporating myths and recounting important sacred events in the Hindu calendar and in the lives of deities and avatāras. Immigrant families hold elaborate and lavish arangetrams (solo debut dance performances) celebrating a significant milestone in a dancer's training. Similarly, learning bhajans (Hindu devotional music) provides an important connection to religion and culture.

Maintaining identity: religious nurture

In order to further reinforce religious values in the lives of their children, Hindu-American families cooperate with other families to provide religious instruction to their children. In some communities with significant Hindu populations bāl vihār classes are sponsored by cultural community centres or by temples. Conversely families get together to host classes in their homes on a rotating basis (Kurien 1998). Each group creates its own curriculum using books, CDs, videos and tapes to cater for the second generation. Although the specific content of the religious instruction varies, the overall focus is on the following: teaching bhajans and ślokas (prayers), including providing English translation for parts incomprehensible to these children; explaining the basic tenets of Hinduism and Hindu values such as the principles of dharma (duty), karma (action and reaction) and saṃsāra (cycle of re-birth), among others; narrating stories and myths from Hindu epics and demonstrating their relevance to the lives and experiences of children growing up in America; explaining the symbolism, significance and meaning underlying pūjā (worship), the different deities, their representations (for example, Lakṣmī represents good fortune, wears red – an auspicious colour – and holds a lotus, a significant flower symbolising Lakṣmī's aquatic origins in her hands); celebrating significant Hindu religious holidays, such as Dīvālī and Holī with children and teaching them the significance and meaning of these holidays.

Maintaining identity: Hindu clubs and camps

In addition to parental teaching, Hindu children born and raised in America have taken specific steps to preserve and maintain their Hindu identity through the formation of Hindu clubs on a few high school and college campuses (Coward 2000). For example, several college campuses have formed local chapters of the Hindu Student Council (Kurien 2005). Students maintain websites, publish newsletters and sponsor religious and secular events. Club activities include performing pūjā, sponsoring guest speakers to lecture on Hinduism, celebrating Hindu holidays, visiting local temples, organising retreats and camps for Hindu-American students, as well as hosting sports events, talent shows and banquets.

Other mechanisms have also helped in the preservation of religion. One is the presence of knowledgeable elders. These are 'transnational' elders (Treas and Mazumdar 2004) who move back and forth between two worlds – India and North America – providing a continuous link between the native and the transplanted community of believers. Their experiential and ritual knowledge makes them excellent storytellers and informal teachers helping in the recitation, translation and transmission of prayers, which are particularly useful for the second generation. Also important is the contact with the native community in India. Through visits to India, to temples, pilgrimage sites, shrines and other sacred spaces, children get first-hand experience of their religious roots. Whether it is bathing in the sacred Gaṅgā at Benares, praying in a Kālī temple at Kālighāt or Dakṣineśvara, or saying prayers in front of the family altar in one's ancestral home in India, religious sightseeing provides memorable experiences and models and helps in the continuance of religion. Additionally, Coward (2000) describes the important role played by the guru in the lives of Hindu Canadians. The presence of enclaves such as Little India in major metropolitan areas (New York and Los Angeles) has also facilitated the preservation of religion. Businesses, stores and institutions cater to a religious clientèle, marketing artefacts such as home shrines, altars, religious icons and statues; and ritual artefacts such as brass and sliver lamps incense, incense stick holders, CDs of prayers and music, religious books and writings (Mazumdar and Mazumdar 2005). Another mechanism, the incorporation of Christian holidays into the Hindu calendar, has, interestingly enough, led to the preservation of the Hindu religion. Some of the secular aspects of Christmas, such as sending greeting cards, setting up Christmas trees and exchanging gifts, are incorporated so that Hindu-American children do not feel left out of Christian celebrations (Gerson 1969). Since Christmas is a national holiday in America, some Hindu families take the opportunity to go to temple. The absorptive, syncretic quality of Hinduism has made this possible for centuries (Singer 1972). Hindus have adopted prophets from other religions (Gautama Buddha and Jesus Christ) into their own pantheon, giving them the exalted status of avatāras (incarnation of Hindu gods, most notably Viṣṇu). Through incorporation and inclusion, Hindu families have been able to reduce the threat of conversion presented by the proselytising religions. These are areas for possible future research and scholarly writing.

Difficulties in practising Hinduism in the diaspora

In the practice of their religion in America, Hindus encounter a number of difficulties. Among these are the following. When their numbers are small, the inability to form a community or raise funds disallows the building of temples of their choosing. Initially, domestic practice substitutes and takes on greater importance. Due to lack of temples children do not have visible models to learn from by seeing and doing. Using rented commercial, educational, entertainment or public buildings enables some practices but disables others. State and local regulations prevent some activities, such as lighting a fire, which requires modifications in prayers and rituals. The tremendous variety in beliefs and practices in Hinduism also leads to problems as, when numbers of followers of one's own belief are insufficient, temple building sometimes necessitates joining forces with and catering to a plurality of groups. For example, many Hindu temples in the US and Canada have taken the uncommon step of including shrines to Viṣṇu, Śiva and other deities to meet the needs of different devotees (see also Coward 2000; Eck 2000). Temples are few, especially large ones offering a full range of services. Not having temples in close proximity restricts those living far away to attending only on weekends or holidays. Many have to make do or attend temples with unfamiliar practices. Even when a community has been formed and sufficient resources are available through pooling, temple building encounters problems with planning approvals and resistance from city dwellers, who, lacking knowledge, are suspicious.

Beyond these problems in the establishment of religion there are other difficulties facing practice. Holidays usually are not attuned to the Hindu calendar, which leads to an inability to follow sacred and auspicious times and compromises in that regard. Explaining the requirements of special events, such as prayers for deceased relatives, and meeting them is even harder. In Canada, as in the United States, many Hindus have had to adjust to death in a hospital, and rely on funeral directors and electric cremation (Coward 2000: 158 ff.). For strict vegetarians, finding uncontaminated food is an arduous job (Mazumdar and Mazumdar 2006). These too are good subjects for further research.

See also: **Altars, domestic; Avatāra; Bhagavadgītā; Bhajan; Bhakti (as Path); Books, comics, newspapers and magazines;**

Calendar; Dance; Deities; Dharma; Diaspora; Dīvālī; Durgā; Fasting; Food; Gaṇeśa; Gaṅgā; Guru; Holī; Image worship; Images and iconography; Internet; Itihāsa; Kālī and Caṇḍī; Karma; Kṛṣṇa; Kuladevatā; Lakṣmī, Śrī; Languages; Makara Saṃkrānti; Mandir; Meditation; Music; Myth; Oṃ; Pūjā; Pativratā and Patiparameśvara; Purity and pollution, ritual; Purohita; Rāma; Religious nurture; Sacred geography; Saṃsāra; Saṃskāra; Sarasvatī; Śiva; Sound Recordings; Sthāpatyaveda; Television and radio; Temple worship; Tīrthayātrā; Tulāsī Utsava; Vārāṇasī; Viṣṇu; Vrata; Yoga

SHAMPA MAZUMDAR AND
SANJOY MAZUMDAR

Further reading

Bhardwaj, S.M. and M.N. Rao. 1998. 'The Temple as Symbol of Hindu Identity in America?' *Journal of Cultural Geography*, 17(2) (Spring–Summer): 125–43.

Buchignani, N., D.M. Indra and R. Srivastiva. 1985. *Continuous Journey: A Social History of South Asians in Canada*. Toronto: McClelland and Stewart Ltd and Ministry of Supply and Services.

Coward, H. 2000. 'Hinduism in Canada'. In H. Coward, J.R. Hinnells and R.B. Williams, eds, *The South Asian Religions in Diaspora in Britain, Canada, and the United States*. Albany, NY: State University of New York Press, 151–72.

Ebaugh, H.R. and J.S. Chafetz (eds). 2000. *Religion and the New Immigrants: Continuities and Adaptations in Immigrant Congregations*. Walnut Creek, CA: Alta Mira Press.

Eck, D.L. 1981. *Darsan: Seeing the Divine Image in India*. Chambersburg, PA: Anima Books.

Eck, D.L. 2000. 'Negotiating Hindu Identities in America'. In H. Coward, J.R. Hinnells and R.B. Williams, eds, *The South Asian Religions in Diaspora in Britain, Canada, and the United States*. Albany, NY: State University of New York Press, 219–37.

Eck, D.L. 2001. *A New Religious America: How a 'Christian country' Has Now Become the World's Most Religiously Diverse Nation*. San Francisco, CA: Harper San Francisco.

Fenton, J.Y. 1988. *Transplanting Religious Traditions: Asian Indians in America*. New York: Praeger.

Gerson, W. 1969. 'Jews at Christmas Time: Role Strain and Strain Reducing Mechanisms'. In W. Gerson, ed., *Social Problems in a Changing World*. New York: Crowell, 65–76.

Khandelwal, M.S. 2002. *Becoming American, Being Indian: An Immigrant Community in New York City*. Ithaca, NY: Cornell University Press.

Kurien, P.A. 1998. 'Becoming American by Becoming Hindu: Indian Americans Take Their Place at the Multicultural Table'. In S. Warner and J. Wittner, eds, *Gatherings in Diaspora: Religious Communities and the New Immigration*. Philadelphia, PA: Temple University Press, 37–70.

Kurien, P.A. 2005. 'Being Young, Brown and Hindu: Identity Struggles of Second Generation Indian Americans'. *Journal of Contemporary Ethnography*, 34(4): 434–69.

Mann, S., D. Numrich and B. Williams. 2001. *Buddhists, Hindus and Sikhs in America*. New York: Oxford University Press.

Mazumdar, S. and S. Mazumdar. 1994. 'Of Gods and Homes: Sacred Space in the Hindu House'. *Environments* 22(2): 41–49.

Mazumdar, S. and S. Mazumdar. 2003. 'Creating the Sacred: Altars in the Hindu American Home'. In J.N. Iwamura and P. Spickard, eds, *Revealing the Sacred in Asian and Pacific America*. New York: Routledge, 143–57.

Mazumdar, S. and S. Mazumdar. 2005. 'How Organizations Interface with Religion: A Typology'. *Journal of Management, Spirituality, and Religion*, 2(2): 199–220.

Mazumdar, S. and S. Mazumdar. 2006. 'Hindu Temple Building in Southern California: A Study of Immigrant Religion'. *Journal of Ritual Studies*, 20(2).

Min, P.G. 2003. 'Immigrants' Religion and Ethnicity: A Comparison of Korean Christian and Indian Hindu Immigrants'. In J.N. Iwamura and P. Spickard, eds, *Revealing the Sacred in Asian and Pacific America*. New York: Routledge, 125–41.

Moore, S.F. and B.G. Myerhoff. 1977. 'Secular Ritual: Forms and Meanings'. In S.F. Moore and B.G. Myerhoff, eds, *Secular*

Ritual. Assen, the Netherlands: Van Gorcum, 3–24.

Narayanan, V. 1992. 'Creating the South Indian "Hindu" Experience in the United States'. In R.B. Williams, ed., *A Sacred Thread: Modern Transmission of Hindu Traditions in India and Abroad.* Chambersburg, PA: Anima, 147–78.

Narayanan, V. 2003. 'Embodied Cosmologies: Sights of Piety, Sites of Power'. *Journal of the American Academy of Religion* 71(3): 495–520.

Ramaswamy, S. and S. Ramaswamy. 1993. *Vedic Heritage.* Saylorsburg, PA: Arsha Vidya Gurukulam.

Rayaprol, A. 1997. *Negotiating Identities: Women in the Indian Diaspora.* Delhi: Oxford University Press.

Richardson, E.A. 1985. *East Comes West: Asian Religions and Cultures in North America.* New York: Pilgrim Press.

Singer, M.B. 1972. *When a Great Tradition Modernizes: An Anthropological Approach to Indian Civilization.* New York: Praeger.

Treas, J. and S. Mazumdar. 2004. 'Kinkeeping and Caregiving: Contributions of Older People in Immigrant Families'. *Journal of Comparative Family Studies,* 35(1): 105–22.

Weightman, B.A. 1993. 'Changing Religious Landscapes in Los Angeles'. *Journal of Cultural Geography,* 14 (Fall–Winter): 1–20.

Williams, R.B. 1998. *Religions of Immigrants from India and Pakistan: New Threads in the American Tapestry.* Cambridge, MA: Cambridge University Press.

Yang, F. and H.R. Ebaugh. 2001. 'Transformations in New Immigrant Religions and Their Global Implications'. *American Sociological Review* 66(2): 269–88.

ANANDA MARG

The Ananda Marg Yoga Society was founded in 1955 in India by Prabhat Ranjan Sarkar, aka Shrii Anandamurti (1921–90). 'Anandamurti' is translated as 'one upon seeing him falls into bliss': he is regarded as a miracle worker and god incarnate. Anandamurti established two monastic orders: the first monk was initiated in 1962, and an order of nuns was established in 1966.

The society teaches a method of meditation, to be practised twice daily, leading jointly to individual salvation and radical social reform. Anandamurti taught a form of tantric yoga, including Aṣṭāṅga Yoga. The latter consisted of two stages: yama and niyama. Yama is said to mean 'that which controls', and both yama and niyama entail control of one's mind and behaviour.

The organisation emphasises seva (service) in conjunction with spiritual practice. In 1965 AMURT (Ananda Marg Universal Relief Team) was founded, initially to assist flood victims, but it subsequently developed a wider social programme, advocating cooperative development between citizens and government. This became part of the society's Education Relief and Welfare Section (ERAWS), which was set up in 1967, and subsequently incorporated the Ananda Marg Universal Relief Team Ladies (AMURTEL) in 1977. AMURTEL aimed at providing healthcare for pregnant and nursing mothers, home employment for women, and the setting up of refugee camps and the provision of aid.

Ananda Marg's social programme is accomplished through PROUT (Progressive Utilisation Theory), which aims to achieve a world government, with a universal language and world army. PROUT teaches human rights and campaigns for integrity in governmental office.

The Indian government regarded Anandamurti as subversive, and in 1971 Sarkar was arrested on a charge of murder, subsequently reduced to incitement to murder. He was condemned to life imprisonment but released in 1978 after a retrial in which he was found not guilty.

See also: **Aṣṭāṅga Yoga; Sarkar, Prabhat Ranjan; Seva; Tantric Yoga**

GEORGE CHRYSSIDES

Further reading

Ananda Marga. 1981. *The Spiritual Philosophy of Shrii Shrii Anandamurti.* Denver, CO: Ananda Marga Publications.

Inayatullah, Sohail. 2002. *Understanding Sarkar: The Indian Episteme, Macrohistory, and Transformative Knowledge*. Leiden: Brill.

ANANDAMAYI MA (b. 1896)

Anandamayi Ma was a Bengali Hindu saint or siddha, born in 1896. As a child, she fell into trances, and people could not tell if she was subject to madness or religious visions. As she grew older, these spontaneous ecstatic states began to be noticed by others, especially at kirtans where people would gather to worship and sing hymns. She was married, but it was a celibate marriage, and her husband later became her disciple.

She never had a guru or belonged to a specific lineage or belief system, yet by the end of her life in 1981 she had hundreds of thousands of followers worldwide. She became known for ecstatic phenomena during her trance states: her body would change size and colour, she would stretch and shrink, roll up into a ball, leap wildly and then appear still as a statue, rolling rapidly on the ground in all directions. Her hair would stand on end, and she would speak in unknown languages. She spent many years as an ascetic (saṃnyāsa), wandering and fasting, with matted hair. She attracted disciples as she travelled, who believed that she spoke with gods and goddesses, that she had supernatural powers (siddhis) and could perform miraculous cures and know their deepest thoughts They called her a goddess and avatāra, but she insisted that she had no identity – that there were trances and states of possession, but she did not identify with any of them. She was the same as she had been at birth, and the rituals she performed were for the sake of her disciples. She was a Hindu holy woman without a formal tradition, whose spiritual status was based almost entirely upon her ecstatic states.

See also: **Avatāra; Guru; Kīrtaṇ(a); Possession; Saṃnyāsa; Saṃpradāya; Siddha**

June McDaniel

Further reading

Bhaiji. 1972. *Mother as Revealed to Me*. Benares: Shree Shree Ma Anandamayee Charitable Society.

Lipski, Alexander. 1977. *The Life and Teaching of Sri Anandamayi Ma*. Delhi: Motilal Banarsidass.

McDaniel, June. 1989. *The Madness of the Saints: Ecstatic Religion in Bengal*. Chicago, IL: University of Chicago Press.

ANANTA

See: **Śeṣa**

ANASŪYĀ

The wife of the sage Atri, one of the seven great sages of Hindu mythology, Anasūyā is renowned for her chastity. She is associated with the birth of Dattātreya, the combined form of Brahmā, Viṣṇu and Śiva. The *Mārkaṇḍeya Purāṇa* recounts that Anasūyā requested that the three gods would become a son to her as the reward for persuading the virtuous wife of a brāhmaṇa to allow the sun to rise in the sky. The brāhmaṇa's wife had been preventing the dawn in order to protect her husband, who was predicted to die that day. A more popular version of the story states that the three goddesses, Sarasvatī, Lakṣmī and Pārvatī were jealous of Anasūyā's reputation for chastity and sent the three gods to seduce her at her husband's hermitage during his absence. The gods demanded that it was a special condition that they could not receive offerings from a clothed person. Anasūyā transformed the gods into newborn babies before they could see her naked body and then suckled them in turn.

See also: **Atri; Brahmā; Brāhmaṇa; Dattātreya; Lakṣmī; Pārvatī; Purāṇas; Sarasvatī; Śiva; Viṣṇu**

Ron Geaves

Further reading

www.suite101.com/article.cfm/mythology_from_India/74280 (last accessed 2 November 2005).
www.avatara.org/dattatreya/story.html (last accessed 2 November 2005).

AṄGIRAS

One of the seven ṛṣis to whom many of the hymns of the Veda are addressed, also regarded as a prajāpati or 'Lord of Creatures', one of the ten progenitors of the human race. He is usually regarded as the father of Bṛhaspati, the sage who became the preceptor of the gods. Aṅgiras is associated with the fire worship of Agni, to the degree that the name is often used as a epithet of Agni or even given to the father of the fire god. In such associations, he is perceived to be the first fire sacrificer and initiator of the sacred ritual to others. As a teacher of brahmavidyā, or sacred knowledge, Aṅgiras and his descendants are associated with light, thus his identification with the planet Jupiter. In later post-Vedic mythology he is regarded as a lawgiver and an astronomer. Interestingly his offspring are regarded as kṣatriyas by birth but brāhmaṇas by vocation, and the Aṅgirasas, as they are known, may have been founders of a school of warrior priests.

See also: **Agni; Brāhmaṇas; Bṛhaspati; Prajāpati; Ṛṣi; Varṇa**

RON GEAVES

Further reading

Stutley, Margaret and James Stutley (eds). 1977. *A Dictionary of Hinduism: Its Mythology, Folklore and Development 1500 BC–AD 1500*. London: Routledge and Kegan Paul.

AṄKĀḶAĪŚVARĪ

Aṅkāḷaīśvarī is popular in Tamil Nadu, where she was described by temple informants as a benign form of Pārvatī. However, according to the *Tamil Lexicon*, the goddess Aṅkāḷaīśvarī, Aṅkāḷaīcuvarī or Āṅkalammaṉ, as she is commonly known, is described as an incarnation of Kālī. Her dual personality is also evident in the essentially benign iconography of this goddess coupled with her close proximity to blood sacrifice and cremation-ground rituals during the biannual Mahā-Śivarātri festival held at her temple. Aṅkāḷaīśvarī is seated with four arms. Her upper right hand holds a ḍamaru, a drum surrounded by a snake. In her lower right is a triśūla (trident), while her upper left holds a snake and her lower left holds the ambiguous small pot of kumkum (red paste), or originally, most likely, a kapāla or (skull).

See also: **Blood sacrifice; Kālī and Caṇḍī; Pārvatī**

LYNN FOULSTON

Further reading

Foulston, Lynn. 2002. *At the Feet of the Goddess: The Divine Feminine in Local Hindu Religion*. Brighton and Portland, OR: Sussex Academic Press.
Meyer, E. 1986. *Aṅkāḷaparamē cuvari: A Goddess of Tamil Nadu, Her Myths and Cult*. Stuttgart: Steiner Verlag Wiesbaden GMBH.

ANNAPRĀŚANA

One of the Hindu childhood saṃskāras or rites of passage, the annaprāśana or the first feeding of cooked food is performed after five to seven months of maternal lactation, or at the time the child's teeth first appear. Generally the descriptions are brief. The primary purpose appears to be to introduce the child to the tastes of solid food. Thus, with recitation of Vedic mantras to the 'Lord of Food' (annapati, *Ṛgveda* 4.12.4–5) and to Agni, giver of long life and splendor (*Ṛgveda* 9.66.19), the father prepares and feeds the child a variety of foods, including meat (goat or partridge – this is rarely done today), fish (also rarely given today) and boiled rice (often cooked in milk or mixed with yogurt, honey and ghee). The mother should eat what is left over. Some authorities recommend fire offerings (homa), gifts to brāhmaṇas and additional benedictory mantra recitation.

See also: **Agni; Agnihotra; Brāhmaṇas; Mantras; Saṃhita; Saṃskāras**

FREDERICK M. SMITH

Further reading

Kane, P.V. 1974. *History of Dharmaśāstra*, vol. 2, pt 1, 2nd edn. Poona: Bhandarkar Oriental Research Institute.

Pandey, R.J. 1969. *Hindu Saṃskāras*. Delhi: Motilal Banardsidass, 90–93.

ANNAPŪRṆĀ

The name of this goddess, after whom the famous mountain is named, means 'full of food' and she represents the aspect of Mahādevī associated with the provision of nourishment by a bountiful and fertile earth. In this capacity, she can be compared with goddesses such as Śrī Lakṣmī who also bestow this-worldly benefits such as prosperity and success. Her iconography reflects her role as provider of food since she is portrayed with a spoon and a cooking pot. Her autumn and spring festivals also reflect her role; in Vārāṇasī the former involves the creation of a mountain of food and the latter the decoration of her image and the temple with green rice sprouts (Eck 1982: 163–64).

See also: **Food; Lakṣmī, Śrī; Mahādevī; Sacred geography; Utsava; Vārāṇasī**

DENISE CUSH AND CATHERINE ROBINSON

Further reading

Eck, D.L. 1982. *Banaras, City of Light*. New York: Alfred A. Knopf.

Kinsley, D. 1986. *Hindu Goddesses: Visions of the Divine Feminine in the Hindu Religious Tradition*. Berkeley, CA: University of California Press.

ANQUETIL-DUPERRON, ABRAHAM-HYACINTHE (1731–1805)

French Orientalist, who studied theology and Oriental languages at the Sorbonne and also at French Jansenist seminaries in Holland. After finding a copy in Paris of an undeciphered Zoroastrian manuscript, Anquetil decided to travel to India to learn the script and language of the text. The result, after six years in India, was his translation of the *Avesta*, published in 1771. While Anquetil did not succeed in his further ambition to learn Sanskrit and to obtain copies of the Veda, his account of his travels in India, prefixed to his translation of the *Avesta*, included many observations on Hindu practices and sacred places, a critique of earlier European accounts of Hinduism and reflections on the best method for studying Indian religions. He did manage to obtain a Persian translation of some *Upaniṣads*, which, in his Latin translation (1801–2), formed the basis of Schopenhauer's knowledge of Indian thought.

See also: **Hinduism, history of scholarship; Schopenhauer, Arthur; Upaniṣads; Veda**

WILL SWEETMAN

Further reading

Anquetil-Duperron, A.-H. 1801–2. *Oupnek'hat*. Paris: Argentorati [Strasbourg: Typis et impensis fratrum Levrault].

Kieffer, J.-L. 1983. *Anquetil-Duperron: L'Inde en France au XVIIIe siècle* [Anquetil-Duperron: India in France in the 18th century]. Paris: Société d'Edition les Belles Lettres.

ANTAḤKARAṆA

The term antaḥkaraṇa, 'internal organ' is a compound formed from antar, 'internal', and karaṇa, 'means of doing, instrument' (from the root kṛ, 'do, make').

According to the *Sāṃkhyakārikās* of Īśvarakṛṣṇa, the internal organ is threefold, consisting of the three internal organs that are the first evolutes of unmanifest Prakṛti in the individual personality: intellect (buddhi), individuality (ahaṃkāra), and mind (manas). From ahaṃkāra with purity (sattva) dominant, evolve, in addition to mind, ten external organs: the five senses and the five organs of action (speech, hands, feet, the organ of generation and the organ of elimination). The internal organ by itself can provide experience of objects in the past, present and future, through memory, thought and imagination, and, in conjunction with an external sense, provides experience in the present. In conjunction with an external organ of action, it formulates the resolution or intention which the external organ carries out.

See also: **Ahaṃkāra; Īśvarakṛṣṇa; Mahat; Manas; Prakṛti; Sāṃkhyakārikās**

PETER M. SCHARF

Further reading

Larson, Gerald James and Ram Shankar Bhattacharya (eds). 1987. 'Sāṃkhya: A Dualist Tradition in Indian Philosophy'. *Encyclopedia of Indian Philosophies*, vol. IV. Princeton, NJ: Princeton University Press; Delhi: Motilal Banarsidass, 621 *sub voce*.

ĀṆṬĀḶ

Āṇṭāḷ is one of the great female mystical poets of the Tamil Vaiṣṇava tradition. She lived in the ninth century, but, as is often the case, her biography is obscured in hagiographical accounts of her actions. Tradition usually affirms that she was found under a plant by the foremost of the Ālvārs, the Brāhmaṇa, Viṣṇucitta.

Her biography informs us that she was offered in marriage to the temple image of Viṣṇu but little is known about this practice in this period. As an adopted daughter of Brāhmaṇa parents, her love for the god may have influenced their decision. It is said that during the marriage ritual in the temple she merged into the image and disappeared. A basic similarity between this narrative and that of Mīrābāī, the North Indian devotee of Kṛṣṇa, can be noted.

Two poems are assigned to her in the canon of Ālvār poetry and in the longer of these, the *Nacchiyar Tirumoli*, a poem of 143 stanzas, she describes the marriage arrangement and the apparition of Viṣṇu coming to claim his bride. Although both poems describe the yearning of Āṇṭāḷ to reach Kṛṣṇa, it is the shorter poem, the *Tiruppavai*, around thirty stanzas, for which she remains well known and loved by Tamils, both the scholarly community and the rural populations. During the month of Marghasirsha, renditions of the poem and religious discourses on its meaning take place in Tamil, Telegu, Kannada and even Hindi in thousands of location across South India. It is said that until recently in South Indian Vaiṣṇava communities, families would not have welcomed brides who could not recite the *Tiruppavai*.

See also: **Ālvārs; Kṛṣṇa; Mīrābāī; Vaiṣṇavism; Viṣṇu**

RON GEAVES

Further reading

Ramanujam, Vimala and M.N. Parthasarathy (eds). 1985. *Sri Andal: Her Contribution to Literature, Philosophy, Religion and Art*. Madras: Sri Ramanuja Vedanta Centre.

ANTYEṢṬI

The antyeṣṭi, the final saṃskāra or rite of passage, is the funeral ceremony as described in the Vedic prescriptive literature. The word means 'the sacrifice' (iṣṭi) at 'the end' (antya), and prepares the embodied being for its journey to Yamaloka, the realm of the dead. Though these rites are to be performed for all, the full rites were performed only for men of the upper three varṇas, brāhmaṇas, kṣatriyas, and vaiśyas. They were performed without mantras for śūdras and women. More extreme exceptions were: young children and unmarried girls, who were often immersed directly in a river without other accompanying rites; renunciants, who were often buried, leaving their purified bodies intact; those who had committed suicide or died an unnatural death; or those who had died away from home, in which case a grass effigy was ritually cremated. The main texts that initially described these are the *Pitṛmedhasūtras* and *Gṛhyasūtras*. Eventually, they found a place in different *smṛti* texts, including compendious dharma texts of the late first millennium and early second millennium CE. The variations in the practices are enormous, betraying differences according to caste, region, religious sect and time period.

When death is drawing near, the individual is placed with the head to the south, the direction of Yama. Mantras are recited and, in modern times at least, water in which tulāsī leaves have been soaked is poured into the individual's mouth. After death, the body is tied to a bamboo litter with the head to the south. The eldest son (assuming the person is elderly) then bathes the body, shaves the head, wraps the body with a new white cloth and covers it with flowers. Pallbearers then carry the litter to the cremation ground (śmaśāna), which is ideally located on the banks of a river, chanting 'Rām Rām satya haiṃ' (at least in Hindi). The early texts prescribe the sacrifice of a bull or goat. This is no longer practised, but one is presented (if possible) to the officiating priest. A suitable place in the cremation ground is then selected for the funeral pyre. After the pyre is prepared, the body is placed on it with the head towards the south. The texts prescribe the kinds of wood to be used, the size of the pyre and other details. It is important to note that electric crematoria are now a regular feature of urban cremation grounds.

The early texts prescribe that the wife of a deceased husband lay down momentarily to his left on the pyre, after which she stepped away accompanied by her son. This is not performed at all today. After the fire is ignited the son circumambulates the pyre three times, sprinkling water on it. In certain cases the son takes a small log or a pair of fire-tongs and strikes the skull, uttering the mantra 'phaṭ!' that allows the spirit (jīva) to escape. After the body is completely incinerated the family members return home. At this time a period of impurity (aśauca) begins, which lasts until the tenth day. During that time of grieving food is not to be cooked at home. After three days the bones are collected (asthisamcaya) and taken to a sacred place, such as the Ganges, for disposal. For eleven days after death, food offerings (piṇḍadāna) are given to the deceased. These provide the spirit with the material for a new spiritual body with which it then passes into the new state. Ritually, the deceased is transformed from a preta or wandering spirit to a pitṛ or deceased ancestor worthy of further regular offerings of śrāddha.

See also: **Brāhmaṇa; Caste; Dharmaśāstras; Jīva; Mantra; Pitṛs; Pradakṣiṇa; Pretas; Sacred Texts; Saṃnyāsa; Saṃskāras; Śrāddha (rites to deceased ancestors); Varṇa; Women's rites; Yama**

FREDERICK M. SMITH

Further reading

Kane, P.V. 1974. *History of Dharmaśāstra*, vol. 4, 2nd edn. Poona: Bhandarkar Oriental Research Institute, 179–333.

Pandey, R.J. 1969. *Hindu Saṃskāras*. Delhi: Motilal Banarsidass, 234–74.

APASMĀRA

Apasmāra (literally, 'forgetting') is the name of the demonic being identified in Hindu mythology with epilepsy. This terminology postdates that of the Gṛhyasūtras, which use the term śva-graha ('seizure by the dog') for this medical condition. In its account of the birth of the child-god Skanda, the *Mahābhārata* (3.219.24–25) describes a demonic Seizer (graha) named Skanda-Apasmāra, who, issuing from Skanda's body, falls to the ground hungry and unconscious. Treatments for epilepsy, which is considered to be possession by Apasmāra, are found in the 'demonology' (bhūta vidyā) sections of such Āyurvedic works as the *Suśrūta Saṃhitā*; and the Apasmāras are mentioned as a class of child-possessing demons in the *Bhāgavata Purāṇa* myth of Kṛṣṇa's slaying of Pūtanā. Apasmāra also figures in Śaiva iconography. In numerous representations of Śiva, the great god's right foot is planted on Apasmāra, who is represented as a boy or dwarf, writhing on his stomach.

See also: **Āyurveda; Gṛhyasūtras; Kṛṣṇa; Mahābhārata; Purāṇas; Pūtanā; Śaivism; Śiva; Skanda**

David Gordon White

Further reading

Rao, T.A.G. 1968. *Elements of Hindu Iconography*, 4 vols. New York: Paragon Book Reprint Corp. (first published 1914).

APSARASAS

'Moving in or between the waters or the clouds'. Female divinities, often translated as 'nymphs'. The *Ṛgveda* introduces the class and first individuals (Urvaśī in 10. 95). Like their companions, the Gandharvas, in Vedic literature the Apsarasas show an ambiguous nature. Both classes share the positive connection to weddings (*Atharvaveda* 4.38.3) and forest trees (*Atharvaveda* 4.37.4) or an earthy odour (*Atharvaveda* 12.1.23), but also are accused of causing madness (*Taittirīya Saṃhitā* 3.4.8) and are included in lists of malicious beings (*Atharvaveda* 4.37). The number and origin of both (for instance of Prajāpati, *Śatapatha Brāhmaṇa* 9.4.1.2) are variously described. Apsarasas can change their shape at will.

From epic times onwards they are regarded as heavenly dancers at Indra's court. On behalf of the gods they often seduce ascetics to weaken their powers. They frequently visit the earth and at times raise families with humans.

See also: **Gandharvas; Indra; Prajāpati; Saṃhitā**

Xenia Zeiler

Further reading

Handique, Krishnakanta. 2001. *Asparases in Indian Literature and the Legend of Urvasi and Pururavas*. New Delhi: Motilal Banarsidass.

ĀRAṆYAKAS

The *Āraṇyakas* are parts of the Veda which stand between the *Brāhmaṇas* and the *Upaniṣads* in terms of their ideas, and probably also chronologically. Like the *Brāhmaṇas* they discuss the meaning of ritual and the powers to be gained by performing and understanding it, particularly the more advanced and rarely performed rituals. Even more than the *Brāhmaṇas*, they emphasise knowledge of the ritual, the cosmos and the human being, using ideas that are developed further in the *Upaniṣads*. The word means 'belonging to the forest or wilderness', the uncultivated land as opposed to the village; it seems that these texts were taught there because they were esoteric and powerful. Like the *Upaniṣads*, they contain injunctions not to teach them to the uninitiated (Gonda 1975: 423–32). Material typical of the *Āraṇyakas* may be found in *Bṛhad-Āraṇyaka Upaniṣad* 1.1 and *Chāndogya Upaniṣad* 1–2 (Roebuck 2003: 13; 109–32), as well as in Keith (1909).

See also: **Brāhmaṇas; Upaniṣads; Veda**

Dermot Killingley

Further reading

Gonda, Jan. 1975. *Vedic Literature.* Wiesbaden: Harrassowitz.

Keith, Arthur Berriedale. 1909. *The Aitareya Āraṇyaka.* Oxford: Clarendon Press.

Roebuck, Valerie. 2003. *The Upaniṣads.* London: Penguin.

ARATĪ

See: **Ārtī**

ARCHERY

See: **Dhanurveda**

ARCHITECTURE

See: **Sthāpatyaveda**

ARDHANĀRĪŚVARA

'The lord who is half female'. Androgynous form combining the characteristics of Śiva and his female energy Pārvatī. According to the *Vāmana Purāṇa* the Ṛṣi Bhṛṅgi refused to worship the goddess along with Śiva. By fusing their bodies to Ardhanārīśvara Śiva forced him to honour both. The Ṛṣi, taking the form of a female bee (Bhṛṅgī), bored a hole through the male–female unity and continued to circumambulate the god alone. In the *Brahmāṇḍa Purāṇa* Śiva became this form by worshipping Śakti.

These origin-myths are often interpreted as illustrations of Śaivism–Śāktism conflicts or amalgamations, respectively. Ardhanārīśvara is understood as the symbol for the breaking of the distinction and limitation of male and female, the completion of both or, more seldom, kāma (love/pleasure).

In iconography, the left is female and the right is male, with the body showing the respective attributes. The first depiction dates from the Kuṣāṇa era, second century CE.

See also: **Kāma; Pārvatī; Purāṇas; Ṛṣi; Śaivism; Śakti; Śāktism; Śiva**

XENIA ZEILER

Further reading

Yadav, Neeta. 2001. *Ardhanarisvara in Art and Literature.* New Delhi: Motilal Banarsidass.

ARJUNA

The third, but most well-known, of the five Pāṇḍava brothers, who were sons of King Pāṇḍu and fought the Kauravas in the battle of Kurukṣetra, whose exploits are told in the *Mahābhārata*. Arjuna, meaning 'white', is also regarded as the son of the god Indra, but this endowment of the Pāṇḍavas with mythic divine paternity needs to be located within the legends of their heroism, chivalry and importance in mythologies associated with Kṛṣṇa bhakti.

Arjuna is believed to have married Draupadī in some accounts, but he also wedded Kṛṣṇa's sister, Subhadrā, Ulūpī, a Nāga princess and later the daughter of the King of Maṇipura; the latter three bore him sons. Although he is known for a number of heroic exploits recounted in the *Mahābhārata*, it is his relationship with Kṛṣṇa for which he is most celebrated. In addition to his marriage to Kṛṣṇa's sister, it also said that he performed the funeral rites for Kṛṣṇa at Dvārakā, after which he is believed to have retired to the Himalayas.

However, it is his role as one of the two protagonists in the *Bhagavadgitā* for which he is famed. The dialogue opens with Arjuna and Kṛṣṇa drawing their chariot between the opposing forces to assess the situation, Kṛṣṇa having agreed not to take sides in the battle but to be Arjuna's charioteer. Arjuna, in spite of his great valour, becomes demoralised on seeing so many figures amongst the enemy who are family members or previous teachers. The moral dilemma is resolved by

Kṛṣṇa in a series of dialogues in which he reassures Arjuna of his duty as a warrior, but goes much further to elaborate on liberation, karma, and salvation through devotion. Most significantly, Arjuna is shown Kṛṣṇa's viśva-rūpa as the omnipresent, all-powerful Supreme Being, which completely transforms the relationship between them. As a result of this experience and his subsequent relationship with Kṛṣṇa, he is known amongst Hindus as an exemplar of devotion.

See also: **Bhagavadgītā; Bhakti; Draupadī; Dvārakā; Indra; Karma; Kauravas; Kṛṣṇa; Kurukṣetra; Mahābhārata; Pāṇḍavas; Pāṇḍu; Subhadrā**

RON GEAVES

Further reading

Dasgupta, Madhusraba. 1999. *Samsad Companion to the Mahābhārata*. Calcutta: Sahitya Samsad.

ARNOLD, SIR EDWIN (1832–1904)

Poet, author and journalist. After studying at King's College, London, and University College, Oxford, Arnold went to India in 1856 as Principal of the Government Deccan College in Pune. He returned to England in 1861, and later became editor of the *Daily Telegraph*. Following his book-length poem on the life of the Buddha, *The Light of Asia* (1879), Arnold published a literary translation of the *Bhagavadgītā*, entitled *The Song Celestial* (1885), based on earlier English translations, in particular that of John Davies (1882). While *The Light of Asia* was the more celebrated of his works, perhaps owing to the greater vogue for Buddhism in late Victorian England, *The Song Celestial* was praised by Gandhi as the best of English translations and it remains perhaps the most widely read English translation of the *Bhagavadgītā*.

See also: **Bhagavadgītā; Hinduism, history of scholarship; Gandhi, Mohandas Karamchand**

WILL SWEETMAN

Further reading

Arnold, E. 1885. *The Song Celestial*. London: Trübner.

Wright, B. 1957. *Interpreter of Buddhism to the West: Sir Edwin Arnold*. New York: Bookman Associates.

ARTHA

Artha as a goal of life refers to the pursuit of wealth and power and was taken by some as the sole goal of human endeavour according to a view also reflected in the *Manusmṛti* (2.224). The *Arthaśāstra* (1.7.6) considers it the primary puruṣārtha: 'Of the three ends of human life, material gain is verily the most important', so says Kauṭilya. 'On material gain depends the realisation of dharma and pleasure'. This apparent primacy of artha manifests itself at both the individual and the collective level. It is a common observation in the gnomic literature of India that both piety and pleasure are within easy reach of the wealthy. The realisation took the more sophisticated form at the collective level that without the existence of the state, and the law and order its existence implied, the pursuit of either virtue or pleasure in an organised way was impossible.

The text which deals explicitly with the system of political economy in ancient India is the *Arthaśāstra*, which tradition unanimously ascribes to Kauṭilya, the prime minister of Candragupta Maurya (fourth century BCE), although the work in its present form is probably later. Polity is described as consisting of seven limbs (saptāṅga): (1) king, (2) ministers, (3) country, (4) forts, (5) treasury, (6) army and (7) allies, in the same spirit as society is described as consisting of the four limbs constituted by the four varṇas. The role of the king is of course central to the scheme of things, a fact also recognised by the *Manusmṛti* (ch. 7).

See also: **Arthaśāstra; Dharmaśāstras; Kauṭilya; Varṇa**

ARVIND SHARMA

Further reading

Kangle, R.P. 1972. *The Kauṭilīya Arthaśāstra*, 3 vols. Delhi: Motilal Banarsidass.
Scharfe, Hartmut. 1989. *The State in Indian Tradition*. Leiden: E.J. Brill.

ARTHAŚĀSTRA

Arthaśāstra is a Sanskrit literary genre and an Indian expert tradition. Artha means 'material wealth' and according to the worldview prevalent in Brahmanism it is one of the three or four aims of human existence (puruṣārthas). The term *śāstra* denotes a compendium or manual. Arthaśāstra in its more technical sense includes economics, law and politics from a comparatively realistic royal perspective and is rather close to the *Nītiśāstras* (political handbooks). The oldest extant and most important treatise of its kind is the *Arthaśāstra* of Kauṭilya or *Kauṭilīya Arthaśāstra*. Although several predecessors of the author are quoted in the text, none of their works seems to have survived. Hardly any other source for investigating ancient India's economic and social history as well as political theory is as rich in material as the *Kauṭilīya Arthaśāstra*. It consists of fifteen books (adhikaraṇa) with 150 chapters (adhyāya) in all. The *Kauṭilīya Arthaśāstra* is written largely in prose, with a few verses. It is a very heterogeneous text, shaped by two different authors, namely Kauṭilya and Viṣṇugupta. The oldest parts of the manual were composed by Kauṭilya himself in 300 BCE. About the third century CE, this *Arthaśāstra* was revised and finally compiled by the author, Viṣṇugupta. Many conceptions of the *Arthaśāstra* tradition recur in the corresponding passages of the *Dharmaśāstras* (legal treatises). The *Kauṭilīya Arthaśāstra* is also considered to have been a model in structure and style for the *Kāmasūtra* of Vātsyāyana. Only two fragmentary commentaries on the *Kauṭilīya Arthaśāstra* have been discovered so far. The *Kauṭilīya Arthasāstra* was first edited in 1909 by R. Shama Sastri. In 1915 the same scholar published an English translation. R.P. Kangle dedicated a work in three volumes (1960–65) to this manual, containing a new edition, an English translation and a study of the text.

See also: **Artha; Brahmanism; Dharmaśāstras; Kāmasūtra; Kauṭilya; Nītiśāstras; Puruṣārthas; Vātsyāyana**

ANNETTE SCHMIEDCHEN

Further reading

Kangle, R.P. (ed./trans.). 1960–65. *The Kauṭilīya Artha Śāstra*, 3 vols. Bombay: University of Bombay (critical edition, English translation, study).
Shama Sastri, R. (ed.). 1909. *The Artha Śāstra of Kauṭilya*. Mysore: Oriental Library Publications (*editio princeps*).
Shamasastry, R. (trans.). 1923. *Kauṭilya's Artha Śāstra*. Trans. R. Shamasastry, 2nd edn. Mysore: Wesleyan Mission Press.

ARTHAVĀDA

In the philosophy of Pūrva Mīmāṃsā, Vedic statements are classified as either vidhi, an injunction or command, or arthavāda, a subordinate or ancillary declaration. Such a declaration may commend or further explain the ritual action in question. Arthavāda can be subdivided into three types: statements that confirm existing knowledge derived from previous experience (anuvāda); statements that must be interpreted figuratively because their literal sense contradicts known truth (guṇavāda); and statements that disclose facts for which there is neither corroboration nor contradiction (bhūtārthavāda). A major concern of Pūrva Mīmāṃsā is to determine which Vedic statements should be classified as vidhi and which as arthavāda.

See also: **Pūrva Mīmāṃsā; Vidhi; Veda**

DENISE CUSH AND CATHERINE ROBINSON

Further reading

Grimes, John. 1996. *A Concise Dictionary of Indian Philosophy: Sanskrit Terms Defined in English*. New and revised edn. Albany, NY: State University of New York Press.

Hiriyanna, M. 1985. *Essentials of Indian Philosophy*. London: George Allen & Unwin.

ĀRTĪ

Ārtī or Āratī is the act of worshipping a deity with light, and is an integral aspect of pūjā, Hindu worship. At the end of the pūjā rituals, the deities being worshipped are made an offering of light. One or, more commonly five, lights are placed on a tray, which is waved in a circular, clockwise motion in front of the deity. The five lights symbolise the five elements of earth, air, fire, water and ether. Together they represent the totality of the cosmos and everything in it. While the ārtī lights are being offered to the deity the priest intones mantras appropriate for the particular god or goddess. He may also ring a small bell in an effort to gain the attention of the gods. Ārtī also refers to the prayers recited or sung during the waving of the ārtī lights. Each deity has his or her own prayer, which honours him or her and reminds the supplicant of his or her greatness. The ārtī ceremony marks the conclusion of the pūjā rituals, after the deities have been honoured. It is at this time that the supplicants offer their prayers up through the medium of the ārtī flame. Agni is the god of fire and in many rituals he is responsible for transferring the prayers and wishes of the human devotees to the divine realm of the gods. This ceremony can be quite intense as it is a time when a link is forged between the divine and human worlds.

After the gods and goddesses have been offered ārtī, the flame is brought round to all those present. The devotees pass their hands over the flames in a gesture that suggests that they are wafting the essence of the flame towards their head. In the same way that the flame was considered to take their prayers towards the gods, the motion of drawing the flame towards the devotees signifies that they are taking the blessings of the divine from the flame. Therefore, to a certain extent, the ārtī flame represents the grace of the particular deity being worshipped. The devotees are then marked with a tilak, a mark between the eyes made of red kumkum or yellow sandal paste representing a third eye. In temples dedicated to Śiva, the devotees are generally offered holy ash (vibhūti), which they smear across their forehead in three horizontal stripes. If the ārtī ceremony has taken place at a temple the devotee might make a small donation of money to the priest, which is placed on the ārtī tray. The priest also distributes prasāda, a further blessing from the deity, which consists of a little of the offerings, usually flowers or fruit, that have previously been given to the deity and are subsequently returned as sacred food.

At some festivals a mass ārtī is celebrated at which many priests wave tiered brass lamps with many small oil lamps set into them. This is a spectacular sight, particularly the ārtīs performed at Haridwar on the banks of the sacred river Gaṅgā (Ganges), where afterwards the devotees launch small lights on leaf boats onto the river at night. The ārtī ceremony also has a more mundane but equally important function. In many temples the mūrti (image) of the main god or goddess is enclosed in a dark chamber situated at the centre of the temple, called a garbhagṛha (womb-house). Since the only light to enter the chamber is through the doorway, which is often linked to a narrow passageway, it is very difficult to see the deity and thereby receive darśana (a blessing bestowed by seeing and being seen). In many temples, the only time that darśana is possible is when the priest illuminates the face of the god or goddesses by performing ārtī.

See also: **Agni; Darśana (worship and practice); Gaṅgā; Image worship; Prasāda; Pūjā; Vibhūti**

LYNN FOULSTON

ARUNDHATĪ

Arundhatī is sometimes described as the wife of Dharma but more often depicted as the consort of the sage Vasiṣṭha and the goddess who personifies the morning star. Her name signifies 'fidelity' and she is usually depicted in iconic form as irenic and austere, holding flowers, leaves and water as offerings to the gods. In other accounts, she is described as the personification of Alcor, the smallest star of the Great Bear, and is associated with conjugal virtue and sometimes invoked in marriage ceremonies. In the *Mahābhārata* it is said that when one loses the ability to see Arundhatī and the Pole Star it is a sign of imminent death. The *Atharvaveda* mentions a plant by the name of Arundhatī which is said to cure serious wounds.

See also: **Dharma; Mahābhārata; Saṃhitā; Strīdharma; Vasiṣṭha**

RON GEAVES

Further reading

Stutley, Margaret and James Stutley (eds). 1977. *A Dictionary of Hinduism: Its Mythology, Folklore and Development 1500 BC–AD 1500*. London: Routledge and Kegan Paul.

ARYA SAMAJ

The Arya Samaj (the 'Noble Society') is a modern Hindu revivalist movement. It was founded by Swami Dayananda Saraswati (1824–83) and his followers in 1875. Dayananda was critical of the 'Hinduism' of his time, advocating a return to the glorious monotheistic religion that he argued that was in India's most ancient texts, the Veda. So the Arya Samaj was first and foremost a religious reform movement, rejecting the polytheism and image worship of contemporary 'Hinduism' in favour of a relatively austere Vedic religion.

The Arya Samaj has also championed social reform. Concerning caste, for example, Dayananda maintained that caste identity should be determined on the basis of the qualities of the individual and not by birth. The history of the Arya Samaj has seen a kind of oscillation on the issue of caste, with radical caste-breaking fervour sliding back into acquiescence to the status quo. One important innovation in this area that is often attributed to the Arya Samaj is the invention of rituals to alter one's caste status. Originally intended to reclaim individuals who had temporarily fallen from caste, these rituals were eventually used to 'reconvert' large social groups, from Islam especially, that were understood to have formerly been 'Hindu'. The most substantial impact of the Arya Samaj on Indian society came in the area of education. In 1886 the Dayananda Anglo-Vedic (or DAV) High School was established in Lahore as a memorial to the recently deceased founder of the Arya Samaj. This initiative appealed to progressive families in India looking for a 'Hindu' alternative to Christian missions, and eventually hundreds of DAV schools were established across north India, including some of the earliest schools for girls. Soon a split developed in the Arya Samaj over education, and other issues as well, and an alternative system of schools was founded beginning in 1902. Dayananda was a very active controversialist, frequently debating with Hindus, Muslims and Christians. His later followers picked up the mantle of defending the Hindu community, with members of the Arya Samaj such as Lala Lajpat Rai and Swami Shraddhanand emerging as important leaders in the Indian nationalist movement. Arya Samajists continued to be active in politics after independence, and contributed to the rising popularity of Hindu nationalism in India in the last two decades of the twentieth century.

Arya Samaj chapters are found almost exclusively in the areas where the Hindi language is spoken in India. The Arya Samaj has also established centres in eastern and southern Africa and more recently in the United Kingdom and North America, though it has largely appealed exclusively to immigrants who came from Arya Samaj families in India in the past few decades. The Arya Samaj has never been a very large group. It is estimated that it had only between 1.5 and 2 million members in 1947 at the end of the British period. Yet the Arya Samaj has been an influential force in the religious, social and political life of modern India.

See also: **Caste; Conversion; Dayananda Saraswati, Swami; Hinduism, modern and contemporary; Lajpat Rai, Lala; Nationalism; Saṃhitā; Shraddhanand, Swami; Women's education**

J.E. LLEWELLYN

Further reading

Graham, J.R. 1965. *The Arya Samaj: a Reformation in Hinduism with Special Reference to Caste*. Ann Arbor, MI: University Microfilms.

Jones, K.W. 1976. *Arya Dharm: Hindu Conciousness in 19th Century Punjab*. Berkeley, CA: University of California Press.

Lajpat Rai, Lala. 1989. *The Arya Samaj: An Account of Its Origins, Doctrines, and Activities, with a Biographical Sketch of the Founder*. Delhi: Renaissance Publishing House.

Llewellyn, J.E. 1998. *The Legacy of Women's Uplift in India: Contemporary Women Leaders in the Arya Samaj*. Delhi: Sage Publications.

ĀRYABHAṬṬA (ĀRYABHAṬA)

A renowned fifth-century astronomer and mathematician probably born in Pāṭaliputra and celebrated as the father of Indian algebra. Known to the Greeks as Andubarius and to the Arabs as Arjabahr, Āryabhaṭṭa's work on algebra remains the bedrock of Indian algebra to the present day. Born in Patna, according to his own writings, dated to 476 CE, he wrote his first book on astronomy at the age of twenty-three. His works include the *Āryāṣtaśata*, the *Dasāgīti-sūtra,* edited by Kern under the title of the *Āryabhaṭiya*, and the *Ārya Siddhānta*. The *Āryabhaṭiya* contains the earliest known account of the decimal place value-system and it is argued that he is the founder of the mathematical system but there are divergent views best represented by Datta and Singh, *History of Indian Mathematics.* He was the first to utilise mathematics in astronomy and argued that the earth was spherical and rotated on its axis. He was also aware that eclipses were the result of the earth's shadow falling onto the moon. Āryabhaṭṭa's significance as a mathematician should not be underestimated and his work was influential for the development of modern algebra and its application to geometry and astronomy. He should not be confused with a later tenth-century astrologer of the same name, who is usually distinguished by the name Laghu Āryabhaṭṭa (Āryabhaṭṭa the Less), who composed the *Mahāsiddhānta*. India's first satellite, launched on 29 April 1975, was named Āryabhaṭṭa in honour of the famed mathematician.

See also: **Jyotiṣa**

RON GEAVES

Further reading

Garg, Ganga Ram. 1992. *Encyclopaedia of the Hindu World Vol. 3*. New Delhi: Concept Publishing Co.

ARYAMAN

'Lord, ruler', 'Aryanhood', 'comrade', 'groomsman'; another suggestion: 'hospitality'.

Along with Varuṇa and Mitra, one of the three chief Ādityas. Mentioned approximately 100 times in the *Ṛgveda*, Aryaman is virtually void of individual or distinguishing characteristics. Among the pre-Vedic Indo-Europeans, he appears as an instance of the chaos-demon.

See also: **Mitra; Saṃhitā; Varuṇa; Vedic pantheon**

MICHAEL YORK

ĀSANA

'Seat', 'place'; 'posture'. In Vedic literature, āsana indicates the offering of a seat to a deity during worship. This rite is part of an elaborate form of pūjā (ritual offering) which includes sixty-four ceremonies called āvāhanas. The use of āsanas as a physical posture is listed in the Veda, the *Upaniṣads*, epic and purāṇic literature, where they are described as conducive to mokṣa (liberation). In *Bhagavadgītā* (6.11), the practice of āsanas is the first method of obtaining the vision (darśana) of the Lord. From the second century CE, with Patañjali's *Yogasūtras*, the term āsana indicates a yogic posture. The āsanas are the third of the eight limbs (aṅga) of the Yoga, one of the six orthodox Hindu philosophical systems (āstika darśanas) (Ṣaḍdarśana). Among the various Yogic schools, Haṭha Yoga greatly emphasises the practice of āsanas as a major technique to achieve self-realisation. In the *Haṭha Yoga Pradīpikā* (1: 19–69) by Svāmī Svātmarāmana (fifteenth century), āsanas are carefully explained. Traditionally āsanas are reputed to be 8,400,000, yet only 32 (or 84) are known to mortals. Yogic postures aim to develop concentration and firmness of mind in order to achieve the experience of unity (samādhī) with the Supreme Principle (Brahman) or, in a theistic sense, God (Īśvara). Meditation while practising yogic posture is described as an effort to transform the immanent reality into transcendence, or to identify one's own self (ātman) with the impersonal absolute (Brahman). Āsanas must be accompanied by the practice of yama (self-restraint), niyama (self-control), prāṇāyama (breath retention), pratyāhāra (sense withdrawal), dhāraṇā (concentration) and dhyāna (meditation). The yogi is required to completely arrest internal and external bodily motions. Every stimulus caused by the dvandvas (the pairs of opposites: heat/cold, hunger/thirst, joy/grief, etc.) must be ignored. A guru only can transmit to his disciple the correct approach to the practice of āsana. The various positions transform the human body into a receptacle of energy (śakti). Therefore the extremity of the limbs must be aligned in order to avoid any possible interruption of the flux of energy. During his training, the disciple's body must adapt itself to a given position for an increasing period of time until a certain degree of comfort is reached. Only then can that particular position be addressed as āsana. From the twentieth century, Yoga – and particularly Haṭha Yoga, the most physical one – spread in the West and gained enormous popularity. The use of āsanas has been dominant, to the point that some schools of Modern Yoga ended up being entirely centred on physical exercise and emended theoretical and spiritual teaching.

See also: **Āstika and Nāstika; Ātman; Bhagavadgītā; Brahman; Darśana; Haṭha Yoga; Īśvara; Meditation; Mokṣa; Patañjali; Pūjā; Purāṇas; Ṣaḍdarśana; Śakti; Upaniṣads; Yoga; Yoga, modern; Yogasūtras**

FABRIZIO M. FERRARI

Further reading

De Michelis, E. 2003. *A History of Modern Yoga. Patanjali and Western Esotericism.* New York and London: Continuum.

Eliade, M. 1958. *Yoga. Immortality and Freedom*. London: Routledge and Kegan Paul.
Stoler Miller, B. (ed.). 1996. *Yoga: Discipline of Freedom. The Yoga-Sūtra Attributed to Patañjali*. Berkeley, CA and London: University of California Press.
Yogendra, J. (ed.). 1988. *Cyclopaedia yoga, vol. 1(Alphabet A–A), with Special Information on Asana*. Bombay: Yoga Institute.

ASCETICISM

See: **Tapas**

ASHRAM

See: **Āśram(a) (Religious Community)**

ASHTANGA VINYASA YOGA

See: **Jois, K. Pattabhi and Ashtanga Vinyasa Yoga**

ASIATIC SOCIETIES

The first learned society for the study of Asia was the Bataviaasch genootschap der Konsten en Wetenschappen (Batavian Society of Arts and Sciences), founded by the Dutch in Batavia (since 1949 Jakarta) in Indonesia in 1778. It was, however, the Asiatick Society (later the Asiatic Society of Bengal), founded in 1784, which was to be most influential for the study of Hinduism. The first president of the Society, and its leading light in its first decade, was Sir William Jones, who in his address to the Society's first meeting identified its objects of study as 'MAN and NATURE; whatever is performed by the one, or produced by the other', within the geographical limits of Asia. From the outset the religions of India formed a significant part of the Society's concerns and several important early works on Hinduism were first published in the Society's journal, *Asiatick Researches*. The Society, itself modelled on the Royal Society of London, quickly inspired imitators elsewhere in India (Bombay 1804) and the wider world. In Europe the first was the Société Asiatique de Paris, founded in 1822, with Silvestre de Sacy as first president. The next several decades saw the founding of many other similar societies, notably the Royal Asiatic Society of Great Britain and Ireland (founded 1823; Royal Charter 1824), the American Oriental Society (1842) and the Deutsch Morgenländische Gesellschaft (1845).

See also: **Asiatick Researches; Jones, Sir William**

WILL SWEETMAN

Further reading

Kejariwal, O.P. 1988. *The Asiatic Society of Bengal and the Discovery of India's Past 1784–1838*. Delhi: Oxford University Press.
Scholarly Societies Project (http://www.scholarly-societies.org/).

ASIATICK RESEARCHES

Founded as the journal of the Asiatic Society of Bengal, *Asiatick Researches* was the first learned journal devoted to the study of Asia. Broad in scope, including also articles on natural history, the journal was an immediate success, and several further editions, some pirated, quickly appeared in Europe, as well as French and German translations. Among the important articles in early volumes were Sir William Jones' annual discourses to the society, the third of which, 'On the Hindus', includes his famous pronouncement on the relationship between Sanskrit and Greek, Latin and the other languages of Europe. Later volumes included important essays by the leading figures of late-eighteenth- and early-nineteenth-century British Orientalism, such as those of H.T. Colebrooke on the Veda, on satī and on the Jains, and those of H.H. Wilson on the *Purāṇas* and on different movements in contemporary Hinduism. From 1788 until its cessation in 1839,

Asiatick Researches ran into twenty volumes and was superseded by the *Journal of the Asiatic Society.*

See also: **Asiatic Societies; Colebrooke, Henry Thomas; Jones, Sir William; Languages; Orientalism; Purāṇas; Sati; Veda; Wilson, Harold Hayman**

WILL SWEETMAN

Further reading

Asiatick Researches. 1788–1839. Calcutta: Printed by Manuel Cantopher at the Honourable Company's Printing Office.

Kejariwal, O.P. 1988. *The Asiatic Society of Bengal and the Discovery of India's Past 1784–1838*. Delhi: Oxford University Press.

ĀŚRAM(A) (RELIGIOUS COMMUNITY)

The Sanskrit word āśrama is commonly anglicised as ashrama. There are two predominant designations of the term āśrama in ancient Indian literature: (1) a hermitage; (2) a religious way of life. The first meaning, which is found in Brahmanical, Buddhist and Jain sources, as well as in non-religious texts, is the most common. It usually refers to the residence of a holy person, but came to refer to a place where people would practise or learn spiritual teachings. According to Buddhist sources, an āśrama (Pāli: assama) was located in the wilderness and housed brāhmāṇas with matted hair, who were married with children and who maintained a household fire. The second meaning of āśrama refers to the Brahmanical institution of designating distinct stages of life for all twice-born males. In more contemporary usages, an ashram can refer to a community that has gathered around a spiritual leader. A number of Hindu reformers, including Vivekananda, Rabindranath Tagore, Mohandas Gandhi and Sri Aurobindo, set up ashrams at the end of the nineteenth and the beginning of the twentieth centuries. Many contemporary ashrams in India have strict rules concerning diet and sexual abstinence, and are devoted to practices like yoga and meditation.

See also: **Buddhism, relationship with Hinduism; Fasting; Gandhi, Mohandas Karamchand; Ghose, Aurobindo; Jainism, relationship with Hinduism; Meditation; Tagore, Rabindranath; Tapas; Vivekananda, Swami**

BRIAN BLACK

Further reading

Flood, Gavin. 1996. *An Introduction to Hinduism.* Cambridge: Cambridge University Press.

Olivelle, Patrick. 1993. *The Āśrama System: The History and Hermeneutics of a Religious Institution.* New York: Oxford University Press.

ĀŚRAMAS (STAGES OF LIFE)

Varṇa and āśrama are two institutions so characteristic of the Hindu social order that the tradition is itself sometimes described as varṇāśrama dharma or the way of life characterised by these two institutions. While varṇa relates to a person's life as a member of a social organisation, āśrama relates the individual's life as such, which is described as undergoing the following four stages: (1) celibate student (brahmacarya), (2) householder (gārhasthya), (3) hermit (vānaprasthya) and (4) renunciant (saṃnyāsa), in that order. Notionally a quarter of one's life is allotted to each stage, as a rule of thumb, but it is the sequence which is of real significance. Its logic is provided by the twofold characterisation of dharma as involving active involvement on the one hand (pravṛtti) and withdrawal on the other (nivṛtti), mentioned in the *Manusmṛti* (12.88–89) and also stated by Śaṅkara in his preface to the commentary on the *Bhagavadgītā*.

An early mention of this scheme is found in the *Chāndogya Upaniṣad* (2.23), which implies three stages. It seems that originally, especially in the period of the *Dharmasūtras*, the various āśramas represented optional lifestyles to choose from for one's entire life. They apparently attained the present sequential formulation only later, in the succeeding period of the *Dharmaśāstras*. It has been plausibly suggested that the doctrine of the four āśramas represents 'Hinduism's' own version of the middle path between the extremes of this-worldliness and other-worldliness.

This template of life offered by the scheme of the āśramas seems to accord well with a human being's biological destiny and has won approval, if not praise, unlike the varṇa system with which it is bracketed and which has attracted considerable criticism.

The scheme of āśramas, although desirable for achieving emancipation, is not essential for it, and Śaṅkara compares them to a saddle etc., which are aids to travelling but not essential for it. There is also some debate about whether this scheme – clearly meant for the male members of the three higher varṇas – applied to women and śūdras. The evidence from Sanskrit literature in general seems to provide evidence of such extended application, although according to *Vāmaṇa Purāṇa* (14.117–18) a brāhmaṇa may pass through all the four āśramas; a kṣatriya the first three; a vaiśya the first two and a śūdra only one, that of the householder.

See also: **Āśram(a) (religious community); Dharma; Dharmaśāstras; Dharmasūtras Śaṅkara; Varṇa**

ARVIND SHARMA

Further reading

Olivelle, P. 1993. *The Āśrama System: The History and Hermeneutics of a Religious Tradition.* New York and Oxford: Oxford University Press.

AṢṬĀṄGA YOGA

Aṣṭāṅga Yoga refers to the practice of Yoga consisting of eight limbs. The term aṣṭāṅga means consisting of eight (aṣṭa) limbs (aṅga). *Yogasūtra* 2.28 states that practice of the eight limbs of yoga destroys impurity, which allows knowledge to shine until one discriminates between one's own intellect, the finest manifestation of Prakṛti in the individual personality, and Puruṣa, the individual self. *Yogasūtra* 2.29 enumerates the eight limbs, and 2.30 and 2.32 their sub-limbs, as follows:

1 yama, 'rules of behaviour'
   a ahiṃsā, 'non-violence'
   b satya, 'truthfulness'
   c asteya, 'non-covetousness'
   d brahmacarya, 'celibacy'
   e aparigraha, 'non-acceptance of possessions'
2 niyama, 'rules of self-conduct'
   a śauca, 'purification'
   b santoṣa, 'contentment'
   c tapas, 'spiritual energy'
   d svādhyāya, 'recitation'
   e īśvarapranidhāna, 'devotion to one's lord'
3 āsana, 'posture'
4 prāṇāyāma, 'settling the breathing'
5 pratyāhāra, 'collecting the senses'
6 dhāraṇā, 'focus of attention'
7 dhyāna, 'meditation, i.e. continuously repeated focus of attention on a single object'
8 samādhi, 'unity of settled focused awareness with an object of attention or without one'

The last three limbs together are called saṃyama 'collection' and are more internal than the previous five. While some schools of Yoga, such at the Transcendental Meditation programme of Maharishi Mahesh Yogi, instruct the practice and culture of all eight limbs simultaneously, others instruct the steps in sequence.

Ashtanga Vinyasa Yoga, so called and taught by Pattabhi Jois at his Ashtanga

Yoga Research Institute since 1948, instructs a vigorous routine of physical exercises synchronised with deep breathing first (3), followed by culture of the behavioural limbs (1–2), followed by prāṇāyāma (2) and then in sequence by the more internal limbs (5–8). The vigorous routine of physical exercises consisting of positions and movements synchronised with inhalation and exhalation (vinyāsa) and directed gaze (dṛṣṭi) which he instructs strengthens the body and sense organs, improves blood circulation and removes toxins as a foundation for controlling the mind, which in turn allows one to culture the first two limbs. The practice of breathing called prāṇāyāma (4), taught after many years of āsana practice, steadies the mind and hence is the foundation for the internal cleansing practices (5–8), which eventually reveal the universal self. Beginning in 1927 Jois studied Ashtanga Yoga under T. Krishnamacharya, who learnt it from his teacher Rama Mohan Brahmachari in the early 1900s.

See also: **Ahiṃsā; Āsana; Brahmacarya; Meditation; Prakṛti; Puruṣa; Tapas; Transcendental meditation; Maharishi Mahesh Yogi; Jois, K. Pattabhi and Ashtanga Vinyasa Yoga; Krishnamacharya, T.; Yoga; Yogasūtras**

PETER M. SCHARF

Further reading

Jois, K. Pattabhi. 2002. *Yoga Mala.* New York: North Point Press.

Scott, John. 2000. *Ashtanga Yoga: The Definitive Step-by-Step Guide to Dynamic Yoga.* New York: Three Rivers Press.

Stern, Eddie and Deirdre Summerbell. 2002. *Sri K. Pattabhi Jois: A Tribute.* New York: Eddie Stern and Gwyneth Paltrow.

ĀSTIKA AND NĀSTIKA

These terms can be translated as 'believer' and 'unbeliever' when used as nouns, or as 'believing' and 'unbelieving' when used as adjectives; nāstika is sometimes translated as 'atheist'. They are derived from Sanskrit *asti*, 'is', and *nāsti*, 'is not', and refer to those who believe in or assert certain religious concepts and those who deny them. What the āstika affirms and the nāstika denies is the Veda, and those beliefs which it authorises: the other world (*para-loka*, the world beyond death), the gods and the efficacy of ritual.

The distinction between āstika and nāstika is used in the classification of systems of thought (Dasgupta 1957: 67f). The well-known set of six systems (the ṣaḍdarśana) are all āstika, since they do not deny the authority of the Veda, though it is a central concern only for the first two, Pūrva Mīmāṃsā and Vedānta. Buddhism, Jainism and the materialist Lokāyata or Cārvāka system are nāstika.

See also: **Buddhism, relationship with Hinduism; Jainism, relationship with Hinduism; Lokāyata; Pūrva Mīmāṃsā; Ṣaḍdarśana; Veda; Vedānta**

DERMOT KILLINGLEY

Further reading

Dasgupta, Surendranath. 1957. *A History of Indian Philosophy, Volume I.* Cambridge: Cambridge University Press.

ASTROLOGY

See: **Jyotiṣa**

ASUNĪTĪ

From asu ('life', 'existence') and nī ('lead', 'guide'). The Vedic Spirit-life goddess, Asunītī is mentioned in the *Ṛgveda* (10.59.5–6) as a life giver, in contraposition to the Nirṛtis, the goddesses of disorder and destruction. Asunītī belongs to a special class of deities which represents personifications of abstract concepts. These are Anumati, 'Favour (of the gods)'; Aramati, 'Devotion'; Asunītī,

'Spirit-life'; Manyu, 'Wrath'; Nirṛti, 'Disorder'; Śraddhā, 'Faith'; and Sūnṛtā, 'Bounty'. Though not clearly described, Asunītī is said to be a benevolent goddess who is invoked when the faculties of experience are asked to return. It is after her intervention that sight, mind (manas), lifetime and breath (prāṇa) are reassembled. Their reconstruction plus the grant of life (jīva) and physical sensation determine the birth of a new living body. Few particulars are known about the modalities of worshipping Asunītī. Her cult seems to be connected with sun worship and the sun god (Sūrya) as shown in *Ṛgveda* in 10.12.4. Due to her relation with the sunlight, Asunītī's benevolence is particularly invoked in order to see the sun again. This makes it likely that she might have been connected to funerary rites (Antyeṣṭi) and deities such as Mṛtyu (Death) and Yama (the god of the dead, son of Vivasvat, the 'Brillant One', an epithet of the Sun) (*Atharvaveda* 18.3.59). As her name indicates, Asunītī has the capacity to lead the souls of the deceased towards the world of the spirits (*Atharvaveda* 8.2.1). In *Ṛgveda* 10.15.14 (the hymn to the fathers), Asunītī is said to be the guide of the 'burned or unburnt', while in the hymn to Agni in *Ṛgveda* 10.16.2 she leads the bodies of the deceased to the realm of the fathers (pitṛloka).

See also: **Agni; Antyeṣṭi; Jīva; Manas; Pitṛloka; Saṃhitā; Sūrya; Yama**

FABRIZIO M. FERRARI

Further reading

MacDonell, A.A. 2002. *A Vedic Reader for Students*. New Delhi: Motilal Banarsidass.

ASURAS

Superhuman beings, usually translated as demons, who are in opposition to gods. However, in spite of their place in mythology as the enemies of the gods, they are often described as possessing good qualities associated with warriors such as valour, generosity and loyalty. In the earliest parts of the *Ṛgveda*, the term is used for the supreme spirit and applied to some of the high deities such as Indra and Agni. The *Taittirīya Brāhmaṇa* acknowledges them as the enemies of the gods but states that they were born from the breath of Prajāpati, but according to the *Viṣṇu Purāṇa* they were created from the groin of Brahmā. The change from god to demon seems to appear for the first time in the last book of the *Ṛgveda* and also in the *Atharvaveda*. It is speculated that the transference may have taken place as a result of divisions between Indian and Persian populations; another theory suggests a linguistic error occurred between asu (breath), sura (god), and a-sura (not god) (Dowson 1968: 28). It is also possible that the division into two sets of powers, respectively representing good and evil, may have been a part of changes taking places in the late-Vedic period concerning the nature of divinity, influenced by contact with Zoroastrianism (Stutley 1977: 23).

In the *Purāṇas* and Epics the asuras are involved in endless struggles with the gods and some of them are prominent figures in epic battles with major deities and avatāras. Foremost amongst them would be Rāvaṇa, the king of Sri Laṅkā, who fought with Rāma after abducting his wife, and Mahiṣa, the buffalo-demon, who was defeated by Durgā. However, by the time of the writing of the *Purāṇas* and Epics asuras were identified with other demonic beings such as rākṣasas. In the older myths, asuras can often perform noble deeds such as that of Āsurī, the demoness who was the first to discover a remedy for leprosy.

See also: **Agni; Avatāra; Brahmā; Brāhmaṇas; Deities; Durgā; Indra; Mahiṣa; Prajāpati; Purāṇas; Rākṣasas; Rāma; Rāvaṇa**

RON GEAVES

Further reading

Dowson, John. 1968. *A Classical Dictionary of Hindu Mythology and Religion, Geography, History and Literature.* London: Routledge and Kegan Paul.

Stutley, Margaret and James Stutley (eds). 1977. *A Dictionary of Hinduism: Its Mythology, Folklore and Development 1500 BC–AD 1500.* London: Routledge and Kegan Paul.

ĀŚVALĀYANA

A pupil of the sage Śaunaka, a celebrated teacher of the *Atharvaveda*. Āśvalāyana was his most noted disciple and the author of noted works on Vedic ritual, most notably the *Śrautasūtras* and the *Gṛhyasūtras*. The former is an elucidation of the sacrificial instructions contained in the *Brāhmaṇas* and the latter is a manual of social and domestic ritual behaviour. The continuation of some elements of Hindu ceremonies with ancient Vedic ritual is often attributed to the *Gṛhyasūtras*. Both works have been published in the *Bibliotheca Indica*. Āśvalāyana was also the founder of a Sākhā of the *Ṛgveda*, one of the many variations of the texts traditionally handed down orally by teachers and leading to the formation of various schools.

See also: **Brāhmaṇas; Gṛhyasūtras; Saṃhitā; Śrautasūtras**

RON GEAVES

Further reading

Ạithal, K.P. 1986. *Non Rgvedic Citations in the Asvalayana Srautasutra: A Study.* Varanasi: Chowkhamba Sanskrit Series Office.

Mohanty, S.S. 1998. *Aspects of Domestic Ceremonies in Asvalayana School: A Study of Vedic Rituals.* Jagatsinghpur, Orissa: Medha Indological Publication.

AŚVINS

'Divine horsemen'. The Vedic divine twins, sons of Dyaus Pitṛ and Pṛthivī. The Aśvins, also known as the Nāsatyas ('children of paradise'?), are exemplary of the Vedic understanding and personification of divine duality. They are foremost to be recognised as Indra and Agni but may also be expressed as Indra and Soma, Indra and Viṣṇu, Indra (Manu) and Yama, Indra and Bṛhaspati, Indra and Pūṣan, Soma and Rudra, Soma and Pūṣan, and Agni and Soma. Like their Greek counterparts, the Dioscuri, the Aśvins are rescuers of those in distress – particularly from the ocean. They are also recognised as divine physicians – able to cure blindness and lameness as well as to rejuvenate. Their joint sister-spouse is Sūryā, daughter of the sun and most likely an instance of the dawn-goddess Uṣas. More central in pre-Vedic Indo-European religiosity, the Aśvins remained as popular figures in Vedic India. A bas-relief of the twins is to be found today in the Dandapāṇīśvara shrine of Vārāṇasī's Viśveśara (Golden) Temple.

See also: **Agni; Bṛhaspati; Dyaus Pitṛ; Indra; Pṛthivī; Rudra; Soma; Uṣas; Vedic Pantheon; Viṣṇu; Yama**

MICHAEL YORK

ATHARVAVEDA

See: **Saṃhitā**

ĀTMAN

The word ātman m., 'breath, spirit, soul, self', derived from reconstructed Proto-Indo-European etmén, 'breath' (Mayrhofer 1956: 73; Pokorny 1959: 39, 345), still occurs in its Proto-Indo-European meaning 'breath' in the *Ṛgveda* (1900–1100 BCE; *Ṛgveda* 7.87.2; 10.92.13), where it is contrasted with the body and sight (*Ṛgveda* 10.16.3) as one of the elements of the person that repair to their corresponding natural elements after death, and where it is contrasted even with the life spirit (asu, *Ṛgveda* 1.164.4). Yet even in this most ancient Indian text, it is used for the universal self, where the sun is called the ātman of all animals and plants (*Ṛgveda* 1.115.1; 7.101.6). It is used for a more abstract entity in contrast with the breath in other Vedic texts (*Atharvaveda* 5.9, etc.), where prāṇa, 'breath', repairs to the wind and ātman to the atmosphere; and for the absolute self in contrast with the human being (puruṣa) (*Aitareya Āraṇyaka* 11.3.2). The term is also used throughout the history of Sanskrit as a reflexive pronoun, 'oneself', and pronominal adjective, 'own'. Additionally, it refers to the essence or nature of a thing, to the torso as opposed to the limbs, to the body, to intelligence and to personality (Böhtlingk and Roth 1852–55: 118–19).

In the *Upaniṣads*, although certain passages still identify the self (ātman) with breath (prāṇa) (*Kauṣītaki Upaniṣad* 2.14; 3.2–3; 3.8), attempts are made to distinguish the self from aspects of individuality commonly conceived to be one's self, such as the body, breath (*Kaṭha Upaniṣad* 5.5), senses, mind, cognition and bliss (*Taittirīya Upaniṣad* 2.1–6; *Praśna Upaniṣad* 4.9). Instead the self is identified as the inner controller (*Bṛhadāraṇyaka Upaniṣad* 3.7.3), the innermost agent and enjoyer of all human faculties of action and experience (*Bṛhadāraṇyaka Upaniṣad* 1.4.7–8; 2.4.11; 2.5.19; 3.7.3; 4.4.17), and the pure subject of all experience that cannot be known as an object (*Bṛhadāraṇyaka Upaniṣad* 2.5.19; 3.4.2; 2.4.14; 4.5.15). Such an individual self referred to by the term ātman is identified with Puruṣa, both explicitly (*Bṛhadāraṇyaka Upaniṣad* 4.3.7) and in its characteristics. Both the ātman and Puruṣa are said to be of a definite small size and to reside in the heart (*Bṛhadāraṇyaka Upaniṣad* 4.3.7; *Praśna Upaniṣad* 3.6; *Chāndogya Upaniṣad* 5.18.1; *Śvetāśvatara Upaniṣad* 5.8–9; *Bṛhadāraṇyaka Upaniṣad* 5.6.1; *Kaṭha Upaniṣad* 4.12–13; 6.17; *Śvetāśvatara Upaniṣad* 3.13). This localised self moves through channels in the body in different states of consciousness, such as dreaming (*Bṛhadāraṇyaka Upaniṣad* 4.3.12–14). Upon death it exits from the body through the crown of the head (*Chāndogya Upaniṣad* 8.6.4; *Taittirīya Upaniṣad* 1.6; *Kaṭha Upaniṣad* 6.16), or through another aperture (*Bṛhadāraṇyaka Upaniṣad* 4.4.2), and transmigrates (*Praśna Upaniṣad* 4.9; *Bṛhadāraṇyaka Upaniṣad* 4.4.3).

The *Upaniṣads* are pre-eminently known, however, for distinguishing the individual self from all limiting characteristics and identifying it with the absolute essence of the world, Brahman. The innermost self that is ordinarily identified as the subject of all one's intellectual and affective experiences and the agent of all one's volition and action is the essence of what is ordinarily perceived to be the external world (*Bṛhadāraṇyaka Upaniṣad* 2.5.1–15, 19; 3.4.1–2; 3.5.1; 4.4.25; *Kauṣītaki Upaniṣad* 1.6; *Māṇḍūkya Upaniṣad* 2). As identified with Brahman and with the cosmic Puruṣa, the individual self is the source and essence of the world; moreover, the self is described as such even under the title of ātman (*Bṛhadāraṇyaka Upaniṣad* 2.1.20; *Taittirīya Upaniṣad* 2.1; 2.6). The ātman creates the world and every aspect of the individual (*Aitareya Upaniṣad* 1.1–3). Its exhalation is all knowledge (*Bṛhadāraṇyaka Upaniṣad* 2.4.10). After creating the world the ātman enters into it (*Taittirīya Upaniṣad* 2.6). It is identical with the whole world (*Bṛhadāraṇyaka Upaniṣad* 1.4.15–16; 2.4.6). It is the lord of all beings (*Bṛhadāraṇyaka Upaniṣad* 2.5.15). In short, viewed as an object, it is all that one ordinarily calls God. Yet it is not an object; it is the single self within every being (*Kaṭha Upaniṣad* 5.10–12). Realisation that the individual self is identical to the essence of the world wins the knowledge and support of all nature (*Praśna Upaniṣad* 4.10–11; *Bṛhadāraṇyaka Upaniṣad* 1.4.15–16; 1.5.20), while the whole world abandons one who considers it as something other than his own self (*Bṛhadāraṇyaka Upaniṣad* 2.4.6).

While upaniṣadic authors describe the self as having wonderful attributes, they frequently state that it is describable only in negative terms (neti neti), such as immortal, ungraspable, indestructible, without attachment, free from the influence of good and bad (*Bṛhadāraṇyaka Upaniṣad* 3.9.26; 4.2.4; 4.4.22; 4.5.15), without distinguishing marks, unthinkable, indescribable, without a second (*Māṇḍūkya Upaniṣad* 7). Categories of extension and location do not apply in the manner of ordinary objects. In contrast to passages that describe the self as localised and mobile, others describe it as omnipresent (*Kaṭha Upaniṣad* 2.22; *Śvetāśvatara Upaniṣad* 3.21; 6.11).

Although Jainism accepts that the individual self (Jīva) is as large as the body it occupies or last occupied, and there is some suspicion that early Vaiśeṣika accepted a localised and mobile self (ātman) (Adachi 1994), the six systems of Indian philosophy (Ṣaḍdarśana) all accept that the self is ubiquitous (Potter 1977: 95–100). While Nyāya, Vaiśeṣika and Pūrva Mīmāṃsā consider the ātman to be the agent responsible for action and the locus of the residual efficacy of action (Karma) (Halbfass 1991: 308), Sāṃkhya, Yoga and Vedānta accept that aspects of the personality mistaken for the self cause action and are the locus of its residues, and that the ātman is entirely unconnected with action. While the others accept that that there are many selves, Advaita Vedānta considers that the multiplicity erroneously perceived in manifest nature is superimposed on the one self.

Upaniṣadic passages that distinguish the ātman from aspects of individuality commonly conceived to be one's self deny that even consciousness belongs to it. Yet consciousness is the most intimate aspect of personal identity, and advocates of Vedānta assert that consciousness is one of the essential properties of Brahman and therefore of the ātman that is identified with it (Brahman-ātman). Cryptic passages deny both consciousness and unconsciousness to the self (*Māṇḍūkya Upaniṣad*). The dilemma is solved upon understanding that the type of cognition that depends upon the duality between knower and known ceases when the subject–object duality itself is transcended upon recognising the identity of everything with one's self (*Bṛhadāraṇyaka Upaniṣad* 2.4.14). While the being conscious of objects ceases, pure consciousness remains.

See also: **Advaita; Brahman; Brahman-ātman; Jainism, relationship with Hinduism; Jīva; Karma; Nyāya; Puruṣa; Pūrva Mīmāṃsā; Saccidānanda; Ṣaḍdarśana; Saṃhitā; Sāṃkhya; Upaniṣads; Vaiśeṣika; Vedānta; Yoga**

PETER M. SCHARF

Further reading

Adachi, Toshihide. 1994. 'On the Size and Mobility of the Atman in the Early Vaisesika'. *Asiatische Studien/Etudes asiatiques: Zeitschrift der schweizerischen Asiengesellschaft/Revue de la Société Suisse-Asie* (ASEA) 48(2): 653–63.

Böhtlingk, O. and R. Roth. 1852–55. *Sanskrit-Wörterbuch*, vol. 1: *Die Vokale* [Sanskrit Dictionary, vol. 1: Vowels]. 1 d: St Petersburg. Reprint: Delhi: Motilal Banarsidass.

Frauwallner, Erich. 1973. *History of Indian Philosophy* [*Geschichte der indischen Philosophie*]. Trans. V.M. Bedekar. Delhi: Motilal Banarsidass.

Halbfass, Wilhelm. 1991. *Tradition and Reflection: Explorations in Indian Thought*. Albany, NY: State University of New York Press.

Mayrhofer, Manfred. 1956. *Kurzgefaßtes etymologisches Wörterbuch des Altindischen*. [*A Concise Etymological Sanskrit Dictionary*], vol. 1. Heidelberg: Carl Winter.

Nakamura, Hajime. 1983. *A History of Early Vedānta Philosophy*. Trans. T. Leggett *et al.* Part One. Religions of Asia Series 1. Delhi: Motilal Banarsidass.

Organ, Troy W. 1964. *The Self in Indian Philosophy*. Studies in Philosophy 2. The Hague: Mouton & Co.

Pokorny, Julius. 1959. *Indogermanisches etymologisches Wörterbuch* [*Indo-European Etymological Dictionary*], vol. 1. Bern and Munich: A. Francke.

Potter, Karl (ed.). 1977. *Encyclopedia of Indian Philosophies*, vol. 2: *Indian Metaphysics and Epistemology: The Tradition of Nyāya-Vaiśeṣika up to Gaṅgeśa*. Delhi: Motilal Banarsidass.

Potter, Karl (ed.). 1981. *Encyclopedia of Indian Philosophies*, vol. 3: *Advaita Vedānta up to Śaṃkara and His Pupils*. Delhi: Motilal Banarsidass.

ATRI

One of the seven mythical sages or ṛṣis of the *Ṛgveda*, whose names are all epithets for fire (Atri literally means 'devourer' or 'eater') and stars of the constellation the Great Bear. Many hymns of the *Ṛgveda* are addressed to him, especially those associated with the praise of Agni, Indra or the Aśvins. In the earliest vedic literature, he is said to be the first of the Āryans to arrive in India and the purohit of the five tribes whose role was to protect the sun against the eclipse demon. In the Epic period, he is considered to be one of the ten prajāpatis or 'Lord of Creatures', one of the ten progenitors of the human race created by Manu. In purāṇic mythology he is considered to be the offspring of Brahmā, having come forth from the god's eyes, and, although destroyed by Śiva's curse, was reborn from the flames after Brahmā performed a fire sacrifice. He is also named as the father of Soma and the ascetic Dattātreya by his wife Anasūyā.

See also: **Agni; Anasūyā; Aśvins; Brahmā; Dattātreya; Indra; Manu; Purāṇas; Purohit(a); Ṛṣi; Saṃhitā; Śiva; Soma**

RON GEAVES

Further reading

Stutley, Margaret and James Stutley (eds). 1977. *A Dictionary of Hinduism: Its Mythology, Folklore and Development 1500 BC–AD 1500*. London: Routledge and Kegan Paul.

AUM

See: **Oṃ**

AUROBINDO, SRI

See: **Ghose, Aurobindo**

AUROVILLE

Auroville is based on Sri Aurobindo's and the Mother's vision. Auroville (City of Dawn), was founded in 1968 as a universal city devoted to human unity, international understanding and service to humanity. Located near Pondicherry in Southeast India, Auroville is an international and experimental community of about 1,700 (as of 2005) individuals from 35 countries devoted to furthering human evolution, peace and harmony. From its inception, Auroville was endorsed by UNESCO and the government of India and has received financial support from various governmental and non-governmental organisations and foundations.

Auroville is laid out in a circular fashion and at its centre is a unique globe-shaped structure known as the Matrimandir. Radiating out from the centre there are four zones: industrial, cultural, residential and international. Residents are engaged in educational research, development of sustainable technologies and agriculture, as well as various cultural and spiritual activities.

See also: **Ghose, Aurobindo; Mother, The**

BAHMAN A. K. SHIRAZI

Further reading

The Auroville Handbook. 2003. Auroville, India: Abundance Publications.

www.auroville.org (accessed 3 March 2006).

AUSTRALASIA, HINDUS IN

Nineteenth century immigration to Australia

Details of religious identification have been collected since the very first population Census held in Australia. However, the detail released from the Census has varied from one Census to another. Until the latter part of the twentieth century, the number of Hindus living in Australia was very small and, in most Censuses, too small to be noted as a separate category.

Australia was not isolated in the days prior to European settlement there. Aboriginal people traded with East Asian communities, particularly with people from Macassar in South Sulawesi (Trudgen 2000). It is quite possible that on some occasions Indian merchants and adventurers made it down to Australia and there are legends which tell of such travels. However, there is little firm evidence of particular journeys or contacts (Bilimoria 1996: 7).

After the cessation of transportation of convicts to Australia, farmers developing pastoral properties looked around for other cheap sources of labour. In 1839, 1,283 indentured Indian labourers were obtained by 111 pastoralists in New South Wales. For example, in 1842 fifty-one coolies from India arrived in Moreton Bay to work on pastoral estates in the Queensland area.

In 1860, Robert O'Hara Burke and John Wills organised a large expedition to cross Australia from south to north. They decided to use camels and organised help in handling camels from some 'Afghans'. These people came from the border between Afghanistan and India. In 1866, Thomas Elder of South Australia imported 122 camels from India to use in transport through the desert terrain, opening up transport to outlying sheep and cattle stations. More camels followed. With the camels came camel drivers, mostly from the same border regions between India and Afghanistan. The majority of these people were Muslims and they built the first Australian mosques in Adelaide and Broken Hill. A few of them were Hindus.

As camels were replaced by road transport, some of these camel drivers resorted to independent hawking of goods around the rural areas. Licences were offered to hawkers in the latter part of the nineteenth century and quite a number of Indians came to hawk materials, utensils and other small goods, most around outlying areas. One firm of Indian Hindu merchants was established in Melbourne operating an opal business which has lasted for more than a century (Bilimoria 1996: 10).

In the mid 1860s, sugar cane cultivation spread in Queensland. The planters were anxious to get cheap labour. Between 1863 and 1904, more than 70,000 workers were brought to Queensland. While the majority of these people were from the Pacific Islands, there were some Chinese, Malays, Singhalese and Indians. They were paid a minimum wage of £6 annually, together with food, shelter, clothing, tobacco and medical care. They cleared the land, ploughed, weeded and cut the sugar cane. Some worked as general labourers. A few women were among them, mostly working as domestic servants. There were not sufficient numbers of these people – nor did they have the freedom – to develop their own religious organisations, however.

While the cheap labour was valued by the plantation owners, others opposed this importation of cheap labour because of the threat to the employment of Europeans. The fact that Asian and Pacific labourers worked for very low wages threatened the conditions of employment for Europeans. There were also fears that these 'aliens' might eventually 'overwhelm' the European population. As early as 1884, the Queensland government announced that the import of cheap 'coloured' labour would cease. The first step was to ban them from being employed in anything but agricultural work. A total ban on non-white immigration was imposed in 1901 by the newly formed federal government under what became known as the 'white Australia' policy.

None of the Hindu groups who came to Australia in the nineteenth century set up any Hindu temples, although a Sikh temple was established by one community in New South Wales. The Hindu labourers, hawkers and merchants may well have practised their religion in private, but there were not enough of them in any one place, nor did they have the wealth, to establish permanent structures for communal worship.

In 1901, Australians born in 'British India' and their descendants numbered approximately 7,637 people (Australian Bureau of Statistics 1901: 121). However, it seems that only a small proportion of these were 'Hindoos' or 'Mahometans', as they are described in the Census. The Immigration Restriction Act 1901 imposed a European language test along with other constraints on any would-be immigrants, even to obtain a permit to enter Australia as a visitor. Even family members of Hindus living in Australia were refused entry. Opportunities for employment of Asians through hawking or farming were restricted. Many Hindus left Australia. Those who died were not replaced through further immigration. Just a few assimilated into the host society and continued to live in Australia. The numbers of Hindus in Australia dwindled. In 1911, the Census recorded just 414 Hindus and by 1933 the number had dropped to just 212 (Hughes 1997: 26).

Early Indian immigration to New Zealand

In New Zealand a similar process occurred, although the number of Indians who emigrated there was much smaller than the number emigrating to Australia. In 1896 there were only forty-six Indians in New Zealand. Most of them worked as hawkers, peddlers or domestic helps. Early in the twentieth century the numbers increased, mostly through 'chain migration' involving the relations and friends of Indians already living in New Zealand. Around 1920 there were sufficient Indians living in New Zealand to form the 'New Zealand Indian Association'.

In 1920 the New Zealand government passed the Immigration Restriction Amendment Act, which allowed them to exclude anyone who was not of British birth from entering New Zealand. Being of British birth was distinguished from being a British subject, and meant that the government could prevent Indians and other non-white British subjects from entering New Zealand. The New Zealand Indian Association wrote to the government:

> we respectfully urge that we are not aliens within the British Common Wealth of Nations . . . to preserve and safeguard the interests of the Indians is to uphold the prestige of the Empire.

But their protests were to no effect. It was not until the latter part of the twentieth century that equality in the criteria for immigration of all Commonwealth citizens to New Zealand was reinstated.

Post-World War II immigration

Following World War II, large numbers of immigrants were welcomed into Australia. The government was anxious to build the population, to develop industry and commerce and to put in place significant infrastructure. But almost all of the immigrants post-World War II were Europeans. In 1973, the Labour government announced that there would be no discrimination against migrants on the basis of colour, race or nationality. Among the first waves of non-European immigrants were refugees from the war in Lebanon. In the latter part of the 1970s many refugees from the war in Vietnam arrived, followed by immigrants from many other parts of Asia.

In the 1980s the Hindu community began to build. Many of the early Hindu migrants came from Fiji. Some of these came via New Zealand. They were attempting to avoid the ethnic tensions which had arisen in Fiji. In Australia, the Fijian community did not succeed in forming its own associations at this time. Nor was it able to build any temples.

In the late 1980s the immigration laws changed again, allowing in people from particular occupational categories – particularly business people. Doctors were also welcomed if they were willing to work in rural areas of Australia. Many Indians responded to these opportunities. Between 1986 and 2001, approximately 80,000 Hindus entered Australia.

Between 1991 and 1996, the Hindu community in Australia grew from 43,000 to 67,000, a growth of more than 50 per cent. This made it the fastest growing of all major religious groups in Australia. The growth continued between 1996 and 2001. An additional 28,000 people brought the total number of Hindus in Australia to 95,473, a growth rate of 42 per cent. While the growth rate during this period was less than that among Buddhists (79 per cent) and a little below that of the Sikhs (45 per cent), it has meant that Hinduism has become one of the larger religious groups in Australia. According to Census figures, the Hindu community is now larger than the Jewish community and larger than many Christian denominations such as the Salvation Army, Jehovah's Witnesses and Seventh-day Adventists.

The patterns of growth in the Hindu community have been similar in New Zealand. In 1971 there were just 3,845 Hindus in New Zealand. The number had grown to 6,078 by 1981. Between 1981 and 1991, the number of Hindus increased to around 18,000. Many of these had been living in Fiji. By 2001 there were almost 40,000 Hindus living in New Zealand, many of the most recent arrivals having arrived directly from India. The Hindus are a larger portion of the New Zealand population (1.1 per cent) than they are of the Australian population (0.5 per cent). In New Zealand the Hindu community is only slightly smaller than the Buddhist community and is twice as large as the Islamic community.

Hindu gurus

Hinduism began to take root in Australia not through immigration but through the visits of Indian gurus. The first Hindu guru to arrive in Australia was Jiddu Krishnamurti, sponsored by Annie Besant's theosophical movement. It had been announced that he would arrive in a miraculous way, walking on water. He disappointed many as he walked ordinarily down the ship's gangway. However, during his visit it is said that he charmed many with his personality (Bilimoria 1989: 24). Krishnamurti returned to Australia several times, the last visit occurring in 1970. A small Krishnamurti Centre in Sydney has continued to hold meetings and distribute video and audiotapes of Krishnamurti's talks and dialogues.

Australia and New Zealand participated in the rise in interest in Eastern religion in the 1960s. These were times of considerable religious and cultural turmoil in Australia and in New Zealand, as in other parts of the Western world. Many turned away from the Christian heritage which had dominated the religious landscape. Some found the Christian traditions spiritually barren, lacking in the experiential dimension. Others abandoned Christianity as they rejected the moral strictures of the churches, particularly what was seen as a restrictive code of sexuality. Many followed the Beatles and other celebrities in looking at what the religions of the East might have to offer.

Several gurus spent time in Australia and New Zealand in the 1960s and 1970s. Among the visitors were:

- Swami Ranganathananda of the Ramakrishna- Vivekanada Mission
- Swami Muktananda of the Siddha Yoga syndicate
- Guru Maharaji of the Divine Light Mission

Swami Venkatesananda and Swami Satyananda Saraswati came on a longer-term basis, establishing ashrams in Western Australia and New South Wales, respectively (Bilimoria 1996: 33–35; Ward and Humphreys 1995: 383–98).

Books on Hinduism found their way into the popular market. Yoga teachers established yoga centres in the suburbs of the cities. Australians joined the throngs of young people visiting India looking for new religious experiences and philosophies.

Hinduism has been taught in the universities mostly in the context of the study of religion. Some universities have taught Sanskrit and others Hindu philosophy (Bailey 1989: 49–56).

The International Society for Krishna Consciousness

The International Society for Krishna Consciousness, popularly known as the Hare Krishna movement, arrived in Australia in 1969. Bhaktivedanta Srila Prabhupada, the founder of the movement, visited Australia several times. Temples were established in several major cities. In the 1970s, it was common to see a small group of Hare Krishnas, mostly European converts, dressed in distinctive Indian-style dress, chanting, dancing and handing out literature through the shopping centres of major Australian cities. The Hare Krishna movement attracted Westerners who were looking for a radical alternative way of life.

While it has not maintained its early growth, the movement has had a continuing presence. In 2003, there were six Hare Krishna temples in the major cities in Australia. The Hare Krishnas also operated eleven restaurants and three rural communities. Approximately 900 people identified themselves with the Hare Krishna movement in the 2001 Australian population Census.

Other Hindu movements

Several other groups of Hindu origin have been formed in Australia and New Zealand. Among them is Elan Vital, formerly known as the Divine Light Mission. Prem Rawat, the founder, first visited Australia in 1972 and established a centre in Melbourne. He has since returned to Australia many times. There is a small group which arranges these visits and promotes the teachings in Australia. However, in the 2001 Census only a handful of people described themselves in a way which linked them directly with the Divine Light Mission or Elan Vital. Similarly, a small group in New Zealand promotes Prem Rawat's teachings (Tiwari 1985: 174).

The Ananda Marg movement was established in Australia in 1972 and in New Zealand in 1973. It captured the attention of some young people as a movement of social protest and reform (Tiwari 1985: 166). It gained notoriety in Australia when, in 1978, three young members of the movement were arrested and convicted for the bombing of a Sydney hotel during the visit of the Indian prime minister. After a special judicial enquiry, the three were pardoned and released in 1985. Ananda Marg has continued to have several small units in various places in Australia, and in the 2001 Australian Census around 100 people identified themselves with the movement. In New Zealand the movement received adverse publicity for its activities during the election in 1975 and support for it declined (Tiwari 1985: 170).

Of greater importance to many Indian Hindus has been the Sai Baba movement, established in Australia in 1980 in Sydney to promote the teaching of Sri Sathya Sai Baba. Since then, centres and groups have been established all around Australia. The New Zealand centre for Sai Baba is in Auckland and groups have been established in three regions: a northern region, a central region and a Bay of Plenty/Waikato region. Weekly or bi-weekly meetings are held in these groups, with larger national conferences from time to time. Many people have been attracted by Baba's teachings about equality and social transformation.

There are a variety of groups which promote Yoga practices and teaching in Australia and New Zealand. Among them are Brahma Kumaris organisation, Krishnamurti centres, Satyananda Yoga Ashrams, Siddha Yoga Meditation Ashrams, the Self Realisation Fellowship, Sri Aurobindo Society, and Sri Chinmoy. Perhaps the most widely known movement is Transcendental Meditation, introduced to Australia in 1961 (Ward and Humphreys 1995: 395) and New Zealand in 1962 (Tiwari 1985: 176). Many thousands of people have been trained in its meditation techniques, and for many these remain helpful as techniques that can be used by people of various religious beliefs. Indeed, the Transcendental Meditation website claims that it requires 'no belief or lifestyle change, is non-religious, is not time consuming'. In 2003, there were twenty-three Maharishi Health Education Centres or Vedic Colleges in Australia and sixteen around New Zealand.

Temple building

In 1974 the first Hindu society, the Sri Mandir Society, was formed in Australia. Initially it had a membership of just 200 people. An old Christian church in the Sydney suburb of Auburn was purchased in 1977 and transformed into the first Australian Hindu temple. It has since been a centre for a variety of Hindu festivals.

The Sri Venkateswara Temple Association was formed in 1978 with the aim of building a temple near Sydney. It was built in Helensburgh, another suburb of Sydney, and consecrated in 1985. This temple has served mostly the Tamil community from Southern India and Sri Lanka. Two other temples have since been built by Tamil Hindus in Australia, another in Sydney and one in Perth.

Another group of Indians, this time from the north, was supported by the India Heritage Research Foundation and began building a Hindu temple in Sydney dedicated to Śiva.

The Hindu Society of Victoria was founded in 1982 and immediately began plans for building a temple. A site was chosen close to the sea, on the outskirts of Melbourne, at Carrum Downs. It was planned that worship at the temple would centre on both Śiva and Viṣṇu, bringing together the two major streams of Hindu ritual tradition. The temple was completed in 1994 at a cost of Aus$1.5 million. It has been a focus for a large portion of the Hindu community in Victoria. Traditional craftsmen, who travelled from India for the task, completed the embellishments of the temple.

However, before this temple was completed, a smaller temple was built and dedicated to Gaṇeśa at the Basin, another suburb of Melbourne, in 1992 (Bilimoria 1996: 38).

In 2003, there were more than thirty Hindu temples in Australia, including six associated with the Hare Krishna movement. Every state capital had at least one temple, except for Hobart, Tasmania. There were four temples in the federal capital, Canberra.

In New Zealand the small Indian community purchased three houses in Auckland in the late 1940s. The site was cleared, and a community hall was built. Named the Gandhi Hall, it was opened in 1955. Led by Shri Rameshbhai N. Patel, religious ceremonies were held each Sunday in the community hall along with festivals such as Dīvālī and Navarātri.

In 1990, a new site was purchased and a prayer hall constructed. Images of Sri Rādhā and Kṛṣṇa were brought from India in 1991. Regular mandir activities were conducted. Construction of a temple began in October 2000 and inauguration ceremonies took place in June 2001.

The Hindu community in Australia

In 2003, the Census recorded that there were 95,473 Hindus living in Australia, constituting around 0.5 per cent of the population. Only 16,571 of them had been born in Australia, the remainder having been born overseas. Out of these, 2,456 were born in Australia and with both parents born in Australia. In other words, of all Hindus in Australia, 83 per cent were immigrants and 15 per cent were first-generation Australians. Only 2 per cent had a longer heritage in Australia.

As the following statistics show, many of the Hindus in Australia were already part of the Indian diaspora and had not come directly from India, but from another country. According to the 2001 Census in Australia, the birthplaces of overseas-born Hindus were as follows:

- 31,938 India
- 19,762 Pacific Islands (almost entirely from Fiji)
- 10,206 Sri Lanka
- 2,251 Malaysia
- 2,241 South Africa
- 1,302 Singapore
- 1,192 United Kingdom
- 1,024 New Zealand

The Hindus living in Australia came from a variety of language groups. A little fewer than 20 per cent of Hindus living in Australia spoke English at home. The most common language among Hindus was Hindi, spoken by 36 per cent, followed by Tamil, spoken by 19 per cent, and another 21 per cent spoke other South Asian languages. Around 860 spoke Punjabi, 600 spoke Indonesian, and between 200 and 300 each spoke Fijian, French and Malay.

The demographic characteristics are typical of a young immigrant community. Most immigrants arrive as single young people in their twenties or thirties, or as young families. In 2001, 69 per cent of Hindus were under the age of 40, compared with 57 per cent of the total Australian population. Only 2,000 Hindus, close to 2 per cent of all Hindus, were aged 70 years or more, compared with 9 per cent of the Australian population.

It has been more common for men than women to emigrate to Australia. Sometimes, men will leave their wives and children in the home country until they have found work and a home in Australia. The process can involve obtaining some Australian qualifications before they are able to work in their chosen profession. Hence, the time before wives and children arrive may be a period of some years. In 2001, the Census found that there were more males than females in the Australian Hindu community, 53 per cent of all Hindus being male.

However, the 2001 Census reported that Hindus had a high rate of marriage, with 63 per cent of all Hindus over the age of 15 being married, compared with 51 per cent of the Australian population. Unlike the wider population, few Hindus were living in *de facto* relationships, and few were separated or divorced; 86 per cent of all married Hindus were married to spouses who identified their religion as Hindu. Of all the major 'world religions', Hindus had the third highest rate of marriage within the religious group, following Islam (90 per cent) and Sikhism (88 per cent). Of those Hindus married to people of other religions, most were married to Catholics, Anglicans or people of no religion.

Most emigrants enter Australia through one of the state capital cities, particularly the two largest, Sydney and Melbourne. Most stay in the capital cities, for it is here that employment is most readily available. In 2001, almost half of all Hindus living in Australia were living in Sydney. Another quarter of them lived in Melbourne; 7 per cent lived in Brisbane, 5 per cent in Perth and around 2.5 per cent each in Adelaide and Canberra. Just 7 per cent of all Hindus lived outside the major state and federal capital cities.

Hindus have not congregated in a few suburbs, as have the Jewish people or, to some extent, Muslims. Part of the reason is that they are not bound to be close to a temple or to other special facilities. Most Hindus have a small shrine at their home where daily worship takes place. Only on special occasions will they go and visit a temple. On the other hand, orthodox Jews have been constrained by the fact that they must live within walking distance of their synagogues. Muslims have looked for those suburbs where they can readily buy halal food and, for many, where they can find work in the factories. Hindu people, however, have spread widely through the middle-class suburbs.

Since the 1980s, Australia has had quotas for an annual intake of refugees and other immigrants accepted on compassionate grounds. Most other immigrants have been accepted because they have fitted certain occupational categories, mostly in certain kinds of business and professions. These immigration regulations had the consequence that most Hindus living in Australia in 2001 had high levels of formal education. Almost one-third of all Hindus 15 years of age or older had university qualifications; 12 per cent of them had postgraduate degrees, compared with just 2.5 per cent of the Australian population as a whole. Indeed, the Hindu community had a higher level of formal education than any other religious community in Australia.

According to the 2001 Census, 13 per cent of Australia's Hindus earnt Aus$1,000 or more per week, compared with just 8 per cent of the wider population. Most Hindu immigrants had been able to find work. In 2001, just 3 per cent of all Hindus stated in the Census that they were unemployed and looking for full-time work, while another 2 per cent were unemployed and looking for part-time work.

The largest portion of Hindus living in Australia were employed as professionals. They were working mainly in property and business services, in health and community services, or in education. Some were associate professionals, for example in nursing, and others were in management and administration. Among others, the most common occupational areas were clerical work and retail sales.

The Hindu community in New Zealand

Among the 39,867 Hindus living in New Zealand, according to the 2001 Census,

- 12,234 were born in the Pacific Islands (most in Fiji)
- 10,743 were born in India
- 1,605 were born in Sri Lanka
- 1,344 were born in South Africa
- 11,142 were born in New Zealand

Hence a total of 71 per cent were immigrants. As in Australia, the majority of those not born overseas would be first-generation New Zealanders.

There were almost equal numbers of men and women in the Hindu community in New Zealand, with men constituting 49.97 per cent of the community. The Hindu community in New Zealand was also more evenly spread in terms of age than the Australian community, reflecting a longer period of immigration. A total of 77 per cent of all Hindus were under 45 years of age in 2001, compared with 66 per cent of the total population. Just 5.3 per cent of Hindus living in New Zealand were 65 years of age or older, compared with 12.1 per cent of the total population (Statistics New Zealand, www/stats.gov.nz: Tables 1 and 209).

Few details are available of the social status of the Hindus *per se* in New Zealand. However, figures based on birthplace give some indications. Of those Indians involved in the workforce at the time of the 2001 Census, 18 per cent were in professional occupations, compared with 15 per cent of Fijians and 14 per cent of the overall population. Indians were over-represented among administrators and managers, although Fijians were under-represented in this occupational category. Fijians were more likely to be clerks or service and sales workers. Few Indians were involved in trades or in other semi- or unskilled occupations, although Fijians were represented in these areas in similar proportions to the overall population.

As in Australia, most Hindus were to be found in the large cities. In 2001 approximately two-thirds of all Hindus in New Zealand were living in Auckland. Another 16 per cent were living in Wellington. Less than 7 per cent of all Hindus were living in the South Island of New Zealand.

Hindu communities in the Australian and New Zealand societies

It has been suggested that many Indian immigrants have expected to leave behind their Hindu traditions upon leaving India. Many of these highly educated people have been attracted to the idea of living in a country which is more secular. Yet, on arrival in the new land, some of these people began to miss elements of their cultural heritage, including their religious festivals and celebrations (Bilimoria 1996: 73).

In building temples, there have been a couple of major hurdles to overcome. The first has been in relation to the Australian community. Planning permits have often been hard to get. Residents have been anxious about having a Hindu temple in their suburb, objecting on grounds of noise, the visual impact and parking problems. There was a plan in Sydney to build one temple largely underground in order to overcome the visual problems. However, the cost of doing this was higher than anticipated and for some time this temple remained incomplete.

Another problem has been reconciling the very different practices and traditions of the members of the Hindu community. Whose gods would be honoured? What suited one group would not suit another. To some extent, compromises have been made as it has not been possible to build a temple for each tradition. Hence, the temple on the outskirts of Melbourne, for example, has been built to honour a range of gods. Nevertheless, the Hindu community has not remained totally united. There are several Hindu temples in Melbourne catering for different groups. For example, another temple has been constructed by the Sri Lankan Hindu community.

In building these temples, workers have often been hired from overseas. Because of the lack of Hindu temple priests in Australia and New Zealand or the opportunities for training them, most priests have been brought out from India. Some of them have had limited English-language skills, and they have not always found it easy to assimilate to the Australian context. In the 2001 Australian Census, twenty Hindus recorded the fact that their major occupation was to care for a religious community. Almost all of these priests had been born overseas. More than half of them were under 40 years of age and none of them received an income above Aus$600 per week. Compared with the Hindu community as a whole, their levels of education were poor, with just three out of the twenty having a university degree and none of them having postgraduate qualifications. These comments do not apply, however, to the purohits who perform life-cycle rituals.

The Hindu communities of Australia and New Zealand are still young. As with other young immigrant communities, it will be a generation or more before they become well established, in terms of having their own training facilities for priests and stable patterns of organisation. It will also take time for them to develop their own patterns of worship and celebration appropriate to the new context.

They may lose younger generations in this process. Second-generation immigrants tend to have a lower level of involvement in their religious heritage. But neither do they relate more easily to other religions or traditions. Many of the second generation do not have the capacity to understand the technical religious language or understand the details of the ceremonies and festivals. In some other religions there has been a marked falling away. Hindus in Australia and New Zealand are very conscious of these problems. They want to pass on their religious and cultural heritage and are looking at ways in which they can effectively do this. How successful they are will be judged by future generations.

See also: **Ananda Marg; Āśram(a) (religious community); Besant, Annie; Brahma Kumaris; Chinmoy, Sri; Darśana (philosophy and theology); Diaspora; Dīvālī; Divine Light Mission; Gandhi, Mohandas Karamchand; Gaṇeśa; Ghose, Aurobindo; International Society for Krishna Consciousness; Krishnamurti, Jiddu; Kṛṣṇa; Maharaj Ji, Guru; Languages; Mandir; Muktananda, Swami; Navarātri; Oceania, Hindus in; Prabhupada, A.C. Bhaktivedanta Swami; Purohit(a); Rādhā; Ramakrishna Math and Mission; Sai Baba (as movement); Sai Baba, Sathya; Siddha Dham; Śiva; Theosophy and the Theosophical Society; Transcendental meditation; Utsava; Viṣṇu; Vivekananda, Swami; Western popular culture, Hindu influence on; Yoga, modern**

PHILIP HUGHES

Further reading

Australian Bureau of Statistics. 1901. *Yearbook Australia*. Melbourne: Commonwealth Government of Australia.

Bailey, G. 1989. 'The Study of Religions in Australia: 2 Indian Religions'. *Australian Religion Studies Review* 2 (3): 49–56.

Bilimoria, P. 1989. *Hinduism in Australia: Mandala for the Gods*. Melbourne: Spectrum Publications with Deakin University Press

Bilimoria, P. 1996. *The Hindus and Sikhs in Australia*. Canberra: Australian Government Publishing Service.

Hughes, P. 1997. *Religion in Australia: Fact and Figures*. Melbourne: Christian Research Association.

Tiwari, K. 1985. 'The Indian Contribution'. In B. Colless and P. Donovan, eds, *Religion in New Zealand Society*, 2nd edn. Palmerston North: Dunmore Press, 160–80.

Trudgen, R. 2000. *Why Warriors Lie Down and Die*. Darwin: Aboriginal Resource and Development Services.

Ward, R. and R. Humphreys. 1995. *Religious Bodies in Australia: A Comprehensive Guide*, 3rd edn. Melbourne: New Melbourne Press.

http://www.archives.govt.nz (accessed 24 April 2006).

http://www.iskcon.com/worldwide/centres/australia.html (accessed 24 April 2006).

http://www.hindunet.com.au/australian-temples.html (accessed 24 April 2006).

http://www.auckindianassoc.org.nz (accessed 24 April 2006).

All figures from the 2001 Australian Census have been taken directly from or derived from customised tables provided to the Christian Research Association by the Australian Bureau of Statistics (ABS), Commonwealth of Australia, Canberra, 2002. Copyright in ABS data resides with the Commonwealth of Australia. Used here with permission. http://www.abs.gov.au.

All figures from the 2001 New Zealand Census table have been taken directly from or derived from tables on the website of Statistics New Zealand: www/stats.gov.nz.

AVALON, ARTHUR

See: **Woodroffe, John**

AVATĀRA

The word 'avatāra' comes from the Sanskrit *ava* + $\sqrt{}$*tṛ*, 'to descend, or cross downwards', and is best translated as 'descent' rather than 'incarnation', which inevitably invites unhelpful comparisons with a doctrine specific to Christianity. It is an idea which is primarily associated with the deity Viṣṇu, and it is first, and most famously, expressed (though without the use of the term itself) in Kṛṣṇa's words in the *Bhagavadgītā*:

> Although unborn and imperishable, although the Lord of creatures, controlling my own nature I come into being by my own miraculous powers of illusion. Whenever there is a decrease of dharma and a rise of adharma, then I send myself forth. For the protection of the good, the destruction of the wicked and the establishment of dharma, I come into being age after age.
>
> (*Bhagavadgītā* 4.6–8)

Although the concept of the supreme and transcendent deity taking a particular finite and temporal form is here associated with Kṛṣṇa, various other avatāras of Viṣṇu come to be identified in the texts, and the generally stated purpose of re-establishment of dharma comes to be linked with the specific task of defeating demons and others who threaten it by their actions. Both the numbers and members of the lists of avatāras that are put forward are fluid, but by the early centuries CE the numbers of times Viṣṇu is stated to have appeared in an avatāra form generally settles to ten (the daśāvatara lists) and the forms which are included, and the deeds they perform, most commonly resolve themselves into the following:

Matsya (the fish): saves Manu from the flood waters which inundate the earth at the time of the universal dissolution (pralaya).
Kūrma (the tortoise): provides the gods and the demons with a foundation for their churning pole when they churn the ocean to release the nectar of immortality.
Varāha (the boar): rescues the earth or, in other stories, the Veda from beneath the waters of the pralaya.
Narasiṃha (the man-lion): manifests himself to overcome the conditions of a boon protecting the demon Hiranyakaṣipu, who is persecuting Viṣṇu's devotee Prahlāda.
Vāmana (the dwarf): tricks the demon Bali into giving away the earth, the heavens and his own freedom by stretching to encompass these in three steps (the third of which lands on Bali's head).
Paraśurāma (Rāma with the axe): rids the world of its corrupt rulers twenty-one times.
Rāma (Rāma Dāśarathi): rescues Sītā from the demon Rāvaṇa.
Kṛṣṇa (or, in some lists, his brother Balarāma): slays the demon Kaṃsa.
Buddha: leads the unorthodox astray.
Kalki (the avatāra yet to come): comes at the end of the fourth world-age (kaliyuga) to rid the world of evildoers and inaugurate the new Golden Age (kṛtayuga).

The concept of the avatāra and the stories of specific avatāras give rise to a number of issues. These focus on: the use and meaning of the term itself (Hacker 1960); the problematic nature of the avatāra's relationship to time and establishment of dharma (Soifer 1991; Biardeau 1976);

the ontological relationship between the individual avatāras and Viṣṇu (particularly in the case of the most complex human avatāras, Kṛṣṇa and Rāma) (Matchett 2001); and the historical processes and purposes involved in the identification of particular figures as avatāras (Brockington 1998).

See also: **Balarāma; Bali; Bhagavadgītā; Buddhism, relationship with Hinduism; Dharma; Kaṃsa; Kṛṣṇa; Manu; Prahlād(a); Rāma; Rāvaṇa; Sītā; Veda; Viṣṇu; Yuga**

LYNN THOMAS

Further reading

Biardeau, M. 1976. 'Etudes de Mythologie Hindoue: bhakti et avatāra'. *Bulletin d'Ecole Française d'Extrême Orient* 63: 111–236.

Brockington, J. 1998. *The Sanskrit Epics.* Leiden: Brill.

Hacker, P. 1960 'Zur Entwicklung der Avatāralehre'. *Wiener Zeitschrift für die Kunde Süd- und Ostasiens und Archiv für indische Philosophie* 4: 47–70.

Matchett, F. 2001. *Kṛṣṇa: Lord or Avatāra?* Richmond: Curzon Press.

Soifer, D. 1991. *The Myths of Narasimha and Vāmana: Two Avatars in Cosmological Perspective.* Albany, NY: State University of New York Press.

For translations of the avatāra myths themselves, see:

Dimmitt, C. and J.A.B. van Buitenen (eds/trans.). 1978. *Classical Hindu Mythology: A Reader in the Sanskrit Purāṇas.* Philadelphia, PA: Temple University Press.

O'Flaherty, W.D. (trans.). 1975. *Hindu Myths.* Harmondsworth: Penguin.

AVVAIYĀR

Avvaiyār, who was a great Tamil female saint-poetess of the Sangam period (300 BCE to 400 CE), is an important figure of early Śaivism in Southern India. Her actual name is unknown since Avvaiyār simply means 'respected old woman'. Though there are said to be several Avvaiyārs, the most famous of them is the one said to have lived in the second century CE. The mythology surrounding Avvaiyār states that she was born of a Brāhmaṇa father and an untouchable mother and that she was abandoned shortly after birth by her parents, and was brought up by a poet who passed by and saw the abandoned child. She had a great talent for poetry and was wise beyond her years. Her poems and sayings against caste are used by modern reformers.

It is said that as a beautiful and intellectually gifted young woman many suitors pestered Avvaiyār, whereas the girl had only time for worship of Gaṇeśa, her favourite deity, and was averse to all worldly pleasures. In her frustration she prayed to the god Gaṇeśa to save her from the attention of young men and she was immediately transformed into an old hag. Her austere life, asceticism, wisdom and piety gained her the status of a saint in a world where mostly only male ascetics were able to make an impact.

See also: **Brāhmaṇa (priest); Caste; Dalits; Gaṇeśa; Poetry; Śaivism; Tapas**

THEODORE GABRIEL

Further reading

Arvanan, Thayammal. 2002. *Avvaiyar – Andru Mudal Indru Varai.* (*Avvaiyar, from Then to Now*). Pondicherry: 'Pachaippasael'.

Arya, Rohit. 2005. 'Avvaiyar, a Great Tamil poet–saint' www.indiayogi.com/content/indsaints/avvaiyar.asp (accessed 24 April).

'Wise Sayings of Avvaiyar'. 2003. *The Hindu*, 26 February.

AYODHYĀ

There are two Ayodhyās, the Ayodhyā of legend that appears in the *Rāmāyaṇa* and the small town in northern Uttar Pradesh. There is considerable controversy whether the present-day town in Uttar Pradesh is the same as that mentioned in the

Rāmāyaṇa. The controversy has led to a longstanding dispute about a plot of land and a sixteenth-century mosque in the centre of present-day Ayodhyā. The dispute centres on claims that Babur, the first Mughal ruler, had the Hindu temple on the site of Rāma's birth destroyed and a mosque erected in its place. Hindu nationalists demanded the destruction of the mosque, generally known as the Babri Masjid, and that a new temple dedicated to Rāma be built in its place. This conflict is known as the Ramjanmabhumi (literally, the birthplace of Rāma) affair. It culminated in December 1992, when a group of Hindu nationalists stormed the Babri Masjid and demolished it. The government of India has effectively delegated to the judiciary the decision as to what happens to the land on which the now destroyed Babri Masjid stood. Nearly a decade and a half after the demolition of the mosque, the issue has still to be resolved. The history of the Ramjanmabhumi issue is long and complex, and in order to understand it fully we have to go back to the mythic time of treta yuga, when, according to the *Rāmāyaṇa*, Rāma was born in Ayodhyā.

Ayodhyā in the *Rāmāyaṇa*

Descriptions of Ayodhyā can be found in both the *Rāmāyaṇa* attributed to Vālmīki and Tulsīdās' later vernacular rendition of the narrative the *Rāmacaritmānas* (The Lake of the Deeds of Rāma). There is an extensive description of Ayodhyā at the beginning of Vālmīki's *Rāmāyaṇa*. Most of the fifth and sixth sarga (part/chapter) of the first book, the *Bālakāṇḍa*, is devoted to an extravagant praise of the wealth and beauty of Ayodhyā and the prosperity and righteousness of its ruler and people. Ayodhyā is identified as the capital of the kingdom of Kosala and is located on the bank of the Sarayu. Kosala was ruled by the Ikṣvāku dynasty, who, Vālmīki states, were descendents of Brahmā.

Vālmīki attributes the founding of Ayodhyā to Manu. However, at the beginning of the main narrative of the *Rāmāyaṇa*, Ayodhyā is ruled by King Daśaratha. Ayodhyā, under Daśaratha's rule, is compared with Indra's Amarāvatī. It is inhabited by beautiful women, mighty warriors and great Brāhmaṇas knowledgeable in the Veda and skilled in the performance of sacrifice. The people of Ayodhyā were happy, righteous and learned, and no citizen lacked riches or was unhappy.

The symbolic importance of Ayodhyā in the narrative of the *Rāmāyaṇa* is indicated by the title of the second book, the *Ayodhyākaṇḍa*. This book traces the early life of Rāma, before he leaves for his fourteen-year exile in the forest. The fortunes of Rāma's life are reflected in the attitudes and disposition of the citizens of Ayodhyā. The people rejoice at the news of Rāma's intended consecration as regent and become totally anguished as Rāma departs for the forest. The description of Ayodhyā after Rāma's departure makes a striking comparison with the earlier description in the *Bālakāṇḍa*. Vālmīki describes Ayodhyā as lacklustre and the people without joy. The people of Ayodhyā are described as being in 'utter agony' without their prince. Ayodhyā once again becomes a place of joy and wealth with the defeat of Rāvaṇa and the return of Rāma.

In Tulsīdās' *Rāmcaritmānas* Ayodhyā acquires a more religious connotation in keeping with the dominant bhakti theme of this vernacular retelling of the epic. In the *Bālakāṇḍa*, for example Tulsīdās suggests 'the beautiful city of Ayodhyā grants men entrance to heaven, it is celebrated through all the worlds as the holiest of holy'. Tulsīdās equates various aspects of the city with parts of the narrative. For example, the episodes of the story are like the groves and gardens on the river banks, the play of the four brothers is equated with the lotus flowers and the divine guests at Rāma's wedding are likened to the fish in the Sarayu. If anything Tulsīdās' panegyric of Ayodhyā is even more extravagant than that of Vālmīki.

The mythic Ayodhyā disappears from view at the end of treta yuga. According to a local legend told by the priests, Ayodhyā was rediscovered in kali yuga by Vikramaditya (Sun of Prowess), an epithet of the Gupta monarch Skandagupta (reigned *c.* 454–467 CE). Vikramaditya is said to have restored Ayodhyā to its former glory. Ayodhyā was sacked by the Muslim invaders during the decline of the Gupta dynasty and only emerges again to view and reassumes its Hindu ethos under the patronage of the Nawabs of Awadh in the eighteenth century (van der Veer 1988: 10). This narrative assumes that the small northern Indian town named Ayodhyā can be identified as being the same place as the town central to the narrative of the *Rāmāyaṇa.*

Ayodhyā in Uttar Pradesh

Ayodhyā is a small town in the northern Indian state of Uttar Pradesh. It is located on the banks of the river Sarayu. Ayodhyā is a fairly typical tīrtha (sacred site), with a multitude of temples, ashrams, and ghāts (places to bathe on the river) spread in and around the town. Ayodhyā is not simply a tīrtha, but is also said to be one of the seven sacred cities (Saptapurī, or Moksapurī 'liberation-cities'). Anyone who dies at one of these seven sacred places is said to be granted liberation. Consequently Ayodhyā attracts pilgrims from all parts of India. Ayodhyā must be considered as being a kṣetra (literally, a field), an area that contains many sacred sites. Many of these places are associated with various events of Rāma's life or devotees of Rāma who, because of their devotions, come to be considered as being holy in their own right. The most sacred location in the town is the contested site of the Ramjanmabhumi. Other sites include Sītā Rasoi, where it is said that Sītā first cooked a meal for Rāma and his brothers, and a small pool where tradition suggests that Rāma and his brothers cleaned their teeth.

Typically, a pilgrim will take a purifying dip in the Sarayu under the guidance of a purohita, a hereditary ritual specialist, on the ghāts. The purohita will also recount many of the mythic narratives of Ayodhyā. These tales include the founding of Ayodhyā by Manu before the first deluge, a tale of the descent of the Sarayu that parallels the myth of the descent of Gaṅgā, the rediscovery of Ayodhyā by Vikramaditya, as well as stories of Rāma. The pilgrim will then visit the various sites scattered around the kṣetra connected with life of Rāma and his brothers and perform pūjā in one or more of the many temples. The most important temples in Ayodhyā are the Kanak Bhavan, in which images of Rāma, Sīta and Lakṣmaṇa are installed, and Hanumanghari, which is dedicated to the popular monkey god Hanumān. It is sometimes claimed that Hanumān is even more revered than Rāma. Hanumanghari is also the main centre for the Vaiṣṇava order the Rāmānandis. Somewhere between 500 and 600 Rāmānandi sādhus reside at Hanumanghari.

All the major Hindu festivals are celebrated in Ayodhyā. However, it is of course festivals associated with the narrative of the *Rāmāyaṇa* that are particularly popular. In the month of Chaitra (March/April) Rāmaṉavamī is celebrated. This festival commemorates Rāma's birthday and approximately half a million pilgrims descend on Ayodhyā. Dīvālī, which is associated with the homecoming of Rāma, is also an important celebration in Ayodhyā. In the month of Kārttik (November/December) pradakṣiṇa parikram, circumambulation of Ayodhyā, also attracts substantial crowds.

Ayodhyā in the Gupta period

Hans Bakker (1986), in his monumental work, argues that present-day Ayodhyā was originally known as Sāketa. The town of Sāketa is mentioned in the Jain canon as a place that was visited by Mahavira and the birthplace of the first and fourth tīrthankaras. Sāketa is also mentioned in the Pali Canon as a place visited by Buddha. Bakker suggests that sometime during the fifth century CE the Guptas relocated their capital from Pātaliputra to Sāketa, which they then renamed Ayodhyā. Sāketa/Ayodhyā then enjoyed a brief period of prosperity before once again disappearing into relative obscurity. Bakker's account is clearly consistent with the local legend that Vikramaditya rediscovered Ayodhyā and restored it to its former glory as the capital of the Ikṣvāku dynasty. The local narrative relates that Vikramaditya was a devotee of Rāma. Whilst seeking the place of Rāma's birth he encounters a man who is totally black on a black horse. Vikramaditya is astonished to see this individual emerge totally white after bathing in the river Sarayu. It transpires that this individual is none other than Prayag, the ruler of tīrthas, who says that he has become black through the absorption of the sins of mortals and that he has been washed clean again through the power of the place, which is none other than the spot where Rāma left the mortal world. Prayag then proceeds to show Vikramaditya the place where Rāma was born (retold in van der Veer 1988: 19).

According to Bakker (1986: 31) Vikramaditya commissioned the building of numerous temples at Sāketa/Ayodhyā and it became a centre for religious teachers. Bakker speculates that Kālidāsa might well have resided in Sāketa/Ayodhyā. Although there is some textual evidence for Bakker's thesis, the archaeological evidence remains equivocal. The earliest of the temples in present-day Ayodhyā do not date from much before the eighteenth century, and as yet no archaeological remains from the Gupta period have been discovered in the centre of Ayodhyā. Nonetheless, shards of grey ware indicate that the site at the centre of the Ayodhyā may well have been occupied in the seventh century BCE.

The Ramjanmabhumi/Babri Masjid controversy

The critical moment in the historical narrative that underlies the dispute about the Ramjanmabhumi is 1528. It is in this year that Mir Baqi, under the orders of the first Mughal emperor Babur, allegedly destroyed the temple that stood on the site of Rāma's birth and built the mosque, which is now known as the Babri Masjid. An inscription inside the mosque clearly attributes the building of the mosque to Mir Baqi by the command of the Emperor Babur in 1528. However, it remains equivocal as to whether or not a Hindu temple was actually destroyed. The Sangh Parivar argue that archaeological evidence from a survey on land adjacent to the Babri Masjid revealed the existence of pillar bases from the eleventh century. Furthermore they suggest that the builders of the mosque in the sixteenth century utilised a number of black stone pillars from a pre-existing Hindu temple (VHP 1990: 2). This archaeological evidence they claim constitutes irrefutable proof that a Hindu temple was destroyed in the sixteenth century and the Babri Masjid was erected in its place.

Twenty-five historians from the Jawaharlal Nehru University in Delhi, including the renowned scholars Sarvepalli Gopal and Romila Thapar, published a short pamphlet in 1989 entitled *The Political Abuse of History*. The rationale underlying this short publication was to completely refute the historical and archaeological evidence mobilised by the Hindu nationalist camp. They suggest that there is no evidence to indicate that there had ever been a Hindu temple on the site of the Babri Masjid. They argue that the narrative that a Hindu temple dedicated to Ramjanmabhumi was destroyed in order to build the Babri Masjid does not arise until the British period. These nineteenth-century histories, they argue, were then utilised by others as genuine historical evidence (Gopal *et al.* 1989 in Noorani 2003, vol. I: 31).

Hindu nationalists suggest that despite the destruction of the Ramjanmabhumi mandir and the building of a mosque, Hindus continued to worship at the site. There does seem to be some evidence for this. William Finch, the first European to visit Ayodhyā, who was in the region some time between 1608 and 1611, reported that Hindu worship was conducted within the compound of the mosque. However, there is no evidence to suggest that Ayodhyā became a significant tīrtha until the eighteenth century. Most of the older temples in Ayodhyā date from this period. After the decline of the Mughal Empire, the Nawabs of Awadh became the dominant power in the region. Ayodhyā was the original administrative centre of the Nawabs. However Safdar Jang (ruled 1722–39), the second Nawab, removed his capital to the nearby town of Faizabad. Patrick Carnegy, in *A Historical Sketch of Tahsil Fyzabad, Zilla Fyzabad*, published in 1870, suggests that it was the removal of the Muslim court that allowed Ayodhyā once again to flourish as a Hindu town and to once again become an important destination for tīrthayātrā. However, van der Veer (1988) suggests that the increasing importance of Ayodhyā as a supra-regional place of pilgrimage was attributable to the patronage of the Nawabs and the commensurate increased wealth of the Hindu community, coupled with the growing prominence of the Rāmānandis.

Communal conflict in Ayodhyā: The British period

The first historical account of a clash between Hindus and Muslims in Ayodhyā occurred in 1855 (although some accounts suggest that this took place in 1853; see Srivastava 1993: 41–42). Ironically this violence was sparked by a claim by local Muslims that there had been a mosque at the site of the Hanumanghari Mandir in the centre of Ayodhyā. This group of Muslims demanded that the temple be opened for prayers. This resulted in a clash with the Rāmānandi nagas of the Hanumanghari Mandir which ended with the death of seventy Muslims (van der Veer 1988: 38).

In 1856 the British annexed Awadh and placed a railing around the Babri Masjid. The mahant of the Hanumanghari Mandir erected a chabutra (platform) just outside the mosque, as a place where Hindus could perform devotions to Rāma. This both physically and symbolically divided Hindus and Muslims, which was clearly commensurate with the British perception of Indian society. In 1885 the mahant filed a petition to build a temple on the site of the chabutra, but this was refused by the British, on the premise that this might incite communal antagonism. Colonel Chamier, the district judge, observed that it was unfortunate that the mosque had been built on land that was sacred to Hindus. However, Chamier observed that because the construction of the mosque had taken place over three centuries before it was then too late to redress any wrong and the only possible course was to preserve the current situation (Noorani 1993: 65). The mahant made a number of unsuccessful appeals against this ruling. What is interesting about this legal case is that it is apparent that the chabutra, and not the Babri Masjid, was considered to be the site of Rāma's birthplace. This case also sowed the seeds of the idea that there was a need for a temple dedicated to Rāma on the alleged site of his birth. This was the first legal case in the long and complex history of litigation that is associated with the Ramjanmabhumi issue.

It is significant that the British perceived Ayodhyā as being essentially a Hindu town, whereas nearby Faizabad was represented as being a Muslim town (Srivastava 1993: 38–39). It was in this period that a number of British colonial scholars published histories that were instrumental in giving credence to the narrative that Babur was responsible for the destruction of a temple dedicated to Rāma and the construction of the Babri Masjid in its stead (see Srivastava 1993; also Gopal *et al.* in Noorani 2003).

At the beginning of the twentieth century, there were a number of clashes between Hindus and Muslims in Ayodhyā. However, these appear not to be directly related to any dispute over the site of the Babri Masjid. The violent confrontations at the beginning of the twentieth century were primarily fomented by the Cow Protection Movement, a pattern that was fairly widespread throughout northern India in this period.

Post-Independence

The conflict over the Ramjanmabhumi/Babri Masjid did not really gain any momentum until the post-Independence period. The critical juncture occurred in December 1949, when images of Rāma and other Hindu deities 'miraculously' appeared in the mosque. Jaffrelot (1996: 93) suggests that there is evidence to indicate that the placing of these images in the Babri Masjid had been carefully planned. The presence of images transformed the nature of the Babri Masjid for many Hindus. According to the controversial scholar Koenraad Elst (2004), architecturally the building remained a mosque, but functionally it became a Hindu temple.

The appearance of these images led to the assertion that Rāma had come to reclaim his birthplace and pilgrims started to flock to Ayodhyā. The presence of images was totally anathema to the Muslim community and was perceived as a defilement of the mosque. This event was the catalyst for the first violence that was directly related to the ownership and nature of the land on which the Babri Masjid stood. Jawaharlal Nehru became involved at this point. Nehru instructed the head of the state government of Uttar Pradesh to ensure that no communal violence ensued. The head of the Uttar Pradesh government in turn instructed the local magistrate, K.K. Nayar, to remove the images from the mosque. Nayar refused to remove the images on the premise that to do so would provoke a riot. There is some evidence to suggest that Nayar was affiliated to the Rashtriya Swayamsevak Sangh; consequently his motivation for not removing the images is somewhat suspect.

Jawaharlal Nehru, fearing that there would be an outbreak of communal violence, ordered that the Babri Masjid be locked and out of bounds. However, a number of carefully selected Hindus from Ayodhyā were permitted to enter the Babri Masjid every year on the anniversary of the appearance of the images. Both the Hindu Mahasabha and the Arya Samaj demanded that the site of the Babri Masjid should be returned to the Hindu community. An akhand kirtan, the continuous singing of devotional songs, was initiated and was intended to continue until the day that Rāma was liberated. The Hindu Mahasabha also tried to utilise the Ayodhyā controversy to mobilise political support. Both Hindus and Muslims filed court proceedings to gain access to the site, thereby continuing the long and complex judicial process that still remains unresolved. The dispute had now become an issue of national, communal, legal, political and religious importance.

The next significant date in the ongoing struggle is July 1984, when the Vishwa Hindu Parishad (VHP) was instrumental in the formation of the Sri Ramjanmabhumi Mukti Yagna Samiti (SRMYS) – the Committee of Sacrifice to Liberate Ram's Birthplace. In September the SRMYS organised a procession from Bihar with the express intention to 'liberate Rāma' and demanded '*tala kholo*' (open the lock). The procession included a truck with large images of Rāma and Sītā under a banner declaring '*Bharat Mata Ki Jai*' – Hail to Mother India, clearly indicating that Rāma has pan-Hindu significance and implying that India is essentially a Hindu nation. The procession arrived in Ayodhyā on the evening of 6 October. The following day a meeting was organised on a vacant lot near the river. Van der Veer (1987: 291) observes that this meeting was only attended by somewhere between 5,000 and 7,000. The meeting was addressed by two office holders of the VHP, who intimated that it was a disgrace that Hindus did not have access to their holy sites. The VHP representatives were followed by a number of local sādhus and religious leaders of various sects from different regions of India. Van der Veer (1987: 293) notes that the most striking aspect of this meeting was that representatives of Śaivism, Vaiṣṇavism and the Śākta traditions all spoke on the same platform without any reference to historical conflicts or metaphysical differences. The following day, the procession peacefully departed to Lucknow to present a petition to the chief minister of Uttar Pradesh. However, the Ayodhyā controversy was overshadowed by the assassination of Indira Gandhi later in October.

In January 1986, a local lawyer lodged a file to have the gates of the Babri Masjid unlocked to enable Hindus to perform pūjā. This was turned down and the lawyer lodged an appeal with the district court at Faizabad. The session judge for the Faizabad district allowed the locks to be removed to allow public access. A crowd of VHP supporters and a television crew were already present when the padlocks were removed forty minutes after the judgment was declared. The televising of the opening of the site led to communal unrest in other parts of northern India. There is some speculation that Rajiv Gandhi had a hand in this rather surprising decision to allow access to the Babri Masjid. One of Rajiv Gandhi's advisers suggested: 'In early 1986 the Muslim Women's Bill was passed to play the Muslim card; and then came the decision on Ayodhyā to play the Hindu card' (cited in Jaffrelot 1996: 371). In February, the SRMYS formed the Ramjanmabhumi Trust specifically to lobby the government to transfer the land on which the Babri Masjid was built in order to build the biggest temple in the world. In response a number of Muslim leaders formed the Babri Masjid Action Committee (BMAC).

In 1987 communal tensions in India became a major issue, and much of this tension was focused on the dispute about sacred space in Ayodhyā. On 25 January Doordarshan, the government-run television station, began to broadcast the *Rāmāyaṇa* as a weekly series. It became the most popular programme ever shown on Indian television. Although no direct causal link can be made between the televising of the epic and increasing communal antagonism, Hindu nationalists were able to exploit the fact that the television series brought the *Rāmāyaṇa* to the forefront of consciousness for millions of Indians.

In March 1987 the BMAC organised a march to Delhi demanding that the status quo be restored in Ayodhyā. The VHP organised a counter-demonstration and communal violence erupted in a number of Indian states. The government of India designated the courts to resolve the dispute in Ayodhyā. This was a delaying tactic by the government and a strategy intended to alienate neither the Hindu nor the Muslim community.

In February 1989 the VHP held a meeting in which it determined to build a temple dedicated to Rāma on the site of the Babri Masjid. It produced a model of the proposed temple and began to collect funds. The VHP came up with a highly inventive scheme that not only raised finance, but also symbolically placed Ayodhyā at the centre of its Hindu nationalist agenda. This scheme was called Ram Shila Puja – pūjā to Rāma's bricks. The shilas were special bricks inscribed with the name of Rāma that were made in various localities throughout India, which would be used as the foundation for the proposed temple. Individuals were asked to sponsor the shilas at a set cost of 1.25 rupees per head or 5 rupees for a small family and 10 rupees for a large family. This sponsorship of the shilas was represented as an act of devotion. The shilas were collected at various local centres, where on 30 September pūjās were performed by representatives of various Hindu groups.

The VHP claims that almost 300,000 Ram Shila pūjās were performed, 11 crore (110 million) people participated in these pūjās and almost 83 million rupees were raised (VHP n.d.b.). The shilas were then aken to divisional centres where mahayagnas were performed. From the divisional centres they were transported to five regional centres. These specially consecrated bricks were then taken from the regional centres in processions accompanied by members of the Bajrang Dal, an extreme wing of the VHP, to converge at Ayodhyā. The intention was to arrive in Ayodhyā to lay the foundation stones in a ceremony referred to as the shilanyas on 9 November, a date determined by astrologers as being particularly auspicious. Many of the processions provoked communal violence en route to Ayodhyā. The chief minister of the Uttar Pradesh government, in consultation with the home minister Buta Singh and representatives of the VHP, authorised the shilanyas to take place on the proviso that the VHP adhered to the legal rulings and respected property rights. However, the Bajrang Dal marked out a site on a disputed piece of land adjacent to the Babri Masjid where the shilanyas took place on 9 November. The first foundation stone was laid by a young dalit, which the VHP (n.d.b.) suggested 'was an explicit example of [the] social equality, social security, and social respect prevalent in Hindu society' and demonstrated that untouchability had no religious sanction.

In January 1990 the VHP announced that the removal of the Babri Masjid and the building of the Ramjanmabhumi mandir should commence in February. Atal Bihari Vajpayee felt that a mobilisation on the Ayodhyā issue would in fact be detrimental to the Bharatiya Janata Party's (BJP) political agenda and requested that the VHP delay any action. The VHP delayed its call for action until June, when it founded another organisation, the Sri Ram Kar Seva Samiti (SRKSS) – the Committee for the Service of Lord Rāma. The SRKSS calls for an army of kar sevaks, volunteers, to March on Ayodhyā in order to begin the construction of the mandir in October. On 25 September L.K. Advani, the then president of the BJP, began his political Rathayātrā from Somnath in a Toyota truck decorated to look like a chariot, intending to arrive at Ayodhyā to inaugurate kar seva. This was a strategy that clearly linked the BJPs political agenda to the Ayodhyā cause. It also drew parallels between the historically verifiable destruction of the temple at Somnath and the far more equivocal case in Ayodhyā.

In October kar sevaks began to congregate in various parts of India to begin their march to 'liberate Rāma'. Advani was arrested in Bihar before he could reach Ayodhyā. A large number of kar sevaks were also arrested on the state border. Nonetheless significant numbers of kar sevaks still managed to reach Ayodhyā. Most were prevented by a police cordon from actually entering the town itself. However, a few kar sevaks managed to break through the cordon and place a saffron flag on one of the domes of the Babri Masjid. In the ensuing violence, as the police tried to maintain control, six kar sevaks were killed. These casualties were represented as being martyrs and consequently the crowd became further inflamed. The following day the kar sevaks stormed the mosque and there were further casualties. The VHP claim that fifty-nine were killed, but official statistics suggest that there were fifteen casualties.

In 1991 the BJP won the Uttar Pradesh elections and formed the state government. It also became the second largest party in the national parliament. The BJP explicitly committed itself to the Ramjanmabhumi cause in its election campaign. Its election manifesto stated that the building of a Shri Ram Mandir on the site of the alleged birthplace of Rāma in Ayodhyā 'is a symbol of our cultural heritage and national self respect' and that this would necessarily entail 'relocating the super-imposed Babri structure' (BJP Election Manifesto 1991, cited in Noorani 2003, vol. 2: 162). References to the construction of a 'Ram mandir' at Ayodhyā can also be found in the BJPs 1996 and 1998 Election Manifestos.

The VHP hoped that this was the breakthrough that they had hoped for. However, the chief minister Kalyan Singh was concerned that if the BJP gave way to the demands of the kar sevaks to have the Babri Masjid torn down in order to build a mandir, the central government would dissolve the state government and impose president's rule. Kalyan Singh came up with a compromise proposal. He acquired a 2.77 acre piece of land adjacent to the mosque for the ostensible purpose of building amenities for tourists and pilgrims. However, the acquisition of this land by the state government was disputed in the courts as it was within the boundaries of land that was still under litigation and therefore it could not be legally acquired. The VHP began to level the site. A ruling by the High Court then prohibited the erection of any permanent structure whilst the various claims about the land were still being considered by the judicial system.

In July 1992, despite the court injunction, kar sevaks began to construct a concrete platform on this disputed piece of land. Narasimha Rao, the head of the Congress-led government, requested the halt of kar seva and organised talks between the VHP and BMAC. These talks broke down and the VHP announced its intention of commencing building the Rāma temple on 6 December. The BJP government of Uttar Pradesh, in a ploy designed to prevent any move by the central government to impose president's rule, assured the Supreme Court that kar seva would be purely symbolic and that no physical construction activity would take place. By the end of November substantial numbers of kar sevaks had converged on Ayodhyā. Nandy *et al.* (1995: 186) suggest that there were 20,000 kar sevaks in Ayodhyā by the end of the month and that this number had reached 200,000 by 6 December. Troops and police were also mobilised and deployed in Ayodhyā. L.K. Advani and M.M. Joshi, both high-ranking officials in the BJP, also made their way to Ayodhyā. Shortly before noon on 6 December a number of kar sevaks broke through the police cordon and stormed the mosque with crowbars, pickaxes and shovels. The demolition of the mosque was undertaken to chants of '*Jai Shri Ram*' – 'Victory to Lord Rāma' – and more aggressive slogans such as '*Ek dhakka aur do, Babri Masjid tod do*' – 'Give one more push and break the Babri Masjid'. By late afternoon the Babri Masjid had been reduced to little more than a pile of rubble.

The destruction of the Babri Masjid sparked off communal confrontations in other parts of India. The government imposed president's rule and the head of the BJP state government in Uttar Pradesh, Kalyan Singh, resigned his post. Several days later a number of prominent leaders of the Sangh Parivar, including L.K. Advani and Bal Thackeray, were arrested on charges of inciting communal violence. Only forty-eight people were indicted on charges relating to the events of 6 December 1992. In 1997 the courts ruled that Advani and the others did have a case to answer. However, in 2001 the sessions judge at Lucknow ruled that the cases against twenty-one of the accused, including Advani and Thackeray, should be dropped on a technical point.

A number of questions about the demolition of the Babri Masjid still remain unanswered. First, was the destruction of the mosque planned in advance? The scholars from the Jawaharlal Nehru University argue that there is clear evidence of preparation and planning for the attack on the Babri Masjid. The official line given by the VHP and BJP is that the tearing down of the mosque was a spontaneous event that was sparked off by the growing frustration of the crowd. The BJP's *White Paper on Ayodhya* argues that if the government and the courts had recognised the symbolic and emotional significance of Ramjanmabhumi and agreed to the compromise of permitting kar seva on the disputed plot of land the razing to the ground of the Babri Masjid would never have taken place. The second question that still remains to be satisfactorily answered is, if the attack on the Babri Masjid was planned, then was the leadership of the Sangh Parivar aware of the plan? Ashis Nandy *et al.* (1995) suggest that Uma Bharati, a BJP Member of Parliament, and Acharya Dharmendra and Sadhvi Ritambra, prominent members of the VHP, were conspicuously active in inflaming the crowd. It is equivocal how much the BJP leaders such as L.K. Advani and Vajpayee knew. Third, the question remains as to how the kar sevaks were so successful in their storming of the Babri Masjid, given the presence of significant numbers of troops and police. Interestingly both the Sangh Parivar and the scholars who oppose Hindu nationalism suggest that there was at least some complicit sympathy for the Ramjanmabhumi movement on the part of the police.

On 16 December 1992 the central government appointed a Commission of Inquiry under a High Court judge to investigate the events and circumstances that led to the destruction of the Babri Masjid. Although this commission received a number of depositions, including one from the then Prime Minister Narasimha Rao, the Commission has not yet submitted a report. In March 2002 the Supreme Court ruled that no religious activity, either 'symbolic or actual', would be permitted on the disputed land (Supreme Court Order 2002, cited in Noorani 2003, vol. 2: 297). The court ruled that the land should be retained by the government, and that it could not lease or hand it over to any interested party until all the various cases of litigation and counter-litigation in respect of the ownership of the land had been decided by the courts. The site on which the Babri Masjid stood and the disputed 2.77 acres of adjoining land remain under guard and the controversy remains unresolved.

See also: **Amarāvatī; Arya Samaj; Āśram(a) (religious community); Bhakti (as Path); Bhārat Mātā; Brahmā; Brāhmaṇas; Buddhism, relationship with Hinduism; Dalits; Daśaratha; Dīvālī; Gaṅgā; Hanumān; Hindu; Hindu Mahasabha; Indra; Jainism, relationship with Hinduism; Jyotiṣa; Kālidāsa; Lakṣmaṇa; Mandir; Manu;**

Nationalism; Pradakṣiṇa; Pūjā; Purohit(a); Rāma; Rāmānandis; Rāmanavamī; Rāmāyaṇa; Rashtriya Swayamsevak Sangh; Rāvaṇa; Sacred animals; Sādhu; Śaivism; Śāktism; Sangh Parivar; Saptapurī; Seva; Sītā; Television and radio; Thackeray, Bal; Tīrthayātrā; Tulsīdās(a); Vaiṣṇavism; Vālmīki; Veda; Vishwa Hindu Parishad; Yajña; Yuga

STEPHEN JACOBS

Further reading

Bakker, H. 1986. *Ayodhya*. Groningen: Egbert Forsten.

Bharatiya Janata Party. 1991. 'The BJP's Election Manifesto'. In A.G. Noorani, ed., *The Babri Masjid Question*, vol. 1. 2003. Delhi: Tulika Books, 162.

Bharatiya Janata Party. 1993. *BJP's White Paper on Ayodhya and the Rama Temple Movement.*

Elst, K. 2004. 'What if Rajiv Gandhi Hadn't Unlocked the Babri Masjid in 1986' http://koenraadelst.bharatvani.org/articles/ayodhya/unlock.html (accessed September 2004).

Godpole, M. 1992. 'Commission of Inquiry Appointed'. In A.G. Noorani, ed., *The Babri Masjid Question*, vol. 2. 2003. Delhi: Tulika Books, 36–37.

Goldman, R. (ed./trans.). 1984. *The Rāmāyaṇa of Vālmīki*, vol. 1: *Bālakāṇḍa.* Princeton, NJ: Princeton University Press.

Gopal, S. (ed). 1993. *Anatomy of a Confrontation: Ayodhya and the Rise of Communal Politics in India.* London: Zed Books.

Gopal, S., R. Thapar *et al.* 1989. 'The Political Abuse of History: Babri Masjid–Ramjanmabhumi Dispute. An Analysis by Twenty Five Historians'. In A.G. Noorani, ed., *The Babri Masjid Question*, vol. 1. 2003. Delhi: Tulika Books, 28–32.

Goyal, S.L. 2002. 'Supreme Court's Order of March 13 2002'. In A.G. Noorani, ed., *The Babri Masjid Question*, vol. 2. 2003. Delhi: Tulika Books, 296–97.

Jaffrelot, C. 1996. *The Hindu Nationalist Movement and Indian Politics: 1925–1990s.* London: Hurst and Company.

Mathur, J. 1992. 'The High Court Strikes Down as Malafide Acquisition of the Land in 1991'. In A.G. Noorani, ed., *The Babri Masjid Question*, vol. 2. 2003. Delhi: Tulika Books, 67–81.

Nandy, A., S. Trivedy, S. Mayaram and A. Yagnik. 1995. *Creating a Nationality: The Ramjanmabhumi Movement and Fear of the Self.* Delhi: Oxford University Press.

Noorani, A.G. 1993. 'Legal Aspects of the Issue'. In S. Gopal, ed., *Anatomy of a Confrontation.* London: Zed Books, 58–99.

Noorani, A.G. 2003. *The Babri Masjid Question: A Matter of National Honour 1528–2003*, vols 1 and 2. Delhi: Tulika Books.

Pannikar, K. 1993. 'A Historical Overview'. In S. Gopal, ed., *Anatomy of a Confrontation.* London: Zed Books, 22–38.

Pollock, S. (trans.). 1986. *The Rāmāyaṇa of Vālmīki*, vol. II: *Ayodhyākaṇḍa.* Princeton, NJ: Princeton University Press.

Prasad, R.C. (ed./trans.). 1999. *Tulasidasa's Shriramcharitamanasa.* Delhi: Motilal Banarsidass.

Shukla, S. 2001. 'Judgement by the Session's Judge: Ayodhya Episode'. In A.G. Noorani, ed., *The Babri Masjid Question*, vol. 2. 2003. Delhi: Tulika Books, 154–59.

Srivastava, S. 1993. 'How the British Saw the Issue'. In S. Gopal, ed. *Anatomy of a Confrontation.* London: Zed Books, 38–58.

van der Veer, P. 1987. 'God Must be Liberated: A Hindu Liberation Movement in Ayodhyā'. *Modern Asian Studies* 21(2): 283–301.

van der Veer, P. 1988. *Gods on Earth: The Management of Religious Experience and Identity in a North Indian Pilgrimage Centre.* London: Athlone Press.

VHP. 1990. *Evidence For the Ram Janmabhoomi Mandir: Presented to the Government of India on December 23 1990 by the Vishva Hindu Parishad.*

VHP. n.d.a. 'Shri Ram Shila Puja Plan' http://www.vhp.org/englishsite/e.Special_Movements/dRanjanambhumi%20Muti/sriramshilapoojaplan.htm (accessed 15 September 2004).

VHP. n.d.b. 'Shilanyas: A Thrill' http://www.vhp.org/englishsite/e.Special_Movements/dRanjanambhumi%20Muti/shilanyas.htm (accessed 16 September 2004).

ĀYURVEDA

Āyurveda, a science (veda) of healthy and long life (āyus), is one of the auxiliary limbs (upaveda) of the Veda imparting instruction on ideas, actions and substances which are life enhancing and which are not. The principles of the theory and practice of Āyurveda (rendered as classical Hindu medicine) are preserved in three Sanskrit texts: *Carakasaṃhitā* (100 CE; Compendium of Caraka), *Suśrutasaṃhitā* (400 CE; Compendium of Suśruta), and *Aṣṭāṅgahṛdaya Saṃhitā* (*c.* 800; 'Eight-part Heart of Medicine' of Vāgbhaṭa).

With some variations, the subject matter in these texts is arranged into eight sections: surgery (śalya); treatment of the eye, ear, nose and throat (śālākya tantra); internal medicine (kayacikitsā); treatment of mental disorders (bhūtavidyā); midwifery and paediatrics (kaumārabhṛtya); toxicology (agadatantra); rejuvenation (rasāyana); and revitalization (vājīkaraṇa).

The day-to-day normal functioning of healthy life as well as pathological changes culminating in death are explained in Āyurveda in terms of three body humours (doṣas: phlegm, 'ṣkapha', bile, 'ṣpitta', and wind, 'ṣvāta') and seven constituents (dhātus): nutrient liquid obtained from digested food, blood, flesh, fat, bone, marrow and semen. Life is deemed to be a productive aggregate of the mind, physical body and conscious self, which are held together in a dynamic equilibrium over the allotted period of 120 years, after which the balance of the humours comes undone and death occurs. Good health prevails provided the humours are maintained in a state of dynamic equilibrium within tolerable limits. However, seasonal variations and unchecked drive for gratification of material pleasures through senses organs (asātmyendriyārtha) constantly threaten this equilibrium.

Āyurveda accordingly lays greater stress on prevention of disease production, and toward that objective prescribes: (1) svasthavṛtta, a regime of seasonally adjusted diet – prescribed with reference to one's class (varṇa), gender and stage of life (āśrama, lifestyles) – physical exercises, rhythmic breathing and meditation; (2) sadvṛtta rules of moral and social hygiene; and (3) habitation in small, self-sufficient communities. The āyurvedic approach to health is thus holistic.

When active medical intervention does become necessary, the physician (vaidya) prescribes medicines (prepared by mixing vegetal, animal and/or mineral matter) to redress the imbalance of the three humours, taking into consideration the specific body type, psychological temperament and attitude of the patient. Familial and community relationships may also figure in the treatment. Healing is also deemed to be a joint enterprise involving active participation of the patient, physician, nurse and medicaments.

Āyurveda continued to flourish in India during the first millennium of the Common Era, when its key doctrines and practices also diffused to regions beyond India: to China and Southeast Asia in the East and to Arab countries in the West. But the fortunes of Āyurveda declined after the Muslims, and following them the British, established political control over most of India during the second millennium.

In post-independence India, however, Āyurveda is rapidly reclaiming its status as a major indigenous medical system thanks to an eclectic policy of encouraging both indigenous and allopathic medicine. Today, it figures prominently in the National Health Network in providing healthcare relief to a population that is faced with chronic poverty and social inequalities. Beyond India, encouraged by indications that Āyurveda could provide relief in certain chronic or stress-related conditions, many Western institutions have embarked on research on the efficacy of Ayurveda as part of a complementary healthcare system.

See also: **Āśramas (stages of life); Gender; Meditation; Upavedas; Varṇa; Veda**

SHRINIVAS TILAK

Further reading

Desai, P. N. 1989. *Health and Medicine in the Hindu Tradition: Continuity and Cohesion.* New York: Crossroad.

Fields, G. 2001. *Religious Therapeutics: Body and Health in Yoga, Āyurveda, Tantra.* Albany, NY: SUNY Press.

Wujastyk, D. 1998. *The Roots of Āyurveda: Selections from Sanskrit Medical Writings.* New Delhi: Penguin.

English translations of the three classical Āyurvedic texts exist in different editions.

AYYAPAN̲

Ayyapan̲ is the deity enshrined in the famous pilgrimage centre of Shabarimala in Kerala. Ayyapan̲ is said to be the progeny of a union of Viṣṇu and Śiva, the consequence of Viṣṇu's Mohinī avatāra (incarnation), in which he took the form of a strikingly beautiful damsel to entice nectar away from the Asuras, who had stolen and run away with it during the churning of the celestial sea of milk (Pilla 1983: 29–30). This symbolises the fusion of Śaivism and Vaiṣṇavism in Southern India. The primary mission of the god was to kill the ferocious demoness Mahiṣī, who was terrorising heaven and the gods. Ayyapan̲ is known by various names, Bhūtanātha (Lord of the Spirits), Manikanta (One who wears a jewel on the neck), Dharma Śāstah (Ruler of Dharma), Hariharaputra (Son of Viṣṇu and Śiva), etc. Usually depicted as riding a tigress and carrying bows and arrows, Ayyapan̲ is evidently a forest or tribal god who has undergone considerable Sanskritisation in later times.

The votaries of the Ayyapan̲ pilgrimage (also known as Ayyapan̲s) have to undergo severe vrata (vows and restrictions) for forty-one days and wear black or dark blue garments and a rudrakśa mala or tulasī mala (garland). They make the arduous journey to the temple on the high hill of Shabarimala, especially for the festival of Makaraviḷakku, which takes place during the winter solstice period.

See also: **Asuras; Avatāra; Dharma; Mohinī; Śaivism; Śiva; Tīrthayātrā; Vaiṣṇavism; Viṣṇu; Vrata**

THEODORE GABRIEL

Further reading

Sekhar, Radhika. 1992. *The Sabarimalai Pilgrimage and Ayyappan Cultus.* New Delhi: Motilal Banarsidass.

Pilla, K. Narayana. 1983. *Sri Bhuthanathasarvaswam.* Kodungallur: Devi Bookstall.

B

BĀDARĀYAṆA (*c.* 100 BC)

Bādarāyaṇa is believed to be the author of the *Brahmasūtras* (*Vedāntasūtra*). Bādarāyaṇa's importance lies in having compiled the views of the early *Upaniṣads* into a work drawn on by later interpreters of the upaniṣadic tradition (Śaṅkara, Rāmānuja) as the most authentic. Bādarāyaṇa has also effectively reflected a diverse philosophical environment. In his critiques of the Sāṃkhya, Vaiśeṣika, Buddhist and Jain doctrines, he presents his own views of non-difference of cause and effect. The effect is perceived only in the presence of the cause: a piece of cloth exists when threads that compose it exist. Cause and effect are more or less the same; the differences are in their functioning. The theory of causality helps in understanding the creation of the world by Brahman, whom Bādarāyaṇa considers the material cause. By his theory of both difference and identity of cause and effect, Bādarāyaṇa fostered the variety of subsequent developments within the Vedānta traditions.

See also: **Brahman; Brahmasūtras; Rāmānuja; Śaṅkara; Sāṃkhya; Upaniṣads; Vaiśeṣika; Vedānta**

EDELTRAUD HARZER

Further reading

(Bādarāyaṇa.) 1904. *Śrī-bhāṣya. The Vedānta Sūtras with the Commentary of Rāmānuja.* Trans. G. Thibaut. SBES 48. Oxford: Clarendon Press.

(Bādarāyaṇa.) 1936. *Brahma-sūtra-bhāṣya. Vedānta-sūtras with the Commentary by Sri Madhwacharya*, 2nd edn. Trans. S. Subha Rao. Tirupati: Sri Vyasa Press.

Bādarāyaṇa. 1962. *The Vedānta Sūtras of Bādarāyaṇa with the Commentary by Śaṅkara.* Trans. G. Thibaut. New York: Dover.

BALADEVA

See: **Balarāma**

BALAK DAS

The eldest son of Guru Ghasas, the founder of the Chhatisgargh Satnamis, who succeeded his father to the leadership of the movement in 1836. Balak Das appears to have been less pious than his father, and more concerned to use the resources of the movement to provoke the higher-caste Hindus in an aggressive and radical campaign against caste discrimination. According to Kenneth Jones, he wore the sacred thread only permitted to the first three varṇas (Jones 1989: 129). His attitude towards the higher castes resulted in his assassination by a group of Rajputs in the 1860s. The immediate consequence of the murder was widespread rioting and social protest and the long-term transformation of the Satnamis from a nineteenth-century low-caste Sant movement to a socio-religious political reaction advocating the rights of the lower castes in India. Balak Das was succeeded by his son Sahib Das. Since then the leadership has remained within the family.

See also: **Caste; Ghasi Das; Sant; Satnamis; Varṇa**

RON GEAVES

Further reading

Jones, Kenneth. 1989. *Socio-Religious Reform Movements in British India, The New Cambridge History of India: Vol. 3.* Cambridge: Cambridge University Press.

BALARĀMA

The elder brother of Kṛṣṇa, sometimes regarded as a partial avatāra of Viṣṇu or the cosmic serpent Ananta or Śeṣa. Balarāma is associated with strength, as suggested by his epithet 'Balabhadra' (whose strength is good), but appears in the *Viṣṇu Purāṇa* linked to irrigation and agriculture, perhaps demonstrating the earlier synthesis of agricultural deities with the historical figure of Kṛṣṇa. The connection with agriculture is also indicated in the god's image which, although showing the usual Vaiṣṇava accoutrements of royalty, also shows him carrying a plough in one of his arms. As a mark of respect to an elder brother, Balarāma stands at the right side of Kṛṣṇa when his image is depicted, but it does not appear alone; nor is he usually worshipped.

The link to Śeṣa is based on the story of Balarāma's death under a banyan tree near Dvārakā, in which it is said that the cosmic serpent came out from his mouth and moved towards the ocean, where it was greeted and garlanded by the ocean-god. Temples to Balarāma in this form once existed but were supplanted by those of Kṛṣṇa as Balarāma was merged into the popular Vaiṣṇava cults to the latter deity in the Middle Ages. In the *Viṣṇu Purāṇa,* Balarāma is the seventh son of Devakī, who is transferred to the womb of Rohiṇī, the queen of Mathurā, in order to save him from the edict of her husband Kaṃsa to destroy all the newborn children of Devakī. In this human form, Balarāma is associated with a number of heroic exploits and married the daughter of King Raivata, who bore him two sons. Alternative accounts of his birth focus on his divine origins and state that he was created along with Kṛṣṇa from two hairs of Viṣṇu's head.

See also: **Avatāra; Devakī; Dvārakā; Kṛṣṇa; Purāṇas; Śeṣa; Vaiṣṇavism; Viṣṇu**

RON GEAVES

Further reading

Dallapicola, Anna. 2002. *Dictionary of Hindu Lore and Legend.* London: Thames & Hudson.

BALI

A powerful Asura king, the grandson of Prahlād, who ruled over the gods and gained dominion of the three worlds as a result of his virtue, valour and penance. He defeated Indra, and the gods turned to Viṣṇu for help. In a famous story, often depicted in Hindu iconography, Viṣṇu was incarnated as a dwarf (Vāmana) and requested from the king a grant of land large enough to be covered by three steps. Bali agreed, but immediately Vāmana expanded to an enormous size and with two steps covered the worlds. The third step was placed on Bali's head and the king was sent down to rule the nether regions. In another variation of the story, Vāmana covers the earth and heaven with two strides but out of respect to Bali's virtue and ancestry leaves him the infernal regions to rule over.

See also: **Asuras; Avatāra; Indra; Prahlād(a)**

RON GEAVES

Further reading

Bunce, Fredrick. 2000. *An Encyclopaedia of Hindu Deities, Demi-Gods, Godlings, Demons and Heroes*, vol. I. New Delhi: DK Printworld.

BASAVA

Basava was a twelfth-century Jain minister of Vijjala, the king who reigned over Kalyāna in the Karnāṭak region of Southern India. Basava possibly founded but certainly developed the Vīraśāiva system, a well-organised and influential Śaiva movement that attracted attention from other parts of India. Basava's teachings were iconoclastic; he was opposed to sacrifices, pilgrimages and image worship, and the movement did not construct temples for worship or acknowledge the authority of the Veda. The only sacred symbol acknowledged was the liṅga. Basava rejected all caste and gender distinctions and encouraged manual labour and simple living, but his views brought a hostile reaction from the local Brāhmaṇas, whose authority he opposed, even going so far as to suggest their replacement by a new order of priests known as jaṅgamas. Contemporary jaṅgamas perform marriage ceremonies and other domestic rites of passage and function as gurus to the community.

The deteriorating relationship with the Brāhmaṇa caste resulted in Basava's exile from the court and the loss of his royal post. Along with the Vīraśāivas, he found himself banished from Kalyāṇa. The Brāhmaṇas vented their outrage on the local Jain community, leading to considerable persecution, and consequently Jain records demonstrate a rather jaundiced view of Basava's religious teachings and behaviour. The best primary source for the teachings of the Vīraśāivas is the *Śūnyasampādane*, written in the vernacular for the common person; however, it contains little that elucidates either the spiritual practices or organisational forms of the movement, other than that it espoused mystical union and rejected asceticism.

See also: **Caste; Guru; Image worship; Śaivism; Saṃskāras; Tīrthayātrā; Veda; Vīraśāiva; Women, status of**

RON GEAVES

Further reading

Nandimath, S.C. 1942. *A Handbook of Viraśaivism*. Dharwar, Delhi: Motilal Benarsidass.
Nandimath, S.C., L.M.A. Menezes and R.C. Hiremath (eds). 1965. *The Śūnyasampādane*, vols 1–3. Dharwar, Delhi: Karnatak University.

BASHAM, ARTHUR LLEWELLYN (1914–86)

English historian and Sanskritist. Basham pursued a literary career before beginning university study at the School of Oriental and Asian Studies (SOAS) in London in 1938, only for his studies to be interrupted by the war. Resuming them after the war, in 1948 he was appointed Lecturer in Ancient Indian History at SOAS. In 1965 he became Professor of Ancient Civilisations at the Australian National

University. His first book, on the *Ājīvikas*, was based on his doctoral research (1951); his second, *The Wonder that Was India* (1954), a wide-ranging survey of Indian history and culture to the twelfth century, has become a classic of its kind and went through many editions. He died in India, where, shortly before, he had accepted the post of Swami Vivekananda Professor of Oriental Studies at the Asiatic Society of Bengal. A work on the development of Hindu thought that had occupied him in his last years was edited by one of his former students and published posthumously (1991).

See also: **Asiatic Societies; Hinduism, history of scholarship; Vivekananda, Swami**

WILL SWEETMAN

Further reading

Basham, A.L. 1954. *The Wonder that Was India*. London: Sidgwick and Jackson.

Basham, A.L. 1991. *The Origins and Development of Classical Hinduism*, ed. K.G. Zysk. New York: Oxford University Press.

BĀULS

'Bāul' literally means 'mad', 'crazy'. According to scholars, at the end of the twelfth century, when the Sena kings who came to power were Vaiṣṇavas, Buddhist influence, which had dominated Bengal until that time, began to wane. The Sahajīya form of Buddhism, which was in vogue in Bengal, came under the influence of Vaiṣṇavism. In the Sahajīya form of Buddhism, the idea of perfect knowledge (prajñā) and its means of attainment (upāya) had already been transformed into symbols of male and female aspects of the absolute reality. When Vaiṣṇavism began to become the dominant religion in Bengal during the twelfth century, these ideas were quickly appropriated by the Vaiṣṇava cult of Radha and Kṛṣṇa. As a result, a new sect known as the Vaiṣṇava Sahajīyas emerged in twelfth-century Bengal. In the thirteenth century, Bengal came under the rule of the Muslim kings, who vigorously began to spread Islam. Some of the Vaiṣṇava Sahajīyas converted to Islam, which gave rise to Muslim Sahajīyas. These Muslims in practice followed Sahajīya rituals but in religious faith followed Islam. The Muslim Sajajīyas found the Sufi mystic tradition particularly attractive as it suited their existing devotional life. Sahajīya spiritual love and Sufi mystic love became integrated into the Muslim Sahajīya movement. This Sufi mysticism together with the Sahajīya cult of spiritual love later on, in the sixteenth century, influenced the Caitanya movement. It is out of this long chain of religious interactions that the movement of the Bāuls was born. These bard singers were mainly influential during the seventeenth century, although some scholars seem to think that they were in existence from the fourteenth century.

See also: **Buddhism, relationship with Hinduism; Caitanya; Kṛṣṇa; Rādhā; Vaiṣṇavism**

PRATAP KUMAR

Further reading

Goswami, B.K. 1965. *The Bhakti Cult in Ancient India*. Varanasi: Chowkamba Sanskrit Series Office.

Ray, Manas. 1994. *The Bauls of Birbhuni: A Study in Persistence and Change in Communication in Cultural Context*. Calcutta: Firma KLM.

BESANT, ANNIE (1847–1933)

Annie Besant (née Wood) was the estranged wife of an Anglican clergyman and had espoused secularism, socialism, trade unionism and the rights of women. At the age of 42 she joined the Theosophical Society after reading H.P. Blavatsky's *The Secret Doctrine* and rapidly took over the intellectual leadership of the movement after Blavatsky's death in 1891. In 1907 she was elected president and threw her remarkable energies into the development of the Society. Its worldwide membership rose from 15,000 when she took office to a peak of over 40,000 in 1929. In the English-speaking world, she encouraged members to engage in social action in such fields as women's suffrage, vegetarianism, alternative medicine, progressive education and the Garden City movement. Throughout the world and in India itself she became an enthusiastic promoter of Hindu thought and culture, learnt Sanskrit, and produced an English translation of the *Bhagavadgītā*. In 1901 she was the driving force behind the establishment of the Central Hindu College in Benares (now Varanasi), which became the Central Hindu University, and continued to work for the establishment of schools and colleges and youth and women's movements in India. Dr Besant encouraged the publication and distribution of textbooks on Hinduism in India, and the dissemination of Theosophical books and journals which popularised Hinduism and the other Asian religions in the Western world. She became an active supporter of independence for India, which she made her home, was president of the Indian National Congress in 1917 and was proprietor of the nationalist newspaper *New India*. She wrote and lectured widely on Indian affairs, theosophy and other causes up to a few years before her death.

See also: **Blavatsky, Helen; Nationalism; Theosophy and the Theosophical Society; Women's movement**

KEVIN TINGAY

Further reading

Nethercot, A.H. 1961. *The First Five Lives of Annie Besant*. London: Rupert Hart-Davies.
Nethercot, A.H. 1963. *The Last Four Lives of Annie Besant*. London: Rupert Hart-Davies.
Prakasa, S. 1969. *Annie Besant*. Bombay: Bhārata Vidya Bhavan.

BHAGAVADGĪTĀ

The *Bhagavadgītā* (Song of the Lord) is located in the sixth parvan of the *Mahābhārata* when the dispute between the Pāṇḍavas and the Kauravas has culminated in the massing of two great armies on the plains of Kurukṣetra. The *Bhagavadgītā*, reported to the old king Dhṛtarāṣṭra by Saṃjaya, the royal bard, vividly evokes the crisis of conscience experienced by Arjuna, the third of the Pāṇḍava brothers, when contemplating the prospect of killing his own kin. The famous warrior, envisaging only evil consequences following from engaging in such a conflict, tells Kṛṣṇa, his charioteer, that he would rather die than kill members of his own family and, sinking down in his chariot, lets his bow fall from his hand. In replying to Kṛṣṇa's stinging rebuke, the troubled Arjuna requests that Kṛṣṇa become his teacher, and it is this teaching, coupled with the theophany in which Kṛṣṇa reveals his divine nature, that eventually convinces Arjuna to fight, now free from doubt and delusion. That teaching covers the nature of the divine and humanity, the supreme goal of life and the path to this goal, but there are many views about what this teaching entails.

Confronting the complexities of the *Bhagavadgītā*, Arvind Sharma poses the question of the text's univalence or multivalence (Sharma 1986: x–xii). He argues that tendencies to regard the *Bhagavadgītā* as either confused and contradictory or systematic and synthetic pay insufficient attention to the overriding imperative to convince Arjuna to fight (Sharma 1986: xvi–xx, xxv–xxvi). In this respect, he concludes that the *Bhagavadgītā* is univalent, irrespective of its multivalence in terms of the specific strategies intended to lead Arjuna to reach the right decision (Sharma 1986: xxvii). Such multivalence has been reflected in the diversity of interpretations offered of the *Bhagavadgītā*. Thus, in his commentary Śaṅkara, the foremost exponent of Advaita Vedānta, upheld the ultimacy of the impersonal absolute and the identity of the one self with the absolute, the aim being realisation of this identity suffused with bliss and achieved through the discipline of knowledge. In contrast, in his commentary Rāmānuja, advocating Viśiṣṭādvaita Vedānta, championed the personal God and the relationship between the individual selves and God, looking towards the selves' communion with God, characterised by love and brought about by grace and devotion.

Moreover, the number of commentaries the *Bhagavadgītā* has generated, including those produced by Vedāntic philosophers and theologians for whom the text is part of the prasthānatrayā (threefold canon), is one indication of the historic importance of the text. Indeed, despite its Vaiṣṇavite credentials, the *Bhagavadgītā* has also attracted Śaivite commentaries, notably Abhinavagupta's *Gītārthasaṃgraha*. An additional indication of the *Bhagavadgītā*'s importance is the way in which the text has inspired other *Gītās*, among them the *Anu-Gītā*, another dialogue between Kṛṣṇa and Arjuna, the *Uddhava-Gītā*, where Kṛṣṇa instructs Uddhava, the *Śiva-Gītā*, where Śiva instructs Rāmā, and the *Devī-Gītā*, where Bhuvaneśvarī instructs Himālaya. Notwithstanding changes in protagonists, the debt owed by these works to the *Bhagavadgītā* is clear in the interaction between the divine teacher and his or her disciple. Further, though the *Bhagavadgītā*'s epic location suggests that its status as smṛti (remembered or traditional literature) is unproblematic, a view endorsed by, for example, Gerald Larson (1975: 661), other scholars have seen its status as approaching that of śruti (heard or revealed literature). This argument is advanced by Thomas Coburn (1984: 448–49), who cites as evidence the text's few variants, its claim to be upaniṣadic and its inclusion in an index to the *Upaniṣads*.

However, the modern period has seen the *Bhagavadgītā* rise to extraordinary popularity, not only in India but globally. Explanations for this differ but there is a measure of agreement that the *Bhagavadgītā* has become *the* Hindu scripture, frequently referred to as the Hindu Bible, and also that it has become a spiritual classic, often featured in prestigious collections of world literature. Eric Sharpe identifies general trends such as the emergence of a new Indian elite in receipt of a Western-style English-medium education as significant but notes factors particular to the *Bhagavadgītā* too: its usefulness in countering Christian propaganda and underwriting an activist agenda and, of course, its brevity (Sharpe 1985: 67–68, 76–77). Insofar as the *Bhagavadgītā*'s history in the West is concerned, the text's accessibility (at least in comparison with the Veda) in the early British era played a part alongside other factors, the revolutions in literacy and typography for instance, leading to interpretations ranging from the academic and historical to the perennialist and mystical. Perhaps, then, the appeal of the *Bhagavadgītā*, to a greater or lesser extent, can be attributed to the text's openness to alternative readings.

Certainly, modern Hindu commentaries have diverged markedly in their accounts of the *Bhagavadgītā*. Bal Gangadhar Tilak (1856–1920) and Mohandas Karamchand Gandhi (1869–1948) both took an activist line, emphasising selfless action, but disagreed over whether violence could ever be justified. For Swami Vivekananda (1863–1902) and Sarvepalli Radhakrishnan (1888–1975), the *Bhagavadgītā*'s inclusivity exemplified the tolerance they attributed to Hinduism. A.C. Bhaktivedanta Swami Prabhupada (1896–1977), founder of the International

Society for Krishna Consciousness, stressed the personal nature of the divine and the primacy of devotion, as well as his place in a lineage originating with Kṛṣṇa himself and to which Caitanya had also belonged. Maharishi Mahesh Yogi (*b.* 1917), founder of Transcendental Meditation, instead asserted the superiority of the impersonal absolute and opposed the subordination of knowledge, insisting throughout that he was following in the footsteps of his own teacher in recovering Śaṅkara's true legacy.

Modern Western commentators have also espoused very different opinions about the meaning and implications of the *Bhagavadgītā*. Rudolf Otto (1869–1937) evinced a fascination with literary critical questions, arguing for the existence of an original form of the text as part of the epic, to which a series of interpolations had been added. These interpolations, he believed, rendered the text's final form, bearing the imprint of Sāṃkhya and Yoga philosophies, the Vedic cult, Vedāntic thought and Vaiṣṇavite devotion, composite and inconsistent. Although he shared Otto's interest in mysticism, R.C. Zaehner (1913–74) rejected the identification of supposed separate strands within the text because he regarded it as unified, expounding a devotional and theistic understanding of its teaching. J.N. Farquhar (1861–1929) and Bede Griffiths (1906–93) reflected upon the *Bhagavadgītā* in the light of their Christian faith, as a prophecy of Christ in the context of fulfilment theology and a confirmation of the Gospel in the context of the equality of religions, respectively. Annie Besant (1847–1933), a leading Theosophist, stressed the universal relevance of the *Bhagavadgītā* and the imperative to act in and for the world, whereas Aldous Huxley (1894–1963) hailed the text as one of the best expressions of the Perennial Philosophy, preferring knowledge to both devotion and action.

In India, the *Bhagavadgītā*'s advent is celebrated in a festival, it is the subject of children's comics and storybooks, constitutes three episodes in B.R. and R. Chopra's television serialisation of the *Mahābhārata* and has become an award-winning Sanskrit feature directed by G.V. Iyer. In the West, since Charles Wilkins' translation was published in 1785, the *Bhagavadgītā* has aroused the interest of writers such as William Blake, Edwin Arnold, T.S. Eliot and E.M. Forster, and, despite its controversially cursory treatment in Peter Brook's stage adaptation of the *Mahābhārata*, versions scholarly and popular continue to appear, not excluding the odd novelisation or even pack of cards. Widely acknowledged as a source of timeless truths, probably dating from the centuries immediately before or after the Common Era, the *Bhagavadgītā* seems to speak authoritatively to each age. Explicitly Hindu in its concepts and terminology, with its composer traditionally thought to be the legendary Vyāsa, the *Bhagavadgītā* seems to transcend its religious and cultural frame of reference. The *Bhagavadgītā* continues to exert a powerful hold over Hindus and non-Hindus alike, ever yielding fresh insights to new seekers moved by the beauty of its poetry and the profundity of its message.

See also: **Abhinavagupta; Advaita; Arjuna; Ātman; Besant, Annie; Bhakti; Books, comics, newspapers and magazines; Brahman; Brahman-Ātman; Caitanya; Deities; Dhṛtarāṣṭra; Farquhar, John Nicol; Film; Gandhi, Mohandas Karamchand; Interfaith/Inter-religious dialogue; International Society for Krishna Consciousness; Jñāna; Karma; Kauravas; Kṛṣṇa; Kurukṣetra; Mahābhārata; Maharishi Mahesh Yogi; Mokṣa; Nationalism; Pāṇḍavas; Prabhupada, A.C. Bhaktivedanta Swami; Prasthānatrayī; Radhakrishnan, Sir Sarvepalli; Rāmā; Rāmānuja; Sacred Books of the East; Sacred texts; Śaivism; Sāṃkhya; Śaṅkara; Śiva; Television and radio;**

Theosophy and the Theosophical Society; Tilak, Bal Gangadhar; Transcendental Meditation; Upaniṣads; Utsava; Vaiṣṇavism; Veda; Vedānta; Vedism; Viśiṣṭādvaita; Vivekananda, Swami; Vyāsa; Wilkins, Sir Charles; Yoga

CATHERINE A. ROBINSON

Further reading

Coburn, T.B. 1984. '"Scripture" in India: Towards a Typology of the Word in Hindu Life'. *Journal of the American Academy of Religion* 52.3: 435–59.

Johnson, W.J. (trans.). *The Bhagavad Gita*. Oxford: Oxford University Press.

Larson, G.J. 1975. 'The *Bhagavadgītā* as Cross-Cultural Process: Toward an Analysis of the Social Locations of a Religious Text'. *Journal of the American Academy of Religion* 43.4: 651–69.

Robinson, C.A. 2005. *Interpretations of the Bhagavadgītā and Images of the Hindu Tradition*. London: Routledge.

Sharma, A. 1986. *The Hindu Gītā: Ancient and Classical Interpretations of the Bhagavadgītā*. London: Duckworth.

Sharpe, E.J. 1985. *The Universal Gītā: Western Images of the Bhagavadgītā*. London: Duckworth.

BHAGAVĀN

Signifying divinity, the Lord or God, the term 'bhagavān' ('The Adorable One') is the first-person nominative form of 'bhagavat' (literally meaning 'having shares'). The term 'bhakti' (devotion), as well as 'bhagavat' or 'bhagavān', derives from the Sanskrit root 'bhaj' ('participate', 'distribute', 'divide', 'apportion'). The term 'bhaga' (also related to 'bhaj') means 'share' or 'portion' in the *Ṛgveda* and is also applied to one of the divine Ādityas ('Āditya Bhaga'). This means that 'bhagavān' signifies 'possessing shares' or 'having a share'; it means the fortunate, powerful, blessed, splendid, venerable, lucky. 'Bhagavān' is the Lord, the holy one, glorious, illustrious. The Bhagavān is one (divine or human) who bestows shares as well as one who 'takes a share in'. In the *Viṣṇu Purāṇa* (e.g. at 6.5.79), six qualities of holiness are listed as belonging to one known as 'bhagavān' (one who possesses 'bhaga'): strength (bala), sovereignty or lordship (aiśvarya), potency or power (śakti), knowledge (jñāna), heroism or virility (vīrya) and splendour (tejas).

The term 'bhagavān' occurs in early Hindu literature. At *Śvetāśvatara Upaniṣad* 5.4, it refers to Rudra-Śiva. Outside Hinduism, it has been applied to the Buddha. It has also been used as a title (meaning 'Blessed One' or 'Venerable') for various sages and spiritual teachers. However 'Bhagavān' is best known as a title of Viṣṇu and Kṛṣṇa.

Throughout the *Bhagavadgītā*, Kṛṣṇa is referred to as 'śrībhagavān' (before he speaks). Thus 'śrī' (a title of respect) is followed by 'bhagavān' ('the beloved one').

The term 'bhāgavata' (meaning 'devoted to' or 'related to' Bhagavān) refers to a devotee of Viṣṇu or a Vaiṣṇava. The *Bhagavadgītā* and *Bhāgavata Purāṇa* are central texts for Bhagavatism. The emotionalist bhakti of the *Bhāgavata Purāṇa* contrasts with the more sober *Bhagavadgītā* and bhakti-yoga teaching. Bhāgavatas regard themselves as benefiting from the Bhagavān's nature (they are devoted to Him, participate in Him, serve Him).

See also: **Bhagavadgītā; Bhāgavatas; Bhakti; Buddhism, relationship with Hinduism; Kṛṣṇa; Purāṇas; Rudra; Saṃhitā; Śiva; Upaniṣads; Vaiṣṇavism; Viṣṇu; Yoga**

MARTIN OVENS

Further reading

Welbon, G.R. 1987. 'Vaiṣṇavism: Bhāgavatas'. In M. Eliade, ed., *Encyclopedia of Religion*. Vol. 15. New York: Macmillan Publishing Company, 172–77.

BHĀGAVATA PURĀṆA

See: **Purāṇas**

BHĀGAVATAS

The religion of the Bhāgavatas initially emerged in the Mathurā region in the north. Even though Vaiṣṇavism traces its origins to the Vedic texts, there is sufficient evidence to believe that early Bhāgavata religion was centred around Vāsudeva–Kṛṣṇa, who was believed to be a popular deity and later came to be identified with the Vedic god Viṣṇu. For instance, in the *Taittirīya Āraṇyaka* (10.1.6) Vāsudeva is identified with Viṣṇu. The biggest resources for the religion of the Bhāgavatas are the *Mahābhārata* and especially the *Bhagavadgītā*.

See also: **Āraṇyakas; Bhagavadgītā; Kṛṣṇa; Mahābhārata; Mathurā; Saṃhitā; Vaiṣṇavism**

PRATAP KUMAR

Further reading

Dasgupta, Shashibusan. 1976. *Obscure Religious Cults*. Calcutta: Firma K.L. Mukhopadhyaya.

De, Sushil Kumar. 1961. *Early History of the Vaiṣṇava Faith and Movement in Bengal from Sanskrit and Bengali Sources*. Calcutta: Firma K.L. Mukhopadhyaya.

Gonda, J. 1993. *Aspects of Early Viṣṇuism*. Delhi: Motilal Banarsidass (first published 1954).

Goswami, B.K. 1965. *The Bhakti Cult in Ancient India*. Varanasi: Chowkamba Sanskrit Series Office.

BHAGAVATĪ

The name Bhagavatī is a generic term for the goddess in Kerala and other parts of South India. There are many Bhagavatīs associated with various towns and villages, and the name of Bhagavatī is often derived from the place name, – e.g. Kotuṅgallūr Bhagavatī, Kaññangād Bhagavatī, Muccilt Bhagavatī or Māppiccri Bhagavatī. Kurup opines that Bhagavatī may be either of local origin or a hypostasis of the prototype pan-Hindu goddess Śakti (Kurup 1973: 22). Some are deified human beings, as in the case of the great female saint Kāṇṇaki whose legend is extolled in Iḷaṅkō Aṭikaḷ's famous epic poem *Cilappatikāram* (Tale of an Anklet).

There are some interesting rituals associated with Bhagavatī. The Kodunagallur Bhagavatī has to be appeased by reciting very obscene words and ditties. The Chengannūr Bhagavatī is said to have periods and during this menstrual phenomenon the priest removes the undergarments draped on the image, examines them for blood and sells them to devotees as sacred mementos (Vaidyanathan 1982: 119).

See also: **Kāṇṇaki; Śakti**

THEODORE GABRIEL

Further reading

Ayrookuzhiel, A.M. Abraham. 1983. *The Sacred in Popular Hinduism*. Bangalore: CISRS.

Kurup, K.K.N. 1973. *The Cult of Teyyam in Kerala*. Calcutta: Indian Publications.

Smith, H.D. and M. Narasimhachary. 1991. *Handbook of Hindu Gods, Godesses, and Saints Popular in Contemporary South India*. Delhi: Sundeep Prakashan.

Vaidyanathan, K.R. 1982. *Temples and Legends of Kerala*. Bombay: Bharatiya Vidya Bhavan.

BHAJAN

'Worship', 'adoration'. The bhajan is a Hindu (mainly Vaiṣṇava) and Sikh devotional song. Although bhajans are grounded in the rāga (melody) and tāla (rhythm) structure of the north Indian classical musical tradition, many of their melodies and lyrics are taken from the devotional popular tradition (bhakti). Episodes from the lives of gods and hagiographic stories of saints and devotees are among the favourite subjects of bhajans. Complex spiritual truths are portrayed in the simple language of the farmers, merchants and other common people of the time. The popularity of the bhajan is due to the spread of the many and diverse bhakti streams from the sixteenth century on. Some of the most revered saints and mystics, such as Kabīr, Tulsīdās, Mīrābāī, Sūrdās, composed bhajans to worship a unique transcendent god differently called Īśvara, Rāma, Kṛṣṇa, Allah, Buddha, etc. Bhajans are generally performed by a small orchestra playing a limited number of musical instruments such as kartāl (wooden clappers), ektāra (one-stringed lute), dotāra (two-stringed lute), harmonium (hand-pumped organ), mañjīrā (cymbals), sitār (lute), ḍholak (small drum), tablā (hand drums), mṛdaṅga (big drum). As in kīrtan, a lead singer and a chorus alternate in singing strophe and refrain. Bhajans cover a broad range of musical styles from the simple chant (dhun) to highly developed performance like ṭhumrī. The structure of bhajan is very conventional. It contains a sthāi (fixed refrain) and numerous antaras (the intermediary part between the refrain and the final development of a musical theme), the last one having a special significance because it contains the colophon (banhitā) with the name and the intention of the author. Although traditional Vaiṣṇava bhajan holds a dominant position, this was influenced by different styles (Sikh kīrtan, Muslim qawwali, etc.) and is now employed in non-religious contexts such as film and pop music.

See also: **Bhakti Movement; Film; Īśvara; Kabīr; Kīrtaṇ(a); Kṛṣṇa; Mīrābāī; Music; Ráma; Sikhism, relationship with Hinduism; Sound recordings; Sūrdās; Tulsīdās(a); Vaiṣṇavism**

FABRIZIO M. FERRARI

Further reading

Beck, G. 2000. 'Religious and Devotional Music: Northern Area'. In A. Arnold, ed., *South Asia: The Indian Subcontinent, Garland Encyclopaedia of World Music*, vol. 5. New York: Garland Publishing, 246–58.

Simon, R. 1984. *Spiritual Aspects of Indian Music*. Delhi: Sundeep Prakashan.

BHAKTI (AS PATH)

The path of bhakti (devotion) is one of three standard, soteriologically efficacious personal orientations, the others being the paths of jñāna (knowledge) and karma (action). All three may be found closely associated in the *Bhagavadgītā*, which has usually been interpreted as exalting one of the three paths above the others (Sharma 1986: xv–xvi, xxii–xxvi). Such interpretations demonstrate that the three paths are generally seen to be, if not mutually exclusive, at least broadly independent.

Bhakti is derived from the verbal root *bhaj-*, 'to share with', and may often be understood non-theologically (Ali 2002). Generally speaking, it indicates a position of dependence *vis-à-vis* another, in which offerings may be made in the hope of grace. In Sanskrit sources the earliest bhakti soteriology appears in the *Śvetāśvatara Upaniṣad* and the *Mahābhārata* (for the precursors to Vaiṣṇavite bhakti, see Solomon 1970), particularly the latter's *Bhagavadgītā* and *Nārāyaṇīya* sections, where exclusive (ananya) devotion is said to be indispensable for direct experience of the god (Sharma 1986: xv–xvi, xxii–xxvi). Rather than the gods having differing arenas of practical jurisdiction, one god was made the focus of all a person's attention. This god, chosen from many, is the Iṣṭadevatā (deity of choice), and such focused attention may result in a vision (darśana) of him or her as he or she truly is.

Bhakti finds its most vibrant textual expression in the south Indian Śaivite and Vaiṣṇavite poetry of the 'bhakti movement', where idioms originally associated with romantic love were used of the person–god relationship. The devotional impulse was incorporated into the orthodox philosophical tradition by various Vedānta philosophers, most prominently

Rāmānuja. In later bhakti traditions the object of devotion may be considered as nirguṇa (without qualities, impersonal and ineffable) or saguṇa (with qualities).

Bhakti, expressed in pūjā (rites of reverence) and pilgrimage, is said to counteract and outweigh the ill effects of neglecting other socio-religious duties. Since such neglect has often been obligatory for many – various traditionally efficacious behaviours being reserved for dvija (twice-born) men – bhakti is easily associated with the subversion of elitisms: it offers a radically universal but personally adaptable religious possibility. As Kṛṣṇa says in the *Bhagavadgītā* (9.30, 32):

> Even a hardened criminal who loves me and none other is to be deemed a saint, for he [or she] has the right conviction . . . . Even people of low origins, women, *vaiśyas*, nay *śūdras*, go the highest course if they rely on me.
>
> (Buitenen 1981: 107)

Bhakti's transcendence of social hierarchy is most clearly demonstrated in the poetry of the north Indian sants, some of whom saw mere utterance of Rāma's name as guaranteeing salvation. As might be imagined, however, bhakti has been readily incorporated into institutional and hierarchical schemes by a wide variety of renunciative and non-renunciative groups.

See also: **Bhagavadgītā; Bhakti movement; Darśana (worship and practice); Dvija; Iṣṭadevatā; Jñāna; Karma; Kṛṣṇa; Mahābhārata; Pūjā; Rāma; Rāmānuja; Śaivism; Sant; Tīrthayātrā; Upaniṣads; Vedānta; Vaiṣṇavism; Varṇa**

SIMON BRODBECK

Further reading

Ali, D. 2002. 'Anxieties of Attachment: The Dynamics of Courtship in Medieval India'. *Modern Asian Studies* 36: 103–39.

Buitenen, J.A.B. van (ed./trans.). 1981. *The Bhagavadgītā in the Mahābhārata: A Bilingual Edition*. Chicago, IL and London: University of Chicago Press.

Sharma, A. 1986. *The Hindu Gītā: Ancient and Classical Interpretations of the Bhagavadgītā*. La Salle, IL: Open Court.

Solomon, T. 1970. 'Early Vaiśṇava *Bhakti* and Its Autochthonous Heritage'. *History of Religions* 10: 32–48.

BHAKTI MOVEMENT

While regarded as historically the last path developed for the attainment of mokṣa, there is evidence of proto-bhakti in the Vedic hymns and, while not specifically mentioned in the *Upaniṣads*, these essential texts do provide the doctrine of grace which is such an essential element for bhaktimarga (Klostermaier 1994: 222–23). The most important classes of texts for inspiration for those who practice bhakti are the Epics and the *Purāṇas*; however, the Sanskrit texts the *Bhagavadgītā* and the *Bhaktisūtras* of Śāndilya, written in the eighth century CE, provide a more philosophical underpinning to the tradition and help reconcile it to Brahmanical Hinduism. However, generally bhakti traditions broke down social barriers concerned with caste and gender distinctions as they promoted a way of salvation that was open to all. Although appropriated on several occasions by Brāhmaṇas, especially in its Vaiṣṇavite manifestations, bhakti has succeeded in becoming the religion of the Indian masses, undermining caste distinctions and providing forms of worship with a common language of ritual practice. In addition to a number of sacred texts, often written in the vernacular, bhakti has inspired thousands of religious poets and mystics whose songs are extremely popular with the masses of rural Indians.

In one of the *Bhaktisūtras*, Śāndilya defines bhakti as intense desire for the Lord from one's whole heart (Klostermaier 1994: 222), and in the other text Narada is quoted as saying that it is supreme love for the Lord, by gaining which an individual is fulfilled and content to the degree that he or she becomes desireless (Klostermaier 1994: 222).

The etymology of the term is varied. It is believed to have originated from *bhaj*, the basic meaning of which is 'to share with'. In a religious context, however, it is often defined as 'to worship' or 'to adore' (Vaudeville 1987: 27) in that it consists of loving devotion towards a personal god, but another possibility is *bhañj* ('to separate'), in that most bhakti traditions are based on the idea of separation from the divine leading to the human existential dilemma, and the consequent suffering only being overcome by reunion with the divine (Klostermaier 1994: 221). Central to bhakti is the cultivation of inner longing, focusing desires for the temporal into one all-consuming passion for reunion with chosen object of worship. The bhakta is intensely aware of this painful separation and seeks to overcome it. Thus the two central themes of bhakti poetry are the pain of separation and the ecstasy of union.

It is claimed that the bhakti tradition began as early as the fourth century BCE in Tamil Nadu, south India, but that it flourished from the twelfth to the eighteenth centuries, moving up through India to develop unique forms in north India, especially the group of religious iconoclasts who came to be labelled Sants. Certainly early poetry shows Tamil devotees singing of their love to either Śiva or Viṣṇu, and by the seventh to ninth centuries CE the tradition was institutionalised sufficiently for large temple endowments to maintain the musicians, dancers and recitals of poetry. In particular, the Nāyaṉmārs (those who adored Śiva) and the Āḻvārs (those who adored Viṣṇu) provided literary contributions in the vernacular that were to form the bedrock of Tamil culture. Other bhakti-poets were to have a similar impact on the development of regional languages and culture, such as the Sikh gurus in the Punjab, Kabīr and Tulsīdās, with regard to Hindi-speaking parts of North India.

The Bhakti tradition has incredible diversity, whereas some bhaktas supported orthodoxy, others fiercely criticised the worship of deities and the outer expression of religiosity, opposing the caste system with complete disregard for social conventions. Some worshipped only a formless divine (nirguṇa bhakti) whereas most used the forms of Śiva, Viṣṇu and the Devī to focus their intense and passionate relation with the divine (saguṇa bhakti). The orthodox bhaktas tended to be south Indian Brāhmaṇas intent on reasserting their authority upon the non-brāhmaṇa populations of south India who were flocking to bhakti, perhaps attracted by the possibilities that it offered as an outlet for social and economic discontent, and by its egalitarianism and outpouring of emotions, all expressed in the vernacular. The most famous of these was Rāmānuja (eleventh century CE), the great critic of Śaṅkara's Advaita Vedānta, who supplied an intellectual link between the bhakti movement and orthodox Brahmanical traditions and the supremacy of the Veda.

Through the means of intense devotion to Viṣṇu, Rāmānuja developed a theistic philosophy that asserted that human beings cannot have knowledge of God outside of God's revelation of himself. Thus salvation comes from God's grace, that is, from above and beyond, rather than the classic liberation model arrived at by realising or achieving Brahman-Ātman unity within. The bhakta's role in his/her salvation comes through loving devotion expressed by worship. According to Rāmānuja, a devotee should cultivate goodwill to all creatures, faith in the Lord's protection, and seek refuge in the Lord as a personal saviour, a sense of helplessness in hope of his favour and, finally, a sense of being a servant striving for the salvation of others (Klostermaier 1994: 229). Along with these qualities, he also listed several prerequisites: certain dietary regulations, which are normally strict vegetarianism, including no garlic or onions; complete disregard for worldly possessions; faithful observation of all religious practices; virtuous behaviour; and the maintenance of a state of equanimity (Klostermaier 1994: 229).

Rāmānuja provided the philosophical basis for bhakti with his commentary on the *Brahmasūtras*, the *Bhagavadgītā* and his critique of Advaita Vedānta. Although maintaining a central emphasis on the surrender of the self (prapatti) negotiated through submission to a personal form of God (Viṣṇu), firm faith in divine protection and human helplessness without grace, Rāmānuja remained strictly orthodox and did not provide the egalitarian and subversive access to Vaiṣṇava bhakti that allowed either low caste or female access.

Although the Śrī Vaiṣṇava tradition which developed in south India remained firmly entrenched in brahmanical traditions, revering a purāṇic version of Viṣṇu and maintaining a controlled and non-ecstatic ritual worship in large temple complexes (Flood 1996: 137), other forms of Vaiṣṇava bhakti were to be less bound by temple formality and caste hierarchy. The Telegu Brāhmaṇa Vallabha (1481–1533) created a new doctrine of salvation known as puṣṭimārga, with a complete emphasis on grace. Vallabha not only took the emphasis away from the saṃnyāsi, promoting a householder's life as the ideal for sanctifying the whole of life, but he proclaimed that Puṣṭimārga was open to all, women and low castes, even those who other schools of Hinduism considered beyond any kind of redemption. Puṣṭimārga was perceived by its founder as the highest form of bhakti, which discredits reason and relies on grace alone, prepared for by the devotee through cultivating love for Kṛṣṇa, surrender to his or her guru and sevā (service) to the form of Kṛṣṇa, known as Śri Govardhana-nāthajī, revealed to Vallabha in an ecstatic vision. The performance of sevā as loving devotion cultivates premā (love) in the devotee's heart and by grace can result in unparalleled bliss, which is then the means to further cultivate selfless action, detachment from the world and absorption into the divine. The highest state of bhakti is represented by the gopīs of Vṛndāvana and they are the model for all followers of Puṣṭimārga (Klostermaier 1994: 254–57).

Other great egalitarian bhaktas are also found amongst the Kṛṣṇa worshippers of north India, notably the traditionally blind Sūrdās (1478–1560) and the woman-saint Mīrābāī, according to legend the wife of a Rajput prince (b. 1550), both of whom wrote countless songs of their devotion, which remain extremely popular to this day. In Surdās' verse we hear the liberating power of bhakti for the oppressed when he sings of elevating the lowly of the world or exclaims that through bhakti even hunters and prostitutes can achieve liberation. It is in Mīrābāī's lovelorn verses that we hear the classic relationship with the Lord exhibited by the bhaktas, that of lover and beloved, borrowing from the language of sensual love, able to draw upon the metaphors of separation and sexual union.

An even more well-known and influential Vaiṣṇava group of movements to draw upon the explicit sexual imagery of Kṛṣṇa's dalliances with the gopīs was to emerge from the ecstatic love of Caitanya Mahāprabhu (1486–1533), regarded to the present day as an avatāra of both Kṛṣṇa and his consort, Rādhā, believed to be the most ardent of the lovers of the incarnate god amongst the cowherds of Vṛndāvana. Caitanya's influence on international bhakti movements that have transcended the borders of India is well known to those Westerners and members of other nationalities who have joined the International Society of Krishna Consciousness (ISKCON), better known as the Hare Krishna movement, who regard him as their founder.

Although not the founder of Bengali manifestations of Kṛṣṇa bhakti, known as Gaudīya Vaiṣṇavism, Caitanya and his immediate disciples (gosvāmin) were able to formulate the theology of the movement and establish Vṛndāvana as a major centre of pilgrimage renowned throughout India and to take the movement beyond its Bengali origins. Initiated into the worship of Kṛṣṇa whilst visiting south India, Caitanya returned to his home, where he drew to him a group of disciples who began to sing in public of their love for the god and to dance ecstatically in the streets. Caitanya himself, on numerous occasions, manifested the conditions of ecstatic consciousness.

Although Gaudīya Vaiṣṇavas recognise the erotic element in the continuous play (līlā) between Kṛṣṇa and Rādhā, and to a lesser extent the other gopīs, inherent within a number of legends such as the rasa-līlā dance, where Kṛṣṇa takes a individual form for each gopī in a woodland dalliance, this love-play is not regarded as worldly, but rather as a manifestation of a pure and perfect experience of intimacy beyond any selfish motivation or fulfilment of carnal desire (Flood 1996: 139). This premā or pure love provides the model for liberation as each devotee not only can hope to achieve the same state of ecstatic experience of divine love-play but also can persuade the divinity to fulfil their every longing through his capacity to respond to their feelings.

The rasa-līlā is performed as a dance by professional troupes throughout India, and its themes of longing, separation and fulfilment have been utilised in a number of poems, the most well known being the *Gītāgovinda* by Jayadeva (twelfth century). Many are written from the perspective of Rādhā and, although they exhibit the outer manifestations of courtly love, to devotees they represent their longing for the Lord. Gaudīya Vaiṣṇavas do not renounce or overcome the emotions but rather sublimate them into an overwhelming relationship with their chosen Lord, whom they regard as the creator of all existence (Flood 1996: 141). Rather than a formal obedience to the injunctions of scripture, the devotee on this path finds a way to salvation based upon an intimate and reciprocated affection that transcends all conventional rules.

However, it is the numerous cults of Śiva that were able to develop forms of bhakti that most challenged the supremacy of the Brāhmaṇas and religious adherence based upon knowledge of sacred texts or performance of rituals and developed a socially critical theology that saw much of India's religion as hypocrisy. Basava (1106–68), although a brāhmaṇa by birth, expressed his reformer's zeal in a challenge to textual knowledge and image worship, scorning those who give food to stone gods or become patrons of temples but persecute the lovers of God (Embree 1988: 348). It is perhaps not surprising that Śaivism was able to develop forms of popular devotion that were subversive. Historically the ancient Śiva cults were not only shaped by synthesis and absorption, but had been able to accommodate a number of local traditions outside the fold of Brahmanic Hinduism and absorb marginal divinities, thus crossing the boundaries of textual orthodoxy and popular religion of the disenfranchised.

Śiva is an ambiguous figure: on the one hand the ultimate ascetic and yogi, he is venerated by the wandering sādhu, for whom he exemplifies strict performance of sādhana and renunciation; on the other hand, he is a dangerous householder, bursting with vitality, partner to the goddess and father of two sons, both popular gods, whose following consists of the dark side of Indian rural life, the goblins, ghosts and spirits of the underworld. He is an impecunious god and many songs exist, sung by the rural landless, victims of feudalism, that describe how his wife maintains the home whilst he is away in low company or smoking ganja (Chitgopekar 1998: 18). It is not surprising to find him the deity of the semi-Hinduised tribes and the lower castes and untouchables. Perhaps he is most popular as the god who can grant offspring, appearing in the symbolic form of the liṅga, who delights in singing and dancing (Chitgopekar 1998: 21). He is the great healer of diseases, the protector of cattle, but retains his ancient Vedic origins where he is feared by both gods and humans. It is not surprising that such qualities would be prized by agricultural communities. However, Śiva has inspired sublime bhakti movements as well as tantric mysticism.

In the bhakti traditions focused around Śiva, some similarities are found with the Vaiṣṇavas. Śiva devotees also draw primarily upon the *Purāṇas*, discovering in their mythologies an exclusivism that regards the god as the sole Lord of creation, with all other gods inferior or subordinate to him, and his worship as the sole means of liberation. As with Viṣṇu, Śiva is believed to have taken several incarnations (twenty-eight as opposed to ten) in order to save his devotees, but these have not taken on the same significance as the avatāras of Viṣṇu, and none have the appeal of Rāma and Kṛṣṇa. Śiva worship also developed its temple forms, with detailed forms of worship focused upon anthropomorphic images of the god and the liṅga. However, Śaiva devotion always retained a place for the ascetic, incorporating Śiva as the Mahāyogi, and to this day most Yogis remain in his following. The hagiography of the god, known for his ambiguous relationship with social conformity, provided a more obviously unconventional outlet for the spiritual aspirations of the dispossessed. Mahādēvyakka, the twelfth-century contemporary of Basava, risked censure for her unconventional life, a naked female wandering ascetic. She uses the same sexual imagery as Mīrābāī but in her poetry we hear a critique of the limitations of householder life for the Hindu woman when she exclaims that husbands who die and decay should be fed to the kitchen fires and only perfect union with the Lord should be sought.

In her verses we hear the classic bhakti themes of separation, longing and consummation in union, and, rather than the espousal of pleasure, the passionate claim that union with the divine provides a pleasure that the world can never match. However, her Śiva is not the god of the temples or of the popular imagination, fulfilling the pragmatic needs of rural existence. Rather, he is closer to the formless, omnipresent Lord of the nirguṇa bhaktas. A similar voice can be heard in the poetry of Lallā, a fourteenth-century Kashmiri woman-saint who also defied convention.

In Lallā's poetry she refers to a unified concentration of breath and mind (Embree 1988: 350–51). The reference to the unification of breath and mind shows that devotion to Śiva has always been closely related to yogic and tantric practices. Both Śaiva and Vaiṣṇava traditions have close links with the goddess or Devī. In purāṇic myths, Śri is the consort of Viṣṇu and is regarded as the primal guru, the origin of the lineage for all Vaiṣṇava gurus. The goddess, also known throughout India as Lakṣmī and associated with fortune and wealth, appears as the various consorts of the human Viṣṇu avatāras, for example, Rādhā and Sītā. However, in Śaiva traditions, the goddess is even more intertwined in its mythology, doctrines and practices. In the tantric systems, the neuter Brahman becomes active as both Śiva and Śakti, the male and female principles. She is not only Śiva's consort as Pārvatī or Umā, but lies dormant in the human being as Kuṇḍalinī awaiting union with Śiva as the primal consciousness through yogic practices.

However, it is probable that goddess worship predated both Viṣṇu and Śiva worship and Devī always had her own exponents of intense bhakti. As with all bhakti traditions, the chosen īśvara is worshipped as the sole or supreme divinity, the bestower of salvation and the principle behind creation. Amongst her own votaries, she is not merely the consort of the two gods; rather they are under her subjection. It is in Bengal that worship of Devī is at its strongest, and it is not surprising to find her most well-known bhaktas writing their praise for her in Bengali, for example Rāmprasād (1718–75), a well-known Śakta poet who influenced Ramakrishna Paramhansa.

Sri Aurobindo, another Bengali, describes her as the consciousness and force of the Divine, and explains that the īśvara, the personal Lord of the Universe, manifests from within her, and that she then takes her place alongside him as a consort (Klostermaier 1994: 293). However, it is probably in Ramakrishna Paramhansa that one finds the most contemporary and fervent of the devotees of the Mother Goddess. The great nineteenth-century syncretist saw himself above all as a Devī bhakta. An ecstatic, he describes the means of realising God as an ecstasy of love and devotion but perceived Brahman as Mother (Nikhilananda 1969: 34). Ramakrishna speaks of his relationship with the goddess in very personal terms, expressing his relationship with her as a child to a mother.

Sometimes Ramakrishna presents us with a significant element of bhakti, where the devotee identifies completely with various relationships in order to get close to the chosen deity. He indicates that the classic roles of the Devī worshipper are child, handmaid or hero (Nikhilananda 1969: 44). The hero role presents once again the transformation of the erotic impulse in bhakti. Ramakrishna describes the heroic attitude as trying to please the goddess with the same passion that a man uses to please a woman during intercourse (Nikhilananda 1969: 44).

Both Śakta and Śaiva forms of bhakti have been able to develop sophisticated theologies, most evident in Tantra and Śaiva Siddhānta; both have been able find acceptance within Vedic orthodoxy, yet they have been able to maintain their place in the hearts of the rural populations and the disenfranchised. They are not always respectable, with the ritual slaughter of animals, the use of intoxicants, the incorporation of sexuality into both doctrine and practice and the use of frenzied dancing and chanting; this is a different form of bhakti from the sublime poetry and worship of the formless essence, but nonetheless worthy of consideration.

The final variety of bhakti that requires consideration is the nirguṇa bhaktas of north India, often described as Sants by both scholars and practitioners. These passionate iconoclasts, with their rejection of the outer forms of both Hindu and Muslim religiosity, whilst collecting adherents from both traditions, rigorously deny the existence or at least the significance of any of the Hindu deities. This begs the question of whether and in what sense they can be identified with Hinduism. The voice of Kabīr (fifteenth century), believed to have been a low-caste weaver from near Varanasi, claimed today by both Hindus and Muslims as their own, scorns the everyday religious conventions that he saw around him, accusing the practitioners of both religions, whether imams, yogis, faqirs or brāhmaṇas, of being deluded hypocrites (Embree 1988: 375).

The same critique of the outer forms of religion can be heard in the poetry of Nanak (b. 1469), believed by the Sikhs to be their historic founder, yet Nanak goes one step further and states that all religious worldviews are mental shackles (Singh *et al.* 1973: 74–75).

Yet despite their virulent critique, the nirguṇa bhaktas remained within the worldview of Indian traditions, in that they accepted the concepts of saṃsāra, karma and final liberation, even though their own experience of salvation was both imminent and immanent, thus providing an eschatology that invariably ignored the afterlife in favour of a liberation found in the present. In addition they must be incorporated into the fold of bhakti, in spite of their criticism of much that other bhaktas would have deemed essential to the worship of their chosen form of the divine, because of their intense love for a personal but formless divinity, both transcendent and immanent in creation, but, above all, found within the heart of the human being.

The Sants' overriding conviction that the divinity resided within all beings, manifested as the Name or Word of God, led them to disregard social barriers in regard to the spiritual quest. All had access to the divine, regardless of caste, gender or religion. It is a way to salvation for everyone, and has been called a 'universal path to sanctity' (Vaudeville 1987) based on inner transformation rather than outer manifestations of religion.

It is with the nirguṇa bhaktas of north India that the path of devotion reached its culmination in inclusiveness and iconoclastic rejection of the outer forms of religion. All the forms of bhakti were theistic and relied upon grace for salvation, giving exclusive worship to their chosen deity as the sole creator of the universe. These aspects of bhakti led to some nineteenth-century writers seeing the influence of Christianity in its development; more plausible is the idea that there was interaction between Hinduism and Islamic mysticism (Embree 1988: 343). However, this influence should not be overstated as the bhakti tradition stays firmly within a Hindu worldview and has its roots in ancient texts that predate both Christianity and Islam.

What is certainly true is that bhakti, especially in its nirguṇa varieties, provided a means for Muslims and Hindus, at least in north India, to find common ground and even to obscure the borders between both worldviews. The Hindu bhakta and the Sufi share together the pain of separation and longing for union. Both are recipients of the grace of God, given as a loving gift to a servant who remains in constant remembrance of the Lord's Name(s). Both can be absorbed into the divine, in a state where all awareness of individual self is lost, the bhakta in the condition of samādhi and the Sufi in the state of fanā.

Sufis themselves were divided between those who recognised the wisdom of the Hindu scriptures and the similarities between bhaktimārga and tasawwuf and others who remained closer to orthodoxy, nervous of the contamination resulting from contact with Hindu beliefs and practices. Some were eclectic and, although remaining loyal to Islam, found more in common with the Hindu bhaktas than the orthodox ulema of Islam, with their emphasis on the exoteric. Others took a very different position towards Hindu beliefs and practices, upholding the exclusive truth claims of Islam.

All Sufis would have had some difficulties with saguṇa bhakti, where worship was directed to an image, especially images believed to be incarnations of God in human form such as the avatāras of Viṣṇu or Śiva. Whereas the worship of form would have raised the suspicions of Muslims, the nirguṇa bhaktas were often perceived as kindred spirits. The medieval north Indian Sants were often familiar with Islamic beliefs and were sympathetic to Sufi tradition. Both shared the idea that God is one, all-pervading reality, essentially without form. Both perceived the divine to be immanent in creation and thus capable of being experienced through indwelling in the human heart/soul. Each practised contemplation or remembrance of the Word or Name(s) of God as the central discipline through which unity with God was achieved. The names were different according to language and culture, were remembered silently in the heart or chanted by the tongue, but essentially Sufi dhikr and the nāma simarān of the Sants performed the same function. The goal of each was continuous remembrance of the divine, and each speaks of a state where the divine takes over and remembers the devotee and effort ceases. The Sants were iconoclasts; they criticised caste, sectarian differences and exterior forms of religion such as sacred languages, scriptures, image worship, fasting, ritual bathing, pilgrimages and asceticism. Sufis were more ambivalent about the external forms of worship as the Islamic shari'a insisted upon several of the above as essentials of revelation. However, they agreed with the Sants that the externals of religion were to no avail if the esoteric path of the heart had not been discovered. The Sants acknowledged the guru as the intermediary between humans and God, and the Sufis were equally adamant that a shaykh or pīr was essential in order to progress towards Allah. Finally, each wrote or sung their poetry and preached their message in the vernacular, reaching out to the common people of both religions.

It is not surprising that Sufis and Sants began to collect followers from different communities, seeing the religion of the heart as overriding religious difference. In rural populations, the Muslim saint was often identified with a Hindu mystic or even a deity. The period of the Mughals brought about a number of new movements, most notably Sikhism. The Sufis seemed to be taking the Hindu ideas closer to Islam, and often the Sufis and the Sants seemed to have more in common with each other than the respective orthodoxies of brāhmaṇa and alim. Figures like Bullhe Shah (1680–1752) and Waris Shah (1730–90) attacked the conventional forms of religions associated with orthodoxy and, like Guru Nanak, claimed to be neither Hindu nor Muslim. To Bullhe Shah, the path of love overrode the law prescribed by either faith (Embree 1988: 486–87).

Thus bhakti introduced a salvation model to Indian ideas of liberation, positing that a close intimacy with the personal divinity was superior to absorption into the transpersonal Brahman. Although accepting the worldview of reincarnation, bhaktas challenged the dominant view of the final goal being an ultimate release from saṃsāra, preferring either an eternal heaven or abode of their chosen Īśvara, or even rejoicing in a return to human life as long as they could remain in perpetual service to the divinity. The focus on this life and the possibility of fulfilment here challenged the traditional eschatology, but, above all these, bhakti has been able to subvert the exclusivism of the Brāhmaṇas and provide a religious path for millions. It continues to introduce new variations, adding to the thousands of saṃpradāyas already created, developing regional cultures, but, above all, provides a path for the common people that acknowledges the body and the emotions, as opposed to the renunciates with their ascetic ideals of world-transcendence. Bhakti has challenged caste and gender, produced its own sacred texts in the vernacular, liberated its adherents from institutionalised religion, establishing a personal relationship with the divine, provided a vast network of local and national deeply venerated holy men and women, installed itself in the daily life of countless Hindus, and there are very few who do not know the ecstatic utterances of the bhakti poets and continue to sing their songs of love and praise.

See also: **Āḻvārs; Bhagavadgītā; Brahman; Caitanya; Ghose, Aurobindo; Gopī(s); International Society of Krishna Consciousness; Kabīr; Kṛṣṇa; Kuṇḍalinī Yoga; Lakṣmī, Śrī;**

Mahādevī; Nāyaṉmār; Pārvatī; Purāṇas; Rādhā; Rāma; Ramakrishna, Sri; Rāmānuja; Śaiva Siddhānta; Śakti; Saṃnyāsa; Śaṅkara; Sant; Sant Sādhana; Sītā; Śiva; Tulsīdās(a); Umā; Vedānta; Viṣṇu; Vṛndāvana

RON GEAVES

Further reading

Chitgopekar, N. 1998. *Encountering Śivaism*. New Delhi: Munshiram Manoharlal.
Embree, A. 1988. *Sources of Indian Tradition*. Albany, NY: Columbia University Press.
Flood, G. 1996. *An Introduction to Hinduism*. Cambridge: Cambridge University Press.
Klostermaier, K. 1994. *A Survey of Hinduism*. New York: State University of New York Press.
Nikhilananda, Swami. 1969. *The Gospel of Ramakrishna*, 5th edn. Madras: Sri Ramakrishna Math.
Singh, T., J. Singh, Kapur Singh, B.H. Singh and Khushwant Singh (trans.). 1973. *The Sacred Writings of the Sikhs*, 3rd edn. London: George Allen & Unwin.
Vaudeville, Charlotte. 1987. 'Sant Mat: Santism as the Universal Path to Sanctity'. In K. Schomer and W.H. McLeod, eds, *The Sants: Studies in a Devotional Tradition of India*. New Delhi: Motilal Banarsidass, 21–40.

BHAKTISIDDHANTA SARASWATI (1874–1936)

Bhaktisiddhanta Saraswati built on the proselytising work done by his father, Bhaktivinoda Thakura, and established the Gaudiya Vaishnava Mission after his death in 1914.

Born in Bengal, he was educated in classical and devotional Hindu teachings, and in Sanskrit and English as well as his mother tongue. As a moderniser, his father imbued in him the value of the printing press as a bṛhat-mṛdanga, a great drum capable of spreading word of Kṛṣṇa throughout India and beyond. Bhaktisiddhanta Saraswati took up this missionary call, sending his first disciple to the West in 1930. He stressed the simplicity and accessibility of Caitanya's teachings, and accepted male candidates for initiation irrespective of caste background, giving them all the status of brāhmaṇa (varṇa). Through his organisation of the Gaudiya Mission he developed the foundations and principles for the Vaiṣṇava movement, which his disciple, A.C. Bhaktivedanta Swami Praphupada, was later to establish worldwide as the International Society for Krishna Consciousness.

See also: **Brāhmaṇas; Caitanya; Gaudiya Vaishnava Mission; International Society for Krishna Consciousness; Prabhupada, A.C. Bhaktivedanta Swami; Varṇa**

KIM KNOTT

Further reading

Bromley, D.G. and L.D. Shinn (eds). 1989. *Krishna Consciousness in the West*. Lewisburg, PA: Bucknell University Press.
Bryant, E.F. and M.L. Ekstrand (eds). 2004. *The Hare Krishna Movement: The Post Charismatic Fate of a Religious Transplant*. New York: Columbia University Press.
Squarcini, F. and E. Fizzotti. 2004. *Hare Krishna: Studies in Contemporary Religion*. Salt Lake City, UT: Signature Books.

BHANDARKAR, RAMKRISHNA GOPAL (1837–1925)

Ramkrishna Gopal Bhandarkar, a significant figure of the late-nineteenth-century Maratha renaissance, was responsible, along with other historians from Maratha and Bengal, for the rewriting of Indian history. Borrowing from the methodology of the British Orientalists, Bhandarkar attempted to reconstruct Indian history before the advent of Islam. In addition to such works as *The Early History of the Dekkan Down to the Muhammaden Conquest*, first published in 1895 and reprinted in 2001, he also translated, edited and published other manuscripts. Considered to be among the elite of India's Sanskrit scholars and Indologists, his scholarship inspired the Bhandarkar Oriental Research Institute in Poona, which remains one of India's most prestigious institutions.

Ironically, because of his relatively uncritical acceptance of the work of British historians, his reputation has been attacked by the supporters of Hindutva. In 2003, the Bhandarkar Oriental Research Institute was ransacked by the Shiv Sena, who destroyed thousands of rare manuscripts; the ostensible reason given was that one of its scholars had been credited in a book apparently critical of Śivaji, the seventeenth-century Maratha Hindu ruler-hero and icon of the supporters of Hindu nationalism. However, more than most, Bhandarkar is responsible for the reclamation of India's history and philosophy, which was part of the process of Independence and the restoration of national pride during the period of British colonisation. Many of R.G. Bhandarkar's works remain in print, including his early attempts to trace the historical origins of India's religious systems, for example his *Vaiṣṇavism, Śaivism and Minor Religious Systems*, first published in 1913 and recently reprinted in 2001 by Munshiram Manoharlal.

See also: **Hinduism, modern and contemporary; Hindutva; Nationalism; Shiv Sena**

RON GEAVES

Further reading

Wagle, N.K (ed.). 1999. *Writers, Editors and Reformers: Social and Political Transformations of Maharashtra 1830–1930*. Delhi: Manohar.

www.bori.ac.in/rgb.htm (accessed 27 October 2005).

BHARAT DHARMA MAHAMANDALA

The 'great society for the religion of India'. A conservative Hindu organisation founded by Pandit Din Dayalu Sharma to promote the a traditionalised vision of sanātana dharma. In particular, the Mahamandala was conceived as a mechanism to provide some form of unitary guidance to the plethora of likeminded local Dharma Sabhas and the various Hindu traditionalist movements established in the latter half of the nineteenth century. The plan for the Mahamandala was first formulated in 1887, and quickly followed by a meeting in the city of Haridwar. Here the need to protect the Hindu social and religious order was emphasised, together with the promotion of Sanskrit and Hindi through traditional education. The Mahamandala also planned to utilise the technique of religious preaching, adopted from Christian missionaries, in order to combat the increasingly popular reform movements represented by the Brahmo Samaj and the Arya Samaj. While the Mahamandala continued to act as the rightful guardian of Hindu tradition, it also conceived of itself as an important instrument through which Hindu practices could be regenerated. Measures were therefore adopted to combat the use of the dowry and to alleviate the conditions in which widows lived. In this regard it may be said that the Mahamandala shared, to some extent, the impetus towards social reform best represented by the Brahmo Samaj. By the early twentieth century the Mahamandala came under the effective control of Swami Gyananda. From its new headquarters in the city of Benares, the Mahamandala then grew in influence over subsequent decades. Funded by a variety of rājas, landholders and merchants, it held periodic conferences to debate issues relating to the preservation and strengthening of Hinduism; developed an extended administrative system of local governing bodies; lobbied the British government on a variety of relevant social and religious issues; and promoted its views within journals such as *Mahamandala Magazine*. In this regard the Mahamandala was largely successful in moulding perceptions of Hindu orthodoxy, in effect foreshadowing organisations such as the Vishwa Hindu Parishad.

See also: **Arya Samaj; Brahmo Samaj; Dharma Sabhas; Gyanananda, Swami; Rājas; Sanātana Dharma; Sharma, Pandit Din Dayalu; Vishwa Hindu Parishad; Widowhood**

MICHAEL S. DODSON

Further reading

Farquhar, J.N. 1967. *Modern Religious Movements in India*. Delhi: Munshiram Manoharlal (first published 1915).

Jones, K.W. 1989. *Socio-Religious Reform Movements in British India*. Cambridge: Cambridge University Press.

BHĀRAT MĀTĀ

Bhārat Mātā, or Mother India, made her first appearance in Bankim Chandra Chatterjee's Bengali nationalistic novel of 1882, *Ānandamaṭh*, translated as *Abbey of Bliss* by B.K. Roy, or *The Sacred Brotherhood* by Julius Lipner. In *Ānandamaṭh*, Bhārat Mātā is worshipped by the Order of Children, who fought the British in the Saṃnyāsa uprising of 1772. In their temple, she appears in three forms. As India of the past, she is Annapūrṇā, the goddess of plenty. In her current state, she is in the form of a naked and dishevelled Kālī. However, Bhārat Mātā also appears in another form, as a ten armed Durgā, resplendent and powerful. This represents India as she could be if she was liberated. Bhārat Mātā has since been adopted by the Hindu nationalists as their patron goddess and her devotional song, *Bande* (or *Vande*) *Mātāram*, 'I Bow to Thee, Mother', has become their anthem.

There are two Bhārat Mātā temples in India, one at Hardwar, built by Swami Satyamiterand Giri, leader of the Vishwa Hindu Parishad (VHP; World Hindu Council), and the other at Vārāṇasī. In the temple at Vārāṇasī, Bhārat Mātā is represented simply as a map of India, whereas at Hardwar she stands majestically in anthropomorphic form, holding stalks of grain in one hand and an auspicious pot of milk in the other. The eight-storey temple, consecrated in 1983, celebrates a variety of deities, nationalistic heroes and various virtuous women, some of whom burnt themselves on their husband's funeral pyre, satī (act of immolation).

See also: **Annapūrṇā; Chatterjee, Bankim Chandra; Durgā; Kālī; Nationalism; Saṃnyāsa; Sati (Faithful wife); Vārāṇasī; Vishwa Hindu Parishad**

LYNN FOULSTON

Further reading

Lipner, Julius J. (trans.). 2005. *Ānandamaṭh, or The Sacred Brotherhood: Bankimcandra Chatterji*. Oxford: Oxford University Press.

McKean, Lise. 1996. 'Bharat Mata: Mother India and Her Militant Matriots.' In J.S. Hawley and D.M. Wulff, eds, *Devi: Goddesses of India*. Berkeley, Los Angeles, CA and London: University of California Press.

BHARATI, SWAMI AGEHANANDA [LEOPOLD FISCHER] (1923–91)

Austrian saṃnyāsī and anthropologist. Born in Vienna, as a teenager Bharati studied Sanskrit and several Indian vernaculars informally with Indian medical students and was received as a Hindu with the name Ramachandra by a travelling Hindu preacher in Vienna in 1939 at the age of 16. In the later stages of the war he served in France with the Free India Legion of the German army. In 1949 he went to India, where he spent two years as a novice with the Ramakrishna Order before being ordained as a saṃnyāsī in the Daśanāmī order. Bharati taught in India at Delhi University and Banaras Hindu University and then in the United States at the Universities of

Washington (from 1956) and Syracuse (from 1961). He was sharply critical of those forms of modern Hinduism prevalent among English-educated, urban Hindus, all of which he believed to derive, directly or indirectly, from Vivekananda.

See also: **Hinduism, history of scholarship; Ramakrishna Math and Mission; Vivekananda, Swami**

WILL SWEETMAN

Further reading

Bharati, A. 1961. *The Ochre Robe: An Autobiography.* London: George Allen & Unwin.

Bharati, A. 1970. 'The Hindu Renaissance and Its Apologetic Patterns'. *Journal of Asian Studies* 29: 267–87.

BHARATIYA JANATA PARTY

Unlike other affiliates of the Rashtriya Swayamsevak Sangh (RSS), the Bharatiya Janata Party (BJP; Party of the Indian People) is a political party. It has participated as a coalition partner in India's national government. Its leader, Atal Bihari Vajpayee, first became the prime minister of India in 1996.

Keshav Baliram Hedgewar and Madhav Sadashiv Golwalkar, the first two leaders of the RSS, both prioritised character building and cultural mobilisation and resisted attempts to involve the RSS in formal political activity. In 1951, however, Golwalkar accepted the formation of the Jana Sangh, a political party organised by RSS members, in response to internal pressure from activists. Deendayal Upadhyaya, the party's most influential ideologue, formulated the political theory of Integral Humanism, with its selective allusions to Gandhian principles of swadeshi and sarvodaya. The Jana Sangh was amalgamated with the Janata Party in 1977.

The Bharatiya Janata Party came into being in April 1980 after the collapse of the Janata government under the premiership of Moraji Desai in July 1979. Like the Jana Sangh before it, the BJP faced the problem of attempting to broaden its appeal beyond that of a Hindu nationalist party without alienating its core support. It attempted to do this by retaining the ideological position constructed for the Jana Sangh by Upadhyaya, now incorporated into the BJP's 'five commitments' to 'Gandhian socialism', 'positive secularism', 'nationalism', 'national integration', 'democracy' and 'value-based politics'. It also presented itself as the heir to the Janata party, which had opposed Indira Gandhi during the period of Emergency. It entered into alliances with other opposition parties, addressed broad socio-economic issues and sought Muslim members. Although it succeeded in attracting a number of Janata politicians not known as Hindu nationalists, the sympathy for Rajiv Gandhi in the 1984 election following the assassination of his mother, Indira Gandhi, ensured the largest majority ever secured by the previously dominant Congress Party. The BJP was subsequently criticised by Hindu nationalists for diluting its politics through alliances with other parties, and the future delivery of the Hindu vote was made conditional upon a commitment to a Hindu nationalist manifesto. In the following two decades, the BJP increased its share of the vote and its number of seats in local and national elections through alliances and by taking up ethno-religious issues. Having benefited from the upsurge in Hindu nationalist feeling in north India following the Shah Bano affair in 1985 and during the Ramjanmabhoomi (Rāma's birthplace temple) controversy in 1992, the violence unleashed by the demolition of the Babri Mosque at Ayodhyā forced the BJP again to review its policies and relationship with the RSS and affiliated organisations, such as the Vishwa Hindu Parishad. From 1993, issues such as corruption in national life, external threats and economic issues took on greater prominence in appeals made by the BJP to the electorate.

See also: **Ayodhyā; Gandhi, Mohandas Karamchand; Golwalkar, Madhav Sadashiv; Hedgewar, Keshav Baliram; Jana Sangh; Nationalism; Rāma; Rashtriya Swayamsevak Sangh; Vishwa Hindu Parishad**

GWILYM BECKERLEGGE

Further reading

Hansen, T.B. 1999. *The Saffron Wave: Democracy and Hindu Nationalism in Modern India.* Princeton, NJ: Princeton University Press.

Jaffrelot, C. 1996. *The Hindu Nationalist Movement and Indian Politics, 1925 – The 1990s.* London: Hurst.

BHARATIYA VIDYA BHAVAN

The Bhavan was founded in 1938 by Dr K.M. Munshi and was inspired by the teachings of Mahatma Gandhi and the Congress Party with regard to India's secular and multicultural constitution. It perceives itself as a secular, non-political organisation open to all regardless of creed, race or sexual orientation, dedicated to promoting Indian arts and culture. However, its attitude towards religion is highly influenced by its founder and his impact on the Hindu renaissance originally started by Rammohan Roy. This can be discerned in the Bhavan's aim to 'revitalise ancient values and reintegrate them in the changing needs of modern times'.

Today there are over 100 branches of the Bhavan in India, including schools, and it has also opened branches outside India. The first of these was opened in London in 1972, where it now flourishes as the largest institute for Indian art and culture outside India.

See also: **Munshi, Kanaiyalkal; Roy, Rammohan**

RON GEAVES

Further reading

www.bhavan.net (accessed 17 October 2005).
www.bhavans.info (accessed 17 October 2005).

BHARTṚHARI

A grammarian-philosopher, Bhartṛhari was one of the greatest and most influential of all Indian thinkers, in spite of not founding a school as such. Little is known of Bhartṛhari's life and even dates. Beside many legends, including that of his identity with the eponymous poet, we have the Chinese pilgrim I-Tsing's manifestly erroneous opinion that he died in 651. He is now generally situated in the fifth or, at the latest, the early sixth century, between the times of Vasubandhu and the younger Dinnāga, who cites him. By his own account, he was a disciple of Vasurāta, who is credited with a revival of the grammatical tradition of Pāṇini and Patañjali (Vyākaraṇa). Apart from a commentary on Patañjali's great work the *Mahābhāsyatīkā*, of which only a fragment survives in a single manuscript, his thought is chiefly known through the three books (kāṇḍa) of his monumental *Vākyapadīya* ('of phrase and word'), whose verses (kārikā) are expounded in a commentary (vṛtti) on the first two books by Harivṛsabha (traditionally identified with Bhartṛhari himself), on which is grafted a tīkā (sub-commentary) by Vṛsabhadeva. There is also a gloss on the second book by Punyarāja and on the third by Helarāja. The three parts deal, respectively, with speech in general (*Brahmakāṇḍa*), the book most imbued with metaphysics, the sentence (*Vākyakāṇḍa*) and the word (*Padakāṇḍa*).

For Bhartṛhari, all knowledge is linguistic and nothing can be known outside language: speech is, above even perception, the primary means of attaining a valid cognition (pramāṇa). That language is, fundamentally, the grammatical structure of Vedic utterance which underpins the universe, itself viewed as the real unfolding of a non-dual absolute, the Śabdabrahman (Brahman-as-word) or a supreme universal (mahāsattā). Thus, the One Supreme Word manifests itself as manifold and remains present in the depths of the consciousness of all living beings in the form of Tradition Intuition (āgama-pratibhā). In the mind, language proceeds in an analogous way, beginning in an inner unitary meaning-bearing reality (sphota), itself identical with the ultimate Word and manifested through sounds (dhvani) which bring about the particularisation in the objective world of a meaning originally universal.

Bhartṛhari's influence culminated in the work of the first great Hindu non-dualist Maṇḍana Miśra.

See also: **Brahman; Pāṇini; Patañjali; Pramāṇas; Veda; Vyākaraṇa**

DANIEL MARIAU

BHĀSA

A Sanskrit dramatist whose prominent works, *Pratimā nāṭaka* and *Abhiṣeka nāṭaka*, drawing upon themes from Vālmīki's *Rāmāyaṇa*, at least indicate that he was born later than the writing of that work and prior to Kālidāsa, who refers to Bhāsa in his works. His work has been overshadowed to a large extent by the later dramas of Kālidāsa, but he is significant in his own right, with twenty-three works attributed to him. In 1922, thirteen of these remained in existence and they showed the significant influence of the *Mahābhārata* (six dramas) and then the *Rāmāyaṇa* (two works) and the *Bṛhatkathā* (three works). The remaining two were drawing upon themes taken from the anecdotes concerning Kṛṣṇa. However, there remains some dispute over the attribution of authorship to all thirteen works.

See also: **Kālidāsa; Kṛṣṇa; Mahābhārata; Rāmāyaṇa; Vālmiki**

RON GEAVES

Further reading

Mani, Vettam. 1993. *Purāṇic Encyclopaedia*. Delhi: Motilal Banarsidass.

BHAṬṬOJI DĪKṢITA

A grammarian, based in Benares, around 1600 CE. His most famous work is the *Siddhānta Kaumudī*, a presentation of and commentary on the sūtras of Pāṇini's grammar that is very widely studied in Indian universities and traditional centres of learning to the present day. Bhaṭṭoji is known to have had several teachers, among whom was the grammarian Śeṣa Kṛṣṇa. After Śeṣa Kṛṣṇa's death, Bhaṭṭoji criticised many of his positions. Descendants and pupils of Śeṣa Kṛṣṇa, took offence, and wrote various treatises critising Bhaṭṭoji. This did not reduce his fame, which also extended into the realm of the 'philosophy of grammar'. Bhaṭṭoji revived the philosophy of grammar after a lull of almost a thousand years, reacting primarily to new ideas that had been introduced by the New Logicians. His reflections are elaborated in two commentaries – a long and a short one – written by his nephew Kauṇḍa Bhaṭṭa.

Bhaṭṭoji and some members of his family received patronage from the rulers of Ikkeri, a small kingdom in the south of the subcontinent.

See also: **Pāṇini**

JOHANNES BRONKHORST

Further reading

Bronkhorst, J. Forthcoming. 'Bhaṭṭoji Dīkṣita on Sphoṭa'. *Journal of Indian Philosophy* 33(1), 2005, 3–41.

BHAVE, VINOBA (1895–1982)

Vinoba Bhave, regarded by Jawaharlal Nehru and Jayaprakash Narayan as Gandhi's spiritual heir (Tandon 1992), is best remembered for the Bhoodan (or land-gift) Movement.

Bhave met Gandhi in 1916, joining the ashram in Ahmedabad. He became involved in the freedom movement and was imprisoned four times between 1923 and 1941, having been nominated by Gandhi as the first satyagrahi in the civil disobedience campaign against India's entry into World War II. After Independence Bhave actively continued working for sarvodaya (welfare for all). In 1970 he retreated to Paunar, spending his remaining years in fasting and meditation (Tandon 1992).

The Bhoodan Movement began when, at a meeting with harijan villagers in Andhra Pradesh, a wealthy landlord offered them 100 acres of land. In this act of generosity Bhave saw a solution to the problems of poverty and landlessness. He and his followers began walking all over India, asking landlords for 10 per cent of their land. The movement achieved immense popularity and estimated donations of 4,227,472 acres of land – a tremendous achievement, although significantly below Bhave's target of 50 million acres (Osborne 1998: 196–97).

The movement gradually changed its emphasis from bhoodan to gramdan (village gift), whereby villagers were asked to relinquish individual ownership in favour of gramraj (collective management). For Bhave, gramdan encouraged villagers to rely on themselves, whereas he maintained that socialism fostered dependence on the state (Kumar 1992: 57).

Bhave's impact is difficult to assess. Much of the donated land was infertile and many of the gramdan villages failed to achieve gramraj. However, Bhave's vision still inspires organisations working with poor and landless people today (such as the Association for Sarva Seva Farms in Tamil Nadu, ASSEFA). Bhave believed that land was a gift from God and that the redistribution of land to the landless was an act not of charity but of justice (Kumar 1992).

See also: **Āśram(a) (religious community); Dalits; Gandhi, Mohandas Karamchand**

CHRISTINA SCHWABENLAND

Further reading

Kumar, S. 1992. *No Destination: An Autobiography*. Devon: Green Books.

Osborne, B. 1998. *Victory to Vinoba*. Delhi: Ajanta.

Ram, S. 1958. *Vinoba and His Mission*. Varanasi: Akhil Bharat Sarva Seva Sangh.

Tandon, V. 1992. *Acharya Vinoba Bhave*. New Delhi: Publications Division, Ministry of Information and Broadcasting, Government of India.

BHEDĀBHEDA

The term bhedābheda refers to a doctrine of Vedāntic philosophy stating that difference and identity can co-exist in intimate relation with each other. While things may appear incompatible, they are in reality in such a relation that a seeming difference is totally unified as well. The doctrine was applied by several philosophers of Vedānta who saw no ultimate contradiction in such things as substance and quality, whole and parts, universal and particular. The doctrine of bhedābheda attempts to resolve the problem posed by the *Upaniṣads* where they sometimes say Brahman is a unity and a single source of all existence and sometimes also say that Brahman is different from the individual self and the objective world. One such instance of an apparent contradiction is *Taittirīya Upaniṣad* 3.1, which states: 'That from which these beings are born, by which being born they live, and into which they pass upon dying – seek to perceive that. That is Brahman'. The view that unity is in non-difference while also encompassing difference implies the pariṇamavāda or the 'theory of transformation'. Discrete things or differences transform and acquire limiting adjuncts, such as a spark separating from a fire, or individual selves (jīvātman) acquiring bodies and sense organs. While these things or individuals appear separate, they still maintain the essence of the source from which they developed, which for living individuals is the Brahman dwelling in them as the highest Ātman and is their Inner Controller.

Compared with other great Vedānta philosophies such as Advaita and Viśiṣṭādvaita, the bhedābheda view was eclipsed in the history of Indian thought. Nevertheless, this view emerged before Bādarāyaṇa, the author of the *Brahmasūtras*, and continued, serving successfully later on as a theological explanation for the relation of the individual with a personal god, such as in the bhakti cult of Kṛṣṇa and Rādhā. The pre-Bādarāyaṇa phase of the bhedābheda doctrine appears in the thinkers Āśmarathya, Auḍulaumi and Kāśakṛtsna, who are known through later authors of the different Vedānta schools. The second phase of the bhedābheda doctrine appears in Lakulīśa, Bhartṛprapañca, Bhāskara and Yādavaprakāśa, the old teacher of Rāmānuja. The extant writings by Bhāskara show a transition from Śaṅkara to Rāmānuja. Bhāskara criticised Śaṅkara's doctine of illusion (māyāvāda), but he accepts monistic doctrines of non-difference from the Absolute. Individual selves are understood to be Brahman, while also limited by adventitious moral and metaphysical imperfections, thus the doctrine is Aupādika Bhedābhedavāda or the 'identity-in-difference concerning limiting adjuncts'. The third phase of bhedābheda appears in the Vaiṣṇava Nimbārka's doctrine of Svābhāvika Bhedābheda, or 'natural identity-in-difference', and the Gauḍiya Vaiṣṇava Caitanya's doctrine of Acintya Bhedábeda or 'inexplicable identity-in-difference'. Nimbārka, who is thought to be post-Rāmānuja, accepts the natural causal relation between Brahman and the individual, and Brahman and the inanimate world. These doctrines are also referred to as Dvaitādvaita or 'dual and non-dual', because they explain Kṛṣṇa as both absolute, transcendent Śakti and, together with Rādhā, as also dual and distinct, lover and beloved.

See also: **Advaita; Ātman; Bādarāyaṇa; Bhakti movement; Brahman; Brahmasūtras; Gauḍiyas; Jīva; Kṛṣṇa; Lakulīśa; Māyā; Nimbārka; Rādhā; Rāmānuja; Śakti; Śaṅkara; Upaniṣads; Vaiṣṇavism; Vedānta; Viśiṣṭādvaita**

ROBERT GOODDING

Further reading

Olivelle, Patrick. 1998. *The Early Upanisads: Annotated Text and Translation*. New York: Oxford University Press, 308–9.

Srinivasachari, P.N. 1972. *The Philosophy of Bhedābheda*. Madras: The Adyar Library and Research Centre.

BHIKṢU

Although the term is frequently associated with Buddhism, its literal meaning is 'one who begs food', and includes world-renouncers (usually male), who have long existed in the Hindu tradition, certainly for many centuries. The *Upaniṣads*' reduced emphasis on ritual was extended by some to entail the renunciation of all worldly action, and the requirements of such world-renouncers are set out in the *Laws of Manu*. These include initiation by one's guru, leaving home after renouncing the life of the householder, chastity, giving up possessions and undertaking spiritual practices aimed at transcending the senses with a view to attaining mokṣa. Also known as a Śramaṇa (literally, one who strives), the bhikṣu seeks to transcend worldly life, including worldly responsibilities (dharma), success (artha) and pleasure (kāma). The Buddhist and Jain tradition made the ascetic tradition more corporate, while differing on the degree of austerity which world-renunciation entailed. Buddhism adopted a 'middle way', while

Jainism adopted a more rigorous asceticism. In the Hindu tradition, renunciation admits of different degrees.

See also: **Artha; Brahmacarya; Buddhism, relationship with Hinduism; Dharma; Dharmaśāstras; Gārhasthya; Guru; Jainism, relationship with Hinduism; Kāma; Manu; Puruṣārthas; Śramaṇa**

GEORGE CHRYSSIDES

Further reading

Doniger, W. (trans.). 1991. *The Laws of Manu*. Harmondsworth: Penguin.

BHĪMA

'Fearful', 'tremendous', 'formidable'. The second-eldest of the five Pāṇḍava brothers is considered to be the son of Vāyu (*Mahābhārata*, Ādiparvan 122). The *Mahābhārata* depicts him as a great, coarse and rough warrior and wrestler in numerous adventures. Being extraordinarily strong since his childhood, he gained the strength of thousands of elephants by a nectar offered to him by Nāgas (snakes) (*Mahābhārata*, Ādiparvan 128). In his fights he killed several opponents, among them the famous wrestler Jīmūta (*Mahābhārata*, Virāṭaparvan 16) and the Rākṣasa Hiḍimba, whose sister Hiḍimbā married him and gave birth to their son Ghaṭotkaca (*Mahābhārata*, Ādiparvan 147–54).

Bhīma frustrated many insidious plans of his great enemy Duryodhana, eldest of the Kauravas, to kill him and the Pāṇḍavas. In their crucial encounter on the eighteenth day of the war the fighting skills of both were evenly matched, but striking an unfair blow Bhīma finally defeated his cousin (*Mahābhārata*, Śalyaparvan 58–59).

See also: **Hiḍimbā; Kauravas; Mahābhārata; Nāgas; Pāṇḍavas; Rākṣasas; Vāyu**

XENIA ZEILER

Further reading

Dange, Sadashiv Ambadas. 1977–2002. *Myths from the Mahabharata*, vols 1–3. New Delhi: Manohar.

BHIMA BHOI

Born in Western Orissa, Bhima Bhoi was most probably an orphan, cared for by a tribal couple. It is said that he composed beautiful songs, although he was completely illiterate. Later he became a disciple of Mahima Gosain, to whom he devoted all his poetry. It is generally accepted that after the death of his guru, Bhima Bhoi founded his own ashram at Khaliapali in 1877. It is there that Bhima Bhoi composed his most beautiful and original part of Satya Mahima Dharma's devotional literature, *Stuticintāmaṇi*, which is still sung today. He also fought against social evils such as caste and ritualised piety and initiated women into his community. Because of his social engagement and poetry he is remembered today as a santa kabi ('holy poet').

See also: **Āśram(a) (religious community); Guru; Poetry; Satya Mahima Dharma; Women, status of**

JOHANNES BELTZ

Further reading

Beltz, Johannes. 2003. 'Bhima Bhoi: The Making of a Modern Saint'. In A. Copley, ed., *Hindu Nationalism and Religious Reform Movements*. New Delhi: Oxford University Press, 230–53.

Mahapatra, Sitakant. 1983. *Bhima Bhoi*. New Delhi: Sahitya Akademi (Makers of Indian Literature).

BHĪṢMA

One of the great heroes of the *Mahābhārata*, in spite of being the war-leader of the Kauravas, the great enemies of the Pāṇḍavas, Bhīṣma literally means 'the terrible', an epithet that may have referred to his prowess in battle rather than his character, which was the epitome of honour and Kṣatriya codes of dharma. Born the son of King Śāntanu and the goddess Gaṅgā, Bhīṣma is also known as Nadija (the river-born) and Gāngeya. When the father of Pāṇḍu and Dhṛtarāṣṭra died, it was Bhīṣma who brought them both up, whilst he acted as regent of their kingdom. A writer of war manuals which set out the codes of chivalry, he taught the children of both Pāṇḍu and Dhṛtarāṣṭra (the Pāṇḍavas and the Kauravas) and tried to counsel moderation between the two families. In the final battle, he was fatally wounded by Arjuna and it is said took fifty-eight days to die as he had the power to prolong life. During this period he delivered a number of discourses on honour, loyalty and service, which are recorded in the *Mahābhārata.*

See also: **Arjuna; Dharma; Dhṛtarāṣṭra; Gaṅgā; Kauravas; Mahābhārata; Pāṇḍavas; Pāṇḍu; Varṇa**

RON GEAVES

Further reading

Dasgupta, Madhusraba. 1999. *Samsad Companion to the Mahābhārata*. Calcutta: Sahitya Samsad.

BHŪTAS (ELEMENTS)

Already in the oldest Indian sources one can notice an avid interest in exploring the universe and the process of its evolution, together with an attempt to reduce the immensity of different phenomena to a limited number of interconnected lines of development and a few basic elements. Besides the idea that everything in the world originated from one beginningless reality (Brahman), into which it will merge again, the notion of five elements, bhūta, from which everything visible is composed and into which everything dissolves became the predominant theory of the *Upaniṣads*, later developed into the Sāṃkhya system to a theory of mahā-bhūtas as the irreducible fountainheads of evolution.

The *Taittirīya Upaniṣad* offers the most detailed early exposition of the original idea of five elements, bhūtas (similar to the Greek archai), together with lists of correspondences in the realms of the physical world and the human person: pṛithvī (earth), apas (water), agni (fire), vāyu (air), akāśa (ether). The Sāṃkhya system coordinates them with smell (gandha), taste (rasa), form (rūpa), touch (sparśa) and sound (śabda). This schema of (māha) bhūtas and their evolution has been widely accepted in Hindu thought also by representatives of schools of thought that reject the other teachings of Sāṃkhya. It has also been of great practical importance in the practical arts, such as architecture.

Bhūta śuddhi, the 'purification of the elements', is an important part of Vaiṣṇava and Śaiva forms of image worship (pūjā). In this ritual the worshipper transforms his gross and subtle body (made up of the five elements) into the body of the deity (which is free from material elements). In line with the pañcabhūta schema the whole universe is considered by many Hindu schools to be fivefold in structure. In many ritual manuals correlations between the bhūtas and deities, colours, symbols, etc. have been developed. One such schema from a Śaiva *Āgama* may serve as illustration (there are numerous alternative schemata in use)

Bhūta	*Form*	*Symbol*	*Colour*	*Bīja-mantra*	*Deity*
Prakriti	Square	Vajra	Gold	La	Brahmā
Apas	Half-moon	Lotus	White	Va	Viṣṇu
Agni	Triangle	Svāstika	Red	Ra	Rudra
Vāyu	Hexagon	Six dots	Black	Ya	Maheśvara
Akāśa	Circle	Point	Translucent	Ha	Sadāśiva

In addition many other things, like the letters of the Sanskrit alphabet, have been correlated to the five mahā-bhūtas.

See also: **Brahmá; Brahman; Image worship; Pūjā; Rudra; Sacred texts; Śaivism; Sāṃkhya; Śiva; Svāstika; Upaniṣads; Vaiṣṇavism; Viṣṇu**

KLAUS K. KLOSTERMAIER

Further reading

Besides the classical texts referred to, a number of contributions in the five-volume *Prakrti: The Original Vision* (1995; gen. ed. Kapila Vatsyayan, published by the Indira Gandhi National Centre for the Arts: New Delhi) offer perspectives on elements: e.g. S.K. Lal. 'Pañcamahābhūtas: Origin and Myths in Vedic Literature'. Vol. 2, 5–21; T.N. Dharmadhikari. 'Bhūtas in Vedic Rituals and Literature'. Vol. 2, 41–62; Prabhakar P. Apte. 'Ritual Sublimation of Elements in Pañcarātra Āgama'. Vol. 3, 11–26; S.S. Janaki, 'Pañcabhūtas in Śaiva Ritual: With Special Reference to Bhūtaśuddhi'. Vol. 3, 37–46; S.P. Sabarathinam. 'Agamic Treatment of Mahābhūtas in Relation to Maṇḍalas and Arts'. Vol. 3, 47–66.

Hume, R.E. (trans.). 1931. *The Thirteen Principal Upanisads*. Oxford: Oxford University Press.

Radhakrishnan, S. (trans.). 1953. *The Principal Upanisads*. London: George Allen & Unwin.

BHŪTAS (LIFE FORMS)

Bhūtas (the 'Deceased') are spirits of the dead who, like pretās (the 'Departed'), have not found peace after death. Because their unhappy postmortem condition is usually due to the failure by the living to ensure their transfer to the World of the Fathers (pitṛloka) and their transformation into ancestors there, the bhūtā-pretā seek to avenge themselves. This they generally do by possessing their living descendents (with nightmares, disease, insanity) and by haunting the world in which they had lived (by disturbing ritual practice, harming crops and livestock, causing accidents, etc.). Although they are weak, these demonic entities are unrelenting, and so must be either combated through various Tantric techniques of exorcism and sorcery or appeased through rites of feeding and veneration. The branch of Āyurveda concerned with psychological disorders, termed bhūta-vidyā – the 'Science of [Combating] Bhūtas – employs the same sorts of Tantric rites to heal 'those whose minds are possessed' (*Suśrūta Saṃhitā'* 1.1.3).

See also: **Āyurveda; Pitṛloka; Pitṛs; Pretas; Tantras**

DAVID GORDON WHITE

Further reading

Freed, R.S. and S.A. Freed. 1993. *Ghosts: Life and Death in North India*. Seattle, WA: University of Washington Press.

BIHAR SCHOOL OF YOGA

See: **Satyananda, Swami and the Bihar School of Yoga**

BIJOY KRISHNA GOSWAMI (1841–99)

Bijoy Krishna was a Bengali Hindu saint or siddha, a Vaiṣṇava practitioner who was not a part of the orthodox tradition of Bengali or Gauḍīya Vaiṣṇavism. Rather he was an ecstatic who could bring large crowds of people into states of intense devotional love.

Bijoy Krishna was born in 1841. He first joined the Brahmo Samaj, and later became a Vaiṣṇava. He would have visions of gods and their actions, which he would act out dramatically. His disciples described him as intoxicated with love, radiating light and bliss, with his visions becoming imprinted on his body, along with mantras and Sanskrit phrases. He would sing and dance at kirtans, calling out to the gods and goddesses that he saw before him. These gatherings would often last for six or seven hours, with people falling into trance, dancing wildly, finding themselves possessed by gods or spirits, trembling and sobbing with joy. Bijoy Krishna became famous as a saint and perfected being – he was called an avatāra or incarnation of Kṛṣṇa by his disciples by the time of his death in 1899.

See also: **Avatāra; Brahmo Samaj; Gauḍīyas; Kirtaṇ(a); Kṛṣṇa; Siddha; Vaiṣṇavism**

JUNE MCDANIEL

Further reading

Basu, Sobharani. 1974. *Modern Indian Mysticism: A Comparative and Critical Study*, vol. 2. Varanasi: Bharat Sadhana Publications.

Kuladananda Brahmacari. 1388 BS. *Sadguru sangha*. Calcutta: Sansad Prakasani (in Bengali).

McDaniel, June. 1989. *The Madness of the Saints: Ecstatic Religion in Bengal*. Chicago, IL: University of Chicago Press.

BJP

See: **Bharatiya Janata Party**

BLAVATSKY, HELENA PETROVNA (1831–91)

The prime founder of the Theosophical Society was born Helena Petrovna Hahn in Ekaterinoslav in the Ukraine in 1831. As a child she took a great interest in the folklore and popular religious practices of the local peasant community, especially in psychic phenomena, magic and shamanism. Three weeks before her seventeenth birthday she was married to Nikifor Blavatsky, a man over twenty years her senior. After a few weeks Helena abandoned her husband and began a series of travels and adventures which resulted in the foundation of the theosophical movement twenty-seven years later.

The life and activities of this curious Russian woman of no formal education have been perpetuated both in writings that have remained in print over the century since her death in 1891 and in a host of organisations expressing what we now call alternative spiritualities from then until the present day. Blavatsky travelled in Europe, the Middle East and Central Asia in search of spiritual wisdom. Contacts with the early Spiritualist movement led her to the United States, where in 1874 she met Henry Olcott, who was also investigating Spiritualism. These two drew together a small group to discuss how they might facilitate the study of occultism and related matters, which in September 1875 was named the Theosophical Society. Blavatsky was appointed as corresponding secretary. The duties of this office were not detailed and it was not continued after Blavatsky's death. Her leadership role in the movement rested on her role as the spokesperson for the Masters of the Wisdom, spiritual teachers whom she claimed to have met in northern India and Tibet, and on the authoritative character of her own writings. The details of Blavatsky's life and teachings have remained controversial to the present day, but she was instrumental in establishing a movement which, amongst other things, presented in accessible form the teachings of Buddhist and Hindu traditions to the Western world. Those of her biographers who have been associated with the theosophical movement, or who have been sympathetic to it, present her as a misunderstood proponent of a recovered ancient wisdom tradition (Barborka 1970; Cranston 1993; Fuller 1988; Kingsland 1928; Murphet 1975). Amongst those who see her essentially as a fraudulent or self-deluded adventuress are Meade (1980) and Washington (1993).

See also: **Olcott, Henry Steel; Theosophy and the Theosophical Society**

KEVIN TINGAY

Further reading

Barborka, G. 1970. *H.P. Blavatsky, Tibet and Tulku*. Adyar: Theosophical Publishing House.

Cranston, S. 1993. *H.P.B. – The Extraordinary Life and Influence of Helena Blavatsky.* New York: G.B. Putnam's Sons.
Fuller, J.O. 1988. *Blavatsky and Her Teachers.* London: East West Publications.
Kingsland, W. 1928. *The Real H.P. Blavatsky.* London: Rider.
Meade, M. 1980. *Madame Blavatsky – The Woman behind the Myth.* New York: G.B. Putnam's Sons.
Murphet, H. 1975. *When Daylight Comes.* Wheaton, IL: Quest Books.
Washington, P. 1993. *Madame Blavatsky's Baboon.* London: Bloomsbury.

BLOOD SACRIFICE

Bali, or blood sacrifice, has been a central Hindu ritual since ancient times, with the *Ṛgveda* describing the great horse sacrifice to the Vedic gods. Animal and human sacrifice have been principally linked to goddess worship. The so-called 'blood chapter' of the *Kālīkā Purāṇa* describes the pleasure that the goddess takes in blood sacrifice, including of humans – as long as they are non-Brāhmaṇa and male. The inclusion of animal sacrifice in ritual is seen as typical of village goddesses, but the goddess's thirst for blood is also made clear in the *Devī Māhātmya* of the *Mārkaṇḍeya Purāṇa*, where Kālī/Cāmuṇḍā swallows the blood of the demon Ratkabīja.

Animal sacrifice is still commonly found in temples to the goddess, such as the famous Kalighat temple in Calcutta, where hundreds of male goats are sacrificed, each with a single stroke of the sword, to ensure a successful pūjā, every Tuesday and Saturday (the days of the goddess). Even those temples where sacrifice is no longer practised often have a sacrificial post, painted vermilion, as a reminder of the goddess's love of blood, which feeds and reinvigorates her.

There has been increasing unease about the practice, famously expressed in Rabindranath Tagore's play *Sacrifice* (1900) and echoed by Gandhi. Currently, a substitute for the sacrificial animal may be used, such as a coconut, a reminder of the tradition of offering the head of the victim, or a large pumpkin, which is split open with a sword. This can be seen as an aspect of toning down the violent, bloodthirsty nature of the goddess, imposing vegetarianism on her. However, the nature of blood, which is both polluting and regenerative, so captures the ambivalent nature of the goddesses like Kālī that it is still found, symbolically, throughout her worship in such details as the repeated use of vermilion in decoration and offerings of her favourite flower, the blood-red hibiscus.

See also: **Devī Māhātmya; Gandhi, Mohandas Karamchand; Kālī and Caṇḍī; Pūjā; Purāṇas; Saṃhita; Tagore, Rabindranath; Varṇa; Vedic pantheon**

CYNTHIA BRADLEY

Further reading

Hardy, F. 1995. *The Religious Culture of India: Power, Love and Wisdom.* Cambridge: Cambridge University Press, ch. 5.

BOOKS, COMICS, NEWSPAPERS AND MAGAZINES

Moveable type printing reached India relatively soon after Gutenberg's innovations: a printing press sent by the Portuguese to Abyssinia by way of Goa never reached its destination and instead remained in India. As a result, the year 1556 saw the first book published on Indian soil – *Doctrina Christiana.* Twenty-two years later a translation of the work into Tamil was printed. Printing of this nature, however, remained largely an activity carried out by missionary presses. It took almost 300 years before Hindu religious texts were made available to the masses in print.

The reason for this delay was largely cultural. As in other religions – like Islam and Buddhism – in Hinduism the spoken word was considered more important and authoritative than the written text (Śabda and mantra). Though the śruti (revealed and heard) and smṛti (composed and committed to memory) texts were written in Sanskrit as early as 600 BCE, they long remained available to the elites and the priestly class only. Later, after the arrival of Muslims in India, translations of these texts were written and copied across India, but in that era circulation was limited to only a select few. However, by the late nineteenth century printing presses (lithographic and moveable type) had begun operating throughout India. Most of these presses belonged to Hindus, who, not surprisingly, printed large numbers of religious texts. Though objections were raised over the undiscriminating dissemination of sacred texts, this marked an irrevocable change in the way that Hindu tradition was transmitted. As a result, a renewed interest developed amongst Hindus of all classes and castes in understanding theological doctrines by reading the original works. Printed works were made available to remote areas and also outside India. Wherever the priestly class was not available, Hindus were now able to follow their traditions by reading various tracts and books along with the sacred texts.

In addition to sacred texts, the teachings of various gurus and philosophers, as well as the popular devotional poetry written in various vernaculars by saints and bhaktas, became available in print. Already in the first half of the nineteenth century, Kolkata (Calcutta) saw a brisk trade in cheap printed versions of Hindu mythological tales. The latter half of the century, however, saw an explosion of publication in major centres, beginning in Kolkata but soon spreading to Chennai (Madras) and Mumbai (Bombay), where the famous Nirnayasagara Press was established. Statistics compiled by the British authorities show a marked preference for religious (mainly Hindu) titles in the last quarter of the century. European-founded publishers such as Kolkata's Baptist Mission Press and the government press in Mumbai also began turning their attention to the Hindu classics.

The printing revolution was not confined to books and pamphlets, but gave rise to another powerful medium: newspapers. By the end of the eighteenth century, newspaper publication began in Kolkata and gradually spread to Chennai and Mumbai, so that by the beginning of nineteenth century there were several dozen papers, all, however, in English. In 1896 the periodical *Prabuddha Bhārata* began publication (and is still published), while around the turn of the century other, shorter-lived periodicals began appearing in Patna, Delhi and Simla. Amongst magazines being published today, *Hinduism Today* enjoys international recognition as representing the Hindu faith. It is produced by a small monastic community based in Hawaii.

Printing in India was not confined to the written word; it also included the printing of images. In this respect two media deserve our attention: posters and comics. Before the beginning of the twentieth century India had many lithographic presses that printed religious material, including posters. However, it was the last century that witnessed a revolution in this area. Publishers of posters, particularly of Hindu deities, but also images of saints and holy places, are found in all regions of India. The publishing firms that produce the highest volume of posters are found in Mumbai, Delhi, Kolkata and Chennai. Posters of deities are displayed by devotees at home and in the workplace. The placement of these posters by Hindus indicates the power these deities are believed to have. For example, at home Rāma with Sītā or Kṛṣṇa with Rādhā occupy places of honour, usually freshly garlanded, in recognition of their domestic significance; at the workplace one may see pictures of Lakṣmī, the dispenser of wealth and fortune, above the cash register; pictures of Sarasvatī, who represents knowledge, may be observed in school libraries; and portraits of Śiva Naṭarāja, a symbol of perpetual dance, often grace the walls of theatres and dance academies. The availability of deity posters in India and the world over in Hindu households has brought some sort of 'unified perception' of the sacred deities. A Hindu living in Montreal will imagine Kṛṣṇa in much the same way as a Hindu in some remote area of Gujarat, thanks to the similar image of a given poster.

English comic strips were a feature of newspapers in India from the beginning of the twentieth century. However, it was in 1967 that the series *Amar Chitra Katha* ('immortal illustrated story') emerged as a popular source of Indian classics in English and other Indian vernaculars. The editor and creator of the series, Anant Pai, conceived the idea of creating comics in Delhi and started publishing them from his India Book House in Mumbai. Since then more than 500 comic books have been published, including the epics of *Rāmāyaṇa* and *Mahābhārata*, biographies of saints, philosophers and freedom fighters, important events in Indian history, and so on. Anant Pai's objective was to educate young minds through the entertaining medium of comics and for this reason *Amar Chitra Katha* has become a vehicle for the spread of Hindu religious awareness. With time *Amar Chitra Katha* has grown into a self-improvement and entertainment empire that encompasses comics, children's books, audio cassettes (sound recordings), magazines, correspondence courses and videotapes.

See also: **Altars, domestic; Americas, Hindus in; Bhakti movement; Brāhmaṇa; Castes; Deities; Gurus; Iconography, modern; Kṛṣṇa; Lakṣmī, Śrī; Languages; Mahābhārata; Mantra; Myth; Poetry; Rādhā; Rāma; Rāmāyaṇa; Śabda; Sacred Geography; Sacred texts; Sarasvatī; Sītā; Śiva; Sound recordings; Tīrthayātrā; Varṇa**

PERWAIZ HAYAT

Further reading

Babb, Lawrence A. 1975. *The Divine Hierarchy: Popular Hinduism in Central India*. New York: Columbia University Press.

Basham, Arthur L. 1968. 'Introduction'. In *Hindu Epics, Myths, and Legends in Popular Illustrations*. London: Fontana/Collins, 219–53.

Blurton, T. Richard. 1998. 'Tradition and Modernism: Contemporary Indian Religious Prints'. *South Asia Research* 8, 1: 47–49.

Darnton, Robert. 2002. 'Book Production in British India'. *Book History* 5: 239–62.

Ghosh, Anindita. 2003. 'An Uncertain "Coming of the Book": Early Print Cultures in Colonial India'. *Book History* 6: 23–55.

Graham, William A. 1987. *Beyond the Written Word: Oral Aspects of Scripture in the History of Religion*. Cambridge: Cambridge University Press.

Hawley, John Stratton. 1995. 'The Saints Subdued: Domestic Virtue and National Integration in of *Amar Chitra Katha*'. In Lawrence A. Babb and Susan S. Wadley, eds, *Media and the Transformation of Religion in South Asia*. Philadelphia, PA: University of Pennsylvania Press, 107–34.

Hoover, Stewart M. 'Media and Religion'. In *ER* (2) 9: 5,805–10.

India Book House. 1986. *Catalogue: Amar Chitra Katha*. Bombay: India Book House.

Inglis, Stephen R. 1995. 'Suitable for Framing: The Work of a Modern Master'. In Lawrence A. Babb and Susan S. Wadley, eds, *Media and the Transformation of Religion in South Asia*. Philadelphia, PA: University of Pennsylvania Press, 51–75.

Pritchett, Frances W. 1995. 'The World of *Amar Chitra Katha*'. In Lawrence A. Babb and Susan S. Wadley, eds, *Media and the Transformation of Religion in South Asia*. Philadelphia, PA: University of Pennsylvania Press, 76–106.

Purohit, B.R. 1965. *Hindu Revivalism and Indian Nationalism*. Sagar, MP: SathiPrakashan.

Smith, Daniel M. 1995. 'Impact of "God Posters" on Hindus and Their Devotional Traditions'. In Lawrence A. Babb and Susan S. Wadley, eds, *Media and the Transformation of Religion in South Asia*. Philadelphia, PA: University of Pennsylvania Press, 24–50.

BRAHMĀ

Brahmā is pre-eminent in Hindu mythology as the god who created the universe out of pre-existing primeval matter. His particular roles are to set the process of creation in motion and to function as the first expression of individuality (ahaṃkāra). His embodiment of individuality is fundamental, but he is depicted as creating in a variety of ways, often through sexual progenation. Where he becomes the symbol of progenation, he is often portrayed as losing control sexually. Many versions of the long myth cycle dealing with the marriage of Śiva and Pārvatī, his wife, show Brahmā losing his semen at the mere sight of Pārvatī's finger or thumb. In some myths he has five heads in order to leer at her when she walks around him, and in an act of violence, demanding subsequent expiation, Śiva cuts off one of these heads. Hence Brahmā's four-headed form that is often depicted in sculpture.

Once the world is created, Brahmā acts primarily in an advisory capacity. In times of crisis, such as when the Earth is overrun with destructive demons, the Earth and the gods will always approach Brahmā, who recommends them to Viṣṇu. It is he, not Brahmā, who always takes decisive action. Yet Brahmā and Viṣṇu form a pair, both operating to preserve dharma, the divinely ordained order of the universe, but do so in different ways, Brahmā through his upholding and dissemination of Vedic knowledge and cosmic dharma, Viṣṇu through the strength of his arm and his ultimate physical defence of dharma, epitomising the cooperation ideally expected to define the relationship between the elite brāhmaṇa and the warrior classes in ancient Indian society.

Brahmā was worshipped widely only from about 600–200 BCE, though few temples to him exist in the present day.

See also: **Ahaṃkāra; Pārvatī; Sanātana Dharma; Śiva; Varṇa; Viṣṇu**

GREG BAILEY

Further reading

Bailey, Greg. 1983. *The Mythology of Brahmā*. New Delhi: Oxford University Press.

BRAHMĀ, DAY OF (BRAHMĀHORĀTRA)

In accordance with the differences in Hindu sources concerning the length of yugas, there are proportionate differences in the reckonings of the length of a Day and Night of Brahmā.

According to the *Manusmṛti* a Day of Brahmā consists of 1,000 divya-yugas, each of which lasts 12,000 human years. However, according to the *Viṣṇu Purāṇa* a Day of Brahmā equals one kalpa (4,320,000,000 human years), consisting of 14 manvantaras (Ages of Manu) and 15 sandhyas (periods of twilight). Each manvantara (and each sandhya) consists of 71 mahā-yugas, totalling 306,720,000 years. Each mahā-yuga (4,320,000 years) consists of four yugas: kṛta- or satya-yuga (1,728,000 years), tretā-yuga (1,296,000 years), dvāpara-yuga (864,000 years) and Kali-yuga (432,000 years). After each Kali-yuga a pralaya (dissolution) follows, equal in length to a mahā-yuga. Similarly, after the completion of a manvantara a period of sandhya (calculated to be of the length of a satya-yuga) follows, during which no manifest creation exists. A Year of Brahmā is equal to 3,110,400,000,000 human years. The Life of Brahmā is made up of 100 years of 360 days each (and an equal number of nights of the same duration) of Brahmā, lasting 311,040,000, 000,000 human years. According to some authorities the Life of Brahmā lasts 108 years, of which 50 have already elapsed. With the completion of a Life of Brahmā the universe disappears together with Brahmā and a new universe with a new Brahmā appears after a hiatus of equal length. According to the *Viṣṇu Purāṇa* one Life of Brahmā equals one Day of Viṣṇu. Assuming again a Life of Viṣṇu to last 100 or 108 years of 360 days each, the resulting figure expressed in human years is nearly impossible to imagine: 3,110,400,000,000,000 years!

See also: **Brahmā; Dharmaśāstras; Kalpas (Time); Manvantara; Pralaya; Purāṇas; Viṣṇu; Yuga**

KLAUS K. KLOSTERMAIER

Further reading

Bühler, G. (trans.). 1886. *The Laws of Manu*, SBE vol. 25. Oxford: Oxford University Press.
Doniger, W. and B.K. Smith (trans.). 1991. *The Laws of Manu*. Harmondsworth: Penguin.
Kane, P.V. 1958. *History of Dharmaśāstra*, vol. 5, pt 1. Pune: BORI.
Prakashanand Saraswati, Swami. 1999. *The True History and the Religion of India: A Concise Encyclopedia of Authentic Hinduism*. Austin, TX: International Society of Divine Love.
Wilson, H.H. 1961 *The Viṣṇu Purāṇa: A System of Hindu Mythology and Tradition*. Calcutta: Punthi Pustak.

BRAHMA KUMARIS

The Brahma Kumaris is a Hindu religious movement founded by Dada Lekraj (1876–1969) in the 1930s and notable for its apocalyptic teachings and largely female membership and leadership. Then in his sixtieth year, Lekhraj began to experience a series of visions of the imminent destruction of the world and the establishment of a post-destruction paradise. These visions became the foundation for a belief system based on the idea that the history of the world consists of repeating 5,000-year cycles. The world is a paradise at the start of a cycle; then ensues moral and physical decline, terminating in destruction. The Brahma Kumaris seek to be reborn in the paradise to come, which requires self-purification by means of a strictly vegetarian diet and celibacy, and the practice of a special type of meditation known as rāja yoga. Membership has been largely female from the start, with early followers being mainly of women from the business community of Hyderabad (now in Pakistan), who found Lekhraj's visions compelling. Having moved to its present headquarters at Mount Abu in Rajastan in 1950, the movement established a pattern of vigorous proselytising. With expansion, it acquired its current structure, which is that of a totally committed and mostly female monastic core surrounded by a much larger lay following. Lay followers attend meditation sessions and other functions at movement centres, which are found in all major Indian cities. The movement has successfully internationalised, and currently claims to have centres in about seventy countries.

See also: **Lekhraj, Dada; Rāja Yoga**

LAWRENCE A. BABB

Further reading

Babb, L.A. 1986. *Redemptive Encounters: Three Modern Styles in the Hindu Tradition*. Berkeley, CA: University of California Press.
Chandar, J. 1977. *The Way and the Goal of Raja* Yoga, 2nd edn. Mt Abu: Prajapita Brahma Kumari Ishvariya Vishva-Vidyalaya.
One Week Course for Attainment of Complete Purity, Peace and Prosperity. n.d. 5th edn. Mt Abu: Prajapita Brahma Kumari Ishvariya Vishva-Vidyalaya.

BRAHMACARYA

The word Brahmacarya literally means a mode of life designed for the realisation of Brahman or the supreme reality.

Celibacy, however, was considered such a key component of this lifestyle that the word itself came to denote a lifestyle characterised by celibacy in all the four religions of Indian origin: Hinduism, Buddhism, Jainism and Sikhism. Celibacy, in the Indian religious imagination, is thought to confer great spiritual powers, a belief which can be traced back to the *Atharvaveda* (11.5.1).

In Hinduism, however, it possesses the primary connotation of the first of the four stages of life into which a human existence has been apportioned, and thus refers to the period of life led as a celibate student prior to embarking on the life of a householder or gṛhastha. During this stage of life one typically resided in the house of the guru, after having undergone the rite of upanayana. Life in this stage largely consisted of tending the sacrificial fires, begging alms and assisting in household chores as one acquired Vedic learning in the devout proximity of the guru. This lifestyle is spelt out in detail in the second chapter of the *Manusmṛti*.

See also: **Brahman; Celibacy; Dharmasāstras; Gārhasthya; Guru; Saṃhitā; Upanayana**

ARVIND SHARMA

Further reading

Kane, P.V. 1974. *History of Dharmaśāstra*, vol. 2, pt 1, 2nd edn. Poona: Bhandarkar Oriental Research Institute.

BRAHMAN

The Sanskrit neuter noun Brahman usually denotes the one supreme, absolute being from which the entire universe develops, which pervades the entire universe, and into which the universe merges when it dissolves, and which, as pure consciousness, is the innermost self (Ātman) of every being. The term also commonly denotes liberation (Mokṣa), vedic text, or the Brāhmaṇa class. Differently accented, the masculine noun brāhmaṇa denotes one who composes or knows Vedic texts; the learned supervisor in certain Vedic ceremonies; or the personal Creator Brahmā. The conception of the absolute differs in various traditions of Vedānta and has a long history of development that spans the entirety of more than three millennia of extant Indian literature. Interpreters in subsequent periods in this history project conceptions they attach to the term Brahman onto its use in vedic texts, and even the most eminent modern scholars disagree over the connotation and etymology of the term, and its interpretation in vedic passages.

In vedic usage the term usually refers to a vedic hymn; that is, to a sacred poetic composition. Oldenberg (1917, vol. 2: 65) characterises it particularly as a sacred formula; Renou (1949) as an enigma or riddle; Thieme (1952: 104, 125) more broadly as a poetic, artistic formulation, the result of the poetic shaping of thought in verbal expression. While they agree that the term brahman denotes a vedic hymn, they disagree concerning its connotation and etymology. Oldenberg (1917, vol. 2: 65) considers that it connotes the aura of magic power that fills the hymn; Renou (1949: 43) the energy or force that promotes, fashions and connects the hymns; and Gonda (1950) their life force or power. Heesterman (1987: 294) agrees that the hymns are so called because they embody this power, or the cosmic principle. Thieme (1952: 98) and van Buitenen (1959) deny that the term connotes any such power or principle in vedic usage. Thieme argued that its basic meaning is 'formation' by demonstrating that it denotes other types of formations besides verbal ones, such as that of an embryo (Thieme 1952: 115). Rather than accepting that the vedic hymns are called brahman because they embody an abstract principle, van Buitenen suggests a converse semantic development from 'sacred formula, hymn' to 'supreme principle' by demonstrating a parallel development in the term akṣara. From meaning just 'syllable' the term akṣara comes to mean also 'the imperishable absolute', with the help of an analysis and etymology a-kṣara, 'not perishing', which, whether correct or not, applies to both meanings. The term brahman underwent a similar semantic development from 'speech' to 'the absolute'.

Although the etymology of the term brahman remains unsettled, the term's grammatical analysis is clear, and certain proposals regarding its etymology deserve attention. The term brahman consists of a stem *brah-* plus an abstract noun suffix *man* (Thieme 1952: 125–26) and is cognate with Middle Iranian *brahm*, 'form', 'appearance', 'style', derived from reconstructed Iranian *brazman* – derived from a reduced reconstructed Proto-Indo-European *b(h)-r/l-gh-*, 'increase', 'grow' (Mayrhofer 1963). While accepting Thieme's exegesis, Mayrhofer (1963) and van Buitenen (1959) doubt Thieme's (1952) proposed derivation from reconstructed Proto-Indo-European *mrég^{u}h-men* related to Greek *bréphos*, 'embryo', *morph-lē*, 'form', derived from Proto-Indo-European *mrelog^{u}h* – from the verb 'to form'. Over Thieme's objection, Mayrhofer allows the possibility of Gonda's (1950: 1ff., 18ff.) proposal that the stem derives from the Sanskrit root bṛh, 'increase', 'grow', even if brahman does mean 'form', 'shape'. This is compatible with the *Nighaṇṭu* classification of brahman under terms for food (2.7) and wealth (2.10), and the identification of Brahmaṇaspati with Bṛhaspati as 'lord of speech', which assumes the identity of brahman with *bṛh*. Also compatible is the reconstruction of Proto-Indo-European *bhlagh-men*, related to Latin *flamen*, 'priest' (Pokorny 1959: 154).

Various hymns of the *Ṛgveda* already identify a Creator, or a fundamental principle at the foundation of existence, independent of the term brahman (Brown 1942: Indra; *Ṛgveda* 10.72: Brahmaṇaspati; 10.81–82: Viśvakarman; 10.90: Puruṣa; 10.121: Prajāpati; 10.129: the one). In *Ṛgveda* 10.125, Speech (Vāc) identifies herself as the pervader of heaven and earth, and, by analogy with the wind, as the creator of all things. The early *Upaniṣads* at once preserve evidence of the use of the term Brahman in the meaning 'speech' and yet generally use the term for the absolute that is the source and essence of everything that exists. *Bṛhadāraṇyaka Upaniṣad* 1.3.21 maintains that Brahman is speech. Yet *Bṛhadāraṇyaka Upaniṣad* 4.1.2, by repeating the same statement in the context of similar identifications of Brahman with breath, sight, hearing, mind and the heart, shows that Brahman has already become established as the absolute at the foundation of everything and that speech and the others are identified with Brahman only insofar as they are understood as the foundation of everything in their respective spheres. So established is Brahman as the absolute in the fifth century CE that Bhartṛhari (similar to *Bṛhadāraṇyaka Upaniṣad* 4.1.2) makes speech the foundation of everything by identifying it as Brahman. The *Bṛhadāraṇyaka* and *Chāndogya Upaniṣads* identify Brahman as Puruṣa, the ancient, unborn, undying, immortal creator of everything, the fearless totality that is filled with everything, beyond duality, real, the highest world where supreme bliss is enjoyed and from which there is no return to Saṃsāra, pure consciousness, the self (Ātman), the inner controller, and the essence of subjective awareness and the objective world.

Later Vedāntins consider the ultimate absolute Brahman to be unqualified (nirguṇa). Because it is beyond the range of speech and thought, it is beyond description in any positive terms whatsoever but is describable only by denying to it various attributes and identifications. It is negatively described as being, for instance, formless, changeless, indivisible and infinite. Yet its essential nature is positively described to be existence, pure consciousness and bliss (Saccidānanda). From the point of view of ignorance, according to Advaita Vedānta, Brahman is conceived with positive qualities (saguṇa) as the immortal, omniscient, omnipotent creator God (see Potter 1981: 74–78). Brahman, which forms the special topic of the *Brahmasūtras*, and its relation to the Ātman are conceived variously in Advaita, Viśiṣṭādvaita and Dvaita Vedānta.

See also: **Advaita; Ātman; Bhartṛhari; Brahmā; Brahman-Ātman; Brāhmaṇa; Brahmasūtras; Dvaita; Indo-European traditions; Languages; Mokṣa; Puruṣa; Saccidānanda; Saṃhitā; Saṃsāra; Upaniṣads; Varṇa; Vedānta; Viśiṣṭādvaita**

PETER M. SCHARF

Further reading

Brown, W. Norman. 1942. 'The Creation Myth of the Rig Veda'. *Journal of the American Oriental Society* 62.2 (June): 85–98.

Brown, W. Norman. 1965. 'Theories of Creation in the Rig Veda'. *Journal of the American Oriental Society* 85.1 (March): 23–34.

Gonda, Jan. 1950. *Notes on Brahman*. Utrecht: J.L. Beyers.

Gonda, Jan. 1989. *Prajāpati's Relations with Brahman, Bṛhaspati and Brahmā*. Amsterdam and New York: North-Holland Publishing Co.

Heesterman, Jan C. 1987. 'Brahman'. In Mircea Eliade, ed., *The Encyclopedia of Religion*, vol. 2: 294–96. New York: Macmillian; London: Collier Macmillian.

Mayrhofer, Manfred. 1963. 'Brāhma'. In *Kurzgefaßtes etymologisches Wörterbuch des Altindischen* [*A Concise Etymological Sanskrit Dictionary*], vol. 2. Heidelberg: Carl Winter, 453–56.

Oldenberg, Hermann. 1917. *Die Religion des Veda*. 2nd edn. Stuttgart: J.G. Cotta. [1 ed Berlin: W. Hertz, 1894. Shridhar B. Shrotri, trans. 1988. *The Religion of the Veda*. 1 ed. Delhi: Motilal Banarsidass.]

Pokorny, Julius. 1959. *Indogermanisches etymologisches Wörterbuch* [Indo-European Etymological Dictionary], vol. 1. Bern and Munich: A. Francke.

Potter, Karl. (ed.). 1981. *Encyclopedia of Indian Philosophies*, vol. 3: *Advaita Vedānta up to Śaṃkara and His Pupils*. Delhi: Motilal Banarsidass.

Renou, Louis. 1949. 'Sur la Notion de "brāhman"'. *Journal Asiatique* 237.1: 7–46.

Thieme, Paul. 1952. 'Brāhman', *Zeitschrift der deutschen morgenländischen Gesellschaft* 102.1: 91–129.

van Buitenen, J.A.B. 1959. 'Akṣara'. *Journal of the American Oriental Society* 79: 176–87.

BRAHMAN-ĀTMAN

Adherents of Advaita, Viśiṣṭādvaita, and Dvaita Vedānta differ concerning the relation that holds between the individual self (Ātman) and the absolute (Brahman). Śaṅkara holds that they are identical: there is just one non-changing absolute. Each individual self is nothing other than the absolute. It appears to be limited and multiple due to the erroneous superimposition of limiting adjuncts on it. The absolute does not evolve into individuals; the distinctions that define individuals don't exist on the level of absolute knowledge. Their apparent reality is unrelated to the reality of the absolute just as the reality of objects in a dream is unrelated to objects in waking. Rāmānuja holds that the absolute is the inner self of individual selves just as individual selves are the inner selves of their bodies. Individual selves are parts that constitute the body of one great being. This one great being evolves the individual selves that constitute its body out of itself in the process of creation, giving parts of itself individual expression. The great being is the material out of which selves and everything else are made. Madhva holds that the supreme god Viṣṇu, with whom Brahman is identified, dwells in the heart of individual selves, which are distinct from, yet subordinate to and dependent upon him.

Commentators describe the views of three ancient sages Bādarāyana mentions in *Brahmasūtras* 1.4.20–22. Raṅgarāmānuja, the Viśiṣṭādvaita commentator on the *Bṛhadāraṇyaka Upaniṣad*, characterises them as follows: Āśmarathya considers that Brahman is the material cause of individual selves; Auḍulomi that individual selves differ from Brahman before liberation but are identical to it afterwards; and Kāśakṛtsna that the supreme self is the inner controller of individuals in the way that an essential property is to the individual of a kind (Nārāyaṇa 1911: 115). Śaṅkara interprets Kāśakṛtsna to assert, rather, non-difference (*Brahmasūtrabhāṣya* 1.4.22).

See also: **Advaita; Ātman; Bādarāyana; Brahman; Brahmasūtras; Dvaita; Madhva; Rāmānuja; Śaṅkara; Upaniṣads; Vedānta; Viśiṣṭādvaita; Viṣṇu**

PETER M. SCHARF

Further reading

Nārāyaṇa, Hari. 1911. *Bṛhadāraṇyakopaniṣat Raṅgarāmānujaviracitaprakāśopetá* (Sanskrit) [*The Bṛhadāraṇyaka Upaniṣad with the Commentary Prakāśa by Raṅgarāmānuja*]. Ānanda Āśrama Sanskrit Series 64. Pune: Ānanda Āśrama.

BRĀHMAṆA (PRIEST)

Brāhmaṇas or Brāhmans have been by birth the priests, scholars, thinkers, writers and systematisers of Hindu culture. They are the class of men responsible for studying, memorising and communicating sacred knowledge. The very ancient cosmogony of the *Hymn to the Puruṣa*, the *Puruṣa Sukta*, already contains the hierarchy of the four varṇas in which the sacerdotal class is identified with the mouth of the Puruṣa. In the Veda, the brāhmaṇa was one of the priests of the solemn Vedic sacrifice, whose function was to oversee the complex unfolding of the rites and recitations. Brāhmaṇa male priests were ritual specialists who sacrificed on behalf of the sacrificer (yajamana) and recited and taught the Vedic texts. They possessed theoretical and practical knowledge, Brāhman, and were responsible for dharma, the sociocosmic order. The union of brāhmaṇa and kṣatriya was recognised as essential for social flourishing. Later *Saṃhitās* and the *Brāhmaṇas* and *Sūtras* enumerate many prerogatives, particularly those referring to the honour (arca) and gifts (dakṣiṇā) due to them. In theory they alone are entitled to receive as well as make gifts. Despite this, the ideal brāhmaṇa of the *Dharmaśāstra* is poor and a false brāhmaṇa is seen as one who converts his religious duties into a trade. The imparting of knowledge or vidyā to the deserving (satpatra) is believed to be the greatest act of public welfare or philanthropy. Brāhmaṇas had to guard themselves against pollution and observe caste restrictions as a matter of religious and moral duty. Some priestly brāhmaṇas still lead a very orthodox style of life, following the śāstric injunctions scrupulously and remaining vegetarian. They are the most likely to perform traditional rituals and saṃskāras. Traditionally the majority of non-priestly brāhmaṇas were landowners and government servants. Today they are doctors, lawyers, engineers, teachers, IT specialists and so on.

See also: **Caste; Dharma; Dharmaśāstras; Saṃhitā; Saṃskāras; Varṇa; Yajña**

ANNA KING

Further reading

Biardeau, M. 1989. *Hinduism: The Anthropology of a Civilisation*. New Delhi: Oxford University Press.
Brockington, J.L. 1991. *The Sacred Thread: Hinduism in Its Continuity and Diversity*. Edinburgh: University of Edinburgh Press.
Carman, J.B. and F.A. Marglin (eds). 1985. *Purity and Auspiciousness in Indian Society* Leiden: Brill.
Carstairs, G.M. 1957. *The Twice-Born: A Study of a Community of High-Caste Hindus*. London: Hogarth Press.
Dumont, L. 1972. *Homo Hierarchicus: The Caste System and Its Implications*. London: Paladin.

Dumezil, G. 1958. 'Métiers et classes fonctionelles chez divers peuples indo-européens'. In *Annales, Economies, Sociétés, Civilisations*, 4 (Oct–Dec): 716–24.
Flood, G. 1996. *An Introduction to Hinduism*. Cambridge: Cambridge University Press.
Fuller, C.J. (ed.). 1996. *Caste Today*. SOAS Studies on South Asia. Delhi: Oxford University Press.
Fuller, C.J. 2003. *The Renewal of the Priesthood: Modernity and Traditionalism in a South Indian Temple*. Princeton, NJ and Oxford: Princeton University Press.
Larson, G.J. 1995. *India's Agony over Religion*. Albany, NY: SUNY.
O'Flaherty, W.D. 1991. *The Laws of Manu*. Harmondsworth: Penguin.
Raheja, G.G. 1988. *The Poison in the Gift: Ritual, Prestation, and the Dominant Caste in a North Indian Village*. Chicago, IL: University of Chicago Press.
Sanderson, A. 1985. 'Purity and Power among the Brahmans of Kashmir'. In M. Carrithers, S. Collins and S. Lukes, eds, *The Category of the Person: Anthropology, Philosophy, History*. Cambridge: Cambridge University Press, 190–216.
Searle-Chatterjee, M. and U. Sharma. 1994. *Contextualising Caste: Post Dumontian Approaches*. Oxford: Blackwell.
Stevenson, S. 1971. *The Rites of the Twice-Born*. New Delhi: Oriental Books Reprint Corporation.

BRĀHMAṆAS (TEXTS)

Brāhmaṇas are collections of prose material contained in the Veda, which discuss Vedic rituals. The word means 'belonging to brahman', or, since the word brahman can mean the Veda, 'belonging to the Veda'; it is the same word as the name of the brāhmaṇa varṇa. The earliest *Brāhmaṇas* are probably the passages of discussion and explanation which are interspersed among the mantras of the *Black Yajurveda Saṃhitā*. In the other Vedas, the *Brāhmaṇas* are handed down separately from the mantras. The longest collection is that of the *White Yajurveda*, the *Śatapatha* ('hundred paths') *Brāhmaṇa* (trans. Eggeling 1882–1900). In time the *Black Yajurveda* also developed a separate collection, the *Taittīrya Bráhmaṇa* (trans. Keith 1914).

The *Brāhmaṇas* do not set out to describe the ritual; this is done in the *Śrautasūtras* and *Gṛhyasūtras*. They assume a knowledge of ritual, and without such knowledge they are difficult to understand. They discuss reasons why a particular ritual (yajña) is performed, sometimes narrating a myth of how it was first performed and what resulted from it. They report the opinions of ritual experts who argue for different ways of performing a ritual, reflecting different ways of understanding it. For instance, some say that the morning offering should be made before sunrise, just as one offers food to a guest before he or she departs. Others say it should be made just after sunrise, as one gives suck to a baby after it is born (Bodewitz 1976: 41–50).

Correct performance of the ritual brings rewards: long life, the birth of sons, freedom from sickness, wealth, existence in a secure world (loka) after death. This power of ritual actions to shape a person's destiny was later generalised to all actions (Tull 1989). Stability in the worlds beyond death is a particular source of anxiety. 'There are deaths in every world, and if he did not make offerings to them, death would seize him in every world' (*Śatapatha Brāhmaṇa* 13.3.5.1; Eggeling 1882–1900, vol. 5: 339). The need to avoid re-death (punar-mṛtyu) led to ideas about re-birth and mokṣa which become clear in the *Upaniṣads*. The idea of stability is associated with the self (ātman), which in this context usually includes the body, though not in a merely physical sense.

To gain the benefits of the ritual one must not only perform it correctly but understand it. Often in the *Brāhmaṇas* we are told that 'he who knows this' – a particular ritual, or a particular way of understanding some aspect of ritual, of the cosmos, or of the human being – gains some benefit such as long life, victory over enemies or even victory over death. The discussions reveal ideas about the self, the cosmos, time, language, as well as ritual itself, which were developed further in the *Āraṇyakas* and *Upaniṣads*. They also contain a wealth of mythology (examples in O'Flaherty 1987), especially about cosmogony, the origins of rituals, and the struggle of the gods and asuras. Myth is used in a creative way, as a means of forming and expressing ideas about these topics. Many of the myths in the *Brāhmaṇas* and *Āraṇyakas* involve Prajāpati, the originator of ritual.

The *Brāhmaṇas* trace correspondences between elements of the ritual and parts of the human being, or parts of the cosmos. Knowledge of these gives the person for whom the ritual is performed (normally a man, but in the mythical prototype of the ritual often a god) control over his body, or over the cosmos. Thus the special fireplace (agni-cayana) built for certain elaborate sacrifices has five layers of earth and five of bricks; these correspond to five mortal parts of a man – hair, skin, flesh, bone, marrow – and five immortal parts – mind, voice, breath, sight, hearing. By correctly building it, Prajápati became immortal, and so does the man for whom this ritual is performed (*Śatapatha Brāhmaṇa* 10.1.3.4–7; Eggeling 1882–1900, vol. 4: 290f.). By building it with 360 stones and 360 bricks, corresponding to the 360 days and nights of the year (according to the Vedic calendar), the gods conquered the year and so became immortal (*Śatapatha Brāhmaṇa* 10.4.3.8; Eggeling 1882–1900, vol. 4: 357). The asuras failed to do so, because they used countless stones and bricks. This exemplifies a recurrent feature of myths about the struggle between the gods and the asuras: the asuras rely on force, but the gods are victorious through their ingenuity and understanding of the ritual.

See also: **Āraṇyakas; Asuras; Ātman; Brāhmaṇa (priest); Deities; Gṛhyasūtras; Karma; Mantra; Mokṣa; Myth; Prajāpati; Saṃhitā; Śrautasūtras; Upaniṣads; Veda; Varṇa; Yajña**

DERMOT KILLINGLEY

Further reading

Bodewitz, H.W. 1976. *The Daily Evening and Morning Offering (Agnihotra) According to the Brāhmaṇas*. Leiden: E.J. Brill.

Eggeling, Julius. 1882–1900. *The Çatapatha-Brâhmana According to the Text of the Mâdhyandina School*, 5 vols. Oxford: Clarendon Press. Reprinted Delhi: Motilal Banarsidass, 1963.

Keith, Arthur Berriedale. 1967. [1914] *The Veda of the Black Yaju School Entitled Taittīrya Sanhitā*. Cambridge, MA: Harvard University Press. Reprinted Delhi: Motilal Banarsidass, 91.

O'Flaherty, Wendy Doniger. 1987. *Tales of Sex and Violence: Folklore, Sacrifice and Danger in the Jaiminīya Brāhmaṇa*. Delhi: Motilal Banarsidass.

Tull, Herman W. 1989. *The Vedic Origins of Karma: Cosmos as Man in Ancient Indian Myth and Ritual*. Albany, NY: State University of New York Press.

BRAHMANISM

Brahmanism is a term that tends to be used by scholars of religion to describe the beliefs and practices represented primarily in the post-Vedic smṛti literature. The name Brahmanism is based on the importance placed on brāhmaṇas, the priestly class, throughout these texts. Similar to Vedism, Brahmanism is a scholarly construct, useful in describing the main tenets articulated by a particular group of Sanskrit texts, yet not to be taken as representing a distinct religion in the social reality of ancient India. Despite the prevalence of the term in secondary literature, various scholars have defined Brahmanism differently. Monier-Williams (1883), for example, delineated three stages of Brahmanism: (1) Ritual Brahmanism, which he associated with the *Brāhmaṇas*; (2) Philosophical Brahmanism, which he associated with the *Upaniṣads*; and (3) Mythological Brahmanism, which he associated with the *Mahābhārata* and *Rāmāyaṇa*. More recently, scholars like Patrick Olivelle (1993) have extended the use of the term Brahmanism to describe beliefs and practices expressed in the *Dharmasūtras* and *Dharmaśāstras*. The following entry, perhaps rather subjectively, follows this extended usage of the term, thus defining Brahmanism as that which accepts the authority of the Vedas, but as finding its unique expression in non-Vedic texts like the *Dharmasūtras, Dharmaśāstras, Rāmāyaṇa* and *Mahābhārata*.

In this way, the difference between Vedism and Brahmanism perhaps can best be understood in relation to the designation of two kinds of authoritative texts in ancient India: śruti (that which is perceived) and smṛti (that which is inferred). As Sheldon Pollock (1997) has demonstrated, both śruti and smṛti claim vedic status. But whereas śruti designates the vedic texts that have remained intact, traditional accounts present smṛti as that which has been remembered from lost vedic sources. In terms of content, śruti is focused primarily on ritual, while smṛti is largely concerned with social interactions. If we differentiate Brahmanism from Vedism along the lines of this textual distinction, we could say, provisionally, that whereas Vedism principally refers to the beliefs and practices found in śruti, Brahmanism is more closely aligned with smṛti. Accordingly, Brahmanism accepts the fundamental ideas of Vedism, including the authority of śruti, but extends its focus beyond the ritual to the entire range of human activities.

The concept of central concern throughout the smṛti literature is dharma. There is no exact equivalent in English for the term dharma; within its semantic range it includes dimensions of the English terms 'religion', 'duty', 'law' and 'justice'. The word first appears in the *Ṛgveda*, where it designates correct ritual action. However, in the smṛti literature, dharma is considered the cosmic order or natural law. It is universal in the sense that it applies to everyone, yet it is context-specific depending upon a person's class (jatidharma), region (deśadharma), family (kuladharma) and other circumstances. The smṛti literature discusses dharma primarily in relation to social obligations, which are considered in exhaustive detail outlining correct behaviour for public practices like marriage, judicial processes and inheritance, as well as private considerations like personal hygiene. The smṛti texts develop two theological constructs that firmly root dharma within the social and the personal realms of a person's life: (1) varṇa, which refers to one's social position; (2) āśrama, which designates one's stages of life. Together these constructs are referred to as varṇāśramadharma.

As first articulated in the *Ṛgveda* (10.90) but expanded and developed in the smṛti literature, there are four varṇas: brāhmaṇa, kṣatriya, vaiśya and śūdra. The first three varṇas constitute the twice-born classes. The designation of twice-born refers to the fact that, in addition to a natural birth, these three classes all have an initiatory birth conducted through Vedic ritual.

A main theme throughout the smṛti literature is the purity of the three twice-born classes, which is developed in the texts by the idea that each group has different innate identities that are to be maintained by prohibiting intermarriage and keeping the classes separate. The concept of dharma is specifically related to varṇa as each group in society was considered to have a particular function or duty (svadharma) which should be strictly followed. According to most texts, the duty of brāhmaṇas was controlling the sacrifice and teaching the Veda; kṣatriyas should be rulers or warriors; vaiśyas should be agriculturalists or merchants; and śūdras should serve the other classes. The importance of performing one's particular class duty is one of the teachings delivered by by Kṛṣṇa to Arjuna in the *Bhagavadgītā* when he says that it is better to do your own dharma poorly than another person's dharma well (3.35). In the context of the *Bhagavadgītā,* Arjuna should fight because it is his obligation as a warrior; if he were to renounce fighting he would be going against his kṣatriya-dharma.

In addition to caste status, Brahmanism designates distinct stages in the life of all members of the twice-born classes. In its classical codification there are four such stages, which are known as āśramas: (1) brahmacārin, Vedic student; (2) gṛhastha, married householder; (3) vānaprastha, retired householder, who retreats to the forest, usually with his wife, lives in a hermitage and continues to maintain the household fires; (4) saṃnyāsin, renouncer who gives up everything to pursue mokṣa. All four of these stages were originally considered as distinct lifestyles before they were codified by brahmanical legal texts into sequential stages of an individual's life. As Patrick Olivelle (1993) has demonstrated, the āśrama system represents a theological construct and does not reflect a social reality in ancient India.

Another important feature of Brahmanism is the ritual status of the king (rājas). Brāhmaṇas claimed for themselves the ritual power to bestow regal authority on the king; yet brāhmaṇas relied on the king for patronage and to legitimise their ritual power. The importance of the king is reflected in a number of smṛti texts where the king is presented as the primary law-giver (Manu in the *Mānava Dharmaśāstra*) or as the principle receiver of teachings about dharma (Yudhiṣṭhira in the *Mahābhārata*).

Brahmanism is often seen by scholars as an attempt to redefine Vedism in response to a number of the social changes that took place during the late Vedic period. Among these social changes was the emergence of the renouncer traditions (śramaṇa culture), including Jainism and Buddhism, which directly challenged some of the fundamental assumptions of Vedism. Two of the ideals most highly esteemed in these movements are vegetarianism and non-violence. Indeed, one of the most vexed issues addressed in the smṛti texts is how to reconcile a ritualism that called for the violent slaughter of domesticated animals with the emerging emphasis on non-violence. Another tension reflected throughout the smṛti literature is between renunciation and the brahmanical institution of maintaining a home with wife, children and a household fire. The smṛti texts offer up a number of different strategies to confront these problems.

See also: **Arjuna; Āśramas (stages of life); Bhagavadgītā; Brahmacarya; Buddhism, relationship with Hinduism; Dharma; Dharmaśāstras; Food; Gṛhasthya; Jainism, relationship with Hinduism; Kṛṣṇa; Mahābhārata; Manu; Mokṣa; Rāja; Rāmāyaṇa; Saṃhitā; Saṃnyāsa; Śramaṇa; Vānaprasthya; Varṇa; Vedism; Yudhiṣṭhira**

Brian Black

Further reading

Flood, Gavin. 1996. *An Introduction to Hinduism.* Cambridge: Cambridge University Press.

Monier-Williams, Sir Monier. 1883. *Religious Thought and Life in India: An Account of the Religions of the Indian Peoples, Based on a Life's Study of Their Literature and on Personal Investigations in Their Own Country, pt 1: Vedism, Brahmanism, and Hinduism.* London: John Murray.

Olivelle, Patrick. 1993. *The Āśrama System: The History and Hermeneutics of a Religious Institution.* New York: Oxford University Press.

Pollock, Sheldon. 1997. 'The "Revelation" of "Tradition": *Śruti, Smṛti,* and the Sanskrit Discourse of Power'. In Siegfried Lienhard and Irma Piovano, eds, *Lex et Litterae:*

Essays on Ancient Indian Law and Literature in Honour of Professor Oscar Botto. Turin: CESMEO.
Roy, Kumkum. 1994. *The Emergence of Monarchy in North India*. Delhi: Oxford University Press.
van Buitenen, J.A.B. 1981. *The Bhagavad Gītá in the Mahābhārata*. Chicago, IL: University of Chicago Press.

BRAHMASŪTRAS (VEDĀNTASŪTRAS, UTTARAMĪMĀṂSĀSŪTRAS)

The *Brahmasūtras* as we know them are ascribed to Bādarāyaṇa (*c.*100 BCE), who seems to represent the culmination of a long tradition of *Brahmasūtra* writers. The *Brahmasūtras* deal with the major upaniṣadic topics in 555 couplets, employing twenty-eight passages from the *Chāndogya-*, *Bṛhadāraṇyaka-*, *Katha-*, *Taittirīya-*, *Kauṣītaki-*, *Muṇḍaka-*, and *Praśna-Upaniṣads*. These couplets are grouped into four chapters, each for a particular purpose: (1) harmonising the various upaniṣadic views with the view of Brahman being the ultimate reality; (2) responding to objections of rivals and refuting their views; (3) prescribing a way to achieve knowledge of Brahman; (4) describing the results of perfect knowledge of Brahman.

Śaṅkara, Rāmānuja, Madhva and others considered this work to contain the most authentic representation of the upaniṣadic teachings in the milieu of a lively philosophical diversity. The *Brahmasūtras* became the basis for the varied Vedānta development and served as a vehicle of dissemination for the Vedānta theologians' own interpretations.

See also: **Bādarāyaṇa; Brahman; Madhva; Rāmānuja; Śaṅkara; Upaniṣads; Vedānta**

EDELTRAUD HARZER

Further reading

(Bādarāyaṇa). 1904. *Śrī-bháṣya. The Vedānta Sūtras with the Commentary of Rāmānuga.* Trans. G. Thibaut. SBES 48. Oxford: Clarendon Press.
(Bādarāyaṇa). 1936. *Brahma-sūtra-bháṣya. Vedānta-sūtras with the Commentary by Sri Madhwacharya*, 2nd edn. Trans. S. Subha Rao. Tirupati: Sri Vyasa Press.
(Bādarāyaṇa). 1962. *The Vedānta Sūtras of Bādarāyaṇa with the Commentary by Śaṅkara*. Trans. G. Thibaut. New York: Dover.

BRAHMAVAIVARTA PURĀṆA

See: **Purāṇas**

BRAHMO SAMAJ (SOCIETY OF BRAHMA)

Originally founded in Calcutta in 1828 by Rammohan Roy, the Brahmo Samaj replaced Roy's previous organisation, the Atmuja Sabha, which he founded in 1815. Influenced by Islam and the post-Enlightenment Christian world, Roy proclaimed a monotheism which rejected the use of mūrtis. The Brahmo Samaj was set up to reinterpret Hindu tradition along these lines, and set up its own premises at Chitpur, Calcutta, in 1830. The organisation's stated aim was the daily congregational worship of the Eternal without the use of images or paintings. The group was non-sectarian, and the *Saṃhitās* and the *Upaniṣads* were used alongside other sacred texts. All were accepted, irrespective of caste, and members became known as the Brotherhood. Roy translated parts of the *Upaniṣads* into Bengali, thus breaking from the tradition of reading sacred texts solely in their original Sanskrit form. The movement worshipped the one God found in all religions, although its rejection of divine emissaries such as prophets and avatāras and its unitarian interpretation of Christianity tended to limit its popular appeal, whether to Hindus, Muslims or Christians. The Samaj also advocated social reform, particularly of the caste system, and of the status accorded to women. Some traditional

Hindus formed a rival organisation, the Dharma Sabha, to oppose the Samaj's activities, fearing that the latter was only a short step away from the Christianity of the Western missionaries.

After Rammohan Roy's death in 1833, the organisation fell into decline: many supporters used mūrtis at home, and lapsed back into traditional practices. However, the organisation experienced a revival a decade later, under Debendranath Tagore, who compiled a book entitled *Brahmo Dharma* (1854), which consisted of a selection of passages from the *Upaniṣads*, together with an outline of the Brahmo Samaj's theology.

The Society experienced schism in 1865. Keshab Chandra Sen, who had joined the Samaj in 1858, had actively supported its programme of social reforms, but was convinced that it was only through Christianity that Hindu society could properly be renewed. Particularly controversial was Sen's insistence that brāhmaṇas should dispense with their sacred threads. Tagore could not accept such changes, and Sen and his supporters formed their own Bharatvarshiya Brahmo Samaj (Society of Brahma of India), while Tagore and his followers renamed themselves the Adi Brahmo Samaj (Original Brahmo Samaj). A further schism occurred within Sen's group, led by Pandit Shivanath Shastri, who formed a breakaway group called the Sadharan (Common) Brahmo Samaj.

Despite its internal quarrels, the various branches of the Samaj made a significant contribution to social reform in India. Consistent with its principles, the Brahmo Samaj afforded a place in which widows could remarry, and in 1881 its branch at Barishal, Bengal, appointed a woman, Manorama Mazumdar, as its preacher.

The society still exists: Indian membership is probably around 5,000, and a branch in London, England, has existed since 1911.

See also: **Avatāra; Caste; Dharma Sabha; Image worship; Roy, Rammohan; Saṃhitā; Sen, Keshab Chandra; Tagore, Debendranath; Upanayana; Upaniṣads; Veda; Widow remarriage; Women, status of**

GEORGE CHRYSSIDES

Further reading

Killingley, D. 1993. *Rammohun Roy in Hindu and Christian Tradition*. Newcastle: Grevatt and Grevatt.

Kopf, D. 1978. *The Brahmo Samaj and the Shaping of the Modern Indian Mind.* Princeton, NJ: Princeton University Press.

BṚHADĀRAṆYAKA UPANIṢAD

See: **Upaniṣads**

BṚHASPATI

The 'lord of might or brightness'. Also known as Brahmaṇaspati ('lord of the word, prayer'), Bṛhaspati is the divine guru of the Vedic gods. His development is largely a priestly creation and reveals an early stage in the eventual brahmanisation of Vedic religion. In this process, he absorbs various myths and feats that originally belonged to either Indra or Agni – including associations with thunder and rain. As such, he is most likely an original manifestation of Dyaus. Like Dyaus, Brahmaṇaspati is called the father of the gods (*Ṛgveda* 2.26.3, 4.50.6). Bṛhaspati's shape-changing ability (*Ṛgveda* 3.62.6) gives rise eventually to the Hindu doctrine concerning avatāras or divine incarnation. In subsequent Hinduism, Bṛhaspati is identified as the planet Jupiter. The moon-god Soma abducts Bṛhaspati's consort, Tara, 'star'.

See also: **Agni; Avatāra; Dyaus Pitṛ; Guru; Indra; Soma; Vedi; Vedic Pantheon**

MICHAEL YORK

BRITISH WHEEL OF YOGA

Established in 1965, the British Wheel of Yoga (BWY) is an association of teachers and practitioners with no binding affiliation to one particular teacher or lineage (unlike most forms of modern yoga in the United Kingdom). Ecumenical in approach, the Wheel is receptive to a wide range of teaching styles and considers itself the 'umbrella organisation' for all yoga in the UK. However, only a small number of yoga schools (such as Viniyoga Britain and Satyananda UK) are officially accredited by the Wheel. In 1995 the British Wheel won recognition from the national Sports Council as the governing body for yoga in the United Kingdom. The Wheel has a distinctive in-house teaching style which aims to make yoga accessible to all, and Wheel teachers put a great emphasis on safety in practice. BWY teacher training courses also have a strong textual and theoretical component.

There is no single publication that summarises the aims, methods and history of the British Wheel. However there is a quarterly journal, *Spectrum* (Sleaford: British Wheel of Yoga), and a website (www.bwy.org.uk/).

See also: **Yoga, modern**

MARK SINGLETON

BUDDHI

See: **Mahat**

BUDDHISM, RELATIONSHIP WITH HINDUISM

The origins of Buddhism can be traced to the historical figure Śākyamuni. Śākyamuni was born into a tribe of Kṣatriyas (the Śākya tribe, hence his appellation Śākyamuni – 'the Sage of the Śākyas'). He is believed to have lived in the sixth or (more likely) the fifth century BCE (although dates vary), in North India. He was born into a noble family in Lumbini, now on the southern border of Nepal. Many myths and legends surround his life, from which it is difficult to extract elements of a biography, but it appears that, as a young man, he decided to leave behind his worldly life and become a homeless wanderer (śramaṇa). His quintessential religious experience came whilst sitting under a Bo tree, at which time he experienced Awakening (bodhi) and thus became the Buddha, the 'Awakened One'. Subsequent to his Awakening experience, according to the textual sources, he spent the next forty-five years wandering the forests and plains of north India teaching his Dharma, his teachings, and gained a large following of disciples.

When Western scholarship first became aware of the Buddhist tradition it was through British connections in India, though Buddhism had long since died out in its country of origin. Its demise is often construed as engendered by the Muslim invasions of the tenth to twelfth centuries, but in fact it was more likely a consequence of numerous co-existent factors. Because of these British links in India, the original educators of the West in matters Buddhistic were brāhmaṇa paṇḍits. On the whole, these brāhmaṇas proffered an idea of the Buddha as an incarnation of Viṣṇu, and it was not until Western scholars (e.g. E. Burnouf and R. Spence Hardy) began to read Buddhist manuscripts and/or visit the countries of Southeast Asia in which Buddhism continues to be the state-sponsored religion – as did T.W. Rhys Davids – that a fuller picture of the Buddhist religion (although, oftentimes, a rather distorted one) began to emerge in the West.

With regard to Buddhism's early relation to Brahmanism, two key themes emerge. First, the notion that Buddhism is a reaction against Brahmanism and, second, the idea that it is, essentially, a revalorisation of its hegemonic counterpart. In contrast to brahmanical essentialism, the Buddha taught a nominalism. For the Buddha, there is no fixed or permanent essence either within the self or underlying the nature of the universe. Instead, the Buddha described the nature of all existence as characterised by anitya (impermanence), anātman (no-self) and duḥkha (unsatisfactoriness, suffering). Further, with regard to causation, the Buddha propagated the law of pratītya-samutpāda (Pali: paṭicca-samuppāda), according to which all phenomena arise in dependence on other conditions, and because of the constant flow of conditions no worldly phenomena have a fixed or permanent essence, but all are in a constant state of change. These views of the Buddha can be seen as a reaction to Brahmanism, as the emphasis on impermanence is a radical juxtaposition to the brahmanical emphasis on essence. Other examples of Buddhism as a reaction against Brahmanism can be found in the Buddha's opposition to the caste system, and there is some evidence that women were treated more favourably within the Buddhist community (Collett forthcoming: 1).

A chapter in the well-known *Dhammapada* on 'The Brāhmaṇa' illustrates Buddhism as both a reaction to and revalorisation of Brahmanism. Here it is said: 'Neither . . . by lineage nor by birth does one become a Brāhmaṇa. But in whom truth and righteousness exist, that one is pure, that one is a Brāhmaṇa' (*Dhammapada* 393). From this radical reinterpretation of religio-social status to the repositioning of saṃsāra in relation to the new Buddhist goal of nirvāṇa, there are many instances of the Buddha appearing to reinterpret old teachings (whether brahmanical or from other traditions) and reinvest them with Buddhistic meaning. A second strong example of the Buddha's revalorisation of Brahmanism is in his ethicisation of the karma (Pali: kamma) doctrine. The Buddha takes the brahmanical notion of karma, efficacious ritual action, and overwrites it with Buddhistic meaning. The Buddha broadened out the meaning of the word karma to mean action in general, rather than its narrow brahmanical sense of ritual action, and within the parameters of his own karma doctrine he links action with (psychological) intention and material consequence, therefore positioning it as a doctrine about ethics and the consequences of moral action.

In the late ancient and medieval period Buddhism, like Hinduism, developed a tantric dimension. It seems most likely that, in this instance, the Buddhists adopted existing Śaivite tantric practices, overwrote them with Buddhistic meaning and circumscribed them with medieval Buddhist philosophies on emptiness (śūnyatā). As a result of this adoption and adaptation, some Hindu deities have found their way into the Buddhist pantheon. The deities associated with a form of Buddhism called Vajrayāna include Bhairava/Mahābhairava, Mahākālā and various female ḍākinīs. These wrathful and semi-wrathful figures are used in Buddhism as a basis for visualisation meditation practice, ritual and chanting. Quintessentially, these figures have come to represent a means for the transformation of negative energy into positive, and therefore are seen as a crucial tool in the adept's quest for Awakening.

As well as the relationship between Hindu and Buddhist tantra during this period, there was also some cross-fertilisation of ideas between the Buddhist Mahāyāna schools and medieval Hindu philosophical schools such as those expressed in Advaita Vedānta. Some similarities are evident in this context in discourse on the nature of self, the nature of existence and the nature of liberation.

Following its inception in India, Buddhism soon spread beyond the borders of the subcontinent, to Sri Lanka, Tibet, Nepal, Burma, Thailand and East Asian countries. In many of these countries Buddhism continues to be the state-sponsored religion, and in each of its meetings with new cultural circumstances and historical situations it has undergone acculturation and partial assimilation with indigenous traditions. This is evidenced in such phenomena as the influence of Taoism and Confucianism on East Asian forms of Buddhism, and the continued incorporation of the occult arts and indigenous and Hindu deities in Southeast Asian traditions. Medieval and modern-day Nepal has seen the emergence of a Hinduised Buddhism and a Buddhist-influenced Hinduism, both of which include worship of a pantheon of deities who are an amalgamation of Hindu, Buddhist and indigenous Nepalese (historical and archetypal) figures. Here the very categories of 'Buddhism' and 'Hinduism' break down, and religious practice incorporates elements of both.

In more recent decades, India has witnessed both sustained practice of Tibetan Buddhism on its soil, in the government's granting of the Tibet-in-exile community in Dharamsala, and a revival of indigenous practice of Buddhism, in the Ambedkarite movement. Dr B.R. Ambedkar was an ex-untouchable who trained as a lawyer, became a formidable force in Indian politics and was a resilient critic of Gandhi. In the 1950s Ambedkar decided to convert to Buddhism, as he considered the emphasis on the caste system within Hinduism an insurmountable problem for the ex-untouchable communities. He converted in 1956, just prior to his death, and following his conversion many other Dalits converted to Buddhism, hence beginning the Trailoka Bauddha Mahāsaṅgha Sahayaka Gana, a movement which continues to flourish today.

See also: **Advaita; Ambedkar, Bhimrao Ram; Brāhmaṇa (priest); Brahmanism; Burnouf, Eugène; Caste; Dalits; Karma; Paṇḍit; Śaivism; Saṃsāra; Śramaṇa; Śramaṇa culture; Tantrism; Varṇa; Viṣṇu**

ALICE COLLETT

Further reading

Collett, A. (forthcoming). 'Buddhism and Gender: Re-framing and Re-focusing the Debate'. *Journal of Feminist Studies in Religion*, Volume 22, Number 2, Fall 2006, pp. 155–158.

von Hinüber, O. and K.R. Norman (eds). 1994–95. *Dhammapada*. Oxford: Pali Text Society.

BÜHLER, GEORG (1837–98)

German Indologist, who has been described as 'the Sanskritist's Sanskritist'. Bühler studied in Göttingen and worked on Sanskrit, primarily vedic, manuscripts in Paris and London from 1858 to 1862 before going to India, where, in 1863, he became Professor of Oriental Languages at Elphinstone College in Bombay. While Educational Inspector for the northern part of the Bombay Presidency from 1868 he compiled a catalogue of manuscripts in libraries of western India, also purchasing many manuscripts for the libraries of Oxford, Cambridge, Berlin and Vienna. Bühler translated four *Dharmasūtras* and the *Manusmṛti* for the *Sacred Books of the East*, and also edited the *Pañchatantra* (1868) and Āpastamba's *Dharmasūtra* (1868–71) for the Bombay Sanskrit Series. Apart from his work on Hinduism he also wrote several pioneering articles on the Jains, based in part on his manuscript researches. From 1881 he was Professor at Vienna, where he founded the *Wiener Zeitschrift für die Kunde des Morgenlandes* (Vienna Journal for Oriental Studies, 1881ff.), edited the *Grundriss der indo-arischen Philologie und Altertumskunde* (Encyclopedia of Indo-Aryan Research) and completed his work on Indian epigraphy (1896).

See also: **Dharmaśāstras; Dharmaśūtras; Jainism, relationship with Hinduism; Hinduism, history of scholarship; Pañcatantra; Sacred Books of the East**

WILL SWEETMAN

Further reading

Bühler, G. 1879–82. *The Sacred Laws of the Aryas*. Sacred Books of the East 2 & 14. Oxford: Clarendon Press.

Bühler, G. 1886. *The Laws of Manu*. Sacred Books of the East 25. Oxford: Clarendon Press.

Jolly, J. 1899. 'Georg Bühler: 1837–1898'. *Grundriss der indo-arischen Philologie und Altertumskunde*, 1, 1 A. Strasbourg: Trübner.
van Buitenen, J.A.B. (ed./trans.). 1973–80. *The Mahābhārata*. Chicago, IL: University of Chicago Press.

BUITENEN, JOHANNES ADRIANUS BERNARDUS VAN (1928–79)

Dutch Sanskritist. Van Buitenen began the study of Sanskrit while at high school, and then studied Asian languages and classical philosophy at the University of Utrecht. His doctoral research was on Rāmānuja's *Gītābhāṣya*, his commentary on the *Bhagavadgītā* (abbreviated translation, 1953), and he later published an edition and translation of Rāmānuja's *Vedārthasamgraha* (1956). During a visit to India from 1953 to 1956, he worked at the Deccan College Research Institute in Pune on the *Encyclopedic Dictionary of Sanskrit* and also arranged to record the performance of a large Vedic ceremony, the *Vājapeya*. After two years in the United States, he returned to Utrecht as Reader in Indian Philosophy before taking up an appointment at the University of Chicago in 1961. While continuing to publish on Indian philosophy and Vedic ritual, in the last decade of his life he began translation of the *Mahābhārata* based on the new critical edition, completing half of it before his death.

See also: **Bhagavadgītā; Hinduism, history of scholarship; Mahābhārata; Rāmānuja**

WILL SWEETMAN

Further reading

Rocher, L. (ed.). 1988. *Studies in Indian Literature and Philosophy: Collected Articles of J.A.B. van Buitenen*. Delhi: Motilal Banarsidass.
van Buitenen, J.A.B. 1953. *Rāmānuja on the Bhagavadgītā: A Condensed Rendering of his Gītābhāṣya*. The Hague: H.L. Smits.
van Buitenen, J.A.B. 1956. *Rāmānuja's Vedārthasamgraha*. Pune: Deccan College Postgraduate and Research Institute.

BURNOUF, EUGÈNE (1801–52)

French Sanskritist and Indologist, an outstanding figure in the study in Europe of the texts of the Buddhist, Hindu and Zoroastrian traditions. He studied Sanskrit with Antoine Léonard de Chézy in Paris, succeeding him at the Collège de France on Chézy's death in 1832. Although best known for his work on Buddhism, Burnouf worked also on the Veda and *Purāṇas*. The preface to his translation of the first nine books of the *Bhāgavata Purāṇa* placed the Purāṇas, hitherto little studied by European scholars, in their Indian literary and religious context. Burnouf also made important suggestions regarding the dating of Hindu texts by reference to the emergence of Buddhism. Among the students in Burnouf's lectures on the Veda were Rudolf von Roth (1821–95), who (with W.D. Whitney) published a critical edition of the *Atharvaveda*, and Friedrich Max Müller, who reported that it was at Burnouf's suggestion that he undertook a critical edition of the *Ṛgveda* with Sāyaṇa's commentary. Burnouf's younger brother, Émile-Louis, was also a Sanskritist and published the first translation of the *Bhagavadgītā* from Sanskrit into French (1861).

See also: **Buddhism, relationship with Hinduism; Hinduism, history of scholarship; Müller, Friedrich Max; Purāṇas; Saṃhitā; Veda; Whitney, William Dwight**

WILL SWEETMAN

Further reading

Burnouf, E. 1840–47. *Le Bhâgavata Purâṇa, ou Histoire poétique de Krĭchna*, 3 vols. Paris: L'Imprimerie Royale.
Windisch, E. 1917. *Geschichte der Sanskrit-Philologie und indischen Altertumskunde* [History of Sanskrit Philology and Research on Ancient India]. Strasbourg: Trübner.

C

CAITANYA

In a short span of forty-eight years, Caitanya spread a wave of Kṛṣṇa-bhakti (devotion to Kṛṣṇa) throughout India, especially in the regions of Bengal, Orissa and Mathura. His life and teachings are recorded in several sixteenth-century Sanskrit and Bengali works, most notably *Caitanya-Bhāgavata* of Vṛndāvana Dāsa Ṭhākura and *Caitanya-Caritāmṛta* of Kṛṣṇadāsa Kavirāja.

Caitanya was born in 1486 as Viśvambhara Miśra, in a village near Navadvīpa, West Bengal. He was the second son of the Vaiṣṇava brāhmaṇa Jagannātha Miśra and his wife Śacī Devī. Viśvambhara mastered vyākaraṇa (grammar) in his youth, and opened his own school. He married Lakṣmīdevī and, after her untimely demise, Viṣṇupriyā. The young scholar-teacher underwent a dramatic transformation when he visited Gayā to perform śrāddha (post-funeral rites) for his father. There, he received dīkṣā (initiation) from Īśvara Purī, and returned to Navadvīpa overcome with ecstatic devotion to Kṛṣṇa. Thereafter, he spent his time performing saṃkīrtana, congregational singing of Kṛṣṇa's names, in the company of other Vaiṣṇavas in Navadvīpa.

At the age of 24, Viśvambhara accepted saṃnyāsa, receiving the name Kṛṣṇa-Caitanya, and began extensive tours of South India, Orissa, Bengal and Vṛndāvana. Wherever he travelled, Caitanya encouraged people to chant the names of Kṛṣṇa constantly and lead a sinless life of devotion to the Lord. He attracted a following from among the intellectual and cultural elite, as well as from low-caste and tribal communities.

Caitanya spent the final eighteen years of his life in Jagannātha Purī, Orissa, ministering to visiting followers, worshipping Rādhā and Kṛṣṇa, discussing passages from the *Bhāgavata Purāṇa* and other bhakti literature with his close associates, and experiencing heightened states of devotional ecstasy. Most biographers are quiet about his death/disappearance, which occurred in 1533.

Even during his lifetime, Caitanya was regarded by his followers as a manifestation of Kṛṣṇa, who descended to teach the religious process for this age – the simple yet profound practice of chanting the holy names. Thus, Caitanya is revered by Gauḍīya Vaiṣṇavas as both bhakta and Bhagavān; that is, as both the ideal devotee, to be emulated by aspirants, and the Lord himself, worthy of worship.

Over the last half-millennium, Caitanya's life and teachings have inspired prolific output in the realms of devotional poetry, aesthetic theory and theology, along with innovations in kīrtana music and Kṛṣṇa art. The pilgrimage town of Vṛndāvana, with its temple architecture and communities, owes much to the work of his Gosvāmī disciples. In modern times, Caitanya's following has grown worldwide, due to the missionary efforts of A.C. Bhaktivedanta Swami Prabhupada and the institution he founded, International Society for Krishna Consciousness (ISKCON).

Although Caitanya directed his immediate disciples to write the canonical texts of the school, he himself wrote only the *Śikṣāṣṭaka*, or 'eight verses of teaching'. He gave special importance to the third: 'Thinking oneself lower than a blade of grass, with more forbearance than a tree, feeling no pride and yet honouring others, one should chant (the name of) Hari constantly'.

See also: **Aesthetics; Bhakti; Dīkṣā; Gauḍīyas; Gayā; International Society for Krishna Consciousness; Jagannātha; Kṛṣṇa; Languages; Music; Prabhupada, A.C. Bhaktivedanta Swami; Purāṇas; Rādhā; Saṃnyāsa; Śrāddha (rites to deceased ancestors); Vaiṣṇavism; Varṇa; Vṛndāvana; Vyākaraṇa**

RAVI M. GUPTA

Further reading

Bhūmipati Dāsa (trans.). 1998. *Śrī Caitanya-bhāgavata of Śrīla Vṛndāvana dāsa Ṭhākura, with English translation of the Gauḍīya-bhāṣya introduction and commentary, life sketch of the author and chapter summaries by Śrī Śrīmad Bhaktisiddhānta Sarasvatī Gosvāmī*, ed. Puṇḍarīka Vidyānidhi Dāsa, 5 vols. New Delhi: Vrajraj Press.

Chakrabarty, R. 1985. *Vaisnavism in Bengal: 1486–1900*. Calcutta: Sanskrit Pustak Bhandar.

De, S.K. 1961. *Early History of the Vaisnava Faith and Movement in Bengal*, 2nd edn. Calcutta: Firma KLM.

Dimock, E.C. (trans.). 1999. *Caitanya Caritāmāta of Kṛṣṇadāsa Kavirāja: A Translation and Commentary by Edward C. Dimock, Jr., with Introduction by Dimock and Tony K. Stewart*. Cambridge, MA: Department of Sanskrit and Indian Studies, Harvard University.

Eidlitz, W. 1968. *Krsna-Caitanya: sein Leben und seine Lehre*. Stockholm: Almquist and Wiksell.

Kapoor, O.B.L. 1978. *The Philosophy and Religion of Sri Caitanya*. Delhi: Munshiram Manoharlal.

Majumdar, A.K. 1978. *Caitanya: His Life and Doctrine*. Calcutta: Jijnasa.

Prabhupada, A.C. Bhaktivedanta Swami 1988. *Teachings of Lord Caitanya, the Golden Avatar*. Los Angeles, CA: Bhaktivedanta Book Trust.

Prabhupada, A.C. Bhaktivedanta Swami (trans.). 1996. *Śrī Caitanya-Caritāmāta of Kṛṣṇadāsa Kavirāja Gosvāmī, with the original Bengali text, roman transliteration, English equivalents, translation and elaborate purports*, 9 vols. Los Angeles, CA: Bhaktivedanta Book Trust.

CAKRAS

See: **Tantrism**

CALENDAR

Almanacs are necessary to identify the correct and auspicious times for making vows, celebrating festivals, offering sacrifices and observing life-cycle rites (Kane 1958: 641). The traditional Hindu calendar is lunar-solar. While the months (māsa) are defined by the moon-cycles, the beginning of the year (varṣa) is fixed by either the solar spring or the autumn equinox. The difference between the year of twelve lunar months and the solar year (amounting to roughly 10.87 days every year) is made up by inserting an intercalary month every third year: the so-called ādhika māsa (additional month).

At the time of India's Independence (1947) about thirty different calendars were in use in India. In order to eliminate the confusion caused by the great variety of traditional calendars and to correlate the Indian calendar with the Gregorian, the government of India established in 1952 a Calendar Commission, which recommended the introduction of an *Indian Reformed Calendar*, valid for the whole of India for official purposes. It became effective with the spring equinox on 22 March 1957, which became New Year's Day: Chaitra 1, 1879 Śaka era. The *Indian Reformed Calendar* separates the Indian months (whose old names have been preserved) from the moon phases and approximates the length of each month to that of the Gregorian calendar.

The traditional Indian calendar, called Pañcāṅgam (Five Limbs), consists of five parts: tithi (lunar day), vāra (solar day), nakṣatra (asterism), yoga (planetary conjunctions) and kāraṇam (influences of stars). Each tithi is subdivided into two kāraṇas, which are either cara (changing) or sthira (fixed). Each of these has a presiding deity, whose influence determines the auspicious or inauspicious character of the time span designated. The *Indian Reformed Calendar* issued by the government in New Delhi also contains basic information on all of these items, but does not offer all the minutiae required for religious and astrological purposes, for which the numerous regional *Pañcāṅgas*, which are published every year from many places, have to be consulted.

Correlation of the *Indian Reformed Calendar* with the Gregorian (Western) Calendar

The months of the *Indian Reformed Calendar* begin on these dates of the Gregorian Calendar:

Caitra (30 days; 31 days in a leap year)	22 March (21 March in a leap year)
Vaiṣākha (31 days)	21 April
Jyeṣṭha (31 days)	22 May
Āsādha (31 days)	22 June
Śrāvana (31 days)	23 July
Bhādrapada (31 days)	23 August
Āśvina (30 days)	23 September
Kārtīka (30 days)	23 October
Mārgaśīrsa (30 days)	22 November
Pauṣa (30 days)	22 December
Māgha (30 days)	21 January
Phālguna (30 days)	20 February

The Indian Calendar knows six seasons (ṛtu):

1 Vasantha (spring), comprising Phālguna and Caitra
2 Grīṣma (summer), comprising Vaiśākha and Jyeṣṭha
3 Varṣa (rainy season), comprising Āsāḍha and Śrāvana
4 Śāradā (autumn), comprising Bhādrapada and Āśvina
5 Hemānta (late autumn), comprising Kārtīka and Mārgaśīrṣa
6 Śiśira (winter), comprising Pauṣa and Māgha

(The *Ṛgveda* mentions only five seasons, leaving out Śiśira, but later texts have six.)

The days of the week (vāra) are:

ravivāra	Sunday (day of the sun)
romavāra	Monday (day of the moon)
maṇgalavāra	Tuesday (day of Mars)
budhavāra	Wednesday (day of Mercury)
guruvāra	Thursday (day of Jupiter)
śukravāra	Friday (day of Venus)
śaṇivāra	Saturday (day of Saturn)

(There is some evidence that in Vedic times there was a six-day week.)

The times for religious festivals are still set according to lunar months. Since in some areas of India, such as Punjab and Orissa, the beginning of the (moon-)month is reckoned from the beginning of the bright fortnight (śuklānta), in others from the beginning of the dark (kṛṣṇanta), there is no India-wide agreement concerning the beginning of a feast day, and thus many problems arise in connection with the setting of popular feasts. The *Rāṣṭriya Pañcāṅga* (annual National Almanac) provides alternative dates for various regions. Regional *Pañcāṅgas* decide the case for each locality.

Each lunar month is divided into two pakṣas: sukla pakṣa (bright half) and kṛṣṇa pakṣa (dark half). Each pakṣa is subdivided into fifteen tithis (moon-days). Dates of festivals are given in the form: māsa/pakṣa/tithi. For example: Kṛṣṇa's birthday is always celebrated on Śrāvana (māsa) Kṛṣṇa (pakṣa) aṣṭami (tithi). According to the *Reformed Indian Calendar*, Kṛṣṇa's birthday is a moveable feast, whose commencement is calculated differently in various parts of India according to the system used locally to determine the commencement of a tithi.

The names of the fifteen moon-days (tithis) in each half-month (pakṣa) are:

1 pratipad
2 dvitīya
3 tṛtīya
4 caturthī
5 pañcami
6 ṣaṣthī
7 saptamī
8 aṣṭamī
9 navamī
10 daśamī
11 ekādaśī
12 dvādaśī
13 trayodaśī
14 caturdaśī
15 pañcadaśī
  a in kṛṣṇapakṣa: amavasya, darśa (new moon)
  b in śuklapakṣa: pūrṇimā (full moon)

Each tithi is divided into thirty muhūrtas ('hours'), each muhūrta into sixty nimeṣas ('minutes'), each nimeṣa into sixty kṣaṇas ('moments', winks of the eye).

For astrological purposes it is important to find the right tithi (and kārana) as well as the appropriate muhūrta for every activity: there are auspicious and inauspicious times for everything and no important enterprise is to be undertaken without ensuring the auspiciousness of the day and hour. Many Hindus even today follow a timetable called Rahu-kā, which identifies auspicious/inauspicious times for every day of the week.

The Jyotiṣa Department of Banaras Hindu University (like many other places in India connected with traditional centres of learning) issues a yearly (traditional) *Pañcāṅga* following the pre-reformed Indian calendar. Its charts for every lunar pakṣa with traditional astronomical/astrological information are widely used by astrologers in India. The central government's *Rāṣṭrīya Pañcāṅga* follows the *Indian Reformed Calendar*. It too offers additional information on lunar tithis, nakṣatras, yogas, kāraṇas and rāśis, which can be also used for astrological purposes. It contains a comparative table showing the beginnings of years in other eras used in some parts of India such as Vikram, Bengali San, Kollam, Kali, Buddha Nirvāna, Mahāvīra Nirvāṇa and Hijra. The year 2004 Common Era corresponded to Śaka 1925/26; Vikram Samvat 2061/62; Bengali San 1411/12; Kollam 1180/81; Kali Yuga 5106/07; Buddha Nirvāṇa 2548/49; Mahāvīra Nirvāṇa 2531/32; Hijra 1424/25.

See also: **Jyotiṣa; Kṛṣṇa; Saṃskāras; Utsava; Vrata**

KLAUS K. KLOSTERMAIER

Further reading

Kane, P.V. 1958. *History of Dharmasastra*, vol. 5, pt 1. Pune: Bhandarkar Oriental Research Institute.

Raṣṭrīya Pañcāṅga, Indian Reformed Calendar. Annual. (Published in English and several

Indian vernaculars.) New Delhi: Director-General of Observatories, Government of India.
Rath, Pt. Sanjay. 2001. 'The Hindu Calendar', http://sanjayrath.tripod.com/Article/hindu_calendar.htm. (accessed 5 August 2003).
Viśva Pañcāṅgam [*Universal Almanac*]. Annual. (Published in Hindī.) Kāśī Hindū Viśva Vidyālaya.

CĀMUṆḌĪ

The goddess Cāmuṇḍī is one of the many forms of the prototype Hindu goddess Śakti, who is particularly worshipped in South India. The word Cāmuṇḍī comes from the place name Chāmuṇḍa in Tulunad. The prime shrine to this goddess is found in the Cāmuṇḍī Hills of Mysore in Karnataka, where the goddess is known as Cāmuṇḍīśwarī and is believed to be associated with Durgā, who slew the fierce demon Mahiṣāsura. A prominent statue of the demon Mahiṣāsura carrying a large sword and a huge serpent stands in the courtyard of the temple. The temple in Mysore also features an enormous statue of Nandi, Śiva's vehicle, who is also worshipped by the devotees who visit the temple. In Kerala, Cāmuṇḍī is worshipped in many forms with the place names prefixed to the name Cāmuṇḍī (Nampoothiri 1990: 21). Cāmuṇḍī is worshipped as both a public goddess and a domestic goddess, and is a popular deity in the teyyam rituals of Keralan low-caste worship (Kurup 1973: 21). Some icons represent Cāmuṇḍī as seated on a black bull somewhat akin to Śiva or Yama.

See also: **Dance; Devī Māhātmya; Durgā; Nandi; Śakti; Śiva; Yama**

THEODORE GABRIEL

Further reading

Kurup, K.K.N. 1973. *The Cult of Teyyam and Hero Worship in Kerala*. Calcutta: Indian Publications.
Nampoothiri, M. Vishnu. 1990. *Tottampattukal* [Tottam Songs]. Kottayam: National Bookstall.

CAṆḌĪ

See: **Kālī and Caṇḍī**

CAṆḌĪDĀSA

A sixteenth-century Bengali poet famed for his songs extolling the love between Rādhā and Kṛṣṇa. Caṇḍīdāsa is regarded by the Bengali Vaiṣṇavas as one of the three original gurus of the easy path or emotional approach (rāgātmika-paddhati), who were believed through their own experience to have attained the same level of passion felt by Rādhā for Kṛṣṇa and to have expressed the emotions of such bhakti in their writings. The other two poets were Vidyāpati and Jayadeva.

The Bengali Vaiṣṇavas revered Caṇḍīdāsa because his works influenced Caitanya, the great Sylheti mystic and early exponent of the Bengali school of Kṛṣṇa bhakti known as Gaudīya Vaiṣṇavism. Caṇḍīdāsa's songs were listened to and sung by Caitanya and remain part of Vaiṣṇava kīrtaṇa in Bengal and elsewhere. Little is known concerning the poet's life, although later centuries have seen the creation of a burgeoning hagiography which includes stories and anecdotes that focus on his unorthodox faith and his sexual liaison with a low-caste woman. However, by the more orthodox Vaiṣṇavas he is regarded as a mystic and lover of Kṛṣṇa who practised Tantric yoga with the assistance of a female partner who was not his wife. Indeed the poet's name would suggest that he was a Śakti devotee and therefore support the tantric connection. The poet is ambiguous about his own caste origins in his poetry but the first modern biography written in 1873 by Ramagati Nyayaratna asserts that he was a Brāhmaṇa, born in the village of Nannur, in the eastern district of Birbhum.

The most famous work attributed to Caṇḍīdāsa is the *Śrīkṛṣṇakīrtaṇa*, a cycle of erotic love poems concerning Rādhā and Kṛṣṇa, discovered at the beginning of the twentieth century. However, the authorship is disputed as the style is markedly different from the existing songs belonging to old Bengali literature, and they are perceived as too erotic for the poet. Consequently a number of scholars posit the idea of a number of authors bearing the name Caṇḍīdāsa.

See also: **Bhakti (as path); Caitanya; Caste; Gauḍīyas; Gurus; Kīrtaṇ(a); Kṛṣṇa; Rādhā; Śakti; Tantrism; Vaiṣṇavism**

RON GEAVES

Further reading

Sen, Sukumar. 1971. *Chandidas*. Makers of Indian Literature Series. New Delhi: Sahitya Akademi.

CAPPĀṆI

Cappāṇi is a minor-ranking male temple guardian in the Madurai area of Tamil Nadu, and particularly in the ancient town of Cholavandan. Cappāṇi occupies his own shrine in the main Aṅkāḷaīśvarī temple in the centre of the town. In other districts he is included in a group of twenty-one deities associated with this goddess. During the bi-annual Śivarātri festival, celebrated in a distinctive manner over two nights at the particular temple, Cappāṇi possesses one of the temple priests. The possessed priest carries a pot decorated with white spots, which contains chicken legs, brandy, eggs, and ghī; things that Cappāṇi likes to eat. Cappāṇi, via his possession of the priest, also takes part in the animal sacrifice that constitutes the climax of this festival as celebrated at this particular Aṅkāḷaīśvarī temple.

See also: **Aṅkāḷaīśvarī; Blood sacrifice; Madurai; Mandir; Possession; Śivarātri; Utsava**

LYNN FOULSTON

Further reading

Foulston, Lynn. 2002. *At the Feet of the Goddess: The Divine Feminine in Local Hindu Religion*. Brighton and Portland, OR: Sussex Academic Press.

Meyer, E. 1986. *Aṅkāḷaparamēcuvari: A Goddess of Tamil Nadu, Her Myths and Cult*. Stuttgart: Steiner Verlag Wiesbaden GmbH.

CASTE

The English word caste is commonly used today to denote any one of the numerous endogamous social groupings of India, despite the fact that it does not correlate with a single term found in the languages of South Asia. Indeed, the origin of the word caste can be traced to the Portuguese traders and voyagers who visited the Indian subcontinent in the sixteenth century. Upon reaching India, the Portuguese were confronted with a complex social order, and they theorised that the basic unit of categorisation for this society was the casta, a Portuguese word meaning clan, tribe or race. The Portuguese used the word casta to refer to what they took to be the foundation of Hindu, Indian Muslim and Indian Christian societal organisation. Yet when the British adopted the Portuguese casta, they limited the scope of their word caste to apply exclusively to the divisions within Hindu society. The word caste, then, must be understood as primarily denotative of groups within Hindu society.

While casta and caste may provide evidence that representatives of the European colonial powers were aware of the hierarchical aspects of Hindu society, the Sanskrit tradition had recognised such stratification since the *Ṛgveda*. What the Europeans saw as castas and castes were most probably the varṇas and jātis of the Hindu populace. Like the word caste, the Sanskrit terms varṇa and jāti together indicate a social category into which an individual is born. In a very basic sense, each of the potentially limitless jātis is grouped under one of the four varṇas, viz. brāhmaṇa, kṣatriya, vaiśya and śūdra. The existence of a peculiarly Indian social structure was noted by foreign observers as early as the fourth century BCE, when Megasthenes documented his visit to the court of Candragupta Maurya in Magadha (modern Bihar) as the ambassador of the Hellenistic emperor Seleucus. Because he was writing for a Greek-speaking audience, Megasthenes refrained from identifying the varṇas and jātis specifically and chose instead to analyse Magadhan society using economic criteria. By contrast, the seventh-century Chinese scholar Xuanzang and the eleventh-century central Asian polymath Alberuni correctly presented a general overview of the varṇa system by identifying the brāhmaṇas as that portion of the population devoted to the maintenance of religion, the kṣatriyas as that portion involved in governance, the vaiśyas as that portion occupied with trade and the śūdras as that portion devoted to service and agriculture. Xuanzang himself further recorded the existence of many other 'classes' – by which he most likely meant the jātis – but he did not venture to elaborate on this point, no doubt for fear of treating an aspect of Hindu society that had effectively defied the skills of even the most illustrious representatives of the Sanskrit tradition.

Caste was, however, not simply an English term expressive of the entities denoted by varṇa and jāti. While the British were the latest in a long line of travellers to the Indian subcontinent who attempted to come to terms with a profoundly complex foreign social reality, they distinguished themselves from their predecessors by integrating their understanding of caste *qua* varṇa and jāti into their administrative framework. As the British became established in India, they oversaw the transformation of caste from one of many characteristics by which Hindus could be variously described into a single descriptive term that sufficed to delimit the entirety of Hindu society, to the near-total exclusion of all other identifying features. While the historical record clearly demonstrates that varṇa and jāti long antedated the advent of British rule, these distinguishing features had never been so universally fundamental to Indian identity as they became in the nineteenth and twentieth centuries.

Worse still, the British notion of caste was informed largely by traditional Sanskrit texts, such as the *Laws of Manu*, that tended both to elevate the brāhmaṇas and to denigrate most severely the śūdras and those groups designated 'untouchable', viz. those Hindus not belonging to any one of the four varṇas. Discrimination and distinction on the basis of caste thus underwent a manner of official valorisation and codification owing to the renewed attention paid by the ruling power to textual artefacts that were, in some cases, more than 2,000 years old by the time they caught the attention of colonial scholars. While there is ample evidence that members of certain varṇas and jātis, as well as untouchables, suffered disadvantages in medieval and early modern India, the British paid caste such documentary attention, through officially sanctioned ethnographies, surveys and censuses, that it achieved a national and even international prominence. As M.K. Gandhi sought to rally Hindus together, members of the lower and untouchable castes began to question their place in Hindu society. Since caste was regarded as central to Hindu identity, it followed that being a Hindu offered little to those millions officially excluded from the privileges afforded the upper castes. To this end, the twentieth-century low-caste reformers E.V.R. Naicker (Periyar) and B.R. Ambedkar fought to free the śūdras and the untouchables from their enforced subservience to the brāhmaṇas. Ambedkar, a Mahar untouchable from Maharashtra, took the most radical approach.

He argued that Hinduism would never afford certain castes and tribes a dignified status, and he enshrined in the Indian Constitution a special right of representation for members of those social groups that had been designated 'scheduled castes', viz. those whose longstanding economic and social disadvantages would entitle them to parliamentary seats, among other things.

Contemporary India continues to be afflicted by difficulties relating to caste. At present, however, much of the conflict concerns the so-called caste Hindus, viz. the members of the four varṇas, and those Hindus who exist outside the four varṇas, viz. the 'scheduled castes' and 'tribes' together with the so-called 'other backward castes'. With the latter allotted a certain percentage of government jobs and places in educational institutions based solely on their outcaste status, a new codification of a modified caste system has taken place. The merits of such reservations notwithstanding, they effectively disprove any contention that caste has disappeared from the Indian subcontinent.

See also: **Ambedkar, Bhimrao Ram; Brāhmaṇa (priest); Dalits; Dharmaśāstras; Gandhi, Mohandas Karamchand; Jāti; Manu; Saṃhitā; Varṇa**

ANONYMOUS

Further reading

Ambedkar, B.R. 1990. *Annihilation of Caste*. New Delhi: Arnold Publishers.

Beal, Samuel. 1906. *Si-Yu-Ki: Buddhist Records of the Western World*, vol. I. London: Kegan Paul, Trench, Trübner & Co. Ltd.

Dirks, Nicholas B. 2001. *Castes of Mind*. Princeton, NJ: Princeton University Press.

Dumont, Louis. 1970. *Homo Hierarchicus: An Essay on the Caste System*, trans. Mark Sainsbury. Chicago, IL: University of Chicago Press.

Lach, Donald F. 1971. *Asia in the Making of Europe*, vol. 1. Chicago, IL: University of Chicago Press.

McCrindle, J.W. 1877. *Ancient India as Described by Megasthenes and Arrian*. London: Trübner & Co.

Mendelsohn, Oliver and Marika Vicziany. 1998. *The Untouchables*. Cambridge: Cambridge University Press.

Rudolph, Lloyd and Suzanne Hoeber Rudolph. 1965. 'Barristers and Brahmans in India: Legal Cultures and Social Change'. *Comparative Studies in Society and History* 8.1: 24–49.

Sachau, Edward. 1964. *Alberuni's India*. Delhi: S. Chand & Co.

Srinivas, M.N. 1962. *Caste in Modern India*. Bombay: Asia Publishing House.

CASTRATION AND EUNUCHS

The Sanskrit term klība of classical texts is generally translated 'eunuch', though, more accurately, this is an umbrella term that can refer to impotent, sterile, castrated, transvestite, genitally mutilated men or hermaphrodites.

In contemporary South Asia, castrated 'third-sex' individuals are known as hijṛā. In hijṛā communities castration is called nirvāṇ (Sanskrit nirvāṇa, 'liberation') and is sometimes performed as a votive ritual before an image of the localised form of the goddess Tripurasundarī, known as Bahucarā, from the Mehsana District in Gujarat. Bahucarā is popularly thought of as the patron deity of modern hijṛā communities. The liminal status of hijṛās as castrated men confers upon them the power to generate and transmit auspiciousness (saubhāgya), but at the same time their ambiguous, non-procreative sexuality is a source of social stigma. In contemporary South Asia hijṛās are socially marginalised, and a large number of them are commercial sex workers. Associations such as the All India Hijra Kalyan Sabha have been formed to address HIV/AIDS awareness and human rights issues in the community.

See also: **Deities, folk and popular; Sex and sexuality**

DAVESH SONEJI

Further reading

Cohen, L. 1995. 'The Pleasures of Castration: The Postoperative Status of *Hijras, Jankhas* and Academics'. In P.R. Abramson and S.D. Pinkerton, eds, *Sexual Nature, Sexual Culture.* Chicago, IL: University of Chicago Press, 276–304.

Doniger, W. 1982. *Women, Androgynes and Other Mythical Beasts.* Chicago, IL: University of Chicago Press.

Doniger, W. 1997. 'Myths of Transsexual Masquerades in Ancient India'. In D. van der Meij, ed., *India and Beyond: Aspects of Literature, Meaning, Ritual and Thought.* Leiden and Amsterdam: International Institute for Asian Studies, 128–47.

Hall, K. 1997. 'Go Suck Your Husband's Sugarcane!: Hijras and the Use of Sexual Insult'. In A. Lina and K. Halls, eds, *Queerly Phrased: Language, Gender, and Sexuality.* New York: Oxford University Press, 430–60.

Hall, K. and V. O'Donovan. 1996. 'Shifting Gender Positions among Hindi-Speaking Hijras'. In V.L. Bergvall, J.M. Bing and A.F. Freed, eds, *Rethinking Language and Gender Research: Theory and Practice.* London: Longman, 228–66.

Kāmasūtra. 2002. trans. W. Doniger and S. Kakar. New York: Oxford University Press.

Lal, V. 1997. 'Not This, Not That: The *Hijras* of India and the Cultural Politics of Sexuality'. *Social Text* 17.4: 119–40.

Nanda, S. 1985. 'The Hijras of India: Cultural and Individual Dimensions of an Institutionalized Third Gender Role'. *Journal of Homosexuality* 11.3–5: 35–54.

Nanda, S. 1994. 'Hijras: An Alternative Sex and Gender Role in India'. In G. Herdt, ed., *Third Sex, Third Gender: Beyond Sexual Dimorphism in Culture and History.* New York: Zone Books, 373–417.

Nanda, S. 1998. *Neither Man Nor Woman: The Hijras of India*, 2nd edn. Belmont, CA: Wadsworth Publishing.

Pattanaik, D. 2002. *The Man Who Was a Woman and Other Queer Tales from Hindu Lore.* New York: Haworth Press.

Preston, L.W. 1987. 'A Right to Exist: Eunuchs and the State in Nineteenth-Century India'. *Modern Asian Studies* 21.2: 371–87.

Preston, L.W. 1997. 'Myths of Transsexual Masquerades in Ancient India'. In D. van der Meij, ed., *India and Beyond: Aspects of Literature, Meaning, Ritual and Thought.* Leiden and Amsterdam: International Institute for Asian Studies, 128–47.

Reddy, G. 2005. *With Respect to Sex: Negotiating Hijra Identity in South India.* Chicago, IL: University of Chicago Press.

CELIBACY

The closest Sanskrit equivalent to the word celibate – which denotes being unmarried, usually because of religious vows, but connotes sexual abstinence – is brahmacārya. But brahmacārya denotes conduct (cārya) for the pursuit of Brahman and connotes many types of renunciation besides sex (such as avoidance of meat, stimulants, intoxicants and emotions). Pāṇini, Kauṭilya and the *Mahābhārata* all refer to female ascetics using terms such as śramaṇā, pravrājitā, tapasī, parivrājikā, saṃnyāsinī, brahmacārinī, munivratā, yoga-siddha and tapas-siddha. Gradually, however, women lost the formal opportunity to follow ascetic paths. Arranged marriage became mandatory for both elite men and elite women, although the former had alternatives (older men, who had fulfilled their family responsibilities, could, for instance, renounce their marriages formally in a ritual of 'dying to this world' and follow spiritual paths).

But celibacy, in the sense of being unmarried and sexually abstinent, was not an 'officially' acceptable choice for elite women. The closest an elite woman could come to a 'legitimate' ascetic life was as a vānaprasthin; both husband and wife, if the husband was willing, withdrew to the forest for spiritual pursuits after fulfilling their family responsibilities. An early example of such a woman is Lopāmudrā. An extreme version, claimed by the modern saint Anandamayi Ma, is the unconsummated marriage. Several analogies to female celibacy also existed. Maidens were supposed to be sexually abstinent (although this had nothing to do with asceticism). As 'widows', elite women were like ascetics but without respect from society.

Lack of scripturally honoured asceticism for women distinguished Hinduism from Buddhism and Jainism, which had monastic orders for women. Despite this official lack of opportunity, some Hindu women did indeed become saints, such as Mīrābāī; they were celibate in the sense of bypassing marriage altogether (as did Āṇṭāḷ), being abandoned (as was Kāraikkāl Ammaiyār), sexually withdrawing from it (as did Anandamayi Ma). Some aspects of women's religiosity were analogous to brahmacārya, moreover, if we use this word informally as chastity in the sense of either renouncing desire for anyone except a husband or maintaining abstinence during rituals, vows and pilgrimages.

Due to the negative legacy for women of male asceticism as superior to the householder stage of life, which sometimes contributed to misogyny, some feminists have encouraged a new hermeneutic. To draw men's and women's religious orientations closer together, they refer to degrees of brahmacārya, or women's temporary brahmacārya, or sexual abstinence as intercourse without passion and only for procreation – the Brahma Kumārī model. In addition, they either promote the bhakti and tantric traditions, believing that women are as capable as men of following spiritual paths toward enlightenment, or remove from brahmacārya the idea of total service to the husband and restore religious connotations of self-control, emotional detachment, and ritual and moral purity (Khandelwal 2001: 162, 171).

One of the biggest changes in modern Hinduism has been the founding of ascetic orders for women or the appointment of female ascetics to head them. Asceticism has become a respectable choice for Hindu women, even though it is rarely chosen.

See also: **Anandamayi Ma; Āṇṭāḷ; Bhakti; Brahma Kumaris; Brahmacārya; Brahman; Buddhism, relationship with Hinduism; Feminism; Jainism, relationship with Hinduism; Kāraikkāl Ammaiyār; Kauṭilya; Lopāmudrā; Mahābhārata; Muni; Pāṇini; Saṃnyāsa; Siddha; Śramaṇa; Tapas; Vānaprasthya; Widowhood**

KATHERINE K. YOUNG

Further reading

Denton, L.T. 1991. 'Varieties of Hindu Female Asceticism'. In J. Leslie, ed., *Roles and Rituals for Hindu Women*. Delhi: Motilal Banarsidass, 211–31.

Kane, P.V. 1968–77 [1930–62]. *History of Dharmaśāstra*, 5 vols, 2nd edn. Poona: Bhandarkar Oriental Research Institute.

Khandelwal, M. 2001. 'Sexual Fluids, Emotions, Morality: Notes on the Gendering of Brahmacharya'. In E.J. Sobo and S. Bell, eds, *Celibacy, Culture, and Society: The Anthropology of Sexual Abstinence*. Madison, WI: University of Wisconsin Press, 157–79.

Marglin, F.A. 1985. 'Female Sexuality in the Hindu World'. In C.W. Atkinson, C.H. Buchanan and M.R. Miles, eds, *Immaculate and Powerful: The Female in Sacred Image and Social Reality*. Boston, MA: Beacon Press, 39–60.

Narayanan, Vasudha. 1995. 'Renunciation and Gender Issues in the Sri Vaisnava Community'. In V.L. Wimbush and R. Valantasis, eds, *Asceticism*. New York: Oxford University Press, 443–58.

Olivelle, Patrick. 1995. 'Deconstruction of the Body in Indian Asceticism'. In V.L. Wimbush and R. Valantasis, eds, *Asceticism*. New York: Oxford University Press, 188–210.

Phillimore, P. 2001. 'Private Lives and Public Identities: An Example of Female Celibacy in Northwest India'. In E.J. Sobo and S. Bell, eds, *Celibacy, Culture, and Society: The Anthropology of Sexual Abstinence*. Madison, WI: University of Wisconsin Press, 29–46.

CELLATTAMMAṈ

The Tamil goddess Cellattammaṉ or Celliyammaṉ, as she is most commonly called in local settlements, has her own temple in Madurai. In her local form she may preside over disease, but she has associations with Kālī, Durgā and Pārvatī. In Madurai she is represented as Mahiṣāsuramardinī (Slayer of the buffalo demon) and is the only outsider deity to enter the sacred Mīnākṣī temple that dominates Madurai. Once a year the movable image of Cellattammaṉ is taken to the Sundarēśvarar (a local form of Śiva) shrine. He rejects her, as he is the consort of Mīnākṣī, and Cellattammaṉ leaves in a rage. When she returns to her own temple she is calmed with a buffalo sacrifice. It is conceived that her encounter with Sundarēśvarar and her subsequent anger are instrumental in re-energising her power. Cellattammaṉ is also connected to another regional goddess, Kāṇṇaki, who is represented in her temple.

See also: **Blood Sacrifice; Durgā; Kālī; Kāṇṇaki; Madurai; Mahiṣa; Mandir; Mīnākṣī; Pārvatī; Śiva; Sundarēśvarar**

LYNN FOULSTON

Further reading

Foulston, Lynn. 2002. *At the Feet of the Goddess: The Divine Feminine in Local Hindu Religion*. Brighton and Portland, OR: Sussex Academic Press.

Van den Hoek, A.W. 1979. 'The Goddess of the Northern Gate: Cellattamman as the "Divine Warrior" of Madurai'. *Asie du Sud: Traditions et changements, Colloques Internationaux du Centre National de la Recherche Scientifique Sèvres, 8–13 Juillet 1978* [*South Asia: Traditions and Changes, International Conferences of the National Centre of Scientific Research, Sevres, 8–13 July 1978*], Proceedings of the 6th European Conference on Modern South Asian Studies: 119–29.

CHANDAS

Dealing with the science of poetic metre, chandas is the technical term assigned to one of the six ancillary branches of Vedic literature (Vedāṅgas) (the other five are śikṣā [phonetics], kalpa [ritual], vyākaraṇa [grammar], nirukta [lexicography] and jyotiṣa [astrology]) and, in some contexts, refers to the sacred Vedic hymns themselves. The various researches and formulations of Vedic poetic metre almost certainly influenced the development, use and analysis of metres found in classical Sanskrit poetry and its commentaries. The *Brāhmaṇa* texts, ancient commentaries and ritual texts concerned with the Vedic hymns seem to contain the earliest treatment of metre, while the defining technical text has the eponymous title *Piṅgalachandaśāstra*, named for its traditional author Piṅgala. The majority of classical Sanskrit metres consist of a determined number of long or short syllables (akṣaracchandas) in individual lines (pāda) of a quatrain divided at a certain point by a caesura (yati). Perhaps the most popular classical meter with a Vedic pedigree is the anuṣtubh metre, simply called śloka in later periods and synonymous with poetic verse itself. Some have speculated that the cultural emphasis on versification is rooted in the sacred nature of Vedic recitation and the mystical significance of the sounds themselves. It is the case that the majority of Sanskrit literature is metrical, including scientific and political texts.

See also: **Brāhmaṇa; Jyotiṣa; Kalpa (ritual); Mantra; Nirukta; Poetry; Saṃhitā; Śikṣā; Sūtra; Vedāṅgas; Vyākaraṇa**

DEVEN M. PATEL

Further reading

Keith, A.B. 1993. *A History of Sanskrit Literature*. Delhi: Motilal Banarsidass.

CHĀNDOGYA UPANIṢAD

See: **Upaniṣads**

CHATTERJEE, BANKIM CHANDRA (1838–94)

Bankim was born into a brāhmaṇa family in a village not far from Calcutta, the capital of British India. After an education which blended Bengali, British and Sanskritic influences, he took employment in the Bengal Civil Service under the British. Here he worked for thirty years, concomitantly developing a career in writing that made him the doyen of Bengali literary figures.

Through his often pioneering writings (especially in *Baṅgadarśan*, the Bengali monthly he edited), Bankim played an important part in shaping the neo-Hinduism of the nationalist movement that developed in Bengal in the late nineteenth century. Influenced by Comtism and utilitarianism, on the one hand, and by the *Bhagavadgītā* on the other, he helped reconstruct certain traditional motifs – notably the concepts of dharma and asceticism, the place of caste (with special reference to the role of women and brāhmaṇas) and certain deities such as the Goddess and Kṛṣṇa – which progressively informed this movement, largely to the exclusion of non-Hindu, especially Muslim, elements. Some of these ideas received intellectual expression in two major Bengali treatises, the *Kṛṣṇacaritra* ('The Life of Krishna', Part I: published 1886, the complete work in 1892), and the *Dharmatattva* ('The Essence of Dharma', 1888). In the first, he depicted a historical Kṛṣṇa shorn of his mythological characteristics, and fit to be the ethical and heroic ideal (a sort of counterpart to Christ) of the diverse Hindu India he envisaged; in the second, he analysed, in a predominantly Hindu context, what makes for rounded, personal development in modern circumstances. How influential these two works were among the intelligentsia is open to debate; what is indisputable is the presiding influence in the nationalist movement, and more generally in Bengal, of his novel *Ānandamaṭh* (published as a book in 1882). Set in the early 1770s, this tells the story of a band of celibate warrior-monks who strive to throw off the foreign yoke of Muslim and British domination. In the process, a new historical order in which the sway of a reconstituted eternal code (sanātana dharma) of the Hindus is envisaged. This novel gave independent India its national song, *Vande Mātaram*, 'I Revere the Mother', where the 'Mother' is iconised as a kind of divinised motherland.

See also: **Brāhmaṇa (priest); Caste; Dharma; Nationalism; Sanātana Dharma; Tapas**

JULIUS LUPNER

Further reading

Bhattācārja, Amitrasūdan. 1991. *Baṅkimcandrajībanī*, Kolkata: Ānanda Publishing Ltd.

Bhattacharya, Sabyasachi. 2003. *Vande Mataram: The Biography of a Song*. New Delhi: Penguin Books India (P) Ltd.

Das, Sisir Kumar. 1984. *The Artist in Chains: The Life of Bankimchandra Chatterji*. New Delhi: New Statesman Publishing Company.

Harder, Hans. 2001. *Bankimchandra Chattopadhyay's Śrīmadbhagabadgītā: Translation and Analysis*. New Delhi: Manohar.

Kaviraj, Sudipta. 1995. *The Unhappy Consciousness: Bankimchandra Chattopadhyay and the Formation of Nationalist Discourse in India*. Delhi: Oxford University Press.

Lipner, Julius. 2005. *Ānandamaṭh, or The Sacred Brotherhood*. New York: Oxford University Press.

Raychaudhuri, Tapan. 1988. *Europe Reconsidered: Perceptions of the West in Nineteenth Century Bengal*. Delhi: Oxford University Press.

CHAUDHURI, NIRAD C. (1897–1999)

Indian journalist and writer. Although his family were members of the Brahmo Samaj, Chaudhuri's account of his early years in Bengal, in his *Autobiography of an Unknown Indian* (1951), provides a rich account of more traditional rural Bengali religious practices at the turn of the century. In *The Continent of Circe*, Chaudhuri provocatively developed the theory that Hindus were not indigenous to India, and that the essential form of Hindu religion had developed prior to the migration of the Indo-Aryans to India, where it had undergone only degeneration. Although somewhat modified, essentially the same view appears in his later monograph on *Hinduism* (1979). His other works include biographies of F. Max Müller (1974) and of Robert Clive (1975). Despite his close association with the nationalist movement in Bengal, Chaudhuri was profoundly Anglophile, and spent the last three decades of his life living in Oxford. Among other honours he received a DLitt from Oxford University in 1990.

See also: **Brahmo Samaj; Hinduism, history of scholarship; Müller, Friedrich Max**

WILL SWEETMAN

Further reading

Chaudhuri, N. 1951. *The Autobiography of an Unknown Indian*. London: Macmillan.

Chaudhuri, N. 1965. *The Continent of Circe; being an essay on the peoples of India.* London: Chatto and Windus.

Chaudhuri, N. 1979. *Hinduism: A Religion to Live By.* London: Chatto and Windus.

CHILD MARRIAGE

In the Vedic period (*c.* 1700–1800 BCE), marriage was based on the consent of adults and culminated in intercourse between a man and a woman who was capable of bearing strong children. But from about the sixth century BCE to the second century CE, the age of marriage in elite circles declined to below puberty, despite the fact that medical (āyurvedic) texts recommend a mature age. (This was not such an issue for lower castes and tribals, who had other customs.) Reasons for child marriage included fulfilment of the following: (1) bridal virginity, which encouraged a reduction of the time available for promiscuity; (2) preventing embryo murders (because menstrual periods represented lost pregnancies); (3) having girls without Vedic schooling (which meant that they were available for marriage); (4) controlling mate selection by arranging marriages to ensure proper subcaste (for brāhmaṇas) and exogamy (a wife from outside the village in north India), and also to facilitate political and economic alliances; (6) integrating brides into new families (young girls being more adaptable and trainable than older ones); (7) avoiding competition due to a lack of qualified young men; and (8) avoiding investment in daughters who were destined to leave home. But despite the norm of arranged marriage, husbands had to be suitable; otherwise, after searching for three years, families allowed girls to find their own mates.

Indian reformers, missionaries and other colonialists criticised child marriage as an uncivilised practice. Because husbands were often considerably older than their brides, some of the latter became young widows and, at least in elite circles, could never remarry. This led to the Hindu Widows' Remarriage Act (1856), which made remarriage legal, and the Indian Penal Code (1860), which made 10 the legal age of marriage. Legislators gradually raised the age. In 1978, the Child Marriage Restraint (Amendment) Act made the minimum age 18 for brides and 21 for grooms. But courts continue to recognise underage marriages (although they sometimes punish those involved) because they know that non-virginal elite girls would find it hard to remarry.

See also: **Āyurveda; Brāhmaṇas; Saraswati, Pandita Ramabai; Virginity; Widow remarriage; Widowhood**

KATHERINE K. YOUNG

Further reading

Altekar, A.S. 1959 [1938]. *The Position of Women in Hindu Civilization*, 3rd edn. Delhi: Motilal Banarsidass.

Mazumdar, S. and S. Mazumdar. 2002. 'Silent Resistance: A Hindu Child Widow's Lived Experience'. In A. Sharma and K.K. Young, eds, *Annual Review of Women in World Religions*, vol. 6. Albany, NY: State University of New York Press, 93–121.

Menski, W. 2003. *Hindu Law: Beyond Tradition and Modernity*. New Delhi: Oxford University Press.

CHINMAYANANDA, SWAMI (1916–93)

Swami Chinmayananda was the founder of the Chinmaya Mission established in 1953 by devotees in India. It has since established branches around the world. Today the Mission is administered by the Central Chinmaya Mission Trust, based in Mumbai and under the leadership of Swami Tejomayanand.

The Chinmaya Mission is known for educational and charitable activities but its main purpose is to promote the teachings of Advaita Vedānta throughout the world by the means of publishing literature and opening centres for teaching. Swami Chinmayananda originally studied law but renounced the world to pursue his spiritual development under the guidance of Swami Sivananda and Swami Tapovanan. Advocating a balance between 'head' and 'heart' which manifested in promoting a lifestyle of study and selfless work, Swami Chinmayananda was part of the Hindu renaissance which combined the influence of Western rationality, Christian charitable work, Vedānta and the cultural values of India into a coherent package able to challenge the influence of the West and which in its own way provided the spiritual values for India's independence.

See also: **Advaita; Hinduism, modern and contemporary; Vedānta**

RON GEAVES

Further reading

Emir, Rudite. 1999. *At Every Breath a Teaching: Stories about the Life and Teachings of Swami Chinmayananda.* London: Chinmaya Publications.

www.chinmayauk.org (accessed 29 October 2005).

CHINMOY, SRI (b. 1931)

Born Chinmoy Kumar Ghose in Shakpura, Chittagong, East Bengal (now Bangladesh), Chinmoy was orphaned at age 12 and entered the Sri Aurobindo Ashram in Pondicherry. On entering the ashram he is believed to have attained nirvikalpa samadhi (an advanced state of enlightenment), and continued with twenty years of spiritual practice. In 1964 he came to the United States, and in 1966 he established the first Sri Chinmoy Center (Aum Centre) in San Juan, Puerto Rico. He became the first director of the United Nations Meditation Group, and in 1970 he initiated meditation sessions at the United Nations Church Center in New York.

Sri Chinmoy is a writer, poet, artist and musician, and has composed some 17,000 devotional songs, 1,700 books of poetry and over 200,000 million 'mystical paintings'. He has given over 500 musical concerts worldwide. Chinmoy's teachings are non-sectarian, drawing on Kṛṣṇa, the Buddha and Jesus of Nazareth. His main theme is 'aspiration', leading to self-transcendence. Chinmoy teaches that God, who is 'infinite consciousness', is within the self, working through the body and the mind. Accordingly, Chinmoy discourages separation from the world, advocating care and improvement of one's body. His followers are vegetarian, abstain from tobacco, alcohol and recreational drugs, and practise physical cleanliness and celibacy. They are encouraged to meditate for fifteen minutes twice daily. Chinmoy describes his path as the 'path of the heart', advocating 'love, devotion and surrender'.

Sri Chinmoy has gained publicity for his biennial World Harmony Run, in which participants run in relays through several countries, carrying torches. The event is designed to improve physical fitness, as well as to encourage world harmony and peace.

In 2005 Sri Chinmoy was reported as having 7,000 followers worldwide in seventy countries, with an estimated 2,000 in the US and 1,500 in Canada.

GEORGE CHRYSSIDES

Further reading

Biography Online. 2006. 'Sri Chinmoy', available at www.biographyonline.net/spiritual/srichinmoy.html (accessed 20 July 2006).

Sri Chinmoy Centre. 2006. 'About Sri Chinmoy', available at http://www.srichinmoycentre.org/ie/sri_chinmoy (accessed 20 July 2006).

United Nations. 1986. *Sri Chinmoy: The Student of Peace.* New York: United Nations.

CHITTRAI

Chittrai is the main festival celebrated at the Mīnākṣī temple that dominates the ancient city of Madurai in Tamil Nadu. It represents the climax to other festivals celebrated at this temple throughout the year. For fourteen days during April and May temple priests and devotees celebrate Mīnākṣī's crowning and her later meeting with Sundarēśvarar, a localised form of Śiva. Mīnākṣī is envisaged as the Pandian queen of Madurai who refuses to marry until she meets her martial equal. When she encounters Śiva he inevitably wins in battle and then marries her, staying in Madurai to rule with her. The tenth day encapsulates the marriage ceremony and is the most important day of the festival. On the eighth day the moveable images of Sundarēśvarar and other deities process around the temple, but on the ninth day of the festival Mīnākṣī processes alone. As she circles the temple, she has various battles with forms of Śiva associated with the compass directions. Christopher Fuller (1980: 344) describes the marriage ceremony that takes place before the images on the last morning, essentially a re-enactment of a brāhmaṇa wedding. While the festival is essentially one that renews the power of Mīnākṣī, David Shulman, cited by Fuller (1980: 344), suggests that the marriage ceremony might be viewed as an 'inversion' of Devī's battle and subsequent defeat of Mahiṣasura, which is the focus of the annual Durgā Pūjā festival, celebrated most elaborately in Kolkata (formerly Calcutta). The festival reinforces the concept underlying the theology of many local or regional goddesses that their wild and aggressive ways can be redirected towards more peaceful tendencies through marriage. Of course, this paradigm does not pertain to all goddesses and, even in the case of Mīnākṣī, her destructive potential is often thinly veiled and controlled.

See also: **Durgā Pūjā; Madurai; Mahiṣa; Mandir; Mīnākṣī; Śiva; Sundarēśvarar; Utsava; Varṇa; Vivāha**

LYNN FOULSTON

Further reading

Fuller, C.J. 1980. 'The Divine Couple's Relationship in a South Indian Temple: Mīnākṣī and Sundareśvara at Madurai'. *History of Religions* 19: 321–48.

Shulman, D. 1976. 'The Murderous Bride: Versions of the Myth of Devī and the Buffalo-Demon'. *History of Religions* 16: 138–46.

CHOUDHURY, BIKRAM (b. 1946)

Born in 1946 in Calcutta, Bikram studied yoga and physical culture in Calcutta with B.C. Ghosh, the bodybuilding brother of Paramahansa Yogananda. He won an all-India yoga competition at the age of 13, and a gold medal in weight lifting at the 1964 Olympics. After his training he taught yoga in Bombay, where he met film star and New Age 'guru' Shirley MacLaine, who invited him to America. He moved to Los Angeles in 1970, establishing his exclusive Yoga College of India in Beverly Hills. His physically demanding yoga system comprises a series of twenty-six āsanas performed twice through in temperatures of at least 100° Fahrenheit. He wrote *Bikram's Beginning Yoga Class* in 1978. In 2003 Bikram, who claims to have brought haṭha yoga to the West, took controversial measures to franchise his brand of yoga, and since then he has taken lawsuits against unauthorised practitioners. His system continues to grow in popularity, with four approved centres in London alone.

See also: **Āsana; Haṭha Yoga; Yoga, modern; Yogananda, Paramahansa**

MARK SINGLETON

Further reading

Choudhury, B. 2003. *Bikram's Beginning Yoga Class*, rev. edn. London: Thorsons.

CIDAMBARAM

Cidambaram, an ancient holy city in Tamil Nadu, south India, is associated with the Hindu god Śiva. He appears in the form of Naṭarāja (King of Dancers) in a huge temple complex that dominates the centre of the city, and has been worshipped here, in this form, since the seventh century CE (Smith 1996: 1). There are said to be five elementary images of Mahādeva (Śiva) in southern India and Cidambaram houses the sky image (Dey 1979: 49). According to the mythology of the Sabhānāyaka (Lord of the Hall) temple (its official name), Cidambaram is equated with the centre of the world, just as Śiva as Naṭarāja is considered to be the Lord of the Universe. In the Naṭarāja image, Śiva performs the dance that represents the creative pulse of life. The ānandatāṇḍava, or dance of bliss, sustains creation and is beneficial to the world, but if Śiva dances more frantically, which he does, according to mythology, with the goddess Kālī, his dance threatens to destroy the world. The mythology from the Naṭarāja temple in Cidambaram states that this was the first place that the dance was performed. It was performed in Cidambaram for the human form of Śeṣa (Viṣṇu's serpent), Patañjali (believed by some to be the author of the *Yogasūtras*) (Mani 1989: 583), and his companion, Vyāghrapāda 'Tigerfoot' (Smith 1996: 31). The sages waited in Cidambaram for Śiva's arrival and in the meantime they worshipped his liṅga (phallic symbol). In contrast to other Śiva temples, at Cidambaram the Naṭarāja image is placed in the sanctum, rather than the liṅga, which is usually the focus of worship.

See also: **Kālī and Caṇḍī; Mandir; Patañjali; Śeṣa; Śiva; Temple worship; Viṣṇu; Yogasūtras**

LYNN FOULSTON

Further reading

Dey, Nando Lal. 1979. *The Geographical Dictionary of Ancient and Mediaeval India*. New Delhi: Cosmo Publications.
Mani, Vettam. 1989. *Purāṇic Encyclopaedia*. Reprint. Delhi: Motilal Banarsidass.
Smith, David. 1996. *The Dance of Śiva: Religion, Art and Poetry in South India*. Cambridge: Cambridge University Press.

CIRCUMAMBULATION

See: **Pradakṣiṇa**

CITTA

Deriving from the Sanskrit verbal root 'cit', the term citta has been used in Hindu texts to refer to thought, consciousness or mental processes in general.

In the *Ṛgveda*, citta and other derivatives of 'cit' occur in association with the mental faculties and organs. Vision, mental perception, intellect, visualisation, imagination, emotion and volitional thought are all indicated. For example, in association with 'hṛd' (the heart, regarded as an organ of emotion, perception and thought), derivatives of 'cit' signify intuitive or emotional thought.

Derivatives of 'cit' (such as citta and cetas) are used in the *Upaniṣads* to signify the process or functioning of consciousness. They are also used in the context of the metaphysical idealism taught in the *Upaniṣads.*

In the Yoga system of Patañjali, citta is used as the equivalent of Sāṃkhya's mahat (the first evolute of prakṛti). Here, citta includes buddhi (intellect), manas (mind) and ahaṃkāra (ego).

See also: **Ahaṃkāra; Mahat; Manas; Patañjali; Prakṛti; Saṃhitā; Sāṃkhya; Upaniṣads; Yoga**

MARTIN OVENS

Further reading

Reat, N.R. 1990. *Origins of Indian Psychology.* Berkeley, CA: Asian Humanities Press.

COEURDOUX, GASTON-LAURENT (1691–1779)

Jesuit who arrived in India in 1732, remaining there until his death. He was the superior of the Madurai, Carnatic and Mysore missions from 1739. Coeurdoux's work represents both the final flowering and the crowning achievement of the first period of Jesuit writing on India, from the arrival of Francis Xavier in 1542 to the suppression of the Society in 1773. Sylvia Murr has shown that the well-known work published by Jean-Antoine Dubois is in fact substantially based on Coeurdoux's *Moeurs et coutumes des indiens* (completed *c.* 1777). Perhaps his most remarkable – certainly his most unjustly neglected – achievement was to have anticipated William Jones' announcement of the common origin of Latin and Sanskrit. In a 1767 letter to Abbé Barthélemy (1716–95), the head of the Académie des Inscriptions et Belles Lettres, Coeurdoux analysed the similarity between Sanskrit and Latin and argued that it could only be explained by supposing that they shared 'une origine commune'.

See also: **Dubois, Jean-Antoine; Hinduism, history of scholarship; Jones, Sir William**

WILL SWEETMAN

Further reading

Murr, Sylvia. (ed.). 1987. *L'Inde philosophique entre Boussuet et Voltaire* [Indian Philosophy from Boussuet to Voltaire], vol. I. *Moeurs et coutumes des indiens* (1777). 'The Manners and the Customs of the Indians', vol. II. *L'Indologie du Père Coeurdoux* [The Indology of Père Coeurdoux]. Paris: École française d'Extrême Orient.

COLEBROOKE, HENRY THOMAS (1765–1837)

English Sanskritist. Colebrooke, who was educated privately, first went to India as a writer in 1782, was later Professor of Sanskrit at the College of Fort William, Chief Justice of the Court of Appeal and a member of the Supreme Council of Bengal. In 1806 he became president of the Asiatic Society of Bengal and, after his return to England in 1814, founded the Royal Asiatic Society in London. Colebrooke's first essay in the *Asiatick Researches*, 'On the Duties of a Faithful Hindu Widow' (1795), is revealing in its choice of subject, indicating the connection between the private researches of men like Colebrooke and their public role as employees of the company which in 1829 would outlaw sati. While in India he also published the first detailed study of the Veda by a European scholar, which was still considered worthy of translation into German as late as 1874, and also essays on the Jains and on Indian astrology and mathematics. His later essays on Hindu philosophy were important sources for G.W.F. Hegel and F. von Schlegel.

See also: **Asiatic Societies; Asiatick Researches; Hegel, Georg Wilhelm Friedrich; Hinduism, history of scholarship; Jainism, relationship with Hinduism; Sati; Schlegel, (Karl Wilhelm) Friedrich von**

WILL SWEETMAN

Further reading

Colebrooke, H.T. 1837. *Miscellaneous Essays*, 2 vols. London: W.H. Allen.

Windisch, E. 1917. *Geschichte der Sanskrit-Philologie und indischen Altertumskunde* [History of Sanskrit Philology and Research on Ancient India]. Strasbourg: Trübner.

CONSECRATION

See: **Abhiṣeka**

CONTRACEPTION

The varying attitudes to contraception rest on the attitude to the function of sexual intercourse. Sex is not seen as inherently sinful as in some puritanical cultures but as a necessary act from the point of view of human physiology and even a sacred part of life (as evident through its incorporation in tantrism). But, as with anything Hindu, it must be engaged in within the ambit of dharma. Therefore, by no means does the use of contraception make extra-marital or casual sex acceptable within dharma.

Sex may be seen to serve three purposes: reproduction, gratification and expression. The viewpoint of the traditionalist is that family units and their expansion are to be encouraged, not limited, so contraception is unthinkable.

While this is the ideal for some, others look to acknowledge the differing picture of reality. To control the increasing population of India, the negative view placed upon abortion leaves only contraception as a realistic choice. In addition, its use is also being encouraged to control the spread of sexually transmitted diseases in India.

The ethical perspectives are plentiful. Some may support, like Roman Catholics do, the withdrawal and rhythm methods, arguing that they are wholly natural. Barrier methods are then seen as artificial means unnaturally preventing the (potential) formation of life. In addition, if emergency contraception is taken, some may hold this to be a form of abortion.

See also: **Celibacy; Dharma; Saṃskārs; Tantrism**

RISHI HANDA

Further reading

Crawford, S. Cromwell. 2003. *Hindu Bioethics for the Twenty-First Century*. Albany, NY: State University of New York Press.

Jackson, Robert and Dermot Killingly. 1991. *Moral Issues in the Hindu Tradition*. Stoke-on-Trent: Trentham Books Limited.

CONVERSION

When dealing with the question of whether one can become Hindu, perceptions on conversion are varied amongst Hindus. In a nutshell, traditionalists argue that one cannot become, but is born Hindu, while modernists argue the contrary and that the adoption of 'Hindu beliefs' allows for conversion into the fold. The difference in opinion is explained by the fact that the two groups are posited in different discourses although each is unaware of this. The argument essentially centres on what it means to be a Hindu, a term which both use but, unknown to them, with different connotations. The term 'Hindu', given by foreigners, is originally descriptive of an ethno-geographical people, disparate by nature. Irrespective of the application of the label, the populace is structured in accordance with varṇa (class) and āśrama (stage of life) and thus one's duty or dharma, governed by these two ordering systems, is of concern for the maintenance of social order. It was thus praxes and the continuation of ancestral customs which defined this ethno-geographical society, and not belief. What we today view as Hindu beliefs were in fact the beliefs of ancient textualists and certain sectarian groups, but they did not speak for all ethno-geographic Hindus; individuals in common society and less literate groups may very well have had their own beliefs. Sectarian traditions may have been founded on personal ideologies, but in this traditionalist discourse 'Hindu' (one living in Hind) refers to an ethno-geographic body of people associated with praxes contingent on their varṇa and āśrama, not belief. On the other hand, the modernist Hindu has adopted the Orientalist's perception of religion, which is grounded in Protestant attitudes and presuppositions. What was once an ethno-geographical culture of Hindus has now been reified into a 'religion' called 'Hinduism'. And with Western models of 'religion' centred on beliefs and faith, and Protestant approaches placing 'scripture' as the locus, being 'Hindu' is defined by doctrines rooted in text.

One can now see how the two groups reach their conclusions. For the traditionalist, one cannot adopt the customary or ancestral practices of a varṇa or jāti (caste), which one can only be born into. Adoption of certain beliefs may allow an individual to join or convert to a formal order or sectarian group brought into being because of its personal doctrine, but they cannot call themselves 'Hindu', the prerequisite of which is the possession, at birth, of immutable class status as 'Hindu' and is concerned with varṇa-āśrama-based praxes and not belief. The modernist, defining 'Hindu' by only certain hegemonic textual doctrines, sees the belief in these ideologies as sufficient to becoming 'Hindu'. Varṇa is relegated to a societal issue and not a 'religious' one. Therein, however, lies the twofold failure to realise that distinctions of 'religious' and 'profane' were absent prior to the Enlightenment, the ideas of which were brought into India through the Orientalists; and that at some point in history 'Hindu' was synonymous with 'Indian'.

Ideology-based orders and sectarian groups indeed proselytised in order to increase numbers, but to proselytise on grounds of being Hindu made no sense, for the customs of one's own ancestors were to be followed, not of someone else's. For this reason, those grounded in their varṇa did not convert to Christianity or Islam, at least not through choice, as it nonsensically meant leaving one's ancestral practices to adopt another's. Today having entered the arena of world religions, 'Hinduism' is seen as a 'religion' like others, and for nationalist Hindus, it is not just a numbers game, but the survival of their civilisation is at stake. While Muslims and Christians are busy seeking converts from Hinduism, modernist Hindus are reciprocating not only by educating Hindus about their 'apologetic fallacies' that all religions lead to the same goal, but by sharing with non-Hindus their heritage and philosophies.

See also: **Āśramas (stages of life); Dharma; Hindu; Hinduism; Jāti; Nationalism; Orientalism; Varṇa**

RISHI HANDA

Further reading

King, Richard. 1999. *Orientalism and Religion – Postcolonial Theory, India and 'The Mystic East'*. London and New York: Routledge.

COOMARASWAMY, ANANDA KENTISH (1877–1947)

Born of a Ceylonese brāhmaṇa father and a British mother, he studied geology in London but is best known as a historian of Indian art and an activist against British imperialism in India and Sri Lanka. Influenced by the Arts and Crafts school in England, Coomaraswamy charged the British with destroying the traditional Ceylonese way of life through their attempts at industrialisation, and sought to revive indigenous artistic traditions through a rediscovery of their religious nature. In *Art and Swadeshi* (1911), he rejected the then prevailing view that Indian sculpture had been shaped by Greek influences transmitted through Gandharan Buddhist art. In a pioneering work, *Rajput Painting* (1916), he demonstrated the existence of a Hindu tradition of miniature painting, distinct from secular Mughal court paintings. Coomaraswamy also wrote on Hinduism and Buddhism, interpreting both as Indian forms of the *philosophia perennis* and dismissing the attempts of European scholars to understand Hinduism as profoundly misconceived (Coomaraswamy 1943: 1).

See also: **Buddhism, relationship with Hinduism; Hinduism, history of scholarship; Image worship**

WILL SWEETMAN

Further reading

Coomaraswamy, A. 1918. *The Dance of Shiva: Fourteen Indian Essays*. New York: Sunwise Turn.

Coomaraswamy, A. 1943. *Hinduism and Buddhism*. New York: The Philosophical Library.

Lipsey, R. 1977. *Coomaraswamy*, 3 vols. Princeton, NJ: Princeton University Press.

COSMOGONY

Questions about the origin of the world have always been of interest to humankind and almost all peoples know traditional accounts of cosmogony. Hindus possess a multitude of stories relating to the creation of the universe and of everything in it. In the *Ṛgveda*, Pṛthivī-Dyaus, Earth-and-Heaven, are worshipped as divinities, the original divine parents. India shares this 'heaven–earth' division and religion with a good many other peoples, who similarly explain the whole world as being originated from a pair of world-parents.

This dualism could not accommodate the numerous new developments in Vedic religion, which uses a basic partition of the universe into tri-loka, 'three-worlds', distinct places for gods, ancestors and men. To each of these three worlds eleven devas were assigned, with various functions.

One hymn in the *Ṛgveda* (10. 82) is addressed to Viśvakarman, 'The One-who-makes-all'. He is called mighty in mind and power, maker, disposer and most lofty presence, the Father who made us, the One beyond the seven ṛṣis (seers).

The two best-known Vedic versions of cosmogony are the *Puruṣa Sūkta* (*Ṛgveda* 10. 90) and the *Nāsadīya Sūkta* (*Ṛgveda* 10.129). The former, true to the Vedic understanding of the yajña (sacrifice) as universally creative act, derives everything from the ritual sacrifice of Puruṣa, a human-shaped first being:

> Thousand-headed was the Puruṣa, thousand-eyed, thousand-footed. He embraced the earth on all sides, and stood beyond the breadth of ten fingers. The Puruṣa is this all, that which was and which shall be. He is Lord of immortality, which he outgrows through (sacrificial) food. One fourth of him is all beings. The three fourths of him is the immortal in heaven.

This Puruṣa begets viraj, the 'widespread', and both together bring forth Puruṣa, the son, who becomes the sacrificial victim of the great sacrifice of the gods. From this great sacrifice originate the verses of the Veda, horses, cattle, goats and sheep. The four classes also have their origin in him, the sacrificial victim.

> The Brāhmaṇa was his mouth, out of his two arms were made the Kṣatriyas, his

two thighs became the Vaiśyas and from his feet the Śūdras were born. From his mind was born the moon, from his eye the sun, from his mouth Indra and Agni, from his breath Vāyu, from his navel the sky, from his head the heaven, from his feet the earth, from his ears the quarters.

We find here the germ of the later Pāñcarātra system, the idea that Viṣṇu is also the material cause of the universe, out of which everything is fashioned.

A more speculative treatment of the topic of creation is found in the *Nāsadīya Sūkta*:

Neither being, nor non-being existed: there was no air, no sky that is beyond it. What was concealed? Wherein? Who was its protector? And was there deep unfathomable water? Death then existed not, nor life immortal, of neither night nor day was there any sign. By its inherent force the One breathed without wind: no other thing existed beyond that. There was at first darkness, by darkness hidden; without distinctive marks, this all was water. Covered by the void, by force of heat (tapas) the One came into being. Desire entered the One in the beginning: it was the earliest seed, the product of thought. The sages searching in their hearts with wisdom found the origin of being in non-being. Who knows for certain? Who shall declare it? From which was it born, and wherefrom came this creation? The gods were born after this world's creation: who can know from where it has arisen? None can know from where creation has arisen and whether he has or has not produced it: he who surveys it in the highest heaven, he only knows – or he may not.

The terms asat, usually translated as 'non-being', and sat, 'being', do not have the meaning of the Greek ón – mēón, which would result in a mutual exclusion. The Indian understanding of these terms permits their co-existence: asat is 'being without specific determination', akin to chaos, whereas sat is 'determined entity, manifest being, order'. The asymmetry of sat and asat, which is, as it were, complementary, is of a fundamental nature like that between chaos and order, as understood by modern science, expressed in terms of entropy and neg-entropy. Sat and asat are the positive and the negative poles, complementary, whose tension produces and maintains the many things. The Hindu notion of creation (sarga) presupposes an uncreated substratum, and concerns more the moulding and ordering of the basic material than its absolute beginning (creatio ex nihilo).

The *Upaniṣads* offer a great variety of theories regarding the origin of the universe. According to the *Bṛhadāraṇyaka Upaniṣad* (1. 1. 4):

In the beginning the atman, the Self, was alone, in the form of a Puruṣa, a male being. He looked around and saw nothing beside himself. He said: 'I am'. He was afraid and he had no joy; he longed for another being. He was as large as a man and woman embracing. He divided himself into two: husband and wife. Thus human beings were created. She turned into a cow – he became a bull. She turned into a mare – he became a stallion. And thus the various kinds of animals came into existence.

The account given here reveals the first traces of the Sāṃkhya system, in which everything owes its origin to the interaction between Puruṣa and Prakṛti, the uncreated principles, one male, the other female, spirit and matter, passivity and activity.

The *Purāṇas* are the main source for the popular traditional Hindu cosmogony. They usually begin with a question to the narrator, requesting him to tell his audience everything about the origin and development of the universe. The narrator complies and launches into often lengthy accounts. The story of creation (sarga) is one of the standard five topics (pañcalakṣana) of *Purāṇas*. The version in *Viṣṇu Purāṇa* (1.2) goes like this:

In the beginning Brahmā was all things, comprehending in his nature the manifest (vyakta) and the non manifest (avyakta). He then came to exist in the form of spirit (Puruṣa) and time (kāla). Next developed the forms of the non-manifest and the manifest. These four – prakṛti (primary matter), Puruṣa (spirit), vyakta (manifest being) and kāla (time) – were the original creations of Viṣṇu and the cause of the origin, the preservation and the destruction of all things. The further detail of the initial evolution of the universe follows the Sāṃkhya account, which makes the disturbance of the equilibrium of the guṇas (constituent principles) responsible for the development of gross and subtle elements, the sense organs and their faculties. A new element appears when the text continues:

> Having combined with each other into one mass they formed an egg (aṇḍa), which gradually expanded like a bubble of water. This vast egg, compounded of the elements and resting on the waters, was the excellent abode of Viṣṇu; and there Viṣṇu, the Lord of the Universe, whose essence is inscrutable, assumed a perceptible form and abided in it in the form of Brahmā. Its shell, vast as the mountain Meru, was composed of the mountains and the interior was filled with the waters of the oceans. In that egg were the continents and the seas and the mountains, the planets and the divisions of the universe, the gods, the demons and humankind.

God, assuming the role of creator, becomes Brahmā and engages in creating the world. As Viṣṇu he preserves the world, and assuming the form of Rudra he swallows it up at the end of a world-age.

> Having thus devoured all things and converted the world into one vast ocean of water, the Supreme reposes on his mighty serpent couch amidst the deep: he awakes after a world-age, and again, as Brahmā, becomes creator.

One can find illustrations of Viṣṇu resting on the world-snake (Śeṣa) with a lotus-stalk issuing from his navel, the four-faced Brahmā, the Creator, sitting cross legged on top of the lotus flower.

Creation is described as Viṣṇu's līlā (play) in order to exclude any (selfish) purpose served by God's activity. After a detailed description of the process of formation of the universe, the *Purāṇa* mentions several unsuccessful attempts by Viṣṇu to create a living being willing to propagate, before present humankind came into existence.

The *Manusmṛti* account of creation is important because of Manu's authority as father of humankind and first law-giver. According to this, in the beginning the world was chaos, without distinguishable forms and attributes, as if in sleep. Then appeared the Svayambhu Bhagavaṇ, the Lord-who-is-of-Himself, invisible and without distinguishing characteristics: he removed the darkness. This paramātman (supreme spirit-soul) was filled with a desire to create beings. He created water and put the seed śakti-rūpī, power-form, into it. This seed shone with the splendour of a thousand suns. It then became an egg, as bright as gold (hiraṇyagarbha): from it issued Brahmā, who shaped all the worlds. He, who is the origin of everything, eternal, of the form of sat and asat, Puruṣa who issued from it, he is called Brahmā. For a whole year he remained in the form of an egg, and then, through concentrated thought (dhyāna), he divided himself into two. From the two halves were created heaven and earth, and space in between them: the eight points of the compass, the place of water and the sea. From the Self he produced mind (manas), containing in him both sat and asat; from this came individuality (ahaṃkāra), with pride and dominion. The *Manusmṛti* enumerates the successive creation of the twenty-four principles from which, according to the Sāṃkhya system, everything is made: mahat, the Great Principle, all entities that contain the three guṇas (constituent principles: sattva, rajas, tamas) in themselves, the five sense organs and so on. The various celestial beings are then created, along with yajña, the sacrifice. For it *Ṛg-*, *Yajur-* and *Sāma-veda* were produced out of Agni, Vāyu and Sūrya. Tapas, heat-power, as well as rati, pleasure, icchhā, desire, and krodha, anger, are created. Dharma and adharma, as well as all other pairs of opposites, like hiṃsa and ahiṃsā (cruelty and kindness), are apportioned by Brahmā unto every being. The origin of the four castes is explained in the same terms as the account in the *Puruṣa Sūkta*. Brahmā divides his body into two parts. Out of the union springs up the first human being, Virāṭ. Virāṭ practises tapas in order to create Prajāpati, who brings forth ten Maharṣis as well as seven Manus, Devas and the various kinds of good and evil spirits: the Yakṣas and Piśācas, Gandharvas and Apsarasas, Nāgas and Garuḍas.

The most complex cosmogony narrative is offered by *Bhāgavata Purāṇa* 3.5, in which traditional mythological motives are combined with the fully developed Sāṃkhya philosophy. It first describes the Lord (Viṣṇu) in his pre-creation existence. Looking around, he could not perceive anything because he alone was. He was, as it were, asat ('non-existent', i.e. unmanifest) because his śaktis (powers) were asleep although his consciousness was awake. The power of he who was looking around in the form of sat and asat is called māyā – through this the Lord created the universe. When the equilibrium of the three guṇas in māyā were disturbed by the influence of kāla, he placed his manly power in the form of the Puruṣa, as his own self, into it. From the Unmanifest impelled by Time, Mahat (the Great Principle) was evolved. From this evolved Aham (the ego-principle), which in its triple form of Adhibhūta (elementary), Adhyāma (spiritual), and Adhidaiva (divine) became the origin of the five gross bhūtas, the five senses of perception and of action (indriyas) and the mind (manas). The process of creation then seemed to be stalling. The text continues after an intermezzo:

> When the Lord saw that his *śaktis* were unable to begin the process of creation of the universe he assumed the form of the Goddess Kala and entered the twenty-three principles (tattvas) – the Mahat, the Aham, the five gross elements, the five subtle elements, the five senses of perception, the five senses of action, and the mind. He connected the disconnected principles into one Puruṣa (a cosmic person).

This being is a part-manifestation of the Supreme being and also called the primeval avatāra: from it the entire creation takes its origin. On this Puruṣa, originally shaped like an egg, gradually individual organs appear:

> There appeared in him a mouth: the god of fire, one of the Lokapālas, whose abode it is, entered it along with his śakti: the organ of speech, through which the jīva is capable of uttering words.

Successively all the other organs appear on the Primeval Puruṣa: the appropriate deities enter these and create the corresponding human faculties. The last of these is

> Citta, the seat of intelligence, the abode of Brahmā, who entered it along with his power, the faculty of intellection, by means of which the jīva distinguishes between right and wrong.

Apparently taking up another creation-story tradition, the *Purāṇa* continues:

> From his head emanated the heavenly world, the earth from his feet and the intermediate world from his navel.

The lengthy account ends with yet another motive, recalling the Vedic *Puruṣa Sūkta* and the *Manusmṛti*:

> From the mouth of the Puruṣa emanated the Vedas, as well as the Brāhmaṇa. From the arms emanated the Kṣatriya order, from the thighs the order of agriculturists and traders, from the feet came the rules for those born to serve.

Hindus in more recent times have attempted to harmonise their ancient cosmogonies with modern scientific findings and have detected many parallels between their traditional accounts of the origin of the universe and modern explanations of the evolution of the universe.

See also: **Agni; Ahaṃkāra; Ahiṃsā; Apsarasas; Ātman; Avatāra; Bhūtas; Brahmā; Brāhmaṇa; Deities; Dharma; Dharmaśāstras; Dikpālas; Dyaus Pitṛ; Gandharvas; Garuḍa; Guṇas; Hiraṇyagarbha; Indra; Jīva; Līlā; Mahat; Manas; Māyā; Meru, Mount; Nāgas; Pāñcarātras; Piśācas; Prajāpati; Prakṛti; Pṛthivī; Purāṇas; Puruṣa; Ṛṣi; Rudra; Saṃhitā; Sāṃkhya; Śeṣa; Sūrya; Tapas; Time; Upaniṣads; Varṇa; Vāyu; Vedism; Viṣṇu; Viśvakarman; Yajña; Yakṣa**

KLAUS K. KLOSTERMAIER

Further reading

Bhāgavata Purāṇa. 1952–60. 2 vols. Text and Translation. Goralchpur: Gita Press.

Bühler, G. (trans.) 1953 *The Laws of Manu,* SBE vol. 25. Oxford: Oxford University Press

Doniger, W. and B.K. Smith. (trans.). 1991. *The Laws of Manu.* Harmondsworth: Penguin.

Griffith, R.T.H. (trans.). 1863. *The Hymns of the Ṛg Veda,* 2 vols. Varanasi: Chowkamba Sanskrit Office.

Hume, R.E. (trans.). 1931. *The Thirteen Principal Upaniṣads.* Oxford: Oxford University Press.

Kuiper, F.B.J. 1983. *Ancient Indian Cosmogony.* New Delhi: Vikas.

Radhakrishnan, R. (trans.). 1953. *The Principal Upaniṣads.* London: George Allen & Unwin.

Saraswati, Swami Prakashanand. 1999. *The True History and the Religion of India.* Austin, TX: Barsana Dham.

Seshadri, R.K. 1990. *Cosmology, God and the Indian Scriptures.* Madras: The Samskrita Academy.

Wilson, H.H. (trans.). 1961. *The Visnu Purana: A System of Hindu Mythology and Tradition.* Calcutta: Punthi Pustak (first published 1840).

COSMOLOGY

The ancient Hindus certainly had a quite accurate knowledge of those parts of India in which they lived, and those parts of Asia to which they ventured forth across the seas, as far as the Philippines, where Sanskrit inscriptions have been found (and perhaps even further). As far as the cosmos was concerned, they situated themselves within a universe much larger than that of other ancient cultures. The models of the universe in various texts differ in a number of substantial details: all of them have mythical Mount Meru at the centre. The *Mahābhārata* has preserved an old version of the world-model in which four dvīpas or continents were arranged around Mount Meru, with the Ocean of Salt as the southern border of the world, and the Ocean of Milk as the northern. The fully developed model of the *Viṣṇu Purāṇa* (2.4; with parallels in other *Purāṇas*) is much more complex: it knows of seven dvīpas surrounded by and surrounding seven concentric oceans. In the centre of this world stands Mount Meru, forming with Jambu-dvīpa the innermost circle. Its boundary is formed by a vast ring of salt water, the lāvaṇa-sāgara, followed by another concentric ring of land and so on, according to the following scheme (to be read from the bottom upwards):

Aṇḍakaṭaha	128	Shell of World Egg
Tamas	128	Darkness
Lokālokaśaila	128	World-No-World Mountains
Kañcanībhumī	128	Land of Gold
Jalasāgara	64	Sea of Sweet Water

Puṣkaradvīpa	64	Blue Lotus Land
Kṣirasāgara	32	Milk Ocean
Śākadvīpa	32	Teak Tree Land
Dadhisāmudra	16	Buttermilk Ocean
Krauñcadvīpa	16	Heron Land
Sarpisāmudra	8	Melted Butter Ocean
Kuśadvīpa	8	Kusa Grass Land
Surāsāmudra	4	Wine Ocean
Śālmadvīpa	4	Silk Cotton Tree Land
Ikṣurasasāmudra	2	Sugarcane Juice Land
Plakṣadvīpa	2	Fig Tree Land
Lāvaṇasāmudra	1	Saltwater Ocean
Jambudvīpa	1	Roseapple Tree Land
	(Total: 510)	

Mount Meru

The numeral indicates the width of each ring of sea or land, using as basic unit the diameter of Jambudvīpa=100,000 yojanas (a yojana is not uniformly defined – here it is about nine English miles). The universe seen horizontally, has to be imagined as consisting of concentric circles, whose centre is Mount Meru, the pivot of Jambudvīpa.

Jambudvīpa consists of twelve parts, one of which is Bhārata-varṣa. Bhārata-varṣa (India) again is divided into nine parts, ruled over by kings from the dynasties descended from Satajit, going back through various illustrious rulers to Pṛthu, from whom the earth (pṛhvi) took her name, since he subdued the earth, levelling it and beginning to cultivate it. Whereas the other eight parts of Jambudvīpa are described as 'places of perfect enjoyment, where happiness is spontaneous and uninterrupted, without vicissitude, without age and death, without distinction of virtue or vice, without any change brought about by the cycle of sages' (*Viṣṇu Purāṇa* 2.2:42–54), Bhārata-varṣa is subject to the deterioration which is brought about by the succession of the four yugas; it knows suffering and death. But it is praised nevertheless as 'the best of the divisions of Jambudvīpa, because it is the land of works' which enable people to gain heaven or even final emancipation (*Viṣṇu Purāṇa* 2.3:1–2). The gods themselves praise the good fortune of those born in Bhārata-varṣa. The description of the several parts of Jambu-dvīpa, which follows in the *Viṣṇu Purāṇa*, contains valuable information about the geography and ethnology of ancient India.

Mount Meru, the Golden Mountain in the centre of Jambudvīpa, plays a large role in Indian cosmology. Its height is given as 84,000 yojanas, its depth below the surface of the earth as 16,000. Its diameter at the summit is 32,000 yojanas and its base 16,000 yojanas 'so that this mountain is like the seed-cup of the lotus of the earth' (*Viṣṇu Purāṇa* 2.2:4–5). From the base of Meru extend mighty mountain ridges; on its summit is the vast city of Brahmā, extending 14,000 yojanas. Around it, at the cardinal points and in the intermediate quarters, is situated the city of Indra and the cities of the other regents of the spheres. The capital of Brahmā is enclosed by the river Ganges (Gaṅgā): issuing from the foot of Viṣṇu and washing the lunar orb, it falls here from the skies, and, after encircling the city, divides into four mighty rivers.

The *Purāṇas* describe in detail not only Jambudvīpa but also the other continents with their geography and history. In the five continents outside Jambudvīpa the lives of men last for five thousand years; they are happy, sinless and enjoy uninterrupted bliss. They have their own system of classes, corresponding to the four varṇas in Bhārata-varṣa, but this division does not result in any friction of any deprivation of one group of people compared with other. In Puṣkara-dvīpa men live a thousand years, free from sickness and sorrow and unruffled by anger and affection. There is neither virtue nor vice, neither killer not slain;

there is no jealousy, envy, fear, hatred; neither is there truth or falsehood. Food is spontaneously produced there. There is no distinction of caste and order, there are no fixed laws, nor are rites performed for the sake of merit. The three *Sāṃhitās*, the *Purāṇas*, ethics, policy and the laws of service are unknown. It is, in fact, a terrestrial paradise where time yields happiness to all its inhabitants, who are exempt from sickness and decay. A Nyagrodha-tree grows on this land, which is the special abode of Brahmā, and he resides in it, adored by devas and asuras. 'Beyond the sea of fresh water is a region of twice its extent, where the land is of gold and where no living beings reside. Thence extends the Lokāloka mountain, which is ten thousand yojanas in breadth and as many in height; and beyond it perpetual darkness invests the mountain all around; which darkness is again encompassed by the shell of the world-egg. Thus the universe with its exterior shall is give hundred million yojanas in extent. It is the mother and nurse of all creatures, the foundation of all worlds, and the principal element. (*Viṣṇu Purāṇa* 2.4:94–8).

The universe as described in Hindu cosmology is geocentric: the earth is the centre of the entire universe, though not its best part as regards enjoyment. It is, however, best suited for work, for the possibilities which it opens to gain the supreme end, liberation. Mount Meru, the centre of the Hindu world, is far away from Bhārata-varṣa. Only later Hindu sects identify the centre of the world with their centres of worship. Śaivites consider Cidambaram as the world-centre, Vaiṣṇavas identify Vṛndāvaṇa with the pivot of the world. The *Purāṇa* accounts are also quite modest when comparing their own country with other countries; the people in other countries are described as materially much better off, they are free from most of the hazards which beset the people of Bhārat.

A vertical section produces the following 'layers' of sheaths of the World-Egg, the brahmāṇḍa:

Satyaloka		
Tapoloka		
Janaloka		
Maharloka		
Svarloka	(Planets)	Regions of the consequences of work
Bhuvarloka	(Sky)	
Bhurloka	(Earth)	

Atala (White)	
Vitala (Black)	
Nitala (Purple)	
Gabhastimat (Yellow)	
Mahātāla (Sandy)	Nether worlds
Sutāla (Stony)	
Pātāla (Golden)	
Śeṣa (the World-Snake)	
Raurava etc.	(28 nārakas or hells)

The cosmos, whose centre is the Earth, extends upwards and downwards in many lokas ('worlds').

Each of the seven nether worlds extends for 10,000 yojanas below the surface of the one preceding: 'They are embellished with magnificent palaces in which dwell numerous dānavas, daityas, yakṣas and great nāgas. The Muni Nārada after his return from those regions to the skies declared amoungst the celestials that pātāla was much more delightful than Indra's heaven.' Below these is Śeṣa, the 'form of Viṣṇu proceeding from the quality of darkness', also called Ananta, the endless one, with a thousand heads, embellished with the svastika. Śeṣa bears the entire world like a diadem upon his head. When Ananta, his eyes rolling with intoxication, yawns, the earth, with all her woods and mountains, seas and rivers, trembles.

The twenty-eight hells 'beneath the earth and beneath the waters' are places of punishment for sinners – specified according to their crimes. 'One who bears false witness or utters a falsehood is condemned to the Raurava hell. One who causes abortion, plunders a town, kills a cow, or strangles a man, goes to the Rodha hell. A Brāhmáṇa murderer, one who steals gold, a drinker of liquor and anyone associating with them goes to the Sukara hell.' Amongst others, there is a special hell, called Asipatravana, into which those fall, who 'wantonly cut green trees.' The text concludes: 'These hells, and hundreds of thousands of others, are the places in which sinners pay the penalty of their crimes. As numerous as are the offences that people commit, so many are the hells in which they are punished: and all who deviate from the duties imposed upon them by caste and stage of life, in thought, word or deed, are sentenced to punishment in the hellish regions.' Frightful as the hells may be – illustrated with gruesome pictures in modern edition of the *Purāṇas* they are temporal, not eternal punishment. After the crime has been atoned for, the sinners are released and can continue their life-journey upwards.

The sphere of the earth in the upward direction 'extends as far as it is illuminated by the rays of sun and moon; and to the same extent the sphere of the sky extends upwards, till the beginning of the sphere of the planets.' The solar orb is situated a hundred thousand yojanas from the earth and that of the moon an equal distance from the sun. At the same interval above the moon occurs the orbit of all lunar constellations. Budha (Mercury) is two hundred thousand yojanas above the lunar mansions. Śukra (Venus) is at the same distance from Budha. Aṅgāraka (Mars) is as far above Śukra; Bṛhaspati (Jupiter) as far from Aṅgāraka, whilst Śani (Saturn) is two hundred and fifty thousand leagues beyond Bṛhaspati. The sphere of the Seven Ṛṣis is a hundred thousand yojanas above Śani, and at a similar height above these is the Dhruva (Pole-star), the pivot of the whole planetary circle. Bhur, Bhuva and Svar form the 'region of the consequence or works' – the region of the works that bring merit is Bhāratāvarṣa alone.

Above Dhruva at the distance of ten million yojanas, lies Mahar-loka, whose inhabitants dwell in it for a kalpa or a day or Brahmā. At twice that distance is Jana-loka, where Sānandana and other pure-minded sons of Brahmā reside. At four times the distance, between the last two, lies the Tapo-loka inhabited by the devas called Vaibhrajas, who fire cannot harm. At six times the distance Satya-loka is situated, the sphere of truth, whose inhabitants will never known death again. Satya-loka, is also called Brahmā-loka, Sectarian texts add above Brahmā-loka, Viṣṇu-loka (or Vaikuṇṭha) and Śiva-loka (or Kailāsa), assigning the supreme place to the deity of their own choice.

The world-egg (with its seven dvīpas and samudras, its seven lokas and its seven nether worlds, Śeṣa and the hells beneath – all within the shall of brahmāṇḍa) is but the centre of a greater universe which is stratified according to the following scheme:

Pradhana-Purusa	(primeval matter and spirit)
mahat	(the first principle)
bhutadi	(the gross elements)
nabhas	(ether)
vayu	(wind)
vahni	(fire)
ambu	(water)
The World-Egg	(earth)

The *Viṣṇu Purāṇa* explains in detail: the world is encompassed on every side and above and below by the shell of the egg of Brahmā, in the same manner as the seed or the wood-apple is encircled by its rind. Around the other surface of the shall flows water, for a space equal to ten times the diameter of the world. The waters are encompassed by fire, fire by air, air by ether, ether by the gross-elments, these by the first-principle. Each of these extends in breadths ten times that layer which it encloses, and the last is enveloped by pradhāna, which is infinite and its extent cannot be enumerated: It is therefore called the boundless, the illimitable cause of all existing things, supreme nature or prakṛti the cause of all world-eggs of which there are thousands, and millions of thousands of millions. Within pradhāna resides puman, diffusive, conscious, and self-irradiating, as fire is inherent in flint. Both are encompassed by the energy of Viṣṇu (Viṣṇu-śakti), which is the case of the separation of the two at the period of dissolution, and the cause of their continuance in existence, as well as of their re-combination at the time of creation.

See also: **Asuras; Brahmā; Deities; Gaṅgā; Indra; Kalpa; Mahābhārata; Meru, Mount; Muni; Nāgas; Nārada; Prakṛti; Pṛthu; *Purāṇas*; Ṛṣi; Śaivism; Śakti; Saṃhitā; Śeṣa; Svastika; Vaiṣṇavism; Varṇas; Viṣṇu, Vṛndāvaṇa, Yakṣas, Yuga**

Klaus K. Klostermaier

Further reading

Ali S.M. 1966. *The Geography of the Purāṇas.* New Delhi: People's Publishing House.

Wilson, H.H. (trans). 1961. *The Viṣṇu Purāṇa: A System of Hindu Mythology and Tradition.* Calcutta: Punthi Pustak (first published 1840).

COURTESANS

In Sanskrit texts, including the Epics, *Purāṇas* and the poems and plays of medieval poets such as Kālīdāsa, nymphs called apsarases ('women in the waters [of the clouds]') can be identified as celestial 'courtesans'. They are all associated with the arts of music and dance, and are often depicted entertaining Indra in his celestial court. Apsarasas such as Raṃbhā, Menakā, Ūrvaśī, Tilottamā and Ghṛtācī thus figure prominently in Sanskrit literature as performers, temptresses, lovers and sometimes mothers. Though they engage in sexual relations with the celestial gandharva musicians, ascetics, kings and humans, their relationships rarely, if ever, culminate in marriage.

In classical Sanskrit poetry, *Dharmaśāstra*, *Kāmaśāstra* and *Alaṅkāraśāstra*, human courtesans are usually called veśyā or gaṇikā. The entire sixth book of Vātsyāyana's *Kāmasūtra* is dedicated to the human courtesan. Vasantasenā of Ujjayinī, the heroine of the Sanskrit play *Mṛcchakaṭikā* ('The Little Clay Cart', attributed to the poet Śūdraka, *c.* fourth century) is among the veśyās of classical India depicted as a virtuous and dignified woman, indicating the socially ambiguous yet tolerated presence of such women. An oft quoted Sanskrit proverb, veśyā darśánaṃ puṇyaṃ pāpa nāśanam ('the sight of a veśyā is meritorious and destroys sin') also points to their status in the Sanskritic imagination.

In terms of social history, several communities of courtesans have traditionally existed in various parts of South Asia. In northern India, courtesans are generally known as tawā'if ('accomplished courtesan') or bāījī ('respected lady'). In Bengal, they are called nacnī ('dancer'), and kaḷāvant ('embodiment of the arts') in Maharashtra.

The figure of the courtesan is sometimes conflated with that of the devadāsī in south India. From the seventeenth century onward in the Tamil and Telegu-speaking parts of India, the same women who danced in temples and temple processions also performed in secular settings such as royal courts and the homes of landed gentry (zamīndārs), and thus could be understood to function as both ritual performers and courtesans.

See also: **Aesthetics; Apsarasas; Dance; Devadāsīs; Dharmaśāstras; Gandharvas; Indra; Kālīdāsa; Kāmasūtra; Mahābhārata; Music; Purāṇas; Rāmāyaṇa; Ujjayinī; Vātsyāyana, Mallanāga**

Davesh Soneji

Further reading

Babiracki, C.M. 2004. 'The Illusion of India's "Public Dancers"'. In J.A. Bernstein, ed., *Women's Voices Across Musical Worlds.* Boston, MA: Northeastern University Press, 36–59.

Banerjee, S. 2000. *Dangerous Outcaste: The Prostitute in Nineteenth Century Bengal.* Calcutta: Seagull Books.

Banerji, P. 1982. *Apsaras in Indian Dance.* New Delhi: Cosmo Publications.

Kadam, V.S. 1998. 'The Dancing Girls of Maharashtra'. In A. Feldhaus, ed., *Images of Women in Maharashtrian Society.* Albany, NY: State University of New York Press, 61–89.

Kāmasūtra. 2002. Trans. W. Doniger and S. Kakar. New York: Oxford University Press.

Masiecewski, A. 2006. 'Tawaif, Tourism, and Tales: The Problematics of Twenty-First-Century Musical Patronage for North India's Courtesans'. In M. Feldman and B. Gordon, eds, *The Courtesan's Arts: Cross-Cultural Perspectives.* New York: Oxford University Press.

Mukul, K. 1994. 'Urdu, Awadh, and the Tawaif: The Islamicate Roots of Hindi Cinema'. In Z. Hasan, ed., *Forging Identities: Gender, Communities, and the State.* New Delhi: Kali for Women, 244–57.

Oldenburg, V.T. 1990. 'Lifestyle as Resistance: The Case of the Courtesans of Lucknow, India'. *Feminist Studies* 16.2: 259–87.

Qureshi, R.B. 2006. 'Female Agency and Patrilineal Constraints: Situating the Courtesan in Twentieth-Century India'. In M. Feldman and B. Gordon, eds, *The Courtesan's Arts: Cross-Cultural Perspectives.* New York: Oxford University Press.

Ramanujan, A.K., V.N. Rao and D. Shulman. 1994. *When God Is a Customer: Telegu Courtesan Songs by Ksetrayya and Others.* Berkeley, CA: University of California Press.

CŪḌĀKARAṆA

One of the Hindu childhood saṃskāras or rites of passage. The cūḍākaraṇa – literally, 'creating a tuft (cūḍā)' by cutting all the hair except a tuft on the top or back of the head – indicates the first cutting of the child's hair. The texts prescribe the performance no sooner than the first birthday and up to three years of age. A barber and a metal razor (alternatively of udumbara wood) are required, and the rite is performed while the child is sitting in the mother's lap. The number of strokes of the razor is prescribed, as well as their direction, all with the goal of leaving an intact tuft. The place of the tuft on the head is a matter of sectarian style; most leave it on the top and back as a topknot (śikha), but others prescribe it for the right side of the head. As usual many mantras are recited, beginning with mantras for Gaṇeśa. However, most of the mantras divinise the razor as well as the entire process. This rite is also prescribed for young girls, though without the recitation of the mantras. This ceremony marks a step in the integration of the child with the Vedic culture of viewing all aspects of nature as divine, exemplified in the interlocking complexity of the Vedic pantheon.

See also: **Gaṇeśa; Mantra; Saṃskāra**

Frederick M. Smith

Further reading

Kane, P.V. 1974. *History of Dharmaśāstra*, 2nd edn, vol. 2, pt 1. Pune: Bhandarkar Oriental Research Institute, 260–65.

Pandey, R.J. 1969. *Hindu Saṃskāras.* Delhi: Motilal Banarsidass, 94–101.

D

ḌĀKIṆĪS

Ḍākiṇīs ('Female Flyers'), who are most often found in Buddhist Tantric traditions, are identical in their characteristics and functions to their Hindu homologues, the Yoginīs. In fact, the earliest inscriptional reference to a Hindu goddess temple in all of South Asia, the 423 CE Gangdhar inscription, evokes the flying Ḍākiṇīs, rather than the Yoginīs. Both Ḍākiṇīs and Yoginīs are possessed of the power of flight, a power fuelled by their consumption of human and animal blood and flesh; and the Buddhist Ḍākiṇīs, like the Hindu Yoginīs, also identified as human sorceresses, play a vital role in the initiation of male practitioners into esoteric Tantric practice. In non-Tantric works such as the *c.* twelfth-century *Tithiḍākinīkalpa*, Ḍākiṇīs are listed together with a host of other demonic entities as principles of childhood diseases. In modern-day parlance, the Hindi dāyan (or dāīn), a cognate of the Sanskrit ḍākinī, is used as a generic term to refer to a female demoness, a human sorceress or simply an 'old hag'.

See also: **Buddhism, relationship with Hinduism; Tantras**

DAVID GORDON WHITE

Further reading

Hermann-Pfandt, A. 1996. 'The Good Woman's Shadow: Some Aspects of the Dark Nature of Ḍākiṇīs and Śākinīs in Hinduism'. In Axel Michaels, Cornelia Vogelsanger and Annette Wilke, eds, *Wild Goddesses in India and Nepal, Proceedings of an International Symposium, Berne and Zurich, November 1994*. Bern: Peter Lang, 39–70.

DAKṢA

Dakṣa is one of the prajāpatis, one of the ten progenitors of the human race created by Manu, and is generally considered to be their chieftain. Regarded also as a son of Brahmā, he is usually associated with creative forces. The *Ṛgveda* contains the enigmatic statement that 'Dakṣa sprang from Aditi, and Aditi sprang from Dakṣa'. This has been interpreted in various ways to mean that the gods spring from each other in an eternal cycle or that Dakṣa is the universal creative energy represented as the power in the sacrifice. This early identification of Dakṣa with the creative energy and priestly abilities to safeguard the sacrifice and ensure contact with the gods is picked up by the Epics and the *Purāṇas*, which describe him as a secondary creator or a ṛṣi who is present at the beginning of each cycle of creation. Some traditions present him as the progenitor of the devas (deities) and ṛṣis.

See also: **Aditi; Brahmā; Deities; Manu; Prajāpati; Purāṇas; Ṛṣi; Saṃhitā**

RON GEAVES

Further reading

Stutley, Margaret and James Stutley (eds). 1977. *A Dictionary of Hinduism: Its Mythology, Folklore and Development 1500 BC–AD 1500*. London: Routledge and Kegan Paul.

DALITS

Dalit (Sanskrit dalita, 'split, broken, crushed') is a general term for the most disadvantaged hereditary groups (caste, jāti) in Indian society (Michael 1999). It includes the Chamars of northern India, the Mahars of Maharashtra, the Paraiyans (whence the English word pariah) of Tamil Nadu, and others. Other groups, such as caṇḍālas, are often mentioned in Sanskrit literature. All these are subject to exploitation and oppression. They are considered by others to be so unclean that their touch, or in some cases even their shadow, is polluting. This pollution is attributed to their occupations, such as leatherworking and other work involving dead cattle, or the distillation of toddy from the sap of the palmyra or other palms, and to their consumption of meat, including beef, and toddy. It applies to all members of a group, whether or not they share the polluting occupation or diet; all are traditionally excluded from housing areas, wells, schools, temples or even roads used by other castes. According to the 1931 census (the last to yield relevant figures), what are now called Dalits were 14.9 per cent of the Indian population, and 21.1 per cent of the Hindu population – over three times as numerous as brāhmaṇas (Schwartzberg 1978: 106).

The name 'Dalit' was made current in the late twentieth century by Dalits themselves, in preference to terms imposed by others, such as asprśya ('untouchable'), avarṇa ('without a varṇa') or pañcama ('fifth [after the four varṇas]'), used in *dharmaśāstra*, 'scheduled castes', used by legislators and administrators in the British period and in independent India, or 'Harijan' ('people of God'), bestowed by Gandhi. The Indian constitution of 1950, drafted under the chairmanship of the Mahar lawyer B.R. Ambedkar, declares 'the enforcement of any disability arising from "untouchability"' to be an offence. This legal provision, though reinforced by the Untouchability Prohibition Act of 1955, is insufficient to protect Dalits from exploitation and violence, including mutilation, rape and murder.

Various forms of positive discrimination for the 'scheduled castes', in education, employment and electoral representation, were introduced in the course of the twentieth century. However, following British theorists who saw caste as a feature of Hindu religion rather than of South Asian society, the Indian legislators ruled that only a Hindu (or, according to later legislation, a Buddhist) could be a member of a scheduled caste. Christians or Muslims of the same origin who suffer the same oppression are excluded from the provisions for protection and positive discrimination (Dushkin 1972: 168).

The category 'Dalit', unlike 'scheduled caste', is independent of religious boundaries, and Dalit Christians have been prominent in movements for Dalit self-assertion and advancement (Prabhakar

1988). Many Dalits refuse to call themselves Hindu and reject Hindu dharma (even as interpreted by reformers such as Gandhi) as an ideology of oppression (Omvedt 1995; Leslie 2003: 53–61). This rejection was expressed dramatically by the mass conversion of Mahars to Buddhism led by Ambedkar in 1956; it has been further provoked by the claims of Hindutva. Some, however, such as the Izhavas of Kerala, led by Narayana Guru (1854–1928) (Jones 1989: 179–82, 203–7), or the Vālmīki Sabha in the Panjab (Leslie 2003), seek to overcome exclusion through 'sanskritisation'.

See also: **Ambedkar, Bhimrao Ram; Brāhmaṇas; Buddhism, relationship with Hinduism; Caste; Dharma; Dharmaśāstra; Gandhi, Mohandas Karamchand; Hindu; Hindutva; Jāti; Purity and pollution, ritual; Varṇa; Vālmīki**

DERMOT KILLINGLEY

Further reading

Dushkin, Leah. 1972. 'Scheduled Daste Politics'. In J.M. Mahar, ed., *The Untouchables in Contemporary India.* Tucson, AR: University of Arizona Press, 165–226.

Jones, Kenneth W. 1989. *Socio-religious Reform Movements in British India.* New Cambridge History of India, III, 1. Cambridge: Cambridge University Press.

Leslie, Julia. 2003. *Authority and Meaning in Indian Religions: Hinduism and the Case of Vālmīki.* Aldershot: Ashgate.

Michael, S.M. 1999. *Dalits in Modern India: Vision and Values.* Delhi: Vistaar.

Omvedt, Gail. 1995. *Dalit Visions: The Anti-Caste Movement and the Construction of an Indian Identity.* Delhi: Orient Longman.

Prabhakar, M.E. (ed.). 1988. *Towards a Dalit Theology.* Delhi: ISPCK.

Schwartzberg, Joseph E. (ed.). 1978. *A Historical Atlas of South Asia.* Chicago, IL: University of Chicago Press.

DAMAYANTĪ

See: **Nala**

DĀNA

Encompassing a wide range of prestations, dāna is understood as a ritually given gift, donation, offering, transfer or endowment. The giver of dāna forges an ephemeral relationship with the recipient and may accumulate merit, transfer the effects of wrongdoing, discharge a debt or ensure a future return. Some types of dāna are given between kin groups of similar social standing; some are made from higher- to lower-caste groups. Some cannot be returned; others cannot be refused. In early vedic literature, dāna is a materially valued item – such as cattle, horses, women servants or gold, generally presented by members of the Kṣatriya to Brāhmaṇas for their role as priestly intermediaries. A particular type of dāna known as dakṣiṇā is regularly presented by the yajamāna, or 'sacrificer', to Brāhmaṇas as compensation for services rendered in performing yajña, 'sacrifice'. Dāna later comes to include bequests of land, thus forming the basis of great wealth for many religious institutions in India. In Buddhism, dāna is counted as one of the key pāramīs, 'perfections', in which giving is formalised as a foundational practice for laypeople, as well as monastics. The practice of giving dāna is not only one of the most important ways for Buddhist householders to accumulate merit, it also ensures the perpetuation of a monastic saṅgha, or 'community', dependent on communally given alms. As both idea and practice, dāna has economic and religious dimensions, and continues to be a central feature of contemporary ritual in India, including those related to the saṃskāras, such as funerary rites and marriage.

See also: **Antyeṣṭī; Brāhmaṇa; Caste; Saṃskāra; Varṇa; Veda; Vivāha**

ANDREA MARION

Further reading

Parry, J. 1986. 'The Gift, the Indian Gift and the "Indian Gift"'. *Man (Journal of the Royal Anthropological Institute)* 21.3: 453–73.

DANCE

Dancing is a vital part of Hindu worship. Dancing in worship might have originated when the early human being, helpless against the furies and ravages of nature, tried to propitiate these forces through song and dance (Goswami 2000: XI). Hindus believe that dance is a gift of the gods to the world. Brahmā is believed to have created a fifth Veda, *Nāṭya Veda*, out of the four *Saṃhitā*, taking its padya (poetic content) from the *Ṛgveda*, music from the *Sāmaveda*, abhinaya (acting) from the *Yajurveda* and the rasa (emotions) from the *Atharvaveda*, and gave it to Bhārata Muni, who wrote the redoubtable *Nāṭya Śāstra*, the seminal treatise for all dancing and acting, with its thirty-seven chapters on dancing, music, dramatic representation, and theatre and stage craft (Govindarajan 1992: 5–6). There is extensive discussion of dance in many *Purāṇas*, such as the *Agni Purāṇa* and *Viṣṇu Purāṇa*. Dance is also a popular and effective medium for the propagation of religious devotion and in addition raises funds for the running of temples. Dance is an indispensable part of all temple festivals.

Śiva and dance

Śiva is the Hindu god of dance. An alternative creation story of the universe states that creation was effected by Śiva setting its first rhythm in motion through his dance. The damaru, or small drum, in his upper right hand produces the sacred sound of creation, the Om (Banerji 1985: 8). Śiva is Naṭarāja, Lord of dance. The eternal dance of Śiva (Śiva taṇḍava) is represented in the Naṭarāja icon, which is full of spiritual symbolism. His lifted right hand represents abhaya (refuge) and his left hand points down to a way out of saṃsāra (the cycle of births and deaths), which is represented by the circle of fire surrounding the dancer. His lifted left foot represents anugraha (blessing) and his right foot stamps down on a dwarf representing ignorance. A more gentle form of dance (lāsya) is said to have been created by Pārvatī, wife of Śiva, and given to human beings. Śiva Naṭarāja is the main deity of the famous Cidambaram temple in south India, which is believed to be at the centre of the universe. The walls of this fourteenth-century structure have 108 sculptures of Bhārata Nāṭyam poses. The famous ancient temples at Bēlūr and Haḷebīd in Mysore are full of dancing sculptures. These temples were scarcely more than dancing pavilions for devotees, who danced on large circular slabs before the image of Viṣṇu.

Viṣṇu is associated with dance in his Mohinī (seductress) incarnation, necessitated by the vicious demon Bhasmāsura, who was granted the boon by Śiva of being able to turn anyone into ashes by touching their head. It is said that the demon tried to test his newly obtained powers on Śiva himself and Śiva fled to Viṣṇu to save him from this predicament. Viṣṇu, in the guise of Mohinī, performed a dance before the demon, who was entranced by the beauty of the dancer and the dance, and, imitating the dancer, touched his own head, rendering himself ashes.

Dance forms in Hinduism

The main dance forms of India are Bhārata Nāṭyam of Tanjore, Kathak of Uttar Pradesh, Manipuri of Manipur State, Assam and Kathākaḷi. All these art forms are permeated by worship of gods and mythology. The Bhārata Nāṭyam always begins with the alarippu, an invocation to the gods. The dance begins with the añjali, a pose of adoration. Manipuri dance, a gentle form, has themes mainly based on episodes from Lord Kṛṣṇa's life.

The origins of Kathākaḷi are traced to the Tantric period, about the fourteenth century CE. The Tantrists recommended dancing and singing at the end of all rituals. They believed that dance was efficacious in arousing Kuṇḍalinī, the coiled energy at the base of the spine.

Rāmanāttam, Kūyāttam, Kṛṣṇanāttam, Cākiār Kūttu, Teyyam and such religious art forms of Kerala contributed to the development of Kathākaḷi, which has the richest gestural code (mudrā) of all Indian dance forms (Pandeya 1943: 28). The themes are taken from Hindu mythology. It is basically a tāṇḍava (fierce dance) and many of the themes tell of the destruction of evil beings and persons. But, unlike in Bhārata Nāṭyam, the performers are male.

Teyyam is a form of ritual dance in Kerala in which elaborately masked and painted performers impersonate gods and deceased heroes. A highly stylised dance accompanied by ecstatic drumming and chanting is the main feature of this ritual of Northern Kerala. The dancing is inspired by the spirit of the deity possessing the ritual specialist, and ends with the return of the spirit to the shrine. The teyyam is a highly significant departure from Brahmanical forms of worship and, though originating from low and untouchable castes of Malabar, is increasingly attended by higher castes. Even brāhmaṇas have a role in this popular ritual.

Kṛṣṇa and dance

The Kṛṣṇa-Rādhā dance of northern India is so familiar that a song is not considered perfect if it does not mention the dance of Kṛṣṇa and Rādhā (Banerji 1985: 34). In the Kṛṣṇa cult sringāra rasa (erotic emotion) is very prominent and the movements depict the spiritual love that exists between Kṛṣṇa and the Gōpikas (cowherdesses), symbolising the close affinity between God and his devotees.

Devadāsīs

The institution of Devadāsīs (literally servants of God) is well known. These were devotional singers and dancers who had dedicated their lives to the service of God in a temple. They were considered to be married to the deity, and since they could never experience widowhood were considered as auspicious and were invited, for instance, to marriage ceremonies. Dancing, music and the arts were considered pleasing to the gods, as can be understood from the notion that Gandharvas, Kinnaras and Apsarasas were an essential part of the heavenly court. The Āpsara is the prototype of the Devadāsī.

Some Devadāsīs were abused by priests of the temple and royal patrons and this led to a stigma being attached to the profession of dance during the British Raj. Efforts were made by overzealous reformers to ban this institution. Respectable families were reluctant to send their daughters for instruction in dance. However, due to the efforts of dedicated performers such as Uday Shankar, Vyjayanthimala, Mrinalini Sarabhai and Balasaraswati (herself a Devadāsī) a change in attitude was brought about and there has been an explosion of interest in dance in recent times.

See also: **Apsarasas; Brahmā; Brāhmaṇas; Brahmanism; Cidambaram; Dalits; Devadāsīs; Gandharvas; Kinnaras; Kṛṣṇa; Kuṇḍalinī Yoga; Mohinī; Mudrā; Music; Myth; Oṃ; Pārvatī; Purāṇas; Rādhā; Sacred texts; Saṃhitā; Saṃsāra; Śiva; Tantras; Utsava; Veda; Viṣṇu; Widowhood**

THEODORE GABRIEL

Further reading

Banerji, Projesh. 1985. *Basic Concepts of Indian Dance*. Delhi: Chaukhamba Orientalia.

Goswami, Kali Prasad. 2000. *Devadasi: Dancing Damsel*. New Delhi: APH Publishing Corp.

Govindarajan, Hema. 1992. *The Natya Shastra and Bharatha Natya*. New Delhi: Harman Publishing House.

Misra, Susheela. 1987. *Invitation to Indian Dances*. New Delhi: Arnold Heinemann.
Pandeya, G.A.C. 1943. *The Art of Kathakali*. Allahabad: Kitabistan.

DARŚANA (PHILOSOPHY AND THEOLOGY)

See: **Ṣaḍdarśana**

DARŚANA (WORSHIP AND PRACTICE)

'A way of seeing' can refer either to a philosophical system or to a school of thought or Darśan, the 'auspicious sight' of the deity, where the worshipper stands in front of the image, or mūrti, to see and be seen by the god. Darśana is a central element common to most worship, where the devotee makes visual contact with the deity, receiving blessings and protection through the eyes of the image. (In this way it can be seen as the counterbalance to the power of the 'evil eye' to do harm, often found in myth.) In most temples the image is kept behind curtains or locked doors, which are only opened at certain times, after the image has been washed, dressed and decorated by the priests. Being able actually to see the image is the climax of worship and the sense of excitement may be heightened by loud drumming and clashing of cymbals.

The experience of darśana depends on the belief that the image actually embodies the deity and is in some sense alive. Devotees will speak of an image being particularly effective (in that it responds to requests) because it is 'most alive'. The fact that this life is found in the eyes is expressed in the importance of the final ceremony of the making of the image, the *prānapatiṣthā*, which literally gives life to the image in the form of giving it eyes, either by painting them in or by adding shiny enamel eyes. Many images, such as the famous Lord Jagannātha of Puri, have disproportionately large eyes as a way of expressing the importance of visual contact with the deity. Aniconic deities, such as the stones found at wayside shrines in Rajastan, may be given large eyes so that they may give darśana.

The concept of darśana is also behind the popularity of pilgrimage, whose importance stems from the idea of the sacred geography of India, with its many holy places connected with the lives of the gods and imbued with their presence. Pilgrims feel that they are taking darśana of the holy place, and the souvenir maps and pictures they buy will be installed in the domestic shrine, where they will be worshipped. This phenomenon, where pictures of powerful places and images retain the power to give and receive darśana, has been extended to the internet, where there are several sites specifically designed as virtual shrines offering darśana.

The experience of darśana is one of bhakti: the devotee is entering into a personal relationship with the deity without intervention from a priest. The priest may well be present, performing the appropriate rituals, but darśana allows the worshipper to approach the deity directly. It is also a reciprocal relationship – it is important to worshippers to have been seen by their god. This moment of contact seems to be the foundation for a developing sense, found notably among urban worshippers, of having a personal relationship with the deity. This relationship transforms the deity, whether previously categorised as 'wild' or 'gentle', into a protective ally.

See also: **Bhakti; Internet; Image worship; Jagannātha; Tīrthayātrā (Pilgrimage); Sacred geography; Saḍdarśana; Shrines, wayside**

CYNTHIA BRADLEY

Further reading

Eck, D. 1985. *Darsan: Seeing the Divine Image in India*. Chambersburg, PA: Anima Books.

Singer, M. 1972. *When a Great Tradition Modernizes: An Anthropological Approach to Indian Civilization*. Chicago, IL: University of Chicago Press.

DAŚAHRĀ

A ten-day festival held in October throughout India which celebrates the victory of good over evil. Mythologically the festival commemorates the victory of Rāma over Rāvaṇa. In north India, where devotion to Rāma is especially strong, for nine days the events of the *Rāmāyaṇa* are enacted by dance companies and actors, but on the final day street processions, with young boys dressed as the two princes, act out the final battle scenes leading to the death of Rāvaṇa. The festival culminates in the destruction by fire of giant effigies of Rāvaṇa, his son Meghnāda and his brother Kumbhakarṇa, who is regarded thoughout India as the epitome of sloth. The effigies are usually full of fireworks, and the child who is acting out the part of Rāma fires into them flaming arrows. In recent times, the festival has also become associated with right-wing Hindu nationalism or Hindutva.

The tenth day of Daśahrā also coincides with the ninth day of Navarātri, the festival associated with the Goddess. In parts of India where goddess worship is particularly strong, such as Bengal, the emphasis is on celebrating Durgā's victory over the buffalo-demon Mahiṣa, and culminates, after nine days of intense worship of the Goddess, in her immersion in water. In Mysore, the occasion is marked by a magnificent procession of richly decorated elephants. In Tamil Nadu, the nine days preceding the final event are given equally to the three goddesses; Lakṣmī, who presides over wealth and prosperity, Sarasvatī, the goddess of learning and the arts, and finally Durgā, considered to be the goddess of fertility. The tenth day is considered auspicious for children to begin education in dance or music and to offer respect to their teachers in these arts.

See also: **Dance; Durgā; Durgā Pūjā; Gandharvaveda; Hindutva; Lakṣmī, Śrī; Mahiṣa; Music; Nationalism; Rāma; Rāmāyaṇa; Rāvaṇa; Sacred animals; Sarasvatī; Utsava**

RON GEAVES

Further reading

www.mangalore.com/festivals/dussera.html (accessed 17 October 2005).

DAŚARATHA

Daśaratha is the father of Rāma, the hero of the *Rāmāyaṇa,* and of his three brothers, Bhārata, Lakṣmaṇa and Śatrughna, born from his three queens, Kausalyā, Kaikeyī and Sumitrā (in the developed form of the text, born as incarnations of Viṣṇu after Daśaratha has performed elaborate sacrifice). As he prepares to install Rāma as his co-ruler, his favourite, Kaikeyī, claims two boons that he has previously granted her and now demands Rāma's exile for fourteen years and her son Bhārata's installation instead. Bound by his promise, Daśaratha reluctantly agrees but angrily repudiates Kaikeyī. Heartbroken, he soon dies in the arms of Kausalyā, Rāma's mother, to whom he turns in his grief. As he dies, he recalls an episode of his youth when, shooting by sound, he killed an ascetic boy by mistake and so orphaned his helpless parents (a favoured episode in folk tellings and in sculpture).

See also: **Lakṣmaṇa; Rāma; Rāmāyaṇa; Śatrughna; Viṣṇu**

JOHN BROCKINGTON

DASGUPTA, SURENDRANATH (1885–1952)

Indian philosopher and historian of philosophy. Dasgupta was born in a part of Bengal that is now Bangladesh, where his great-grandfather ran a college offering instruction in Kāvya (poetry), Vyākaraṇa, Nyāya, Vedānta and Āyurveda. He studied first in Calcutta, receiving a doctorate in 1920. He then went to Cambridge, where he earned a second doctorate in Western philosophy and was appointed lecturer. During his time in Cambridge, he published the first volume of the work which was to occupy him throughout his life, his *History of Indian Philosophy* (1922–55). He also published monographs on Patañjali (1920) and Yoga (1930), and edited *A History of Sanskrit Literature* (1947). After his return to India he was principal of the Sanskrit College and, from 1942–45, professor at the University of Calcutta. He was offered the Professorship of Sanskrit at Edinburgh University, but was unable to take it up due to ill health. He died before being able to complete a planned two-volume account of his own philosophy; a brief version of it had been published in 1936.

See also: **Āyurveda; Nyāya; Patañjali; Poetry; Vedānta; Vyākaraṇa; Yoga**

WILL SWEETMAN

Further reading

Dasgupta, S.N. 1920. *The Study of Patañjali*. Calcutta: University of Calcutta.

Dasgupta, S.N. 1922–55. *A History of Indian Philosophy*. Cambridge: Cambridge University Press.

Dasgupta, S.N. 1930. *Yoga Philosophy in Relation to Other Systems of Indian Thought*. Calcutta: University of Calcutta.

Dasgupta, S.N. (ed.). 1947. *A History of Sanskrit Literature*. Calcutta: University of Calcutta.

DATTA VIDYARTHI, PANDIT GURU (d. 1890)

Hindu reformer and leading advocate of the militant Gurukul wing of the Arya Samaj. Guru Datta Vidyarthi was at the centre of the debate which would split the Arya Samaj in the 1880s. In essence, Vidyarthi and the 'militants' considered the Arya Samaj founder Dayananda Saraswati to be a divinely inspired ṛṣi (prophet), and his principal work, *Satyārth Prakāś* ('an illumination of truth'), to be an unquestionable religious text. The internal debate came to head over the issue of the leadership of the Dayananda Anglo-Vedic College in Lahore, as the Gurukul militants desired a revision of the curriculum to reflect their views, with Vidyarthi as the institution's principal. While the moderates eventually succeeded in retaining control of the college, the Gurukul wing subsequently expanded its activities into preaching and the 'conversion' of Indians to their brand of the Arya religious worldview. Among Vidyarthi's more memorable contributions to Arya Samaji literature was his attempt to authoritatively establish the 'true meaning' of the *Ṛgveda*, considered by Arya Samajis as the urtext of Hinduism. Vidyarthi objected to European Orientalist depictions of this text as constituted by natural myths, and so translated the Veda to support the Arya Samaj view that it recorded early elements of Hindu scientific achievement and hence supported claims to an advanced Hindu nationhood. His essays were collected for posthumous publication in *The Wisdom of the Rishis* (Lahore, n.d.).

See also: **Arya Samaj; Orientalism; Saṃhitā; Dayananda Saraswati, Swami**

MICHAEL S. DODSON

Further reading

Jones, K.W. 1989. *Socio-Religious Reform Movements in British India*. Cambridge: Cambridge University Press.

Prakash, G. 1999. *Another Reason: Science and the Imagination of Modern India*. Princeton, NJ: Princeton University Press.

DATTĀTREYA

The son of Atri and Anasūyā, who is variously regarded as the teacher of the

Asuras or the preceptor of non-Aryan tribal peoples, and thus regarded as ritually impure. His sons were Soma, Datta and Durvāsas, each of whom is believed to have received a portion of the divine essence, inherited from their father's association with the trimūrti, the triad form of the gods Brahmā, Viṣṇu and Śiva. Dattātreya's identification as a partial incarnation of the three major deities of classical Hindusim may have been an early attempt to synthesise competing cults. Dattātreya remains an object of devotion in contemporary India and is often associated with Advaita Vedānta. Iconographically, he appears as the three gods of the trimūrti sitting or standing with each other with their customary emblems and vāhanas. Alternatively he can be depicted with three heads (one for each god) and accompanied by four dogs and a bull.

See also: **Anasūyā; Asuras; Atri; Brahmā; Soma; Śiva; Trimūrti; Vāhanas; Vedānta; Viṣṇu**

RON GEAVES

Further reading

Stutley, Margaret and James Stutley (eds). 1977. *A Dictionary of Hinduism: Its Mythology, Folklore and Development 1500 BC–AD 1500*. London: Routledge and Kegan Paul.

DAYA MATA, SRI

The president of the Self-Realisation Fellowship started by Yogananda Paramhansa in Los Angeles in 1920 to promote the teachings of Kriyā Yoga. Known as the Sanghamata (Mother of the Society), Daya Mata was one of the group of American women who dedicated their lives to the teachings of Yogananda Paramhansa and went on to join his monastic order. Since 1955, she has remained head of the order of monks and nuns, many of whom work as her assistants and secretaries. Through others, she remains the guiding force of the network of Ashram communities throughout the world. She spent over twenty years with Yogananda Paramhansa, including eleven years in Encinitas when he was working on his two books, *Autobiography of a Yogi* and the *Second Coming of Christ*. Otherwise her primary residence as been the Mother Centre in Mt Washington, which she first entered as a young girl and which remains her 'home' to this day.

See also: **Āśram(a) (religious community); Kriyā Yoga; Self-realisation Fellowship; Yogananda, Paramhansa**

RON GEAVES

Further reading

www.yogananda-srf.org (accessed 27 October 2005).

Daya Mata. 1998. *Only Love: Living the Spiritual Life in a Changing World*. Los Angeles, CA: Self-Realization Fellowship Publishers.

DAYA, SISTER (1882–1955)

Georgina Jones was the daughter of a Nevada senator and an adherent of theosophy before meeting Swami Paramananda of the Boston Vedanta Centre. In 1921, she took the name Sister Daya and became a Vedantin minister. As one of Paramananda's prominent women disciples, Sister Daya made an energetic contribution to the growth of the movement in America.

Together with Gayatri Devi, Paramananda's niece, Sister Daya was chosen in 1940 by the Boston and Ananda Ashrama Vedanta communities to succeed Swami Paramananda as their leader. Swami Virajananda, then president of the Ramakrishna Math and Mission, rejected this proposal and subsequently withdrew recognition from these two centres. Sister Daya continued as a leader of the independent Order of Ramakrishna

Brahmavadin, which was created as a result of this dispute.

See also: **Ramakrishna Math and Mission**

GWILYM BECKERLEGGE

Further reading

Daya, Sister. 1976. *The Guru and the Disciple: My Life with Swami Paramananda*. Cohasset, MA: The Vedanta Centre.

DAYANANDA SARASWATI, SWAMI (1824–83)

Swami Dayananda Saraswati was the founder of the Hindu revivalist movement the Arya Samaj. Raised in a Brahmāṇa family in Gujarat, Dayananda had a traditional education. Discontented with life in the world, Dayananda ran away from home as a young man and was initiated as a saṃnyāsin. After studying with various teachers, Dayananda met Virjanand, a blind saṃnyāsin who instilled in him a revulsion for contemporary 'Hinduism', but also a burning desire to revive India's glorious ancient religion. After unsuccessful attempts to start Sanskrit schools, Dayananda and his followers formed the Arya Samaj in 1875 to realise his vision of religious revitalisation.

In many ways Dayananda's understanding of the history of the religions of India, an ancient golden age followed by centuries of decline, was similar to the opinions of the British Orientalists of his time. Yet Dayananda maintained that his teaching was based upon the oldest strata of the literature of the Veda, the *Saṃhitā*. By novel methods of interpretation, Dayananda attempted to demonstrate that Vedic theology was monotheistic, with those texts praising a single almighty and unchanging God. To prove this contention, Dayananda wrote and published a complete commentary and translation into Hindi of the *Yajurveda* and a partial commentary on the *Ṛgveda*, making those texts available to the general public in a way that was unprecedented. Dayananda was also a strident advocate of social reform. He rejected widow immolation and criticised restrictions on widow remarriage, for example, and he championed education for girls as well as boys. Dayananda was also a very active controversialist, frequently engaging in public debate with Hindu, Muslim and Christian religious leaders. A tireless preacher, writer and activist, Swami Dayananda Saraswati was one of the most influential figures in nineteenth-century India.

See also: **Arya Samaj; Hinduism, history of scholarship; Orientalism; Saṃhitā; Saṃnyāsa; Sanskrit; Sati; Widow remarriage; Women's education**

J.E. LLEWELLYN

Further reading

Dayanand Saraswati. 1978. *Autobiography of Dayananda Saraswati*, ed. K.C. Yadav. Delhi: Manohar.

Dayanand Saraswati. 1989. *Light of Truth: Or, An English Translation of the Satyarth Pradash*, trans. Chiranjiva Bharadwaja. Delhi: Sarvadeshik Arya Pratinidhi Sabha.

Jordens, J.T.F. 1993. *Dayananda Saraswati: His Life and Ideas*. Delhi: Oxford University Press.

Llewellyn, J.E. 1993. *The Arya Samaj as a Fundamentalist Movement: A Study in Comparative Fundamentalism*. Delhi: Manohar.

DECCAN EDUCATION SOCIETY

The Deccan Education Society was founded in 1884 and now constitutes twenty-seven institutions in India, ranging from pre-primary through to higher education. The educational focus is on science, technology, commerce and medicine. Its origins go back to 1880 in the founding of the New English School in Poona, created by the efforts of Vishnu Krishna Chiplonkar, Bal Gangadhar Tilak, Gopal

Ganesh Agarkar and Mahadavrao Namjoshi, all stalwarts of the Indian freedom struggle.

Believing that India's entry into the modern world could only be achieved by education, they went on to establish the Deccan Education Society in 1883 with the intention of providing continuity and permanence to the vision of private education of a high standard begun with the establishment of the school. In 1884, Gopal Krishna Gokhale and Dhonde Keshav Karve built the first college of the Deccan Education Society, charged with the vision to promote national regeneration through the means of education.

In 1885, the Deccan Education Society established Fergusson College, named after its first patron, Sir James Fergusson, Governor of Bombay from 1880–85 and inaugurated by its first principal, William Wordsworth, the grandson of the poet. Fergusson College expanded rapidly, aided by contributions from Deccan royalty, and remains one of India's foremost education institutions, now incorporating the Institute of Management Development and Research, opened in 1974.

The Deccan Education Society succeeded in developing a modern education system for Indians, combining the best of British education techniques available in India with a sense of Indian nationalism. It was the first institution to provide such an education for Indians independently of the British or Christian-controlled schools, from the very beginning displaying the symbols of Hinduism such as the Hanuman temple incorporated into the grounds of Fergusson College. The ethos of the society is manifested in the combination of English educators and Hindu patriots who made up its founding body.

See also: **Gokhale, Gopal Krishna; Hanumān; Karve, Dhonde Keshav; Tilak, Bal Gangadhar**

RON GEAVES

Further reading

Jones, Kenneth. 1989. *Socio-Religious Reform Movements in British India, The New Cambridge History of India*, vol. 3.1. Cambridge: Cambridge University Press.

www.fergusson.edu (accessed 17 October 2005).

DEITIES

For Hindus, the Divine is both one and many. A rich mythopoetic culture personalises and sanctifies very many aspects of human life and the natural world, including concepts, feelings and inspirations. Almost every human activity and every local area or group of people has its patron deities. These are all woven together in a complex web. One deity can be revealed in many different forms; conversely, different deities can merge into each other, by sharing epithets or myths. They are related by kinship ties (which can vary in different parts of India) or are seen as devotees of each other. New deities can emerge, to reflect changing historical and social situations or theological and philosophical developments.

Behind this 'polytheism' is an underlying unity. According to one's philosophical view or darśana, the Supreme Being may be thought of either as personal or as the impersonal Brahman, but in either case its 'own form' (svarūpa) is beyond conception; it is nirguṇa, 'without qualities'. That which *can* be imagined is God-with-form (saguṇa), for which the Sanskrit word used is deva or devatā. This is related to Latin 'deus' and hence to English 'deity', but tends to signify 'a god', for the devas are plural. If Hindus use the word 'God' in English, with an initial capital, they usually refer to one of the 'high' or 'great gods' (mahā deva), or to the supreme Brahman.

For the deities are not all equal: they do not express the One-beyond-form to the same degree. There is a divine hierarchy. Lesser divinities are 'parts' (amśa), like rays from the sun, while the 'high gods', in this analogy, are the sun itself: the perfect form through which Supreme Being communicates itself. Another analogy might be concentric circles: the 'higher' divinities are the more inclusive – and therefore the greater the number of forms (rūpa) in which they can appear to their devotees. It is lesser deities who are restricted to one or a few forms. Interwoven with this division is another one: that between local and India-wide relevance. Again, the more inclusive or 'higher' the divinity, the wider the geographical spread of his/her significance.

Most Hindus hold as the prime focus of their devotion their Iṣṭadevatā (chosen divinity). It is usually a form of one of the three 'high' deities, Viṣṇu, Śiva or Mahādevī (the Great Goddess), who each have their retinue of family, servants or incarnations (avatāra). Thus Hindus describe themselves as Vaiṣṇava, Śaiva or Śākta, respectively (Śākta from Śakti, meaning 'power' or 'energy', the most important epithet of the Goddess). In practical terms these three divinities replace the older, classical 'trinity' or trimūrti of Brahmā, Viṣṇu and Śiva, each presiding over three cosmic functions of creation, preservation and destruction.

Worship of deities

Deities are worshipped in temples, in the home, in the workplace, at pilgrimage sites, in wayside shrines. They reside in their prescribed iconographic images (pratimā, mūrti) or in aniconic symbols – Śiva's liṅga, Viṣṇu's śāligrama (a stone containing fossil molluscs), a plant, a jar or some other object. Especially in tantric sects, the power of a deity resides in particular sounds (mantras) and even letters (akṣara), and geometric diagrams (yantras). Sometimes divinity may be present in a natural object, a tree or a river, a mountain or a rock. A particular deity may be worshipped at any time, but they also have their special days of the week or lunar fortnight, and their seasonal festivals.

Deities are categorised as 'pure' or 'impure', the latter being those that receive animal sacrifice. Public worship of 'pure' (Sanskritic) deities is performed exclusively by male brāhmaṇa priests, while worship of domestic deities is performed by women of the household. 'Impure', local or folk deities are mediated by non-brāhmaṇa priests of either sex. The basic pattern of worship of any deity involves presenting offerings, as to an honoured guest. In the standard pūjā there are sixteen ingredients, including food offerings which are shared with the worshippers as prasāda ('grace' of the deity). The major deities have their own scriptures, myths and manuals for worship, though most branches of Hinduism acknowledge the Veda as their foundational text.

Ancient origins

Modern Hinduism is a synthesis of different historical traditions. The most dominant has been that derived from the *Saṃhitā*, the oldest texts of the sacred Sanskrit language. But there have been other sources as well. The Dravidian languages spoken mostly in south India have had their own traditions and deities, and there is a vast substratum of local and tribal divinities, varying from region to region. There is much speculation that some deities may have roots in the ancient Indus Valley culture which flourished in northern and western India from around 2500 BCE to around 1800 BCE. Examples of its script on steatite seals and copper plates have been subjected to intensive study, but still remain largely impenetrable; and consequently the iconographic figures associated with the script remain equally mysterious. Identifications are suggestive, though speculative; none is unambiguously connected to later Hindu religious images. For example, one seal image depicting a figure seated in what looks like a yoga position has been tentatively named a 'proto-Śiva' but its similarity to the later iconography of that deity remains a matter of subjective judgement. It seems at least probable that many local forms of the Devī worshipped throughout India – and clearly not reflected in the male-dominated pantheon of the vedic hymns – may have very ancient roots in the Indus Valley culture.

Vedic divinities

With some recent exceptions, scholarly consensus has been on discontinuity between this pre-historic civilisation and the oldest literature in Sanskrit. The *Ṛgveda* – first of the four *Saṃhitā* – is a collection of hymns believed by many scholars to have been composed in modern Punjab around 1500–1200 BCE, but there is clearly an older tradition behind them. There are over a thousand hymns associated with a ritual sacrifice to gods who represent natural phenomena – sky, earth, winds, storm, fire and sun – among many other things. There are close connections to the *Avesta* of ancient Iran, and this may suggest that some early Vedic divinities were brought to India by Indo-European tribes entering from the northwest.

The Vedic gods are at war with enemies called daitya, dānava and other names which eventually came to signify 'demon'. (The demons were called asura later on, but originally this was a name for a class of gods.) Throughout later Hinduism this war between gods and demons continues, which is why the deities are always depicted with their characteristic weapons. Mythically it represents the conflict between good and evil – or, rather, between enlightenment and ignorance – but perhaps it sometimes reflected historical political conflicts.

The *Saṃhitā* contain subtle and profound metaphysical concepts which have continued to underlie later Hinduism. Their gods represent natural phenomena but they always 'mean' other things as well. They are hypostases (mythical personifications) of social, moral and metaphysical principles, like Varuna, who represents the moral order as well as the overarching sky, and Mitra, his companion, whose name means 'friend'. These belong to a group of sky gods called ādityas, sons of Aditi, 'the primordial'. The gods are said to be thirty-three in number – eleven each belonging to the 'three worlds' of earth, atmosphere and the heavens – but in fact there are far more. The 'three worlds' are the realms of mortal existence which worshippers seek to transcend in a quest for immortality. Later this quest is seen as freedom from rebirth in the illusory realms of saṃsāra.

Among gods of the atmosphere, Indra, the Storm, is king of the gods. His most famous exploit is to defeat the drought demon Vṛtra. In later Hinduism he stands for royalty, but also sometimes the senses, for he is very much 'of this world'. A group called Maruts are stormy winds and young warriors. The Rudras (howlers) are the storm in its destructive aspect, with their wild leader Rudra, who becomes the 'high God' Śiva later on. Agni, the personified sacred fire, connects the human and divine worlds. There are several solar deities, associated with the sun's different aspects. Its journey across the sky is represented by Sūrya in his chariot drawn by seven horses (reproduced in the famous thirteenth-century sun temple at Konarak). Sāvitṛ represents the glowing light before dawn and after sunset, and like Agni he is a god of inspiration. He continues to be invoked in the Gāyatrī mantra recited by observant Brāhmaṇas three times a day at sunrise, noon and sunset. Viṣṇu 'the pervader', is praised in the Veda for taking three giant steps which encompass the three worlds, and represent the sun's ascent to the zenith. The most important female divinities are Uṣas, the Dawn, depicted as a young married woman; Rātrī, night in its benevolent aspect; Pṛthivī, the earth; and, more important later on, Vāc, speech, who became identified with Sarasvatī. These are just a few examples from a vast pantheon.

In later Hinduism, Indra and the Vedic gods represent an old order that has passed away. Always apparently closer to personified abstractions than to personal divinities, these deities diminished in importance relative to the ritual and metaphysical concepts they embodied. They were eventually 'demythologised' and interiorised, especially in the *Upaniṣads.* New divinities were placed above them – or were seen as encompassing them: Prajāpati, 'the progenitor', and Puruṣa, the cosmic 'Person'. The Brahman of the sacrifice – the power of invocation, or prayer itself – came to be seen as the absolute principle behind all that exists. Personified as Brahmā, he becomes the creator god. In later Hinduism he is inferior to his transcendent neuter form, but he remains the creator of this world and its cycles of time. Brahmā or Prajāpati is seen as the supreme divinity in late vedic texts.

'High gods' and 'classical Hinduism'

Historical dating of ancient Indian texts and therefore of theological and philosophical developments is uncertain, but by around the second century BCE a new kind of divinity seems to have arisen: personal gods who inspired devotion in followers who looked to them for salvation from the three worlds – by now understood as the round of saṃsāra and rebirth. The Vedic deities having been transcended by the absolute Brahman, the latter in turn is 'encompassed' by two personal 'high gods', Viṣṇu and Śiva. Meanwhile the Vedic religion was being spread east and south through the Indian subcontinent by kings and emperors who looked to its brāhmaṇa priesthood to authenticate their rule – and their deities. In consequence many local traditions contributed to the ongoing synthesis that constitutes 'classical Hinduism'. This process is sometimes called 'sanskritisation': local deities are absorbed into the 'Vedic' mainstream through the medium of Sanskrit and 'purification' through brahmanical forms of worship.

Both Viṣṇu and Śiva emerged out of the conceptual background of Vedic religion, but the cult of the latter seems to have absorbed many non-Vedic elements – especially the liṅga, the 'fertility symbol' that has become his characteristic 'mark' or 'sign' (the meaning of liṅga in Sanskrit). Both of these divinities absorb the names, deeds and attributes of many others – an example of their 'encompassing' nature that we noted at the beginning. Viṣṇu, whose three strides cover earth, atmosphere and highest heaven, became identified with Puruṣa, the 'cosmic Person'. Among other new names he acquired the epithet bhagavat ('blessed') and in the *Bhagavadgītā* he reveals himself in his human incarnation, Kṛṣṇa, as the awe-inspiring great Being whose body is the whole universe. Meanwhile Rudra, too, has developed from his fearsome Vedic role, and starts to be addressed as Śiva, the kindly, the auspicious – perhaps at first an apotropaic epithet – and in the *Śvetāśvatara Upaniṣad* is addressed as the one God above all others. In both these early theistic texts Viṣṇu and Śiva are associated with yoga, although there are already different kinds of yoga. But it is Śiva who eventually becomes known as Lord of Yoga (Yogeśvara) as an ascetic practice. Myth and theology focused on these two deities were developed in the Epics and *Purāṇas,* scriptures which took shape over a very long period from about mid-first millennium BCE to the middle of the first millennium CE.

In iconography, 'high gods' are depicted with at least four hands (sometimes more), whereas lesser gods and mortals have only two. All are identified by distinguishing marks of dress or accoutrements. Viṣṇu carries his cakra or discus – a weapon of war, but also the sun's disk – a conch shell, a mace and a lotus. He wears a crown signifying that he is Lord of the World (Jagannātha). Śiva is associated with his trident weapon, the crescent moon in his hair, a snake and a tiger skin. His hair is piled in the matted locks of the ascetic and his skin is pale from sacred ash (vibhūti), with which, as a yogi, he smears his body. Also signifying his connection with yoga, his third eye in the middle of the forehead indicates inner sight or enlightenment. These are the most common features of a complex and varied iconography.

In Vaiṣṇavism, Śiva is usually acknowledged as a lesser deity, and vice versa in Śaivism. These two Hindu 'religions' each incorporate different sects and mirror each other, for their theology, ritual and devotion run in parallel. In both, the cosmos unfolds out of the Deity in stages, in each of which he is known by different names, which also correspond to different levels of consciousness in yoga. Śiva has five faces (pañcānana); Viṣṇu has four vyuhas, or emanations, and many incarnations (avatāra). At the end of each era, or kalpa, the cosmos is destroyed and recreated out of the Deity in his svarūpa – his 'own', or real, form, which is also nirrūpa, beyond form or concept.

Viṣṇu and Śiva are each praised in a 'hymn of a thousand names' (sahasranāma) – indicative of the infinite number of forms these protean deities may take. Their names are different, for their cults are quite distinct, though they also complement each other – as signified by Viṣṇu's dark complexion and Śiva's white colour. The former, as Preserver, is concerned with cosmic and social order and sovereignty. (His two most important incarnations are kings.) Śiva the Destroyer retains something of his Vedic identity as Outsider. As the great Yogi he lives on society's fringes and destroys the world-illusion through meditation and asceticism. Yet paradoxically, Śiva the Ascetic is also Śiva the Erotic, the consort of the Great Goddess. (This is not as contradictory in Hindu thought as it might appear at first sight, for both involve mastery of the sexual force.)

These two 'high', or 'encompassing', Gods are worshipped in distinct local forms in important temples throughout the subcontinent, where they are closely identified with a particular place. For example, Śiva is Naṭarāja (Lord of dance) at the great temple at Cidambaram; Viṣṇu is Viṭhoba at Pandharpur in Maharasthra; Venkateśvara in the mountain shrine at Tirupati in Andhra; at Srirangam in Tamil Nadu he is Anantaśāyin, the Lord lying upon the cosmic waters. Each shrine has its own myths, often recorded in its own local *purāṇa* (*sthalapurāṇa*) and belongs to an India-wide pilgrimage route. Śiva is worshipped in twelve major pilgrimage sites from south to north where his hidden 'liṅga of light' (jyotirliṅga), is said to reside. Thus local and universal (India-wide) traditions of a deity are interconnected.

In the devotional or Bhakti movements, which arose from around the seventh century CE, again there are both Śaiva and Vaiṣṇava sects, each teaching devotion to one of these deities as the most immediate or even exclusive means to mokṣa or salvation. In devotional hymns in vernacular languages there is often a local emphasis: it is Śiva or Viṣṇu worshipped in a particular place who is being addressed. The hymns express a personal relationship of intimacy and tenderness. Bhakti is also central to the worship of Kṛṣṇa and Rāma, Viṣṇu's avatāras and the many forms of Devī.

Devī or Śaktī

In contrast to Vedic religion, in 'Hinduism' feminine divinity becomes prominent.

Each member of the male pantheon has a consort who represents his feminine aspect but is also worshipped independently. Brahmā is accompanied by Sarasvatī – a river in the Veda, now Goddess of learning; she rides a swan and carries a musical instrument or a book. Viṣṇu has two consorts, Lakṣmī or Śrī, who represents wealth and well-being, and Bhūdevī, the earth. Lakṣmī's invariable emblem is the lotus, on one of which she sits while holding another in her hand. Sometimes she is shown being bathed by two elephants. Both she and Sarasvatī have eight names expressing their different aspects. It is Śiva's consort, however, who is the Great Goddess as an independent cosmic principle. She has innumerable forms: as wife of Śiva, she is Pārvatī or Umā. This pair are the divine lovers for Śaivism, as Rādhā and Kṛṣṇa are for Vaiṣṇavism. Their marriage is celebrated at the Śivarātri festival. Their love creates the universe; for erotic desire is a form of the divine energy that wants to bring the world into existence, just as its opposite, ascetic withdrawal, seeks to eliminate it. Śiva combines the opposites: as archetypal ascetic, he burns the god of desire (Kāma) with his third eye. Pārvatī, however, persuades him to bring him back to life again! The divine pair appear together under different names in different localities, where often it is the Goddess who is the more prominent. For example at the big temple at Madurai, in south India, the Goddess Mīnākṣī (historically a patron deity of the ancient Pāndya kingdom) is married to Śiva in the form of Sundareśvara (Lord of beauty).

It is mostly when she fights the demons on her own that Devī becomes Mahādevī, the Great Goddess, independent of her consort. Her place in the pantheon is first reflected in a long poem called *Devī Māhātmya* (fourth century CE). It tells how the male gods projected from themselves their female energies or aspects (their śaktis) and these coalesced into an awe-inspiring martial goddess. She fights the 'great demon' Mahiṣa, who takes the form of a buffalo. During the battle the Goddess emanates from herself even fiercer female forms, including 'the black one', Kālī, who emerges from her angry countenance. Kālī is mostly a Tantric goddess (see below).

The Great Goddess incorporated fierce or martial female divinities in many parts of India. For example, she is Vindhyavāsinī – 'dweller in the Vindhya' mountains – in western India. Her most India-wide name is Durgā, and her most important festival the 'nine nights' of the Goddess (Navarātri) in the autumn. Durgā is portrayed as a beautiful young woman with many arms holding a variety of weapons, riding a lion and attacking a buffalo, from whose head emerges the figure of a man. But iconography does not always reflect how a deity is experienced. In Bengal, where she is especially important, Durgā is seen as a young married daughter, returning on a visit from her husband's home, accompanied by her four children, Sarasvatī and Lakṣmī and Śiva's two sons (see below). Although a form of Śiva's consort Pārvatī, she is not usually portrayed alongside her husband.

The Great Goddess has her own 'hymn of a thousand names'. In parts of South India she is worshipped as Lalitā, a beautiful, erotic goddess who defeats the demon Bhāndāsura. Lalitā dwells in the mythical city of Śrīpura – notionally at the heart of her emblem the Śrī Cakra, the geometric 'diagram' which is the focus of her worship. As the 'encompassing' Goddess, Mahādevī incorporates innumerable local goddesses, who are often addressed simply as 'Mother' (Mā).

Viṣṇu's avatāras and Śiva's family

All deities can have incarnations; but it is Viṣṇu who specially takes incarnation in order to save the world from evil (part of his role as 'Preserver'). There are several lists of his avatāras, but the most common one has ten, among whom the two most important are Rāma, the king of Ayodhya, and Kṛṣṇa, who spoke the *Bhagavadgītā* to Arjuna. The story of the kidnapping of Rāma's wife, Sītā (incarnation of Lakṣmī), by Rāvana, demon king of Sri Lanka, and her husband's expedition to rescue her is told in the *Rāmāyaṇa*. Kṛṣṇa is a king in the *Mahābhārata* and military ally of the Pāndava brothers; but in later texts he has another character as the delightful child (Bāla Kṛṣṇa) growing up in the idyllic forest of Vṛndāvana and as the irresistible divine lover of Rādhā and the cowherd women (the gopīs). The two avatāras have their own iconography; Kṛṣṇa is blue in colour, most typically portrayed as a graceful youth playing a flute; or else as a playful child. Rāma, a graceful young warrior, carries a large bow. They are each worshipped by their devotees as a full expression of the Supreme Being in human form (pūrnavatāra).

Paradoxically, it is Śiva the ascetic who is father of the Hindu 'holy family'. His two sons are elephant-headed Gaṇeśa and Skanda Kumāra, usually portrayed with a peacock and a long spear. They both have many different names, myths and local and historical traditions. In Tamil-speaking areas of south India and Sri Lanka, the latter is worshipped as a 'high god', where he is also known as Subramanya and Murukaṉ. He has two wives: Devasenā, whose name reflects his identification with Skanda, the army commander of the Vedic gods, and Vaḷḷi, a local forest maiden. They reflect his dual character: he is both martial and a god of romantic love. As Kumāra, he is portrayed as a handsome young bachelor. As Kārttikeya, he was born with six heads and nourished by the six kṛttikās (the Pleides) in the lunar month of Kārttik, when his major festival is held. Historically Kārttikeya was a presiding deity of rulers and the warrior classes.

Gaṇeśa or Gaṇapati, the remover of obstacles, and hence 'lord of beginnings', is the widely popular elephant-headed deity whose shrine is present in most temples. Representing 'success', he is invoked at the start of enterprises. Possibly his elephant nature results from fusion of a local animal-deity with Gaṇapati, the 'general' of Śiva's host of gaṇas, his semi-demonic entourage. But his myths tell how, born by parthenogenesis from Pārvatī alone, he lost his human head during a battle with his 'stepfather', but was restored by being given an elephant's head in its place. He has a jovial, gentle nature. His major festival (Gaṇeśacaturthi) is especially important in Maharashtra, where the nationalist leader B.G. Tilak gave the name Gaṇapati ('lord of hosts') a political significance as lord of 'the masses'. He has many different local forms and aspects.

Divinities in the tantras

In the Tantric sects, which flourished from around the tenth century onwards, we see a proliferation of images of terrifying and sometimes grotesque deities, often with multiple arms wielding weapons. Best known of these is the naked Kālī standing upon her husband Śiva's chest, holding an axe and a severed head, and other gruesome accoutrements. This image, like that of other Tantric deities, is deliberately inauspicious, designed to represent what is most threatening in the natural world and in human nature. Many of them are understood as the inauspicious or fearsome aspects of otherwise benevolent 'high gods'. It is part of the latter's 'encompassing' role that they absorb both kinds of attributes, for the nature of a high deity is to transcend the opposites of 'duality'.

There are Tantric cults of Viṣṇu; but the Tantric deity above all is Śiva, logically continuing his Vedic role as the cosmic outsider; while Mahādevī the

Great Goddess has both benevolent and fierce aspects. The violence of Hindu deities is directed against the demons, but in Tantric cults violent or erotic divinities are part of a complicated philosophy that has both magical and mystical dimensions. The most widespread Tantric form of Śiva is Bhairava (whose name means 'fearful'), while the Goddess is Bhairavī. In Tantric Śaktism the latter has ten forms, called the mahāvidyās, or ten great forms of knowledge, of which some are auspicious, some inauspicious. Her sometimes terrifying iconography does not prevent the Tantric Goddess from being seen as a protective and salvific mother attracting tender devotion, for example from the famous Bengali saint Sri Ramakrishna

Minor divinities and other supernatural beings

The distinguishing feature of a 'high god' is that he/she can bestow mokṣa, liberation from rebirth in saṃsāra ('the wandering'). Hindus also acknowledge divinity, however, in lesser or partial forms. A second 'tier' rules over specific departments. Those we have already met as consorts and 'family' of the high deities are worshipped independently during their special festivals and prayed to for practical aims: Sarasvatī is patron deity of arts, music and learning; Lakṣmī is prayed to for success in business or for prosperity and general well-being. Viśvakarman ('world maker') is the divine architect in the Veda, another form of Brahmā the creator. He too has his own festival, and nowadays is adopted as patron deity of engineers. In parts of rural India, Gaṇeśa and Durgā are connected to agriculture.

Another 'tier' forms the retinue of the higher gods, and they are worshipped alongside them, or in side shrines: for example, Hanumān, the monkey god, devoted servant of Rāma who helped him in his quest for Sītā, represents the ideal bhakta or devotee. Rāma's three faithful brothers are lesser or partial incarnations of Viṣṇu, while the dark Kṛṣṇa has his pale brother Balarāma, who holds a plough. All deities have a vāhana ('vehicle'), usually a bird or animal on whom they ride. Those of the high gods are specially honoured: Viṣṇu's great 'eagle' Garuḍa, and Śiva's white humped-back bull, Nandi, stand guard facing their shrines. Deified legendary devotees and sages like Nārada and Viśvāmitra might also appear in the retinue.

Another class of minor divinities represent aspects of the cosmos and natural world: such as the nine planets (navagraha), worshipped as astrological forces; the nakṣatras, the lunar mansions; and eight dikpālas, guardians of the directions. Yama, guardian of the south, is also the dread judge of the dead. Kubera, who guards the north, is god of riches; he is chief of another group of supernatural beings, the yakṣas, not exactly deities but elemental forces of the earth, who guard its treasures. They are similar to the nāgas, serpent-like beings who inhabit the waters. The great rivers of India are all goddesses, especially the sacred Gaṅgā and Yamunā. Since nationalist times, India itself has become a goddess – Bhārat Mātā.

Divinity is spread throughout and within the visible world so that almost anything can become a theophany, a mediation of at least one aspect of the divine. Like saints and angels in the monotheistic religions, the lesser divinities are prayed to for specific purposes and help to make the cosmos an inhabited, companionable place.

Local and folk divinities

Particular minor deities preside over the domestic sphere and the family, the fields and crops. Diseases and other calamities are represented by folk deities, usually goddesses, whose worship is apotropaic.

Śītalā ('the cool one') is goddess of smallpox and fevers generally. Manasā, the snake goddess, protects from snakebite.

Deities mentioned so far have a place in the India-wide Sanskritic pantheon. In particular geographical areas the picture can look very different, for there are very many deities whose worship belongs principally or solely to that region. Some of these, again, will be regarded as local forms of the 'high gods' of the wider pantheon. Others will be lesser divinities representing specific aspects of life. Every village has its grāmadevatā, who guards its boundaries, and its mātṛkā, or 'mother', who, like the Great Goddess, can have benevolent or fearsome attributes. Away from urban centres, deified local heroes and local folk divinities mediated by non-brāhmaṇa priests and by women are usually more important than the Sanskritic, brahmanical pantheon. Some of these will be 'impure' deities who accept animal sacrifice. Others will communicate through 'possession' cults where they are called upon for healing and prophecy.

Exclusion

The 'divine hierarchy' also reflects the 'pure/impure' dichotomy of the caste system, and religious exclusion is connected to the social and economic oppression of Dalit groups. So-called 'untouchables' have traditionally been banned from the shrines of 'pure' (Sanskritic) deities, although government legislation attempts to counteract this. In local or folk religions, however, a Dalit can be a priest or act as 'shaman' for a whole village or wider community. In some Bhakti and Tantric sects Dalits have made significant contributions to wider Hinduism.

Divinised saints

The divine and human realms intermingle, for humans can 'rise' to divine status, even as deities can 'descend' into human incarnation. The steadily growing importance of the guru has led to many preceptors and saints being seen as incarnations of Viṣṇu, Śiva or Devī and, increasingly in modern times, as independent embodiments of Brahman. Examples range from the philosopher Śaṅkarā (seen as an incarnation of Śiva), through Swami Narayan or Sri Ramakrishna in the nineteenth century, to many modern and contemporary avatāras, who embody the divine in its fullness for their followers. Among the enlightened saints are some, such as Ravidās and Vālmīki, who belonged to Dalit castes.

Conclusion

The deities are important for all branches of Hindu culture, which cannot be appreciated without them: the visual arts, dance, music, astrology, yoga and the traditional 'sciences' are closely connected to them. They reflect human nature in all its aspects, along with the world in which humans find themselves. The devotee can relate to the divine as parent, child, king, master, lover or intimate friend, but ultimately all images are transcended by the deity in his/her unknowable 'own form'.

See also: **Aditi; Aesthetics; Agni; Arjuna; Asuras; Balarāma; Bhagavadgītā; Bhakti; Bhārat Mātā; Brahmā; Brahman; Caste; Dalits; Dance; Darśana; Dikpālas; Durgā; Gaṇeśa; Gaṇeśacaturthi; Gaṅgā; Garuḍa; Gāyatrī mantra; Grāmadevatās; Guru; Hanumān; Image worship; Indra; Indus Valley civilisation; Iṣṭadevatā; Itihāsa; Jagannāta; Jyotiṣa; Kālī and Caṇḍī; Kalpa; Kāma; Kubera; Lakṣmī, Śrī; Languages; Madurai; Mahābhārata; Mahādevī; Mahāvidyās; Mahiṣa; Manasā; Mantra; Maruts; Mātṛkās; Mīnākṣī; Mitra; Mokṣa; Murukaṉ; Music; Nāgas; Nandi; Nārada; Narayana, Swami; Navagrahas (Planets); Pāṇḍavas; Pārvatī;**

Prajāpati; Pṛthivī; Pūjā; Purāṇas; Puruṣa; Rādhā; Rāma; Ramakrishna, Sri; Rāmāyaṇa; Rāvana; Ravidās(a); Rudra; Śaivism; Śakti; Saṃhitā; Saṃsāra; Śaṅkara; Sarasvatī; Sītā; Śītalā; Śiva; Śivarātri; Skanda; Stars; Subramanya; Sūrya; Tantras; Tilak, Bal Gangadhar; Time; Tīrthayātrā (Pilgrimage); Trimūrti; Umā; Upaniṣads; Uṣas; Vaiṣṇavism; Vālmīki; Varuṇa; Vedāṅgas; Vedic Pantheon; Vibhūti; Viṣṇu; Viśvakarman; Viśvamitra; Vṛndāvana; Vṛtra; Yajña; Yakṣas; Yama; Yantra; Yoga; Yogi

KATHLEEN TAYLOR

Further reading

Bhattacharji, S. 2000. *The Indian Theogony: Brahma, Visnu, Siva*. New Delhi: Penguin Books.
Bunce, F.W. 2000. *An Encyclopaedia of Hindu Deities, Demi-Gods, Godlings, Demons and Heroes*. New Delhi: D.K. Printworld.
Daniélou, A. 1964. *Hindu Polytheism*. New York: Bollingen Foundation.
Das, Alokparna. 2002. *Prominent Hindu Deities Myths and Meanings*. Delhi: Indu Prakashan.
Eck, Diana L. 1998. *Darśan: Seeing the Divine Image in India*. New York: Chichester.
Harshananda, Swami. *c.*1981. *Hindu Gods and Goddesses*. Madras: Ramakrishna Math.

DEITIES, DOMESTIC AND FAMILY

Also known as kuladevatās or jātidevatās.

This class of gods and goddesses differs from personal deities (iṣṭadevatās) and village deities (grāmadevatās) in that they belong to the abode of a kin rather than to a single individual or a community. The kuladevatās are associated with the ancestral place of a family. Domestic and family deities can belong either to the local tradition or to the official pantheon, as in the case of the pañca devatās ('five deities'): Śiva, Viṣṇu, Devī (the Goddess), Sūrya and Gaṇeśa. When a family or part of it moves from its original location, an altar to the kuladevatās is built in the new house and the family deities are represented by an earthen pot (kumbha; Kumbhamātā) which contains the ancestral earth. The worship of the kuladevatās takes place at the performance of saṃṣkāras (rites), scheduled or occasional festivals and celebrations. It is generally performed in the house by the householder (gārhasthya) or the family priest (purohit). The domestic cult of the kuladevatās requires the offering of the sixteen customary items : (1) offering of a seat; (2) water to wash the feet; (3) water to drink; (4) water to wash hands and face; (5) light food; (6) water to rinse mouth and hands; (7) bath; (8) clothes; (9) ornaments; (10) scent; (11) flowers; (12) incense; (13) light; (14) food; (15) additional water to rinse the mouth; and (16) salutations. Domestic and family deities are also celebrated by undertaking vows (vratas) and through the recitation of liturgical manuals (*paddhatis*) and sections from the epics (*Rāmāyaṇa, Mahābhārata*). The building of temples in honour of kuladevatās has recently become a widespread phenomenon in India as well as in the countries of the Hindu diaspora.

See also: **Diaspora; Gaṇeśa; Gārhasthya; Grāmadevatā; Iṣṭadevatā; Itihāsa; Kumbhamātā; Mahābhārata; Mahādevī; Purohit; Rāmāyaṇa; Saṃskāras; Śiva; Sūrya; Viṣṇu; Vrata**

FABRIZIO M. FERRARI

Further reading

Fuller, C. 2004. *The Camphor Flame. Popular Hinduism and Society in India*. Princeton, NJ and Oxford: Princeton University Press.
Kulke, H. 1992. 'Tribal Deities at Princely Courts: The Feudatory Rajas of Central Orissa and Their Tutelary Deities (Istadevatas)'. In S. Mahapatra, ed., *The Realm of the Sacred. Verbal Symbolism and Ritual Structures*. Calcutta and New York: Oxford University Press, 56–78.

DEITIES, FOLK AND POPULAR

Undoubtedly of ancient origin, folk and popular deities remain an integral part of local Hindu religion. They are represented in many ways, most often by a tree, a stone, a pot or perhaps as a sacrificial stake, like the male deity Pōtu Rāju, who occupies a place in many goddess shrines and temples. Generally, male deities occupy the position of guardian or watchman at the numerous goddess temples or shrines that characterise local worship. Many goddesses personify disease, particularly the smallpox goddess Śītalā in north India and Māriammā in the south, who are most often approached for their curative powers. Since the eradication of smallpox, these goddesses now preside over other ailments such as chickenpox and measles. Individual goddesses may be popular in a particular region, such as Mīnākṣī in Tamil Nadu or Maṅgaḷā in Orissa. The ancient practice of snake (nāga) worship is particularly popular in south India, though it is practised all over India. Many folk or popular deities were once human. Particularly popular, especially in Rajasthan, are satī mātās (women who ended their lives on their husband's funeral pyre) and vīras or heroes (whose lives ended gloriously in battle), who are now believed to be powerful deities (Fuller 1992: 49). The festivals of folk or popular deities, especially those of the goddesses, are often extremely unorthodox. Possession, blood sacrifice and fire walking are important and characteristic forms of worship, as is pulling a festival cart attached to the devotees' back with hooks or piercing the cheeks or tongue with metal skewers. Over time, the nature of some folk deities has been softened as they have had the most unorthodox aspects of their character and worship Brahmanised, bringing them more into line with the pan-Indian deities, who generally abstain from meat eating and are served by brāhman priests.

See also: **Blood sacrifice; Māriammā; Mīnākṣī; Śītalā**

LYNN FOULSTON

Further reading

Fuller, C.J. 1992. *The Camphor Flame: Popular Hinduism and Society in India*. Princeton, NJ: Princeton University Press.

DEITIES, VILLAGE AND LOCAL

Village deities, or grāmadevatā, most properly refers to the protective gods and goddesses that inhabit India's villages. Local deities, including folk and popular divine beings, have a huge number of different names, forms and characteristics, even in one settlement. A brāhmaṇa priest seldom serves them, and their worship is generally less orthodox than that of the major Hindu deities. In many areas of India, particularly Tamil Nadu and Orissa, female deities are more prevalent than males. Goddesses in particular are fond of blood sacrifices. In some instances, the deities may have different names but similar characteristics. Conversely, a group of deities may share the same or a strikingly similar origin myth. They are distinguished from the more famous pan-Indian deities such as Śiva, Viṣṇu, Lakṣmī and Pārvatī in the way they are represented. Alongside the other deities are localised forms of the great gods and goddesses. In Tamil Nadu, for instance, Viṣṇu is often portrayed as Perumāl and Gaṇeśa appears as Vināyaka. These deities have an iconography and mythology that locate them among the people who worship them. In each settlement there may be just one or many deities, a factor not necessarily dependent on population size. Local deities may be peculiar only to one settlement, perhaps giving their name to or receiving their name from it, or may be known throughout a whole region. There seems to be a more intimate relationship between these deities and their devotees: they know each other well as their lives are inextricably entwined. While the pan-Indian deities may be considered more intrinsically pure, and certainly more orthodox, they remain at the periphery of village/local life, paid homage to when required but not necessarily sharing the daily lives of the masses.

See also: **Blood sacrifice; Deities, folk and popular; Gaṇeśa; Grāmadevatās; Lakṣmī, Śrī; Pārvatī; Śiva; Viṣṇu**

LYNN FOULSTON

Further reading

Foulston, L. 2002. *At the Feet of the Goddess: The Divine Feminine in Local Hindu Religion*. Brighton and Portland, OR: Sussex Academic Press.

Fuller, C.J. 1992. *The Camphor Flame: Popular Hinduism and Society in India*. Princeton, NJ: Princeton University Press.

DEMERIT

See: **Pāpa**

DESIKACHAR, T.K.V. AND VINIYOGA

Son of T. Krishnamacharya, Desikachar first trained as a structural engineer before making yoga his vocation in the early 1960s. In 1976 he established the Krishnamacharya Yoga Mandiram (KYM) in Chennai to propagate the teachings passed on to him by his father. His method is therapeutic in emphasis, with each student being treated one to one, using yoga techniques adapted to suit their particular requirements. Synchronised breathing and movement and logically progressive sequences of postures (vinyāsa krama), combined with a significant element of chanting, are characteristic of his teaching. Formerly known as 'Viniyoga', Desikachar (2004) recently insisted that his method should simply be designated 'yoga', and has asked his teachers to no longer use the former term. He has made a significant contribution to the development and propagation of modern yoga worldwide.

See also: **Krishnamacharya, T.; Yoga; Yoga, modern**

MARK SINGLETON

Further reading

Desikachar, T.K.V. 1998. *Health, Healing and Beyond*. New York: Aperture.

DEUSSEN, PAUL JAKOB (1845–1919)

German Indologist and historian of philosophy. Studied theology, philosophy, philology and Sanskrit at Bonn, Tübingen and Berlin before teaching at the universities of Geneva, Berlin and Kiel. His account of Vedānta was based on the *Brahmasūtras* and Śaṅkara's commentary on them. His translation of sixty *Upaniṣads* was published in 1897. His magnum opus, a general history of philosophy (1894–1917), devoted three volumes each to Indian and to European philosophy. His view of Indian philosophy was strongly coloured by his reading of Schopenhauer, to whom he had been introduced by his classmate and friend Friedrich Nietzsche, and for whom in turn he became an important source of information on Indian religions.

See also: **Brahmasūtras; Hinduism, history of scholarship; Śaṅkara; Schopenhauer, Arthur; Upaniṣads; Vedānta**

WILL SWEETMAN

Further reading

Deussen, P. 1883. *Das System des Vedânta: nach den Brahma-Sûtras des Bâdarâyaṇa und dem Commentare des Çankara über dieselben*. Leipzig: Brockhaus. [Charles Johnston (trans.). 1912. *The System of the Vedânta according to Bâdarâyana's Brahmasûtras and Çankara's Commentary Thereon*. Chicago, IL: Open Court.]

Deussen, P. 1894–1917. *Allgemeine Geschichte der Philosophie mit besonderer Berücksichtigung der Religionen*. [General History of Philosophy with Special Consideration for Religion] Leipzig: Brockhaus.

Deussen, P. 1897. *Sechzig Upanishad's des Veda*. Leipzig: Brockhaus. [V.M. Bedekar and G.B. Palsule (trans.). 1980. *Sixty Upanisads of the Veda*. Delhi: Motilal Banarsidass.]

Deussen, P. 1922. *Mein Leben*. Leipzig: Brockhaus.

DEV SAMAJ

The 'Divine Society,' an organisation aimed at the reform of Hinduism, was established by Pandit Shiv Narayan Agnihotri in February of 1887 in the Punjab. Originally conceived as an extension of the Brahmo Samaj, Agnihotri increasingly moulded the teachings of the Dev Samaj so as to place himself at the centre of all religious practice. Agnihotri considered himself to be the only valid guru (spiritual preceptor) – the one whose state of religious enlightenment was sufficient to guide others on the same path. In this regard, Agnihotri became in large measure a god himself, and hence the object of worship at Dev Samaj services. Agnihotri then became known as Mahāmānanīya Pūjanīya Śrī Deva Guru Bhagavān ('most reverend, most worshipful, most exalted, divine teacher, blessed lord'). Yet the Dev Samaj was not simply an extension of Agnihotri's ego, nor was it a purely religious organisation, for it also advocated a radical programme of social reform. For example, Dev Samajis were encouraged to live as householders and to take ten prescriptive vows, which committed them to follow a strict regime of teetotal vegetarianism, absolute honesty and purity in social and sexual relations. Moreover, like many of the religious reform movements of this time, Dev Samajis eschewed the trappings of caste and the differential treatment of women. For example, inter-caste dining and marriage were encouraged by the Dev Samaj, as was widow remarriage. The Dev Samaj was, moreover, active in the promotion of female education, establishing a school for this purpose in Firozpur district in 1899. While the Dev Samaj's membership was never as large as that of the Brahmo Samaj, for example, it did boast numerous adherents among the Punjab's educated elites and, as such, did possess some measure of social influence. The principal tenets of the Dev Samaj are outlined in Agnihotri's principal Hindi work, the multi-volume *Dev Śāstra*.

See also: **Brahmo Samaj; Caste; Guru; Shiv Narayan Agnihotra, Pandit; Widow remarriage; Women, status of; Women's education**

MICHAEL S. DODSON

Further reading

Farquhar, J.N. 1967. *Modern Religious Movements in India*. Delhi: Munshiram Manoharlal (first published 1915).

Jones, K.W. 1989. *Socio-Religious Reform Movements in British India*. Cambridge: Cambridge University Press.

DEVADĀSĪS

The Sanskrit term devadāsī literally means 'female servant (dāsī) of God (deva)'. While the term is found in some medieval Sanskrit textual genres, in the nineteenth century it became a generic way of referring to a variety of women defined by their non-conjugal sexuality. The evocation of the Sanskrit term devadāsī in public discourses on social purity effaced the obvious differences between the various communities and furthered the political aim of outlawing their lifestyles, a task accomplished in 1947, the year India became independent.

These communities can be broadly divided into: (1) Dalit women dedicated to village goddesses such as Yellamā (called jogin, jogati, basavi, mātaṅgi, yellammadāsī, in Kannada, Marathi and Telegu); and (2) elite women 'dedicated' to brahmanic deities such as Śiva, Viṣṇu or Murukaṉ in various parts of India (usually called tēvaṭiyāḷ in Tamil, bhogam in Telegu, kuṭikkāri in Malayalam, mahari in Oriya and bhāviṇ or kaḻāvant in Konkani and Marathi).

Women belonging to the elite communities often lived in matrifocal households, were specialists in the performance of music and dance, and performed in temples, royal courts and at public and private social events. Some women in these communities underwent a ritual marriage (often called a 'dedication') to a temple deity. These 'dedicated' women held rights to tax-free land and held ritual privileges in the temple. Even women who belonged to such families but were not dedicated were active performers and participated in the matrifocal household and kinship structures.

In the colonial period these women's identities were conflated with those of secular female performers from northern India (called 'Nautch Girls', from the Hindi nāc, 'dance') and prostitutes, and in the Orientalist imagination they became the focus of European novels, travelogues and films. At the nexus of colonial modernity and emergent nationalism in the early twentieth century, the social, aesthetic and religious lives of these women were irrevocably transformed in the name of social reform. Their art forms were appropriated and sanitised in a nationalist endeavour to define India's classical heritage, and they emerged on the contemporary stage as 'spiritual' arts for the middle class.

See also: **Dalits; Dance; Murukaṉ; Music; Nationalism; Orientalism; Śiva; Viṣṇu; Yellamā**

DAVESH SONEJI

Further reading

Bradford, N.J. 1983. 'Transgenderism and the Cult of Yellamma: Heat, Sex and Sickness in South Indian Ritual'. *Journal of Anthropological Research* 39.3: 307–22.

Epp, L.J. 2000. *'Violating the Sacred'? The Social Reform of Devadasis Among Dalits in Karnataka, India*. PhD Dissertation, Department of Anthropology, York University.

Kersenboom, S. 1987. *Nityasumangali: Devadasi Tradition in South India*. Delhi: Motilal Banarsidass.

Marglin, F.-A. 1985. *Wives of the God-King: The Rituals of the Devadasis of Puri*. Delhi: Oxford University Press.

Orr, L.C. 2000. *Donors, Devotees, and Daughters of God: Temple Women in Medieval Tamilnadu*. New York: Oxford University Press.

Parker, K.M. 1998. '"A Corporation of Superior Prostitutes": Anglo-Indian Legal Conceptions of Temple Dancing Girls, 1800–1914'. *Modern Asian Studies* 32.3: 559–633.

Soneji, D. 2004. 'Living History, Performing Memory: *Devadasi* Women in Telegu-Speaking South India'. *Dance Research Journal* 36.2: 30–49.

Srinivasan, A. 1985. 'Reform and Revival: The Devadasi and Her Dance'. *Economic and Political Weekly* 20.44: 1869–76.

Whitehead, J. 1998. 'Community Honor/Sexual Boundaries: A Discursive Analysis of Devadasi Criminalization in Madras, India, 1920–47'. In J.E. Elias *et al.*, eds, *Prostitution: On Whores, Hustlers, and Johns*. New York: Prometheus Books, 91–106.

DEVAKĪ

Devakī is revered as the mother of Kṛṣṇa in early and medieval Sanskrit texts, including the *Mahābhārata* and the *Bhāgavata Purāṇa*. According to the latter, Devakī and her husband Vasudeva become Kṛṣṇa's parents after performing extreme austerities in a previous life and then praying to Viṣṇu for a son like himself. But, since there can be no likeness of the Supreme God, Viṣṇu himself took birth as their child, not only in his incarnation as Kṛṣṇa but as previous avatāras as well. As the son of Vasudeva and Devakī at the end of the Dvāpura Yuga, Kṛṣṇa's life is threatened by Devakī's brother, Kaṃsa, who hears a prophecy that the eighth child of Devakī will slay him. Terrified, Kaṃsa agrees to spare Devakī's life provided that the couple give him all their children immediately after birth so that he can murder them and thereby protect himself. Following this agreement, Kaṃsa imprisons them both and kills Devakī's first six children, until the seventh, Balarāma, is transferred from Devakī's womb to that of Rohinī, another of Vasudeva's wives. Kṛṣṇa then becomes Devakī's eighth foetus, and is born in his divine four-armed form bearing conch, discus, mace and lotus, but after explaining the purpose of his incarnation he assumes the form of an ordinary baby in their arms. Though Kṛṣṇa then spends his infancy and youth with his foster parents in Vraja, he eventually returns to Mathurā, kills Kaṃsa, and liberates his adoring parents from prison. Less popular in devotional poetry and practice than Kṛṣṇa's foster mother, Yaśodā, Devakī nevertheless remains an object of great reverence due to her unique relationship with Kṛṣṇa.

See also: **Balarāma; Kaṃsa; Kṛṣṇa; Languages; Mahābhārata; Mathurā; Purāṇas; Viṣṇu; Yaśodā; Yuga**

TRACY COLEMAN

Further reading

Bryant, Edwin F. (trans.). 2003. *Krishna: The Beautiful Legend of God. Śrīmad Bhāgavata Purāṇa. Book X.* London: Penguin Books.

DEVAMATA, SISTER (1867–1942)

Laura Glenn, who took the name Sister Devamata, was one of the pioneers of the American Vedanta movement. A graduate who had lived in Europe, she attended Swami Vivekananda's lectures and joined the New York Vedanta Society in 1899 in the face of her wealthy family's disapproval. She became the disciple and assistant of Swami Paramananda, the founder of the Boston Vedanta Society. She travelled to India in 1907–9, where, under the guidance of Swami Ramakrishnananda, she met Sarada Devi and other direct disciples of Sri Ramakrishna. She related her experience of living in Madras in *Days in an Indian Monastery* (1927). On her return to the United States, she resumed her work with Swami Paramananda and continued to write and to lecture.

See also: **Ramakrisna Math and Mission; Ramakrishna, Sri; Sarada Devi; Vivekananda, Swami**

GWILYM BECKERLEGGE

Further reading

Jackson, C.T. 1994. *Vedanta for the West: The Ramakrishna Movement in the United States.* Bloomington and Indianapolis, IN: Indiana University Press.

DEVĪ MĀHĀTMYA

'Glorification of the Great Goddess'. A seven-hundred verse Sanskrit poem interpolated in the *Mārkaṇḍeya Purāṇa* (81–93), the *Devī Māhātmya* (sixth century CE) is one of the major Śākta scriptures. Also, it is the first text in which the Goddess appears as the object of an independent cult and is no longer the feminine form of male deities. The narration includes three myths. The first describes the fight between Viṣṇu and the asuras (demons) Madhu and Kaiṭabha after the dissolution of the Universe. The two asuras arose from the dirt in Viṣṇu's ear while he was in yogic sleep. Brahmā saw them and invoked the Goddess, who promptly woke Viṣṇu. After a 5,000–year battle, the demons were killed and Viṣṇu built the universe out of their marrow. The second myth tells the slaying of the buffalo-demon Mahiṣa. After practising severe austerities, he obtained invincibility and defeated the devas. But the gods united their powers and created Durgā, who fought against Mahiṣāsura for nine days (navarātri) and defeated him on the tenth, the victorious one (vijayadaśamī). The third myth, possibly extraneous to Vedic culture, narrates the struggle between the goddess and the two asura brothers Śumbha and Niśumbha. After the demons drove the devas out, Durgā assumed her most fierce aspect, Kālī, who slew Caṇḍa and Muṇḍa, the two asura generals (hence her title Cāmuṇḍā), and then let a Śakti rise from each of her forms and killed both Śumbha and Niśumbha.

See also: **Asuras; Brahmā; Durgā; Durgā Pūjā; Kālī and Caṇḍī; Mahiṣa; Purāṇas; Śakti; Veda; Viṣṇu**

FABRIZIO M. FERRARI

Further reading

Coburn, T.B. 1991. *Encountering the Goddess. A Translation of the Devī-Māhātmya and a Study of Its Interpretation*. Albany, NY: State University of New York Press.

Humes, C.A. 2000. 'Is the Devi Mahatmya a Feminist Scripture?' In A. Hiltebeitel and K.M. Erndl, eds, *Is the Goddess a Feminist? The Politics of South Asian Goddesses*. Sheffield: Sheffield Academic Press, 123–150.

DHANURVEDA

Dhanurveda, used specifically to refer to the art of archery and, more generally, the art of warfare, forms one of the four supplementary texts to the Veda, or Upavedas, that deal with essentially non-religious knowledge

The art of archery is praised in the *Ṛgveda* in a hymn to war weapons and the bow and arrow were regarded as the correct weapon of the kṣatriya but the Dhanurveda is more closely connected to the *Yajurveda*. It is believed that Dhanurveda was first revealed to the sages Bhṛgu and Viśvāmitra but other famous Vedic exponents were Droṇa and Paraśurāma. Various contemporary Indian martial arts, for example Thang-ta in East India (Manipur) and Kalaripayattu (Kerala), are believed to be derived from ancient Dhanurveda systems of self-defence. The high point of Kalaripayattu, believed to have been passed down from Paraśurāma through a lineage of teachers, was from the thirteenth to eighteenth centuries, but it was banned by the British in 1793. Today it is enjoying a revival as part of a south Indian cultural renaissance.

See also: **Droṇa; Saṃhitā; Upavedas; Varṇa; Veda**

RON GEAVES

Further reading

Vasishtha's Dhanurveda Samhita. 1991. Text with English translation. J.P. Publishing House.

www.veda.harekrsna.cz/encyclopaedia/prana.htm (accessed 23 March 2006).

DHARMA

The polysemic word dharma can be traced back to the *Ṛgveda*, which even anticipates the forms sanātana dharma (as sanatā dharmāṇi in 3.3.1) and svadharma (as svadharman in 3.21.2). Derived from the root dhṛ, which means to uphold, it constitutes that which makes a thing what it is, either descriptively or prescriptively, and denotes the law of its being. Its primary meanings include: (1) individual religious ordinances or rights (*Ṛgveda* 3.17.1, etc.); (2) the whole body of religious duties (*Aitareya Brāhmaṇa*. 7.17); (3) justice (*Bṛhadāraṇyaka Upaniṣad* 1.4.14); (4) moral virtues to be practised by all human beings (*Arthaśāstra* 1.3.13; *Manusmṛti* 6.92; 10.63); (5) duties specific to one's varṇa (*Manusmṛti* 1.107); (6) duties specific to one's āśrama (*Chāndogya*

Upaniṣad 2.23); (7) duties specific to groups or people as in the expressions strīdharma (duties of women), rājadharma (royal duties), etc.; (8) duties specific to an Age, called yugadharma (*Manusmṛti* 1.85–86); (9) duties common to all human beings, called sāmānya or sādhāraṇa or sāmāsika dharma (*Manusmṛti* 6.92; 10.63); (10) that which is conducive to well-being both here and hereafter (*Vaiśeṣika Sūtra* 1.1.2).

The word dharma has also been used to render the English word 'religion' into the Indian languages, thereby narrowing its connotation. The term 'secular state', for instance, has been designated in the Hindi text of the Indian Constitution as dharma-nirapekṣa-rājya, or a state which is neutral in terms of dharma. This is tantamount to translating the word secular as 'God-less'; unless one is conscious that the word dharma does duty here for the English word 'religion', its connotation of this expression would be hedonistic. Hence it has been proposed that the word dharma-nirapekṣa-rājya should be replaced by the word saṃpradāya-nirapekṣa-rājya, or state neutral as to sect (saṃpradāya) in keeping with the fact that the term 'secular state' arose in a context of Christian sectarian conflict. Deep conceptual difficulties underlie these translation problems, which even carry political implications and have coloured the way the word 'secular' has been understood or not understood in India. There are three strong associations the word 'religion' has in English which do not carry over to dharma: that a religion (1) is conclusive – is final, as the one and only religion; (2) is exclusionary – in that only those who subscribe to that particular religion shall be saved; and (3) is separative – in that one who belongs to one religion cannot belong to another at the same time. In Dharmic discourse these are characteristics of a 'sect' (saṃpradāya) rather than 'religion' (dharma).

The word dharma plays a key role in Hindu axiology, as expressed in the doctrine of the four goals of human life (puruṣārtha) collectively called caturvarga or puruṣārtha-catuṣṭaya. In this respect the usual order in which these four goals are enumerated – dharma, artha, kāma and mokṣa – is doubly significant. To note this double significance one needs to put a mental comma after the first three and view them as representing 'ordinary norms' in contradistinction to the fourth, which may be described as the 'extra-ordinary norm', following Franklin Edgerton. Mokṣa represents the goal of moving beyond saṃsāra, or the world of empirical manifestation, altogether and therefore stands in a class by itself; the other three norms or goals apply to the world as ordinarily lived – the world as saṃsāra. In relation to mokṣa as a goal, dharma serves as a means, implying that a basic plinth of moral living is required for any soteriological structure to rest on. It is for this reason that when sometimes only three goals of life are mentioned – dharma, artha and kāma, then mokṣa is deemed to be subsumed under dharma. However, while the role of dharma is foundational in relation to mokṣa, it is regulative in relation to kāma and artha. That is to say that although all the four goals of life may be independently followed, the pursuit of desires (kāma) and the pursuit of wealth and power (artha) should be subject to moral norms, although they are ends worthy of being followed on their own.

Such dharma or virtue, however, to which life should be subject, may not always be a straightforward matter and its determination requires subtlety. Moreover, dharma has to be constantly assessed and understood afresh as no two moral situations are absolutely alike. Hence the constant discussion about dharma, or what is the right thing to do, in Hindu texts. The course of virtue may be sublime but it is not obvious, and sometimes it may even prove to be counterintuitive. In any case complications could be caused by such factors as the following:

(1) Norms of conduct presuppose normal conditions; exceptional circumstances may call for exceptions. These cases are covered by the category of āpad-dharma or conduct appropriate in a crisis; thus Viśvāmitra is famously known to have eaten dogmeat in a famine.
(2) Times change, and conduct appropriate in one age may be deemed inappropriate in another. Thus the practice of levirate (niyoga) was considered appropriate in former times but is deemed inappropriate in Kali-Yuga (yugavarjya), although Swami Dayananda Saraswati (1824–83) tried to revive it.
(3) Times may change even within a yuga, in the spirit of 'new occasions teach new duties, time makes ancient good uncouth'.
(4) Dharma pertains to the spirit rather than the letter, hence taking Dharmic injunctions literally may result in loss of dharma. A sage who told the literal truth to a group of robbers about the direction in which their potential victims had fled earnt the karmic guilt of their death and ended up in hell.

See also: **Arthaśāstra; Āśramas (stages of life); Dayanand(a) Saraswati, Swami; Niyoga; Puruṣārthas; Saṃpradāya; Strīdharma; Varṇa; Yuga**

ARVIND SHARMA

Further reading

Kane, P.V. 1968–77. *History of Dharmaśāstra*, 2nd edn, 5 vols. Poona: Bhandarkar Oriental Research Institute.

Matilal, B.K. 1989. *Moral Dilemmas in the Mahābhārata*. Shimla: Indian Institute of Advanced Study, in association with Motilal Banarsidass, Delhi.

DHARMA SABHA

An 'assembly' for the promotion or preservation of 'dharma'. In the pre-colonial era, it is thought that such assemblies, which were constituted by a group of learned brāhmaṇas, sought to interpret the precepts of the *Dharmaśāstras* in a variety of religious and civil matters. These could include, for example, issues relating to the duties and privileges of a caste group or the inheritance of a paternal estate. The decisions of the Dharma Sabha could, therefore, be utilised within the regulation of caste disputes or could in fact be applied as the actual law administered within the civil or criminal judiciary of a given region. In the early nineteenth century, however, the character and function of the Dharma Sabha changed dramatically, as it instead became an institution closely linked with the Indian movement to protect and revive a conception of sanātana dharma ('eternal religion') based in the tenets of the Veda and *Purāṇa*s. As such, the Dharma Sabha was imbued primarily with a cultural relevance within a colonial context, rather than simply a juridical one. The Dharma Sabhas of the nineteenth century were usually composed of a variety of individuals, including the traditional brāhmaṇa intelligentsia, often together with members of the emerging middle class (known as the bhadralok in Bengal), who worked jointly to promote a 'return' to a more orthodox form of Hinduism. Primarily, it was the perception that the norms and values of Hinduism were coming under threat from Christian missionaries and British liberal reformers, as well as from Indian reformers such as Rammohan Roy and Dayananda Saraswati, which drove this 'revival' of a 'traditional' Hinduism through the mechanism of the Dharma Sabha.

Such a revival, however, needs to be understood not simply as a 'return' to older beliefs and practices, but rather as an active re-making, or re-interpretation, of the cultural significance of Hindu practices and the tenets of Sanskritic knowledge systems in the light of the changes wrought upon Indian society by British political hegemony. Indeed, it may be argued that the Dharma Sabhas played a significant role in the actual construction, or perhaps systematisation, of many modern Hindu religious norms and practices. Moreover, those associated with the Dharma Sabhas were amongst the earliest proponents of a newly articulated and overtly political Hindu identity – an identity clearly opposed to much of British cultural and, by extension, political intervention in the subcontinent.

The earliest example of the nineteenth-century incarnation of the Dharma Sabha can be found in Calcutta. It was here that the liberal governor-general William Bentinck (1828–35) attempted to impose wide-ranging cultural and religious reforms upon Indian society. In particular, Bentinck's desire to abolish the rite of sati (the immolation of a widow on her husband's funeral pyre) as a necessary 'humanitarian' intervention in degraded Hindu 'superstition' provoked furious debate among Calcutta-based intellectuals. Reformers such as Rammohan Roy agreed with the government's position, arguing that sati was indeed an aberration within Hindu religious practice. In contrast, intellectuals such as Radhakant Deb and Ramkamal Sen, who were associated with the Calcutta Dharma Sabha (founded in 1830–1 explicitly as a reaction against Bentinck's policies), argued for the validity of sati on the basis that it was clearly sanctioned in the Sanskrit texts. As such, they deplored the colonial government's 'interference' in matters of essentially religious concern. In essence, the Calcutta Dharma Sabha attempted to draw upon the authority of scriptural 'tradition' to define Hindu religious practice and insulate it from the variety of radical reformers present in Calcutta at the time. To make their views known, the Dharma Sabha submitted petitions to government and also published in a variety of media, including pamphlets, to shape public opinion. Yet the Calcutta Dharma Sabha was not simply concerned with the issue of sati, for its members also worked to promote the increased representation of Indians in the civil service, as well as the uplift of the poor.

By the later half of the nineteenth century, the Dharma Sabha had become a widespread organisational mechanism by which the interests of 'Hindu orthodoxy' were promoted in India. Often the immediate impetus for the formation of a Dharma Sabha during this period was the perceived threat of missionary activity or Hindu reform. In Benares, for instance, the presence of Dayananda Saraswati, and in particular his attacks upon the authority of purāṇic texts and practices as valid expressions of 'Hinduism', spurred the establishment of the Kashi Dharma Sabha in about 1869. Indeed, in that same year the paṇḍits associated with the Dharma Sabha met Dayananda in a now-famous debate (śāstrārtha) on the subject of the validity of image worship. Yet the members of the Dharma Sabha also undertook a variety of other activities intended to establish their views of Hindu religious orthodoxy. In each case, reference to canonical Sanskrit texts and the respect in which the organisation's preeminent paṇḍits were held were the keys to authorising this particular vision. For example, members of the Kashi Dharma Sabha issued vyavasthās ('pronouncements') on contentious points of religious practice, such as the validity of Brahmo marriage and issues of ritual procedure.

Many of the Dharma Sabhas which were established in India during the late nineteenth century held only local or regional influence, and may have been short-lived responses to particular perceived cultural 'threats'. The establishment of the Bharat Dharma Mahamandala in 1887 by Pandit Din Dayalu

Sharma, however, provided an overarching infrastructure through which these local assemblies were able to extend and fortify their cultural influence. By the early twentieth century, the Dharma Sabha had indeed become a sophisticated mechanism for the propagation of Hindu 'orthodoxy' through annual meetings and melas (fairs), publication, debate and the lobbying of government.

See also: **Bharat Dharma Mahamandala; Brahman; Caste; Dayananda Saraswati, Swami; Dharma; Dharmaśāstras; Image worship; Purāṇas; Roy, Rammohan; Sanātana Dharma; Sati; Sharma, Pandit Din Dayalu; Veda**

MICHAEL S. DODSON

Further reading

Dalmia, V. 1997. *The Nationalization of Hindu Traditions: Bharatendu Harischandra and Nineteenth-Century Banaras.* Delhi: Oxford University Press.

Kopf, D. 1969. *British Orientalism and the Bengal Renaissance: The Dynamics of Indian Modernization, 1773–1835.* Berkeley, CA: University of California Press.

DHARMAŚĀSTRAS

From the early centuries CE onwards, the prose *Dharmaśāstras*, belonging to the Vedic ancillary literature of the *Kalpasūtras*, gave way to *Dharmaśāstras* in verse form. In contrast to the *Dharmasūtras*, the *Dharmaśāstras* no longer belong to a specific Vedic school and so are not linked with particular ritual traditions, but concentrate on the study of dharma in its broadest sense. Their rules are intended to be authoritative for everyone – not just those belonging to a particular school – and enlarge the range of dharma, in content as much as in scope, alongside the specialisation which made it an independent discipline.

Certain disciplines became independent of the system of competing ritual schools early on: first grammar (vyākaraṇa – no grammatical treatise surviving belongs to a Vedic school), then astronomy (jyotiṣa), then dharma. To secure acceptance, such works were ascribed divine origin and given the names of ancient sages. Thus the earliest and best-known *Dharmaśāstra*, the *Mānavadharmaśāstra* or *Manusmṛti* ('Laws of Manu'), is assigned to Manu Vaivasvata, traditionally the first mortal king; in its present form, though, it probably belongs to around the second century CE.

Some scholars consider it a reworking of an old *Dharmaśāstra* originally attached to the *Kalpasūtra* of the Mānava school (part of the Maitrāyaṇī school of the Black Yajurveda), but serious divergences between certain rules of *Manusmṛti* and the rituals of the Mānava school tend to invalidate this hypothesis. Among its sources was in fact the *Gautamadharmasūtra.* The work itself does not claim to be the direct revelation of Manu but the exposition made by Bhṛgu, the great sage, of the law of Brahmā, as he had heard it from the mouth of Manu. The *Manusmṛti* should thus be attributed, not to Manu, but to Bhṛgu, or at least should be considered as Bhṛgu's recension of the *Mānavadharmaśāstra*, as some late texts actually call it.

The contents of the *Manusmṛti* may serve as a sample of the genre. Its four main divisions, identified by Olivelle (2005), deal with the creation of the world, sources of dharma, the dharma of the four varṇas, and the law of karma, including rebirth, but these are rather obscured by the traditional division into twelve chapters. The first and last chapters are in many ways parallel, forming a frame to the rest. Chapter 1 opens with the great sages coming to Manu and asking him to expound the dharmas of all the castes, to which Manu replies by describing the creation of the world by Brahmā and his own birth; it then establishes the law of karma and locates within it the creation of the various classes of beings. The last chapter returns to the law of karma to explain how, depending on their past deeds, individuals are reborn as various classes of beings, particularly humans and animals.

Chapters 2–6 treat the same topics as the older texts and in the same order as most of them. Chapter 2, after expounding the sources of dharma (the whole Veda, the tradition and practice of those who know the Veda, the usages of virtuous men and self-satisfaction or conscience), lists the main saṃskāras (rites of passage) from birth to initiation and details the conduct of the brahmacārin (celibate Vedic student). Chapter 3 deals with the householder (gṛhastha), marriage and śrāddha (funerary and memorial rituals); chapter 4 describes the householder's means of livelihood, miscellaneous rules of daily life, Vedic study, the moral framework of life, the avoidance of sin and preparation for the third stage of life; chapter 5 deals with forbidden food, ritual impurity and mourning, purification of individuals and objects, and the duties of women. Chapter 6, which is much the shortest, deals with the last two stages of life but a significant development is seen: whereas the *Dharmasūtras*, while recognising the four styles of life (āśrama), presented them as options open to the student after he has completed his basic education, here they are definitely presented as successive stages.

Chapters 7–9 diverge most from the *Dharmasūtras* and in fact have analogies with the *Arthaśāstra* of Kauṭilya. Chapter 7 deals with rājadharma, the proper way for a king to rule; Manu here often encroaches on the field of politics, showing the important place that brāhmaṇas had gained in kings' counsels. Chapters 8 and 9 are more original (and generally considered late additions to the work), being devoted to the regulation of private litigation submitted to royal justice, including rules of procedure and evidence, especially ordeals. The king's duties envisaged include administering justice, which approaches pure law but still seeks to impose graded punishment according to the offender's varṇa. This section concludes with a brief account of the duties of vaiśyas and śūdras.

Chapter 10 then deals with mixed castes, the rules of occupation in relation to caste, and occupation in time of distress (āpaddharma). In his theory of mixed castes, Manu proposes an elaborate system of marriages between varṇas, producing in their various combinations the many castes (jāti), which were by then the actual social divisions rather than the four classes (varṇa), and which were in many cases occupational groups or guilds that had adopted the closed pattern of endogamy typical of a jāti; the scheme is artificial but it brings the theory into line with actual practice while appearing to do the opposite. It is here too that Manu lists the warlike peoples on the fringes of Indian culture, including the Yavanas, Śakas and Pahlavas, as lapsed kṣatriyas who have lost their status through neglect of dharma, and by this legal fiction opens up the possibility of their reception into the Aryan community again by adopting orthodox behaviour and performing appropriate expiatory sacrifices; thus their actual status as rulers (*c.* second century BCE to second century CE) can be given religious approval, provided they acknowledge the brāhmaṇas as religious leaders. The *Manusmṛti* may be a theoretical textbook but the practicalities of life are not overlooked, and this is an attitude which has in fact marked later Indian legal theory as well.

The concept of āpad (distress) recognises the inevitability of human shortcomings, providing both an ideal standard and more practical guidance. Manu lays down – here and elsewhere – first a few general principles and then a whole series of exceptions. For example,

Manu declares that brāhmaṇas should study the Veda and vaiśyas should trade; in extremity, however, a brāhmaṇa may engage in trade, but not in all the things that vaiśyas trade; he may not sell sesame seed, for example, but in certain circumstances he may sell it, and, finally, if he does sell it in the wrong circumstances, he will become a worm sunk in dog's urine (10.75–91). The apparent inconsistencies are in fact more nearly a recognition of reality.

The whole of chapter 11 reflects the attitudes of the *Dharmasūtras*, while the part on penances and the classification of sins has many analogies with another early *Dharmaśāstra,* the *Viṣṇusmṛti.* Chapter 12 returns to the same kind of topics as chapter 1. It begins with a classification of the acts resulting from the various human conditions, explains how the three guṇas influence transmigration, specifies the penalties in the next life awaiting those who commit culpable actions and, by contrast, enumerates the deeds which secure supreme bliss. For brāhmaṇas these are austerity and sacred knowledge, that is, knowing the Veda and dharma.

There are many parallels to verses of Manu in both the *Mahābhārata* and the *Rāmāyaṇa*, probably borrowed from a common source in the earlier parts but also, especially in Mbh.13, showing knowledge of our present text of Manu or something very like it. In some respects, for example the attitude to ahiṃsā, Manu belongs to a period of transition, in which older and later doctrines are found side by side. It is an attempt at reaffirming the older tradition while reorienting it around new values, and is a prime example of the brāhmaṇa response to the crisis undergone by orthodoxy in the previous few centuries. While Manu is still largely a textbook about how human life should be lived, later *Dharmaśāstras* come closer to being purely legal textbooks. Besides the *Viṣṇusmṛti*, major *Dharmaśāstras* after Manu are those of Yājñavalkya and Nārada, which date from the Gupta period (fourth to sixth centuries CE) or later.

See also: **Ahiṃsā; Arthaśāstra; Āśramas (stages of life); Brahmā; Brahmacaryā; Brāhmaṇas; Dharma; Dharmaśāstras; Gārhasthya; Guṇas; Jāti; Jyotiṣa; Kalpasūtras; Karma; Kauṭilya; Mahābhārata; Manu; Rāja; Rāmāyaṇa; Saṃskāras; Śrāddha; Varṇa; Veda; Vivāha; Vyākaraṇa; Women, status of; Yājñavalkya**

JOHN BROCKINGTON

Further reading

Derrett, J.D.M. 1973. *Dharmaśāstra and Juridical Literature.* Wiesbaden: Harrassowitz.

Kane, P.V. 1962–75. *History of Dharmaśāstra,* 5 vols. Poona: Bhandarkar Oriental Research Institute.

Lariviere, Richard W. (ed. and trans.). 2003. *The Nāradasmṛti,* 2nd edn. Delhi: Motilal Banarsidass.

Lingat, Robert. 1973. *The Classical Law of India.* Berkeley, CA: University of California Press.

Olivelle, Patrick (ed. and trans.). 2005. *Manu's Code of Law: A Critical Edition and Translation of the* Mānava-Dharmaśāstra. New York: Oxford University Press.

Rocher, Ludo. 1993. 'Law Books in an Oral Culture: The Indian *Dharmaśāstras*'. *Proceedings of the American Philosophical Society* 137: 254–67.

Wezler, Albrecht. 1982. 'Manu's Omniscience: On the Interpretation of Manusmṛti II.7'. In G.-D. Sontheimer and P. K. Aithal, eds, *Indology and Law: Studies in Honour of Professor J. Duncan M. Derrett.* Wiesbaden: Franz Steiner Verlag, 79–205.

DHARMASŪTRAS

The *Dharmasūtra*s are the earliest literature of dharma. Unlike the verse *Dharmaśāstra*s which succeeded them, they are in the concise prose typical of *sūtras.* They are included among the *Kalpasūtras,* and attached to schools of the Veda, although they are not primarily concerned with ritual. Topics include the sources of dharma, upanayana, Veda study, the āśramas (but not as a succession of four stages) (Olivelle 1993: 73–93), food, purity, means of livelihood, marriage, succession, property, the dharma of women, penances, punishments and duties of a king. As with all Vedic texts, their chronology is very uncertain. As a rough estimate they can be placed around the second half of the last millennium BCE, starting with the *Gautama Dharmasūtra* around 600 BCE (Kane 1968–77, 1: 19–142).

See also: **Āśramas (stages of life); Dharma; Kalpasūtras; Upanayana; Veda**

DERMOT KILLINGLEY

Further reading

Kane, Pandurang Vaman. 1968–77. *History of Dharmaśāstra (Ancient and Mediæval Religious and Civil Law)*, 2nd edn, 5 vols (vols 1, 2 and 5 bound in two parts each). Poona [Pune]: Bhandarkar Oriental Research Institute (1st edn 1930–62).

Olivelle, Patrick. 1993. *The Āśrama System: The History and Hermeneutics of a Religious Institution.* New York: Oxford University Press.

DHENUKA

A ferocious anthropophagous demon living in the Talavan forest, near Vṛndāvana.

According to the myth (*Harivaṃśa* 69; *Bhāgavata Purāṇa* 10. 15; *Viṣṇu Purāṇa* 5. 8), Dhenuka was killed by the hand of Balarāma, who went in the palm grove with Kṛṣṇa to pick up some fruit. The two brothers were attacked by Dhenuka in the form of an ass who started violently kicking Balarāma in the chest with his hooves. The hero grasped the demon by the heels and started to whirl him around until he was dead. The carcass of the ass was then cast on to the top of a palm tree. Several ass-demons came to vindicate Dhenuka but they were all killed in the same way and the trees were burdened with dead asses. According to Vaiṣṇava devotees, the killing of Dhenuka by Balarāma represents the victory of truth over ignorance and the acknowledgement of one's spiritual identity.

See also: **Balarāma; Kṛṣṇa; Vaiṣṇavism**

FABRIZIO M. FERRARI

Further reading

Bryant, E.F. 2003. *Krishna: The Beautiful Legend of God: Srimad Bhagavata Purana, Book X*. London: Penguin.

DHṚTARĀṢṬRA

The eldest son of King Vicitravīrya and half-brother to Pāṇḍu. Born blind after his mother could not bear to look upon the frightening visage of the sage Vyāsa who fathered the child on the king's behalf, he was not considered fit to rule and was replaced on the throne by Pāṇḍu. Dhṛtarāṣṭra eventually attained the kingdom after his childless brother renounced it and retired to the Himālayas, cursed by a sage to die if ever he attempted to have intercourse. Dhṛtarāṣṭra had 100 sons, known collectively as the Kauravas, by his wife Gāndhārī, who was delivered of a great ball of matter that was divided and placed in a hundred jars to gestate. It is after both brothers renounced the throne due to their respective afflictions that their sons began to compete with each other for the right to rule, thus leading to the conflict known as the *Mahābhārata*. The *Bhagavadgītā* begins with the literary device of the king's minister and charioteer Sanjaya recounting to the blind Dhṛtarāṣṭra the events on the battlefield. The king and his wife outlived the conflict and eventually died in a forest fire.

See also: **Bhagavadgītā; Kauravas; Mahābhārata; Pāṇḍu; Vyāsa**

RON GEAVES

Further reading

Dasgupta, Madhusraba. 1999. *Samsad Companion to the Mahābhārata*. Calcutta: Sahitya Samsad.

DHYĀNA

See: **Meditation**

DIASPORA

Hindu populations are gradually growing in several countries despite the conventional curbs on travelling overseas. We can divide worldwide Hindus into five categories: Hindus living in India and Nepal; Hindus who are outside India and Nepal but are not migrants (e.g. Hindus in Bangladesh and Pakistan); Hindus who are migrants but have been living in their homelands for many generations (e.g. in Fiji, Guyana, Sri Lanka, Trinidad and Tobago, Surinam, Republic of South Africa and Kenya); recent migrants (e.g. in Australia, Canada, the UK, the USA) and temporary migrants to countries like UAE and Oman. In the first category, 80.5 per cent (Census of India 2001) of India's population, i.e. 827,578,869 were Hindus, and in the Himalayan kingdom of Nepal Hindus constitute about 90 per cent of its population (adherents.com). In the second category, about 18.5 million Hindus are among the original inhabitants of Bangladesh, Pakistan, Bhutan and (historically) Afghanistan. The majority of these live in Bangladesh. In the third category, about 8 million people travelled to distant lands during the nineteenth and the early part of the twentieth centuries. Among them, there is a sizeable number who migrated again to another country and thus became twice-migrants. This included Hindus who migrated from Uganda to Western countries in 1972, those who migrated from the sugar plantation nations to Western countries like Canada and the United States, and those Surinamese Hindus who chose to migrate to the Netherlands at the time of Surinam's independence in 1975. In the fourth category, the largest number of Hindu migrants is living in the United States (approx. 1.5 million), followed by the United Kingdom (approx. 559,000 according to the 2001 UK Census). In the last category, many workers, traders and engineers have been working in the Middle Eastern countries without much hope of settling there permanently and with many constraints on practising their culture there. Hindus in each category have different cultural and political issues confronting them. In the nineteenth and twentieth centuries, migration of Hindus into many countries around the globe has given their community a transnational character, with all the ensuing adaptations and changes.

The expatriate Hindus' political success in the sugar plantation countries, their professional success in the Western nations and their financial success in many of their new homelands have been remarkable, thus bringing them recognition in India and abroad. The rise of many Hindus of Indian origin to the premiership and presidency in their new homelands, the brilliance of Indian minds in recent Nobel laureates in medicine, economics and literature, the high socio-economic profile of overseas Hindus in information technology, medicine, engineering, research and in business in general are making these overseas Hindus a well-recognised community. Their somewhat stable social family structure has also earnt them the status of model minority in some parts of the world. Such an extraordinary success in their new homelands has been united with the recent generation of their connection with rising India through Pravasi Bharatiya Divas, new investment opportunities in India and the prospect of regaining their Indian citizenship without losing their own. This seems to be engendering a renewed psychological and emotional tie with India and is recharging their buoyancy in their religious, social and cultural values.

Hinduism abroad

The establishment of transnational Hinduism in countries outside the Indian corridor has resulted from three major factors – migration of Hindus to different countries, preachers of Hinduism and Western individuals who have been fascinated by some aspect of Hinduism. The most noteworthy factor is the dispersion of millions of Hindus in many countries. Second, the visits of many exponents of Hinduism have inspired both Hindus and non-Hindus in many parts of the world. The visit of Swami Vivekananda in the United States in 1893, followed by more recent teachers (Paramhansa Yogananda, Maharishi Mahesh Yogi, Prabhupada A.C. Bhaktivedanta Swami, Swami Muktananda and many others), contributed significantly in sowing and nurturing the seeds of Hindu thought in many countries. In addition, Western thinkers – humanists Ralph Waldo Emerson and Henry David Thoreau, the founder of the Theosophical Society Madame Blavatsky, the theoretical physicist Julius Robert Oppenheimer, the German philosopher Schopenhauer and many others – have been greatly influenced by the *Bhagvad-gītā* and the *Upaniṣads*. These thinkers in turn have reinforced the confidence of the Hindu diaspora in its own heritage and have also influenced many Westerners.

As physical emblems of their religion, Hindus outside India have created many temples and religious centres. As of 2006, there were 716 temples and centres according to a database created by the Harvard University's Pluralism Project. These institutions include temples for worshipping and performing rituals, self-help centres for practising yoga and meditation and ashrams for philosophical discourses. Most of the temples accommodate multiple deities for catering to the needs of diverse Hindu communities living in their areas. There are a few temples where Jains and Sikhs have also joined hands in sharing the same premises. Although Hindus from the northern and southern parts of India have often built separate temples, all Hindu devotees visit each other's temples occasionally to pay their homage. Many Hindu temples, especially in Western countries, have an attached cultural centre where the local communities disseminate various aspects of the Hindu culture to members of their younger generations. These cultural aspects crisscross their religion in interesting ways. Imparting instruction in such classical lore is considered an essential part of preserving their religious traditions.

Most Hindus have a small temple in their homes where they have a few images of their favourite deities. A widespread ritual that one can see in many families is paying obeisance to deities during morning and/or evening hours and to a lesser extent reciting ārtī – a standard prayer. Some houses have a full room dedicated to the family deities. It is common to find the images of Lord Buddha and Guru Nanak included in these Hindu temples and sometimes one can also see an image of Jesus Christ placed side by side.

Most Hindu families periodically perform religious worship with relatives and friends, often known as pūjā. Recitation from a holy book, worshipping the deities, and singing devotional songs often mark such occasions. Elaborate food is often served as prasāda (literally meaning divine grace) after the pūjā. One can see people from diverse sects coming together to partake in the pūjā and staying for a meal and the accompanying socialisation. Such events thus expose everyone to each other's way of worshipping. Children and older members of the family are also invited. In such get-togethers the broad ethnic and religious identity of every Hindu is reinforced. Also, one can see some sort of standardisation developing in the ways of conducting worship. For example, the recitation of *Rāmacaritamānasa* is becoming the most frequent form of doing pūjā among Punjabi- and Hindi-speaking Hindus in many countries.

The role of *Rāmacaritamānasa* in the preservation of Hinduism in sugar plantation colonies merits special mention. Indentured labourers and their descendants looked upon this book as their ultimate holy book and they listened to the versified story of Rāma and his divine acts with rapt attention and reverence. The language in which *Rāmacaritamānasa* is written is Avadhi and its recitation has a conventional melody to it. Listening to its recitation used to be a common community pastime in the earlier generations and it thus played a seminal role in preserving Hinduism there. It was especially true in the wake of the activities of Christian evangelism which were widespread in all these colonies. These labourers understood Avadhi as it was close to their own heritage languages. The prevalence of *Rāmacaritamānasa* in many other Hindu communities around the world is a more recent phenomenon and is interesting from the viewpoint of language. Very few of these devotees really understand the language in which *Rāmacaritamānasa* is written but reciting it and listening to it is simply a part of their religiosity.

One interesting aspect of pūjā gatherings is the role of one's ethnic language in inviting guests. It is easy to see on such occasions that most invitees are from the same speech community, provided the community's local demographics permit this. One can also observe that Punjabi and Hindi communities are often indistinguishable. In such assemblies, it is impossible to distinguish between Hindus, Jains and clean-shaven Sikhs. A few other Sikhs can also be seen. All of the guests, irrespective of their religious orientation, show reverence for the religious performances and they intermingle freely for socialisation. This sort of intermingling, to whatever extent it may be, is bringing Hindus and others together into a more cohesive community. Sometimes in some families one can also see a few others who are Christians, Jews and Muslims. In Guyana and Trinidad, one sees some Muslim members of the immediate community participating in such Hindu pūjā ceremonies. If a host family cannot find a sufficient number of guests from their own local speech community it will invite Hindus from other speech communities in the area. Compatibility in socioeconomic status does play its usual role in the selection of all guests. In India, in most cases, the process of selecting one's guests from one's own speech community happens automatically due to the linguistic organisation of states. However, in the case of overseas Hindu communities, it is interesting to see how language and culture continue to play a combined role (cf. Fisher 1980).

Most of the religious literature is available in everyone's traditional language, written in its traditional script. In some homes, one can find a few things in Sanskrit in Devanagari script. In the case of some religious groups like Sathya Sai Baba centres, where the congregations are drawn from across linguistic boundaries, the religious literature of devotional songs is often in Hindi and Sanskrit languages but always scripted in Roman. They also have some devotional songs in English which they recite with Indian tunes. Many families would also have some devotional songs and ārtī in Roman script in order to accommodate members of the younger generation, who have often lost a functional knowledge of their heritage language and almost always the knowledge of the script in which their heritage language is written.

Rituals in Hindu diaspora

Over thousands of years, Hindus in their motherland amassed many religious beliefs and rituals. When leaving India for relocation in other countries they took their beliefs, notions of ritual practices, their holy books and some limited supplies for performing rituals. They also carried with them their non-material culture in the form of food habits, languages and their notions of family, caste system, social customs, festivals and pilgrimage, etc. Out of all these aspects of their culture, elements related to religion have been attested to as the best-preserved constituents and the heritage language as the least-preserved constituent (Gambhir 1988).

Rituals, especially in the diaspora context, fulfil a useful function of preserving an attachment with the heritage culture. The variation that one sees from region to region is overwhelming. Jhungare (2004), following earlier anthropologists, maintains a useful distinction between 'Great Traditions' and 'Little Traditions' for discussing the Hindu religious traditions in Minnesota, USA. For a variety of reasons, the 'Little Traditions' gradually submit themselves to Sanskritisation. An empirical analysis shows that, overall, both types of beliefs that have been part of the religious and cultural traditions of transnational Hindu communities undergo changes. Activities that need to happen publicly are affected much more than the intramural activities. The establishment of Hindu temples and having a native priest there to manage religious procedures allow many rituals to continue for a generation or two but sooner or later these rituals are considerably simplified. The first-generation members show more knowledge about the performance of rituals but elaborate aspects are gradually lost over generations. The reasons for the gradual loss include absence of training for subsequent generations of priests, no easy availability of many items for performing rituals and the lack of permission to perform certain activities due to property insurance constraints in some countries. Another factor that is contributing to the simplification process is the changing lifestyle of people everywhere.

Even in the first generation of Hindu immigrants, most families seem to perform fewer saṃskāras ('standard rituals') than they did in their mother country. Two prominent saṃskāras that continue to be performed for obvious reasons are the wedding ceremony and the final rite, though with many changes associated with them. Whether in the Caribbean or North America, both of these rituals have shorter durations. They have also incorporated some local customs in them. In weddings in the USA, for example, the inclusion of bridesmaids, speeches by siblings and friends about the bride and bridegroom's accomplishments (often interspersed with a humorous commentary), DJs and dances, etc. are new elements in wedding ceremonies. In intramural rituals, the performance of havan ('fire-worship') is becoming more symbolic, with the help of a candle etc. rather than with agni ('sacred fire'). The restriction on the use of fire inside buildings due to insurance regulations is the main reason for this type of change. Many other customs such as barāt ('bridegroom's processions') with all the music and fanfare, stealing the bridegroom's shoes, ghaṛaulī (prevalent in some regional weddings only), ḍolii ('bride's caravan') and welcoming the newly-weds with elaborate rituals at the entrance of the house are often not seen, especially in urban settings. Similarly, religious rituals at the time of death have also been greatly simplified and/or changed. The cremation of dead bodies, particularly in Western countries, is in electric crematoria. Once again, speeches in honour of the departed soul can be seen in Western settings and bereavement in the form of crying publicly is unusual. Jacobsen (2004) provides interesting details of re-creating new places of pilgrimage by the Sri Lankan Hindu community in Norway. Similar re-creations have also happened in the Caribbean countries where Hindus live in large numbers.

Both in the mother country and in new homelands around the world, there are some families, and in them some individuals, who are deeply engrossed in the performance of elaborate religious rituals. These are usually 'ones pursuing the path of devotion predominantly'. These include some women who do not work outside the home. Such devotees often pursue a complex path of performing rituals on a daily basis. They will give a bath to their deities every day, change their clothes, clean their jewellery and will provide food to them before they serve food to their family members or to themselves. There are others who regard their family deities so reverentially that they take them along during their travels. On the other end of the spectrum there are some Hindus who consider themselves 'ones pursuing the path of knowledge predominantly' and observe minimum rituals in their day-to-day lives. They are more interested in understanding their scriptures on an intellectual level. Most people lie in between these two extremes. Many Hindus in this middle class are showing stronger signs of offering brief prayers and minimum rituals. They are trying to incorporate yoga and meditation as a means of contributing to their material and spiritual well-being.

A new group of Hindu gurus in the West are adding a new dimension to the performative dimension of Hinduism. Many of these gurus are engrossed in elaborate rituals. A.C.Bhaktivedanta Swami Prabhupada's International Society for Krishna Consciousness (ISKCON) is an important example of this. Their disciples, both Westerners and Indians, can be seen performing rituals in a comprehensive way. Swami Dayananda Saraswati's Arsha Vidya Gurukulam in the Pocono Mountains of Pennsylvania is another such place. Although philosophical discourses on Advaita Vedānta and the *Bhagavadgītā* dominate their activities, on special occasions they perform elaborate rituals in a temple on their premises. The temple is dedicated to Sri Medha Dakshinamurthi and Gaṇeśa and has two resident priests to take care of all religious procedures.

However, looking beyond this, it is likely that members of the second and subsequent generations will visit these places less frequently and will be less open to elaborate religious practices. With online ārtīs, pūjā and explanation of many rituals, there seems to be easy access to many rituals. The Hindu students on college campuses in the US, for example, benefit from such online descriptions in English and thus celebrate Hindu festivals like Dīvālī on their campuses. The new multimedia technology will certainly have some impact on later generations in the use and preservation of some of these rituals.

Caste among overseas Hindus

The caste system is very intricately woven in Hindu society in India and Nepal and many consider it an integral part of Hinduism. Within a class (varṇa) there are many castes (jāti). Although social interaction between different classes is considerably reduced in urban settings in India, marriage outside one's caste is more of an exception. In rural areas, social interaction between higher castes and lower-caste members is often limited to work settings. There are some marriages between the middle two castes – kṣatriyas and vaiśyas – but marriages of brāhmaṇas and śūdras are more or less within their own communities.

In the overseas communities, these social demarcations have been breached significantly from very early on for very practical reasons. In the context of sugar plantation colonies, the concept of 'jahājī bhāī' (bonding produced by travelling together in the same ship) overtook class considerations. The size of the total Hindu community in any one place is often too small and the size of classes and castes within that community is further undersized. Religious interaction and finding life partners within one's own small community have often been difficult. In countries like Guyana, Trinidad and Surinam in the Caribbean area and in African countries, Hindus have based their decisions of marriage and other social interaction more on socioeconomic factors than on any caste-related factors. In these overseas communities, little consciousness about classes and almost none about castes remains. Some priests are still recognised as brāhmaṇas because of their connection with priestly roles. A similar situation has been reported regarding Mauritius and Fiji. A northern and southern divide has also been reported for Fiji (Buchignani 1980) and a similar divide also seems to exist in Mauritius. In Mauritius, there is some evidence that the caste system is re-emerging in a limited way and this is due to the increasing interaction between the peoples of Mauritius and India. In the United States, the Kannada Hindu community is another interesting example of the disappearance of caste boundaries. Personal interviews with some Hindu Karnataka families reveal that the low-caste Liṅgāyats, who used to bury their dead bodies in India, have started cremating them in the USA for two reasons. First, it costs less to cremate than to bury a dead body in the USA and, second, Hindu Brāhmaṇa priests who will not perform rituals in the house of a lower-caste member in India are reported to be available to perform any rituals in their houses in the United States. Personal interviews also report marriages between individuals of these different castes of Kannada Hindus.

In the first generation of Hindu immigrants in the United States notions of caste may exist conceptually to some extent but in the second generation its importance is positively reduced. In a face-to-face interaction within a group of about twenty Hindi-speaking Hindu men and women, I found that theoretically almost everyone preferred their children to marry within their own castes. Realising, however, that this may not be possible given the small size of the community, people were clear about their second preference – a Hindu who speaks the same Indic language as they do. When pressed further, their consensus on the third preference was a Hindu from the northern region of India and the fourth preference was any Hindu. In the continuing dialogue, it became clear that if the children are going to marry someone outside the Hindu community the parents' first preference would be a white person of Jewish or Christian background. Someone in the group echoed the thoughts of everyone in the group when he threw his hands in the air and said that, beyond the fourth possibility, whatever happens will happen but they don't want to think about it. Everyone also agreed with the idea that parents in general had very little control in determining the choice of spouse for their children. I also met with about twenty-five second-generation college-bound young men and women separately and it became clear that they did not have the same caste considerations as their parents would have in the selection of their future spouse. About 50 per cent said with a smile on their faces that they wanted to see their parents happy and they would do their best to keep their ideas and instructions in mind to the extent possible.

Neo-sects of Hinduism

Many new sects have emerged both in and outside India. These are founded by gurus who interpret Hindu scriptures and principles to their followers. Most of the neo-sects that originated in India also have their chapters, in the form of religio-social movements, in many other countries. These include the Arya Samaj, Ramakrishna Mission, Sri Chinmoy Mission, Sathya Sai Baba centres, Baba Muktananda's Siddha Yoga Foundation, Radhasoami Satsang Beas and the two Swaminarayan sects. Many other sects originated in the West with a Western following but have gradually attracted Indian immigrants also to their fold. Some of these are Swami Yogananda's Self-Realisation Fellowship, Maharishi Mahesh's Transcendental Meditation, Prabhupada's ISKCON, Swami Ram's Himalayan Institute, Swami Dayananda Saraswati's Arsha Vidya Gurukulam and Swami Tadatmananda's Arsha Bodha Center. There are many more such organisations that have surfaced all over the world. Many of the ashrams founded by these spiritual gurus provide a retreat where rich Hindu devotees can go and participate in the activities. Many families are often happier with this new crop of religious centres as the gurus can explain matters related to Hindu scriptures and the Hindu way of life in English, which their children can also understand. An institution like Art of Living, which is not religious, often combines its activities with Hindu philosophical concepts and Sanskrit recitations.

One important aspect that is peculiar to temples and ashrams in Western communities is the direct way of soliciting donations. In India and Nepal this is often not the case. However, particularly in the Western world, inevitable high insurance costs, mortgage payments, salaries of priests, the cost of importing images from India, etc. contribute to the high costs of maintaining such facilities and thus necessitate such solicitations. Some money is also collected through unsolicited donations which devotees make when they visit such centres but this is often not enough to defray all the expenses of maintaining them.

The role of the media and internet in diaspora Hinduism

In many parts of the world morning broadcasts on most of the Indian television channels available through satellites are dedicated to religious discourses by Hindu saints. In more recent times, TV channels like Āsthā and Sanskār are presenting Hinduism in all its facets round the clock. Thousands of CDs and CD-ROMs present devotional songs sung in the melodious voices of first-class artists. These also bring home religious discourses and virtual visits to places of pilgrimage. The role of the internet in disseminating information has proven extraordinary in internationalising almost all aspects of Hinduism. Ranging from the concrete to the conceptual, the exquisite architectural photographs of the Akshardhām temple in New Delhi, the information about the demolition of a Hindu temple in Malaysia, vandalism inflicted on a temple in Minnesota in the United States or else the presentation of a Hindu viewpoint on terrorism in a symposium in Washington, DC – anything happening in any part of the world, once posted on the web or distributed through listserves, becomes available to the global community almost instantly. There are literally thousands of websites covering almost all possible aspects of Hinduism – from rituals to philosophy and from providing information of a local temple to international conferences. There are also websites like Beliefnet.com, which is distributing the wisdom of all religions, including Hinduism. Powerful search engines like Google sort such information with the greatest alacrity, within seconds. As a result, the explosion of information and the synergy of communication are promoting interconnectivity among Hindus of the Indian diaspora by creating open platforms for the sharing of ideas, discussions and rejoinders.

Assertive Hinduism

This is a relatively recent phenomenon in the history of Hinduism that is emerging both in India and in the overseas communities, and one is reinforcing the other. Many Hindu organisations and their members believe that it is important for them to organise politically in order to survive in the world in which they are living. They believe that there are many political and religious forces that would otherwise swallow them. Their financial success is infusing in them the confidence to assert their religious identity and, if need be, to fight for it intellectually, politically and legally. The California school textbook battle in early 2006 is a glaring example of this. The presentation of a Hindu viewpoint in a symposium on terrorism held in Washington, DC, in the early months of 2006 is another example of such assertive Hinduism. Rejoinders to Indic scholarship in universities have also happened in the recent past. There are emerging Hindu intellectuals, especially in Western countries, who contest publicly any writings that they perceive as demeaning to Hinduism. It is interesting that most academics perceive such Hindus as fundamentalists and, on the other hand, Hindus who are engaged in this intellectual battle perceive all such academicians as leftist in their political orientation. A constant battle of ideas is evident between these two groups. The term, Hindutva, is used to express this belligerent form of Hinduism. The term was coined in India and has travelled abroad to refer to hard-line Hindus overseas.

The Hindu Education Foundation (http://www.hindueducation.org/intro.html) and the Infinity Foundation (http://www.infinityfoundation.com/index.shtml) are among the leading organisations which are holding an intellectual dialogue with American academics in South Asian studies. In the words of the former, 'Hindu Education Foundation, an educational project by concerned Indians and Hindus in the USA, strives to replace ... various misconceptions with correct representation of India and Hinduism. Such a true representation becomes necessary in a changing world that continues to be plagued by religious misunderstanding, intolerance, hate and violence.' The Infinity Foundation of Princeton, New Jersey, is leading an intellectual battle with South Asian academics in the US. In its own words, it 'seeks to create dialogue that breaks out of the dualities of anti- and pro-globalization forces, of the right vs. the left, of secularism vs. religion, of science vs. spirituality, of economic growth vs. ecological preservation'. Many other organisations have also cropped up at the national or local level. The Educators Society for the Heritage of India (http://www.eshiusa.org/), for example, is a relatively recent organisation in the New Jersey area and has been very active on the educational front to make sure that what is being taught in school textbooks represents Hinduism in a positive light. They want to ensure that what is being taught to their young children triggers positive images of their religious and cultural heritage.

On another level, institutions such as Hindu Svayamsevak Sangh and Vishwa Hindu Parishad have been vigorously pursuing the organisation of Hindus as a political force around the world. These organisations have existed for a much longer time than any other organisation mentioned above. These are subsidiaries of Rashtriya Swayamsevak Sangh (RSS) in India and draw tremendous support from there, especially in the form of visits from their emissaries from time to time. They inspired the creation of Hindu student councils on many American campuses and they organise camps for Hindu youth. They work vigorously to bring all likeminded forces onto common platforms. They have a tough battle with academicians in the West, who often look upon these organisations as fanatical and opposed to minorities in India. In terms of their local chapters around the world, these two organisations are much more organised than any other Hindu organisation engaged in these hard-line efforts.

Religion and ethnic identity

For most Hindu immigrants, their religion plays a very important role in the formulation of their ethnic identity. An active or passive connection with some god of the Hindu pantheon, participation in family pūjā events, observance of Hindu festivals and to some extent the political aspects of the religion contribute heavily to the structure of their ethnicity as Hindus. For many, vegetarianism also contributes to the formulation of Hindu ideals.

The composition of ethnic identity for the second generation, however, takes a different course. At least for those who are situated in the midst of dominant Western cultures, there is more that goes into the composition of their ethnic identity. It stems from their peer culture, weaker identity with their parents' motherland and stronger identity with the country they have been brought into. From all the observations and many personal interviews, it seems that the religious component continues into the second generation but in a somewhat weakened form. For them, religious practices, visits to Hindu temples and the performance of rituals are considerably simplified and somewhat universalised. Some aspects of Hinduism, however, which have sunk deep down in their psyche have become a permanent part of their worldview. One such aspect is the respect for different modes of worship, whether it is for various modes of worship within Hinduism or outside Hinduism. Even those who are not religious personally seem to be anchored in such a notion.

There are various institutions in the diaspora context that contribute substantially to the reinforcement and nurturing of many notions of Hinduism in its members. Such institutions include Hindu temples, Sunday schools and religious camps organised for youngsters. The notion of religion is thus enforced through many cultural activities. This seems to be true of all religions and Hinduism is no exception. Depending on their previous orientation, their current resources and the availability of source-personnel, Hindu immigrant communities continue to try hard to retain the traditions of their art and culture in their new homelands. These cultural facets are apparently not connected with religion but it seems they do contribute to their religious identity. Young girls learning classical dance need to make salutations to Śiva, Sarasvatī or some other god or goddess. The stories on which such dances are based are almost always rooted in Hindu mythology. There is hardly any aspect of traditional Indian culture that has no links with Hinduism. It may be meditation, Haṭha yoga, Āyurveda or even the study of Sanskrit language. Both insiders and outsiders perceive them to be closely connected with Hinduism.

See also: **Advaita; Africa, Hindus in; Agni; Americas, Hindus in; Antyeṣṭi; Ārtī; Arya Samaj; Āśram(a) (religious community); Australasia, Hindus in; Āyurveda; Bhakti; Blavatsky, Helena; Brāhmaṇas; Buddhism, relationship with Hinduism; Caste; Chinmoy, Sri; Dance; Dayananda Saraswati, Swami; Deities; Dīvālī; Emerson, Ralph Waldo; Europe, Hindus in; Food; Gaṇeśa; Guru; Haṭha Yoga; Hindutva; Image worship; International Society for Krishna Consciousness; Internet; Jainism, relationship with Hinduism; Jāti; Jñāna (as path);**

Maharishi Mahesh Yogi; Mandir; Meditation; Muktananda, Swami; Myth; Nepal, Hindus in; Oceania, Hindus in; Politics; Pūjā; Radhasoami Satsang; Rāma; Ramakrishna Math and Mission; Rashtriya Swayamsevak Sangh; Religious nurture; Saṃskāra; Sarasvatī; Sai Baba, Sathya; Self-Realisation Fellowship; Sikhism, relationship with Hinduism; Śiva; Sound Recordings; Southeast and East Asia, Hindus in; Sri Lanka, Hindus in; Swami Narayana Sampradaya; Television and radio; Tīrthayātrā; Transcendental Meditation; Utsava; Varṇa; Vishwa Hindu Parishad; Vivāha; Vivekananda, Swami; Yoga; Yogananda, Paramhansa

SURENDRA GAMBHIR

Further reading

Buchignani, N. 1980. 'Accommodations, Adaptation, and Policy: Dimensions of the South Asia Experience in Canada'. In Victor Ujimoto and Gordon Hirabayashi, eds, *Visible Minorities and Multiculturalism: Asians in Canada*. Toronto: Butterworths, 121–50.

Eck, D.L. 2000. 'Negotiating Hindu Identities in America'. In H. Coward, J.R Hinnells and R.B. Williams, eds, *The South Asian Religious Diasporas in Britain, Canada, and the United States*. Albany, NY: State University of New York Press.

Fisher, M.P.D. 1980. *Indians of New York City*. Columbia, Missouri: South Asia Books.

Gambhir, S.K. 1988. 'The Modern Indian Diaspora and Language'. In Peter Gaeffke and David Utz, eds, *The Countries of South Asia: Boundaries, Extensions and Interrelations – Proceedings of the South Asia Seminar University of Pennsylvania*. Philadelphia, PA: Dept of South Asia Regional Studies, University of Pennsylvania.

Jacobsen, K.A. and P. Pratap Kumar (eds). 2004. *South Asians in the Diaspora – Histories and Religious Traditions*. Leiden and Boston, MA: Brill.

Jhungare, Indira. 2004. 'The Hindu Religious Traditions in Minnesota'. In Knut A. Jacobsen and P. Pratap Kumar, eds, *South Asians in the Diaspora – Histories and Religious Traditions*. Leiden and Boston, MA: Brill.

Morris, H.S. 1968. *The Indians in Uganda*. London: Weidenfeld and Nicolson.

Schwartz, B.M. (ed.). 1967. *Caste in Overseas Communities*. San Francisco, CA: Chandler Publishing Company.

Stuart-Fox, D. J. 2002. *Pura Besakih – Temple, Religion and Society in Bali*. Leiden: KITLV Press.

Williams, Raymond Brady (ed.). 1992. *A Sacred Thread: Modern Transmission of Hindu Traditions in India and Abroad*. Chambersberg, PA: Anima Publications.

www.pluralism.org. The Pluralism Project, Harvard University.

DIASPORA, ANCIENT AND MEDIEVAL PERIODS

Europe and the Near East

Trade relations between India and the West go back to the hoary antiquity of Harappa and Sumer. At later times Indian wares arrived in the Mediterranean via South Arabia. The Achaemenid Persia annexed the Indus Valley and in Xerxes' army Indian soldiers went as far as Greece. But as far as intellectual contacts are concerned, there is hardly anything worth mentioning for the ancient Near East and pre-Alexander Greece. During the past 200 years many speculations of influence have been offered for Pythagoras, Parmenides, Empedocles, Heraclitus, Plato, etc., but nothing remains after critical examination.

The great turning point in Indo-Western relations was the Indian expedition of Alexander the Great. Though it affected only a limited area of northwest India and was soon forgotten by Indians, it revealed at least some of India's culture and religion to the West. The meeting with Gymnosophists of Taxila led to a living literary tradition of these naked ascetics, extending far into the Middle Ages. But this tradition knew no doctrines; just their hard asceticism was greatly admired.

After Alexander, the intellectual contacts are often hard to show definitely, but not non-existent. There were active relations in trade and politics, with resident or visiting merchants and diplomats. Soon after Alexander, the Seleucid ambassador Megasthenes gave an account of Indian brāhmaṇas and mendicants and related some legends about early history. His text – preserved only in fragments – tends to interpret everything in a Greek light. Thus, according to him, the main gods of India were Heracles and Dionysus (perhaps Kṛṣṇa and Śiva), whose correct identification has long puzzled scholars.

From the Maurya period to the Muslim conquest the area of modern Afghanistan belonged to the Indian cultural sphere. The coins of the Indo-Greek rulers (second to first centuries BCE) show a curious mixture of religions: Greek, Iranian, local and Hindu. The area soon became a stronghold of Buddhism, but the last dynasty before the Muslim rule, the Śāhis, were Hindus.

At least two Greek philosophers visited India, Anaxagoras and Pyrrho participated in Alexander's campaigns, and Pyrrho's Sceptic asceticism was supposedly learnt in India. Much later Sextus Empiricus was familiar with some standard examples of Indian philosophy.

Flavius Philostratus told of Apollonius of Tyana and his fantastic voyage to the mountain of Gymnosophists. The text, however, is full of details borrowed from earlier literature and the Gymnosophists behave and talk like Greek philosophers.

The early centuries CE saw the development of many new doctrines. They were often of a syncretic nature, deriving elements from Egypt, Mesopotamia, Iran, etc. India was probably involved, but even with Gnosticism there is hardly any direct evidence. One Gnostic philosopher, Syrian Bardesanes, came across an Indian embassy on the way to Rome and gave a new account of India and its religion, including a description of Śiva. The Indian layer in Manichaeism is clear, but mainly Buddhist. Neo-Platonism and its relations to Indian thought is an eternal question. Plotinus intended to go to India, but did not. There are clear doctrinal similarities, but no certainty.

The general idea of the intellectual and religious life in India remained vague. There was probably some good information available, but there was also a definite lack of interest and few were familiar with it. In the Middle Ages, India had become a distant fairyland to Europeans. Muslims, though keenly interested in Indian science (astronomy, mathematics, medicine), had no interest in Indian religion and philosophy (with a few notable exceptions such as al-Bīrūnī).

Southeast Asia

Active relations between India and Southeast Asia started at least two millennia ago. There was active trade, even a mission, but no colonisation or large-scale migration. Although Southeast Asia was certainly not a primitive vacuum as was sometimes supposed, the impact of Indian culture was soon felt and in the fifth century it had reached even the remotest regions. But the resulting culture was Indianising, not Indian. Both north and south India participated in this development.

In Southeast Asia it is often difficult to discern between Hindu and (Mahāyāna) Buddhism. Important testimony is given by epigraphy (often in Sanskrit) and archaeology. There are temples (Angkor), images of Buddha and Viṣṇu, Śiva liṅgas. Systems of writing were derived from India. Sanskrit influence was particularly strong in the Mon, Khmer and Champa states, but it was felt as far as the Philippines.

On the mainland, Theravāda Buddhism finally took the upper hand in the thirteenth century, but court ritual remained Hindu (Thailand, Cambodia). Folklore and forms of theatre (puppet) have preserved much Hindu literary tradition (*Rāmāyaṇa*, *Pañcatantra*).

In Indonesia the most striking example of Indianising culture is perhaps the Old Javanese (Kavi) literature, with Indian themes (often from the *Mahābhārata*) and Indian (Sanskrit) vocabulary. Here, too, Hinduism and Buddhism were rivals, but from the thirteenth century on both lost their position with the Islamisation of Indonesia and the Malay Peninsula. Buddhism disappeared and only Bali remained vigorously Hindu until modern times. Still, Indian elements are easily detected in traditional forms of government, vocabulary, shadow theatre, etc.

Central and East Asia

Northwards, too, Indian cultural influence played an important role, but this was almost entirely Buddhist. It was carried through Central Asia to China (and further to Korea and Japan), also to Tibet and Mongolia. With Buddhism many elements of Indic culture were carried: astronomy and mathematics, medicine, artistic expression. In this way, some Hindu mythic elements are found even in modern Japan. The amalgamation of Indian cultural influence was especially strong in Tibet, where Indian classics of grammar, aesthetics, etc. were translated and studied.

Since 400 CE important information on (Buddhist) India is offered in the travel accounts of Chinese Buddhist monks (Faxian, Xuanzang, etc.) who travelled in India visiting holy places and collecting manuscripts.

See also: **Aesthetics; Brāhmaṇas; Buddhism, relationship with Hinduism; Languages; Mahābhārata; Rāmāyaṇa; Southeast and East Asia, Hindus in; Viṣṇu**

KLAUS KARTTUNEN

Further reading

Halbfass, W. 1988. *India and Europe. An Essay in Understanding.* Albany, NY: State University of New York Press.

Karttunen, K. 1989. *India in Early Greek Literature.* Studia Orientalia 65. Helsinki: Finnish Oriental Society.

Karttunen, K. 1997. *India and the Hellenistic World.* Studia Orientalia 83. Helsinki: Finnish Oriental Society.

Sarkar, H.B. 1985. *Cultural Relations between India and Southeast Asian Countries.* Delhi: Indian Council for Cultural Relations and Motilal Banarsidass.

Sarkar, H.B. 1986. *Trade and Commercial Activities of Southern India in the Malayo-Indonesian World.* 1. Calcutta: Firma KLM Private Limited.

DIKPĀLAS (REGENTS OF DIRECTIONS) AND LOKAPĀLAS (WORLD PROTECTORS)

Hindus hold the eight directions of space to be presided over and guarded by eight deities: Indra (East), Agni (Southeast), Yama (South), Nirṛti (Southwest), Varuṇa (West), Vāyu (Northwest), Kubera (North), Iśāna (Northeast). These are Vedic deities that were worshipped long before the later mainstream traditions of Vaiṣṇavism, Śaivism or Śāktism became prominent. Texts like the *Bṛhat saṃhitā*, the *Āgamas* and the *Viṣṇudharmottara Purāṇa* provide detailed description of these figures, which are also frequently represented in sculptures in and on temples, either singly or as groups. Extensive summary descriptions and illustrations of these can be found in Gopinath Rao (1914).

Dikpālas/Lokapālas are sometimes also identified as Dik-gajas, 'elephants of the (eight) directions', associated with the above-named deities as their vahanas (vehicle): Airāvata (Indra), Puṇḍārika (Agni), Vāmana (Yama), Kūmuda (Nirṛti), Añjana (Varuṇa), Puṣpadanta (Vāyu), Sarvabhauma (Kubera) and Supratika (Iśāna). They are often depicted together with these.

The Dikpālas play a role in astrology, where the positioning in their quarters determines influences on persons and events. In astronomy/astrology Sūrya (sun), Śukra (Venus), Śani (Saturn) and Śaṣi (Moon) are called Dikpālas of the East, West, South and North, respectively.

See also: **Agni; Airāvata; Indra; Jyotiṣa; Kubera; Purāṇas; Sacred texts; Śaivism; Śāktism; Sūrya; Vāhanas; Vaiṣṇavism; Varuṇa; Vāyu; Vedic pantheon; Yama**

KLAUS K. KLOSTERMAIER

Further reading

Gopinath Rao, T.A. 1914. *Elements of Hindu Iconography*, vols 2–3. Delhi: Motilal Banarsidass (reprint 1993).

DĪKṢĀ

Dīkṣā is a ceremony of initiation, usually into a particular method of practice or into a particular saṃpradāya. When a person decides to become an ascetic, they first need to find a guru who is willing to take them on. After a period of instruction, they may be deemed ready, by the guru, to undertake full initiation, or dīkṣā, into that particular order. In the case of would-be ascetics, their dīkṣā marks the end of their old life and the beginning of a new one. Therefore, many of the rituals performed symbolise that. The detail of the dīkṣā ceremony may differ from group to group, but there are common features. The initiates conduct their own cremation by lying for a short while on a funeral pyre that they, themselves, have constructed. They then set fire to the pyre, a symbolic gesture that indicates that they have departed their old life and will sever all ties with it. Their body may be shaved, and following the cremation they may immerse themselves in water and take a few steps in a state of nakedness. This represents their birth into a new life. Perhaps the most important part of the dīkṣā ceremony is the guru's passing on of a secret mantra, which is whispered into the initiate's ear. This should not be divulged to anyone else unless the newly initiated saṃnyāsin one day becomes a guru. When saṃnyāsins die, they are not cremated but are buried instead since their cremation has already taken place.

See also: **Antyeṣti; Guru; Mantra; Saṃnyāsa; Saṃpradāya**

LYNN FOULSTON

Further reading

Klostermaier, Klaus K. 1994. *A Survey of Hinduism*, 2nd edn. Albany, NY: State University of New York Press.

DĪVĀLĪ

Falling during October–November, Dīvālī is a pan-Indian celebration known as the 'festival of lights'. Many Vaiṣṇava purāṇic myths are associated with Dīvālī, including Sītā's rescue and the return of Rāma to Ayodhyā; the triumph of Vāmana over Bali; and the victory of Kṛṣṇa over Nārakāsura. However, in contemporary north India, this festival primarily honours the goddess Lakṣmī, and symbolically reinstates her as a benign and beneficent force in the new year. Ritualised gambling occurs on the night of the new moon, and many businesses treat the occasion as the end of the fiscal year, closing the books and performing elaborate ceremonies to usher in a prosperous new year. In this capacity, Gaṇeśa, the remover of obstacles, and Kubera, the god of wealth, share honours with Lakṣmī on this cycle of new beginnings. Commencing with Dhan Teras (Kārttika, kṛṣṇa pakṣa 13), Dīvālī is celebrated as a cluster of festival days, of which the most important is Lakṣmī Pūjā, which falls on amāvasyā, the new moon night of Kārttika (Kārttika, kṛṣṇa pakṣa 15). Against the dark absence of the moon, fireworks are exploded to create noise and light, dispelling inauspiciousness, and homes are adorned with sparkling clay lamps known as dīyās so that

Lakṣmī will be enticed to enter the home and bestow blessings in the coming year. Friends, families and neighbours distribute sweets; and clothing, cash and other gifts are presented to both domestic and public servants. The night following Lakṣmī Pūjā is celebrated as Govardhan Pūjā (Kārttika, śukla pakṣa 1) in honour of Kṛṣṇa, and the last night, Bhāī Dūj (or Yama Dvitīyā) commemorates the relationship between brothers and sisters. The celebration of Dīvālī shows great regional variation, such as in Bengal, where devotional emphasis centres on the goddess Kālī.

See also: **Ayodhyā; Calendar; Gaṇeśa; Kālī; Kṛṣṇa; Lakṣmī, Śrī; Purāṇas; Rāma; Sītā; Utsava; Vaiṣṇavism**

ANDREA MARION PINKNEY

Further reading

Babb, L.A. 1975. *The Divine Hierarchy: Popular Hinduism in Central India.* New York: Columbia University Press.

DIVINE LIFE SOCIETY

Swami Sivananda arrived in Rishikesh in 1924, which he described in his autobiography (Sivananda 1995: 21) as a holy place inhabited by mahātmas. Rishikesh is not considered to be a tīrtha as such. Tīrtha literally means 'to cross over' and connotes a ford and refers to pilgrimage places. However, thousands of pilgrims do flock to Rishikesh as it is the gateway to a number of very important pilgrimage places. In 1934 Sivananda settled in a spot overlooking the Ganges that was eventually to become the ashram and the headquarters of the Divine Life Society (DLS). In 1936 Sivananda established the Divine Life Trust Mission to 'systematically carry on the Divine Mission on a large scale' (Sivananda 1995: 43).

He established a publication business, began a monthly journal and founded the Yoga Vedanta Forest University (later called the Yoga Vedanta Forest Academy) in order to disseminate his spiritual ideas. As service was an integral aspect of Sivananda's teaching, he established a hospital. Over the years a number of branches of the Divine Life Society were founded in India and abroad. A bhajan hall and temple dedicated to Viśvanāth (literally 'Lord of the Universe' – a form of Śiva) were built on the ashram in the early 1940s.

In 1963 after the death of Swami Sivananda, Swami Chidananda (b. 1916), one of Sivananda's leading devotees, was appointed president of the DLS. In his inaugural speech Chidananda (1963) suggested that 'the DLS is veritably Gurudev himself'. Gurudev is a widely used epithet for Sivananda, indicating that he is regarded as a true Guru, and is therefore God.

The motto of the DLS is 'Serve, Love, Meditate, Realise', indicating that karma yoga, bhakti yoga, rāja yoga and jñāna yoga are all integral to the teaching of Sivananda. The DLS claims to be nonsectarian. The stated aims of the DLS are: to disseminate spiritual knowledge; to establish and run schools; to help the deserving; and to establish and run medical dispensaries. The DLS continues to publish a vast amount of literature, both titles by the prolific Sivananda and works by his disciples, such as the current president, Swami Chidananda. The Yoga Vedanta Forest Academy continues to run residential courses, which include lectures on subjects such as the *Upaniṣads* as well as practical instruction in yoga āsanas and meditation. The DLS continues to run and finance the Sivananda Charitable Hospital and several leper colonies as well as other charitable ventures. The DLS also has two websites: http://www.divinelifesociety.org and http://www.dlshq.org/.

See also: **Āśram(a) (religious community); Bhajan; Gaṅgā; Śiva; Tīrthayātrā (Pilgrimage); Upaniṣads**

STEPHEN JACOBS

Further reading

Chidananda, S. 1963. 'Talk Given by Swami Chidananda'. *Divine Life* 25(8): ii–vii.

Divine Life Society. 1983. *Swami Sivananda and the Divine Life Society*. Sivanandanagar: The Divine Life Society.

Divine Life Society. 1986. *Companion to the Divine Life Society Branch Personnel*. Sivanandanagar: The Divine Life Society.

Divine Life Society. 1994. *The Divine Life Society: Handbook of Information*. Sivanandanagar: The Divine Life Society.

Sivananda, S. 1995. *Autobiography of Swami Sivananda*. Sivanandanagar: The Divine Life Society.

DIVINE LIGHT MISSION

A defunct but historically significant new religious movement, Divine Light Mission was founded in 1971 in England after the visit of Maharaji, then known as Guru Maharaj Ji, to London. During the early years of the 1970s, Divine Light Mission experienced phenomenal growth and attracted the attention of both the media and scholars. Created to promote the teachings of Maharaji, Divine Light Mission rapidly became a movement composed predominantly of counterculture youth that spread through Britain, North America, France, Germany, Holland, Switzerland, Spain, Portugal, Italy, Scandinavia, Japan, South America and Australasia.

However, it was in the USA that the movement attracted the largest numbers of adherents and by 1973 it was estimated that 50,000 people had been shown the four techniques collectively known as Knowledge. Although open to all, the movement displayed a number of characteristics that showed apparent Sant Mat origins. These included strict vegetarianism, guru bhakti, and an idiom of teaching associated with the language of medieval nirguṇa sants. In addition, the movement was spearheaded by a renunciate order of Indian mahātmas and an inner circle of full-time volunteers who had committed themselves to a celibate lifestyle within communal ashrams.

During the 1980s, as the young Guru Maharaj Ji came of age, certain major transformations took place. Divine Light Mission was disbanded and the teachings moved away from the counterculture milieu and concerted efforts were made by Maharaji, dropping the title 'Guru', to remove the outer trappings of Indian culture and doctrine that had accompanied the arrival of the teachings from their place of origin in northern India. The ashrams were closed, the majority of the Indian mahātmas were returned to India and the focus of the efficacy of the techniques to provide inner fulfilment was emphasised as a universal panacea to human existential thirst outside any religion or culture.

Maharaji has continued to promote the benefits of the experience of Knowledge throughout the world and has succeeded in establishing his message in over eighty countries. Since the 1980s, he has utilised the assistance of several national organisations, known as Elan Vital, to manage his activities. However, Elan Vital itself was to grow immensely in the last two decades of the twentieth century. Although, unlike Divine Light Mission, it never displayed the characteristics of a religious movement, it had its own problems of institutionalisation, lack of spontaneity and inflexibility common to bureaucratic structures. In the first years of the twentieth-first century, Maharaji once again began a process of deconstruction, dismantling the over-hierarchical structures of the organisation, leaving it toothless except as a vehicle for dealing with official bodies such as in the hiring of halls, legal frameworks, health and safety issues, rights of volunteers and the financial management of donations to support the promotion of the teachings.

A new organisation was created by Maharaji and named the Prem Rawat

Foundation (TPRF). The Foundation provides a range of publicity materials and seeks opportunities for Maharaji to speak at public engagements such as university departments, non-governmental organisations and business conventions. These events are independent of those organised by individuals or organisations such as Elan Vital who have benefited from practising Maharaji's teachings. The Foundation website states that 'The Prem Rawat Foundation is dedicated to promoting and disseminating the speeches, writings, music, art and public forums of Prem Rawat'.

See also: **Bhakti (as path); Maharj Ji, Guru; Sant; Sant Sādhana**

RON GEAVES

Further reading

Geaves, R.A. 2004. 'From Divine Light Mission to Elan Vital and Beyond: An Exploration of Change and Adaptation'. *Nova Religio*, March: 45–62.

DIVORCE

Conceptually, marriage (vivāha), divorce and remarriage are intertwined. The traditional, elite type of marriage, 'gift of a daughter' (kanyādāna), was a sacrament (saṃskāra). The *Manusmṛti* (16.28) defines the purpose of marriage as 'Offspring, rites prescribed by Law, obedient service, the highest sensuous delights, and procuring heaven for oneself and one's forefathers – all this depends on the wife' (Olivelle 2004: 157). Marriage was supposed to be lifelong and monogamous, although the *Dharmaśāstras* allow exceptions for those who refuse to perform the mandatory rituals; are infertile; commit adultery; convert to some other religion; suffer from mental illness, leprosy or venereal disease; join religious orders; go missing for seven years; or commit crimes such as rape, sodomy or bestiality. Unjust abandonment, however, meant going to hell or, in the case of a husband, being reborn as a barren woman. Despite a general fairness to both parties, some passages are unfair to women; women, for instance, could be abandoned for merely being quarrelsome. It is difficult to know what was meant by the word tyāga, which denotes leaving, abandoning or renouncing. Did it refer to a wife who left home? Did it refer to a couple who abandoned intercourse because the husband had taken on a second wife? The general principle was that elite husbands had to maintain their estranged wives (who were not allowed to remarry) either in the home or, more rarely, in separate quarters after receiving some property.

Manu does not mention divorce, although he prescribes strict penances for those who abandon their life partners, but *Arthaśāstra* 3.15–18 and *Nāradasmṛti* 12.96–97 allow divorce. Divorce was less problematic for low castes, because their weddings were contractual rather than sacramental and often involved minimal public ritual. But whether weddings combined scriptural (brahmanic) rituals and local customs (often those of women) or were based merely on local customs, Hindu marriage (or divorce for those who were allowed it) was ultimately defined by families, castes or village councils. Only as a last resort did feuding couples use courts to resolve their disputes (vyavahāra).

Initially, the British avoided upsetting Hindus and refrained from reforming marriage or introducing divorce. But gradually legal changes to the understandings of marriage took place. These included the Hindu Widows Remarriage Act, 1856, the Indian Divorce Act, 1869, the Hindu Women's Rights to Property Act, 1937, the Hindu Married Women's Right to Separate Residence and Maintenance Act, 1946, the Hindu Marriage Disabilities Removal Act, 1946, a series of Hindu divorce acts at the state level around the time of independence and, most importantly, after independence the

Hindu Marriage Act, 1955, with amendments in 1964, and the Marriage Laws (Amendment) Act, 1976. The latter made it possible for either the husband or wife to petition for divorce. Grounds for divorce include the following: voluntary sexual intercourse with another person; cruelty; desertion for two years; the religious conversion of one spouse; joining an ascetic order; mental disorder of a degree that prevents normal life; incurable leprosy; and venereal disease.

Divorce is problematic even today. Despite new laws, it is sometimes hard to know if a marriage has even taken place given the lack of a state registration system and the variety of local customs. Because India cannot offer the security of a welfare state, judges try pragmatically to preserve marriages, if the wives agree; otherwise, wives would have few resources on which to survive (Menski 2003: 308–15).

See also: **Arthaśāstra; Dharmaśāstras; Saṃskāras; Vivāha; Widow remarriage; Women's rites**

KATHERINE K. YOUNG

Further reading

Diwan, P. 1983. *Family Law: Law of Marriage and Divorce in India*. New Delhi: Sterling.

Harlan, L. and P.B. Courtright, (eds). 1995. *From the Margins of Hindu Marriage: Essays on Gender, Religion, and Culture*. Oxford: Oxford University Press.

Kane, P.V. 1968–77 [1930–62]. *History of Dharmaśāstra*, 5 vols, 2nd edn. Poona: Bhandarkar Oriental Research Institute.

Kohli, H.D. 2000. *Hinduism and Divorce from Dharmaśāstras to Statutory Law: A Critical Study*. Delhi: Decent Books.

Menski, W. 2003. *Hindu Law: Beyond Tradition and Modernity*. New Delhi: Oxford University Press.

Nicholas, R.W. 1995. 'The Effectiveness of the Hindu Sacrament (Saṃskāra): Caste, Marriage, and Divorce in Bengali Culture'. In L. Halan and P.B. Courtright, eds, *From the Margins of Hindu Marriage: Essays on Gender, Religion and Culture*. New York: Oxford University Press, 137–59.

Olivelle, P. 2004. *The Law Code of Manu*. Oxford: Oxford University Press.

Owen, M. 1996. *A World of Widows*. New Jersey: Zed Books.

Pothen, S. 1986. *Divorce: Its Causes and Consequences in Hindu Society*. New Delhi: Shakti Books.

DOW, ALEXANDER (*c.* 1735–79)

Soldier in the East India Company's Bengal army from 1760 until his death in 1779. Dow's *History of Hindostan* (1768–71, and later editions), a free translation from Persian of Muhammad Qasim Firishtah's *Gulshan-i Ibrahimi* (1606–7), included extensive observations of his own, notably 'A Dissertation Concerning the Customs, Manners, Language, Religion and Philosophy of the Hindoos', which gave extended quotations from purāṇic sources and an account of the Nyāya of Gautama. Dow's account of Hinduism, like those of other British writers on Hinduism of the period who shared his inclination toward deism, stressed the basically monotheistic character of Hinduism and praised the purity of its moral code. In the period prior to the Sanskrit scholarship of those associated with the Asiatic Society of Bengal, Dow's *History* was widely read, and it was an important source of Voltaire's knowledge of Hinduism. French translations of his 'Dissertation' appeared separately in 1769 and 1771.

See also: **Asiatic Societies; Hinduism, history of scholarship; Nyāya**

WILL SWEETMAN

Further reading

Dow, A. 1768–71. *The History of Hindostan; from the earliest account of time, to the death of Akbar; translated from the Persian of Mahummud Casim Ferishta of Delhi; together with a dissertation concerning the religion and philosophy of the Brāhmaṇas.*

London: Printed for T. Becket and P.A. De Hondt.
Marshall, P.J. (ed.). 1970. *The British Discovery of Hinduism in the Eighteenth Century.* Cambridge: Cambridge University Press.

DOWRY

Dowry likely had its origin in the brahmanical type of elite marriage called 'gift of a daughter' (kanyādāna), accompanied by a woman's wealth (strīdhana) in the form of voluntary gifts that were made by her parents and kin during the wedding rituals. According to the *Manusmṛti* 9.194, women had six kinds of property. As an expression of affection by her birth family and its desire for her well-being and material comfort, these marked the transition to her new home but also provided her with economic security in case of adversity. An elite woman feared the latter, because she did not work outside the home, had no inheritance rights and therefore depended entirely on her husband's family. During her lifetime, a woman had complete control, jural right, over her woman's wealth (strīdhana); when she died, that passed to her heirs.

Veena Oldenburg argues that the practice of dowry changed dramatically during the colonial period, when crushing taxes led some families into extreme debt and loss of land. Families tried several solutions: having more sons (achieved in part by female infanticide) to increase income; and appropriating a woman's dowry to pay off debts. The fact that finding good husbands became more competitive, because now higher education and civil service were desired, contributed to families' need for additional income to offer larger dowries. Thus, dowry appropriation was not the direct cause of infanticide or bride burning, but rather a symptom of underlying economic changes caused by colonial rule (Oldenburg 2002).

Whatever the reasons, there was demand for reform. Dowry became illegal due to the Dowry Prohibition Act of 1961. But still it spread secretly and exploited legal loopholes. By 1978, women's organisations began to use the words 'dowry death' and 'dowry murder' for the killing of brides by husbands or in-laws after extortion of more money and goods. This exposed the crimes that had been camouflaged as accidents or suicides. In 1986, the Dowry Prohibition (Amendment) Act introduced S.304-B into the Indian Penal Code to penalise perpetrators of dowry deaths, which were defined as unnatural deaths within seven years of marriage, preceded by cruelty and in connection with any demand for dowry. If this situation led to a bride's suicide, then it, too, was deemed a dowry death.

See also: **Infanticide; Sati; Women's education**

KATHERINE K. YOUNG

Further reading

Das, M. 1984. 'Women Against Dowry'. In M. Kishwar and R. Vanita, eds, *In Search of Answers: Indian Women's Voices from Manushi*. London: Zed Books, 178–83.
Garg, H.S. 1990. *Bride Burning (Crime Against Women): Social, Criminological and Legal Aspects.* New Delhi: Sandeep Publications.
Jethmalani, R. (ed.). 1995. *Kali's Yug: Empowerment, Law, and Dowry Deaths.* New Delhi: Har-Anand Publishers.
Kane, P.V. 1968–77 [1930–62]. *History of Dharmaśāstra*, 5 vols, 2nd edn. Poona: Bhandarkar Oriental Research Institute.
Kumari, R. 1989. *Brides Are Not for Burning: Dowry Victims in India.* New Delhi: Radiant Publishers.
Leslie, J. 1998. 'Dowry, "Dowry Deaths" and Violence Against Women: A Journey of Discovery'. In W. Menski, ed., *South Asians and the Dowry Problem, GEMS No. 6.* Stoke on Trent: Trentham Books Limited, 21–35.
Mathew, A. 1990. 'Dowry and Its Various Dimensions'. In L. Devasia and V.V. Devasia, eds, *Women in India: Equality, Social*

Justice and Devleopment. New Delhi: Indian Social Institute, 79–88.
Menski, W. (ed.). 1998. *South Asians and the Dowry Problem, GEMS No. 6*. Stoke on Trent: Trentham Books.
Menski, W. 2003. *Hindu Law: Beyond Tradition and Modernity.* New Delhi: Oxford University Press.
Oldenburg, V.T. 2002. *Dowry Murder: The Imperial Origins of a Cultural Crime.* Oxford: Oxford University Press.
Olivelle, P. 2004. *The Law Code of Manu.* Oxford: Oxford University Press.
Paul, M.C. 1986. *Dowry and Position of Women in India: A Study of Delhi Metropolis.* New Delhi: Inter-India Publishers.
Rudd, J.M. 1994. *Dowry-murders in India.* Michigan State University: Women in International Development.
Sen, M. 2002. *Death by Fire: Sati, Dowry Death and Female Infanticide in Modern India.* New Brunswick, NJ: Rutgers University Press.
Stone, L. and C. James. 1997. 'Dowry, Bride Burning and Female Power in India'. In *Gender in Cross-cultural Perspective*, eds. C.B. Brettell and C.F. Sargent. Upple Saddle River: Prentice Hall, 270–79.
Umar, M. 1998. *Bride Burning in India: A Socio-Legal Study.* New Delhi: A.P.H. Publishing Corporation.

DRAMA

The most common word for drama in Indic languages is derived from the Sanskrit root naṭ (to dance, to perform). In Sanskrit it gives us the word nāṭya (mimetic representation/drama), while a specific genre of play comes to be known as nāṭaka. Nāṭya comprises verbal and physical expression articulated through dialogue, music and a stylised gestural vocabulary. For this reason, it is often difficult to make clear distinctions between the practices of dance and drama in India. Ritual drama (and dance) is a pan-Indian phenomenon and takes many guises. Most of these performances are undertaken by devotees or specialised performers and are built around the familiar narratives of the *Purāṇas*, *Mahābhārata* and *Rāmāyaṇa*, adapted to reflect local concerns and shaped to the needs of a particular local deity (Richmond 1971: 123). Performers of such ritual drama are often set apart by birth (hereditary performers), age (prepubescent boys) and almost always through observances of rules of ritual purity. Religious theatre traditions flourish in regional 'folk' performance cultures such as Rām Līlā (The Play of Rāma) in Northern India and in equally localised dramatic forms such as Kūṭiyāṭṭam nurtured within the temple precincts.

For the Orientalists, beginning with Sir William Jones (1746–94 CE), Sanskrit theatre as exemplified in Kālidāsa's *Abhijñānaśākuntalam* (The Recognition of Śakuntalā) was both the theatre of the Hindus and, by extension, a national (Indian) theatre. Jones thus conceived a homogenous entity that he called 'Hindu Theatre' largely from his brahmanical textual sources rather than observance of lived, vernacular performance cultures. Equating Hindu with Indian, Jones made the ubiquitous claim that Hindu theatre was a national theatre because it charted the vagaries of Indian empire, from its glory days to its fall with the arrival of the Muslims (Dalmia 2006: 28–29).

Textual sources for Sanskrit drama

The earliest (and certainly most iconic) extant textual source for drama is the Sanskrit dramaturgical manual the *Nāṭyaśāstra* (Treatise on Drama), attributed to Bhārata. It was, however, in all likelihood composed around the second century by a number of different authors. The *Nāṭyaśāstra* is made up of thirty-six chapters that discuss everything from the origin of drama (Chapter 1), through aesthetics (Chapters 6 and 7) to the way and manner in which a theatre ought to be built and protected. While the opening narrative on the origin of drama establishes the religious, ritual and social dimensions of drama, the chapters on aesthetics become foundational to a number of philosophical schools, most importantly that of the Kashmiri Śaiva philosopher Abhinavagupta (tenth century).

The mythic origin of drama

The *Nāṭyaśāstra* opens with an account of the origin of drama. In the narrative, Bhārata (the sage to whom the text is attributed) is approached by a group of sages lead by Ātreya who desire to know how he came to compose a treatise that is equal to the Vedas. Bhārata replied that Brahmā created Nāṭya at the behest of the gods as a tool to rectify the avarice and moral decay that gripped the world. They also requested that it encapsulate the Veda and yet remain accessible to those prohibited from either listening or learning from them. Brahmā created the Nāṭya Veda, judiciously incorporating various elements of the Veda. He then returned the text to the gods and bid them practise it well. However, they demurred, insisting that they lacked the qualifications of stern mind and discerning intellect to undertake so daunting a task. It was only then that Brahmā taught it to Bhārata, who in turn taught it to his sons.

Eventually, when Bhārata informed Brahmā that they were ready to perform drama, he suggested the occasion of Indra's flag festival. The play showcased the gods' victory over the demons and the gods, pleased with the performance, showered the actors with gifts. The demons, however, were not so pleased and disrupted the performance by freezing the movements, speech and memory of the performers. When Bhārata reported the interruption to Brahmā and requested protection from further such interruptions, the god directed that a theatre protected by various celestial beings should be built. Brahmā then asked the demons why they wished to destroy drama. The demons responded saying that Nāṭya portrayed them in an unfair light and its purpose was to glorify the gods while humiliating the demons. To this Brahmā replied that the Nāṭya Veda is meant to reveal both the negative and the positive and is but the *representation* of the three worlds, its ways, circumstances and emotions. He further insists that there is no knowledge that is not contained in Nāṭya. The chapter ends with an exhortation that a sacrifice must be performed to the stage before any performance commences.

Kūṭiyāṭṭam

Kūṭiyāṭṭam (dance/performing together or combined performance) is a ritual drama tradition preserved since the tenth century in select temples in Kerala, south India. It is considered to be the only example of surviving Sanskrit theatre and its repertoire consists of the plays of several important Sanskrit dramatists such as Bhāsa, though Kālidāsa is notably absent. Kūṭiyāṭṭam is performed by a high-caste group of male performers known as Chakyārs and female performers known as Naṅgyārs. Percussionists who comprise the orchestra are the only accompaniment to the performance. Kūṭiyāṭṭam takes place over several nights and is performed in a specially designated theatre area known as Kūttambalam (the Drama/Dance Stage) that faces the main shrine and is located within the temple compound. As Farley Richmond has pointed out, the very location of the stage asserts its ritual purpose as visual sacrifice (Richmond 1971: 123–24).

Rām Līlā

Rām Līlā is perhaps the best-known Indian folk ritual drama and the Rāmnagar Rām Līlā is arguably its most extravagant manifestation. Rām Līlā performed by amateur actors is an enactment of the

Rāmāyaṇa, to commemorate Rāma's victory over Rāvaṇa. Prepubescent boys play the roles of Rāma, Lakṣmaṇa and Sītā and the same boys may do so every year until they reach puberty. For the duration of the Rām Līlā performance the boys are thought to embody Viṣṇu and his consort and are treated with appropriate reverence and humility. They are carried on the shoulders of priests so that their feet do not touch the ground and the lay audience may not touch them. Within the performed narrative of the Rām Līlā, the episode of Rāma's reunion with his brother Bhārata's, Sītā's trial by fire and Rāma's defeat of Rāvaṇa are by far the most important (Kapur 1990).

See also: **Abhinavagupta; Asuras; Bhāsa; Brahmā; Deities; Hindu; Indra; Jones, Sir William; Kālidāsa; Lakṣmaṇa; Languages; Mahābhārata; Orientalism; Purāṇas; Rāma; Rāmāyaṇa; Rāvaṇa; Sītā; Veda; Viṣṇu**

ARCHANA VENKATESAN

Further reading

Dalmia, Vasudha. 2006. *Poetics, Plays and Performances: The Politics of Modern Indian Theatre*. New Delhi: Oxford University Press.

Kapur, Anuradha. 1990. *Actors, Pilgrims, Kings and Gods: The Ramlila at Ramnagar*. Calcutta: Seagull Press.

Rangacharya, Adya. 1986. *Natyasastra (English Translation with Critical Notes)*. Bangalore: IBH Prakashana.

Richmond, Farley. 1971. 'Some Religious Aspects of Indian Traditional Theatre'. *Drama Review* 5.2: 23–131.

DRAUPADĪ

One of the central characters in the *Mahābhārata*, she is variously described as the daughter of Drupada, the king of Pancala, and an embodiment of the primal goddess Śrī, born from sacrificial fire. A cousin of the Pāṇḍavas, she is sometimes regarded as married to Arjuna or his elder brother Yudhiṣṭhira. Yet, in the *Mahābhārata* and elsewhere, she is married to all five brothers, a polyandrous custom that is generally found only amongst Himālayan tribes. The *Mahābhārata* declares that Draupadī was won by Arjuna when he became the champion in a feat-of-arms contest. However, on their return home, the brothers declared to their mother that they had made a great acquisition. Before seeing Draupadī, she requested that the brothers share equally and it would have been wrong to disobey a mother's request. The sage Vyāsa came up with the solution that Draupadī should be shared by the brothers, spending time with each brother in turn.

It was Draupadī's humiliation at the hands of the Kauravas, especially Duḥśāsana and Duryodhana, which helped to cause the war between the two groups of cousins. Foolishly, Yudhiṣṭhira allowed himself to be drawn into a rigged gambling match with the Kauravas in which he lost all his possessions, the kingdom he shared with his brothers and finally Draupadī. Declared a slave-girl, she refused to do menial tasks and was dragged into the public arena in front of all the chieftains. Duryodhana tried to seat her on his knee but Duḥśāsana attempted to remove her sari and veil. None of the assembled men came to her rescue, the Pāṇḍavas restrained by Yudhiṣṭhira' s acknowledgement of his gambling debts. Draupadī turned to the absent Kṛṣṇa in prayer and miraculously her garments were restored as rapidly as they were removed. Many of the Pāṇḍavas vowed to take revenge on her dishonour, a vow later fulfilled in the battle of Kurukṣetra. Draupadī accompanied her five husbands into exile and was later instrumental, through complaining to Kṛṣṇa, in seeking revenge.

See also: **Arjuna; Duryodhana; Kauravas; Kṛṣṇa; Mahābhārata; Pāṇḍavas; Vyāsa; Yudhiṣṭhira**

RON GEAVES

Further reading

Dasgupta, Madhusraba. 1999. *Samsad Companion to the Mahābhārata*. Calcutta: Sahitya Samsad.

DROṆA

One of the central characters and heroic figures in the *Mahābhārata*, whose name means 'bucket' or 'pot', an appellation that was given because his birth was attributed to his father, the sage Bhāradvāja, ejaculating into a pot after being entranced by a beautiful nymph. Droṇa was married to Kripā, the half-sister of Bhīṣma, and was employed as a guru of martial skills to both the Kaurava and Pāṇḍava princes, the protagonists in the war. During the titanic struggle between the two sides, he kept faith with the Kauravas, although he was immensely respected by the Pāṇḍavas as both an ācārya and a brāhmaṇa who had been their teacher. After the death of Bhīṣma, he took command of the Kaurava forces and was eventually slain using unfair means by Dhṛṣṭadyumna, an act which was considered to be highly sinful. The *Mahābhārata* records that Droṇa ascended to heaven like the sun. It was the presence of such figures as Droṇa on the opposing side that helped throw Arjuna into moral confusion and provide the backdrop for the dialogue with Kṛṣṇa that constitutes the *Bhagavadgītā*.

See also: **Arjuna; Bhagavadgītā; Bhīṣma; Guru; Kauravas; Kṛṣṇa; Mahābhārata; Pāṇḍavas**

RON GEAVES

Further reading

Dasgupta, Madhusraba. 1999. *Samsad Companion to the Mahābhārata*. Calcutta: Sahitya Samsad.

DUBOIS, JEAN-ANTOINE (1765–1848)

A secular French priest of the Missions Étrangères, Dubois left France for India in 1792. After his return to Europe he published *Letters on the State of Christianity in India*, in which he argued that caste rendered the conversion of Hindus 'impracticable'. He published also a translation of the *Pañcatantra* and a work on brahmanical cosmogony. He is best known, however, for a work published under his name in English in 1817 as *Description of the Character, Manners and Customs of the People of India; and of Their Institutions, Religious and Civil*. The work, republished in French and English several times during the nineteenth and early twentieth centuries and still in print in India, is, however, not his own but largely based on a late eighteenth-century work by Gaston-Laurent Coeurdoux.

See also: **Coeurdoux, Gaston-Laurent; Hinduism, history of scholarship; Pañcatantra**

WILL SWEETMAN

Further reading

Dubois, Jean-Antoine. 1817. *Description of the Character, Manners and Customs of the People of India; and of Their Institutions, Religious and Civil.* London: Longman.

Dubois, Jean-Antoine. 1823. *Letters on the State of Christianity in India, in Which the Conversion of the Hindoos Is Considered as Impracticable.* London: Longman.

Dubois, Jean-Antoine. 1826. *Le Pantcha-Tantra ou les cinq ruses, fables du brahme Vichnou-Sarma* [The Pancatantra or the Five Ruses, Fables of the Brahman Vishnu-Sharma]. Paris: J.-S. Merlin.

DUMONT, LOUIS (1911–98)

French anthropologist and sociologist, who offered an analysis of Indian society by postulating a series of oppositions which organise the values of Indian religion: between the world-renouncer and the man-in-the-world; purity and impurity; and the brāhmaṇa and the king, or between religious status and political power. Dumont saw Indian society as holistic and traditional, in contrast to the individualism which he took to be characteristic of the modern West. Dumont's critics have been as numerous as his work has been influential; among other things he is charged with representing only one of a number of Indian perspectives (an elite, 'top-down', brahmanical view).

See also: **Brāhman; Caste; Hinduism, history of scholarship; Rāja**

WILL SWEETMAN

Further reading

Collins, S. 1989. 'Louis Dumont and the Study of Religions'. *Religious Studies Review* 15: 14–20.

Dumont, L. 1966. *Homo hierarchicus: Essai sur le système des castes*. Paris: Gallimard. [English translation, 2nd edn, 1980. *Homo Hierarchicus: The Caste System and Its Implications*. Chicago, IL: Chicago University Press.]

DUPERRON

See: **Anquetil-Duperron, Abraham-Hyacinthe**

DURGĀ

Durgā is one of the most popular goddesses in the contemporary Hindu pantheon. She is related to the goddess Ambā/Ambikā (Mother) in terms of iconography and certain nurturing aspects of her character. However, Durgā is also associated or identified with Kālī/Caṇḍī and Pārvatī, and has three primary mythological and cosmic roles. She is, first and foremost, understood and worshipped as a defender of the dharmic order, an all-powerful warrior goddess who manifests unsurpassed martial skills to confront various demonic threats to the world. Second, she is identified as a consort of Śiva (through her identification with Pārvatī) and, more specifically, as a mother goddess; four deities being regarded as her children at her main festival, Durgā Pūjā: Gaṇeśa, Kārttikeya (Skanda), Lakṣmī and Sarasvatī. Third, for many Hindus, Durgā is worshipped as the Māhādevī (Great Goddess), the Supreme Being and ultimate reality that transcends all others. This final understanding of Durgā is closely interrelated with the universal female 'power' of Śakti and the Śākta tradition of goddess devotion.

Historically, rulers throughout India have practised rituals and worship associated with Durgā in order to gain victory in battle; and figures such as the Pāṇḍava brothers and Rāma have sought the protection and favour of the Goddess prior to their major military campaigns. However, it was not until the sixth century CE that the first goddess-centred text to establish the all-inclusive nature of feminine power became accessible in a part of the *Mārkaṇḍeya Purāṇa*. Originally consisting of Chapters 81 to 93 of the *Mārkaṇḍeya Purāṇa*, it is the *Devī Māhātmya* (Specific Greatness of the Goddess) or *Durgā Saptaśatī* (Seven Hundred Verses to Durgā) that introduces the stories of Durgā as a protector of the dharmic order (see Coburn 1988, 1992). In the first of these stories it is the power of Durgā as Mahāmāya (great illusion) that permits Viṣṇu to defeat the demons Madhu and Kaiṭabha. In the second two stories, it is Durgā who directly confronts and defeats the demons in battle, Mahiṣa the buffalo demon, in the first instance, and the demon brothers Śumbha and Niśumbha, in the second. It is from these latter two stories that most of the contemporary iconography and characterisation of Durgā are derived.

In the story of Durgā's battle with Mahiṣa, it is explained that the Goddess emerges from the collective energies (tejas) of the male deities in order to defeat a foe who is invulnerable to the power of men, although not the power of women. She is provided with weapons and other items by the gathered gods, including a trident from Śiva, a discus from Kṛṣṇa, a conch and noose from

Varuṇa, a staff from Yama, a spear from Agni and a lion (or sometimes tiger) mount from Himavat, and then proceeds, with a loud bellow of pleasure, to enter combat with Mahiṣa and his army of demons (Coburn 1992: 40–42). In most of her iconographical representations, this is the primary image of Durgā: she is astride her mount, wielding in eight or ten arms her arsenal of weapons, confidently fighting and dispatching her demonic enemy. She is typically presented as beautiful and serene in the midst of battle, dressed usually in red, but it is notable that she also possesses a 'hot', fierce and bloodthirsty nature, exhibiting great anger, passion and intoxication at certain points during her confrontations with the demons.

Durgā's behaviour and gender identity, as outlined in the *Devī Māhātmya*, is significant insofar as it diverges radically from that of the normative model of the 'good woman' in Hindu society. Durgā excels in the stereotypically male role of a warrior; she is wholly detached from the duties of the female householder; and she is also an autonomous woman, acting independently of male direction, who simply generates female helpers from within her own being, including the wild and bloodthirsty Kālī and Mātṛkās (Mothers), whenever she requires assistance. Unlike the goddesses Lakṣmī, Sarasvatī and Sati, who are exemplars of virtue, the activities of Durgā do transgress the 'natural' dharmic order of what is acceptable in terms of what is prescribed for the female. While it is emphasised in the *Devī Māhātmya* that Durgā is both beautiful and compassionate, lustrous and quite clearly sexually desirable, she is also independent and steeped in the highly undesirable pollutants of blood and death. Durgā, therefore, possesses an ambiguous, paradoxical and often terrifying character. She is a goddess who balances world-supporting and salvific powers with a pattern of behaviour that marks her as an outsider or, at minimum, as existing on the periphery of the dharmic order. The precise manner in which worshippers reconcile these attributes is difficult to ascertain; some scholars have claimed that it is these very ambiguities and liminal qualities that contribute to the Goddess's appeal (Kinsley 1988: 97), while feminist scholars have debated whether Durgā and the *Devī Māhātmya* empower women or are principally antifeminist in character (Humes 2000: 123–50).

Durgā's origins doubtless lie in many different directions. It has been suggested that some aspects of her character, her dangerous and passionate nature, may be traced to the indigenous, non-Aryan peoples and tribes of the Indian subcontinent. As befits her ambiguous 'outsider' status, Durgā is often associated with the fringes of 'civilised' Vedic society, notably the Himālaya and Vindhya mountains of northern India and the tribal peoples, such as the Śabaras, who dwell there (Kinsley 1988: 99). Another important aspect of Durgā's character is the connection with fertility and fertility rituals evident at her yearly festival. Durgā Pūjā is celebrated most elaborately in Kolkata (Calcutta), where the temporary pandals (pavilions) that house the images of her slaying the demon completely take over the city. Durgā worship may and ideally ought to entail blood sacrifice, echoing her fierce and bloody nature, but northern Indian practices tend to emphasise the familial aspects of Durgā, while it is the southern Indian practices that stress the dangers and dharmic ambiguities of her character.

See also: **Agni; Asuras; Blood sacrifice; Dharma; Durgā Pūjā; Gaṇeśa; Kālī and Caṇḍī; Kṛṣṇa; Lakṣmī, Śrī; Māhādevī; Mahiṣa; Mātṛkās; Pāṇḍavas; Pārvatī; Purāṇas; Purity and pollution, ritual; Rāma; Sacred geography; Śakti; Śāktism; Sarasvatī; Sati; Śiva; Skanda; Varuṇa; Viṣṇu; Women, Status of; Yama**

PAUL REID-BOWEN

Further reading

Coburn, T.B. 1988. *Devī-Māhātmya: The Crystallization of the Goddess Tradition*. Delhi: Motilal Banarsidass.

Coburn, T.B. 1992. *Encountering the Goddess: A Translation of the Devī-Māhātmya and a Study of Its Interpretation*. Delhi: Sri Satguru Publications.

Humes, C.A. 2000. 'Is the Devi Mahatmya a Feminist Scripture?'. In A. Hiltebeitel and K. M. Erndl, eds, *Is the Goddess a Feminist? The Politics of South Asian Goddesses*. Sheffield: Sheffield Academic Press, 123–50.

Kinsley, D. 1988. *Hindu Goddesses: Visions of the Divine Feminine in the Hindu Religious Tradition*. Berkeley, CA: University of California Press.

DURGĀ PŪJĀ

Also known as Navarātri, the great festival celebrating the victory of the goddess Durgā over the demon Mahiṣāsura, as described in the *Devī Māhātmya* of the *Mārkaṇḍeya Purāṇa*. It takes place in the bright half of Āśvina (September/October) and is traditionally said to commemorate Rāma's worship of Durgā before going to Laṇkā to rescue Sītā from the clutches of Rāvaṇa. The festival is particularly popular in West Bengal, where it grew in importance under the British, with the prominent families of Calcutta holding increasingly ostentatious festivities to enhance their status. These families still hold traditional pūjās but Durgā Pūjā is now a truly popular festival, at least as important for its social as for its religious aspects. The streets are filled with decorative lights and temporary, but highly elaborate and beautiful, pāndāls (shrines with images of Durgā) which are the focus of much sightseeing and competitions.

The festival starts on ṣaṣṭhī, the bright 6th of Āśvina, when the goddess is welcomed, the rituals themselves beginning on śapṭamī, the 7th. Aṣṭamī, the 8th, is the most important day ritually, when victory over Mahiṣāsura is celebrated with ritual, mantras and sacrifice of black goats or a substitute such as chalkumro, a large pumpkin. On nabamī, the 9th, Durgā is offered food, and on the last day, daśamī, she returns to her home in Mount Kailash and the clay images are taken with great ceremony to the river where they are immersed.

Although Durgā Pūjā centres on the struggle and victory of a powerful goddess, its imagery has become that of a married daughter returning to her natal home, her followers feeling like a sorrowing family when she leaves. The images in the pāṇḍāls show her on her lion spearing the demon, but her expression is gentle and she looks increasingly like a Hollywood film star. This is symptomatic of an evolving view of the goddesses traditionally classified as 'fierce' and independent becoming 'sweeter' and gentler in the minds of their devotees.

See also: **Devī Māhātmya; Durgā; Film; Purāṇas; Rāma; Rāmāyāṇa; Sītā**

CYNTHIA BRADLEY

Further reading

Rodgrigues, H. 2003. *Ritual Worship of the Great Goddess: The Liturgy of Durga Puja with Interpretation*. Albany, NY: SUNY Press.

DURGARAM MANCHHARAM, MEHTAJI (1809–78)

Influential in the founding of the Manav Dharma Sabha along with Dadoba Pandurang, Manchharam Mehtaji Durgaram was typical of the product of Western education and missionary activity introduced into Gujarat in the second and third decades of the nineteenth century. Often educated in Bombay in elite schools and colleges, students such as Mehtaji Durgaram went on to become headmasters and teachers of government schools in the surrounding region. In the specific example of Mehtaji Durgaram, he was appointed headmaster of the Surat Government School in 1830 and subsequently of the Surat English School in 1834.

The influence of Western education provided the impetus for a rational criticism of contemporary Indian society, and Mehtaji Durgaram joined with a like-minded group of educated Gujaratis to challenge the religious practices and beliefs of rural India. They first created the Pustak Prasarak Mandali (Book Propagation Society) in 1842, utilising the lithograph for the dissemination of their views, and subsequently, in 1844, they founded the Manav Dharma Sabha.

See also: **Pandurang, Dadoba; Manav Dharma Sabha**

RON GEAVES

Further reading

Jones, Kenneth. 1989. *Socio-Religious Reform Movements in British India, The New Cambridge History of India: Vol. 3.1*. Cambridge: Cambridge University Press.

DURYODHANA

Duryodhana is the leader of the hundred sons of King Dhṛtarāṣṭra and his wife Gāndhārī, born from the aborted foetal mass which Vyāsa divided and placed in pots of ghī until their birth; he is regarded as an incarnation of the demon Kali, 'strife'. These malicious brothers are commonly called the Kauravas, in contrast to their cousins and hated rivals from youth, Pāṇḍu's sons, the Pāṇḍavas. Dhṛtarāṣṭra, though blind, succeeded his older brother Pāṇḍu and Duryodhana succeeds him in turn at Hāstinapura, forcing Yudhiṣṭhira, Pāṇḍu's oldest son, to establish Indraprastha. The disputed succession eventually leads to warfare between the cousins. Its most significant cause is the dicing match to which Duryodhana challenges Yudhiṣṭhira (won for him by the crooked Śakuni); Duryodhana's offensive gesture of baring his left thigh to Draupadī (on top of his brother Duḥśāsana's attempt to strip her) fuels her and the Pāṇḍavas' thirst for vengeance. Duryodhana is killed by Bhīma, who breaks that thigh with his mace.

See also: **Bhīma; Dhṛtarāṣṭa; Draupadī; Kauravas; Pāṇḍavas; Vyāsa; Yudhiṣṭhira**

JOHN BROCKINGTON

Further reading

Gitomer, David. 1992. 'King Duryodhana: The *Mahābhārata* Discourse of Sinning and Virtue in Epic and Drama'. *Journal of the American Oriental Society* 112.

DVAITA

The Dvaita Vedānta school of Indian philosophy was the third of the Vedānta movements that emerged in medieval south India. It is similar to the Viśiṣṭādvaita school of Rāmānuja in its theistic devotionalism. The god Viṣṇu is held as supreme and independent of all other things in reality. The school's founder, Madhva (1238–1317 CE), also taught a pluralistic realism where all individuals and material objects have a real existence separate from each other and from God, but are dependent on God. This idea verges on pragmatism in the modern sense of the term by viewing separate objects as real, distinct entities. Like Viśiṣṭādvaita, the Dvaita school also positioned itself as a reaction against the teaching of the Advaita Vedānta school of Śaṅkara that sensory reality is an illusion.

Madhva's Dvaita school draws on the *Brahmasūtras* of Bādarāyana, the *Upaniṣads*, the *Bhagavadgītā* and the *Bhāgavata Purāṇa*. Rather than focusing on the nature of ātman, or 'self' and its relation with the divine Brahman, as put forth in the normative textual tradition of the *Upaniṣads*, Madhva focused in the nature of Brahman. Furthermore, while Dvaita shares the devotional aspect of theism with Viśiṣṭādvaita, Dvaita diverges from Viśiṣṭādvaita in viewing God as completely svatantra, or 'independent' and separate from things in the universe, rather than being in a relationship of apṛthak-siddhi, or 'inseparability'. Madhva's doctrine is thus completely dvaita or 'dualist', where all things in creation and human individuals possess viśeṣas, or 'particularities', separate from the one transcendent real divine. Individual jīvas, or souls, come to know the true nature of reality by realising that they are totally asvatantra, or 'dependent' on the independent divine. Individual jīvas are still nonetheless real in themselves, while being finite and dependent on a higher divine being. Madhva interprets those textual passages speaking of unreality to mean that the dependent beings and objects in the world lack any reality compared with the independent reality of God. In a dualistic world, therefore, it makes good pragmatic sense to believe in the reality of persons and objects, because that is what we regularly perceive and live with when using distinct objects in our daily existence, and dualities are everywhere, yet no two things are exactly alike. Thus the notion of bhedábheda, or 'difference and non-difference', takes on special importance in Dvaita Vedānta. But for Dvaita, the notion of difference is ultimately significant.

Knowledge in the realistic world of Dvaita is also apprehended in regard to the difference between objects. One can know something if it is in space and time, and standing in reference to some other object. Thus the real is the same as the empirical. In contrast to Advaita, for which the experience of the rope-snake is illusory, an unreal object is also empirically valid since it was experienced at some place and time. The only absolute distinction in ontology is between the reality of God and everything else that depends on God. Knowledge is true insofar as it corresponds with external reality. True knowledge for Dvaita is the real facts we see in space and time. This epistemology depends on three pramāṇas: the accurate perception (pratyakṣa) of the senses, perfect reasoning through inference (anumāna) and authoritative testimony through either reliable scripture (āgama) or a person who is trustworthy and entitled to transmit the knowledge (āpta). Perception is believed to give intrinsically self-valid knowledge by means of the sakṣin, or 'witness', to which Dvaita gives a unique definition. The sakṣin is one of the seven senses including manas or the 'internal organ'. The sakṣin is thought to perceive true knowledge intuitively, as well as through the senses and the manas that has weighed the knowledge in relation to other knowledge. After the perception of the senses and the assessment of manas, truth is at last directly known by the sakṣin. The manas as the internal organ of sense is thus simply an aid to knowing, while the sakṣin, like God, is of the nature of sentience itself. Knowledge is not, however, a quality of the self. It is, rather, a transformation occurring in the manas, which is in contact with an object through the senses. The self is thought to possess and be connected to the knowledge, yet stands apart as an agency, because it commences the process of knowing an object in the other senses. Error occurs in the manas and not in the sakṣin, owing to a flawed apprehension of an object. It is simply perceiving things that are unreal and do not exist in the present, imposing them on the real.

Liberation (mokṣa) for Dvaita is brought through the intense love of God (bhakti), combined with the knowledge of God (jñāna) on the part of the aspirant and finally granted by God's prasāda, 'grace'. After long, arduous preparation in the traditional means of śravaṇa, 'Vedic study', manana, 'reflection' and nidhidyāsana, 'meditation', the aspirant to liberation comes to the correct knowledge of God and realises more and more deeply his dependent relationship with God. Ultimately, God chooses to reveal himself to the aspirant, and the aspirant realises the nature of God and his own true nature through God's reflection, the bimba/pratibimba 'image and reflection', in his mind. He does not of course realise his equivalence with God as in Advaita. Because there are differences between all individual jīvas, not all have the same chances of liberation through knowledge and devotion. Some with evil tendencies would of course not be fit to receive God's grace. There is thus a notion of predestination in Dvaita and it has an elitist view of liberation. There is no real institution of saṃnyāsa or 'renunciation' as such. Further, as in Viśiṣṭādvaita, there is no jīvanmukti or 'liberation in life' as such. The aspirant must maintain a continual observance of prescribed rituals for the duration of his life even though he may have aparokṣajñāna or 'immediate knowledge' of God.

See also: **Advaita; Ātman; Bādarāyana; Bhagavadgītā; Bhakti (as path); Bhedābheda; Brahman; Brahmasūtras; Jīvanmukti; Jīva; Jñāna (as path); Madhva; Mokṣa; Pramāṇas; Prasthānatrayī; Purāṇas; Rāmānuja; Sakṣin; Saṃnyāsa; Śaṅkara; Upaniṣads; Vedānta; Viśiṣṭādvaita; Viṣṇu**

ROBERT GOODDING

Further reading

Sharma, B.N.K. 1986. *The Philosophy of Madhvācārya*. Delhi: Motilal Banarsidass.
Sharma, B.N.K. 1979. *Madhva's Teachings in His Own Words*, 3rd edn. Bombay: Bharatiya Vidya Bhavan.
Sharma, Deepak 2003. *An Introduction to Mādhva Vedānta*. Ashgate World Philosophies Series. Aldershot and Burlington, VT: Ashgate Publishing Ltd.

DVAITĀDVAITA

See: **Bhedābheda**

DVĀRAKĀ

The modern city of Dwārkā (ancient name: Dvārakā or Dvāravatī), situated on the westernmost point of the Kathiawad (Saurashtra) peninsula in the modern Indian state of Gujarat, is built near the submerged ruins of the ancient capital city of Lord Kṛṣṇa. Dvārakā (literally 'gateway') has been a centre for Vaiṣṇava and Śaiva Hindus for centuries and is the only city that is both one of the four principal pilgrimage stops (dhāms) for Hindus (along with Puri, Badarīnāth and Rāmeśvaram) and also stands as one of the seven most sacred cities of ancient India. It is home to several important temples. The site of the sixteenth-century Dwarkadisha temple (also known as Jagatmandir or Shri Krishna Temple) is supposed to have been the place where Viśvakarman, the architect of the gods, constructed a lavish residence for Lord Kṛṣṇa and his 16,000 queens. Vajranābha (a grandson of Lord Kṛṣṇa) is said to have built the first temple at this location. A significant home of one of the twelve jyotirliṅgas of Lord Śiva is the Nāgeśvara Mahādeva temple about ten kilometres from the town. Also, one of the four original monasteries (maṭha) to house monks of the Daśanāmī sect was established in Dvārakā by the Advaita Vedānta master Śaṅkara. In the ancient lore, Dvārakā (perhaps modern Beyt Dwārkā, a small island thirty kilometres off of the coast of the new city, or the submerged and recently excavated ruins found nearby) became important as a wealthy and auspicious city founded by Lord Kṛṣṇa upon his departure from Mathurā. The city's sacred geography includes memorials to the place where Lord Kṛṣṇa's wife Rukminī was punished by being separated from her husband by the sage Durvāsas, where Lord Viṣṇu (bearing the epithet 'Wheel-Nārāyaṇa', cakranārāyaṇa) appeared on the earth as a stone marked with a wheel on, and the pond (modern gopī-tālav) where Kṛṣṇa met the gopīs (milkmaids) during their visits to Dvārakā. The city is also a place where sages Sanaka, Marīcī, Atri and Aṅgiras performed penances.

See also: **Advaita; Aṅgiras; Atri; Kṛṣṇa; Maṭha; Mathurā; Rāmeśvara; Rukminī; Śaivism; Śaṅkara; Tirthayātra (Pilgrimage); Vaiṣṇavism; Viśvakarman**

DEVEN M. PATEL

Further reading

Bhardwaj, Surinder Mohan. 1983. *Hindu Places of Pilgrimage in India: A Study in Cultural Geography.* Berkeley, CA: University of California Press.

Rao, S.R. 1999. *The Lost City of Dvaraka.* New Delhi: Aditya Prakashan.

DVIJA

Dvija, 'one who is twice-born', and dvijāti, 'one who has two births', are synonymous Sanskrit terms for male members of the three higher varṇas, viz. the brāhmaṇas, kṣatriyas and vaiśyas. When these brāhmaṇas, kṣatriyas and vaiśyas reach the ages of 8, 11, and 12, respectively, they are initiated into Vedic study through a ceremony known as upanayana, investiture with the sacred thread, at which point they are said to be born a second time. While their initial birth involves their biological parents, in this case they are said to be born from sacred knowledge. The upanayana ceremony also marks the moment when brāhmaṇas, kṣatriyas and vaiśyas become responsible for acting in accordance with the dictates of their varṇa and their stage in life. Prior to this, they may act more or less as they please without incurring any moral taint. Dvijas/dvijātis are often placed in opposition to members of the fourth varṇa, the śūdras, who are designated as ekajati, 'having a single birth', since the study of the Veda is forbidden to them.

See also: **Āśrama (stages of life); Brāhmaṇa; Upanayana; Varṇa; Veda**

ETHAN KROLL

Further reading

Dumont, Louis. 1970. *Homo Hierarchicus: An Essay on the Caste System.* [Mark Sainsbury, trans.] Chicago, IL: University of Chicago Press.

Ghurye, G.S. 1932. *Caste and Race in India.* London: Kegan Paul, Trench, Trubner & Co., Ltd.

Kane, Pandurang Vaman. 1941. *History of Dharmasastra*, vol. 2. Poona: Bhandarkar Oriental Research Institute.

Smith, Brian K. 1994. *Classifying the Universe.* Oxford: Oxford University Press.

DYAUS PITṚ

'Bright father', the 'divine'. The Vedic Zeus-cognate and personification of the bright sky. Dyaus Pitṛ is the father of the devas, the Vedic gods. He is frequently coupled with the earth as Dyāvāpṛthivī, the all-encompassing universe. Throughout the *Ṛgveda*, Dyaus remains a shadowy figure, unlike his Greek and Roman counterparts, and appears to be replaced by his more dynamic counterpart and offspring, Indra, the god of thunder and lightning and, in essence, the personification of Dyaus' virility. The pre-Vedic, Indo-European conflict between the devas and asuras becomes increasingly obscured in the Veda and later Sanskrit literature, and in the *Ṛgveda* itself, Dyaus is sometimes given the epithet asura, as are various devas as well. Other epithets that most likely first belonged to Dyaus before later emerging as separate figures include Rudra, Bṛhaspati and Parjanya ('thunderer'). The underlying Dyaus hypostasis, however, is the fertility principle that counters the stagnation, aridity and sterility sponsored or embodied by the antithetical asuras.

See also: **Asuras; Bṛhaspati; Indra; Rudra; Vedic pantheon; Vedism**

MICHAEL YORK

E

ECOLOGY

The attitudes to nature found in Hinduism are as multifaceted as the tradition itself, and, as in other traditions, the various visions are sometimes in conflict. While India today boasts what is perhaps the world's largest environmental movement (Peritore 1993), we should not expect to find examples of contemporary environmental awareness in pre-modern Hinduism. Traditional attitudes range from reverencing of nature as a manifestation of divinity through dismissal of the world as illusory (māyā) and insignificant (tuccha) in relation to authentic spiritual existence. What is not found – except perhaps as approximated in certain passages in the courtly literature – is the late modern concern for nature as nature, valued in itself for its beauty and diversity. In thinking about Hindu approaches to nature, caution must be taken to avoid reading contemporary concerns into ancient texts, which often results in romanticisation.

Despite the sometimes violent nature of their sacrificial milieu, the Veda contains hymns venerating aspects of nature as deities: Earth (Pṛthivī), Dawn (Uṣas), Fire (Agni) and others. In the sacred Gāyatrī mantra, generations of Hindus have paid homage to the sun and proclaimed their connectedness with 'earth, atmosphere, and heaven' (*Bṛhadāraṇyaka Upaniṣad* 6.3.6). The *Upaniṣads* set forth the notion – important when differentiating the Hindu vision from that of Abrahamic monotheism – of the one ultimate Being that becomes the universe, rather than creating it as an external product. As the *Chāndoyga Upaniṣad* (3.14.1) asserts, 'All this is Brahman'.

In the later theistic, devotional traditions of Hinduism, particularly in the Vaiṣṇavism of Rāmānuja, one finds the striking image of the world as the body of God. The earth is divinised as Bhū Devī ('Goddess Earth'), and Lord Viṣṇu himself is said to descend as avatāra to rescue her from destruction by demonic forces. Thus, devout Vaiṣṇavas ask Earth in their daily prayers to forgive the ill treatment of the touch of their feet. Indeed, pious Hindus regard the land of India itself as a goddess – Mother India (Bhārat Mātā). She is criss-crossed by pilgrimage routes connecting holy places, many associated with rivers, mountains and other natural features, giving India a kind of sacred geography. The *Bhagavadgītā* echoes the notion of God embodied in nature and recommends further a frugal lifestyle in which one devotes oneself to 'preserving the world' (loka-saṃgraha) and the 'welfare of all beings' (sarva-bhūta-hita). The theologian Vallabha teaches in his *Siddhāntamuktāvalī* that, just as no one would worship Gaṅgā Devī (Goddess Ganges) as deity only and fail to reverence her embodiment in the holy river, so no one who worships the supreme being, Kṛṣṇa, should devalue the world, which is his cosmic embodiment. Hindu law books (*Dharmaśutras* and *Dharmaśāstras*) contain numerous edicts that might now be considered as eco-friendly, involving protection of land, trees, rivers and so on, particularly as the duty of kings.

The notion of the sacred river is illustrative of some of the problematics of the Hindu understanding of the sacrality of nature. To take the most famous example, the Ganges is not only a river, she is indeed a goddess and, as such, an object of pious veneration. She is not only inherently pure, but also powerfully purifying. Bathing in the Ganges is spiritually cleansing: it relieves one of karmic and other religious impurities going back lifetimes. Ganges water is a purifying substance, bottled and distributed for ritual use all over India and abroad. Residents of Banaras, who bathe daily in the river's waters, say that since Mother Gaṅgā is purifying she cannot be polluted. Of course, the Ganges is polluted. Hindu awareness of a distinction between ritual purity and physical cleanliness means that something can be ritually pure but physically dirty, and vice versa. The religious perceptions of devout pilgrims and clerics may actually make it more difficult to mobilise action to clean up the Ganges. The problems caused by divergences between religious, scientific and political conceptions of the river's 'pollution' have been explored by Alley (1998, 2002).

Further dimensions of this complexity have been explored by Nagarajan (1998), who has studied the ecological implications of South Indian kōlam, ritual designs applied by women on the ground in worship of the goddess Earth. Nagarajan notes that human–nature interactions are embedded in complex cultural webs, so that what may appear 'ecological' to the outsider may not be understood that way from within. She offers the notion of 'intermittent sacrality' to explain how, for example, villagers can begin the day by honoring Earth as a goddess but later throw refuse on the same spot. Awareness of sacrality is not, and perhaps cannot be, sustained: the sacrality of a given aspect of nature may wax and wane or the ritual relationship that recognises that sacrality may lapse.

It is clear that, in the Hindu context, to say that an aspect of nature is sacred is not automatically and unambiguously an ecological plus. Indeed, as Alley, Nagarajan and others have noted, to sacralise nature could paradoxically undermine ecological consciousness, particularly if, as is often the case with maternal goddess imagery, it portrays nature as protecting, cleansing and forgiving – powerfully needing no protection from humans in return.

It is often claimed that Hinduism's unitary vision of the world as Brahman involves the sacralisation of the entire cosmos. This is less true than one might suppose. The prestigious Non-dualist or Advaita school of thought, in its classical formulation, achieves its monism not by divinising the world, but by eliminating it, as māyā, from the realm of the real. Dualism is often portrayed as a purely Western affliction, but Advaita and other Hindu theologies in fact involve a hierarchical dualism of God/world, spirit/

matter, soul/body that is not much different. Adherents must practice 'discrimination' (viveka) between these elements, characterised as 'the eternal and the non-eternal'. Although theistic Hindu doctrine, unlike Advaita, recognises the reality of multiplicity, it also displays a tendency to denigrate physical existence in favour of the more highly valued spiritual body (siddha-deha) and supramundane worlds (śuddha-sattva, go-loka, etc.). The ultimate religious goal for most Hindus is of course mokṣa, defined as 'liberation' of the individual from rebirth in the natural world (saṃsāra). This world-transcending aspiration is supported by the classical Hindu idea of declining cosmic ages (yuga), which predicts that the world for thousands of years hence will inevitably slide into increasing levels of moral, social and environmental chaos. Together, these elements further sharpen the spirit/matter dualism and – to whatever extent they are taken seriously – provide potential disincentives to ecological activism.

It may well be ecologically fruitful that Hinduism regards all beings, 'from [the god] Brahmā down to a blade of grass', as having equal spiritual potential, as being equally ensouled by ātman. This is among the considerations underlying the Hindu ethics of nonviolence (ahiṃsā) and vegetarianism. Still, the tradition does not escape a pronounced anthropocentricism. All humans were once, in their long chain of existences, incarnated as animals and even plants. There is a hierarchy of births, however, and human birth is the highest, even superior to birth as a god, because only humans, with rare exceptions, may attain mokṣa. On the other hand, humans who commit evil deeds are threatened by the law books with rebirth in 'lowly wombs', i.e. those of animals or insects.

The ecological problematics identified here are by no means intended to obscure the many affirmations of nature in Hinduism, even less to suggest that contemporary Hindus are not free to creatively reconfigure their traditions in the light of urgent needs of the present day. Hindu scholars have, in fact, already begun to do so. For example, Sherma (1998) has suggested that the Tantric traditions of Hinduism, with their doctrine of world and matter as fully real expression of the divine śakti (creative energy), may provide an antidote to the dualistic, world-negating tendency mentioned above.

See also: **Advaita; Agni; Ahiṃsā; Ātman; Bhagavadgītā; Bhakti Movement; Bhārāt Mātā; Blood Sacrifice; Brahmā; Brahman; Dharmaśāstras; Dharmasūtras; Gaṅgā; Gāyatrī Mantra; Karma (Law of Action); Kṛṣṇa; Māyā; Mokṣa; Pṛthivī; Purity and Pollution, Ritual; Rājā; Rāmānuja; Śakti; Saṃsāra; Tantrism; Tīrthayātra; Upaniṣads; Uṣas; Vaiṣṇavism; Vallabha; Vārāṇasī; Viṣṇu; Yuga**

LANCE NELSON

Further reading

Alley, Kelly D. 1998. 'Idioms of Degeneracy: Assessing Gaṅgā's Purity and Pollution'. In Lance E. Nelson, ed., *Purifying the Earthly Body of God: Religion and Ecology in Hindu India*. Albany, NY: State University of New York Press, 297–330.

Alley, Kelly D. 2002. *On the Banks of the Gaṅgā: When Wastewater Meets a Sacred River*. Ann Arbor, MI: University of Michigan Press.

Chapple, Christopher Key, and Mary Evelyn Tucker (eds). 2000. *Hinduism and Ecology: The Intersection of Earth, Sky, and Water*. Cambridge, MA: Harvard University Press.

Feldhaus, Anne. 1995. *Water and Womanhood: Religious Meanings of Rivers in Maharashtra*. New York: Oxford University Press.

James, George A. (ed.). 1999. *Ethical Perspectives of Environmental Issues in India*. New Delhi: A.P.H. Publishing.

Nagarajan, Vijaya Rettakudi. 1998. 'The Earth as Goddess Bhū Devī: Toward a Theory of "Embedded Ecologies" in Folk Hinduism'. In Lance E. Nelson, ed., *Purifying the Earthly Body of God: Religion and Ecology in Hindu India*. Albany, NY: State University of New York Press, 269–95.

Nelson, Lance E. (ed.). 1998. *Purifying the Earthly Body of God: Religion and Ecology in Hindu India.* Albany, NY: State University of New York Press.

Peritore, N. Patrick. 1993. 'Environmental Attitudes of Indian Elites: Challenging Western Postmodernist Models'. *Asian Survey* 33 (August): 304–818.

Sherma, Rita Dasgupta. 1998. 'Sacred Immanence: Reflections of Ecofeminism in Hindu Tantra'. In Lance E. Nelson, ed., *Purifying the Earthly Body of God: Religion and Ecology in Hindu India.* Albany, NY: State University of New York Press, 89–131.

EDGERTON, FRANKLIN (1885–1963)

American Sanskritist and comparative philologist. Edgerton studied at Cornell University, the Universities of Munich and Jena, and at Johns Hopkins University, teaching at the last and at the University of Pennsylvania (1913–26) before being appointed Professor of Sanskrit at Yale, where he remained until his retirement in 1953. In 1953–54 he was visiting Professor of Indology at Banaras Hindu University. Edgerton's early research was on Vedic linguistics; he published an edition of the sixth book of the Kashmirian *Atharvaveda* and a series of articles on the philosophical material in the *Atharvaveda* and on upaniṣadic thought. In 1924 he published a reconstruction of the lost original text of the *Pañcatantra.* In 1937, Edgerton replaced Moriz Winternitz (1863–1937) as the only non-Indian scholar invited to contribute to the Pune critical edition of the *Mahābhārata.* Although Edgerton's greatest work is perhaps his grammar and dictionary of Buddhist Hybrid Sanskrit (1953), in relation to Hinduism he is best known for his works on the *Bhagavadgītā* (1925, 1944a).

See also: **Bhagavadgītā; Hinduism, history of scholarship; Pañcatantra; Saṃhitā**

WILL SWEETMAN

Further reading

Edgerton, F. 1924. *The Pañcatantra Reconstructed*, 2 vols. New Haven, CT: American Oriental Series.

Edgerton, F. 1925. *The Bhagavad Gita or the Song of the Blessed One.* Chicago, IL: Open Court.

Edgerton, F. 1944a. *The Bhagavad Gītā Translated and Interpreted*, 2 vols. Cambridge, MA: Harvard Oriental Series.

Edgerton, F. 1944b. *The Sabhāparvan, Being the Second Book of the Mahābhārata*. Poona: Bhandarkar Oriental Research Institute.

Edgerton, F. 1953. *Buddhist Hybrid Sanskrit Grammar and Dictionary*, 2 vols. New Haven, CT: William Dwight Whitney Linguistic Series.

EIDLITZ, WALTHER (1892–1978)

Austrian expressionist poet, playwright and novelist, who studied in Vienna before serving in the First World War. A converted Jew, after the *Anschluß* (the annexation of Austria by Nazi Germany) Eidlitz went to India, where he remained from 1938 until 1946. Although interned by the British for most of this period, he met Swami Sadananda Dasa, whom he described as his teacher. In 1950 Eidlitz returned to India and spent two further years with Sadananda in Navadvipa and Puri. He then settled in Sweden, where he wrote of his experiences in India (1952). Among other publications on India was his major work on Caitanya (Eidlitz 1968). This book combined a retelling of the myths of Kṛṣṇa, drawing on Eidlitz's skills as a novelist in order 'to bring the sources to life', with extensive translations of the same sources in a more exact manner. It includes also a short analysis of the psychology of bhakti and an account of Caitanya's place in the Kṛṣṇa tradition.

See also: **Bhakti (as path); Hinduism, history of scholarship**

WILL SWEETMAN

Further reading

Eidlitz, W. 1952. *Unknown India; A Pilgrimage into a Forgotten World*. London: Rider. [Originally published in Swedish, *Den glömda världen: en bok om det okända Indien* (Stockholm, 1948)].

Eidlitz, W. 1968. *Kṛṣṇa-Caitanya: Sein Leben und seine Lehre* ('Kṛṣṇa-Caitanya: his life and his teaching'). Stockholm: Almqvist & Wiksell.

Raabe, P. 1992. *Die Autoren und Bücher des literarischen Expressionismus* ('The Authors and Books of Literary Expressionism'). Stuttgart: Metzler.

EKAŚṚṄGA

See: **Avatāra**

ELEMENTS

See: **Bhūtas (Elements)**

ELIADE, MIRCEA (1907–86)

Romanian historian of religions. After studying at the University of Bucharest, Eliade studied Indian philosophy with S.N. Dasgupta at the University of Calcutta from 1928 to 1932. After his return to Romania, he published his first scholarly book, entitled *Yoga: Essai sur les origines de la mystique indienne* (1933; revised English version, 1958), having already published fiction on Indian themes. The nature, extent and significance for his scholarly work of Eliade's involvement with Romanian fascist and anti-Semitic movements during the 1930s and the Second World War have been the subject of extensive discussion in recent scholarship. After the war Eliade taught in Paris, and from 1958 until his death was Professor at the University of Chicago. Although much of his later scholarly output was, in keeping with his understanding of the nature of religion and the task of the history of religions, concerned primarily with questions of general significance, Hinduism continued to serve as a source of examples of religious ideas and structures that he took to be common patterns in all religions.

See also: **Dasgupta, Surendranath; Hinduism, history of scholarship**

WILL SWEETMAN

Further reading

Eliade, M. 1958. *Yoga, Immortality and Freedom*. London: Routledge & Kegan Paul.

Eliade, M. 1978–85. *A History of Religious Ideas*, 3. vols. Chicago, IL: University of Chicago Press.

Rennie, B. (ed.). 2001. *Changing Religious Worlds: The Meaning and End of Mircea Eliade*. Albany, NY: State University of New York

EMERSON, RALPH WALDO (1803–82)

American poet, essayist and leader of the Transcendentalists. Emerson's engagement with Indian thought is most apparent in his journals and letters, rather than his published works, but one of his poems ('Brahma') has clear Hindu themes, being based on a verse found in both the *Bhagavadgītā* and the *Katha Upaniṣad*, and an early essay entitled 'The Over-Soul' has been seen as expressing ideas similar to those found in the *Upaniṣads*, although it was written before Emerson had read them. While Emerson's enthusiasm for Hindu thought is undoubted, its influence on him was more limited and it has been argued that Hinduism served primarily as a confirmation of his existing beliefs (Sharpe 1985: 26). Emerson not only drew attention to Asian thought in America but even, Lawrence Buell argues, shaped the views of Asian writers such as D.T. Suzuki who played a more direct role in transmitting Asian thought to the West.

See also: **Bhagavadgītā; Hinduism, history of scholarship; Upaniṣads**

WILL SWEETMAN

Further reading

Buell, L. 2003. *Emerson*. Cambridge, MA: Harvard University Press.
Goodman, R.B. 1990. 'East–West Philosophy in Nineteenth-Century America: Emerson and Hinduism'. *Journal of the History of Ideas* 51: 625–45.
Sharpe, E.J. 1985. *The Universal Gītā: Western Images of the Bhagavadgītā, a Bicentenary Survey*. London: Duckworth.

ETHICS

Most people define ethics in connection with what one ought to do. Some people are more specific, defining it in connection with 'doing no harm' and 'doing good'. Either way, ethics has two roots. First is human freedom. Although it allows adaptation, freedom does create problems. It must be curtailed by cultural preferences for some behaviours to bridge the oppositions that structure human existence: the individual versus the community, life versus death, and order versus chaos. Second is the experience of fear and awe when faced with nature – that is, the cosmic other. This, too, provokes people to prefer some behaviours rather than others in the quest to establish order. Authority supports these and rejects others. In this way, culture is the necessary counterpart of nature in organising human existence. So, ethics is a fundamental and universal feature of human existence.

The Hindu word that encompasses not only ethics but also religion and law is dharma: that which sustains and holds up the realms (dharati lokān iti). Because it assumes that specific acts are necessary to maintain order – cosmic, natural and social – dharma includes many things not generally included in modern Western ethics. These include piety and even, when used in the plural, the customs that characterise caste duty. 'It has been repeatedly emphasized that the concept of dharma is so difficult to define because it ignores or transcends differences which are essential or irreducible for Western understanding – differences between fact and norm, cosmos and society, physics and ethics, etc.' (Halbfass 1988: 312–13). But the same can be said of most pre-modern views of ethics, including those of Judaism and Christianity.

The roots of dharma appeared first in two Vedic ideas. One of these was ṛta (proper, right, fit, divine law, righteousness, law), which refers by extension to the universal order (the rhythm of the seasons, the movement of the planets, the migration of the animals and so forth). The other was ṛṇa (the debts that one must repay). These were like the premises of other early civilisations. Nature and even the cosmos were energised or animated by supernatural forces – often personified as deities, demons and minor spirits – that needed people to rejuvenate them periodically in the form of sacrificial offerings. The latter channelled energy, as life force, back to those supernatural forces, helping them to maintain order. Despite this interdependence – supernatural forces needed energy from people, and people needed energy from them – this was by no means a straightforward ritual proposition. Correctly performed rituals would uphold the cosmos, but personified supernatural forces had their idiosyncrasies; people sometimes had to flatter or beg them into acting on their behalf. The system contributed in no small way to ideas of what people should do, the linchpin of ethics, to ensure the necessary cosmic balance and prevent gaps in their support of it (sometimes construed as cosmic or social holes that they had to plug). To counteract any human lapses, Varuṇa, with his thousand eyes, watched for misdeeds and punished sins. Other deities, such as Rudra, punished them with diseases.

By the classical period, Hindus used several clusters of meaning to define dharma. These included: (1) upholding or sustaining; (2) religious ordinances and rites, which came to include not only mandatory Vedic rituals but also saṃskāras to mark the stages of life (āśramas), vows (vratas) and rites of expiation (prāyaścitta); (3) fixed principles or rules of conduct; (4) merit acquired by performing religious rites; (5) all religious and moral duties; (6) conduct appropriate to caste or stage of life; and (7) the fundamental characteristics of someone or something (light and heat being the sun's dharmas, for instance, flow and cleansing the water's, protection the king's and so forth). Despite this apparent heterogeneity, the underlying idea of dharma remained normative ordering. This explains the Hindu emphasis on orthopraxy rather than orthodoxy. Royal support for a just society now became more central to the meaning of dharma than brahmanical ritual, although royal legitimation via the aśvamedha (a complicated and costly ritual that sacrificed many animals but culminated in the sacrifice of a white stallion) linked the king with both cosmos and society. Dharma not only limited the king's power but also legitimated his use of it to protect society.

The *Dharmaśāstras*, in good scholastic tradition, further classify the vast topic of dharma: acts that are required daily (nitya), ones that are required occasionally (naimittika), ones that are optional (kāmya) and ones that are prohibited (pratiṣiddha). The first two refer mainly to Vedic rituals that are mandatory for brāhmaṇas; the third is open to anyone who wants to fulfil a mundane or supermundane personal desire; the fourth includes both universal prohibitions (such as abortion except when the mother's life is in danger) and those specific to particular groups. Another classification divides dharma into sāmānya and viśeṣa. Sāmānya, or common dharma according to the famous rule-giver Manu (who lived some time between the second century BCE and second century CE), includes nonviolence (āhiṃsa), truthfulness, not stealing, purity and restraint of the sense organs. This became a standard list, to the extent that anything can be called standard in Hinduism. By contrast, viśeṣa, or particular dharma, includes right acts (including rituals). Hindus determine these according to sex, caste, stage of life, occupation and region. In addition, they classify rules, rank rules (krama) and identify exceptions (apavāda). Because dharma acknowledges many different norms inherent in viśeṣadharma, normativity and orthopraxy have never led to homogeneity. And yet there has been an underlying coherence. Wilhelm Halbfass concludes that dharma is conceptually similar to Sanskrit grammar, which is 'a domain of "normative empiricism," an exemplary structure of rules and exceptions, complex and infinitely differentiated, yet irreducibly one and unique . . . . We may also refer to the use of the word *sādhu*, "good," "correct," which signifies both the grammatically "correct" forms of words and persons who are "good" insofar as their behavior conforms to the norms of *dharma*' (Halbfass 1988: 320).

In the classical period, the four sources of authority for dharma, in descending order, were śruti (revealed, heard), smṛti (remembered), sadācāra (right behaviour) and ātmanastuṣṭi (contentment). The first two are types of scripture that anchor regulations in the sacred. The last, personal conscience provides scope for adaptation to new situations. But even scriptures provide such scope. For one thing, they have internal contradictions, because they represent cumulative traditions that authors can exploit. Moreover, smṛti remains an open canon, which means new texts can be written with new norms to suit the times. Sadācāra, when it represents custom at the local level, can legitimate behavioural norms that are different from those prevailing elsewhere.

Hindu ethics are informed not only by the *Dharmaśāstras* but also by the *Mahābhārata* and *Rāmāyaṇa*. These place the dry lists of earlier texts into dramatic narratives that explore moral complexity and ambiguity. In the *Mahābhārata*, dharma is broader in scope than ever before. Of great importance are intention, with its underlying psychology, and remorse – perhaps in imitation of Buddhism. Performance traditions carry these ideas to the people. So do didactic animal tales such as the *Pañcatantra* and the *Subhāṣitas* or ethical maxims. These have become familiar to many people over the centuries.

Dharma is one side of a coin, karma the other. Karma, too, includes ritual. As the law of karma, though, it focuses more on personal behaviour and personal destiny. From the time of the *Upaniṣads*, cosmic cycles have microcosmic parallels. Each sentient being – consisting of soul (ātman), life principle (jīva), and body (deha/śarīra) – undergoes cycles of birth, death and rebirth on account of primal ignorance or desire. 'Hence there is this saying: "He's made of this. He's made of that". What a man turns out to be depends on how he acts and how he conducts himself. If his actions are good, he will turn into something good. If his actions are bad, he will turn into something bad. A man turns into something good by good action and into something bad by bad action. And so people say: "A person here consists simply of desire"' (*Bṛhadāraṇyaka Upaniṣad* 4.4.8; Olivelle 1998: 65). This puts primary ethical responsibility on the individual. But there are ways around this seemingly inexorable law: rites of expiation (prāyaścittas), for instance, or, if they fail, the grace of a supreme deity who eliminates these negative effects (pāpa) altogether.

People are extremely complex mosaics defined by preordained categories, each with mandatory behaviours that are coded by even more specific virtues with their underlying rules. Moreover, these norms are tempered by karmic legacies that contribute to one's own destiny (svabhāva). Norms tempered by personal karma create a rich moral palette and constitute the public, 'worldly' self (ahaṃkāra). Viśeṣa ethics are position relative – not in the postmodern sense of everyone having freedom to define both a distinctive self and 'the good', but in the sense of considering context and fostering creative adjustments. Hindus are like poets, therefore, who submit to the constraints of metres and semantics but play subtly with them to express personal insights. This expresses rasa (a word that refers in medical works to the organic substance created by digesting food, which circulates through the body to nourish it, and in dramatic texts to aesthetics). Rasa brings both vitality and refinement to ethics.

Hindus relate this moral aesthetic to ethics and spirituality by seeking enlightenment in one of three ways: the way of action (karmayoga), the way of knowledge or (jñānayoga) or the way of devotion (bhaktiyoga). Religious paths reduce the passions that create karma and keep people bound within the cycles of birth, death and rebirth. To stop the causality, they must eliminate desires, which propel the chain of cause and effect (epitomised in the *Bhagavadgītā*'s concept of naiṣkāmyakarmayoga, behaviour that is indifferent to results). P.V. Kane puts it this way: 'In the midst of countless rules of outward conduct there is always insistence on the necessity to satisfy the inner [person] ... (āntara-puruṣa) .... The reason given for cultivating ... virtues ... is based upon the philosophical doctrine of the one Self being immanent in every individual as said in the word "tat tvamasi" [that art thou]. This is the highest point reached in Indian metaphysics and combines morality and metaphysics' (Kane 1968–77: 2. 7). The root metaphor for this is 'crossing the ocean of saṃsāra' to liberation (mokṣa) on the other shore.

This explains how the classical world-view could be summarised as the four puruṣārthas, or goals, of human life: dharma, artha, kāma and mokṣa. Dharma begins the list, not only because it places ethical restraints on artha (the accumulation of wealth, governance and economics) and kāma (pleasure and sexuality), but also because it provides an ethical foundation for paths that lead to liberation by purifying the mind, eliminating egotism and developing virtues.

During the colonial period, Christian missionaries criticised Hinduism for lacking ethics. It was morally corrupt, they said, and therefore mistreated women, created the castes and so on. Because Hinduism had no supreme God who embodied moral perfection, placed too much emphasis on myth and imagination, had a cyclical view of time and was world-negating (a position popularised by Albert Schweitzer), it had no ethics and, therefore, no power to motivate reform.

In the nineteenth century, Hindus responded to these criticisms in several ways, including reform and creative hermeneutics. After India's independence, they linked socialist reforms with growing nationalism. By the early twenty-first century, they were creating a second round of creative hermeneutics. Consider how Mahesh Mehta argues his case: 'To reply to these objections, *mokṣa* or Brahman-relation is not transcendence or rejection of the world as such, but only of worldliness, of the false, deluded, self-bound attitude toward the world . . . . It actually designates freedom from egocentricity, which seeks to appropriate the world exclusively for itself . . . In the state of *jīvan-mukti*, the *dharma* returns and reasserts itself. A *jīvanmukta*, or any advanced renunciant, whole-heartedly engages in *loka-saṅgraha* or world welfare (Gītā III.25, IV.23) and indefatigably acts in the world for the deliverance of all creatures from *duḥkha*' (Mehta 2005: 99). Put otherwise, 'spiritual bliss and the welfare of the world' (ātmaśreyase jagathitāya ca) can be simultaneous.

Many of these general ethical principles characterise more specific ethical paradigms. Consider the relation between dharma or karma and medical ethics. In classical Āyurveda (medical) works, for instance, Hindus extended the notion that dharma upholds and sustains the world to include rituals and right actions to sustain the body by balancing the various forces that act on it and by preventing any holes or gaps. Because health is necessary to fulfil the goals of life, for instance, activities that ensure it are morally good and therefore dharmic. Many Hindus, in fact, consider health the root of dharma itself (and therefore of the other puruṣārthas, legitimate aims of life). Moreover, the law of karma explains birth defects, diseases, forms of suffering that resist medical treatment, and untimely death. Hindus relate right acts to good diet, exercise, adequate sleep, avoiding psychological stress, sexual moderation and so forth. Just as Hindus strive for harmony in society, nature and the cosmos, they strive for harmony in the physical, psychological, social, ethical and spiritual dimensions of life: past karma, diet, season, personal habits, temperament, caste, age, occupation, spiritual level and even astrological signs – all contribute to personal harmony.

In response to predictions of ecological disaster because of erosion, air and water pollution, and deforestation, some Hindu religious leaders have argued that Hinduism has many resources to support 'eco-dharma'. The divine expresses itself through nature in the following forms: the soul (ātman), energy (śakti), breath (prāṇa), and the five elements of material nature (mahābhūtas). Hindus are sympathetic to animals, moreover, because the latter have souls. They worship some (such as cows and serpents, nāgas) and believe that others are the vehicles of deities. Some Hindus express their concern for animals by being vegetarian or protecting animals, moreover, in other ways. Hindu are sympathetic to rivers in general, because these purify, and to some rivers in particular (such as the Sarasvatī and Gaṅgā), because these are sacred. They remember scriptural verses that praise water for its capacity to eliminate disease and sustain the body and believe that wisdom means using it properly (*Ṛgveda* 1.23). Hindus care for all trees, too, but especially for sacred trees such as the pippala and tulasī. They offer flowers (such as lotuses, marigolds and chrysanthemums) and fruits (bananas, coconuts and mangoes) in worship. And they revere other plants for their medicinal properties (turmeric, curry leaves). Hindus emphasise the importance of being in harmony with creation. Some people go further, in fact, by claiming that hell awaits those who kill creatures, pollute wells, ponds and tanks, and destroy gardens (*Padmapurāṇa bhūmikhaṇḍa* 96.7–8). Others believe in living abstemiously according to the dharmic obligation of supporting the welfare of all creation. Many worship, moreover, the Earth as Bhū Devī. Some Hindus have become activists; they stop the construction of dams that harm the environment, for instance, and protect trees. And some temples have become eco-conscious. Tirupati-Tirumalai, for instance, has encouraged people to plant trees as acts of devotion. In short, Hinduism can provide many traditional resources for environmentalists. But other activists point out that Hindus must be re-educated to reactivate their resources before it is too late; pollution is rampant.

The classical Hindu view of ethics influenced warfare, too, because dharma regulated artha (statecraft, which included warfare). A war was dharmic (dharmayuddha) if both its means and ends (self-defence, say, or the establishment of justice according to public standards) were righteous. The latter included clarity (discussing matters before the battle to ensure that the fight would be between equals); discrimination (restricting battles to particular places, times and participants, which protected women, children, the aged, the ill, priests, teachers, military support staff and all other peaceful citizens); containment (delegitimating ego and greed as motivations); establishing war as a duel, ideally, which would not involve a 'cast of thousands'; prudence (maintaining a link between brāhmaṇas and kṣatriyas to ensure that the latter would not use state power against the former); fairness (not continuing to fight if the enemy became panic-stricken, disabled, had broken weapons or showed signs of being willing to surrender); and reconciliation after victory (reinstating the defeated king and allowing defeated peoples to maintain their customs and laws as long as they recognised the suzerainty of the victorious king).

These specific types of ethics uphold ideas of order, balance, tolerance, minimalisation of violence, purity and restraint of the sense organs, all of which are said to belong to the Hindu way of life.

See also: **Abortion; Aesthetics; Ahaṃkāra; Āhimsa; Artha; Āśramas (stages of life); Ātman; Āyurveda; Bhagavadgītā; Bhakti (as path); Brāhmaṇas; Buddhism, relationship with Hinduism; Caste; Dharma; Dharmaśāstras; Gaṅgā; Halbfass, Wilhelm; Jīva; Jīvanmukta; Jñāna (as path); Kāma; Kane, Pandurang Vaman; Karma (as path); Karma (Law of Action); Mahābhārata; Manu; Mokṣa; Nāgas; Nationalism; Pañcatantra; Pāpa; Prāyaścitta; Puruṣārthas; Rāmāyaṇa; Rudra; Sacred animals; Sacred geography; Sacred texts; Śakti; Samsāra; Saṃskāras; Sarasvatī; Śarīra; Tulasī; Upaniṣads; Varṇa; Varuṇa; Vrata**

KATHERINE K. YOUNG

Further reading

Barlingay, S.S. 1998. *A Modern Introduction to Indian Ethics*. Delhi: Penman Publishers.

Chapple, C.K. 1993. *Nonviolence to Animals, Earth, and Self in Asian Traditions.* Albany, NY: State University of New York Press.
Coward, H.G., J.J. Lipner and K.K. Young (eds). 1989. *Hindu Ethics: Purity, Abortion, and Euthanasia.* Albany, NY: State University of New York Press.
Crawford, C.S. 2003. *Hindu Bioethics for the Twenty-first Century.* Albany, NY: State University of New York Press.
Creel, A. 1977. *Dharma in Hindu Ethics.* Calcutta: Firma KLM Private.
Halbfass, W. 1988. *India and Europe: An Essay in Understanding.* Albany, NY: State University of New York Press.
Heesterman, J.C. 1978. 'Veda and Dharma'. In W.D. O'Flaherty and J.D.M. Derrett, eds, *The Concept of Duty in South Asia.* New Delhi: Vikas Publishing House, 80–95.
Heim, M. 2005. 'Differentiations in Hindu Ethics'. In W. Schweiker, ed., *The Blackwell Companion to Religious Ethics.* Malden, MA: Blackwell, 341–54.
Hiltebeitel, A. 2001. *Rethinking the Mahābhārata: A Guide to the Education of the Dharma King.* Chicago, IL: University of Chicago Press.
Hopkins, E.W. 1924. *Ethics of India.* New Haven, CT: Yale University Press.
Kane, P.V. 1968–77 [1930–62]. *History of Dharmaśāstra*, 5 vols, 2nd edn. Poona: Bhandarkar Oriental Research Institute.
Matilal, B.K. (ed.). 1989. *Moral Dilemmas in the Mahābhārata.* Shimla: Indian Institute of Advanced Study.
Mehta, M.M. 2005. 'Dharma and Mokṣa: Conflict, Continuity, and Identity'. In A. Vohra, A. Sharma and M. Miri, eds, *Dharma: The Categorial Imperative.* New Delhi: DK Printworld, 88–103.
Monius, A. 2005. 'Origins of Hindu Ethics'. In W. Schweiker, ed., *The Blackwell Companion to Religious Ethics.* Malden, MA: Blackwell, 330–40.
O'Flaherty, W.D. 1978. 'The Clash Between Relative and Absolute Duty: The Dharma of Demons'. In W.D. O'Flaherty and J.D.M. Derrett, eds, *The Concept of Duty in South Asia.* New Delhi: Vikas Publishing House, 96–106.
Olivelle, P. (trans.). 1998. *Upaniṣads.* New York: Oxford University Press.
Perret, R.W. 1998. *Hindu Ethics: A Philosophical Study.* Honolulu, HI: University of Hawaii Press.
Perret, R.W. 2005. 'Hindu Ethics?' In W. Schweiker, ed., *The Blackwell Companion to Religious Ethics.* Malden, MA: Blackwell, 323–29.
Prabhu, J. 2005. 'Trajectories of Hindu Ethics'. In W. Schweiker, ed., *The Blackwell Companion to Religious Ethics.* Malden, MA: Blackwell, 355–67.
Vohra, A., A. Sharma and M. Miri (eds). 2005. *Dharma: The Categorical Imperative.* New Delhi: DK Printworld.
Young, K.K. 2004. 'Hinduism and the Ethics of Weapons of Mass Destruction'. In S. H. Hashmi and S. P. Lee, eds, *Ethics and Weapons of Mass Destruction: Religious and Secular Perspectives.* New York: Cambridge University Press, 277–307.

ETYMOLOGY

See: **Nirukta**

EUROPE, HINDUS IN

Basic structures

Hinduism in Europe is a plural and highly heterogeneous phenomenon. Hindus living in European countries come from diverse countries such as India, Sri Lanka, Surinam, Trinidad and the Fiji Islands. Furthermore, Western converts in new religious movements such as the International Society for Krishna Consciousness (ISKCON), Transcendental Meditation and the Rajneesh movement of the late Bhagwan Shree Rajneesh have broadened the category of 'Hindu' beyond the Indian ethnicity. The so-called 'Indian' or 'migrant Hindus' have created their own homes away from home, bringing with them a diversity of ethnic styles and cultural patterns. Kinship, caste, region of origin, affiliation to a religious subtradition (saṃpradāya) and ethnicity differentiate the estimated one million Hindus living in Europe in the early twenty-first century.

The current presence of Hindus and Hindu traditions in Europe is primarily the result of several waves of numerically strong immigrations. During the 1950s and early 1960s, large numbers of South Asians came to Britain in order to fill the labour shortage in British post-war industry. The 1960s and early 1970s saw the arrival of Hindu women and children in the course of family reunion. This process was accompanied by the flight of East African Asians to Britain in the wake of the 'Africanisation' policies. From 1975, on the eve of the independence of Surinam (former Dutch Guyana), about 80,000 to 100,000 Surinamese Hindustanis have settled in the Netherlands. And since the mid-1980s about 200,000 Tamils from Sri Lanka, the majority of them Hindus, have found refuge in various Western countries in Europe. In addition, during the 1970s and 1980s Hindu-related groups and movements won converts and supporters though their actual numbers remained much lower than reported by the media and highlighted by anti-cult groups.

Early encounters

Before the actual arrival of Hindu people to Europe, India and reified 'Hinduism' were allocated an idealised and romanticised place in European imagination. Britain as colonial power in India became instrumental in introducing Hindu ideas and concepts in Europe. British Orientalists of the late eighteenth century translated and edited Indian sacred texts, such as the *Bhagavadgītā* and Kālidāsa's classic Sanskrit play *Śakuntalā*. Starting from William Jones (1736–94), the famous founder of the Royal Asiatic Society in Calcutta in 1784, up to Friedrich Max Müller (1823–1900), the diligent editor of the *Sacred Books of the East* (50 vols, 1879 ff.), India and the Orient in general became the coherent 'Other' in European imagination and self-definition. In Germany, romanticists glorified India as the locus of purity, innocence and original religiosity. The idealisation lasted a long time, even up to the 1960s' enthusiasm for India and its spirituality.

During the nineteenth and early twentieth centuries, only a small number of Indian professionals, traders and students came to Europe and even fewer settled there, mainly in Britain. The reformer and spokesman Vivekananda (1863–1902), having delivered his famous lecture at the World's Parliament of Religions in Chicago 1893, toured the United States and Europe (1893–97 and 1899–1900). His Ramakrishna Mission, founded in 1897, sought to spread Indian spirituality in the West. In addition, through the reinforcement of Indian intellectuals such as Sarvepalli Radhakrishnan (1888–1975) in the first half of the twentieth century, 'Hinduism' came to be seen purely in terms of a refined philosophy. This particular focus in the interpretation of the few elite intellectual Neo-Vedāntists acquired hegemonic status. It neglects and disregards, however, all forms of so-called common or popular Hindu traditions as practised by the vast majority.

The entry will outline the developments country by country. Different developments and varied compositions of Hindu 'communities' will become apparent, due to a country's specific historical and juridical situation. An emphasis is laid on Great Britain, the Netherlands and Germany. Eighty per cent of Hindu people in Europe live in these countries and numerous studies make possible a reliable reconstruction of the local histories.

Great Britain

Until the 1950s few Hindus had come to Britain; the total number of Asian residents in 1945 did not exceed 7,000 persons. Most of these individuals were skilled or semi-skilled professionals, among them doctors, merchants, sailors and students. Following this pioneer stage, the 1950s and early 1960s saw a considerable influx of immigrants from the Indian subcontinent and the Caribbean. British industry offered a variety of employment opportunities, though immigrants were mainly relegated to the lowly status of cheap labour in the least desired jobs. During this period, immigration statistics listed almost exclusively men, most of them in their twenties to forties. Emigration from India was mainly conducted from the North West Indian states of Punjab and Gujarat, both regions with longstanding traditions of migration. The migrants predominantly intended to stay abroad for only a few years. By all accounts, their aim was to earn and save money and to invest this for their future in India.

In addition to Indian workers, Hindu Tamils from Sri Lanka and Indo-Caribbeans from Trinidad and Guyana had arrived in London and the industrial regions. The latter were the first to set up a Hindu cultural society in Britain, the Hindu Dharma Sabha in 1957. This body hired public halls in south London for the celebration of major Hindu festivals. Likewise, in Bradford, Gujarati Hindus set up the Bharatiya Mandal (Indian Association) in 1957. Since the mid-1960s the pattern of migration has changed considerably. Stimulated by the increasingly restrictive Immigration Acts during the 1960s, family reunification started on a grand scale. The arrival of wives, children and further relatives via chain migration transformed the character of each community. The all-male households changed to family and kinship households. The money saved was invested to purchase houses, if possible in those districts where a certain number of fellow Hindus already resided. Apparently, the nature of settlement pointed to the fact that Britain was more and more accepted as a new home. The sojourners became settlers; the myth of return declined.

The arrival of East African families of Indian descent marks the second main event during this phase. Due to nationalist policies of Africanisation, about 9,600 Hindus from Kenya, 28,000 from Uganda and some further thousands from Tanzania and Zambia came to Britain during the period 1967–73. These by then twice migrants had had previous experiences of establishing social and religious institutions, as their caste groups had crystallised into formal caste associations in East Africa. These African Indians came to Britain in complete family units and quickly employed their organisational skills to re-establish their institutions in their new environment. A proliferation of cultural societies and places of worship occurred. Typically, the first Hindu temple was established in Coventry in 1967 by Gujaratis from Kenya, followed by a temple in Leicester in 1969 and a Swami Narayana temple in Islington (London) in 1970. As a consequence of the rapidly increasing number of institutions, religious practices and observances became intensified.

After the end of mass immigration in 1973, the proliferation of religious organisations and activities continued. Furthermore, the emergence of the second generation led to initiatives to provide mother-tongue classes, form youth groups and adapt to the British lifestyle. Calculations estimated that there were 82 Hindu temples in 1978, growing to more than 100 four years later. The temples were established in adapted private houses or in converted churches. During the 1980s and early 1990s the number of Hindu places of worship grew to some 300, supplemented by more than 400 local and nationwide cultural and religious organisations. A concentration of temples and societies can be found in Greater London and in the conurbations of the Midlands. In particular, in Leicester, where according to the 2001 Census one person in seven is Hindu, almost 100 Hindu associations and temples exist.

Statistics regarding the number of Hindus living in Britain vary; nevertheless they underscore a continuous increase in the figure. In 1975 some 307,000 Hindus had settled in Britain, rising to 357,000 Hindus among the 1,271,000 South Asians in 1984. Estimates for the early 1990s run to some 400,000–440,000 Hindus. The results of the 2001 Census give the number of Hindus in England and Wales as 552,421 (1.06 per cent of the population), providing reasonable grounds for an estimate of 600,000–620,000 Hindus for the whole of Britain.

The vast majority of Hindus came from the Punjab and Gujarat, either directly or via East Africa. Hindus of Gujarati background make up about 70 per cent of the British Hindu population. Far from being a homogeneous ethnic group, the Gujarati population is subdivided according to local origin, caste and sectarian affiliation. The remaining 30 per cent of the Hindu population is made up of Hindus of Punjabi descent (15 per cent) and other Indian states. In addition, from 1983 onwards an increasing number of Tamil refugees from Sri Lanka applied (mostly in vain) for asylum. Their number is estimated at 35,000, four out of five being Hindu. The construction of a South Indian-styled temple with a typical gopuram is underway in East Ham (London), though several Tamil Hindu temples already exist. The number of Indo-Caribbean and Indo-Fiji immigrants is somewhat lower than the that of Tamils. Nevertheless, Caribbean and Fijian Hindus have set up their own societies and their typical style of Hindu temple.

In addition to these South Asian Hindus, Hindu-related groups, as mentioned earlier, became established in Britain. Their followers are mainly Western converts. Although temples and centres of Sathya Sai Baba and ISKCON are increasingly visited by Indian Hindus, an apparent difference in these two forms of religiousness nevertheless exists. The legal quarrel which threatened to shut down the Bhaktivedanta Manor temple of the Krishna Consciousness Movement during the 1990s, however, brought the two strands closer together and fostered a considerable solidarity for the Krishna Consciousness Movement among British South Asian Hindus. The impact and influence of this convert-based movement have been classified as an 'Iskconisation of British Hinduism' (Nye 1998).

In terms of religious affiliation, the vast majority of Britain's Hindus consider themselves to follow the Sanātana Dharma understanding of Hindu practices and ideas. In this line, numerous temples became organised in the National Council of Hindu Temples (a registered charity, founded 1978). Most of these temples are involved in Vaiṣṇava traditions. However, one also finds Śaiva Hindus such as Sri Lankan Tamils and further regionally based Hindu traditions and specific saṃpradāya. According to Raymond Williams, the Vaiṣṇava Swami Narayana movement was 'the largest and perhaps the fastest growing' (Williams 1984: 187). Almost as an empirical confirmation of this assumption, the Swaminarayan Hindu Mission in Neasden (North West London), inaugurated in 1995, was Britain's first traditionally built Hindu temple. This huge marble mandir is by far the biggest and most splendid temple of Europe's Hindu diaspora.

The Netherlands

Up to the early 1970s, less than 2,000 Hindus, mainly from Surinam (named Dutch Guyana until 1948), were resident in the Netherlands. As the date of independence of the Netherlands' last colony in South America approached (1975), a third of the Caribbean country's population, more than 100,000 Creoles, Javanese, Africans and so-called Hindustanis, descendants of former indentured workers from India, left for the Netherlands. Among the Hindustanis ('Indians'), Hindus made up 76 per cent, Muslims 20 per cent and Christians 4 per cent. The bulk of migrants came in 1974 and 1975, and again in 1980, the last year for Surinamese to apply for Dutch citizenship. The number of Surinamese Hindus in the Netherlands rose from 2,500 in 1971 to 24,000 in 1976 and almost 40,000 in 1981. Since then, a steady increase of about 2–3 per cent per year is observable. The Central Bureau for Statistics stated the number of Hindus, including also Indian, Tamil Sri Lankan and Western Hindus, to be 71,000 in 1993 and 95,000 in 2002. This is 0.6 per cent of the population in the Netherlands.

The Hindus from Surinam brought with them their particular form of 'Caribbean Hinduism', evolved during the nineteenth and early twentieth centuries. Its characteristics are an attenuation of the caste system and an expansion of the brāhmaṇa's ritual and social influence. Brāhmaṇa priests were able to establish themselves as constituting the sole authority in carrying out rites and interpreting the texts. From the 1920s, this dominant position came under threat as missionaries of the Hindu reform movement, the Arya Samaj, gained popularity among Guyanese Hindus. Emigration transplanted these two factions, shaping Surinamese Hindu presence in the Netherlands along the numerically stronger brahmanical, so-called Sanātana Dharma and the smaller, though well-organised, Arya Samaj strands.

The Dutch government's policy of deconcentration of the migrant flow resulted in the dispersal of the Hindustanis into small pockets all over the country. The priests were forced to travel to their clientele, ever more so as the extended families had been split up. During their short visits, only the performance of the rituals was possible, and no time remained for more intense personal and family-related care as was practised in Surinam. A situation evolved 'in which the pandits become free entrepreneurs in the market of religion, vying with each other to attend to as many clients as possible' (van der Burg and van der Veer 1986: 523).

Since its inception, Hinduism has been weak in the Netherlands in terms of organisation. Though state policy helped to set up a number of welfare organisations and cultural foundations, personal struggles for prestige and distrust among the priests hindered the establishment of effective organisations. The brahmanical priests became organised in a council in 1977, whereas the followers of the Arya Samaj had organised a national society as early as 1964. The latter, however, was more or less confined to the region of The Hague. Consequently, a new nationwide Stichting Federatie Arya Samaj Nederland was set up in 1987. In 1994, there were about 90 brahmanical or Sanātana Dharma priests, 71 of them organised in the priesterraad (board of priests). The number of Arya Samaj priests is estimated to be about 40. Only a few of the priests work on a full-time basis, most of them having an ordinary job or having retired.

In addition to the national organisation, according to Jan P. Schouten's stocktaking in 1991, the Arya Samaj had 26 regional societies and foundations, which maintained three temples in Utrecht, Amsterdam and The Hague. Likewise, the Sanātana Dharma was organised in three national and 40 regional societies, maintaining 16 temples. As such, Hinduism in the Netherlands had become denominationalised into Sanātana Dharma and Arya Samaj. A concentration of Hindu activities can be found in Amsterdam and The Hague, where numerous Hindu societies and temples of both factions can be found. The temples are placed in residential houses, offering regular services, mainly on Sundays.

In the shadow of Surinamese Hinduism, some other groups of Hindus live in the Netherlands. A few thousand Tamil Hindus, all refugees from Sri Lanka, have found asylum there. They maintain Śaivaite temples in Den Helder, Harleen and Roermond. An estimated 10,000 Hindus were among the 12,500 Indian citizens residing in the Netherlands in 2002. In addition to these South Asian and the Surinamese Hindus, there are quite a number of Hindu-related groups. Amongst the 27 groups and movements listed by Schouten in 1994, the Krishna Consciousness Movement and the Sathya Sai Baba tradition are the most active and established ones. Both have been met with increasing interest by Surinamese Hindus too.

Germany

The presence of Hindu people and communities in Germany is relatively recent. However, the establishment of the German branch of the Theosophical Society in 1884 and the invitations to the poet Rabindranath Tagore in 1921 and 1930 to lecture in Germany are of interest. Both point to the glorified picture of India and Indian religiosity, prominent in Germany since the late eighteenth century.

During the period from the 1950s to the 1970s, the number of Hindus coming to Germany rose slowly. They were mainly medical students from West Bengal, but also doctors, scientists, technicians and merchants from various parts of North India. These individual professionals and academics were mainly men from the urban, upper middle classes. Quite a number married German women. Staying in Germany for several decades, they became well established as businessmen, professors or senior physicians. Many of them adopted German nationality. In late 2002, 41,200 registered Indians (70 per cent male) and an estimated 1,000 illegal entrants and asylum seekers from India lived in Germany. These included a number of Indian Christians, estimated at about 10,000, mainly from Kerala. Though most are financially well off, the established Indian Hindus have built only a few places of worship situated in private houses. A temple in Frankfurt am Main, the only Indian Hindu temple so far, was short-lived.

A much smaller though much better organised group of Hindu people can be found among refugees from Afghanistan, arriving from 1980 onwards. Among the 93,000 Afghan people living in Germany in late 2002 – about 25,000 with German citizenship – a minority of about 5,000 were Hindus. In Afghanistan, the approximately 35,000 Hindus formed a prosperous, urban minority, many of them working as traders in Kabul. Their skill in surviving in the Afghan diaspora was successfully transplanted to Germany, even more so as the forced migration occurred in whole family and kinship units. These migrants established several cultural societies and spacious, richly decorated temples in Hamburg, Frankfurt and Cologne (two temples). The temples are occasionally visited by Indian Hindus and Sikhs too.

The numerically strongest and currently most visible Hindu community in Germany is formed by Tamil people. Since the escalation of the Sinhalese–Tamil war in Sri Lanka in 1983, about 300,000 Sri Lankans have left for Canada and 200,000 for Europe. In Germany, up to late 2002, about 60,000 men and their families had taken refuge as asylum seekers. Among these were approximately 45,000 Hindus, almost all Śaivas. The Tamil refugees have established South Asian shops and founded cultural societies in various cities and towns. These organise Tamil language, music and dance classes. Additionally, since the late 1980s many Hindu temples have been founded, numbering 25 places of worship in early 2003. These well-organised temples are situated in cellars and flats, some in former industrial storerooms or halls. Apart from their religious importance for the carrying out of pūjā, life-cycle rituals and festivals, these temples also function as socio-cultural meeting points. A few temples have started to celebrate the annual temple festival with a public procession, thus bringing the gods and Hindu tradition to wider notice. The first to have done so was the Sri Kamadchi Ampal temple in Hamm, Westphalia, in 1993. The attendance at the festival grew from a few hundred to 4,000 in 1996 and 12,000–15,000 in 2002. These public processions also enable Hindu participants to perform bodily austerity practices known from South Asia, such as women carrying a heavy fire pot or doing prostrations, and men rolling on their sides around the temple or performing the kavāti dance (dancing with a yoke on the shoulders, decorated with peacock feathers). Some of these dancers have been pierced with hooks in their backs and had a spear pricked through their cheeks. Since its inception, the festival of the Sri Kamadchi Ampal temple has grown nearer to established South Asian patterns each year. Additionally, the temple's head priest, Sri Paskarankurukkal, succeeded in building a huge South Indian-style temple on the outskirts of Hamm. It was financed by donations from devotees and the installation ceremony took place in July 2002, generating enthusiastic interest from the media and many German people.

Less prominent in the public perception are those Germans who have converted to a Hindu tradition. These Western Hindus, in groups such as the Krishna Consciousness Movement, Ananda Marga, Transcendental Meditation and the Rajneesh Movement, might be estimated at some 7,000–8,000 people. They come together in numerous local groups to pursue devotional acts or meditation, no longer provoking public debates as in the 1970s and 1980s. As in Great Britain, though on a smaller scale, the Krishna movement attracts some interest among Indian and Tamil Hindus. In general, the approximately 100,000 Hindus living in Germany are a heterogeneous, little visible religious minority, though this has started to change considerably due to the dedicated efforts from within the Tamil Hindu fold.

Switzerland

As in Germany, Tamil Hindus make up the majority of Hindu people living in Switzerland. In late 2001, some 38,000 Tamils were registered as asylum seekers or residents with permission to stay. According to Christopher McDowell's study, 87 per cent of the Tamil refugees coming from 1983 to 1991 were Hindus (McDowell 1996: 119). The 2000 Census gives the number of Hindus living in Switzerland as 27,800, 92.5 per cent of them of non-Swiss nationality. Similar to the developments in Germany, the 1990s were a time of temple proliferation. In early 2003, Tamil Hindus had built 19 temples, the majority located in the German speaking cantons (West and North Switzerland). One of the most prominent and spacious temples, the Sri Sivasubrahmanyam temple (founded 1994) in Adliswil (near Zurich) stages a public procession attended by some 3,000 visitors. As in the circumambulation festival at the Sri Kamadchi Ampal temple in Germany, devotees perform various kinds of bodily demanding and severe practices. In addition to these new religious places, Tamils – both Hindu and Christian – tend also to visit Catholic Marian shrines. Most famous among these is the statue of the Black Madonna at Einsiedeln, central Switzerland. The community of non-Asian, Western Hindus is rather small and organised in a variety of centres and circles. Among them, the Sathya Sai Baba, with four Seva centres (local groups for study and social service), and the Swiss Krishna Community, with its beautiful shrine room at the Zurich Krishna temple, are quite active, attracting the few Indian Hindus living in Switzerland also.

Austria

Austria is a peculiar case compared to the other countries. Due to the restrictive state policy against foreigners, few Indian and very few Tamil Sri Lankan people reside there. The 2001 Census states that there are 3,600 Hindus, made up of 1,800 Austrians and 1,800 foreigners. In Vienna the Indians formed two organisations, the Hindu Community in 1980 and the Hindu Mandir Association in 1990. These two tend not to cooperate and appear to be rivals. Both maintain a Hindu temple in North Indian style in converted buildings. In 1998, the Hindu Religious Society of Austria, an organisation formed by Indian and Western Hindus, acquired the status of a juridical community. As such, the society received a status similar to established Christian churches, unlike them not supported by the state. Despite ambitious plans according to the society's rules, activities remain at a low level due to personnel shortages. However, developments have just begun and it is too early to point to first results. Neo-Hindu groups with Western followers are, compared to the few migrant Hindus, strong and well organised. A recent survey pointed to 14 different groups (Hutter 2001: 53), the number of members in groups such as Sathya Sai Baba, the Sri Chinmoy movement, ISKCON, Omkarananda Ashram and Sahaja Yoga equalling that of Indian Hindus.

France

In France some 10,000 Gujarati Hindus have settled, many of them refugees from Uganda. In addition, an estimated 40,000–60,000 Hindu Tamil refugees have found asylum and established temples in Paris and some cities. In particular, in the Parisian district La Chapelle, a 'petite Jaffna' with Tamil shops, societies and temples, has developed.

Portugal

Despite Goa being Portugal's Indian colony until 1961, the present Hindu community originates from Mozambique. Mozambique was a Portuguese colony from 1507 to 1974. At the time of independence, most Indian people fled the country due to the 'Africanisation' policy, bringing some 4,000–5,000 Hindus to Portugal. These Hindus, almost all Gujaratis, settled mainly in the capital Lisbon, especially in the poor districts of Quinta da Holandesa and Quinta da Montanha. During almost 30 years of residence, a few became affluent as tradesmen, doctors or technicians; the majority, however, remained in low-paid occupations. In the mid-1990s the number of Hindus was estimated at some 8,000, only about 500 of whom lived outside the Lisbon area.

As in other countries, Hindus in Portugal strive to retain and preserve their Hindu identity through public festivals, domestic rituals and supplementary classes for the children. Temples have been established in Lisbon, Porto and Faro. The Comunidade Hindú, founded in 1982, organises religious, cultural, educational and recreational activities. This organisation is also promoting the building of an impressive Hindu temple in Lumiar, a district near the centre of Lisbon. The temple, its construction having started in 1989, is designed to be accompanied by a spacious socio-cultural centre. A special problem for the Hindus in Portugal, however, stems from the fact that their children grow up speaking Portuguese as their mother tongue, which makes communication with Hindus elsewhere in Europe and India rather difficult.

Denmark

In Denmark, Sri Lankan Hindus make up 90 per cent of the approximately 9,000 Hindus present in early 2003. The approximately 8,000 Tamil Hindus are scattered all over Denmark. In the small town of Herning, 70 km West of Aarhus, Tamils inaugurated the first Danish Hindu temple in a top-floor flat above a fitness centre in 1994. Fairly soon it became obvious that the temple, dedicated to Vinayagar (Skt. Gaṇeśa), was too small and it was moved to a former factory in an industrial area outside Herning. The installation of the deities took place in 1996. In the same year, a young Tamil woman, Lalitha Sripalan, and her husband started a temple for the goddess Śrī Apirāmi Ampāḷ in a rebuilt house in the small town of Brande (also in Jutland). However, as the publicly performed procession attracted more than a thousand participants, neighbours started to complain. Lalitha Sripalan agreed to leave the town and converted a former farmhouse into the new Sree Abirami Amman Temple in 2000. The distinctive character of this temple is that worship is conducted three times a day by the young, non-trained and non-brāhmaṇa woman herself. Furthermore, when necessary, Lalitha Sripalan is possessed by Śrī Apirāmi Ampāḷ and becomes the medium of the goddess and an embodiment of śakti (cosmic energy, power). In this trance state Lalitha Sripalan, alias Śrī Apirāmi Ampāḷ, is able to heal and to perform divinations. Though she is not acknowledged by brāhmaṇas, the fame of the female medium has spread all over Denmark, and Tamils from Norway, Sweden, Germany and even Canada come to attend the annual temple festival. Finally, in Denmark there are also a few hundred Hindus from North India and members of and sympathisers associated with Hindu-related groups, especially the Krishna Consciousness Movement.

Norway

In Norway, again, the majority of Hindus is made up of Tamil refugees from Sri Lanka. They opened the Sri Sivasubramanyar temple in Oslo in 1998 and maintain a rented assembly hall in Bergen. Services (pūjā) and festivals are conducted on a regular basis according to brahmanical rules. Knut Jacobsen identified some 75 per cent of the 10,000 South Asian Hindus in Norway as Tamils (Jacobsen 2003). The remaining 2,500 Hindus are made up of North Indian Hindus, among them also several hundred Gujaratis who came as refugees from Uganda. Both Indian and Tamil Hindus have founded societies to retain linguistic and cultural bonds.

Sweden

In Sweden, due to the fact that an overwhelming majority of both Indian and Tamil Sri Lankan immigrants acquired Swedish citizenship, reliable figures are hard to find. Calculations based on Census statistics suggest about 12,000 Indian people, some 3,000 of these Gujarati refugees from Uganda, and approximately 6,000 Sri Lankan Tamil people in 2000. Near Stockholm, the Tamil Hindus opened the Sri Vinayagar temple (in Tamil: Cuvitaṉ Cirī Citti Vināyakar Ālayam) in a converted house in 2000. Indian Hindus maintain several cultural societies.

Eastern European countries

In Eastern European countries no South Asian Hindu communities have been traced, only some individual Hindus who work there as professionals. As in most West European countries, Hindu-related groups such as the Krishna Consciousness Movement, Brahma Kumari, Transcendental Meditation and Sri Chinmoy have been able to gather a small following.

Concluding remarks

The developments and histories of Hindu traditions vary considerably in European countries. Also, obviously 'Hinduism' does not compose a monolithic block or uniform shape, either in Europe as a whole or in a specific country. Though Britain has the largest number and longest history of permanently settled Hindus in Europe, it cannot claim to be representative and exemplary of Europe at large. Whereas Indian Hindus, mainly Vaiṣṇava from North India, dominate the British situation, as they do in Portugal and Sweden, in continental Europe Tamil Śaivas and Śaktas have taken the lead. An exception, nevertheless, is the Netherlands, where Surinamese Hinduism in its particular Caribbean form is strongest. In most of Europe, convert Hindu groups have remained numerically less significant.

Contacts between the different Hindu traditions, strands and communities are few, though this differs from country to country. In general, regional-linguistic and 'sectarian' temples have been set up. Only where too few Hindus of like language, tradition and caste live have temples been formed by two or more religious-cultural groups on a collaborative basis (e.g. in Leeds and Edinburgh). However, fusion gave way to fission as soon as the number of supporters and financial resources enabled the creation of a place of worship in a particular tradition. In Europe, in contrast to the USA, eclectic pan-Hindu or 'ecumenical' associations and temples are rather the exception than the rule.

Practising Hindu devotion, fasts, lifecycle rites, storytelling and much more at home is still paramount for the continuation and handing on of the specific tradition to the next generation. However, given that temples in India have acquired an important function and integral role within Hindu traditions, their importance in the European diasporas – once established – seems to have further increased. In addition to functioning as a place of worship, the diasporic temple has become the physical and psychological focal point for the Hindu population in a region. The temple also serves as a supplementary school, a community centre, sometimes as a sports activity centre like the Shree Krishna Temple in Coventry, built in 1992. In general, a temple is a social place to meet fellow Hindus. The temple makes 'Hinduism' experiential and provides it with a visible and concrete point of reference, both for the Hindus themselves and for the non-Hindus. This became most apparent with the inauguration of the Shree Swaminarayan mandir in London in 1995 and the Sri Kamadchi Ampal alayam (temple) in Hamm in 2002. In both countries, national and international media reported enthusiastically on the traditionally styled temples. Such prestigious temples highlight that Hindus and Hindu traditions in Europe are in the process of change. No longer exclusively relegated to small back-door places of worship, Hindus have started to enter the mainstream. Acquiring visibility and public recognition, through both well-attended processions and the building of spectacular temples, Hindus have a presence in the public sphere. European societies have become plural in religious terms, and Hindu traditions form an increasingly vigorous part of this pluralism. And as the Hindu deities of old take residence in new homes, the migrants and their offspring consider Europe as their new and permanent home as well.

See also: **Ananda Marga; Arya Samaj; Asiatic Societies; Brahma Kumaris; Caste; Chinmoy, Sri; International Society for Krishna Consciousness; Jones, Sir William; Mandir; Müller, Friedrich Max; Orientalism; Paṇḍit; Pūjā; Radhakrishnan, Sir Sarvepalli; Rajneesh, Bhagwan Shree; Rajneesh Movement; Ramakrishna Math and Mission; Sacred Books of the East; Sahaja**

Yoga; Sai Baba, Sathya; Śaivism; Śakti; Saṃpradāya; Saṃskāra; Sanātana Dharma; Tagore, Rabindranath; Theosophy and the Theosophical Society; Transcendental Meditation; Vaiṣṇavism; Vivekananda, Swami

MARTIN BAUMANN

Further reading

Ballard, R. (ed.). 1994. *Desh Pardesh: The South Asian Presence in Britain*. London: Hurst.

Baumann, M. 1998. 'Sustaining "Little Indias": The Hindu Diasporas in Europe'. In G. ter Haar, ed., *Strangers and Sojourners: Religious Communities in the Diaspora*. Leuven: Uitgeverij Peeters, 95–132.

Baumann, M., B. Luchesi and A. Wilke (eds). 2003. *Tempel und Tamilen in zweiter Heimat. Hindus von Sri Lanka im deutschsprachigen und skandinavischen Raum* [Temple and Tamils in their Second Home: Hindus from Sri Lanka in German-speaking and Scandinavian Localities]. Würzburg: Ergon.

Coward, H., J.R. Hinnells and R.B. Williams (eds). 2000. *The South Asian Religious Diaspora in Britain, Canada, and the United States*. Albany, NY: SUNY.

Halbfass, W. 1988. *India and Europe. An Essay in Understanding*. Albany, NY: SUNY.

Hutter, M. (ed.). 2001. *Buddhisten und Hindus im deutschsprachigen Raum* [Buddhists and Hindus in the German-speaking Region]. Frankfurt: Lang.

Jackson, R. and E. Nesbitt. 1993. *Hindu Children in Britain*. Stoke-on-Trent: Trentham.

Jacobsen, K. 2003. 'Settling in Cold Climate: Tamil Hindus in Norway'. In M. Baumann, B. Luchesi and A. Wilke, eds, *Tempel und Tamilen in zweiter Heimat. Hindus von Sri Lanka im deutschsprachigen und skandinavischen Raum* [Temple and Tamils in their Second Home: Hindus from Sri Lanka in German-speaking and Scandinavian Localities]. Würzburg: Ergon, 363–77.

Knott, K. 1991. 'Bound to Change? The Religions of South Asians in Britain'. In S.Vertovec, ed., *Aspects of South Asian Diaspora*, Papers on India, vol. 2, pt 2. Delhi: Oxford University Press, 86–111.

Knott, K. 1997. 'The Religions of South Asian Communities in Britain'. In J.R. Hinnells, ed., *A New Handbook of Living Religions*. Oxford: Blackwell, 756–74.

Knott, K. 2000. 'Hinduism in Britain'. In H. Coward, J.R. Hinnells and R.B. Williams, ed., *The South Asian Religious Diaspora in Britain, Canada, and the United States*. Albany, NY: SUNY, 89–107.

McDowell, C. 1996. *A Tamil Asylum Diaspora: Sri Lankan Migration, Settlement and Politics in Switzerland*. Oxford: Berghahn Books.

Nye, M. 1995. *A Place for our Gods: The Construction of a Temple Community in Edinburgh*. Richmond: Curzon.

Nye, M. 1998. 'Hindus Old and New: Problem of Sacred Space in Britain'. In E. Barker and M. Warburg, ed., *New Religions and New Religiosity*. Aarhus: Aarhus University Press, 222–42.

Schouten, J.P. 1991. 'Nieuwe wegwijzer in hindoeïstisch Nederland' [New Guide to Hindu Netherlands]. *Religieuze bewegingen in Nederland* 23: 49–97.

Schouten, J.P. 1994. 'Nederlandse hindoes op zoek naar hun wortels. Een schets van de Brahmarishi Mission' [Netherland Hindus in Search of their Roots: A Sketch of the Brahmarishi Mission]. *Religieuze bewegingen in Nederland* 29: 99–121.

Thomas, T. 1993. 'Hindu Dharma in Dispersion'. In G. Parsons, ed., *The Growth of Religious Diversity. Britain from 1945*, vol. 1: *Traditions*. London: Routledge, 173–204.

van der Burg, C.J.G. 1993. 'Surinam Hinduism in the Netherlands and Social Change'. In R. Barot, ed., *Religion and Ethnicity: Minorities and Social Change in the Metropolis*. Kampen: Kok Pharos, 138–55.

van der Burg, C.J.G and P.T. van der Veer. 1986. 'Pandits, Power and Profit: Religious Organization and the Construction of Identity among the Surinamese Hindus'. *Ethnic and Racial Studies* 9.4: 514–28.

van der Veer, P.T. 1996. 'Authenticity and Authority in Surinamese Hindu Ritual'. In D. Dabydeen and B. Samaroo, eds, *Across the Dark Waters: Ethnicity and Indian Identity in the Caribbean*. London and Basingstoke: Macmillan, 131–46.

van Dijk, A. 1996. 'Hinduismus in Suriname und den Niederlande' [Hinduism in Surinam and the Netherlands]. *Zeitschrift für Missionswissenschaft und Religionswissenschaft* 80.3: 179–97.

Vertovec, S. 2000. *The Hindu Diaspora: Comparative Patterns.* London: Routledge.
Williams, R.B. 1984/2001. *A New Face of Hinduism: The Swaminarayan Religion.* Cambridge: Cambridge University Press.7

EUTHANASIA

Through a study of the texts, one sees a changing attitude to euthanasia over the ages. In the Vedic literature, one finds that it is a long life that is encouraged and, with this ideal in mind, terminating one's life does not make sense. This attitude to longevity is maintained over the course of history, arguably so as to remain true to the Vedic ideal, but occasions do arise when self-willed death is seen as acceptable, such as an heroic death when a warrior is captured, an honour death where a captured woman would kill herself to protect her honour, a widow death where the wife would throw herself on her husband's funeral pyre, and euthanasia. As the *Upaniṣads* fall within the Vedic tradition, with their awareness of the misery of saṃsāra or the transient world, they still do not speak of ending life. The śāstric texts are vehemently against suicide, but self-willed death is permitted in a case where an individual is so ill that he or she is beyond medical assistance, or is so old that the person has no desire for life's pleasures. But a fine line was acknowledged between euthanasia and suicide, and it was the individual's responsibility to make sure, through intention, that it was not the latter. Given that dharma is concerned with the welfare of the collective, by the turn of the first millennium CE thinkers began to encourage the prohibition of euthanasia, perhaps because the act was becoming a problem for society.

Ethically speaking, life, especially human life, is not only considered sacred, but its attainment a rarity given the abundance of possible life forms. Although there is the principle of ahiṃsā (non-violence), which is notably fluid in application, the law of karma would discourage any self-willed termination, for one would have to wait for the karmically allotted time to meet death. The aged and the ill may find ways of getting around this by refusing to eat under the pretext of fasting, but, ultimately, the individual's conscience must decide whether his or her act is euthanasia, austerity or suicide.

See also: **Ahiṃsā; Dharma; Dharmaśāstras; Karma (Law of Action); Saṃsāra; Sati; Upaniṣads; Veda**

RISHI HANDA

Further reading

Coward, Harold G., Julius J. Lipner and Katherine K. Young. 1991. *Hindu Ethics.* Delhi: Sri Satguru Publications.
Crawford, S. Cromwell. 2003. *Hindu Bioethics for the Twenty-First Century.* Albany, NY: State University of New York Press.
Menski, Werner. 2001. 'Hinduism'. In Peggy Morgan and Clive Lawton, eds, *Ethical Issues in Six Religious Traditions*, 4th edn. Edinburgh: Edinburgh University Press, 1–54.

F

FARQUHAR, JOHN NICOL (1861–1929)

British missionary and Orientalist. After studying at Oxford, Farquhar went to India as a teacher with the London Missionary Society in 1891. He learnt Bengali and Sanskrit and was later Professor of Comparative Religion in the University of Manchester. Eric Sharpe argues that, although a leading proponent of 'fulfilment' theology – which saw other religions as raising questions which are only satisfactorily answered in Christianity (1913) – Farquhar was able to separate his scholarship on Hinduism from his theological and missionary work. Nevertheless, in a pamphlet on the *Bhagavadgītā* ('The Age and Origin of the Gita', Madras, 1904) Farquhar sought to disprove the historicity of Kṛṣṇa's discourse in contrast to the New Testament record of Christ's words. Farquhar insisted on the need for missionaries to study Hinduism historically and himself published surveys of modern Hindu, mainly nineteenth-century Bengali, movements (Farquhar 1915) and Hindu texts to 1800 (Farquhar 1920).

See also: **Bhagavadgītā; Kṛṣṇa**

WILL SWEETMAN

Further reading

Farquhar, J.N. 1913. *The Crown of Hinduism*. London: Oxford University Press.

Farquhar, J.N. 1915. *Modern Religious Movements in India*. New York: Macmillan.

Farquhar, J.N. 1920. *An Outline of the Religious Literature of India*. London: Oxford University Press.

Sharpe, E.J. 1965. *Not to Destroy but to Fulfil: The Contribution of J.N. Farquhar to Protestant Missionary Thought in India before 1914*. Lund: Gleerup.

FASTING

Fasts are performed in virtually every arena of Hindu practice. Saṃnyāsis make public displays of fasts, demonstrating their varying degrees of renunciation and ascetic prowess. Housewives undertake vows (vrata) that entail the relinquishing of certain foods for specific periods of time, while traditionally observant widows often follow dietary restrictions. Fasting plays an important role for any Hindu preparing to undergo a ritual initiation and for family members of those participating in life-cycle sacraments (saṃskāras). In the practice of yoga, fasts famously serve hygienic purposes of cleansing and purifying the body. Acts of fasting, whether gestural or extreme, are closely associated with Hindu tradition in the global arena of world religions.

Ancient scriptural traditions depict fasting as a mark of virtue and as a means of achieving success. Brahmanic liturgies frequently prescribe fasts, ranging from token food taboos to elaborate degrees of renunciation. Purāṇic myths celebrate dramatic performances of fasts among a wide array of renunciative physical austerities. Contemporary popular practice conforms to such ideals, and fasting persists as a ubiquitous feature of Hindu identity formation.

The names of days of the week are predicated on fasts. The Sanskritic term for each day ends in '-var' (literally, 'fast') and this usage prevails even on secular calendars in most Indian languages today. This means that for the literally inclined, who might choose to keep etymologies in mind, each day can serve as a reminder of the deity to be honoured by a fast. Indeed the Hindu calendar prescribes specific fasts based on the lunar cycle. Some vrata vows entail increasing and decreasing the number of grains of rice to be consumed according to the waxing and waning of the moon for a full lunar cycle. This is not an end in itself, but serves as a device for meditation (somewhat similar to a rosary or prayer beads) and as a way of exercising self-discipline. Hindu almanacs schedule frequent fasts in relation to calendrical festivals that highlight the opposite of fasting, namely feasting.

The act of fasting is complex and saturated with signifiers. To fast is to use one's body as vessel of sacrifice. Fasting is a ritual technique, and the body becomes an instrument of power and efficacy. Fasting is believed to enhance through denial, and one gains by not getting. By not consuming, one accrues energy to expend. The Hindu view of this process does not imply, as in Western traditions, any kind of separation of mind and body wherein one gives up physical comfort to gain mental or spiritual strength. On the contrary, a Hindu fasts for the holistic benefit of the complex self that is at once mind and body, that is simultaneously spiritual force and physical entity – a self embracing both duty and responsibility, ethical codes within genetic substance.

While some, like Gandhi, have observed fasts for idealised purposes, sometimes extending into the realm of political strategy, many, perhaps most, associate fasting with more mundane aspects of worldly gain. There are countless instances of fasts undertaken to persuade a deity to grant a wish such as the healing of a loved one, success in a commercial venture, passing of school exams, conceiving sons or daughters, or coping with financial hardship.

Through the growing global popularity of numerous schools of yoga, Āyurvedic medicine and traditional Indian arts, Hindu ideals of fasting have become increasingly fashionable. Whether ritualised according to tradition or not, occasional fasting has emerged as an important element in neo-Hindu circles everywhere.

See also: **Āyurveda; Calendar; Food; Gandhi, Mohandas Karamchand; Meditation; Purāṇas; Saṃnyāsa; Saṃskāra; Vrata; Widow remarriage; Yoga**

SANDRA ROBINSON

Further reading

Khare, R.S. 1976. *The Hindu Hearth and Home*. Durham, NC: Carolina Academic Press.

Mukerji, A.C. 1916. *Hindu Fasts and Feasts.* Allahabad: The Indian Press.

Pearson, A.M. 1996. *Because It Gives Me Peace of Mind: Ritual Fasts in the Religious Lives of Hindu Women.* Albany, NY: State University of New York Press.

Sivananda. 1947. *Hindu Fasts and Festivals and Their Philosophy.* Rishikesh: Sivananda Publication League.

FEMINISM

Women's mobilisation during the nineteenth century and the first half of the twentieth was the root of Indian feminism. Following the development of second-wave feminism in the West, beginning in the 1960s, it became more self-consciously feminist and campaigned for greater awareness of women's problems and women's rights.

By the 1970s, feminists realised that progress had been too slow. Many joined radical leftist movements, therefore, including political parties. These included the following: the Communist Party of India; the Marxist and the (Maoist) Progressive Organisation of Women, which began in Hyderabad but influenced the Purogami Stree Sangathana (Progressive Women's Organisation) in Pune; and the Stree Mukti Sangathan (Women's Liberation Organisation) in Bombay. Accompanying these developments was agitation on behalf of landless labour and the anti-caste dalits (formerly untouchables) in Andhra and Maharashtra, trade unions and student protests. Groups such as the Self-Employed Women's Association (in Gujarat), the Nav Nirman movement (also in Gujarat), and the Shahada movement (in Maharasthra) protested against rising prices, exploitive labour and male alcoholism that led to violence against women. As many as 20,000 women demonstrated. They sometimes found inspiration or support in international movements. The Maoists, for instance, used a slogan from the Chinese revolution: 'Third World Women Hold Up Half the Sky'. The dalit organisation Mahila Samta Sainik Dal (League of Women Soldiers for Equality) gained insights from the American black power movement. After the Emergency (1975–77), which shut down many of these movements, socialist women in the Janata Party formed the Mahila Dakshata Samiti (Women's Self-Development Organisation) and renewed agitation in parts of the country such as Bihar.

In the late 1970s, some urban, middle-class women's groups on the political left began to call themselves feminist. Although some continued to agitate in political parties and trade unions, others did so autonomously. Only women's groups, they said, could present an adequate critique of organisational hierarchy. Some found inspiration in the United Nations, 1975 being International Women's Year. Others, especially in Delhi (Mahila Dakshata Samiti, Stri Sangharash and Nari Raksha Samiti) continued or began campaigns against dowry and the related crime of wife-burning. This resulted in a new law against dowry crimes in 1980, which was modified in 1983 by the Criminal Law (Second Amendment) Act. Indian feminists pressed also for better legislation against rape, drawing national attention to cases such as the Mathura rape case (1979) and the Suman Rani case (1988). In the process, they developed new organisations such as the Forum Against Rape, later renamed the Forum Against Oppression of Women (Bombay), and networks for mobilisation across the country.

Although laws were improving life for women, implementation was still slow. Feminists turned increasingly in the 1980s, therefore, to educating women about their rights and promoting the rhetoric of agency rather than victimisation. This involved establishing women's centres and women's studies in colleges and universities, literacy and audio-visual information campaigns, mock courts, neighbourhood groups, street theatres, rewritten scriptural stories, renewed interest in traditional symbols of the heroic woman (vīrāṇgaṇā) or the goddess Kālī, and national magazines such as *Manushi* founded by Madhu Kishwar. Social activists continued for both old and new causes. The latter included environmental problems (the Chipko movement), sati (the Roop Kanwar case), sex selection and the need for a common law (the Shah Bano case).

Feminism, with its tremendous range from rural to urban movements and from reform to radical strategies, was not without its critics. With the growing movement of Hindu nationalism, sometimes known as fundamentalism, feminism came under attack for opposing Hinduism, the family, and regional religious practices (an argument used by supporters of sati in Rajasthan).

See also: **Dalits; Dowry; Kālī and Caṇḍī; Kishwar, Madhu; Sati; Women's movement**

KATHERINE K. YOUNG

Further reading

Bhasin, K. and N.S. Khan. 1986. *Some Questions on Feminism and Its Relevance in South Asia*. New Delhi: Kali for Women.

Brouwer, J. 1999. 'Feminism and the Indigenous Knowledge System in India: An Exploration'. In R. Indira and D.K. Behera, eds, *Gender and Society in India*, vol. 1. New Delhi: Manak Publications, 14–30.

Grimes, J. 1993. 'Feminism and the Indian Goddess: Different Models'. In N. Smart and S. Thakur, eds, *Ethical and Political Dilemmas of Modern India*. New York: St Martin's Press, 126–43.

Hiltebeitel, A. and K. Erndl (eds). 2000. *Is the Goddess a Feminist: the Politics of South Asian Goddesses*. New York: New York University Press.

Kunjakkan, K.A. 2002. *Feminism and Indian Realities*. New Delhi: Mittal Publishers.

Mankekar, P. 2003. 'Off-Centre: Feminism and South Asian Studies'. In J. Assayag and V. Benei, eds, *At Home in Diaspora: South Asian Scholars and the West*. Bloomington, IN: Indian University Press, 52–65.

Mohanty, C.T., A. Russ and L. Torres (eds). 1992. *Third World Women and the Politics of Feminism*. Bloomington, IN: Indiana University Press.

Ratté, L. 1985. 'Goddesses, Mothers, and Heroines: Hindu Women and the Feminine in the Early Nationalist Movement'. In Y.Y. Haddad and E.B. Findly, eds, *Women, Religion and Social Change*. Albany, NY: State University of New York Press, 351–76.

Ray, B. 2002. *Early Feminists of Colonial India: Sarala Den Chaudhurani and Rokeya Sakhawat Hossain*. Toronto: Oxford University Press.

Sen, S. 2002. 'Towards a Feminist Politics? The Indian Women's Movement in Historical Perspective'. In K. Kapadia, ed., *The Violence of Development: The Politics of Identity, Gender and Social Inequalities in India*. New York: Zed Books, 459–524.

Sugirtharajah, S. 2002. 'Hinduism and Feminism: Some Concerns'. *Journal of Feminist Studies in Religion* 18.2: 97–104.

FESTIVALS

See: **Utsava**

FILLIOZAT, JEAN (1906–82)

French Indologist who first qualified as a medical doctor and continued to practice medicine for some years after beginning his study of India with Sylvain Lévi. His first Indological publication traced the spread of Indian medical thought into Central and East Asia. In the same year appeared the first of two volumes, co-edited with L. Renou (1949–53), offering a comprehensive account of classical Indian civilisation, to which Filliozat contributed accounts of Buddhism and of Indian history to the seventh century. From 1952 Filliozat was Professor of Indian Languages and Literature at the Collège de France, and he was director of the French Institute of Indology in Pondicherry from its foundation in 1955 until

1977, where he emphasised collaboration with Indian paṇḍits. He stressed the connections between yoga and Indian medical systems, and rejected the theory of its shamanic origins. Among his publications are translations from Sanskrit, Tamil, Pāli and Tibetan; he also published several articles relating to the history of European study of India and its religions.

See also: **Buddhism, relationship with Hinduism; Paṇḍit; Renou, Louis; Yoga**

WILL SWEETMAN

Further reading

Filliozat, J. 1949. *La Doctrine classique de la médecine indienne: ses origines et ses parallèles grecs.* Paris: Imprimerie nationale. [Trans. Dev Raj Chanana. 1964. *The Classical Doctrine of Indian Medicine: Its Origins and Its Greek Parallels.* Delhi: Munshiram Manoharlal.]

Filliozat, J. 1991. *Religion, Philosophy, Yoga: A Selection of Articles by Jean Filliozat.* Delhi: Motilal Banarsidass.

Renou, L. and J. Filliozat. 1949–53. *L'Inde classique: manuel des études indiennes*, 2 vols. Paris: Payot.

FILM

Introduction

Over the last century, cinema has established itself in India as the dominant form of public culture and is now recognised as a unique form of cinema with a global audience. Among the many distinctive features of Indian cinema are its unique genres, chief of which are those which can be loosely labelled 'religious'.

The religious genres and their popularity

With the first all-Indian film, *Raja Harischandra* (1913), D.S. Phalke created one of the categories or genres of films that are unique to Indian cinema, all of which were established during the early days and may be loosely labelled 'religious' from their titles alone: the mythological, the devotional and the Muslim social. Through these genres filmic ways of viewing religious symbols and practices became part of the visual culture of India.

The mythological

The mythological may recount the story of gods and goddesses or draw on other stories of heroes and heroines from the large repository of Hindu myths. The pan-Indian version of Indian mythology of these films could feed into the creation of national culture and religion. India's founding genre, the mythological, made as a nationalist gesture in response to Western Biblical films, was one of the most productive. The imagery of the mythological film is enmeshed with other visual forms, in particular the representations of 'calendar art', that is, popular prints of gods and goddesses produced in the new medium of chromolithography, which in turn had drawn on the new national art, both of which had earlier affected stage presentations. Phalke also drew on the iconic image of early photography, whose frontality in turn had developed from conventions of miniature painting via the Company School and Ravi Varma.

These films have to grapple with the problem of realism in cinema. Geeta Kapur (1993) argues that their demand for iconicity and illusionism rather than reality is, in part, to compensate for the descent of the gods into realism. The films give much time to the depiction of miracles, while iconicity is reinforced by the manifestation of pre-modern ways of looking in the cinema, notably that of darśana ('seeing'). Although this genre faded in the rise of the more omnibus social genre of the 1940s and 1950s, it had a brief resurgence in the 1970s, when it famously popularised a new goddess,

Santoṣī Mātā, in the film *Jai Santoshi Maa* (1975). In the late 1980s, the government relaxed its restrictions on the depiction of religion on television, where the mythological had a phenomenal success in the new form of religious soaps, whose impact on Indian politics has been well documented (Rajagopal 2001).

The devotional film

The devotional genre foregrounds stories of the sants, drawing on India's rich premodern bhakti traditions ('loving devotion to God'), creating new visual relays of looks between the audience, the devotee and the divine. The 1936 film *Sant Tukaram* was the first Indian film to win an award at the Venice Film Festival. The devotional presents historical figures, the medieval singer-saints who are associated with the traditions of bhakti, where the devotee's deeply personal and emotional relation to the deity is often expressed in song. The films historicise bhakti, presenting it as the religion of the people, emphasising its origins outside Brahmanical religion, in its introduction of vernacular languages and its inclusion of low castes and women, rather than the Sanskritised forms which later developed, often drawing analogies with the popular nationalism of Mohandas Karamchand Gandhi.

The secular film

While religious and other genres remained popular after Independence, they were largely eclipsed by the epic melodrama (Rajadhyaksha 1993), the omnibus genre of the social film, which is set in contemporary society, where a central protagonist seeks to incorporate his romantic love into his family and to fulfil his kinship duties, sometimes with clear references to mythological stories. The social is made in the melodramatic mode, where traditional hierarchies and the concepts of the sacred are transposed to the domain of nationhood and its key icons to make it a 'secular' genre, upholding Nehruvian ideology, where secularism is not an absence of religion but a separation of religion and culture from politics, as suggested by Chatterjee (1993). Perhaps the most popular and important secular film is Mehboob Khan's *Mother India* (1957), which combines nationalist allegory with the noble struggle of India's rural women. The social does not show a plurality of religions but the Hindu norm, as does the public sphere in general in India, which is full of religious signs and practices presented as culture.

The 1990s: secularism and Hindutva

The social genre has remained dominant in India, as 'secularist' politics have continued to dominate up to the 1990s. The Hindu–Muslim riots of 1992 represent a turning point of sorts in Indian filmmaking. For example, *Amar, Akbar, Anthony* (1977) depicted three brothers separated on Independence Day under a statue of Gandhi, one raised as a Muslim, one Hindu and the other Christian; the innocent message of the film, that despite their religion they are still blood brothers, suddenly seemed to belong to a more naive age.

It would be surprising were the Hindi films from the 1990s onwards, produced and consumed by the new middle classes, not to manifest Hindutva ideology, just as nationalist and Nehruvian ideologies dominated earlier films. However, many argue that these films espouse only 'Indian values' (Dwyer 2000), which may be hard to distinguish from Hindutva, as both include religiosity (mostly Hindu) and patriotism. Thus, while Hindi film in the 1990s onwards places a great emphasis on Hindu family values, expresses anti-Pakistan sentiments and represents Muslims and other religious minorities in a problematic manner, there are very few films which show anything that can be said to be explicitly Hindutva in ideology.

Other media

The 1990s saw the rise of Hindu nationalism, which was simultaneous with a media invasion (satellite and cable television since 1991), a communications revolution (the mobile phone and the internet) and a flood of Western brands into India. The Bharatiya Janata Party (BJP, the political party of Hindutva) and its allies harnessed the media via televised religious soap operas, popular visuals and cheap technology such as the music cassette to get its message across. Religious soaps that may not have set out with a political agenda or been overtly chauvinistic have been used by Hindutva supporters to foment nationalism.

It may be that film gives better access to the public imagination than any other art form in India. The secularist epic gained precedence because of the fear of disunity and separation, but started to fall apart in the 1970s with the break-up of an uneasy coalition between dominant groups. Politicised Hinduism is alien unless couched in the language of devotion to Rāma. Indian cinema shows an underlying, perhaps even a pre-modern religiosity, with respect for all religions, and allows great scope for thinking about contemporary beliefs and practices. One of its more recent offerings, *Veer-Zaara* (2004), attempted to minimise the divide between India and Pakistan by portraying a love story between a Sikh and Muslim.

See also: **Bhakti Movement; Bharatiya Janata Party; Brahmanism; Caste; Darśana; Gandhi, Mohandas Karamchand; Hindutva; Images and iconography; Internet; Myth; Nationalism; Rāma; Sacred languages; Sangh Parivar; Sant; Santoṣī Mātā; Sound recordings; Television and radio; Western popular culture, Hindu influence on; Women, status of**

RACHEL DWYER

Further reading

Chatterjee, Partha. 1993. *The Nation and Its Fragments: Colonial and Postcolonial Histories.* Delhi: Oxford University Press.

Dwyer, Rachel. 2000. '"Indian Values" and the Diaspora: Yash Chopra's Films of the 1990s'. *West Coast Line*, Autumn; and in Parthiv Shah, ed., *Figures, Facts, Feelings: A Direct Diasporic Dialogue.* Catalogue to accompany a British Council exhibition, November: 74–82.

Dwyer, Rachel. 2006. *Filming the Gods: Religion and the Hindi Film.* London: Routledge.

Hansen, Thomas Blom. 1999. *The Saffron Wave: Democracy and Hindu Nationalism in Modern India.* Princeton, NJ: Princeton University Press.

Kapur, Geeta. 1993. 'Revelation and Doubt: Sant Tukaram and Devi'. In T. Niranjana *et al.* eds, *Interrogating Modernity: Culture and Colonialism In India.* Calcutta: Seagull, 19–46.

Rajadhyaksha, Ashish. 1993. 'The epic melodrama: themes of nationality in Indian cinema.' *Journal of Arts and Ideas*, 35–6: 55–70.

Rajadhyaksha, Ashish and Paul Willemen. 1999. *An Encyclopaedia of Indian Cinema,* 2nd edn. London: British Film Institute.

Rajagopal, Arvind. 2001. *Politics After Television: Hindu Nationalism and the Reshaping of the Public in India.* Cambridge: Cambridge University Press.

Vasudevan, Ravi. 2000. 'The Politics of Cultural Address in a "Transitional" Cinema: A Case Study of Indian Popular Cinema'. In C. Gledhill and L. Williams, eds, *Reinventing Film Studies.* London: Arnold; New York: Oxford University Press, 130–64.

FIVE M'S

See: **Pañcamakāra**

FOETICIDE

In pre-modern medical (Āyurveda) and ethical/legal (*Dharmaśāstra*) texts, words for abortion denote active killing (hatyā, vadha). These texts classify abortion as a great crime (mahāpātaka) – in the same category as murder – because it causes untimely death and robs the foetus of its human status, which provides the best opportunity for a better rebirth or even liberation. They require the punishment of abortionists by loss of caste (which amounts to social and economic ostracism) or by a heavy fine. But they make a clear exception for abortion to save a pregnant woman's life and a more ambiguous exception for abortion when pregnancy is the result of rape, intoxication or manipulation.

In 1971, the central government legalised abortion during the first twenty weeks of pregnancy – and even after that if a woman's life or mental stability is threatened, if the foetus is deformed or if the pregnancy is the result of rape or incest. The law does not permit abortion for economic and social reasons. Not many Hindus have commented on this law, despite the fact that it clearly rejects the traditional Hindu position. After the development of new technologies for sex selection, which made abortion of female foetuses more common in regions that already practised infanticide or neglected the health of girls, the central government outlawed this technology. But that has not stopped the practice.

See also: **Abortion; Āyurveda; Caste; Dharmaśāstras; Infanticide; Mahāpātakas**

KATHERINE K. YOUNG

Further reading

Crawford, S.C. 1995. *Dilemmas of Life and Death: Hindu Ethics in a North American Context*. Albany, NY: State University of New York Press.

Gupta, J.A. 2004. 'Practices in India'. In Spiros Simitis, ed., *Der Umgang mit vorgeburtlichem Leben in anderen Kulturen*. Berlin: Nationaler Ethikrat, 63–76.

Khana, S.K. 1995. 'Prenatal Sex Determination: A New Family Building Strategy'. *Manushi* 86: 23–29.

Lipner, J.J. 1989. 'The Classical Hindu View on Abortion and the Moral Status of the Unborn'. In H.G. Coward, J.J. Lipner and K.K. Young, eds, *Hindu Ethics: Purity, Abortion, and Euthanasia*. Albany, NY: State University of New York Press, 41–69.

Mehta, P.S. 2000. *Numbers, at What Cost?* Jaipur: Consumer Unity and Trust Society.

Miller, B.D. 1985. *Prenatal and Postnatal Sex-selection in India: The Patriarchal Context*. Lansing, MI: Michigan State University Press.

Ramasubban, R. and S. Jejeebhoy (eds). 2000. *Women's Reproductive Health in India*. Delhi: Rawat Publications.

Reddy, D.V.N. 1994. 'Amniocentesis'. In C. Chakrapani and S. Viyaya Kumar, eds, *Changing Status and Role of Women in Indian Society*. Delhi: M.D. Publications, 127–34.

Sharma, R.K. 1992. *Some Aspects of Professional–Client Relationship: Sterilization and Abortion*. Delhi: Konark Publishers.

Sripati, C. 1994. *India's Abortion Experience*. Denton, TX: University of North Texas Press.

Young, K.K. 2004. 'The Status of the Fetus in Scriptural Hinduism'. In Spiros Simitis, ed.,*Der Umgang mit vorgeburtlichem Leben in anderen Kulturen*. Berlin: Nationaler Ethikrat, 51–61.

FOOD

Food is woven into the very fabric of Hinduism: it is incorporated into ritual and myth; it regulates society and social behaviour and exemplifies complex Hindu philosophies. For example, classic texts such as *Manusmṛti* (1.15; 12.24–53), the *Dharmasūtras* (Āpastamba 1.17.14–28; Vasiṣṭha 14.33) and the *Bhagavadgītā* (17.7–10) make specific mention of the three guṇas and the foods categorised by them.

According to the philosophy of the guṇas, Hindus are recommended to follow a pure diet consuming only sāttvic foods. These include milk, yoghurt, vegetables, pulses, ghee butter and some sweet products, and are recommended to bring about the pure state of mind and nature essential for devotion to God. A tāmasic diet, which includes garlic, onion, meat and fish lead to a dark state of mind, spiritual ignorance and physical lethargy.

A rājasic diet includes excessively hot and spicy food that may lead to an overexcited state of mind and misery; alcohol and drugs lead to altered consciousness (also rājasic) and likewise prohibit the development of a spiritual relationship with God.

The natural extension of the philosophy of the guṇas is the widespread practice of vegetarianism throughout Hinduism particularly in the Vaiṣṇava and bhakti traditions. Vegetarianism, initially a brahmanic ideal, has evolved into far more than a dietary custom; it has become a focal point of Hindu values based upon the doctrine of ahiṃsā and consequently relates directly to the concepts of both dharma and karma. It should be stressed, however, that not all Hindus are strict vegetarians, especially in the diaspora.

Types of food indicate types of Hinduism; for example, many saṃpradāyas characteristically advocate a strict vegetarian diet, prohibiting the consumption of eggs, onions, garlic and mushrooms as well as many modern emulsifiers and flavourings. The Swami Narayana Sampradaya's texts and religious literature, e.g. *Shikshāpatri* (79,106,138), *Vachanāmritam* (G1.18,30), and the International Society for Krishna Consciouness' (ISKCON) *Bhagavad Gītā As It Is* (17.6–11), regulate many aspects of religious life, from fasting and hospitality to domestic diet purity, the offering of food to God and seasonal variations in diets.

To further fulfil their 'food dharma' devotees from various bhakti traditions make elaborate food offerings to Kṛṣṇa several times a day. The food is prepared with care, devotion and the purest sāttvic ingredients. When ready, the untasted food is presented to Kṛṣṇa, who is then invited to come and eat. The invitation will be accompanied by bhajans or thāls (devotional songs accompanying the preparation of the offerings) and, once Kṛṣṇa has eaten, the food becomes sanctified, transformed from mundane bhoga to sacred prasādam, which may now be consumed by the devotee. The prasādam is said to satisfy one's hunger, both physically and spiritually.

The preparation and offering of food, either to the deities in the home shrine or at the temple, allows many Hindus to serve God (Seva) and to express their sense of devotion and love. This can be an individual or collective act that cements the relationship between the devotee and God.

An alternative categorisation of food contrasts Pakkā, that which is cooked in clarified butter and hence pollution resistant, and Kaccā, that which is boiled in water and prone to pollution outside one's immediate hearth and relations. Such classification is related to people and commensal relationships between castes.

Food maintains caste distinction and hierarchy through concepts of ritual purity and pollution; put simply, a brāhmaṇa, being ritually and therefore socially pure, would be unable to consume food prepared by a śūdra, who is considered ritually and therefore socially impure. However, all castes can accept the food prepared by a brāhmaṇa. Often the concept of caste pollution, transmitted through food, is predicated on the nature of an individual's occupation within Hindu society and one's occupation is invariably predicated upon one's caste.

Caste distinction is also eroded by food. Amongst bhakti devotees in the UK, for example, when it comes to the preparation, offering and consumption of food during religious festivals, the individual takes precedence over caste and class and throughout the diaspora the same broad processes have been in evidence (Vertovec 2000: 111). As far as food and caste being inseparable socially, culturally and religiously in theory, the practice of caste-based commensality seems to have lessened considerably.

Food is a vivid expression of continuity and change both in India and throughout the Hindu diaspora, communicating distinctive Hindu worldviews and vividly reflecting the religious essence and experience of Hindus on both a personal and a collective level. During the main Hindu festivals and pilgrimages, especially in the Vaiṣṇava traditions, food becomes an important vehicle for devotion. Braj, in the Mathurā region of India, plays host to thousands of pilgrims gathering to partake in the great offering of specially prepared food or Annakūt to Kṛṣṇa and to Mount Govardhana. For many pilgrims it is an emotional time heightened by the sense of grace bestowed upon them through the consumption of the divine food left over by Kṛṣna (Toomey 1992: 119).

On the day after the Dīvālī festival, similar scenes are witnessed at temples throughout the diaspora, the most impressive being at the Swami Narayana temple in Neasden, North West London, where 45,000–55,000 Hindus from various traditions gather to witness a spectacular Annakūt. During this Annakūt a vast array of individual handmade offerings, as many as 1500, are placed at the feet of the samprādaya's Guru Mūrtis, the largest devotional food offering outside India. Once the food has been offered, consumed and sanctified by the Mūrtis it is distributed as prasādam throughout the community and for many this Annakūt prasādam has especially sacred qualities.

Such festivals have encouraged pilgrimage to this and several other temples in the area, each with their own Annakūts. Throughout the diaspora today, such devotional activity centred around food as well as a distinctive religious food culture have lead to an increased awareness of Hinduism amongst the host communities in Europe, North America, Africa and Australasia, and this in turn has lead to a strengthening of Hindu religious identity in general.

See also: **Africa, Hindus in; Ahiṃsā; Altars, domestic; Americas, Hindus in; Australasia, Hindus in; Bhagavadgītā; Bhajan; Bhakti movement; Brahmanism; Caste; Dharma; Dharmaśāstras; Diaspora; Dīvālī; Europe, Hindus in; Govardhana; Guṇas; Image worship; International Society for Krishna Consciouness; Karma; Kṛṣṇa; Mathurā; Purity and pollution, ritual; Saṃpradāya; Seva; Swami Narayana Sampradaya; Vaiṣṇavism**

MARTIN WOOD

Further reading

Dave, H.T. (trans.). 1996. *The Vachanāmritam.* Ammedabad: Swaminarayan Aksharpith.

Dave, H.T. (trans.). 2001. *The Shikshāpatri.* Ammedabad: Swaminarayan Aksharpith.

Doniger, W. (trans.). 1991. *The Laws of Manu.* London: Penguin.

Mascaro, J. 1962. *The Bhagavad Gītā.* London: Penguin.

Olivelle, P. (trans.). 1996. *Upaniṣads.* Oxford: Oxford University Press.

Olivelle, P. (trans.). 1999. *The Dharmasūtras.* Oxford: Oxford Univerity Press.

Prabhupada, A.C. (trans.). 1989 *Bhagavad Gītā As It Is.* Hong Kong: Bhaktivedanta Book Trust.

Toomey, P. 1992. 'Mountain of Food, Mountain of Love: Ritual Inversion in the Annakūta Feast at Mt Govardhan'. In R.S. Khare, ed., *The Eternal Food.* Albany, NY: State University of New York.

Vertovec, S. 2000. *The Hindu Diaspora.* London: Routledge.

FRAUWALLNER, ERICH (1898–1974)

Austrian Indologist. Frauwallner studied philology, Indology and Iranian languages at the University of Vienna, where he was appointed Professor of Indo-Iranian Studies in 1939. After early work on the *Upaniṣads*, he concentrated especially on Buddhist logic, learning Tibetan and Chinese in order to read works no longer extant in Sanskrit, and later Japanese in order to read the works of Japanese scholars. After the Second World War he was forced to retire and, although later restored to his professorship, noted in the introduction to his general history of Indian philosophy that his circumstances had forced him to write a less ambitious work than he had planned. He also published on Hindu philosophy, including Vaiśeṣika, the history of which he had reconstructed in the second volume of his history, and Mīmāṃsā, particularly in connection with Buddhism. He published also translations of selected Śaiva, philosophical texts which were prepared as part of the more comprehensive history of Indian philosophy he had hoped to write.

See also: **Hinduism, history of scholarship; Pūrva Mīmāṃsā; Śaivism; Upaniṣads; Vaiśeṣika**

WILL SWEETMAN

Further reading

Frauwallner, E. 1953–56. *Geschichte der indischen Philosophie.* Salzburg: Müller. [English translation by V.M. Bedekar. 1973. *History of Indian Philosophy.* Delhi: Motilal Banarsidass.]

Frauwallner, E. 1962. *Aus der Philosophie der śivaitischen Systeme* [From the Philosophy of the Śaiva System]. Berlin: Deutsche Akademie der Wissenschaft zu Berlin.

Oberhammer, G. 1976. 'Erich Frauwallner (28.12.1898–5.7.1974)'. *Wiener Zeitschrift für die Kunde Südasiens* XX: 5–19.

FUNERAL

See: **Antyeṣṭi**

G

GAṆA(S)

The gaṇas ('horde', 'host') are a class of supernatural entities, encountered in Hindu mythology from the beginning of the common era, most often in association with Śiva or Gaṇeśa (the 'Lord of the Horde'). Servants, messengers, guardians or warriors of these gods, gaṇas are generally portrayed as impish, dwarfish, deformed or animal-headed beings. The iconography and functions of the gaṇas parallel those of the Yakṣas, with particular figures, such as Puṣpadanta, 'Flower-Tooth', and Gaṇeśa himself straddling the two categories. While they are sometimes portrayed as destructive (in certain Śaiva Purāṇas, they form a part of the spectral horde of Vīrabhadra when he destroys Dakṣa's sacrifice) or obstructive, they are most often depicted as benevolent beings that intercede with gods on the behalf of the humans who propitiate them. Certain Tantric traditions describe various means by which a human may become a gaṇa or a Lord of the Gaṇas (gaṇanātha), through devotion to Śiva, alchemical practice, inititation or other means.

See also: **Dakṣa; Gaṇeśa; Purāṇas; Śaivism; Siddha; Śiva; Yakṣas**

DAVID GORDON WHITE

Further reading

Thapan, A.R. 1997. *Understanding Gaṇapati: Insight into the Dynamics of a Cult*. Delhi: Manohar.

GĀṆAPATYAS

The name of various sectarian groupings focused on the worship of the god Gaṇapati, better known as Gaṇeśa. A South Indian inscription of about 1160 mentioning six sects, among which the Gāṇapatyas would be included, is certain evidence of their existence. It is likely Gaṇeśa only becomes an important god in the tenth and eleventh centuries, a date fitting well with the composition of the *Śaṅkaradigvijaya*, a hagiography of Śaṅkara. Approximately six sectarian groups associated with the god are recorded in this text, but later literature provides little to fill in the missing details. It mentions sects of Gaṇeśa called Ucchiṣa Gaṇapati, Heramba Gaṇapati, Haridra Gaṇapati, Mahāgaṇapati, Saṃtāna, Navanīta and Svara Gaṇapati. They are just six amongst many names of the god and little other information is given about the names or the specific rituals of devotion associated with them.

Apart from this text, anything else we know comes from inference based on brief mentions in certain texts, a large body of literature dealing with rituals for the worship of this god, and the huge numbers of images and temples associated with him. But this is different from saying that all the worshippers were members of, or associated with, specific sectarian groups centred on the worship of particular forms of Gaṇeśa or around individual gurus professing a direct connection with the god. This conclusion is also supported when it is considered that the large body of likely gāṇapataya literature is Tantric in nature, therefore highly restricted in access.

From the middle of the sixteenth century onwards the worship of Gaṇeśa becomes very popular in the state of Maharashtra and from there spreads, with the expansion of the Maratha empire, to most parts of India, especially to the South. Maharashtra witnesses the creation of the so-called Aṣavināyakas, or the eight sacred places for Gaṇeśa located in a circle around the city of Poona. These became important pilgrimage centres for the worship of Gaṇeśa and gave rise to a large body of popular literature about the god composed in Marathi. Certain prominent families, especially those associated with the lineage of Morayā Gosavī (1610–59), built shrines to the god in the town of Cincvad. From the early eighteenth century Peshwa rulers of Poona took Gaṇeśa as their protective deity.

Two *Purāṇas*, the *Gaṇeśa* and *Mudgala,* both of which became popular in elite circles by the late sixteenth century, may be texts of these sects, as could be the *Atharvaśiras Upaniṣad* and a number of little studied late *Tantras* centred on Gaṇeśa. Of these the *Gaṇeśa Purāṇa* is undoubtedly the most important. It has been summarised several times into Marathi and translated at least once into Tamil and Hindi, making it available for people who lack access to the Sanskrit version of the text. However, most of the people who will read this text are not members of Gaṇeśa sects but just worshippers of the god who worship other gods as well.

See also: **Gaṇeśa; Guru; Purāṇas; Śaṅkara; Tantras; Tantrism**

GREG BAILEY

Further reading

Thapan, A. 1997. *Understanding Gaṇapati. Insights into the Dynamics of a Cult*. New Delhi: Manohar.

GĀNDHĀRĪ

One of the characters of the *Mahābhārata* and a princess of the ancient kingdom of Gāndhāra. The daughter of King Subala, Gāndhārī was married to the blind Dhṛtarāṣṭra, the father of the Kauravas. In sympathy with her husband's blindness she always wore a bandage over her own eyes. The story of the birth of her 100 sons recounts that they were created from a shapeless lump delivered after two years of pregnancy. The lump of flesh was divided into 101 pieces and placed in jars by the sage Vyāsa, who had originally provided the blessing for Gāndhārī's wish to have 100 sons, after being touched by her hospitality. The first son to develop in a jar was Duryodhana, and after the birth of ninety-nine other sons, a sole daughter, Duhṣalā, was born. Gāndhārī died with her husband in a forest fire, both surviving the conflict of the *Mahābhārata.*

See also: **Dhṛtārāṣṭra; Kauravas; Mahābhārata; Vyāsa**

RON GEAVES

Further reading

Dasgupta, Madhusraba. 1999. *Samsad Companion to the Mahābhārata*. Calcutta: Sahitya Samsad.

GANDHARVA(S)

In the *Ṛgveda*, a mostly singular and beneficial being living in the region of heaven or atmosphere (*Ṛgveda* 9. 86.36; 8. 77.5). He, for instance, guards the Soma (*Ṛgveda* 9. 83.4) and is parent of the first human couple (*Ṛgveda* 10. 10.4), but also has mystical power over women and may possess them (*Ṛgveda* 10. 85.40f.).

From the *Atharvaveda* onwards the Gandharvas are regarded as a class, characterised by contrary features. Described as either half-animal (often half-bird) beings or beautiful men, they are connected, together with their female counterparts, the Apsarasas, with gambling (*Atharvaveda* 7. 109.5) or may cause insanity. But they also know the best medicines (*Atharvaveda* 8. 7.23), and several gods are called Gandharva (*Taittirīya Saṃhitā* 1. 4.7).

In epic and purāṇic literature the Gandharvas are the celestial musicians. Keeping their ambiguous nature, they are depicted as radiant and healing as well as haunting and maddening beings.

See also: **Apsarasas; Mahābhārata; Purāṇas; Rāmāyaṇa; Saṃhitā; Soma**

XENIA ZEILER

Further reading

Wayman, Alex. 1997. *The Vedic Gandharva and Rebirth Theory*. New Delhi: Manohar.

GANDHARVAVEDA

Gandharvas, singers and musicians to the gods, appear throughout Vedic and later Sanskrit mythological and poetic literature. In classifications of Vedic literature, gandharvaveda is listed as an Upaveda (subordinate) of the *Sāmaveda*. It is most often used to refer to the music or texts of the earliest periods, particularly that of the *Nāṭyaśāstra*, a compendium on theatre, music and dance dated between 200 BCE and 200 CE. The term is occasionally used to evoke classical music or music in sacral Hindu contexts, but the standard terms for music are gīta (Sanskrit, 'song') and saṃgīta ('sung together'). The latter is defined in early sources as a combination of melody, drumming and dance and in later usage refers to India's formal or classical music (Rowell 1992: 9). A sizeable body of writings in Sanskrit and later in Persian and colloquial languages make up the textual sources of Indian musicology, called saṃgītaśāstra.

Recitations of Vedic and post-Vedic texts, particularly the elaborate tones of sāmaveda recitation, are considered to be the earliest practices of formal music in India (Howard 1977). The ritual potency of sound and the use of hand gesture to express melodic and rhythmic material are characteristics of Indian music dating to this period. Beginning about the ninth century, the influence of Tantra, a branch of meditational and ritual practice that permeated Hindu and Buddhist thought, appears in music texts. Discussions of primordial sound, nāda, as the substance of reality and nāda brahman (sound as the single reality) became a philosophical foundation for music (Beck 1995: 81–85). Beginning about the twelfth century, the aesthetics and mystical ideals of bhakti devotionalism and Islamic Sufism deeply informed music practices. Lyrics of human and divine love, longing and desire expressed an aesthetic that was both mystical and pan-sectarian. Saint poets of the bhakti period all over the subcontinent composed songs, many of which remain in the repertoire of Hindustānī (north Indian classical) and Karṇāṭak or Carnatic (south Indian classical) and bhajan (devotional) music today (Viswanathan and Allen 2004: 42ff.; Ruckert 2004: 55). The temple, the court and the salon were institutions that supported thousands of hereditary musicians, from the highest-caste kalāvant ('carrier of art') to the bhāṇḍ (jester) and the devadāsī (courtesans) until their displacement in the nineteenth and twentieth centuries.

The main feature of India's classical music is rāga, 'colouring' or 'passion'. Each rāga consists of a set of scale tones with prescriptions relating to sequence, phrasing, ornaments and rest (Ruckert and Widdess 2000: 64–88; Bor 1999: 1–9). Rāgas are performed in composed and improvised sections as prescribed for a variety of genres. Main contemporary classical genres are khayāl, dhrupad and ṭhumrī in north India and kriti, varṇam and rāgam-tānam-pallavī in South India. Lyrics consist of a range of topics, from the ritual and meditational virtues of music to devotional and erotic love. India's classical metrical system is tāla ('clapping the hands'). It consists of a cycle of counts maintained through a performance, within which compositions and improvisations are set. The complex subdivisions of the tāla cycles and the multiple layering of rhythm and melody are prominent features of Indian classical music (Clayton 2000). The aesthetics and stylistic changes of Indian music reflect all the factors that affect urban cultural history. Threads of continuity from the earliest periods of chant and ecstatic devotionalism are traceable. Also traceable are musical reactions to modern social, economic and political processes. Classical music survives in contemporary India with the patronage of corporate sponsors, but it is dwarfed by popular music, whose markets support a thriving recording industry in India and abroad (Arnold 2000: 525–70).

See also: **Bhajan; Bhakti; Brahman; Buddhism, relationship with Hinduism; Caste; Dance; Devadāsīs; Mudrā; Music; Sound recordings; Tantras; Upavedas**

ALLYN MINER

Further reading

Arnold, Alison. (ed.). 2000. 'Mass Media and Contemporary Musical Exchange'. In *South Asia: The Indian Subcontinent. Garland Encyclopedia of World Music* 5. New York: Garland Publishing, 525–70.

Beck, Guy L. 1995. *Sonic Theology: Hinduism and Sacred Sound*. Delhi: Motilal Banarsidass.

Bor, Joep. (ed.). *c.*1999. *Raga Guide: A Survey of 74 Hindustani Ragas*. Netherlands: Nimbus Records.

Clayton, Martin. 2000. *Time in Indian Music: Rhythm, Metre, and Form in North Indian Rāg Performance*. Oxford and New York: Oxford University Press.

Howard, Wayne. 1977. *Sāmavedic Chant*. New Haven, CT: Yale University Press.

Rowell, Lewis Eugene. 1992. *Music and Musical Thought in Early India*. Chicago Studies in Ethnomusicology. Chicago, IL: University of Chicago Press.

Ruckert, George. 2004. *Music in North India: Experiencing Music, Expressing Culture*. Global Music Series. New York: Oxford University Press.

Ruckert, George and Richard Widdess. 2000. 'Hindustani Raga.' In Alison Arnold, ed., *South Asia: The Indian Subcontinent*, Garland Encyclopedia of World Music 5. New York: Garland Publishing, 5: 64–88.

Viswanathan, T. and Matthew Harp Allen. 2004. *Music in South India: Experiencing Music, Expressing Culture*. Global Music Series. New York: Oxford University Press.

GANDHI, MOHANDAS KARAMCHAND (1869–1948)

Social reformer, political and religious leader, Gandhi was born on 2 October 1869 in Porbandhar, Gujurat. He was called 'Mahatma' (great soul), and his activities and goals were informed by a philosophy of life or worldview which reflected Jain teachings as well as Hindu ethics and metaphysics. He was the author of *The Story of My Experiments with Truth* (1927) and *Satyāgraha in South Africa* (1938).

From an early age, Gandhi was inspired by, and adhered to, ideals of truthfulness, love, courage and integrity. His background and upbringing ensured the development of key values, attitudes and practices, including religious toleration and vegetarianism. Among early influences were the gentle character and deep religiosity of his mother, Putlibai; his father was chief minister (diwan) of Porbandhar. Gandhi's parents were devotees of Viṣṇu (and belonged to the vaiśya, merchant varṇa). Family friends and the local community exposed him to Islamic, Jain and Zoroastrian teachings.

Gandhi was a reserved and unremarkable pupil at school. Married at 13 to Kasturbai (arranged by the parents), it was agreed that he should become a lawyer. He set out to study in London, leaving Bombay on 4 September 1888.

The young Gandhi studied the *Bhagavadgītā*, which he regarded as his lifelong companion, 'the universal mother'. He was interested in the New Testament (especially the Sermon on the Mount) and Buddha, reading Sir Edwin Arnold's *The Light of Asia*. He was not inspired by the Old Testament.

Gandhi was called to the Bar on 10 June 1891 and returned to India. In 1893 he took up an offer to work in South Africa, where, in response to injustices suffered by Indians, he developed his method of non-violent struggle or resistance, satyāgraha. Translated literally as 'holding on to Truth' (i.e. devotion to or zest for Truth) or 'Truthforce', satyāgraha involved commitment to ahiṃsā (non-violence, non-injury) and self-suffering. For Gandhi, ahiṃsā signified positive compassion or love of all beings rather than mere avoidance of harm. Through love, sympathy and endurance, he strove to induce a realisation or feeling of justice in the conscience of the opponent or wrongdoer.

Returning to India in 1915, Gandhi soon used satyāgraha methods against British rule. Suffering periods of imprisonment, he succeeded in undermining British authority, leading major movements from 1920 (including the 'non-cooperation' and Quit India movements). India achieved independence (with Pakistan) in 1947.

Gandhi's core beliefs echoed Advaita Vedānta – he identified ultimate reality with God or Truth (satya), which he conceived as non-dual. 'Glimpses' of Truth are possible through 'faith' (which he likened to a 'sixth sense'). His identification of our inner essence or soul (ātman) with God is the metaphysical basis of his dedication to harmlessness and egoless service of others. His commitment to the 'good of all' (sarvodaya) and equality led to concern for the treatment of women and untouchables (who, for Gandhi, were children of God, harijans) within Indian society. He also pursued Hindu–Muslim unity but was slain by a Hindu extremist on 30 January 1948.

Gandhi is an iconic and unique figure; his historic achievements, moral example, values and methods continue to inspire and provoke debate.

See also: **Advaita; Arnold, Sir Edwin; Ātman; Bhagavadgītā; Dalits; Jainism, relationship with Hinduism; Nationalism; Varṇa; Viṣṇu**

Martin Ovens

Further reading

Bondurant, Joan V. 1988. *Conquest of Violence: The Gandhian Philosophy of Conflict*. Princeton, NJ: Princeton University Press.

Chatterjee, Margaret. 1983. *Gandhi's Religious Thought*. Notre Dame, IN: University of Notre Dame Press.

GANDHIJAYANTI

Gandhijayanti is a celebration of the birthday of the great Indian political leader Mohandas Karamchand Gandhi on 2 October. In India the day is marked by activities commemorating Gandhi's cherished ideals. This may involve multi-faith prayer, symbolising Gandhi's pluralistic stance on religions and his promotion of inter-faith harmony. Prayers are said in a public event by Hindu, Muslim and Christian priests and representatives of other faiths. Volunteers may sweep streets, and other cleaning of public places is undertaken to signify both Gandhi's attitude to cleanliness and self-help as well as opposition to the categorisation of people engaging in such menial duties as 'untouchables'. Spinning cloth on the spinning wheel or thread from cotton on the takli may be carried out in memory of Gandhi's economic vision of cottage industries and self-subsisting activity by Indians, in contrast with establishing heavy industries.

A march to the seaside may be undertaken in remembrance of Gandhi's famous Dandi March of 11 March 1930, a demonstration of opposition to the British Raj's unjust salt law. The singing of songs dear to Gandhi's heart, such as *Vande Mataram*, *Vaishnava Janato* and *When I Survey the Wondrous Cross*, will also be part of the meeting's programme.

See also: **Bhārat Mātā; Chatterjee, Bankim Chandra; Dalits; Gandhi, Mohandas Karamchand**

THEODORE GABRIEL

Further reading

Fischer, L. 1997. *The Life of Mahatma Gandhi*. London: HarperCollins.

GAṆEŚA

Gaṇeśa (or Gaṇapati) means 'Lord of the hosts' or 'Lord of the gaṇas', divine beings and people of Śiva. The god with the big belly and the elephant head is the god of wisdom and the giver of favours. For all undertakings – be it an inauguration of a new house, a wedding, an opening of a shop or the starting of a journey – Gaṇeśa needs to be called upon first for assistance, and he is called Vighneśvara, 'the Lord of obstacles'. As the god of all successful enterprises, he must be worshipped before all religious ceremonies. Today Gaṇeśa is venerated all over India on Gaṇeśacaturthī.

Very little is known about Gaṇeśa's origin as a deity, though his half-human half-elephant nature may point to animistic origins. The Vediv texts mention a Gaṇapati but lack evidence that it signifies the elephant-headed god that we know. Was he first a tribal god who was later incorporated into the Brahmanic pantheon?

Gaṇeśa's mythic origin is given in the *Purāṇas*. According to the *Skanda Purāṇa*, the *Devī Purāṇa* and the *Mahābhāgavata Purāṇa*, Gaṇeśa was shaped by the goddess Pārvatī from her own body. He was supposed to guard her house during her daily bath. One day, not knowing that Śiva was Pārvatī's husband, Gaṇeśa refused to admit him. In his rage, Śiva cut off Gaṇeśa's head. When Pārvatī discovered the torso of her mutilated son, she insisted furiously that Śiva restore Gaṇeśa's original form. Unfortunately he could not find the missing head. Instead he promised to take the head of the first being he encountered. This was an elephant.

The *Bṛhaddharma Purāṇa* tells another version of the story, in which Pārvatī, after conceiving a child, asked the planet Śani (Saturn) to look at him. In spite of the devastating effects of his glance, Śani obliged. Immediately the child's head burnt to ashes. The god Brahmā suggested then that Pārvatī replace the head with the head of the first being she could find, which was an elephant.

In terracotta, stone sculptures or on paintings, Gaṇeśa appears with an elephant head, with two, four or more hands. His possessions are axe, conch, goad, noose, lotus flower and rudrākṣa chaplet. He is often shown plunging his trunk into a bowl filled with sweets, of which he is very fond. A serpent circles his waist. His divine vehicle (vāhana) is the mouse (or rat). With his broken tusk he is said to have written the *Mahābhārata* dictated by Vyāsa.

See also: **Brahmā; Gaṇas; Gaṇeśacaturthī; Mahābhārata; Navagrahas (Planets); Purāṇas; Pārvatī; Saṃhitā; Śiva; Vyāsa**

JOHANNES BELTZ

Further reading

Courtright, Paul B. 1985. *Ganesha, Lord of Obstacles, Lord of Beginnings*. New York and Oxford: Oxford University Press,

Martin-Dubost, Paul. 1997. *Ganesha: The Enchanter of the Three Worlds*. Mumbai: Franco-Indian Research Project for Indian Cultural Studies.

Pal, Pratapaditya. (ed.). 1995. *Ganesha. The Benevolent*. Mumbai: Marg Publications.

Thapan, Anita Raina. 1997. *Understanding Ganapati, Insights into the Dynamics of a Cult*. New Delhi: Manohar.

Potter, K.H. and S. Bhattacharyya (eds). 1994. *Encyclopedia of Indian Philosophies, Volume Six, Indian Philosophical Analysis: Nyāya-Vaiśesika from Gangeśa to Raghunātha Śiromani*. Princeton, NJ: Princeton University Press, 86.

GAṆEŚA PURĀṆA

See: **Purāṇas**

GAṆEŚACATURTHĪ

Gaṇeśacaturthī designates the fourth day of the lunar month Bhādrapada and is the starting point of a ritual dedicated to the god Gaṇeśa. In Maharashtra this festivity was traditionally celebrated exclusively by brāhmaṇas and limited to their houses as well as to the royal courts. The Gaṇeśa festival as we know it today was invented only at the end of the nineteenth century. In 1893 Bal Gangadhar Tilak called on his Hindu brethren to withdraw their participation in the Muslim Moharram festival that commemorates the martyrdom of Muhammad's grandson. Guided by the idea of a popular festival with a procession, he decided to organise a similar event for Hindus. In 1893 the first Sarvajanika Gaṇeśa Utsava took place in Pune. Gaṇeśa should help to overcome the gap between the brāhmaṇas and non-brāhmaṇas, establish unity and brotherhood among Hindus, and manifest their cultural and religious identity distinct from the colonial rule.

The organisation of the festival is based on maṇḍalas, local associations of volunteers, and financed by private donations. On the first day, huge maṇḍapas (pavilions or booths for Gaṇeśa-mūrtis) are constructed. On the tenth and last day of the festival the statues are taken out into the streets in a final procession and immersed in rivers, ponds or the ocean.

Today the Gaṇeśa festival is not only popular in many parts of India: through globalisation, diaspora Hindu communities celebrate this festival in France, Switzerland, England and the United States.

See also: **Diaspora; Gaṇeśa; Image worship; Tilak, Bal Gangadhar; Utsava; Varṇa**

JOHANNES BELTZ

Further reading

Courtright, Paul B. 1985. *Ganesha, Lord of Obstacles, Lord of Beginnings*. New York and Oxford: Oxford University Press.

Fuller, C.J. 2001. 'The Vinayaka Caturthi Festival and Hindutva in Tamil Nadu'. *Economic and Political Weekly*, May 12: 1.607–16.

Kaur, Raminder. 2003. *Performative Politics and the Cultures of Hinduism, Public Uses of Religion in Western India*. New Delhi: Permanent Black.

GAṄGĀ

For Hindus in India and abroad, the river Gaṅgā (Ganges) is sacred. She is a

Mother, Goddess, purifier and sustainer of all life. Some of the most important centres of Hindu spiritual learning and healing have developed along the banks of the Gaṅgā and her tributaries and mark the sources of her sacred power today. The Gaṅgā is also a key source of water for the basin which spans one million square kilometres in India, Nepal and Bangladesh. As her headwaters drain through the slopes of the Himalayas and generate a sediment load unequalled in the world, the Gaṅgā nourishes agriculture, industry, municipalities, human cultural practices and ecological and hydrological systems.

Hindu religious leaders, devotees and pilgrim service providers describe Gaṅgā as a goddess who absolves worldly impurities and rejuvenates the cosmos with her purificatory power. She is also a mother who cleans up human sin and mess with loving forgiveness. Gaṅgā's powers are cited in the *Ṛgveda*, *Rāmāyaṇa*, *Mahābhārata*, *Purāṇas* and *Māhātmyas* and inscribed in temple sculpture and art. The *Ṛgveda* describes Gaṅgā's character as a life force and goddess. In the *Mahābhārata*, Gaṅgā takes anthropomorphic forms as the daughter of Bhāgīratha, mother of Bhīṣma and wife of Śaṃtanu. Purāṇic inscriptions outline how a bath in the Gaṅgā cures ailments, makes impure people pure and leads to mokṣa or final liberation. Devotees express these beliefs and sentiments through ritual practices of ablution or snāna and in oblations to ancestors and deities performed on the riverbank and in temples across the basin and the world. Hindus also show their respect to the Goddess in oil lamp rituals (āratī) performed on the riverbank at numerous locations.

Hindus describe Gaṅgā's purificatory power by relating the story of her descent from the cosmic realm, loosely following the main events of the Gaṅgā-avataraṇa in the *Rāmāyaṇa*. In various versions of this story, a devotee named Bhāgīratha called Gaṅgā down to earth to purify the ashes of King Sagara's 60,000 sons, who were burnt for their precociousness by a powerful monk. Gaṅgā descended on the locks of Lord Śiva, followed Bhāgīratha from the Himalayas across the plains and purified the ashes of the King's sons near the Bay of Bengal. In another rendition of her descent, the *Bhāgavata Purāṇa* relates how Viṣṇu in his incarnation (avatāra) as a dwarf asked for three strides of land from Bali, the Chief of the Demons. Thinking the dwarf's stride would be limited, Bali granted the wish. But then the dwarf (who was really Viṣṇu) grew exponentially and extended three legs across this world, the heavens and the netherworld in the strides allotted by Bali. The toe of one foot scratched the highest tip of the cosmic egg encapsulating this world, and out of this crack Gaṅgā flowed and washed down Viṣṇu's foot. When washing over Viṣṇu's foot, she absorbed the dirt and sins of the whole world, all the while remaining pure and unpolluted by sin. In these ways, Gaṅgā's descent is intricately related to Brahmā, Viṣṇu and Śiva, and Gaṅgā herself is called tripathagā (the union of three paths or aspects).

Gaṅgā's immanent form as water (jala) is a central element of Hindu ritual practices. Bathing or snāna in the river stream is an essential component of daily ritual for residents and pilgrims living in or visiting sacred cities along the river. Hindus immerse the ashes or bones of the cremated in the Gaṅgā to ensure their safe journey to the realm of the ancestors. Uses of Gaṅgājala for pūjā (offerings to deities), jalābhiṣeka (pouring of Gaṅgājala over a Śiva liṅga) and other worship rituals performed in homes and temples affirm the eternal essence of the river. Devotees also celebrate her purificatory power and abiding grace in the festivals of Gaṅgā Daśāhara and Gaṅgā Saptamī.

While devotees note the exceptional power of the river's qualities and flow, less faithful Hindus, scientists and followers of other religious persuasions think the Gaṅgā is polluted and, in some reaches, almost dead. For at least two and a half millennia, the Gaṅgā served as the main waterway for long-distance trade and transportation, and today carries the liquid and solid waste of numerous cities situated along the riverbank. The river reaches out to over 45 million people residing in the basin, and after feeding agriculture, industry and urban and rural drinking water needs, receives the return flow of these uses in the form of waste. Of the many sources of pollution finding their way to the river stream – urban and industrial wastewater, surface run-off from agricultural fields, landfills and dump sites, and human cultural practices – three-fourths of the load comes from the discharge of untreated municipal and industrial sewage generated in the large cities hugging the banks.

However, devout Hindus continue to believe in Gaṅgā's purifying power and do not think that she can be overpowered by the world's dirtiness. This continued faith in the river also derives from the way devotees attribute feminine and motherly qualities to her power, to explain her role in housekeeping, cleaning up and forgiveness. For example, Hindus in the sacred urban complex of Vārāṇasī (Banāras) explain that Gaṅgā, as a good mother, cleans up the messes her children make and forgives them lovingly. In this way, she cleans up other kinds of dirtiness people bring to her and excuses dirty behaviour with maternal kindness. She is forgiving rather than angry about human dirtiness. However, environmentalists argue that by attributing a forgiving nature to Gaṅgā Hindus may undermine pollution prevention activities that require citizen involvement. This approach may also provide a cover for municipalities and industries that avoid compliance with regulatory measures and the responsibility for treating their own waste before dumping it into the river. Hindus do link morality to the dirtiness produced by humans and find both degenerate, but they do not believe that Gaṅgā participates in the sin-game (pāp-līlā) of humans. This means that as she carries away human waste she is unaffected by the sins of humans; she is not motivated to retaliate. She did, after all, descend to earth to wash away those very misdeeds. So in this degenerate age, the kali yuga, her purificatory power is even more essential to human salvation and will likely remain that way in the future.

See also: **Altars, domestic; Brahmā; Devī Māhātmya; Gaṅgā Daśāhara; Mahābhārata; Pūjā; Purāṇas; Rāmāyaṇa; Saṃhitā; Śiva; Temple worship; Vārāṇasī; Viṣṇu; Yuga**

KELLY. D. ALLEY

Further reading

Alley, K.D. 1998. 'Idioms of Degeneracy: Assessing Gaṅgā's Purity and Pollution'. In Lance Nelson, ed., *Purifying the Earthly Body of God: Religion and Ecology in Hindu India*. Albany, NY: State University of New York Press, 297–330.

Alley, K.D. 2002. *On the Banks of the Gaṅgā: When Wastewater Meets a Sacred River*. Ann Arbor, MI: University of Michigan Press.

Central Pollution Control Board. 1995. *Status of the Industrial Pollution Control Programme Along the River Gaṅgā (Phase-I)*. New Delhi: Central Pollution Control Board.

Chapple, C.K. and M.E. Tucker. 2000. *Hinduism and Ecology*. Cambridge, MA: Harvard University Press.

Darian, S.G. 2001. *Ganges in Myth and History*. Varanasi: Motilal Banarsidass.

Eck, D. 1982. *Banaras: City of Light*. New York: Alfred Knopf.

Eck, D. 1982. 'Gaṅgā: The Goddess in Hindu Sacred Geography'. In John Stratton Hawley and Donna Mane Wulff, eds, *The Divine Consort: Radha and the Goddesses of India*. Boston, MA: Beacon Press, 166–93.

Feldhaus, A. 1995. *Water and Womanhood*. New York: Oxford University Press.

Markandya, A. and M.N. Murty. 2000. *Cleaning-up the Ganges: A Cost Benefit Analysis of the Gaṅgā Action Plan*. Delhi: Oxford University Press.
Peavey, F. 1995. 'Questions for the Ganges'. *Whole Earth Review*, Summer 86.
Shukla, A.C. and A. Vandana. 1995. *Gaṅgā: A Water Marvel*. New Delhi: Ashish Publishing House.
Stille, A. 1998. 'The Ganges' Next Life'. *New Yorker*, 19 January: 73 (43).
Tagare, G.V. (trans.). 1976. *Bhāgavata Purāṇa*. Trans. and annotated by G.V. Tagare. Part II (Skandas 4–6). Delhi: Motilal Banarsidass.
Tripathi, A.S.K. (ed.). 1991. *Kasi Khanda*, 2 parts. Varanasi: Sampurnanand Sanskrit University.

GAṄGĀ DAŚĀHARA

Gaṅgā Daśāhara, a festival commemorating the birthday of the Ganges River, is celebrated on the tenth day of Jyeṣṭhā or Jeth (May–June) at Vārāṇasī. The most popular legend about her birth is that she fell to earth, but was caught in Śiva's hair. Ganges, or mother Gaṅgā, is the first among India's holy rivers, sacred from her source down through such famous tīrthas as Haridvāra, Prayāga and Kāśī – also called Vārāṇasī (anglicised as Banaras) – until she reaches the estuary in the Bay of Bengal. The water of the Ganges is considered a source of purification for the body and soul. The celebration includes bathing, alms-giving (dāna) and making offerings to Gaṅgā. Traditionally, it has been maintained that the sins of ten births will be removed from a worshipper who places ten kinds of fruits on his or her head and immerses him or herself in the river. The festival is also celebrated outside India: in Trinidad, it has acquired much importance, having been celebrated there since the nineteenth century.

See also: **Dāna; Gaṅgā; Haridvāra; Jyeṣṭhā; Prayāga; Purity and pollution, ritual; Sacred geography; Śiva; Tīrthayātrā; Utsava; Vārāṇasī**

PERWAIZ HAYAT

Further reading

Arya, S.N. 2004. *History of Pilgrimage in Ancient India AD 300–1200*. New Delhi: Munshiram Manoharlal.
Crooke, W. 'Ganga, Ganges'. *ERE* VI: 177–79.
Gupta, Shakti M. 1996. *Festivals, Fairs and Fasts of India*. New Delhi: Clarion Books.
Klostermaier, K.K. 1994. *A Survey of Hinduism*, 2nd edn. Albany, NY: State University of New York Press.
Oakley, E.S. 1905. *Holy Himalaya*. Edinburgh and London: Oliphant.

GAṄGEŚA UPĀDHYĀYA

Gaṅgeśa was one of the most important and influential philosophers of the Nyāya school. He is associated with the inauguration of the Navya-Nyāya or 'New Logic' tradition. However the origin of Navya-Nyāya is usually traced to Udayana.

The most recent scholarly opinion is that Gaṅgeśa flourished *c.*1320 CE, a date supported by authorities such as Matilal. He lived in Mithilā, northern India. According to tradition he had several wives, one daughter and three sons. The philosopher Vardhamāna was one of the sons.

Gaṅgeśa is renowned as the author of the seminal text *Tattvacintāmani* ('The Jewel of Reflection on Reality'). This work has four chapters on the means of knowledge (accepted by Nyāya): perception, inference, comparison and speech. It is concerned with definitions and is marked by great precision and rigour. Gaṅgeśa had a realist ontology (a commitment to the existence of objects independent of consciousness).

See also: **Nyāya; Udayana**

MARTIN OVENS

Further reading

Phillips, S.H. and N.S.R. Tatacharya (trans.). 1998. *Gaṅgeśa's 'Jewel of Reflection on Reality,' the Perception Chapter*. Delhi: Motilal Banarsidass.

Potter, K.H. and S. Bhattacharyya (eds). 1994. *Encyclopedia of Indian Philosophies, Volume Six, Indian Philosophical Analysis: Nyāya-Vaiśesika from Gangeśa to Raghunātha Śiromani*. Princeton, NJ: Princeton University Press.

Further reading

Kane, P.V. 1974. *History of Dharmaśāstra*, 2nd edn, vol. 2, pt 1. Poona: Bhandarkar Oriental Research Institute, 201–07.
Pandey, R.J. 1969. *Hindu Saṃskāras*. Delhi: Motilal Barnarsidass, 48–59.

GARBHĀDHĀNA

The first of the saṃskāras, or Hindu rites of passage, the rite of impregnation, literally the 'placing (ādhāna) (of semen) into the womb (garbha)'. The husband was to approach his wife when she was in the most fertile days of her menstrual cycle (generally the fourth to sixteenth days after menstruation, avoiding in particular the eighth, thirteenth, fourteenth and fifteenth days). After considerable ritualisation, including elaborate dress and mantra recitation, the couple was to have sexual intercourse. If the union was not successful in generating pregnancy, then it was to be repeated every month until fertilisation. Although in general the purpose of this rite was to generate a good and powerful son, daughters also figured in the ritual calculus: even nights were deemed desirable for generating sons, and odd nights for daughters. The *Ṛgveda* well expresses the divinisation that the garbhādhāna is supposed to actualise:

> Let Viṣṇu prepare the womb, let Tvaṣṭṛ grind out the form, let Prajāpati sprinkle the seed and Dhātṛ place the embryo for you. O Sinīvālī, place the embryo; O Sarasvatī, place the embryo. May the Aśvins, the twin deities with garlands of blue lotuses, place the embryo for you. That which the Aśvin twins with their golden fire-churning sticks churn out, let us invoke that embryo of yours so that it is born in the tenth month.
>
> (*Ṛgveda* 10.184)

See also: **Saṃhitā; Saṃskāras**

FREDERICK M. SMITH

GARGA

Garga is the name of a number of mythological and historical characters. One was an ancient sage whose descendants, known as the Gārgas or Gārgyas, considered to be kṣatriya by birth but brāhmaṇa by vocation and achievement, were renowned ṛṣis, one of them being a priest to Kṛṣṇa and the Yādavas. The *Viṣṇu Purāṇa* comments that 'from Garga sprang Sina; from them were descended the Gārgas and Sainyas, Brāhmans of Kṣatriya race'. Garga is believed to be descended from Viṣṇu and became the preceptor of the Yādavas and it was on his advice that Kṛṣṇa was sent to learn from the sage Sāṃdīpani. Another Garga was a famed astronomer and one of the earliest writers on the subject. Along with the Nāga architect Śeṣa, he was instrumental in creating the Nāgara style of architecture and painting (sthāpatyaveda).

See also: **Brāhmaṇa; Jyotisa; Kṛṣṇa; Purāṇas; Ṛṣi; Sthāpatyaveda; Varṇa; Viṣṇu**

RON GEAVES

Further reading

Mani, Vettam. 1993. *Puranic Encyclopaedia*. Delhi: Motilal Benarsidass.

GĀRGĪ

Gārgī is a woman who appears in the *Bṛhadāraṇyaka Upaniṣad* (3.8.1–12) as one of the participants in a debate which takes place in the court of Janaka, the learned King of Videha. She challenges Yājñavalkya, the principal contestant, with regard to the nature of the imperishable

Brahman. Her first question concerned the underlying reality of existence, the power that is present throughout both the created order and the dimension of time. Known fully as Gārgī Vācaknavī, indicating she was the daughter of Vacaknu, her significance is that she demonstrates the intellectual knowledge and education of upper-class women in the late Vedic period, who often took part in philosophical and literary debates, in contrast with later times when the study of Vedic literature was forbidden to women.

See also: **Brahman; Janaka; Yājñavalkya**

RON GEAVES

Further reading

Stutley, Margaret and James Stutley (eds). 1977. *A Dictionary of Hinduism: Its Mythology, Folklore and Development 1500 BC–AD 1500*. London: Routledge and Kegan Paul.

GĀRHASTHYA

The stage of life during which one leads the life of a householder is the second of the four stages of life in the Hindu scheme of things. In the famous convocation passage in the *Taittirīya Upaniṣad* (1.11) the student is exhorted not to sever the continuity of the family line. The student thus marries after completing his studies and raises a family. The texts provide the details of how marriage should be arranged, the qualities to look for in a bride and so on. The details of the lifestyle pertaining to this āśrama are provided in the third chapter of the *Manusmṛti*, which also regards this stage of life as the best of the four because the other three depend on it (6.89–90).

One lives the life of a gṛhastha to discharge the three debts (ṛṇas) which one owes to the gods, the sages and the ancestors, also extended to include what one owes to human beings and to all creatures as well. These account for the five mahāyajñas (or great sacrifices) the householder is expected to perform thrice daily: by tending the sacrificial fires he discharges his debt to the gods (devayajña); by studying the scriptures he discharges his debt to the sages (brahmāyajñā); by offering oblations to the ancestors he discharges his debt to them (pitṛyajña); by welcoming guests he discharges his debt to fellow human beings (mānuṣayajñā); and by offering food to animals he discharges his debt to all living beings (bhūtayajña).

See also: **Āśrama (stages of life); Dharmaśāstras; Pitṛs; Upaniṣads; Vivāha; Yajña**

ARVIND SHARMA

Further reading

Kane, P.V. 1974. *History of Dharmaśāstra*, vol. 2, pt 1, 2nd edn. Poona: Bhandarkar Oriental Research Institute.

GARUḌA

A garuḍa is a fabled bird-like figure that is also depicted as half-human and appears in countless stories in the *Mahābhārata* and the *Purāṇas*. In the oldest texts, probably derived from pre-Aryan sources, Garuḍa is associated with the rays of the sun and the wind. As a devourer of serpents, the Garuḍa mantra is still considered as a powerful destroyer of disease and poison. In popular religion he is invoked as a healer of snakebite but he is also considered to represent the esoteric meaning of the Veda and thus crosses into Brahmanic as well as village forms of Hinduism.

More significantly, as the king of the birds he is the sacred mount (vāhana) of Viṣṇu and associated with the qualities of courage. In iconography he is usually depicted with an upper body of a predatory bird with wings and a lower body of a man, sometimes crowned. When shown with four arms, he carries an umbrella and a pot of nectar (amṛta) and his lower arms demonstrate reverence and worship.

See also: **Mahābhārata; Mantra; Purāṇas; Sacred animals; Vāhanas; Veda; Viṣṇu**

RON GEAVES

Further reading

Stutley, Margaret and James Stutley (eds). 1977. *A Dictionary of Hinduism: Its Mythology, Folklore and Development 1500 BC–AD 1500*. London: Routledge and Kegan Paul.

GARUḌA PURĀṆA

See: **Purāṇas**

GAUḌAPĀDA (sixth century CE)

The first clear example of the Advaita (non-dualist) philosophy within the Vedānta tradition. Śaṅkara cites Gauḍapāda approvingly on a number of occasions, describing him as his supreme teacher (paramaguru). The Śaṅkarācarya tradition has generally understood this in terms of a direct lineage, seeing Gauḍapāda as the teacher of Govindācarya, Śaṅkara's teacher.

Gauḍapāda is said to said to have written a commentary on the *Saṃkhyakārikās* but is most revered as the author of the *Māṇḍūkyakārikās* (otherwise known as *Gauḍapādakārikās* or *Āgamaśāstra*), a short text comprising 215 verses outlining the philosophy of non-dualism. The text comprises four chapters (the last of which amounts to almost half of the entire work). Chapter 1 (on 'Tradition') functions as an indirect commentary upon the *Māṇḍūkya Upaniṣad*, with its verses interspersed between the prose of the *Upaniṣad*. Chapters 2 and 3 (on 'Falsity' and 'Non-Duality') outline the central themes of the non-dualist philosophy, arguing that the world is essentially an illusion (māyā), and that the final truth is that no change or origination has in fact ever taken place (ajātivāda). The entire text, especially the final chapter ('The Peace of the Firebrand') is replete with Buddhist philosophical terminology and shows awareness of key Mahāyāna Buddhist philosophical texts and ideas. The text probably originated from the sixth century CE and was composed at a time and in a region where Mahāyāna Buddhist ideas were prevalent.

See also: **Advaita; Buddhism, relationship with Hinduism; Guru; Māyā; Śaṅkara; Śaṅkarācarya; Upaniṣads; Vedānta**

RICHARD KING

Further reading

King, Richard. 1995. *Early Advaita Vedānta and Buddhism: the Mahāyāna Context of the Gauḍapādīya-kārikā*. Albany, NY: State University of New York Press.

GAUDIYA VAISHNAVA MISSION

In the 1880s the teachings and practices of the sixteenth-century mystic Caitanya began to receive renewed attention. Caitanya Vaiṣṇavism had been in decline in Bengal and was revived principally by an English-educated magistrate, Bhaktivinoda Thakura (1838–1914), following his study of the *Bhāgavata Purāṇa* and *Caitanya-caritāmṛta*. He began a journal to disseminate the teachings of Caitanya in 1881 and translated and published many texts, which he sent to scholars in and beyond India. As a moderniser, he stood out against caste distinctions, yet remained uncompromising in his adherence to Caitanya tradition. He passed his mission on to his son, and it was he, Bhaktisiddhanta Saraswati, who formally organised the movement and carried forward the work of printing, publishing and spreading Caitanya's teachings about Kṛṣṇa. Like his father he looked beyond India, and sent preachers to the West, the most successful of whom was A.C. Bhaktivedanta Swami Prabhupada, founder of the International Society for Krishna Consciousness, an international development of Gauḍīya Vaiṣṇavism.

See also: **Bhaktisiddhanta Saraswati; Caitanya; International Society for Krishna Consciousness; Prabhupada, A.C. Bhaktivedanta Swami; Purāṇas**

KIM KNOTT

Further reading

Bromley, D.G. and L.D. Shinn (eds). 1989. *Krishna Consciousness in the West*. Lewisburg, PA: Bucknell University Press.

Rosen, S.J. (ed.). 1992. *Vaisnavism: Contemporary Scholars Discuss the Gaudiya Tradition*. New York: Folk Books.

Squarcini, F. and E. Fizzotti. 2004. *Hare Krishna: Studies in Contemporary Religion*. Salt Lake City, UT: Signature Books.

GAUḌĪYAS

Bengali Vaiṣṇavism teaches different levels or stages of devotion: Vaidhi Bhakti is the result of studying the religious texts such as *Śrīmadbhāgavatam*; Rāgānuga Bhakti is the result of inward feeling and attachment to Kṛṣṇa; this Rāgānuga Bhakti matures into what is known as Bhāva Bhakti. This kind of devotion gives rise to intimate personal feeling and it may develop through the grace of God. The Bhāva Bhakti further develops into Prema Bhakti, i.e. personal love for Kṛṣṇa. According to Bengali Vaiṣṇava philosophy, Kṛṣṇa has three powers: Svarūpa Śakti, the power of his inner nature; Jīva Śakti, the power to produce creatures; and Māyā Śakti, the power to create the material world. The Svarūpa Śakti is characterised by three attributes: Sat (Existence), Cit (Pure Consciousness) and Ānanda (Bliss).

Another important aspect of Bengali Vaiṣṇavism is the idea of 'rasa'. It has to do with the emotion that the devotee goes through in his or her expression of love for God. It is considered as the culmination of determinants (vibhavas) experiences (anubhavas), moods (bhāvas) and involuntary emotions (sancaribhāvas). There are nine rasas: Śanta, Dasya, Śakhya, Vāstalya, Madhura, Śṛngāra, Vātsalya, Prema and Kāma. The bhakti poets of Bengal have used a variety of these moods to express their love of God. The *Bhāgavata Purāṇa* is considered to be the best expression of these nine rasas. The bhakti poets of Bengal have also used an interesting type of poetry known as Padāvali, series of songs. These series of songs are supposed to be arranged in a sequence leading up to the ultimate bliss. Devotees are encouraged to sing these songs in an effort to seek the ultimate bliss.

See also: **Bhakti; Jīva; Māyā; Purāṇas; Saccidānanda; Śakti; Vaiṣṇavism**

PRATAP KUMAR

Further reading

Chakravarti, S.C. 1969. *Philosophical Foundation of Bengal Vaiṣṇavism: A Critical Exposition*. Calcutta: Academic Publishers.

Dasgupta, Shashibusan. 1976. *Obscure Religious Cults*. Calcutta: Firma KLM.

De, Sushil Kumar. 1961. *Early History of the Vaiṣṇava Faith and Movement in Bengal from Sanskrit and Bengali Sources*. Calcutta: Firma K.L. Mukhopadhyaya.

Dutt, Lal Kanai. 1963. *The Bengal Vaishnavism and Modern Life*. Calcutta: Sribhumi Publishing Co.

Gonda, J. 1993. *Aspects of Early Viṣṇuism*. Delhi: Motilal Banarsidass.

Goswami, B.K. 1965. *The Bhakti Cult in Ancient India*. Varanasi: Chowkamba Sanskrit Series Office.

Majumdar, A.K. 1969. *Caitanya: His Life and Doctrine*. Bombay: Bharatiya Vidya Bhavan.

Mukhopadhyaya, Durgadas. 1990. *Religion, Philosophy, and Literature of Bengal Vaiṣṇavism*. Delhi: BR Publishing Corporation.

GAUTAMA

See: **Nyāyasūtras**

GAYĀ

Gayā is an ancient pilgrimage centre in the state of Bihar in north-eastern India and a number of important temples can be found in and around the town. For example, there are three sun temples, as this area was originally part of the Magadha region, where worship of the sun god, Sūrya, was practised. The most important of the sun temples is the Dakṣinārka Temple, which houses an image that represents the sun god dressed in the style of an Iranian warrior and is considered by many to confirm the link with central Asia and the Aryans. However, the town is best known as a predominantly Vaiṣṇavite pilgrimage centre and the Viṣṇupada Temple is one of the most sacred temples dedicated to Viṣṇu, with a rock said to bear the imprint of his foot: it is a Piṇḍa Dāna Vedī (a site of offerings to the ancestors). The great Vaiṣṇavite teachers Rāmānuja and Madhva are associated with the Viṣṇupada Temple. There is also an ancient temple dedicated to Śiva at Gayā, the Prapitāmaheśyara Temple, dating from the eleventh century CE. Worship of the goddess Śakti is also represented at Gayā and the Maṅgalā Gourī Temple is believed to mark one of the places where a part of the body of Kālī fell when she was dismembered. Śakti is represented by the symbol of a breast at Maṅgalā Gourī and embodies benevolence and nourishment. The site, believed to be where Siddhartha Gautama gained enlightenment as the Buddha whilst sitting under a pipal tree, can also be found on the outskirts of Gayā at Bodh Gaya. During the reign of the emperor Aśoka the site was marked off and the Mahābodhi Temple was then built there. It is visited by Buddhist and Hindu pilgrims and Śiva and Gaṇeśa are both represented in the temple.

See also: **Buddhism, relationship with Hinduism; Gaṇeśa; Image worship; Indo-European traditions; Kālī and Caṇḍī; Madhva; Mandir; Rāmānuja; Śakti; Śiva; Sūrya; Tīrthayātrā; Vaiṣṇavism; Viṣṇu**

VIVIENNE BAUMFIELD

Further reading

Basham, A.L. 1975. *The Wonder that Was India*. London: Collins.

GĀYATRĪ MANTRA

Strictly, Gāyatrī is the name of a verse metre in both Vedic and Sanskrit (Śikśā, Vedānga). It consists of three eight-syllable pādas ('feet'), forming a line and a half-line. The word Gāyatrī, however, is commonly used to refer to a particular verse in that metre, which is the most famous and sacred of all Vedic mantras. It is addressed to Savitr, the deity who empowers Sūrya, the Sun. Traditionally kept secret from all except the twice-born castes, it may be translated thus: 'Let us meditate upon that longed for splendour of the god Savitar who when pondered upon will urge us onward'. The Gāyatrī mantra is recited, especially by observant brāhmaṇās, three times a day, at morning, noon and evening. When a young brāhmaṇa boy is invested with his yajñopavīta ('sacred thread') in a special ceremony (Upanāyana), he is also initiated into the Gāyatrī mantra.

Images of Gāyatrī as a minor goddess can sometimes be seen. She is portrayed sitting on a lotus, with many arms and several heads, and carries the weapons and insignia of Lakṣmī, Pārvatī and Viṣṇu, including axe, discus and conch.

See also: **Brāhmaṇās; Caste; Dvija; Lakṣmī, Śrī; Mantra; Pārvatī; Śikṣā; Sūrya; Upanayana; Vedāṇgas; Viṣṇu**

JOHN R. MARR AND KATHLEEN TAYLOR

Further reading

Frawley, D. 1994. *Wisdom of the Ancient Seers: Mantras of the Rig Veda*. Delhi: Motilal Banarsidass.

Gopinath Rao, T.A. 1910. *Elements of Hindu Iconography.* Madras: Law Printing House.
Macdonell, A.A. 1910. *Vedic Grammar.* Strasburg: Trübner (section on metre).

GENDER

Many modern scholars contrast the words *sex* (the biological characteristics of maleness and femaleness that define people as men or women) and *gender* (the cultural interpretations of these definitions). Hindu notions of gender as sanctioned patterns of identity and templates of behaviour, like those of other cultures, give meaning and order to life. Deeply embedded in language and worldview, gender pervades ways of perceiving, classifying and thinking about primary experience. Becoming self-conscious about it can fundamentally shift meaning and identity (as feminists argue) but cannot eliminate all residual gendered aspects of language and somatic awareness.

Hinduism has both positive and negative views of women. In traditional Hinduism as defined by smṛti works, gender informed women's identity by stressing that they should produce many sons, an ideal that went back to the blessing of the bride in *Ṛgveda* 10.85.45. The rites of passage (saṃskāras) in elite groups included one during pregnancy (puṃsavana) to create a male foetus or to change the sex of a female one. Scholars call this androcentric orientation found in some texts 'son preference'. It was the result of several factors, which, if considered one by one, initially had some legitimate functions, but when consolidated created problems.

All societies have used culture in binding fathers to mothers and children; that link has always been a weak one, after all, given men's lesser role in the reproductive cycle. Hinduism did this by stressing the father's identification with the children that were most like him. According to *Śatapatha-Brāhmaṇa* 5.2.1.10, men became complete by having sons through whom they would be reborn. Sons (putra) were also important in delivering their fathers from hell (put) (*Manusmṛti* 9. 138), a (false) etymology that nonetheless made men feel dependent on their sons (although there could be substitutes if they had no sons). Perhaps because people realised that male foetuses and infants are more vulnerable than female ones – more are lost in pregnancy and the first few years of life – some parents pampered their sons and, when resources were few, provided them with better food and medical attention than their daughters. Like other religions that supported patrilocal and patrilineal social structures (the most common type in the anthropological record), so did mainstream Hinduism. This meant placing a premium on sons. The consolidation of public religious, political and economic power in male hands intensified this son preference and led to androcentrism in some circles, sometimes even misogyny. In some elite groups, the result of all this relegated many women to the domestic sphere, although modern reforms have been addressing these problems.

But gender is a complex topic in Hinduism. Other elite women were not subject to these ideals found in smṛti texts. Some belonged to regional traditions of matrilineality and cross-cousin marriage (vivāha), in which women had a strong position. Others were bhakti saints who had left a marriage or bypassed it altogether to pursue love of God; in some of these traditions, even married women were viewed by their religious communities as the pre-eminent devotees because of their 'natural' womanly love of a male god (Āṇṭāḷ, Mīrābāī). By contrast, in goddess traditions female devotees had a special relationship with the supreme deity because of shared characteristics. Many Hindu communities are not sexually polarised, moreover, perhaps because women dominate the domestic domain.

Besides, women have their own intimate culture, religious activities, forms of authority and interpretations of negative scriptural passages; women mercilessly deride men, moreover, in folk songs, stories and rituals. Adding to this complexity is the fact that some were Tantric gurus or adepts; some military heroines; some, such as temple women and courtesans, were outside the norms of marriage altogether; and most low-caste and tribal women did not face the restrictions of smṛti texts. In many of these circles, there is the popular maxim that a daughter is equal to a hundred sons.

No discussion of this topic is complete without definitions of gender that do not fit into the standard categories. Some 'intersex' people are known as hijras. That word denotes a physical inability to function sexually as men and therefore includes both hermaphrodites and eunuchs. Formal initiation into the hijra community involves castration. Hijras wear clothing normally assigned to women, worship goddesses and perform publicly as women (dancing and singing at family celebrations of the birth of a son or on other auspicious occasions). Other intersex people have no doubt remained 'hidden', but that is changing due to the gay liberation movement.

See also: **Āṇṭāḷ; Bhakti; Homosexuality; Lesbianism; Mīrābāī; Motherhood; Sacred texts; Saṃhitā; Saṃskāras; Vivāha; Women's rites**

KATHERINE K. YOUNG

Further reading

Bannerji, H., S. Mojab and J. Whitehead (eds). 2001. *Of Property and Propriety: The Role of Gender and Class in Imperialism*. Toronto: University of Toronto Press.

Chakravarti, U. 1999. 'Beyond the Altekarian Paradigm: Towards a New Understanding of Gender Relations in Early Indian History'. In K. Roy, ed., *Women in Early Indian Societies*. New Delhi: Manohar, 72–81.

Nanda, S. 1994. 'Hijras: An Alternative Sex and Gender Role in India'. In G. Herdt, ed., *Third Sex, Third Gender: Beyond Sexual Dimorphism in Culture and History*. New York: Zone Books, 373–417.

Olivelle, Patrick. 2004. *The Law Code of Manu*. Oxford: Oxford University Press.

GENETIC ENGINEERING

The arrival of technological advancements brings an unprecedented angle into the debate in Hindu medical ethics. While Āyurveda has in the pre-technological era been concerned with working with and within the boundaries set by Mother Nature, man-made technology has empowered humans with the ability to override her wishes. Thus, from one point of view, the sceptic may justify his or her opinion by claiming that one's physical condition is karmic, and it is within the jurisdiction of natural law and not through tampering with nature that any attempts to rectify the situation should be attempted. For others, this fatalistic attitude is not acceptable, and given that Āyurveda has been evolving, it is within the evolution of medical science, one could argue, that technology feels at home. Caution would need to be exercised, though, keeping in mind the karmic effects of any decision given the relatively recent and unprecedented appearance of modern medical technology.

What, in the Hindu ethical discourse, is of prime importance, however, is arguably the motivation behind the engineering. If it is simply for the purpose of healing or rectifying some health problem, one may suggest that any principled means of treatment is justified as life and well-being are paramount in fulfilling one's dharma. If the basis is, however, vanity and therefore correction rather than cure, then this could be argued to be against the decision of Mother Nature and one's karma. If nature is played with for selfish gains, then upsetting the cosmic balance would result in negative reactions. From a spiritual point of view, any concerns regarding vanity only encourage the ego. The function of the body, then, is as a vehicle to enact one's dharma and to facilitate union with the divine.

While ahiṃsā (non-violence) is an important concept amongst Hindus, implying that all creatures have the right to life, some would not dismiss the use of animals for the welfare of humans on the grounds that humans are higher than animals on the spiritual and evolutionary scale. The death of an animal to save the life of a human is seen as a sacrificial act. For others, however, their commitment to vegetarianism and ahiṃsā would make them think twice about how far they would be prepared to sacrifice another life for theirs or how much they would avoid animal products to avoid impurity. But in no situation does Hindu ethics allow for the death of an animal for materialistic reasons or those of vanity.

See also: **Ahiṃsā; Āyurveda; Dharma; Karma; Medical ethics**

RISHI HANDA

Further reading

Crawford, S. Cromwell. 2003. *Hindu Bioethics for the Twenty-First Century*. Albany, NY: State University of New York Press.

GEOGRAPHY

See: **Sacred geography**

GHASI DAS (1756–1836)

Ghasi Das is a well-known guru of the state of Chhatisgarh. After initiation into the practice of Satnām following a pilgrimage to Jagannāth, he gave up working as an agricultural labourer and began to preach. The movement that developed from his teachings is known as the Satnām Panth or Satnamis. In the nineteenth century his followers constituted up to one-sixth of Chhatisgarh's population, preaching social equality and worship of the formless as manifested in Satnām. They opposed all ritual worship of the pantheon of Hindu gods and maintained a strict regime of no alcohol, meat or tobacco.

Ghasi Das' teachings were opposed to caste and need to be seen in the context of the social and religious order of the state of Chhatisgarh, which contained a high proportion of scheduled castes and tribal peoples dominated by a minority of brāhmaṇas who worshipped Rāma. The Satnamis, along with Ravidāsis and Kabīrpanthis, formed a non-violent religious opposition to oppression which was to provide resistance against the British. The paraṃparā, led by hereditary gurus, remains popular with religious centres in Bhandar and Girod.

See also: **Jagannātha; Rāma; Ravidās(a); Satnamis**

RON GEAVES

Further reading

Jones, Kenneth. 1989. *Socio-Religious Reform Movements in British India, The New Cambridge History of India: Vol. 3.1*. Cambridge: Cambridge University Press.

GHOSE, AUROBINDO (1872–1950)

Aurobindo Ghose, also known as Sri Aurobindo, is often claimed to be one of twentieth-century India's foremost philosophers, poets and spiritual figures. At age 7 he was sent to England, where he mastered Western classical literature and languages. He returned to India at age 21 and soon mastered classical Indian literature and languages as well. He was active in the Indian independence movement until 1910, when he moved to Pondicherry to pursue his spiritual work.

From 1910 to 1950 his spiritual practice focused on the reconciliation of the spiritual and material realities, with the ultimate goal of utilising the most powerful spiritual forces (the Supermind) to accelerate and transform human evolution. He proclaimed that the current human state of consciousness is merely a transitional state with endless potential for spiritual development and called for the integration of Eastern and Western cultural and knowledge traditions.

Sri Aurobindo rejected the notion of the illusoriness of the phenomenal world and recognised spiritual and material realities as equally real dimensions of a whole and indivisible spectrum of reality. He reconciled several major schools of Vedānta with the essential teachings of the Tantric approach, thus synthesising a comprehensive approach known as Integral Yoga, emphasising a balanced approach to spiritual development with equal emphasis on knowledge/wisdom, love/compassion and action.

He stressed the purposefulness of human life on earth as the embodiment of spirit and taught that human suffering stems from ignorance and unconsciousness due to disharmony between the physical, emotional, mental and spiritual dimensions. He rejected the world-negating as well as individualistic approaches to spiritual development as escapism and embraced embodied spirituality and the reintegration of the feminine Divine.

His most notable works in prose are *The Life Divine*, *The Synthesis of Yoga*, *Essays on the Gita* and *The Human Cycle*. His poetic magnum opus is titled *Savitri*.

See also: **Auroville; Māyā; Mother, The; Nationalism; Tantrism; Vedānta**

BAHMAN A.K. SHIRAZI

Further reading

Ghose, Aurobindo. 1992. *The Synthesis of Yoga*. Pondicherry: Sri Aurobindo Ashram Press.

Ghose, Aurobindo. 1993. *Savitri: A Legend and a Symbol*. Pondicherry: Sri Aurobindo Ashram Press.

Ghose, Aurobindo. 1997. *Essays on the Gita*. Pondicherry: Sri Aurobindo Ashram Press.

Ghose, Aurobindo. 1997. *The Human Cycle*. Pondicherry: Sri Aurobindo Ashram Press.

Ghose, Aurobindo. 1997. *The Life Divine*. Pondicherry: Sri Aurobindo Ashram Press.

GĪTAGOVINDA

A Sanskrit poem by Jayadeva (Bengal, late twelfth century CE) about Kṛṣṇa (text and translation, Miller 1977). The title means 'Kṛṣṇa sung'; Govinda is one of Kṛṣṇa's many names. Little is certain about Jayadeva, but he was patronised by King Lakṣmaṇa-sena, who ruled Bengal 1179–*c.*205. It is said that he became a devotee of Jagannātha, the form of Viṣṇu worshipped at Purī in Orissa.

It tells of Kṛṣṇa and Rādhā, his favourite among the gopīs (cowherd women) who loved him during his boyhood in Vṛndāvana. It uses the conventions of Sanskrit love poetry: the separation of lovers, the different moods of the girl and their final union. Different verses are spoken by Kṛṣṇa, Rādhā, a woman messenger, a confidante of Rādhā and a narrator. Each of the twelve cantos (sarga) includes up to four songs, called prabandha, using rhyme and a strong metrical beat, quite unlike the unrhymed metres usual in classical Sanskrit. Each song has its tāla (rhythm) and rāga (musical mode). The poem thus links the learned kāvya tradition of poetry with the more popular tradition of the stotra. Near the end of each song Jayadeva mentions his own name – a link with vernacular devotional poets such as Kabīr.

The poem has become part of the tradition which uses the gopīs' love for Kṛṣṇa to express bhakti (devotion), as in the *Bhāgavata Purāṇa* (Hardy 1983). It strongly influenced the Caitanya, Vallabha or Puṣṭi Mārga, and Sahajiyā forms of Vaiṣṇavism. The Sahajiyās, a group in seventeenth-century and eighteenth-century Bengal which emphasised sexual love as an expression of bhakti (Dimock 1966), regarded Jayadeva as their chief teacher. There have been many imitations, some substituting Rāma and Sītā, or Śiva and Pārvatī, for Kṛṣṇa and Rādhā. The first song, in praise of the ten avatāras of Viṣṇu, is widely used in worship.

See also: **Bhakti; Caitanya; Gopī(s); Jagannātha; Jayadeva; Kabīr; Kṛṣṇa; Pārvatī; Poetry; Rādhā; Rāma; Sacred texts; Sītā; Śiva; Vaiṣṇavism; Vallabha; Vṛndāvana**

DERMOT KILLINGLEY

Further reading

Dimock, Edward C., Jr. 1966. *The Place of the Hidden Moon: Erotic Mysticism in the Vaiṣṇava-Sahajiyā Cult of Bengal*. Chicago, il: University of Chicago Press.
Hardy, Friedhelm. 1983. *Viraha-bhakti: The Early History of Kṛṣṇa Devotion in South India*. Delhi: Oxford University Press.
Miller, Barbara Stoler. 1977. *Love Song of the Dark Lord: Jayadeva's Gitagovinda*. New York: Columbia University Press.

GLASENAPP, (OTTO MAX) HELMUTH VON (1891–1963)

German Indologist. Born the son of a prominent banker in Berlin, while studying at Tübingen Glasenapp switched from law to Indology under the influence of the works of P. Deussen, H. Oldenberg and Richard von Garbe (1857–1927). He was Professor at Königsberg from 1928 until the end of the war, and thereafter at Tübingen. His early research was on Jain philosophy and on Madhva. He published important overviews of several major Indian religions which were widely read in Germany and translated into several European and Indian languages. He published also on Vallabha and Śaṅkara, on Sanskrit and north Indian vernacular literature and on the influence of Indian thought on German philosophy and literature. His travels in India are described in his autobiography. A full list of publications is included in a volume edited by his students for his seventieth birthday.

See also: **Deussen, Paul Jakob; Hinduism, history of scholarship; Jainism, relationship with Hinduism; Madhva; Oldenberg, Hermann; Śaṅkara; Vallabha**

WILL SWEETMAN

Further reading

Glasenapp, H. von. 1922. *Der Hinduismus: Religion und Gesellschaft im heutigen Indien* [Hinduism: Religion and Society in Contemporary India]. Munich: Wolff.
Glasenapp, H. von. 1964. *Meine Lebensreise: Menschen, Länder und Dinge, die ich sah* [My Life's Journey: People, Countries and Things Which I Saw]. Wiesbaden: F.A. Brockhaus.
Moeller, V., W. Nölle and J.F. Sprockhoff (eds). 1962. *Von Buddha zu Gandhi: Aufsätze zur Geschichte der Religionen Indiens* [From Buddha to Gandhi: Essays on the History of the Religions of India]. Wiesbaden: Harrassowitz.

GODSE, NATHURAM VINAYAK (1912–49)

Nathuram Vinayak Godse was born into a Chitpavan brāhmaṇa family in Pune, Maharashtra. Godse fell under the influence of V.D. Savarkar, also a Marathi Chitpavan brāhmaṇa, while a student and subsequently joined the Rashtriya Swayamsevak Sangh and the Hindu Mahasabha. Disillusioned with Madhav Sadhasiv Golwalkar's policy of cultural mobilisation rather than political activism, Godse left the Rashtriya Swayamsevak Sangh in 1942 to form the Hindu Rashtra Dal, a militant and aggressive organisation committed to Savarkar's ideology.

Godse assassinated Mahatma Gandhi on 30 January 1948 and was executed in

1949. Although hostile to Gandhi's policies, he maintained that he was not motivated by personal animosity. He was particularly outraged by Gandhi's role in pressuring India's government to compensate Pakistan for losses suffered during Partition, and mistrusted the challenge to brahmanical values, and thus the status of his own caste, which ran through Gandhi's social and religious thinking.

See also: **Gandhi, Mohandas Karamchand; Golwalkar, Madhav Sadashiv; Hindu Mahasabha; Rashtriya Swayamsevak Sangh; Savarkar, Vinayat Damodar**

GWILYM BECKERLEGGE

Further reading

Sharma, A. 1993. 'Gandhi or Godse? Power, Force and Non-Violence'. In N. Smart and S. Thakur, eds, *Ethical and Political Dilemmas of Modern India*. London: Macmillan Press Ltd, 15–29.

GOKHALE, GOPAL KRISHNA (1866–1915)

Gopal Krishna Gokhale was a Hindu reformer, nationalist, teacher, economist, legislator and statesman. Born in a poor Chitpavan brāhmaṇa family in the coastal Ratnagiri district of Maharashtra, he graduated from Elphinstone College, Bombay, in 1884. Having joined the Deccan Education Society he then taught at its Fergusson College in Pune, initiating a lifelong championing of free universal education for all Indians, Hindu and Muslim alike, but most specially for women. Having strenuously mastered the English language, he contributed to *Mahratta*, the journal founded in 1881 by Tilak and, from 1888, to the English sections of *Sudharak*.

Crucially, he became M.G. Ranade's assistant in 1887, which marked his political awakening and consolidated his belief in moderation and the pursuit of a nationalist agenda through constitutional means. He then became editor of the *Quarterly*, the journal of the Poona Sarvajanik Sabha, a body created to mediate between the government and the governed. When in 1895 the Sabha was taken over by the radical Tilak, Gokhale rejoined Ranade to form the Deccan Sabha. As an economist, he was a forceful critic of the disastrous impact of British policies on the Indian economy. However, he resisted the lure of the Swadeshi and the Boycott movements, started in 1905, which vowed to abstain from purchasing any British manufactured goods, seeing that the rebuilding of an indigenous economy could only be achieved through a gradual process grounded above all in the spread of education, the acquisition of technical expertise but also the abolition of the caste system – and, in particular, untouchability – and nothing less than the eradication of religious rivalries. That programme greatly inspired Gandhi, who had been supported by Gokhale in his South African struggles and Satyāgraha (truth force, i.e. non-violent resistance) and whom, also attracted by the man's spartan lifestyle, he called rajaguru: his master, with no hyperbole. A member of the Congress since 1889, Gokhale steadily became a major influence on the party, stamping it with his political moderation and thus turning it into a respectable channel of Indian opinion for the British.

Elected in 1902 to the Imperial Legislative Council, law-abiding cooperation, in his view, could be the only successful framework for a constructive critique of British power that would eventually lead, first, to an Indianisation of the administration, for which he vigorously campaigned, and, eventually, to freedom for India in a secular democracy, with parliamentary rule, a Congress ideal which was to determine the nature of the Indian state to this day, as implemented in due course by Gandhi and Jawaharlal Nehru. A devout Hindu, Gokhale was thus the farsighted forefather of a secular independent India, a dream that was left for Gandhi to fulfil.

See also: **Brāhmaṇa; Caste; Dalits; Gandhi, Mohandas Karamchand; Nationalism; Ranade, Mahadev Govind; Tilak, Bal Gangadhar; Women's education**

DANIEL MARIAU

Further reading

Heimsuth, C.H. 1964. *Indian Nationalism and Hindu Social Reform*. Princeton, NJ: Princeton University Press.

GOLWALKAR, MADHAV SADASHIV (1906–73)

Madhav Sadashiv Golwalkar, the second sarsanghchalak (supreme leader) of the Rashtriya Swayamsevak Sangh (RSS), succeeded its founder, K.V. Hedgewar, in 1940. Raised in Nagpur and a one-time lecturer at Banaras Hindu University, Golwalkar gained an early reputation for his spirituality. His standing as the RSS's most influential thinker stems from *We or Our Nation Defined* (1939), which owed much to V.D. Savarkar. Golwalkar's later theory of 'positive Hinduism' (1954), with its stress upon service, illustrated the no less important influence of the Ramakrishna movement. Credited with rehabilitating the RSS after the assassination of Mahatma Gandhi, Golwalkar unintentionally fostered the autonomy and political activism of the RSS's affiliates through his creation of the post of pracharak (regional organiser). He played a major part in the formation of the Vishwa Hindu Parishad in 1964.

See also: **Gandhi, Mohandas Karamchand; Hedgewar, Keshav Baliram; Ramakrishna Math and Mission; Savarkar, Vinayat Damodar; Vishwa Hindu Parishad**

GWILYM BECKERLEGGE

Further reading

Jaffrelot, C. 1996. *The Hindu Nationalist Movement and Indian Politics, 1925 to the 1990s*. London: Hurst.

GONDA, JAN (1905–91)

Dutch Indologist and philologist. Born in Gouda and educated at the Universities of Utrecht and Leyden, Gonda first studied classical and Indo-European linguistics. From 1932 until his retirement he was Professor of Sanskrit and Indo-European Linguistics at the University of Utrecht; until 1950 he was also Professor of Malay and Javanese Linguistics and Literature, and many of his early publications were in this field. Later he concentrated primarily on Sanskrit linguistics and Vedic religion, especially ritual, and literature. A prolific scholar, he published hundreds of specialist articles and numerous books, including a comprehensive history of Hinduism in two volumes (1960–63), and other works on aspects of Vedic religion and literature (1970, 1975). Gonda was editor and also contributed volumes to two important multi-volume reference works, the *History of Indian Literature* and the Indian section of the *Handbuch der Orientalistik* (Handbook of Oriental Studies).

See also: **Languages; Vedism**

WILL SWEETMAN

Further reading

Ensink J. and P. Gaeffke (eds). 1972. *India Maior. Congratulatory Volume Presented to J. Gonda*. Leiden: E.J. Brill.
Gonda, J. 1960–63. *Die Religionen Indiens. I. Veda und älterer Hinduismus. II. Der jüngere Hinduismus* [The Religions of India. I. Veda and early Hinduism. II. Later Hinduism]. Stuttgart: Kohlhammer.
Gonda, J. 1970. *Visnuism and Śivaism: A Comparison*. London: Athlone Press.
Gonda, J. 1975. *Vedic Literature (Saṃhitās and Brāhmaṇas)* (*A History of Indian Literature* I, 1). Wiesbaden: Harrassowitz.

GOPĪ(S)

The cowherd women enamoured of Kṛṣṇa, first described in the *Harivaṃśa* in a brief passage significantly elaborated in the later *Bhāgavata Purāṇa*, the gopīs are extolled as exemplary lovers of God, willing to forsake everything for Kṛṣṇa and totally absorbed in bhakti, devotion. Due to their ardent attachment to Kṛṣṇa, who is essentially ultimate reality, and their perfect meditation on him during times of painful separation, the gopīs attain salvation, and their path of passionate love thus becomes paradigmatic for later devotional traditions, especially Gauḍīya Vaiṣṇavism. The most famous gopī is Rādhā, Kṛṣṇa's special beloved, but the amorous devotion of all the gopīs who meet Kṛṣṇa in Vṛndāvana is said to symbolise the deep longing of human beings for God.

See also: **Bhakti; Gaudiya Vaishnava Mission; Harivaṃśa; Kṛṣṇa; Purāṇas; Rādhā; Vṛndāvana**

TRACY COLEMAN

Further reading

Bryant, Edwin F. (trans.). 2003. *Krishna: The Beautiful Legend of God. Śrīmad Bhāgavata Purāṇa. Book X.* London: Penguin Books.

Coleman, Tracy. 2002. 'Suffering Desire for Krishna: Gender and Salvation in the *Bhāgavata Purāṇa*'. *Journal of Vaishnava Studies* 10.2: 39–50.

Journal of Vaiṣṇava Studies 5.4 Fall. 1997. Focus on Kṛṣṇa and the Gopīs.

GORAKHNĀTH(A)

Circa eleventh century Goraksanātha, in Sanskrit, was a historical founder of the Nāṭha Yoga tradition (saṃpradāya), whose followers are variously known as Siddha(perfect)-yogin, Nātha-siddha, Gorakhnāthi in Hindi or Jogi throughout Northern India, also, for short, Nāthā (Master, Lord). They have also been nicknamed kāṇphata, 'split ears' after their custom of piercing their ears so as to wear large and heavy hoop earrings (kuṇḍala). Apart from numerous legends found in the ballads and songs that are the first documents of some northern vernaculars such as Bengali, nothing is known of the life and whereabouts of Gorakhnāth, whose dates are also disputed. Gorakhnāth is held by tradition to be the disciple of Matsyendranāth, an equally elusive figure who may have been the same person as Mīnanāth or even Lūipa (all names relating to 'fish'), who all, including Gorakh, count among the eighty-four Perfect Ones (mahāsiddha or siddhācārya) also revered by the Sahajiyā Tantric Buddhists and celebrated in the old Bengali *Caryāpada* (Songs on the Conduct). Matsyendra's own guru, however, was none other than the supreme one (paramaguru), Ādinātha, the Primordial Lord, Śiva himself, from whom proceed all teachings. Thus, the Nāthayogin call themselves Śivagotra, 'Śiva's family' or Śiva-Gorakh, since Gorakh is viewed as an incarnation of Śiva and worshipped as such in a number of temples, including the one in the city named after him, Gorakhpur, in eastern Uttar Pradesh.

Of the many works attributed to Gorakhnāth, in Sanskrit, Hindi or Rajasthani, or a mixture of those, and which all expound aspects of practices of the 'yoga of violent effort' (haṭha yoga), only a few can be attributed to him directly. Of those, the most important is the *Siddhasiddhāntapaddhati* (Manual of the Doctrines of the Siddhas), its clear attribution confirmed by the later manuals of the tradition, including the *Hathayogapradīpikā* (The Little Lamp of Haṭha Yoga).

The manual, in six chapters (Upadeśa: Teachings), accounts for how the material world proceeds from the Nameless (Anāmā) or ultimate reality through its creative Energy (Śakti) as a series of six 'bodies' (Piṇḍa), of which only the last emerge as gross materiality, much as speech emerges from an undifferentiated meaning-sound (Nāda) into the plurality of phonemes. The subtle body is then analysed, including its centres of energy or cakra, of which there are nine (against the classical six or seven). The non-difference between macrocosm and microcosm – the body – is then discussed, the visible body being the revealed form (kula) of the un-revealed Śakti (akula) present in the body in a dormant form that the yogin is to awaken and make rise through the cakras until the body enters a state of equivalence/equipollence (samarasa) with the ultimate reality, in which it then merges non-dually, a state of eternal bliss and freedom. That state is the achievement of deathlessness, only possible through the grace of the guru. The final chapter enumerates the characteristics of an avadhūta yogin, a perfected being in complete control over psyche and body and indeed all natural laws. Thus, the SSP expounds the method that results in physical immortality through a reversal of all natural processes.

Along with his teacher, Gorakhnāth remains to this day the Supreme exemplar of the fully realised yogin, an immortal reappearing at will to perform miracles emulated by his Siddha successors, the supreme Lord-Guru (Gurunāth) celebrated in a vast hagiographical literature.

See also: **Buddhism, relationship with Hinduism; Guru; Haṭha Yoga; Kāṇphata Yoga; Kuṇḍalinī Yoga; Matsyendranāth; Mudrā; Nāṭh(a) Yoga; Śakti; Saṃpradāya; Siddha; Śiva; Tantrism**

DANIEL MARIAU

Further reading

Banerjea, A.K. 1962. *Philosophy of Gorakhnath*. Gorakhpur: Mahant Dig Vijai Nath Trust. Reprinted Delhi, 1983.

Briggs, G.W. 1938. *Gorakhnāth and the Kānphata Yogis*. Calcutta and London: Y.M.C.A. Publishing House and Oxford University Press. Reprinted Delhi, 1973.

Kuvalayananda, Swami (trans.). 1964. *Goraksa-Śataka*. Lonavla: Kaivalyadhama S.M.Y.M. Samiti.

GOTRA

Gotra is a Sanskrit term that referred to individuals, primarily brāhmaṇas, who could trace their lineage to a common ancestor. Estimates given in Sanskrit texts on the precise number of these gotras ranged widely, from four in the *Mahābhārata*, through eight in the *Baudhayana Dharmaśūtra*, to 18 in the *Balambhatti* and 3 million in the *Pravaramanjari*. The Sanskrit term pravara, or illustrious ancestor, was inexorably linked to the concept of gotra, since within each gotra were subcategories affiliated with three, or less frequently two or five, pravaras. Pravaras thus served to delimit further communities of related individuals. Determinations of a person's gotra and pravara were particularly significant for the institution of marriage, since a marriage between two individuals of the same gotra and pravara was prohibited and thus considered to be null and void. These marriages were very likely forbidden because they were regarded as incestuous. That members of the same gotra and pravara were considered as quasi-kinsmen is further borne out by the fact that gotra played a role in inheritance law, since some Sanskrit jurists held that the property of a man who died without sons or daughters should devolve to members of his gotra.

See also: **Brāhmaṇa; Mahābhārata**

ETHAN KROLL

Further reading

Brough, John. 1953. *The Early Brahmanical System of Gotra and Pravara*. Cambridge: Cambridge University Press.

Kane, Pandurang Vaman. 1941. *History of Dharmasastra*, vol. 2. Poona: Bhandarkar Oriental Research Institute.

Zimmer, Heinrich. 1914. *Studien zur Geschichte der Gotras*. Berlin.

GOVARDHANA

Mount Govardhana (literally, Mountain of cow dung wealth (Toomey 1992: 123)) is a sacred hill located in Braj, Mathurā area. Its significance lies in a narrative taken from the earliest texts *Bhāgavata Purāṇa* dealing with the life of Kṛṣṇa in the region (Vaudeville 1976). As a young boy, Kṛṣṇa persuaded the local cow-herding villagers to make their annual food offerings to him instead of Indra as usual. Indra loosed a deluge to punish the villagers but Kṛṣṇa simply lifted the mountain upon his little finger, sheltering them and their cows.

Lavish devotional food offerings are made annually at the site, and in ISKCON temples, to commemorate this occasion. Mount Govardhana has been a focus of pilgrimage since the sixteenth century, when Vallabha and Caitanya, the preceptors of Puṣṭi Marga and the Gauḍīya saṃpradāyas, established residences at either end of the hill.

See also: **Caitanya; Food; Gauḍīyas; Kṛṣṇa; Indra; International Society for Krishna Consciousness; Mathurā; Puṣṭi Mārga; Saṃpradāya; Vallabha**

MARTIN WOOD

Further reading

Prabhupada, A.C. Bhaktivedanta Swami. 2002. *Kṛṣṇa: The Supreme Personality of Godhead Part One*. Germany: Bhaktivedanta Book Trust.

Toomey, P. 1992. 'Mountain of Food, Mountain of Love: Ritual Inversion in the Annakuta Feast at Mount Govardhan'. In R.S. Khare, ed., *The Eternal Food*. Albany, NY: State University of New York Press.

Toomey, P. 1994. *Food From the Mouth of Krishna: Feasts and Festivals in a North Indian Pilgrimage Centre*. Delhi: Hindustan Publishing Corporation.

Vaudeville, C. 1976. 'Braj Lost and Found'. *Indo-Iranian Journal* 18: 195–213.

GOVINDA BABA

An influential figure in the development of the Satya Mahima Dharma, a religious movement founded by Mahima Gosain promoting the worship of the one God, known as Alekh Param Brahma. Mahima Gosain met Govinda Baba whilst travelling in Orissa on his preaching tours in the 1860s. With his message of a revived Hinduism, he needed the skills of a good organiser to establish a movement that would function as a vehicle for the message and provide the continuity required for the teachings to continue after the founders. Govinda Baba was able to supply these organisational talents and during the 1860s and 1870s the movement grew in size and strength but antagonised local brāhmaṇas as it opposed their practises. A third pioneer devotee, Bhima Bhoi, established the new stronghold of the movement in his Khalialpali Ashram in 1877 until his death in 1895. The Satya Mahima Dharma continues to exist in Orissa as a socio-religious movement in opposition to the Hinduism of the higher castes.

See also: **Āśram(a) (religious community); Bhima Bhoi; Brāhmaṇa; Mahima Gosain; Satya Mahima Dharma**

RON GEAVES

Further reading

Jones, Kenneth. 1989. *Socio-Religious Reform Movements in British India, The New Cambridge History of India: Vol. 3.1*. Cambridge: Cambridge University Press.

GRĀMADEVATĀS

Grāmadevatās, or village deities, are the gods and goddesses that protect the settlement to which they belong. The majority of grāmadevatās are female, with any male deities holding a position of inferiority. The relationship between the community and its goddess is very close, for in some places a representative of the village is ritually married to the goddess. Another way that this connection is made is in the way the goddess is characterised. Sometimes she is depicted as only a head, with the village considered her body. Grāmadevatās are most often symbolised by a tree or a stone. Sometimes at the centre of the settlement or standing guard at its periphery, the village goddess is generally independent of male control, and is often offered blood sacrifices. Although the grāmadevatās protect the village or hamlet to which they are connected, they may also be seen as the cause of epidemics or other disasters.

See also: **Blood sacrifice; Deities, village and local**

LYNN FOULSTON

Further reading

Fuller, C.J. 1992. *The Camphor Flame: Popular Hinduism and Society in India*. Princeton, NJ: Princeton University Press.

GRAMMAR

See: **Vyākaraṇa**

GṚHADEVĪ

'Household goddess'. The story of Gṛhadevī, also known as Jarā, a rākṣasī, is told in *Mahābhārata* 2.13–18. Gṛhadevī is worshipped to obtain welfare, offspring and good fortune and is depicted as a graceful young woman surrounded by children. Her images are found on the walls of the houses as they bring prosperity. The worship of Gṛhadevī includes offerings of essences, flowers, edibles and objects of enjoyment. If not properly worshipped, the goddess is believed to cause decay and destruction. Such power is found in the *Mahābhārata* (2.17.1), where she tells Kṛṣṇa that she was created to destroy the Dānavas (a class of demons). The name of Gṛhadevī is particularly linked to the birth of the heir of king Bṛhadratha of Magadha. The king was married to two twin sisters who gave birth half a baby each. Jarā/Gṛhadevī united the two half-corpses and the revived baby was called Jarāsandha ('United-by-Jarā') (*Bhāgavata Purāṇa* 9.22: 8).

See also: **Mahābhārata; Purāṇas; Rākṣasas**

FABRIZIO M. FERRARI

GṚHYASŪTRAS

The *Gṛhyasūtras* are a group of texts composed in Sanskrit that describe household rituals. Most probably composed between 600 and 300 BCE, they describe a number of simple domestic rites that were performed around the household fire by the head of the family and prescribed for all twice-born classes. Additionally, the *Gṛhyasūtras* contain instructions for maintaining the household fire that was kindled at marriage and was maintained throughout a person's life. Generally there are two types of domestic ritual described in the texts: (1) saṃskāras: the consecration rites that cover all the important phases of human life, including rites for birth, initiation, marriage and death; (2) rituals that accompany festivals, performances and particular occasions. These would include rites to be performed when building a house, looking after cattle and ploughing fields, as well as rituals for getting rid of enemies, warding off disease, and not getting lost in the woods. In addition to containing instructions for how to perform these rituals, the *Gṛhyasūtras* instruct the practitioner on which Vedic mantras to recite to accompany ritual actions. Despite the similar orientation among the *Gṛhyasūtras*, they are not uniform from text to text: they differ as to which mantras they prescribe, as well as in their organisational structure. The *Gṛhyasūtras*, together with the *Śrautasūtras* and the *Dharmasūtras*, are collectively called the *Kalpasūtras* and they have all been preserved as part of the corpus of their respective Vedic schools. Sūtra, which literally means 'thread', is a textual genre that consists of short aphorisms and presents the essence of a doctrine in a compact form. Unlike the *Śrautasūtras*, the *Gṛhyasūtras* are less complicated and not as closely related to the Vedic texts about rituals. Whereas the śrauta rituals required three fires, the gṛhya rituals required just one fire.

See also: **Mantra; Saṃskāra; Utsava; Veda**

BRIAN BLACK

Further reading

Flood, Gavin. 1996. *An Introduction to Hinduism*. Cambridge: Cambridge University Press.

Gonda, Jan. 1977. *A History of Indian Literature: The Ritual Sūtras*. Wiesbaden: Harrassowitz.

Jamison, Stephanie. 1996. *Sacrificed Wife: Sacrificer's Wife*. New York: Oxford University Press.

Patton, Laurie. 2005. *Bringing the Gods to Mind: Mantra and Ritual in Early Indian Sacrifice*. Berkeley, CA: University of California Press.

GRIFFITH, RALPH THOMAS HOTCHKIN (1826–1906)

English Sanskritist. Educated at Oxford, where he studied classics before becoming University Boden Sanskrit Scholar under H.H. Wilson. In 1853, after four years' teaching in England, Griffith went to India where he remained for the rest of his life. He was at first Professor of English Literature, and later Principal (1861–78), of Benares College. Griffith's scholarly work was devoted to translation. Already before reaching India he had begun to publish translations of selections from Indian epic and dramatic literature. In India he completed a full translation of the *Rāmāyaṇa* (1870–74), and in retirement he published verse translations of each of the four collections of Vedic hymns. Although modern scholars have found Griffith's translations unsatisfactory, they have nevertheless usually conceded their literary quality, and his translations of the *Atharva* and White *Yajurveda* remain the only complete translations into English.

See also: **Hinduism, history of scholarship; Rāmāyaṇa; Saṃhitā; Wilson, Harold Hayman**

WILL SWEETMAN

Further reading

Griffith, R.T.H. 1870–74. *The Ramayan of Valmiki*, 5 vols. London: Trübner.

Griffith, R.T.H. 1889–92. *The Hymns of the Rigveda, Translated with a Popular Commentary*, 4 vols. Benares: E.J. Lazarus.

Griffith, R.T.H. 1893. *The Hymns of the Sāmaveda, Translated with a Popular Commentary*. Benares: E.J. Lazarus.

Griffith, R.T.H. 1895–96. *The Hymns of the Atharvaveda, Translated with a Popular Commentary*, 2 vols. Benares: E.J. Lazarus.

Griffith, R.T.H. 1899. *The Texts of the White Yajurveda, Translated with a Popular Commentary*. Benares: E.J. Lazarus.

GUÉNON, RENÉ-JEAN-MARIE-JOSEPH (1886–1951)

French occultist, traditionalist and scholar of religions. As a young man Guénon was attracted to and entered several occultist orders before being initiated as a sufi by Shaykh 'Abd al-Raḥmān 'Illaysh al-Kabīr in 1912. Although he remained a Muslim, and lived in Egypt from 1930 until his death, Guénon espoused belief in the essential unity of all religions which represent true forms of the Primordial Tradition, the philosophia perennis. Guénon, who claimed also to have been instructed by Hindu masters, described his first book as an introduction to the study of Hindu doctrines; nevertheless, much of it is taken up with an account of

Guénon's conception of tradition and a critique of the modern West's departure from it. He also wrote on Vedānta, from which he thought all other Hindu systems were derived, and on Theosophy, for Guénon 'a confused and barely coherent syncretism' (1945a: 316). Guénon's view of Hindu society as hierarchical, in opposition to the illusory individualist egalitarianism of the West, influenced Louis Dumont; his account of the philosophia perennis in Hinduism was taken up by Ananda Coomaraswamy.

See also: **Coomaraswamy, Ananda Kentish; Dumont, Louis; Hinduism, history of scholarship; Theosophy and the Theosophical Society; Vedānta**

WILL SWEETMAN

Further reading

Guénon, R. 1921. *Le Théosophisme: Histoire d'une pseudo-religion* [Theosophism: the history of a pseudo-religion]. Paris: Nouvelle Librairie Nationale.

Guénon, R. 1945a. *Introduction to the Study of Hindu Doctrines*. London: Luzac. (First published in French, as *Introduction générale à l'étude des doctines hindoues*, 1921).

Guénon, R. 1945b. *Man and His Becoming According to the Vedānta*. London: Luzac. (First published in French, as *L'Homme et son devenir selon le Védānta*, 1925).

Guénon, R. 2001. *Studies in Hinduism*. Ghent, NY: Sophia Perennis. (First published in French, *Études sur l'hindouisme*, 1966).

GUṆAS

The term guṇa refers to two types of entities current in Indian thought: qualities and constituents. Vaiśeṣika formally enumerates and describes the former in its second category of the Six Categories, and the common use of the term in literature in the sense 'good characteristic' derives from it. The characteristics that objects have are due to being endowed with certain qualities. *Vaiśeṣikasūtras* 1.1.5 enumerates seventeen types of qualities: colour (rūpa), taste (rasa), odour (gandha), tangibility (sparśa), number (saṃkhyā), size (parimāṇa), distinction (pṛthaktva), conjunction (saṃyoga), disjunction (vibhāga), remoteness (paratva), proximity (aparatva), cognition (buddhi), pleasure (sukha), pain (duḥkha), desire (icchā), aversion (dveṣa) and effort (prayatna). Commentators add another seven, most of which are indicated elsewhere in the *Vaiśeṣikasūtras*: weight (gurutva 1.1.28), fluidity (dravatā 2.1.6), viscidity (sneha 2.1.2), sound (śabda 2.1.24), disposition (saṃskāra 4.1.8), and merit (dharma) and demerit (adharma) (6.2.17).

Sāṃkhya considers some of these types of properties, in particular colour, taste, odour, tangibility and sound, to be constituent components of objects, rather than mere attributes of them, and refers to them by the term tanmātra, 'merely that, basic element'. At the same time, Sāṃkhya uses the term guṇa to refer to the three fundamental constituents of Prakṛti: sattva, 'purity'; rajas, 'passion'; and tamas, 'dullness'. Sattva is characterised by pleasure, has illumination as its purpose, and is buoyant and illuminating; rajas is characterised by displeasure, has activity as its purpose, and is stimulating and mobile; and tamas is characterised by dejection, has restraint as its purpose, and is heavy and obstructive. These constituents belong to and influence every layer of Prakṛti from the unmanifest to the gross elements, including all the faculties of the personality, which, though apparently subjective, are evolutes of objective nature. Teleologically motivated by Puruṣa, the guṇas inseparably undergo transformation and interaction by mutually supporting or repressing each other (*Sāṃkhyakārikās* 11–16). Sattva and tamas are opposed in being light versus dark; yet they are alike in being inactive as opposed to rajas, which is active. Hence virtue, knowledge, dispassion and power are the pure form of the intellect, while vice, ignorance, passion and infirmity are its dull form; that is, the buddhi with sattva predominant is virtuous, knowledgeable, dispassionate and powerful, but with tamas predominant is bad, stupid, emotional and weak (*Sāṃkhyakārikās* 23). With sattva predominant, Ahaṃkāra evolves into the apparently subjective faculties of the person, namely mind, senses and organs of action, while with tamas predominant it evolves into obviously material components of the person and nature, namely the subtle and gross elements that compose the body and objects of experience (*Sāṃkhyakārikās* 25). Different proportions of the guṇas account for the variety of internal and external differences (*Sāṃkhyakārikās* 27, 36, 38). They even account for differences between supernatural, human and subhuman orders of beings; they have, respectively, sattva, rajas and tamas predominant (*Sāṃkhyakārikās* 54). The various dispositions (a full fifty varieties are enumerated in *Sāṃkhyakārikās* 46–51) brought about in the intellect by varying proportions of the three guṇas in turn dispose a person to rise or fall, to rest content in unmanifest nature or to delve into its manifestations, to meet with success or failure in action, and to tend toward freedom or be further bound in the cycle of transmigration (*Sāṃkhyakārikās* 44–45).

See also: **Mahat; Prakṛti; Puruṣa; Sāṃkhya; Sāṃkhyakārikās; Vaiśeṣika; Vaiśeṣikasūtras**

PETER M. SCHARF

GURU

A term of tremendous import in the Hindu tradition, the word 'guru' has a basic sense of 'heaviness'. Technically, it seems to have been originally applied to a venerable man who performed the various Vedic rites (saṃskāras) for a young boy and instructed him in the Veda. Traditionally, the young student (śiṣya) lived in the guru's house and was treated as a son, a system of ancient education generally known as the gurukula system. It later comes to signify a host of personal teachers learned in a particular scriptural or secular subject (dance, music, etc.). For example, many religious sects and social organisations within the larger Hindu fold are often headed by a chief guru, whose authority remains the final word on most doctrinal and administrative matters. The *Mahābhārata* offers a verse that lists five distinct gurus: mother, father, teacher, the sacred fire and the soul (ātman). The deep significance of the teacher–student relationship in Hindu consciousness cannot be overstated and is pointedly celebrated during the holy full moon in the month of Āṣāḍha (roughly falling in July–August), popularly known as Guru Purṇimā. The term guru also applies to the planet Jupiter (Bṛhaspati), anthropomorphically rendered in Hindu mythology as the teacher of the devas.

See also: **Ahaṃkāra; Ātman; Bṛhaspati; Dance; Deities; Music; Saṃskāra; Śiṣya; Veda**

DEVEN M. PATEL

Further reading

Freke, Timothy. 1998. *The Wisdom of the Hindu Gurus.* Boston, MA: Journey Editions.

Swami Sivananda. 1974. *Bliss Divine.* Rishikesh: Divine Life Society.

GYANAMATA, SRI

One the first female disciples of Yogananda Paramhansa, the founder of the Self-Realisation Fellowship. She is regarded as one of the saints of the movement. She was one of the group of early American disciples of the guru, along with Sri Daya Mata, who remains President of the Society. Born Edith Bisset, Yogananda first met her in Seattle in 1924 when he was on his way to Alaska. She remained a significant figure in the Seattle branch of the movement and was also among the small inner circle of devotees who ran the international headquarters of the Self-Realisation Fellowship in Los Angeles. She joined the monastic order in 1932 and was renamed 'Gyanamata' by Yogananda. The story of her life and her personal letters to Yogananda Paramhansa, including his replies, are available in her autobiography, entitled *God Alone*.

See also: **Daya Mata, Sri; Guru; Self-Realisation Fellowship; Yogananda, Paramhansa**

RON GEAVES

Further reading

Sri Gyanamata. 1920. *God Alone: The Life and Letters of a Saint*. Los Angeles: Self-Realisation Fellowship Press.

GYANANDA, SWAMI

The second leader of the Bharat Dharma Mahamandala organisation, who took over from the founder Din Dayalu Sharma in 1902 and succeeded in consolidating the organisation into an all-India movement representing an orthodox Hinduism which safeguarded the interests of the brāhmaṇas. In 1903 Swami Gyananda moved the organisation's headquarters to Vārāṇasī and by the 1930s there were over 950 branches throughout India. The organisation began as the Ganga Dharma Sabha in Haridvāra, where it sought to establish Hindu unity and respect for the cow, the Gaṅgā river, places of Hindu pilgrimage and the Brāhmaṇa priesthood. In its early years it established sanctuaries for cows and Sanskrit schools. It later promoted its views at major religious fairs, where it performed the fire sacrifices or havan amongst gatherings of brāhmaṇas. Today the organisation represents the interests of those who consider themselves orthodox Hindus and exists to defend Hinduism from government intervention and perceived Muslim encroachment and maintain the purity of performance of Hindu rituals.

See also: **Agnihotra; Bharat Dharma Mahamandala; Brāhmaṇas; Gaṅgā; Haridvāra; Sacred Animals; Sharma, Pandit Din Dayalu; Tīrthayātrā; Vārāṇasī**

RON GEAVES

Further reading

Jones, Kenneth. 1989. *Socio-Religious Reform Movements in British India, The New Cambridge History of India: Vol. 3.1*. Cambridge: Cambridge University Press.

H

HACKER, PAUL (1913–79)

German Indologist, specialising in the study of Vedānta, the *Purāṇas* and modern Hinduism. After early research on the Advaita of Śaṅkara and his disciples (1951), Hacker lectured in Germany and, for a little more than a year, in India before being appointed professor at Bonn in 1955. In 1963, shortly after converting to Roman Catholicism, he became professor at Münster, where he remained until his retirement in 1978. While continuing to work and publish on philosophical topics related to Advaita, including comparative philosophy, Hacker also conducted research on the *Purāṇas* (1960) and on modern Hinduism (1995). He was sharply critical especially of Neo-Vedāntic thinkers such as Vivekananda and Radhakrishnan, whom he saw as masking an 'inclusivist' claim to superiority beneath an apparent tolerance which in reality served only as a device to maintain 'the fiction of unity' among the diverse religious traditions which constitute modern Hinduism.

See also: **Advaita; Purāṇas; Radhakrishnan, Sir Sarvepalli; Śaṅkara; Vedānta; Vivekananda, Swami**

WILL SWEETMAN

Further reading

Hacker, P. 1951. *Untersuchungen über Texte des frühen Advaitavāda* [Investigations of the texts of early Advaitavāda]. Wiesbaden: Steiner in Komm.

Halbfass, W. (ed.). 1995. *Philology and Confrontation: Paul Hacker on Traditional and Modern Vedānta.* Albany, NY: State University of New York Press.

HALBFASS, WILHELM (1940–2000)

German philosopher and Indologist. Halbfass studied philosophy at Göttingen, and his first book, published in 1968, was on Cartesian ontology. His work on Indian philosophy began also with ontology, in the Vaiśeṣika darśana (1992). Halbfass's masterly *Indien und Europa*

(1981; English translation 1988) provided not only a history of the intellectual encounter between India and Europe, particularly strong in its treatment of eighteenth- and nineteenth-century German thought, but also a philosophical account of the significance of that encounter and the prospects for a comparative philosophy that is genuinely both philosophical and comparative. The consequences for Hindu self-understanding of a world dominated by European modes of thought were examined by Halbfass in a collection of essays (1991) which extended the treatment of the Indian side of the encounter between India and Europe. Halbfass argues for a traditional Hindu identity founded on a commitment to the Veda which, however, underwent significant reinvention in the modern period.

See also: **Hinduism, history of scholarship; Orientalism; Vaiśeṣika; Veda**

WILL SWEETMAN

Further reading

Halbfass, W. 1988. *India and Europe: An Essay in Understanding*. Albany, NY: State University of New York Press.

Halbfass, W. 1991. *Tradition and Reflection: Explorations in Indian Thought*. Albany, NY: State University of New York Press.

Halbfass, W. 1992. *On Being and What There Is: Classical Vaiśeṣika and the History of Indian Ontology*. Albany, NY: State University of New York Press.

Franco, E. and K. Preisendanz (eds). 1997. *Beyond Orientalism? The Work of Wilhelm Halbfass and Its Impact on Indian and Cross-cultural Studies*. Amsterdam: Rodopi.

HALLESCHE BERICHTE

The *Hallesche Berichte* ('Halle Reports') are a series of letters, essays and diaries written by Lutheran missionaries in South India and published in Germany. The first reports were published in 1708 under the title *Merckwürdige Nachricht aus Ost-Indien* [Remarkable news from East India]. Two years later further reports appeared as the first 'instalment' in the first of nine volumes later given the title *Der königlichen dänischen Missionarien aus Ost-Indien eingesandte ausführliche Berichte* [Detailed reports sent by the Royal Danish Missionaries from India] (Halle, 1710–72). The reports provided a wealth of information about south Indian society, culture and natural history, but were especially important for their description of Hinduism. Particularly noteworthy is the so-called 'Malabarian [i.e. Tamil] Correspondence', which consists of ninety-nine letters written by Hindus in response to questions about Indian religion and society, translated and annotated by the missionaries. The reports were partially translated into Dutch, English, French and Latin and formed an important source for knowledge of Hinduism in eighteenth-century Europe.

WILL SWEETMAN

Further reading

Bergunder, M. 1999. 'Die Darstellung des Hinduismus in den Halleschen Berichten' [The representation of Hinduism in the Hallesche Berichte]. In *Missionsberichte aus Indien im 18. Jahrhundert* [Mission reports from India in the 18th century], ed. M. Bergunder. Halle: Verlag der Franckeschen Stiftungen zu Halle, 111–25.

Liebau, K. (ed.). 1998. *Die malabarische Korrespondenz: tamilische Briefe an deutsche Missionare; eine Auswahl* [The Malabarian Correspondence: Tamil letters to German missionaries; a selection]. Sigmaringen: Thorbecke.

HANS RAJ, LALA (1864–1938)

Lala Hans Raj was one of the most charismatic leaders of the Arya Samaj and an eminent social reformer and educationist. Born into a Punjabi Khatri family, he was attracted to the reform movement while studying in Lahore in the early 1880s.

Through his relentless fundraising efforts he contributed significantly to the establishment of the Dayananda Anglo Vedic (DAV) High School in 1886, which was to become the Samaj's most successful educational institution. He served as headmaster from the outset and became principal of the college section three years later. When the Samaj split in 1893 Hans Raj – meanwhile the respectful title 'Mahatma' had been conferred on him – became leader of the so-called moderate faction, stressing the importance of English education at the expense of Sanskrit and tolerating a non-vegetarian diet. After leaving the prospering DAV College in 1912 he became primarily engaged in social reform and philanthropical activities, namely famine and earthquake relief. After Swami Shraddhanand he was the second prominent Arya Samaj leader to be involved in the controversial śuddhi (reconversion) campaigns of the 1920s. He died in Lahore in 1938.

See also: **Arya Samaj; Conversion; Dayananda Saraswati, Swami; Languages; Shraddhanand, Swami**

HARALD FISCHER-TINÉ

Further reading

Jijñāsu, P.R. (ed.). 1986. *Mahātmā Haṃsrāj Granthāvalī*, 4 vols. Dillī: Govindrām Hasānand.

HANUMĀN

Hanumān first appears in the *Rāmāyaṇa* as the exiled Vānara (monkey) ruler Sugrīva's minister, although in later texts his service to Sugrīva is superseded by service to Rāma. He leaps to Laṅkā, enters Rāvaṇa's palace and searches for Sītā until finally he discovers her in the aśoka grove. He reveals himself to Sītā and establishes his identity by producing Rāma's ring, in return for which she gives him a jewel as a token to take to Rāma. Popular later is the episode during the battle when Hanumān goes to the Himālayas to fetch healing herbs; not recognising which are needed, he uproots the entire mountain and carries it back to Laṅkā – a demonstration both of his enormous strength and of his simple-mindedness. He is regularly called the son of the Wind – a metaphor for his speed and legerdemain.

Later Hanumān typically is celibate, which ties in with his unusual strength, given Indian views on the link between sexual continence and power, which undoubtedly underlie his frequent description and depiction as wearing a tightly bound loincloth, with its implication of restrained sexuality. He is also the patron deity of wrestlers, for whom Hanumān is the embodiment of both energy and devotion, śakti and bhakti.

Loving devotion is the aspect most prominent in vernacular retellings of the *Rāmāyaṇa*. The best known is the *Rāmcaritmānas* of Tulsīdās. Himself the humble servant of Rāma, he displays a particular fondness for Hanumān and stresses his devotion to Rāma. Tulsīdās develops the story of the necklace that Sītā presents to Hanumān: Hanumān accepts it but begins to crush each pearl in his jaws and, when challenged, explains that he is looking for the name of Rāma inside. Ultimately this gives rise to the motif of his tearing open his chest to reveal the Name of Rāma (or Rāma and Sītā enthroned) on his heart, a favourite subject for Kālīghāt painters and still commonly found in modern colour prints of Hanumān.

The appeal of Hanumān to Hindu militancy may be one factor in a recent vogue for erecting colossal images of Hanumān. But more significant for his current popularity is his role as an easily propitiated intermediary, his ability to 'get things done' as the fixer, and his providing access to the more remote Rāma, which accounts for the common remark that there are more shrines nowadays to Hanumān than to Rāma.

Strongman, wrestler, fixer, magician – all are Hanumān. Yet above all he is the loyal servant. His strength, his loyalty, his devotion are all laid at Rāma's feet, limited as they are by the volatility of his monkey nature; but he is also Sugrīva's wise adviser, the trusted messenger between Rāma and Sītā, the learned grammarian, needing to be seen in human terms. Hanumān's dual nature is a major key to his appeal. His monkey nature aligns him with the more inconsistent sides of human nature, while at the same time his constancy as a devotee supplies a model for the ordinary worshipper.

See also: **Bhakti; Himālayas; Rāma; Rāmāyaṇa; Rāvaṇa; Sacred animals; Śakti; Sītā; Sugrīva; Tulsīdās(a)**

JOHN BROCKINGTON

Further reading

Brockington, John. 2004. 'Hanumān in the Mahābhārata'. *Journal of Vaishnava Studies* 12.2: 129–35.

Brockington, John. 2007. 'Vālmīki's Portrayal of Hanumān'. In Petteri Koskikallio and Aska Parpola, eds, *Proceedings of the 12th World Sanskrit Conference*, vol. 2, New Delhi: Motilal Banarsidass.

Bulcke, C. 1959. 'The Characterization of Hanumān (a Bird's-eye View of Its Evolution)'. *JOIB* 9: 393–402.

Goldman, R.P. and Sally J. Sutherland Goldman. 1994. 'Vālmīki's Hanumān: Characterization and Occluded Divinity in the *Rāmāyaṇa*'. *Journal of Vaishnava Studies* 2.4: 31–54.

Keul, Istvān. 2002. *Hanumān, der Gott in Affengestalt: Entwicklung und Erscheiningsformen seiner Verehrung* [Hanumān, the god in ape form: the growth and manifestation of his worship]. Berlin and New York: Walter de Gruyter.

Lutgendorf, Philip. 1993–94. 'My Hanuman is Bigger than Yours'. *History of Religions* 33: 211–45.

Lutgendorf, Philip. 1997. 'Monkey in the Middle: The Status of Hanuman in Popular Hinduism'. *Religion* 27: 311–32.

Lutgendorf, Philip and J. Moussaieff Masson. 1981. 'Hanumān as an Imaginary Companion'. *Journal of the American Oriental Society* 101: 355–60.

Sutherland Goldman, Sally J. 1999. 'A Tale of Two Tales: The Episode of Hanumān's Childhood in the Critical Edition'. *Purāṇa* 41: 132–53.

HANUMĀNJAYANTĪ

Hanumānjayantī is a regional festival marking the birthday of Hanumān, the monkey god widely venerated throughout India, especially for his devotion to Rāma. Hanumān's deeds of valour and selfless service are recorded in the *Rāmāyaṇa* when he assists in the conquest of Sri Lanka, but it is Tulsīdās' medieval version, written in Hindi, that placed Hanumān, a monkey-warrior, as the epitome of devotion. Hanumān requests not to be freed from saṃsāra, but rather to be reborn endlessly to serve his lord when he incarnates in human form. Thus the most common depiction of Hanumān in Hindu iconography is as a kneeling monkey-warrior at the feet of Rāma, Lakṣmaṇa and Sītā.

The festival is held in March/April on the full moon of Caitra and is a significant occasion for brahmacārins, wrestlers and body-builders. Hanumān is described in mythology as the son of Vāyu, the wind-god, and a celebrated ascetic and grammarian. He also exists as the caste deity of wrestlers and wandering acrobats, and is revered by a number of lower-caste groups.

The popularity of the festival is most obvious in rural areas as Hanumān is worshipped in folk tradition as a deity with magical powers and the ability to conquer evil spirits. There are many temples to Hanumān in India but he is also often present in temples dedicated to other deities, as his valour and martial prowess make him an ideal choice as a gatekeeper deity protecting the sacred space.

The festival is often marked with melās or fairs set up near to Hanumān temples and with recitations of the *Rāmāyaṇa* and other material honouring Hanumān both in the home and temple. Traditionally the devotees will visit Hanumān temples and apply a tilak of red powder to their foreheads from the image of Hanumān. According to the legend, Sītā applied red powder to her head and informed Hanumān that this would ensure long life for her husband. Hanumān then smeared his entire body with red powder, in an effort to ensure Rāma's immortality.

See also: **Brahmacarya; Deities, folk and popular; Hanumān; Lakṣmaṇa; Mandir; Rāma; Rāmāyaṇa; Pativratā and Patiparameśvara; Saṃsāra; Sītā; Tulsīdās(a); Utsava; Vāyu**

RON GEAVES

Further reading

Brown, Alan. (ed.). 1986. *Festivals in the World Religions*. London: Longman, 121.

Dowson, John. 1968. *A Classical Dictionary of Hindu Mythology and Religion, Geography, History, and Literature*. London: Routledge and Kegan Paul.

Stutley, M. 1985. 'Hanuman'. *The Illustrated Dictionary of Hindu Iconography*. London: Routledge.

www.hindutemple.org.uk/festivals/hanuman_jayanti.htm.

HARE KRISHNAS

See: **International Society for Krishna Consciousness**

HARIDVĀRA

One of the seven holy cities or places of tīrthayātra (pilgrimage) mentioned in the *Mahābhārata*. It is on the river Gaṅgā, just below Rishikesh, in north-east Uttar Pradesh, and located at the beginning of the Himalayan foothills, the Uttarakhāṇḍ region mentioned in the *Rāmāyaṇa*, where the ice cold waters of the river first touch the plains. It is also one of the sites of the Kumbha Melā, probably the largest religious gathering in the world, attracting up to 15 million pilgrims, which occurs every twelve years in the town as it revolves between Allahabad, Ujjain, Haridvāra and Nasik.

The Gaṅgā tīrtha sites, which include Vārāṇasī, are especially auspicious as it is believed that they are most efficacious in removing sins in this kali yuga, and Haridvāra is a place where bathing is believed to bring salvation. The city, one of the oldest in India, is also famous for the celebration of Vaisakhi and Durgā Pūjā. The surrounding area contains many aśramas and temples, especially to the south of the town; and the bathing area, Hari-ki-Pauri, the principal bathing ghāṭ, is a renowned gathering place for sādhus and contains a footprint of Viṣṇu embedded in the wall. Situated at the bottom of thirty-nine steps, the original ghāṭ was very narrow and resulted in several disasters as pilgrims stampeded to the river. It has now been rebuilt to avoid such situations occurring. The locality also contains the famous goddess temples of Caṇḍi Devī, Māyā Devī, Mānasā Devī and Gaṅgādwara.

As one of the only gateways to the Himālayas the town has had historical strategic importance and is known as Māyāpūr, Gaṅgādwara, Kapila and Moyulo in various ancient travelogues. It is also referred to as the 'capital of Śiva' at the time of the Moghul dynasties. Haridvāra is associated with numerous legends connected with Śiva's first wife, Satī, and is believed to be the place where she committed suicide after her husband was not invited to attend a yajña held by King Dakṣa at the same site.

However, it is most sacred, because as one of the sites for the Kumbha Melā it is believed to contain one of the four drops of amṛta which spilled when Viṣṇu stole the nectar of immortality from the demons at the beginning of creation, as it was regarded as too precious to be given over to them. The next Kumbha Melā in the town will take place in 2010. At the last Kumbha Melā in Haridvāra, held in 1998, the organisers expected over 150 million to bathe in the river over the three and a half months that the festival lasted. The bathing ghāṭ at Hari-ki-Pauri is famous for its adornment with coloured lights and around 500,000 people bathed in the Gaṅgā at the ghāṭ on the opening day of the festival alone. Haridvāra is also the location of a special Kumbha Melā, known as the Ardh Kumbha, which takes place additionally halfway through the twelve-year cycle.

See also: **Durgā Pūjā; Gaṅgā; Kumbha Melā; Mahābhārata; Mandir; Rāmayāna; Sādhu; Śiva; Tīrthayātra; Vaiśākhi; Vārāṇasī; Viṣṇu; Yajña; Yuga**

RON GEAVES

Further reading

Davidson, Linda and David Gitlitz. 2002. *Pilgrimage from the Ganges to Graceland*, vol. 1. Santa Barbara, CA: ABC-Clio.

HARIJANS

See: **Dalits**

HARIŚCANDRA

The legend of King Hariścandra is originally told in the *Mārkaṇḍeya Purāṇa* but still grips the imagination of contemporary Hindus through dance, film, song and even comic strips for children. Although today the story is often perceived in ethical terms and associated with honesty and integrity under trial from overwhelming forces – this meaning influenced Gandhi, who was told the tale in his childhood – the earlier significance of Hariścandra's trials places the legend closer to the tribulations of Job and the relationship between God and his perfect devotee.

Though a king, Hariścandra sacrificed everything, including his kingdom. Even when poverty stricken and working as an attendant at the funeral ghāṭs, he demanded payment of half his wife's sari when she brought their own son for cremation. The stories of kings such as Hariścandra and Janaka were popular as examples of devotion to the mediaeval bhaktas and demonstrated that it was possible to live in the world and remain completely committed to the life of God-consciousness. They probably appeared in the *Purāṇas* as a part of contested authority between brāhmaṇas and kṣatriyas.

See also: **Bhakti; Books, comics, newspapers and magazines; Brāhmaṇas; Dance; Film; Gandhi, Mohandas Karamchand; Janaka; Music; Purāṇas; Varṇa**

RON GEAVES

Further reading

Dimmitt, Cornelia and J. van Buitenen (eds). 1978. *Classical Hindu Mythology.* Philadelphia, PA: Temple University Press.

HARIVAMŚA

The *Harivaṃśa* has been subject to fundamental changes in its literary history. The popular version with more than 16,000 ślokas (verses) has been reduced in the Critical Edition (Poona 1969–71) to little more than 6,000 śloka*s*. Probably from the outset conceived as a supplement (khila) to the *Mahābhārata*, the *Harivaṃśa* embedded the courtly and military events reported in the epic in the overall frame of cosmic development. Thus as a type of literature it is both a supplement to an epic and the model for an important part of the older *Purāṇas*, the purāṇapañcalakṣaṇa. The core of the *Harivaṃśa* has been enlarged in two directions: at the end by a relatively short passage dealing with gloomy future prospects; and in the middle by extensive additions concerning divine interventions in worldly affairs, especially regarding another *Mahābhārata* hero, Kṛṣṇa. This process of Kṛṣṇaisation, which is also discernible in the *Mahābhārata*, has changed the nature of the *Harivaṃśa* profoundly. It came to be a Kṛṣṇa epic, possibly conceived as an equivalent to the older Rāma epic, the *Rāmāyaṇa*. Kṛṣṇa, however, is described in the *Harivaṃśa* mainly as a juvenile arch-enemy of the demonic despot Kaṃsa, and as such shows remarkably little connection with the hero of the same name in the *Mahābhārata.* As a human manifestation of Nārāyaṇa-Viṣṇu, he is regarded at the same time as one element in a whole series of divine manifestations intervening in worldly processes. Various accounts of such divine manifestations are to be found in several passages and these mirror a certain phase in the development of the Viṣṇuite prādurbhāva doctrine which later culminated in the classical avatāra mythology.

See also: **Avatāra; Kaṃsa; Kṛṣṇa; Mahābhārata; Purāṇas; Rāma; Rāmāyaṇa; Viṣṇu**

HORST BRINKHAUS

Further reading

Brockington, J. 1998. *The Sanskrit Epics.* Leiden: Brill.

HAṬHA YOGA

Haṭha yoga, literally the 'discipline of force', emerged in Northern India as part of the developments that can be termed Tantra. It is a form of yoga that has particular associations with the Kāṇphata or Nātha Yogīs. G.W. Briggs (1938) lists forty-seven works of the nātha school. Four have been translated into English: the *Gorakṣa Śataka*, dating from the twelfth or thirteenth century; the *Haṭha Yoga Pradāpikā*, dated around the fifteenth century CE, which borrowed from the *Śataka* and reconciles haṭha and rāja yoga; the *Gheraṇḍa Saṃhitā*, shorter than the *Haṭha Yoga Pradāpikā*, from which it borrows, and compared to which it has more emphasis on health and personal hygiene; and the *Śiva Saṃhitā*, the latest of the four texts and Vedāntic in orientation, attempting to explain haṭha yoga in terms that the orthodox (smārta) brahmanical tradition could accept.

Haṭha yoga is the method or discipline of forcing effects onto the subtle body, and particularly onto the dormant kuṇḍalinī energy, by means of physical exercises. The texts provide instructions on cleansing the nāḍīs, or subtle channels, and awakening and directing the kuṇḍalinī energy. Kuṇḍalinī ('the coiled feminine one') is the dormant form of the divine creative consciousness, śakti.

Before the prāṇa (respiration) can enter the suṣumna (the subtle channel that runs the length of the spine), kuṇḍalinī, who blocks the entrance, must be awakened and taken up. When the prāṇa is in the suṣumna, the mind becomes still. Nevertheless, stillness of mind and the accompanying freedom from karmic effects do not constitute liberation; for this the yogin has to raise the kuṇḍalinī (and along with it the prāṇas) to the sahasrāra at the top of the head and be able to hold her there as long as he wills. To do this he must first pierce the cakras (lotuses/discs), each of which is a barrier to be overcome, especially the granthis (knots), where the power of māyā is particularly strong. At each cakra, a particular bliss is experienced and certain powers are gained. Also, the cakras through which kuṇḍalinī passes on her upward journey become laya (dissolved); she recreates them only on her return. By constant practice of the yoga techniques for rousing kuṇḍalinī and uniting the prāṇas, the yogin is able to pierce all the cakras and drink the divine nectar exuding from the sahasrāra. If the yogin is unfortunate enough to die before he has succeeded in raising the kuṇḍalinī to the sahasrāra, his efforts are not in vain, because he begins his next life still possessing the benefits he has gained. Haṭha yoga texts also claim that the guidance of the guru is essential, and that the awakening of kuṇḍalinī is accomplished through the grace of the guru.

Thus, an outline of this yoga would be as follows. One must first find a guru who will accept one as a disciple and bestow a formal initiation. Following this, the disciple should practice the haṭha yoga techniques and purify the nāḍīs. Then, at an appropriate time, the guru will enable the disciple to awaken the kuṇḍalinī and begin the practice of laya yoga, which begins when kuṇḍalinī is roused and the prāṇas are taken into suṣumna; at this stage concentration proper begins and the disciple is able to attain samādhi.

See also: **Gorakhnāth(a); Guru; Kāṇphata Yoga; Laya Yoga; Māyā; Nāth(a) Yoga; Śakti; Tantras; Vedānta; Yoga**

PETER CONNOLLY

Further reading

Briggs, G.M. 1938/1982. *Gorakhnāth and the Kāṇphata Yogīs*. Delhi: Motilal Banarsidass.

HAZRA, RAJENDRA CHANDRA (1905–82)

Indian Sanskritist and purāṇic scholar. Hazra was born in what is now Bangladesh, in the district of Dhaka, and studied Sanskrit at Dhaka University under Sushil Kumar De (1890–1968). He received his PhD in 1936 for his 'Studies in the Purāṇic Records on Hindu Rites and Customs' (published under the same title in 1940), in which he sought to reconstruct the history of purāṇic texts and determine their earlier forms on the basis of quotations from them in other works. Hazra's focus on individual *Purāṇas* distinguished his work from other, mainly German, scholarship on the *Purāṇas* which prioritised individual passages repeated in different *Purāṇas*. Hazra lectured at the University of Dhaka until 1951, receiving a DLitt in 1947 for the first volume of his *Studies in the Upapurāṇas*, later moving to the Sanskrit College in Calcutta, where he retired as Professor in 1972.

See also: **Hinduism, history of scholarship; Purāṇas**

WILL SWEETMAN

Further reading

Bailey, G. 2003. 'The Purāṇas'. In A. Sharma, ed., *The Study of Hinduism*. Colombia, SC: University of South Carolina Press, 139–68.

Hazra, R.C. 1940. *Studies in the Purāṇic Records on Hindu Rites and Customs*. Dacca: Dacca University.

Hazra, R.C. 1958–63. *Studies in the Upapurāṇas*, 2 vols. Calcutta: Sanskrit College.

HEALING

Healing is not particularly prominent in Hindu mythology. Dhanvantari, the divine physician (vaidya), is said to be one of the 'nine gems' (navaratna) churned by the gods from the milky ocean, and the Aśvins, horse-faced twins, are also mentioned as divine physicians. However, none of these figures have an elaborate mythology or iconography to compare with, for example, the 'medicine-Buddha'. The most striking mythological connection between Hinduism and healing is perhaps the idea that measles and smallpox are manifestations of the goddess, who 'possesses' persons in the form of these diseases. Āyurveda, or classical Indian medicine, has relatively few religious elements, although it does recognise 'possession' as a particular syndrome requiring the services of specialist exorcists. The related South Indian system of Siddha medicine is more explicitly Hindu, incorporating Tantric elements into its theory and practice. The twentieth century saw the transformation, both in India and elsewhere, of yoga from a spiritual exercise into a kind of health therapy. The phenomenon of 'tantric healing' is a Western invention that does not correspond to any established Hindu tradition.

The connection between Hinduism and healing is much more evident at the popular level. Pilgrimages are often undertaken in order to heal various kinds of illnesses, and textual sources indicate that this is an ancient practice. Famous and not so famous temples specialising in the cure of particular diseases are to be found throughout South Asia. Hindus often take vows to particular gods, of the form: 'If you heal my illness, then I will worship you in such-and-such a manner'. Local healing cults throughout the subcontinent often involve pilgrimage, vows and special forms of worship, together with diagnosis by oracles temporarily possessed by deities or other supernatural beings.

See also: **Aśvins; Āyurveda; Mandir; Myth; Popular and vernacular traditions; Possession; Siddha; Tantrism; Tīrthayātra; Vrata; Yoga**

WILLIAM SAX

Further reading

Kakar, Sudhir. 1982. *Shamans, Mystics and Doctors: A Psychological Inquiry into India and Its Healing Traditions.* New York: Knopf.

HEDGEWAR, KESHAV BALIRAM (1889–1940)

Keshav Baliram Hedgewar, or 'Doctorji', was born into a brāhmaṇa family in Nagpur. Inspired by Bal Gangadhar Tilak, he became involved as a student in the nationalist movement, forging links with revolutionary groups in Bengal while completing his medical training.

Hedgewar's views were shaped by a convergence of influences that flowed from the Arya Samaj, through the Hindu Sabha, led in Nagpur by Balkrishna Shivram Moonje, Hedgewar's mentor and former aide of Tilak, and ultimately into the Hindu Mahasabha (founded in 1915). Convinced that Hindus had become demoralised by centuries of foreign rule, Hedgewar created the Rashtriya Swayamsevak Sangh in 1925 to train volunteers to protect the interests of Hindu communities. Insisting on its character-building role, Hedgewar resisted merging it with the Hindu Mahasabha. He is regarded as one of the architects of Hindutva ideology.

See also: **Arya Samaj; Hindu Mahasabha; Hindutva; Nationalism; Rashtriya Swayamsevak Sangh; Tilak, Bal Gangadhar**

GWILYM BECKERLEGGE

Further reading

Deshpande, B.V. and S.R. Ramaswamy. 1981. *Dr. Hedgewar the Epoch-Maker: A Biography.* Bangalore: Sahitya Sindhu.

HEGEL, GEORG WILHELM FRIEDRICH (1770–1831)

German philosopher. Not directly a scholar of Hinduism, Hegel's importance lies rather in his being the first major European philosopher to acknowledge the claims of Indian thought, or, perhaps more accurately, the claims made on behalf of Indian thought by other European scholars, above all representatives of German Romanticism such as F. von Schlegel. From 1822 until his death Hegel, professor of philosophy at Berlin, studied closely the most recent European works on India and China, the most important for his understanding of Hinduism being the works of H.T. Colebrooke and Wilhelm von Humboldt's account of the *Bhagavadgītā*. Hegel interprets

Hinduism as a 'religion of substance' which neglects the particularity of objects in the world in favour of the assertion of the ultimate unity of all in Brahman. In Brahman Indian thought has discovered the true ground of religion and philosophy but has failed to understand it, failed to recognise itself in it, and therefore failed to grasp its relationship to the concrete particulars of the world. These then are left to themselves and flourish in an uncontrolled and chaotic manner, typified for Hegel by the 'excesses' of Indian mythology and iconography. Where individuality is recognised, it is not affirmed but rather denied. Thus for Hegel the highest point of Indian religion is also its essential flaw: the denial of the self and meditative withdrawal from the world which he took to be the ultimate goal of Indian religion.

See also: **Bhagavadgītā; Brahman; Colebrooke, Henry Thomas; Hinduism, history of scholarship; Orientalism; Schlegel, (Karl Wilhelm) Friedrich von**

WILL SWEETMAN

Further reading

Hegel, G. 1825–26. *Vorlesungen über die Geschichte der Philosophie*, 2nd edn, ed. J. Hoffmeister. Leipzig: Meiner. [English translation by E.S. Haldane and F.H. Simson, *Lectures on the History of Philosophy*. London: K. Paul, Trench, Trübner, 1892–1896.]

Rothermund, D. 1986. *The German Intellectual Quest for India*. New Delhi: Manohar.

HIḌIMBĀ (OR HIḌIMBĪ)

Sister of the demon (rākṣasa) Hiḍimba encountered by the Pāṇḍava princes in the forest area south of Vārṇāvata shortly after their escape from the burning wax house. Bhīma kills her attacking brother – a cannibal who is said to have yellow eyes – and, at his mother Kunti's behest, marries Hiḍimbā, who had fallen in love with him and had tried to save the Pāṇḍavas from her brother's cruel intention to eat them. Bhīma and Hiḍimba's child is the celebrated warrior Ghaṭotkaca, whom Karṇa kills during the great *Mahābhārata* war. A temple in honour of Hiḍimbā, who has been variously deified as a manifestation of Durgā or Kālī, was erected by Mahārāja Bahādur Singh in the year 1553 CE near the town Dunghri (in modern Himachal Pradesh). Even today, a festival in her name is celebrated at the popular temple.

See also: **Bhīma; Durgā; Kālī and Caṇḍī; Kuntī; Mahābhārata; Pāṇḍavas; Rākṣasas; Utsava**

DEVEN M. PATEL

Further reading

Chaudhury, P.C. Roy. 1981. *Temples and Legends of Himachal Pradesh*. Bombay: Bharatiya Vidya Bhavan.

Garrett, John. 1999. *A Classical Dictionary of India*. New Delhi: DK Printworld.

HIMĀLAYAS

The Himālayas, the largest mountain range on earth, are associated in the Hindu world with ascetics, places of pilgrimage, gods and other supernatural beings. They are above all holy mountains where religious pilgrimage and other activities are thought to be particularly fruitful and, according to the *Skanda Purāṇa*, 'as the Sun dries the morning dew, so are the sins of man dissipated at the sight of the Himālayas'.

In particular, the Himālayas are associated with the great Hindu god Śiva, from whose hair the sacred river Ganges emerges, and who lives on Mt Kailash with his divine spouse Pārvatī, 'the mountain-born'. The actual location of Mt Kailash is debatable, although since the late nineteenth century it has been identified with a mountain in Western Tibet near Lake Manasarovar, from near whose base the holy rivers Satluj,

Brahmaputra and Indus arise, along with the Karnili, a tributary of the Ganges.

The great Indian epic *Mahābhārata* mentions several important places in the Himālayas, for example Badrikashram (presumably equivalent to Badrinath; see below) and Svargarohini, where the Pāṇḍavas climbed into heaven at the end of their lives. Both Vālmīki's and Tulsīdās's *Rāmāyaṇa*s mention the Himālayas, and indeed the latter begins at Lake Manasarovar. In the 'Bengali Rāmāyaṇa' of Krittibas, Rāmā visits Lake Manasarovar, where he has an important encounter with the goddess Durgā.

Beginning in the eighth, but especially from the tenth to the thirteenth centuries, religious teachers and translators regularly traversed the Himālayas, bringing Indian Buddhism to Tibet, and periodically reforming it. This was also the period during which a syncretic Hindu–Buddhist tradition associated with powerful beings (the 'eighty-four Siddhas') flourished in the Himālayas. Such exchanges slowed with the gradual closing of Tibet to the outside world, and stopped altogether with the Chinese invasion of 1951.

The Himālayas have always been thought of as an ideal location for spiritual practice. Places like Rishikesh at the foot of the Himālayas are filled with ashrams offering instruction in yoga and other forms of meditation, which attract Hindus and non-Hindus from all over the world.

Many important Hindu places of pilgrimage are found in the Himālayas. These are concentrated in the former Hindu kingdom of Garhwal, in the present-day Indian state of Uttaranchal in the central Himālayas. They include Badrinath, sacred to Viṣṇu and one of the four so-called dham or 'abodes' situated at the corners of kite-shaped India; Kedarnath, which is one of the twelve jyotīrliṅga, or 'liṅgas of light', associated with the great god Śiva; Gangotri, at the source of the Ganges River; and Jamnotri, at the source of the Jamuna River. Other important Himālayan places of pilgrimage include Muktinath in Nepal, which is visited by both Hindus and Buddhists; Pashupatinath in Kathmandu, which is the royal temple of the reigning Shah dynasty; the ice-liṅga at Amarnath in Kashmir, which, like Kedarnath, is one of the twelve jyotīrliṅga, and is the object of a large annual pilgrimage fair; and the goddess temples Jwalamukhi and Cāmuṇḍā Devī in Himachal Pradesh.

With the rapid growth of tourism in the past few decades, pilgrimage activity in the Himālayas is increasing dramatically, as it is elsewhere in India. It remains to be seen if the fragile Himālayan environment can withstand this onslaught.

See also: **Āśram(a) (religious community); Buddhism, relationship with Hinduism; Gaṅgā; Mahābhārata; Meditation; Pāṇḍavas; Pārvatī; Purāṇas; Rāmāyaṇa; Sacred geography; Śiva; Tīrthayātrā (Pilgrimage); Tulsīdās(a); Vālmīki; Viṣṇu**

William S. Sax

Further reading

Bhardwaj, Surinder Mohan. 1973. *Hindu Places of Pilgrimage in India: A Study in Cultural Geography.* Berkeley, CA: University of California Press.

Gutschow, Niels, Axel Michaels and Charles Ramble (eds). 2003. *Sacred Landscapes of the Himalayas.* Vienna: Verlag der Österreichischen Akademie der Wissenschaften.

HINDU

The genesis of 'Hindu' and 'Indian'

The most widely accepted meaning of the term 'Hindu' in the pre-modern period of Indian history was a person or thing of Indian origin. Both words, Hindu and Indian, used interchangeably in some travel accounts, were coined by outsiders. The River Indus was known in Sanskrit as 'Sindhu', and the Persians, who found difficulty in pronouncing an initial s, called it 'Hindu' – a word which, as Heinrich von Stietencron explains, was applied to the River Indus and the area beyond it (Stietencron 2001: 33). Sharma, citing Jackson, claims that the term 'Hindu' appears first in the Persian *Zend Avesta* in the phrase 'Hapta Hindu', meaning Seven Rivers and referring to the people beyond the Indus river (Sharma 2002: 2) Thus, for the Persians, the 'Hindus' were the local or indigenous inhabitants who lived in the vicinity of the Indus river. Later still, the term Hindu was extended in meaning to include native inhabitants of the entire subcontinent. In the meantime, the Greeks, who invaded and settled in parts of northern India in the third century BCE, coined the word India. Borrowing the Persian word Hindu for the Indus river, they called it Indos and the country through which it flowed, India. Thereafter the terms Hindu or Indian were synonymous, indicating the people and their place of origin or the things, such as language, customs or artefacts, associated with them (Basham 1954: 1; Basham 1975: vii; Stietencron 2001: 33–34). Sharma, citing Raychaudhuri, identifies the earliest 'datable' use of the term 'Hidu' (Hindu) to an inscription of Darius I, dated *c.*518–515 BCE (Sharma 2002: 2). It is clear that the origin of the term was ethno-geographic and an element of this meaning remains. However, the term Hindu eventually came to indicate the follower of a particular Indian religion. This transition is complex and is a matter given much attention by many scholars.

Subsequent Arab and European travellers and commentators on Indian society had a ready-made interchangeable terminology. For example, if the translation is correct, the eighth-century Arab commentator Al Masudi referred to Indians in one part of his description and to Hindus in another (Elliot and Dowson 1867: 1.19–20). This practice was followed by Arab and Muslim travellers writing about India from the tenth to the thirteenth centuries (Elliot and Dowson 1897: 1.27–8, 97–8), also by European observers of a later date. Among these were François Bernier and Jean Baptiste-Tavernier, the well-known French travellers and commentators on India in the seventeenth century, and the Dutch adventurer Mandelslo, who, referring to the king of Cambay in about 1662, described him as a 'Pagan' 'Hindou' or 'Indian' (Bernier 1916: 300, 302, 325, 333; Tavernier 1977: 1.237, 2.146). At least one Englishman, John Ovington, followed the same trend in his account of his visit to Surat in 1689, referring to Indians in some parts of his book and to 'Hindoes' in another (Ovington, 1929: 85, 183, 190, 195, 199, 201, 204, 219–20).

Reference to Hindus as the people inhabiting Hindustan or India, and the use of the term 'Hindu' in a territorial, racial, social and cultural sense appear to have persisted right through the eighteenth and nineteenth centuries and even at a time when the more purely religious definition of the Hindu as a follower of Hinduism was becoming more popular. Indeed, a belief that the Hindus (who may or may not have been seen as the very earliest inhabitants of India) were the founders of a distinctive civilisation preceding the Muslim incursions was the basis of a considerable literature in the early colonial period. Orientalist scholars such as Sir William Jones, Alexander Dow and William Robertson and governors and administrators such as John Malcolm and Mountstuart Elphinstone all thought and wrote about the history of the Hindu people and the nature of Hindu civilisation, including their language, religion and social institutions. But, though religion was discussed, the Hindu was not defined solely on the grounds of his or her religious allegiance (Elphinstone 1849; Davies and Malcolm

1970; Marshall 1970; Robertson 1804). The comparison was more between the Hindus and people of other ancient civilisations such as Egypt, Greece or Rome than it was between Hindus and the followers of other faiths. In other words, nationality, residence or citizenship rather than religion continued as the primary focus and basis of definition.

This territorial, racial and general cultural notion of the Hindu continued to be reflected in nineteenth-century individual comment (Oddie 2003) and in English and French dictionary definitions, even when the specifically religious idea of the Hindu as 'the follower of Hinduism' was becoming increasingly popular. British dictionaries, even in the middle of the nineteenth century, continued to insist on a basic territorial and racial definition. Thus, according to *Barclay's Universal English Dictionary*, published in 1848, Hindus, who inhabited India, were referred to as 'gentoos' – gentoo being a Portuguese term for gentile or heathen (Barclay 1848; Grose 1772: 231; Hamilton 1828: 2.724). In the words of the author of the entry in the *Imperial Dictionary*, published in 1851, 'Hindoo' or 'Hindu' referred to a native of 'Hindoostan or Hindostan' (Ogilvie 1851) The similarity in the meaning of 'Hindu' and 'Indian' is implied in other contemporary observations of the time. Thus, according to James Forbes, author of *Oriental Memoirs*, the 'Hindoos' were 'the aborigines of Hindostan' (Forbes 1834: 1.236). However, while dictionaries limited themselves to the territorial and racial definition, the notion of 'the Hindu' was beginning to change. Colange, in *The People's Encyclopedia*, published in 1875, described the Hindu as 'a native of Hindostan', but then, in an article on Hindustan, made three significant points: (1) the great bulk of the inhabitants of Hindustan are Hindus; (2) they are followers of the Brahmanical religion; and (3) they are separate and different from the Muslims (Colange 1875). The comment on their religion was the increasingly important ingredient and an indication of the way in which the concept of the Hindu was beginning to develop.

The Hindu in Hindu self-understanding

The idea of the Hindu developed only as a result of the interface between insiders and outsiders. There was a pressing need for Persians, Greeks, Arabs and, later, for Europeans to develop a term which could be used to describe and to begin to understand India's people, who, like other foreigners, appeared to be so different from themselves. Apparently for some Muslim commentators the Hindus were a classic example of 'the Other', a potent reminder that they were everything Muslims were not. This point was made abundantly clear in the early years of the eleventh century when the Muslim scholar and traveller Alberuni, who accompanied Mahmud into northern India, declared to the readers of his account that they should always bear in mind that 'the Hindus' were different from Muslims in their language and in all other aspects (Embree 1971: 17–22). Furthermore, in the author's view, Muslims believed in nothing in which Hindus believed 'and vice versa'. Alberuni perceived that Hindus saw themselves as different from the Muslim outsiders as they called them mleccha (impure) and avoided intermarriage and even eating with them, making it clear that they considered this would make them impure. Lastly, adverting to what he claimed were the peculiarities of the Hindu 'national character', he remarked that to them their religion, nation, country, etc. were superior, leading to Alberuni's assessment of them as 'vain' and 'haughty' (Embree 1971: 17–22). According to Sachau, cited in Sharma, Alberuni referred to Hindus as 'our religious antagonists' (Sharma 2002: 7).

Cerainly, during the period of the Delhi Sultanate (*c*.1200–1526) the term 'Hindu' was used both in a regional and a religious sense.

If, then, this is an outsider's labelling and summation of India's people, how did they describe themselves? When did they begin to adopt the outsider's terminology and to think of themselves as Hindus and what did they think being a Hindu actually meant?

These issues have been explored in the author's recent paper on the development of Hindu self-understanding (Oddie 2003). Suffce it to say that, according to Cynthia Talbot, the earliest evidence of non-Muslims adopting the designation Hindu so far discovered is in Andhra where inscriptions dating from 1513 CE onward refer to the title 'Sultan among Hindu Kings', assumed by several Indian rulers of the Vijayanagara empire (Talbot 1995). Arguably, an increasing awareness of being Hindu is apparent before colonial interaction in Bengali Vaiṣṇava texts dating from the first half of the sixteenth to the second half of the eighteenth century, in the period roughly coinciding with Mughal rule in Bengal. However, according to Joseph O'Connell, who has analysed this material, the term Hindu usually refers to a social rather than a religious group and was often used in the broad social and cultural sense to distinguish the local Bengalis and their customs from Muslim residents and their practice and style of life. There is, according to O'Connell, no great emphasis on differences in religion or a sense that Hindus generally were the followers of a different religion from Muslims (O'Connell 1973: 342). This is obviously a complex question.

What Sumit Sarkar describes as 'the communalist assumption' of Hindus and Muslims as two distinct 'hostile' groups (an assumption clearly reflected in British histories of India written during the nineteenth century) has long been questioned and effectively undermined (Sarkar 1983: 59–60). The lack of a sense of a clear polarity between Muslims and Hindus in eleventh-century Sind is, for example, also apparent in other parts of India during the pre-colonial period – especially at the grassroots level. Indeed, recent studies of the nature and spread of Islam in Bengal and south India suggest that Muslim converts, who were mostly drawn from the lower castes, greatly modified imported Islamic teaching and practice, adapting it to their own pre-existing (so-called Hindu) lifestyle and views of the world. Furthermore, Hindus, following a variety of different cults and religious traditions, mixed easily with others influenced by the teachings and customs associated with Muhammad (Bayly 1989; Eaton 1994).

Evidence relating to Hindu feeling in western India in the seventeenth century, especially during the period of Aurangzeb's rule, however, suggests that there was a deepening divide between Hindus and Muslims. In his discussion of Hindu responses to the Muslim presence in Maharashtra, Balkrishna Gokhale has drawn attention to the comments of Ram Das (1608–81), the great Marathi exponent of militant bhakti who maintained a close contact with Śivajī. Here there is some evidence of a Hindu–Muslim polarity, and of a feeling on the part of Hindus that their gods and ritual practices were different from those of Muslims and that Hindus suffered from severe and unwarranted religious discrimination (Gokhale 1984).

While there is, then, evidence that some Hindus during the pre-colonial period began to think of themselves as belonging to a broad-based Hindu religious community, the predominance and intensity of feeling were perhaps dependent on location. For instance, Mahmud of Ghazi's 1025 attack on Somnath, including the destruction of temple deities, precipitated a clear divide between Hindus and Muslims (Sharma 2002: 6–7). In his survey of evidence related to religious identity in the pre-colonial period, Gottschalk is critical of the view that such identities were solely the product of imperialism on the grounds that communal antagonisms were already present, while continuing to place emphasis on the power of imperialism to exacerbate tensions between Hindus and Muslims (Gottschalk 2000: 18–24).

Hindus as followers of 'the Hindu religion'

The division between foreign religious traditions and the 'insiders' was perhaps later reinforced by the activity of Protestant missionaries, whom it was believed were in league with a foreign power. It was this activity and apparent collusion with the colonial state that appeared to present a peculiar threat to the Hindu dharma, deities and way of life. In their preaching and propaganda activity of the first half of the nineteenth century, Protestant missionaries constantly bracketed all Hindus together in a system of religion which was different from Islam and opposed to Christianity. Hindus were repeatedly challenged to think comparatively and of themselves as participants with all other Hindus in a unified India-wide (and unacceptable) system of belief and practice. The consequence of this approach was to concentrate attention on the differences between religious traditions defined as 'Hinduism', Christianity or Islam, rather than on differences within. An aggressive style of missionary preaching, conversion to Christianity and fear of conversion, heightened by apparent government support of missionaries, created a growing concern among elites and others that Hindu society was in considerable danger, perhaps even on the verge of collapse. The feeling that there was a need for greater unity, defensive measures and reform to meet all of these threats is reflected in the rise of numerous Hindu defence and reform associations. But not only was a consciousness of being Hindu greatly developed; so too was the idea of being a Hindu through religious conviction. The term 'dharma' was already coming to be used in a less social and more religious sense to match up with Christian terminology and meet the pressure to accept the Christian belief system. And, while in opposing Christianity Hindus were often concerned with pollution and loss of status, religious beliefs were bound up with caste and other forms of social practice and were never far beneath the surface in the Hindu–Christian encounter. Furthermore, it was the specifically religious or doctrinal issues that the middle- or high-caste converts to Christianity continued to emphasise in what were usually highly publicised statements about the reasons for their decision to join the Christian community. What mattered for them, they argued, was not being a Christian for social reasons, but because they no longer believed in Hindu doctrine and teachings.

The Hindu in the colonial context and census

During the British colonial period the term 'Hindu' was certainly appropriated and utilised by builders of empire for varied and multifarious purposes; even so, some recent research suggests that the first Europeans to use the term were not eighteenth-century Orientalist scholars or British officials, but mostly travellers and merchants, such as the Frenchmen Bernier and Tavernier and the English merchant John Ovington, who visited India in 1689 (Bernier 1916: 325; Tavernier 1977: 1.237; Ovington 1929: 219). Also noteworthy was Edward Terry, the English East India Company's chaplain at Surat, who, drawing attention to the religious practices of the people of 'Indostan', calling them 'Hindoos', described them as 'Gentiles' and 'idolaters' (Foster 1968: 307). In this case Terry, like Bernier, appears to have borrowed the term directly from Indian sources.

The question of who is a Hindu arose in official circles with the introduction of census surveys in India during the second half of the nineteenth century. Early tabulations, such as those which appeared in the Madras Presidency district reports published in the 1850s, divided the population into the three general categories of Hindu, Muslim and Christian, with the clear implication that the term 'Hindu', like 'Muslim' and 'Christian', was a religious rather than a racial category. District-level surveys were followed by broader presidency or state-level enquiries conducted in several parts of British India, and finally by the introduction of the first all-India decennial census. All of these and subsequent census reports included sections on religion, though from the 1930s onwards social, occupational and economic enquiries began to assume a much greater importance. While they continued to include figures on people's religious affiliation, these tables are swamped by the findings on other issues and are not discussed systematically anywhere in the general report. Nevertheless, it was the census, especially during the period 1871 to 1931, which constantly reinforced the missionary and broader view that the Hindu was, first and foremost, a follower of Hinduism.

In assuming that religion was a basic trait and fundamentally important for the understanding and management of Indian society, the census commissioners broke with the tradition followed in the United Kingdom where religion was not usually taken into account in census reports. The only time religion was investigated by the state in Britain was in 1851, when an attempt was made to assess the extent of religious observance in England and Wales, together with the relative strengths of denominational allegiance (Watts 1998: 2.22). British policy in India, therefore, probably reflects the long-held European view that India was 'the most religious country in the world' (Hutton 1933: 386; Inden 1992: 82). The people's religion was not only recorded on a regular basis, but was also presented as the most important and fundamental division in Indian society. This meant that other categories such as age, sex, housing, education and sometimes even economic activity were broken down into the basic religious categories (Jones 1981: 73–101).

Having once introduced religion and Hindu as categories in census reports, superintendents discovered that the idea of the Hindu as a follower of the Hindu religion was extremely problematic. First, as Wilfred Cantwell Smith and others have shown, a concept of 'religion' was a European and Christian construct and, as a foreign and imported term, it created considerable confusion, if not in the minds of enumerators, then among the people themselves. People, it was reported in the *Census of British India, 1881*, could not tell whether they belonged to any particular religion (Indian Census Commissioner 1883: 1.17). All they knew, they said, was their caste, or which deities were important to them. Reflecting on the problem in the report for 1911, the commissioner remarked that apart from 'Muhammadanism' and Christianity there was no 'definite creed'. Instead, he identified the word 'dharma' as corresponding most closely to the word 'religion', although it indicates 'conduct more than creed' (Gait 1913: 1.113). Similar comments were made by census officials elsewhere, underlining the difficulties of classifying Hindus as followers of any particular system of beliefs. Writing in his report for the *Census of India, 1921*, the Superintendent of Census Operations, Madras, went so far as to claim that those classified as Hindu were not familiar with the term in reference to their religion (Boag 1922: 13.57).

Organisers of the census not only struck difficulties with the idea of Hindus having a religion, but faced problems in trying to separate Hindus from followers of other systems. What was 'Hinduism' and how did Hindus differ from adherents of other religions? As with missionaries, their search for a definition of Hinduism was long and hard, and one which remained inconclusive. And yet without it it was difficult to say which beliefs about God or ideas of religion a Hindu was supposed to follow. According to Risley, who summarised some of these definitions in his report for the *Census of India, 1901*, they ranged from a suggestion that 'Hinduism' was a system of conduct to the view that 'Hinduism', as a religion, might be applied to those who 'accept' the 'Brahmanic Scripture' (Risley and Gait 1903: 1.357). Gradually, however, for practical and applied purposes and out of deep frustration, officials began to devise a definition not of what 'Hinduism' was, but of what it was not. 'Hinduism' was, according to this view, the residuum, what was left after all the other religions had been taken out. Accordingly, Hindus were the people who remained after Sikhs, Buddhists, Jains and others had been siphoned off. However, this train of reasoning raised further questions. How far, for example, was it possible to distinguish Jain from Hindu religious beliefs, or tribal from low-caste Hindu views? This was not merely an academic issue but one which had serious social consequences.

The census, social conflict and Hindu identity

Bernard Cohn has discussed the role of the census in 'objectification' and in affecting the way in which Indian subjects thought about themselves and their position in society (Cohn 1990). The census was a catalyst which stimulated considerable social ferment and indigenous debates about who was a Hindu and who was not.

(1) Since the difference between the religious beliefs of some 'Hindus' and tribals was unclear, this gave rise to numerous disputes among the people themselves. For example, according to the census commissioner of the Central Province, his survey of 1881 seemed to suggest that there was among 'aboriginal' peoples 'a general desire' to be classified as belonging to 'the Hindoo religion'. And while in the feudatory states the preponderance of 'aboriginal tribes' enabled them to have recognised 'their religious leaning', they were less fortunate in the British districts. There, according to the superintendent, 'orthodox' Hindus employed as enumerators were reluctant to include 'the hill races' in their records of 'Hindoo by religion' (Indian Census Commissioner 1883: 1.18–19).

(2) The same high-caste manipulation of census returns and pressure on the depressed classes are apparent in the case of low-caste groups seeking recognition and acceptance within Hindu society. Referring to the results of the census of 1891 the commissioner remarked that there was a distinct unwillingness to include the lowest strata of society within the Hindu grouping in some parts of the country (Indian Census Commissioner 1892: 1.158).

The growth of democracy and the Hindu need for numbers

Political developments soon began to affect the attitude of the Hindu elites. With the rise of the nationalist movement, the gradual introduction of democratic institutions and the growing competition with Muslims for representation in legislative councils, it became increasingly important for Hindus to overcome their traditional reluctance to include tribals and outcastes within the boundaries of a Hindu community. An early indication of this new inclusive Hindu approach was apparent in 1911 during an official pre-census investigation into which castes should be classified as Hindu. The enquiry, which also happened to precede the appointment of Hindu and Muslim representatives to the new Legislative Councils, highlighted the issue of the relative strength of the Hindu and Muslim communities and generated considerable discussion. Some Hindus, already anxious about the community's future, feared that the debates would lead to the exclusion of certain classes from the category of Hindu and would thus react unfavourably on their political importance (Gait 1913: 1.116). Thereafter, political considerations, bound up with the definition of 'the Hindu', remained as one of the central issues throughout the rest of the colonial period.

European views and Hindu fears of annihilation

The rise of a new Hindu consciousness, assertiveness and desire for redefinition arose from a profound sense among Hindus that they were under threat or even in danger of annihilation. Linked with what Kenneth Jones has described as the negativity 'of Hindu consciousness' was the Hindu's acceptance and internalisation of British depictions of Hindu character (Jones 1998: 65–80). European comments on the character of Hindus, especially during the first half of the nineteenth century, were generally far from complimentary. Much of the comment, including remarks in the best-selling contemporary accounts of India, such as those in James Mill's *The History of British India* and in William Ward's (1815) *History, Literature, and Mythology of the Hindoos*, was very largely negative (Mill 1826; Ward 1990; cf. Grant 1812–13). One exception was Sir Thomas Munro's well-known panegyric in response to a question in the House of Commons (Bearce 1961: 124–25). Two of the most significant criticisms (often made in justification of missionary effort or in favour of some form of colonial rule) were as follows: the Hindus, enslaved for centuries by the twin evils of despotism and priest-craft, were weak and effeminate, incapable of resisting invaders, dependent and in need of the European's helping hand. The second assessment, not entirely unrelated to the first, was that the Hindus were morally 'depraved', the victims of irrational belief, worshippers of idols and immoral gods, prone to unrestrained selfishness, 'leading to discord', cruel in their socio-religious practices (such as sati and hook-swinging), sexually immoral and harsh and unjust in their treatment of women.

It was this type of indictment of the Hindu character that was, to a greater or lesser extent, accepted by educated Hindus. Hence, Hindu reform and revival movements and the new and aggressive forms of political agitation were designed, amongst other things, to reinvent the Hindu – to reassert his manliness, to show his rationality and, in many cases, to abolish socio-religious 'evils' and demonstrate the Hindus' concern for charity, welfare and the upliftment of women.

The need to save Hindus from extinction, let alone rehabilitate their image or change their attitude, was made abundantly clear in the census reports, which showed the proportion of Hindus in the community in steady decline. This was partly as a result of defections to Christianity and Islam, but also because of the superintendents' policy of identifying new communities which were extracted from the Hindu category. In a series of letters published in the *Bengalee* in 1909, U.N. Mukherji referred to the Hindus as 'A Dying Race'. He painted a disturbing picture of decline, as they slipped from a majority to a minority and were faced with the possibility of extinction, as conversion and differential growth rates overwhelmed them (Jones 1998: 70–73; Sarkar 1997: 286–88). In an argument which was echoed by Hindu nationalist leaders elsewhere, he held that it was the Hindus' own fault. Their physical weakness and lack of aggression, their lack of unity and especially their lack of concern for the despised untouchables (who understandably were susceptible to conversion to alien faiths), these and other evils all contributed to Hindu decline and the threat of extinction.

Communalism nationalism and the new Hindu

One reaction to these threats of decline, including fear of increasing Muslim power, was to attempt to rally, unify and consolidate the Hindu community – a measure which, combined with a similar response on the part of Muslims, was bound to exacerbate communal feeling. Linked with this was a second response – to break with Congress policy and form specifically Hindu religio-political organisations in order to further protect Hindu interests.

A subtle change in census terminology helped to disseminate the idea that what mattered at least as much as the individual's religious belief was membership of an identifiable religious 'community'. The Hindu, so long problematic as a believer, was now a Hindu by virtue of his or her 'community'. The reasons for this transition (apparent in the language of the *Census of India, 1931*) are much the same as the reasons for the rise and development of the Hindu Mahasabha. British policies stressing the differences between Muslims and Hindus, economic and political rivalry and other factors already mentioned greatly increased tensions in the late nineteenth century. These tensions in the 1880s resulted in an increasing number of communal riots that became even more serious, frequent and widespread in the decades leading up to India's independence. Moreover, influenced by the idea that India was essentially a religious country, and especially by the communal developments of the late nineteenth and early twentieth centuries, historians and bureaucrats (perhaps interested in demonstrating that India could not do without the British) consolidated the communal view of Indian history. Further, as Pandey and others have so clearly shown, they imposed a modern all-India communal interpretation upon earlier riots and disturbances, which were clearly the result of other local or non-religious factors (Pandey 1992). Therefore, the modern communalistic-minded Hindus who became more prominent in the twentieth century appear to have been as much a creation of historical views and writing as they were of other factors affecting the relationship between Hindus and Muslims.

The rise of nationalism and progress towards the creation of a democratic state automatically raised questions about what role 'religion' should play in the newly independent India. With the growth of communalism and the increasing likelihood of a British withdrawal, Hindus became increasingly divided about the future. The dominant Congress view was that, though they were in a majority, Hindus should join with Muslims and other minorities in the formation of a secular state in which all citizens of whatever religious persuasion would have equal rights and opportunities. The opposing view was put by V.D. Savarkar and members of the Hindu Mahasabha. His basic policy was to create a system of Hindu dominance by redefining 'the Hindu' and, if not eliminating Muslims and Christians as components of India's population, then relegating them to an inferior position within the Hindu-dominated state.

In contrast to the way in which the census developed, namely to create more and more categories of 'religion' at the expense of the Hindu population, Savarkar, one of the leaders of the Hindu Mahasabha and an exponent of Hindutva, suggested a reversal – the re-inclusion in the Hindu population of a number of minority groups. 'Who is a Hindu?' he asked. A Hindu, he concluded, is one who looks upon India as 'the land of his forefathers', who is descended from Hindu parents, who follows a sect or religious system developed in India (India being 'the land of its revelation') and who has inherited a common culture, language, laws, customs, folklore and history. Hence the Jains, Buddhists and Sikhs are all Hindus who give to India their total allegiance. On the other hand, Muslims and Christians have all the essential qualifications but one, the inability to see India as 'their Holyland'. For them the focus of their faith is outside India (Savarkar 1964: 6.66–91).

In 1921, shortly before this was written, an Indian journal suggested a revival of the old and original territorial meaning of Hindu. All Indians, it was suggested, should call themselves Hindus, irrespective of their particular religion. Savarkar and the Hindu Mahasabha, however, were not quite so generous. They feared, in particular, the growth of Muslim power and influence, and needed the support of other groups which, for some time during the colonial period, had been regarded as outside the Hindu system; they suggested their incorporation in a larger Hindu fold – but one which would continue to exclude Muslims and Christians.

See also: **Bhakti; Basham, Arthur Llewellyn; Buddhism, relationship with Hinduism; Caste; Dalits; Deities; Dharma; Gauḍīyas; Hindu Mahasabha; Hinduism; Hinduism, history of scholarship; Hinduism, modern and contemporary; Hinduvta; Idolatry; Jainism, relationship with Hinduism; Jones, Sir William; Nationalism; Orientalism; Purity and pollution, ritual; Sati; Savarkar, Vinayat Damodar; Sikhism, relationship with Hinduism; Vaiṣṇavism; Women question; Women, status of**

GEOFFREY A. ODDIE

Further reading

Barclay, James. 1848. *Barclay's Universal English Dictionary*, new edn. London: James. S. Virtue.

Basham, A.L. 1954. *The Wonder that Was India*. London: Sidgwick and Jackson.

Basham, A.L. (ed.). 1975. *A Cultural History of India*. Oxford: Clarendon Press.

Bayly, Susan. 1989. *Saints, Goddesses and Kings. Muslims and Christians in South Indian Society, 1700–1900*. Cambridge: Cambridge University Press.

Bearce, G.D. 1961. *British Attitudes towards India*. Oxford: Oxford University Press.

Bernier, François. 1916. *Travels in the Moghal Empire, AD 1656–1688*. Trans. Irving Brock. London: Oxford University Press.

Boag, G.T. 1922. *Census of India, 1921, vol. XIII, pt 1– Report*. Madras: Superintendent, Government Press.

Cohn, B.S. 1990. 'The Census, Social Structure and Objectification in South Asia'. In B.S. Cohn, ed., *An Anthropologist among the Historians and Other Essays*. Delhi: Oxford University Press, 224–54.

Colange, L. (ed.). 1875. *The People's Encyclopedia*. London: John G. Murdoch.

Davies, W. and John Malcolm. 1970 [1823]. *A Memoir of Central India*, 2 vols. Delhi: Sagar Publications.

Eaton, Richard M. 1994. *The Rise of Islam and the Bengal Frontier, 1204–1760*. Delhi: Oxford University Press.

Elliott, H.M. and J. Dowson. 1867. *The History of India as Told by Its Own Historians*, vol. 1. London: Trubner & Co.

Elphinstone, Mountstuart. 1849 [1841]. *The History of India*, 3rd edn. London: John Murray.

Embree, Ainslie T. 1971. *Alberuni's India*. Trans. Edward C. Sachau. Abridged edn. New York: W.W. Norton & Co.

Forbes, James. 1834. *Oriental Memoirs*, vol. 1. London: Bentley.

Foster, William (ed.). 1968. *Early Travels in India, 1583–1619*. Reprint. Delhi: S. Chand & Co.

Frykenberg, R.E. 1991 [1989]. 'The Emergence of Modern Hinduism'. In G.D. Sontheimer and H. Kulke, eds, *Hinduism Reconsidered*. New Delhi: Manohar, 29–49.

Gait, Edward. 1913. *Census of India 1911*, vol. 1. Calcutta: Office of the Superintendent of Government Printing, India.

Gokhale, B.G. 1984. 'Hindu Responses to the Muslim Presence in Maharashta'. In Y. Friedman, ed., *Islam in* Asia, vol.1. Boulder, CO: Westview Press, 146–73.

Gottschalk, Peter. 2000. *Beyond Hindu and Muslim: Multiple Identity in Narratives from Village India*. New York: Oxford University Press.

Grant, Charles. 1812–13. 'Observations on the State of Society among the Asiatic Subjects of Great Britain'. In *Parliamentary Papers*, X, Paper 282: 1–112.

Grose, J.H. 1772. *A Voyage to the East Indies*. London: Printed for S. Hooper.

Hamilton, W. 1828. *The East India Gazetteer*, vol. 2. London: Printed for Parbury, Allen.

Hutton, J.H. 1933. *Census of India, 1931, vol. 1, pt 1– Report*. Delhi: Superintendent, Government Press.

Inden, R. 1992. *Imagining India*. Cambridge, MA, and Oxford: Blackwell.

Indian Census Commissioner. 1883. *Census of British India, 1881, vol. 1, pt 1– Report*. London: Indian Government.

Indian Census Commissioner. 1892. *Census of India, 1891, vol. 1, pt 1– Report*. London: Indian Government.

Jackson, A.V. Williams. 1922. 'The Persian Dominions in Northern India Down to the Time of Alexander's Invasion'. In E.J. Rapson, ed., *Ancient India*. Cambridge: Cambridge University Press, 319–44.

Jones, K.W. 1981. 'Religious Identity and the Indian Census'. In G. N. Barrier, ed., *The Census in British India: New Perspectives*. Delhi: Manohar, 73–101.

Jones, Kenneth W. 1998. 'The Negative Component of Hindu Consciousness'. In G.A. Oddie, ed., *Religious Traditions in South Asia. Interactionand Change*. Richmond: Curzon Press, 65–80.

King, Richard. 1999. *Orientalism and Religion. Postcolonial Theory, India and 'the Mystic East'*. London and New York: Routledge.

Marshall, P.J. (ed.). 1970. *The British Discovery of Hinduism in the Eighteenth Century*. Cambridge: Cambridge University Press.

Mill, James. 1826. *The History of British India*, 6 vols, 3rd edn. London: Baldwin, Cradock & Joy.

O'Connell, J.T. 1973. 'The Word "Hindu" in Gauḍiya Vaiṣṇava Texts'. *Journal of the American Oriental Society* 93(3): 340–44.

Oddie, Geoffrey A. 2003. 'Constructing "Hinduism": The Impact of the Protestant Missionary Movement on Hindu Self-Understanding'. In Robert Eric Frykenberg, ed., *Christians and Missionaries in India. Cross Cultural Communications since 1500*. Grand Rapids, MI: William B. Eerdmans; London: RoutledgeCurzon, 155–82.

Ogilvie, John. (ed.). 1851. *The Imperial Dictionary English Technological and Scientific: Adapted to the Present State of Literature, Science and Art; on the Basis of Webster's English Dictionary*, vol. 1. London: Blackie and Son.

Ovington, J. 1929. *A Voyage to Surat in the Year 1689*, ed. R.G. Rawlinson. London: Oxford University Press.

Pandey, Gyanendra. 1992. *The Construction of Communalism in Colonial North India*. Delhi: Oxford University Press.

Raychaudhuri, Hemchandra. 1996. *Political History of Ancient India*. With a commentary by B.N. Mukherjee. Delhi: Oxford University Press.

Risley, Herbert Hope and Edward Gait. 1903. *Census of India 1901, vol. 1, pt 1– Report*. Calcutta: Office of the Superintendent of Government Printing, India.

Robertson, William. 1804 [1791]. *An Historical Disquisition Concerning the Knowledge Which the Ancients had of India*, 4th edn. London: T. Cadell.

Sarkar, Sumit. 1983. *Modern India, 1885–1947*. Madras: Macmillan India.

Sarkar, S. 1997. 'Indian Nationalism and the Politics of Hindutva'. In D. Ludden, ed., *Making India Hindu*. Delhi: Oxford University Press, 286–88.

Savarkar, V.D. 1964 [1923]. *Essentials of Hindutva*, vol. VI. Poona: Samagra Savarkar Wangmaya.

Sharma, Arvind. 2002. 'On Hindu, Hindustān, Hinduism and Hindutva'. *Numen* 49: 1–36.

Smith, W.C. 1991. *The Meaning and End of Religion*. Minneapolis, MN: Fortress Press.

Stietencron, Heinrich von. 2001. 'Hinduism: On the Proper Use of a Deceptive Term'. In Gunther-Dietz Sontheimer and Hermann Kulke, eds, *Hinduism Reconsidered*. New Delhi: Manohar, 32–53.

Talbot, Cynthia. 1995. 'Inscribing the Self: Hindu-Muslim Identities in Pre-Colonial India'. *Comparative Studies in Society and History* 37.4: 692–722.

Tavernier, John-Baptiste. 1977. *Travels in India*, 2 vols, 2nd edn. Trans. U.N. Ball. Delhi: Munshiram Manoharlal.
Ward, William. 1990 [1815]. *History, Literature, and Mythology of the Hindoos*, 3rd reprinted edn. Delhi: Low Price Publications.
Watts, Michael. 1998. *The Dissenters*, vol. 2. Oxford: Clarendon Press.

HINDU HISTORY, CULTURE AND CIVILISATION

It may be impossible to define 'Hinduism' as one religion, but it makes perfect sense to speak of a Hindu culture and a Hindu civilisation. Over thousands of years there grew on the Indian subcontinent a distinctive culture embracing all spheres of human activity. In the wider ethno-geographical sense, this Hindu culture is shared by Buddhists, Jains and others, who at some time rejected certain features of Brahmanic religion that now characterise the narrower 'religious' sense in which the word Hindu is conventionally used. Hindu culture later spread to large parts of South-East Asia: from Sri Lanka and Burma to Indonesia and as far as the Philippines.

There will hardly be any other major region on earth in which a people has developed such a close symbiosis of religion, culture and nature: the life-cycle, the change of the seasons, the founding of a village or town, the building of a house or a temple, labour in the fields and in workshops, the arts and the sciences, social structures and political institutions – all became facets of Hindu civilisation. It needed many generations to integrate many local cultures, but once developed it proved resilient enough to withstand foreign influences and to absorb elements of other cultures without giving itself up.

The origins of Hindu culture

Hindus, in the narrower 'religious' sense, call their tradition Vaidika dharma. 'Vedic' acquired in the course of time a host of cultural connotations over and beyond the designation of a set of the most ancient literary composition. The Hindu cultural heartland was the Āryavārta, the 'country of the noble'. Its way of life was to serve as model for the followers of the Vaidika dharma. *Itihāsa-Purāṇa*, a vast narrative literature that claims to be as ancient in its beginnings as the Veda, and which has served as a repository for ancient Indian history, has preserved tales of the beginnings of Hindu culture and civilisation, including long lists of ruling dynasties that go back several thousand years. Vyāsa, the arranger of the Veda and author of the *Mahābhārata*; Manu, the forefather of the Hindus and the author of the most important Hindu law book, the *Manusmṛti*; Bhārata, the first king of India; and Pṛthu, the first royal promoter of agriculture – all feature prominently in these works.

Although more recent scholarship has not tended to perpetuate the Orientalist stereotype that Hindu culture was ahistorical in character, the question of origins remains controversial. Given striking linguistic, cultural and religious similarities between Europe and India, it has seemed necessary to explain how these came about. One explanation was of an Aryan invasion of India, introducing Vedic culture to the subcontinent. Where once the discovery of the Indus Valley Civilisation was interpreted as substantiating this hypothesis, few now regard the theory as plausible. Some scholars advocate more peaceful migration, settlement and integration, while others identify Vedic culture as indigenous to India.

India the Hindu Holy Land

Hindu culture and civilisation, including religion, were from the very beginning closely tied to the geography of India. The Mātrī-bhūmī, 'Mother India', has an emotional connotation for Indians: the distinctive physical features of the country are directly associated with the gods and goddesses of Hinduism, the religious practices and the eschatological expectations of the Hindus. The Gaṅgā, the Yamunā, the Narbadā, the Kaverī – to mention only a few of the mighty rivers of India – are not only reservoirs of water and means of transportation, but also sources of inspiration and ritual purification. They are divine entities who invite worship and along their banks there are thousands of tīrthas, places where pilgrims in large numbers congregate to obtain supernatural blessings and spiritual benefits. India's mountains, the mighty Himālayas, the Vindhyas, the Ghāṭs, the Nilgiris, or single peaks like Gaurī-Śaṅkara or Aruṇācala – again, to select only a very few – are not only the abodes of gods, but have also been sanctified by thousands of ṛṣis and samṇyāsins since ages immemorial. Numberless pilgrims, individually or in groups, have climbed over dangerously high mountain passes to reach remote sacred places like Amarnath and Kedarnath associated with Śiva. Ancient and mediaeval India was dotted by numerous sacred groves – large areas where the gods were believed to dwell and where nobody could harm a living being with impunity. Countless temples, big and small, embellish India's landscape, visibly transforming the country into a holy land, where gods dwell among humans.

Hindu word-culture

The most ancient monuments of Hindu culture are the Vedic hymns. The *Ṛgveda*, the most representative of the four *Saṃhitās*, contains a *Vāc-sūkta*, a hymn in praise of the Word, worshipped as goddess, almighty and everlasting. For thousands of years brāhmaṇas memorised and recited the Veda as an accompaniment to sacrifices and other rituals.

The pride of place in the world of Brahmanic knowledge always belonged to the study of the Word (Vāc), which from early on was seen as imbued with divine power. The brāhmaṇas who preserved and investigated the Word occupied the highest social rank. Sanskrit, the (refined) language of the Veda and of higher learning, was considered a gift of the gods. The Vedāṅgas of Śiksā (phonetics) and of Nirukta (etymology) as well as of Vyākaraṇa (grammar) and Chandas (metrics) relate to the study of language, followed by a large number of later works that go into the intricate detail of linguistic problems.

Religiously authoritative Hindu literature in Sanskrit, the sacred language of India, has come down through the ages mainly in two major streams: the *Vedas* and the *Āgamas*. The first is the literature of the religious professionals, only to be studied by brāhmaṇas. The Vedas comprise the *Saṃhitās*, the *Brāhmaṇas*, the *Āraṇyakas* and the *Upaniṣads*. These books contain what is required for the performance of Vedic rituals. It was the prerogative of the brāhmaṇas alone to perform these. The second genre is the literature for the people at large, accessible to all castes. It comprises besides the great Epics (*Rāmāyaṇa* and *Mahābhārata*) and the *Purāṇas* a large number of so-called 'sectarian' texts – *Āgamas*, *Saṃhitās*, *Tantras* – expositions of doctrines and ritual practices with the appropriate stories about gods and saints and which are shared only by members of specific worship traditions (saṃpradāyas). They contain creation narratives, the histories of kings and patriarchs, the myths of gods and goddesses, edifying stories, wisdom of life, eschatological lore. Both kinds of literature contain, besides religious, many secular elements which are integral to their religious purpose.

Based on these stories, famous poets and playwrights like Kalidāsa and Bana (fifth or sixth century CE) produced dramatic literature of a high order in Sanskrit, and poet-saints like Tulsīdāsa and Kambha (sixteenth century CE) created popular vernacular versions of the classics, which are performed in hundreds of places to this very day in India, not to mention the countless films that take their stories from *Itihāsa-Purāṇa*. Love and respect for the word were not confined to a small literary elite: so-called 'illiterate' villagers and townspeople often could recite from memory hundreds of verses of the *Rāmcaritmānas* and season conversation with words of wisdom from Kabīr or Sūrdās.

'Vedic', the language of the most ancient literary documents of Hinduism, the Vedic hymns, is an archaic form of Sanskrit, the 'refined language', which was standardised around 600 BCE by the grammarian Pāṇini. With his *Aṣṭādhyayī* he created a Sanskrit grammar on linguistic principles unrivalled to this day. Not only did he organise the sounds of the language along empirical lines, but he derived its vocabulary from some 100 verbal roots and formulated about 4,000 interrelated rules that covered the entire complex language.

Sanskrit was called Deva-vani, the 'language of the gods', a sacred language, to be used only by persons of higher rank. It became the language of Hindu scholarship as well as Hindu religious literature: the Epics, the *Purāṇas*, the *Āgamas*, the *Tantras* are all composed in Sanskrit, albeit not always in conformity with Pāṇini's grammar. Not by coincidence did the 'heretical' Buddhists and Jains use Prakrits, 'natural' languages, whose vocabularies have strong affinities to Sanskrit, but which were not considered 'sacred' by the brāhmaṇas. When the popular bhakti movements became the predominant form of Hinduism, the vernaculars became the preferred linguistic medium. Most of the bhakti poets came from backgrounds which precluded the knowledge of Sanskrit and their songs and hymns were composed for the ordinary folk of their own neighbourhoods. Thus languages like Tamil, Mahratti, Telegu, Avadhi, Punjabi, Brajbhasa, Bengali and others acquired a large religious literature that was also used in certain forms of worship. The South Indian Śri Vaiṣṇavas in particular felt so strongly about the Tamil compositions of the Aḷvārs that they considered them equal to the Sanskrit texts and used them side by side with Sanskrit in temple worship. While Sanskrit continued to be the preferred medium of Hindu scholarship (even now there are conferences where Hindu paṇḍits read to each other papers in Sanskrit and where debates are conducted in Sanskrit), Tamil (in South India) as well as Hindi (in North India) and Bengali (in Eastern India) were used to write scholarly and theological treatises as well. With the development of virtually all the major vernaculars into literary languages, all were adopted as vehicles for religious instruction: Sanskrit religious texts have been translated into all the major Indian languages and original compositions in these are becoming the main source for ordinary people.

Hindu ritual culture

Public and private rituals were a main feature of early Vedic culture and regarded as indispensable for the well-being of society and individuals. The praxis and the theory of the yajña (sacrifice) reached such sophistication that it can justly be called a science. Hundreds of intricate and interrelated rules had to be observed by the performers of major yajñas and the construction of the required altars (vedis) required the solution of many arithmetical and geometrical problems.

The routine of nitya karmas (fixed or obligatory rituals) structured the course of the year and determined the life-cycle, thus creating a framework that supported communities and families. The change of seasons was accompanied by rituals; so were the stages in the development of persons: public offerings ensured the fertility of fields and domestic animals, home rituals accompanied birth, adolescence, marriage and death. Naimittika karmas (occasional or non-obligatory rituals) were available to give spiritual support in special circumstances and additional comfort to individuals. In later centuries, when the worship of Great Gods like Viṣṇu and Śiva associated with images and temples became the predominant form of religion, the old Vedic rituals were not given up. Besides the more popular pūjās, the ritual veneration of the image-presence of the deities in temples and homes, the performance of Vedic rites in connection with saṃskāras (sacraments) continues to this very day: Vedic hymns are still recited at upanayana (initiation), vivāha (marriage) and antyeṣṭi (last rites). Hindu temples celebrate daily, monthly and yearly festivals which structure time on a personal and public level. Many Hindus participate daily in temple pūjās, partaking of prasādam (consecrated food), and major temple festivals are great public events for every village and town. In addition the performance of numerous private rituals, such as rangoli (colourful artistic patterns of auspicious designs made daily of flower petals or coloured flour in front of the main entrance of a home), mūrti-bhoga (offering the meal to the image of the deity of the house before partaking of the food) or evening ārtīs (circling a plate with burning pieces of camphor before the image of the deity), not only fills the days and weeks with religious meaning but spills over into other daily activities: the laying of tables for eating, the arrangement of flowers for decorations, the production of cloth or pots or baskets – a sense of ritual aesthetic infuses the work of the humblest craftsman, showing in the ornamental patterns of everyday rattan furniture, the elegant shapes of utility vessels, the colour combinations of traditional textiles.

An important part of ritual culture was also music. The Vedic hymns had to be recited according to a definite pattern of pitches; if these were missed, the recitation was invalid. Later both instrumental and vocal music was developed with a sophisticated system of rāgas as the basis of musical improvisation. Music, later also joined by ritual dance, became an indispensable ingredient of temple worship and each court and temple employed professional musicians. Artistic training, lasting twelve years, was considered a sādhana, a 'path' leading to enlightenment. Even today's performances of Indian classical music and classical dance have an aura of worship: not only do they usually begin with an invocation, but the pieces performed frequently take their inspiration from Hindu mythology and end with a prayer. The audiences attend these artistic events in an attitude of reverence and religious awe.

Hindu socio-political culture

Hindu culture had from its very beginning a socio-political orientation expressed in the varṇāśrama dharma. It was built on the assumption that humans were not created equal and that their birth in different varṇas defined their various rights and duties. The brāhmaṇas, who claimed to have been born from the original Puruṣa's mouth, were the custodians of the sacred word and the teachers of humankind, the highest in rank. The kṣatriyas, born from the chest of the primeval being, were destined to be rulers and warriors, entitled to support from those of the lower ranks. The vaiśyas, born from the Puruṣa's belly, businesspeople and artisans, farmers and clerks, had to provide the necessities of life for society at large. The śūdras, originating from the feet, were there to serve the upper three varṇas, who alone were entitled to receive the saṃskāras that made them dvijātis (twice-born). The atiśūdras, the people below the status of śūdras, also called untouchables were outside the pale of Hindu society proper: they were relegated to work that was considered ritually polluting such as dealing with carcasses, cleaning latrines and disposing of the dead. They were not allowed to dwell in the village proper or to use the community well or other amenities reserved for caste people. The four varṇas (and the atiśūdras) were each aligned with a very large number of jātis (literally: birth-lines, often translated as sub-castes) that observed ranking between themselves. Commensality and marriage connections were determined not only according to varṇa but also according to jāti.

Duties were not only assigned according to varṇas, but also according to āśramas, stages in life. Largely reflecting the ideal of the brāhmaṇas, a male twice-born was to spend the first twelve years after upanayana as a student, living with a reputable teacher; he was then to marry and procreate children, to support his family through his work and to fulfil his ritual duties. When his children were grown up, he was to leave the village community and give up his work and involvement in the world to live as a vānaprastha, a forest-dweller with a life of simplicity and meditation. The last stage was that of a saṃnyāsin, a homeless pilgrim visiting holy places until death relieved him of the burden of his body. While relatively few people followed this schema strictly, it gave a spiritual orientation to society at large and established saṃnyāsa as an institution that became greatly respected: millions of men and women at any given time have chosen renunciation as a lifestyle and devoted themselves to the pursuit of spirituality.

Hindu dharma also includes rājyadharma, statecraft, the theory and practice of government. The *Śāntiparvan* of the *Mahābhārata* has long sections devoted to this topic. The famous Kauṭilya *Arthaśāstra* ascribed to the Prime Minister of Chandra Mauryagupta (321–293 BCE) not only contains Machiavelli-like political advice to rulers, but also gives a detailed description of a well-ordered professional bureaucratic administration. While a kingdom's rule was usually in the hands of kṣatriyas (or rulers who got their varṇa corrected to that status), brāhmaṇas had great influence as advisers and ministers. There are examples of regicide, like that of King Venu, instigated by brāhmaṇas who ousted rulers that did not observe Hindu dharma. It was one of the aims of the Hindu jāgaran that began in the early twentieth century to re-establish a Hindu-rāṣṭra, a Hindu dominion. The Hindu Mahasabha, the first modern Hindu political party, founded in 1909 by Pandit Madan Mohan Malaviya, a one-time Vice-Chancellor of Benaras Hindu University, proclaims in its manifesto: 'Hindus have a right to live in peace as Hindus, to legislate, to rule themselves in accordance with Hindu genius and ideals and establish by all lawful and legal means a Hindu State, based on Hindu culture and tradition, so that Hindu ideology and way of life would have a homeland of its own'.

Hindu reformers from Rammohan Roy to Mahatma Gandhi have criticised the failings of the Hindu caste system: while some wanted to abolish caste altogether, others fought against the notion of untouchability and strove to integrate the untouchables into caste society. The Indian constitution abolished untouchability, but not caste. The former untouchables, now calling themselves dalit (oppressed), have created numerous organisations fighting for socio-economic improvements.

Hindu artistic high culture

Besides the omnipresent deśī, the 'country' or popular culture, created by ordinary village and townspeople, in which virtually everybody freely participated in daily life, India also possessed a great wealth of mārga, 'high-road' or high culture, produced by professional artists under the patronage of royal courts in many parts of the country.

The story of Hindu mārga-saṇskṛti begins with the Mauryas, who established an empire in North-west and Central India that lasted from 323 to 183 BCE. If the ascription of the *Arthaśāstra* to Kauṭilya, the Prime Minister of Candragupta Maurya, is correct, the Maurya Empire must not only have possessed an extensive and well-organised administration and a flourishing economy, but also developed arts and crafts. The best-known Maurya descendant, Emperor Aśoka (269–232 BCE) proclaimed the Buddha's message in pillar and tablet inscriptions. One of these pillars, erected in Sarnath, the legendary place of the Buddha's first sermon, was topped by the famous Lion capital that appears on the official seal of the Republic of India: perfectly sculpted, highly polished sandstone figures of four lionheads whose torsos merge in the centre.

The Kuśānas, invaders from the northwest, who founded a large empire in Northern India in the early first century CE, continued this tradition and supported Buddhist establishments in their realm. Under their patronage a school of sculpture developed in Mathurā, which in later centuries produced some of the finest works of Indian art. During that time – possibly unrelated to the Kuśāna rulers – major cave-sanctuaries came into existence in various parts of India, such as the famous Caitya-hall of Karle, not far from today's Mumbai: a huge cave, decorated in imitation of large wooden structures with rows of ornamental columns and curved roof ribs.

Under the Imperial Guptas (320–540 CE), whose empire comprised large parts of Northern, Eastern and Central India, Hindu dharma experienced a major renaissance. Under their protection brāhmaṇas launched a major campaign to win the people back from Buddhism and Jainism. The Guptas built temples, encouraged the composition of *Purāṇas* and the cultivation of Sanskrit literature that elaborated themes from the epics. This time is often called the 'Golden Age' of Indian culture. During that time the most exquisite Buddha sculptures were produced in the workshops of Mathurā as well as the world-famous paintings in the Ajanta caves. The huge reliefs of Viṣṇu and his avatāras in the Udayagiri caves as well as freestanding monumental Varāhas (boars) owe their creation to Gupta patronage.

After the disintegration of the Gupta Empire, many smaller kingdoms arose in various parts of India. They too patronised the arts and left behind enduring monuments. Thus the local rulers of Vidarbha (now part of Maharashtra) supported in the late eighth century the magnificent rock-cut temples of Aurangabad and Ellora, to mention only the most famous, and under the contemporary Kalachuris' patronage the large cave temples and sculptures of Gharapuri (Elephanta) in the Bay of Bombay were created. The builder of the famous temple complex in Bhubhanesvara (Orissa) is unknown, but the Candellas built (in the twelfth century) about a hundred temples in their capital city, Khajuraho, in Bundelkhand, some of large dimensions and exquisitely decorated. In South India the Pallavas (*c.* 300–888 CE), later supplanted by the Colas (*c.* 846–1279 CE), ruling over the country along the Kaveri, established themselves as major powers and patrons of Hindu religion and art. Not only were magnificent temples such as the shore temple in Mammalapuram and the Kailāsanātha temple in Kanci built under the Pallavas, but Hindu culture reached out to Southeast Asia, whose languages and arts still show strong Hindu influence. The rule of the Colas became famous not only through the building of major temples like the Bṛhadeśvara in Tanjore or the

Naṭarāja in Cidambaram; they were also responsible for major irrigation schemes in the Kaveri river region. Under their patronage exquisite sculptures of Hindu gods and goddesses were created that became world famous. Smaller but locally important kingdoms, patronising various Hindu traditions, were emerging in the Middle Ages in the Deccan: Rāṣṭrakutas, Hoyśalas, Yādavas, Kakatīyas and others, all of them patrons of religion and the arts.

Many of the large temple cities like Śriraṅgam, Madurai, Tirupati, Kañcīpura, Rāmeśvara and others were built with the support of a long list of royal patrons over many centuries: while the latest additions were made by the eighteenth-century Nāyaks, earlier structures go back to Pandyas, Pallavas, Colas and other local rulers.

Buddhist and Jain rulers as well as rich businesspeople also added to the wealth of architectural and artistic monuments in India: suffice it to mention Ajanta, with its famous cave paintings, the complex of stūpas at Sanchi, Mount Abu, with its delicately carved marble temples, or the giant Mahabali statue at Śravanabelgola.

The rulers of the Vijayanāgara Empire, flourishing from 1336 to 1565 in South India, at a time when almost all of India was under Muslim rule, were lavish patrons of Hindu culture and left a large legacy of beautiful temples.

The early Muslim invaders stripped jewellery and precious metals from Hindu temples. Later Muslim invaders, in an effort to eliminate 'idolatry', not only looted but also destroyed Hindu temples and images. Between *c.*1000 and 1500 CE temples were razed to the ground, mosques were built where temples had stood, images were smashed and institutions of learning were destroyed. Under the enlightened rule of Akbar 'the Great' (1556–1605 CE), who aimed at uniting India politically and culturally, Hindus enjoyed considerable freedom to rebuild their temples and Hindu culture was appreciated again. Akbar invited Hindu scholars to religious discourses and debates, enjoyed listening to Hindu musicians and had his miniaturists illustrate the great Hindu epics. One of his grandsons, Darah Suko, translated the *Upaniṣads* into Persian. Another one of his grandsons, however, who prevailed in the competition for the throne, Aurangzeb (1658–80), again repressed Hindus and razed many temples that his predecessors had allowed to be built.

The arrival of the British East India Company and subsequently British imperial rule had a significant but ambivalent impact on Hindu culture and civilisation. It is this impact that some have suggested was responsible for the creation of 'Hinduism'. The British government adopted a nominal policy of non-interference but this could be interpreted differently – did it mean maintaining a strictly neutral stance towards religions, thus allowing Christian missionary activity, or continuing to discharge the duties traditionally performed by a ruler, thus patronising indigenous religious institutions? On the one hand, the British government was persuaded by the famous Minute of Macauley (1835) to promote Western (English language) education in India. On the other hand, the British government adopted a policy of non-interference with the indigenous religions and even paid the salaries of priests in major temples. Some British officials helped restore famous temples and established the first museums of Indian art. The British established a Sanskrit College in Vārāṇasī and encouraged the editing and translating of important Hindu texts by Indian as well as Western scholars.

While Jawaharlal Nehru, the first Prime Minister of India (1947–64), advocated secular socialism and state-promoted industrialisation – he called the big steel mills and the hydroelectric dams the 'new temples of the new India' – under his successors Hindutva became a major issue. Whereas in former centuries Hindu rulers built temples and supported religious endowments, today it is largely businesspeople and industrialists, together with the followers of famous gurus, who patronise Hindu culture and who help found new temples all over India. Altogether, during the half-century since Independence, more new Hindu temples have been built in India than in the five hundred years before. The largest and best known is probably the Birla Temple in New Delhi, but new temples are seen in all large cities and in many smaller places too. There is, by now, also a sizeable diaspora of over 25 million Hindus who live outside India, many of whom have become rich in South east Asia, in Europe, in North America, in Africa, in Australia and in Oceania. Hundreds of Hindu temples have been built in these places, often replicas of famous Indian temples, with Hindu priests performing Hindu ceremonies. The Vishwa Hindu Parishad, the World Association of Hindus, founded in 1964 in Bombay, is active in India as well as in the diaspora, promoting its interpretation of Hindu culture.

Hindu religious culture

The Vedic religion was family based: the individual branches (śakhas), of which the Veda consists, were preserved and continued in individual families, who exercised hereditary offices in public yajñas. The home was also a centre for religious exercises: the sacred hearth-fire was not allowed to die out. Husband and wife together had to perform the domestic rituals. Families were responsible for performing the life-cycle rituals (saṃskāras). Young boys, during their first āśrama, moved into the families of their gurus, who taught them while they also served the family. The role of the guru was always important but it reached greater prominence when specific worship communities (saṃpradāyas) developed under the leadership of charismatic personalities, who often claimed to be the embodiment of a deity. These religious leaders (acāryas) also exercise great influence on Hindus at large. They not only regulate the lives of their followers but also interpret and reinterpret sacred texts and traditional teachings. There is no central authority which all Hindus would recognise as such and there is no single name by which all Hindus would worship the deity.

Not only are many gods and goddesses invoked in Vedic hymns; even Indra, often considered the greatest, is called upon under a variety of names and titles. Consequently, it is not possible to articulate a creed to which all Hindus would subscribe or even to find a single doctrine or practice common to all Hindus. Modern compilations, often by Western converts to a particular Hindu group, that claim to offer a 'Hindu Catechism', i.e. a normative and systematic presentation of the articles of faith of Hinduism, are artificial and idiosyncratic attempts that try to give universal validity to the teachings of their particular sect. The closest to a common foundation of Hindu beliefs is the nominal acceptance of the Veda as revealed, and a general agreement on the factual reality of karma and rebirth. Looking at the many different ways in which the Veda is understood by various Hindu schools and the controversies among Hindus about strategies to cope with karma and rebirth, even those minimal foundations seem somewhat shaky.

Rather than attempting to list beliefs shared by all Hindus and establish a kind of common creed of Hinduism, it is more meaningful to study the literatures of specific saṃpradāyas and learn what their followers believe and think. The authoritative books of particular schools within Vaiṣṇavism, Śaivism or Śāktism narrate in great detail their specific teachings on God and creation, human life and salvation, heavens and hells, commandments and prohibitions. Each saṃpradāya exercises fairly strict control over doctrines taught and practices permitted.

Reprimand, or even excommunication of non-conformers, is not unheard of.

India has never known the division between philosophy and theology that has characterised much of modern Western intellectual history. Thus it is natural for Hindus with an enquiring mind philosophically to analyse and investigate the teachings of their traditions, and professional philosophers with a Hindu background do not hesitate to deal with ultimate issues in a religiously meaningful way. Among the philosophies, several take the Veda as their basis, considering it their task not to create new truths but to interpret the revealed texts. Thus Pūrva Mīmāṃsā investigates the injunctions of the vedic literature relating to ritual; it does not question them but attempts to get at their precise structure and meaning. Vedānta (also called Uttara Mīmāṃsā) is essentially a reflection on portions of the *Upaniṣads*, presupposing their intrinsic truth, a truth that could not be obtained through unaided human reason. The task which the Vedāntins set themselves is not to question or dissect the truth of upaniṣadic utterances but to make sure that they are properly understood. When Hindu scholars debate matters of religion the point is not to argue for or against the content of a scriptural statement but to ascertain an assertion as scriptural.

Hindu darśanas (philosophical systems) are not mere abstract systematic verbal constructs but also sādhanas, paths for the realisation of the highest purpose of life. Among the qualifications required for beginning philosophical study is the earnest desire to find liberation from the sufferings of saṃsāra, caused by ignorance (avidya) concerning the true nature of reality.

Hindu educational institutions and curricula

The well-organised publicly as well as privately sponsored ancient Indian universities – the most famous were Takṣaśīla (Taxila) in the Punjab, Nalanda and Vikramasila in Mithila (Bihar), already considered venerable institutions at the time of Gautama the Buddha – with thousands of teachers and tens of thousands of students, taught not only the Veda and the Vedāṅgas, but also the 'eighteen sciences', later supplemented by the 'sixty-four arts'. The basic curriculum included śabda-vidyā (linguistics), śilpasthāna-vidyā (arts and crafts), cikitṣa-vidyā (medicine), hetu-vidyā (logic and dialectics) and adhyātma-vidyā (spirituality). The Hindus called their most ancient and most venerated scripture Veda (from the verbal root vid-, to know). Vidyā, from the same root, designated knowledge acquired in any subject (a medical doctor was called a Vaidya), particularly that of the highest reality/truth taught by the *Upaniṣads*. The term śāstra (from the root sas-, to order) became the most general designation for 'science' (in the sense of French science or Italian scienza): authoritative, systematic teaching, ranging from Dharmaśāstra, the exposition of traditional law, through Vāstu-śāstra, city planning and architecture, to Kāma-śāstra, the teaching of luxurious living.

High ethical standards were expected from both students and teachers. A student not only had to pass stringent examinations to prove his aptitude for the subject of study, but also had to live an austere life according to traditional ideals of higher learning. A medical student, for instance, had to take an oath of initiation and a professional oath at the end of his training period, expressing his determination to follow the code of ethics of his calling.

Traditional Hindu thought is characterised by a holistic vision. Instead of breaking experience and reality up into isolated and unrelated fragments, thinkers looked at the whole and reconciled tensions and seeming contradictions within overarching categories. The *Ṛgveda* speaks of a universal ṛta, an ordering principle comprising physical nature as well as the moral law. The *Upaniṣads* strive to teach Brahma-vidyā, the knowledge of an all-embracing reality principle. In life Hindus were striving for a balance of values, expressed in the four puruṣārthas, 'aims of life': while it was important to acquire wealth (artha) and to enjoy life (kāma), one had to practise morality and religion (dharma) and also seek final emancipation (mokṣa) in order to lead a fulfilled life.

Religion was not separated from other aspects of life. Texts dealing with medicine or agriculture contain religious regulations and admonitions. The study of Nyāya (logic and epistemology) was undertaken to achieve mokṣa (spiritual emancipation). The notion of ātman (conscious self) was applied to humans, animals and plants. Many Indian scientists even today show an interest in religious issues, and Hindu spiritual leaders frequently draw on modern sciences to illustrate their instructions. According to the Veda, only one-quarter of Reality is accessible to the senses (which also include manas, instrumental reason). Super-sensual reality revealed itself to the ṛṣis, the composers of the Vedic *sūktas*. The *Upaniṣads* know an ascending correlation of subject/consciousness and object/reality: only the lowest of four stages (jāgarita) concerns sense perception of material objects. The three higher levels of reality are intuited through meditative introspection, which culminates in the insight: Ātman is Brahman, i.e. Spirit-Self alone is Supreme Reality. Taxila was destroyed by the Huns in the fifth century CE, Nalanda and Vikramasila by Afghans in the late thirteenth century CE.

Hindu sciences

The central ritual of Vedic culture was the yajña (sacrifice of material objects according to fixed rules). Young brāhmaṇas had to train for many years to learn to perform yajña, which involved, besides the priest and the patron, devas, the deities of earth, space and heaven, who were invited to attend. It was offered on altars built with specifically produced bricks arranged in a prescribed geometric pattern, performed at astronomically fixed times. The altar was conceived as a symbol of the human body as well as of the universe: one text relates the 360 bricks of an altar to the 360 days of the year and the 360 bones in the human body. The building of altars of different configurations, and more so their change in shape and volume, as required in certain rituals, involved a sophisticated geometry. *Śulvasūtras* (part of *Kalpasūtras*, ritual texts) provided the rules for constructing a variety of shapes of altars and their permutations. (Abraham Seidenberg, reputable historian of science and author of such groundbreaking works as *The Ritual Origin of Geometry* and *The Ritual Origin of Counting*, maintains that the Vedic *Sulvasūtras* exhibit an original algebraic geometry, older and more advanced than early Egyptian, Babylonian or Greek geometry.) The exact timing of the performance of the sacrifices was determined by those conversant with the movement of the stars. Jyotiṣa, one of the six early Vedāṅgas (auxiliary sciences of the Veda), reveals a good deal of astronomical knowledge. Astronomical knowledge of a fairly high order was required to determine the right time for the performance of Vedic yajñas. One of the Vedāṅgas, the Jyotiṣa, explains how to determine the positions of sun and moon at solstices and of the new and full moon in the circle of the twenty-seven nakṣatras.

Like geometry, other fields of Indian mathematics developed out of the requirements for the Vedic yajña. The *Yajurveda Saṃhitā* knows terms for numbers up to 1014 – by comparison the highest number named by the Greeks was myriad (104). The *Pañcaviṃśa Brāhmaṇa* has terms for 1 (eka), 10 (daśa), 100 (śata), 1,000 (sahasra), 10,000 (ayuta), 100,000 (niyuta), 1,000,000 (prayuta), 10,000,000 (arbuda), 100,000,000 (nyarbuda), 1,000,000,000 (samudra), 10,000,000,000 (madhya), 100,000,000,000 (anta) and 1,000,000,000,000 (parārdha). Later on the Indians coined terms for numbers up to 1,023 and 1,054. Algebra, in spite of its Arabic name, is an Indian invention, and so are zero and the decimal system, including the 'Arabic' numerals. The names of some great Indian mathematicians and some particulars of their accomplishments are known. Thus Aryabhata I (fifth century CE), a link in a long chain of unknown earlier master mathematicians, knew the rules for extracting square and cubic roots. He determined the value of π (i.e. pi) to four decimals and developed an alphabetical system for expressing numbers on the decimal place-value model. His *Āryabhaṭīya* was translated into Latin (from an Arabic translation) by a thirteenth-century Italian mathematician. Brahmagupta (seventh century CE) formulated a thousand years before the great European mathematician Euler (1707–83) a theorem based on indeterminate equations. Bhaskara II (twelfth century) is the author of the *Siddhānta-Śiromani*, a widely used text on algebra and geometry. Hindus have continued to show great aptitude for mathematics. Recently the South Indian mathematician Ramanujan (1887–1920), practically untutored, developed the most astounding mathematical theorems.

The *Atharvaveda* (by some considered the oldest among the four *Saṃhitās*) contains invocations relating to bodily and mental diseases. Its Upaveda, the Āyurveda, 'life-science', was cultivated systematically from early on. It was mainly oriented towards preventing diseases and healing through herbal remedies, but it also later developed other medical specialties. Good health was not only considered generally desirable, but also prized as a precondition for reaching spiritual fulfilment. Medicine as a 'charity' was widely recommended and supported by the rulers. Two Indian medical handbooks, the result of centuries of development, became famous in the ancient world far beyond India: the *Cāraka-saṃhitā* and the *Suśruta-Saṃhitā*.

Āyurveda was also applied to animals and plants. There is an ancient *Vṛksāyurveda*, a handbook for professional gardeners, and a *Gavāyuraveda* for veterinarians of cattle. Other texts deal with veterinary medicine relating to horses and elephants. Ancient India also had hospitals as well as animal clinics. Gośalas, places in which elderly cattle are provided for, are still popular in some parts of India. Āyurveda was the source of much of ancient Greek and Roman, as well as medieval Arabic, medical knowledge. The scientific value of Āyurvedic pharmacology is being recognised today by major Western pharmaceutical companies, who are applying for worldwide patents on medicinal plants discovered and described by the ancient Indian Vaidyas.

The ancient Indus Valley civilisation exhibits a high degree of architectural achievement. The well laid-out cities, the carefully built brick houses, the systems of drainage and the large water tanks reveal the work of professional town planners and builders. This tradition was continued and enhanced in later centuries, especially in connection with the building of temples to provide abodes for the deity. No village or city was deemed suitable to be inhabited without a temple. Careful selection and preparation of the building site preceded the building activity proper. The edifice had to be constructed according to an elaborate set of rules that took into account not only structural engineering and quality of materials but also the circumstances of caste and the religious affiliation of the builder. The Upaveda of Sthāpatyaveda was expanded into a professional Vāstu-śāstra and Śilpśāstra. Elaborate handbooks like the *Mānasāra* and the *Mayamata* provide detailed artistic and religious canons for the building of temples and the making of images.

The Gandharvaveda, music (vocal and instrumental) and dance, was eagerly cultivated. Both were intimately connected with the temple and temple worship. Classical Indian music developed out of Vedic chanting. The subtle laws of sound worked out by Indian musicians, the long and systematic training they had to undergo and the care they had to exercise in performing their art are notable features of the art form.

Sāṃkhya offers a general theory of evolution based on the interactive polarity of nature/matter (prakṛi) and spirit/soul (puruṣa). All reality is subsumed under five times five principles (tattvas) originating from one substratum (pradhāna), covering all possible physical, biological and psychological categories. It shows the interconnections between the various components of our world in order to unravel the evolutionary process (which is seen as the cause of all unhappiness and misery) and to return to the changeless bliss of spirit-existence. The twenty-five categories to which Sāṃkhya reduces the manifold world became widely accepted in Hindu thought. The yoga system of Patañjali is wholly based on it. The *Purāṇas* also accept it as their philosophical basis, with one amendment: prakṛti and puruṣa are overarched by Īśvara, a personal creator-maintainer-saviour God.

Vaiśeṣika, another one of the six orthodox darśanas, offers a theory of atomism more ancient than that of Democritus, and a detailed analysis of viśeṣas, qualities, differences, after which the system is called. The *Vaiśeṣikasūtras* describe the formation of physical bodies from atoms (anu) through dyads (dvyāṇuka) and triads (tryāṇuka) in a strict cause–effect series. The positioning of the atoms determines the qualities of a body. Vaiśeṣika also developed the notion of impetus – a concept that appeared in Western science only in the fourteenth century. In Vaiśeṣika the relation of science to religion is less clear than in the case of Sāṃkhya. However, the other darśana with which it has been paired, Nyāya, concerned with epistemology and logic, declares that such analysis is necessary for obtaining spiritual liberation.

Among the subjects of the ancient Indian university curriculum we find adhyātma-vidyā, the science relating to spirit. As the most important level of Reality, Brahman was the subject of the highest science, employing personal experience (anubhava), a coherent epistemology (yukti) and the exegesis of revealed utterances (śruti or śabda). The *Upaniṣads* mention thirty-two vidyās, paths leading to the goal of all science. The knowledge aimed at through these was of a particular kind, involving a transformation of the student: 'One who knows brahman becomes brahman'. The ideas of the *Upaniṣads* were further developed into the systematics of Vedānta philosophy, laid down mainly in commentaries (bhāṣyas) on the *Brahmasūtras* ascribed to Badarayana (second century BCE). From Śaṅkara (eighth century CE), through Rāmānuja (eleventh century) to Madhva (thirteenth century) the greatest minds of India have endeavoured to cultivate that science that concerns itself with the eternal reality of the spirit. Yoga too, in the form systematised by Patañjali (raja yoga), is proceeding 'scientifically' by analysing the world of experience in terms suitable for spiritual enlightenment and describing experiential steps to be taken to find enlightenment.

See also: **Acāryas; Africa, Hindus in; Aḷvārs; Americas, Hindus in; Antyeṣṭi; Āraṇyakas; Artha; Arthaśāstra; Ārtī; Āśrama(s) (stages of life); Ātman; Australasia, Hindus in; Āyurveda; Bhakti; Brahman; Brāhmaṇas; Brahmanism;**

Buddhism, relationship with Hinduism; Chandas; Cidambaram; Dalits; Dance; Deities; Dharmaśāstras; Diaspora; Dvija; Europe, Hindus in; Film; Gandharvaveda; Gandhi, Mohandas Karamchand; Gaṅgā; Gārhasthya; Guru; Himālayas; Hindu Mahasabha; Hinduism; Hindutva; Image Worship; Indo-European traditions; Indra; Indus Valley civilisation; Īśvara; Itihāsa; Jainism, relationship with Hinduism; Jāti; Jyotiṣa; Kabīr; Kalidāsa; Kalpasūtras; Kāma; Kāmāsūtra; Kāñcīpura; Karma; Languages; Madhva; Madurai; Mahābhārata; Malaviya, Pandit Madan Mohan; Manas; Mandir; Mathurā; Mokṣa; Music; Nirukta; Nyāya; Oceania, Hindus in; Orientalism; Paṇḍit; Pāṇini; Patañjali; Prakṛti; Prasāda; Pūjā; Purāṇas; Puruṣa; Puruṣārthas; Pūrva Mīmāṃsā; Rāgas; Rāja; Raja Yoga; Rāmānuja; Rāmāyaṇa; Rāmeśvara; Roy, Rammohan; Ṛṣi; Sacred Geography; Sacred Texts; Ṣaḍdarśana; Śaivism; Śāktism; Saṃhitā; Sāṃkhya; Saṃnyāsa; Saṃpradāya; Saṃsāra; Saṃskāra; Śaṅkara; Śilpaśāstras; Śiva; South-East and East Asia, Hindus in; Śulvasūtras; Sūrdās; Tamil Veda; Tantras; Tīrthayātrā; Tulsīdās(a); Upanayana; Upaniṣads; Utsava; Vaiśeṣika; Vaiṣṇavas, Śri; Vaiṣṇavism; Vānaprasthya; Vārāṇasī; Varṇa; Veda; Vedāṅgas; Vedānta; Vedic pantheon; Vedi; Vedism; Viṣṇu; Vishwa Hindu Parishad; Vivāha; Vyākaraṇa; Vyasa; Yajña; Yamunā; Yoga

KLAUS K. KLOSTERMAIER

Further reading

Basham, A.L. 1954. *The Wonder that Was India*. New York: Macmillan (numerous reprints).

Bose, D.M., S.N. Sen and B.V. Subbarayappa (eds). 1984. *A Concise History of Science in India*. New Delhi: Indian National Science Academy.

Flood, G. (ed.). 2003. *The Blackwell Companion to Hinduism*. Oxford: Blackwell Publishing.

Harle, J.C. 1987. *The Art and Architecture of the Indian Subcontinent. The Pelican History of Art*. Harmondsworth: Penguin Books.

Heimann, B. 1964. *Facets of Indian Thought*. London: Allen and Unwin.

Klostermaier, K. 1994. *A Survey of Hinduism*, 2nd edn. Albany, NY: State University of New York Press.

Majumdar, R.C. (gen. ed.). 1951ff. *The History and the Culture of the Indian People*, 11 vols. Bombay: Bharatiya Vidya Bhavan (reprints and later editions of individual volumes). *The Cultural Heritage of India*, 6 vols. Calcutta: Ramakrishna Mission Institute of Culture. Originally published 1937ff (numerous reprints of later, enlarged editions of individual volumes).

Mittal, S. and G. Thursby (eds). 2004. *The Hindu World*. New York and London: Routledge.

Pande, G.C. (ed.). 1999. *Science and Civilization in India*. Delhi: Oxford University Press

Ramanathan, V. 2004. *Hindu Civilization and the Twenty First Century*. Mumbai: Bharatiya Vidya Bhavan.

Seidenberg, A. 1983. 'The Geometry of the Vedic Rituals'. In Frits Staal, ed., *Agni: The Vedic Ritual of the Fire Altar*, vol. II. Berkeley, CA: Asian Humanities Press, 95–126.

Singhal, D.P. 1969. *India and World Civilization*, 2 vols. East Lansing, MI: Michigan State University Press.

HINDU MAHASABHA

The Hindu Mahasabha was an institution that aimed to represent the political interests of 'Hindus' in India between the 1910s and 1960s. Because of the inherent difficulty of defining the Hindu community, it attempted to encompass a very wide range of reformist and 'orthodox' institutions and movements. Although initially an umbrella forum, the Hindu Mahasabha offered a limited electoral challenge to the Congress during the system of 'dyarchy' in the 1920s. By the 1930s and 1940s, the Mahasabha was easily marginalised by the Congress in elections. Nevertheless, through its ideologies and in the nature of its leadership, it retained an important influence in Indian politics – a position which has made it one of the obvious ancestors of contemporary Hindu nationalism.

The Hindu Sabhas and Mahasabha developed in the context of an early twentieth-century colonial state, pre-occupied with defining the subcontinent by ethnographies of religious community. The first Hindu Sahaik Sabha was established in Lahore in 1906 with the vague objective of promoting broad Hindu interests. From 1909, the mood was more one of reaction to Congress' failure to promote Hindu self-assertion. The prime mover here was Lala Lal Chand, who, at the time of separate representation for Muslims in the 1909 Morley-Minto reforms, encouraged moderate communal appeals to government on behalf of the 'Hindu community'. Colonial enumeration further provoked this communal politics. The 1911 Census challenged assumptions that the Hindu community could contain India's diverse low-caste and tribal religious traditions. Hindu institutions reacted by encouraging popular enumeration: the Arya Samaj galvanised the reconversion of low-caste Muslim converts 'back' to Hinduism in the śuddhi campaigns. The national network of Hindu Sabhas – under the umbrella of the Hindu Mahasabha – was given a new urgency. At the heart of this communal politics was a fear of an apparently organised Indian Islam. But its popular scope was limited. The first all-India Hindu Sabha – the precursor to the Hindu Mahasabha – was only formed in 1915. Like its satellite organisations, it was a middle-class organisation of educated elites, little concerned with mass politics.

Partly because of these political weaknesses, the much more successful Congress movement appropriated some of the Mahasabha leadership. An important figure in this respect was Madan Mohan Malaviya, who rejuvenated the Hindu Mahasabha in 1921. The 1920s was the first decade in which the Mahasabha took an active role in local and Legislative Council elections, by extending and reorganising its institutional framework, in parallel with the Congress. The support of Swami Shraddhanand from 1923, with his movements for śuddhi and sangathan (organisation), more clearly defined the Mahasabha's trajectory. Throughout this decade it promoted a system of broad Hindu culture, highlighting cow protection, Hindi as a national language, swadeshi and service to widows and untouchables.

Although electorally very weak in most of India in the 1930s, the Hindu Mahasabha was taken seriously by the colonial state as a communal party. For example, it was present at the first Round Table Conference in 1930, represented by B.S. Moonje, Nanak Chand and N.C. Kelkar. This position of privilege was again encouraged in the 1940s as the Raj sought support in its war effort. Hindu Sabhas in some parts of India responded to the war by organising Hindu Defence Committees. But this apparent national strength was superficial and in important areas of the subcontinent it was seriously divided. In Uttar Pradesh in the early 1940s, followers of V.D. Savarkar (president of the Mahasabha from 1937), were split off from a pro-Congress group under Maheshwar Dayal Seth. Savarkar redefined the Hindu nation in his work *Hindutva* (1923), by shifting the emphasis away from religious identity and by encouraging the notion of a broad Hindu culture and 'race'.

The Mahasabha's association with extremism and social conservatism after independence led to its marginalisation in the era of Nehruvian secularism. It retained a political presence in areas where it had support from conservative nobles and princes, such as Madhya Pradesh. But more fruitful in the long term was S.P. Mookerjee's approach to Mahasabha leaders to set up a new Hindu nationalist party away from the old Mahasabha – the Bharatiya Jana Sangh in 1951, the forerunner of the Bharatiya Janata Party.

See also: **Arya Samaj; Bharatiya Janata Party; Caste; Hindutva; Jana Sangh; Malaviya, Pandit Madan Mohan; Nationalism; Politics; Sacred animals; Savarkar, Vinayat Damodar**

William Gould

Further reading

Gordon, Richard. 1975. 'The Hindu Mahasabha and the Indian National Congress, 1915 to 1926'. *Modern Asian Studies* 9(2).

Jaffrelot, Christophe. 1996. *The Hindu Nationalist Movement and Indian Politics, 1925 to the 1990s: Strategies of Identity-building, Implantation and Mobilisation (with Special Reference to Central India)*. London: Hurst.

Jones, Kenneth. 1973. *Arya Dharm: Hindu Consciousness in 19th Century Punjab.* Berkeley, CA: University of California Press.

Pandey, Gyanendra. 1992. *The Construction of Communalism in Colonial North India*. Delhi and Oxford: Oxford University Press.

Zavos, John. 2002. *The Emergence of Hindu Nationalism in India*. Delhi and Oxford: Oxford University Press.

HINDUISM

Introduction

The history of what we now call 'Hinduism' goes back to the Indus Valley, to Harappan urbanisation and culture *c.*2600–1700 BCE and to the composition of the ancient Vedic hymns compiled from about 1500 to 500 BCE. Subsequent developments, which saw the compilation of the *Upaniṣads, Dharmaśāstras*, epics and other brahmanical texts, also witnessed the rise of Buddhism, Jainism and other movements which, among other things, questioned the brāhmaṇas' authority and the validity of some of their basic teachings. Added to these developments was the rise of regional forms of religion, sectarian and devotional cults focusing on the worship of specific deities such as Viṣṇu and Śiva and other movements, some of which had little relationship with Vedic or other elite forms of religion. However, scholars are divided over the origin of Hinduism as a concept. Some argue that in the sense the term is now used, it is modern and shaped by colonialism (Frykenberg 2005; King 1999), though others regard it as pre-dating the imperial era by centuries or millennia (Lorenzen 2005; Sweetman 2005). In his survey of these arguments, Pennington endorses constructionist claims that Hinduism was a product of colonial conditions, but qualifies this by observing both that its modernity is not without religious parallel and that the concept is not discontinuous with the past (Pennington 2005: 168–72).

It soon becomes apparent that what we refer to as 'Hinduism' represents a complex interplay of beliefs and practices. Various scholars have identified and examined the apparent absence of religious unity and cohesion among Hindus in India during the pre-colonial period. Studies such as those of Nainar Jagadeesan (1997: 230–9), Heinrich von Stietencron (1995: 51–81) and Sanjay Subrahmanyam (1996: 44–80) highlight the extent of religious diversity and fragmentation that prevailed among Hindus at least up until the later stages of Mughal rule. Especially well documented is the intensity of the Vaiṣṇavite–Śaivite conflict in south India, which, it has been argued, is best envisaged as between two mutually exclusive and distinctive 'religions'. Furthermore, when Muslims made initial contact with Hindus (in the northwest in about the ninth century CE) there is little or no evidence of a Hindu–Muslim conflict along religious lines (Wink 1990: esp. 196–201). In many cases, Muslim immigrants collaborated with the locals so that any alliance system that emerged tended to cut across the foreign versus indigenous peoples division. In other words, rivalry was between class or special interest groups rather than between clearly defined religious communities.

These findings, which stress the lack of clearly demarcated religious boundaries between Hindus and Muslims during much of the pre-colonial period, are in line with other studies of intercultural and religious contact. Richard Eaton (1994: 77–82, 269–81), Susan Bayly (1989), Gyan Pandey (1992) and others suggest a picture which at the religious level is less about violent conflict and antagonism between the two so-called 'communities' and more about intermingling and peaceful accommodation. In many cases Hindus and Muslims attended the same shrines and festivals and borrowed religious rituals and ideas from each other. However, there is also evidence suggesting that, after the earlier stages of Islamic conquest and settlement, Hindus in different parts of India gradually became conscious that there were general differences between them, as 'insiders' or residents of India, and the foreigners (Oddie 2003: 155–82). This feeling is reflected not only in south Indian inscriptions (Talbot 1995: 692–722), but also in Bengali Vaiṣṇava texts of the second half of the sixteenth century (O'Connell 1993: 340–433). The latter suggests a greater Hindu awareness of material and other 'secular' lifestyle differences between themselves and Muslims – a sense of difference which extended to aspects of religion as well. A consciousness of being Hindu even in some religious or sacral sense was intensified, especially in western India, as a result of Aurangzeb's policies of discrimination against non-Muslims (Gokhale 1984: 146–73).

European perceptions of religion in India

Cultural contacts and changing European perceptions of religion in South Asia from the sixteenth to the end of the eighteenth centuries have been explored at the more general level by a range of scholars, including Marshall (1970), Schwab (1984), Halbfass (1988) and Inden (1992: 85–130). Other accounts, including those of travellers, merchants and missionaries, reporting on religious affairs in the subcontinent make it clear that they accepted the idea that there were four religions in the world – Judaism, Islam, Christianity and Paganism or Heathenism (Oddie 2006: 13–14, 39–66). Hindus, apart from 'Moors' or Muslims, were commonly referred to as 'pagans', 'idolaters', 'heathens' or 'gentiles'. However, as time progressed it became more clearly apparent that Indian forms of paganism were not necessarily the same as, for example, those in the Americas, China or other parts of the world. For this reason there was a need for a term which would encapsulate what was seen as distinctive in Indian 'paganism' or 'religion'. Terms such as Indian or Hindu religion were used and this led to the development of a less clumsy or simpler expression, 'Hindu(-ism)' or, in other words, that form of religion peculiar to the Hindus. The term 'Hinduism' emerged at least as early as the 1780s. Charles Grant, who subsequently became a director of the English East India Company, used it in correspondence with his friend Thomas Raikes in 1787 and again in his *Observations on the State of Society among Asiatic Subjects of Great Britain*, written chiefly in 1792 (Morris 1904: 110). Thereafter, terms such as Indian heathenism, paganism or idolatry continued to be used, but alongside 'Hinduism' – a term which gradually became more popular and widely accepted in Europe during the early decades of the nineteenth century.

Emergence of a dominant paradigm

A key factor in European attempts to understand and evaluate other religions was their idea of 'religion' itself (J.Z. Smith 1998: 271–72; Fitzgerald 2000: 3–33). The history and character of Christianity, and to a lesser extent that of other

Semitic religions (Judaism and Islam), provided European commentators with ideas about how to interpret and assess what they discovered in the new worlds of East and West. There were certain features seen to be prominent in Christianity, which, it was assumed, were the norm and universal in all religions. As in Christianity so in Hinduism. Christianity had its recognisable external attributes, its creeds, doctrines or statements of belief and also its philosophical treatises justifying the faith. It had its priesthood and rituals and, crucially, interpreters of sacred texts. It had the one book, the Bible, commentaries and literature. It had its own ecclesiastical structures, papacy and councils, churches, monasteries and other forms of organisation. Furthermore, in spite of divisions within, there was still a clear idea of boundaries between what was considered 'Christian' and what was not. Thus for most European observers, religions, like material objects, could be clearly differentiated from each other and, if necessary, arranged in a hierarchy, with 'true' religion' at the top while other religions (depending on the extent of their 'evils') were relegated to the ranks below.

Hinduism as Brahmanism

Influenced by their deep-seated presuppositions about the essential nature of religion, European travellers, Jesuits, Oriental scholar-administrators and Protestant missionaries all tended to adopt an elitist top-down view of Hinduism (Oddie 2006; Zupanov 1999: 1–42, 116, 145). The first thing, in their view, was to find text or texts equivalent to the Bible, the discovery of which would give Europeans an idea of Hindu belief, doctrines and teaching. In following this procedure it was seen as important to consult the custodians of religion, the priests or paṇḍitas, who, like priests, ministers and scholars in the West, were supposed to have knowledge of the essentials of the faith. This meant that Europeans usually approached brāhmaṇas and, in doing so, consolidated their textual bias and adopted an even more exclusive top-down interpretation of Indian religion and society. It was this view, sometimes known as Brahmanism, which became the dominant paradigm and for most Europeans the key to their understanding of Hinduism. Hinduism was Brahmanism, and Brahmanism was Hinduism. It was an India-wide unitary 'system' invented and controlled by the priestly and scholarly elite – a form of religion in which the lower classes had no autonomy and perhaps few independent views of their own. Conditioned and held in place through the caste system, they had no option but to submit to the tyranny and oppression of brāhmaṇa control. Forgetful of the origins of the early Jesus movement, European writers minimised the importance of oral tradition and, when faced with the phenomenon of popular religion, were usually inclined to dismiss it as an inadequate copy of 'the real thing' or simply as superstition. It was also as a result of the development of these top-down views of Indian society that many European commentators came to the conclusion that the brahmanical notion of pantheism (the belief that all, including the material universe, is God) was the key to understanding Hindu religion.

Some European critics of the dominant paradigm

The dominant paradigm, emphasising the uniform, monolithic form of Hinduism, was not without its critics as Europeans gained an increasing knowledge of India's religious activity, literature and diverse population. Among the dissidents were missionaries, Oriental scholars and especially census commissioners concerned with the beliefs and attitudes of the entire Hindu population.

First, there were increasing doubts that pantheism (linked with notions of Vedānta) was 'the essence' of the Hindu faith. Some missionaries, like Robert Caldwell, were struck by the absence of pantheistic views among the people they had most contact with in south India as well as in some parts of the north. Doubts about the extent to which pantheism was influential among Hindus were also fuelled by the Europeans' growing familiarity with Tamil and Marathi poetry and with their recognition of the importance of bhakti (Oddie 2006: 270, 283). This was the tradition of loving devotion to a personal deity – a form of worship usually based on a sense of difference between God and the individual. Indeed, missionary claims that bhakti could be considered almost as a separate religion were reinforced by Monier-Williams, who stressed its distinctiveness in his writings towards the end of the nineteenth century (Sharma 2002: 83–84). However, Monier-Williams did bring together the elements that are drawn together in later studies of Hinduism in his 1877 book *Hinduism*, which Lorenzen (2005: 59–60) identifies as 'a standard model', with an outline which contemporary scholars follow (Basham, Sen and Hopkins).

Second, there was growing recognition of the importance of regional differences. As a result of the spread and development of the Protestant missionary movement outside the main European centres of power and activity, the missionaries became increasingly aware of regional diversity and critical of works, like those of William Ward, which gave the impression that a description of Hinduism in Bengal could be applied to other parts of the subcontinent. However, other early writers, such as William Buyers, who likened Ward's correspondence in India to an inhabitant of Yorkshire being representative of Europeans in general, pointed out the anomaly in such a view (Buyers 1840: 2). An awareness of diversity, which was becoming apparent in missionary publications, is also reflected at least to some extent in non-missionary scholarly writing. For example, in his work on the religious sects of the Hindus, H.H. Wilson remarked that the term 'Hindu religion' was used to designate religious diversity (Wilson 1828: 1). Moreover, this sense of diversity was further encouraged by the introduction of the Indian census (beginning at the British India level in 1871), which emphasised regional and other differences within Hinduism.

Impetus to the same idea was also given by linguistic developments as well as by the publication of specialist regional studies of religion and society during the second half of the nineteenth century. Sir William Jones and others had espoused the idea that, apart from tribal languages, all the rest, including those of the south, were derived from Sanskrit. However, there was increasing recognition that south Indian languages, including Tamil, belonged to a separate family group. With this conviction was the growth of the idea that Tamils had evolved their own distinctive religious system as seen in Śaiva Siddhānta. Indeed, some observers, such as G.U. Pope, argued that Śaiva Siddhānta was a religion completely separate from Hinduism (Arooran 1980: 14–26; Oddie 2006: 278–9).

Third, there remained the vexed question of layers or stratification within Hinduism. Most proponents of the dominant paradigm had always recognised that there were at least two layers within Hinduism, namely elite and popular religion. The question was: were these the only levels and was there any relationship between them? Ward, Duff, James Mill and others argued that these were differences within the one gigantic system held together though brahmanical power and control. However, later scholars, including James Murray Mitchell (author of *Hinduism Past and Present*), concluded that this idea was much too simplistic. Having begun with the conventional idea of a unified system of Hinduism, he discovered bhakti, which he felt was something altogether different. Then, in later life, he suggested that Hinduism was a three-tiered system, at least in Maharashtra (for details of Mitchell's changing views, see Oddie 2006: 281–4). This type of argument continues and is reflected in discussions of 'great and little traditions' (Cohn 1971: 4–5) and in the work of the anthropologist Lawrence Babb (1975), who places some emphasis on local systems which interpenetrate with wider beliefs and practice.

Certainly among missionaries there was a growing conviction, apparent at the turn of the century, that there was no ultimate unity or coherence in Hinduism. For example, in one of its resolutions passed in 1889 the Madras Missionary Conference (a well-attended ecumenical organisation) declared that the religion of India alluded to by the term 'Hinduism' had never represented simply one religion (*Free Church of Scotland Quarterly Paper*, CXXII, March 1890). Writing in his book *New Ideas in India*, published in 1906, the Rev. John Morrison, who was teaching in Calcutta, remarked that those who study 'Hinduism' quickly discover that there is no one doctrine and no single 'canonical book' (Morrison 1906: 151).

Assumptions about the unity and coherence of Hinduism were also questioned in the census reports. In 1901 the report quoted, among others, Sir Alfred Lyall, who declared that Hinduism pertained to those who 'accept the Brahmanic Scriptures' (Risley and Gait 1903: 357). The problem with that definition was that it ignored many others who called themselves Hindus, or who were classed in the census as Hindus, but who had little or nothing to do with brāhmaṇas. Ten years later, and as if in reply to Lyall's comments, the census commissioner, referring to the Central Provinces and Bihar, noted that many do not accept the authority of the Veda or worship the 'great Hindu Gods' and are not served by brāhmaṇa priests (Gait 1913: 117). These comments are all the more striking as anti-brāhmaṇa feeling in the Central Provinces and Bihar was almost certainly not as strong as in the south.

There was not only a tendency among census commissioners to reject an all-embracing brahmanical model of Hinduism, but also a reluctance to make any statements about its coherence or common characteristics. Indeed, the technique employed was to avoid any kind of positive identification. Thus Hindus, or followers of Hinduism, were the people who remained after Muslims, Christians, Sikhs and others had been assigned to their particular categories within the census (Gait 1913: 113–14). Taking the same approach in 1921, the census commissioner explained that Hinduism had no single concept to distinguish it from other Indian religions (India Census Commissioner 1921–24: 108). The Hindu 'residuum' is a most 'heterogeneous mixture', remarked Gait in his report of 1911. He described it as encompassing monotheism, polytheism, those who worship Viṣṇu, Śiva or the Mother Goddess, while others offer blood sacrifices to their tutelary deities in contrast to those opposed to all injury (Gait 1913: 114)

Edward Said and the reinterpretation of 'Orientalism'

Linked with this issue of European responses to Hinduism are debates about 'Orientalism'. In his influential study entitled *Orientalism: Western Conceptions of the Orient*, Edward Said (1978) argued that there was a clear relationship between European power and expansion on the one hand and the way in which Europeans depicted the Orient on the other. The world, he argued, was polarised into two camps, Europe and the

Orient – the Orient being depicted by Europeans as 'the other', as the place where peoples and cultures were not only different from but inferior to those of the West. The evolution and construction of these European views, he argued, was (and still is) designed to justify European conquests and exploitation of other countries, often in the guise of their 'civilising mission'.

The term 'Orientalism' was originally used to describe the work of eighteenth- and nineteenth-century scholars and administrators who studied Oriental texts and languages and who were sympathetic to Indian and other forms of Oriental civilisation. However, as a result of Said's reassessment the term 'Orientalism' became popular, referring negatively to the West's exploitation and 'misunderstanding' of the East. This popularity, according to David Smith (2003: 89), was a result of the need for a word to sum up such an idea, but the choice was 'unfortunate'.

While there can be no doubt that Europeans have often expressed negative views of Oriental religions, there are some problems with Said's very general theory (Oddie 1994: 27–42; King 1999: 96–117; D. Smith 2003: 85–101). First, the growth of Western knowledge and depictions of the Orient was never a completely independent process free from the influence of Oriental or Asian views of the Orient. For example, Europeans writing about Hinduism in the eighteenth and nineteenth centuries often relied on the work and insights of paṇḍitas and other Indian consultants (Rocher 1994; Oddie 2006).

Second, Said tends to conflate missionary and all other European activities in the Orient with the process of colonisation. As Porter's work makes abundantly clear, this type of argument ignores the independent origin of a number of different European movements, only one of which was the drive to found and develop empires (Porter 2004). In a sweeping and somewhat simplistic argument, Said ignores the different agendas of different groups of Europeans connected with the Orient.

Third, Said's argument overlooks differences in European attitudes even during the so-called colonial era. If some Europeans thought of the Orient, including its peoples and religions, as completely 'other', this was not necessarily the case with Western missionaries (Oddie 1994: 40–41; Oddie 2006).

Fourth, Said's thesis leaves little room for changes in attitude which took place during the period of colonial rule. Outstanding examples of this are the development of more sympathetic attitudes towards Hinduism among missionaries at the turn of the century and also the positive views of Theosophists and anthropologists who lived or worked in the Orient prior to the ending of colonial rule. Lastly, Orientalist attitudes were not confined to Europeans and are clearly apparent in, for example, brahmanical representations and attitudes to untouchables and even Europeans, whom they described as mlecchas – foreigners or barbarians who were distinctly inferior (Pollock 1993: 76–133).

The Indian reaction to critical views of Hinduism

Changing theories of Hinduism as an India-wide religion have also been apparent among its Western-educated Hindu adherents. While their main concern has been to understand the Hindu tradition from their own perspective, in some cases their objective has also been to counter European arguments, to reform what is understood as Hinduism and to change it to meet their own needs or restore Indian religion to what it is thought to have been, its pristine purity. Those promoting their own models of the Hindu religion often denied that certain 'objectionable' scriptures, ideas or customs were a part of authentic tradition. The net effect was to excise carefully the corrupted parts and rearrange boundaries, reducing the extent of what was regarded as genuine Hinduism. In his writings in English, published primarily for European consumption, Rammohan Roy, for example, drew a distinction between 'the real Hindooism' and the superstitious practices that deformed 'the Hindoo religion' and that had nothing to do with 'the pure spirit of its dictates' (Oddie 2003: 162). Dayananda Saraswati, founder of the Arya Samaj, adopted a similar approach, strictly limiting what he regarded as the genuine faith. Basing his arguments on his own distinctive interpretation of the Veda, he preached a purified Hinduism – one that, as Jones has pointed out, rejected the popular *Purāṇas*, polytheism, idolatry, the role of brāhmaṇa priests, pilgrimages, nearly all rituals and the ban on widow remarriage – practically all that is commonly known as 'contemporary Hinduism' (Jones 1989: 96).

These and other early 'purist' views of Hinduism led to differences between early reformers on the one hand and some of the most influential religious and nationalist leaders of a later date. The real Hinduism was, according to Rammohan Roy and Dayananda, known and practised only by a minority of Hindus. In contrast to these views were the opinions of some of the later religious leaders, including Swami Vivekananda (1863–1902), Mahatma Gandhi (1868–1948) and leaders of the All-India Hindu Mahasabha founded in 1915 – all of whom took a more inclusive approach as to who should be included within the ranks of Hinduism. For a recent discussion of Vivekananda's policy of divorcing caste from religion and of opening up the 'treasures' of the Veda to low-caste and outcaste Hindus, see Brekke (2002).

Gandhi, like Vivekananda, reverted to the early district census definition of Hinduism as something which included both Buddhism and Jainism (Jordens 1998: 151), with Vivekananda going so far as to claim, in 1894, that apart from the 2 million Christians and 60 million Mohammedans 'all the rest' (222 million) were Hindus, according to *The Complete Works of Swami Vivekananda* (Vivekananda 1991–92: 1.331). The Hindu nationalist Hindu Mahasabha adopted much the same approach. Sikhs, Jains, Buddhists and Parsis attended the session held in Benares in 1823 (Jones 1981: 445) and later summaries of those within 'Hinduism' included not only those groups but untouchables and Hindus overseas. Furthermore, śuddhi was developed into a true conversion ritual that could, theoretically, make inclusion within the fold of Hinduism accessible to all (Jones 1981: 464–65). Thus, while prominent Hindu leaders steadily expanded the notion of 'Hindu' and 'Hinduism', the British in control of the census tended to go in the opposite direction, identifying and defining newer categories.

One reason for the increasing Hindu desire to appropriate and claim as Hindus other members of the population was the rise of nationalism. Some British officials were already arguing that, because of its religious and other divisions, India was unsuited for independence. For those who, like Gandhi, worked for the Indian National Congress and a secular state it was essential, therefore, to justify demands for self-government and unify opposition to British rule. Gandhi's focus was on the need for national and Hindu–Muslim unity rather than on the need to protect the Hindus' special interests or expand the Hindu community. He was, however, forced to defend his already enlarged and inclusive idea of Hinduism as a result of the communal award of 1932. In his view the effect of the award, which promised untouchables separate electorates and which prompted his epic fast, would have been to 'vivisect' Hinduism (Brown 1977: 313).

While Gandhi was driven to defend his view that untouchables were a part of the Hindu community, leaders of the Hindu Mahasabha such as Parmanand and Savarkar needed Hindu unity in order to stave off the threat, especially, of Muslims. The stress placed by Gandhi and other Congress nationalists on the need to unify all religious groups was replaced by the Hindu nationalists' stress on the primacy of Hindus. One of the reasons for this was a long-term sense of insecurity. There was a widespread perception that Muslims were backed by the British and would also stop at nothing in communal disturbances and in the way they treated Hindus in Muslim native states. The role of the Sabha, therefore, became increasingly to protect and defend Hindu interests. The need for unity and to preserve and increase the number of Hindus, was seen as paramount, the twin objectives of śuddhi or reconversion and sangathan or unity among all Hindus coming to symbolise the hopes as well as many of the fears of the Hindu community (Jones 1981: 455; see also the report of Lala Lajpat Rai's presidential address in Mitra 1925: 378–82) .

While Hindu religious leaders, such as Vivekananda, Savarkar and Gandhi, had much in common in their inclusive approach as to who were Hindus, their ideas of the essence or nature of Hindu religion were different. Vivekananda and Gandhi insisted on the importance of the inner process of spiritual growth rather than on something which might be defined primarily through its outward characteristics, such as doctrine, rituals, institutions and practice. In this sense, their focus and basic definitions of Hinduism and religion were very different from those of the census commissioners, missionaries and of other commentators who, when speaking of Hinduism, were influenced by the conventional enlightenment ideas of religion as an objective 'system'. Thus, for Vivekananda 'religion' in India meant 'realisation' (Vivekananda 1991–92: 3.377). 'The East', he said on another occasion, was looking 'inward' and the West 'outward' for God (ibid.: 375). The basic core of these ideas he expressed at the Parliament of Religions in Chicago in 1892. For the Hindu, he said, the diversity of religious beliefs and practices constituted simply attempts, by the soul, to 'realise the Infinite' (ibid.: 1.331). Each religion, he argued, was determined by the condition of its birth and association, and each of these marked 'a stage of progress' towards the ultimate goal (ibid.: 17) Certainly Vivekananda was not uncritical of attitudes and practice in contemporary Hinduism such as temple rituals and caste taboos and regulations (Raychaudhuri 1998: 11–15), but these things he regarded as irrelevant and sometimes harmful distractions – impediments to the attainment of the ultimate goal.

Gandhi's views, which were gradually evolved through his experience in South Africa as well as in India, were in some ways similar to those of Vivekananda, although Jordens' recent well-researched study of Gandhi's religion does not place much emphasis on Vivekananda's influence. In *Hind Swaraj*, written at the end of 1909, Gandhi declared that when he talked of 'religion' he was not referring to 'formal' or 'customary religion', but was instead referring to the fundamental impetus that informed all religions, bringing the adherents before 'their maker' (Jordens 1998: 74). Further, while in his definition of Hinduism in a lecture to Europeans in 1905, and in subsequent publications, he linked his own and Hindu views with Advaita, he also began to develop his own idea of the inner life (Jordens 1998: 69, 83). This was his view that the essence of religion is moral action, namely the action of one who 'truly adores God' and who finds fulfilment in 'the happiness of others' (Jordens 1998: 70, 84, 146). Hence, both he and Vivekananda chose to emphasise the importance of the inner journey and the individual's realisation of the presence of God – a process which it was possible for persons of any religion to achieve.

By way of contrast, Savarkar and the Hindu Mahasabha (the largest of the Hindu nationalist organisations to rival the secular-based Indian National Congress) continued to place their emphasis on externals, on an identifiable Hindu community, on category and numbers, on śuddhi and on adherence to the doctrine of the sanctity of the Hindu homeland. Like the Muslim League, Hindu nationalists demanded a religiously defined state structured on the basis of external categories, religious boundaries and a view of 'religion' remarkably similar to European views of religion in the Enlightenment.

Recent scholarly debates

The European and Indian views of Hinduism discussed above were, in many cases, the views of commentators who, far from being dispassionate, were interested in promoting a cause or special agenda. Some were practitioners promoting Hinduism, some opponents all too ready to expose its weaknesses, while others were administrators or people anxious to use it for some political or other extraneous purpose. But what of the views of modern professional scholars, those who certainly are not without prejudice but who profess some kind of commitment to objectivity?

One view of Hinduism which has long been current, and is reflected in works such as those of K.M. Sen (1961) and R.C. Zaehner (1966), is a modified view of Hinduism as Brahmanism. A top-down interpretation of Indian religion which privileges brāhmaṇa texts and philosophy, it is based on certain unquestioned assumptions about the influence of brahmanical ideas and practice. One of these assumptions is that all those who call themselves Hindus believe in reincarnation and karma and the need for mokṣa or liberation. Such a view does not take into account the belief systems and practices of popular Hinduism. Referring to beliefs among Hindus in the village he studied in Hyderabad, S.C. Dube commented that he found 'very few' who were concerned with or understood the concept of 'salvation' (Dube 1967: 91). However, bhakti and karma yoga are fitted into a comprehensive unitary model embracing all followers of Hinduism.

By way of contrast with these views, other modern scholars have proposed a variety of alternative interpretations. For example, instead of attempting to look at Hinduism as a unified system some of them argue that there are several different 'Hinduisms', or independent traditions in Hindu religion. Indeed, Heinrich von Stietencron goes as far as to suggest that Hinduism as a culture or civilisation contains a number of religions, regarding Vaiṣṇavism, Śaivism and Śāktism, comparable with Judaism, Christianity and Islam, as religions in their own right (Stietencron 2001: 33, 46–47). A different perspective proposed by Gabriella Eichinger Ferro-Luzzi is to reject the idea that concepts have to be based upon common features and clear boundaries. Instead she argues for a 'family resemblance' model of Hinduism where there are patterns of similarity but no central core (Ferro-Luzzi 2001: 294–95, 298).

Modern developments in organisation, belief and practice

Reference has already been made to the rise and development of religious reform and revival movements during the nineteenth century. Protestant missionaries in particular had a considerable impact on Hindu ideas of Hinduism and in stimulating the rise of Hindu reform and revival movements. One of the reasons for this is that the missionaries were seen increasingly as part of the imperial presence. Numerous Hindu organisations were established with the specific idea of adopting some Christian ideas and values or rejecting them altogether. Almost all were impressed with missionary forms of organisation, methods of publicity and evangelism and were determined to counteract what they saw as the threat of Christian conversion, encouraged by an evil axis of missionaries and government officials. The other major factor, helpful for higher-caste Hindus galvanised by a feeling that their entire society was under siege, was certain pro-Hindu aspects of government policy. As Robert Frykenberg (2003) and others have pointed out, British rulers not only participated in the maintenance and conduct of Hindu festivals and institutions such as maṭhas and temples but also created supra-local forms of Hindu organisation. Policies in relation to Hindu maṭhas, temples and festivals were often decided at the provincial or at the all-India level. While, therefore, some Hindus were suspicious of government motives and policy, the organisational framework and potential for state activity and outreach in modern Hinduism were greatly strengthened, not only through the imitation of missionary methods but also through the government's centralised higher-level support and management of Hindu institutions.

Alongside these developments were the increasing ability of Indians to communicate through English (which became a lingua franca), the rise of a Western-type newspaper industry with India-wide interests, a greater ease of travelling and other improvements which helped facilitate communication at a provincial and all-India level. The Western educated elites especially became better informed and more aware of the wider pro- and anti-Hindu forces (as seen, for example, in the Christian missionary movement) operating in different parts of the country and in the attitude of Europeans overseas. One consequence of these trends, in conjunction with the introduction of the Indian census, was that Hindus were becoming more self-consciously 'Hindu'. Indeed, it is quite possible that this sense of being Hindu in some vague religious sense was the chief factor, or most important common characteristic, uniting Hindus in Hinduism.

In the twentieth century Hinduism expanded rapidly overseas, especially as a result of the Indian diaspora, to countries such as Britain, Europe, Canada and the United States. New movements such as the International Society for Krishna Consciousness (ISKCON) (Gelberg 1989: 138–61) and those associated with Sathya Sai Baba (Babb 1986: 159–201) and other gurus place considerable emphasis on bhakti and inner devotion and are also inclusive in membership. They demonstrate very clearly that Hinduism is now an international movement which, in some of its manifestations, willingly embraces Europeans.

The modern nationalist interpretation of Hinduism

A final issue relating to the emergence of new forms of Hinduism is that version of it which has resulted from the deliberate reinvention of tradition – a form of religion which is now a part of the functioning ideology of Hindu nationalism. This new system can perhaps be seen as an attempt by members of the wealthy middle-class elite, including politicians, to invent a tradition which reinforces their hegemony and suits their social and economic as well as religious needs. The emphasis in recent decades has been on the uniform and monolithic nature of Hinduism. In tandem with this, Hindu nationalists have tended to look back at an 'imagined' golden age of Hinduism which is envisaged as being free from interference from 'outsiders'. A stronger insistence on what is Hinduism and what is not is combined with a stress on the primacy of selected texts or passages of scripture. The term 'Hindutva', or Hinduness, is used to distinguish between those with a legitimate claim to be included in the Hindu fold, i.e. Sikhs, Buddhists and Jains, as opposed to those who do not regard India as their sacred motherland.

According to Jaffrelot, a well-known scholar of Hindu nationalism, the mobilisation of opinion in the 1989 national election campaign involved a combination of traditional symbolism alongside the retelling of old myths and the invention of new rituals (Jaffrelott 1996: 388). One of the most powerful of these myths or symbols is Rāma (hero of the *Rāmāyaṇa*), who was put forward by Hindu nationalists as 'the angry Hindu', a national and all-India symbol of strength and power. An increasingly standardised version of local and regional variations of the *Rāmāyaṇa*, the attempt to promote Rāma as a symbol for all Hindus (and not merely for Vaiṣṇavism) and agitation for the rebuilding of the Hindu temple at Ayodhyā, the 'birthplace' of Rāma, can all be seen as recent attempts to standardise Hinduism and to provide dominant nationalist groups with symbols they can manipulate.

See also: **Advaita; Americas, Hindus in; Arya Samaj; Ayodhyā; Basham, Arthur Llewellyn; Bhakti (as path); Bhakti movement; Brāhmaṇas; Brahmanism; Buddhism, relationship with Hinduism; Caste; Dalits; Dayananda Saraswati, Swami; Dharmaśāstras; Diaspora; Europe, Hindus in; Gandhi, Mohandas Karamchand; Guru; Hindu; Hindu Mahasabha; Hinduism, history of scholarship; Hinduism, modern and contemporary; Indus Valley civilisation; International Society for Krishna Consciousness; Itihāsa; Jainism, relationship with Hinduism; Jones, Sir William; Karma (as Path); Languages; Mandir; Mokṣa; Monier-Williams, Sir Monier; Nationalism; Orientalism; Paṇḍit; Pope, George Uglow; Popular and vernacular traditions; Purāṇas; Rāma; Rāmāyaṇa; Sai Baba, Sathya; Śaiva Siddhānta; Śaivism; Śakti; Śāktism; Saṃhitā; Savarkar, Vinayat Damodar; Sikhism, relationship with Hinduism; Śiva; Temple worship; Tīrthayātrā; Upaniṣads; Utsava; Vaiṣṇavism; Veda; Vedānta; Viṣṇu; Vivekananda, Swami; Widow remarriage; Wilson, Harold Hayman**

GEOFFREY A. ODDIE

Further reading

Arooran, K.N. 1980. *Tamil Renaissance and Dravidian Nationalism, 1905–1944*. Madurai: Koodal.

Babb, Lawrence A. 1975. *The Divine Hierarchy: Popular Hinduism in Central India*. Columbia, SC: Columbia University Press.

Babb, L.A. 1986. *Redemptive Encounters. Three Modern Styles in the Hindu Tradition*. Berkeley, CA: University of California Press.

Basham, A.L. 1954. *The Wonder that Was India*. London: Sidgwick and Jackson.

Bayly, S. 1989. *Saints, Goddesses and Kings. Muslims and Christians in South Indian Society 1700–1900*. Cambridge: Cambridge University Press.

Brekke, T. 2002. *Makers of Modern Indian Religion in the Late Nineteenth Century*. Oxford: Oxford University Press.

Brown, J.M. 1977. *Gandhi and Civil Disobedience. The Mahatma in Indian Politics 1928–34*. Cambridge: Cambridge University Press.

Buyers, W. 1840. *Letters on India*. London: Snow.

Cohn, Bernard S. 1971. *India: The Social Anthropology of a Civilization*. Princeton, NJ: Prentice Hall.

Dube, S.C. 1967. *Indian Village*. Bombay: Allied Publishers.

Eaton, R.M. 1994. *The Rise of Islam and the Bengal Frontier, 1204–1760*. Delhi: Oxford University Press.

Ferro-Luzzi, Gabriella Eichinger. 2001. 'The Polythetic-Prototype Approach to Hinduism'. In Gunther-Dietz Sontheimer and Hermann Kulke, eds, *Hinduism Reconsidered*. New Delhi: Manohar, 294–304.

Fitzgerald, T. 2000. *The Ideology of Religious Studies*. New York and Oxford: Oxford University Press.

Frykenberg, Robert Eric. (ed.). 2003. *Christians and Missionaries in India. Cross Cultural Communications since 1500*. Grand Rapids, MI: William B. Eerdmans; London: RoutledgeCurzon

Frykenberg, Robert Eric. 2005. 'Constructions of Hinduism at the Nexus of History and Religion'. In J.E. Llewellyn, ed., *Defining Hinduism: A Reader*. London: Equinox, 125–46.

Gait, Edward. 1913. *Census of India 1911*, vol. 1. Calcutta: Office of the Superintendent of Government Printing, India.

Gelberg, S.J. 1989. 'Krishna and Christ: ISKCON's Encounter with Christianity in America'. In H. Coward, ed., *Hindu Christian Dialogue. Perspectives and Encounters*. Delhi: Motilal Banarsidass, 138–61.

Gokhale, Balkrishna Govind. 1984. 'Hindu Responses to the Muslim Presence in Maharashtra'. In Yohanan Friedmann, ed., *Islam in Asia*, vol. 1. Boulder, CO: Westview Press, 146–73.

Halbfass, W. 1988. *India and Europe. An Essay in Understanding*. Albany, NY: State University of New York Press.

Hopkins, Thomas J. 1971. *The Hindu Religious Tradition*. Encino, CA: Dickenson Publishing Co.

Inden, R. 1992. *Imagining India*. Cambridge, MA, and Oxford: Blackwell.

India Census Commissioner. 1921–24. *Census of India 1921*, vol. 1. Calcutta: Office of the Superintendent of Government Printing, India.

Jaffrelott, C. 1996. *The Hindu Nationalist Movement in India*. New York: Columbia University Press.

Jagadeesan, N. 1997. *History of Sri Vaishnavism in the Tamil Country (Post-Ramanuja)*. Madurai: Koodal.

Jones, K.W. 1981. 'Politicized Hinduism: The Ideology and Program of the Hindu Mahasabha'. In R.D. Baird, ed., *Religion in Modern India*. Delhi: Manohar, 447–80.

Jones, K.W. 1989. *Socio-Religious Reform Movements in British India*. Cambridge: Cambridge University Press.

Jordens, J.T.F. 1998. *Gandhi's Religion. A Homespun Shawl*. New York: St Martin's Press.

King, Richard. 1999. *Orientalism and Religion. Postcolonial Theory, India and 'the Mystic East'*. London and New York: Routledge.

Klostermaier, Klaus K. 1994. *A Survey of Hinduism*, 2nd edn. Albany, NY: State University of New York Press.

Llewellyn, J.E. (ed.). 2005. *Defining Hinduism: A Reader*. London: Equinox.

Lorenzen, David N. 2005. 'Who Invented Hinduism?' In J.E. Llewellyn, ed., *Defining Hinduism: A Reader*. London: Equinox, 52–80.

Marshall, P.J. (ed.). 1970. *The British Discovery of Hinduism in the Eighteenth Century*. Cambridge: Cambridge University Press.

Mitra, N.N. (ed.). 1925. 'All-India Hindu Mahasabha – The Presidential Address'. In *Indian Quarterly Register*, vol. 1 (January–June), 1&2: 377–86.

Morris, H. 1904. *The Life of Charles Grant*. London: John Murray.

Morrison, John. 1906. *New Ideas in India During the Nineteenth Century*. Edinburgh: George A. Morton.

O'Connell, Joseph T. 1993. 'The Word "Hindu" in Gaudiya Vaishnava Texts'. *Journal of the American Oriental Society* 93: 340–43.

Oddie, Geoffrey A. 1994. '"Orientalism" and British Protestant Missionary Constructions of India in the Nineteenth Century'. *South Asia* XVII(2): 27–42.

Oddie, Geoffrey A. 2003. 'Constructing "Hinduism": The Impact of the Protestant Missionary Movement on Hindu Self-Understanding'. In Robert Eric Frykenberg, ed., *Christians and Missionaries in India. Cross Cultural Communications since 1500*. Grand Rapids, MI: William B. Eerdmans; London: RoutledgeCurzon, 155–82.

Oddie, Geoffrey A. 2006. *'Imagined Hinduism' British Protestant Missionary Constructions of Hinduism. 1793–1900*. Delhi: Sage.

Pandey, G. 1992. *The Construction of Communalism in Colonial North India*. Delhi: Oxford University Press.

Pennington, B.K. 2005. *Was Hinduism Invented? Britons, Indians, and the Colonial Construction of Religion*. New York: Oxford University Press.

Pollock, S. 1993. 'Deep Orientalism? Notes on Sanskrit and Power Beyond the Raj'. In Carol A. Breckenridge and Peter van der Veer, eds, *Orientalism and the Postcolonial Predicament. Perspectives on South Asia*. Delhi: Oxford University Press, 76–133.

Porter, Andrew. 2004. *Religion versus Empire? British Protestant Missionaries and Overseas Expansion, 1700–1914*. Manchester and New York: Manchester University Press.

Raychaudhuri, T. 1998. 'Swami Vivekananda's Construction of Hinduism'. In W. Radice, ed., *Swami Vivekananda and the Modernization of Hinduism*. Delhi: Oxford University Press, 11–15.

Risley, Herbert Hope and Edward Gait. 1903. *Census of India 1901, vol. 1, pt 1 – Report*. Calcutta: Office of the Superintendent of Government Printing, India.

Rocher, Rosane. 1994. 'British Orientalism in the Eighteenth Century: The Dialects of Knowledge and Government'. In Carol A. Breckenridge and Peter van der Veer, eds, *Orientalism and the Postcolonial Predicament. Perspectives on South Asia*. Delhi: Oxford University Press, 215–249.

Said, Edward W. 1978. *Orientalism. Western Conceptions of the Orient*. London: Routledge and Kegan Paul.

Schwab, R. 1984. *The Oriental Renaissance. Europe's Rediscovery of India and the East, 1680–1800*. New York: Columbia University Press.

Sen, K.M. 1961. *Hinduism*. Harmondsworth, Middlesex: Penguin.

Sharma, K. 2002. *Bhakti and the Bhakti Movement*. New Delhi: Munshiram Manoharlal.

Smith, B.K. 2005. 'Questioning Authority: Constructions and Deconstructions'. In J.E. Llewellyn, ed., *Defining Hinduism: A Reader*. London: Equinox, 102–24.

Smith, D. 2003. *Hinduism and Modernity*. Malden, USA and Oxford: Blackwell.

Smith, Jonathan Z. 1998. 'Religion, Religions, Religious'. In M.C. Taylor, ed., *Critical Terms for Religious Studies*. Chicago, IL: University of Chicago Press, 269–84.

Sontheimer, Gunthur-Deitz and Hermann Kulke (eds). 2001. *Hinduism Reconsidered*. Delhi: Manohar.

Stietencron, Heinrich von. 1995. 'Religious Configurations in Pre-Muslim India and the Modern Concept of Hinduism'. In Dalmia Vasudha and Heinrich Von Stietencron, eds, *Representing Hinduism: The Construction of Religious Traditions and National Identity*. Delhi: Sage, 51–81.

Stietencron, Heinrich von. 2001. 'Hinduism: On the Proper Use of a Deceptive Term'. In Gunther-Dietz Sontheimer and Hermann Kulke, eds, *Hinduism Reconsidered*. New Delhi: Manohar, 32–53.

Subrahmanyam, Sanjay. 1996. 'Before the Leviathan: Sectarian Violence and the State in Pre-Colonial India'. In Kaushik Basu and Sanjay Subrahmanyam, eds, *Unravelling the Nation: Sectarian Conflict and India's Secular Identity*. Delhi: Penguin Books, 44–80.

Sweetman, Will. 2005. 'Unity and Plurality: Hinduism and the Religions of India in Early European Scholarship'. In J.E. Llewellyn, ed., *Defining Hinduism: A Reader*. London: Equinox, 81–98.

Talbot, Cynthia. 1995. 'Inscribing the Self: Hindu–Muslim Identities in Pre-Colonial India'. *Comparative Studies in Society and History*. 37.4: 692–722.

Thapar, Romila. 2001. 'Syndicated Hinduism'. In Gunthur-Deitz Sontheimer and Hermann Kulke, eds, *Hinduism Reconsidered*. Delhi: Manohar, 54–81.

Vivekananda, Swami. 1991–92. *The Complete Works of Swami Vivekananda*, vol. 1, 3. Mayavati memorial edn. Calcutta and Borne End: Advaita Ashrama and Ramakrishna Vedanta Centre.

Wilson, H.H. 1828. 'Sketch of the Religious Sects of the Hindus'. In *Asiatick Researches* XVI: 1–136.

Wilson, H.H. 1832. 'Sketch of the Religious Sects of the Hindus'. In *Asiatick Researches* XVII: 169–313.

Wink, A. 1990. *Al Hind. The Making of the Indo-Islamic World, vol. 1: Early Medieval India and the Expansion of Islam 7th to 11th Centuries*. Delhi: Oxford University Press.

Zaehner, R.C. 1966. *Hinduism*. London, New York and Toronto: Oxford University Press.

Zupanov, I.G. 1999. *Disputed Mission. Jesuit Experiments and Brahmanical Knowledge in Seventeenth-Century India*. New Delhi: Oxford University Press.

HINDUISM, HISTORY OF SCHOLARSHIP

In studying Hinduism, we are studying a rich and varied tradition (or, in the opinion of many, related traditions) with a heritage of serious and sophisticated self-reflection. Hindus and their religion have also been the object of others' curiosity since antiquity, and classical works such as that of Megasthenes, a Greek ambassador at the court of the Mauryas at the start of the third century BCE, served as scholarly sources until early modern times. Hence, even though there is considerable debate about the concept of Hinduism and its applicability to the premodern period, beliefs and practices now regarded as constituting Hinduism were studied and described in the medieval period by both Buddhist and Muslim writers. From the fifth century Chinese Buddhist pilgrims travelled to the 'Middle Kingdom' (i.e. India) to visit sites associated with the Buddha and to collect Buddhist scriptures. Fa-Hsien (fl. 399–418) and Hsüan-tsang (*c.*596–664) were among those who left accounts of their travels which make mention of some Hindu practices, especially caste. More detailed works were written by Muslims, among which the most notable early work is that of the central Asian scholar al-Bīrūnī (973–1051), whose account of India (*Kitāb al-Hind* [1030]; Sachau 1888) has been described as the first objective study ever made of a foreign culture. Al-Bīrūnī studied Sanskrit and translated Patañjali's *Yogasūtras* into Arabic. The presence of Islam in South Asia gave rise to a series of further works on India and its religions by Muslims, culminating in the *Ā'īn-i Akbarī* of Abū al-Fazl 'Allāmī (1551–1602), a minister at the court of the emperor Akbar (1542–1605). Some of these works also served as sources for the later study of Hinduism during what has been called the 'Persian interlude' in European Indology in the later eighteenth century, most notably the 1657 translation of the *Upaniṣads* into Persian by Dārā Shikūh (1615–59), brother of the emperor Aurangzeb (1619–1707), under the title *Sirr-i Akbar* ('The Great Secret'). In the Latin translation of A.H. Anquetil-Duperron, published in 1801–02, this was the main source of A. Schopenhauer's knowledge of the *Upaniṣads*. This entry will, however, be concerned primarily with the scholarly study of Hinduism by European writers since the early modern period.

Between the arrival of Vasco da Gama in Calicut in 1498 and the start of British colonial rule in India in 1765, the most impressive studies of Indian religions were written by clergymen, both missionaries and chaplains to the different European trading companies in India. Missionary interest in Indian religions was of course connected with interest in converting Indians. After some early success in converting mainly low-caste groups, towards the end of the sixteenth century some missionaries of the Society of Jesus (Jesuits) began to argue that a new strategy was required to overcome the resistance of high-caste Hindus to conversion. The strategy required that the missionaries 'accommodate' or 'adapt' themselves to a high-caste lifestyle so far as this was not incompatible with Christian doctrine. In practice the strategy meant changes to the missionaries' lifestyle, from their dress and diet to the adoption of Indian terms such as prasāda and pūjā for elements of Christian worship. The leading proponent of the strategy, Roberto de Nobili, argued that differences in doctrine among Hindus who shared the practices accommodated by the missionaries meant that these practices had only a social, and not a religious, significance. The strategy nevertheless gave rise to a fierce controversy which was the spur for the production of many works in the early seventeenth century which provided accounts of Hindu beliefs and practices in the context of arguments for or against the strategy. Some of these works, particularly those of de Nobili himself, were based upon a thorough knowledge of Indian languages and reveal an advanced understanding of Hindu traditions. Although few were published, the circulation of such works in manuscript contributed to the development of Jesuit knowledge of these traditions which in turn made possible some outstanding later works. Other missionary works on Hinduism from this period were drawn upon, usually without acknowledgement, in works published by other authors. The most notable example is the work of Augustinian friar Agostinho de Azevedo, on which Diogo do Couto (1542?–1616) based his account of Hindu religious beliefs and practices in the fifth of his *Décadas da Ásia* (1612). An exception among the predominantly clerical authors of this period is François Bernier (1620–88), whose work, unlike that of other travel writers, was based on an extended stay of ten years in India.

Among Protestants, the English and Dutch chaplains Henry Lord (dates unknown, fl. 1620–30) and Abraham Roger (d. 1649), produced books which, unlike more general works which included descriptions of India's religions alongside descriptions of its geography, economy, flora and fauna, take the religions of India as their primary subject. Both Lord's *A Display of Two Forraigne Sects in the East Indies* (1630) and Roger's *De Open-Deure tot het Verborgen Heydendom* (The Open Door to Hitherto Concealed Heathenism, 1651) give accounts of regional (respectively, Gujarati and Tamil) traditions, which are based not on first-hand knowledge of Indian languages but on observation and discussions with informants. The first Protestant author to produce work of a standard comparable to that of the Jesuits is the German Pietist Bartholomäus Ziegenbalg (1682–1719). A missionary in the Danish enclave of Tranquebar, on the south-east coast of India, Ziegenbalg wrote two major and numerous smaller works, which drew on his extensive knowledge of Tamil religious literature. His works, especially his last work, the *Genealogie der malabarischen Götter* (Genealogy of Malabarian Gods, 1713), are notable for his insistence that Hindus, despite their many images of different gods, are essentially monotheists. Although neither of his major works on Hinduism was published in the form he wrote it until the twentieth century, both works were known to and used by a variety of writers during the eighteenth and nineteenth centuries. The first writer to use Ziegenbalg's works was a French Protestant convert, Mathurin Veyssière de La Croze (1661–1739), who included extensive extracts from Ziegenbalg's manuscripts in his *Histoire du christianisme des Indes* (1724). La Croze exemplifies the polemic strategy known as 'paganopapism', the identification of parallels between non-Christian religions and Roman Catholicism in order to discredit the latter. Toward the end of the eighteenth century, an edition of the *Genealogie* appeared anonymously under the title *Beschreibung der Religion und heiligen Gebräuche der malabarischen Hindous* (Description of the Religion and Sacred Customs of the Malabarian Hindus, 1791) which, in the alterations to Ziegenbalg's text, reflected the Enlightenment ideal of an objective account of other religions. Accounts by Ziegenbalg and many of his successors in the Tranquebar mission reached European audiences more directly in the form of the *Hallesche Berichte* (1710–72), a series of reports from the mission published throughout the eighteenth century from Halle in Germany.

During the eighteenth century Jesuit authors continued to produce works of outstanding quality on Indian religions, some of which continued to be motivated by the debate over accommodation, which continued even after the pope ruled against the strategy in 1744. Many of these took the form of letters published in the long-running series *Lettres édifiantes et curieuses* (1702–76). As in the previous century, other Jesuit works were published in encyclopaedic works or collections of travel writing. Thus, for example, Jean Venant Bouchet's *Relation des erreurs qui se trouvent dans la religion des gentils malabars* (Account of the Errors Found in the Religion of the Malabar Gentiles) appeared in 1723 in Bernard Picart's *Cérémonies et coutumes religieuses de tous les peuples du monde* under the title 'Dissertation historique sur les dieux des indiens orientaux'. The two most significant results were, however, not to appear until after the dissolution of the Society of Jesus in 1773.

The first of these is the *Moeurs et coutumes des indiens* of Gaston-Laurent Coeurdoux, which in many ways represents the culmination of more than two centuries' Jesuit study of Hinduism. Completed by 1777, Coeurdoux's work was again not published directly but served as the primary source for Jean-Antoine Dubois' *Hindu Manners, Customs and Ceremonies*, first published under the auspices of the English East India Company in 1816, and republished to wide acclaim several times during the nineteenth century. The other work is the *Ezour-Vedam* (1778), which purported to be a translation from Sanskrit of an ancient commentary on the Veda, but was in fact a work of Christian apologetics perhaps best understood as a continuation of the idea of 'adapting' Christianity to an Indian context. Although a copy of the *Ṛgveda Saṃhitā,* obtained by the Jesuit Jean Calmette, had been received in Paris in 1731, it remained unread, and the *Ezour-Vedam* was received enthusiastically as offering for the first time a detailed account of the content of the Veda, which had long been reported to contain the most ancient, and therefore the purest, doctrines of Hinduism. Particularly enthusiastic were critics of Christianity, such as Voltaire, who saw the work as disproving the uniqueness of Christianity. Doubts about the provenance of the work surfaced as early as 1782, and by the early eighteenth century it had become, for critics of the Jesuits, a prime example of their duplicity. The authorship of the work remains uncertain; nevertheless, the predominance of Jesuits among the likely candidates for a work which, whatever its motive, demanded considerable knowledge of Indian religious texts, is testament to the depth and breadth of Jesuit knowledge of Hindu belief and practice in the eighteenth century.

As the balance of power in India shifted increasingly toward the British in the later eighteenth century, so accounts of Hinduism by British authors began to predominate. Mid-eighteenth-century British works such as those of J.Z. Holwell and Alexander Dow are very much the work of amateur gentlemen scholars and appear, even by the standards of their time, somewhat eccentric. Holwell was proud to call himself a 'Christian Deist', and he found in Hinduism confirmation of the Deist position, set out most influentially by the English diplomat Edward Herbert (1583–1648; from 1629 Lord Herbert of Cherbury), that all religions of the world shared certain 'common notions' concerning the existence of God, our religious and moral obligations and life after death. Holwell expanded Herbert's five common notions to fourteen, introducing a series of claims about the fall of angelic beings which allowed him to identify a belief in reincarnation as one of the 'primitive truths' common to all religions. Since at least the early seventeenth century, evidence of Hindu belief in reincarnation, together with the practice of vegetarianism, which was thought to arise from it, had given rise to speculation about connections between Egyptian, Indian and Greek religious beliefs, much of which centred on the figure of Pythagoras. If most writers attributed the source of these ideas to Egypt, Holwell was not alone in arguing that the Egyptians had 'stolen' the idea of reincarnation from the Hindus, along with the other 'common notions': the doctrines of 'the unity of the Godhead, the immortality of the soul, a general and particular

Providence, and a future state of rewards and punishments' (Holwell 1765–71: 1.16).

Dow was a soldier in the East India Company's Bengal Army from 1760 until his death in 1779, and therefore experienced at first hand the origins of British colonial rule when the Company was granted the diwani of Bengal and Bihar in 1765. In 'A Dissertation Concerning the Origin and Nature of Despotism in Hindostan', published in the second edition of his *History of Hindustan* (1772), he argued that in their ready acceptance of hierarchy Hindus were predisposed by their religion to accept 'the government of foreign lords' (Dow 1772: xxxv). This idea, which can be found in various forms in the writings of Western writers as far back as Aristotle, was developed by Karl Marx (1818–83) into a full-blown theory of 'Oriental despotism'. While few writers went as far as Dow in using images of 'mild', 'obedient' and 'effeminate' Hindus to justify colonial domination, the connection between colonial rule and the study of Hinduism by British writers in the next several decades is undeniable. One exception to the predominance of British authors in the later eighteenth century is A.H. Anquetil-Duperron, a Frenchman who was the first European to travel to India primarily in order to study its religions and who, perhaps not coincidentally, became increasingly critical of British colonial rule.

Many of the works which were to appear toward the end of the eighteenth century and at the start of the nineteenth were sponsored by the East India Company and some were explicitly intended to serve its needs. The first of these is the compilation from the *Dharmaśāstras* drawn up in Persian by eleven paṇḍits at the request of Warren Hastings (1732–1818), governor-general of Bengal, who commissioned Nathaniel Halhed (1751–1830) to translate the work into English (*A Code of Gentoo Laws*, 1776). The need for such a work arose from the Company's policy of governing Hindus and Muslims, so far as possible, in accordance with their existing laws. Halhed included in his preface an extract from the *Bṛhadāraṇyaka Upaniṣad*, translated from Dārā Shikūh's Persian translation of the *Upaniṣads*, which he later translated in full but never published. Like Holwell, and to much criticism, Halhed argued for the great antiquity of Hinduism.

The East India Company also sponsored the first published direct translation from Sanskrit of an Indian religious work: Charles Wilkins' translation of the *Bhagavadgītā*, arguably chosen not so much for its importance to Hindus as for its adaptability to the deistic inclinations of those involved in the production of the translation. Both the relevance of this work to the colonial rulers of Bengal and their wider cosmopolitan and enlightened aspirations are spelt out by Hastings in a widely quoted letter which was prefixed to the translation: 'Every accumulation of knowledge, and especially such as is obtained by social communication with people over whom we exercise a dominion founded on the right of conquest, is useful to the state: it is the gain of humanity' (Hastings in Wilkins 1785: 13). The cosmopolitan inclinations of the group around Hastings, expressed in Hastings' letter as the belief that the world 'in respect of the general diffusion and common participation of arts and sciences may be considered as one community' (Hastings in Wilkins 1785: 7), were reinforced by William Jones' argument that the similarity between Sanskrit and Latin could only be explained by their having had a common source. Jones was not the first to have noticed the similarity, but his discussion of it stimulated a series of developments which were to have a profound impact on European study of Hinduism in the nineteenth century and beyond.

Jones was the first president and leading light of the Asiatick Society (later

Asiatic Society of Bengal), founded in 1784 for the study of 'the history, civil and natural, the antiquities, arts, sciences and literature of Asia'. In addition to his translations of the *Manusmṛti* (*Institutes of Hindu Law, or, the Ordinances of Menu*, 1794) and other Sanskrit works (including the *Gītagovinda*, the *Īśa Upaniṣad* and some works of Kālidāsa), Jones' annual discourses to the society, later published in its journal *Asiatick Researches*, did much to shape Europe's view of Hinduism. Jones' work reflects both the profound Indophilia of many scholars connected with the Asiatic Society and the concern to integrate what was learnt of Hinduism with a biblical chronology of humankind. The widely shared perception among British scholars that Hinduism was a religion much in decline from a glorious past was expressed by Jones when he wrote that 'how degenerate and abased so ever the Hindus may now appear ... in some early age they were splendid in arts and arms, happy in government, wise in legislation, and eminent in various knowledge' (Jones 1807: 3.82). The most distinguished among Jones' successors as President of the Asiatick Society was H.T. Colebrooke (1765–1837), who, after his return to Europe, also founded the Royal Asiatic Society of Great Britain and Ireland. His essay 'On the Vedas' (first published in *Asiatick Researches* in 1805) was the first detailed scholarly account of them by a European scholar, and his later essays on the philosophy of the Hindus remained, in the view of Wilhelm Halbfass, unrivalled for much of the century (Halbfass 1988: 84).

Although important work on Hinduism continued to be produced in India throughout the nineteenth century, already in the early decades of the century it can be seen that the centre of gravity of the European study of Hinduism is beginning to shift from India to Europe. Among the factors which contributed to this, the most important are changes in colonial attitude and policy toward India and Indology and the gradual accumulation in Europe's libraries and universities of Indian, especially Sanskrit, texts and expertise in reading them. As the British consolidated their power in India – the Marathas, the last significant force able to oppose them, were defeated in 1818 – the Indophilia of Hastings and the circle around him, with its emphasis on understanding Indian languages and culture, gave way to a more aggressive assertion of European intellectual, cultural and religious superiority. Representative of this trend is James Mills' *History of British India* (1817), which included a long essay on the Hindus. Although an employee of the East India Company, Mill never visited India and knew no Indian languages. Drawing on theories of the progressive development of civilisation common among writers of the Scottish Enlightenment, Mill allocated India and Hinduism to an early and relatively unsophisticated stage in the development of human civilisation. Throughout the *History* Mill conducted a sustained attack on the legacy of Hastings, Jones and other 'Orientalists' who had stressed the importance of knowledge, and even love, of Indian language and culture among those who sought to rule India. Mill's work influenced those (known as 'Anglicists') who argued that instead of supporting the study of India, the East India Company should devote its efforts to educating Indians in English and in 'European' sciences. In a rearguard action, long after the Orientalists had lost the battle, H.H. Wilson published a fifth edition (Mill 1858) of Mill's work, seeking in his preface and footnotes to counter the tendency of the work which he described bluntly as evil.

The same period saw a general hardening of attitudes towards Hinduism, especially, perhaps, on the part of missionaries. Indicative of this is the campaign against sati, which was eventually banned in British India in 1829. While accounts of sati had been a staple feature of accounts of Hinduism at all levels of sophistication since classical times, earlier accounts had often mixed admiration for the fortitude and devotion of Hindu widows (often in contrast to the cowardice of their menfolk) with disgust at the brutality of their fate and the religion which ordained it. The difference in tone between Colebrooke's scholarly account 'On the Duties of a Faithful Hindu Widow' in 1795 and the outraged account of the 'Burning of Widows Alive' by the missionary William Ward (1769–1823) in his multi-volume *A View of the History, Literature and Mythology of the Hindoos* (1817–20) is perhaps evident from their titles alone. Missionary contempt for Hinduism may not be unrelated to the reluctance (surprising to those who perceived Hinduism as a 'primitive' religion) of Hindus to convert. Despite such contempt and the resultant tendency to focus on the grotesque, it is arguable that missionaries gave a fuller picture of Hinduism than scholars who represented Hinduism on the basis of the texts of the literate elite, ignoring what they regarded as the later corruption of an originally pure tradition.

In the early decades of the nineteenth century the study of India began to find an institutional footing in Europe for the first time, with the establishment of the first chair of Sanskrit in Europe, at the Collège de France, in 1815 (first held by Antoine-Léonard de Chézy (1775–1832)) and the foundation of the Société Asiatique de Paris in 1822 and the Royal Asiatic Society in London in 1824. By virtue of its location in Europe, such study was bound to be almost exclusively textual, and, while it was to lead, later in the century, to lasting monuments in the European study of Hinduism such as critical editions of the *Ṛgveda* (1849–74 and 1861–63) and the massive translation project *Sacred Books of the East* (1879–1910) under the editorship of F. Max Müller, the image of Hinduism which emerged from such studies was inevitably partial. The early nineteenth century was also the period in which Hinduism, and India more generally, briefly caught the attention of philosophers of the first rank. Among these are Friedrich von Schlegel, brother of the Indologist August Wilhelm Schlegel (1767–1845), and G.W.F. Hegel. Schlegel studied Sanskrit in Paris and his work *Über die Sprache und Weisheit der Indier* (On the Language and Wisdom of the Indians, 1808) reflects both the Romantic enthusiasm for India as the cradle of humanity (inspired in part by the evidence in British works of linguistic links with Europe and the idea of a 'golden age') and the gradual waning of that enthusiasm. For Hegel, Hinduism demanded attention less for itself than because of the universalistic pretensions of his philosophy; as a result his work, although influential, cannot be considered to have contributed directly to the advancement of European understanding of Hinduism.

In India in the later nineteenth century, an important motivation for the study of Hinduism remained the pragmatic requirement that the colonial state understand those it sought to rule. This was particularly the case after the 1857 'Mutiny', which many Europeans attributed to their failure to understand the 'religious prejudices' of the Indians. As part of the reorganisation of government after the abolition of the East India Company in 1858, attempts were made to organise and systematise knowledge of different Indian religious and ethnic groups, and especially of customs related to caste, alongside and on the same model (if not the same budget) as other forms of imperial knowledge of India, such as the Survey of India, which sought to produce high-quality accurate maps of the whole of India. Although regional surveys and gazetteers had been produced from the beginnings of British rule in India, often on the model of earlier Mughal works, from the 1860s efforts were made to standardise the categories used in such surveys and to coordinate them with those used in the censuses of India carried out every ten years from 1871. The inevitable difficulties in using standardised categories for castes which differed from region to region resulted in the production of prose reports on the religious beliefs and practices of different groups to supplement the statistical data. The culmination of these efforts was the vast 119-volume *Imperial Gazetteer of India* (1907–09) and its ethnographic counterpart, Herbert Risley's *The People of India* (1908). Risley (1851–1911) was Commissioner for the 1901 Census and subsequently director of the Ethnological Survey of India. Risley's true passion, however, lay in anthropometry and racial science. For Risley, India was the perfect place to test racial theories because caste restrictions on marriage had preserved racial characteristics which had elsewhere been lost through racial mixture. Risley used his office to gather measurements of the heads of members of different castes, from which could be calculated a 'nasal index' which would allow a precise determination of the origins of each caste in terms of seven racial 'types' and the formulation of general laws. The background to Risley's thinking is Aryan race theory, which, from its beginnings in the identification of the link between Sanskrit and Latin, had become during the course of the nineteenth century a key piece of evidence in the reconstruction of the early history of India. This theory postulated that the Veda had been brought to India by a Sanskrit-speaking race who called themselves ārya, conquering the darker-skinned inhabitants of India and imposing the caste system upon them. Expressions of this theory varied to some degree, but it was widely used to explain the diversity of Hindu religious belief and practice. In its cruder forms, it was used to explain the degeneration of Hinduism from its original purity. While the idea of lighter-skinned, civilising conquerors had an obvious appeal to the British as a precedent for their actions in India, the theory was not without appeal to Indians, both to those who saw it as an opportunity to claim kinship with their 'Aryan brothers' and to those who wished to use it to expose the illegitimacy of both brahmanical and British dominance.

New evidence was introduced to this debate in the 1920s by the archaeological excavation of an ancient civilisation in the Indus Valley, which had flourished around 2500 BCE prior to both the date accepted by most scholars for most of the material in the Veda and the postulated Aryan invasion of India. The interpretation of this civilisation remains contested, the most serious difficulty being that no one has yet been able to decipher the script found on many of its artefacts in a way that would command consensus among scholars.

In the twentieth century new explanatory frameworks emerged in the attempt to understand the interaction between the tradition embodied in the Sanskrit texts of Hinduism and the variety of everyday Hinduism. In 1952 the sociologist M.N. Srinivas coined the term 'Sanskritisation' to describe the process by which low castes had improved their status by becoming vegetarian and teetotal and by adopting, so far as possible, the customs, rites and beliefs of the locally dominant caste, often but not always the brāhmaṇas. While this process is by no means only recent, Srinivas argued that the introduction of Western technology and political forms had accelerated the spread of Sanskrit norms. Borrowing terms from Robert Redfield, Milton Singer characterised this process as one of the ways in which the 'great tradition' of Sanskritic Hinduism interacted with the 'little tradition', or traditions, of vernacular Hinduism.

Subsequent scholars have refined this analysis, pointing out that this is not a one-way process and the many different regional Hindu traditions in India have exerted an influence on the Sanskritic tradition that need not always be understood pejoratively as the degeneration of that tradition.

The period following Indian independence in 1947 saw an increase in anthropological studies of particular communities, often village communities. While such studies usually included discussion of the role of religious values and practices, they were not typically concerned to understand these within the wider context of historic and contemporary Hinduism. Louis Dumont attempted to bring together the insights of classical, textual and anthropological fieldwork, including his own study of a South Indian subcaste, in a book on the caste system, *Homo Hierarchicus* (1966; English translation 1970). T.N. Madan has commented that almost all recent sociologists of India have been influenced by, even if they have not agreed with, his approach (Madan 1999: 475).

Friedhelm Hardy (1990: 148–49) has suggested that in the second half of the twentieth century significant advances in understanding Hinduism, especially regional traditions and individual monotheistic traditions, have resulted from the study of Hindu theology. Following pioneering work in the first decades of the twentieth century by H.W. Schomerus (1879–1945) on Śaiva Siddhānta and Rudolf Otto on Vaiṣṇavism, and supported by the production of critical editions and English translations of the *Purāṇas* and other post-Vedic scriptures, the history and theology of many of these traditions have been examined in a series of works, including, for example, Hardy's own work on the Sri Vaiṣṇavas, and A.K. Ramanujan's work on the Vīraśāivas. Following the emergence of gender as an important analytical category, feminist scholars in particular have been interested in the theology of the Hindu goddesses and in the effects of idealised representations of the feminine in the lives of Hindu women. The scholarly study of Hindu Tantra, initiated by John Woodroffe in the early years of the century, has been taken further by both textual scholars and those who are initiates of the tradition they study.

Although the focus of Edward Said's *Orientalism* (1979) was the representation, especially in literary works since the nineteenth century, of Islam and the Middle East, his suggestion that imperialism enabled and was enabled by the study of Asian cultures was quickly applied in other contexts, including the study of Hinduism. As well as forcing a re-evaluation of much of the work mentioned above, Said's conception of Orientalism has led to examination of the role of colonial interests in the formation of religious identities, above all in the conception of Hinduism itself. A number of scholars, notably R.E. Frykenberg (1991) and Heinrich von Stietencron (1991), have argued that the term represents the imposition by European scholars of an artificial conceptual unity onto diverse traditions which are better understood as separate religions. This, in turn, has provoked further controversy, with some scholars arguing that, though the term Hinduism is recent and is Western in origin, the concept of a single pan-Indian religion may be found earlier in both European and Indian sources (e.g. Lorenzen 1999; Sharma 2002) and the term itself is in use as early as 1787 (Oddie 2003: 156–57). It would not be an exaggeration to suggest that this debate has dominated scholarship for some time, not least because it raises issues about the provenance of religion itself (e.g. W.C. Smith 1978). Scholars (e.g. Staal 1982; Fitzgerald 2000) have denied the applicability and usefulness in India, or in Asia more generally, of the term 'religion' at all, arguing that it presupposes a distinction between the religious and the non-religious which, while characteristic of modern Western thought, is not found in traditional Indian thought. Notwithstanding, efforts have been made both to defend Hinduism as a religion (e.g. Ferro-Luzzi 1991) and to criticise the premises on which Hinduism may be denied this status (e.g. Sweetman 2003). In this respect, disagreements about the nature of Hinduism reflect wider disagreements within the study of religions about the category of religion itself (e.g. J.Z. Smith 1982).

See also: **Anquetil-Duperron, Abraham-Hyacinthe; Asiatic Societies; Asiatick Researches; Bhagavadgītā; Coeurdoux, Gaston-Laurent; Colebrooke, Henry Thomas; Dharmaśāstras; Dow, Alexander; Dubois, Jean-Antoine; Dumont, Louis; Gītagovinda; Halbfass, Wilhelm; Hallesche Berichte; Hegel, Georg Wilhelm Friedrich; Hinduism; Holwell, John Zephaniah; Indus Valley Civilisation; Jones, Sir William; Kālidasā; Lettres édifiantes et curieuses; Müller, Friedrich Max; Nobili, Roberto de; Orientalism; Otto, Rudolf; Patañjali; Pūjā; Purāṇas; Ramanujan, Attipat Krishnaswami; Sacred Books of the East; Śaiva Siddhānta; Saṃhitā; Schlegel, (Karl Wilhelm) Friedrich von; Schopenhauer, Arthur; Srinivas, Mysore Narasimhachar; Tantras; Upaniṣads; Vaiṣṇavas, Śrī; Vaiṣṇavism; Veda; Wilson, Harold Hayman; Woodroffe, John; Yogasūtras**

WILL SWEETMAN

Further reading

Béteille, A. 1996. 'Caste in Contemporary India'. In C.J. Fuller, ed., *Caste Today*. Oxford: Oxford University Press, 150–79.

Dow, Alexander. 1772. 'A Dissertation Concerning the Origin and Nature of Despotism in Hindostan'. In *History of Hindustan*, 2nd edn. London: T. Becket and P.A. De Hondt.

Ferro-Luzzi, G.E. 1991. 'The Polythetic–Prototype Approach to Hinduism'. In G.-D. Sontheimer and H. Kulke, eds, *Hinduism Reconsidered*. Delhi: Manohar, 187–95.

Fitzgerald, Timothy. 2000. *The Ideology of Religious Studies*. Oxford: Oxford University Press.

Frykenberg, Robert E. 1991. 'The Emergence of Modern "Hinduism" as a Concept and an Institution: A Reappraisal with Special Reference to South India'. In G.-D. Sontheimer and H. Kulke, eds, *Hinduism Reconsidered*. Delhi: Manohar, 29–49.

Halbfass, W. 1988. *India and Europe: An Essay in Understanding*. Albany, NY: State University of New York Press.

Hardy, F. 1990. 'Turning Points in the Study of Indian Religions: Hinduism'. In U. King, ed., *Turning Points in Religious Studies: Essays in Honour of Geoffrey Parrinder*. Edinburgh: T. & T. Clark, 145–55.

Holwell, J.Z. 1765–71. *Interesting Historical Events, Relative to the Provinces of Bengal and the Empire of Indostan*, 3 vols. London: Printed for T. Becket and P.A. Hondt.

Jones, W. 1807. *The Works of Sir William Jones. – With a Life of the Author, by Lord Teignmouth*, vol. 3. London: Printed for John Stockdale & John Walter, 24–46.

Kejariwal, O.P. 1988. *The Asiatic Society of Bengal: and the Discovery of India's Past 1784–1838*. Delhi: Oxford University Press.

Kopf, D. 1969. *British Orientalism and the Bengal Renaissance: The Dynamics of Indian Modernization, 1773–1835*. Berkeley, CA: University of California Press.

Lorenzen, D.N. 1999. 'Who Invented Hinduism?' *Comparative Studies in Society and History* 41.4: 630–59.

Madan, T.N. 1999. 'Louis Dumont (1911–1998): A Memoir'. *Contributions to Indian Sociology* 33: 473–502.

Marshall, P.J. (ed). 1970. *The British Discovery of Hinduism in the Eighteenth Century*. Cambridge: Cambridge University Press.

Mill, J. 1817. *The History of British India*, 3 vols. London: Baldwin, Craddock & Jay.

Mill, J. 1858. *The History of British India (with Notes and Continuation by H.H. Wilson)*, 10 vols. London: James Madden.

Müller, F. Max. 1878. *Lectures on the Origin and Growth of Religion as Illustrated by the Religions of India*. London: Williams and Norgate.

Oddie, G.A. 2003. 'Constructing Hinduism: The Impact of the Protestant Missionary Movement on Hindu Self-Understanding'. In R.E. Frykenberg, ed., *Christians and Missionaries in India: Cross-Cultural Communication since 1500*. Richmond: Curzon, 155–82.

Sachau, E.C. 1888. *Alberuni's India: An Account of the Religion, Philosophy, Literature, Geography, Chronology, Astronomy, Customs, Laws and Astrology of India about AD 1030*. London: Trübner.

Schwab, Raymond. 1984. [1950] *The Oriental Renaissance*. Trans. G. Patterson-Black and Victor Reinking. New York: Columbia University Press.

Sharma, A. 2002. 'On Hindu, Hindustān, Hinduism, Hindutva'. *Numen* 49.1: 1–36.

Sharpe, E.J. 2003. 'The Study of Hinduism: The Setting'. In A. Sharma, ed., *The Study of Hinduism*. Colombia, SC: University of South Carolina Press, 20–55.

Smith, J.Z. 1982. *Imagining Religion: From Babylon to Jonestown*. Chicago, IL and London: University of Chicago Press.

Smith, W.C. 1978. *The Meaning and End of Religion*. London: SPCK.

Staal, Frits. 1982. 'The Himalayas and the Fall of Religion'. In D.E. Klimberg-Salter, ed., *The Silk Route and the Diamond Path: Esoteric Buddhist Art on the Trans-Himalayan Trade Routes*. Los Angeles, CA: UCLA Art Council, 38–51.

Stietencron, Heinrich von. 1991. 'Hinduism: On the Proper Use of a Deceptive Term'. In G.-D. Sontheimer and H. Kulke, eds, *Hinduism Reconsidered*. Delhi: Manohar, 11–27.

Sweetman, W. 2003. '"Hinduism" and the History of "Religion": Protestant Presuppositions in the Critique of the Concept of Hinduism'. *Method & Theory in the Study of Religion* 15.4: 329–53.

Trautmann, T.R. 1997. *Aryans and British India*. Berkeley, CA: University of California Press.

Wilkins, C. 1785. *The Bhăgvăt-Gēētā or Dialogues of Krēēshnă and Ărjōōn In Eighteen Lectures; With Notes*. London: C. Nourse.

HINDUISM, MODERN AND CONTEMPORARY

This article will examine the development of Hindu traditions during the modern and contemporary period. This is of course a period of dramatic global change, and it is no surprise to note that Hindu traditions, like other traditions, have developed and been transformed in quite startling ways. The entry seeks to make sense of these developments by putting them in the broader contexts of historical process and social change. It also seeks to explore the meaning of some terms which have become common currency in the context of modern Hindu traditions: terms such as reform, revival, renaissance, neo-Hinduism and, indeed, Hinduism itself. We need to be careful when we use these terms, as they have emerged in contexts of political contestation and sometimes reflect the influence of particular relations of power. Exploring their meaning is one way of understanding how such relations of power operate.

Locating the modern

Although there has been plenty written on particular movements, figures and themes of modern Hinduism (see, for instance, Beckerlegge 2000; Dalmia and von Steitencron 1995; Kaviraj 1995), there is rather less available on the idea of modern Hinduism and how it has emerged (although the issue has recently been addressed to some extent in Smith 2003). This is partly because it is difficult to encompass the complexity of changes during this period.

It may also be because it is difficult, and indeed controversial, to locate the period of modernity. A traditional approach is to mark the beginning of modernity in India as the beginning of British colonial domination over the subcontinent. There are several problems with this approach. In the first instance, it gives the impression that the British arrived in India and assumed control in a straightforward fashion, with a clearly delineated policy of modernisation. In reality, the British domination of India was a slow and uneven development – variously felt in the economic, military and political spaces of subcontinental life over a period of more than two centuries – before the assumption of crown control in 1858. Prior to this date, control was exerted in the name of a commercial trading company, the East India Company. The Company grew in power through a series of micro-level strategies, rather than any grand plan of ruling the whole region. These strategies were often geared towards enabling the British to merge into the landscape, disrupting the values and perspectives of social and political life in the locality as little as possible. This policy of non-interference would, it was assumed, enable the Company to trade effectively in a region where vast profits were to be made. In this perspective, the image of the British 'bringing modernity' to India in the late eighteenth century must be modified, as the historical processes associated with colonial control were by no means clear cut.

In addition, we need to be wary of any image of 'Western' modernity contrasted with 'Eastern' tradition. This is a classic polarisation or 'othering', which we may associate with Edward Said's notion of Orientalism (1995). As a structure of knowledge, Orientalism imputes inverse qualities to the 'non-West' as a means of affirming the progressive qualities of the post-Enlightenment West. In this formulation, the image of the modernising, progressive force of British colonialism imputes an image of stagnancy and regression to the subcontinent. This enormously powerful image has in recent years been countered by significant historical work on the late Mughal period (e.g. Eaton 2000) and the eighteenth century (e.g. C.A. Bayly 1990), in which processes of social mobility and change have been emphasised. This work suggests that the East India Company became part of a more general social and economic dynamism during this period. The Company, then, may be seen as a feature of processes of modernisation in which local economies were becoming more clearly integrated into a developing world system of economic interactions.

This points us towards a concept that may indeed help us to pin down the beginning of the 'modern period' as it impacts on Hinduism. This concept is globalisation. If we define globalisation as an ongoing process of the integration of worldwide markets, with all the social and cultural interactions which are implied by this, then we are beginning to ground the idea of the modern period in a useful analytical context.

What, then, does this process of globalisation mean for the myriad network of Hindu traditions? Two themes emerge as central. First, there is the whole theme of interaction. Globalisation is a process which encourages both social and geographical mobility, and mobility increases interaction. So, for example, during the eighteenth century brāhmaṇas from the South came increasingly to Benaras, and their interaction with local brāhmaṇas produced a rejuvenation of brahmanic tradition in the city (Bose and Jalal 1998: 55). More generally, the eighteenth century saw the emergence and development of the concept of 'religion' as we understand it today; that is, religion as an objective category through which it is possible to classify a whole range of human activities and thoughts. This category only becomes meaningful through the realisation (or, perhaps more precisely, reification) of the idea that there are other sets of practices and thoughts which may be classified as of the same kind. This comparative approach, which was so crucial to colonial understandings of Hinduism, again emerges out of processes of interaction.

The second key theme associated with globalisation is the development of new public spaces, spaces in which to articulate the new concepts emerging out of interaction. Social mobility is again significant here, as the development of newly powerful social classes demanded the development of new ways of expressing power. In addition, new technologies meant that new forms of communication became available – as we shall see, these have proved enormously influential in the articulation of a religion called Hinduism in the modern and contemporary period.

Conceptions of Hinduism and changes in Indian society in the eighteenth and nineteenth centuries

If social mobility was a key feature of the eighteenth-century subcontinent, this was partly a reflection of the dynamism of power relations in the wake of the collapse of Mughal authority. The Maratha Empire was one of several flourishing kingdoms which expanded during this period. Expansion was accompanied by the development of powerful mercantile and banking castes taking advantage of the new trading opportunities emerging in this era of economic dynamism (S. Bayly 1999: 65–73). In the northern plains armed ascetic monastic orders gained considerable prominence and political authority. They gained power through their role as merchants, bankers and soldiers, and were also significant in giving opportunities to lower-caste individuals to change their economic and social status (Pinch 1996: 23–30). All these developments led to greater interaction across the subcontinent and beyond, and so encouraged the emergence of supra-local religious identities.

The activities of the East India Company contributed to this dynamic. At the same time, the Company's preferred strategy of non-interference in indigenous cultural and religious practices ironically tended to institutionalise these rapidly shifting developments. Hence, when he became governor of Bengal in 1772, Warren Hastings declared that British administrators had to 'adapt our regulations to the manners and understandings of the people . . . adhering as closely as we are able to their ancient uses and institutions' (quoted in Cohn 1985: 289). Locating these 'ancient uses and traditions' led to a textualisation of Hindu traditions, on the assumption that texts (the more ancient the better) would contain the most authentic versions of what were on the face of it rather degenerate religious beliefs and practices, replete with superstition. Orientalist scholars and missionaries (particularly after they gained official permission to operate in Company territory in 1813) were highly instrumental in articulating and promoting this textualisation of Hindu traditions. It could be argued that their work consolidated the development of supra-local religious identities noted above. On the other hand, it could be argued that this development was a qualitative shift, in its insistence on the embodiment of the 'real' tradition of Hinduism in texts. Some scholars have argued that this development was so influential that it constituted the invention of Hinduism as a religion (Frykenberg 1993; see also the essays by von Stietencron, Thapar and Frykenberg in Sontheimer and Kulke 2001).

Focusing on the written texts of the Hindu tradition was certainly significant in relation to the development of new public spaces during the nineteenth century. This is because one of the key ways in which these public spaces were opening up was the increasing circulation of the printed word, through pamphlets, cheaply produced books and newspapers. The newspaper industry expanded rapidly, and debates over issues related to religion were frequently articulated within this forum (Talbot 2000: 60–71). The proliferation of advanced printing technology in the second half of the nineteenth century led to the development of new focal points of Hindu devotionalism. This point is demonstrated graphically by the story of the *Rāmcaritmānas*. This sixteenth-century Hindi version of the *Rāmāyaṇa* grew into a ubiquitous feature of north Indian Hinduism over the course of the late nineteenth and early twentieth century. The Gita printing press in Gorakhpur, established in the early 1920s, was highly instrumental in propelling this text into the heart of north Indian Hindu homes through its production of cheap editions with commentary and illustrations (see Lutgendorf 1991: 61–63). This was in fact part of a broader strategy employed by the Gita Press to popularise what were perceived as key Hindu texts; not just the *Rāmcaritmānas* but also the purāṇic texts and especially the *Bhagavadgītā* were produced with Hindi translations sold at below cost price. The Press continues to have a major influence over the tenor of contemporary north Indian devotional Hinduism.

In the early colonial period no one was more influential in demonstrating how to capitalise on the development of a print culture than the renowned social commentator Rammohun Roy. Having settled in Calcutta, the hub of the British Indian Empire and the focal point for processes of globalisation affecting eastern India, Rammohun became part of an emerging urban intelligentsia, interpreting and commenting on the rapid changes affecting the city and society more generally. Much of Rammohun's published output was directed towards refuting missionary criticism of indigenous religious practices. This resulted in the generation of a series of debates in print – such as that which ensued after the publication in 1820 of his provocative rationalist text *The Precepts of Jesus* – which effectively established a public arena for the examination of social, religious and cultural issues. As an arch-rationalist, Rammohun used this public arena to expose what he perceived to be the superstitious aspects not only of Christianity but also of Hinduism. He wrote extensively in his Bengali journal *Sambad Kaumudi* on the status of women in Hindu society, and was, during the 1820s, increasingly vocal in his support for the campaign against the practice of sati.

This campaign was partially responsible for what is commonly cited as the first real act of 'reform' of Hinduism in the modern era, the legal prohibition of sati in 1829. One needs to be cautious with this idea of reform in nineteenth-century India, because it has historically been underpinned by some specific epistemological assumptions. The classic, Orientalist image of Hinduism during this period is as a degenerate system, which could only be revitalised by the intervention of modernisers inspired, inevitably, by the reforming zeal of European Protestantism (Zavos 2000: 39–41). In fact reform has been a constant refrain within Hindu traditions over a period of some three millennia (Jones 1989: 1–14), and it is difficult to see how the concerns of nineteenth-century reformers – such as caste, the status of widows and even sati – differed from those of earlier eras. In fact, the idea that sati was to be eradicated in the interests of modernity is quite problematic. The East India Company's own records demonstrate that the closer you got to that focal point of modernity in India, Calcutta, the more common the incidence of sati became (Nandy 1975)! The concept of globalisation may help us to understand this evidence. The popularity of sati may be seen as part of a movement to *traditionalise* Hindu practices as a means of protecting an emerging sense of Hindu identity in the context of increased interaction. And in fact it is here that the idea of nineteenth-century reform as distinctive begins to attain some substance. As this sense of Hindu identity began to emerge amongst particular social classes – those classes most involved in the interactions and public spaces implicit in the process of globalisation – debates ensued about the quality of this identity. How should the *idea* of Hinduism be fashioned as a feature of the modern world? In response to this question, attitudes of 'progressive reform' and 'traditional defence' began to crystallise into political positions in the emerging public spaces of modernity.

Nothing demonstrates this point more clearly than the group which was established in 1831 in order to demonstrate against the outlawing of sati, the Calcutta Dharma Sabha. This Sabha was a creation of the same intelligentsia (bhadralok) of which Rammohun Roy was a part. Its main weapon in its stated aim of defending Hindu tradition was to formulate petitions and memorials addressed to authority, and articulated as public documents, through the press as well as through the machinery of the modern state. It developed a structure which was able to wield these weapons effectively – namely the structure of a modern organisation, with a chairman, a secretary, financial records, membership lists and so on (Zavos 2000: 45). This organisational form set a critical precedent for the development of modern Hinduism. It became the established, legitimate form through which individuals and social groups could articulate their concerns about their 'religion'. In the development of modern Hinduism, the traditional institutions of authority – the saṃpradāyas, gurus and ṛṣis, brāhmaṇa paṇḍits and caste elders – have sometimes had less influence than these modern organisations. Indeed, as we shall see, very often these traditional sources of authority have reinvented themselves through these structures of modernity in order to gain a new sense of authority in relation to the modern concept of Hinduism.

In Calcutta in the 1830s and 1840s the Dharma Sabha became the model for the first self-consciously reforming organisation of modern Hinduism: the Brahmo Samaj. Although the Samaj had initially been established by Rammohun in 1828 as the Brahmo Sabha, it was not until the early 1840s that the organisation was properly instituted by Debendranath Tagore. From this point on, the Samaj began to expand, opening branches across British India. This expansion reflected the migration of English-educated middle-class Bengalis across the growing Empire, in search of positions in government service. The Samaj was particularly strong in Punjab, which had been annexed by the British in 1856. It also experienced a series of splits, the most significant inspired by the rather messianic leadership of Keshab Chandra Sen, whose radical pronouncements on the issue of caste grated with the more reflective, cautious approach of Tagore. Sen's Samaj developed in the 1860s into a fairly aggressive proselytising organisation, but in general it remained very much a high-caste Bengali concern wherever branches were established, and its ability to effect change in the wider world of Hinduism was consequently limited. Indeed, this limitation has led some authors to criticise the academic emphasis on organisations like the Brahmo Samaj and other so-called reforming bodies as unrepresentative of the development of modern Hinduism (Bharati 1970; Lutgendorf 1991; Smith 2003).

Hindu movements in the late nineteenth century

Although there is some substance to this criticism, we do have to acknowledge that in the second half of the nineteenth century organisations echoing the form of the Dharma Sabha and the Brahmo Samaj proliferated across British India. The Dev Samaj, the Prarthana Samaj, the Veda Samaj, the Arya Samaj, numerous Sanatana Dharma Sabhas and the Bharat Dharma Mahamandala are all examples of organisations which emerged in the public arena during this period. The latter two emerged as self-conscious defenders of 'orthodoxy'. The former all represented some form of reformist position in relation to the idea of Hinduism.

The Arya Samaj in particular emerged as a powerful force in north India. Its founder, Swami Dayananda Saraswati, developed a creed based on the absolute authority of the Veda as the 'true' scripture of Hinduism. According to Dayananda, any religious practice or belief not found in the Veda was an accretion which true Hindus would dispense with. In particular, the idea of jāti was perceived as an accretion, and should be replaced by a system of merit-based varṇa, as located by Dayananda in the *Yajurveda*. This proved to be an enormously popular approach amongst upwardly mobile middle castes, particularly in Punjab, where Brahmanism was relatively weak. It was also attractive to aspiring lower castes and untouchables, many of whom sought entry to a higher status through the Samaj's innovative use of śuddhi, or purification, rituals. The latter development was often violently resisted by higher castes, and even by many members of the Arya Samaj.

Some lower-caste and untouchable groups instead developed their own organisations in opposition to what were perceived as high-caste monopolies like the Arya Samaj. In Maharashtra the low-caste activist Jotirao Phule established the Satyashodak Samaj (Truth-seeking Society) in 1873. The Samaj assumed the form of a modern organisation in the manner of its high-caste counterparts. Yet it positioned itself in direct opposition to the idea of Hinduism. As Phule stated in 1882, 'if our learned Aryans really want to build unity amongst all of the people, and improve the country, then they will have to get rid of this vile religion of winners and losers' (quoted in O'Hanlon 1985: 267).

To Phule, then, despite all the public activity and institutional modernisation associated with Hinduism, it was still a 'vile religion of winners and losers'. Like many low-caste activists, Phule appears to have regarded the idea of modern Hinduism as little more than a public image which disguised a plethora of age-old and thoroughly deplorable social practices. As well as again calling into question the idea of 'reform', Phule's viewpoint helps us to problematise some other terms often associated with late nineteenth-century Hinduism: 'renaissance' and 'revival'. Advances in 'print capitalism' had undoubtedly led to the development of new forms of public culture in India. The work of Bankim Chandra Chatterjee is indicative, for example, of new forms of literary expression in Bengal, which may conceivably be perceived as 'renaissant', although it would be more accurate to describe it as a Bengali, rather than a Hindu, renaissance. In Benaras, Bharatendu Hariscandra was in the 1870s attempting to project the image of a homogeneous Hindu religion by consolidating key Vaiṣṇavite doctrines (Dalmia 1997). But this was as far removed from a 'revival' of past practices as Dayananda's conception of 'Vedic religion'. In reality these were responses to the particular circumstances of modernity at work in various regions of India in the later nineteenth century. As with any other time, the way people expressed their values and beliefs has to be placed in the context of a range of specific historical developments. To characterise them as indicative of a Hindu renaissance or revival runs the risk of projecting religions as having their own kind of history, almost outside human agency. In addition, the identification of Hinduism as 'a religion', comparable to and experiencing the same patterns of development as other 'religions', is a highly problematic notion. We need to bear in mind that during this period the idea of Hinduism as a religion is still crystallising within the context of the development of particular social classes in India, heavily involved in the processes of interaction – economic, social, cultural and political – signified by globalisation.

Hinduism in politics and political Hinduism

It is to the area of political interaction in the late nineteenth and early twentieth century that I will now turn. As they became increasingly articulated in the public spaces of the colonial state, ideas about Hinduism were implicated in a new kind of politics emerging in this context: the politics of representation. This kind of politics was partly driven by the development of nationalist consciousness. The Indian National Congress, established in 1885, was the most prominent of a host of organisations claiming to represent the interests and opinions of Indians, or of one or another section of the Indian people. These organisations sought to influence the policies of the government or, increasingly, to oppose the idea of the colonial state altogether. Much like the religious Samajes and Sabhas described above, these organisations developed mostly in middle-class contexts and their social base was, despite their representative claims, generally very narrow. One way of legitimising these representative claims, then, was to engage with what was perceived as popular culture. Hence elite nationalists like Bal Gangadhar Tilak and Aurobindo Ghose articulated their political concerns using a variety of Hindu motifs. From the 1890s onwards, Hinduism was therefore a consistent feature of mainstream nationalist politics. In the 1920s its role was given a new dimension by Mohandas Karamchand Gandhi, who articulated politics as a religious imperative, and the nationalist goal of independence as a mere stepping-stone on the path to spiritual liberation (mokṣa).

Running parallel to and closely interwoven with these developments was the growth of a specifically Hindu politics: a politics which sought to represent the interests and opinions of Hindus within the colonial state. This kind of politics emerged partly out of the prominence of modern organisations seeking to establish ideas about what it meant to be a Hindu, such as those outlined above. It was also encouraged by structures of Orientalist knowledge within the institutional culture of the colonial state, which sought naturally to categorise Indians in terms of definite religious affiliations. A significant example of this institutional culture is the All-India Census, which was first taken in 1871. Religious classification in the census implicitly invoked the idea of discrete religious communities, 'fenced off' from one another with definite boundaries. Despite the difficulty experienced by Census enumerators in acquiring statistics on this basis, there is no doubt that this projected image of religious communities was enormously influential. The Census was a published document, debated and discussed at length in the press and in pamphlets. In political terms, the invocation of an identifiable Hindu community through the 'science' of statistical enumeration (however vague this 'science' may have been in practical terms) was a further encouragement to the representation of this community. The government compounded the tendency in the first decade of the twentieth century by formally recognising the Muslim community as a viable political bloc in the so-called Morley-Minto Reform package. This established what became known as the 'communal principle' at the heart of the developing polity. Influential Hindu organisations – in particular the Arya Samaj and the Bharat Dharma Mahamandala – were not slow to take up the challenge of representing the Hindus in the same manner that the Muslim League, established in 1906, claimed to represent 'the Muslims'. Together these organisations established a series of 'Hindu Sabhas' which emerged in the 1920s as the

Hindu Mahasabha, a major political organisation which projected itself as the voice of 'the Hindus' in the run-up to independence and was the platform for the career of major Hindu politicians such as Pandit Madan Mohan Malaviya and Vinayat Damodar Savarkar.

The Mahasabha provided a significant arena for the development of what has become known as Hindu nationalism, that ideology which seeks to present Hindu-ness as synonymous with the 'true' culture of India, and Hindus as the only 'real' Indians. This is a major force in contemporary Hinduism, both in India and in the diaspora. I will return to it presently.

Before leaving the specifically political sphere, however, we do need to consider the development of non-elite articulations of Hinduism as politics. So far we have looked at middle-class groups and their attempts to project themselves as representative of broader constituencies. As the economy and in particular the urban areas of India developed, a broader network of social classes gained access to and asserted themselves within the arenas of interaction associated with globalisation. One way in which this assertion was expressed towards the end of the nineteenth century was through cow protection. This issue galvanised trading, banking and landowning castes in particular, and involved other sections of the population through a myriad of caste and local community based structures of mobilisation and enforcement (see Pandey 1990). As an issue, cow protection was not new during this period, but what was new was its increasing articulation as a 'religious right' of Hindus, in legal terms, and its promotion through modern organisations, Gaurakshini Sabhas, using modern forms of communication. Care needs to be taken not to present cow protection as a single movement during this period. Numerous fragmentary interests were involved. On the other hand, it is certainly the case that it was employed as a means of invoking the idea of the Hindu community. As one government officer noted in relation to leaflets distributed by a Gaurakshini Sabha in 1893, 'some cartoons represent the cow about to be slaughtered by a butcher and all the different castes of Hindus standing around and crying out to him to desist' (D.F. McCracken, quoted in Zavos 2000: 86).

Cow protection did, of course, frequently lead to violence. Indeed, in the developing towns and cities, in particular, the pressures of social change, deprivation and economic uncertainty led to the development of many dynamic political movements in which religious forms of identity and religious practice were implicated. A strident, martial Hindu culture developed, through which poor, śūdra castes adapted Hindu symbols such as the cow, institutions such as the Rāmlīlā and especially Hindu festivals such as Holī in order to express the virtues and triumphs of the poor in a Hindu milieu (Gooptu 2001: 211–21). Amongst urban untouchables, an egalitarian form of bhakti devotionalism emerged as an expression of opposition to the caste hierarchy (Gooptu 2001: 151). Such developments demonstrate the vibrant dynamism of what we might understand as religious identity, adapting and being fashioned in order to make sense within the multiple contexts of modern urban life. Ideological developments amongst untouchables crystallised in the emergence of Adi Hindu Sabhas in Uttar Pradesh, the Ad Dharm movement in the Punjab and the Adi Dravida movement in southern India. In the 1930s and 1940s the great untouchable leader Bhimrao Ram Ambedkar capitalised on these developments in order to build a solid political constituency. In this sense, the relationship between politics, Hinduism and related religious identities was not just driven by the concerns of high-caste Hindu nationalists. The implication of the myriad traditions we might understand as Hinduism with issues of social and political status means that this relationship in the modern world is implicit.

Universalist spiritualism and global identity

As well as these social and political pressures, modern Hinduism has been deeply influenced by a further aspect of its development in the nineteenth century. This might be termed universalist spiritualism – the idea that Hinduism is in a unique position to teach the world about the inner truths of reality, the cosmos and the concept of the divine. This approach can be linked to Rammohun Roy's defence of Hinduism against missionary criticism through a rationalist interpretation of Advaita Vedānta, the first manifestation of what is often understood as 'neo-Vedānta' (Halbfass 1988: 222). In this conception, different religions – Christianity, Islam and also Vaiṣṇavism, Śaivism and so on – are perceived as different approaches to the one divine reality. Advaita Vedānta is, however, the most pure and the most effective of these approaches; the one which comes closest to understanding the nature of that reality, and, furthermore, the one which is able to encompass all others through the totality of its vision of the cosmos. What is significant about this attitude is perhaps not so much its insistence on the truth of Vedānta, but its reinterpretation of tradition as a means of engaging with modernity, in the specific context of colonial domination.

This point is illustrated by the visit of Swami Vivekananda to the self-styled World Parliament of Religions held in Chicago in 1893. Vivekananda was an English-educated bhadraloki Calcuttan who, having flirted with the Brahmo Samaj, turned in the 1880s to the prominent mystic Sri Ramakrishna. For a generation of disaffected middle-class Bengali youth, Ramakrishna had begun to represent an image of Indian spirituality which was the antithesis of Western rationalism. It is this attitude which Vivekananda took to Chicago. At the World Parliament he projected Advaita Vedānta as an expression of Hindu spirituality, and offered it as a salvific counterpoint to the material prosperity and consequent spiritual wasteland of the West. The offer was enthusiastically received. Certain Americans and Europeans had already become actively interested in Indian religions as an alternative to the Christian churches. Prominent amongst these were Colonel Henry Steel Olcott and Madame Helena Blavatsky, who together set up the Theosophical Society in 1875, an influential organisation in both India and the West (van der Veer 2001: 55–82).

Vivekananda's success in presenting the universal spirituality of Hinduism in the West enabled him to return to India having raised considerable sums of money. With this he was able to purchase land in Calcutta and establish an organisation in the name of his guru, Ramakrishna. The Ramakrishna Math and Mission was, at the time, a unique blend of traditional Hindu institution and modern organisation. It projected itself as a saṃpradāya, yet at the same time it developed, as the name suggests, into an organisation with an active mission in the modern world, practising social service (seva) of various kinds as a divine duty and aiming to 'spread the word' of spiritual reality in an increasingly dehumanised, materialist society. Like other organisations examined in this entry, the Math and Mission was established in a systematic fashion, a well-managed modern structure in a modern world. As it established branches both in India and in the West, the Mission began to accumulate wealth through contributions from supporters and followers of its cause. Through a message of selfless spirituality, therefore, this modern organisation with a traditional inflection established a position of considerable wealth and sociopolitical influence. It remains a major force in modern Hinduism and is often cited as a key example of what has become known as 'neo-Hinduism'. This rather vague term is associated with those we have looked at earlier, such as 'reformist' or 'renaissant' Hinduism. It has been used by the influential Sanskrit scholar Paul Hacker as a means of distinguishing between those who have reinterpreted Hindu ideas around Western models and those whose interpretation of ideas remains primarily structured around indigenous models of thought (Hacker 1978; Halbfass 1990: 219–20). This distinction has been criticised as, amongst other things, essentialising and undermining the dynamism of the tradition (Beckerlegge 2000: 76–78). But there is a sense in which the image of universalism and tolerant spirituality associated with Vivekananda, and with later exponents of the universal or sanātana dharma of Hinduism such as Aurobindo Ghose and Sarvepalli Radhakrishnan, offers something distinctive which may be described as 'neo-Hinduism'. This is a kind of self-conscious 'opening out' of Hindu ideas to the world, on the basis that such ideas of tolerance and universalism have a global significance, and are globally applicable, regardless of the constraints of dharma with which they are traditionally associated in India (Halbfass 1992: 51–55).

This idea is certainly implemented in a variety of contexts across India and further afield. It could also be claimed that the Ramakrishna Math and Mission *has* become a template, to a greater or lesser extent, for a plethora of organisations which dominate contemporary Hinduism. The Swami Narayana Sampradaya, Sathya Sai Baba, the Divine Life Society, the Rajneesh Movement, the International Society for Krishna Consciousness (ISKCON), the Radhasoami Satsang, the Brahma Kumaris; these are all organisations which operate both in India and abroad and have a stake in what the anthropologist Lise McKean has called 'the business and politics of spirituality' (McKean 1996: 1). Her characterisation reflects the fact that the idea of Hindu spirituality has become integrated as a feature of our globalised world, as a kind of oppositional rhetoric which is nevertheless heavily implicated in the developing power of transnational capital (McKean 1996: 10). At the heart of this development has been the emergence of 'modern gurus' – religious teachers who emphasise the need to 'revitalise' spirituality, who use modern methods of communication to propagate their message and who regularly travel to different parts of the world in order to preach, raise funds and consolidate their organisations (van der Veer 1994: 136–37).

Having a global presence is one way, of course, to demonstrate the global significance of Hindu spirituality. It is also a means of servicing the ritual and spiritual needs of what during the twentieth century became an enormous Indian diaspora. Indian communities can now be found across the globe, from Trinidad to Tooting. The religious commitment of these communities is often perceived as a means of preserving cultural identity in a non-Indian environment (Vertovec 2000). As second and third generations emerge, new ways of articulating this identity are fashioned. Modern gurus and their organisations are undoubtedly instrumental in fashioning these new identities, helping to propagate the image of tolerant spiritualism as the 'essence' of Hinduism.

One highly significant actor in this process has been the Vishwa Hindu Parishad (VHP; World Hindu Council). This organisation was initiated in 1964 by an archetypal modern guru, Swami Cinmayananda, under the guidance of the Hindu nationalist Rashtriya Swayamsevak Sangh. The avowed objective of the VHP was to develop a unified image of

Hindu dharma in the context of diverse traditions (not just those recognised as Hindu, but also Sikh, Buddhist, Jain traditions – those that are seen as indigenous to India) and to consolidate this image both in India and across the diaspora communities. The VHP has grown rapidly to occupy a central position in the political and cultural spaces of Hinduism. It manufactures an image of modern Hinduism which combines the rhetoric of tolerant spirituality with the martial traditions of Hindu nationalism. The unifying agenda of the VHP leads it to propagate certain festivals and figures as emblematic of Hindu-ness, or Hindutva. Rāma and Rāmanavamī are especially significant, particularly as the figure of Rāma has been progressively reinvented as a martial hero, defending the honour of Hinduism. The VHP has also laid particular emphasis on the sacred geography of Bhārata (India) and the idea of pilgrimage (yatra) associated with it. This has led to the significant opening of a temple to Bhārat Mātā, Mother India, in Hardwar (McKean 1996). This temple is in many ways emblematic of the invented traditions of modern Hinduism.

With the advance of globalisation, and in particular the process of time–space compression associated with it, such images as those described here have had a major impact on how Hindus conceive of their religion. The internet has become a major force in the propagation of Hinduism, with sites such as the Global Hindu Electronic Networks (GHEN; http://www.hindunet.org) and Hinduism Today (http://www.hinduismtoday.com) delivering ideas about Hinduism to a worldwide audience. Television productions of the *Rāmāyaṇa* and *Mahābhārata* have also been major forces in propagating particular versions of these multi-faceted epics as authoritative, and so representative of modern Hinduism.

There is no doubt that in the contemporary period there is a strong compulsion to homogenise the many traditions of Hinduism and that to a certain extent the processes associated with globalisation have encouraged this trend. This is, in a sense, a natural progression from the nineteenth-century idea of Hinduism as 'a religion', comparable to other religions in the world. Certainly, amongst many people around the globe, the concept of Hinduism as one of five or six world religions is seen as an unremarkable, uncontestable fact. At the same time, however, the new public spaces of the globalised world have opened up the possibility for the articulation of dissonance and resistance to this homogenised view. Bhakti has always provided a channel to articulate this kind of resistance in recognisable Hindu idioms, and this remains the case. Dalit (untouchable) and low-caste groups have been particularly significant in challenging the hegemony of homogenised Hinduism in recent times, developing alternative theologies which are characterised by the acknowledgement of diversity (Ilaiah 1996). The voice of the dalit is now to be heard on the internet, providing a significant counterpoint to sites such as GHEN (see, for example, http://www.dalitstan.org). Women too provide an independent voice which is engaged in challenging this hegemony: the women's publishing house Manushi and the work of its editor Madhu Kishwar are key examples of the way in which this voice is being expressed (see also Kishwar 1998).

The modern religion we call Hinduism may in fact be characterised by the tensions between centripetal and centrifugal forces which are identifiable in this complex set of traditions. At times, Hinduism is a religion which is clearly recognisable and comparable with other religions around the world. At other times it appears to evade this comparison and challenge the whole category of religion as an analytical tool for understanding the way humans behave in the world.

Because of this, it holds a critical position for our understanding of religious practice in the twenty-first century, as well as our understanding of how processes of globalisation are impacting on our world.

See also: **Advaita; Arya Samaj; Bhakti; Bharat Dharma Mahamandala; Blavatsky, Helena; Brahma Kumaris; Brahmo Samaj; Caste; Chatterjee, Bankim Chandra; Cinmayananda, Swami; Dalits; Dayananda Saraswati, Swami; Dev Samaj; Dharma; Divine Life Society; Gandhi, Mohandas Karamchand; Ghose, Aurobindo; Guru; Hacker, Paul; Hariścandra; Hindu Mahasabha; Hinduism; Holī; International Society for Krishna Consciousness; Jāti; Kishwar, Madhu; Mahābhārata; Malaviya, Pandit Madan Mohan; Mokṣa; Swami Narayana Sampradaya; Nationalism; Olcott, Henry Steel; Orientalism; Paṇḍit; Prarthana Samaj; Radhakrishnan, Sir Sarvepalli; Radhasoami Satsang; Rajneesh movement; Rāma; Ramakrishna Math and Mission; Ramakrishna, Sri; Rāmanavamī; Rāmāyaṇa; Rashtriya Swayamsevak Sangh; Roy, Rammohan; Sacred geography; Sai Baba (as movement); Sai Baba, Sathya; Saṃpradāya; Sati; Savarkar, Vinayat Damodar; Sen, Keshab Chandra; Tagore, Debendranath; Television and radio; Theosophy and the Theosophical Society; Tilak, Bal Gangadhar; Tīrthayātrā (Pilgrimage); Varṇa; Veda Samaj; Vishwa Hindu Parishad; Vivekananda, Swami; Widowhood; Women, status of**

JOHN ZAVOS

Further reading

Bayly, C.A. 1990. *Indian Societies and the Making of the British Empire*. Cambridge: Cambridge University Press.

Bayly, S. 1999. *Caste, Society and Politics in India from the Eighteenth Century to the Modern Age*. Cambridge: Cambridge University Press.

Beckerlegge, G. 2000. *The Ramakrishna Mission: the Making of a Modern Hindu Movement*. New Delhi: Oxford University Press.

Bharati, A. 1970. 'The Hindu Renaissance and its Apologetic Patterns'. *Journal of Asian Studies* 29(2): 267–88.

Bose, S. and A. Jalal. 1998. *Modern South Asia: History, Culture, Political Economy*. London: Routledge.

Cohn, B. 1985. 'The Command of Language and the Language of Command'. In R. Guha, ed., *Subaltern Studies IV*. New Delhi: Oxford University Press, 276–329.

Dalmia, V. 1997. *Nationalisation of Hindu Traditions: Bharatendu Harischandra and Nineteenth Century Benaras*. Oxford: Oxford University Press.

Dalmia, V. and H. von Steitencron (eds). 1995. *Representing Hinduism: the Construction of Religious Traditions and National Identity*. New Delhi: Sage.

Eaton, R. 2000. *Essays on Islam and Indian History*. New Delhi: Oxford University Press.

Frykenberg, R.E. 1993. 'Constructions of Hinduism at the Nexus of History and Religion'. *Journal of Inter-disciplinary History* 23(3): 523–50.

Gooptu, N. 2001. *Politics of the Urban Poor in Early Twentieth Century India*. Cambridge: Cambridge University Press.

Hacker, P. 1978. 'Aspects of Neo-Hinduism as Contrasted with Surviving Traditional Hinduism'. In L. Schmidthausen, ed., *Kleine Schriften*. Wiesbaden: Franz Steiner, 580–608.

Halbfass, W. 1988. *India and Europe*. Albany, NY: State University of New York Press.

Halbfass, W. 1990. *India and Europe: An Essay in Philosophical Understanding*. Delhi: Motilal Banarsidass.

Halbfass, W. 1992. *Tradition and Reflection: Explorations in India Thought*. Delhi: Satguru Publications.

Ilaiah, K. 1996. *Why I Am Not a Hindu: A Sudra Critique of Hindutva Philosophy, Culture and Political Economy*. Calcutta: Samya.

Jones, K. 1989. *Socio-Religious Reform Movements in British India*. Cambridge: Cambridge University Press.

Kaviraj, S. 1995. *Unhappy Consciousness: Bankimchandra Chattopadhyay and the Formation of Nationalist Discourse in India*. New Delhi: Oxford University Press.

Kishwar, M. 1998. *Religion at the Service of Nationalism and other Essays*. New Delhi: Oxford University Press.

Lutgendorf, P. 1991. *The Life of a Text: Performing the Ramcaritmanas of Tulsidas.* Berkeley, CA: University of California Press.
McKean, L. 1996. *Divine Enterprise: Gurus and the Hindu Nationalist Movement*. Chicago, IL: University of Chicago Press.
Nandy, A. 1975. 'Sati: A Nineteenth Century Tale of Women, Violence and Protest'. In V.C Joshi, ed., *Rammohun Roy and the Process of Modernisation in India*. New Delhi: Vikas Publishing.
O'Hanlon, R. 1985. *Caste, Conflict and Ideology: Mahatma Jotirao Phule and Low Caste Protest in Nineteenth Century Western India.* Cambridge: Cambridge University Press.
Pandey, G. 1990. *Construction of Communalism in Colonial North India*. New Delhi: Oxford University Press.
Pinch, W. 1996. *Peasants and Monks in British India*. Berkeley, CA: University of California Press.
Said, E. 1995. *Orientalism*. London: Penguin.
Smith, D. 2003. *Hinduism and Modernity.* Oxford: Blackwell Publishing.
Sontheimer, G. and H. Kulke. 2001. *Hinduism Reconsidered.* New Delhi: Manohar.
Talbot, I. 2000. *India and Pakistan: Inventing the Nation*. London: Arnold.
van der Veer, P. 1994. *Religious Nationalism: Hindus and Muslims in India*. Berkeley, CA: University of California Press.
van der Veer, P. 2001. *Imperial Encounters: Religion and Modernity in India and Britain*. Princeton, NJ: Princeton University Press.
Vertovec, S. 2000. *The Hindu Diaspora: Comparative Patterns.* London: Routledge.
Zavos, J. 2000. *Emergence of Hindu Nationalism in India*. New Delhi: Oxford University Press.

HINDUTVA

A number of Hindu nationalist organisations, including Shiv Sena and the groups affiliated to the Rashtriya Swayamsevak Sangh, have been founded on a commitment to defend and foster Hindutva ('Hinduness'). Elements of this ideology can be traced back to the Hindu Mahasabha, secret societies committed to freeing India from British rule, and to the less direct influence of the Arya Samaj.

The concept of Hindutva was formulated by Vinayat Damodar Savarkar (1883–1966), who was greatly influenced by Giuseppe Mazzini's role in the making of the modern Italian state. Savarkar encouraged revolutionary activities in India through Abhinav Bharat, a secret society he created in 1904. Revolution and cultural nationalism lay at the heart of his ideas, first expressed comprehensively in his *Indian War of Independence 1857* (1908), which portrayed Hindus and Muslims fighting together against the British. Svarāj (self-rule) and svadharma (the individual's own obligations) were identified as principles underlying Indian resistance. By the 1920s India's Muslims had replaced the British as the enemy of Hindus in Savarkar's writing, reflecting increasing communal violence and competition. In his classic statement of Hindutva ideology, *Hindutva: Who Is a Hindu?* (1923), Savarkar defined Hindutva as the culture of the 'Hindu race', of which Hinduism, the religion, is but an element. Rejecting 'Hinduism' as an alien concept, he defined Hindu dharma as the religion practised by Hindus as well as Sikhs and Buddhists. He portrayed India as a holy land, sanctified by the deities and Hindu martyrs, and its people as a nation (rāṣṭra) bound together by blood and a common culture preserved by Sanskrit and Hindi, in spite of differences in caste. Savarkar's ideas have been adopted by a range of Hindu nationalist ideologues, including Keshav Baliram Hedgewar and Madhav Sadhasiv Golwalkar.

Proponents of Hindutva have sought to promote the identification of national identity with the religious and broader cultural heritage of Hindus. Measures taken to achieve this end have included attempts to 'reclaim' individuals judged to have taken up 'alien' religions, the pursuit of social, cultural and philanthropic activities designed to strengthen awareness of Hindu belonging, and direct political action through various organisations, including recognised political parties such as the Bharatiya Janata Party (BJP). Such expressions of political 'Hinduism' have proved controversial, having been blamed for contributing to the growth of communal violence in the period leading to Indian Independence and subsequently in post-Independence India under a secular constitution, for example during the controversy over the contested site at Ayodhyā in 1992. Faced with economic uncertainty and internal and external threats to national security, however, many Hindus have responded positively to the political appeal of Hindutva ideology, as indicated by the increasing power of the BJP over the closing decades of the twentieth century and its role as a coalition partner in India's national government. However, the 2004 election result suggested that the secular ideals of the Congress Party retained their appeal.

See also: **Abhinav Bharat Society; Arya Samaj; Ayodhyā; Bharatiya Janata Party; Buddhism, relationship with Hinduism; Dharma; Golwalkar, Madhav Sadashiv; Hedgewar, Keshav Baliram; Hindu Mahasabha; Nationalism; Rashtriya Swayamsevak Sangh; Sangh Parivar; Sanskrit; Savarkar, Vinayat Damodar; Shiv Sena; Sikhism, relationship with Hinduism**

G. Beckerlegge

Further reading

Jaffrelot, C. 1996. *The Hindu Nationalist Movement and Indian Politics, 1925 to the 1990s*. London: Hurst.

McLean, L. 1996. *The Divine Enterprise*. Chicago, IL and London: University of Chicago Press.

Zavos, J. 2000. *The Emergence of Hindu Nationalism in India*. New Delhi: Oxford University Press.

HIRAṆYAGARBHA

'Golden embryo'. One of the names developed in later Vedic times for the abstract supreme being or the primordial cosmic egg that produces the desiring/creative spirit of the universe. Hiraṇyagarbha's only mention in the *Ṛgveda* occurs at 10.121.1 as the one lord of what exists, a philosophic name for the sun. Part of the ascending monistic tradition of Brahmanic/Hindu reflection, he occurs in the *Atharvaveda* (e.g. 4.2.8 as the golden-coloured germ that emerges from the primordial waters) and in the *Brāhmaṇas* (e.g. *Taittirīya Saṃhitā* 5.5.1.2 as identified with Prajāpati). Eventually he becomes a name of the Trimūrti Brahmā.

See also: **Atharvaveda; Brahmā; Brāhmaṇas; Prajāpati; Ṛgveda; Trimūrti; Vedic pantheon; Vedism**

Michael York

HIRAṆYAKAŚIPU

'Golden-seated', 'golden-robed'. A Daitya ruler famous for his ruthlessly accumulated wealth and power and for his impiety. Declaring himself lord of the three worlds, Hiraṇyakaśipu even claimed Indra's throne, protected by a boon Brahmā had formerly granted. It secured his absolute power and rulership, and assured that no god or created being could kill the Daitya either indoors or outdoors, neither during the day nor at night, either on earth or in the atmosphere, or through weapons (*Bhāgavata Purāṇa* 7.3–4.3).

According to the *Bhāgavata Purāṇa* (7.5.33–7.55), Hiraṇyakaśipu himself provoked his fall by cruelly persecuting his son Prahlāda for his unwavering Vaiṣṇava faith. Protected by Viṣṇu, Prahlāda survived all of his father's attacks, who finally was killed by the Narasiṃha avatāra (incarnation) of the god in a situation complying with all details of Brahmā's boon (*Bhāgavata Purāṇa* 7.8–9; *Śiva Purāṇa*, Rudrasaṃhitā 43). In the differing *Viṣṇu Purāṇa* version (1.15.140–20.39) father and son are reunited.

See also: **Brahmā; Indra; Purāṇas; Śiva; Vaiṣṇavism; Viṣṇu**

XENIA ZEILER

Further reading

Soifer, Deborah A. 1991. *The Myths of Narasimha and Vāmana: Two Avatars in Cosmological Perspective.* Albany, NY: University of New York Press.

HITOPADEŚA

See: **Pañcatantra**

HOLĪ

A Hindu festival held in February/March, or the Hindu month of Phālguṇa, that involves all the community. Although the festival is traditionally marked by the lighting of bonfires on the evening before, in which pieces of coconut are sacrificed and the flames circumambulated, it is the throwing of coloured dyes or water on each other for which the festival is more famous. On the day of Holī, everybody engages in throwing coloured water or powder dyes on each other, both within family groups and in the streets. Behaviour can be very robust, with large groups of young men colouring everyone in sight. The festival is also marked by the reversing of traditional social authority patterns; women are allowed to rebuke and insult their husbands, sometimes publicly in groups on the streets; students can be rude to their teachers and small children will often throw mud and even rubbish at adults passing by. The atmosphere is one of abandonment and gaiety but can easily become quite aggressive and competitive.

There are similarities to the idea of carnival in the West but the festival has a number of explanations concerning its origins. Generally these are associated with the demoness Holikā, who ate a child every day. One day it was the turn of a poor widow to offer her only son to be eaten. However, a sādhu advised all the children of the area to gather together and abuse the demoness. Holikā died of shame and rage. In recent times, Holikā seems to have been linked with the demon-king Hiraṇyakaśipu and the story of the child devotee Prahlād. This may be a part of the process of legitimising the festival by linking it to a legend associated with Viṣṇu. In diaspora, Hindus celebrate the festival in a more restrained fashion, lighting bonfires and reciting prayers, but rarely with the displays of abandonment or the spraying of coloured dyes.

See also: **Diaspora; Hiraṇyakaśīpu; Prahlād(a); Sādhu; Utsava; Viṣṇu**

RON GEAVES

Further reading

Klostermaier, Klaus. 1989. *A Survey of Hinduism.* Albany, NY: State University of New York.

HOLWELL, JOHN ZEPHANIAH (1711–98)

Born in Dublin, Holwell spent thirty years in Bengal with the East India Company. In his time, he was famous (now infamous) for his exaggerated account of his incarceration during the occupation of Calcutta by the Nawab of Bengal in 1756 (the 'Black Hole of Calcutta' incident). He later published, in different parts and over several years, a historical work (1765–71) which included an account of 'the religion of the Gentoos' based upon a text identified by Holwell only as the 'Chartah Bhade Shastah' (i.e. *Śāstra* of the four *Vedas*). While not a scholarly work even by the standards of his immediate successors among British Orientalists, Holwell's book is nevertheless notable for his insistence that Hindus were monotheists and that their religion represented the original revelation of God at creation. The book, with its implication of the superiority of Hinduism, was eagerly received among heterodox thinkers in Europe, and was quickly translated into German and French.

See also: **Hinduism, history of scholarship**

WILL SWEETMAN

Further reading

Holwell, J.Z. 1765–71. *Interesting Historical Events, Relative to the Provinces of Bengal and the Empire of Indostan*, 3 vols. London: Printed for T. Becket and P.A. Hondt.

Marshall, P.J. (ed.). 1970. *The British Discovery of Hinduism in the Eighteenth Century*. Cambridge: Cambridge University Press.

HOMOSEXUALITY

Homosexuality is mentioned in the *Dharmaśāstras* and Epics, Āyurvedic texts and Kāmaśāstra. Brāhmaṇic textual tradition, with its clear emphasis on reproductive sexuality and patriliny, generally condemns homosexual activity. Texts such as the *Manusmṛti* for example, mention fines and expiation rituals for homosexual activity. In most textual contexts, female–female sexual relations are more severely punished than male–male relations.

However, it appears that the sparse references to homosexuality in such literature reflect more the purpose of these texts than the social history of homosexual activity in South Asia. The *Kāmasūtra* of Vātsyāyana, by contrast, is one of the few Sanskrit sources that affirms same-sex relations in the context of discussing varieties of sexual experience. Its ninth chapter, called Auparisṭaka, 'Oral Sexual Activity', mentions persons of a third nature (tritīya prakṛti), some of whom engage in same-sex activity.

Under British colonialism, homosexual activity was officially criminalised when anti-sodomy laws were written into the Indian Penal Code (IPC). In 1860, under Lord Macaulay, the Indian Law Commission instituted Section 377, which reads: 'intercourse against the order of nature with any man, woman or animal shall be punished with imprisonment for life . . . and shall also be liable to fine'. In contrast to the brahmanic laws that involved temporary forms of punishment for such offences, the IPC and legal modernity reified the condemnation of homosexual activities in a new way. Today, many Hindu right-wing organisations, such as the Rashtriya Swayamsevak Sangh (RSS), that attempt to uphold fixed visions of 'Hindu morality' construct homosexuality as foreign to Hinduism and attribute its presence in India to Muslims and the British.

Queer scholars and activists are searching for alternative voices in both Sanskrit and vernacular literary and ritual contexts. The works of Ruth Vanita (2000, 2002), for example, attempt to locate spaces of same-sex intimacy in traditions such as bhakti to demonstrate instances of Hinduism's diversity and flexibility on the subjects of gender and sexuality. Organisations such as the Gay and Lesbian Vaishnava Association Inc. (GALVA) provide networking and religious support for queer persons who identify as Hindu.

See also: **Āyurveda; Dharmaśāstras; Lesbianism; Mahābhārata; Rāmāyaṇa; Rashtriya Swayamsevak Sangh; Sex and sexuality; Vātsyāyana Mallanāga**

DAVESH SONEJI

Further reading

Aldrich, R. 2003. *Colonialism and Homosexuality*. New York: Routledge.

Bacchetta, P. 1999. 'When the (Hindu) Nation Exiles Its Queers'. *Social Text* 61: 141–66.

Kāmasūtra. 2002. Trans. W. Doniger and S. Kakar. New York: Oxford University Press.

The Law Code of Manu. 2004. Trans. P. Olivelle. New York: Oxford University Press.

Sharma, A. 1993. 'Homosexuality and Hinduism'. In A. Swidler, ed., *Homosexuality and World Religions.* Valley Forge, PA: Trinity Press International, 47–80.

Sweet, M.J. and L. Zwilling. 1993. 'The First Medicalization: The Taxonomy and Etiology of Queerness in Classical Indian Medicine'. *Journal of Homosexuality* 3.4: 595–96.

Vanita, R. and S. Kidwai. 2000. *Same-Sex Love in India: Readings from Literature and History.* New York: St Martin's Press.

Vanita, R. (ed). 2002. *Queering India: Same-Sex Love and Eroticism in Indian Culture and Society.* New York: Routledge.

Vanita, R. 2005. *Love's Rite: Same-Sex Marriage in India and the West*. London: Palgrave Macmillan.

www.galva108.org, The Gay and Lesbian Vaishnava Association Inc. (accessed 20 October 2005).

HUMAN RIGHTS

Scholars have often denied the applicability of human rights to Hinduism because of its prevailing social hierarchy, preference for groups over individuals and emphasis on duty. But the following arguments could be made for the idea that human rights have been known to Hindus.

First, the idea of autonomy, on which the concept of human rights is usually based, is at the heart of the law of karma ('as you sow, so you shall reap'), which is a recognition by Hindus of the human capacity for self-determination and the idea that justice is impartial. Just as the theory of autonomy acknowledges self-determination as a universal human *capacity* rather than a property of action (because acts can always be coerced for good or bad reasons), so too does the law of karma. Just as human rights recognise limits made necessary by the rights of others and the needs of society, so too does the law of karma. Just as individuals are the ultimate source of value for human rights, so too are they according to the law of karma. It is only in human form that one can seek liberation, after all, and liberation is defined as realisation of the true self (ātman), which is within all. And just as autonomy needs agency (self-consciousness, desire, intention and action), so does the law of karma. Second, Hinduism acknowledges that 'the general rule, in the absence of express provision to the contrary, is equal distribution' (samam syād-aśrutitvāt). Third, Hinduism acknowledges that there are universal human rules/virtues (sāmānya-dharma), such as non-violence, truthfulness, non-stealing, celibacy, renunciation of possessions and self-control. Its first rule, for instance, is the negative right of non-injury/non-killing (ahiṃsā). Its second rule, truthfulness, has been linked with justice and human rights following *Bṛhadāraṇyaka Upaniṣad* 1.4.14, which says that righteousness/justice (dharma) is truth (satyam). Like those advocates of human rights who argue that rights are of practical importance primarily because of the duties they imply (which presupposes the correlativity between rights and duties), so too Hinduism accepts this correlativity but generally approaches it from the side of duties. Parents have a duty, for instance, to marry off their children in order of age; the correlative, though implicit, idea is that all people have a right to marry. Or the husband's family, should he die before his wife, has a duty to support his wife; the correlative right, of course, is that she has a right to support.

Even with its emphasis on duties, which have imposed constraints that might seem onerous from today's standards, Hinduism has always provided exceptions. Self-defence, for instance, is an exception to the negative right of non-injury. Saṃnyāsa (renunciation to pursue spiritual goals through radical autonomy) is an exception to the norm of life within society, regulated by duties and rights based on family and caste. Reform is an exception to religiously prescribed norms, moreover, if unrighteousness prevails. Hinduism, for instance, allows revolution against an unrighteous king who makes the people hate him. Although admitting that rights and duties are correlative and even interchangeable, A. Sharma argues that the language of rights, which has antecedents in Hinduism, is preferable today to duties, because the idiom of duties has not been balanced in Indian history with rights and state protection of individual freedom (Sharma 2003: 144–52).

See also: **Ahiṃsā; Āśrama; Ātman; Dharma; Ethics; Karma; Saṃnyāsa; Upaniṣads**

KATHERINE K. YOUNG

Further reading

Beckerlegge, G. 1990. 'Human Rights in the Ramakrishna Math and Mission: "For Liberation and the Good of the World"'. *Religion* 20: 119–37.

Carman, J.B. 1988. 'Duties and Rights in Hindu Society'. In L.S. Rouner, ed., *Human Rights and the World's Religions*, 113–28. Notre Dame, IN: University of Notre Dame Press.

Kumar, P. 1997. 'The Role of Hinduism in Addressing Human Rights Issues in South Africa'. *Dialogue and Alliance* 11:1: 80–93.

Martin, N.M. 2003. 'Rights, Roles, and Reciprocity in Hindu Dharma'. In J. Runzo, N.M. Martin and A. Sharma, eds, *Human Rights and Responsibilities in the World Religions*. Oxford: Oxford University Press, 267–82.

Panikkar, R. 1982. 'Is the Notion of Human Rights a Western Concept?' *Diogenes* 120: 75–102.

Prabhu, J. 1998. 'Dharma as an Alternative to Human Rights'. In S.K. Maity, U. Thakur and A.K. Narain, eds, *Studies in Orientology: Essays in Memory of Prof. A.L. Basham*. Agra: YK Publishers, 174–79.

Pushparajan, A. 1983. 'Harijans and the Prospects of their Human Rights'. *Journal of Dharma* 8: 391–405.

Rai, L.D. 1995. *Human Rights in the Hindu–Buddhist Tradition*. Jaipur: Nirala Publications.

Sharma, A. 2003. *Hinduism and Human Rights: A Conceptual Approach*. Oxford: Oxford University Press.

I

ICONOGRAPHY, MODERN

The makers of Hindu temples and sacred images traditionally traced their lineage back to Viśvakarman. The regulation of their craft was linked to specialist castes and the principles governing their work were laid down in the *Śilpaśāstras*. Although some early examples of decorative art and mural and miniature painting beyond the confines of temples were devoted to secular subjects, many motifs were taken from religious and mythological sources. The interaction with Islamic artistic traditions during the Mughal period (sixteenth–eighteenth century CE) resulted in vibrant, regional schools of art. From the eighteenth century CE, this fusion of Hindu and Muslim artistic conventions influenced and was influenced by European styles of painting, inaugurating changes in popular Hindu iconography that have been influential to the present day.

During the nineteenth century, increased access to European-style painting, new forms of technology, new tastes and new markets had a profound impact upon Hindu artistic forms, including religious iconography, and resulted in distinctive schools of Indian art. Technological innovations included printing presses and chromolithographic reproduction, which replaced woodcuts, photography and the means to achieve mechanised mass production. By the 1880s, such was the speed of change in Bengal, where the British presence was most felt, that lithographic prints and oleographs had virtually supplanted more traditional styles of painting.

The first chromolithographic press in India was started in Calcutta by the Calcutta Art Studio in 1878 and was followed by that established in the Bombay region in 1894 by the south Indian painter Raja Ravi Varma (1848–1906). Ravi Varma had been exposed to Indian courtly traditions of painting as a child and had closely observed the techniques of European oil painting. His pictures of Hindu deities and scenes from popular devotional narratives combined traditional Hindu aesthetic sensibilities and iconographic conventions with European techniques, and with the emphasis upon naturalism that characterised the genre of European history painting and depictions of Biblical scenes. Where previously German firms, already involved in the production of erotica and Roman Catholic prints, had manufactured some Hindu devotional pictures, Ravi Varma and his German collaborator succeeded in creating an all-India market for his paintings.

By the end of the nineteenth century, the colour prints produced by Ravi Varma and the presses in Calcutta had captured the popular art market and because of the style of production were becoming more uniform. The new and realistic settings chosen for devotional pictures owed much to the interiors of the dwellings of contemporary wealthy Hindus, with their neo-classical columns and European furnishings, and to European landscapes. At the same time, features of the older symbolism – the use of bright blue when depicting certain deities and the incorporation of multiple limbs – were retained, particularly by the Calcutta Art Studio. Vivid colours, quasi-medieval costumes, rounded goddesses with faint, enigmatic smiles and glistening landscapes with swans and lotuses soon characterised the genre. The faces of the deities took on an increasingly asexual appearance as a result of their full form and composed features, an impression strengthened by long hair and ornamentation. These pictures continue to occupy a central place in the devotional lives of countless Hindus, whether as posters or on calendars. During the campaign for independence, Ravi Varma's Western-influenced style fell out of favour with the intelligentsia, and more assertive and ferocious embodiments of the nationalist cause in the form of the Mother Goddess were popularised.

Several other important centres for the creation and distribution of poster art emerged during the twentieth century, including the Sri Devi Art Studio established by C. Kondiah Raju at Kovilpatti in 1944. The increasingly standardised portrayal of the deities in devotional prints has influenced the depiction of mythological subjects in the Indian cinema, for example Saṇtoṣī Mā-(tā), in the hugely popular serialisations of the *Rāmāyaṇa* in the late 1980s and then the *Mahābhārata* on Doordarshan (the state television service), and more recently on the internet. As sympathy for the Hindutva movement grew in India during the last quarter of the twentieth century, representations of Rāma, in particular, were transformed to emphasise more militant and militaristic characteristics. The consolidation of a sizeable Hindu diaspora during the twentieth century created conditions that encouraged the standardisation of Hindu iconography in media designed for global circulation. The popular *Amar Chitra Katha* comic series, with its instantly recognisable depictions of deities and great personalities, has become widely used by communities outside India to introduce their children to Hindu myths and a Hindu understanding of India's history. The process of drawing upon both Indian and European artistic conventions continues in movements such as the International Society for Krishna Consciousness (ISKCON), which publishes richly illustrated texts.

The arrival of photography in India during the 1840s reinforced the growing tendency towards realism in the portraiture of artists like Ravi Varma, further contributing to the standardisation of popular iconographic representations. It also enabled devotees to photograph the great religious personalities of the latter part of that century and subsequently. It thus gave rise to traditions of 'photo iconography' centred upon popular Hindu gurus, for example Ramakrishna and Sathya Sai Baba, and leaders, such as Mahatma Gandhi, in which the photographic image has shaped subsequent representations in other media, including 'bazaar art'.

Mass production, the availability of new materials and the effects of consumerism and globalisation continue to affect the production and situating of mūrti (sacred images). Precious metal, bronze and clay have given way to ceramics and plastic, and pictures of deities and teachers have been reproduced on items as diverse as key fobs, tiles and fridge magnets. Representations of the divine are now manufactured for acquisition as souvenirs, whether by Hindu or foreign tourists, as much as for their original use as cultic objects. The deities in their festival tableaux have not been immune from the influence of Hollywood cinema.

See also: **Aesthetics; Caste; Diaspora; Gandhi, Mohandas Karamchand; Guru; Hindutva; Image worship; International Society for Krishna Consciousness; Mahābhārata; Mandir; Rāma; Ramakrishna, Sri; Rāmāyaṇa; Sai Baba, Sathya; Saṇtoṣī Mātā; Śilpaśāstras; Viśvakarman**

GWILYM BECKERLEGGE

Further reading

Babb, L.A. and S.S. Wadley (eds). 1995. *Media and the Transformation of Religion in South Asia*. Philadelphia, PA: University of Pennsylvania Press.

Beckerlegge, G. 2001. 'Hindu Sacred Images for the Mass Market'. In G. Beckerlegge, ed., *From Sacred Text to Internet*. Aldershot: Ashgate, 57–116.

IDOLATRY

Idolatry is often solely narrowed to mean the worship of statues, as practised, by and large, by non-monotheists, but the term may be more accurately extended to the worship or adoration of anything. In fact, many mystics hold idolatry to be the veneration of anything other than the divine, irrespective of how the devotee wishes to portray Him or Her. In religious contexts, the term idolatry possesses negative undertones propelled by the cultural imperialism of monotheism: the idol is seen as that of a 'false' god and it is only the formless deity that has the potential for divine legitimacy. It is thus necessary to understand this form of worship from the perspective of the Hindu.

When the devotee engages in what appears to be the worship of a statue or a picture, he or she participates in mūrti pūjā, literally 'the worship of the form' and not of the statue *per se*. The clichéd and perhaps apologetic interpretation of this practice, which suggests that the statue is not the object of worship but an aid to worship, holds true to some extent, but the devotional sentiment may be taken a step further. What the outsider sees is not what is in the mind and heart of the mūrti pūjāka, the one who engages in mūrti pūjā. The bhakti or devotion expressed by the sincere devotee is subjectively transformative in that the statue is not actually a statue; for the devotee, it is the very manifestation of his or her deity. The mūrti does not simply enable the devotee to focus, but to serve his or her Lord in person. To the outsider, this appears as the worship of carved stone, but just as one sees a loved one in a photograph and not the ink and paper used to create the image, the devotee sees through the material used to make the statue, and instead perceives his or her Lord alone. Thus the devotee's bhakti can in principle, transform any object into the mūrti of a deity for the devotee, if the heart of the devotee perceives it as such. One may argue that it is the experience of bhakti that then matters, and not necessarily the object of devotion; the mūrti simply facilitates this bhakti.

The mandir is not just a building containing a statue, but is seen as the temple of an indwelling living deity. When a mūrti is formally installed in a mandir, the prāṇa pratiṣṭhā ceremony of infusing the life force of the deity into the statue is undertaken. This is performed according to a strict protocol through the recitation of sacred formulae. The mūrti must then be seen as living, treated respectfully and worshipped daily in accordance with formal ritual procedure. The difference in the two personal and formal approaches perhaps stems from mūrti pūjā's dual origins in both folk worship and Tantrism.

Historically speaking, iconography of deities has been present ever since pre-Vedic days and continued to exist in the popular and vernacular traditions. Vedic ritualists, however, concerned with the performance of fire sacrifices had no need for anthropomorphic imagery but focused on the powers and functions of the devas, the cosmic archetypes. While the *Upaniṣads* centred on the nature of the Self (Ātman) as Brahman, emerging theistic sects equated their deities with the manifest forms of Brahman and developed their own mūrtis and temples. In the *Gṛhyasūtras*, a set of rules for householders, pūjā refers to the honouring of brāhmaṇas invited to ceremonies. The same ritual procedure was used for the ritual worship of the deity through the mūrti once the practice was later incorporated into the Brahmanical system. Popular worship focused on the relation between the deity and the devotee and thus any representation was appropriate. Tantrism, though, which emphasised the characteristics of the image as revealing the attributes of the deva, resulted in the standardisation of the images of the deities along with a new understanding of the relationship between the powers of the deity and the devotee.

See also: **Agnihotra; Ātman; Bhakti; Brahman; Brāhmaṇas; Deities; Gṛhyasūtras; Image worship; Indus Valley civilisation; Mandir; Popular and vernacular traditions; Pūjā; Tantrism; Upaniṣads**

RISHI HANDA

Further reading

Hopkins, Thomas J. 1971. *The Hindu Religious Tradition*. Belmont, CA: Wadsworth Publishing Company.

Kantikar, Helen and Duncan Macpherson. 1999. *Accessing Hinduism*. London: Melisende.

IMAGE WORSHIP

Image worship is a widely prevalent practice in Hinduism. It has blossomed and survived through the centuries of its manifold growth and spread beyond India's borders into Tibet, China, Japan and the Southeast Asian countries through travelling and migrating Buddhists and Hindus. Today, image worship is engaged in both in urban areas and in villages. In recent years it has been televised widely in channels watched avidly by Indians living abroad. The practice also survives in the numerous temples (mandir) scattered throughout India and quietly exists in household shrines, in dashboards of taxi cabs, lorries, long-distance buses, in shops and tea-shacks. In fact, in spite of strong pronouncements made by highly respected systems of philosophy originating in India calling the Divine formless (e.g. Advaita Vedānta), it can be said that image worship is still one of the defining characteristics of Hinduism. This is because of the Hindu belief that the Formless expresses itself through forms, that it is indeed immanent in all that is, including the is-not. Non-being and being generate each other, are contained in each other. Together, they make a whole, which continuously becomes manifest in perceptible forms. As manifestations of the creative power, all forms are divine. To be is to be divine, at least in theory. Debate about the role and status of image worship emerged as a major theme of modern Hindu discourse, probably reflecting the prominence attached to critiques of idolatry in Christian missionary polemic. Swami Dayananda Saraswati of the Arya Samaj opposed image worship on the grounds that it was not found in the Veda, famously recalling an incident during the Śivarātri vigil when he was troubled by the sight of mice running over the image of Śiva and unable to accept that God would permit this defilement.

In contrast, Swami Vivekananda was not prepared to condemn image worship since he emphasised the tolerance and inclusivity of Hinduism, which meant that even less sophisticated forms of belief and practice were worthy of respect, in the process attacking those reformers who inveighed against image worship because they were condemning a form of devotion necessary to others.

Moreover, it is still possible to find examples of Christian denunciation of image worship. A broadcast made by Pat Robertson with his son, Gordon Robertson, went as far as to identify what they regarded as idolatry as the cause of India's ills, causing considerable offence and prompting a defensive reaction that tended to present image worship in symbolic terms.

The word 'image' can be understood in many ways. Images can mean 'reflections', akin to what is known as 'pratibimba' in Sanskrit. Reflections can appear in the mirror, in water or against light, as shadows. In each case, it is understood that the reflection is a mere image of the real object and hence not real in the same sense as the object itself. It cannot perform the same functions as the object itself. Hence, the images are treated as somewhat unreal, more like appearances than as reality. Yet that they are also real in some sense is undeniable. Even as images, they can wreak havoc and destruction through their power of creating illusions. Avidya (ignorance), māyā (illusion) and bhranti (error) are powerful forces in life, even though they recede when true knowledge dawns. They are built into our knowledge system, a system that brings into play several factors interacting with each other and building upon each other. Most of these factors are either completely or partially beyond our control. For instance, visual perception depends on the condition of our eyes, how the object is lit, at which time of the year it is being perceived, from which angle, etc. When we deal with reflections, the additional factor of a medium through which the object is perceived is introduced and its effect upon our perception has to be reckoned with. We may perceive an object knowing it to be a mere reflection, or we may erroneously think of the image as the real object. When the Hindu worships the image, neither of these processes takes place. When the image is known to be a simple reflection, it is easily seen as not the real object and not placed on the altar. Sultan Alauddin Khilji saw queen Padminī's image in the mirror, as the purdah regulations did not permit a direct encounter. What he saw infatuated him and led him through a series of acts to win the queen 'in person'. The image of the queen was not what he worshipped. He went after the real Padminī. In contrast, when the lion in Aesop's fables saw his own image in the well he mistook it for a real lion, was angered by what he saw and jumped to his death. Likewise, in Plato's 'Allegory of the Cave', the shadows on the wall of the cave are perceived as real objects by the cave dwellers, who have no access to the real objects casting the shadows from outside the cave. In the last two instances, the image is perceived as the real object due to an inescapable condition built into the system of knowledge of the respective perceivers. In order for the animal or the cave dwellers to tell the image from the real object, things will need to happen. Only then can they be set free and stopped from suicidal leaps and enchained existence. The Hindu, however, does not need to be 'delivered' from a similar situation. Image worship is the worship not of an appearance, but of what is genuinely real or as real as things can get to any human being.

In a sense, all human beings can be seen as images of the divine. The father and the mother become the supreme deities. Devotion to them is experienced as a fulfilling religious emotion and may be considered enough for a spiritual life as the divine spirit resides in our parents. In the same vein, our children are images of God. The qualities of innocence, joy, trust and unconditional devotion to parents that we find in the children are recognised as divine. The child we hold in our arms is the same as the Baby Kṛṣṇa. Tending to our baby is a complete religious activity. It brings us joy, makes us responsible, opens our hearts to all other children. Similarly, loving one's spouse can be a religious function if one is able to see in one's partner a loving companion for life. If the partners fulfil their vows to each other, then they have fulfilled a religious obligation. Our involvement with our friends can also be considered a sacred affair. A friend is an image of the Divine. Thus, dāsya, or service to parents, vātsalya, or affection for children, prema, or love for a partner, the bonds of brotherhood and sisterhood that we may feel for our friends, are all divine experiences. It is because we are thus able to see what is human as divine that at times of great sorrow, when we need to reach out to the source of superhuman strength, we are able to cry out to the Divine as our Father or Mother, Friend or Saviour, hold it close to our hearts as we do a baby, to rejuvenate our afflicted selves.

Once the world is perceived as created in the image of God, the entire order of nature becomes worthy of worship. Animals of all kinds, members of the plant kingdom, rocks and stones, mountains and rivers, the sky, the air, the waters, the earth, the heavenly bodies, the day and the night are all seen as bearing the imprint of the Divine. Hymns are sung in their praise, propitiations offered and tender, loving care is bestowed upon them. The thought that the world is an image of the Divine is not, however, the reason why images are built and worshipped by the Hindus. This philosophy simply clears the way for such worship by declaring that there is nothing unholy about form, multiplicity, change or mutability. It further suggests a way to connect the formless with what has form, the one with the many, the universal with the particular, by using the parent–child analogy. It provides a philosophical basis for nature worship, animism and polytheism.

The origin, persistence and celebration of image worship are significantly connected with the idea of manifestation. The image is worshipped because the deity manifests itself through that image. Particular deities manifest themselves through particular images. This does not necessarily mean that the Hindu is a polytheist. It is widely understood that the different deities are manifestations of the same supreme deity in various roles. Just as the same individual is capable of being multiple without losing his/her identity, the Divine also can undergo different experiences and express its different moods, functions and acts in different visible images. The settings, shapes, postures and facial expressions may change accordingly. The worship of multiple images can cohabit quite comfortably in the mind of a Hindu with the belief that in the ultimate analysis there is only one Divine Spirit. We call this One Divine by many names in recognition of our different needs. In fact, a Hindu has the right to choose any particular deity as his or her very own to worship. This chosen deity is known as Iṣṭadevatā. However, each person knows that the numerous deities chosen by the numerous people are really one and the same. The many deities simply represent the many ways in which people have sought refuge in the same source of strength and compassion. It is the one indestructible quality which manifests itself in particular forms. When that ground of all, namely Being, becomes discernible by us in a particular object, that object is seen as worship-worthy. Any existent thus qualifies for worship. At the hour of worship, however, we need to go through a conscious process of deliberation and choice. The image worshipper goes though a mental process resulting in the recognition of a particular form as divine for the purpose of that specific act of worship. When the image is built, the worshipper has to ceremoniously instil life into it. The ceremony involves purification with substances such as honey or ghee, the installation of a number of deities into the various parts of the image, and prāṇa pratīṣṭhā, which involves the recitation of mantras to give prāṇā, or vital breath, to the image. The final act is the opening of the eyes, after which the image is considered to be 'live'. Without this ceremony, the image remains an artefact, as venerable as any other piece of nature, even if it is a spectacular piece of art. The Divine Spirit must be invited to take residence in the image or else be discovered, through the grace of God, to be pre-existent in it, before it begins to be worshipped. At the end of worship, the invoked spirit may be bade goodbye, and clay images are often immersed in the waters in order to return to the earth what is from the earth. The Citmayī (one whose essence is consciousness) appeared as Mṛnmayī (one who is made of dirt) to the devotee to establish a bond with her 'earthy' child. The straw, the clay, the rocks, the metals that make the image are, by Hindu logic and philosophy, all divine. But worship is an act of love, connected to the insecurities of our mortal existence in need of benediction and support. The Hindu experiences fulfilment in the act of worship when an image that is alive with the presence of the Divine is placed in front of the eyes and the heart, much in the same manner that our being is quieted when we can behold and hold our dear ones in our presence. The fact that the devotee pours out his devotion on one particular locus does not clash with the belief that the Divine is omnipresent. Thus, it is with volition that the devotee looks upon the image as a manifestation, consecrates it and proceeds to offer the worship. The Divine is here, there and everywhere. In his book *Yaksas: Essays in Water Cosmology*, Ananda Coomaraswamy refers to this characteristic of Being as the dual nature of Brahman as being 'in a likeness and not in any likeness'.

When trying to understand image worship, the idea of manifestation has to be looked at carefully. Every existent, animate or inanimate, manifests the Divine. It is, is no longer and becomes again, in accordance with the laws of its own being and of being in general. Each being can be said to manifest the principles of birth, growth, decay and rebirth. When an image is worshipped, however, the Great Root of all being is specifically invited to take its seat in the image, to manifest itself in the little set-up. There is a process of double manifestation involved here. One is spontaneous, taking place with no human intervention, as God manifest in creation. The other occurs through the special call of the worshipper. The image becomes religiously meaningful because the devotee gives it that meaning. We see the image as housing God, and hence cherish it. Worship is a two-party affair. The devotee plays as important a role in it as the deity. Rabindranath Tagore expressed this sentiment in the lines: 'but for me, Oh Lord of the three worlds, all your love would be meaningless' (*Geetabitan*). The same truth is expressed in the following lines: 'If I die, Oh Goddess of the Three-cities, there will be no one to call your name'.

Thus it is that the Hindus believe that the One Divinity manifests itself in plural forms, in images of stone, clay, metals, through strokes of the artist's brush, in photographs and in all live creation. In undergoing this process of manifestation, the manifesting power subjects itself to the principles of subjective limitations that characterise anything created: (1) its experience can last only for a limited period of time and can occur only in succession; (2) it can be in only one place at a time; (3) it can attend to only a few things at a time; (4) it is limited to the confines of its own way of knowing; (5) it is subject to the confusion-creating powers of Māyā. These limitations are called prapañcas, or marks of finitude. While subjecting itself to prapañca, the Manifesting Spirit yet remains ultimately free and identical with itself. The manifestation is an 'ābhasā', a 'glimpse' of what is manifested, without the latter being exhausted or affected by the process. The Divine is essentially formless and invisible, and yet, as constantly manifesting, is always recognisable in the manifest.

See also: **Advaita; Altars, domestic; Arya Samaj; Brahman; Buddhism, relationship with Hinduism; Coomaraswamy, Ananda Kentish; Dayananda Saraswati, Swami; Idolatry; Images and iconography; Iṣṭadevatā; Kṛṣṇa; Mandir; Mantra; Māyā; Ṛṣi; Sacred animals; Sacred geography; Śiva; Śivarātri; Southeast and East Asia, Hindus in; Tagore, Rabindranath; Television and radio; Veda; Vivekananda, Swami**

KARABI SEN

Further reading

Bakshi, Dwijendra Nath. 1979. *Hindu Divinities in Japanese Buddhist Pantheon: A Complete Study*. Calcutta: Benten Publishers.

Beswick, Ethel. 1993. *The Hindu Gods*. New Delhi: Crest Publishing House.

Coomaraswamy, Ananda K. 1993. *Yaksas: Essays in Water Cosmology*. Oxford: Oxford University Press.

Eck, D.L. 1985. *Darśan: Seeing the Divine Image of India*, 2nd rev. enlarged edn. Chambersburg, PA: Anima Books.

Eliade, Mircea. 1952. *Images and Symbols*. London: Harvill Press.

Kinsley, David. 1997. *Hindu Goddesses: Visions of the Divine Feminine in the Hindu Religious Tradition*. Berkeley, CA: UC Press.

Pal, Pratapaditya. 1978. *The Ideal Image: The Gupta Sculptural Tradition and its Influence*. New York: Asia Society.

Rajan, V.J. 1995. 'Using TV, Christian Pat Robertson Denounces Hinduism as "Demonic": Evangelist Opposes Freedom of Religion, Says It's Time to Convert India and Wants to Keep Hinduism Out of US'. *Hinduism Today* (July); www.geocities.com/CapitolHill/7027/htoday.html (accessed 25 May 2006).

Rao, Gopinath T.A. 1985. *Elements of Hindu Iconography*. 2nd edn. Delhi: Motilal Banarasidass.

Richards, G. (ed.). 1985. *A Sourcebook of Modern Hinduism*. Richmond: Curzon Press.

Rose, H.A. 1986. *Hindu Gods and Goddesses*, ed. S.P. Gulati. Delhi: Amar Prakashan.

Satpathy, Sarbeswar. 1991. *Sakti Iconography in Tantric Mahavidyas*. Calcutta: Punthi Pustak.

Shastry, Ramaswamy. 1922. *Hindu Culture: An Exposition and a Vindication*. Madras: S. Ganesan

Singh, Chitralekha and Prem Nath. 1995. *Hindu Goddesses*. New Delhi: Crest Publishing House.

Singh, R.S. 1993. *Hindu Iconography in Tantrayana Buddhism*. New Delhi: Ramanda Vidya Bhawan

Smith, H. Daniel and M. Narasimhachary. 1991. *Handbook of Hindu Gods, Goddesses and Saints*. New Delhi: Sandeep Prakashan.

Tattvabibhusan, Sitanath. 1898. *Hindu Theism*. Calcutta: GGM Brothers.

IMAGES AND ICONOGRAPHY

Images of the various Hindu deities are not only found in temples and shrines but can be found in virtually all Hindu shops, offices, homes and on the dashboards of trucks and buses. These images can be found in a staggering array of differing forms such as colourful lithographs, wood, stone and brass sculptures, plastic models and stucco work.

The earliest carved images on the subcontinent are images of yakṣas and yakṣis dating from the third century BCE. These images of animistic spirits, often in the form of snakes, are associated with fertility and are often found near pools and the bases of trees, and can still be found throughout India today. The earliest images of Hindu gods are some bas relief carvings of the deities Indra and Sūrya found at a Buddhist monastic retreat at Bhājā, near Bombay, from the second century BCE. Images did not really flourish until the Gupta period (fourth to seventh century CE), which is often called the Golden Age of Indian Art. During this period we also see the construction of the first stone temples and it is likely that it is during this period that images became important focal points of religious practice.

There are three main categories of sacred images, which may be termed formal, informal and natural icons. An informal icon might be little more than a large rock, usually painted orange and frequently with large stylised staring eyes. Other informal icons might have features that make them clearly recognisable as one or other of the many Hindu deities. For example, rudimentary images of Hanumān as rocks roughly carved in the form of a monkey carrying a mace and painted orange can be found in many parts of India. Natural icons are specific natural objects that are associated with a particular deity. Examples of natural icons include the ice liṅga that form each year in the Amarnath cave in Kashmir and śāligrāmas, fossil stones found in some Himalayan rivers that are said to be a manifestation of Viṣṇu.

Formal icons on the other hand are made according to strict conventions which govern posture, colour, number of arms, sacred objects which are held, mudrās (gestures) and appropriate vāhana (animal mount/vehicle). Each of these prescribed elements of the image has a specified range of meanings. For example, Śiva's triśūla (trident) on the macrocosmic level represents the three guṇas and consequently suggests that Śiva fulfils the functions of Creator, Preserver and Destroyer. On the microcosmic level the triśūla represents the three principal nāḍis (the subtle channels that conduct prāṇa): iḍā, pingalā and suṣumnā (Daniélou 1991: 216).

Not only do all the prescribed elements have to be present but there are very precise measurements that determine the iconometric proportions of each image. The formulas for the making of images are found in a number of texts known as the *Śilpaśāstras*. Details of iconography can also be found in the *Purāṇas*, and in particular the *Viṣṇu Purāṇa*.

The image has to be beautiful for it to be an effective focal point for religious devotion. The definition of what is beautiful is defined in the *Śilpaśāstras*. Only if the iconometric proportions are accurate does the image become tenable as a place for the deity to reside (Michell 1988: 73). The basic unit of measurement in the construction of an image is known as a tala, which is the distance between the hairline and the lower jaw. The *Śilpaśāstras* also specify the exact process for making images. For example, in making the brass image of Śiva Naṭarāja (Lord of the Dance), utilising a lost wax process, there are detailed instructions on how to prepare the wax, the clay that is used to coat the initial model and the recipe for the alloy (Pillai *et al.* 2002).

Each particular deity is also represented in numerous different manifestations. For example, the *Mudgala Purāṇa* lists thirty-two names of Gaṇeśa. Although there seem to be no iconographical details given in the text, these names have assumed clearly delineated iconographical forms. For example, Bāla Gaṇapati is traditionally represented as seated, with four arms and holding a banana, a mango, sugar cane and a jackfruit, whereas Vīra Gaṇapati is represented with sixteen arms, each holding a weapon, such as a discus, sword and trident. Different forms visually represent differing aspects of the deity. The fruit in the image of Bāla Gaṇapati represents fertility and abundance and the weapons held by Vīra Gaṇapati represent the discriminating powers of the mind, both characteristics associated with Gaṇeśa.

Furthermore each image suggests a bhāva, a mood or state of being, according to the form that it takes. Hindu iconography has developed a system of conventions that evoke certain feelings. These conventions are often determined by the relationship between vertical, horizontal and diagonal lines. For example, the lines of the image of Viṣṇu reclining on the cosmic serpent Śeṣa are predominately horizontal, evoking a sense of tranquillity and harmony; whereas a stress on diagonal lines, such as in the image of Durgā slaying Mahiṣa the Buffalo demon, suggests action and dynamism. The linear orientation of the image is also related to the elements. So a horizontal line is associated with water, whereas a diagonal line is related to the wind (Baumer 1995).

The image of the deity in the temple is known as mūrti or arcāvatāra. Both of these terms suggest that the infinite, which transcends all form, takes on a defined and limited shape for the sake of the devotee. The image therefore is not simply a representation or a symbol, but is considered to be the deity. In Vaiṣṇavism the mūrti is considered to be one of the five forms of the deity.

There are two main forms of temple images. There are images that are permanently installed and utsava mūrti, processional images. Many of the beautiful brass images that are displayed in museums of Indian art throughout the world are in fact designed and made to be carried outside the temple on special festival occasions. Often these images are carried around on wooden carts known as rathas. The image and the processional vehicle are elaborately decorated. The most famous of these processional festivals is the Rathayātrā in Puri dedicated to Jagannātha. In addition temporary images are sometimes also important features of certain festivals. For example, in Bengal large images of Durgā are constructed of unfired clay and placed in the street during Durgā Pūjā. These images are then destroyed and remade each year.

See also: **Buddhism, relationship with Hinduism; Deities; Durgā; Durgā Pūjā; Gaṇeśa; Guṇas; Hanumān; Indra; Jagannātha; Mahiṣa; Mandir; Mudrā; Mūrti; Purāṇas; Ratha Yātrā; Śeṣa; Śilpaśāstra; Śiva; Sūrya; Utsava; Vaiṣṇavism; Viṣṇu; Wayside shrines; Yakṣas**

STEPHEN JACOBS

Further reading

Baumer, B. 1995. 'Lines of Fire, Lines of Water: The Elements in Śilpaśāstras'. *The Agamic Tradition and the Arts*; http://www.ignca.nic.in/ps_03012.htm (accessed 1 October 2004).

Burton, T.R. 1992. *Hindu Art*. London: British Museum Press.

Daniélou, A. 1991. *The Myths and Gods of India*. Rochester, VT: Inner Traditions.

Eck, D. 1981. *Darśan: Seeing the Divine Image in India*. Chambersburg, PA: Anima Books.

Grimes, J. 1995. *Ganapati: Song of the Self*. Albany, NY: State University of New York Press.

Michell, G. 1988. *The Hindu Temple: An Introduction to its Meaning and Form*. Chicago, IL: University of Chicago Press.

Mookerjee, A. 1985. *Ritual Art of India*. London: Thames and Hudson.

Pillai, R.M., S.K.G. Pillai and A.D. Damodaran. 2002. 'The Lost-Wax Casting of Icons, Utensils, Bells and Other Items in South India'. *JOM*; http://www.tms.org/pubs/journals/JOM/0210/Pillai-0210.html (accessed 1 October 2004).

INDO-EUROPEAN TRADITIONS

Indo-European (IE), a term borrowed from comparative linguistics, refers to a particular group of languages, including Sanskrit, Latin and Greek, which descend from a common origin. This IE proto-language was unwritten, but can be partially reconstructed by comparing its descendants. Where and when it was spoken is controversial, but many favour the south Russian steppes *c.*3500 BCE. Spreading from there, it differentiated into various branches, among them Indo-Iranian, which itself branched into Avestan (the original language of Zoroastrian scriptures) and Sanskrit. Since culture is largely transmitted in and alongside language, the question soon arose how far the linguists' model applies to traditions – to belief systems, narratives, customs, etc. Though vigorously promoted by the copious and erudite work of Georges Dumézil (1898–1986), IE cultural comparativism has remained controversial, and most specialists in particular branches of IE studies prefer to ignore comparisons extending outside their specialism. Dumézil's approach has found only a few continuators, and its place in pedagogy remains minimal.

Over the last decade the view that Indo-European languages came to India from outside has been attacked by 'Aryan Indigenists', many of them Indian, who see it as reflecting colonialist prejudice. In their turn the revisionists are attacked as being ignorant of comparative philology and motivated by nationalism (JIES 2002). However, use of a common origin framework for cultural comparativism does not depend on the geographical location of the common origin.

Dumézil's theory of the three functions in IE ideology focuses on a particular triadic pattern pervasive in the older or more traditional parts of the IE world and rare elsewhere. Within such triads each item relates to one of the following principles: (1) sovereignty and the manipulation of the sacred; (2) force or war; (3) fecundity with its conditions and consequences. These principles can be conceptualised as three distinct bundles of ideas which together constitute an ideology used to classify or organise many areas of social life. Where the pattern occurred, the order in which the principles were represented typically reflected a ranking, so the principles were named first, second and third.

In Hinduism the most important manifestation of the ideology was the twice-born varṇas: brāhmaṇas represent the first function, kṣatriya (or rājanya), the second and vaiśya, the third (the śūdra being seen as descendants of the dāsa aboriginals subjugated by immigrant Aryans). But Dumézil recognised many other manifestations. One was a set of Vedic gods – Mitra-Varuṇa, Indra, the twin Aśvins, a grouping attested occasionally in the Saṃhitā and also in a fourteenth century BCE Hittite treaty; here two of the functions are represented by paired beings. Another example was the set of gods who father the five Pāṇḍava brothers in the *Mahābhārata*: Dharma; Vāyu and Indra (both second function); and again the Aśvins. Different manifestations often 'harmonise' with each other. Thus, when the brothers adopt disguises, the son of Dharma chooses a brāhmaṇa role while the twins take vaiśya roles. Manifestations also occur in ritual and law, and Manu's eight modes of marital union (Vivāha) are seen by Dumézil as an expansion of three basic modes – by dowry (kanyādāna, first function), capture (second) and purchase (third).

Manifestations of the ideology may be inherited as such from the IE proto-culture or may be created within their own branch of the tradition in the light of the inherited ideology. Thus, according to Dumézil, the twice-born varṇas continue a division of labour already present in the proto-culture (though not necessarily in the form of social classes), while the Pāṇḍava pentad was created by Indian bards who transposed an inherited theological structure into epic form. Moreover, he (and others, e.g. Bruce Lincoln) have proposed an IE origin for cultural elements that stand outside the three functions. For instance, linguists have long known that the names of Vedic Dyaus, Greek Zeus and Latin Ju(-piter) go back to 'Dyeus' (the inverted commas here indicating a reconstruction), and comparison with the Norse god Heimdall shows that the *Mahābhārata* hero Bhīṣma, incarnation of Dyaus, retains features that once belonged to 'Dyeus'. Surprisingly – given their relative dates of fixation – the *Mahābhārata* offers more to cultural comparativism than do the allusive hymns.

Recent work by Allen argues that Dumézil's trifunctionalism is a compressed model of an ideology that was actually pentadic. Expressed in terms of social roles, the full model would recognise king, priest, warrior, producer, serf. As seen by the twice-born, king and serf are both outsiders, the serf being excluded from cultic life and the king representing totality, transcending or standing outside social divisions. Though the king is sometimes said to be kṣatriya and hence inferior to brāhmaṇas, his separation from kṣatriyas at his inauguration (rājasūya) better represents his basic position. This approach recognises a fourth function relating to Otherness but split into valued and devalued aspects, and it modifies Dumézil's definition of the first function by transferring sovereignty to the valued aspect of the fourth (which also covers creators and founders). The śūdra are interpreted, not as tacked on to an earlier triad, but as filling a devalued slot present in the original ideology (a slot which also covers enemies, demons and destroyers). In general, where Dumézil looks for triads liable to elaboration, the newer model looks for pentads liable to contraction and blurring.

Applied to the *Mahābhārata*, the pentadic model has led to: (1) reanalyses of structures treated by Dumézil (Pāṇḍava brothers, modes of marital union); (2) recognition of new contexts manifesting the ideology (Kaurava generals); (3) some direct comparisons with Greek epic (Arjuna's marital history is cognate with Odysseus'). Probably, indeed, contrary to Dumézil's transposition theory, both epic traditions go back to proto-IE heroic narratives. IE origins have also been suggested for, among other things, the patterning of cosmic time (yugas) and features of yoga and Sāṃkhya doctrine. Though they involve similar methods to IE comparativism, Veda-Avesta comparisons naturally reach back no further than Indo-Iranian.

Scholarly consensus on Hinduism's debt to its IE roots (as distinct from substrate influences and independent developments) will need much further work, but the field offers exciting prospects.

See also: **Arjuna; Aśvins; Bhīṣma; Dharma; Indra; Kauravas; Mahābhārata; Mitra; Nationalism; Pāṇḍavas; Saṃhitā; Sāṃkhya; Sanskrit; Varṇa; Varuṇa; Vivāha; Yoga; Yuga**

NICK ALLEN

Further reading

Allen, N.J. 2000. *Categories and Classifications.* Oxford: Berghahn (esp. references).

Dumézil, G. 1968–73. *Mythe et épopee*, 3 vols [Myth and epic]. Paris: Gallimard (esp. vol. 1, pt I).

Dumézil, G. 1979. *Mariages indo-européens* [Indo-European marriages]. Paris: Payot.

JIES. 2002. (Multiple authors.) 'The Indo-Aryan Migration Debate'. *Journal of Indo-European Studies* 30: 273–409.

Lincoln, B. 1986. *Myth, Cosmos and Society.* Cambridge, MA: Harvard University Press.

Puhvel, J. 1987. *Comparative Mythology.* Baltimore, MD: Johns Hopkins University Press.

Sergent, B. 1997. *Genèse de l'Inde* [Genesis of India]. Paris: Payot.

INDRA

'Lord'; 'man'. The Vedic personification of thunder/lightning and the fertilisation principle of nature. Whereas the features of sky brightness and lightning remained integral to such Dyaus' cognate corollaries as the Greek Zeus and Roman Jupiter, in India the thunder expression of virility emerged as an independent and separate figure, namely Indra, king of the gods. Indra's central feat is the defeat of the rain-withholding dragon Vṛtra, thereby insuring the fertility and prosperity of the lands for humanity. His standing epithet is vajrin, 'bearer of the thunderbolt' (e.g. *Ṛgveda* 10.83.6). As the champion-god *par excellence*, Indra's other enemies include Tvaṣṭṛ, Tvaṣṭṛ's son Viśvarūpa, and even Varuṇa. There is always an implicit if not explicit enmity between Indra and the asuras – exemplified in particular by the Ādityas, the sons of Aditi. It is through this opposition that the anti-humanistic expressions of Brahmanic Hinduism are developed. As early as the *Yajurveda*, the asura Viśvarūpa is converted into a Brāhmaṇa, making Indra's former heroic act an instance of the unforgivable sin of brahmanicide. Vṛtra too comes to be declared a Brāhmaṇa. In subsequent literature, Indra is forever losing his throne to an usurping asura, thereby paving the way for the emergence and super-intervention of the Trimūrti-figures of Śiva and Viṣṇu.

In the Vedic as opposed to the Hindu characterisation of Indra, the rain-god is a full expression of victorious humanity. He is often paired with a supporting figure (Agni, Viṣṇu, Pūṣan), and his alliance with the intoxicating Soma is especially stressed. *Ṛgveda* 6.59.2 names the lightning-god Indra and the fire-god Agni as twins. Elsewhere, the one is identified as the other. In essence, Indra and Agni are the divine twins, or Aśvins – expressing ultimately both the immortal and mortal aspects of human nature. While Indra's name is compared by some with the word indu, 'drop', suggesting Soma, it is more likely to be a cognate of the Greek anēr (genitive, andros), 'man'. Indra's attendants are the rain-assistants, the Maruts. Among the epithets ascribed to Indra, we find that of savitṛ (*Ṛgveda* 2.30.1, 3.33.6), which emerges later as the solar stimulator god Savitṛ.

Other popular Indra epithets are Śakra, 'mighty one' (e.g. *Ṛgveda* 1.10.5, 4.16.6), and Śacīpati, 'lord of might', 'husband of Śacī' (e.g. *Ṛgveda* 3.60.6) – the personification of strength being considered Indra's consort. In later literature, Indra and Śacī's child is Jayanta, 'victory'. The essential corpus of Indra's mythology survives through the Hindu gods of Śiva and Śiva's son Kumār/Skanda/Kārttikeya. The feminine personification of divine energy, now known as Śakti, is usually identified as Śiva's consort Durgā. Indra himself has been relegated to being one of the eight world-protectors (Lokapālas) – most prominently as the guardian of the direction of the east.

See also: **Aditi; Agni; Asuras; Aśvins; Durgā; Dyaus Pitṛ; Śiva; Skanda; Soma; Trimūrti; Tvaṣṭṛ; Varuṇa; Vedism; Viṣṇu**

Michael York

INDRA DEVI (1900–2002)

Born Eugenie Vasilievna Peterson in 1900 in Latvia, she married a Czech commercial attaché and in 1930 travelled to India, where she studied yoga, first with Kuvalayananda and later with Krishnamacharya. For seven years she ran, with Krishnamacharya's blessing, a yoga school in Shanghai. Then in 1946 she sailed for America, where she started teaching yoga to Hollywood stars such as Gloria Swanson and Greta Garbo. During the 1960s she visited Soviet Russia and briefly taught yoga to government officials in the Kremlin. In 1966 she met Sai Baba and formulated a new practice based on this encounter called 'Sai Yoga'. She died in Buenos Aires in 2002. Sometimes referred to as 'the First Lady of American Yoga', Indra Devi did much to make yoga accessible to the West. Her early practical books, like *Forever Young, Forever Healthy* (1953, based on her time with Krishnamacharya) and *Yoga for Americans* (1959), present yoga primarily as a regime of physical and mental health, divested of mystical trappings.

See also: **Krishnamacharya, T.; Kuvalayananda, Swami and Kaivalyadhama; Sai Baba, Sathya; Yoga; Yoga, Modern**

MARK SINGLETON

Further reading

Devi, I. 1955. *Forever Young, Forever Healthy*. Blackpool: A. Thomas.

INDRA JĀTRĀ

While this autumnal festival continues to be celebrated in several places in India and Nepal, it is only Kathmandu that celebrates the festival in a fashion that adheres closely to the ritual prescriptions laid out in classical Sanskrit-language texts. The earliest reference to the origin of this festival is found in *Mahābhārata* I.57, in which Indra has King Vasu raise a wooden pole, still the festival's central object, as a reminder of his royal dharma. The Nepalese origin story focuses, rather, on the humiliation of the marginally royal Indra, arrested by the citizens of the Kathmandu Valley for stealing the parijat flower. The Kathmandu performance incorporates an amazing variety of ritual elements, many of which are carried out via a series of urban processions, that serve to construct royal power, humiliate the thief Indra, display the protective power offered by Bhairav and the living goddess Kumārī, and remember the recently departed ancestors.

See also: **Indra; Kumārī Jātrā; Mahābhārata; Pitṛs; Utsava**

MICHAEL BALTUTIS

Further reading

Toffin, Gerard. 1992. 'The Indra Jātrā of Kathmandu as a Royal Festival: Past and Present'. *Contributions to Nepalese Studies* 19: 73–92.

INDRAPRASTHA

Literally meaning 'Indra's station', Indraprastha is the capital city of the Pāṇḍavas in the *Mahābhārata*. The Pāṇḍavas built Indraprastha, which lies along the Yamunā River, on an uncultivated tract of forested land which was given to them by their uncle King Dhṛtarāṣṭra in an attempt to avoid the inevitable conflict between the Pāṇḍavas and his own sons, the Kauravas. The *Mahābhārata* recounts that Kṛṣṇa and Arjuna burned down the Khāṇḍava forest, paving the way for the construction of the capital city, where King Yudhiṣṭhira would perform his consecration ceremony (rājasūya), proclaiming himself the most powerful king. Despite these grand beginnings, Indraprastha was only the Pāṇḍava capital city for a brief period, as after emerging victorious in the great Bhārata war the Pāṇḍavas claimed the Kaurava capital city of Hāstinapura for themselves. Some archaeologists claim that the excavation site at Purānā Qilā, in present-day Delhi, represents the ruins of Indraprastha.

See also: **Arjuna; Dhṛtarāṣṭra; Indra; Kṛṣṇa; Mahābhārata; Pāṇḍavas; Yudhiṣṭhira**

BRIAN BLACK

Further reading

van Buitenen, J.A.B. 1973. *The Mahābhārata, 1. The Book of the Beginning*. Chicago, IL: Chicago University Press.

van Buitenen, J.A.B. 1975. *The Mahābhārata, 2. The Book of the Assembly Hall; 3. The Book of the Forest*. Chicago, IL: Chicago University Press.

van Buitenen, J.A.B. 1978. *The Mahābhārata, 4. The Book of Virāṭa; 5. The Book of the Effort*. Chicago, IL: Chicago University Press.

Fitzgerald, James L. 2004. *The Mahābhārata, 11. The Book of Women; 12. The Book of Peace: Part One*. Chicago, IL: Chicago University Press).

INDUS VALLEY CIVILISATION

Discussions of the origins of Hinduism until the early twentieth century had one obvious starting point: the Veda of the Aryans. The term Aryan derives from the Sanskrit 'ārya', which means 'noble' and is used to designate the people whose religious world is reflected in the *Ṛgveda*. However, as much of Hinduism is not prefigured in the Veda, the discovery of the Indus Valley Civilisation was greeted with great excitement. The cities of Harappa and Mohenjo-Daro, part of the Indus Valley Civilisation, were uncovered by Sir John Marshall and his team during the 1920s. These urban settlements were located in the basin of the Indus river, which flows through present-day Pakistan. They flourished from approximately 2500 BCE to 1700 BCE, although the beginnings of the civilisation itself have been dated to the Neolithic Period (7000–6000 BCE). Both cities had a huge acropolis and rectangular city plans, with Mohenjo-Daro also sporting a Great Bath. Later archaeological findings uncovered over 1,000 more sites, including Kot Diji, Amri, Kalibangan, Mehrgarh and Lothal, as well as an impressive palace in Mudigak, Afghanistan. The cultural unity between the cities has been demonstrated in architecture, pottery and writing, and archaeologists have now categorised the various historical strata into Pre-Harappan, Early Harappan, Mature Harappan and Late Harappan.

C.F. Oldham (1893) first tried to parallel the *Ṛgveda* land of Sapta Sindhu, or 'Seven Rivers', with some empirical paleogeology. The Sarasvatī (between the Yamunā and the Sutudri or Sutlej) was considered the most distinct in majesty (*Ṛgveda* 4:61.13) and Oldham thought that this may be the dry riverbed of Hakra, which, according to local legends, once flowed through the desert to the sea. After the discovery of the Indus Valley Civilisation, Sir Aurel Stein (1942) mapped out various Harappan sites along the banks of the Hakra and his discoveries raised many questions about the relationship between the Vedic Aryans and the Indus Valley residents: if this river was indeed the Sarasvatī of the *Ṛgveda*, could the Aryans have lived at the same time as, or even been related to the citizens of, the Indus Valley Civilisation? Some scholars thought that the Indus Valley Civilisation held the key to the indigenous culture that had existed prior to the presumed Aryan invasion. A variant of this view posits Aryan migrations, though here too the Aryans tend to emerge as dominant. In religious terms, this suggests that indigenous beliefs and practices filtered into and interacted with an exogenous Vedic heritage. An alternative view identifies continuities between the Indus Valley Civilisation and the Aryans, according to which the former was an early version of Vedic culture. The religious implications of this view turn on the wholly indigenous roots of Hinduism rather than appealing to an incoming Indo-European ideology.

Although such speculations are interesting, they are problematic because both the Aryan and the Indus Valley civilisations are ancient and we cannot accurately judge the nature of the religion or culture from those times. The discussion has also taken a political dimension in the post-colonial period, with many Indian scholars hoping that the Indus Valley Civilisation can demonstrate that the Aryans came from India, rather than from outside, as most Western scholars think. However, one should be wary of misinterpreting why certain scholars have questioned the status quo; they are not necessarily working with a nationalist agenda in mind, but are, rather, questioning the standard hypotheses about this highly speculative area of study (Bryant 2001).

It is often argued that the difference between the Aryan and Indus Valley civilisations is that the Aryans were nomadic, pastoral and horse-centred: it is generally thought that they introduced the domestic horse into the country. On the other hand, there is some evidence to support the indigenist interpretation in reports of horse remains having been found at a number of Indus sites. If confirmed, this would suggest that the Indus Valley Civilisation was Aryan. Of course, both the nature of the remains and the role of the horse as an Aryan cultural marker have been questioned.

Other findings, including seals, figurines, beads and pottery, have encouraged a lively debate about the relationship between the Vedic texts, early Hinduism and the Indus Valley Civilisation. Of particular importance are the female figurines and the 'Paśupati' seal, which have all been paralleled to later Indian religious ideas. The female figurines, typically made out of terracotta, may have been statues of goddesses (not necessarily relating to Hindu deities) and the 'Paśupati' seal has been interpreted as a prototype of the god Śiva, in his form as the Lord of animals (Hiltebeitel 1978). The figure's posture, seated with knees out and feet joined, may also indicate an early form of yoga and his moon-shaped hair could resemble the horns of a bull-god. The discovery of 'phallic'-shaped stones has also caused some scholars to wonder if there was a prototype of Śiva in his representation as the liṅga, but again we must be wary of trying to associate an unknown ancient object with a much later form of religious practice.

An undeciphered system of writing has been uncovered on a number of the steatite seals and copper plates, and it is hoped that once this script is understood the debate can be resolved. The problem is that neither the script nor the language is known, and no bilingual inscription has yet been found. Parpola (1994) attempted to find parallels between this script and the known language Dravidian; if he is successful, then that would prove that the Indus language was unrelated to Sanskrit, which is part of the Indo-Iranian tradition and the language of the Veda. Another scholar, Kak (1987), began with the Brahmi script instead, and he believes that this has produced evidence of the Sanskrit genitive case marker, but again we must be wary of presuming that either scholar has approached the script correctly. Until more samples are uncovered or a bilingual inscription is found, it is doubtful that the script will be properly deciphered.

Between 1800 and 1700 BCE, the Indus Valley Civilisation declined relatively quickly. It is now presumed that environmental considerations, such as a change in rainfall patterns, led to the abandonment of the major cities. The smaller towns and villages survived longer, although most were probably evacuated before 1500 BCE, which is the approximate dating for the Aryan 'invasions'. In Mohenjo-Daro a number of skeletons were found on the top strata and some scholars, such as Wheeler, claimed that these deaths were the result of early Aryan invaders, but this version of events has been largely superseded.

See also: **Indo-European traditions; Languages; Saṃhitā; Śiva; Veda; Yamunā; Yoga**

ANGELA QUARTERMAINE

Further reading

Bryant, E. 2001. *The Quest for the Origins of Vedic Culture: The Indo-Aryan Migration Debate*. Oxford: Oxford University Press.

Feuerstein, G., S. Kak and D. Frawley. 1995. *In Search of the Cradle of Civilization: New Light on Ancient India*. Wheaton, IL: Quest Books.
Hiltebeitel, A. 1978. 'The Indus Valley "Proto-Siva", Re-examining Through Reflection on the Goddess, the Buffalo, and the Symbolism of the Vahanas'. *Anthropos* 73.5–6: 767–79.
Kak, S. 1987. 'On the Decipherment of the Indus Script: A Preliminary Study of Its Connections with Brahmi'. *Indian Journal of History of Science* 22.1: 51–62.
Kulke, H. and D. Rothermund. 1998. *A History of India*, 3rd edn. London and New York: Routledge, 16–29.
Marshall, J. 1931. *Mohenjo-Daro and the Indus Civilisation*, 3 vols. London: Oxford University Press.
Oldham, R.D. 1893. 'The Sarsawati and the Lost River of the Indian Desert'. *Journal of the Royal Asiatic Society*, 1893: 49–76.
Parpola, A. 1994. *Deciphering the Indus Script*. Cambridge: Cambridge University Press.
Renfrew, C. 1987. *Archaeology and Language: The Puzzle of Indo-European Origins*. London: Jonathan Cape.
Stein, Aurel. 1942. 'A Survey of Ancient Sites Along the "Lost" Sarasvati River'. *Geographical Journal* 99(4), April: 173–82.
Wheeler, M. 1953. *The Indus Civilisation: The Cambridge History of India Supplementary Volume*. Cambridge: Cambridge University Press.

INFANTICIDE

Many elite Hindu communities practised son preference for both religious and secular reasons. Sons had to perform their father's cremation rituals (śrāddha), for instance, although some lawgivers allowed a daughter or other relative to do this if there were no son. Despite the traditional Hindu taboo on abortion except to save the lives of mothers, infanticide – especially of deformed, mentally impaired or female foetuses – was once very common in some areas. Whereas some scholars have attributed infanticide to Hindu son preference, this view has been challenged by one empirical study (Oldenburg 2002) of the Punjab, which showed that infanticide became common in the colonial period mainly for economic rather than religious reasons. Infanticide involved either direct killing or neglecting diet and healthcare, which enabled the parents, at least technically, to abide by the ethical principle of ahiṃsā. Although illegal, infanticide continues today in some communities, contributing, along with abortion after sex-determining tests, to sex selection, which results in fewer girls than boys in the society.

See also: **Abortion; Śrāddha**

KATHERINE K. YOUNG

Further reading

Kane, P.V. 1968–77 [1930–62]. *History of Dharmaśāstra*, 5 vols, 2nd edn. Poona: Bhandarkar Oriental Research Institute.
Oldenburg, V.T. 2002. *Dowry Murder: The Imperial Origins of a Cultural Crime*. Oxford: Oxford University Press.
Purewal, T. 2003. 'Re-producing South Asian Wom(b)en: Female Feticide and the Spectacle of Culture'. In N. Puwar and P. Raghuram, eds, *South Asian Women in the Diaspora*. New York: Berg, 137–56.
Sen, M. 2002. *Death by Fire: Sati, Dowry Death and Female Infanticide in Modern India*. New Brunswick, NJ: Rutgers University Press.
Saxena, R.K. 1975. *Social Reforms: Infanticide and Sati*. New Delhi: Trimurti Publications.

INITIATION

See: **Upanayana**

INTEGRAL YOGA

See: **Satchidananda, Swami and Integral Yoga**

INTER-FAITH/INTER-RELIGIOUS DIALOGUE

The word 'inter-faith' is used in varying ways to cover several different, if related, activities. Some people use 'inter-faith' –

with or without a hyphen – to emphasise a sense of fellowship and cooperation between religions, in contrast to 'multi-faith' or 'inter-religious', which are more neutral terms. Others prefer two words – 'inter faith' – to highlight the distinctiveness of each faith tradition. Usually the word 'interfaith' refers to the coming together of people who belong to different faith communities, which is how it is understood here, but other people use it to refer to a new spirituality which draws upon the great religions of the world but is independent of any of them.

At the 1893 Parliament of the World's Religions, which is usually taken to mark the start of organised interfaith activity, Swami Vivekananda (1863–1902), a follower of Sri Ramakrishna, said he was proud to belong to a religion which accepted 'all religions as true', and quoted from the *Bhagavadgītā*, which says, 'Whosoever comes to Me, through whatsoever form, I reach him'. Many Hindus, during the last hundred years, have been active in interfaith organisations and today, like others, they recognise the importance of inter-religious understanding and cooperation. Hindu speakers at the Parliament of the World's Religions, held in Chicago in 1893, also included two members of the Brahmo Samaj, B.B. Nagarkar and P.C. Mozoomdar, author of *The Oriental Christ*, and other Hindus of various institutional and traditional affiliations. The Parliament's centenary in 1993 was marked by a big international gathering, *Sarva-Dharma-Sammelana*, held at Bangalore, and by a Parliament in Chicago, which adopted 'A Declaration Toward a Global Ethic', affirming the moral values shared by the great religions. Many Hindus participated, including Swami Chidananda Saraswati, of the Divine Life Society, Rishikesh, Satguru Sivaya Subramuniyaswami, Publisher of *Hinduism Today*, Mata Amritanandamayi, renowned Hindu guru, leading members of the Ramakrishna Order and C.V. Devan Nair, from Singapore, who is a devotee of Sri Aurobindo. Another Parliament was held at Cape Town (1999), which was attended by many Hindus from South Africa and overseas. A further Parliament took place in Barcelona in 2004.

The twentieth century saw the development of many local, national and international interfaith organisations, in which Hindus were usually active, many of whom had been influenced by Gandhi, who stressed the underlying unity of religions and who included readings from all scriptures in the devotions at his ashram. The oldest international interfaith organisation is the International Association for Religious Freedom (IARF), in which members of the Brahmo Samaj have been active since its inception in 1900. In 1936 the explorer and mystic Francis Younghusband (1863–1942) founded the World Congress of Faiths (WCF), in which the Hindu philosopher Sarvepalli Radhakrishnan (1888–1975) played a leading role. The World Conference on Religion and Peace (WCRP) developed from a symposium held in New Delhi in 1968, at which Sri Jayaprakash Narayan, the veteran Sarvodaya worker, and Dr R.R. Diwakar of the Gandhi Peace Foundation played an active role. Many Hindus are active in the United Religions Initiative (URI) and in the Indian-based World Fellowship of Inter-Religious Councils (WFIRC). International interfaith organisations work co-operatively through the International Interfaith Centre (IIC) at Oxford.

Hindus play their part in national interfaith organisations, such as the Inter Faith Network for the UK and the North American Interfaith Network, as well as in local groups in India and the West. Several religious communities have agencies for interfaith work, and environmental and peace organisations now often have a multi-religious membership. Leading Hindu swamis and scholars contribute to a wide variety of interfaith activities and people of all religions are usually welcome at Hindu ashrams and centres.

Initially interfaith dialogue met with considerable opposition. Many religions define their identity by differentiating themselves from others by dress, diet or beliefs, so fraternising with members of other religions was considered disloyal by fellow believers and inter-faith marriages still cause problems. Christian missionary activity made many Hindus suspicious that dialogue might be misused to win converts. The emphasis of some Hindus on the underlying unity of all religions made some Christians and other believers uneasy, fearing that in inter-faith dialogue they would be expected to discard their traditional claim to a unique revelation. Some scholars in the study of religions were at first unsympathetic because they felt the interfaith movement glossed over the real differences between religions and that it distorted objective study by trying to create an artificial unity.

Attitudes gradually changed in the last decades of the twentieth century. European and North American societies had become increasingly multi-religious, so it became important to understand and respect the beliefs and practices of new arrivals. At the same time there was a renewed interest in 'Eastern' spirituality. Gradually, despite the uneasiness of traditional religions, the interfaith movement opened its doors to new spiritual movements, such as the International Society for Krishna Consciousness (ISKCON). Recently some politicians and many in the media – even if they themselves are not personally religious – have recognised the importance of religious dialogue if there is to be peace among the nations and social cohesion. At the same time, increasing numbers of religious leaders are distancing themselves from religious extremism and intolerance and speaking with a common voice on urgent moral issues and on the need for peace, relief of poverty and protection of the environment.

See also: **Āśram(a) (religious community); Bhagavadgītā; Brahmo Samaj; Divine Life Society; Gandhi, Mohandas Karamchand; Ghose, Aurobindo; Guru; International Society for Krishna Consciousness; Radhakrishnan, Sir Sarvepalli; Ramakrishna, Sri; Ramakrishna Math and Mission; Vivekananda, Swami**

MARCUS BRAYBROOKE

Further reading

Braybrooke, M. 1992. *Pilgrimage of Hope: One Hundred Years of Interfaith Dialogue.* London: SCM Press.

Braybrooke, M. 1998. *Faith and Interfaith in a Global Age.* Grand Rapids, MI: CoNexus Press; Oxford: Braybrooke Press.

Küng, H. and K.J. Kuschel (eds). 1993. *A Global Ethic.* London: SCM Press.

Race, A. 2001. *Interfaith Encounter.* London: SCM Press.

Seager, R.H. (ed.). 1993. *The Dawn of Religious Pluralism, Voices from the World's Parliament of Religions, 1893.* La Salle, IL: Open Court.

Storey, Celia and David Storey (eds). 1994. *Visions of an Interfaith Future, Proceedings of Sarva-Dharma-Sammelana, Bangalore 1993.* Oxford: International Interfaith Centre.

INTERNATIONAL SOCIETY FOR KRISHNA CONSCIOUSNESS

The International Society for Krishna Consciousness (ISKCON) or Hare Krishna movement has centres in eighty-six countries and publications in seventy languages. It is a modern, globalised branch of a Bengali movement, the Gaudiya Vaishnava Mission. ISKCON's founder, Swami Bhaktivedanta (Prabhupada A.C. Bhaktivedanta Swami), took Caitanya's teachings to the West in 1965, and formed the organisation after attracting young Americans eager for Indian spirituality and disaffected by contemporary values and war in Vietnam.

He introduced his followers to what were to become key features of ISKCON: the chanting with beads of the mahā mantra – 'Hare Kṛṣṇa, Hare Kṛṣṇa, Kṛṣṇa Kṛṣṇa, Hare Hare, Hare Rāma, Hare Rāma, Rāma Rāma, Hare Hare' – the four regulative principles (no meat, fish or eggs, no intoxicants, sex only for the procreation of children and no gambling), lively worship of Kṛṣṇa and Rādhā in the temple and in public devotional chanting, the preparation and eating of vegetarian food in the name of Kṛṣṇa, and the study of scripture such as the *Bhagavadgītā* and *Bhāgavata Purāṇa*.

The beliefs and practices of Krishna Consciousness were taken by the Swami's new devotees across North America to San Francisco, Buffalo, Boston and Montreal, and then to England in 1968. There they captured the imagination of the Beatles, particularly George Harrison, who helped them to produce a chart-topping record of the Hare Kṛṣṇa mantra. The devotees preached in Europe, Australia and Africa, and also in India, where, as young white brāhmaṇas (varṇa) in Indian attire, they were met with both interest and suspicion.

In 1977, after the death of the founder, the administration of ISKCON passed to its Governing Body Commission, and the spiritual leadership became the responsibility of eleven initiating gurus, a number of whom failed to live up to ISKCON's moral and spiritual principles and were later removed from office. The focus in the 1980s on the exalted role of the celibate male – whether young brahmacaris, saṃnyāsis or gurus – and the emerging culture of gender separation and animosity to family life often led to the undermining of women and to a lack of protection for children. These problems led in later years to disputes within the movement and even to court action over child abuse. Current leaders have accepted the need for greater equality and accountability.

By the mid-1990s the early focus on internal affairs and an engagement with the wider world only for financial support and missionary outreach had given way to greater openness in terms of public education, relations with the diaspora, food distribution and participation in interfaith dialogue. A social change occurred as single devotees married and had children. The movement grew in new areas, particularly in Eastern Europe following the fall of Communism.

An ISKCON devotee's spiritual objective is to serve and remember Kṛṣṇa at all times and in all activities, whilst the movement's goal is to follow Caitanya's call to spread Kṛṣṇa consciousness to every town and village.

See also: **Bhagavadgītā; Brahmacarya; Caitanya; Diaspora; Gaudiya Vaishnava Mission; Guru; Kṛṣṇa; Mantra; Prabhupada, A.C. Bhaktivedanta Swami; Purāṇas; Rādhā; Saṃnyāsa; Varṇa**

KIM KNOTT

Further reading

Bryant, E.F. and M.L. Ekstrand (eds). 2004. *The Hare Krishna Movement: The Post Charasmatic Fate of a Religious Transplant*. New York: Columbia University Press.

Knott, K. 1986. *My Sweet Lord*. Wellingborough: Aquarian Press.

INTERNET

Hinduism on the internet is an important and developing area of religious representation and activity. Although the early phases of Hindu religious representation on the internet and world wide web were primarily conducted by members of the Hindu diaspora within North America and Europe, recent developments in internet accessibility in India have allowed for much greater levels of online activity and www representation within the country itself.

The internet medium is being utilised in a number of ways in relation to Hinduism. This includes online environments where people can engage in discussions concerning Hindu religious traditions and practices, websites that provide information about Hinduism, and interactive websites that provide the opportunity for people to connect with gurus and to conduct rituals at sacred Hindu temples.

Online discussion areas, bulletin boards and chat rooms

Early discussions of Hinduism first appeared on the internet within the Usenet public Bulletin Board Systems (BBS) in the 1980s. Although non-Hindus initiated most of the early conversations concerning the Hindu religion, by 1985 a group called net.nlang.india was established on Usenet for discussions concerning all things relating to Indian culture. The primary purpose of this group was to provide an online environment where people from India living in the United States could get news from home, get information concerning restaurants in different cities, talk with others about their life in the diaspora and also discuss their religion, which was primarily Hinduism but also included a number of other traditions.

By the 1990s, as the Usenet network expanded, a number of groups were renamed and placed in new categories. Net.nlang.india became a culture group (soc.culture.indian) and was used to discuss any issues related to India but not necessarily any particular religious tradition. In an attempt to establish an online area specifically for discussing Hinduism, the Hindu Student Council sponsored two discussion groups that were created and maintained by Ajay Shah (an immigrant to the US who was working on a PhD in chemistry at the University of Mississippi). The purposes of these new groups (alt.hindu and soc.religion.hindu) were to allow for the creation of online communities and discussion networks based specifically upon Hindu religious traditions. This created a moderated environment with the goal of bringing the Hindu community from around the world together on one communications platform (Zaleski 1997: 220–26). The newsgroups also became an online environment that provided sacred Hindu scriptures (such as the *Bhagavadgītā*) online to those who requested them. This allowed for diaspora workers in foreign countries (where these works were forbidden) the opportunity to read and discuss their sacred texts.

Some of the most popular discussion areas for Hinduism on the internet include soc.culture.indian, soc.culture.indian.delhi and alt.religion.hindu.

Although there is a significant amount of online discussion in these groups, access in India is restricted due to a number of economic, technological and social factors. By 2001, internet access in India was still restricted by a government monopoly on telecommunications and the average cost for twenty hours of monthly internet access was approximately 17 per cent of GDP per capita, making India the 63rd (out of 72) most expensive country in which to maintain internet access. By 2002, India had a relatively small percentage of its population with regular internet access (1.6 per cent) and less than 1 per cent of the population owned their own personal computer. However, internet access in India continues to climb at an incredible rate. From 2000 to 2005 online activity in the country increased by 912 per cent and it is now estimated that 4.5 per cent of the population has regular internet access.

Hinduism on the world wide web

There are currently thousands of websites that represent various aspects of the Hindu religious traditions. Of all the religious based websites represented on the world wide web, the 'Hinduism' category is consistently one of the top five largest groups. These sites range from amateur home pages to professional websites developed by temple organisations. Many of these sites provide information; however, a large number are now providing interactive services, such as online pūjā and interactive rituals.

Due to the diversity and complexity of Hinduism, there are a wide range of websites related to this topic. Categories used for classifying Hinduism sites on the world wide web include: 'Approaches', which contains websites detailing Advaita Vedānta, Ganapath, Śaiva, Śakta, Tantra, Vaiṣṇava and Yoga practices; the 'Religious Texts' category, which includes websites containing information, translations, audio files and MP3 downloads of the *Bhagavadgītā*, *Mahābhārata*, *Purāṇas*, *Rāmāyaṇa*, *Upaniṣads*, *Saṃhitā* and *Yogasūtras*; the 'Gods and Goddesses' category, which includes websites devoted to (or providing information about), Brahmā, Devī (Māhādevī), Durgā, Gaṇeśa, Kālī, Kṛṣṇa, Śrī Lakṣmī, Lalitā Tripurasundarī, Rāma, Sarasvatī, Śiva, Skanda, Vaiṣṇo Devī and Viṣṇu; a category for 'Gurus and Saints', which contains hundreds of websites devoted to specific religious teachers and scholars and their philosophies. There is also a large grouping of websites under the category of 'Temples'. The temple category is broken down by country and provides websites for Hindu temples in the diaspora as well and temples within India.

A number of websites are also now providing interactive services, which include virtual pilgrimages and also ritual services at 'wired' temples throughout India. An early example of this form of activity occurred in 1998, when the world wide web was still relatively new. At that time, 20,000 people a day were going online from outside India to witness Durgā Pūjā in Kolkata (Calcutta). This online broadcasting of religious festivals became so popular that in January of 2001 the Kumbha Melā festival was broadcast online on an even larger scale, not particularly for people in India but rather for those in the diaspora. The live broadcasting of the event was sponsored by the Himalayan Institute (a Hindu Ashram in Northern Pennsylvania) and used to promote their religious website.

Other interactive services available on the world wide web include the ability to have specific rituals conducted at sacred temples almost anywhere in India. One of the first websites to offer this service was www.Saranam.com. The service began online in 1999 and of those participating 80 per cent were Hindus living outside India. The goal of the website is to 'do whatever it takes to help Hindus around the world meet their own needs in the realm of religion, spirituality, morality and the Hindu value system'. Although the site provides a number of services and items, including gifts, music and books, they state that 'Best of all you can order for pujas to be performed in your favorite Indian temple'. To confirm that the ritual has been conducted, the pūjā receipt, offerings, pūjā certificate, sacred ash or even a video recording is sent to the customer.

See also: **Advaita; Americas, Hindus in; Āśram(a) (religious community); Bhagavadgītā; Brahmā; Diaspora; Durgā; Durgā Pūjā; Europe, Hindus in; Gaṇeśa; Guru; Kālī and Caṇḍī; Kṛṣṇa; Kumbha Melā; Lakṣmī, Śrī; Mahābhārata; Mahādevī; Mandir; Purāṇas; Rāma; Rāmāyaṇa; Sacred texts; Śaivism; Śakti; Saṃhitā; Sarasvatī; Śiva; Skanda; Tantra; Tīrthayātrā; Upaniṣads; Utsava; Vaiṣṇavism; Vaiṣṇo Devī; Viṣṇu; Yoga; Yogasūtras**

CHRISTOPHER HELLAND

Further reading

Zaleski, J. 1997. *The Soul of Cyberspace*. San Francisco, CA: HarperEdge.

ĪŚĀ UPANIṢAD

See: **Upaniṣads**

ISKCON

See: **International Society for Krishna Consciousness**

IṢṬADEVATĀ

'Personal deity'. A god or a goddess chosen by an individual as the main deity to worship. The cult of personal deities is similar to that of family deities (kuladevatās), chosen by a single family and linked to the house where the fire is kept, or village deities (grāmadevatās), who protect a whole community and its land. The name of the iṣṭadevatā should be the first word pronounced by a householder at dawn, before daily activity begins, while during the deva-yajña ('sacrifice to the deity') invitations to the iṣṭadevatā must precede any other rites. The iṣṭadevatās developed in post-Vedic times as a natural necessity of the people to have tutelary gods to whom they could refer. The cult of iṣṭadevatās is classified as belonging to the bhakti mārga ('path of devotion') and is centred on the worship of the divine as saguṇa (with attributes) in contrast to nirguṇa (without attributes).

See also: **Bhakti (as path); Deities; Deities, domestic and family; Deities, village and local**

FABRIZIO M. FERRARI

Further reading

Lipner, J. 1998. *The Hindus*. London and New York, Routledge.

Kulke, H. 1992. 'Tribal Deities at Princely Courts: The Feudatory Rajas of Central Orissa and Their Tutelary Deities (Istadevatas)'. In S. Mahapatra, ed., *The Realm of the Sacred. Verbal Symbolism and Ritual Structures*. Calcutta and New York: Oxford University Press, 56–78.

ĪŚVARA

In Hindu literature, terms deriving from the Sanskrit verbal root 'īś' ('to have power') have been used to apply to deity or signify the 'Lord'. These include 'īśvara', 'īśa' and 'īśāna'. 'Īśvara' occurs in various compound titles such as 'Maheśvara' ('Great Lord'), 'Amareśvara' ('Immortal Lord'), 'Parameśvara' ('Supreme Lord'), and 'Yajñeśvara' ('Lord of sacrifice').

In the *Ṛgveda*, 'īśāna' ('master' or 'ruler') occurs in connection with gods such as Indra and Soma, signifying special powers or achievements. In the *Atharvaveda* 'īśvara' is the title of the cosmic being Puruṣa (called the 'lord', īśvara, of immortality) and is used to indicate the power or 'lordship' of Vedic gods. The *Upaniṣads* contain teachings relating to the supreme Lord (referred to by the terms 'īśvara', 'īśa' and 'īśāna'). In the theistic *Śvetāśvatara*, the Lord (Īśa) is the ruler and source of the universe. The world is due to God's creative power of māyā. This *Upaniṣad* has been associated with Śaivism; it identifies Brahman with Rudra.

The *Upaniṣads* have been interpreted as describing the ultimate reality Brahman in two ways. On the one hand it is acosmic, without qualities, beyond description; on the other it is full of qualities and cosmic. Thus, in Śaṅkara's Advaita, there is 'higher' (para) Brahman (the impersonal, distinctionless absolute) and 'lower' (apara) Brahman (saguṇa, with qualities) or God (Īśvara). The Lord (īśvara, parameśvara) is Brahman associated with name and form (nāma-rūpa); God's 'lordship' (īśvaratva), omniscience and omnipotence exist in relation to limiting conditions (upādhi) only (which are ultimately unreal). By contrast, Rāmānuja identifies Brahman with the immanent God (matter and souls are God's real body); he attempts to harmonise absolutism and personal theism (Viśiṣṭādvaita).

The supreme Lord (parameśvara) of the *Bhagavadgītā*, the lord of all beings (bhūtānām īśvarah), is an object of devotion or worship as well as the basis of reality.

In his Yoga system, Patañjali uses the term 'īśvara' to refer to his conception of God as a special puruṣa; his God is not the cause, creator, preserver or destroyer of the universe.

See also: **Advaita; Bhagavadgītā; Brahman; Indra; Māyā; Patañjali; Puruṣa; Rāmānuja; Rudra; Śaivism; Saṃhitā; Śaṅkara; Soma; Upaniṣads; Vedic Pantheon; Viśiṣṭādvaita; Yoga**

MARTIN OVENS

Further reading

Sullivan, H.P. 1987. 'Īśvara'. In *Encyclopedia of Religion*, ed. M. Eliade. New York: Macmillan Publishing Company, 7: 498–99.

ĪŚVARAKṚṢṆA

Īśvarakṛṣṇa (*c.*350–450) is the author of the *Sāṃkhyakārikā* in a line of teachers of Sāṃkhya (Larson and Bhattacharya 1987: 136). According to the Chinese translation of his work by Paramārtha in 557–69 CE, he was a Brāhmaṇa of the Kauśika gotra 'family' (Larson and Bhattacharya 1987: 149) and, according to the *Jayamaṅgala* (*c.*600–800 CE), a wandering monk (Larson and Bhattacharya 1987: 287). His work, while preceded by informal expositions on Sāṃkhya, represents the most ancient extant source and the definitive exposition of the philosophical school.

See also: **Brāhmaṇa; Gotra; Sāṃkhya; Sāṃkhyakārikās**

PETER M. SCHARF

Further reading

Larson, Gerald James and Ram Shankar Bhattacharya (eds). 1987. 'Sāṃkhya: A Dualist Tradition in Indian Philosophy'. *Encyclopedia of Indian Philosophies*, vol. IV. Princeton, NJ: Princeton University Press; Delhi: Motilal Banarsidass.

ITIHĀSA

A Sanskirt word that literally means 'so, indeed it was', itihāsa (iti ha āsa) is an account of the past. In post-Vedic texts it came to refer to a genre of narrative literature that includes aspects of the Western categories of history, myth, legend and epic. The *Mahābhārata* is the text that most exemplifies the genre, although the *Rāmāyaṇa* is sometimes considered itihāsa. Along with the *Dharmaśāstras* and *Purāṇas*, itihāsa is one of the three genres of literature that constitute smṛti. The larger category of itihāsa-purāṇa, which can be translated as 'ancient history', includes the *Mahābhārata*, the *Rāmāyaṇa* and the eighteen *Mahāpurāṇas*. The earliest textual reference to itihāsa is found in the *Atharvaveda* (15.6.4), where it appears in the compound itihāsa-purāṇa. The term appears on its own for the first time in the early *Upaniṣads* (BU 2.4.10; CU 3.4.1–2), where it seems simply to refer to tales and legends.

See also: **Dharmaśāstras; Mahābhārata; Purāṇas; Rāmāyaṇa; Saṃhitā; Upaniṣads**

BRIAN BLACK

Further reading

Fitzgerald, James L. 2004. *The Mahābhārata, 11. The Book of Women, 12. The Book of Peace: Part One.* Chicago, IL: Chicago University Press.

Flood, Gavin. 1996. *An Introduction to Hinduism.* Cambridge: Cambridge University Press.

Pollock, Sheldon. 1989. 'Mīmāṃsā and the Problem of History in Traditional India'. *Journal of the American Oriental Society* 109(4): 603–10.

IYENGAR, B.K.S. AND IYENGAR YOGA (b. 1918)

Born in 1918 at Bellur, Karnataka, Iyengar lived and studied with his brother-in-law T. Krishnamacharya for three years before moving to Pune in 1937. Dedicating himself to the intensive practice and teaching of āsana, Iyengar established himself as a respected international authority, instructing such well-known figures as J. Krishnamurti and Yehudi Menuhin. It was largely through Menuhin's influence that Iyengar became known in the West. He is renowned for his exacting teaching style, precision of alignment and his innovative use of props to help students understand movements and positions. There is a strong medical and remedial component to his teaching. In 1966 he published *Light on Yoga*, which remains a standard encyclopaedic work on āsana. In 1973 he established the Ramamani Iyengar Memorial Yoga Institute in memory of his wife, who died earlier the same year. Iyengar himself has now largely retired from teaching, and classes at the Institute are run by his daughter Geeta and son Prashant. Iyengar Yoga is probably the most popular form of Modern Postural Yoga taught in the West today.

See also: **Āsana; Krishnamacharya, T.; Krishnamurti, Jiddu; Yoga, modern**

MARK SINGLETON

Further reading

Iyengar, B.K.S. 1965. *Light on Yoga*. London: Allen and Unwin.

J

JAGANNĀTHA

A unique form of Kṛṣṇa worshipped in the large temple complex at Purī in Orissa which probably began life as a Buddhist centre. The temple has no caste restrictions and demonstrates adaptations of the Buddhist 'three jewels' into Hindu worldview. The temple contains three mūrtis, Jagannātha, his brother Balarāma and his sister Subhadrā. The temple, built in the eleventh century CE, is regarded as one of the four holiest places in India. The highlight of the worship of Jagannātha takes place at the festival of Ratha Yātrā in June when the deity is enthroned on a temple-shaped cart and pulled through the streets by hundreds of ecstatic devotees, accompanied by smaller chariots containing his brother and sister. The English word 'juggernaut' is derived from Jagannātha. The image is unlike the usual depictions of Kṛṣṇa as a baby or attractive youth and is a crudely carved lump of wood. There are numerous legends that explain this phenomenon.

See also: **Balarāma; Buddhism, relationship with Hinduism; Image worship; Kṛṣṇa; Mandir; Ratha Yātrā; Subhadrā; Utsava**

RON GEAVES

Further reading

Stutley, Margaret and James Stutley (eds). 1985. *A Dictionary of Hinduism*. London: Routledge and Kegan Paul, 122–23.

JAIMINI

'Jaimini' has been the name of different authors and personages within the Hindu tradition. For example, among various 'Jaiminis' are a writer of a work of astrology and a Kanarese author. The name is also associated with the *Sāmaveda*; in the *Mahābhārata*, 'Jaimini' is one of five disciples of Vyāsa. However, 'Jaimini' is perhaps most familiar as the name of an ancient sage in the tradition of Pūrva Mīmāṃsā, one of the six schools of Hindu philosophy (Ṣaḍdarśana).

The *Mīmāṃsāsūtras* attributed to 'Jaimini' form the basis of Pūrva Mīmāṃsā. However it is evident that he was not the first Mīmāṃsā thinker. There is reference in the *Mīmāṃsāsūtras* to earlier teachers such as Ālekhana, Ātreya, Lāmbukāyana and Bādari. Another early Mīmāṃsā teacher named 'Jaimini' has also been indicated.

It has been maintained that Mīmāṃsā debates arose as the complexity of sacrificial ritual increased. There was a need for proper interpretation of the Vedic injunctions involving sacrifice so that doubts concerning the correct performance of sacrifices could not arise. Hence it is possible that a number of attempts were made to formulate rules for interpreting the Veda. On this view, Jaimini's scheme is the sole surviving attempt; perhaps it was superior to other efforts.

The date of the composition of the *Mīmāṃsasūtras* is uncertain but it has been placed around the second century BCE. The *sūtras* defend Vedic authority and dharma, and have been understood as representing a response to heterodox teachers such as the Buddha who attacked Vedic ritual and undermined Vedic authority. There are no accounts or details of Jaimini's life. His date is uncertain due to a lack of historical data. Various dates up to around 200 CE have been suggested and argued for, many scholars placing him well before the common era, perhaps around 400 BCE.

See also: **Buddhism, relationship with Hinduism; Dharma; Jyotiṣa; Mahābhārata; Mīmāṃsāsūtras; Pūrva Mīmāṃsā; Ṣaḍdarśana; Saṃhitās; Veda; Vyāsa; Yajña**

MARTIN OVENS

Further reading

Dwivedi, R.C. (ed.). 1994. *Studies in Mīmāṃsa*. Delhi: Motilal Banarsidass.

JAINISM, RELATIONSHIP WITH HINDUISM

Jainism is a śramaṇa tradition. It rejects the authority of the Veda, instead investing its religious authority in the Tīrthankaras, omniscient preceptors who have conquered saṃsāra. 'Tīrthankara' means 'ford-maker', their teachings providing a crossing to mokṣa from saṃsāra. Tīrthankaras are also called Jinas, meaning 'conqueror', hence the term 'Jainism'. Twenty-four Jinas appear during every half of a cosmic cycle; the most recent was Vardhamāna Mahāvīra, who lived and taught in Bihar, north-west India. Textual evidence establishes him as a contemporary of the Buddha, which places him in the fifth century BCE. Jains do not regard Mahāvīra as the founder of Jainism, but as one in a lineage of omniscient gurus. Nevertheless, Mahāvīra provides a point of historical origin for Jainism, which means that, although it has sectarian division (principally Śvetāmbara, 'white-clad', and Digambara, 'sky-clad'), Jainism does not mirror the fluid pluralism of Hinduism.

On a secular level Jain society in India is organised by caste and sect. Interaction and marriage between sects and castes is uncommon, although intermarriage between Jains and Hindus of the same caste occurs, the marriage ceremony itself being very similar to the Hindu ceremony. Interaction between sects is more commonplace amongst diaspora communities (East Africa, Europe, North America). There are an estimated 3 million Jains worldwide.

On a religious level Jainism rejects the hierarchy of the Hindu caste system. Mahāvīra's Jainism sprang from the fertile social and religious changes occurring during the fifth and sixth centuries BCE. A kṣatriya by birth, Mahāvīra evaded his prescribed social duties in favour of renunciation and asceticism. This is a clear message of opposition to the then dominant tradition of ritual sacrifice in a polytheistic worldview officiated exclusively by the brāhmaṇas. Jain philosophy is more akin with that of the *Āraṇyakas* and *Upaniṣads*. Jainism subscribes to the fundamental philosophy expounded in these early texts that the soul (ātman) is trapped in saṃsāra and needs to liberate itself from the binding effects of karma in order to achieve mokṣa. However, there are some several differences in the way that Jainism and Hinduism deliver this philosophy.

Significantly, Jainism does not have a concept of Brahman. This means that it does not engage in the dvaita/advaita debate that has enriched Hindu philosophy because for Jains the ātman does not merge into 'oneness' with Brahman. The Jain universe is dualistic, consisting of consciousness – a quality unique to the soul – and that which is not conscious – matter, space, time, motion and non-motion. The liberated soul (siddha) retains its individualism and resides in the topmost part of the universe known as siddhaloka. The concept of individualism needs qualifying; to achieve mokṣa the soul has to be rid of any vestiges of ego, so anything reminiscent of personality and gender is lost.

Karma is also interpreted differently by Jainism and Hinduism. Both religions perceive karma as the central mechanism of bondage in saṃsāra through a perpetual cycle of actions generating reactions that influence the circumstances of one's future incarnations. For Jains the binding quality of karma has almost literal connotations because it is believed to be physical – very fine particles that stick to the soul, like dust on a mirror, weighing it down in saṃsāra and obscuring its true nature of omniscience and bliss.

Another important difference between Hinduism and Jainism is the concept of ātman. Both religions regard ātman as an eternal soul that is reincarnated through countless embodiments until it finally achieves liberation and release from saṃsāra. Jainism combines with ātman the concept of ubiquitous jīva (life monads) that permeate the entire cosmos. Some jīva are incarnated in sophisticated life forms, such as humans, through every conceivable type of animal and plant life, to simple air and water bodies. Irrespective of their incarnation, all jīva are sentient, which means they are self-aware and capable of experiencing suffering.

An understanding of Jain beliefs about the relationship between karma and jīva explains the soteriological motivation behind Jainism's rigorous commitment to ahiṃsā (non-violence); for example, they are strict vegetarians and mendicants sweep the path ahead of them to avoid stepping on insects. Harmful actions are believed to attract the most potent types of karma, therefore ahiṃsā is practised meticulously because sentient beings (jīva) pervade the entire cosmos and so are at constant risk of harm. So, whereas Hindu ethics are associated through the concept of dharma with combined social and religious obligations, Jainism's moral framework is exclusively and inextricably linked to its soteriology.

Mahāvīra established a substantial, celibate mendicant community from the outset that continues today. Jainism teaches that karma is purged from the soul prematurely through asceticism and that free-floating karma is avoided through non-action and non-attachment. Consequently Jain mendicants have minimal possessions and are prohibited from staying in one place for more than three consecutive nights (with the exception of the monsoon season). Inevitably, the survival of these wandering mendicants depended upon lay followers, so that Jain mendicant and lay communities developed in tandem. Although the guru–disciple relationship is central to Jainism, its form differs to that encountered in Hinduism because mendicants' peripatetic lifestyles preclude, to a certain extent, a sustained relationship with lay individuals. The laity engage in guru-bhakti through, amongst other practices, devotional singing that praises the spiritual triumphs of Jinas, siddhas and living mendicants. Mendicants are venerated equally because all embody the religious ideal (although in practice lay Jains sometimes revere a favourite mendicant as their special guru).

Most Jain sects (two exceptions are Sthānakvāsī and Terāpanthi) engage in temple worship where pūjā is performed before Jina images. Superficially this resembles Hindu pūjā – the image is bathed and offerings placed before it – but importantly Jain worship of the Jinas is not transactional. The Jinas have transcended worldly affairs and so cannot reciprocate the worshipper's devotion. The objective of worship is to imbibe the Jina's qualities by veneration and emulation. Offerings are not gifts to the Jinas, but 'given up' in the spirit of asceticism. Hence Jain mendicants do not have a tradition of temple worship because, by definition, they have nothing to give up.

See also: **Advaita; Ahiṃsā; Āraṇyakas; Ātman; Brahman; Brāhmaṇas; Buddhism, relationship with Hinduism; Caste; Dharma; Diaspora; Dvaita; Guru; Jīva; Karma; Mokṣa; Pūjā; Saṃsāra; Siddha; Śramaṇa; Śramaṇa Culture; Varṇa; Upaniṣads; Veda**

EMMA SALTER

Further reading

Babb, L.A. 1996. *Absent Lord. Ascetics and Kings in a Jain Ritual Culture.* Berkeley, Los Angeles, CA and London: University of California Press.

Cort, J.E. 2001. *Jains in the World.* Delhi, New York and Oxford: Oxford University Press.

Dundas, P. 2002. *The Jains.* London: Routledge.

Jaini, P.S. 1998. *The Jaina Path of Purification.* Delhi: Motilal Banarsidass.

JANA SANGH

The Akhil Bharatīya Jana Sangh (literally: All India People's Party), a Hindu fundamentalist organisation, was founded in 1951 by Dr Shyama Prasad Mukherji as a forum of opposition to the Indian National Congress, from which he had resigned as one of the prominent leaders and Cabinet minister in the Nehru government. Its ideological roots and mass base can be found in the Rashtriya Swayam Sevak Sangh (RSS; National Voluntary Service Association), which described itself as a social rather than a political organisation, especially after it was temporarily banned after the assassination of Gandhi. The Jana Sangh was, therefore, more or less the political wing of the RSS. Many Jana Sangh office holders were also RSS office holders. Its sway was mainly in the Hindi-speaking areas of the northern and central regions. The main objective of the Jana Sangh was to rebuild India on the basis of Indian culture and tradition and claim back the age-old values of Indian life which it deemed Indian society was fast losing due to the introduction of Western values in the guise of modernism (Puri 1980: 6). While inspired by the past, it claimed to be forward looking and was neither leftwing nor rightwing in the Western political sense. The reunification of India – Akhandha Bharat – was an objective and it rejected the notion of India as a federation of states, as stated in the Indian constitution, but considered it as Bhārat Māta (Mother India), the original pre-partition India, undivided and unitary. Any talk of multiculturalism was also anathema for them. To its members Indian culture, like the land, was one and indivisible. It also supported Hindi as the national language, probably because of its close links to Sanskrit, the religious language of Hinduism. The Indian National Congress was accused of forgetting all that was good and profound in Hindu culture and ideals, and also of appeasing the Muslims. The Congress and other critics denounced the Jana Sangh as a backward-looking and communalistic party, which would take India back to the Middle Ages.

The party had some electoral success, especially in collaboration with socialist parties opposed to the Congress, and in 1977 they formed the Janata Sangh (People's Union). Due to internal struggles for power the Bhāratīya Janata Party (BJP) Indian People's Party was formed in 1980, viewing itself as a truly egalitarian organisation based on the cornerstone of Gandhian socialism (Malik and Singh 1995: 37). This development spelt the demise of the Jana Sangh as a viable force in Indian society and politics.

See also: **Bhārat Māta; Bhāratīya Janata Party; Gandhi, Mohandas Karamchand; Hindutva; Rashtriya Swayamsevak Sangh; Sacred geography; Sacred languages**

THEODORE GABRIEL

Further reading

Puri, Geetha. 1980. *Bharathiya Jana Sangh: Organisation and Heritage*. New Delhi: Sterling Publishers

Malik, Yogendra and V.B. Singh. 1995. *Hindu Nationalists in India*. New Delhi: Vistaar Publications.

JANAKA

Raja Janaka of Videha appears as the father of Sītā in the lengthy description of her marriage to Rāma that appears in both Vālmīki's and Tulsīdās's *Rāmayaṇa*. The king had promised to give his beautiful daughter in marriage only to a suitor who could lift and pull the bow of Śiva which was in his possession. Many warriors, demons and kings come to win Sītā's hand but they all fail to lift the bow, except for Rāma, who pulls it so hard it snaps in two and thus brings upon himself the rage of Parāśurāma.

Janaka also appears in a number of stories recounted in the nirguṇa bhakti tradition, all concerned with the nature of renunciation. The stories usually follow the motif of a brāhmaṇa's son or a sadhu coming to Janaka's opulent court for instruction in knowledge of the Self. The disillusioned renunciates complain that they can learn nothing amidst such wealth. Janaka, by a series of devices, according to the various versions of the story, shows that renunciation is an internal quality, where worldly action is pursued but simultaneously the attention is maintained on the ātman within. Thus the householder is privileged over the saṃnyāsa in mediaeval Sant traditions.

See also: **Ātman; Bhakti; Brāhmaṇa; Gṛhasthya; Rāma; Rāmayaṇa; Sadhu; Saṃnyāsa; Sant; Sītā; Śiva; Tulsīdās(a); Vālmīki**

RON GEAVES

Further reading

Klostermaier, Klaus. 1989. *A Survey of Hinduism*. New York: State University of New York.

JANMĀṢṬAMĪ

Janmāṣṭamī is the celebration of Kṛṣṇa's birth. 'Janma' means 'birth' and 'aṣṭamī' means 'the eighth day', referring to Kṛṣṇa's birth on the eighth day of the dark fortnight in the month of Śravana. By the Western calendar, Janmāṣṭamī falls in August or early September. Janmāṣṭamī, though technically a Vaiṣṇava festival, is celebrated throughout India and surrounding countries by members of various Hindu religious denominations.

On Janmāṣṭamī, devotees of Kṛṣṇa rise early and spend the day absorbed in prayer and meditation, often fasting until midnight. The primary festivities of the day are devotional singing and scriptural reading about Kṛṣṇa, particularly the traditional stories surrounding his birth and childhood. Midnight, the hour at which Kṛṣṇa was born, marks the climax of the festival, with an ārtī, a ceremony of worship, and kīrtaṇa, devotional song. Many elaborate food items and presents are offered to Kṛṣṇa at midnight and are thereafter served to all guests and celebrants. Throughout the day celebrants partake of darśana of the mūrti form of Kṛṣṇa, which is decorated elaborately with flowers and fine ornaments. An abhiṣeka bathing of Kṛṣṇa's mūrti in fruit juices and milk products is also common among the festivities. The pastimes of Kṛṣṇa are frequently re-enacted in dramas and portrayed in traditional Indian dance.

This festival specifically celebrates Kṛṣṇa's identity as a young cowherd boy in Vṛndāvana. Vaiṣṇava devotees of Kṛṣṇa aspire to one day partake in the reality of Kṛṣṇa's life in Vṛndāvana, which is characterised by eternal cognisance and joy.

Janmāṣṭamī has enjoyed ardent loyalty from Hindus in the diaspora. Bhaktivedanta Manor, a Vaiṣṇava temple in North London, houses the largest Janmāṣṭamī festival outside India, drawing around 60,000 celebrants to its annual celebration. Also, in 2005, Janmāṣṭamī was celebrated for the first time in the House of Commons, in the British Parliament.

See also: **Abhiṣeka; Ārtī; Dance; Darśana; Diaspora; Drama; Fasting; Image worship; International Society of Krishna Consciousness; Kīrtaṇ(a); Kṛṣṇa; Utsava; Vaiṣṇava; Vṛndāvana**

CLAIRE ROBISON

Further reading

Andrews, Ross. 'The Festival of Janmastami'. Watford: ISKCON Educational Services.

Rosen, Steven J. 2006. *Introduction to the World's Major Religions: Hinduism*. Westport, CT: Greenwood Press.

JĀTAKARMA

Literally, 'birth ceremonies', which constitute an important rite of passage (saṃskāra). These wide-ranging ceremonies begin about a month before birth and continue intermittently through the delivery of the child. As with other saṃskāras, these rites are driven by mantric meaning and ritual precision, and, like the others, are variable depending on the Gṛhya or Dharma texts followed. The arrangements should be made a month prior to the expected date of delivery. At this time a room in the south-east portion of the house is consecrated and named sūtikā-bhavana, 'maternity house'. A day or two before delivery the expectant mother, accompanied by other experienced women, enters the sūtikā-bhavana, which has been ritually protected. She performs appropriate worship to gods, brāhmaṇas and cows, with accompanying music and recitation. This is designed to facilitate safe delivery. If the delivery is successful a fire is lit in the room and offerings made. The fire, the mantras and the offerings are believed to be good for the health of the mother and child and to drive away untoward spirits. After ten days this sūtikā-bhavana fire is to be replaced with a more enduring domestic fire. The main jātakarma ceremony is performed just before severing the umbilical cord. This consists, first, of the medha-janana, the ritual of 'production of intelligence'. In this rite the father, accompanied by recitation of mantras, feeds the newborn child, with the ring finger of his right hand holding a small golden rod, a small quantity of ghee or ghee mixed with honey (though some texts prescribe sour milk, rice, barley or even hairs of a black bull). Then the āyuṣya ceremony is performed. This is designed to bring long life to the child. Mantras are recited in the right ear or by the navel of the child. Following this a brief rite meant to bestow strength on the child is performed. The umbilical cord is then severed, the mother cleaned and expiatory mantras are recited to ward off wayward spirits and prevent unseen diseases.

See also: **Brāhmaṇas; Mantra; Sacred animals; Saṃskāra**

FREDERICK M. SMITH

Further reading

Kane, P.V. 1974. *History of Dharmaśāstra*, 2nd edn, vol. 2, pt 1. Poona: Bhandarkar Oriental Research Institute, 228–34.

Pandey, R.J. 1969. *Hindu Saṃskāras*. Delhi: Motilal Banarsidass, 70–77.

JAṬĀYU

Jaṭāyu is the aged vulture who, in the *Rāmāyaṇa,* becomes the friend of Rāma during his forest exile and, when Rāvaṇa arrives and abducts Sītā, first berates him for his misdeed and then seeks to prevent him by force. Jāṭāyu is no match for Rāvaṇa and falls dying to the earth, where soon afterwards he is found by Rāma and Lakṣmaṇa as they begin their search for Śītā. Jaṭāyu manages to gasp that it is Rāvaṇa who has abducted Sītā and expires. Rāma then cremates his body. Later the Vānaras (monkeys) in their seach for Śītā are advised by Jaṭāyu's brother, Saṃpāti.

See also: **Lakṣmaṇa; Rāma; Rāmāyaṇa; Rāvaṇa; Sacred animals; Sītā**

JOHN BROCKINGTON

Further reading

Bose, Mandakranta. (ed.). 2004. *The Rāmāyaṇa Revisited.* New York: Oxford University Press.

Brockington, John. 1985. *Righteous Rāma: The Evolution of an Epic*. Delhi: Oxford University Press.

Brockington, John. 1998. *The Sanskrit Epics* (Handbuch der Orientalisk 2.12). Leiden: Brill.

Brockington, John and Mary Brockington (trans.). 2006. *Steadfast Rāma: An Early Form of the Rāmāyaṇa*. London: Penguin Books.

Brockington, Mary. 1997. 'The Art of Backwards Compostion: Some Narrative Techniques in Vālmīki's Rāmāyaṇa'. In Mary Brockington and Peter Schreiner, eds, *Composing a Tradition.* Proceedings of the First Dubrovnik International Conference on the Sanskrit Epics and Purāṇas, 99–110.

Bulcke, Camille. 1950. *Rāmkathā: utpatti aur vikāś* [The Rama story: origin and spread]. Prayāg: Hindā Pariṣad Prakāśan.

Goldman, Robert P. (gen. ed.). 1984–. *The Rāmāyaṇa of Vālmīki: An Epic of Ancient India*. Trans. Robert P. Goldman *et al.* Princeton, NJ: Princeton University Press.

Goldman, Robert P. and Sally J. Sutherland Goldman. 2004. 'Rāmāyaṇa'. In Sushil Mittal and Gene Thursby, eds, *The Hindu World*. New York: Routledge, 75–96.

Lutgendorf, Philip. 1990. 'Ramayan: The Video'. *Drama Review* 34: 127–76.

Lutgendorf, Philip. 1991. *The Life of a Text: Performing the Rāmcaritmānas of Tulsīdās.* Berkeley, CA: University of California Press.

Lutgendorf, Philip. 1995. 'Interpreting Rāmrāj: Reflections on the *Rāmayaṇ*, Bhakti and Hindu Nationalism'. In David N. Lorenzen, ed., *Bhakti Religion in North India*. Albany, NY: SUNY Press, 253–87.

Richman, Paula. (ed.). 1991. *Many Rāmāyaṇnas: The Diversity of a Narrative Tradition in South Asia.* Berkeley, CA: University of California Press.

Richman, Paula. 2001. *Questioning Rāmāyaṇas: A South Asian Tradition.* Berkeley, CA: University of California Press.

Theil-Horstmann, Monika. (ed.). 1991. *Rāmāyaṇa and Rāmāyaṇas* (Khoj – A Series of Modern South Asian Studies 3). Wiesbaden: Harrassowitz.

JĀTĪ

Jātī is a Sanskrit term that best represents the concept of caste by designating a social group into which a person is born. Although Sanskrit authors held out the possibility that a person could change his or her jātī in subsequent births, the jātī into which one was born was, to all intents and purposes, regarded as immutable. Unlike the varṇa system, which provided a very general, theoretical framework for the division of Indian society into the brāhmans, the kṣatriyas, the vaiśhyas and the śudras, the proliferation of jātīs conformed to the social realities of ancient and medieval India. Consequently, in contrast with the four varṇas, the number of jātīs was neither fixed nor limited. Sanskrit authors attempted to root the evolution of the jātīs in a theory that took the four varṇas into account. Although members of a particular varṇa were ruled by the principle of endogamy, according to which they could only marry and cohabit with a member of the same varṇa, it was argued that, at some point in the past, there had been a varṇa-samkara, an intermingling of the members of various varṇas. The offspring of such unions, belonging neither to the varṇas of their fathers nor to those of their mothers, were said to have constituted new social categories, namely jātīs. Regardless of their origins, jātīs were ultimately connected to the four varṇas, with the result that dozens of diverse, endogamous social groups in various regions of India could all be said to belong to one of the varṇas, irrespective of their striking differences. Nevertheless, the fourfold system of varṇas could not completely contain the multiplicity of jātīs, for jātīs whose members were considered impure, who were later referred to as untouchables, dalits or harijans (God's children), could not be ascribed to any one of the varṇas. Because the notion of jātī was considered incompatible with the humanist spirit of modernity, numerous reformers in the nineteenth and twentieth centuries tried unsuccessfully to eliminate it from Indian society. Today, the Constitution of India acknowledges that jātī does exist, but it affords protection against discrimination on that basis.

See also: **Brāhmaṇas; Caste; Dalits; Varṇa**

ETHAN KROLL

Further reading

Dumont, Louis. 1970. *Homo Hierarchicus: An Essay on the Caste System*. Trans. Mark Sainsbury. Chicago, IL: University of Chicago Press.

Galanter, Marc. 1963. 'Law and Caste in Modern India'. *Asian Survey* 3(11): 544–59.

Ghurye, G.S. 1932. *Caste and Race in India*. London: Kegan Paul, Trench, Trubner & Co., Ltd.

Kane, Pandurang Vaman. 1941. *History of Dharmasastra*, vol. 2. Poona: Bhandarkar Oriental Research Institute.

Smith, Brian K. 1994. *Classifying the Universe*. Oxford: Oxford University Press.

Srinivas, M.N. 1962. *Caste in Modern India and Other Essays*. Bombay: Asia Publishing House.

JAYADEVA (TWELFTH/ THIRTEENTH CENTURY)

Vaiṣṇava poet and saint. Born in the village of Tindubilva (Kindavila), believed to be the Kenduli diversely located in Bengal, Orissa, Bihar or as far away as Gujarat, Jayadeva spent his career as court poet (kavi) for King Laksmanasena (reigned *c.*1180–1202) at Vijayapura in western Bengal. His masterpiece, the *Gītagovinda* (Song of the Cowherd), was completed by the end of the twelfth century and has remained to this day a major influence on literature, art and religion, a feature of many festivals and daily devotion. Initiating a new phase of development in the tradition of Kṛṣṇa-bhakti, the focus of the poem is the relationship between Kṛṣṇa and his lover, Rādhā, here promoted to quasi – if not wholly – divine status. The only other protagonist is the Sākhi, Rādhā's friend, confidante and go-between. The story is a simple one: Kṛṣṇa is seduced by Rādhā but she is subsequently estranged, hurt by his dalliance with the gopīs, the cowherds' womenfolk. Kṛṣṇa comes to regret his behaviour, while both lovers pine for each other, in the memory of their passionate embraces. Thanks to Kṛṣṇa's repentance and to the Sākhi's intercession, the lovers are reconciled and finally reunited, the sadness of separation triumphantly overcome in lovemaking. The tale unfolds through twelve cantos in which the spoken narration alternates with twenty-four songs set in specified musical modes (rāgas) and rhythm-patterns (tāla) which reinforce the moods and states of mind evoked in the verses. The poem has also always been performed in dance, according to different traditions, especially during religious festivals.

The *Gītāgovinda* being a gem of unabashedly explicit erotic poetry has never detracted from its being primarily interpreted in mystical terms as depicting the love between the human soul, represented by Rādhā, and God-Kṛṣṇa; the agony of their separation and their final communion. Thus, unconditional devotion (bhakti) is expressed in erotic terms while, in return, human love is seen to be grounded in divine delight, confirming the primacy and universality of love. The religious dimension of the poem accounts for Jayadeva being esteemed as a saint rather than a poet, all the more so in that it is the hagiographic stories about his life, rather than his work, that are known throughout India, mostly by those with no Sanskrit. The poet is depicted as a wandering ascetic that God wills to marry the beautiful Padmāvatī, so that he may learn the ways of human love while remaining an otherworldly householder, guru to many, including the king. This accounts for his presence at court, where his wife is then brought, the couple exemplifying the love between Rādhā and Kṛṣṇa, or Viṣṇu and Śrī Lakṣmī, in a play of mirrors where God is equally devoted to humans. Many legends associate Jayadeva with Purī in Orissa and its famous Jagannātha temple, where his words are sung daily, an auspicious sound and meritorious act, so that even the retelling of his life stories is itself an act of bhakti.

The *Gītagovinda* is one of the summits of Sanskrit literature and Sir William Jones' translation of 1792 was among the very first renderings of Sanskrit into English to be published.

See also: **Bhakti (as path); Dance; Gopī; Guru; Jones, Sir William; Kṛṣṇa; Lakṣmī, Śrī; Rādhā; Vaiṣṇavism; Viṣṇu**

DANIEL MARIAU

JHĀ, SIR GANGANATHA (1871–1941)

Indian Sanskritist, born in Darbhanga and raised in an orthodox brāhmaṇa family. He studied at Queen's College, Banaras, and then at Allahabad University, where his DLitt on the Prabhākara, a hitherto little-studied Pūrva Mīmāṃsā philosopher, was the first research degree in Sanskrit to be awarded. Jhā taught at Muir College, Allahabad, before becoming first Indian principal of the Banaras Sanskrit College in 1917. From 1923 to 1932 he was Vice-Chancellor of Allahabad University. He translated and commented on several Mīmāṃsā texts, including the *Mīmāṃsāsūtras* of Jaimini (a partial edition, with translation and commentary, in the *Sacred Books of the Hindus* series), the *Śābara-bhāṣya* and the *Ślokavārttika*. Among his other published works are a translation of Mammaṭa's *Kāvya-Prākaśa* (a work on poetics), and translations and editions of other philosophical (especially Nyāya) and legal texts.

See also: **Hinduism, history of scholarship; Pūrva Mīmāṃsā; Sacred Books of the East**

WILL SWEETMAN

Further reading

Jha, G. 1911–15. *The Pūrva Mimāmsa Sūtras of Jaimini* [Sacred Books of the Hindus, vol. 10]. Allahabad: Panini Office.

Jha, G. 1920–26. *Manusmrti: The Laws of Manu with the Bhāsya of Medhātithi*. Calcutta: University of Calcutta.

Jha, G. 1925. *Kavyaprakasha of Mammata*. Allahabad: Indian Press.

JĪVA

The term jīvā (adj. 'living, alive'; m. 'life, individual soul'), a nominal formed from the Sanskrit root jīv ('live') derived from reconstructed Proto-Indo-European g^u^i̯u̯ (Mayrhofer 1956: 440; Pokorny 1959: 468) cognate with English quick, begins to be used to refer to the individual soul even in the *Ṛgveda*, where the immortal jīva is contrasted with the mortal body (*Ṛgveda* 1.164.30), and in the early *Upaniṣads*, where the body endowed with the jīva dies while the jīva does not die (*Chāndogya Upaniṣad* 6.11.3). Still charged with its etymological meaning here, it does not vie with the terms Puruṣa and Ātman as a conventional term for the individual soul until the latest of the early *Upaniṣads* (third to first centuries BCE). *Kaṭha Upaniṣad* 4.5 states that the lord does not seek to hide himself from the one who sees his own soul (ātmānam jīvam) as the lord. While here it is still possible to take the term ātman as the conventional term for the individual self and jīva as an adjective, and so to translate ātmānam jīvam, 'the living self' instead of 'his own soul', as has Olivelle (1998: 393), *Śvetāśvatara Upaniṣad* 5.9–10 provide an unambiguous case of the term jīva used conventionally for the individual self. The first verse describes the jīva as one ten-thousandth the size of the tip of a hair, yet as infinite. The next adds that, being gender-free itself, it adopts the gender of whatever body it inhabits. The passage describes the individual self as unencumbered by specific dimension and other bodily characteristics, just as numerous Upaniṣadic passages that use the terms Puruṣa and Ātman do.

Later philosophical texts, especially in Vedānta and exclusively in Jainism, prefer this term to refer unambiguously to the individual self over the terms Ātman and Puruṣa, which may be used to refer to a cosmic person, to Brahman, or to the supreme God.

See also: **Ātman; Brahman; Jainism, relationship with Hinduism; Puruṣa; Saṃhitās; Upaniṣads; Vedānta**

PETER M. SCHARF

Further reading

Grimes, John A. 1996 [1988]. *A Concise Dictionary of Indian Philosophy: Sanskrit Terms Defined in English*. Albany, NY: State University of New York Press.

Mayrhofer, Manfred. 1956. *Kurzgefaßtes etymologisches Wörterbuch des altindischen [A Concise Etymological Sanskrit Dictionary]*, vol. 1. Heidelberg: Carl Winter.

Olivelle, Patrick. 1998. *The Early Upaniṣads: Annotated Text and Translation*. South Asia Research. Oxford: Oxford University Press.

Pokorny, Julius. 1959. *Indogermanisches etymologisches Wörterbuch [Indo-European etymological dictionary]*, vol. 1. Bern; Munich: A. Francke.

JĪVANMUKTA

The term 'jīvanmukti' means liberation (mokṣa or mukti) while living, and the term 'jīvanmukta' refers to an individual who has achieved liberation or release while embodied. The concept of jīvanmukti is associated with several Hindu schools, including Śaṅkara's Advaita Vedānta, Sāṃkhya, Kashmiri Śaivism and Śaiva Siddhānta.

Mokṣa is generally characterised as the supreme goal of the Hindu; it is release from transmigration or the cycle of births and deaths (saṃsāra); it is transcendence of pain and suffering, and ultimate or perfect freedom.

However, Hindu religious and philosophical traditions have expressed different views on the exact nature of liberation and how to attain it. Thus the possibility of jīvanmukti has been debated. The attainment of liberation on the death of the physical body is associated with many devotional forms of Hinduism. Schools which teach that liberation is due to a discriminating knowledge, such as Advaita and Sāṃkhya, have admitted the doctrine of jīvanmukti.

Śaṅkara interpreted the *Upaniṣads* from the standpoint of strict non-dualism (advaita). For him the sole ultimate reality is the non-dual Self (Ātman), which is identified with Brahman. Thus reality is distinctionless, bereft of plurality. Transmigratory life is based on the erroneous identification of the Self and not-self (mind, body, senses). So the ultimate goal of the Advaita discipline is discrimination (viveka) of the true nature of the Self from the not-self superimposed on it. Liberation is cessation of superimposition, removal of ignorance (avidyā), knowledge of ātman (ātmavidyā). To awaken to the true nature of our Self is to be liberated 'here and now' (jīvanmukti). Although the enlightened person is aware of his embodied state, there is no belief in plurality. The body continues for the detached, dispassionate jīvanmukta just as the potter's wheel spins for a period of time after the potter's hand has been withdrawn. The death of the physical body results in 'final release' (videhamukti).

See also: **Advaita; Ātman; Brahman; Kashmiri Śaivism; Mokṣa; Śaiva Siddhānta; Śaivism; Sāṃkhya; Samsāra; Śaṅkara; Upaniṣads**

MARTIN OVENS

Further reading

Fort, A.O. 1998. *Jīvanmukti in Transformation: Embodied Liberation in Advaita and Neo-Vedānta*. Albany, NY: SUNY Press.

JÑĀNA (AS PATH)

The path of jñāna (knowledge), epitomised by the Vedāntic philosopher Śaṅkara, is one of three standard, soteriologically efficacious personal orientations, the others being the paths of bhakti (devotion) and karma (action). In soteriological contexts the term jñāna indicates an apprehension that is not merely discursive but contains an additional intuitive or experiential aspect.

The importance of jñāna can be traced back textually as far as the early Vedic brahmodya, a riddling or debating contest (Kuiper 1960). In the period of the Brāhmaṇas, ritual officiants speculated about the hidden significance of the ritual and the ultimate basis of its power: elaborate systems were devised, correlating elements from macrocosmic and microcosmic domains, and the knower of such esoteric patterns was extolled as superior to the assiduous ritual performer. In the *Upaniṣads* this trend continues, with particular emphasis (retained in most subsequent Hindu soteriological discourse) on the knowledge of ātman, the essential constituent of the human being, famously equated with Brahman, the essential constituent of the cosmos (*Bṛhadāraṇyaka Upaniṣad* 1.4:10, 2.5:19, 4.4:5; *Chāndogya Upaniṣad* 6.8–16; *Māṇḍūkya Upaniṣad* 2). Two important developments take place at this stage, both of which are shared by early groups of śramaṇas, Buddhists and Jains, and have often been explained with reference to influences from outside the Vedic tradition. First, there is the idea of saṃsāra, a continuing and unsatisfactory succession of lives, and of mokṣa (nirvāṇa in Buddhism), the end of such a succession; second, there is the idea that renunciation (saṃnyāsa) of the householder lifestyle accompanies any successful attempt to bring mokṣa about. Special knowledge is the essence of the salvation process: incipient knowledge leads one to renounce, allowing specialised pursuit of the fuller knowledge required to obviate rebirth.

The path of jñāna is thus usually associated with the renunciation of social dharmas, these being seen as dependent on desire (kāma), most fundamentally the desire for children. Several innovations attempted to counter the renunciative tendency. The institution of four successive āśramas (life stages) accommodated a period of renunciation at the end of an otherwise orthodox social career, and the *Bhagavadgītā*'s theory of non-attached action made soteriological progress available even to those currently engaged in socio-economic life. Despite these innovations, renunciation remains the paradigm of the path of jñāna; but, equally, because of these innovations we cannot view the path of jñāna as travelled only by renouncers. The pursuit of jñāna may be full time or part time, and, if part time, may take place in series or in parallel with other pursuits.

Jñāna is sought by many and varied methods. The path usually involves initiation into an organisation (however loose) of jñāna-seekers, and participation in the generational guru/śiṣya (master/disciple) tradition of education. Different organisations focus on different combinations of methods, including various meditative techniques, and recitation and contemplation of mantras and texts, Vedic or otherwise. Descriptions of the jñāna being sought also vary, as does the place that the idea of enlightenment holds in the inner lives of those concerned.

See also: **Āśramas (stages of life); Ātman; Bhagavadgītā; Bhakti; Brahman; Brāhmaṇas; Buddhism, relationship with Hinduism; Dharma; Guru; Jainism, relationship with Hinduism; Kāma; Karma (Law of Action); Mantra; Mokṣa; Saṃnyāsa; Saṃsāra; Śaṅkara; Śiṣya; Śramaṇas; Upaniṣads; Vedānta**

SIMON BRODBECK

Further reading

Kuiper, F.B.J. 1960. 'The Ancient Aryan Verbal Contest'. *Indo-Iranian Journal* 4: 217–81.

JOIS K. PATTABHI AND ASHTANGA VINYASA YOGA

K. Pattabhi Jois was born in 1915 in Kowshika, Karnataka State. He studied yoga with T. Krishnamacharya from 1927 onwards, and in 1937 began teaching at the Yoga Department of the Mysore Sanskrit College, where he remained until his retirement in 1973. From the early 1970s onwards he began to teach Westerners and today his system is extremely popular, especially in Britain and America. Jois claims that his system, known as 'aṣṭāṅga vinyāsa yoga', derives from a manuscript, *Yoga Kurunta*, discovered by Krishnamacharya in the 1930s in a Calcutta library. It is an intensely physical practice, in which a seamless flow of postures is combined with special breathing (ujjayi prāṇāyāma), gaze points (dṛṣṭi) and energetic body-locks (bandha). There are six increasingly challenging 'series', which can take up to two hours each to complete.

New postures are taught only when the student is deemed ready. Pattabhi Jois wrote a book explaining the Primary Series in 1958, entitled *Yoga Māla*. The demanding aerobic nature of this form has made it a favourite in Western-style fitness clubs and gyms.

See also: **Krishnamacharya, T.; Yoga; Yoga, modern**

MARK SINGLETON

Further reading

Jois, Sri K. 1999. *Yoga Mala*. New York: Eddie Stern/Patanjali Yoga Shala.

JONES, SIR WILLIAM (1746–94)

British judge, already a renowned linguist and Orientalist scholar before his arrival in India in 1783, having published translations from Persian, Arabic and Turkish works and been elected a fellow of the Royal Society in 1772. It is nevertheless largely for his study of Sanskrit and his translations from it, especially of *Śakuntalā*, a play of Kālidasā (1789), and the *Manusmṛti* (1794), undertaken in India that he was celebrated in his lifetime and is remembered now. His anniversary discourses to the Asiatic Society of Bengal were perhaps the primary reason for the wide circulation of the society's journal, the *Asiatick Researches*; those of most importance for the study of Hinduism are 'On the Gods of Greece, Italy, and India'

(1785) and 'On the Hindus' (1786). The latter contains his famous announcement of the relationship between Indian and European languages which contributed, together with the other works of Jones and his collaborators, to the extremely positive late eighteenth-century attitudes to India and its religions which Thomas Trautmann has characterised as 'Indomania'.

See also: **Asiatick Researches; Asiatic Societies; Dharmaśāstras; Hinduism, history of scholarship; Kālidasā**

WILL SWEETMAN

Further reading

Cannon, G. and K.R. Brine. 1995. *Objects of Enquiry: The Life, Contributions, and Influences of Sir William Jones (1746–1794)*. New York: New York University Press.

Jones, W. 1789. *Sacontalā; or, The Fatal Ring: An Indian Drama*. Calcutta: Printed and sold by Joseph Cooper, for the benefit of insolvent debtors.

Jones, W. 1794. *Institutes of Hindu Law: or, The Ordinances of Menu*. Calcutta: Printed by order of the Government.

Trautmann, Thomas R. 1997. *Aryans and British India*. Berkeley, CA: University of California Press.

JUNG, CARL GUSTAV (1865–1961)

Psychologist, born in Switzerland and trained as a medical doctor before working closely with Sigmund Freud (1856–1939). Jung's study of Yoga – for him not only the school of thought systematised by Patañjali but a general term for all forms of South and East Asian religious traditions – came largely after his break with Freud in 1913. Although doubtful of the benefits of Eastern forms of religious practice for those shaped by the fundamentally different cultural heritage of the West, Jung found in Hindu symbolism, and especially the use of *maṇḍalas*, both confirmation of and inspiration for some of the central themes of his psychoanalytic thought concerning the archetypes of the collective unconscious which structure our experience. In the concept of *prāṇa,* Jung found confirmation of his own conception of the libido as a neutral psychic energy, as opposed to Freud's reduction of it to sexual instinct. His work has influenced later scholars of Hinduism, including M. Eliade and W. Doniger.

See also: **Eliade, Mircea; Hinduism, history of scholarship; Patañjali; Yoga**

WILL SWEETMAN

Further reading

Coward, H. (ed.). 1985. *Jung and Eastern Thought*. Albany, NY: SUNY Press.

Clarke, J.J. 1994. *Jung and Eastern Thought: A Dialogue with the Orient*. London: Routledge.

JYEṢṬHĀ

The cult of the goddess Jyeṣṭhā goes back to at least to the time of the *Baudhāyana Gṛhyasūtra*, in which her worship is described. However, the earliest use of the term jyeṣṭhā ('female eldest') in Hindu literature is in the *Atharvaveda*, where the lunar mansion jyeṣṭhā (the star Antares), is so-called because it is jyeṣṭhā-ghnī, 'she who strikes down the eldest son'. This dire association carries over into the circa sixth-century CE designation of Jyeṣṭhā as the 'cruellest month' in the Indian luni-solar calendar, falling in the hot season months of May–June. These death-laden associations make Jyeṣṭhā a dire and dread goddess, identified in the *Padma Purāṇa* as Alakṣmī ('Inauspicious'), the elder sister and negative mirror-image of the auspicious Lakṣmī, goddess of prosperity. Her worship is widely attested throughout South Asia, especially in south India, where numerous medieval sculptures portray her astride an ass and holding a winnowing broom and a crow-banner, attributes that also link her to the goddesses Śītalā and Dhūmāvatī.

See also: **Alakṣmī; Mahāvidyās; Purāṇas; Saṃhitās; Śītalā**

DAVID GORDON WHITE

Further reading

Rao, T.A.G. 1968. *Elements of Hindu Iconography*, 4 vols. New York: Paragon Book Reprint Corp. (first published 1914).

JYOTIṢA

Jyotiṣa (astrology) is the assignation of meaning to celestial events and the traditions of learning associated with this practice. In India, astrology and astronomy are together traditionally known as jyotiṣa, or the 'science of light', itself one of the six vedāṅgas, the subjects necessary to a proper understanding of the Veda. Jyotiṣa originated as a means of calculating the sacred calendar. The *Vedāṅga Jyotiṣa* was the first known astrological/astronomical text, which was primarily a manual for the determination of auspicious times for performing religious rituals. Traces of early astrology are found in the Vedic hymns, though it is difficult to reconstruct the earliest Indian astrology. It appears that, at least in the first millennium BCE, a lunar 'zodiac' of twenty-seven nakṣatras, conforming to the twenty-seven days of the sidereal lunar month, was in use. Complete lists of the twenty-seven nakṣatras appear in the *Atharvaveda* and *Yajurveda*. Intense contact between India and the West during the Hellenistic period, from 300 BCE, resulted in the introduction of a distinctive and complex astrology, including the use of horoscopes, charts of the heavens calculated for an exact time and place. There is considerable controversy concerning the extent to which this astrology was indigenous or was imported.

Astrology remains a vital part of Indian culture and is intertwined with both sacred and mundane life. Although there are significant regional differences of practice, chiefly between the north and south, astrologers are consulted on every aspect of life, notably marriage, health and career. The dominant style is predictive, although the point of making forecasts is to manage the future either by harmonising one's behaviour with celestial patterns or by making direct appeals to the relevant deities via pūjās. The planets may function both as influences and signs of divine intent, and the procedures for interpreting their meaning are exceedingly complex. Although, traditionally, astrology was chiefly a priestly or hereditary practice, increasingly it may be taught and practised like any other discipline; in the late 1990s the nationalist Bharatiya Janata Party government instituted jyotiṣa as a university discipline, against much opposition from prominent secularists.

See also: **Bharatiya Janata Party; Pūjā; Saṃhitā; Veda; Vedāṅgas; Vivāha**

NICHOLAS CAMPION AND DENNIS HARNESS

Further reading

Pingree, David. 1978. *The Yavanajataka of Sphujidhvaja*, vols. 1 and 2. Cambridge, MA: Harvard University Press.

K

KABANDHA

A demon, formerly known as Viśvāvasu, whose name literally means 'headless trunk'. Kabandha's most well-known appearance in the literature occurs in the *Rāmāyaṇa*, where he attacks Rāma and Lakṣmaṇa while they wander in the forest in search of Sītā. After the two brothers cut off his hands, kill him and burn his body, the demon's former self (that of a Gandharva prince known as Viśvāvasu) rises from the corpse and advises Rāma to find Sugrīva in order to help locate Sītā. The epithet 'kabandha' originates in a story that recounts an arrogant Viśvāvasu (who has been granted immortality by Lord Brahmā as a reward for his penance) as an enemy of Indra. Lord Indra squeezes his head and thighs into his body as punishment, thus leaving him in his hideous form. Pleading with the king of the gods for some relief, Indra predicts that he will recover his previous form when Lord Rāma and Lakṣmaṇa cut off his hands. Another story has it that it was the sage Sthūlaśiras who granted him the favour of being liberated at the hands of Rāma.

See also: **Brahmā; Gandharva; Indra; Lakṣmana; Rāma; Rāmāyaṇa; Sītā**

DEVEN M. PATEL

Further reading

Mani, Vettam. 2002. *Purāṇic Encyclopaedia*. Delhi: Motilal Banarsidass.

KABĪR

Kabīr (1398–1448), a low-caste weaver, was a North Indian sant who lived in Vārānasī. He is claimed by both Hindus and Muslims but it is probable that his family converted to Islam one or two generations prior to his birth. Hindu traditions claim that he was a disciple of the Vaiṣnava Rāmānanda, although this would seem unlikely as the latter was born a century earlier. Written in a colloquial oral style Hindi, Kabīr's poetry rejects the outer forms of worship as found in Islam and Hindu practices, rejecting the authority of both Veda and Qur'an, holding to the Sant ideal that sacred books are not necessary to human salvation. Along with the rejection of sacred texts, rituals and knowledge, Kabīr also lambasts as hypocrites the brāhmaṇas and imams, claiming that they are in ignorance of God. Kabīr's poetry remains popular in Northern India, made known to the people through song, and to the literate through the English translation of Rabindranath Tagore entitled *One Hundred Poems of Kabir*, first published in 1915 and still available. In this work Kabīr is identified as a mystical poet, but for other Indians of low-caste status his critique of caste enables him to be adopted as a figurehead of their aspirations for social and political reform. The largest and oldest collection of poems attributed to Kabīr appears in the sacred text of the Sikhs, the *Guru Granth Sāhib*, and some Sikh traditions even claim that he was the guru of Nanak. The second source is the *Bijak*, the sacred text of the Kabīrpanthis, the religious movement which has developed around Kabīr and his teachings. Western scholarship has thrown some doubt on the authenticity of all the poems attributed to the sant, noting the variation of style and content, but he remains the epitome of the Northern Indian medieval sant, uncompromisingly worshipping a formless God with intense bhakti (devotion), attacking and challenging orthodoxy and hypocrisy in a unique, fearless style resonant with religious iconoclasm.

See also: **Bhakti (as path); Brāhmaṇas; Guru; Rāmananda; Sant; Sikhism, relationship with Hinduism; Tagore, Rabindranath; Vaiṣṇavism; Vārāṇasī; Veda**

RON GEAVES

Further reading

Hess, Linda. 1983. *The Bijak of Kabīr.* San Francisco, CA: North Point Press.

Vaudeville, Charlotte. 1974. *Kabir*, vol. I Oxford: Clarendon Press.

KAIVALYA

The term kaivalya, 'isolation' (derived from kevala, 'alone, isolated'), adopted from Jain usage, is used in Sāṃkhya and Yoga for the state of the Puruṣa, free of contact (saṃyoga) with Prakṛti and in late Vedānta texts (*Kaivalya Upaniṣad*, Tantavaraya Cuvamikal's (1408–1534) *Kaivalyanavanītam*) for liberation (mokṣa). The *Sāṃkhyakārikās* use the terms apavarga, 'separation' (*Sāṃkhyakārikā* 44), and vimokṣa, 'liberation' (*Sāṃkhyakārikās* 56–58), as synonyms for kaivalya to state that it results from knowledge residing in the intellect, and that Prakṛti instigates her entire manifestation for the purpose of the liberation of each Puruṣa. Original nature, though insentient, engages in activity for the purpose of the separation of the self from her, as well as for the purpose of the self's enjoyment of her. Once the knowledge of the distinction between the self and nature is established in the intellect, nature ceases to act because she no longer serves any purpose for the self (*Sāṃkhyakārikā* 66, 68; *Yogasūtra* 4.34). When the pure knowledge arises, complete and alone (kevala, *Sāṃkhyakārikā* 64), so that the Puruṣa is silent, pure witnessing consciousness, and Prakṛti is the insentient actress who merely appears to be conscious when she assumes the role of the intellect and the other faculties of an individual personality, then Prakṛti withdraws, like a dancer from the stage when she has finished her performance (*Sāṃkhyakārikā* 51). The machinery of the personality and subtle body persists until the destruction of the gross body. Although the self and nature are in fact distinct all along, the fact that the Puruṣa has not seen her prompts her to act, and once he has seen her she desists. In the state of kaivalya, disinterested (upekṣaka) in her act, he sees nature only in her original unmanifest form, retired from her manifest roles, though she continues to act for others.

See also: **Jīvanmukta; Mokṣa; Prakṛti; Puruṣa; Sāṃkhya; Sāṃkhyakārikās; Upaniṣads; Vedānta; Yoga; Yogasūtras**

PETER M. SCHARF

Further reading

Mahadeva Sastri (trans.). 1898. *Amritabindu and Kaivalya Upanishads*. Madras: Printed by Thompson and Co.

Swami Ramanananda Saraswathi (trans.). 1965. *Kaivalya Navaneeta (The Cream of Emancipation): An Ancient Tamil Classic*. Tiruvannamalai: T.N. Venkataraman.

KAIVALYADHAMA

See: **Kuvalayananda, Swami and Kaivalyadhama**

KĀLAMUKHAS

See: **Śaivism**

KALHAṆA

A twelfth-century poet and author of the *Rājataraṅgiṇī* (The River of Kings), a verse history of Kashmir. Traditionally considered to be a Kashmiri Śaivite with an interest in Buddhism, his erudition would certainly suggest someone with the learning associated with the brāhmaṇa castes. He is best known through his work the *Rājataraṅgiṇī*, written in Sanskrit and completed in 1148–49 CE. The colophon at the end of each book tells us that Kalhaṇa was the son of Canpaka, a famed minister of Kashmir.

The *Rājataraṅgiṇī* comprises eight books containing over 6,000 verses. The work is significant in the contemporary period as it provides a link between present Kashmir and its past and therefore can be utilised for Kashmiri nationalism and identity. It provides an historical record and a mass of detailed information concerning the conditions of ancient Kashmir. It is primarily set within the time period of Kalhaṇa's own life and provides an account of political life and the poet's opinions of political representatives. Kalhaṇa witnessed the dynastic changes brought about through the revolution of King Harsa's two brothers Uccala and Sussala, who were opposed to the heavy taxation of the king's later reign and his persecution of the landed aristocracy. The princes partitioned the territory but the period of their rule was one of civil war and strife. Writing in the reign of King Jayasimha, the son of Sussala, Kalhaṇa looks back critically on the period of strife and assesses the political problems of Kashmir.

See also: **Brāhmaṇa; Caste; Buddhism, relationship with Hinduism; Kashmiri Śaivism; Nationalism**

RON GEAVES

Further reading

Dhar, Somnath. 1978. *Kalhana*. New Delhi: Sahitya Akademi.

KĀLĪ AND CAṆḌĪ

Kālī, translatable as 'the dark one' (and Caṇḍī, 'the fierce, passionate'), is the Hindu goddess whose name and iconography has probably extended the furthest beyond its original Indian context. Today most popularly worshipped in Bengal, Kālī has had devotees throughout the Indian subcontinent for many centuries and her name and image are recognisable to large numbers of people across the contemporary Hindu diaspora. This widespread awareness of Kālī is, in part, explicable in terms of her unique countenance and her strong associations with destruction and violence.

Typically Kālī is depicted icongraphically as a terrifying emaciated woman; her skin is black, her hair is long and tangled, her eyes are red and her mouth has a long lolling tongue. She is naked except for a macabre set of adornments: a necklace of skulls or freshly decapitated heads, a skirt of severed arms and jewellery made from the corpses of infants. In her four arms she carries a bloody cleaver and a severed head and she is most commonly depicted standing on the prone body of Śiva, who is as lifeless as a corpse. Kālī represents dynamic energy, while Śiva is consciousness. At first sight Kālī looks terrifying but her iconography is symbolic of her protective role as the destroyer of evil, with her sword being used to cut the ties of bondage and so offer liberation. She also makes the signs of one who confers boons and offers protection. Kālī will look after those who approach her in the attitude of a child. In Bengal, where she is most widely worshipped, devotional songs and poems that extol her motherly aspect are popular. Conversely, she is also portrayed in a state of frenzy or extreme intoxication, her wildness being a defining attribute of her character. Indeed it has been postulated that Kālī represents, and can assist one in understanding, those aspects of life that are uncontrollable and on occasion disrupt the order of dharma (Kinsley 1996: 83–84).

Mythologically and textually, Kālī first appears during the seventh century CE. She plays an important role in the *Devī Māhātmya*, where she appears as a manifestation of the rage of the goddess Durgā in her battles against two demon generals, Caṇḍa and Muṇḍa, and the great demon Raktabīja. In these conflicts the demon generals are slain by Kālī in a particularly brutal and swift fashion, while Raktabīja is killed by the goddess draining him of blood, to stop him replicating himself, and devouring him. An element of Kālī's character is her hunger for blood and her preference for dwelling in or near places of death and decay, such as battlefields and cremation grounds. However, Kālī is also closely connected with transcendent knowledge and in this respect is the foremost of the ten Mahāvidyās, a collection of goddesses who offer liberating knowledge to their devotees. In the *Liṅga Purāṇa* Kālī emerges from the goddess Pārvatī in order to defeat another demon, Dāruka. While her power is used to defeat evil it is can be a menace to the cosmos if left unchecked, and only the intervention of Śiva is understood to be capable of curtailing her destructive activity (Kinsley 1988: 118–19).

Kālī is a goddess who embodies and intimately embraces the worldly realities of blood, death and destruction. Historically, she has been associated with the boundaries of civilisation, with criminality and pollution, and with the dynamic female energy of Śakti. She is the preeminent goddess of the left-handed Tantrism (Kinsley 1988: 122–24) and, for her devotees, she can promote an understanding of the cycle of birth, death and rebirth (saṃsāra) that may ultimately lead to liberation (Kinsley 1996: 82–84). It is noteworthy, too, that Kālī has proved to be of value to many women in the contemporary world – both Hindu and non-Hindu – as a potent resource for personal and political liberation and, specifically, as a feminist symbol of uncontrolled female power (Gupta 1992).

In Bengal, Kālī has been important as the goddess most closely associated with nationalism. Appearing in Bankim Chandra Chatterjee's famous novel *Ananda Maṭh* (Abbey of Bliss), she represents India under oppression but who, nevertheless, has the power to free herself.

See also: **Chatterjee, Bankim Chandra; Devī Māhātmya; Dharma; Diaspora; Durgā; Images and iconography; Mahāvidyās; Mokṣa; Mudrā; Myth; Pārvatī; Purāṇas; Raktabīja; Śakti; Śaktism; Saṃsāra; Śiva; Tantric Yoga; Tantrism; Women's movement**

PAUL REID-BOWEN

Further reading

Gupta, L. 1992. 'Kali, the Savior'. In P.M. Cooey, W.R. Eakin and J.B. McDaniel, eds, *After Patriarchy: Feminist Transformations of the World Religions*. New York: Orbis Books, 15–38.

Kinsley, D. 1988. *Hindu Goddesses: Visions of the Divine Feminine in the Hindu Religious Tradition*. Berkeley, CA: University of California Press.

Kinsley, D. 1996. 'Kali: Blood and Death Out of Place'. In J.S. Stratton and D.M. Wulff, eds, *Devī: Goddesses of India*. Berkeley, CA: University of California Press, 77–86.

Kinsley, D.R. 1997. *Tantric Visions of the Divine Feminine: The Ten Mahāvidyās*. Berkeley, CA: University of California Press.

McDermott, Rachel Fell and Jeffrey J. Kripal (eds). 2003. *Encountering Kālī: In the Margins, at the Center, in the West*. Berkeley, CA: University of California Press.

KĀLIDĀSA

Kālidāsa is considered by many North Indians to be India's greatest poet and dramatist. He is attributed authorship of the poetical works the *Raghuvamśa*, *Śakuntalā*, *Vikramorvaśi*, *Meghadūta*, *Ritu-sanhāra*, *Nalodaya* and the *Kumārasambhava*. His most well-known dramatic works are the *Śakuntalā*, *Vikramorvaśi* and the *Mālavikāgnimitra*, especially the first of these, which was translated by Sir William Jones and was instrumental in bringing Sanskrit to the serious attention of European scholars and literati. The *Śakuntalā* was praised by Goethe for the beauty of its language and all of Kālidāsa's works have been translated into the major European languages.

Very little is known about Kālidāsa; although his life is embellished by legends known throughout North India, even his birth date is uncertain. Some argue that he was born in the fourth century CE and was a member of the court of King Candra-Gupta II. However, there is considerable disparity between the views of scholars, ranging from dating him to the reign of Vikramāditya of Ujjayinī, which began in 56 BCE, to the sixth-century CE reign of Harśa Vikramāditya. The uncertainty over his birth date has led some scholars to argue that there was more than one Kālidāsa and that the name was a honorary title for an esteemed court poet.

As with many Indian religious figures who expressed themselves in poetry, the most reliable way of penetrating through the hagiography to the biography of Kālidāsa is not via the narratives but through his own descriptions in his poems and dramatical works. Kālidāsa's writings inform the reader that he was a well-educated and well-travelled brāhmaṇa who observed the high court manners and behaviour associated with his background. He indicates that he was a devotee of Śiva but also offers praise to Viṣṇu and there are no signs of any exclusive or partisan loyalty to his chosen Īśvara.

See also: **Brāhman; Deities; Drama; Īśvara; Jones, Sir William; Poetry; Sanskrit**

RON GEAVES

Further reading

Stutley, Margaret and James Stutley (eds). 1977. *A Dictionary of Hinduism: Its Mythology, Folklore and Development 1500 BC–AD 1500*. London: Routledge and Kegan Paul.

KALKI

See: **Avatāra**

KALPA (RITUAL)

Kalpa (ritual) is one of the six Vedāṅgas, auxiliary Vedic sciences. Its main purpose is to elucidate the rules for conducting Vedic ceremonies, found in the *Brāhmaṇas*. Along with the other five Vedāṅgas, it served to ensure that rituals were correctly performed as this was crucial to their effectiveness and ritual itself was the core of Vedic religion. The centrality of ritual performance continues to be a major feature of the Hindu tradition.

See also: **Brāhmaṇas; Kalpasūtras; Veda; Vedāṅgas; Vedism**

DENISE CUSH AND CATHERINE ROBINSON

KALPA (TIME)

Both Hindu and Buddhist thought consider the creation of the cosmos to be an eternally changing and continuous process, in which universes also come and go, being created, evolved and then finally devolved to reappear again. Thus both religions deal with vast sweeps of cyclical time. The longest unit of time is the Kalpa, the period between the origin of the universe, its dissolution and the period in which all matter returns to seed form in the cosmic ocean, representing the undifferentiated condition of the cosmos before the emergence of form. This period of time is known in Hinduism as 'a day and night of Brahmā' and is said to consist of fourteen manvantaras (reign of a Manu or patriarch), each lasting 4,320,000,000 human years plus and equivalent time for the night of Brahmā.

Each Kalpa is divided into four yugas, decreasing in length of time from the first (Kṛta or Sat Yuga) to the last (Kali Yuga), as they descend from unrighteousness to righteousness. The full cycle of the Yugas, consisting of 4,320,000 years, is known as Mahā-yuga or Manvantara. One thousand of these cycles make up a day of Brahmā and, when combined with their own periods of twilight gestation, make up a complete Kalpa. One hundred Kalpas is said to be the lifespan of Brahmā, but this does not end creation, it only indicates that the gods themselves are manifestations of Brahman and not immortal. There are some variations on the above timescale, but all subscribe to the idea of cycles of creation and cosmic dissolution and the gradual decline of the world situation as righteousness declines. The major difference concerns whether a deity is involved in the process or not.

See also: **Brahmā; Brahman; Manvantara; Yuga**

RON GEAVES

Further reading

Stutley, Margaret and James Stutley (eds). 1977. *A Dictionary of Hinduism: Its Mythology, Folklore and Development 1500 BC–AD 1500*. London: Routledge and Kegan Paul.

KALPASŪTRAS

This term distinguishes the sūtras of the Vedic schools, composed from around 600 BCE, from other sūtras (Winternitz 1927: 271–82; Gonda 1977). It includes *Śrautasūtras*, *Gṛhyasūtras*, *Dharmasūtras* and *Śulvasūtras*. Each of them belongs to a particular school or saṃhitā of the Veda and represents the practice of that school; this is less true of the *Dharmasūtras*, which are less concerned with ritual. They are not śruti or revealed sacred texts, but smṛti or traditional texts, being ascribed to particular authors. The author's patronymic is usually included in the title, for instance the *Āśvalāyana Śrauta Sūtra* of the *Ṛgveda* or the *Kātyāyana Śulva Sūtra* of the White *Yajurveda*. Not every school has all four kinds of sūtra. Some have an additional category of *Pitṛmedhasūtra*s, 'rules for ancestral offerings' (Gonda 1977: 469).

Kalpasūtra is also the title of a Jain text attributed to Bhadrabāhu.

See also: **Āśvalāyana; Dharmasūtras; Gṛhyasūtras; Jainism, relationship with Hinduism; Kātyāyana; Pitṛs; Sacred Texts; Saṃhitā; Śrautasūtras; Śulvasūtras; Sūtra; Veda**

DERMOT KILLINGLEY

Further reading

Gonda, J. 1977. *The Ritual Sūtras*. Wiesbaden: Harrassowitz.

Winternitz, M. 1927. *A History of Indian Literature,* vol. I. Trans. S. Ketkar. Calcutta: University of Calcutta.

KĀMA (DEITY)

With a parrot as his vehicle, Kāma, the god of love, dwells on the moon with his co-wives, Rati and Prītī, divine embodiments of 'sensual pleasure' and 'affection', respectively. Bearing a quiver of five flower-tipped arrows and a bow of sugarcane strung with bees, Kāma greatly resembles Eros or Cupid, as he aims his incendiary shafts without regard to caste, social standing or propriety. The *Matsya Purāṇa* recounts how Kāma, along with Vasanta, the personification of springtime, famously united Śiva and Pārvatī at the behest of Indra. Unfortunately, when Kāma aroused the erotic passion of Śiva he also incurred his fiery wrath, and was immediately incinerated. Bereaved Rati lamented her husband's death so bitterly that Śiva relented and reconstituted Kāma in an invisible, yet omnipresent form. Accordingly, Kāma is also known as Anaṅga, the 'body-less one', as well as Kāmadeva, Madana and Pradyumna.

See also: **Indra; Pārvatī; Purāṇas; Rati; Śiva**

ANDREA MARION PINKNEY

Further reading

Stutley, M. 1985. *An Illustrated Dictionary of Hindu Iconography.* London and Boston, MA: Routledge & Kegan Paul.

KĀMA (DESIRE)

The word kāma appears with several meanings in Hinduism. It appears first in the most general sense of desire, especially for worldly pleasure and then for sexual desire as the chief manifestation of it. At the theological level it denotes the personification of such desire in the God of Love, often depicted with his wife Rati (sex and especially sexual delight), with Tṛṣṇā (longing) figuring as daughter. He is also called Anaṅga, or without a visible body, on account of an episode in which he tried to disturb Śiva while the latter was engaged in meditation, thereby provoking him into reducing him to ashes with a flash of his third eye. Rati's importunity secured his life – but in invisible form. Kāma is often equated with the Buddhist Māra, who was also defeated by the Buddha with less drastic consequences. Kāma is often depicted as equipped with flower-tipped arrows, named after vernal blossoms. He bears a makara (a sea-monster) in his standard.

Kāma enjoys a secure place in Hindu axiology as one of the goals of human endeavour, thus representing at one level the pleasures of the senses, at another sex and at yet another the urbane pleasures of life such as art, music and literature. The *Kāmasūtra* of Vātsyāyana (*c.* fourth century CE) offers the necessary guidance in the matter. Although concerned with kāma, it recommends its pursuit in harmony with other goals of life, such as artha and dharma, especially when kāma is kept within moral bounds, that is, is regulated by dharma. Kṛṣṇa even identifies himself with such morally uncensured kāma in the *Bhagavadgītā* (7.11).

Kāma also has an etiological and teleological sense which is related to but surpasses these connotations. It is mentioned in the famous Nāsadīya hymn as the principle of cosmic creation (*Ṛgveda* 10.129.4), while kāma, not as carnal or mundane love, but as love of God, secures liberation. Morally it could also mean the desire for righteousness, for it is hard to interpret its occurrence in the *Taittirīya Brāhmana* as the son of Dharma and the Śraddhā otherwise. According to the *Yājñavalkyasmṛti* (1.7) such pious desire is a source of dharma itself. The school of Hindu materialism called Lokāyata or Cārvāka considers kāma and artha as the sole goals of life, and artha also only as an ancillary goal of life because it secures kāma. The view that kāma is the primary goal of life is also echoed in the *Manusmṛti* (2.224). However, although one of the four goals of life, it is apparent that it can be brought into relation with the other three as well.

See also: **Artha; Dharma; Kāmasūtra; Kṛṣṇa; Lokāyata; Puruṣārthas; Rati; Śiva; Śrāddhā; Vātsyāyana Mallanāga**

ARVIND SHARMA

Further reading

Doniger, Wendy and Sudhir Kakar. 2002. *Kāmasūtra*. Oxford: Oxford University Press.

KĀMADHENU

The sacred 'wish-fulfilling cow', Kāmadhenu is also known as 'Surabhi', 'Nandinī', and 'Śabalā'. According to the *Purāṇas* and the Vālmīki *Rāmāyaṇa*, she is both the daughter and wife of the sage Kaśyapa and the progenitor of all cattle that exist in the world today. Kāmadhenu presides over the world of cattle (goloka) and her powers as a goddess allow her to fulfil all the wishes of her caretaker. There may be more than a single Kāmadhenu and her most famous appearances in various texts include her role in sage Vaṣiṣṭha's āśrama (*Vālmīki Rāmāyaṇa*) during a war of attrition with king Viśvāmitra, her being produced from the churning of the ocean of milk, and her birth from Lord Kṛṣṇa's side and the creation of the famed ocean of milk (kṣīrasāgara) (*Devī Bhāgavata*). There are several instances where Kāmadhenu is the object of theft and recovery between duelling factions. One account has Kāmadhenu being murdered by a wayward prince named Satyavrata (well known as Triśanku) and her flesh being eaten during a famine.

See also: **Māhābhārata; Purāṇa; Rāmāyaṇa; Vālmīki**

DEVEN M. PATEL

Further reading

Mani, Vettam. 2002. *Purānic Encyclopaedia*. Delhi: Motilal Banarsidass.

KĀMASŪTRA

Composed in approximately the third century CE, the *Kāmasūtra* of Vātsyāyana Mallanāga is the oldest extant Indian text on erotics and is the foremost representative of the *kāmaśāstra* genre. Kāma, or 'erotics', is considered alongside dharma, 'civic comportment', and artha, 'material concerns', as one of the three classically prescribed trivarga, or 'trio of goals', prioritised according to one's place in the varṇāśramadharma system. Although the *Kāmasūtra* has often been misunderstood as pornographic, its style is more typically śāstric than titillating, characterised by taxonomies, definitions and normative injunctions. Written primarily in prose aphorisms, the *Kāmasūtra* is similar to the slightly older *Arthaśāstra* of Kauṭilya, the premier text on statecraft. Aimed at the young male urbanite known as the nagārika, the chief objective of the *Kāmasūtra* is to study heterosexual relationships. However, it also discusses male and female homoeroticism, gender roles and the experience of courtesans, while perceptively integrating a feminine perspective. The *Kāmasūtra* guides the reader through all stages of intimate relations, providing practical advice on how to become both sexually and emotionally mature. The text opens with a review of common knowledge, moves through an encyclopaedic classification of sexual union and then devotes chapters to courtship, marriage and extra-marital affairs, describes the protocol to be adopted with sex professionals and closes with an overview of magic and sex aids. The 1893 translation ascribed to Sir Richard Francis Burton introduced the *Kāmasūtra* to English-speaking audiences. However, the text was produced in large part by two Indian scholars, Bhagavanlal Indrajit and Shivaram Parashuram Bhide, with further assistance from Forster Fitzgerald Arbuthnot. Although the Burton edition is an exemplar of the Victorian temper, it is an unreliable source for understanding the mores of the text and its long history of reception, as it mingles Vātsyāyana's root text with the thirteenth-century commentary of Yaśodhara Indrapāda, the *Jayamaṅgalā*, produced a thousand years later.

See also: **Artha; Āśram(a) (religious community); Courtesans; Dharma; Homosexuality; Kauṭilya; Puruṣārthas; Sex and sexuality; Varṇa; Vātsyāyana Mallanāga**

ANDREA MARION PINKNEY

Further reading

Doniger, W. and S. Kakar (eds and trans.). 2002. *Kamasutra*. New York: Oxford University Press.

KAṂSA

The tyrant ruler of Mathurā, described in the Epic literature as a demon incarnation sometimes identified as the dānava (a type of demon) Kālanemi, who personifies the wheel of time. The son of Ugrasena, and a cousin of Devakī, the mother of Kṛṣṇa, Kaṃsa is best known for his attempts to murder the newborn Kṛṣṇa. Living always in fear of revenge or retribution after deposing his father, Kaṃsa was alarmed by a prophecy that he would be killed by the eighth child of Devakī. Consequently, he tried to destroy her children, but he failed to kill the seventh son, Balarāma, who was smuggled away to Gokula, the idyllic rural district where he was later joined by Kṛṣṇa. On the birth of Kṛṣṇa the parents fled with their newborn child, but Kaṃsa ordered the slaughter of all healthy male children. The tyrant king was finally killed by Kṛṣṇa.

See also: **Balarāma; Devakī; Kṛṣṇa**

RON GEAVES

Further reading

Walker, Benjamin. 1968. *Hindu World*. London: George Allen & Unwin.

KAṆĀDA

Kaṇāda is the name of the author of the *Vaiśesikasūtras*, the foundational text of the Vaiśesika school of Hindu philosophy. He is also known as Ulūka or Aulūka, Kanabhuj, Kanabhaksa and Kāśyapa. The Vaiśesika system is also named after him, Aulūka darśana (view or philosophy of Kaṇāda).

Kaṇāda has been regarded as a mythical or legendary personage. Various legends or stories about this ancient author have centred on his name. Kana means 'grain', so Kaṇāda has been analysed as 'grain-eater', signifying that Kaṇāda led an ascetic life, feeding on grains plucked from the fields. One story (from *Life of Harivarman*, fifth century CE) relates that Kaṇāda led a nocturnal life and that his appearance frightened young women, so he ventured into mills in secret to feed on pieces of corn from rice-bran. Hence Kaṇāda's other names, Kanabhuj or Kanabhaksa ('rice-grain eater') and Ulūka ('owl', due to Kaṇāda's habit of meditating during the day and seeking food at night). Another story relates that the Vaiśesika teaching was revealed to Kaṇāda by the god Mahādeva or Śiva (who manifested in the form of an owl); hence arose Kanada's name Ulūka.

Kana also means a 'particular' or 'particle', thus the name Kaṇāda signifies one who lives or feeds on the philosophy of particularity. Vaiśesika derives from the term 'viśesa' ('distinction' or 'distinguishing feature'); viśesa is one of the categories (padārtha) treated in the system. The Vaiśesika school emphasises pluralism, realism, uniqueness, difference and diversity.

Kaṇāda has also been analysed as 'eater of atoms'. It signifies Kaṇāda's reduction of reality to the smallest possible atomic units or divisions. The Vaiśésika system is well known as teaching a doctrine of atomism.

The roots of Vaiśesika are ancient and obscure. The date of the composition of the *Vaiśesikasūtras* is uncertain; it has been placed between the first and third centuries CE.

See also: **Vaiśeṣika; Vaiśeṣikasūtras**

MARTIN OVENS

Further reading

Potter, K.H. (ed.). 1977. *Encyclopedia of Indian Philosophies, Volume Two, Indian Metaphysics and Epistemology: The Tradition of Nyāya-Vaiśesika up to Gangeśa*. Princeton, NJ: Princeton University Press.

KĀÑCĪPURA

Kāñcīpura was the capital of the Pallava dynasty from at least the fifth century CE onwards and remains to this day an important city in northern Tamil Nadu. In more recent times it has become famous as a centre of silk weaving. Also known as kāmakotī pītha, it is the site of one of the four great Śaiva maṭha, or monasteries, whose head or 'abbot' is known as the Śankarācārya. The heads of these maṭhas are the closest one gets in traditional Hinduism to any idea of a Patriarch.

From ancient times Kāñcīpura was divided into three sections: Śivakāñci, Viṣṇukāñci and Jinakāñci – 'Kanchi of the Jains'. This last division is on the far side of a dried-up river course from the other two, at about 5 km distance, and is nowadays known as Tirupparutikkunran. Pallava remains here consist of two Jain temples, one of which was still in use in the seventeenth century. Śivakāñci is the larger of the two other divisions and since medieval times has had two cult centres: the temple of Kāmāksī, who can be regarded as the tutelary Goddess of the city, and her consort Śiva as Ekāmreśvara ('Lord of the Mango Tree'). Kāmāksī's temple is by far the more vibrant and this deity is to Kāñcīpura what the Goddess Mīnākṣī is to Madurai. It is significant that Kāmākṣī has her own separate temple rather than simply a shrine within the Śiva temple. In Pallava times the focus of Śiva's cult was a temple now on the north-west outskirts of the city, where he is worshipped as Kailāsanātha ('Lord of Kailāsa'). Built in the eighth century, this is a fine example of Pallava architecture and has some striking sculptures. There has been a similar shift of focus in Viṣṇukāñci also, where the ninth-century Pallava Viṣṇu temple has been superseded by the great medieval Varadarāja Temple, which is the centre of the 'northern' group of South Indian Śrī Vaiṣṇava worship.

In modern times the authorities at the kāmakotī pātha have established a Hindu university on the outskirts of Kāñcīpura on the lines of the Śri Venkateśvara university near the Vaiṣṇava shrine of Tirupati.

See also: **Jainism, relationship with Hinduism; Madurai; Mandir; Maṭha; Mīnākṣī; Śaiva; Śaṅkarācārya; Śiva; Śrī Vaiṣṇavas; Sthāpatyaveda; Vaiṣṇavism; Viṣṇu**

JOHN R. MARR AND
KATHLEEN TAYLOR

Further reading

Michell, G. 1989. *The Penguin Guide to the Monuments of India,* vol. 1. London: Viking.

KANE, PANDURANG VAMAN (1880–1972)

Indian Sanskritist and legal scholar. Kane was born to a Citpāvan brāhmaṇa family in Maharashtra and studied at Bombay University. After some years teaching he began to practise law at the Bombay High Court in 1911, and was Professor of Law at the Government Law College from 1917–23. He was Fellow (1919–28) and later Vice-Chancellor (1947–49) of Bombay University, and in 1953 was nominated by the President of India to be a member of the Indian parliament. Kane's first major work on Sanskrit literature was his *History of Sanskrit Poetics* (1923). Kane's many articles cover a wide range of Sanskrit literature and he published also a short monograph on Pūrva Mīmāṃsa. His *magnum opus* is, however, undoubtedly his monumental *History of Dharmaśāstra*, researched over a period of thirty-five years and offering an authoritative and comprehensive account, in over 6,500 pages, of Hindu legal literature from 600 BCE to 1800 CE.

See also: **Dharmaśāstras; Pūrva Mīmāṃsa**

WILL SWEETMAN

Further reading

Kane, P.V. 1923. *History of Sanskrit Poetics.* Bombay. 3rd rev. edn, Delhi: Motilal Banarsidass, 1961.

Kane, P.V. 1930–62. *History of Dharmaśāstra*, 5 vols. Poona: Bhandarkar Oriental Research Institute.

Kane, P.V. 1997. *Professor Kane's Contribution to Dharmaśāstra Literature*, ed. S.G. Moghe. Delhi: DK Printworld.

KĀṆṆAKI

Kāṇṇaki is a Tamil goddess who appears as the heroine of the *c.* fifth-century Tamil epic *Cilappatikāram*, or *Tale of an Anklet*. Kāṇṇaki is the long-suffering wife of Kōvalan, who is beguiled by Mātavi, a courtesan, and consequently leaves Kāṇṇaki. Unfortunately, Kōvalan is wrongly accused of stealing the Queen's anklet, which happens to be the same as that belonging to Kāṇṇaki. On hearing of Kōvalan's death, Kāṇṇaki goes to the palace and clears his name. In her rage she famously rips off her left breast and throws it at the city of Madurai, which then burns to the ground. Her act is viewed as an indication that a woman's power is most potent in her breasts. Kāṇṇaki is considered a form of the goddess Pattini, who is popular in Sri Lanka.

See also: **Madurai**

LYNN FOULSTON

Further reading

Parthasarathy, R. (trans.). 1993. *The Cilappatikāram of Iḷaṅkō Aṭikaḷ: An Epic of South India.* New York: Columbia University Press.

KĀṆPHATA YOGA

Kāṇphata (literally, 'split eared') is a term commonly employed to refer to the followers of Gorakhnāth(a), who are also known as Nātha Yogīs (nātha means 'lord'). Members of this group are noted for their practice of haṭha yoga. The name 'kāṇphata' comes from their ritual of splitting the cartilage of the ears during initiation and the subsequent wearing of large earrings, some of which are so heavy that their weight has to be taken by a string passed over the head. All are devotees of the god Śiva and they display distinctively Śaivite marks on their bodies, most common of which is the tripuṇḍ(ra) – three broad horizontal bands drawn with ashes, clay or sandalwood paste. All fully initiated yogīs, who take the title of nātha during the final initiation, are attached to a monastery and, thereby, a subsect of the order. Within the order, caste divisions are not observed, perhaps a testimony to the movement's low-caste origins – Kāṇphatas were originally regarded by orthodox brāhmaṇas as untouchables. The nātha practice of burying rather than cremating dead yogīs and not employing the services of brāhmaṇas for such rituals further separates the Kāṇphatas from orthodox Brahmanism, as does the movement's early associations with Buddhism.

See also: **Brāhmaṇas; Buddhism, relationship with Hinduism; Gorakhnāth; Haṭha Yoga; Śiva; Smārta**

PETER CONNOLLY

Further reading

Briggs, G.W. 1938/1982. *Gorakhnāth and the Kāṇphata Yogīs*. Delhi: Motilal Banarsidass.

KAṆVA

Several sages are named Kaṇva but a number of hymns of the *Ṛgveda* are attributed to one of their number who is also described on occasions to be one of the celebrated seven ṛṣis. The name also occurs in a number of other Vedic texts and one of the maṇḍalas, the eighth book, of the *Ṛgveda* is attributed to the descendants of Kaṇva, known as the Kaṇvas. However, one passage of the *Atharvaveda* views the family with hostility. Kaṇva is also described in the *Śatapatha Brāhmaṇa* (18.5, 4:13) as the sage who raised Śakuntalā, the mother of Bhārata, as his daughter in his hermitage at Nādapit. His name is given to one of the two known texts of the latter work.

See also: **Brāhmaṇas; Ṛṣi; Saṃhitā**

RON GEAVES

Further reading

MacDonnell, A. and A. Keith. 1967. *Vedic Index of Names and Subjects*, vol. 1. Varanasi: Motilal Banarsidass.

KANYĀKUMĀRĪ

Kanyākumārī ('Virgin Goddess') refers to the southernmost tip of India and to the Goddess whose temple stands there. Also known by its Anglicised name 'Cape Comorin', it is located at the confluence of the Arabian Sea, the Bay of Bengal and the Indian Ocean.

Though the site is mentioned in medieval works such as the *Brahmavaivartapurāṇa*, three late texts – two Tamil *sthalapurāṇas* called *Kaṇāiyākumarittalapurāṇam* and *Cucīntirastalapurāṇam* and a Sanskrit text called *Kanyākṣetramāhātmya* – provide textual sources for the popular mythology of Kanyākumārī. In the Tamil versions of the narrative, Śiva promises to marry the goddess after she has won him by performing asceticism. The wedding is scheduled at the seashore for midnight, but while accompanying Śiva as part of his wedding retinue, Nārada takes on the form of a rooster and announces dawn. The wedding party turns back, thinking that the auspicious time for the wedding has passed. The Goddess, still in her bridal finery, waits until the real dawn and is devastated when Śiva does not appear. In anger, she curses the wedding paraphernalia, which becomes sand and shells on the shore. At this time the demon Bāṇāsura, who has secured a boon that he can only be slain at the hands of a virgin, sees the Goddess and lusts after her. Furious at his advances, she slays him. She then settles on the shore, forever longing for union with Śiva, in the form of the virgin Goddess Kanyākumārī.

In the early part of the twentieth century, the site of Kanyākumārī and the Goddess were scripted into an anti-Sanskritic Tamil nationalist past. Taking their cue from nineteenth-century European ideas about a mega-continent called 'Lemuria', Tamil nationalists claimed that millions of years ago this mega-continent (comprised of present-day Australia, Africa and South Asia) was called Kumarikanṭam. This was identified as the 'cradle of civilisation' and the home of the first two academies (caṅkams) of classical Tamil literature. Invoking the figure of the Goddess Kanyākumārī, they claimed that she stood at the shore to prevent a further disintegration of the mega-continent, and that her tears of sorrow produced the Indian Ocean. Kanyākumārī also came to represent the embodiment of the Tamil language itself, pure and virginal, never 'married' to another linguistic family.

See also: **Nārada; Śiva; Virginity**

DAVESH SONEJI

Further reading

Mahalingam, N. and S. Sekaran. 1991. *Concise Form of Concept of Kumari Kandam*. Madras: International Linguistic Centre.

Ramaswamy, S. 1997. *Passions of the Tongue: Language Devotion in Tamil India, 1891–1970*. Berkeley, CA: University of California Press.

Ramaswamy, S. 2004. *The Lost Land of Lemuria: Fabulous Geographies, Catastrophic Histories*. Berkeley, CA: University of California Press.

Shulman, D. 1980. *Tamil Temple Myths: Sacrifice and Divine Marriage in the South Indian Śaiva Tradition*. Princeton, NJ: Princeton University Press.

KĀPĀLIKAS

The Kāpālikas (or Kapālins) were a Tantric Hindu religious sect or group who followed a vow based on a myth that tells how the god Śiva cut off one of the five heads of the god Brahmā and then undertook a penance to atone for this crime of 'killing' a brāhmaṇa (brahmahatyā). The essence of this penance, known as the 'Great Vow' or 'Mahāvrata', was to wander about as an ascetic living on alms collected in a skull bowl (kapala). For Śiva, this bowl was made from Brahmā's own cut head. Human Kāpālikas are described as Śaivite ascetics who should wear six insignia (mudrā) consisting of four special ornaments, ashes (vibhūti) smeared on their bodies and a sacred thread. They were also expected to carry a skull bowl and a club (khaṭvāṅga) on which a skull was impaled.

The historical evidence for the existence of human Kāpālikas is basically of two sorts. One the one hand they appear as either cruel villains or as slapstick fools in many plays and stories, written mostly in Sanskrit. The most interesting depictions found in such texts appear in Kṛṣṇamiśra's *Prabodhacandrodaya*, Mahendravarman's *Mattavilāsa* and the hagiographies of the famous theologian Śaṅkara. On the other hand, the Kāpālikas are mentioned in several inscriptions, in a few cases as donors or donees, and in several religious texts, most notably Sanskrit texts by Rāmānuja and Yāmuna.

The doctrine of the Kāpālikas is sometimes called Somasiddhānta ('the doctrine of Soma'). Several texts claim that that Soma here refers not to the famous Vedic god and sacred drink Soma, but to the bliss of the sexual union of the god Śiva and his wife Uma, Śiva as sa-Umā or 'with Uma'. This suggests some relationship with the symbology of sexual union common in many Tantric texts. Unfortunately little other information exists about the nature and contents of Somasiddhānta.

See also: **Brahmā; Brāhmaṇa; Mudrā; Rāmānuja; Sacred thread; Śaivism; Śaṅkara; Śiva; Soma; Tantras; Tapas; Umā; Vedic pantheon; Vibhūti; Yāmuna**

DAVID LORENZEN

Further reading

Dyczkowski, Mark S.G. 1988. *The Canon of the Saivagama and the Kubjika Tantras of the Western Kaula Tradition*. Albany, NY: State University of New York Press.

Lorenzen, David N. 1991. *The Kapalikas and Kalamukhas: Two Lost Saivite Sects*, 2nd rev. edn; Delhi: Motilal Banarsidass.

Lorenzen, David N. 2000. 'A Parody of the Kapalikas in the *Mattavilasa*'. In David Gordon White, ed., *Tantra in Practice*. Princeton, NJ: Princeton University Press, 81–96.

KAPILA

The *Sāṃkhyakārikas* (Verses on Sāṃkhya) form the earliest available complete work of classical Sāṃkhya (one of the six schools of Hindu philosophy). Its author was Īśvarakṛṣṇa (fourth to fifth century CE). According to tradition, Kapila is the name of the founder of the Sāṃkhya system.

At *Sāṃkhyakārika* 69, Īśvarakṛṣṇa refers to a sage who explained and 'enumerated' the Sāṃkhya philosophy. According to Īśvarakṛṣṇa, this sage (identified by tradition as 'Kapila') passed on the Sāṃkhya teaching to Āsuri, who transmitted it to Pañcaśikha (who expanded and spread it). Commentators on Īśvarakṛṣṇa's kārikas suggested possible lines of Sāṃkhya teachers (from Pañcaśika to Īśvarakṛṣṇa). Īśvarakṛṣṇa was regarded as having simplified the old system after a period of several centuries.

In Sāṃkhya literature, Kapila has been described as a compassionate, wise ascetic, heaven-born, endowed with power, knowledge, virtue and renunciation. He has been called one of the seven great seers or sages (sapta mahāṛṣi), the others being Voḍhu, Āsuri, Pañcaśika, Sanātana, Sanaka and Sananda. For Vācaspati Miśra, Kapila was an incarnation of Viṣṇu, obtained total knowledge from Maheśvara and was born at the dawn of creation. Another account relates that, with the aid of an 'artificial mind' (nirmāṇacitta), Kapila, as a 'primal wise man', taught Āsuri Sāṃkhya wisdom.

There are doubts about possible linkages between references to Kapila in earlier Hindu literature and later Sāṃkhya writings. In the *Ṛgveda* and *Upaniṣads*, 'kapila' is a term for a colour. But at *Śvetāśvatara Upaniṣad* 5.2, 'kapila' (as a colour reference) is connected to a seer born at the dawn of creation, possibly linking to Rudra.

There are various references to Kapila in the *Bhagavadgītā* and *Mokṣadharma* of the *Mahābhārata*. In the *Bhagavadgītā*, there is reference to Kapila as a 'perfected one' (siddha). In the *Moksadharma*, Kapila is connected to Viṣṇu, Śiva and Agni.

See also: **Agni; Bhagavadgītā; Īśvarakṛṣna; Mahābhārata; Ṛṣi; Rudra; Ṣaḍdarśana; Saṃhitā; Sāṃkhya; Sāṃkhyakārikas; Siddha; Śiva; Upaniṣads; Vācaspati Miśra; Viṣṇu**

MARTIN OVENS

Further reading

Larson, G.J. and R.S. Bhattacharya. 1987. *Encyclopedia of Indian Philosophies, Vol. 4, Sāṃkhya: A Dualist Tradition in Indian Philosophy*. Delhi: Motilal Banarsidass.

KĀRAIKKĀL AMMAIYĀR

Kāraikkāl Ammaiyār ('the venerable mother of Kāraikkāl') (sixth century), named Puṇitavati, is perhaps the earliest Tamil Śaivite saint-poetess. Legend has it that she was the daughter of a prosperous merchant of Kāraikkāl, a flourishing sea port in South India. Even as a young girl Puṇitavati ('the immaculate one') was devoted to Śiva, and her marriage to Paramaṭattaṉ did not affect this devotion. Overawed by her miraculous powers, which he took to be a manifestation of divine śakti, Paramaṭattaṉ left her. She turned to Śiva as her only refuge, imploring him to transform her beautiful body into a ghastly one, thereby indicating her severance with the world as well as subverting patriarchal expectations of feminine beauty and social norms. She prayed that Śiva would liberate her from this earthly life. Her devotional poetic compositions in praise of Śiva, *Aṟputa-t-tiruvantati* (Wonderful Songs) and *Tiruviraṭṭai maṇimālai* (Splendid Songs) are part of Śaivite scriptures.

See also: **Śaivism; Śakti; Śiva**

SHARADA SUGIRTHARAJAH

Further reading

Zvelebil, Kamil V. 1995. *Lexicon of Tamil Literature.* Leiden: E.J. Brill, 334–35.

KARMA (LAW OF ACTION)

The term karman in Sanskrit means simply 'action' or 'deed'. The nominative singular karma in English refers to the quality of deeds as determining the quality of subsequent experience: good and bad deeds cause subsequent enjoyment and suffering, respectively, to their agent, possibly in a subsequent state of existence. The concept of karma combines ideas of natural causality, ethics and transmigration (O'Flaherty 1980: xi) in an ethically committed retributive causality (Halbfass 1991: 301). It serves both to justify present circumstances on the basis of past actions and to exhort present actions on the grounds of their future effects (O'Flaherty 1980: xi). Integral to life in saṃsāra, it is developed as the counterpart and stepping-stone to mokṣa (Halbfass 1991: 295).

Origins

Scholars sharply disagree over the origins of the concept of karma. Bland repetitions that the theory is not found in the Vedas (Halbfass 1991: 291) lead to Obeyesekere's (1980, 2002) imagining karma's historical roots in tribes indigenous to the Ganges river valley prior to the immigration of Indo-European-speaking peoples. Against them, Tull (1989) argues in favour of the Vedic origins of karma. Certainly already in the hymns of the *Ṛgveda* is found the expectation that the quality of subsequent experience and existence is determined by the quality of prior deeds (e.g. *Ṛgveda* 1.24.9; 1.24.12–15; 10.100.7; 10.164.3).

Integral to the concept of karma, the concept of rebirth is first explicitly articulated in the early *Upaniṣads* (*Bṛhad Āraṇyaka Upaniṣad* 6.2; *Chāndogya Upaniṣad* 5.3–10; *Kauṣītaki Upaniṣad* 1). Two paths are delineated for the performers of good deeds. By one, they reach the moon, where they dwell with their ancestors until their store of merit is exhausted (Tull 1989: 31), whereupon they reincarnate on earth in accordance with their previous deeds (*Chāndogya Upaniṣad* 5.10.7). By the other, those with special knowledge reach Brahman and are free of reincarnation. The immediate reincarnation of minute creatures on Earth constitutes a third path. *Bṛhad Āranyaka Upaniṣad* 4.4.4–5 describes reincarnation in accordance with the quality of one's deeds. Obeyesekere (1980; 2002: 8) argues that Vedic thinkers here adopt an unfamiliar idea of rebirth and ethicise it. Conversely, Tull (1989: 105) argues that the Brāhmanic concept of the realisation of ritual acts in the afterlife is extended to acts in general, and Halbfass (1991: 305) argues that the need to justify empirically falsified instances of the correspondence of rewards to deeds motivates appeal to their satisfaction prior to birth and after death.

Indian theories of transmigration vary in the length of time and mode of experience between earthly births. While Jains allow no more than a few moments between births, and Buddhist Vaibhāṣikas up to seven weeks (Jaini 1980: 229–30), *Purāṇas* allow long sojourns in heaven and hell prior to rebirth (O'Flaherty 1980: 14–18). *Purāṇas* (*Garuḍa Purāṇa*, *Pretakalpa*) and *Dharmaśāstra* texts (*Mānavadharmaśāstra* 12; Rocher 1980) describe in detail reward and punishment for acts in various heavens and hells between births, and in varieties of earthly incarnations. Yoga and Advaita texts range births from Brahmā down to tufts of grass.

Philosophical schools develop systematic theories of karma utilising the basic components of causality, ethical retribution and rebirth. Vaiśeṣika and Pūrva Mīmāṃsā both develop the mechanism of an unobservable deposit that preserves the efficacy of action until it manifests its effect. The former extends its concept of adṛṣṭa, 'unseen', used to fill empirical gaps in natural causality, to ethical behaviour (Halbfass 1991: 315). The latter introduces apūrva, 'new', an invisible deposit that sustains the soul after death in another world, to establish an unobservable causal link between the performance of a sacrifice and the sacrificer's enjoyment of heaven after death (Halbfass 1991: 309). Yoga and Advaita Vedānta offer the most rigorous treatment of karma, the former supplying more detail regarding the karmic mechanism, the latter regarding the process of rebirth (Potter 1980: 259).

The karmic mechanism in classical yoga

Active states of consciousness, including bodily, vocal and mental acts and experiences, generate corresponding impressions that reside in the subtle body. These impressions are of two types (*Yogasūtrabhāṣya* 3.18). Vāsanās, 'dispositions', cause subjective states such as memory and afflictions. Karmāśaya, 'action deposit', in the form of merit (dharma) and demerit (adharma) resulting from good and bad action, ripens into pleasurable or painful objective conditions of experience, length of life and future birth. Action performed under the influence of the afflictions is good, bad or mixed (*Yogasūtra* 4.7) and produces corresponding karmāśaya, which contributes to corresponding experience. When karmāśaya ripens by presenting objective conditions, it causes corresponding vāsanās to manifest subjective states such as memories, habits and afflictions. Thus the karmāśaya and vāsanās together produce the subjective experience of the person. Influenced by the vāsanās, the individual is disposed to respond to the circumstances in certain ways. In this way, past experience determines future action.

Free will versus fate

A number of texts, including epics, the *Yoga Vāsiṣṭha* (Chapple 1986), medical texts (Weiss 1980: 90–96) and Theravāda advocates of karma (Halbfass 1991: 322; McDermott 1980: 180), reject the role of karma in determining intention and decision. In Yoga, however, vāsanās determine a person's will (Potter 1980: 256; Larson 1980: 307). While the self in Yoga is free, there is no free will.

The causal cycle of impressions and actions is terminable through the practice of Yoga, but the intention to practise Yoga is itself an act of the intellect which is within the field of nature (Larson 1980: 307–9, 315). Meditation weakens the afflictions and Samādhi displaces afflicted impressions by unafflicted ones, thereby preventing them from being made manifest by aggravating objective circumstances. Action undertaken without the influence of afflictions produces no karmāśaya. Free of the influence of afflictions, the intellect becomes filled with knowledge of the discrimination between Prakṛti and Puruṣa, establishing the conditions for Kaivalya. Yet even this liberation from the cycle of karma is brought about by the causal activity of nature, not by any activity of the self (*Sāṃkhyakārikā* 62). The intellect, part of nature, presents the realisation of the freedom of the self to the self that is ontologically already free.

Karma transfer and group karma

Certain karma theories allow exceptions to a uniform rule of correspondence between the quality of acts and the quality of experience. There are less formal discussions of karma shared by a group, transferred to ancestors or children, or to other parties in interaction (O'Flaherty 1980: 3–37; Long 1980: 38–60). Even systematic presentations allow results of acts to vanish without retribution. Yoga allows that the latent impressions of acts subsumed by impressions of more dominant acts and postponed for fruition in future lives may be parched and rendered fruitless in the state of Kaivalya. Devotional traditions allow God or other compassionate beings to forgive acts (Hart 1980: 133).

Systematic presentations of karma deny karma transfer and the mollification of karmic effects in group karma (Potter 1980: 263). Buddhists, for instance, require that the karma of each individual involved be in confluence with that of every other participant in the situation so that each participant experiences exactly what is properly due (McDermott 1976; 1980: 175). Jains allow that an individual soul can experience results only of actions which it has itself performed (Jaini 1980: 235–36). Instances of forgiven or surrendered karma should be viewed as compensated for or transcended rather than transferred.

See also: **Advaita; Bhakti (as path); Brahmā; Brahman; Buddhism, relationship with Hinduism; Dharmaśāstras; Itihāsa; Jainism, relationship with Hinduism; Kaivalya; Karma (as path); Meditation; Mokṣa; Prakṛti; Purāṇas; Puruṣa; Pūrva Mīmāṃsā; Saṃhitā; Saṃsāra; Saṃskāra; Upaniṣads; Vaiśeṣika; Vedānta; Yoga**

PETER M. SCHARF

Further reading

Bronkhorst, Johannes. 2000. 'Karma and Teleology: A Problem and Its Solutions in Indian Philosophy'. *Studia philologica Buddhica, Monograph series 15*. Tokyo: International Institute for Buddhist Studies of the International College for Advanced Buddhist Studies.

Chapple, Christopher. 1986. *Karma and Creativity.* Albany, NY: State University of New York Press.

Egge, James R. 2002. *Religious Giving and the Invention of Karma in Theravada Buddhism.* Richmond: Curzon.

Halbfass, Wilhelm. 1991. *Tradition and Reflection: Explorations in Indian Thought.* Albany, NY: State University of New York Press.

Hart, George L., III. 1980. 'The Theory of Reincarnation among the Tamils'. In Wendy Doniger O'Flaherty, ed., *Karma and Rebirth in Classical Indian Traditions.* Berkeley, CA: University of California Press, 116–33.

Jaini, Padmanabh S. 1980. 'Karma and the Problem of Rebirth in Jainism'. In Wendy Doniger O'Flaherty, ed., *Karma and Rebirth in Classical Indian Traditions.* Berkeley, CA: University of California Press, 217–38.

Larson, Gerald James. 1980. 'Karma as a "Sociology of Knowledge" or "Social Psychology" of Process/Praxis'. In Wendy Doniger O'Flaherty, ed., *Karma and Rebirth in Classical Indian Traditions.* Berkeley, CA: University of California Press, 303–16.

Long, Bruce J. 1980. 'The Concepts of Human Action and Rebirth in the *Mahābhārata*'. In Wendy Doniger O'Flaherty, ed., *Karma and Rebirth in Classical Indian Traditions.* Berkeley, CA: University of California Press, 38–60.

McDermott, James Paul. 1976. 'Is There Group Karma in Theravāda Buddhism?' *Numen* 23: 67–80.

McDermott, James Paul. 1980. 'Karma and Rebirth in Early Buddhism'. In Wendy Doniger O'Flaherty, ed., *Karma and Rebirth in Classical Indian Traditions.* Berkeley, CA: University of California Press, 165–92.

McDermott, James Paul. 1984. *Development in the Early Buddhist Concept of Kamma/Karma.* New Delhi: Munshiram Manoharlal.

Neufeldt, Ronald W. 1986. *Karma and Rebirth: Post-classical Developments.* Albany, NY: State University of New York Press.

O'Flaherty, Wendy Doniger. (ed.). 1980. *Karma and Rebirth in Classical Indian Traditions.* Berkeley, CA: University of California Press.

Obeyesekere, Gananath. 1980. 'The Rebirth Eschatology and Its Transformations: A Contribution to the Sociology of Early Buddhism'. In Wendy Doniger O'Flaherty, ed., *Karma and Rebirth in Classical Indian Traditions.* Berkeley, CA: University of California Press, 137–64.

Obeyesekere, Gananath. 2002. 'Imagining Karma: Ethical Transformation in Amerindian, Buddhist, and Greek rebirth'. *Comparative Studies in Religion and Society 14.* Berkeley, CA: University of California Press.

Potter, Karl. 1980. 'The Karma Theory and Its Interpretation in Some Indian Philosophical Systems'. In Wendy Doniger O'Flaherty, ed., *Karma and Rebirth in Classical Indian Traditions.* Berkeley, CA: University of California Press, 241–67.

Rocher, Ludo. 1980. 'Karma and Rebirth in the Dharmaśāstras'. In Wendy Doniger O'Flaherty, ed., *Karma and Rebirth in Classical Indian Traditions.* Berkeley, CA: University of California Press, 61–89.

Tull, Herman Wayne. 1989. *The Vedic Origins of Karma: Cosmos as Man in Ancient Indian Myth and Ritual.* Albany, NY: State University of New York Press.

Tull, Herman Wayne. 2004. 'Karma'. In Sushil Mittal and G. R. Thursby, eds, *The Hindu World.* New York: Routledge, 309–31.

Weiss, Mitchell G. 1980. 'Caraka Saṃhitā on the Doctrine of Karma'. In Wendy Doniger O'Flaherty, ed., *Karma and Rebirth in Classical Indian Traditions.* Berkeley, CA: University of California Press, 90–115.

KARMA (AS PATH)

The path of karma (action) is one of three standard, soteriologically efficacious personal orientations, the others being the paths of jñāna (knowledge) and bhakti (devotion).

The emphasis on action as a soteriological prerequisite is seen in the earliest parts of the *Ṛgveda*, where hymns and fire-offerings to the gods are deemed necessary in order to ensure a long, healthy and successful life. As the tradition developed, the ritual was seen as a system capable of manipulating the world in any number of ways, as detailed by the *Brāhmaṇas*, *Śrautasūtras* and *Gṛhyasūtras.*

Texts of the late Vedic period introduce the view that ritual action leads to rebirth within saṃsāra unless accompanied, or even replaced, by esoteric knowledge. Residence in ritually attained heavens was criticised as temporary, and although rituals such as the agnicayana offered new varieties of salvation (Tull 1989), the *Upaniṣads* and the new nāstika religions of Jainism and Buddhism disparaged conventionally motivated ritual performance.

Hereafter, two different developments maintained the ancient view of sacred, saving action. The first, epitomised by the Pūrva Mīmāṃsā school, emphasised the irresponsibility of ritual neglect. According to Jaimini (*c.*200 BCE), the uncreated Veda exists in order that people preserve the correct structure and operation of the cosmos, through ritual action. Attainment of heaven by individual practitioners is merely a byproduct of the ritual, a concession to human motivation. Since the Pūrva Mīmāṃsā did not admit the possibility of mokṣa until about the seventh century CE, the Pūrva Mīmāṃsā kept the Vedic ritual tradition alive through a fundamentalist approach to Vedic exegesis.

The second development was the theory of non-attached or disinterested action. Though visible in the *Kauṣītakī Upaniṣad*, this theory is famously associated with the *Bhagavadgītā*, in which Kṛṣṇa tells Arjuna that he must do his kṣatriya duty and fight. Although this might seem to be an activity productive of dire karmic consequences, these may be avoided by acting without desire or aversion, in the knowledge of the difference between puruṣa and prakṛti, and with faith in Kṛṣṇa as the true agent of all acts. Thus allowing jñāna and bhakti to purify the actor's motivation, the text insists on a basic ritual calendar and on the dharmas laid down in the *Dharmaśāstras.*

The result of this is a soteriology of dispassionate (hence karmically neutral) fulfilment of one's own dharma. The power of dharmic propriety is shown by many instances of the satyakriyā (truth-act) in narrative literature, in which a person works miracles by announcing his or (often) her spotless dharmic record (Brown 1972). Although soteriological emphasis upon dharmic activity has usually favoured the status quo, what constitutes one's dharma may nonetheless be reinterpreted, as shown by Tilak's call for anti-colonial insurgence on the basis of the *Bhagavadgītā*.

See also: **Arjuna; Āstika and Nāstika; Bhagavadgītā; Bhakti; Brāhmaṇas; Buddhism, relationship with Hinduism; Dharma; Dharmaśāstras; Gṛhyasūtras; Jaimini; Jainism, relationship with Hinduism; Jñāna (as path); Kāma; Kṛṣṇa; Mokṣa; Prakṛti; Puruṣa; Pūrva Mīmāṃsā; Saṃsāra; Śrautasūtras; Svarga; Tilak, Bal Gangadhar; Upaniṣads; Veda; Yajña**

SIMON BRODBECK

Further reading

Brown, W.N. 1972. 'Duty as Truth in Ancient India'. *Proceedings of the American Philosophical Society* 116: 252–68. Reprinted in R. Rocher, ed., *India and Indology: Selected Articles by W. Norman Brown*. Delhi: Motilal Banarsidass, 1978, 102–19.

Tull, H.W. 1989. *The Vedic Origins of Karma: Cosmos as Man in Ancient Indian Myth and Ritual*. Albany, NY: State University of New York Press.

KARṆA

One of the major figures in the *Mahābhārata*, who fought with the Kauravas, in spite of being the half-brother of the Pāṇḍavas. He had already discovered that his natural mother was Kuntī, who had abandoned him at birth to avoid the stigma of a premarital lapse with Sūrya, the sun-god, but his intense enmity with Arjuna influenced his decision as he wished to fight his rival in the battle.

Karṇa was raised by a childless couple, Nandana, a charioteer, and his wife Rādhā, on the banks of the Yamunā river. He was endowed with supernatural strength and a commanding presence. He possessed Indra's javelin that killed whosoever it was directed towards and received celestial earrings and an invulnerable suit of armour from his natural father. In spite of these divine gifts, he was humiliated by Draupadī, who refused his hand because of his presumed lowly birth. After a number of encounters with Arjuna, he was crowned Rāja of Anga by Duryodhana. He eventually met his death in combat at the hands of Arjuna.

See also: **Arjuna; Draupadī; Duryodhana; Indra; Kauravas; Kuntī; Mahābhārata; Pāṇḍavas; Sūrya**

RON GEAVES

Further reading

Dasgupta, Madhusraba. 1999. *Samsad Companion to the Mahābhārata*. Calcutta: Sahitya Samsad.

Stutley, Margaret and James Stutley (eds). 1977. *A Dictionary of Hinduism: Its Mythology, Folklore and Development 1500 BC–AD 1500*. London: Routledge and Kegan Paul.

KARṆAVEDHA

One of the Hindu childhood saṃskāras, or rites of passage, the karṇavedha, or 'piercing the ears' of the child, is performed very early. Some texts prescribe it as early as the tenth, twelfth or sixteenth day after birth, others after a year. Most agree that it should be performed before teething. The right ear of a boy is pierced first, while the left ear of a girl is pierced first. Types of needles – gold, silver or copper – are prescribed depending on the desired goal or the varna of the child. Vedic mantras which glorify the ear and its capacity for hearing bliss or auspicious utterances are recited. After this brief ritual, the father must feed brāhmaṇas.

See also: **Brāhmaṇas; Mantra; Saṃskāra; Varna**

FREDERICK M. SMITH

Further reading

Kane, P.V. 1974 *History of Dharmaśāstra*, 2nd edn, vol. 2, pt 1. Poona: Bhandarkar Oriental Research Institute, 254–55.

Pandey, R.J. 1969. *Hindu Saṃskāras*. Delhi: Motilal Banarsidass, 102–05.

KĀRTTIK

Kārttik is the second lunar month of the traditional two-month autumn season, falling around October–November. The month of Kārttik derives its name from the Kṛttikā constellation (the Pleiades) because Kārttik's full moon generally appears in conjunction with the Kṛttikā asterism. Kārttik is a sacred month concerned primarily with the worship of Viṣṇu, Lakṣmī and the plant-goddess Tulsī, who is supposed to be honoured daily during Kārttik. The key religious injunction of the month is the Kārttik vrata, or vow, whose central observance is daily, predawn ritual bathing in a public body of water, such as a river, throughout the month. Many important holidays fall during Kārttik, including Karvā Cauth, Divālī and the Tulsī-vivāha. The eleventh day of Kārttik's bright half also marks the end of the cāturmāsa, the inauspicious four-month rainy season when Viṣṇu sleeps on his cosmic ocean, and the return of both Viṣṇu's sovereignty and the earth's auspiciousness.

See also: **Divālī; Lakṣmī; Stars; Tulsī-vivāha; Viṣṇu; Vrata**

TRACY PINTCHMAN

Further reading

Pintchman, Tracy. 1999. 'Kārttik as a Vaiṣṇava *Mahotsav*: Mythic Themes and the Ocean of Milk'. *Journal of Vaiṣṇava Studies* 7.2: 65–92.

KĀRTTIKEYA

See: **Skanda**

KARVE, DHONDE KESHAV (1858–1962)

Dhonde Keshav Karve was born in Sheravali, a small village in Maharashtra, and against all the odds became professor of mathematics at Ferguson College in Bombay. Married to a widow in 1893, he dedicated his life to the improvement of the socio-economic, educational and spiritual status of women, particularly the conditions of widows and their right to remarry. In order to further his work with women, he founded the *Maharshi Karve Stree Shikshan Samstha* in Pune, which remains active in education across India, collaborating to found a number of higher education institutions for women. Dhonde Keshav Karve also founded the first college for women and the first university for women, the SNDT University in Bombay. His efforts as an educator resulted in educational institutions for women covering the entire spectrum, ranging from pre-primary schools to post-graduate, engineering, vocational and professional colleges. In 1958 he was awarded the Bharat Ratna, the highest civilian award of India.

See also: **Widow remarriage; Woman question; Women's education**

RON GEAVES

Further reading

Chandavarkar, G.L. 1970. *Dhondo Keshav Karve (Builders of modern India)*. Govt. of India, Ministry of Information and Broadcasting.
Karve, Dhondo Keshav. 1936. *Looking Back*. India: Hindu Widows' Home Association.

KASHMIRI ŚAIVISM (TRIKA)

The expression 'Kashmiri Śaivism' is somewhat confusing since it commonly denotes only one of the schools, sects and ritual Śaiva traditions that have flourished in the region, that of the non-dualist Trika (Triad) school which developed there from the early ninth century. Other forms of the cult of Śiva in Kashmir included the influential doctrine of the dualist Śaiva Siddhānta, the cult of the

Śrīvidyā ('Holy Science', a practice related to Kuṇḍalinī yoga) – which was also later adopted by the Trika – Krama Śaivism, the mystical cult of Kālī, as well as the very popular devotion to the couple formed by Svaccandabhairava (a terrifying form of Śiva) and his consort Aghoreśvarī (the 'non-terrifying' Lady, i.e. ferocious goddess).

By now effectively extinct, the Trika grew as a distinct entity by the ninth century on the basis of three kinds (one of its many triads) of textual sources: *Āgama*, *Spanda* and *Pratyābhijñī*.

The *Āgamaśāstra*, a kind of canon of ancient treatises, form the common foundation of all Śaiva schools, wherever they are found, not solely in Kashmir but particularly in South India and also in Bengal, and are written usually in Sanskrit but also in diverse vernaculars, principally Tamil. The *Āgama* ('that which has come down') are the same kind of literature as the *Saṃhitā* or the *Tantra* of other sects; that is, religious tractates of non-Vedic origin. In the case of the Trika, however, the *Śaivāgama* are composed in Sanskrit and, like the Veda, are viewed as eternal, being derived from the Transcendent Word (parā vāc) identical with the ultimate reality, Śiva himself, of whom they are a manifestation in the form of meaningful sound, crystallised into the morphophonemes of Sanskrit. That Supreme Word/Śiva is but pure and free spontaneity, earning the Trika the alternative name of Svātantryavāda, doctrine of autonomy, or of freedom.

The *Āgamaśāstra* comprise again three categories of texts: *Āgama* proper, *Tantra* and the *Śiva Sūtra*. That latter collection of very obscure aphorisms is regarded as a direct revelation of Śiva to the seer Vasugupta (early ninth century) in the form of a rock inscription, with the aim of reviving an enfeebled doctrine. Chronologically the last text of the *Āgamaśāstra*, the *Śiva Sūtra* is the foundational scripture of the Trika, and Vasugupta the first historical teacher of the school. Of the many commentaries on the *Śiva Sūtra*, the most notable is the *Vimarśinī* by Kṣemarāja (eleventh century).

Vasugupta is also credited with the inauguration of the *Spanda* category of texts with the *Spandakārikās* (Stanzas on the Vibration), which was more probably authored by his disciple, Kallata. The main theme of this type of literature is a cosmology whereby the differentiation of the universe is caused by a vibration (spanda) in the Supreme Consciousness (caitanya) through Śiva's Energy (śakti), who unfolds the indefinitely diversified manifestation of the One while never becoming different from her transcendent source – hence the non-dualistic outlook of the school.

The *Pratyābhijñāśāstra* was initiated by Somānanda (ninth century) with his *Śivadṛṣṭi* and further systematised by his disciple Utpaladeva. This doctrine of Recognition will come to form the very heart of Trika teaching thanks to its sublime formulation in the works of the great Abhinavagupta (late tenth century), notably his *Vimarśinī* commentary on the *Īśvarapratyabhijña* (*Karikā*) of Utpaladeva, later condensed by Abhinava's disciple, Kṣemarāja. The 'recognition' in question is that of one's true nature as the manifestation of the ultimate transcendent Source, a salvific experience.

The last significant work in the creative phase of the Trika is the *Viveka* commentary by Jayaratha (thirteenth century) on Abhinavagupta's *Tantrāloka*. The literature of the school eventually comes to a close with the works of Śivopādhyāya in the eighteenth century.

Extremely diverse in its outlook, practices and doctrines, the Trika cannot be said to have formed a system. However, viewed through the lens of the works of its most notable exponent, Abhinavagupta, a coherence emerges, mostly due to his genius. Apart from enlightening commentaries, Abhinava left the most important independent treatise, the vast

Tantrāloka, which he later condensed into *Tantrasāra* where he presents an original interpretative synthesis of the teachings of his school.

The uncreated supreme Lord, supreme Self, ultimate Word, sovereign in his absolute freedom, principle of infinite light, Śiva, is both transcendent and immanent. One with his Energy (śakti), Śiva projects himself into what becomes the universe, reflecting his light into all levels of manifestation, through which his radiance becomes progressively dimmer without, however, being totally obscured. The cosmos is thus pervaded with divine light/consciousness and therefore never alienated from its fount. Consequently the world cannot be illusory, being grounded in the ultimate reality, and it is viewed as a real transformation of the divine, an illumination (ābhāsa). The universe is but a reflection of the reflection of Śiva in his śakti; hence yet another name for the school, ābhāsavāda, the 'doctrine of reflection'. That process of transformation evolves through thirty-six categories (tattva) or hypostases, from the most fundamental, śivatattva, out to the basest cosmic element, Earth. The śivatattva is pure spirit (cinmātra), though endowed with three powers: creative will (icchā), cognition (jñana) of the relations between all objects and between objects and himself, and activity (kriyā), the ability to take any form he wishes. Śiva's refulgence (prakāśa) is nevertheless beyond even pure emptiness (śūnyātiśūnya).

The emanation of Śiva as cosmos is an eternal alternation of expansion and contraction, the universe being periodically reabsorbed into its principle as an effect of the Lord's pulsating energy (spanda). That energy is present in the depth of the human body in the form of Kuṇḍalinī, who is both a principle of limitation or self-forgetfulness, a force of enslavement and a force of liberation.

Among the many schemes attempting to describe the complexities of cosmic unfolding, one of the most arresting is that which views the primordial vibration in terms of phonic energy (vākśakti) taking the form of sound (nāda), which from a subtle, unheard state progressively materialises into the phonemes of Sanskrit and thence into words and their corresponding objects, in a process that derives the signified form from the signifier, according to the principle that speech precedes its object and is the energy that underpins it. That conception is close to the Sāṃkhya's satkāryavāda, according to which the effect is pre-existent in its cause.

Closer to Vedic thought than to that of the grammarian philosophers, Abhinavagupta conceives of the Word, or Speech (vāc), as being manifested on four levels; the supreme Word (parā vāc), original Speech, universal ground of meaning and Śiva's feminine Energy, free from sequence, imperishable, subtle and undifferentiated, descends into the stage of paśyantī (seer), where the first lineaments of differentiation and phonemes begin to emerge, then madhyamā (median/intermediary), where duality is fully established in words, and finally vaikharī (gross), fully audible, where full sentences are formed and empirical objects find their full distinctiveness. All levels being rooted in the supreme Word, which is both the source of existence and the origin of language, language itself becomes the privileged epistemic means.

Since all beings are identical with Śiva even while under the spell of māyā and because of the impurities of the soul, they remain unaware of their true identity. The path to deliverance consists in a radical change of perspective through a sudden direct intuition (pratibhā) of their true reality, the 'recognition' that 'I am him'. On this subject, the fourteenth century *Sarvadarśanasaṃgraha* (Compendium of all Viewpoints) offers this illustration: a girl falls in love with a boy she has never met upon hearing of his shining qualities. When she meets him, however, she feels disappointed since those qualities are not in evidence. Upon longer acquaintance, she comes to perceive his qualities; she has recognised/acknowledged them, is dazzled and finally finds happiness.

That experience of clear insight and bliss is that of the coincidence of the individual's waking consciousness with the omniscient boundless self, Śiva, and results in a state of liberation-in-life (jīvanmukti). What is instrumental to the awakening of the intuition of oneness is the initiation (dīksā) by the guru, which opens the soul to the descent of divine grace (anugraha) and marks the beginning of spiritual discipline (sādhana).

Although the *Vijñānabhairava*, a foundational *Tantra*, describes some 112 types of discipline or yoga, the Trika broadly focuses on four paths to liberation. The highest and rarest of these 'means' (upāya) is the attainment of the goal without any means at all (paropāya), instantaneously, through a sudden overwhelming burst of divine grace. The Śambhāvopāya, the 'means of Śambhu (Śiva)' is the second path, where intense devotion (bhakti) rushes the yogin into a state of complete identification with Śiva. Śāktopāya, the 'path of Energy', is that of the power of gnosis (jñānopāya), relying on an extreme intensity of emotion to descend, with the help of the guru, into the energies of the depths where, fused with kuṇḍalinī śakti, a lightning ascent into the non-dual state (nirvikalpa) is triggered. Finally there is the 'way of the common man' (naropāya), living in the world and who cannot aspire to liberation-in-life (though that may well occur) but, through practices of yoga, supplemented by rituals and the grace of the guru, seeks to purify his mind as a preparation for the higher paths. It is in the last two paths that the process of initiation is paramount.

Apart from its supremely intricate philosophy and soteriology, the Trika is also a system of tantric ritual and worship, closely associated with the mysticism of Krama Śaivism and largely focused on the transcendent goddess Kālī as manifested in the divine triad Aparā, Parāpara and Parā, as well as eight mother deities immanent in both divine and human females associated with clans (kula) of followers and with the particular spiritual lineage from the supreme Śiva down to one's own teacher, and thus also defines a type of sādhana which is specific to a lineage of tantric gurus.

See also: **Abhinavagupta; Bhakti; Dīksā; Jīvanmukta; Kālī and Caṇḍī; Kuṇḍalinī Yoga; Languages; Māyā; Sacred texts; Śaiva Siddhānta; Śaivism; Śakti; Sāṃkhya; Śiva; Tantras; Veda; Vyākaraṇa; Yoga**

DANIEL MARIAU

Further reading

Abhinavagupta: Essenza dei Tantra [*Tantrasāra*]. 1960. Introduction, trans. and notes by Raniero Gnoli. Torino: Boringhieri.

Abhinavagupta: Luce delle Sacre Scritture [Tantrāloka] di Abhinavagupta. 1972. A cura di Raniero Gnoli. Torino: U.T.E.T.

Śiva Sūtras, The Yoga of Supreme Identity. 1979. Trans. Jaiyadeva Singh. Delhi: Motilal Banarsidass.

KATARAGAMA

See: **Skanda**

KAṬHA UPANIṢAD

See: **Upaniṣads**

KĀTYĀYANĪ

A celebrated grammarian who followed after Pāṇini and wrote the vārttikas, critical notes on his aphorisms which also complete and correct Pāṇini's work and adapt them to classical Sanskrit. In addition to his work on Pāṇini he wrote the *Śrautasūtras*, explaining the Brāhmaṇa text of the White *Yajurveda*. He is also associated with the *Sarvānukramanī*, a work in sūtra form that provides the first words of every *Ṛgveda* hymn and the number of verses and metres. Another figure by the same name was attributed authorship of a *Dharmaśāstra*, and may help explain the uncertainty over placing Kātyāyana's period. Max Müller identified him as living in the second half of the fourth century BCE but there is considerable disagreement, with dates ranging from the third century to the first half of the second century BCE. A story in the *Kathāsaritsāgara* states that Kātyāyana was an incarnation of the demigod Puṣpadanta, the guardian elephant of the north-west direction and one of the attendants of Śiva. It is believed that after being guilty of indiscretion through overhearing an intimate conversation between Śiva and Pārvatī, he was reborn as a human being and the greatest of the grammarians. He is regarded as one of the Nine Gems of the court of King Vikramaditya.

See also: **Brāhmaṇa; Dharmaśāstras; Müller, Friedrich Max; Pāṇini; Pārvatī; Śrautasūtras; Saṃhitā; Sūtra; Śiva; Vyākaraṇa**

RON GEAVES

Further reading

Kapoor, Subodh. (ed.). 2000. *The Hindus: Encyclopaedia of Hinduism*, vol. 3. New Delhi: Cosmo Publications.

KAURAVAS

The generic family name given to the 100 sons of the blind king Dhṛtarāṣṭra, born as a result of a blessing by the sage Vyāsa and given to Gāndhārī, his barren wife. They were known as the Kauravas after the name of their common ancestor, Kuru. Their leader was the eldest, Duryodhana, who ascended the throne after his father renounced it. The *Mahābhārata* describes Duryodhana as malicious and dishonourable, lacking in the noble attributes required of a prince, but in doing so is setting the scene for the conflict between the Kauravas and their hated opponents and cousins the Pāṇḍavas. The conflict began as a result of jealousy and ambition after Dhṛtarāṣṭra received the Pāṇḍavas at court and even named the eldest, Yudiṣṭhira, as his heir. The culmination of the conflict was the great battle fought at Kurukṣetra, which came to symbolise the struggle between the forces of good and evil.

See also: **Dhṛtarāṣṭra; Gāndhārī; Kurukṣetra; Mahābhārata; Pāṇḍavas; Vyāsa; Yudiṣṭhira**

RON GEAVES

Further reading

Dasgupta, Madhusraba. 1999. *Samsad Companion to the Mahābhārata*. Calcutta: Sahitya Samsad.

KAUṢĪTAKĪ UPANIṢAD

See: **Upaniṣads**

KAUṬILYA

Kauṭilya is the name of the 'author' of the Kauṭilīya *Arthaśāstra*, a Sanskrit manual on statecraft. Kauṭilya is sometimes regarded as the 'Indian Machiavelli'. We know very little about the personal history of Kauṭilya, also called Cāṇakya, a brāhmaṇa from Gandhāra, who lived in the late fourth century BCE. The traditional view is that Kauṭilya, as an influential minister of Candragupta Maurya, destroyed the power of the Nanda dynasty and placed his king on the throne of Magadha. The Kauṭilīya *Arthaśāstra* has given rise to frequent controversies about its authorship, its authenticity and its age. It is the oldest extant *Arthasāstra*, but the text probably grew over time (Trautmann 1971: 186). It was decisively shaped by two authors (Scharfe 1993: 67–77), the earlier of them being named Kauṭilya in one of the introductory verses of the book. The latter of the two is called Viṣṇugupta in the concluding stanza.

See also: **Artha; Arthaśāstra; Brāhmaṇa; Rājā**

ANNETTE SCHMIEDCHEN

Further reading

Scharfe, H. 1993. *Investigations in Kauṭalya's Manual of Political Science*, 2nd, rev. edn of 'Untersuchungen zur Staatsrechtslehre des Kauṭalya'. Wiesbaden: Harrassowitz.

Trautmann, Th.R. 1971. *Kauṭilya and the Artha Śāstra. A statistical investigation of the authorship and evolution of the text*. Leiden: Brill.

KENA UPANIṢAD

See: **Upaniṣads**

KEŚĀNTA

The keśānta, or first shaving, is one of the Hindu educational saṃskāras, or rites of passage. After performing the upanayana and receiving the sacred thread, the Vedic student was expected to maintain physical and mental purity. One of the physical requirements of this was regular shaving of the hair on the head and the body. Hair was considered a powerful substance to be retained by renunciant mendicants, but it was also considered dangerous and impure for householders, who were required to shave their beard and often their heads. The Vedic tradition was decidedly a householder tradition; thus, Vedic students were required to shave their head and beards and keep their nails trimmed. These were excess impure substances that had to be regularly cut. In this way the keśānta attends to the notion that bodily maturity exacts extra demands on the system of ritual purity.

According to most ritual authorities this saṃskāra was performed when the student reached the age of 16. The procedure agrees substantially with that of the cūḍākaraṇa, the rite in which the hair was initially cut between ages one and three. In the keśānta the boy sits next to his mother rather than on her lap, the beard is shaved in addition to the head (excepting the topknot) and, like the cūḍākaraṇa, the hair and the cut nails were thrown into water. The rite is also called godāna because the ritual also requires that the student (or his family) present a cow (go) as a gift to his teacher, and other gifts to the barber. At the end of the ritual the student takes a vow of silence and observes certain austerities for a year.

See also: **Brahmacarya; Cūḍākaraṇa; Dāna; Guru; Gārhasthya; Sacred animals; Saṃnyāsa; Saṃskāra; Upanayana**

FREDERICK M. SMITH

Further reading

Kane, P.V. 1974. *History of Dharmaśāstra*, 2nd edn, vol. 2, pt 1, 402–05. Poona: Bhandarkar Oriental Research Institute.

Pandey, R.J. 1969. *Hindu Saṃskāras*. Delhi: Motilal Banarsidass, 143–45.

KINNARAS

Literally meaning 'deformed man', the Sanskrit term 'kinnara' has also come to refer to a stringed musical instrument and has been used as an epithet of the god of wealth, Kubera. The most common reference to the term, however, concerns an obscure class of semi-divine musicians (also known as kiṃpuruṣas), often described as holding a stringed instrument (vīnā) in their hands. Although usually presented as a strictly male coterie with horse heads and human bodies that sing and play music in Kubera's court, there are also occasional allusions to beautiful Kinnara women. The Kinnaras are supposed to have been created from the arms of Lord Brahmā. The name Kinnara generally appears in long lists with other divine and demonic beings, such as Gandharvas, Apsarasas and Rākṣasas. They are said to live on the 'golden-peaked mountain' known as hemakuṭa.

See also: **Apsarasas; Brahmā; Gandharvas; Kubera; Rākṣasas**

DEVEN M. PATEL

Further reading

Dimmit, Cornelia and J.A.B van Buitenen, (eds and trans.). 1978. *Classical HinduMythology: A Reader in the Sanskrit Purāṇas*. Philadelphia, PA: Temple University Press.

KĪRTAṆ(A)

'Repetition', 'mentioning'. More specifically, the kīrtan is a kind of devotional congregational song. The kīrtan is a product of the Vaiṣṇava devotional tradition but it is also performed by the Sikhs during the recitation of their holy book, the *Guru Granth Sahib*. The kīrtan can be performed by singers alone or be accompanied by instruments such as ḍholak (drum), jhāñjhas (cymbals) and harmonium. Spontaneous or professional groups (maṇḍalas) are made of males and females from any caste and social strata. The kīrtan thus differs from classical music, where the performers belong to a lineage (guru-śiṣya-paramparā) and follow a fixed melodic structure (rāga). Two forms of kīrtan can be distinguished. The nām-kīrtan is a repetition of Viṣṇu's name(s). The leader and the chorus alternate and accelerate the rhythm until a climax is reached. If the song uninterruptedly repeats, it is called akhaṇḍa-kīrtan, 'unbroken' kīrtan. The līlā-kīrtan opens with an invocation (also working as a refrain) and then describes the dalliances of Kṛṣṇa with Rādhā and the gopīs. In both instances, loudness is sought and power is embedded in sound, not in meaning. Although the *Bhāgavata Purāṇa* is considered the spiritual source of kīrtan, its structure is developed from the *Gītagovinda*, a Sanskrit poem by Jayadeva (twelfth century CE). Many famous kīrtanas appeared in the fourteenth century, but only in the sixteenth century, with the spread of new devotional movements and the teachings of Caitanya and Vallabha, was the kīrtan adopted as a ritualistic tool. With time, kīrtan adapted to different styles (dhrupada, ṭhumrī, ṭappā), modes (rāgas) and rhythms (tālas). In its contemporary form the kīrtan is influenced by pop and jazz music, it is employed in film industry and has been adopted by different sects and religious cults as a form of meditation.

See also: **Bhakti; Bhakti movement; Caitanya; Caste; Gītagovinda; Gopī(s); Guru; Jayadeva; Kṛṣṇa; Music; Paramparā; Purāṇa; Rādhā; Sikhism, relationship with Hinduism; Śiṣya; Vaiṣṇavism; Vallabha**

FABRIZIO M. FERRARI

Further reading

Beck, G. 2000. 'Religious and Devotional Music: Northern Area'. In A. Arnold, ed., *South Asia: The Indian Subcontinent (Garland Encyclopaedia of World Music, Vol. 5)*. New York: Garland Publishing, 246–58.

Gobind Singh, M. 1982. *Indian Classical Music and Sikh Kirtan*. New Delhi and Oxford: IBH.

Slawek, S. 1988. 'Popular Kirtan in Benares: Some "Great" Aspects of a Little Tradition'. *Ethnomusicology* 32(2): 77–92.

KISHWAR, MADHU

Madhu Kishwar is widely acclaimed as a contemporary scholar-activist working for women's rights and social change. She has rejected the label 'feminist', focused on the distinctiveness of Indian women's problems and sought solutions that will work specifically in India. She thinks that women should have more choices. A reform, according to Kishwar, should build confidence and self-esteem and avoid reliance on authoritarian methods. As the founder and long-time editor of *Manushi* (a journal on women and society, which began in 1978), she has provided a forum for women's first-hand accounts of their lives and problems – especially those of the poor – and has reported herself on events at the grassroots level. Her activism has made her a critic of urban and educated elites, who have little knowledge of the problems faced by ordinary people. In her own words:

> One of the most important things I have learnt is that even the most well-meaning efforts to help improve people's lives can end up in disaster if you do not take people's actual lives, dilemmas and perceptions sufficiently seriously, or if you fail to understand the effects of any particular effort at change on other parts of a complex social situation.
>
> (Kishwar 1999: 2–3)

Kishwar's activism led to many thought-provoking editorials, which were later printed in anthologies such as *Gandhi and Women* (1985); *Religion at the Service of Nationalism and Other Essays* (1998); and *Off the Beaten Track: Essays on Gender Justice for Indian Women* (2001). In recent years, she has turned her attention to the impact of globalisation on Indian society. This independent thinking is characteristic of her *Deepening Democracy: Challenges of Governance and Globalization in India* (2005). She is currently a Senior Fellow at the Centre for Studies in Developing Societies in New Delhi, India.

See also: **Women, status of**

KATHERINE K. YOUNG

Further reading

Kishwar, Madhu. 1999. *Off the Beaten Track: Rethinking Gender Justice for Indian Women*. New Delhi and New York: Oxford University Press.

KOŚA

The term 'kośa' (translated as 'sheath' or 'cover') signifies enfoldment. It pertains to a doctrine of the envelopment of the soul in successive 'cases' or 'sheaths'.

The *Taittirīya Upaniṣad* teaches five levels of the soul which came to be called 'kośa' in later literature. The first layer or sheath is the 'food-made', which represents the physical body.

Some Advaita thinkers identified the next three sheaths as making up the 'subtle body' (the transmigrating aspect of the soul). These include the 'mind-made soul', which is indicated as 'different from' and 'within' the 'breath-made soul'. Similarly, the 'consciousness-made soul', representing pure consciousness, is 'different from' and 'within' the mind-made soul.

The fifth sheath is the 'soul made of bliss' (ātmā ānanda-maya), the ultimate level or core of the soul.

In the *Taittirīya Upaniṣad* each level of the soul is fivefold. For example, truth, order, faith, yoga and 'the great' are the five parts of the consciousness-made soul.

See also: **Advaita; Upaniṣads**

MARTIN OVENS

Further reading

Reat, N.R. 1990. *Origins of Indian Psychology*. Berkeley, CA: Asian Humanities Press.

KOSAMBI, DAMODAR DHARMANAND (1907–66)

Mathematician, Sanskritist and historian. Although best known as a mathematician, Kosambi also published editions of Bhartṛhari's *śatakas* and Vidyākara's Sanskrit anthology, the *Subhāśitaratnakośa*. He wrote extensively on Indian history, from a perspective that was fundamentally but not rigidly Marxist, seeking to move away from the dynastic histories favoured by colonial historians and to develop an understanding of different stages in India's history. His Marxist perspective is apparent in his claim that the *Bhagavadgītā*'s message of obedience to a god is to be understood within the context of the feudal relationship between a lord and his retainers. Similarly, he explained the decline of Buddhism and the revival of Hinduism in economic terms. Kosambi also revised Henry Clarke Warren's edition of the *Visuddhimagga* of Buddhaghosa, a Pāli Buddhist text.

See also: **Bhagavadgītā; Bhartṛhari; Hinduism, history of scholarship**

WILL SWEETMAN

Further reading

Kosambi, D.D. 1948. *The Epigrams Attributed to Bhartrhari.* Bombay: Bharatiya Vidya Bhavan

Jha, D.N. 1973. 'D.D. Kosambi'. In S.P. Sen, ed., *Historians and Historiography in Modern India.* Calcutta: Institute of Historical Studies, 121–32.

KRAMRISCH, STELLA (1898–1993)

Austrian art historian. Kramrisch studied in Vienna, where her interest in India, first awakened by reading the *Bhagavadgītā* in translation, was further stimulated by Wassily Kandinsky (1866–1944) and Rudolf Steiner (1861–1925). In 1919 Kramrisch received her doctorate for research on early Buddhist sculpture in India. While lecturing in Oxford, she met Rabindranath Tagore, who invited her to teach at Santiniketan. She subsequently taught at the University of Calcutta, at the Courtauld Institute in London and at the University of Pennsylvania (1950–69). She was curator of Indian art at the Philadelphia Museum (1954–72) and Professor of Indian Art at New York University (1964–82). Her most important contributions to the study of Hinduism were her 1946 book *The Hindu Temple*, a definitive study of the development of Hindu temple architecture, and an exhibition 'Manifestations of Shiva', which she curated in 1981 with an accompanying book, *The Presence of Śiva*, in which she retold the myths associated with Śiva in the *Saṃhitās* and the *Purāṇas.*

See also: **Bhagavadgītā; Hinduism, history of scholarship; Purāṇas; Saṃhitās; Tagore, Rabindranath**

WILL SWEETMAN

Further reading

Kramrisch, S. 1946. *The Hindu Temple*, 2 vols. Calcutta: University of Calcutta.

Kramrisch, S. 1981. *The Presence of Śiva.* Princeton, NJ: Princeton University Press.

Miller, B.S. 1983. 'Stella Kramrisch: A Biographical Essay'. In B.S. Miller, ed., *Exploring India's Sacred Art: Selected Writings of Stella Kramrisch.* Philadelphia, PA: University of Philadelphia Press, 3–34.

KRISHNA PREM, SRI

Born Ronald Nixon, a former fighter pilot in the British Royal Flying Corps during the First World War, Sri Krishna Prem had first become interested in Buddhism and the Pali language whist studying at Cambridge University. After graduation, he accepted a post as Reader in English at Lucknow University. It was here that he came under the influence of Theosophy as a result of contact with the university vice-chancellor, Dr Chakravarti. His first guru was Monica Chakravarti, also known as Yashoda Ma after her renunciation of householder life, who initiated him in 1924. Both were initiated into Gauḍīya Vaiṣṇavism by Bal Goswami at Vrindāvan, but Sri Krishna Prem experienced difficulties with the conservative attitudes prevalent amongst Vṛndāvana brāhmaṇas, and with Yashoda Ma established their own ashram in Almora. After her death, he continued to maintain the centre himself until his own demise in

1965, when he was succeeded by Sri Madhava Ashish (born Alexander Phipps). Sri Krishna Prem was respected throughout India for his knowledge of Indian philosophy and adherence to the principles of the lifestyle of Hindu renunciation, and was the first Western Hindu guru to have Indians as disciples.

See also: **Āśram(a) (religious community); Brāhmaṇa; Buddhism, relationship with Hinduism; Gaudiya Vaishnava Mission; Guru; Saṃnyasa; Theosophy and the Theosophical Society; Vṛndāvana**

RON GEAVES

Further reading

Sri Krishna Prem. 1976. *Initiation into Yoga: An Introduction to the Spiritual Life*. Wheaton, IL: Theosophical Publishing House.

KRISHNAMACHARYA, T. (1888–1989)

Born in 1888 in Muchukundapuram, Karnataka. Krishnamacharya began learning Sanskrit and yoga before the age of five and later in life received the highest degrees in all six orthodox schools of thought. From 1915 he spent seven years near Mount Kailash in the Himālayas studying yoga and its applications under the instruction of Sri Ramamohan Brahmachari. The Maharaja of Mysore heard of Krishnamacharya's skill in healing and, in 1933, gave him a wing of the Jaganmohan Palace to teach in. He remained there until 1950, when the yoga school closed due to lack of interest. In 1952 he was invited to Chennai by a leading jurist and in 1976 the Krishnamacharya Yoga Mandiram was created, gaining governmental recognition in 1983. Krishnamacharya died in 1989 aged 101 years.

Krishnamacharya taught several of the twentieth century's most important Modern Yoga teachers, such as B.K.S. Iyengar (his brother-in-law), Sri K. Pattabhi Jois, Indra Devi and T.K.V. Desikachar (his son). The very distinct styles of each of these figures reflect the breadth and complexity of Krishnamacharya's own teaching history. His primary resource remained the *Yogasūtra* of Patañjali, but he constantly drew on his vast knowledge of the Indian philosophical traditions and Āyurveda. In a vision at the age of 16 he received an important yoga text by the ninth-century Vaiṣṇava sage Nathamuni (from whom his family are said to be descended), called *Yoga Rahasya*. Krishnamacharya is a key figure in the contemporary renaissance of āsana practice. Noteworthy is his notion of vinyāsa krama (the proper sequencing of āsana with suitable counterposes) and his insistence on individually tailored practice. He authored books on yoga in Sanskrit, Telegu and Kannada, such as *Yoga Makaranda* in 1935.

See also: **Āsana; Āyurveda; Desikachar, T.K.V. and Viniyoga; Himālayas; Indra Devi; Iyengar, B.K.S. and Iyengar Yoga; Jois, K. Pattabhi and Ashtanga Vinyasa Yoga; Patañjali; Ṣaḍdarśana; Vaiṣṇavism; Yoga, modern; Yogasūtras**

MARK SINGLETON

Further reading

Krishnamacharya, T. 1998. *Śri Nāthamuni's Yogarahasya*. Chennai: Krishnamacharya Yoga Mandiram.

Sjoman, N. 1996. *The Yoga Tradition of the Mysore Palace*. New Delhi: Abhinav Publications.

KRISHNAMURTI, JIDDU (1895–1986)

The life of Jiddu Krishnamurti falls into two distinct parts. The child of poor brāhmaṇa parents, he lived near to the headquarters of the Theosophical Society in Adyar, Madras (now Chennai), where his father worked in an administrative capacity. The Theosophical leader Annie Besant and her associate C.W. Leadbeater perceived hitherto unnoticed spiritual potential in the child and arranged for him to receive a European-style education. In 1911 the Order of the Star in the East was founded by the Theosophists to prepare for the coming of a World Teacher. Though technically not part of the Theosophical Society, the movement attracted wide support from its membership as well as from elsewhere. In the period from 1925 to 1929 Krishnamurti's teachings began to challenge the messianic expectations of the Order's followers. In 1929 he dissolved the Order of the Star, as it become, and severed all his links with the Theosophical Society.

From that time until his death he devoted himself to lecturing and writing. He taught that no religion, no teacher, no organisation could mediate the truth to seekers of it. He did, however, attract to himself a body of followers whose support permitted him to live the life of an independent spiritual teacher.

Though as critical of Hinduism as he was of any other tradition, he did espouse the centrality of self-enquiry as the basis of the spiritual life, in common with other Indian teachers from ancient times to the present day.

He was instrumental in the establishment of schools in India, England and the United States where his philosophy was embodied in the educational practice. Since his death the Krishnamurti Foundation has ensured that his writings and the texts of his many talks and lectures continue to be available for future generations.

See also: **Besant, Annie; Theosophy and the Theosophical Society**

KEVIN TINGAY

Further reading

Jayakar, P. 1986. *Krishnamurti – A Biography.* San Francisco, CA: Harper & Row.

Lutyens, M. 1990. *The Life and Death of Krishnamurti.* London: John Murray.

Vernon, R. 2000. *Star in the East.* London: Constable.

KRIYĀ YOGA

The 'Yoga of action' is expounded in the second book of the *Yogasūtras.* That discipline is the convergence of three elements: ascesis (tapas), study/utterance of sacred texts (svādhyāya) and devotion to the Lord (Īṣvara-pranidhāna), which serve to promote the cultivation of states of ecstasy (samādhi) through countering the five causes of affliction (kleśa) that are obstacles to their realisation. The five imperfections are: ignorance (kleśa), attachment to the ego (asmitā), passionate attachment (rāga), hatred/aversion (dvesa) and the will to live/fear of death (abhiniveśa). All causes of affliction are rooted in ignorance/nescience. Kriyā Yoga is the central teaching of Patañjali and not, as often believed, a simple preparation for the eight-limbed discipline (astāngayoga); it encompasses the whole of yoga practice.

Vācaspati Miśra's sub-commentary on the *Yogasūtras* identifies the yoga of action as renunciation of all action and its fruits (niskāmakarmayoga) preconised in the *Bhagavadgītā*, while Vijñānabhiksu says that Kriyā Yoga is but one of the three disciplines described in that text, alongside the yogas of gnosis (jñāna) and of devotion (bhakti).

In modern literature, the term kriyāyoga at times erroneously designates the practice of haṭha yoga.

See also: **Aṣṭāṅga yoga; Bhagavadgītā; Haṭha yoga; Patañjali; Vācaspati Miśra; Vijñānabhikṣu; Yogasūtras**

DANIEL MARIAU

KṚṢṆA

One of the most popular deities in the Hindu pantheon, Kṛṣṇa is depicted in three major forms throughout his long and diverse history in Indian religions: (1) as the warrior prince, Vāsudeva and Mādhava, advisor to the Paṇḍavas in the *Mahābhārata* battle and benevolent ruler of Dvārakā; (2) as the playful child and adolescent lover Gopāla and Govinda in the Sanskrit Purāṇas and vernacular poetry, celebrated throughout India in popular expressions of devotion; and (3) as the Supreme Lord, Nārāyaṇa, Viṣṇu and Bhagavān, who creates the entire cosmos and grants mokṣa (liberation) to those devotees who unconditionally adore him.

The Sanskrit term kṛṣṇa means 'black' or 'dark', perhaps indicating his association with the Kali Yuga, for it was precisely Kṛṣṇa's death in 3102 BCE, shortly after the end of the *Mahābhārata* war, which marked the onset of this darkest and most degenerate of ages according to the classical Hindu view of cyclical history. Though archaeological evidence has been cited in support of this traditional date, current scholarship suggests the ninth century BCE as a probable time for the core events described in the *Mahābhārata*, political struggles in which a historical Kṛṣṇa may have been engaged. Scholars have thus proposed that a prince and martial hero named Kṛṣṇa later became deified, as a once minor cult of devotion became more prominent, but such claims are difficult to substantiate given Kṛṣṇa's obscure origins in ancient history. The pre-Buddhist *Chāndogya Upaniṣad* mentions 'Kṛṣṇa, the son of Devakī' (3.17.6–7) without further elaboration, but Pāṇini includes a sūtra referring to persons showing preference for Vāsudeva, among other objects of devotion, a reference indicating the possible roots of the Bhāgavata movement by the fifth century BCE (Brockington 1998: 257). Mention of those devoted to Vāsudeva and Baladeva (also called Saṃkarṣana), Kṛṣṇa's elder brother, is also found in the Pāli Buddhist canon and in Patañjali's second-century BCE *Mahābhāṣya*. A number of inscriptions also attest to the worship of Kṛṣṇa and Saṃkarṣana between 200 BCE and the early Common Era.

Epic and purāṇic literature

Not until the epic *Mahābhārata*, composed between 400 BCE and 400 CE, do we find sustained textual accounts of Kṛṣṇa's rise to divine supremacy. The son of Vasudeva, king of the Vṛṣṇis, Kṛṣṇa is a member of the royal warrior class and known by his patronymic Vāsudeva. As a kṣatriya, Vāsudeva Kṛṣṇa becomes advisor to the righteous Pāṇḍavas as they vie with their Kaurava cousins over sovereignty of the Kurukṣetra kingdom in northern India. In this role, Kṛṣṇa often resorts to unscrupulous means to advance his cause, but justifies such cunning by emphasising that his actions – and the battle altogether – ultimately uphold dharma (cosmic order). This focus on dharma becomes especially prominent in Kṛṣṇa's most famous discourse, the *Bhagavadgītā*, where he urges Arjuna to engage in battle and thereby fulfil his own dharma (duty) for the sake of social and universal order. Whenever dharma decays and its opposite, adharma, flourishes, Kṛṣṇa himself takes birth in age after age to protect the virtuous, destroy the wicked and establish dharma firmly (4.7–8). However, not only must Arjuna fight the war and thus fulfil his dharma, but he must act without attachment and in the spirit of sacrifice, devoting all his actions to Kṛṣṇa in order to attain salvation by becoming one with Kṛṣṇa, who unveils his awesome divinity in a wondrous and terrible theophany in Chapter 11. In the *Bhagavadgītā*, Kṛṣṇa therefore reveals himself to be not only the sovereign lord of dharma, but likewise the lord of mokṣa and the gracious God of bhakti (devotion) simultaneously. Such bhakti is not the passionate attachment and adoration we find in later *Purāṇas* and vernacular poetry, but rather the disciplined devotion of the supreme Lord, whose radical freedom from karma nevertheless entails deep concern for social harmony and personal dharma.

In referring to his own purposeful birth in age after age, Kṛṣṇa articulates an early version of the classical avatāra theory, according to which the supreme God incarnates himself in order to restore the balance between good and evil on Earth. Although in the *Baghavadgītā* it is Kṛṣṇa himself who periodically becomes incarnate in various forms, in the *Mahābhārata* more generally, and specifically in the *Nārāyanīya*, it is Nārāyaṇa who takes birth as Vāsudeva Kṛṣṇa, an identification that establishes continuity with earlier Vedic literature. It is unclear, however, exactly how the later connection between Nārāyaṇa, Vāsudeva and Viṣṇu was made, but texts beginning with the *Viṣṇu Purāṇa* emphasise that Kṛṣṇa is explicitly an avatāra of Viṣṇu, perhaps due to Dravidian influence, given the emphasis on Viṣṇu in South Indian Vaiṣṇavism. This explicit avatāra relationship between Viṣṇu and Kṛṣṇa is not yet articulated in the *Mahābhārata*, though in response to the theophany Arjuna twice addresses Kṛṣṇa as Viṣṇu in the vocative, and the *Harivaṃśa* includes a few verses that either state or intimate Kṛṣṇa's hidden identity as Viṣṇu.

Though he is known throughout the *Mahābhārata* as the son of Vasudeva and Devakī, we have no detailed descriptions of Kṛṣṇa's much-celebrated childhood and adolescence until the *Harivaṃśa*, a supplement to the *Mahābhārata* that perhaps attained its final form in the early centuries of the Common Era. Here for the first time we find the popular tales of Kṛṣṇa's youth in the cowherd community of Braja, where Vasudeva hides the infant Kṛṣṇa with his foster parents Nanda and Yaśoda in order to protect him from Kaṃsa. In the idyllic forests of Vraja, the youthful Kṛṣṇa Gopāla performs many extraordinary deeds, such as taming the serpent Kāliya, lifting Mount Govardhana and effortlessly slaying several demons which the evil Kaṃsa has dispatched to kill him, all of which feats have been depicted iconographically and performed dramatically for nearly two millennia. The charming Kṛṣṇa also frolics with the amorous gopīs in Vṛndāvana, thus depicted for the first time in what will become his most celebrated persona, though the episode is described only briefly in the *Harivaṃśa*.

How the cowherd Gopāla became associated with the princely Vāsudeva of the *Mahābhārata* is a historical problem that has long perplexed scholars. Though the *Mahābhārata* occasionally refers to Kṛṣṇa's pastoral youth, such passages lack detail and development, and some scholars therefore consider them to be later interpolations to the epic, inserted as the rustic Gopāla was incorporated into brahmanical Sanskrit mythology. Scholars then further speculate that Kṛṣṇa Gopāla was at least a minor deity for a tribe of nomadic herdsmen known historically and in the *Mahābhārata* as the Ābhīras, who lived in the region of Mathurā during the time the epic and its supplemental *Harivaṃśa* were likely compiled. Why this fusion would have occurred – if in fact it did – remains a mystery in the history of religions, but nevertheless marks a significant beginning for Kṛṣṇa's development as the supreme God who is intimately accessible to those who worship him.

By the time of the *Viṣṇu Purāṇa* in roughly the fifth century CE, Kṛṣṇa is explicitly identified as an avatāra of Viṣṇu and is thus portrayed in detail in Book 5, following descriptions of Viṣṇu's previous incarnations. Although Viṣṇu is clearly regarded as supreme throughout the text, a number of passages point to the supremacy of Vāsudeva, Hari and Kṛṣṇa, by virtue of their identification with Viṣṇu, who is likewise recognised as Brahman. In this respect, the soteriology of the *Viṣṇu Purāṇa* closely follows the *Bhagavadgītā*, where contemplation of and devotion to Vāsudeva bestow the ultimate reward: liberation from fear, suffering and saṃsāra (perpetual transmigration). In the *Bhagavadgītā*, Kṛṣṇa specifies the worship of himself as one among many various spiritual paths, but it is the highest of paths, alone leading to the supreme goal. The same hierarchy of salvific means is found in the *Viṣṇu Purāṇa*, but many passages identify Kṛṣṇa as the *sole* path to salvation: 'Without having propitiated Vāsudeva, who will attain *mokṣa*?' (1.4.18). Again bhakti is identified as either the most efficacious or the only means to salvation, and, following the *Bhagavadgītā*, the *Viṣṇu Purāṇa* advocates a contemplative form of bhakti, one by which the devotee knows everything including himself as Kṛṣṇa. The same theme is found in the later and far more influential *Bhāgavata Purāṇa*, a text of obscure origins perhaps composed some time between the sixth and eighth centuries CE. Here one finds a similar emphasis on Vāsudeva's divine form becoming the entire world, so that the entire universe is known as a cosmic incarnation of Kṛṣṇa. Within this theological context, the goal is to realise the unity of everything and everyone in Kṛṣṇa, a unity that leads to the important ethical concept of equal regard, earlier articulated in the *Bhagavadgītā* 5.18, where Kṛṣṇa says that sages look with equal regard upon learned brāhmaṇas, cows, elephants, dogs and even outcastes. Seeing Kṛṣṇa everywhere thus allows one to wish for the welfare of all, without harbouring enmity towards even those who are hostile. Though the *Viṣṇu* and the *Bhāgavata Purāṇas* are filled with praise for devotees who embody this yogic equilibrium, both texts admit that because of the extreme difficulty of attaining this perfect wisdom, such enlightened ones are rare. As a result, this particular soteriology has been less influential on later Vaiṣṇava traditions, where the emphasis instead falls on a passionate and salvific attachment to Kṛṣṇa's charming human form and delightful stories.

In both the *Viṣṇu* and the *Bhāgavata Purāṇas*, accounts of Kṛṣṇa's life from birth to death are central to the narratives, and in contrast to the earlier *Harivaṃśa*, here the theological significance of his relationships with people is elaborated at length. Having witnessed a number of Kṛṣṇa's astonishing deeds, the cowherds in Vraja become confused about his nature and even ask him who he is, but, in the *Viṣṇu Purāṇa*, Kṛṣṇa never reveals his essential identity. As a result, the intimacy with Kṛṣṇa that his parents, friends and lovers all experience is premised on a fundamental ignorance of Kṛṣṇa's divine being, but this does not preclude their attainment of salvation. Indeed, the gopīs who rush from their homes to dance and play with their beloved Kṛṣṇa in the forest are liberated by the joy of beholding him, and those who are unable to reach him physically are freed from saṃsāra by their ceaseless and painful contemplation of him in separation. In the *Bhāgavata Purāṇa*, in fact, the stunning claim is made that any intense emotion directed towards Kṛṣṇa leads to salvation – be it desire, hatred, fear, affection or genuine devotion (7.1.29). Truly novel is such a claim that all the passions can be an efficacious path to salvation. The efficacy of intense emotion, moreover, is closely connected to the concept of māyā in the *Bhāgavata*, because it is precisely by means of māyā, Kṛṣṇa's power of divine illusion, that he enters into creation, embodied in human form and becomes son, friend, brother, lover, enemy, husband and father, fully participating in society as if he were just like all others. Being ignorant of his divinity, however, people perceive him as a mere human being – however extraordinary – and then love him or hate him accordingly. Māyā is therefore a necessary illusion insofar as it allows the supreme God to be known and loved intimately, through which intimate attachment one attains freedom from saṃsāra.

Such consistent emphasis on bhakti, jñāna (salvific knowledge) and mokṣa does not, however, eclipse the significant of dharma in the *Viṣṇu* and the *Bhāgavata Purāṇas.* Indeed, both texts repeatedly claim that Kṛṣṇa becomes incarnate to protect the world and uphold dharma, and to provide through his own actions a model of dharmic behaviour – hence Kṛṣṇa's portrayal as the perfect kṣatriya, and as the ideal husband and father who begets ten sons and one daughter, following earlier Vedic injunctions, with each of his 16,008 beautiful wives. To be sure, the ultimate goal stressed in both texts is release from saṃsāra, but only *after* one has fulfilled one's dharma. To this end, the *Bhāgavata* articulates two further means of final release, both of which inform contemporary devotional practice. The first is chanting the various names of Kṛṣṇa, for by pronouncing the name of him whom fear itself fears, the powerless one, having fallen into the grisly cycle of transmigration, is immediately liberated (1.1.14). The second involves the text itself: At the beginning of the first skandha it is said that when Kṛṣṇa left the earth and returned to his own abode the light of the *Bhāgavata Purāṇa* appeared for those who had lost their sight (1.3.45). Then in the twelfth and final skandha the narrator claims that a man hearing and contemplating the text with devotion will surely be liberated (12.13.18), for there is no path across the terrible ocean of saṃsāra other than listening to the sweet stories of the Lord's līlā, his divine play (12.4.40). Frequently throughout the text, therefore, devotees express a deep longing to hear the accounts of Kṛṣṇa's deeds again and again, so the stories are thus retold and reheard by those who never tire of chanting and listening – even today, wherever devotees of Kṛṣṇa gather.

Vernacular poetry

Diverse evidence suggests that Kṛṣṇa was worshipped in South India even before Caṅkam poets writing in the first to third centuries CE refer to him as Māyōn, the 'dark one', as his Sanskrit name also signifies. Somewhat later, the Vaikuṇṭha Perumāl Temple clearly reveals that by 770 CE royal patronage supported the worship of Kṛṣṇa and the recounting of his marvellous deeds, for this temple, constructed by a Pallava emperor in Kāñcīpuram, west of modern Chennai, includes numerous sculpted panels depicting Kṛṣṇa's līlā as described in the *Bhāgavata Purāṇa* (Hudson 1993, 1995), thereby publicly displaying Kṛṣṇa's significance as an incarnation of Viṣṇu.

That Kṛṣṇa is an avatāra of Viṣṇu is never forgotten by South Indian Vaiṣṇavas, who celebrate his divine exploits along with the heroic acts of Rāma and all Viṣṇu's other incarnations, manifestations of the Lord's grace and of his compassionate desire to relieve suffering. Kṛṣṇa as gracious avatāra is thus praised in the popular songs of the Āḻvār saints who wrote in Tamil and lived in South India between the sixth and tenth centuries CE. Periyāḻvār, Āṇṭāḷ and Nammāḻvār, for example, all sang of Kṛṣṇa and were among the earliest devotees to express their devotion in highly emotional and passionate verses, thereby inaugurating the popular bhakti movement that spread through the entire subcontinent within several centuries. Periyāḻvār often expresses maternal emotions and adores the baby Kṛṣṇa, thereby identifying with Kṛṣṇa's foster mother Yaśoda, whose example of devoted care for the child Kṛṣṇa provides the model for one of the most popular modes (or moods) of devotion in India today. The ninth-century Āṇṭāḷ, on the other hand, assumed the persona of a gopī and adored Kṛṣṇa passionately as her lover and husband. The only woman Āḷvār, Āṇṭāḷ sings of Kṛṣṇa with intense erotic emotion, longing for union with him and suffering deeply in separation. It is said that her devotion was so pure and powerful, in fact, that in the end she merged bodily with the iconic body of Viṣṇu housed in the famous temple of Śrīraṅgam near modern Tirucchirapali. Her long beautiful songs are still used in ritual settings, especially by unmarried girls longing for a husband and a happy marriage, though few women today actually worship Kṛṣṇa with such erotic passion.

Somewhat later in eastern India a long, lyrical Sanskrit poem appeared that reveres Kṛṣṇa as God yet depicts him quite differently from earlier literature. This poem is Jayadeva's twelfth-century *Gītagovinda*, subsequently influential throughout all of India. Here Kṛṣṇa is again acknowledged as the Supreme Being who takes birth in age after age in order to protect the righteous and destroy the wicked, and he is again portrayed as the supreme lover and beloved. But in relation to his favourite beloved, Rādhā, Kṛṣṇa's nature changes radically, for not only does Rādhā adore Kṛṣṇa as her lover and her lord, but Kṛṣṇa likewise adores Rādhā passionately. Indeed, theirs is a mutually passionate and intimate relationship in which the supreme Lord himself loves Rādhā deeply and longs for her intimate company. What is more, Kṛṣṇa actually suffers in Rādhā's absence, as he ashamedly regrets his infidelity among other gopīs and then begs her forgiveness. Wounded by his love and professing deep devotion, he later dresses and ornaments Rādhā, after they have made love, as Rādhā triumphs over the Lord himself due to the power of her unswerving devotion. Popular among all audiences, the *Gītagovinda* has long been incorporated into rituals at the famous Jagannātha Temple in Puri, Orissa, where Jayadeva composed the poem, and it is still dramatised in classical Indian dance, especially Odissi style.

Among the many poets who seized upon this erotic devotional aesthetic were Caṇḍīdāsa and Vidyāpati, writing in Bengali and Maithili, respectively, in roughly the late fourteenth to early fifteenth centuries. Often singing from the perspectives of Rādhā or one of her friends and hoping to experience her perfect devotion to Kṛṣṇa, these well-known poets celebrate not only the incomparable bliss and rapture attained in loving Kṛṣṇa, but also the excruciating suffering that devotees experience in loving a God who is fickle and distant. Both likewise speak of Rādhā and Kṛṣṇa being metaphysically one but physically separate in order to taste the sweet pleasures of love. This concept of sameness in difference (bhedābheda) is central for a group of devotees called the Vaiṣṇava-sahajiyās, whose theology and rituals derive from this metaphysics and thus focus on realisation of Kṛṣṇa and Rādhā as united in the devotee himself. Influenced by Tantra, the rites of the Vaiṣṇava-sahajiyās involve sexual rituals and culminate in the existential experience of Rādhā and Kṛṣṇa's eternal bliss. It is unclear how the Vaiṣṇava-sahajiyās might have been historically linked to the famous Bengali saint Caitanya, who lived his later years at the Jagannātha Temple, but Gauḍīya Vaiṣṇavas claim that Caitanya was an avatāra of Rādhā and Kṛṣṇa in a single body.

In north-western India, notable are the popular songs of two devotees, Sūrdās and Mīrābāī, both of whom might have lived in the sixteenth century. Little is known of Sūr's historical circumstances, but his poems about Kṛṣṇa the child and lover reveal both the joys and sorrows associated with Kṛṣṇa bhakti. In a plaintive mood, Sūr frequently styles himself a gopī, in love with the beautiful Kṛṣṇa but cruelly deserted by him, though in other poems he assumes the joyful persona of

Kṛṣṇa's loving foster mother. It is said that Sūr was a disciple of Vallabha, the Vaiṣṇava saint who established the popular Puṣṭi Mārga, but his songs are nonsectarian and are sung today throughout north India in various settings, including dramatic performances of Kṛṣṇa's divine exploits in Vṛndāvana. Because hagiographies claim Sūr himself was blind, the poet is especially beloved of the blind in India today, though the hagiographical claim is impossible to verify historically. The Rajasthani princess Mīrābāī likewise styled herself a gopī, and legend claims that since her childhood she sought none but Kṛṣṇa Giridhara – the Holder of Mount Govardhana – as her husband. But married against her will to a prince from a Rajput family, Mīrā encountered many obstacles as a woman in love with Kṛṣṇa. Having refused to consummate her marriage and bow down to the deity of her in-laws, Mīrā eventually joined a group of itinerant devotees and travelled to Vṛndāvana, thereby defying her strīdharma, which is why today she is considered both an extraordinary devotee and a non-exemplary woman, precisely because she failed to fulfil her duties as a devoted wife and mother (Harlan 1995). But betrothed to only Kṛṣṇa in her heart, she finally journeyed to Dvārakā, where she merged bodily with Kṛṣṇa's icon in the temple and thus attained her heart's desire.

Icons and rituals

Images of Kṛṣṇa are ubiquitous in India. In exquisite paintings, on mass-produced glossy posters and cards, and in centuries-old icons, Kṛṣṇa is seen in homes and in temples, on the streets and in the markets, in private cars and public taxis, in his many adorable forms. As a child Kṛṣṇa is often shown eating butter from a pot, while freshly churned butter drips down his face and arms. He is likewise portrayed killing various demons known from the Tenth Book of the *Bhāgavata Purāṇa*, especially the many-headed serpent Kāliya, whom Kṛṣṇa heroically banishes from the river Yamunā. Among the other famous deeds frequently depicted is his lifting of Mount Govardhana while all the cows and the entire cowherd community of Vraja, hiding underneath, take shelter from the torrential rains loosed by the angry god Indra. Common also are images of Kṛṣṇa with remarkably happy cows, and in the tribhaṅga pose with his flute named Muralī, the instrument with which he summons the gopīs in the night. Famous, too, are images of Kṛṣṇa performing the circle dance with the gopīs after multiplying himself in order to dance with each impassioned woman individually. Perhaps most popular, however, are the images of Kṛṣṇa and his favourite gopī, Rādhā, shown together in the moonlit forest, sometimes taking shelter during the monsoon rains, sometimes playfully wearing each other's clothes or clothing each other with lotus petals. Often Kṛṣṇa is portrayed in submission to Rādhā, bowing at her feet or decorating her long beautiful tresses with lotus flowers. Less frequently one sees images of Kṛṣṇa and Arjuna in their majestic chariot drawn by four white horses, engaged in the frightful Mahābhārata battle.

When an icon has been properly installed in a home or in a temple, it becomes the very body of God. Kṛṣṇa is therefore fully present in such settings and thus served accordingly by devotees who perform appropriate rituals. It is said that Kṛṣṇa descends due to compassion, for his presence in various icons allows his devotees to actually see him and love him and serve him. Sometimes such service takes the form of a simple home pūjā, in which devotees offer water, flowers and various foods. Sometime daily rituals are elaborate and highly formalised, beginning when Kṛṣṇa is awakened in the morning and continuing throughout the day, with specific rituals at precise times, until Kṛṣṇa is finally put to bed, often with lullabies. Because Kṛṣṇa actually resides in the images, it is necessary that he be bathed, fed and dressed, and thereby treated as a special guest, who often wears abundant jewels and fresh flower garlands. Devotees also entertain Kṛṣṇa with songs of praise, not only in temples, but wherever they may gather to sing his glories and chant his holy names. Called kīrtaṇa or bhajana in Sanskrit, these social gatherings sometimes continue long into the night, with devotees singing and dancing to the melody of flutes and to the beat of drums and small cymbals, and perhaps a harmonium. Often they sing songs in vernacular languages, such as Bengali, Tamil, Hindi or Kannaḍa, which open the worship of Kṛṣṇa to everyone, sometimes through regional folk performances.

Kṛṣṇa's deeds are also dramatised in performances called rās līlā in Vṛndāvana, where children portray Kṛṣṇa, Rādhā and all of the characters involved in Kṛṣṇa's līlā. As in his icons, Kṛṣṇa becomes truly present in such dramas, embodied in the actors, who are thus treated as Rādhā and Kṛṣṇa and all their friends throughout the rās līlā, which continues for several weeks during the monsoons of July and August. Kṛṣṇa is also present to devotees who, through meditative identification with a specific character in mythic Vraja, enter Kṛṣṇa's cosmic play and thereby play a part in the eternal drama. Such devotees attain salvation through their emotional identification with an exemplary devotee from Vraja, who may be one of Rādhā's intimate friends serving Rādhā and Kṛṣṇa during their blissful love-play. The ultimate goal of such devotional techniques, first elaborated in the sixteenth century by Rūpa Gosvāmin, is the direct and spontaneous participation in the same, a state defined precisely as salvation by those who see constant and passionate adoration of Kṛṣṇa as the ultimate experience of ultimate reality.

Festivals and pilgrimages

Since its rediscovery in the sixteenth century and subsequent development by the Vallabha and Gauḍiya saṃpradāyas, Vṛndāvana has been a popular place of pilgrimage for devotees of Kṛṣṇa. The site of Kṛṣṇa's famous dalliance with the gopīs, this small dusty town south of Delhi becomes crowded with hundreds of thousands of pilgrims every year, especially in the weeks preceding Jaṇmāṣṭamī, Kṛṣṇa's birthday, celebrated in August or September, now not only in India but in the West as well. It is the city of Mathurā, however, Kṛṣṇa's birthplace, which remains the cosmic centre of this significant festival. The original temple no longer remains, but twenty-first-century pilgrims can still descend into a small room said to mark the very place of Kṛṣṇa's birth nearly 5,000 years ago. Like the cell in which Kṛṣṇa was born to his parents, imprisoned by Kaṃsa, the room is dark and small, but packed with pilgrims who are deeply moved upon seeing the image of Kṛṣṇa. In temples worldwide devotees likewise gather on Jaṇmāṣṭamī, often while fasting until midnight, when Kṛṣṇa is finally unveiled, beautified by countless flowers and glorious new clothes.

Pilgrims also descend by the hundreds of thousands upon the city of Puri in Orissa during the monsoon season of June and July for the annual Ratha Yātrā, the Car Festival, in which the Jagannātha form of Kṛṣṇa, along with his sister Subadrā and his brother Balabhadra, is transported through the streets in a grand chariot for all to behold. During the procession the deities are available to everyone equally, irrespective of class distinctions and conventional social boundaries, and everyone reaches for the ropes that pull the chariot, for touching the ropes bestows emancipation, it is said. The festival therefore signifies Kṛṣṇa's willingness to bless even those who are traditionally forbidden to enter the temple. So great is Jagannātha's compassion, moreover, that he likewise travels through the streets even in foreign cities such as New York, Boston and Denver, among other urban centres in the West that now have Kṛṣṇa temples, some associated with the International Society for Krishna Consciousness (ISKCON; commonly known as the Hare Krishna movement). For centuries Kṛṣṇa has demonstrated similar regard for those denied access to temples, and stories abound about his graceful interactions with even outcastes. In Udupi, Karṇātaka, for example, devotees claim that Kṛṣṇa's image in the temple turned 180 degrees in order to face his beloved devotee Kanakadāsa, who peered lovingly at Kṛṣṇa through a crack in the temple wall because his low-caste status prevented his entry. Today a small window at the rear of the temple is named for Kanakadāsa, and his devotional songs in Kannaḍa are still popular throughout Karṇātaka. This same temple and its eight surrounding monasteries are visited yearly by numerous pilgrims hoping to see Bala Kṛṣṇa with his diamond crown, an icon that was allegedly saved during the submersion of Dvārakā, then found by the thirteenth-century Vaiṣṇava saint Madhva, who subsequently installed it in the temple. Devotees also claim that the temple deity in Guruvayur, Kerala, another major pilgrimage site, was saved when Dvārakā was submerged after Kṛṣṇa abandoned his earthly form and returned to the heavenly Vaikuṇṭha. Dvārakā itself, on the coast of Gujarat, also attracts countless pilgrims, as does Vraja, where devotees make a long and arduous journey through the forests every year, visiting various sites where Lord Kṛṣṇa once played with all his friends and lover and thereby made the entire space sacred.

See also: **Āḷvār; Āṇṭāḷ; Arjuna; Avatāra; Bhagavadgītā; Bhajan; Bhakti; Bhedābheda; Brahman; Caitanya; Caste; Dance; Devakī; Dharma; Dvārakā; Gaudiya Vaishnava Mission; Gītagovinda; Gopī(s); Govardhana; Harivaṃśa; Image worship; Images and iconography; Indra; International Society for Krishna Consciousness; Jagannātha; Jaṇmāṣṭamī; Jayadeva; Jñāna; Kaṃsa; Karma; Kaurava; Kīrtaṇ(a); Kurukṣetra; Līlā; Madhva; Mahābhārata; Mathurā; Māyā; Mīrābāī; Mokṣa; Nammāḻvār; Paṇḍavas; Pāṇini; Patañjali; Pūjā; Purāṇas; Puṣṭi Mārga; Rādhā; Rāma; Ratha Yātrā; Saṃpradāya; Saṃsāra; Sanskrit; Strīdharma; Subhadrā; Tantrism; Upaniṣads; Vaiṣṇavism; Vallabha; Varṇa; Viṣṇu; Vṛndāvana; Yamunā (River); Yaśodā; Yuga**

TRACY COLEMAN

Further reading

Primary Sources in Translation

Bhattacharya, Deben. 1963. *Love Songs of Vidyāpati*, ed. W.G. Archer. London: George Allem & Unwin Ltd.

Bryant, Edwin F. (trans.). 2003. *Krishna: The Beautiful Legend of God. Śrimad Bhāgavata Purāṇa. Book X*. London: Penguin Books.

Dehejia, Vidya. 1990. *Āṇṭaḷ and Her Path of Love: Poems of a Woman Saint from South India*. Albany, NY: SUNY Press.

Dimmock, Edward, C. and Denise Levertov. 1967. *In Praise of Krishna: Songs from the Bengali*. Garden City, NY: Doubleday.

Miller, Barbara Stoler. 1977. *Love Song of the Dark Lord, Jayadeva's Gitagovinda*. New York: Columbia University Press.

Miller, Barbara Stoler. 1986. *The Bhagavad-Gita, Krishna's Counsel in Time of War*. New York: Bantam Books.

Narasimhan, Chakravarthi V. 1998. *The Mahābhārata, An English Version Based on Selected Verses*. New York: Columbia University Press.

Ramanujan, A.K. 1981 *Hymns for the Drowning: Poems for Viṣṇu by Nammāḻvār*. Princeton: Princeton University Press.

Tagare, Ganesh Vasudeo. 1976–78. *Bhāgavata Purāṇa*. Ancient Indian Tradition and Mythology Series, vols. 7–11, ed. J.L. Shastri. Delhi: Motilal Barnarsidass.

van Buitenen, J.A.B. 1974–78. *The Mahābhārata*, 3 vols. Chicago, IL: University of Chicago Press.

Wilson, H.H. 1980 [1840]. *The Viṣṇu Purāṇa: A System of Hindu Mythology and Tradition.* Reprint, Delhi: Nag Publishers.

References

Archer, William G. 1957. *The Loves of Krishna in Indian Painting and Poetry.* London: George Allen & Unwin Ltd.

Brockington, John. 1998. *The Sanskrit Epics.* Leiden: Brill.

Case, Margaret H. 2000. *Seeing Krishna: The Relgious World of a Brahman Family in Vrindaban.* Oxford: Oxford University Press.

Dimock, Edward C. 1989. *The Place of the Hidden Moon: Erotic Mysticism in the Vaiṣṇava-sahajiyā Cult of Bengal*, 2nd edn. Chicago, IL: University of Chicago Press.

Entwistle, A.W. 1987. *Braj: Centre of Krishna Pilgrimage.* Gronigen Oriental Studies, 3. Groningen: Egbert Forsten.

Goswami, Shrivatsa. 2001. *Celebrating Krishna.* Vrindavan: Sri Caitanya Prema Samsthana.

Haberman, David. 1988. *Acting as a Way of Salvation: A Study of Rāgānugā Bhakti Sādhana.* New York: Oxford University Press.

Hardy, Friedhelm. 1983. *Viraha-Bhakti: The Early History of Kṛṣṇa Devotion in South India.* Delhi: Oxford University Press.

Harlan, Lindsey. 1995. 'Abondoning Shame: Mīrā and the Margins of Marriage'. In Lindsey Harlan and Paul B. Courtright, eds, *From the Margins of Hindu Marriage: Essays on Gender, Religion and Culture.* New York: Oxford University Press, 204–27.

Hawley, John Stratton. 1981. *At Play with Krishna: Pilgrimage Dramas from Brindavan.* Princeton, NJ: Princeton University Press.

Hein, Norvin. 1972. *The Miracle Plays of Mathurā.* New Haven, CT: Yale University Press.

Hein, Norvin. 1986. 'A Revolution in Kṛṣṇaism: The Cult of Gopāla'. *History of Religions* 25.4: 296–317.

Hiltebeitel, Alf. 1990. *The Ritual of Battle: Krishna in the Mahābhārata.* Albany, NY: SUNY Press.

Hudson, Dennis. 1993. 'Vāsudeva Kṛṣṇa in Theology and Architecture: A Background to Śrīvaiṣṇavism'. *Journal of Vaiṣṇava Studies* 2.1: 139–70.

Hudson, Dennis. 1995. 'The *Śrimad Bhāgavata Purāṇa* in Stone: The Text as an Eighth-century Temple and Its Implications'. *Journal of Vaiṣṇava Studies* 3.3: 137–82.

Matchett, Freda. 2001. *Krishna, Lord and Avatāra: The Relationship between Krishna and Vishnu.* Richmond: Curzon Press.

Rosen, Steven, J. (ed.). 1996. *Vaiṣṇavī: Women and the Worship of Krishna.* Delhi: Motilal Banarsidass.

Vaudeville, Charlotte. 1996. *Myth, Saints and Legend in Medieval India.* Compiled by Vasudha Dalmia. Delhi: Oxford University Press.

KṚṢṆAJAYANTI

See: **Janmāṣṭamī**

KṢATRIYA

See: **Varṇa**

KṢETRA

The term 'kṣetra' means 'field' and has been used to refer to the body or matter. Combined with 'jña' (the 'knower'), the term 'kṣetrajña' ('field-knower') signifies the soul or self.

In the *Chāndogya Upaniṣad* 8.3.2, the term 'aksetrajña' ('one who does not know the field') is used to mean one who does not know the locality or area of the country one is in. Such a person might pass over hidden treasure but not find it, just as all creatures go on day by day without finding the truth, the world of Brahman, within them. In the *Mahābhārata*, 'kṣetra' is applied ordinarily to refer to a field of endeavour or subject, so 'kṣetrajña' is an expert, one who knows one's subject.

In the *Bhagavadgītā* 13.1, Kṛṣṇa defines 'kṣetra' as 'body', śarīra (and in 13.5–6 describes it in Sāṃkhya terms as prakṛti together with its modifications). For Śaṅkara fruits of action are reaped in it just as fruits are reaped in a field.

See also: **Bhagavadgītā; Brahman; Kṛṣṇa; Kṣetrajña; Mahābhārata; Prakṛti; Sāṃkhya; Śaṅkara; Śarīra; Upaniṣads**

MARTIN OVENS

Further reading

Minor, R.N. 1982. *Bhagavadgītā: An Exegetical Commentary*. New Delhi: Heritage Publishers.

KṢETRAJÑA

The term 'kṣetrajña' means 'field-knower' or 'knower of the body'. It has been used to refer to the individual self, soul or spirit and is associated with the development of Sāṃkhya.

'Kṣetrajña' occurs in the *Upaniṣads*, the *Mokṣadharma* portion of the *Mahābhārata*, Aśvaghosa's *Buddhacarita* (Acts of the Buddha) (first to second century CE) and the *Carakasaṃhitā* (Caraka's Compendium) (first century CE). It is a synonym for 'puruṣa' in classical Sāṃkhya.

The *Katha*, *Maitrī* and *Śvetāśvatara Upaniṣads* contain Sāṃkhya-Yoga terminology and concepts. In the theistic *Śvetāśvatara*, God is the ruler of primordial nature and the field-knower (pradhāna-kṣetrajña-pati). 'Kṣetrajña' also appears in the context of the monism of the *Maitrī*.

The *Bhagavadgītā* takes up the terminology of 'field' and 'field-knower' in Chapter 13. This chapter is known as the 'yoga of the distinction of field and field-knower' (kṣetra-kṣetrajña-vibhāga-yoga). Kṛṣṇa introduces the 'field-knower in all fields' as Himself. God is above the field and field-knower. Thus, as Rāmānuja says, God knows all 'fields' and all 'knowers of the field'.

See also: **Bhagavadgītā; Mahābhārata; Puruṣa; Rāmānuja; Sāṃkhya; Sāṃkhya-Yoga; Upaniṣads**

MARTIN OVENS

Further reading

Larson, G.J. 1998. *Classical Sāṃkhya: An Interpretation of its History and Meaning.* Delhi: Motilal Banarsidass.

KṢETRAPĀLA, KṢETRASYA PATI AND KṢETRASYA PATNĪ

The landscape of village India is dotted with kṣetrapālas ('field guardians'), kṣetrasya patis ('lords of the fields') and kṣetrasya patnis ('mistresses of the field'), whose role is to protect the village, land, crops and livestock from demonic entities. In these settings, these divinities are generally represented as naturally occurring stones, perhaps sprinkled or smeared with vermilion powder or paste. Since the medieval period, this role has been reified into a figure named Kṣetrapāla which, according to the *Agni Purāṇa*, is sculpted onto the south-east corner of temples. Kṣetrapāla's iconography, as seen on the circa tenth-century Khajuraho temples, is similar to that of Bhairava or other fierce forms of Śiva. Kṣetrapāla is also found on the north-west or north-east corners of certain Tantric yantras, and both Kṣemarāja's eleventh-century commentary to the *Netra Tantra* and the thirteenth-century *Śrimatottara Tantra* prescribe the making of blood sacrifice (bali-dāna) to the multiple kṣetrapālas.

See also: **Blood sacrifice; Purāṇas; Śiva; Yantra**

DAVID GORDON WHITE

Further reading

T. A. Gopinath Rao. 1999. *Elements of Hindu Iconography*, 2 vols. Madras: Law Road Printing House, 1914–16; New Delhi: DK Publishers, vol. 2, part 2.

W. Crooke. 1968. *The Popular Religion and Folk-Lore of Northern India*, 2 vols. London: A. Constable and Co., 1896; Delhi: Munshiram Manoharlal, vol. 1.

KUBERA

Also known as Vairāvaṇa, Dhanapati and Dhanada.

The god of riches, Kubera (Kuvera) has little in the way of Hindu mythology. He is first found in the *Yajurveda* (8.10.28) as an aboriginal earth-spirit. In the *Mahābhārata*, he appears as Gaviputra Vaiśrāvana – a mental son of Pulastya, himself a mind-born son of Brahmā. Deserting his father, Kubera went to Brahmā, who rewarded him with immortality and made him the lord of wealth, gold and jewels. Lanka became his capital, and he received the aerial chariot Puṣpaka. Both capital and chariot were seized by the Rākṣasa Rāvaṇa until the latter was killed by Rāma. In the *Rāmāyaṇa*, Kubera appears as Pulastya's grandson. After 1,000 years of austerities, Brahmā makes him the god of riches and Lokapāla or guardian of the north. Kubera is also considered the king of Yākṣasas, perpetually hungry demonic beings. Iconographic representations of the pot-bellied Kubera frequently depict him astride a mongoose which is vomiting jewels. Otherwise, his mount is an elephant, and his attributes include a club, moneybag, pomegranate and water-vessel.

See also: **Brahmā; Mahābhārata; Rāma; Rāmāyaṇa; Rāvaṇa**

MICHAEL YORK

KUBJIKĀ

Kubjikā, the 'Female Hunchback', is a Tantric goddess whose cult likely originated in the Koṅkana region of present-day coastal Maharashtra and Goa in the tenth century CE. An extensive corpus of Tantric literature – often referred to as the *paścimāmnāya* (the 'western transmission' or 'latter transmission'), mostly dating from the eleventh to fourteenth centuries, is devoted to the worship of this goddess. Nearly every one of the thousands of manuscripts of the principal Kubjikā scriptures (the *Kubjikāmata, Manthānabhairava Tantra* and *Saṭsāhasra Tantra*) and ancillary texts were written in Nepal, and it is in the Kathmandu Valley that the cult of this goddess continues to thrive, as a form of esoteric Śaktism specific to the Newar community there. While much of Kubjikā's imagery is of a piece with that of the 'archetypal' Tantric goddess Kālī, one element of her mythology appears to be unique: it is by licking her own vulva (whence her hunchbacked form) that she generates the universe.

See also: **Kālī and Caṇḍī; Śakti; Tantras**

DAVID GORDON WHITE

Further reading

Dyczkowski, M. 2001. *The Cult of the Goddess Kubjikā: A Preliminary Comparative Textual and Anthropological Survey of a Secret Newar Goddess.* Stuttgart: Steiner Verlag.

KULA

Kula is a Sanskrit term designating a large, interconnected group of kinfolk residing in a common territorial space. The kula was of particular importance for ancient and medieval India because its customs were given the status of laws governing its members. So vital was the preservation of these customs to the maintenance of social stability that the *Bhagavadgītā* (1.40–1) linked the collapse of society to the initial destruction of mores of the kula. Thus, the kula was an autonomous unit whose functioning was not to be impeded by the king or his authorities. Owing to the kula's status as a legal body, the term kula came to denote a manner of family/village tribunal. These tribunals were the courts of first resort. If litigants were from the same familial grouping, the tribunal would be comprised of representatives from a single family; if they were from different families, the tribunal would consist of representatives from both families. In either case, the decision of the kula was to be regarded as law, although the right of appeal to higher authorities was preserved in most cases.

See also: **Bhagavadgītā**

ETHAN KROLL

Further reading

Kane, Pandurang Vaman. 1973. *History of Dharmasastra*, vols 2 and 3. Poona: Bhandarkar Oriental Research Institute.

Mookerji, Radhakumud. 1919. *Local Government In Ancient India*. Oxford: Clarendon Press.

Thaplyal, Kiran Kumar. 1996. *Guilds in Ancient India*. New Delhi: New Age International Limited.

KULADEVATĀ

Every Hindu traditionally worships a kuladevatā ('tutelary clan deity') in addition to his or her grāmadevatās ('local, village deities') and iṣṭadevatā ('chosen deity'). Unlike the chosen deity, one's kuladevatā is determined by the extended family or clan into which one is born, the kuladevatā (or the female kuladevī) generally being a deified ancestor. Like grāmadevatās, kuladevatās will often be worshipped in the form of a simple unhewn stone, located at a specific site associated with the ancestral home of the families who worship it. Strictly speaking, kuladevatās cannot be moved from their ancestral homes, for which reason persons who change residence will often make an annual 'pilgrimage' back to the place of their kuladevatā. However, rituals do exist for the transfer of the kuladevatā from its original worship support to a portable vessel (often a clay pot), to ensure a continuity of worship. While kuladevatās are often worshipped daily in the home, their most important worship ceremonies take place annually or on the occasion of specific life-cycle rites (saṃskāras) at their original ancestral shrines.

See also: **Grāmadevatās; Iṣṭadevatā; Saṃskāra; Tīrthayātrā (Pilgrimage)**

DAVID GORDON WHITE

KUMĀRA

See: **Skanda**

KUMĀRĪ JĀTRĀ

The Kumārī Jātrā of Kathmandu, Nepal, consists of three gruelling urban chariot processions, conveying the three 'living divinities' – Gaṇeśa, Bhairav and Kumārī – through the three major divisions of the city. While in other Nepalese cities Kumārī makes her primary appearance during Dasain/Durgā Pūjā, her Kathmandu jātrā represents the most dramatic days of the Indra Jātrā festival, celebrated one month earlier. Each procession is accompanied by an assortment of traditional masked dances telling of the goddess' ultimate power to defeat cosmic evil and modern military displays reminding the crowd of the associated power of the king and his army. On the festival's final day she fulfils her role as the source of the king's royal power, giving her blessing to the reigning king in the form of a red tika, a blessing she will subsequently bestow on the general public, thus bringing to a close the festival that jointly celebrates both her and Indra.

See also: **Durgā Pūjā; Gaṇeśa; Indra Jātrā; Rāja; Utsava**

MICHAEL BALTUTIS

Further reading

Allen, Michael R. 1975. *The Cult of Kumari: Virgin Worship in Nepal.* Kathmandu: INAS, Tribhuvan University.

KUMBHA MELĀ

The Kumbha Melā, probably the largest religious gathering in the world, attracting up to 15 million pilgrims, revolves between Allahabad, Ujjain, Haridvāra and Nāsik on a twelve-year cycle. Haridvāra is also the location of a special Kumbha Melā, known as the Ardh Kumbha, which takes place additionally halfway through the twelve-year cycle. It was estimated that 50 million people attended in 2001.

Khumbha means a 'pot' or 'vessel' for containing water and the name originates in the legends associated with the Melā, which go back to the creation myth where the devas (deities) and asuras churn the cosmic ocean of milk, bringing up various precious objects. One of these was a pot containing amṛta, the nectar of immortality, and it was claimed by the asuras, but Viṣṇu stole it from them as it was regarded as too precious to be given over to demons. Whilst flying away with the amṛta to take it to the abode of the gods, he spilled four drops in the cities that became the sites of the Kumbha Melā. However, the festival always takes place when the sun stands in the astrological house of Aquarius, also known as Khumbha.

The festival is renowned not only for the mass bathing that takes place in the various sacred rivers that pass through each location but also for the gatherings of sādhus that congregate there. One of the famous features of the festival is the procession of all the major saṃpradāyas (religious orders) of Hinduism. It is also used as an opportunity to meet in council and make new decisions concerning changes in their rules or discuss controversial issues that may have arisen. In the nineteenth century, conflicts would sometimes break out over rank, but today thousands of male and female renunciates join the procession, in which an assigned place has been allotted according to precedence.

See also: **Asuras; Deities; Haridvāra; Jyotiṣa; Nāsik; Sādhu; Saṃpradāya; Utsava; Viṣṇu**

RON GEAVES

Further reading

Jackson, R. 1986. 'Hindu Festivals'. In *Festivals in World Religions*, Alan Brown, ed. on behalf of SHAP Working Party. London: Longman, 104–39.

KUMBHAMĀTĀ

Kumbhamātā is the goddess of pots. In local festivals and worship a brass or clay pot often represents the goddess. During many local goddess festivals, the goddess is invoked into a pot, which then becomes the repository for her power and represents her throughout the festival proceedings. The pot is also a symbol of fertility. Auspicious pots as symbols figure prominently at Hindu marriages.

See also: **Pūjā; Utsava; Vivāha**

LYNN FOULSTON

Further reading

Stutley, M. and J. Stutley. 1977. *A Dictionary of Hinduism: Its Mythology, Folklore and Development 1500 BC–AD 1500*. London and Henley: Routledge & Kegan Paul.

KUṆḌALINĪ YOGA

Tantric practices to effect the awakening of the female divine Energy (Śakti), who, as Kuṇḍalinī ('She who is coiled [upon herself]'), rests dormant or latent in the base of the human body and, then, the process of mastering her upward movement in the body through 'centres of energy' (cakra) until, beyond the top of the head, a last cakra is reached where a merging occurs of the individual and the supreme Consciousness.

The exercises, associated with older techniques of Haṭha Yoga, presuppose a complex system of theology, cosmology and subtle physiology variously articulated in different schools.

First is the immutable supreme Consciousness, the ultimate reality which, in a tantric context, is usually identified as Śiva. However, it is his consort, his Energy, Śakti, who accounts for the existence of this relative, dynamic and transient universe, the world of multiplicity and change, and, as she unfolds its manifestation through elements of decreasing subtlety, she undergoes a process of gradual forgetfulness of the primal consciousness of which she is an emanation until she comes to rest in materiality, the cosmic element Earth. Then, at the end of a cosmic cycle, Śakti reascends through the subtle elements until she is reabsorbed back into Śiva. After a rest, the period of procession and dissolution recommences in an eternal rhythm of expansion and contraction.

Since the human individual, as microcosm, is a replica of the whole cosmos, Śakti, the sustaining force of all creation, comes to reside in the element Earth, in the base (mūla) of each individual's spine. The spine itself represents the *axis mundi* in the same way as Mount Meru is the pivot of the cosmos and the vertical link between earth and heaven. However, the human body (śarīra) in question is not just the gross (sthūla) material body but also the invisible body of subtle (suksma) matter that supports it. That body is irrigated by an incalculable number of rivers (nāḍī) or channels of vital energies (prāna), of which Kuṇḍalinī is the fount. Along the spine run two central channels, Piṅgalā to the right and Idā to the left, with contrasting functions which correspond to the dyadic opposites (dvandva) with which we construct our world: high/low, bright/dark, etc. The moon presides over Idā and the sun over Piṅgalā. These two nāḍī are intertwined around another, central one, the Suṣumnā, which alone connects the base of the axis with its summit but remains ordinarily empty. The task of the yogin is, with attending his visualisations and sounding of mantras and through his mastery over the movement of the energies (prāṇāyāma) to collect them and concentrate their collected, sharpened might on the point where the Kuṇḍalinī blocks the entrance to Suṣumnā, awaken her and release her to shoot up the central channel, where, having pierced through a number of energy-centres ('wheels': cakra), she emerges, like a diver to the surface, into the light of immortal Consciousness in the 'thousand-petalled lotus' (sahasrāra padma).

Each cakra corresponds to a cosmic element, has its own 'seed-mantra', is visualised as a lotus and a coloured diagram. Each also has its own presiding deity and corresponds to a level of cosmic manifestation, up to the highest heaven. The ascending sequence is as follows:

1 The base cakra is mūlādhāra ('base support'), by the anus, associated with the cosmic element Earth, represented by a yellow square and a four-petalled lotus; its seed-mantra (bīja) is LAM.
2 Above, near the genitals, is svādhisthāna ('self-founding'), corresponding to Water, symbolised by a white crescent and a six-petalled lotus. Its bīja is VAM.
3 Manipūraka ('fulfilling jewel') is level with the navel, associated with Fire, viewed as a red inverted triangle and a ten-petalled lotus. Its bīja is RAM.
4 The anāhata ('unstruck sound') or heart cakra correlates to Air and is YAM.
5 The viśuddhi ('purification') or throat cakra corresponds to Ether, the subtlest of elements, is a golden white or bluish circle, a lotus with sixteen petals and its syllable is HAM.
6 Above the level of the eyebrows is the ajñā ('authority'), a cakra which transcends all cosmic elements and is the place of dissolution of the mental principle (manas) into the principle of individuation (ahamkāra) and the principle of intelligence (buddhi/mahat). Ajñā illuminates all lower cakra and shows, like a lamp, the way to the brahmarandra ('hole of the brahman'), where the Energy will leave the skull. Called mahant ('majesty'), represented by an inverted moon-bright triangle and a two-petalled lotus, its mantra is Oṃ, the holiest of

utterances. Ajñā is a watershed, the acme of cosmic manifestation.

7 The ultimate cakra is sahasrāra ('thousand rays'), beyond all categories, formless though represented by a thousand-petalled lotus; it is also beyond the reach of mantras, being their silent source. Situated twelve digits above the apex of the head, it is the place of the union between Śiva and Śakti, eternal salvation.

Apart from the extensive literature on Haṭha Yoga, including that of the Nāthayogin, the most influential and detailed account of Kuṇḍalinī Yoga is found in the *Satcakranirūpana* (Mirror of the Seven Cakra), which forms the sixth chapter of Pūrnānanda's *Śritattvacintāmani* (sixteenth century), on which there is a commentary by Kālīcarana. The SCN has been very loosely translated by Arthur Avalon in his *The Serpent Power* (London, 1918).

See also: **Ahaṃkara; Gorakhnāth; Haṭha Yoga; Mahat; Manas; Mantra; Meru, Mount; Nāth(a) Yoga; Oṃ; Śakti; Śiva; Tantrism**

DANIEL MARIAU

Further reading

Silburn, Lilian. 1983. *La Kundalinī ou l'énergie des profondeurs*. Paris: Les Deux Océans.

KUNTĪ

Also known as Pṛthā, Kuntī was given by her father, Śūra, a Yādava king, to his childless cousin Kuntibhoja. Through the use of a secret mantra given to her by the ṛṣi Durvāsas, she was able to give birth by invoking Sūrya, the sun-god. The child was born secretly to avoid scandal and adopted by the charioteer Adiratha, who named him Vasusena, later to be called Karṇa, who figures in the *Mahābhārata* as the lifelong rival of Arjuna. Later Kuntī married Pāṇḍu and produced three sons, Yudhiṣṭhira, Bhīma and Arjuna. It was only at the culmination of hostilities between the Pāṇdavas and Kauravas, and the death of Karṇa at the hands of Arjuna, that Kuntī announced the former was her son. After the war, Kuntī accompanied the blind king, Dhṛtarāṣṭra and his wife Gāndhārī to the hermitage in the forest and was killed along with them in a forest fire.

See also: **Arjuna; Bhīma; Dhṛtarāṣṭra; Gāndhārī; Karṇa; Kauravas; Mahābhārata; Mantra; Pāṇdavas; Pāṇḍu; Ṛṣi; Sūrya; Yudhiṣṭhira**

RON GEAVES

Further reading

Dasgupta, Madhusraba. 1999. *Samsad Companion to the Mahābhārata*. Calcutta: Sahitya Samsad.

KUPPUSWAMI SASTRI, S. (1880–1943)

Indian Sanskritist and philosopher. Kuppuswami Sastri was born in the district of Tanjore, in Tamil Nadu, and received a traditional education in Sanskrit (covering Vedānta, Nyāya and Pūrva Mīmāṃsa as well as Vyākaraṇa) while also attending an English-medium school. He studied law at the Universities of Madras and Trivandrum, but before qualifying as a lawyer was appointed Principal of the Sanskrit College at Mylapore. He was later Principal of Tiruvayyāru Sanskrit College and finally Professor of Sanskrit at Presidency College, Madras, until his retirement in 1935. He was also curator of the Madras Government Oriental Manuscripts Library, and published in many volumes descriptive catalogues of its collections. He published also a primer of Indian logic, based on the Nyāya synthesis of Annambhaṭṭa (*c.*1650), and an edition of the *Dhvanyā-*

loka with Abhinavagupta's commentary and his own, as well as editions of several other texts in the *Journal of Oriental Research* and the *Madras Oriental Series*, both of which he founded and edited. The Kuppuswami Sastri Research Institute in Chennai (Madras) is named after him.

See also: **Abhinavagupta; Hinduism, history of scholarship; Nyāya; Pūrva Mīmāṃsa; Vedānta; Vyākaraṇa.**

WILL SWEETMAN

Further reading

Janaki, S.S. 1981–85. *Professor Kuppuswami Sastri Birth-centenary Commemoration Volume*, 2 vols. Madras: Kuppuswami Sastri Research Institute.

Kuppuswami Sastri, S. 1932a. *A Primer of Indian Logic According to Annambhaṭṭa's Tarkasaṃgraha*. Madras: Varadachary.

Kuppuswami Sastri, S. 1932b. *Dhvanyālokaḥśrīmadanandavardhanakṛtaḥ*. Madras: Balasubrahmanya Aiyar.

KŪRMA

See: **Avatāra**

KŪRMA PURĀṆA

See: **Purāṇas**

KURUKṢETRA

Literally meaning 'the field of the Kurus', Kurukṣetra is best known in the *Mahābhārata* as the battlefield where the Kauravas and Pāṇḍavas fight their eighteen-day war. Kurukṣetra is mentioned in the first line of the *Bhāgavadgītā*, where it is described as a dharmic field, implying a moral outcome for the Bharata war. First mentioned in the Brāhmaṇas, as the place where the gods perform their sacrifices, it came to refer more generally to the territory of Kuru-Pañcāla. It was named after King Kuru, who had ploughed the field for many years in an attempt to seek a boon from Indra, who eventually rewarded the king's efforts by proclaiming that kṣatriyas who died in battle there would go straight to heaven. Also, throughout the *Mahābhārata* and subsequent literature, Kurukṣetra is described as one of the foremost pilgrimage sites. Kurukṣetra is in modern-day Haryana, about 85 miles northeast of Delhi.

See also: **Bhāgavadgītā; Brāhmaṇas; Indra; Kauravas; Mahābhārata; Pāṇḍavas; Tīrthayātrā (Pilgrimage); Varṇa.**

BRIAN BLACK

Further reading

van Buitenen, J.A.B. 1973. *The Mahābhārata, 1. The Book of the Beginning*. Chicago, IL: Chicago University Press.

van Buitenen, J.A.B. 1975. *The Mahābhārata, 2. The Book of the Assembly Hall, 3. The Book of the Forest*. Chicago, IL: Chicago University Press.

van Buitenen, J.A.B. 1978. *The Mahābhārata, 4. The Book of Virāṭa, 5. The Book of the Effort*. Chicago, IL: Chicago University Press.

Fitzgerald, James L. 2004. *The Mahābhārata, 11. The Book of Women, 12. The Book of Peace: Part One*. Chicago, IL: Chicago University Press.

KUVALAYANANDA, SWAMI (1883–1966) AND KAIVALYADHAMA

Born in Dabhoi in Gujarat. An important figure in the modern 'renaissance' of yoga, Kuvalayananda first learnt combat techniques and gymnastics from the nationalist physical culturist Rajaratna Manik Rao of Baroda. He then studied yoga with Paramahansa Shri Madhvadasji (1789–1921) and with this guru's blessings established his teaching and research institute, Kaivalyadhama, in Lonavla (near Mumbai) in 1921. For Kuvalayananda, yoga could best be propagated by coordinating it with modern sciences and making it applicable to everyday life. The techniques of yoga, he felt, should be empirically tested to prove their efficacy as healing methods. Using the paraphernalia of modern science, he and his group of researchers set about measuring the physiological effects of āsana (posture), prāṇāyāma (breath control), kriya (physical purification) and bandha (internal body 'locks'), and used their findings to develop therapeutic approaches to disease. The institute still exists and continues to treat large numbers of patients through yoga. Swami Kuvalayananda died in 1966.

Kuvalayananda's work was extremely influential in creating the modern-day conception of yoga as a healing science. Many of the most renowned yoga teachers of the time, such as Sivananda and Krishnamacharya, visited Kaivalyadhama to learn about Kuvalayananda's work. In 1937 Yale University sent K.T. Behanan to undertake a scientific evaluation of yoga under Kuvalayananda's guidance. Kaivalyadhama's literary output was, and remains, prodigious. Of particular note are the review *Yoga Mimāṃsa* – at once cutting-edge scientific journal and practical illustrated instruction manual – which began to appear in 1924; and the 'Popular Yoga' book series, including *Āsana* of 1931 and *Prāṇāyāma* of 1932.

See also: **Guru; Shivananda, Swami; Yoga; Yoga, modern**

MARK SINGLETON

Further reading

Alter, J. 2004. *Yoga in Modern India, Between Science and Philosophy.* Princeton, NJ: Princeton University Press.

L

LAJPAT RAI, LALA (1865–1928)

Lajpat Rai was one of the key figures of the early Indian nationalist movement. He became a member of the Arya Samaj while studying in Lahore in the early 1880s and soon emerged as a leader of the organisation's moderate faction. In addition to his commitment to social and religious reform he also became active politically from the early 1890s after joining the Indian National Congress. He developed leanings towards the 'extremists' in the freedom movement, opting for boycott of imported goods and open resistance to British rule. His staunch anti-colonial stance was responsible for his being imprisoned and transported to Burma by the colonial government in 1907–08. From 1914–20 he was in exile in the USA to escape renewed arrest by the British.

Remaining rooted in the cultural revivalism of the Arya Samaj, his political creed oscillated between a broader pluralist vision of the Indian nation and a more narrowly defined Hindu nationalism. His engagement in the Hindu Mahasabha in the 1920s brought him closer to the latter position in the final years of his life. Lajpat Rai died in November 1928.

See also: **Arya Samaj; Hindu Mahasabha; Nationalism**

HARALD FISCHER-TINÉ

Further reading

Nanda, B.R. (ed.). 2003–04. *The Collected Works of Lala Lajpat Rai*, 3 vols. New Delhi: Manohar.

LAKṢMAṆA

In the *Rāmāyaṇa* Lakṣmaṇa is the full brother of Śatrughna (both sons of Sumitra) and attaches himself to his oldest brother Rāma as his loyal companion and servant. He is regularly the foil to Rāma's character, excitable where Rāma is calm (and vice versa), suspicious where Rāma is trusting, and generally there to voice emotions and views that it would not be appropriate for Rāma himself to express.

When the Śūrpaṇakhā propositions the brothers and then attacks Sītā, Lakṣmaṇa punishes her with mutilation. When he refuses to leave Śītā after Rāma has left to pursue the golden deer, she denounces his motives and he reluctantly goes after Rāma, only to be blamed by him for deserting her. He plays a leading role in the battle against Rāvaṇa and kills Indrajit, Rāvaṇa's son and foremost warrior. Just before Rāma's own death, Lakṣmaṇa immolates himself in the river Sarayū.

See also: **Rākṣasas; Rāma; Rāmāyaṇa; Rāvaṇa; Śatrughna; Śītā**

JOHN BROCKINGTON

Further reading

Goldman, R.P. 1980. 'Rāmaḥ Sahalakṣmaṇaḥ: Psychological and Literary Aspects of the Composite Hero of Vālmīki's Rāmāyaṇa'. *Journal of Indian Philosophy* 8: 149–89.

LAKṢMĪ

See: **Lakṣmī, Śrī**

LAKṢMĪ PŪJĀ

Śrī Lakṣmī is worshipped throughout the year, particularly in shops and by businessmen but also has her own festival, Lakṣmī Pūjā. In Northern India, in particular, Lakṣmī is worshipped on the full moon after Durgā Pūjā or Daśahrā. Many people worship Lakṣmī at home, using small images purchased from a stall or in the form of an earthen lid or plate painted with an image of Lakṣmī seated on a lotus attended by two females and her owl vehicle. The image of Lakṣmī is installed in the house and rice flour patterns of her feet are drawn on the floor. Alakṣmī (ill fortune) is driven out of the back door at night in the hope Lakṣmī will enter through the front. Bengali families traditionally recite the legend of Kojagarī Lakṣmī, in which a king has his adherence to righteousness (dharma) tested by the goddess Lakṣmī. The goddess is worshipped with lights, incense, flowers and songs during the night.

As well as worship of Lakṣmī in the home, many beautifully decorated clay statues of Lakṣmī are created for community worship, especially in Bengal and Orissa. The Lakṣmī images are generally two-armed, sometimes with a cornucopia in her left hand while her right is held in a boon-granting gesture with the palm facing towards the devotee and the fingers pointing downwards. She is usually pink or golden coloured, wearing a red sari and decorated with tinsel or pith. In Bhubaneswar, the capital of Orissa, the most predominant form of Lakṣmī at the 2002 pūjā was of Gaja Lakṣmī. This image represents Lakṣmī's associations with fertility, as two elephants on either side of her pour water on her with their trunks. The showers of water, according to David Kinsley, represent fertilising rains (Kinsley 1987: 22). The priests bring the images to life in the morning by performing the eye-opening ceremony (in which the eyes are repainted) and, using mantras, they ask the goddess to occupy the image. After one day, Lakṣmī Pūjā is over and the numerous images of the goddess of prosperity are immersed in the waters of a nearby river or pond.

See also: **Alakṣmī; Daśahrā; Dharma; Durgā Pūjā; Lakṣmī, Śrī; Mantra; Pūjā; Sacred animals; Utsava**

LYNN FOULSTON

Further reading

Kinsley, D.R. 1987. *Hindu Goddesses: Visions of the Divine Feminine in the Hindu Religious Tradition*. Delhi: Motilal Banarsidass.

Mohanty, B. 1998. 'Lakṣmī and Alakṣmī: The Kojagari Lakṣmī *vratkatha* of Bengal'. *Manushi* 104: 9–11.

LAKṢMĪ, ŚRĪ

The name Lakṣmī and its homonym Śrī refer to an ancient goddess who appeared in vedic literature and is still worshipped by Hindus. Both terms mean 'beauty' and 'prosperity'. The goddess has always been worshipped in her own right. A long hymn to Śrī Lakṣmī is appended to the fifth book of the *Ṛgveda*, but is a later text. She is described here as the swift-moving deity who brings wealth and prosperity. She symbolises fertility and beauty, which associates her with the lotus flower.

She is associated with agricultural prosperity. This is symbolised by her iconography as seated on a lotus and being lustrated by two elephants pouring water over her head. These elephants closely resemble rain clouds. In many parts of north and east India she is worshipped as the goddess of grains, especially of paddy; hence her annual festival in this region is observed in autumn when paddy ripens in the fields and harvesting time approaches. However, the theme of consecration also shows her as the supreme ruling power.

Śrī Lakṣmī is always associated with royal power and fortune. Lakṣmī represents the cosmic sovereign power that sustains the creation and all creatures. Many purāṇic mythologies underscore that she personifies cosmic opulence. The *Mahābhārata* describes her association with various divine royalties, Indra being predominant among them. When the demon Bali became the greatest power in the world and defeated Indra, Lakṣmī went over to the victor; but later, aided by Viṣṇu's strategic advice, Indra won her over again.

When Viṣṇu/Nārāyaṇa became the dominant cosmic God, Lakṣmī became associated with him. She left Indra because of his weak position and hid under the cosmic ocean. To regain her, both gods and demons churned the ocean. When she reappeared, she went straight to Viṣṇu and stayed with him as his divine power. Her aspect of the supreme royal power is represented by her Mahā Lakṣmī image.

As the independent deity presiding over sovereign power and well-being, she is still worshipped as Śrī in the Tantric cult of Lalitā. In this cult she is venerated by the three powerful cosmic gods, Brahmā, Viṣṇu and Śiva. The śaktis or divine powers of these three gods are Her three manifestations viz. Sarasvatī, Lakṣmī (the lesser one) and Pārvatī (respectively). The supreme Śrī Lalitā is the transcendental divinity, and although in Tantric tradition she is associated with Śiva, he is conspicuously absent from her iconography. This shows her wielding weapons, which somehow merge into the sweet weapons of the god Kāma, losing their lethal quality. She wields a sword and a noose and carries a bow and five arrows. However, the bow is only a sugar-cane bow and the arrows are made of five types of flower, heralding the approach of spring.

Lakṣmī is worshipped by Hindus more frequently than any other deity. Hindu women adore her and propitiate her for the good of their families in all aspects. She is almost omnipresent in Hindu family shrines and receives daily offerings. Although she is royal power and fortune, Lakṣmī naturally does not remain constant to a single individual for long, and as a consequence has earnt the epithet 'fickle'. For women she is the epitome of graceful beauty, loyalty to husband and loving kindness to all.

See also: **Bali; Brahamā; Indra; Kāma; Lakṣmī Pūjā; Mahābhārata; Pārvatī; Purāṇas; Sacred animals; Saṃhitā; Sarasvatī; Śiva; Tantrism; Utsava; Viṣṇu; Women's rites**

SANJUKTA GUPTA

Further reading

Kinsley, D.R. 1987. *Hindu Goddesses: Visions of the Divine Feminine in the Hindu Religious Tradition*. Delhi: Motilal Banarsidass.

LAKṢMĪ-NĀRĀYAṆA

Lakṣmī-Nārāyaṇa is a composite figure, combining the goddess Lakṣmī and the god Nārāyaṇa. Nārāyaṇa became identified with Viṣṇu at an early period and is widely adored as the cosmic sovereign deity who sustains the creation and governs it according to the sacred and universal law (ṛta). Powerful kings erected temples and pillars in veneration of Viṣṇu Nārāyaṇa. Nārāyaṇa represents the supreme divinity, the model of royal authority that is powerful, just and beneficial. Lakṣmī, being the divine embodiment of royal power and prosperity, naturally became Nārāyaṇa's essential power (śakti), hypostatised as the goddess and mythologised as Nārāyaṇa's spouse. Nārāyaṇa as the protector of all creatures incarnated himself again and again in this world. As his essential power, Lakṣmī accompanied him on these occasions and reappeared on earth in various forms. The most important and popular of these are Sītā and Rādhā. In some Tantric Vaiṣṇava cults Lakṣmī and Nārāyaṇa are regarded as a two-in-one divinity, and this idea is depicted in the symbolic figure of their combined (hermaphroditic) image, Lakṣmī-Nārāyaṇa.

See also: **Avatāra; Lakṣmī; Rādhā; Rāja; Śakti; Sītā; Tantrism; Vaiṣṇavism; Viṣṇu**

SANJUKTA GUPTA

LAKULĪŚA

Lakulīśa – also called Nakulīśa – was the founder of the important Śaivite sect known as the Pāśupatas. Although various Sanskrit texts allude to or tell stories about Lakulīśa, this information is not consistent enough, or sufficient, to construct a solid historical biography. The earliest mention appears in Kauṇḍinya's commentary on the *Pāśupata-sūtra*. Kauṇḍinya says that the Lord took the body of a Brāhmaṇa and came to earth at Kāyāvataraṇa (literally, 'the [place of] the body's descent'). He then went to the city of Ujjain, where he imparted the sūtras to a disciple named Kuśika. Texts that describe Lakulīśa's life in somewhat more detail include the *Vāyu Purāṇa*, the *Liṅga Purāṇa*, the *Kāravāṇa Māhātmya* and a few inscriptions found at temples once used by the Pāśupatas. These texts state that Brāhmaṇa in whom Śiva became incarnate was Lakulīśa. The place known as Kāyāvataraṇa is now identified with the modern village of Karvan in Gujarat, about 30 km north of the city of Baroda.

The dates of Lakulīśa are difficult to establish. The earliest clearly dated inscription to mention him seems to be one of 971 CE from the Ekliṅgjī temple near Udaipur. Literary and sculptural evidence suggests, however, that he lived at least several centuries earlier. An inscription of 380 CE, during the reign of the Gupta king Candragupta II, mentions a donation of two liṅgas to a temple in Mathurā by the Māheśvara (i.e. Śaivite) teacher Uditācārya. Uditācārya is described as the tenth in descent from Bhagavat Kuśika. If this Kuśika is the same as Lakulīśa's disciple Kuśika, Lakulīśa can be assigned to the first half of the second century CE. Unfortunately the Mathurā inscription does not specifically mention either Lakulīśa or the Pāśupatas.

Sculptural representations of Lakulīśa are found in many medieval Śaivite temples. He is usually seated and holds a club (lakula or laguṇa). Hence Lakulīśa is literally 'the Lord (īśa) who has a club'. The presence of these sculptures in these temples strongly suggests that the temples were once associated with the Pāśupatas. In the southern Karnataka region the Kālāmukhas, a sect derived from the Pāśupatas, also revered Lakulīśa. Kālāmukha inscriptions frequently mention a text known as the *Lakulīśāgama*, but this text no longer survives.

See also: **Brāhmaṇa; Mathurā; Pāśupatas; Purāṇas; Śaivism; Śiva**

DAVID LORENZEN

Further reading

Lorenzen, David N. 1991. *The Kapalikas and Kalamukhas: Two Lost Saivite Sects*, 2nd rev. edn. Delhi: Motilal Banarsidass.
Pasupata-sutra. 1940. Ed. R. Ananthakrishna Sastri. Trivandrum: University of Travancore.

LANGUAGES

There is no single language in which Hindu rituals are conducted, Hindu texts composed or Hindu teachings transmitted. For these purposes, different Indian languages may be used by different Hindus, or some other language such as English. Sanskrit, the ancient language in which the Veda and many other texts are composed and many rituals are performed, has a special place; but some Hindus explicitly reject the use of Sanskrit.

India as a linguistic area

The subcontinent of India, divided by natural barriers such as mountains and deserts, and with authority and prestige centred in different places at different times, and often at the same time, has a very diverse linguistic geography. Post-independence India alone has fifteen official languages: Assamese, Bengali, Gujarati, Hindi, Kannada, Kashmiri, Malayalam, Marathi, Oriya, Panjabi, Sanskrit, Sindhi, Tamil, Telegu and Urdu. Among these, Hindi is also the national language of India, Urdu of Pakistan, and Bengali of Bangladesh. (Urdu is similar to Hindi in its grammar, but takes much of its vocabulary from Arabic, Persian and Turkish.) Sanskrit has a unique (though not undisputed) position: unlike the other official languages it does not belong to a particular region, and its speakers are counted in thousands rather than millions. English is much used in education, law, politics and commerce. Hindi, the language of a large part of the north, has become increasingly used throughout India since its adoption as the national language.

This list of official languages gives only a faint indication of the actual linguistic diversity. Each of these languages has several dialects, and dozens of languages are excluded from the list; some of these, such as Maithili in Bihar and Konkani in Maharashtra, are similar enough to one or other of the official languages to be thought of, rightly or wrongly, as dialects of them, while others are totally unrelated. Nor does language vary only from place to place; the same town or village may have speakers of different languages living near each other but with some social distance between them, while bilingualism is common. For instance, a town in Bihar may have speakers not only of Hindi but of Maithili, Bengali, English or Santali (a 'tribal' language unrelated to Hindi), as well as people who speak two or more of these languages, using them for different purposes. Outside India, in the Himalayan countries of Nepal, Sikkim and Bhutan, Nepali is widely spoken, together with other languages (Schwartzberg 1978: 100, 234f.).

The most widely spoken languages of South Asia belong to two main language families: Indo-Aryan and Dravidian. The Indo-Aryan languages include Hindi, Bengali, Gujarati, Marathi, Nepali, Sinhala (spoken in Sri Lanka) and Sanskrit. (Romany, brought to Europe by migrants from South Asia, is also an Indo-Aryan language.) The main Dravidian languages are Tamil, Telegu, Kannada and Malayalam, all spoken in South India; there are also small areas further north where other Dravidian languages are spoken, and even an isolated Dravidian language, Brahui, in Pakistan. Languages of other families are also found in South Asia, but they are not much spoken by Hindus (except for English).

Some features are shared by South Asian languages of different language families. Like any group of languages that have been spoken in one area for centuries, they have many words in common, borrowed from each other. They also have features of syntax in common, and some phonetic features which can be noticed even without understanding a word of these languages. Most notable are the 'retroflex' sounds, similar to t, d and n but pronounced with the tip of the tongue curled back to touch the palate; these are the sounds written ṭ, ḍ and ṇ in this encyclopedia and in other books. They occur not only in South Asian languages but in some South Asian varieties of English.

The Indo-Aryan language family (Masica 1991) is part of a larger family that has been known since the nineteenth century as the Indo-European family, because it includes nearly all the languages of Europe as well as those of the greater part of India; it also includes the Iranian family, which is very closely related to Indo-Aryan. Written records of extinct Indo-European languages in Asia Minor and Central Asia show that the geographical extent of this language family is greater than the name implies. Similarities between Sanskrit and European languages, already pointed out by Coeurdoux and others, led Sir William Jones to postulate a common ancestor language (Robins 1967: 134f.). Systematic comparison has enabled historical linguists to reconstruct many features of this postulated ancestor language, now called Proto-Indo-European. However, such comparison cannot tell us where Proto-Indo-European was spoken, or when or by whom. Such questions are still debated by historical linguists and archaeologists, while in India and the Hindu diaspora many non-specialists, and some specialists, argue that the Indo-Aryan languages are indigenous to the subcontinent, not brought from outside as has been the scholarly consensus for over a century (Bryant 2001).

On such questions, much nineteenth-century thought was vitiated by unjustified assumptions. First, the history of languages was confused with the history of races, which themselves were thought of in an essentialist way which is now discredited; speakers of related languages were assumed to be related by 'blood' (i.e. genetically). The word ārya, by which the composers of the Vedic hymns referred to their own people (and which later referred to the three upper varṇas), was used by nineteenth-century linguists to form the name of the Indo-Aryan languages; the term Aryan was also often used to refer to what we now call the Indo-European languages. From this use came the notion of an 'Aryan race', to which contemporary speakers of Indo-European languages, both European and South Asian, belonged – or at least those of them in whom 'Aryan blood' had not been corrupted by 'miscegenation' (Poliakov 1974; Trautmann 1997).

Sanskrit studies, especially Vedic studies, received a powerful impulse from this sense of a common heritage; it was felt most strongly in Germany, influenced by the ideas of nationhood of Johann Gottfried Herder (1744–1803) and other Romantics, and was promoted in Britain by Max Müller. South Asia, especially the north-west, where the Veda was composed, gained prestige as the cradle of European culture. Further developments of the idea of an 'Aryan race' were more sinister, and in the twentieth century they became part of the ideology of Nazism.

Related to the confusion between language and race is the assumption that geographical movement of languages necessarily involves the migration of large numbers of people. Progress in the comparative study of the Indo-European languages, especially in the 1860s and 1870s, showed that the Indo-Aryan and Iranian families shared some important innovations and that the Indo-Aryan languages had most probably entered the subcontinent from outside (Bryant 2001: 68–72). This reasonable linguistic inference led to the theory of an 'Aryan invasion', in which hordes of Indo-Aryan speakers entered from the north-west, displacing or subjugating the indigenous population by military force. This theory, which has little or no support in Vedic literature and is difficult to reconcile with archaeology (Bryant 2001: 197–237), goes far beyond the linguistic evidence on which it is based. Conquest is not the only mechanism by which a language can move from one place to another (Renfrew 1987: 120–44).

Much has been said, but little is certain, about the language of the Indus Valley culture. It has often been thought to be a Dravidian language; this has been supported by analysis of the Indus Valley inscriptions, and also by the likelihood that Dravidian languages were once more widespread than now (Parpola 1993).

Sanskrit

Sanskrit, the oldest of the Indo-Aryan languages, has a special place in Hinduism as the language of the Veda and of Vedic rituals. Some of these, such as the marriage rituals, are widely practised; others less so or not at all. It is also used in many non-Vedic rituals, and in non-Vedic religious poetry and other texts. Indeed, it is hardly possible for a text in any other language (except English) to be current outside the region of that language. Sanskrit, though first spoken in the north-west, has for over two millennia been known, if only to a few, or only partially, throughout the Hindu world, including the Hindu diaspora. It does not belong exclusively to those who are Hindu by religion; Buddhist, Christian, Islamic and Zoroastrian texts have been written in or translated into Sanskrit.

Sanskrit was used over an increasing area of South Asia from *c.*1500 BCE. In the Hindu kingdoms it was used not only in religious contexts but as the language of learning in all subjects, as a medium for poetry, drama and other literature, and for official purposes such as decrees, diplomatic documents and inscriptions. (The earliest inscriptions, however, from the third century BCE onwards, are in other languages; Sanskrit inscriptions are known only from the second century CE.) A scholar of Sanskrit, known as a paṇḍita in Sanskrit, paṇḍit in Hindi or English, would hope to receive royal patronage; paṇḍitas were usually brāhmaṇa men, though non-brāhmaṇa paṇḍitas, and women scholars (paṇḍitā), are not unknown. Patronage of paṇḍitas continued under some of the Muslim rulers, and in British India they found employment as private teachers and consultants on various branches of learning, in colleges and universities, and in the law-courts as experts on Hindu law.

A few people in India still receive their education through the medium of Sanskrit and can converse in it with each other; it is also used as a source of new words for new concepts in Indian languages, as Latin and ancient Greek are used for European languages, so that a speaker of any Indian language knows some Sanskrit words, albeit in adapted forms. It is the language of many Hindu rituals and of those Hindu religious texts which are authoritative throughout India. Today, ritual is the context in which Sanskrit is most commonly heard. The word paṇḍit nowadays often denotes a religious functionary, and is translated 'priest', because the decline of royal and government patronage has left the conduct of rituals as the commonest source of employment for paṇḍits.

People who use Sanskrit today, most of whom are brāhmaṇas, have learnt it only as a second (or subsequent) language. This situation has obtained for over two thousand years; it is already reflected in the grammar of Patañjali (see below) in the second century BCE (Deshpande 1993: 33). Any simple answer to the question of whether Sanskrit is a 'living' or a 'dead' language, therefore, is bound to be misleading. It is nobody's mother tongue, but it is used in creative writing, reading, letters and conversation. In some cases it is the most natural and convenient way for two people from different regions to communicate, though Hindi and English are more commonly used for this purpose. Its classical form was fixed by the ancient grammarians, but already in Patañjali's time there were vernacular forms of Sanskrit, influenced by different regional languages, as there still are (Deshpande 1993: 29f.; 33–51). As with other languages, new words have constantly been added to the vocabulary.

Sanskrit has not always been the name of this language. The grammarian Pānini (see below), in the fifth century BCE, uses two terms for different forms of the language he describes: bhāsā, literally 'language', for Sanskrit as spoken in his time, and chandas, which means 'ritual utterance' and also 'metre', for the closely related, but different, forms found in the Veda. It was probably around the first century CE that the language came to be called saṃskṛta, later Anglicised as Sanskrit. The adjective saṃskṛta, related to saṃskāra, means 'processed, made fit for some purpose'; when applied to a person, it can mean 'ritually purified' or 'well-educated, cultured'. When applied to the language we call Sanskrit, it implies that this is the language that is used by cultured people and is fit to use when dealing with the gods – for those who accept certain assumptions about culture and fitness. We will see below that some Hindus reject those assumptions.

The language of the Veda, especially the earliest parts of the *Saṃhitā*, differs considerably in grammar and vocabulary from the language of classical Sanskrit literature (composed from about the first century CE). Some Western writers have therefore restricted the term 'Sanskrit' to the classical language, calling the language of the Veda 'Vedic' and using 'Old Indian' to cover both. However, it is more usual now to call them both 'Sanskrit', distinguishing between 'Vedic Sanskrit' and 'classical Sanskrit'. There is no firm boundary between the two, since the language of the later parts of the Veda becomes progressively closer to classical Sanskrit. Some varieties of Sanskrit are neither classical nor Vedic, such as the Sanskrit of the *Mahābhārata* and *Purāṇas*, 'vernacular Sanskrit' written or spoken by people who have not fully mastered classical Sanskrit (Deshpande 1993: 3351) and Buddhist Hybrid Sanskrit, mentioned below.

The prestige of Sanskrit was disputed already by some early Buddhists, who insisted that the words of the Buddha should be transmitted not in Sanskrit but in the vernacular language of each region (Deshpande 1993: 7). However, some Buddhists did write Sanskrit; indeed, the earliest known classical Sanskrit poet, apart perhaps from Vālmīki and some inscriptions, was a Buddhist, Aśvaghosa, in the first or second century CE. Buddhist philosophers such as Nāgārjuna (second century CE?), used Sanskrit in similar ways, with similar methods of argumentation, to Hindu philosophers such as Śaṅkara. While Aśvaghosa showed considerable learning in the brahmanical tradition, including grammar, some Buddhist texts are written in a form of Sanskrit known as Buddhist Hybrid Sanskrit, which does not follow the norms of the grammarians and is strongly influenced by other languages (Edgerton 1953).

The vernacular languages

Ancient India had several languages that are clearly related to Sanskrit; these are known as Prakrits, from the Sanskrit word prākṛta, meaning 'natural, unprocessed, ordinary'. In the terminology of historical linguistics, these languages are 'Middle Indo-Aryan', while Sanskrit is 'Old Indo-Aryan'; they are the ancestors of the 'New Indo-Aryan' languages such as Hindi and Bengali, known from around the beginning of the second millennium CE. A further development of Middle Indo-Aryan, known from the middle of the first millennium CE is Apabhraṃśa (Sanskrit for 'falling away'). This term, like Prakrit, covers a variety of dialects which stand between the Prakrits and the New Indo-Aryan languages.

Pali, the language of the Theravāda Buddhist texts, is a form of Prakrit; the inscriptions of the emperor Aśoka (third century BCE) are in three different forms of Prakrit. Other kings, not supporters of Buddhism as Aśoka was, used Prakrit in their inscriptions. Prakrit was gradually replaced in inscriptions by Sanskrit from the second to the fifth centuries CE. Jains also wrote in Prakrit; the insistence on the use of vernacular languages by the Buddhists and Jains represents a rejection of the prestige and authority of the brāhmaṇas, their sacred texts and their learned language.

However, Buddhist writers began to use Sanskrit some time around the first century CE; Jains did so later, during the second half of the first millennium. The increasing use of Sanskrit is partly due to the increasing influence of brāhmaṇas in the courts of kings; but it also had the practical advantage of being a standardised language which varied little geographically or over time (Burrow 1973: 60). Further, while Prakrit in its various forms could claim to be the vernacular in North India, in the Dravidian-speaking south it was no less foreign than Sanskrit.

The Dravidian language family was named by the nineteenth-century scholars, using a Sanskrit name, dravida, which denotes the Tamil people, country and culture and which is related to the name tamil (Mayrhofer 1956–80, 2: 73). Tamil, like Prakrit, was used in inscriptions before Sanskrit, and it has a literary tradition of its own going back to the first century CE or earlier, independent in its origins from Sanskrit. Records of the other Dravidian languages begin later. The presence of words of Dravidian origin in Sanskrit shows that Sanskrit was in contact with Dravidian speakers throughout its history. The Dravidian languages also took many words from Sanskrit, and despite the independent origins of Tamil literature, some Sanskrit influence can be found even in the earliest period. Many of the great writers of Sanskrit literature lived in the South, and probably spoke a Dravidian language before learning Sanskrit. Some wrote in both Sanskrit and Tamil; others thought only Sanskrit was worthy of attention. From 1916 a movement for pure Tamil, closely allied to the anti-brāhmaṇa movement, sought to exclude all Sanskrit words from Tamil.

Apart from such deliberate purism, the vernacular languages used by Hindus contain many words, especially nouns, taken straight from Sanskrit, with no change except in the pronunciation. Such words are called tatsama, 'the same as that'. If a word is derived from Sanskrit but in a changed form, such as Hindi ghī, from Sanskrit ghṛta, 'ghee', it is a tadbhava, 'originating in that'.

Vernacular literature and bhakti

The use of vernacular languages for literature appears to have spread hand in hand with the spread of the bhakti movement from the sixth or seventh century CE. The earliest surviving vernacular bhakti poetry is in Tamil, which was already a literary language. The appearance of a spread from south to north may be deceptive, because we do not know what preceded our earliest records of each region and language (Lorenzen 2004: 196). However, while the bhakti traditions of different regions and languages are to some extent independent of each other, they have features in common which amount to a rejection of the structures of the brahmanical tradition in Sanskrit. These features, besides the use of the vernacular itself, include the prominence of non-brāhmaṇa leaders, teachers and poets, the higher (though by no means equal) representation of women among them, the sanctity of regional holy places and disregard of, or even contempt for, brāhmaṇas, their rituals and their texts. In each case, except for Tamil with its longstanding tradition, it was the bhakti poets and those who recited their poems who established the vernacular as a literary language.

The Tamil poets – the Vaiṣṇava Āḻvārs and the Śaiva Nāyaṉmār – were followed in the eleventh century by the Vīraśaiva or Liṅgāyat poets, further north, using another Dravidian language, Kannada. Further north again, beginning in the thirteenth century, came the Vaiṣṇava poets who used Marathi. Among them Nāmdev, perhaps in the fifteenth century (his biography is very uncertain, as is the authorship of the works attributed to him), used Hindi as well as Marathi. Here at least we can speak of vernacular bhakti poetry passing from one region and language to another.

In the north, however, the picture is complicated by the presence of a group of bhakti traditions, known from the fifteenth century onwards, which while using vernacular languages are closely linked to Sanskrit literature and brahmanical norms. Varadharmī bhakti (Lorenzen 2004: 199–203), as its name implies, asserts the values of dharma as handed down in the *Dharmaśāstras*, in particular the division of society into four varṇas, which provides the theoretical underpinning for caste; unlike the forms of bhakti mentioned above, its leaders are brāhmaṇa men, not śūdras or women. It includes Tulsīdās, whose *Rāmcaritmānas*, a retelling of the *Rāmāyaṇa* in Avadhi (a dialect of Hindi), remains popular in recitation and dramatic performance even though its language is no longer easily understood. It also includes the Kṛṣṇa-worshipping traditions of Vallabhācārya and Caitanya. Vallabhācārya wrote in Sanskrit, but a Hindi poet, Sūrdās, is said to have been his disciple. Caitanya founded the Bengali Vaiṣṇava tradition which was brought to the West by the International Society for Krishna Consciousness (ISKCON). He was a preacher, not an author, but his disciples produced a mass of literature in Bengali and in Sanskrit. Hagiographical works about Caitanya introduced a new genre into Bengali literature (De 1961: 34).

Until modern times, literature in the vernacular languages was almost all in verse. In Sanskrit, however, prose was composed from the *Brāhmaṇas* onwards.

Non-Indian languages

Sanskrit was the only language for communication between regions throughout South Asia until Persian was introduced by the Muslim dynasties who ruled a varying area from the thirteenth century CE. The *Mahābhārata* and *Rāmāyaṇa* were translated into Persian for the seventeenth-century Mughal emperor Akbar, and the *Upaniṣads* for his great-grandson Dara Shikoh. Though Persian is associated with Islamic culture, it was learnt by some Hindus, especially those who were employed by the Muslim dynasties as administrators, generals or paṇḍits. With the gradual establishment of British rule from the middle of the eighteenth century, English became increasingly used, though Persian remained the official language of the law courts until 1837.

English, whose special place has been mentioned, has religious functions. Vivekananda, Radhakrishnan and others read, wrote and lectured extensively in it, developing new forms of Hindu thought for English-educated Hindus and for people whose background is outside Hinduism. The use of English in India has facilitated the export of Hindu movements to the English-speaking world. In the diaspora, and also in urban India, rituals conducted in Sanskrit are often interpreted in English, as are sermons in South Asian vernaculars. The vocabulary of Hindu English includes not only loan-words from Sanskrit and other South Asian languages, but English words used in special senses: *realisation* in the sense of intuitive knowledge of Brahman, christening for muṇḍan, or candle for the oil lamp used in pūjā. The vocabulary of ISKCON abounds in such words, e.g. planet for loka, pastimes for līlā, demigod for deva.

Writing

Most of the languages of South Asia (and also Tibetan and Thai) are written in a family of scripts called Indic. The earliest form is the Brāhmī script used in the inscriptions of the emperor Aśoka in the third century BCE. The Indic scripts used in different regions of South Asia, though differing in the shapes of the characters, are all constructed on the same principles. These include the use of a single character to represent a consonant followed by the vowel a, which in Sanskrit is the commonest vowel. Marks are added to the character if the consonant is followed by any other vowel, or by no vowel.

The regional scripts were formerly used not only for the regional languages but also for Sanskrit. The introduction of printing in the late eighteenth century CE led to some standardisation, and Sanskrit is now usually written in the form of Indic script called Devanāgarī, which is also used for Hindi and Marathi.

Arabic script is also used in South Asia, for Urdu and other languages used mainly by Muslims. Roman script is used not only for English but for many tribal languages. It is used when writing South Asian words or names in an English context, and in the diaspora it is often used for religious texts. The standard transcription with diacritics, as used in this encyclopedia, is sometimes used, especially by ISKCON, but often Anglicised spelling is used (see 'How to read Sanskrit words' below).

In Hindu culture the sounds of language are more important than its representation in writing, and texts are often preserved and transmitted orally.

Theories of language

The Sanskrit tradition has a long history of theory about language (Kunjunni Raja 1963). In Vedic thought, Vāc ('speech') is a goddess and language is a manifestation of an undifferentiated transcendent utterance, sometimes identified as the sacred syllable oṃ (Killingley 1986). The importance of speech in ritual led to a concern to recite the Veda accurately and with understanding. Four of the Vedāṅgas, which were part of the training of a Vedic priest, were concerned with language: phonetics (śikṣā), grammar (vyākaraṇa), etymology (nirukta) and metre (chandas).

From early in the last millennium BCE, phoneticians observed the workings of the speech organs with an accuracy and completeness which were not achieved in Europe until Sanskritists such as Whitney made them known in the late nineteenth century (Allen 1953). In the fourth or fifth century BCE, Pāṇini codified the grammar of Sanskrit in about four thousand brief rules. He, and the predecessors whom he mentions, seem to have developed their treatment of grammar as a system of ordered rules from the rules governing Vedic ritual (Staal 1989). His work was built on in the second century BCE by Patañjali (perhaps not the same as the author of the *Yogasūtras* of Patañjali), who quotes extensively from another commentator, Kātyāyana.

Etymology is represented by Yāska's *Nirukta*, which is a commentary on the *Nighaṇṭu*, a set of lists of Vedic words. Yāska, who lived some time before Pāṇini, follows a very influential theory that nouns are derived from verbs. His work includes many interpretations of verses from the *Ṛgveda*. This kind of etymology is not concerned with the historical derivation of words; indeed, words are considered constant (nitya), not products of history. Rather, it brings out the meaning of a word by linking it to other, similar words. Thus the name of the god Pūṣan, associated with cattle, is explained as puṣṭi, 'prosperity', because cattle are prosperity (*Śatapatha Brāhmaṇa* 3.1.4.9; Eggeling 1882–1900: vol. 2.22). Such discussions of the meanings of words are frequent in the *Brāḥmaṇas*, which also contain discussions on phonetics, grammar and metre. Piṅgala's *Chandasūtras* deals with both Vedic and classical metre.

The importance of language for ritual is reflected in Pūrva Mīmāṃsā. This school, in line with its view that the purpose of the Veda is to enjoin rituals, holds that the primary use of language is to command. Words are inherently connected to the things they denote; this follows from the idea that the Veda is eternal (D'Sa 1980; Clooney 1990). Vedānta is concerned with statements, not commands, the most important parts of the Veda being its statements about Brahman. For Śaṅkara, a statement such as 'I am Brahman' is only figuratively true, since it imposes on Brahman attributes of myself which do not belong to it; absolute truth is inexpressible, and such statements can only lead to it through a gradual unpeeling of layers of falsity. For Rāmānuja such statements are literally true, since all words, besides their primary sense, refer to Brahman, which is the self of the universe. Madhva goes further: all words refer primarily to Brahman (Lott 1980: 66–92).

Nyāya rejects the idea that the connection between word and meaning is inherent: some meanings are assigned by God, and others by human convention, such as those of proper names or words for newly discovered things. Since its concern is with padārthas, 'meanings of words, things that words denote', Nyāya uses language as a means for finding truth. The grammarians, too, insisted on the necessity of language for cognition. Grammar, though not listed among the six systems (ṣaḍdarśana), was developed as a system leading to salvation by Bhartṛhari. A key concept in this system is sphoṭa, 'bursting forth', which refers to the total meaning of an utterance, existing in the speaker's mind before it is uttered and appearing in the hearer's mind when it is understood, but not identical with the words or their sequence (Coward and Kunjunni Raja 1990).

Sanskrit for non-Sanskritists

One function of Sanskrit is as a source of words in English, and in other languages (most of them nouns, but a few adjectives), for talking about Hindu concepts or other concepts that originated in South Asia. Some of these words are used more or less commonly in English, e.g. Buddha, guru, karma, mahārāja, mahātma, mantra, nirvāna, rāja, swastika (svastika), yoga, which passed into English during the period of British rule in South Asia. These words have become English with no change of form (except that diacritic marks are not used); in Sanskrit terminology, explained above, they are tatsamas. Some tatsamas have undergone slight changes such as the omission of final a (which is not pronounced in Hindi or most other New Indo-Aryan languages), e.g. ashram (āśrama), avatar (avatāra), or are spelt differently from the scholarly convention, e.g. pundit (paṇḍita), Sanskrit (saṃskṛta). Many Sanskrit words relating to religion were popularised in English by Theosophy, the Vedānta Societies, and later by the upsurge of interest in South Asian religion from the 1960s onwards, together with ISKCON, Transcendental Meditation and other movements. In more technical contexts such as religious education, a much larger lexicon of South Asian terms is used, and most of these are Sanskrit words, as are most of the names of deities and many of the names of human persons found in this encyclopedia and other books on the subject.

A few words used in English are not tatsamas, however, e.g. ārti, dīvālī and ghee (or ghī), all from Hindi (the tatsama dīpāvalī is less well known than the tadbhava dīvālī, but is used in English by Tamils). Some names of deities are not tatsamas, e.g. the Tamil names Aiyaṉār, Māriammā, Murukaṉ.

Since different languages are spoken by Hindus in different regions of South Asia, it would be possible to use the vocabulary of those languages to talk about the ideas and practices current in those different regions. This is what anthropologists often do in studies of particular localities. However, while it would have the advantage of keeping our terminology as close as possible to that of the people we are talking about, it would obscure the relationships between concepts in different regions. For instance, if we find Hindi speakers talking of dharm, Bengalis of dhormo, and Tamils of tharumam, it is useful to know that these are all tatsama forms of the same Sanskrit word dharma. When we are talking of Hindu culture or religion in general rather than that of a particular region, it is useful to have a master key to stand for all these words, and that key is provided by the Sanskrit word. Similarly, Sanskrit deva can stand for Hindi dev, Bengali deb and Tamil thevar; or Sanskrit veda for Hindi ved, Bengali bed and Tamil vetham. This is very useful, so long as we are careful not to suppose, or imply, that the Sanskrit form or meaning of a word is superior to the form or meaning in a vernacular language, or that the vernacular word is a 'mispronunciation' or 'corruption'.

Since we use Sanskrit words so extensively, it is useful to know something about how they are formed. The rest of this section gives a few hints on the commoner features.

How to read sanskrit words

One source of difficulty in reading Sanskrit words is that besides the omission of diacritics there are other differences between the Anglicised spelling used in non-specialised contexts and the transcription used by specialists. The sound transcribed ṣ is spelt sh (e.g. Lakṣmī/Lakshmi), and ś is spelt either s or sh (e.g. Śiva/Siva or Shiva). The sound c is spelt ch (e.g. cakra/chakra), ṛ is spelt ri (e.g. Kṛṣṇa/Krishna) and v may be spelt w (e.g. svāmi/swami). Some words which are transcribed as ending in -an or -in may have the final n omitted, e.g. karman/karma, yogin/yogi. (This final -n does not occur in all contexts in Sanskrit; it is part of the stem of the word but does not occur in all its inflectional forms.) Some words which are transcribed as ending in a have the final a omitted, as mentioned above, e.g. Rāma/Ram.

Sometimes the long vowels (transcribed with the diacritic ā, ī, ū) are spelt with double letters, e.g. Sītā/Siitaa or Seetaa; pūjā/pooja or poojaa.

Among Tamils, t (which is pronounced with the tip of the tongue between the teeth like the English th- sound) is often spelt th, e.g. mukti/mukthi. Some words are written with the Tamil endings , -m, -n, e.g. liṅga/liṅgam; Kṛṣṇa/Krishnan. There are many other variations in form and spelling which reflect the different pronunciation of Sanskrit words in different South Asian languages.

Many Sanskrit words are formed by adding a suffix to the end of another word. The suffix -in (also written -i) means 'one who has, possesses, is characterised by'; e.g. yogin/yogi, 'one who has yoga, one who practises yoga'; saṃnyāsin/sannyasi, 'one characterised by saṃnyāsa, renouncer'. The suffix -ī (replacing a final a) forms feminine nouns: yoginī, 'woman who practises yoga'; devī, 'female deva, goddess'. Most feminine nouns end in either ī or ā.

Other words are formed by adding a prefix before a word. The prefix a- (an- before a vowel) means 'not, non, un-'; for example, hiṃsā, 'violence', ahiṃsā, 'non-violence'; ārya, 'Aryan', anārya, 'non-Aryan'; mṛta, 'dead', amṛta, 'immortality; life-giving drink'. The prefix sa- means 'having, possessing, with', and niḥ- (or nis-, niś-, niṣ-, nir- depending on the sound that follows) means 'without', e.g. saguṇa, 'with qualities', nirguṇa, 'without qualities'.

A word can be formed from another by changing the vowel in the first syllable (a→ā; i→ai; u→au; ṛ→ār); this change is called vṛddhi. A word formed in this way means 'belonging to, descended from, following, devoted to' the referent of the first word; for example Bhārata, 'descendent of Bharata'; brāhmaṇa, 'belonging to Brahman; bhāgavata, 'belonging to or devoted to Bhagavat (a name of Viṣṇu)'; Vaidika, 'belonging to the Veda, Vedic'; Śaiva, 'devoted to Śiva'; Vaiṣṇava, 'devoted to Viṣṇu'; Bauddha, 'Buddhist'; paurāṇika, 'teller of stories from the Purāṇas'; ārṣa, 'belonging to the ṛṣis'; smārta, 'following the smṛti'.

An important feature of Sanskrit is its facility for combining two or more nouns or adjectives into a longer unit, called a compound (samāsa), which functions in some ways like a phrase and in some ways like a word. Some elements which occur in many compounds will become familiar during the study of Hinduism; for example mahā, 'great', in Mahā-bhārata, 'the great story (of the descendants) of Bharata'; mahā-rāja, 'great king'; Mahā-devī, 'great goddess'; Mahā-rāṣṭra, 'great country' (name of a state in western India); śāstra, 'book of instruction, science', in Dharma-ṣāstra, 'science of dharma'; Śilpa-śāstra, 'book on craftsmanship'. Many titles of books are compounds; so are many personal names and place names. The beginnings and ends of the words in a compound may be obscured by changes known as sandhi; for example, pūrṇāvatāra, 'full avatāra' (pūrṇa 'full' + avatāra); rāmeśvara (rāma + īśvara, 'lord'); yajurveda (yajuṣ, 'ritual utterance', + veda).

The Indic scripts do not have capital letters or italics. Until the nineteenth century they were written without spaces between words, and they do not use hyphens in compounds as in the paragraph above. You may therefore find the same phrase transcribed variously, for instance *dharmaśāstra, Dharma-śāstra or Dharma Śāstra.*

See also: **Ahiṃsā; Āḻvārs; Ārti; Āśram(a) (religious community); Avatāra; Bhakti movement; Bhartṛhari; Brahman; Brāḥmaṇas; Buddhism, relationship with Hinduism; Caitanya; Caste; Coeurdoux, Gaston-Laurent; Deities; Dharma; Dharmaśāstras; Diaspora; Dīvālī; Drama; Guṇas; Guru; Indus Valley Civilisation; International Society for Krishna Consciousness; Jainism, relationship with Hinduism; Jones, Sir William; Karma; Kṛṣṇa; Lakṣmī, Śrī; Līlā; Madhva; Mahābhārata; Mantra; Māriammā; Müller, Friedrich Max; Nāyaṉmār; Nirukta; Nyāya; Oṃ; Paṇḍit; Pāṇini; Patañjali; Poetry; Politics; Pūjā; Pūrva Mīmāṃsā; Purāṇas; Radhakrishnan, Sir Sarvepalli; Rāja; Rāma; Rāmānuja; Rāmāyaṇa; Religious education; Ṛṣi; Sacred texts; Śaivism; Saṃhitā; Saṃnyāsa; Saṃskāra; Śaṅkara; Sītā; Śiva; Smārta; South Indian political movements; Svāstika; Theosophy and the Theosophical Society; Transcendental Meditation; Tulsīdās(a); Upaniṣads; Vaiṣṇavism; Vallabha; Vālmīki; Vīraśāivas; Vedāṅgas; Vedānta; Veda; Viṣṇu; Vivekananda, Swami; Western popular culture, Hindu influence on; Whitney, William Dwight; Yāska; Yoga; Yogasūtras; Yogi**

DERMOT KILLINGLEY

Further reading

Allen, W.S. 1953. *Phonetics in Ancient India*. London: Oxford University Press.

Bryant, Edwin. 2001. *The Quest for the Origins of Vedic Culture*. New York: Oxford University Press.
Burrow, T. 1973. *The Sanskrit Language*. London: Faber and Faber.
Clooney, Francis X. 1990. *Thinking Ritually: Rediscovering the Pūrva Mīmāṃsā of Jaimini*. Vienna: Institut für Indologie der Universität Wien.
Coward, Harold G. and K. Kunjunni Raja. 1990. *The Philosophy of the Grammarians (Encyclopedia of Indian Philosophies, vol. 5)*. Princeton, NJ: Princeton University Press.
D'Sa, Francis X. 1980. *Śabdaprāmāṇyam in Śabara and Kumārila: Towards a Study of the Mīmāṃsā Experience of Language*. Vienna: Institut für Indologie der Universität Wien.
De, Sushil Kumar. 1961. *Early History of the Vaiṣṇava Faith and Movement in Bengal*, 2nd edn. Calcutta: K.L. Mukhopadhyay (first published 1942).
Deshpande, Madhav M. 1993. *Sanskrit and Prakrit: Sociolinguistic Issues*. Delhi: Motilal Banarsidass.
Edgerton, Franklin. 1953. *Buddhist Hybrid Sanskrit*. New Haven, CT: Yale University Press.
Eggeling, Julius. 1882–1990. *The Satapatha Brāhmana*, 5 vols. Oxford: Clarendon Press.
Killingley, Dermot. 1986. 'Om: The Sacred Syllable in the Veda'. *A Net Cast Wide: Investigations into Indian Thought in Memory of David Friedman*. Newcastle upon Tyne: Grevatt & Grevatt, 14–33.
Kunjunni Raja, K. 1963. *Indian Theories of Meaning*. Madras: Adyar Library.
Lorenzen, David N. 2004. 'Bhakti'. In Sushil Mittal and Gene Thursby, eds, *The Hindu World*. New York: Routledge, 185–209.
Lott, Eric. 1980. *Vedantic Approaches to God*. London: Macmillan.
Masica, C.P. 1991. *The Indo-Aryan Languages*. Cambridge: Cambridge University Press.
Mayrhofer, M. 1956–80. *Kurzgefasstes etymologisches Wörterbuch des Altindischen* [A concise etymological Sanskrit dictionary]. Heidelberg: Carl Winter, Universitätsverlag.
Parpola, Asko. 1993. *Deciphering the Indus Script*. Cambridge: Cambridge University Press.
Poliakov, Léon. 1974. *The Aryan Myth: A History of Racist and Nationalist Ideas in Europe*. Translated by Edmund Howard. London: Chatto Heinemann.
Renfrew, Colin. 1987. *Archaeology and Language: The Puzzle of Indo-European Origins*. London: Jonathan Cape.
Robins, R.H. 1967. *A Short History of Linguistics*. London: Longmans.
Schwartzberg, J.E. (ed.). 1978. *A Historical Atlas of South Asia*. Chicago, IL and London: University of Chicago Press.
Staal, Frits. 1989. *Rules without Meaning: Ritual, Mantras and the Human Sciences*. New York: Lang.
Trautmann, Thomas R. 1997. *Aryans and British India*. Berkeley, CA: University of California Press.

LAW, INCLUDING CRIME AND PUNISHMENT

There is no specific word for law in Hinduism; this concept lies embedded in the larger one of dharma and overlaps in meaning with the closely related ones of religion and ethics. It is a kind of sacred law, therefore, with metaphysical foundations for rightness, obligation and retribution based on the concepts of ṛta, dharma, and karma.

Ṛta, already a key concept in the *Ṛgveda*, the earliest text of Hinduism, is the universal and set order of things at the foundation of the cosmos (natural law) but also the ideal and just order for human society. Because of the free will of human beings, the latter must be regulated by deities such as Varuṇa and Yama through impartial rewards and punishments and supported by Vedic rituals and ethical actions. This concept of impartial justice gives Hindu religion, ethics and law a rational basis.

Initially, dharma (from the verbal root dhṛ, to uphold or support) was the aspect of ṛta that presupposed human moral choice and regulation. By the classical period, dharma was divided into two types: sāmānya (general moral principles such as non-violence, truthfulness, not stealing, celibacy, renunciation of possessions, self-control) and viśeṣa (duties related to caste, stage of life, gender, age, regional custom and so forth). As a legal concept, dharma has referred to commands and prohibitions with penalties enforceable by judicial action.

Karma (literally, action) referred in the Vedic period (*c.* fifteenth century BCE–sixth century CE) to properly performed rituals; improper performance, displeasing to the deities and dangerous to cosmic order, constituted sin. In *Bṛhadāraṇyaka Upaniṣad* 4.4.5, it came to mean the principle of moral causation: 'As you sow, so shall you reap'. More specifically, each action (which came to include thoughts and words) created a potency (bhāvanā) that would be manifested either immediately or in the future. When the potency was right, proper, good or meritorious, it was dharma, or puṇya; when wrong, improper, bad or unmeritorious, it was adharma, or pāpa. The corollary of the law of karma is the theory of rebirths (saṃsāra) in heavens, hells or back again on earth (as human, animal, plant).

The law of karma is one of retribution. It is not deterministic, however, for human beings have free will and can decide whether to commit good or bad acts, which can influence the general direction of destiny. They can choose also to neutralise or 'expiate' bad karma by rituals, confessions, austerities, recitations or gifts.

In addition, the law of karma has a societal dimension. The past acts of all individuals collectively determine the social context and set limiting conditions within which acts take place. In other words, the will of this generation creates possibilities for future generations.

By the classical period (*c.* sixth century BCE–sixth century CE), sources for Hindu law included, in descending order of authority: the Veda, the most ancient, 'heard' scripture, believed to be eternal and without human authorship (śruti); a vast 'remembered' collection of secondary scriptures with human authorship (smṛti); the behaviour of good people, that is, the norms of local tradition (sadācāra), and personal conscience (ātmatuṣṭi). Reason, too, was a source. According to Bṛhaspati and Nārada, for instance, legal decisions should not be based merely on scripture, for without reason dharma is diminished.

Especially important for the topic at hand is the category of smṛti, which includes the *Dharmasūtras* (short aphorisms composed between 800 and 100 BCE); the *Arthaśāstra* (*c.*300 BCE–100 CE); and the *Dharmaśāstras* (expansion and refinement of the content of the *Dharmasūtras*). Most important among the latter are the works of Manu (*c.*200 BCE–100 CE), Yājñavalkya (*c.*100–300 CE), Nārada (*c.*100–400 CE) and commentaries on these such as those of Medātithi (800–900) and Kullūka (*c.*1100–1200) on Manu, of Viśvarūpa (*c.*800–900) and Vijñāneśvara (the *Mitākṣarā*) (*c.*1100–1200) on Yājñavalkya, and of Asahāya (*c.*600–700) on Nārada. There were also digests that tried to synthesise the various positions and specific treatises, such as the *Dāyabhāga* (*c.*1000–1100) by Jīmūtavāhana on partition and succession. Legal topics were classified as eighteen from the time of Manu and included recovery of debt, sale without ownership, non-payment of wages, theft, assault, partition and inheritance (all the branches of modern jurisprudence, although Indian law focused on the family and its joint property). After the twelfth century, the distinctions among religion, ethics and law grew, with law becoming more like today's civil law and some texts distinguishing law – duties enforceable by secular authorities (vyavahāra) – from religion (ācāra) and ethics (prayaścitta).

Law was said to have 'four feet': complaint, reply, proof and decision. In addition, it was described as dharma (by admission, statement of truth), evidence (vyavahāra), usage (caritra) or order of the king (rājaśāsana). Legal logic was derived primarily from rules of ritual that were systematised by Mīmāmsā. Many legal transactions involved ceremonies for which participants had to have competency. There were organisations to interpret justice and resolve disputes. Among these were village councils (pañcayats), assemblies of brāhmaṇas (pariṣads) and royal courts (sabhās/samitis).

Hindu law is distinctive among the legal systems of world religions for: (1) its pluralism and tolerance (which cause it to respect local customs and the rights of dissenting religions but also create ambiguity, with its encyclopaedic classifications, regarding what is normative); (2) its flexible ordering of categories (krama) by various authors; and (3) its frequent use of poetry.

The corpus as a whole reflects the values of brāhmaṇas (the intellectual and priestly class), who wrote the texts and protected their own interests (albeit within limits created by duties). They made sure that kings were bound by dharma (unlike Roman emperors, who were above the law). Kings had specific legal duties such as ordering punishments (daṇḍa) at four levels (local verbal censure, royal or court verbal censure, fine and bodily or painful punishment). In addition, they were pre-eminently responsible for guarding the state and its prosperity. To do that, they regulated agriculture, trade, ownership of property, the retribution of crimes and the rehabilitation of wrongdoers.

Although Hindu law was ostensibly conservative, there were many hermeneutical strategies by which change could be accommodated: adding new texts with new values to the sacred corpus; declaring that something was implicit in śruti (which could give authority to a later practice); using allegory or some other level of meaning to circumvent archaic practices; arguing that practices belonged to former ages (yuga); and so forth. The advent of Islamic rule and law around the eleventh century and British rule and law several centuries later ended the flexibility of Hindu law. It retreated into itself and rigidified, especially in personal law. But because colonial policy officially recognised the existing laws, which led to translation of the Hindu *Dharmaśāstras* and judicial consultations with paṇḍits to define Hindu laws, there was a kind of revival but also distortion because a few texts such as that of Manu dramatically increased in authority and local custom was ignored. Gradually, however, modern Western law made inroads through secular legal education and the development of public (state) legislative and judicial institutions. The result is called 'Anglo-Indian' law. It is based on standardisation, the creation of legal statutes (except for personal law, which has been left to religious communities, except that the state might intervene to reform Hindu law) and the writing of a constitution at the time of Independence. All this has created the full range of modern substantive law, case law, legislation, codes, judicial review and human rights, but has also created, in turn, cognitive dissonance with traditional Hindu law and local customs.

See also: **Arthaśāstra; Brāhmaṇas; Dharma; Dharmaśāstras; Dharmasūtras; Ethics; Karma (Law of Action); Manu; Pāpa; Puṇya; Sacred Texts; Saṃhitā; Saṃsāra; Upaniṣads; Varuṇa; Yājñavalkya; Yama; Yuga**

KATHERINE K. YOUNG

Further reading

Agarwal, D.N. 1993. *Hindu Law*. Allahabad: University Book Agency.

Day, T.P. 1982. *The Conception of Punishment in Early Indian Literature*. Waterloo, Ontario: Canadian Corporation for Studies in Religion with Wilfrid Laurier Press.

Derrett, J. 1963. *Introduction to Modern Hindu Law*. Oxford: Oxford University Press.

Derrett, J. 1968. *Religion, Law and State in India*. New York: Free Press.

Derrett, J. 1976–78. *Essays in Classical and Modern Hindu* Law, 4 vols. Leiden: E.J. Brill.
Galanter, M. 1989. *Law and Society in Modern India*. Delhi: Oxford University Press.
Glenn, H.P. 2000. *Legal Traditions of the World*, Oxford: Oxford University Press.
Mayne, John. 1991. *Mayne's Treatise on Hindu Law and Usage*, 13th edn, rev. by A. Kuppuswami. New Delhi: Bharat Law House.
Kane, P.V. 1968–77. *History of Dharmaśāstra (Ancient and Medieval Religious and Civil Law in India)*, 2nd edn, 5 vols. Poona: Bhandarkar Oriental Research Institute.
Lingat, R. 1967/1998. *The Classical Law of India*. Trans J.D.M. Derrett (with additions). Delhi: Oxford University Press.
Nanda, V.P. and S.P. Sinha (eds). 1996. *Hindu Law and Legal Theory*. New York: New York University Press.
Rocher, L. 1977–78. 'Hindu Conceptions of Law'. *Hastings Law Journal* 29: 1,283–305.

LAYA YOGA

The 'yoga of absorption' is not a separate discipline but stands for the highest reaches of haṭha yoga, consisting in the dissolution of the mind, or rather the cognitive, affective and conative mental processes and the merging of the psyche with the ultimate reality, resulting in an experience of perfect bliss. Laya is the experience that mirrors at the individual level the reversal of the process of cosmic emergence until the entire universe (prapañca), with all its sustaining energies, as 'endowed with parts' (sakala), is reabsorbed into the supreme Self 'devoid of parts' (nirkala).

The *Haṭhayogapradīpikā* (*The Little Lamp of Haṭhayoga*), an authoritative text of the tradition traced back to Gorakhnāth, puts it this way:

> 'When breathing-in and breathing-out are entirely suspended, when the perception of sensory objects has ceased and there is no longer any movement or mental activities, there indeed is the triumph of the yogins' resorption (laya). . . . The psyche is absorbed in the object of contemplation. Eternal Nature (prakṛti, in its aspect of nescience), from which proceed both the cosmic elements and the sensory faculties, and also that Energy (śakti, as gnosis) of all living beings are both reabsorbed into That which possesses no distinguishing marks (i.e. the brahman)'
>
> (*Haṭhayogapradīpikā* 4.31–33).

The text goes on to say that laya consigns the entire cosmos to oblivion; in other words, it is emancipation, deliverance-in-life (mokṣa, jīvanmukta). Another text, the *Yogaśikha-Upaniṣad* (1.134–36), concurs with the *Haṭhayogapradīpikā*, while the *Yogatattva-Upaniṣad* (23) views laya yoga as a state of unceasing meditation on the 'Lord devoid of parts' while attending to all mundane activities such as walking, sleeping and eating.

See also: **Brahman; Haṭha Yoga; Gorakhnāth; Jīvanmukta; Mokṣa; Prakṛti; Śakti; Upaniṣads; Yoga**

DANIEL MARIAU

LEKHRAJ, DADA (1876–1969)

Dada Lekhraj was the founder of the Brahma Kumari movement. A wealthy jeweller born near the city of Hyderabad in Sind, at the age of 60 he began to have visions in which he foresaw the imminent destruction of the world. His visions attracted followers, mostly women from wealthy business families, who became the nucleus of the future Brahma Kumari movement. His teachings stressed the need for devotees to prepare for the world's end by means of self-purification and the practice of a special type of yoga. So prepared, movement members would survive to enjoy a paradisiacal age following the catastrophe. The movement he founded survived his death and has established centres throughout India and in many other countries.

See also: **Brahma Kumaris; Yoga**

LAWRENCE A. BABB

Further reading

Babb, L.A. 1986. *Redemptive Encounters: Three Modern Styles in the Hindu Tradition*. Berkeley, CA: University of California Press.

Chander, J. 1981. *Adi Dev: The First Man*. Translated by Shanta Trivedi. San Francisco, CA: Brahma Kumaris World Spiritual University.

LESBIANISM

As with male homosexuality, Brahmanic textual attitudes toward female homosexuality generally condemn it and find it a punishable offence. However, in some texts female homosexual activity is more severely reprimanded than male homosexual activity. In the *Manusmṛti* (8.369–70), for example, a virgin who manually penetrates another virgin is fined and receives lashes, while a (non-virginal) woman who penetrates a virgin is punished by either having her head shaved or two fingers cut off, and is also paraded around town on a donkey. A central concern in these types of passages is the protection of the young woman's virginity and her marriageable status, which follows the internal logic of Brahmanic perspectives on both marriage and the essentially procreative functions of female sexuality.

Medical texts use terms such as nārīṣaṇḍhi to delineate a masculine woman who engages in female–female sexual activity (*Caraka Saṃhitā* 4.2.17–21), but posit this, along with male impotence, sterility and homosexuality, as a vikṛti or 'abnormality'.

The *Kāmasūtra* uses words such as puruṣarūpiṇī ('a woman in the form of a man') and svairiṇī ('independent woman'), and these are often used in the context of female homosexual activity. This is described in detail in *Kāmasūtra* 2.8.11–41, in which one woman penetrates another using a device, or apadravya. Aside from these textual sources, there is scant evidence of the social histories of Hindu women who have sex with women in South Asia.

While some activists, such as Giti Thadani (1996), have attempted to read female–female sexual desire into Vedic and Epic Sanskrit materials, others have looked for homosocial female spaces in vernacular texts (Vanita 2001) in an attempt to locate a place for female–female love in the Hindu context. In 1996, Deepa Mehta's film *Fire*, which depicted a female–female sexual relationship developing between two sisters-in-law in modern Delhi, caused considerable controversy among some Hindu groups and initiated a new public debate on homosexuality and Hinduism.

See also: **Brahmanism; Dharmaśāstras; Film; Homosexuality; Kāmasūtra; Sex and sexuality; Veda; Virginity**

DAVESH SONEJI

Further reading

Olivelle, P. (trans.). 2004. *The Law Code of Manu*. New York: Oxford University Press.

Penrose, Walter. 2001. 'Hidden in History: Female Homoeroticism and Women of a "Third Nature" in the South Asian Past'. *Journal of the History of Sexuality* 10.1: 3–39.

Thadani, G. 1996. *Sakhiyani: Lesbian Desire in Ancient and Modern India*. New York: Cassell.

Vanita, R. 2001. 'At All Times Near: Love Between Women in Two Medieval Indian Devotional Texts'. In F.C. Sautman and P. Sheingorn, eds, *Same-Sex Love and Desire Among Women in the Middle Ages*. New York: Macmillan.

Vanita, R. 2005. 'Born of Two Vaginas: Love and Reproduction Between Co-Wives in Some Medieval Indian Texts'. *Gay and Lesbian Quarterly* 11: 4, 547–77.

LETTRES ÉDIFIANTES ET CURIEUSES

First published in Paris in thirty-four volumes from 1702 to 1776, the *Lettres édifiantes et curieuses* consist primarily of letters written by members of the Society of Jesus (Jesuits) involved in missionary work in Asia and the Americas. Although the letters from China and the Americas were more celebrated, among those from India are several which made significant contributions to the contemporary European knowledge of Hinduism, in particular a letter from Jean François Pons in 1740 which gave an account of Nyāya, Vedānta and Sāṃkhya that was not surpassed until the following century, and two long letters from Jean Venant Bouchet which presented much that was new about Hindu beliefs and practices, despite his determination to find evidence that they were either borrowed from biblical sources or demonically inspired. Even the Jesuits' critics (including John Lockman, who provided an English translation that is in every sense partial) were forced to acknowledge the importance of the letters. A later edition (1781–84) collected most of the letters from India in seven volumes.

See also: **Hinduism, history of scholarship; Nyāya; Sāṃkhya; Vedānta**

WILL SWEETMAN

Further reading

Le Gobien, C. *et al.* (eds). 1702–76. *Lettres édifiantes et curieuses, écrites des missions étrangères par quelques missionaires de la Compagnie de Jésus* [Edifying and remarkable letters, written from the foreign missions by several missionaries of the Society of Jesus], 34 vols. Paris: Chez Nicolas Le Clerc (some later volumes published by Jean Barbou and by P.G. Le Mercier).

Lockman, J. 1743. *Travels of the Jesuits into Various Parts of the World: Compiled from their Letters. Now first attempted in English. Intermix'd with an account of the Manners, Government, Religion & c. of the several nations visited by those Fathers: With Extracts from other Travellers, and miscellaneous notes*, 2 vols. London: Printed for John Noon.

Rétif, A. 1951. 'Brève Histoire des *Lettres édifiantes et curieuses*' [A Brief History of the Edifying and Remarkable Letters]. *Neue Zeitschrift fur Missionswissenschaft* 7: 37–50.

LĪLĀ

A Sanskrit term meaning 'sport' or 'play', līlā as an influential theological concept appears in *Brahmasūtra* 2.1.33, an ambiguous verse where the author likens God's creation to play and perhaps thereby implies God's radical spontaneity and freedom. Later traditions employ the term līlā to describe not only divine creativity but also God's specific deeds in the world and beyond, such as Śiva's cosmic dancing and Kālī's wild unpredictable behaviour. In Vaiṣṇava traditions, theologians similarly describe the worldly deeds of Viṣṇu's avatāras, particularly Rāma and Kṛṣṇa, but in this context divine play is clearly motivated by a concern for dharma. While such emphasis on dharma may seem to conflict with līlā defined as playful activity, a close reading of foundational texts such as the *Bhāgavata Purāṇa* reveals that both blissful play and moral purpose are consistently expressed even in the mischievous Kṛṣṇa's līlā.

Apart from cosmic creation and divine exploits, līlā also refers to entertaining religious dramas called *Rās līlā* and *Rāmlīlā*, plays depicting the divine play on earth of Kṛṣṇā and Rāma, respectively. In contrast to the līlā in which God plays various roles when incarnate in human form, in the dramatic līlās human beings re-enact the divine līlā, for the purpose of remembering specific deities and realising their graceful presence on stage as the human actors temporarily become the gods they imitate. While such staged dramas entertain popular audiences throughout India, other forms of remembrance require constant meditation on the divine līlā, a practice which eventually enables the devotee not only to see the divine līlā unfolding before his eyes, but also to participate actively in the līlā as part of the deity's entourage. Beyond such esoteric practices, however, exists divine līlā, which allows gods and humans to play together, for a moment or for eternity, and is thus a manifestation of God's emancipating grace.

See also: **Avatāras; Brahmasūtras; Dharma; Kālī and Caṇḍī; Kṛṣṇa; Purāṇas; Rāma; Śiva; Viṣṇu**

TRACY COLEMAN

Further reading

Coomaraswamy, A.K. 1941. 'Līlā'. *Journal of the American Oriental Society* 61: 98–101.

Dimock, E.C. 1989. 'Līlā'. *History of Religions* 29(2): 159–73.

Haberman, D. 1988. *Acting as a Way of Salvation: A Study of Rāgānugā Bhakti Sādhana*. New York: Oxford University Press.

Haberman, D. 1994. *Journey Through the Twelve Forests: An Encounter with Krishna*. New York: Oxford University Press.

Lutgendorf, P. 1991. *The Life of a Text: Performing the Ramcaritmanas of Tulsidas*. Berkeley, CA: University of California Press.

Sax, W.S. (ed.). 1995. *The Gods at Play: Līlā in South Asia*. New York: Oxford University Press.

LIṄGA

See: **Śiva**

LIṄGA PURĀṆA

See: **Purāṇas**

LIṄGAŚARĪRA

The term liṅga, 'mark, sign', is used in the *Sāṃkhyakārikās* of Īśvarakṛṣṇa for the subtle body consisting of eighteen evolutes of Prakṛti, namely the thirteen faculties (karaṇa) and the five basic elements (tanmātra). In this use, in other texts, liṅga appears compounded with the term śarīra, 'body'. The subtle body, which is insentient, seems to be sentient due to conjunction with the sentient Puruṣa (*Sāṃkhyakārikā* 20). Although composed at the beginning of creation, it is unable to convey experience without a gross body. It enters a womb and, along with the semen and blood born of the father and mother, and the gross elements, develops specific gross bodies. Not destroyed when the gross body perishes after death, it transmigrates, housing the dispositions that determine its next specific gross body and subsequent experience (*Sāṃkhyakārikās* 38–42). It decomposes into its constituent elements and becomes unmanifest when the experiences set in motion by the dispositions cease and the gross body perishes after the distinction between Puruṣa and Prakṛti is finally established in the intellect.

See also: **Antaḥkaraṇa; Īśvarakṛṣṇa; Prakṛti; Puruṣa; Sāṃkhyakārikās**

PETER M. SCHARF

Further reading

Powell, Arthur Edward. 1956. *The Causal Body and the Ego*. London: Theosophical Pub. House; Wheaton, IL: Theosophical Press.

LIṄGĀYATS

See: **Vīraśaivas**

LOKAPALAS

See: **Dikpālas (Regents of Directions) and Lokapālas (World Protectors)**

LOKĀYATA

The term lokāyata is provided various derivations, of which the most convincing is lokeṣu āyataḥ, 'prevalent among the people' (Dasgupta 1940: 514–15). By the end of the fourth century BCE it refers to a particular school of thought mentioned by Kauṭilya (*Arthaśāstra* 1.1) and by the mid-second century BCE there existed a doctrine with a commentary called *Bhāgurī* (Dasgupta 1940: 515–16). Several works in other schools in the seventh to fourteenth centuries CE cite aphorisms they attribute to the preceptor of the gods, Bṛhaspati, and associate with Lokāyata, and one mentions two divergent commentaries on them (Dasgupta 1940: 516).

Also known as Lokāyatika and Cārvāka, Lokāyata was a materialist school of thought whose doctrines are extant only in accounts presented in the texts of other schools for the purpose of refutation. Vedic, Jain, Buddhist and Hindu texts and the epics and didactic texts all refer to a number of heretical doctrines that license immorality and hedonism by denying ethical retribution and its presuppositions. *Śvetāśvatara Upaniṣad* (third to first century BCE), for example, begins by referring to time, inherent nature, necessity, chance and material elements as among the possible causes of people happening upon their particular circumstances of enjoyment and suffering (*Śvetāśvatara Upaniṣad* 1.2). The Buddhist canon's presentation of the teaching of Ajita Kesakambalī corresponds quite closely with the doctrines of Lokāyata (Dasgupta 1940: 521–22). These doctrines are given a lively presentation in the first chapter of Mādhava's *Sarvadarśanasaṃgraha*, 'Compendium of all Views' (*c.* 1331 CE). Validating only what can be directly perceived, they deny any continued existence of personal experience, soul or karma beyond the dissolution of the physical body into the four elements, earth, water, fire and air. Hence they deny any grounds for ethical behaviour and conclude that wealth (artha) and pleasure (kāma) are the sole aims of man.

See also: **Artha; Arthaśāstra; Bṛhaspati; Buddhism, relationship with Hinduism; Itihāsa; Jainism, relationship with Hinduism; Kāma; Karma; Kauṭilya; Pramāṇas; Puruṣārthas; Ṣaḍdarśana; Upaniṣads; Veda**

PETER M. SCHARF

Further reading

Chattopadhyaya, Debiprasad. 1959. *Lokāyata: A Study in Ancient Indian Materialism.* New Delhi: People's Publishing House. Reprint 1985.

Chattopadhyaya, Debiprasad and Mrinalkanti Gangopadhyaya. 1990. *Cārvāka/Lokāyata: An Anthology of Source Materials and Some Recent Studies.* New Delhi: Indian Council of Philosophical Research in association with Ṛddhi-India, Calcutta.

Cowell, Edward B. and Archibald Edward Gough. 1882. *The Sarva-darśana-saṃgraha of Mādhavāchārya: or Review of the Different Systems of Hindu Philosophy.* London: Trübner & Co. (Delhi: Motilal Banarsidass, 2000.) 2–11.

Dasgupta, Surendranath. 1940. *A History of Indian Philosophy,* vol. 3. Cambridge: Cambridge University Press. Reprint 1961, 512–50.

Frauwallner, E. 1973. *History of Indian Philosophy,* Vol. 2, (trans.) V.M. Bedekar. Delhi: Motilal Banarsidass.

Hiriyanna, Mysore. 1932. *Outlines of Indian Philosophy.* London: George Allen and Unwin. (Delhi: Motilal Banarsidass, 1993.) 101–7, 187–95.

Shastri, Dakshinaranjan. 1930. *A Short History of Indian Materialism, Sensationalism and Hedonism.* Calcutta: The Book Company.

Shastri, Hara Prasad. 1925. *Lokāyata.* University of Dacca Bulletin 1. London: Oxford University Press. (Reprinted in *Lokāyata and Vrātya.* Naiheti, India: Haraprasad Shastri Gavbeshana Kendra, Calcutta: available with Firma K.L. Mukhopadhyay, 1982.)

LOPĀMUDRĀ

The wife of the sage Agastya, described in the *Mahābhārata* as the embodiment of wifely virtue and devotion. She is also known as Kauṣītakī and Varapradā, with a hymn in the *Ṛgveda* attributed to her authorship. However, she is more commonly known as Lopā (loss) mudrā (beauties) as a result of her unique birth. It is stated in post-Vedic mythological literature that Agastya created her out of the most beautiful parts of different animals in order to manufacture a woman according to his desire. After her creation she was stealthily introduced into the court of the king of Vidarbha, who later adopted her. When she reached marriageable age, Agastya claimed her hand and the king agreed, with some reluctance. Her name describes the loss suffered by each of the animals which contributed to her creation.

See also: **Mahābhārata; Saṃhitā**

RON GEAVES

Further reading

Dasgupta, Madhusraba. 1999. *Samsad Companion to the Mahābhārata*. Calcutta: Sahitya Samsad.

Stutley, Margaret and James Stutley (eds). 1977. *A Dictionary of Hinduism: Its Mythology, Folklore and Development 1500BC–AD1500*. London: Routledge and Kegan Paul.

M

MACDONELL, ARTHUR ANTHONY (1854–1930)

Born in India of Scots parents, Macdonell attended school and university in Germany, studying Sanskrit and comparative philology at Göttingen, before winning an exhibition at Corpus Christi, Oxford, where he also held the Boden Sanskrit scholarship. After lecturing in German and Sanskrit at Oxford, Macdonell returned to Germany to work with Rudolf von Roth (1821–95), receiving a PhD in 1885 from Leipzig University for an edition of the *Sarvānukramaṇī* of Kātyāyana, a late Vedic work on etymology. He then returned to Oxford as deputy to M. Monier-Williams, succeeding him as Boden Professor of Sanskrit and Keeper of the Indian Institute in 1899. Macdonell's most important publications were all related to the study of the Veda (Macdonell 1897, 1904; Macdonell and Keith 1912). His edition and translation of the *Bṛhad-devatā* of Śaunaka, an index of Vedic deities, served as a reference work for Vedic scholars throughout the twentieth century. He also published several textbooks, as well as works on broader topics addressed to a wide audience (Macdonell 1900, 1925).

See also: **Hinduism, history of scholarship; Monier-Williams, Sir Monier; Veda**

WILL SWEETMAN

Further reading

Macdonell, A.A. 1886. *Kātyāyana's Sarvānukramaṇī of the Rigveda*. Oxford: Clarendon Press.

Macdonell, A.A. 1897. *Vedic Mythology*. Strasbourg: Trübner.

Macdonell, A.A. 1900. *A History of Sanskrit Literature*. London: Heinemann.

Macdonell, A.A. 1904. *Bṛhad-devatā, Attributed to Śaunaka*, 2 vols. Cambridge, MA: Harvard University Press.

Macdonell, A.A. 1925. *Lectures on Comparative Religion*. Calcutta: University of Calcutta.

Macdonell, A.A. and A.B. Keith. 1912. *Vedic Index of Names and Subjects*. London: John Murray.

MADHVA

Madhva (*c.*1238–1317 CE) was the founder of the Dvaita school of Vedānta. He was born in the Tuḷunāḍu area in the village Pājaka, near Uḍupi in the South Kanara district of the modern Karnataka state, to Śivaḷḷi brāhmaṇa parents. Southern Karnataka in Madhva's time was very pluralistic, with other theologies such as Advaita and Viśiṣṭādvaita, and other religions such as Jainism and Vīraśaivism. The *Madhvavijaya*, a hagiography by Madhva's follower Nārāyaṇa Pāṇḍitācārya, gives some details about his early life. Epigraphical evidence and other records survive at the maṭhas, or monasteries, dedicated to Dvaita.

Tradition says that after having his upanayana at about age seven, and following the course of study in subsequent years, Madhva took saṃnyāsa an early age and received the name Pūrṇaprajña. He continued his study of the contemporary Vedānta theologies, particularly Advaita, and became deeply dissatisfied with this view. He then sought to bring about a new theology based on his own theistic realism, founding a new religious tradition. He developed his polemic against Advaita on a debating tour in South India and returned to Uḍupi to begin his prodigious literary career. He composed numerous works, including commentaries on the *Mahābhārata*, the *Bhagavadgītā* and the *Upaniṣads*. His greatest work is the *Anuvyākhyāna* based on the *Brahmasūtras*. Madhva later took debating tours to North India, gathering many converts, and became the first in a lineage of Madhva gurus that has continued for 700 years until the present. His followers founded the Āṣṭa-Maṭhas in Uḍupi, which also have endured until the present.

See also: **Advaita; Bhagavadgītā; Brahmasūtras; Brāhmaṇa; Dvaita; Guru; Jainism, relationship with Hinduism; Mahābhārata; Maṭha; Saṃnyāsa; Upanayana; Upaniṣads; Vedānta; Viśiṣṭādvaita**

ROBERT GOODDING

Further reading

Sharma, B.N.K. 1981. *History of the Dvaita School of Vedānta and Its Literature*, 2nd edn. Delhi: Motilal Banarsidass.

Sharma, Deepak. 2003. *An Introduction to Mādhva Vedānta*. Ashgate World Philosophies Series. Aldershot and Burlington, VT: Ashgate Publishing Ltd.

MĀDRĪ

The sister of the King of Madras and, along with Kuntī, one of the two wives of King Pāṇḍu, who sired the Pāṇḍavas. Mādrī was the mother of the twins Nakula and Sahadeva, but their paternity was alleged to have been by Nāsatya, one of the twin Aśvins, the divinities who appear in the sky before the dawn in a golden carriage drawn by horses or birds. In some accounts of the story it is said that Nakula and Sahadeva were incarnations of the Aśvins. The *Mahābhārata* recounts that Dhṛtarāṣṭra was not allowed to ascend the throne as he was blind and Pāṇḍu replaced him. However, he later renounced the kingdom as a result of a curse and retired to the Himalayas, and it is there that his two wives bore him five sons. Pāṇḍu died in the mountains and Mādrī became a sati on the funeral pyre of her husband.

See also: **Dhṛtarāṣṭra; Kuntī; Mahābhārata; Nakula; Pāṇḍavas; Pāṇḍu; Sahadeva; Sati**

RON GEAVES

Further reading

Dasgupta, Madhusraba. 1999. *Samsad Companion to the Mahābhārata*. Calcutta: Sahitya Samsad.

MADURAI

Madurai is an important city that stands on the banks of the Vaigai River in Tamil Nadu, but is dominated by the huge and spectacular Mīnākṣī temple that is at its sacred heart. It is one of the oldest cities in southern India, with a history that stretches back over many years. It was once known as Madhupuri, or City of Nectar, in reference to the divine nectar that fell from Śiva's hair at the place where the city now stands. It is also reputed to be one of the holy places or pīṭhas (seats) where parts of the goddess fell, in this case her eyes, where the Mīnākṣī temple now stands (Dey 1979: 128). Madurai is a place of pilgrimage in its own right, but is also on the ancient pilgrimage route to Rāmeśvara, one of the four holiest places in India.

Madurai is immortalised in the Tamil epic of Iḷaṅkō Aṭikaḷ, called *Cilappatikāram* (*The Tale of an Anklet*), in which the goddess Kaṇṇakī tears off her breast and throws it at the city, burning it to the ground with the fierce heat that had built up in her breast. Her dramatic action was prompted by the unjust killing of her husband by the king of Madurai.

See also: **Kaṇṇakī; Mandir; Mīnākṣī; Rāmeśvara; Sacred geography; Satimacr; (Goddess); Śiva; Tīrthayātrā (Pilgrimage)**

LYNN FOULSTON

Further reading

Dey, Nando Lal. 1979. *The Geographical Dictionary of Ancient and Mediaeval India*. New Delhi: Cosmo Publications.

Foulston, Lynn. 2002. *At the Feet of the Goddess: The Divine Feminine in Local Hindu Religion*. Brighton and Portland, OR: Sussex Academic Press.

Parthasarthy, R. (trans.). 1993. *The Cilappatikāram of Iḷaṅkō Aṭikaḷ: An Epic of South India [The Tale of an Anklet]*. New York: Columbia University Press.

MAGIC

Magic consists of those rituals or observations which attempt to manipulate the natural world or alter the course of future events. It typically represents a body of knowledge with its own set of methods, which can be employed by magic experts to control forces undetectable to scientists, such as spirits or mystical powers. It is often used as a negative label symbolising hidden or forbidden wisdom, somehow separate from religion. In *The Golden Bough*, James Frazer claimed that magic was the earliest stage of humanity's religious development: humans originally believed that they could manipulate the impersonal power of the universe and later, when magic failed, they became dependent on prayers and sacrifice instead. The final stage of human development came when humans were frustrated with religious practices and turned to science.

However, the relationship between magic, religion and science is far more complex than Frazer's analysis allows. For instance, prayers need not be considered a means of communicating with the divine, but rather attempts to plead for a course of action favourable to the individual. The acts of meditation or yoga can also be said to have magical qualities, since one's mind constantly focuses on a specific object or being for the purposes of self-realisation. Some Indian ascetics conduct secret rituals to gain boons from a particular deity, which can then be used to manipulate the natural world for the purposes of gaining mokṣa or to provide support within the local community.

One must be wary of employing the term 'magic' in this broad fashion, though, because practitioners of certain faiths will disagree with its applicability. For example, the charismatic leader Sathya Sai Baba would not claim to use magic, because that suggests he partakes in a dangerous activity; he prefers the term 'miracle', because this suggests purity of action.

See also: **Meditation; Mokṣa; Sai Baba, Sathya; Tapas; Yoga**

ANGELA QUARTERMAINE

Further reading

Frazer, J. 1922. *The Golden Bough: A Study in Magic and Religion.* London: Macmillan.
Harvey, G. 2000. 'Introduction'. In G. Harvey, ed., *Indigenous Religions: A Companion.* London: Cassell.
Swallow, D.A. 1982. 'Ashes and Powers: Myth, Rite and Miracle in an Indian God-man's Cult'. *Modern Asian Studies* 16: 123–58.
Thrower, J. 1999. *Religion: The Classical Theories.* Edinburgh: Edinburgh University Press.

MAHĀBHĀRATA

The *Mahābhārata* (*Mbh*) is the longer of the two great Sanskrit epics of Classical Hinduism (the other being the *Rāmāyaṇa*). It is a huge work, several times longer than the *Iliad* and *Odyssey* put together, and is an encyclopaedic compendium of myths and teachings, famously claiming to include everything there is to know. The text is broken up into eighteen books, or parvas, which are subdivided into chapters and verses, and there is also a system of division into 100 minor books. The epic has the status of smṛti but is also called the Fifth Veda, thus emphasising its importance to the tradition. Both dating and authorship of the text are controversial. Tradition ascribes its authorship to Vyāsa, the Arranger, who is said to have also compiled the Veda, and gives it a date of around 3000 BCE. Scholarship has been more conservative in its dating, with the consensus placing it somewhere between 400 BCE and 400 CE, although there is still much debate within this band (J. Brockington 1998; Hiltebeitel 2001). Equally debated is the question of the text's compilation. Few scholars accept the traditional idea of a single author and agree that the text is a compilation of several hands, but there is considerable difference of opinion as to the process and timespan of the compilation and the corresponding coherence of the text (Biardeau 1968–71; J. Brockington 1998; Goldman 1977). There are several different versions of the *Mahābhārata* but most scholarship now uses the Critical Edition of the text (Sukthankar *et al.* 1933–59). The first five books of the Critical Edition have been translated into English (van Buitenen 1973–78). There is also a translation of the Calcutta edition of the Northern Recension (Roy and Ganguli 1970) and there are several abridgements of the story in English (Narasimhan 1965; Rajagopalachari 1978). More recently the Clay Sanskrit Library is working with International Scholars to produce a series of new translations that are 'readable and accurate'.

The structure of the *Mahābhārata* is complex, with a base narrative (the story of the great battle between two branches of the Kuru lineage); framing narratives outside that (the settings in which the story is told); and sub-narratives within it that give the epic its encyclopaedic nature (myths, teachings, etc. told to the protagonists at various points in the story). The base narrative begins with the events leading up to the dynastic conflict between two sets of royal cousins, the Kauravas and the Pāṇḍavas. The seeds for the conflict are sown when Bhīṣma, who should have succeeded his father Śaṃtanu as king, renounces his right to the kingdom and, in doing so, throws into chaos the line of succession, the well-being of the kingdom and the natural order of the cosmos itself. The rights of succession get increasingly complex over the next two generations: Śaṃtanu's new heir dies childless, so two sons are begotten by proxy on his widows. The older of these, Dhṛtarāṣṭra, is blind, and the younger brother Paṇḍu, becomes king. He, too, is unable to beget children so his wife Kuntī gives him children fathered by the gods: Yudhiṣṭhira, the oldest, by Dharma; Bhīma by Vayū; Arjuna by Indra; and the twins, Nakula and Sahadeva, fathered on Kuntī's co-wife Mādrī, by the Aśvins. Pāṇḍu dies before Yudhiṣṭhira comes of age and the kingdom passes into the regency of Dhṛtarāṣṭra. Dhṛtarāṣṭra's oldest son, Duryodhana, is deeply resentful of Yudhiṣṭhira and attempts to wrest the kingdom from the Pāṇḍavas in various ways (Book 1). These culminate in a crooked game of dice in which Yudhiṣṭhira loses the kingdom and his freedom, along with that of his brothers and their polyandrous wife Draupadī. Although Draupadī manages to overturn this defeat, Duryodhana challenges Yudhiṣṭhira to a second game and, losing this, the five brothers and their wife are forced into thirteen years of exile in the forest, the last of which must be spent in hiding (Book 2).

The Pāṇḍavas undergo many adventures in the forest and the stories that are told to them at various points in their sojourn make up much of the substratum of additional myths in the epic (Book 3). The thirteenth year is spent in disguise at the court of a neighbouring king, Virāta, but once again the issue of succession is clouded: the Pāṇḍavas believe they remained hidden for the full year but Duryodhana claims they were discovered before the year was completed and must undergo another thirteen years in exile (Book 4). Despite Yudhiṣṭhira's reluctance to cause bloodshed, war becomes inevitable and the two sides muster their allies (Book 5). In a famous episode Kṛṣṇa agrees to act as the charioteer of Arjuna, and it is in this guise that he delivers the teachings contained in the *Bhagavadgītā* on the eve of the battle. The battle itself is cataclysmic and involves the whole of the world as the epic knows it. The fighting lasts for eighteen days and charts a steady decline from chivalrous and properly conducted warfare (Books 6–9) into massacre of sleeping warriors at its conclusion (Book 10). The Pāṇḍavas survive to regain the kingdom, but stand as victors on a battleground strewn with the corpses of an entire generation of warriors (Book 11).

Following the lengthy teachings of Bhīṣma, who remains alive but mortally wounded (Books 12 and 13), Yudhiṣṭra conducts a horse sacrifice (Book 14) and the epic draws to a close with the deaths of the main protagonists: Kuntī, Dhṛtarāstra and his wife Gāndhārī in a forest fire (Book 15); Kṛṣṇa by the arrow of a huntsman (Book 16); and the Pāṇḍavas themselves, who die one by one on a pilgrimage to the Himālayas (Book 17). Only Yudhiṣṭhira does not die, but, as reward for his perfect dharma, ascends to heaven in a chariot. There he sees Duryodhana treated with great honour but when he asks for his brothers and Draupadī he is conducted to hell, where they are in torment. Yudhiṣṭhira renounces his own place in paradise to be with them and, this final test of dharma completed, the Pāṇḍavas all go to heaven (Book 18).

This brief summary of the story should begin to give some idea of the themes and concerns which dominate the *Mahābhārata.* The first of these is the complex and ambiguous nature of dharma. A recurrent refrain in the epic is that dharma is subtle and difficult to know and this is illustrated by the narrative events: the complexity of the rights of succession; Yudhiṣṭhira's uncertainty about engaging in the violence embedded in kṣatyria dharma; Kṛṣṇa's role in the epic; and the twists and darkness at the end of the story. The nature of dharma is also reflected upon in the didactic portions of the *Mahābhārata*, not least in the *Bhagavadgītā*, which is in many ways a distillation of the central epic concerns. Another important theme is the nature and duty of the king. Again, Yudhiṣṭhira is central to this: he is the Dharma King and his actions and dilemmas give rise to much teaching on the subject, especially by Bhīṣma in the largely didactic Books 12 and 13. Finally, the pervasive and inexorable nature of fate and time is a recurrent theme in the epic, both in terms of individuals and in terms of the cosmos and its journey through the cycle of the yugas.

See also: **Arjuna; Aśvins; Bhagavadgītā; Bhīṣma; Dharma; Dhṛtarāṣṭra; Draupadī; Duryodhana; Gāndhārī; Himālayas; Indra; Itihāsa; Kṛṣṇa; Kauravas; Kuntī; Mādrī; Nakula; Pāṇḍavas; Pāṇḍu; Rāmāyaṇa; Sacred texts; Sahadeva; Varṇa; Vāyu; Veda; Vyāsa; Yajña; Yudhiṣṭhira**

LYNN THOMAS

Further reading

Biardeau, M. 1968–71. 'Études de mythologie Hindoue: Cosmogonies purāṇiques'. [Studies in Hindu Mythology: Purāṇic Cosmogonies]. *Bulletin de l'Ecole française d'Extrême Orient* 54 (1968): 19–45; 55 (1969): 59–105; 58 (1971): 17–89.

Biardeau, M. 1976–78. 'Études de mythologie Hindoue: Bhakti et avatāra'. [Studies in Hindu Mythology: Bhakti and Avatāra]. *Bulletin de l'Ecole française d'Extrême Orient* 63 (1976): 111–263; 65 (1978) 87–238.

Brockington, J. 1998. *The Sanskrit Epics*. Leiden: Brill.

Brockington, M. 2002. *Stages and Transitions: Temporal and Historical Frameworks in Epic and Purāṇic Literature. Proceedings of the Second Dubrovnik International Conference on the Sanskrit Epics and Purāṇas*. Zagreb: Croatian Academy of Sciences and Arts.

Brockington, M. and P. Schreiner. 1999. *Composing a Tradition: Concepts, Techniques and Relationships: Proceedings of the First Dubrovnik International Conference on the Sanskrit Epics and Purāṇas*. Zagreb: Croatian Academy of Sciences and Arts.

Gitomer, David. 1992. 'King Duryodhana: The *Mahābhārata* Discourse of Sinning and Virtue in Epic and Drama'. *Journal of the American Oriental Society* 112.

Goldman, R. 1977. *Gods, Priests and Warriors: The Bhṛgus of the Mahābhārata*. New York: Columbia University Press.

Hiltebeitel, A. 2001. *Rethinking the Mahābhārata: A Reader's Guide to the Education of the Dharma King*. Chicago, IL: University of Chicago Press.

Johnson, W.J. (trans.). 1998. *The Sauptikaparvan of the Mahabharata: The Massacre at Night*. Oxford: Oxford University Press.

Katz, R. 1989. *Arjuna in the Mahabharata: Where Krishna Is, There Is Victory*. Columbia, SC: Univeristy of South Carolina Press.

Narasimhan, C.C. 1965 *The Mahābhārata: An English Version Based on Selected Verses*. New York: Columbia University Press.

Rajagopalachari, C. 1978. *Mahabharata*. Bombay: Bharatiya Vidya Bhavan.

Roy, P.C. and K.M. Ganguli (trans.). 1970. *The Mahabharata of Krishna-Dwaipayana Vyasa*, 12 vols, 2nd edn. Calcutta: Oriental Publishing Company.

Scheuer, J. 1982. *Śiva in the Mahābhārata*. Paris: Presses Universitaires de France.

Sukthankar, V.S, S.K. Belvalkar, *et al.* (eds). 1933–59. *The Mahābhārata: For the First Time Critically Edited*, 19 vols. Poona: Bhandarkar Oriental Research Institute.

van Buitenen, J.A.B. (ed. and trans.). 1973–78. *The Mahābhārata*, 3 vols. Chicago, IL: University of Chicago Press.

MAHĀDEVĀ

See: **Śiva**

MAHADEVAN, TELLIGYAVARAM MAHADEVAN PONNAMBALAM (1911–83)

Philosopher and scholar of Advaita Vedānta. Educated at a school of the Ramakrishna Math and Mission and at the University of Madras, where he gained a doctorate for research on Vidyāraṇya, Mahadevan taught in two south Indian colleges before returning to the University of Madras as head of the Department of Philosophy in 1943, remaining there, excepting a visiting professorship at Cornell University in 1948–49, until his retirement in 1976. Under his leadership the department was upgraded in 1964 to a Center for Advanced Study in Philosophy, with a special emphasis on Advaita, later being renamed the Radhakrishnan Institute. The heart of Mahadevan's philosophical thought was the Advaitic thought of Śaṅkara. Advaita was not only a scholarly concern for Mahadevan, and he was close to Ramana Maharishi and Candrashekhara Sarasvati, the Śaṅkarācārya of Kancipuram, publishing books on both.

See also: **Advaita; Hinduism, history of scholarship; Ramakrishna Math and Mission; Ramana Maharishi; Śaṅkara**

WILL SWEETMAN

Further reading

Balasubramanian, R. 1998. *T.M.P. Mahadevan*. Delhi: Munshiram Manoharlal.

Mahadevan, T.M.P. 1938. *The Philosophy of Advaita with Special Reference to Bhāratītīrtha-Vidyāraṇya*. London: Luzac.

Mahadevan, T.M.P. 1940. *Outlines of Hinduism*. Madras: Madras Law Journal Press.

Mahadevan, T.M.P. 1952. *Gauḍapāda: A Study in Early Advaita*. Madras: University of Madras.

MAHĀDEVĪ

Mahādevī literally means Great Goddess and is a term or title that applies to the inclusive, immanent and transcendent concept of the divine feminine in Hindu thought. Mahādevī is eulogised as the ultimate mother, as the creator of the world, being also the powerful force behind creation, Ādya-Śakti (Primordial Power). The name Mahādevī can quite comfortably be interchanged with other names such as 'Mother Goddess' or simply, and most commonly, Devī, 'Goddess'. As well as being the Mother Goddess, Devī is also envisaged as a divine warrior who protects her creation from any evil forces that might threaten its stability. Mahādevī appears in many forms, both benign and terrible, that represent the many aspects of her all-encompassing character.

The development of the idea of Mahādevī

In the early period of Hindu religion, such as the Vedic period, goddesses were presented as distinct deities, their function, mythology and iconography having no perceptible connection. For instance, the goddesses in the Vedic hymns, Uṣas (the Dawn), Pṛthivī (Mother Earth), Vāc/Vāk (Speech), Rātrī (Night), Aditi (Mother of the Gods), and the many goddesses that were simply the wives of the gods, appear unconnected. Similarly, the goddesses that appeared later in the epics, the *Mahābhārata* and the *Rāmāyāṇa*, such as Gangā (River Ganges), Śrī Lakṣmī, Durgā and Sītā, to name but a few, were also presented as individuals with no apparent underlying connection. Of particular importance to the later concept of Mahādevī was the concept of a connection between God, referred to as Brahman (a term without gender) or ultimate reality, and the totality of all cosmic manifestation. The all-embracing nature of Brahman formulated in the *Upaniṣads* gave rise to an idea, fundamental to later Hindu thought, that everything, whether divine or human, was in its deepest essence identical, thereby establishing a connecting factor, the ātman or permanent essence, in all life. In this respect, the gods and goddesses were envisaged as manifest aspects of Brahman's nature; that is, ultimately beyond human comprehension.

In the *Purāṇas*, which characterise the classical period of Hinduism, individual goddesses, such as Pārvatī, Śrī Lakṣmī and Sarasvatī gradually came to be portrayed as embodying śakti (divine power or energy) and in so doing embraced a fundamental commonality. One way this idea was conveyed in a number of the non-Śākta *Purāṇas* (texts in which a/the goddess is not the primary deity) was that a particular goddess was depicted as the source of all other goddesses. In the *Brahmavaivarta Purāṇa*, for example, the primary goddess of the text, Rādhā, was described as being one-fifth of prakṛti (primary or primordial matter) along with Durgā, Lakṣmī, Sarasvatī and

Sāvitrī. The text goes on to explain that all female beings, including local goddesses and mortal women, were, to various degrees, parts of Rādhā, as prakṛti. All these forms were simply parts of the one energetic source, in this case referred to as Mūlaprakṛti (the primordial material source of the universe). However, despite Rādhā being considered the source of other feminine beings, she was still regarded as an aspect of, and subject to, her male partner, Kṛṣṇa. Similar ideas were presented in various purāṇic texts but no single goddess was selected as consistently being the source of the others. The choice of primary goddess in each text was dictated by the preference of its author.

The *Purāṇas* were not the only textual sources to lead toward a more metaphysical conception of a Great Goddess; tantric texts have also been influential in elevating the status of the divine feminine. The concept of a supreme goddess, representing śakti, the power of the universe, and on an equal footing with the male principle, Śiva, was fundamental in Tantra. In tantric thought, in order to create, ultimate reality or Brahman produces two principles, Śiva and Śakti. The Śiva aspect represents cosmic consciousness, puruṣa, or the male principle, whereas Śakti is conceived of as creative power, prakṛti, the cosmic force of nature, the female principle. Their union creates the cosmos and all it contains, and though Śiva and Śakti represent opposing forces they are, nonetheless, indivisible. Tantra envisages Śiva-Śakti, in its unmanifest state as being like a 'grain of gram' with Śiva and Śakti described as two seeds entwined under a single sheath (Woodroffe 1987: 228). Therefore, in tantric thought goddesses and women, to a greater or lesser degree, are regarded as embodying the śakti principle. In addition to their elevated status, many tantric goddesses have a distinctly unorthodox nature, encouraging their devotees to imbibe impure substances or perform unorthodox practices, most commonly the pañcamakāra or five Ms (mada, wine; matsya, fish; māṃsa, meat; mudrā, parched grain, considered an aphrodisiac; and maithuna, sexual intercourse). They do this in an effort to conquer their desires and aversions, ultimately hoping to gain full control of, and to transcend, their ego. Many tantric goddesses, or goddesses that are popular in tantric worship, such as Kālī and Tārā and the Mahāvidyās, accept blood sacrifices. This unorthodox nature is also evident in Śākta texts as the character of the Great Goddess that developed was not simply benign and orthodox but was also terrible and unorthodox.

The idea of a Mahādevī was first articulated in the *Devī Māhātmya*, 'Glory of the Divine Mother' (also known as the *Durgā-Saptaśatī*, 'Seven hundred verses to Durgā'). It is the most significant and popular goddess text, in which we are offered a vision of a supremely powerful goddess whose deepest essence is the basis of all other goddesses. Implicitly, she is the basis of all power. Although she was created by the combined powers of the gods, the Goddess that the gods produced immediately established herself as a powerful entity in her own right. Conceptualised as the Mahādevī, her role as cosmic protector is the basis of the text's mythological narrative. During various battles fought against the asuras (demons), Devī is constantly addressed by different names such as Durgā (Beyond Reach) Ambā (Mother) or Caṇḍī (Violent and Impetuous One) which point to her multifarious powers. Devī also produces various śaktis from her own body, powerful goddesses that aid her in her fight against the demons and who also represent different aspects of her character.

The most detailed and profound expressions of Mahādevī are transmitted most comprehensively by the Śākta *Purāṇas*. The texts that are available in printed form are the *Devī Purāṇa*, the

Mahābhāgavata Purāṇa, the *Kālika Purāṇa* and the *Devī-Bhāgavatam Purāṇa*; of these four, only the last two have been translated into English. These *Purāṇas* were probably written to spread Śāktism (the cult of goddess worship) and to offer various conceptions of Devī (Hazra 1979: 16). By far the largest and perhaps the most comprehensive Śākta *Purāṇa* is the *Devī-Bhāgavatam Purāṇa*, which provides a kind of encyclopaedic mix of goddess mythology, ritual practice and metaphysical discussion. It was written as a Śākta response to the Vaiṣṇava (cult of Viṣṇu) *Bhāgvata Purāṇa* (Brown 1990: x) and offers a development of the ideas formulated in the earlier *Devī Māhātmya*. It includes versions of the *Devī Māhātmya* legends and retells a number of well-known purāṇic myths, but from a Śākta perspective. Of significance is the retelling of Devī's initial appearance, which in the original version of the *Devī Māhātmya* attributes her birth to the combined power and anger of the gods. In the *Devī-Bhāgavatam Purāṇa* account, no such male intervention is acknowledged as Devī appears by her own volition from a blinding light in response to the gods' devotion and propitiation of her. As well as the title Mahādevī, she is also called Parameśvarī (Supreme Ruler) and Viśvādhikā (She who transcends the world) and is often praised as the dynamic or energetic aspect of ultimate reality or Brahman.

The nature of Mahādevī

Although the Goddess is described in many different ways, as an all-encompassing power or as individual female deities, the fundamental nature of all goddesses is the same. Mahādevī, and in the purāṇic texts goddesses in general, is closely associated with three important principles, māyā (illusion), prakṛti (primary or primordial matter) and śakti (power or energy). The conceptual understanding of māyā and prakṛti is important throughout Hinduism, not just in connection with the divine feminine. Both māyā and prakṛti in many contexts have rather negative connotations but in their association with goddess theology become positive powers. According to the philosophy of Śaṅkara's Advaita Vedānta, māyā had wholly negative implications, in that it prevented individuals from seeing the identity between Brahman and the Self (Ātman), fooling them into incorrectly perceiving the world around them as real. This erroneous belief led to attachment to the material world, a path leading away from mokṣa (liberation from the cycle of birth and death, saṃsāra) rather than towards it. By contrast, in Śākta thought māyā was perceived as a positive creative force, a necessary tool for the Goddess to use and one that was not separate from her essential nature. Hence, Devī claims: 'I imagine into being the whole world, moving and unmoving, through the power of my Māyā, Yet that same Māyā is not separate from me; this is the highest truth' (*Devī Gītā* 3.1). Goddess theology does not dispute the falseness and impermanence of the world, but instead declares that it is both real and unreal because it exists but is 'not what it appears to be' (Brown 1998: 15), for when the individual soul attains enlightenment the world no longer has any substance. In the Śākta view, there is a more intimate relationship between Mahādevī and the world as she not only creates it but also enters into it. Therefore, despite the fact that many of the ideas advanced in the *Devī-Bhāgavatam Purāṇa*, and the *Devī Gītā* ('Song of the Goddess') in particular, are strongly influenced by Advaita philosophy, they represent a more positive view of the world and its creation. Māyā enables the Goddess, who in reality is beyond conception, to provide accessible forms of herself, with which her devotees can interact, for the Śākta texts, despite being metaphysically based, promote bhakti (devotion) as a means to liberation.

Another important aspect of the Mahādevī that is inseparably linked with śakti and māyā is her association with prakṛti (primordial matter), the principle underlying the manifest world. Prakṛti, like māyā, in many schools of thought has rather negative connotations. In order to understand its original meaning and to see how it is changed in Śākta theology, it is necessary to examine its genesis in perhaps the oldest school of philosophical thought, Sāṃkhya. Sāṃkhya envisaged everything as originating from two principles, consciousness (puruṣa) and primordial matter (prakṛti). Prakṛti was the source and the means of manifestation of the material world in which individual souls were ensnared, or, more correctly, considered themselves to be trapped. Prakṛti, or material nature, essentially consisted of three attributes (guṇas): sattva (purity, goodness, the illuminating principle), rajas (activity, passion, the energetic principle) and tamas (darkness, inertia, dullness). Prakṛti was a binding force and one that had to be overcome before the individual soul could be liberated. However, prakṛti was an essential principle of manifestation as without it puruṣa was inert. In Śākta theology prakṛti is endowed with positive associations as its non-difference from matter is emphasised along with the reality of māyā, regarded as a creative power rather than as illusion. The Goddess's appearance in the world, by means of her prakṛti and māyā, is to offer a source of liberation to the souls, who in essence are no different from her own being, offering them an object of devotion and a source of knowledge that can lead them beyond the physical world that surrounds them.

In the *Devī Māhātmya*, the terrible and ferocious side of Mahādevī appears most prominent. Since the text is dominated by various battles between the Goddess and the demons, she is most often portrayed as the ultimate divine warrior queen. Even at times when she is called mother, her martial aspect is thinly veiled. During one episode, she creates a group of seven goddesses from herself, referred to as the Mātṛkās (Mothers), and ironically the battle that ensues is one of the bloodiest in the text. In many myths, the angry aspect of Mahādevī or of individual goddesses represents a positive force, for instance the appearance of Kālī as a transformation and extension of Devī's anger, a force that separates from her, becoming a goddess in her own right. During a battle with the demons, Kālī is able to defeat two formerly invincible demons that had so far prevailed against Devī in her less fierce aspect. The dynamic and protective aspects of Mahādevī juxtaposed with her compassionate and maternal incarnations are an indication of her essentially transcendent nature. She is often described in apparently contradictory terms, for instance when she is praised as beautiful and grotesque, as the source of liberating knowledge and of ignorance, and as being martial and maternal. The opposing poles of her nature offer a glimpse of her ultimate transcendency.

While the *Devī Māhātmya* is the most recited and best-known of the Śākta texts, the *Devī-Bhāgavatam Purāṇa*, in its 18,000 verses, provides the most comprehensive depiction of the nature of Mahādevī. In this text, she is clearly presented as the supreme power of the universe, as Para-Śakti. Her many names provide a glimpse of her multifarious nature. She is Mahāmāyā (Power of Illusion), Deveṣī (Ruler of the Gods), Parabrahmaika (the One Brahman); as well as these grand incarnations she is also Kumārī (Virgin or Maiden), Ramaṇīyāṅgī (Beautiful of Limb), but one of her most prolific forms is Bhuvaneśvarī (Ruler of the Universe) (Brown 1998: 325–33). While the aspect of Mahādevī that is most prominent in the *Devī Māhātmya* is her forceful, often terrible, warrior nature, the *Devī-Bhāgavatam Purāṇa* concentrates on her compassionate side. However, though her benign nature might dominate the text, her terrible side is not dismissed, nor is it negated. Mahādevī is clearly understood to consist of both aspects. Nowhere is this more evident than in her revelation of her cosmic form at the request of the gods.

In the *Devī Gītā* portion of the *Devī-Bhāgavatam Purāṇa*, Devī shows her cosmic form in much the same way as Kṛṣṇa revealed his cosmic form in the *Bhagavadgītā* ('Song of the Lord'). What appears first is Mahādevī's terrible form, described as 'thousands of blazing rays, licking with its tongue, producing horrible crunching sounds with its teeth, spewing fire from its eyes, holding various weapons, heroic in stature, making mush of Brahmans and Kṣatriyas for its food' (*Devī Gītā* 3.35–36). Even though the gods had requested this vision, its appearance overawed them and they quickly implored her to show them her beautiful, benign and auspicious form instead. In this respect, the gods' preference for Mahādevī's auspicious aspect perhaps parallels Devī's human devotees, many of whom feel most comfortable with her beautiful and auspicious forms.

At first glance, the two totally opposed forms of Mahādevī might indicate that she has an ambivalent character. However, this is not the case as the combination of benign and terrible qualities in her character underlies her most fundamental features, namely that 'She *is* the world in the form of a great being' (Kinsley 1986: 149). Just as the world is a source of nourishment, as represented by Annapūrṇā (She who is full of food), Śākambharī (She who bestows vegetables) and Jagaddhātrī (She who supports the world), it can also be a source of destruction, represented by Bhairavī (The Terrible) and Kālarātri (Night of death). Similarly, śakti, the underlying essence of Mahādevī, is not purely creative, but also embodies destructive tendencies.

The *Devī-Bhāgavatam Purāṇa* clearly envisions Mahādevī as being independent of male control, for though it is at pains to offer various, often diametrically opposed forms, of the One Goddess they are all feminine. The masculine aspect, personified by the gods, especially the trimūrti, Brahmā, Viṣṇu and Śiva, who generally represent the world creator, preserver and destroyer, respectively, are presented as 'mere instruments' of the Goddess. Since the trimūrti are integral to Hinduism in general, their existence cannot simply be negated. In the Śākta texts, and the *Devī-Bhāgavatam Purāṇa* in particular, they are wholly subject for their existence to the power of the Goddess. She ridicules their claims of power, declaring: 'it is I that make you dance like inert wooden dolls as My mere instruments. You are merely My functions. I am the Integral Whole' (*Devī-Bhāgavatam Purāṇa* 12. 8. 81). From the outset, the text makes it clear that the Goddess in her transcendent form is the basis from which the gods have arisen. In this respect, Mahādevī is equated with Brahman, the formless and genderless ultimate reality, and, as such, she is herself, beyond masculine and feminine distinctions. However, unlike the rather lofty and inaccessible conception of Brahman that was formulated in the *Upaniṣads*, the Goddess, mainly through her creative maternal nature, her heroic deeds, and her great compassion, remains engaged with the world as its creator and saviour. These are perhaps the most important qualities of Mahādevī, and are aspects that appear to dominate her character. Despite being perceived as the source of the world, and indeed as the world, she is not distant from it. Through her intimate relationship with prakti, māyā and śakti, the Goddess infuses her creation with herself. She is eternally accessible to her devotees, who are encouraged to worship her, as a child adores its mother. Similarly, like a mother, Devī offers protection, promising to manifest herself whenever she is needed. In this respect, the many goddesses who are subsumed into her character represent her presence in the world, being always available to her devotees.

As well as being a creator and protector, Mahādevī also represents and offers divine knowledge of the sort that leads to liberation. Many of the Śākta texts stress the importance of bhakti (loving devotion) as a means to liberation through the goddess. Her terrible manifestations, in particular, encourage her devotees to face up to the realities of life such as death and suffering, which are inseparable from birth and happiness. Within this context, but most popular in tantric worship, is the concept of the Mahāvidyās, ten forms of the goddess who represent supreme or transcendent knowledge. One Śākta text, the *Mahābhāgavata Purāṇa*, contains the oldest account of the Mahāvidyās. Their inclusion is bound up in the account of the goddess Satī's immolation, an important myth in each of the Śākta *Purāṇas*. On first appearance, the goddess Satī appears to be simply a pure, benign goddess, the consort of Śiva. However, this is only one side of her inherently dualistic character, for according to the Satī myth in the *Mahābhāgavata Purāṇa* she also has another, more profound aspect to her nature. Satī was anxious to go to her father's sacrifice although she had not been invited. She tried unsuccessfully to persuade Śiva to give his permission for her to go. When her supplication failed, Satī decided to remind Śiva exactly who she was. It is important that when she revealed her power its initial personification was in the form of Kālī, a fierce goddess, who seems on the surface to be the antithesis of the pure, benign Satī. Confronted by her fierce form, Śiva tried to turn away from her, but she produced other forms until the Mahāvidyās surrounded him. The text clearly shows that though Satī most often chooses to present herself as the consort of Śiva, content to carry out his wishes, in reality she is the power underlying the entire cosmos, subject to the will of no one and encompassing all duality.

Expressions of Mahādevī

Not all expressions of the underlying essence of the divine feminine are found solely in textual sources. A more practical and tangible expression of this idea is evident in the worship of numerous goddesses across India at places referred to as śākta pīṭhas or (seats of the goddess). India is a sacred land and is punctuated by many sacred places, though most of them are not directly connected with one another. The development of the śākta pīṭha notion is important because it indicates that not only is there an underlying correspondence between many goddesses, but their collective essence infuses the land. By worshipping the goddesses at the śākta pīṭhas, the devotee can tap into the power of the Mahādevī.

Although different goddesses are worshipped at each site, according to mythology they have all originated from the dismemberment of one goddess, Satī. The chain of events that led to the death of Satī and, consequently, the creation of the śākta pīṭhas began in the divine realm, where it was decided that Śiva was in need of a wife to necessitate the continuation of creation. Devī agreed to be born as the daughter of Dakṣa, one of the mind-born sons of Brahmā, in order to become Śiva's wife (*Kālikā Purāṇa* 1. 7. 1–3). When Dakṣa organised a grand sacrifice he invited all the gods, and according to some texts all creatures, but neglected to invite Śiva and his wife Satī. On discovering her father's slight of her husband and herself, Satī became very angry and immolated herself, according to some versions of the myth in his sacrificial fire, or in the *Kālikā Purāṇa*, by her own power. When he learnt of Satī's death, Śiva flew into a terrible rage and destroyed Dakṣa's sacrifice. Becoming inconsolable at the death of Satī, he put her body on his shoulder and wandered about with it like a madman. The other gods, Brahmā and Viṣṇu, were fearful of Śiva in this state and resolved to remove Satī's body in the hope of lessening Śiva's anger and grief. They entered the body and disposed of it piece by piece (*Kālikā Purāṇa* 1.18.39–40); or, as is recounted in another source (*Devī-Bhāgavatam Purāṇa* 7.30), Viṣṇu cut it from Śiva's shoulder with his arrows or discus. The places where the various parts of Satī's body fell became known as the śākta pīṭhas, and as such are now considered especially powerful places of goddess worship. In a practical sense, this idea has given coherence and added meaning to the many places of goddess worship scattered across India that at one time were disparate. Although there is no decisive list of how many pieces of Satī fell to earth or their exact location, it does not seem particularly important. To what extent individual places are defined is less important than grasping the idea of the interconnectedness of the goddesses and the earth that this myth expresses and promotes.

Although Mahādevī, especially in the form of different goddesses, changes from text to text, her underlying nature stays the same. Similarly, she may be envisaged in many different ways in different parts of India. In Assam she is the goddess Kāmākhyā, who in her most famous temple is represented by a cleft in the rock, regarded as her yoni (female generative organ). Although she is to a certain extent a regional goddess (prolific only in Assam), she also represents the creative aspect of the supreme goddess. In Bengal she is most often Kālī, Durgā or the disease goddess Śītalā. In Tamil Nadu Devī is most commonly known as Māriammā, Mīnākṣī or Kalīammā. Whatever the individual mythology and iconography of each goddess is, underlying her individuality, the presence of Mahādevī remains. Consequently, various social groups construct her identity in the ways that are most meaningful to them, and as a result India is teeming with goddesses belonging to different caste groups or related to a particular geographical area. One goddess in particular, Vaiṣṇo Devī, whose cave temple in the mountains of Jammu and Kashmir draws thousands of pilgrims each year, clearly embodies Mahādevī's 'manyness and oneness' (Rohe 2001: 56). Vaiṣṇo Devī is represented by three piṇḍis (small, round rocky outcrops) that are described by her priests as Mahā-Sarasvatī, Mahā-Lakṣmī and Mahā-Kālī. There seems no clear conception among her devotees about who Vaiṣṇo Devī (whose name simply identifies her as a pure, vegetarian goddess with some relationship to Viṣṇu) actually is. She is described as Mahādevī, either the power of Mahā-Sarasvatī, Mahā-Lakṣmī and Mahā-Kālī, or as being separate from them. Poster art identifies Vaiṣṇo Devī as a Durgā-type figure, seated on a tiger, brandishing various weapons in her eight hands. In whatever way Vaiṣṇo Devī is conceived of, each pilgrim creates his or her own meaning from their encounter with her. The Vaiṣṇavite (devotee of Viṣṇu) might see her as an incarnation of Lakṣmī, the Śaivite (devotee of Śiva) may see her as a form of Durgā and the Śākta may simply see Vaiṣṇo Devī as the Mahādevī, personified in many forms. All Hindu goddesses operate on two levels. They are individuals in that they have their own iconography and a mythology that in many cases is individual to themselves, but as each goddess is a manifestation of Mahādevī, as such, they all have the same underlying essence. It is this combination of individuality and cosmic correspondence that allows the Goddess to be both available and yet beyond human conception, to live among her people despite being their ultimate source.

See also: **Aditi; Advaita; Asuras; Ātman; Bhagavadgītā; Bhāgvatas; Bhakti; Blood sacrifice; Brahmā; Brahman; Devī Māhātmya; Durgā; Gaṅgā; Guṇas; Hazra, Rajendra Chandra; Kālī and Caṇḍī; Kramrisch, Stella; Kṛṣṇa; Lakṣmī, Śrī; Mahābhārata; Mahāvidyās; Māriammā; Mātṛkās; Māyā; Mīnākṣī; Mokṣa; Pañcamakāra; Pārvatī; Prakṛti; Pṛthivī; Purāṇas; Puruṣa; Rādhā; Rāmāyāṇa; Sacred geography; Śaivism; Śakti; Saṃhitā; Sāṃkhya; Saṃsāra; Śaṅkara; Sarasvatī; Sītā; Śītalā; Śiva; Tantras; Tārā; Trimūrti; Upaniṣads; Uṣas; Vaiṣṇavism; Vedānta; Woodroffe, John**

LYNN FOULSTON

Further reading

Brown, C. Mackenzie. 1974. *God as Mother: A Feminine Theology in India; An Historical and Theological Study of the Brahmavaivarta Purāṇa*. Hartford, VT: Claude Stark.

Brown, C. Mackenzie. 1990. *The Triumph of the Goddess: The Canonical Models and Theological Visions of the Devī-Bhāgavata Purāṇa*. Albany, NY: State University of New York Press.

Brown, C. Mackenzie. 1998. *The Devī Gītā – The Song of the Goddess: A Translation, Annotation, and Commentary*. Albany, NY: State University of New York Press.

Coburn, T.B. 1988. *Devī-Māhātmya: The Crystallization of the Goddess Tradition*. Reprint of 1984 edn. Delhi: Motilal Banarsidass

Coburn, T.B. 1991. *Encountering the Goddess: A Translation of the Devī-Māhātmya and a Study of Its Interpretation*. Delhi: Sri Satguru Publications.

Dutt, K. Guru. 1975. 'Shakti Worship in India'. *Religion and Society (Bangalore)* 22: 47–62.

Hazra, R.C. 1979. *Studies on the Upapurāṇas, vol. 2: Śākta and Non-sectarian Upapurāṇas*. Reprint of 1963 edn. Calcutta: Sanskrit College.

Kinsley, D.R. 1986. *Hindu Goddesses: Visions of the Divine Feminine in the Hindu Religious Tradition*. Delhi: Motilal Banarsidass.

Kinsley, D.R. 1997. *Tantric Visions of the Divine Feminine: The Ten Mahāvidyās*. Berkeley, CA: University of California Press.

Kramrisch, Stella. 1975. 'The Indian Great Goddess'. *History of Religions* 14/4: 235–65.

Pintchman, T. 1994. *The Rise of the Goddess in the Hindu Tradition*. Albany, NY: State University of New York Press.

Pintchman, T. (ed.). 2001. *Seeking Mahādevī: Constructing the Identities of the Hindu Great Goddess*. Albany, NY: State University of New York Press.

Rohe, M.E. 2001. 'Ambiguous and Definitive: The Greatness of Goddess Vaiṣṇo Devī'. In T. Pintchman, ed., *Seeking Mahādevī: Constructing the Identities of the Hindu Great Goddess*. Albany, NY: State University of New York Press, 55–76.

Shastri, B. (trans.). 1991–92. *Kālikā Purāṇa*, vols 1–3. Delhi: Nag Publishers.

Swami Vijnanananda (trans.). 1986. *The Śrīmad Devī-Bhāgavatatam*, 3rd edn. New Delhi: Munishiram Manoharlal.

Woodroffe, Sir John. 1987. *Śakti and Śākta: Essays and Addresses*. Reprint 9th edn. Madras: Ganesh and Company.

MAHĀDEVĪ, AKKA (TWELFTH-CENTURY)

Akka Mahādevī, a Kannada bhakti saint, poetess and rebel of the Vīraśaiva movement, was born in Udutadi in Karnataka. Her initiation into Śiva worship at a very early age is said to have marked the moment of her spiritual birth. She was given in marriage to the wealthy local king, Kauśika, a non-believer, who fell in love with her. The marriage was short-lived. She defied notions of 'feminine behaviour' by leaving her husband, even discarding her garments and wandering about covered only in her long tresses. After being subjected to a severe test she was admitted into the company of saints. She came to be known as Akka, 'elder sister'. She is said to have finally merged into Śiva's image at Śrīśaila, thus ending her mortal life, in her early twenties. Her mystical longing for Śiva is expressed in her vacanas, or lyrical poems.

See also: **Bhakti; Śiva; Strīdharma; Vīraśaivas**

SHARADA SUGIRTHARAJAH

Further reading

Dabbe, V. and R. Zydenbos. 1989. 'Akka Mahadevi'. In *Manushi*, Tenth Anniversary Issue, nos. 50, 51 and 52 (January–June): 39–44.

Ramanujan, A.K. 1973. *Speaking of Siva*. Harmondsworth: Penguin.

MAHĀLAYA

See: **Pitṛpakṣa**

MAHĀPĀTAKAS

Mahāpātaka (literally, great 'falling down') refers in smṛti texts to great crimes. Lists of these vary but usually include incest, murdering a brāhmaṇa, drinking liquor, stealing a brāhmaṇa's gold, having sexual relations with a guru's wife and associating with perpetrators of these crimes. Some smṛtis, such as the *Viṣṇu Dharmasūtra* view the types of incest as even more serious crimes (called atipātakas). By contrast, upapātakas (literally, secondary 'falls' – that is, minor crimes) include wrong speech (bragging, accusing, denouncing, reviling); lack of reverence (toward parents, wife, son); improper bodily acts (forbidden food and drink); theft; improper employment; adultery; unlawful presents; forgetting the Veda; breaking a vow of chastity; studying irreligious books; and offending a guru.

Hindu morality and law focus on acts, which they classify in various ways (formal and informal, daily and occasional, enjoined and prohibited, and so forth). They relate acts, in turn, to the law of karma – 'as you sow, so you reap' – which means that every act will receive its exact retribution. Because no act is amoral, a wrong one cannot be excused; rather, it must be the result of bad karma. There are, however, degrees of responsibility (related to degrees of intentionality, such as evil design, criminal intent, compelling motive and submission to coercion, and therefore degrees of guilt, with corresponding penalties). An unintentional sin (pāpa) could be expiated by prayers or mantras, for instance a minor civil infraction by a fine. But a serious crime could be expiated only by corporal punishment or, in the case of murder, by capital punishment and condemnation to hell – although capital punishment was prohibited, according to prohibitions called Kalivarjya (things to be avoided in the Kaliyuga, a time when only one-quarter of the righteous remained according to the theory of the four yugas), from the tenth century. Ignorance, along with senility and retardation, however, were not punished by society.

See also: **Guru; Karma (law of action); Mantra; Pāpa; Sacred texts; Varṇa; Veda; Yuga**

KATHERINE K. YOUNG

Further reading

Day, T.P. 1982. *The Conception of Punishment in Early Indian Literature.* Waterloo, Ontario: Canadian Corporation for Studies in Religion with Wilfrid Laurier Press.

Glucklich, A. 1994. *The Sense of Adharma*. Oxford: Oxford University Press.

Herman, A.L. 1976. *The Problem of Evil and Indian Thought*. Delhi: Motilal Banarsidass.

Kane, P.V. 1968–77. *History of Dharmaśāstra (Ancient and Medieval Religious and Civil Law in India)*, 2nd edn, 5 vols. Poona: Bhandarkar Oriental Research Institute, esp. vol. 4.

MAHARAJ JI, GURU (PREM RAWAT)

Born in 1958, the youngest son of Sri Hans Ji Maharaj, Guru Prem Rawat was instructed into the four techniques known as 'Knowledge' by his father at the age of six. He took on the challenge of continuing his father's work to promote self-knowledge and inner fulfilment after his death in 1966.

The young Maharaji toured India speaking to large audiences whilst continuing to attend school. In June 1971 he accepted an invitation to come to London. The arrival of the 13-year-old guru attracted considerable media attention. After speaking at several locations in London and addressing the participants at the first Glastonbury festival, Maharaji travelled to the USA. As a result of his success in America and Europe, he decided to finish his education and devote himself fully to his activities.

Since the 1970s Maharaji has continued to tour the world and his teachings have been established in over eighty countries. A number of scholars have written about Maharaji, usually placing him as part of the Sant Mat tradition, with historic links to the Radhasoamis. However, Maharaji's historical background links him to the satgurus (true teachers whose teachings have become known in Northern India as Advait Mat, now a cluster of panths (groups of disciples) who perceive themselves as originating from Totapuri, the teacher of Ramakrishna (Geaves 2006)).

The most effective way to analyse Maharaji and his activities, especially his continuous deconstruction of organisations and movements created around the world to promote his teachings, is to compare him to the solitary sant master owing no allegiance to any religion (Geaves 2004). He certainly refutes any connection to Hinduism and has worked hard to remove any accretions to his teachings that originated in his Indian background. His own emphasis has always been on the centrality of experiential knowledge and the role of a living master to inspire and encourage the thirst that leads to such knowledge. Maharaji's mode of teaching and delivery of his message provide an insight into the iconoclasm, universalism, spontaneity and renewal that were a feature of the medieval solitary sants before the message became institutionalised after their deaths. However, he is also an important figure in any assessment of emergent forms of spirituality in contemporary Western society.

See also: **Guru; Radhasoami Satsang; Ramakrishna, Sri; Sant**

RON GEAVES

Further reading

Geaves, R.A. 2004. 'From Divine Light Mission to Elan Vital and Beyond: An Exploration of Change and Adaptation'. *Nova Religio* 7(3) (March): 45–62.

Geaves, R.A. 2006. 'From Totapuri to Maharaji: Reflections on a (Lineage) Parampara'. In Anna King, ed., *Indian Religions: Renaissance and Renewal*. London: Equinox.

MAHARISHI MAHESH YOGI (b.1911 or 1918?)

Founder of Transcendental Meditation (TM), the Maharishi Mahesh Yogi was born in Jabalpur, India. Little is known of his early life. His original name was either Mahesh Prasad Varma or J.N. Srivastava (it is not known which), and 'Maharishi' – 'great seer' – is an assumed title.

In 1940 he gained a degree in physics from Allahabad University, after which he studied under Swami Brahmananda Saraswati (1869–1953, aka Guru Dev) in Śaṅkara's Advaita Vedānta tradition. After Guru Dev's death, the Maharishi became a recluse for two years, after which he completed his first book, *The Beacon Light of the Himalayas* (1956), which introduced TM.

In 1957 the Maharishi founded the Spiritual Regeneration Movement (SRM) in Madras, and later brought the TM technique to the West, lecturing in the USA in 1959 and in Britain in 1960. The following year he began to train others to teach TM, and in 1963 published his key text *Science of Being and Art of Living*, which is still used within the organisation. The Maharishi set up a number of organisations to utilise TM, linking it with education, management, medicine and politics: for example the International Academy of Meditation (founded in 1966), the Students International Training Society (SITS) (1968) and the Maharishi International University (MIU) in the USA (1971). The Science of Creative Intelligence (1971) was devised to link modern Western science with ancient Vedic knowledge, and his Maharishi Ayur-Veda Panchakarma Programme, as well as the Maharishi Vedic Vibration Technology, offers treatments for various medical conditions. In 1992 the TM organisation established the Natural Law Party (NLP) in the USA and Europe, with the aim of achieving world peace and practising conflict-free politics.

See also: **Advaita; Āyurveda; Transcendental Meditation; Veda**

GEORGE CHRYSSIDES

Further reading

Forem, Jack. 1974. *Transcendental Meditation: Maharishi Mahesh Yogi and the Science of Creative Intelligence*. London: Allen and Unwin.

MAHĀŚIVARĀTI

See: **Śivarātri**

MAHAT

Mahat, 'great', is the first evolute of Prakṛti in classical Sāṃkhya. It is probably so called by adapting the term mahān ātmā, 'great self', used in Upaniṣadic cosmology (*Kaṭha Upaniṣad* 3.10–11, 6.7–9; Larson 1969: 102–3), which derives from Vedic creation mythology of the absolute taking birth as its own first creation (Larson 1969: 98). Mahat in an individual is buddhi, 'intellect', the faculty of determination (adhyavasāya) (*Sāṃkhyakārikā* 23). It determines the nature of objects presented to it by the other faculties of knowledge and perception and decides courses of action to be carried out by the organs of action, accomplishing all of the experience of the Puruṣa (*Sāṃkhyakārikā* 35–37). It is the locus of the eight pure and impure dispositions virtue and vice, knowledge and ignorance, dispassion and passion, and power and infirmity, by seven of which the Puruṣa is bound and by the second of which, i.e. knowledge, it distinguishes the difference between Puruṣa and Prakṛti which finally liberates the Puruṣa from Prakṛti.

See also: **Prakṛti; Puruṣa; Sāṃkhya; Sāṃkhyakārikās; Upaniṣads**

PETER M. SCHARF

Further reading

Larson, Gerald James. 1969. *Classical Sāṃkhya: An Interpretation of its History and Meaning*. Delhi: Motilal Banarsidass.

MAHĀVIDYĀS

The term Mahāvidyā literally means 'Great knowledge' and refers to ten goddesses, often referred to as the Dasamahāvidyās, who have been identified as a group since the tenth century CE. Their names and the order in which they appear may vary but the following list represents their most common formation, in which Kālī, the most important Mahāvidyā, usually comes first: Kālī (The Black Goddess), Tārā (The Goddess Who Guides Through Troubles), Tripura-Sundarī or ṣoḍaśī (She Who Is Lovely in the Three Worlds), Bhuvaneśvarī (She Whose Body Is the World), Chinnamastā (The Self-decapitated Goddess), Bhairavī (The Fierce

One), Dhūmāvatī (The Widow), Bagalāmukhī, literally 'face of a crane' (The Paralyser), Mātaṅgī (The Outcaste) and Kamalā or Śrī Lakṣmī (The Lotus Goddess) (Kinsley 1997). The Mahāvidyās are an odd collection of goddesses, including the auspicious and the inauspicious and those who are well known and those who are little known beyond the group. There is only one known temple (in Kolkata) to the Mahāvidyās collectively, though some, such as Kālī, Tārā and Kamalā (Śrī-Lakṣmī), do have their own temples. As a group, they are most often depicted on the walls of goddess temples or on posters. They are mostly independent and, with the exception of Kamalā, are fierce goddesses. Although they do not neatly fit into any one category, they represent transcendent, liberating knowledge, embodying both creative and destructive aspects of existence, and perhaps making their devotees aware of the less comfortable facts of life. The Mahāvidyās are essentially tantric goddesses who are closely linked with the acquisition of magical powers. Their fundamental form is as a mantra (a sacred spoken formula) through which the devotee aims to identify with one of the goddesses. As a group, the Mahāvidyās also represent the benign and terrible aspects of the Mahādevī (The Great Goddess).

See also: **Kālī and Caṇḍī; Lakṣmī, Śrī; Mahādevī; Mantra; Tantrism**

LYNN FOULSTON

Further reading

Kinsley, D.R. 1997. *Tantric Visions of the Divine Feminine: The Ten Mahāvidyās*. Berkeley, CA: University of California Press

MAHĀVRATA

While mahāvrata, meaning 'great observance' in Sanskrit, is used in a variety of contexts, the term has unique usage in the context of Vedic literature.

There, the Mahāvrata is a communal festival celebrating a new vegetation and harvest cycle, and it takes place at the end of the year-long gavāmayana rite, which follows the course of the sun throughout the year. Because there is some evidence the Mahāvrata was performed on the day of the winter solstice, where the daily position of the sun begins to move auspiciously northwards, the Vedic Mahāvrata has been linked to the contemporary winter solstice festival of Makara saṃkrānti. The rite finds elaborate mention in the *Aitareya Āraṇyaka*, and is also described in detail in the *Āpastamba* and *Kauṣika Śrautasūtras.* The performance of the rite is quite unique among Vedic rituals, in that it includes a high degree of female participation, as well featuring a great proportion of 'folk' elements, such as dancing and drumming, the use of obscene language and even ritual intercourse – all of which suggests that this rite is a Vedic ritualisation of an older indigenous fertility festival.

See also: **Āraṇyakas; Makara saṃkrānti; Śrautasūtras; Utsava; Veda**

TRAVIS L. SMITH

Further reading

Keith, A.B. 1908. *The Śāṅkhāyana Āraṇyaka: With an Appendix on the Mahāvrata.* London: Royal Asiatic Society.

MAHEŚVARA

See: **Śiva**

MAHIMA GOSAIN

Somewhere around 1828, Mukunda Das arrived in Kapilas in Orissa and began to practise yogic sādhana. During this period he disagreed with the local brāhmaṇas, arguing that their rituals were unnecessary for the worship of the only true reality, the nirguṇa aspect of the divine, who he named Alakh. After decades of practising tapas, alternatively moving between Kapilas and other districts of Orissa, preaching his simple message of nirguṇa bhakti to the rural populations, it is believed that he attained mokṣa on his death in 1876. The movement is significant for its work amongst the lower-caste populations of Orissa and its critique of brāhmaṇa hegemony and the corruption endemic at the shrine of Jagannātha.

Later, known as Mahima Gosain, he attracted a number of saṃnyāsi disciples who travelled throughout the state, staying only one night in each place. In this way, the movement spread. Today, the centre of the Satya Mahima Dharma is Joranda, attracting thousands of devotees to a three-day melā which takes place annually on Maghā Pūrṇimā, when multitudes of Mahima saṃnyāsis gather at Mahima Gosain's samādhi, revering him as a modern avatāra.

See also: **Avatāra; Jagannātha; Tapas**

RON GEAVES

Further reading

Jones, Kenneth. 1989. *Socio-Religious Reform Movements in British India, The New Cambridge History of India: Vol. 3.1*. Cambridge: Cambridge University Press.

MAHIṢA

The demon Mahiṣa is usually presented mythically and iconographically as possessing a buffalo form and battling the goddess Durgā. This conflict is detailed in the *Devī Māhātmya* (500–600 CE) and, more expansively, in the *Devī Bhāgavata Purāṇa* (1000–1600 CE). These myths recount how, as a reward for the performance of severe austerities, Mahiṣa is granted by Brahmā (or the Mahādevī in the *Bhāgavata Purāṇa*) the boon of invulnerability to the power of men. So imbued, and commanding a vast army of demons, Mahiṣa then proceeds to overthrow the rule of the gods. It is only the intervention of the goddess Durgā, Mahiṣa's superior in combat and unaffected by his boon, that ultimately saves the world and re-establishes order. Depicted iconographically as early as the first century BCE (Coburn 1988: 227–28), the slaying of a buffalo-demon by a warrior goddess continues to be ritually enacted during the festival of Durgā Pūjā.

See also: **Asura; Brahmā; Devī Māhātmya; Durgā; Durgā Pūjā; Mahādevī; Purāṇas; Utsava**

PAUL REID-BOWEN

Further reading

Coburn, T.B. 1988. *Devī Māhātmya: The Crystalization of the Goddess Tradition*. Oxford: Molital Books.

MAITREYĪ

The wife of the ṛṣi, Yājñavalkya, who was taught philosophy and religion by her husband, and which is recorded in the form of a dialogue in the *Śatapatha Brāhmaṇa*. She is regarded as one of the most learned and virtuous women of ancient India and is mentioned on many occasions in the *Purāṇas*. She was noted for being more interested in learning the nature of the self than wearing jewellery, and when Yājñavalkya advised her at the time of his departure from home on one occasion that she could not hope to attain immortality by riches, she immediately replied that she was not interested in anything that could not liberate from death and asked him to reveal such knowledge. Significantly, she initiates the dialogue and is then taught the secrets of self-knowledge by her husband. Maitreyī and Gārgī provide fascinating insights into the status and position of educated women in the early *Upaniṣads*.

See also: **Gārgī; Yājñavalkya**

RON GEAVES

Further reading

Deshpande, Uma. 1992. 'Position and Status of Women in Early Upaniṣads', *Position and Status of Women in Ancient India Vol. II*, ed. L.K. Tripathi, Varanasi: Banaras Hindu University, 27–39.

MAKARA SAṂKRĀNTI, TIL SAṂKRĀNTI, LOHRI

Makar saṃkrānti is the winter solstice on the month of Pauṣa (December–January). The day of makara saṃkrānti represents the transition of the sun from the tropic of Cancer to the tropic of Capricorn, its passage form Dhanu (Sagittarius) to Makara (Capricorn) and its ascent from Dakṣinayāṇa (the Southern station) to Uttaranayāṇa (the Northern station). Makara saṃkrānti is observed as an auspicious day celebrating the beginning of spring and the new harvest. In *Bhagavadgīta* 10: 31, Kṛṣṇa identifies himself with the makara. One of the greatest pilgrimages related to makara saṃkrānti takes place at Gaṅgāsāgara (West Bengal), where the Ganges enters the sea. Makara saṃkrānti – Pongal in South India – is preceded by lohri (the 'bonfire festival'), which marks the culmination of winter and celebrates fertility. The day of makara saṃkrānti, famous as the 'kite festival', is alternatively called til saṃkrānti for the usage of sesame (til) for preparing sweets, food and oil for oblations.

See also: **Pongal**

FABRIZIO M. FERRARI

Further reading

Deb, S. 2001. *Encyclopaedia of Fairs & Festivals in India: With Select Rituals, Vows, Holy Cities, Temples and Pilgrim Centers.* Delhi: Raj Publications.

MĀL

Māl, also popularly known as Māyon, Perumāḷ and Tirumāl, is most popular in South India, in particular Tamil Nadu. Māl or Māyon appears in the Tamil, Saṅgam literature. The word Māl means 'Great' or 'Great Man' and is associated with Viṣṇu. Māyon means 'dark-coloured person' and is the Tamil equivalent of the word kṛṣṇa, meaning 'black'. Māl or Māyon is associated with two deities, Kṛṣṇa and Viṣṇu, particularly in his Nārāyaṇa aspect. Māl appears in the devotional poetry of the Āḻvārs (Tamil saint-poets), who named numerous Vaiṣṇava temples that contain his statues. In the main, worship of Māl in his various forms is devotional in nature. Māl as Perumāḷ (Esteemed Person) or Tirumāl (Tiru being the equivalent of Śrī, an honorific title) appears in many local settlements as the most common form of Viṣṇu. In this form he is associated with a particular location by the addition of a place name. For instance, Jenaka Perumāḷ has a large and probably the oldest temple dedicated to him in the town of Cholavandan, a place originally called Jenakaipuri.

See also: **Āḻvārs; Kṛṣṇa; Mandir; Poetry; Vaiṣṇavism; Viṣṇu**

LYNN FOULSTON

Further reading

Foulston, L. 2002. *At the Feet of the Goddess: The Divine Feminine in Local Hindu Religion.* Brighton and Portland, OR: Sussex Academic Press.

Klostermaier, K.K. 1994. *A Survey of Hinduism*, 2nd edn. Albany, NY: State University of New York Press.

http://philtar.ucsm.ac.uk/encyclopedia/hindu/ascetic/mal.html (accessed 25 April 2006).

MALAVIYA, PANDIT MADAN MOHAN (1861–1964)

Lawyer, journalist, politician, educationalist and social reformer. Allahabad-born into a family of Sanskrit scholars from Malwa, he graduated from Calcutta University in 1884. After his LL.B in 1891, he worked as a lawyer until 1909 while contributing to several newspapers – in Hindi and English – devoted to the nationalist movement, a strand of his career that eventually culminated in his chairmanship of the *Hindustan Times* (1942–46). Having attended sessions of the Indian National Congress since 1886, he was elected its president in 1909 and 1918, as well as in 1932 and 1938, both the latter times while under arrest.

Often differing sharply from the views of Gandhi, opposed to the Non-Cooperation movement and in favour of moderate activism through constitutional means, he nevertheless participated in the Salt Satyagraha and facilitated the Gandhi–Irwin Pact of 1931.

Having founded a number of associations for the defence of Hindu interests and campaigned against cow-slaughter, he became a co-founder of the powerful All-India Hindu Mahasabha (1910), a counterweight to the All-India Muslim League (1906), acting twice as its president. The Mahasabha, inspired in part by the Arya Samaj, was, from the early 1920s, to promote the movements of śuddhi (reconversion to Hinduism from Islam or Christianity) and of Sangatham (calling for Hindu unity).

His most lasting legacy has been the establishment of the Banaras Hindu University (founded in 1916 and opened in 1921), of which he became vice-chancellor (1919–38) and then rector, until his death.

See also: **Arya Samaj; Gandhi, Mohandas Karamchand; Hindu Mahasabha; Nationalism; Sacred animals**

DANIEL MARIAU

MANAS

The term manas in Indian thought often has a much more specific sense than its translation 'mind' does. In classical Sāṃkhya, manas is one of the three first evolutes of Prakṛti that comprise the internal organ (antaḥkaraṇa). While the buddhi is the faculty of judgement and the ahaṃkāra the individuality, the manas, the first evolute of ahaṃkāra with purity dominant, is the intentional (sāṃkalpika) faculty of attention that directly engages with each of the five senses and five organs of action, while yet serving as a transparent conveyance of experience to the self like the other faculties (*Sāṃkhyakārikā* 27). According to the *Jayamaṅgala* (*c.*600–800 CE) commentary on this verse, the manas is transparent and it is the intellect that determines the nature of the object. According to Vācaspati Miśra (*c.*841 or 976 CE) in his *Tattvakaumudī*, however, the senses present the manas with bare awareness (ālocanamātra *Sāṃkhyakārikā* 28), while the manas is constructive (*Sāṃkhyakārikā* 27). It not only passes perception to the intellect but constructs an object qualified by general and specific properties.

In contrast to the specific use of the term in Sāṃkhya, the term manas is used in Yoga synonymously with Citta for the mind. According to Vaiśeṣika, manas is one of nine fundamental types of substance.

See also: **Ahaṃkāra; Antaḥkaraṇa; Buddhi; Citta; Prakṛti; Sāṃkhya; Sāṃkhyakārikās; Vācaspati Miśra; Vaiśeṣika; Yoga**

PETER M. SCHARF

Further reading

Larson, Gerald James and Ram Shankar Bhattacharya (eds). 1987. 'Sāṃkhya: A Dualist Tradition in Indian Philosophy.' *Encyclopedia of Indian Philosophies*, vol. IV. Princeton, NJ: Princeton University Press; Delhi: Motilal Banarsidass, 49–73.

MANASĀ

The snake goddess of eastern India. Her principal function is to protect from snake bite, so she is worshipped mostly in the month of Śrāban (July–August), when the monsoon rains have brought snakes out into the open. Manasā's origin in myth has her as the daughter of Śiva, coming to earth to establish her worship among humans, which she does easily amongst the lower castes but with more difficulty with the upper. She is often worshipped in the form of a rounded earthenware pot, ghaṭ, or a chali, an elaborate piece of pottery decorated with snakes' heads. Although she is traditionally a typical 'wild' goddess, independent (she is separated from her husband Jaratkāru), ugly and cruel, there are now gentler images of her, adorned with snakes but without the powerful 'poison eye' she has in her origin myth, and described by her worshippers as beautiful.

See also: **Caste; Śiva**

CYNTHIA BRADLEY

Further reading

Maity, P.K. 1966. *Historical Studies in the Cult of the Goddess Manasa (a Socio-cultural Theory).* Calcutta: Punthi Pushtak.

Smith, W.L. 1980. *The One-eyed Goddess: A Study of the Manasa Mangal.* Stockholm: Almquist and Wiksell.

MANAV DHARMA SABHA

The organisation founded on 22 June 1844 by Dadoba Pandurang, Mehtaji Durgaram and a small circle of friends after the conversion of a Parsee student to Christianity and the resulting outrage of members of his own community and Hindus. Although it began as a reaction to conversion to Christianity, there is no doubt that the intellectual elite attracted to the movement in Surat were themselves influenced by their education in English schools and contact with missionary teaching. However, rather than promote a brahmanical or purāṇic Hinduism in opposition to Christian and Western influence, they chose to reform Hinduism, espousing monotheism with an anti-ritual, anti-image worship and anti-caste message based upon Dadoba Pandurang's seven principles, which later became the foundation of the more successful accultурative Paramahansa Mandali, founded in Bombay.

In some ways, the Manav Dharma Sabha was the forerunner for the contemporary Indian rationalist movements, as it engaged in similar strategies to publicly denounce as charlatans miracle workers, magicians or those who claimed to be able to perform supernatural feats through mantra incantation. Its members were critical of the caste system but did little to challenge brāhmaṇa orthodoxy on the matter. Although their meetings were open to the public and the ideals disseminated through literature and articles, they were not able to have a major impact in transforming society, rationalising popular religion or changing the views of the dominant brāhmaṇa leadership. However, the organisation formed the prototype for the more successful Paramahansa Mandali and the Prarthana Society. The organisation went into terminal decline in 1852 after Mehtaji Durgaram left for Rajkot, having already lost Dadoba Pandurang in 1846.

See also: **Caste; Durgaram Manchharam, Mehtaji; Image worship; Pandurang, Dadoba; Paramahansa Mandali**

RON GEAVES

Further reading

Jones, Kenneth. 1989. *Socio-Religious Reform Movements in British India, The New Cambridge History of India, Vol. 3.1.* Cambridge: Cambridge University Press.

MAṆḌALA

See: **Yantra**

MANDIR

'A place for dwelling in'. Mandir is not adequately translated by 'temple' since it also includes 'shrine'. Nor should it be conceived as the Hindu equivalent of a church. A mandir is an enclosed sacred space that houses one or more images of a god or goddesses. It is believed that a deity or powerful being has taken up residence in the image, usually after consecration, though it may be self-manifest. A mandir may be no larger than a niche in a wall or it may have attached halls, courtyards and passages, and be an architectural marvel as large as a town. It is primarily a home for a god or gods, though large mandirs are used for congregational gatherings during festivals. The use of mandirs for congregational gatherings is increasing among Indians overseas. Weddings do not normally take place in mandirs, but in the home, as does a great deal of religious activity, in front of the domestic shrine for example.

The main activity of the priest, or worshipper, in the mandir is to honour the deity in the image. Offerings are generally fruits or sweetmeats, though in some regions and among some communities blood sacrifices are offered. Worship is usually an individual act. The 'visible' remains of the edible offerings may be presented to the worshipper who has come to see and partake of the power present in the image (darśana), partly through this consuming of the 'leftovers' of the deity. Honour may also be shown by the use of incense, flowers, ringing of bells and movement of vessels with flames (ārtī). Music may be played, and there may be hymn singing, chanting of the names of God or uttering of discourses. There are often annual festival days for the particular form of deity with decorations and processing of the central image. Nearby may be a well or tank for bathing. There are many regional variations in temple architecture, especially between the North and South India.

Mandirs are usually privately owned by particular families, lineages or communities, though in some regions they are owned by trusts controlled by the state government.

Mandirs and image worship appear not to have been part of Vedic or early Brahmanic traditions, and only became common from the fifth century of our era. Over time some mandirs became fabulously wealthy from donations of land, gems and gold. In various periods mandirs have been looted, or even destroyed in a show of dominance, by rival chiefs and kings from neighbouring or far-off regions of the subcontinent or by dynasties from the more barren lands of Central Asia. Throughout South Asian history there have been anti-mandir movements, often originating among low-status groups. In the 1990s certain political parties and groups began to use the slogan 'Mandir not Mandal' (Bharatiya Janata Party). This was an appeal to traditional religious attachments in an attempt to counter low-caste pressures for expansion of reserved quotas of jobs and university places, as advocated by the Mandal Commission.

See also: **Abhiṣeka; Altars, domestic; Ārtī; Bharatiya Janata Party; Blood sacrifice; Darśana; Image worship; Sthāpatyaveda; Temple worship; Veda; Vivāha**

MARY SEARLE-CHATTERJEE

Further reading

Fuller, Chris. 1992. *The Camphor Flame: Popular Hinduism and Society in India*. Princeton, NJ: Princeton University Press.

Klostermaier, K.K. 1994. *A Survey of Hinduism*. Albany, NY: State University of New York.

MĀṆḌŪKYA UPANIṢAD

See: **Upaniṣads**

MAṄGALĀ

Maṅgaḷā, meaning Auspicious, is the most popular regional goddess in Orissa.

She was originally associated with disease, especially smallpox, but now is more often associated with chickenpox, dysentery, cholera and measles, especially in children. Maṅgaḷā's most important incarnation is at Kakatpur, where she is strictly vegetarian and access to her temple is denied to non-Hindus. This incarnation of Maṅgaḷā is instrumental in finding the dārus, 'sacred trees', used to make the new images of Jagannātha (an incarnation of Viṣṇu), Balarāma, his brother, and Subhadrā, his sister, at the Navakalevara ritual held every twelve years in Puri. A pamphlet, the *Maṅgaḷā Mahāpurāṇa*, produced and sold in Kakatpur, provides details of Maṅgaḷā's associations with Durgā.

See also: **Balarāma; Durgā; Jagannātha; Subhadrā; Viṣṇu**

LYNN FOULSTON

Further reading

Eschmann, A., H. Kulke and G.C. Tripathi (eds). 1978. *The Cult of Jagannāth and the Regional Tradition of Orissa*. New Delhi: Manohar.

Foulston, Lynn. 2002. *At the Feet of the Goddess: The Divine Feminine in Local Hindu Religion*. Brighton and Portland, OR: Sussex Academic Press.

Trinath Pattnaik. n.d. *Mā Maṅgalā Mahāpurāṇa*. Orissa: Sri Sarada Store (purchased in Kakatpur).

MĀṆIKKAVĀCAKAR

Although not listed as one of the sixty-three Nāyaṉmār, the impassioned Tamil devotee-poets of Śiva who lived between 600 and 900 CE, Māṇikkavācakar is the most esteemed of Śaiva poet-saints and is customarily included in their number. According to legendary accounts he was the minister of Varaguna II (862–85), though some datings place him as early as the sixth century as a court official in Madurai. Tradition states that he departed from the court to live a life of meditation and devotion at Cidambaram, where he is believed to have entered the inner sanctum of the temple and merged with the form of Śiva. There is no doubt of his place in Śaiva Siddhānta, in which he is often regarded as the summation of Tamil Śaiva mysticism. He is the author of two important works. The first, the *Tirukkvaiyār* (*Sacred Garland*) is a 400-stanza poem which describes the love between Śiva and the soul. However, it is the second, the *Tiruvācakam* (*Sacred Sayings*), which is considered to be an exposition of Śaiva Siddhānta in fifty-one hymns. Māṇikkavācakar describes the soul's journey through the various forms of existence to human life, where it is possible to obtain salvation though Śiva's manifestation as the guru. He also recounts his own visions, in which he describes an all-encompassing being of Śiva who is neither male or female but is both immanent and transcendent, creator and creation. Devotion is described as worship of Śiva, which is the highest form of religious observance, and salvation takes place in mystical union with the god. The two works together form the eighth *Tirumurai*, the sacred compilation of poems that has canonical status in the Śaiva Siddhānta tradition.

See also: **Bhakti movement; Cidambaram; Guru; Madurai; Nāyaṉmār; Śaiva Siddhānta; Śiva**

RON GEAVES

Further reading

Duniwila, Rohan. 1985. *Saiva Siddhanta Theology*. Delhi: Motilal Banarsidass.

Flood, Gavin. 2003. 'The Saiva Traditions'. In *The Blackwell Companion to Hinduism*. Oxford: Blackwell, 200–28.

MANTRA

A mantra is a text that is spoken or sung as a ritual act. Such acts of speech are believed to have inherent power and to be of superhuman origin (Gonda 1977: 67;

Padoux 1990: 1–29). They can affect the physical world, for instance by removing impurities, curing diseases or overpowering enemies. There are Vedic and non-Vedic mantras.

The words used in ritual are spoken of in the Vedic hymns as objects, fashioned by processes such as weaving or building: 'May the thread not break as I weave insight' (*Ṛgveda* 2, 28, 5). They can be offered to deities or used to achieve goals (Deshpande 2004: 507): 'I have brought praises to you like a herdsman' (*Ṛgveda* 1, 114, 9). In the Veda, mantras are contained in the *Saṃhitā*; they are also often mentioned in the *Brāhmaṇas* by quoting their opening words (pratīka).

The most frequently recited Vedic mantra is the Gāyatrī Mantra or Sāvitrī Mantra (*Ṛgveda* 3, 62, 10), recited at morning and evening twilight as part of smārta practice: 'Let us meditate on the excellent splendour of [the sun-god] Savitṛ; may he stir our thoughts!'. After sipping water, holding the breath, sprinkling himself with water and offering water to the sun, the practitioner mutters the mantra in a low tone (japa), prefacing it with the syllable oṃ and the sacred utterances (vyāhṛti) bhūḥ, bhuvaḥ, svaḥ ('earth, atmosphere, sky'). The whole ritual is called saṃdhyā, 'twilight', and further elements have been added to it (Kane 1968–77, II: 302–4, 312–21; Gonda 1980: 226). It has become a mark of the smārta tradition, and the teaching of this mantra, as a minimal token of knowledge of the Veda, is often included in the *upanayana* (Kane 1968–77, II: 683).

Vedic mantras are only to be heard by twice-born men; according to Manu, they are omitted in the life-cycle rituals of women and śūdras (*Mānusmṛti* 2, 66; 10, 127). However, this rule is not strictly followed, and Vedic mantras can be heard in marriage rituals and on other occasions.

The imparting of a mantra (usually non-Vedic) is an important part of initiation into a saṃpradāya, making the new member a pupil of a guru (and so forming a link in a succession of pupils and gurus going back to the saṃpradāya's supreme deity, who first revealed the mantra (Fuller 1992: 164)). Some of these mantras are in verse, like the well-known Hare Kṛṣṇa mantra (hare kṛṣṇa hare kṛṣṇa kṛṣṇa kṛṣṇa hare hare, hare rāma, hare rāma, rāma rāma hare hare), a series of names in the vocative case; others are in prose, such as namaḥ śivāya, 'homage to Śiva', or oṃ namo nārāyaṇāya, 'homage to Nārāyaṇa' (Gonda 1977: 247; 285). The monosyllables called 'seed mantras' (bīja-mantra) are important both in Tantrism and in Pāñcarātra (Gonda 1977: 69). Other mantras are used by magicians known as mantra-speakers (mantra-vādin) to cure diseases, control spirits or inflict harm (Fuller 1992: 237)

Some ancient Vedic interpreters held that mantras were meaningless, a view rejected but still reported by the Pūrva Mīmāṃsā theorists. In Vedic rituals, though not in smārta rituals, the performer should understand the mantras (Kane 1968–77, IV: 51).

See also: **Brāhmaṇas; Dharmaśāstras; Dvija; Gāyatrī Mantra; Guru; Kṛṣṇa; International Society for Krishna Consciousness; Manu; Oṃ; Pāñcarātras; Pūrva Mīmāṃsā; Saṃhitā; Saṃpradāya; Smārta; Tantrism; Upanayana; Varṇa; Vivāha**

DERMOT KILLINGLEY

Further reading

Babb, Lawrence A. 1975. *The Divine Hierarchy: Popular Hinduism in Central India.* New York: Columbia University Press.

Deshpande, Madhav M. 2004. 'Bhāṣā'. In Sushil Mittal and Gene Thursby, eds, *The Hindu World.* New York: Routledge, 505–30.

Fuller, C.J. 1992. *The Camphor Flame: Popular Hinduism and Society in India.* Princeton, NJ: Princeton University Press.

Gonda, J. 1977. *Medieval Religious Literature in Sanskrit* (History of Indian Literature, vol. 2, fasc. 1). Wiesbaden: Harrassowitz.

Gonda, Jan. 1980. *Vedic Ritual: The Non-solemn Rites* (Handbuch der Orientalistik, Abteilung 2, vol. 4, Abschnitt 1). Leiden: E.J. Brill.

Kane, Pandurang Vaman. 1968–77. *History of Dharmaśāstra (Ancient and Mediaeval Religious and Civil Law)*, 2nd edn, 5 vols (vols 1, 2 and 5 bound in two parts each). Poona [Pune]: Bhandarkar Oriental Research Institute (1st edn 1930–62).

Padoux, A. 1990. *L'Image divine: Culte et méditation dans l'hindouisme.* [The Divine Image: Cult and Meditation in Hinduism.] Paris: Editions du Centre National de la Recherche Scientifique.

MANU

Manu is a mythical figure in the early Sanskrit literature, sometimes regarded as the father of the human race or as one of the very ancient sages (ṛṣi). He also appears as a king in the 'golden age' (kṛtayuga) and as a semi-divine being who received the human laws and regulations from the god Brahmā himself. *Manusmṛti* (The Law Book of Manu) and *Mānava Dharmaśāstra* (The Legal Treatise Belonging to Manu) are the titles of a famous work which was historically the most influential of all the extant *Dharmaśāstras.* It is almost impossible to say who composed the *Manusmṛti.* One motive of the unknown author(s) in naming this work after the mythical Manu and to suppress his/their own identity may have been to invest the treatise with the reputation of great antiquity and authority. The present *Manusmṛti* is put into the mouth of Bhṛgu, Manu's son. The text is divided into twelve chapters (adhyāya) and consists of 2,694 verses (śloka). The *Manusmṛti* contains earlier and later strata as well as conflicting doctrines. It focuses on varṇa and āśrama rules, rites of passage (saṃskāras), duties of men and women, duties of the king (Rājā), righteous conduct and penance, civil and criminal law and many other topics from the perspective of orthodox Brāhmaṇism. Writers from the second century CE onwards looked upon the *Manusmṛti* as the most authoritative manual on dharma. The *Manusmṛti* seems to be older than Yajñavālkya and Nārada, since the rules of juridical procedure are incomplete in Manu as compared with the two others. The *Manusmṛti* had numerous commentators; the earliest commentary is that of Medātithi, which was composed *c.*900 CE. The *Manusmṛti* was first published in India in 1813, and it has been translated into English several times. The best-known translations are perhaps those of G. Bühler and W. Doniger.

See also: **Āśrama; Brahmā; Brāhmaṇism; Bühler, Georg; Dharma; Dharmaśāstras; Medhātithi; Nārada; Rāja; Ṛṣi; Sacred Books of the East; Sacred texts; Saṃskāra; Strīdharma; Varṇa; Yajñavālkya; Yuga**

ANNETTE SCHMIEDCHEN

Further reading

Bühler, G. (trans.). 1886. *The Laws of Manu* Sacred Books of the East, vol. 25. Oxford: Clarendon Press.

Doniger, W. and B.K. Smith (trans.). 1991. *The Laws of Manu.* London: Penguin Books.

Mandlik, V.N. (ed.). 1886. *Mānavadharmaśāstra* (Institutes of Manu). With the commentaries of Medhātithi, Sarvajñanārāyaṇa, Kullūka, Rāghavānanda, Nandana and Rāmachandra, and an appendix. 3 vols. Bombay: Ganpat Krishnaji's Press.

MANVANTARA

Age or period of Manu. There is no unanimity in Hindu literature with regard to the length allotted to a Manvantara, or with regard to their number. According to *Manusmṛti* I 63, a Manvantara comprises one-fourteenth of a Day of Brahmā or 4,320,000 human years. Fourteen Manvantaras constitute one full Day of Brahmā. Each of the fourteen periods is presided over by its own Manu. We are currently living in the seventh Manvantara, with seven more to come before the end of the current Day of Brahmā. The first Manu was Manu Svāyambhuva, who produced the ten Prajāpatis ('Progenitors' of famous human races). He is also the author of the *Manusmṛti*, arguably the most important Hindu code of laws. The present Manu, born from the sun, is the creator of the now-living race of human beings. He was saved from the great flood by Viṣṇu in the form of a fish (*Matsya-avatāra*). He is also the founder of the solar race of kings who ruled over Ayodhyā. The names of the fourteen Manus are not identical in all sources. The most widely accepted list reads: (1) Svāyambhuva, (2) Svārociṣa, (3) Auttami, (4) Tāmasa, (5) Raivata, (6) Cākṣusa, (7) Vaivāsvata, (8) Sāvarṇi, (9) Dakṣasāvarni, (10) Brahmasāvarṇi, (11) Dharmasāvarṇi, (12) Rudrasāvarṇi, (13) Raucya-daivasāvarṇi and (14) Indrasāvarṇi. The first six Manus belong to the past, the last seven to the future.

See also: **Avatāra; Ayodhyā; Dharmaśāstras; Manu; Prajāpati; Viṣṇu;**

KLAUS K. KLOSTERMAIER

Further reading

Bühler, G. (trans.). 1886. *The Laws of Manu*. Sacred Books of the East, vol. 25. Oxford: Oxford University Press.

Doniger, W. and B.K. Smith. 1991. *The Laws of Manu*. Harmondsworth: Penguin.

Kane, P.V. 1958. *History of Dharmaśāstra*, vol. V, pt I. Pune: BORI.

MĀRIAMMĀ

Māriammā or Mariyammaṉ is one of the most important South Indian village goddesses, who to a large degree maintains her position outside the brahmanical religious system, with non-brāhmaṇic priests serving at her shrines. By the local villagers she is considered to be one of the 'mothers' (ammā), with them interpreting the first element of her name either as 'rain' or 'smallpox'. According to various mythological traditions, she was a woman who recovered from smallpox and therefore became venerated as goddess. Another tradition tells that she did not recover from smallpox but was reborn as a demoness who brings this disease to the villagers. Another aspect focuses upon the goddess' connection with rain – asking her during a festival in April to go to the mountainous western area to bring rain from there with her return in early June. Māriammā is usually depicted as a beautiful young woman, but sometimes mixed up both in iconography and worship with the furious goddess, thus leading to her identification with Durgā or Kālī in the 'great tradition'. As a result, in recent decades there occurred a change as brahmanical priests also began to serve at her shrines, but the goddess' festivals also added new ritual elements like the use of chariots for processions, which originally were not part of Māriammā's festivals. One important element within festivals for the goddess is the fire-walking ceremony. Originally a village goddess, Māriammā is also highly venerated in Hindu diasporas in Southeast Asia and the Caribbean because rural South Indians went there as contract workers in the nineteenth century, focusing around her as the main goddess, whom they sometimes also call Kālīammā.

See also: **Americas, Hindus in; Deities, village and local; Diaspora; Durgā; Kālī and Caṇḍī; Religious specialists; South and East Asia, Hindus in**

MANFRED HUTTER

Further reading

Foulston, Lynn. 2002. *At the Feet of the Goddess: The Divine Feminine in Local Hindu Religion*. Brighton and Portland, OR: Sussex Academic Press.

Hindu Endowment Board (ed.). 1996. *Sri Mariamman Temple*. Singapore: Hindu Endowment Board.

Whitehead, H. 1921. *The Village Gods of South India.* Madras: Oxford University Press.
Younger, P. 2002. *Playing Host to Deity. Festival Religion in the South Indian Tradition.* Oxford: Oxford University Press, 95–106, 133–43.

MĀRKAṆḌEYA

A sage, the son of Mṛkaṇḍa, reputed to be the author of the *Mārkaṇḍeya Purāṇa* and feted for his austerities and longevity. He is the principal narrator of the *Mārkaṇḍeya Purāṇa*, written in a style in which Mārkaṇḍeya tells a succession of legends first told by sages in reply to questions by the ṛsi Muni.

The *Mahābhārata* contains an incident in which Mārkaṇḍeya becomes terrified by a deluge which engulfs the earth and calls upon Viṣṇu to save him. The god invites the sage to enter his mouth and take shelter. Inside Viṣṇu, Mārkaṇḍeya discovers all the gods, demigods and the whole world. When he emerges he finds that Viṣṇu remains in his child-form. The story in which swallowing denotes the loss of the limits of individuality, oneness with the deity and the attainment of a special kind of knowledge is more famously repeated in Arjuna's vision of Kṛṣṇa within the *Bhagavadgītā*.

See also: **Arjuna; Bhagavadgītā; Mahābhārata; Purāṇas; Viṣṇu**

RON GEAVES

MARRIAGE

See: **Vivāha**

MARUTS

From mā-rodīh, 'weep not'. Vedic storm-gods, adorned with golden jewellery (i.e. lightning), sons of Rudra and Pṛśnī (the 'mottled', the storm-cloud or mountainous extension of earth) and assistants of the rain-god Indra. Also known as the Rudras, the Maruts personify rain as the semen of the sky-lord Dyaus Pitṛ, which fertilises Pṛthivī, the earth. In *Ṛgveda* 10.78.7, the Maruts are likened to the rays of Uṣas, the goddess of the dawn.

See also: **Dyaus Pitṛ; Indra; Pṛthivī; Rudra; Uṣas; Vedism**

MICHAEL YORK

MAṬH(A)

The term maṭha is most closely associated with the work of Śaṅkara, to whom is attributed the organisation of saṃyāsins into maṭhas, or permanent monastic communities in four regions representing the points of the compass: Badrikāśrama in the north, Rāmeśvara in the south, Jagannātha Puri in the east and Dvārakā in the west. He is also credited with the grouping of saṃyāsins into ten cohorts or daśanāmis linked to the four maṭhas. The development of settled monastic communities as opposed to the tradition of saṃyāsins having no fixed place to live and being discouraged even from congregating as a group is thought to have been a response to the development of communities of Buddhist monks. Some people have doubted whether the establishment of the maṭhās and the grouping into the daśanāmis was actually completed by Śaṅkara and suggest a later date for these developments. Advaitin maṭhas are usually linked to temples and the best-known use of the term maṭha in the West is the Ramakrishna Math founded by Swami Vivekananda in the late nineteenth century, which has sites all over India as well as in England and the USA.

See also: **Advaita; Buddhism, relationship with Hinduism; Mandir; Ramakrishna Math and Mission; Saṃnyāsa; Śaṅkara; Vivekananda, Swami**

VIVIENNE BAUMFIELD

Further reading

Flood, G. 2005. *An Introduction to Hinduism.* Cambridge: Cambridge University Press.

Hirst, J.S. 2005. *Shankara's Advaita Vedanta*. London: RoutledgeCurzon.

MATHURĀ

Popularly known as Brajbhoomi, Mathurā is one of India's Saptapurī (seven sacred cities), in Uttar Pradesh, on the west bank of the Yamunā River, 141 km from Delhi and 54 km from Agra.

An ancient city, it was the capital of the Shursen region, and became a centre for Buddhism and Jainism during the Mauryan Empire (fourth to second centuries BCE). The Mathurā school of art flourished from the twelfth(?) to the second centuries BCE, specialising in Buddhist images made from local red sandstone. In the second century BCE the city came under Indo-Greek rule, and subsequently Indo-Scythian (first century BCE).

In 1018 Mahmud of Ghanzi assumed control of the city, destroyed Hindu and Buddhist shrines and established Muslim rule. Sikandar Lodhi did further damage in 1500, and in 1661 Aurangzeb ordered the destruction of the Kesava Dev Temple and built the Jama Masjid on its site. In 1757 Ahmed Shah Abdali burnt the city down and in 1804 it came under British rule.

Mathurā is best known as the legendary birthplace of Kṛṣṇa, at the site of the Keshav Dev Temple. The main temple is the Dwarkadheesh Temple, built in 1814 or 1815 by Set Gokuldass Parikh of Gwalior and dedicated to Kṛṣṇa. The Shri Kṛṣṇa Janma Bhoomi contains Kaṃsa's prison, and the Vishram Ghaṭ on the River Yamunā is said to be the place where Kṛṣṇa rested after killing King Kaṃsa.

Ten kilometres to the north of Mathurā is Vṛndāvana, where Kṛṣṇa is believed to have lived. On the road to Vṛndāvana lies the Gītā Mandir, built by the Birla family; this temple contains scenes of Kṛṣṇa's life and the entire *Bhagavadgītā* is inscribed on a pillar. Govardhan Hill is 26 km away and commemorates the story of Kṛṣṇa lifting the mountain with his little finger to protect the inhabitants from Indra's storms.

See also: **Bhagavadgītā; Buddhism, relationship with Hinduism; Indra; Jainism, relationship with Hinduism; Kaṃsa; Kṛṣṇa; Mandir; Saptapurī (Seven Sacred Cities); Vṛndāvana**

GEORGE CHRYSSIDES

Further reading

Sharma, Aruna 2006. *History of Mathura c.200 BC–AD 300*. New Delhi: Om Publications.

MĀTṚKĀS

Of the many goddesses described and worshipped within the Hindu pantheon, those referred to as the Mātṛkās (or Mothers) are some of the oldest and least clearly defined. First appearing in a textually accessible form in the *Mahābārata*, the Mātṛkās are portrayed as a particularly dangerous and inauspicious group of deities. Initially associated with the story of the god Kārttikeya's birth, they are presented both as threats to the young god's life and also as figures who are subsequently adopted by him as mothers. In these and other accounts, the Mātṛkās are described as possessing a terrifying appearance: they are violent and wild in their behaviour; they consume blood, flesh and intoxicants; they dwell in the wilderness or inauspicious places; and they are often depicted as dark skinned and speaking strange languages. Although some of these goddesses are named, there is little clear sense of any of the Mātṛkās possessing a distinct individual character. Rather, their numbers are usually indeterminate and large, and they are defined as a form of collective identity.

It is likely that the Mātṛkās of the *Mahābārata* are closely related to or represent the many village goddesses of the Indian subcontinent. One of the defining features of the Mātṛkās is the danger that they present to children, including expectant mothers, and it is common practice throughout rural India to worship local goddesses in order to protect one's children from the various threats that they embody, principally diseases. The references to Mātṛkās in the *Mahābārata* as being of dark complexion and speaking strange languages establish a plausible connection between them and the various village goddesses of the non-Aryan peoples of India (Kinsley 1988: 155). It is only during the post-epic period (post-400 CE), and in particular through the development of the *Purāṇas*, that the Mātṛkās are drawn more thoroughly into the Brāhmaṇic tradition.

Referred to many times in the *Purāṇas*, it is probably in the *Devī Māhātmya* that one encounters the most comprehensive account of the Mātṛkās as allies of the gods. Appearing in the story of a battle between the Mahādevī (Great Goddess) and the demons Śumbha and Niśumbha, the Mātṛkās are individually named as personifications of the female energy of seven male deities: Brahmāṇī (alt. Brāhmī) emerges from Brahmā, Māheśvarī from Śiva, Kaumārī from Kārttikeya, Vaiṣṇavī from Viṣṇu, Vārāhī and Nārasiṃhī from avatāras of Viṣṇu (though in other versions Cāmuṇḍā is included instead of Nārasiṃhī) and Aindrī (alt. Indrāṇī) from Indra (Coburn 1992: 63–65). These Mātṛkās retain their earlier violent and bloodthirsty natures, but their powers are deployed principally in the service of dharma. From this juncture onwards it is difficult to discern a consensus view of the nature of the Mātṛkās; sometimes they are numbered as seven, sometimes eight or sixteen. Often they are named and related to male deities, but more often they retain their independence. For most contemporary Hindus it is arguable that the Mātṛkās constitute a large but indeterminate number of goddesses who manifest a range of frightening qualities. Most notably they are figures of menace and, specifically, they are a danger to children and must be appeased.

See also: **Asuras; Avatāra; Brahmā; Brahmanism; Deities, village and local; Devī Māhātmya; Indra; Mahābārata; Mahādevī; Purāṇas; Śakti; Saptamātṛkās; Śiva; Skanda; Viṣṇu**

PAUL REID-BOWEN

Further reading

Coburn, T.B. 1992. *Encountering the Goddess: A Translation of the Devī-Māhātmya and a Study of Its Interpretation*. Dehli: Sri Satguru Publications.

Kinsley, D. 1988. *Hindu Goddesses: Visions of the Divine Feminine in the Hindu Religious Tradition*. Berkeley, CA: University of California Press.

MATSYA

See: **Avatāra**

MATSYENDRANĀTH(A)

Matsyendranāth(a), also known as Mīnanāth(a) and Macchendernāth, is one of the founding figures of the Kāṇphata or Nātha Yoga movement. He was an older contemporary of Gorakhnāth(a), who, according to a number of accounts, was Matsyendranātha's most eminent disciple. Briggs dates both men between the eleventh and twelfth centuries CE, though he also raises the possibility of the seventh to eighth centuries CE and offers evidence in support of this. Matsyendranātha is the patron saint of Nepal, though his origins obviously lie elsewhere as he is said to have gone to Nepal at the request of the Buddha. He is often identified with the bodhisattva Avalokiteśvara (Lokeśvar) and is named in the Buddhist lists of tantric adepts (siddha). Matsyendranātha was, therefore, perhaps a Buddhist tantric teacher who converted to Śaivism. He is reputed to have heard Śiva impart instructions on gaining liberation to Pārvatī whilst in the form of a fish, hence the name Matsya/Mīna (fish).

See also: **Gorakhnāth; Kāṇphata Yoga; Pārvatī; Śiva**

PETER CONNOLLY

Further reading

Briggs, G.W. 1938/1982. *Gorakhnath and the Kanphata Yogis*. Delhi: Motilal Banarsidass.

MĀYĀ

Māyā is best known as the illusion that deludes jivas (individual selves) and as a key component of the doctrines of the Advaita school of Vedānta, sometimes disparagingly called māyāvāda (the School of Illusionism), founded by Śaṅkarācārya in the eighth century. Though this definition as illusion is significant and cannot be discounted, it should not supplant the meaning of the term as it was first found in the Vedas. Māyā appeared over 100 times in the *Ṛgveda*, denoting a mysterious creative power that was employed by devas and asuras for both favourable (sumāya) and unfavourable (durmāyu) purposes. Māyā also designated some sort of power, ability and capacity enabling its possessor to act in extraordinary ways. By means of māyā, Indra was able to transform himself and to defeat the demon Vṛta (*Ṛgveda* 6.47.18). Indra even conquered the māyā of Śuṣṇa by means of his own māyā (*Ṛgveda* 1.11.7). In these earliest instances, the meaning of māyā went beyond simply illusion.

The term acquired epistemological connotations in the *Upaniṣads*. In *Śvetāśvatara Upaniṣad* 4.9–4.10, for example, māyā referred to an illusory power and was linked to Brahman and the creation of the world. Though Śaṅkarācārya himself used the term infrequently, his followers often referred to māyā and held that it was responsible for the creation of a perception of difference when there was actually unity. They reinforced this notion as they developed Advaita doctrines. Individuals, deluded by māyā, thus perceived the universe, namely Brahman, incorrectly as differentiated and as having distinct entities. Māyā was deemed anirvacanīya (indescribable) by the Advaitins, thereby affirming the mysteriousness of its nature. In this context, māyā was primarily an epistemological concept. Such usage was not exclusively philosophical, as it is also found in texts predating the Advaita school such as the *Mahābhārata*. For instance, Draupadī stated that her husband Yudhiṣṭhira was deluded by God's māyā (*Mahābhārata* 3.31.33).

This usage was not the only way that māyā was employed in post-Vedic Hinduism. Several schools of philosophy, including the Viśiṣṭādvaita and Madhva schools, held māyā to have significant ontological, rather than epistemological, import. Rāmānujācārya, who founded the Viśiṣṭādvaita school of Vedānta in the eleventh century, proclaimed that māyā was the marvellous and enigmatic creative power of Brahman from which the entire universe was produced. In this case, māyā had an explicitly ontological significance rather than an epistemological one. For Madhvācārya, the founder of the thirteenth-century school of Vedānta, māyā had both ontological and epistemological connotations: it was identified with prakṛti, the material stuff from which the universe evolved, as well as being the deceiving power which created ignorance of the nature of God in jīvas.

Hence, māyā is a creative power that makes possible the generation of the marvellous and extraordinary. Though illusion and deception must be included among these possibilities, māyā is not limited to them alone. Throughout its wide semantic range, māyā serves to account for the inexplicable and the ineffable.

See also: **Advaita; Asuras; Brahman; Deities; Indra; Jīva; Madhva; Mahābhārata; Prakṛti; Ramanuja; Saṃhitā; Śaṅkara; Upaniṣads; Vedānta; Viśiṣṭādvaita; Yudhiṣthira**

DEEPAK SARMA

Further reading

Deutsch, Eliot. 1980. *Advaita Vedānta: A Philosophical Reconstruction.* Honolulu, HI: University of Hawaii Press.

Devanandan, Paul David. 1950. *The Concept of Māyā.* London: Lutterworth Press.

Doniger, Wendy. 1984. *Dreams, Illusions, and Other Realities.* Chicago, IL: University of Chicago Press.

Gonda, Jan. 1965. *Change and Continuity in Indian Religion.* The Hague: Mouton.

Goudriaan, Teun. 1978. *Māyā Divine and Human.* Delhi: Motilal Barnarsidass.

Reyna, Ruth. 1962. *The Concept of Māyā from the Vedas to the 20th Century.* New York: Asia Publishing House.

Shastri, Prabhu Dutt. 1911. *The Doctrine of Māyā in the Philosophy of the Vedānta.* London: Luzac.

MEDHĀTITHI

A Vedic ṛṣi and, according to the *Viṣṇu Purāṇa*, one of the ten sons of King Priyavrata, who upon dividing the world into seven continents appointed Medhātithi to rule over Plakṣadvipa. According to the *Ṛgveda*, he received a visitation from Indra in the form of a ram. He is also mentioned in the *Purāṇas* as being the sage who gave Arundhatī to Vasiṣtha in marriage after obtaining permission from Brahmā. Medhātithi is associated with the myths of Arundhatī. In a previous life as Sandhyā, full of remorse at infatuating Brahmā and the Manasāputra sages, she jumped into the sacrificial fire lit by Medhātithi for his yajña. She went to the kingdom of Sūrya, the sun-god. She was reborn out of Medhātithi's sacrificial fire as a child and named by the sage as Arundhatī, who brought her up and ensured that she was educated in all the arts and Vedic sciences.

See also: **Arundhatī; Brahmā; Indra; Purāṇas; Sūrya; Yajña**

RON GEAVES

Further reading

Krishna Iyer, Kolar and Chikkerur Dheerendra Acharya. 2003. *The Great Men and Women of Puranas.* New Delhi: Munshiram Manoharlal.

MEDICAL ETHICS

Compared to his Roman Catholic counterpart, the Hindu medical ethicist has, on the one hand, his own apparent problems and limitations but, on the other, a degree of ethical flexibility and a practical appreciation of life's relativities. The Catholic has a central authority in the form of the Vatican and the Pope prescribing immutable laws governing what is seen as ethical and moral. The Hindu, on the other hand, has no such location or head, and while there are ancient dharma texts, sometimes contradictory, these are authorial opinions and are not binding on all of Hindu society. But all is not lost. While the Hindu ethicist does not possess absolute authoritative mandates, he certainly draws from hegemonic philosophical ideas as his yardstick for determining the right thing to do in a medical case. Thus, notions such as karma, ahiṃsā (non-violence), punarjanma (rebirth) and dayā (compassion) all contribute towards the ethicist's sense of dharma. Based on these, ultimately his conscience has to be the judge. This indeed places the burden of responsibility on him much more, but allows him to resolve 'dharma dilemmas' with more fluidity than someone with prescriptive absolutes, as real-life issues, especially in the medical profession, are seldom black and white.

One of the ancient medical texts, the *Cārakasaṃhitā* composed by Cāraka, presents what he feels are attributes necessary to being a physician, and the idea that adhering to ethical principles distinguishes the genuine ones from the 'quacks'. Cāraka's 'Oath of Initiation' is key to medical ethics in Āyurveda and, while it resembles the Hippocratic Oath in manners such as commitment to the good of the patient, it has its own Indian characteristics such as belief in the doctrine of karma, practising celibacy, bearing arms, abstaining from meat, not assisting social and political anarchists, etc.

See also: **Ahiṃsā; Āyurveda; Celibacy; Dharma; Dharmaśāstras; Karma**

RISHI HANDA

Further reading

Crawford, S. Cromwell. 2003. *Hindu Bioethics for the Twenty-First Century*. Albany, NY: State University of New York Press.

MEDICINE

See: **Āyurveda**

MEDITATION

The Sanskrit word most usually translated 'meditation' is dhyāna, which is a state of contemplative absorption. This is the name of the penultimate stage in Patañjali's eightfold (aṣṭāṅga) yoga, and leads to samādhī, the state of complete absorption in the supreme Brahman. But when the word 'meditation' is used in English it more often denotes the different methods by which the mind becomes steadied so that it reaches the state of dhyāna. These, Hindus often call sādhana and they are very varied. While the former term is related to dhī (insight) and implies inward vision, the latter is related to the verb 'to strive' and implies an active form of practice. The word yoga is also used; here, however, the familiar physical postures of haṭha yoga are only a preliminary, for the real aim is control of the mind. This means withdrawing it from external objects so that it concentrates on increasingly subtle layers of inward consciousness, until, leaving even these behind, it reaches a still and timeless state that transcends thought and is conceived as immersion in divine consciousness. In more devotional meditation the aim is loving union with the deity.

The most common tool for focusing and transforming the mind is repetition of a mantra, which can be a simple phrase or prayer, or merely a word of a single syllable. Mantras usually contain the name or epithet of a deity. Other methods use external or internal visual images, sometimes accompanied by mantra repetition. These could include a geometric diagram called yantra which encapsulates the power of a deity or could be a simple object like a candle flame. A picture of a deity or a guru, first contemplated externally, then inwardly in the heart, is one form of devotional meditation.

Another frequently used tool is prāṇāyāma, usually translated 'breath control', but the word prāṇa really refers to the life-force itself, directed and controlled through the breath. Prāṇāyāma involves holding the in-breath and the out-breath for increasing lengths of time. On a physiological level this can induce a trance state. Ultimately in the Hindu view the aim is to gain complete control over the breath-flow (an achievement of only the most advanced yogi) in order to immerse mind and body in the supreme source of life, the Ātman-Brahman. In most forms of meditation, however, prāṇāyāma is just one more method of stilling the mind.

Intense concentration on and visualisation of the body are involved in practices using the kuṇḍalinī force, believed to lie dormant at the base of the spine and to rise with increasing concentration through six cakras, or 'neural centres', until it reaches the centre of spiritual awakening at the crown of the head. Visualisation of these cakras, according to prescribed forms, is accompanied by mantra and prāṇāyāma.

Naturally practices and aims vary. Most gurus teach their own adaptation of one or more of these general methods, and all of the well-known teachers have produced their own guides to practice. There is consequently a wealth of literature on meditation, but few general studies.

See also: **Aṣṭāṅga Yoga; Brahman; Guru; Haṭha Yoga; Kuṇḍalinī Yoga; Mantra; Patañjali; Tantrism; Yantra; Yoga; Yogi**

KATHLEEN TAYLOR

Further reading

Bader, J. 1990. 'The Nature of Meditation'. In *Meditation in Śankara's Vedānta.* New Delhi: Aditya Prakashan, 25–44. (A more philosophical overview of the principles and comparison with Western ideas of 'contemplation'.)

Gidoomal, R. and R. Thomson. 1997. *A Way of Life: Introducing Hinduism.* London and Sydney: Hodder & Stoughton. (An easy general introduction that includes meditation.)

MEERA, MOTHER (1960–)

Mother Meera was born in Southern India in 1960 to a poor village family and received only a minimal education. By her own account, she often had mystical experiences throughout childhood, and a direct communication with gods and divine beings. She describes all her spiritual learning and preparation as coming directly from these deities. She was taken by Venkat Reddy, her uncle and a follower of Aurobindo, to the Sri Aurobindo āśram in Pondicherry, and questioned by elders about her insights and experiences, which were accepted as authentic. She declared herself an avatāra, a 'goddess in human form', 'having ninety percent of the powers of a god', a claim accepted then and now by many of her followers, which launched her spiritual teaching career. She is also widely perceived as an incarnation of the divine mother.

Meera then travelled to Thalheim, Germany, married a German and began to receive thousands of followers from all over the world to her darśanas, held in the basement of her house. Up to 200 followers at a time are admitted to the darśanas. Each person comes up in turn to kneel before Mother Meera and make eye contact, which is held to be the moment when the spiritual transmission happens. Unusually, the entire ceremony is conducted in silence. Many people report profound religious experiences.

Problems arose when in 1995 Meera instructed a devotee, Martin Goodman, to write an official biography. During his research in India, he discovered that Mother Meera had received six months of intensive tuition from Venkat Reddy prior to the visit to Pondicherry. This preparation had allegedly not been declared, and threw into doubt the divine provenance of her learning. It also seems that she has interests in real estate in India and Germany. Goodman was threatened with legal action if he did not destroy the book. Eventually it was published by Harper San Francisco, despite the threats. There has also been a high-profile falling out with Andrew Harvey, a noted scholar of All Souls, Oxford, and author of a hagiographic book about her, when she refused to bless his homosexual relationship and he accused her of being homophobic – a charge strongly denied by her and many followers.

See also: **Āśram(a) (religious community); Avatāra; Darśana; Ghose, Aurobindo**

ELIZABETH PUTTICK

Further reading

Goodman, Martin. 1998. *In Search of the Divine Mother.* London: HarperCollins.

MEMORIAL RITES

See: **Śrāddha (rites to deceased ancestors)**

MERIT

See: **Puṇya**

MERU, MOUNT

Mount Meru holds a central position in Hindu cosmology and is mentioned in the *Mahābhārata* and several *Purāṇas* (Itihāsa). It is believed to be at the centre or axis of the universe, the Brahmāṇḍa or World Egg, and around it is the first of the several concentric circles of which the universe is comprised, viz. Jambu Dvīpa or the Earth. Since many *Purāṇas* depict the sun as circling Mount Meru every day it is identified by some scholars as the North Pole.

Mount Meru is the abode of gods, and in particular of Brahmā, who has a golden city at its summit. The *Mahābhārata* gives a clear description of the splendours of the mountain, covered with gems and with its slopes full of gold and other precious minerals. Some myths seem to identify Meru with Kailāsa, the abode of Śiva. Gandharvas, Yakṣas, Apsarasas and great divine sages are all believed to reside on Meru.

The mountain is huge and depicted in the *Mārkaṇḍeya* and *Viṣṇu Purāṇas* as being 84,000 yojanas (3,360,000 miles) in height and its base at a depth of 16,000 yojanas (640,000 miles) below the earth. The base is supported by the great celestial serpent Vāsuki. The mountain is lotus shaped, its top being double the diameter of its base, giving it the name 'the lotus or seed cup of the earth'.

See also: **Apsarasas; Cosmology; Gandharvas; Itihāsa; Mahābhārata; Purāṇas; Sacred geography; Śiva; Vāsuki; Yakṣa**

THEODORE GABRIEL

Further reading

O'Flaherty, W. 1975. *Hindu Myths*. Harmondsworth: Penguin Books.

METRE

See: **Chandas**

MEYKAṆṬAR

A thirteenth-century Tamil saint and devotional writer whose book *The Realization of Knowledge of Śiva* (*Śivajñānabodham*) played a crucial role in the development and systemisation of Śaiva Siddhānta. It is the basic text of the *Śaiva Siddhānta Śāstras*, also known as the *Meykandar Śāstras*. These latter contain fourteen works, but the most important is the *Sivajñānabodham*, comprising twelve aphorisms divided into four groups approximately corresponding to Bādarāyaṇa's *Brahmasūtras*. In brief, the twelve aphorisms can be summarised as the following: Śiva is the cause of the creation as well as its dissolution; the world continuously comes into being after each dissolution; only the soul is eternal and distinct from any part of the physical world; Śiva's first task is the salvation of all souls. These are followed by various expositions on the nature of the soul, including aphorisms on the real and the unreal, how the soul obtains knowledge and how it is purified. Finally Meykaṇṭar deals with how the soul can reach the shelter of Śiva and discover that the invisible and unknowable can be worshipped as visible and knowable through the form of Śiva. Meykaṇṭar is the first of the Tamil Śaivite saints to formalise and put into systematic form the intense devotional tradition expounded by the Nāyaṉmārs, the poet-saints of Śiva bhakti. His work was developed by Arulnandi (1253) in his *Śivajñānasiddhiyār* and Umāpati (1306) in his two treatises, the *Śivapirakāśam* and the *Sañkalpanirākaraṇam*.

See also: **Bādarāyaṇa; Bhakti movement; Brahmasūtras; Nāyaṉmār; Śaiva Siddhānta; Śiva; Umāpati Śivācārya**

RON GEAVES

Further reading

Duniwila, Rohan. 1985. *Saiva Siddhanta Theology*. Delhi: Motilal Benarsidass.

MĪMĀṂSĀSŪTRAS

Ascribed to the ancient sage Jaimini, the *Mīmāṃsāsūtras* (Aphorisms on Mīmāṃsā) form the foundational text of the Pūrva Mīmāṃsā school of Hindu philosophy.

The date of the composition of the *Mīmāṃsāsūtras* is uncertain. It has been placed around the second century BCE. It contains more than 2,500 sūtras and there are twelve 'books' (*adhyāya*), each of which is divided into several chapters (pāda). The work considers around 1,000 topics.

The Pūrva Mīmāṃsā school developed as commentaries and subcommentaries were written on the *Mīmāṃsāsūtras*. Śabara (or Śabarasvāmin) is the author of the earliest preserved commentary (bhāsya) which became an important basis for later philosophical developments. Śabara's date is also uncertain; he has been placed between the third and sixth centuries CE.

Concerned with interpretation of Vedic ritual, the *Mīmāṃsāsūtras* begin by defining the subject matter, 'dharma' ('duty,' 'righteousness,' what ought to be done), as that which is indicated by Vedic injunctions as conducive to the highest good. Dharma is not amenable to perception or other means (it is known only from the Veda).

See also: **Dharma; Jaimini; Pūrva Mīmāṃsā; Ṣaḍdarśana; Sūtra; Veda**

MARTIN OVENS

Further reading

Jha, G. (trans.). 1933–36. *Śābarabhāsya*. Gaekwad's Oriental Series 66, 70, 73. Baroda: Oriental Institute.

MĪNĀKṢĪ

Mīnākṣī the 'fish-eyed' goddess is most popular in Tamil Nadu, where she resides in a magnificent temple that dominates the centre of the ancient city of Madurai. Legend states that Mīnākṣī (originally called Thadadhagai) was born from a sacrificial fire to a Pandyan king because the goddess Pārvatī had agreed to be born as his wife's daughter. The child was unusual because she had three breasts. A divine voice spoke to the king, telling him to bring her up as if she were his son, assuring him that the third breast would disappear when she met her future husband (Balaram Iyer 1994: 11). Thadadhagai became the successor to her father's throne and a supreme warrior who was without equal until she met Śiva. Before him she became shy, her ferocity dissipated and her third breast disappeared. After their marriage, the god and goddess entered their temple as Mīnākṣī and Sundarēśvarar.

At the seventeen-day Chittrai festival, celebrated annually, the images of Mīnākṣī and Sundarēśvarar are taken through the streets of Madurai and their marriage ceremony is enacted (Fuller 1992: 190). Mīnākṣī is unusual in that, though she is Śiva's wife, she has her own sanctum and is worshipped before her husband, only being worshipped with him during their annual festival. After the festival, Mīnākṣī reverts to her independent character. Mīnākṣī is a very beautiful benign-looking goddess who holds a parrot, a symbol of peace and happiness. She was probably a popular regional goddess. Despite her ritual purity and orthodoxy, it seems likely that animal sacrifices were once offered in her temple for, periodically, Mīnākṣī is presented with a pumpkin smeared with a red paste (kumkum) that represents, when cut, a sacrificial head (Fuller 1992: 97).

See also: **Chittrai; Madurai; Pārvatī; Śiva; Sundarēśvarar**

LYNN FOULSTON

Further reading

Balaram Iyer, T.G.S. 1994. *History and Description of Sri Meenakshi Temple*, 8th edn. Madurai: Sri Karthik Agency.

Fuller, C.J. 1992. *The Camphor Flame: Popular Hinduism and Society in India*. Princeton, NJ: Princeton University Press.

MĪRĀBĀĪ (*c.*1498–1546)

Mīrābāī was one of India's greatest and most loved saints. Born at Mertā in Western Rajasthan, only child of the local clan chief, Ratna Singh of the Rāthor caste, she lost her mother in infancy and was brought up by her uncle, son of Virāmdeva. In 1516 she married Bhojraj, Mahārānā Sāngā, the ruler of Mewar, and thus went to dwell in the great fortress of Chittaur (Chittorgarh), where a temple dedicated to her still stands. When she was widowed only five years into her marriage, her father-in-law became her protector, but after his death she became for years the butt of his family's hostility, as is documented in many of her poems, and also in contemporary poems, as well as hagiographic literature. Her behaviour, public singing of devotional songs and her taste for the company of Vaiṣṇava holy men was judged scandalous not only in view of the mores of the time but also because the tutelary deity of the royal family was Durgā. Having escaped several murder attempts through, she believed, the intervention of Kṛṣṇa, she moved first to Ajmer then to Vṛndāvana and Puṣkara, evading the 1534 sack of Chittaur by Bahādur Shāh. She later visited a number of pilgrimage centres, including Benares (Vārāṇasī) and then apparently retired to the major Kṛṣṇa temple at Dvāraka in Kathiawar, where she died at the end of the 1540s, miraculously absorbed, it is said, into the main icon, a not unusual metaphor for final emancipation.

Mīrā (bāī is honorific) composed a number of devotional poems (pada), which from the seventeenth century were collected in diverse anthologies (alongside the work of other poets). Many texts attributed to her match neither her style, her theology nor her language, old rājasthnī, a dialect close to braj which is closely associated with Kṛṣṇa devotionalism. Further, so great was her appeal that her poems were early translated into many northern Indian vernaculars. The most reliable modern edition (by Achārya Parasurām Caturvedi, Prayāg, 1964) contains 201 pādas expressing her spiritual endeavour (sādhana) in her very distinctive poetic voice.

Like those of all bhakti poets of the period, Mīrā's poems are designed to be sung, which determined the versification so as to match specific rhythm-cycles (tāla). Each pāda is also associated with one of the Hindustani melodic patterns (rāga) in order to generate in singer and audience particular emotions; no fewer than seventy rāgas, also relating to times of the day and the year, were used to that effect. Mīrā was not only a great poet but also an accomplished musician.

The religious world of Mīrā is that of bhakti, in her case the passionate surrender to the love of Kṛṣṇa, intensely personal and erotic, focused on the mutual relationship between lover and beloved, involving a complete renunciation of the world. The depth of that love is expressed in the joy of mystical union but also, and often, in longing and the suffocating anguish of separation, evoking an astonishing variety of psychological situations and emotions.

Mīrā's poetry still guides, informs and sustains people's devotion, be they Vaiṣṇava or not, literate or not, throughout India and the diaspora.

See also: **Bhakti movement; Diaspora; Durgā; Dvāraka; Kṛṣṇa; Languages; Music; Poetry; Tīrthayātrā; Vaiṣṇavism; Vārāṇasī; Vṛndāvana**

DANIEL MARIAU

Further reading

Alston, A.J. (trans.). 1980. *The Devotional Poems of Mirabai.* Delhi: Motilal Barnarsidass.

MITRA

'Friend', 'contract'. A quasi-solar Āditya usually paired in a dvandva formulation with Varuṇa. Unlike his Iranian and Roman counterparts, Mitra as an independent personage is insignificant: only one Ṛgvedic hymn is dedicated to him (3.59). Commenting on *Ṛgveda* 1.2.7, Sāyana describes Mitra presiding over the day, Varuṇa over the night. One theory holds that the dvandvic union of Mitra and Varuṇa (Mitrāvaruṇā) possibly represents an apotropaic application of the title 'friend' to the otherwise frightening and dangerous Varuṇa.

See also: **Varuṇa**

MICHAEL YORK

MOHA, RĀGA, DVEṢA

Moha, 'delusion', rāga, 'attachment', and dveṣa, 'aversion', are the three principal psychological obstacles to freedom (mokṣa) in Vedānta (Potter 1981: 317) and are mutually associated in the causal chain that supports erroneous experience in Buddhism (Dasgupta 1922–55, 2: 143). While some passages count attachment (here icchā) and aversion as the source of the delusion concerning pairs of opposites that keeps beings in the cycle of transmigration (Saṃsāra) (*Bhagavadgītā* 7.27; van Buitenen 1981: 101), moha is associated with ignorance in Nyāya-Vaiśeṣika and is at the root of other defects such as rāga and dveṣa (Potter 1977: 234). Similarly, moha is counted as one of the five fundamental misconceptions in Sāṃkhya (*Sāṃkhyakārikā* 48) and is associated with the identification of the self (Puruṣa) with the instruments of cognition that are evolutes of nature (Prakṛti) in Yoga (*Yogasūtra* 2.6). Rāga is the disposition to pursue pleasure (*Yogasūtra* 2.7) and its opposite is dveṣa, the disposition to avoid sorrow (*Yogasūtra* 2.8).

See also: **Mokṣa; Nyāya-Vaiśeṣika; Puruṣa; Prakṛti; Sāṃkhya; Saṃsāra; Vedānta**

PETER M. SCHARF

Further reading

Dasgupta, Surendranath. 1922–55. *A History of Indian Philosophy,* 5 vols. Cambridge: Cambridge University Press.

Potter, Karl. (ed.). 1977. *Encyclopedia of Indian Philosophies,* vol. 2, *Indian Metaphysics and Epistemology: The Tradition of Nyāya-Vaiśeṣika up to Gaṅgeśa.* Delhi: Motilal Banarsidass.

Potter, Karl. 1981. *Encyclopedia of Indian Philosophies,* vol. 3, *Advaita Vedānta up to Śaṃkara and His Pupils.* Delhi: Motilal Banarsidass.

Prithipaul, K. Dad. 1972–73. 'Moha in Hindu Religious Thought'. *VBQ* (*Vishvabharati Quarterly,* Santiniketan) 38.4: 132–60.

Prithipaul, K. Dad. 1988. *Moha: A Study in the Metaphysics of Error in the Brahmanical Tradition.* Madras: Southern Publications.

van Buitenen, J.A.B. (trans.). 1981. *The Bhagavadgītā in the Mahābhārata: A Bilingual Edition.* Chicago, IL: University of Chicago Press.

MOHINĪ

While the gods (devas) and demons (asuras) are fighting among themselves over the nectar (amṛta) that has been harvested from the churning of the primordial ocean of milk (kṣirasāgara), Lord Viṣṇu appears as the beautiful Mohinī (literally, 'a captivating woman') and seduces the demons long enough for the gods to run off with the nectar. Lord Śiva falls in love with Mohinī (really Lord Viṣṇu) and their offspring is known as Śāstā (or Ayyappaṉ or Hariharaputra), who is the presiding deity of the Śabarimala temple in eastern Kerala. Another name of the child is Ayenār, who is also one of the several major 'village deities' (grāmadevatās) worshipped in South India for the protection of rural society from natural and supernatural calamities. The classical Indian dance form known as Mohinīattam draws inspiration from this figure of Mohinī, especially her role in the above story and her (again Lord Viṣṇu) saving of Lord Śiva from the demon Bhasma by performing a dance known as 'the dance for the liberated one' (muktanṛtya).

See also: **Asuras; Ayyappan̲; Dance; Deities; Grāmadevatās; Śiva; Viṣṇu**

DEVEN M. PATEL

Further reading

Garrett, John. 1999. *A Classical Dictionary of India*. New Delhi: DK Printworld.

Mani, Vettam. 2002. *Purāṇic Encyclopaedia*. Delhi: Motilal Banarsidass.

MOKṢA

The word mokṣa means liberation, which first occurs in verb forms of the root muc, before yielding the abstract form mokṣa, or mukti or vimukti – forms which are then found in all the four 'religions' of India: Hinduism, Buddhism, Jainism and Sikhism. It is usually rendered by the word 'liberation' in English and constitutes the counterpart to 'salvation' in the Abrahamic religions.

If mokṣa means liberation, then such questions as liberation for whom, liberation for what and liberation from what naturally arise. The answer provided by the various religions of Indian origin at one level is essentially similar: mokṣa, or liberation, is attained by the jīva, or the embodied being; mokṣa is for bliss or perfect and permanent happiness and mokṣa constitutes freedom from being trapped in the endless cycle of birth and death, in which one is continually reborn in accordance with one's karma and in which the experience of supreme felicity which comes from transcending the karmic involvement in saṃsāra is denied one. There is also broad agreement that the jīvas' involvement in this process of saṃsāra is beginningless (anādi) and would continue without end until happily terminated by mokṣa. The school of Hindu materialism known by such names as Lokāyata Svabhāvavāda, or Cārvāka, however, constitutes an exception here. According to this school the doctrine of reincarnation and therefore mokṣa is a myth; so also the idea of dharma or righteousness, as the universe lacks the kind of moral supervision implied by the concepts of karma and dharma. The only goal worth pursuing is that of kāma or worldly pleasures, which are secured through artha or material gain. The more sophisticated version of this school acknowledges analogues to dharma and mokṣa. It does not accept dharma as embodying morality but it accepts rājadharma or the system of law and order imposed by the king because violation of it brings punishment, which compromises the goal of achieving kāma or pleasure. Similarly, although Hindu materialists discard the idea of rebirth they do concede that as a human being one must face death and that one could distinguish usefully between a painful and a relatively painless or 'good death'. Dying in pleasant circumstances (as embodied in the American expression 'what a way to go') is then taken to be the counterpart to mokṣa.

Each school of Hindu philosophy likewise has its own conception of mokṣa. According to the Nyāya school of thought, so long as the soul is in contact with the body, the body, on account of the sense organs, is liable to experiences which may be pleasant or unpleasant. Hence, in order to be liberated the soul must be free of the body and the senses. In such a state it cannot experience pain, pleasure or even consciousness. Hence this state is called apavarga and described in Nyāya as one of total cessation of pain, rather than as involving the positive experience of joy. Hence mokṣa is the cessation of duhkha, or suffering, which comes from cessation of rebirth in any form. The process is explained in the *Nyāyasūtra* (1.1.2) as follows: knowledge removes ignorance, ignorance once removed dispels desire, aversion and error which give rise to karma; when they end karma ends, and end of karma means end of rebirth. The knowledge which sets this salvific chain in motion is the knowledge of the sixteen philosophical and logical categories (padārthas) such as pramāṇas etc. The school of Hindu philosophy known as Vaiśeṣika also presents a similar picture of the state of release, but the knowledge which brings about such release is the knowledge of the seven padārthas or categories listed in this system as: (1) dravya (substance); (2) guṇa (qualities); (3) karma (activity); (4) sāmānya (generality); (5) viśeṣa (particularity); (6) samavāya (inherence); and (7) abhāva (non-existence). The categories whose knowledge leads to liberation are largely epistemological in the case of Nyāya and ontological in the case of Vaiśeṣika.

Unlike the schools of Nyāya and Vaiśeṣika, the third school of Hindu philosophy, that of Sāṃkhya, accepts consciousness as the defining attribute of the soul. This system, unlike the previous two, brings all of matter into the category of prakṛti, and mokṣa in this school consists of liberating the self, characterised by pure consciousness (puruṣa), from prakṛti. When the puruṣa releases its 'aloneness' (kaivalya) from prakṛti, it is liberated from pain. In Sāṃkhya also one does not experience pleasure in this state, because in this system pleasure is associated with one of the three guṇas of prakṛti which the puruṣa transcends; nevertheless there is the peace which comes from realising one's own true nature. This experience can be had even in this life according to Sāṃkhya and is called jīvanmukti or embodied liberation, while in the systems of Nyāya and Vaiśeṣika such liberation represents a post-mortem state. According to Sāṃkhya the soul remains in the body after liberation in life but is not bound by it. The fourth school of Hindu thought, called Yoga, largely shares the metaphysical principles of Sāṃkhya and is distinguished by the greater attention it pays to the process for bringing about the separation of puruṣa from prakṛti. Eight such steps are spelt out in the system: (1) yama (five rules such as abstention from killing etc.); (2) niyama (five rules for cultivating moral virtues, like purity etc.); (3) āsana (meditational posture); (4) prāṇāyāma (breath control); (5) pratyahāra (withdrawal of the senses from sense objects); (6) dhāraṇā (holding the mind in this state); (7) dhyāna (concentration); and (8) samādhi or states of absorption resulting in cessation of mental modifications, when the self abides in its essential pure consciousness. This is kaivalya. There is, however, one major point of difference between the schools of classical Sāṃkhya and Yoga. Sāṃkhya is atheistic but Yoga accepts the existence of God, like the schools of Nyāya and Vaiśeṣika.

The fifth school of Hindu philosophy, namely Mīmāṃsā, is ritualistic in its orientation and interprets karma to mean not action in general but ritual action. It classifies such ritual actions into three categories: (1) nitya karma, or obligatory actions, and naimittika karma, or occasional rites, also obligatory; (2) niṣiddha karma, or forbidden actions; and (3) kāmya karma, or volitional rituals prompted by desire. As mokṣa comes from neutralising karma, Mīmāṃsā recommends the following procedure to obtain the desired result: it recommends the performance of nitya and naimittika karma, and abstention from niṣiddha karma, so that no bad karma accrues through acts of omission and commission, respectively. It also recommends avoiding kāmya karma so that no good karma is generated. The absence of both good and bad karma neutralises the operation of karma. One is thus liberated from saṃsāra.

The sixth and the most influential school of Hindu thought is Vedānta. It offers a philosophical interpretation of the Vedas, as distinguished from Mīmāṃsā, which is oriented towards a ritualistic orientation of it. Several systems of Vedānta have evolved over the centuries on account of its popularity as a philosophical school. The views of three such systems: Advaita Vedānta, Viśiṣṭādvaita Vedānta and Dvaita Vedānta, are summarised below.

According to Advaita Vedānta, nirguṇa Brahman represents the sole spiritual reality and one attains mokṣa when one realises that one's own self (ātman) is identical with it. It is the illusion of one's separateness from it which is the cause of one's bondage in saṃsāra. Once this illusion is overcome, liberation is obtained. The illusion is overcome when one listens to this insight carefully (śravaṇa), reflects on it constantly (manana) and meditates on it deeply (nididhyāsana). If this course of spiritual practice is successfully followed, knowledge of this identity (jñāna) brings about a liberative transformation of one's understanding of oneself and the world. Such mokṣa can be obtained in a premortem state. The most celebrated exponent of this school is Rāmānuja (*c.*788–820 CE).

According to Viśiṣṭādvaita Vedānta, the ultimate reality about the world is represented by saguṇa Brahman or God, and the universe and the souls are inseparable from it and comprised within it in a state of utter dependence. When the ātman realises its true relationship with God in complete devotion, mokṣa is achieved through God's grace. Such mokṣa, however, is a postmortem state. The most celebrated exponent of this school is Rāmānuja (1017–1137).

According to Dvaita Vedānta, the ultimate reality is saguṇa Brahman or God as Viṣṇu, while the universe and the individual souls are quite distinct from it and utterly dependent on it. Liberation is achieved by God's grace and represents a postmortem state. The most celebrated exponent of this school is Madhva (1199–1278).

Apart from Hinduism, Buddhism also accepts the concept of mokṣa, although the preferred word for it is nirvāṇa. According to Buddhism, human beings do not possess any underlying permanent essence such as the ātman, although such an assumption pervades Hinduism. Ātman is not a part of the solution but a part of the problem. Once one realises that one's sense of the ego is merely a figment of the imagination without any objective counterpart, one discovers the true nature of things and is liberated from saṃsāra and karma. And such a state can be achieved while alive.

Jainism also possesses its own concept of mokṣa. Karma consists of very fine particles of matter according to Jainism, which actually invade the soul and weigh it down, just as dust might penetrate an orb of light. Through a life of rigorous asceticism it is possible to purge the soul of such matter, as well as prevent it from accumulating fresh matter. When it achieves this state the soul rises to the top of the universe and dwells there in bliss, forever freed from the trammels of karma and rebirth.

Buddhism and Jainism are atheistic religions; mokṣa in Sikhism is, by contrast, located in a firmly theistic worldview. The soul is trapped in the world from beginningless time, having lost sight of God; by constantly remembering God one finally realises him and achieves mokṣa in this very life. Such a life consists of five spiritual stages: the first is represented by pious living (dharam khaṇḍ); the second by knowledge (giān khaṇḍ); the third by effort (saram khaṇḍ); in the fourth one receives the grace of god (karam khaṇḍ) and finally one attains to the truth of God (sach khaṇḍ).

Another perspective on mokṣa is provided not by the final point of liberation but by focusing on the initial point of the seeker seeking such liberation. This involves a shift in our focus from the end represented by mokṣa to the means by which it is achieved.

The human personality with its various components provides a good starting point for mapping out the various paths of mokṣa. One may begin with the initial observation that the human being obviously functions in this world with the awareness of possessing a body and a mind. Any spiritual technique which enables this person to forge a link with the ultimate reality, which produces a liberative outcome or mokṣa, could be called a yoga. The word yoga also means union – so any path which united the spiritual seeker with his or her spiritual goal could be called a yoga.

Haṭha Yoga is that form of yoga which takes the body as the starting point and enables one to achieve mokṣa by making the dormant spiritual energy lying coiled up at the bottom of the spine like a serpent (called kuṇḍalinī) move through it to the head, at which point mokṣa is attained. This path to mokṣa visualises certain nodal points along the spine as part of its spiritual cartography. Five of these correspond to the divisions of the vertebral column: mūlādhāra (cervical); svādhiṣṭhāna (dorsal); maṇipūraka (lumbar); anāhata (sacral); and viśuddha (coccygeal). The sixth is placed between the eyebrows (ājñā) and the seventh at the top of the head (sahasrāra).

Rāja Yoga, on the other hand, begins with the mind but deals with it only in its most general aspect. It then takes the seeker through the eight stages already discussed earlier, which are:

- Samādhi
- Dhyāna
- Dhāraṇā
- Pratyahāra
- Prāṇāyāma
- Āsana
- Niyama
- Yama.

The system also distinguishes between various forms of samādhi which are:

sāsmita sānanda savicāra savitarka	} saṃprajñāta samādhi

At the savitarka stage, the mind (citta) works with an object of the physical world, such as an image. In the next stage (savicāra), the mind catches hold of its subtle essence. The process gets subtler in the sānanda stage, when one focuses on the sense itself doing the seeing, and this leads one to the ego behind the sense in the sāsmita stage. As it proceeds further the mind also becomes freed from its habitual individuation by the ego, when it turns out to be nothing but pure consciousness shining by itself in the state of asaṃprajñāta samādhi.

So far we have used the body and the mind in their broadest sense as our starting point. Just as one could use a physiological function as the starting point for mokṣa, the way Tantra uses sex, or Laya Yoga uses sound, one could also similarly use psychological functions as the starting point. One could thus conceivably use cognition itself for this purpose, but typically the three functions of the psyche which have been utilised for this function are thinking, feeling and willing.

The use of thinking as a spiritual avenue points in the direction of Jñāna Yoga or the path of knowledge. It will be obvious that the Hindu schools of Nyāya, Vaiśeṣika and Sāṃkhya made extensive use of this method but it is the method used by Advaita Vedānta par excellence.

The use of feeling as a spiritual avenue points in the direction of Bhakti Yoga, which was utilised by theistic Yoga and

Table 1

Mode of worship	Mode of relation	Mode of liberation
1. *Caryā* External worship	*Dāsa-mārga* Servant-master	*Sālokya* Residence in God's world
2. *Kriyā* Intimate service to God	*Sat-putra-mārga* "Good" son-father	*Sāmīpya* Proximity to God
3. *Yoga* Mental concentration on God	*Sakhā-mārga* Friend-to-friend	*Sārūpya* Having same form as God
4. *Jñāna* Knowledge of God	*San-mārga* Path of truth	*Sāyujya* Union with God

the schools of Viśiṣṭādvaita and Dvaita Vedānta. The last two represent the form of Hindu theism known as Vaiṣṇavism but Hindu Śaivism has also made extensive use of devotion. Bhakti Yoga uses human emotional relationships as paradigms for the divine and the school of Śaiva Siddhānta enables one to draw up a diagram which posits correlations between modes of worship, emotional attitudes, modes of disciple and modes of salvation (see Table 1). Willing as a third function of the psyche points in the direction of Karma Yoga.

According to Karma Yoga, mokṣa can be achieved by continuing to live and act in the world as we usually do but changing the spirit in which we perform these daily duties. Our activities in the world are usually motivated by desire, but if we begin performing them out of a sense of impersonal duty rather than personal desire the very karma which normally binds us to saṃsāra will take us out of it and ensure that we achieve mokṣa. Such selfless action through which mokṣa is achieved is called niṣkāma-karma. It is one of the major paths advocated in the *Bhagavadgītā*.

See also: **Advaita; Āsana; Artha; Bhagavadgītā; Bhakti; Brahman; Dharma; Dvaita; Guṇa; Haṭha Yoga; Jīva; Kaivalya; Kāma; Karma (as path); Karma (Law of Action); Laya Yoga; Lokāyata; Madhva; Nyāya; Nyāyasūtras; Nyāya-Vaiśeṣika; Prakṛti; Pramāṇas; Puruṣa; Pūrva Mīmāṃsā; Rāja Yoga; Śaiva Siddhānta; Śaivism; Sāṃkhya; Vaiśeṣika; Vaiṣṇavism; Vedānta; Viśiṣṭādvaita; Viṣṇu; Yoga**

ARVIND SHARMA

Further reading

Klostermaier, Klaus K. 1984. *Mythologies and Philosophies of Salvation in the Theistic Traditions of India*. Waterloo, Ontario: Wilfred Laurier University.

Mahadevan, T.M.P. 1971. *Outlines of Hinduism*. Bombay: Chetana.

MONIER-WILLIAMS, SIR MONIER (1819–99)

English Indologist born in Bombay, son of the surveyor-general of the Bombay presidency. For most of his life named simply Monier Williams, in 1889 he adopted his Christian name as a second surname. After studying at Oxford and the East India Company's Haileybury College, Monier-Williams had intended to go to India as a writer for the East India Company, but the death of his younger brother resulted in him remaining in England and returning to Oxford, where he studied Sanskrit under H.H. Wilson. In 1844 he was appointed professor at Haileybury and in 1860 succeeded Wilson as Boden Professor of Sanskrit at Oxford. The appointment was controversial, and widely held to be due to the suspicion that his rival, F. Max Müller, a much more liberal Christian than Monier-Williams, represented the sort of continental scholarship which had given rise to David Strauss' *Life of Jesus* and Ludwig Feuerbach's *Essence of Christianity*, recently translated into English by George Eliot. Monier-Williams also made a virtue of his personal familiarity with India, in contrast to the more strictly textual approach of German scholarship. Thus in 1882 he published one of the first accounts of the Swami Narayana Sampradaya and an edition and translation of the *Śikṣāpatrī*, a copy of which he himself had received from an ācārya of the saṃpradāya in India in 1876. His orientation is also demonstrated in his 1872 Sanskrit–English dictionary, which is notorious for its rather insufficiently acknowledged dependence upon the Sanskrit–German dictionary (1855–75) of Rudolf von Roth (1821–95) and Otto von Böhtlingk (1815–1904). Ladislav Zgusta comments that whereas Roth and Böhtlingk's dictionary treated Sanskrit literature as a closed canon, Monier-Williams worked with an open canon where, arguably, Sanskrit was a living language (Zgusta 1988: 160). Most of Monier-Williams' other works were intended for the instruction of students or the wider public and include several introductory works on Indian religions and an anthology of Sanskrit literature in translation (Monier-Williams 1875) which had three editions in two years. Monier-Williams was instrumental in the foundation of the Oxford Indian Institute and in raising money in India for it.

See also: **Hinduism, history of scholarship; Müller, Friedrich Max; Swami Narayana Sampradaya; Saṃpradāya; Wilson, Harold Hayman**

WILL SWEETMAN

Further reading

Monier-Williams, M. 1875. *Indian Wisdom, or, Examples of the Religious, Philosophical and Ethical Doctrines of the Hindus*. London: W.H. Allen.

Monier-Williams, M. 1877. *Hinduism*. London: SPCK.

Monier-Williams, M. 1882. 'The Vaishṇava Religion, with Special Reference to the Śikshā-patrī of the Modern Sect Called Svāmi-Nārāyaṇa'. *Journal of the Royal Asiatic Society* XIV: 289–316.

Zgusta, Ladislav. 1988. 'Copying in Lexicography: Monier-Williams' Sanskrit Dictionary and Other Cases (Dvaikośyam)'. *Lexicographica* 4: 145–64.

MOTHER, THE (MIRRA ALFASSA) (1878–1973)

An extraordinary mystic and spiritual leader, the Mother was Sri Aurobindo's spiritual collaborator. As a child she had a series of spiritual experiences leading to her realisation of the Divine. She was also an accomplished artist, musician and writer. In 1914 she met Sri Aurobindo and six years later joined him in Pondicherry, where she stayed for the rest of her life to collaborate with him in his spiritual mission aimed at the complete transformation of human consciousness.

The Mother oversaw the daily activities of Sri Aurobindo Ashram, founded the International Centre of Education and in 1968 founded Auroville, an experimental international community devoted to human unity. The Mother's spiritual work was concerned with the activation of the highest human spiritual potential and the transformation of the physical body at the cellular level. Her complete writings are compiled in *The Collected Works of the Mother* and *The Mother's Agenda*.

See also: **Āśram(a) (Religious Community); Auroville; Ghose, Aurobindo**

BAHMAN A. K. SHIRAZI

Further reading

Mother, The. 1972–80. *The Collected Works of the Mother*. Pondicherry, India: Sri Aurobindo Ashram Press.

Mother, The. 2002. *The Mother's Agenda.* New York: Institute for Evolutionary Research (1st edn 1981).

Ghose, Aurobindo. *The Mother.* Pondicherry, India: Sri Aurobindo Ashram Press.

MOTHERHOOD

In pre-modern Hinduism, as in many contemporary circles, motherhood was the raison d'être of womanhood. As the *Manusmṛti* (9.96) says, 'Women were created to bear children, and men to extend the line; therefore, scriptures have prescribed that the Law is to be carried out in common with the wife' (Olivelle 2004: 161). According to *Taittirīya Upaniṣad* (1.11.2), one's mother is a deity. According to *Mahābhārata* (12.109.15–16), moreover, venerating a mother is ten times as important as venerating a father. Because mothers nourish children within their wombs, bear them painfully and care for infants lovingly, mothers are the supreme refuges and protectors (*Mahābhārata* 12.258.20). Even personal suffering is involved (Kuntī as the ideal, long-suffering mother (*Mahābhārata* 1.138.15–19)). Matricide is a heinous sin, according to *Mahābhārata* (12.258.39), although, according to the *Rāmāyaṇa*, Bhārata's desire to kill his mother Kaikeyī, whom he blames for his father's death, is barely held in check (*Rāmāyaṇa* 2.74.7). The mother's high status is best described by the *Manusmṛti* (2.145): 'The teacher is ten times greater than the tutor; the father is a hundred times greater than the teacher; but the mother is a thousand times greater than the father' (Olivelle 2004: 34). The childless woman is pitiful, by contrast, her condition being a result of sin. Her husband may marginalise her by taking another wife or even abandoning her.

Anthropologists and psychiatrists, too, have documented motherhood as the defining feature of the pre-modern Hindu woman's identity. The girl-child is socialised into the role of motherhood, especially by puberty rituals that celebrate her fertility. After marriage, pregnancy eliminates the fear of infertility and dramatically enhances her status in the extended family. She receives extra care and attention. She gets even more after returning to her natal home for several months before delivery.

Hindus traditionally praised mothers, especially mothers of sons. A common blessing was 'May you be the mother of many sons'. Hinduism attached great importance to sons for religious, economic, social and political reasons.

Despite all this praise for mothers, other attitudes appear in mythology, theology and anthropological accounts. Because patrilineal solidarity takes precedence over conjugal solidarity, women sometimes compensate for lack of emotional intimacy with their husbands by transferring unfulfilled love to their children, especially their sons. This situation is exacerbated because of late weaning and constant maternal attention during the early years. The effect on sons can be overwhelming. In fact, it can give rise to feelings of being engulfed and seduced, which have their mythic counterparts in mothers and goddesses who are both caring and rejecting, loving and angry. All this, in turn, might contribute later to ambivalence towards women.

See also: **Dharmaśāstras; Divorce; Gender; Kuntī; Mahābhārata; Rāmāyaṇa; Upaniṣads; Women, status of; Women's rites**

KATHERINE K. YOUNG

Further reading

Falk, Nancy E. 1998. '*Shakti* Ascending: Hindu Women, Politics, and Religious Leadership During the Nineteenth and Twentieth Centuries'. In R.D. Baird, ed., *Religion in Modern India*. New Delhi: Manohar, 298–334.

Jeffery, P., R. Jeffery and A. Lyon (eds). 1989. *Labour Pains and Labour Power: Women and Childbearing in India.* London: Zed Books.

Kakar, S. 1979. *Inner World: A Psychoanalytic Study of Childhood and Society in India.* Delhi: Oxford University Press.

Khanna, M. 2000. 'Paradigms of Female Sexuality in the Hindu World'. In E. Ahmed, ed., *Women and Religion,* vol. 4: *Desire and Resistance.* Lahore: Heinrich Böll Foundation, 119–252.

McDonald, M. 1987. 'Rituals of Motherhood among Gujarati Women in East London'. In R. Burghart, ed., *Hinduism in Great Britain: The Perpetuation of Religion in an Alien Cultural Milieu.* New York: Tavistock Publishers, 50–66

Olivelle, P. 2004. *The Law Code of Manu.* Oxford: Oxford University Press.

Reynolds, H.B. 1980. 'The Auspicious Married Woman'. In S.S. Wadley, ed., *The Powers of Tamil Women.* Syracuse, NY: Syracuse University, 35–60.

Sankar, P. 1992. 'The Rites of Passage in Hinduism: Sacraments Relating to Birth'. *Ecumenism* 108: 4–6.

Shah, S. 1995. *The Making of Womanhood: Gender Relations in the Mahābhārata.* Delhi: Manohar.

Stork, H. 1991. 'Mothering Rituals in Tamil Nadu: Some Magico-Religious Beliefs'. In J. Leslie, ed., *Roles and Rituals for Hindu Women.* London: Pinter, 89–105.

Thompson, Catherine. 1983. 'Women, Fertility and the Worship of Gods in a Hindu Village'. In Pat Holden, ed., *Women's Religious Experience.* Totowa, NJ: Barnes and Noble, 113–31.

MUDRĀ

Mudrā, originally 'insignia' or 'seal' (as of a court official), came to designate hand gestures in ritual, theatre and iconography. A mudrā is a symbolic representation of some concrete object, abstract idea or action, which in some forms of ritual (especially in Tantrism) is part of an elaborate act of mimesis. Like mantra, to which it is closely connected in the ritual context, mudrā has the power to make the sacred actively present. According to Abhinavagupta, mudrā, mantra and dhyāna (mental image) are the three essential features of tantric practice, corresponding to the body, speech and mind of both deity and practitioner (*Tantrāloka* 15.259). Some tantric mudrās are secret, either as part of esoteric rituals or as secret signs by which members of a sect recognise each other. Others are common to all forms of pūjā to the deities.

Ritual mudrās are used for purification – of practitioner, site and offerings (a very simple example is snapping of the fingers to ward off potentially destructive demonic influences); also as means of invoking the deity; and for presenting offerings, especially of an abstract or inner kind (such as the worshipper's own self). They are also used in interior meditation, to identify the practitioner with the deity, and in the process of cosmic creation and dissolution that lies at the heart of tantric practice. The power of different deities can be placed upon parts of the practitioner's body by means of special mudrās known as nyāsa.

Mudrā has subsidiary meanings, deriving from its primary one as sign or symbol. It can signify the female partner of the tantric practitioner, who is the 'seal' or representative of the supreme Śakti, the Goddess. This is probably the original reason for the inclusion of mudrā among the five Ms or pañcmakāra in tantric 'circle worship' (cakra pūjā), along with wine, meat, fish and sexual intercourse. But in this special context mudrā signifies grain or parched rice.

The hand gestures used in dance were called hasta in the classical texts but are often referred to as mudrā today. Special gestures identify divinities or are stylised representations of natural objects, and are used to portray a narrative. In iconography sometimes the hand postures of the various deities which convey a theological message are called mudrā, although this is more usual in a Buddhist context. Common to all deities are the two gestures of reassurance (abhaya) and giving (dāna).

Mudrā or mudrā-bandhana is also the term used to designate certain body postures used in tantric forms of yoga in order to arouse the kuṇḍalinī force within the body.

See also: **Abhinavagupta; Buddhism, relationship with Hinduism; Dāna; Dance; Kuṇḍalinī Yoga; Mantra; Pañcamakāra; Pūjā; Śakti; Tantrism; Woodroffe, John**

KATHLEEN TAYLOR

Further reading

Avalon, A. 1989. *The Serpent Power*. Madras: Ganesha.

Gupta, S., D.J. Hoens and T. Goudriaan. 1979. *Hindu Tantrism*. Leiden: Brill.

White, David. 2003. *Kiss of the Yogini: 'Tantric Sex' in Its South Asian Contexts*. Chicago, IL: Chicago University Press.

MUKTANANDA, SWAMI (1908–82)

Swami Muktananda initiated thousands of Indians and Westerners (including a number of celebrities) into his school of Siddha Yoga meditation. He had previously wandered around India as a monk for several years, studying with various teachers, eventually becoming a disciple of Bhagavan Nityanada. On the guru's death he claimed the succession and powers. His main teaching methods were śakti patā initiation (awakening kuṇḍalinī energy), meditation and yoga.

In 1970 Muktananda moved to the United States, at the invitation of the American teacher Baba Ram Dass. He taught there until his death, and was generally well regarded. Later, however, allegations of sexual misconduct, assaults and gun possession surfaced (disputed by his followers). He left thirty-one āśrams and numerous meditation centres around the world.

Muktananda appointed his son Nityananda and daughter Gurumayi Chidvilasananda as his successors, but after a leadership struggle between them Gurumayi emerged the victor. The movement has an active programme of teaching and events in its headquarters in the US and around the world.

See also: **Āśram(a) (religious community); Guru; Kuṇḍalinī Yoga; Meditation; Śakti; Siddha; Yoga**

ELIZABETH PUTTICK

Further reading

Muktananda, Swami. 1976. *Selected Essays*. New York: Harper & Row.

MÜLLER, FRIEDRICH MAX (1823–1900)

German Sanskritist and comparative philologist. Müller was born in Dessau and studied Sanskrit, comparative philology and philosophy at Leipzig, Berlin and Paris. His early works include German translations of the *Hitopadeśa* (1844) and Kālidāsa's *Meghadūta* (1847). In 1846 he went to England, where he was to remain for the rest of his life, eventually becoming something of a celebrity scholar. With the support of the East India Company, Müller began his critical edition of the *Ṛgveda* with Sāyaṇa's commentary, which, sometimes to the chagrin of other Sanskritists, was to occupy him for almost the next three decades. In 1850 he began lecturing on modern languages at Oxford, and in 1854 became a full professor. After the death of H.H. Wilson, Müller applied for the Boden Chair of Sanskrit but, for reasons as much political and religious as scholarly, this went instead to M. Monier-Williams. In 1868 a chair in comparative philology was created for him, the first to be established by the University itself rather than by private or royal endowment. Already in 1856, Müller had summed up his theory of the origins of religion in myth by suggesting that 'mythology is a disease of language' in which '*nomina* became *numina*'. In the last decades of his life, during which he edited the *Sacred Books of the East*, comparative mythology and the study of religion became his primary interests. Where he had once been concerned to demonstrate the properly scientific nature of the study of language, he now advocated the establishment of a 'science of religions' (Müller 1873). The religions of India, and the Veda in particular, were of the greatest importance to this endeavour, as they represented the first stage of human religion, in which the attribution of divinity to natural phenomena could still be seen in the literal meanings of the names of the Vedic gods (Müller 1878). Although he never visited India, it is there that Müller retains his celebrity, being both honoured, in the names of streets and of German cultural institutes (elsewhere in the world named for Goethe), and reviled, as an agent of the East India Company, paid to destroy Hinduism by translating its scriptures in a demeaning way.

See also: **Hinduism, history of scholarship; Kālidāsa; Monier-Williams, Sir Monier; Sacred Books of the East; Saṃhitā; Veda; Wilson, Harold Hayman**

WILL SWEETMAN

Further reading

Bosch, L.P. van den. 2002. *Friedrich Max Müller: A Life Devoted to the Humanities*. Leiden: Brill.
Müller, F.M. 1849–74. *Rig-Veda Sanhita, the Sacred Hymns of the Brahmans: Together with the Commentary of Sayanacharya*, 6 vols. London: William H. Allen.
Müller, F.M. 1873. *Introduction to the Science of Religion*. London: Longmans, Green.
Müller, F.M. 1878. *Lectures on the Origin and Growth of Religion as Illustrated by the Religions of India*. London: Williams & Norgate.
Stone, J.R. (ed.). 2002. *The Essential Max Müller: On Language, Mythology and Religion*. New York: Palgrave Macmillan.

MUṆḌAKA UPANIṢAD

See: **Upaniṣads**

MUNI

The word Muni usually refers to a sage or ascetic or someone endowed with great spiritual powers. The *Kaṭha Upaniṣad* (1.4) speaks of a Muni as having transcended earthly desires and concentrating on the ātman. Hence a Muni is a person who has advanced far on the path to mokṣa (liberation) or enlightenment or has attained it. Such a person's focus is on the inner being, which is identical to Brahman or the ultimate reality, rather than on matters to do with the temporal world and, therefore, is one who has abandoned all earthly desires and thoughts which bind one to the finite world. Such people are often bound by a vow of silence. The word has been applied to such illustrious sages as Agastya, Kaśyapa and Bhṛgu. The term has been used to denote female ascetics as well. The word most probably arises from the Sanskrit term mauna (silence).

See also: **Agastya; Ātman; Brahman; Mokṣa; Ṛṣi; Upaniṣads**

THEODORE GABRIEL

Further reading

Flood, G. 1998. *An Introduction to Hinduism*. New Delhi: Oxford University Press.

MUNSHI, KANAIYALKAL (1887–1971)

More commonly known as Kulapati K.M. Munshi, he was one of the significant figures of the Hindu renaissance that flourished in the first half of the twentieth century. He came under the influence of Sri Aurobindo whilst studying law at Baroda College. His passion for India's independence led him to join Annie Besant's All India Home Rule League in 1916 and then to become a member of the Indian National Congress. He took part in the Salt Satyagraha in 1930 and was imprisoned by the British for his political activities on more than one occasion.

After independence he enjoyed a successful political career, serving as Home Minister in the first Congress government and Food and Agricultural Minister in 1950. From 1952 to 1957 he was governor of the state of Uttar Pradesh. However, in spite of his political activity, K.M. Munshi's passion was for Indian culture; he founded the Bharatiya Vidya Bhavan in 1938 and devoted himself to its development as India's foremost cultural institution. In addition he was a successful novelist writing in Gujarati.

See also: **Besant, Annie; Bharatiya Vidya Bhavan; Gandhi, Mohandas Karamchand; Ghose, Aurobindo; Hinduism, modern and contemporary**

RON GEAVES

Further reading

http://bhavans.info/vision/munshi.asp (accessed 27 October 2005).

Kulkarni, K.M. 1983. *K.M. Munshi (Builders of Modern India)*. Government of India, Ministry of Information and Broadcasting.

MŪRTI

See: **Image worship; Iconography, modern**

MURTI, TIRUPATTUR RAMASESHAYYER VENKATACHALA (1902–86)

Indian philosopher. Born to a South Indian brāhmaṇa family, Murti's early studies were interrupted by his active participation in the nationalist movement under Gandhi's leadership, including a period of five months' imprisonment. From 1925 Murti studied both Sanskrit and the Western philosophical tradition, receiving a BA, MA and later DLitt from Banaras Hindu University and the titles of Śāstri and Ācārya from Banaras Sanskrit College. Although best known for his work on Buddhism (1955, 1960), especially Mādhyamika, Murti also wrote on Advaita Vedānta, co-authoring a work on the Vedāntic theory of ignorance, and on Indian philosophy of language. His work is distinguished by his mastery of both traditional Indian and Western philosophical approaches, and creative philosophical thinking on the basis of sound historical scholarship, summed up in his personal statement 'The Philosophy of Spirit' (1952; reprinted in Coward 1983).

See also: **Advaita; Gandhi, Mohandas Karamchand; Hinduism, history of scholarship; Vedānta**

WILL SWEETMAN

Further reading

Coward, H.G. (ed.). 1983. *Studies in Indian Thought: Collected Papers of Professor T.R.V. Murti*. Columbia, SC: South Asia Books.

Coward, H.G. 2003. *T.R.V. Murti*. Delhi: Munshiram Manoharlal.

MURUKAṈ

An ancient Tamil god of war generally supposed to have pre-dated the cultural and religious influence of Sanskrit traditions. However, most studies of the god acknowledge that the present-day cult of Murukaṉ is heavily influenced by a synthesis of early Tamil religious formations and the Vedic god of war, variously known as Skanda, Kumāra or Kārttikeya. As the latter figure was assimilated into Śaivite traditions, appearing as Śiva's second son, the contemporary figure of Murukaṉ demonstrates the continuity between tribal folk-religion, scriptural religions, oral traditions and inter-regional cults that is ubiquitous in India. However, any study of Murukaṉ and his devotees demonstrates that it is better to perceive the above categories as complementary and part of an organic whole than as exclusive of each other.

It is certainly true that Murukaṉ is the most important of the deities worshipped amongst Tamils, not only religiously but also as a repository for the strong Tamil urge to define themselves culturally and ethnically as distinctly separate from Sanskritic influences. The ancient Caṅkam (Sangam) literature expressed in the Tamil language invokes a powerful bhakti tradition firmly based in this-worldliness rather than ascetic rejection. The principal recipient of Caṅkam bhakti is Murukaṉ, who is simultaneously the god of love and war. Rather than the transcendent message of Brahman-ātman unity found in the *Upaniṣads*, Murukaṉ devotees contact the god through possession, often achieved by frenzied dancing under the guidance of a shaman-type figure. Early texts suggest there may have been blood sacrifice and strong followings of young women possessed by the god. This is no longer evident amongst devotees, but witnesses of the annual festivals to the god at any of his temples or major pilgrimage centres will see processions of young men who lacerate themselves. Pilgrimage groups are still led by non-brāhmaṇa shaman-type figures who have the power to be possessed and excite others into possession states. Murukaṉ bhakti still retains a wild and frenzied element distinctly different in tone to ritual temple worship associated with Brahmanical traditions.

Later Murukaṉ was absorbed into the Hindu pantheon through identification with Skanda, which allowed for his entry into more sedate and ritualised brāhmaṇa-led worship, but in reality the legends of Skanda are assimilated into the earlier Murukaṉ mythologies and remain more often a unique blending of folk religion and scriptural tradition in which possession dominates as the major expression of contact with the sacred. This is assisted by Skanda's own assimilation into Śiva lore, appearing as one of the god's two offspring. The identification with Śiva allows for a syncretism with mainstream Sanskrit-origin traditions but allows for the 'wildness' of original Murukaṉ worship to remain intact through Śiva's own affiliation to the outcaste, the disreputable and the supernatural.

Murukaṉ is generally depicted as a young androgynous male accompanied by his vāhana, a peacock, and possibly accompanied by his two consorts, although Valli, his main consort, who has a devotional following of her own, is more likely to be depicted as a spear. Where absorbed into Śaivite tradition, the iconographic images are more likely to be that of a child-Śiva figure influenced by the god's representation as a renunciate yogi. Sometimes he is found on Śiva's lap, either alone or accompanied by Gaṇeśa.

See also: **Bhakti; Blood sacrifice; Brahman-Ātman; Dalits; Gaṇeśa; Possession; Śaivism; Sanskrit; Śiva; Skanda; Tapas; Tīrthayātrā; Upaniṣads; Vāhanas; Yogī**

RON GEAVES

Further reading

Klostermaier, Klaus. 1989. *A Survey of Hinduism*. Albany, NY: State University of New York.

MUSIC

From Veda chanting to the devotional songs of the great bhakti saints, from lullabies to the upper reaches of classical performance and to the soundtracks of 'Bollywood' films, music pervades all of Hindu culture, high and low, sacred and profane, and is at the heart of all, bar the most severely ascetic, Hindu religious traditions. As the Greek historians saw it, India is the original land of music, revealed there by Dionysus (i.e. Śiva). Classed as an ancillary science to the Veda, musical theory is also called Gandharvaveda, the science of the celestial beings who are musicians and dancers to the gods. Indeed, music is deemed to have been created by Brahmā as the fifth Veda, which, unlike the four others, would be accessible to people of all social classes (*Nāṭyaśāstra* 1.12–17). The generic term for performance arts, Saṃgīta, encompasses dance and the dramatic arts, singing and instrumental music, all viewed as complementary means of conveying meaning, emotions and feelings. Further, since the ultimate reality is 'in the form of sound' (nādabrahman), music is a manifestation of the divine and, conversely, musical meditation (nādopasana) is a means of emancipation, i.e. a yoga as well as its end; it is also said to fulfil all four goals of human life (puruṣārthas): duty, wealth, pleasure and salvation.

Apart from the rules concerning Vedic psalmody, the earliest extant authority on performance arts remains the *Nāṭyaśāstra* (*c.*100 CE), a treatise on 'acting' attributed to the ancient sage Bhārata which is clearly a compilation of earlier teachings and which has received numerous commentaries, notably by Abhinavagupta (tenth century) and Nānya Deva (eleventh century). Also ancient is the *Gītālaṃkara* (The Ornament of Song), also attributed to Bhārata, whereas the most influential treatise, the *Saṃgīta Ratnākara* (Music's Mine of Jewels), is from the twelfth century. There is an immense literature on music, not only in Sanskrit but also in Persian as well as Indian vernaculars. Western study of Indian music was initiated by William Jones in his *Music of India* (Jones and Willard 1793), which draws on the main old sources.

Vedic chant

Each collection of the Vedic texts is chanted in different ways, of which the notation is probably the oldest on record. The *Ṛgveda* is psalmodised on three tones: anudātta (median/unraised), udātta (raised) and svarita (accented). In the written text, anudātta is represented by a horizontal stroke under the syllable, udātta has no accent and svarita has a vertical line above the syllable, thus: a̱, a, à.

The *Yajurveda* is chanted on four or five tones, while the *Sāmaveda* uses a full scale of seven tones indicated by rising digits, while the phoneme Ra above a syllable doubles its duration. Thus, the hymns of the *Sāmaveda* are sung and its psalmody is fully musical.

One of the preoccupations of Vedic ancillary sciences geared towards the oral preservation of the hymns has been metre and prosody which stipulate the arrangement of long and short syllables (mātrā) into rhythmic patterns. For the purpose of textual transmission the 'continuous' (saṃhitā) chanting is underpinned by techniques of memorisation such as the word-by-word (pada) reciting where the effects of euphony (saṃdhi) that fuse words together are suspended, restoring grammatical endings. There are a number of types of exercise called vikṛti, such as the krama (tramping), where words are enunciated in couples and repeated in the order ab/bc/cd/de, etc. A more complex vikṛti is Jatā (braid), where words are uttered in the order ab/ba/ab/bc/cb/bc, etc. Learnt in this way the phonetically correct texts have been preserved even if the meaning has been lost.

There are different branches (Śākhā) of Vedic chanting, with great variations of singing style. The *Sāmaveda* has also five main different singing styles (gāna), with countless variants, which, unlike the schools of Ṛk and Yajus chanting, are now virtually extinct.

Classical music

As attested by all ancient treatises, there once was a single musical system in use throughout India. A distinction between a northern and a southern tradition appeared during the Delhi Sultanate, as evinced in the *Saṃgīta Sudhākara* by Haripala of Deogir, written *c.*1310 CE.

Here for the first time appear the terms Karnataka and Industhani to designate the southern and northern systems, respectively. The main difference between the two was the strong influence Persian music exercised in the North, while what was retained was thought of as the 'authentic' (deśya) tradition, although in fact the ancient, pre-Muslim material (mārga: path) had already been replaced by what was termed 'provincial' (deśī) practice.

The common background is a conception of musical sound (nāda) as emerging from an inner 'unstruck' sound (anahāta nāda), a mystical vibration, divine origin of the universe and perceived only by advanced yogins. Audible nāda is classified, according to its timbre, as emanating from the human voice, a plucked instrument, a bowed instrument, a membranophone or a metallic surface. Another classification differentiates, for a singer, between sounds originating in the navel, the chest, the head, the throat and the mouth. Sonic intervals may also be sonant (vādī), consonant (samvādī) or assonant (anuvādī).

The basic material of music-making is a series of seven degrees (saptaka) or tones (svara), which themselves encompass twenty-two microtones, or śruti. The svaras are known by and solmisated with the first syllable of their full name: Sa, Ri, Ga, Ma, Pa, Dha, Ni. Of these seven, only Sa and Pa, the tonic and dominant in the diatonic scale, are invariable. The other five notes each possess two variants: in northern terminology these are komal, which is flat-ish, and tivra, which is sharp-ish, resulting in the theoretical series of the twelve: SA, k.ri, T.ri, k.ga, T.ga, k.ma, t.ma, PA, k.dha, t.dha, k.mi, k.ni. The southern tradition has a parallel nomenclature.

Melody and rhythm

Indian music is modal and monodic and, from two tonal systems, śadjagrāma and madhyamagrāma (scales differentiated by tuning and microtonal distribution), were derived seven plagal sequences each: the mūrchhanā, which lost their usefulness when, by the twelfth century, the ancient fixed-tone harp was displaced by lute-like instruments with moveable frets. In the North, ten modal scales (thāta) were later identified as forming the basis for the large number of musical modes, or rāgas, which are the melodic language of India. In the South, seventy-two melakartas are identified as parent scales to the rāgas.

A rāga is not only a specific zigzagging ascending and differently descending scale, but it encapsulates an autonomous musical order characterised by melodic phrases and ornaments, by a certain way of bridging intervals and by two characteristic notes called vādī (speaking) and samvādī (co-speaker) which are the anchors of the melody. Above all, a rāga is designed to arouse in the hearer a particular emotional state in which performer and audience commune. The moods generated by the rāgas have been the subject of a large amount of poetry and also miniature paintings (rāgamalikā) which bring out the association of each rāga with a time of the day or night and the seasons.

Rhythm (tāla) is the other major component of musical expression and the Indian science and aesthetics of rhythm is the most complex and sophisticated of any music. Metre and rhythm are related since they both use strong, weak and silent beats combined into intricate sequences to form, in the specific case of music, a cyclic formula that encompasses a number of bars or time-units (mātrā: metre) which themselves contain a number of beats (akṣara: syllable). Apart from the numerical element of time-keeping, each beat is further characterised by a syllable (thekā) that denotes a specific drum-stroke (thus differentiating the colours of two tāla which may be numerically identical). For example, the northern Eka tāla runs as shown in Table 2.

Table 2

Mātra	1	2	.	3	4	5	6	.	7	8	9	10	.	11	12
Thekā	dhin	dhin		dhāge	trika	tū	nā		kat	tā	dhāge	trika		dhin	nā

Karnatic music, which is far more elaborately systematised than the Hindusthani, possesses a theoretical (i.e. potential) number of 108, later reduced into a system of 35 tālas in current use.

Main forms of classical music

Classical music is both composed and improvised. In the North as in the South there are generally two main movements in the performance of a rāga. The first is an elaborate improvised prelude called ālāpana or ālāp, where the performer systematically explores all the degrees and intervals of a rāga in relation to its tonic. The ālāp is metrical but does not conform to a tāla. Once the character and mood of the rāga is established, then either a composition or a tāla-based improvisation may follow.

The Dhrupad, perfected at the court of Akbar, is the grandest of northern styles. It consists of an ālāp then a dhruva (fixed form) that manifest the rāga, followed by a composition on a four-line poem (pāda) set to rhythmic variations. A simpler form of Dhrupad is the Dhamar.

Khyāl (fantasy) has been called the Indian bel canto; it is a northern style, elegant and virtuosic, allowing for melodic ornamentations (tāna) and bendings of pitch (gamak) that are forbidden in the austere Dhrupad. Khyāl takes two forms, usually performed in succession: the slow, grave and serene vilambita and the fast, exhilarating druta. The most widely appreciated genre, Khyāl, like the Dhrupad is sung by both Hindus and Muslims.

Thumrī, based on intense love poetry, is a kind of light music usually – though not always – practised by women, mostly using rāgas derived from folk music. The Ghazal, sung in Urdu, is a Muslim relative of the Thumrā and is often tinged with mysticism.

Until the mid-twentieth century, when the All India Radio replaced local grandees as the new patron of musicians, diverse singing styles (gayaki) were associated with schools (gharana) at a number of courts, such as the Patiala gharana, resulting in marked differences in interpretation that have now been largely blended or become optional.

In the South, music composed in notation (kṛti: work) and mostly devotional has largely predominated and has formed the anchor for improvisation. However, the most eagerly anticipated element in any concert is the rāgam-tānam-pallavi. Unlike much of Karnatic music, this is almost entirely improvised, with a long initial ālāpana (rāgam) that begins in the lower register and builds up the rāga. Tānam introduces a free rhythmic pulse and finally the pallori section is set to a tāla as complex as possible – a delightful challenge to both musicians and audience. Southern music has a galaxy of famous composers, among whom the saint Tyāgarāja (1767–1847) is pre-eminent.

Instruments

In parallel with the classification of the types of sounds, India's some 500 musical instruments are grouped into four categories: strings (tata), wind (suśira), skin-drums (vitata) and other percussion (ghana). Yet the primary instrument remains the voice, so that melody instruments mostly imitate or echo its inflections.

Along with the ancient harp, which had been eclipsed by the twelfth century, the oldest, most important and revered string instrument is the vīṇā, a kind of large lute with two resonators, usually with seven strings. There are different types of vīṇā but the main two are the northern Rudra vīṇā, named after Śiva, its mythical inventor, and the southern Sarasvatī vīṇā (from its association with the goddess). Far more common nowadays in the North is the sitār, designed in the fifteenth century by Amir Khusru and perfected in the seventeenth. A sitār – another lute – possesses four main melodic strings with two side strings sounding the tonic and dominant, used for rhythmic effect. A number of sympathetic strings also enrich the tone. A bowed instrument, the sarangī, was, until the mid-twentieth century when it found a vocation as a soloist, mainly used in the North for the accompaniment of singers, a role taken by the violin in the South.

Wind instruments comprise a variety of flutes, straight (vaṃsa), or transverse (muralī), and a kind of oboe, the śahnāī in the North and the larger nāgasvaram in the South.

The main percussion instruments are the mṛdanga, a double-headed horizontal barrel-shaped drum already mentioned in the *Ṛgveda* (5.33–36), and mostly used in the South. A large northern version is the noble pakhāvaj, used in the Dhrupad, while, cut into two vertical single-headed timbals, this becomes the tablā, ubiquitous in the North.

To underpin the playing of the voice or other instruments, the tānpūrā is a sitār-looking fretless drone which provides the constant buzzing of the tonic and dominant (and sometimes sub-dominant) of the rāga played; it is usually sounded for a while before a performance to attune the ear of the audience.

Folk instruments are simple variations on the above.

Folk, devotional and film music

Classical music is for a learned audience and has only become widely available in the last century, through the broadcastings of All India Radio, the availability of recordings and the novelty of public concerts. If 'classical' music is like Sanskrit, with a pan-Indian though socially limited reach, folk music would be like the vernaculars, with only regional appeal. There is an enormous diversity of local folk traditions which address the concerns of their people: life's events and their attendant emotions, the rhythms of rural life and of festivals, the stories of Hindu mythology and, of course, sheer entertainment.

Of greater range are the devotional songs of the great bhakti saints which fuel people's religious sentiments. Called kīrtan, abhang or, more commonly, bhajan, the songs of Mīrābāī, Sūrdās, Jñānadeva and many others, including, in Bengal, the songs of Rabindranath Tagore, are widely known and loved.

The most important recent development has been the birth of a cinema industry in Bombay, Calcutta and Madras and, particularly, of cinema sound in the 1930s. Apart from 'art-cinema', Indian films are overwhelmingly musicals, and, from crude beginnings, the composition of film music as well as the skills of singers have increased in sophistication and it is that kind of Indian music that has achieved a truly global reach.

See also: **Abhinavagupta; Bhakti; Brahmā; Dance; Drama; Film; Gandharvaveda; Jones, Sir William; Mīrābāī; Myth; Puruṣārthas; Rudra; Saṃhitā; Sarasvatī; Śiva; Sound recordings; Sūrdās; Tagore, Rabindranath; Television and radio; Tyāgarāja; Upavedas; Utsava; Veda; Yogi**

DANIEL MARIAU

Further reading

Bhatkande, Pt. V.N. 1917. *A Short Survey of the Music of Upper India.* Bombay. Reprint 1934.

Danielou, A. 1949–54. *Northern Indian Music*, 2 vols. London: Halcyon Press.
Jones, William and N.A. Willard. 1793. *Music of India.* Reprint Calcutta, 1962.
Kaufmann, W. 1968. *The Rāgas of North India.* Bloomington, IN: Indiana University Press.
Nijenhuis, E.Te. 1974. *Indian Music: History and Structure.* Leiden: E.J. Brill.
Sambamoorthy, P. 1958–69. *South Indian Music*, 6 vols. Madras: Indian Music Publishing House.

MUTTAPAṈ

Muttapaṉ is a popular deity of low-caste Hindu groups in Northern Kerala, where he is worshipped in teyyam rituals in which ritual practitioners don elaborate costumes and through song and dance invoke the spirit of the deity into themselves. Muttapaṉ is in reality a duo of gods, the Valiya Muttapaṉ and the Cheriya Muttapaṉ, who through a process of Sanskritic hermeneutics of the Muttapaṉ legend is now believed to be the pan-Hindu gods Viṣṇu and Śiva, incarnated together. Muttapaṉ's role is to rescue the low-caste and tribal populace from the oppression of high-caste rulers of the land (Karunasagar 1995: 27–29.)

The origins of Muttapaṉ are in the hill tracts of Northern Kerala, where he, like the other popular Keralan god Ayyapaṉ, was found on the banks of the Payyāvūr river by the brāhmaṇa ruler of Ayyankara.

The popularity of Muttapaṉ has now transcended state boundaries and even national boundaries, and pilgrims from all over south India and of all castes throng the teyyam worship in Muttapaṉ shrines.

See also: **Ayyapaṉ**; **Brāhmaṇa**; **Caste; Dance; Possession; Śiva; Varṇa; Viṣṇu.**

THEODORE GABRIEL

Further reading

Karunasagar. 1995. *Bhagavān Srī Muttappan.* Kaṇṇūr (Kerala): Sadguru Sēvā Sadanam.
Nambudiripad, Usha. 2001. *Kunnattur Paadi, God's Own Land.* Ellarenji (Kerala): Karakkattedam.

MYTH

Sources

Myths are generally assumed to be texts, more specifically verbal texts (though images can be texts too), and usually written verbal texts (though so much of mythology is orally transmitted). These assumptions start us off on the wrong foot in the study of Hindu mythology, and they land us in the middle of a historical debate about the relationship between two bodies of material, one in Sanskrit and the other not. The Sanskrit texts began with the *Ṛgveda*, *c.*1500 BCE, flourished right through the late medieval period (ending in about 1500 CE) and are still being composed in many parts of India. The non-Sanskrit texts probably begin well before 2500 BCE and also continue to the present day. Scholars of India used to speak of the culture of the Veda entering India from somewhere in Europe (from what was called Indo-European or Indo-Germanic or Indo-Aryan culture) in an invasion, or (more recently) a migration, but in any case this was assumed to be the base onto which other things were added in the course of Indian history, rather than, as is obvious from world history, the something that was added to a pre-existing base. That base has been the silent partner of Hinduism, allowing us to hear it only at those relatively late historical moments when it broke into the Sanskrit club. Yet it is the fons et origo of Hindu mythology; new myths arose in the non-Sanskrit world, found their way into the Sanskrit world and, often, left it again, to have a second life among the great vernacular mythologies of India. The only way we can tell the story is to begin with those texts that left a literary record – the Sanskrit texts – but to acknowledge, right from the start, from the *Ṛgveda*, the presence of something else uniquely Indian (or, rather, non-Indo-European) at the heart of these texts. The Vedic people may never have been in direct contact with the civilisation of the Indus Valley in its prime, but the religion of the Indus culture probably influenced them.

The *Ṛgveda* contains many Indo-European elements, such as the worship of male sky gods with sacrifices and the existence of the old sky god Dyaus, whose name is cognate with those of the classical Zeus of Greece and Jupiter of Rome ('Father Jove'). The Vedic heaven, the 'world of the fathers', resembled the Germanic Valhalla and seems also to be an Indo-European inheritance. The Vedic god Varuṇa, later an unimportant sea god, is cognate with the Greek sky god Ouranos and appears in the *Ṛgveda* as sharing many features of the Zoroastrian Ahura Mazda ('Wise Lord'); the hallucinogenic sacred drink soma corresponds to the sacred haoma of Zoroastrianism. But even in the earlier parts of the *Ṛgveda* the religion had already acquired numerous specifically Indian features, along with many words borrowed from the non-Sanskritic, Dravidian languages of India, and these features may well stem from the influence of the indigenous inhabitants. Some of the Vedic gods have no clear Indo-European or Indo-Iranian counterparts. On the other hand, the goddess Saraṇyu (probably cognate with the Greek furies called the Erinues), to whom one Vedic hymn is dedicated and whose mythology continued to be central to later Hinduism, may be an atavism from the worship of goddesses that pre-date patriarchal Indo-European mythology.

Vedic cosmogony and cosmology

Some of the Vedic creation myths have strong Indo-European parallels, while others do not. Of the former sort, some texts view creation as procreation: the personified heaven, Dyaus, impregnates the earth goddess, Pṛthivī, with rain, causing crops to grow on her. Also closely related to certain Norse myths, in particular, is another myth recorded in the last book of the *Ṛgveda*, the 'Hymn of the Cosmic Man' (*Puruṣasūkta*, 10.90): the universe was created out of the parts of the body of a single cosmic man (Puruṣa) when the gods sacrificed and dismembered his body at the primordial sacrifice. From him the four classes (varṇas) of Indian society were created: the priest (brāhmaṇa) emerging from the mouth, the warrior (rājanya) from the arms, the peasant (vaiśya) from the thighs and the servant (śūdra) from the feet of the primeval victim. Yet in Indo-European myths there are only three classes, to which myth-makers in India added the fourth; and in the earlier myths the kings are in the first tier, but they slip down, without a murmur, into the second tier together with the other warriors in the vedic hymn.

Generally speaking, Vedic gods share many characteristics: several of them (Indra, Varuṇa, Viṣṇu) are said to have created the universe, set the sun in the sky, and propped apart heaven and earth. All of them are bright and shining, and all are susceptible to human praise. Some major gods were clearly personifications of natural phenomena, and for these deities no clearly delineated divine personalities were perceived. Indra, Agni and Soma are the three most frequently invoked gods. Indra, the foremost god of the Vedic pantheon, is a god of war and rain, who granted human fertility and agricultural plenty, aid against demons and victory against human enemies. Agni (a cognate of the Latin ignis, 'to ignite') is the deified fire, particularly the fire of sacrifice, and Soma is the intoxicating or hallucinogenic drink of the sacrifice, or the plant from which it is pressed; neither is greatly personified. Agni, fire, appears in the sacrificial fire, in lightning or hidden in the logs from which fire can be drilled. As the fire of sacrifice, he is the mouth of the gods and the carrier of the oblation, the mediator between the human and the divine orders.

The principal focus of Vedic literature is the sacrifice, which in its simplest form can be viewed as a ritualised banquet to which a god is invited to partake of a meal shared by the sacrificer and his priest. The invocations mention, often casually, the past exploits of the deity. The offered meal gives strength to the deity to repeat his feat and to aid the sacrificer. Ṛta – the truthfulness that governed the alliance between humans (and between humans and gods) – was necessary to maintain the physical and moral order of the universe and was the central concept of Vedic morality, in many ways the antecedent of dharma. Varuṇa, with Mitra (related to the Persian god Mithra, 'the friend') presides over the observance of ṛta. Thus Varuṇa is a judge before whom a mortal may stand guilty, while Indra is a king who may support a mortal king. The worshipper would ask Varuṇa for forgiveness, for deliverance from evil committed by oneself or others and for protection.

Although there are many demons (Rākṣasas), no one god embodies the evil spirit; rather, many gods have their devil within, inspiring fear as well as trust. Among the perpetually beneficent gods are the Aśvins (horsemen), who are helpers and healers and often visit the needy. Apart from Earth, the other goddesses of importance in the text of the *Ṛgveda* are Uṣas (Dawn), who brings in the day and thus is said to bring forth the Sun, and Vāc, the personification of speech (particularly the speech of ritual recitation).

In the later Vedic period, the ṛgvedic gods and their myths gave way to a pantheism of Prajāpati ('Lord of Creatures'), the deified sacrifice or ritualised deity, the patron of procreation in popular belief, who, with his consort Vāc (Speech), is said to have begotten the world. In the course of the Vedic period Puruṣa fused with Prajāpati, who emerged as the creator god and in many respects as the highest divinity, the immortal father even of the gods, whom he transcends and encompasses. In the *Ṛgveda*, mythology begins to be transformed into philosophy; for example, 'in the beginning was the nonexistent, from which the existent arose' (*Ṛgveda* 10.72.2). But even the reality of the nonexistent is questioned: 'then there was neither the nonexistent nor the existent' (*Ṛgveda* 10.129). Such cosmogonic speculations continue, particularly in the older *Upaniṣads*, the *Mahābhārata* and the *Rāmāyaṇa*.

The Vedic gods lost their sacrificial importance and true mythological meaning, but they survived as figures of myth and legend in the *Mahābhārata* and the *Rāmāyaṇa*, the two great Sanskrit epics, composed between 300 BCE and 300 CE. The Prajāpati of the *Upaniṣads* became popularly personified as the god Brahmā, who creates all classes of beings and dispenses boons. Of far greater importance is Kṛṣṇa. In the *Mahābhārata* he is a hero, a leader of his people and an active helper of his friends. His biography as it is known later is not worked out; still, the text is the source of early Kṛṣṇaism. Not everyone considered Kṛṣṇa a god, but he is sometimes identified with Viṣṇu and occasionally clearly identified as the supreme deity; he reveals the *Bhagavadgītā*, a discourse on dharma (law, justice and morality) and the immortality of the soul, to prince Arjuna, simultaneously revealing his own tremendous divine form. Later, as one of the most important of the incarnations of Viṣṇu, Kṛṣṇa undergoes a complex development as an incarnate god, and many idyllic myths are told of his boyhood, when he plays with and loves young cowherd women (gopīs) in the village while hiding from an uncle who threatens to kill him. But this complex figure has a shadow side. Even in the *Mahābhārata*, where it is said that Kṛṣṇa becomes incarnate in order to sustain dharma when it wanes and to combat adharma (forces contrary to dharma), he himself commits a number of deeds in direct violation of the warrior ethic and is indirectly responsible for the destruction of his entire family. This adharmic shadow is also cast in the purāṇic idyll, because the gopīs he woos are the wives of other men. Śiva, in the *Mahābhārata*, is far more remote than the instantly accessible Kṛṣṇa, and Śiva is hailed as the supreme god in several myths recounted of him, notably his destruction of the sacrifice of Dakṣa.

The *Mahābhārata* is rich in information about sacred places, and it is clear that making pilgrimages and bathing in sacred rivers constituted an important part of religious life. Occasionally these sacred places are associated with sanctuaries of gods. There are also frequent accounts of mythical events concerning the particular place and enriching its sanctity. Numerous descriptions of pilgrimages (tīrthayātrā) give the authors opportunities to detail local myths and legends. In addition to these, countless edifying stories shed light on the religious and moral concerns of the age.

The *Rāmāyaṇa* identifies Rāma as another incarnation of Viṣṇu. Like Kṛṣṇa in the *Mahābhārata*, Rāma is not always aware of his divinity, but that is the nature of incarnation: to be human is, in part, to forget that you are divine. The divinity of Rāma's wife, Sītā, is more thoroughly veiled but equally evident: Sītā is born not from human parents but from a furrow in the Earth, and she returns to the Earth, which opens up to receive her, after she bears Rāma twin sons. Though not as long as the *Mahābhārata*, the *Rāmāyaṇa* contains a great deal of comparable religious material in the form of myths, stories of great sages and accounts of exemplary human behaviour. But Rāma, like Kṛṣṇa, has a shadow side. His killing of the monkey-king Vālin in violation of all rules of combat and his banishment of the innocent Sītā (when he learns that his people are criticising him for taking back a woman whom the demon Rāvaṇa has held capture for many years) are troublesome to subsequent tradition. These problems of the 'subtlety' of dharma and the inevitability of its violation remained the locus of philosophical argument throughout Indian history.

Apart from their influence as Sanskrit texts, the *Mahābhārata* and the *Rāmāyaṇa* have made an enormous impact throughout South Asia and Southeast Asia in the form of vernacular and oral versions that have continually retold their stories, and their influence on art has been profound. Even today, the epic stories and tales are part of the early education of all Hindus; a continuous reading of the *Rāmāyaṇa* is an act of great merit, and a popular enactment of the Hindi version by Tulsīdās is an annual event across northern India. Television, radio and film versions of both stories, as well as retellings in the form of comic books, have also been extraordinarily popular. And the myths come alive in ritual, as well: Draupadī, the heroine of the *Mahābhārata*, is worshipped as a goddess in South India.

The Purāṇas

The *Purāṇas* (traditionally said to be eighteen, though there are more) are often voluminous texts that treat in encyclopaedic manner the myths, legends and genealogies of gods, heroes and saints, as well as instructions for the performance of many rituals. Many deal with the same or similar materials. With the epics, with which they are closely linked in origin, the *Purāṇas* became the scriptures of the common people; they were available to everybody, including women and members of the lowest order of society (śūdras), and were not, like the Veda, restricted to initiated men of the three higher orders. The origin of much of their contents may well have been non-brahmanic, but they were accepted and adapted by the brāhmaṇas.

The *Purāṇa* texts present an elaborate mythical cosmography. There are three levels: heaven, earth and the netherworlds. Earth consists of seven circular continents, the central one surrounded by the salty ocean and each of the other concentric continents by oceans of other liquids. In the centre of the central mainland stands the cosmic mountain Meru; the southernmost portion of this mainland is Bhārata-varṣa, the old name for India. Above earth there are seven layers in heaven, at the summit of which is the world of Brahmā (Brahmā-Loka); there are also seven layers below earth, the location of hells inhabited by serpents and demons of various kinds.

According to one of many purāṇic versions of the story of the origin of the universe, in the beginning the god Nārāyaṇa (identified with Viṣṇu) floated on the snake Ananta ('Endless') on the primeval waters. From his navel grew a lotus, in which the god Brahmā was born reciting the four Vedas with his four mouths and creating the 'Egg of Brahmā', which contains all the worlds. Other cosmogonies refer to other demiurges, or creators, like Manu (the primordial ancestor of humankind). At the other end of the spectrum, the Fire of Time or Doomsday (Kala) periodically destroys the world at the close of every eon. Sometimes the destruction is specifically attributed to the god Śiva, who dances the taṇḍava dance of doomsday and destroys the world.

Yet this end is not an absolute end but a temporary suspension (pralaya), after which creation begins again in the same fashion. For purāṇic myths develop around the notion that each eon consists of four yugas or world ages, named after the four throws, from best to worst, in a dice game: Kṛta Yuga (the Golden Age), Tretā, Dvāpara and Kali (the present, degenerate age). At the end of the Kali Yuga the universe is destroyed and created again at the start of the next Kṛta Yuga. So, too, on the individual human level, after death a soul returns to be born again. The soul, on departing, may go either of two ways: the Way of the Flame, which brings it through days, bright fortnights and eventually to Release from the world altogether, or union with Brahman (ultimate reality); or the Way of the Smoke, through nights, dark fortnights, eventually back to earth clinging to raindrops. If the soul happens to alight on a plant that is subsequently eaten by a man, the man may impregnate a woman and thus the soul is reborn as a human. (If an animal eats the plant, the soul is born as an animal.) In parts of India, popular belief has modified the transmigration doctrine by the assumption that the soul of the deceased reappears in a child born in the same family within a year after the person's death. Many Hindus believe that virtue will improve their lot in a subsequent existence, but they do not seem to strive for final union with Brahman. Here, and elsewhere, a workaday religion meant to meet the requirements of everyday life exists alongside a higher religion understood only by the brāhmaṇas, who are called on to officiate on important occasions.

The trinity: Śiva, Viṣṇu and Devī

While some of the Vedic gods play bit parts in the *Purāṇas*, other gods, previously of less official significance, take centre-stage. Some texts speak of Brahmā, Viṣṇu and Śiva as a trinity, but in fact Brahmā does not play in the same league as Viṣṇu and Śiva. Brahmā appears in the *Purāṇas* primarily to appease over-powerful sages and demons by granting them boons and to carry out the periodic creation of the world, usually at the behest of one (or more than one) of the actual trinity of purāṇic Hinduism: Viṣṇu, Śiva, and Devī (the Goddess).

Viṣṇu is worshipped in his own right and with his consort Lakṣmī (Good Fortune) or Śrī, the lotus goddess, granter of beauty, wealth and good luck, who came forth from the ocean when gods and antigods churned it in order to recover from its depths the ambrosia or elixir of immortality. At the beginning of the commercial year people worship her for success in personal affairs. Viṣṇu's emblems are the lotus, club, discus (as a weapon) and a conch shell, which he carries in his four hands. But Viṣṇu is also worshipped through his avatāras (incarnations, literally 'descents'), of which the human kings Rāmā and Kṛṣṇa are the most important.

Śiva is an ambivalent god who is dreaded for his unpredictable attacks but also invoked for his fierce protection of his devotees. Śiva interrupts his yoga and his asceticism (tapas) to marry Pārvatī ('Daughter of the Mountain [Himālaya]'). His combination of the roles of lover and ascetic grows out of the ancient conviction that by his very chastity an ascetic accumulates (sexual) power that can be discharged suddenly and completely to produce marvellous results. Ascetics engaging in erotic and creative experiences are a familiar feature in Hinduism, and the element of teeming sexuality in mythological thought counterbalances the Hindu bent for asceticism. Śiva's marriage with Pārvatī is a model of conjugal love, the divine prototype of human marriage, sanctifying the forces that carry on the human race. The couple are often worshipped in the form of the liṅga, or phallus, of Śiva surrounded by the yoni, or womb, of Pārvatī.

As for the Goddess, she first enters the Sanskrit world full grown from the vernacular sources, like Athena from the head of Zeus; the Glorification of the Goddess in the *Mārkaṇḍeya Purāṇa* (probably composed in the early centuries of the common era) tells how, in order to kill a powerful buffalo demon (Mahiṣa), who had scornfully refused to include women in the list of people who could not kill him, the gods contributed all of their special powers (śaktis) to create Devī. She first charmed Mahiṣa into proposing marriage to her and then demanded that he conquer her before wedding her; she killed him, thus releasing the anthropomorphic demon from his buffalo body. Devī is also worshipped as Pārvatī, the wife of Śiva; as Mother (Ambā), black and destructive (Kālī), and well-nigh inaccessible (Durgā); and as each of the many local goddesses.

Manaṣa, a snake goddess, is worshipped in Assam and Bengal to ward off snakebites and secure prosperity. She is personified in a plant of the same name or in a stone carved into the shape of a female seated on a snake; a day in the rainy season, when reptiles are most dangerous, is devoted to her priestless worship. In literary works she is eulogised as the Great Mother, who is expected to give a prosperous journey through life and, to a certain extent, is also Sanskritised by being identified with epic snake demons. Among other female deities are tutelary goddesses of young children and women in childbed: Ṣaṣṭhī, 'the Sixth', is worshipped on the sixth day after birth (the day on which, if the newborn child is still alive, he or she is likely to survive) and is represented by a compost pile of cow dung or earth that is placed in the birth room. (Her vehicle is a cat.) Caṇḍī, a fierce form of the goddess Durgā, lives in trees and is propitiated by lumps of earth.

Local myths

There is great diversity in local mythologies throughout South Asia. Local mythologies, expressed in vernacular literature, oral tradition, folklore and folk and tribal arts, derive from the most ancient times and have influenced both Vedic and Purāṇic mythology. Purāṇic mythology became what it is by continuously assimilating myths not previously known or accepted, so that the line between local and pan-Indian mythology (sometimes, rather misleadingly, referred to as the Little and Great Traditions, respectively) is apt to be arbitrary. The Sanskrit tradition of Purāṇic mythology includes many deities who continue to have an independent existence on a local level. Many local myths and rituals are absorbed into the Sanskrit tradition by a specific association with a major god; divine manifestations of purely local interest are associated with the higher mythology by becoming a local manifestation of a pan-Indian god, such as the footstep of Rāma or the bathing place of Sītā. The Maharashtrian god Viṭṭhoba is identified with a manifestation of Viṣṇu and thus assured a place in the pan-Indian tradition, and in North India the village goddess Naurtha is associated with the widely celebrated festival of Navāratrī ('Nine Nights'). Conversely, an incident of the pan-Indian tradition may be adopted and adapted on the local level: Satī, the wife of Śiva, is said to have committed suicide when her father, Dakṣa, dishonoured Śiva; Śiva carried her corpse all around India, mad with grief, until Viṣṇu dismembered the corpse with his discus; where each piece landed, a base of the Goddess's power (or Śākta Pīṭha) arose as a place of worship. Often local gods are adopted into the family of an older, established god or goddess. Thus the god Gaṇeṣa is made the son of Śiva, as is Kumāra Kārttikeya, the war god, who arose from the South Indian war god Murukan̲. Hanumān, the monkey god, becomes an all-Indian god as a helper and devotee of Rāma. The tribes of Chota Nagpur (Bihar state), the Santal (West Bengal and Bihar states), the Toda in the Nilgiri Hills (Tamil Nadu state) and many others have rich mythologies of their own, which often incorporate gods or plots from the *Purāṇas.*

Minor spirits of local provenance often retain much of their original character even when taken up by Sanskrit texts. The Yakṣas guard great treasures but are dangerous to deal with; Vetalas, ghoulish pranksters, haunt corpses; and ghosts (Bhūtas and Pretas, literally 'has-beens') possess people who fail to take the proper precautions. An example of the fusion of general and local Hindu institutions is the conviction that ghosts and demons who trouble people anywhere in India are warded off by performing a ceremony in honour of the deceased at Gaya in modern Bihar state.

Nāgas and Nāginīs, cobras or creatures which are cobra from the waist down and anthromorphic from the waist up, are guardians of underground treasurers. Sacred snakes, especially cobras, are given offerings, usually saucers of milk – partly to avert the danger of snakebite, partly to propitiate them with the aim of obtaining rain, fertility or children; to that end women worship snake stones or erect stone figures of cobras. Every joint family of the Coorgs in Karnataka state and most other peoples have a snake deity of their own that is said to embody their welfare. Here and there, brāhmaṇas officiate in this ritual, which usually takes place in small sanctuaries in private gardens.

The awe and mystery of the jungle and mountains are often personified as forest 'Mothers' or mountain deities, represented by piles of stones or branches of trees to which every passerby contributes an offering. Mother Earth is a great goddess whose marriage (with the Earth god or the Sun) is festively celebrated and whose annual period of impurity is observed by a cessation of all agricultural activities. Though Purāṇic mythology also recognises the existence of these spirits, they operate primarily on the local level.

Many myths have developed around great ascetics capable of fantastic feats;

people seek their benevolence and fear their curses. Practically gods on earth, they have amassed tremendous powers that they do not hesitate to use. The sage Kapila, meditating in the netherworld, burned to ashes 60,000 princes who had dug their way to him. Another sage, Bhagīratha, brought the Ganges River down from heaven (where she is the Milky Way) to revive them from their ashes and, in the process, created the ocean. The Ganges came down reluctantly, cascading first onto the head of Śiva and meandering through his matted locks, in order to break her fall, which would have shattered the Earth. Another great sage, Agastya, on one occasion drank and digested the ocean (in which certain noxious demons were hiding). When the Vindhya mountain range would not stop growing, Agastya crossed it to the south and commanded it to cease growing until his return; he still has not returned, and is credited with bringing Sanskrit civilisation to South India. Viśvāmitra, a king who became a brāhmaṇa, created a duplicate universe with its own galaxies to spite the gods.

A local hero can easily be assimilated to a god by identifying him with an incarnation of a god. So, too, great religious teachers are considered manifestations of the god of their devotional preaching, and their lives become part of mythology. The founder of a sect is often deified as an incarnation of a god: the philosopher Śaṅkara (*c.*788–820) as an incarnation of Śiva, the religious leader Rāmānuja (d. CE 1137) as an incarnation of Nārāyaṇa-Viṣṇu, and the Bengal teacher Caitanya (1485–1533) as an incarnation of Kṛṣṇa and his beloved Rādhā simultaneously.

Sacred places, usually rivers and fords, have powers to reward the pilgrim that are often described in local legends. The great rivers are of particular sanctity in India, and the Ganges is the greatest of them all. Confluences are particularly holy, and the Ganges' confluence with the Yamunā at Allahabad is the most sacred spot in India. Another river of importance is the Sarasvatī, which loses itself in desert; it was personified as a goddess of eloquence and learning, the wife of Brahmā.

Every temple and sanctuary has its own myths telling how it was founded and what miracles were wrought there. The same is true of famous places of pilgrimage, usually at sacred spots near and in rivers. Vṛndāvana (Brindaban), on the Yāmuna, is held to be the scene of the youthful adventures of Kṛṣṇa and the cowherd wives. Gāyā, is especially sacred for the funerary rites that are held there. And there is no spot in Vārāṇasī (Benares) along the Ganges that is without its own mythical history.

A striking feature in the religion of South India is the propitiation of usually local female deities of varied and ambivalent character, to whom almost every village dedicates a shrine or other sacred place. These deities are thought to be particularly skilled in dealing with the facts of village life, such as diseases of the inhabitants and their cattle. Special cholera and smallpox goddesses are the subject of elaborate stories; the worshipper invokes the goddess to come and give him just a kiss, leaving a pockmark that is the sign of her grace – and an assurance that the worshipper is now immune to the disease. Māriammā is the smallpox goddess throughout South India; in Bengal, she is called Sītalā, 'The Cool One', because she brings fever. These mothers, from whom all good and bad luck emanate, are almost universally worshipped with animal sacrifices, and the priestly ministrants (pūjāri) officiating in their rituals belong to the non-brāhmaṇa groups. The goddesses may be represented by various symbols (stone pillars, sticks, clay figures) that need not be permanent. Most of their shrines are small brick buildings or stone platforms under a tree. Offerings of rice, fruit and flowers may be made every day or on fixed days; although there is often a fixed annual festival, it is not uniformly celebrated and no calendar of festivals is established. An exception to this is the male deity Aiyannār, who in the countryside of Tamil Nadu state is worshiped as the watchman and patron of the villages but also is implored to grant children and other blessings. He is a vegetarian and therefore ranks as socially superior to the female village goddess with whom he has entered into a complementary relationship. Aiyannār is worshipped either as a village deity or in a temple dedicated to Śiva, where he is regarded as Śiva's son. Śiva himself is also worshipped and given a consort, who, though considered a manifestation of Durgā, has various names according to the tradition of temple or village.

Incarnations and vehicles

Two concepts that evolved in Purāṇic mythology have facilitated the absorption of local elements: avatāra and vahana (vehicle).

The concept of avatāra expresses the belief that in times of trouble a god, notably Viṣṇu, incarnates himself as a man or hero to set matters right. A local deity may be regarded as the avatāra of an all-Indian god like Viṣṇu, and so may a local hierophany (manifestation of the sacred) such as a South Indian 'icon-incarnation' (arcāvatāra), in which Viṣṇu 'descends' into a local icon. One of Viṣṇu's avatāras even incorporates the human founder of another religion: the Buddha. The classical number of the avatāras is ten, ascending from animal form to fully anthropomorphic manifestations in a quasi-Darwinian manner. These are: the Fish (Matsya), Tortoise (Kurma), Boar (Varāha), Man-Lion (Narasiṃha), Dwarf (Vāmana), Rāma-with-the-Axe (Paraśurāma), King Rāma, Kṛṣṇa, Buddha and the future incarnation Kalki.

Animals, which loom so large among the avatāras of Viṣṇu, also play an important role in the mythology of other gods in the form of vāhanas (literally 'vehicles' or 'mounts'). Every god has an entourage of his own, which includes a favourite mount, and this facilitates many local associations. Viṣṇu's mount is the eagle Garuda, arch-enemy of snakes; Śiva's is the bull Nandi, whose worship may go back to the ancient Harappan civilisation; and the Goddess rides on a lion (often represented, after the demise of lions in India, as a tiger). The animal represents the power of the god in the world; wherever there is a bull, Śiva is present. It also represents an essence of the god; the bull represents Śiva's power of fertility. Gaṇeśa, an elephant-headed god, has a bandycoot (a very large rodent) for his mount, not because an enormous elephant would ride on a rat (even a very large rat) but because rats, like elephants, remove all obstacles in their paths and Gaṇeśa is the remover of obstacles, worshipped at the beginning of any enterprise. (He is also the god of intellectuals, scribes, and merchants: elephants are rightly famous for their wisdom.)

Another sort of vehicle plays an important part in local mythologies, and that is the horse. In Orissa, terracotta horses are given to various gods and goddesses to protect the donor from inauspicious omens, to cure illness or to guard the village. In West Bengal, clay horses are offered to all the village gods, male or female, fierce or benign, though particularly to Dharma Thakur, the sun god. At Kenduli in Birbhum, clay horses are offered on the grave of a Tantric saint named Kangal Kshepa, and Bengali parents offer horses when a child first crawls steadily on its hands and feet like a horse. In Tamil Nadu, as many as 500 large clay horses may be prepared in one sanctuary, most of them standing between 15 and 25 feet tall (including a large base), and involving the use of several tons of stone, brick and either clay, plaster or cement. They are a permanent part of the temple and may be renovated at ten- to twenty-year intervals; the construction of a massive figure usually takes between three to six months. In Balikondala, votive horses, or thakuranis, are provided as vehicles for the gods to ride at night to protect the fields and visit the infirm; and there are terracotta horses in the Śaivite temple on the edge of the village. New horses are constantly set up, while the old and broken ones are left to decay and return to the earth of which they were made. This simple ritual resonates with the grander concept, so basic to Hindu mythology, of the cyclic regeneration of all things.

See also: **Agastya; Agni; Agnihotra; Arjuna; Aśvins; Bhagavadgītā; Bhakti (as path); Bhūtas; Books, comics, newspapers and magazines; Brahmā; Brahman; Brāhmaṇa; Buddhism, relationship with Hinduism; Caitanya; Dakṣa; Dharma; Draupadī; Durgā; Dyaus; Film; Gaṇeṣa; Gaṅgā; Garuda; Gopī(s); Hanumān; Indo-European traditions; Indra; Indus Valley Civilisation; Itihāsa; Kālī and Caṇḍī; Kapila; Kṛṣṇa; Lakṣmī, Śrī; Languages; Mahābhārata; Mahādevī; Mahiṣa; Manaṣa; Mandir; Manu; Māriammā; Meru, Mount; Nāgas; Nandi; Pārvatī; Prajāpati; Pretas; Pṛthivī; Purāṇas; Puruṣa; Rādhā; Rākṣasa; Rāma; Rāmānuja; Rāmāyaṇa; Rāvaṇa; Sacred animals; Sacred geography; Śaivism; Śakti; Saṃhitā; Śaṅkara; Sarasvatī; Satī (Goddess); Sītā; Śītalā; Śiva; Skanda; Soma; Tantrism; Tapas; Television and radio; Tīrthayātrā (pilgrimage); Tulsīdās(a); Upaniṣads; Uṣas; Utsava; Vāhana; Vārāṇasī; Varṇa; Varuṇa; Veda; Vedic pantheon; Viṣṇu; Viśvāmitra; Vivāha; Vṛndāvana; Yakṣa; Yoga; Yuga**

WENDY DONIGER

Further reading

Bhattacharji, Sukumari. 1970. *The Indian Theogony: A Comparative Study of Indian Mythology from the Vedas to the Puranas*. London: Cambridge University Press.

Calasso, Roberto. 1998. *Ka: Stories of the Mind and Gods of India*. New York: Alfred Knopf.

Doniger O Flaherty, Wendy. 1975. *Hindu Myths: A Sourcebook, Translated from the Sanskrit*. Harmondsworth: Penguin Classics.

van Buitenen, J.A.B. and Cornelia Dimmitt. 1978. *Classical Hindu Mythology*. Philadelphia, PA: Temple University Press.

Mani, Vettam. 2002. *Puranic Encyclopedia: A Comprehensive Work with Special Reference to the Epic and Puranic Literature*. Delhi: Motilal Banarsidass.

N

NACIKETAS

Naciketas appears in the *Kaṭha Upaniṣad* as the child who is accepted as a disciple by Yama, the god of Death. Having been sent to Death for irritating his father, Naciketas is kept waiting on the threshold by the god. In recompense, the god offers him three boons. The significant one is the third, when Naciketas asks how death may be conquered. At this point Yama begins to teach him, thus initiating the guru/disciple (śiṣya) relationship, a central motif of the *Upaniṣads.* At first, the god tries to dissuade the child from the question by offering him a very long life. But Naciketas is not to be sidetracked, answering that all things which are created must eventually die, however long their duration. The boy is insistent that he wants to overcome death. Eventually Yama responds that it can only be done by realisation of the eternal through contemplation of the Self (ātman), achieved by yoga, which is defined as control of the senses.

See also: **Ātman; Guru; Upaniṣads; Yama; Yoga**

RON GEAVES

Further reading

Flood, Gavin. 1996. *An Introduction to Hinduism.* Cambridge: Cambridge University Press.

NĀGA(S)

The mythical semi-divine serpents, 1,000 in number, who were the offspring of Kadru, created to populate the regions below the earth, where they are said to rule in magnificent splendour. The Nāgas are depicted as half human and half cobra. However, the term is also used generally for snakes, especially the hooded cobra, which is totemic to Śiva and often appears wrapped around his neck in iconography of the god. It can also be used for devotees of snake-cults which are found in South India, Bengal and Assam. Many village households in these regions will have stone images of serpents and groves that are maintained for snakes. Failure to propitiate household serpents can result in family sickness. Serpent festivals are held in these regions, known as nāga-pañcami, in which representations of serpents are worshipped and milk is poured into snakes' holes. Snakes are also propitiated for fertility.

See also: **Sacred animals; Śiva, Utsava**

RON GEAVES

Further reading

Stutley, Margaret and James Stutley (eds). 1977. *A Dictionary of Hinduism: Its Mythology, Folklore and Development 1500 BC–AD 1500*. London: Routledge and Kegan Paul.

NĀGĀPAÑCAMĪ

The fifth day of the bright half of the month of Śrāvaṇa (July/August) when the festival of snakes is celebrated. The Nāgāpañcamī presents both sacred and profane aspects, the former being related to serpent worship, the latter to joyful celebrations. Some rituals are observed all over the subcontinent but regional ways of worship make of Nāgāpañcamī one of the most variegated festivals of India. This is related to the worship of Gaṇeśa, Manasā and other regional deities. Tilling the soil is absolutely forbidden during Nāgāpañcamī as snakes are believed to be the protectors of the harvest. Women prepare sweets, draw serpent-like diagrams, wash their head and wear wet clothes. Devotees fast, pay a visit to the snake pits in the morning, leave offerings (milk, sweets, etc.) and offer prayers for the well-being of their families. Snake charmers are special guests in temples as well as in private houses.

See also: **Gaṇeśa; Manasā; Sacred animals; Utsava**

FABRIZIO M. FERRARI

Further reading

Deb, S. 2001. *Encyclopaedia of Fairs & Festivals in India: With Select Rituals, Vows, Holy Cities, Temples and Pilgrim Centers*. Delhi: Raj Publications.

NAIDU, SAROJINI (1879–1949)

Sarojini Naidu was the daughter of scientist, philosopher, and linguist Aghornath Chattopadhyaya (founder of Nizam College in Hyderabad, which pioneered English education and women's education) and Barada Sundari Devi (a Bengali poetess). She was sent first to school in Madras, where she excelled, and later to King's College in London and Girton College in Cambridge (with a scholarship from the Nizam, who was impressed by the fact that she had written a play in Persian). Frail health prevented her from continuing her education. A poetess, she published several books with Indian themes: *The Golden Threshold* (1905), *The Bird of Time* (1912) and *The Broken Wing* (1917). At a time when inter-caste marriages were forbidden, the brāhmaṇa Sarojini married a non-brāhmaṇa physician, Govindarajulu Naidu, and had four children. She turned her attention to liberation from British rule and the liberation of women through the development of women's education. With Mohandas K. Gandhi, whom she called 'Mickey Mouse' – she had a wicked sense of humour – she participated in the Salt March and was jailed on many occasions. She went to England in 1919 as a member of the All-India Home Rule Deputation, presided over the Indian National Congress at Kanpur (1925) and was President of the National Women's Conference for many years. She went to the United States in 1928 to promote the message of non-violence and participated in the Round Table Summit in 1931. After Independence, she became the governor of Uttar Pradesh. She died in 1949. Her birthday is celebrated as women's day in India.

See also: **Ahiṃsā; Gandhi, Mohandas Karamchand; Nationalism; Women's movement**

KATHERINE K. YOUNG

Further reading

Naidu, S. 1969 [1928]. *The Sceptred Flute: Songs of India*. Allahabad: Kitabistan.

Sengupta, P. 1966. *Sarojini Naidu: A Biography*. London: Asia Publishing House.

NAIDU, SRIDHARALU

Sridharalu Naidu was a South Indian brāhmaṇa from Cuddalore who first brought the message of the Brahmo Samaj to South India. In the early 1860s, after selling his property in order to live in Calcutta for one year studying Bengali, Sanskrit and Brahmo Samaj teachings, he returned to the South, intending to establish the movement. However, it was not until Keshab Chandra Sen visited Madras in 1864 that the movement's ideals were transferred to South India through the vehicle of the Veda Samaj.

At the end of the 1860s, Sridharalu Naidu arrived in Madras and took over the leadership of the fledgling organisation, developing it into an uncompromising version of Brahmo Samaj ideals, performing the first marriage that followed Samaj rituals in 1872. Through his travels and organisational skills, he succeeded in establishing branches of the movement throughout South India until his tragic death in a carriage accident in 1874.

See also: **Brahmo Samaj; Sen, Keshab Chandra; Veda Samaj**

RON GEAVES

Further reading

Jones, Kenneth. 1989. *Socio-Religious Reform Movements in British India. The New Cambridge History of India: Vol. 3*. Cambridge: Cambridge University Press.

NAKULA

One of the five sons of King Pāṇḍu, known collectively as the Pāṇḍavas. Nakula and Sahadeva were the twin sons of Pāṇḍu's second wife, Mādrī, but mythology ascribes their paternity to Nāsatya, one of the twin Aśvins. In some accounts, it is said that Nakula and Sahadeva were the incarnations of the Aśvins. The *Mahābhārata* informs us that Nakula was trained in the art of warfare, especially the management of horses, by Droṇa. He later entered the service of the King of Virāṭa and became his master of horse. He was married to Karenumatī, a princess of Chedi, and they had a son named Niramitra.

See also: **Droṇa; Mādrī; Mahābhārata; Pāṇḍavas; Pāṇḍu; Sahadeva**

RON GEAVES

Further reading

Dasgupta, Madhusraba. 1999. *Samsad Companion to the Mahābhārata*. Calcutta: Sahitya Samsad.

NALA

The King of Niṣada, who was married to Damayantī, the daughter of Bhīma. In many ways, their story echoes some of themes picked up and developed in the saga of the central protagonists, the Pāṇḍavas and Kauravas. In the *Mahābhārata* account, Niṣada and Damayantī had fallen in love after hearing tales of each other's virtues and beauty. Bhīma held a svayaṃvara where kings, princes and gods gathered to win his daughter's hand. Nala had met the gods and promised to obey their will and they commanded him to inform Damayantī that she must choose one of them. The gods took on the form of Nala but the princess was able to recognise the real Nala. However, Kali, the personification of the Kali-Yuga, had arrived late for the svayaṃvara, and resolved to ruin the king through his weakness for gambling. Nala lost everything and ended up wandering in the forest naked. After great privation and the pangs of separation, he was reconciled with Damayantī. The story is a well-known tale of romance, intrigue and the final triumph of love, known throughout India and also told in the epic poem the *Nalodaya*.

See also: **Bhīma; Kauravas; Mahābhārata; Pāṇḍavas; Svayaṃvara; Yuga**

RON GEAVES

Further reading

Dasgupta, Madhusraba. 1999. *Samsad Companion to the Mahābhārata*. Calcutta: Sahitya Samsad.

Dowson, John. 1978. *A Classical Dictionary of Hindu Mythology*. London: Routledge and Kegan Paul.

NĀMAKARAṆA

The baby-naming ceremony, one of the most important Hindu saṃskāras, or rites of passage. This saṃskāra constitutes the introduction of the infant to the public, enabling the baby to be identified by name. Because of the importance of name in Sanskritic culture, this saṃskāra assumes great significance. According to most of the ritual authorities, this is to be performed on the tenth or twelfth day after the birth of the child, though this could be extended up to the first birthday under unusual circumstances. The house is cleaned and ritually purified, the mother and baby are bathed, the baby is wrapped in a new cloth, its head is wetted and then it is handed over to the father. He then makes certain offerings, touches the breath of the child and utters certain mantras, which contain empty slots to add the name(s) of the baby, in the right ear of the child. The rules for giving both a public name and a secret name are extensive. The primary name could be that of a deity, the lunar asterism under which the child was born or the deity of the month in which the child was born. In practice, ancestral names are frequently given and naming conventions have differed from region to region. Numbers of syllables were also important, as was the phonological structure of the name. Because of the importance of the child's initial identification in the world, guests are often invited to this ceremony.

See also: **Mantra; Saṃskāras**

FREDERICK M. SMITH

Further reading

Kane, P.V. 1974. *History of Dharmaśāstra*, 2nd edn, vol. 2, pt 1. Poona: Bhandarkar Oriental Research Institute, 234–54.

Pandey, R.J. 1969. *Hindu Saṃskāras*. Delhi: Motilal Banarsidass, 78–85.

NAMASKĀR(A)

The namaskāra, literally an act of homage, is the traditional Hindu gesture of salutation – to gods, friends, family and general acquaintances. A namaskāra may take the form of the word itself (namaskāra or namaste), broadly in the sense of 'my respects to you'. A namaskāra may also involve a prāñjalī, placing together right and left hands from the palm to the fingertips, slightly cupped, and raised either to the level of the head or the heart. This form of the namaskāra as a gesture of greeting has been widely adopted in many parts of the world. It is perhaps equivalent to the handshake or the formal bow in its silent conveyance of respect and humility. The pervasive practice of saluting the sun (sūrya-namaskāra) is known to all students of haṭha yoga.

See also: **Yoga**

DEVEN M. PATEL

Further reading

Sivananda, Swami. 1974. *Bliss Divine*. Rishikesh: Divine Life Society.

NAMASTE

See: **Namaskār(a)**

NAMMĀḺVĀR

'Our āḻvār', one of the greatest among the āḻvārs, was born in a śūdra household probably in the ninth century CE, in Kurukur, renamed Āḻvār Tirunagari, near Tirunelveli. It is said that when he refused to eat, his parents abandoned him at the feet of a Viṣṇu image in the local temple. He then walked to a tamarind tree nearby and sat silently meditating for a long time – this tree still remains there as a place of worship. Eventually Maturakavi, who was to become his disciple, discovered him there and posed a very intricate question to him. Then, for the first time, Nammāḻvār, who by then was 35 years old, broke his silence, and from then on began to sing his rapturous hymns in praise of Viṣṇu. The *Tiruvāymoḻi*, *Tiruviruttam* and *Periyatiruvantati* are among his most famous works. Nammāḻvār is also known under the names of Māran, Caṭakōpaṉ or Pārāṅkuśa.

See also: **Āḻvārs; Sudra; Varṇa; Viṣṇu**

ANNA L. DALLAPICCOLA

Further reading

Dehejia, V. 1988. *Slaves of the Lord. The Path of Tamil Saints*. New Delhi: Munshiram Manoharlal.

Ramanujan, A.K. 1981. *Hymns for the Drowning. Poems for Viṣṇu by Nammalvar*. Princeton, NJ: Princeton University Press.

NANDI

The milk-white bull figure that is the vāhana (mount) of Śiva and always present in the front of Śiva temples, sometimes possessing his own room for those who come to offer worship to his image. Nandi normally resides facing towards Śiva's image in the outer hall of the temple, either lying down with his left leg bent as if about to rise or standing up. His name means 'the happy one' and he is often depicted as a highly decorated and benign figure, giving little indication of the more usual aspects of the bull as a symbol of fertility and strength found in bull cults. However, Nandi may have been the theriomorphic form of Śiva, who has his own worship throughout North and South India as a fertility god. As the mount of Śiva, the great renunciate and yogi, the bull figure, usually associated with virility and even ferocity, may indicate the god's conquest of his own passions; in short, he has mastered instinctive animal behaviour.

In the *Vāyu Purāṇa*, Nandi is said to be the son of Kaśyapa and Surabhi, but this may be an example of appropriation of older myths by the Śiva cults, as Surabhi also gave birth to Nandīnī, the Vedic cow of great plenty that came out of the churning of the cosmic ocean and was given to the sage Vasiṣṭha. Nandi is the chief of the attendants of Śiva and carries a staff of office indicative of his high position, which also makes him the guardian of all four-footed animals. He is regarded as a mythical teacher of music and dance and is the accompanying musician for Śiva's cosmic dance. In his anthropomorphic form as Nandīkeśvara, a human with a bull's head, he achieves complete identification with Śiva, merging the two forms.

See also: **Dance; Music; Purāṇas; Sacred animals; Śiva; Vāhanas; Vasiṣṭha**

RON GEAVES

Further reading

Bunce, Fredrick. 2000. *An Encyclopaedia of Hindu Deities, Demi-Gods, Godlings, Demons and Heroes*, vol. I. New Delhi: DK Printworld.

NĀRADA

Nārada is a divine sage (ṛṣi) who appears throughout Sanskrit literature. He is a messenger of the gods and conveys the divine will to the mortals. Nārada is also the name of the 'author' of one of the *Dharmaśāstras* (legal treatises), the *Nāradasmṛti* (The Law Book of Nārada). It is doubtful whether the *Nāradasmṛti* was composed by a single individual; most probably the text grew over time. The *Nāradasmṛti* is unique in the corpus of Sanskrit legal literature, as it is the only manual on dharma which is exclusively dedicated to juridical matters. The *Nāradasmṛti* is younger than the *Manusmṛti* (The Law Book of Manu), and belongs to the fourth century CE. The *Nāradasmṛti* itself claims to be an extract of a more comprehensive version of the *Manusmṛti*. A critical edition and an English translation by Lariviere were published in 1989.

See also: **Dharma; Dharmaśāstras; Manu; Ṛṣi**

ANNETTE SCHMIEDCHEN

Further reading

Lariviere, R.W. (ed. and trans.). 1989. *The Nāradasmṛti*. Critically edited with an introduction, annotated translation and appendices. Part 1: Text; Part 2: Translation. Philadelphia, PA: University of Pennsylvania.

NARASIṂHA

See: **Avatāra**

NĀRĀYAṆA

See: **Viṣṇu**

NARAYANA GURU (1854–1928)

Narayana Guru, a scholar, ascetic and yogi, was the spiritual leader of the Izhavas, a community in Kerala who, though dalits whose traditional occupation is making toddy, have a tradition of literacy. In 1887 he consecrated a shrine of Śiva, following it with many others, notably one to Sarasvatī, goddess of learning, in 1912. He wrote in Malayalam, Tamil and Sanskrit, calling his doctrine advaita but giving this word his own interpretation, summed up in his slogan 'One caste, one religion, one God' (Samuel 1977; Jones 1989: 179–82, 203–7). By consecrating temples, and by using the Sanskrit tradition and language, he asserted that these did not belong exclusively to brāhmaṇas. His advocacy of Sanskritisation contrasts sharply with those dalit leaders who reject the Sanskrit tradition.

In 1903 his followers formed the Sri Narayana Dharma Paripalana Yogam ('union for fostering Narayana's doctrine'), for which he prescribed a plan for the reform of the Izhavas which emphasised education, technological development and Hindu religious practices such as temple worship, monasticism and reverence for the guru. It promotes schools, libraries and hospitals.

One disciple, Nataraja Guru (1895–1973), eschewed these social concerns, interpreting Narayana's message as purely spiritual. Nataraja, like many modern Hindu thinkers, expressed his ideas in a commentary on the *Bhagavadgītā* (Nataraja Guru 1961).

See also: **Advaita; Bhagavadgītā; Brāhmaṇas; Dalits; Guru; Hinduism, modern and contemporary; Mandir; Sarasvatī; Śiva; Yogi**

DERMOT KILLINGLEY

Further reading

Jones, Kenneth W. 1989. *Socio-religious Reform Movements in British India* (New Cambridge History of India, 3.1). Cambridge: Cambridge University Press.

Nataraja Guru. 1961. *The Bhagavad Gita: A Sublime Hymn of Dialectics Composed by the Ancient Sage-Bard Vyasa*. Bombay: Asia Publishing House.

Nataraja Guru. 1968. *The Word of the Guru*. Ernakulam, Kerala: Paico Publishing House.

Samuel, V. Thomas. 1977. *One Caste One Religion One God: A Study of Sree Narayana Guru*. Delhi: Sterling.

NARAYANA, SWAMI (1781–1830)

Swami Narayana (Sahajanand Swami) was a Hindu reformer in Gujarat in the early nineteenth century. He was born in Chhapia, near Ayodhyā, of brāhmaṇa parents. Orphaned at 11 years old, he then spent seven years as an ascetic wandering student. His travels took him to Gujarat, where he was initiated into a band of Vaiṣṇava sādhus who followed the tradition of Rāmānuja. He soon became leader and from 1802 until his death attracted followers, initiated sādhus and established temples in Gujarat. His followers placed images of him in temples beside those of Kṛṣṇa and Viṣṇu and gave him the title of Lord Swami Narayana as founder of the Swami Narayana Sampradaya.

He established five principal vows for householders: (1) not to steal, (2) not to commit adultery, (3) not to eat meat, (4) not to drink intoxicants and (5) not to take food from persons belonging to a caste lower than one's own. He initiated sādhus with more stringent vows: (1) strict celibacy, (2) renunciation of family ties, (3) renunciation of attachment to objects of the senses, (4) a holy poverty and (5) avoidance of the pride of ego. He advocated the protection and uplift of women by attacking the practices of female infanticide, widow burning (sati) and large dowries. He established separate precincts in temples for women and permitted some celibate women to reside in the temples. He also opposed the British trade in opium.

He produced or inspired several texts sacred to followers: (1) *Shikshapatri*, a Sanskrit work of 212 verses containing regulations for personal conduct; (2) *Vachanamritam*, a collections of sermons in Gujarati; (3) *Satsangijivan*, a multi-volume compendium of teachings, history and legends; and (4) *Lekh*, a text that established two administrative dioceses of Vadtal and Ahmedabad, over which he appointed his two nephews as ācāryas.

See also: **Ācarya; Ayodhyā; Brāhmaṇa; Caste; Celibacy; Dowry; Kṛṣṇa; Rāmānuja; Religious specialists; Sādhus; Saṃpradāya; Sati; Swami Narayana Sampradaya; Tapas; Vaiṣṇavism; Viṣṇu; Women, status of**

RAYMOND BRADY WILLIAMS

Further reading

Williams, R.B. 2001. *An Introduction to Swaminarayan Hinduism*. Cambridge: Cambridge University Press.

NĀSIK

Situated on the banks of the sacred river Godāvarī in the north-west of the modern Indian state of Maharashtra, Nāsik has been an important Hindu pilgrimage spot and an ancient centre of trade and commerce. Its place in ancient lore is largely on account of its connection with the *Rāmāyaṇa*'s sacred geography. Nāsik lies in the heart of the famous Pañcāvatī grove in the Daṇḍaka forest that served as home for an exiled Rāma, Lakṣmaṇa and Sītā. There is also the Rāmeśvara temple and the nearby bathing tank known as Rāmakuṇḍ to commemorate the place where Rāma performed the last rites for his deceased father Daśaratha. One etymology of the name Nāsik traces it to the Sanskrit word nāsikā (meaning nose), claiming it to be the spot where Lakṣmaṇa disfigured the nose of the demon Rāvaṇa's sister Śurpanakhā. Another story traces the city back to a time when Lord Brahmā performed penance there while seated in the lotus position (padmāsana); thus another ancient name for the place, Padmāsana. Yet another legend has it that Lord Viṣṇu rid the place of three demons, who were 'thorns' (kaṇṭaka), as it were, in the side of the world, and therefore the region now known as Nāsik was once called

Trikaṇṭakā. Nāsik's most significant modern role from a religious point of view rests on its playing host to the triennial Kumbha Melā. Also, some 30 km from Nāsik is the famous hilltop Tryambakeśvara temple, which houses one of Lord Śiva's twelve jyotirliṅgas and also stands near the spot where the river Godāvarī issues forth. Other temples near the Godāvarī include the Sundaranārāyaṇa and Kampaleśvara temple, where Lord Śiva is said to have come to take a penitential bath to cleanse himself from the sin of decapitating one of Lord Viṣṇu's heads in anger. Nāsik holds significance for Buddhists and Muslims as well. The Pāṇḍu Caves (sculpted from the third millennium BCE to the seventh century CE) contain numerous murals, sculptures and engravings of Buddha and Bodhisattvas. More recently, Nāsik held special significance for the Mughals, who named the place Gulshanabad. It was during the Peshwa period that the city was renamed Nāsik.

See also: **Brahmā; Buddhism, relationship with Hinduism; Haridvāra; Kumbha Melā; Lakṣmaṇa; Prayāga; Rāma; Rāmāyaṇa; Rāvaṇa; Sītā; Śiva; Tīrthayātra (Pilgrimage); Ujjayinī; Viṣṇu**

DEVEN M. PATEL

Further reading

Bhardwaj, Surinder Mohan. 1983. *Hindu Places of Pilgrimage in India: A Study in Cultural Geography*. Berkeley, CA: University of California Press.

Hebner, Jack. 2003. *Kumbha Mela* (Veda Files). La Jolla, CA: Mandala Publishing Group.

NĀSTIKA

See: **Āstika and Nāstika**

NĀTH(A) YOGA

Nātha Yoga is the ascetic discipline developed in Northern India largely on the basis of the teaching of Gorakhnāth. Its goal is the realisation of the practitioner's identity with Śiva, the ultimate reality, and the method leading to that end is Haṭha Yoga (yoga of violent effort), which enables one to vanquish death through exercises of 'corporeal culture' (kāya sādhana) which operate a cleansing of the body from all the impurities that are the cause of death and thus help transubstantiate the mortal body into an immortal one in a state of liberation-in-life (jīvanmukti). That goal can also be attained through the practice of alchemy (rasāyana), which was the exclusive means used by other groups of Siddhas (Perfected Ones), the Māheśvara and Raseśvara Siddhas, often mentioned in the Nātha literature. Mādhava, in his fourteenth-century *Sarvadarśanasaṃgraha* (Compendium of all the View-points) even opines that alchemy is itself a branch of Haṭha Yoga.

The Nātha-yogins have always existed on the far margins of brahmanical orthodoxy, often claiming, with perhaps some justification, that their praxis is even older than the Veda. Consequently, this group tends to be indifferent to Hindu social hierarchy and mores. Their dead, instead of being cremated, as is the norm, are buried sitting in a meditative posture. Cannabis (siddhi) is also widely used. Vilified by the orthodox, the Nāthas have also been widely feared since their yoga is believed to endow them with paranormal powers, including that of overcoming gravity, hence the ability to fly through all worlds and the capacity of making themselves as small – and therefore invisible – or as huge and mighty as they wished.

In Nātha Yoga the body is viewed as mirroring the cosmos and as being twofold. Below the navel is the domain of Śakti, the universal Energy and consort of Śiva who governs the world of change, dominated by bhoga (enjoyment, experience). Above the navel is the domain of Śiva himself and the blissful peace of tyāga (renunciation). The material body is only, however, the gross aspect of an ordinarily invisible body, the sūksma śarīra, or subtle body, which is irrigated by some 72,000 channels of energy (nāḍī), of which ten to fourteen are particularly important, though, of those, the two most significant ones are, as the two snakes of a caduceus, twined round the axis of the body. To the left of the spine is Idā and to the right is Piṅgalā, also known, respectively, as Gaṅgā and Yamunā, after the great rivers of North India and representing the moon (candra) and the sun (sūrya), i.e. night and day, those corresponding in turn to the vital energies prāna and apāna, centripetal inspiration and centrifugal expiration. The symbolism of the rivers is clear: the holiest site in India is the confluence of the Ganges and the Yamunā (Prayāg), into which also flows the invisible river, the Sarasvatī. That last is equipollent with the central vertical channel of energy, the suṣumnā nāḍī, also called path of Brahman (brahma-mārga). The yogi's task is to gather all the energies dispersed in his body, to focus them onto the base of his spine where the universal Śakti lies dormant, awaken her and make her ascend through the previously empty suṣumnā, passing through (according to the source) seven to nine centres of energy (cakra), each one conferring particular powers until, twelve digits above the skull, the ultimate cakra is reached, where the sun becomes one with the moon, Śakti is reunited with Śiva and emancipation is attained. The whole process is accompanied by the utterance of sacred syllables, or bāja mantra, which, apart from governing each cakra, also enable the practitioner to become increasingly attuned to the divine sound-vibration (śabda) until a state of 'uttering-non uttering' (ajāpajapa) is reached where the mantra is reabsorbed into its unmanifested origin and the 'unstruck sound' (anāhata nāda) vibrates unimpeded through the whole being. When liberation from the bonds of death has been conquered, the yogin is said to be in a state 'beyond duality and non-duality'. The liberated ascetic is then in a state of 'innateness' (sahajā-avasthā) and is termed an avadhūta, one who has severed all ties.

The literature of Nātha Yoga is extensive and, apart from a few works deemed to be by Minanātha, begins with some twenty treatises attributed to Gorakhnāth, chief among which is the *Siddha-Siddhānta Paddhati* (Guide to the Doctrine of the Siddhas). Many tractates of Haṭha Yoga, such as the *Haṭhayoga-pradīpikā*, explore similar territory, as well as a number of late *Yoga Upaniṣads.*

See also: **Brahman; Brahmanism; Gaṅgā; Gorakhnāth; Haṭha Yoga; Jīvanmukta; Kundalinī Yoga; Mantra; Śakti; Siddha; Śiva; Upaniṣads; Veda**

DANIEL MARIAU

Further reading

Banarjea, A.K. 1962. *Philosophy of Gorakhnath, with Gorakha-Vacana-Sangraha.* Gorakhpur: Mahant Dig Vijai Nath Trust.

Mallik, Smt. Kalyani. 1954. *Siddha-Siddhānta-Pddhati and Other Works of the Nātha Yogīs.* Poona: Oriental Book House.

NATIONALISM

This entry will examine the relationship between Hindu traditions and the concept of nationalism in modern India. The relationship is somewhat controversial and contested, and takes a variety of forms. As well as exploring some manifestations of the relationship in colonial and postcolonial India and beyond, the entry will raise issues and reflect on what the specific case of Hindu traditions can tell us about the relationship between religion and nationalism in general. As is often the case, the Hindu traditions push at the boundaries of the concept of religion, challenging our assumptions about the status of such traditions in the modern world.

Nationalism: what does it mean?

In the first instance, let us briefly consider the meaning of the concept of nationalism. Despite the insistent claim to antiquity by particular nationalisms, it is, objectively speaking, a relatively modern concept. Most commentators agree that it has its roots in post-Enlightenment Europe and/or the Americas, drawing on the emergence of Cartesian secular rationalism, the development of capitalist modes of production and the concomitant rise of new social forces to political power. The French Revolution provides an emblematic signifier (although the revolution itself was inspired partly by the American Declaration of Independence in 1776): a bourgeois revolution, sweeping away the established, divinely ordained structures of power and replacing them with a form of government legitimised by its claim to represent the sovereign people (however attenuated that idea of representation may have been). The idea of the French nation came to be seen as the expression of the collective will of the French people, a political community with collective interests which superseded identifiers of class, region and even – or perhaps especially – faith. As such, nationalism emerged precisely as a form of political consciousness appropriate to the progressive character of modernity. Freed from the oppressive restraints of feudalism, parochialism and superstition, the people who constituted the nation realised their own potential by acting as a collective unit, in the context of a rational legal state constructed ostensibly to serve their interests. In doing so they came increasingly to express themselves through a homogeneous cultural consciousness: that is, nationalism.

Two key points emerge from this understanding of nationalism. First, nationalism develops primarily as a form of community consciousness. It is, in Benedict Anderson's durable phrase, 'an imagined political community . . . inherently limited and sovereign' (Anderson 1991: 6). The emphasis in Anderson's characterisation is on the world of the imagination; it is here that the idea of the nation is constructed, invoked by a network of symbols which encapsulate the character and extent of the community. This form of consciousness has emerged as a fundamental feature of the modern world. As another key theorist of nationalism, Ernest Gellner, has noted, 'a man must have a nationality as he must have a nose and two ears' (Gellner 1983: 6). Significantly, both Anderson and Gellner see this form of consciousness as *superseding* the dominance of worldviews based upon religion. The culture of nationalism is seen as providing value and meaning in the new secular spaces of modernity; the same kind of value and meaning provided by religious cultural systems in previous eras. In this understanding, then, religion is perceived as typically traditional (premodern), whilst nationalism is perceived as typically modern.

Second, nationalism emerges as a form of consciousness in a specifically European framework. Its modernity is linked to the modernity of capitalist development both in European colonies in America (dubbed by Anderson the 'creole pioneers' of nationalism) and in Europe itself. The universal implication of nationalism noted by Gellner therefore must be seen as the result of ongoing processes and dynamics of interaction: the processes of European expansion, first into the Americas; the dynamic interaction between American colonies and Europe, which produced independence movements in the former and bourgeois ruptures in the latter; and further processes of European expansion in the nineteenth and early twentieth century. As the European powers took control of territory across the globe during this later period, they (more or less unwittingly) brought with them this specifically 'modern' capitalist form of political consciousness. In another of Anderson's oft-quoted phrases, models of nationalism were 'pirated' 'by widely different, and sometimes unexpected hands' (Anderson 1991: 67). In the hands of the colonised, the models were used to create vibrant anti-colonial nationalisms which ushered in the postcolonial world. Problems arose, however, because the modernity of the colonised was truncated, left incomplete by the social and economic violence of colonial domination. As a result, the forms of nationalism which arose in these contexts have also at times been perceived as incomplete – in particular, it is in these contexts that 'ethnic' or 'religious' nationalism has been most virulent: a form of nationalism which hybridises modern and traditional forms of communal consciousness.

An example of this kind of approach is that taken by the theorist Anthony Smith. He notes that ethnic nationalism has emerged in colonial contexts as a result of what he calls 'dual legitimation' (Smith 1971). The intelligentsia in a colonised society accept the authority of their traditional culture, but they also accept the authority of the scientific (Western) state: a dual legitimation. One response to this dual legitimation is 'objectification', through which indigenous tradition is objectified by the intelligentsia and then reinvented as a 'modern' tradition. By focusing on the regeneration of this objectified tradition, a return to its 'essence', the intelligentsia is able to both affirm and supersede the existing tradition – the process is thus legitimised by reference to both sources of authority.

As we shall see, this kind of approach appears to resonate with the development of nationalist consciousness in India in the nineteenth century. But we also need to be aware that these ways of understanding nationalism have been heavily criticised by postcolonial theorists such as Partha Chatterjee (1986, 1993) and Peter van der Veer (1994). In particular these writers have challenged the idea of a straightforward dichotomy between tradition and modernity: opposing these two, they argue, oversimplifies what are highly complex and multi-layered phenomena, and privileges one form of (dominant) political organisation as archetypally modern. One key element of this critique is to reconceptualise nationalism in a colonial context as characterised by diversity and heterogeneity, rather than homogeneity. Because anti-colonial nationalism emerged as a form of resistance to European powers and European ideologies, it was never a flat 'derivative discourse', to use Partha Chatterjee's phrase, 'pirated' from the models of European nationalism. Rather, it developed as a modern, multiform idea, in which a range of identities – including religious identities – had potentially modern, resistant functions. Resistant, that is, not just against domination by European colonial powers, but also against the modernisation paradigm associated with the Western model of nationalism. One advantage of this approach is that rejecting the dichotomy between tradition and modernity, and acknowledging the potential diversity of nationalism as a form of consciousness, enables reflection on a variety of ways in which 'Hinduism' has been implicated with nationalism over the past century or so, without the pejorative subtext of flawed hybridity which so often accompanies discussion of the relationship between religion and nationalism. As we examine developing nationalist consciousness, we should bear this critique in mind.

Nineteenth-century developments in 'Hinduism' and 'Nationalism'

The nineteenth century witnessed the rapid development of modern 'Hinduism'.

Various modern-style organisations – for example, in Bengal in the 1830s and 1940s, the Brahmo Samaj and the Dharma Sabha – were influential in this process. They contributed to the emergence of 'Hinduism' as an objective phenomenon, in which it was possible to identify defining characteristics, even if there was persistent conflict over what exactly these characteristics were. It is widely understood that such organisations developed as a form of cultural resistance to colonial rule. In the context of Christian missionary comment on indigenous religious practices, which was almost invariably derogatory, they provided an institutional basis on which to engage with this critique in the new public spaces of colonial rule. A classic example is provided by Rammohan Roy's 'Dialogue Between a Christian Missionary and Three Chinese Converts' (1982), in which he lampoons the attempts of a hapless Christian missionary to explain the contradictions of the doctrine of the Trinity to some Chinese 'coolies' blessed with the art of logical argumentation. This was part of a strategy designed to demonstrate the irrationality of Christian doctrine when compared to the sublime rationalism of Vedānta as propagated by the Brahmo Samaj. Swami Dayananda Saraswati, the founder and spiritual leader of the Arya Samaj, was similarly committed to the public explanation of 'Hinduism's' superiority – not just to Christianity, but to other perceived religious systems as well. Most famously, Swami Vivekananda took the idea of the superiority of 'Hinduism' to the West. In 1893 he spoke in Chicago at the self-styled 'World Parliament of Religions'; here he explained how India's spiritual traditions could provide salvation to the Western world, which had become manifestly alienated due to the extent of capitalist development.

This kind of approach is indicative of what Partha Chatterjee (1993: 6) sees as a conceptualisation of two 'domains' by indigenous thinkers during this period: the 'outer' domain of materialism – economy, statecraft, science and technology – which was dominated by the West; and the 'inner' domain of the spirit – the home, the family, culture, religion – in which India maintained a superior status. This recognition of spiritual superiority – exemplified by Vivekananda – was critical to the development of nationalist consciousness in India. It provided a key stimulus to the emergence of a national culture, and this ensured that 'Hinduism' had a major role in the fashioning of this culture. It is easy to apply Smith's notion of dual legitimation in this context, in the sense that 'traditional' culture is presented as being regenerated and given status in relation to the ravages of 'modernity'. At the same time, it is important not to oversimplify the idea of 'traditional culture' here: Hindu traditions are diverse and frequently contradictory, and this quality is apparent in the multiple ways in which Hindu-ness is related to nationalism during this period. The Brahmo Samaj, the Arya Samaj, Vivekananda's Ramakrishna Math and Mission, not to mention such bodies as the Bharat Dharma Mahamandala – these organisations presented radically different interpretations of what constituted Hindu tradition, and their attempts to represent 'Hindu spirituality' in the modern world have always been hotly contested. So, in consonance with our postcolonial critics mentioned above, we need to remember that a variety of ideas about Hindu tradition fed into discourse about Indian nationalism towards the end of the nineteenth century. Not surprisingly, the forms of nationalism which emerged were also diverse.

One tendency which all these organisations had in common was their engagement with modern forms of communication in their attempts to assert their position. In particular, they demonstrate an acute awareness of the power of the printed word, producing tracts and newspapers which discussed key issues and affirmed community identity. This tendency reflects the significant intervention of what Benedict Anderson terms 'print capitalism' (Anderson 1991: 37–46). According to Anderson, the commodification of the printed word as a feature of capitalist expansion is a key signifier of nationalist consciousness, because it persistently invokes a community beyond the locality, which is nevertheless limited by its linguistic scope. Nothing exemplifies this point more clearly than the development towards the end of the nineteenth century of Hindi and Urdu as distinct languages which invoked Hindu and Muslim religious groups, respectively, in North India – groups which were increasingly to be articulated as nations (see King 1994).

The key political organisation of Indian nationalism – the Indian National Congress – emerged in 1885 somewhat against the grain of these developments in cultural consciousness. In its first few years it was dominated by an approach which sought to capture the air of an official opposition to the colonial government. Its statements were couched in a quasi-parliamentary language and it directed its attention towards the state, despite its rather weak claim to represent the 'Indian people'. Almost immediately, this approach to nationalism was challenged by competing voices amongst the indigenous elite, as well as by non-elite groups who questioned the right of elites to represent 'the people'.

A useful example of the former is provided by the development of the Gaṇapati, a political event in Maharashtra. At the beginning of the 1890s, this popular regional festival was largely a family-based occasion, in which an image of Gaṇeśa was ceremonially brought to and worshipped in the house, before being immersed in a local water source. By 1894, and partly at the instigation of the Pune publicist and emerging nationalist leader Bal Gangadhar Tilak, the festival had begun to take on significance at a different level in certain urban localities. Large Gaṇeśa images were constructed by neighbourhood groups. These images were then taken out in public procession, accompanied by groups singing songs with a topical content, before being immersed dramatically at the climax of the procession. This development demonstrates the way in which Hindu symbols and Hindu events were invoked and reinvented as part of the cultural repertoire of emerging nationalism. The culture of secular parliamentarianism, associated with the early Congress, became one amongst many voices feeding into the national movement at this time.

Equally significant at this time were challenges from non–Hindu elite groups to Congress' claim to represent 'the Indian people'. Non-brāhmaṇa groups, for example, confronted Congress as early as 1889 by staging an alternative gathering at the time of the annual Congress meeting. Congress was attacked precisely because of the high caste profile of its members (O'Hanlon 1985: 285). Some Muslim groups were also opposed to the Congress on the basis that it was representative of a particular high-caste Hindu sector of society. Syed Ahmed Khan's Aligarh movement, which in other ways self-consciously embraced the challenge of colonial modernity, was resolutely opposed to the Congress on this basis. Indeed, Syed's conceptualisation of the Muslim qaum (community) in India was in many ways an alternative use of the nation concept – the Muslim nation within the territorial limits of India. Here we can again see the way in which nationalism was emerging as a concept with diverse, contested meanings within the context of colonialism.

Gandhi and nationalism in the late colonial period

Perhaps as a result of this diversity, the Congress movement emerged in the twentieth century as a very broad umbrella-like organisation, accommodating a variety of different views of the nation. One of the most significant of these views was that of Mohandas Karamchand Gandhi. For Gandhi, nationalist politics was an appropriately dharmic mode of action in the kali yuga: the dark era, in which moral disorder (adharma) was rampant. 'No Indian who aspires to follow the way of true religion,' Gandhi commented, 'can afford to remain aloof from politics' (quoted in Parekh 1989: 92). Gandhi's approach to 'Hinduism' was based on a form of Advaita Vedānta, in which Brahman was conceptualised as absolute truth (satya), and the relationship between Brāhman and Ātman was perceived as that between absolute and relative truth. In the kali yuga, religion had become degenerate, the truth had been obscured: a situation encapsulated by illusion (māyā) of colonial rule, through which a handful of British bureaucrats and soldiers were able to dominate the great mass of the Indian people. Politics was perceived as a progressive unveiling of this māyā; a demonstration of truth through non-violent action. By following the path of ahīṃsa, Gandhi envisioned the purification of the spirit (ātmaśuddhi) of India, a complete moral regeneration – a form of liberation which was characterised rather controversially by Gandhi as Rāmarājya, by which he meant to invoke a concept of righteous, moral rule, in the manner of the rule of Rāma in the *Rāmāyaṇā* (although Gandhi's use of the concept by no means sanctioned monarchy as a form of government; it was, rather, he said, 'rule of the people'; see Lutgendorf 1991: 380–81).

The great mass mobilisation campaigns of Indian nationalism in the 1920s and 1930s were conducted within the framework provided by this ambitious vision. At the same time, however, a strain of militant secularism was becoming increasingly prominent within the Congress movement, which characterised national liberation in the classic liberal democratic sense – the creation of a nation-state governed by the rule of law, in which issues of culture and religion would be ushered into the private sphere. Jawaharlal Nehru, the first prime minister of Independent India, in many ways represented the emergence of this particular idea of nationalism. Some scholars have suggested that it was precisely this development in the 1920s which produced the idea of communalism – violent, immutable antagonism between religious groups – as the antithesis of nationalist modernity (see Pandey 1990). Such a view of discursive development in Indian politics certainly enables us to see the emergence of one particular form of nationalism in a less teleologically loaded fashion: that is, Hindu nationalism.

The emergence of Hindu nationalism

As we have seen, nationalist politics in India during the late nineteenth and early twentieth century was partly articulated through religious imagery and religious ideas. As we reflect back on the ideas discussed initially about the development of nationalism in a colonial context, we can understand why this may be the case. Furthermore, if we take into account that ideas of Hindu-ness as a form of religious identity were also developing rapidly during this period amongst the emerging professional and bureaucratic classes, we can see that the overlapping of these ideas with ideas of national identity almost inevitably came to be a powerful force in Indian politics. This can be seen across the political spectrum in India; for example, strong ideas about the 'Hindu community' as the core of the nation are plainly evident amongst sections of the Congress both before and after Independence.

As early as the 1910s, however, a formal political structure for the development of this kind of idea was developing in northern India, particularly in Punjab and the central plains around Delhi, Lucknow and Banaras. Local-level Hindu Sabhas emerged seeking to protect what they perceived as the common interests of Hindus (Zavos 2000: 112). These Sabhas provided the momentum for the first 'Hindu Conference', which was held in Lahore in 1909. The conference looked to forge a 'common nationality' amongst Hindus, and to provide a broader platform for the political representation of 'Hindu interests', particularly in light of the Congress' perceived inability to fulfil this role (for an account of the conference, see Zavos 2000: 118–21). These developments fed into the formation of the All Indian Hindu Mahasabha, which was to become fully active in the 1920s as a political party.

Throughout this period of early development, the lines of opposition between Hindu nationalism and Congress nationalism were only very vaguely drawn. This is demonstrated particularly by the fact that many prominent figures in the Congress and the Indian national movement more generally were also involved in the developing Sabha movement. The Punjabis Lala Lajpat Rai and Swami Shraddhanand were important figures in both the Congress and the emerging Hindu nationalist movement in Nagpur. But perhaps the most famous of these 'crossover' figures was V.D. Savarkar, the president of the Hindu Mahasabha between 1937 and 1943. In earlier years, Savarkar had written a significant Indian nationalist text about the 1857 rebellion against the British (Savarkar 1947). He had also been transported for life to the penal colony of the Andaman Islands in 1910 for his part in a conspiracy to assassinate two British officials. In the classically heroic Indian nationalist context of this incarceration, Savarkar was to produce what was to become a seminal text of Hindu nationalism: *Hindutva/Who Is a Hindu?* (Savarkar 1989). This short and rather verbose text outlined the basis of Hindu nationalism not in religion, but in Hindutva, or Hindu-ness, a feeling of cultural oneness based on the sacralisation of the geography of India, which purported to encompass all those religious and cultural systems – Buddhism, Jainism, Sikhism, Vaiṣṇavism, Śaivism and even (nominally) forms of low-caste practice – which had emerged on the subcontinent. Savakar's text presented the 'Hindu race' as a strong, martial people, who had been struggling for a thousand years or more with various foreign invaders from the north and west, first of all, of course, Muslims and much more recently Christians.

This idea of Hindus as a martial race may be seen as a response to the popularity of Gandhian nationalism, with its key principle ahiṃsā, or non-violence (Jaffrelot 1996: 45–46). The apotheosis of this contrast is the assassination of Gandhi in 1948 by a militant Hindu nationalist, Nathuram Godse, on the basis of his 'weak' accommodationist approach towards the new state of Pakistan. But martial 'Hinduism' needs also to be recognised as having its own developing history in urban India, deriving from dialogue and contestation between a variety of caste-based and 'neo-Hindu' ideologies. For example, low-caste Yadavs began to establish a strident public profile in Lucknow and other towns of the northern plains in the 1920s. Yadav caste associations laid great emphasis on the historic martial status of their caste group. Such ideas blended and clashed with those of organisations like the Arya Samaj and the Hindu Sabhas (inspired by high-caste 'reformers' and 'revivalists') during the 1920s and 1930s to produce a kind of discourse of martial Hinduism, through which a variety of social groups struggled for power (Gooptu 2001: 221–43).

In central India, it was this discourse of martial Hinduism which provided the framework for the founding of the Rashtriya Swayamsevak Sangh (RSS) in 1925. The leading figure in this development was a Deshastha Brāhmaṇa called K.V. Hedgewar, who had previously been involved in the local Congress organisation in Nagpur city. According to RSS legend, Hedgewar conceived of the RSS as a 'non-political' organisation dedicated to 'character-building' (Deshpande and Ramaswamy 1981: 81). His vision was to recruit mostly high-caste boys and young men in order to produce a vanguard organisation dedicated to the transformation of Hindus into a strong, self-confident, organised people, capable of resisting the debilitating influence and outright aggression of 'foreign' interlopers in Indian society. The RSS is based on small, localised units (shakhas) which have acted as the building blocks of the organisation. Shakhas have a relatively high profile in localities, meeting once or twice a day in whatever open space is available; conducting a series of physical games, marching, singing and discussion groups; and marking itself out through its uniform of khaki shirts, white shorts and black caps. Each shakha is led nominally by a full-time worker (pracharak) but is comprised of volunteers (swayamsevaks) from the locality. Shakhas began to proliferate across Maharashtra and northern India in the 1930s and 1940s, and have since spread across the nation. There are now estimated to be around 20,000 shakhas, providing a daily focus for the lives of several million Hindu boys and men (Bhatt 2001: 113).

This formidable expansion, primarily amongst the urban middle- and lower-class, high- or middle-caste groups (Jaffrelot 1996: 46–49), is indicative of the resonance of this form of Hindu nationalism, based on the martial tendencies we saw expressed in Savarkar's *Hindutva/Who Is a Hindu?* Both Hedgewar and his successor as leader (sarsanghchalak) of the RSS, Madhav Sadashiv Golwalkar, further developed ideas of Hindutva along these lines. Golwalkar in particular elaborated in print on the idea of the sacred geography of Bhāratavarśa (the land of India), and the threats to the Hindu nation posed variously by Muslims, Christians, Secularists and Communists. In more recent times these themes have come together in the campaigns to 'liberate' features of this sacred geography – most famously in Ayodhyā, where the sixteenth-century Babri Masjid was eventually destroyed in 1992 by Hindu nationalists claiming that it was sited on the birthplace of Lord Rāma.

A Hindu nationalist 'family'

One of the most distinctive features of the RSS as an organisation has been its ability to establish a network of affiliated organisations working in different areas of social and political life. This network is known as the Sangh Parivar, or Sangh 'family'. In 1936 the Rashtriya Sevika Samiti (National Women's Organisation) was formed as the first affiliate of the RSS. In 1948 the Akhil Bharatiya Vidyarthi Parishad (All India Students Council) was formed, and since then a proliferation of organisations has emerged, working in such areas as labour, tribal welfare, farming, teaching (for details of some of the major organisations, see Bhatt 2001: 114–15). Each of these organisations has been nurtured by RSS pracharaks, seconded from the 'parent' organisation, but has also drawn in non-RSS activists working in that particular field. Perhaps the two most prominent fields in which the Sangh has established organisations have been politics and religion.

The Sangh launched a political party in 1951, the Bharatiya Jana Sangh. The Jana Sangh did not perform particularly strongly in elections and was eventually absorbed into the anti-Congress Janata Party, which ruled for two years following the Emergency period, 1975–77. As the Janata coalition collapsed in 1979, the key Jana Sangh members, Atal Behari Vajpaypee and Lal Krishnan Advani, became convinced that a Hindu nationalist party could become a major political force in the country. They thus established the Bharatiya Janata Party (BJP; Indian People's Party) in 1980. This party has since emerged as one of the most powerful political parties in India.

In the field of religion, the Sangh launched the formidable Vishwa Hindu Parishad (VHP; World Hindu Council) in 1964. This organisation aims to present a united front of Hindu religious leaders and to provide some 'baseline' values which define Hindu-ness. The VHP's website defines the idea of Hindu as embracing 'all people who believe in, respect or follow the eternal values of life – ethical and spiritual – that have sprung up in Bharat'. One can see clearly the echoes of Savarkar's conception of Hindutva here. The VHP has been very active in opposing conversions amongst marginal groups such as tribals and dalits; policing, as it were, the borders of 'Hinduism'. It also projects itself as having a global mission to promote 'Hinduism' as a 'World Religion'. As a result, it has been the most active of the Sangh organisations amongst the diaspora communities. In places like the Caribbean, the United States and the United Kingdom, the VHP has attempted to provide a focal point for Hindu communities (see Vertovec 2000). The VHP UK website, for example, states that it aims to support 'activities that promote unity among Hindus' and ensure the 'correct portrayal of Hindus by the media'. This kind of activity has been remarkably successful, particularly amongst second-generation migrants, partly because a homogenised vision of 'Hinduism' is perceived as a kind of cultural expression of migrant identity (Vertovec 2000; Sarhadi Raj 2000).

The state, secularism and 'Hinduism' in post-Independence India

The Sangh Parivar has emerged and blossomed within the framework of a post-Independence state in which secularism has been established in a rather equivocal fashion. Although many of the key figures in the framing of the Constitution of India – notably Jawaharlal Nehru and B.R. Ambedkar – were committed to the idea of a national political space in which religion would play no part, they were equally committed to the protection of minorities whose religious identities had been reinforced by the traumatic communal violence which had accompanied the partition of the subcontinent between India and Pakistan. As a result, religious identity maintained a formal position in political life (through, for example, the retention of separate codes of personal law for different religious groups).

This formal status has only served to reinforce the continued existence of the variety of approaches to the idea of nationalism fashioned within the context of colonialism. Indeed it is fair to say that the Indian state has always been caught between the desire to produce a strongly centralised nation-state, on the European model, and the need to accommodate strong community identities by devolving power on a loose federal model (the argument has been made particularly strongly in Jalal 1995). This dilemma was apparent, for example, in the Centre's approach to South Indian movements in the 1950s, which sought to gain greater autonomy for a series of cultural and linguistic identities. Tamil nationalism in particular, with its strongly anti-Brahmanical flavour, has challenged the visions of the nation fashioned by northern elites. Ironically, the main Tamil movement in the 1960s and 1970s, the Dravida Munnetra Kazhagham (DMK), operated with a strongly secularist rhetoric, and was critical of northern nationalism precisely because of its perceived elision with high-caste 'Hinduism'. This perhaps serves to illustrate the way in which a series of different identities continue both to contest and to become intermingled across the discursive space of nationalism in India.

From the time of Independence, Hindu nationalism has been a significant presence in this space. In the first few years of freedom, political parties such as the Hindu Mahasabha and the Ramrajya Parishad competed with the Jana Sangh for Hindu nationalist votes. Partly because of its organisational resources, however, the Sangh Parivar has become increasingly dominant over the past three decades. In particular, the VHP has launched a series of campaigns which have provided the basis for the elaboration of a plethora of symbolic evocations of the Hindu nation. The geographical and social unity of Hindutva was evoked, for example, by the Ekatmata Yajna in 1983. Three major processions crisscrossed India, starting and finishing at symbolic, sacred spots such as Somnath and Kanyakumari. The procession converged at Nagpur, the geographical heart of India and the headquarters of the RSS. The processions carried images of Gaṅgā and Bhārata Mātā (Mother India) and along the way they distributed Ganges water (Gaṅgāpāṇi). To symbolise the unity of castes, scheduled castes (dalits) were asked to carry the water in the processions. Increasingly, the deity and hero of the *Rāmāyaṇa*, Rāma, has been co-opted as the central focus of Hindu nationalist symbolism (Kapur 1993). The dispute over Rāma's 'birthplace' (janmabhūmi) in Ayodhyā mentioned earlier has provided the key vehicle for this development. The campaign to destroy the Babri Masjid and build a magnificent temple to Rāma can be seen as a precise articulation of the ideology of a martial race asserting itself and reclaiming its rightful possessions from 'foreign invaders'. Images of Lord Rāma both as a boy, 'caged' in the Masjid and as a bold and brave young adult with a mighty bow, the archetypal martial Hindu, have been produced in videos and poster art as a central feature of the campaign. The idea of Rām(a)rājya evoked here has very different connotations to those noted earlier as associated with Gandhi.

Such strongly articulated cultural visions of the Hindu nation have had an inevitable impact on the political process in India. Intense communal violence has been associated with the Ayodhyā campaign throughout. The BJP has undoubtedly been involved in and capitalised upon the campaign. Indeed the period since the destruction of the Masjid in 1992 has witnessed the steady rise to power of the party until the elections held in 2004. The exigencies of power, however, had nevertheless constrained the ability of the BJP to implement a Hindutva agenda – a point symbolised by the continued dispute over whether and when to built the Rām(a)janmabhūmi temple.

This constraint has resulted in tensions emerging amongst different sections of the Sangh Parivar. Such tensions serve to remind us that Hindu nationalism has throughout its history been a loose set of ideas rather than a homogeneous ideology. It is much broader, indeed, than the already very broad umbrella of the Sangh Parivar. Such organisations as the Shiv Sena in Maharashtra, for example, subscribe to what is at times a particularly virulent form of Hindu nationalist, anti-minority rhetoric, which is combined with its equally virulent Marathi chauvinism.

The Congress has also incorporated elements of Hindu nationalism into its political stance at various times, as have other political parties. The Tamil party the All-India Annadurai Dravida Munnetra Kazhagam (AIADMK), for example, has in recent times been promoting a form of Hindu nationalism in the South. Outside the ambit of formal politics, various Vaiṣṇava movements in areas like Gujarat, and in the Gujarati diaspora, have adopted elements of Hindu nationalist ideology as a feature of their approach to social and political questions. Some authors have also noted the way in which ideas associated with Hindu nationalism have become part of 'commonsense' views of the world in parts of India, amongst particular social classes (see Dutta 1993). At the same time, we need to bear in mind that such ideas are continually challenged in an Indian context. The emergence of an assertive, politically powerful dalit identity, for example, is persistently threatening to the idea of the Hindu nation (see Omvedt 1995; Zavos 2001). Equally, the tendency of significant elements within Hindu nationalism to articulate a more homogenised view of Hindu religions is undermined by the continuing diversity within the Hindu traditions. Indeed, attempts to homogenise in themselves tend to increase trends of 'heterogenisation', of assertive diversity (van der Veer 1994: 15). This point, which van der Veer makes about the modernisation paradigm which is associated with Western-style nationalism, is equally relevant in the context of modern 'Hinduism'. As aspects of modernity, both 'Hinduism' and nationalism may produce heterogeneous forms of identity which will, amongst other forms of identity, challenge what are currently the politically predominant homogenising tendencies of Hindu nationalism.

See also: **Advaita; Ahiṃsā; Ambedkar, Bhimrao Ram; Arya Samaj; Ayodhyā; Bharat Dharma Mahamandala; Bharatiya Janata Party; Brahmo Samaj; Buddhism, relationship with Hinduism; Dalits; Dayananda Saraswati, Swami; Dharma Sabha; Diaspora; Gandhi, Mohandas Karamchand; Gaṇeśa; Gaṇeśacatūrthi; Gaṅgā; Godse, Nathuram Vinayak; Golwalkar, Madhav Sadashiv; Hedgewar, Keshav Baliram; Hindu Mahasabha; Hinduism, modern and contemporary; Hindutva; Jainism, relationship with Hinduism; Jana Sangh; Lajpat Rai, Lala; Māyā; Rāma; Ramakrishna Math and Mission; Rāmarājya; Rāmāyaṇā; Ramarajya Parishad; Rashtriya Sevika Samiti; Rashtriya Swayamsevak Sangh; Roy, Rammohan; Śaivism; Sangh Parivar; Savarkar, Vinayat Damodar; Shiv Sena; Shraddhanand, Swami; Sikhism, relationship with Hinduism; South Indian political movements; Tilak, Bal Gangadhar; Vaiṣṇavism; Vedānta; Vishwa Hindu Parishad; Vivekananda, Swami; Yuga**

JOHN ZAVOS

Further reading

Anderson, B. 1991. *Imagined Communities: Reflections on the Origin and Spread of Nationalism*. London: Verso.

Bhatt, C. 2001. *Hindu Nationalism: Origins, Ideologies and Modern Myths*. Oxford: Berg.

Chatterjee, P. 1986. *Nationalist Thought and the Colonial World: A Derivative Discourse?* London: Zed.

Chatterjee, P. 1993. *The Nation and Its Fragments: Colonial and Postcolonial Histories*. Princeton, NJ: Princeton University Press.

Deshpande, D.V. and S.R. Ramaswamy. 1981. *Dr. Hedgewar: The Epoch Maker*. Bangalore: Sahitya Sindhu.

Dutta, P.K. 1993. "Dying Hindus": Production of Hindu Communal Common Sense in Early 20th Century Bengal'. *Economic and Political Weekly* 28, 25: 1,305–19.

Gellner, E. 1983. *Nations and Nationalism*. Oxford: Blackwell.

Gooptu, N. 2001. *Politics of the Urban Poor in Early Twentieth Century India*. Cambridge: Cambridge University Press.

Jaffrelot, C. 1996. *The Hindu Nationalist Movement and Indian Politics, 1925 to the 1990s*. London: Hurst & Co.

Jalal, A. 1995. *Authoritarianism and Democracy in South Asia*. Cambridge: Cambridge University Press.

Kapur, A. 1993. 'Deity to Crusader: The Changing Iconography of Ram'. In G. Pandey, ed., *Hindus and Others: The Question of Identity in India Today*. New Delhi: Viking Penguin, 74–109.

King, C. 1994. *One Language, Two Scripts: The Hindi Movement in Nineteenth Century North India*. New Delhi: Oxford University Press.
Lutgendorf, P. 1991. *Life of a Text: Performing the Ramcaritmanas of Tulsidas*. Berkeley, CA: University of California Press.
O'Hanlon, R. 1985. *Caste, Conflict and Ideology: Mahatma Jotirao Phule and Low Caste Protest in Nineteenth Century Western India*. Cambridge: Cambridge University Press.
Omvedt, G. 1995. *Dalit Visions: The Anti-Caste Movement and the Construction of Indian Identity*. Hyderabad: Orient Longman.
Pandey, G. 1990. *Construction of Communalism in Colonial North India*. New Delhi: Oxford University Press.
Parekh, B. 1989. *Colonialism, Tradition and Reform: An Analysis of Gandhi's Political Discourse*. New Delhi: Sage.
Roy, R. 1982. 'Dialogue Between a Christian Missonary and Three Chinese Converts'. In J.C. Ghosh, ed., *English Works of Raja Rammohan Roy*, vol. 4. New Delhi: Cosmo, 911–13.
Sarhadi Raj, D. 2000. 'Who the Hell Do You Think You Are? Promoting Religious Identity among Young Hindus in Britain'. *Ethnic and Racial Studies* 23,3: 535–58.
Savarkar, V.V. 1947. *The Indian War of Independence 1857*. New Delhi: Rajdhani Granthnagar.
Savarkar, V.V. 1989. *Hindutva/Who Is a Hindu?* Bombay: S.S. Savarkar.
Smith, A.D. 1971. *Theories of Nationalism*. London: Duckworth.
van der Veer, P. 1994. *Religious Nationalism: Hindus and Muslims in India*. Berkeley, CA: University of California.
Vertovec, S. 2000. *The Hindu Diaspora: Comparative Patterns*. London: Routledge.
Zavos, J. 2000. *Emergence of Hindu Nationalism in India*. New Delhi: Oxford University Press.
Zavos, J. 2001. 'Conversion and the Assertive Margins: An Analysis of Hindu Nationalist Discourse and the Recent Attacks on Indian Christians'. *South Asia* 24,2: 73–89.
http://www.vhp.org/englishsite/a-origin_ growth/birthofvhp.htm (accessed 21 November 2003).
http://www.vhp-uk.com/activities.php (accessed 21 November 2003).

NAVAGRAHAS (PLANETS)

The observation of the planets and their movements, as well as the belief in their influence on persons and events, goes far back in Indian history. Graha, the Sanskrit word for planet, is derived from the root gṛh- to grasp, to seize, to lay hold of. There is literary evidence for the ancient Indians' knowledge of planets and their orbits by 1900 BCE, which was expressed in the form of myths. The Epics and Purāṇas are filled with episodes that narrate in great detail the good and evil influences of the planets. Later astronomical literature offers fairly precise observations and calculations of the movements of the planets and their conjunctions. The full list of planets (together with their influence) as employed even today in Indian astrology (jyotiṣa) appears in texts like the *Bṛhatsaṃhitā* and *Rājamārṭanda*. In the geocentric Hindu universe the sun and moon also figure as planets, in addition to those recognised today as such.

Each of the nine planets has many names in Sanskrit literature:

1 Sun: sūrya, ravi, bhanu, savitṛ, bhāskara, arka, prabhākara, etc.
2 Moon: candra, indu, candramas, soma, śāsī, niśākara, etc.
3 Mars: aṅgāraka, kuja, bhauma, vakra, lohitāṅga, rudhir, etc.
4 Mercury: budha, bodhan, vibhud, kumāra, rājaputra, saumya, etc.
5 Jupiter: guru, bṛhaspati, vākpati, girīśa, suri, etc.
6 Venus: śukra, bhṛgu, bhṛgusūta, sītā, kavi, kavyā, etc.
7 Saturn: sanaiśvara, sauri, sūryaputra, maṇḍa, asita, śani, etc.
8 Rahu: tamaḥ, agu, asura, svarbhanu, dānava, surāri, etc.
9 Ketu: sikin, brahmasūta, dhumravarna, etc.

While the first seven coincide with the heavenly bodies known universally, the last two are peculiarly Indian: Rahu, the ascending node, represented as a head (whose body is Ketu) that swallows the moon; and Ketu, the descending node, represented as a trunk (to which Rahu is the head) from which the moon is emitted again. (Ketu may also mean a comet, or a meteor.)

The planets are associated with colours, deities, directions, varṇas, body parts, habitats, flavours, saṃhitās, etc.

The following list is incomplete, but representative:

1 Sun: red, Agni, East, kṣatriya, bones, temple, copper, pungent.
2 Moon: white, Varuṇa, Northwest, vaiśya, blood, watery place, jewels, salty.
3 Mars: dark red, Karttikeya, South, *Sāmaveda*, kṣatriya, marrow, fireplace, gold, bitter.
4 Mercury: green, Viṣṇu, North, *Atharvaveda*, śūdra, skin, playground, bronze, mixed.
5 Jupiter: yellow, Indra, Northeast, *Ṛgveda*, brāhmaṇa, fat, treasury, silver, sweet.
6 Venus, variegated, Indrāṇī, Southeast, *Yajurveda*, brāhmaṇa, semen, bedroom, pearl, sour.
7 Saturn: dark, Prajāpati, West, caṇḍāla, muscles, dust-hole, iron, astringent.

Astrological predictions are based on the movements of the planets through twelve houses (rāśis).

The planets also have amongst each other natural friends and enemies.

Planet	*Friend*	*Enemy*	*Indifferent*
Sun	Moon, Mars, Jupiter	Venus, Saturn	Mercury
Moon	Sun, Mercury	none	Mars, Jupiter, Venus, Saturn
Mars	Sun, Moon, Jupiter	Mercury	Venus, Saturn
Mercury	Sun, Venus	Moon	Mars, Jupiter, Saturn
Jupiter	Sun, Moon, Mars	Mercury, Venus	Saturn
Venus	Mercury, Saturn	Sun, Moon	Mars, Jupiter
Saturn	Mercury, Venus	Sun, Moon, Mars	Jupiter

The influence of a planet is determined by place, direction, activity and time. A planet is considered powerful when it is in its own house, or in its friend's house. For more details the ample astrological literature of India, ancient and contemporary, has to be consulted. The traditional Indian science of Jyotiṣa embraces both astronomy and astrology and is also taught at university-level institutions in India. Since the establishment of birth horoscopes is still almost universal in India, there is much scope for professionals in Jyotiṣa, who also have begun working with computers to produce kundlis (personal astrological charts).

Viṣṇu Purāṇa (2.11–12) describes the movements of the planets with their respective rathas ('chariots'). The Sun, which reflects the energy of Viṣṇu, 'perpetually revolves, affording delight to the gods, to the progenitors, and to humankind'. The chariot of Candra (Moon) has three wheels and is drawn by ten horses. The chariot of Budha (Mercury) is composed of the elements air and fire and is drawn by eight horses. And so forth. 'Eight black horses draw the dusky chariot of Rahu, and once harnessed are attached to it forever' (2.12.21). The eight horses of the chariot of Ketu are dusky red like lacquer or the smoke from burning straw.

See also: **Agni; Brāhmaṇa; Caste; Deities; Indra; Jyotiṣa; Mahābhārata; Prajāpati; Purāṇas; Rāmāyaṇa; Saṃhitā; Varṇa; Varuṇa; Viṣṇu**

KLAUS K. KLOSTERMAIER

Further reading

Kak, S.C. 1993. 'Planetary Periods from the Rigvedic Code'. *Mankind Quarterly* 33.

Kak, S.C. 1996. 'Knowledge of Planets in the Third Millennium BCE'. *Quarterly Journal of the Royal Astronomical Society* 37: 709–15.

Kane, P.V. 1958. *History of Dharmasastra*, vol. 5, pt 1. Pune: BORI.

Wilson, H.H. (trans.). 1996. *The Visnu Purana: A System of Hindu Mythology and Tradition.* Calcutta: Punthi Pustak. First published 1840.

NAVALAR, ARUMUKA (1822–79)

Arumuka Navalar was born Arumuka Pillai, but is better known as Arumuka Navalar ('the learned'). He was renowned for three things: his significant role in reviving Śaivism in Sri Lanka, his contribution to Tamil prose and his involvement in the Tamil Bible translation. Navalar's religious and literary activities need to be seen against the nineteenth-century evangelical missionary critique of Śaivism. It was the persistent missionary attack on Śaivism that caused Navalar to mount a vigorous defence of it. With his knowledge of the Bible he was able to demonstrate that Śaiva temple practices, ridiculed by missionaries, were similar to those described in the Hebrew Scriptures. He wrote profusely, and his religious tracts and booklets, such as *Śaiva-tūṣaṇa-pariharam* (The Absolute Abolition of the Abuse of Śaivism), were aimed at his fellow Śaivites, urging them to study their own tradition so that they could defend themselves against any religious abuse and rectify misconceptions about Śaivism.

See also: **Hinduism, modern and contemporary; Śaivism; Sri Lanka, Hindus in; Temple worship**

SHARADA SUGIRTHARAJAH

Further reading

Hudson, D.D. 1992. 'Arumuga Navalar and the Hindu Renaissance Among the Tamils'. In Kenneth W. Jones, ed., *Religious Controversy in British India: Dialogues in South Asian Languages.* Albany, NY: State University of New York Press.

NAVARĀTRI

See: **Durgā Pūjā**

NĀYAṈMĀR

Nāyaṉmār (sing.) in Tamil means, literally, 'leader'. The plural, Nāyaṉmār, is the collective term given to the sixty-three saints of Tamil Śaivism who are often referred to in Tamil simply as 'the sixty-three'. They lived between approximately the sixth and eleventh centuries CE at a time when bhakti (devotion) was a prominent form of religious expression. They were responsible for a vast body of Tamil devotional poetry in twelve collections or 'books' known as *Tirumurai*. The twelfth collection, *Periyapurāṉam*, by Cekkilar, consists of the hagiographies of these Śaiva saints and was probably written around 1150 CE.

By far the most important part of these twelve 'books' are the first seven, known collectively as 'the Garland of God' (*Tevāram*). They are the work of three Nāyaṉmār: Tirunānacampantar, Appar and Suntarar (all dated to around the eighth century CE). They are mostly site-specific praises of the God Śiva at a large number of temples, the majority in Tamil Nadu, with a few in Sri Lanka, and are a storehouse of information on the mythology of Śiva at various places, both the well-known pilgrimage sites such as Cidambaram and Madurai, and the less well known, such as Cīrkāli (close to the former). Each poem consists usually of eleven or twelve stanzas (four-line verses) that are distinguished one from another by an internal head-rhyming system. The last verse of each poem, in the manner of much medieval poetry in India, Persia and central Asia, contains the name of the poet – his 'signature'. Book Eight contains two works, the well-known poem in praise of Śiva, called *Tiruvācakam*; and *Tirukkovaiyar*, a collection of mystical love poetry addressed to the God at Cidambaram. Books Nine, Ten and Eleven of the *Tirumurai* consist of other miscellaneous Śaiva devotional poems.

It must be stressed that none of these poems is part of a liturgy in the sense that the Veda is part of a liturgy. But in recent years the custom has grown up of non-brāhmaṇa priests called pantāram, or otuvār ('chanter'), who sing the *Tevāram* relevant to that particular site as an accompaniment to temple ritual. The melodies used, called in Tamil pan, are supposedly those of ancient Tamil music. Effectively, however, they are cast in rāgas of contemporary South Indian classical music.

Thanks to the *Periyapurānam* we know much of the traditional hagiographies of these saints. By far the most voluminous relates to the author of the first three books of *Tevāram*, Tirunānacampantar, who lived around the eighth century CE. On being temporarily abandoned in the temple at Cīrkāli by his over-devout father at the age of two and a half, he cried to the God and Goddess out of hunger. Fed by the Goddess Pārvatī with milk from her breast drawn into a golden cup, he jumped for joy and sang his first *Tevāram* verses. Unfortunately his reported work is coloured by the twelfth-century bigotry of Tamil Śaivites towards the Jains, and his story includes an episode which leads to the impaling of a number of Jains. This, together with one core episode each from the lives of the sixty-three Nāyaṉmār, is documented in a narrative frieze in the temple at Dārāsuram, which was built around 1150 by the Chola king Rajaraja II. The remarkably close parallels between this frieze and the *Periyapurānam* are our best evidence for the date of the latter.

(Note: spellings are transliterations from Tamil. Alternative Sanskrit spellings exist for Tirunānacampantar/Tirunānasambandhar.)

See also: **Bhakti; Cidambaram; Jainism, relationship with Hinduism; Madurai; Mandir; Music; Pārvatī; Śaivism; Śiva; Veda**

JOHN R. MARR AND KATHLEEN TAYLOR

Further reading

Marr, John Ralston. 1985. *The Eight Anthologies: A Study in Early Tamil Literature*. Madras: Institute of Asian Studies.

Zvelebil, K. 1973. *The Smile of Murugan: Tamil Literature in South India*. Leiden: Brill.

NEPAL, HINDUS IN

Many of the difficulties in providing a coherent definition for the loosely organised group of practices, texts, narratives and communities commonly referred to as Hinduism in India apply also to the situation in Nepal, the largely Hindu nation immediately to the north. As in India, this difficulty in categorisation is produced by the lack of a strict delineation amongst variant practices that may or may not be termed Hindu; by immigrating peoples who have been retroactively fitted into the predominant Hindu caste hierarchy; and, especially in Nepal, by the overlapping of Buddhist and Hindu religious sites, practitioners and ritual officiants.

The modern nation of Nepal, which has retained its essential shape since the late eighteenth century, is often divided into three geographic zones. In the northern high Himalayas, an area that shares a border with Tibet, the Bhotiya people share various religious systems: forms of shamanistic healing rites performed by the jhankri, as well as monastic and non-monastic forms of Vajrayāna Buddhism. In the centre of the middle hills sits the Kathmandu Valley, a site whose residents have for approximately two thousand years utilised and incorporated into their religious lives both Hindu and Buddhist artistic, ritual and social forms. And in the south along the border with India runs the Tarai, a fertile strip of land running the length of the country in whose western area one finds Lumbini, the birthplace of the historical Buddha, and in the east Janakpur, the birthplace of Sītā, the wife of Rāma.

The relatively small area of the Kathmandu Valley contains one of the widest varieties of religious forms in the country. This is due in part to its somewhat idyllic location as a historic refuge for Hindu kings and would-be kings fleeing from their north Indian enemies, and in part to its position on old trade routes between India and Tibet. While the historicity of the first kingdoms in the valley and the religions that they sponsored is somewhat difficult to establish, the earliest inscriptions found in the valley, those of the Licchavi King Amsuvarma from the mid-fifth century, refer in their iconography not only to Buddha, who was already being worshipped in the valley, but also to the prominent Hindu deities Nārāyaṇa (Viṣṇu) and Paśupati (Śiva). Temples to these two deities remain some of the most frequented sites of the valley, Paśupati also serving as the foremost site for the cremation of the dead.

The very visible presence of Buddhism in the valley prevents us from being able to clearly demarcate that which is strictly Hindu. While two Buddhist stūpas located on the outskirts of the city of Kathmandu – Svayambhu to the west and Boudha to the north-east – serve the city's current Tibetan population, Svayambhu and its proximate Haritī shrine also serve as significant ritual sites for the valley's Buddhist Newar population, where vegetarian offerings are frequently made to the ancestors. Though Buddhism is traditionally seen to be anti-caste, Newar Buddhists comprise an integral part of the Newar caste system, a system that resembles, but is not parallel to, that of India: the top of this system is split into two branches, one headed by Buddhist monk-priests (Vajrācārya) and just below them Śākya and the other by Hindu brāhmaṇa priests (Rājopādhyaya). Those who utilise members of one or both of these two religiously authoritative groups as religious specialists represent the members of the approximately twenty-five Newar castes, very few of which, however, can be absolutely defined as either Hindu or Buddhist.

The forms of Hinduism found in Nepal resemble those in India. Festivals of Kṛṣṇa's birthday (Janmāṣṭamī, Holī, Durgā Pūjā (Nep. Dasain) and Dīvālī (Nep. Tihar) are celebrated in ways that resemble their Indian counterparts. Also, Hindu deities are enshrined and given pūjā both in large central temples (many containing a Śiva liṅga) and small street shrines (frequently of Gaṇeśa) throughout the cities of the Kathmandu Valley. Even more intensely than Indian villages, however, these cities function as self-contained ritual units, and it is the Newar people, a religiously Hindu though Tibeto-Burman-speaking ethnic group of long standing in the valley, who ritually maintain these cities. In addition to the regular performance of rites by Newar families, lineages, social organisations and neighbourhoods, each of these social units possessing its own specified geographic marker, the city itself is enacted as a ritually meaningful unit of space for festivals of major importance. Thus, during Dasain (New.

Mohani), Newars twice daily visit the open-air pīṭha of the eight Mātṛkās, shrines that sit outside and define the boundaries of the city proper and house not an image of the goddess but a set of aniconic stones. This festival also sees an intense concentration on several ritual elements that permeate the Hinduism of the Newars: the presence of masked dancers who take on the personae of Bhairava, the goddesses, and their attendants; the performance of animal sacrifice and the display of blood; and the subsequent consumption of meat and liquor in the form of organised feasts (New. bhwae, Skt. bhoj) by all of the social units mentioned above.

While the streets and neighbourhoods of the three major cities of the valley contain predominantly Buddhist images, stūpas and now-domesticised Newar monasteries (Skt. vihāra, Nep. bahal), each city also possesses a central royal square containing numerous Hindu temples and images situated around the city's old palace. Adjoining each palace is a temple to the goddess Taleju, who is seen as a manifestation of Durgā and the tutelary deity of the Newar Malla dynasty, a loosely related group of Newar families ruling Nepal from the early twelfth century until 1768. Due to her intimate connection with royalty, her temples are restricted to foreigners and her temple in Kathmandu is only open to Hindus on the ninth day of Dasain. It is also on the evening of this day that hundreds of animals are sacrificed as a blood offering to Taleju inside the courtyard adjoining her temple, thus re-enacting the story of Durgā's slaying of the buffalo demon. Royalty itself is embodied by both the king of Nepal, or by his traditional representative, and the local Kumārī, the young girl and 'living goddess' (jīvit devī), who is herself seen as an incarnation of Taleju and the representation of the glory (śrī) and power (śakti) of the king. While at many festivals she merely observes the proceedings, she is worshipped most intensely during Dasain, when she interacts most closely with the king and the general populace. And during Indra Jātrā in Kathmandu, she goes out in procession through the city and gives ṭīkā to the king, thus providing a public reaffirmation of his divine right to rule.

Though not as unique to Nepal as Taleju, it is Bhairava, who might be said to be the central deity of Hindu Nepal. Bhairava has major temples and festivals in all of the major Newar cities of the valley, and the 'split-eared' Kāṇphata yogis who have Gorakhnāth as their guru perform their initiation rites in front of Bhairava. His most dramatic manifestations, however, occur during festivals that do not bear his name. During the Indra Jātrā of Kathmandu, it is the masks and beer pots of Bhairava that are put on display throughout the city; following the procession of Kumārī through the upper half of the city, young men will fight for a taste of the life-bestowing beer that flows through his large golden mask, displayed in the royal square within sight of the festival's centrally raised pole. And it is during the solar new year's festival of Bisket Jātrā in Bhaktapur that his own pole is raised and lowered, signalling the beginning of the new year, and that his chariot bearing a representative cross-section of the city's population is pulled through the city and crashed together with that of his consort Bhadrakālī.

See also: **Blood sacrifice; Brāhmaṇa; Buddhism, relationship with Hinduism; Caste; Dīvālī; Durgā; Durgā Pūjā; Gorakhnāth; Holī; Image worship; Indra; Janmāṣṭamī; Kṛṣṇa; Mahiṣa; Mātṛkās; Pāśupatas; Pūjā; Rāja; Rāma; Sītā; Śiva; Utsava; Viṣṇu**

MICHAEL BALTUTIS

Further reading

Allen, Michael. 1975. *The Cult of Kumari: Virgin Worship in Nepal.* Kathmandu:

Tribhuvan University, Institute for Nepalese and Asian Studies.
Gellner, David N. and Declan Quigley. 1999. *Contested Hierarchies: A Collaborative Ethnography of Caste among the Newars of the Kathmandu Valley, Nepal*. Oxford: Oxford University Press.
Levy, Robert I., with the collaboration of Kedar Raj Rajopadhyaya. 1990. *Mesocosm: Hinduism and the Organization of a Traditional Newar City in Nepal*. Berkeley, CA: University of California Press.

NEW RELIGIOUS MOVEMENTS, HINDU ROLE IN

The New England literary movement known as Transcendentalism (1836–60), including such figures as Ralph Waldo Emerson, Frederic Henry Hedge, George Ripley, Amos Bronson Alcott, Henry Thoreau, Margaret Fuller and Theodore Parker, among others, represents an early example of engagement with Hindu ideas. Espousing a romantic view of the individual and intuition as the highest form of apprehension, Transcendentalism abandoned the rationalism of Unitarianism and other Protestant denominations to seek new forms of vitality in religious thought – incorporating, especially through Emerson, Hindu notions concerning the immanence of God in nature, the natural harmony interlinking all forms of life and the mystical propensity of the individual. Emerson's poem 'Brahma' has become one of the Transcendental classics – reflecting the illusion of life and death as espoused in the *Bhagavadgītā*. Thoreau, likewise, championed a naturalistic mysticism that stressed the individual against materialistic civilisation. His essay 'Civil Disobedience' was one of the inspirations behind Gandhi's formulation of satyagraha, or non-violent resistance. In the United States itself, Transcendentalism became a leading instigator behind the American or Western Metaphysical Tradition, with its concern for healing and its emphasis on the reality and immanence of the spiritual. Accordingly, much American metaphysical thought directs itself toward the understanding that evil and negativity are illusions of the mind. Jesus Christ is no longer considered the supreme redeemer of a fallen humanity but functions instead as the most achieved exemplar of the discovery and realisation of the inner self's divinity.

This non-ontological nature of illness and negativity (including poverty) became the springboard, through the healing work of Phineas Parkhurst Quimby (1802–66), Mary Baker Eddy (1821–1910) and Emma Curtis Hopkins (1853–1925), of what subsequently coalesced as the New Thought movement. Essentially an American phenomenon, New Thought argues that new ways of thinking are necessary to free the individual from the delusions of disease and deficiency – reminiscent of the Hindu doctrine but not using the language of māyā concerning the illusory appearance of the world. Accepting the mental-spiritual as the sole reality, New Thought stresses that evil is an aberrational product of the mind alone. But by affirming that the underlying reality is one of pure goodness and light, New Thought differs from the Vedāntic perception of the total transcendence of all attributes by the Absolute or Brahman as the ultimate reality. New Thought concentrates instead on humanity's incorrect thinking obscuring the original understanding of the illusory nature of the physical world. Nevertheless, New Thought, influenced by the Western Metaphysical Tradition shares with some forms of Indian philosophy a fundamental rejection of the reality of the world. But at the same time, New Thought and the Western Metaphysical Tradition tended not to advocate asceticism, substituting a wishful mysticism which emphasised the attainment rather than rejection of such worldly goals as success, health, wealth, happiness and self-realisation.

But if New Thought represents a diffuse expression of Hindu ideas, a more direct connection between Hinduism and the West occurred through Swami Vivekananda (1863–1902) – disciple and spokesperson of Sri Ramakrishna (1836–86), the Bengali saint and mystic. Vivekananda represented Hinduism in the World Parliament of Religions held in Chicago in 1893. He was particularly welcomed because not only was his level of education, articulation and sophistication for someone from the East largely a surprise to Americans and others, but also because he presented a form of Hinduism that was attractive to a Western audience. After the Parliament, Vivekananda made a tour of the United States and Europe to establish the international branch of the Ramakrishna Math and Mission. He founded the Ramakrishna–Vivekananda Center in New York City. The monastic order is dedicated to chastity, poverty and charity, and it has played a major foundational role in the dissemination of Hindu concepts and practices within Western culture.

Nevertheless, apart from the successes of Vivekananda's missionary efforts, Hindu influences have persisted in the Western Metaphysical Tradition itself. Beside New Thought, another major aspect of the American cultic milieu has been Spiritualism – a movement that is frequently dated to the experiences of the Fox sisters in 1848 and dedicated to mediumistic communication with departed spirits. As a movement, Spiritualism has developed through the seminal works of the visionary Emanuel Swedenborg (1688–1772), the hypnotist Franz Anton Mesmer (1734–1815) and the magnetic healer Andrew Jackson Davis (b. 1826). The movement also attracted the controversial Russian ex-patriot Helena Petrovna Blavatsky (1831–91), who had travelled from her native country to India and then to Great Britain and the United States, where she developed her mediumistic propensities. However, as she came increasingly under the influence of both Hinduism and Buddhism, Blavatsky broke with Spiritualism to found with Henry Steel Olcott and William Quan Judge the Theosophical Society in New York in 1875. Later, the headquarters of Theosophy were moved to Adyar in India.

Whereas Spiritualism seeks contact in the afterlife with former family or friends who have lived on earth, Theosophy is concerned with receiving occult wisdom from ascended masters that Blavatsky referred to collectively as the Great White Brotherhood – arguably an adaptation of the bodhisattvas of Buddhism but equally the enlightened ṛṣis, sages and mahātmās of Hinduism. It is chiefly through Theosophy that such Hindu concepts and practices as reincarnation, karma, ākāṣic (etheric) worlds, higher spiritual beings, avatāras, yoga and meditation have reached the West. Blavatksy's Theosophy holds that spiritual progression is achieved through meditative and yogic practice along with assistance from spiritual masters. Reincarnation is understood much as it is in Hinduism, namely as affording the possibility for spiritual growth and eventual samadhī or mokṣa, or, in theosophical terms, allowing repeated opportunities through which to overcome lower-plane attachment. One's future life is simply determined by the spiritual achievements of the present life.

With Blavatsky's death, leadership of the Theosophical Society of America passed to Annie Besant (1847–1933). In 1895, Judge led a schism in the movement and established the Theosophical Society in America as a separate organisation. With the guidance of Charles Leadbeater (1854–1934), Besant formally recognised the Indian religious figure Jiddu Krishnamurti (1895–1986) as the physical vehicle of the world teacher Bodhisattva Avatar in 1925. This in turn precipitated the rupture of the Theosophical Society with Rudolf Steiner (1861–1925), one of the 1902 founders of the German Theosophical Association, proceeding to found his separate movement, which he named Anthroposophy in its attempt to explain the world in terms of the nature of humanity. Krishnamurti had been placed at the head of the Order of the Star of the East, which was created to be his vehicle. However, in 1929 Krishnamurti dissolved the Order and repudiated the Theosophical Society's contentions regarding his preordained position. Henceforth, though maintaining loose theosophical connections, he remained unaffiliated to any institutionalised religion and chose to be an independent spiritual teacher. He stressed personal spiritual responsibility for the individual and denied all restrictive mental and religious dogmas, though maintaining a basically Advaitin view. He advocated the concerted effort of self-observation, rather than any alleged religious authority of the guru or spiritual master, as what leads to the freedom of enlightenment. In 1969 the Krishnamurti Foundation, based on the popularity of his teachings, was founded in Ojai, California, on land originally purchased for Krishnamurti by Besant.

Krishnamurti, along with such figures as Steiner, Sri Aurobindo and the mature Guru Maharaj, all teach or have taught a secularised version of Eastern spirituality and insight that stems more broadly from Hinduism. By contrast, following more closely in the tradition established by Blavatsky, if not part of that tradition itself, the Maharishi Mahesh Yogi (Transcendental Meditation), Swami Muktananda (Siddha [Yoga] Dham of America), the earlier Guru Maharaj Ji (Divine Light Mission/Elan Vital), Bhagwan Shree Rajneesh/Osho (Rajneesh Movement), Paramhansa Yogananda (Self-Realisation Fellowship) or such Westerners as Baba Ram Das (Hanuman Foundation), Ma Jaya Bhagavati (Kashi Ashram), Da (Bubba) Free John/Adidam (Johannine Daist Community/the Religion of Adidam) and John-Roger Hinkins (MSIA) all promote various Eastern meditative practices that aim toward the ultimate mystical or spiritual release that is the ultimate goal of traditional Hinduism. Following more directly in the theosophical tradition of Blavatsky herself, however, there are the teachings of Alice Bailey and such related spin-offs as Guy and Edna Ballard's 'I AM' Religious Activity, Mark and Elizabeth Clare Prophet's Summit Lighthouse/Church Universal and Triumphant, Benjamin Creme's Tara Centre and even, to an extent, Edgar Cayce's Association for Research and Enlightenment, among others.

Alice Bailey (1880–1949), through a series of 'visitations', was led from her native England to the Theosophical Society in Pacific Groves, California, in the early 1920s. She became a Theosophist, and her first book, *Initiation, Human and Solar*, reputedly dictated through Djwhal Khul or D.K. (Blavatsky's Djual Khool), was enthusiastically received by the Society. In time, however, through difficulties with Annie Besant, Alice and her husband Foster Bailey became marginalised and then broke with the Society to form their own organisations: the Lucifer Trust in 1922, later renamed the Lucis Trust, the Arcane School (founded in 1923), the New Group of World Servers (founded in 1932), the Triangles in 1937 and the Men of Goodwill (since 1950, World Goodwill). Bailey follows but elaborates on Blavatsky's teachings concerning the divine hierarchy, the seven (cosmic) rays and evolution to higher levels. Her basic thrust is to concentrate on loving service to humanity, with the power of the divine hierarchy channelled through established meditation groups. Bailey's central importance was that she was one of the first spiritual leaders to stress the coming 'New Age' and the imminent return of the spiritual master, Christ Maitreya. She is also known for her prayer the Great Invocation, in which the power of the cosmic or divine hierarchy is visualised funnelling down to earth.

Through Alice Bailey's writings many Hindu and Buddhist concepts became familiar in the West. The Arcane School and the Lucis Trust continue the fused Hindu–Buddhist theosophical notions of karma, reincarnation, the divine plan and the spiritual hierarchy. Bailey's theosophical cosmology parallels the six cakras of the human body: (1) Shamballa/Sanat Kumara (the highest energy centre, in which the will of God is to be known); (2) the spiritual hierarchy; (3) the heart cakra, in which Christ is at the hierarchy's heart, where God's love is encountered; (4) the new group of world servers; (5) men and women of goodwill everywhere; and (6) the physical centres of distribution – London, Darjeeling, New York, Geneva and Tokyo.

The teachings of Alice Bailey, especially as interpreted by the American David Spangler (1945–), inform the key ideas behind the inspiration of the contemporary centre of spiritual education and personal transformation, the Findhorn Foundation in Forres, Scotland. The wider Findhorn Community, of which the Foundation is the legally established charity trust, recognises Alice Bailey as a prophet of the New Age movement. Findhorn offers adult holistic educational programmes and courses that aim to develop interrelationships between the environment, economics, social life and spiritual principles. Though these are presented without dogma or creed, the New Age thought of Bailey permeates these Findhorn endeavours and reveals their underlying Hindu-derived theosophical origins.

Following in the same theosophical tradition is Elizabeth Clare Prophet's Church Universal and Triumphant (CUT), which was originally the Summit Lighthouse and was founded by Mark Prophet (1918–73) in 1958 when he reputedly received a mandate from the Ascended Master El Morya to become the new Messenger of the Great White Brotherhood. Following Mark's death, his widow Elizabeth (1939–) assumed the title of Guru Ma and leadership of the movement. According to CUT, Ascended Masters are those who have assumed the Christ-Mind and thereby transmuted more than half of their karma – being thus able to inhabit the spirit planes that exist beyond the lower material worlds (the physical, emotional, mental and etheric). As Jesus Christ was the cosmic teacher for the Piscean Age that is now coming to an end, so Saint Germain will assume the same role for the now dawning Age of Aquarius. Both pivotal figures are incarnations of the Word as Viṣṇu, the Son of God. In addition, the śakti or twin soul counterpart of Saint Germain is Portia, the goddess of justice or opportunity. In fusing Eastern spiritual concepts (e.g. karma, reincarnation) with Christianity, CUT has produced a dualistic schema of the cosmos that differs from the monistic tendencies of the influential Vedānta philosophy. Evil is a cosmic reality and will be eventually sealed off from the I AM THAT I AM for all eternity.

Although largely atypical, the Church Universal and Triumphant is part of the diffuse collection of modern-day spiritualities known as New Age. In contrast to the Prophets' conservative injunctions against everything from fluoride and sucrose to marijuana, rock 'n' roll music and homosexuality, the wider laissez-faire New Age movement has little in the way of doctrine, boundary determination or fundamental sexual puritanism. Two key Hindu players who have had an impact upon the development of New Age in the West are the Maharishi Mahesh Yogi (*c.*1918–) and Bhagwan Shree Rajneesh/

Osho (1931–90). The Maharishi became a Western household name in the 1960s when the Beatles visited him in Rishikesh, India, to learn his technique of Transcendental Meditation. It is arguable that the Maharishi's practice played a seminal role in the development of the Human Potential Movement in the 1960s and 1970s, as well as the fitness, holistic and self-help fashions of the 1980s. The guru sponsors the meditative concept of 'critical mass' by which, it is argued, the square root of 1 per cent of a community meditating collectively can reduce or eliminate violence, hostility and other forms of negativity. Even more colourful than the Maharishi was Rajneesh, who claimed never to have subscribed to any particular religious faith but nevertheless to have received samādhi at the age of 21. He founded an ashram in Poona in 1974 and, flouting traditional Hindu usage, named his promiscuous followers saṃnyāsins. In 1981 Rajneesh moved to the United States and established the Rajneeshpuram settlement, before being deported from the country by Federal authorities in 1987. Subsequently, Rajneesh declared that he was a Buddha and assumed the new name of Osho. His best-known practice is Dynamic Meditation – beginning with strenuous physical activity, concluding with silence and celebration and designed to lead the individual to overcome repression, lower personal inhibition, develop a state of emptiness and attain enlightenment. Rajneesh/Osho's teachings comprise a form of monism that stresses the presence of God in everything and everyone. In keeping with Hindu understanding, people, even at their worst, are considered to be divine.

Another controversial Hindu Indian figure on the Western New Age scene is Prem Pal Singh Rawat, or Guru Maharaj Ji (1957–), who, at the age of 9, succeeded his father as leader of the Divine Light Mission, established in India in 1960. Following in the teacher–disciple Sant Mat tradition, and with his recognition as the latest satguru, Maharaj Ji taught spiritual realisation through the technique of satsaṅg or meditation. His followers were known as 'premies', and they lived for the most part in drug-, alcohol- and meat-free ashrams. Maharaj Ji began a world tour in 1971, but the combination of his youth and fondness for Rolls-Royce cars, plus the hierarchical control of his ashrams, attracted much public dissent. Following his marriage to his 24-year-old secretary at the age of 16, his mother deposed him as head of the Mission. He has renamed the remnants of his following Elan Vital and has progressively eliminated the Indian and Hindu elements from his teachings. He lives today as a private person with his family in the United States, and those who practise his 'techniques of knowledge' number approximately 75,000 and are to be found throughout Britain, the United States, Europe and Australia, as well as Africa. Also incorporating a Hindu–Sikh fusion of ideas, other Sant Mat traditions in the form of various Radhasoami groups exist in both India and the West. The largest is Radhasoami Satsang Beas. They all trace their origins to Soamiji Maharaj (Shiv Dayal Sahib, 1818–78), who founded the tradition in Agra in 1861.

Also in the Sant Mat tradition was John Paul Twitchell (1908/1912?–71), a disciple of Kirpal Singh, founder of Ruhani Satsang. Twitchell developed a form of surat śabda yoga as a series of physical exercises and spiritual practices aiming to allow soul-travel beyond physical limitations to the impersonal and infinite source of all life (ECK: Spirit or the Cosmic Current). In the late 1960s, John-Roger Hinkins (1934–), a former student of ECKANKAR, which is centred on Twitchell's understanding of the divine essence of God to be found within each of us, founded MSIA (pronounced 'messiah'), or the Church of the Movement of Spiritual Inner Awareness. Hinkins has established in Los Angeles the Prana (Purple Rose Ashram of the New Age) Theological Seminary and College of Philosophy. MSIA techniques include aura balancing, light studies and becoming aware of one's programmed responses.

Both Maharaj Ji and MSIA as well as Maharishi Mahesh Yogi are indicative of the New Age Movement of spiritualities and especially the Hindu contribution to its characteristic eclecticism. Consequently, throughout the movement as a whole, the concepts of karma and reincarnation as well as 'higher beings' or Ascended Masters are part of the lingua franca. New Age spirituality will speak of cakras not only of the human body but also of the earth, in terms of geomantic nodal points and vortices of transcendent powers. Increasingly, in the New Age concern with health – not only spiritual and mental but especially physical – there is a growing interest in Āyurveda among the huge range of practices imported from various traditions as well. Typical of psycho-physical therapy of the kind that New Age incorporates is Aura-Soma, developed by Vicky Hall in 1984 and described as a form of 'soul' therapy based on the use of bottled coloured oils for purposes of self-empowerment and the ability of the individual to become a co-creator of his or her future. In its eclectic reappropriation of spiritual idioms from various religious practices, New Age has been influenced by Hinduism as much if not more than any other religiosity, although the resultant mix may often bear little resemblance to any form of Hindu orthodoxy. Nevertheless, this Hindu resource within New Age stems both from Theosophy (Mary Farrell Bednarowski, in fact, considers New Age largely a recasting of Theosophy into a modern idiom) and the 1960s countercultural popularity of such figures as Maharishi Mahesh Yogi and Maharaj Ji.

Another influential figure in the counterculture's fascination with Hinduism is former drug-guru Richard Alpert (1933–), who, after travelling to India and encountering Bhagwan Sri Nityananda's disciple Neem Karoli Baba, returned to the West as Baba Ram Das to promote 'meditation-in-action', a vegetarian diet and self-transformative social action. Another Western Hindu activist, also claiming Neem Karoli as her spiritual guru, is Ma Jaya Bhagavati, who maintains Kashi Ashram in Sebastian, Florida. Ma was particularly prominent in the 1993, 1999 and 2004 revivals of the Parliament of the World's Religions, which, unlike the 1893 parliament, is a true multi-faith dialogue between all religions on an equal footing – one in which Hinduism itself has assumed a high profile.

Ram Das and Ma Jaya are contemporary Western illustrations of a more authentic, non-theosophical Hindu presence in the West – one which in particular is part of the popular impact of yoga beyond its Indian homeland. The Indian Hindu saint pioneering yoga in the West was Paramhansa Yogananda (1893–1952), who in 1925 established the international headquarters of the Self-Realisation Fellowship in Los Angeles to promote Kriyā Yoga meditation. Likewise, Ramana Maharshi (1879–1950), an Advaitin teacher who stressed that the ultimate purpose of life is self-realisation, has disseminated orthodox jñāna yoga from his Sri Ramanasramam centre of south India to California, New York, Nova Scotia, Italy and elsewhere throughout the world.

Another popular form of yogic practice is kuṇḍalinī yoga. Nityananda had founded the Ganeshapuri Ashram north-east of Mumbai/Bombay in 1949 as the centre for Siddha Yoga. Involved with both Ram Das and Werner Erhard, Nityananda-initiate Kashmiri Śaivite Swami Muktananda (1908–82) made world tours to Europe, America and/or Australia in 1970, 1974 and 1978 to establish hundreds of meditation centres. The Siddha [Yoga] Dham Associates Foundation was created in 1975. Muktananda's innovation, however, has been his stress on śaktipata initiation so that the kuṇḍalinī that resides at the base cakra can be aroused directly through the grace of the guru rather than strictly through the individual's own effort. This can occur through touch or simply by thought. Consequently, Muktananda promoted the notion of darśana, or the seeing of one's guru, as more important than advance through meditation itself, a practice that is followed by Ma Jaya as well. Muktananda designated Chidvilasananda (1956), known as Gurumayi, and her brother Swami Nityananda (1963–) as his successors. Nityananda renounced his saṃnyāsin vows and position in 1985, leaving his sister in control of the Siddha Dham despite his subsequent resumption of celibate status in 1989. Adi Da Samraj (Franklin Albert Jones, 1939–) is another initiate of Muktananda who acknowledged Adi Da's yogic liberation in the late 1960s/early 1970s. By 1986, Adi Da recognised his own divine self-'Emergence' as a 'World-Teacher'. Maintaining retreat centres in California, Hawaii and Fiji, Adi Da's devotees accept their guru as the promised 'God-Man' of the New Age. Another follower in the tradition of Muktananda is Harbhajan Singh Khalsa Yogiji (1929–), aka Yogi Bhajan, who established his Western Sikh movement in Los Angeles in 1969. Although not strictly Hindu, Yogi Bhajan focuses on kuṇḍalinī and tantric forms of yoga.

Some other influential Hindu figures in the West include both Sathya Sai Baba (1926–) and Hamsah Manarah (Gilbert Bourdin, 1923–98). Sai Baba affirms the truth and unity of all faiths as well as the ecumenical/interfaith elements of worship. Most Western devotees reject the label 'Hindu' and, denying that Sai Baba is a Hindu figure, emphasise instead his universal mission as a 'world teacher'. The movement concentrates on humanitarian service through 6,500 Sathya Sai Baba centres in over 137 countries. By contrast, Hamsah Manarah was a much different leader, similar in some respects to Ramakrishna in being initiated into various world religions, but in this case founding a colourful but much persecuted monastic centre, Cité Sainte de Mandarom Shambhasalem, in Castellane, France. The religion of Aumism recognises Hamsah Manarah as the Cosmoplanetary Messiah. Nevertheless, despite the Hindu input, the Aumists consider themselves, like the followers of Sai Baba, to include and transcend all particular religious expression. Two further Hindu or partially Hindu-derived movements found in the West are the Brahma Kumaris and the Aum Shinrikyo of Asahara Shoko (1955–). Asahara incorporated a blend of Hindu deities and yoga with the prophecies of Nostradamus and the Christian millenarian expectation of Armageddon. His Japanese-based movement that shot to fame through its involvement with the Tokyo subway sarin gas attack maintains additional membership in Russia, the United States, Germany and Sri Lanka. The Brahma Kumari World Spiritual Organisation, largely administered by women and teaching Rāja Yoga, was founded by Dada Lekhraj (Prajapita Brahma 1876–1969).

In particular contrast to figures like Asahara and Hamsah Manarah and their theosophical-like teachings concerning a divine cosmic hierarchy, the influential but secularised form of Hinduism is found chiefly in the post-Order of the Star of the East Krishnamurti and Sri Aurobindo (1872–1950). Both have nevertheless emphasised Hindu notions of oneness and growth. Whilst Adi Da holds that he is a conjunction with and rebirth of Swami Vivekananda, Aurobindo claimed that much of his inspiration came simply from communication with the deceased Vedāntic master. Aurobindo taught the practice of Integral Yoga (not to be confused with the Integral Yoga of Swami Satchidananda), a right-hand Tantric deep meditation based on quieting the mind in order to encounter the spaceless and timeless Brahman. Perhaps more importantly, Aurobindo's vision of spiritual consciousness as manifested in social reconstruction became the impetus behind the founding of the planned community model of Auroville in Pondicherry, India. This in turn has led to various educational centres being established chiefly in the United States. Aurobindo's disciple Haridas Chaudhuri founded the California Institute for Integral Studies in San Francisco. Within the framework of progressive education, students and Auroville residents are encouraged to serve 'Divine Consciousness'. Aurobindo's teachings have provided a substantial impetus and grounding behind New Age aspirations for the emergence of a 'planetary consciousness'. Linked to Aurobindo and Mira Richards (the Mother, 1878–1973), Aurobindo's spokesperson, is the popular Hindu guru Mother Meera (1960–), now residing in Germany. Known as a silent avatāra of the Divine Mother, Meera grants darśana but does not advocate meditation since, she contends, it can lead to spiritual pride. Operating without ashram or other external paraphernalia, she offers personal and silent service.

Consequently, Hindu influences on new religious movements range from those of traditional Eastern practice and ideas to those of the theosophical synthesis. Both have been seminal in the range of spiritual ideas which make up the New Age movement, but both exercise a popular impact that exists beyond the cultic milieu and reaches into mainstream society as well. Whether there is concern for personal growth and physical well-being through yoga or for a social evolution based on the spiritual insight concerning the oneness of humanity and ultimate reality, the social and consciousness transformations currently being sought in the West owe much of their seminal inspiration to Hinduism.

See also: **Advaita; Āśram(a) (religious community); Auroville; Avatāra; Āyurveda; Besant, Annie; Bhagavadgītā; Blavatsky, Helena; Brahma Kumaris; Brahman; Buddhism, relationship with Hinduism; Darśana; Divine Light Mission; Emerson, Ralph Waldo; Gandhi, Mohandas Karamchand; Ghose, Aurobindo; Guru; Homosexuality; Karma; Kashmiri Śaivism; Krishnamurti, Jiddu; Kriyā Yoga; Kuṇḍalinī Yoga; Lekhraj, Dada; Maharaj Ji, Guru (Prem Rawat); Maharishi Mahesh Yogi; Māyā; Meditation; Meera, Mother; Mokṣa; Muktananda, Swami; Olcott, Henry Steel; Radhasoami Satsang; Rāja Yoga; Ram Das; Ramakrishna Math and Mission; Ramakrishna, Sri; Ramana Maharshi; Ṛṣi; Sai Baba (as movement); Sai Baba, Sathya; Śakti; Saṃnyāsa; Sant Sādhana; Satchidananda, Swami and Integral Yoga; Satsaṅg; Siddha Dham; Sikhism, relationship with Hinduism; Soamiji Maharaj; Tantrism; Theosophy and the Theosophical Society; Transcendental Meditation; Vedānta; Viṣṇu; Vivekananda, Swami; Yoga; Yogananda, Paramhansa**

MICHAEL YORK

Further reading

Barker, Eileen. 1989. *New Religious Movements: A Practical Introduction*. London: Her Majesty's Stationery Office.

Bednarowski, Mary Farrell. 1989. *New Religions and the Theological Imagination in America*. Bloomington, IN: Indiana University Press.

Sullivan, Bruce M. 1997. *Historical Dictionary of Hinduism*. London: Scarecrow.

York, Michael. 1995. *The Emerging Network: A Sociology of the New Age and Neo-pagan Movements*. Lanham, MD: Rowman & Littlefield.

York, Michael. 2004. *Historical Dictionary of New Age Movements*. Lanham, MD: Scarecrow.

NIMBĀRKA (d. 1162?)

Nimbārka was the leader of a Vedāntic school of thought supporting the Kṛṣṇa-Rādhā cult of Vaiṣṇavism known as Svābhāvika Bhedābheda, or 'natural identity-in-difference', and also known as Dvaitādvaita. He is thought to have been a Telegu brāhmaṇa flourishing just after Rāmānuja and living mostly in Vṛndāvana. His compositions include a commentary on the *Brahmasūtras* entitled the *Vedāntapārijātasaurabha* and a statement of the essence of his system in the *Daśaślokī* or 'Ten Stanzas'. Nimbārka accepted the reality of Brahman, the animate individual self (jīva) and the inanimate world (jagat) existing in a relation of natural cause and effect. Brahman as Kṛṣṇa is the Inner Controller of both the individual, whose nature is cognition and enjoyer, and the world, which is the object of enjoyment.

See also: **Bhedābheda; Brahman; Brāhmaṇa; Brahmasūtras; Jīva; Kṛṣṇa; Rādhā; Rāmānuja; Vaiṣṇavism; Vedānta; Vṛndāvana**

ROBERT GOODDING

Further reading

Aghrawal, Madan Mohan. 1977. *The Philosophy of Nimbārka*. Sadabad (Mathura): Usha Agharwal.

Mishra, Umesha. 1966. *Nimbārka School of Vedānta*. Allahabad: Tirabhukti Publications.

NIRṚTIS

Nirṛtis are the three Vedic goddesses of disorder (nir-ṛta). The Nirṛtis are identified with destructive forces (*Ṛgveda* 10.36. 2, 4; 10.59. 1–4) and are invoked by those who seek their enemies' destruction (*Atharvaveda* 7.70). They represent every evil aspect of the nature. Men offer black pulses and black scarves (*Yajurveda* 1.8.1) to keep them away. A black hornless cow is offered in the house of the sacrificer's neglected wife (*Yajurveda* 1.8.9) and the oblation of fire is made on an altar of black bricks (*Yajurveda* 5.2.4). From post-Vedic times, Nirṛti, one of the Nirṛtis, became prominent. Nirṛti (the wife/daughter of Adharma, Disorder) is associated with old age, barrenness and disease (*Atharvaveda* 2.10; 3.11. 2; 7.53.3). Along with Mṛtyu (Death), she is the regent of the southern direction (*Yajurveda* 4.2.5). Inauspicious animals like owls and pigeons are her vehicles (*Atharvaveda* 6.27; 6.29).

See also: **Saṃhitā; Vedic pantheon**

FABRIZIO M. FERRARI

Further reading

Kinsley, D. 1986. *Hindu Goddesses: Vision of the Divine Feminine in the Hindu Religious Tradition*. Berkeley, CA and London: University of California Press.

NIRUKTA

The word nirukta in Sanskrit means 'explained'. In Indian religion it denotes etymologies that lend association and meaning to religious or philosophical terms. In this sense it is one of the six sciences or branches of knowledge (Vedāṅgas) employed in the elucidation of the Veda. It comes to have a more general application as a way of expanding the meaning of any name or term to arouse knowledge: nirukta are smṛti remembered, rather than śruti, or heard. The term is used first in Yāska's *Nirukta*, dating from around the fourth century BCE, which provides a commentary on the Veda. This work acknowledges earlier commentators on the subject but is the first text to treat etymologies in a systematic way. It divides words into four kinds, noun, verb, preposition and participle, and argues that all words can be reduced to their elements, called roots. So Viṣṇu is described as pervading, through the root viṣ, to pervade. Yāksa made significant contributions to etymology, philology and semantics in the modern sense, at a time when such disciplines were unknown in other parts of the world. Two modern stances, however, can limit an appreciation of his and others' nirukta. The first is that they should be assessed only for philological or historical accuracy. This kind of understanding does not accord with the ancient perception of the connectivity of language: two, three or more nirukta may be applied to one term without invalidating any of the others. The second is the low status modern culture accords to puns, despite their endless popularity. In ancient India etymologies based upon affinities between words were held in high esteem for revealing hidden associations between phenomena. In this sense nirukta, as a means of decoding sacred texts, came to be seen as providing a special and sometimes esoteric understanding of the divine.

See also: **Languages; Sacred texts; Veda; Vedāṅgas; Viṣṇu**

SARAH SHAW

Further reading

Kahrs, E. 1998. *Indian Semantic Analysis: The Nirvacana Tradition*. Cambridge: Cambridge University Press.

NIṢKRAMAṆA

One of the Hindu childhood saṃskāras, or rites of passage, the niṣkramaṇa, or first 'outing' of the child, was performed, according to most authorities, in the fourth month after birth. The ritual authorities do not all agree on the procedures, and some of the ritual schools do not include it at all. In this initiation of the child to the outside world, the father takes the child outside and makes him look at the sun or the moon, or both if possible. The father recites Vedic mantras that glorify the sun and homologise it with the eye, emphasising that the divine sun with its hundreds of rays dispels the darkness. He then offers rice cooked in milk, and other substances, to the sun. Alternatively, the mother bathes the child, after which both parents take him out to see the young but waxing moon on the third lunar day of the third month after birth. Following this the father makes offerings to the lunar deities.

See also: **Mantra; Saṃskāras**

FREDERICK M. SMITH

Further reading

Kane, P.V. 1974. *History of Dharmaśāstra*, 2nd edn, vol. 2, pt 1. Poona: Bhandarkar Oriental Research Institute, 255–56.

Pandey, R.J. 1969. *Hindu Saṃskāras*. Delhi: Motilal Banarsidass, 86–89.

NĪTIŚĀSTRAS

Nītiśāstras are Sanskrit works that deal with ethics and politics. One of the oldest *Nītiśāstras* is believed to have been written by a contemporary of Alexander, Acārya Viṣṇugupta (fourth century BCE), styled Cānakya, but better known as Kauṭilya. His compilation on morals, ethics and everyday wisdom was called the *Arthaśāstra*. The historical background of this particular *Nītiśāstra* is the division of the Indian subcontinent into a number of kingdoms called the Mahājanapādas and the inability of the regional rulers to unify to counter foreign attack. Cānakya made successful attempts to bring together a major part of these small regional kingdoms under the hegemony of Candragupta Maurya, the founder of the Maurya dynasty. Indian history records this as one of the subcontinent's most progressive ages, which in contemporary popular understanding is attributed to the implementation of the principles of Nītiśāstra (the science of conduct, especially statecraft).

Two other authors who composed treatises on Nītiśāstra are Kamandaka and

Śukracārya. Of the two, Kamandaka's work, tentatively dated around the fourth century CE, mentions Cānakya in its invocation and refers to him as one of the original teachers of Nītiśāstra.

The other popular texts which are categorised under the heading of Nītiśāstra are *Pañcatantra* and *Hitopadeśa*. Both these texts are a collection of short stories like Aesop's fables, illustrating wise and foolish conduct.

See also: **Artha; Arthaśāstra; Ethics; Kauṭilya; Pañcatantra; Politics**

ABHISHEK GHOSH

Further reading

Kangle, R.P. (ed./trans.). 1960–65. *The Kauṭilīya Artha Śāstra*, 3 vols. Bombay: University of Bombay (critical edition, English translation, study).

NIVEDITA, SISTER (1867–1911)

Born Margaret Elizabeth Noble in Ireland, Nivedita is renowned for her work on girls' education in India. She worked as a teacher in Ireland, but, having experienced doubts concerning the Christian faith, began to read about Buddhism. In 1895 she met Swami Vivekananda at the home of Lady Isabel Margesson and found him a source of inspiration. In 1897 she departed for Calcutta, arriving on 12 January 1898, where she began learning Bengali. She received the name Nivedita (literally, 'one who is dedicated') on receiving initiation on 25 March 1898.

In November of the same year Nivedita opened her girls' school in Calcutta; originally called the Nivedita School, it is now subsumed under Shri Sarada Math. She assisted with relief work during the plague in Calcutta in 1899, and later in the same year went back to Europe for the purpose of fundraising. She attempted to counter some of the misconceptions about India that had been perpetrated by Christian missionaries. Returning to India in 1901 Nivedita worked with Christine Greenstidel, from Germany, and extended her educational work to include women as well as girls. Famous visitors to her school included Ramsay Macdonald and Mahatma Gandhi.

Following Vivekananda's death in 1902, Nivedita felt a renewed responsibility to work in the service of India, working with the Indian independence movement. She introduced the national anthem, 'Vande (or Bande) Mataram' in her school, in preference to the British one. She encouraged indigenous Bengali art, providing funding for the art of Rabindrananth Tagore, Nandalal Bose and Asita Haldar. She forged links with members of the Brahmo Samaj, and Rabindranath Tagore found her a source of inspiration. Other close contacts with political leaders included Surendranath Bannerjea, Rama Chandra Dutt, Aurobindo Ghose, Gopalakrishna Gokhale and Bipin Chandra Pal.

See also: **Brahmo Samaj; Gandhi, Mohandas Karamchand; Ghose, Aurobindo; Gokhale, Gopal Krishna; Tagore, Rabindrananth; Vivekananda, Swami; Women's education**

GEORGE CHRYSSIDES

Further reading

Nivedita, Sister. 1910/1987. *The Master as I saw Him*, 14th edn. Calcutta: Udbodhan Office.

NIYOGA

Niyoga (literally, that which is joined together) was the intercourse of a childless widow and a man (usually the brother-in-law), with the permission of elders, for the sake of producing up to two children. This exception to adultery, common in *Mahābhārata* accounts of sonless royal families (largely due to death in battle), was carefully bounded by rules.

omparatively young, willing women practised niyoga – out of duty and ritually, not lustfully; otherwise, they were punished severely. From the beginning, this practice created ambiguity and debate over permissible substitutes for brothers-in-law, the status of sons so conceived and so on. By the first centuries CE, some authors condemned niyoga. Their position was reiterated in a list of prohibitions from the tenth century called Kalivarjya (things to be avoided in the Kaliyuga, a time when only one-quarter of righteousness remained according to the theory of the four yugas). After that, it was rarely mentioned.

See also: **Mahābhārata; Yuga**

KATHERINE K. YOUNG

Further reading

Crawford, S.C. 2003. *Hindu Bioethics for the Twenty-first Century*. Albany, NY: State University of New York Press.

Dhand, A. 2000. 'Poison, Snake, the Sharp Edge of a Razor: Yet the Highest of Gurus: Defining Female Sexuality in the Mahabharata'. Unpublished thesis, McGill University, Montreal.

Kane, P.V. 1968–77. *History of Dharmaśāstra (Ancient and Medieval Religious and Civil Law in India)*, 2nd edn, 5 vols. Poona: Bhandarkar Oriental Research Institute, esp. vol. 2.

Sharma, A. 2002. *The Hindu Tradition: Religious Beliefs and Healthcare Decisions* [handbook]. Religious Traditions and Healthcare Decisions Series. Park Ridge, IL: Park Ridge Centre.

van Buitenen, J.A.B. (trans. and ed.). 1973. *The Mahābhārata: 1. The Book of the Beginning*. Chicago, IL: University of Chicago.

Young, K.K. 2007. *A History of Medical Ethics*, eds R.B. Baker and L.B. McCullough. Cambridge: Cambridge University Press.

NOBILI, ROBERTO DE (1577–1656)

Of aristocratic Italian birth, de Nobili is perhaps the greatest of all missionary scholars of Hinduism. Arguing that caste was essentially a social, rather than religious, institution, he pioneered in India the method of 'adaptation' of Christianity to prevailing social norms that had earlier been practised in the Jesuit missions in China. For de Nobili this meant adopting as much of the lifestyle of a brāhmaṇa as was compatible with Christianity, including dress, diet and restrictions on contact with those of lower caste. The method both required and enabled a profound study of Hinduism. A prolific author, who left writings in six languages (Tamil, Telegu, Sanskrit, Latin, Portuguese and Italian), several of his works on Hinduism are concerned with the defence of his methods against critics within and beyond the Society of Jesus. Like many other Christian authors on Hinduism, de Nobili was particularly drawn to Advaitic forms of Hindu thinking, which were seen as less polytheistic and less concerned with image worship. Many of de Nobili's works which were long thought to have been lost have been rediscovered and published by S. Rajamanickam, SJ.

See also: **Advaita; Hinduism, history of scholarship**

WILL SWEETMAN

Further reading

Amaladass, A. and F.X. Clooney (eds and trans.). 2000. *Preaching Wisdom to the Wise: Three Treatises by Roberto de Nobili*. Saint Louis, MO: Institute of Jesuit Sources.

Rajamanickam, S. (ed.). 1971. *Roberto de Nobili on Adaptation* [1619. *Narratio Fundamentorum quibus Madurensis Missionis Institutum caeptum est et hucusque consistit*]. Trans. J. Pujo. Palayamkottai: De Nobili Research Institute.

Saulière, A. 1995. *His Star in the East*. Madras: De Nobili Research Institute.

NYĀYA

Nyāya is one of the six traditional systems of Hindu philosophy. Its metaphysical teachings relate to the Vaiśeṣika school. It accepts karma and liberation (mokṣa). The word 'Nyāya' signifies argumentation, method or reasoning and indicates the school's preoccupation with problems and themes of logic and epistemology. With origins in the ancient tradition of debate (vāda), the Nyāya school developed over many centuries and has generated a vast literature. It teaches four distinct means or instruments of valid knowledge (pramāṇas): perception (pratyakṣa), inference (anumāna), comparison or analogy (upamāna), and verbal knowledge or testimony (śabda).

Modern scholarship on Nyāya has led to increasing awareness of its teachings, one focus being the relation of Nyāya to Western philosophy in the Analytic tradition.

Nyāya texts and authors

The *Nyāyasūtras* form the basic text of the school and the *Nyāyabhāṣya* (Commentary on Nyāya) of Pakṣilvāmin Vātsyāyana (fifth century CE) is the earliest surviving commentary on it. Vātsyāyana was responding to the critique of the means of knowledge (pramāṇas) by the Buddhist philosopher Nāgārjuna (second century CE). He sought to defend Nyāya realism (everyday objects such as trees and chairs are directly perceived) and established a philosophical basis for later Nyāya thinkers and their engagement with Buddhist critics.

The *Nyāyavārttika* (Supplementary Commentary on Nyāya) of Uddyotakara (sixth century CE) is a response to the critique of Vātsyāyana by the Buddhist logician Dignāga (*c.*480–*c.*540 CE). A Pāśupata teacher, Uddyotakara developed Nyāya theism. Later, Udayana contributed arguments for God's existence in his *Nyāyakusumāñjali* (Handful of Nyāya Flowers). Vācaspati Miśra commented on Uddyotakara's *Nyāyavārttika*, producing the *Nyāyavārttikatātparyatīkā* (Commentary on the True Intention of the Nyāyavārttika). The *Nyāyavārttikatātparyapariśuddhi* (Clarification of the True Intention of the Nyāyavārttika) of Udayana is a commentary on Vācaspati's text.

The *Nyāyamañjarī* (Cluster of Nyāya Blossoms) by Jayanta Bhatta (ninth century) is an example of an independent classical Nyāya work. The *Nyāyasāra* (Essence of Nyāya) is a work of Bhāsarvajña (tenth century).

Gaṅgeśa Upādhyāya, author of *Tattvacintāmaṇi* (Jewel of Reflection on the Nature of Things), established the Navya-Nyāya ('New Logic') school. Important later Nyāya thinkers include Raghunātha (fifteenth to sixteenth century) and Gadādhara (seventeenth century).

Epistemological teachings

The realistic Nyāya regards objects of valid knowledge as existing independently of the knower and the cognitive process. The distinct factors in our knowledge include the subject (pramātṛ) and object (prameya), the state of cognition (pramiti) and the four means of knowledge (pramāṇa). Valid knowledge (pramā) for Nyāya corresponds to reality; it is right apprehension of an object (yathārthānubhavaḥ) or an object revealed as it is. It leads to 'successful activity' (pravṛttisāmarthya).

Whereas perception, inference, comparison and testimony deliver valid knowledge, memory (smṛti) and 'tarka' ('hypothetical reasoning' or 'conditional proof') are not accepted as separate sources of valid knowledge. For example, in the case of memory no new knowledge is provided; it reproduces previous experience. As a representative rather than presentative cognition, memory cannot be valid. Doubt (saṃśaya), error (viparyaya) and illusion (bhrama) are further instances of invalid knowledge. In the case of error there is no correspondence to reality; it is misapprehension.

Perception is defined in the *Nyāyasūtras* as non-erroneous cognition resulting from sense–object contact. The mind (manas) and self (ātman) have a role in the perceptual process; that is, perception involves self–manas contact and manas–sense contact. The mind mediates between the self and senses. Thus in the case of the perception of a pencil, the manas carries the impressions arising from the contact of the sense organs and pencil to the self, and the knowledge 'that is a pencil' arises.

There are two stages in perception. The earlier stage is 'indeterminate' (nirvikalpa) perception, which is mere sensation or apprehension of an object as an uncharacterised 'something'. The second is 'determinate' (savikalpa) perception, which is perceptual knowledge or judgement, clear perception of an object with its qualities or attributes. For Vātsyāyana, determinate perception is perceiving an object with its name. For Gaṅgeśa Upādhyāya, indeterminate perception is non-relational apprehension of an object without association of name, genus, etc.

Nyāya distinguishes between 'ordinary' (laukika) and 'extraordinary' (alaukika) perception. There are two kinds of ordinary perception, 'internal' (mānasa) and 'external' (bāhya). In external perception, there is contact between external objects and the five sense organs. Mind (manas), or the 'internal organ', has its own objects; in internal perception there is contact between mind and states or processes such as pain (duḥkha), pleasure (sukha), cognition, desire (icchā), aversion (dveṣa) and so on. Extraordinary perception includes perception of universals (sāmānyalaksaṇā), cognition through association (jñānalaksaṇā) and yogic perception (yogaja).

Inference is knowledge (māna) which follows or arises after (anu) other knowledge. Essential to inference is 'vyāpti' or 'avinābhāvaniyama' (the major premise, 'universal connection' or 'invariable concomitance'). For example, due to knowledge of the universal connection between smoke and fire, the presence of smoke on the hill leads us to conclude that there is a fire on the hill. A key feature of Nyāya inference is its stress on the 'example' (dṛṣtānta). Scholars have emphasised Nyāya's concern for material truth as well as formal validity. The classical Nyāya form of inference or syllogism is as follows:

1 The hut has fire.
2 Because it smokes.
3 Whatever smokes has fire (e.g. a kitchen).
4 This hut also smokes.
5 Therefore this hut has fire.

Here, hut is the minor term (pakṣa), fire is the major term (sādhya) and smoke is the middle term (liṅga or hetu). The first statement is the thesis or proposition to be proved (pratijñā). The second is the 'reason' (hetu). The third member (avayava) of the syllogism indicates the universal concomitance, plus an example (udāharaṇa). The fourth statement is the 'application' (upanaya) and the fifth is the conclusion (nigamana).

Concerning the remaining pramāṇas, comparison is the means by which we acquire knowledge of something based on its similarity to another thing already known; it is knowledge of the connection between a word and its denotation. 'Śabda' concerns authoritative verbal testimony, apprehension of the meaning of a statement of a trustworthy person (āptavākya); it includes the Veda and ordinary linguistic communication.

See also: **Ātman; Buddhism, relationship with Hinduism; Karma; Manas; Mokṣa; Nyāyasūtras; Pāśupatas; Pramāṇas; Udayana; Vācaspati Miśra; Vaiśeṣika; Vātsyāyana, Pakṣilavāmin; Veda**

MARTIN OVENS

Further reading

Matilal, B.K. 1986. *Perception: An Essay on Classical Indian Theories of Knowledge.* Oxford: Clarendon Press.

Vattanky, J. 1993. *Development of Nyāya Theism.* New Delhi: Intercultural Publications.

NYĀYALĪLĀVATĪ

The *Nyāyalīlāvatī* (The Charm of Nyāya) is an independent work in the Vaiśeṣika tradition of Hindu philosophy. The author, Vallabha or Vallabhācārya, may have lived in the first half of the twelfth century.

Little is known about the life of Vallabha. He may have studied in Banaras. His work was named after his wife, Līlāvatī.

Nyāyalīlāvatī has four chapters and seventy-five sections. Vallabha analyses the Vaiśeṣika categories and subcategories in the first chapter (which is the longest, consisting of fifty-eight sections). He devotes eighteen sections to the theory of knowledge, which, according to Matilal (1977), may have inspired Gaṅgeśa to write the *Tattvacintāmaṇi* (Jewel of Reflection on Reality). Vallabha defends the Vaiśeṣika system of categories against various objections in the fourth chapter.

Important philosophers of the Navya-Nyāya ('New Logic') school were attracted to the *Nyāyalīlāvatī* and several commentaries and subcommentaries were written on it.

See also: **Gaṅgeśa Upādhyāya; Nyāya; Vaiśeṣika**

MARTIN OVENS

Further reading

Matilal, B.K. 1977. *Nyāya-Vaiśesika, A History of Indian Literature*, vol. 6: *Scientific and Technical Literature.* Wiesbaden: Otto Harrassowitz.

NYĀYASŪTRAS

The *Nyāya Sūtras* (Aphorisms on Nyāya) form the root text of the Nyāya school of Hindu philosophy. The author of the *sūtras*, and founder of Nyāya, is usually referred to as 'Gautama' or 'Gotama' but the date and identity of this personage have never been established.

According to the commentator Pakṣilavāmin Vātsyāyana, the founder of Nyāya was 'Akṣapāda' (literally meaning 'eyes in his feet'). It has been suggested that an Akṣapāda mentioned in the *Brahmāṇḍa Purāṇa* was the author of the final version of the *Nyāyasūtras.*

Scholars have proposed that the text of the *Nyāyasūtras* built up in stages. Suggested dates for the final form have ranged from the second to the fourth centuries CE.

The *Nyāyasūtras* are divided into five chapters or 'books' (adhyāyas) and each chapter has two sections. Topics include the means of valid knowledge (perception, inference, comparison and verbal testimony) and the syllogism.

See also: **Nyāya; Pramāṇas; Purāṇas; Vātsyāyana, Paksilavāmin**

MARTIN OVENS

Further reading

Jha, G. (trans). 1984. *The Nyāya-Sūtras of Gautama with the Bhāsya of Vātsyāyana and the Vārtika of Uddyotakara, Indian Thought.* Delhi: Motilal Banarsidass, 4–11.

NYĀYA-VAIŚEṢIKA

Nyāya and Vaiśeṣika are two of the six traditional schools of Hindu philosophy. Closely intertwined, they reflect a realist and analytical tradition of thinking.

Vaiśeṣika concentrated on physics and metaphysics or ontology: it was concerned to describe reality. Nyāya thinkers concentrated on logic and epistemology or theory of knowledge: they were concerned to analyse knowledge of reality.

Vaiśeṣika is viewed as 'similar philosophy' (samānatantra) to Nyāya; they are often described as 'allied' or 'sister' schools. In this connection scholars usually indicate standpoints and doctrines shared by the schools, including realism (with respect to, for example, things and relations), pluralism, atomistic cosmology and theism.

However, differences between the schools have been highlighted. Umesh Mishra listed nineteen points of disagreement between Nyāya and Vaiśeṣika. Among these disagreements are Nyāya admitting four means of knowledge (pramāṇas) and Vaiśeṣika accepting only two. Many of the differences between the schools have been regarded as minor.

It has been maintained that a similar background in relation to the philosophy of nature explains the similarity between classical Nyāya's ontology and that of Vaiśeṣika. Scholars have pointed to the presence of classical Vaiśeṣika ontology in the historically later parts of the *Nyāyasūtras.* In their early history the schools developed independently in the sense that they continued with their own authors, texts and commentators, although scholars have traced mutual influences and borrowing of doctrines as far back as Praśastapāda (possibly sixth century CE), author of the *Padārthadharmasaṃgraha*, and Uddyotakara (sixth century), author of the *Nyāyavārttika* (Supplementary Commentary on Nyāya).

The fusion of Vaiśeṣika and Nyāya (and hence the syncretistic school now referred to as 'Nyāya-Vaiśeṣika') has been traced to Udayana (author of commentaries on works of both systems) and a common affiliation to Śaivism. An example of a syncretistic text attempting to combine both schools is Varadarāja's twelfth-century *Tārkikarakṣā* (In Defence of the Logician).

See also: **Nyāya; Nyāyasūtras; Padārthadharmasaṃgraha; Pramāṇas; Śaivism; Udayana; Vaiśeṣika**

MARTIN OVENS

Further reading

Potter, K.H. (ed.). 1977. *Encyclopedia of Indian Philosophies, Indian Metaphysics and Epistemology: The Tradition of Nyāya-Vaiśeṣka up to Gangeśa.* Delhi: Motilal Banarsidass.

O

OCEANIA, HINDUS IN

The time of arrival of the first Hindus in Oceania is speculated to be around the last two decades of the eighteenth century. The British brought the first Hindus from India to Australia and Fiji to work as labourers in the sugar and cotton plantations. Later on, these Hindus stayed on and currently make up a sizable percentage of the population in Fiji (http://www.statsfiji.gov.fj/).

One of the first organised Hindu groups in Fiji, where the Hindu population has been larger than any other country in Oceania, was the Arya Samaj and they began by establishing schools and their periodical *Fiji Samachar* in 1923. Two of the first legislators, Vishnu Deo and Parmanand Singh, were staunch preachers of the Arya Samaj movement, but their ideologies differed from the general Hindu sentiments as they denounced the various deities and criticised idol worship. The Arya Samaj also promoted the idea of forced conversion of Muslims back to Hinduism, leading to its unpopularity among many sections of Fijian society. According to 1996 census information the majority of Hindus in Fiji are described as 'Sanatan' (http://www.statsfiji.gov.fj/Social/religion_stats.htm)

The Arya Samaj later inspired the formation of Kisan Sangh, a Hindu farmer wing actively involved with Fijian politics, mobilising the freedom movement from the colonial government. The Arya Samaj also inspired the formation of Maha Sangh, a political group, formed around the mid-1940s, which encouraged the Hindus in Fiji to fight against the colonial government.

Since the 1960s and 1970s, some of the New Religious Movements have put down roots in Oceania. One of the popular gurus, especially in New Zealand and Fiji, is Sathya Sai Baba of Puttaparthi. However, lately the number of his followers has declined due to negative publicity in the media. Another popular influence has been the International Society for Krishna Consciousness (ISKCON), which has been very active since the 1970s. Based on the Gauḍīya Vaiṣṇava tradition, this movement has lately attracted a huge number of Hindus all over Oceania and has been actively proselytising among the non-Hindus of Oceania.

See also: **Arya Samaj; Australasia, Hindus in; Deities; Conversion; Guru; Idolatry; Image worship; International Society for Krishna Consciousness; Sai Baba (as movement); Sai Baba, Sathya; Sanātana Dharma; Vaiṣṇavism**

ABHISHEK GHOSH

Further reading

Jacobsen, Knut A. and P. Pratap Kumar (eds). 2004. *South Asians in the Diaspora*. Leiden: Brill Academic Publishers.

Rukmani, T.S. (ed.). 1999. *Hindu Diaspora: Global Perspectives*. Montreal: Concordia University.

http://www.statsfiji.gov.fj/ (accessed 31 July 2006).

http://www.statsfiji.gov.fj/Social/religion_stats.htm (accessed 31 July 2006).

OLCOTT, HENRY STEEL (1823–1907)

Colonel Henry Steel Olcott was co-founder (with H.P. Blavatsky) and first President of the Theosophical Society. He was responsible for the constitutional and structural development of the Society as a worldwide body. He encouraged a Buddhist revival in Ceylon (now Sri Lanka), with particular emphasis on the establishment of Buddhist schools. He also worked to bring about dialogue between different schools of Buddhism in Asia. In India he promoted the revival of Sanskrit studies and Hindu schools, libraries, journals and encouragement of Indian arts and crafts. In 1897 he established the Adyar Library at the new headquarters of the Theosophical Society near Madras (Chennai). He encouraged the acquisition of Oriental books and manuscripts which formed the basis of a collection which continues to be a centre of excellence in the field to the present day.

See also: **Blavatsky, Helena; Theosophy and the Theosophical Society**

KEVIN TINGAY

OLDENBERG, HERMANN (1856–1920)

German Sanskritist and historian of religions. Oldenberg trained in classical and Sanskrit philology at Berlin, and was professor at Kiel from 1889 and Göttingen from 1908. Although perhaps best known for his work on Pāli Buddhist texts, Oldenberg worked also on Vedic texts, especially the hymns of the *Ṛgveda Saṃhitā* and the *Gṛhyasūtras,* translations of which he contributed to the *Sacred Books of the East.* He was among the first to use ethnographic data in understanding Vedic textual material. Oldenberg, who died before the excavations began in the Indus Valley which first seriously put an Aryan migration into question, opened his account of the religion of the Veda (Oldenburg 1894) with an emphatic statement of the then dominant theory of the migration of the Aryans into India and their resultant dissociation from the 'healthy manliness' of the Western nations through mixing with the 'dark-skinned primitives of India' (Oldenburg 1988: 1). Among Oldenberg's later publications are works on the *Upaniṣads*, the *Brāhmaṇas* and the *Mahābhārata*.

See also: **Brāhmaṇas; Gṛhyasūtras; Hinduism, history of scholarship; Mahābhārata; Sacred Books of the East; Saṃhitā; Upaniṣads**

WILL SWEETMAN

Further reading

Oldenberg, H. 1886–92. *The Grihya-sutras, Rules of Vedic Domestic Ceremonies*, 2 vols (*Sacred Books of the East*, 29 and 30). Oxford: Clarendon Press.

Oldenberg, H. 1894. *Die Religion des Veda.* [The Religion of the Veda] Berlin: W. Hertz.

Oldenberg, H. 1897. *Vedic Hymns* (*Sacred Books of the East*, 46). Oxford: Clarendon Press.
Oldenberg, H. 1988. *The Religion of the Veda.* Trans. S.B. Shrotri. Delhi: Motilal Banarsidass Publishers.

OṂ

The sacred syllable ॐ 'Oṃ', or 'Aum', has an important role in a variety of Hindu rituals and practices and is represented by one of the most recognisable symbols in Hinduism. Oṃ is taught and elaborated upon in the *Upaniṣads.* It has been taken to symbolise the totality of the manifested world and Brahman itself; it is the 'primal' or 'primordial' sound.

Oṃ has been called 'ekaksara' ('the one syllable' or 'the imperishable one') and 'praṇava' (signifying a droning utterance). A combination or contraction of three sounds ('a', 'u' and 'm'), its utterance generates a solemn, humming vibration. Oṃ has been taken to represent various groups of three, for example Brahmā ('a'), Viṣṇu ('u') and Śiva ('m').

Oṃ has been referred to as a prayer or mantra in itself or the 'seed' (bīja) of all mantras. It is used for blessings and invocations; it is uttered at the beginning and end of prayers and meditation. Its articulation at the conclusion as well as the beginning of a lesson on the Veda (or recitations of passages from the Veda) preserves the knowledge gained and ensures that the merit will not be lost.

The symbol of Oṃ is omnipresent in Hindu society. As well as finding a place in family shrines and holy sites, it features in a range of everyday, practical contexts; thus it may be worn on the body or found at the head of letters. Moreover, Oṃ is articulated in the course of daily, routine activities; thus it is uttered before the start of the working day or when setting out on a journey.

Among *Upaniṣads* containing teachings on Oṃ are the *Chāndogya*, *Taittirīya* and *Mundaka.* In addition the *Māṇḍūkya Upaniṣad* treats the symbolism of the sacred syllable. It teaches four states of consciousness of the soul and relates them to Oṃ and its constituent elements or sounds. The *Māṇḍūkya* begins by declaring that the past, present and future are included in Oṃ and that whatever is beyond 'threefold time' is also Oṃ. The first element of the sacred syllable ('a') corresponds to the waking state. The dream state corresponds to the second letter, 'u'. And the third element of Oṃ ('m') relates to the state of dreamless or profound sleep. Transcending the three states is 'the fourth' (caturtha), which in Gaudapāda's *kārikās* (verses) on the *Māṇḍūkya* is known as 'turīya' (this came to be the standard term). In his commentary on the *Māṇḍūkya*, Śaṅkara says that the fourth is the pure ātman (Self) beyond speech and mind, representing the bliss of non-duality, the final dissolution of the world. It is represented by a dot in the symbol of Oṃ, separated from waking, dream and dreamless sleep (represented by three curves) by an arc or semi-circle.

Meditation on Oṃ is meditation on the different levels of consciousness and being. Śaṅkara takes up the Upaniṣadic imagery of an arrow (the empirical self) shot into the target (turīya). Oṃ is the bow that enables the 'arrow' ('sharpened' by meditation) to unite with the imperishable reality.

See also: **Ātman; Brahmā; Brahman; Gauḍapāda; Mantra; Śaṅkara; Śiva; Upaniṣads; Veda; Viṣṇu**

MARTIN OVENS

Further reading

Hume, R.E. (trans.). 1995. *The Thirteen Principal Upanishads.* Oxford: Oxford India Paperback.

ONAM

The Onam festival marks the Malayali new year. It is centred on tiruvōṇam, the twenty-first lunar asterism in the solar month of Cinnam (August–September). Mythologically, it celebrates the annual recreation of the orderly kingdom ruled over by Mahabali, a demon king dethroned by Vāmana, the dwarf avatāra of Viṣṇu. Mahabali promised Vāmana as much land as he could cover in three paces, whereupon Viṣṇu bestrode the whole of heaven, sky and earth. Even so, Mahabali ('great sacrifice') honoured his bargain, and achieved redemption in return for this demonstration of devotion and generosity.

Onam is commonly described as a harvest festival, but is celebrated publicly in many different ways throughout Kerala, often involving forms of competitive display, such as boat races on the Pampa river at Aranmulla, dance-dramas at Cheruthuruthy and elephant processions at Trichur. Above all, it is celebrated domestically. Children construct floral seats outside their homes to house the deity Onattappan during his annual visit. Migrant workers return home for feasting, just as ancestor spirits (pitṛs) are believed to do, and household heads distribute presents to family members. Landlords and other patrons also exchange gifts with their labourers and hereditary artisans.

Despite its Hindu associations, Onam is celebrated by all communities, which is largely why it has come to be officially represented as the defining Kerala state festival. Innumerable websites managed by Non-Resident Indians show that it serves as a synecdoche of cultural identity for the Malayali diaspora overseas, too. Its close mythological links with notions of dharma also make it a potent political symbol, susceptible of various interpretations and hence capable of validating a diverse array of political projects. Officially sponsored Onam celebrations generally seek to represent pluralism, equality and social justice as defining features of Malayali society and culture.

See also: **Calendar; Dance; Dharma; Diaspora; Drama; Pitṛs; Utsava; Viṣṇu**

ANTHONY GOOD

Further reading

Kurup, A.M. 1977. 'The Sociology of Onam'. *Indian Anthropology* 7: 95–110.

Osella, F. and C. Osella. 2001. 'The Return of King Mahabali: The Politics of Morality in Kerala'. In C.J. Fuller and V. Bénéï, eds, *The Everyday State & Society In Modern India*. London: Hurst & Company, 137–62.

Tarabout, G. 1986. *Sacrifier et Donner à Voir en Pays Malabar: les fêtes de temple au Kerala (Inde du sud): étude anthropologique*. [Sacrifice and Display in Malabar: An Anthropological Study of Temple Festivals in Kerala, South India]. Paris: Ecole française d'Extrême-Orient.

Thurston, E. and K. Rangachari. 1987 [1909]. *Castes and Tribes of Southern India*, vol. V. New Delhi: Asian Educational Services, 371–76.

ORANGE PEOPLE

See: **Rajneesh Movement**

ORIENTALISM

The Orientalism debate

In 1978 Edward Said (1935–2003), professor of comparative literature at Columbia University, published his influential work *Orientalism. Western Conceptions of the Orient*. In this study Said offered an analysis of Orientalism as a discourse founded upon a binary opposition between 'East' and 'West'. His book offered a sweeping critique of Western notions of 'the Orient' and the ways in which Orientalism has legitimated the colonial aggression and political supremacy of Western nations. According to Said, there are three dimensions to the phenomenon he calls 'Orientalism'. First, we have what one might call the everyday meaning of the term, denoting the academic study of the Orient. Second, Orientalism represents a specific mindset or 'style of thought' that divides the world up into a rigid dichotomy between 'East' and 'West'. Third, the term, as he uses it, refers to the corporate institution authorised to dominate, control and subjugate the peoples and cultures of the East (Said 1978: 2–3). For Said all three dimensions are intertwined by virtue of the complicity between Western discourses about the Orient and Western colonialism. Orientalism therefore denotes a 'Western style for dominating, restructuring, and having authority over the Orient' (Said 1978: 3).

Orientalism and Indology

The legacy of Said's work can be seen in the birth of postcolonial studies and colonial discourse analysis, fields of study and approaches that have now extended their influence beyond literary studies to the arts and humanities in general. Edward Said's examples were mainly taken from the West Asian (or 'Middle Eastern') context, no doubt a reflection of his own Palestinian origins, and it has been left to others to explore the implications of his work further afield. In such a context the study of South Asian history and culture has come under increasing scrutiny in terms of the issues of the ongoing reproduction of colonialist tropes about Asians and their cultures. In recent years, with the publication of Willhelm Halbfass' work *India and Europe. An Essay in Understanding* (1988), Ronald Inden's *Imagining India* (1990) and Richard King's *Orientalism and Religion* (1999), the Orientalist problematic has been discussed in relation to the study of Hindu religion and philosophy.

Ronald Inden (1986, 1990) argues that Indology (the study of ancient Indian texts) has tended to portray Indian thoughts, institutions and practices as aberrations of 'normative' (that is, Western) modes of living. Such scholarship, he suggests, places Hindus in a subjugated position as objects and has often based itself upon a systematic study of Hindu sacred literature as the key to uncovering the essential features of 'the Indian mind'. Such accounts also tend to carry with them the claim, on the part of the Western scholar, to be able to intuit the specific 'nature' or 'essence' of Indian culture in a way that may not be discernible to the indigenous Indian subject under analysis. Of course it has always been the aim of good scholarship, whether Western or Indian, to consider the big picture rather than lose oneself in the specifics, and this has been one of the key tasks of specialists seeking to study the long history of movements, cultures and traditions. Richard G. Fox (1992: 144–45) criticises Inden for his condemnation of 'all South Asian scholarship as Orientalist'. Fox (and others such as Wilhelm Halbfass) argues that Inden replicates the same tendency to stereotype in his own portrayal of Orientalist scholarship that he attributes to Orientalist accounts of India. Inden's analysis, however, like Said's before him, has clearly touched on a raw nerve in contemporary scholarship and the issues he brings up are unlikely to go away. Particularly important is Inden's call for a rejection of essentialist approaches to the study of India that seek to speak about entire cultures and traditions in homogeneous terms, as in references to 'the Hindu mind' or 'Hindus believe this' or 'Hindus do that'.

Debating the Bengali Renaissance

Such has been the influence of Edward Said's work in this area that the term 'Orientalism' is most often used today as a pejorative term denoting a Western colonialist attitude towards Asian culture in general. However, Orientalism in the purely descriptive sense of 'the academic study of the Orient' (the first of Said's three aspects of the total phenomenon of

Orientalism) has a specific meaning and origin in the context of the study of India, referring to the academic discipline that came into existence with the founding of the Asiatic Society of Bengal in 1784. It is the work of members of the Asiatic Society, led by Sir William Jones, judge of the East India Company, that has been credited by many as the primary catalyst in what has become known as 'the Bengali Renaissance' – a burgeoning intellectual interest in Hindu culture and an accompanying reformist spirit amongst the Bengali intelligentsia of the nineteenth century.

David Kopf, a historian of this period, criticises Said explicitly for 'dropping names, dates and anecdotes' and for adopting a method that is 'diametrically opposed to history' (Kopf 1980: 499). In contrast to what he sees as Said's excessively negative account of Western scholarship on the East, Kopf argues that the early Orientalists were in fact 'men of social action, working to modernise Hindu culture from within' (ibid.: 502). The real target of Said's critique, Kopf argues, should be groups like the Anglicists, led by the redoubtable Thomas B. Macauley, for whom 'a single shelf of a good European library was worth the whole native literature of India and Arabia'. However, Kopf appears to be misreading Said's thesis here. For Said, whether approving or critical in its appraisal, Orientalist discourse is based upon the questionable premise that there is an unbreachable dichotomy between 'East' and 'West'. All Orientalist discourses are implicated in wider political contexts and the problem with the Orientalist approach from Said's perspective is *systemic* rather than a question of the positive or negative attitudes expressed towards India by individual Orientalists.

Nevertheless, Kopf emphasises the dispute between the Anglicists and the Orientalists to show that many Orientalists were in many respects 'pro-Indian' and therefore, in Kopf's eyes at least, free from a Western colonial agenda. It is here that Ronald Inden's analysis makes an important intervention in the debate. Inden describes the 'affirmative Orientalism' that Kopf appeals to here as 'the Loyal Opposition'. Such approaches reproduce romantic stereotypes of India grounded in a deep affection for, and sometimes even a firm belief in the superiority of, Indian culture. Such romantic Indophilia, however, generally fails to challenge the idea that India is a kind of the mirror-opposite of Europe. According to Inden, in such cases we are still in the realm of talking about cultural 'essences' and a binary opposition between East and West. Such approaches still involved the projection of stereotypical ideas about India that serve to distinguish the British coloniser from the colonised subject, however well intentioned and 'positive' some of these images may have been at the time.

One of the problems with much of the debate surrounding 'Orientalism' has been the tendency for some to treat it as a purely Western phenomenon or 'disease'. This has led to a misreading and misappropriation of Said's thesis as somehow authorising 'insider' perspectives alone. From this standpoint one encounters a characteristic dismissal of any analysis or criticism offered by Western 'outsiders' (now pejoratively labelled 'the Orientalists') as irredeemably implicated in a colonialist agenda. This simplistic appropriation of Said's thesis in many ways perpetuates the binary opposition that he sought to displace. It also obfuscates issues of power and authority within such 'insider communities', as summarised in the question 'who speaks for Hinduism?'

Ironically, such approaches also tend to reinforce the myth that the indigenous 'Oriental' has no agency in the construction of Orientalist forms of knowledge. In response to such accounts Richard King (1999) draws attention to the role of indigenous brahmanical elites in the construction of Orientalist notions of Hinduism. Similarly, Buddhist scholar Charles Hallisey has argued that we should see the construction of Orientalist knowledge about Asia as the result of a localised process of *intercultural mimesis*. This refers to the subtle lines of cultural negotiation, mirroring and replication that take place when Western Orientalists and native informants interact to produce 'authentic knowledge' about India. Hallisey argues that we should avoid the tendency to 'interpret Orientalist representations as being primarily embedded in European culture', by paying attention to the local production of meaning (Hallisey 1995: 50). In this way a more nuanced understanding of the complex relations between coloniser and colonised in the production of Orientalist knowledge can be gained.

Is 'Hinduism' a colonial invention?

The notion of 'Hinduism' is of relatively recent provenance and the usefulness of this category has become a key debating point in recent scholarship on Hindu traditions. The word 'Hindoo' (Hindu) is the Persian variant of the Sanskrit sindhu (referring to the Indus river) and was used by the Persians to denote the people of that region. Indigenous use of the term by the native populations of India seems to exist in the fifteenth and sixteenth centuries, but this seems to be largely a result of interaction with Persian Muslims and does not seem to have meant anything more than a term to denote 'indigenous' or 'native' peoples (for a counter view, see Lorenzen 1999, where it is argued that Hindu self-consciousness can be found as early as the fourteenth century). Through such contacts 'Hindu' came to be contrasted with much older terms such as 'mleccha', denoting foreigners. In the eighteenth century it was common to find references to 'Hindoo Christians' or 'Hindoo Muslims' and there appears to have been no explicitly 'religious' connotations to the term (Frykenberg 1991: 131). Amongst Europeans the term gradually supplanted earlier words such as 'Gentoos' (an alternative to 'heathen) and 'Banians' (a reference to the merchant classes of Northern India).

The coining of the term 'Hinduism' to denote a system of beliefs and practices common to 'the Hindus' does not appear to have emerged until the late eighteenth to early nineteenth century. Rammohan Roy, founder of the Brahmo Samaj, one of the emerging Hindu reformist movements of the nineteenth century, and often called 'the father of modern India', is perhaps the first Hindu to use the term, in 1816, at the same time as his first visit to the Baptist missionaries of Serampore. Geoffrey Oddie notes that the term had already been employed by Charles Grant (an evangelical Christian and later to be director of the East India Company) in correspondence as early as 1787. Similarly, in an entry in his diary in February 1801, the Baptist missionary William Ward refers to a pamphlet directed against 'Hindooism' composed by an Indian convert to Christianity. The term 'Hinduism' (if not necessarily *the idea* underlying it, namely that there is a single 'Hindoo religion') first seems to have appeared in a Protestant missionary context and entered the Hindu popular lexicon through reformist (and Christian-influenced) figures such as Roy. The spread of the term and the reification that its popularised usage encouraged became highly significant in the struggle for social, political and moral authority in a British colonial context. It provided a basic category for the British colonial administration to make sense of the panoply of Hindu movements and practices, a foil for Christian missionaries to debate and decry, and a rallying point for colonised and subalternised Hindus. Later the term and its homogenising associations would play a crucial role in mobilising anti-colonialist struggles against the British and in forging a modern 'Hindu' national identity in nineteenth- and twentieth-century India.

One of the debates that has emerged from consideration of the history of the term 'Hinduism' has focused upon the question of its usefulness as a way of understanding the pre-colonial history of Indian culture. In terms of Western scholarship, historian David Kopf (1980: 502) praises the systematisation of Hinduism from 'an amorphous heritage into a rational faith' as a gift offered by the Western Orientalists to the Hindu people. Richard King (1999), however, has argued that the modern construction of 'Hinduism' as a unified religious tradition should be seen as largely inspired by the Christocentric presuppositions of the nineteenth-century Orientalists. This is not, however, to diminish the role of indigenous Hindus in the development of this concept. The artifice of modern Hinduism is built upon a much older legacy of brahmanisation – a process of assimilation and colonisation of non-brahmanical forms of Indian religion into the brahmanical fold that has been occurring for centuries. The form that the newly homogenised Hinduism took in the late nineteenth and early twentieth centuries was further consolidated by the desire to build a sense of national identity amongst Hindus seeking to challenge and then move beyond British imperial control of India. The indigenous Indian examples of brahmanisation and the Hindu search for swaraj (home rule) are important for a number of reasons. First, they demonstrate that native Indians were not passive recipients of Western Orientalist discourses but in fact were actively involved in the discursive and non-discursive processes which led to the rise of 'Hinduism' as a dominant ideological and explanatory construct in the modern era. Second, such examples also illustrate the sense in which totalising discourses and the impulse towards universalisation are by no means exclusively Western ideological trends. Indeed, what we now call the 'world religions' are precisely those universalising ideologies, filtered through a Eurocentric conception of history and inflected according to local cultural specificities and modes of expression (King 1999; Fitzgerald 2000; Masuzawa 2005).

There have been two ways in which the colonial encounter between Hindus and Europeans has contributed to the modern construction of 'Hinduism' – first, Western Orientalist emphasis tended to locate the core of Indian religiosity in specific Sanskrit texts. More generally, under the influence not only of Western Orientalists and colonial administrators but also the Hindu reformist movements that emerged as powerful voices in the nineteenth century, there has been a tendency to define Indian traditions in a way that reflects contemporary Western understandings of religion – with Christianity as the paradigmatic example of a religion (see Balagangadhara 1994). This is clearly linked to the cultural, political and economic shifts precipitated by European colonial expansion in South Asia. The result was the development of a variety of hybrid 'modernisations' in the emerging nation-states of Asia that sought to respond in their own ways to the challenge of Western models of modernity. These trends relate to the rise of what has been called 'the Bengali Renaissance' in India, and can be seen in parallel developments such as the 'modernist' spirit of the Meiji Restoration of late nineteenth-century Japan. The reconfiguration of such societies in terms of a now universalised category of 'religion' and of 'world religions' (Masuzawa 2005) has had a profound impact upon such societies and our own general sense of 'world history'.

In the specifically Indian context, Western associations of 'religion' with adherence to a specific sacred text (the Bible) contributed to a textualisation of modern

Indian religion. This is not to deny that Indian culture has its own literary traditions; rather, it is to emphasise the sense in which Western presuppositions about the role of sacred texts in religious traditions predisposed Orientalists to emphasise such texts as the *essential* foundation for understanding the Hindu people as a whole. The Protestant assumptions of the early missionaries and Western Orientalists meant that they immediately instigated a search for the Hindu equivalent of the Bible, convinced that all religions must have a sacred text as its doctrinal centrepiece. This search for a single point of scriptural origin led to an early scholarly emphasis upon the Veda (pioneered most notably by Max Müller through his *Sacred Books of the East* series). The focus on the Veda was based largely on the grounds of its obvious antiquity and its centrality to the brahmanical traditions of India. Others, with more of an interest in the more devotional (bhakti) elements of later Hindu practice focused upon the Epics or on the *Bhagavadgītā*. It was the latter, part of Chapter 6 of the great Hindu Epic the *Mahābhārata* and a key scriptural source for the various Vedānta schools, which came to the fore in many circles. William Jones, for instance, recommends that those who wish 'to form a correct idea of Indian religion and literature' should 'begin by forgetting all that has been written on the subject, by ancients and moderns, before the publication of the *Gita*' (Jones 1799: 363).

An example of the impact of Orientalist scriptocentrism upon Indian society can be seen in the establishment of a pan-Indian system of law by Sir William Jones. In his role as Supreme Court Judge in India, Jones initiated a project to translate the *Dharmaśāstras* based upon his belief that these texts represented the established law of the Hindu people. The problem with such an approach is that the texts themselves were composed by and representative of a priestly elite (the *brāhmaṇa* castes) within society and not of Hindus *in toto*. Thus, even within these texts, one will be hard pushed to find the idea of a unified Hindu community to which all law must apply universally. Rather, what one finds is an acknowledgement of a diversity of local, occupational and caste contexts in which different customs or rules applied.

Under colonial rule, Western claims about the decadence and corruption of contemporary Hindu religious practice created an opportunity for certain indigenous elites to assert their authority and authenticity under the rubric of 'reforming Hinduism'. Some of these figures emerged from the new middle classes that were developing as a direct result of the colonial reconfiguration of Indian society. Rammohan Roy (1772–1833) is a good example of this. Others represented responses from older traditions of brahmanical scholarship (the various paṇḍits) and ritual practitioners (brāhmaṇas) such as Ishwar Chandra Vidyasagar (1820–91). Whatever the different shades of their approaches and interpretations, the Hindu reformists of the nineteenth century exploited the growing perception that 'Hinduism' – understood as the religion of the Hindu people as a whole – required a reformation in order to meet the challenges of modernity. The Western Orientalist and missionary emphasis upon the decadence of contemporary Hinduism in relation to its glorious (textual) past resonated with the widespread indigenous belief, deriving from the *Purāṇas*, that humans were currently living in the age of kali yuga – an era of inevitable cultural and moral decline. What distinguished the Hindu reformists, however, was a general belief in – a conversion of sorts to – the project of modernity. In other words, the perceived decline of Hindu traditions was no longer seen as a cosmic inevitability, and Hindus could reform their traditions by returning to the golden age of previous eras. This 'missionary' spirit amongst the

Hindu reformists took up the challenge offered by Western Christian missionaries in India, but not in the direction that the missionaries had hoped, choosing to reform their own traditions rather than convert to another.

Alongside moves towards a homogenised account of Hindu traditions based upon an appeal to sacred scriptures there still remained the vexing question for Orientalists, colonial administrators and Hindu reformists alike of how to make sense of the multitude of popular or folk practices of Hindus' relation to the sacred texts of Brahmanism. Convinced of the superiority of text and belief over practice (something that is not easy to establish in an Indian context), many of the early Western Orientalists and missionaries criticised Hindu practices of their day for failing to 'live up to' or conform to the standards found in Hindu sacred texts. The problem with such an approach, of course, is that it misreads the role and significance of Hindu sacred texts. It also constitutes a failure to understand that the great diversity of Indian movements and schools is the product of a rich and pluralistic network of traditions, rather than a problem of nonconformity to scriptural injunctions.

Recent debates about the construction of 'Hinduism' have sought to pay attention to the role played by indigenous movements and figures in the development of this term as a corrective to the tendency to see change in modern Indian society as merely a product of Western colonial interests (King 1999; Pennington 2005). Accounts that portray the development of modern Hinduism as the simple imposition of a set of Western terms and presuppositions onto a largely passive indigenous population reproduce the same 'Orientalist' problematic that scholars such as Said sought to displace. Thus, increasing attention has turned to the role played by key indigenous Indian elites (most notably the scholarly elites of brahmanical circles) and the emerging new middle classes in British-ruled India (such as those involved in what has been called 'the Bengali Renaissance') in contributing to the emergence of this new construction of 'Hinduism' in the modern period. This is no more clear than in the prominence given to Vedānta in the nineteenth and twentieth centuries as representative of some kind of underlying theology of Hinduism which could then be engaged with (either constructively or apologetically) by Western philosophers and theologians (see King 1999: ch. 6). Moreover, noted Indian historian Romila Thapar (1985: 14–22) has argued that in the modern period we have witnessed the rise of a form of 'Syndicated Hinduism' that merges elitist brahmanical beliefs and ritual practices, elements of Christian and Islamic conceptions of religion and a political and nationalistic consciousness of itself. This, she suggests, is 'being pushed forward as the sole claimant of the inheritance of indigenous Indian religion' (Thapar 1985: 21). This modern construction of Hinduism

> seeks historicity for the incarnations of its deities, encourages the idea of a centrally sacred book, claims monotheism as significant to the worship of deity, acknowledges the authority of the ecclesiastical organisation of certain sects as prevailing over all and has supported large-scale missionary work and conversion. These changes allow it to transcend caste identities and reach out to larger numbers.
>
> (Thapar 1985: 22).

On similar grounds, Richard King (1999: 107) has argued that, while the term is useful (and indeed indispensable) for the study of modern Indian consciousness:

> it remains an anachronism to project the notion of 'Hinduism' as it is commonly understood into pre-colonial Indian history. Before the unification begun under imperial rule and consolidated by the

> Independence of 1947 it makes no sense to talk of an Indian 'nation', nor of a religion called 'Hinduism' which might be taken to represent the belief system of the Hindu people.
>
> (King 1999: 107)

Not all scholars, however, have been so willing to accept the contemporary post-colonial deconstruction of the category of 'Hinduism'. Will Sweetman (2003a, 2003b), Brian Pennington (2005) and David Lorenzen (1999, reprinted 2006), for instance, have challenged the idea that 'Hinduism' is a modern colonial invention. Lorenzen argues, for instance, that one can find evidence of indigenous consciousness of a 'Hindu religion' in India as early as the fifteenth century. Similarly, Julius Lipner (1996) argues that scholars should retain the term 'Hinduism' whilst avoiding an essentialist reading of the term. Lipner suggests that while Hinduism may not necessarily denote a single religion (in a Western sense of the term) it does accurately pinpoint the 'dynamic polycentrism' of Hindu culture. Thus, he suggests, 'Hinduism' is more like a multi-branched Banyan tree. Others such as Wilhelm Halbfass (1988) have appealed to the universality of the concept of Dharma in pre-modern Hindu thought as a counterpoint to the claim that 'Hinduism' is a modern Orientalist construction, though he admits that 'we cannot reduce the meanings of dharma to one general principle' (Halbfass 1988: 333).

One view on much of nineteenth-century Orientalist scholarship emphasised an underlying unity to Hindu beliefs and practices and this reflected a perspective conditioned by Western Christian presuppositions about what constitutes a religion. An alternative approach might be to argue that Hinduism is indeed a 'religion' but not in the sense that this term has been used by Westerners – that is, as a unitary and exclusivist phenomenon. Arvind Sharma, for instance, has argued that if one takes Hindu notions of 'Dharma' as the primary model for discussing what 'religion' in India would look like, then one finds evidence of polycentricity and an inclusivist approach to other traditions that actively challenges Western notions of religion. This would then make sense of the existence of such things as 'Hindu Christians' or 'Hindu Muslims' before the advent of British colonialism, since, on this understanding of 'the Hindu perspective', embracing the tradition of another does not require one to give up one's own. Gauri Viswanathan (2003: 28) also offers an important methodological warning to those so keen to deprive Hinduism of its unity as a 'religion'.

The notion that modern Hinduism represents a false unity imposed on diverse traditions replays a Western fascination with – and repulsion from – Indian polytheism. In this enduring perception, the existence of many gods must surely indicate they were the basis of many smaller religions and therefore to describe them under the rubric of 'Hinduism' as if they constituted a single religious system must be false, a distortion of heterogeneous religious practices. The reluctance of many scholars to call Hinduism a religion because it incorporates many disparate practices suggests that the Judeo-Christian system remains the main reference point for defining religions.

See also: **Asiatick Societies; Bhakti (as path); Brahmanism; Brahmo Samaj; Buddhism, relationship with Hinduism; Caste; Dharmaśāstras; Halbfass, Wilhelm; Hindu; Hinduism; Hinduism, history of scholarship; Hinduism, modern and contemporary; Itihāsa; Jones, Sir William; Languages; Mahābhārata; Müller, Friedrich Max; Nationalism; Popular and vernacular traditions; Purāṇas; Roy, Rammohan; Sacred Books of the East; Sacred texts; Varna; Veda; Vedānta; Vidyasagar, Ishwar Chandra; Yuga**

RICHARD KING

Further reading

Balagangadhara, S.N. 1994. *'The Heathen in His Blindness …': Asia, the West and the Dynamic of Religion*. Leiden: E.J. Brill.

Fitzgerald, Timothy. 2000. *The Ideology of Religious Studies*. Oxford: Oxford University Press.

Fox, Richard G. 1992. 'East of Said'. In Michael Sprinker, ed., *Edward Said: A Critical Reader*. Oxford: Blackwells.

Frykenberg, R.E. 1991. 'The Emergence of Modern "Hinduism" as a Concept and an Institution: A Reappraisal with Special Reference to South India'. In Günter D. Sontheimer and Hermann Kulke, eds, *Hinduism Reconsidered*. New Delhi: Manohar Publications.

Halbfass, Wilhelm. 1988. *India and Europe. An Essay in Understanding*. Albany, NY: State University of New York Press.

Hallisey, C. 1995. 'Roads Taken and Not Taken in the Study of Theravada Buddhism'. In Donald Lopez, ed., *Curators of the Buddha*. Chicago, IL: University of Chicago Press, 31–62.

Inden, Ronald. 1986. 'Orientalist Constructions of India'. *Modern Asian Studies* 20.3.

Inden, Ronald. 1990. *Imagining India*. Oxford: Basil Blackwells.

Jones, Sir William. 1799. *The Works of Sir W. Jones*, 6 vols, ed. A.M. Jones, with a discourse on the life and writings of Sir W. Jones, by Lord Teignmouth. London.

King, Richard. 1999. *Orientalism and Religion: Postcolonial Theory India, and 'the Mystic East'*. London: Routledge.

Kopf, David. 1980. 'Hermeneutics versus History'. *Journal of Asian Studies* XXXIX.3, May.

Lipner, Julius J. 1996. 'Ancient Banyan: An Inquiry in to the Meaning of "Hinduness"'. *Religious Studies* 32: 109–26.

Lorenzen, David N. 1999. 'Who Invented Hinduism?' *Comparative Studies in Society and History* 41: 630–59.

Lorenzen, David N. 2006.*Who Invented Hinduism?: Essays on Religion in History*. New Delhi: Yoda Press.

Masuzawa, Tomoko. 2005. *The Invention of World Religions or How European Universalism Was Preserved in the Language of Pluralism*. Chicago, IL: University of Chicago Press.

Oddie, Geoffrey. 2003. 'Constructing "Hinduism": The Impact of the Protestant Missionary Movement on Hindu Self-Understanding'. In Robert E. Frykenberg, ed., *Christians and Missionaries in India. Cross-Cultural Communication since 1500*. London: RoutledgeCurzon, 155–82.

Pennington, Brian K. 2005. *Was Hinduism Invented? Britons, Indians and the Colonial Construction of Religion*. Oxford: Oxford University Press.

Said, Edward W. 1978. *Orientalism: Western Conceptions of the Orient*. London: Routledge & Kegan Paul.

Sweetman, Will. 2003a. '"Hinduism" and the History of "Religion": Protestant Presuppositions in the Critique of the Concept of Hinduism'. *Method and Theory in the Study of Religion* 15: 329–55.

Sweetman, Will. 2003b. *Mapping Hinduism. 'Hinduism' and the Study of Indian Religions 1600–1776*. Halle: Franckesche Stiftungen zu Halle.

Thapar, R. 1985. 'Syndicated Moksha?' *Seminar* 313 (September): 14–20.

Viswanathan, Gauri. 2003. 'Colonialism and the Construction of Hinduism'. In Gavin Flood, *The Blackwell Companion to Hinduism*. Oxford: Blackwells, 23–44.

OSHO

See: **Rajneesh, Bhagwan Shree**

OTTO, RUDOLF (1869–1937)

German Christian theologian and historian of religions, especially of Hinduism. Otto's understanding of religion proceeds from a characteristically German Protestant emphasis on the primacy of religious experience – for Otto, the experience of the holy which is at once a source of fear in the face of its overwhelming power and of fascination and attraction as wholly different to anything else in our experience. Otto described several occasions on which he himself experienced this feeling, the last in 1927 before a statue of Śiva on Elephanta Island (Alles 1996). In his comparative work, Otto sought to show how Christian and Hindu mysticism, e.g. Śaṅkara and Meister Eckhardt (Otto

1926), and devotional theism (Otto 1930) developed in parallel in response to this basic religious experience. He also translated and commented on numerous Hindu texts, notably the *Bhagavadgītā* (Otto 1934, 1935), to which he applied the methods developed in biblical criticism in an attempt to determine its 'original' form.

See also: **Bhagavadgītā; Hinduism, history of scholarship; Śaṅkara**

WILL SWEETMAN

Further reading

Alles, G.D. (ed.). 1996. *Autobiographical and Social Essays*. Berlin: Mouton de Gruyter.

Otto, R. 1926. *West-östliche Mystik*. Gotha: L. Klotz. [B.L. Bracey and R.C. Payne (trans.). 1932. *Mysticism East and West: A Comparative Analysis of the Nature of Mysticism*]. New York: Macmillan.

Otto, R. 1930. *Die Gnadenreligion Indiens und das Christentum*. Gotha: L. Klotz. [F.H. Foster (trans.). 1930. *India's Religion of Grace and Christianity Compared and Contrasted*.] New York: Macmillan.

Otto, R. 1934. *Die Urgestalt der Bhagavad-Gita*. Tübingen: J.C.B. Mohr.

Otto, R. (trans.). 1935. *Der Sang des Hehr-Erhabenen: Die Bhagavad-Gita*. Stuttgart: W. Kohlhammer.

Turner, J.E. (trans.). 1939. *The Original Gita: The Song of the Supreme Exalted One*. London: Allen and Unwin.

OUTCASTES

See: **Dalits**

P

PADĀRTHADHARMASAṂGRAHA

Praśastapāda's work *Padārthadharmasaṃgraha* (Compendium of the Characteristics of the Categories) marks a major development in the philosophy of the Vaiśeṣika school. It became Vaiśeṣika's standard text and many important commentaries were written on it.

The date of Praśastapāda is uncertain. Various scholars (such as Frauwallner, Stcherbatsky and Keith) have argued for different dates from the fourth to the sixth centuries CE.

The *Padārthadharmasaṃgraha* is called a 'commentary' (*bhāsya*) on the *Vaiśeṣikasūtras* and is also known as *Praśastapādabhāsya* (Praśastapāda's Commentary). However, it is not a commentary in the strict sense: it does not, for example, follow the order of the *sūtras*.

For Praśastapāda, the supreme good results from true knowledge of the similar and dissimilar characteristics of the six categories (padārthas). He adds seven qualities to Kaṇāḍa's list of seventeen and introduces theories of the creation and dissolution of the world, including a concept of a Creator God (Maheśvara) (Śiva).

See also: **Frauwallner, Erich; Kaṇāḍa; Padārthas; Śiva; Vaiśeṣika; Vaiśeṣikasūtras**

MARTIN OVENS

Further reading

Peeru Kannu, S. 1992. *The Critical Study of Praśastapādabhāsya.* Delhi: Kanishka Publishing House.

Potter, K.H. (ed.). 1977. *Encyclopedia of Indian Philosophies*, vol. 2: *Indian Metaphysics and Epistemology*: *The Tradition of Nyāya-Vaiśesika up to Gangeśa*. Princeton, NJ: Princeton University Press.

PADĀRTHAS

Vaiśeṣika outlines six fundamental categories of things in the realm of scientific discourse (padārthas): substance (dravya), quality (guṇa), action (kriyā), generality (sāmānya), particularity (viśeṣa) and inherence (samavāya), to which is added a seventh category: non-existence or absence (abhāva). Substances include atoms (paramāṇu) and composites of the four types of elements: earth, water, fire and air, and also include space, time, direction, soul and mind. Substances are the substrates of members of the next two categories, namely of qualities (guṇas) and actions (kriyā). Members of these first three categories, that is, qualities and actions as well as substances, exist and can be the substrates of general properties and particularities. On one extreme, they are the substrates of the universal existence (sattā). On the other, because the ultimate simples of these classes, namely earth atoms, water atoms, individual souls, etc., even if identical to each other in every other respect, are unique: they are the substrates of ultimate particularities (viśeṣa). It is due to advocating these last that the philosophical school is termed Vaiśeṣika. Inherence is the relation by which a generality or particularity is present in a substance, quality or action.

See also: **Guṇas; Vaiśeṣika**

PETER M. SCHARF

Further reading

Halbfass, Wilhelm. 1992. *On Being and What There Is: Classical Vaisesika and the History of Indian Ontology.* Albany, NY: State University of New York Press.

PAÑCAMAKĀRA

The pañcamakāra are a set of five terms beginning with the Sanskrit letter ma, whose referents constitute what may be termed the five esoteric sacraments of Hindu Tantra. The five are māṃsa (flesh), matsya (fish), madya (spirituous liquor), mudrā (the female consort in sexual intercourse) and maithuna (sexual fluids). Interpretations of these last two terms have varied over history, with recent commentators and scholars preferring to read mudrā as 'salty food' and maithuna as 'sexual intercourse'. However, many Hindu and Buddhist Tantras refer to mudrā as the Tantric consort (she is often called karma-mudrā, the 'Action Seal', in Buddhist sources); and maithuna is often described as a substance to be consumed in early Hindu sources. In certain early Hindu sources, it is a set of three, rather than five, makāras that are named, with all three (madya, māṃsa and maithuna) described as substances to be consumed. Several late Tantric works propose non-trangressive, non-polluting substitutes (pratinidhis) for the original five.

See also: **Buddhism, relationship with Hinduism; Mudrā; Tantras**

DAVID GORDON WHITE

Further reading

White, D.G. 2003. *Kiss of the Yogini: 'Tantric Sex' in Its South Asian Contexts.* Chicago, IL: University of Chicago Press.

PĀÑCARĀTRAS

Virtually all the various Vaiṣṇava traditions follow one or other Pāñcarātra ritual texts which claim to have originated with Viṣṇu himself. The popularisation of the Pāñcarātra ritual was credited to the work of the South Indian Vaiṣṇava teachers Yāmuna and Rāmānuja. While Yāmuna wrote a text in defence of the Pāñcarātra rituals (*Āgamaprāṇya*), Rāmānuja not only made use of Yāmuna's work in his *Śrībhāṣya* (where Rāmānuja defends the Pāñcarātra rituals), but also vigorously propagated those ritual rules and procedures in various South Indian Vaiṣṇava temples. The traditional biographers of Rāmānuja indicate his work in this regard and point out that he succeeded in introducing these rituals in most temples except in the Śrī Venkateśvara temple in Tirupati (Andhra Pradesh) and the Padmanābha temple in Trivendrum (Kerala).

Some of the important Pāñcarātra texts are *Sāttvata, Jayākhya* and *Pauṣkara*

Saṃhitās (known as the Triad). The others include *Ahirbudhnya, Īśvara* and *Śrīpraśna Saṃhitā* and the *Lakṣmī Tantra*. Only *Ahirbudhnya Saṃhitā* (Otto Schrader) and the *Lakṣmī Tantra* (Sanjukta Gupta) have been studied by contemporary scholars, although Daniel Smith managed to compile a comprehensive descriptive bibliography of the Pāñcarātra texts. The influence of the Pāñcarātra texts on the Vaiṣṇava theology and philosophy is certainly beyond question.

See also: **Rāmānuja; Vaiṣṇavism; Viṣṇu; Yāmuna**

PRATAP KUMAR

Further reading

Neevel, W.G. 1977. *Yāmuna's Vedānta and Pāñcarātra: Integrating the Classical and the Popular.* Missoula, MT: Scholars Press.

Schrader, Otto. 1916. *Introduction to the Pāñcarātra and the Ahirbudhnya Saṃhitā.* Madras: The Adyar Library and Research Centre.

Smith, H.D. 1980. *A Descriptive Bibliography of the Printed Texts of the Pāñcarātrāgamas*, vols 1 and 2. Baroda: Oriental Institute.

Varadachari, V. 1982. *Āgamas of South Indian Vaiṣṇavism.* Madras: Prof. M. Rangacharya Memorial Trust.

PAÑCATANTRA

The *Pañcatantra* is a collection of stories, in Sanskrit prose interspersed with verses (translations Olivelle 1997; Rajan 1993). It exists in many versions of different length but following the same outline. It has five chapters; hence the title (*pañca* 'five'; *tantra* 'warp; principle'). Each chapter tells a story whose characters tell each other stories, whose characters may in turn tell more stories, each story teaching a lesson which is summed up in a verse. The book begins with a story about a teacher, Viṣṇuśarman, who undertook to teach a king's three ignorant sons in six months, and did so by telling them these stories. It calls itself a *Nītiśāstra* – a book of instruction in conduct, particularly the conduct that makes a successful king. Many of the characters are animals, with human characteristics: noble but vain lions, treacherous tigers, manipulative jackals, meddlesome monkeys, quick-witted hares. Others are people: kings, brāhmaṇas, thieves, farmers, carpenters and ingeniously adulterous wives. The stories show a hazardous world in which the prudent and knowledgeable prosper while the foolish and the trusting are cheated or eaten.

It was written some time before the sixth century CE, when it was translated into Pahlavi (Middle Persian). This version, now lost, was soon translated into Syriac, and later into Arabic. From the Arabic came versions in European languages, starting with Greek in the eleventh century. Besides the versions in Sanskrit, there are many in the vernacular languages of India. The individual stories are part of folk literature, and some of them have been found in China, South-East Asia, Africa and Europe.

Some time between the ninth and fourteenth centuries Nārāyaṇa, a Bengali, wrote a new Sanskrit version, the *Hitopadeśa* ('useful teaching'). He recast the five chapters into four, added stories from other sources, and inserted many verses from the literature of *nīti*.

See also: **Brāhmaṇas; Nītiśāstras**

DERMOT KILLINGLEY

Further reading

Olivelle, Patrick. 1997. *The Pañcatantra* (World's Classics series). Oxford: Oxford University Press

Rajan, Chandran. 1993. *The Panchatantra* (Penguin Classics series). New Delhi: Penguin Books India

PĀṆḌAVAS

The five sons of King Pāṇḍu, who appear in the *Māhabhārata* as one of the two groups of rival princes who dispute the succession to the vacant kingdom of Hastināpura after the abdication of Pāndu and his blind brother, Dhṛtarāṣṭra. The names of the princes are Yudiṣṭhira, Bhīma, Arjuna, Nakula and Sahadeva. Arjuna was to achieve pre-eminence as the warrior-prince to whom the *Bhagavadgītā* is revealed by Kṛṣṇa. However, Yudiṣṭhira, the eldest, is also renowned for his wisdom and sense of justice. The Pāṇḍavas passed twelve years exiled in the forest after Yudiṣṭhira was tempted to gamble away their share of the kingdom in a crooked dice game with the Kauravas. On return from exile they were still not given their rightful heritage and thus the great battle took place at the plain of Kurukṣetra, north of Delhi. The religious geography of Northern India is full of sacred sites that mark the presence of the Pāṇḍavas whilst they wandered in exile.

See also: **Arjuna; Bhagavadgitā; Dhṛtarāṣṭra; Kauravas; Kṛṣṇa; Kurukṣetra; Māhabhārata; Pāṇḍu; Yudiṣṭhira**

RON GEAVES

Further reading

Dasgupta, Madhusraba. 1999. *Samsad Companion to the Mahābhārata.* Calcutta: Sahitya Samsad.

PAṆḌIT(A)

In Sanskrit paṇḍita means learned one. A paṇḍit is a scholar and/or a teacher, especially a brāhmaṇa versed in Sanskrit and the different branches of sacred knowledge. The title paṇḍit is given as a recognition of learning to those priestly brāhmans who have a reputation for Sanskritic learning and who are engaged in traditional ways of Sanskritic teaching and learning, especially the memorisation and transfer of traditional knowledge. There are still paṇḍits who teach students under the traditional system of guru-śiṣya paraṃparā. The appellation paṇḍit is also in practice the title of respect given to priests and brāhmaṇas of all kinds (whether learned or not), and to any person who has achieved excellence in any traditional field of learning (such as Āyurveda, Yoga and Vedic astrology) or the arts (e.g. classical music, poetry and dance). Today the paṇḍit may be a private scholar, a university teacher or a publicly recognised intellectual or legal adviser. Pandita Ramabai Saraswati (1858–1922) was one of the first women to be awarded the title Paṇḍitā in recognition of her great learning. The title paṇḍit is also bestowed on eminent Western scholars (e.g. Dr David Frawley is also known as Pandit Vamadeva Shastri).

See also: **Brāhmaṇa; Dance; Jyotiṣa; Music; Paraṃparā; Poetry; Yoga**

ANNA KING

Further reading

Monier-Williams, M. 1899. *A Sanskrit–English Dictionary: Etymologically and Philologically Arranged with Special Reference to Cognate Indo-European Languages.* Oxford: Clarendon.

Sarasvati, Svami Chandrasekharendra. 1991. *Voice of the Guru: The Guru Tradition.* Bombay: Bharatiya Vidya Bhavan.

PĀṆḌU

Literally 'the pale', King Pāṇḍu was the half-brother of Dhṛtarāṣṭra, the father of the Kauravas. The ruler of Hastināpura, he was the father of the Pāṇḍavas, the two sets of cousins being the central protagonists of the Hindu epic the Mahābhārata. The great struggle or war that gives its name to the epic was for dominion over the kingdom formerly ruled by Pāṇḍu.

The epic recounts that two widows were made pregnant by the great ascetic Vyāsa, who bore a terrifying visage. The woman who gave birth to Dhṛtarāṣṭra was so terrified that she turned away from Vyāsa and her son was born blind. Her sister was so frightened that she turned white and gave birth to a pale son, thus the name 'Pāṇḍu'. On coming of age, Dhṛtarāṣṭra was not allowed to ascend the throne as he was blind and Pāṇḍu replaced him. However, he later renounced the kingdom as a result of a curse and retired to the Himalayas, where he died. It is there that his wives bore him five sons. Dhṛtarāṣṭra returned to the throne after his brother's departure and sired over one hundred offspring known collectively as the Kauravas.

See also: **Dhṛtarāṣṭra; Kauravas; Mahābhārata; Vyāsa**

RON GEAVES

Further reading

Dasgupta, Madhusraba. 1999. *Samsad Companion to the Mahābhārata.* Calcutta: Sahitya Samsad.

PANDURANG, ATMARAM (1823–98)

Dr Atmaram Pandurang was educated at Elphinstone College in Bombay, where he was a member of the Students' Literary and Scientific Society, founded in 1848. He later became influenced by Justice Mahadev Govind Ranade in Bombay, the founder of the Prarthana Samaj. Along with Pandita Ramabai Saraswati, S.P Kelkar and S.P. Pandit, Atmaram Pandurang was one of the principal advocates of the movement.

The Prarthana Samaj was founded in Bombay in 1867, inspired by Rammohan Roy (b. 1772) and his influential organisation the Brahmo Samaj and its offshoot, the New Dispensation, founded by Keshab Chandra Sen. The organisation was not as radical as the Brahmo Samaj, essentially focusing on recognition of widow marriage, women's education and disapproval of caste restrictions. Its members encouraged caste intermarriage and commensality. Through the efforts of its founder, Justice Ranade, Atmaram Pandurang and the other three founding figures, the Prarthana Samaj was widespread through Maharashtra, where it promoted a rational monotheistic religion devoted to social reform.

See also: **Brahmo Samaj; Roy, Rammohan; Saraswati, Pandita Ramabai; Sen, Keshab Chandra**

RON GEAVES

Further reading

Jones, Kenneth. 1989. *Socio-Religious Reform Movements in British India, The New Cambridge History of India*, vol. 3.1. Cambridge: Cambridge University Press.

PANDURANG, DADOBA (TARKHADAR)

Renowned grammarian and the first chairman of the Students' Literary and Scientific Society, founded in 1848 at Elphinstone College in Bombay. Dadoba Pandurang was responsible for the Marathi section of the society, known as Upayukta Jnanprasarak Sabha. In 1842, he co-founded the Pustak Prasarak Mandali (Book Propagation Society) with Manchharam Mehtaji Durgaram, and in 1844 the same collaboration created the Manav Dharma Sabha. The latter organisation only lasted eight years, as Dadoba Pandurang returned to Bombay in 1846 and with a small circle of friends began the Parahamahansa Mandali, an organisation that gave final form to the ideals of the earlier movements. Like his collaborator, Manchharam Mehtaji Durgaram, Dadoba Pandurang began his career as a headmaster of a government school (Bombay Normal School) after imbibing the ideals of Western-style education at the Bombay Native School. The influence of Western education provided the impetus for a rational criticism of contemporary Indian society, especially the religious practices and beliefs of rural India.

See also: **Durgaram Manchharam, Mehtaji; Manav Dharma Sabha; Paramahamsa Mandali**

RON GEAVES

Further reading

Jones, Kenneth. 1989. *Socio-Religious Reform Movements in British India, The New Cambridge History of India*, vol. 3.1. Cambridge: Cambridge University Press.

PĀṆINI

Pāṇini is the author of the *Aṣṭādhyāyī*, the unrivalled authoritative text on Sanskrit grammar, provisionally dated from the fourth century BCE. Vyākaraṇa, or 'grammar', is categorised as one of the primary six Vedāṅgas, or 'limbs of the Veda', and is considered ancillary Vedic literature. This status is derived from grammar's capacity to regularise and conserve the Sanskrit language, thus ensuring the correct transmission of the sacred words of the Veda. One of the remarkable features of the *Aṣṭādhyāyī* is its notational method, which allows the complex grammar of Sanskrit to be defined with utmost brevity. Using 'dummy' letters as equivalents to 'real' grammatical items, Pāṇini's system functions algebraically, with hyper-brief formulae describing verbal conjugation, inflection and so on, eliminating the need to provide full forms of words as they occur in speech. Such succinctness, however, comes at some cost; study of the *Aṣṭādhyāyī* is considered a discipline autonomous from grammar, and despite the aid of important commentaries such as the *Mahābhāṣya* traditionally attributed to Patañjali (second century BCE), debate among Pāṇinian scholars concerning the interpretation of particularly cryptic aphorisms continues to this day. Other works attributed to Pāṇini include the *Dhātupāṭha*, a catalogue of verbal roots; the *Gaṇapāṭha*, which categorises words according to grammatical patterns; the *Liṅgānuśāsana*, a consideration of grammatical gender; and the *Śikṣā*, a teaching text. References to the grammarian may be found in the *Aṣṭādhyāyī* itself, and legends appear in sources as varied as the *Pañcatantra*, the *Kathāsaritsāgara* of Somadeva and the eleventh-century *Bṛhatkathāmañjarī* of Kṣemendra. The son of Pāṇina and Dākṣī, Pāṇini was born in Śalātura, a village near modern Peshawar, Pakistan. Reputed to be a poor student, Pāṇini is said to have repaired to the Himālayas to become an ascetic, where the basic structure of Sanskrit grammar was revealed to him by Śiva.

See also: **Himālayas; Pañcatantra; Śiva; Veda; Vedāṅgas; Vyākaraṇa**

ANDREA MARION PINKNEY

Further reading

Cardona, G. 1997. *Panini, His Works and Its Traditions*. Delhi: Motilal Banarsidass.

PĀPA

Pāpa means demerit or actions that conduce towards sorrow. An alternative translation is evil. Just as virtuous action produces merit (puṇya), so evil or sinful action (or the failure to discharge prescribed duties) produce pāpa. It is possible to expiate demerit in much the same ways as it is possible to gain merit, for example by undertaking pilgrimage (tīrthayātrā) or other merit-making activities.

See also: **Puṇya; Tīrthayātrā (pilgrimage)**

DENISE CUSH AND CATHERINE ROBINSON

PARAMAHAMSA MANDALI

Described as a radical socio-religious society (Jones 1989: 140), the Paramahamsa

Mandali was founded in 1849 by Dadoba Pandurang and a small group of companions. Dadoba Pandurang had returned to Bombay in 1846 after playing a significant part in the Manav Dharma Sabha. The new organisation was formed on the basis of the ideals already framed within the Manav Dharma Sabha, which were essentially those written by Dadoba Pandurang in 1843 in his book *Dharma Vivechan*. The seven principles which acted as the guiding light of both organisations were that only God is worthy of worship, that genuine religion is always based on love and good moral conduct, that spirituality is universal, that every human being has the right to freedom of thought, that speech should be consistent with reason, that knowledge should be available to everyone and that the only caste is membership of the human race (Jones 1989: 139).

The organisation met in secret but membership was predominantly made up of young educated Brāhmaṇas who were either residents of Bombay or had migrated to the city in search of its English educational system. As with the earlier Manav Dharma Sabha, the members rejected the caste system, image worship, brahmanical authority and rituals. Thus it can be placed as part of the Hindu renaissance, influenced by Western rationalism and Christianity, but determined to introduce reforms to the existing religion rather than convert to the religion of the colonisers.

In the secret meetings, members took part in prayer and study, but on initiation to the organisation had to eat food prepared for them by members of the lower castes. The secretive nature of the organisation meant that little influence was brought to bear upon Hindu orthodoxy, and on publication of the members' names in 1860, after the theft of their records revealed the nature of the initiation ceremony, the movement collapsed completely.

See also: **Manav Dharma Sabha; Pandurang, Dadoba**

RON GEAVES

Further reading

Jones, Kenneth. 1989. *Socio-Religious Reform Movements in British India. The New Cambridge History of India*, vol. 3.1. Cambridge: Cambridge University Press.

PARAṂPARĀ

Method of transmission of knowledge from guru to disciple (śiṣya), principally in the Saṃpradāya tradition. Such transmission is oral, not written. The Saṃpradāya tradition is generally traced back to Rāmānanda; the process of paraṃparā can be linked to other 'summit' teachers, such as Madhva or Caitanya. At times the principal teacher can be a Hindu high god: thus, Kṛṣṇa gives teachings to Arjuna, later written down in the *Bhagavadgītā*, and Rāmā instructs Hanumān verbally. The guru and disciple are generally, though not necessarily, male.

Although generally associated with the unaltered and uninterrupted transmission of spiritual knowledge, paraṃparā can refer to the transmission of other types of knowledge and skill relating to the arts (painting, dance, music) or education. It is believed that teachings of the Veda were delivered in this way. The meaning of the word *Upaniṣad* ('sitting near') implies a guru-śiṣya paraṃparā. Paraṃparā is used in the Guru-Śiṣya tradition, and also Gauḍīya Maṭh, from which the International Society for Krishna Consciousness (ISKCON) emerged.

The rationale of paraṃparā serves to ensure that the transmitted knowledge is authentic, and that it is transmitted exclusively to appropriate students, who have the qualities of respect for their guru and commitment. The technique is not only used to ensure that advanced or esoteric knowledge is transmitted exclusively to those who are eligible; it is employed to transmit material that cannot be handed down in written form: for example the sound of a mantra or an artistic technique such as musical expression.

The disciples' eligibility to receive instruction is often marked by an initiation ceremony, in which the disciple typically presents a gift to the guru (gurudakṣina) before receiving the knowledge.

See also: **Arjuna; Bhagavadgītā; Caitanya; Dance; Gauḍīyas; Guru; Hanumān; Kṛṣṇa; Madhva; Music; Rāmā; Rāmānanda; Saṃpradāya; Śiṣya; Upaniṣads; Veda**

GEORGE CHRYSSIDES

Further reading

Abhishiktananda, Swami. 1974. *Guru and Disciple.* London: SPCK.

Saraswati, Baidyanath. (ed.). 2001. *The Nature of Living Tradition: Distinctive Features of Indian Parampara.* New Delhi: DK Printworld.

PARĀŚARA

A ṛṣi who is believed to have written a number of the hymns in the *Ṛgveda*; however, the disagreements over the dates of his life, ranging from the fourteenth century BCE to the sixth century BCE, would suggest that there may have been more than one sage known by the same name. Parāśara is also known as a writer on *Dharmaśāstra* and is often cited in books of law. The *Mahābhārata* states that he was the grandson of Vasiṣṭha but the *Nirukta* claims that he was the son of the same sage. It is also stated that he fathered the twenty-eighth Veda-Vyāsa, Kṛṣṇa-dvaipāyana, the legendary compiler of the *Mahābhārata*, through his liaison with Satyavatī, the daughter of the Apsaras Adrikā. The *Viṣṇu Purāṇa* states that Parāśara received many boons from Pulastya, one of which was the gift to be the author of a summary of all the *Purāṇas.* It claims that he was a disciple of Kapila who taught the *Viṣṇu Purāṇa* to his pupil Maitreya.

See also: **Apsarasas; Dharmaśāstras; Kapila; Mahābhārata; Nirukta; Purāṇas; Saṃhitās; Vasiṣṭha; Vyāsa**

RON GEAVES

Further reading

Walker, Benjamin. 1968. *Hindu World*, vol. 2. London: George Allen & Unwin.

PARAŚURĀMA

See: **Avatāra**

PARGITER, FREDERICK EDEN (1852–1927)

English Sanskritist. Although his degree was in mathematics, Pargiter was Boden Scholar of Sanskrit at Oxford in 1872. He joined the Indian Civil Service in 1875 and was sent to Bengal, where he worked for thirty-one years, retiring in 1906 as judge of the High Court in Calcutta. He was president of the Asiatic Society of Bengal in 1903–05 and vice-president of the Royal Asiatic Society from 1916. While in India he published a translation of the *Mārkaṇḍeya Purāṇa*, which appeared in instalments in the Asiatic Society's *Bibliotheca Indica* series from 1888. In retirement in Oxford he combined the study of Indian epigraphy with further work on the *Purāṇas*, and published two works on the historical material contained in the *Purāṇas* (Pargiter 1913, 1922).

See also: **Asiatic Societies; Hinduism, history of scholarship; Purāṇas**

WILL SWEETMAN

Further reading

Pargiter, F.E. 1904. *The Mārkaṇḍeya Purāṇa.* Calcutta: The Asiatic Society.

Pargiter, F.E. 1913. *The Purāṇa Text of the Dynasties of the Kali Age with Introduction and Notes*. London: Oxford University Press.

Pargiter, F.E. 1922. *Ancient Indian Historical Tradition*. London: Oxford University Press.

PARIKṢIT

A grandson of Arjuna and father of Janamejaya, who, according to the *Mahābhārata*, succeeded to the throne of Hastināpura after the abdication of Yudhiṣṭhira at the end of the conflict. The *Mahābhārata* states that he was born dead after being killed in the womb of his mother, Uttarā, by Aswatthāman, but was restored to life by Kṛṣṇa, who blessed him. His death is described in the *Bhāgavata Purāṇa*, where it is recounted that the king died from a snakebite after offending a hermit. In preparation for his death, he retired to the banks of the Gaṅgā, where the complete *Bhāgavata Purāṇa* was recited to him. In revenge, his son, Janamejaya, a famous performer of the horse-sacrifice, attempted to exterminate the race of Nāgas, who only survived through the intervention of the sage Āstika.

See also: **Arjuna; Gaṅgā; Kṛṣṇa; Mahābhārata; Nāgas; Purāṇas; Yajña; Yudhiṣṭhira**

RON GEAVES

Further reading

Dasgupta, Madhusraba. 1999. *Samsad Companion to the Mahābhārata*. Calcutta: Sahitya Samsad.

Stutley, Margaret and James Stutley (eds). 1977. *A Dictionary of Hinduism: Its Mythology, Folklore and Development 1500 BC–AD 1500*. London: Routledge and Kegan Paul.

PĀRVATĪ

Pārvatī is the daughter of the deities Himavat, who is the personification of the Himālaya mountains, and Menā. Her name is translatable as 'she who is of the mountains' and her epithets expand on this association by describing her, variously, as the daughter or mistress of the mountains. Pārvatī's primary characteristics are those of a devoted mother and wife (Pativratā). Indeed, through her relationship with her husband Śiva and their children, she may be understood as the model of the ideal female householder.

Mythologically and historically, Pārvatī is mentioned first by name during the epic period in the *Mahābhārata* as dwelling with Śiva in the Himālayas. Prior to this there is only a reference in the *Kena Upaniṣad* to one of her alternative names, Umā Haimavatī, as an intermediary between Brahman and the gods (Kinsley 1988: 36). It is not until the *Purāṇas* that detailed stories of Pārvatī's activities become available. From the outset, Pārvatī's life story is closely entwined with that of the god Śiva. Often identified as the reincarnation of Śiva's first wife, Satī, it is seemingly Pārvatī's destiny to marry Śiva. Indeed, the primary role of Pārvatī may be said to be to draw Śiva away from the practices of the ascetic and renouncer into the world of the householder, with all of its requisite duties. Described as dark skinned and beautiful, Pārvatī does not simply seduce Śiva in these stories; she secures his agreement to marriage by proving herself to be his equal in the performance of austerities. They have two children, Kārttikeya (Skanda) and Gaṇeśa, with whom they are depicted as engaged in happy and harmonious family life.

Besides her exemplification of the householder ideal, Pārvatī has numerous other associations and attributes. She is viewed as a representation of female energy, śakti, and, such is the intimacy between Śiva and Pārvatī, she is often characterised as the embodiment of Śiva's śakti. This close interrelationship is illustrated further through the Ardhanārīśvara, a hermaphroditic image/concept of a body comprising Śiva on the right and Pārvatī on the left, which signifies the absolute union and interdependence of the two deities (Kinsley 1988: 50). She is also linked with the warrior goddesses Durgā and Kālī, both of whom, it is explained, emerge from her when there is great need or a threat to the world. More typically, though, she is a model of devotion, her commitment to Śiva serving as paradigm for loving religious devotion to any deity.

See also: **Ardhanārīśvara; Bhakti; Brahman; Durgā; Gaṇeśa; Gārhasthya; Himālayas; Kālī and Caṇḍī; Mahābhārata; Pativratā and Parameśvara; Purāṇas; Śakti; Satī; Śiva; Skanda; Tapas; Umā Haimavatī; Upaniṣads**

PAUL REID-BOWEN

Further reading

Kinsley, D. 1988. *Hindu Goddesses: Visions of the Divine Feminine in the Hindu Religious Tradition*. Berkeley, CA: University of California Press.

PĀŚUPATAS

The earliest literary reference to a Śaiva sect is to be found in Patañjali's commentary on the grammar of Pāṇini, where he mentions the Śiva bhāgavatas – devotees of Śiva. This was in the second century BCE. Although the Pāśupatas are not mentioned by name, the reference is probably to them as they are the oldest of the various Śaiva movements in India. The first specific reference comes in book twelve of the *Mahābhārata* (349.64). There, the Paśupata system is said to have been founded by Śiva Srikaṇtha, consort of Umā. Paśupata Śaivism is sometimes referred to as the Lakulīśa, after an important teacher of the sect, though some scholars, for example K.C. Pandey (1954), differentiate the early Paśupata from the Lakulīśa version because the latter appears to teach a 'dualism-cum-nondualism' (dvaitādvaita) ontology whereas the former subscribed to a dualistic (dvaita) one. Pandey locates Lakulīśa in the second century by allowing twenty-five years per generation. This assertion's basis is epigraphical evidence from a pillar inscription at Mathura dating from the time of Candragupta II, around 380 CE, which refers to one Uditacarya, the eleventh teacher of the Pasupatas after Lakulīśa.

Most of our information about the sect comes from much later works, however, primarily the *Sarvadarśanasaṃgraha* of Mādhava (fourteenth century CE) and the *Paśupata Sūtras* with Kauṇḍinya's commentary. Kauṇḍinya is reputed to have lived between the fourth and sixth centuries CE. We learn from these texts that the five fundamental categories of the system are as follows:

1 The lord (pati), sometimes called the cause (kārana);
2 The effect (kārya), which has three subclasses:
   - the stuff of the universe (pāsa or kāla);
   - the soul (paśu);
   - cognition or knowledge (vidya).
3 Contemplative exercise (yoga).
4 Conduct or religious activity (vidhi).
5 The end of suffering (duhkhānta).

The essence of Paśupata theology is that God is in control; it is his grace that releases souls from suffering. God's grace works through guidance on yoga and vidhi. Paśupata is the only Śaiva system to subscribe to the Sāṃkhya teaching of twenty-five categories (tattva) of existence. All the others adopt the later thirty-six-category scheme, which functions to transform the dualistic ontology of Sāṃkhya into a monistic one by adding eleven additional categories to the twenty-five of Sāṃkhya. This is further testimony to the antiquity of the system.

See also: **Dvaita; Mahābhārata; Pāṇini; Patañjali; Śaivism; Sāṃkhya; Śiva**

PETER CONNOLLY

Further reading

Pandey, K.C. 1954/1986. *An Outline History of Saiva Philosophy.* Delhi: Motilal Banarsidass.

PATAÑJALI

Patañjali, the author of the grammatical treatise called the *Mahābhāṣya*, an extensive commentary on Pāṇini's *Aṣṭādhyāyī* and Kātyāyana's *vārtika*s, 'brief notes' on it, wrote *c.*150 BCE. To him is attributed authorship of the *Yogasūtras*, and thereby the founding of the systematic study of Yoga, and a recasting of the Āyurvedic medical treatise *Carakasaṃhitā* (Raghavan 1983: 89–90). He is traditionally thought to be the incarnation of Śeṣa, the serpent on whom Viṣṇu lies, and he is the subject of a late work, *Patañjalicarita* (*The Deeds of Patañjali*), in eight chapters (sarga), by Rāmabhadradīkṣita, the son of Yajñarāma Dīkṣita (Raghavan 1983: 11.90–91). Scholarly opinion is divided, however, as to whether the works on Yoga were composed by the same author as those on grammar.

See also: **Pāṇini; Śeṣa; Viṣṇu; Yoga; Yogasūtras**

PETER M. SCHARF

Further reading

Raghavan, V. 1983. *New Catalogus Catalogorum: An Alphabetical Register of Sanskrit and Allied Works and Authors*, vol. 11. Madras: University of Madras.

PATIVRATĀ AND PATIPARAMEŚVARA

In pre-modern Hinduism, pativratā denoted a woman who performed vows (vratas) for her husband (pati), a key concept of the good wife in elite circles (and those that imitated them). In Indian vernaculars, the term is often patiparameśvara, which means she who has her 'supreme lord as her husband'. The ostensible purpose of the vow to a husband was to ensure his health, welfare and longevity (and by extension that of the family). Its deep structure, like that of other vows, was an implicit contract (though cosmicised and sacramentalised as marriage). A wife's duties included the following: having children (especially sons), preparing food, providing sexual and other pleasures for her husband, managing the household, and doing housework and childcare. A husband's duties included being a progenitor and providing economic support, protection and marital security. Sometimes, this implicit contract was adjusted to a religious context: service to and praise of a deity with the hope that he or she would reciprocate by supporting the implicit contract (strīdharma).

Highly ritualised, the vow began with a formal declaration of intention (saṃkalpa). It continued with fasting or other acts of renunciation, which created a power that the wife could use directly for her own purpose but also indirectly to pressurise either her husband or the deity to act on her behalf. Besides fulfilling her side of the contract, or barter, the power generated by this vow could even generate control over her husband. At least, this was how Draupadī explained her control over five husbands (*Mahābhārata* 3.223.37). Seeing husbands as gods was like other forms of apotheosis in Hinduism (such as seeing brāhmaṇas or kings as gods on earth and women as incarnations of Śrī Lakṣmī). But whereas the husband's apotheosis was permanent, the wife's was often limited to ritual and festival contexts. The outcome of pativratā was a fusion of a woman's social role as wife (strīdharma) with her own spirituality in connection with ritual, yoga, devotion and service. This was her religious path to a better rebirth – especially a vacation in some lower heaven (svarga) – or even liberation in the supreme heaven (Vaikuṇṭha or Kailāsa).

Today, pativratā lives on in some Hindu communities. But feminists emphasise its contribution to oppressive androcentrism.

See also: **Draupadī; Lakṣmī, Śrī; Mahābhārata; Strīdharma; Vrata**

KATHERINE K. YOUNG

Further reading

Hess, L. 1999. 'Rejecting Sita: Indian Responses to the Ideal Man's Cruel Treatment of His Ideal Wife'. *Journal of the American Academy of Religion* 67.1: 1–32.

Leslie, J. 1989. *The Perfect Wife: The Orthodox Hindu Woman According to the Stridharmapaddhati of Tryambakayajvan*. New York: Oxford University Press.

McDaniel, J. 2003. *Making Virtuous Daughters and Wives: An Introduction to Women's Brata Rituals in Bengali Folk Religion*. Albany, NY: State University of New York Press.

McGee, M. 1991. 'Desired Fruits: Motive and Intention in the Votive Rites of Hindu Women'. In J. Leslie, ed., *Roles and Rituals for Hindu Women*. 71–88. London: Pinter Publishers, 71–88.

Narayanan, V. 1991. 'Hindu Perceptions of Auspiciousness and Sexuality'. In J. Becher, ed., *Women, Religion and Sexuality: Studies on the Impact of Religious Teachings on Women*. Geneva: World Council of Churches Publications, 64–92.

Olivelle, P. 2004. *The Law Code of Manu*. Oxford: Oxford University Press.

Patton, L. 2002. *Jewels of Authority: Women and Text in the Hindu Tradition*. Oxford: Oxford University Press.

Pearson, A.M. 1996. *'Because it Gives Me Peace of Mind': Ritual Fasts in the Religious Lives of Hindu Women*. Albany, NY: State University of New York Press.

Shah, S. 1995. *The Making of Womanhood: Gender Relations in the Mahābhārata*. Delhi: Manohar.

Wadley, S.S. 1983. 'Vrats: Transformers of Destiny'. In E.V. Daniel and C. Keyes, eds, *Karma: An Anthropological Inquiry*. Berkeley, CA: University of California Press, 147–62.

PĒCCIYAMMA

Pēcciyamma or Pēcciyamman is pervasive in the Madurai area of Tamil Nadu and possibly throughout the region. Her name is said, locally, to originate from pēccu, 'speech', a reference to her speaking to people in their dreams. However, she has a possible association with pēy or demons, for according to the *Tamil Lexicon* pēcci is a corruption of pēycci, meaning 'demoness' or 'a woman possessed by a demon'. She is perhaps an example of a goddess who straddles the divide between the gods and demons. In one small town near to Madurai, Pēcciyamman is considered to be fierce at one temple, benign at another and a combination of both at another. Pēcciyamman also changes her character from day to day. Every Friday, at a small backstreet temple in Madurai, one of the pūjāris (religious specialist) beautifully decorates the goddess with sandal paste, flowers, ornaments and new clothes. A radical transformation follows, as a fierce looking goddess with fangs and a lolling tongue re-emerges as a benevolent and smiling goddess.

See also: **Madurai; Religious specialists**

LYNN FOULSTON

Further reading

Foulston, L. 2002. *At the Feet of the Goddess: The Divine Feminine in Local Hindu Religion*. Brighton and Portland, OR: Sussex Academic Press.

PHULE, JOTIRAO (1827–90)

Jotirao Phule was a pioneering and influential low-caste radical who reconstructed Hindu as well as Maharashtrian myths and legends. He believed brāhmaṇas had conspired to oppress the low castes by creating a fatalistic culture and expensive rituals, and that the brāhmaṇas' traditional role of controlling access to education had been reinforced under British rule through their new role as civil servants, with jobs far in excess of their numbers. He stressed the unity of all non-brāhmaṇa groups as tillers of the soil and defenders of land and thus paved the way for later anti-brāhmaṇa movements. He was the first writer to use the 'Aryan invasion' theories of Max Müller for radical purposes, by presenting brāhmaṇas as the alien conquerors. He described Brahmā and Paraśurama, not as Gods, but as historical figures who led the onslaught on the indigenous peoples. The 'untouchables' were those who were banished due to their role as defenders. Śivaji, the Maratha warrior (now often represented by the Hindu right as anti-Muslim) was presented by Phule as an anti-brāhmaṇa leader. Phule was from a prosperous low caste, but not untouchable. He was deeply committed to the welfare of all. He set up schools for women, including unmarried mothers, as well as for 'untouchables'. He was an early advocate for the remarriage of widows. Educated by Christian missionaries, he was influenced by their Protestant anti-clericalism and by their view that belief should be shaped by scripture. He refused to convert, being also deeply influenced by the deists and the writing of Thomas Paine, as well as by the traditions of his region. He wanted freedom from the British but considered that a true patriotism would concern itself with social injustice. He published plays, tracts, stories and ballads and created an alternative Hindu calendar.

See also: **Avatāra; Brahmā; Brāhmaṇas; Caste; Dalits; Müller, Friedrich Max; Shiv Sena; Widow remarriage; Women question; Women's education**

MARY SEARLE-CHATTERJEE

Further reading

O'Hanlon, Rosalind. 1985. *Caste Conflict and Ideology: Mahatma Jotirao Phule and Low Caste Protest in Nineteenth Century Western India.* Cambridge: Cambridge University Press.

Omvedt, Gail. 1995. *Dalit Visions: Tracts for the Times.* London: Sangam.

PILGRIMAGE

See: **Tīrthayātrā (Pilgrimage)**

PIḶḶAI LOKĀCĀRYA (1264–1369)

One of the two major figures of Viśiṣṭādvaita Vedānta after the death of Rāmānuja (d. 1137). The other is Vedānta Deṣika, and they are, respectively, considered to be responsible for the founding of the Southern (Teṇkalai) and Northern (Vaṭakalai) divisions of the Viśiṣṭādvaita school, although these schools did not develop fully until the eighteenth century. The Southern (Teṇkalai) school believes that the soul should give up all effort and throw itself on complete dependence upon the saving grace of Viṣṇu. For this reason it is known as the school of the kitten, who is carried by the mother, as opposed to the school of the monkey, who has to hold on to its parent.

Piḷḷai Lokācārya taught during the second half of the thirteenth century and wrote in a highly Sanskritised Tamil known as Maṇipravāḷa. Collectively entitled the *Aṣṭādaśarahasya*, his works consist of eighteen works, of which the *Tattvatreya*, the *Arthapañcaka* and the *Śrivacanabhūṣaṇa* are well known. In addition to his views on complete dependence, he also elaborated upon and defended worship of the deity through the temple image (arcā) consecrated to receive the divine spirit and consequently an incarnational form. He also put forward the argument that Śri, or the Goddess, was only a subordinate deity unable to liberate beings, a function of Viṣṇu alone, but significant as an intercessor to the God. His final major contribution to Vaiṣṇavite philosophy lies in his categorisation of souls. The usual three types of jīva are baddha (those who are bound), mukta (those who are free from bondage) and nitya (those who are eternally free). To these three categories Piḷḷai Lokācārya added mumukṣus (those which desire liberation) and kevalas (those who desire the bliss of the individual self without rebirth). The latter category was probably under the influence of Jainism.

See also: **Image worship; Jainism, relationship with Hinduism; Jīva; Rāmānuja; Vaiṣṇavism; Viśiṣṭādvaita; Viṣṇu**

RON GEAVES

Further reading

Colas, G. 2003. 'History of Vaiṣṇava Traditions: An Equisse'. In G. Flood, ed., *The Blackwell Companion to Hinduism*. Oxford: Blackwell, 229–70.

Srinivasa Chari, S.M. 1994. *Vaiṣṇavism*. Delhi: Motilal Banarsidass.

PIŚĀCAS

The tormented souls of dead people, unable to become either pretas or pitṛs. When the śrāddha rituals are not performed, or are performed imperfectly, the psyche of the deceased turns into a constantly hungry and thirsty being. This condition is due to the predominance of tejas (heat) in the subtle body of his/her new existence. The piśācas are named only once in Vedic literature (*Ṛgveda* 1.133.5), while they appear quite often in epic (their birth from the cosmic egg is told in *Mahābhārata* 1.1.33) and Purāṇic literature. They appear as vampires who capture the vital fluids and devour the inner organs of their victims by entering through orifices. The piśācas live in cremation grounds (śmaśānas) and wander in the hope of eating corpses. Despite the lack of a proper cult, piśācas are offered liquor, meat, black scarves, insects and sesame seeds during rituals of exorcism (piśācamocana).

See also: **Itihāsa; Mahābhārata; Pitṛs; Pretas; Purāṇas; Saṃhitā; Śrāddha**

FABRIZIO M. FERRARI

Further reading

Bhattacharyya, N.N. 2000. *Indian Demonology. The Inverted Pantheon*. Delhi: Manohar.

Filippi, G.G. 1996. *Mrtyu. Concept of Death in Indian Tradition*. Delhi: D.K. Printworld.

PITṚLOKA

'World of forefathers'. The purpose of the still widely performed śrāddha ceremonies is the transformation of the person of a deceased father into a pitṛ (ancestor) and to settle him in pitṛloka, the dwelling place of the forefathers, and not expose him to the fate of wandering the earth as a restless preta (ghost). As a pitṛ he not only enjoys the bliss of the heavenly abode but is also qualified to receive worship as a deva. While śrāddha and ancestor veneration have been practised from the earliest Vedic religion until the present day, the understanding of the nature of pitṛloka has undergone many changes in the course of time.

Purāṇic tradition identifies the original pitṛs with the Prajāpatis, the progenitors of human races and the sons of gods. Brahmā, by way of penance, had ordered the devas, who had ceased to worship him, to receive instruction from their sons in matters of proper worship and devotion: the devas then had to call their sons 'fathers' – the first generation of pitṛs (*Matsya Purana* 1.13; *Viṣṇu Purana* 3.14).

There are seven classes of pitṛs, three of which, namely the Vairājas, the Agniśvāttas and Varhiṣads, are called amūrttya (without bodily form), composed of mental, non-material substances, who are able to assume at will any form. The four other classes, namely the Sukālas, the Āngirasas, the Suṣvadhas and the Somapās, are called mūrttya (embodied). The *Harivaṃśa Purana* offers detailed information on the genealogies of all these seven classes of forefathers and their progeny, including their places of residence.

According to the *Ṛgveda*, all good brāhmanas for whom proper last rites had been performed dwelt in pitṛloka, ruled over by Yama, who was the first mortal to find the path to immortality. *Ṛgveda* (9.113) calls pitṛloka 'the deathless, undecaying world, wherein the light of heaven is set and everlasting luster shines'. The supplicant prays: 'Make me immortal in that realm, where they move even as they list, in the third sphere of inmost heaven where lucid worlds are full of light.' Further, the place is described as 'the region of the radiant moon, where food and full delight are found', the region 'where happiness abounds' and where 'all wishes are fulfilled' (trans. Griffiths 1963). Although later Hindu tradition understands pitṛloka as a place of transit, from which the deceased return to the world of saṃsāra to strive to achieve full liberation (mokṣa), it appears that the *Vedas* considered it a place of eternal enjoyment for those who had found the 'right way'.

The Vedas divide the year into Uttarāyāna (Northern course), also called Devayāna, the Path of the Gods, and Dakṣiṇayāna (Southern course), called Pitṛyāna, the Path of the Fathers. The first comprises the six months from winter to summer solstice, when the length of the days increases, the second those from summer to winter solstice, when the length of day decreases. According to the *Upaniṣads*, sages who meditate instead of offering sacrifices pass at death into the light, from there into the day, then into the half-month of the waxing moon, then into the six months in which the sun travels northward, from these to devaloka, from there into the sun, into lightning: they are led to Brahma-loka, from which there is no return. Brāhmaṇa householders who observe the rites pass at the time of dying into smoke, from smoke into night, the half-moon of the waning moon, from there to the six months during which the sun travels southward, from there to pitṛloka, from there into the moon. They must return again to be reborn in a human body (*Bṛhadāraṇyaka Upaniṣad* 5.2.15).

Hindu eschatology is a mixture of Vedic and Purāṇic ideas and thus among Hindus today various notions of the nature of pitṛloka are entertained, following diverse traditions.

See also: **Brahmā; Deities; Mokṣa; Pitṛs; Pretas; Saṃhitā; Śrāddha; Vedism**

KLAUS K. KLOSTERMAIER

Further reading

Griffiths, R.T.H. 1963. *The Hymns of the Ṛgveda Translated with a Popular Commentary*, 2 vols, 4th edn. The Chowkchamba Sanskrit Studies Vols. 24 and 25. Varanasi: The Chowkchamba Sanskrit Series Office.

Macdonell, A.A. 1963. *Vedic Mythology, Encyclopedia of Indo-AryanResearch*, ed. G. Bühler, vol. III, 1A. Reprint. Varanasi: Indological Book House.

Radhakantadeva, R. 1961. 'Pitrloka'. *Sabdakalpadruma*, vol. 3, 147. Reprint. Varanasi: Chaukhamba Sanskrta Granthamala No. 93.

PITṚPAKSA

The death rituals (antyeṣṭi) are only part of a long process whereby a deceased person is separated from this world and incorporated into the world of the ancestors (Kane 1968–77, IV: 334–551). Following the funerary rites, there is a series of other rituals performed for deceased ancestors (pitṛ) designated śrāddha. These include not only those rituals performed shortly after death and annually on the anniversary of the death but also a festival when all ancestors are remembered. The mahālaya ('great abode') śrāddha is in the dark half of the month Bhādra, around October, which is called pitṛpakṣa, 'half-month of the ancestors'. Generally, the ritual takes place on the day of the pitṛpakṣa corresponding to the day of the half-month on which the person died, but some categories of the deceased are allotted different days (Stevenson 1920: 327f.).

See also: **Antyeṣṭi; Pitṛs; Śrāddha.**

DERMOT KILLINGLEY

Further reading

Kane, Pandurang Vaman. 1968–77. *History of Dharmaśāstra (Ancient and Mediæval Religious and Civil Law)*, 2nd edn, 5 vols (vols 1, 2 and 5 bound in two parts each). Poona [Pune]: Bhandarkar Oriental Research Institute (1st edn 1930–62).

Stevenson, Mrs [Margaret] Sinclair. 1920. *The Rites of the Twice-Born*. London: Oxford University Press.

PITṚS

'Father'; 'ancestor', 'forefather'. When someone dies, he is transformed into preta, a 'voyager', a departed. Only after the correct performance of the śrāddha rituals (the last of the saṃskāra rites following antyeṣṭī) is the deceased integrated into the pitṛloka, the abode of the ancestors. The śrāddha ritual, with its tangible and intangible donations, is made both to ensure the transformation of the deceased into ancestor and to grant protection to the living. In fact, if rituals are not properly performed, the preta becomes a piśāca and in this form he/she will torment the living. The śrāddha rites are performed by the sapiṇḍas (those who have at least one ancestor in common back to the seventh generation), but according to the *Manusmṛti* (9.106) it is the eldest son of the deceased who will take care of the transformation into pitṛ. The ten days following the cremation of the body are crucial in that a subtle body will be given to the deceased, the yātanā śarīra ('suffering body'). During a ritual called piṇḍa-pitṛ-yajña, the soul (jīva) of the deceased is fed with the piṇḍas, sweet balls made of barley flour, ghee, sugar, milk, peas, butter and sesame seeds. Ten piṇḍas are offered to him, each of them representing a different part of the body. Now the deceased is a preta. He will rest in this form for ten lunar months. After this period, the eldest son of the dead is guided by a brāhmaṇa in performing the sapiṇḍī-karaṇa, a special śrāddha rite. A mixture of water, various essences and black sesame seeds is poured into four earthen vessels. Three of them represent the father, the grandfather and the great-grandfather of the deceased, while the fourth one is the new pitṛ. With this ritual, the preta is eventually transformed into an ancestor.

See also: **Antyeṣṭī; Brāhmaṇa; Dharmaśāstras; Piśāca; Pitṛloka; Pretas; Saṃskāra; Śrāddha**

FABRIZIO M. FERRARI

Further reading

Filippi, G.G. 1996. *Mrtyu. Concept of Death in Indian Tradition*. Delhi: DK Printworld.

PLANETS

See: **Navagrahas (Planets)**

PODDAR, HANUMAN PRASAD (b. 1892)

Born in 1892 in Bengal, Hanuman Prasad Poddar was one of the significant figures of the Hindu renaissance in the first half of the twentieth century. Originally inspired by the various movements to free India from British colonialism, he spent twenty-one months under house arrest because of his close connections with a number of Bengali revolutionaries. During this time he experienced a profound spiritual transformation which led to his undertaking the editorship of the Hindu periodical *Kalyāṇ*. The magazine was used to promote a moral and social awakening based on the values of Indian religions, philosophy and culture.

Although a social activist at the forefront of relief and charity work, he was also renowned as a spiritual figure, attracting large numbers who sought his guidance and counsel. However, his most significant and abiding activity was the creation of the Gita Press in Vārāṇasī, which published Hindu sacred texts, such as the *Bhagavadgītā*, the *Upaniṣads* and the *Rāmāyaṇa*, in Sanskrit with Hindi translation. The books were mass-produced and continue to sell millions of copies throughout India.

See also: **Bhagavadgītā; Hinduism, modern and contemporary; Rāmāyaṇa; Upaniṣads; Vārāṇasī**

RON GEAVES

Further reading

Verma, Braj Lal. 1987. *Hanuman Prasad Poddar*. Publications Division, Government of India.

www.freeindia.org/dynamic (accessed 1 November 2005).

POETRY

In all major Indian languages poetry is used as a form of religious expression and this often intermingles with devotional songs popular at every level of society. The most usual form of expression for the more popular religious works has always been verse, in part reflecting the substantially oral status of these works and their access through recitation. Much of this, however, is not called poetry in Indian languages. Though the *Mahābhārata* is composed in metrical verse it is called itihāsa, translating roughly as 'legend', whereas Vālmīki, author of the *Rāmāyaṇa* is called ādikavi, or 'the original poet', and has been respected by later commentators as 'composing' what becomes the high style of poetry called *kāvya*. The latter does not perform any religious function and was never composed for religious purposes even though the subject of *kāvyas* often derives from the two epics. In contrast to all of this are the prose works, dating from the early Vedic period, which are normally presenting technical data, or, in the Common Era, take the form of scholastic commentaries on earlier texts.

The problem with defining the vast bulk of Sanskrit literature as poetry is that it is composed in metrical verse forms containing four feet and a standard number of syllables measured by the so-called heaviness or lightness of the syllable. Both Sanskrit epics are substantially composed in two metres called anuṣṭubh and triṣṭubh, which recur in later literature, added to by some longer metres usually found in actual poetry. Whilst the variations in metre become very obvious in oral recitation, the poetic function achieved by verse tends to be sublimated by the content and the intense repetition of the verse. The ubiquity of the anuṣṭubh metre in religious texts of all kinds and genres, where the intention is not to produce beauty of expression, means that a text cannot be regarded as poetry simply because it is produced in metrical form as opposed to prose form. Generic types do not necessarily coincide with poetic forms, though the later Sanskrit scholars of poetics did make distinctions between types of texts based on the form of those texts. The same applies to Tamil religious poetry, which is composed in several rather complex metres, but this differs in some measure from the Sanskrit poetry in that it can be set to music, sung and be understood by a popular audience.

Recitation of poetry has been important since the earliest recorded history of Sanskrit literature. The *Ṛgveda* is the earliest Sanskrit text and is composed in a variety of metres. These poems are hymns which were sung, probably to music, in sacrifices, performed in order to venerate particular gods. There is also evidence of competitions between specialists in poetry in regard to composition, where the actual gift of poetic composition was regarded as being inspired by the power of sacrality epitomised in the name Brahman. As such, a ritual context for the use of poetry was established from a very early period.

Following the earliest strata of Vedic literature most texts were composed in prose until the two great Sanskrit epics. Following them, most other mythological texts, especially the *Purāṇas*, were composed in a similar metre to what is found in both of the epics. The ubiquity of the anuṣṭubh metre used here must have created an emphasis on any other metre that happened to come up in the text. This is especially so in the *Purāṇas* where what are called ornamental metres are used, often placed at the end of chapters or particular narrative units in order to mark boundaries or create emphasis. Often poetry is used to present a hymn of praise to a particular god. Such poems are called stotras and, though embedded within the standard anuṣṭubh metre, they can easily be extracted and used for singing hymns of devotion to the particular god to which they are directed. This has led to the production of several complete selections of stotras which almost function like hymnbooks. An example is this verse from a stotra to Gaṇeśa found in the *Gaṇeśapurāṇa*:

To him who has the form of the supreme Brahmā,
Who has the form of bliss and consciousness,
Who has the form of the bliss of truth,
The Lord of the gods, the supreme Lord,
The ocean of qualities, Lord of the qualities,
Beyond the qualities, the Lord,
To Mayūreśa, the primeval,
We have bowed! We have bowed!
To him who should be praised by the world,
The one, the supreme syllable Oṃ,
The supreme cause of the qualities,
Who is free from transformation,
Protector of the world, its destroyer,
Its creator, to him,
To Mayūreśa, the primeval,
We have bowed! We have bowed!
(*Gaṇeśapurāṇa* 2, 123, 40–41)

Tamil religious literature also has long epics such as the *Manimekalai* and the *Cilapattikāram* composed in fairly consistent metres and so paralleling the Sanskrit epics in allowing the content to override the verse form in importance. However, this situation is reversed in the poems of the so-called Nāyaṉmār, worshippers of Śiva and the Āḻvārs, worshippers of Viṣṇu. They composed collections of poems such as *Tevarām* and the *Divyaprabandham* between the seventh and tenth centuries of the Common Era. These are uniformly devotional in content and, whilst they can be of considerable theological sophistication, they are still sung to the accompaniment of music and are easily understood at a popular level.

Although most is known about poetry in the two great canonical languages, Sanskrit and Tamil, poems which can be sung as devotional songs (bhajans) exist in all major Indian vernacular languages. Groups of devotees walk around the streets singing bhajans as an expression of their devotion and in order to gain good karma. Thus the poems assume an important role in religious observance, almost as important as the devotional impulse in those who compose them.

See also: **Āḻvārs; Gaṇeśa; Mahābhārata; Nāyaṉmār; Purāṇas; Rāmāyaṇa; Śiva; Vālmīki; Veda; Viṣṇu**

GREG BAILEY

Further reading

Cutler, Norman. 1987. *Songs of Experiences. The Poetics of Tamil Devotion.* Bloomington, IN: Indiana University Press.

Lienhard, S. 1984. *A History of Classical Poetry. Sanskrit-Pali-Prakrit.* Wiesbaden: Otto Harrassowitz.

POLITICS

Until the terms Hinduism and Hindu expressed a collective community (albeit an artificial one even today), it is difficult to relate abstract religious principles to political activity. Nevertheless, religious traditions of the subcontinent were clearly tied to political processes. From the time of the early republics and monarchies of the seventh century BCE through to the Gupta dynasty and the Pallavas in the South in the early Middle Ages, kingly authority appropriated the divine for political legitimacy, for example in the rājasuya – a ritual of royal consecration. So too did religious authority regulate the secular. Around the beginning of the Common Era, the hitherto secular epics – the *Rāmāyaṇa* and *Mahābhārata* – were given a divine significance. The most important addition in this respect was that of the *Bhagavadgītā* to the *Mahābhārata*. This hymn synthesised the secular duties of war with a sense of the morality of action as based in the concept of Dharma, through the actions of Arjuna and Kṛṣṇa. The divinity of the king was emphasised in brahmanical sources for clear reasons of state: daṇḍa (punishment) and dharma (a notion of social order) were crucial in a political world based on a continual fear of anarchy, as expressed in Kauṭilya's *Arthaśastra*.

Religious authority could also serve to invert traditional power structures. The sects that emerged from Buddha and Mahavira from the sixth century BCE were distinguished from brahmanical power by, among other things, their qualified rejection of traditional social stratifications and their stress on lower strata of society. Buddha, for example, used a popular language, Magadhi, instead of Sanskrit and his followers were drawn mainly from mercantile, artisan and cultivating communities. Since both Mahavira and Buddha preached non-violence, there was little place, in theory, for the authority of the kṣatriya warrior ruler. However, royal patronage remained crucial. Indeed, an important reorganisation of Buddhism occurred under the rule of Aśoka in *c.*250 BCE. In the rock and pillar edicts of Aśoka we have a clear exposition, through the principle of Dharma (Dhamma), of an officially sponsored code of social conduct, involving toleration and non-violence. This state policy was designed to overcome sectarian and regional conflict and was probably motivated by a response to religious heterogeneity. Such a notion of state-sponsored religious toleration was to have an important bearing on later, modern expositions of Indian secularism.

Other movements contributed to the separation between officially sponsored Brahmanism and popular religions in the political life of the subcontinent. From the eighth and ninth centuries CE there were attempts to systematise Vedic philosophy and religion, to endow it with wider meanings for communities across the subcontinent. The earliest serious movement to reform in this sense was probably that of the Keralan brāhmaṇa Śaṅkara, which came to be known as Vedānta. Śaṅkara's movement worked through a series of richly endowed maṭhas, allowing it to spread in a monastic form. Around the same time, in South India, a range of popular Bhakti (devotional) cults served to distinguish official and state-sponsored Brahmanism from the religious traditions of subjects. In later centuries royal patronage was extended to such cults. But political and social protest in India could always be exercised through popular sects and movements, such as the Liṅgāyats – a sect which attacked the religious hypocrisy of Brahmanical dominance.

The temple formed the meeting point for these two levels of religious activity in medieval India. In a practical sense it also served to delineate Hindu society and to provide the space and infrastructure for local political activity. Unclean castes were excluded from the temple, but general village assemblies – sabhas – composed of smaller committees, would use temples as meeting centres. The priesthood acted as arbitrators in village administration. A large community of dependents aside from this priesthood might rely upon the temple and so its finance, whether through royal or local patronage, remained crucial despite the theoretical irrelevance of the authority of the warrior-cum-ruler, and as such was central to the stability of Indian societies. The temple was also the centre of formal education in Sanskrit, serving to divorce learned subjects from everyday life, but defining educated elites in each region. The significant temple towns, being centres of great wealth and offering opportunities for pious Islamic iconoclasm, also determined the character of Afghan invasions in India in the early eleventh century. For example, between 1010 and 1026, the invasions of Mahmud of Ghazni were directed to Mathura, Thanesar, Kanauj and Somnath.

The Islamic impact on India's spiritual geography has had significant political implications right through to the present day, colouring contemporary political views of India's Muslim invaders and settlers. The notion of a 'model Hindu Kingdom' was set up through the Vijayanagar Empire in the fourteenth century in response to Muslim power in North India. The invasion of the Turkified Mongol, Babur, the first Mughal ruler, through to the last successful descendant of that dynasty, Aurangzeb, was marked by alternating policies of accommodation and iconoclasm: Akbar turned his back on Islamic orthodoxy by abolishing a discriminatory poll tax for non-Muslims and by attempting to instate what has been described as a syncretic state religion. The openness of Akbar to religious diversity led to him to perform certain Hindu rites, although he never allowed himself to be publicly viewed as an anti-Islamic apostate. Aurangzeb restored Islamic orthodoxy between 1658 and 1707. This, combined with his policy of destroying newly constructed temples and his conflict with the Hindu Marathas, has led him to be painted in a hateful light by Hindu fundamentalists and compared with James II of England in less discriminating colonial accounts.

As the British East India Company expanded across the subcontinent, the project of establishing legal systems to underpin British authority served to politicise an as yet ill-defined 'Hinduism'. Hastings' plan for the administration of Bengal in 1772 attempted to parallel śāstric law with ecclesiastical law in England. This meant that British courts in India came to rely on vyavasthas (written opinions) from recognised paṇḍits. William Jones subsequently produced a code of Hindu law in 1784, which paved the way for the 'discovery' of what it thought were Hinduism's essential traditions and texts. In this early colonial discourse on Hinduism there was a constant tension. On the one hand were attempts to find order and homogeneity and a basis for political authority in the subcontinent's indigenous religious practices. On the other were efforts to denigrate Hinduism as a degenerate, chaotic cacophony of primitive forms of animism. James Mill's *A History of British India* (1818) exemplified the second more critical voice in this discourse. The *History* set out phases of Hindu and Muslim history and described the former as primitive despotism – the antithesis of Whiggish political and social progress. The tension between these colonial views encouraged a range of Indian responses, some of which resulted in political and religious institutions seeking to define and limit the meaning of Hinduism. This struggle to define and thereby politicise Hinduism was encouraged still further with the British proclamation of religious neutrality in 1858, which effectively placed religion at the centre of Victorian ideas of Indian rights and privileges.

For most of the nineteenth century, however, it is difficult to generalise colonial thinking about Hinduism, even though it tended to create a more concrete political sense of Hindu community. This difficulty extends into the late nineteenth century, when writers and administrators attempted to systematise 'scientific' knowledge about the subcontinent. The European literature setting out with the project of investigating Hinduism and the Hindu people is complex and varied. Taking into account the significant shifts in this writing over at least three centuries, and the heterogeneous nature of European responses to the subcontinent, it seems inappropriate to describe it as a clearly defined discourse. But there were some outstanding trends: Victorian scholarship was fascinated by what appeared to be an ethnographical battleground, in which caste and tribe were commonly researched in terms of racial hierarchies. And in a large number of these accounts 'caste' was represented as an essential institution of the Hindu. For writers such as Walter Elliot, William Hutton and Herbert Hope Risley, respectively, racial categorisation could be based around notions of nationality and political organisation amongst 'castes', racial collisions between 'Aryan' invaders and 'aboriginal' tribes, or even in the physiognomy of Indians (Bayly 1995). The discourse was divided and varied, being part of other academic interactions about racial theory taking place in Europe. In India, the idea of divided ethnicities described by writers and administrators also served a general political purpose and suited the imperial state. Yet in its attempt to investigate essential characteristics of castes and tribes, often as racial groups, the need to describe 'national' types became urgent.

What this discussion dating back to the late eighteenth century did help to produce amongst Indians, then, was a struggle, sometimes through race, sometimes through culture, to define Hindus as a community, and from there as a nationality. Where groups began to comprehend political roles and identities that corresponded to religious identities, such political roles were often derivative of, or at least based in, a dialogue between European writers and administrators and Indian reformers. The most obvious case here is the discussion of a Hindu 'nation', to which we will turn shortly. Constructions of nationality were based on a set of interactions between Indians and European political theorists, and grew out of similar interactions to those surrounding religious reform. And it was through Indian movements to reform or to revive religious traditions and to form organisational frameworks to drive such movements that the first concrete and generalised Indian discussions of Hindu identity emerged in the nineteenth century.

The Brahmo Samaj, founded in 1828 by Rammohan Roy in Calcutta, represented perhaps the first such reforming organisation. By the 1840s, under the leadership of Debendranath Tagore, the Samaj was transformed into a movement which confronted the challenges to what it saw as consolidated Hindu religious sentiment, by resisting the activities of missionaries in Bengal. Hot on the tail of the Brahmo Samaj, parallel institutions developed to uphold alternative discourses of Hindu orthodoxy – in 1831 the Calcutta Dharma Sabha was formed with a programme explicitly directed against alleged state interference in Hindu religious practices – in this case Bentinck's sati decree. This two-stranded development of reformist and orthodox institutions was to run through the infant national political institutions such as the Indian National Congress in the late 1880s and 1890s. But before the foundation of that body in 1885, reformers and orthodox had already formed their own institutions, which were to transcend local politics. The Arya Samaj, founded in 1875 by Swami Dayananda Saraswati, was perhaps the most successful and politically notorious Hindu reform movement of this period, despite its activities being concentrated in the Punjab and western Uttar Pradesh. Projecting the Veda as the 'book' of Hinduism – the textual challenge to Islam and Christianity – propagating monotheism and caste reform, the Arya Samaj was popular amongst early twentieth-century nationalists, attracted by the idea of a single Hindu canon and a nationally encompassing faith. It was partly through the Arya Samaj and leaders such as Lala Lajpat Rai that the modernising dreams of educated middle-class Congressmen were associated with new notions of Hindu community. Equally important in political terms were orthodox institutions, which shadowed Hindu reformist organisations. The most significant were the Sanatan Dharma Sabhas and their umbrella organisation, the Bharat Dharma Mahamandala, founded in 1887. Orthodox bodies in this period were deliberately modelled along modern political lines, with annual sessions and representative delegates, akin to the Congress itself. They set out to define and defend Hindu orthodoxy with the support of wealthy Hindu patrons and Rājas.

Around the turn of the century, as Westernised political institutions were being developed, a new discourse on Hinduism itself began to emphasise the essentially 'modern' characteristics of Hindu community. This process was not just championed by the Arya Samaj. Political thinkers and journalists feeding off the burgeoning Indian-language presses contributed to a rich and widening public sphere of debate on Hinduism and Hindu identity. Probably the most important thinkers in this respect were the literary figures Bankim Chandra Chatterjee in Bengal and Hariscandra Bharatendu in Banaras. Both contributed to a sense of an all-encompassing Indian Hindu identity, based on ideas of the linguistic, cultural and political bases of Hindu unity, as a challenge or response to Western modernity. Both did so within the framework of reformist–orthodox discussions on Hinduism, with Hariscandra Bharatendu promoting a modern image of Hindu orthodoxy. This literary activity was also built around a new public sphere in the development of 'national' languages and the promotion of Hindi. In response to the championing of Urdu by North Indian Muslim landed elites in the late nineteenth century, the promotion of Hindi as a language of government, and eventually as a national tongue, fed into the parallel communal assertions of Hindus and Muslims, helping to shape their identity symbols.

It was not only in discussion and debate that Hinduism and Hindu identity were shaped through a response to modernity. The idea of a unified Hindu community and nation went hand in hand with political institution building. These institutions, in their turn, were built around the particular political conditions of a rapidly transforming colonial state. The Raj in India sought to limit the parameters of political debate and political participation to collaborating elites. But as the imperial power attempted to adapt to new international pressures for political and constitutional advance around the time of the Great War, it was forced to widen its political net, seeking out new collaborators who would have political clout with a predetermined set of

Indian communities. Indian leaders and popular politicians both responded and reacted to this process. As early as the very modest local government reforms of the 1880s and 1890s, Indian leaders had realised the political urgency of reaching wider popular constituencies. And since the parameters of political debates and notions of political representation had already been set out in terms of religious community (and the numerical values attached to community – a process developed by the colonial census from 1871), appeals to wide religious identities became an integral part of popular political appeal. Bal Gangadhar Tilak exploited the popular Gaṇapati festival in Maharashtra in the 1890s, infusing the festival with a new political significance. With Curzon's partition of Bengal in 1905, embattled Bengali Hindu leaders attempted to broaden their protest by building a swadeshi movement of foreign boycotts. This was an explicitly economic response to Lancashire cloth which was infused with rhetoric of the spiritual sanctity of all things indigenous to Indian soil. In the inter-war period, as we shall see below, leaders of the ostensibly 'secular' Congress were also to toy with the idea of popular politics through religious sentiment and appeals to national, 'Hindu' symbols.

More explicitly, political movements were built around a struggle to define a Hindu constituency in direct response to colonial notions of political representation. In 1910, the census commissioner E.A. Gait attempted to clarify how a Hindu population might be recorded, and his 'circular' formed the basis of the 1911 Census. The colonial view was to challenge the assumption of high-caste Hindus that Hinduism could contain India's diverse low-caste and tribal religious traditions. Although not the sole cause of it, the colonial census helped to strengthen moves within Hindu institutions for popular enumeration. It gave a spur to the unprecedented movement of the Arya Samaj of reconversion of low-caste Muslim converts 'back' to Hinduism, in the śuddhi or purification campaigns. It helped to galvanise the Samaj leader Swami Shraddhanand to develop his notion of Hindu sangathan (organisation) in response to the idea of Hindus as 'a dying race' by the late 1910s and 1920s. Perhaps most significantly, it fed into the development of a national network of political institutions with the broad purpose of promoting the political interests of India's Hindu communities – the Hindu Sabhas – under the umbrella of the Hindu Mahasabha. This organisation, although insignificant in electoral terms, was to be an important forerunner to modern Hindu nationalist parties after 1947.

The first Hindu Sabha was founded in Lahore in 1906 with the general and poorly defined objectives of promoting broad Hindu interests. Although later organised along similar institutional lines to the Congress, the Hindu Sabhas from 1909 were initially set up in reaction to Congress's failure to promote Hindu self-assertion. The prime mover here was Lala Lal Chand, an Arya Samaj leader who critiqued the whole basis of Congress's composite nationalism in the context of separate electorates for Muslims in the 1909 Morley Minto reforms. Instead of a direct challenge to colonialism, moderate communal appeals to government on the behalf of the 'Hindu community' were to be the basis of the Sabha programme. The significance of the period from 1909 was that the Hindu Sabha movement set up for the first time an explicitly political agenda for the community interests of 'Hindus', however ill defined and loose that community might be, and despite the Sabha's fitful existence up to the 1920s. It was not until 1915 that an all-India Hindu Sabha was formed – the precursor to the Hindu Mahasabha – and compared to the Arya Samaj its purpose appeared vague. This organisational and political weakness was to have important implications for the much more successful Congress movement, which was repeatedly compared with the Sabhas in the Indian press. In the inter-war years the Congress was intermittently appropriated by part of the leadership, and thereby in some areas of India by some of the ideologies of the Hindu Sabha movement. The result was that the notion of a Hindu political interest was to gain a much wider currency than simply through the elitist and somewhat vague channels of the Hindu Mahasabha and its satellites.

The figure perhaps most clearly illustrative of this trend of the Congress appropriating 'Hindu' leadership was Pandit Madan Mohan Malaviya. This lawyer, agent of great Hindu patrons and planner and founder of the Banaras Hindu University, rejuvenated the Hindu Mahasabha in 1923. Importantly, the Mahasabha reappeared in the very new context of more strident post-war nationalist politics, Gandhian reorganisation of the Congress, the resurgence of Hindu–Muslim violence in North India and the continued moves of the Arya Samaj to promote śuddhi. The 1920s were the first decade in which the Hindu Mahasabha took an active role in local and Legislative Council elections, by extending and reorganising its institutional framework. The 1920s were also a decade in which symbols of communal mobilisation helped to generate increasingly frequent opportunities for conflict between Hindus and Muslims in the towns and cities of North India. Cow slaughter and 'music before mosques', the clashes of religious festivals, often became the foci for this violence. These assertions of Hindu identity were implicitly, sometimes explicitly, tied into elections and political representation. Riots in 1924 in Lucknow, in Allahabad in 1926 and in Kanpur in 1927 were linked into municipal and, by extension, provincial politics and the electoral process. There were new ideological directions too. Swami Shraddhanand further developed the notion of Hindu sangathan, through a stress on self-discipline and brahmacārya and proposals to build a 'Hindu Rashtra Mandir', or Hindu national temple. His activities and those of the Arya Samaj too were increasingly associated with the Hindu Mahasabha movement as a whole.

This entrance of a new 'Hindu' voice into Indian politics was not without its challengers. Symbols of Hindu unity and assertion were used for the social and political assertion of a range of social groups. For example, in Kanpur the Adi-Hindu Sabha represented the rights of low-caste Hindus in Kanpur to present themselves as the true defenders of Hinduism (see Gooptu 2001). Although not in any sense coordinated, there had been a tradition of low-caste opposition to these brāhmaṇa-dominated Hindu movements, which went back at least to the low-caste reformer Jotirao Phule. This Maharashtran challenger to Tilak founded the Satyashodak Samaj ('Truth Seeking Society') in 1873, which publicised the idea of the śūdras and ādi-śūdras as the kṣatriyas of a previous era (O'Hanlon 1985). What is interesting about a number of these challenges is that they largely worked within the framework of Orientalist and nationalist assumptions about Hindu community, inverting the meaning of caste, but rarely challenging the existence of a 'Hindu' communal voice.

Yet the idea of a distinctively 'Hindu' politics in the subcontinent was really made possible in the 1920s and 1930s, ironically by the very success and amorphousness of the Indian National Congress itself and the nature of its own religious publicity. There were practical and ideological reasons for this. Malaviya, along with a host of other leaders active in the Hindu Sabhas or Arya Samaj, was subsumed within the Congress during the Non-Cooperation movement of 1920–22.

With the political successes of the Congress in the 1930s, it seemed to many of these leaders that longstanding exclusion from the Congress Party framework might amount to political isolation. Gandhi's philosophy of satyāgraha (literally, 'truth force') and ahiṃsā and the very style of his ascetic approach clearly brought selected Hindu symbols into the practice of agitational politics. In some cases, Gandhi's manipulation of popular Hindu symbolism was more explicit: references to 'Ramrajya', ongoing movements to assert the role of untouchables within the Hindu community, celebrations of the all-embracing, tolerant and absorbent nature of Hinduism, was easily associated in some Muslim minds with the programme of the Hindu Mahasabha. The whole notion of satyāgraha volunteering was to have an important impact on extreme Hindu nationalist institutions. But Gandhi was perhaps less important in generating this ambiguity in Congress politics than other leaders in the movement. Whereas Gandhi was adamant that national and religious identity should be independent variables, the programmatic manipulation of Hindu symbols had important effects as Congress rapidly extended its political mobilisation (and lost some of its control) through Civil Disobedience in the 1930s. Other leaders within the Congress were more directly and easily associated with Hindu mobilisation, despite the secular image of the All India Congress Committee: P.D. Tandon, Sampurnanand and Balkrishna Sharma in Uttar Pradesh, for example, in different ways expressed a notion of Hindu political mobilisation. A host of other local leaders in this important region of India manipulated festivals and melās or appropriated Hindu symbolism and rhetoric throughout the 1930s and 1940s. A comparable process occurred in the Bengal Congress in the 1940s (Chatterji 1994). It was with some justification, by viewing this symbolic politics at least, that the Muslim League was able to claim from the late 1930s that the Congress was largely a 'Hindu' party.

Running alongside these developments in nationalist politics and reacting to them was a more explicit Hindu nationalist orientation within the Hindu Mahasabha, and the emergence of a militant volunteer movement for Hindu sangathan, the Rashtriya Swayamsevak Sangh (RSS), in 1925. The latter party was relatively insignificant at the time of its appearance, and the Hindu Mahasabha was still very weak in electoral terms. But the ideological development of Hindutva by V.D. Savarkar (a Chitpavan brāhmaṇa from Maharashtra) in 1923, and his subsequent leadership of the Hindu Mahasabha from 1937 were later to have enormous significance for Indian politics. Savarkar presented a new definition of the Hindu nation, by shifting the emphasis away from religious identity and by setting up the notion of a broad Hindu culture and Hindu 'race'. The RSS was allegedly founded by Dr Keshav Baliram Hedgewar, and was based on an organisation of shakhas, or centres, aimed particularly at transforming the lives of the young through systems of physical culture and ideological indoctrination in secret proceedings. Its recruitment occurred (and still occurs today) largely amongst small-town high-caste communities, and its khaki shorts-wearing volunteers were often prominent both in social service work and at the scenes of communal violence.

That violence reached its peak in 1946–48, as the 'two-nation' theory and the prospect of the formation of Pakistan generated support for Hindu extremist parties. But in the aftermath of the violence and the assassination of Gandhi by a member of the RSS in January 1948 Nehruvian secularism gained the ascendant against a 'right wing' of the Congress under Patel and Tandon. The RSS was banned, and despite the subsequent formation of the Bharatiya Jana Sangh in 1951 out of the old Hindu Mahasabha and Congress right, Hindu identity politics was something of a dead letter until the 1980s. By that stage, the context had changed dramatically: growing regionalism and regionalist parties and the Mandal Commission proposals for caste-based quotas in government and education generated support for a revived high-caste party of 'national unity' which opposed the forces of 'national disintegration'. It wasn't just the newly modelled Bharatiya Janata Party (BJP) in 1981 which set out to adopt this national unity strategy, or the more extreme Shiv Sena in Bombay. Rajiv Gandhi and the Congress also played the 'Hindu' card in the 1984 elections, following the assassination of his mother, Indira Gandhi, by her own Sikh bodyguards in October 1984 and the subsequent anti-Sikh riots.

One central point of Rajiv's Hindu symbolism was the disputed Ayodhyā Babri Masjid (mosque), which he reopened – a mosque claimed by Hindu parties to be constructed on the site of a temple celebrating the birthplace of the god Rāma. The temple–mosque dispute had been simmering since Independence. But there was inconsistency in Congress's promotion of religious politics too, indicative of its declining authority and helplessness in the face of political and regional challenges. Rajiv Gandhi pushed through a deeply conservative Muslim Women's Bill to placate Muslim opinion. By the end of the 1980s, forty years of Congress rule began to crumble. The victory of the Janata Dal in the 1989 elections, which implemented the Mandal Commission recommendations on caste reservations in the midst of the Ayodhyā dispute, paved the way for the rise of the BJP and its associated Hindu institutions under the umbrella of the Sangh Parivar.

An important member of the Parivar, the Vishwa Hindu Parishad (VHP; World Hindu Council), founded in 1964 against the perceived threat from Christian missionary activity, spearheaded an agitation to 'rebuild' the temple at Ayodhyā on the eve of the election in 1989. This move was supported by the BJP through one of its key leaders, L.K. Advani, who undertook a rathyātrā – a journey by chariot across India. Two years later, with a BJP government in office in Uttar Pradesh, crowds spurred on by the VHP, RSS and Bajrang Dal tore down the Babri Masjid, helping to generate further Hindu–Muslim rioting across India. The VHP is underpinned by a sense of Hindu insecurity which links both to fears of conversion and to a more deep-seated desire to build a national Hindu church. Since its foundation the VHP had attempted to endow Hinduism with a sacred book and to provide a church and ecclesiastical structure along the lines of the Semitic faiths. Since the 1980s the VHP and Sangh Parivar as a whole have been very quick to take advantage of the popularisation of electronic, television and audio and video media – a communications revolution that has arrived on the back of economic liberalisation in India (Rajagopal 2001).

Once the BJP was finally able to lead the formation of a government at the centre in India in 1998 and 1999, its Hindutva ideologies were watered down. The need to maintain alliances with regional parties to stay in power and to challenge the only other serious contender at the centre – the Congress – are the main factors responsible for this shift. It is a change that has threatened to drive a wedge between the BJP and its traditional allies in the VHP and RSS. But despite this moderation and the promises of stabilised relations with Pakistan in 2003, the presence of a BJP government did little to ease international relations in South Asia. In 1998 both India and Pakistan tested nuclear devices and were intransigent in the face of the Comprehensive Test Ban Treaty. Nor has the passion surrounding

Ayodhyā died down. In one of the saddest episodes of post-1947 Indian politics, the year 2002 was marred by a state-sponsored pogrom of Gujarat's Muslim minority. Again, the violence was originally linked to the Babri Masjid at Ayodhyā. The initial attacks were carried out in response to a Muslim assault on a train carriage carrying Hindu activists from the site of the demolished mosque.

To understand the rise of Hindu nationalism in India in recent decades it is important to consider the crisis of Congress legitimacy in the 1970s and 1980s, against the context of an opening economy, threats of regional disintegration and the maturation of caste-based politics. But this does not provide a full explanation. It is still necessary to study how and why Indian secularism was so easily contested by Hindu parties, exposing its essential fragility. And to chart the history of Indian secularism, it is necessary to consider why notions of Hindu identity have entered political movements across the spectrum – even those that have outwardly championed the secular state.

See also: **Ahiṃsā; Arjuna; Arthaśastra; Ayodhyā; Bhagavadgītā; Bhakti; Bharat Dharma Mahamandala; Bharatiya Janata Party; Brahmacārya; Brāhmaṇa; Brahmo Samaj; Buddhism, relationship with Hinduism; Caste; Chatterjee, Bankim Chandra; Dalits; Dayananda Saraswati, Swami; Dharma; Gandhi, Mohandas Karamchand; Gaṇeśa; Hedgewar, Keshav Baliram; Hindu; Hindu Mahasabha; Hinduism; Hinduism, modern and contemporary; Hindutva; Indo-European traditions; Indus Valley Civilisation; Jainism, relationship with Hinduism; Jones, Sir William; Karma (as path); Kauṭilya; Kṛṣṇa; Lajpat Rai, Lala; Mahābhārata; Malaviya, Pandit Madan Mohan; Mandir; Maṭha; Nationalism; Orientalism; Paṇḍit; Phule, Jotirao; Rāja; Rāma; Rāmāyaṇa; Rashtriya Swayamsevak Sangh; Roy, Rammohan; Sacred animals; Sacred languages; Sangh Parivar; Śaṅkara; Sati; Savarkar, Vinayat Damodar; Shiv Sena; Tagore, Debendranath; Tilak, Bal Gangadhar; Varṇa; Veda; Vedānta; Vīraśāivas; Vishwa Hindu Parishad; War and peace**

William Gould

Further reading

Bayly, Susan. 1995. 'Caste and "Race" in the Colonial Ethnography of India'. In Peter Robb, ed., *The Concept of Race in South Asia.* Delhi and Oxford: Oxford University Press, 189–204.

Chatterji, Joya. 1994. *Bengal Divided: Hindu Communalism and Partition, 1932–1947.* Cambridge: Cambridge University Press.

Gooptu, Nandini. 2001. *The Politics of the Urban Poor in Early Twentieth Century India.* Cambridge: Cambridge University Press.

O'Hanlon, Rosalind. 1985. *Caste, Conflict, and Ideology: Mahatma Jotirao Phule and Low Caste Protest in Nineteenth-century Western India.* Cambridge: Cambridge University Press.

Rajagopal, Arvind. 2001. *Politics after Television: Hindu Nationalism and the Reshaping of the Public in India.* Cambridge: Cambridge University Press.

PONGAL

The pongal (or poṅkal) ritual, celebrated particularly by Tamils, involves the ceremonial, open-air cooking of rice, often with added jaggery or nuts, by auspicious, fertile married women (sumaṅkali). Pongal has a milky, pudding-like consistency, because it is made from raw grain, not the parboiled variety used in daily cuisine, which is not washed to remove excess starch. The cooking process is special too, and every step, especially the moment of coming to the boil, is marked by prolonged kuruvai trills from the cook and her neighbours. Some is offered to a deity, the rest shared out and consumed by members of the social unit involved.

Both materially and conceptually, pongal is a process. 'Pongal' itself is a verbal noun ('boiling', 'overflowing', 'flourishing'). This state is brought about by fire, in accordance with the idea that red or hot substances bring about transformations, whereas whiteness is linked to stasis (Beck 1969: 556). Pongal cooking seems in fact to be the archetype of South Indian transformational symbolism, as regards both agriculture and cosmology.

In Tamil Nadu, the rite occurs in two distinct contexts: just outside the home during the Pongal festival at the start of the month of Tai (mid-January); and outside village goddess temples during their annual festivals. Tai Pongal marks the winter solstice, when the sun begins its progress northwards. Goddess Pongal marks her movement into the body of her hereditary medium during the festival, exemplifying the common ritual association between Hindu deities and round pots of consecrated water.

The Tamil festival calendar is enmeshed within the cycle of rice cultivation, which has always been economically and culturally crucial to the Tamil region (Fuller 1992). For most areas dependent upon tank irrigation, the growing season extends from mid-Purattasi (October) until mid-Tai (February). Although Tai Pongal is often described as a harvest festival, the cooking process encapsulates this entire rice-growing cycle. Thus, raw rice is placed in a pot of water, just as seed grain is strewn over flooded fields; both pot and field represent the womb of the goddess (Biardeau 1972: 186); the heating of rice in the pot corresponds to the ripening crop in the fields, the boiling to the harvest, and so on. Tai Pongal is also partly an offering to the sun (Reiniche 1979: 66ff.) to enlist its aid in drying out the ripening crop or as a first-fruits offering.

See also: **Calendar; Deities, village and local; Food; Utsava; Women's rites**

ANTHONY GOOD

Further reading

Beck, B.E.F. 1969. 'Colour and Heat in South Indian Ritual'. *Man* (n.s.) 4: 553–72.

Biardeau, M. 1972. *Clefs pour la pensée hindoue* [Keys to Hindu Thought]. Paris: Seghers.

Fuller, C.J. 1992. *The Camphor Flame: Popular Hinduism and Society in India*. Princeton, NJ: Princeton University Press.

Good, A. 1983. 'A Symbolic Type and Its Transformations: The Case of South Indian Ponkal'. *Contributions to Indian Sociology* (n.s.) 17: 223–44.

Reiniche, M.-L. 1979. *Les Dieux et les hommes: Etude des cultes d'un village du Tirunelveli, Inde du Sud* [Gods and Men: A Study of Worship in a Tirunelveli Village, South India]. Paris and the Hague: Mouton.

POPE, GEORGE UGLOW (1820–1908)

English missionary and scholar of Tamil. Pope first went to India as a Wesleyan missionary in 1839, later joining the Church of England, in which he was ordained as a priest in 1848. Much of Pope's work as a missionary was in the field of education. After his return from India, Pope became Lecturer in Tamil at Oxford from 1886 until his death. He published editions and translations of several major religious texts in Tamil, including the *Tirukkuṛaḷ*, ascribed to Tiruvaḷḷuvar and the first complete translation of the *Tiruvācakam* of Māṇikkavācakar, part of the Śaiva canon *Tirumuṛai*. Pope found it 'not improbable' that Tiruvaḷḷuvar had been influenced by Christian ideas introduced to him by Armenian traders in Mylapore (later scholars have argued that beyond its pragmatic and empirical moral code it reflects mostly a Jaina point of view).

See also: **Hinduism, history of scholarship; Māṇikkavācakar; Nāyaṉmār**

WILL SWEETMAN

Further reading

Copley, A. 1997. 'George Uglow Pope Contra Vedanayagam Sastriar: A Case Study in the

Clash of "New" and "Old" Mission'. In G. Oddie, ed., *Religious Conversion Movements in South Asia: Continuities and Change, 1800–1900*. Richmond: Curzon, 173–227.

Pope, G. U. 1886. *The 'Sacred' Kurral of Tiruvalluva-Nayanar with Introduction, Grammar, Translation, Notes, Lexicon, and Concordance*. London: Henry Frowde.

Pope, G. U. 1900. *The Tiruvāçagam, or, Sacred Utterances of the Tamil Poet, Saint, and Sage Manikka-Vaçagar*. Oxford: Clarendon Press.

POPULAR AND VERNACULAR TRADITIONS

General features

The traditions of popular Hinduism are generally non-textual, with their data transmitted *orally*, through vernacular songs, sayings, spells and the routinised expressions that comprise performative possession; *visually*, through specific types of imagery; and *gesturally*, through a wide variety of ritual observances. Its principal practices – of venerating superhuman entities through feeding and of attempting to communicate with the same through a variety of ritual divination techniques and controlled or uncontrolled possession – rarely require the mediation of religious specialists. When such are required, these are generally of a 'shamanic' type and are often persons from low-caste or 'tribal' backgrounds – the Ojhas of Uttar Pradesh, Bhopās of Rajasthan, Baigas of Madhya Pradesh, Cāmis of Tamil Nadu, Balians of Bali, etc.

The deities (devas or devatās in much of South Asia; bhūtas and kalas in Bali) of popular Hinduism are embodied either through the human body itself (in possession) or through elements found in both the natural surroundings and local human culture – stones, trees, living water, wells, food grains, ashes, cow dung, paint, powder, rope, household or agricultural implements, etc. They may permanently or intermittently inhabit these 'supports' of their own accord, be induced to enter into them for the duration of a rite, or have rudimentary bodies constructed out of them – bodies that are 'fed' and sometimes made to 'grow' by the layering of organic or inorganic matter into an abstract or anthropomorphic form.

These deities are worshipped in the domestic space of the home or at their 'place' (sthāna) – the site where they manifest themselves in a village or urban neighbourhood, the fields or the wild. These tutelary gods of the place (grāmadevatās) are the most universal objects of worship in popular Hinduism. Often simply called 'Mother' (Māṃ in Hindi; Ammaṇ in Tamil), 'Father' (Bāp in Hindi), Grandmother (Aijmā in Nepali) or 'Chief' (Ṭhakur), grāmadevatās incorporate every life-form, substance, structure and energy that make up a given locale, including the living, the dead, plant and animal life, houses, fields, watercourses and stones. The deity is the community, just as the community is the deity (Huyler 1999: 102). In addition to their daily veneration for the continued protection of the community, grāmadevatās also become the objects of occasional or votive rites, for example when the foundation for a new home or public building is being laid or a well being dug, or when the seasonal work of planting and harvesting crops commences.

Shrines of popular Hindu deities are generally minimalist, often nothing more than a stone or rudimentary image placed on a slab beneath a tree (when the tree itself is not the object of worship). They may also be temporary structures, erected for the duration of a particular rite. A multiplicity of deities will often be present at a shrine, clustered together in a variety of ways that are often indicative of the intricate network of symbiotic relationships that obtain between the human, the divine, the demonic and the dead in traditional South Asian societies. The deities of popular Hinduism are, before all else, multiple, veritable hordes of supernatural entities that often belong to families, clans or lineages whose kinship structures are patterned after those of human society. Female deities – Goddesses (devīs), Mothers (mātrs or mātṛkās), Female Seizers (grahaṇīs), Female Dryads (yakṣiṇīs, ḍakkinīs), Female Serpents (nāginīs), the divinised heroines called Faithful Wives (satīs) and the demonised Female Dead (bhūtnīs), etc. – have a far greater presence in popular traditions than in the more male-deity-oriented devotional cults of 'classical Hinduism'.

While many of these divine families or aggregates are classified into named and numbered groups – the ubiquitous Seven Sisters and Sixty-four Sorceresses (cauṃsāṭ yoginī); the Seven River Nymphs (sāti āsarā) of Maharashtra; the Fifty-two Virile Heroes (bāvan bīr) and Fifty-two Horrifics (bāvan bherūmjī) of Rajasthan; the Fifty-six Removers (chappan vināyaka) of Vārāṇasī, etc. – they are more often a numberless aggregate. Such is particularly the case with the demonic or unhappy dead (bhūta-preta in much of North India; pēy in Tamil Nadu etc.), who, although relatively weak, can wreak havoc when they seek to avenge themselves on their living families or fellow townsmen, whom they hold responsible for their often untimely deaths as well as their unsettled postmortem condition. Especially dangerous and vindictive are the ravening spirits of women who have died in childbirth or as the result of male abuse (chuḍels in much of North India; yakṣīs in Kerala; kichkinnis in Nepal, etc).

In this respect, many of the deities of popular Hinduism are 'family gods', deceased members of an extended family or clan-group who are venerated in order that they protect, rather than torment, their living relatives. Here, one's tutelary family or clan deity (kuladevatā in northern South Asia; kulam tēvam in Tamil Nadu; digu dyah in the Kathmandu Valley) will often be an idealised ancestor that has been 'domesticated', through a worship cult, from a source of affliction into a protector of the households of the extended family unit. In this respect, one may view the pantheon of popular Hindu deities as an unbroken continuum of beings, shading from the living to the dead, the auspicious to the noxious, and the divine to the demonic.

The Hindus in Bali have multiple household shrines, in which the ancestors, guardians of the living family, tutelary deities, etc. each have their particular place of worship, specialised offerings, etc. One of these shrines, called the sanggah pengijeng, is often connected with a group of four deities called the kanda empat, the four divines siblings of every Balinese Hindu. As such, it is a family shrine in the sense that it serves to honour the spiritual (niskala) family whose lineage, even whose very substance, interpenetrates that of the physical (sakala) human family. Although the members of this group of four have names that link them to high gods of 'classical Hinduism', their functions are identical to those of the kuladevatās and grāmadevatās of South Asia, as they inhabit both the bodies of their human families and the immediate surroundings of the human community: cemeteries, rivers, stones and trees. Their behaviour also verges on the demonic, inasmuch as they eat the corpses of persons whose death rites were carried out at the wrong time, people who sleep at noon or walk around after sunset, or people who cut or climb trees on inauspicious days. Each of the four kanda empat has four modes of being, and each of the four has twenty-seven 'young', making for a divine family (nyama bajang) of 108 members (Eisemann 1989–90, 1: 5, 273).

As in this Balinese case, the multiple clans or families of popular Hindu deities are considered to be arrayed behind a leader or headman (or mistress), whom people will venerate in order that s/he control his or her minions. This sort of relationship is described in the *circa* tenth-century Kashmiri *Netra Tantra*, whose precepts continue to apply down to the present. In its nineteenth chapter are a series of instructions (verses 61–80) for persons afflicted by individual supernatural entities from one or another family (kula). In each case, one is to make offerings to the leader of that family: to the Lord of Obstacles (Vighneśa) for the Removers (vināyakas), the Lord of Deceased (Bhūteśvara) for the Deceased (Bhūtas) and Seizers (Grahas), the Ruler of the Demons (Rākṣodhipa) for the Demons (Rakṣasas), and Bhairava for the eight classes of multiple female beings 'born from a divine womb' (devayonayaḥ), etc. When satisfied by the offering made to them, these leaders bring the assaulting entity under control. In present-day north India, Bhairava, Narasiṃha and Hanumān (often called Bālājī) are termed Bhūtnāthas ('Lords of the Deceased') and venerated in precisely this role. The same dynamic is found in coastal Andhra Pradesh, where Vīrabhadra, who is identified as a fierce form or portion of the high god Śiva, is called upon to control hordes of lesser vīrabhadras, the wrathful spirits of dead infants. In these contexts, worship or veneration (pūjā) is rarely performed in a spirit of devotion (bhakti) and no bond of love links the human practitioner to the object of his or her practice. The goal is rather one of manipulation, control, or coercion and it is the ritual efficacy of the sacrificial offering with its attendant mantra – or simply the fact of satiating the hunger of the object of worship with a gift of often non-vegetarian food (bali in South Asia; caru in Bali) – that is effective in nearly every case.

Possession is extremely frequent in popular Hindu traditions. On the one hand, the generally malevolent beings one seeks to control often manifest themselves by possessing their human victims, penetrating their minds and bodies and thereby causing sickness, miscarriage, nightmares, insomnia, insanity and death. On the other, controlled possession, by a 'shaman-type' religious specialist, is a prime means of combating the same. In Rajastan, for example, Bhopās will induce Bherūṃ-jī (Bhairava) to possess them in order to exorcise the malevolent deities or entities (especially the bhūta-preta) that posses their clients, either by frightening them off with threats or cajoling them with promises. Here, it is generally understood that possession is the sole means that these relatively weak entities have for communicating their desires to the living. Once their will is made known – through dream interpretation, induced possession or various divination techniques – a solution is negotiated that is equitable to both parties. The possessing deity, or bhūta-preta needs – food, a worship cult, shrine, etc. – are satisfied, in exchange for which it ceases tormenting the living. In addition to appeasing them, popular religious specialists will resort to a number of prophylactic techniques for warding off these malevolent beings, including the use of protective mantras, amulets, threads and nails to bind, immobilise and nail them down somewhere outside the boundaries of the human body and the inhabited space of the topocosm. Very often, the principles of 'sympathetic magic' are operative here. So, for example, the smallpox goddess is called Sītalā ('Cooling') in north India, even though the prime symptom of her possession is the eruption of burning pustules or pox; and ritual treatment for smallpox entails, among other things, plunging her worship image into cold water and then having the patient drink a sip of that water. However, not all instances of possession are unwelcome or harmful. Benevolent deities may possess their devotees, giving them healing powers or the power to walk across a fire pit unscathed (Foulston 2002: 141–9).

Here popular Hinduism may be termed 'pragmatic' religion, concerned with finding solutions to real life problems, as opposed to the 'transcendental' goals of devotional religion (liberation from the cycle of rebirth, union with the divine). In the latter case, the adoration offered by devotees to the high gods of their tradition, in the controlled atmosphere of a religious festival or periodical ritual observance, is proactive. Conversely, the religious practices of popular Hinduism are generally reactive, with deities being propitiated because they have already erupted into people's bodies, households, herds, fields and forests. Once appeased – fed with sacrificial oblations, offered a shrine or gratified with offerings of flowers, aromatics and fineries – they become nurturing, protective and life-giving.

Popular Hinduism – in fact, popular South Asian religion in general – is also pragmatic in the sense that it is nonsectarian. On the one hand, Hindus will not hesitate to venerate the tomb (dargah) of a Muslim Saint (pīr) if that saint's charismatic power (baraka) to heal and resolve human problems is well known. On the other, the same local or regional god may be venerated as a Muslim pīr by one community and a Hindu deity by another, as in the case of Gugga Pīr (also known as Gugga Chauhan, Guru Gugga and Gugga Nāth), who is worshipped for protection against snakebite by persons from all religious backgrounds throughout much of western and central India. Similarly, the bhūtanātha Bhairava is widely worshipped for pragmatic reasons by North Indian and Nepali Hindus, Buddhists, Jains, Sikhs and Muslims alike. Deities such as these, both Hindu and non-Hindu, become the foci of regional pilgrimage networks and religious festivals (melās), each having its own specific religious specialists and clienteles.

'Popular Hinduism' and 'classical Hinduism'

In all these respects, popular Hinduism is to be distinguished from the elite traditions of 'classical Hinduism', which is textual, Sanskritic, monotheistic, translocal and transcendental. Yet it would be a mistake to assume, as most scholars and many South Asians have done since the colonial period, that the practices associated with popular Hinduism are limited to rural, low-caste, illiterate society. In spite of the fact that, since the advent of bhakti, 'monotheistic' devotion to one's chosen deity (iṣṭadevatā) – nearly always identified with a translocal 'high god' such as Viṣṇu, Śiva or the Great Goddess Mahādevī – has been the hallmark of transcendental Hindu practice, Hindus have never ceased to venerate their family gods and local gods. Every Hindu has a kuladevatā, by simple virtue of belonging to an extended family; and every locale, including urban neighbourhoods in such translocal pilgrimage centres as Vārāṇasī, has its grāmādevatās. In Vārāṇasī, these include local goddesses – often identified with Śitalā, whose shrines are located at the base of nīm (margosa) trees – as well as networks of local gods venerated as the eight Bhairavas, the fifty-six Vināyakas, etc.

Every Hindu, male or female, urban or rural, literate or illiterate, high-status or low-status, will venerate one or another of the 'popular' goddesses of childbirth – often with offerings of blood or some blood substitute to ensure easy delivery and ward off complications, which are seen as the work of the unhappy or demonic dead – from pre-parturition until usually six days after birth. The cult of the ancestors, all of them family gods, is central to the religious life of every Hindu; and all Hindus will venerate a bhūtanātha when the unhappy dead begin to haunt their dreams or trouble their waking lives. In times of particular adversity, high-status Hindus from the 'pure castes' will go so far as to call upon local religious specialists to make an offering on their behalf to said deities, whose taste for impure blood offerings is well known. Translocal but non-scriptural gods like the dire Śani (the planet Saturn) are worshipped for pragmatic reasons by Hindus from every walk of life, with their shrines often attracting greater numbers of worshippers (on Saturday, in the case of Śani) than the high gods of 'classical Hinduism'.

While it is the case that the multiple deities of popular Hinduism have historically been the objects of a virtually universal veneration, the same cannot be said for the high gods, apart from those who appear in localised forms. Whereas all Hindus have worshipped the multiple deities of the lower echelons of the pantheon from the time of the *Arthaveda*, only relatively cosmopolitan high-status Hindus have exclusively engaged in the devotional propitiation of the Hindu high gods. For nearly all other Hindus, the gods at the apex of the divine hierarchy have always been distant. Down to the present day, even those cases in which temples to Rāma, Śiva or Durgā are found in rural settings, it may only be the high-status members of village society who worship the high god of that temple, for the simple reason that they may be considered to be too lofty and majestic to be concerned with the problems of the little man. The same holds for the great all-Indian temples and pilgrimage sites of the exalted gods of bhakti: they do not draw the rural masses (and it should be recalled that over 80 per cent of India's Hindus live in its 650,000 villages). Until very recent years, a Hindu villager's conceptual horizons did not extend far beyond the boundaries of his or her own village and fields, and many continue to live in such a spatially circumscribed universe. And, in spite of the fact that the transportation and communications revolutions are pushing back the boundaries of that space, every Hindu – including the traditional exponents of translocal, transcendent forms of Hinduism – comes from *somewhere*, and continues to venerate family and local gods that remain linked to a specific clan group and tied to the soil of a specific place. For all these reasons, the term 'popular Hinduism' ought to be applied to the *entire* Hindu population of South and Southeast Asia, because every Hindu is always already a person from a particular family and place.

More than this, the use of the term 'classical Hinduism' is quite arbitrary, since there is nothing intrinsically normative about bhakti-style monotheistic devotion to a high god. This is the case for a number of reasons, beyond the simple question of numbers. The first of these is methodological. As Christopher Fuller has observed, models of Hinduism that favour translocal, Sanskritic, transcendental styles of belief and practice as the 'Great Tradition' – in contradistinction to the 'Little Tradition' of popular, local, vernacular, pragmatic forms of the same – 'primarily connote a Brahmanical standard for evaluation, a paradigm of the normatively most distinguished or prestigious'. However, scholars who embrace such models commit 'a stock anthropological error convert[ing] an indigenous, ideological distinction into an analytical concept, and then apply[ing] it to the empirical evidence to try to divide what is actually united by common underlying themes and principles' (Fuller 1992: 27–28). The Brahmanical standard of Sanskritic Hinduism, while neither monolithic nor unchallenged, becomes enshrined as normative, and, following a tautological form of reasoning, 'classical Hinduism' is reduced to what modern-day brāhmaṇas and their imitators think and do (or say they do), to the institutions they patronise, the gods they worship, etc.

Clearly, such two-tiered essentialist models of the 'Great Tradition' or of 'classical' and 'popular' Hinduism are unsatisfactory. A compelling alternative, which has been convincingly presented by Richard Cohen (1998: 361) on the subject of fifth-century images of Buddhist deities at the Ajanta Caves in Maharashtra, is to make a distinction between 'local' and 'translocal' deities and their respective worship forms and clienteles. The divine is always emplaced for the simple reason that people live, work and worship in places, places that have always already been inhabited by deities particular to those locales. The deities are therefore justified in demanding worship, if only because the territory of every human settlement, building, well and path originally belonged to them.

The same rule in fact applies to the worship sites of the translocal gods of Hinduism: at any given great temple or pan-South Asian pilgrimage site, the translocal god will always be identified by his or her local name, and the worship cult at that site will be marked by the local setting and its pantheon. Thus, although from a translocal perspective grounded in the Purāṇic Śakta mythology it is, in essence, the same Great Goddess (Mahādevī) who is present at both the massive temple of Mīnākṣi at Madurai in Tamil Nadu and Vaiṣṇo Devi in Jammu, pilgrims and devotees will call these goddesses by their particular site-specific names and approach them in different ways, based on the local mythology, pantheon, topography, history and so forth. In this context, translocal gods have always also had specific local identities. The converse – of a local god having a translocal identity – also occurs, for example in the identification, through mythological discourse, of numerous local Bhairavas of Rajastan and the Kathmandu Valley with Kāśī Kāl Bhaironāth, the principal Bhairava of Vārāṇasī, whose temple is a mandatory stopping place for pilgrims to that city. In fact, it is through just this sort of historical process that various local deities have come to be identified with or *as* translocal gods.

In spite of the fact that all of the translocal Hindu gods are local when they are venerated in their particular temples, shrines and pilgrimage sites (Tīrthas), they may nonetheless be perceived to be purely translocal, universal and unalterable when viewed through the lens of Sanskrit mythology, elite doctrine or meditative practice. This is the worldview of Hindus whose devotional styles are purely translocal, for whom the godhead is a single essence manifesting in multiple images, forms and names. This is a minority worldview, however, which can only be wholly embraced by those Hindus whose religious life is not anchored to a particular locale; that is, Hindus with a cosmopolitan lifestyle and sense of place. These are of three types: (1) brāhmaṇa and other high-status groups whose place at the top of the socio-religious hierarchy has always afforded them an all-encompassing god's-eye view of the universe from the elevated centre of the Hindu pantheon; (2) persons who are itinerant by profession or avocation (traders, merchants, member of certain religious orders); and (3) persons recently 'displaced' through urbanisation and emigration.

The history of Hindu deities

Now, in the present-day Indian (but not Nepalese or Indonesian) contexts of Hindu reform, neo-bhakti and exclusivist claims concerning the hindutva of a highly Brahmanaised body of doctrines, worship styles and religious institutions – and in the light of the growing grassroots support for such an exclusivist position – one might be tempted to allow that bhakti-style devotionalism to a unique translocal god does indeed constitute 'classical Hinduism' and the 'Great Tradition' in every sense of the term. These traditions are not, however, ahistorical, and those forms of Hinduism that may appear to be normative for a growing number of Indians in the early twenty-first century become entirely relativised when viewed through the lens of historical change.

To begin, none of the high gods of classical Hinduism enjoyed a worship cult in the Veda that is in any way comparable to their place in their modern-day translocal traditions. Yet, fully half of the hymns in the *Arthaveda* are devoted to protection against demonic entities that are the sources of disease and other sources of human unhappiness, and to precisely the sorts of multiple deities and religious practices that have prevailed, without a break, down to the present day, in local Hindu traditions. The nymphs of the *Arthaveda* played the same roles and were propitiated in the same ways in the first millennium BCE as are the Seven River Nymphs in present-day Maharastra.

Furthermore, certain deities of present-day popular Hinduism were once high gods of translocal cults patronised by kings and other high-status Hindus. A prime example, is Ṣaṣṭhī ('She of the Sixth'), who is identified in the *Mahābhārata* as the spouse of the epic war-god Skanda. Ṣaṣṭhī is also identified with Śri, the goddess of royal sovereignty in the *circa* third-century BCE *Mānava Gṛhyasūtra*, and whose image figures on coins minted in the Kushan and Yaudheya periods as well as on royal temple sculptures for over a thousand years – from Kushan-era images down to at least the eleventh century of the Common Era at Khajuraho. Ṣaṣṭhī is today regarded as a 'folk goddess', worshipped in village settings as a stone beneath a tree. To call Ṣaṣṭhī a goddess of popular Hinduism on the basis of present-day norms is inappropriate in the light of her earlier status as a royal, translocal goddess, and it remains the case that her worship cult has remained unchanged for over two thousand years, a claim that cannot be made by many of the gods.

Since the time of Pāṇini, Hindu textual traditions have commonly referred to the multiple deities of popular Hinduism as laukika devatās, a term having basically the same semantic field as the Buddhist vyantara devatās ('intermediate deities', as opposed to enlightened bodhisvattvas) and the Jain devas (gods, as opposed to tīrthaṇkaras or jinas). A number of sources from the beginning of the Common Era identify the devatās with Yakṣas. When one examines early data on the yakṣas, one finds that both they and their female counterparts, the Yakṣiṇīs, played the same roles in the past as do the local gods of modern-day South Asia and Indonesia. The male Yakṣas and female Yakṣiṇīs that protect the villages, cities, sacred groves, rivers, pools and mountains with which they were identified were the most ubiquitous deities of the Kushan and Gupta periods. Yakṣas and Yakṣiṇīs were carnivorous and had great appetites, as the *Rāmāyaṇa* makes clear in its etymology of their name, which, derived from the imperative form of the root yakṣ, would mean 'may we gobble' (yakṣāmah). However, the *Dhātupāṭha*, a list of ancient verb-roots ascribed to Pāṇini, glosses the verb yakṣayate as simply meaning 'to worship, honour', in the light of which the Yakṣas were simply 'the worshipped'.

Because their shrines were frequently located at the base of trees, the term Yakṣa has often been translated as 'Dryad', and the early iconography of Yakṣiṇīs nearly always represents these as lithe female figures entwined in trees that have burst into blossom from their simple fecundating touch. Female deities like the smallpox goddesses Śitalā and Māriammā – the medieval and modern heiresses of the Yakṣiṇīs – continue to be offered food in shrines at the bases of trees, which they inhabit and 'possess' like the human bodies they also frequently afflict, although they may also occupy shrines or temples. The ancient Yakṣas' and Yakṣiṇīs' proclivity for possessing humans is underscored in the earliest mythic account described in epic, āyurvedic and tantric literature. Standard treatments for Yakṣa possession, found in all of these sources, include blood offerings made at the base of trees and the tying of protective threads around the arms and legs of the afflicted.

According to these sources the child-god Skanda is himself intimately related to these hungry, angry female deities who possess and destroy those who neglect to worship them. Another child-god whose mythology is linked to the same is Kṛṣṇa, whose slaying of the female demon (rakṣasī) Pūtanā is also attested in the *Mahābhārata.* According to the *Bhāgavata Purāṇa* version of this story, when the cowherding women of Vraja find Pūtanā's massive body lying dead on the ground beside the infant Kṛṣṇa, they wave a cow-tail brush over him, bathe him in bovine urine and, using cow dung, write the names of Viṣṇu over his twelve limbs to protect him. They then utter mantras over each of his limbs as they evoke the various demonic minions of childhood diseases against which their spells are meant to protect him. Among those mentioned are the ḍākinīs, Ghouls, Dryads, Protectors, Vināyakas, Mothers and the male Epilepsy Demon (Apasmāra). Whereas, however, these practices and the multiple deities who are their objects are extremely ancient and have continued virtually unchanged down to the present day, the *Bhāgavata Purāṇa* is a chronicle of the post-Gupta age elevation of the cult of a local cowherding god named Kṛṣṇa-Gopāla to translocal status, through his identification with the Vedic god Viṣṇu.

Like all of the multiple devatās, the Yakṣas and Yakṣiṇīs of these pre-colonial traditions would, when worshipped with offerings of food, protect from the very same afflictions that they otherwise inflict on humans. The ravening Yakṣiṇīs, when satisfied, protect human foetuses and infants; and Yakṣas who were the cause of epidemics protected against the same when worshipped. The Yakṣas and Yakṣiṇīs were also considered to be powerful oracles and possessors of spells, charms and magic, and most especially as supernatural agents of virility and endowers of genitalia. This last feature appears to correspond to the configuration of Yakṣa shrines: the basic constituents of a Yakṣa caitya were a flat platform or clay brick, a conical aniconic representation of the Yakṣa or a colossal anthropomorphic image of the same, sometimes accompanied by an enormous phallus. Much of the early iconography of the emerging high god Śiva, most particularly his representation as a great anthropomorphic figure emerging in bas-relief from a massive liṅgam, is likely derived from earlier representations of Yakṣas. In a more general sense, the most powerful and prestigious images of the high Hindu gods – which are naturally occurring or self-generating rather than fashioned according to normative iconographic precept, and in which those gods are naturally present – are identical to those local Yakṣa-type deities: Śiva's svayambhu liṅgams; Viṣṇu's śālagrāmas and the Great Goddess' piṇḍis (in northwestern India) are all simple unhewn stones.

In fact, the origins of all of the translocal gods of classical Hinduism, as well as their worship forms and cultic practices, can be traced back to Yakṣa-type cults of local deities. Independent of their mythologies, each of the high gods of 'classical Hinduism' originally came from elsewhere. Each began as a local tutelary deity, worshipped without devotion or the protection of a particular people, territory and way of life, and was identified either as a Yakṣa, serpent, mountain, river or some other specific element of a given local landscape, before being elevated, through the mythologising efforts of emergent sectarian groups, to the high status of a high god of bhakti, during the first millennium of the Common Era.

These translocal gods are all composites of pre-existing local, regional or sectarian deities. The divine person of Viṣṇu, for example, was composed by north Indian Bhāgavata sectarians who concatenated the mythologies and attributes of a heroic Yādava warrior named Kṛṣṇa from the Dvārakā region of Gujarat, a local pastoral deity named Kṛṣṇa Gopāla from the Mathurā region of Uttar Pradesh, a god of abundance named Vāsudeva, a Vedic solar deity named Viṣṇu and a deified sage named Nārayaṇa. Later, Tamil Āḻvārs, the original exponents of bhakti in South India, would identify Mayon, a local 'black' deity with the black god of the north (the name Kṛṣṇa also means 'black'). Following an interpretive strategy that became the modus operandi of Purāṇic commentators in particular, what were originally names of independent local or regional deities became reduced to the multiple names or epithets of the one transcendent Viṣṇu. Similarly, nearly everyone of the avatāras of Viṣṇu has its own regional and historical antecedents, which originally had no intrinsic connection with Viṣṇu, but with whom they later became identified in Sanskritic textual traditions.

This sort of strategy, of identifying local deities with translocal high gods, is particularly transparent in the Kathmandu Valley, where the multiple local mothers (māīs) and grandmothers (ajimās) of indigenous, pre-Tantric traditions have been incorporated, over the centuries, into maṇḍalas of Tantric deities, with whom they have been identified. Nearly always, these local goddesses retain their local identities in open-air shrines (pīṭhas, 'mounds'; or maiti gharas, 'mother houses') located on the peripheries of their communities, at which they are most often worshipped as simple stones; while their translocal identities, as Tantric goddesses belonging to a pantheon of Tantric high gods, are the object of worship in a lineage house (deochems) within the inhabited area of the community, where they are often represented in ways that correspond to the iconographic programme of the Tantric texts. Nepalis recognise the relationship between these local and the translocal goddesses, and refuse to deem that the cult of either is more normative than, or superior to, the other. Here as elsewhere in the Hindu world (with the possible exception of recent diaspora Hindus cut off from a sense of 'place'), the pantheons and worship practices of local gods constitute the mainstream, as they have for over two thousand years.

See also: **Āḻvārs; Apasmāra; Avatāra; Āyurveda; Bhāgavatas; Bhakti; Bhūtas; Blood sacrifice; Buddhism, relationship with Hinduism; Caste; Dākiṇīs; Deities; Deities, domestic and family; Deities, folk and popular; Deities, village and local; Diaspora; Durgā; Dvārakā; Grāmadevatās; Gṛhyasūtras; Hanumān; Hindutva; Iṣṭadevatā; Jainism, relationship with Hinduism; Kṛṣṇa; Kula; Kuladevatā; Madurai; Magic; Mahābhārata; Mahādevī; Mantra; Māriammā; Mathurā; Mīnākṣī; Nāgas; Navagrahas; Pāṇini; Pēcciyammā; Possession; Pūjā; Purāṇas; Pūtanā; Rākṣasas; Rāma; Rāmāyaṇa; Religious specialists; Śakti; Saṃhitās; Shrines, wayside; Sikhism, Relationship with Hinduism; Sītalā; Śiva; Skanda; Ṣaṣṭhī; Tantras; Tīrthayātrā; Vaiṣṇo Devī; Vārāṇasī; Varṇa; Viṣṇu; Yakṣa**

DAVID GORDON WHITE

Further reading

Cohen, R.S. 1998. 'Nāga, Yakṣiṇī, Buddha: Local Deities and Local Buddhism at Ajanta'. *History of Religions* 37: 360–400.

Eisemann, F. Jr. 1989–90. *Bali, Sekala and Niskala*, 2 vols. Berkeley, CA: Periplus Editions.

Foulston, L. 2002. *At the Feet of the Goddess: The Divine Feminine in Local Hindu Religion*. Brighton and Portland, OR: Sussex Academic Press.
Fuller, C. 1992. *The Camphor Flame, Popular Hinduism and Society in India*. Princeton, NJ: Princeton University Press.
Huyler, S.P. 1999. *Meeting God, Elements of Hindu Devotionalism*. New Haven, CT: Yale University Press.
Misra, R.N. 1981. *Yakṣa Cult and Iconography*. Delhi: Munshiram Manoharlal.
Nabokov, I. 2000. *Religion against Self. An Ethnography of Tamil Rituals*. New York: Oxford University Press.
Sontheimer, G.D. 1989. *Pastoral Deities in Western India*. Trans. Ann Feldhaus. New York: Oxford University Press.
Tiwari, J.N. 1985. *Goddess Cults in Ancient India [with special reference to the first seven centuries A.D.]*. Delhi: Sundeep Prakashan.
Vaudeville, C. 1999. *Myths, Saints and Legends in Medieval India*. Delhi: Oxford University Press.

POSSESSION

Possession is an important aspect of local religious practice, being the pivotal ritual in many festivals. Possession by a deity is generally desired and may be invoked by the mortal, whereas possession by an unhappy spirit is not desirable and can be harmful. Possession provides the deity (generally a goddess) with a direct means of communication with their devotees and is generally dependent on the will of the goddess. For example, in Orissa a local woman is regularly considered to be possessed by the goddess Saṇtoṣī Mātā. In her role as the vehicle of the goddess's power she is able to heal those that are sick and give advice to those who are in need of it (Foulston 2002: 145–49). Possession by Saṇtoṣī Mātā appears to be a feature of local worship in the Bhubaneswar area, although she would not normally be considered a local goddess. In the case of possession by a deity, the person who is possessed may be regarded as being specially chosen. Possession is also a prominent feature of local worship in Tamil Nadu and the term for it, iṟaṅku, means to 'descend'. The person on which the deity is thought to have descended is then referred to as a cāmyāṭi, or 'god-dancer' (Diehl 1956: 177). There are those who claim that they are in control of a range of negative spirits by the use of mantras. They inflict an undesirable possession onto their unfortunate victims and then offer to exorcise the spirit for them for a price (Foulston 2002: 97–98).

In both Orissa and Tamil Nadu, possession is common on three main occasions, particularly during goddess festival proceedings. Often the first occasion is during the ceremony that invokes the power of the goddess into a symbolic pot or śakti kalasam (kumbhamātā). The second occasion is during the main procession, if there is one, around the temple, during which the pūjāri and other key figures may become possessed. Perhaps the most important occasion when possession takes place is at the climax of the festival, particularly if a fire walk or a blood sacrifice is the central ritual. The beating of a metal gong most often brings on the possessed state.

Possession represents a key aspect of many festival proceedings, but P.J. Claus has recorded evidence of at least one festival at which possession is the focus (Claus 1975: 47–58). In the Siri festival celebrated in South Kanara District, Mysore, the goddess and her descendants possess those, including different caste groups, who have assembled for the festival. The most experienced participants consider themselves to be possessed by Siri herself. As far as I am aware, this focus on mass possession is rare, with the more common occurrence being that possession only happens to a select few, most commonly to the attendant pūjāri.

See also: **Blood sacrifice; Caste; Deities; Kumbhamātā; Mandir; Mantra; Religious specialists; Śakti; Saṇtoṣī Mātā; Utsava**

LYNN FOULSTON

Further reading

Claus, P.J. 1975. 'The Siri Myth and Ritual: A Mass Possession Cult of South India'. *Ethnology* 14.1: 47–58.

Diehl, C.G. 1956. *Instrument and Purpose: Studies in Rites and Rituals in South India.* Lund: C.W.K. Gleerup.

Foulston, Lynn. 2002. *At the Feet of the Goddess: The Divine Feminine in Local Hindu Religion.* Brighton and Portland, OR: Sussex Academic Press.

PRABHUPADA, A.C. BHAKTIVEDANTA SWAMI

Prabhupada, A.C. Bhaktivedanta Swami, or more simply 'Prabhupada' as he was known to his followers, founded the Hare Kṛṣṇa movement. At his death in 1977 he was head of a global religious organisation with centres in America, Europe, Asia, Africa and Australasia, and with an active presence in his homeland of India. He was guru to thousands of devotees and known by many as a populariser of devotional Hinduism centred on love of Kṛṣṇa. He was author of some fifty books, including *Bhagavadgītā as It Is* and *Kṛṣṇa*, copies of which had been distributed in airports, streets and bookshops around the world.

Born Abhay Charan De in Bengal in 1896, he encountered the Gauḍīya Vaiṣṇava Mission, a movement inspired by the teachings of Caitanya, whilst working as a chemist. He was initiated by Bhaktisiddhanta Saraswati in 1932, and, on his advice, began to write in English about love of Kṛṣṇa, founding the magazine *Back to Godhead* in 1944. After retiring from work and family responsibilities, he entered the saṃnyāsa order in 1959 and took the name Bhaktivedanta Swami. He began the lengthy task of translating and commenting upon the *Bhāgavata Purāṇa*, and then took the bold move in 1965 of taking the message of devotion to Kṛṣṇa to the West. In New York his unusual and uncompromising appearance and beliefs struck a chord with young people disenchanted with the religion and values of their parents. Within the first year he had attracted many young men and women, given them the Hare Kṛṣṇa mantra and the status of brāhmaṇa, taught them skills of preaching and public chanting, imparted Bengali Vaiṣṇava culture, and formed the new international organisation the International Society for Krishna Consciousness (ISKCON).

His achievements are recorded in the devotional biography *Śrīla Prabhupāda-līlāmṛta* and he is remembered daily in ISKCON temples. Throughout his life he remained a sincere devotee of Kṛṣṇa and an ardent servant of his guru. He has since been widely acknowledged for his effective global transmission of Kṛṣṇa consciousness.

See also: **Bhagavadgītā; Bhaktisiddhanta Saraswati; Caitanya; Gaudiya Vaishnava Mission; Guru; International Society for Krishna Consciousness; Kṛṣṇa; Mantra; Purāṇas; Saṃnyāsa; Varṇa**

KIM KNOTT

Further reading

Bromley, D.G. and L.D. Shinn (eds). 1989. *Krishna Consciousness in the West.* Lewisburg, PA: Bucknell University Press.

Bryant, E.F. and M.L. Ekstrand (eds). 2004. *The Hare Krishna Movement: The Post Charismatic Fate of a Religious Transplant.* New York: Columbia University Press.

Squarcini, F. and E. Fizzotti. 2004. *Hare Krishna: Studies in Contemporary Religion.* Salt Lake City, UT: Signature Books.

PRADAKṢIṆA

Pradakṣiṇa is the movement around a sacred object, a god, temple or even oneself with the intent to honour, worship, bond and reaffirm one's elevated status. Symbolising the duality inherent in Hindu religious thought, pradakṣiṇa means pursuit, yet the attainment of one's destination, and quest as well as fulfilment, as circumambulation is performed upon completion of one's journey or attainment of the desired destination. Passageways to allow circumambulation are part of most temples and allow the worshipper to circle around all deities in a clockwise direction. According to Hindu scriptures, Gaṇeśa won a contest with his brother, who challenged him to circumambulate the universe, a task which Gaṇeśa completed in an instant by circumambulating his parents. Pradakṣiṇa is performed in the clockwise direction so as to keep the deity always on the right, and the circular motion signifies that god is in the centre of our universe; while circumambulating, all devotees are equidistant from god at the centre, at all points of the circle. After the completion of a pūjā, a devotee is asked to circumambulate him/herself in order to commemorate the supreme divinity within.

See also: **Gaṇeśa; Mandir; Pūjā; Temple worship**

KOKILA RAVI

Further reading

Chakrabarti, Vibhuti. 1990. *Indian Architectural Theory*. London: Routledge.

PRAHLĀD(A)

The legendary figure of Prahlād is a significant inspirational presence in Vaiṣṇava bhakti traditions as he refused to give up his love for Viṣṇu and worship his own father, the demon-king Hiraṇyakaśīpu, even when under severe physical and mental pressure. The story becomes emblematic of standing up for your faith even when persecuted and also of the certainty of protection to those who show one-pointed devotion. Eventually Viṣṇu manifested as the half-man, half-lion avatāra known as Narasiṃha, who rescued Prahlād from his father by destroying the demon-king and thus saving the world.

Although festivals associated with the rescue of Prahlād are regional or located within various Vaiṣṇava saṃpradāyas, in recent times this has become associated with the all-India festival of Holī as some versions of the story state it was Hiranyakaśīpu's demon sister Holikā who was killed by Narasiṃha when called upon by the king, who had failed in his own efforts to murder his son as he was under the protection of Viṣṇu's grace.

See also: **Avatāra; Bhakti; Holī; Hiraṇyakaśīpu; Saṃpradāya; Utsava; Vaiṣṇavism; Viṣṇu**

RON GEAVES

Further reading

Stutley, Margaret and James Stutley (eds). 1977. *A Dictionary of Hinduism: Its Mythology, Folklore and Development 1500 BC–AD 1500*. London: Routledge and Kegan Paul.

PRAJĀPATI

The name of the most important god in the *Brāhmaṇas*, texts dating roughly from 800 to 500 BCE, and precursor to the later god Brahmā. Meaning 'Lord of progeny' this god is primarily associated with four interrelated themes: the creation of the universe, sexual procreation, the power residing in the sacrifice, and certain ascetic practices. Sometimes he is presented as being androgynous, at other times he procreates with the help of a female principle. Uniformly he is connected with various totalities, such as the year and the sacrifice, and this associated him with the metaphysical speculations contained in the *Brāhmaṇas*. His importance is gauged by his widespread appearance in mythology, but it cannot be ascertained if he was worshipped as a popular god, although this may be implied by his invocation in small-scale rituals associated with marriage and childbirth.

See also: **Brāhmaṇas; Brahmā; Tapas**

GREG BAILEY

Further reading

Gonda, J. 1986. *Prajāpati's Rise to Higher Rank*. Leiden: Brill.

PRAKṚTI

The term prakṛti, 'original nature', is derived from the preverb pra, 'pre', compounded with a derivate of the root kṛ, 'do, make', and refers to the original material out of which an object is fabricated, i.e. its material cause. The fabricated object that is its effect is termed vikṛti, 'transformation'.

In the dualist ontology of Sāṃkhya, Prakṛti is one of the two fundamental types of entities, the other being Puruṣa. Prakṛti is the original material out of which the entire universe has developed. Its evolutes include not only physical objects and the bodies of living beings but also the entire personality. Only individual selves (Puruṣas), consisting solely of pure consciousness, are distinct from Prakṛti and are not its evolutes. The one unmanifest Prakṛti manifests itself for each Puruṣa, teleologically motivated to allow each Puruṣa to experience nature and ultimately to attain isolation from nature (Kaivalya). In the interest of Puruṣa, unmanifest Prakṛti, which consists of the three Guṇas sattva, 'purity', rajas, 'passion', and tamas, 'dullness', swells into Mahat 'the great', which takes the form of the intellect (buddhi) as the subtlest constituent of an individual, and sprouts into Ahaṃkāra, 'individuality'. Ahaṃkāra, in turn, with sattva predominant transforms into Manas, the five senses: hearing, touch, sight, taste and smell; and the five organs of action: speech, hands, feet, reproductive organs and anus; and with tamas predominant, it transforms into the five basic elements (tanmātra): sound, contact, form, fluid and fragrance (*Sāṃkhyakārikā* 25). The five basic elements transform into the five gross elements (mahābhūta): space, wind, fire, water and earth. The seven evolutes of the original Prakṛti Mahat/buddhi, Ahaṃkāra, and the five basic elements all have further evolutes; hence, together with the original they are termed the eight prakṛtis. Different balances of the three Guṇas develop forms of the intellect (buddhi) called dispositions (bhāva) that dispose the individual to different types of thought and activity (*Sāṃkhyakārikā* 23).

All of the evolutes of nature, being effects, are transient, finite, changing, conglomerate and dependent. In contrast, unmanifest Prakṛti is eternal, infinite, inactive, independent and, although consisting of the three fundamental constituents, is unitary because they are inseparable. Prakṛti consists of the three fundamental constituents, is insentient, objective, common to numerous witnessing selves and evolvent, in contrast to the selves, which are sentient, subjective, private and non-changing (*Sāṃkhyakārikā* 10–11).

While the Puruṣa, conceptualised as masculine, is merely an inactive witness to all the experience that Prakṛti channels through the faculties of knowledge and ultimately through the intellect for the Puruṣa to experience, Prakṛti, conceptualised as feminine, undertakes every aspect of the activity. She even performs the act of cognition of the distinction between the self and nature that sets the Puruṣa free. Her activity is compared with that of a dancer for an audience and a servant for an unrequiting master (*Sāṃkhyakārikā* 59–60).

Although in Sāṃkhya Prakṛti is insentient, she is deified in Hinduism under her own name, and as the female consorts of principal deities, Durgā or Pārvatī, the wife of Śiva, Śrī or Lakṣmī, the wife of Viṣṇu, and Sarasvatī, the consort of Brahmā. Although in classical Sāṃkhya Prakṛti is a fundamental element distinct from multiple Puruṣas, her appearance as these female consorts and her appearance in Tantra as Śakti, 'power', of a transcendent God recall the proto-Sāṃkhya traditions that consider Prakṛti the first development of a universal transcendent being.

See also: **Ahaṃkāra; Brahmā; Durgā; Guṇas; Kaivalya; Lakṣmī, Śrī; Mahat; Manas; Pārvatī; Puruṣa; Śakti; Sāṃkhya; Sāṃkhyakārikās; Sarasvatī; Śiva; Tantrism; Viṣṇu**

PETER M. SCHARF

Further reading

Jacobsen, Knut A. 1999. *Prakṛti in Sāṃkhya-yoga: Material Principle, Religious Experience, Ethical Implications.* New York: Peter Lang.

PRALAYA

'Dissolution (of the world)'. Traditional Hindu cosmology presupposes an endless cycle of periodic creations and dissolutions of the universe. *Viṣṇu Purāṇa* 6.2:3–6.5 speaks of three kinds of pralaya, also known as prasamjara or pratisarga: the first one is called naimittika pralaya ('occasional') and occurs at the end of a kalpa, coinciding with a Night of Brahmā, to be followed by a new Day of Brahmā. The second is called prākritika pralaya ('material') and occurs at the end of a Life of Brahmā, after two Parārddhas (two times seventeen years), ending one Day of Viṣṇu. The third is called atyantika pralaya ('final'), terminating all notions of time and individual existence. The text describes in great detail the processes involved in each of these. In naimittika pralaya all the worlds are burnt up and absorbed by Viṣṇu, who then reposes for a thousand kalpas (One Night of Brahmā) on Śeṣa (the world-snake) in the midst of the original ocean. 'Awaking, at the end of his night, the unborn Viṣṇu, in the form of Brahmā, creates the universe anew' (*Viṣṇu Purāṇa* 6.4:8). In prākritika pralaya, after the dissolution of all entities, the elements (bhutas) are absorbing each other till unformed prakṛti (primary matter) alone remains. This pralaya also involves the Egg of Brahmā (brahmāṇḍa) and eventually prakṛti itself is dissolved in Puruṣottama (Supreme Person). The Life of a Brahmā is equal to a Day of Viṣṇu, who after an equally long Night begins to issue Brahmā again to begin another world cycle. Atyantika pralaya results in the complete and final absorption of jīvas (living souls) into Viṣṇu.

In addition to these three, the *Agni Purāṇa* mentions a fourth, nitya pralaya: the constant death of those that were born in this world – the end of their individual bodily existence.

See also: **Brahmā, day of; Jīva; Kalpa; Prakṛti; Purāṇas; Śeṣa; Viṣṇu**

KLAUS K. KLOSTERMAIER

Further reading

Klostermaier, K.K. 1994. *A Survey of Hinduism*, 2nd edn. Albany, NY: State University of New York Press.
Wilson, H.H. (trans.). 1961. *The Viṣṇu Purāṇa: A System of Hindu Mythology and Tradition.* Calcutta: Punthi Pustak. First published 1840.

PRAMĀṆAS

The term pramāṇa is one of several epistemological terms that derive from the preverb pra, 'pre', plus the root mā, 'measure'. A pramāṇa, 'valid means of knowledge', is the direct cause by which a knower (pramātṛ) arrives at correct knowledge (pramā) of an object to be known (prameya). Correct knowledge is differentiated from memory, which arises exclusively from impressions of past experience, and from incorrect cognition. According to Nyāya, there are four pramāṇas: perception (pratyakṣa), inference (anumāna), analogy (upamāna) and testimony (śabda). Perception, which results in non-verbal, invariant and determinate perceptual knowledge, consists in contact of a normally functioning sense organ with an object. Non-conceptual (nirvikalpaka) perception, in which the mere existence of the object is apprehended, precedes conceptual perception (savikalpaka), in which the object is recognised as what it is, qualified by certain qualifiers. Inference is the knowledge that an object (pakṣa) is the substrate of a property (sādhana, 'ground of proof'), invariably accompanied by a second property (sādhya, 'object to be proven'), as induced from other examples (udāharaṇa) by previous experience, and results in the inferential knowledge (anumiti) that the object has the second property. One infers, for example, that the mountain has fire on it by seeing that it has smoke on it and recalling that smoke is invariably accompanied by fire, just as it is in the kitchen. Analogy is the means of arriving at new knowledge of an object by comparing its properties with those of a known object. For example, one determines that a previously unencountered animal is a Gayal because one observes that it has certain features which one recalls having been informed that a Gayal shares with a cow. Verbal testimony is instruction by a reliable witness (āpta-upadeśa).

Pūrva Mīmāṃsā and Advaita Vedānta accept non-perception (anupalabdhi) and presumption (arthāpatti) as additional independent pramāṇas. (Prabhākara (*c.* 700 CE) only the latter.) Non-perception is the means by which one knows that something is missing. Presumption is the postulation of a cause because of the impossibility of accounting for facts otherwise. For example, one presumes that Devadatta eats at night because he is plump but does not eat during the day. Although Paurāṇikas, 'Narrators', count concurrence (saṃbhava) and tradition (aitihya) as independent means of knowledge and Tāntrikas, 'adherents of Tantrism', count gesture (ceṣṭā) (Śukla 1985: 49), Nyāya subsumes tradition under testimony and the other two under inference (Potter 1977: 227, 354, 408). Moreover, it subsumes presumption under inference, and non-perception under perception, inference or testimony (Potter 1977: 178, 408). Sāṃkhya, Yoga, Viśiṣṭādvaita and Dvaita Vedānta do not recognise analogy as an independent means of knowledge. Vaiśeṣika and Buddhism consider the relation between a speech form and the object it denotes to be established by inference and hence subsume testimony under inference (Prasad 2000: 23–38). Lokāyata denies even inference on the grounds that perception can establish only probabilities, not the invariable relations on which inference depends (Smart 1964: 220; King 1999: 129; Mohanty 2000: 16–17). Some non-naive-realist philosophers – including Buddhists who hold that only momentary unique particulars are real on one extreme and Advaita Vedāntins who hold that only Brahman is real on the other – accept the ultimate reality only of non-conceptual perception (King 1999: 156–59).

See also: **Advaita; Brahman; Buddhism, relationship with Hinduism; Dvaita; Lokāyata; Nyāya; Pūrva Mīmāṃsā; Sāṃkhya; Tantrism; Vaiśeṣika; Viśiṣṭādvaita; Yoga**

PETER M. SCHARF

Further reading

Bartley, Christopher. 2005. *Indian Philosophy A–Z*. New York: Palgrave Macmillan.

Jwala Prasad. 1987. *History of Indian Epistemology*. New Delhi: Munshiram Manoharlal.

King, Richard. 1999. *Indian Philosophy: An Introduction to Hindu and Buddhist Thought*. Washington, DC: Georgetown University Press.

Matilal, Bimal Krishna. 1971. *Epistemology, Logic, and Grammar in Indian Philosophical Analysis*. Janua Linguarum, studia memoriae

Nicolai van Wijk dedicata, ed. C. H. van Schooneveld, series minor 111. The Hague: Mouton.

Mohanty, J.N. 1988. 'A Fragment of the Indian Philosophical Tradition – Theory of Pramāṇa'. *PEW* 38.3 (July): 251–60.

Mohanty, J.N. 2000. *Classical Indian Philosophy.* Part I: *Theory of Knowledge (Pramāṇa Śāstra)*, 9–38. Lanham, MD, Boulder, CO, New York and Oxford: Rowman & Littlefield.

Phillips, Stephen H. and N.S. Ramanuja Tatacharya. 2004. *Epistemology of Perception: Gaṅgeśa's Tattvacintāmaṇi: Jewel of Reflection on the Truth (about Epistemology): The Perception Chapter: Pratyakṣa-khaṇḍa: Transliterated Text, Translation, and Philosophical Commentary.* Treasury of the Indic Sciences. New York: American Institute of Buddhist Studies.

Potter, Karl. (ed.). 1977. *Encyclopedia of Indian Philosophies, vol. 2: Indian Metaphysics and Epistemology: The Tradition of Nyāya-Vaiśeṣika up to Gaṅgeśa.* Princeton, NJ: Princeton University Press.

Prasad, K.S. 2000. *The Philosophy of Language in Classical Indian Tradition.* Hyderabad Studies in Philosophy 2. New Delhi: Decent Books.

Sastri, Kuppuswami S. 1932. *A Primer of Indian Logic: According to Annambhaṭṭa's Tarkasaṃgraha.* Madras: Kuppuswami Sastri Research Institute.

Satprakashananda, Swami. 1965. *Methods of Knowledge: Perceptual, Non-perceptual, and Transcendental: According to Advaita Vedānta.* London: George Allen and Unwin.

Simonnsson, Nils. 1977. 'Knowledge and Means of Knowledge'. *Studia Orientalia* 47 (Aalto Felicitation Volume): 207–17.

Smart, Ninian. 1964. *Doctrine and Argument in Indian Philosophy.* Muirhead Library of Philosophy, ed. H.D. Lewis. London: George Allen and Unwin.

Śukla, Candradhara (ed. and trans.). 1985. *Annambhaṭṭaviracitaḥ tarkasaṃgrahaḥ ācāryacandrajasiṃharacitaḥ padakṛtyayutaḥ* (Annambhaṭṭa's *Tarkasaṃgraha* with Candrajasiṃha's *Padakṛtya*). [Sanskrit and Hindi.] Gokul Das Sanskrit Series 14. 4d. Varanasi: Caukhambha Orientalia.

Varadachari, K.C. 'A Critique of the Pramāṇas'. *Journal of the Ganganath Jha Research Institute* 5.2: 93–119. Allahabad.

PRĀṆĀYĀMA

See: **Aṣṭāṅga Yoga**

PRARTHANA SAMAJ

Ideologically influenced by the Bengali Brahmo Samaj, the Prarthana Samaj (Prayer Society) was an influential theistic Hindu reform movement in Western India in late nineteenth and early twentieth century. The Bombay Presidency (roughly corresponding to today's Indian states Maharashtra and Gujarat) witnessed the emergence of a small English-educated Hindu elite in the first three decades after it had come under British rule in 1818. Particularly high-caste Hindus (mostly Chitpavan and Saraswat brāhmaṇas) in the urban centres of Bombay, Poona, Ahmadabad and Surat were attracted by the newly created educational institutions, which soon became the centres of debate on religious, scientific and social issues. However, the first attempts to create synthetic reform organisations reconciling brahmanical Hindu belief with elements of Western thought and Christian theology – the Manav Dharma Sabha and the Paramahamsa Mandali founded in the 1840s – were short-lived secret societies with a very limited impact. It was only after the Brahmo Leader Keshab Chandra Sen visited Bombay in 1864 and 1867 that things took off. Under the impact of the Bengali reformer, Dr Atmaram Pandurang founded the Prarthana Samaj in 1867 as the city's reformist Hindu intelligentsia's forum for religious and social reform. Dozens of branches were opened in other cities and towns of western and, to a lesser extent, southern India in the following two decades. In organisational terms, the Samaj was modelled after the pattern of a modern association, complete with a managing committee and an extensive catalogue of rules and by-laws. Its religious doctrine was based on the premise that there was truth in every religion, as long as it accepted that there was only one God. Accordingly, Christian and Buddhist texts were read together with brahmanical and bhakti scriptures during the weekly prayer meetings, while idol worship was strictly refuted.

Perhaps more important than its iconoclastic zeal and the efforts in religious syncretism was the society's programme of social reform. The full catalogue of nineteenth-century Hindu reform movements can be found on the Prarthana Samaj's agenda, namely the fight for widow remarriage and female education and the crusade against child marriage and the oppressive features of the caste 'system'. Unlike its immediate predecessors, the Samaj managed to translate its ideology into practice: it opened educational institutions of various kinds and maintained orphanages, reading rooms and libraries. In 1906 a leading member of the society founded a 'Depressed Classes Mission' for the upliftment of the region's 'untouchable' population.

However, contrary to the more radical reform initiatives of the Brahmo and the Arya Samaj, the members of the Prarthāna Samaj were always anxious not to alienate brahmanical orthodoxy, which was extremely powerful in their regional stronghold Maharashtra. Moreover, the movement itself retained an elitist character as its members were almost exclusively drawn from an intellectual urban elite shaped by their own high-caste background – a fact which helps to explain the moderate and paternal outlook of the reformers in the sensitive issues of caste and women's uplift. Perhaps the most important impact of the Samaj lay in providing a religious and intellectual stimulus as well as a rallying point for the region's emerging political leaders and social reformers like M.G. Ranade, R.G. Chandavarkar, V.R. Shinde and Pandita Ramabai Saraswati.

Being a product of the specific socio-cultural configuration of the late nineteenth century, the movement gradually declined in importance in the subsequent decades.

See also: **Brahmo Samaj; Buddhism, relationship with Hinduism; Caste; Idolatry; Image worship; Inter-faith/Inter-religious Dialogue; Manav Dharma Sabha; Pandurang, Atmaram; Paramahamsa Mandali; Ranade, Mahadev Govind; Religious education; Saraswati, Pandita Ramabai; Sen, Keshab Chandra; Varṇa; Widow remarriage; Widowhood**

HARALD FISCHER-TINÉ

Further reading

Jones, K.W. 1989. *Socio-religious Reform Movements in British India.* Cambridge: Cambridge University Press.

PRASĀDA

In contemporary Hindu practice, prasāda, 'substantiated grace', is a material substance endowed with divine favour that is ingested, worn or applied to the body by the devotee. Along with having darśana, 'visual audience', receiving prasāda is one of the major acts of worship for Hindus, either at pilgrimage sites or at local shrines. In many ritual settings, prasāda is the end result of an exchange between a god and an individual: a gift called naivedya is presented to the deity; while it is being 'consumed' by the deity it becomes bhogya; the product left over, prasāda, bestows spiritual benefits upon the recipient. The offering that becomes prasāda changes according to region and divine preference: in Bengal, black male goats are regularly presented to Kālī; a particular sweetmeat, the laḍḍū, is known to be Gaṇeśa's favourite; and leaves of the bilva tree are preferred by Śiva. Yet, prior to its instantiation in ritual practice, prasāda is generally understood in the Sanskrit literary tradition as a mood or disposition which can be a force behind events. As a 'mood' of the divine, prasāda is characterised by generosity and benevolence – it often results from propitiation, and may bring about the fulfilment of a devotee's wishes. When present between people, prasāda encompasses a broader set of exchanges, including: the legacy conferred by ancestors upon their descendants; the generosity extended by a sovereign to his subjects; or the guidance given by a guru to his disciples. From the earliest Vedic literature to the heterodox writings of the Buddhists and Jains, the meaning of prasāda varies significantly according to literary genre and period. It is in Purāṇic literature, however, that a transition is discernible from the conception of prasāda as abstract to physical – as a tangible substantiation of divine temper.

See also: **Buddhism, relationship with Hinduism; Darśana; Gaṇeśa; Guru; Jainism, relationship with Hinduism; Kālī and Caṇḍī; Puraṇas; Śiva; Veda**

ANDREA MARION PINKNEY

Further reading

Fuller, C.J. 1992. *The Camphor Flame: Popular Hinduism and Society in India*. Princeton, NJ: Princeton University Press.

PRAŚĀSTAPĀDA

See: **Padārthadharmasaṃgraha**

PRAŚNA UPANIṢAD

See: **Upaniṣads**

PRASTHĀNATRAYĪ

The Prasthānatrayī (triple foundation) is the primary collection of textual resources upon which the theologians of the Vedānta system base their teachings. The texts that comprise the Prasthānatrayī are the *Upaniṣads*, the *Bhagavadgītā* and the *Brahmasūtras* or *Vedāntasūtras* of Bādarāyaṇa. There are many *Upaniṣads*, only a few of which are regarded by Vedāntins as sufficiently authoritative to warrant inclusion in the Prasthānatrayī. Śaṅkara comments on or refers to the *Aitareya*, the *Bṛhadāranyaka*, the *Chāndogya*, the *Īśā*, the *Jabala*, the *Kaṭha*, the *Kauṣītakī*, the *Kena*, the *Māṇḍūkya*, the *Muṇḍaka*, the *Piṅgala*, the *Praśna*, the *Śvetāśvatara* and the *Taittirīya*. These are the texts (with the possible addition of the *Maitrāyaṇāya* (*Maitrī*) and the *Mahānarāyana*) that constitute the *Upaniṣad* section of the Prasthānatrayī. Only these *Upaniṣads* have the status of Śruti (revelation); the *Bhagavadgītā* and the *Brahmasūtras* are classed as Smṛti (tradition).

The Vedānta theologians interpret the Prasthānatrayī on the basis of one fundamental presupposition: that all the teachings contained within it are compatible with each other. Indeed, the *Brahmasūtras* itself were composed primarily to demonstrate that, despite impressions to the contrary, the various *Upaniṣads* taught essentially the same doctrine. The task of all post Bādarāyaṇa Vedāntins was to expand this into a coherent interpretation of the Prasthānatrayī as a whole, a task that led to the creation of innovative hermeneutical strategies and, ultimately, to versions of Vedānta that were fundamentally incompatible with each other, e.g. Śaṅkara's monistic (advaita) interpretation, Rāmānuja's quasimonistic (viśiṣtādvaita) interpretation and Mādhva's dualistic (dvaita) interpretation.

See also: **Advaita; Bādarāyaṇa; Bhagavadgītā; Brahmasūtras; Dvaita; Mādhva; Rāmānuja; Śaṅkara; Upaniṣads; Vedānta; Viśiṣṭādvaita**

PETER CONNOLLY

Further reading

Nakamura, H. 1983. *A History of Early Vedanta Philosophy*. Delhi: Motilal Banarsidass.

PRAYĀGA

The ancient city of Prayāga (literally, 'a sacrificial ground') was near the present Allahabad (so rechristened as 'the City of God' by Mughal emperor Akbar) in the modern Indian state of Uttar Pradesh. Prayāga is believed to be the site where the three holy rivers Gaṅgā, Yamunā and the (invisible) Sarasvatī come together in what is known as the sacred 'confluence of three rivers (literally, braids of hair)' (triveṇī-saṅgam), bathing in which ensures liberation (mokṣa). Lord Śiva takes residence in Prayāga in the form of Someśvara, while Lord Viṣṇu resides here as Veṇumādhava. Ancient lore of the place contends that Lord Brahmā performed a sacrifice in Prayāga at the beginning of time and that the Vedic deities Soma, Varuṇa and Prajāpati took birth here. Such is the holy resonance of this spot that both earthly joy and liberation are available to those who live and die here, thus earning it the title of 'king of all pilgrimage centres' (tīrtharāja). Prayāga's contention as the holiest of all Hindu pilgrimage spots may be supported by the fact that every twelve years it is the site of the 'Great Kumbha Melā' (mahākumbhamelā), where millions of seekers and saints converge to ritually bathe. Every six years Prayāga is the location for the 'Half Kumbhamelā' (ardhakumbhamelā), while every year (excepting the times for the kumbha melā) it hosts the Māghamelā, a January–February bathing festival that the *Brahma Purāṇa* praises as equal to the performance of millions of Vedic sacrifices. In addition to its significant connection with the triveṇī-saṅgam, Prayāga is also thought to have been the location for the āśramas of the sages Bharadvāja and Durvāsas, as well as an important place of learning for Indian philosophers such as Buddha, Kumārilabhaṭṭa, Śaṅkara, Caitanya, Vallabha, Rāmānanda and Dayānanda. The ancient city of Prayāga has held significance for Hindu, Buddhist, Muslim and British political rulers for the past thousands of years and has also been the home of several post-Independence Indian prime ministers and numerous other leaders. It was in Allahabad that Mahātmā Gandhi first proposed his campaign to liberate India from British rule through non-violent resistance.

See also: **Ahiṃsā; Āśram(a) (religious community); Brahmā; Buddhism, relationship with Hinduism; Caitanya; Gandhi, Mohandas Karamchand; Gaṅgā; Indus Valley Civilisation; Kumbha Melā; Mokṣa; Prajāpati; Purāṇas; Rāmānanda; Śaṅkara; Sarasvatī; Śiva; Soma; Tīrthayatrā (Pilgrimage); Vallabha; Varuṇa; Veda; Vedic Pantheon; Viṣṇu; Yajña; Yamunā**

DEVEN M. PATEL

Further reading

Dubey, D.P. 2001. *Prayaga: The Site of Kumbha Mela (in Temporal and Traditional Space)*. Delhi: Aryan Publishers.

Bhardwaj, Surinder Mohan. 1983. *Hindu Places of Pilgrimage in India: A Study in Cultural Geography*. Berkeley, CA: University of California Press.

PRĀYAŚCITTA

Prāyaścitta (literally, the thought of going forth – that is, of death) refers to death by fasting as punishment and, by extension, to any kind of atonement or expiation that purges major sins (mahāpātakas), minor ones (upapātakas) or the negative effects of accidental events. Prāyaścittas can be inflicted by deities; the assembly of learned men (pariśad), the king or the self. Penalties include capital punishment (prohibited from the tenth century in the Kalivarjya, which refers to things to be avoided in the Kaliyuga, a time when only one-quarter of righteousness remained according to the theory of the four yugas); excommunication; branding; tonsure; yogic restraints (fasting; sleeping on the ground; eating only leaves, roots and fruits; begging for alms); performing vows (vrata) and fire rituals (homa); going on pilgrimage; reciting Vedas, mantras or the names of deities; presenting gifts to brāhmaṇas; and cultivating virtues. Whereas prāyaścitta were once popular, they are today uncommon; only gifts, pilgrimages and recitations remain.

See also: **Mahāpātakas; Tīrthayātrā (Pilgrimage); Varṇa; Veda; Vrata; Yuga**

KATHERINE K. YOUNG

Further reading

Day, T.P. 1982. *The Conception of Punishment in Early Indian Literature.* Waterloo, Ontario: Canadian Corporation for Studies in Religion with Wilfrid Laurier Press.

Glucklich, A. 1994. *The Sense of Adharma.* Oxford: Oxford University Press.

Herman, A.L. 1976. *The Problem of Evil and Indian Thought.* Delhi: Motilal Banarsidass.

Kane, P.V. 1968–77. *History of Dharmaśāstra (Ancient and Medieval Religious and Civil Law in India)*, 2nd edn, 5 vols. Poona: Bhandarkar Oriental Research Institute, esp. vol. 4.

PREMIS

See: **Divine Light Mission**

PRETAS

Literally, 'deceased', the term preta is used to refer to the ethereal state of existence experienced by all recently dead human beings that precedes either rebirth, reunion with ancestors or departure to another realm of being. It is very important that funeral rituals are observed absolutely correctly to avoid the possibility of the soul remaining earthbound and becoming a preta rather than passing on to the next life in the cycle of rebirth.

However, the term is generally used for beings who were not able for some reason to find their way out of this world and remain bound and restless, haunting places and disturbing the living. Most villages will be populated by ghosts, generally the troubled spirits of people who have died violently, in strange circumstances or by suicide. Ghosts will usually trouble those who might have been involved in the death, although there is considerable evidence to suggest that they are activated in households where there is a sense of grievance or unfulfilled lives. House ghosts are generally benign, but those that haunt ponds, trees or fields are not.

There are a number of experts who are able to exorcise pretas. Religious explanations commonly state that the preta failed to fulfil a vow to a divinity, and in such cases the chosen expert will be a devotee of the respective deity, who will show the person disturbed by the ghost how to complete the vow on its behalf. Other specialists involved in exorcism are the village ohja and religious functionaries concerned with village deities. All of these specialists able to deal with supernatural possession or haunting are usually members of low castes and operate as another layer of rural religious life below the brāhmaṇa ritual priests. However, there are also specialist texts that provide mantras for dealing with pretas such as the *Garuḍa Purāṇa.*

See also: **Antyeṣṭi; Pitṛs; Possession; Purāṇas**

RON GEAVES

Further reading

Stutley, Margaret and James Stutley (eds). 1977. *A Dictionary of Hinduism: Its Mythology, Folklore and Development 1500 BC–AD 1500*. London: Routledge and Kegan Paul.

PRONUNCIATION

See: **Śikṣā**

PṚTHĀ

See: **Kuntī**

PṚTHIVĪ

The 'broad [one]'; the 'broad [expanse]'. The Vedic name for the earth as the mother of the gods (devas). Pṛthivī is usually coupled with the sky-lord Dyaus in a dvandva (dual compound): Dyāvāpṛthivī, 'heaven and earth'. The one Ṛgvedic hymn addressed to her alone (5.84) portrays her as an atmospheric deity concerned with the production of rain. She is most likely to be identified with Pṛśni, the 'storm-cloud' mother of the Maruts. Invariably, throughout the *Ṛgveda*, Pṛthivī's motherhood is emphasised. Although in later portions of the *Ṛgveda* Pṛthivī and Aditi are occasionally conflated, they originally represent telluric and anti-telluric forces, respectively.

See also: **Deities; Dyaus Pitṛ; Maruts; Saṃhitā; Vedic Pantheon; Vedism**

MICHAEL YORK

PŪJĀ

Pūjā literally means worship or homage. The term generally refers to the ritual of honouring or worshipping one or more Hindu deities. Pūjā is most often directed towards a statue or mūrti of the deity, but may be directed towards a pictorial image. It is the most important and widely practised daily ritual of the majority of Hindus. This ritual enables the devotee to establish a relationship with their preferred deity. Many of the ceremonies conducted during pūjā are ways of honouring the deities or treating them as respected guests. The deity is made comfortable, bathed, adorned with jewellery, dressed in clean clothes and anointed with fragrant sandal paste. They may be offered a seat and given food to eat, entertained with singing and delighted with the aroma of incense, the air around them purified by the use of a camphor flame. The offerings appeal to the five senses, of smell, sight, hearing, touch and taste. By making offerings during the pūjā ritual, the devotee may seek to gain favour from the deities, though most often the rites are performed simply as an act of devotion. The blessing of the deity is received by the devotee in the form of a tilak – a mark between the eyes made of red kumkum or yellow sandal paste representing a third eye – or through the prasāda given at temples, which usually consists of some blessed foodstuff. During the pūjā rituals, ārtī (the offering of a flame and prayers) represents the climax of the proceedings.

As Hindus believe that Brahman as ultimate reality pervades the whole cosmos, anywhere can be a sacred place, therefore Hindu worship is not confined to the temple. However, temple worship is an integral aspect of Hinduism, but is not as widely practised as pūjā in the home at the domestic altar. Devout Hindus would perform a simple pūjā in the home twice a day, in the morning and in the evening.

Pūjā in the home and at the temple is a ritual undertaken to honour the deities installed there. The rituals performed might be simple or complex; at home, for instance, a simple pūjā consists of the home deities being bathed and decorated and offered water, incense, light, food and prayers. The head male of an orthodox brāhmaṇa family might perform this type of pūjā on behalf of the family. He may also recite the many names of the chosen deity, to remind the family of the many attributes of God, or he may recite passages from the Vedas. The purpose of the ritual is to make the mind pure by concentrating on God. Therefore, before starting the pūjā ritual, each member of the family would have a bath and put on clean clothes. This signifies that they are clean on the outside, ready to be cleansed within.

In the temple, pūjā is normally more elaborate, performed by one or more priests rather than by the devotee him- or herself. However, pūjā in the temple is generally undertaken on an individual basis rather than as a congregation. There is no commitment to attend a temple regularly and many Hindus only visit the large temples on special occasions, preferring instead to worship at home or at a local shrine. However, communal worship takes place periodically, at the many yearly Hindu festivals, and on these occasions pūjā at the temple is more elaborate and is performed many times during the festival. Although pūjā is a ritual in itself, during the festivals it is a core ritual within a larger group of ceremonies. On these occasions pūjā may be conducted by a number of priests who follow the complicated formulas set out in various texts such as the *Āgamas*, and is undertaken on behalf of many people rather than the individual. During the major festivals, great numbers of people come to take darśana, to see and be seen by the primary deity. Through pūjā, the devotees are able to communicate with the deities, who are believed to be full of sacred power, offering their prayers and receiving a blessing in return.

Pūjā became popular during the later purāṇic age (300–750 CE). This period is characterised by theism and the popularity of temple building. Gradually, pūjā replaced the Vedic sacrifice yajña as the core ritual. Unlike the Vedic yajña, which was performed solely by priests and was often undertaken for the purpose of propitiating the gods and maintaining the natural order of life, pūjā in its simplest form can be performed by anyone and is most often an expression of gratitude and honour rather than to placate a deity. The popularity of pūjā was increased further after the *Bhagavadgītā* sanctified it as the core of Bhakti, loving devotion (to a personal god or goddess), a legitimate path to God when Kṛṣṇa declared that he would accept any offering, however humble, if that offering was made in the spirit of devotion (*Bhagavadgītā* 9.26).

It is not only gods and goddesses who are honoured by pūjā rituals. Pūjā is offered on many occasions, such as in honour of school or college teachers, of one's guru, at marriages, to celebrate a birth or commemorate a death and during some festivals, in the form of kumārī pūjā, the worship of young girls as representatives of Śakti, the Goddess.

See also: **Altars, domestic; Ārtī; Bhagavadgītā; Bhakti; Brahman; Darśana; Hindu; Image worship; Kṛṣṇa; Prasāda; Sacred texts; Śakti; Temple worship; Yajña**

LYNN FOULSTON

Further reading

Johnson, W.J. (trans.). 1994. *The Bhagavad Gita*. Oxford and New York: Oxford University Press.

Michaels, A. 2004. *Hinduism: Past and Present*. Princeton, NJ: Princeton University Press.

PUṂSAVANA

'Bringing forth a male child'. A pre-natal saṃskāra, or rite of passage, this ceremony is generally prescribed for the third or fourth month after conception, generally before the foetus begins moving, when the moon is passing through a male lunar asterism (nakṣatra). Its purpose was to animate the foetus, assuring the birth of a son. The Vedic mantras used in this ritual, found in the *Atharvaveda*, dictate that a son be produced. In addition to the mantra recitation, the early texts suggest that a herbal substance was given to the pregnant wife. The second-century CE Āyurvedic text of Suśruta says that three or four drops of the juice of a banyan fruit, or a mixture of milk with a number of herbs, should be inserted into the right nostril of the wife. In the late Vedic period, from approximately the fifth century BCE to the turn of the Common Era, this rite was the occasion for a minor celebration. It is still occasionally performed today among certain Brāhmaṇa families of South India.

See also: **Āyurveda; Brāhmaṇa; Saṃskāra**

FREDERICK M. SMITH

Further reading

Kane, P.V. 1974. *History of Dharmaśāstra*, 2nd edn, vol. 2, pt 1. Poona: Bhandarkar Oriental Research Institute, 218–20.

Pandey, R.J. 1969. *Hindu Saṃskāras.* Delhi: Motilal Banarsidass, 60–63.

PUṆYA

Puṇya means merit or actions that conduce towards happiness. The term derives from the root puṇ, to act virtuously. Various actions are performed with the hope of gaining merit such as going on pilgrimage (tīrthayātrā) and other forms of devotional observance.

See also: **Bhakti; Tīrthayātrā (Pilgrimage)**

DENISE CUSH AND CATHERINE ROBINSON

PURĀṆAS

One of the most important bodies of sacred literature in Hinduism, the *Purāṇas* number some hundreds of texts dating from the early centuries of the Common Era almost up until the present day. They are composed in Sanskrit and Tamil, plus most of the vernacular languages. *Purāṇas* exist in Jainism and arguably in Buddhism in the form of avadāna literature, and have for almost two millennia provided a literary/oral instrument for communicating the central aspects of the Hindu culture from the elite to the mainstream of society and back again. Hindu *Purāṇas* are divided within the tradition into eighteen 'Great *Purāṇas*' and eighteen 'Lesser *Purāṇas*', though it is difficult to know on what principles this classification is based, especially since different *Purāṇas* are included in different lists of the respective types.

As cultural artefacts the *Purāṇas* have been transmitted to us in both manuscript and oral form as a large set of individual texts, all appearing to be highly derivative of other literary sources. Of the best-known *Purāṇas*, scores of manuscripts, usually only a few hundred years old, can be found in manuscript collections. Some *Purāṇas*, especially the *Bhāgavata*, and individual parts of *Purāṇas* continue to be recited and commented upon in oral performances. Elsewhere, extracted portions from named *Purāṇas* are quoted, sometimes several times in different texts, by the medieval encyclopedists of society and ritual in single-authored collections known as *Nibandhas*. Finally, scenes from Purāṇic mythology have been, and continue to be, depicted in sculpture and in paintings in illustrated manuscripts. In studying the *Purāṇas* it is possible to look at all these components of Purāṇic expression individually, but collectively they are expressions of a broader cultural perspective.

In this sense the *Purāṇas* function as a method of codifying a particular view of reality. Their method of creation, transmission and reception defines a distinctive way of presenting religious and social data in a manner accessible to people of various classes and levels of education. What is presented is clearly central to how Hindu culture is to be defined, otherwise the genre would not have survived until the present day. And though it is likely that the *Purāṇas* are accorded a particular status because they were composed in Sanskrit, their influence within Hindu society has been a consequence of the ease with which they could also be composed and transmitted in vernacular languages, a trend that continues. Some of the more technical contents of the *Purāṇas* – those dealing with mineralogy, grammar or poetics, and composed in the typical *sūtra* style of scientific literature – would be comprehensible only to a very learned and small audience. Not so the myths, which are part and parcel of a person's acculturalisation and are as well known in the vernacular as they are in Sanskrit forms. What this means is that the *Purāṇas* are as much a process of education as they are distinct literary texts arising from this process.

The word purāṇa means 'old, primeval, ancient', and so denotes a distant past somehow reaching into the present. A Sanskrit etymology of the word purāṇa breaks the word up into purā, 'old', and nava, 'new', with the intention of placing stress on the capacity of *Purāṇas* to preserve the old and integrate the new. A traditional view of society and culture is always being renewed by the new, whilst the new is always being anchored in the traditional past. Their traditional status, traditional because each *Purāṇa* is a collection of tales from the past, is confirmed by the attribution of their authorship to the mythical figure Vyāsa. The *Purāṇas* declare their own composition to come from the famous sage Vyāsa at an indeterminate time in the past, the same figure also being attributed with the composition of the *Mahābhārata*. As such the *Purāṇas* are a received body, traditionally derived from an original *Purāṇasaṃhitā* (*Viṣṇupurāṇa* 3, 6, 15) or 'Collection of *Purāṇas*'. This was a much larger text than the extant *Purāṇas*, which were reduced in size in order to make them comprehensible by mankind. The initial recitations of many of the *Purāṇas* are all localised in the Naimiṣa forest, where the bard Lomaharṣaṇa recites them individually to assembled sages. This effectively gives one standard of fictional recitation which all the *Purāṇas* share and enables contemporary reciters to stand within this mythic world of the Naimiṣa forest, at least for that specific time when engaged in their recitation.

Transmission

Purāṇas have always been communicated through oral recitation, though contemporary evidence suggests individual parts of any given *Purāṇa* were recited rather than the entire text. In the manner in which these texts are recited, there is a substantial level of compositional and commentarial activity taking place at the same time. This has been empirically verified in recent work on oral composition in India. But the *Purāṇas* and other early Sanskrit texts also allude to recitations of themselves in royal courts and villages. Empirical studies show there is no decisively fixed form of a *Purāṇa* from which a reciter cannot deviate. This does not mean that in a recitation the reciter will not repeat portions of what he knows, but that he will feel no compunction in embellishing existing material to make it more exciting to an audience, easier to understand or more specifically relevant to the particular geographical region in which the people live. When such changes are incorporated into different manuscript versions of any given *Purāṇa*, they give the impression that new material, occasionally massive, has been added over time to the individual recitational tradition of that *Purāṇa*. The problem is that it is virtually impossible to date additions (or excisions) and it is foolhardy to investigate the *Purāṇa* as a particular text composed and set in one form at one particular time. Any study, even of recent manuscripts, of the *Mahā Purāṇas* demonstrates widespread variance in content, and even size, and this must have been much greater in oral recitation, where a given text would have been composed only in parts over a month.

For students of *Purāṇas* this means the distinction between oral and written versions of texts must be taken very seriously in defining what it means to speak of a given *Purāṇa* and what it means to speak of the *Purāṇa* genre as such. The genre must include both oral and written forms of expression, the former in deference to the still living tradition of Purāṇic recitation. An example of such a recitation in Gujarat illustrates perfectly the necessity of focusing on the manner of dissemination of the texts:

> The neighbourhood flocks to hear the kathā, as the Purāṇic recital is called; the public square in front and the windows of the surrounding houses are turned into an auditorium for the occasion. The bhaṭ [reciter] recites an ākhyān [mythic narrative]; explains many parts of it; adds a flourish here, a touch there, to move or tickle the audience; improvises new stories and introduces lively anecdotes. The audience sits, hour after hour, absorbed in the recital. The description of a Purāṇic incident or character in the mouth of a competent bhaṭ, assumes a fresh form, and a contemporary colour.
>
> (Munshi, cited in Rocher 1986: 59)

Purāṇic tales are inculcated into Indian homes by the parents of children, especially of those living in high-caste communities. By the time they are adults many Indian children will know in outline many of the Purāṇic tales and these will be reinforced in temple iconography and occasionally in film and television production. This raises the question of the kind of reality Purāṇic recitation and tales represent within Hindu culture, not unlike the kind of distorted mirror of reality advertising presents to a Western television audience. To term a phrase, Purāṇic culture is broader simply than the presence of a collection of texts each bearing the name *Purāṇa*.

Ordering purāṇic contents

The contents of the *Purāṇas* mark the full development of Hinduism as a set of ideas and practices centred above all on the belief in, and practice of devotion to, a personal god, but not neglecting the ritual and ascetic elements of religious activity. A theory and practice of devotion is already implied in earlier Buddhist texts and the *Mahābhārata*, but it is brought to full expression in the *Purāṇas* and continues up until the present day. As texts they are best known for the huge body of mythology they contain, a combination of material going back to the *Vedas* and the *Mahābhārata* mixed with material that sometimes cannot be traced back to texts earlier than the particular *Purāṇa* in which it appears. Any reader of even just one *Purāṇa* will be astonished at the richness of the mythological narratives they contained. Individual *Purāṇas* do focus on individual gods rather than others, though they always operate in the presence of the complete pantheon of gods, recognisable from the *Vedas* onwards, and the themes brought up in the myths are as important as the gods who appear in them. Focus on an individual god is most obvious in the case of the *Viṣṇu* and the *Bhāgavatapurāṇas*, where Viṣṇu is unambiguously advanced as the supreme deity of the universe, a role accorded to Śiva in the *Śiva*, *Brahmavaivarta* and *Liṇgapurāṇas*. Other *Purāṇas* focus on Sūrya, Gaṇeśa or the generalised mother goddess called Devī. Still others such as the *Vāmana* and the *Kūrma*, though named after avatāras of Viṣṇu, seem to treat Viṣṇu and Śiva equally. This mode of classification has been recognised within the Purāṇic tradition itself, where a classification into sāttvic (= Viṣṇu), rājasic (= Brahmā) and tāmasic (= Śiva) (guṇas) is sometimes seen. But like so many other classifications within the *Purāṇas*, the actual evidence of the texts themselves defies any attempt to mirror precisely anything like the image of what these classifications might produce.

If there is an originality in the *Purāṇas* it lies in the manner in which they combine and order the material they collect from elsewhere. Two controlling strategies are of fundamental importance within the genre and its development of a particular poetics, and these do command a degree of originality. The first is the occurrence of a distinctive and well-known set of topics dealing with every aspect of cosmogony and cosmology; and, the second, the ubiquitous presence of a system of devotion called bhakti. Whilst bhakti occurs in every *Purāṇa* in many different ways, not every *Purāṇa* has cosmological and cosmogonic tracts. In a sense this does not matter, however, since it is the tradition associated with the name *Purāṇa* that is important and a Purāṇic audience, even one not learned in Sanskrit, knows the *Purāṇas* are all about the things of the past, of which creation and destruction of the universe are two such topics. Any given *Purāṇa*, therefore, is part of the system of knowledge where these subjects are taken as givens. These subjects give a clear emphasis within a rich body of what could otherwise be seen as extraneous material.

Cosmology and cosmogony are classified into the traditional five characteristics of the Purāṇic genre, characteristics determining a set of contents as much as the way these contents interact. Though a number of *Purāṇas* list the five characteristics, they do not draw the equation between them and the definition of *Purāṇa* as a genre. This is only done in the synonymic dictionary, the *Amarakośa*. The five characteristics are shown in Table 3. These offer a complete context for the mythological acts presented in the Purāṇic narratives. Many *Purāṇas* contain a whole series of creation myths which encompass the creation and destruction of the universe, activities associated prominently with the gods Brahmā and Śiva. Such narratives are highly complex and cover up to twenty chapters in those *Purāṇas* where they occur. It is believed that the myths of creations and destruction encode normative social and religious behaviour and that the narratives have also been structured around the different stages of yogic activity as the yogin enters and leaves the advanced meditational state called samādhi.

Table 3

sarga	cosmogony
pratisarga	cosmogony and cosmology
Vaṃśa	genealogies of kings
manvantara	histories of the world during a period of one patriarch
Vaṃśānucaritam	legends of the reigns of kings

As many as fourteen worlds are described and the creation itself proceeds from the Supreme Being in an evolutionary scheme involving up to twenty-five principles. It is possible to recognise the philosophical underpinning to this when it is realised that the principal role of the creator god, Brahmā, in these creation myths is to establish a sense of individuality, of which he is the divine symbol. Once established, the description of creation proceeds with the sequential emergence of the various species of beings, including humans, animals, gods and demons, and further subdivides the creation of humans into the four basic social classes.

All Purāṇic texts are also predicated on the universal occurrence in South Asia of a set of religious precepts and practices associated with devotion to an object of devotion, usually a god/goddess or a holy man/woman. Whilst the early historical development of the theory and practice of devotion remains vague, the *Purāṇas* were the earliest Hindu texts to depict the devotional tendency in its fullest possible form. Myths extolling devotion as a practice, hymns of devotions to gods and descriptions of devotional practices are found everywhere in the *Purāṇas*, and a text such as the sumptuous *Bhāgavata Purāṇa* could be described as a devotional meditation on the god Kṛṣṇa. A reader of an entire *Purāṇa* could easily become lost in the devotional material, such is its expanse, yet there are implicit controls on the way the genre develops and encapsulates this material.

These controls are best illustrated in a myth which occurs hundreds of times in the *Purāṇas*, and can also be found in the first eleven chapters of the *Bhagavadgītā*. A summary of one myth from the fourteenth century *Gaṇeśa Purāṇa* (2, 134, 7–40) is typical.

There was a heavenly musician named Krauñca who accidentally struck a sage with his foot and was cursed to become a rat which would be used as a vehicle by Gaṇeśa, who would eventually give him spiritual liberation.

He was reborn in the hermitage of Parāśara as a huge rat, terrifying everyone in the hermitage and eating all the corn. All the sages of the hermitage became worried about who would get rid of the rat, but Gaṇeśa, living there as a boy, said he would make him the vehicle on which he would ride. Immediately he released a noose and bound the rat in the underworld. He became frightened, wondering who would be able to do this to him. Gaṇeśa proceeded to pull him around with his mind, and as soon as the rat saw him he praised the god using a hymn of devotion and declared himself to be auspicious.

When he heard the speech Gaṇeśa became pleased, realising the rat had become his devotee. Then he offered him any wish he liked and the rat asked to serve Gaṇeśa. In turn Gaṇeśa asked the rat to become his vehicle. He climbed on him but was too heavy for him and so the rat asked him to lessen his weight and Gaṇeśa did so.

Though many details are left out here, the contents can be divided into the following nine stages, each of which summarises a body of content placed upon an axis of transformation of a person from non-devotee to devotee. Any name can be given for these two positions. Here the names are Krauñca and Gaṇeśa, respectively.

1 Introduction.
2 Spiritual ignorance of the future devotee.
3 Beginning of spiritual realisation for the future devotee.
4 Demonstration of the god's grace.
5 'Conversion' of the devotee.
6 Demonstration of the devotee's devotion.
7 The god offers grace to his devotee.
8 The devotee reaffirms devotion by accepting the grace.
9 The devotee performs specific activities as an expression of devotion.

In the Krauñca myth the first two stages are demonstrated in the rat's appearance and disruption of the hermitage, the third and fourth in the capturing of the rat and his sight of the boy/god. This can be understood as a favour on the part of the god. The fifth and sixth stages mark the conversion of the devotee, the actual transformation of his status and the demonstration of devotion by the offering of the short hymn. Stages seven and eight are crucial in marking the formalisation of the devotional relationship by the offering and receiving of a boon. Krauñca's decision to become the god's vehicle is, finally, a devotional act and the most obvious way in which his devotion will henceforth be expressed.

The large bulk of Purāṇic myths function to fill out aspects of each of these stages. This applies even if the particular myths do not appear superficially to be dealing with the subject of devotion. All the Purāṇic creation myths, for example, which involve the presentation of some highly technical material, also provide some theology of the principal god associated with the origin of the act of creation. Information of this kind is of normative value for the devotees of that god, as is the large body of myths where all the gods appear. For instance, the myths where Viṣṇu appears as an avatāra always depict his capacity to provide spiritual liberation to his devotees and to protect the world from physical and moral danger, thus demonstrating both spiritual and material concerns. The large body of *dharmaśāstra* material, consisting of descriptions of life-cycle rituals and specified behaviour for the higher classes, summaries of devotional rituals, instructions for royal behaviour, etc., could be seen as an expression of the type of social activity of the devotee, who must continue to live in society as well as participate in an individual/collective relationship with the deity.

The final four stages of the myth encompass the practical expression of the devotee's devotion and so include such topics as ritual, recitation of lists of names of the god, pilgrimage, recitation of mantras and so on, all of which are comprehensively represented in the Purāṇic narrative outside of the actual myths themselves. Much of the non-mythological material in these texts is taken up with this kind of data. As well as covering the practical applications of devotion, the final stages also require for the devotee the presentation of the maximum possible knowledge about the deity. Accordingly, they can produce theological statements, discussions about the functions performed by the god in the Purāṇic creation myths or even biographies of deities like those of Kṛṣṇa found in the *Viṣṇu* and the *Bhāgavata Purāṇas* and of Gaṇeśa in the *Brahmavaivarta Purāṇa*. The full textual manifestation of such a semantic frame requires a large narrative, though it is certainly possible for its presence to be made evident in small fragments.

Given that this devotional poetics will normally generate mythic as well as homiletic narratives, its shaping influence on a particular text will produce various kinds of subtexts, including myths and more formal descriptions of rituals and rules of conduct in daily life. It is especially in respect of the latter that the lived world intersects with the mythological world because many of the rituals described would have been personally witnessed by the audience of a Purāṇic recitation. In that sense the *Purāṇas* are anchored in a world of myth as well as in the empirical world. For 500 years from about 1200 CE the *Purāṇas* were used as sources of quotations by the writers of the huge social and religious digests collectively called *Nibandha*. The material they select relates mainly to prescribed social behaviour (*dharmaśāstra*) and ritual (pūjā, vidhi), examples of which they sometimes illustrate with myths. Because of this tendency to be selective in quoting them, the *Purāṇas* have sometimes been described as *dharmaśāstras*. This they are clearly not, though it is a further confirmation of the eclectic nature of the texts that they can be regarded as such.

Content

Even a mere summary of some of the main *Purāṇas* gives some idea of their content, but in no sense can it be said to exhaust their richness. The *Garuḍa Purāṇa*, for example, has a long section on mineralogy and the *Agni Purāṇa* contains sections on Sanskrit grammar, theories of poetry and medicine. The control on content lies more at the level of the genre than at the level of individual texts and the recitations which are the expression of the genre. This gives to the audience of the genre an expectation that it will be communicating the image of a world defined by the five traditional Purāṇic characteristics, the received body of Hindu mythology, the devotional theology of bhakti and the ritual and social practices associated with bhakti.

Of all the *Purāṇas*, the *Viṣṇu* preserves most faithfully the description of the Purāṇic narrative in terms of the five characteristics and seemingly in the sequence with which the contents of the characteristics logically flow. This requires the text to begin with a set of narratives describing the creation of the universe, then of the various classes of beings, and of the seven continents, including Jambudvīpa or India. The various hells are described as well as some heavenly bodies. After that come the periods of Manus, or patriarchs – those figures from whom groups of humans and others are created – the creation of the *Veda* by Vyāsa, the development of the rules pertaining to the social classes and normative stages of life, life-cycle rituals and of Viṣṇu himself turning certain heretical groups away from the *Veda*. Next comes a description of royal lineages deriving from the lunar and solar dynasties. This in turn is followed by the long section dealing with the birth and life of Kṛṣṇa, one of Viṣṇu's most important avatāras. The final section of the text is devoted to three types of dissolution of the world systems, including personal liberation from existence. Viṣṇu is attributed as the supreme deity in the universe in this text, which may have been composed around 300 CE.

The *Śiva Purāṇa* is voluminous, containing 477 chapters in one recension, much shorter in another, and tends to be dated by its individual parts rather than as a text in its entirety. It contains examples of all the myths associated with the five characteristics, but is dominated by myths associated with Śiva himself and especially of his family, including his two wives, Satī and Pārvatī. One of its books deals with the theology of the liṅga, the representation of Śiva as a penis; whilst another lists and describes twelve important liṅgas, their locations and the myths associated with them, thereby localising certain aspects of what is found in the text. Another book collects together many of the rituals associated with Śiva, containing much material associated with the Śākta sect, and still others contain philosophy associated with Śiva and the manner in which liberating knowledge – jñāna – can be obtained by means of the worship of Śiva. It is significant that this *Purāṇa* has been printed in substantially different lengths, with some versions leaving out complete books which are found in the other versions. Sections of this text date until as late as 1000 CE.

The *Vāmana Purāṇa* is one of several mixed *Purāṇas* in the sense that it is not obviously sectarian in the manner of the *Viṣṇu* and the *Śiva Purāṇas*. In total its ninety-five chapters do not contain much material pertaining to the five characteristics, but they contain a version of the famous myth where Viṣṇu is incarnated as a boar and of Viṣṇu's demon devotee Prahlāda. But there are also versions of the destruction of Dakṣa's sacrifice and the transformation of the demon Andhaka into a devotee of Śiva. Both are myths where Śiva plays the most prominent role of all the gods. Yet because of the similar positions they play in their respective myths, the composers of the text seem to have brought together mythic material inviting a comparison between the two gods. In addition, the *Vāmana* contains a description of pilgrimage places and some chapters detailing life-cycle rituals and others used in the annual ritual calendar. It may have reached its present form by about 1000 CE.

The *Bhāgavata Purāṇa* is probably the best known of all *Purāṇas* and is still extensively recited and has always been a canonical text of the International Society for Krishna Consciousness (ISKCON). It is composed in a form of Sanskrit filled with archaic language designed to convey an appearance of antiquity and it may also contain elements translated from medieval Tamil. It contains twelve sections, covers the five characteristics and in its famous tenth book deals with the childhood and youth of Kṛṣṇa, and especially his erotic games with the cowgirls living in the bucolic environment of Mathurā in Central India. This section shares a strong inter-textual relation with the earlier *Harivaṃśa*, but has also been a fundamental inspiration to collections of poetry about this god composed in both Hindi and Tamil, and is also represented pictorially in some of the many illustrated manuscripts of this text. In earlier books it presents descriptions of the lineages of kings and the dynasties associated with them, the relationship between them and actual royal lineages being quite difficult to determine, yet confirming the importance of the *Purāṇas* in creating their own mythical worlds which mirror the historical world around them. It may be dated to some time during the ninth century CE.

The *Skanda Purāṇa* stands alone within the genre because it appears in so many versions, one as long as 87,000 verses, another recently discovered manuscript as short as 8,000 verses. Skanda is the name of one of Śiva's two sons and it might function as one of the factors around which material was placed into it. In this sense it is probably a Śaivite *Purāṇa* and contains the famous *Kāśī-khaṇḍa*, which provides a geographical and ritualistic tour of the holy city of Vārаṇāsī, listing many of the sacred ghaṭs located on the Ganges and including myths which explain why these places have attracted a sacrality. Dating to between the eighth and fifteenth centuries CE, this text is known more for its individual components than for its totality, but this is not a problem for the Purāṇic tradition. Even its written forms are highly fluid and do not prevent new material being placed into the tradition of manuscripts and oral recitations of the *Skanda Purāṇa*.

Many Upapurāṇas (lesser *Purāṇas*) are associated with gods other than Viṣṇu and Śiva. Examples are texts such as the *Saura Purāṇa*, associated with the worship of the god Sūrya, and the *Gaṇeśa Purāṇa*, one of two *Purāṇas* centred on the important god Gaṇeśa. It is divided into two books and reinterprets many myths found in earlier *Purāṇas*, placing Gaṇeśa in pivotal roles in the plot in order that his role as the god who creates and removes obstacles is brought out. The *Purāṇa* attempts to give a full account of the worship of the god and a whole set of myths associated with his birth on Earth as a boy in order to kill certain marauding demons. Possibly composed in the fourteenth century, it is best known in summaries composed in modern Indian languages and sold at stalls outside of temples and popular bookshops.

Purāṇas as History

For many Indian scholars the *Purāṇas* have been regarded as historical records relevant to political history, but especially to religious history. King lists, where the names sometimes allude to actual historical figures, occur in the fifth section of the *pañcalakṣaṇa* narratives of several *Purāṇas*, though the utility of this for the exact reconstruction of dynastic histories has often been doubted. As a record of change in religious belief and sectarian development the body of literature has often been praised. Individual *Purāṇas* are described as having evolved over a period of several centuries, and because they have always been accepted as texts lacking a final fixed form, they have facilitated the efforts of sectarian groups, often associated with Viṣṇu and Śiva, to include new theological ritual material associated with their specific gods and to incorporate it into the continuing recitational and manuscript tradition of given *Purāṇas*. European scholars have also traced changes in theological perceptions of a particular god by studying changes in specific myths associated with that god.

Their use as sources for the extraction of historical data masks another dimension of Purāṇic contents, their function as texts providing a history of something, whether this is the biography of a god or the narrative of the creation and end of the world. Both are presented within particular timeframes and are regarded as referring to events which have occurred in the past (cosmogony) or whose influence continues to the present day (myths of the gods). Such histories are not the kind of empirical/interpretative histories produced by professional historians, nor are they the summaries of recent events that every person holds in his or her mind to the extent that this understanding of past events is influential in respect of daily life. Rather, they are coherent alternative histories existing elsewhere in the thought-world of Hindu culture, the contents of which – especially the events associated with the lives of individual gods – come to life in recitations and at religious festivals.

This particular historical sense has led on to the development of specific expressions to Purāṇic sub-genres. Such are the *māhātmyas* and the *Sthalapurāṇas*. Usually short texts, they are entirely Purāṇic in their mixture of mythic narrative with instruction in the śāstric style. They are centred on the description of a particular sacred place; the most sacred cites such as Vārāṇasī have many such, but every South Indian sacred town has its own *māhātmya*. All describe how the location became sacred and develop a 'sacred history', expressed in mythological language, of the activities of the particular god, usually Śiva, who has brought about the sacrality of a particular location. They are accessible because they are short, associated with a specific subject and often summarised in print form in vernacular languages.

See also: **Avatāra; Bhagavadgītā; Bhakti; Brahmā; Buddhism, relationship with Hinduism; Cosmogony; Cosmology; Dakṣa; Dharmaśāstras; Gaṇeśa; Guṇas; International Society for Krishna Consciousness; Jainism, relationship with Hinduism; Jñāna; Kṛṣṇa; Mahābhārata; Mahādevī; Manu; Mathurā; Pārvatī; Pūjā; Śakti; Sati; Śiva; Skanda; Sūrya; Vārāṇasī; Veda; Vidhi; Viṣṇu; Vyāsa**

GREG BAILEY

Further reading

Bailey, Greg. 1995. *The Gaṇeśa Purāṇa*, vol. I: *The Upāsanākhaṇḍa*. Wiesbaden: Otto Harrassowitz.

Chakrabarti, K. 2001. *Religious Process: The Purāṇas and the Making of a Regional Tradition*. New Delhi: Oxford University Press.

Doniger, W. (ed.). 1993. *Purāṇa Perennis. Reciprocity and Transformation in Hindu and Jaina Texts*. Albany, NY: State University of New York Press.

Hazra, R.C. 1940. *Studies in the Purāṇic Records on Hindu Rites and Customs*. Dacca University. Reprint, Delhi: Motilal Banarsidass, 1975.

Rocher, L. 1986. *The Purāṇas*. Wiesbaden: Otto Harrassowitz.

PURITY AND POLLUTION, RITUAL

The concepts of ritual purity and pollution in dharmaśāstra are inexorably linked, since a form of purification must take place after every polluting event to restore an individual to his or her former state of purity. Moreover, pollution is virtually impossible to avoid, since it can be associated with birth, death, eating and so on. Therefore, a person's life must be marked by a constant cycle of pollution, the elimination of that pollution through some action, and an ultimate, though temporary, restoration to purity. It is impossible to impress upon a modern reader the degree to which these matters concerned the most illustrious ancient and medieval scholars writing in Sanskrit, and it is rare indeed to find a digest devoted to the discussion of dharma, moral law, that does not examine purity and impurity in extensive detail, for these were aspects of dharma that impacted upon the daily lives of the members of the Vedic community, the brāhmaṇas, the kṣatriyas, the vaiśyas, and the śūdras, to a far greater degree than the coronation of a king, the administration of ordeals or the constitution of a court. Purity, or śuddhi, was of particular importance because it was a necessary condition for the performance of activities enjoined by the Veda, and it thus affected the Brāhmaṇas most strongly, since they were responsible for the organisation of the Vedic ritual. The death of a child, for example, would deprive the father of śuddhi, incapacitating him with respect to his ritual duties. He would then become impure for a specific period of time, after which he would be restored to śuddhi through a ritual bath. In addition to individual persons, objects could also become impure by coming in contact with certain substances, or by being touched or looked at by various persons or animals. They could, however, be restored to purity through various practices, such as being immersed in fire in the case of metal pots, and through the application of various materials, such as cow dung and water in the case of a polluted house. Food, too, could become polluted, but the prescription for such cases was fairly straightforward, and generally involved throwing away the affected portion.

See also: **Dharma; Dharmaśāstras; Varṇas; Veda**

ETHAN KROLL

Further reading

Dumont, Louis and D. Pocock. 1959. 'Pure and Impure'. *Contributions to Indian Sociology* 3: 9–39.

Kane, Pandurang Vaman. 1971. *History of Dharmasastra*, vol. 4. Poona: Bhandarkar Oriental Research Institute.

Marglin, Frederique Apffel. 1977. 'Power, Purity and Pollution: Aspects of the Caste System Reconsidered'. *Contributions to Indian Sociology (NS)* 11(2): 244–70.

Mines, Diane Paull. 1989. 'Hindu Periods of Death "Impurity"'. In McKim Marriott, ed., *India Through Hindu Categories*. New Delhi: Sage Publications, 103–30.

Orenstein, Henry. 1968. 'Toward a Grammar of Defilement in Hindu Sacred Law'. In Milton Singer and Bernard Cohn, eds, *Structure and Change in Indian Society*. Chicago, IL: Aldine Publishing Company, 115–31.

PUROHIT(A)

Purohita or purohit literally means one who is appointed or 'placed in front', one who holds a charge or commission, i.e. is appointed to an office (purodha) of the Court (*Ṛgveda*, VII.83.4). The purohit's function was to counsel and to protect the king by his magical powers (cf. Stutley and Stutley 1977). He became the chief officiant at the consecration (rājāsuya) of a new king, and at all important sacrifices, such as the aśvamedha (horse sacrifice). The most notable purohit in post-Vedic times was Kauṭilya, the minister of the emperor Candragupta Maurya and of his grandson. The word is now used to indicate the family priest, whose function is almost entirely devoted to presiding over or performing specific rites. The purohit performs religious (dharmic) rites for his patrons (jājmān; in Sanskrit yajamana) to mark life-cycle events such as birth, initiation and marriage. He employs all kinds of ritual and mantras to put his clients in touch with the divine in order to create well-being, cure disease and defer death. Traditionally each family had its purohit and the relationship between purohit and jājmāna was permanent, personal and hereditary. In many regions these hereditary relationships with patron households have broken down so that priests now work in a competitive open market.

See also: **Kautilya; Mantra; Saṃskāra; Yajña**

ANNA KING

Further reading

Diehl, C.G. 1956. *Instrument and Purpose: Studies on Rites and Rituals in South India*. Lund: CWK Gleerup.

Fuller, C.J. 1992. *The Camphor Flame: Popular Hinduism and Society in India*. Princeton, NJ: Princeton University Press.

Fuller, C.J. 2003. *The Renewal of the Priesthood*. Princeton, NJ and Oxford: Princeton University Press.

Heesterman, J.C. 1985. *The Inner Conflict of Tradition: An Essay in Indian Ritual, Kingship and Society*. Chicago, IL: Chicago University Press.

Madan, T.N. 1987. *Non-renunciation: Themes and Interpretations of Hindu Culture.* Delhi: Oxford University Press.
Monier-Williams, M. 1899. *A Sanskrit–English Dictionary: Etymologically and Philologically Arranged with Special Reference to Cognate Indo-European Languages.* Oxford: Clarendon.
Stutley, M. and J. Stutley. 1977. *A Dictionary of Hinduism: Its Mythology, Folklore and Development 1500 BC–AD 1500.* London and Henley: Routledge and Kegan Paul.
Wiser, W.H. 1969. *The Hindu Jajmani System.* Lucknow: Lucknow Publishing House. First published 1936.

PURUṢA

The term puruṣa, 'man, person', is used in the *Puruṣasūkta* (*Ṛgveda* 10.90; *Atharvaveda* 19.6) to refer to the cosmic being that comprises the entire manifest and unmanifest universe. Puruṣa is absolute essential being that manifests itself in every aspect of expressed nature. Puruṣa, as the seat of all deities, is identified with Brahman (*Atharvaveda* 11.8.32) and with the creator Brahmā who emerges from the golden egg, Hiraṇyagarbha (*Mānavadharmaśāstra* 1.11). The individual self is identified with this cosmic self located in the sun (*Yajurveda* 40.17, *Chāndogya Upaniṣad* 3.19.1–4) in the early expressions of Vedānta. Later, Puruṣa is identified with the supreme deity, either Viṣṇu (*Bhagavadgītā* 11.38) or Śiva.

In contrast to the identification of the individual self with a sentient essence, source and creator of the world called puruṣa, classical Sāṃkhya and Yoga call the many individual selves puruṣa but sharply distinguish these silent witnesses from Prakṛti. Īśvarakṛṣṇa argues that the material cause of the world is insentient because the cause has the same character as its effect (*Sāṃkhyakārikā* 14). Hence there is no agent who creates it; rather, creation is motivated teleologically to satisfy the purpose of the enjoyment and ultimate liberation of Puruṣas.

In classical Sāṃkhya and Yoga, Puruṣas are non-agents (akartṛ, *Sāṃkhyakārikā* 19), neither material cause nor effect (*Sāṃkhyakārikā* 3); they are the ones for whose purpose nature is active (*Sāṃkhyakārikās* 31, 36; *Yogasūtra* 2.21). There are many of them (*Sāṃkhyakārikā* 18; *Yogasūtra* 2.22), they are conscious, do not consist of the three Guṇas, are not objects but only subjects of experience (*Sāṃkhyakārikā* 11), are neutral (*Sāṃkhyakārikā* 19) enjoyers (bhoktṛ, *Sāṃkhyakārikā* 17), knowers (jña, *Sāṃkhyakārikā* 2), experiencers (draṣṭṛ) and witnesses (sākṣin, *Sāṃkhyakārikā* 19). Puruṣas exist in private isolation (kaivalya) (*Sāṃkhyakārikā* 19) rather than being, like Prakṛti, an object common (sāmānya) to many experiencing subjects (*Sāṃkhyakārikā* 11). Yet in contact with Prakṛti they seem to be active by mistaking Prakṛti's activity for theirs. In conjunction with Prakṛti, each conscious Puruṣa experiences the sorrow caused by aging and death until the cessation of the subtle body (Liṅgaśarīra) (*Sāṃkhyakārikā* 55; *Yogasūtra* 2.17). The insentient intellect (Mahat/buddhi), which passes for the sentient self due to ignorance, presents all experience to the Puruṣa, including the ultimate knowledge that discriminates Puruṣa from Prakṛti (*Sāṃkhyakārikā* 37). When this pure knowledge arises complete and alone in the intellect, Puruṣa is established as independent in the state of Kaivalya and sees Prakṛti, who desists from manifestation (*Yogasūtra* 4.34), in her true unmanifest state (*Sāṃkhyakārikās* 64–65).

While Patañjali's *Yogasūtras* generally concur with the Sāṃkhya characterisation of Puruṣa, it differs in two important details. First, while Īśvarakṛṣṇa does not consider dispassion (vairāgya) to contribute to attaining Kaivalya, Patañjali considers it a means to destroy ignorance (*Yogasūtra* 1.12) and considers the highest form of dispassion, lack of interest in the Guṇas, to result from the knowledge of

Puruṣa (1.16). Second, Patañjali considers that God is a specific Puruṣa untouched by affliction and Karma, that he is omniscient, primordial and that worship of him contributes to the destruction of ignorance that leads to Kaivalya (*Yogasūtras* 1.23–26).

See also: **Brahmā; Brahman; Dharmaśāstras; Guṇas; Hiraṇyagarbha; Īśvarakṛṣṇa; Kaivalya; Karma (Law of Action); Liṅgaśarīra; Mahat; Patañjali; Prakṛti; Saṃhitā; Sāṃkhya; Sāṃkhyakārikās; Śiva; Upaniṣads; Vedānta; Viṣṇu; Yoga; Yogasūtras**

PETER M. SCHARF

Further reading

Brown, W. Norman. 1931. 'The Sources and Nature of Puruṣa in the *Puruṣasūkta*'. *Journal of the American Oriental Society* 51: 108–18.

Brown, W. Norman. 1965. 'Theories of Creation in the Rig Veda'. *Journal of the American Oriental Society* 85.1 (January–March): 23–34.

Larson, Gerald James. 1969. *Classical Sāṃkhya: An Interpretation of Its History and Meaning*. Delhi: Motilal Banarsidass, 84–85, 89–94.

PURUṢĀRTHAS

Hindu axiology accepted a fourfold classification of the valid goals of human endeavour (puruṣārtha), after an initial period of debate, namely kāma (pleasure), artha (material gain), dharma (righteousness) and mokṣa (liberation) in ascending order of valuation. Another sequence places dharma at the head, implying that it is regulative and productive of kāma and artha, and preparatory for mokṣa. This discontinuity in its role confirms a divide in this set of goals between dharma, artha and kāma, collectively known as trivarga, which are objects of pursuit within the world of mundane existence, and mokṣa, which catapults one out of such existence. The first three are sometimes described as ordinary norms in relation to which mokṣa may be referred to as the extraordinary norm.

One pursues the goals of sensory pleasure and material gain even instinctively, so their inclusion among the goals of human endeavour can only be justified in terms of their conscious pursuit. This is confirmed by the fact that textual guidance is provided for such conscious pursuit of each puruṣārtha. The most famous text for kāma is the *Kāmasūtra* of Vātsyāyana (*c.* fourth century CE) and for artha the *Arthaśāstra* of Kauṭilya, placed by tradition in the fourth century BCE but probably later in the form we have it. It is obvious from these texts themselves that they are representative of their genre. For the practice of dharma, an object of detailed attention in the tradition, a host of works, classified into *dharmasūtras* or aphoristic works and *dharmaśāstras* or metrical works, are available of which the *Āpastamba Dharma Sūtra* and the *Mānava-Dharma-Śāstra* or *Manusmṛti* are particularly well known. There is no mokṣaśāstra as such in symmetry with the rest but the whole range of the texts of Hindu philosophical schools or darśanas naturally fall in this category.

The fourfold classification is accepted by Jainism, but, according to one Hindu view, Buddhism differs from it in focusing on the last two puruṣārthas at the expense of the first two, thus subordinating the worldly to the transcendental.

'Hinduism' prefers to emphasise the harmonious pursuit of all the puruṣārthas, as exemplified by the definition of dharma at its broadest in the *Vaiśeṣika sūtras* 1.1.2 as that which secures both material (abhyudaya) and spiritual (niṣśreyasa) ends. All this and heaven too!

The fourfold classification of human endeavour is useful both descriptively and prescriptively and implies a non-reductive approach to life. Thus the main Hindu critique of Freudian psychology would be that it mistakenly reduces the whole of life only to kāma; and of Marxism that it similarly tries to reduce the whole of life to artha. The Hindu scheme would prevent such a univaluation and all the problems that result from such reductionism.

See also: **Artha; Arthaśāstra; Buddhism, relationship with Hinduism; Dharma; Dharmaśāstras; Kāma; Kāmasūtra; Kauṭilya; Jainism, relationship with Hinduism; Mokṣa; Ṣaḍdarśana; Vaiśeṣikasūtras; Vātsyāyana, Mallanāga**

ARVIND SHARMA

Further reading

Sharma, A. 1982. *The Puruṣārthas: A Study in Hindu Axiology.* East Lansing, MI: Asian Studies Center, Michigan State University, Occasional Paper No. 32.

Sharma, A. 1999. 'The Puruṣārthas: An Axiological Exploration of Hinduism'. *Journal of Religious Ethics* 27:2 (Summer): 223–56.

PŪRVA MĪMĀṂSĀ

Pūrva Mīmāṃsā is one of the six schools of Hindu philosophy. The term 'mīmāṃsā' means 'investigation' and 'revered thought'; it signifies the investigation and interpretation of Vedic injunctions. 'Pūrva' means 'prior', so 'Pūrva Mīmāṃsā' means 'First Reflection', a reasoned or critical enquiry into the early part of the Veda. The school seeks to justify Vedic ritualism and provide rules of interpretation of Vedic injunctions.

Pūrva Mīmāṃsā is regarded as 'allied' to the Vedānta school. The Veda is the basis of both systems; and both are concerned to interpret Vedic texts. Pūrva Mīmāṃsā concerns the earlier part of the Veda (the *Brāhmaṇas* and *Saṃhitā* portion), known as 'Karmakāṇḍa' (i.e. the part concerning action, rites, sacrifices, rituals). Thus the school is also known as 'Karma-Mīmāṃsā'. Vedānta concerns the *Upaniṣads*, the later part of the Veda, known as 'Jñānakāṇḍa' (i.e. the portion concerning knowledge of ultimate reality). Thus Vedānta is also known as 'Uttara-Mīmāṃsā' (Later or Final Investigation) and 'Jñāna-Mīmāṃsā'.

As it is concerned with defending Hindu dharma as a whole, Pūrva Mīmāṃsā is also called 'Dharma-Mīmāṃsā'. 'Dharma' refers to proper conduct, performing prescribed rituals, living according to rules, observing custom and etiquette. One's 'duty' as enjoined by the Veda signifies moral and religious duties as well as the virtue to be attained on their performance.

Pūrva Mīmāṃsā is characterised by pragmatism, realism and empiricism. Spiritual freedom and happiness do not depend on metaphysics, mystical insight or yogic practice; they simply follow from performing actions enjoined by the Veda.

Mīmāṃsā texts and authors

About the fifth century BCE, the authority of the Veda was being undermined by heterodox thinkers. Vedic priests reacted by seeking to resolve problems such as contradictions or inconsistencies apparent in the scriptures. Hence Mīmāṃsā developed as an exegetical enterprise.

The *Mīmāṃsāsūtras* attributed to Jaimini form the textual basis of the school. Regarded as a response to the challenge of non-orthodox teachers such as the Buddha, it is concerned to defend the Veda as eternal and authoritative. Jaimini sets out by declaring his theme as 'dharma' (signifying 'duty' or 'righteousness'), defined as that which is indicated or enjoined by the Veda as conducive to human good. Dharma is known only from the Veda; perception and other means of knowledge (pramāṇas) are restricted to the here and now (and do not relate to the future, the transcendental, the afterlife or heaven). For Jaimini, the Veda is the reliable means of knowledge of dharma because it is authorless, the eternal word.

The oldest surviving 'bhāsya', or commentary on Jaimini's *sūtras*, was written by Śabara (possibly fifth century CE). Mīmāṃsā literature refers to earlier commentators such as Bhavadāsa and Upavarṣa but their works have been lost (apart from quotes from Upavarṣa in Śabara's commentary). Śabara's work is a response to the establishment of schools of Buddhist idealism (Vijñānavāda and Śūnyavāda). He sought to counter the Buddhist threat to Vedic ritual and realism by undermining idealist assumptions. Among his philosophical contributions was his attempt to establish the soul as permanent and independently real.

Major philosophical developments followed on from the work of Śabara. Kumārila Bhaṭṭa (seventh century CE) is often referred to as the most important and influential Mīmāṃsā thinker. His works include the *Ślokavārtika* (Exposition or critical gloss on the Verses), which is a commentary on Śabara's commentary on Jaimini's *sūtras* 1.1, the *Tantravārtika* (Exposition on Sacred Science), which is a commentary on Śabara's commentary on Jaimini's *sūtras* 1.2–4, 2 and 2), and the *Tupṭīkā* (Full Exposition), a commentary on Śabara's commentary on Jaimini's *sūtras* 4–9. Kumārila was reacting to the growth of Buddhism and the decline of Vedic religion. His deep knowledge of Buddhism enabled him to attack its rejection of the Vedic system. Another major Mīmāṃsā philosopher, Prabhākara (seventh century CE), was the author of *Bṛhatī* (Large Commentary), a commentary on Śabara's commentary.

Due to many significant differences between Kumārila and Prabhākara, their work led to the emergence of two Mīmāṃsā sub-schools, known as the 'Bhāṭṭa' and 'Prābhākara' schools, respectively. Important thinkers of the Bhāṭṭa school who wrote commentaries on Kumārila's commentary include Pārthasārathi Miśra (tenth century), author of *Nyāyaratnākara* (Abode of Logic Jewels); Sucarita Miśra (tenth century), author of *Kāśikā* (Shining); Someśvara Bhāṭṭa (twelfth century), author of *Nyāyasudhā* (Nectar of Logic); and Khaṇḍadeva (seventeenth century). Although associated with Advaita, Maṇḍana Miśra (eighth century) was also interested in Kumārila's thought. An important thinker of the Prābhākara school was Śālikanātha Miśra (ninth century), author of *Ṛjuvimalā* (Straight and Free from Blemishes), a commentary on Prabhākara's *Bṛhatī*.

Pūrva Mīmāṃsā was associated with atheism; the eternal Veda is uncreated, authorless; the universe is eternal. Jaimini admitted Vedic deities but omitted the notion of a supreme God. Kumārila produced arguments against God's existence and necessity. However, around the eleventh century another school of Mīmāṃsā emerged. Established by Murāri Miśra, it is known as 'Seśvara Mīmāṃsā' and admitted God's existence.

Philosophical teachings

As indicated above, Mīmāṃsā's task of interpretation, its concern to defend Vedic authority, tradition and dharma, led to discussion of various philosophical issues. Mīmāṃsā teaching involves epistemological and metaphysical doctrines as well as philosophy of language and meaning (the school has been referred to as 'vākyaśāstra' or 'theory of language').

The metaphysics of the Bhāṭṭa and Prābhākara schools was realist and pluralist. Ontologically, the Bhāṭṭas accepted five types of entity: substance (dravya), universals (sāmānya), action (karma), quality (guṇa) and negation (abhāva). The Prābhākaras accepted eight types: resemblance (sādṛśya), number (sāṃkhyā), inherence (samavāya) and power (śakti), plus the Bhāṭṭa list but without negation.

Kumārila accepted six means of valid knowledge: perception (pratyakṣa), inference (anumāna), verbal testimony (śabda), comparison (upamāna), presumption (arthāpatti) and non-perception (anupalabdhi). Prabhākara rejected non-perception (as he rejected the reality of 'absence' (abhāva)).

Mīmāṃsā contributed the celebrated doctrine of the intrinsic validity or self-validity of knowledge (svataḥprāmāṇya-vāda). For Kumārila all cognitions present themselves as true but are considered false if their causes are found to be defective or if other cognitions overturn them. As the authorless Veda is eternal, cognitions arising from it are true. Perception, inference, etc. do not contradict cognitions of Vedic injunctions.

According to Mīmāṃsā, as the Veda is eternal, so language in general is eternal (nitya). Words, letters, the meanings of words (as universals) and the relation between word and meaning are all eternal.

See also: **Advaita; Brāhmaṇas; Buddhism, relationship with Hinduism; Dharma; Karma; Jaimini; Mīmāṃsāsūtras; Pramāṇas; Saṃhitā; Upaniṣads; Vedānta; Vedic Pantheon**

MARTIN OVENS

Further reading

Dwivedi, R.C. (ed.). 1994. *Studies in Mīmāṃsā*. Delhi: Motilal Banarsidass.

Jha, G. (trans). 1983. *Ślokavārttika*. Delhi: Sri Satguru Publications.

PUṢṬI MĀRGA

The Puṣṭi Mārga ("Path of Grace") or Vallabha sampradāya is the tradition of Kṛṣṇa devotion founded in the early 16th century by Vallabhācārya (1479–1531?). The Puṣṭi Mārga has been one of the most dominant forms of sectarian devotion, and the leading sect of Kṛṣṇa devotion, in Western India – from Mumbai to Braj, spanning Gujarat and Rajasthan—since the mid-16th century. The Puṣṭi Mārga has three touchstones: a special initiation called brahmasambandha, a highly developed notion of sevā, and the deity Śrīnāthjī. The brahmasambandha (literally, connection, sambandha, with the absolute, Brahman) empowers the devotee to recite the two mantras peculiar to the sect and to perform sevā, or selfless service, to Kṛṣṇa according to standards of the sect. Though most of the worship performed by members of the sect consists of sevā to an embodied form of Kṛṣṇa (Ṭhākurjī) that resides in the house, any devotee is also eligible to travel to Nathdvara in Rajasthan, to worship the manifesttion of Kṛṣṇa known as Śrīnāthjī.

One of the unique features of the Puṣṭi Mārga is the importance of the descendants of Vallabhācārya (Vallabh kul) to the growth and development of the sect. No sect or system of teachings in India has been so thoroughly dominated by a single family, sustained over at least fourteen generations, as found in the Pusti Mārga. Indeed, Vallabh kul members maintain the exclusive right to conduct the brahmasambandha initiation. Probably during the time of Vallabhācārya's grandchildren, the seven sons of Viṭṭhalnāthjī, Vallabhācārya's younger son (1516–86), it was established that brahmasambandha could only be performed by male members of the Vallabh kul. At present there are over two hundred male descendants of Vallabhācārya and at least five million devotees. What is perhaps surprising is that there have been very few sectarian schisms, in spite of considerable internecine rivalry over the centuries. This is due largely to the fact that, irrespective of occasional differences in doctrinal emphasis, members of the Vallabh kul have remained remarkably loyal to the teachings and memory of Vallabhācārya and Viṭṭhalnāthjī.

The sect is divided into seven houses or pīṭhas spread through Gujarat, Rajasthan, and Braj, established by the seven grandsons of Vallabhācārya. All have special svarūps or manifestations of

Kṛṣṇa distributed by Viṭṭhalnāthjī to his sons just before his death. The sect is nominally headed by a member of the First House, a descendent of Viṭṭhalnāthjī's first son, Giridharjī, called the Tilkāyat ("leader, chief"), who is the custodian of the Śrīnāthjī temple at Nathdvara. While the Tilkāyat enjoys extra prestige, in fact he has no real authority over any of the other members of the Vallabh kul. The understanding implicit among devotees is that Vallabhācārya was a partial manifestation of Kṛṣṇa, specifically the mukhāvatāra or incarnation of the mouth of the Lord, a divinity his descendants are believed to inherit exclusively. Accordingly, the devotee is expected to revere his or her own guru within the Vallabh kul as equal to and identical with the Lord Himself.

As noted, the primary form of devotion in the Puṣṭi Mārga is individual sevā to a svarūp of Kṛṣṇa. This may be a small carved image of Śrīnāthjī, a stone (called Girirāj) from Govardhan Hill in Braj, a type of stone called śālagrāma, a hand-painted picture of Śrīnāthjī, or a memento presented by a member of the Vallabh kul. The objective of individual sevā is to develop an intimate personal relationship with the Lord, based on intense love for Him.

Among the general rules for sevā are maintenance of a high state of personal purity, preparation of appropriate food offerings, ornamentation (śṛṅgāra) of the svarūp, and mindfulness of the daily schedule and yearly calendar into which Kṛṣṇa's activities are divided. The Puṣṭi Mārga probably possesses the most highly developed musical tradition of all India's Vaiṣṇava sects, the purpose of which is to enable the devotee to sing to the Lord. All of these accoutrements assist the devotee's entrance into the divine līlā, which is to say into the life of Kṛṣṇa as depicted in the *Bhāgavata Purāṇa* and interpreted by the preceptors of the Puṣṭi Mārga. In this divine (alaukika) comportment, one establishes a loving relationship with the Lord. The prototypes for such a relationship are the 84 main disciples of Vallabhācārya and the 252 (84 x 3) disciples of Viṭṭhalanāthajī. But within the general rules there is considerable scope for variation, for the individual to develop his or her own style of sevā that generates the proper rasa or archetypal mood that in turn results in a more transparent bhāva or inner experience of the Lord's grace (kṛpā, anugraha). The final goal of devotional practice is entrance into a state of nirodha, cessation of worldly activity after death and eternal participation in the līlās of Kṛṣṇa.

See also: **Bhakti movement; Brahman; Guru; Kṛṣṇa; Kula; Līlā; Mantra; Purāṇas; Sampradāya; Sevā; Vallabha (Vaiṣṇava Theologian); Vaiṣṇavism**

FREDERICK M. SMITH

Further reading

Barz, Richard. 1976. *The Bhakti Sect of Vallabhācārya*. Faridabad: Thomson Press.

Bennett, Peter. 1993. *The Path of Grace: Social Organization and Temple Worship in a Vaishnava Sect*. Delhi: Hindustan Publishing Corporation.

Bennett, Peter. 1993. "Krishna's Own Form: Image Worship and Puṣṭi Mārga." *Journal of Vaiṣṇava Studies* 1.4: 109–34.

Gaston, Anne-Marie. 1997. *Krishna's Musicians: Musicians and Music Making in the Temples of Nathdvara, Rajasthan*. New Delhi: Manohar.

Shah, Jethalal G. 1969. *Shri Vallabhacharya: His Philosophy and Religion*. Nadiad, Guj.: Pushtimargiya Pustakalaya.

Smith, Frederick M. 1993. "The Saṃnyāsanirṇaya, a Suddhādvaita Text on Renunciation by Vallabhācārya." *Journal of Vaiṣṇava Studies* 1.4: 135–56.

Smith, Frederick M. 1998. "*Nirodha* and the *Nirodhalaksaṇa* of Vallabhācārya." *Journal of Indian Philosophy* 26.6: 589–651.

Toomey, Paul. 1994. *Food from the Mouth of Krishna: Feasts and Festivities in a North Indian Pilgrimage Centre*. Delhi: Hindustan Publishing Corporation.

PŪTANĀ

Pūtanā ('Stinky') is the name of a demoness widely attested in Hindu traditions since the time of the *Mahābhārata*, in which she is named as one of the seven female Seizers (grahāṇis) that arose following the birth of Skanda. Her name likely refers to the pustulant sores whose eruptions are the symptoms of chicken pox; with the arrival of smallpox from Europe in the sixteenth century, her imagery and mythology gradually fused with those of Śītalā, the goddess of smallpox. Pūtanā is explicitly identified with childhood diseases in the Āyurvedic literature, which describes her as a terrifying and odoriferous demoness, clad in filthy garments and inhabiting empty, broken-down buildings. Pūtanā figures in the mythology of the childhood of Kṛṣṇa, who sucks the life out of her when she, having disguised herself as a beautiful woman, offers him her poisoned breast. Very often portrayed as a bird, Pūtanā is classified in a variety of sources as a Rākṣasī (Demoness), Piśācī (Female Flesh-Eater), Yoginī, Mātṛka (Mother) or Female Seizer.

See also: **Āyurveda; Kṛṣṇa; Mahābhārata; Mātṛkas; Piśācas; Rākṣasas; Śītalā; Skanda**

DAVID GORDON WHITE

Further reading

White, D.G. 2003. *Kiss of the Yogini: 'Tantric Sex' in its South Asian Context.* Chicago, IL: University of Chicago Press.

R

RĀDHĀ

Though her origins are obscure, Rādhā becomes one of the most celebrated figures in Vaiṣṇava poetry and theology after she emerges in Jayadeva's twelfth-century *Gītagovinda* as the extraordinary gopī who is Kṛṣṇa's special beloved. In this famous Sanskrit song, Rādhā embodies the perfection of erotic passion, and despite her jealousy after Kṛṣṇa's initial infidelity, she eventually triumphs when Kṛṣṇa regrets his wanton ways, begs her forgiveness and professes an ardent and faithful love that ensures the mutuality of their relationship. Subsequent to the *Gītagovinda*, which concludes with the lovers' joyful union, later vernacular poetry in northern and eastern India frequently emphasises Rādhā's pain and sorrow in separation from Kṛṣṇa, either because of Kṛṣṇa's dalliance with other gopīs or because the married Rādhā must return to her husband after transgressing her strīdharma for a secret tryst with Kṛṣṇa. Despite the emphasis on separation, however, poets and theologians, particularly in the Gauḍīya tradition, have understood Rādhā and Kṛṣṇa as eternally and metaphysically one, but physically separate in order to savour the pleasures of love. In this context, devotees envision Rādhā not only as Kṛṣṇa's rustic cowherd lover and divine eternal consort, but also as his hlādinī śakti, his power of blissful enjoyment. In this capacity Rādhā is worshipped by devotees aspiring to enjoy the ultimate bliss of bhakti, for only Rādhā symbolises utterly perfect love and thereby provides inspiration for Vaiṣṇavas seeking to perfect their own devotion to Kṛṣṇa.

See also: **Bhaktī; Gauḍīyas; Gītagovinda; Gopī(s); Jayadeva; Languages; Śakti; Strīdharma; Vaiṣṇavism**

TRACY COLEMAN

Further reading

Hawley, J.S. and D.M. Wulff (eds.). 1986. *The Divine Consort: Rādhā and the Goddesses of India.* Boston, MA: Beacon Press.

Journal of Vaiṣṇava Studies 8.2, Spring 2000; 10.1 Fall 2001. Focus on Śri Rādhā, Parts One and Two.

Miller, B.S. (trans.). 1977. *Love Song of the Dark Lord, Jayadeva's Gītagovinda*. New York: Columbia University Press.

RADHAKRISHNAN, SIR SARVEPALLI (1888–1975)

A South Indian brāhmaṇa who held professorships in the Universities of Mysore and of Calcutta before becoming the first Spalding Professor of Eastern Religions and Ethics at Oxford in 1936, the first Asian to hold any professorial chair at Oxford. He was later Vice-President (1952–62) and then President of India (1962–67). Radhakrishnan identified *the* Hindu view of life – the title of his best-known work – with Advaita Vedānta, his interpretation of which was influenced by his extensive study of European idealism. Despite the definite article in his title, the book extols the openness of Hindu thought, in contrast to the perceived rigidity of dogmatic Christianity. In addition to numerous works on Indian thought, Radhakrishnan also published translations of several Hindu texts, including the *Upaniṣads*, *Bhagavadgītā* and the *Brahmasūtras*.

See also: **Advaita; Bhagavadgītā; Brahmasūtras; Hinduism, history of scholarship; Upaniṣads**

WILL SWEETMAN

Further reading

Killingley, D.H. 1989. 'Radhakrishnan (1888–1975): The First Professor of Eastern Religions and Ethics at Oxford'. *Asian Affairs* 20: 25–36.

Radhakrishnan, S. 1939. *Eastern Religions and Western Thought*. London: Oxford.

Radhakrishnan, S. 1927. *The Hindu View of Life*. London: Allen & Unwin.

Radhakrishnan, S. 1923–27. *Indian Philosophy*. London: Allen & Unwin.

Schilpp, P.A. (ed.). 1952. *The Philosophy of Sarvepalli Radhakrishnan*. New York: Tudor.

RADHASOAMI SATSANG

Radhasoami is a prominent religious movement of northern India promoting a spiritual discipline suitable for non-mendicants. One of its two main branches is centred in Agra, where the movement originated, and the other in Punjab, where it has been strongly influenced by Sikhism. These have given rise to numerous sub-branches. The movement's founder was a holy man of Agra named Shiv Dayal Singh (1818–78), also known as Soamiji Maharaj. The son of a Punjabi moneylender, he came under the influence of Tulsi Sahib of Hathras, a regionally important holy man. Though married, he was childless, and spent his life mainly in meditation and as a religious teacher. His Agra house became a gathering place for spiritual seekers, to whom he taught his own special techniques of meditation, and he opened his congregation to the public in 1861.

Drawing chiefly from the religious milieu of such poet-saints as Kabīr and Nānak, Radhasoami teachings blend Hindu devotionalism, Tantric imagery and some elements of Islamic mysticism. A person's true self is an emanation of the formless Supreme Being (known as Radhasoami) that has become estranged from its origin and true nature and languishes in the cycle of death and rebirth under layers of coarse mind and body. Redemption is a journey in which the self, propelled by an inwardly focused spiritual practice known as surat-śabda-yoga (secret and revealed only to initiates), ascends to a reunion with the Supreme Being through a succession of layers of the cosmos that can be reached from within the body itself. This journey can be successfully undertaken only under the guidance of a spiritual master, a true guru. The poetic compositions of some of the Radhasoami masters describe the experiences of such an ascent in language both vivid and esoteric.

Radhasoami teachings place great stress on the indispensability of a devotee's connections with a true and living guru, and this relationship is a major focus of Radhasoami religious culture. A congregation of followers of a particular guru is known as a satsaṅg (in this context meaning 'good company'). These groups are notoriously vulnerable to succession disputes, because the question of who is a 'true' guru is always to some degree open and contestable, especially when a guru with a flourishing following leaves the world. This accounts for the highly ramified structure of the Radhasoami world. The movement's Agra branch has produced two settled communities, one at Soami Bagh and the other at Dayal Bagh, along with several other sub-branches. The main Punjabi branch is headquartered at Beas, where a famed religious centre has arisen. It and some of its numerous offshoots have been notably successful in attracting international followings.

See also: **Guru; Satsaṅg; Sikhism, relationship with Hinduism; Tantrism**

LAWRENCE A. BABB

Further reading

Babb, L.A. 1986. *Redemptive Encounters: Three Modern Styles in the Hindu Traditions.* Berkeley, CA: University of California Press.

Gold, D. 1987. *The Lord as Guru: Hindi Saints in Northern Indian Tradition.* New York: Oxford University Press.

Juergensmeyer, M. 1991. *Radhasoami Reality: The Logic of a Modern Faith.* Princeton, NJ: Princeton University Press.

RĀHU

The 'Seizer'. After the churning of the Ocean, Viṣṇu turned himself into Mohinī to distribute the amṛta. The asuras were enchanted by the forms of Mohinī allowing the devas to take the ambrosia. Meanwhile Svarbhabu, one of the asuras, sat between Sūrya (Sun) and Candra (Moon) to get some nectar. Both of them recognised him and called Viṣṇu/Mohinī, who beheaded him. But Svarbhabu did not die as he was able to swallow a bit of amṛta. His head was given a serpent body and became Rāhu, the eclipse demon, whose revenge is to eat the sun and the moon (*Bhāgavata Purāṇa* 5.24. 1–3; 8.9. 25–26; *Mahābhārata* 1.19). On his torso was put a serpent head and he became Ketu, the ṛṣi. Rāhu, the sky-demon (Abhrapiśāca), son of Vipracitti and Siṃhikā, holds the south-western quarter of the sky and rides a cart pulled by eight black stallions (*Viṣṇu Purāṇa* 2.11. 20–22).

See also: **Asuras; Deities; Mahābhārata; Mohinī; Purāṇas; Ṛṣi; Sūrya; Viṣṇu**

FABRIZIO M. FERRARI

Further reading

Danielou, A. 1991. *The Myths and Gods of India: The Classic Work on Hindu Polytheism from the Princeton Bollingen Series.* Rochester, VT: Inner Traditions International.

RĀJA

The word rāja, which has entered the English language, is one of great antiquity. It is applied to the gods in the *Ṛgveda* but also to the human king Sudās, the victor in the Battle of the Ten Kings (*Dāśarājña* 7.83.6). It is derived from the root rāj, 'to shine forth'; its derivation from rañjayati or one who pleases the people, although appealing and popular, is not grammatically accurate. Its abstract form rājya is the Sanskrit word which comes closest to the concept of state.

The origin of kingship as an institution signified by the word was the object of speculation in ancient India, and can be traced to the need for electing a military leader to lead battle, according to the *Aitareya Brāhmaṇa* (1.14). Other accounts trace it to divine appointment (*Taittirīya*

Upaniṣad 1.5) or to a special civil compact with the subjects, as in the Buddhist account of the *Mahāsammata* (*Dīghanikāya* 3.93), while other accounts, principally found in the *Mahābhārata*, combine or contain elements of both. All these are obviously attempts to answer the key question posed by Yudhiṣṭhira in the *Mahābhārata*: the king is like any other human being, so what is it that makes him a king over them?

The doctrine of the divinity of the king (as distinguished from the divine right of kings or of divine kingship) is often propounded (*Manusmṛti* 7.8), sometimes making the king into a virtual pantheon (7.4–5). A bad king similarly is said to be composed of demonic elements so that the description of the king as a divinity contains a figurative element in it. One hears of deposed kings (*Śatapatha Brāhmaṇa* 12.9.3.1–2), and two well-known kings, Rudradāman (*c.*150 CE) and Gopāla (*c.*750 CE), were elected to royalty.

The basic role of the king was to provide protection to the people. He was allowed to tax the subjects in return for this service and the *Mahābhārata* permits him to be killed like a mad dog if he failed in this duty. He also protected the varṇāśrama system, as symbolising political and social order. Subjects typically registered their protest against the failure to maintain such order or to offer protection 'by voting with their feet' and moving out of the king's realm.

See also: **Āśramas; Brāhmaṇas; Buddhism, relationship with Hinduism; Dharmaśāstras; Mahābhārata; Saṃhitā; Upaniṣads; Varṇa; Yudhiṣṭhira**

ARVIND SHARMA

Further reading

Kane, P.V. 1973. *History of Dharmaśāstra*, vol. III, 2nd edn. Poona: Bhandarkar Oriental Research Institute.

Scarfe, Hartmut. 1989. *The State in Indian Tradition*. Leiden: E.J. Brill.

RĀJA YOGA

Rāja Yoga – literally, the 'royal' or 'kingly' yoga – is based on the *Yogasūtras* of Patañjali and is one of the four paths to Samādhi outlined in some sources: the other three are karma-yoga, jñāna-yoga and bhakti-yoga. In Rāja Yoga there are eight levels or practices, known as the eight limbs or aṣṭāṅga:

1	Yama	self-restraint in the conduct of your life as it affects others
2	Niyama	self-restraint in the conduct of your inner, spiritual life (tapas)
3	Āsana	physical exercise designed to integrate the mind and the body
4	Prāṇāyāma	breath and mind control
5	Pratyāhāra	a preliminary state of meditation where the senses are abstracted
6	Dhāraṇā	concentration
7	Dhyāna	meditation
8	Samādhi	uninterrupted contemplation of reality

The stages of āsana and prāṇāyāma are characteristic of Rāja Yoga and together are sometimes known by the term Haṭha Yoga. Rāja Yoga makes use of terms drawn from the Sāṃkhya philosophy and shares many aspects of its metaphysics; indeed references to Rāja Yoga will sometimes use the term Sāṃkhya Yoga as a synonym. However, Rāja Yoga is not atheistic, as is classical Sāṃkhya. Swami Vivekananda was an advocate of Rāja Yoga, which he made popular in America when he taught classes there during his visits to Chicago, New York and San Francisco in the late nineteenth century.

See also: **Āsana; Bhakti (as path); Haṭha Yoga; Jñāna (as path); Karma (as path); Patañjali; Sāṃkhya; Sāṃkhya-Yoga; Tapas; Vivekananda, Swami; Yogasūtras**

VIVIENNE BAUMFIELD

Further reading

Vivekananda, Swami. 1907. *The Complete Works of Swami Vivekananda*, vol. 1. Calcutta: Advaita Ashrama.

RAJNEESH, BHAGWAN SHREE (1930–90)

Bhagwan Shree Rajneesh, or Osho, was the founder and leader of the Rajneesh movement. He was the most significant guru during the 1970s counterculture and pioneered the synthesis of Eastern mysticism with Western psychology. He also created many new meditations and therapies, widely used by psychotherapists and New Age teachers, of which the best known is Dynamic Meditation.

Osho was born Rajneesh Mohan Chandra into a Jain business family in northern India. He claimed to have become enlightened in 1953 while a philosophy professor at the University of Jabalpur. In the 1960s he became a well-known ācārya in Bombay, eventually taking the title Bhagwan Shree Rajneesh and initiating his disciples as saṃnyāsins. In 1976 he moved to Pune and set up an ashram, which attracted many thousands of Indian and Western seekers, including leaders of the human potential movement.

Osho produced no formally coherent philosophy, despite his academic background; rather, he delighted in inconsistency and contradiction. He is sometimes placed in India's antinomian Tantra tradition, and lectured extensively on Tantra and other mystical traditions, particularly Zen Buddhism and Sufism. Part of his appeal lay in his modernisation of these teachings, which he synthesised with the work of Western writers such as Wilhelm Reich, Friedrich Nietzsche and D.H. Lawrence.

Throughout his career, Osho caused controversy, initially by his polemical talks on politics and sexuality, continually challenging the mores of Hindu and Western society. He became notorious after moving his headquarters to the United States in the 1980s. Although he personally withdrew into silence and reclusion, his deputies became embroiled in various legal battles. Osho himself was arrested on immigration charges but released later, and returned to the ashram in Pune. Here he resumed his spiritual programme, and died in 1990.

Osho's reputation initially declined after the American debacle, but has now risen to the point where he is increasingly being recognised in India and the West as a major spiritual teacher of the twentieth century, at the forefront of the current 'world-accepting' trend of spirituality based on self-development.

See also: **Āśram(a) (religious community); Buddhism, relationship with Hinduism; Guru; Meditation; Rajneesh Movement; Saṃnyāsa; Tantras**

ELIZABETH PUTTICK

Further reading

Osho. 2001. *Autobiography of a Spiritually Incorrect Mystic*. New York: St Martin's Press.

RAJNEESH MOVEMENT

The Rajneesh Movement, now known as the Osho Movement, was one of the largest and most influential New Religious Movements (NRMs) of the 1970s, founded by the charismatic guru Osho. In its heyday it had approximately 200,000 members, although active membership is now much lower. Its headquarters is in Pune in western India, with around twenty other main centres and many communities worldwide.

The movement originated in Bombay in the late 1960s, when Osho was attracting enormous crowds to his public talks and began to initiate his closest followers as saṃnyāsins. Unlike the ancient Hindu tradition of world-renunciation, Osho reinterpreted 'neo-sannyas' as a life-affirmative spiritual path requiring the renunciation of the ego, symbolised by taking on a new Sanskrit name, wearing orange and a mala (string of prayer beads). Osho's innovative blend of personal charisma, Indian mysticism and Western humanistic psychology attracted thousands of seekers from the intelligentsia, counterculture and Human Potential Movement. By the late 1970s 'sannyas' (as it was called by disciples) had become the most popular and fashionable Eastern-based NRM.

Osho founded an ashram in Pune in 1976, and the next five years were the movement's heyday. The ashram offered a programme of meditation and therapy, lectures and darśana, and work, which would nowadays be considered holistic in its integration of mind, body and spirit. Rajneesh therapy is now recognised as a pioneering approach to psychotherapy and self-development, which has influenced other therapies and encouraged other Eastern-based NRMs to integrate therapy with spiritual praxis. The movement was famous for its ultra-liberal attitude to sexuality, drawing on Tantric tradition to develop an approach of sacred sexuality. Again, this is now an approved praxis in other NRMs and New Age groups. However, the main draw for seekers was the prospect of enlightenment, and Osho offered an essentially traditional, if somewhat 'left-hand', path to liberation, drawing on the Tantric, upaniṣadic and Buddhist teachings. In common with many other Indian gurus, his main method was śakti-patā, the direct transmission of energy and spiritual transformation from the guru to the disciple.

The most dramatic stage of the history of the Osho Movement unfolded after the move in 1981 to Rajneeshpuram, a huge ranch in Oregon, USA. Osho intended to build a city, but the project became bogged down in planning applications, leading to prolonged legal battles and hostility from neighbours. Many saṃnyāsins left in disillusionment, and Osho himself withdrew from public appearances. Finally, the acting leader, Sheela, left suddenly, and Osho was arrested on charges including immigration offences and tax evasion. He was deported, and returned with his closest disciples to the Pune ashram. The multi-million-dollar ranch was used to pay off creditors.

Osho lived quietly in Pune until his death in 1990, leaving no spiritual successor. Osho Commune International, as the movement is now known, is directed by a group called the Inner Circle. There are still many resident members and short-term visitors, though considerably fewer than in Osho's lifetime. However, the therapy and meditation centre is flourishing, and has become a popular destination on the international New Age circuit. The Osho Movement is now recognised for its creative and pioneering role within contemporary alternative spirituality and self-development, and Osho's books are being reissued by mainstream publishers in the USA and Britain.

See also: **Āśram(a) (religious community); Buddhism, relationship with Hinduism; Darśana; Meditation; New Religious Movements, Hindu role in; Rajneesh, Bhagwan Shree; Saṃnyāsa; Tantras; Tapas; Upaniṣads**

ELIZABETH PUTTICK

Further reading

Puttick, Elizabeth. 1997. *Women in New Religions.* Basingstoke: Macmillan Press.

RAKṢA BANDHAN

An annual festival, more commonly and affectionately known as 'Rakhi' in Northern India, where sisters tie coloured threads to the right wrist of their brothers, praying for their long life and happiness; brothers, in turn, promise to be their sisters' lifelong protectors. At the same time, vermilion tilak marks are applied between the brother's eyebrows, sweets are placed in the mouth and they sing ārtī and offer prāṇam. Afterwards gifts are exchanged. Friends can also perform the ceremony. It is said that in medieval India if a woman tied a rakhi to the wrist of any man he was beholden to protect her as a religious duty and defend her honour. Brāhmaṇa priests will also tie rakhis to the wrists of attendees at their temples. Literally, rakṣa means 'protection' and bandhan means 'to tie'. According to ancient traditions, it was the practice to offer sacred verses from the Veda over the threads and sanctify them with rice and durva grass. The protection offered lasted for one year and kept a person free from sin and safe from disease. Today, sisters outdo each other to buy threads that are entwined with silver and gold, ornaments and even jewellery. The rakhis carry good wishes, but may carry a connotation of a sister's anxiety about leaving the household at the time of her marriage to live with her groom's family, and thus remind her brothers of the lifelong imperative to come to her aid if she is troubled.

According to tradition, the festival is said to have originated in a battle between the devas and asuras, described in the *Bhaviṣya Purāṇa*, which resulted in the god Indra feeling depressed. His wife Sachā took a thread and tied it to his hand, reciting mantras for his protection and well-being. The festival occurs during the full moon of the month of Śravana (July–August).

See also: **Asuras; Brāhmaṇa; Deities; Indra; Mantra; Purāṇas; Utsava; Veda**

RON GEAVES

Further reading

Brown, Alan. (ed.). 1986. *Festivals in the World Religions*. London: Longman, 126–27.

www.raksha-bandhan.com (accessed 31 October 2005).

RĀKṢASAS

Demon. The Rākṣasas are dark-complexioned monstrous beings with dazzling lolling tongues and fire-eyes. They can be invisible and take whatever form they want, especially that of inauspicious animals (dogs, hyenas, owls, vultures, etc.). Rākṣasas are night creatures who possess their victims by entering through their mouths. They live on the cremation grounds, in jungles or next to rivers and are particularly feared as they try to impede the correct arrangements of sacrifices. The Rākṣasas are described in the *Mahābhārata*, *Rāmāyaṇa* and the *Purāṇas* as enemies of order (ṛta). They were produced by Brahmā's foot but are also indicated as the progeny of the ṛṣi Pulastya (*Manusmṛti* 1.35–37). In the *Rāmāyaṇa*, the king of the Rākṣasas, Rāvaṇa, is the kidnapper of Sītā, Rāma's wife. According to nineteenth- and early twentieth-century theories, the Rākṣasas were identified with pre-Aryan people.

See also: **Brahmā; Dharmaśāstras; Mahābhārata; Purāṇas; Rāma; Rāmāyaṇa; Rāvaṇa; Ṛṣi; Sītā**

FABRIZIO M. FERRARI

Further reading

Bhattacharyya, N.N. 2000. *Indian Demonology. The Inverted Pantheon*. Delhi: Manohar.

RAKTABĪJA

Raktabīja, or Raktavāja, means 'Red seed', 'Blood drop' and is one of the Asuras fighting against Mahādevī and her emanations in their battle against the Asuras Śumbha and Niśumbha (*Devī Māhātmya* 5–10; *Devī Bhāgavata Purāṇa* 5). From every drop of blood Raktabīja lost after being wounded by the Mātṛkās (mothers) an accurate replica arose, whose shed blood again formed new ones. The rapidly increasing number of Asuras terrified the gods. But Mahādevī instructed her emanation Kālī (Cāmuṇḍā) to dry up Raktabīja by drinking the blood he shed by the strike of her weapons. The goddess did so and also swallowed the already emerged Asuras alive, not allowing one drop of their blood to fall. Mahādevī then attacked Raktabīja with a variety of different weapons and, finally, supported by the blood-drinking Cāmuṇḍā, killed him (*Devī Māhātmya* 8.39–62; *Devī Bhāgavata Purāṇa* 5).

The *Vāmana Purāṇa* (17–21) and *Devī Bhāgavata Purāṇa* (5) also depict him as the rebirth of Mahiṣa's father Rambha (Buffalo demon).

See also: **Asura; Cāmuṇḍā; Devī Māhātmya; Kālī and Caṇḍī; Mahādevā; Mahiṣa; Mātṛkās; Purāṇas**

Xenia Zeiler

Further reading

Coburn,Thomas B. 1988. *Devi Mahatmya: The Crystallization of the Goddess Tradition.* New Delhi: Motilal Banarsidass.

Coburn,Thomas B. 1992. *Encountering the Goddess: Translation of the Devi Mahatmya and Its Interpretation.* New Delhi: Motilal Banarsidass.

RAM DASS (b. 1931)

Born Richard Alpert, he collaborated at Harvard University with Timothy Leary on research into psilocybin and LSD; both were dismissed in 1963 for their experiments. Leary continued to advocate the use of drugs for spiritual purposes, but Alpert travelled to India in 1967, where he met Neem Karoli Baba (d. 1973), who gave him the name of Ram Dass, meaning 'servant of God'. In 1974 he became acquainted with Joya Santanya, who predicted that he would become a world teacher.

Ram Dass' teachings are eclectic, drawing on Hindu bhakti, focused on Hanumān, the cakras, Buddhism (particularly Vipassana, as well as its Tibetan and Zen forms), the teachings of Jesus, Sufism and Judaism. He advocates the validity of different spiritual paths: world-renunciation, the use of mantras, Tantric Yoga and psychedelic experience, contending that the answer to life's meaning lies within oneself. He does not claim to be an enlightened master or even a guru.

In common with Neem Karoli Baba, he teaches the importance of love and sevā (service to humankind), and this is expressed in a number of practical projects which he has initiated. Particularly noteworthy is the Hanuman Foundation (incorporated in 1974), from which emerged his Prison Ashram Project and his Dying Project. The former aims to provide spiritual guidance for detainees, while the latter offers support to the dying and the bereaved. Ram Dass co-founded the Seva Foundation, an international relief organisation.

Ram Dass' first book was *Be Here Now* (1971). *The Only Dance There Is* (1976) and *Grist to the Mill* (1977) are based on Neem Karoli Baba's teachings, and *Miracle of Love* (1979) recounts stories of his life. In 1997 Ram Dass suffered a serious stroke, which left him partially paralysed. This experience enabled him to write *Still Here: Embracing Aging, Changing and Dying* (2000), and he continues to teach and publish extensively.

See also: **Bhakti (as path); Buddhism, relationship with Hinduism; Guru Hanumān; Mantra; Seva; Tantric Yoga**

George Chryssides

Further reading

Alpert, Richard (Baba Ram Dass). 1992. *Be Here Now.* Boulder, CO: Hanuman Foundation.

Alpert, Richard (Baba Ram Dass). 1976. *The Only Dance There Is.* New York: J. Aronson.

RĀMA

Rāma is the hero of the *Rāmāyaṇa* and its portrayal of him as the ideal prince and warrior prompts the gradual understanding of Rāma as an avatāra of Viṣṇu and eventually as supreme deity himself; an alternative view stresses the theme of the divine king in Indian thought as the key to Rāma's divinity (on this view, present from the earliest phases of the epic). The core narrative, the second to sixth books, reflects the interests and concerns of the warrior aristocracy (the kṣatriya class), and Rāma is a martial hero whose actions are accepted without question as necessary and for that reason as justified; his general prowess means that he is frequently compared to Indra, the battle chief of the Vedic gods, and indeed occasionally Rāma and Lakṣmaṇa are compared to Indra and Viṣṇu, respectively, reflecting their relative status in Vedic literature. However, his adherence to ethical values is equally outstanding (he is frequently called the best of upholders of dharma').

Rāma's moral status comes from his willing submission to his apparently arbitrary exile, which leads him ultimately to his greatest deed, the killing of Rāvaṇa, who is presented by Vālmīki as a slave to lust and later quite naturally seen as the embodiment of evil, defeated by good in the person of Rāma. When Kaikeyī abruptly demands his banishment, Rāma accepts his father Daśaratha's reluctant decree with absolute submission and with the calm self-control which regularly characterises him.

As his moral elevation is increasingly emphasised, various episodes receive a moralistic gloss, to eliminate the possibility of moral lapses on his part; so, for example, his killing of the Vānara chief Vālin while the latter is fighting his brother Sugrīva, with whom Rāma has made a pact, is elaborately justified, as are his martial activities to protect the hermits while they go about their religious activities (basically in terms of his duty as a prince to uphold law and order). Throughout most of the earlier expansions Rāma is still viewed as human but as a particularly moral figure, so that his linking with Indra becomes increasingly problematic, as Indra's morals come into question. But at the end of the sixth book, in a passage which is transitional to the outlook of parts of the first and seventh books (and may belong with them in date), following Agni's restoration of Sītā to Rāma with her reputation vouched for by his intervention, the major gods, headed by Brahmā, assemble to praise Rāma for his exploit in defeating Rāvaṇa (by now transformed into a threat to the stability of the universe) and to reveal his divinity to him in a series of identifications with various deities (Nārāyaṇa, Varāha, Brahmā and Indra among them, before an identification with Viṣṇu), but this recognition is expressed in terms of identity and not yet as incarnation.

The growing veneration shown to Rāma is then reflected in the first and seventh books, which include not only material presenting Rāma as divine but also narratives enhancing the status of his opponent Rāvaṇa and so indirectly of Rāma, the only person able to defeat him. The purpose of the first book is to narrate Rāma's birth, youthful exploits and marriage, and generally to provide a framework for the narrative; at the gods' request, Viṣṇu agrees to become incarnate as Daśaratha's four sons as the only means of destroying Rāvaṇa, the evil king of Laṅkā. The last book is set in Ayodhyā after Rāma's victorious return to rule in Ayodhyā, but the first half details Rāvaṇa's genealogy and his previous misdeeds (making him into an adversary of the gods), while the rest of the book deals with events after Rāma's installation; these include Rāma reluctantly ordering Sītā's exile to Vālmīki's hermitage (placing public opinion above his own feelings for his wife) and the birth of the twins, Kuśa and Lava, at Vālmīki's hermitage. Eventually, after a long and prosperous reign (rāmarājya, 'Rāma's ideal rule'), Rāma settles the kingdom on his sons, publicly immolates himself in the river Sarayū (thus returning to his form as Viṣṇu) and is welcomed to heaven by Brahmā.

The account of Rāma is further developed in the *Purāṇas* and the later Sanskrit *Rāmāyaṇas*, which give a Vedāntin slant to the emerging bhakti emphasis. The *Adhyātma Rāmāyaṇa* includes a motif which becomes common in later retellings, that those killed by Rāma are thereby blessed. Already in Kampan's Tamil *Irāmāvatāram,* appearing in the wake of the impassioned bhakti poetry of the Āḻvārs, there is something of the emphasis on the name of Rāma, later so significant. The *Rāmcaritmānas* of Tulsīdās is notable for its vision of Rāma's righteous rule and the saving power of his name, as well as for its use as the base text for the Rāmlīla, which is performed annually in so many locations across North India and which has clearly played a major part in the popularity of the Rāma story and in particular in its broad appeal beyond sectarian boundaries.

In the Vālmīki *Rāmāyaṇa* Rāma was often called 'Rāma, the best of upholders of dharma', and the narrative was conditioned both by dharma and by the reaction of the characters to its requirements. In many later adaptations Rāma comes to be recognised as the embodiment of dharma, the ideal ruler, promoting justice and the welfare of his subjects and exemplifying perfect filial obedience: a model of putting dharma into practice. Although dharma can be imposed for a time by external pressures, its mainstay is the individual's free choice, as in Rāma's willing submission to his exile. In the ideal world of rāmrāj (rāmarājya, 'Rāma's righteous rule') evil in the form of premature death, the overturning of the social order and so on are all abolished and dharma reigns supreme. It is no surprise, therefore, that various political parties have appropriated the Rāma story and in particular the concept of rāmrāj for their own purposes, from the Ramarajya Parishad (Rāma's Reign Party) through to the Bharatiya Janata Party (Indian People's Party) and the Ramjanmabhumi (Rāma's birthplace) agitation.

See also: **Agni; Āḻvārs; Avatāra; Ayodhyā; Bhakti (as path); Bharatiya Janata Party; Brahmā; Daśaratha; Dharma; Indra; Lakṣmaṇa; Purāṇas; Rāmāyaṇa; Rāmarājya; Ramarajya Parishad; Rāvaṇa; Sītā; Sugrīva; Tulsīdās(a); Vālmīki; Varṇa; Vedānta; Vedic pantheon; Vedism; Viṣṇu**

JOHN BROCKINGTON

Further reading

Brockington, John. 1985. *Righteous Rāma: The Evolution of an Epic.* Delhi: Oxford University.

Brockington, John. 2000. 'The names of Rāma'. In Greg Bailey and Mary Brockington, eds, *Epic Threads: John Brockington on the Sanskrit Epics.* New Delhi: Oxford University Press, 265–79.

Pollock, Sheldon. 1984. 'The Divine King in the Indian Epic'. *Journal of the American Oriental Society* 104: 505–28.

Pollock, Sheldon. 1985. 'Rāma's Madness'. *Weiner Zeitschrift für die Kunde Südasiens* 29: 43–56.

Veer, Peter van der. 1995. 'The Politics of Devotion to Rāma'. In David N. Lorenzen, ed., *Bhakti Religion in North India.* Albany, NY: SUNY Press, 288–305.

RAMAKRISHNA MATH AND MISSION

The Ramakrishna Math and Mission were founded by Swami Vivekananda, following his return to India from the West in 1897, to propagate the message of Sri Ramakrishna, to promote harmony between religions and to raise the spiritual and material conditions of the Indian people. Belur Math was established in 1899 as a permanent Maṭh ('monastery') for those of Ramakrishna's devotees who had entered saṃnyāsa in his name. This has remained the headquarters of both the Ramakrishna Math and Ramakrishna Mission. Although the Math and Mission remain legally separate, both function as one under the authority of the president of the Ramakrishna Math.

The combined movement's earliest centres developed in Bengal and the region around Madras (Chennai), where Vivekananda had been most active. Other centres, which had been founded independently by admirers of Vivekananda, also became absorbed within the movement, and this ad hoc process has continued to the present day. Vivekananda's protracted stays in the United States and England in 1893–97 and 1899–1900 led to the creation of Vedanta Societies in New York and California and of a short-lived circle of supporters in London, which was later re-established. The movement currently maintains, excluding Belur Math, 146 branches, including separate Math and Mission centres and combined centres, 110 of these being within India. Outside India, the largest concentration is to be found in Bangladesh, with the remaining centres scattered globally. The designation 'Vedanta Society/Centre' is reserved for centres outside South Asia. Centres are required to be financially independent and are run by a Swami-in-charge, supported by other saṃnyāsins and brahmacārins, local devotees and employees. Membership of the Mission is not restricted on religious or ethnic grounds, and applications for training for entry into the Math are considered from those not Hindus by birth.

The Ramakrishna movement's centres do not actively proselytise but offer worship and other cultic activities, including the celebration of religious festivals from a range of traditions, as well as programmes of lectures and classes. Some centres are major publishers of the movement's literature. In less materially developed countries, the Math and Mission also engage extensively in sevā activities (organised service to humanity), providing educational and medical facilities and training in rural development. The movement follows Vivekananda in claiming that Ramakrishna sanctioned service to human beings as embodiments of the divine, elevating this practice to the status of a sādhana (form of spiritual training), even though many of Ramakrishna's earliest followers disputed this interpretation of their master's priorities. The movement's humanitarian work has been recognised by national governments and international agencies, and in 1998 the Ramakrishna Mission was awarded the Gandhi Peace Prize by the Indian Government. The twin thrusts of the movement's work are summed up in the motto, chosen by Vivekananda, 'For liberation and the good of the world'.

See also: **Brahmacarya; Gandhi, Mohandas Karamchand; Hinduism, modern and contemporary Ramakrishna, Sri; Saṃnyāsa; Sevā; Vivekananda, Swami**

GWILYM BECKERLEGGE

Further reading

Beckerlegge, G. 2000. *The Ramakrishna Math and Mission: The Making of a Modern Hindu Movement.* New Delhi: Oxford University Press.

Gambhirananda, Swami. 1983. *History of the Ramakrishna Math and Mission*, 3rd rev. edn. Calcutta: Advaita Ashrama.

RAMAKRISHNA, SRI (*c.*1834/36–86 CE)

Ramakrishna has become associated with an outlook characterised by the acceptance of all religions as paths leading to the same goal, which stemmed from his experiments with various Hindu, Muslim and Christian disciplines and practices. He attracted the interest of prominent Hindus and European scholars, and consequently his direct and indirect influence has been considerable within and beyond Hinduism.

Born Gadadhar Chattopadhyay and brought up in Kamarpukur, north of Calcutta (Kolkata), Ramakrishna developed a reputation as a child for falling into altered states of consciousness. He spent some thirteen years at the Kālī temple at Dakṣineśvar under different religious guides in an intense quest for God-realisation. He remained at Dakṣineśvar until shortly before his death from cancer in 1886, and was joined by his wife, Sarada Devi, and a nucleus of young disciples, led by Swami Vivekananda, who later established the Ramakrishna Math and Mission in Ramakrishna's name. A partial record of Ramakrishna's spontaneous discourses, as recalled by Mahendranath Gupta ('M'), was later published as *The Gospel of Sri Ramakrishna (Srisriramakrishnakathamrita)*.

The Ramakrishna Math and Mission, under the influence of Vivekananda, has portrayed Ramakrishna as an Advaitin, deriving universal themes and a justification for organised philanthropy from Ramakrishna's teaching. The centrality of Tantra and the worship of Śakti to Ramakrishna's religious life and his repeated warnings to his male followers to shun 'women and gold', however, have been emphasised in other accounts of Ramakrishna's thinking, which have stressed the difficulty of recovering evidence of any intention on Ramakrishna's part to found a movement.

See also: **Advaita; Hinduism, modern and contemporary; Kālī and Caṇḍī; Ramakrishna Math and Mission; Śakti; Sarada Devi; Tantrism; Vivekananda, Swami**

GWILYM BECKERLEGGE

Further reading

Kripal, J.J. 1995. *Kali's Child: The Mystical and the Erotic in the Life and Teachings of Ramakrishna.* Chicago, IL and London: University of Chicago Press.

Sarkar, S. 1993. *An Exploration of the Ramakrishna Vivekananda Tradition.* Shimla: Indian Institute of Advanced Study.

RAMAKRISHNA UTSAVA

Ramakrishna Utsava is a festival in celebration of the birth of the Bengali mystic Ramakrishna. Ramakrishna was born in Calcutta (now Kolkata) on 20 February. Each year on his birthday a procession starts from the Dakṣineśvar Kālā temple, where Ramakrishna lived, and proceeds through the main streets of Kolkata. This festival is celebrated primarily in Bengal but also wherever branches of the Ramakrishna Math and Mission have been established, both in India and abroad.

See also: **Kālī and Caṇḍī; Ramakrishna, Sri; Ramakrishna Math and Mission; Utsava**

LYNN FOULSTON

Further reading

Woodward, P. (ed.) with R. El Droubie and C. Gould. 1998. *Festivals of the World.* RMEP.

RAMANA MAHARSHI (1879–1950)

Ramana Maharshi, named Vēṅkataraman, is a widely known Hindu sage and a contemporary exemplar of the Advaitic tradition. Born in Tiruchuli in Tamil Nadu, Ramana attained spiritual enlightenment at the age of 17. His teachings were derived, not from books or a human guru, but from his own spiritual experience. On realising that the Self is unaffected by the death of the body, his fear of death vanished. He was drawn to the sacred hill, Arunachala, in Tiruvannamalai, where he spent most of his time in silent meditation, and an ashram bearing his name came into being. Ramana's silence, his compassionate gaze and touch transformed the lives of many. He taught that we can realise the Self within us by following the direct path of self-enquiry ('Who am I?').

See also: **Advaita; Āśram(a) (religious community); Ātman**

SHARADA SUGIRTHARAJAH

Further reading

Natarajan, A.R. 2002. *Timeless in Time: Sri Ramana Maharshi. A Biography.* Bangalore: Ramana Maharshi Centre for Learning.

Osborne, A. (ed.). 1964. The *Collected Works of Ramana Maharshi.* London: Rider.

RĀMĀNANDA

Born around the beginning of the fourteenth century in Prāyaga, Rāmānanda is significant for opening up Vaiṣṇavite devotion to all castes and including women, thus challenging the brāhmaṇa domination of worship that went back to Rāmānuja. In other respects there were similarities between the two in that Rāmānanda and his order also worshipped Śrī, the consort of Viṣṇu, but in the form of Sītā, the wife of Rāma.

In the present time, Rāmānanda's saṃpradāya remains one of the largest in India and the connection to Rāmānuja remains in the similarity of the order. The Rāmānuja saṃpradāya is known as Śrī Vaiṣṇavas, whereas Rāmānanda's is called Śrī-saṃpradāya. The monks, as is usually the case in Vaiṣṇavite traditions, are known as vairāgis and its main centre, known as bara sthāna, is in Ayodhyā, the legendary birthplace of Rāma. Today, the order, although attended by large numbers of ecstatic groups of the uneducated, no longer maintains the egalitarian ethos of the founder, and it restricts priesthood in its temples to male brāhmaṇas, although there are a few nuns remaining in the monastic order.

The sect observes an ideal of a master–servant relationship with the divine, personified as Rāma, in which Hanumān is epitomised as having the perfect relationship with the Lord through dedicated service. For this reason, the monks' names are suffixed by dāsa (servant) and usually the name of Rāma is burnt into their skin as part of the initiation rite. Rāmānanda is not known to have written anything and the sect draws upon the teachings contained in Tulsīdās' Hindi version of the *Rāmayāṇa*, the *Rāmacaritamānasa*.

Traditionally, the famous nirguṇa bhakti sant Kabīr (1398–1448) is said to have been a disciple of Rāmānanda, although the dates cause some difficulties as Kabīr was born a century later.

See also: **Ayodhyā; Bhakti movement; Brāhmaṇa; Caste; Hanumān; Kabīr; Rāma; Rāmānandīs; Rāmānuja; Saṃpradāya; Sītā; Śrī Vaiṣṇavas; Tulsīdās(a); Vairāgya; Vaiṣṇavism; Viṣṇu**

RON GEAVES

Further reading

Schomer, K and W.H. McLeod. 1987. 'Introduction'. In K. Schomer and W.H. McLeod, eds, *The Sants: Studies in a Devotional Tradition of India.* New Delhi: Motilal Banarsidass, 1–21.

RĀMĀNANDIS

A Vaiṣṇava order (saṃpradāya) whose foundation is attributed to Rāmānanda.

Rāmānandis worship Rāma and have their centre in Ayodhyā, where they settled in the eighteenth century. One of the most widespread of saṃpradāyas, Rāmānandis consider themselves an original stream of Vaiṣṇava bhakti. Rāmānanda (*c.*1400–70) – though mentioned as the adiguru ('first teacher') – is a little-known figure. He is believed to have been the teacher of Kabīr and Ravidās, while sectarian texts like the *Śrī-Bhakti-Māla* (the 'Garland of Devotion') (sixteenth century) look at him as the spiritual descendent of

Rāma and Rāmānuja. Rāmānandi ascetics are called vairagis, 'those who practice passionlessness', and are divided in three orders: (1) nāgas, (2) tyāgis and (3) rasikas. They observe celibacy (brahmacarya) and removal of passion (vairāgya), but while the latter is a sedentary group which emphasises ritual, the worship of Rāma with attributes (saguṇa) and the respect of hierarchical rules, the former observe a more radical discipline. They wander half-naked, with matted hair and besmeared with ashes, practise hard penances and semen retention, smoke hemp and hardly observe caste regulations. The main difference between them and Śaiva ascetics is the meditation on the name of Rāma. Both in Ayodhyā and in other Rāmānandi centres, rasikas are more successful: their path, which closely reflects Vaiṣṇava bhakti, represents a more acceptable religious attitude, respectful of social rules and hierarchical structures.

See also: **Ayodhyā; Bhakti movement; Brahmacarya; Guru; Kabīr; Rāma; Rāmānuja; Ravidās(a); Śaivism; Saṃpradāya; Tapas; Vaiṣṇavism**

FABRIZIO M. FERRARI

Further reading

Burghart, R. 1978. 'The Founding of the Rāmānandi Sect'. *Ethnohistory* 25: 121–39.

Burghart, R. 1983. 'Wandering Ascetics of the Rāmānandi Sect'. *History of Religions* 22: 361–80.

Veer, P. van der 1988. *Gods on Earth: The Management of Religious Experience and Identity in a North Indian Pilgrimage Centre.* London: Athlone.

Veer, P. van der 1989. 'The Power of Detachment: Disciplines of Body and Mind in the Rāmānandi Order'. *American Ethnologist* 16: 458–70.

RĀMANAVAMĪ

This festival, literally 'Rāma's ninth', commemorates the birth of Rāma at noon on the ninth day of the bright half (when the moon is waxing) of the lunar month Caitra, which generally falls in March or April. It closes a period of nine nights (navarātra) which is the spring counterpart of the better-known autumn navarātra or navarātri which falls six months later (Durgā Pūjā, Daśahrā; Babb 1975: 132, 140). Rāmanavamī marks the approach of the hot season; in Andhra Pradesh this may be marked by giving fans to brāhmaṇas (Christian 1982: 259, 265).

According to the Sanskrit prescriptive texts, the day is marked by a vrata. This requires the worshipper to abstain completely from food, to remain awake all night, listening to stories and songs about Rāma, and to donate a gold image of Rāma (Kane 1968–77: 5.84–88). However, these practices are not usually followed, though some eat only fruit and abstain from sex (Stevenson 1920: 289). The main observances are in temples of Rāma, at noon, the time of his birth, when pūjā may be done to an image of the baby. There are recitations of the *Rāmāyaṇa* (in the Hindi-speaking region, Tulsīdās' *Rāmcaritmānas*), music, especially bhajans, and distribution of ginger sweets, as for a human birth. In some regions there are dramas about Rāma, or an image carried through the streets. The festival is most frequented at Ayodhyā, Rāma's birthplace, and at other places of pilgrimage associated with him, such as Nāsik, Tirupati and Rāmeśvara.

See also: **Ayodhyā; Bhajans; Brāhmaṇas; Calendar; Daśahrā; Durgā Pūjā; Nāsik; Pūjā; Rāma; Rāmāyaṇa; Rāmeśvara; Tulsīdās(a); Vrata**

DERMOT KILLINGLEY

Further reading

Babb, Lawrence A. 1975. *The Divine Hierarchy: Popular Hinduism in Central India.* New York: Columbia University Press.

Christian, Jane M. 1982. 'The End Is the Beginning: A Festival Chain in Andhra

Pradesh'. In Guy R. Welbon and Glenn E. Yocum, eds, *Religious Festivals in South India and Sri Lanka*. Delhi: Manohar.

Kane, Pandurang Vaman. 1968–77. *History of Dharmaśāstra (Ancient and Medieval Religious and Civil Law)*, 2nd edn, 5 vols (vols 1, 2 and 5 bound in two parts each). Poona [Pune]: Bhandarkar Oriental Research Institute (1st edn 1930–62).

Stevenson, Mrs [Margaret] Sinclair. 1920. *The Rites of the Twice-Born*. London: Oxford University Press.

RĀMĀNUJA (d. *c.*1137)

Rāmānuja was the leading theologian of the Viśiṣṭādvaita, or 'qualified non-dualist', Vedānta school. He was a Tamil brāhmaṇa and received his early training in the *Brahmasūtras* of Badarāyaṇa in Kañcīpuram from Yādavaprakāśa, who at the time espoused the Bhedābheda school of Vedānta. Traditional accounts say that Rāmānuja disagreed with his teacher, believing Yādavaprakāśa to be influenced by the Advaita view. He left him to find another teacher devoted to the theistic Vaiṣṇava faith of the Tamil Āḻvārs. He shifted his loyalty to Yāmunācārya, an earlier exponent of what later would be called Viśiṣṭādvaita. Yāmunācārya also was the head of an important site of the Āḻvār devotional faith, the Śrīraṅgam temple. Yāmunācārya died before they could meet and Rāmānuja believed it was one of Yāmuna's posthumous wishes that he compose the *Śrī Bhāṣya* commentary on the *Brahmasūtras*, opposed to Advaita according to the Śrī Vaiṣṇava view. Rāmānuja became a priest at the Śrīraṅgam temple and his former teacher Yādavaprakāśa converted and became Rāmānuja's pupil.

Rāmānuja became estranged from his wife and entered saṃnyāsa. At this time he took control of the maṭha at Śrīraṅgam and instituted many reforms. Rāmānuja later took extensive pilgrimages through south and north India. Tradition says in the late eleventh century a Śaivite Cōḷa king persecuted the Vaiṣṇava faith and Rāmānuja was forced to flee to Karṇāṭaka. Upon returning to Śrīraṅgam about twelve years later, he took complete control of the temple and finished his *Śrī Bhāṣya*. Other texts that are accepted undisputably as his are the *Vedārthasaṃgraha* and *Bhagavadgītā Bhāṣya*.

See also: **Advaita; Āḻvārs; Badarāyana; Bhagavadgītā; Bhedābheda; Brāhmaṇa; Brahmasūtras; Maṭha; Śaivism; Saṃnyāsa; Śrī Vaiṣṇavas; Tīrthayātrā; Vaiṣṇavism; Viśiṣṭādvaita; Vedānta**

ROBERT GOODDING

Further reading

Lott, E.J. 1976. *God and the Universe in the Vedāntic Theology of Rāmānuja*. Madras: Rāmānuja Research Society.

Ramakrishnananda, Swami. 1965. *Life of Sri Ramanuja*, 2nd edn. Madras: Sri Ramakrishna Math.

RAMANUJAN, ATTIPAT KRISHNASWAMI (1929–93)

Poet, translator and folklorist. Born into a Tamil Śrī Vaiṣṇava brāhmaṇa family living in Karnataka, he initially studied English language and literature at the University of Mysore and taught at several colleges in India before studying theoretical linguistics at Deccan University and Indiana University, receiving his doctorate on Kannada grammar from the latter in 1963. From 1962 he taught at the University of Chicago. As well as his own poetry, he published translations from ancient Tamil Caṅkam poetry (Ramanujan 1967, 1985) and from the poems of the Kannada Vīraśāivas (Ramanujan 1973) and the Tamil Āḻvārs (Ramanujan 1981), and he collected and published Indian folktales (Ramanujan 1991). He also published essays on many aspects of Indian literature, bhakti, symbolism and folklore, some of which have been collected (Dharwadker 1999).

See also: **Āḻvārs; Hinduism, history of scholarship; Vīraśaivas**

WILL SWEETMAN

Further reading

Dharwadker, V. (ed). 1999. *The Collected Essays of A.K. Ramanujan*. Delhi: Oxford University Press.

Ramanujan, A.K. 1967. *The Interior Landscape: Love Poems from a Classical Tamil Anthology*. Bloomington, IN: Indiana University Press.

Ramanujan, A.K. 1973. *Speaking of Śiva*. Harmondsworth: Penguin.

Ramanujan, A.K. 1981. *Hymns for the Drowning: Poems for Viṣṇu, by Nammāḻvār*. Princeton, NJ: Princeton University Press.

Ramanujan, A.K. 1985. *Poems of Love and War*. New York: Columbia University Press.

Ramanujan, A.K. 1991. *Folktales from India*. New York: Pantheon Books.

RĀMARĀJYA

Rāmarājya (Rāma's reign) was inaugurated on Rāma's return to Ayodhyā, as recounted in the *Rāmāyaṇa*. This period of peace, prosperity and happiness under the archetypal just and wise ruler has been extolled in later popular texts such as the *Rāṃ(a)acaritamānas(a)*.

The ideal of Rāmarājya and the figure of Rāma have taken on more recent connotations with the rise of the Hindutva movement and the Rām(a)janmabhūmi/Babri Masjid conflict in 1992 centred upon the city of Ayodhyā. Rāma and his utopian kingdom have become symbols of resistance against perceived threats to the values of India's Hindu population. Campaigning to restore the ideal of Rāmarājya has become a symbolic expression within Hindutva ideology of the struggle to establish the Hindu rāṣṭra (the national Hindu state) in India.

See also: **Ayodhyā; Hindutva; Nationalism; Rāma; Rāmāyaṇa**

GWILYM BECKERLEGGE

Further reading

Lutgendorf, P. 1995. 'Interpreting *Ramraj*: Reflections on the *Ramayana*, Bhakti and Hindu Nationalism'. In D. Lozenzen, ed., *Bhakti Religion in North India*. Delhi: Manohar.

RAMARAJYA PARISHAD

The Ramarajya Parishad, founded in 1948 by Swami Karapatri, was one of the many Hindu fundamentalist organisations to emerge during the British colonial regime in India, no doubt as a reaction to the critique of Hinduism by Christian missionaries of the period and the political domination by an alien 'Christian' power. The Ramarajya Parishad, unlike some of the other Hindu organisations such as the Arya Samaj or the Jana Sangh, did not seek to reform Hindu society as a reaction to Christian and British critique, but was the most orthodox of all the Hindu rightist parties of the day (Puri 1980: 11). The Parishad took the days of the mythological king Rāma (avatāra of Viṣṇu) as the ideal for society and governance and had the objective of recreating those glorious days in modern India. It sought to enforce cow protection and ban alcoholic drinks and had a vision of an economy based on barter. These ideals seem suspiciously similar to those propagated by Mahātma Gandhi, who also used the phrase Rāmarājya (Kingdom of Rāma) to describe his vision of an ideal society, though not in a totally Hindu context as the Ramarajya Parishad did.

The Ramarajya Parishad was elitist in that its leadership mainly rested on the Hindu aristocracy (Andersen and Damle 1987: 16) and it did not obtain a hold on the Indian masses as some of the reform-oriented and more broad-based Hindutva parties did. After 1962 it ceased to be a viable political force.

See also: **Arya Samaj; Avatāra; Gandhi, Mohandas Karamchand; Hindutva; Jana**

Sangh; Rāma; Rāmarājya; Sacred animals; Viṣṇu

THEODORE GABRIEL

Further reading

Andersen Walter, K. and Shridhar Damle. 1987. *The Brotherhood in Saffron*. Boulder, CO: Westview Press.
Puri, Geetha. 1980. *Bharatiya Jana Sangh*. New Delhi: Sterling Publishers.

RĀMĀYAṆA

The *Rāmāyaṇa* is one of the two long narrative poems in Sanskrit which are commonly called the Sanskrit epics; in their developed forms the *Rāmāyaṇa* (almost 20,000 verses long in its Critical Edition) and the *Mahābhārata* (which is more than three times as long) are among the most extensive literary works in the world. The *Rāmāyaṇa* tells the story of prince Rāma, ranging from accounts of intrigue at court to wanderings among hermits in the forest, and culminating in the great battle when the Rākṣasa Rāvaṇa is defeated and punished for his abduction of Rāma's wife, Sītā.

Indian tradition unanimously holds that the original version was composed by Vālmīki and transmitted orally. Most Western scholars also accept that it was originally composed orally, and transmitted for several centuries by oral recitation, but opinions vary about the date of composition. The version now extant was most probably composed between about 500 BCE and 300 CE, during which period it was also committed to writing. There are two main lines of transmission of the extant text, the Northern and Southern recensions, within which more regional versions developed in the different scripts later used to write the text, although there was much mutual influence. In its complete form, the poem comprises seven books (kāṇḍas).

The coherence of the core narrative shows it to be the conception of a single creative intelligence, an author, despite its blurring by the amplifications and modifications of later generations of redactors. The author was clearly an excellent poet, who planned his plot carefully. Though traditionally named as Vālmīki, in reality we know nothing about this original author, apart from what little his work reveals. He was familiar with the geography and political set-up of the central Gaṅgā region at a period before the rise there of large-scale monarchies and with the interests and pursuits of the kṣatriya class, for whom warfare and hunting in the surrounding forests were important. He composed in a distinct dialect of Sanskrit. He may have used earlier brief lays in composing his masterpiece but there is no trace whatsoever in the Veda of the Rāma story and very little of any of its characters: two characters (Sītā and her father Janaka) have names found in Vedic literature but nothing suggests that this is other than a coincidence. Several peripheral characters have roots in Vedic literature, but their inclusion merely demonstrates that they were still well known to both storytellers and their audiences, not that the story of Rāma as such has any prehistory.

Transmission of the *Rāmāyaṇa* and *Mahābhārata* in their oral stages was altogether different from the exactness of Vedic recitation. Both began, and continued for several centuries, as the preserve of the warrior kṣatriya class, recited for their entertainment by bards or sūtas, before being taken over by brāhmaṇa redactors. Meaning, not sound, was crucial, and additions and modifications were freely made.

The bards and itinerant ballad-singers who recited the *Rāmāyaṇa* from memory undoubtedly felt the need to embellish it with further ornament and to complete it by inserting short stories, descriptive digressions, eulogies of local places and other geographical descriptions in response to popular taste and the expectations of their audience; another motive was to explain the reasons for characters' actions which seemed questionable by later moral standards. A further stage in this expansion was to add both a precursor and a sequel around the five core books: the Childhood Book (*Bālakāṇḍa*) and the Further Book (*Uttarakāṇḍa*), which have generally been recognised as relatively late, revealing the fact by considerable differences of style and language, as well as outlook.

This later material, naturally, was composed in the diction and style of the teller's own day, alongside the earlier material that he felt unable to omit and retained largely unmodified. The text of the *Rāmāyaṇa* did not become relatively fixed until perhaps the Gupta period (fourth to sixth centuries CE), a period of consolidation of the high culture, nearly a thousand years after the composition of its core.

The religious pattern found in the early *Rāmāyaṇa* is one of older deities and of rituals based on sacrifice leading to heaven, rather than the newer patterns of worship, usually seen as leading to liberation (mokṣa – the term is absent from the *Rāmāyaṇa*). Indra is the most prominent god, as both the leader of the gods and the performer of various heroic deeds. Yama appears next most frequently because of his role as king of the dead (a role incompatible with the later concept of saṃsāra); a common formula refers to dispatching warriors to Yama's realm. Varuṇa too still appears, mainly as the lord of the ocean, but also linked with Indra, reflecting an early stage in their relative importance. Garuḍa is mentioned more often than, and independently of, Viṣṇu. In general, the opposition between gods and anti-gods shows a Vedic or immediately post-Vedic pattern very different from that of later Hinduism.

However, deities are mentioned much more often in the first and last books, when religious influences were increasing. In particular Brahmā, the creator deity, shows an almost fivefold increase from the basic narrative, and his granting of boons as a reward for asceticism becomes an element in the narration of several events. But, whereas he suffers a marked decline in importance thereafter, Viṣṇu and Śiva, who are also more frequently mentioned, become increasingly significant from now on and soon appear as protectors of the other gods. In particular, Rāma becomes identified with Viṣṇu.

Testimony to the text's significance is provided by the wide variety of art forms in which the story has been expressed over the centuries. Non-verbal presentations of the story are found in temple sculptures and narrative friezes, paintings and dance. Besides the numerous later literary versions, it is perpetuated in retellings by storytellers, puppet plays, the Rāmlīlā (a form of popular dramatic presentation analogous to the Western medieval mystery plays) and – at the end of the twentieth century – a hugely popular, long-running television serial.

See also: **Brahmā; Brāhmaṇa; Deities; Gaṅgā; Garuḍa; Indra; Itihāsa; Mahābhārata; Mokṣa; Rākṣasas; Rāma; Rāvaṇa; Saṃsāra; Sītā; Śiva; Vālmīki; Varṇa; Varuṇa; Viṣṇu; Veda; Yama**

JOHN BROCKINGTON

Further reading

Bose, Mandakranta. (ed.). 2004. *The Rāmāyaṇa Revisited.* New York: Oxford University Press.

Brockington, John. 1985. *Righteous Rāma: The Evolution of an Epic*. Delhi: Oxford University Press.

Brockington, John. 1998. *The Sanskrit Epics* (Handbuch der Orientalisk 2.12). Leiden: Brill.

Brockington, John and Mary Brockington (trans.). 2006. *Steadfast Rāma: An Early Form of the Rāmāyaṇa*. London: Penguin Books.

Brockington, Mary. 1997. 'The Art of Backwards Compostion: Some Narrative

Techniques in Vālmīki's Rāmāyaṇa'. In Mary Brockington and Peter Schreiner, eds, *Composing a Tradition* (Proceedings of the First Dubrovnik International Conference on the Sanskrit Epics and Purāṇas), 99–110.
Bulcke, Camille. 1950. *Rāmkathā: utpatti aur vikāś* [The Rama story: origin and spread]. Prayāg: Hindā Pariṣad Prakāśan.
Goldman, Robert P. (gen. ed.). 1984–. *The Rāmāyaṇa of Vālmīki: An Epic of Ancient India*. Trans. Robert P. Goldman *et al.* Princeton, NJ: Princeton University Press.
Goldman, Robert P. and Sally J. Sutherland Goldman. 2004. 'Rāmāyaṇa'. In Sushil Mittal and Gene Thursby, eds, *The Hindu World*. New York: Routledge, 75–96.
Lutgendorf, Philip. 1990. 'Ramayan: The Video'. *Drama Review* 34: 127–76.
Lutgendorf, Philip. 1991. *The Life of a Text: Performing the Rāmcaritmānas of Tulsīdās.* Berkeley, CA: University of California Press.
Lutgendorf, Philip. 1995. 'Interpreting Rāmrāj: Reflections on the *Rāmayaṇ*, Bhakti and Hindu Nationalism'. In David N. Lorenzen, ed., *Bhakti Religion in North India*. Albany, NY: SUNY Press, 253–87.
Richman, Paula. (ed.). 1991. *Many Rāmāyaṇnas: The Diversity of a Narrative Tradition in South Asia.* Berkeley, CA: University of California Press.
Richman, Paula. 2001. *Questioning Rāmāyaṇas: A South Asian Tradition.* Berkeley, CA: University of California Press.
Theil-Horstmann, Monika. (ed.). 1991. *Rāmāyaṇa and Rāmāyaṇas* (Khoj – A Series of Modern South Asian Studies 3). Wiesbaden: Harrassowitz.

RĀMEŚVARA

The island of Rāmeśvara, between India and Śrī Laṅkā, is one of the four dhāmas. Because of its associations with Rāma and Śiva, it is a popular place of pilgrimage for Śaivas and Vaiṣṇavas alike. The presiding deity is called Śrī Rāmanāhasvāmi or Śrī Rāmaliṅgam, and his consort is known as Śrī Parvathavardhinī. According to tradition, before the battle against Rāvaṇa, Rāma fashioned an earthen liṅga (a phallic symbol representing Śiva) on the seashore, worshipped it and was promised victory by the god. After having defeated and killed Rāvaṇa, Rāma returned to Rāmeśvara with Sītā, where he found a great number of sages awaiting him. However, he felt as if a shadow followed him, and the sages explained to him that having killed Rāvaṇa he had committed the most heinous of sins, brahmanicide. To purify himself Rāma sent Hanumān to Kailāsa to request from Śiva a liṅga which he could install on Gandhamādana hill. As he was slow in returning, Sītā fashioned a sand liṅga, which Rāma then worshipped. When Hanumān arrived, Rāma deeply regretted what had happened, and asked him to pull out and discard the sand liṅga. Despite Hanuman's efforts the liṅga, obviously of divine origin, could not be shifted. The second liṅga was then set beside the first, and both were worshipped. The main temple on the island, dedicated to Śiva, is supposed to have been founded by Rāma; however, the core of the present temple is attributed to the Pāṇḍya period (*c.* seventh to thirteenth centuries). It has been greatly extended and renovated during the following centuries, mainly under the patronage of the Sethupatis. The island is dotted with a number of sacred places, among which are the Gandhamādana hill and Dhanuśkoṭi, 'bow notch', the place from which Rāma allegedly destroyed the bridge built by his allies, to prevent any further invasion of Laṅkā.

See also: **Hanumān; Rāma; Rāvana; Sacred geography; Śaivism; Sītā; Śiva; Sri Lanka, Hindus in; Tīrthayātrā (Pilgrimage); Vaiṣṇavism**

ANNA DALLAPICCOLA

RANADE, MAHADEV GOVIND (1842–1901)

Leading social and religious reformer, a founding member of the Indian National

Congress and justly called 'father of the renaissance' in western India, Ranade was born into a brāhmaṇa family, then educated at Elphinstone College (Bombay) and Edinburgh before joining the Civil Service's Education department in 1866. Appointed to the judiciary in Poona (Pune) in 1871, he slowly gained promotion and, after several stints as member of the Bombay Legislative Council, his career culminated in the post of puisne judge of the Bombay High Court.

Ranade's publications reflect the eclectic range of his interests, which encompassed history, politics, economics, religion and social reform, as well as German and Marathi literature. Seeking to promote the cause of female education, he founded the Deccan Education Society, the body which later saw the foundation of Fergusson College in Poona, where the young Gokhale was to teach before becoming Ranade's assistant.

Founder in 1861 of the Widow Remarriage Association, Ranade campaigned for the actual implementation of the Act of 1856, which allowed widows to marry, a deed abhorrent to conservative Hindus; he also pressed for legislation to expunge child marriage and this resulted in the Age of Consent Bill of 1890. That, however, did not deter the great man from taking an 11-year-old girl as his second wife, an action not untypical among many a high-minded reformer and symptomatic of the dislocation then felt between the old and the new.

Prevented by his official position from engaging directly in politics and a moderate who believed that, in spite of the injustice of alien domination, Indians had much to learn from the British, Ranade was not a resolute opponent of their rule and, against more militant leaders, stood up for the promotion of Indian interests through constitutional measures, a strategy that was to be followed by his disciple Gokhale. Ranade's advocacy of conciliation and cooperation was to have a considerable impact on the policies of Congress, while at the same time instilling a new national consciousness in the people.

Alongside social reform, Ranade was an apologist for religious regeneration, since, in his words, 'If your religious ideas are low and grovelling, you cannot succeed in social, economical and political spheres'. However, for him, reformation did not consist in a break from the past but rather in a critical re-evaluation of deep-seated beliefs and habits, since one never starts with a clean slate. Reformation is like 'completing a half-written sentence'. Ranade's liberal attitude led to heated debate with conservative brāhmaṇas over the interpretation of the texts of Hindu Law.

A man of immense energy, of vast and profound learning, of toleration and compassion and a visionary nation-builder, Ranade has been called, with little hyperbole, a ṛṣi for modern times.

See also: **Brāhmaṇa; Child marriage; Deccan Education Society; Dharmaśāstras; Gokhale, Gopal Krishna; Hinduism, modern and contemporary; Prarthana Samaj; Ṛṣi; Widow remarriage; Women's education**

DANIEL MARIAU

Further reading

Jagirdar, P.J. 1971. *Mahadeo Govind Ranade.* New Delhi: Publications Division, Ministry of Information and Broadcasting, Government of India.

Ranade, Mahadeo Govind. 1961. *Rise of the Maratha Power.* Reprint. New Delhi: Publications Division, Ministry of Information and Broadcasting, Government of India.

RASHTRA SEVIKA SAMITI

The Rashtra Sevika Samiti (Society of Servants of the Nation) was established in Wardha, present-day Maharashtra, in 1936. It is strongly associated with the

Rashtriya Swayamsevak Sangh, established at nearby Nagpur in 1925. The key architect of the Samiti was Laxmibai Kelkar (1905–78, also known as Mausiji). The 1930s were a period of intense politicisation in India, with many women taking full part in direct action campaigns associated with Congress and M.K. Gandhi, as well as other forms of political action. Kelkar herself had been a Gandhian activist, but at least one of her sons was a member of the Sangh, and in the mid-1930s she proposed that women should also be allowed to join the organisation.

K.B. Hedgewar, the supreme leader of the Sangh, resisted the idea of female membership. He had fashioned this organisation from its inception as a kind of brotherhood, drawing on male-centric high-caste models such as brahmacarya. The Samiti emerged as a kind of compromise between Kelkar's ambition and Hedgewar's reservations. It was established as a 'sister' organisation of the Sangh, echoing its organisational set-up and modes of practice, yet maintaining a separate institutional existence and membership. As such it relates to the Sangh in a somewhat different way from other components of the so-called Sangh Parivar, the 'family' of organisations, which have generally been set up by and continue to run with the involvement of seconded pracharaks (full-time workers) from the 'parent' organisation. Indeed the Samiti appears to have seconded its own pracharikas in order to develop the role of women in key Sangh organisations such as the Bharatiya Janata Party and the Vishwa Hindu Parishad.

The Samiti claims an all-India membership of about 1.5 million women, and it engages in particular in social welfare and educational activities – perceived as critical to the development of Hindu consciousness. Ideologically, the Samiti has elaborated the Hindutva valorisation of the mother (mātṛśakti, the power of the mother), producing an image of active womanhood which combines the well-known tropes of the dutiful wife (strīdharma pativratā varṇa) and the nurturing mother with images of dynamic kṣatriya queens and wise female ascetics. The images proclaim an active role for women in the development of the Hindu nation – a role which has manifested itself in the engagement of women in situations of communal violence, noted recently in relation to both the Ayodhyā campaign and the violence in Gujarat in 2002.

See also: **Ayodhyā; Bharatiya Janata Party; Brahmacārya; Gandhi, Mohandas Karamchand; Hedgewar, Keshav Baliram; Hindutva; Nationalism; Pativratā and pati-parameśvara; Rashtriya Swayamsevak Sangh; Sangh Parivar; Strī dharma; Varṇa; Vishwa Hindu Parishad**

JOHN ZAVOS

Further reading

Bacchetta, P. 1999. 'Militant Hindu Nationalist Women Re-imagine Themselves: Notes on Mechanisms of Expansion/Adjustment'. *Journal of Women's History* 10(4): 125–47.

Sarkar, T. 1993. 'The Rashtrasevika Samiti and Ramjanmabhoomi'. In G. Pandey, ed., *Hindus and Others: The Question of Identity in India Today*. New Delhi: Viking Penguin, 24–45.

RASHTRIYA SWAYAMSEVAK SANGH

The Rashtriya Swayamsevak Sangh (RSS; the National Volunteer Corps) was founded in 1925 by Keshav Baliram Hedgewar and has been led by four successive sarsanghchalaks (supreme leaders) to date. It has numerous closely linked affiliates, known collectively as the Sangh Parivar ('sangh family'). Although the RSS maintains that it is a cultural organisation, its ideals and the political activities of many of its individual members and affiliates have made it a controversial organisation since its foundation. It has been accused of intensifying communal tensions within India through its promotion of Hindutva ideology.

Influenced by V.D. Savarkar and his own experience as a member of the Nagpur Hindu Sabha, Hedgewar created the RSS to provide character-building training for those committed to protecting the Hindu rāṣṭra (nation) in the face of a perceived threat from India's Muslims. Beginning in Nagpur, the embryonic RSS required its members to attend a traditional gymnasium (akhara), where exercise, instruction and Hindu worship took place. The first shakha (branch), the basic unit of the RSS, was inaugurated in Nagpur in 1926. Members of the RSS took an oath before the bhagva dhwaj (the saffron flag of Shivaji, the seventeenth-century Maratha ruler). Hedgewar also devised their characteristic uniform of khaki shorts, cap and white shirt. By 1927, RSS units had become actively involved in protecting Hindu districts during outbreaks of communal violence. There were approximately 500 shakhas and a women's affiliate, the Rashtra Sevika Samiti, by the end of the 1930s.

Under the leadership of the second sarsanghchalak, Madhav Sadashiv Golwalkar, the RSS gained in popularity as it gave physical protection and aid to Hindu refugees who crossed into India on Partition in 1947. After the assassination of Mahatma Gandhi in 1948 by Nathuram Godse, a onetime member of the RSS, the organisation was banned for approximately a year and several of its leaders, including Golwalkar, were imprisoned. During this period, pracharaks (local organisers) became increasingly important in maintaining the underground survival of the movement. The post of pracharak, answerable directly to the sarsanghchalak and originally created by Golwalkar to bind the regions closer to the central leadership, became instrumental in aiding the growth of the organisation's many affiliates. The political party the Bharatiya Janata Party (BJP) and the Vishwa Hindu Parishad, called into existence by Golwalkar to encourage unity between Hindu religious groups, are the most widely known of these affiliates. The Akhil Bharatiya Vidyarthi Parishad (a student movement) and the Bharatiya Mazdoor Sangh (a labour organisation), two of the Rashtriya Swayamsevak Sangh's largest and most influential affiliates, also date from this period. The RSS has subsequently become increasingly involved in humanitarian and educational projects through its affiliates, and has supported campaigns to 'reclaim' those it believes to have been lost from Hinduism to other religions. Its affiliates have also been active in the Hindu diaspora.

The increasing organised social and political activism of the RSS and its affiliates was encouraged by the third sarsanghchalak, Balasaheb Deoras. During his leadership the Akhil Bharatiya Vanavasi Kalyan Ashram was created to work in tribal areas, together with Seva Bharati to promote educational initiatives among scheduled castes. The movement played a prominent role in the opposition to Indira Gandhi's government during the period of Emergency, 1975–77, and in the destruction of the Babri Masjid and the ensuing violence at Ayodhyā in 1992. The direct and indirect political influence of the RSS has grown with the popularity of the BJP since the 1980s, culminating in the BJP's participation in coalitions that have formed India's national government until the early twenty-first century.

See also: **Ayodhyā; Bharatiya Janata Party; Diaspora; Gandhi, Mohandas Karamchand; Godse, Nathuram; Golwalkar, Madhav Sadashiv; Hedgewar, Keshav Baliram; Hindutva; Rashtra Sevika Samiti; Sangh Parivar; Savarkar, Vinayat Damodar; Vishwa Hindu Parishad**

GWILYM BECKERLEGGE

Further reading

Andersen, W.K. and S.D. Damle. 1987. *The Brotherhood in Saffron: The Rashtriya Swayamsevak Sangh and Hindu Revivalism.* Boulder, CO and London: Westview Press.

Jaffrelot, C. 1996. *The Hindu Nationalist Movement and Indian Politics, 1925 to the 1990s.* London: Hurst.

RATHA YĀTRĀ

The 'journey of chariots'. Ratha Yātrā/ Jagannātha is held in honour of Kṛṣṇa as Jagannātha ('Lord of the Universe'), in Puri (Orissa) during Āṣāḍha (June–July). The story of Jagannātha and the Ratha Yātrā appears in the *Padma-*, *Brahmā-* and other *Purāṇas*, but the earliest account is in the *Skanda Purāṇa* (Vaiṣṇava Khaṇḍa). Viśvakarman was shaping a wooden box to keep the bones of Kṛṣṇa, who had been killed by a hunter while roaming in form of a deer. But as he was interrupted he left his work unfinished. Only after Brahmā's intervention was the log given a soul (hence the title Dārubrahmā, the 'Wooden Lord'). During the festival, three wooden slabs representing Kṛṣṇa, his brother Balarāma and his sister Subhadrā are brought in procession on enormous carts pulled by hundreds of devotees. Every twelve years, these are burnt and new mūrtis are carved from a neem tree.

See also: **Balarāma; Brahmā; Image worship; Kṛṣṇa; Purāṇas; Subhadrā; Viśvakarman**

FABRIZIO M. FERRARI

Further reading

Kulke, H. and B. Schnepel (eds). 2001. *Jagannath Revisited: Studying Society, Religion and the State in Orissa.* Delhi: Manohar.

RATI

Rati, a divine embodiment of 'sensual pleasure', is a minor goddess who dwells on the moon as the co-wife of Kāma, the god of love, along with her rival Prītī, the embodiment of 'affection'. Rati is perhaps best known for her role in saving Kāma from Śiva's wrath. As recounted in the *Matsya Purāṇa*, Kāma caused Śiva to fall in love with Pārvatī, only to be burnt to ashes by the fervid deity. Rati's bitter lament persuaded Śiva to reconstitute Kāma. In another version, Rati held Indra responsible for the death of her husband; in recompense, Indra promised that Kāma would be returned to her in the person of Pradyumna, a son of Kṛṣṇa and Rukmiṇī, and that she would be reunited with him as his wife Māyāvatī. In Indian aesthetic theory, rati is the basic emotion (sthāyibhāva) which underlies the poetic sentiment (rasa) of love or passion (śṛṅgāra).

See also: **Kāma (Deity); Kṛṣṇa; Pārvatī; Purāṇas; Rukmiṇī; Śiva**

ANDREA MARION PINKNEY

Further reading

Hawkley, J.S. and D.M. Wulff. 1996. *Devi: Goddesses of India.* Berkeley, CA: University of California Press.

RĀVAṆA

Rāvaṇa, the Rākṣasa ruler and king of Laṅkā, is presented from the start in the *Rāmāyaṇa* as a slave to lust and later on as the embodiment of evil. His sister Śūrpaṇakhā rouses him to action by narrating not so much her own woes as Sītā's beauty. He oustsd his half-brother Kubera; he quarrels with his brother Vibhīṣaṇa when he advises Sītā's return; he and his son Indrajit seek to defeat Rāma and his army by various underhand means. As Rāma's status rises, so Rāvaṇa's might is magnified and much of the last book of the *Rāmāyaṇa* then recounts his past exploits: defiance of the gods, lifting of Mount Kailāsa, asceticism leading to a boon of invulnerability (except from humans) and his abduction of various females, culminating in his rape of Rambhā, for which he is cursed that his head will shatter if he uses force on another woman.

See also: **Kubera; Rāma; Rākṣasas; Rāmāyaṇa; Sītā; Tapas**

JOHN BROCKINGTON

Further reading

Brockington, J. 1985. *Righteous Rāma: The Evolution of an Epic*. Delhi: Oxford University Press.

Brockington, J. 1998. *The Sanskrit Epics* (Handbuch der Orientalistik 2.12). Leiden: Brill.

Brockington, Mary. 2001. 'Indian Ogres: Tradition Versus Artistry'. In Hilda Ellis Davidson and Anna Chaudhri, eds, *Supernatural Enemies*. Durham, NC: Caroline Academic Press.

Brockington, Mary. 2003. 'Who Was the Golden Deer? Narrative Inconsistency in the Abduction of Sītā'. In Renata Czekalska and Halin Marlewicz, eds, *2nd International Conference on Indian Studies: Proceedings* (*Cracow Indological Studies* (4–5): 73–84). Kraków: Ksiegarnia Akademicka.

Goldman, R. and J. Masson. 1969. 'Who Knows Rāvaṇa? – A Narrative Difficulty in the *Vālmīki Rāmāyaṇa*'. *Annals of the Bhandarkar Oriental Research Institute* 50: 95–100.

Hospital, Clifford. 1985. 'Rāvaṇa in Epic and Purāṇa'. *Purāṇa* 27: 352–70.

Hospital, Clifford. 1991. 'Rāvaṇa as Tragic Hero: C.N. Srikantan Nayar's Laṅkālakṣmī'. In Monika Thiel-Horstmann, ed., *Rāmāyaṇa and Rāmāyaṇas*. Wiesbaden: Harrassowitz, 85–102.

RAVIDĀS(A)

Ravidās, also known as Raidās, was a religious poet and 'saint' who lived in the city of Benares or Vārāṇasī in northern India some time around 1500. He is said to have been one of a group of five non-brāhmaṇa disciples (the others being Kabīr, Pīpā, Dhanā and Sen) of the brāhmān saint Rāmānanda. These five, especially Kabīr and Ravidās, offered devotion to a formless, or nirguṇa, God. In their view, this God is higher and more authentic than the visible, or saguṇa, forms of God worshipped by most Hindus. For this reason, the religious current to which Kabīr and Ravidās belonged is often called nirguṇā. Although most present-day followers of Kabīr and Ravidās now consider themselves to be Hindus, the religion of Guru Nānak and the Sikhs is also closely associated with this nirguṇī current. The religious songs in Hindi attributed to Ravidās are still sung throughout northern India.

Ravidās belonged to the caste of leatherworkers known as Chamars. Since the Chamars handle dead animals, including dead cows, they are considered to be a particularly low caste. Many songs attributed to Ravidās allude to the cruel treatment he received from brāhmaṇas and other higher-caste persons. Most devotees of Ravidās have been Chamars. In recent years these devotees have begun to organise themselves both as a religious sect and as a social movement. The annual celebrations of the birth anniversary of Ravidās in Benares and other cities are now an important expression of low-caste religious, political and social solidarity.

The earliest detailed account of Ravidās' life is the *Raidās paracāī* of Anantadās, a Hindi text written sometime around 1590. Although this text and other later descriptions of Ravidās' life are more hagiographical than historical, it is reasonable to accept that Ravidās was a Chamar from Benares who became a popular religious poet and singer and was somehow associated with Rāmānanda and with Kabīr. The *Raidās paracāī* claims that Ravidās was originally a worshipper of the Goddess, but that Kabīr convinced him that the formless, nirguṇa God was superior to all visible saguṇa forms of God. Many of the legends about

Ravidās tell how he overcame the opposition of brāhmaṇas, who objected to a Chamar taking up a successful religious vocation. One popular legend tells how a queen from Rajasthan came to Benares and became Ravidās' disciple.

See also: **Caste; Deities; Jāti; Kabīr; Purity and pollution, ritual; Rāmananda; Sant Sādhana; Sikhism, relationship with Hinduism; Vārāṇasī; Varṇa**

DAVID LORENZEN

Further reading

Callewaert, Winand M. and Peter G. Friedlander. 1992. *The Life and Works of Raidas*. New Delhi: Manohar.

Hawley, John Stratton and Mark Juergensmeyer. 1988. *Songs of the Saints of India*. New York: Oxford University Press.

Lorenzen, David N. 1996. *Praises to a Formless God*. Albany, NY: State University of New York Press.

RELIGIOUS EDUCATION

'Hinduism' features within the religious education programmes for schools in a number of countries (such as Denmark, England, Finland, Norway, Scotland, South Africa, Sweden and Wales), in at least the final years of secondary education and often throughout the school years. 'Religious education' in this context refers to a non-confessional approach of learning about Hinduism in classes composed of students from many religions or none, rather than religious nurture of Hindu children. This non-confessional, multi-faith approach to the subject is currently a minority option for state-funded school systems worldwide, as most opt either to omit religious studies from the curriculum (e.g. USA) or to include confessional religious education either in the tradition deemed to be that of the nation or in separate faith groups. Nevertheless, in faith-based confessional contexts syllabuses might include study of Hinduism as part of a course on 'world religions' (e.g. Catholic schools in Ontario, Canada). In addition, some aspects of Hinduism might be studied as part of courses in history, geography, social studies or philosophy.

The following account is based largely on the example of England, although an examination of syllabuses and textbooks from other countries reveals that it is representative. The motivation for studying Hinduism at school is twofold. First, in a country where there is a substantial Hindu minority, or in a world where the Hindu tradition affects the lives of hundreds of millions of people, it is important to know and understand the beliefs and customs of one's neighbours. Second, the study of Hinduism can contribute to the pupil's own spiritual, moral, social and cultural development. Hindu pupils can see their own tradition valued by the school and non-Hindu children can benefit from considering such teachings as ahiṃsā or dharma (in the sense of duty) as applicable to their own lives, or deepen their reflection on their own beliefs and values where they agree with or differ from the Hindu tradition, e.g. reincarnation and afterlife beliefs.

Syllabus compilers select aspects of Hinduism suitable for the target age of pupils. In England, pupils might study Hinduism systematically once or twice in their school career, or might encounter Hinduism several times as part of cross-religious work on themes such as festivals. Children aged from about 5 to 7 years old would concentrate on aspects of the tradition that can be directly experienced by the senses, such as pictures and statues of popular deities (Gaṇeśa is a firm favourite with the youngest children), worship and shrines, or festivals such as Dīvālī. No clear division is made between 'religion' and 'culture' so that Indian clothes such as the sari and Indian food might also feature in the topic. Family life, respect for all living things and stories which appeal to children, such as that of Rāma and Sītā, are common features. Pupils aged 8 to 11 years might explore the gods and the concept of God in more detail, study family ceremonies such as those connected with birth and marriage, or look at practices such as meditation, temple worship and pilgrimage, sacred sites and how Hindu beliefs affect daily life. Secondary school students aged 11 to 14 might look in more depth at concepts central to a 'Hindu' worldview, such as saṃsāra, mokṣa and karma, as well as a selection of practice such as worship, rites of passage, scriptures or festivals. They may look at notable Hindus, such as Gandhi. Students aged 14 to 16 might look at the variety of Hindu philosophies such as the various forms of Vedānta, caste and Hindu perspectives on a number of contemporary social and ethical issues such as gender and sexism, human rights or environmental issues. At ages 16, 17 and 18 there are public examinations in religious education, which might include an optional paper on the Hindu tradition, or aspects of Hinduism might be taught as part of a more general course.

The selection of material by syllabus writers has led to the accusation that a reified 'school Hinduism' has been constructed that bears little resemblance to the diverse complexity of the tradition as practised, and which reflects the history of biased 'Orientalist' scholarship by non-Hindus. Religious educators have tried to counteract this by stressing diversity, by arranging for pupils to visit temples and meet Hindus, and by producing textbooks that are based on ethnographic research with Hindu children rather than a watered-down version of dated scholarship. A good example of this is the Warwick Religious Education Project (e.g. Wayne and Everington 1996).

The selection of material is influenced not only by the history of Western scholarship but also by the diaspora community itself, which may have either a regional bias (English Hindus are mostly of Gujarati or Punjabi descent) or an interest in portraying a particular version of the tradition. For example, there was some controversy surrounding the publication of a book for school religious education by the UK branch of the Vishwa Hindu Parishad in 1996 (with a revised edition in 1998) which takes a definite stand on contested issues such as the indigenous origins of the tradition (Vishwa Hindu Parishad (UK) 1998).

Because of either outsider stereotypes or insider partiality, and depending on the teacher and resources used, 'Hinduism' as taught in schools may well not reflect either the rich diversity of the tradition or the latest scholarly research. However, even if the knowledge and understanding of 'Hinduism' gained from religious education classes is partial or stereotyped, it provides a good basis for further explorations, and if it includes encounters with members of the Hindu community it will be authentic for at least some members of the tradition. Conversations with school pupils in England reveal that 'Hinduism' is one of the religions that they enjoy – for the younger ones the colourful iconography and wealth of stories is attractive, and for older students ideas like reincarnation and the place of animals appeal. The main complaints are trying to remember the difficult Sanskrit vocabulary, and the sheer diversity and complexity of 'Hinduism' compared with the school versions of other traditions they study.

See also: **Ahiṃsā; Caste; Dharma; Diaspora; Dīvālī; Gaṇeśa; Gandhi, Mohandas Karamchand; Karma; Meditation; Mokṣa; Orientalism; Rāma; Religious nurture; Sacred geography; Sacred texts; Saṃsāra; Saṃskaras; Sītā; Temple worship; Tīrthayātrā (pilgrimage); Utsava; Vedānta; Vishwa Hindu Parishad**

DENISE CUSH

Further reading

Cush, D. and C. Robinson. 2000. 'Teaching about Hinduism: Classroom Teaching'. In W.K. Kay and L.J. Francis, eds, *Religion in Education*, vol. 3. Leominster, MA: Gracewing, 307–19.

Vishwa Hindu Parishad (UK). 1998. *Explaining Hindu Dharma*, 2nd edn. Thornton Heath: Vishwa Hindu Parishad

Wayne, E. and J. Everington (with D. Kadodwala and E. Nesbitt). 1996. *Hindus*. Oxford: Heinemann.

RELIGIOUS NURTURE

Religious nurture consists of the processes by which values, beliefs and practices are passed on and adapted from generation to generation. In view of the contested, diverse and fluid character of the Hindu tradition no summary account can represent the nurture of young Hindus worldwide.

For the majority of Hindus, nurture involves copying older relatives of the same sex. It occurs principally at home and in the wider family and community, rather than through formal provision such as special classes, and much of it is gender-specific.

Informal nurture

Informal nurture can be understood in terms of saṃskāra. This means both that children are 'processed' by rites of passage, such as nāmakaraṇa (naming) and cūḍākaraṇa (mundan in Hindi), i.e. ceremonial shaving of first hair, and that they are deeply influenced (conditioned) by their families' attitudes and expectations. Although they do not remember their own nāmakaraṇa, mundan, etc. they learn through participating in the saṃskāras of family members. For example, in the build-up to a wedding children acquire familiarity with assumptions about families' relative status and with the roles inherent in particular family relationships, e.g. the responsibilities of a bride's māmā (mother's brother). They learn about giving and receiving the gifts appropriate to particular relationships and they experience the jubilation of the bridegroom's companions on the way to the marriage and the grief of the bride's family and the bride at her departure, in addition to roles (serious or playful) that a child may be asked to play. Photographs and videos of weddings reinforce this informal learning.

Similarly, daily worship and annual festivals are part of many young Hindus' formative experience. A parent may put an infant's hands together and encourage her or him to say 'Jay' (a respectful greeting) in front of religious pictures. Later the child may become aware that a parent is observing a vrata and refraining from certain foods on a particular day of the week or month. In most families at least one member will practise devotion by lighting a dīvā (wick lamp), praying in front of a domestic shrine, repeating sacred syllables (such as names of deities or a mantra) with the help of beads, reading from a religious text or visiting a mandir to 'receive darśana'. Children are likely to be involved in pūjā to mark life-cycle rites and festivals. They hear the stories associated with particular celebrations.

Children learn too how to address and refer to others (both kin and fictive kin), with relationship words which convey affection and respect, e.g. (Hindi) 'māsī' for mother's sister or friend.

Caste

Caste used to determine children's nurture to a great extent. A potter's son and a carpenter's would learn different skills and the family's focus of religious devotion would also correspond to caste as well as local variation. In the twenty-first century many children's nurture is still inseparable from their parents' occupation, although this may not be directly related to caste.

In previous centuries, in the years between their mundan and upanayana (janeu ceremony) boys of brāhmāṇa caste would learn the Sanskrit necessary for conducting religious rites. Some would receive this instruction from a guru (teacher) in a gurukula (school).

Schooling in India

Access to state education in India is open to all regardless of caste, and it is 'secular' in the sense that all faiths are respected and that there are no specially designated religious education classes. However, aspects of Hindu tradition are integral to the calendar and the curriculum – there will be a holiday for Dīvālī, for example, elementary Sanskrit is taught and curriculum books include stories from Hindu tradition.

Supplementary classes

Formal religious nurture refers to the organised perpetuation of Hindu tradition through regular classes. Such provision is particularly characteristic of the diaspora in countries such as the United Kingdom and the United States. Parents in non-Hindu societies are concerned that the wider community does not reinforce Hindu culture. Supplementary classes are usually held at the weekend in a venue such as a school or a community centre. The curriculum may include tuition in an Indian language such as Gujarati, Hindi or Telegu, as parents consider this necessary for fuller participation in religious events and for making a stronger connection with India as well as for communication with relatives. There may be classes in music (tablā, harmonium, sitar, singing) and training in drama and dance (in regional or filmī styles) for cultural events which are held to mark festivals. Some children learn more classical dance styles such as Bhārata Nāṭyam and kathak.

Teachers of some supplementary classes prepare young Hindus to take part in competitions and to enter public examinations in Hinduism. Residential camps and gatherings for young people are sometimes arranged, and these stimulate students' interest in their tradition and affirm their sense of identity as Hindus.

Saṃpradāya

The content of devotional material in classes and camps will depend upon the organisation responsible. In some cases classes are established by the committee of a mandir or by followers of a saṃpradāya. Jackson and Nesbitt (1993: 154–58) illustrate the distinctive character of classes organised by the International Society for Krishna Consciousness (ISKCON) and by devotees of Sathya Sai Baba, as well as the informal nurture in Puṣṭi Mārga families (Jackson and Nesbitt 1993: 115–18). Pocock (1976) and Brear (1992) describe the formal nurture of young Gujaratis in Swami Narayana families.

Shakha

Nurture may have a political character. Since 1925 an all-male Hindu nationalist organisation, the Rashtriya Svayamsevak Sangh (National Volunteer Corps), has provided training through daily gatherings of each 'branch' (shakha) and through its camps (shabir). The shakha meeting combines prayer, physical exercise and ideological study. The members are divided into sections according to age: 6–10, 10–14, 14–28 and 29 and older. Outside India some Hindu cultural activities for young Hindus are organised by the related organisation Hindu Svayamsevak Sangh.

Research in the UK shows that many young Hindus are eager for opportunities for more structured learning. They are keen to discuss issues and seek answers to questions that arise in a plural, fast-changing society, there is interest in spirituality and they intend to encourage a sense of Hindu identity in the next generation. In the diaspora especially the internet increasingly contributes to nurture as a resource for information on Hindu tradition and a means of contact with individuals and organisations.

See also: **Brāhmaṇa; Cūḍākaraṇa; Dance; Darśana; Diaspora; Dīvālī; Drama; Guru; International Society for Krishna Consciousness; Internet; Jāti; Languages; Mandir; Music; Nāmakaraṇa; Narayana, Swami; Pūjā; Rashtriya Swayamsevak Sangh; Sai Baba, Sathya; Saṃpradāya; Saṃskāra; Upanayana; Varṇa; Vrata**

ELEANOR NESBITT

Further reading

Brear, D. 1992. 'Transmission of a Swaminarayan Hindu Scripture in the British East Midlands'. In R.B.Williams, ed., *A Sacred Thread: Modern Transmission of Hindu Traditions in India and Abroad*. Chambersburg, PA: Anima, 209–27.

Jackson, R. and E. Nesbitt. 1993. *Hindu Children in Britain*. Stoke on Trent: Trentham.

Pocock, D. 1976. 'Preservation of the Religious Life: Hindu Immigrants in England'. *Contributions to Indian Sociology* 10.2: 341–65.

RELIGIOUS SPECIALISTS

Religious specialists in Hinduism today range from powerful all-India figures like the Śaṅkarācāryas of the four monastic centres of Sringeri, Puri, Dvārakā and Badrinath, and global gurus like Sathya Sai Baba and Amritanandamayi, to brāhmaṇa priests, scholarly paṇḍits and ascetics, astrologers, exorcists, sorcerers, magicians, shamans, Tantric and Āyurvedic practitioners and New Age healers. Most religious specialists understand their roles and functions as timeless and governed by tradition and paraṃparā. Nevertheless, they, like millions of Hindus, are caught up in a tide of rapid change and the interplay of influences at work on society as a whole. Hindu revivalism, economic liberalisation and the growing prosperity of diasporic Hindus have had strong implications for their status and standing. Political ideology, government policies, administrative procedures and the decline of anti-Brahmanism have also been potent forces in shaping the prosperity and respect accorded them. The new media, particularly the internet, are today providing sites where the role of religious specialists is actively debated and where their services are advertised. A purely textual understanding of the roles of religious specialists will not enable us to understand this complexity. This discussion will indicate the historical development of the roles of priests and other religious specialists, but its principal emphasis will be to give some indication of their changing character and contemporary diversity.

Brāhmaṇas and priests

Brāhmaṇas or brāhmans are the traditional priests of Hinduism. Their superiority within the caste structure depends upon their traditional command of learning as given by their right to learn (adhyayana) and teach (adhyāpana), to sacrifice (yajana) and to preside over the sacrifices of others (yājana), and to give (dāna) and receive gifts (pragrahana or pratigraha). Brāhmaṇas have come to be partly assimilated with renouncers, so that the brāhmaṇa who carries out rituals for others and who receives gifts or payments is often seen as inferior to the brāhmaṇa who does not serve at all or is a scholar or teacher. The ideal brāhmaṇa should lead an austere life and regard ritual and teaching as a form of worship rather than as a livelihood or business. There are therefore constraints in the matter of earning by yājana and pratigraha. Moreover, teaching should be practiced as vidyā-dāna (the gift of learning) and its divine aspect safeguarded (cf. Sarasvati 1991: 68).

Brāhmaṇa priests have often been regarded in India with ambivalence. This ambivalence is ancient and has roots in sacred texts, but during the colonial period British administrators and missionaries often dismissed both priests and faqirs as parasitic and exploitative. Among professional brāhmaṇas, the poorest are often those connected with Vedic learning, temple service and religious functions. Ritual specialists who are attached to small, poor temples or shrines are often ill paid and receive little real respect. In post-Independence India there were periods when the way of life of many religious specialists, brāhmaṇa temple and pilgrimage priests, for example, seemed anachronistic and destined to disappear.

Throughout India brāhmaṇas are the family priests (kul purohita) of the upper castes and traditionally perform their ritual functions with a variety of other specialists, the barber, the washerman, etc. They are ritual technicians, specialists in performing rites that involve, refer to or derive from sacred literature and as such are bound to the world and the social order (Babb 1975: 210). They are called upon by their jajmāns (patrons) to preside over life-cycle rituals (saṃskāras) and other domestic rites because of their knowledge of text and ritual purity, but their presence is not essential to the rites as such. Among priestly brāhmaṇas, there are traditionally status gradations which correspond to the rank of the castes they serve (cf. Dumont 1972: 143). Similarly those who patronise brāhmaṇa priests gain prestige. More recently the presence of the brāhmaṇa priest at ceremonies may depend more upon the desire to have him there and the ability to pay than upon caste status (Babb 1975: 75). Traditionally priests received donations in kind, a fixed quantity of grain at harvest time and obligatory presents (often of money) at the time of major festivals and family ceremonies. They are also paid dakṣiṇa for particular ritual services. A brāhmaṇa priest is almost indispensable at the time of marriage celebrations (vivāha), but he may also perform other common life-cycle rituals, for example the naming ceremony on the tenth or twelfth day after birth (nāmakaraṇa), the shaving of the head ceremony (cūḍākaraṇa), investiture with the sacred thread (upanayana) and the death ritual (antyeṣṭi). He will also perform rituals for the health and moral and spiritual wellbeing of his clients.

There are also ritual specialists who deal with the pollution of death, witchcraft, malevolent ghosts (bhūta-preta), etc. These specialists often belong to low brāhmaṇa subgroups. Thus different kinds of caste specialist handle different aspects of the disposal of the physical remains of the dead, the posthumous fate of the soul and the purification of mourners (cf. Parry 1994: 4). The pure brāhmaṇa performs the ritual for the benign ancestor (pitṛ) and accepts pure offerings. The inauspicious Mahābrāhmaṇa funeral priests who embody or represent the preta perform the ritual for the preta and accept the impure donations of death. They participate in the death pollution (sutak) which afflicts their patrons and are in many contexts treated much like untouchables. The untouchable Dom funeral attendant superintends the cremation of the physical remains of the deceased. In parts of India low-caste specialists (e.g. Ḍakauts and Vedpatras) accept the inauspicious donations which rid the donor of the afflictions of the planet Saturn and those made at the time of eclipses, astronomical conjunctions that are said to be caused by the planets Rāhu and Ketu swallowing the sun and moon. Such donations are often believed to transfer sins and impurities away from the donor to the receiver and are therefore hard to 'digest'.

Pan-Hindu pilgrimage centres are densely settled by all kinds of religious specialists, priestly and ascetic, who transmit both śāstric (Sanskritic/Āgamic) and laukik (folk, popular) knowledge to their clients. Among the most highly respected are the learned paṇḍits and ascetics who are the guardians of Hindu textual traditions and act as the specialists and final authority in anything that concerns the textual tradition (dharmadhikārī). They cultivate, preserve and promote the classical cultural traditions (cf. Vidyarthi 1961: 91). While there are Sanskrit universities and pāthaśālās in India, there are also paṇḍits who still teach students under the traditional system of guru-śiṣya paramparā (Saraswati 1975: 19; Sarasvati 1991: passim). For example, Vārāṇasī has several universities that teach Sanskrit studies and Hindu philosophy, and pāthaśālās that transmit under the tutelage of a brāhmaṇa guru knowledge of the sacred scriptures and an ability to recite the Vedic mantras.

In such centres a large sacerdotal class caters particularly to the religious needs of pilgrims. At the core of traditional patterns of pilgrimage are the tīrtha purohitas or paṇḍās, who often claim to be autochthonous and whose relationships with their jajmāns continue from generation to generation. Their main duties are to tell the stories of the place, keep genealogical records, look after their pilgrims and perform rituals for them. These may be attenuated rites, which generally include pūjā and piṇḍa dāna (the offering of rice balls to departed ancestors). Some pilgrims also come for prāyaścitta (purification). Pilgrimage priests have often been attacked and criticised for their ignorance of the Sanskrit texts and of karmakāṇḍa. However, today, while many young paṇḍās have left their traditional occupation, a growing commitment to education means that some working paṇḍās have degrees and qualifications in Sanskrit. In pilgrimage centres like Haridvāra the paṇḍās 'own' many communities, regions or even states and regard it as their right to receive their dāna and dakṣiṇa. Their hereditary monopoly of donations is increasingly challenged by the multiplication of ashrams and the opening up of the priesthood. It should also be noted that ethnographers have noted the violence and stratagems of paṇḍās at particular tīrthas (cf. van der Veer 1988; Parry 1994).

There are many other religious specialists in the great pilgrimage centres of India. There are, for example, the karmakāṇḍīs, who make their living by performing rituals for others. These rituals may include the ordinary rituals performed by the paṇḍās but they may also refer to Vedic rituals – yajña, abhiṣeka and saṃskāra rituals. At jal tīrthas (water tīrthas) ghāṭiyās generally look after pilgrims' clothes when they bathe and put tilak marks on the foreheads of their clients. They may also help the pilgrims to perform pūjā of various kinds. They accept donations (dāna) at the ghāṭs on the Ganges, a practice which the *Śāstras* condemn, and as a result their profession is considered low. Unlike the paṇḍās, the karmakāṇḍīs, ghāṭiyās and pūjāris are not traditionally endogamous; nor do they adhere to their occupation hereditarily. The institution of paṇḍās often creates allied groups, for example gumāśtās (paid servants), bhandars and yātrawals (pilgrim 'hunters'). Associated with the brahmanic ritual complex are the florists, the barbers, the boatmen and the sellers of pūjā material and of articles required for the mortuary rites.

Religious specialists who function primarily as astrologers (jyotiṣī), preachers and storytellers (kathāvācaks), palmists or healers operate everywhere in India. The kathāvācaks transmit knowledge of the *Purāṇas* and the Epics by their oral retellings, and before the advent of modern media were crucial in maintaining continuity with the past. A few, like Morari Bapu, travel the world preaching, drawing vast crowds. Astrologers remain of great significance in the lives of many Hindus. They draw up the horoscopes of children after birth, and are consulted on all manner of occasions to determine the most auspicious times to undertake rituals, pilgrimage, business ventures, etc. They have a particularly important function at the time of marriage. Politicians often consult astrologers, and more generally the tradition of spiritual adviser to the ruler goes back to the Vedic notion of purohita, 'standing before the king' (Smith 2003: 168). Possibly the most infamous and colourful of modern astrologers is Chandraswami (b. 1949). A Tantric astrologer, he was the guru of Narasimha Rao (prime minister 1991–96).

Temple functionaries

Pūjāris, or temple priests, may be self-employed or employed by the temple management. In general they are not a hereditary group, although there are cases of priests possessing hereditary rights and privileges. Some priests own the temples in which they officiate, but often they are paid servants and their services can be dispensed with by the temple authorities. In most brahmanic shrines the brāhmaṇas are priests but there are cases of non-brāhmaṇas acting as priests. The temples of great deities like Viṣṇu and Śiva tend to attract more high-caste worshippers and are served by brāhmaṇa priests or pūjāris who make only vegetarian offerings and use Sanskrit as the ritual language.

The pūjāri is responsible for regular public worshipping (pūjā) of the gods before their images. One of his most important duties is to ensure the purity of the temple complex. He performs the daily rituals of the temple, leads hymn singing, offers oblations into the sacred fire and distributes the food offered during the worship as prasāda. He will also maintain the temple's ritual cycle, which includes periodic festivals such as Dīvālī, Holī, Navarātrī (Durgā Pūjā), etc. The temples of many other deities are patronised by low castes. They generally have non-brāhmaṇa priests who make both vegetarian and non-vegetarian offerings (bali) and use vernacular languages in ritual.

Research in the Mīnākṣī temple at Madurai shows that the brāhmaṇa priests who serve Mīnākṣī and Sundareśvara seldom worship the little deities enshrined near the temple (e.g. C.J. Fuller 1992: 96–99). In all Mīnākṣī temple rituals, the food offered to the gods is vegetarian and animal sacrifices are never performed, though certain vegetable sacrifices are understood as surrogate blood sacrifices. By contrast, Cellattammaṉ, a village goddess who is worshipped nearby, is served by non-brāhmaṇa priests who sacrifice pigs to the goddess. The great deities' independence is partly institutionalised in the ritual domain because the two categories of deities have separate priesthoods and different modes of worship. Nevertheless, both systems uphold brahmanic hegemony (C.J. Fuller 1992: 99).

Brāhmaṇa priests may sometimes preside over sacrifices to fierce goddesses like Kālī, Durgā and Caṇḍī while a non-brāhmaṇa beheads the sacrificial animals. However, in a reversal of orthodox brahmanical Hinduism, brāhmaṇas who act as priests in Tantric temples may participate in ritual violence. At Tarapith temple in Bengal, which is dedicated to Tārā, several goat sacrifices occur almost every day. In this temple, which is governed by the *Tantras*, brāhmaṇa priests decapitate the animals and afterwards offer some of the blood to the goddess in a short pūjā. Tantrism's fundamental premise is the reversal of conventional religious values, so that what is normally proscribed as impure, inauspicious and abominable is eulogised as pure, auspicious and desirable. Hence the formula for Tantric rituals which require the offering of meat, fish, alcohol and parched grain and involve worshipping the goddess in the form of a naked woman with whom devotees have sexual intercourse (C.J. Fuller 1992: 87).

Sherma (2000: 48) claims that popular Śāktism functions in terms of a 'theology of reciprocity' which revolves round a reciprocal relationship between worshipper and deity. It gives rise to the conventional male priest-mediated temple-centred tradition, which continues to be the most visible and accessible form of Śāktism. In contrast, the Tantric ritual performed by the individual worshipper involves a 'theology of identification' between self and the Divine. It is designed to evoke a sense of sacred presence and heighten the awareness of Śakti within one's own mind–body complex. Sherma argues that there is a correlation throughout Hindu history between the rise of movements that emphasise the feminine divine and the emergence of female religious teachers and preceptors. She notes that that the majority of contemporary Hindu women gurus of international status are primarily worshippers of the Great Goddess (Sherma 2000: 49).

Women priests

Today there are attempts being made to set up schools of karmakāṇḍa which are inclusive and which abandon or reinterpret the hereditary jajmāni system. There are sometimes tensions when reformist movements initiate low castes or women with the sacred thread and permit them to conduct ritual as this hits at the hereditary monopoly of those brāhmaṇas who feel that they have an ancestral entitlement. Women, like śūdras and untouchables, were traditionally ineligible to hear the recitation of the Veda. They were not invested with the sacred thread and have rarely exercised a priestly role. Women were seen as impure at the time of menstruation and childbirth and were not permitted to visit temples, take part in religious rites or prepare the family food. Death was particularly inauspicious for the woman whose husband died before her. Women did not make arrangements for funerals or perform the last rites (antim saṃskāra). Nevertheless, the lack of a priestly role does not mean that women were unimportant, particularly in the domestic sphere, and a few women did find an escape from conventional roles in religion. Female ascetics left their families to seek god. Devadāsīs, dancers who served the gods of Hindu temples, were trained in the arts of dancing, singing and ritual. However, their identification with prostitution attracted the attention of reformers from the 1870s onwards (Forbes 1996/1999: 182) and the Devdasi Act of 1919 made the institution technically illegal.

Today, despite resistance, widespread changes are taking place. Increasing numbers of women are recognised for their knowledge of Sanskrit, the Veda and other scriptures. This trend has been growing since the nineteenth century when the Arya Samaj led by Lal Devraj began to teach girls to recite the Veda and perform Vedic rituals. Other groups also promoted this tradition (e.g. Sarada Devi Mission, Brahma Vidya Mandir, Kanya Kumari Sthan and Udyan Mangal Karalaya) (Young 2002: 28). Moreover, in large cities like Pune, Chennai and Mumbai women priests (strī purohitās) are performing rites at religious ceremonies, marriages, thread initiations and cremations. Women pioneers have established themselves as highly qualified priests in towns like Hyderabad and Kolkata. In urban areas where priesthood has become a profession like any other, the gender of the practitioner is increasingly irrelevant. Women, no longer exclusively defined by concepts such as purity and pollution or auspiciousness and inauspiciousness, may find that the demand for women priests outstrips that for men. The Arya Samaji Arya Pratinidhi Sabha organises courses throughout the world (e.g. in North America and South Africa), which train both men and women for the Vedic priesthood. The Vishwa Hindu Parishad (VHP) has also invested much energy in training programmes for paṇḍits and priests. It was reported in the *Times of India* 1999 that in a major step towards gender parity and social justice the VHP had offered to train women of all castes to become priests.

Dalit priests

The Supreme Court declared in 2002 that any Hindu, regardless of caste, has a right to officiate as a priest, either in temples or at ceremonies. This annihilated formally the millennia-old birth-based caste rights and privileges. However, it is unlikely that the temples of India, whether at Tirupati, Puri, Vaishno Devi, Ujjain or the millions of small temples, will open up the job of priest to people of all castes. The Indian Constitution states that public temples must be open to all Hindus whatever their class or caste. However, even today, dalits are not infrequently forbidden entry to Hindu temples or shrines administered by brāhmaṇas on the grounds that they would pollute them.

Thus by no means all who officiate as priests in Hinduism are brāhmaṇas. Dalits, who have been traditionally denied access to temples and other holy places, have been forced to build their own temples and shrines. Their priests and gurus are often drawn from among themselves (cf. Lipner 1994: 115–16). The ideologies and theologies developed by dalit leaders today show how far they have come from being harijans. *Why I Am Not a Hindu* by Kancha Ilaiha (1996) shows an activist's understanding of the power of rituals to construct an oppressive hierarchy. He claims that dalitbahujans (dalits and backwards classes) are concerned with their own village gods and goddesses and local deities, who have nothing in common with the gods and goddesses of the Hindu pantheon (Ilaiah 1996: 71–101). Ilaiah Kancha also asserts that in the relationship between the Hindu priest and the dalitbahujans there is no spirituality. The relationship is that between exploiter and exploited (Ilaiah 1996: 23). For Kancha Ilaiah and many other dalit activists, the desire to incorporate dalits and tribals into a Hindu social system simply reveals the desire to maintain a hegemonic social structure.

Priests, shamans and healers

Hinduism is frequently portrayed in terms of a system that is highly abstract, philosophical and speculative. Less well-known features of popular Hinduism are ignored. Thus the literature on Hinduism often neglects fundamental religious concerns of many Hindus (cf. Dwyer 2003: 140). One of these concerns is supernatural affliction, as well as its avoidance, treatment and cure. Research carried out by Dwyer, Opler (1958), Babb (1975), C.J. Fuller (1992), Parry (1994) and Assayag and Tarabout (1999) appears to confirm this view (cf. Dwyer 2003: 141). Scholars have often made a sharp distinction between two types of practitioner – the ritual expert on the one hand and the curer on the other, the latter being referred to by a large variety of terms such as shaman, exorcist, diagnostician, oracle, diviner, magician and prophet.

Babb (1975: 179) distinguished between the more prestigious textual complex in the hands of the hereditary priests, usually brāhmaṇas, who are exemplars of ritual purity, and the local complex in the hands of ritualist-exorcists, often shamanistic, whose status is achieved rather than ascribed and whose origins are generally in the lower castes. The Baiga, for example, is a type of priest-exorcist who specialises in diagnostics, healing and the worship of village deities. He is the priest of the village deities, who are less demanding of purity and may be dealt with in a less elaborated ritual style. The Baiga has a special relationship with these deities, who warn him in dream of disease or misfortune coming to the village. The deities enter directly into the world and affairs of human beings. They are likely to possess their worshippers, while the goddess voluntarily enters the body of human beings in the form of illness. Neglecting them may result in mutual neglect or even angry retaliation. The Baiga also has knowledge of protective and curative mantras that give him access to, and a degree of control over, certain benevolent and harmful deities and spirits, and is able to cure illnesses attributed to witchcraft or possession by malignant ghosts.

Dwyer challenges this dichotomous understanding by an analysis of the roles played by the priests and healers in the famous temple of Mehndipur near Bharatpur in Rajasthan. He finds that their roles are different though overlapping. While the priests are pre-eminent and their practices ritually superior, the hierarchical relationship between priests and healers is based upon interdependence and complementarity. Both provide services that are often said by pilgrims to be crucial for sufferers afflicted by spirits or other malevolent supernaturals. The priest ensures communion between pilgrim and deity, while the bhagat or healer brings divinity directly into relation with the sufferer.

Different regions of India have their own unique cultures, rituals, art, music, dance and theatre. In South India, for example, in art forms such as teyyam or muṭīyēṯṯu the deity is really present, and Tantric rituals and practices become the basis for healing. Features of Sanskrit theatre are combined with ritual arts whose essential features are possession and an earthy ecstatic religion. The agency which enables the rites to take place effectively is divine, not human (cf. Caldwell 1999: passim.; Freeman 1993; F. Fuller 1993).

Kakar interestingly argues that Indian society is organised round the primacy of the therapeutic, and that paradigms of illness are often metaphysical, psychological and social rather than exclusively biomedical (Kakar 1984: 277). In this respect, healers from many religious traditions on the subcontinent display strong similarities. Healing cults surrounding charismatic pīrs (wise elders) or saints often cut across the division between Muslim, Sikh and Hindu. Three groups of therapists are discerned by Kakar. First, there are the traditional physicians: the vaids of the traditional Indian system of medicine, Āyurveda; siddhas, saints who have knowledge of healing or who have acquired supernatural powers; and the hakīm, practitioners of the Islamic medical tradition (unāni). Second, there are the palmists, astrologers, herbalists, diviners, sorcerers and a variety of shamans whose therapies draw upon both classical and folk and popular sources. Third are the ascetic and lay specialists who trace their lineage in the various ancient spiritual traditions of India.

Ascetics

There are two aspects of brahmanic revelation: organisation of the world and renunciation of the world (cf. Biardeau 1989: 29). Post-Vedic texts reveal a turning away from the ritual religion of the Veda despite the dogma that the Veda remains authoritative. Increasingly the religious goal is identified as liberation (mokṣa) from the eternal cycle of rebirth (saṃsāra). From the sixth century BCE onwards Jainism and Buddhism were also influential in extolling the renouncers. It is often said that the ritual specialist is engaged in activity which links him to the cosmic moral order of the universe and to the worldly duties of the householder (gārhasthya). The ascetic who has relinquished the world is primarily concerned with the fourth aim of humanity, mokṣa, and with the goal of liberation. While this may be generally true, we find that many married priests practise renunciation, while celibates of all kinds work in the world. In fact the renouncer who 'leaves' the world does not escape complementarity with others who are in the world. Renouncers are dependent on their lay devotees for alms, acknowledge a duty to teach the dharma and generally interact freely and frequently with householders. For their part, members of the general public often seek out the assistance of the ascetic in their own lives, both materially and spiritually. Some are initiated into a spiritual order by an ascetic who becomes the householder's guru. Wandering sādhus also attract crowds of people eager for their darśana. For many Hindus the power of renunciation, especially sexual renunciation, is associated with the acquisition and control of power which may be used to heal. Through the heat of his or her austerities the ascetic acquires super-abundant potency. The blessings of an aghorī sādhu (traditionally regarded as necrophagous), for example, are often believed to bestow benefits including wealth, healing and fertility (cf. Parry 1994: 259).

During the Hindu Renaissance, the role of the ascetic came under great scrutiny. Vivekananda, while proclaiming Ramakrishna's teachings, put much greater emphasis on service and mission. Today the drift to settled communities like those of the Ramakrishna Math and Mission continues. Many ascetics now live permanently in maths or maṭhas (monasteries), ashrams or āśramas (religious communities) or akhāṛas (headquarters of monastic orders). Orders of ascetics like the powerful Daśnāmi orders, whose members have historically played a great role in trade, military engagements and as landlords, are also changing. While the role of militant sādhus (Nāgas) has become a matter of pageantry, they nevertheless continue to uphold traditional values and to protect properties, temples and shrines. Many traditional monasteries, such as those of the Smārtas, Śrī Vaiṣṇavas, Madhvas and Liṅgāyats (Vīraśāivas), use their wealth and prestige to promote education and social welfare.

Today Hindu asceticism is adapting itself to the redefinition of the role of women and the demand for equal rights. The number of female ascetics remains much smaller than that of males but they are increasingly visible and powerful. In the past the ascetic tradition has often excluded women, identifying them with sexuality, worldliness and domesticity (Sherma 2000: 27). Renunciation was seldom considered acceptable for young women, whose destiny was wifehood and motherhood. Female ascetics belonged to traditional ascetic orders but remained under the protection of men. Today self-confidence among Indian women, particularly among the urban middle classes, is strengthening. Now women ascetics become the leaders of their orders or start new ones. A few head wealthy global organisations. Others run private schools and oversee property. Some female renouncers (known popularly as Mātājis, 'Mothers') are self-supporting through their healing and ritual activities and are often well respected and sought after in their communities (Erndl 2000: 94).

Increasingly women are coming to the fore as gurus, maṇḍaleśvars (spiritual preceptors) and ācāryas (religious teachers). Some leaders of important saṃpradāyas have transferred their spiritual authority to a woman when they died. Sarada Devi, the Mother, Daya Mata, Godaveri Mataji, Gayatri Devi and Gurumayi Chidvilasanda all inherited the mantle of renowned male gurus. In 1954 the Sri Sarada Math was founded as a female ascetic order. Run by female ascetics who give saṃnyāsa to other women, it is a very special 'symbol of women's rise to strength', symbolising a soft revolution against male hegemony, while simultaneously remaining traditional (cf. Rustau 2003: 166). Among the Brahma Kumaris, daughters of Brahmā, leadership is invested in a group of nine women known as dadis, sisters. Some women worshipped as the godhead have achieved international recognition: Anandamayi Ma (1896–1982), Amritanandamayi Ma (b. 1954) and Meera Devi or Mother Meera (b. 1960). Three of the main female leaders of the Bharatiya Janata Party (BJP) – Vijayraje Scindia, Sadhvi Rithambara and Uma Bharati – present themselves as celibate, with the associations of purity, spiritual power and morality (Young 2002: 24).

Gurus

The spiritual abodes or ashrams of gurus may be a tiny cave or a palatial personal growth resort, but the importance of the guru cannot be overstated. The teacher or guru is the dispeller of darkness and an enlightened being who has realised the true nature of reality. The function of the guru is to enable the celā or śiṣya (disciple) to discover his or her true nature, to conquer his senses and to make him free. For many Hindus there is no one higher than the guru and it is devotion to the guru that takes the devotee across the ocean of saṃsāra. The guru himself or herself need not be learned or teach systematically, and may be beyond any notion of character and conduct. The guru's may be a world of inner experience. However, the guru may also be an ācārya, someone who lives a disciplined life according to the acaras, customs and practices governed by the śāstra and saṃpradāya to which he belongs.

Today in India there are many gurus (generally renouncers) who follow traditional teachings. Charismatic godmen with international followings have been active since the 1960s. Many have mediated Hindu traditions to the West. They include Maharishi Mahesh Yogi, Guru Maharaj Ji (now often known simply as Prem Ravat), Bhagwan Shree Rajneesh/Osho, Maharaj Charan Singh of the Radhasoami Satsang and Sathya Sai Baba. Some of these gurus are internationally venerated and have influential devotees and organisations which are immensely powerful. Sathya Sai Baba, the most popular of all living gurus, has strong ethical and philosophical teachings, which are quite traditional, and a strong humanitarian programme. Other gurus have established their organisational centres outside India. For example, Swami Chidvilasananda or Gurumayi (1955–), the successor to Swami Muktananda, is based in New York State but visits her ashrams in India and gives śaktipat dīkṣā (the transmission or bestowal of grace or divine śakti) to thousands of devotees each year.

A spiritual renaissance in the 1990s produced gurus like Sri Sri Ravi Shankar, Mata Nirmala Devi of Sahaja Yoga and Kerala's Mata Amritanandamayi, who have built institutional empires. Such gurus appeal to middle-class devotees, who value the choice, freedom and flexibility offered, and whose own skills and capabilities are used to enable the organisation to grow (Warrier 2003: 272). Sri Sri Ravi Shankar, for example, has an international following, and his foundation Art of Living (AOL) claims to be the world's largest non-governmental organisation. The Amritanandamayi Mission likewise owns and manages schools, orphanages, management and engineering colleges and computer training institutes (Warrier 2003: 256).

According to some media commentators (see *India Today*'s cover story in July 2003; Chopra and Raval 2003) the global gurus of the 1960s and 1990s have been succeeded by a plethora of new gurus who are 'trendy, urbane and educated', and who use contemporary and modern language to give ancient philosophy life. Their spirituality is less about liberation in the next life than mind–body–spirit harmony in this. Such gurus often claim to combine the best of Eastern wisdom and Western knowledge. Thus Pandit Rajmani Tigunait PhD, the successor to Swami Rama and spiritual head of the Himalayan Institute, stresses a holistic approach to health and well-being and advocates the natural way to stress-free living. There also appears to be something of a spiritual globalisation. Teachings combine elements of Haṭha Yoga, meditation, Yoga philosophy, psychology, Tantra and mantra, Āyurveda, astrology, palmistry, Vāstu (the art or science of building), gemology, aura healing, tarot cards and graphology.

Contemporary changes and diasporic Hinduism

The rapid social changes in contemporary India in education, employment, economic liberalisation and consumerism, communications, media and global accessibility have had huge impact on the status and function of many religious specialists. The rise of Hindu nationalism and the political preoccupation with religion and religious concerns have gone hand in hand with attempts to promote brahmanical Sanskritic Hinduism. Fuller, in his excellent study of the renewal of the priesthood, shows how nationalist modernity and religious traditionalism mutually reconstruct and reinforce each other. Religious specialists have been caught up in the multidimensional process of modernisation. There have been in many states attempts to improve priestly education and ritual performance. Commitment to a notion of Sanskritic education as professional training by many priestly and ascetic communities and the interplay between traditionalist and modernist attitudes to their professions are transforming some specialists into 'authentic representatives of modern Indian society' (C.J. Fuller 2003: 167). Two critical factors have assisted this transformation: first, the growth of an Indian urban prosperous middle class which is prepared to spend money on rituals and, second, the development of an affluent Indian diaspora which has offered opportunities for priests to work abroad. They have done much to reverse the demoralisation experienced by many religious specialists in the post-Independence era and generated a rethinking of tradition.

In diasporic Hinduism tremendous vitality and energy have been expended in building temples. This in turn has generated a great demand for trained priests. In the United States many of these priests serve deities in multi-use ecumenical temples where priests and devotees drawn from very different devotional traditions worship together. However, the internal heterogeneity of Hinduism may also lead to 'retraditionalisation' rather than changes or innovations (e.g. in Europe). In some countries (e.g. Malaysia or East African states) the trend towards regional-linguistic, sectarian and caste-based temples is marked (see, e.g. Baumann 1999: 59–79; Younger 1999: 367–85). Where Hindus have links with aggressively Hindu organisations like the VHP, the Rashtriya Swayamsevak Sangh (RSS), and the BJP, there is often a unifying approach to the diverse Hindu ethnic and religious groupings. Such an approach emphasises the role of religious specialists in transmitting values, Hindu mores and customs to the younger generation.

The roles of diasporic priests, ascetics, astrologers, etc. are being shaped not only by the particular needs of the immigrant communities, but by the values and structures of the host community. There is constant change and adaptation. For example, in Canada and the USA, Hindu worship is often congregational, and held on Sundays. Children may attend Sunday school programmes. Perhaps more fundamentally, the Hindu way of life changes so as to be perceived as a discrete faith in the modern Western sense (Baumann 1999: 71). As Brockington comments, the character of the tradition changes 'as it becomes something consciously learnt about rather than absorbed naturally, with a concomitant shift from practice to doctrine' (Brockington 1992: 188). Today there are guides and networks in New York, Toronto and London which assist non-resident Indians (NRIs) in selecting Hindu astrologers and priests just as they would find entertainment, cultural associations, dentists, grocery stores, gurdwārās and temples, travel agents, etc. There are Hindu societies and centres for Hindus in most continents of the world. Those in the USA, UK and Canada often provide religious, cultural and social services and have Sunday programmes which include havan (a sacrificial ceremony in which burnt offerings are made) and pūjā, bhajans, pravacan (religious discourse, sermon) and bhoj (offering of food, feast). And while the language of paṇḍit, jajmān (sacrificer or ritual patron), dāna and dakṣiṇa may remain the same, the functions and even rituals are often reinterpreted in countries where Hinduism is not the dominant faith. In countries like Australia organisational structures have developed partly in response to the growing appeal of Hinduism, yoga and meditation among the youth in the larger community. Increasingly, ashrams, mandirs and yoga centres have their own websites which include profiles of religious specialists. They give information on how to book a priest for private functions and suggest minimum amounts of dakṣiṇa to be offered to the priest for pūjās, marriage ceremonies, etc.

In previous generations Hindus who settled outside India were often acutely conscious of their need for trained priests who could perform pūjā and life-crisis rituals. This has given great impetus to training courses for priests. Organisations like the Hindu Heritage Pratishthan have initiated the training of priests who are brāhmaṇas, have studied Sanskrit and possess a working knowledge of English. Today it is still common in the UK and America for trained brāhmaṇa priests to come from India with knowledge of Sanskritic mantras and experience of performing rituals in India. They increasingly possess qualifications which show mastery of the scriptures. In some temples the tendency is for English-speaking priests to be preferred where possible and they are valued for their ability not only to perform the rituals, play the harmonium and sing bhajans but to nurture community projects and programmes. The residential priest may combine the roles of a religious teacher (ācārya), domestic priest (purohita), temple priest (pūjāri), ritual specialist (karmakaṇḍīn), funeral priest (mahāpatra), astrologer (jyotiṣī) and possibly healer (Baumann 1999: 69). He may be requested to perform the rites of passage for the entire community. He may also teach religious classes and Sanskrit, or take classes in Hindi, Kannada, Gujarati, Tamil, etc. He may even become a central community figure, taking on the role of hospital chaplain, media spokesperson and interfaith representative. In some large temples, however, the priest's role remains a more or less exclusively ritual one; members of the elected management committee become the principal spokespersons for the community. In countries where Hinduism is not dominant, global saṃpradāyas like the International Society for Krishna Consciousness (ISKCON) often speak nationally on behalf of Hindus in general. ISKCON prides itself on its standard of worship and has developed an elaborate training college for priests. Western devotees are initiated as brāhmaṇas, wear the sacred thread and tilak (Vaiṣṇava mark on forehead) and take care of the deities in the temples. They also have ascetics who are the initiating gurus.

Paradoxically there has also been a specialisation of function. In many areas pūjās, homas and other Hindu ceremonies are performed by paṇḍits who advertise regionally and nationally. Astrologers promote themselves to an international market as consultants for life charts, forecasts, compatibility matches, astrological problems and gemology. In Britain there are marriage consultants who will advise on every aspect of the ceremonies, including the appointment of the priest. There are also professional Indian funeral directors who will make all the funeral arrangements, book the services of a priest and arrange for the disposal of the ashes of the dead. Ashes may be stored in their chapel of rest or scattered in a crematorium garden of rest or in a river. One comprehensive service includes the delivery of ashes worldwide and the dispersal of ashes in the River Ganges.

The circumstances that push large numbers of Hindus into religious occupations and act as barriers to the aspirations of millions of others are slowly being challenged. In India lower-caste Hindus, and particularly dalits, are finding a voice. More Hindu women who become religious specialists have real choices and multiple role models from which to choose. Diasporic Hindus in countries like Britain and America have increasing access to visiting religious specialists, from Vedic scholars to Arya Samaji activists. The role of the enlightened guru is often assuming increasing importance in meeting the challenge of restructuring traditional ritual and pūjā. As remarkable is the steady multiplication worldwide of indigenous teachers and practitioners of yoga, Sanskritic learning, Āyurveda, astrology, karmakāṇḍa, Tantra. There are also inspired teachers of drama, film, music and dance who draw greatly upon Hindu religion, iconography and mythology.

See also: **Abhiṣeka; Anandamayi Ma; Antyeṣṭi; Arya Samaj; Āśram(a) (religious community); Āyurveda; Bhajan; Bharatiya Janata Party; Bhūtas; Brahmā; Brāhmaṇas; Brahmanism; Buddhism, relationship with Hinduism; Caste; Cūḍākaraṇa; Dalits; Dāna; Darśana; Devadāsī; Dharma; Diaspora; Dīvālī; Durgā; Durgā Pūjā; Dvārakā; Gārhasthya; Guru; Haridvāra; Haṭha Yoga; Hinduism, modern and contemporary; Holī; International Society for Krishna Consciousness; Internet; Jainism, relationship with Hinduism; Jyotiṣa; Kālī and Caṇḍī; Madhva; Madurai; Maharaj Ji, Guru (Prem Rawat); Maharishi Mahesh Yogi; Mandir; Mantra; Maṭha; Meditation; Mīnākṣī; Mokṣa; Motherhood; Muktananda, Swami; Nāmakaraṇa; Nationalism; Paṇḍit; Paraṃparā; Pitṛs; Pretas; Pūjā; Purāṇas; Purohita; Radhasoami Satsang; Rāhu; Rajneesh, Bhagwan Shree; Ramakrishna, Sri; Ramakrishna Math and Mission; Rashtriya Swayamsevak Sangh; Religious nurture; Sādhu; Sahaja Yoga; Sai Baba, Sathya; Śakti; Śāktism; Saṃhitā; Saṃnyāsa; Saṃpradāya; Saṃsāra; Saṃskāra; Śaṅkarācāryas; Sarada Devi; Śiṣya; Śiva; Strīdharma; Tantras; Tārā; Tīrthayātrā; Upanayana; Vārāṇasi; Vīraśāivas; Vishwa Hindu Parishad; Viṣṇu; Vivāha; Vivekananda, Swami; Women's rites; Yoga**

ANNA KING

Further reading

Assayag, J. and G. Tarabout (eds). 1999. *La Possession en Asie du Sud: Parole, corps, territoire*. [Possession in South Asia: Speech, Body, Territory]. Paris: Editions de L'Ecole des Hautes Etudes en Sciences Sociales.

Babb, L.A. 1975. *The Divine Hierarchy: Popular Hinduism in Central India*. New York: Columbia University Press.

Baumann, M. 1999. 'The Hindu Diasporas in Europe and an Analysis of Key Diasporic Patterns'. In T.S. Rukmani, ed., *Hindu Diaspora: Global Perspectives*. Montreal: Department of Religious Studies, Concordia University, 59–79.

Biardeau, M. 1989. *Hinduism: The Anthropology of a Civilisation*. New Delhi: Oxford University Press.

Brockington, J. 1992. *Hinduism and Christianity*. London: Macmillan Press.

Caldwell, S. 1999. *Oh Terrifying Mother: Sexuality, Violence and Worship of the Goddess Kali*. New Delhi: Oxford University Press.

Cenkner, W. 1983. *A Tradition of Teachers: Sankara and the Jagadgurus Today*. Delhi: Motilal Banarsidass.

Chopra, A. and S. Raval. 2003. 'Guru Chic'. *India Today* (14 July) 11(28): 10–17.

Davis, R.H. 1991. *Ritual in an Oscillating Universe: Worshipping Siva in Medieval India*. Princeton, NJ: Princeton University Press.

Diehl, C.G. 1956. *Instrument and Purpose: Studies on Rites and Rituals in South India*. Lund: CWK Gleerup.

Dumont, L. 1972. *Homo Hierarchicus: The Caste System and Its Implications*. London: Paladin.

Dwyer, G. 2003. *The Divine and the Demonic: Supernatural Affliction and Its Treatment in North India*. London: RoutledgeCurzon.

Erndl, K.M. 2000. 'Is Shakti Empowering for Women? Reflections on Feminism and the Hindu Goddess'. In A. Hiltebeitel and K.M. Erndl, eds, *Is the Goddess a Feminist: The Politics of South Asian Goddesses*. Sheffield: Sheffield Academic Press, 91–103.

Falk, N.A. 1995. '*Shakti* Ascending: Hindu Women, Politics and Religious Leadership during the Nineteenth and Twentieth Centuries'. In R.D. Baird, ed., *Religion in Modern India*, 3rd edn. New Delhi: Manohar, 298–334.

Flood, G. 1996. *An Introduction to Hinduism*. Cambridge: Cambridge University Press.

Forbes, G. 1996/1999. *Women in Modern India*. Cambridge: Cambridge University Press.

Freeman, J.R. 1993. 'Performing Possession: Ritual and Consciousness in the Teyyam Complex of Northern Kerala'. In H. Bruckner, L. Lutze and A. Malik, eds, *Flags of Fame: Studies in South Asian Folk Culture*. Delhi: Manohar, 109–38.

Fuller, C.J. 1979. 'Gods, Priests and Purity: On the Relation Between Hinduism and the Caste System'. *Man* (n.s.) 14: 459–76.

Fuller, C.J. 1984. *Servants of the Goddess: The Priests of a South Indian Temple*. Cambridge: Cambridge University Press.

Fuller, C.J. 1992. *The Camphor Flame: Popular Hinduism and Society in India*. Princeton, NJ: Princeton University Press.

Fuller, C.J. 2003. *The Renewal of the Priesthood*. Princeton, NJ and Oxford: Princeton University Press.

Fuller, F. 1993. 'Pierced by Murugan's Lance: The Symbolism of Vow Fulfilment'. In L.B.Boyer, R.M. Boyer and S.M. Sonnenberg, eds, *The Psychoanalytic Study of Society: Essays in Honor of Alan Dundes*, vol. 18. Hillsdale, NJ: Analytic Press, 277–98.

Hiltebeitel, A. and K.M. Erndl (eds). 2000. *Is the Goddess a Feminist: The Politics of South Asian Goddesses*. Sheffield: Sheffield Academic Press.

Ilaiah, K. 1996. *Why I Am Not a Hindu: A Sudra Critique of Hindutva Philosophy, Culture and Political Philosophy*. Calcutta: Samya.

Kakar, S. 1984. *Shamans, Mystics and Doctors: A Psychological Inquiry into India and Its Healing Traditions*. Hemel Hempstead: Unwin Paperbacks.

Leslie, I.J. (ed.). 1991. *Roles and Rituals for Hindu Women*. Delhi: Motilal Banarsidass.

Leslie, I.J. 2003. *Authority and Meaning in Indian Religions: Hinduism and the Case of Valmiki*. Aldershot: Ashgate.

Lipner, J.S. 1994. *Hindus: Their Religious Beliefs and Practices*. London: Routledge.

Madan, T.N. 1987. *Non-renunciation: Themes and Interpretations of Hindu Culture*. Delhi: Oxford University Press.

Monier-Williams, M. 1899. *A Sanskrit–English Dictionary: Etymologically and Philologically Arranged with Special Reference to Cognate Indo-European Languages*. Oxford: Clarendon.

Opler, M.E. 1958. 'Spirit Possession in a Rural Area of Northern India'. In W. Lessa and E. Vogt, eds, *Reader in Comparative Religion*. Evanston, IL: Row, Peterson & Co., 553–56.

Pandey, R.B. 1969. *Hindu Samskaras: Socio-religious Study of the Hindu Sacraments*. Delhi: Motilal Banarsidass.

Parry, J. 1994. *Death in Banaras*. Cambridge: Cambridge University Press.

Rustau, H. 2003. 'The Hindu Woman's Right to *Samnyasa*: Religious Movements and the Gender Question: The Sri Sarada Math and the Ramakrishna Sarada Mission'. In A. Copley, ed., *Hinduism in Public and Private: Reform, Hindutva, Gender, and Sampradaya*.

New Delhi: Oxford University Press, 143–72.

Sarasvati, Svami Chandrasekharendra. 1991. *Voice of the Guru: The Guru Tradition*. Bombay: Bharatiya Vidya Bhavan.

Saraswati, B. 1975. *Kashi: Myth and Reality of a Classical Cultural Tradition*. Simla: Indian Institute of Advanced Study.

Sharma, A. (ed.). 2002. *Women in Indian Religions*. New Delhi: Oxford University Press.

Sherma, R.D. 2000. '*Sa Ham* – I Am She: Woman as Goddess'. In A. Hiltebeitel and K.M. Erndl, eds, *Is the Goddess a Feminist: The Politics of South Asian Goddesses*. Sheffield: Sheffield Academic Press, 24–51.

Smith, D. 2003. *Hinduism and Modernity*. Oxford: Blackwell.

Srinivas, M.N. 1965. *Religion and Society among the Coorgs of South India*. London: Asia Publishing House.

van der Veer, P. 1988. *Gods on Earth: The Management of Religious Experience and Identity in a North Indian Pilgrimage Centre*. London: Athlone Press.

Vidyarthi, L.P. 1961. *The Sacred Complex of Hindu Gaya*. Bombay: Asia Publishing House.

Warrier, M. 2003. 'The *Seva* Ethic and the Spirit of Institution Building in the Mata Amritanandamayi Mission'. In A. Copley, ed., *Hinduism in Public and Private: Reform, Hindutva, Gender, and Sampradaya*. New Delhi: Oxford University Press, 254–89.

Wiser, W.H. 1936. *The Hindu Jajmani System*. Lucknow: Lucknow Publishing House.

Young, K. 2002. 'Women and Hinduism'. In A. Sharma, ed., *Women in Indian Religions*. New Delhi: Oxford University Press, 3–37.

Younger, P. 1999. 'Behind Closed Doors: The Practice of Hinduism in East Africa'. In T. S. Rukmani, ed., *Hindu Diaspora Global Perspectives*. Montreal: Concordia University, 367–85.

RENOU, LOUIS (1896–1966)

French Sanskritist and historian of religions. Renou first studied Sanskrit alone, and then with Sylvain Lévi. He received his doctorate for work on the Vedic hymns and on Ptolemy's geography of India. He was professor of Sanskrit at Lyon from 1925 to 1928 and afterward at the École des Hautes Études in Paris and the Sorbonne. A prolific scholar who contributed to many fields, Renou's primary concerns remained with the *Ṛgveda* and Vyākaraṇa. He insisted that the Vedic hymns be understood on their own terms, rather than by reference to later commentarial literature or to their social context, of which, he wrote, we know virtually nothing. Although left incomplete at the time of his death, his prose translation of the *Ṛgveda* into French (Renou 1955–69) includes more than 600 hymns. Among his works on Vyākaraṇa are a translation of Pāṇini's grammar (Renou 1948–54) and a Sanskrit grammar (Renou 1930).

See also: **Hinduism, history of scholarship; Pāṇini; Saṃhitā; Veda; Vyākaraṇa**

WILL SWEETMAN

Further reading

Renou, L. 1930. *Grammaire sanscrite* [Sanskrit Grammar]. Paris: Librairie d'Amérique et d'Orient Adrien-Maison-neuve.

Renou, L. 1948–54. *La Grammaire de Pāṇini: Traduite du Sanskrit avec des extraits des commentaires indigènes* [Pāṇini's grammar: translated from Sanskrit with extracts from Indian commentaries], 3 vols. Paris: C. Klincksieck.

Renou, L. 1954. *The Civilization of Ancient India*. Calcutta: Susil Gupta. Originally published in French, 1950.

Renou, L. 1955–69. *Etudes védiques et pāṇinéennes* [Vedic and Pāṇinian studies]. Paris: E. de Boccard.

ṚGVEDA

See: **Saṃhitā**

RISHIKESH

See: **Divine Life Society**

RITES OF PASSAGE

See: **Saṃskāras**

RITUAL

See: **Kalpa (Ritual)**

ROHIṆĪ

The 'Red One'. Rohiṇī is the female counterpart of Rohita, the Sun (*Atharvaveda* 13.1. 22–23). Often addressed with typical solar titles such as Sūryā, Rohiṇī is one of the minor figures of Vedic and Purāṇic Hinduism. There are various traditions on Rohiṇī. She is the mother of Kāmadhenu, the holy cow of abundance, and is called the protectress of cattle and offspring (*Atharvaveda* 1.22. 3). Rohiṇī is the ninth of the twenty-seven daughters of Dakṣa who got married to Candra (the Moon) and are thence identified with the twenty-seven lunar asterisms (nakṣatras). Rohiṇī, also called Tārā (a star of the Taurus constellation), gave birth to Budha (Mercury) (*Viṣṇu Purāṇa* 4.6). She is a benevolent deity and according to the Vaiṣṇava tradition she can be either one of the vidhyādevīs, the goddesses of knowledge headed by Sarasvatī, or the mother of Balarāma (*Bhāgavata Purāṇa* 9.24.45–46).

See also: **Balarāma; Dakṣa; Kāmadhenu; Purāṇas; Sacred animals; Saṃhitā; Sarasvatī; Sūryā; Vaiṣṇavism; Vedism**

FABRIZIO M. FERRARI

Further reading

Danielou, A. 1991. *The Myths and Gods of India: The Classic Work on Hindu Polytheism from the Princeton Bollingen Series.* Rochester, VT: Inner Traditions International.

ROY, RAMMOHAN (1772–1833)

Hindu reformer and founder of the Brahmo Samaj, Roy studied Hindu philosophy at the University of Benares, and was particularly attracted to the notion of God as Brahman, as found in the *Upaniṣads*, in contrast to the plurality of iconic forms of the divine. Roy's aniconic monotheism was equally inspired by Islam and Christianity.

Roy was employed by the East India Company from 1804 to 1814, during which time he wrote his first book, *A Gift to Monotheists.* At the age of 42 he settled permanently in Calcutta, where he devoted himself to religious and political affairs. Roy became actively involved in educational reform, favouring a Western curriculum, and widening of access, since he was opposed to the caste system. Roy also endeavoured to raise the status of women, opposing satī, polygamy and the marriage of young girls.

Roy translated the *Upaniṣads* and other Vedic writings into English. These translations inspired Max Müller to learn Sanskrit, in order to study the original texts. Roy is also renowned for his work *The Precepts of Jesus – The Guide to Peace and Happiness*, an anthology of harmonised Gospel passages. The book outraged Christian missionaries, largely because Roy, being a rationalist, omitted all miracle stories from the collection.

In 1815 Roy founded the Atmuja Sabha ('Society of the Spirit'), subsequently Brahmo Samaj, in 1828: this was a forum for Indians and Europeans, as well as Hindus, Christians and Muslims. Roy came to England in 1831 as a representative of Akhbar II, the ex-Emperor of Delhi, and returned in 1833, hosted by Unitarians in Bristol. On this visit he contracted meningitis, and died in the same year. He was buried at Arnos Vale Cemetery in the city and in 1997 a statue was erected in his honour.

See also: **Brahman; Brahmo Samaj; Caste; Child marriage; Hinduism, modern and contemporary; Languages; Satī; Upaniṣads; Women, status of**

GEORGE CHRYSSIDES

Further reading

Killingley, D. 1993. *Rammohun Roy in Hindu and Christian Traditions.* Newcastle upon Tyne: Grevatt and Grevatt.

Robertson, Bruce C. (ed.). 1999. *The Essential Works of Rammohan Roy.* New Delhi: Oxford University Press.

ṚṢI

A general term for a 'seer' or 'sage', the word ṛṣi is often applied in the earlier literature of Hinduism to one of a set of important Vedic visionaries who literally saw with a special psychic perception the sacred mantras upon which they meditated and finally communicated in the form of the Veda. A traditional Sanskrit verse identifies a ṛṣi as a celibate performer of penance who controls his senses, is able to bless and curse, and is firmly devoted to telling the truth. In some contexts, ṛṣis seems to constitute a class of creative beings wholly distinct from gods, demons and men. As a class, they are further subdivided into brāhmaṇa seers (brahmārṣi), royal seers (rājarṣi) and divine seers (devarṣi). Although one tradition indicates that there are about 48,000 ṛṣis, the seven major ones of the Veda include Atri, Gautama, Bharadvāja, Vaṣiṣṭha, Viśvāmitra, Jamadagni and Kaśyapa. These seven ṛṣis are believed to constitute the astronomical constellation of the Great Bear, known as the 'seven ṛṣis' (saptarṣi). Different lists occur in later texts such as the *Mahābhārata*. Traditional Vedic ṛṣis often lived alone or in aśrāmas with their wives, children and disciples.

See also: **Āśrām(a) (religious community); Atri; Brāhmaṇa; Mahābhārata; Mantra; Vaṣiṣṭha; Veda; Viśvāmitra**

DEVEN M. PATEL

Further reading

Mani, Vettam. 2002. *Purāñic Encyclopaedia.* Delhi: Motilal Banarsidass.

RUDRA

The 'weeping' or 'red' one. The howling or furious ruler of the tempest or storm in Vedic mythology. Most likely an early theonym of the sky-god Dyaus, Rudra personifies the destructive or violent aspects of nature. He is frequently identified with Agni, the fire-god (both are known as Kṣetrapati or 'lord of the field'; *Ṛgveda* 4.57.1; 7.35.10), but his strongest affinities would appear to be with Indra, the lightning-lord. Rudra's consort is known as either Rodasī or Pṛśnī, and the latter is named as mother of Rudra's sons and Indra's attendants, the Maruts. In the *Yajurveda*, Rudra appears as Paśupati or 'lord of beasts or cattle'. In the later *Brāhmaṇas*, he becomes Mahādeva, both protector and hunter of cattle. He is also identified as Vāstoṣpati ('lord of the house') in the *Taittirīya Saṃhitā* (3.4.10.3). In an obscure myth, Rudra is the archer who interrupts the primordial incest myth involving Dyaus or Prajāpati with his daughter Uṣas. From the spilled semen, the gods create Vāstoṣpati. The Rudra prototype is a major forerunner of the Hindu Śiva, the Trimūrti destroyer. As an epithet, however, śiva ('propitious') belonged originally to the Vedic Rudra.

See also: **Agni; Brāhmaṇas; Dyaus Pitṛ; Indra; Maruts; Prajāpati; Śiva; Trimūrti; Uṣas; Vedic pantheon; Vedism**

MICHAEL YORK

RUKMIṆĪ

The wife of Kṛṣṇa and mother of Pradyumna. The story of Rukmiṇī is told in Epic (*Mahābhārata*, *Harivaṃśa*) and Purāṇic (*Viṣṇu*, *Bhāgavata*, *Padma*, *Skanda Purāṇas*) literature. Rukmiṇī was the daughter of Bhiṣmāka, king of Vidharbha, whose eldest son, Rukmi, decided to marry her to King Śiṣupāla of Cedi. But Rukmiṇī had fallen in love with Kṛṣṇa. Bhiṣmāka was too old to oppose his son's will and so the marriage was arranged. Rukmiṇī sent a brāhmaṇa-messenger to Dvārakā, where Kṛṣṇa was living, to let him know about her love and threatened to commit suicide if married to Śiṣupāla. Kṛṣṇa acknowledged the exceptional qualities of Rukmiṇī and decided to marry her. A kidnapping was arranged for the day before her marriage but Śiṣupāla discovered the trick and a fight took place. Eventually Kṛṣṇa, with the help of Balarāma, defeated him. The two brothers brought Rukmiṇī to Dvārakā, where the marriage was celebrated.

See also: **Balarāma; Brāhmaṇa; Dvārakā; Harivaṃśa; Itihāsa; Kṛṣṇa; Mahābhārata; Purāṇas**

FABRIZIO M. FERRARI

Further reading

Bryant, E.F. 2003. *Krishna: The Beautiful Legend of God: Srimad Bhagavata Purana, Book X*. London: Penguin.

S

ŚABDA

Śabda, 'word', carries philosophical as well as straightforward connotations. The term Śabda Brahman, in a similar way to Greek Logos, implies an absolute or divine principle that bestows meaning on language itself, being prior to the spoken words of all languages. Śabda exists on many levels, from the articulated sound of a word, through the subtle levels of mental conception, to the initial creative ideation (sṛṣṭi kalpana) of divine consciousness. At this level śabda is mantra – whether the cosmogenic sounds of the Veda, or the seed-syllables (bīja mantra) of the *Tantras*, which in a literal sense are envisaged as 'spelling out' the cosmos as sonic emanation from the divine mind. Śabda in the sense of 'signifier' is coupled with its object artha – that which is signified. On a metaphysical level, śabda thus corresponds to divine language with the universe as its object or 'meaning' (artha).

See also: **Brahman; Mantra; Tantras; Veda**

KATHLEEN TAYLOR

Further reading

Avalon, A. 1989. *Garland of Letters.* Madras: Ganesh.

Padoux, A. 1990. *Vāc: The Concept of the Word in Selected Hindu Tantras.* Albany, NY: SUNY Press.

SACCIDĀNANDA

Exponents of Vedānta consider that the essential nature of Brahman is existence (sat), consciousness (cit) and bliss (ānanda). As the absolute, indivisible, infinite, unchanging, eternal one without a second, Brahman is the ultimate existent. It is not composite; nor is it subject to relations, change, origination or destruction. Yet it is not a particular existing thing beside which there might be another, or beyond which there might be something else, even non-existence. All entities derive their existence from it and depend upon it without diminishing it or compromising its transcendence. Nor is it an object of awareness by an experiencing subject because its essential nature is consciousness. As pure consciousness it is the subject of all awareness, of all experience of any kind. As the subject of all consciousness it cannot be grasped as an object of consciousness. It is that by which everything else is known or experienced. In this sense it is the inner self (Ātman) of all beings. The essence of all knowers and objects of knowledge, it is yet beyond the distinction between knower, known and process of knowing. Beyond any distinctions, it is completely full, without any gaps. Hence its nature is absolute bliss, infinitely more blissful than the highest human joy (*Bṛhadāraṇyaka Upaniṣad* 4.3.33; *Taittirīya Upaniṣad* 2.8). Bliss is the innermost of five layers or sheaths successively identified with brahman after food (anna), breath (prāṇa), mind (manas) and consciousness (vijñāna), from each of which all beings are born, by means of which they live, and into which they pass upon death (*Taittirīya Upaniṣad* 2.5–9; 3.1–6). Although Śaṅkara appears reluctant to accept bliss as an essential property of Brahman because the experience of joy requires faculties of perception and hence depends upon distinctions that do not belong to Brahman, other Advaita Vedāntins defend bliss as simply fullness (Potter 1981: 75–76).

See also: **Advaita; Ātman; Brahman; Śaṅkara; Upaniṣads; Vedānta**

PETER M. SCHARF

Further reading

Potter, Karl. (ed.). 1981. *Encyclopedia of Indian Philosophies, vol. 3: Advaita Vedānta up to Śaṃkara and His Pupils.* Delhi: Motilal Banarsidass.

SACRED ANIMALS

A great number of animals are significant in Hinduism. Some, like the goat and the buffalo, are sacrificial animals – which is also a kind of sanctity – while for others their sanctity prohibits their killing (at least by the communities that hold them sacred). Many animals have mythical representatives or ancestors, especially among the 'vehicles' (vāhana) of the deities, whose iconography usually depicts them upon their own special animal, like Garuḍa, the great bird with a human face who carries Viṣṇu, variously described as part man and part eagle or vulture. Another mythical bird is haṃsa, the divine swan or goose, the vehicle of Brahmā, and his consort Sarasvatī, and symbol of the soul and the breath: the divine element within the material body. In the waters, Viṣṇu rests upon the many-headed snake Ananta ('endless') or Śeṣa ('the remainder'), who represents the vast waters of chaos before and after the universe exists. Ananta is king of the nāgas, mythical cobra-like beings whose paradise lies beneath the waters. Shrines to cobras, usually at the foot of a tree, are common in folk religion, where they are propitiated to protect against snakebite; but the primary association of snakes is with water and fertility, and offerings are made to the nāgas by women seeking to become pregnant. Their festival (Nāgapancāmi) occurs during monsoon time in the month of Śrāvan (July–August).

Śiva, too is associated with the cobra, which he wears across his body as his 'sacred thread', or as a garland round his neck. His symbolic liṅga in his shrines is encircled by a snake. It is not only fertility but the ambivalent nature of the snake that he rules over: it is both the life force and the source of poison.

Śiva's vehicle, however, is his faithful white hump-backed bull Nandi. The bull, associated with strength and virility, is appropriate to this deity's dual nature as god of procreation and also of ascetic control of the senses. The bull is a symbol of strength and pre-eminence in the Vedic hymns and important Vedic gods are sometimes compared to it, especially Indra. Though once a sacrificial animal, it is no longer killed – unlike the buffalo, which is sacrificed at festivals to the goddess Durgā.

The most sacred of all animals is of course the cow, identified with the nourishing character of Earth as the Great Mother. Its sanctity probably derives from its importance as a sacrificial animal in the Vedas, which in turn was connected to its economic significance as an index of wealth; but at least by the time of the *Dharmaśāstras* the killing of a cow had become a heinous sin. Not only the animal itself but all its products are sacred and health-giving. Thus the 'five products' (pancagava) of the cow – milk, curd, melted butter (ghi), dung and urine – are all highly auspicious. No deity has the cow for a vehicle, but she has natural associations with Lakṣmī, goddess of prosperity, and Kṛṣṇa, who carries the epithet Gopāla ('cowherd') from his rustic life in Vṛndāvana.

Monkeys and apes are traditionally believed to be of semi-divine origin, with male deities as their ancestors. The former are specially revered in Vaiṣṇavism, because under their king, Sugriva, they aided Rāma in his battle with the demon king of Sri Lanka. Folk shrines to Hanumān the monkey-deity are a very common sight in India. Divine messenger of the monkey army, he is the devoted disciple of Rāma. Son of Vāyu the wind-god, he has the immense strength of the storm. Far from being 'cute', these divine monkeys are awe-inspiring creatures.

Lions and tigers – not always distinguished in iconography – are vehicles of the Goddess, most famously Durgā. The lion is also connected to Viṣṇu in his incarnation as Narasiṃha, the man-lion, who was born to kill the demon Hiraṇyakaśipu. Lions were symbols of royalty and empire from ancient times, as evidenced by the pillars set up by the Mauryan emperor Aśoka. Tiger-deities occur in folk religion, sometimes as the form taken by deceased local heroes – or villains.

Also associated with royalty is the elephant, whose ancestor is Airāvata, the milky-white elephant of Indra, king of the gods. In the Vedic hymns it is told how the elephants once were clouds, who lost their wings and were confined to earth – hence their connection with rains and fertility. Elephants were the traditional animals for royal processions, and are still used to pull the moveable temple images of the gods on certain festivals.

Another royal animal from Vedic times is the horse, seven of whom draw the chariot of Sūrya, the sun-god, while the vedic horse-sacrifice (aśvamedha) was the greatest yajña performed by a conquering king. Consequently the horse became a symbol of the cakravartin, the 'wheel-turning' emperor who conquers in all the directions.

Smaller, more humble, animals also have their sacred aspects. The mouse or rat (musika) is honoured as the vehicle of elephant-headed Gaṇeśa. The reason for this surprising association has caused much speculation but perhaps is best understood to derive from them both being overcomers of obstacles, one on a large scale, the other on a small scale. Rats were traditionally regarded as sources of trouble (vighna) and therefore propitiated; but the mouse is also symbol of the inner self or ātman, who is hidden within all beings.

The frog, as an aquatic creature, is associated with water and fertility, along with the snake and the more mighty elephant. Frogs are worshipped in the month of October with offerings of rice and ghi and sprinkled with water.

The goat is the prime sacrificial animal. The word aja, meaning a female goat, also means 'unborn' and so it becomes the symbol of unmanifested nature (prakṛti) in philosophy. In the Vedic hymns, a goat draws the chariot of the deity Pusān, who has an agricultural connection.

These are a few among a great number of animals that have symbolic significance through being associated with the deities or for their own innate qualities. With some, worship is apotropaic, to ward off the troubles they bring; for others the desire is to acquire their attributes, such as strength or fertility; but underlying all is the power of mythic association that bestows on the animal a rich variety of meanings.

See also: **Airāvata; Brahmā; Deities; Durgā; Gaṇeśa; Garuḍa; Hanumān; Hiraṇyakaśipu; Indra; Kṛṣṇa; Lakṣmī, Śrī; Nāgapañcami; Nāgas; Nandi; Prakṛti; Rāma; Saṃhitā; Sarasvatī; Śeṣa; Śiva; Sūrya; Vaiṣṇavism; Viṣṇu**

KATHLEEN TAYLOR

Further reading

Majupuria, T.C. 1991. *Sacred Animals of Nepal and India.* Lashkar: M. Devi.

SACRED BOOKS OF THE EAST (1879–1910)

Series conceived by the editor F. Max Müller as a scholarly replacement for popular anthologies of sacred texts and intended to serve as the basis for a new 'science' of the comparative study of religions. Alongside other massive late-Victorian publishing ventures, such as the *Oxford English Dictionary* and the revised translation of the Bible, the series helped establish the prestige of Oxford University Press. Of the fifty volumes (including an index) of the series, twenty-one provide translations of Hindu texts, including selections from the *Saṃhitās*, the *Śatapatha Brāhmaṇa*, the *Upaniṣads*, several *Dharmasūtras*, *Vedāntasūtras* (*Brahmasūtras*), *Gṛhyasūtras* and the *Bhagavadgītā.* Both the emphasis on textual sources and the selection of texts chosen have been seen as evidence of a specifically Protestant bias in the study of Hinduism but the series nevertheless undoubtedly served to advance and to disseminate knowledge of Hinduism.

See also: **Bhagavadgītā; Brahmasūtras; Dharmaśāstras; Dharmasūtras; Gṛhyasūtras; Hinduism, history of scholarship; Müller, Friedrich Max; Saṃhitā; Upaniṣads**

WILL SWEETMAN

Further reading

Girardot, N.J. 2002. 'Max Müller's Sacred Books and the Nineteenth-Century Production of the Comparative Science of Religions'. *History of Religions* 41(3): 213–50.

Müller, F.M. (ed.). 1879–1910. *The Sacred Books of the East*, 50 vols. Oxford: Clarendon Press.

SACRED GEOGRAPHY

Hindu cosmology maintains that the earth, Jambudvīpa, is the innermost of the seven ring-like continents separated one from the next by seas. The earth is divided into various regions; the one to its extreme south is Bhārata, or India. Bhārata-varṣa, or Bhārata khaṇḍa, is one of the early names of India, derived from the great patriarch Bhārata. Bhārata-varṣa embraces the whole of the subcontinent, north of the Vindhya range. Although the name refers to Bhārata, the most important notion, on which sacred geography is grounded, is the reverence for the divine feminine and the sacrality of the land itself, identified with the goddess Pṛthivī. A number of hymns dedicated to her, as the epitome of stability and provider of fertility and inexhaustible abundance, are to be found in the *Ṛgveda Saṃhitā*. Later, the *Devī-bhāgavata-Purāṇa* (7.33.21–41) speaks of the mountains as Devī's bones, the rivers as her veins, the trees and forests as her hair. The notion of the earth as a personified goddess continues and plays a pivotal role in later Hindu mythology. Bhudevi, 'the goddess who is the earth', becomes an integral part of Vaiṣṇava mythology and iconography. However, the idea of the Indian subcontinent being a goddess, is vividly expressed in the myth of Satī, whose charred remains fall bit by bit on the ground, thus establishing the Śakti pīṭhas, 'seats of the goddess'. Each pīṭha represents either one of her limbs or her ornaments. The number of pīṭhas varies between four and 108, according to the various traditions. When the totality of the pīṭhas is considered, it reveals the existence of a goddess who unifies the subcontinent. In other words, the goddess Satī becomes the Indian subcontinent, the living great goddess, Mahādevī, from which emanate all local goddesses worshipped at the various pīṭhas. India is thus not so much Satī's burial ground but, rather, Devī's living body.

The conviction that the earth, i.e. the Indian subcontinent itself, is not only a goddess but a mother to all Indians is at the foundation of the cult of Bhārat Mātā, 'Mother India'. As her children, all Indians are expected to protect her and face hardships and sacrifice for her. Bankim Chandra Chatterjee's (1838–94) novel *Ānandamaṭh*, written in late nineteenth-century Bengal, is probably among the earliest and most popular literary expressions of this idea, and had a momentous impact on the independence movement, which at that time was gaining momentum. Independent India still clings to the theme of Bhārat Mātā as a goddess. In it, Chatterjee includes his famous poem 'Bande Mātāram' ('Vande Mātāram'), a hymn to the goddess in which he describes how the Mother's name rouses the heart of all the regions of the subcontinent, how it echoes in the peaks of the Vindhyas and the Himālayas and mingles with the murmur of the water of its rivers and is chanted by the waves of the sea. In 1911 Rabindrath Tagore composed the national anthem, 'Jana Gana Mana', very similar in wording to 'Vande Mātāram'. Vārāṇasī and Haridvāra each have a temple dedicated to Bhārat Mātā. At Vārāṇasī, in the place of an anthropomorphic image of the goddess, there is a large, coloured relief map of the Indian subcontinent, to which pilgrims pay respectful homage. There are also anthropomorphic images of Bhārat Mātā: a young crowned woman, with long flowing hair carrying the Indian flag in the left hand, and with the right in a blessing gesture. Behind her is the lion, her conveyance. Both goddess and lion are surrounded by a halo of flames. Or, on the other hand, there is a goddess holding a vessel full of milk in one hand and sheaves of grain in the other.

The concept of India being a sacred land is mirrored in its innumerable sacred mountains, rivers and lakes, either having some physical peculiarity or connected to some momentous mythical event narrated either in the epics or in the *Purāṇas*, both classic or the local *Sthālapurāṇas*. These are tīrthas, literally a place where one can ford a river; it is here that the pilgrim can get in touch with the divine, crossing over from everyday life to a higher realm. It is difficult to ascertain how a given site becomes a tīrtha. In many cases, however, the awesome or remote location may have played a determinant role in its development. Long journeys to distant sites, as, for instance, in the notoriously arduous pilgrimage through the forest to the Ayyappaṉ temple at Sabarimalai at the border between Tamil Nadu or Kerala; or the equally difficult trek to Amarnath in Kashmir, where the devotee worships the liṅga-shaped ice block in a cave indicate that both geographic location as well as natural peculiarities such as the ice liṅga are inextricably connected with the sanctity of the place. The holy location, with all its mythical associations, rather than the temple, motivates the pilgrim's visit. Pilgrimage is one of the important religious duties of a Hindu. Although some of the tīrthas are of special sanctity for Śaivas, e.g. Srisailam (Kurnool dst. Andhra Pradesh), some for Vaiṣṇavas, e.g. Tirumalai (Chittoor dst. Andhra Pradesh), and others for Śāktas, e.g. Kamakhya near Gauhati (Assam), there are no sectarian distinctions. Indeed, Hindus will visit shrines dedicated to different deities and offer their homage to non-Hindu holy places such as the Basilica of Our Lady at Velankanni (Thanjavur dst., Tamil Nadu) or the tombs of Muslim saints, such as that of Sikander Shah at Tirupparankunram, near Madurai (Tamil Nadu) or the shrine of Gesūdarāz at Gulbarga (Karnataka). The following seven cities are the most important tīrthas are: in the north, Ayodhyā, capital of Rāma, Mathurā, birthplace of Kṛṣṇa, Haridvāra, at the source of the Ganges, and Vārāṇasī, the city of Śiva; in central India Ujjain, sacred to Śiva; in the west Dvāraka, the capital of Kṛṣṇa; and in the south, Kāñcīpuram, sacred both to Viṣṇu and Śiva. It is said that a pilgrimage to any of these places ensures liberation from rebirth.

Of these, Vārāṇasī, the spiritual capital of India, is the first and foremost. As all the gods dwell in Vārāṇasī, so all the tīrthas are present there. In other words, Vārāṇasī is the summa of all that is sacred in the subcontinent and pilgrimage there is as good as a pilgrimage to all Indian tīrthas. The layout of the town itself symbolically recreates the whole Indian sacred geography, the dhāmas, 'divine abodes', the jyotirliṅgas, 'liṅgas of light', the seven holy cities and other relevant tīrthas. Purāṇic commentators note that these tīrthas are to be found in their respective locations but only in their partial and gross form. However, it is only in Vārāṇasī that they assume their full potential and subtle form.

Four main pilgrimage sites, the four dhāmas, mark the four cardinal points of Indian sacred geography. Badarinath, Uttar Pradesh, in the Himālayas, a site dedicated to Viṣṇu in his dual form of Nara-Nārāyaṇa, in the north; Puri, Orissa, sacred to Jagannātha in the east; Rāmeśvaram, Tamil Nadu, an island situated between India and Sri Lanka, where Rāma worshipped Śiva after the defeat of Rāvaṇa, in the south; Dvāraka, Gujarat, the capital of Kṛṣṇa, situated at the north-western tip of the Saurashtra peninsula overlooking the Arabian Sea in the west.

A number of mountains and mountain ranges are revered as sacred because of the deities dwelling on their peaks and the sages populating their caves and forests, or because they provided a site for some mythical incident. The most celebrated are the Himālayas, which play a conspicuous role in mythology and culture. A number of myths are set on the Himālayas, involving gods, semi-divine beings and ṛṣis. According to a famous legend, the Vindhyas, dividing the northern and the southern part of the subcontinent, were mightier than the Himālayas, but they bowed respectfully before the sage Agastya on his way to the south of the country, and thus lost their height for ever. Again, according to legend, the Sahyadri (Western Ghats) are reputed to be the abode of malevolent spirits. They became known as Sahya, 'enduring', because they were the last to be engulfed when most of the earth was submerged by the flood. Paraśurāma wanted some land for the brāhmaṇas and requested the god Varuṇa to retreat, then a narrow strip of land emerged. Paraśurāma pinched it with his fingers, creating the Malaya hills of Malabar, stretching from the Nilgiris to Kanyakumari. The Mahendra, the Eastern Ghats, were once a continuous chain of high ranges ruled by kings who opposed the gods for a long time. The gods eventually hacked the hills, destroyed their peaks and subdued their inhabitants. There are other mountain ranges, as well as innumerable hills and peaks, which are endowed with special sanctity. The most famous of them is the Kailāsa, abode of Śiva. Devotees regard the Kailāsa as the Śivaliṅga itself. It takes two or three days for the pilgrims to perform a circumambulation of the mountain (*c.*40 km). At the foot of the Kailāsa is the Manasarovara lake, where the wild geese migrate in the breeding season and at the beginning of the monsoon. It is said that the right hand of Satī has fallen there. The most important among the mythical mountains are the golden Meru or Sumeru, the pivot of the universe, located in the Himālayas and believed to be the abode of the gods. The celestial Gaṅgā descends from the heaven upon its summit before flowing to earth in four streams, each directed to the four cardinal points. Yet another mountain of mythical relevance is the Mandara, which served as a churning stick at the time of the Churning of the Ocean and which was supported by Viṣṇu as Kūrma.

Apart from mountains and ranges which are of pan-Indian importance, there are a large number of mountains and individual hills whose sanctity is celebrated in local *Sthālapurāṇas.* Among these is Sivagiri in the Palani Hills, near Dindigul (Tamil Nadu), sacred to Subrahmanya in his form as Daṇḍapāni, 'bearer of the staff'. It is said that a number of siddhas, conversant in medicine and alchemy and endowed with supernatural powers, used to live in the caves and forests of the Palani Hills. Perhaps one of the most famous hills of peninsular India is Tirumalai, near Tirupati in Chittoor district (Andhra Pradesh), sacred to Veṅkateśvara, known in north India as Bālājī. This impressive mountain, rising dramatically 700 metres above Tirupati, is part of a small range of seven hills which in the popular imagination represent the seven hoods of the cosmic serpent Śeṣa. Nestled among them is the temple, which is visited by an average of 10,000 pilgrims a day. On a smaller scale, in the extreme south of India, between Nagercoil and Kanyakumari, is Agastyamalai, the mountain of Agastya, where the sage is believed to dwell.

In the north, near Mathurā, is the Govardhana hill, which Kṛṣṇa lifted on the small finger of his hand to protect the herdsmen from the deluge unleashed by Indra. In the Aravalli range of western Rajasthan, particularly important is the Arbuda, popularly known as Abu. The sage Vasiṣṭha is believed to have lived here, and according to tradition this is the place where the Rajputs emerged from the fire pit. Abu is considered a sacred place by the Jains, and the eleventh-century Solanki rulers built the famous Dilvara temples. At a short distance from Dilvara is Acalgadh, site of many temples, one of which is said to contain a toe of Śiva. Apart from Abu, other mountains are connected to Jainism: Girnar in Junagadh, associated with Neminatha, the twenty-second tīrthankara, and Shatrunjaya, near Palitana in Kathiawad, associated with Ṛṣabhanatha, the first tīrthankara. In the south, both the hills at Sravana Belgola, in Karnataka, are connected with Bhadrabāhu, the head of the Digambara Jains, who migrated there with a group of followers in the third century BCE.

Along with the mountains, rivers play a pivotal role in Indian sacred geography. Although officially there are only seven sacred rivers, practically all expanses of water receive homage as the givers of life and fertility. First of all there are the Gaṅgā, the Jumna or Yamunā and the Sarasvatī, the most sacred three among the seven, at whose confluence is situated Prayaga, followed by the Godavari, Narmada, Indus and Kaveri. As expected, the names on this list vary: according to some traditions the Indus and the Kaveri are substituted with the Tapti and the Krishna. Occasionally, in the southern states of the subcontinent the Tungabhadra finds a place among the holy seven. There is no doubt that according to Hindu tradition the Gaṅgā is the most sacred river on earth, originating from the sky and flowing to earth through the penance of Bhagīratha and the grace of Śiva. Furthermore, she is the sister of Pārvatī and the second wife of Śiva and she is his cooling 'liquid Śakti'. Although not as sacred as the Gaṅgā, because there is some uncertainty about her wedded state, the Yamunā is reputed to be the daughter of the sage Kalinda and was once dragged her from bed by Balarāma. On her banks lie Indraprastha, Delhi, the holy sites connected with Kṛṣṇa's childhood and youth, Vṛndāvana and Mathurā, Agra and, at the confluence with the Gaṅgā, Prayaga. The Sarasvatī, often mentioned in Vedic literature, has its sources in the Himālaya, but at a certain point of its course she disappears in the sands of the desert, and is believed to rise up from her subterranean course at Prayaga and join her waters with those of the Gaṅgā and the Yamunā. Many legends have been woven around her disappearance. The Godavarī, also called Goda, 'cow-giver', because reputedly the sage Gautama revived with its water a cow he had accidentally killed, is known as the Gaṅgā of the Deccan. It has its source at Tryambaka, near Nasik, the site of one of the twelve jyotirliṅgas; it flows through the Deccan plateau and fans out in a huge delta in the Bay of Bengal. It is said that originally the river divided into seven branches before it met the sea. Of these only four still remain and it is recommended that whoever desires offspring should bathe in them in succession. The Narmada starts from the Amarakantaka hill in the eastern Vindhya, a place renowned for religious suicide. Those who drown themselves or fast to death there are said to obtain liberation. The water of the Narmada is so sacred that it is believed that one's sins are obliterated at the mere sight of it. The Kaveri, the Gaṅgā of the south, has been an inexhaustible source of inspiration in Tamil poetry. There are a number of myths related to the origin of the Kaveri. The most popular story, narrated at Talakaveri at the source of the river, in the Kodagu mountains, tells how Agastya married the Kaveri and placed her in his kamaṇḍalu (water jar). One day, accidentally, a crow tipped over the pot and the Kaveri flowed out of it. The story is also popular in Tamil Nadu, and because of the connection with Agastya, an important figure in Tamil culture, the Kaveri became the symbol of Tamil language, literature and culture. Along its course are a number of holy sites; the most renowned is the sacred island of Srirangam, on which is the Raṅganātha temple. The Tapti is personified as the daughter of Sūrya and Chaya. The *Mahābhārata* narrates the love of Saṃvarṇa, a descendant of Bhārata for Taptī, and the birth of their child, Kuru, after whom the Kauravas were named (*Adi Parva* 7.89.40). The Krishna or Kistna has its source in mount Sahya on the Mahabalesvar plateau and reputedly was originated by the sweat of Śiva. Its chief tributary is the Bhima, on whose banks are Alandi, associated with the Maratha saint Jñānadeva (1275–96), and Pandharpur, with its celebrated temple dedicated to Viṭṭhoba.

Sacred geography is not only defined by mountains and rivers, but by other manifestations of the deities, such as the 108 Śakti pīṭhas and the twelve jyotirliṅgas, scattered throughout the subcontinent. It should be noted, however, that the location of some is not consistently identified. Among the most popular jyotirliṅgas are: the Kedareśa, a shapeless formation at Kedarnath in the Himālayas, the Mahākāleśvara (Mahākāla) at Ujjainī, the Mallikārjuna at Srisailam (Kurnool dst.), Omkareśvara on an island in the Narmada. In addition to the twelve jyotirliṅgas are the five elemental liṅgas in South India: the earth liṅga at Kāñcīpuram, the water liṅga at Jambukesvaram on Srirangam island, the fire liṅga at Arunachalam (Tiruvannamalai), the air liṅga at Kalahasti, and finally the ether liṅga at Cidambaram.

These holy places, in turn, are connected with other sites: deities are carried in procession from one temple to another according to the ritual calendar, thus strengthening the spatial and religious links between holy sites. Some places are connected to the career of a single deity, such as, for instance, the six tīrthas sacred to Murukaṉ, scattered through Tamil Nadu. Nine temples, known collectively as Nava Tirupati, in the Tambraparni basin are associated with various aspects of Viṣṇu and the career of some of the Aḷvārs. Another group of nine temples around Kumbakonam is dedicated each to one of the nine planets (Navagrahas).

In the last twenty-five years or so there has been a surge in affluence and in the numbers of pilgrims touring India. What was once an arduous journey is now made easier by the availability of trains, buses and aeroplanes. With the increased presence of visitors there is a standardisation of the 'services' offered at the various tīrthas, which, in the long run, might destroy the tīrtha's individuality. Among the visitors are the NRI (non resident Indians), for whom India is still a sacred space, with temples revered for generations by members of their own families. Although some 9 million Indians live outside India, and some of them have been severed from the subcontinent for the past 150 years, there is still a deep respect, if not reverence, for the land of their ancestors. Temples, religious and cultural institutions abroad, generally served by Indian swamis flown in for this purpose, and the strong ties between the motherland and those abroad demonstrate that diaspora Indians still look to India as the source of spiritual authority and inspiration.

See also: **Agastya; Aḷvārs; Avatarā; Ayodhyā; Ayyappaṉ; Bhārat Mātā; Brāhmaṇas; Chatterjee, Bankim Chandra; Cidambaram; Diaspora; Dvārakā; Gaṅgā; Haridvāra; Himālayas; Image worship; Indra; Itihāsa; Jagannātha; Jainism, relationship with Hinduism; Kāñcīpura; Kauravas; Kṛṣṇa; Languages; Madurai; Mahābhārata; Mahādevī; Meru, Mount; Murukaṉ; Navagrahas (Planets); Pārvatī; Pṛthivī; Purāṇas; Rāma; Rāmeśvara; Rāvaṇa; Ṛṣi; Śaivism; Śakti; Saṃhitā; Sati; Śesa; Siddha; Śiva; Subramanya; Sūrya; Svāmi; Tagore, Rabinandrath; Tīrthayātrā; Ujjainī; Vārāṇasī; Vaiṣṇavism; Varuṇa; Vasiṣṭha; Veda; Viṣṇu; Vṛndavāna; Yamunā**

ANNA DALLAPICCOLA

Further reading

van Buitenen, J.A.B. (ed. and trans.). 1973. *The Mahabharata. 1. The Book of the Beginnings*. Chicago, IL: University of Chicago Press.

Dallapiccola, A.L. 2002. *Dictionary of Hindu Lore and Legend*. London: Thames & Hudson.

Eck, D. 1983. *Banaras: City of Light*. Princeton, NJ: Princeton University Press.

Kinsley, D. 1986. *Hindu Goddesses: Visions of the Divine Feminine in the Hindu Religious Tradition*. Berkeley, Los Angeles, CA and London: University of California Press.

Vertovec, S. 2000. *The Hindu Diaspora*. London and New York: Routledge.

Vettam, Mani. 1979. *Puranic Encyclopedia*. Delhi: Motilal Banarsidass.

Vijnanananda, Swami (trans.). 1986. *Srimad Devi Bhagawatam*. New Delhi: Oriental Books Reprint Corporation.

Walker, B. 1968. *Hindu World*. London: Allen & Unwin.

SACRED TEXTS

Hinduism (if Hinduism can be characterised at all as a single entity) is characterised by the importance of texts of all kinds: prose and verse, written and oral, spoken and sung (whether by a single specialist or by a crowd), archaic and vernacular, stable and fluid. This entry discusses the place of texts in Hinduism, explains some categories of texts and gives references to those described elsewhere in this encyclopedia.

Written and oral, stable and fluid

The word 'text' here refers to any utterance, long or short, which can be repeated in more or less the same form on different occasions. There is a tendency (reinforced by the terminology of mobile phones) to restrict the term text to utterances recorded in writing, whether in handwritten, printed or electronic form. However, this restriction is inappropriate when dealing with Hindu culture, where some texts exist independently of writing, being transmitted orally from one speaker to another. Apart from the Indus Valley script, it seems that writing appeared in India around the middle of the last millennium BCE and was only later used for sacred texts. Some of these, the Vedic texts (except for some later ones), existed at a time when there is no evidence that writing was known. Others, handed down in local communities, only become known outside those communities if they are recorded in writing or electronically by some outside observer. Texts, understood in this wide sense, exist in all the languages that are used by Hindus (including English and other languages of countries outside South Asia).

Many cultures possess ritual texts that are extremely stable: they must always be recited in exactly the same form – the same words in the same order, even in some cases with the same inflections of the voice – otherwise the recitation will be offensive, ineffective or even disastrous. This is the case with Vedic texts. Other texts are fluid: different reciters or scribes, or the same one on different occasions, may vary the text by omitting or adding material or changing some words. Improvised variation may be expected as part of the reciter's art. This has happened extensively with the *Mahābhārata* and *Rāmāyaṇa*, which vary greatly in different parts of South Asia. Whether a text is stable or fluid is a separate matter from whether it is written or oral. There are hundreds of manuscripts and four printed editions of the *Mahābhārata,* all different from each other, while the texts of the Veda have remained unchanged, though they were transmitted orally for centuries before being written.

That a text should be preserved unchanged without the use of writing conflicts with the findings of literary historians and anthropologists about the nature of oral literature. Much valuable research on the oral transmission of texts has been done in cultures where oral texts are fluid (Chadwick and Chadwick 1932–40; Lord 1960; Ong 1982). A typical orally transmitted text such as a ballad or an epic exists as a multitude of performances, each of which is not an exact repetition of any previous performance but is partly improvised. This accounts for the many recensions and countless variations of the *Mahābhārata*, for instance. Though the oral transmission of the Veda in ancient and modern times is well attested (Scharfe 2002: 8–37, 240–51), some theorists (mainly from outside Indian studies) have doubted that it could have been transmitted unchanged without the aid of writing. An anthropologist has argued that the idea of a stable text can only exist in a literate society and that therefore the Vedic texts cannot have acquired a fixed form before writing was known (Goody 1987).

Part of his argument is that in a literate society the school situation decontextualises memory by separating learning from doing (Goody 1987: 189). But in India this was, and is, achieved without the use of writing, by separating the process of learning the Veda from the situation of the yajña in which the texts would be employed. The learning process is a ritual in itself, as is the practice of self-study (svādhyāya) in which the Veda-knower recites the texts he has learnt. Oral transmission of a stable text demands much mental labour and a class of persons who spend a large part of their lives on it. It was achieved by brāhmaṇās, whose status depended on their knowledge; the transmission of Buddhist texts was achieved similarly, by monks (Warder 1970: 205, 294).

The possibility of a stable oral text means that some observations of Paul Ricoeur (1981: 147; cf. Graham 1987: 15) have to be modified in a Hindu context. He argues that the act of writing at once constitutes the text and separates it from speech, and thus from the context in which the words were originally uttered and in which they had meaning. The task of hermeneutics, according to Ricoeur, is to recontextualise the text in the interpreter's own world. But in the Hindu view the Veda and other texts are not separated from speech and are constituted as texts without being written. The Veda is itself speech, a manifestation of the original speech uttered at the origin of the universe (oṃ); it is sometimes called śabda-brahman, 'Brahman as sound'. The primacy of speech over writing applies not only to the Veda but to the Epics, *Purāṇas*, *Tantras* and other texts, which are handed down in manuscripts but recited orally (Carpenter 1992). Recontextualisation, giving a text a new meaning in a new context, did indeed occur in ancient India, as is shown by commentaries (see below), but it had occurred already in the *Brāhmaṇas* and texts such as Yāska's *Nirukta*, quite independently of writing.

While the Vedic texts have been kept stable by a tightly controlled technique of oral transmission, other texts depended either on less stable methods of oral transmission or on perishable manuscripts, or both, until printing became widespread in the nineteenth century. Many classical Sanskrit texts have been handed down in fairly reliable manuscript form, while more popular texts such as the *Pañcatantra* exist in many versions, both manuscript and printed, in different regions, reflecting the unrestrained inventiveness of anonymous storytellers. The *Mahābhārata*, *Rāmāyaṇa*, *Purāṇas* and other smṛti texts are similarly fluid. Some vernacular collections have a relatively stable tradition, while others, such as the poems of Kabīr, have many versions. Some scholars have attempted to reconstruct an original form of such a text, comparing the readings of different manuscripts according to the methods of textual criticism. Others object that these methods are inappropriate to texts that have always existed in many variants reflecting regional and ideological differences. The debate continues between those who seek the original text through the variant versions and those for whom these versions themselves are the proper object of study (Narayana Rao 2004: 110–03).

In the nineteenth century, printing changed the situation, privileging particular versions of hitherto fluid texts and making Vedic texts, traditionally the preserve of twice-born males who had received upanayana, available to anyone. In the twentieth century, broadcasting and recording changed the situation again. Sound recordings have joined with printed books of mantras in making specialist reciters unnecessary (Bühnemann 1988: 96). The versions of the *Rāmāyaṇa* and *Mahābhārata* on television (Brockington 1998: 510–13) have privileged particular versions more effectively than printed editions could do.

While some narratives have found comparatively stable literary form in the *Mahābhārata*, *Rāmāyaṇa* and *Purāṇas*, popular storytelling remains fluid. An important religious narrative genre is the vrat-kathā, told to a group of people performing a vrata. The telling of the story, which tells how the vrata was instituted and what rewards are gained by keeping it, is an essential part of the traditional form of a vrata. Now, however, the storyteller may be replaced by a videotape (Jackson and Nesbitt 1993: 65–70).

The diligence with which texts are preserved, and the reverence shown to those who remember them, both in the Vedic textual tradition and in less formal traditions, bears witness to the importance of speech in Hindu thought (Graham 1987: 67–77). But despite the primacy of speech and the prominent vocal element both in Vedic ritual and elsewhere, in non-Vedic ritual writing has a place alongside speech. Mantras are painted inside and outside temples; the character representing oṃ can be seen in domestic shrines as a metal sculpture, and on some temples as a neon sign. This character, and others representing 'seed mantras', are inscribed on sacred diagrams (yantras). The whole of Tulsīdās' *Rāmcaritmānas* is inscribed on the walls of a modern temple in Vārāṇasī, and Valmīki's *Rāmāyaṇa* in another in Ayodhyā (Brockington 1998: 506n.). Many temples display a printed copy of the *Ṛgveda Saṃhitā*, not as a resource for reading but as an object of veneration, on the lines of Sikh veneration of the Ādi Granth.

What do we mean by 'sacred texts'?

The category of 'sacred texts' is a convenient way of separating those texts which have a clearly religious function in a particular tradition from those which do not. In this entry, for instance, we deal with texts which are used in ritual or which convey religious ideas or precepts, such as the Veda, the *Dharmaśāstra*, the poems of the Āḻvārs and Nāyaṉmār, the mantras spoken or chanted in worship, bhajan songs or books of instruction such as the *Śikṣpatrī* of Swami Narayana. We are not concerned with texts such as the *Pañcatantra* or the *Kāmasūtra*, which are clearly not sacred, though they are included in this encyclopedia because of their relevance to Hindu culture. Nor are we concerned with most classical poems or modern novels, although many of them contain mythological material or convey important ideas such as karma or purity. On the other hand, we are concerned with the *Mahābhārata* and the *Rāmāyaṇa*, because they not only tell stories but are repositories of religious teachings and mantras, and are recited and represented dramatically on ritual occasions.

The study of Hindu texts in Sanskrit and other languages in the nineteenth and much of the twentieth century has left a valuable legacy of editions, translations and other work. But that tradition of scholarship encouraged, and to some extent was driven by, an assumption that each religion had its 'Bible' or 'scriptures', having a similar function to that of the Bible (in theological principle if not in observable practice) in Protestantism. This assumption, typified by Müller's *Sacred Books ofthe East* series, overlooks the different ways in which texts may be used in different traditions (Timm 1992: 2) and the different ways in which their authority or sanctity may be understood.

The category of 'sacred texts' or 'scripture' is (like 'the sacred' itself) imposed from the outside, not necessarily current among participants. We may understand it as texts which are 'perceived in some sense as a prime locus of verbal contact with transcendent truth, or ultimate reality' (Graham 1987: 68). They may be understood to be such because they are spoken by an especially enlightened person such as Vālmīki or by a multitude of such persons, such as the Vedic ṛṣis or a group of bhakti poets, or by a deity such as Śiva; or they may be believed to be eternal and independent of any author, which in the Pūrva Mīmāṃsā view is the guarantee of the authority of the Veda.

Some texts proclaim their own sacredness by promising rewards for hearing or reciting them, or forbidding teaching them to unauthorised people (e.g. *Bhagavadgītā* 18, 67–78; *Śvetāṣvatara Upaniṣad* 6. 22f.). But a text may be marked as sacred not by its contents but by the way it is used: whether or not it is recited in ritual situations, whether it is treated as a source of truths or moral imperatives, whether written copies of it or oral recitations of it are venerated or defended from pollution. To speak of sacred texts implies that there is a group of people for whom those texts are sacred (W.C. Smith 1993: 17f.).

Different texts are sacred for different groups of Hindus, and in different ways. What is for convenience called a 'sect' in Hinduism may be defined by adherence to a text (Renou 1953: 91–99). The term sect roughly corresponds to Sanskrit saṃpradāya, 'tradition'; it does not imply something which diverges from a church or from social norms, as it may in a European context. Even where the founder of a saṃpradāya left no literary work, literary activity both in the vernacular and in Sanskrit followed in later generations. This was the case with the Vaiṣṇava tradition founded by Caitanya, where the group known as the six Gosvāmins of Vṛndāvana wrote Bengali and Sanskrit works which became authoritative for the saṃpradāya. Even the Bāuls, who have no known founder and no hierarchy, have their undefined and changeable corpus of songs.

Śruti and smṛti

While 'sacred texts' or 'scripture' is not an indigenous category, there are important ways in which Hindus themselves have classified such texts. We may take first the division into śruti, 'hearing, revelation', and smṛti, 'memory, tradition'. Śruti is the Veda; it is eternal, and was perceived by ancient ṛṣis by supranormal means. Smṛti texts have human authors, even if these were much wiser than human beings in the present age can be. Since the boundaries of the Veda are not fixed, the term śruti does not refer to a definite canon of texts. Indeed, the word was not always restricted to the Veda; *Manusmṛti* (12.95) condemns 'śrutis which are outside the Veda', probably Buddhist and Jain texts (Olivelle 2005: 234, 349).

The term smṛti is still less precise. It includes the *Kalpasūtras*, but these are not typical of smṛti texts, being part of the Vedic ritual system. What are usually understood by the term are the *Mahābhārata*, *Rāmāyaṇa*, *Dharmaśāstras*, *Purāṇas*, *Āgamas* and *Tantras*. None of these is a firmly defined set, and there can be disputes over whether a text is genuine. Such texts are typically framed by a dialogue in which a mythical figure receives instruction from another, the status of these figures giving authority to the teachings. In some cases, notably the *Mahābhārata*, dialogues are framed within dialogues to give a succession of instructors and listeners. Their literary form thus situates them in the context of verbal instruction from an authoritative speaker to an attentive listener, a situation repeated by a succession of speakers and listeners down to the present reciter and his audience. While śruti makes audible the eternal speech at the origin of the universe, smṛti makes its hearers indirect recipients of verbal communication from the divine.

Unlike the Vedas, which have to be protected from being heard by unauthorised people (such as non-twice-born men, or women) and recited in a set ritual manner in the precise form in which they have been learnt, the smṛti texts are publicly recited, the reciter often interspersing a vernacular translation. Though such recitation has been facilitated by manuscripts and even more by printing, it is as speech that most people experience the text. The reciting of *Purāṇas* is an essentially oral performance, but is the work of a highly literate specialist, the paurāṇika, who not only recites the text but comments on it, drawing on other texts as he does so. Such a performance overrides the distinction between oral culture and literate culture (Singer 1972: 150–55; cf. Narayana Rao 2004: 103f., 114f.).

Traditionally, the authority of smṛti is derived from that of śruti, since the promulgators of smṛti had thorough knowledge of the Veda. Manu says that the second source of dharma, after the Veda itself, is the tradition (smṛti) and conduct of those who know it (*Manusmṛti* 2, 6). The *Mahābhārata* claims to have been composed by Vyāsa, the redactor of the Vedas, after he had compiled them (*Mahābhārata* 1.1.52). 'The epics (*itihāsa*) and Purāṇas should be used to strengthen the Veda, for the Veda fears an unlearned man, lest he should harm it' (*Mahābhārata* 1.1.204). The *Bhāgavata Purāṇa* repeats the story: Vyāsa composed the *Mahābhārata* because the Vedas were beyond the reach of women, śūdras and nominal brāhmaṇās (those who do not fulfil the true nature of brāhmaṇas by studying the Veda) (*Bhāgavata Purāṇa*, 1.5.25). But it adds a sequel: Vyāsa still felt dissatisfied, and eventually composed the *Bhāgavata Purāṇa* to teach worship of Kṛṣṇa (*Bhāgavata Purāṇa* 1.4. 26–31; 1.7.6–8).

Historically, the connection of smṛti to śruti becomes increasingly tenuous as we proceed from *Kalpasūtras* through *Dharmaśāstras* and epics to *Purāṇas*, *Agamas* and *Tantras*. This historical difference is recognised within the tradition by reference to the four yugas, the frame on which historical time is traditionally constructed. The Vedas could be fully followed only in the Kṛta age; in the Dvāpara age they were in danger of being lost, which is why Vyāsa arranged them. In the present Kali age, when brāhmaṇas who should preserve them are degenerate and the status of the kṣatriyas who used to be patrons of the yajña has been usurped by upstarts, the Vedas are little known and little understood; the smṛti texts, which contain the meaning of the Vedas, have taken their place. Certain practices which are enjoined in Vedic texts are said to be forbidden in the Kali age (kali-varjita). These include animal sacrifice and niyoga, or levirate: the custom whereby the wife of a man who dies without an heir has intercourse with his brother to conceive a son for her deceased husband.

The view that smṛti in general, or any particular smṛti text such as the *Bhāgavata Purāṇa*, contains the meaning of the Veda does not mean that particular phrases in the one can be related to phrases in the other. Rather, it expresses a conviction that both contain the ultimate truth.

The most widely printed smṛti text today is the *Bhagavadgītā*, of which there have been hundreds of translations and commentaries since the late nineteenth century. Long before then it inspired many imitations, some of which are included in *Purāṇas*, such as the *Gaṇeśagītā* or the *Devīgītā*, while the *Anugītā* is included in the *Mahābhārata* itself (Gonda 1977: 271–76). The *Bhagavadgītā* is used as a text for religious classes, and is also much used in death rituals, although some paṇḍits disapprove of this (Firth 1997: 84, 87).

Many smṛti texts support the worship of a particular deity, Śiva, Viṣṇu or Śakti, but are known and accepted by worshippers of other deities. This is true of many of the *Purāṇas*. On the other hand, there are texts which are specific to one or other of these deities, variously known as *Āgama*s, *Tantra*s and *Saṃhitās*. The term āgama, meaning 'tradition', can refer generally to texts giving instruction in ritual life and the quest for salvation, but it is used especially for those which teach Śiva as the supreme deity. *Tantra* can also be used in a general sense, but is especially applied to texts on the worship of Śakti. The word *saṃhitā* has several applications, but two main ones: the *Saṃhitā*s of the Veda; and the class of texts devoted to Viṣṇu called the *Pāñcarātra Saṃhitās*. Although three terms, *Āgama*, *Tantra and Saṃhitā*, are often associated respectively with Śaivism, Śāktism and Vaiṣṇavism, none of them is restricted to any of these three. However, the particular texts that they denote are in most cases exclusively Śaivism, Śāktism or Vaiṣṇavism (Gonda 1977).

Mantra, vidhi, arthavāda

Another classification, developed in Pūrva Mīmāṃsā, divides portions of the Veda into mantra, vidhi and arthavāda. A mantra is a text that is spoken or sung as a ritual act. A vidhi, usually translated 'injunction', is a passage that tells ritual practitioners what to do and how to do it. Arthavāda, literally a 'statement of purpose', gives the reasons for performing the ritual in a particular way; in effect, it covers all those passages of the Veda which are neither mantra nor vidhi. Mantras are to be found in the *Saṃhitās*, but are also frequently quoted in the *Brāhmaṇas* and *Āraṇyakas*; vidhi and arthavāda are to be found in the *Brāhmaṇas, Āraṇyakas* and *Upaniṣads*.

This classification refers to Vedic texts, but the term mantra is used extensively outside the Vedic context. The terms vidhi and arthavāda are less used, but non-Vedic texts can similarly be divided into parts that are used in ritual, parts which prescribe and parts which provide motivation for ritual action.

Sanskrit texts and vernacular texts

The śruti and smṛti texts referred to above are all in Sanskrit, and the sound of Sanskrit is familiar, through its use in ritual, to many Hindus who do not know the language; but there are sacred texts in all Indian languages. The use of texts in vernacular languages was fostered by bhakti, with its emphasis on the relation of devotee and deity, which obviates the need for the brāhmaṇa and his ritual texts in Sanskrit. We need not suppose, however, that the earliest available bhakti texts, from the sixth-century Tamil poems onwards, were the first vernacular texts ever. The example of the Buddhist and Jain texts, composed from the outset in vernacular languages, suggests that Sanskrit's monopoly in the religious sphere had long been challenged.

Besides the bhakti poems there are countless vernacular *Purāṇas*, some of them translated or adapted from Sanskrit, some totally independent (Rocher 1986: 72–77). There are many vernacular versions of the *Rāmāyaṇa* which adapt the story to regional and didactic concerns, such as Kampan's Tamil version *Irāmavatāram*, or Tulsīdās's Hindi *Rāmcaritmānas*. These, especially the latter, are not only recited but presented in the dramas called *Rāmlīlā*, particularly at Daśahrā (Brockington 1998: 505–07; Lutgendorf 1991). Dramatisation of the *Mahābhārata* is less common, but dramas centred on Draupadī are performed in South India and Sri Lanka (Brockington 1998: 507; Hiltebeitel 1988–91; Tanaka 1991).

Some bhakti traditions make the rejection of Sanskrit texts quite explicit, as in the story of the Marathi poet Nāmdev, who caused a buffalo to recite the Veda (Ranade 1961: 71). The idea of the fifth Veda, and the idea that smṛti texts such as the *Bhāgavata Purāṇa* (see above) contain the meaning of the Veda, was extended to vernacular texts with concepts such as the Tamil Veda. On the other hand, in many traditions the production of vernacular texts has been followed by texts in Sanskrit: for instance, the Tamil poems of the Āḻvārs were followed by the Sanskrit works of Yāmunācārya, Rāmānuja and others. Here the change from the vernacular to Sanskrit was accompanied by a change from an emotional to an intellectual form of bhakti (Hardy 1983: 36–43); but the Āḻvārs were also followed by the *Bhāgavata Purāṇa*, which, being in Sanskrit, made emotional bhakti accessible outside the Tamil-speaking region.

Vernacular texts are necessarily regional, though this does not prevent their being translated or imitated in neighbouring languages; poems attributed to Kabīr, for instance, occur in Panjabi and Bengali versions as well as in Hindi. The

Telegu songs of Tyāgarāja (1767–1847) are sung throughout South India and in parts of the diaspora, but hardly known elsewhere (Jackson 1991). Sanskrit was the only language in which texts could be made accessible thoughout the Hindu world until English became increasingly used in the course of the nineteenth century. The English publications of Vivekānanda (a Bengali), Gandhi (a Gujarati), Radhakrishnan (a Tamil) and others show the importance of English in the development of a non-regional, non-sectarian Hinduism. Hindi, as the national language, has gained ground from English as an all-India language in the past fifty years.

While vernacular texts are regional by their nature, some Sanskrit texts are also regional or even local. Besides those belonging to locally based saṃpradāyas, there are texts belonging to places of pilgrimage or temples: *Sthala-Purāṇa*s ('purāṇas of the place, local purāṇas') giving the story of the origin of the place's sanctity and rules for visiting it, and *Māhātmya*s ('glorifications') extolling the local deity and the benefits to be gained at it. These two categories overlap, and examples are found in Sanskrit and vernacular languages (Rocher 1986: 71f.; Gonda 1977: 276–81).

Vernacular texts are not always comprehensible to their readers or hearers; it is not only Sanskrit that is used in ritual without being fully understood. The language of the Tamil bhakti poems is not modern spoken Tamil, but they are still regularly chanted in temples. Tulsīdās' *Rāmcaritmānas* may have owed its popularity initially to its being in language familiar to its hearers, but it continues to be recited in its original, now archaic form, its value lying in its sanctity rather than its accessibility.

Prose and verse

Most of the texts we are concerned with are in verse, but many mantras of the *Yajur veda*, and all the *Brāhmaṇas*, are in prose (remarkable as the first examples of prose in any Indian language); so are the *Āraṇyakas* and some of the *Upaniṣads* and the *Kalpasūtras*. The non-Vedic sūtras are also in prose. The *Mahābhārata* and *Purāṇas* are almost entirely in verse, with some passages in prose. Verse was and is used extensively in Sanskrit literature, including technical works such as the *Sāṃhyakārikās*, the foundation text of the Sāṃkhya system. By far the commonest verse form is the śloka, a stanza of thirty-two syllables divided into four quarters. It is flexible and easy to use, unlike the other metres used in the elaborate literature known as kāvya (see below). Ślokas are used even for quite unpoetic subjects, and have been composed by countless anonymous contributors to the *Purāṇas* and other texts, as well as by known poets.

Sanskrit prose was used in theological works such as Rāmānuja's *Vedārtha-saṃgraha* ('Compendium of the meaning of the Veda'), and for the vast literature of commentaries discussed below. Outside the category of sacred texts, it was used for narrative works such as the *Pañcatantra*, for drama and for other literary works.

In the vernacular languages, little was written in prose before the nineteenth century, except for letters and similar documents. The bhakti poems are in verse, though in some, such as the Kannaḍa vacans and the Marathi abhangs, the verse form is free. From 1816, Rammohan Roy and his Hindu and Christian opponents published prose works in Bengali and English as contributions to religious controversies, which had formerly been exclusively conducted in Sanskrit. Roy remarked in his earliest work that many people were unable to read Bengali prose and gave some brief hints on how to do so (Killingley 1982: 12; Das 1966: 131f.). Throughout the nineteenth century newspapers, novels and other innovations fostered the use of prose in the vernacular languages. Together with English, these were used in prose works of religious instruction and controversy, such as Swami Narayan's *Vacanāmṛta* ('Immortality in words') in Gujarati, Dayananda Saraswati's *Satyārtha Prakāśa* ('Light of truth') in Hindi, or Vivekānanda's works in English.

Kāvya

The term kāvya is sometimes translated 'poetry', though it can be in prose. It is a class of Sanskrit literature which requires considerable literary education to compose and to appreciate. It includes many literary forms, from one-verse epigrams to plays, prose novels and verse epics. It was developed under the patronage of kings, but continues even now, though few are sufficiently learned to enjoy it. The earliest surviving examples are inscriptions, from the second century CE onwards, and the *Buddha-carita* ('Life of the Buddha'), composed by Aśvaghoṣa in the first or second century. The *Rāmāyaṇa* is celebrated as the original kāvya, though the only passages in which it calls itself such are considered late by textual scholars, and it lacks the stylistic elaboration typical of kāvya (Brockington 1998: 23, 361). Unlike smṛti and other texts, kāvya strictly follows the norms set out by Pāṇini and other grammarians, and uses elaborate metres and stylistic ornaments described in literary manuals.

Though kāvya in general falls outside the category of sacred texts, it contains many references and allusions to myths, so that a detailed knowledge of mythology, as well as other subjects, is needed to appreciate it. Kāvya works commonly begin with a prayer or invocation of a deity. Some are built on mythological narratives, such as Kālidāsa's *Kumārasaṃbhava* on the birth of Skanda, or take up stories from the epics, such as his play *Śakuntalā.*

Some kāvya works are devotional throughout: examples are the *Gītagovinda* and the *Karṇāndana* ('Delight of the ears'), a poem from the Rādhāvallabhī saṃpradāya, which was founded by the poet's father, Hita Harivamśa, and centred on Kṛṣṇa's lover, Rādhā (Gonda 1977: 25–29; Entwistle 1987: 168). A particularly interesting example is the *Kuñcitāṅghri-stava* ('Hymn of praise to [Naṭarāja's] curved foot'), composed by Umāpati Śivācārya around 1300 CE. Each of its 313 verses ends with a refrain referring to Śiva's foot uplifted in the dance, approaching it through an ingenious and evocative interweaving of mythological, theological and philosophical ideas (D. Smith 1996).

Stotra

A popular kind of religious text, both Sanskrit and vernacular, is the stotra, a hymn of praise to a deity (Gonda 1977: 232–70). Many stotras are in very simple Sanskrit, using rhyme and a metre with a strong recurrent beat, unlike the śloka or the metres used in kāvya, often with a refrain. Several stotras are attributed to Śaṅkara (Mahadevan 1980; Hirst 2005: 24f.). The songs included in the *Gītagovinda* are stotras. The poem *Bande Mātaram* by Bankim Chandra Chatterjee, originally praising Bengal as a mother-goddess but modified to refer to India, is another example, so simple in its grammar that a reader who knows Bengali or Hindi can understand much of it (Lipner 2005).

A particular form of stotra is the nāma-stotra, essentially a list of names, epithets and descriptions of a particular deity (Gonda 1977: 268–70; Gonda 1970: 67–76). An early example is the *Śata-rudrīya* ('[hymn] of a thousand Rudras'), included in the *Black Yajur veda* (*Vājasaney Saṃhitā* 4, 5), and still recited in temples of Śiva. It invokes Rudra by many names and epithets, interspersed with prayers (Gonda 1970: 70f.; Gonda 1977: 241; translated Keith 1914: 353–62). Other well-known examples are the *Viṣṇu-sahasra-nāma* ('Thousand names of Viṣṇu'; Raghavan 1958: 421–36) and the *Lalitā-sahasra-nāma* ('Thousand names of the voluptuous [Goddess]') in the *Brahmāṇḍa Purāṇa*.

Commentary

In the Hindu tradition, texts are there to be commented on. Some commentaries, often called ṭīkā, merely explain difficult words; the term for a more substantial commentary is bhāṣya. Some, like Sāyaṇa's commentaries on Vedic texts, Śaṅkara's commentaries on the *Upaniṣads* or the many commentators on the *Manusmṛti* or *Mānavadharmaśāstra*, account for every word, on the principle that nothing in the original text is without purport. Certain texts, such as the *Brahmasūtras* and the *Bhagavadgītā,* have been commented on many times from different and often conflicting points of view; part of the commentator's task is to refute rival interpretations. A commentary, especially on a sūtra, may be an authoritative text in its own right, with sub-commentaries by members of the same school of thought refining the meaning of the first commentary in the light of further developments in the school. It has been suggested that the existence of substantial commentaries is a measure of the theological importance of a text, though a text which is religiously inspiring but not theologically weighty may attract little or no comment (Clooney 2003: 461). Besides Sanskrit commentaries, there are vernacular commentaries, for instance Tamil commentaries on Tamil texts (Hardy 1983: 244f.), and we have already mentioned oral commentaries on *Purāṇas*.

See also: **Āḻvārs; Āraṇyakas; Arthavāda; Ayodhyā; Bāuls; Bhagavadgītā; Bhāgavatas; Bhajan; Bhakti; Blood sacrifice; Brahman; Brāhmaṇas; Brahmasūtras; Buddhism, Relationship with Hinduism; Caitanya; Chatterjee, Bankim Chandra; Dalits; Daśahrā; Dayananda Saraswati, Swami; Dharmaśāstras; Diaspora; Draupadī; Gandhi, Mohandas Karamchand; Gītagovinda; Hinduism; Indus Valley Civilisation; Jainism, relationship with Hinduism; Kabīr; Kāmasūtra; Kalpasūtras; Karma; Kṛṣṇa; Languages; Mahābhārata; Mandir; Mantra; Manu; Müller, Friedrich Max; Narayana; Nāyaṉmār; Niyoga; Oṃ; Pañcatantra; Paṇḍit; Pāṇini; Purāṇas; Pūrva Mīmāṃsā; Rādhā; Radhakrishnan, T.; Rāmānuja; Rāmāyaṇa; Roy, Rammohan; Ṛṣi; Rudra; Sacred Books of the East; Śakti; Saṃhitā; Sāṃkhya; Saṃpradāya; Śaṅkara; Sāyaṇa; Sikhism, relationship with Buddhism; Śiva; Skanda; Sound recordings; Sri Lanka, Hindus in; Sūtra; Tamil Veda; Tantras; Television and radio; Tīrthayātrā (Pilgrimage); Tulsīdās(a); Umāpati Śivācārya; Upanayana; Upaniṣads; Vaiṣṇavism; Valmīki; Vārāṇasī; Veda; Vidhi; Viṣṇu; Vivekānanda, Swami; Vrata; Vṛndāvana; Vyāsa; Yajña; Yantra; Yāska; Yuga**

DERMOT KILLINGLEY

Further reading

Brockington, John. 1998. *The Sanskrit Epics* (Handbuch der Orientalistik, Abteilung 2, vol. 12). Leiden: Brill.

Bühnemann, G. 1988. *Pūjā: A Study in Smārta Ritual*. Vienna: University of Vienna, Institute for Indology.

Carpenter, David. 1992. 'Bharthari and the Veda.' In Jeffrey R. Timm, ed., *Texts in Context: Traditional Hermeneutics in South Asia*, 17–32. Albany, NY: State University of New York Press.

Chadwick, H.M. and N.K. Chadwick. 1932–40. *The Growth of Literature*, 3 vols. Cambridge: Cambridge University Press.

Clooney, Francis. 2003. 'Restoring "Hindu Theology" as a Category'. In Gavin Flood, ed., *The Blackwell Companion to Hinduism*. Oxford: Blackwell, 460f.

Das, Sisir Kumar. 1966. *Early Bengali Prose: Carey to Vidyasagar.* Calcutta: Bookland.

Entwistle, Alan W. 1987. *Braj: Centre of Krishna Pilgrimage.* Groningen: Egbert Forsten.

Firth, Shirley. 1997. *Death, Dying and Bereavement in a British Hindu Community.* Leuven: Peeters.

Gonda, Jan. 1970. *Notes on Names and the Name of God in Ancient India.* Amsterdam: North-Holland.

Gonda, Jan. 1977. *Medieval Religious Literature in Sanskrit* (History of Indian Literature, vol. 2, fasc. 1). Wiesbaden: Harrassowitz.

Goody, Jack. 1987. *The Interface between the Written and the Oral.* Cambridge: Cambridge University Press.

Graham, William A. 1987. *Beyond the Written Word: Oral Aspects of Scripture in the History of Religion.* Cambridge: Cambridge University Press.

Hardy, F.W. 1983. *Viraha-bhakti: the early history of Kṛṣṇa devotion in South India.* Delhi: Oxford University Press.

Hiltebeitel, Alf. 1988–91. *The Cult of Draupad,* 2 vols. Chicago, IL: University of Chicago Press.

Hirst, J.G. Suthren. 2005. *Śaṅkara's Advaita Vedānta: A Way of Teaching.* London: RoutledgeCurzon.

Jackson, William James. 1991. *Tyāgarāja: Life and Lyrics.* Madras: Oxford University Press.

Jackson, R. and E. Nesbitt. 1993. *Hindu Children in Britain.* Stoke-on-Trent: Trentham Books.

Keith, Arthur Berriedale (trans.). 1914. *The Veda of the Black Yajus School Entitled Taittiriya Sanhita: Translated from the Original Sanskrit Prose and Verse,* 2 vols numbered in one sequence (Harvard Oriental Series vols. 18 and 19). Cambridge, MA: Harvard University Press. Reprinted Delhi: Motilal Banarsidass, 1967.

Killingley, Dermot. 1982. *The Only True God: Works on Religion by Rammohun Roy.* Newcastle upon Tyne: Grevatt & Grevatt.

Lipner, Julius J. 2005. *Ānandamaṭh, or The Sacred Brotherhood: Bankim Chatterji: Translated with an Introduction and Critical Apparatus.* New York: Oxford University Press.

Lord, Albert B. 1960. *The Singer of Tales.* Cambridge, MA: Harvard University Press.

Lutgendorf, Philip. 1991. *The Life of a Text: Performing the Rāmcaritmānas of Tulsīdas.* Berkeley, CA: University of California Press.

Mahadevan, T.M.P. 1980. *The Hymns of Śaṅkara,* rev. edn. Delhi: Motilal Banarsidass (1st edn Madras, 1970).

Narayana Rao, Velcheru. 2004. 'Purāṇa'. In Sushil Mittal and Gene Thursby, eds, *The Hindu World.* New York: Routledge, 505–30.

Olivelle, Patrick. 2005. *Manu's Code of Law: A Critical Edition and Translation of the Mānava-Dharmaśāstra.* Oxford: Oxford University Press.

Ong, Walter J. 1982. *Orality and Literacy: The Technologizing of the Word.* London and New York: Methuen.

Raghavan, V. (trans.). 1958. *The Indian Heritage: An Anthology of Sanskrit Literature,* 2nd edn. Bangalore: Indian Institute of World Culture.

Ranade, Mahadev Govind. 1961. *The Rise of the Maratha Power.* Delhi: Publications Division, Ministry of Information and Broadcasting, Government of India (first published Bombay: Punalekar, 1900).

Renou, Louis. 1953. *Religions of Ancient India.* London: Athlone Press.

Ricoeur, Paul. 1981. *Hermeneutics and the Human Sciences.* Ed. and trans. John B. Thompson. Cambridge: Cambridge University Press.

Rocher, L. 1986. *The Puranas.* Wiesbaden: O. Harrassowitz.

Scharfe, Hartmut. 2002. *Education in Ancient India* (Handbuch der Orientalistik, Section 2, vol. 16). Leiden: Brill.

Singer, Milton. 1972. *When a Great Tradition Modernizes: An Anthropological Approach to Indian Civilization.* London: Pall Mall Press.

Smith, David. 1996. *The Dance of Śiva: Religion, Art and Poetry in South India.* Cambridge: Cambridge University Press.

Smith, Wilfred Cantwell. 1993. *What Is Scripture? A Comparative Approach.* Minneapolis, MN: Fortress Press.

Tanaka, Masakazu. 1991. *Patrons, Devotees and Goddesses: Ritual and Power among the Tamil Fishermen of Sri Lanka.* Kyoto: Kyoto University Institute for Research in Humanities.

Timm, Jeffrey L. (ed.). 1992. *Texts in Context: Traditional Hermeneutics in South Asia.* Albany, NY: State University of New York Press.

Warder, A.K. 1970. *Indian Buddhism.* Delhi: Motilal Banarsidass.

SACRED THREAD

See: **Upanayana**

ṢAḌDARŚANA

The Sanskrit term Ṣaḍdarśana, 'six views', refers to the six systems of Indian philosophy Nyāya, Vaiśeṣika, Sāṃkhya, Yoga, Pūrva Mīmāṃṣā and Vedānta (Uttara Mīmāṃsā). The term itself is a compound of ṣaṣ, 'six', and darśana, 'view', the latter of which derives from the root dṛś, meaning 'see', with its implications of conceptual knowledge as well as perceptual observation. In philosophical expositions, authors refer to the correct view (samyag-darśana) versus a wrong view (mithyā-darśana), or to the view of one tradition of thought as opposed to that of another. Growing out of circles of oral debate, systematic presentations of various topics were summarised in treatises consisting of sūtras, 'short aphorisms', which were memorised and transmitted with commentary, initially oral and later written. Argumentation in commentaries on received sūtra texts and their commentaries, and in later instructional manuals and verse summaries, typically took the form of the presentation and criticism of an opponent's point of view followed by the exposition of one's own. Other terms used to refer to points of view, sciences and traditions of thought include dṛṣṭi, 'view' (also from the root dṛś), from which is derived Pālī diṭṭhi, most conspicuous in Buddhism, tantra 'system', mata 'thought', siddhānta 'conclusion', śāstra 'discipline', vāda 'exposition', vidyā 'science' and naya 'worldview'.

The long history of documenting various views in India shows considerable variety in the number, range and arrangement of views included. Early texts such as the *Upaniṣads*, epics and the Buddhist canon list various views. Bhartṛhari's *Vākyapadīya* (late fifth century) uses the term darśana to refer to schools of thought including Vaiśeṣika and (Pūrva-) Mīmāṃsā (Halbfass 1988: 268), and Cāttanār's Buddhist Tamil verse epic *Maṇimekhalai* (500 CE) includes a list of six systems of thought (Varadachari 1971). Jains and Vedāntins composed doxographies in order to explain, justify and demarcate their own doctrines as encompassing and transcending contrasting views (Halbfass 1988: 355). While the oldest extant Sanskrit doxography (Halbfass 1988: 264), the Jain Haribhadra's *Ṣaḍdarśanasamuccaya* (eighth century), includes six systems of thought, as its title, *Compendium of Six Views*, announces, it does not give a separate treatment of Vedānta and closes with an exposition of the Lokāyata. The *Sarvasiddhāntasaṃgraha* (Compendium of All Conclusions), falsely attributed to Śaṅkara (Halbfass 1988: 535, n.7), surveys ten schools of thought, including Lokāyata, Jainism, Buddhism and the view of Vyāsa as author of the *Mahābhārata*. The most famous doxography, Mādhava's *Sarvadarśanasaṃgraha* (Compendium of All Views) (*c.*1331 CE), surveys sixteen schools of thought, treating Dvaita and Viśiṣṭādvaita separately, and including in addition Pāśupata, Śaiva, Śāiva Siddhānta and Pāṇini's grammatical school. Only in recent centuries did recognition of the list of the six systems that share acceptance of Vedic authority become standard (Halbfass 1988: 353). These form three pairs. Nyāya and Vaiśeṣika deal primarily with epistemology and ontology, respectively; the soteriological schools of Sāṃkhya and Yoga share a dualist evolutionary ontology; and the two Mīmāṃsās ground themselves in the exegesis of Vedic texts concerning ritual duty (Dharma) and Brahman, respectively. These six contrast with Buddhism, Jainism and Lokāyata in that the latter deny Vedic authority.

See also: **Astika and Nāstika; Bhartṛhari; Brahman; Dharma; Dvaita; Itihāsa; Jainism, relationship with Hinduism; Lokāyata; Mahābhārata; Nyāya; Pāṇini; Pāśupatas; Pūrva Mīmāṃṣā; Śāiva Siddhānta; Śaivism; Sāṃkhya; Śaṅkara; Sūtra;**

Upaniṣads; Vaiśeṣika; Vedānta; Viśiṣṭādvaita; Vyāsa; Yoga

PETER M. SCHARF

Further reading

Bartley, Christopher. 2005. *Indian Philosophy A–Z*. New York: Palgrave Macmillan.

Bedekar, V.M. (trans.). 1973. *History of Indian* Philosophy, 2 vols. By Erich Frauwallner. Delhi: Motilal Banarsidass.

Cowell, Edward B. and Archibald Edward Gough. 1882. *The Sarva-darśana-saṅgraha of Mādhavāchārya: Or Review of the Different Systems of Hindu Philosophy*. London: Trübner & Co., 2–11. [Delhi: Motilal Banarsidass, 2000.]

Dasgupta, Surendranath. 1922–55. *A History of Indian Philosophy*, 5 vols. Cambridge: Cambridge University Press.

Grimes, John A. 2004. 'Darśana'. In Sushil Mittal and Gene Thursby, eds, *The Hindu World*. London: Routledge, 531–52.

Halbfass, Wilhelm. 1988. *India and Europe: An Essay in Understanding*; ch. 15, 'Darśana, Ānvīkṣikī, Philosophy', 263–86; ch. 19, 'The Sanskrit Doxographies and the Structure of Hindu Traditionalism', 349–68. Albany, NY: SUNY Press.

Hiriyanna, Mysore. 1932. *Outlines of Indian Philosophy*. London: George Allen & Unwin. [Reprint: Delhi: Motilal Banarsidass, 1993.]

King, Richard. 1999. *Indian Philosophy: An Introduction to Hindu and Buddhist Thought*. Washington, DC: Georgetown University Press.

Müller, Max. 1952 [1899]. *Indian Philosophy*, 4 vols. Calcutta: S. Gupta. [1st edn. London: Longmans, Green and Co.]

Raju, P.T. 1985. *Structural Depths of Indian Thought*. SUNY Series in Philosophy. Albany, NY: State University of New York Press.

Varadachari, V. 1971. 'Treatment of the Schools of Religion and Philosophy in the Maṇimekhalai'. *Sri Venkatesa University Oriental Journal* 14: 9–26.

SĀDHU

Sādhu is an ascetic who abandon the duty of everyday life to seek mokṣa. The word sādhu comes from the Sanskrit root sadh-, 'to accomplish', 'to finish', and indicates a man or a woman (sādhvī) who follows a certain sādhana. The instructions for such practice vary according to the order (saṃpradāya) and usually are meant to reach perfection (siddhi). As long as the ascetic has not reached this state, she or he is a sādhakaśī, a practitioner. Sādhus live in a non-ritual state: they wander homeless, earn a living by begging, wear sectarian marks and tend to behave in an anti-social manner. Vegetarian alimentation is not compulsory; nor is celibacy. Many sādhus eat meats and consume liquors and intoxicants. The presence of gharbari-sādhus (ascetic householders) is accepted within some saṃpradāyas, while others have sexual intercourse with female disciples (śiṣī). When they die, sādhus are generally not cremated but buried. Their tombs (samādhi) can become centres of pilgrimage.

See also: **Mokṣa; Saṃpradāya; Saṃnyāsa; Tīrthayātrā (Pilgrimage)**

FABRIZIO M. FERRARI

Further reading

Olivelle, Patrick. (ed.). 1992. *Saṃnyāsa Upaniṣads. Hindu Scriptures on Asceticism and Renunciation*. Oxford: Oxford University Press.

Tripathi, B.D. 2004. *Sadhus of India: The Sociological View*. Varanasi: Pilgrims.

SAHADEVA

The youngest of the five sons of King Pāṇḍu, known collectively as the Pāṇḍavas. Sahadeva and his twin brother Nakula were the twin sons of Pāṇḍu's second wife, Mādrī, but mythology ascribes their paternity to Nāsatya, one of the twin Aśvins. In some accounts, it is said that Sahadeva and Nakula were the incarnations of the Aśvins. The *Mahābhārata* informs us that Sahadeva studied astronomy with Droṇa and was learned in the subject. However, he was also skilled in the farming of cattle. He was married to Vijayā and they had a son named Suhotra.

See also: **Aśvins; Droṇa; Mādrī; Mahābhārata; Nakula; Pāṇḍavas; Pāṇḍu**

RON GEAVES

Further reading

Dasgupta, Madhusraba. 1999. *Samsad Companion to the Mahābhārata*. Calcutta: Sahitya Samsad.

SAHAJA YOGA

Sahaja Yoga was founded in 1970 by Sri Mataji Nirmala Devi (b. 1923), who is known as Mataji or the Divine Mother. She was born into a Protestant family in central India, but Sahaja Yoga is in many ways a traditional Hindu path. Mataji was originally a disciple of Osho, but fell out with him and set up her own movement. She teaches mainly in Britain and India, but also has disciples worldwide and travels extensively. The movement claims approximately 20,000 members worldwide, half in India, but is not growing.

Sahaja Yoga is unusual in being founded and led by a woman, but the movement is not feminist and leadership positions are held almost exclusively by men. Mataji herself is believed to be the Supreme Goddess by her followers, and she claims to be an incarnation avatāra of the śakti. As Lakṣmi, the wife of the god Viṣṇu, she is the model of the ideal wife, upon which female disciples are expected to model themselves – meek, submissive and 'feminine'.

Photographs of Mataji are also used as symbols in meditation.

Sahaja means spontaneity and the basis of Sahaja Yoga is spontaneous union with the divine through kuṇḍalinī yoga. It is believed that with Mataji's help kuṇḍalinī can be awakened in anyone. When it happens, practitioners are said to feel a cool breeze on the palms of their hands and above their heads. The praxis is primarily devotional and concern has been expressed at the high level of commitment demanded by Mataji.

There have been no public scandals, but there are allegations of financial misdemeanours, sexual abuse, threatening and violent behaviour towards ex-members and critics. There is also concern about separation of children from their parents and overly strict discipline at the movement's school in India, although it is not compulsory for children to be educated there.

See also: **Avatāra; Bhakti; Kuṇḍalinī Yoga; Lakṣmī, Śrī; Rajneesh, Bhagwan Shree; Śakti; Tantras; Viṣṇu; Yoga**

ELIZABETH PUTTICK

Further reading

Palmer, Susan and Charlotte Hardman (eds). 1999. *Children in New Religions*. Rutgers University Press.

SAI BABA (AS MOVEMENT)

The Sai Baba Movement denotes the following of Sathya Sai Baba, a contemporary Hindu religious leader and miracle-worker. Born in 1926 in Puttaparthi (Andra Pradesh) and regarded by his followers as an avatāra (an incarnation of God), he is one of contemporary India's most renowned religious figures. He claimed to be a reincarnation of Sai Baba of Shirdi, and also to be a dual incarnation of the Hindu deity Śiva and his consort Śakti. Especially popular among India's urban middle and upper classes, he also has a significant international following.

The religious and ritual culture of the movement is based on the premise of Sathya Sai Baba's divinity. His devotees regard his discourses as divinely originated and treat his person with ritual attitudes appropriate for images of deities. Many devotees (and even non-devotees) keep his pictures or images as objects of worship in their household shrines and regard him as a watchful and protective presence in their lives, even when he is not physically present. Devotees believe his divinity to be manifested in miracles, and his reputation for miracle-making power is undoubtedly a major element in his personal charisma. Although he is famous for miracles of all kinds, he specialises in alleged materialisations of objects and substances, which devotees treat as his power-charged blessing in physical form. He is especially noted for his materialisation and distribution of sacred ash. This practice echoes his connection with Shirdi Sai Baba, also famous for distributing miraculous ash, and reiterates his link with Śiva, a deity associated with ashes in myth and ritual. A spin-off of his materialisation of ash is the alleged oozing of sacred ash from his pictures in some devotees' homes. Sathya Sai Baba's teachings are drawn from a generalised ecumenical Hinduism and are unremarkable. He encourages meditation, but does not promote a special system of his own. Among his most important teachings is the essential truth of all religions and the need for interreligious tolerance and understanding.

His devotees do not constitute an organised sect, and devotion to him can be expressed at varying levels of intensity, from placing his picture on one's dashboard or in one's family shrine to regular pilgrimage to Puttaparthi. Although the movement is not a bounded group, an entity called Central Shri Sathya Sai Trust acts as an institutional core. Under its umbrella, various subsidiary organisations manage the movement's main ashram at Puttaparthi and other centres, and undertake a variety of charitable, social service, publishing and educational activities.

See also: **Avatāra; Magic; Meditation; Sai Baba, Sathya; Sai Baba, Shirdi; Śakti; Śiva; Tīrthayātrā (Pilgrimage); Vibhūti**

Lawrence A. Babb

Further reading

Babb, L.A. 1986. *Redemptive Encounters: Three Modern Styles in the Hindu Tradition.* Berkeley, CA: University of California Press.

Klass, M. 1991. *Singing with Sai Baba: The Politics of Revitalization in Trinidad.* Boulder, CO: Westview Press.

Swallow, D.A. 1982. 'Ashes and Powers: Myth, Rite and Miracle in an Indian God-Man's Cult'. *Modern Asian Studies* 16: 123–58.

White, C.S.J. 1978. 'The Sai Baba Movement: Approaches to the Study of Indian Saints'. *Journal of Asian Studies* 31: 863–78.

SAI BABA, SATHYA (b. 1926)

Sathya Sai Baba is a contemporary Hindu religious leader and miracle-worker. Born in Puttaparthi, a remote village of Andra Pradesh, at the age of 13 he proclaimed himself to be a reincarnation of Sai Baba of Shirdi, after which his reputation as a holy man and performer of miraculous cures and materialisations spread rapidly, at first within South India and then beyond. In June of 1963, after eight days of apparent self-cured illness, he announced that he was an incarnation of the deity Śiva and his consort Śakti in a single body, and added that there would be a total of three Sai incarnations, all in the spiritual lineage of Bharadvaja. Shirdi Sai Baba was Śakti alone; Sathya Sai Baba is Śiva and Śakti together, and still to come is an incarnation of Śiva alone, who will be in Karnataka state and known as Prem Sai. Sathya Sai Baba has acquired a large following, especially among middle- and upper-class urbanites, and is currently a religious figure of national importance in India. At the foundation of his charisma is his reputed miraculous power, and he is especially famous for materialisations of sacred ash and other items. His teachings are eclectic, with a strong emphasis on inter-religious harmony. Under his direction and in his name, his followers have created a number of organisations engaged in religious, charitable and educational endeavours.

See also: **Sai Baba (as movement); Sai Baba, Shirdi; Śakti; Śiva; Vibhūti**

LAWRENCE A. BABB

Further reading

Babb, L.A. 1986. *Redemptive Encounters: Three Modern Styles in the Hindu Traditions*. Berkeley, CA: University of California Press.

Murphet, H. 1975. *Sai Baba: Man of Miracles*. Madras: Macmillan Company of India.

Swallow, D.A. 1982. 'Ashes and Powers: Myth, Rites and Miracle in an Indian God-Man's Cult'. *Modern Asian Studies* 16: 123–58.

White, C.S.J. 1972. 'The Sai Baba Movement: Approaches to the Study of Indian Saints'. *Journal of Asian Studies* 31: 863–78.

SAI BABA, SHIRDI

Sai Baba of Shirdi was a saint and miracle-worker who achieved great fame in life and continued to be the focus of a devotional cult after his death in 1918. His place and date of birth unknown, he settled in the Maharashtrian town of Shirdi in 1858. Having been refused permission to live in a Hindu temple, he took up lifelong residence in an abandoned mosque. His persona was that of a Muslim mendicant, but his teachings blended Islamic and Hindu elements and his devotees were mostly Hindu. He famously used ashes from a perpetually burning fire as a means of blessing his devotees and performing healing miracles. A sizeable pilgrimage complex devoted to his worship exists in Shirdi today.

See also: **Mandir; Sai Baba (as movement); Sai Baba, Sathya; Tīrthayātrā (Pilgrimage); Vibhūti**

LAWRENCE A. BABB

Further reading

Rigopoulos, A. 1993. *The Life and Teachings of Sai Baba of Shirdi*. Delhi: Sri Satguru Publications.

White, C.S.J. 1972. 'The Sai Baba Movement: Approaches to the Study of Indian Saints'. *Journal of Asian Studies* 31: 863–78.

ŚAIVA

See: **Śaivism**

ŚAIVA SIDDHĀNTA (ŚUDDHA ŚAIVA)

Today, Śaiva Siddhānta is a school of Śaiva thought and practice which is associated with southern India, in particular with the state of Tamil Nadu. Yet this sect, which venerates the god Śiva, was one of the most influential in the pan-Indian spread of Śaiva devotional worship in the medieval period. Literally, a siddhānta is a 'conclusive doctrine', and thus the term Śaiva Siddhānta makes explicit reference to the elaborate theological doctrines which define the tradition. Around the ninth century CE this philosophical school began to distinguish itself from general Śaivism and presented itself as Śuddha Śaiva, or 'pure Śaivism', another term for the siddhānta school. Soon after this period, evidence for Śaiva Siddhānta temples and monasteries is found concentrated in Tamil Nadu, but also as widely spread as the modern states of Madhya Pradesh, Andhra Pradesh, Gujarat, Rajasthan, Maharastra, Orissa and even some parts of Southeast Asia. The most popular subsect of Siddhānta Śaivism was known as the Mattamayūra, whose teachers served as advisors for kings of prominent regional and trans-regional dynasties, such as the Kalachuris and the Colas.

The popularity and spread of this sect was due in large part to its focus on state-sponsored temple worship, evolving countless works on temple construction and guidelines for ritual worship, along with an elaborate and consistent set of theological doctrines. These are largely contained in the genre of texts known as the Śaiva (and Raudra) *Āgamas*, of which there are said to be twenty-eight primary 'root' texts (*mūlāgama*) and around 200 subsidiary texts (*upāgama*). These texts were considered authoritative, 'revealed' literature for the Siddhāntins, along with the Vedic *Saṃhitā*s (with a special focus on the *Śatarudrīya* of the *Yajurveda*) and *Upaniṣads* (in particular the *Atharvaśiras Upaniṣad*) of mainstream brahmanism. Uniquely among Śaiva sects, the Siddhāntins also accept as authoritative a series of Tamil texts in addition to these Sanskrit works: a set of devotional poems known as the *Tirumurai* and a collection of thirteenth- to fourteenth-century theological treatises known as the *Meykaṇṭaśāstras*. Of these, however, the *Āgama*s are generally given the most weight in the tradition. Additionally, many of the *Śaiva Purāṇas* bear the imprint of being composed and/or redacted by Siddhānta scholars, making a substantial portion of the popular and scholarly understanding of classical Śaivism a product of Siddhānta doctrine.

The strong priestly and scholarly emphasis of this sect allowed for an elaborate and remarkably consistent doctrinal framework. A dualistic system of thought (as opposed to the monistic doctrines of the Trika philosophical system, for example), Siddhānta ontology is based on the discrete and eternal existence of three categories of entities: the singular Lord (pati), a plurality of individual souls (paśus, or 'creatures') and the infinite forms and permutations of physical and mental matter which comprises the material universe (pāśa, or 'fetter'). The basic problem of human suffering is due to the fact that the essentially pure individual soul is bound to impure matter through the habitual performance of agentive action (karma). It is through the grace (prasāda) of Śiva, the 'Lord of Creatures' (Paśupati), that liberation from this bind is possible – and this grace is attainable through the fourfold methodology laid down in the Śaiva *Āgamas*: knowledge (jñāna), ritual (kriyā), conduct (caryā) and discipline (yoga). Known as the four 'feet' (pada) of Śaiva praxis, these categories are thought to comprise the contents of an *Āgama* text. The central theme of Śaiva Siddhānta practice, however is devotion to Śiva, a doctrinal focus that in many ways parallels (and likely bears the influence of) developments in bhakti theologies of contemporaneous Vaiṣṇava sects.

See also: **Bhakti (as path); Brahmanism; Jñāna; Karma (Law of Action); Kashmiri Śaivism; Mandir; Purāṇas; Sacred texts; Śaivism; Saṃhitā; Śiva; Upaniṣads; Vaiṣṇavism**

TRAVIS L. SMITH

Further reading

Davis, R. 1991. *Ritual in an Oscillating Universe: Worshipping Śiva in Medieval India*. Princeton, NJ: Princeton University Press.

ŚAIVISM

Śaivism is a term that broadly comprises a diverse set of doctrines, practices and representations that relate to the great Hindu divinity Śiva. It refers not to a single cult or religion, but rather a collection of systems that have shared historical connections. Strictly speaking, a Śaiva is not simply a worshipper of Śiva, which could apply to any individual who reverences Śiva within a general framework or Hindu devotionalism, but rather refers to an initiate into one or another of the Śaiva lineages, subscribing to some degree to the theological and practical strictures of that system.

History and origins

The history of the worship of Śiva is traceable only in part via the history of the individual Śaiva sects, given the fact that the evidence for Śiva far pre-dates concrete evidence of any organised sect. According to many scholars, 'Śaivism' has roots in the Indus Valley Civilisation, where pictorial representations on seals suggest an ithyphallic 'proto-Śiva' seated in a yogic position. Whether or not this figure indeed has any historical connection to the classical Śiva is debatable at best, but the fact that this is much debated in scholarly literature provides an occasion to evaluate those features which are supposed to be characteristic of Śiva and his worship.

Śiva is closely associated with the liṅga, which is overwhelmingly his most common aniconic representation. Considered a phallic symbol, the cylindrical or conical form is a symbol of generative power common to many cultures. Certainly by the period of the *Purāṇas* and the post-Vedic classical Hindu tradition, the connection between Śiva and the liṅga is firmly established. Because of this strong association, some scholars speculate that several derogatory references in the *Ṛgveda* to śiśna-devāḥ, which may mean '[those who worship the] phallus-god', is early textual evidence of Śiva worship. In any case, the classical worship of Śiva has strong ties to both ascetic yoga practices and lineages, as well as to the liṅga – perhaps in the context of indigenous fertility cults. Both of these elements are peripheral to the early Vedic social and religious world, which focused on the performance of the fire sacrifice and on a relatively fixed pantheon of gods in connection to that.

The crucial link between the extra-Vedic elements of Śaivism and the Vedic tradition lies in the Vedic deity Rudra ('The Howler'). Both traditional and modern scholars have sought to explore the extent to which the great Lord Śiva of the classical Hindu tradition can be identified with the Vedic divinity Rudra. Characterised as a fierce (ugra) and powerful warrior god, Rudra is prayed to in several hymns partially or fully dedicated to him in the *Ṛgveda* (1.43, 1.114 and 2.33). He is a hunter who howls and possesses sharp and dangerous weapons. The *Ṛgveda* descriptions do not offer much detail beyond these, except that he is also described as having braided or matted hair (kapardin) and being of ruddy or tawny colour. Rudra is also famously invoked in the *Taittirīya Saṃhitā* of the *Kṛṣṇa-Yajurveda* and the *Vājasaneyi Saṃhitā* of the *Śukla-Yajurveda*, in a section known to both as the *Śatarudrīya* ('The Hundred Epithets of Rudra'), an extended invocation of Rudra which many later Śaiva traditions hold in high esteem. Here Rudra is described with a number of epithets that become prominent later in classical religious understandings of Rudra-Śiva. He is praised, for example, as the 'lord of animals' (paśupati), the 'mountain-dweller' (giriśa), 'the peaceful' (śambhu; śaṅkara), and 'blue-throated' (nīlakaṇṭha), among other appellations. All of these epithets become extremely common in the classical Śaiva religious traditions, and many develop specific mythological associations as well. In general, Rudra is worshipped as a fierce god responsible for storms, famine, disease and natural disasters; he is propitiated primarily to calm his violent, destructive nature and to show instead his 'compassionate face' (dakṣiṇaṃ mukham), which grants favours and offers protection from all these dangers. Although Rudra is infrequently described with the epithet Śiva in these early Vedic texts, explicit identification of Rudra and Śiva seems to first occur in the *Śvetāśvatara Upaniṣad* (sixth century BCE?), apparently the first textual source in which Rudra and Śiva occur as alternative names of a single being.

Sects and doctrines

The development of mainstream Śaivism might be usefully understood as an extended negotiation between the extra-Vedic world-renouncing ascetic traditions, indigenous worship customs and beliefs, and the hegemonic, pan-Indian brahmanical tradition which reverenced the Vedas, their auxiliary *śāstras* and their varṇa-based hierarchical social structure. In examining the major Śaiva sects, it is possible to see this negotiation played out in the varying socio-historical contexts in which these sects were active. Still, except for the relatively consistent and coherent sect of the Śaiva Siddhāntins, it is extremely difficult to separate the strands of Śaiva sects, given the interpenetration of their doctrines and practices. Although scholars often distinguish between 'Purāṇic' and 'non-Purāṇic' Śaivism, with the former thought of as a 'general' form of Śaivism somehow distinct from the specialised, initiation-based practice of particular sects (usually divided into the atimārga and mantramārga paths, on which more will be said below), this distinction is difficult to establish. While it is generally true that the Purāṇic Śaivism tends towards aligning Śaiva practice with normative brahmanical models, in particular the traditional varṇāśramadharma framework, this is true of much of sectarian Śaivism as well, including some varieties which emphasise the paradigm of the socially transcendent ascetic. Moreover, the Śaiva-based *Purāṇas* themselves frequently, if not universally, bear the influence of sectarian Śaivism, and in at least some cases bear evidence of having been composed or significantly redacted by sectarian Śaiva scholars. It is therefore necessary to understand the fluidity of Śaiva sectarianism: even when certain textual sources tend to clearly demarcate sects and doctrines, in all likelihood the complex web of Śaiva lineages and practices were on the whole quite amorphous, being alternately related to and distinguished from each other, as well as being alternately related to and distinguished from smārta brahmanical praxis.

Though it is not possible to reliably tie its composition to a particular historical sect or lineage, the aforementioned *Śvetāśvatara Upaniṣad* is the earliest expression of what could be termed a Śaiva theology. And as this text is more a hymnic praise of Śiva than a systematic theological treatise, it is not possible to derive specific doctrinal tenets from it. The Rudra-Śiva of the *Śvetāśvatara Upaniṣad* is presented as the absolute (non-dualistic) principle and the primal cause, and again is held to be the god of gods, the recipient of prayers and worship, and the great bestower of boons. He is attained by tapas, and his worship leads to the removal of all worldly bondage. These elements of Śiva adoration and worship are easily recognisable in the more developed doctrines of the later Śaiva schools.

Classically there are four sects of Śaivism, although there is an extraordinary amount of uncertainty and divergence of opinion even as to which these four were and what constituted their individual doctrines and practices. One commonly cited list of the four major sects distinguishes the Pāśupata, the Śaiva Siddhānta or Śuddha Śaiva, the Kālāmukha and the Kāpālika. Within this fold, a further distinction is sometimes made in Śaiva scriptures (*Āgama*) between the 'Outer Path' (atimārga) and the 'Path of Mantras' (mantramārga). The 'outer path' is for ascetics interested in freeing themselves from the cycle of saṃsāra, while the 'path of mantras' is open to all aspirants (ascetics and householders) who seek eventual salvation and the attainment of special powers (siddhi) and sensual pleasures (bhoga) in worlds along the way to liberation. The atimārga is thought to transcend the traditional system of the four classes and stages of life (varṇāśramadharma). Each of these paths requires an initiation into the specific practices in order to be a recognised participant in the tradition. The various sects are generally understood to be complementary to one another, although one or another is usually said by its expounders to contain the most complete exposition of the Śaiva way.

The Pāśupatas seem to be the oldest distinct sect of Śaivism and emerge around the second century BCE. Evidence for their existence is in the *Mahābhārata* (300 BCE?–300 CE?) and in a possible reference in the *Mahābhāṣya* of the grammarian Patañjali. There, the sect is called that of the Śiva-bhāgavatas, and it mentions their dedication to extreme ascetic practices, and their wandering about with iron tridents (the trident or triśūla being the favorite weapon of Śiva – to this day, Śiva temples commonly feature a trident on their peak). Patañjali also mentions the worship of images of Śiva (as well as those of Skanda and Viśākha) in homes. This seems to indicate the two interrelated modes by which Śaivism developed: the ascetic traditions and the lay devotional traditions. It was the emergence of Pāśupata Śaivism, it is reasonable to assume, which first effectively consolidated the two and began the systematic integration between the popular folk worship of Śiva and the ascetic yoga Śiva cults. And, despite the traditional assertion that Pāśupata Śaivism, being within the division of the atimārga, was universally opposed to the varṇāśramadharma ideology of mainstream brahmanism, it is probable that this sect was also responsible for integrating previously marginal or antinomian Śiva-based asceticism – and, with it, Śiva himself – into the brahmanical fold. That particular Pāśupata lineages were able to build a popular, pan-Indian cult around the worship of Śiva was likely due in part to their receiving support from the imperial Guptas (300–550 CE). Although the Guptas were primarily Vaiṣṇavas, they also supported Śaiva temples and monastic institutions, and it appears that most of these were of Pāśupata affiliation. In this way, the Pāśupatas became the early architects of a pan-Indian, temple-based Śaivism. In the south in particular, Śaivism became the dominant state-sponsored religious expression, culling patronage from several other regional dynasties, and largely supplanting both Buddhism and Jainism.

The 'pure' (śuddha) Śaiva doctrine is also known as Śaiva Siddhānta. This sect emerged from the earlier Pāśupatas and at least by the ninth century CE emerged as the dominant Śaiva sect. Although the evidence of the precise nature of the historical relationship between these two sects is sparse, they appear to be closely enough related to speculate that the Pāśupatas died out only in that their institutions became merged into those of the Siddhāntins, and into general Purāṇic Śaivism. With the Siddhānta school, the more extreme ascetic traditions were generally backgrounded in favour of a temple- and laity-based institutional framework, which elaborated an extensive philosophical and practical textual canon, along with supporting a strong priestly and scholarly tradition. The Siddhānta cult became dominant in much of India, although its survival in the north was short-lived, due in large part to the Turko-Afghan military incursions from the north-west from the tenth century CE and the eventual establishment of Islamic state governance in the north with the establishment of the Delhi Sultanate in 1206. The north had also featured another closely related brand of Śaivism, known as the Trika school (often referred to in recent discourse as Kashmiri Śaivism), which gained popularity from about the ninth century.

The southern Siddhāntins were greatly influenced by the Śaiva devotional saints, known as Nāyaṉmār, of the Kāveri river basin, who composed ecstatic devotional poetry to Lord Śiva in Tamil. Collections of these hymns, which were originally composed between the seventh and tenth centuries, were to be incorporated into the Śaiva Siddhānta canon, along with other scholarly treatises in Tamil.

The historical connection between the Pāśupatas and the Śaiva Siddhāntins can be seen in their doctrinal continuities. In both, the universe is considered to be composed of three distinct and eternal entities: the Lord (pati), individual souls (paśu) and matter (pāśa). The basic problem of human existence is that the soul is bound to matter, due to the influence of mala (impurity), which is accumulated through agentive action (karma). It is through the grace of Lord Śiva, attainable through the four categories of practice laid down in the Śaiva *Āgamas*, that an individual soul is released from this bondage of impurity and thus matter. The overarching theme of Śaiva practice is devotion to Śiva, the theological exposition of which parallels certain Vaiṣṇava doctrines, to which the Śaiva sects have significant historical relations. The practice of cultivating devotion towards Śiva might be said to constitute the core of normative Śaiva theology.

The Kālāmukhas are often considered a class of ascetics within the Pāśupata fold (specifically, followers of a branch of that sect known as the Lākula, named after a Śaiva teacher and reformer called Lākulīśa), who practised more transgressive forms of worship to Śiva in the extreme ascetic mode of the atimārga. This group also considered to have been the precursor of the Liṅgāyat sect, which emerged in the thirteenth century CE around the modern-day Indian state of Karnataka.

The sect known as the Kāpālikas likely refers to a cluster of ascetic traditions centring around various aspects of the cult figure of Bhairava, considered to be a particularly fierce form of Śiva. On the other hand, most occurrences of the term Kāpālika were likely etic references to any form of 'skull-bearing' (kāpālin) ascetic of Śaiva strain.

Conclusion

If Śaivism and Vaiṣṇavism are considered the two dominant streams of Hindu thought and practice, the two might be usefully distinguished beyond their centring around the worship of different supreme godheads. To be sure, the two are parallel in many ways: both develop similar theological constructions (especially those which focus on bhakti as the most effective means to salvation) and both meta-traditions can be viewed in some way to be the result of the interaction of Veda-centred brahmanical orthodoxies with a diverse array of local, regional and indigenous practices. Yet Śaivism, and indeed, Śiva himself, retained more of an extra-Vedic character. This is evident in the importance of the figure of the ascetic or yogi, who theoretically transcends social categorisations. It is also preserved in the importance of the Tantric elements of mantra and magic, which in general are more prevalent in Śaivism than in Vaiṣṇavism. This is not to say that Śiva and Śaiva practice is universally, or even largely, considered to be heretical or outside the pale of Vedic orthodoxy – on the contrary, the success of Śaivism is largely due to its conformity to this hegemonic model. Yet the preservation of these counter-normative elements is noteworthy, and is responsible for the distinctive nature of the diverse traditions known collectively as Śaivism.

See also: **Agnihotra; Āśramas; Bhakti (as path); Brahmanism; Buddhism, Relationship with Hinduism; Indus Valley Civilisation; Jainism, relationship with Hinduism; Kāpālikas; Karma; Kashmiri Śaivism; Lakulīśa; Liṅga; Mandir; Mantra; Nāyaṉmār; Pāśupatas; Patañjali; Purāṇas; Rudra; Sacred texts; Śaiva Siddhānta; Saṃhitā;**

Saṃnyāsa; Saṃsāra; Siddha; Śiva; Skanda; Smārta; Tapas; Upaniṣads; Vaiṣṇavism; Varṇa; Veda; Vedic pantheon; Vīrāśāivas; Yoga; Yogi

TRAVIS L. SMITH

Further reading

Bhandarkar, R.G. 1982. *Vaiṣṇavism, Śaivism and Minor Religious Systems.* Poona: Bhandarkar Oriental Research Institute.

Chattopadhyaya, S. 1970. *Evolution of Hindu Sects up to the time of Saṃkaracarya.* New Delhi: Munshiram Manoharlal.

Mittal, S. and G. Thursby. 2004. *The Hindu World.* New York: Routledge.

SĀKṢIN

There are different theories regarding the ontological status/nature of the Sākṣin in Indian philosophy. Śaṅkara believed that the Sākṣin is the same as the Ātman or the universal self in the individual (jīva). It is the witness of all cognitions. Vācaspati held an almost similar view. Jīva is the Ātman as conditioned by the mind–body, while the pure, unconditioned Ātman which is the witness of jīva's functions is the Sākṣin. The later Vedāntins deviated from the above. According to *Dharmarājādhvarīndra*, Sākṣin is the Ātman as conditioned by the antaḥkaraṇa (internal organ/mind) in the way an upadhi (title) does a person, without entering into the latter's being, whereas in the case of jīva, it is qualified by the mind in the manner a viśeṣaṇa (adjective) does an object. Antaḥkaraṇa is not separable from jīva, but it is from Sākṣin. The *Kaumudī* believes the Sākṣin to be a special mode of God, which permits the self to act or not act, itself remaining an indifferent spectator. The *Tattvaśuddhi* believes the Sākṣin to be Brahman. It only appears to belong to jīva. According to Vidyāranya, Sākṣin is the unchanging consciousness, the ground of all bodies (gross/subtle), giving them their self-identity. It is the inactive spectator in jīva, falsely identified with jīva. The *Tattvapradīpīkā* holds that the Sākṣin is Brahman, the ground of all jīvas, but wrongly identifies itself with them.

See also: **Ātman; Brahman; Jīva; Śaṅkara; Vācaspati Miśra; Vedānta**

KARABI SEN

Further reading

Sinha, Jadunath. 1952. *Indian Philosophy,* vol. 2. Delhi: Motilal Banarsidass.

ŚĀKTA

See: **Śāktism**

ŚAKTI

Śakti is defined in Monier-Williams' Sanskrit dictionary as 'power, ability, strength, might, effort, energy, capability' and 'capacity for' or 'power over' (Monier-Williams 1993: 1,044). The term śakti has wide connotations but most simply it means power or energy. In its most abstract sense, śakti refers to the energetic principle of ultimate reality, conceptualised as primordial power. Śakti is principally associated with the feminine, and the innumerable goddesses that are an integral part of Hindu religious expression personify śakti in a tangible form. The derivation of such an idea was formulated over many centuries, with ideas drawn from many sources.

The Indus Valley Civilisation

The Indus Valley Civilisation was highly sophisticated. Many scholars have assumed that goddess worship was prevalent because in practically all the houses of Mohenjo-daro and Harappa terracotta female figurines were found. Many had smoke-blackened headdresses, suggesting that they may have been used for ritual purposes (Agrawala 1984: 29). The many artefacts found in the houses and the numerous seals that appear to portray female deities, particularly the one depicting a female figure with a tree issuing from her womb, seem to point towards a predominant goddess cult. However, we should be cautious in assuming that this putative cult is the precursor of goddess worship in India today. Undoubtedly there may be links, but goddess worship as it is now has evolved over a vast period and represents the culmination of many influences.

The Vedic period

The oldest texts in which Hindu goddesses are mentioned are the *Veda Saṃhitās*. The most accessible knowledge of Vedic goddesses comes from the *Ṛgveda* (Royal Knowledge) and from the less frequently translated *Atharvaveda* (Knowledge of Incantations). At first glance, the Vedic goddesses seem to have had little importance, as there were not many female deities of any consequence. Few goddesses had any hymns dedicated solely to them, but, of these, Uṣas, goddess of the Dawn, was the most often praised. However, the Vedic goddesses, though they may not have been as famous or widely praised as the male deities such as Indra and Agni, subtly pervaded the Vedic religious worldview, personifying such important aspects as Mother Earth (Pṛthivī), Mother of the Gods (Aditi), Night (Rātrī) and Speech (Vāc/Vāk). The goddess Vāc as the personification of Speech is an important goddess despite the fact that she disappeared after the Vedic period. Vāc is mentioned often in the Vedas, but one particular hymn addressed to her, the *Devī-sūkta*, has remained an important part of later goddess theology. Thus in *Ṛgveda* 10. 125. 6, Vāc claims: 'I bend the bow for Rudra that his arrow may strike and slay the hater of devotion. I rouse and order battle for the people, and I have penetrated Earth and Heaven'. In this hymn, Vāc is presented as a powerful and pervasive energy, as immanent and transcendent, bestowing her power on gods and humans alike. This element of Vāc's nature eventually evolved into a more developed theology. Her most important characteristics were assimilated into the personality of Sarasvatī, who, despite being a relatively unimportant river goddess in the Vedas, eventually became known as the Goddess of Wisdom and Learning, often referred to as Mother of the Vedas.

Many of the goddesses of the Vedic period are simply the wives of the gods, with little or no distinct function. These goddesses had no individual name of their own, instead taking their husband's name, but with a feminine suffix, so Indrāṇī, for example, is the wife of Indra. At first glance, there does not seem to be any deep philosophical meaning underlying the function of these goddesses. Yet, on closer examination, particularly of the role of Indrāṇī, there may be a suggestion of the later conception of śakti as divine power. Indrāṇī is addressed in one *Ṛgvedic* hymn (10. 159) as Śacī Paulomī, and presented essentially as a deification of Indra's deeds of power (Das 1934: 12). It is very interesting that here is the notion that power and energy are not necessarily things that are inherent within a deity; there is a separation between the two. It seems evident that this process of thinking, of seeing power as a separate entity from the deity, started with the use of the term śacī, meaning 'the rendering of powerful or mighty help, assistance, aid', especially of the 'deeds of Indra' (Monier-Williams 1993: 1,048). These ideas must have had some influence on subsequent thought, for in later texts, as the notion of śakti as divine power became more clearly defined, the wives of the gods started to personify their husband's power. Despite Vāc's association with power, and the inference that the wives of the gods, particularly Indrāṇī, to a certain extent embodied their power, it was only after considerable philosophical speculation that a developed concept of śakti, as powerful feminine divinity, the universal energetic force, was articulated. Only after the idea of a connection underlying the universe was formulated did the concept of an underlying feminine unity develop. It is generally accepted that it was not until the medieval or classical period that the total identity between the goddesses and śakti came to full fruition.

Vedānta-Upaniṣadic/Later Vedic

Although goddesses did not figure prominently in the Upaniṣads, ideas formulated at that time were important to the later concept of śakti. The conceptual notion of śakti that is advanced in the Śākta texts (those in which the Goddess is the primary deity) is based on the concept of an Absolute or ultimate reality, most commonly referred to as Brahman, a term without gender. The *Upaniṣads* contain some of the most fundamental and profound religious ideas that became the basis of many aspects of later Hindu thought. One such idea is the concept of a correspondence between God, referred to as Brahman or ultimate reality, and the totality of all cosmic manifestation. The all-encompassing nature of Brahman gave rise to a major theory that everything, whether divine or human, was in its essence the same – thereby establishing a connecting factor, the ātman or permanent essence, in all life. Since Brahman was considered neither male nor female, it was not surprising that, at that point, there was an absence of any emphasis on the divine feminine. The earlier upaniṣadic texts posited a vision of a transcendent Absolute that could be neither described nor known, except through jñāna (intuitive knowledge). However, the later *Upaniṣads*, in particular the *Śvetāśvatara*, provided a more accessible representation of the Absolute, presenting the notion of a manifest (saguṇa) aspect of Brahman, without, however, negating the underlying unity between the essence of Brahman and the essence of the manifest world. In the *Śvetāśvatara Upaniṣad*, Brahman was portrayed as the manifest Lord or Īśvara, making a theistic relationship possible between deity and devotee.

The classical period

Slowly, an increase in literature with a predominantly theistic standpoint appeared, the most important being the epics, the *Mahābhārata*, '*The Great (mahā) Story of the Bhāratas*', containing the *Bhagavadgītā* and the *Rāmāyaṇa*, perhaps the most famous Hindu scripture. They are supplemented by a huge body of material concerned primarily with myth and legend, the *Purāṇas*, that asserted the supremacy of individual deities. This period is generally referred to as the classical period of Hinduism. The purāṇic texts built on the unifying foundation established in the *Upaniṣads*, but tended to express the supremacy of a particular god, equating him in his unmanifest (nirguṇa) form with Brahman. In this context, the myriad deities of the classical period were considered aspects or manifestations of Brahman. While the majority of purāṇic texts predominantly offered a male deity, most commonly Viṣṇu or Śiva, as the supreme deity, the later *Śākta Purāṇas* were dedicated to the goddess.

In most *Purāṇas* the goddesses were primarily presented as consorts of the gods. In the *Kūrma Purāṇa*, for instance, the goddess Śrī or Lakṣmī was presented as appearing at the churning of the ocean of milk. She is clearly subordinate to Viṣṇu as he 'takes possession' of her (*Kūrma Purāṇa* 1.1.30). However, Śrī Lakṣmī is presented as the means of Viṣṇu's power, described by him as 'that great Śakti (potency) of my form' (*Kūrma Purāṇa* 1.1.34). A close connection between the goddess and her consort's powers of creation is established through her embodiment of three significant principles – śakti (energy), prakṛti (primordial or primary matter) and māyā (illusion) – thereby establishing a relationship between female divinity and creative power. It is as a personification of his energy that the goddesses are associated with the principal god's creative function, being addressed, or referred to, as prakṛti. However, in this purāṇic context the goddess, while she may be considered the source of the manifest world, is always considered a part of, or subject to, the will of her consort. It would appear that, despite the fact that an individual goddess was addressed by the name Śakti, śakti as a quality was possessed by both male and female deities, with an overt identity between female divinity and cosmic energy yet to be established.

The metaphysical concept of śakti

Two texts, the earlier *Devī Māhātmya* and the later *Devī-Bhāgavatam Purāṇa,* significantly changed the way that the divine feminine was perceived. The first and most popular goddess-centred text is the *Devī Māhātmya*, originally a section of the *Mārkaṇḍeya Purāṇa*. The importance of this text and its uniqueness are apparent in its independence from the parent text. It is in this text that the concept of an all-inclusive Goddess or Mahādevī (Great Goddess) is fully elucidated. Within a mythical framework of the Goddess' martial deeds is the assertion that she is ultimate reality, an idea transmitted by inference rather than in direct terms. Mythically, in order to conquer the asuras (demons) that threatened the very existence of the devas (gods), a supremely powerful goddess was created from the combined anger of the gods (*Devī Māhātmya* 2.9–12). The vital power that emanated from the gods took shape in feminine form, and from then on was accepted as the Mahādevī, a supreme goddess in her own right. She is entirely separate from the gods, the embodiment of śakti, and is able to produce further powers of her own. When her work is done, she disappears but does not return to her source, the gods. The text reinforces the conceptual notion of a Great Goddess, Mahādevī, the embodiment of power in all its myriad forms by the many epithets used to address the Goddess. Apart from the term Devī, the most common name of the Goddess is Caṇḍī or Caṇḍikā, meaning 'violent and impetuous one', a name used here for the first time in a Sanskrit text, and possibly formulated specifically for this incarnation of divinity (Coburn 1986: 163–64). Caṇḍikā as a name is most apt for the martial deeds of the Goddess, presenting her in a forceful and often unorthodox manner, with her penchant for drink and acceptance of blood offerings.

One of the most interesting facets of Devī's character in the *Devī Māhātmaya* is her independence and her challenge to the stereotypes of goddesses. The Goddess here, most often identified as Durgā the demon slayer, does not depend on a male consort and successfully manages male roles herself. In battle, for instance, she does not fight with male allies; if she needs assistance, she creates female helpers, like Kālī, from herself. Her role as a personification of śakti also differs from that of the other purāṇic goddesses, for rather than lending her power or śakti to a male consort, she *takes* power from the gods, particularly at her creation, when they 'surrender their potency to her' (Kinsley 1986: 97).

The *Devī Māhātmaya* makes clear that the Goddess cannot be easily categorised. The Goddess so carefully outlined in the text leaves the reader in no doubt of the fluidity of her character, for she is the personification of all aspects of energy, described as simultaneously creative, preservative and destructive (*Devī Māhātmya* 1.56–58). The all-encompassing Mahādevī in this text represents all aspects of power and energy, both positive and negative, as she is described as devī (goddess) and asurī (demoness). The Devī of the *Devī Māhātmya* is fully equated with ultimate reality, presented as the power behind the functions of the trimūrti, the triad of deities – Viṣṇu, Śiva and Brahmā – who are responsible for the preservation, dissolution and creation of the universe respectively (*Devī Māhātmya* 1.59). Devī originated at a time of cosmic crisis and, consequently, her role seems very similar to that of Viṣṇu in his many avatāras (incarnations). Just as Viṣṇu promised to manifest himself in order to protect the cosmic balance, Devī, too, promises to return if her help is needed again (*Devī Māhātmya* 12.36).

Śakti in the *Devī-Bhāgavatam Purāṇa*

By far the largest and perhaps the most comprehensive Śākta *Purāṇa* is the *Devī-Bhāgavatam Purāṇa*, compiled five to ten centuries after the *Devī Māhātmya* and representing a 'justification or vindication of the Goddess tradition, as well as an elaboration of it' (Brown 1990: ix). It presents a Śākta response to a variety of purāṇic strands of thought. The *Devī Gītā*, which comprises skandha (book) 7, chapters 30–40 of the *Devī-Bhāgavatam Purāṇa*, is based on the style of the *Bhagavadgītā*, but is presented from a Śākta perspective. The *Devī-Bhāgavatam Purāṇa* also encompasses a version of the *Devī Māhātmya* and retells a number of purāṇic myths. The text is more consistently metaphysically orientated than the earlier *Devī Māhātmya*, frequently eulogising the Goddess as the 'Eternal' and 'Ever Constant Primordial Force' (*Devī-Bhāgavatam Purāṇa* 3.30.28) who is the power behind all other deities.

It is also significant that in the *Devī-Bhāgavatam Purāṇa* the Great Goddess is consistently portrayed as independent of any male authority and control. Indeed, it is the gods who are completely subject to the will of Devī, being totally reliant on her power. The Goddess of the *Devī-Bhāgavatam Purāṇa* is repeatedly portrayed as eternal, the basis of everything and identical with Brahman. Referred to as Ādya or Primordial Śakti, the Goddess is explicitly shown to be the source of all goddesses, from the highest to the lowest forms. The higher forms represent the major facets of her power or energy and correspond with the three strands or constituents of all existence, sattva (purity, goodness, the illuminating principle), rajas (activity, passion, the energetic principle) and tamas (darkness, inertia, dullness), the three guṇas, encompassing both positive and negative energies. As sattva she is Mahā-Lakṣmī, as rajas she is Mahā-Sarasvatī and as tamas she is Mahā-Kālī. However, Devī is also described as being beyond all form, described as nirguṇa (without guṇas or unmanifest) and as such is beyond human comprehension. In order to offer liberation to her devotees, Devī becomes saguṇa (with guṇas or manifest) in a form that can be known and appreciated in the world.

In the *Devī-Bhāgavatam Purāṇa* the essential character of the Mahādevī encompasses both prakṛti (material nature), in its unmanifest and manifest forms, and puruṣa (pure consciousness) – the dual realities of Sāṃkhya philosophy. Unlike Sāṃkhya and other schools of thought, particularly Advaita Vedānta, the *Devī-Bhāgavatam Purāṇa* portrays prakṛti in a more positive light: as an integral feature of the Goddess' power. Similarly, the concept of māyā (illusion) is also presented positively rather than negatively, as a fundamental energy necessary in the act of creation. There is an interesting and important difference between the conception of māyā in the *Bhāgavata Purāṇa*, in which Viṣṇu is the supreme deity, and that in the *Devī-Bhāgavatam*

Purāṇa. Whereas in the *Bhāgavata Purāṇa* Viṣṇu is the 'controller and possessor of māyā', the Goddess of the *Devī-Bhāgavatam Purāṇa*, as well as wielding the power of māyā, actually *is* māyā (Brown 1998: 87). There appears to be a much more intimate relationship in the *Devī-Bhāgavatam Purāṇa* between the Goddess and the workings of the cosmos, for as Viṣṇu and Śiva resort to their respective śaktis for assistance, Devī resorts to no one but herself.

Śakti Personified by the pan-Indian goddesses

The most visible expression of śakti is in the personification of the many goddesses. The countless Hindu goddesses can be divided into roughly two types, Brahmanical and consequently orthodox, pan-Indian goddesses or local goddesses. The first group, referred to as pan-Indian, are generally known across India and are in the main Brahmanical, though some do have unorthodox tendencies. These goddesses generally have well-developed mythologies, are given textual credence and are most often found anthropomorphically presented in temples, large and small. Goddesses such as Śrī Lakṣmī, who represents the power of good fortune and wealth, or Sarasvatī, the goddess of learning and wisdom, have become recognisable outside India. However, Kālī is by far the most famous Hindu goddess and is often erroneously referred to as the goddess of death and destruction. Although Kālī is associated with death and does have destructive tendencies, she represents a far wider power that includes liberation and protection. Obviously there are significant differences between Lakṣmī and Sarasvatī and goddesses like Kālī and Durgā, who personify the benign and terrible aspects of śakti, respectively. In much Hindu thought, all deities are aspects of the one Brahman, the origin of everything, including the negative aspects of life. There is no single concept of an all-benevolent God or Goddess and a separate power of evil. Whatever goddesses appear to be on the outside, ultimately they embody śakti, divine power or energy. In this respect, the pan-Indian goddesses represent the positive and negative, or benign and terrible aspects of śakti. On one hand, there are those goddesses that personify the essentially benign aspects of śakti, the power of devotion, wisdom, love or compassion, etc. In contrast to the essentially benign goddesses are those who are best described as essentially fierce. These goddesses personify the more dynamic powers of protection and the destruction of evil; they require their devotees to face up to their fears and in return offer the salvific power of liberation. An important point to bear in mind is that the goddesses are *essentially* benign and *essentially* fierce. The benign goddesses are not wholly benign, for there may be a fierce element to their characters. Likewise, the fierce goddesses have a benign side to their personalities. The dual nature of the goddesses highlights the dualism and opposition that are a characteristic of divine power or indeed any power or energy. For instance, the power of fire, necessary to maintain life, can and does at times destroy life. Similarly, the power that made creation possible is the same power that will periodically destroy, or perhaps more correctly dissolve, life, transforming it into an unmanifest state once more.

The benign aspect of śakti

The numerous aspects of the divine feminine show the infinite facets of her nature. The essentially benign goddesses reward their devotees with divine grace. Among these orthodox goddesses are Rādhā, the lover of Kṛṣṇa; Gaurī, the golden one; Sītā, the devoted and faithful wife of Rāmā; Sarasvatī, the goddess of wisdom and learning; Śrī Lakṣmī; the wife of Viṣṇu, goddess of good fortune and wealth; and Pārvatī, the wife of Śiva, who represents the ultimate devotee. Generally, these goddesses are very beautiful and pleasing to look at. They are eminently approachable, coaxing the devotee to form a close and loving relationship with the divine. In a very gentle way, the essentially benign goddesses show the devotee how to follow their dharmic path (individual moral and religious duty), helping them to overcome obstacles along the way. These goddesses above all offer the devotee the power of love and grace, and there need not be any apprehension on the part of the devotee in approaching them. The majority of benign goddesses are the consorts of various gods. In this role, they represent their husband's power as his śakti. They are generally portrayed as significantly smaller than their husband and often shown in a subservient role; for example, Lakṣmī is often depicted rubbing Viṣṇu's feet. In their role as wife, the benign goddesses convey many paradigmatic features such as support and faithfulness, often representing the supreme devotee. In this respect, they are conceived of as ideal role models for Hindu women in general.

The fierce aspect of śakti

The essentially fierce goddesses, such as Kālī, Durgā and Caṇḍī, represent the more dynamic personifications of śakti. It is in the character and symbolism of these goddesses that the most profound insight into the cosmic expression of power is found. The fierce goddesses seem to break all taboos and bring their devotees face to face with the dark side of divinity. In many cases, the power of the benign goddesses is subtle, whereas that of the fierce goddesses is blatant. They are clearly powerful in their own right and seem to delight in showing off that power. They are in essence independent, even if they are described as married. Kālī and Tārā, if they are depicted with their husbands, are usually shown to be in the dominant position, often engaged in sexual intercourse. Kālī is the most obvious example of this symbolism as she is generally portrayed standing on top of Śiva's prone body. One of the most common representations of the fierce goddesses is that of the divine warrior, as is commonly epitomised by the goddess Durgā. In this capacity, the goddesses have a protective role and act as destroyers of evil, usually represented in the shape of a demon. In a general sense, both Durgā and Kālī represent the power of protection. These goddesses will protect anyone who can come before them in the attitude of a child or with a humble spirit.

While Durgā conforms outwardly to the Brahmanical ideal of womanhood, being depicted with a beautiful face and many arms wielding various weapons, Kālī stands firmly on the margins of acceptability, outside what is generally acknowledged as orthodox. Her terrifying outward appearance, naked but for a garland of severed heads and a skirt of severed limbs, holding a sword, a severed head and standing on Śiva in a cremation ground, has led many to misunderstand her completely. Consequently, Kālī is the most grossly misrepresented Hindu goddess. Portrayed in the West as the goddess of death and destruction, her positive and subtle attributes have been conveniently discarded in favour of her more dramatic characteristics. However, the sword that Kālī holds is not just for the destruction of evil but also to sever the many ties that bind the egotistical person to this world.

Śakti personified by local goddesses

To the vast number of Indians who live in India's numerous villages and towns, the local deities, goddesses in particular, are more important than the deities of the Hindu pantheon. Many villages do have shrines and festivals for Brahmanical deities but they are often known by different names; for instance, Śiva in Madurai in south India is called Sundarēśvarar. The local population may also place an emphasis on different characteristics than would be normal in mainstream Hinduism, since local goddesses are concerned with the issues that are important to their devotees. While goddesses such as Durgā and Kālī are eternally fighting demons and restoring cosmic order, local goddesses protect their caste group, communicate the whereabouts of lost cattle and find suitable jobs and husbands for their supplicants. They represent a different aspect of śakti, which is grounded in the mundane, a readily available power source for the inhabitants of the settlement that they reside in.

Local goddesses are often treated as though they bear no relationship to the Brahmanical goddesses or to the conception of śakti that all goddesses personify. While it is true that local goddesses cannot simply be considered the local equivalents of pan-Indian goddesses, there is, nevertheless, a basic comprehension that all goddesses represent divine power and, furthermore, that between all goddesses there is some underlying correspondence. According to textual sources, local goddesses are just as much manifestations of the Mahādevī as the Brahmanical, pan-Indian goddesses. The *Brahmavaivarta Purāṇa* and the *Devī-Bhāgavatam Purāṇa* both express the idea that all goddesses spring from one reality. According to the *Devī-Bhāgavatam Purāṇa* (9.1.58), 'Every female in every Universe is sprung from a part of Śrī Rādhā or part of a part'. In fact, the pan-Indian goddesses themselves have numerous manifestations, a point emphasised in the *Kūrma Purāṇa* (1.12.64) in the chapter in praise of Pārvatī. One epithet of the goddess is Ekānekavibhāgasthā, meaning 'stationed in one as well as in many divisions'. It is likely that the often used phrase 'all the mothers are one' may have its genesis in these basic correlations.

In local settlements, there is generally interplay between the pan-Indian and local goddesses, in which attempts may be made to Brahmanise, Sanskritise or Hinduise a local goddess. This process reduces a goddess' overtly local characteristics, such as the acceptance of blood sacrifice and, instead, moulds her character to resemble more closely those of pan-Indian or Brahmanical deities. One part of this process has been termed 'spousification' (Gatwood 1985: 2), in which an independent goddess is ritually married, either temporarily, annually or – if fully Hinduised – permanently, to an established god, usually Śiva. Conversely, some pan-Indian goddesses have been localised, being endowed with names and forms that are more popular, with their myths relating them to the local settlement or area.

There seems to be an intimate relationship between local deities and their devotees: they know each other well as their lives are inextricably entwined. While the pan-Indian deities may be considered more intrinsically pure, and certainly more orthodox, they remain at the periphery of local life, paid homage to when required but not necessarily sharing the daily lives of the masses. Arguably, it is local goddesses that are most important in the daily workings of Hindu life. The day-to-day concerns of the population are most readily addressed to the goddesses close by. They are always ready to concern themselves with the problems of their devotees, no matter how trivial, and they have the power necessary to rectify them. Therefore, local goddesses personify the most immediate and accessible aspect of śakti, a world away from the metaphysical workings of śakti on the cosmic plane.

While many ancient cultures have clearly had a belief in the power of a Mother Goddess, very few of those belief systems are still extant. What is fascinating about Hinduism is that it has an ongoing tradition of goddess worship, which now we have moved into the twenty-first century is no less vital and alive.

See also: **Aditi; Advaita; Agni; Asuras; Ātman; Avatāra; Bhagavadgītā; Blood sacrifice; Brahmā; Brahman; Devī Māhātmya; Dharma; Durgā; Grāmadevatās; Guṇas; Indra; Indus Valley Civilisation; Īśvara; Jñāna; Kālī and Caṇḍī; Kṛṣṇa; Lakṣmī, Śrī; Māyā; Mahābhārata; Mahādevī; Monier-Williams, Sir Monier; Pārvatī; Prakṛti; Pṛthivī; Purāṇas; Puruṣa; Rādhā; Rāma; Rāmāyaṇa; Śāktism; Saṃhitā; Sāṃkhya; Sarasvatī; Sītā; Śiva; Sundarēśvarar; Tantrism; Tārā; Trimūrti; Upaniṣads; Uṣas; Vedānta; Viṣṇu**

LYNN FOULSTON

Further reading

Agrawala, P.K. 1984. *Goddesses in Ancient India*. New Delhi: Abhinav Publications.

Basham, A.L. 1982. *The Wonder That Was India*. Reprint of 1967, 3rd revised edn. London: Sidgwick and Jackson.

Brown, C. Mackenzie. 1974. *God as Mother: A Feminine Theology in India: An Historical and Theological Study of the Brahmavaivarta Purāṇa*. Hartford, VT: Claude Stark.

Brown, C. Mackenzie. 1990. *The Triumph of the Goddess: The Canonical Models and Theological Visions of the Devī-Bhāgavata Purāṇa*. Albany, NY: State University of New York Press.

Brown, C. Mackenzie. 1998. *The Devī Gītā – The Song of the Goddess: A Translation, Annotation, and Commentary*. Albany, NY: State University of New York Press.

Coburn, T.B. 1986. 'Consort of None, Śakti of All: The vision of the *Devī-Māhātmya*'. Reprint of 1982 edn. In J.S. Hawley and D.M. Wulff, eds, *The Divine Consort: Rādhā and the Goddesses of India*. Berkeley, CA: Berkeley Religious Studies Series, 153–65.

Coburn, T.B. 1991. *Encountering the Goddess: A Translation of the Devī-Māhātmya and a Study of Its Interpretation*. Delhi: Sri Satguru Publications.

Das, S.K. 1934. *Sakti, or Divine Power: A Historical Study Based on Original Sanskrit Texts*. Calcutta: University of Calcutta.

Gatwood, L.E. 1985. *Devī and the Spouse Goddess: Women, Sexuality and Marriage in India*. New Delhi: Manohar Publications.

Griffith, R.T.H. 1991. *The Hymns of the Ṛgveda*. Reprint of 1973 revised edn. Delhi: Motilal Banarsidass.

Kinsley, D.R. 1986. *Hindu Goddesses: Visions of the Divine Feminine in the Hindu Religious Tradition*. Delhi: Motilal Banarsidass.

Monier-Williams, Monier. 1993. *A Sanskrit–English Dictionary*. Reprint of 1899 edn. Delhi: Motilal Banarsidass.

Tagare, V.G. (trans.). 1981. *Kūrma Purāṇa*, vols 1–2. Delhi: Motilal Banarsidass.

Vijnanananda, Swami (trans.). 1986. *The Śrīmad Devī-Bhāgavatatam*, 3rd edn. New Delhi: Munishiram Manoharlal.

ŚĀKTISM

Derived from śakti ('power', 'energy', 'strength').

A religious system grounded in the worship of the goddess as the supreme principle. Together with Vaiṣṇavism and Śaivism, Śāktism is one of the major branches if the Hindu tradition. The goddess of the Śākta tradition embodies all possible aspects of reality. She is described as a compassionate mother and a vengeful destroyer; she is the ultimate refuge and the scariest of the deities; she is a peaceful housewife but also a fierce warrior; she is truth and illusion. Finally, she is both a transcendent principle and an immanent presence. Śākta goddesses are protective figures but some derive power mostly from their position as anti-models at the fringes of the Hindu society. Many Śaktis are the exact opposite of the ideal woman (pativratā) emphasised in the *Dharmaśāstras*: good daughter, pious wife and loving mother. Sanskrit and vernacular literature as well as oral regional lore describe them as ambiguous figures. They are generally unmarried and even though they are called mothers they are not functional mothers. If they are worshipped as healers, they can inflict diseases. They live in impure environments and deal with impure matters. Their occupations are generally believed to be unsuitable for women. Their behaviour (sexual aggressiveness, rage and voraciousness), look (dishevelled hair, nakedness), ornaments (severed heads, human corpses) and companionship (impure animals, low-caste or tribal people) are sordid. Śaktis are in a constant state of pollution and so are their devotees. Human and animal sacrifices, alcoholic offerings and use of intoxicants are required to satisfy them. Notwithstanding that, Śaktis are widely known as mothers. In this form, Śāktas recognise the essence of their power.

Theology

Śākta theology can be divided in two forms: (1) the Śrī-kula ('family of the Goddess Śrī') follows the *smārtasūtras* (smārta, orthodox treatises grounded in *smṛti*) and is strongest in South India; (2) the Kālī-kula ('family of Kālī') openly rejects the Brahmanic tradition and prevails in Northern and Eastern India. Apart from these differentiations, Śākta theology agrees with the Advaita (non-dualistic) and Vedānta doctrines of a supreme principle (Brahman) as the cause and the origin of everything.

Basically monistic, Śākta theology looks at the Devī (goddess; Mahādevī) as the eternal Brahman which embodies sat (existence), cit (consciousness) and ānanda (bliss) (saccidānanda). She generates the sensible world by virtue of māyā (illusion). But unlike Advaitins and Vedāntins, Śāktas describe māyā as a conscious force which reflects the various aspects of the great goddess. The Vedāntic theory of the acintya-bhedābheda-vāda (the 'inconceivable difference-non difference' between the worshipper and the worshipped) is ignored while Vedānta admits the divine origin of the human being, though maintaining its substantiality on an inferior/dependent level, the goddess of the Śāktas manifests her power through māyā, but at the same time she is Māyā. The Devī – though ontologically identified as Brahman – is also her various manifestations, whether illusory or not. The worship of the goddess in Śākta cults is a theistic expression of devotion towards a personal deity and not an abstract philosophical undetermined principle. Although some Śākta texts and philosophers admit that Śakti and Brahman are basically the same, practical discrepancies remain. While Advaita (non-dualism) and Dvaita (dualism) schools, respectively, stress the identity or non-identity of the object with the subject, Śāktas ground their theology on the freedom from dualism and non-dualism (dvaitādvaita vivarījīta).

Although some similarities can be observed with other bhakta saṃpradāyas (devotional schools), Śāktas stress the importance of dichotomies as a way to reach perfect knowledge and obtain liberation. Renunciation (mukti) is valid only if validated by the experience and the enjoyment (bhukti) of worldly affairs, while knowledge (vidyā) can be obtained only through the capacity of recognising illusion. According to orthodox Hindu systems (āstika darśanas) like Sāṃkhya, prakṛti (nature) is determined by the combination of three qualities (guṇas): sattva (brightness, virtue), rajas (activity, passion) and tamas (obscurity, inertness, ignorance). But for Śāktas – who do not always recognise the presence of tamas in the creation of the gross elements and the subtle bodies (*Devī Gīta* 2: 35–42) – the ultimate reality is the goddess who appears according to its own desire (icchā), action (kriyā) and knowledge (jñana) in a twofold aspect: śakti, the active force, which is female, and puruṣa, the inactive matter, which is male. Feminine dynamism dominating the inert matter is posed at the origin of the creative process and embodied in multitudinous goddesses who are ultimately reconciled in one.

Origin and development

The cult of the goddess as Śakti has its roots in non-Vedic culture and, possibly, in pre-Vedic times. The study of the socioeconomic structure and beliefs of South Asian scheduled tribes (ādivāsīs), together with the analysis of the remnants of non-Vedic cultures such as those which flourished in the Indus Valley, bears witness to the existence of non-Vedic female deities. In Vedic literature there are no major goddesses. Indeed, in the *Ṛgveda* many goddess are named and praised, yet their role is never central. Aditi, the Vedic mother of the gods, Pṛthivī, the goddess of earth, Uṣas, the goddess of dawn, Rātrī, the goddess of night, Vāc, the goddess of speech, Sarasvatī, a river goddess, Lakṣmī the goddess of abundance, and Iḍā, the goddess of milk/butter oblation, are personifications of rituals and/or natural forces, while Indrāṇī, Rudrāṇī, etc. are simply the female counterparts of major gods. Yet notwithstanding the predominance of a male-dominated pantheon, the *Ṛgveda* (10. 125) presents one of the earliest hymns in which a goddess is independently praised and worshipped: the *Devī-sūkta* (also present with slight variations in *Atharvaveda* 4. 30). The hymn is dedicated to Vāc (the Word), a goddess described as the Queen who gives birth and maintains both human beings and gods. Śāktas have in great consideration the *Devī-sūkta*, which is still employed as an invitation before animal sacrifices and at the end of the homayajña (fire oblation) in honour of various goddesses.

The post-Vedic period

The post-Vedic emergence and affirmation of goddesses is not a new element. Vedic literature acted as a sort of interlude between non-Vedic goddesses and post-Vedic female deities. The cult of the Devī in South Asia is not recorded because only the Sanskrit tradition had a written literature but Sanskrit was not a universal language. When the merging of the Vedic culture with other traditions was established and Sanskrit became a literary lingua franca, the great tradition moved on to accept goddesses. In this sense, Sanskrit literature allowed regional forms of worship (mostly feminine-centred) to develop into institutional cults. During the post-Vedic period, marked by the birth of a variety of religious streams (Vaiṣṇava, Śaiva but also Buddhism and Jainism), the presence of goddess worship is well attested. Kālī, Durgā, Ambikā (the Mother), etc. easily found their place in new forms of religion. Although Śaktis are still described as dangerous entities, living in impurity and worshipped by fierce tribes through obscene rituals (*Mahābhārata* 4.6. 18), it is in this period that they start to acquire a domesticated aspect. Thanks to the popularity of the cult of Pṛthivī (the Earth) and her association with the god Viṣṇu, other female deities started to be worshipped in a milder and gentler form. Vaiṣṇava scriptures individuate their own śaktis (*Viṣṇu Purāṇa* 3.46. 17, 7.5. 31), while the cult of Sītā, the heroine of the *Rāmāyaṇa*, increases in popularity. In the *Mahābhārata* too, the role of Draupadī, wife to the five Pāṇḍavas, underlines the transformative attitude of female worship. Not by chance are both Draupadī and Sītā regarded as originated by earth female deities. The rising of new social patterns (integration of fringe populations into Brahmanical society) and substantial economic modifications (development of agriculture and trades) determined the domestication and acquisition of non-Vedic goddesses. But many areas remained peripheral and inaccessible, a fact which ensured the maintenance of

Śaktis' most obscure and dreadful side. From the end of the third century, along with the definition of a proper theology, three worshipping paths can be clearly identified: the devotional (bhakti mārga), the Tantric (tāntrika mārga) and the folk/tribal one.

The devotional path

Devotion to the goddess is at the core of every form of Śāktism: philosophy, theology, literature, sculpture, etc. The bhakti mārga presents close analogies with Vaiṣṇava and Śaiva systems, yet in this case the efforts of the devotees are entirely centred on the figure of a female supreme deity. The relation between a bhakta (devotee) and the goddess can be spontaneous (e.g. the goddess somehow appears to the devotee) or already established (e.g. the goddess is the family-protecting deity). In each case it is a personal and emotional tie which generally does not require the presence of a guru. The goddess is worshipped with attributes (saguṇa) or without attributes (nirguṇa). In the former, the relationship is instituted between a parental figure and a child. The devotee worships his or her Śakti either as a mother/mistress or as child/young daughter. In the latter, the goddess is pictured as an ocean which contains sat, cit and ānanda, each of them developing into a different power. These are sandhinī-śakti (power of existence), saṃvit-śakti (power of consciousness) and hlādinī-śakti (power of bliss). According to the nature of the devotee, a number of states or moods (bhāvas) can be experienced: such bhāvas are the ultimate task of the devotional path. The *Devī-Bhāgavata Purāṇa* (7.37.24–25) describes the highest degree of devotion (para-bhakti) in quasi-Vaiṣṇava terms. The repetition of name and focus on the image and the attributes of the goddess are emphasised. The recitation of the Lalitā Sahasranāma (the 'thousand names of the Goddess Lalitā'), a hymn interpolated as the thirty-sixth chapter of the *Lalitopākhyāna* (the 'story of Lalitā') at the end of the *Brahmāṇḍa Purāṇa* (tenth century), represents one of the most widespread forms of devotional worship of the Devī. Because of its relative freedom from doctrinal bondage and lack of instructions from a guru, the outcome of the devotional approach has been long compared with the ecstatic phenomena present in other devotional streams, either Hindu or not. The complete abandon of the bhakta who experiences the condition of divine madness is considered the greatest attainment.

The Tantric path

This peculiar formula can be dated back to the tenth century CE, when customary practices such as pūjā (tangible offering), bolidāna (sacrifice) and meditation (dhyāna) were still performed in accordance with Brahmanical instructions and other saṃpradāyas' observances, yet they gradually became integrated into a corpus of esoteric scriptures: the Tantras. By stressing the importance of initiation (dīkṣā), secrecy, guru–śiṣya-bandhana (teacher–disciple relationship) and erotic symbolism, Tantras developed a twofold path of worship. On the one hand there is the dakṣinācāra (right-hand method): the devotee considers the goddess as supreme principle and ultimate goal and stresses contemplation. On the other hand, there is vāmācāra (left-hand method), where great emphasis is given to ritual practice (sādhana), with special reference to pañcamakāras (or pañcatattva), the five Ms: mudrā (gestures), māṃsa (meat), maithuna (sexual intercourse), matsya (fish) and madya (liquor). Śākta Tantras are imbued with Yoga, which happens to be an extremely articulate discipline. It involves diverse techniques, both mental and physical. The former include meditation, the repetition of name(s) of the goddess (japa), the spell of mantras and the focus on yantras. The latter are bodily positions and exercises aimed at awakening inner power. This is called kuṇḍalinī śakti and is presented as a serpent curled three and a half turns around the lowest cakra ('discus', here 'subtle centre') of the body. Bodily energy is dispersed in many channels (nāḍis) and the major among them, iḍā and piṅgalā, represent worldly duality. By letting śakti conflux at the base of suṣumnā, the principal nāḍi, which runs parallel to the spinal cord, kuṇḍalinī starts her awakening process and moves on to pierce all the seven cakras. According to Śākta Yoga, each cakra is associated with a particular goddess. The sādhaka (practitioner) must learn how to focus on her and then be united with her before moving to the next stage. The śaktis are Dākinī on the mūlādhāra cakra (perineum), Rākinī on the svādhiṣṭhāna cakra (genitals), Lakṣmī on the maṇipura cakra (navel), Kākinī on the anāhata cakra (heart), Śākinī on the viśuddha cakra (throat), Hākinī on the ājñā cakra (between the eyebrows) and Nirvāṇa Śakti on the sahasrāra cakra (above the head). When kuṇḍalinī has penetrated all the cakras (sat-cakra-bheda), the devotee has obtained perfect worship (siddhāntācāra) and becomes a jīvanmukti, 'liberated while alive'. The dichotomies of the material world are no more an issue and, finally, having given up all bondages, the Śākta reaches the stage of kaulācāra, the closest one to perfect knowledge and the state of divinity.

The folk/tribal practice

Śāktism is one of the most common forms of worship among Hindu low-caste and tribal people. South Asian tribes show an overt worship of the divine feminine, yet tribal goddesses are rather different from the Devīs of devotional and yogic Śāktism. The cult of folk/tribal goddesses is grounded in shamanic practices, particularly linked to ancestral forms of worship of the earth as the mother who nurtures the community and the abode of the dead. In tribal and folk contexts the power of goddesses is absolute because it is non-dependent. The essential traits of folk/tribal goddesses can be summarised by considering that:

1 They often have no defined iconography. Mostly represented as darkish stone slabs (śīlās), tribal goddesses are the custodians of the tribe's heritage. When an anthropomorphic rendering is given, they are not the beautiful maidens or pious wives of Brahmanical Hinduism. Rather, they are imaged as dark, ugly and, often, old.
2 They are regarded as the mothers of the village. This includes non-Hindu people like ādivāsīs, Muslims and Christians.
3 They make show of a gendered ritualism based on both tangible offerings and self-offerings (fasting, self-tortures, etc.).
4 Their worship sometimes requires the ritual killing of a victim.
5 Their behaviour is highly unstable. Goddesses are protective-cum-malign. They can be hungry (hot) or satisfied (cold).
6 They grant tangible benefits (fertility, good harvesting, wealth, removal of diseases, etc.) rather than spiritual relief or ultra-mundane experiences.
7 They do not require a priestly caste. On the one hand, pūjāris (non-brahmanical priests) are recruited among the lowest strata of the Hindu traditional hierarchy (carpenters, scavengers, blacksmiths, winemakers, etc.). On the other, ādivāsī people employ shamans, healers and oracles of both sexes.

Possession is one of the most common traits in folk/tribal Śāktism. These episodes – often leading to trance phenomena – allow individuals to deal with the goddess in order to satisfy personal or collective requests. Possessions can be observed on the occasion of a scheduled festival (utsava) or big celebration, when many devotees are simultaneously possessed, or as spontaneous occurrences (dream, pathological or temporary possessions). In tribal environments it is possible to find possession specialists: male and female shamans. Shamans seek direct contact with the goddess(es) in order to obtain tangible relief for the community, to placate the dead or to understand what the deity requires. Folk/tribal Śāktism is still a living religion in peripheral rural areas. Brahmanical elites and governmental educational programmes have both attempted to discourage (often with the use of violence) many of these practices in that they represent 'popular superstitions'. Nevertheless, worshipping protective-cum-malign goddesses as living mothers remains at the very base of the religious practice and experience of great strata of the Indian population.

The establishing of Śākta literature

Only from the fourth century CE, with the consolidation of a more intimate relation between Śiva and the goddess Śakti, does religion become an established reality in South Asia. Śāktas are no longer at the margin. Instead, their doctrine, religious practices and literature develop in more and more complex and original forms. Early *Purāṇas* indulge in myths on the goddess, particularly those of Śiva's and Viṣṇu's consorts. The *Vāyu Purāṇa* (third to fifth century CE) is one of the first to mention the myth of Satī, one of the most important for the Śaktis, while in the *Viṣṇu Purāṇa* (fourth century CE) great emphasis is given to the goddess as Śrī, Nārāyaṇī or Lakṣmī. But along with the incorporation of a constructive mythology of the goddess, Śaktis continue to display their fierce nature. Terrifying goddesses are mentioned in an increasing number of *Purāṇas* as well as in the epic. At the end of the first millennium CE this association became the object of great inspiration. With the birth of new forms of worship grounded in traditional schools but focused on esoteric teachings and scriptures, the Tantras, the worship of the goddess develops new approaches. Tantras differ from other sectarian scriptures in that they reject the authority of the Veda. The earliest of them were written shortly before the tenth century CE. Both Śaivas and Śāktas consider Tantras as revelation. Usually they are built in a dialogical form and, according to the structure, they can be *Āgamas* or *Nigama*. In the former instance, Śiva acts as a guru and imparts knowledge through the questions posed by the Devī. In the latter, it is the goddess who shows the ways to succeed in sādhana. Śaiva *Tantras* have been divided in 28 *Āgamas* and 108 *Upāgama* (secondary *Āgamas*), while Śākta *Tantras* are traditionally believed to be 77 *Āgamas*. Although they might include myths of different origin, they do not develop a specific subject. They generally deal with practical methods to gain supernatural powers and be united with the goddess: alchemy, mantra, yantra, mudrā, japa, dhyāna, yogic practices and magic. Tantric gurus, practitioners and yogins contributed to the acquisition of antisocial practices, most of them inherited by the lore of tribal people, in Śākta esoteric scriptures. Hence the birth of a whole literary imagery in which the Śākta practitioner indulges in dangerous sexual dalliances with outcaste or tribal women clearly substituting for the great goddess. Between the fourth and the tenth century CE, mainly in remote eastern areas (Bengal, Orissa and Assam), collective forms of worship of the goddess appeared. Among these the most popular are the saptamātṛkās (the 'seven mothers') and the dasa-mahāvidyās (the 'ten supreme [forms of] knowledge'). In the *Devī Māhātmya*, as well as in other Sanskrit sources, the seven mothers are identified with goddesses who are produced in moments of crisis from the bodies of major gods. These are Vaiṣṇavī from Viṣṇu, Brahmāṇī from Brahmā, Kaumarī from Kārttikeya (Skanda), Aindrī (or Indrāṇī) from Indra, Maheśvarī from Śiva, Narasiṃhī from Narasiṃha and Vārāhī from Varāha. But in the *Devī Māhātmya* (8.22) the seven mothers are inscribed in a larger myth, possibly of non-Vedic origin, and the most powerful deity is Kālī, a śakti produced by the great goddess herself: Durgā. Further, Durgā admits that all these goddesses are just different aspects of her and eventually she absorbs them, including Kālī, into herself (*Devī Māhātmya* 10.2–5).

The cult of the dasa mahāvidyās is more articulate. The ten manifestations of the great goddess are usually compared to the ten incarnations (avatāras) of Viṣṇu. These are Kālī, Tārā, Tripura-Sundarī (also called Ṣoḍāśī), Bhuvaneśvarī, Chinnamastā, Bhairavī, Dhūmāvatī, Bagalāmukhī, Mātaṅgī and Kamalā. There are no written sources on the origin of this cult (Kinsley 1997: 22). According to the *Mahābhāgavata Purāṇa* (which refers to itself as *Pārvatī Gīta*) and the *Bṛhaddharma Purāṇa* (both composed in eastern India around the fourteenth century CE) these goddesses are manifestations of Satī, who uses them to control Śiva. In the *Devī-Bhāgavata Purāṇa* (7.28) the ten mahāvidyās spring out from the body of Mahādevī (the 'Great Goddess') in order to fight demons. More generally, they are celebrated in written and oral lore as manifestations of Śiva's wives (Satī, Pārvatī) or independent śaktis (Durgā, Kālī) who try to restrain or dominate a male figure, usually Śiva, and eventually embody the Universe in all its aspects. With the spread of these myths, Śaktis reinforce their antisocial aspect but at the same time they strengthen a theological approach which stresses the unity of the primordial feminine principle in a multiform and ambiguous way.

The medieval period

Between the eleventh and the sixteenth century, Śāktas had to face the arrival and establishment of the Muslims and the massive popularity of Vaiṣṇava devotional schools. During this period, Śaivism became even more blended with Śākta doctrine. The development of Tantrism favoured this process. Although Śākta and Tantra literature often overlap, it has to be maintained that *Tantras* can be Vaiṣṇava, Śaiva, Bauddha (Buddhist) and Śākta. Śākta Tantric texts have been continuously arranged according to sectarian motivations rather than a theoretical approach. Early *Tantras* were divided according to the pīṭha schema, i.e. the geographical location of the holy site of pilgrimage related to the myth of the dismemberment of Satī to which the text refers. A later classification simply divides Tantric texts into four āmnāyas (lines of transmission): Trika (worshipped deities: Parā, Aparā, Parāparā, the threefold aspect of the Devī), Krama (worshipped deity: Kālī), the Kubjikā (worshipped deity: Kuṇḍalinī) and Śrīvidyā (worshipped deity: Tripura-Sundarī or Lalitā). Whatever their origin, Śākta Tantric texts agree in describing Śiva as a limit and a restraint, while Śakti personifies both the power to create and the power to free from the bondage of the material world. The centrality of the female power had a great impact on contemporary theological and philosophical speculations. Buddhist *Tantras* developed their own ritual practice around the duality expressed by prajña (knowledge) and upāya (method), the female and male principles. Vaiṣṇava ideas too have been greatly influenced by Śāktism. The cult of Jagannātha in Orissa emphasised the presence of Subhadrā among her brothers Kṛṣṇa and Balarāma.

Rādhā developed a multiform character too. In the *Bhāgavata Purāṇa* (ninth to eleventh century), in the *Gītagovinda* of Jayadeva (twelfth century), in the *Brahmavaivarta Purāṇa* (thirteenth century) and in the many devotional *Padāvalīs* ('lines' or 'series' of verses) especially written by Vaiṣṇava *Gauḍiyas* and *Sahajiyās* (Sahaja Yoga), Rādhā became the focus of new speculations and, in some instances, like the Rādhāvallabhis, the actual object of goddess worship.

From the fourteenth century onwards, great production of Śākta texts can be observed. These are divided in *gītas* (praise to the goddess), *māhātmyas* (ritual manuals), *Upaniṣads* and *Purāṇas.* Although the first two might overlap in some respects, every scripture maintains its own peculiar traits. Between the twelfth and the fifteenth century the eight Śākta *Upaniṣads* were written: *Tripura-*, *Bahvricha-*, *Saubhagya-Lakṣmī-*, *Sarasvatī-Rahasya-*, *Tripura-Tāpinī-*, *Devī-*, *Bhāvana-* and *Sītā-Upaniṣad*. A ninth one, the *Annapūrṇā Upaniṣad*, is occasionally mentioned. The most important Śākta *Purāṇas* are also written in this period: the *Kālikā Purāṇa*, the *Devī-Bhāgavata Purāṇa* and the *Devī Purāṇa*. These texts offer a variegated description of the patterns of worship of the Devī. Ritual theological speculations and regional beliefs are given and explained through a number of myths. Great emphasis is also given to the goddess as a primordial force (Ādya-Śakti), and the importance of the śākta pīṭhas (holy sites) as places of pilgrimage (tīrthayātrā) is established. Śākta texts and Śākta Tantra continued to be written in the seventeenth and eighteenth centuries yet they assume a more speculative structure. A rich literature of commentaries is also issued. *Tantras* and *Purāṇas* are interpreted and debated and the whole Tantric corpus is arranged in five *subhāgamas* (practice for knowledge and liberation), sixty-four *kaulāgamas* (practices to gain supernatural powers) and eight *miśrāgamas* (meant for both liberation and magic purposes) (Bhattacharyya 1974: 187). The Śrīvidyā theological school of South India is particularly active in this period. Its philosophical implant maintains a monistic metaphysics which identifies the ultimate reality with the Devī (here called Lalitā-Tripurasundarī), and even though its scriptures develop from the texts of the Śrīkula, it reflects the Advaita tradition of Śaṅkara (788–820 CE). Great theologians like Bhāskarācārya and Nāgoji Bhaṭṭa (seventeenth century) contributed to make of the Śrīvidyā one of the most prolific Śākta schools. Among the major scripture of the Śrīvidyā, it is worth mentioning the *Yoginīhṛdaya* (*c.* eleventh century), a speculative treatise which was followed by many commentaries in the seventeenth and eighteenth centuries.

Modern and contemporary Śāktism

From the second half of the eighteenth century, Śāktism undergoes a period of great change. Poets like Rāmprasād Sen (*c.*1718–75) and Kamalākānta Bhaṭṭāchārya (*c.*1769–1821) describe in their verses their love for a goddess who is infinite love and terrible wrath, but who always represents the ultimate shelter, the mother. On the one hand, it is possible to observe the definitive incorporation of the figure of Kālī, together with Durgā and Pārvatī/Umā in the Śākta common imagery. On the other, Śāktism acquires a new social façade. The myths of the goddess are employed as models for social struggles (emancipation of women, widow remarriage, the fight against arranged marriage and the struggle for independence). Śaktis become models of virtue, especially in Bengal, where the local Renaissance gives birth to a new season of Śākta literature. Śākta themes happened to be employed at all levels in the arts. Even non-Śākta thinkers and artists such as Bharatcandra Ray (1712–60),

Nilakantha Mukhopadhyaya (1841–1912), Girish Candra Ghose (1844–1912), Dasarathi Ray (1807–57), Michael Madhusudan Datta (1824–73), Rabindranath Tagore (1861–1941) and Najrul Islam (1899–1976) somehow adhered to this trend. But the affirmation of Śāktism was not always free from problems. The worship of the goddess, especially in her ugly and terrible forms, remained linked to her antisocial and impure origins. For this reason, esoteric practitioners seeking supernatural powers, such as revolutionaries, nationalists and criminals too, looked at the Śaktis as their personal deities.

The duality of the goddess remains vivid in Indian culture. She is both the goddess of the Thugs (the cult of stranglers who worshipped Kālī) and the inspiring mother of Rammohan Roy (1772–1833) and Bankim Chandra Chatterjee (1838–94). Also, with the advent of Marxist ideologies in the nineteenth century, Śāktism and Tantrism start to be considered as 'liberating philosophies', a role which is still greatly debated (Urban 2003: 200). Along with the politicisation of Śāktism, the cult of the goddess gained international acknowledgement thanks to the contribution of saints and mystics like Sri Ramakrishna (1836–86), Aurobindo Ghose (1872–1950) and Swami Vivekananda (1863–1902). Ramakrishna, heir to the tradition of Rāmprasād Sen, developed a mystic approach to the goddess which allowed him to theorise the identity of all form of religions. Both the transcendent and the immanent reality are embodied by the figure of the great mother Kālī. Ramakrishna's teaching was further developed by Vivekananda, who employed the Śākta common imagery and the Vedāntic theories in a more practical way, transforming Śāktism into a humanitarian and universal religion. Śākta Tantrism was at the base of other teachers like Vāma Kṣepā (*c.*1843–1911), who developed Ramakrishna's universalistic approach according to the Tantras, and Sri Aurobindo, who saw in the Śaktis the only way to experience both the transformation and the consequence of transformation in order to transcend and attain liberation in all its possible meanings.

In the twentieth century new forms of Śāktism emerged, particularly in Diaspora Hinduism and within new forms of religions. The cult of the goddess has been interpreted from a number of viewpoints: feminism, psychoanalysis, structuralism, postmodernism, etc. Ultimately, with the increasing diffusion of the World Wide Web Śāktism has become a global phenomenon. Yoga books and teachers explaining how to awaken kuṇḍalinī and Tantra-inspired sex manuals can be found everywhere. The social and political exploitation of Śākta imagery (Śaktis as symbols of military power or self-determination) and massive employment of the Devī iconography in the advertising business are common phenomena in India. In this milieu the goddess of the Śāktas still conserves her original ambiguity and – in a broader context – remains the mother of everybody.

See also: **Aditi; Advaita; Astika and Nāstika; Avatāras; Balarāma; Bhakti; Bhedābheda; Blood sacrifice; Brahmā; Brahman; Brahmanism; Buddhism, relationship with Hinduism; Chatterjee, Bankim Chandra; Devī Māhātmya; Dharmaśāstras; Diaspora; Dīkṣā; Draupadī; Durgā; Ghose, Aurobindo; Guṇas; Guru; Indus Valley Civilisation; Internet; Jagannātha; Jainism, relationship with Hinduism; Jīvanmukta; Kālī and Caṇḍī; Kṛṣṇa; Kuṇḍalinī Yoga; Lakṣmī, Śrī; Languages; Mahābhārata; Mahādevī; Mahāvidyās; Mantra; Māyā; Nationalism; Pañcamakāra; Pāṇḍavas; Pārvatī; Pativratā and Patiparameśvara; Possession; Pṛthivī; Pūjā; Purāṇas; Rādhā; Ramakrishna, Sri; Rāmāyaṇa; Roy, Rammohan; Religious specialists; Saccidānanda; Sacred Texts; Saḍdarśana; Sahaja Yoga; Śaivism; Śakti;**

Saṃhitā; Śaṅkara; Sāṃkhya; Saṃpradāya; Saptamātṛkās; Sarasvatī; Satī; Sītā; Skanda; Smārta; Subhadrā; Tagore, Rabindranath; Tantras; Tantrism; Tīrthayātrā (Pilgrimage); Umā; Upaniṣads; Uṣas; Utsava; Vaiṣṇavism; Veda; Vedānta; Viṣṇu; Vivekananda, Swami; Yantra; Yoga; Yogi

FABRIZIO M. FERRARI

Further reading

Berkson, C. 1995. *The Divine and Demoniac: Mahisa's Heroic Struggle with Durgā*. Delhi: Oxford University Press.

Bhattacharyya, N.N. 1974. *History of the Śākta Religion*. Delhi: Munshiram Manoharlal.

Brooks, D.R. 1992. *Auspicious Wisdom. The Texts and Traditions of Srividya Sakta Tantrism in South India*. Albany, NY: State University of New York Press.

Brown, C.M. 1999. *The Devī Gita. The Song of the Goddess*. Delhi: Sri Satguru Publications.

Carrin, M. 1999, 'The Sacrifice of Femininity: Female Sacredness at the Hindu/Tribal Frontier in Bengal'. In Harald Tambs-Lyche, ed., *The Feminine Sacred in South Asia*. Delhi: Manohar, 114–33.

Coburn, T.B. 1991. *Encountering the Goddess. A Translation of the Devī-Māhātmya and a Study of Its Interpretation*. Albany, NY: State University of New York Press.

Erndl, K.M. 1993. *Victory to the Mother. The Hindu Goddess of Northwest Indian Myth, Ritual, and Symbol*. Oxford and New York: Oxford University Press.

Erndl, K.M. 2000. 'Is *Shakti* Empowering for Women? Reflection on Feminism and the Hindu Goddess'. In A. Hiltebeitel and K.M. Erndl, eds, *Is the Goddess a Feminist? The Politics of South Asian Goddesses*. Sheffield: Sheffield Academic Press, 91–103.

Gourdiaan, T. and S. Gupta. 1981. *Hindu Tantric and Śākta Literature*. Wiesbaden: Otto Harrasowitz.

Gupta, S. 1992. 'Women in the Śaiva/Śākta Ethos'. In Julia Leslie, ed., *Roles and Rituals for Hindu Women*. Delhi: Motilal Banarsidass, 193–210.

Hazra, R.C. 1963. *Studies in the Upa Purāṇas*, vol. 2: *Śākta and non-Sectarian Upa Purāṇas*. Calcutta: Sanskrit College.

Kinsley, David R. 1997, *Tantric Vision of the Divine Feminine. The Ten Mahavidyas*. Berkeley, CA: University of California Press.

Kripal, J.J. 1995. *Kālī's Child. The Mystical and the Erotic in the Life and Teachings of Ramakrishna*. Chicago, IL and London: University of Chicago Press.

McDaniel, J. 2004. *Offering Flowers, Feeding Skulls. Popular Goddess Worship in West Bengal*. Oxford and New York: Oxford University Press.

McDermott, R.F. and J.J. Kripal. 2003. *Encountering Kālī in the Margins, at the Center, in the West*. Berkeley and Los Angeles, CA: University of California Press.

McLean, M. 1998. *Devoted to the Goddess. The Life and Work of Ramprasad*. Albany, NY: State University of New York Press.

Pintchman, T. 1994. *The Rise of the Goddess in the Hindu Tradition*. Albany, NY: State University of New York Press.

Urban, H.B. 2003. *Tantra: Sex, Secrecy, Politics, and Power in the Study of Religion*. Berkeley, CA and London: University of California Press.

Warrier, A.G. (ed.). 1975. *The Śākta Upaniṣads*. Madras: Adyar Library and Research Centre.

Wendell, B. 1977. *Myth, Cult and Symbols in Śākta Hinduism: A Study of the Indian Mother Goddess*. Leiden: E.J. Brill.

White, D. 2003. *The Kiss of the Yogini. 'Tantric Sex' in its South Asian Context*. London and Chicago, IL: Chicago University Press.

Woodroffe, J. 1998. *Sakti and Śākta*. Madras: Ganesh & Co.

SALIG RAM, RAI

An influential successor of Shiv Dayal Singh, the founder of the Radhasoami traditions. Amongst the six successors, Rai Salig Ram was arguably the most successful, and his satsang, established in Peepal Mandi, Agra, attracted more disciples than his own guru and arguably eclipsed even the efforts of Jaimal Singh in the Punjab.

More than anyone, Rai Salig Ram established the Radhasoamis as a distinct religious tradition. Not only publishing his guru's main text, *Sar Bachan*, he went on to develop the teachings into a coherent theology that separated Radhasoami from other mediaeval nirguna bhaktis such as Kabīr or Nānak. He argued that Shiv Dayal Singh was the first complete incarnation of God to appear on the earth and was thus presenting a new message to the human race. Not all the rival successors agreed with this interpretation but David Lane argues that Rai Salig Ram was the St Paul of Radhasoami traditions, providing the coherence for the development of an autonomous religion (see David Lane, http://vclass.mtsac.edu940/adiem/guru1.htm).

See also: **Bhakti; Kabīr; Radhasoami Satsang**

RON GEAVES

Further reading

Jones, Kenneth. 1989. *Socio-Religious Reform Movements in British India, The New Cambridge History of India: Vol. 3.1*. Cambridge: Cambridge University Press.

Lane, David, http://vclass.mtsac.edu940/adiem/guru1.htm.

SAMĀDHI

See: **Aṣṭāṅga Yoga**

SAMĀVARTANA

This saṃskāra, or rite of passage, marks the end of the period of studentship (brahmacarya), making it a type of graduation ceremony, after which the student returns to his home before entering the next phase of life, that of becoming a married householder (gṛhasthin). The main rite is a ceremonial bath, or snāna, and the graduate was called a snātaka, one who has completed this bath. The dharma texts list three types of snātaka: the vidyā-snātaka, who has completed the entire course of study but has not remained in residence at the guru's house for the entire prescribed period (usually sixteen years); the vrata-snātaka, who has observed all his vows (vrata) and spent the required number of years at the guru's house but has not completed the course of study; and the ubhaya-snātaka, the best of the students, who has both completed (ubhaya) the full course and has remained with the guru for the full term.

The ritual begins with the student spending the morning shut in a room. According to the *Bharadvāja-Gṛhyasūtra*, this is because he has built up such great lustre from his studies that the sun would be insulted by his presence. Then he emerges, grasps the feet of his guru and pays his respects to the guru's fire by placing some fuel on it. Eight vessels of consecrated water, some of them scented, have been prepared for his grand bath. He then casts off into water the accoutrements of his studentship, including his belt, his deerskin and his staff. He then cleanses himself thoroughly, shaves, cuts his nails, dons new undyed white garments, bathes with the prepared water and receives flowers, garlands, ornaments, collyrium, earrings, umbrella, turban, shoes and a mirror. The teacher then feeds him a mixture of honey, ghee and yogurt (madhuparka), and the student gives the teacher a large payment. The snātaka then proceeds to a learned assembly on a chariot or an elephant. He is now prepared for his future as a householder among the learned. In recent historical times, the samāvartana has become absorbed into either the upanayana or the marriage ceremonies (vivāha), and most of these rites are not performed or are performed symbolically.

See also: **Brahmacarya; Gārhasthya; Gṛhyasūtra; Guru; Saṃskāra; Vivāha; Vrata**

FREDERICK M. SMITH

Further reading

Kane, P.V. 1974. *History of Dharmaśāstra*, 2nd edn, vol. 2, pt 1. Poona: Bhandarkar Oriental Research Institute, 405–15.

Pandey, R.J. 1969. *Hindu Saṃskāras.* Delhi: Motilal Banarsidass, 146–52.

SĀMAVEDA

See: **Saṃhitā**

SAṂHITĀ

Saṃhitā, meaning 'collection', refers to the text of a Veda as handed down by a particular school of reciters. It usually excludes the *Brāhmaṇas, Āraṇyakas* and *Upaniṣads*, so that the *Ṛgveda Saṃhitā*, for instance, consists of the hymns only. There is only one saṃhitā of the *Ṛgveda*, though in ancient times there were five. The *Sāmaveda* has three, though two of them differ only a little, and the *Atharvaveda* two. The *Black Yajurveda* has three, containing not only the words spoken in the ritual but brāhmana material as well. In the *White Yajurveda* there are two recensions of the *Vājasaneyi Saṃhitā* (Gonda 1975: 16, 313, 272, 318; Howard 1977: 10).

The *Ṛgveda Saṃhitā* has attracted special interest as the oldest text in any Indian language and one of the world's monuments of ancient poetry. It is a collection of 1,028 poems (*sūkta*), conventionally called 'hymns', of around ten verses on average, and in most cases addressed to a particular deity. The special term for these verses is ṛc; hence the name *Ṛgveda*. There is no satisfactory complete English translation; Griffith (1889–92), in verse, is dated, but there are selections (Bose 1966; O'Flaherty 1981). The *Sāmaveda Saṃhitā* also contains hymns, but its most important part is not the verses, 95 per cent of which are selected from the *Ṛgveda*, but the tunes (sāman) to which they are sung. The sāmans are still sung, though the music may have changed over the centuries (Howard 1977). The *Yajurveda Saṃhitā* contains ritual utterances (yajuṣ), some in verse but most in prose. The *Atharvaveda Saṃhitā* (trans. Whitney 1905) is a collection of hymns, with some prose pieces, used in private rituals for cures, fertility of humans, animals and crops, victory, the infliction of harm on enemies and so on.

Most of the *Ṛgveda Saṃhitā*, unlike the *Yajurveda* and *Sāmaveda,* is not arranged with reference to ritual, but with reference to families of ṛṣis. It is divided into ten maṇḍalas (literally 'circles', but conventionally called 'books'), and each of maṇḍalas 2–7 is a collection of hymns revealed, or from a historical point of view composed, by members of a particular lineage of ṛṣis. Only maṇḍala 9 appears to have been compiled for a particular ritual context, the pressing of soma.

The *saṃhitā-pāṭha* of a Vedic text is the version in which it is recited (or written) continuously, as distinct from the *padapāṭha* ('word recitation'), in which the words are separated to clarify their grammatical forms. The word saṃhitā is also used in the titles of some non-Vedic texts, such as the *Pāñcarātra Saṃhitās* and the *Bhat Saṃhitā*, a work on jyotiṣa. The *Bhāgavata Purāṇa* refers to itself as a *saṃhitā*.

See also: **Āraṇyakas; Brāhmaṇas; Jyotiṣa; Pāñcarātras; Purāṇas; Ṛṣi; Soma; Upaniṣads; Veda**

DERMOT KILLINGLEY

Further reading

Bose, Abinash Chandra. 1966. *Hymns from the Vedas.* Bombay: Asia Publishing House.

Gonda, Jan. 1975. *Vedic Literature.* Wiesbaden: Otto Harrassowitz.

Griffith, Ralph T.H. 1889–92. *The Hymns of the Ṛgveda: Translated with a Popular Commentary*, 4 vols. Benares: E.J. Lazarus. New edition ed. J. L. Shastri, vol. 1, Delhi: Motilal Banarsidass, 1973.

Howard, Wayne. 1977. *Sāmavedic Chant.* New Haven, CT: Yale University Press.

O'Flaherty, W.D. 1981. *The Rig Veda: An Anthology of One Hundred and Eight Hymns: Anthology.* Harmondsworth: Penguin.

Whitney, William Dwight. 1905. *Atharva-Veda Saṃhitā: Translated with a Critical and Exegetical Commentary*, 2 vols. Cambridge, MA: Harvard University Press. Reprinted Delhi, Motilal Banarsidass, 1962.

SĀṂKHYA

Sāṃkhya is one of the six systems of Indian philosophy (Ṣaḍdarṣana). The fundamental dualism described in its definitive classical presentation in the *Sāṃkhyakārikā* of Īśvarakṛṣṇa contrasts with the absolute monism of Advaita Vedānta and the idealism and nihilism of certain Buddhist schools. The assertion that the cause of the universe is insentient (*Sāṃkhyakārikā* 14) and is instigated to create for multiple passive witnessing selves (*Sāṃkhyakārikā* 31) contrasts with the attribution of agency to an omnipotent creator by Nyāya and theistic Hinduism. With all of these it has engaged in debate since its earliest systematic presentations and has been rejected as unorthodox and heretical. Yet its distinction between a silent witnessing transcendent consciousness and an active insentient manifest nature is represented by numerous theistic movements in India by the pairing of male and female deities. It has deeply influenced Śaiva, Śākta and Tantric doctrines and practices, and even the ideals of dispassion depicted in Vaiṣṇava texts such as Śrīdhara's commentary on the *Bhāgavata Purāṇa*.

Classical Sāṃkhya

Knowledge of manifest (vyakta) nature, unmanifest (avyakta) nature and the knower is necessary in order for a person to destroy suffering that arises from bodily, natural or supernatural causes finally and completely. Technology based upon empirical science, such as medical treatment, and on religious scripture, such as sacrifices, succeeds only in temporarily eliminating specific sources of discomfort. Three means of knowledge (Pramāṇas) are accepted as valid: direct perception (dṛṣṭa), inference (anumāna) and the verbal testimony of a reliable source (āptavacana). While direct perception and inference based upon it provide knowledge of manifest nature, inference based upon analogy and verbal testimony are accepted as valid means of evidence concerning objects beyond the range of direct perception. Knowledge of entities beyond direct perception, such as the unmanifest material cause of manifest nature, is thereby justified by inferring causes from their effects. The effect exists in its material cause prior to its manifestation. In this manner it is possible to attain knowledge of the ultimate causes of human experience in order to eliminate suffering completely and finally.

Human experience is the effect of the manifestation of unmanifest original nature (Prakṛti). Prakṛti manifests for the purpose of allowing each of many selves (Puruṣa) to experience nature and ultimately to attain isolation from nature (kaivalya). While the Puruṣa, conceptualised as masculine, is merely an inactive witness to all the experience that Prakṛti channels through the faculties of knowledge and ultimately through the intellect for the Puruṣa to experience, Prakṛti, conceptualised as feminine, yet insentient, undertakes every aspect of the activity, teleologically motivated to supply Puruṣa's experience and ultimate liberation. Not only does she perform what appears to be objective and external to the body, but her evolutes constitute all the faculties of the personality that appear to be subjective due to ignorance. These include the intellect (mahat/buddhi), the individuality (ahaṃkāra) and the mind (manas), which comprise the internal organ (antaḥkaraṇa), and the senses, organs of action and the basic elements. All these together constitute the subtle body (liṅgaśarīra). Basic elements evolve the gross elements that constitute the body and external material objects.

By virtue of conjunction with a Puruṣa, the intellect, which is an insentient evolute of Prakṛti, seems to be conscious; and the Puruṣa, which is indifferent and inactive, seems to act, which is solely a function of Prakṛti. The faculties of experience present all experience to the intellect, which is the finest evolute of insentient Prakṛti, which in turn presents them to the sentient silent witness, Puruṣa. Through various proportions of the three guṇas, Prakṛti manifests various dispositions in the intellect (mahat/buddhi) which dispose a person to be good or bad, smart or stupid, dispassionate or emotional, and powerful or weak. Fifty varieties of dispositions create tendencies in the person towards various experiences and various behaviour during life. Housed in the subtle body, after death they are carried through transmigration to determine the structure of a new body and the experiences of the next life in a cycle of death and suffering (saṃsāra).

Prakṛti, however, conducts not only those activities that bind Puruṣa but also those that liberate him. The knowledge of the distinction between the self and nature that ultimately allows him to attain kaivalya is one of the functions of the intellect. When this knowledge is established in the intellect, the same nature that manifests to provide enjoyment to the self desists from manifestation to free the self from suffering.

The term

The meaning of the term sāṃkhya ('knowledge, deliberation, number': sam, 'together, complete', + khyā, 'see, know', pass. 'appear', caus. 'make known, tell') has been variously interpreted to mean relating to knowledge, discernment (Eliade 1969: 367) or enumeration (Larson and Bhattacharya 1987: 3, 48). While the philosophical system is concerned with the enumeration of basic constituents, such as the three guṇas, and the twenty-five constituents of Prakṛti, its ultimate goal, kaivalya, is contingent upon thorough knowledge of Prakṛti and its discrimination from Puruṣa.

Pre- and proto-Sāṃkhya

A number of ideas present in systematic classical Sāṃkhya can be traced to ancient Indian philosophical speculation in Vedic hymns and *Upaniṣads*, but Sāṃkhya is first mentioned, along with Yoga, as a means to liberation from bondage in *Śvetāśvatara Upaniṣad* 6.13 (*c.*400–200 BCE). At about the beginning of the Common Era, the *Carakasaṃhitā*, the *Mokṣadharma Parvan* (12.168–320) and *Bhagavadgītā* in the *Mahābhārata*, and Aśvaghoṣa's *Buddhacarita* present early and less systematised versions of Sāṃkhya and Yoga doctrines. Many passages differ in essential details from classical Sāṃkhya. For instance, *Carakasaṃhitā* and the statements of Pañcaśikha in the *Mokṣadharma Parvan* identify unmanifest Prakṛti with a single Puruṣa, departing from the essential dualism of the classical system.

Early and late Sāṃkhya

Texts claim Kapila as the founding sage, and mention a number of teachers that precede Īśvarakṛṣṇa. Some of them are associated with cited passages and stories; others are known only by their names. Medieval Sāṃkhya works (*c.*1350–1500 CE) include the brief *Tattvasamāsasūtra* and the *Sāṃkhyasūtra*, consisting of 527 sūtras, on both of which commentaries were composed. Aniruddha (1464 CE) composed the *Sāṃkhyasūtravṛtti* (*c.*1500 CE), upon which draws Vijñānabhikṣu's synthetic *Sāṃkhyapravacanabhāṣya* (*c.*1550–1600 CE).

See also: **Advaita; Ahaṃkāra; Antaḥkaraṇa; Bhagavadgītā; Guṇas; Īśvarakṛṣṇa; Kaivalya; Kapila; Liṅgaśarīra; Mahābhārata; Mahat; Manas; Nyāya; Prakṛti; Pramāṇas;**

Purāṇas; Puruṣa; Ṣaḍdarṣana; Śaivism; Śāktism; Saṃhitā; Sāṃkhyakārikās; Saṃsāra; Tantrism; Upaniṣads; Vaiṣṇavism; Vedānta; Vijñānabhikṣu; Yoga

PETER M. SCHARF

Further reading

Ballantyne, James Robert (trans.). 1865. *The Sāṃkhya Aphorisms of Kapila: With Illustrative Extracts from the Commentaries*. Calcutta: Baptist Mission Press.

Dasgupta, Surendranath. 1922. *A History of Indian Philosophy*, vol. 1. Cambridge: Cambridge University Press, 208–73.

Edgerton, Franklin. 1924. 'The Meaning of Sāṃkhya and Yoga'. *American Journal of Philology* 45.1: 1–46.

Edgerton, Franklin. 1965. *The Beginnings of Indian Philosophy*. Cambridge, MA: Harvard University Press.

Eliade, Mircea. 1969. *Yoga: Immortality and Freedom*. Trans. Willard R. Trask [from the French, *Le Yoga: Immortalité et Liberté*. Paris: Librairie Payot, 1954]. Bollingen Series 56. 2nd edn. Princeton, NJ: Princeton University Press [1st edn. New York: Pantheon Books, 1958].

Hulin, Michael. 1978. *Sāṃkhya Literature. A History of Indian Literature*, ed. Jan Gonda, vol. 6, pt. 3, fasc. 3. Wiesbaden: Otto Harrassowitz.

Johnston, E.H. 1937. *Early Sāṃkhya: An Essay on its Historical Development According to the Texts*. London: Royal Asiatic Society.

Keith, Arthur Berriedale. 1918. *The Sāṃkhya System: A History of the Sāṃkhya Philosophy*. Calcutta: Association Press; London and New York: Oxford University Press.

Larson, Gerald James. 1969. *Classical Sāṃkhya: An Interpretation of its History and Meaning*. 1st edn. Delhi: Motilal Banarsidass. 2nd rev edn. Santa Barbara, CA: Ross/Erikson, 1979; Delhi: Motilal Banarsidass.

Larson, Gerald James and Ram Shankar Bhattacharya (eds). 1987. *Sāṃkhya: A Dualist Tradition in Indian Philosophy*. Encyclopedia of Indian Philosophies, vol. IV. Princeton, NJ: Princeton University Press; Delhi: Motilal Banarsidass.

van Buitenen, J.A.B. 1956. 'Studies in Sāṃkhya (I)'. *Journal of the American Oriental Society* 76: 153–57.

van Buitenen, J.A.B. 1957. 'Studies in Sāṃkhya (II)'. *Journal of the American Oriental Society* 77: 15–25.

van Buitenen, J.A.B. 1957. 'Studies in Sāṃkhya (III)'. *Journal of the American Oriental Society* 77: 88–107.

SĀṂKHYA-YOGA

Sāṃkhya is one of the six schools of Indian philosophy (ṣaḍdarśana) and its development as a system of thought is attributed to Kapila in the sixth century BCE. The term sāṃkhya is associated with concepts such as enumeration based on calculation and more generally discernment, and the main preoccupation of sāṃkhya is the distinguishing of Prakṛti (Matter) from Puruṣa (Spirit or Consciousness). In its classical form sāṃkhya is considered to be an atheistic philosophy; in the *Bhagavadgītā*, for example, the doctrine of sāṃkhya is seen more generally as the discipline of knowledge, the means to attaining enlightenment, and is associated with Jñāna Yoga. The use of the term yoga is itself rather fluid in texts such as the *Bhagavadgītā* and this can be confusing when trying to consider specific schools or approaches to yoga from the more general use of the term as simply a method or means. Consequently we have the association of Sāṃkhya-Yoga with both Jñāna Yoga and Rāja Yoga and at the same time discussions which oppose Yoga (as a particular form of spiritual discipline) with Sāṃkhya as an atheistic school of philosophy. However, the metaphysical view of Sāṃkhya with the idea of refining understanding through discernment in order to achieve kaivalya (aloneness or the awareness of Puruṣa) has close parallels with Rāja Yoga.

See also: **Bhagavadgītā; Jñāna (as path); Kaivalya; Kapila; Prakṛti; Puruṣa; Rāja Yoga; Ṣaḍdarśana; Sāṃkhya**

VIVIENNE BAUMFIELD

Further reading

Raju, P.T. 1971. *The Philosophical Traditions of India*. London: George Allen and Unwin.

Zimmer, H. 1969. *Philosophies of India*. Princeton, NJ: Princeton University Press.

SĀṂKHYAKĀRIKĀS

The *Sāṃkhyakārikā* of Īśvarakṛṣṇa is the definitive text of classical Sāṃkhya, perhaps dating from as early as the second century CE but probably *c.*350–450 CE (Larson and Bhattacharya 1987: 136). Together with a commentary, it was translated into Chinese by Paramārtha 557–69 CE (Eliade 1969: 369). The text consists of 72–73 kārikās, 'verses', in Ārya metre, though 63, 72–73 may be later additions (Larson and Bhattacharya 1987: 151). Early commentaries on it include the *Sāṃkhyasaptativṛtti*, 'comment on the seventy verses on Sāṃkhya' (sixth century). Verses 71 and following relate that Īśvarakṛṣṇa summarised the doctrines of a longer work, no longer extant, that either dealt with ṣaṣṭitantra, 'sixty topics', or was so called. Major commentaries on it include the *Yuktidīpikā* (*c.*510–750) and Vācaspati Miśra's *Tattvakaumudī* (*c.*976 CE).

See also: **Īśvarakṛṣṇa; Sāṃkhya; Vācaspati Miśra**

PETER M. SCHARF

Further reading

Bhattacharya, Ram Shankar. (ed.). 1966. *Sāṃkhyadarśana*. Varanasi: Bharatiya Vidya Prakasana.

Bhattacharya, Ram Shankar. 1967. *Sāṃkhyakārikā*. Varanasi: Motilal Banarsidass.

Colebrooke, Henry Thomas (trans.). 1837. *The Sāṃkhya Kārikā or Memorial Verses on the Sāṃkhya Philosophy: With the Bhāṣya or Commentary of Gaurapāda* [sic]. Trans. Horace Hayman Wilson. Oxford: Oriental Translation Fund of Great Britain and Ireland.

Davies, John (trans.). 1957. *The Sānkhya Kārikā of Iswara Krishna: An Exposition of the System of Kapila with Original Sanskrit Texts*. 2nd edn. Calcutta: Susil Gupta.

Eliade, Mircea. 1969. *Yoga: Immortality and Freedom*. Trans. Willard R. Trask [from the French, *Le Yoga: Immortalité et Liberté*. Paris: Librairie Payot, 1954]. Bollingen Series 56. 2nd edn. Princeton, NJ: Princeton University Press [1st edn 1958].

Jha, Ganganath (trans.). 1934. *The Tattvakaumudī: Vāchaspati Miśra's Commentary on the Sāṃkhya-kārikā*, 2nd rev. edn. Pune: Oriental Book Agency.

Larson, Gerald James and Ram Shankar Bhattacharya (eds). 1987. Sāṃkhya: A Dualist Tradition in Indian Philosophy. *Encyclopedia of Indian Philosophies*, vol. IV. Princeton, NJ: Princeton University Press; Delhi: Motilal Banarsidass.

Mainkar, T.G. (ed. and trans.). 1964. *The Sāṃkhya-kārikā: With the Commentary of Gauḍapāda*. Pune: Oriental Book Agency.

Srinivasan, Srinivasa Ayya. (ed.). 1967. *Vācaspatimiśra's Tattvakaumudī: ein Beitrag zur Textkritik bei kontaminierter Uberlieferung*. Alt- und neu-indische Studien 12. Hamburg: Cram, de Gruyter & Co.

Suryanarayana Sastri, S.S. (ed. and trans.). 1973. *The Sāṃkhyakārikā of Īśvara Kṛṣṇa*. Madras: University of Madras.

Wezler, Albrecht and Shujun Motegi (eds). 1998. *Yuktidipika: The Most Significant Commentary on the Samkhyakarika*. Alt- und neu-indische Studien 44. Stuttgart: Steiner.

SAṂNYĀSA

The word saṃnyāsa literally means to cast aside and is used in this literal sense in the *Bhagavadgītā* (e.g. 5.13). Its literal sense, however, often yields to the more conventional sense of the fourth stage of life in the Hindu scheme of things, which is entered upon by casting away the domestic fires, or, figuratively, the bonds of domestic life, in favour of wandering alone. Thereafter a person passes his life absorbed in the contemplation of the ultimate reality until his death (*Manusmṛti* 6.96). Equanimity in all circumstances in the basic virtue to be cultivated in this stage of life (*Manusmṛti* 6.44). It is possible to enter this stage of life immediately after the first, that of brahmacarya, in exceptional circumstances, as in the case of the famous Śaṅkara (*c.* eighth century CE).

Renunciation of the world in search of the ultimate is stated or implied in the *Chāndogya* (2.23) and *Bṛhadāraṇyaka* (2.4.1) *Upaniṣads* but it is not clear if this implies saṃnyāsa as a settled stage of life. Its formal enumeration as the fourth stage is first found in the *Jābālopaniṣad* (4). A few debated points within the Hindu tradition regarding saṃnyāsa pertain to: (1) whether only brāhmaṇas are entitled to it or male members of all the three higher castes; (2) whether, in theory or practice, it is permitted to śūdras and women; (3) whether one follows set rules like those of any stage of life or is set free from all rules whatever; and (4) whether formal saṃnyāsa is necessary for mokṣa or whether internal renunciation suffices.

See also: **Bhagavadgītā; Brahmacarya; Brāhmaṇas; Śaṅkara; Upaniṣads; Varṇa; Women, status of**

ARVIND SHARMA

Further reading

Kane, P.V. 1974. *History of Dharmaśāstra*, vol. II, pt II, 2nd edn. Poona: Bhandarkar Oriental Research Institute.

Marcaurelle, Roger. 1993. *Śankara and Renunciation: A Reinterpretation*. Albany, NY: State University of New York Press.

Olivelle, P. 1992. *The Saṃnyāsa Upaniṣads: Hindu Scriptures on Asceticism and Renunciation*. New York and Oxford: Oxford University Press.

SAṂPRADĀYA

A saṃpradāya is a distinct religious tradition; its central teachings have been handed down from the original founder, a guru or possibly deity, through a lineage of spiritual successors, all of whom have shaped the religious lives of its devotees. Saṃpradāya can be translated as that which 'is handed over' (Eschmann 2001: 111), and although the term sect is often used as a rough equivalent (Flood 1996: 34), this tends to refer to the Christian notion of heterodoxy. Whilst many saṃpradāya advocate social and doctrinal change, including transgressing caste and gender barriers, it is the very absence of a centralised Hindu orthodoxy that enables saṃpradāyas to become accepted Hindu traditions, often attaining some measure of orthodoxy (Eschmann 2001: 111).

The individuals who establish the lineage of spiritual leadership will be worshipped for their divine personality, wisdom and ability to bestow divine grace upon their devotees. The line of guru succession is crucial in establishing spiritual authenticity for the saṃpradāya (Flood 1996: 34), with gurus acting as the bearers of distinct teachings and interpreters of the traditions' scriptures for the lay communities. Many of a saṃpradāya's religious activities will revolve around the monastic order, which often resides at the established centre of worship.

Many saṃpradāya are established on a regional basis and, whilst some might be classed as New Religious Movements or recent social reform movements, many claim direct and venerable roots from their founding saints or gurus. The teachers of Śaṅkaras' saṃpradāya, established in the ninth century, continue to pass on his ideas today in Puri and Kāñcīpura, whereas the teachings of Madhva (thirteenth-century) have been passed on to the International Society for Krishna Consciousness (ISKCON) via the charismatic Bengali Vaiṣṇava Caitanya (1385–1533). The Puṣṭi Mārga continue to take refuge in Kṛṣṇa as taught by another sixteenth-century Bhakti Vaiṣṇava, Vallabha, hugely popular in North India and the Gujarat region (Dwyer 1994: 172).

Most saṃpradāyas recognise and refer to the classical scriptures and philosophical schools. Saṃpradāya will, however, distinguish themselves by commenting upon and reinterpreting the scriptures found within the Hindu canon. Many saṃpradāya compile their own specific literature, often written in regional languages, introducing new elements and thoughts in their texts, for example Swami Narayana Sampradaya, who produced the *Śikṣāpatrī* (Eschmann 2001: 114).

See also: **Bhakti; Caitanya; Caste; Guru; Kāñcīpura; International Society for Krishna Consciousness; Kṛṣṇa; Madhva; Puṣṭi Mārga; Śaṅkara; Swami Narayana Sampradaya; Vaiṣṇavism; Vallabha**

MARTIN WOOD

Further reading

Dwyer, R. 1994. 'Caste, Religion and Sect in Gujarat'. In R. Ballard, ed., *Desh Pardesh*. London: Hurst and Co.

Eschmann, A. 2001. 'Religion, Reaction and Change'. In G.-D. Sontheimer and H. Kulke, eds, *Hinduism Reconsidered*. Delhi: Manohar.

Flood, G. 1996. *An Introduction to Hinduism*. Cambridge: Cambridge University Press.

Williams, R. 2001. *Swaminarayan Hinduism*. Cambridge: Cambridge University Press.

SAṂSĀRA

The term saṃsāra literally means 'passage', as in passing through a succession of states. The common translation is 'cycle of lives' or transmigration. This concept is closely related to two other concepts: karma and Mokṣa (liberation). The concept of a cycle of lives is shared with Buddhism and Jainism.

This concept may have originated in the fear of repeated death. The earliest notions of life after death in the Vedic hymns seem to suggest that life was followed by an afterlife. However, fears that this too might have an end may have led to speculations of repeated death and birth. By the time of early *Upaniṣads*, speculation centred on the idea that different fates pertained to different individuals.

In the *Chāndogya Upaniṣad*, after death the ātman (self) is accompanied by prāṇa (breath) and subtle matter. Two possibilities for passage were available: one passage was directed by the way of the fathers (pitṛyāna), the other by the way of the gods (devayāna). The way of the fathers was the view of basic transmigration: the self of the deceased went up from the smoke of the funeral pyre to the moon, transferred to the clouds, rained on the earth, became a seed in the ground, which became food, which in turn was eaten and became semen in men, who procreated by means of this semen. The other passage, called 'of the gods', leads past the clouds, past the known universe, beyond the sun, to a special place without sorrow, pain or concern. From here there was no return.

The accompaniments of the transmigrating self have been studied, for example, by the Sāṃkhya teachers, who defined them as a subtle body (sūkṣmaśarīra or liṅgaśarīra). There are some different opinions on the composition of the subtle body, but basically it was described as formed from the internal (intellectual and mental) faculty (antaḥkaraṇa) and the cognitive sensory apparatus, along with karmic impressions. Some do not subscribe to this view, but, rather, believe that a life is repeated according to a person's merit or demerit alone. That means that only the karmic impressions are operational.

The formulation of the basic premise of fear of repeated lives led to the search for freedom from these vicissitudes. In order to determine an escape from the repetitions of life, it was necessary to identify a cause for this cycle. The cause was found in not knowing the things as they are, and therefore a person engaged in an indiscriminate action, either physical, mental or vocal, could commit some inconsequential acts. Action was stimulated by desire and desire arose again from ignorance of the state of affairs.

Any act (karma) of an ordinary mortal will accrue effects which will be positive, negative or even neutral. These karmic effects function as seeds for the subsequent formation of an individual's future life. Everything in this universe repeats itself in one form or another. It is the contingency of the effects which will determine the quality of the future life. Once born, one is always subject to death; once dead, one is subject to new birth and so on. Many view the repetition of these endless cycles as terrifying.

Two distinct responses to redeath/rebirth can be observed in the history of Hindu thought. The first response, prescribed renunciation of acting in the world and the world itself as the solution. Renunciates have experienced a vision in which they perceive that they themselves are part of the larger cosmos, that in fact they are identical with it. Thus the individual self (ātman) aimed at experiencing the vision of being the same with the universe (Brahman) and nothing else, with, as a result, no desires, no drives, no goals of possessions, no passions, no bereavement, no loss, no existential anxiety, no depression. One is rewarded with the ultimate freedom from all desire, disappointment and fear. This can be accomplished on one's own, with great self-reliance and without an outside agency. While effort could be supported with the help of a teacher, this is still an effort, exerted by the individual.

Another response to the effort of resolving the difficulty of repeated lives was less demanding in that it sought direct assistance from God. This immediately signalled dependence on an agency outside oneself. This view gradually deemphasised the fear of and the belief in repeated lives (saṃsāra) to adherents of several different traditions, Vaiṣṇava, Śaiva, etc., who incorporated such views in the folds of their own beliefs.

Among the Vaiṣṇava theologians, such as Rāmānuja, saṃsāra was the ultimate source of unhappiness. Only God could guide the self out of the entanglement with the busy and perpetually turbulent mundane world. To reach freedom (mokṣa) away from this world and its tedious repetition of becoming and perishing requires a complete self-surrender (prapatti). An even stronger stress on the role of God's grace was emphasised by another Vedāntin, Vallabha. He placed great importance on service (sevā) to God, as a family man with family values. He denounced ascetic ways toward liberation as no longer practicable. His way is known as the way of grace (Puṣṭi Mārga). Devotion is also the means in other religious traditions, such as the Śaiva Siddhānta. Here, in particular, there were various well-developed forms of devotion directed to one's Lord as a child to one's parent, as a lover, as a pupil to one's teacher, etc.

The concept of saṃsāra was originally linked with the idea that this world is unsatisfactory. The cause of an individual's bondage to saṃsāra is karma. However, with proper focus one could direct one's actions and therefore a person was the maker of his own destiny to a great extent. With the development of theistic tendencies, the force of karma was diminished by surrender and service to the Lord. He could take care of everything. This became the means to freedom from the repeated cycle of lives and their mundane existence in the world hurrying past.

See also: **Antaḥkaraṇa; Ātman; Brahman; Karma; Mokṣa; Puṣṭi Mārga; Rāmānuja; Śaiva Siddhānta; Śaivism; Sāṃkhya; Sevā Upaniṣads; Vaiṣṇavism; Vallabha; Vedānta**

EDELTRAUD HARZER

Further reading

Halbfass, Wilhelm. 2000. *Karma und Wiedergeburt in indischen Denken*. [Karma and Rebirth in Indian Thought] Kreuzkingen: Hugendubel.

Neufeldt, Ronald. (ed.). 1986. *Karma and Rebirth: Post Classical Developments.* Albany, NY: SUNY.
O'Flaherty, Wendy Doniger. (ed.). 1983. *Karma and Rebirth in Classical Indian Traditions.* Delhi: Motilal Banarsidass.
Prasad, Narayana. 1994. *Karma and Reincarnation.* New Delhi: DK Printworld (P) Ltd.
Singh, Balbir. 1989. *Karma and Reincarnation.* Bangalore: Arnold Publishers.

SAṂSKĀRAS

The Sanskrit word saṃskāra is related to the word Sanskrit itself. They derive from the verbal root 'kṛ', with the prefix 'sam-', meaning 'to refine, embellish, purify, put together in an orderly fashion'. Saṃskṛta, a participial form of this verb, indicates, in its most common usage, the Sanskrit language, 'perfected, sanctified, polished, well ordered', while a saṃskāra is a 'sacred, sanctifying, purifying' event, notably such a ceremony or ritual. More specifically, saṃskāras are rites of passage prescribed by an array of brahmanical ritual and dharma texts, the number of which varies from text to text. These rites can be dated in their present form to the first few centuries BCE, where they are first described (and prescribed) in detail in texts on domestic ritual composed during that period called *Gṛhyasūtras*. They are further elaborated in a variety of *Dharmaśāstra* or *smṛti* texts of the first millennium and early second millennium CE. In more recent historical times, handbooks called *prayogas* or *paddhatis*, which inscribe the local performative and textual variants, have been employed almost exclusively, rather than the classical texts.

Their status as rites of passage is directly addressed by Śabarasvāmin, the great fourth- or fifth-century CE commentator on the *Mīmāṃsāsūtras* of Jaimini. Commenting on Jaimini 3.1.3, Śabara states that when something comes into being (specifically a ritual) that renders a person suitable (yogya) for a certain purpose, it is called a saṃskāra; it 'refines' or ripens a person. This is amplified a few centuries later by Kumārila, the most important theoretician of the Pūrva Mīmāṃsā school of ritual exegesis, who wrote in his *Tantravārtika* (on Jaimini 3.8.9) that such suitability (yogyatā) works in two ways: it eliminates defects (doṣa) and generates positive attributes (guṇa). Such defects and attributes are physical as well as mental, as 'refinement' in the Vedic ritual system distinctly considers purification and sanctification to be enacted on physical objects as well as the mind. Thus, saṃskāras are ritual actions that 'refine' the body and mind, conferring on the individual eligibility (adhikāra) to advance through the demarcations of Hindu lifestyle patterns, such as the acquisition of a name, the beginning or end of Vedic study, marriage and death.

The number of saṃskāras ranges from eleven to forty in the various *Gṛhyasūtra* and *smṛti* texts in which they are prescribed. Very few of the texts agree on a single list, though a few appear in all the texts, including the baby-naming ceremony (nāmakaraṇa), the first feeding of solid food (annaprāśana), the initiation into Vedic study (upanayana), the return home after the conclusion of Vedic study (samāvartana) and the marriage ceremony (vivāha). Not all the texts admit the postmortem rites (antyeṣṭi) into the category of saṃskāra, though most of them do. The most canonical number is sixteen, spanning the human life from conception to death. Saṃskāras may be divided into five categories: pre-natal, childhood, educational, marriage and postmortem. The following discussion covers a number of the most commonly discussed saṃskāras.

The first is the garbhādhāna, the 'placing (of semen) into the womb'. The purpose of this was to generate a good and powerful son. The husband was to approach his wife when she was in the most fertile days of her menstrual cycle (generally considered the fourth to sixteenth days after menstruation) and, after considerable ritualisation, including elaborate dress and mantra recitation, the couple was to have intercourse. If the union was not successful in generating pregnancy, then it was to be repeated every month until fertilisation. If successful, the next saṃskāra to be performed was the puṃsavana, the 'vitalising', 'animating' or 'quickening' of a son. This is generally prescribed for the third or fourth month after conception when the moon is passing through a male lunar asterism (nakṣatra). As with all the saṃskāras, the puṃsavana consists of a number of brief rites and recitations of Vedic text. The third saṃskāra was the sīmantonnayana, the ritual parting of the hair of the pregnant wife. This rite, to be performed in the fourth or fifth month of pregnancy, was distinctly expiatory and purificatory, designed to confer prosperity on the wife. It was widely believed that certain possessing demonesses called bālagrahas or 'childsnatchers' could inhabit the pregnant mother or the foetus, and this saṃskāra in part protected against this.

The next series of saṃskāras consisted of those performed on the child, from birth to age 8 or 12. It is important to note that both male and female children were given saṃskāras up to the upanayana, the rite of initiation into Vedic education. The educational saṃskāras were limited to males belonging to one of the three upper varṇas or classes: brāhmaṇas, kṣatriyas and vaiśyas, the priests and ritualists, the ruling class and military, and the mercantile classes, respectively. Labourers or śūdras and those outside the varṇa system were excluded. The fourth saṃskāra is a series of rites called jātakarma, 'birth rituals'. These ceremonies should begin about a month before birth, and require a number of interlocking and related rites, including ritual preparation of the room in which the delivery takes place, the presence of priests to recite mantras at the time of severing the umbilical cord, rites conferring intelligence (medhājanana), long life (āyuṣya) and strength on the child, and general exorcistic rites. The fifth saṃskāra is the nāmakaraṇa, the baby-naming ceremony, which is the first truly public ceremony of the child's life. Naming was of the greatest importance in India. Though naming conventions have differed from one region and linguistic area to another, similarities were expressed in the brahmanic rites of naming. These included, variously, a 'secret' name, a name similar to the first letter of the lunar asterism under which the child was born, the name of the deity presiding over the month, or the name of a deity associated with the family. Numbers of syllables were prescribed depending on the desired merit of the child. For example, the *Āśvalāyana Gṛhyasūtra* (1.15.5) states that, 'If one desires fame (for the child), then his name should consist of two syllables; if one desires that the child be brilliant in mantras, then the name should have four syllables'. The timing was also important. The usual days prescribed were the tenth, eleventh or twelfth day after birth, but other options were there as well, including the hundredth day or the first birthday.

Other childhood saṃskāras were the first outing of the child (niṣkramaṇa), the first feeding of solid food (annaprāśana), the first haircutting (cūḍākaraṇa) and the piercing of the ears (karṇavedha). The niṣkramaṇa, with a ritual sendoff of the newborn into the world, with full regalia, took place from the twelfth day after birth to four months after, according to different texts. The annaprāśana occurred after six or seven months of maternal lactation. In this ceremony different kinds of food were prescribed corresponding to different goals the parents envisioned for the child. The usual food was yoghurt or rice mixed with honey and ghee, but other foods, including meat, were possible. This was performed to the accompaniment of Vedic mantras. The cūḍākaraṇa was performed between the first and third birthdays. It was closely tied in with notions of the power and symbolic significance of hair and the competing notion that it was a necessary impurity that had to be cut off occasionally. Usually not all the hair was cut off, leaving a remnant topknot, often as a sectarian mark. The karṇavedha was performed quite early, some texts prescribing it as early as the tenth, twelfth or sixteenth day after birth, others after a year. All agree that it should be done before teething. The type of needles – gold, silver or copper – was prescribed depending on the desired goal or the varṇa of the child.

The educational saṃskāras included, first, the optional and fairly infrequently performed ceremony at the time of learning the alphabet (vidyārambha), generally prescribed for the child at five years of age. More important was the extensive ritual performed at the commencement of Vedic study, the so-called 'thread ceremony' (upanayana), in which the child received the sacred thread, to be worn over the left shoulder and under the right arm (this was reversed during the performance of postmortem rituals), and a ritual staff (daṇḍa). The child was also initiated into the recitation of the Gāyatrī mantra (*Ṛgveda* 3.62.10), was taught the elements of the saṃdhyā, the daily rites to be performed at dusk, dawn and sometimes midday, and given first instructions in the care of a sacred fire. This was a major festive occasion. Guests were invited and the expense was often quite high, much of it dakṣiṇā, or payment to the initiating ritualists. This was to be performed at age eight for brāhmaṇas, eleven for kṣatriyas, and twelve for vaiśyas. In fact, it was done any time after the age of 8 for any of the members of these three varṇas, though historically it was almost always preformed on brāhmaṇas and less frequently on others. Its great importance was in large part because it represented the commencement of the first true stage of life, the brahmacarya-āśrama, the period of studentship.

After the conclusion of Veda study, which was prescribed to last eight to twelve years (though for some it was of much briefer duration and for others much longer), a ceremony was performed that marked the student's return home (samāvartana), a graduation of sorts.

The most complicated and extended saṃskāra was the marriage ceremony, which had a large number of textual, geographical and community variants. It could last from a few hours to a few days in length, depending on the number and duration of rites that were strung together. This represented the introduction to the second stage of life, that of the married householder (gṛhasthya-āśrama). That marriage was ritualised in ancient India is already evident in the *Ṛgveda* (10.85), where the marriage of Sūryā, the daughter of the sun, is celebrated with Soma, the moon. Though the marriage ceremony gradually grew in complexity, in most cases it retained a few basic elements, and in nearly all cases Vedic mantras were recited. This is not to say, however, that throughout India, across all caste and varṇa lines, the same Vedic mantras are recited, as there was variation even here. The basic elements that have in general been retained are, among others, the giving away of the bride by the father or another male member of the family (kanyādāna), the circling of the fire three or four times (agnipariṇaya, agnipradakṣiṇam), the act of taking seven steps around the fire, hand in hand (saptapadī), and a grain offering into the sacred fire (lājāhoma), which is emblematic of the householder's life. In recent historical times, the moment at which the marriage becomes formally constituted is the saptapadī, though this is not so specified in the classical literature. The giving of the marriage necklace (maṅgal-sūtra) by the groom to the bride is not part of the ancient ceremony, though it has become an essential part of the marriage ceremony in recent historical times.

The cremation and other accompanying obsequies constitute the final rite of passage, to the realms of Yama, the various states of the deceased. As such, death is not regarded as the opposite of life, but of birth; it is a stage of life to be entered through a rite of passage. These rites are also very complicated, requiring a trained class of ritual officiant, along with others, usually of a hereditary caste, trained in the care of the deceased. The deceased is also nourished on a regular basis through daily rites called śrāddha, up to the tenth or twelfth day when the spirit of the dead (preta) is ritually transformed into a deceased ancestor (pitṛ) eligible for annual śrāddha offerings.

The most complicated saṃskāras are, not surprisingly, the ones that are most frequently performed, namely the birth ceremonies, the Vedic initiation, the marriage and the funerary rites. All of these, especially the marriage, have ritual mechanisms and structures that allow for nearly unlimited regional variants to accumulate. It is also important to note that the transitions of life according to the prescribed changes in the life stages (āśramas), from childhood through student (brahmacarya-āśrama) to householder (gṛhasthya-āśrama) to forest dweller (vānaprasthya-āśrama) to full renunciate (saṃnyāsa-āśrama), are not all marked by rites of passage. The reason, it appears, is that saṃskāras were not regarded as appropriate for the trajectory into renunciation, but were definitive household and social rituals, including the postmortem rites.

See also: **Annaprāśana; Antyeṣṭi; Āśram(a) (religious community); Brahmacarya; Brāhmaṇas; Cūḍākaraṇa; Dharmaśāstra; Garbhādhāna; Gārhasthya; Gāyatrī mantra; Gṛhyasūtras; Karṇavedha; Mantra; Mīmāṃsāsūtras; Nāmakaraṇa; Niṣkramaṇa; Pitṛs; Pretas; Puṃsavana; Sacred languages; Samāvartana; Saṃhitā; Saṃnyāsa; Sīmantonnayana; Soma; Śrāddha; Upanayana; Vānaprasthya; Varṇa; Vidyārambha; Vivāha; Yama**

Frederick M. Smith

Further reading

Kane, P.V. 1974. *History of Dharmaśāstra*, vol. 2, pt 1, 2nd edn. Poona: Bhandarkar Oriental Research Institute, 188–267.

Michaels, Axel. 2004. *Hinduism Past and Present*. Princeton, NJ: Princeton University Press, 74–77.

Pandey, Raj Bali. 1969. *Hindu Saṃskāras*. Delhi: Motilal Banarsidass.

SANĀTANA DHARMA

This Sanskrit term has emerged as significant in 'Hinduism' in the modern and contemporary period. From the late nineteenth century onwards, it has developed a set of meanings which have a particular resonance for Hindus, mostly related to the projection of 'Hinduism' as an objectified way of being religious, as distinct from other ways of being religious extant in the modern world. It may be translated rather generally as 'eternal religion' or 'eternal order' (Klostermaier 1994: 31, 607), and this translation may indeed reflect its more contemporary usage by Hindus as a kind of synonym for 'Hinduism' – albeit a synonym which signifies particular claims for that religion. However, the meaning of this term has developed over the specified period, reflecting the dynamic changes that have been a feature of modern Hinduism itself.

Several authors have noted that sanātana dharma does have a presence in premodern Hindu contexts. Both Halbfass (1990: 344) and Lutgendorf (1991: 363) note its presence in the Epics as a kind of formulaic phrase, intended, as Halbfass notes, 'to emphasise the obligatory nature of social and religious rules'. In Vālmīki's *Ayodhyākāṇḍa*, for example, Ramā proclaims, 'for that is the eternal dharma', both as an explanation for his brother's guardianship of the throne of Ayodhyā and for his own obedience to his parents (Lutgendorf 1991: 363, n. 53). During the nineteenth century, we can detect a shift in meaning, such that it is possible, as Halbfass notes, for paṇḍits to claim that they are members or followers of sanātana dharma, implying that the latter constituted a defined group or set of beliefs to which one adhered. This meaning, as he says, 'exhibits the influence of the European concept of religion' (Halbfass 1990: 344).

Perhaps the best example of this kind of usage is provided by the census. The colonial authorities instituted a decennial census across India in 1871. The census included questions related to religious identity. In 1891 the Punjab Census superintendent noted that a large number of respondents to a question about sect affiliation described themselves as 'Sanathan-dharmi' (quoted in Zavos 2001: 113), a clear indication of the developing usage of the term. But what exactly was signified here? What, in other words, were the qualities of the group or set of beliefs being defined? The superintendent gives us a clue, when he goes on to comment that 'the term is generally used now-a-days in contradistinction to the Aryas, and there are numerous societies and clubs which under this title do what they can to maintain the orthodox faith' (quoted in Zavos 2001: 114). What we have here, then, is the term being used as an indicator of 'orthodoxy', in the context of the 'reformism' of the Arya Samaj, an organisation which was particularly strong in Punjab during this period. Orthodoxy is a problematic concept in the Hindu traditions, because of the implication of centralised, controlling institutions, as in the Christian tradition. This kind of institution is not evident in the Hindu traditions. Some authors have nevertheless identified the operation of regional orthodoxies on the basis of the dominance of certain castes and saṃpradāyas (see Eschmann 1997: 112). The idea of sanātana dharma as it was expressed in the late nineteenth century, however, was to project a pan-Hindu notion of orthodoxy. Its reference point was precisely the idea of 'the Hindu religion' and the perceived threats posed to it by reformers like the Arya Samaj, Christian missionaries, assertive low-caste groups and others.

During this period, a plethora of groups known as Sanātana Dharma Sabhas emerged to promote this idea of orthodoxy, and these were generally associated after 1887 with an umbrella organisation which attempted to project an all-India profile, the Bharat Dharma Mahamandal. These were modern organisations which drew the bulk of their support from the same middle-class groups that supplied recruits and sympathisers to reforming organisations (Zavos 2001: 115). Figures such as Pandit Din Dayalu Sharma were prominent in this movement, which worked to preserve a necessarily vague notion of what constituted 'proper custom' whilst at the same time resisting the 'bad custom' associated with reforming organisations (Jones 1998: 237). Significantly, Sanatana Dharmis or 'Sanatanists', as they became known, were influential in launching and consolidating Hindu political organisations such as the Hindu Mahasabha (Zavos 2001).

As the idea of the Hindu religion became more politically significant in the early years of the twentieth century, the idea of sanātana dharma as orthodoxy, the defender of Hindu tradition, began to be superseded by the more combative thrust of Hindu nationalism. Subsequently sanātana dharma began to develop a new, though related, inflection. This was the idea of 'true' or 'eternal' religion, promoted by figures such as the philosopher president, Sarvepalli Radhakrishnan, and based on Advaita Vedānta. Radhakrishnan saw a key role for sanātana dharma in the modern world: 'those who overlook this perennial wisdom, the eternal religion behind all religions, this sanatana dharma, this timeless tradition', he stated, 'are responsible for the civilised chaos in which we live. It is our duty to get back to this central core of religion, this fundamental wisdom which has been obscured and distorted in the course of history by dogmatic and sectarian developments' (Radhakrishnan 1952: 80). Sanātana dharma here invokes a worldview which, in its universalism, tolerance and timelessness (having, unlike other world religions, no founding figure like Jesus, Mohammad, Buddha, etc.), actually envelops other traditions. As Halbfass aptly states, this idea of sanātana dharma provides a 'transcending context' for other religions (Halbfass 1990: 346); they become manifestations (or sometimes, more forcefully, distortions) of the divine order which is extant in the timeless Veda.

In this sense, sanātana dharma may be associated with a strain of 'neo-Hinduism' which defines itself self-consciously in relation to other religions. As a result, it has a particular significance amongst the Indian diaspora, where temples are frequently named as 'Sanatan Dharma mandirs'. It is also advocated strongly by the Vishwa Hindu Parishad (World Hindu Council) as a kind of primordial ethos, relevant for all humanity (Bhatt 2000: 569). It is therefore implicated in the 'world mission' of 'Hinduism', which has increasingly come to be expressed as an adjunct of Hindu nationalist ideology. More generally, one may associate sanātana dharma in contemporary usage with the vision of the future of Hinduism as a universal religion; as one author has expressed it, 'a truly new world religion', potentially the dominant religion of the twenty-first century (Klostermaier 1994: 475).

See also: **Advaita; Arya Samaj; Bharat Dharma Mahamandal; Caste; Diaspora; Hindu Mahasabha; Hinduism, modern and contemporary; Languages; Nationalism; Paṇḍit; Radhakrishnan, Sir Sarvepalli; Ramā; Rāmāyaṇa; Saṃpradāya; Sharma, Pandit Din Dayalu; Vālmīki; Veda; Vishwa Hindu Parishad**

JOHN ZAVOS

Further reading

Bhatt, C. 2000. 'Dharmo Rakshati Rakshitah: Hindutva Movements in the UK'. *Ethnic and Racial Studies* 23(3): 559–93.

Eschmann, A. 1997. 'Religion, Reaction and Change: The Role of Sects in Hinduism'. In G. Sontheimer and H. Kulke, eds, *Hinduism Reconsidered*. Delhi: Manohar, 108–20.

Halbfass, W. 1990. *India and Europe: An Essay in Philosophical Understanding.* Delhi: Motilal Banarsidass.

Jones, K. 1998. 'Two Sanatan Dharma Leaders and Swami Vivekananda'. In William Radice, ed., *Swami Vivekananda and the Modernisation of Hinduism*. New Delhi: Oxford University Press, 224–43.

Klostermaier, K. 1994. *A Survey of Hinduism.* Albany, NY: State University of New York Press.

Lutgendorf, P. 1991. *Life of a Text: Performing the Ramcaritmanas of Tulsidas.* Berkeley, CA: University of California Press.

Radhakrishnan, S. 1952. 'The Religion of the Spirit and the World's Need'. In Paul Schilp, ed., *The Philosophy of Sarvepalli Radhakrishnan*. New York: Tudor Publishing Company, 3–82.

Zavos, J. 2001. 'Defending Hindu Tradition: Sanatana Dharma as a Symbol of Orthdoxy in Colonial India'. *Religion* 31: 109–23.

SANGH PARIVAR

The term Sangh Parivar (literally, family union) is used to denote a group of Hindu fundamentalist organisations associated with the Rashtriya Swayamsevak Sangh (RSS). These are the Bharatiya Janata

Party (BJP), the Vishwa Hindu Parishad (VHP), Bajrang Dal and Durga Vahini.

The RSS (euphemistically named National Volunteer Corps) is a militant Hindu organisation formed in the 1920s that was most probably a reaction against the increasing political mobilisation of the Muslims of India, communal violence, cultural contrasts between Hindus and non-Hindus and the apparent failure of Gandhi's independence movement to secure freedom from colonial rule. Their roots are in Maharashtra, though the founder, Dr K.B. Hedgewar, came from Nagpur in Madhya Pradesh. Protection of the cow, promotion of Hindi and the Devanagari script and caste reforms were some of the aims of the organisation, which sought to unite Hindus on a platform of militant anti-Muslim sentiment. Revitalisation of Hindu youth was sought by establishing gymnasiums (akhara) which, significantly, started on the Daśahrā festival of 1925, a festival marking the killing of Rāvaṇa by Rāma the avatāra. The RSS took a kṣatriya (warrior) rather than the ascetic model of Hinduism propagated by Gandhi (Andersen and Damle 1987: 29). Lāthis (long batons), khaki dress and caps became almost symbols of the movement. Recruitment of RSS cadres is mainly from these gymnasia. Though apolitical it has considerable impact on communal politics in India, especially through its political wing, the Jana Sangh, later to be replaced by the Bharatiya Janata Party (Indian People's Party) (Malik and Singh 1995: 36).

Founded in 1966 by Shivram Shankar Apte, a senior RSS activist, the VHP (World Hindu Congress) may be deemed to be the intellectual and religious front of the RSS. It seeks to provide a single religious platform for all the Hindus in the world. Its activities are particularly aimed at the Hindu diaspora and it is strongest in the USA and the UK. The VHP wishes to consolidate Hindu society and ensure the preservation of Hindu spiritual and ethical values in modern times, especially in Hindus abroad, where they may be more likely to lose such values. Though it is opposed to the infiltration of Western culture it does not shirk the tools of science and is not against the use of Western liberal democratic concepts for Hindu cultural self-assertion and eventual takeover of the government of India to form a Hindu nation-state. Like the RSS, it sees the Christians and Muslims of India as 'the other' and its vehement anti-Semitic sentiment is evinced in its organisation of the destruction of the Babri Masjid on 6 December 1992 and seeking to construct a temple in the Ramjanmabhumi (birthplace of Rāma) on the site in Ayodhya.

The Bajrang Dal (Bajrang is the birthplace of Lord Kṛṣṇa) is the youth wing of the VHP formed in 1986 and is known for its militancy and readiness to use violence to realise its aims (Katju 1998: 143). One of the most traumatic incidents was the burning to death of an Australian medical missionary, Graham Staines, and his two sons in 1999, reportedly by Bajrang Dal activists. A former head of the Bajrang Dal once stated that a warlike situation existed in India comparable to the confrontation between Rāma and Rāvaṇa. Working under the orders of the VHP, the Bajrang Dal's members are sometimes described as the storm troopers of the VHP

The Durga Vahini is the female counterpart of the Bajrang Dal. It is formed by wives and female family members of RSS and VHP activists, who keep an eye on Hindu women of their locality and are trained in martial arts for self-defence. A strong family structure and domestic harmony are emphasised and an awareness of larger national responsibility nurtured in Hindu women.

See also: **Ayodhyā; Bharatiya Janata Party; Daśahrā; Gandhi, Mohandas Karamchand; Hedgewar, Keshav Baliram; Jana**

Sangh; Rāma; Rashtriya Swayamsevak Sangh; Rāvana; Vishwa Hindu Parishad

THEODORE GABRIEL

Further reading

Andersen, Walter, K. and Shridhar D. Damle. 1987. *The Brotherhood in Saffron.* Boulder, CO: Westview Press

Goel, Sitha Ram. 1997. *Whither Sangh Parivar?* New Delhi: Voice of India.

Katju, M. 1998. *The Vishva Hindu Parishad and Hindu Nationalism 1964 to 1996*. PhD thesis. London: University of London.

Malik, Y.K. and V.B. Singh. 1995. *Hindu Nationalists in India: The Rise of the Bharatiya Janata Party.* New Delhi: Vistaar Publications.

Sathyamurthy, T.V. 1996. *Region, Religion, Caste, Gender and Culture in Contemporary India.* New Delhi: Oxford University Press.

ŚAṄKARA

Śaṅkara (eight to ninth centuries CE) is the best-known Advaita Vedānta thinker. He was the first in a series of medieval theologians to reinterpret Bādārāyaṇa's *Brahmasūtras.* By commenting on the main *Upaniṣads,* Śaṅkara streamlined the teaching of the *Upaniṣads.* He also commented on the *Bhagavadgītā* from the *Mahābhārata*. The work *Upadeśasāhasrī* is considered his own work.

Postulating only one reality, Brahman, Śaṅkara's theory has been called non-dual (a-dvaita). This Brahman can be viewed in two ways: (1) Brahman with attributes – here Brahman can be characterised as satcidānanda, real, conscious and joyous; (2) Brahman as empty of any characterisations – this resembles the Buddhist understanding of the ultimate reality as being empty (śūnya). Similarly, Śaṅkara's proposition of a two-tiered reality also seems similar to concepts in Buddhism. Śaṅkara proposed one level of reality, the highest, Brahman, which is without content or characterisation; the other conventional level is real in as much as it enables us to aim toward the highest reality. In proposing a two-tiered reality, Śaṅkara viewed the conventional level as being superimposed on the ultimate. Our seeing, hearing, etc. of the manifoldness of the world around us occurs because of our ignorance and inability to see the true state of Brahman. The superimposition works like this: we can see a snake and become truly frightened, running away hastily, although there is only a piece of old, discarded rope on the ground. We have superimposed a snake on the rope. Here the mundane level of reality does have an existence; it is not false: the snake has been part of our experience elsewhere at another time.

Śaṅkara's interpretation of upaniṣadic ideas has become most influential, primarily by the activism of the nineteenth-century reformers, or rather renovators, of the ancient Indian tradition. Unwittingly, they may have considered a form of monism rooted in ancient ideas as the best form of renewal of their own tradition, paving the way for Advaita Vedānta to become popular and respected to the present day.

See also: **Advaita; Bādarāyaṇa; Bhagavadgītā; Brahman; Brahmasūtras; Buddhism, relationship with Hinduism; Mahābhārata; Upaniṣads; Vedānta**

EDELTRAUD HARZER

Further reading

Deutsch, E. 1973 *Advaita Vedānta. A Philosophical Reconstruction.* Honolulu, HI: University Press of Hawaii.

Gupta, B. 1998. *The Disinterested Witness. A Fragment of Advaita Vedānta Phenomenology.* Evanston, IL: Northwestern University Press.

Mahadevan, T.M.P. 1976. *The Philosophy of Advaita.* New Delhi: Arnold-Heineman Publishers.

Potter, K. 1981. *Advaita Vedānta up to Śaṅkara and His Pupils.* Princeton, NJ: Princeton University Press.

ŚAṄKARĀCĀRYAS

Śaṅkara, the famous exponent of Advaita Vedānta, often referred to as Śaṅkarācārya (Śaṅkara the Teacher), succeeded in establishing four orders of sādhus, thus formalising Hindu renunciation (saṃnyāsa) with codes of practice and a hierarchy of leadership. To this day, the leaders of the four orders, also called Śaṅkarācāryas, located in the north, south, east and west of India remain influential figures, often regarded as the official spokesmen for nationwide Hinduism. Most Śaivite renunciate orders authenticate their lineage by going back to Śiva in legendary time through Śaṅkara in historical time.

See also: **Advaita; Sādhu; Śaivism; Saṃnyāsa; Śaṅkara; Śiva**

RON GEAVES

Further reading

Flood, Gavin. 1997. *An Introduction to Hinduism*. Cambridge: Cambridge University Press.

SANSKRIT

See: **Languages**

SANT

In common parlance in North India, Sant is used in reference to an apparent succession of thousands of holy men and women upholding sanātana dharma from the beginning of time to the present. In this context, little attempt is made to differentiate the variety of competing traditions and worldviews with which individual sants may be associated. Thus the term sant mahātma is seen as a binding force of enlightened knowers of truth.

However, in the strictest sense sant should be used to refer to an individual devotee of nirguṇa Brahman, forming part of the phenomenon defined by scholars as the Sant tradition, which arose in the medieval period and continued to have manifestations through to the present. Charlotte Vaudeville provides the best description of a sant, as:

> a holy man of a rather special type, who cannot be accommodated in the traditional categories of Indian holy men – and he may just as well be a woman. The Sant is not a renunciate. . . . He is neither a *yogi* nor a *siddha*, practices no *asanas*, boasts of no secret *bhij mantras* and has no claim to magical powers. The true *Sant* wears no special dress or insignia, having eschewed the social consideration and material benefits which in India attach to the profession of asceticism. . . . The *Sant* ideal of sanctity is a lay ideal, open to all; it is an ideal which transcends both sectarian and caste barriers.
>
> (Vaudeville 1987: 36–37)

Vaudeville is describing a Sant in a more specialised sense than in everyday usage, and her point is that the Sant figure cannot be assimilated into other traditions of Indian holy people. However, such ideal Sant figures are rare, and even though iconoclastic, on their death a process of institutionalisation usually occurs that can over the generations display all the usual outer manifestations of Hindu piety.

In Sikhism, the term Sant is used to describe a devout follower of the teachings of the Gurus who has succeeded in attracting his or her own group of disciples, often leading to sectarian offshoots. These figures often display all the manifestations of a guru, but the designation of Sant avoids the problematic label of guru, which in orthodox Sikh traditions can only be applied to the succession of ten human Gurus, the sacred text, the *Guru Granth Sahib*, and also the community, the Khalsa Panth. Indeed, the first Sikh Guru, Guru Nanak, has been regarded by some scholars as a member of the Sant tradition, though this has also been rejected out of hand.

See also: **Brahman; Guru; Sanātana Dharma; Sant Sādhana; Sikhism, relationship with Hinduism**

RON GEAVES

Further reading

Vaudeville, Charlotte. 1987. 'Sant Mat: Santism as the Universal Path to Sanctity'. In K. Schomer and W.H. McLeod, eds, *The Sants: Studies in a Devotional Tradition of India*. New Delhi: Motilal Banarsidass, 21–40.

SANT SĀDHANA

A number of scholars have identified the Sant tradition from amidst the bhaktas of North India. Charlotte Vaudeville, in answer to the question 'who were the *Sants*?', argues that they were drawn from the lower strata of both Hindu and Muslim society and expressed themselves, often in poetry, in the vernacular, often contributing to the development of several literary languages (Vaudeville 1987: 21). However, this definition does not fully differentiate the Sants from saguṇa bhaktas, worshipping the various forms of a personal divinity available from the Hindu pantheons. In addition, the Muslim variants need to be distinguished from Sufis, who often shared the above characteristics. Also not all Sants were illiterate, poor or uneducated, as in the case of the Sikh gurus.

Vaudeville was very explicit and accurate in her definition of Sant tradition by identifying the key features of its sādhana. She states:

> All the Sant poets stress the necessity of devotion to and practice of the Divine Name (*satnāma*), devotion to the Divine Guru (*satguru*) and the great importance of the 'company of the sants' (*satsaṅg*). The Name, the Divine Guru and the *Satsaṅg* are the three pillars of the Sant *sādhana*.
>
> (Vaudeville 1987: 31)

The Sants place the emphasis on the human body not as a means of sense pleasure, but as a unique vehicle for inner revelation. Consequently, while the knowledge of an inner experience of the indwelling divine is available, there is little emphasis on rites, rituals, dogmas or places and objects of worship. Those to whom the experience is available tend to be iconoclastic, and this marks the Sant tradition, with its uncompromising nirguṇa bhakti, out from the general milieu of bhakti, albeit they are bhaktas in that they conceive of the absolute being as a personal God to be adored (Klostermaier 1994: 225).

Sants can also be identified by their attempts to verbalise the experience of the immanent divine, by nature indefinable, resorting to a symbolic language comprised of metaphors. Investigation of their writings reveals that four metaphors are being used repeatedly. Their experience of the divine is veiled in various images of light (prakash), sound (nad brahman or anahat), nectar (amrit), and finally the Word (shabd brahman) or Name of God (satnam) (Geaves 2004).

In many respects, the Sant tradition could be defined by its contemplation upon the Name or Word of God, through which it is believed that the ego can be overcome and unity with the Divine realised. Nanak, the founder of Sikhism and along with Kabīr one of the foremost nirguṇa bhaktas, states: 'The Yogi meditates on the fearless and pure Lord. Night and day he remains awake and embraces affection for the true Name' (*Sri Guru Granth Sahib* 1991: 223) For Ravidās, the low-caste shoemaker-sant, now virtually the patron-saint of those that struggle against caste inequalities, everything is contained in contemplation of the Name:

> The contemplation of Thy Name is my worship of Thee:
> This is also my ablution in the holy waters,

For, without Thy Name, everything is an
illusion, O God.
(*Sri Guru Granth Sahib* 1991: 664–65)

The song goes on to mention and reject virtually all the common forms of traditional Hindu temple worship in favour of this one practice. However, the Sants also acknowledge the satguru (true teacher) as the intermediary between humans and God, even though it is not always apparent whether the guru is human or some aspect of the immanent divinity which is self-revealing. Tradition usually allocates them to a human guru, with the notable exception of Nanak.

The key characteristics of the Sants has to be their rejection of all externals of religion in favour of direct experience of the inner divine and transformation of the person. Kabīr and Nanak repeatedly reject the outer forms of both Muslim and Hindu religiosity. Kabīr states:

My satguru has shown me the way
I have given up all rites and ceremonies
I bathe no more in holy rivers
No longer do I ring the temple bells,
Nor do enthrone a divine image.
(Tagore 2002: 108)

Today, a number of traditions exist that trace their roots back to one or more followers of the Sant sādhana, most notably Sikhism. Some of these are relatively modern nineteenth- or twentieth-century movements claiming allegiance to contemporary Sant masters, for example the Radhasoamis, Sant Nirankaris, Advait Mat and the various organisations that promote the teachings of Prem Rawat worldwide. A fascinating question raises itself with the existence of these movements; that is, how does a tradition develop complete with rituals, doctrines, sacred texts, pilgrimages and institutional lineages of gurus from such extraordinary iconoclasts?

Sant sādhana undergoes its own process of institutionalisation, which goes through the following stages:

1 The solitary figure, such as Kabīr, Nanak or Ravidās, can become a line of masters whose authority is derived from their own personal charisma and remain focused on individual experience. An institutionalised paraṃparā need not develop if a strategy of separating the material inheritance from the spiritual inheritance is developed.
2 As stated by Gold (1987), a lineage can develop in which the dominant focus of spiritual power is still contained in the living holy man but the institutionalisation process develops alongside charismatic authority. Such a lineage develops into a paraṃparā.
3 A panth where the teachings of the past Sant(s) are claimed to be represented, but the dominant focus of spiritual power now resides in ritual forms and scripture is officiated over by a mahant who looks after the ritual and administration. The mahant's charisma is clearly derived from his position and his traditional connection to the original Sant (Gold 1987: 85).
4 A panth can develop around the samādhi of the deceased Sant, in which the focus of worship manifests as veneration of the deceased master. Although the shrine will be administered by successors of the sant (either by blood relatives or mahants), their authority derives from the spiritual presence of the dead Sant embodied in the remains and within the follower's heart. The samādhi panths are more loosely knit organisations than sectarian institutions and can provide the inspiration for new forms of the tradition to emerge as a result of contact with the blessings of the deceased master (Geaves 2003: 25).

All of these stages of Sant sādhana create a web of movements that continue to influence the development of contemporary Indian religion and form an alternative means of devotional practice and hope of salvation that remains in a competitive and uneasy relationship with orthodoxies. Living Sants continue to arise, anti-brahmanical, anti-caste and universalist in their understanding of the relationship between the human and the divine. The Sant tradition has been called the universal path to sanctity (Vaudeville 1987) and some modern variants have succeeded in bringing this path on to an international stage, attracting followers from a range of cultures and religious backgrounds.

See also: **Caste; Kabīr; Maharaj Ji, Guru (Prem Rawat); Paraṃparā; Radhasoami Satsang; Ravidās(a); Sant; Satsaṅg; Sikhism, relationship with Hinduism**

RON GEAVES

Further reading

Geaves, R.A. 2003. 'From Totapuri to Maharaji: Reflections on a (Lineage) Parampara'. *Indian Religions: Renaissance & Renewal.* London: Luzac.

Geaves, R.A. 2004. 'From Founder to Institution: Metaphors of Experience and the Sant Tradition'. *Journal of Indian Philosophy and Religion* 9.

Gold, D. 1987. *The Lord as Guru: Hindu Sants in the Northern Indian Tradition.* Oxford: Oxford University Press.

Klostermaier, K. 1994. *A Survey of Hinduism.* Albany, NY: State University of New York.

Sri Guru Granth Sahib. 1991. Trans. *Gurbachan Singh Talib.* Patiala: Punjab University.

Tagore, Rabrindranath (trans.). 2002. *Songs of Kabir.* Boston, MA: Weiser Books.

Vaudeville, Charlotte. 1987. 'Sant Mat: Santism as a Universal Path to Sanctity'. In K. Schomer and W. H. McLeod, eds, *The Sants: Studies in a Devotional Tradition of India.* New Delhi: Motilal Banarsidass, 21–40.

SAṆTOṢĪ MĀTĀ

Saṇtoṣī Mātā, or Santoṣī Mā, the Mother of Satisfaction, became popular after the release of the 1975 film *Jai Santoshi Maa*, 'Glory to the Mother of Satisfaction'. In it, she appeared as the saviour of her long-suffering devotee, Satyavatī, who endures cruelty at the hands of her in-laws. Santoṣī Mā made an immediate impact on the audiences, who showered offerings of flowers and rice at the screen and set up shrines to the goddess outside the cinema (Kabir 2001: 115). Although there is no origin myth contained in the pamphlets outlining her worship, probably written in the 1950s, the film portrays her as the daughter of Gaṇeśa. Before the film's release, she was worshipped in Jodhpur but was not widely known elsewhere (Hawley and Wulff 1996: 3). On posters, Santoṣī Mā appears pale-faced, dressed in red, seated in the lotus position, holding a trident, a sword, a bowl of jaggery (unrefined sugar), gesturing that her devotees have no fear. Her worship, which consists of offering jaggery and chickpeas while undertaking a fast for sixteen consecutive Fridays, is relatively cheap and easy for anyone to perform. The only restriction is that no onions, lemons, garlic or anything sour are to be eaten on Friday. Through such worship, devotees hope to have their wishes fulfilled. The popularity of Santoṣī Mā may well be due to her aptness for the present age, in which the demons who in mythology threatened the gods have been replaced by ruthless landlords or grasping relatives.

Santoṣī Mā is worshipped across north India but seems particularly popular in Orissa. Worshipped in Bhubaneswar and in the surrounding villages, this essentially orthodox goddess is sought out for her ability to heal devotees by taking possession of a local woman, a form of religion generally confined to local deities (Foulston 2002: 145–49).

See also: **Film; Gaṇeśa; Deities, village and local**

LYNN FOULSTON

Further reading

Foulston, L. 2002. *At the Feet of the Goddess: The Divine Feminine in Local Hindu Religion*. Brighton and Portland, OR: Sussex Academic Press.
Hawley, J.S. and D.M. Wulff (eds). 1996. *Devī: Goddesses of India*. Berkeley, CA: University of California Press.
Kabir, Nasreen Munni. 2001. *Bollywood: The Indian Cinema Story*. London: Channel 4 Books.

SAPTAMĀTṚKĀS

The Saptamātṛkā ('Seven Mothers') first appear in Hindu religious imagery and the Purāṇic literature in about the fourth century, as the female energies (śaktis) and consorts of a set of brahmanic male gods. Although the names of the goddesses listed in this group vary, the list is generally comprised of Brāhmī, Vaiṣṇavī, Māheśvarī, Kaumarī, Vārāhī, Indrāṇī and Cāmuṇḍā, who is exceptional inasmuch as she is portrayed as independent of any male divinity, the śakti of no one. Multiple independent Mothers (Mātṛs) were worshipped in India long before the emergence of this standard set, which was introduced with the advent of Śāktism, the sectarian cult of the Great Goddess Mahādevī introduced in the *Devī Māhātmya* ('Glorification of the Goddess') portion of the *Mārkaṇḍeya Purāṇas*. In Śākta traditions, the Saptamātṛkā are so many hypostases of the Great Goddess. According to iconographic evidence, the devotional cult of the Saptamātṛkā was relatively short-lived, persisting for about seven centuries before it was totally eclipsed by the cult of the Great Goddess. However, the group remained important in Hindu Tantric traditions, in which the Saptamātṛkā were propitiated as the leaders of clans of lesser female deities.

In earlier non-sectarian traditions a host of often nameless Mothers were universally worshipped, mainly in connection with the childhood diseases, childbirth complications and psychological disorders of which they were considered to be the multiple sources. An early mythological attempt to systematise these Mothers is found in the *Mahābhārata* (3.207–3.219) account of the birth child-god Skanda, which identifies seven Mothers, together with Skanda himself and his 'brother' Skanda-Apasmāra, as a group who torment children up to the age of 16 unless they are propitiated with offerings of food, incense, etc. This set of seven Mothers, together with two male divinities, informs many early iconographic representations of the Saptamātṛkā, who are flanked by two male figures, comprised of some combination of Skanda, Gaṇeśa, Vīrabhadra or some other form of Śiva.

In later iconography, Gaṇeśa becomes the sole male deity that is so represented.

See also: **Apasmāra; Cāmuṇḍā; Devī Māhātmya; Gaṇeśa; Mahābhārata; Mahādevī; Purāṇas; Śakti; Śiva; Skanda**

DAVID GORDON WHITE

Further reading

Harper, K.A. 1989. *The Iconography of the Saptamatrikas: Seven Hindu Goddesses of Spiritual Transformation*. Lewiston, NY: Edwin Mellen Press.

SAPTAPURĪ (SEVEN SACRED CITIES)

The term saptapurī ('the Seven Cities') is a grouping of important pilgrimage centres spread across the Indian subcontinent. The seven cities are usually given as: Kāśī (Vārāṇasī; Benares), Kāñcī (Kāñcīpura; Conjeevaram), Māyā (Haridvāra; Haridwar), Ayodhyā (Ayodhya), Dvārāvatī (Dvārāka; Dwarka), Mathurā and Avantikā (Ujjayinī; Ujjain). Of these, Kāśī or Vārāṇasī is often given pride of place, although the relative ranking of pilgrimage sites is extremely fluid, with the highest praise being bestowed variously according to different sources.

Little is known of the origin of grouping these sites together beyond the existence of a single popular Sanskrit verse, one that is sometimes erroneously attributed to the *Mahābhārata*. This verse identifies these cities as unique among other holy places, in that they possess the power to grant release (mokṣa) from the cycle of rebirth if one dies there. Pilgrimage to other sacred places might accumulate merit and confer other benefits to the pilgrim, but only these seven cities guarantee final release merely by dying within their bounds. For this reason they are also referred to as mokṣa-purīs, or 'liberation-cities'. Also implicit is the concept that the cities are not simply considered holy because of the presence of one or more sacred sites within their boundaries; instead, each cityscape is itself a sacred 'zone' (kṣetra) that possesses an abundance of individual tīrthas. That is to say, the sacred aura is not confined to particular shrines, temples, holy tanks or groves, but rather pervades the entire place.

The saptapurī concept is comparable to other groupings, such as the twelve jyotirliṅgas, the fifty-one 'seats' of Śakti (Śakti-pīṭhas), the seven rivers of India (sapta-sindhu) and the four 'abodes' (Hindi: cār-dhām). Such groupings are illustrative of the shared sense of sacred geography amongst sometimes disparate regional and sectarian traditions of Hinduism.

See also: **Ayodhyā; Dvārakā; Haridvāra; Kāñcīpura; Kṣetra; Mahābhārata; Mathurā; Mokṣa; Sacred geography; Śakti; Śiva; Tīrthayātrā (Pilgrimage); Ujjayinī; Vārāṇasī**

TRAVIS L. SMITH

Further reading

Eck, D. 1983. *Banāras: City of Light*. New York: Columbia University Press.

SARADA DEVI

Born in 1853 CE and named Saradamani, Sarada Devi came to be regarded as the Holy Mother of the Ramakrishna movement and a member, with Sri Ramakrishna and Swami Vivekananda, of its 'Spiritual Trinity'. Sarada Devi was married to Ramakrishna in 1859, but only joined him at Dakshineshwar temple in 1872. Devotees maintain that their relationship was celibate and entirely spiritual, Ramakrishna worshipping his wife as the Devī, or Mother Goddess.

After Ramakrishna's death, caring for Sarada Devi became an important act of devotion for several of Ramakrishna's disciples. Women disciples from the United States and London also sought her out. Photographs taken in their company provided the popular iconographic image of Sarada Devi. She died in 1920 and her thoughts, as recorded from her conversations, were later published as a 'Gospel'. The Sarada Math for women was founded in 1954.

See also: **Deities; Ramakrishna Math and Mission; Ramakrishna, Sri; Vivekananda, Swami**

GWILYM BECKERLEGGE

Further reading

Nikhilananda, Swami. 1962. *Holy Mother*. New York: Ramakrishna–Vivekananda Center.

SARASVATĪ

An ancient Indian goddess, who according to the Veda was created from the body of Brahmā in order to create the worlds. Brahmā then became infatuated with the beauty of his own creation and it is said that because of his lustful desire to stare at her he grew several heads. Brahmā coupled with her and made love for a hundred years within a pavilion that was also inside a lotus. It is said that from their intercourse the two primal human beings (Manu) were created, who shared in their father's nature.

The goddess Sarasvatī is usually depicted as a young, pale-skinned woman depicted with either two or four arms. As the goddess of the arts, speech and learning, and also believed to be the originator of the Sanskrit language, she plays a vīṇā and carries a book (a symbol of learning) and a string of prayer beads (a symbol of mantric power). Sometimes she may be depicted with a weapon such as a mace, discus or spear in her fourth hand. Her usual vāhana is a swan (haṃsa), a symbol of knowledge and purity. In some regions of India, notably the Deccan, her mount becomes the ram rather than the swan, and in some places rams are still sacrificed to her.

In Vedic times, Sarasvatī was personified as a river which flowed through north-west India, and of the twenty-five rivers mentioned in the *Ṛgveda* seems to have been the most renowned, described as the 'best of mothers, the best of rivers and the best of goddesses'. The *Manusmṛti*, the great text of orthodox dharma, actually geographically defines the location of 'right behaviour', the place where all men are guided by the brāhmaṇas, as the land between the sacred rivers, Sarasvatī and the Dṛṣadvatī. As a river-goddess, Sarasvatī was associated with fertility and purification, and as with many sacred rivers, all who bathe in her waters and perform acts of worship on her banks are guaranteed to be cleansed of impurities. Today, the Sarasvatī has dried up due to the extreme desert conditions of her course, but the riverbed can still be traced. The river is often mistaken for the modern Sarasvatī, which flows down into the sands of Patiala.

Sarasvatī, like other manifestations of the goddess, who are depicted as consorts of major deities in the Hindu pantheon, is benign. In modern India she is often found in schoolrooms, smiling serenely down on the children. She always appears independently, and Brahmā, her consort, seems to have little involvement in her worship. Other examples of her image occur wherever there are cultural centres, seats of learning, gatherings of musicians, artists or poets.

See also: **Brahmā; Brāhmaṇas; Dharmaśāstras; Image worship; Languages; Manu; Saṃhitā; Sacred geography; Vāhana; Veda**

RON GEAVES

Further reading

Stutley, M. 1985. 'Sarasvatī'. *The Illustrated Dictionary of Hindu Iconography*. London: Routledge.

Stutley, Margaret and James Stutley (eds). 1985. *A Dictionary of Hinduism*. London: Routledge and Kegan Paul, 270.

SARASVATĪ CULTURE

See: **Indus Valley Civilisation**

SARASVATĪ PŪJĀ

Sarasvatī Pūjā, also called Vasant Pañcamī or Śrī Pañcamī, is a holiday dedicated to the goddess Sarasvatī. It marks the first day of spring, which comes in India during the month of Māgha (January–February). In some areas of India the goddess is also worshipped during Aśvina (September–October).

Sarasvatī is the beautiful goddess of wisdom, speech and the arts. She is traditionally shown dressed in white, symbolising purity, with four arms. In one hand is a sacred text; a lotus of knowledge or a rosary is in the second; with the third and fourth she plays a musical instrument, the vīṇā. She is accompanied by her mount, a white swan. Sarasvatī gives intellectual and artistic inspiration, and is the main goddess for writers and musicians. She is 'the flowing one', who was originally a river goddess and now represents the flow of wisdom. She is also called the Mother of the Veda, in her role as Vāc, or divine speech.

There are many rituals dedicated to Sarasvatī performed on her Pūjā day.

There are special chants, the Sarasvatī Vandana, and worship rituals with offerings of sweet fruits, incense and flowers. Schoolbooks are offered to her, and in West Bengal schoolchildren dedicate their pens to her so that they may never write wrong answers on tests. Children are taught their first words on this day, and schools are closed for regular classes but often hold special literary events.

There are regional differences in the holiday – in north-western India people worship Sarasvatī as the consort of Brahmā or Gaṇeśa, or as the attendant of Gaṇeśa, while in West Bengal she is the daughter of Śiva and Durgā. In the Punjab, her holiday is associated with the ripening of the mustard crop, and people cook spiced yellow rice in celebration, do bhangra folk dances and fly kites, while in West Bengal women dress in yellow saris and make special desserts and craftsmen make beautiful statues of the goddess. In medieval India, kings and rulers would have debates and poetry contests on the holiday, and writers were rewarded. Today it is an auspicious first day of school, the beginning of a life of wisdom.

See also: **Brahmā; Durgā; Gaṇeśa; Sarasvatī; Śiva; Vāhanas; Veda**

JUNE MCDANIEL

Further reading

Bahadur, Om Lata. 1997. *The Book of Hindu Festivals and Ceremonies*. New Delhi: UBS Publishers.

Ghosh, Niranjan. 1984. *Sri Sarasvati in Indian Art and Literature*. Delhi: Sri Satguru Publications.

Singh, Chitralekha and Prem Nath. 1999. *Hindu Festivals, Fairs and Fasts*. New Delhi: Crest Publishing House.

SARASWATI, PANDITA RAMABAI (1858–1922)

Saraswati, Pandita Ramabai grew up in a non-conventional household. Her father was Anant Sastri, a Chitpavan brāhmaṇa. He had taught Sanskrit and scriptures (except the *Veda*) to his child bride and later to his children, including Ramabai. This act, for which he was punished by other brāhmaṇa, caused him to take his family to a retreat and then to wander about India. When their parents died in 1874 during a famine, Ramabai and her brother continued to travel, maintaining themselves by the recitation of Sanskrit texts. During this time, Ramabai began to argue that the scriptures did not support women's slavery to their husbands, taboos on Vedic education for women or sati (self-immolation after the husband's death).

As a 20-year-old, Ramabai became a sensation in Calcutta because of her learning, beauty and high birth. She was even awarded titles for being learned (paṇḍita and saraswati) after being examined by professors at the University of Calcutta. After several more years of travel, her brother died. She became a leader in the campaign for women's rights, attracting both Hindus (including members of the Brahmo Samaj) and the British establishment. She married a lower-caste Brahmo Samaji lawyer named Bipin Behari Medhavi and had a daughter, Manoramabai.

After studying English in Poona, Pandita Ramabai established the Aryamahila Samaj in 1882 to promote female education. Hoping to study medicine, she went with her daughter to England, funding this trip by sale of her book *Strī-dharma-nīti* (Precepts on the duties of women). In England she worked with Indologists such as Friedrich Max Müller and Christian leaders. Eventually, she became an Anglo-Catholic (which provoked consternation back in India). Due to the decline of her hearing, she stopped hoping to study medicine and turned instead to education. She went to the United States and raised money for her projects, calling attention to her work in 1888 by publishing *The High-Caste Hindu Woman* and meeting various missionary and university organisations.

Returning to India in 1889, Ramabai opened a home for widows called Sharada Sadan (Home of Learning) in Poona. Whereas she had earlier maintained a policy of religious neutrality, she now promoted Christianity. After several famines in parts of India and a plague in Poona, she rescued more widows. Needing more room, she created a new establishment outside Poona, renaming it Mukti (liberation) and made it a place to educate and train 'Indian female village evangelists' (although she welcomed Hindus as well). In 1898 she returned to the United States, again to raise funds but also to give Manoramabai a Western education. After they returned to India yet again and worked on women's problems, Manoramabai died unexpectedly in 1921, and the grieving Ramabai herself died nine months later.

See also: **Brāhmaṇa; Brahmo Samaj; Müller, Friedrich Max; Saṃhitā; Sati; Widowhood; Women's education**

KATHERINE K. YOUNG

Further reading

Arles, N. 1999. 'Pandita Ramabai: An Appraisal from a Feminist Perspective'. *Bangalore Theological Forum* 31.1: 64–86.

Bapat, R. 'Pandita Ramabai: Faith and Reason in the Shadow of East and West'. In V. Dalmia and H. von Stientencron, eds, *Representing Hinduism: The Construction of Religious Traditions and National Identity.* New Delhi: Sage Publishers, 224–52.

Blumhofer, Edith L. 2003. '"From India's Coral Strand": Pandita Ramabai and U.S. Support for Foreign Missions'. In D.H. Bays and G. Wacker, eds, *Foreign Missionary Enterprise at Home: Explorations in North American Cultural History.* Tuscaloosa, AL: University of Alabama Press, 152–70, 296–99.

Kosambi, M. 1995. *Pandita Ramabai's Feminist and Christian Conversions: Focus on Stree Dharma-neeti.* Bombay: Research Centre for Women's Studies, SNDT Women's University.

Ramabai, P. 2000. *Pandita Ramabai through Her Own Words: Selected Works.* Ed. and trans. M. Kosambi. New Delhi: Oxford University Press.

Ramabai, P. 2003. *Pandita Ramabai's American Encounter: The Peoples of the United States 1889.* Ed. and trans. M. Kosambi. Bloomington, IN: Indiana University Press.

Ramabai Sarasvati, P. 1976 [1988]. *The High-Caste Hindu Woman.* Westport, CT: Hyperion Press.

ŚARĪRA

The term 'śarīra' (translated as 'body') signifies that which wastes away or perishes. In the *Ṛgveda* 'tanū' is the term used most commonly for 'body', but 'śarīra' does occur and is used to mean 'physical body'. Later, in post-Upaniṣadic theories of human nature, the terms 'liṅga-śarīra' ('sign-body') and 'sūkṣma-śarīra' ('subtle body') are used to refer to the transmigrating aspect of the soul. The terms 'sthūla-śarīra' and 'kāraṇa-śarīra' refer to concepts of the 'gross body' and 'causal body', respectively.

Views of the body are expressed in systems such as Sāṃkhya, Nyāya-Vaiśeṣika and Viśiṣṭādvaita. For Śaṅkara the appearance of the individual soul is due to the non-dual ātman undergoing apparent delimitation by the gross physical body and the more permanent liṅga-śarīra. He regards the subtle body (which is inferred but not perceived) as the repository of the impressions of past acts and experiences; it is a combination of the vital functions, senses, mental faculties and powers of activity.

See also: **Ātman; Liṅgaśarīra; Nyāya-Vaiśeṣika; Saṃhitā; Sāṃkhya; Śaṅkara; Viśiṣṭādvaita**

MARTIN OVENS

Further reading

Reat, N.R. 1990. *Origins of Indian Psychology.* Berkeley, CA: Asian Humanities Press.

SARKAR, PRABHAT RANJAN (b. 1921)

Born in Bihar in 1921, Prabhat Ranjan Sarkar worked as a railway employee until 1955, when he underwent a spiritual transformation and formed the organisation known as Ananda Marg (the Path of Bliss). From this date forward he would be more commonly known by the epithet given to him by his followers, Shrii Shrii Anandamurti. In 1958 he founded the Progressive Utilisation Theory, known as PROUT, which ran as a political party, standing for one world government with a unified world language, at the 1967 and 1969 Indian elections. The political venture was not successful and Prabhat Ranjan Sarkar turned his full attention to Ananda Marg (AM), forming a number of offshoots such as the AM Education and Welfare Section, the AM Board of Education, the AM Degree College and the AM Institute of Technology. Espousing a combination of humanism, rationalism influenced by the West and more traditional Tantric and Yogic practices, he was able to attract disciples from across the world. In 1971 he was arrested for conspiracy to murder and spent three years in prison. Eventually he was exonerated and released. During the incarceration, he further formulated his ideas into a coherent path to perfection.

See also: **Ananda Marg; Tantrism; Yoga**

RON GEAVES

Further reading

Dhara, G. 1986. *Prabhat Ranjan Sarkar: Poet, Author, Philosopher.* Vermont: Ananda Marg Publications.

www.prout.org/sarkar.ht (accessed 27 October 2005).

SATCHIDANANDA, SWAMI AND INTEGRAL YOGA

Born in 1914 in Coimbatore, South India, he worked in business until the death of his wife, at which point he turned his attention more and more to the study of yoga, reading Ramakrishna, Vivekananda and Sivananda and studying with such figures as Ramana Maharshi. In 1949 he moved to Rishikesh to study with Swami Sivananda, taking saṃnyāsa and the name Satchidananda. In 1953 he established a Divine Life Society ashram in Sri Lanka, as well as an orphanage and a medical dispensary, and participated in a movement to open all Hindu temples there to the untouchable castes.

He arrived in the USA in 1966 and set up the Satchindananda Ashram, Yogaville, Virginia, for the teaching of 'Integral Yoga'. He became a cult figure in the American counterculture with his speech at the Woodstock Festival in 1969. In 1970 he published his primer *Integral Yoga Hatha*, in which he summarised the teachings of Sivananda. He regularly appeared on television and in interfaith dialogue. Throughout the 1970s he lectured and travelled regularly, authoring a large number of books, such as *Blessed Are They ...* (1974) and *Beyond Words* (1977). His teaching emphasises the unity of all religions. He died in 2002 in Tamil Nadu, India.

See also: **Āśrama; Caste; Mandir; Ramakrishna, Sri; Ramana Maharshi; Saṃnyāsa; Vivekananda, Swami; Yoga; Yoga, modern**

MARK SINGLETON

Further reading

Satchindananda, Sw. 1977. *Living Yoga: The Value of Yoga in Today's Life.* New York: Gordon and Breach.

SATI

If derived from the present participle of the verbal root as (to be), then sati (sometimes anglicised as 'suttee') denotes a perfect or true act. When the noun ends with a long i, it refers to a woman who truly exists, a perfect female being. One example would be satī pārvatī, (the best woman, Pārvatī). This refers to Pārvatī, Śiva's wife, whose name in a previous incarnation had been Satī). But if derived from the adjective sat (good), then satī is the good woman. Sati came to connote the perfect or good wife's ritual self-immolation either on her husband's funeral pyre, sahagamana (going together with one's husband), or by herself if he had already been cremated elsewhere, anugamana (following one's husband). A woman's power (śakti), which had developed over a lifetime of austerities, was magnified by this final extraordinary act. The conflagration destroyed her bad karma, which had caused her husband's death, and replaced it with good karma. It transformed her into the epitome of an auspicious woman or a goddess, in fact a giver of both mundane and supra-mundane boons.

The act of sati was ritualised and became analogous to a wedding – bridal dress, procession and sacred fire – but with the vow (saṃkalpa) at the beginning rather than the climax. It became analogous also to other forms of self-willed death: heroic warriors facing death in battle, servants who had pledged ultimate loyalty and yogis burying themselves alive. In addition, sati drew meaning from the Hindu religious idioms of sacrifice (yajña) and devotion (bhakti).

Although the Vedic goals of life included longevity and natural death, self-willed death and sati developed in warrior (and some religious) circles. The first textual description of sati is by the Greek Diodorus, who describes how the Indian general Ceteus, fighting in Asia Minor in 316 BCE, fell in battle and was cremated together with his two wives. The *Mahābhārata* has several examples, but it is more common in texts by some medieval authorities who formally legitimated sati as long as rules prevailed. They did not allow pregnant women and those with young children to perform sati, for instance, tested women to make sure that their decisions were voluntary and prevented them from using drugs to dull the pain.

Though legitimated in some circles, however, sati was decried in others. Among those who condemned the practice were the seventh-century poet Bāṇa, the tenth-century commentator (on Manu) Medhātithi, the author of the *Mahānirvāṇa-tantra*, and various Śrī Vaiṣṇava authors. But the tenth-century Kalivārjya prohibitions did not forbid it, even though they forbade other forms of self-willed death, which had become popular. The British initially accepted it, because they did not want to inflame Hindu sentiments after the revolt of 1854. By the late nineteenth century, though, missionary critiques were convincing the British that sati was tantamount to homicide or suicide. Hindus themselves had looked into the matter and decided that sati was not central to Hinduism. After consultation with Indian reformers such as Rammohan Roy, the British outlawed sati (Regulation XVII of 1829). Since Indian independence, sati has remained illegal, although it still occurs now and then. In 1987 Roop Kanwar ignited not only herself but also a national debate over whether sati was a crime against women (as feminists argued) or a legitimate expression of Hinduism freed from colonial restraints (as some Hindu nationalists thought).

See also: **Bhakti; Mahābhārata; Manu; Medātithi; Pārvatī; Śakti; Satī (Goddess); Śiva; Vaiṣṇavas, Śrī; Yajña; Yogi**

KATHERINE K. YOUNG

Further reading

Courtright, P.B. 1995. 'Sati, Sacrifice, and Marriage: The Modernity of Tradition'. In L. Halan and P.B. Courtright, eds, *From the Margins of Hindu Marriage: Essays on*

Gender, Religion and Culture. New York: Oxford University Press, 184–203.

Datta, V.N. 1988. *Sati: A Historical, Social and Philosophical Enquiry into the Hindu Rite of Widow Burning*. London: Sangam Books.

Hawley, J.S. 1994. *Sati, the Blessing and the Curse: The Burning of Wives in India*. New York: Oxford University Press.

Leslie, J. 1991. 'Suttee or Sati: Victim or Victor?' In J. Leslie, ed., *Roles and Rituals for Hindu Women*. London: Pinter, 173–91.

Mani, L. 1998. *Contentious Traditions: The Debate on Sati in Colonial India*. Berkeley, CA: University of California Press.

Nandy, A. 1995. 'Sati in the *Kali Yuga*: The Public Debate on Roop Kanwar's Death'. *The Savage Freud and Other Essays on Possible and Retrievable Selves*. Princeton, NJ: Princeton University Press, 32–52.

Pederson, P. 1991. 'Ambiguities of Tradition: Widow-burning in Bengal in the Early Nineteenth Century'. In A.W. Geertz and J.S. Jensen, eds, *Religion, Tradition and Renewal*. Aarhus: Aarhus University Press, 67–78.

Phadke, H.A. 1996. 'Sati: A Historiographical Survey of the Practice of Widow Immolation in Ancient India'. In C. Margabandhu and K.S. Ramachandran, eds, *Spectrum of Indian Culture: Professor S.B. Deo Felicitation*, vol. 2. Delhi: Agam Kala Prakashan, 305–15.

Rajan, R.S. 1993. *Real and Imagined Women: Gender, Culture and Postcolonialism*. New York: Routledge.

Ray, A.J. 1985. *Widows Are Not for Burning: Actions and Attitudes of the Christian Missionaries, the Native Hindus, and Lord William Bentinck*. New Delhi: ABC Publishing House.

Roy, B.B. 1987. *Socioeconomic Impact of Sati in Bengal and the Role of Raja Rammohun Roy*. Calcutta: Naya Prakash.

Sharma, A. with A. Ray, A. Hejib and K.K. Young. 1988. *Sati: Historical and Phenomenological Essays*. Delhi: Motilal Banarsidass.

Singh, S. 1989. *A Passion for Flames*. Jaipur: RBSA Publishers.

Spivak, G. 1985. 'Can the Subaltern Speak? Speculations on Widow-Sacrifice'. *Wedge* 7–8: 120–30.

Sugirtharajah, S. 2001. 'Courtly Text and Courting Sati'. *Journal of Feminist Studies in Religion* 17.1: 5–32.

van den Bosch, L.P. 1995. 'The Ultimate Journey: Sati and Widowhood in India'. In J.N. Bremmer and L.P. van den Bosch, eds, *Between Poverty and the Pyre: Moments in the History of Widowhood*. New York: Routledge, 171–203.

Weinberger-Thomas, C. 1999. *Ashes of Immortality: Widow-burning in India*. Trans. J. Mehlman and D.G. White. Chicago, IL: University of Chicago Press.

SATĪ (FAITHFUL WIFE)

See: **Sati**

SATĪ (GODDESS)

Satī is the daughter of Dakṣa and the first wife of the god Śiva. Devī (the goddess) agreed to be born as the daughter of Dakṣa, one of the mind-born sons of Brahmā, in order to become Śiva's wife (*Kālikā Purāṇa* 7. 1–3). She is very closely associated with the goddess Pārvatī, Śiva's second wife, who is often described as her reincarnation. For many Hindus, Satī is a model of the devoted wife (Pativratā and Patiparameśvara) but also fulfils a number of other important mythic roles in her relationship with Śiva. Her story is told in the *Mahābhārata* and in various *Purāṇas*.

Satī is portrayed as pursuing Śiva with the intention of marrying him, an activity that is significant because of Śiva's tendency to detach himself from the world and its duties and pleasures. Indeed Satī's central mythic role may be viewed as that of drawing Śiva away from his world-denying austerities (tapas), which can be a grave threat to the world if taken to excess, and causing him to creatively engage with the world. Described as very beautiful, it is not Satī's physical appearance that ultimately ignites Śiva's desire (Kāma) but her ability to perform austerities and overcome the various challenges that Śiva sets before her. Śiva agrees to marry Satī and, somewhat grudgingly, also acquiesces to a complex marriage ceremony, presided over by Brahmā. It is at this ceremony that a dislike for Śiva emerges in Dakṣa and the seeds of a tragedy are sown. Some years after the marriage, Dakṣa organises a great ritual sacrifice (yajña) that is noteworthy because of its exclusion of Satī and Śiva from the proceedings. Although Śiva is unmoved by this omission, Satī is at first irritated by this slight to her husband and then furious when her father refuses to recant. Such is Satī's indignation and rage that she burns herself to death by kindling an inner fire through her yogic power. Śiva is then enraged and destroys the sacrifice.

Some of the later versions of this event add an important element that became an established aspect of Satī's mythology in relation to Śāktism, the dismemberment of her body by Viṣṇu. These versions of the Dakṣa myth claim that Śiva was so distraught at Satī's death that he placed her lifeless body on his shoulder and in his grief threatened the world. The other gods, Brahmā and Viṣṇu, were fearful of Śiva in this state and resolved to remove Satī's body in the hope of lessening Śiva's anger and grief. They entered the body and disposed of it piece by piece (*Kālikā Purāṇa* 18.39–40) or, as is recounted in another source (*Śrīmad Devī Bhāgavatatam* 7.30), Viṣṇu cut it from Śiva's shoulder with his arrows or discus. Satī's body parts fell to earth. This has provided orthodox status for many geographical sites of goddess worship across India, known widely as the seats of the goddess (śākta pīṭhas). The famous Kālī temple in Kolkata (formerly Calcutta), Kālīghāt, is said to be where Satī's big toe fell. Perhaps the most important of the śākta pīṭhas is at a mountain called Kamagiri in Kamrupa (Assam) where the yoni (vagina) of Satī fell and is now known as Kamakhya.

Satī's suicide has been associated with the practice of widow burning (sati), whereby wives would throw themselves onto the funeral pyres of their husbands. However, given that the relationship between these activities is not symmetrical – Śiva does not die – it is doubtful that the myth legitimates the practice (Kinsley 1988: 40–41). Rather, Satī is more typically understood as a model of faithful, albeit extreme, devotion, and a goddess who mediates the powers of the world-renouncing Śiva and the worldly concerns of Dharma and Kāma.

See also: **Brahmā; Dakṣa; Dharma; Kālī and Caṇḍī; Kāma; Mahābhārata; Mandir; Pārvatī; Pativratā and Patiparameśvara; Purāṇas; Śāktism; Sati; Śiva; Strīdharma; Tapas; Tīrthayātrā; Vaiṣṇo Devī; Viṣṇu; Yajña**

PAUL REID-BOWEN

Further reading

Kinsley, D. 1988. *Hindu Goddesses: Visions of the Divine Feminine in the Hindu Religious Tradition.* Berkeley, CA: University of California Press.

Shastri, B. (trans.). 1991–92. *Kālikā Purāṇa*, vols 1–3. Delhi: Nag Publishers.

Vijnanananda, Swami (trans.). 1986. *The Śrīmad Devī Bhāgavatatam*, 3rd edn. New Delhi: Munishiram Manoharlal.

SATNAMIS

Although the term 'Satnami', meaning those who follow the true Name of God, has been used by various sectarian movements within Sikhism, it first appears as an appellation for a religious movement outside Sikhism in the late seventeenth century during the reign of Aurangzeb, under the guruship of Jagivan Das, a native of Awadh. Muslim sources indicate that the movement was made up of lower-caste Hindus drawn from the ranks of sweepers and tanners but also carpenters and goldsmiths. The sect was destroyed by an army sent by Aurangzeb.

A later manifestation of Satnamis appeared in Chhatisgarh, a district of Central Provinces, under the inspiration of Guru Ghasi Das between 1820 and 1830. As with the earlier sect of Jagivan Das, the Satnamis were known for their piety, indifference to the world, devotion to their guru, rejection of practices associated with the veneration of images, worship of a formless deity as the supreme reality and a belief in equality based on the immanence of the divine as the indwelling Satnam. The latter functioned as a critique of caste and provided the religious doctrines for the formation of socio-political movements in opposition to the caste system and as rallying points for lower-caste resistance to Brāhmaṇa hegemony.

The Chhatisgarh Satnamis continue to exist as an important religious and political movement for the Chamars of the region. The original religious organisation of the sect provides the structures for a tight-knit social movement. In addition to the guru, now the hereditary lineages of Ghasi Das, at the head of the panth, there are mahants who control community activities over specified regions containing a number of villages, a bhandari who represents the authority of the guru at the level of a single village and acts as a religious functionary (Dube 2001). In addition to the organisational structures, Satnami villages are recognised by white flags. Individual Satnamis are distinguished by the wearing of a kanthi (wooden beads), the janeu (sacred thread) and total abstinence from tobacco, alcohol and meat.

See also: **Ghasi Das**

RON GEAVES

Further reading

Dube, Saurabh. 2001. *Religion, Identity and Power Among a Central Indian Community, 1780–1850*. New Delhi: Vistaar Publications.

ŚATRUGHNA

In the *Rāmāyaṇa* Śatrughna is the full brother of Lakṣmaṇa; both are Daśaratha's sons by Sumitra (indeed twins in the birth story in the late first book). While Rāma and Bhārata play the chief roles, Lakṣmaṇa and Śatrughna each attach themselves to one of their half-brothers as loyal but subservient companions. As Bhārata's companion, Śatrughna has very minor role until the final book, where he conquers the Asura Lavaṇa and founds the city of Madhurā (Mathurā).

See also: **Asura; Daśaratha; Lakṣmaṇa; Rāma; Rāmāyaṇa**

JOHN BROCKINGTON

Further reading

Bose, Mandakranta. (ed.). 2004. *The Rāmāyaṇa Revisited.* New York: Oxford University Press.

Brockington, John. 1985. *Righteous Rāma: The Evolution of an Epic*. Delhi: Oxford University Press.

Brockington, John. 1998. *The Sanskrit Epics* (Handbuch der Orientalisk 2.12). Leiden: Brill.

Brockington, John, and Mary Brockington (trans.). 2006. *Steadfast Rāma: An Early Form of the Rāmāyaṇa*. London: Penguin Books.

Brockington, Mary. 1997. 'The Art of Backwards Composition: Some Narrative Techniques in Vālmīki's Rāmāyaṇa'. In Mary Brockington and Peter Schreiner, eds, *Composing a Tradition* (Proceeding of the First Dubrovnik International Conference on the Sanskrit Epics and Purāṇas), 99–110.

Bulcke, Camille. 1950 *Rāmkathā: Utpatti Aur Vikāś* [The Rama story: origin and spread]. Prayāg: Hindī Pariṣad Prakāśan.

Goldman, Robert P. (gen. ed.). 1984–. *The Rāmāyaṇa of Vālmīki: An Epic of Ancient India*. Trans. Robert P. Goldman *et al.* Princeton, NJ: Princeton University Press.

Goldman, Robert P. and Sally J. Sutherland Goldman. 2004. *Rāmāyaṇa. In The Hindu World,* eds Sushil Mittal and Gene Thursby. New York: Routledge, 75–96.

Lutgendorf, Philip. 1990. 'Ramayan: The Video'. *Drama Review* 34: 127–76.

Lutgendorf, Philip. 1991. *The Life of a Text: Performing the Rāmcaritmānas of Tulsīdās.* Berkeley, CA: University of California Press.
Lutgendorf, Philip. 1995. 'Interpreting Rāmrāj: Reflections on the *Rāmayaṇ*, Bhakti and Hindu Nationalism'. In David N. Lorenzen, ed., *Bhakti Religion in North India*. Albany, NY: SUNY Press, 253–87.
Richman, Paula (ed.). 1991. *Many Rāmāyaṇnas: The Diversity of a Narrative Tradition in South Asia.* Berkeley, CA: University of California Press.
Richman, Paula. 2001. *Questioning Rāmāyaṇas: A South Asian Tradition.* Berkeley, CA: University of California Press.
Theil-Horstmann, Monika (ed.). 1991. *Rāmāyaṇa and Rāmāyaṇas* (Khoj – A Series of Modern South Asian Studies 3). Wiesbaden: Harrassowitz.

SATSAṄG

Satsaṅg literally signifies the 'company of truth', but the term has several overlapping meanings used more specifically within the sant and bhakti traditions of northern India. Charlotte Vaudeville defines Sant as a distinct tradition on the basis of their emphasis on satnam, satsaṅg and satguru. She states:

> whether they be born Saiva, Vaisnava, or Muslim, all the sant poets stress the necessity of devotion to and practice of the Divine Name (*satnama*); devotion to the Divine Guru (*satguru*) and the great importance of the company of the Sants (*satsaṅg*). The Name, the Divine Guru and *satsaṅg* are the three pillars of the Sant *sādhana*.
>
> (Vaudeville 1987: 31)

Charlotte Vaudeville identifies one meaning of satsaṅg; however, Sat (truth) in Indian traditions usually refers to that which is both eternal and changeless. It is one of the qualities of Brahman (supreme being), along with Cit (consciousness) and Ānand (bliss). Thus, in this context, satsaṅg is used in the context of an experience of the changeless and eternal immanence of Brahman, especially manifested as the personal Lord indwelling the human heart.

The adherents of both nirguṇa (formless) and saguṇa (form) variations of bhakti emphasised the importance of the company of fellow bhaktas for inspiration and maintaining focus in the face of material and mental distraction. Rāmakrishna (d. 1886) stated: 'if you are in bad company, then you will talk and think like your companions. On the other hand, when you are in company of devotees, you will think and talk only of God' (Nikhilananda 1969: 67). This communal aspect of bhakti traditions is another meaning of satsaṅg. Thus it has come to signify a gathering of devotees. Both listening to spiritual discourse and singing the praises of the divine are regarded as satsaṅg. Tulsīdās, the author of the *Rām(a)cari(a)tmānas(a)*, encapsulates these various meanings in the discourse of Rāma, the avatāra of Viṣṇu, to the low-caste woman Bhilni when he praises her devotion:

> Now I tell you the nine forms of devotion; please listen attentively and cherish them in your mind. The first in order is fellowship with the saints and the second is marked by a fondness for My Stories. The fourth type of devotion consists in singing My praises with a guileless purpose. The seventh sees the world full of Me without distinction and reckons the saints as even greater than Myself.
>
> (*Rāmcharitmānas*· 281–82)

However, despite this connection with medieval and contemporary Sant and bhakti traditions, the term is common parlance in Northern India, used to refer to a religious discourse or a gathering of people brought together to listen to such a discourse and participate in communal worship.

See also: **Avatāra; Bhakti; Brahman; Rāma; Rāmakrishna; Sant; Tulsīdās(a); Viṣṇu**

RON GEAVES

Further reading

Nikhilananda, Swami. 1969. *The Gospel of Rāmakrishna*, 5th edn. Madras: The Rāmakrishna Math.

Rāmcharitmānas. Arānya-Kānda, Varanasi: Gita Press.

Vaudeville, C. 1987. 'Sant Mat: Santism as the Universal Path to Sanctity'. In K. Schomer and W.H. McLeod, eds, *The Sants: Studies in a Devotional Tradition of India*. New Delhi: Motilal Banarsidass.

SATYA MAHIMA DHARMA

Mahima Dharma (the 'dharma of the divine glory') is a religious tradition of Orissa which goes back to a historic person called Mahima Swami (or Mahima Gosain). He is said to have appeared in Puri in 1826. Dissatisfied with the ritualised idol worship of Lord Jagannatha, he left Puri and travelled to the Kapilas hills near Dhenkanal, where he engaged himself in severe yogic practices. In 1862 he became a siddha and started preaching a new dharma. He is said to have attained samādhi in 1876. Under his first disciple, Govinda Baba, and the dissident saint poet Bhima Bhoi, the movement shifted away from the coastal region towards the central and western parts of Orissa. Spreading also to other states (Madhya Pradesh, Andhra Pradesh, West Bengal, Assam), people from different regions and socio-cultural backgrounds joined as followers. Since then, several monastic as well as lay currents and competing associations have emerged and various regional centres (Joranda, Khaliapali) have been established. Mahima Dharma is a popular ascetic movement which considers the void, śūnya, as the divine principle, opposing as such any idol worship. The void can only be venerated through fire or its manifestation in the sun, traits which link Mahima Dharma to the nirguṇa bhakti tradition.

See also: **Bhakti; Bhima Bhoi; Dharma; Idolatry; Image worship; Jagannātha; Siddha; Yoga**

JOHANNES BELTZ

Further reading

Banerjee-Dube, Ishita. 2001. 'Issues of Faith, Enactment of Contest: The Founding of Mahima Dharma in Nineteenth-Century Orissa'. In H. Kulke and B. Schnepel, eds, *Jagannath Revisited*. New Delhi: Manohar, 149–77.

Banerjee-Dube, Ishita and Johannes Beltz (eds). Forthcoming. *Routinization of Charisma: New Studies on Mahima Dharma*. New Delhi: Manohar Publishers.

Eschmann, Anncharlott. 1978. 'Mahimā Dharma: An Autochtonous Hindu Reform Movement'. In A. Eschmann, H. Kulke and C.G. Tripathi, eds, *The Cult of Jagannath and the Regional Tradition of Orissa*. New Delhi: Manohar, 375–410.

SATYABHĀMĀ

One of Kṛṣṇa's four principal wives, who bore him ten sons, Bhānu, Subhānu, Swarbhānu, Prabhānu, Bhānumat, Chandrabhānu, Brihadbhānu, Atibhānu, Srībhānu and Pratibhānu. She was the daughter of the Yādava prince Satrājita, and it is recounted in the *Viṣṇu Purāṇa* that she accompanied Kṛṣṇa to the heavenly abode of Indra. While there she persuaded him to take away the Pārijāta tree which belonged to Indra's wife, Śacī. The tree was said to be one of the five produced at the churning of the Ocean and it was claimed by Indra. According to the *Viṣṇu Purāṇa*, the scent of the tree pervaded all the worlds. The theft of the tree led to the fight between the two gods in which Indra was defeated. Kṛṣṇa removed the tree to Dvārakā but after his death it was returned to Indra's heaven.

See also: **Dvārakā; Indra; Kṛṣṇa; Purāṇas**

RON GEAVES

Further reading

Bunce, Fredrick. 2000. *An Encyclopaedia of Hindu Deities, Demi-Gods, Godlings, Demons and Heroes*, vol I. New Delhi: DK Printworld.

SATYANANDA, SWAMI (b. 1923) AND THE BIHAR SCHOOL OF YOGA

Born in Almora, Uttar Pradesh, in 1923. Between 1943 and 1955 he was a saṃnyāsin at Sivananda's ashram in Rishikesh. He founded the Bihar School of Yoga in Munghir (Bihar) in 1964 with the intention of propagating the transnational message of yoga from 'door to door' and 'shore to shore'. For the next twenty years he travelled extensively around the world promoting yoga. His teaching is a synthesis of traditional haṭha yoga techniques and the insights of modern medicine and psychology, and includes a large therapeutic component. A typical class consists of a series of gentle āsana, followed by prānāyāma and a deep relaxation technique called yoga nidrā, pioneered (and since trademarked) by Satyananda himself. Satyananda also formulated a distinctive system of therapeutic āsana called the 'pawanmuktāsana series'. Alongside haṭha yogic methods, the Satyananda method incorporates significant elements of bhakti yoga (ritual devotion) and karma yoga (conceived as selflessly undertaken work).

Satyananda retired in 1988 to devote himself to sādhana practice, and handed over the running of the Munghir centre to his disciple, Swami Niranjanananda. In 1994 this latter founded the Bihar Yoga Bharati, a 'gurukul university' for teaching and researching yoga. Among some eighty books written by him, Satyananada's encyclopedic *Asana Pranayama Mudra Bandha*, first published in 1966 (the same years as Iyengar's *Light on Yoga*) and revised regularly ever since, is the most important and influential.

See also: **Āsana; Āśrama; Bhakti; Haṭha Yoga; Iyengar, B.K.S. and Iyengar Yoga; Karma; Saṃnyāsa; Yoga**

MARK SINGLETON

Further reading

Aveling, H. 1994. *The Laughing Swamis.* Delhi: Motilal Banarsidass.

Satyananda, Sw. 1996. *Asana Pranayama Mudra Bandha*, rev. edn. Munger, Bihar: Bihar School of Yoga.

SAVARKAR, VINAYAT DAMODAR (1883–1966)

Although he was not a religious authority in the traditional sense, V.D. Savarkar's writings had an impact on contemporary notions of Hindu identity that can hardly be overestimated. He was born into a family of Chitpavan Brāhmaṇas in Nasik District in Maharashtra in 1883. Already during his high school days he became involved in anti-colonial revolutionary societies modelled in the image of Mazzini's 'Young Italy'. After graduating in law in Bombay he went to England in 1906 to complete his education. In London he came in contact with the leading revolutionary nationalist figures among the Indian expatriate community, who confirmed him in his view that terrorist violence was a legitimate means in the anti-colonial struggle. As a result, Savarkar was arrested in 1910 for being involved in the murder of a British official and sentenced to a long imprisonment, which he served first in the Andaman Islands and later in Ratnagiri (Maharashtra). While in prison, he wrote his famous pamphlet *Hindutva – Who Is a Hindu?* In an attempt to overcome internal divides and sectarianism within the Hindu community, Hindutva (Hinduness) was defined by attachment to the geographical entity of India, bonds of blood and a shared culture rather than religious belief. According to Savarkar, the ultimate aim of Indian nationalism had to be the creation of a Hindu Rashtra (Hindu state). Savarkar's overarching definition of such a nation-state's only legitimate citizens – broad enough to include Sikhs, Jains and Buddhists but excluding Muslims and Christians – was welcomed by the Hindu nationalist movement, who were looking for clear boundaries of their constituency.

When Savarkar became President of the Hindu Mahasabha after his release from 1937 to 1944, he managed to transform the organisation into a radical party according to his motto 'Hinduise all politics and militarise Hindudom', but remained rather unsuccessful in elections. Instead, his glorification of military strength and 'manhood', his outspoken admiration for Nazi Germany and his radical verbal attacks against Muslims soon brought him accusations of fascism. In 1948 he was tried for being involved in the murder of Mohandas Karamchand Gandhi by a Hindu fanatic (Nathuram Godse), but was eventually acquitted.

Although Savarkar himself was somewhat less visible in the political field of post-Independence India, the exclusive cultural nationalism of his Hindutva concept remains a seminal influence for the ideology of the Hindu right even in the twenty-first century.

See also: **Bharatiya Janata Party; Buddhism, relationship with Hinduism; Gandhi, Mohandas Karamchand; Godse, Nathuram Vinayak; Hindu Mahasabha; Hindutva; Jainism, relationship with Hinduism; Sikhism, relationship with Hinduism; Varṇa**

HARALD FISCHER-TINÉ

Further reading

Bhatt, C. 2001. *Hindu Nationalism, Origins, Ideologies and Modern Myths.* Oxford and New York: Berg.

SĀVITRĪ

Sāvitrī was the daughter of King Aśvapati of Madra, born by the grace of the goddess Sāvitrī, to whom her father had made offerings for eighteen years. When she had reached an age to marry, her father sent her out into the world to select a husband. She chose Satyavat, an exiled prince living with his mother and blind father in the forest, despite the prophecy that her husband-to-be would die within the year. Performing penances in preparation for the day of Satyavat's death, on that day Sāvitrī accompanied her husband and held him in her arms as he died. Yet, when Yama arrived to collect Satyavat's soul, she followed the god of death and won from him a number of boons, the only exclusion being her husband's life. Her first wish was that her father-in-law would recover his eyesight, her second that her father-in-law would reclaim his throne and her third that her own father would have one hundred sons. Her next wish was that she and her husband would also have one hundred sons. This required that Satyavat be released and Yama duly restored him to her. Sāvitrī's story is told in the *Mahābhārata* (3.42.277–83) and retold in numerous contexts, both textual and ritual.

Sāvitrī is generally acknowledged to exemplify the pativratā (husband-vowed) ideal of the devoted and faithful wife who worships her husband as a god (patiparameśvara). However, members of the Indian women's movement have appealed to her, for example, in opposing child marriage and identified in her qualities other than loving service of her husband, such as courage, initiative and determination.

See also: **Child marriage; Feminism; Mahābhārata; Pativratā and Patiparameśvara; Woman question; Women's movement; Yama**

CATHERINE ROBINSON

Further reading

Leslie, I.J. 1989. *The Perfect Wife: The Orthodox Hindu Woman according to the Strīdharmapaddhati of Tryambakayajvan*. Delhi: Oxford University Press.

Robinson, C.A. 1999. *Tradition and Liberation: The Hindu Tradition in the Indian Women's Movement*. Richmond: Curzon Press.

SĀVITRĪ (VERSE)

See: **Gāyatrī Mantra**

SĀYAṆA (1320–87)

Also known as Sāyaṇācārya, a celebrated grammarian and hermit, who wrote the *Vedārthaprakaśa*, a commentary on the *Ṛgveda*, a work, which along with Yāska's *Nirukta*, is believed to have saved the Indians from the plight of losing the ability to comprehend the Veda after changes were made in language and grammar, although some modern commentators blame the loss of scholarship on the chaos caused by the Muslim invasions of South India. He also wrote a commentary on the *Yajurveda*, the *Taittirīya Brāhmaṇa* and *Taittirīya Āraṇyaka* and all eight *Brāhmaṇas* of the *Samaveda*. He was fortunate to be able to work under the protection of the kings of the Sangama dynasty who carved out the Vijayanagara empire, which was able to withstand Muslim encroachment into South Indian territory.

He was the brother of Mādhavācārya, the prime minister of Vīra Bukka Rāya, the Rājā of Vijayanagara (1350–79), in Karnatak. They both wrote commentaries on the *Saṃhitās* and *Brāhmaṇas* and also original works on grammar and law. They elaborated on Madhva's philosophy of Dvaita Vedānta. In all these works, the two brothers were assisted by the king, a great patron of literature, who invited to the court a number of learned brāhmaṇas to assist in their endeavours. In all, Sāyaṇā and Mādhavācārya served as ministers to several kings of the Sangama dynasty, including Harihara I, Bukka, Kampa, Sangama II and Harihara II. Sāyaṇā, however, was more than a scholar and was a noted warrior and patron of the arts.

In addition to the above philosophical and grammatical works, Sāyaṇā also compiled anthologies of verses taken from the *śāstras* (entitled *Subhaita-sudhanidhi*) and also technical works on poetics, the most celebrated being the *Alamkara sudhanidhi*.

See also: **Āraṇyakas; Brāhmaṇa; Brāhmaṇas; Dvaita; Madhva; Nirukta; Saṃhitā; Veda; Yāska**

RON GEAVES

Further reading

Kapoor, Subodh. 2000. *Encyclopaedic Dictionary of Hinduism*. New Delhi: Cosmo Publications.

Modak, B.R. 1995. *Sayana: Makers of Indian Literature*, Delhi: Sahitya Akademi.

SCHLEGEL, (KARL WILHELM) FRIEDRICH VON (1772–1829)

Unlike his elder brothers Carl August, a soldier who died in Madras in 1789, and August Wilhelm, who taught Sanskrit while Professor at the University of Bonn, Friedrich Schlegel (from 1815 von Schlegel) neither travelled to India nor held a permanent academic post. After studying law, philology, history and philosophy at Göttingen he studied Sanskrit with Alexander Hamilton (1762–1824) in Paris for two years, and began to read the texts on which he based his 1808 work on Indian language and philosophy. While Schlegel's initial enthusiasm for the study of India was fired by the belief, typical of German Romanticism of the time, that India was the source of everything, this book marked the end of his enthusiasm for

India and serious commitment to its study (Halbfass 1988: 75). Instead Schlegel sought to show how Hinduism embodied the gradual degradation of original divine revelation. Unlike most European scholars of his time, Schlegel regarded Advaita Vedānta as the lowest rather than the highest expression of Hindu thought.

See also: **Advaita; Hinduism, history of scholarship**

WILL SWEETMAN

Further reading

Halbfass, W. 1988. *India and Europe: An Essay in Understanding*. Albany, NY: State University of New York Press.
Rothermund, D. 1986. *The German Intellectual Quest for India*. New Delhi: Manohar.
Schlegel, F. 1849. 'On the Language and Wisdom of the Indians' (*Über die Sprache und Weisheit der Inder*, 1808). In *The Aesthetic and Miscellaneous Works of Friedrich Von Schlegel*, trans. E.J. Millington. London: H.G. Bohn, 465–95.

SCHOPENHAUER, ARTHUR (1788–1860)

German philosopher. Although perhaps finally more interested in Buddhism, Schopenhauer was profoundly attracted to Hindu thought, and especially the *Upaniṣads* in the Latin translation of A.H. Anquetil-Duperron. The extent of influence of Indian thought on Schopenhauer's own thought, particularly as represented in the first edition of his major work, *The World as Will and Representation* (1818), remains controversial; although he explicitly denies that his thought may be found in the *Upaniṣads*, he also admitted that it would have been impossible for him to have formed his own ideas without the ability to draw upon the *Upaniṣads*, Plato and Kant at the same time (Halbfass 1988: 107). There are, however, clear parallels, especially in the idea of māyā (illusion, the world of appearances) and Schopenhauer's rejection of linear time and a teleological view of history. Ultimately, however, Schopenhauer's attraction to Indian thought seems inseparable from his rejection of Judaism, Christianity and G.W.F. Hegel. His reception of Indian thought influenced that of Friedrich Nietzsche (1844–1900) and Richard Wagner (1813–83).

See also: **Anquetil-Duperron, Abraham-Hyacinthe; Hegel, Georg Wilhelm Friedrich; Hinduism, history of scholarship; Māyā; Upaniṣads**

WILL SWEETMAN

Further reading

Halbfass, W. 1988. *India and Europe: An Essay in Understanding*. Albany, NY: State University of New York Press.
Schopenhauer, A. 1958. *The World as Will and Representation*. Trans. E. Payne. Indian Hills, IA: Falcon's Wing.

SCHRADER, (FRIEDRICH) OTTO (1876–1961)

Otto Schrader was a German Indologist. After doctoral research on Buddhist and Jaina philosophy, Schrader continued to work on Buddhism before being appointed as director of the Adyar Library of the Theosophical Society in Madras. While in Madras he studied also the South Indian Dravidian languages and travelled widely in India collecting manuscripts for the library, the scholarly reputation of which he is credited with establishing. During his internment by the British in the First World War Schrader learnt Thai and Tibetan. After the war he returned to Germany and was appointed Professor of Indology at the University of Kiel. He edited the Kashmir recension of the *Bhagavadgītā*, on the basis of manuscripts he had himself collected. He published a critical edition of the minor

Upaniṣads. His book on Hinduism for A. Bertholet's *Religionsgeschichtliches Lesebuch* (1930) included extracts of Sanskrit and Tamil bhakti religious texts.

See also: **Bhagavadgītā; Hinduism, history of scholarship; Upaniṣads**

WILL SWEETMAN

Further reading

Schrader, Otto. 1916. *Introduction to the Pāñcarātra.* Ed. R.D. Ramanujacarya. Madras: Adyar Library.

Schrader, Otto. 1930. *The Kashmir Recension of the Bhagavadgītā.* Stuttgart: Kohlhammer.

Schrader, Otto. 1930. *Der Hinduismus*, 2nd edn. Tübingen: Mohr.

Stache-Rosen, V. 1990. *German Indologists.* New Delhi: Max Müller Bhavan.

SCIENCE

Indian civilisation, Vedic and onwards, was no stranger to scientific inquiry, be it directed towards an understanding of material or spiritual phenomena. While the orthodox traditions treat the sacred texts as divinely revealed, modern analyses treat them as milestones in human understanding and discovery. It is this attitude which allows for the possibility of the texts being legitimate conclusions of scientific experimentation, even on spiritual issues.

Studies on the presence of science in Vedic and later literature seem to reveal that the ancients were knowledgeable in a number of areas. They were versed in astronomy and its sibling astrology, they knew that gravitation was caused by the earth, the speed of light with reasonable accuracy, that light is split up into seven colours, the shape of the earth, heliocentricity, medicine, surgery, including plastic, the origins of the natural elements, embryology, physiology, zoology, electricity, transport technology such as submarines, ships, space travel, aviation, chemical science, including alchemy, and a form of atomic (aṇu) theory through the Vaiśeṣika system. There is no doubting that a great number of the subjects in this list indeed have historical verisimilitude, yet one wonders to what extent some of the conclusions in various studies have been construed to fall in parity with modern science simply to give apologetic legitimacy to ancient Hindu civilisation. Nevertheless, mathematics has always played a prominent role in Hindu society and it is from the ancient Indians that the world obtained the concepts of zero, infinity and the decimal system. What the Western world calls Arabic numerals were in fact born in India and given to the Arabs, as was algebra. The Indians also knew geometry, trigonometry and other areas of mathematics.

There are parallels with modern physics and certain Indian philosophical ideas. The origins of the universe were speculated upon, with the final declaration in the *Ṛgveda* that whence it came nobody knows. Later, texts talk of the golden egg or womb (hiraṇyagarbha), a single point from which the universe comes forth at the big bang. The arrival of elaborate systems of time result in the idea of an infinite number of creations (ṣṛṣthi), each lasting a kalpa (4.32 million years) and each ending with a big crunch which triggers off dissolutions (pralaya) for the same duration.

Newton's third law of physics echoes the moral doctrine of karma in that every action has an equal and opposite reaction. In fact, karma has been referred to as the law of conservation of moral energy. While the law of conservation of energy in physics holds that energy cannot be created or destroyed, only transferred from one form to another, the opening verse to the *Iśā Upaniṣad* expresses the same with regard to Brahman (Ultimate Reality).

The conclusions of Vedānta resonate well with a number of ideas within theoretical physics. First, Einstein's special relativity suggests that matter is a form of energy. Vedānta holds that all that is manifest is ultimately the consciousness that is referred to as the Brahman. Second, the unified field theory, the 'holy grail' sought within quantum physics, as an attempt to combine all the forces and particle interactions into a single theoretical framework is no less than monistic. In the case of Advaita Vedānta, the plurality that one finds present in the manifest world is only apparent, for all is reducible to the monistic Brahman. In addition, many within present-day quantum physics theorise that the fundamental building block of all matter is the superstring. It is vibrating at different modal frequencies that results in different particles. Saṃkhya cosmology in similar ways also holds that all matter is composed of three building blocks, the three guṇas, and it is the manner in which these three combine that determines the nature of the material entity.

See also: **Advaita; Brahman; Guṇas; Hiraṇyagarbha; Kalpa; Karma; Pralaya; Sacred texts; Saṃhitā; Saṃkhya; Upaniṣads; Vaiśeṣika; Vedānta**

RISHI HANDA

Further reading

Iyengar, T.R.R. 1997. *Hinduism and Scientific Quest*. New Delhi: D.K. Printworld (P) Ltd.

Jitatmananda, Swami. 2004. *Modern Physics and Vedanta*. 5th edn. Mumbai: Bharatiya Vidya Bhavan.

Krishnaji. 1995. *Science and Technology in the Vedas*. Delhi: Nag Publishers.

Vartak, Padmakar Vishnu. 1995. *Scientific Knowledge in the Vedas*. Delhi: Nag Publishers.

SELF-REALISATION FELLOWSHIP

Originally founded in India, the Self-Realisation Fellowship's (SRF) teachings derive from its founder-leader, Swami Paramhansa Yogananda (1893–1952). Yogananda was taught by Sri Yukeswar (1855–1936), a student of Lahiri Mahasaya (1828–95), and claimed a paraṃparā (lineage of disciplic succession) going back to Mahavatar Babaji, said to have been born in the third century CE and to be still alive. Mahavatar Babaji is said to have been the originator of kriyā yoga, the spiritual practice taught by Yukeswar, Yogananda and the SRF.

Yogananda met Yukeswar in 1910; he joined his order of swamis in 1914 and founded the Yagoda Satsanga Society of India in 1917. The society is still known by this name in India. Yogananda visited Boston in 1920 to attend the International Congress of Religious Liberals; his address, 'The Science of Religion', still remains a key text. Two years later, he established a Western branch, with an ashram near the city. In 1935 he returned to the USA to give a lecture tour, attracting large crowds.

The methods of kriyā yoga remain confidential, being disclosed only to students who have received dīkṣā (initiation). The practice involves meditation, breath control and withdrawal of the senses, leading ultimately to the state of samādhi. The techniques are said to be 'scientific', being empirical and experiential, and to lead to a personal experience of God. Although Yogananda came from a neo-Vedānta monist tradition, his teachings allowed his disciples to engage in bhakti, worshipping God in a personal form, and he sought to attain a harmony between Hindu devotion and Christianity. Yogananda's life and teachings are set out in his *Autobiography of a Yogi* (1946), a spiritual classic, now translated into eighteen languages.

See also: **Āśram(a) (religious community); Āṣṭāṅga Yoga; Bhakti; Meditation; Paraṃparā; Svāmi; Vedānta; Yogananda, Paramhansa**

GEORGE CHRYSSIDES

Further reading

Yogananda. 1987. *The Science of Religion.* Los Angeles, CA: Self-Realisation Fellowship.
Yogananda. 1990. *Autobiography of a Yogi.* Los Angeles, CA: Self-Realisation Fellowship.

SEN, KESHAB CHANDRA (1838–84)

Born into a Vaiṣṇavite family, Sen joined the Brahmo Samaj in 1858, under Debendranath Tagore's leadership, but caused a schism within the organisation in 1865. Sen took the Brahmo Samaj's ideas outside Bengal, creating forums for discussion, establishing schools, working for famine relief and championing women's rights, particularly advocating the remarriage of widows and women's education.

Sen attracted several younger men into the movement and formed a society known as Sangat Sabha. Some of their ideas were more radical than those of Tagore: in particular, Sen and his followers held that the brāhmaṇas' practice of wearing a sacred thread was inconsistent with the principles of the Brahmo Samaj, and exhorted them to remove them. Sen's followers seceded to form their own separate group, known as the Nabad-Bidhan ('New Dispensation') Samaj.

In contrast with the original Brahmo Samaj's attempts to create an aniconic form of religion that could be shared by Hindus, Christians and Muslims, Sen became increasingly drawn to Christianity, introducing elements such as praying to Christ for the forgiveness of sins. Sen combined such elements of Christian devotion with Hindu bhakti notions, introducing singing processions and samkirtan (a form of preaching associated with Caitanya), claiming a 'New Dispensation' in which elements of various world religions became blended. Furthermore, Sen's supporters held him in increasing esteem, reportedly referring to him as 'Master' and even 'Saviour'. Numerous supporters believed that the Samaj was seriously compromising its original principles, and left.

In 1878 further controversy arose when Sen allowed his 13-year-old daughter to marry the Prince of Cooch Behar, contrary to his principles of outlawing child marriages. This caused most of his followers to leave, and Pandit Shivanath Shastri formed a breakaway group called the Sadharan (Common) Brahmo Samaj.

See also: **Bhakti; Brahmo Samaj; Caitanya; Kīrtan; Tagore, Debendranath; Vaiṣṇavism; Widow remarriage**

GEORGE CHRYSSIDES

Further reading

Kasinath, Kayal. 1998. *Keshub Chunder Sen: A Study in Encounter and Response.* Calcutta: Minerva Associates.

ŚEṢA

The thousand-headed serpent (nāga), upon whose coils Viṣṇu reclines and sleeps at the end of every cosmic cycle of creation, before awakening and starting the process of creation once again. In Hindu iconography, the multi-headed cobra floats upon an ocean of water or milk representing the undifferentiated condition of the cosmos before the emergence of form. Śeṣa is also known as Ananta, meaning 'endless' or 'infinite', and in some mythologies is said to be formed from the residue of the universe after the cosmic destruction at the end of each cycle of creation. In other accounts he is an animal form of Viṣṇu, whose fiery breath destroys the world at the end of time. The universe is thus reduced to ashes, which sink into the cosmic ocean and provide the residue for re-creation. In some interpretations of the mythology Śeṣa represents time itself and his many coils are the endless cycles of creation. Śeṣa is also the king of the nāgas.

See also: **Images and iconography; Nāgas; Sacred animals; Viṣṇu**

RON GEAVES

Further reading

Stutley, Margaret and James Stutley (eds). 1977. *A Dictionary of Hinduism: Its Mythology, Folklore and Development 1500 BC–AD 1500*. London: Routledge and Kegan Paul.

SEVĀ

Prior to the early nineteenth century CE, the meaning of sevā, 'serving' or 'honouring', had been virtually synonymous with that of pūjā (worship). Sevā thus had typically been performed for a deity and the deity's mūrti in a temple, and for the guru and other devotees. Such activity has been and remains central to bhakti religion and to Vaiṣṇavism in particular.

Since the early nineteenth century CE, a number of Hindu movements, for example, the Swami Narayana Sampradaya, Radhasoami Satsang and Ramakrishna Math and Mission, have invested the concept of sevā with a wider sense of serving those in need. Such groups have drawn to varying degrees upon elements from traditional Hindu philanthropy, Christian charitable institutions and forms of social service in the United States and Europe. This expanded form of sevā has come to be regarded as a universal obligation, even for those classed as sādhus and saṃnyasīs, and its recipients in many cases are no longer confined to followers of the same movement. Its practice is commonly justified on the basis of a theological or philosophical identification of those in need with divinity or ultimate reality as, for example, in Vivekananda's Neo-Vedantin ethic. In addition to responding to natural disasters, recent expressions of sevā include the maintenance of extensive, permanent institutions providing education, healthcare, welfare and social development. Organisations committed to the ideals of Hindutva have used sevā to strengthen Hindu values and build support for the Hindu rāṣṭra (nation). The Swami Narayana movement and the Rashtriya Swayamsevak Sangh and its affiliates have promoted ambitious sevā programmes through their presence in the Hindu diaspora.

See also: **Bhakti; Diaspora; Guru; Hindutva; Mandir; Pūjā; Radhasoami Satsang; Ramakrishna Math and Mission; Rashtriya Swayamsevak Sangh; Sādhu; Saṃnyāsa; Swami Narayana Sampradaya; Vaiṣṇavism; Vivekananda, Swami**

GWILYM BECKERLEGGE

Further reading

Beckerlegge, G. 2005. *Swami Vivekananda's Legacy of Service.* New Delhi: Oxford University Press.

Jones, K.W. 1989. *The New Cambridge History of India III.1: Socio-religious Reform Movements in British India.* Cambridge: Cambridge University Press.

Williams, R.B. 2001. *An Introduction to Swaminarayan Hinduism.* Cambridge: Cambridge University Press.

SEVEN SACRED CITIES

See: **Saptapurī (Seven Sacred Cities)**

SEX AND SEXUALITY

Hindu mythology explores all dimensions of sexuality, recognising the libido as central to life and pleasure (although most Hindus attribute its more unconventional expressions to deities or demons). The classical Hindu notion of kāma, which encompassed pleasure in general and sexual pleasure in particular as one of the four legitimate goals of human life (puruṣārthas), incorporated ancient Vedic celebrations of the good life and of pleasure. Kāma, however, was somewhat different for men and women. For most elite Hindu women, kāma was a positive good only in the context of marriage (vivāhā); for many elite men, however, it was tolerated even outside marriage despite the tradition's general presumption of monogamy. Extramarital affairs sometimes led to polygamy or long-term liaisons with temple and court performers (who had another kind of elite, albeit somewhat ambiguous, status). Vātsyāyana's *Kāmasūtra* explores all things sexual and pleasurable to educate elite townsmen on how to transform the crude sexual act into a refined, mutual eroticism. This includes explicit instructions on how a man should tenderly guide his new wife during her first intercourse, on types of love play and on emblems of passion such as nail and teeth marks – all of which the text pedantically classifies. Indian poets, too, explored sexual themes (except for actual intercourse) with charming frankness.

Hinduism recognises not only the pleasurable and powerful aspects of sex but also its useful aspect in producing progeny. Because householders needed children to fulfil their debts to ancestors and deities, they followed rules that governed the proper time in a woman's monthly cycle for intercourse (ṛtukāladharma) and endured penalties or atonements (prāyascitta) for ignoring it.

Hindus based negative views of female sexuality on the following. As in other cultures, men's awareness that they were born of women and depended on them in early life contributed to ideas of male inferiority, which they disguised or overcame with expressions of male superiority and misogynistic views of women's innate inferiority (such as their innate promiscuity) as antidotes. Hindus located manhood pre-eminently in semen. Retaining it increased a man's power. By releasing it, he passed this power to a woman. Even when viewed as a duty for the sake of progeny, doing so connoted a sacrifice (which implied that intercourse was a negative act). This problem was compounded by observing that women could replace their bodily fluids (blood, breast milk) and hence their power (śakti) automatically. It was partly to retain semen that Gandhi and neo-Hindu groups advocated sexual abstinence as the preferred method of contraception.

Son preference, too, caused men to take a dim view of female sexuality. The *Āyurveda*s (medical texts) and *Dharmaśāstra*s prescribed ways to have sons, because fathers needed them to perform funeral and other rituals. This ritual requirement – along with the need for sons to maintain a patrilocal and patrilineal social structure, with its corollary of caring for parents in their old age and the need for sons to perform various economic and political functions – contributed not only to son preference but also to the devaluation of daughters in some circles.

As a negative force, the libido must be converted into spiritual power through a religious path, many Hindus believed, which produced another reason for negative views of female sexuality. The ascetic critique of sexuality presents it as the cause of pollution, death, evil and enslavement due to the cycles of death and rebirth (saṃsāra) (*Mahābhārata* 13.40.5–12; *Mārkaṇḍeya-purāṇa* 49.28–29). These ascetics (*The Law Code of Manu* 2:213–15; 9:15) believed that women were innately promiscuous. Some authors, however, gave the latter a more positive spin. In the *Mahābhārata*, for instance, Bhangasvana refuses to be transformed back into a man; she prefers to remain a woman, because women experience greater pleasure in sexual intercourse than men do (*Mahābhārata* 13.12.47). Similarly, Tantra rejected ascetic misogyny by claiming that sexual intercourse, whether a physical act (left-handed Tantra) or meditation on the act (right-handed

Tantra), was the means to liberation. In fact, some tantric authorities believed that women were the best gurus.

See also: **Āyurveda; Dharmaśāstras; Dowry; Foeticide; Gandhi, Mohandas Karamchand; Gender; Infanticide; Kāma; Kāmasūtra; Mahābhārata; Myth; Pativratā and Patiparameśvara; Prāyaścitta; Purāṇas; Puruṣārthas; Śakti; Saṃsāra; Strīdharma); Tantrism; Vātsyāyana Mallanāga; Virginity; Vivāhā**

KATHERINE K. YOUNG

Further reading

Harlan, L. and P.B. Courtright (eds). 1995. *From the Margins of Hindu Marriage: Essays on Gender, Religion, and Culture*. Oxford: Oxford University Press.

Kumari, R. 1988. *Female Sexuality in Hinduism*. Delhi: Joint Women's Programme by ISPCK.

Khandelwal, M. 2001. 'Sexual Fluids, Emotions, Morality: Notes on the Gendering of Brahmacharya'. In E.J. Sobo and S. Bell, eds, *Celibacy, Culture, and Society: The Anthropology of Sexual Abstinence*. Madison, WI: University of Wisconsin Press, 157–79.

Marglin, F.A. 1982. 'Types of Sexual Union and their Implicit Meanings'. In J.S. Hawley and D.M. Wulff, eds, *Divine Consort: Radha and the Goddesses of India*. Berkeley, CA: Graduate Theological Union, 298–315.

Nanda, S. 1994. 'Hijras: An Alternative Sex and Gender Role in India'. In G. Herdt, ed., *Third Sex, Third Gender: Beyond Sexual Dimorphism in Culture and History*. New York: Zone Books, 373–417.

Narayanan, V. 1991. 'Hindu Perceptions of Auspiciousness and Sexuality'. In J. Becher, ed., *Women, Religion and Sexuality: Studies on the Impact of Religious Teachings on Women*. Geneva: World Council of Churches Publications, 64–92.

O'Flaherty [Doniger], W. 1980. 'Sexual Fluids in Vedic and Post-Vedic India'. *Women, Androgynes, and Other Mythical Beasts*. Chicago, IL: University of Chicago Press, 17–61.

Olivelle, P. 2004. *The Law Code of Manu*. Oxford: Oxford University Press.

Rao, K.L.S. 1995. 'Sexual Morality and Family Values: A Gandhian Perspective'. *Dialogue and Alliance: A Journal of the International Religious Foundation* 9: 20–26.

Reynolds, H.B. 1980. 'The Auspicious Married Woman'. In S.S. Wadley, ed., *The Powers of Tamil Women*. Syracuse, NY: Syracuse University, 35–60.

Shah, S. 1995. *The Making of Womanhood: Gender Relations in the Mahābhārata*. Delhi: Manohar.

Sharma, A. 1993. 'Homosexuality and Hinduism'. In A. Swidler, ed., *Homosexuality and World Religions*. Valley Forge, PA: Trinity Press International, 47–80.

Sutherland, S.J.M. 1992. 'Seduction, Counterseduction, and Sexual Role Models: Bedroom Politics and the Indian Epics'. *Journal of Indian Philosophy* 20: 243–51.

Thompson, C. 1983. 'Women, Fertility and the Worship of Gods in a Hindu Village'. In *Women's Religious Experience*, ed. P. Holden. Totowa, NJ: Barnes and Noble, 113–31.

SHANKAR MISRA, BRAHM

Also known as Maharaj Saheb, Brahm Shankar Misra was a disciple and disputed successor to Rai Salig Ram, who was himself one of the key figures in the development of the Radhasoami lineage. Preaching in the first decade of the twentieth century, he did not immediately announce himself as the legitimate successor of his guru. The space of one or two years in which he reflected upon his right to succeed was later developed into the concept of an interregnum, a period of time when no satguru (true teacher) is publicly manifest. The idea of an interregnum would have modified the teaching of Shiv Dayal, the founder of Radhasoami, who promoted the more usual Sant Mat tradition of the need for a living master or satguru.

Highly educated, Brahm Shankar Misra is famous for his failed attempt to reunite all the various Radhasoami factions by the creation of the Central Administrative Council in 1902 in Agra. Although supported by Shiv Dayal

Singh's younger brother, Partap Singh, and other prominent Agra satsangis, the attempt to reunify led to even more schisms.

See also: **Guru; Radhasoami Satsang; Salig Ram, Rai; Sant**

RON GEAVES

Further reading

Jones, Kenneth. 1989. *Socio-Religious Reform Movements in British India, The New Cambridge History of India: vol. 3.1*. Cambridge: Cambridge University Press.

SHARMA, PANDIT DIN DAYALU (b. 1863)

An advocate of conservative Hindu 'orthodoxy' in northern India. Pandit Din Dayalu Sharma is best known as the founder of the Bharat Dharma Mahamandala, an umbrella organisation designed to unite the variety of Dharma Sabhas formed during the later nineteenth century. Devoted to the protection of sanātana dharma and Hindu varnāśramadharma, he was active during his lifetime in establishing a significant number of Sanskrit schools, including a Sanskrit College in Delhi in 1899, as well as goshālās (rest homes for cows) and Dharma Sabhas. Among his initial forays into conservative Hindu religious politics was the 1886 founding of the Gau Varnashrama Hitaishini Ganga Dharma Sabha, an organisation intended to protect the sacred cow, the Hindu social order, and the river Ganges against such Hindu reformist institutions as the Arya Samaj. In 1887 he became the nascent Bharat Dharma Mahamandala's chairman, and later its secretary. He withdrew from active involvement with the organisation in 1902.

See also: **Āśram(a) (religious community); Arya Samaj; Bharat Dharma Mahamandala; Dharma; Dharma Sabha; Gaṅgā; Sacred animals; Sanātana Dharma; Varṇa**

MICHAEL S. DODSON

Further reading

Jones, K.W. 1989. *Socio-Religious Reform Movements in British India*. Cambridge: Cambridge University Press.

SHIV DAYAL, SWAMI

See: **Soamiji Maharaj**

SHIV NARAYAN AGNIHOTRA, PANDIT (1850–1929)

Founder of the Hindu reformist organisation the Dev Samaj ('Divine Society'). Pandit Shiv Narayan Agnihotra joined the Brahmo Samaj in 1873 in Lahore. He soon became a prominent member, speaking and publishing widely on the issues of marriage reform and vegetarianism. Yet following his entrance into the Brahmo form of saṃnyāsa (worldly renunciation) in 1882, he left the Brahmo Samaj and in 1887 founded his own religious organisation, the Dev Samaj. Here his teachings increasingly began to depart from Brahmo ideals. For example, Agnihotra emphasised the importance of the guru (spiritual preceptor) in religious practice. But not just any guru. Agnihotra believed that he alone had achieved a sufficiently enlightened state (the 'Complete Higher Life') to instruct his followers in their spiritual path. In this regard, Dev Samajis were to undertake the worship of Agnihotra and he was to serve as the focus of all religious practice. He was later known as Bhagvan Devatma.

See also: **Food; Guru; Vivāha**

MICHAEL S. DODSON

Further reading

Jones, K.W. 1989. *Socio-Religious Reform Movements in British India*. Cambridge: Cambridge University Press.

SHIV SENA

Shiv Sena is a militant provincial organisation that, while initially based on Maharashtrian ethnicity, has now allied itself to Hindutva organisations such as the Rashtriya Swayamsevak Sangh (RSS) and the Bharatiya Janata Party (BJP) and adopted a distinct anti-Muslim and anti-Western stance. It was founded in 1966 by Bal Thackeray, an erstwhile political cartoonist, and was perhaps a response to the large influx of professionals and other jobseekers from other Indian regions to Mumbai (Bombay), the headquarters of Shiv Sena. Though it had once demanded the closing of the borders of Maharashtra to other Indians, it has never made, like the Punjabis, the Nagas or the Kashmiris, a demand to secede from India. It has often gone on a rampage against South Indians in Mumbai and also against Muslims in the wake of the Babri Masjid incident, and its ideology on the whole is crude and insensitive and against the egalitarian and secular ideals of the nation of India.

The name Shiv Sena originates from King Śivaji, a ruler of Maharashtra well known for his defiance of the powerful Mughal emperor Aurangzeb. The martial overtone of the organisation is evident from the term Sena (army) in its title and the fact that the members call themselves Sainiks (soldiers). Recently they have stated that Shiv Sena means not only the army of Śivaji but also that of Śiva, the Hindu god, thereby taking on a Hindu as well as a Maharashtrian identity (Banerjee 2000: 150). They have therefore taken an antagonistic stance to Muslims and Pakistan, the latter demonstrated by their digging up of cricket grounds in Delhi to prevent the Pakistani cricket team playing against India. Their avowed aim is to unite the youth of India against oppression and injustice, but they themselves have oppressed ethnic and religious minorities in Maharashtra.

Shiv Sena was until 1999 a political force in Maharashtra, and in 1995 in alliance with the BJP it formed the government in the state. Manohar Joshi, the erstwhile chief minister of Maharashtra, was a Shiv Sena sainik.

See also: **Ayodhyā; Bharatiya Janata Party; Hindutva; Rashtriya Swayamsevak Sangh; Śiva; Thackeray, Bal**

THEODORE GABRIEL

Further reading

Eckert, Julia M. 2002. *The Shiv Sena and the Politics of Violence*. Oxford: Oxford University Press.

Banerjee, Sikata. 2000. *Warriors in Politics: Hindu Nationalism, Violence and the Shiv Sena in India*. Boulder, CO: Westview Press.

Purandare, Vaibhav. 1999. *The Sena Story*. Mumbai: Business Publications.

SHIVANANDA, SWAMI (1916–63)

Born in 1916 as P.V. Kuppuswami Iyer in Tamil Nadu, he received a Western education and served as a doctor among Indians in British Malaya from 1913 to 1923. Learning about different religious traditions (besides Hinduism, mainly Christianity, Malay Islam and Chinese Buddhism), he gave up his worldly career and moved to Rishikesh to pursue spiritual matters. There he lived an austere life, gaining the saṃnyāsā name Swami Shivananda. In 1936 he founded the Divine Life Society. Shivananda's teaching and practice are rooted in Hindu devotional and yogic traditions but focus on a common set of unity of all religious traditions. Thus he addresses modern Hindus as well as Western disciples. At his death in 1963 he left the Divine Life Society to the leadership of Swami Chidananda (b. 1916).

See also: **Bhakti movement; Divine Life Society; Saṃnyāsā**

MANFRED HUTTER

Further reading

Maharaj, S.S.V. (ed.). 1985. *Sivananda. Biography of a Modern Sage.* Freemantle: Divine Life Society.

Sivananda, Sri Swami. 1974. *Sadhana. A Textbook on the Psychology and Practice of the Techniques to Spiritual Perfection.* Sivanandanagar: Divine Life Society.

Sivananda, Sri Swami. 1976. *Divine Nectar.* Delhi: Motilal Barnasidass.

SHRADDHA RAM PHILLAURI, PANDIT (1837–81)

Among the first prominent expounders of a return to 'orthodox' Hinduism in the Punjab during the nineteenth century. Much of his time was spent travelling that region, preaching a form of traditionalised Vaiṣṇavism with a particular emphasis upon 'pure' social and ritual practice, rather than a specific religious doctrine per se. In particular, he advocated the wearing of Tulsi beads, a tilak (sectarian marking) upon the forehead and the abandonment of alcohol consumption, gambling, etc. Shraddha Ram was also involved in the establishment of numerous dharma sabhas, temples and rest houses for pilgrims in northern India. As a declared defender of sanātana dharma ('eternal religion'), he was also particularly opposed to the reformist agenda of the Arya Samaj leader Dayananda Saraswati. Shraddha Ram's best-known work, the 1876 tract *Dharma Rakśā* ('the defence of religion'), emphasised the Sanskrit textual basis of Hindu belief and practice.

See also: **Arya Samaj; Dayananda Saraswati, Swami; Dharma Sabha; Languages; Mandir; Sanātana Dharma; Tīrthayātrā (Pilgrimage); Vaiṣṇavism**

MICHAEL S. DODSON

Further reading

Jones, K.W. 1989. *Socio-Religious Reform Movements in British India.* Cambridge: Cambridge University Press.

SHRADDHANAND, SWAMI (1857–1926)

Shraddhanand (known as Munshiram before he took saṃnyāsa in 1917) was one of the most charismatic leaders to emerge from the Hindu reform movement Arya Samaj. From the late 1880s onwards he was conspicuously active in religious and social reform and nationalist politics.

He was born into the Khatrī caste in a Punjab village in 1857. Under the influence of Swami Dayananda Sarasvati he converted to Aryanism and eventually dropped his career as a lawyer to devote his life entirely to the cause of the movement. When the Samaj split in 1893, Munshiram became the leader of the so-called radical wing, trying to check Westernisation by advocating vegetarianism and the introduction of a system of education largely based on Hindu tradition. His educational visions materialised in the Gurukul Kangri (founded in 1902), a school combining a modern curriculum with a thorough knowledge of Sanskrit and Hindu patriotism. The institution was supposed to educate a highly motivated avant-garde of 'social engineers' who would prepare the masses for Indian self-rule.

Reacting to the political turmoil in 1919 and the growing tensions between Hindus and Muslims in subsequent years, Shraddhanand left the Gurukul and dropped his concept of evolutionary nation-building for a direct involvement in politics. He became active in the Indian National Congress (leading a satyāgraha campaign in Delhi) and the Hindu Mahasabha. He vigorously advocated the strengthening and organisation (saṅgaṭhan) of the Hindu community by abolishing untouchability and practising śuddhi, the reclamation of Hindus who had previously been converted to Islam. His reconversion campaigns and his anti-Islamic rhetoric made him a target for radical Muslims, and he was murdered by a zealot in December 1926. His 'martyrdom' eventually turned him into an icon of early Hindu nationalism. Throughout his career he had been a prolific writer on religious, social and political topics in Hindi, Urdu and English.

See also: **Arya Samaj; Caste; Conversion; Dayananda Saraswati, Swami; Gandhi, Mohandas Karamchand; Hindu Mahasabha; Languages; Nationalism; Religious education; Saṃnyāsa**

HARALD FISCHER-TINÉ

Further reading

Bhāratīya, B. (ed.). 1987. *Svāmī Śraddhānand Granthāvalī* [collected works of *Svāmī Śraddhānand*], 11 vols. Dillī: Govindrām Hasānand.

Jordens, J.T.F. 1981. *Swāmī Shraddānanda. His Life and Causes.* Delhi: Oxford University Press.

SHRINES, WAYSIDE

Wayside shrines are prolific throughout the Indian subcontinent and worship at them is an integral aspect of religious practice for the majority of the population. They are found most extensively punctuating the rural landscape of India, though towns and cities also have their share of individually placed, small shrines dedicated to one of the many Hindu gods and goddesses. Wayside shrines are most commonly associated with the countryside and the worship undertaken at them generally consists of simple acts of devotion.

Wayside shrines and the deities who inhabit them are numerous and very individual. Many are dedicated to goddesses but certainly not all of them. While most wayside shrines are small, commonly a three-sided house-type structure installed under a tree, others, particularly in Tamil Nadu, are huge and imposing. They rise out of the often featureless landscape, their outer wall painted with the characteristic red and white stripes that indicate a sacred place, perhaps with an enormous garishly painted horse carrying a local hero turned god. In complete contrast is the often deified red-earth termite mound, its only decoration a faded flower garland. Other wayside deities have no shrine but are simply represented by a stone that may be carved or, as many are, without feature. Whether large or small, they all receive periodic worship from the people who have adopted them as their own, or from people passing by them. As India is a sacred land to the Hindus, it is natural that its landscape should be inhabited by so many sacred places.

The veneration of snakes (nāgas) is a common feature of worship across India but is perhaps most pervasive in south India. In particular, a snake goddess called Nākamāl (popular in Tamil Nadu) is often installed within the temple complex. Most commonly, snake worship is practised at the many wayside shrines at which nāga stones are placed, often at the base of trees. These stones are stylised depictions of the cobra, associated with nīm trees in particular. Snakes occupy an ambiguous position in Indian culture, having both sacred and profane associations. On one hand, they are feared (not surprisingly as many people die each year from snakebites), yet, conversely, they are also deified as the power of fertility. In this capacity, snakes are inextricably linked both to trees and to pātāla (the netherworld), to which they were assigned guardianship. The nāga resting place and doorway to this world is very often among the roots of trees or, in the case of some Nākamāl shrines, via a specially made snake house. Snakes are considered powerful creatures and are offered milk and eggs in order to divert their potential to cause trouble or to persuade them to offer their help in matters of infertility.

Many wayside shrines, not just those dedicated to snakes, are known for their power in granting children and are visited, mostly by women hoping for offspring.

These shrines are immediately obvious as the women tie red and yellow threads to the tree, if there is one, or simply to the edge of the shrine. Often little wooden cribs are also offered and tied, in the hope that the goddess will provide the baby to occupy them. Similarly, other deities are famous for their healing powers, evident from the offerings of small pottery or silver-foil arms and legs which are presented in the hope that the deity will heal the devotee.

Deities who offer various sorts of protection or who offer a public service, such as finding lost cattle, are installed in wayside shrines. Probably the most common are those deities whose shrines are at the sides of many roads. They are most commonly offered incense, perhaps a camphor flame or some flowers by travellers who wish for protection during their journey. Some deities have been installed specifically at locations where many accidents have occurred. One such goddess, Kumkum Kāliammā, was installed next to a particularly dangerous road bend where she is now worshipped, bathed and decorated once a month by the local population. They claim that since her installation there have been no accidents on her stretch of road. Periodically worshipped for their protection of the town or village water supply, many deities occupy wayside shrines that are situated next to ponds or water tanks.

In Rajasthan, some wayside shrines are dedicated to local satīs (virtuous wives) who ended their lives on their husband's funeral pyre and were deified subsequently. They are generally offered worship for their protective powers. The Saptamātṛkās (Seven Mothers) or Saptakaṇṇimār (Seven Virgins), as they are known in Tamil Nadu, are prolific among the wayside shrines in north and south India. Although they are very popular, the names of the seven goddesses change from place to place. However, they, like many of the other wayside deities, are approached primarily for their protection. While most deities are simply worshipped with offerings of light, incense, flowers or sometimes a coconut, some deities, usually goddesses, might also be offered an annual blood sacrifice.

It is often unclear what specific function individual wayside shrines have as some are situated away from any obvious feature. Even here, evidence of worship is clear in the dried flowers and smoke-blackened pedestal where camphor tablets have been lit. Most often worship at wayside shrines is undertaken on an individual basis, rather than communally. Since the deities are generally in the open, rather than in a closed temple, and are not attended by a priest, the devotee interacts directly with the god or goddess. Therefore worship, which may be simply the lighting of an incense stick or might involve offerings that are more lavish, may take place at any time.

See also: **Blood sacrifice; Nāgas; Saptamātṛkās**

LYNN FOULSTON

Further reading

Foulston, L. 2002. *At the Feet of the Goddess: The Divine Feminine in Local Hindu Religion*. Brighton and Portland, OR: Sussex Academic Press.

Fuller, C.J. 1992. *The Camphor Flame: Popular Hinduism and Society in India*. Princeton, NJ: Princeton University Press.

Whitehead, H. 1983. *The Village Gods of South India*. Reprint of 1921 edition. New Delhi: Cosmo.

SIDDHA

Siddha ('Perfect Being') is a term employed in Hindu Tantra to denote a practitioner of the inner circle of Tantric virtuosi who, by taking higher initiations involving transactions in the sexual fluids of Yoginīs, has transformed himself into a demigod. Similar terminology is found in

Hindu haṭha yoga traditions, where the means to the end of self-divinisation involve the consumption of nectar (amṛta) in the form of yogically refined bodily fluids. In Hindu alchemy, one became a siddha by ingesting the transmuted sexual fluids of Śiva and the Great Goddess Mahādevī, in their mineral forms of mercury and sulphur. All these medieval traditions presuppose the existence of a class of siddha demigods whose elevated rank and atmospheric station one could attain through sexual, yogic and alchemical practice. In all three traditions, humans who so perfected themselves entered into the lineages or families of the immortal, ever youthful, invulnerable, demigod siddhas, whose mythology often identifies them with mountains.

See also: **Haṭha Yoga; Mahādevī; Śiva; Tantrism**

DAVID GORDON WHITE

Further reading

White, D.G. 1996. *The Alchemical Body: Siddha Traditions in Medieval India*. Chicago, IL: University of Chicago Press.

SIDDHA DHAM

An ashram in the Himālayas, Siddha Dham lies between two famous pilgrimage sites at Kedarnath (believed to be Śaṅkara's samādhi) and Badrinath. The site is sometimes used for teaching by Param Mahasiddha Awatar Sri Alakhpuriji, who is said to be an immortal ṛṣi, one of the four great siddhas from Satya Loka. Alakhpuriji is the guru of Paramyogeshwar Sri Devpuriji, who is believed to be an incarnation of Śiva. There are held to be seven such ṛṣis, who dwell in Satya Loka, the highest level of reality, and serve as protectors of the world and are capable of appearing on earth in a variety of visible or invisible forms.

See also: **Āśram(a) (religious community); Ṛṣi; Siddha; Śiva; Śaṅkara; Tīrthayātrā (Pilgrimage)**

GEORGE CHRYSSIDES

Further reading

Moorthy, K.K. 1995. *That Lord Siva to Be Adored: A Mini-compendium of 300 Saivate Shrines*. Tirupati, Andhra Pradesh: Message Publications.

Sen Gupta, Subhadra. 2002. *Badrinath and Kedarnath: The Dhaams of the Himalayas*. New Delhi: Rupa.

SIKHISM, RELATIONSHIP WITH HINDUISM

The creation of the categories Hinduism and Sikhism is in itself problematic, as any analysis of the relationship between those that define themselves as Hindus and as Sikhs needs to take into account the politics of colonialism and its impact on shaping contesting arenas for discrete religious traditions in post-colonial India. During the nineteenth century, not only did the British increasingly define Indian populations according to religious affiliation for political purposes, but the creation of European-style schools was also according to religious affiliation. In the Punjab, instead of the common Punjabi language, Hindi and Urdu were adopted as the vehicle for instruction for Hindus and Muslims, whilst Punjabi was maintained for Sikhs (Tatla 1999: 17). In addition, the efforts of Christian missionaries to convert people caused a reaction of religious revivalism, helping to define discrete religious boundaries. At the same time the neo-Hindu reform movement the Arya Samaj was reclassifying Sikhism as a sect of Hinduism, leading to a backlash in which newly emerging Khalsa movements (Singh Sabhas) countered with the assertion that 'Sikhs are not Hindus' (Tatla 1999: 17).

The creation of the Khalsa in 1699 by the last human guru, Gobind Singh, in which his followers were given unique identity markers (the well-known five Ks, often perceived to be the external signs of Sikh allegiance), provided the possibility for the followers of the gurus (gurmat) to see themselves as distinct from other communities in India. Guru Gobind Singh's apparent attempt to create a separate identity has to be seen in the context of the increasingly difficult relations with the Mughal Empire.

Earlier, Sikhism's monotheism had been more likely to be sympathetically perceived by Muslims, but after the emperor Akbar's death in 1606 the Mughal court was to move closer to Muslim orthodoxy. In the ensuing struggle for power, Guru Arjan gave his blessing to Khusrau, only to see him defeated by his brother Jehangir. The victor of the Mughal throne arrested the Sikh guru and had him put to death in Delhi. From this time forward, gurmat relations with the empire remained strained. The ensuing martyrdom of the ninth Guru, Teg Bahadur (1621–75), who was also the father of Gobind Singh, led to increasing militarisation of the panth and a period of violent struggle with the declining Mughals, too weak to take on a resurgent Marattha rebellion.

However, even after Guru Gobind Singh's period, the followers of gurmat and other Indian expressions of religion maintained an ambiguous relationship. Certainly the creation of the Khalsa brotherhood provided Sikhs with an outward identity that was clearly distinct from those of Hindus and Muslims, but the opposition and estrangement from the Mughal authorities, it could be argued, also pushed Sikhs back to reaffirm their roots as being within the fold of ancient Indian worldviews.

The code of discipline proclaimed by Guru Gobind Singh forbade the eating of meat that had been slaughtered using the Muslim ritual and sexual intercourse with Muslim women. 'Muslim' was to become a powerful symbol of otherness, but paradoxically not all the Guru's followers were comfortable with Khalsa identity making a clean break from wider Indian culture and religion (Oberoi 1994: 68) The attempt to avoid contact with Muslims was accompanied by Guru Gobind Singh sending a number of his followers to study Hindu sacred texts in Vārāṇasī under brāhmaṇa guidance. It is also evident from the resistance of Sikhs in Delhi belonging to the brāhmaṇa and Khatri castes that acceptance of the Khalsa identity was not universal (Oberoi 1994: 62).

However, it is the content of Sikhism's second sacred text, the *Dasam Granth*, attributed to Guru Gobind Singh, that is most ambiguous concerning relations that Sikhs maintained with myths and cosmologies located in the *Purāṇas*. The text acknowledges the avatāras of Viṣṇu and the myths of the Goddess and appears to endorse the view that Guru Gobind Singh and Guru Nanak were avatāras. Contemporary Khalsa discourse largely ignores the existence of the *Dasam Granth* as its content provides embarrassing evidence of a single pool of hagiography and myth (Oberoi 1994: 97) rather than discrete worlds of Hindu and Sikh existing in the eighteenth century, exactly when many Sikhs argue that they were emerging as a unique religious and ethnic grouping.

At the same time as Khalsa Sikhs were creating separate rites of passage, religious rituals, unique dress codes, a distinct scriptural tradition and a separate sense of identity from both Islam and Hinduism, other Sikhs were keen to promote their continuity with an eternal revelation as manifested in the Hindu ideal of sanātana dharma (the eternal truth) (Oberoi 1994: 92). They argued that there were other ways of demonstrating Sikh identity than Khalsa allegiance. These categories of Sikh are often known as sahajdhārī and it is not surprising that they embraced the *Dasam Granth* as paradigmatic for their religious culture. When it came to defining identity, the solution was simply that a Sikh was anyone who accepted the teachings of Guru Nanak (1469–1539), the historic founder of Sikhism. Those who adhered to this position became known as Nanakpanthis (McLeod 1987: 243).

Nanak appears to have been brought up a Hindu, even though the stories of his early life indicate close contact with various Muslims who lived in the locality. However, it is said that he rejected the sacred thread ceremony when aged 10, and in his writings contained in the Guru Granth Sahib, Nanak criticises purity and pollution requirements, varṇāśramdharma and the efficacy of popular practices such as bathing, pilgrimage, mantra repetition and temple ritual as means for achieving liberation or union with the divine. In addition to his critique of popular practices and the role of brāhmaṇas, Guru Nanak was also equally suspicious of the practices of yogis and sādhus. However, it is important to note that Guru Nanak was equally critical of the formalism of Islam.

On emerging from the river Beas after his encounter with the divine, Nanak made his famous enigmatic utterance:

> There is no Hindu and no Mussulman so whose path should I follow? I shall follow God's path. God is neither Hindu nor Mussulman and the path which I follow is God's.
>
> (Singh 1979: 45)

However, Nanak's apparent critique of aspects of Indian religiosity and lack of Vedic underpinning to the teachings has not ruled out his appropriation by Hindus. For Brahmanical orthodoxy, it certainly means that his teachings, like those of the Buddha, are unorthodox (Nāstika) and place personal reasoning and experience above tradition. Yet there is a category of Indian religious life into which Nanak's life and teachings fit comfortably. Guru Nanak's poetry demonstrates a remarkable symmetry with a number of individuals, most notably Kabīr, who are exponents of a nirguṇa bhakti, flourished in medieval north India and have been grouped together and labelled as sants (McLeod 1968: 157; Cole and Sambhi 1995: 7).

Sant devotion insists that liberation is found within and is independent of the outer forms of religion. God is one all-pervading reality, essentially without form and discovered through intense one-pointed recollection of his name (satnām) existing as divine reality within all human beings. This path to union was achieved with the help of the company of like-minded seekers (satsaṅg) and the grace of the true teacher (satguru). Although critical of the outward forms of religiosity, the medieval sants are viewed as part of the diversity of the Hindu worldview, expressing a message in vernacular language that is more akin to the Upaniṣadic tradition than the worldview of the *Purāṇas*, Epics or the typical worship of countless devatās (minor deities). However, it should be noted that Khalsa Sikhs have never been happy with this association as it seems to undermine the distinctive revelation given to Guru Nanak and the independence of the Sikh faith (Cole and Sambhi 1995: 7).

Clearly, Khalsa has become the normative Sikh identity in the twentieth and twenty-first centuries, especially since the Indian army's assault on the Golden Temple complex in 1987 and the consequent assassination of Indira Gandhi, resulting in the Delhi riots, in which thousands of Sikhs were slaughtered by Hindus. The late twentieth century saw a polarisation and increasingly rigid compartmentalisation of both communities but there remain tens of thousands of Sikhs, especially in rural Punjab, who are indistinguishable from Hindus except for their own claim to be Sikhs. Their homes contain Hindu images, they acknowledge caste distinctions and observe purity and pollution rules, and place their Sikhism within the context of non-historical epic time gleaned from purāṇic legends and myths. They worship alongside others of nominal Hindu or Muslim allegiance, who are equally uncertain or careless of discrete religious boundaries, within popular rural Punjabi cultic milieux such as Baba Balaknath or Sakhi Sarvar (Oberoi 1994: 147ff.; Geaves 1998). In spite of the increasing Khalsa hegemony throughout the nineteenth and twentieth centuries, other forms of demonstrating Sikh identity remain much closer to the reality of what has come to be labelled as Hinduism and continue to challenge the dominant discourse of separate Sikh identity and cause discomfort to those who would like to maintain an unproblematic history of the development of a distinct Sikh identity. Hindus may regard Sikhism as part and parcel of Hindu dharma, but Sikhs, on the other hand, have never been completely clear about their own relationship with Hinduism, ranging from those who assert an aggressive position of separation, both politically and in regard to religious identity, to others who eclectically blend the two traditions and many who have not even considered that there is any differentiation to be blended.

The political arena in which Sikhs have lived as a small minority, although concentrated in the relatively small area of west Punjab, alongside a vastly numerically dominant Hindu population of independent India, has resulted in a struggle for identity. Since 1947 Sikhs have developed an increasing conviction that India is a Hindu country in which Sikh identity is threatened by absorption into Hinduism. The struggle for separate Sikh religious and political identity took place against a background of increasing communalism within all India's religious communities in the second half of the twentieth century, but the relationship between Hinduism and Sikhism has fluctuated dramatically from the origin of Sikh religious teachings with the birth of Guru Nanak (1469–1539) to the present time.

See also: **Arya Samaj; Āśram(a) (religious community); Āstika and Nāstika; Avatāras; Brāhmaṇa; Buddhism, relationship with Hinduism; Caste; Guru; Image worship; Kabīr; Mahādevī; Mandir; Mantra; Nationalism; Purāṇas; Sādhu; Sanātana Dharma; Sant; Sant Sādhana; Satsaṅg; Tīrthāyatra (Pilgrimage); Upanayana; Upaniṣads; Vārāṇasī; Varṇa; Veda; Viṣṇu; Yogi**

RON GEAVES

Further reading

Cole, W.O. and P.S. Sambhi. 1995. *The Sikhs: Their Religious Beliefs and Practices.* Brighton: Sussex Academic Press.

Dogra, R.C. and G.S. Mansukhani. 1996. *Encyclopaedia of Sikh Religion and Culture.* New Delhi: Vikas Publishing House.

Geaves, R.A. 1998. 'Baba Balaknath: An Exploration of Religious Identity'. *Diskus* 5.1.

McLeod, W.H. 1968. *Guru Nanak and the Sikh Religion.* London: Oxford University Press.

McLeod, W.H. 1987. 'The Development of the Sikh Panth'. In K. Schomer and W.H. McLeod, eds, *The Sants: Studies in a Devotional Tradition of India.* New Delhi: Motilal Banarsidass, 229–50.

Oberoi, H. 1994. *The Constructions of Religious Boundaries.* Chicago, IL: University of Chicago Press

Singh, G. 1979. *A History of the Sikh People.* New Delhi: Allied Publishers.

Tatla, D.S. 1999. *The Sikh Diaspora: The Search for Statehood.* London: UCL Press.

ŚIKṢĀ

The science of phonetics that ensures that the sacred recitation of the Veda that takes place in brahmanic ritual is correctly pronounced. The system of phonetics developed was sophisticated and included not only correct pronunciation but also the value of each letter, its accent and the proper method of articulation.

Śikṣā does not exist in isolation, but is part of an interwoven system of six disciplines known as the Vedāṅgas, or limbs of the Veda, that between them governed the performance of the Havan, the Vedic sacrifice. The other five are: Chaṇdas, which is closely linked to Śikṣā, as it deals with the use of the appropriate metre; Nirukta, or etymology, which seeks to ascertain the origins and meanings of the words used in the chants; Vyākaraṇa, the correct grammar; and, finally, Jyotiṣa and Kalpa, respectively astronomy and ceremony, which deal with finding the auspicious days for undertaking the sacrifice and the correct ritual actions.

The fact that four of the Vedāṅgas, including Śikṣā, deal with the language of the sacrifice indicates the significance given to the ritual words of the Veda and their import beyond that of interpretation. Pronunciation was particularly significant and many treatises exist on the subject. The words themselves carry power and recitation must be faultless, or the mantras, or Vedic hymns, may lose their impact to transform or bless.

See also: **Chaṇdas; Jyotiṣa; Kalpa; Mantra; Nirukta; Saṃhitā; Veda; Vedāṅgas; Vyākaraṇa; Yajña**

RON GEAVES

Further reading

Dowson, John. 1978. *A Classical Dictionary of Hindu Mythology*. London: Routledge & Kegan Paul.

ŚILPAŚĀSTRA(S)

'Craft manuals', a distinctive body of Sanskrit literature pertaining to the arts and crafts, give insights into the interface between theory and practice in the Indian arts. Compiled by various authors in different places and historical periods, they are regarded as anthologies of prescriptive rules. Since, however, there are discrepancies between the theory and the practice, the *śilpaśāstras* are to be seen, rather than as prescriptive texts, as the theoretical basis of artistic activity, which the craftsmen can interpret in different ways. The intention of this impressive literary output was probably to collect all possible information on image-making, painting and iconography to help future artists to achieve the same degree of excellence as those of the past. The authors, who had no practical knowledge of the arts, based their prescriptions on the observation of extant material, as well as on the experience of the craftsmen.

The *śilpaśāstras* generally contain a detailed section on the canon of proportions for fashioning images, and sections on painting, sculpture, the iconography of the various deities and other topics of interest such as observations on the physiognomy of men and women, on auspicious and inauspicious marks on persons, animals and objects, and much more.

Probably the earliest of these works is the *Nāṭya śāstra*, attributed to Bhārata (*c.* fourth century CE). Although mainly devoted to dance and music, it has many references to painting and sculpture and it is seminal to the understanding of the arts of India. The *Citralakṣaṇa* of Nagnajit, dated between the fourth and the fifth century CE, is one of the most relevant texts on painting, dealing principally with the correct proportions for the rendering of the image of the cakravartin and the origin of painting. The most famous among the early texts is the *Viṣṇudharmottara Purāṇa*; its date is still debated (*c.*450–650 CE). Among the numerous topics in this work, the section on painting, the citrasutra, is particularly renowned. Several chapters dealing with iconography appear in the *Agni Purāṇa* (eighth to ninth century), while the

Āgamas and the *Tantras* are particularly rich sources for the study of iconography.

Connected with the *śilpaśāstras* are the *Vastu śāstras*, treatises on architecture, which deal with town planning, building of temples and private mansions. Thus, the *Mayamata* (*c.* ninth to twelfth century CE) deals extensively with the selection of the site, the rituals before the beginning of the construction, the building materials and carefully describes various types of buildings. Some of the texts, for example the *Mānāsara* (*c.* tenth to twelfth century CE), also have sections on the fashioning of objects for the use of the ruler and courtiers.

Among the important works on architecture, arts and crafts are the *Samarāṅagana Sūtradhara* of King Bhoja of Dhara (eleventh century), Bhuvanadeva's *Aparājitapṛcchā* (*c.* twelfth century), which, although mainly focusing on architecture, has some chapters on painting; the *Mānasollasā* or *Abhilaṣitārtha Cintāmaṇi*, an encyclopaedic work containing chapters on painting and sculpture by Someśvaradeva, a king of the Western Chalukya (*c.* twelfth century); and the *Śilparatna*, by Śrīkumāra, king of Kerala, dated to the mid-sixteenth century.

See also: **Aesthetics; Dance; Images and iconography; Music; Purāṇas; Sacred texts; Tantras**

A.L. DALLAPICCOLA

Further reading

Dallapiccola, A.L. (ed.). 1989. *Shastric Tradition in the Indian Arts.* Stuttgart: Franz Steiner.

Goswamy, B.N and A.L. Dahmen-Dallapiccola. 1976. *An Early Document of Indian Art. The Citralaksana of Nagnajit.* New Delhi: Manohar.

SĪMANTONNAYANA

One of the Hindu pre-natal saṃskāras, or rites of passage, the sīmantonnayana, or 'parting of the hair (of a woman) upwards', occurs during the fourth or fifth month of pregnancy. This rite celebrated the pregnancy, as the wife was garlanded and generally feted. The ritual was, as usual, accompanied by a number of Vedic mantras. More ritually significant, however, this rite was expiatory and purificatory, warding off certain minor possessing demonesses (bālagrahas, or 'childsnatchers') that could inhabit the pregnant mother or the foetus. The wife is seated on a bull's hide or comfortable seat. Then the husband recites mantras and parts his wife's hair three times from front to back (hence 'upwards' first with a number of unripe fruits, next with a porcupine quill with three white spots, and finally with three braided strands of kuśa grass. Finally, the husband orders two lute players to praise King Soma.

See also: **Saṃskāra; Soma**

FREDERICK M. SMITH

Further reading

Kane, P.V. 1974. *History of Dharmaśāstra*, 2nd edn, vol. 2, pt 1. Poona: Bhandarkar Oriental Research Institute, 222–26.

Pandey, R.J. 1969. *Hindu Saṃskāras.* Delhi: Motilal Banarsidass, 64–69.

ŚIṢYA

A common term for 'student', the word śiṣya literally means 'one fit to be taught'. The word itself is often related to the system of ancient Indian education that involved a close personal relationship between the teacher (guru) and the student (śiṣya). The *Upaniṣads* generally seem to identify the śiṣya as a boy between the ages of 8 and 16 who, after being properly accepted as pupil, lived with his guru's family until his formal graduation. As reciprocity for the guru's imparting of knowledge and affection, the śiṣya was expected to express his devotion to the guru through constant willingness to serve and obey.

See also: **Guru; Upaniṣads**

DEVEN M. PATEL

Further reading

Sivananda, Swami. 1974. *Bliss Divine*. Rishikesh: Divine Life Society.

SĪTĀ

Sītā is Rāma's wife in the *Rāmāyaṇa* and from the start they are seen as models of conjugal fidelity, but she is not just the submissive wife. When she persuades him to let her accompany him into exile, she proclaims both her confidence in his ability to protect her and her duty to be with him. Their mutual affection tends to be more explicit in later elaborations, sometimes revealed incidentally but sometimes the focus of a whole episode, as when Sītā delivers her moral homily urging Rāma to lay aside his arms in the forest and adopt a non-violent lifestyle, and he responds by urging his duty as a kṣatriya to defend the weak (the hermits among whom they are living) against aggressors (the Rākṣasas). Again, she persuades him to indulge her desire for the golden deer, against his better judgement. But her devotion to Rāma prompts both her vigorous but erroneous denunciation of Lakṣmaṇa's motives, when he refuses to leave her after Rāma has pursued the golden deer, and her defiant and scornful rejection of Rāvaṇa's advances, both when he first approaches and throughout her captivity. While Sītā is captive, Hanumān reveals himself to her, establishing his identity by producing Rāma's ring, but she refuses to escape with him, wishing to be freed by Rāma in person, and she gives him a jewel as a token for Rāma.

Sītā is a more independent and rounded figure in Vālmīki's work than in later versions or in the popular view. Rāma's harsh rejection of her following Rāvaṇa's defeat was developed in response to growing emphasis on his moral elevation. For in the version now extant later qualms about Sītā's virtue cause Rāma to spurn her coldly, saying – for the first time – that he undertook the war simply to vindicate his family honour, not for her sake. In desperation, Sītā immolates herself on a pyre but Agni hands her back to Rāma, unharmed and exonerated. Sītā herself is now portrayed as more submissive, both here and when he later banishes her.

They live happily for a time but gossip about Sītā's virtue while a prisoner of Rāvaṇa compels Rāma reluctantly to order her exile to Vālmīki's hermitage. Vālmīki gives her sanctuary and she gives birth to her sons Kuśa and Lava. Subsequently, after Kuśa and Lava are recognised by their singing of the Rāma story, Sītā is recalled and publicly reaffirms her purity by calling on the Earth to swallow her; the Earth embraces Sītā and disappears with her; Rāma mourns her loss, using a golden statue of her as a substitute at sacrifices.

An important theological development found in the *Kūrma Purāṇa* is the illusory Sītā created by Agni when Sītā prays to him just before Rāvaṇa seizes her, taken by him to heaven and then restored to Rāma through the fire-ordeal: this development – safeguarding the real Sītā's purity – then recurs in the *Adhyātma Rāmāyaṇa*, Tulsīdās's *Rāmcaritmānas* and elsewhere. Sītā is worshipped jointly with Rāma by the Rāmānandis and some other groups.

See also: **Agni; Hanumān; Lakṣmaṇa; Pativratā and Patiparameśvara; Purāṇas; Rākṣasas; Rāma; Rāmānandis; Rāmāyaṇa; Rāvaṇa; Strīdharma; Tulsīdās(a); Vālmīki; Varṇa**

JOHN BROCKINGTON

Further reading

Brockington, John. 1985. *Righteous Rāma: The Evolution of an Epic*. Delhi: Oxford University Press.

Brockington, John. 1998. *The Sanskrit Epics* (Handbuch der Orientalistik 2.12). Leiden: Brill.

Brockington, John. 2000. 'The Names of Sītā'. In Greg Bailey and Mary Brockington, eds, *Epic Threads: John Brockington on the Sanskrit Epics*. New Delhi: Oxford University Press, 280–87.

Bulcke, Camille. 1952. 'La Naissance de Sītā' [Sītā's birth]. *Bulletin de l'École Française d'Extrême-Orient* 46: 107–17.

Dimmitt, Cornelia. 1982. 'Sītā: Fertility Goddess and *Śakti*'. In John Stratton Hawley and Donna Marie Wulff, eds, *Divine Consort: Rādhā and the Godesses of India*. Berkeley, CA: Graduate Theological Union; Delhi: Motilal Banarsidass, 210–23.

Doniger, Wendy. 1997. 'Sita and Helen, Ahalya and Alcmena: A Comparative Study'. *History of Religions* 37: 21–49.

Hiltebeitel, Alf. 1980–81. 'Sītā *Vibhūṣitā*: The Jewels for Her Journey'. *Indologica Taurinensia* 8–9: 193–200.

Narayana Rao, Velcheru. 2004. 'When Does Sītā Cease to be Sītā? Notes toward a Cultural Grammar of Indian Narratives'. In Mandakranta Bose, ed., *The Rāmāyaṇa Revisited*. New York: Oxford University Press, 219–41.

Pauwels, Heidi. 2004. '"Only You": The Wedding of Rāma and Sītā, Past and Present'. In Mandakranta Bose, ed.,*The Rāmāyaṇa Revisited*. New York: Oxford University Press, 165–218.

Singaravelu, S. 1982. 'Sītā's Birth and Parentage in the Rama Story'. *Asian Folklore Studies* 41.2: 235–43.

Sutherland, Sally J. 1989. 'Sītā and Draupadī: Aggressive Behaviour and Female Role Models in the Sanskrit Epics'. *Journal of the American Oriental Society* 109: 63–79.

Sutherland, Sally J. 1992. 'Seduction, Counter Seduction, and Sexual Role Models: Bedroom Politics and the Indian Epics'. *Journal of Indian Philosophy* 20: 243–51.

ŚĪTALĀ

The smallpox goddess of North and East India, also known as Olācandi and Olābibi, a Muslim name, used also by Hindu followers. (Her equivalent in South India is Māriammā). Although Śītalā manifests herself in the heat and pustules of smallpox, her name means 'Cool One' and she has to be pleased in worship by means of 'cooling' offerings of cold food and branches of the neem tree. Iconographically, she is shown riding a white donkey, with a broom in one hand (with which to scatter the water in the pot at her feet) and a winnowing fan on her head. She is accompanied by Jvarasur, the fever demon, and her serving woman, Rāktabāti, 'the Bloody One'. Tradition has it that Śītalā was born from the cooling embers of the sacrificial fire and was named by Brahmā. She came to earth, where she gained worshippers first among the lower castes, only winning over the king after killing vast numbers of his subjects with poisoned lentils.

Her popularity has withstood the eradication of smallpox, and her remit has widened to include other spotty diseases, such as measles. She is particularly worshipped in the hot pre-monsoon season, a time of great risk of epidemic disease, by women hoping to protect their children from illness. Asking for the protection of Śītalā is not incompatible with seeking the help of a doctor – they operate in different realms, both of which are powerful. Although she is traditionally seen as a rural 'folk' goddess, Śītalā's status is sometimes enhanced by being linked to Kālī, as at the Feringhee Temple in Calcutta, or by being seen as one of the saptamātṛkās, the seven sisters, as in the Belgachia district of Calcutta. At her urban temples, Śītalā is not seen as a fierce, disease-bringing goddess, but as a gentle, kind friend who gives general protection in the lives of her devotees.

See also: **Brahmā; Kālī and Caṇḍī; Māriammā; Saptamātṛkās**

CYNTHIA BRADLEY

Further reading

Egnor, M. 1984. 'The Changed Mother or What the Smallpox Goddess Did When

There Was No More Smallpox'. *Contributions to Asian Studies* XVIII: 24–45.
Mukhopadhyay, S.K. 1994. *Cult of the Goddess Sitala in Bengal: An Enquiry into Folk Culture.* Calcutta: Firma KLM Private.
Wadley, S. 1980. 'Sitala: The Cool One'. *Asian Folklore Studies*: 39.1: 33–62.

ŚIVA

Similar to Viṣṇu and Devi (Mahādevi) in her various forms, Śiva (literally, 'the auspicious one') is for many Hindus the Supreme Lord (mahādeva or maheśvara), responsible for the creation, preservation and destruction of the universe. For others Śiva is understood as the third aspect of the three-personed God (trimūrti) that renders Brahmā responsible for creation, Viṣṇu for the task of preservation and Śiva as the cosmic destroyer. Some schools of thought consider Śiva to be the formless absolute reality whose nature is pure consciousness, perhaps analogous to the Brahman principle of the *Upaniṣads* itself. Envisioned as the greatest of meditators (yogīn/yogi), the supreme dancer (naṭarāja) and, among other forms, the Lord of creatures (paśupati) in the *Purāṇa* literature, Śiva has rich and complex iconic and aniconic representations in the popular Hindu imagination to match the complexity of this godhead. Standard iconography of Lord Śiva portrays him as a yogī meditating in utter solitude on Mount Kailāsa, his favourite abode. With long, matted hair, he is either naked or wearing animal skins, his body is covered in ashes and adorned with snakes. In the locks of his hair rests a crescent moon and through his hair flows the river Gaṅgā. He has a third eye on his forehead and his blue-black throat is often garlanded with snakes and sacred beads known as 'the eyes of Rudra' (rudrāska). While meditating, he is often shown seated on a tiger skin. Nearby lies his special weapon, the three-pronged spear (triśūla), and mendicant's bowl. For devotees, each of these features of Lord Śiva holds special symbolic significance that is often tied up with various stories told about Śiva in the epics. When artists render the aspect of Lord Śiva as a family man, he is often visualised in domestic scenes with his wife, the goddess Pārvatī, and his two sons Kārttikeya (often alternatively referred to as Skanda or Murukaṉ) and Gaṇeśa (or, often, Gaṇapati). Also near him is pictured his vehicle, devotee and bodyguard, the bull Nandi.

A very famous representation of Śiva, originally popularised by the influential Śaiva Siddhānta (or Śuddha Śaiva) schools of orthodox Śiva devotionalism, depicts him as Naṭarāja, lord of the dance. In this form of cosmic dancer, encircled by a ring of flames, Lord Śiva has four arms and is shown to dance ecstatically with his left leg raised and crossing his lower body, while the foot of the other leg crushes a dwarf symbolising destructive negligence (apasmāra). In one hand he holds a drum (damaru) that when shaken emanates the creative energy of the universe; in another hand he balances a plate of fire, symbolic of cosmic destruction (sambhāva) and inner purification; another hand strikes a pose of fearlessness and protection (abhaya-mudrā) for those who take refuge in him; one hand points towards the feet in the 'elephant gesture' (gaja-mudrā), signalling for devotees to humbly seek the grace (prasāda) of the spiritual teacher (guru). The face of Śiva, in this and practically every other representation, remains immutably placid in the midst of his dynamic activity.

Śiva's fierce aspect emerges in his role of dispensing punishment to the wicked. A popular early story of Śiva, depicted in countless representations, but perhaps most famously in the cave sculptures at Elephanta, concerns his punishment of his own demonic son Andhaka. Miraculously produced from a drop of sweat of Śiva, Andhaka is born blind and inauspicious, and is thus given away in adoption to demons (asuras). The rejected offspring grows and eventually becomes powerful through the practice of intense austerities, seeking to dominate the world, oppress the gods and obtain all pleasures. Not knowing his parents, he lusts after his mother, Pārvatī, Śiva's consort, a crime for which Śiva chastises and confronts him. After a long and bloody battle in which all the gods and demons take part, Śiva kills Andhaka by impaling him on his trident and holding him aloft – the dramatic iconic representation of this episode. Andhaka is later resuscitated and becomes a devout follower of Śiva, adopting the name Bhṛṅgi.

When Lord Śiva is represented aniconically, it is most often in the extremely popular form known as liṅga, literally meaning 'mark' or 'characteristic', but also suggesting a phallic dimension, perhaps connected with Śiva's procreative associations. Some hold that the liṅga placed within a circular base representing the female generative organ (yoni) is a symbolic union of Śiva with the creative energy of the universe (śakti), imagined as feminine. In some representations, four or five faces of Śiva emerge from the liṅga. Important sites where Śiva is believed to actually manifest in the world (for example, as Viśvanātha at Vārāṇasī or as Mahākālśvara at Ujjayinī) are centred around the Śiva liṅga envisioned as a column of radiant light (jyotir-liṅga).

The story of the primordial jyotirliṅga is told in many *Purāṇas*. Brahmā and Viṣṇu are vainly arguing about which of the two is greater, and amidst their dispute a dazzling, awe-inspiring column of light (jyotirliṅga) appears before them. Brahmā assumes the form of a swan and flies upwards, seeking the upper limit, while Viṣṇu assumes his boar form and burrows through the ground, in search of its root – both exhaust themselves and admit that this mysterious entity is greater than both. Śiva then reveals himself and explains that this is his divine liṅga form, and the two rivals sing inspired praises of his absolute supremacy.

The phallic aspect of the liṅga is confirmed by at least one common story which also purports to explain the origin of liṅga worship. Once, Śiva was wandering through the forest as a naked ascetic and came upon a hermitage where a group of great sages were performing sacrifices. The sight of the naked Śiva disturbed the minds of the sages' wives, who immediately were overcome by lust and began to follow the mendicant around as he wandered. For this offence, the sages cursed Śiva so that his phallus would drop to the ground. When it did, however, it grew to an immense size and pierced the very earth, penetrating deep into the subterranean realms and causing the entire universe to tremble. Śiva, finally revealing himself as the supreme deity, curses the sages for their impertinence, forgiving them only on the condition that he be worshipped by them, and by all beings, in his phallic form – that of the liṅga.

The various representations of Lord Śiva tend to underscore the primary qualities of the divinity: on the one hand, Śiva is a celibate yogī who dwells aloof from human society, ever absorbed in meditation; on the other hand, he exhibits a powerful erotic energy that is potentially destructive and dangerous. In sharp contrast with his rival Viṣṇu, who is consistently imagined as protective and beneficial, and embodying qualities consistent with orthodox norms, Śiva's identity is inherently paradoxical. He is both peaceful and wildly destructive, ascetic and erotic, a warrior and world-renouncer, the supreme divinity and yet shunned by all other gods. As Rudra (also see below) he is the ultimate hunter, and yet is also praised as the protector of all animals (paśupati). Furthermore, as the supreme embodiment of knowledge, Śiva is also identified as the great guru of the universe, and all teachers in the world are said to bear a spark of Lord Śiva.

One important question that traditional and modern scholars have sought to trace is the extent to which the great Lord Śiva of the epics, ancient lore (*Purāṇa*) and other literature of the classical Hindu tradition can be identified with the Vedic divinity Rudra ('the Howler'). Rudra is prayed to in several hymns partially or fully dedicated to him in the *Ṛgveda* (1.43, 1.114 and 2.33). In these, Rudra is characterised as a fierce (ugra) and powerful warrior god, energetic, with strong limbs and bearing weapons. He is a hunter who howls and possesses sharp and dangerous weapons. The *Ṛgveda* descriptions do not offer much detail beyond these, except that he is also described as having braided or matted hair (kapardin) and being of ruddy or tawny colour. Rudra is also famously invoked in the *Taittirīya Saṃhitā* of the *Kṛṣṇa-Yajurveda* and the *Vājasaneyi Saṃhitā* of the *Śukla-yajurveda*, in a section known to both as the *Śatarudrīya* ('The Hundred Epithets of Rudra'), an extended invocation of Rudra which many later Śaiva traditions hold in high esteem. Here Rudra is described with a number of epithets that become prominent later in classical religious understandings as Rudra-Śiva. He is praised, for example as the 'lord of animals' (paśupati), the 'mountain-dweller' (giriśa), 'the peaceful' (śambhu; saṅkara) and 'blue-throated' (nīlakaṇṭha), among other appellations. All of these epithets become extremely common in the classical Śaiva religious traditions, and many develop specific mythological associations as well. In general, Rudra is worshipped as a fierce god responsible for storms, famine, disease and natural disasters; he is propitiated primarily to calm his violent, destructive nature and to show instead his 'compassionate face' (dakṣiṇaṃ mukham), which grants favours and offers protection from all these dangers. Although Rudra is infrequently described with the epithet śiva in these early Vedic texts, explicit identification of Rudra and Śiva seems to first occur in the *Śvetāśvatara Upaniṣad* (sixth century BCE?), apparently the first textual source in which Rudra and Śiva occur as alternative names of a single being.

Rudra is held apart from the other gods of the Vedic pantheon, and the classical Rudra-Śiva retains this feature. Rudra is described as being excluded from partaking of the sacrificial offerings, instead demanding the unclean leftovers (ucciṣṭha) of the other gods' shares. When the gods attained heaven, Rudra remained behind. Even in the classical traditions Śiva represents – in sharp contrast to Viṣṇu and his avatāras – extra-Vedic, heterodox and even antinomian elements. If Viṣṇu takes on the qualities of benevolence, orthodoxy and 'preservation' (sthiti) of the world, Śiva embodies more disruptive forces, and his relationship with the pantheon of Hindu deities is more complex and contested.

Illustrative of this is one of the most frequently cited Śiva stories, having variants in the *Mahābhārata* and in various *Purāṇas*; it concerns the emergence – or rather the intrusion – of Śiva into the pantheon of Vedic gods through his destruction of the sacrifice of the Vedic seer Dakṣa. Satī (later reborn as Pārvatī), the daughter of the Dakṣa, weds Śiva against the will of her father, who apparently bristles at the unorthodox and erratic behaviour of Śiva – wearing no clothes, besmearing his body with ashes and consorting with unsavoury and frightful characters (Śiva's gaṇas; see below). When Dakṣa performs a Vedic fire-sacrifice (yajña), he purposely does not invite Śiva. While Śiva himself is characteristically unperturbed by this slight, Satī is deeply insulted by her father's insolence and immolates herself through her yogic power. Suddenly stricken with grief and rage, Śiva attacks the sacrifice in a frightening form called Vīrabhadra, physically assaults the invited Vedic gods and, finally, dramatically beheads Dakṣa himself. Śiva eventually resurrects Dakṣa through his power, and then becomes a permanent recipient of shares of Vedic sacrifices, thus establishing himself as a deity not only equal to the more orthodox or accepted Vedic deities, but actually superior in power to all of them, and supreme. This story seems to demonstrate the process by which a deity once peripheral to Vedic religious tradition makes an entry into it and becomes the focus of devotional cults. But even if other deities have extra-Vedic origins or influences, few retain such associations as dramatically as does Śiva.

Many other stories glorifying Śiva occur in the *Mahābhārata*, *Rāmāyaṇa* or one of the several *Purāṇas* dedicated to Śiva, such as the *Liṅga Purāṇa* and the *Śiva Purāṇa*. Some of the other important myths that highlight Śiva's nature as the supreme divinity include his drinking of the poison (halāhala) produced from the primal churning of the ocean, in order to save humanity from destruction. He keeps the poison in his throat so as not to destroy the three worlds which are said to reside in his belly. For his trouble, Śiva's throat is darkened and he is thereby called 'the blue-throated one' (nīlakaṇṭha) by his devotees. He also famously incinerates Kāmadeva, the god of love, when the latter attempts to break Śiva's sexual continence so that he may accept Pārvatī as his wife and thereby produce a child to defeat the demon Tāraka. He eventually does accede to the marital entreaties of the goddess Pārvatī, but not before rendering the god of love 'bodiless' (anaṅga) for his indiscretion by burning him to ashes with a wrathful glance from his, Śiva's, third eye. Śiva is also responsible for destroying the divinely created and otherwise impregnable triple-city (tripura) of the demons with a single flaming arrow, and thus acquires the epithet of 'Destroyer of the Triple City' (tripurāntaka).

Even beyond the Dakṣa myth and his general unrefined characteristics there is much about Śiva that is unorthodox. As the great yogī, he is a model for extreme forms of asceticism, and indeed it is certain that several ascetic/yogic traditions, in particular those which would become amalgamated to form the influential Pāśupata sect, were responsible for the early rise of the Śiva cult. His association with snakes perhaps ties Śiva to the cults of nāga worship prevalent in ancient Indian popular praxis but peripheral to mainstream brahmanical Hinduism. Even more prominently than this, Śiva is imagined as consorting with a retinue of outlandish beings known as his gaṇas ('hordes'). They are frequently described in colourful terms: possessing deformed bodies and faces or with animal heads; as voracious eaters of flesh, characterised by brutish conduct and a general lack of civilised refinement. It is also apparent that there is a measure of ethnic 'othering' in these descriptions: traditional characterisations of the gaṇas can be said to be exaggerated representations of ethnic others, and the devotional or totemic objects of worship, which are incorporated as subordinates to the Great God in the Śaiva universe.

In a related vein, Śiva is further associated with other elements or even inimical to orthodox brahmanical caste society. In one story, Śiva punishes Brahmā for lusting after his daughter by cutting off the fifth head of the latter (who is universally imagined as catarmukha, or four-headed) with the nail of his left thumb, and the sin arising from that most heinous crime of murdering a brāhmaṇa makes the head attach to his hand. Śiva must wander around thousands of years as a skull-bearer (kapālin) until his sin is expiated. This is the prototype for skull-bearing Śaiva ascetics, who are enjoined to undertake the macabre practice of using a human skull as a begging bowl, and shows the inherent tension between the ascetic Śaiva traditions and brahmanical orthodoxy, epitomised by Brahmā, the prototypical brāhmaṇa. Śiva is also said to be the bhūta-nātha, lord of departed spirits, cementing his ties to cults of death and spirit possession.

These more extreme forms of unorthodox associations relate to the character of Bhairava, often considered to be a particularly fierce aspect of Śiva, but sometimes imagined as an independent deity – or sometimes a general class of deities – though with strong Śaiva associations. Bhairava is considered a Tantric deity and is specifically connected with death and the iconography of the cremation ground. As such he is often propitiated with blood sacrifice, alcohol and ritual sex, and usually depicted with a sword and a wild dog as a vehicle. Bhairava thus represents the most extreme, unorthodox and transgressive aspects of Śiva and exists on the fringes of mainstream, orthodox Śaivism.

Despite these fierce and unorthodox characteristics, much of Śiva worship has sought to emphasise his benevolent and normative aspects. The Śaiva Siddhānta traditions, for example, although having historical origins in extreme ascetic and Tantric traditions of Bhairava worship, came to be centred upon the worship of benevolent forms of Śiva, such as the eternally placid Sadāśiva principle, and the youthful, silent guru Dakṣiṇāmūrti. Such forms of Śaiva theology and practice were perhaps more amenable to the emergence of state-sponsored religious organisation, featuring elaborate temple worship and systematic guidelines for priestly and lay conduct.

See also: **Agnihotra; Asuras; Avatāra; Brahmā; Brahman; Brāhmaṇa; Brahmanism; Caste; Dakṣa; Gaṇeśa; Gaṅgā; Guru; Image worship; Images and iconography; Itihāsa; Kāpālīkas; Mahābhārata; Mahādevi; Mandir; Nāgas; Nandi; Pañcamakāra; Pārvatī; Pāśupatas; Possession; Purāṇas; Rāmāyaṇa; Rudra; Śaiva Siddhānta; Śakti; Saṃhitā; Sati; Skanda; Tantrism; Trimūrti; Ujjayinī; Upaniṣads; Vāhanas; Vārāṇasī; Vedic pantheon; Viṣṇu; Yajña; Yoga; Yogi**

TRAVIS L. SMITH

Further reading

Gonda, J. 1970. *Viṣṇuism and Śaivism: A Comparison*. London: Athlone Press.
Kramrisch, S. 1981. *The Presence of Śiva*. Princeton, NJ: Princeton University Press.
O'Flaherty, W. 1981. *Śiva: The Erotic Ascetic*. New York: Oxford University Press.

ŚIVA PURĀṆA

See: **Purāṇas**

SIVANANDA YOGA

See: **Vishnudevananda and Sivananda Yoga**

ŚIVARĀTRI

Śivarātri may be observed on the fourteenth day of any waning lunar fortnight (caturdaśi) by devotees who keep a fast and have darśana, 'visual audience', at a local Śaiva temple. However, on the fourteenth day of the dark half of Phālgun (February–March), the final month of many Hindu calendars, the pan-Indian festival known as Mahāśivarātri, or the 'great night of Śiva', is celebrated. Mahāśivarātri is particularly important in major Śaiva centres such as Banāras, or Vārāṇasī, where devotees visit the Kāśī Viśvanātha temple to receive darśana of the jyotirliṅga, 'liṅga of light', which is understood to be a manifestation of Śiva in the form of a luminous pillar. While almost all other Hindu festivals are observed in the daytime, the celebration of Mahāśivarātri at night commemorates

Śiva's appearance on the cusp of the Kali Yuga, the 'age of folly', and appeals for his protection in dark times. Ritual practices associated with Śivarātri include: having darśana at a local temple; keeping a fast and all-night vigil; and making offerings such as leaves of the bilva tree, milk and water to a śivaliṅga, the aniconic and ithyphallic representation of the deity. Some devotees also commemorate Śiva's predilection for a mild intoxicant prepared from the hemp plant, known as bhāṅg. Small balls of this substance are offered to Śiva, and are then consumed as the festival's special prasāda, or 'substantiated grace'. Married women may celebrate the wedding of Śiva and Pārvatī on Mahāśātri by keeping a fast and venerating a śivaliṅga in order to ensure the well-being of their spouses, while unmarried girls may also perform a special pūjā, 'devotional rite', with thoughts turned to their future bridegroom.

See also: **Calendar; Darśana; Pūjā; Śaivism; Yuga**

ANDREA MARION PINKNEY

Further reading

Babb, L.A. 1975. *The Divine Hierarchy: Popular Hinduism in Central India.* New York: Columbia University Press.

SIX CATEGORIES

See: **Padārthas**

SKANDA

Skanda is first mentioned in the Saṃhitās, where he appears as the god of war, and cults that worshipped him appear as early as the second century BCE. However, as a seventh-century bas-relief in Mammalipuram on the South East Tamil Nadu coast demonstrates, he is absorbed into Śaivism, where he appears as the elder of Śiva's two sons sitting on the god's knee alongside Gaṇeśa. Also known as Kārttikeya, his birth and exploits are recounted in the Purāṇic texts, especially the *Skanda Purāṇa*, where he is definitely established within the framework of Śiva and Pārvatī mythology. The *Śiva Purāṇa* contains a complete section describing Skanda's birth, as a result of Śiva's disturbance from meditation by the gods, who wished the god of war to be born in order to defeat a powerful demon. Śiva is sexually attracted to his consort Pārvatī; however, the semen is said to have taken a circuitous route to her womb via Agni and Gaṅgā (Chitgopekar 1998: 77). Thus Skanda is known as the son of Śiva, Agni and Gaṅgā. In the *Śiva Purāṇa*, he is described as a 'boy of beautiful and tender limbs, a model for all boys' (Chitgopekar 1998: 78), and he is usually depicted as a renunciate child-warrior whose vehicle is a peacock. However, the Kārttikeya variation often depicts him as multi-headed.

Although never achieving the popularity of Gaṇeśa, a number of local cults have flourished, often associated with possession, with their own distinctive mythologies and ritual practices; these in turn have been universalised through the process of Sanskritisation (Geaves 1999: 43–47). Thus Skanda is known by a number of names in the different regions of India, the most common being Kartek and Baba Balaknath in the Punjab and Balnath in Gujarat. Historically, he has also been known as Mahāsena, Kumāra, Gūha, Viśākha and Ṣavadana (Geaves 1999: 45). However, the most significant manifestation of Skanda has to be Murukaṉ, the pre-eminent god of the Tamils. Although pre-dating the Aryan gods, Murukaṉ is depicted in the child-form of the son of Śiva, the god of war, and his vehicle is the blue-feathered peacock associated with all the forms of Skanda.

See also: **Agni; Gaṇeśa; Gaṅga; Murukaṉ; Pārvatī; Purāṇas; Śaivism; Śiva**

RON GEAVES

Further reading

Chitgopekar, N. 1998. *Encountering Śivaism*. New Delhi: Munshiram Manoharlal.

Geaves, R.A. 1999. 'The Authentication of a Punjabi Regional Folk Cult'. *Scottish Journal of Religious Studies* 20(1): 37–50.

SKANDA PURĀṆA

See: **Purāṇas**

SKANDA ṢAṢṬI

A seven-day temple festival occurring in October–November. This is a popular South Indian festival more accurately associated with Murukaṉ or Subramanya, and demonstrates the common belief that those two deities are perceived as forms of Skanda, especially in the Tamil-speaking regions of India. The seven days of the festival correspond to the key events in the mythical life of the deity, believed to be the elder son of Śiva, and mark his birth, maturation, his defeat of evil forces personified as demons and his marriage to his two consorts, Devasenā and Vallī (Jackson 1986: 138). In this respect, the South Indian forms of Skanda vary from the Northern manifestations, where Skanda is generally regarded as a brahmacārya.

The festival ritually reproduces bringing the god into existence, including dressing and ornamentation. On the seventh day he is ritually married to his consorts and then processed through the streets. The procession is one of the highlights of the Tamil calendar and demonstrates both the strength of Murukaṉ/Subramanya popular devotion and the close association of the deity with expressions of Tamil cultural identity (Jackson 1986: 138).

See also: **Brahmacārya; Murukaṉ; Śiva; Skanda; Subramanya**

RON GEAVES

Further reading

Jackson, R. 1986. 'Hindu Festivals'. In *Festivals in World Religions*. Produced by SHAP Working Party. London: Longman, 104–39.

SMART, RODERICK NINIAN (1927–2001)

British philosopher and phenomenologist of religion, born in Cambridge and educated in Glasgow, where his father was Regius Professor of Astronomy. From 1945 to 1948 Smart was in the Intelligence Corps of the British Army, during which time he learnt Chinese and spent a year in Sri Lanka. He then studied Classics and Philosophy at Oxford; he held appointments in Philosophy at University College Wales, Yale, London and (briefly) Banaras Hindu University before becoming Professor of Theology at Birmingham University in 1961. In 1967 he was appointed Professor in the Department of Religious Studies at Lancaster University, the first to be established in the United Kingdom. From 1976 he held concurrently professorships at Lancaster and the University of California, Santa Barbara. In *Doctrine and Argument in Indian Philosophy* Smart sought to give an account of the major Indian philosophical thinkers and traditions which understood their philosophy as related to their religious practices and the experiences associated with them. His method was a reaction and challenge to contemporary trends in Western analytic philosophy, which Smart found lacking in concern for context and overly Eurocentric. A 1965 essay for the *Listener*, a magazine with a broad readership, entitled 'The Unknown Hinduism of Christianity', characteristically reversed the interpretive thrust of Western models for understanding Hinduism, in this case Raimundo Pannikar's *The Unknown Christ of Hinduism* (1964). The emphasis on holistic understanding of a tradition anticipates his later elaboration of a model for understanding different religions and worldviews through their several dimensions, which, though intimately related in practice, may be distinguished in analysis. Smart's work was notable for his concern and capacity for a broad dissemination of the results of scholarly work on Hinduism and other religions and worldviews, through textbooks (Smart 1973, 1978, 1989), encyclopedia articles and a television series, *The Long Search*. In his role as founding co-chair, and later president, of the Shap Working Party on World Religions in Education, Smart was influential in shaping the teaching of Hinduism in schools.

See also: **Hinduism, history of scholarship; Religious education**

WILL SWEETMAN

Further reading

Religion. 2001. 31/4: 317–86 (special issue on Smart's life).

Smart, N. 1964. *Doctrine and Argument in Indian Philosophy*. London: Allen & Unwin. (2nd rev. edn, Leiden: Brill, 1993).

Smart, N. 1973. *The Phenomenon of Religion*. London: Macmillan.

Smart, N. 1978. 'The Making of Early Hinduism', 'Classical Hindu Philosophy' and 'Hindu Patterns of Liberation'. *Man's Religious Quest*. Milton Keynes: Open University Press.

Smart, N. 1989. *The World's Religions*. Cambridge: Cambridge University Press.

Wiebe, D. and P. Masefield (eds). 1994. *Aspects of Religion: Essays in Honour of Ninian Smart*. New York: Peter Lang.

SMĀRTA

The word smārta means 'belonging to smṛti', sometimes opposed to śrauta, 'belonging to śruti'. It applies to practices authorised by texts such as the *Kalpasūtras* and *Dharmaśāstras* (including the dharma passages of the *Mahābhārata*) and the *Purāṇas*. The *Dharmasūtra*s and *Gṛhyasūtra*s are grouped together as *Smārtasūtra*s (Renou 1963: 168). Typical smārta practices include the use of Vedic mantras, especially the Gāyatrī deities grouped in one shrine, the pañcāyatana: Śiva, Viṣṇu, Devī, Sūrya, Gaṇeśa (Hopkins 1971: 119–21; Pathak 1987). Such practices are largely confined to brāhmaṇas, and in South India, especially Tamil Nadu, smārta brāhmaṇas are a distinct group, associated with Śiva worship and the authority of the Śankarācāryas.

Smārta is often translated as 'orthodox', but this implies that other practices or persons are heterodox, whereas if Hinduism has orthodoxy at all, it has many orthodoxies.

See also: **Brāhmaṇas; Devī; Dharma; Dharmaśāstras; Dharmasūtras; Gaṇeśa; Gāyatrī; Gṛhyasūtras; Kalpasūtras; Languages; Mahābhārata; Mantra; Purāṇas; Sacred texts; Śaṅkarācārya; Śiva; Sūrya; Viṣṇu**

DERMOT KILLINGLEY

Further reading

Gonda, J. 1980. *Vedic Ritual*. Leiden: Brill.

Hopkins, Thomas J. 1971. *The Hindu Religious Tradition*. Encino, CA: Dickenson.

Kane, Pandurang Vaman. 1968–77. *History of Dharmaśāstra (Ancient and Mediaeval Religious and Civil Law)*, 2nd edn, 5 vols (vols 1, 2 and 5 bound in two parts each). Poona [Pune]: Bhandarkar Oriental Research Institute (1st edn 1930–62).

Pathak, Vishwambar Sharma. 1987. *Smārta Religious Tradition*. Meerut: Kusumanjali Prakashan.

Renou, Louis. 1963. 'Sur le Genre du sūtra dans la littérature sanskrite' ['On the sūtra genre in Sanskrit literature']. *Journal Asiatique* 151: 165–216.

SMṚTI

See: **Sacred texts**

SNĀNA YĀTRĀ

Snāna Yātrā is one of the twelve yātrās or outdoor festivals celebrated in honour of

Jagannātha, an Oriya regional icon of Kṛṣṇa in Puri. This festival includes the ceremonial public bathing of the three images of Jagannātha and his divine siblings Baladeva (Balarāma) and Subhadrā by the priests of the temple. Legends say that this day commemorates the actual installation day of these ancient images and is considered to be the birthday of Jagannātha. It takes place between June and July according to the local lunar calendar.

This festival continues to the next outdoor festival, the chariot festival or Ratha Yātrā. Between these two yātrās, Jagannātha is said take rest for a fortnight, since he gets high fever from the public bath. The temple remains closed to all pilgrims for a fortnight and the priests utilise this time to repair and paint the wooden images for the next festival.

See also: **Balarāma; Jagannātha; Kṛṣṇa; Mandir; Ratha Yātrā; Tīrthayātrā (Pilgrimage); Utsava**

ABHISHEK GHOSH

Further reading

Eschmann A., H. Kulke and G.C. Tripathy (eds). 1978. *The Cult of Jagannath and the Regional Tradition of Orissa*. Bonn: German Research Council.

Tripathy, Gaya Charan. 2004. *Communication with God.* New Delhi: Aryan Books.

SOAMIJI MAHARAJ

The name given by his devotees to Shiv Dayal Singh, the founder of the Radhasoami movements, who is also known under the more formal titular epithet of Param Purush Puran Dhani Radhasoami. Born in Agra in 1818, he is believed to have shown remarkable spiritual competency from the age of 5. His parents and other close relatives were devotees of Tulsi Sahib, the eighteenth-century reviver of the Sant Mat tradition. Followers of the Satsang Beas branch of Radhasoami believe Soamiji Maharaj first received initiation into the secrets of Surat Shabd Yoga from Tulsi Sahib, whilst the Soami Bagh and Dayal Bagh branches claim that he was born fully enlightened and did not require a guru.

Certainly, all Radhasoamis believe Soamiji Maharaj to be the Sant Satguru of the era, even the incarnation of the Supreme Being, known as Radhasoami, which also refers to the Name of God conceived as the anahat shabd or 'sound current'. Following the death of Soamiji Maharaj in 1878, the movement split into various branches, most of which resulted from divisions over the Satguru's successor.

See also: **Guru; Radhasoami Satsang**

RON GEAVES

Further reading

Juergensmeyer, M. 1991. *Radhasoami Reality.* Princeton, NJ: Princeton University Press.

www.radhasoami-faith.in (accessed 29 October 2005).

SOCIAL EVILS

See: **Woman question**

SOMA

'Pressed juice'; later 'moon'. Personification of the central intoxicant of the Vedic yajña ritual – producing amṛta, the draught of immortality for the gods; curative medicine for mortals. In the *Ṛgveda* an entire maṇḍala (the ninth) is dedicated to Soma. He is especially linked with Indra, the champion-god, and in *Ṛgveda* 9.85.3 he is recognised as Indra's soul. Both Indra and Viṣṇu are known as madapatī ('lords of intoxication') whose consumption of soma is essential for their destruction of Vṛtra (6.69.3). *Ṛgveda* 9.38.5 acknowledges Soma as a child of Dyaus. The myth of Soma's being brought to earth by an eagle appears to be an ancient Indo-European derivative. In time, Soma became increasingly identified as the moon. As such, he is the first husband of Sūryā (*Ṛgveda* 10.85.40). Soma is named today as the Lokapāla of the north-east.

See also: **Dyaus Pitṛ; Indra; Lokapāla; Vedic Pantheon; Vedism; Viṣṇu; Yajña**

MICHAEL YORK

SOMADEVABHAṬṬA

A Kashmiri priest and the author or compiler of an eleventh-century collection of over 350 stories, fables and anecdotes known as the *Kathāsaritsāgara* (Ocean of the Streams of Stories), originally translated into English by C.H. Tawney and published by the Asiatic Society of Bengal. Written in Sanskrit, the work is purported to have been ordered by Queen Sūryamatī, the wife of the king of Kashmir. With similarities to the *Arabian Nights*, it is divided into 124 chapters and highly influenced by the Buddhist Jataka tales. There are several stories that describe violent orgies performed on behalf of Durgā. It also contains 'Twenty-Five Tales of a Vampire' (*Vetālapañcaviṃśati*), which describes how a king is hoodwinked twenty-five times by a storytelling demon who tricks him into answering a question whilst absorbed in the tales. As a result the king has to return again and again to a cemetery from whence he has been commanded by an ascetic to bring down a corpse hanging in a tree. To visit a graveyard carries dangers of ritual defilement and psychic risks from the Tantric rites carried out there. The collection of tales clearly draws upon local Kashmiri Tantric and Śākta influences, as well as Buddhist and Muslim popular genres of storytelling.

See also: **Asiatic Societies; Buddhism, relationship with Hinduism; Durgā; Śākta; Tantrism**

RON GEAVES

Further reading

Kapoor, Subodh. (ed.). 2000. *The Hindus: Encyclopaedia of Hinduism*, vol. 4. New Delhi: Cosmo Publications.

SOUND RECORDINGS

In Hindu belief, sound itself is said to be imbued with divine properties and the correct tonal chanting of mantras or verses is central to Hindu ritual. These chanting tones are thought to have given rise to a whole system of music which rests on hundreds of melodic structures known as rāga(s). Vocal music is considered the highest form of music in India and even instruments are graded according to their ability to ape the many nuances of the human voice. Even in non-religious performances of classical song, whether dhrupad (pure, austere style) or khyāl (a more ornate and imaginative style), the song texts are usually religious. But where devotional music is concerned, vocal music really comes into its own, not only because it is performed by a human voice but also because it is the only kind of music in which the praises of God can be verbalised.

While verses from the scriptures, especially those from the *Bhagavadgītā* and the *Upaniṣads*, are also sung in prescribed tunes for ritual worship, they do not evoke as intense an emotional response from listeners as do the bhajans (poetic hymns) of the bhakti movement.

In the South Asian bhakti tradition, song is the prime ritual of divine worship. In performing it, the singer feels a spiritual oneness with the Divine, establishing a direct and personal connection with God. Listeners, for their part, tune into the performer's feeling and can reach heightened levels of spiritual awareness.

Given the importance of song and of the vocalised glorification of God within the tradition of devotional religion, it is not at all surprising to find that the Indian bhakti movement was spread by poet-singers rather than theoreticians. Their verses, memorised and sung at first in the streets, rather than in the temples, were nearly always in the local spoken dialects as opposed to the literary Sanskrit of the scriptures. Bhakti was a tradition based on loving devotion to God, implying a deeply personal relationship between Creator and created, incorporating two concepts within the general idea of bhakti: to love and to serve.

The recital of bhajans (Hindu devotional hymns) has a dual function: to literally sing the praises of God and also to serve, or to please the Divinity by making music. The bhajan hence becomes an offering to God.

There are, literally, thousands of bhajans – including those composed for Bollywood films – but the same favourites get recorded and performed again and again. Bhajans can be about a number of deities – whether in praise of Hanumān or Gaṇeśa, but those pertaining to Kṛṣṇa (and his consort Rādhā) are among the most popular, with the lyrics usually being recited in the persona of the ever-pining Rādhā, who epitomises the concept of virāha (separation from the Beloved).

Among household names for bhajans, by far the most popular are those of mystic poet-saints like Kabīr (1440–1518), Sūrdās (1483–1563), Tulsīdās (1532–1623) and, especially, Mīrābāī, princess-turned-mystic of Mewar (1498–1547). These songs are usually in the nirguṇa (formless, all-pervading God) mode as opposed to the saguṇa (God with form and qualities). These have been sung by a number of leading vocalists, arranged and re-arranged numerous times in different classical rāgas (melodic structures), although as a genre bhajan is categorised as semi-classical. Among the all-time classics: Sūrdās's *Bhramargīt* (or the songs of the buzzing bee), Kabīr's *Guru Mahīma* (a collection of songs on the greatness of the Guru) and the all-time favourite virāha bhajans of Mīrābāī, on the trials and tribulations of being in love with an elusive, unseen God, exemplified by Kṛṣṇa. Another mystic poet and devotee of Kṛṣṇa, Narsi Mehta of Gujarat (1414–1481), has the honour of being the author of Mahatma Gandhi's personal favourite bhajan – one that was used on the soundtrack of Richard Attenborough's 1981 film *Gandhi*. Narsi Mehta describes the attributes of a perfected human being: 'The true human is one who understands the pain of others.'

The verses of all of these poets have not only proved timeless but have cut across religious boundaries so that it is quite normal to find Kabīr's words sung within shabads (holy verses) of the Sikhs while poems about Kṛṣṇa, notably those by Mīrābāī, have a place of pride in qawwāli (songs of the Muslim Sufi mystics). More recently, there has also been a resurgence of Havēli Saṅgeet (temple music) as composed by Vallabha (in the 1500s) and popularised by vocalist Pandit Jasraj.

Although recorded music came to India early in the twentieth century and the advent of the gramophone was advertised using Hindu religious icons like Sarasvatī (Goddess of Music) as well as other deities, the earliest recordings were those by courtesans who sang thumri(s) (light-classical, often ribald songs), as no self-respecting serious classical musician would consent to being recorded. This situation changed gradually, but the highest-selling recordings were always those from films rather than of serious classical performers. In the early part of the twenty-first century, with the growth of a large and mostly prosperous Indian diaspora in the West, things seem to have come full circle and recordings of good-quality classical (and especially devotional) music are in huge demand. British-based recording companies like Navras confirm an increase in their devotional music output and sales, while Sona Rupa's output, whether Hindi or Gujarati, is almost entirely devotional.

In the past, Hindu devotional songs were memorised by being heard over and over again in the temple. Many of these songs are structured so as to allow a chorus refrain with which everybody may join in. At pūjā(s) and other domestic devotional rituals the same pattern was followed, with an invited singer leading the way while guests provided the chorus. These days, with high-quality, professionally recorded bhajans (available through virtually every street-side stall, record store and numerous sites on the internet) live singers have mostly been replaced by the CD player.

See also: **Americas, Hindus in; Bhagavadgītā; Bhajan; Bhakti movement; Europe, Hindus in; Film; Gandhi, Mohandas Karamchand; Gaṇeśa; Guṇas; Guru; Hanumān; Kabīr; Kṛṣṇa; Languages; Mandir; Mantra; Mīrābāī; Music; Pūjā; Rādhā; Sarasvatī; Sikhism, relationship with Hinduism; Sūrdās; Tulsīdās(a); Vallabha**

JAMEELA SIDDIQI

Further reading

Das, G.N. 1991. *Couplets from Kabir (Kabir Dohe)*. New Delhi: Motilal Banarsidass Publishers.

Farrell, G. 1997. *Indian Music and the West*. Oxford: Clarendon Press.

Khan, Inayat. 1991. *A Sufi Message of Spiritual Liberty, vol. 2: The Mysticism of Sound and Music*. Dorset: Element.

King, Anna S. and John Brockington (eds). 2005. *The Intimate Other. Love Divine in Indic Religions*. New Delhi: Orient Longman.

Sethi, V.K. 1979. *Mira The Divine Lover. Dera Baba Jaimal Singh*. Punjab: Radha Soami Satsang Beas (Mystics of the East Series).

Subramanian, V.K. 1996. *Sacred Songs of India*. New Delhi: Abhinav Publications.

Thielemann, S. 1999. *The Music of South* Asia. New Delhi: APH Publishing Corporation.

Discography

Pandit Shivkumar Sharma and Swami Chidanandji Maharaj. *Upanishad Amrut*. Vocals by Shankar Mahadevan and Devaki Pandit. NAVRAS NRCD 3501–2 (with Hindi interpretation) and 3503–4 (with English interpretation). The two-disc sets contain detailed notes and translations extracted from the book *The Upanishads* by Alistair Shearer and Peter Russell.

Pandit Jasraj. *Havēli Saṅgeet*. NAVRAS NRCD 3511 & 3516 (2 vols) including translations and liner notes by Dr Rupert Snell (vol. 1) and author (vol. 2).

Pandit Bhimsen Joshi. *Bhakti Sangeet, Bhajans of Mira bai and Tulsidas*. NAVRAS NRD 0099.

Pandit Ajoy Chakrabarty, A. Hariharan and Suresh Wadkar. *Bhakta Triveni*. NAVRAS NRCD 3505 (featuring the bhajans of Surdas, Tulsidas and Brahamanand).

Pandit Channulal Mishra. *Krishna – From the Heart of Benaras*. NINAAD NCCD 0024.

Pandit Ulhas Kashalkar. *Bhakti Gunjan*. NAVRAS NRCD 3514, including liner notes and text translations by the author.

Ustad Ghulam Mustafa Khan. *Sur Dhwani*. NAVRAS NRCD 0097. Tracks 4 and 5 – Ganesh Stuti (Song in praise of Lord Ganesh) in Raga Desh.

Ustad Sayeeduddin Dagar. *Inde: Chant Dhrupad de la Dagarvani. Musique du Monde (Music from the World)* 1984912.

Ustad Fahimuddin Dagar. *Raga Kedar*. Jecklin JD 635–2.

Chiranji Lal Tanwar and Suman Yadav. NAVRAS NRCD 3015. *Mewar Ree Mira, Devotional Songs of Mira Bai*. Detailed liner notes and translations by Harshwardhan Singh Rathore.

Lakshmi Shankar. *Divine Love – The Songs of Mira Bai*. NAVRAS NRCD 3515. With detailed liner notes, transliteration of original song texts and translations by author.

Lakshmi Shankar. *Bhakti Ras*. NAVRAS NRCD 0056. Includes bhajans by Brahmanand, Mira Bai, Surdas and Narsi Metha's 'Vaishnava jan to tene kehiye'.

Lakshmi Shankar. *Amrut Ras. Songs from the Devotional Tradition*. AUDIOREC 1055–2. With original song texts with detailed liner notes, translations and transliterations by Dr Rupert Snell.

Purshotam Das Jalota. *Praising Krishna, Ashtachhap Poets*. AUDIOREC 1013–2. With original song texts with detailed liner notes, translations and transliterations by Dr Rupert Snell.

Purshotam Das Jalota. *Songs of Surdas, The Bhramargit*. AUDIOREC 1011–12. With original song texts with detailed liner notes, translations and transliterations by Dr Rupert Snell.

Purshotam Das Jalota. *Songs of Kabir, Call of the Divine*. AUDIOREC 1012–2. With original song texts with detailed liner notes, translations and transliterations by Dr Rupert Snell.

Various Instrumentalists. *Divinity – A Musical Odyssey*. SONA RUPA SRCD 026. (Instrumental adaptations of ten of the most popular bhajans of all time.)

Hema Desai and Ashit Desai. *Bhakti Smaran, Hindi Devotional Songs*. SONA RUPA SR021.

Devotional songs in films

The most memorable ones have music by Naushad Ali, lyrics by Shakeel Badayuni and the voice of Mohammad Rafi.

'Man Tarpat Hari Darshan ko aaj', in Raga Malkauns (from the film *Baiju Bawra*, 1952).

A great favourite, unfolding Radha's love for Krishna, is 'Madhuban mein Radhika naache re', in Raga Hameer (from the film *Kohinoor*, 1960).

The story of Radha's first encounter with Krishna is told in a lilting Raga Gaara sung by Lata Mangeshkar: 'Mohe punghat pe nandlal chherd gayo re' (from the film *Mughal-e-Azam*, 1960).

Indian film music may be tracked through CDs of the film title.

SOUTH INDIAN POLITICAL MOVEMENTS

The South Indian Dravidian movements originated in opposition to the domination of brāhmaṇas in the social and political arenas of the region. Anti-Brahmanism was a prominent issue in the south, unlike in Northern India, where the major issue was the Muslim community. As early as 1914 the Justice Party had been formed to counter brāhmaṇa domination, but after its defeat at the hands of the Indian National Congress in 1932 the remnants of the Justice Party came together as the Dravida Kazhagam (DK), of which the chief proponent was a radical and enterprising figure, E.V. Ramaswami Naickke, known as Periyar ('the respected big man'). Periyar's victory over the popular congress leader K. Kamaraj in local elections in Virudhanagar in 1967 was symbolic of the ascendancy of the DK in Tamil Nadu politics. The movement was characterised by fervent opposition to casteism, of which Periyar had bitter experiences when he attended a Congress leader's training camp called Gurukala. Here low- and high-caste members were forced to eat in separate dining halls. (Diehl 1977: 25). Therefore, in 1925 Periyar left the Congress Party and formed the DK. Periyar attacked not only brāhmaṇa domination but also the domination of Northern Indians and was even anti-Hindu in his campaigns. The Rāmāyaṇa, for instance was characterised as an epic extolling the victory of Aryans over the Dravidians (Sathya Murthy 1996: 558) and the DK even penned a counter-epic Rāvaṇāyaṇa extolling Rāvaṇa. In 1953 Gaṇeśa images were smashed. In 1948 the introduction of Hindi as a compulsory language in school curricula was opposed and in 1952 Hindi signs in railway stations and other public places were tarred over by DK activists. The opposition to Northern Indian domination in India went to the extent of a demand for a separate Dravida homeland, or Dravidasthan. In 1957 a copy of the Indian constitution was burnt and activists threatened to burn a map of India and the Indian National flag.

Differences emerged between Periyar and another rising DK leader, C.N. Annadurai, who later became chief minister of Tamil Nadu in 1967. Known as Aṇṇa ('elder brother'), Annadurai split from Periyar and formed the Dravida Munnetra Kazhagam (DMK; Dravidian Progress Movement) in 1949. It was more accommodating to the central government in Delhi and indeed is now a constituent of the coalition governing India. Its followers consider Brahmanism to be a religious rather than an ethnic issue, and subscribe to a pragmatic agnostic humanism rather than anti-Hinduism.

In 1972 a breakaway faction called the Anna DMK (ADMK) was formed when the DMK leader Karunanidhi refused a ministership to the extremely popular and charismatic M.G. Ramachandran (known as MGR), a famous matinee idol of Tamil cinema (Shankar 2002: 69). MGR alleged rampant corruption in the Karunanidhi government. The DMK and the ADMK are fervently opposed to each other in spite of a more or less common ideology. The present government in Tamil Nadu is led by the ADMK under another former film star, J. Jayalalitha.

See also: **Brāhmaṇas; Brahmanism; Caste; Gaṇeśa; Rāmāyaṇa; Rāvaṇa.**

THEODORE GABRIEL

Further reading

Diehl, Anita. 1977. *E.V. Ramaswami Naicker – Periyar.* Lund: Esselte Studium, 1.

Sathya Murthy, T.V. (ed.). 1996. *Region, Caste, Gender, and Culture in Contemporary India.* Delhi: Oxford University Press.

Shankar, Kalyani. 2002. *Gods of Power, Personality Cult and Indian Democracy.* Delhi: Macmillan India Ltd.

SOUTHEAST AND EAST ASIA, HINDUS IN

General introduction

In contemporary Southeast and East Asian countries Hinduism is a minority religion which has recruited its adherents mainly from migrating Indians and their offspring for several generations. Today the most important Southeast Asian countries with Hindus are Malaysia and Singapore, with a dominance of Tamil-speaking Hindus, and Indonesia, though there the Balinese Hindus are to be treated separately, as they should not be reckoned as 'Hindus in the diaspora'. The different Hindus in Myanmar and Thailand are also of interest. In other countries or territories – like the Philippines, Vietnam, Hong Kong or Japan – Hindus are mainly expatriate Indians with limited numbers. Thus the Hindu diaspora in Southeast and East Asia comprises both Indian citizens and people of Indian origin; the latter still keep contact with their Indian homeland but they also want to contribute to the process of nation-building and of integrating into their 'new' country. The total number of Hindus in Southeast and East Asia can be estimated at about 6 million people (including about 3 million Balinese Hindus).

Historical background

The earliest contacts between India and Southeast Asia may date back as far as the middle of the fourth century BCE. When trade was established during the following centuries, this led to the settlement of Indians on the Southeast Asian mainland and on the islands. In the course of such migration processes, small waves of Indian population groups reached Southeast Asia by land and by sea, also bringing an influence of Indian culture to these areas. Generally speaking, G. Coedès (1968) called this process 'Indianisation', which brought not only Hindu but also (Indian) Buddhist thought to Southeast Asia. In the course of the centuries, Hindu (and Buddhist) dominated states originated in Southeast Asia (cf. de Casparis and Mabbett 1992: 286–322; Narayanan 2005). The first one was, according to Chinese sources, Funan in Southern Vietnam and Cambodia during the third century CE. Also the earliest

Sanskrit inscriptions from Southeast Asia date back to that period, referring to a dynasty in Campa (modern Vietnam). From the fifth century onwards Hindu (and Buddhist) kingdoms were established in the Indonesian archipelago, the Srivijaya kingdom spreading from its centre in Palembang (Sumatra) far to the east of the archipelago, but also reaching the mainland up to Thailand. Later on, focusing on central Java, the kingdom of Majapahit exercised its power over the islands, also including present-day Malaysia. The archaeological site of Prambanan (eighth century) in central Java is still today an impressive expression of Hinduism in those days. Since the turn of the first to the second millennium CE, Hinduism has also reached the island of Bali, continuing there until the present day (Howe 2001). On the mainland, Hindu (and Buddhist) kingdoms partly intertwined in syncretistic ways flourished from the fifth century in Cambodia, introducing there the importance of the devaraja-cult ('god-king cult'); the architecture of some of the famous temples in Angkor (tenth to twelfth centuries) has clearly been inspired by Hindu concepts. Also, in present-day Myanmar the Hindu-based kingdom of Sri Ksetra (third to tenth centuries) is worth mentioning. Starting roughly in the thirteenth century, Hinduism began to decline, due to the increasing dominance of Theravada Buddhism on the mainland and due to the advent of Islam in the Malay archipelago from the fourteenth century onwards.

For present-day Hinduism this historical overview has relevance for the Hindu diaspora in a threefold manner: On a literary level, one has to mention those widely spread traditions of the *Rāmāyaṇa* which create a general awareness of Hindu values also among non-Hindu people. *Rāmāyaṇa* representations, either through shadow play (wayang) in the Malay world, *Rāmāyaṇa* performances on the stage or by dance and visual representations of stories from the epic on murals or reliefs, are widespread, based on local versions that range from Myanmar via Thailand, Laos and Cambodia up to the Philippines, but are also known on the islands of Java and Bali in Indonesia (Sachithanantham 2004). A further slight connection between the historical background and present-day societies with Hindu minority groups can be seen in traditions of a royal Hindu-Brahmanical cult, which – although it has gone through changes in the course of time – still survives in brahmanical ceremonies in the royal cult in Thailand and Cambodia or in installations of (royal) officials in various Malay sultanates. There exists a third link between historical Hinduism and contemporary Hindus, but it is restricted to Indonesia. The Balinese (and partly Javanese) Hindus in recent decades began to unite various Hindu traditions in Indonesia both by focusing on the Hindu heritage in Southeast Asia and by referring to India again. But it must be mentioned that this special Balinese situation should not be generalised for other Hindus.

The starting point for most of the contemporary Hindus has been the political change from the last decades of the eighteenth century onwards. During those days, mainly in the fields of plantation and industrial development, contract workers were engaged in the Southeast Asian parts of 'British India', mainly present-day Myanmar, Malaysia and Singapore. North Indian low-skilled workers were brought to Myanmar and South Indians to Malaysia and Singapore. Also the Netherlands acquired Indians in limited numbers for their colonial island of Sumatra (Indonesia). Those workers should have been employed only for several years and it was planned that they should return to India. But most of those first-generation workers stayed much longer in their new workplace and sought marriage with women who migrated from

India to Southeast Asia for that reason. The origins of the Hindu community in the former British crown colony of Hong Kong also reach back to the middle of the nineteenth century; the first Hindus were employed there by the British for defence reasons, but they soon became important intermediaries for trading between the Chinese people and British interests in Middle Eastern and African countries. Thus we can assume that the oldest communities of Hindus of Indian origin reach back now for six generations in those countries. Later Indian Hindus migrated also to Thailand and the Philippines, and to Vietnam for economic reasons. The Philippines came into the scope of Indian migrants from the last years of the nineteenth century, after the USA had taken possession of the Philippines, and some Indians went there – partly via Singapore or Hong Kong – to make their fortune. Thailand also was reached by Hindus during the late nineteenth century, namely by Tamils who migrated from Penang and peninsular Malaysia to the South of Thailand first and then went on to Bangkok because of better economical opportunities. From the 1940s North Indians, mainly from the Punjab and from Uttar Pradesh, arrived in Thailand. The most recent but minor migrations started several decades ago, when some Indians went to Taiwan, Japan and the Republic of Korea; even though they established some associations or religious institutions in these countries, their number is almost negligible in relation to the total population of the countries.

The situation in different Southeast and East Asian countries

The political independence of India as well as of former colonies after the Second World War brought a change, as the Hindus in the independent states had to rearrange their 'diasporic' status, seeking a balance between being members or citizens of their 'new' country in its process of nation-building and also keeping in touch with the Indian roots of the (fore)fathers. Thus the idea of 'diaspora' mainly began to emerge only after Independence, because Hindus were no longer part of 'India', but they had to integrate in their new society by holding on to their Hindu tradition.

Malaysia

Of the total population of Malaysia today 6.3 per cent, or 1,600,000 people, are Hindus, who together with roughly 310,000 Indian Muslims and 45,000 Sikhs make up the Indian population group there. The main centres of Hinduism in Malaysia are located along the western coast of the peninsula, still resulting from the migrations there during the colonial period. Today Hindus are especially concentrated on the island of Penang in the north, in the capital Kuala Lumpur and in Melacca, a very high percentage of them being Tamils (cf. Collins 1997; Gabriel 2000).

Originally many Hindus in Malaysia had a rural South Indian background and venerated a local 'village' goddess. The most prominent among them was Māriammā, a goddess associated with smallpox, being originally honoured by non-brahmanical cults. In Malaysia, mainly workers at plantations were her followers, but her identification with Kālī and Durgā led to her integration into the Śaiva pantheon. Therefore, for several decades she has been the main female deity in Malaysia; her most important temple in Kuala Lumpur's Chinatown is also the starting point for the procession during the Tai Pusan festival, celebrated every year in January or February, which leads to the Batu Caves with the temple of Subramanya or Murukaṉ. He is one of the two sons of Śiva. For Hindus in Malaysia he nowadays takes a leading position as a god who can remove all evil with his lance, and his adherents can gain part of his strength by practising asceticism and taking vows (vrata) – not only in the course of the Tai Pusan festival, but also through regular service in his temples. The second son of Śiva, Vināyaka Ganeśa, is held in high esteem, not only by Tamils of South Indian origin but also by those from Sri Lanka. The common philosophical background for many Tamils in Malaysia is Śaiva Siddhānta, but Swami Shivananda is also held in high esteem by many Hindus there. It is interesting to note the adherence of Chinese people, who especially in Penang regularly frequent Vināyaka's temple there, but Chinese are also attracted in reasonable numbers by the Satya Sai Baba movement (Kent 2005).

A special Hindu group worth mentioning are the Melacca Chitties. They were Indians, who arrived at the Malacca Sultanate in the sixteenth century, but they have long since accustomed themselves to Malay culture, due to early marriages with local Malay women. In spite of their closeness to Malay culture – they only use the Malay language – they still practise their Hindu wedding ceremonies, hold to Śaiva Hinduism and focus in their own Chitty temple on the worship of Māriammā as their main goddess. The climax of this worship is reached in May at the 'Pesta Datuk Charchar' for Māriammā. Because of their declining number (only 300–400 persons) they now face the problem of needing the assistance of the Hindu mainstream on the one hand to survive as a religious community, while wanting to keep apart from this mainstream in order not to lose their own identity (Ramanathan 2001: 89–90).

Although Malaysia guarantees freedom of religion, in recent years Hindus in Malaysia have had to struggle against general efforts to Islamise Malaysia; this not only leads to general disadvantages for Hindus as a minority, but during recent years cases of (forced) conversion to Islam (and to some fundamental Christian denominations) can be observed. This brings upset to the Hindu community, which is also economically less established than the Chinese minority in Malaysia. Therefore, recently, representatives of the Malaysia Hindu Sangam have taken successful steps to raise the social and religious welfare of Hindus (cf. Hutter 2005a). The activities aim not only to give Hindus a new self-confidence in their own religion, but also to bring them onto a par with other religions in Malaysia by improving the community on religious, educational, social and economic grounds alike.

Singapore

Currently about 8 per cent of the inhabitants of Singapore are Indians and among them 55 per cent, or 140,000 persons, are Hindus, mostly of Tamil origin. Still today an area called 'Little India' is the centre for Hindus in Singapore (Siddique and Puru Shotam 1990), concentrating around the Sri Perumāḷ Temple. Viṣṇu-Perumāḷ and Mahālakṣmi Āṇṭāḷ are venerated as the main deities. The Sri Perumāḷ Temple is also the starting point for the Tai Pusan festival. The main procession of the festival leads from this temple to the Thandayuttapani temple, dedicated to Subramanya-Murukaṉ. This temple is run by a group of Chettiars, originally money-lenders from the Chennai area in South India. The oldest temple in Singapore is dedicated to Śri Māriammā, located in the centre of the city in Chinatown. The Māriammā Temple is the focus for the Thimithi festival with the fire-walking ceremony, held every year in October or November. All these three 'main' temples – as well as Singapore's twenty-four temples in general – traditionally have their own group of worshippers, but in recent decades a change has occurred and connections between the temples have begun to emerge. This has led to some kind of common 'Hindu consciousness' among the different ethnic and devotional Hindu groups there.

By Singaporean society and by the Singaporean government, Hindus are reckoned as 'Indians', parallel to the other ethnicities, namely Chinese, Malays and 'Others', meaning mainly Eurasians (cf. Sinha 1993; Hutter 2005b). To keep religious and social harmony among these ethnicities, one can easily observe that regulations are introduced by official institutions to shape uniformity among Hindus. Both the Hindu Endowments Board (established in 1968) and the Maintenance of Religious Harmony Act (from 1992) are instruments to regulate religious harmony on the part of the government. On the side of the Hindus this sometimes leads to some restrictions: at the main festivals it is mandatory to follow an exact route for the processions which take the deities out of their temples and lead them to another temple. Also the use of some percussion instruments has partly been limited in order to reduce forms of so-called 'superstition' or everyday Hinduism, based on local or rural traditions. Thus we see attempts at change to shape a sophisticated and unified Hinduism which fits into modern Singaporean society. To some degree this creates an artificial Hinduism, which on the one hand is of course accepted by most Hindus in Singapore because it brings a common bond to 'all' Hindus in Singapore, allowing them to be both Hindus and Singaporean citizens and thus to be on the same level as the other ethnic groups. But, on the other hand, such a unified Hinduism focusing on Tamil Hinduism faces differences with other 'Indians', especially from the north, who favour Vaiṣṇavite traditions more than the Śaivite options of the Tamils. In conclusion, Hinduism in Singapore is currently still a Tamil- and Śaiva-dominated tradition, but – especially among younger people – philosophical access to a new interpretation of Sanskrit scripture is also gaining ground.

Indonesia

'Hinduism' in modern Indonesia comprises different peoples (Ramstedt 2004), namely first the Balinese, who make up about 55–60 per cent in Indonesia, then the Javanese, who define themselves as 'Hindu' partly as a symbol of Javanese identity by referring back to the pre-Islamic Javanese culture. Other groups that must be mentioned are ethnic groups like the Toraja, the Karo-Batak and the Ngaju-Dayak, who accepted 'Hinduism' in the 1970s and in the early 1980s because all Indonesians have to belong to one of the five acknowledged religions. In order to avoid being 'non-religious', 'superstitious' or 'animistic', these ethnic groups, who had their own local religions, chose 'Hinduism' as their religion. The total number of all these Hindus is 5,700,000 people, but only a minority is of Indian origin. The Tamils number about 30,000, who have settled in Indonesia for three to five generations now, mainly in the area of Medan in the north of Sumatra. Starting in the 1950s North Indians (mainly Hindu Sindhis or Sikhs) came to Jakarta to engage in the textile industries, but they are of a rather limited number. Thus, in a very strict sense, diasporic Hinduism in Indonesia refers only to this limited number of Tamils and Sindhis.

Tamil Hindus still keep close to Tamil rituals, focusing on Śaiva traditions (Vignato 2000). Thus, this Hindu community has always been close to Hindus in Malaysia, having economic bonds with them, and with Tamil Hindus from Indonesia also seeking work with better-off Hindus in Kuala Lumpur or Penang. However, they still stick to Tamil rituals, and connections to Tamil Nadu in South India have been kept until now, thereby at the same time focusing on ritual, philosophical, diet and ethnic differences with

Balinese and other Indonesian Hindus. In this way the Tamil community is a rather closely knit group; Tamils who settle in Jakarta still refer to Medan as their origin, thus not interacting with Sindhi Hindus in Jakarta. Tamil Hinduism in Indonesia can best be compared to Malaysia – with the main deities being Māriammā and Subramanya-Murukaṉ.

The Sindhi Hindus are also Śaiva, but are a community of their own with the Śiva Mandir in the north of Jakarta as their main temple (Mani 1993: 115–17; Thapan 2002: 172–77). Besides worshipping the main gods of North Indian Śaivism, they also share some saints with the Sikh tradition, thus in some respects having more in common with Sikhs than with Tamil Śaivas. On Monday, an auspicious day for the Sindhi Hindus, they gather at the Śiva Mandir for religious ceremonies; the temple also serves as the focus for the cultural identity of the Sindhis.

The position of Hinduism in Indonesian society depends on Indonesian politics regarding the belief in 'one God'. In order to attain the status of an acknowledged religion, Hinduism had to subscribe to this doctrine, thus leading to some unifying trends headed by the – Balinese-dominated – Parisada Hindu Dharma Indonesia. On the one hand – more for the Tamils than for the even smaller Sindhi community – this leads to occasional tensions between the different 'Hindu' groups, but on the other hand this also brings some aspects of 'Indianisation' to the Balinese-dominated Hinduism. The beginning of this development reaches back as far as the 1920s, but it became more visible in the 1950s with the necessity to shape an organised body for 'Hinduism' as the acknowledged religion. Due to this change, some Balinese Hindus – and in the last two decades mainly also Hindus of the younger generation – began to focus more on philosophical and doctrinal aspects of the religion, in parallel with questioning its ritualistic aspects. Neo-Hindu thoughts, meditation techniques and Indian-based movements like the Ramakrishna Mission, the International Society for Krishna Consciousness (ISKCON) or the Satya Sai Baba mission gained ground among Hindus in Indonesia. Thus, one can say that, although the number of Hindus of ethnic Indian origin in Indonesia is negligible, such new developments not only bring Hindus in Indonesia closer to India again, but also a type of 'new' diaspora comes into existence, by establishing bonds with India again.

Myanmar

About 3–4 per cent of the 48 million inhabitants of Myanmar are people of Indian origin, mostly descendants of Bengalis, Uttar Pradeshis, Tamils and Telegu, who came to Myanmar during the British colonial rule (1885–1948). A good number of the Bengalis are Muslims, while the others are Hindus. In the aftermath of the political changes in Myanmar in 1962, about 1 million Indians had to leave the country. Nowadays, about 800,000 Hindus live in Myanmar, mainly in the areas around cities like Yangon (mostly Tamils), Mandalay (all ethnic Indian groups) and in the Bago district (mainly at Toungoo and Zeyawaddy, especially Uttar Pradeshis), but also in smaller numbers in other areas (Tin Maung Maung Than 1993: 599–612).

Although the Hindu community in Myanmar is made up of different Indian ethnicities, one has to observe that most of the temples are no longer organised along ethnic lines. The important Śrī Kālī Temple in Yangon (established in the 1870s) was originally run by Tamil Chettiars, but the temple management board has, for some time, been made up of Chettiars, Tamils, Gujaratis, Bengalis, Telegus and even one person from the Oriya community. A similar situation can be observed in most other temples; notable exceptions of temples which foster the religious needs of only one ethnic group are rare (e.g. the Sri Perumāḷ temple, with all services only in Tamil, or the Śrī Mahīlakṣmī Temple, mainly for Gujaratis, both in Yangon). Among the Hindus in Myanmar, such situations lead to some commonalities of Hinduism, which means that a wide spectrum of general festivals are celebrated by all Hindus. Thus Durgā Pūjā/Navarātri, Dīvālī, Mahāśivarātri and Holī are of general importance. Most temples also hold regular worship twice a day.

As the majority of the people of Myanmar see Hinduism as being close to Buddhism, Hindu temples are also visited by Myanmar Buddhists. The All Myanmar Hindu Central Board, as an umbrella organisation, also serves as a representative of Hindu matters to the Myanmar government. Together with organisations like the Sanatana Dharma Swayamsevak Sangh, it is engaged in fostering the welfare of the Hindu community. Thus, in general, Hindus experience religious harmony with the majority of the society of the country and with the government. Occasionally subtle forms of racial discrimination against Hindus appear, because of their Indian origin and for historical reasons. However, by and large, the Hindu diasporic community manages to live without tensions between Myanmar nationalism and the maintenance of its religious roots in India. In order not to lose the bonds with India, Hindus in Myanmar welcome organisations inspired by contemporary Hinduism in India like the Ramakrishna Mission, the Satya Sai Baba movement or the activities of the Arya Samaj.

Thailand

Among Thailand's 65 million inhabitants there are only 100,000 Hindus, who have been immigrating to Thailand for three or four generations. About 75 per cent of them live in Bangkok; the others are concentrated in Chiang Mai and in some other places in the north. Nowadays the Hindu community is mainly made up of Tamils, Punjabis, Gujaratis and Hindi-speaking people originating from Uttar Pradesh in India, but there is no umbrella organisation to cover all these groups or to represent Hinduism in Thailand as a common body. According to the different ethnic backgrounds, we can also observe religious differences among the Hindus in Thailand (Sachdeva 1996; Malik 2003).

The Śrī Māriammā Temple in Bangkok is one of the oldest Hindu temples there, established by Tamils. Besides the Tamil Hindus, up to 95 per cent of people who come to the temple are Thai, offering garlands, coconuts or incense. Hinduism is seen by most Thai people either as an offshoot of Buddhism or only as some kind of ritual, but not as a separate religion. Similar observations can be made in other Hindu temples, too. The Viṣṇu Mandir in central Bangkok caters mainly for people whose origins reach back to Uttar Pradesh in India, and the temple is headed today by the Chief Hindu Priest of Thailand. Regarding ethnic differences among the Hindu community, the Punjabis should also be mentioned. They outnumber the other Hindus and have established the Hindu Samaj with the Dev Mandir, mainly for the religious needs of this ethnic group. The Hindu Samaj also runs a school, but most schoolchildren are Thai, while Hindu children are usually sent by their parents either to Christian (meaning Western) schools in Thailand or to schools in India. Because of the school, the Dev Mandir also attracts Thai Buddhists to the rituals. Punjabis have a further Dev Mandir in Chiang Mai.

The Devasthana Bosth Brahmana, as the royal Hindu temple in a Buddhist country, is of special interest. The Rajaguru, as its main priest, is not only the head of the Thai court brāhmaṇas whose ancestors came from India, but conducts all the rituals in this brāhmaṇa temple in the Thai language, serving mainly the official cult for the royal family, and the coronation ceremonies or the yearly ploughing ceremony. There are about twenty such Thai Brāhmaṇas, eleven of them being employed by the royal household. These royal Brāhmaṇas can be seen as a survival of the ancient devaraja-cult now included in the Buddhist kingdom (Kuanpoonpol 1990). For the Hindu community in Thailand, the ceremonies in the temple are of minor importance, despite the efforts of the present Rajaguru to establish links between the Thai Brāhmaṇas and the Śaiva Śaṅkarācārya in Kanchipuram in South India in order to improve religious knowledge of Hinduism in Thailand.

Hindus do not face problems within Thai society on a social level. Problems which Hindus, as a minority in Thailand, are aware of result from other causes. There are sorrows about a further decline of knowledge of Hinduism, because due to mixed marriages younger Hindus do not differentiate between Buddhism and Hinduism – usually at the cost of Hinduism. Further problems focus on the lack of financial means to keep up the temples or to run Hindu institutions to offer services for religious education in a wider sense. Thus, older Hindus complain that among the younger generation interest in the religion of their ancestors is waning, and therefore the fear is expressed that Hinduism might be extinguished in Thailand within a generation or two.

Philippines

It is difficult to estimate the number of adherents of Indian religions in the Philippines, but taking Hindus and Sikhs together one can roughly reckon on about 28,000 people. They are either of Punjabi or of Sindhi origin and started arriving in the Philippines at the end of the nineteenth century. The Punjabis now make up about 60 per cent, and the other 40 per cent are Sindhis. Three-quarters live in Manila and its surroundings, and Santiago in the north of the island Luzon is the second largest town with inhabitants of Indian origin, mostly Punjabi Sikhs. The number of Hindus, mostly Sindhis, is at the most 7,000–8,000.

In 1929 the first gurudwara was built in Manila, fostering the religious needs of both Sikhs and Hindus, but with a clear preference for Sikhs. Therefore in 1962 Sindhis established a temple for themselves, but still kept within the temple precincts statues of the Sikhs' Gurus and Hindu deities and saints alike, namely Kṛṣṇa and Rādhā, Śiva, his bull and his liṅgam, and Viṣṇu with his consort. The Guru Granth Sahib is also displayed in the temple hall in a prominent position. For prayers and recitations during the ceremonies, a Sikh Granthi is employed, and during ceremonies both Sikh bhajans and Vedic hymns are recited by the community. Thus, one must concede that the Hindu temple in Manila is half gurudwara and half mandir, sometimes creating confusion among diasporic Hindus who migrate to Manila because of this blend of different traditions, which is unusual for Hindus who do not have a Punjabi or Sindhi background. To keep up religious contacts with other Hindus, the temple tries to welcome priests, svāmis or lecturers from India, but also from Thailand and Singapore, thus opening up to some Hindu pluralism. Some Sindhi Hindus are also attracted by Radhasoami masters or by the Satya Sai Baba movement (Rye 1993; Thapan 2002).

Generally speaking, both the Punjabi and Sindhi communities are in a good economic position, but they are not well integrated into Philippine society, having a slightly negative image as 'Bumbai', a term referring to Bombay/Mumbai in India, even though most of the Hindus/Indians in the Philippines do not originate from that Indian metropolis. The other problem faced by the community occasionally originates from the Christian majority in the Philippines, who sometimes look down on Hindus as superstitious, which leads to attempts to convert Indians to Christianity, with more success among Sindhi Hindus than among Punjabi Sikhs. In part, these problems can be attributed to the limited religions and cultural education and socialisation of Hindu children, which leaves them estranged from their tradition and vulnerable to Christian influences.

Other countries

Despite the impressive archaeological sites which prove Cambodia's historical connections with Hinduism, at present there are no Hindu communities; the same is the case with Laos. In Vietnam the number of Hindus is less than 1,000, but four temples are still functioning in Ho Chi Minh City. They are run by Tamils who stayed in Vietnam after the political changes of 1975, when many Indians left the former South Vietnam (cf. White 1994). In Hong Kong, Hindus (mainly Sindhis, Punjabis and Tamils) settled down during the nineteenth century under British rule, and they held an economically important position as trade intermediaries between China and (British) India until recent times. Now they still maintain two temples and a variety of ethnic-based associations. In Japan 3,000–4,000 Indian Hindus have been living as expatriates for the last few decades, celebrating the Holī and Dīvālī festivals, but no large temple has been established yet. For two decades mainly Sindhis who are engaged in the textile trade have settled in South Korea's capital Seoul, establishing Hinduism by celebrating festivals like Holī and Dīvālī and – comparable to Japan – working as intermediaries of Indian culture in East Asia. But, generally speaking, Hinduism does not play an important role in those countries.

Conclusion

Hinduism in Southeast and East Asia can best be labelled as 'unity and diversity', at least in those countries where there is a substantial number of Hindus. Efforts to reach unity depend upon factors like the religious politics practised by the state or the dominant society, as can clearly be seen – always with different motivation – in Malaysia, Singapore and Indonesia. But the process of creating a unified 'Hinduism' in these countries also depends upon the dominance of either Islam in Malaysia and Indonesia or of Chinese culture in Singapore. Thus, creating a common 'Hindu identity' also serves for the diaspora community as a sign of strength to keep their own religious and cultural traditions alive. But though widely accepting the necessity of creating such a common bond of Hinduism, the various ethnic groups among Hindus in these three countries also lay an accent on their own local and ethnic tradition, which they want to uphold. Trying to reach a balance between unity and diversity will be the future task for Hindus in Malaysia, Singapore and Indonesia. Focusing on unity can give them strength as a diaspora and minority religion against the majority, but it will also be necessary to allow pluralistic approaches in order to avoid separating the community.

A different religious situation is found in Buddhist countries like Thailand and Myanmar. Here it has been less necessary to further Hindu unity, mainly because Buddhists think Hinduism is similar to their religion. At a first glance, this looks like an advantage for the diaspora situation of Hindus, as no tensions arise therefrom. But it must not be overlooked that there is also the danger of being absorbed into Buddhism. Therefore, Hindus here will have to find a balance between being too assimilated into the Buddhist-dominated society and upholding the differences of their own religious and cultural traditions against the common Indian heritage with the Buddhist surroundings. In the other countries treated in this entry, the number of Hindus is so small that the communities always have to struggle for survival, evident also in the fact that on an organised level they only have a low profile, especially in East Asia; in the Philippines there is also the threat of conversion to Christianity, which the Sindhi community has to face.

The label 'unity and diversity' not only describes the situation of the Hindu communities, but it also brings another facet to the discussion of diaspora, namely the relationship of Hindus to India. On the one hand, the communities can always refer back to their origins in India, partly still genealogically, but at least by keeping contacts with the doctrinal concepts and centres of Hinduism in India. But on the other hand it is necessary to distinguish themselves from India as a political unity, because the Hindus, other than during the colonial periods when they all were part of India, now are citizens or inhabitants of independent states which are proud of their own nation-building. Hindus in the diaspora as part of these nations, therefore, must also necessarily pronounce their diversity from India and the Indian nation.

See also: **Āṇṭāḷ; Arya Samaj; Brāhmaṇas; Buddhism, relationship with Hinduism; Deities, village and local; Diaspora; Dīvālī; Drama; Durgā; Durgā Pūjā; Gaṇeśa; Holī; International Society for Krishna Consciousness; Kālī and Caṇḍī; Kṛṣṇa; Lakṣmi, Śrī; Languages; Māl; Mandir; Māriammā; Meditation; Murukaṉ; Rādhā; Rāmāyaṇa; Sai Baba (as Movement); Śaivism; Sanātana Dharma; Shivananda, Swami; Sikhism, relationship with Hinduism; Śiva; Subramanya; Svāmi; Tai Pusan; Temple worship; Vaiṣṇavism; Viṣṇu; Vrata**

Manfred Hutter

Further reading

Coedès, G. 1968. *The Indianized States of Southeast Asia.* Honolulu, HI: East–West Center Press.

Collins, E.F. 1997. *Pierced by Murugan's Lance. Ritual, Power and Moral Redemption among Malaysian Hindus.* DeKalb, IL: Northern Illinois University Press.

de Casparis, J.G. and I.W. Mabbett. 1992. 'Religion and Popular Beliefs of Southeast Asia Before c. 1500'. In N. Tarling, ed., *The Cambridge History of Southeast Asia*, vol. 1. Cambridge: Cambridge University Press, 276–339.

Gabriel, T. 2000. *Hindu and Muslim Inter-religious Relations in Malaysia* (Studies in Religion and Society 47). Lewiston, ME: Edwin Mellen Press.

Howe, L. 2001. *Hinduism and Hierarchy in Bali.* Oxford: James Currey.

Hutter, M. 2005a. 'Hindus in der muslimisch geprägten Gesellschaft Malaysias'. In E. Franke and M. Pye, eds, *Religionen Nebeneinander.* Münster: LIT Verlag.

Hutter, M. 2005b. 'Kollektive Hindu-Identität in Singapore vor dem Hintergrund staatlich geförderter Multikulturalität'. In G. Distelrath, H.D. Ölschleger and H.W. Wessler, eds, *Zur Konstruktion kollektiver Identitäten im modernen Asien*. Bonn: Bier'sche Verlagsanstalt.

Kent. A. 2005. *Divinity and Diversity. A Hindu Revitalization Movement in Malaysia.* Copenhagen: NIAS Press.

Kuanpoonpol, P. 1990. 'Court Brahmans of Thailand and the Celebration of the Brahmanic New Year'. *Indo-Iranian Journal* 33: 21–51.

Malik, R. 2003. 'Thailand Hinduism'. *Hinduism Today*, July/August/September; available at http://www.hinduismtoday.com/archives/2003/7-9/18-27_thailand.shtml (accessed 21 February 2006).

Mani, A. 1993. 'Indians in Jakarta'. In *Indian Communities in Southeast Asia*, eds K.S. Sandhu and A. Mani. Singapore: Times Academic Press, 98–130.

Narayanan, V. 2005. 'Hinduism in Southeast Asia'. In J. Lindsay, ed., *Encyclopedia of Religion*, 2nd edn, vol. 6. New York: Thomson Gale, 4,009–14.

Ramanathan, K. 2001. 'The Hindu Diaspora in Malaysia'. In T.S. Rukmani, ed., *Hindu*

Diaspora. Global Perspectives. New Delhi: Munshiram Manoharlal Publishers, 81–122.
Ramstedt, M. (ed.). 2004. *Hinduism in Modern Indonesia. A Minority Religion between Local, National, and Global Interests.* London: RoutledgeCurzon.
Rye, A.S. 1993. 'The Indian Community in the Philippines'. In K.S. Sandhu and A. Mani, eds, *Indian Communities in Southeast Asia.* Singapore: Times Academic Press, 708–74.
Sachdeva, M. 1996. *The Hindu Samaj.* Bangkok: Managing Committee of the Hindu Samaj.
Sachithananthan, S. 2004. *The Ramayana Tradition in Southeast Asia.* Kuala Lumpur: University of Malaya Press.
Siddique, S. and Puru Shotam, N. 1990. *Singapore's Little India. Past, Present, and Future.* Singapore: Institute of Southeast Asian Studies.
Sinha, V. 1993. 'Hinduism in Contemporary Singapore'. In K.S. Sandhu and A. Mani, eds, *Indian Communities in Southeast Asia.* Singapore: Times Academic Press, 827–47.
Thapan, A.R. 2002. *Sindhi Diaspora in Manila, Hong Kong, and Jakarta.* Quezon City: Ateneo de Manila University Press.
Tin Maung Maung Than. 1993. 'Some Aspects of Indians in Rangoon'. In K.S. Sandhu and A. Mani, eds, *Indian Communities in Southeast Asia.* Singapore: Times Academic Press, 585–624.
Vignato, S. 2000. *Au Nom de l'hindouism. Reconfigurations ethniques chez les Tamouls et les Karo en Indonésie.* Paris: L'Harmattan.
White, B.-S. 1994. *Turbans and Traders. Hong Kong's Indian Communities.* Hong Kong: Oxford University Press.

ŚRADDHĀ (FAITH)

Conventionally and appropriately translated as 'faith', Śraddhā is a state of mind necessary for the effective performance of Vedic ritual. It involves both confidence in the fruits of the ritual and determination to perform it.

There is a Vedic hymn to Śraddhā (*Ṛgveda* 10.151; Griffith 1973: 642; O'Flaherty 1981: 70; Panikkar 1977: 180) addressing her as a goddess by whom fire is kindled and offerings made, who is invoked at morning, noon and sunset. 'With a wish of the heart one finds *Śraddhā*; with *Śraddhā* one finds wealth' (verse 4): thus Śraddhā is something that follows from a wish and enables one to fulfil it by performing ritual. In *Kaṭha Upaniṣad* 1.2 (Roebuck 2003: 273; Olivelle 1993: 223), it is Śraddhā, zeal for the proper performance of the ritual, which prompts Naciketas to question the value of his father's gift of cows.

Sanskrit commentators often explain Śraddhā as the mental attitude of the āstika. Rāmānuja's commentary on *Bhagavadgītā* 17.2 calls it 'zeal in a course of action, based on confidence that it will produce a desired result'. Vyāsa's commentary on *Yogasūtra* 1.20, following Buddhist precedents, explains it as serenity of mind (cetasa saṃprasāda), this being necessary for reaching the yogin's desired goal (Hacker 1963).

In the *Mahābhārata* and *Viṣṇu Purāṇa*, Śraddhā is the daughter of Dakṣa and wife of Dharma. Śraddhā is often manifested in generosity to brāhmaṇas. In the past and present millennia, when the great Vedic rituals have rarely been performed, the commonest occasions for gifts to brāhmaṇas are the periodical offerings to the dead, performed on the twelve days following a death and annually on the anniversary and in the pitṛpakṣa. These occasions are called śrāddha, which means literally 'belonging to śraddhā'. These two words are distinguished by the position of the long vowel 'ā'.

See also: **Āstika and Nāstika; Bhagavadgītā; Brāhmaṇas; Buddhism, relationship with Hinduism; Dakṣa; Languages; Mahābhārata; Pitṛpakṣa; Purāṇas; Rāmānuja; Saṃhitā; Saṃskāra; Śrāddha; Upaniṣads; Yogasūtras**

DERMOT KILLINGLEY

Further reading

Griffith, Ralph T.H. 1973. *The Hymns of the Ṛgveda: Translated with a Popular Commentary*, new edn, ed. J.L. Shastri. Delhi:

Motilal Banarsidass. First published 4 vols., Benares, 1889–92.
Hacker, Paul. 1963. 'Śraddhā' (in German with English summary). *Wiener Zeitschrift für die Kunde Sud- und Ostasiens* 7: 151–89. Reprinted in P. Hacker, *Kleine Schriften*, Wiesbaden: Franz Steiner, 1978, 437–75.
O'Flaherty, Wendy Doniger. 1981. *The Rig Veda: An Anthology*. Harmondsworth: Penguin.
Olivelle, Patrick. 1993. *Upaniṣads*. Oxford: Oxford University Press.
Panikkar, Raimundo. 1977. *The Vedic Experience: Mantramañjarī: An Anthology of the Vedas for Modern Man and Contemporary Celebration*. London: Darton, Longman and Todd.
Roebuck, Valerie. 2003. *The Upaniṣads*. London: Penguin.

ŚRĀDDHA (FESTIVAL)

See: **Pitṛpakṣa**

ŚRĀDDHA (RITES TO DECEASED ANCESTORS)

Śrāddha is a term indicating rites to deceased ancestors that occur after the conclusion of the funerary rites (antyeṣṭi). The word is derived from another similar word, śraddhā, meaning faith, in the sense of confidence, conviction and trust. The dharma texts thus explain that śrāddha is a rite in which the performer makes offerings to the ancestors (pitṛs), and gifts of food and other material to the officiating priests, with the trust, confidence and faith that it will reach the ancestor and substantially benefit him or her.

The texts prescribe many different kinds of śrāddha, most of them calendrical. Because of the widespread acceptance of the need for and efficacy of śrāddha, as well as its many varieties, a vast literature developed dedicated to its explication. The initial sources were the *Pitṛmedha-Sūtras* (ancillary to some of the *Śrautasūtras*) and *Gṛhyasūtras* of approximately 500–100 BCE. A few centuries later they began to be replaced by the smṛtis, beginning with the *Manusmṛti* of approximately the second century CE and, a millennium later, the encyclopaedic digests (nibandhas) on dharma. These were supplemented by the copious commentaries on these dharma texts, and eventually by the Purāṇas, which were in continuous production from the fourth to the nineteenth centuries and which increasingly adopted the visage of narrativised dharma texts. In addition, the literature includes numerous independent treatises on śrāddha and incalculable numbers of performance manuals (prayogas and paddhatis) on śrāddha keyed to different sectarian, textual and regional practices. These may be found in virtually every corner of India, in libraries great and small, and in the hands of priests who specialise in śrāddha.

The elements of śrāddha include offerings of rice flour balls (piṇḍa) to the father, paternal grandfather, paternal great-grandfather and to the three orders of superintending ancestral deities with whom they were identified, the Vasus, the Rudras and the Ādityas, respectively. Particularly important were offerings of black sesame seeds and water, in different patterns and with different mantras. As with other sacrificial rituals, śrāddhas were classified as nitya, obligatory for certain days, naimittika, performed on irregular special occasions, and kāmya, performed with certain special desires in mind. Śrāddhas were occasions on which great physical purity was to be maintained, and which served as community feasts. Thus, the texts, beginning with Manu, contain long lists of people of different occupations, physical attributes and provenance, who were regarded as impure and were therefore to be excluded from the feasts, which is to say from the community of the deceased. Just as important were certain people regarded as auspicious for this occasion, including ascetics, yogins and certain numbers of brāhmaṇas, who represent the Viśvedevas, the collective of deities – the larger the number of brāhmaṇās, the greater the reward.

The earliest śrāddha is prescribed for the thirteenth day after death, after the deceased has been transformed from a preta (wandering spirit) into a pitṛ (an 'ancestor') by the ritual effects of the extended funerary rites (antyeṣṭi). The Vedic literature describes only a few kinds of śrāddha: the piṇḍapitṛyajña, or 'sacrifice to the deceased ancestor of rice flour balls', offered by those who have established the Vedic śrauta fires (āhitāgni); the monthly (pārvaṇa-)śrāddha, prescribed for the new moon day; the mahāpitṛyajña, or 'great sacrifice to the ancestors'; and aṣṭakā śrāddha, to be performed on the eighth day (aṣṭakā) of the lunar cycle. The elaborate ritual of the pārvaṇa-śrāddha served as the model for all others, including the important sapiṇḍīkaraṇa, the rite in which the deceased is accepted into the community of pitṛs, and the ekoddiṣṭa-śrāddha, in which only the deceased person is to be invoked. Both of these may be performed for women as well as men. Eventually, śrāddha was to be performed every year for a deceased ancestor (pratisaṃvatsara-śrāddha), on the day on which the individual died.

See also: **Antyeṣṭi; Brāhmaṇas; Dharmaśāstras; Gṛhyasūtras; Mantra; Pitṛs; Pretas; Purāṇas; Saṃnyāsa; Śraddhā; Śrautasūtras; Viśvedevas**

FREDERICK M. SMITH

Further reading

Kane, P.V. 1974. *History of Dharmaśāstra*, 2nd edn, vol. 4. Poona: Bhandarkar Oriental Research Institute, 334–551.

ŚRAMAṆA

Derived from the verb śram ('to become tired or exhausted'; 'to make an effort, to strive for') and etymologically related to the word āśrama, śramaṇa is a Sanskrit word that can refer to a number of different types of ascetics. In Buddhist and Jain literature śramaṇa specifically refers to a non-Brahmanical ascetic and there is often a distinction made between brāhmaṇa and śramaṇa. This distinction was also made by the Greek historian Megasthenes, as well as the Aśokan inscriptions, which advised that both groups should be treated with respect and should receive donations. However, as Patrick Olivelle points out (1993: 14), the word goes back to Vedic sources, where it refers to an elite group of ṛṣis who pursued a particularly strenuous lifestyle. In later Vedic literature śramaṇa is one of several terms that designates a renunciate whose lifestyle features a combination of a number of ascetic practices, including austerity, breathing techniques, yoga, and an itinerant lifestyle.

See also: **Brāhmaṇa; Ṛṣi; Veda**

BRIAN BLACK

Further reading

Flood, Gavin. 1996. *An Introduction to Hinduism*. Cambridge: Cambridge University Press.
Olivelle, Patrick. 1993. *The Āśrama System: The History and Hermeneutics of a Religious Institution*. New York: Oxford University Press.

ŚRAMAṆA CULTURE

During the sixth and fifth centuries BCE in India, new religious groups of homeless wanderers began to appear. The exact origins of these new forms of religious life remain locked in the shadows of the past, although three theories exist as to how the new religious groups formulated. There is some evidence that this Śramaṇa culture emerged as a result of changing social conditions. During this period in Northern Indian social life there was a change to urbanisation and a move away from village culture. It is possible that the traditions of Śramaṇas arose out of these changes in the social nexus. The other two competing views of the origins of the Śramaṇa communities argue either that the new forms of religious life and thought grew out of Vedic developments or that they emerged quite apart from Vedic civilisation and culture. The date (or dates) at which Śramaṇa culture died out, or passed its heyday, can be only approximated as there is variation with regard to the various traditions of Śramaṇas and, indeed, Śramaṇa-like religious people exist in India to the present day. But, suffice to say, Śramaṇa culture was at its height between *c.* sixth to fifth centuries BCE and *c.* second to fourth centuries CE.

The word 'śramaṇa' comes from a Sanskrit word which means both 'to become tired or exhausted' and 'to make an effort, to strive for'. Śramaṇa is an action noun and thus implies the action of making effort, toiling, striving. The Pali word 'samaṇa' comes form the same root but its meaning also encompasses a second root whose meaning includes the sense of 'to be quiet or calm, to cease or extinguish'. This second meaning captures the goal of striving for the Buddhist Śramaṇa tradition and exemplifies how the striving implied by the term is circumscribed by religious goals for all Śramaṇa traditions.

Śramaṇas were, basically, groups of homeless wanderers who renounced the world to live a simple life without possessions or social responsibilities. They wandered from place to place, begging for food and either wearing rags, simple garments or going about naked. The main Śramaṇa groups were the Buddhists, the Jains, the Ājīvikas, followers of the *Upaniṣads* and various smaller sects such as the Materialists (Lokāyata) and the Sceptics. The reasoning behind the adoption of this new way of (religious) life differed in detail for each group or movement but, essentially, was founded on the belief that it is through renunciation that true religious liberation (mokṣa) could be attained.

Gavin Flood suggests three basic characteristics of all Śramaṇa traditions, which are that, first, action leads to rebirth and suffering; second, detachment from action, or non-action, leads to freedom; and, third, complete detachment and ergo freedom can be achieved through ascetic and other methods of practice (Flood 1996: 77). Whilst it is the case that these are the main points of similarity between the various traditions, it is also the case that it is on these very points that they differ. The notion of action (karma) and its consequences and, more broadly, how karma fits into the soteriological picture reveal significant contrasts between the various traditions. The various views on this are described in the Buddhist texts of the *Dīgha Nikāya* and *Majjhima Nikāya*, although each view is not related to its particular Śramaṇa group (*Dīgha Nikāya* i.47–86; *Majjhima Nikāya* iii.207–15). Second, there is, again, a strong point of dissimilarity in the types of practices thought to lead to liberation. Most of the Śramaṇa traditions believed in some form of asceticism (tapas). Asceticism refers to types of practices engaged in by some members of some Śramaṇa traditions, but other Śramaṇa traditions and individual Śramaṇas believed in forms of practice other than the practice of austerities. The Buddha propagated a 'middle way' between the extremes of ascetic practice on the one hand and the indulgent worldly life of luxury on the other. The relationship between asceticism and Śramaṇism is that all forms of asceticism are included under the rubric of Śramaṇism, but not all Śramaṇism is ascetic.

Each Śramana group had a different relationship to Brahmanism, and many of these relationships changed over time, as did the relations between Śramaṇa groups. Also, here, regional or geographical relational variations should be taken into consideration. Buddhist literature sometimes indicates animosity between Śramaṇas and Brāhmaṇas, while at other times it describes cordial relations. Patañjali, on the other hand, indicates only hostility between the two factions. In his grammatical treatise he gives 'śramaṇa-brāhmaṇā' as an example of a compound expressing hostile relations, along with 'cat and mouse', 'snake and mongoose' and 'dog and fox' (Jaini 1970: 42); whilst Dharmakīrti, a seventh-century Buddhist monk, disparages both Brāhmaṇas and ascetics (Jaini 1970: 41). The overall relationship between the Śramaṇa traditions and Brahmanism should be considered as one of radical new movements which inverted the Vedic world. Celibacy was advocated by the Śramaṇas over marriage, and this is a crucial act which undermines Brahmanical emphases on familial and hereditary relations. For the Brāhmaṇa, the son is the father's self, ritual is concerned with ancestral worship and it is family that transforms the individual into a complete person. Countervailing procreation, in favour of anti-familial ways of life, was indeed a challenge to Brahmanical tradition. The new movements also promoted the wilderness over village or urban life, economic inactivity over economic productivity, ritual inaction over ritual performance and financial and material instability over residential stability (Olivelle 1992: 39ff.).

The Buddhists, Jains, Ājīvikas and other smaller Śramaṇa sects were invariably considered to be quite separate from, and outside, hegemonic Brahmanism. The *Upaniṣads*, however, had a more complex relationship. Although Upaniṣadic thought is, in certain regards, as much a departure from the Vedic worldview as that of the Buddhists and the Jains, it should be seen as more an intra-traditional subversion than an inter-traditional inversion. The *Upaniṣads* are traditionally considered to be part of the Vedic corpus. The *Upaniṣads* do not wholly reject Brahmanical tradition, but work within it and perhaps are best understood as a development of it, sometimes referred to as heterodoxy in contrast to Brahmanical orthodoxy and orthopraxy, other times as a tradition of 'orthodox renunciation' (Flood 1996: 90–92). Essentially, Upaniṣadic philosophy can be seen as an internalisation of the Brahmanical ritual action of the sacrifice. Whereas Brahmanism focused on (the benefits and significance of) external action, the *Upaniṣads* promoted a quietist spirit of internal reflection. Although the *Upaniṣads* imitate and promulgate Śramaṇa values, it is unclear whether the *Upaniṣads* (or their oral or textual precursors) were composed within a particular renunciate group or simply reflect the influence of Śramaṇa ideologies on Brahmanism.

See also: **Brāhmaṇas; Buddhism, relationship with Hinduism; Jainism, relationship with Hinduism; Karma (Law of Action); Languages; Mokṣa; Patañjali; Śramaṇa; Tapas; Upaniṣads; Vedism; Yajña**

ALICE COLLETT

Further reading

Flood, Gavin. 1996. *An Introduction to Hinduism*. Cambridge: Cambridge University Press.

Jaini, Padmanabh S. 1970. 'Ṣramaṇas: Their Conflict with Brāhmaṇical Society'. In Joseph W. Elder, ed., *Chapters in Indian Civilization*, vol. I. Dubuque, IA: Kendall Hunt Publishing Company.

Ñāṇamoli, Bhikkhu and Bhikkhu Bodhi (trans.). 1995. *Majjhima Nikāya* [he Middle Length Sayings of the Buddha: A New Translation of the Majjhima Nikāya]. Boston, MA: Wisdom Publication.

Olivelle, Patrick. 1992. *Saṃnyāsa Upaniṣads* [*Saṃnyāsa Upaniṣads: Hindu Scriptures on Asceticism and Renunciation*]. With an introduction by Patrick Olivelle. Oxford: Oxford University Press.

Walsh, Maurice (trans.). 1995. *Dīgha Nikāya* [The Long Discourses of the Buddha: A Translation of the Dīgha Nikāya]. Boston, MA: Wisdom Publication.

ŚRAUTASŪTRAS

The *Śrautasūtras* are a group of Sanskrit texts that describe the large-scale, public Vedic rituals. Most probably composed between 700 and 500 BCE, they are called 'śrauta' because they discuss rites that appear in the 'śruti', another name for the Veda. As such, they follow closely the Vedic ritual literature, especially the Brāhmaṇas, in terms of which rituals they describe and the instructions for how to perform them. However, as opposed to the Brāhmaṇas, the *Śrautasūtras* do not discuss the meaning or origin of the rituals, but focus on how they should be performed. Accordingly, the *Śrautasūtras* contain important information for a number of aspects of Vedic ritual practice: (1) an inventory of different types of rituals; (2) the time when particular rituals should be performed; (3) the actions of the priests and other ritual actors; (4) the utensils that are used; (5) the mantras that are spoken during the ritual and when they should be recited; (6) how to prepare the ritual ground; (7) appropriate donations to the priests. The *Śrautasūtras* categorise all the Vedic rituals into three groups: (1) the full-moon sacrifice; (2) more elaborate animal sacrifices; (3) the soma sacrifices. This three-fold division is shared by almost all the sūtra literature. The *Śrautasūtras*, together with the *Gṛhyasūtras* and the *Dharmasūtras*, are collectively called the *Kalpasūtras* and have all been preserved as part of the corpus of their respective Vedic Schools. Sūtra, which literally means 'thread', is a textual genre consisting of short aphorisms that present the essence of a doctrine in a concise form that is often incomprehensible without a commentary. In comparison with the *Gṛhyasūtras*, the *Śrautasūtras* are more closely based on the Veda. Whereas the gṛhya rituals required just one fire, the śrauta rituals required three to five fires.

See also: **Brāhmaṇas; Dharmasūtras; Gṛhyasūtras; Kalpasūtras; Soma; Veda**

BRIAN BLACK

Further reading

Gonda, Jan. 1977. *A History of Indian Literature: The Ritual Sūtras*. Wiesbaden: Otto Harrassowitz.

Flood, Gavin. 1996. *An Introduction to Hinduism*. Cambridge: Cambridge University Press.

Jamison, Stephanie. 1996. *Sacrificed Wife: Sacrificer's Wife*. New York: Oxford University Press.

Patton, Laurie. 2005. *Bringing the Gods to Mind: Mantra and Ritual in Early Indian Sacrifice*. Berkeley, CA: University of California Press.

ŚREṆI

Śreṇi is a Sanskrit term that was used to designate an association of artisans or tradesmen of different castes who were engaged in the same occupation, such as weaving or shoemaking. Śreṇis were powerful economic entities, and legal texts explicitly warned officials and rulers alike against interfering in their affairs. The śreṇis used this autonomy to ensure the financial well-being of their members by exerting a monopolistic control over the market. They could ensure that wages were kept sufficiently high by setting prices, could exclude competition by purchasing large quantities of raw materials, and could even restrict the supply of goods and services provided by their members. They minimised the risks of doing business, since financial burdens, such as the cost of protecting goods in transit, and rewards, such as profit, were to be shared equally among members. And they ultimately provided a form of pension, since a portion of the profits would be distributed among those members who had become old or infirm and among the widows of those who had died.

ETHAN KROLL

Further reading

Kane, Pandurang Vaman. 1941. *History of Dharmasastra*, vol. 2. Poona: Bhandarkar Oriental Research Institute.

Majumdar, Ramesh Chandra. 1918. *Corporate Life in Ancient India*. Calcutta: Calcutta University.
Mookerji, Radhakumud. 1919. *Local Government in Ancient India*. Oxford: Clarendon Press.
Thapyal, Kiran Kumar. 1996. *Guilds in Ancient India*. New Delhi: New Age International Publishers.

SRI LANKA, HINDUS IN

Sri Lankan Hinduism is a composite tradition. Its origins, which are pre-Buddhist, could be traced from the middle of the first millennium BCE. In the course of its development it has interacted closely with Buddhism and exerted a considerable influence over it. The kings of Sri Lanka have generally supported Hinduism and exercised a custodial function over its institutions and traditions. Learned brāhmaṇas were appointed as chief priests and masters of Vedic rituals at the royal court. Hinduism came under the impact of Christianity from the sixteenth century onwards. The Hindu revival led by Arumuka Navalar in the nineteenth century was a response to Protestant Christian evangelism.

In the Eastern Province Hinduism has co-existed with Islam since medieval times. Hindus are the second largest community in the island. Until recent times Hinduism was predominant in the north-east as a result of periodic migrations from South India which consolidated the early Tamil presence on the island. In modern times, Hindu communities have emerged in the plantations in the central parts of the island, in Colombo and several other towns in the Western and Central Provinces. In this era, the influx of South Indian Tamils was associated with the British Raj and the imperial economy. Hinduism is taught as a subject in schools, colleges and universities. The occasions of Tai-Poṅkal (Pongal), Śivarātri and Dīvālī are national public holidays.

The Hindus of Sri Lanka are mostly Śaivites. The cult of Śiva was widely prevalent before the introduction of Buddhism. It flourished in a multicultural setting and it had votaries among diverse ethnic groups. There are references to many individuals called Śiva in the ancient chronicles and inscriptions. During the course of its development in the island, Śaivism was influenced by developments in South India. In beliefs, doctrines and ideology, Śaivism as practised among the Tamils in India and Sri Lanka exhibited almost identical characteristics. It is basically a religion of bhakti or devotion to a personal God. The transcendent, eternal and omniscient Śiva is also conceived as the Supreme Divinity, who is beneficent, compassionate and constantly engaged in providing relief to devotees and in promoting their spiritual advancement and liberation. Besides, there is a considerable measure of diversity because of the assimilation of folk cults and practices of local or regional provenance.

The sacred literature of Śaivism is of four categories: Veda, *Āgamas*, the *Tirumuṟai* and the Śaiva Siddhānta treatises. Śaivism, which adopted the Vedic tradition during the early stages of development, has maintained a close association with specialists in Vedic learning and rituals. In the Śaiva tradition the expression vētam refers to the *Upaniṣads* because the theology of Śaivism is founded on their metaphysical thought. The *Āgamas*, which were compiled as manuals expounding the doctrines, rituals and practices of the principal cults of Hinduism in their post-Vedic phase of development, are of the utmost relevance. Their main focus is on the worship conducted in temples. Traditionally they consist of four parts, of which three are devoted to the description of rituals while the fourth one contains an exposition of Śaiva theology. According to tradition, there are twenty-eight texts called *Āgamas* pertaining to

Śaivism. Among these, the *Kāmika-Āgama* and the *Kāraṇa-Āgama* were used in the temple establishments on the island. Copies of these texts in the form of palm-leaf manuscripts are still found in the temples of Jaffna and Trincomalee.

In the region of Batticaloa, the reformist school of Vīraśaivism had exerted a considerable influence over the older tradition. Kurukkaḷs, who were matrilineal and matrilocal in their social organisation, performed the priestly functions there according to the principles of the *Vīrākamam*. The theology of this text is non-dualistic.

The *Tirumuṟai* is a large compendium of Tamil literature on Śaivism comprising texts of diverse proportions composed in the period between the fifth and thirteenth centuries. It is divided into twelve books. They include texts and poems of four categories: (1) the *Tēvāram* and other types of devotional hymns; (2) the *Tirumurukāṟṟuppaṭai* of Nakkīrar, which contains a description of the cult of Murukaṉ; (3) the *Tirumantiram* of Tirumūlar; and (4) the *Periyapurāṇam* and other texts extolling the life and work of the Nāyaṉmār who were the exponents of the bhakti school.

The study and exposition of the Veda and *Āgamas*, which are in Sanskrit, is the concern of a brāhmaṇa elite specialising in rituals. The *Tirumuṟai* is of the utmost importance to the Tamil Śaivites. The texts in this collection are intelligible and easily accessible. They epitomise the beliefs, thought and spirit of Śaivism and are recited with an intensity of devotion at temples, in homes and in schools. It is through them that the devotees realise the presence of Śiva in greater measure than by any other means.

In Śaivism there is a plurality of divinities. The cults of the Mother Goddess (Mahādevī), Skanda and Gaṇeśa had been assimilated so thoroughly in the early centuries of the Common Era that they have become inseparable. In Sri Lanka, Hindu temples (mandir) are found in large numbers. In every village and town inhabited predominantly by Hindus there are many temples dedicated for the worship of Piḷḷaiyār (Gaṇapati), Skanda/Murukaṉ and Amman (the mother Goddess). Usually brāhmaṇas conduct worship in them. They also conduct domestic rites, wedding ceremonies and post-funerary rites.

There are also temples of Kālī, Aiyannār, Vīrapattirar and Vairavar all over the entire north-eastern region. The priests at these temples are often not brāhmaṇas and some of these temples are managed and supported by some specific communities or castes. The form of worship and rituals conducted at these shrines could be non-āgamic. Rituals are conducted with solemnity and during times of worship emotions of piety and ecstasy are evoked among the participants.

Kings, princes and chieftains endowed the historic temples of Kōnēśvaram, Munnēśvaram and Tāntōnṟīśvaram with extensive lands. They were allocated to temple functionaries who were obliged to render service daily or periodically according to necessity. The arrangements made in medieval times have been largely disrupted. Yet, at Munnēśvaram, Tampalakāmam, Verukal and Kokkaṭṭiccōlai ancient traditions survive in a modified or muted form. Elsewhere, monetary contributions by pious devotees are the mainstay of economic support.

Participation at festivals (utsava), fasts and vows (vrata), pilgrimages (tīrthayātrā) and recital of sacred texts are the manifestations of religiousness among the Hindus. The Hindu calendar determines the dates and the specific times for the performance of religious activities. Worship is conducted at several sessions each day. There are five sessions of worship at the leading temples, whereas in small shrines with limited means worship is conducted once or twice daily. In the Hindu calendar there are many days in the year which have a religious significance. On such occasions there is a large congregation of devotees and the activities assume the character of a festival in all the major temples. The New Year, Pongal, Śivarātri, Dīvālī, Kantacaṣṭi, Tiruvempāvai and Āṭi-Āmāvācai are among such occasions. The annual festival is conducted usually for ten days on a grand scale with a great deal of pomp and pageantry.

There was considerable Hindu influence in the development of Buddhist art and architecture. The Indian *Śilpaśāstra* texts, the *Mānasāra* and the *Mayamata* were used on the island. The *Vaijayanti-Tantra* was another such text. The artisan communities affiliated to the Nānādesi merchants introduced it. Only a few medieval Hindu temples have survived in ruins. The Hindu temples of Polonnaruva are in the Chola style. The sanctum of the Munnēśvaram temple is the remnant of a medieval structure in the Vijayanāgara style. Modern Hindu temples, with the exception of Ponnampalavāṇēśvaram in Colombo, are buildings of brick construction. The entrance towers, some of which are imposing, are in the late Nāyaka style of Dravidian architecture.

The design and ornamentation of Buddhist temples exhibit traces of Hindu influence. The shrine of Upulvan at Devinuvara and the Nālanda Geḍigē are two stone temples constructed on the model of Hindu temples of the Pallava period. The Thūpārāma and other great temples of Polannaruva are in a hybrid style combining elements of Hindu architecture. The temples of Laṅkātilaka and Gaḍalādeniya in the Kandy district exhibit the characteristics of Hindu architecture in great measure. The design of the pillars, niches and ornamental motifs on the superstructure of modern Buddhist and secular buildings exhibits the characteristics of Hindu architecture in varying degrees.

It is not only architectural styles that are shared between Buddhism and Hinduism but also the deities themselves. This can be seen in the dēvālēs, which are Buddhist shrines to the four guardian deities of Lanka – Skanda, Viṣṇu, Pattini and Natha. The first two of these figures are well-known Hindu deities; Pattini is a deity from South Indian Buddhism and Natha is identified with the bodhisattva Avalokiteśvara. As well as separate shrines to these deities, gods such as Viṣṇu, Skanda and Gaṇeśa are frequently to be found in ancillary shrines within Buddhist temples.

In the eleventh and twelfth centuries a local school of bronze casting was developed on the inspiration provided by the Chola style. A large number of Hindu bronzes of exquisite design have been unearthed from the ruins of temples at Polonnaruva and Anuradhapura.

The life and work of Arumuka Navalar led to the revival of Hinduism in the nineteenth century. He had come under the influence of Christian missionaries and derived from his association with them the inspiration for reviving and reforming the religion of his ancestors. He adopted all the methods of the missionaries. He established a printing press and published Hindu and other Tamil texts in large numbers. He established schools and conducted a series of lectures on Śaivism, education and ethics. Inspired by his work the Hindu elite inaugurated and sustained a movement for religious awakening and social advancement.

In the same century, the Hindu revivalist and reform movements in India further inspired the Hindu community. In this respect the life and work of Swami Vivekananda are particularly significant. He had visited Colombo, Jaffna and Trincomalee and his visits were memorable events. In the twentieth century the Ramakrishna Mission was established in Colombo, under the guidance of Swami Vipulananda. He established a number of Hindu schools in the Eastern Province and contributed considerably to the progress of Tamil learning and innovative thinking in relation to human rights and social justice. In recent times the Chinmaya Mission, the Brahma Kumaris and the devotees of Sri Satya Sai Baba have captivated the imagination of many Hindus. A commitment to ethical values, co-existence and social awareness seems to have been developed among their followers.

There are several Hindu organisations. The All Ceylon Hindu Congress, the Vivekananda Society and the Tirukketisvaram Restoration Society are the most important and influential ones with a long history of achievement. There are also a number of youth organisations functioning at the provincial and local levels. There are many schools for providing training in the arts of dance and music. The Ramanathan Academy of Fine Arts, currently affiliated to the University of Jaffna, and the Vipulananda College of Dance and Music were established for the purpose of cultivating and promoting these arts.

See also: **Bhakti; Brahma Kumaris; Brāhmaṇa; Buddhism, relationship with Hinduism; Calendar; Caste; Dance; Dīvālī; Gaṇeśa; Hinduism, modern and contemporary; Kālī and Caṇḍī; Languages; Mahādevī; Mandir; Murukaṉ; Music; Nāyaṉmār; Pongal; Popular and vernacular traditions; Ramakrishna Math and Mission; Sacred texts; Sai Baba, Sathya; Śaiva Siddhānta; Śaivism; Saṃskāra; Śilpaśāstras; Śiva; Śivarātri; Skanda; Sthāpatyaveda; Temple worship; Tīrthayātrā; Upaniṣads; Utsava; Veda; Vīraśāivas; Viṣṇu; Vivekananda, Swami; Vrata**

S. PATHMANATHAN

Further reading

Arunachalam, P. 1916. 'Polonnaruva Bronzes and Siva Worship and Symbolism'. *Journal of the Royal Asiatic Society* (Ceylon Branch) xxiv, no. 68, 1915–16: 189–222.

Arunachalam, P. 1937. *Studies and Translations*. Colombo: Colombo Apothecaries Ltd.

Coomaraswamy, A.K. 1914. *Bronzes from Ceylon Chiefly in the Colombo Museum*. Colombo: Colombo Museum.

Godakumbura, C.E. 1960. *Polonnaruva Bronzes*. Colombo: Department of Archaeology.

Harrigan, Patrick (ed.). 2003. *Glimpses of a Heritage, 2nd International Hindu Conference Souvenir*. Colombo: Ministry of Hindu Affairs.

Indrapala, K. 2005. *The Evolution of An Ethnic Identity: The Tamils in Sri Lanka*. Sydney: MV Publications.

Pathmanathan, S. 1987. 'Hinduism and Buddhism in Sri Lanka Circa A.D. 1300–1600: Some Points of Contact between Two Religious Traditions', *Kalyāṇi: Journal of Humanities and Social Sciences of the University of Kelaniya*, ed. A. Liyanagamage, vols 5 and 6, 1986–87: 78–112.

Pathmanathan, S. 1990. 'Murukaṉ the Divine Child: The Kantacuvāmi temple at Nallūr', *Lanka 5* (Uppsala, Sweden): 80–102.

Pathmanathan, S. 1999. *Temples of Siva in Sri Lanka*. Colombo: Chinmaya Mission of Sri Lanka.

Pathmanathan, S. 2004. *Īlattu ilakkiyamum varalārum* (History and Literature of Īlam). Colombo: Kumaran Book House.

Pathmanathan, S. 2005. *Ilaṅkaiyil intu camayam* (Hinduism in Sri Lanka). Colombo: All Ceylon Hindu Congress in Collaboration with Kumaran Book House.

ŚRĪ VAIṢṆAVAS

The tradition that developed around the Āḻvārs and the later Sanskritic tradition through the contributions of Nāthamuni, Yāmuna and Rāmānuja developed into what has become popularly known as Śrī Vaiṣṇavism. This is particularly because of the special place given to Śrī-Lakṣmī in the overall scheme of salvation of the devotee. There has been a long history of the debate around the goddess Śrī-Lakṣmī beginning around the thirteenth century between two prominent theologians, viz. Vedānta Deśika and Piḷḷai Lokācārya, and finally culminating in the division of the

Śrī Vaiṣṇava community into northern and the southern traditions in the eighteenth century. The terms northern and southern have nothing to do with north India and south India, but rather they have to do with the two temples towns from where the two theologians came. While Vedānta Deśika came from Kāñcīpuram, which is in the northern part of Tamil Nadu, Piḷḷai Lokācārya came from the southern town of Śrīrangam. While Deśika wanted to attribute equal status to the goddess on a par with Viṣṇu, Lokācārya attributed a secondary status to her in the scheme of salvation. Regardless of the debate, both the southerners and the northerners consider themselves Śrī Vaiṣṇavas because of the special place of Śrī-Lakṣmī in their theology. The popular caste name that is often mentioned in this context, namely Ayyangar, needs some clarification. While Śrī Vaiṣṇava is a generic term that includes all those who belong to that tradition regardless of caste distinctions, the term Ayyangar refers to the brāhmaṇa community of this tradition.

See also: **Āḻvārs; Brāhmaṇa; Kāñcīpura; Lakṣmī, Śrī; Rāmānuja; Piḷḷai Lokācārya; Vaiṣṇavism; Viṣṇu; Yāmuna**

PRATAP KUMAR

Further reading

Carman, J.B. 1974. *The Theology of the Ramanuja: An Essay in Interreligious Understanding.* New Haven, CT and London: Yale University Press.

Jagadeesan, N. 1977. *History of Śrī Vaiṣṇavism in the Tamil Country: Post Rāmānuja.* Madurai: Kodal Publishers.

Kumar, P. Pratap. 1997. *The Goddess Lakṣmī: The Divine Consort in South Indian Vaiṣṇava Tradition.* Atlanta, GA: Scholars Press.

Narayanan, Vasudha. 1987. *The Way and the Goal: Expressions of Devotion in Early Śrī Vaiṣṇava Tradition.* Washington, DC: Institute for Vaishnava Studies & Centre for the Study of World Religions, Harvard University.

ŚRĪHARṢA

Śrīharṣa (twelfth century CE) was an important post-Śaṅkara dialectician of Advaita Vedānta who is famed for his *Khaṇḍana-Khaṇḍa-Khādya* ('Khaṇḍana' signifies his method of destructive criticism), a polemical work attacking the Nyāya, realist teachings. Śrīharṣa criticises and rejects the definitions (given by Nyāya and others) of right cognition (pramā), means of knowledge (pramāṇa: perception, inference, etc.) and the categories (padārtha: quality, substance, etc.). For Śrīharṣa, the reality of things cannot be established because all definitions involve the fallacy of circular argument, as in the case of attempting to define knower, known and knowledge. Difference is due to ignorance (avidyā) and is ultimately unreal – the ultimate truth of non-duality cannot be contradicted. Pure consciousness (to be realised) is beyond the rational intellect. The world of experience is indescribable – it is indefinable (neither real nor unreal); it is phenomenal and false. The *Khaṇḍana-Khaṇḍa-Khādya* was commented upon by Nyāya and Advaita thinkers. Śrīharṣa is also of interest with respect to his view of, and relation to, Buddhism (especially śūnyavāda, teaching on emptiness).

See also: **Advaita; Buddhism, relationship with Hinduism; Nyāya; Śaṅkara; Vedānta**

MARTIN OVENS

Further reading

Granoff, P.E. 1978. *Philosophy and Argument in Late Vedānta: Śrī Harṣa's Khandana-khandakhādya.* Dordrecht: D. Reidel Publishing Co.

SRINIVAS, MYSORE NARASIMHACHAR (1916–99)

Sociologist and social anthropologist who studied in Bombay with G.S. Ghurye and in Oxford with A.R. Radcliffe-Brown and E.E. Evans-Pritchard. In his early work,

Srinivas applied Radcliffe-Brown's structural-functional analysis to the Coorgs, a South Indian group with strong martial traditions who consider themselves kṣatriyas, coining the term 'Sanskritisation' to describe the process by which such groups adopted the customs, rites and beliefs of castes of higher ritual status. The concept (and its relation to other processes at work in Indian society such as Westernisation and secularisation) was clarified in a later essay in which he acknowledged that the usefulness of the term is greatly limited by both its complexity and its looseness. Srinivas was a leading advocate of the participant observation fieldwork which characterised many studies of Indian villages in the post-Independence period. The understanding of caste, especially as it undergoes change, which emerged from such work he regarded as an important corrective to that based on textual sources concerned with the four varṇas.

See also: **Caste; Hinduism, history of scholarship; Varṇa**

WILL SWEETMAN

Further reading

Shah, A.M., B.S. Baviskar, and E.A. Ramaswamy (eds). 1996. *Social Structure and Change*, vol. I: *Theory and Method – An Evaluation of the Work of M.N. Srinivas*. New Delhi: Sage.

Srinivas, M.N. 1952. *Religion and Society among the Coorgs of South India*. Oxford: Clarendon Press.

Srinivas, M.N. 2002. *Collected Essays*, ed. A.M. Shah. New Delhi: Oxford University Press.

ŚRUTI

See: **Sacred texts**

STARS (JYOTI, TARA, NAKSATRA)

Jyotiṣa (from jyoti, one of the Sanskrit words for 'star', meaning light, bright), the Indian word for astronomy/astrology, is among the oldest Vedic disciplines of learning. Its practice pre-dates the ancient *Lagadha Jyotiṣa*, one of the six *Vedangas*, which by internal evidence has been dated *c.*1300 BCE. The importance of Jyotiṣa derives from the necessity of finding the right time for the offering of the Vedic yajñas (sacrifices) and the performance of other religious rituals: the right time was determined by astronomical conjunctions, which had to be carefully observed. One reference in the *Ṛgveda* reflects astronomical observations that were made *c.*4500 BCE and another one in the *Śatapatha Brāhmaṇa* points to *c.*2300 BCE. Tāra, another word used for star, like jyoti, also means bright, shining. Nakṣatra, meaning 'imperishable', can designate (1) an individual star; (2) one of the twenty-seven equal parts into which the zodiac was divided; (3) an asterism consisting of one or more stars.

The oldest list of nakṣatras begins with the Kṛttikas (Pleiades), which were then associated with the spring equinox. *Satapatha Brāhmaṇa* 11.1.3,7 says: 'Other *nakṣatras* contain one star, or two or three or four stars, but these Kṛttikas are many; the sacrificer reaches plenty; therefore one should set up sacred fires on Kṛttika. These Kṛttikas indeed do not swerve from the East, while all other *nakṣatras* do swerve from the eastern direction.' Archaeo-astronomers have calculated that the observation referred to in this passage was made *c.*2300 BCE. The Kṛttikas do indeed 'swerve from the eastern direction' – like all other nakṣatras, though, that takes a long period of time – *c.*900 years elapse before the next nakṣatra becomes the point of reference for the spring equinox. The spring equinox had already shifted to the Ardra nakṣatra by the time of classical Hindu writings and has now reached Aśleṣa. The names of some of the twenty-seven (or in other sources twenty-eight) nakṣatras have changed over the ages. A complete list of the old and new names, together with the attribution of gender and presiding deity can be found in Kane (1958).

Under the influence of Greek astronomy (around the fourth century CE) the so-called Siddhānta calendar was adopted (the best known work of this genre is *Sūryasiddhānta*). The older division into 27 (28) nakṣatras became obsolete and was replaced by the zodiac, divided into 12 rāśis, each extending over 2½ nakṣatras. The 12 rāśis correspond to the 12 signs of the zodiac as used today in the West: Meṣa (Aries), Vṛṣabha (Taurus), Mithuna (Gemini), Karka (Cancer), Simha (Leo), Kanyā (Virgo), Tūla (Libra), Vṛścika (Scorpio), Dhanuṣ (Sagittarius), Makara (Capricorn), Kumbha (Aquarius), and Mīna (Pisces). They are identified with the limbs of the Kālapuruṣa ('the person made time', i.e. time imagined as having a human shape); in astrology particular constellations are related to the health or disease of specific limbs of the (human) body.

A famous name in later Jyotiṣa is that of Vārahamīhira (fifth/sixth century CE), author of the *Pañcasiddhāntika* and the *Bṛhatsaṃhitā*, which contains much information pertaining not only to astronomy but also to astrology. Individual nakṣatras were associated with auspiciousness and inauspiciousness relating to various enterprises: these allowed prognostications to determine the appropriate time for vratas (vows) and religious ceremonies. In course of time a Nakṣatra-vidyā arose which is close to what we call astrology.

A great role in Indian astronomy as well as in mythology was played by Dhruva ('firm'), the polestar. According to legend, Dhruva is the immortalised form of a faithful and constant seeker of Viṣṇu. *Viṣṇu Purāṇa* 2.12 positions Dhruva above the Seven Ṛṣis (Great Dipper) and says: 'the space between the Seven Ṛṣis and Dhruva, the third region of the sky, is the splendid Viṣṇu-pāda (path of Viṣṇu) and the abode of the saintly ascetics who are cleansed from every evil. In this portion of the heavens the splendid Dhruva is stationed and serves as the pivot of the atmosphere. On Dhruva rest the seven great planets and on them depend the clouds.' And: 'The chariots of the planets are fastened to Dhruva by aerial cords. The orbs of all the planets, asterisms and stars are attached to Dhruva and travel accordingly in their proper orbits, being kept in their places by their respective bands of air. As many as are the stars, so many are the chains that secure them to Dhruva; and as they turn round, they cause the pole-star also to revolve.' Dhruva is fixed in the celestial porpoise, which provides for its immobility. He was believed to be the unmoving pivot of the starry sky. However, over long periods of time also the position of the star considered the pole-star is changing. While the Vedic Dhruva was Alpha Draconis, the Dhruva of the *Purāṇas* was Beta Ursae Minoris, and the polestar of today is Alpha Ursae Minoris.

See also: **Brāhmaṇas; Purāṇas; Ṛṣi; Saṃhitā; Varāhamihira; Viṣṇu; Vrata; Yajña**

KLAUS K. KLOSTERMAIER

Further reading

Kak, S.C. 2000. *The Astronomical Code of the Ṛg veda*. Delhi: Munshiram Manohar Lal.

Kane, P.V. 1958. *History of Dharmaśastra*, vol. V, pt I. Pune: BORI.

Pande, G.C. (ed.). 1999. 'Development of Astronomy between the Vedanga Jyotiṣa and Aryabhata'. *Science and Civilization in India.* Delhi: Oxford University Press.

Sarma, K.V. (ed. and trans.). (n.d.). *Siddhānta Darpanam* by Nilakantha Somayajin. Adyar/Madras: Adyar Library and Research Centre.

STHĀPATYAVEDA (ARCHITECTURE)

It is difficult to find an exact Sanskrit equivalent for 'architecture'. Sthāpatyaveda (a sthapati is a traditional architect), often classed as one of the Upavedas, applies to the diverse body of texts treating the subject of building, though it is probably a less familiar term than *Vāstuśastra* ('treatises on dwellings') or *Vāstuvidya* ('knowledge of dwellings'), the latter implying the traditional theory or body of knowledge about architecture, not exclusively textual. Taken as a whole, the corpus of canonical texts deals with building design and construction, notably for towns, houses, palaces (houses for kings) and temples (houses for gods), interweaving such matters as orientation, proportion and choice of materials with mythological passages and with detailed instructions for rituals. The tradition is subject to contemporary popularisation, in the same way as Chinese feng shui. Scholarship, however, has so far been unable to show how the texts, for which no early illustrations survive, might provide an explanation of how traditional buildings in South Asia were actually designed and made, still less how their complex architectural forms can be understood. Buildings themselves provide surer answers to these questions.

To define 'Hindu architecture' is also problematic, even setting aside the vexed question of defining Hinduism. Certainly Hindu temples must qualify, along with maṭhas (Śaivite monasteries). It is inappropriate to divide sacred from secular, however, if we consider the related treatment given in the texts to temples, towns and residences, or that in medieval India (*c.* fifth to thirteenth centuries CE) the establishment of temples was expected of kings and played an integral role in state formation. Before labelling all early Indian architecture as Hindu, it should be borne in mind that, apart from the ancient vestiges of the Harappan civilisation, the oldest surviving architecture in the subcontinent, in which the roots of the later traditions can be traced, consists of the earlier stūpas, halls of worship (caitya halls) and monasteries (viharas) of the Buddhists, dating from about the second century BCE onwards. This architecture, in turn, cannot be called purely Buddhist, in that it clearly reflects a broader tradition. From around the fifth century CE, as worship of deities housed in shrines became predominant, the emerging temple architecture is not exclusively Hindu: the same styles are found in Jain temples and later Buddhist structures. With the arrival of Islam in South Asia, guilds of masons adapted their traditions to Muslim patronage, creating new 'Indo-Islamic' forms which, in their turn, were adopted for use in Hindu, Jain and Sikh monuments.

A number of the Brahmanical and Jain temples surviving from between the fifth and eighth centuries CE are rock-cut cave temples, developing from the earlier rock-cut tradition of the Buddhists. By the beginning of the seventh century structural temple architecture in stone or brick was well established, and had become differentiated into two main branches, the Nāgara and the Drāviḍa, the former belonging mainly to northern regions of the subcontinent, the latter mainly to the south. These categories can loosely be called 'styles', or 'orders', but 'architectural languages' is perhaps a more suitable term, in that the Nāgara and Drāviḍa traditions provide a range of components, a 'vocabulary', and establish different ways of putting these together. The shrine proper – the dark sanctuary where the principal image of the deity is housed, together with the superstructure towering above it – is the most important part of a temple. Organised around its cardinal axes, it is centralised and symmetrical, displaying architectural expression mainly on the exterior. A Nāgara shrine is most immediately recognisable by its curved spire (sikhara), single or multiple, and a Drāviḍa one by its tiered, pyramidal outline.

In terms of structure, the two classical languages of temple architecture use piled-up masonry, beams and corbelling, rather than arches and true domes. This architecture can be characterised as one based on imagery, as the masonry is articulated in terms of forms derived from timber construction, even if the details of wooden buildings become abstracted once translated into stone or brick. Typically, a temple design is conceived as composed of numerous smaller temples or shrines, arranged hierarchically at various scales, embedded within the whole or within one another. Often these elements are combined in ways that suggest a process or centrifugal emission and expansion. The resulting architectural patterns invite analogies with hierarchies of deities and their sequences of emanation. Despite the impression sometimes gained from texts that the rules for building temples are rigid, the medieval traditions were never static, and created an astounding variety of designs.

Nāgara and Drāviḍa traditions, though concentrated in what is now India, spread throughout most of the subcontinent and influenced related but distinct traditions in Southeast Asia. Kashmir developed its own kind of stone temple, while traditions of building wooden temples with pitched roofs evolved in the rainy regions of the Himalayan foothills and Kerala. From around the fifteenth century, Islamic rule in much of India resulted both in the disruption of earlier traditions and the infusion of new forms into temple designs. Yet Nāgara and Drāviḍa forms have periodically been revived. In recent years, not least among the Hindu diasporas worldwide, there has been an increasing demand for new 'traditional' temples. Drāviḍa temples are now designed mainly by sthapatis from Tamil Nadu, Nāgara ones especially by the Sompura caste from Gujarat. These traditional architects stress their credentials in terms of their ancient professional lineage and of their knowledge of traditional texts. They copy medieval forms, but adapt construction methods and planning to new climates and needs, notably to more congregational modes of worship than are traditionally accommodated in temples.

See also: **Buddhism, relationship with Hinduism; Caste; Diaspora; Image worship; Indus Valley Civilisation; Jainism, relationship with Hinduism; Mandir; Śaivism; Sikhism, relationship with Hinduism; Upavedas**

Adam Hardy

Further reading

Chakrabarti, V. 1998. *Indian Architectural Theory: Contemporary Uses of Vastuvidya*. London: Curzon.

Hardy, A. 1995. *Indian Temple Architecture: Form and Transformation*. Delhi: IGNCA and Abhinav Publications.

Hardy, A. (Forthcoming). *The Temple Architecture of India*. Chichester: Wiley Academy.

Michell, G. 1988. *The Hindu Temple: An Introduction to its Meaning and Forms*. Chicago, IL: University of Chicago Press.

Tadgell, C. 1990. *The History of Architecture in India*. London: ADT Press.

STRĪDHARMA

Strīdharma refers to women's (strī) religious rituals, duties, gender roles, and rules of decorum (dharma). Theoretically, it brings together duties according to class and stage of life (varṇa-āśrama-dharma) with those that are common to all women (strīdharma), although many authors have focused on the latter.

In classical and medieval Hindu works, an elite woman's life-cycle had three phases: maidenhood, marriage and sometimes widowhood or sati (self-immolation after her husband's death). An elite man's life-cycle, by contrast, had four phases: studentship (brahmacarya), marriage (gārhasthya), modified asceticism in the context of marriage (vānaprasthya) and renunciation of marriage and life as a wandering ascetic (saṃnyāsa). During maidenhood, strīdharma emphasised the preservation of virginity, training to be a good wife and some religious education. During the householder stage – with its threefold goals (trivarga) of duty/ritual/ethics (dharma), wealth (artha) and desire/pleasure (kāma) – elite women had to marry. They became sahadhārmiṇīs, those who performed dharma together with their husbands, especially the mandatory Vedic rituals for the deities and those for bearing sons (because a man could not fulfil his debt to the deities and ancestors without performing these). By extension, a married woman had to ensure the well-being of her husband and family by being faithful (pativratā), maintaining the household, educating the children and respecting her parents-in-law.

Mothers and other women in the extended family socialised young girls into this ideal of womanhood by drawing on praise of ideal wives such as Umā, Satī, Pārvatī, Sāvitrī, Anusūya, Draupadī (*Mahābhārata* 3.222.15–35; 13.134.32ff.) and Sītā (*Rāmāyaṇa* 2.39.23b, 24a etc.) or by recounting traditional stories about women performing vows (vrata-kaṭhās). An elite woman's dharma changed after menopause. She could either ignore some rules or join her husband, after receiving his permission, in vānaprasthya. But if her husband decided to become a wandering ascetic, her strīdharma was anomalous; accompanying him was out of the question. In fact, he ritually 'cremated' all his social identities (such as being a husband) and therefore became 'dead' to his wife. Nevertheless, strīdharma required her to continue being a good wife. The content of strīdharma changed, once again, if her husband died. At this time, some elite women had two choices: sati, self-immolation on her husband's funeral pyre – a rare choice even in elite circles but praised all the same – or widowhood, with its ascetic-like regimens. By choosing the latter, she could expect the family to help her not only in expiating the bad karma that had caused her husband's death in the first place but also in creating good karma for her husband, herself and others in the future. According to other authorities such as Parāśara, however, women could remarry.

Sometimes, descriptions of strīdharma were based on the premise that women's inherent nature (svabhāva) is sinful, promiscuous, fickle, impure or even dangerous; therefore it required self-control through the performance of strīdharma or the control of others (such as their husbands or the senior women in their families). Through strīdharma, women not only neutralised the negative effects of their svabhāva but also earnt merit for more auspicious rebirths and even deification (*Mahābhārata* 13.124.21). But some scriptural passages and women's own oral traditions viewed the inherent nature of women positively: as auspicious embodiments of goddesses such as Śrī Lakṣmī and, when married, as 'half the bodies' of their husbands. Moreover, Hindu women were often powerful matriarchs in the domestic sphere.

Pre-modern Hindu traditions had additional female orientations. Some women were heroic figures (warriors and queens) (vīraṇgaṇās). Others were elite courtesans (gaṇkās) and temple women (devadāsīs). And still others, especially in the lower castes and tribes, were sometimes powerful complements to their husbands or independent.

In some traditional circles even today, the ideals of strīdharma inform a Hindu woman's self-concept. But aspects of this ideal are changing. Hindus outlawed sati and child marriage in the nineteenth century, introduced divorce, encouraged widows to remarry and exposed the androcentric bias of scriptures and customs. Still, instruction booklets on wifely duties (*strī-smṛti*) and premarital instruction on a bride's future duties are common.

See also: **Artha; Brahmacarya; Child marriage; Devadāsīs; Dharma; Divorce;**

Draupadī; Gārhasthya; Kāma; Lakṣmī, Śrī; Mahābhārata; Parāśara; Pativratā and patiparameśvara; Pārvatī; Rāmāyaṇa; Saṃnyāsa; Sati; Sītā; Sāvitrī; Umā; Vānaprasthya; Virginity; Widowhood

KATHERINE K. YOUNG

Further reading

Kane, P.V. 1968–77 [1930–62]. *History of Dharmaśāstra*, 5 vols, 2nd edn. Poona: Bhandarkar Oriental Research Institute.

Knott, K. 1996. 'Hindu Women: Destiny and Stridharma'. *Religion* 26: 15–35.

Harlan, L. and P.B. Courtright (eds). 1995. *From the Margins of Hindu Marriage: Essays on Gender, Religion, and Culture.* Oxford: Oxford University Press.

Leslie, J. 1989. *The Perfect Wife: The Orthodox Hindu Woman According to the Strīdharmapaddhati of Tryambakayajvan*. Delhi: Oxford University Press.

McDaniel, J. 2003. *Making Virtuous Daughters and Wives: An Introduction to Women's Brat Rituals in Bengali Folk Religion*. Albany, NY: State University of New York Press.

Narayanan, V. 1991. 'Hindu Perceptions of Auspiciousness and Sexuality'. In J. Becher, ed., *Women, Religion and Sexuality: Studies on the Impact of Religious Teachings on Women*. Geneva: World Council of Churches Publications, 64–92.

Pearson, A.M. 1996. *'Because It Gives Me Peace of Mind': Ritual Fasts in the Religious Lives of Hindu Women*. Albany, NY: State University of New York Press.

Shah, S. 1995. *The Making of Womanhood: Gender Relations in the Mahābhārata*. Delhi: Manohar.

Young, K.K. 1983. 'From Hindu *Strīdharma* to Universal Feminism: A Study of the Women of the Nehru Family'. In P. Slater and D. Wiebe, eds, *Traditions in Contact and Change*. Waterloo, Ontario: Wilfred Laurier Press, 87–104.

SUBHADRĀ

Subhadrā is Kṛṣṇa's sister and Arjuna's wife, whose story is told in the *Mahābhārata*. It is Kṛṣṇa who persuades Arjuna to take her as his wife, carrying her away from Dvārakā when Balarāma had intended to bestow her hand upon Duryodhana, leader of the Kauravas. She later gave birth to a son, Abhimanyu, whose own son, Parikṣit, succeeded Yudhiṣṭhira to the throne and for whom she was appointed regent. She is accorded pride of place in worship of Kṛṣṇa as Jagannātha, in which her image and that of Balarāma are enshrined alongside Jagannātha in the temple at Puri and paraded about in the Ratha Yātrā festival.

See also: **Arjuna; Balarāma; Duryodhana; Dvārakā; Jagannātha; Kauravas; Kṛṣṇa; Mahābhārata; Mandir; Parikṣit; Ratha Yātrā; Utsava; Yudhiṣṭhira**

CATHERINE ROBINSON

Further reading

Dallapiccola, A.L. 2002. *Dictionary of Hindu Lore and Legend*. London: Thames and Hudson.

Shah, S. 1995. *The Making of Womanhood: Gender Relations in the Mahābhārata*. New Delhi: Manohar.

SUBRAMANYA

Subramanya is difficult to separate from Murukaṉ, the pre-eminent god of the Tamil people who dates back to the pre-Vedic period as an ancient god of war. Certainly, in most instances, the two names are interchangeable, however Subramanya seems to be more commonly used by the Tamil communities of Sri Lanka and Murukaṉ, in Tamil Nadu. It is sometimes proposed that Subramanya is the Sanskritised version of Murukaṉ, associated with Śiva and his son Kartikeya, who is himself assimilated from the Vedic deity, Skanda, the North Indian god of war. However, many Tamil Hindus also worship Murukaṉ, and regard him to be the son of Śiva and brother of Gaṇapati.

It is clear that 'Subramanya' has an ancient heritage. The Subramanya Swami temple at Tirupparankundram near

Madurai in Tamil Nadu, a cave temple known to date back at least to 200 BCE, is mentioned in Sangam literature of that period, and some of the temple inscriptions are dated to the same period.

The Subramanya temple at Tirupparankundram is known as one of the six sacred sites to the god, which are named Aru Padai Veedu and mark famous legendary events in his life. The other five are Tiruchendur, Palani, Swami Malai, Tiruttani and Pazhamuthircolai but the stories associated with these pilgrimage sites are well known to the devotees of Murukaṉ, who frequent them in their millions. Of interest, though, are the legends associated with Tirupparankundram and Swami Malai, where, respectively, Subramanyam/Murukaṉ married the daughter of Indra and taught the mantra oṃ to his father Śiva. Both these stories would suggest assimilation of the ancient Tamil god of war into the Vedic pantheon, and in the latter case his spiritual superiority over Śiva. This would appear to confirm the view that, historically, Murukaṉ becomes known as Subramanya after some kind of Sanskritisation process. The dating of the Subramanya Swami temple at Tirupparankundram does not detract from this theory as Sanskritisation of Tamil Nadu would have taken place prior to the second century BCE. Yet Subramanya is mentioned as a Vedic deity and endowed with the title 'Svāmi'. The other deity to be known by this nomenclature is Kumāra, a proto-divinity of Skanda. The *Skanda Purāṇa* also identifies Subramanya as Skanda, the Vedic war-god.

However, it must be kept in mind that although such distinctions are significant to the scholar of ancient Tamil religious history, they are unlikely to be so crucial to the student of contemporary Murukaṉ bhakti, who will find the two names used synonymously by devotees for the same deity sharing the same iconographic characteristics, the same two consorts, riding on a peacock, performing identical legendary feats, perceived as the offspring of Śiva and visited by pilgrims at the same temple sites. This is borne out in the diaspora context, where the Subramanya temple and ashram in Skanda Vale, South Wales, has become a weekend pilgrimage centre for British Tamil populations, who perceive no distinction between the mūrti installed therein and Murukaṉ.

See also: **Āśram(a) (religious community); Bhakti; Diaspora; Indra; Madurai; Murukaṉ; Oṃ; Śiva; Skanda; Svāmi; Tīrthayātrā (Pilgrimage)**

RON GEAVES

Further reading

Bunce, Fredrick. 2000. *An Encyclopaedia of Hindu Deities, Demi-Gods, Godlings, Demons and Heroes*, vol. I. New Delhi: DK Printworld.

ŚUDDHA ŚAIVA

See: **Śaiva Siddhānta**

ŚŪDRA

See: **Varṇa**

SUGRĪVA

Sugrīva is the younger brother of Vālin, both sons of the Vānara ruler Ṛkṣarajas (monkey), in the *Rāmāyaṇa.* He comes to the throne when Vālin is apparently killed by an asura (demon) but is ousted again when Vālin returns. His minister is Hanumān, with whose help he makes common cause with Rāma, when he arrives on his search for Sītā, promising aid in the search and military help in return for help against Vālin. Rāma kills Vālin and installs Sugrīva as Vānara king. After some delay, Sugrīva redeems his promise, search parties are sent and the Vānara armies assist Rāma in the battle against Rāvaṇa.

See also: **Asuras; Hanumān; Rāma; Rāmāyaṇa; Rāvaṇa; Sacred animals; Sītā**

JOHN BROCKINGTON

Further reading

Srinivasan, S.A. 1984. *Studies in the Rāma Story: On the Irretrievable Loss of Vālmīki's Original and the Operation of the Received Text as Seen in Some Versions of the Vālin-Sugrīva Episode*, 2 vols (Alt- und Neu-indische Studien, 25). Wiesbaden: Franz Steiner.

ŚULVASŪTRAS

The *Śulvasūtras*, or 'rules of the cord', give instructions for the measurement and construction, by means of stakes and cords, of the various sacrificial sites used in the Vedic rituals. They comprise one of the four divisions of the *Kalpasūtras* and are the work of various authors, the oldest of the *Śulvasūtras* being dated to *c.*600 BCE. Certain Indus Valley Civilisation altars appear to have been constructed according to the rules described in the *Śulvasūtras* and, as Frits Staal saw when filming an Agnicayana ritual in Kerala in 1975, many of today's altars continue to be so constructed.

Sacrificial sites, such as the elaborate, bird-shaped Agnicayana altar, incorporated symbolic links with the physical dimensions of the sacrificer, with the cosmos and with relevant mythic events. Accurate correspondences were crucial to the efficacy of the sacrifice. Thus mathematically precise instructions for preparing the dimensions of the altar are elaborately expounded in the *Śulvasūtras*, including theoretical treatments of topics such as the relation of geometrical measurements in quadrilaterals, equi-area transformation of figures and famously an early statement of Pythagoras' Theorem.

The *Śulvasūtras*' mathematical content has been cited (and debated) as an indication of India's sophistication in the ancient period, paralleling that of ancient Greece and Europe, and believed by some to be the inspiration for certain European 'discoveries' in mathematics and astronomy through cultural transmission by the Arabs.

See also: **Indus Valley Civilisation; Kalpasūtras; Science**

JESSICA FRAZIER

Further reading

Bag, A.K. and S.N. Sen. 1983. *The Śulvasūtras of Baudhāyana, Āpastamba, Kātyāyana and Mānava*. New Delhi: Indian National Science Academy.

Hayashi, T. 2003. 'Indian Mathematics'. In G. Flood, ed., *The Blackwell Companion to Hinduism*. Oxford: Blackwell.

Seidenberg, A. 1986. 'The Geometry of Vedic Rituals'. In Frits Staal, ed., *Agni: The Vedic Ritual of the Fire Altar*, vol. 2. Delhi: Motilal Banarsidass, 95–126.

Thibaut, G.F. 1984. 'On the Shulvasutras' and 'Baudhayana Shulvasutras'. In D. Chattopadhyaya, ed., *Mathematics in the Making in Ancient India*. Calcutta: K.P. Bagchi.

SUNDARĒŚVARAR

Sundarēśvarar is a localised form of the Hindu god Śiva. He resides in Madurai as the husband of the Tamil goddess Mīnākṣī. Legend states that Mīnākṣī was unbeaten in battle until she met Śiva in the form of Sundarēśvarar. Since Mīnākṣī is considered to be a form of Pārvatī, the only appropriate husband for her is Śiva. Unusually, the great temple complex that dominates the city is dedicated and named for the goddess rather than her male partner. Although the pair are considered married, Sundarēśvarar has a separate sanctum from Mīnākṣī. However, images of the pair are brought each evening to spend the night together. Their meeting, consequent battle and ensuing marriage are celebrated in spectacular style at the annual Chittrai festival.

See also: **Chittrai; Madurai; Mandir; Mīnākṣī; Pārvatī; Śiva; Utsava**

LYNN FOULSTON

Further reading

Fuller, C.J. 1992. *The Camphor Flame: Popular Hinduism and Society in India*. Princeton, NJ: Princeton University Press.

SŪRDĀS

A Sant bhakta whose songs remain popular in Northern India. He lived from 1478 to 1560 approximately and according to tradition was blind from birth. However, some scholars have interpreted the sant's affliction as spiritual blindness, to which he often refers. Yet in Hindi the word sūrdās is synonymous with physical blindness. One possible solution is that Sūrdās used his physical blindness as a metaphor for spiritual blindness.

His poetry was prolific and his couplets are still sung as bhajans throughout Hindi-speaking India. His magnum opus was the huge collection known as *Sūrsāgar* (Sūr's ocean), which recreates the tenth canto of the *Bhāgavata Purāṇa*. Sūrdās wrote in the Hindi dialect known as Braj Bhāshā, common to the region of Braj, south of Delhi, where it remains a living language to this day.

As with all the Sant poets, Sūrdās sings of the efficacy of remembrance of the divine name (nāma) and love of the personal God in assisting devotees to cross the ocean of the mundane world (saṃsāra) and achieve salvation (mokṣa). In particular, Sūrdās addresses his devotion to the form of Kṛṣṇa; however, it is not certain that he was a devotee of that deity, but rather used the name to refer to the omniscient and ever-present Lord of the Universe, the personal God of the Sants. Although life is regarded as painful in the poetry, there is always an optimistic note in that salvation is possible through the grace of loving deity. Sūrdās' poems are marked by an intense awareness of temporality, the joy of loving God and an intimate relationship with his Lord, to the point where he upbraids God for hiding his presence. Some of Sūrdās' poems are included in the *Guru Granth Sahib*, the sacred writings of the Sikhs.

See also: **Bhajan; Bhakti; Kṛṣṇa; Sant; Sant Sādhana; Sikhism, relationship with Hinduism**

RON GEAVES

Further reading

Hawley, John Stratton. 1987. 'The Sant in Sur Das'. In K. Schomer and W.H. McLeod, eds, *The Sants: Studies in a Devotional Tradition of India*. New Delhi: Motilal Banarsidass, 214.

SŪRYA

'Sun'. The Vedic sun-god, offspring of Dyaus Pitṛ; (*Ṛgveda* 10.37.1). The dawn-goddess Uṣas is recognised as his spouse (7.75.5). Sūrya receives scarcely more than a handful of hymns in the *Ṛgveda*, although he is extolled as far-seeing (7.35.8) and all-seeing (1.50.2), the arouser of humans (7.63.4), the ender of darkness for all (7.63.1) and the one who drives away illness and nightmares (10.37.4). In the *Ṛgveda*'s tenth mandala (10.170.4), he is given the epithet viśvakarman ('all-creating'), but he is also named as the guru of the asuras (8.90.12). The ambivalence of Sūrya's relationship to either the asuras or devas stems in part from the fact that, along with rain, he is the most contested prize. Indra steals a wheel from the sun's chariot to aid a mortal (1.175.4; 4.30.4), but otherwise he is generated by Indra (2.12.4). Elsewhere, Sūrya is a form of Agni whom the gods place in heaven (10.88.11). Although not a prominent deity in contemporary Hinduism, he is frequently conflated with Viṣṇu as Sūrya Nārāyaṇa. He is considered the guardian of the south-west. Under the name Savitṛ, he features in the Gāyatrī mantra, the daily morning prayer of many Hindus.

See also: **Agni; Asuras; Devas; Dyaus Pitṛ; Gāyatrī mantra; Guru; Indra; Uṣas; Vedic pantheon; Vedism; Viṣṇu**

MICHAEL YORK

SŪTRA

Sūtras are brief rules in Sanskrit giving instruction in a technical subject. The word often appears in the titles of texts, such as the *Brahmasūtras* or *Vedāntasūtras*. Each of these texts sets out its subject comprehensively but very briefly in a series of rules. The word sūtra denotes either the individual rule or the whole work, so such works can be referred to either in the plural (e.g. 'the *Brahmasūtras*') or in the singular ('the *Brahmasūtra*'). It means literally 'thread'; the sūtras are threads holding the fabric of the subject together. Śaṅkara describes the *Vedāntasūtras* as threads on which the upaniṣadic passages to which they refer are strung like flowers (commentary on *Brahmasūtra* 1.1.2; Thibaut 1904, 1: 17). The translation 'rule' is better than the older translation 'aphorism', which suggests a statement which, though brief, is comprehensible and independent of a context. A sūtra often has to be understood with reference to one or more preceding sūtras (Gonda 1977: 466).

Brevity is a higher priority than clarity in the composition of sūtras; the grammarian Patañjali says that a sūtra author rejoices more over the saving of one mātrā (a theoretical unit representing the time taken by a short vowel) than the birth of a son. Many sūtras consist of only two or three words, though they can be much longer, particularly if they include quotations. They are scarcely comprehensible without the commentaries which accompany them. Partly for this reason, the commentary itself became an important literary form in which authoritative texts were composed, such as Śaṅkara's, Rāmānuja's and Madhva's commentaries on the *Brahmasūtras*.

The practice of composing sūtras seems to have arisen in the context of the training of Vedic priests; the oldest sūtras are those closely connected with the Veda, known as *Kalpasūtras*. Different Vedic schools have their particular sūtras, closely related to the *Brāhmaṇas* of each school. Some passages of the *Brāhmaṇas* are in the style of sūtras, so the boundary between *Brāhmaṇa* and sūtra is somewhat arbitrary. Generally, however, sūtras are brief while *Brāhmaṇas* are discursive. The student would memorise the sūtras, and the teacher would afterwards explain them; such explanations would originally have been improvised, but they became the model for the commentaries which were written later. Reading a sūtra text without the commentary is thus rather like reading a lecture handout without hearing the lecture. The highest achievement of precision and brevity in the sūtra genre is the *Aṣṭādhyāyī* ('[treatise] in eight lessons') of Pāṇini, in which the grammar of Sanskrit in all its detail and variety is described in about 4,000 sūtras arranged in a systematic order, so that the rules on which the interpretation of any given rule depends always occur before it, never after it (Staal 1989, 2003).

Many sciences, and many schools of theology or philosophy, have their fundamental texts in sūtra form, the meaning of the sūtras being explained in an authoritative commentary. In the case of the *Brahmasūtras*, the foundation of Vedānta, there are several commentaries, such as those of Śaṅkara, Rāmānuja, Madhva and Vallabha, each using the authority of the sūtras to support a different theology. Pūrva Mīmāṃsā, Nyāya, Vaiśeṣika and Yoga are each founded on a set of sūtras attributed to an ancient ṛṣi. Sāṃkhya, unlike these five, has as its authority a verse text, the *Sāṃkhyakārikās*. There is the *Sāṃkhyasūtras*, attributed to the ṛṣi Kapila; but this is a relatively late text, unknown before the fourteenth century CE (Dasgupta 1957: 222; Hulin 1978: 153). It may have been composed to bring Sāṃkhya into line with the rest of the *Ṣaḍdarśana*.

The *Arthaśāstra*, the *Nāṭyaśāstra* (on dance, music and drama), the *Kāmasūtra* and two medical texts, *Suśrutasaṃhitā* and *Carakasaṃhitā,* are partly in sūtra form, though they also include passages of commentary and verses. The *Lokāyatasūtras*, attributed to Bṛhaspati, are not extant. There is a *Bhaktisūtra* attributed to Nārada and another attributed to Śāilya. The *Śivasūtra* (Dyczkowski 1992; Singh 1979) is a ninth-century text of Kashmiri Śaivism in sūtra form. But in general the sūtra form was replaced by verse as a medium for fundamental texts.

The Buddhists and Jains used the word sutta, the Pali or Prakrit form of the Sanskrit word sūtra, in a different sense, referring to texts which are often long and repetitive, quite unlike the sūtras described above.

See also: **Arthaśāstra; Brāhmaṇas; Brahmasūtras; Bṛhaspati; Buddhism, relationship with Hinduism; Dharmasūtras; Jainism, relationship with Hinduism; Kalpasūtras; Kāmasūtra; Kapila; Kashmiri Śaivism; Madhva; Nyāya; Pāṇini; Patañjali; Pūrva Mīmāṃsā; Rāmānuja; Ṛṣi; Ṣaḍdarśana; Sāṃkhya; Śaṅkara; Upaniṣads; Vaiśeṣika; Vallabha; Vedānta; Veda; Yoga**

DERMOT KILLINGLEY

Further reading

Dasgupta, Surendranath. 1957. *A History of Indian Philosophy*, vol. 1. Cambridge: Cambridge University Press.

Dyczkowski, Mark S.G. 1992. *The Aphorisms of Śiva: The Śivasūtra with Bhāskara's Commentary, the Vārttika*. Trans. with exposition and notes. (SUNY Series in Tantric Studies). Albany, NY: State University of New York Press.

Gonda, J. 1977. *The Ritual Sūtras*. Wiesbaden: Harrassowitz.

Hulin, M. 1978. *Samkhya Literature*. Wiesbaden: Harrassowitz.

Renou, Louis. 1963. 'Sur le Genre du sūtra dans la littérature sanskrite' [On the sūtra genre in Sanskrit literature]. *Journal Asiatique* 251: 165–216.

Singh, Jaideva. 1979. *Śiva Sūtra: The Yoga of Supreme Identity*. Delhi: Motilal Banarsidass.

Staal, Frits. 1989. *Rules without Meaning: Ritual, Mantras and the Human Sciences*. New York: Lang.

Staal, Frits. 2003. 'The Science of Language.' In Gavin Flood, ed., *The Blackwell Companion to Hinduism*. Oxford: Blackwell, 348–59.

Thibaut, George. 1904. *The Vedânta-Sûtras with the Commentary by Saṅkarâkârya*, 2 vols. Oxford: Clarendon Press. Reprinted Delhi: Motilal Banarsidass, 1962.

SVĀMI

The word Svāmi literally means 'owner of oneself' in Sanskrit and denotes someone who has achieved mastery of the self and achieved enlightenment through self-knowledge. Usually, a svāmi is a saṃnyāsin and the title is added to the person's name as a sign of respect and to indicate that they are a teacher with specialist knowledge. Although Svāmis have achieved liberation they remain committed to the service of others as teachers and guides to enlightenment. In recent times the best known Swamis in the West have been the monks of the Ramakrishna Math, who take on the title in addition to a new name to denote their particular path of enlightenment, e.g. Swami Vivekananda, the enlightened master (Swami) of the bliss (ānanda) of discernment, and (viveka) or Swami Shivananda, the enlightened master of the bliss of Śiva.

See also: **Ramakrishna Math and Mission; Saṃnyāsa; Shivananda, Swami; Śiva; Vivekananda, Swami**

VIVIENNE BAUMFIELD

Further reading

Flood, G. 2005. *An Introduction to Hinduism*. Cambridge: Cambridge University Press.

SVARGA

Svarga or heaven has a number of different senses in the Hindu tradition. For Śabara, a Mīmāṃsā commentor, svarga was unquestionably real but defied description. In Vedic practice the correct performance of sacrificial rituals required by the Veda was believed to secure a heavenly existence after death. Sometimes svarga was identified with pitṛloka (the world of the pitṛs or ancestors), though generally there was a differentiation between the two. Although svarga can mean specifically Indra's paradise, in later developments other deities have their own heavens, including Viṣṇu's Vaikuṇṭha and the Śaivite Śivaloka. Whether to attain such heavens is also to attain mokṣa is an area of disagreement since, whereas the Vaikhānasas regard mokṣa as entry to Vaikuṇṭha, Śivaloka may be viewed as the destiny of the householder (gārhasthya), as mokṣa is for the initiate. This relates to another complexity in understanding the meaning and implications of svarga as beliefs have changed from those that characterised the early Vedic period, centred on one life, to those that emerged subsequently, centred on reincarnation.

See also: **Cosmology; Deities; Gārhasthya; Indra; Mokṣa; Pitṛloka; Pitṛs; Pūrva Mīmāṃsā; Śaivism; Vaikhānasas; Vedism; Veda; Viṣṇu**

DENISE CUSH AND CATHERINE ROBINSON

Further reading

Flood, Gavin. 1996. *An Introduction to Hinduism.* Cambridge: Cambridge University Press.
Gächter, Othmar. 1983. *Hermeneutics and Language in Pūrva Mīmāṃsā: A Study in Śabara Bhāsya.* Delhi: Motilal Banarsidass.

SVĀSTIKA

Among the most ancient symbols of the world, the svāstika has had special significance for Hindu life for millennia. The name itself derives from the auspicious Sanskrit expression for greeting someone or for expressing good wishes for well-being. The symbol is shaped like a cross of even length, with the edges of the four arms turned in either a clockwise or counterclockwise direction. Ubiquitously found in Hindu homes and businesses, at festivals, on cattle and in sacred sites of every variety, the svāstika retains its primary spiritual resonance and apparently decorative function. As its origins are buried in obscurity, hosts of interpretation about its symbolic significance have arisen. Some of these include its centrality in the Vedic ritual (although its appearance on the Indian scene seems to date back to the earlier Indus Valley Civilisation), its implications in the development of the solar calendar and its wide association with the worship of the sun, Lord Gaṇeśa and various other gods and goddesses.

See also: **Calendar; Gaṇeśa; Indus Valley Civilisation; Vedism**

DEVEN M. PATEL

Further reading

Weger, Robert R. 1998. *The Swastika: A History.* Lafayette, CA: Trebor Regew And Associates.

SVAYAṂVARA

The svayaṃvara, literally 'self choice', is the selection of a husband by the bride. Thus, it departs from the legal forms of marriage discussed in the Sanskrit dharma literature. Certain dharma texts do, however, accord it legality. This is the case if the parents have been unable to locate a husband for the girl or when the parents have died and there is no competent guardian. If the girl chooses her husband without her parents' permission she must return to them all her ornaments, and the husband is not obligated to pay bride-price (śulka), a sum given by the husband or his family for the bride. (This was a predecessor of the opposite practice, begun in the late first millennium CE, of the bride's family giving the husband's family a sometimes large sum of money and/or goods for the privilege of marrying into his family. This is the 'dowry system', and is sometimes confused with the earlier practice because the same word, śulka, was often used for it.) The svayaṃvara is often romanticised in the Sanskrit epics, at least for kṣatriyas. Examples, all of which are of intelligent and discriminating girls from royal families who pursue the highest ideals of dharma, include the svayaṃvaras of Sāvitrī (*Mahābhārata* 3.277ff.) and Damayantī (*Mahābhārata* 3.54ff.). In the Raghuvaṃśa, the poet Kālidāsa describes the svayaṃvara of Indumatā. The only case of a svayaṃvara that is recognised as historically verifiable is found in Bilhaṇa's Vikramāṅkadevacarita, where he describes the svayaṃvara of Candralekhā, the daughter of the Śilāhāra prince of Karahāṭa (Karad in North Kanara district of Karnataka), who, in the latter half of the eleventh century, chose Āhavamalla or Vikramāṅka, the Cālukya king of Kalyāṇa.

See also: **Itihāsa; Kālidāsa; Sāvitrī; Varṇa; Vivāha**

FREDERICK M. SMITH

Further reading

Kane, P.V. 1974. *History of Dharmaśāstra*, 2nd edn, vol. 2, pt 1. Poona: Bhandarkar Oriental Research Institute, 523–24.

Parpola, Asko. 'Sāvitrī and Resurrection'. In Asko Parpola and Sirpa Tenhunen, eds, *Changing Patterns of Family and Kinship in South Asia. Studia Orientalia* 84 (1998): 167–312.

ŚVETĀŚVATARA UPANIṢAD

See: **Upaniṣads**

SWAMI

See: **Svāmī**

SWAMI NARAYANA SAMPRADAYA

The Swami Narayana Sampradaya is a rapidly growing, wealthy Hindu movement developing from a early nineteenth-century reform movement in Gujarat led by a sādhu called Swami Narayana. It grew steadily among Gujaratis in the Bombay Presidency during British rule, and then expanded and became a transnational movement during the twentieth century in East Africa, the United Kingdom, North America and Australasia as part of a resurgence of neo-Hinduism.

Swami Narayana (Sahajanand Swami, 1781–1830) began to teach and gather followers in Gujarat in 1802 following a period of wandering throughout India as an ascetic student. He was born in Chhapia, near Ayodhyā, to brāhmaṇa parents. He was initiated into the Vaiṣṇava tradition of Rāmānuja and undertook to reform the teachings and practice of Hinduism in Gujarat during a period of division and social turmoil.

He established strict standards for sādhus: (1) celibacy; (2) renunciation of family ties and previous social status; (3) avoidance of attachment to objects of the senses; (4) holy poverty; and (5) overcoming prideful ego. The sādhus resided in temples, but travelled in villages, always in pairs, to teach and attract followers. Initiation (dīkṣā) of lay followers included a vow, 'I give over to Swaminarayan my mind, body, wealth and the sins of previous births', water poured over the right hand and the repetition of the Swami Narayana mantra. Their vows are to avoid eating meat, avoid all intoxicating drinks and drugs, avoid adultery and never defile oneself or others. Sādhus avoid all contact with women, and women remain separate from men in temples and organise their own religious activities.

Sahajanand Swami adopted two nephews and appointed them as ācāryas of the two dioceses in Ahmedabad and Vadtal. Lineal descendants from his family continue as ācāryas – Tejendraprasad in Ahmedabad and Ajendraprasad in Vadtal. They operate independently and oversee the temples and sādhus and world-renouncers (approximately 775 in Ahmedabad diocese and 1,468 in Vadtal). Their wives act as religious specialists for women. Ācārya Tejendraprasad and his son, Koshalendraprasad, have been active in organising and visiting temples abroad in the International Swaminarayan Satsang Organisation (ISSO) and the International Swaminarayan Satsang Mandal (ISSM).

Schism in the twentieth century resulted in the Bochasanwasi Akshar Purushottam Sanstha (BAPS), the Swaminarayan Gadi, the Yogi Divine Society and the Anoopam Mission. BAPS is the largest and fastest growing both in India and abroad. It began when Swami Yagnapurushdas (1865–1951) left the temple in Vadtal in 1906. He taught that Swami Narayana is always manifest in the world in the person of his chief devotee. The current leader is Narayanswarupdas (Pramukh Swami, b. 1921) who is accepted as guru and revered as divine. He initiates sādhus and directs the work of approximately 700 sādhus. BAPS is noted for large new cultural centres (e.g. Akshardham in Gandinagar and in Delhi) and temples in India and abroad (e.g. Neasden in North London and Bartlett in Chicago).

See also: **Ayodhyā; Brāhmaṇa; Celibacy; Diaspora; Dīkṣā; Guru; Mantra; Narayana, Swami; Rāmānuja; Sādhu; Saṃpradāya; Vaiṣṇavism; Women, status of; Women's rites**

RAYMOND BRADY WILLIAMS

Further reading

Williams, R.B. 2001. *An Introduction to Swaminarayan Hinduism*. Cambridge: Cambridge University Press.

SWASTIKA

See: **Svāstika**

T

TAGORE, DEBENDRANATH (1817–1905)

Father of Rabindranath Tagore. Debendranth Tagore joined the Brahmo Samaj in 1843. Brought up as a Kālī devotee, Tagore underwent a profound spiritual experience in 1835 and converted to a strict aniconic monotheism. Tagore revitalised the Samaj, which had made little progress since Rammohan Roy's death. He introduced new elements of worship and compiled the *Brahmo-upadeśa* – an anthology of readings from the *Upaniṣads*.

Faced with a challenge from Christian converts about the Samaj's doctrine of the infallibility of the Veda, Tagore sent four students to Benares to study the Veda, and later visited the city himself in 1847. The Samaj abandoned the doctrine in 1850, affirming that no religious text was to be held as infallible.

Following the schism created by Keshub Chunder Sen, Tagore continued to lead the society, which was renamed the Adi Brahmo Samaj.

See also: **Hinduism, modern and contemporary; Kālī and Caṇḍī; Roy, Rammohan; Tagore, Rabindranath; Upaniṣads; Veda**

GEORGE CHRYSSIDES

Further reading

Tagore, D. 1914. *The Autobiography of Maharshi Devendranath Tagore*. London: Macmillan.

TAGORE, RABINDRANATH (1861–1941)

Born in Calcutta, Rabindranath Tagore was the son of Debendranath Tagore, Indian reformer and leader of the Brahmo Samaj. His grandfather, Dwarakanath Tagore, was a friend of Rammohan Roy. Tagore exerted immense influence on the modernisation of India and gained considerable reputation as a poet, novelist, musician, artist and painter, as well as a reformer and critic of British colonialism.

In 1870 Tagore came to England to study law, but returned to India after only a year, becoming a prolific and highly influential writer. Between 1893 and 1900 he composed seven books of poetry. Of particular importance is Tagore's *Gitanjali, Song Offerings* (1912), which consists of English translations, in prose, of his own Bengali poems, including *Gitanjali*, composed in 1910. W.B. Yeats and Ezra Pound expressed great enthusiasm for them and they gained him the Nobel Prize for Literature in 1913. In 1915 Tagore received a knighthood from King George V. He renounced it in 1919, following the massacre of 400 demonstrators at Amritsar by British troops.

Tagore founded Shantiniketan ('Abode of Peace') in 1901 – a school which aimed to combine traditional Indian and modern Western education. This became Vishva-Bharati University in 1924.

Tagore's ideology was based on the *Upaniṣads*, and in particular their monism. A member of the Brahmo Samaj, he believed in one formless deity, with whom the soul could recognise its oneness. Personal purity should therefore be cultivated as a means of service to others: the divine oneness should find expression in the political sphere, with a new world order based on 'unity consciousness'. Although Tagore was an important influence on Gandhi, he found little support for his own ideological values. However, between 1916 and 1934 he undertook considerable international travel, from Persia to the Far East, where he propagated his ideal of uniting East and West.

See also: **Brahmo Samaj; Gandhi, Mohandas Karamchand; Hinduism, modern and contemporary; Roy, Rammohan; Tagore, Debendranath; Upaniṣads**

GEORGE CHRYSSIDES

Further reading

Robinson, A. and Krishna Dutta. 1997. *Rabindranath Tagore: The Myriad-minded Man*. London: Bloomsbury.

Thompson, E.J. 1921. *Rabindranath Tagore: His Life and Work*. Calcutta: Association Press.

TAI PUSAN

Tai Pusan is celebrated at the beginning of the month Tai (January–February) after the Pongal festival in the Tamil area. It focuses on Murukaṉ, remembering the young god's ascetic behaviour and the conquest of his (own) passions. The god's virility and strength, symbolised in his vēl (spear), will be shared with his devotees during the festival. While only of limited importance among Hindu festivals in India, Tai Pusan is the main festival for Hindus in Malaysia and Singapore since the 1930s. Every year several hundred thousand people gather for the festival at the Batu Caves in the vicinity of Kuala Lumpur (but also on Penang island and in Singapore), approaching the god's chariot and doing penance all the way up to the Murukaṉ temple. Displaying the minority Hindu religion in public against a Muslim Malay or Chinese influenced Singaporean society, the festival won huge acceptance as a symbol for Hindu identity in Southeast Asia.

See also: **Diaspora; Murukaṉ; Pongal; Southeast and East Asia, Hindus in; Utsava**

MANFRED HUTTER

Further reading

Clothey, F.W. 1978. *The Many Faces of Murukaṉ*. The Hague: Mouton Publishers, 117–20, 138–42.

Collins, E.F. 1997. *Pierced by Murugan's Lance*. DeKalb, IL: Northern Illinois University Press, 62–88.

TAITTIRĪYA UPANIṢAD

See: **Upaniṣads**

TAMIL VEDA

Śri Vaiṣṇavas consider the entire collection of Tamil devotional poems of Āḻvārs (poet-saints), in praise of Lord Viṣṇu, called *Nālāiyrativviya-pirapantam*, or *Divya Prabandha* (The Sacred Collection of Four Thousand Verses), as the Tamil Veda. These hymns are said to have been revealed to Nātamuni, the first Śri Vaiṣṇava teacher, who compiled them around 900 CE. What is significant is that the term Veda, normally associated with the Sanskrit Veda and sometimes used for other Sanskrit texts such as the *Mahābhārata*, is, for the first time, used for a work in a vernacular medium.

While all the poems of Āḻvārs in the *Divya Prabandha* are considered revelatory, *Tiruvāymoḻi* (Sacred Utterance), by the poet-saint Nammāḻvār (eighth/ninth century), is accorded a pre-eminent place. *Tiruvāymoḻi*, the last and most important of the four works of Nammāḻvār, is a mystical poem of 1,102 verses and expresses Nammāḻvār's deep longing to be united with the Lord Viṣṇu, who is said to have revealed himself to Nammāḻvār. For Śri Vaiṣṇavas, divine revelation is not restricted to the Sanskrit Veda or Vedic seers, nor exclusively revealed through the medium of Sanskrit, but is also seen as manifesting itself through the twelve Āḻvārs, principally through Nammāḻvār. *Tiruvāymoḻi* is often spoken of as 'the Tamil or Dravida Veda'. It is neither a copy nor a translation of the Sanskrit Veda. It is regarded as a revealed text and on a par with the *Sāmaveda*; both are seen as equally valid. Some of the poems were set to music, and even to this day they are chanted in Śri Vaiṣṇava temples and homes.

See also: **Āḻvārs; Languages; Mahābhārata; Nammāḻvār; Saṃhitā; Śrī Vaiṣṇavas; Veda; Viṣṇu**

SHARADA SUGIRTHARAJAH

Further reading

Carman, J. and V. Narayanan. 1989. *The Tamil Veda: Pillan's Interpretation of the Tiruvaymoli*. Chicago, IL: University of Chicago Press.

Sundram, P.S. (trans.). 1996. *The Azhwars: For the Love of God. Selections from the Nalayira Divya Prabandham*. New Delhi: Penguin.

TANTRAS

Broadly conceived, the *Tantras* are the scriptures of the Hindu Tantra; in other words, Hindu Tantra as a tradition is named after its scriptural canon. Not all textual sources on Hindu Tantra call themselves *Tantras*, however; nor is it the case that all Hindu works with *Tantra* in their titles have Tantra as their subject matter. On the one hand, many Hindu Tantric scriptures call themselves *Āgamas*, *Saṃhitās*, *Yāmalas*, *Matas*, etc.; on the other, the *Pañcatantra*, a celebrated collection of animal tales and fables, has nothing to do with Hindu Tantra.

Like most other South Asian scriptural traditions, many of the Hindu *Tantras* are compilations, collections of spells and ritual instructions literally strung together (texts are called granthas, 'knottings' of usually palm-leaf pages, whose knots could be opened to insert additional leaves), with new material interleaved as their compilers saw fit to add new material. This is particularly apparent in works like the *Netra Tantra*, which clearly began as a collection of data from multiple sources on demonology. In a later phase of redaction, the patently polytheistic demonological data became interspersed with passages on the efficacy of the amṛteśa ('Lord of Immortality') mantra and the supremacy and unicity of Śiva, in his Amṛteśa or Mṛtyuñjaya form. One sees a similar process at work in the Tantric canon specific to the goddess Kubjikā. Scriptures such as the *Manthānabhairava Tantra* and *Gorakṣa Saṃhitā* borrow massive chunks of text from one another, as well as from the root *Tantra* of the Kubjikā tradition, the *Kubjikāmata*, and other Tantric texts.

Hindu Tantric literature is divided into two major corpora: (1) 'revealed' works of anonymous authorship, most often having the form of dialogues between two supreme divinities, usually a form of Śiva or Viṣṇu and his consort (Kālī, Kubjikā, Lakṣmī etc.); and (2) 'signed' works by a single author, which comprise commentaries, compendia or guides to the doctrines and practices found in the revealed Tantric literature. This ancillary tradition is often referred to as Tantra Śāstra, the 'Science of Tantra'. The most important works in both of these categories were committed to writing in the eighth to twelfth centuries CE. However, in the course of the many Tantric revivals that have taken place in South and Southeast Asia – in north-east India and Nepal in particular, between the fourteenth and sixteenth centuries – new *Tantras* have continued to be compiled down to the present day. While the vast bulk of the Tantric canon is written in Sanskrit, much of the more recent Tantric literature is written in the Bengali, Hindi and other vernacular languages/dialects.

In spite of the fact that its teachings are the revelations of supreme beings, the Tanric canon is – like the epic and purāṇic literature – considered to be smṛti (tradition) rather than śruti (heard or revealed). While certain of the early *Tantras* (such as the *Kriyākālaguṇottara*) are non-sectarian compendia of magical spells, charms and demonological practices, the great bulk of the Hindu Tantric canon is sectarian, of either Vaiṣṇava, Śaiva or Śākta-Śaiva (also termed Kaula) orientation. Many of the most important Vaiṣṇava *Tantras* are called *Saṃhitās* ('compendias'), such as the *Jāyākhyā Saṃhitā* and *Ahirbudhnya Saṃhitā*, but some are also called *Tantras*, such as the *Lakṣmī Tantra*. The works of the Śaiva Tantric canon are referred to as either *Āgamas, Tantras* or *Saṃhitās* (for example, the *Mṛgendrāgama* has also been called the *Mṛgendra Tantra* and the *Mṛgendra Saṃhitā*). It is with the Śākta-Śaiva canon that the greatest variety of titles are found. Whereas the majority of revealed Śakta works are called '*Tantras*', a wide range of other titles are found: *Kaulajñāna Nirṇaya*, *Śrītantrasadbhāva*, *Siddhayogeśvarīmata*, *Jayadratha Yāmala*, *Tripurā Upaniṣad*, etc. *Tantras* reserved for the 'inner circle' of Śākta-Śaiva practitioners are classified under the heading of '*Kaula Tantra*'. Significant portions of certain *Purāṇas* – the *Agni Purāṇa* and *Kālikā Purāṇa* in particular – contain data that are identical to those found in the sectarian *Tantras*; and the canons of Hindu alchemy and Haṭha Yoga also lie within the purview of Tantric literature.

In a number of *Tantras* and Tantric commentaries, one finds various unsystematic attempts to systematise the literature of the revealed Tantric canon. While the content of the lists one encounters is somewhat arbitrary, there is a certain uniformity in them, which is comparable to that of the many lists of the eighteen *Mahāpurāṇas*.

Thus one encounters the canonical numbers of 108 *Pāñcarātra Saṃhitās*, 28 Śaiva *Āgamas* and 64 Śākta-Śaiva *Tantras*. Several traditions subdivide the Tantric canon into the Left (Vāma), Right (Dakṣiṇa), and Established (Siddhānta) currents. Other classificatory schemata include the four Seats (Pīṭhas) of revelation of the Śākta-Śaiva *Tantras* and the five Transmissions (āmnāyas) of the *Tantras* that streamed from Śiva's mouth. Abhinavagupta (Fl. 975–1025 CE), the great Trika commentator, subdivides the Śākta-Śaiva canon into 10 dualist Śaiva *Āgamas*, the 18 intermediate *Rudra Āgamas* and the 64 non-dualist *Bhairava Āgamas*. Similarly, while there are multiple discussions of the normative contents of a Hindu Tantra (like the *pañcalakṣaṇa* of the *Purāṇas*), few Tantric scriptures ever truly respect said norms. A striking example is the theoretical division of the *Āgamas* into four categories (pādas) of ritual practice (kriyā), customary behaviour (caryā), higher knowledge (vidyā) and concentration (yoga); in fact, very few *Āgamas* respect this division, with most devoting nearly all of their content to the first two.

Whereas the Sanskrit of the revealed Tantric texts is generally poor, that of the signed works of Tantra Śāstra is highly grammatical and polished. This ancillary literature is subdivided into many categories, including commentaries (*vṛttis*), philosophical treatises (*śāstras*), step-by-step ritual guides (*paddhatis*), scriptural digests (*nibandhas*), ritual or doctrinal monographs (*prakaraṇas*), hagiographical tracts, hymns of praise (*stotras*), theoretical treatises on mantras (*mantra śāstras*), etc. The length of these works ranges from a few short verses to such massive compendia as the Śākta-Śaiva *Tantrāloka* ('Elucidation of the Tantras') of Abhinavagupta and the 1095 CE Śaiva *Somaśambhupaddhati* of Somaśambhu, which are thousands of verses in length.

See also: **Abhinavagupta; Haṭha Yoga; Itihāsa; Kālī and Caṇḍī; Kashmiri Śaivism; Lakṣmī, Śrī; Languages; Mantra; Nepal, Hindus in; Pañcatantra; Purāṇas; Sacred texts; Śāktism; Śiva; Southeast and East Asia, Hindus in; Tantrism; Vaiṣṇavism; Viṣṇu**

DAVID GORDON WHITE

Further reading

Gonda, J. 1977. *Medieval Religious Literature in Sanskrit*. History of Indian Literature, II, 1. Wiesbaden: Harrassowitz.

Gouriaan, T. and S. Gupta. 1981. *Hindu Tantric and Śakta Literature*. History of Indian Literature, II, 2. Wiesbaden: Harrassowitz.

TANTRIC YOGA

Although, strictly speaking, Tantric Yoga consists of the practice of Kuṇḍalinī Yoga, the term 'yoga' also generally denotes a spiritual endeavour of any kind, which may be more accurately termed sādhana. From a Tantric perspective, the religious path runs along seven modes corresponding to the degree of ability and the disposition of the devotee or aspirant (sādhaka). Practitioners are divided into three groups and progress from beasts (paśu) to heroes (vīra) and eventually to celestials (divya).

The seven modes of spiritual observance and attainment (ācāra, conduct) are: Veda, Vaiṣṇava, Śaiva, Dakṣiṇa, Vāma, Siddhānta and Kaula. Vedācāra consists in following the Vedic path of rituals and sacrifices with its corresponding observances. The Vaiṣṇavācāra or mode of Viṣṇu is the path of bhakti, intense devotion. The Śaivācāra or mode of Śiva adds gnosis (jñāna) to devotion, and the Dakṣiṇācāra, or mode of the right or auspicious side or hand, which may also encompass the three precedents, is the traditional worship of the goddess Devī, or Śakti.

The common characteristic of these lower stages of sādhana is that its devotees follow the brahmanical dharma by observing the rules that govern the social hierarchy (varṇa) and the stages of life (āśrama). Although the followers of the dakṣiṇācāra are Śākta, it is only with the practices belonging to the vīra, who are fully in control of their senses, that we enter the domain of Tantra proper, so that many sources conceive of only two types of ācāra: Dakṣiṇa and Vāma, 'right hand' and 'left hand'.

Vāmācāra, the 'practice of the left (hand)', which is far more ancient than the Dakṣiṇācāra, is associated with the Kaula, a term derived from kula (family). A Kaula is an initiate who belongs to the 'family' of the goddess, which is nothing less than her divine manifestation throughout the whole cosmos, microcosmically present in the worshipper as Kuṇḍalinī Śakti, the coiled Energy whose awakening and upward thrust carry the devotee to his union with Śiva (Kuṇḍalinī Yoga).

That union, which is a state of liberation-in-life (jīvanmukti) is, it is said, what characterises the true Kaula.

The Kaula rite involves partaking of the five pañcamakāras ('makers of the sound Ma'), also called the 'five substances' (pañcatattva) – that is, madya (alcohol), maṃsa (meat), matsya (fish), mudrā ('gesture'; here: parched grain) and maithuna (sexual intercourse), respectively linked with the cosmic elements of fire, air, water, earth and ether. For the paśu, these transgressive substances/actions are replaced by suitable substitutes. For the divya the substances are purely symbolic. Thus only the vīra are expected to enact the rite literally. Taking place at night, among a circle (cakra) of adepts, male and female, regardless of caste, the rite is presided over by a 'Lord of the cakra' (Cakreśvara) sitting with his female partner (Śakti) in the centre of a circle formed by the participants. The female partner may be one's own wife (adya śakti: primal śakti), someone else's (parastrī) or common property (sādhāranī). Since the first case is associated with 'Vedic practice' the last two, being antinomian, tend to be preferred. The consecrated woman becomes a Śakti and may be enjoyed (bhogyā) or worshipped (pūjyā).

Dakṣiṇācāra is also known as Samayācāra (conventional or established practice). This method was conceived in the sixteenth century by Lakṣmīdhara – whose commentary on chapter 9 of the *Saundaryalaharī* forms its classic exposition – in reaction against the older antinomian practices of the Vāmācārin (see above). The main focus of the system is a highly sophisticated internal worship of the Great Goddess under her aspect of Tripurā, the Goddess of 'the triple city' represented by the Śrī-yantra (or Śrī-cakra, or again Tripurā-cakra), a diagram that symbolises the body of the Goddess in the form of nine imbricated triangles, focused on a point that marks the centre of the labyrinth (bindu-drop); five triangles pointing downwards are aspects of the feminine Śakti and four pointing upwards represent those of male Śiva. The intersections of the lines come to form forty-three triangles: the nine original ones resulting in an additional thirty-four secondary triangles, all encircled by two lotuses of eight and sixteen petals contained in a triple circle within a triple square representing the Earth as Fortress (bhūpura), its walls pierced by four gates opening towards the four cardinal points. Each element of the diagram is also associated with powerful syllables and mantras, themselves deities called Mātṛkas (mothers). The building of the cakra (circle) or maṇḍala, whether manually or mentally, is a sacred gnosis (vidyā) and its esoteric complex ritual necessitates an initiation (dīkṣa).

In practice, the distinction between a 'right-handed' and 'left-handed' method is not clear cut and some traditions use both, viewing them in terms of different forms of spiritual attainment. What matters is the experiential knowledge derived from participation in ritual activity usually allied with yoga praxis, both part of the group of disciplines which form a tantric sādhana (spiritual endeavour).

See also: **Āśramas (stages of life); Bhakti; Caste; Dharma; Dīkṣā; Jñāna; Kuṇḍalinī Yoga; Mantra; Mātṛkās; Pañcamakāra; Pūjā; Śaivism; Śakti; Śāktism; Śiva; Tantrism; Vaiṣṇavism; Varṇa; Veda; Viṣṇu; Yantra; Yoga**

DANIEL MARIAU

Further reading

Gupta, S., D.J. Hoens and T. Gourdriaan. 1975. *Hindu Tantrism*. Leiden/Cologne: E. J. Brill.

TANTRISM

General principles

Since its origins in the seventh century, Hindu Tantra has essentially consisted of a body of ritual techniques for accessing the energies of multiple, often female, supernatural entities as instruments of power, for one's own this-worldly empowerment (bhukti), the attainment of supernatural enjoyments (siddhis) and liberation in the form of self-deification (jīvanmukti). Humans in particular are empowered to realise these goals through strategies of embodiment – that is, of causing the divine energies to become concentrated in one or another sort of template, grid or other diagrammatic transfer medium – prior to their projection onto the individual microcosm. These strategies presuppose a vision of the universe and of the human individual as nexuses of a divine energy (Śakti) that, flowing through the multiple female deities of the Hindu Tantric pantheon, proliferates outward from the godhead, generally represented as a divine pair in sexual union. Such a representation discloses the widespread doctrine that kāma (love, pleasure, desire), in every sense of the term, is productive of the Tantric practitioner's goals: in order to obtain power, enjoyment and liberation one must first desire them, making the creative channelling of desire – through Hindu Tantric ritual – the supreme path to power.

The ritual tools and techniques of Hindu Tantra are of three principal types: (1) mantras, acoustic formulas that, when enunciated properly under the proper conditions, control the multiple supernatural entities of the Tantric pantheon and transform mundane worship media into nectar, the divine fluid that courses through the bodies of the extended families of the gods, gurus and Tantric initiates; (2) techniques of possession, by means of which the divine is moved to act through one's own body through a variety of techniques, including nyāsa, in which divinities are embodied through their mantras, and samāveśa, the meditative 'co-penetration' of practitioner and divinity; and (3) the gratification and coercion of the Tantric gods through 'tribute' (bali), with or without the transformative medium of fire. All require initiation (dīkṣā) into the practice by a teacher (guru, ācārya) who has undergone consecration (abhiṣeka) and who constitutes the pivotal link in a lineage of teachers and disciples (paraṃparā) that goes back to the divine revealer of the Tantric mantras, rituals and attendant doctrines.

The Tantric pantheon – which is simultaneously a flowchart of Śakti, gnosis and the sexual fluids of the divine – is often mapped onto a circular geometric grid known as a maṇḍala, on the concentric circles (cakras) of which are simultaneously arrayed: (1) a hierarchy of divine, demonic, human or animal beings; (2) garlands or piled-up aggregates of phonemes (mantras), which constitute the vibratory energy levels of those beings; (3) the written characters of the hieratic Sanskrit alphabet, which are the graphic cognates of those phonemes; and (4) the elemental building blocks or categories (tattvas) of Tantric metaphysics. As grids for mapping the invisible onto the visible, maṇḍalas are the post-Vedic equivalents of the Vedic fire altar, multivalent diagrams for charting space–time, the vault of heaven, the territory of a kingdom and the subtle human body. The Tantric practice of the maṇḍala easily morphs itself into other media, including worship supports (Śiva liṅgams, divine images, consecrated vessels of water or liquor); the architectural plans of temples, palaces and houses; the mapping of urban space; the choreography of festival dances, etc.

Viewed from above, the Tantric maṇḍala appears as a flat circular diagram, with the centre usually occupied by the dyad of the supreme godhead in its male and female aspects, the divine in essence and manifestation. Maṇḍalas are, however, three-dimensional figures, raised at the centre, such that movement from the periphery toward the centre is at once centripetal and ascendant. The Tantric maṇḍalas that represent this vertical thrust the most dramatically are the manifold depictions of the subtle or yogic body, which are so many side-views of the Tantric universe, projected upon the human microcosm. In both cases, such diagrammatic renderings are tools (yantras) for the practitioner to use, both for identification with the supreme godhead and for manipulation of the multiple deities, energies, mantras, etc. that mediate the relationship between the divine and the human. The lines and circles of these maṇḍalas are so many conduits for the flow of divine energy, being and gnosis – a flow that is simultaneously one of vital fluids, phonemes, photemes and beings – streaming downward and outward through a succession of emanated male and female deities and demigods into 'superhuman' gurus and their human disciples.

Nearly all of these elements of Tantric practice are also found in Vedic ritual; however, the divinities, mantras, worship media and rituals of Hindu Tantra are non-Vedic, based in non-Vedic scriptures and often performed by persons unfit for Vedic initiation. For those Tantric practitioners to whom the Vedic rites have been accessible (mainly high-status householders, such as the smārta brāhmaṇa practitioners of Śrīvidyā in present-day Tamil Nadu), the Tantric rites are a complement to Vedic practice, which has afforded them a more potent ritual access to the goal of liberation. As such, many elements of Tantric ritual have been adopted and adapted over the centuries by orthodox Hindus in their domestic worship, in the public temple ritual of the great Hindu gods and as an esoteric complement to their exoteric Vedic practice. Certain practitioners have classified their practices as 'right-handed', in distinction to the 'left-handed' practices involving the consumption of prohibited foods and sexual intercourse.

Hindu Tantra may be viewed as the early medieval combination of a number of pre-existing strands of practice, including the South Asian demonological tradition (already attested in the *Atharvaveda*, Āyurvedic literature and Hindu and Buddhist mythology), elements of local or popular and vernacular traditions and the innovation, by emerging religious orders and sects (such as the early Pāśupatas), of bodies of new, non-Vedic rituals and doctrines. Much of the medieval Tantric synthesis was developed by religious specialists in the employ of feudal kings who, often hailing from low-caste or foreign backgrounds, sought to legitimate their rule through consecration rites denied them by the Vedic orthodoxy. As a result, much of Hindu Tantric practice involves the ritual transformation of the individual self into the idealised persona of a trans-individual god-king who creates and controls a pantheon of divine and demonic vassals from his royal palace, located at the raised centre of his utopian maṇḍala.

While the special needs of the feudal South Asian kings were the most important impetus behind many of the innovations of this medieval tradition, very few Hindu Tantric practitioners have in fact been kings, and so it is that there exists a wide range of Tantric doctrines, practices and goals that are reflective of the needs, aspirations, worldviews and concerns of a variety of social actors. In rural South Asia and Hindu Indonesia 'shaman-type' Tantric specialists serve their generally low-status clientèles by controlling the demonic hordes that invade the human body, domestic sphere and agricultural environment through induced possession by Tantric 'Lords of Spirits' (Bhūtanāthas), exorcism, sorcery, charms, spells, blood offerings and other ritual techniques. These popular traditions are local, limited to the relationships that obtain between the living, the demonic dead and supernatural entities of a restricted geographical area and set of kinship relations. This pragmatic approach, which remains extremely widespread in all of South Asia and Hindu Indonesia, is basically a sort of reactive damage control that requires no theoretical apparatus or doctrinal rationale. A significant portion of the early Hindu Tantric literature is devoted to this type of demonological practice and in certain texts, like the *Netra Tantra*, it is possible to excavate an original stratum of practice, with successive overlays of metaphysical doctrine relating practice to the transcendental goal of human salvation.

It is only among Hindu Tantric elites – kings, royal chaplains, the aristocracy (including the brāhmaṇa patricians of medieval Kashmir) and high-status specialists – that Hindu Tantric doctrine has borne a significant relationship to practice. As such, Tantric doctrine is generally reflective of the particular concerns of high-status Hindus: power relationships among human and superhuman agents, the balance between purity and power, soteriology, ontology, metaphysics, etc. Such concerns constitute the content of most of the Hindu Tantric canon, which, dating from about the eighth century CE, was written by and for these elites in the learned medium of Sanskrit. The doctrinal systems presented in these works are always sectarian, identifying this or that form of the Great Goddess, Viṣṇu or Śiva as the supreme godhead, standing at the apex of a divine hierarchy whose lesser divinities are specifically Śākta, Vaiṣṇava or Śaiva. The cults of these three high gods have defined the sectarian landscape of elite forms of Hindu Tantra. Principal among these sects, whose texts have constituted the open-ended canon of Hindu Tantra, are: (1) the Vaiṣṇava Pāñcarātras, whose Man-Lion initiation (nārasiṃhā dīkṣā) of kings gained them entrance into the royal courts of much of medieval India; (2) the Śaiva Siddhāntins, whose influence has extended over the entire Indian subcontinent and Hindu Indonesia; and (3) the many Śākta-Śaiva schools and sects that emerged out of Kashmiri Śaivism – the Krama, Trika and Śrīvidyā (which went on to thrive in Tamil Nadu and Nepal) sects, as well as the Śākta Kubjikā cult, which likely arose in the Koṅkaṇa region of western India, but which has mainly flourished in Nepal. Finally, north-eastern India has seen a post-fourteenth-century Tantric revival, which has combined the cult of Kṛṣṇa with those of Śākta goddesses, in the Sahajiyā and other regional traditions.

The cults of certain Tantric divinities have been shared in common by several sects, with their rituals being interpreted from multiple metaphysical perspectives. This was particularly the case with the cults of Svacchanda Bhairava and the goddess Kālī in Kashmir, as well as that of Tripurāsundarī in Kashmir, Tamil Nadu and Nepal. It is in these sectarian contexts that Hindu Tantric mythology comes to the fore, to describe through narrative the complex and often gender-bending relationships between the supreme godhead, his or her male and female aspects and the entire created universe. In the mythology of Kubjikā (the 'Crooked' Goddess), for example, the universe is the outpouring of energy and bliss that arises when she licks the vitalising fluid from the liṅgam (phallus) located at the centre of her own yoni (vulva). Much of the imagery of Tantra – the sculpted and painted images of gods and goddess, superhuman and demonic entities, as well as human practitioners, often in sexual union – also flows from the myriad pantheons, metaphysics and mythologies specific to the various Tantric sects.

Rather than focusing on the relationship between the one and the many, Hindu Tantric doctrine primarily focuses on the bipolar relationship between the one and the One, i.e. between the initiated human practitioner (epitomised by the consecrated king) and the supreme godhead. This relationship, which is often theorised on the basis of a metaphysics of 'identity-in-difference' (bhedābheda), views the multiple deities of the Tantric pantheon as so many intermediaries between or obstructions to the fusion of – or at least an intimacy between, in the case of dualist forms of Tantra – these two poles, a fusion that is tantamount to salvation.

When the goal of practice shifts from supernatural enjoyments and power in the world to soteriology, its focus becomes less one of controlling multiple supernatural beings as independent entities and more one of realising that the said entities are all internal to the transcendental Self of the godhead with which one is identifying. As such, Hindu Tantric metaphysics is emanationist, a great chain of being linking the mundane to the supermundane. Grounded in the twenty-five categories (tattvas) of Śāṃkhya philosophy, nearly every Hindu Tantric metaphysical system posits thirty-six categories, which are simultaneously identified with divine hierarchies, states of consciousness, vibrational levels of mantric sound, subtle sites within the yogic body, the construction of worship supports and guru-disciple lineages, etc. When such emanationist systems are combined with the concept of identity-in-difference, it becomes possible to internalise the elements of Tantric ritual and enact the external practices of manipulating and ingesting sacrificial oblations, purification and protection of the body and the site, etc. through visualisation, meditation, the silent pronunciation of mantra and yogic practice. Yoga as we know it today in fact gradually emerged out of the internalisation of Tantric practice, in the ninth to twelfth centuries. Here, the internalised practice of embedding mantras in the vital breaths (prāṇas) gave rise to a 'mapping' of the subtle channels of the human body and the gradual elaboration of a microcosmic yogic system whose structure and dynamics encapsulated the bipolar relationships obtaining between the male and female and mundane and super-mundane aspects of the godhead in the universal macrocosm. In some Tantric traditions, the internalised feminine is represented as the Kuṇḍalinī, 'she who is coiled', a serpentine nexus of Śakti that, awakened from her sleep at the base of the subtle body, rises upward along the spinal column to unite with her male counterpart, Śiva, in the cranial vault.

Hindu Tantric theologies may be dualist (as in the case of Śaiva Siddhānta and Pāñcarātra traditions), with the soteriological goal of becoming like god or intimately close to god; or non-dualist (as in the case of Kashmiri Śaivism in particular), with the goal of becoming god. In every case, salvation is realised through a combination of ritual practice, gnoseological insight and devotion to god. Through a set of transformative rituals, the practitioner becomes progressively incorporated into his community, and moves ever closer to liberation, as he remounts the hierarchy of being back to its divine source (Davis 1991: 10). In the dualist Śaiva Siddhānta system, ritual practice effects the removal of the ontological substance, called 'primordial stain' (mala), that differentiates the godhead (pati) from its creatures (paśu). In certain of the refined doctrinal systems of Kashmiri Śaivism – as innovated by Abhinavagupta and his disciple Kṣemarāja in particular – ritual 'practice' becomes increasingly internalised into a set of meditation techniques involving visualisation, mantra repetition and gnoseological exercises. Here, ritual doing becomes abstracted into ritual knowing – often through a rigorous meditative analysis of the mantric phonemes – with the final goal being the expansion of the practitioner's individual consciousness into a trans-individual god-consciousness, in which one sees the world and the entire

Hindu Tantric pantheon of beings and energies as 'I' rather than 'that'.

The royal pivot

Like Buddhist Tantra and Jain Tantra, which emerged in the same early medieval period, Hindu Tantra comprised an innovative adaptation, of elements from a preexisting Indian religious substratum, to a changing socio-political landscape. The substratum in question was the South Asian demonological tradition, widely attested since the time of the *Atharvaveda*, in which humans find themselves pitted against hordes of supernatural entities in pandemonium. This worldview, which persists down to the present day in South Asian popular religion, perceives all human misfortune to be the result not of the ripening of karma, but rather of the nefarious activities of a bewildering variety of multiple demonic beings who invade, possess, sicken, madden and destroy their victims. The changing socio-political landscape in question was the collapse of South Asian imperial formations (the Guptas, Pratīharas, etc.), which issued into a long period of political instability, military adventurism and the ruralisation and feudalisation of royal power.

Hindu Tantra coalesced, as a new paradigm of religious power in the world, around the person of the feudal king, who patronised Tantric specialists in order that their non-Vedic rites transform him into a living god on earth. These specialists were of two principal types, the one 'shamanic' and the other 'clerical'. The first group comprised non-institutional religious specialists from the king's rural power base, whose combined practices of induced possession, exorcism, sorcery and sacrifice afforded them mastery over powerful hordes of supernatural entities, the energies of which they appropriated and channelled for the benefit of their royal clients. The second group, most often comprised royal chaplains and preceptors from the Hindu religious orders and temple priesthoods, adapted and invented non-Vedic rituals for the consecration, legitimation and ultimately the deification of kings who often hailed from low-caste (and therefore illegitimate, according to orthodox theories of polity) backgrounds.

As Ronald Davidson has convincingly argued, the new synthesis forged by these religious specialists was one that simultaneously effected the divinisation of kings – who assumed the positions of Tantric gods or their incarnations and manifestations at the centres of vast maṇḍalas of supernatural beings – and the concomitant feudalisation of divinity, wherein the gods became perceived as warlords and feudal kings. A wealth of historical data – textual, inscriptional, artistic and architectural – supports the thesis that between the seventh and twelfth centuries (and in some cases down to the colonial period), many if not most of the royal houses of the Hindu world, in India, Nepal, Indonesia and other kingdoms of Southeast Asia, embraced Tantra. As such, the paradigm of feudal lordship became the model for *all* Hindu Tantric practice, through which every practitioner, regardless of his station in life, could be transformed into a superhuman cosmocrat, controlling a universe of which he was, through his identity with the god at the centre of the maṇḍala, the creator, preserver and destroyer.

Diagrammatic representations of the universe as a clan (kula) of interrelated beings, as an 'embodied cosmos', Tantric maṇḍalas have their origins in South Asian models of royal polity. In fact, long prior to its religious usages, the original referent of the term 'maṇḍala' was an administrative unit or county in ancient India. The allied notion of the king as cakravartin – as both he who turns (vartayati) the wheel (cakra) of his kingdom or empire from its centre and he whose chariot wheel has rolled around its perimeter without obstruction – is also ancient, going back to the late Vedic period. Central to these constructions of kingship is the notion that the king, standing at the centre of his kingdom (from which he also rules over the periphery), mirrors the godhead at the centre of his realm, his divine or celestial kingdom. However, whereas the godhead's heavenly kingdom is unchanging and eternal, the terrestrial ruler's kingdom is made so through the 'utopia' of the maṇḍala. As such, the idealised, 'constructed kingdom' of the maṇḍala is the template between real landscapes, both geographical and political, and the heavenly kingdom of the godhead, with the person of the king as god on earth constituting the idealised microcosm.

More pragmatic theories of royal polity, such as the 'circle of kings' of the circa first-century CE *Arthaśāstra*, situate the king – the ruler of a maṇḍala of power, territory and family relations – at the centre of a constantly shifting nexus of allies and enemies, which he manipulates in order to maintain his dominance. Such models corresponded more closely to the actual situation, on the ground, of medieval South Asian power relations, in which the relationships between vassals and overlords were constantly being overturned through warfare, alliances, subterfuge and marriage. This period, which was marked by a ruralisation of the ruling classes throughout much of South Asia, saw kings reinforcing their socio-economic links with agrarian society through marriage with its daughters, and by embracing the cults of rural tutelary deities, most often in the form of kuladevīs, the clan goddesses of the land, considered to be the source of all life (and death) in an agrarian society. This strategy enters into the political theory of the 1131 CE *Mānasollāsa* – an encyclopedia attributed to the Cāḷukya ruler Someśvara III, which adds śakti (power) to the *Arthaśāstra*'s list of the multiple components of the circle of kings. According to this source, a king's śakti, which takes the form of his 'command' (ājñā), controls all of the other elements in his circle of power relations. The intimate, even sexual, nature of the king's relationship to his clan goddess is underscored in a number of ways, through her identification with both his queen and Śrī, the goddess of sovereignty, and through the maṇḍala of the royal household. From Nepal to Tamil Nadu to Bali, the clan goddess resided within the royal palace, which was at once the dwelling of a royal warrior, a goddess temple and the place of the royal bedchamber. As such the god-king and his goddess-wife would have been models both of and for the divine dyad at the heart of the Hindu Tantric maṇḍalas.

Hindu Tantric clans and Hindu Tantric sex

Throughout its history, the most distinctive feature of Hindu Tantra has been a body of sexual practices proper to an inner circle of elite practitioners (sādhakas), often called the Kaula. Accession to this inner circle has required special initiations and a greatly intensified ritual life that has strongly challenged conventional purity-based notions of selfhood in Hindu thought. In return, this transgressive and dangerous path has afforded greatly accelerated results, particularly in the attainment of supernatural powers. It is, therefore, on the basis of these Kaula practices – particularly involving the ingestion of the five Tantric 'sacraments' (pañcamakāra) – which give the tradition its specificity, that Hindu Tantra may best be understood. All of the other elements of Hindu Tantric practice – the ritual use of maṇḍalas, mantras and mudrās (body postures); invocation of the guru (gurusmaraṇa); rites of purification (bhūtaśuddhi) and protection (digbandhana); visualisation (dhyāna); the worship of terrible or benign divinities (pūjā) with water libations (tarpaṇa), blood sacrifice (bali) and fire offerings (homa); induced possession (āveśa); sorcery (ṣaṭ-karmāṇi), etc. – may be found elsewhere, in Vedic, devotional or popular Hindu traditions.

Many elements of Kaula practice have their origins in the relationship between the feudal king and his clan goddess. Like human families and feudal relations, these goddesses always belong to clans or families (kulas) governed by male or female overlords (pradhānas, nāthas, adhipatis) who are themselves subservient to the supreme authority of the god-king or the goddess to whom the king is symbolically wed. The pair formed by the god-king and his clan goddess-queen at the heart of their royal maṇḍala is homologous to that of the bipolar Hindu godhead, as may be glimpsed through a comparison of a medieval Indonesian royal consecration rite with the final ritual moment of the Tantric purification rite of bhūtaśuddhi. In the former, narrativised in a twelfth-century Old Javanese poem entitled *Smara-Dahana* ('The Incineration of Eros'), royal consecration transforms the king and his queen into the dyad at the centre of their maṇḍala, which regenerates the universe with the nectar of their union: identified with Śiva and Umā, the royal pair shower the nectar of their sexual bliss upon humanity. Bhūtaśuddhi, the rite of self-purification that is the necessary preliminary to every Tantric worship ritual, is described in innumerable Hindu Tantras as the meditative incineration of the five ontological elements of one's material (sense of) self with the 'fire' of śakti. Following this, the microcosmic maṇḍala of the practitioner's body is saturated and rejuvenated by the nectar of the sexual union of the Great Goddess and her male partner (usually Śiva), rendering it pure and consubstantial with the divine. In both cases, the sexual fluids flowing from the godhead at the elevated centre of the maṇḍala vivify the cosmos.

In the light of these parallel data, the maṇḍala may be seen as constituting both a genealogical table and a flowchart of power relations among a vast extended family. It is for this reason that the 'inner circle' of Hindu Tantric practitioners, the Hindu Tantric virtuosi, often referred to themselves as the clan (kula), 'sons of the clan' (kula-putras) or 'generated from the clan' (kaula). Here, the clans in question were families of divine beings, which humans could access through special Tantric initiations. It is in this context that the multiple local and regional goddesses of the South Asian landscape were appropriated into Kaula practice. These petulant female divinities, represented as supernatural hybrids between the human, animal, bird and plant worlds, were by turns terrible and benign with regard to humans, who traditionally worshipped them with blood offerings and animal sacrifice. Known by a variety of names in pre-existing popular and scriptural traditions – Nymphs (Apsarasas), Demonesses (Rākṣasīs), Female Seizers (Grahaṇīs), Mothers (Mātṛkās), Female Dryads (Yakṣīs), etc. – these divine females began to be called Yoginīs in the sixth or seventh century CE, with dozens of temples being erected for their propitiation by Hindu kings between the ninth and twelfth centuries. More than any other element of Hindu Tantra, it is the Kaula cult of the Yoginīs and its attendant practices that give this tradition its specificity.

Like the kuladevīs of the medieval South Asian socio-political landscape, the Yoginīs were located at the fringes of the Tantric maṇḍalas, at the boundary line between the superhuman and the human. As such, they were the prime means of ingress (kaulagocarā) into the clan lineages, globally referred to as the Kaula, with initiation taking the form of sexual transactions with Yoginīs who were also identified with male practitioners' human ritual consorts. That is, the Yoginīs of the Hindu Tantric traditions were at once regarded as flesh and blood women with whom male practitioners interacted and the devouring supernatural entities that were the objects of their worship cults. In the secular literature, these Yoginīs were often portrayed as sorceresses or witches, ambiguous, powerful and dangerous figures that only a heroic male would dare to approach, let alone attempt to conquer. It is for this reason that the fully initiated male practitioners of the Kaula termed themselves Champions or Virile Heroes (Vīras); alternatively, they referred to themselves as Perfected Beings (Siddhas).

On certain nights of the lunar month and solar year, Kaula practitioners would assemble on cremation grounds, or at Yoginī temples, Clan 'Mounds' (pīṭhas), 'Clan-Mountains' (kula-parvatas), or 'Fields' (kṣetras). These gatherings, called 'Minglings' (melakas), involved the union of female and male initiates, of Yoginīs whose presence and interaction with their male counterparts were the sine qua non of Kaula practice. Wild percussive music (of drums, cymbals and bone rattles) and dance were an important feature of these minglings, with the Yoginīs descending from the sky to join their male consorts awaiting them on the ground. The Yoginīs' power of flight was fuelled by the human and animal flesh that comprised their diet; however, the Siddhas or Vīras, by virtue of their own practice, were able to offer the Yoginīs a more subtle and powerful energy source: this was their semen (vīrya), the distilled essence of their own bodily constituents. Gratified by such offerings, the Yoginīs would offer their form of grace to these male virtuosi. Instead of devouring them, they would offer them a counter-prestation of their own sexual discharge, something these male partners would have been as needful of as the Yoginīs were of male semen.

This male requirement stemmed from an altogether different set of needs than those of the Yoginīs, however. According to the Hindu Tantric worldview, the godhead externalised himself (or herself) in the form of a series of female emanations, a cluster of (often eight) goddesses, who in turn proliferated into the multiple circles of feminine energies (often sixty-four) that were their Yoginī entourage. These semi-divine Yoginīs and the human women who embodied them therefore carried in their bodies the sexual fluid of the godhead, called the 'clan fluid' (kula-dravyam), 'clan nectar' (kulāmṛta), 'vulval essence' (yonitattva), the 'command' (ājñā), the 'real thing' (sadbhāva), or simply 'the fluid' (dravyam) or 'the clan' (kula). While this fluid essence of the godhead flowed naturally through these female beings, it was absent in males. Therefore, the sole means by which a male could access the flow of the supreme godhead at the elevated centre of the maṇḍala was through the Yoginīs who formed or inhabited its outer circles. It was therefore necessary that male practitioners be 'inseminated', or more properly speaking 'insanguinated', with the sexual or menstrual discharge of the Yoginīs – rendering the 'mouth' of the Yoginī their sole conduit to membership in the clan and all its perquisites. For all of these reasons, the ingestion of the Yoginī's sexual emissions was the defining feature of Kaula initiation rites. Here, the 'mouth' of the Yoginī was her vulva, and 'drinking female emissions' (rajapāna) the prime means to fulfilling these male needs. As such, the 'Tantric sex' practised by the Kaula practitioners mainly involved *drinking* the menstrual or ejaculatory emissions of the Yoginīs.

Too transgressive for the great majority of Tantric practitioners, the sexual practices of the Kaula virtuosi are described in a small minority of Tantric scriptures. Such have nonetheless been factored into broader Tantric theory, through the psychologisation of the practice. Here, it is argued that the sexual, violent and impure Kaula practices are so many means for effecting a breakthrough from one's limited conventional, caste-bound persona to expansive, trans-individual god-consciousness. Relatively late in the history of Hindu Tantra, these transactions in sexual fluids became internalised, with the male and female partners being located in the cranial vault and lower abdomen, respectively. In this system, semen that was retained within the body and potentiated through yogic practice became a male practitioner's 'fuel' for self-transformation, the accumulation of supernatural powers and ultimately self-deification.

Hindu Tantra in the absence of royal patronage

The rise and fall of Hindu Tantra as the religious 'mainstream' is directly linked to the rise and fall of its royal patrons. In north and central India, Hindu Tantra thrived as the royal cultus under the Kalacuri, Somavaṃśi, Chandella, Cāḷukya and other kings, until their lands fell under Muslim rule in the twelfth century. In other parts of the north, Hindu royal houses that survived as vassals of the Mughals and other Muslim rulers have remained Tantric in much of their public ceremonial down to the present day, especially during the great festival of Daśahrā/Durgā Pūjā/Navarātri, in which the marriage between the titular king and his royal kuladevī is ritually re-enacted. In Kashmir, an entrenched brāhmaṇa aristocracy managed to preserve the Tantric tradition in its householder practice well into the twentieth century, in spite of the loss of Hindu royal patronage there between 1320 and 1819 CE. In north-eastern South Asia, Tantra did not emerge until the early sixteenth century, with the rise of the Hinduised rulers of the Ahom and Koch kingdoms of Assam. Tantra in Bengal, a curious hybrid of devotion to Kālī and Kṛṣṇa and extreme forms of ritual practice, emerged in about the same period, but was never a mainstream tradition (although it was enough of a brahmanic religious fashion in the early twentieth century to excite the imagination of John Woodroffe (aka A. Avalon, the father of Western Tantric studies). On the island of Bali in Indonesia, which remained under the control of Hindu rulers from the tenth century well into the nineteenth century, a certain form of Tantra remains the mainstream form of religious practice. The same is the case in the Kathmandu Valley, whose state religion was Tantric from the early Malla period (early thirteenth century) down to the beginning of the twenty-first century when Parliament declared Nepal to be secular, and where Tantra permeates every aspect of religious life at every level of society.

Without the royal patronage it enjoyed in the medieval period, Hindu Tantra would never have emerged as a distinct religious phenomenon in India. By the same token, Hindu Tantra loses its distinctiveness, and becomes reabsorbed into the broader substrata of Asian religious practice, when the institution of kingship disappears. It is for this reason that Hindu Tantra has continued to thrive in the Kathmandu Valley under the rulers of the current Shah dynasty; and it is for this reason that Hindu Tantra all but disappeared from the Indian landscape when the last maharajas of India lost their royal temporal power in the colonial and post-colonial periods. When the royal centre of Hindu Tantra is missing, it becomes bifurcated into two sorts of practice, which, while they retain certain elements of the original Tantric synthesis, become increasingly indistinguishable from other non-Tantric forms of Hindu religiosity. On the one hand, elite Tantric specialists, generally from high-status groups, tend to turn their energies toward perfecting the rituals and liturgies for which Tantra's telos and real-world goal of power in the world is no longer viable. Here, Hindu Tantra becomes a set of obscure special teachings (viśeṣaśāstra) that complements, without supplanting them, exoteric orthodox Veda-based doctrine and practice. Caste-based concerns for ritual purity predominate, and external ritual becomes progressively formalised, internalised and semanticised into an idealised and intellectualised spiritual exercise. The goal of self-deification remains, but it too comes to resemble the soteriological goals of non-Tantric practice, i.e. liberation. It is in this context that the impressive literary edifice of *Tantra Śāstra*, Tantric exegesis, must be understood. Tantric 'mysticism', which has served as the basis for the quietistic meditative practices of high-status Hindu householders whose ideal of purity prohibits transactions in the defiling substances of Tantric sacrifice and sexual rites, is made up of second-order reflections not unique to Tantra, and which in fact have, over time, brought Hindu Tantra back into the fold of more traditional, and usually conventional, non-Tantric forms of Hindu precept and practice. In the end, Hindu Tantra becomes domesticated and fully absorbed into householder practices that are Tantric in name alone.

On the other hand, those who have continued to pursue the Tantric goal of power in the absence of a royal patron have done so, of necessity, for their own survival, prestige or profit. However, in the absence of royal patronage these sorts of practice become indistinguishable from those of popular Hinduism. It is in this context that many (generally high-status) Hindus in India today deny the relevance of Tantra to their tradition, past or present, identifying what they call 'tantra-mantra' as so much mumbo-jumbo. Without the feudal king as its pivot, Hindu Tantra becomes absorbed back into the two principal Hindu religious styles from which it originally sprang: translocal, proactive, transcendental, Sanskritic, monotheistic devotional practice on the one hand; and local, reactive, pragmatic, vernacular, polytheistic worship without devotion on the other.

See also: **Abhinavagupta; Abhiṣeka; Agnihotra; Altars, Domestic; Apsarasas; Arthaśāstra; Āyurveda; Bhedābheda; Blood sacrifice; Brāhmaṇa; Buddhism, relationship with Hinduism; Daśahrā; Dīkṣā; Durgā Pūjā; Guru; Jainism, relationship with Hinduism; Kālī and Caṇḍī; Kāma; Karma; Kashmiri Śaivism; Kṛṣṇa; Kubjikā; Kula; Kuladevatā; Kuṇḍalinī; Languages; Magic; Mahādevī; Mahāvidyās; Mantra; Mātṛkās; Mudrā; Nepal, Hindus in; Pañcamakāra; Pāñcarātras; Paraṃparā; Pāśupatas; Popular and vernacular traditions; Possession; Rāja; Rākṣasas; Religious specialists; Śaiva Siddhānta; Śaivism; Śakti; Śāktism; Saṃhitā; Śāṃkhya; Siddha; Śiva; Smārta; Southeast and East Asia, Hindus in; Tantras; Tarpaṇa; Temple Worship; Umā; Vaiṣṇavism; Viṣṇu; Woodroffe, John; Yakṣa; Yantra; Yogī; Yoga**

David Gordon White

Further reading

Davidson, R. 2002. *Indian Esoteric Buddhism: A Social History of the Tantric Movement*. New York: Columbia University Press.

Davis, R. 1991. *Ritual in an Oscillating Universe: Worshiping Śiva in Medieval India*. Princeton, NJ: Princeton University Press.

Gupta, S., D.J. Hoens and T. Goudriaan. 1979. *Hindu Tantrism*. Handbuch der Orientalistik, 2.4.2. Leiden: Brill.

Hooykas, C. 1964. *Āgama Tīrtha, Five Studies in Hindu-Balinese Religion*. Amsterdam: N.V. Noord-Hollandsche Uitgevers Maatschappij.

Michaels, A., C. Vogelsanger and A. Wilke (eds). 1996. *Wild Goddesses in India and Nepal, Proceedings of an International Symposium, Berne and Zurich 23 November 1994*. Bern: Peter Lang.

Sanderson, A. 1995. 'Meaning in Tantric Ritual'. In Anne-Marie Blondeau and

Kristofer Schipper, eds, *Essais sur le rituel, III*. Louvain-Paris: Peeters, 15–95.
Slusser, M.S. 1982. *Nepal Mandala, A Cultural Study of the Kathmandu Valley*, 2 vols. Princeton, NJ: Princeton University Press.
White, D.G. (ed.). 2000. *Tantra in Practice*. Princeton, NJ: Princeton University Press.
White, D.G. 2003. *Kiss of the Yogini: 'Tantric Sex' in Its South Asian Contexts*. Chicago, IL: University of Chicago Press.

TAPAS (ASCETICISM)

Tapas literally means 'heat' and is used in the sense of 'inner heat' to convey the concept of an essential psychic energy or spiritual fervour, a great force that can achieve extraordinary results. It is associated with the practice of asceticism, in which the ascetic learns to control tapas through the practice of self-mortification. In the *Ṛgveda* tapas is linked to the soma ritual, in the *Atharvaveda* to the heat of the sun and in the yogic tradition it is one of the niyamas (observance of self-control) described in the Yogasūtras of Patañjali. The heat and power of tapas can be generated and stored up through focused, disciplined effort and from earliest times this has involved austerities such as extremes of heat and cold in order to purify the body, for example the practice of the Five Fires where an ascetic builds fires at each point of the compass and sits in the middle exposed to the full heat of the sun, the fifth fire. The potency of this energy is evident in the *Taittīriya Upaniṣad*, where it describes how the Great Being performed tapas and having done so was able to create the world, and there is a reference in the *Ṛgveda* to Indra having gained heaven through tapas.

In the *Purāṇas* the concept of tapas extends the Vedic idea of the power of the sacrifice (yajña), so that the accumulation of tapas can force the gods to grant a boon and the power accrued by an ascetic can be so great that it can subvert the balance of cosmic power and so risks destroying the world. There are many purāṇic and epic stories involving Indra trying to prevent ascetics from accumulating too much tapas by distracting them and tempting them to expend their psychic energy physically through lust or greed. Stories of Śiva develop the idea of tapas as a powerful force that can create and also destroy and in which the discipline of the ascetic both generates and controls the energy. One of the best known of these stories can be found in the *Saura Purāṇa*, in which the ascetic Śiva destroys Kāma (the god of love/desire) and then revives him. The story exemplifies the complex interplay between desire and renunciation (saṃnyāsa) in the creation and sustaining of the world and the role of tapas as the driving force that can be used both positively and negatively. The story also illustrates how the accumulation of tapas, even by demons, can be used to bargain with the gods and force them to grant boons (O'Flaherty 1975).

Tapas willingly expended through the focused discipline of the ascetic is thought to negate, literally 'burn off', negative energies and so to be a means of clearing a path to spiritual evolution. Being without attachments and living a life of renunciation can only be maintained through the control of tapas. However, the extent to which tapas is controlled through self-mortification varies within the different Indian traditions. Some schools of thought advocate extreme forms of privation, whilst others temper the practices and incorporate tapas into more routinised forms of observance such as periodic fasting. The *Bhagavadgītā*, for example, counsels a moderate approach to tapas and advises against taking the discipline to extremes. Within the Buddhist tradition, it is recorded that Gautama Buddha saw tapas as representing another form of desire, albeit a desire for renunciation, and so without value in the attainment of higher wisdom.

Whilst there are references to forms of ascetic discipline from the very earliest texts it is above all in the practice of yoga that the method of discipline necessary to accumulate and control tapas is developed.

See also: **Bhagavadgītā; Buddhism, relationship with Hinduism; Fasting; Indra; Itihāsa; Kāma; Patañjali; Purāṇas; Saṃhitā; Saṃnyāsa; Soma; Śiva; Upaniṣads; Yajña; Yoga; Yogasūtras**

VIVIENNE BAUMFIELD

Further reading

Edgerton, F. 1974. *The Bhagavad Gita*. Cambridge, MA: Harvard University Press.
O'Flaherty, W.D. 1975. *Hindu Myths*. London: Penguin Classics.

TĀRĀ

Particularly celebrated in Tibetan Buddhism, where she belongs to the family of the Buddha Amitābha and is associated with both Amoghasiddhi and the bodhisattva Avalokiteśvara, the goddess Tārā ('star') is, in that context, a saviour figure, the gentle and youthful essence of compassion. Her cult, promoted in Tibet by the missionary Atīśa (eleventh century), probably originated in Bengal, where she may have started her career as a tribal deity later turned into a fierce tantric goddess then associated, if not identified, with Kālī (of whom she is sometimes an emanation), as attested in the devotional poetry of Ramprasād Sen (eighteenth century) and popular iconography, where the two deities are practically indistinguishable.

Apart from an older but weaker tradition found in the *Viṣṇu Purāṇa*, where she appears as the wife of Bṛhaspati, tutor to the gods, the most prominent role of Tārā (or Tarakā) is as one of the ten mahāvidyās, the transformations of the Great Goddess which represent aspects of both transcendent knowledge and supernatural power and of which, alongside Kālī, she is the most significant. In marked contrast to the mainstream Tibetan figure, the Hindu Tārā, in her main form as Ugratārā (Tārā the powerful/terrible), exhibits terrifying power, represented garlanded in several bleeding human heads, standing near naked on a corpse, with protruding tongue and bared fangs, demanding blood sacrifices. In the *Tārā-Tantra* she is worshipped according to the rites of left-hand Tantra and is also particularly connected with rituals of subjugation.

See also: **Blood Sacrifice; Buddhism, relationship with Hinduism; Kālī and Caṇḍī; Mahāvidyās; Purāṇas; Tantric Yoga; Tantrism**

DANIEL MARIAU

TARPAṆA

Śrāddha tarpaṇa is an essential component of the śrāddha (propitiation of the ancestors) ceremony and is also performed on special days as Amāvāsya (new moon), or as part of yajur upakarma (the annual thread ceremony). The Sanskrit root word tṛp means 'to please or gratify' and the tarpaṇa is performed to please gods, ancestors or sages. The process of tarpaṇa involves the pouring of water mixed with grass (kuśa) and sesame seeds (for ancestors) as a libation. During the tarpaṇa ceremony, the sacred thread is worn in three different positions depending on the class of being worshipped – resting on the left shoulder for the gods, straight down the neck for the ancestors and on the right shoulder for the sages. In a normal tarpaṇa, the gods are first propitiated, then the ṛṣis and finally the pitṛs (ancestors), starting with the most recently deceased forefathers belonging to the paternal side, who are offered libations, followed by the ancestors on the maternal side. Since water is a neutral source, it can be easily converted into other suitable food sources – nectar for those pitṛs who enter heaven, grass for those who inhabit the animal world and rice for those who enter earth. The tarpaṇa ceremony is also performed as part of the annual śrāddha ceremony and during Pitṛpaksa, when tarpaṇa is performed every day for a fortnight to propitiate the ancestors. Kāṇḍarṣi tarpaṇa is performed during yajur upakarma to gratify the Kāṇḍa ṛṣis who revealed the Veda, and this tarpaṇa, being an important ritual, eventually became part of the daily worship regime.

See also: **Pitṛpaksa; Pitṛs; Ṛṣi; Śrāddha; Veda**

KOKILA RAVI

Further reading

Stevenson, Sinclair. 1920. *The Rites of the Twice-Born*. London: OUP.

TELANG, KASHINATH TRIMBAK (1850–93)

Kashinath Trimbak Telang, a distinguished judge and oriental scholar, graduated from Elphinstone College, Bombay, and went on to practise law in 1872. In 1889 he accepted a seat on the high court bench and was elected president of the Bombay branch of the Royal Asiatic Society. He was appointed by the British to head a commission to investigate the educational system of India, for which activity he was awarded the CIE (Commander of the Indian Empire) in 1882. As an educationalist, he was syndic of the University of Bombay from 1881 and vice-chancellor from 1892 until his death the following year.

A renowned linguist, Kashinath Trimbak Telang contributed to the literature of his own native Marathi, but it was in Sanskrit that he achieved excellence. His knowledge of Indian languages enabled him to become an expert on classical Hindu law and he also translated the *Bhagavadgītā*, *The Laws of Manu*, the *Dharmasūtras*, the *Sanatsujātīya*, the *Anugītā* and some of the works of Śaṅkara into English. His translation of the *Bhagavadgītā* remains a standard work.

See also: **Asiatick Societies; Bhagavadgītā; Dharmasūtras; Manu; Śaṅkara**

RON GEAVES

Further reading

Telang, Kashinath Trimbak. 1895. *Telang's Legislative Council Speeches: With Sir Raymond West's Essay on His Life*. Delhi: India Print Press.

TELEVISION AND RADIO

Lawrence Babb argues that new forms of mass communication such as radio and television have crucially altered the very nature of religious change in South Asia (Babb 1995: 1). The nature of this change may be understood in two important ways. First, beginning with the introduction of printing technology in the sixteenth century and its later spread across South Asia, mass media have influenced the mobility of religious symbols. New forms of mass media close physical distance and also bridge previously insurmountable social barriers. The mobility is thus not just spatial, but also social as new means of communication democratise religious symbols, often because these symbols become 'disembedded' from their religious traditions (Babb 1995: 4). Second, the availability of these new media has the perhaps unintended consequence of veering towards standardisation. Complex myths translated into comic-book form for the purpose of inculcating young Indian children in their glorious past may erase resistant narrative threads and through sheer volume of production and consumption standardise a simplified story. However, while television and film may have moved in this direction, other forms of mass media such as audio cassettes and lithographs have also added to the diversity of the religious landscape (Babb 1995: 5).

Radio

Radio broadcasts began in India in 1927 with private transmitters in Bombay (present-day Mumbai), who later expanded into Calcutta (present-day Kolkota). It was swallowed by the central government in 1935 and began operating under the name of the Indian Broadcasting Service. In 1936 the name was changed to that by which it is still known, All India Radio (AIR). From its formative years, the purpose of radio was a point of contention. For London, radio presented the possibility of reaching beyond rising nationalist movements to the rural masses, while Delhi was torn between seeing broadcasting as mere entertainment unworthy of an entire department and as a high-value medium (Lelyveld 1994: 113).

It was under B.V. Keskar, a Maharashtrian brāhmaṇa and Minister for Information between 1950 and 1962 that music became a vehicle to articulate a national (Hindu) identity. For Keskar, Indian music had suffered under the apathy of British imperialism and the hedonistic ignorance of North Indian Muslim rulers. He asserted that two significant developments occurred in Indian music because of Muslim rulers. First, music developed under Muslim patrons ignorant of its Sanskrit moorings, divorced from its anchor in Hindu civilisation and cultivated in exclusive and secret schools (gharānas). Second, under Muslims (and taken up later by the British), Indian music was artificially bifurcated into Hindustāni and Karṇāṭak. To Keskar, the purpose of the radio was to re-establish the unity of Indian music and to propagate it as means to inculcate (Hindu) nationalist ideology (Lelyveld 1994: 116–18). Vallabhai Patel, Minister for Information and Broadcasting from 1946, instituted a five-year plan to nationalise music. Under his and Keskar's watchful eye, they implemented policies to ensure that Hindu music prevailed outside the denigrating influence of courtesan culture encouraged by Muslim patrons and from which high-minded Hindus had turned away in disgust. The most telling move in this campaign to purify Indian music and return it to its religious roots was an enforced ban on performers and musicians who hailed from courtesan families (Lelyveld 1994: 118–19).

Television

Moving images in the form of television and film have had an enormous impact in South Asia, especially in their ability to transmit complex messages to non-literate audiences. One cannot divorce the Indian film industry from that of television, particularly in the ways these media intersect with religion. While television has been around for a number of decades – the first television centre was commissioned in Delhi in 1959 – it was only in the years following the serialised *Rāmāyaṇa* in 1987–88 that the medium began to realise its full potential. Though in 1986 two other mini-series – *Vikram aur Vetal* (*Vikram and the Vampire*) and *Krishna Avatar* – based on mythology were transmitted, the television *Rāmāyaṇa* represented the first time that television was utilised to transmit a major cultural text (Babb 1995: 13–15). Up until that point, television was 'conceptualized as a service to the nation rather than as personal entertainment' (Lutgendorf 1990: 132), embodied through stilted news reading and a dry selection of cultural programmes.

Ramanand Sagar's *Rāmāyaṇa*

On 25 January 1987 the government-run television network Doordarshan premiered a serialised adaptation of the

Rāmāyaṇa. It ran for over a year – the series concluded on 31 July 1988 – for forty-five minutes every Sunday morning at 9.30 a.m. The television version of the *Rāmāyaṇa* was produced by a Mumbai film producer Ramanand Sagar, with little-known actors taking on the lead roles: Rāma was played by Arun Govil, Lakṣmaṇa by Sunil Lahiri and Sītā by Dipika Chikhlia. Though primarily based on the *Rāmacaritamānasa* and the Vālmīki *Rāmāyaṇa*, his television version acknowledged several other *Rāmāyaṇas*, including the Tamil, Bengali and an Urdu version. As such, Sagar's television adaptation of the epic asserted the motif of the *Rāmāyaṇa* as an all-India tradition and a symbol of national unity (Lutgendorf 1990: 129–34).

The television *Rāmāyaṇa* became a national phenomenon, with reports of audiences worshipping their television sets, empty streets on Sunday mornings and *Rāmāyaṇa*-related news appearing on a regular basis in local newspapers (Lutgendorf 1990: 136). However, the serial was savaged in the Hindi- and English-language press for its crude sets, its plodding narrative style and its laughable special effects. But the greatest fear was that Sagar's *Rāmāyaṇa* would displace other versions of the epic to create a standardised, homogenous *Rāmāyaṇa*, especially at it was sponsored by the state-run television network. Such a version, it was feared, emphasised the values of a dominant social group and created a hegemonic version that ironed out cultural diversity. While Lutgendorf sees the validity in this point of view, he also argues against such a reading and makes the case that audiences will regard the Sagar *Rāmāyaṇa* as simply another version and will continue to discuss its merits and flaws (Lutgendorf 1990: 165–70).

The television *Rāmāyaṇa* condensed many of the political problems of the period while anticipating the rise of Hindu nationalism. During the period of its telecast, the issue of Rām Janmabhūmi in Ayodhyā grew in importance. This movement argued for demolishing a mosque, the Babri Masjid, to build a temple to Rāma in its place. Battle scenes in the television epic were seen as models for Hindu militancy, while the serial itself began to echo Hindu nationalist themes. With viewers for the epic at unprecedented numbers, the Bharatiya Janata Party (BJP) could fearlessly declare that it was no longer possible to deny the importance and significance of the Ayodhyā issue (Rajagopal 2001: 30). It temporarily allowed audiences to forget the deep divisions across society as they viewed an epic tale of sacrifice and heroism that created a golden past. Hindu nationalism then argued that this perfect past could be re-created through sufficient political will (Rajagopal 2001: 278).

See also: **Avatāra; Ayodhyā; Bharatiya Janata Party; Books, comics, newspapers and magazines; Courtesans; Film; Hindu; Iconography, modern; Kṛṣṇa; Lakṣmaṇa; Languages; Music; Nationalism; Rāma; Rāmāyaṇa; Sītā; Sound recordings; Vālmīki; Varṇa**

ARCHANA VENKATESAN

Further reading

Babb, L. 1995. 'Introduction'. In L. Babb and S. Wadley, eds, *Media and the Transformation of Religion in South Asia*. Philadelphia, PA: University of Pennsylvania Press, 1–18.

Gupta, Partha Sarathi. 1995. *Radio and the Raj: 1921–47*. Calcutta: K.P. Bagchi and Company publishing for Centre for Studies in Social Sciences.

Lelyvand, David. 1994. 'Upon the Subdominant: Administering Music on the All-India Radio'. *Social Text* 39: 111–27.

Lutgendorf, Philip. 1990. 'Ramayan: The Video'. *Drama Review* 34.2: 127–96.

Rajagopal, Arvind. 2001. *Politics After Television: Hindu Nationalism and the Reshaping of the Public in India*. Cambridge: Cambridge University Press.

TEMPLE WORSHIP

Temple worship is an important expression of theistic Hinduism. However, it did not become widespread until about the sixth century CE. Temple worship was rarely mentioned in the early Purāṇas, but became a major theme of the later purāṇic texts. The temple is the home of the gods and goddesses, a place in which they are treated as kings and queens who receive their loyal subjects. Whereas worship at the domestic altar is a relatively simple and intimate affair, which the devotee practises daily, temple worship is much more elaborate and is a form of worship that, for some people, is practised only on special occasions. Nevertheless, the basic rituals used to honour the deities are essentially the same for home or temple worship. In the home the devotee offers pūjā directly to the chosen deities, whereas in the temple the pūjā is performed by a priest or, in some temples, a pūjarī (a non-brāhmaṇa priest). The temple and the act of worship within it represent the meeting between humans and the divine.

Temples usually house a number of deities but are dedicated to one primary deity. For example, the enormous Mīnākṣī temple in Madurai, South India, houses many gods and goddesses, many of whom have their own priests and their own forms of worship, but at the heart of the temple is the sanctum the garbhagṛha (womb-house), a small windowless room at the centre of the temple the roof of which points up to the heavens, where the mula mūrti (immovable image) of the primary deity is installed. This is the sacred nerve-centre of the temple. This is the most sacred space in the temple and the one towards which the most intense worship is directed. However, whatever deity the temple is dedicated to, the devotee will always find a statue of Gaṇeśa (the elephant-headed god who is the Remover of Obstacles). Gaṇeśa is always the first deity to be worshipped and, therefore, he is usually placed inside the main door and to the left since temple deities are generally worshipped in a clockwise direction.

Pūjā is the main daily ritual carried out in the temple by the priests, for the deities should be worshipped at least once a day. However, many temples perform pūjā many times a day. Generally there are no formal services, though the deities do have periods when they receive worshippers and periods when they are enclosed in their sanctums, such as for taking their meals and for rest. Similarly, there are times of the day, particularly in the larger temples, when the priests regularly perform pūjā, such as in the early evening and first thing in the morning. However, throughout the day there is a constant stream of people coming in and out of the temple with offerings for the deities.

Temple worship is a very noisy affair as there is a constant bustle and continuous noise from the temple bells that people ring as they enter the temple in order to attract the attention of the deities. As the priests make the offerings and perform ārtī, the offering of light that is the core ritual of pūjā, they recite Sanskrit mantras or hymns from the Vedas. In some temples, the only time the devotee can really see the deity is when the priest offers the ārtī flame before the face of the god or goddess. Many sanctums are rather dark, situated at the end of a passageway, a place that only the priests are allowed to enter. Therefore the devotee is kept at a distance from the deity and can only truly take darśana (have sight of the deity and consequently his or her blessing) during ārtī. Some areas of the larger temples may be places of quiet contemplation, but whether noisy or tranquil, temples provide an opportunity for Hindus to come and communicate with their gods. In most cases it is through the medium of the temple priests, who act as intermediaries between the worshipper and the deity, taking the offerings, giving them to the deities and returning the prasāda (a part of the offering that has been blessed by the god or goddess) to the devotee. Temple worship provides the devotee with a temporary respite from the world. The passage into the temple represents not only a route from the secular world outside to a sacred world within, but, on a metaphysical level, a journey into the self. The temple provides a means of contact between divinity and humankind and, as such, is a place of transcendence where the purifying power of divinity can infuse the devotee through the rituals they perform while there.

The temple is often the focus of festival worship, where many people will gather to witness and participate in special temple rituals. Abhiṣeka (the ritual bathing of a deity in various substances) is a ritual generally performed only in the temple, most often during festivals. Many festivals can only be celebrated at the larger temples that have the room to store the necessary festival paraphernalia. The core ritual of many festivals is the decoration and procession of an utsava mūrti (movable image) of the main temple deities. In order that they may be paraded around the temple they must have a suitable vehicle, typically a wooden representation of the animal that they are usually depicted with, on which to ride. The procession of a decorated image of the deity around the streets surrounding the temple is a common festival ritual for deities throughout India. The procession of the beautifully decorated image around the temple is a time when barriers are broken down, as those who might normally be excluded from the temple have a chance to receive darśana. There is clearly a blurring of the distinctions between the sacred temple and the normally profane town in which it is situated, most noticeable in the removal of the festival participants' shoes during the procession.

See also: **Abhiṣeka; Altars, domestic; Ārtī; Brahman; Darśana; Gaṇeśa; Image worship; Mantra; Mīnākṣī; Prasāda; Pūjā; Purāṇas; Saṃhita; Utsava**

LYNN FOULSTON

THACKERAY, BAL (b. 1927)

The controversial Maharashtrian Leader, Bal Thackeray, was born on 23 January 1927 in Mumbai (Bombay), the son of a reputed social reformer, Keshav Sitaram Thackeray. He started his career as a political cartoonist in the *Free Press Journal* and had considerable skills in political and social satire. Thackeray started his own satirical journal, *Marmik* (literally, *Satire*), in 1960. In his cartoons and satirical articles in *Marmik*, Thackeray campaigned for 'a sons of the soil' policy in Mumbai, in which he exhorted Maharashtrian employers and the local government to employ only Maharashtrians. Thackeray's campaign culminated in the formation of Shiv Sena (Śivaji's Army) on 19 June 1966, named after King Śivaji, a popular iconic figure in Maharashtrian history, who had valiantly opposed the religiously bigoted Mughal Emperor Aurangzeb. Initially the organisation claimed to be apolitical (Purandare 1999: 41), but it eventually joined the Bharatiya Janata Party in contesting provincial elections in Maharashtra.

Shiv Sena was implicated in the Mumbai riots following the destruction of the Babri Masjid in Ayodhyā by Hindu Nationalists, and in particular the Sangh Parivar. Many of his critics portray him as a fascist, and Salman Rushdie's character Raman Fielding in his novel *The Moor's Last Sigh* is a thinly disguised caricature of Bal Thackeray.

See also: **Ayodhyā; Bharatiya Janata Party; Nationalism; Sangh Parivar**

THEODORE GABRIEL

Further reading

Eckert, J. 2002. *The Shiv Sena and the Politics of Violence*. New Delhi: Oxford University Press.

Purandare, V. 1999. *The Sena Story*. Mumbai: Business Publications Inc.

THEOSOPHY AND THE THEOSOPHICAL SOCIETY.

The Theosophical Society was founded in 1875 in New York by Helena P. Blavatsky and Henry S. Olcott. The founders soon moved to India, where the headquarters of the movement were established at Adyar, now a suburb of Chennai (Madras). The objectives of the Society were:

1 To form a nucleus of the Universal Brotherhood of Humanity without distinction of race, creed, sex, caste or colour.
2 To encourage the study of Comparative Religion, Philosophy and Science.
3 To investigate unexplained laws of Nature and the powers latent in man.

Behind these objectives lay the belief of Blavatsky that she had discovered in journeys though Asia the existence of a secret wisdom tradition which was the source and origin of religion. She averred that underlying the beliefs and practices of the great world faiths there was an esoteric or hidden body of doctrine. This had been preserved through the ages by a succession of adepts or Masters of the Wisdom. Two of those masters had, she claimed, selected her to present these teachings to a Western world, where they had long been suppressed by the Christian church, and to the adherents of the faiths of Asia, who had forgotten them. Blavatsky published two major works – *Isis Unveiled* (1877) and *The Secret Doctrine* (1888) – as well as a number of more accessible books (*The Key to Theosophy*, *The Voice of the Silence*) and a very great number of contributions to theosophical and other periodicals. Her writings have been kept in print until the present time and have enjoyed a sale far beyond the membership of the theosophical movement.

Blavatsky died in 1891, having attracted a great deal of attention in India, Europe and the USA. Amongst the converts to the movement was the charismatic figure of Annie Besant. On the passing of Olcott in 1907 she was elected president and threw her remarkable energies into the development of the Society. Its worldwide membership rose from 15,000 when she took office to a peak of over 40,000 in 1929. The dominance of her personality and that of her associate C.W. Leadbeater led to disputes over the interpretation of theosophy and to the formation of other groups. The Theosophical Society (Point Loma, later Pasadena) and the United Lodge of Theosophists claimed to preserve the original teachings of Blavatsky. From 1912 Mrs Besant and other leading Theosophists proclaimed the significance of J. Krishnamurti as a spiritual teacher.

Since 1945 the Society's membership has declined in the Western world but has continued to be of some significance in India, where it might be seen as a universalist reform movement within 'Hinduism'.

The doctrines of theosophy teach a scheme of spiritual evolution which underlies physical evolution. Human beings are seen as the embodiments of sparks of the divine which journey back to their origin through a series of incarnations. The Law of Karma is the mechanism which controls the circumstances of each successive life. Amongst those who reach a high stage of moral and spiritual development are those Masters who attempt to assist their 'younger brethren' through the work of the Theosophical Society and other movements. Theosophists are enjoined to follow a disciplined life of meditation, with vegetarianism and abstention from alcohol and drugs being held up as ideals. The Society stresses, however, that membership is open to all who can subscribe to the three objectives noted above and that no doctrines or beliefs are binding upon members.

The Theosophical Society had a profound influence on the popularisation of both esoteric thought and the basic teachings of Hinduism and Buddhism in the Western world. Much of the thought and practice of the contemporary New Age movement can be traced back to its activities in the period from 1875 to 1925.

See also: **Besant, Annie; Blavatsky, Helena; Karma (Law of Action); Krishnamurti, Jiddu; Olcott, Henry Steel**

KEVIN TINGAY

Further reading

Campbell, B. 1980. *The Ancient Wisdom Revived.* Berkeley, CA: University of California Press.

Faivre, A. 1994. *Access to Western Esotericism.* New York: State University of New York Press.

Nethercot, A.H. 1961. *The First Five Lives of Annie Besant*. London: Rupert Hart-Davies.

Nethercot, A.H. 1963. *The Last Four Lives of Annie Besant*. London: Rupert Hart-Davies.

Ransom, J. 1938. *A Short History of the Theosophical Society.* Adyar: Theosophical Publishing House.

THIBAUT, GEORG FRIEDRICH WILHELM (1848–1914)

German Sanskritist. Born in Heidelberg, Thibaut studied there and in Berlin. He worked as an assistant to F. Max Müller on his critical edition of the *Ṛgveda Saṃhitā* before being appointed in 1875 Anglo-Sanskrit professor (from 1879 principal) at the Benares Hindu College. He was later professor (from 1888) and principal (from 1895) at Muir College in Allahabad, before serving as registrar of Calcutta University from 1907 to 1913. Thibaut translated, in collaboration with Indian paṇḍits, a series of philosophical and mathematical texts, including the Brahmasūtras, with the commentaries of Śaṅkara and Rāmānuja (published in the Sacred Books of the East). In his writings on Indian astronomy and mathematics, Thibaut defended the view that they were indigenous sciences, seeing Greek influence only at a late period.

See also: **Brahmasūtras; Hinduism, history of scholarship; Müller, Friedrich Max; Rāmānuja; Sacred Books of the East; Śaṅkara**

WILL SWEETMAN

Further reading

Thibaut, G. 1889. *Astronomie, Astrologie und Mathematik* (*Grundriss der indo-arischen Philologie und Altertumskunde*, Band 3, Heft 9) [Astronomy, Astrology and Mathematics (Encyclopedia of Indo-Aryan Research, vol. 3, issue 9)]. Strasborg: Trübner.

Thibaut, G. 1904. *The Vedanta Sutras*, 3 vols. (Sacred Books of the East, vols 34, 38, 48). Oxford: Clarendon Press.

TĪJ

The festival of Tīj celebrated in July–August rejoices in the start of the monsoon rains in Northern India. It is a swing festival at which brothers and husbands tie swings in the trees for the pleasure and enjoyment of their sisters or wives. It is a time of much happiness and merriment as the monsoon rains are welcomed with much anticipation. Although celebrated throughout northern India, Tīj is particularly popular in Rajasthan, Punjab and Uttar Pradesh. The festival probably has ancient origins as its connections with fertility might suggest. It is also associated with Pārvatī, who performed severe ascetic penances in order to win Śiva as her husband. In Jaipur, in particular, the associations with Pārvatī are celebrated by parading her image through the city with much pomp and ceremony.

See also: **Pārvatī; Śiva; Utsava**

LYNN FOULSTON

Further reading

Woodward, P. (ed.) with R. El Droubie and C. Gould. 1998. *Festivals of the World*. Norwich: RMEP.

TILAK, BAL GANGADHAR (1856–1920)

Born into a middle-class Chitpavan brāhmaṇa family in Maharashtra (today's Ratnagiri District), Bal Gangadhar Tilak became a strong opponent of the British administration and fighter for svarājya (independence). As the editor and later owner of *Kesarī* and *Mahratta*, two local Marathi newspapers, Tilak used journalism as a weapon to struggle against colonial rule. '*Svarājya* is my birth right and I shall have it' (Sunthankar 1993: 556) became his famous patriotic slogan.

In 1893 Tilak organised the first Gaṇeśa Festival in Pune in order to unite the Hindu masses. In a similar move, Tilak remembered in 1885 Śivaji's coronation of 1674 and initiated an annual Śivaji Festival.

Tilak strongly criticised the Indian National Congress for its conformism and inactivity. In 1907, after a split in the Congress about co-operating with the British, he founded his own Indian Nationalist Party. In 1916 at the Lucknow Congress, Tilak and his group finally rejoined the Congress Party.

Though not involved directly in any violent attack, Tilak was accused several times of terrorist activities and imprisoned by the colonial government.

Tilak wrote several books dealing with the Vedas: *Orion* (1893), *Research into the Antiquity of the Vedas* (1893), *The Arctic Home of the Vedas* (1903) and *The Chaldean and Indian Vedas* (1918). In his writings he glorified the antiquity of the Hindu civilisation and its profound philosophy, age and scientific character. Tilak claimed that the Vedic civilisation was the oldest in the world, being as such the Mother of all civilisations. His greatest work is his *Śrīmad Bhagavadgītā Rahasya* or *Karmayogaśāstra*, which is a commentary on the *Bhagavadgītā*.

For his patriotic fervour, Tilak is still remembered as Lokamanya ('honoured by the people'), the 'Father of Indian Unrest' and the 'Maker of Modern India'.

See also: **Bhagavadgītā; Gaṇeśacatūrthī; Nationalism; Saṃhitā; Varṇa**

JOHANNES BELTZ

Further reading

Richards, Glyn. (ed). 1996 [1985]. *A Source Book of Modern Hinduism*. Richmond: Curzon Press.
Sharma, Arvind. 2002. *Modern Hindu Thought: The Essential Texts*. New Delhi: Oxford University Press.
Sunthankar, B.R. 1993. *Maharashtra 1858–1920*. Bombay: Popular Book Depot.

TIME (KĀLA)

Time has been a major preoccupation of Hindus. Finding the 'right time' was essential for the agricultural work-cycle as well as the performance of sacrifices (yajñas), which had to be synchronised with the movements of the heavens. The *Ṛgveda* speaks of the rotating wheel of time as having twelve spokes and connects the seasons with the ingredients of the all-important sacrifice. In a more reflective way the *Maitri Upaniṣad* (6–15) muses: 'Time cooks all things in the great self. He who knows in what time is cooked is the knower of the Veda.' In the *Mahābhārata* time appears as fate (daiva) or even death. Time is seen as provider both of happiness and of misery; its effects are considered inescapable. In the *Puraṇas* time is introduced as one of the uncreated principles (tattvas), on a par with pradhana (matter) and puruṣa (spirit), emerging from the non-manifested universal being (avyakta). Time also takes on the role of a demiurge (secondary creator). By being dissociated from time, Brahman remains totally transcendent and is not connected with the evils of the world, all subject to time – transience being one of the most fundamental failings. According to the *Yogavāsiṣṭa Rāmāyaṇa* time is the root cause of both the creation and the destruction of the universe. By means of niyati (fate) time also controls the course of history. Time is compared to an actor, who appears on the stage, disappears and reappears again to perform a play. In the *Bhagavadgītā*, when Kṛṣṇa reveals his divine nature to Arjuna, he says: 'Time am I, world-destroying, fully matured, engaged in subduing the world.' Everything in this world is preordained; all events happen by necessity, with or without human cooperation. From the *Mausalyaparvan*, one of the last sections of the *Mahābhārata* and which is characterised by a deep sense of doom, we learn that the heroes 'met with destruction, impelled by time'. Time, in an embodied form, is wandering about the earth: 'It looked like a man of terrible and fierce aspect – none else but the destroyer of all creatures.' The evil deeds which the protagonists committed and which earnt them their sad fate are ascribed to 'the perverseness of the hour that had come upon them'.

Time emerges as a major issue for theoretical reflection in the darsaṇas. In Vaiśeṣika, which is a thoroughly atomistic system, time (kāla) is listed as one of nine basic substances (dravya). It is described as 'of three kinds, being characterised by creation, sustention and destruction' (*Saptapadārthī* 16; Gurumurti 1932: 18). Nyāya deals with time in the context of 'valid cognition'. It accepts the Vaiśeṣika notion of time as a substance and attempts to work out the epistemological implications. It holds that 'perception and the rest cannot be regarded as instruments of cognition on account of the impossibility of connecting them with any of the three points of time' (*Nyāyasūtras* 2.1. 37–39; Jha 1939: 154–66). Against the Buddhist teaching of momentariness, the Naiyaikas assert the substantial reality of the present:

> If there is no present time, then past and future are inconceivable, as they are relative to that. Time is not conceived in relation to space but in relation to action. It is the actually existing connection of the object and the action, which present time indicates. On the basis of this we have the notion of past and future, which would not be conceivable if the present did not exist.
>
> (*Nyāyasūtras* 2.1.40–41; Jha 1939: 167–79)

Viśiṣṭādvaitins consider the universe to be 'the body of God' and thus invest it with a degree of reality hardly paralleled anywhere else. Also, time acquires a substantiality of its own as the manifestation of God's eternity and omnipresence. According to the *Yatīndramatadipīkā*, a Vedāntic text, what is called time (kāla) is a particular inert substance devoid of the three guṇas, eternal and all pervasive, the basis for such terms as 'simultaneous', 'immediate', 'long', etc. Time itself is the material cause of existence-in-time. While undivided time is eternal, its effects are non-eternal. Time is an instrument in the divine līlā (sport): in his avatāras the Lord appears as subject to time, while in reality he is independent of time.

According to Śaṅkara's Advaita Vedānta, the a-temporal Brahman is the only reality. One of the preliminary qualifications for Vedānta study is nitya-anitya-vāstu-viveka: the capacity to discriminate between what is timeless and what is subject to time. Manifoldness, the result of evolution in time, is produced by ignorance. Time does not possess an independent reality of its own; it is only associated with events in time. Citsukha, a twelfth-century Advaitin, refutes the reality of time by pointing out that it can neither be perceived by the eye or by touch nor apprehended by mind; it cannot be inferred either, because there are no perceptual data from which to start. Notions such as prior and posterior, succession and simultaneity, quickness and duration do not indicate the nature of time itself. Since the self can be regarded as the cause of manifestation of time in events and things in accordance with their varying conditions of appearance, it is unnecessary to introduce the existence of a new category called time. Prior and posterior do not need time as an explanation: they may be regarded as the impressions produced by a greater or lesser quantity of solar vibrations. There is therefore no need to admit time as separate category since its apprehension can be explained on the basis of our known data of experience.

Patañjali, defining the end and purpose of Yoga as 'the cessation of all time-conditioned fluctuations (vṛttis) of consciousness', endeavours to lead the practitioner to a transcendence of time and space (*Yogasūtra* 1.2). Since the ultimate condition is one of timelessness, time cannot be an aspect of reality. 'Temporality' is a figment of the mind; however, the moments which cause the perception of time are real. One gains metaphysical knowledge by concentrating (samyama) on the sequence (krama) of moments (kṣaṇa). As the commentator Vyāsa explains, 'Just as the atom (paramāṇu) is the smallest particle of matter (dravya) so a moment (kṣaṇa) is the smallest particle of time (kāla)'. Physically a kṣaṇa is the amount of time which an atom in motion takes to cross a space equalling the space it occupies. The sequence of such moments cannot be combined into a 'thing'. Notions like 'hours' or 'days' are mental combinations. Time (kāla) is not a real thing but is based on changes in the mind. The moment, however, is a real thing in itself and constitutive of the sequence. The sequence is constituted by an uninterrupted succession of moments. Past and future can be explained on the basis of change. The world which exists in this moment undergoes instant change. Patañjali accepts the notions of present, past and future. Unlike the present, however, past and future do not exist in manifest form. When, in the progress of Yoga the stage of consciousness called dharmamegha (dharma-cloud) is reached, the sequence of changes comes to an end and the sequence can no longer sustain even a kṣaṇa. In dharmamegha samādhi a Yogi reaches a zero-time experience, which leads to timeless Kaivalya ('aloneness', final emancipation).

See also: **Advaita; Arjuna; Avatāras; Bhagavadgītā; Brahman; Guṇas; Kaivalya; Kṛṣṇa; Līlā; Mahābhārata; Meditation; Nyāya; Patañjali; Puraṇas; Puruṣa; Rāmayāna; Ṣaḍdarśana; Saṃhitā; Śaṅkara; Upaniṣads; Vaiśeṣika; Vedānta; Viśiṣṭādvaita; Yajña; Yoga**

KLAUS K. KLOSTERMAIER

Further reading

Balslev, A.N. 1983. *A Study of Time in Indian Philosophy*. Harrassowitz: Wiesbaden.

Coward, H. 1982. 'Time (Kāla) in Bhartrihari's Vākyapādīya'. *Journal of Indian Philosophy* 10: 277–87.

Gurumurti, D. 1932. *Saptapadarthi of Sivaditya*. Adyar: Theosophical Publishing House.

Hari Shankar Prasad. 1984. 'Time and Change in Samkhya-Yoga'. *Journal of Indian Philosophy* 12: 35–49.

Jha, G. (trans.). 1939. *Gautama's Nyāyasūtras: A System of Indian Logic with Vātsyāyana-Bhasya*. Poona: Oriental Book Agency.

Klostermaier, K.K. 1984. 'Time in Patañjali's Yogasutra.' *Philosophy East and West* 34/2:205–10

Klostermaier, K.K. 1986. 'Dharmamegha Samadhi'. *Philosophy East & West* 36/3:253–62.

Klostermaier, K.K. and S.M. Macey (eds). 1994. *Encyclopedia of Time*. New York and London: Garland.

TĪRTHAYĀTRĀ (PILGRIMAGE)

Overview

Pilgrimage in Hinduism, as in other religious traditions, is the practice of journeying to sites on earth where religious powers, knowledge or experiences are deemed especially accessible to human beings. The ongoing practice of Hindu pilgrimage is rooted in ancient scriptural charters from multiple Sanskrit sources. A plethora of devotional literature in regional vernacular languages also praises the auspicious nature of numerous sacred places. Both classical Sanskrit texts and present-day vernacular pamphlets advertise pilgrimage as an easy and populist practice. In this it is explicitly opposed, on the one hand, to elaborate, costly fire sacrifice, which only the rich and high-born can accomplish, and, on the other, to yoga or asceticism, which only the spiritual elite have the inner strength to pursue. Even poor and low-ranking persons and even women – many texts declare – can perform and benefit from pilgrimage. With its origins over 3,000 years ago, the practice of pilgrimage is increasingly popular throughout India, facilitated by ever-improving transportation networks. Movement over actual kilometres, whether five or 500, is conceptually critical to pilgrimage, for religious journeys are not just about visiting sacred places but about leaving home.

In Sanskrit and most Indian languages the word for pilgrimage is tīrthayātrā – literally a journey to a river ford or a place where it is possible to cross. The concept of a ford is associated with pilgrimage centres not simply because many are located on riverbanks, but because these centres are metaphorically 'crossing places' (Eck 1982: 34). The entire range of human existence, sometimes referred to as the 'ocean of experience', must be crossed before the goal – whether union with divinity or ultimate liberation – is attained. Pilgrims also travel to sacred sites in order to seek divine help in reaching the other side of particular worldly troubles. Whether on a finite or eternal scale, pilgrimage lore promises easy crossings at tīrthas.

Hindu thought internalises pilgrimage and its meanings in a variety of ways. The language of travels on the surface of the earth may stand for spiritual quests undertaken within a motionless body and a meditative mind. Virtues such as truthfulness and chastity are described as tīrthas of the mind. Some yogic texts prescribe directing the breath through subtle channels from one interior tīrtha to the next, thus envisioning the body as a microcosm of India's sacred geography and ultimately of the cosmos (Gold 1988: 295; Varenne 1976: 211).

In general, popular Hinduism sustains a tension between faith in the supreme efficacy of external ritual action and denial of all but internal realities. Ideas about pilgrimage similarly encompass glorification of the fruits of journeys and firm scepticism about the worth of such efforts. To visit sacred places, view the deities in temples and bathe in holy rivers or lakes is valued highly, but pilgrims engaged in costly journeys often articulate a strong sense that travel is no golden road to spiritual success. The River Ganges is the paradigmatic holy river whose waters, Sanskrit texts proclaim, wash away all human sins and bestow salvation. But a rhymed proverb from Rajasthan instructs: 'If your heart is clean and whole, Ganges flows in your mixing bowl' (Gold 1988: 289).

Textual and geographic dimensions of Hindu pilgrimage

According to textual scholars, the earliest reference to pilgrimage in Hindu scripture is found in the *Ṛgveda*. This is a very brief verse, open to more than one interpretation: 'Indra [a member of the Vedic pantheon] is the friend of the wanderer; therefore, wander.' From this one derives the sense that God approves of journeying, but not necessarily that there are particular places upon the earth to which it is especially beneficial to travel.

Numerous later texts, including the epic *Mahābhārata* and several of the mythological *Purāṇas*, elaborate on the capacities of particular sacred places and rivers to grant boons to those who visit them or bathe in their waters. The multi-volume *Mahābhārata* contains an entire section entitled 'The Tour of the Sacred Fords' devoted to pilgrimage and its rewards.

The blessings to be gained from visiting sacred places are called tīrthaphal: literally, the 'fruits of tīrthas'. Some of the fruits promised to pilgrims in the *Mahābhārata* as well as other early works are fulfilment of worldly desires, among which health, wealth and sons are the three most frequently mentioned. Other benefits available to those who visit sacred centres have to do with cleansing the soul in preparation for existence after death. For example, according to Kane's helpful, topically ordered compendium of Sanskrit laws and instructions on many ritual practices, more than one *Purāṇa* and the *Mahābhārata* promise to pilgrims the erasure of countless bad deeds (Kane 1953: 586, 630).

For the purified human soul, these texts may promise the transitory delights of heaven or the ultimate life aim in classical Hinduism: freedom (mokṣa) from the cycle of birth and death (saṃsāra). Hindu pilgrimage has also been associated since ancient times with rituals performed to ensure the well-being of the spirits of recently deceased kin and ancestors. Today's pilgrims transport ashes of their relatives to submerge in the Ganges and other holy rivers, and offer food and water to ancestral spirits at these sites.

Major texts on pilgrimage inevitably include caveats to qualify the otherwise unlimited spiritual benefits conferred by tīrthayātrā. Narayana Bhatta's *The Bridge to the Three Holy Cities*, a sixteenth-century treatise which cites lavishly from earlier sources, advises that impure hypocrites, even if they have 'bathed in all the *tīrtha*s', remain sinful. This treatise concludes vividly by pointing out that fish may spend their entire lives swimming in sacred rivers but nonetheless fail to reach heaven (Salomon 1985: 206–07).

The geography of pilgrimage, as many social scientists have observed, unites diverse regions of the South Asian subcontinent, transcending linguistic, cultural and political boundaries. Because of shared elements in ritual structures, a pilgrim from western Rajasthan will not feel alienated in the eastern pilgrimage town of Purī, even though the spoken language, the landscape and climate, the deities' names and appearances and the food offerings would all be markedly different from those the pilgrim knows at places closer to home. Moreover, pilgrimage works to propagate practices among diverse regions: images, stories and tales of effective or attractive ritual acts circulate along with pilgrims.

While Sanskrit sources lay out a pan-Hindu sacred geography and describe both appropriate behaviours for pilgrims and the many rewards to be reaped from visiting 'crossing places', regional languages propagate a still vaster literature in praise of particular spots, their mythic origins and miraculous potential. Texts that glorify sacred places are known both as *sthala purāṇa*s ('ancient stories of sites') and *sthāna-māhātmya*s ('greatness of places'), often simply shortened to *māhātmya*s ('greatnesses').

Historical and mythological elements have converged to create several traditionally associated sets of sacred centres. One widely recognised grouping is the 'four places' (cār dhām) founded at sites in the four cardinal directions: Badrināth or Kedārnāth in the north, Dvārakā in the west, Purī in the east and Rāmeśvaram in the south. No single mythic origin story links these four, but they are associated with monastic institutions established by Śankara and promoted today by bus tours. A pilgrim who visits all four of these sites has virtually circumambulated India.

Other sets of geographically scattered but mythologically linked sites include the four kumbha melā, or 'pitcher fair' cities – Haridvāra, Nāsik, Prayāga and Ujjayinī – where drops of the nectar of immortality spilled to earth from a pitcher when the demons battled the gods for possession of it (Feldhaus 2003: 129; Hausner 2007); the 12 jyotirliṅgas or 'lingas of light', tīrthas sacred to Śiva; and the fifty-one Śakti Pīṭhas, sites dedicated to the Goddess. In the myth chartering this set of places Śiva wildly mourns his first wife Satī while carrying her corpse on his shoulder. To put an end to this cosmically disruptive situation, Viṣṇu shatters her body to bits with his discus, and each body part falls to earth at a different site (Feldhaus 2003: 127–33; Sircar 1973).

There are also singularly important pan-Hindu centres. Foremost among these in the north is Vārāṇasī or Kāśī (called Banaras under colonialism), understood by many to be the most sacred tīrtha of all. Others include: Ayodhyā, associated with Rāma; Vṛndāvana, associated with Kṛṣṇa; Vaiṣṇo Devī, an immensely popular goddess shrine in the mountains; and Gayā, a prime place for ancestor offerings located very near to Bodhgaya of Buddhist fame. This proximity is no accident, for several crucial events in the Buddha's biography took place at Hindu pilgrimage sites. Over the centuries and into the present these continue to attract Buddhist pilgrims from around the globe. Hindus visiting Gayā rarely miss a visit to Bodhgaya's magnificent Buddhist temples.

In South India, sacred places of renown include: the Śaiva temple in Cidambaram, Tamil Nadu; the goddess Mīnākṣī's temple in Madurai; the Ayyapan̲ shrine at Sabari Malai, which is the object of major annual pilgrimages from all over South India; and Tirupati in Andhra Pradesh, where Lord Venkaṭeśwāra is worshipped by followers of Viṣṇu, Śiva and the Goddess. Tirupati is said to be the wealthiest pilgrimage centre in India, its annual income 'second only to the Vatican' among religious institutions (Naidu 1993: 16; Khanna 2003: 159).

At regional and local levels, there are untold thousands of places with deep religious significance for the devotees who visit them. Often the lore of regional shrines links their mythic origins and miraculous potency to major pan-Hindu geography. For example, a pervasive concept is of a hidden Ganges river or gupt Gaṅgā that flows as an underground source into local ponds and rivers, bestowing upon them sanctity equal to that of the original Ganges. While some may have literal faith in a subterranean Ganges river, pilgrimage is never just about geophysical reality. Diasporic Hinduism has developed new pilgrimage destinations on different continents and displayed a capacity to sacralise landscapes far from India (Narayanan 2003).

Most pilgrimage centres hold periodic religious fairs called melās to mark auspicious astrological moments or important anniversaries calculated according to the lunar calendar. Fairs always generate an increased influx of pilgrims, often accompanied by flourishing trade and a profusion of cultural performances including dramas, epic recitations and collective devotional singing.

The Kumbha Melā, or 'Pitcher Fair', takes place every three years, rotating among its four designated sites in twelve-year cycles. Demographically, the full Kumbha Melā is spectacular and receives extensive international press coverage (Llewellyn 2001). In April 1998 about 10 million pilgrims came to Haridvāra in the course of the melā, which stretches over several weeks, with a few climactic moments for auspicious bathing when attendance surges. Nandan's account of his work as a government servant responsible for keeping order and providing amenities for the January 2001 Kumbha at Prayāga (Allahabad) speaks of an anticipated 30 million people bathing on the most auspicious dark moon day (Nandan 2002: 16).

Melās exist on much more modest scales as ubiquitous elements of India's rural religious landscape. Many regional shrines which are sleepy little places most of the year have their annual moments as lively and crowded centres of pilgrimage and trade. At some shrines smaller melās may occur as frequently as once or twice a month, on days that, according to the lunar calendar, are dedicated to a particular deity.

Pilgrimage sites are often located in spots of great natural beauty. Clean air, clear water and lush greenery are all attributes thought to be pleasing to deities as well as humans. Modern environmental activists draw on the mythology of sacred landscapes to inspire Hindu populations to adopt sustainable environmental practices (Prime 1992). Various theological interpretations intersect with civil engineering strategies when activists tackle the nature of pollution on sacred ground and how to deal with it (Alley 2002; Haberman 2000).

Approaches to the study of Hindu pilgrimage

Social scientists, religionists and Indologists bring many different perspectives and questions to the study of Hindu pilgrimage, resulting in an illuminating array of descriptions and interpretations. We may usefully identify four aspects of pilgrimage which have particularly commanded scholarly attention: (1) mythological origins of sacred sites and textual prescriptions for ritual practices; (2) subcontinental and regional pilgrimage networks as cultural integrators; (3) sacred centres as nexuses where pilgrims, priests, world-renouncers and merchants all flourish and interact; and where varieties of artistic and religious expressive traditions and performances are concentrated; (4) pilgrims' individual experiences and motivations at home, 'on the road' and in tīrthas. Few studies of pilgrimage limit themselves to only one of these dimensions and few cover all four equally. Many attend to one or two elements as central concerns, ignoring or merely touching on others.

Mythological origins and textual prescriptions

Mythic narratives surround every holy place, great or small, not only explaining the origins of its holiness, but often enumerating the wonderful things that have happened there ever since these origins because of a persisting divine presence. Texts also proclaim cyclical auspicious astrological moments of a particular tīrtha's heightened grace-granting capacities. Studies that focus on scriptural charters and rules for pilgrimage may concentrate on Sanskrit sources or draw on regional, vernacular literatures as well. Many textual studies are also ethnographically grounded – Eck's (1982) pathbreaking work on Banaras exemplifies this mixture.

The priests with whom pilgrims interact in sacred places recount the major chartering stories as part of the pilgrimage experience. To hear a priest recite the story of how a particular site gained its sacrality while present in that very location allows pilgrims to incorporate landscapes of meaning into their personal lives through narrative. The same stories are generally available in one or more local vernacular languages in printed inexpensive pamphlets sold at stalls that line the walks leading to any sacred site of sufficient magnitude to support such business. Moreover, the same oral and written sources – priests and pamphlets – advise and instruct pilgrims on just what to do while visiting particular temples, shrines or named bathing sites on riverbanks. Every holy place, unless it is very tiny indeed, has multiple recommended activities.

At pan-Hindu pilgrimage centres, origin stories often involve the deeds of pan-Hindu deities: usually Viṣṇu, Śiva and the Goddess, although they are most likely known by regional names specific to a particular tīrtha. In Purī, for example, Viṣṇu/Kṛṣṇa is worshipped as Jagannāth; in Kāśī Śiva is Viśvanāth; in Madurai the Goddess is 'fish-eyed' Mīnākṣī. Often the narratives surrounding any complex sacred site are themselves complex and multiple. Kāśī, the city of light, has many names and for each name there is a chartering story (Eck 1982: 25–33).

To take one relatively straightforward tale as an example of an origin myth reaching back to Sanskrit sources, consider the pan-Hindu holy city of Puṣkar in Rajasthan (Khanna 2003; Mishra 1999). Puṣkar is famed for its lake, the only large body of fresh water in this arid region. It is also known for its unique dedication as the only pilgrimage place in India where the deity Brahmā – important in myth and art but rarely worshipped – is considered the central presiding god. A streamlined version of the story of Puṣkar's greatness (*Puṣkar māhātmya*) as told in the *Padma Purāṇa* goes as follows: Brahmā decides to hold a sacrifice at the place where a lotus flower he is holding falls to earth. The flower creates divine waters where it strikes the ground; thus Puṣkar lake comes into being. The sacrifice is readied, just at the time of the year when Puṣkar's melā will henceforth be held annually.

Problems arise because sacrificial rituals ideally should be performed by married couples and Brahmā's consort, Sāvitrī, is late arriving from heaven (she is waiting for some other goddesses to join her). So, the story goes, Brahmā decides to marry any other girl who is handy, in order to commence the ritual before the astrologically fixed, supremely auspicious moment elapses. A local Gūjar (cowherding) girl is hurriedly purified for a hasty divine marriage by passing her through the body of a cow; she is renamed Gāyatrī, from the word gāy, for cow.

After the ritual is more or less complete, Sāvitrī arrives and is furious. She delivers a series of curses upon all concerned, the most interesting one being that no one will worship Brahmā anywhere on earth except here in Puṣkar (which of course describes the way things really are). Sāvitrī then precipitately departs for a nearby hilltop. The long climb to Sāvitrī's elevated temple is an important excursion for Puṣkar pilgrims, especially women, usually after they have visited her estranged consort Brahmā's temple, centrally located in the flat part of town. Sāvitrī's darśana is said to ensure for any woman that her husband will outlive her, a conventional desire for every Hindu wife. Gāyatrī also is enshrined on another hill. The entire city of Puṣkar is said to have over 400 temples.

These events, stripped down to bare essentials, are only the opening episodes of a long and complex tale about Puṣkar's significance as it has risen and fallen, been lost and rediscovered, over many centuries. The tale of Puṣkar's greatness also charters the enormous crowds who descend every year upon Puṣkar melā. After the sacrifice had been accomplished, so a later episode instructs, Puṣkar became so holy that the worst sinners could get to heaven just by bathing there. Thus heaven suffered overcrowding and, worse still, the gods complained that mortals no longer had any reason to practise morality, since it had become so easy to get to heaven. Brahmā therefore removed the tīrtha of Puṣkar from the earth to the sky, and decreed that it would only return to earth between the eleventh day of Kārttik and the full moon – the period of Puṣkar melā. Even so, pilgrims visit Puṣkar year-round.

Shulman (1980) and Feldhaus (1995) draw on Sanskrit as well as vernacular *māhātmyas* and *sthala purāṇas* from Tamil and Marathi, respectively, to explore regional pilgrimage mythology. Shulman describes the origins and miracles of sacred places in Tamil Nadu and points to some pervasive themes, echoing Puṣkar's, of ritual sacrifice and of deities' marital unions. Feldhaus explores those texts praising holy places along sacred rivers in Maharashtra to highlight motifs of femininity, agricultural plenty, natural abundance (fish) and human fertility. Feldhaus unites her textual work with ethnographic observations and oral traditions to show how narratives about places and the miracles they promise (or the disasters they threaten) are meaningful elements integrated into individual life histories.

Subcontinental and regional pilgrimage networks as cultural integrators

Bhardwaj, a cultural geographer, also unites fieldwork with textual sources to look at multiple spatial aspects of pilgrimage in his classic study *Hindu Places of Pilgrimage in India* (1973). Bhardwaj suggests that the 'tour of the sacred fords' as depicted in the epic *Mahābhārata* provides 'a clockwise circular pilgrimage of *India*' (Bhardwaj 1973: 42; emphasis his). That is, in a period when India had no existence as a unified political entity, pilgrimage routes made it a religio-cultural entity. Thirty years after Bhardwaj, cultural geographers fruitfully continue to explore the relation between pilgrimage routes described in texts and those that can be mapped on the ground. Singh and Khan draw on epic and purāṇic sources to pose some analogies between cosmological vision and the establishment of a 'moral landscape' on earth (2002: 1–65).

Just as an idea of subcontinental unity might emerge from pan-Hindu journeys, regional consciousness is created by regional pilgrimage practices.

Feldhaus calls the Hindu penchant to create numbered sets of pilgrimage centres an 'arithmetic of Place' and points to the ways such arithmetic works at the pan-Hindu level (Feldhaus 2003: 127). In Maharashtra she sees 'connected places', also in sets, as sources of regional consciousness. Networks of trade were often congruent with networks of pilgrimage. Historians Sen (1998: 32–38) and Yang (1998: 112–60) provide richly documented historical accounts of the links between commerce, religious journeys and fairs in North India in the eighteenth and nineteenth centuries.

Sacred centres

Major pilgrimage sites are always centres of ritual action. To some degree they are equally centres of commerce and art; of political manoeuvres and spiritual instruction. While pilgrimage is paradigmatically a householder's practice, holy places are magnets for holy persons, and have been since ancient times. World-renouncers are highly visible in most tīrthas, residing permanently, temporarily or intermittently in spiritual retreats, called āśramas. Sometimes encounters with renouncers may be a major element in a householder's pilgrimage. Such personages may deliver teachings and promise blessings, but often merely the sight (darśana) of them is considered a spiritual benefit for pilgrims, in the same fashion as is the sight of a deity's image. The Kumbha Melās are famous occasions for world-renouncers from various sects and localities all over India and Nepal to assemble in one place. These holy persons, with their matted hair, ash-smeared skin and sectarian markings, as well as the religious discourses and general blessings they deliver, are a major attraction of the Kumbha for Indian Hindus and also for foreign seekers (Hausner 2007).

Hausner's recent research uses ethnographic and textual sources to consider the nature of the relationship between wandering renouncers and the holy places where they may temporarily, or permanently, reside. Khandelwal's study (2004) of women renouncers in āśramas located near the pilgrimage centre of Haridvāra illuminates gendered aspects of world renunciation in relation to spiritual and physical journeys. Widows sometimes move to spiritual retreats in pilgrimage centres motivated by a desire for a spiritually focused life similar to renunciation and sometimes are encouraged to go by relatives who do not wish to support them.

Pilgrims needs priests to perform rituals on their behalf. At a subtler level, but one several scholars have explored, pilgrims wish through meritorious gift-giving to ritual experts and beggars to spend money for the benefit of their souls (Gold 1988; Parry 1994). Often the various services provided to pilgrims are highly institutionalised in pilgrimage centres, and the right to perform them is divided and inherited within priestly families. Pilgrims also need to purchase offerings, not to mention fulfil their own bodily needs while on pilgrimage, which leads to flourishing businesses not directly connected with ritual in pilgrimage towns.

Parry (1994) and van der Veer (1988) present ethnographic studies of priests and of interactions between priests and pilgrims in the important North Indian pilgrimage centres of Ayodhyā and Vārāṇasī, respectively. Van der Veer's work deals with an institutionalised monastic group, the Rāmānandi sādhus, as well as with householder brāhmaṇa pilgrimage priests. Both treat the intersection of religion and business in the work of priestly experts who guide pilgrims through crucial ritual moves, extracting both fees and gifts from them. Van der Veer tends to focus more on chronicling the political and economic jostlings of priestly lineages, while Parry tries to integrate the transactional aspects of priestly life with moral and cosmological meanings.

Pilgrimage centres are often centres of artistic production. Sometimes particular styles of art are associated with particular holy cities. For example, large paintings based on Kṛṣṇa mythology called pichvāīs are traditionally produced only in Nāthdvāra, a town sacred to Śrī Nāthjī, whose distinctive stone icon appears in some but not all of these paintings (Lyons 2004). Theatrical traditions also flourish in sacred cities, especially those dedicated to Rāma and Kṛṣṇa. The lives of those deities are staged in performances where entertainment and religious instruction fluidly merge. Hein's *Miracle Plays of Mathura* (1972) and Hawley's *At Play with Krishna* (1981) are classic studies of the theatre of pilgrimage. Although Vārāṇasī is often thought of as Śiva's tīrtha, it also has a grand Rām Līlā tradition (Hess 1983; Schechner 1985: 151–212).

Pilgrimage intermingles deeply with a given territory's political economy (Balzani 2001; Sax 1991). The temple of Jagannāth Purī in Orissa offers a fascinating case of divinity, kingship and regional politics in mutual construction, as Banerjee Dube's (2001) finely documented historical study reveals.

Intense religious emotions connected with sacred place are subject to unscrupulous manipulation for political ends, as ongoing conflict surrounding the pilgrimage centre of Ayodhyā demonstrates. On 6 December 1992 militant Hindus destroyed a mosque in Ayodhyā which they claimed had been constructed centuries ago at the very spot where Rāma was born. Engaged scholars have attempted to trace historically and to comprehend analytically the causality of conflict still haunting Ayodhyā (Dube 2004: 164–76; Nandy *et al.* 1997; Pandey 1993).

Conflict and destruction are not by any means the normal outcome when Hindu pilgrims' destinations overlap with those belonging to other religious traditions. Recent work has focused on sacred places in India characterised by many centuries of harmonious interactions and peacefully shared among different religious communities (Roy Burman 2002; Sikand 2003).

Pilgrims' experiences and motivations

Every aspect of Hindu pilgrimage already discussed contributes to pilgrims' motivations to travel and their experiences while journeying. Mythic charters, of course, promise the blessings that attract pilgrims and guide them on their way. The existence of networks defining sacred geographies influences where and how pilgrims travel. While in sacred centres, pilgrims interact with priests, renouncers, vendors and artists in many different fashions, often taking home with them some tangible product of the places visited as a memento, along with oral stories and intangible inner experiences.

It is difficult to study pilgrimage experience without participating in it to some degree; hence academics who study pilgrimage often produce accounts that are more evocative and literary than most social-scientific or religio-historical writings. These hybrid products combine analysis with a personal voice. One of the earliest pilgrimage experience accounts which perhaps provided a model for many that followed is Irawati Karve's '"On the Road": A Maharashtrian Pilgrimage' (1988), published originally in Marathi in 1951 and in English in 1962. Karve (1905–70) was an anthropologist, educated in Germany, whose other publications include far more traditional works on kinship and social structure, as well as some more purely literary endeavours. Her pilgrimage piece uniquely unites deeply personal reflections with a sociological perspective. The foot pilgrimage to Paṇḍharpūr in which Karve participated has been a favourite subject for authors interested in Hindu pilgrimage (Mokashi 1987; Stanley 1992; Vaudeville 1999: 199–220).

Another classic ethnographic study is Daniel's brilliantly rendered narrative and semiotic analysis of his participation in another famous annual foot pilgrimage – this one to the shrine of Lord Ayyapaṉ at Sabari Malai in Kerala. The Sabari Malai pilgrimage is one in which the ritual seems deliberately designed to dissolve separate identities, as pilgrims all take on a single name and share intense physical hardship, achieving at the journey's end a near ecstatic sense of union (Daniel 1984: 245–87; Sekar 1992).

Gold (1988), Haberman (1994) and Sax (1991) all travelled with pilgrims and participated in pilgrimage rituals; each brings to life diverse landscapes, routes, rituals, mythologies and motivations. Sax describes a Himalayan region where the goddess Nandadevī lives as the mountain's daughter and her devotees participate with her when she journeys, in palanquins, from her natal village to the mountaintop home of her husband, Lord Śiva. Haberman describes his participation in the Ban-Yātrā, an annual, 200-mile circuit of the landscape of Kṛṣṇa's enchanted childhood and youth, in an account that fluidly merges personal experience, historical context and mythological narrative. Gold describes three types of pilgrimage originating from a Rajasthan village, and the ways pilgrims link these journeys with different visions of what happens to the human soul after death. Focused on pilgrimage as a round trip, Gold's study includes rituals of departure and return and the ways pilgrims share the fruits of their journeys with those who remained behind.

Practices, themes and meanings in Hindu pilgrimage

A few persistent and pervasive themes emerge from the rich and diverse scholarship on Hindu pilgrimage and the multifaceted nature of pilgrimage experience:

1 Pilgrimage often effects a sense of unified geographic, cultural and religious identity, whether on subcontinental or regional scales.

2 Pilgrimage characteristically combines worldly and spiritual aims and experiences. At a broad level, tīrthas are centres for commerce as well as places where the ultimate human aim is attainable. They are equally sites where ritual and art unite to create vivid, sensuous experiences beyond the everyday.
3 Pilgrimage is related to death in multiple ways. One major motivation for Hindu pilgrimage, chartered in Sanskrit texts, is to perform rituals on behalf of recently deceased kin as well as to make offerings to collective ancestors. Pilgrimage is most often undertaken in old age; it prepares the soul for a more permanent removal from home, whether this is thought of as death itself or as a detached mode of life appropriate to the elderly.
4 Pilgrimage is associated with world-renunciation in multiple ways. Renouncers wander; renouncers often wander to holy places, where pilgrims encounter them, seeking their blessings and teachings. While on the road, pilgrims often emulate renouncers by undertaking ascetic practices, including limited diets and celibacy.
5 Tales of deities are embodied in landscapes of meaning; pilgrims' journeys are expressions of devotion and offer unique access to gods and goddesses through physical participation in their biographies. Because the mythic landscape of pilgrimage is also a geological and biophysical landscape, environmental themes in the late twentieth and early twenty-first century have intersected with pilgrimage – whether it is concern to redress the deforestation of Kṛṣṇa's childhood home or prevent industrial and sewage pollution of the eternally pure Ganges river.
6 Although recent political events have shown that sacred places can be sites of violent conflict, throughout India's long history of religious pluralism many sacred places have been peacefully shared by devotees from different traditions.
7 Pilgrimage may be internalised as a quest for virtues or enlightenment. For example, truthfulness, patience, self-restraint, compassion and chastity are all proclaimed as tīrthas in which a person may metaphorically bathe. Simultaneously, the value of travel to sacred sites, baths in holy rivers and the performance of ritual actions at auspicious times and places have endured throughout millennia of Hindu thought.

See also: **Agnihotra; Āśram(a) (religious community); Ayodhyā; Ayyapaṉ; Brahmā; Brāhmaṇas; Buddhism, Relationship with Hinduism; Calendar; Cidambaram; Dāna; Darśana; Diaspora; Drama; Ecology; Gaṅgā; Gayā; Gāyatrī; Haridvāra; Indra; Jagannātha; Jyotiṣa; Kane, Pandurang Vaman; Kṛṣṇa; Kumbha Melā; Madurai; Mahābhārata; Mīnākṣī; Mokṣa; Nāsik; Prayāga; Purāṇas; Rājā; Rāma; Sacred animals; Sacred geography; Sādhu; Śaivism; Śakti; Saṃhitā; Saṃnyāsa; Saṃsāra; Śankara; Satī; Śrāddha; Tapas; Ujjayinī; Vedic pantheon; Vivāha; Vṛndāvana; Widowhood; Yoga**

ANN GRODZINS GOLD

Further reading

Alley, K.D. 2002. *On the Banks of the Ganga: When Wastewater Meets a Sacred River*. Ann Arbor, MI: University of Michigan Press.

Balzani, M. 2001. 'Pilgrimage and Politics in the Desert of Rajasthan'. In B. Bender and M. Winer, eds, *Contested Landscapes: Movement, Exile and Place*. New York: Berg, 211–24.

Banerjee Dube, I. 2001. *Divine Affairs: Religion, Pilgrimage and the State in Colonial and Postcolonial India*. Shimla: Indian Institute of Advanced Study.

Bhardwaj, S.M. 1973. *Hindu Places of Pilgrimage in India: A Study in Cultural Geography*. Berkeley, CA and London: University of California Press.

Daniel, E.V. 1984. *Fluid Signs: Being a Person the Tamil Way*. Berkeley, CA: University of California Press.

Dube, S. 2004. *Stitches on Time: Colonial Textures and Postcolonial Tangles*. Durham, NC: Duke University Press.

Eck, D. 1982. *Banaras: City of Light*. Princeton, NJ: Princeton University Press.

Feldhaus, A. 1995. *Water and Womanhood: Religious Meanings of Rivers in Maharashtra*. New York: Oxford University Press.

Feldhaus, A. 2003. *Connected Places: Region, Pilgrimage, and Geographical Imagination in India*. New York: Palgrave Macmillan.

Gold, A.G. 1988. *Fruitful Journeys: The Ways of Rajasthani Pilgrims*. Berkeley, CA: University of California Press.

Haberman, D. 1994. *Journey through the Twelve Forests*. New York: Oxford University Press.

Haberman, D. 2000. 'River of Love in an Age of Pollution'. In C. K. Chapple and M.E. Tucker, eds, *Hinduism and Ecology*. Cambridge, MA: Harvard University Press, 339–54.

Hausner, S.L. 2007. *Wandering in Place: The Social World of Hindu Renunciation*. Bloomington, IN: Indiana University Press.

Hawley, J.S. 1981 *At Play with Krishna: Pilgrimage Dramas from Brindavan*. Princeton, NJ: Princeton University Press.

Hein, N. 1972. *The Miracle Plays of Mathura*. New Haven, CT: Yale University Press.

Hess, L. 1983. '*Ram Lila*: The Audience Experience'. In M. Thiel-Horstmann, ed., *Bhakti in Current Research, 1979–1982*. Berlin: Dietrich Reimer, 171–94.

Kane, P.V. 1953. *History of Dharmashastra*, vol. 4. Poona: Bhandarkar Oriental Research Institute.

Karve, I. 1988 [1951]. 'On the Road: A Maharashtrian Pilgrimage'. In E. Zelliot and M. Berntsen, eds, *The Experience of Hinduism: Essays on Religion in Maharashtra*. Albany, NY: SUNY Press, 142–73.

Khandelwal, M. 2004. *Women in Ochre Robes: Gendering Hindu Renunciation*. Albany, NY: State University of New York Press.

Khanna, A.N. 2003. *Pilgrim Shrines of India: Mythology, Archaeology, History and Art*. New Delhi: Aryan Books.

Llewellyn, J.E. 2001. The Kumbh Mela home page, available at http://courses.smsu.edu/jel807f/kumbhmela.html (accessed 1 June 2005).

Lyons, T. 2004. *The Artists of Nathadwara: The Practice of Painting in Rajasthan*. Bloomington, IN: Indiana University Press.

Mishra, R. 1999. *Holy Pushkar: A Pilgrim's Journey in Quest of Lord Brahma*. New Delhi: Kanishka Publishers.

Mokashi, D.B. 1987. *Palkhi: An Indian Pilgrimage*. Albany, NY: SUNY Press.

Naidu, T.S. 1993. *The Sacred Complex of Tirumala Tirupati*. Madras: Institute of South Indian Studies.

Nandan, J. 2002. *Mahakumbh: A Spiritual Journey*. New Delhi: Rupa and Company.

Nandy, A., S. Trivedy, S. Mayaram and A. Yagnik. 1997. *Creating a Nationality: The Ramjanmabhumi Movement and Fear of the Self*. Delhi: Oxford University Press.

Narayanan, Vasudha. 2003. 'Hinduism'. In G. Laderman and L. Leon, eds, *Religion and American Cultures*. Santa Barbara, CA: ABC-CLIO, 97–109.

Pandey, G. (ed.). 1993. *Hindus and Others: The Question of Identity in India Today*. New York: Viking.

Parry, J.P. 1994. *Death in Banaras*. Cambridge: Cambridge University Press.

Prime, R. 1992 *Hinduism and Ecology: Seeds of Truth*. New York: Cassell.

Roy Burman, J.J. 2002. *Hindu–Muslim Syncretic Shrines and Communities*. New Delhi: Mittal Publications.

Salomon, R. (ed. and trans.). 1985. *The Bridge to the Three Holy Cities: The Sāmānyapraghaṭṭaka of Nārāyaṇa Bhaṭṭa's Tristhalīsetu*. Delhi: Motilal Banarsidass.

Sax, W. 1991. *Mountain Goddess: Gender and Politics in a Hindu Pilgrimage*. New York: Oxford University Press.

Schechner, R. 1985. *Between Theater and Anthropology*. Philadelphia, PA: University of Pennsylvania Press.

Sekar, R. 1992. *The Sabarimalai Pilgrimage and Ayyappan Cultus*. Delhi: Motilal Banarsidass.

Sen, S. 1998. *Empire of Free Trade: The East India Company and the Making of the Colonial Marketplace*. Philadelphia, PA: University of Pennsylvania Press.

Shulman, D.D. 1980. *Tamil Temple Myths: Sacrifice and Divine Marriage in the South*

Indian Śaiva Tradition. Princeton, NJ: Princeton University Press.

Sikand, Y. 2003. *Sacred Spaces: Exploring Traditions of Shared Faith in India*. New Delhi: Penguin Books India.

Singh, J.P. and M. Khan. 2002. *Mythical Space, Cosmology and Landscape: Towards a Cultural Geography of India*. Delhi: Manak Publications.

Sircar, D.C. 1973. *The Śākta Pīṭhas*. Delhi: Motilal Banarsidass.

Stanley, J. 1992. 'The Great Maharashtrian Pilgrimage'. In E.A. Morinis, ed., *Sacred Journeys: The Anthropology of Pilgrimage*. Westport, CT: Greenwood Press, 65–88.

van Buitenen, J.A.B. (ed. and trans.). 1976. *Mahābhārata*, vol. 2. Chicago, IL: University of Chicago Press.

van der Veer, P. 1988. *Gods on Earth: The Management of Religious Experience and Identity in a North Indian Pilgrimage Centre*. London: Athlone Press.

Varenne, J. 1976. *Yoga and the Hindu Tradition*. Chicago, IL: University of Chicago Press.

Vaudeville, C. 1999. *Myths, Saints and Legends in Medieval India*. Delhi: Oxford University Press.

Yang, A. 1998. *Bazaar India: Markets, Society, and the Colonial State in Gangetic Bihar*. Berkeley, CA: University of California Press.

TRANSCENDENTAL MEDITATION/ INTERNATIONAL TM SOCIETY

Founded by Maharishi Mahesh Yogi (b. 1911? or 1918?), the Transcendental Meditation (TM) organisation began 1957 in Madras as the Spiritual Regeneration Movement. After being brought to the USA it became the American Foundation for the Science of Creative Intelligence in the USA, with two main wings: the International Meditation Society – targeted at the public – and the Students International Meditation Society (SIMS).

The TM technique is a form of Rāja Yoga, which aims to promote 'knowledge-based action' which will bring the world to perfection. Derived from Patañjali's *Yogasūtras*, it seeks to combine his three methods: dhāranā (concentrating one's attention), dhyāna (meditation) and samādhi (final rest, consciousness of the transcendent). Its declared aim is to reconcile the 'inner Absolute' and the 'physical world', a power taught by Patañjali but lost through time. In modifying Patañjali's techniques, the Maharishi has particularly the gṛhastha (householder) in mind, rather than monastics. TM thus offers pragmatic benefits, including better health, increased efficiency, improved relaxation, reduced effects of ageing and an improved ability to cope with life's problems. This is reportedly achieved through the reduction of the metabolic rate during meditation.

The practice involves the use of a mantra, which is given at an initiation ceremony, to be used by the student for two twenty-minute periods each day. TM emphasises the importance of a teacher in transmitting the mantra, since the meditation is said to rely on the mantra's 'sound vibration', which can only be transmitted orally. There is a fee, said to be equivalent to a week's typical wage, with reduced rates for those undergoing education. TM does not claim to be a religion, but a powerful life tool, the effects of which are scientifically verifiable. TM refers to a number of scientific studies which appear to support its claims.

Alleged benefits are societal as well as individual. In the 1970s the Maharishi began to teach the 'one percent' principle: if 1 per cent of a community practised TM, there would be fewer accidents, less crime, improved educational standards, better economic prosperity and various other benefits. On a global level, TM can help to contribute to world peace, since violence is said to be reduced where TM practice is concentrated. This societal effect is known as TM's 'field effect' or 'Maharishi effect'. To attain such effects,

100 practitioners are needed in a population of 1 million, but proportionally fewer for larger populations. Later, the Maharishi taught that such effects were better accomplished by his 'siddhis', advanced spiritual powers which are practised collectively in designated centres, for example in Washington DC and the 'Dome' in Skelmersdale, England. The 'siddhi programme', devised in 1976, involves 'yogic flying' and claims to afford increased paranormal powers, including the ability to levitate. Patañjali's *Yogasūtras* teach that there are fifty-two siddhis that accompany enlightenment.

See also: **Gārhasthya; Maharishi Mahesh Yogi; Mantra; Patañjali; Rāja Yoga; Siddha; Yogasūtras**

GEORGE CHRYSSIDES

Further reading

Maharishi Mahesh Yogi. 1995. *Science of Being and Art of Living: Transcendental Meditation*. Harmondsworth: Penguin.

Russell, Peter. 1978. *The TM Technique*. London: Penguin.

TRIKA

See: **Kashmiri Śaivism**

TRIMŪRTI

The word trimūrti means 'three forms' and is essentially a theological concept developed probably after the beginning of the Christian era. It is used extensively in the *Purāṇas* (third century CE) and serves two functions. Initially, it systematises the three functions of creation, preservation and destruction of the universe around the gods Brahmā, Viṣṇu and Śiva. Second, it enables the obscure neuter godhead Brahman to be manifested in physical form in these three gods. Usually, one of the three gods, with the exception of Brahmā, is said to be the equivalent of Brahman, but takes the form of the three gods in order to enter the creation and perform the appropriate cosmogonic functions. The trimūrti was never worshipped, though there do exist images of the individual gods in the three forms of the trimūrti.

See also: **Brahmā; Brahman; Purāṇas; Śiva; Viṣṇu**

GREG BAILEY

Further reading

Bhattacharji, S. 1970. *The Hindu Theogony*. London: Cambridge University Press.

TULĀSĪ

Tulāsī, the basil plant, is revered as both a sacred plant and a goddess. Tulāsī is aligned with purifying, liberative values as well as auspicious worldly values. The *Padma Purāṇa*, for example, claims that those whose dead bodies are burnt with Tulāsī wood are liberated from the effects of negative karma, and it praises all parts of the plant as capable of purifying sins. Tulāsī leaves are used in Āyurvedic medicine to treat illness and promote physical well-being, and food consumed with Tulāsī leaves is rendered suitable for consumption even by deities. Tulāsī is especially important to Vaiṣṇavas. Various *Purāṇas* portray Tulāsī as Viṣṇu's consort and a form of Lakṣmī, Viṣṇu's wife and goddess of auspiciousness, or Vṛndā, a devoted wife of a powerful demon. Viṣṇu breaks Vṛndā's chaste powers through deception in order to ensure divine defeat of Vṛndā's husband. In the autumn the *Tulāsī-vivahā*, Tulāsī's marriage to Viṣṇu or Kṛṣṇa, is performed in Hindu homes and temples all over India.

See also: **Āyurveda; Karma; Kṛṣṇa; Lakṣmī, Śrī; Pativratā and Patiparameśvara; Tulāsī-vivahā; Vaiṣṇavism; Viṣṇu**

TRACY PINTCHMAN

Further reading

Simoons, Frederick J. 1998. *Plants of Life, Plants of Death*. Madison, WI: University of Wisconsin Press.

TULĀSĪ-VIVAHĀ

This ritual enacts the marriage of Tulāsī to Viṣṇu or Kṛṣṇa. Tulāsī, the basil plant, is also considered a goddess very dear to Viṣṇu, and on this day she becomes his bride. The Tulāsī-vivahā takes place on the eleventh or twelfth day of the bright half of the Hindu lunar month of Kārttik (October–November) and marks the beginning of the Hindu marriage season in India. In many Hindu homes and temples a full marriage rite is performed using a Tulāsī plant and an icon of Viṣṇu or Kṛṣṇa, and the celebration of the divine wedding may take place over several days, drawing to a close on the fifteenth day of Kārttik, the full moon that marks the end of the month. The Tulāsī-vivahā is especially important to Hindu women, who may spend several days preparing for the wedding, singing wedding songs, gathering items to be used in the wedding and purchasing gifts for the divine couple.

See also: **Kṛṣṇa; Tulāsī; Viṣṇu; Vivāha**

TRACY PINTCHMAN

Further reading

Narayan, Kirin. 1997. 'Sprouting and Uprooting of Saili: The Story of the Sacred Tulsi in Kangra'. *Manushi* 102: 30–38.

TULSĪDĀS(A) (1532–1623)

The greatest of all Hindi poets, Tulsīdās, was probably born at Sōrōñ, Bāndā district, in 1532 (although traditional hagiographies would, improbably, prefer 1503). Soon abandoned by his parents due to inauspicious astral conjunctions, he was eventually 'adopted' by the ascetic Narharīdās, himself a disciple of Anantānand and therefore in the lineage (saṃpradāya) of the great reformer Rāmānanda (fifteenth century), who preached a religion of devotion (bhakti) to members of all classes and both sexes. The first part of his life may have been spent in Rājāpur, where he married Ratnāvalī and had a son who died early. Separated from his wife he then made a number of pilgrimages, lived for a while in Ayodhyā, where he began, in 1574, his Hindi version of the *Rāmāyaṇa*, which he finished in Vārāṇasī, where he finally settled then died in 1623.

With the exception of a single poem to Kṛṣṇa, the *Kṛṣṇgītāvalī*, the entire output of Tulsīdās is devoted to the cult of Rām (Sanskrit: Rāma). However, the *Gītāvalī*, *Vinayapatrikā*, *Dohāvalī* and *Kavitāvalī*, major works as they may be, are put in the shade by the greatest masterpiece of Northern Indian vernacular poetry, the *Rāmacaritamānas* (The Lake of the Life of Rām), justly esteemed as 'the Bible of Northern India'. This structurally uneven poem in seven books was composed in a simple and flowing language, a branch of Eastern Hindi, the Brāj Bhāsā, which, at the time, was considered an uncouth medium and thus attracted the ire of the local scholars to its author. Far from the secular hero of Vālmīki's epic, the prevalent medieval opinion made of Rāma an incarnation (avatāra) of Viṣṇu and in Tulsīdās' poem all the characters, including the god's foes, the Rāksasas and their chief Rāvaṇa, are his devotees, all perfect beings even if under a curse. The lesson is that deliverance is at hand for everyone, as bhakti, loving devotion to God, is the surest path to salvation since it alone can ensure the defeat of Māyā, the cosmic power of nescience. Rām is the master of Māyā, personified and identified with his wife, Sītā. Through her, the universe is created, in which beings are trapped in ignorance and ceaseless rebirths. In turn, for the devotee in whose heart God dwells, divine grace will effect salvation, although those devoid of bhakti will be emancipated even in spite of themselves – the thoughtless utterance of God's name is enough to trigger deliverance. Thus, Rām is the supreme Deity descended to earth for the salvation of humankind. The theology of Tulsīdās is not an original one but a very effective and successful synthesis of a varied heritage of Hindu religious thought, firmly within the bounds of brahmanical orthodoxy and sealing in Northern India the process of integration of bhakti that Rāmānuja had initiated in the South five centuries earlier. Composing the story of Rām in the vernacular, Tulsīdās made theology accessible to the common people and their religiosity was recognised as valid by the orthodox.

See also: **Avatāra; Ayodhyā; Bhakti movement; Bhakti (as path); Brahmanism; Kṛṣṇa; Languages; Māyā; Rākṣasas; Rāma; Rāmananda; Rāmānuja; Rāmāyaṇa; Rāvaṇa; Saṃpradāya; Sītā; Tīrthayātrā (Pilgrimage); Vālmīki; Vārāṇasī; Viṣṇu**

DANIEL MARIAU

Further reading

Growse, F.S. 1978. *The Ramayana of Tulsidas*, rev. edn. Delhi: Motilal Banarsidass.

TVAṢṬṚ

Demiurgic 'fashioner'. Vedic craftsman-god. The celestial smith Tvaṣṭṛ's epithet 'omniform' is also the name of his son Viśvarūpa/Triśiras, a three-headed monster, who is slain by Indra – suggesting the necessary shattering of stagnant totality or the cosmic void for divine growth and creation to occur. Indra's hostility to Viśvarūpa, Varuṇa and Vṛtra extends to Tvaṣṭṛ as well (*Ṛgveda* 4.18.9–12), only here the opposition is framed as one chiefly over soma rights. As the husband or alter ego of Aditi (cf. *Atharvaveda* 6.81.3), Tvaṣṭṛ is the presumed father of the Ādityas, the asurian antigods inimical to the devas. Like the Greek Hephaistos, Tvaṣṭṛ is the maker of the gods' weapons – in particular the invincible vajra or thunderbolt belonging to Indra.

See also: **Indra; Soma; Varuṇa; Vedic Pantheon; Vedism**

MICHAEL YORK

TWICE BORN

See: **Dvija**

TYĀGARĀJA (1767–1847)

Tyāgarāja was a South Indian musician, poet and saint. He was born in Tiruvārūr, in Tañjāvūr (Tanjore) district in Tamil Nadu, but his family soon moved to Tiruvaiyāru, twenty miles (or thirty kilometres) to the north, where he spent nearly all his life. They were Telegu-speaking smārta brāhmaṇas, devoted to Rāma, to whom Tyāgarāja's songs are addressed. He was married, but became a saṃnyāsin shortly before his death. Himself an object of worship, he has been called an avatāra of Nārada, of Śiva or of Vālmīki. He composed some 600 songs in Telegu and fifty-one in Sanskrit (selected translations in Jackson 1991). The songs are called kṛti, literally meaning 'making, composition', a term which can have a general sense but here refers to a distinct poetic and musical form, having an opening which recurs as a refrain (pallavi), an elaboration of it (anupallavi) and one or more verses (caraṇa). Besides devotion to Rāma, with many mythological references to Rāma and other foms of Viṣṇu, his themes include music as an expression of the divine and the way to mokṣa. He became better known in the twentieth century (Jackson 1994) and is now celebrated as one of the masters of Karnatak music (in the context of music Karṇāṭak, earlier spelt Carnatic, refers to South India as a whole, not just the Kannada-speaking region and state of Karnataka). Festivals, including pūjā to his image as well as performances of his songs, are held at Tiruvārūr and Tiruvaiyāru, and also at over a hundred places in North America, where he is a focus of regional loyalty and artistic endeavour (Hansen 1996).

See also: **Americas, Hindus in; Avatāra; Brāhmaṇas; Diaspora; Mokṣa; Music; Nārada; Pūjā; Rāma; Saṃnyāsa; Śiva; Smārta; Utsava; Vālmīki; Viṣṇu**

DERMOT KILLINGLEY

Further reading

Hansen, Kathryn. 1996. 'Peforming Identities: Tyāgarāja Music Festivals in North America'. *South Asia Research* 16: 155–74.

Jackson, William James. 1991. *Tyāgarāja: Life and Lyrics.* Madras: Oxford University Press.

Jackson, William James. 1994. *Tyāgarāja and the Renewal of Tradition.* Delhi: Motilal Banarsidass.

U

UDAYANA

Udayana (eleventh century CE), who had the patronage of the king of Tirabhukti (modern Bihar) and a school in Mithilā, is one of the most important philosophers in the development of Nyāya, the realist system of thought.

In his *Ātmatattvaviveka* (Discrimination of the Reality of the Self), Udayana defended the existence of Ātman (enduring or eternal soul) against the attack of Buddhist philosophers (who taught impermanence and thus denied a permanent soul or self). The conflict between the realist Nyāya and Buddhism had been longstanding. Udayana defended realism through the defence of ātman. Udayana also defended theism, presented in the *Nyāyakusumāñjali* (Handful of Nyāya-Tree Flowers). He offered nine arguments for the existence of God. One relates to order and design – the world must have an efficient cause (God). Others relate to the Veda, the supply of motion to the atoms and so on. Udayana also studied Vaiśeṣika and wrote a commentary on Praśāstapāda's *Padārthadharmasaṃgraha* (Kiranāvalī), in which he discussed the problem of 'class' (varṇa).

See also: **Ātman; Buddhism, relationship with Hinduism; Nyāya; Padārthadharmasaṃgraha; Vaiśeṣika; Varṇa; Veda**

MARTIN OVENS

Further reading

Swami Revi Tirtha (trans.). 1946. *The Nyāyakusumāñjali of Udayanācarya*. Adyar: Adyar Library.

UDDĀLAKA ĀRUṆI

The son of Aruṇa, a Kurupañcālas brāhmaṇa, who, like his father, was a famed teacher of the Veda. He is referred to in the *Śatapatha Brāhmaṇa*, the *Bṛhadāraṇyaka Upaniṣad* and the *Chāndogya Upaniṣad* on a number of occasions. The *Bṛhadāraṇyaka Upaniṣad* (6.3,7) states that he was the teacher of Yājñavalkya. However, he is most well known for taking instruction from Pravāhaṇa Jaivali, a local rāja, who initiates him into a teaching that is described as never taught previously to brāhmaṇas. The story and the teaching are described in the *Bṛhadāraṇyaka Upaniṣad* (6.2, 1–2) and occur after Uddālaka Āruṇi's son, Śvetaketu Āruṇeya, visits the settlement of the rāja and is asked whether his father has fully instructed him. Śvetaketu Āruṇeya replies in the affirmative but cannot answer five questions put to him by the king. Uddālaka Āruṇi cannot answer the same questions on the return of his disgruntled son and goes to Pravāhaṇa Jaivali and formally requests to be accepted as a disciple.

See also: **Brāhmaṇa; Brāhmaṇas; Rāja; Upaniṣads; Veda; Yājñavalkya**

RON GEAVES

Further reading

Stutley, Margaret and James Stutley (eds). 1977. *A Dictionary of Hinduism: Its Mythology, Folklore and Development 1500 BC–AD 1500*. London: Routledge and Kegan Paul.

UJJAYINĪ

The modern city of Ujjain, situated on the sacred river Śiprā in the north-east Mālwa region (ancient name: Avanti) of the modern Indian state of Madhya Pradesh, lies a short distance southward from the celebrated ancient city of Ujjayinī, which itself was originally known as Avantikā. The ancient city (perhaps as old as 2000 BCE) ranks among the seven traditional cities that grant its dwellers liberation (mokṣa) and has had several historical phases of importance in Hindu consciousness, stemming from its role in ancient lore up until the present day. The change of its name from Avantikā to Ujjayinī ('city of victory') has been linked with Lord Śiva's vanquishing of the demon Duṣaṇa at the behest of the Avanti inhabitants. The legend has it that Lord Śiva then took permanent residence here at the renowned Mahākīleśvara temple, site of one of the twelve jyotirliṅgas. According to the *Mahābhārata*, Lord Kṛṣṇa and Sudāma were educated in Ujjayinī at the āśrama of Ṛṣi Sāndīpani. Known to the ancient Greeks as Ozene, the city was on the lucrative trade route between Mesopotamia and Egypt for centuries. The prosperity, beauty and overall auspicious nature of the city are alluded to in many Sanskrit works, including Śūdraka's play *Mṛcchakaṭika* and the famous short poem *Meghadūta* by master poet Kālidāsa, who himself may have been a resident of the city at some point. Aside from its connection with King Vikramarka, whose name marks the beginning of an oft-used era of time-keeping in India (vikrama samvat) at the year 57 BCE, and King Candragupta II (aka Vikramāditya), who ruled in Ujjayinī during the fifth century, Ujjayinī has been a centre for many political regimes throughout history. It has continued to be a centre for Sanskrit learning for at least the last millennia and still remains important for Hindu astronomers and geographers, who consider the city to run through the first meridian used to calculate longitude; Jaipuri king Jai Singh built a Veda Śāla (still active) here in 1730 to facilitate astronomical research. Today, Ujjayinī remains as one of the four loci for the Kumbha Melā, a massive gathering of pilgrims and holy men, and an important centre for traditional arts and literature.

See also: **Āśram(a) (religious community); Drama; Jyotiṣa; Kālidāsa; Kumbha Melā; Languages; Mokṣa; Poetry; Śiva**

DEVEN M. PATEL

Further reading

Bhardwaj, Surinder Mohan. 1983. *Hindu Places of Pilgrimage in India: A Study in Cultural Geography*. Berkeley, CA: University of California Press.

UMĀ

Umā is an alternative name or an appellation of the goddess Pārvatī favoured in several of the *Purāṇas*. Although uncertain in translation, the name signifies the 'splendour' or 'light' of Pārvatī. Referred to first in the *Kena Upaniṣad* as Umā Haimavatī, daughter of the Himālayas, she is presented as fulfilling a particularly important role by channelling information between the absolute reality of Brahman and the gods (Kinsley 1988: 36). Through her later identification with Pārvatī, Umā is a wife of Śiva and a goddess who manifests a range of maternal characteristics. She is a model of the female householder ideal, but also a goddess who can emanate violent and combative goddesses such as Durgā and Kālī.

See also: **Brahman; Durgā; Gārhasthya; Himālayas; Kālī and Caṇḍī; Pārvatī; Purāṇas; Śiva; Upaniṣads**

PAUL REID-BOWEN

Further reading

Kinsley, D. 1988. *Hindu Goddesses: Visions of the Divine Feminine in the Hindu Religious Tradition*. Berkeley, CA: University of California Press.

UMĀPATI ŚIVĀCĀRYA

An early fourteenth-century devotee and scholar of Śaiva Siddhānta who is regarded in that tradition as the fourth in the lineage of the Tirukkayilāya paramparā succeeding Arulnandi, who in turn had developed the systematisation begun by Meykaṇṭar. He was born and raised in the Cidambaram Naṭarāja temple and performed the rituals to the deities blending both Vedic and Āgamic conventions but also took regular Śaivite initiation from Maṟaijñāna-Sambandhar, whose descendants at Cidambaram still revere him as an illustrious predecessor. Very little is known about his life outside hagiographical accounts contained in the traditional biographies found in the *Pārthavanamāhātyma* and the *Umāpativijaya*, both written in Sanskrit. These works refer to miracle stories in the vicinity of Cidambaram and refer to him alternatively as Umāpati Śivām, Umāpati Devar and occasionally Koṟṟavañgudi Umāpati Śivām. It is by his works that he is best known. In the *Śivapirakāśam* (The Light of Śiva) he further developed the exposition of Śaiva Siddhānta begun in Arulnandi's and Meykaṇṭar's standard works. In the *Sañkalpanirākaraṇam* (The Repudiation of Doubts) he refuted the movements who were opposed to the doctrines of the Siddhānta, especially those who denied the superiority of the strict non-dualism espoused by the school. He also wrote on the topic of grace in four treatises, a popular anthology of the *Āgamas* with commentary entitled the *Śataratnasañgraha* (Collection of a Hundred Gems) and a commentary on the *Pauṣkara Āgama*.

See also: **Cidambaram; Meykaṇṭar; Paraṃparā; Sacred texts; Śaiva Siddhānta; Śaivism**

RON GEAVES

Further reading

Janaki, S.S. (ed). 1996. *Śrī Umāpati Śivācārya: His Life, Works and Contribution to Śaivism*. Chennai: Kuppuswami Sastri Research Institute.

UNTOUCHABLES

See: **Dalits**

UPANAYANA

Receiving the Sacred Thread (yajñopavīta). The upanayana or initiation into the status of the 'twice-born' (dvija) is the most important of the Hindu saṃskāras, or rites of passage. The word upanayana means literally 'leading or taking near', which indicates taking the young boy near to the teacher (guru) for instruction or introducing the boy to the life of celibate studentship (brahmacarya). In common parlance this is known as the 'thread ceremony', indicating the receipt of the sacred thread (yajñopavīta), one of the most important and unquestionably the most visible of the many elements of this complex ritual. The sacred thread consists of three strands, each consisting of three cotton threads, knotted together in one place, which are to be worn at all times by the initiate. Normally it is to be looped over the left shoulder and under the right arm (upavīta), indicating activity in the service of the gods. This is to be reversed (prācīnavīta) when performing rites for deceased ancestors (antyeṣṭi or śrāddha). The third position for it is looped around the neck and over the chest. where it is secured with both thumbs in the region of the heart (nivīta). This form is employed during water offerings to sages (ṛṣi-tarpana), sexual intercourse, saṃskāras of one's children except when fire ritual (homa) is performed, going to the toilet or carrying a corpse.

As indicated, the individual initiated becomes a member of the twice-born, enabling him to perform and otherwise participate in a large number of Sanskritic rituals; indeed, the upanayana has become the most characteristic marker of brahmanical culture. It is restricted to members of the three upper classes (varṇa): brāhmaṇas (priests and educators), who should undergo upanayana at eight years of age; kṣatriyas (ruling classes and warriors), who should receive the upanayana at age 11; and vaiśyas (mercantile classes), who should take this initiation at age 12. However, historically there has been a great deal of flexibility, as children as young as 5 have received the upanayana and adults as old as 24, depending on the type of education given. Ordinarily girls were excluded, including by Manu. However, certain texts, notably the *Hārīta Dharmasūtra* (quoted in the *Smṛticandrikā*), permit girls who may be students of sacred lore (brahmavādinī) to undergo the upanayana at age 8 and study the Veda up to puberty.

The ceremony begins with the child taking a ritual bath. Then he dresses as an ascetic and appears before his teacher (guru, ācārya), who presents him with a new upper garment, a staff and his sacred thread. The initiate then is instructed in the recitation of the Gāyatrī mantra (*Ṛgveda* 3.62.10) and the basic elements of the saṃdhyā rituals, to be performed twice or thrice daily from then on. The student was then instructed in care of the sacred fire (agniparicaya) and the correct method of begging for alms (bhikṣā), which was a regular feature of studentship regardless of the means of the student's family.

In recent historical times, the upanayana has been performed only by orthodox Hindus and, with few exceptions, only by members of the brāhmaṇa varṇa. The initiate then is instructed in the recitation of the Gāyatrī mantra (*Ṛgveda* 3.62.10) and the basic elements of the saṃdhyā rituals, the obligatory offerings of water accompanied by mantra recitation that are to be to be performed twice or thrice daily from then on, at the 'junctures' (saṃdhyā), viz. dawn, dusk and (optionally) midday.

See also: **Ācārya; Agnihotra; Antyeṣṭi; Brahmacarya; Brāhmaṇas; Dharmaśāstras; Dharmasūtras; Dvija; Gāyatrī Mantra; Guru; Mantra; Manu; Ṛṣi; Saṃnyāsa; Saṃskāra; Śrāddha; Varṇa; Veda; Women's education**

FREDERICK M. SMITH

Further reading

Kane, P.V. 1974. *History of Dharmaśāstra*, 2nd edn, vol. 2, pt 1. Poona: Bhanarkar Oriental Research Institute, 268–314.

Pandey, R.J. 1969. *Hindu Saṃskāras*. Delhi: Motilal Banarsidass, 111–40.

UPANIṢADS

The *Upaniṣads* are among the most significant sacred texts of India, embodying ideas about the nature of the individual and of the universe which have remained central to the philosophy of Hinduism.

The word upaniṣad (from Sanskrit upa-ni-sad-, 'to sit down close to'), has traditionally been taken to mean 'a session of teaching', referring to the student sitting at the guru's feet. Recently, this interpretation has been questioned. Within the texts themselves the word upaniṣad generally seems to be used for a secret inner name or meaning, or sometimes for a hidden correspondence (bandhutā, or kinship), e.g. between macrocosm or microcosm (Olivelle 1996: 303). In practice there is a considerable overlap between these concepts. The texts known as *Upaniṣads* are indeed often based around one or more sessions of teaching, though not always between people who are in a formal teaching relationship. Frequently, too, the content of the teaching involves the revelation of a hidden name or correspondence, and these revelations are indeed intended to be confidential. 'One should not teach this to anybody who is not a son or a student', says the *Bṛhadāraṇyaka* of a powerful piece of ritual (Bṛhadāraṇyaka 6.3.12), and much the same is said of the whole of teaching of the *Śvetāśvatara* (6.22). So it appears that, from an early date, the word upaniṣad, whatever its original sense, was capable of bearing all these shades of meaning.

There are several hundred works called *Upaniṣads*, composed in Sanskrit over a number of centuries. The traditional number is 108, but not all lists include the same 108. J.L. Shastri's collection (Shastri 1970) contains 188. But the term is primarily used for a series of some twelve to fourteen 'principal' or 'major' *Upaniṣads*, generally accepted by Hindus as having the status of śruti. Those more or less universally accepted are the *Īśā* (or *Īśāvāsya*), *Bṛhadāraṇyaka*, *Chāndogya*, *Taittirīya*, *Aitareya*, *Kauṣītakī*, *Kena*, *Kaṭha*, *Śvetāśvatara*, *Muṇḍaka*, *Praśna* and *Māṇḍūkya Upaniṣads*: all of these but the *Kauṣītakī* have commentaries by Śaṅkara, who, however, referred to the *Kauṣītakī* (among others) without writing a commentary on it. In addition many would include the Maitrī (*Maitrāyaṇa*/*Maitrāyaṇīya*) and/or the *Mahānārāyaṇa* among the 'principal' group. (The names of the *Upaniṣads* often vary slightly in form and spelling.)

The *Upaniṣads* are regarded as the culminating part or end of the Veda (hence 'Vedānta'), completing the sequence of *Saṃhitā*, *Brāhmaṇa* and *Āraṇyaka*. The earliest of them, at least, must have been composed and transmitted orally: in the context of Hindu sacred texts, the words 'text' and 'literature' are not restricted to something written down. The act of memorising them is still regarded as a meritorious act, and many Hindus, especially those interested in Vedānta, know portions of them by heart.

The composition of the *Upaniṣads* is traditionally attributed to the ancient sages whose teachings are recounted within the texts themselves. Some of these sages, such as Yājñavalkya in the *Bṛhadāraṇyaka* and Uddālaka Āruṇi in the *Chāndogya*, come across as vivid personalities. Of others we learn next to nothing: Śvetāśvatara, for example, seems not to be known apart from one mention in the *Upaniṣad* to which he gave his name.

Dating the *Upaniṣads*

As with so many ancient Indian texts, the date of the *Upaniṣads* is debatable, and the matter has been complicated in recent years by nationalistic imperatives to date all developments in South Asia earlier than their equivalents elsewhere in the world. There is little archaeological evidence with a direct bearing on this subject: none of the kings or leaders mentioned in the *Upaniṣads* seems to have left us coins or inscriptions, though one of the names, Ajātaśatru, is mentioned independently elsewhere, in early Buddhist literature. The most that can be said is that the material culture described in the early *Upaniṣads* appears fully compatible with what is known of the city-based culture of the sixth to fifth centuries BCE, and is very different from the pastoral way of life that forms the background to the Vedic hymns (Roebuck 2000: xxxix).

The usual academic view, which places the *Saṃhitās* around 1500–1000 BCE and the *Brāhmaṇas* from 1000 BCE on, would date the principal *Upaniṣads* over a period of centuries from about 700 BCE (for the early prose *Upaniṣads*) to near the beginning of the Common Era (for the *Māṇḍūkya* and *Praśna*) and perhaps even later for parts of the *Maitrī*, which seems to refer to astronomical concepts that were probably not known before the second century of the Common Era. *Maitrī* 6.14 seems to refer to the twelve-sign zodiac, and to the navāṃśas – ninths of signs, which are also quarters of nakṣatras (lunar mansions) – which reconciled the imported zodiac with the indigenous system of twenty-seven lunar mansions. This would place the passage in Pingree's 'Greco-Babylonian' period, *c.*200–400 CE (Pingree 1981: 9.10–11). The mention of Ketu alongside Śani and Rāhu in 7.6 seems to belong to an even later period, but could so easily have been interpolated that it probably has little bearing on the dating of the rest of the text.

It is relatively easy to place the *Upaniṣads* in a plausible order of composition among themselves. The *Bṛhadāraṇyaka* and *Chāndogya* are generally agreed to be the oldest, followed by the *Taittirīya*, *Aitareya* and *Kauṣītakī*. All are mainly in prose, with verse for passages of summary or for heightened moments of teaching: all maintain a close connection with the earlier Vedic material and the ritual of the sacrifice (yajña). Both the *Bṛhadāraṇyaka* and *Chāndogya* seem to share concerns with the early Buddhist texts of the Pāli Canon, and can even be seen as having a debate with them (and among themselves) about the nature of the universe and the nature and place within it of the human individual (Gombrich 1990).

The *Kena*, *Mahānārāyaṇa*, *Kaṭha*, *Śvetāśvatara* and *Muṇḍaka* seem to form a second group. The *Kena* and *Mahānārāyaṇa* are in a mixture of verse and prose, the others almost entirely in verse. The latter three share verses among themselves, while the *Kaṭha* and *Śvetāśvatara* also share verses with the *Bhagavadgītā*. Many scholars would also place the *Īśā* in this group, though in view of its short length and the large number of verses it shares with the *Bṛhadāraṇyaka* it is very hard to date, and could equally well be placed in the early group.

The *Praśna*, *Māṇḍūkya* and *Maitrī* return to the mainly prose format of the early *Upaniṣads*, but contain ideas that seem to be later, for example in their understanding of the sacred syllable Oṃ, which they analyse into its individual sounds, each with its own symbolism. The *Maitrī*, in particular, shows clear signs of having been composed in written form, though drawing upon a body of much earlier oral material, including a *Brāhmaṇa*-like core that bears a clear relation to the *Taittirīya*. The terminology of what are presumed to be the later passages shows influence from, and reaction against, Buddhism (von Buitenen 1962: 6–7 disputes the extent of this, but see also Ranade and Belvalkar 1927: 124–30).

So perhaps we can place the composition of the early prose *Upaniṣads* around 700–400 BCE (though all containing some material that is considerably earlier); the verse *Upaniṣads* around 400 to 200 BCE; and the *Māṇḍūkya* and *Praśna* shortly before the beginning of the Common Era.

The *Maitrī* as we have it may date from as late as the second or third century CE. But the whole matter remains highly speculative. For those who regard the *Upaniṣads* as śruti, the date is perhaps irrelevant, since the teachings contained in them are viewed as beyond human origin and not tied to a particular period of history.

The 'later' or 'minor' *Upaniṣads* include the Yoga *Upaniṣads*, Saṃnyāsa *Upaniṣads* and sectarian Vaiṣṇava, Śaiva and Śākta *Upaniṣads*, dedicated to particular deities. (These categories appear not to be original, but to have been given for convenience by later scholars.) The latter groups tend to contain strong devotional and/or Tantric elements. Most accessible in translation are the Saṃnyāsa ('renunciation') *Upaniṣads*, twenty texts on the way of life proper to renunciants (Olivelle 1992). On internal evidence, these seem to have been composed over a period from early in the Common Era to around the twelfth century CE (Olivelle 1992: 10–11). The *Upaniṣad* as a category of texts clearly proved very durable, and there are examples which reflect most of the movements of Hindu religious history, with works of that title still being composed into the latter half of the last millennium. These later *Upaniṣads* would not generally be regarded as śruti, except by followers of the particular sects for which they were composed.

It is worth noting that the *Bhagavadgītā* is sometimes called the '*Bhagavadgītā Upaniṣad*', based as it is around a series of confidential teachings imparted by Kṛṣṇa to Arjuna.

Background

Each *Upaniṣad* is assigned to one of the four *Saṃhitās*, and often to a specific line of learned priests who handed on the tradition of that *Veda*. In the case of the early group of *Upaniṣads*, the relationship with the earlier strata of the tradition is generally a close one, often with a considerable overlap in content. For example, the *Bṛhadāraṇyaka Upaniṣad* is, as its name applies, an *Āraṇyaka* as well as an *Upaniṣad*: it shares many chapters with the *Śatapatha Brāhmaṇa* of the *Yajurveda*. The *Chāndogya*, as befits a *Sāmaveda* text, is much concerned with the symbolism of the Udgītha, the chanting by the udgātṛ priest at the sacrifice. The *Taittirīya* and *Aitareya* form part of the *Taittirīya* and *Aitareya Āraṇyakas*, respectively, and are attached to the Brāhmaṇas of the same name. The *Īśā*, uniquely, actually forms part of the *Saṃhitā* of its *Veda*.

In the case of the middle period *Upaniṣads*, the connection may be looser. The famous frame story of the *Kaṭha*, telling how the boy Naciketas came to receive teaching from Death himself, is expanded and reinterpreted from a passage in the *Taittirīya Brāhmaṇa* (3.9.8); but the *Mahānārāyaṇa* and *Śvetāśvatara*, assigned to the same lineage, appear not to show any special closeness to it. (The latter certainly quotes from the *Yajurveda*, but perhaps no more than from the other *Saṃhitās*.)

With the later *Upaniṣads* of the principal group, and those composed afterwards, there seems to have been a tendency to allot those that did not have an obvious home to the *Atharvaveda*. (In the case of the *Muṇḍaka* and *Praśna*, however, the link is a genuine one, since their teachings are attributed to sages of the *Atharvaveda* tradition.)

In recent years there has been a tendency to re-emphasise the relationship of the *Upaniṣads* to the earlier parts of the Vedic tradition: while important, this should not lead us to underestimate their originality. It is clear that there were great changes in society and attitudes between the Vedic hymns and the Upaniṣadic period. The authors of the *Saṃhitās* seem on the whole to have found earthly existence enjoyable, and sought blessings in this world: victory, wealth, health, sons.

They hoped for an afterlife, in the realm of the ancestors, not too different from what they knew on earth. The ritual of the sacrifice was a way of securing these blessings by pleasing the gods.

In the *Brāhmaṇas*, the sacrifice seems to take on a life of its own. By performing the ritual, it is thought that the priests are not merely securing blessings for the patron of the sacrifice (yajamāna) and for themselves, but helping to maintain the world in being. In the *Āraṇyakas* and the early *Upaniṣads*, the sacrifice is still central, but the process is becoming internalised, so that instead of having to be performed in the physical world, it can now be practised as a form of contemplation, with the elements of the sacrifice represented in symbolic form within the mind and body of the worshipper.

The change may have been caused in part by the difficulty and expense involved in commissioning one of the great sacrifices, and perhaps also by a growing emphasis on non-violence, which led some to reject the slaughter of animals that formed a part of many forms of yajña. But behind this lay a growing sense that the desire to win worldly goods, or even heavenly realms, was ultimately futile, since life in any world could never become totally satisfactory. People began to wonder what would happen to those living in a heavenly realm if the sacrifices ceased, or if the meritorious action (karma) that had placed them there was used up. Would they die again there, and fall back to this world or a lower one? Stability (pratiṣṭhā), not only finding a world, but remaining secure in it, became a preoccupation, while the fear of 're-death' (punarmṛtyu), already found in the *Brāhmaṇas*, clearly contributed to the growth of concepts of repeated births and reincarnation.

Influential in the growth of the new ideas were the śramaṇas, wandering ascetics who had left the household life and all its concerns, which included the formal religion of the sacrifice. The Śramaṇa culture helped to inspire a number of schools which rejected the authority of the Veda: notably Buddhism and Jainism, but also others which have not survived to the present, such as that of the Ājivikas. But there were also śramaṇas within the Vedic fold, who played an important part in the development of the *Upaniṣads*. Śramaṇas, unlike the sacrificial priests, did not have to be members of the brāhmaṇa varṇa: it has often been noted that, like the Buddha and Mahāvīra, several of the teachers in the early *Upaniṣads* were kṣatriyas; while others, such as Raikva in *Chāndogya* 4.1–3, an uncouth man found 'under a cart, scratching a rash', are of unspecified but perhaps not very reputable background. Notable in this context is the story of Satyakāma ('Lover of Truth') Jābāla (*Chāndogya* 4.4), in which the fact that the boy does not know who his father is counts for less than the honesty with which he explains his predicament.

In the *Bṛhadāraṇyaka*, we also find two women who are learned in spiritual matters: Maitreyī, one of Yājñavalkya's wives (Bṛhadāraṇyaka 2.4, 4.5), and Gārgī Vācaknavī, a brāhmaṇa woman who takes part in a public debate (Bṛhadāraṇyaka 3.6, 3.8) and clearly regards herself as the equal in learning of any of the male sages present apart from Yājñavalkya himself.

The śramaṇas perhaps helped to give the *Upaniṣads* their subversive aspect, a willingness to question the assumptions of Vedic religion and society. Hints of this can already be found in the *Saṃhitās* themselves, notably in the speculations of *Ṛgveda*, Book 10: 'Whence this creation has arisen, the one who looks down on it, in the highest heaven, only he knows – or perhaps he does not know' (*Ṛgveda* 10.129; trans. O'Flaherty 1981: 25–26). *Atharvaveda*, Book 15 celebrates the Vrātya, an ascetic living outside the norms of society, perhaps a forerunner of the śramaṇa. But clearly by the period of the early

Upaniṣads increasing numbers of men (and a few women) were beginning to say, like the ancients quoted by Yājñavalkya (*Bṛhadāraṇyaka* 4.4.22): '"What is offspring to us, when the self (Ātman) is our world?" For desire for sons is desire for wealth, and desire for wealth is desire for worlds: both are merely desires.'

Teaching of the *Upaniṣads*

Many have sought to sum up the teaching of the *Upaniṣads* in simple terms, on the following lines: human beings (and indeed all other sentient beings) are caught up in Saṃsāra, the round of existence, in which they die and are reborn time after time in consequence of their actions (karma). Distinct from, and unaffected by, the changing nature of the individual is the self (ātman), the unchanging reality within every being. The corresponding reality within the universe is Brahman, the absolute. Liberation (mukti, mokṣa) is the freeing of the ātman from saṃsāra: for some, but by no means all, Hindus, this is seen as a union of ātman with brahman, or a realisation of their essential identity. It is indeed in this form that Upaniṣadic thought has been absorbed into Hinduism. However, the position within the *Upaniṣads* themselves is much more fluid, and the way in which the terminology is used is complex, and changes over time. Often, too, we find older and newer concepts side by side.

Both ātman and (especially) brahman are terms with a complex history before they are used in the *Upaniṣads.* Ātman is the reflexive pronoun in Sanskrit, equivalent to 'myself', 'yourself', 'themselves', etc., regardless of the gender or number of beings or things referred to. In the *Brāhmaṇas*, it often refers to the body. Brahman, related to bṛhat, 'great', may originally have meant 'power', particularly the power of sacred speech, viewed as an attribute of the brāhmaṇa varṇa. It could refer to the essence of that varṇa, 'priesthood', as contrasted with kṣatra, 'royalty', the essence of the kṣatriya; or to a particular instance of sacred speech, some wise or powerful saying. In the *Upaniṣads*, these earlier senses of the word continue to be used alongside the more specialised one, and it is sometimes a matter of controversy which we are meant to understand on a particular occasion.

In the early *Upaniṣads*, in particular, the inner reality of each being may be called Puruṣa, 'man', 'person', either as well as, or instead of, ātman, and both terms can be used on a macrocosmic, as well as a microcosmic, level. The *Bṛhadāraṇyaka* (1.4.1) describes the primal man, Prajāpati: 'In the beginning this was self (ātman), in the likeness of a person (puruṣa)'. Some of the texts envisage a series of puruṣas or ātmans, of increasingly subtle form, from the physical body to the inmost self (*Taittirīya Upaniṣad*, 2.2–5).

In *Bṛhadāraṇyaka*, Chapter 3, the concepts of karma and reincarnation are introduced as something new and secret. In the course of a great debate between brāhmaṇas, one Jāratkārava Ārtabhāga asks Yājñavalkya what happens to a person when the body dies. Yājñavalkya says that this is not a matter to be discussed in public, and leads Ārtabhāga apart from the others: 'What they spoke of was action. One becomes good by good action, evil by evil action' (Bṛhadāraṇyaka 3.2.13). In 4.4.3–5 the theme is developed: 'As a caterpillar (more accurately, grass-leech), reaching the end of a blade of grass and taking the next step, draws itself together, so the self, dropping the body, letting go of ignorance and taking the next step, draws itself together. As one acts, as one behaves, so does one become.'

Deities

As ideas about the world and human beings changed, so too did ideas about the role of the gods and demons (devas and asuras). Often in the early prose *Upaniṣads*, the gods are treated as beings not entirely dissimilar in kind to ourselves: more powerful and radiant, but not intrinsically wiser. Demons, too, are not necessarily evil. In Bṛhadāraṇyaka Upaniṣad 5.2, gods, human beings (manuṣya: children of Manu) and demons appear as three branches of the same family, the descendants of Prajāpati, each with its own strengths and weaknesses. Prajāpati acts as the teacher of all, and each group hears the teaching in accordance with its needs.

Frequently, 'the gods', collectively, are the human faculties and sense organs. This draws upon a tradition of correspondences, found in the *Brāhmaṇas*, in which the eye or sense of sight corresponds to the sun (and the god Āditya/Surya), the mind to the moon (and Candra/Soma), the breath to the wind (and Vāyu) and so on. (The Vedic literature makes no clear distinction between the cosmic forces and the deities associated with them.) A number of myths are told to account for the relationship between the two forms of the devas, and to explain why the cosmic forms are pure and apparently deathless while those within the human being are flawed and subject to death. The *Aitareya* (Chapters 1–3) tells how the sense organs broke out of the primal man, like an egg hatching, and how the various devas, seeking food, flew down and settled on the ocean of existence to inhabit the man.

Where individual deities are mentioned, they are generally those prominent in the Vedas: Agni, Sūrya, Indra, Rudra, among the gods, and Aditi and Vāc (Speech), among the goddesses. There is rarely any implication that gods, as gods, can help human beings to become free of saṃsāra: in fact they may have a vested interest in keeping us there, nurturing them with sacrifices. According to *Bṛhadāraṇyaka* 1.4.10, human beings are like domestic animals for the gods: 'As many animals are useful to a man, so each man is useful to the gods. When even one animal is taken away, one does not like it, let alone when many are. So the gods do not like it when human beings know this [i.e. that "I am Brahman"].'

In the middle period *Upaniṣads*, we see the beginnings of a more devotional attitude to the gods. The *Kena Upaniṣad* has a remarkable story in which Brahman, usually treated as an abstraction, appears as a mysterious entity (Yakṣā) and confounds the pride of the gods. Brahman has won a victory for the gods (presumably over the demons), on which the gods are now congratulating themselves. Though Agni boasts of being able to burn anything, and Vāyu of being able to blow anything away, neither can affect a blade of grass set before him by Brahman. When Indra runs up to Brahman, it disappears, and in its place appears a most beautiful woman, Umā Haimavatī, perhaps the earliest reference to this goddess. Here she appears as a symbol of wisdom, teaching the nature of Brahman to the gods.

In the *Kaṭha*, the supreme reality, as well as being a puruṣa, 'a thumb in length, in the midst of the self', is identified with several deities, including Aditi (Kaṭha 4.7), and especially with Agni (Kaṭha 4.8). The *Śvetāśvatara* contains the earliest explicit mention of bhakti in the *Upaniṣads* (*Śvetāśvatara* 6.23), commending the seeker 'who has the highest devotion to the god/And to his guru as to the god'. Unusually, the supreme being in this *Upaniṣad* is called deva, and in its distinctive version of the Sāṃkhya philosophy, the deva is placed above the puruṣa and Prakṛti of classical Sāṃkhya. The deva is identified with the solar god Savitṛ but above all with Rudra, who already bears the title and many of the attributes of Śiva. In *Śvetāśvatara* 6.18, 20, the poet speaks of going for refuge to the deva, and roundly declares that without knowledge of him liberation from sorrow is not possible.

At the other end of the philosophical spectrum, the *Māṇḍūkya Upaniṣad* describes the cosmos in non-dualist (Advaita) terms, and seems to give no role to a god. Through Gauḍapāda's commentary, the *Māṇḍūkya Kārikā*, it becomes one of the major sources of Advaita philosophy.

In the *Maitrī* we already see the theology of Hinduism in its classical form: it makes several references to the Trimūrti as 'Brahmā, Rudra and Viṣṇu', and pays particular regard to Viṣṇu, under this name and as Nārāyaṇa.

Content and style

The *Upaniṣads* generally do not teach through statements of dogma, but through stories, riddles and puns: for 'the gods seem to love the mysterious, and hate the obvious' (*Bṛhadāranyaka* 4.2.2). Many of the most original passages of teaching take the form of dialogue, sometimes formal instruction and sometimes debate between rival sages.

The heart of the *Chāndogya Upaniṣad* is a dialogue (Chapter 6) between Uddālaka Āruṇi and his son Śvetaketu, who appears here and elsewhere in the *Upaniṣads* (*Bṛhadāraṇyaka* 6.2, *Kauṣītakī* 1.1–2) as a callow young man, proud of his education but in need of his father's instruction to bring him genuine wisdom. Uddālaka teaches him the nature of ātman through a series of lessons. For example, he asks Śvetaketu to bring him a banyan fruit, to break it open and then to break one of the tiny seeds he finds inside it.

> 'What do you see there?' he asks.
>
> 'Nothing.'
>
> 'On this subtle part – the subtle part which you do not see – rests the great banyan tree. This subtle part is what all this has as self. It is truth: it is the self. You are that, Śvetaketu.'
>
> (*Chāndogya* 6.12)

The repeated saying (tat tvam asi), taken as affirming the identity of ātman and Brahman, has become one of the most quoted teachings of the *Upaniṣads*. (This traditional understanding has been questioned by Olivelle (1996: 349), though on grounds that I do not find entirely convincing (Roebuck 2000: 423)).

Influence

It is impossible to overestimate the importance of the *Upaniṣads* for the development of Hindu thought. All schools of Vedānta, whether Dvaita, Advaita or Viśiṣṭādvaita, have been concerned to show that their ideas are founded in the *Upaniṣads*, with the *Brahmasūtras* shaping their interpretation within that tradition. The fact that the *Upaniṣads* teach by symbolism and suggestion rather than dogmatic statement means that different interpretations are often possible. Śaṅkara and Madhva wrote commentaries on the *Upaniṣads*, while Rāmānuja drew on the *Upaniṣads* in his commentary on the *Brahmasūtras* and his other works. The process continued into more recent times, with philosophers such as Radhakrishnan and Aurobindo Ghose writing their own commentaries on the *Upaniṣads*. Gandhi was a great admirer of the *Īśā* in particular, saying: 'If all the Upanishads and all the other scriptures happened all of a sudden to be reduced to ashes, and if only the first verse of the Ishopanishad were left intact in the memory of Hindus, Hinduism would live for ever' (Gandhi 1977: 259).

The *Upaniṣads* have also been influential in the development of other traditions. Ideas developed in them were taken further in the Sāṃkhya philosophy. Outside Hinduism, it is clear that, for example, the Buddhist formulation of the concept of 'not-self' (anātman, Pāli anattā) is in some respects a criticism of the Upaniṣadic concept of ātman (Gombrich 1990: 13–15).

Their influence outside South Asia has probably been greater than that of any Hindu text apart from the Bhagavadgītā. The earliest translation into a European language was Anquetil Duperron's *Oupnek'hat*, a Latin version published in two volumes in 1801–02, of which the philosopher Schopenhauer said, 'It has been the most rewarding and the most elevating reading which (with the exception of the original text) there can possibly be in the world. It has been the solace of my life, and will be of my death' (quoted in Hume 1995: 461). To the modern reader, this reaction may seem surprising: the *Oupnek'hat* is not a direct translation from the Sanskrit, but from a seventeenth-century Persian translation commissioned by the Mughal prince Dara Shukoh, which contains a large amount of commentarial material embedded in the text. As well as much Islamic terminology derived from Dara Shukoh's version (devas appear as 'fereschtehha', angels and asuras as 'djenian', djinns), it introduces quirks of its own, such as the classical Greek definite article to denote the singular and plural where this is not clear from the Latin. Sir William Jones, who pointed out the deficiencies of the Dara Shukoh version, did not himself translate the *Upaniṣads*, apart from the *Īśā* and brief extracts from the *Bṛhadāraṇyaka* and *Maitrī* (Jones 1807: 365–66, 370–79).

Such was the degree of padding in Anquetil's version that when Rammohan Roy's more reliable versions of four *Upaniṣads* appeared, in 1816–19, some supposed that they must have been abridged (Lanjuinais 1823). In the middle of that century, scholarly translations into European languages began to appear, for example the works of E. Röer in English and of L. Poley in French and German. (Both were prolific translators: see, for example, Röer 1850–56; Poley 1835, 1847.) By the end of the century, the versions of major scholars such as P. Deussen (Deussen 1897) and Max Müller (Müller 1962) made the 'principal' *Upaniṣads* readily available to readers without knowledge of Sanskrit, and enabled their ideas to gain currency in the West, where they had a powerful effect on those interested in occult or theosophical ideas. The poets W.B. Yeats and T.S. Eliot both show their influence. The former, though not himself a Sanskritist, produced a translation of extracts in collaboration with Shree Purohit Swami (Purohit Swami and Yeats 1937), while the latter, who in 'The Waste Land' makes explicit reference to *Bṛhadāraṇyaka* 5.2, was a good enough Sanskritist to read the texts in the original.

Translations have continued to be produced, some aiming at scholarly accuracy and original research, others, in the tradition of the commentators, at expressing the spiritual experience of the translators. The *Upaniṣads* continue to be admired and studied both in India itself and among students of Yoga and Vedānta through the rest of the world. This worldwide spread of interest in them bears witness to the power and universality of much of their teaching: a remarkable journey for a group of texts composed in the first millennium BCE and which were intended not to be taught to anyone who was not a son or a student.

See also: **Aditi; Advaita; Agni; Ahiṃsā; Anquetil-Duperron, Abraham-Hyacinthe; Āraṇyakas; Arjuna; Asuras; Ātman; Bhagavadgītā; Bhakti; Brahmā; Brahman; Brāhmaṇa; Brahmasūtras; Buddhism, relationship with Hinduism; Buitenen, Johannes Adrianus Bernardus van; Deities; Deussen, Paul Jakob; Dharma; Dvaita; Food; Gandhi, Mohandas Karamchand; Ghose, Sri Aurobindo; Guru; Hindutva; Indra; Jainism, relationship with Hinduism; Jones, Sir William; Jyotiṣa; Kṛṣṇa; Madhva; Maitreyī; Manu; Mokṣa; Müller, Friedrich Max; Nationalism; Oṃ; Prajāpati; Prakṛti; Puruṣa; Radhakrishnan, Sir Sarvepalli; Rāmānuja; Roy, Rammohan;**

Rudra; Sacred texts; Śaivism; Śāktism; Saṃhitā; Sāṃkhya; Saṃnyāsa Upaniṣads; Saṃsāra; Śaṅkara; Śiva; Soma; Śramaṇa; Sūrya; Tantrism; Theosophy and the Theosophical Society; Trimūrti; Uddālaka Āruṇi; Umā; Vāyu; Vaiṣṇavism; Varṇa; Veda; Vedānta; Viśiṣṭādvaita; Viṣṇu; Women, status of; Yajña; Yājñavalkya; Yakṣas; Yoga

VALERIE J. ROEBUCK

Further reading

Anquetil Duperron, A.-H. 1801–02. *Oupnek'hat*, 2 vols. Strasbourg.

Deussen, P. Sechzig. 1897. *Upanishads des Veda* [Sixty Upanishads of the Veda]. Leipzig: Brockhaus.

Gandhi, M.K. 1977. *Collected Works of Mahatma Gandhi*, 90 vols, vol. 64. Delhi: Publications Division, Government of India.

Gombrich, R. 1990. 'Recovering the Buddha's Message'. In T. Skorupski, ed., *The Buddhist Forum*, vol. I. London: School of Oriental and African Studies; Delhi: Heritage Publishers.

Hume, R.E. 1995. *The Thirteen Principal Upanishads Translated from the Sanskrit*, 2nd edn, revised. Reprint, Oxford India Paperback. Delhi: Oxford University Press (first published 1877).

Jones, Sir William. 1807. *The Works of Sir William Jones: With the Life of the Author by Lord Teignmouth*, vol. 13. London.

Lanjuinais, Jean-Denis (Comte de). 1823. *Journal Asiatique* III: 243–49.

Müller, F.M. 1962. *The Upaniṣads*, 2 vols. Reprint. New York: Dover (first published 1879, 1894).

O'Flaherty, W.D. 1981. *The Rig Veda*. Harmondsworth: Penguin Classics.

Olivelle, P. 1992. *Saṃnyāsa Upaniṣads: Hindu Scriptures on Asceticism and Renunciation*. Oxford and New York: Oxford University Press.

Olivelle, P. 1996. *Upaniṣads*. Oxford and New York: Oxford University Press.

Pingree, D. 1981. *Jyotiśāstra: Astral and Mathematical Literature*. A History of Indian Literature, vol. 6, fasc. 4. Wiesbaden: Harrassowitz.

Poley, L. 1835. *Kathaka-Oupanichat; extrait du Yadjour-Véda, traduit du Sanskrit en français* [Kathaka-Oupanichat (Kaṭha Upaniṣad); extract from the Yadjour-Véda (Yajurveda), translated from the Sanskrit into French]. Paris: Dondey-Dupr.

Poley, L. 1847. *H. Th. Colebrooke's Abhandlung über die heiligen Schriften der Indier, aus dem Englischen übersetzt, nebst Fragmenten der ältesten religiösen Dichtungen der Indier* [H. Th. Colebrooke's treatise on the holy writings of the Indians, translated from English, together with fragments of the oldest religious literature of the Indians]. Leipzig: Trübner (includes German translations of *Kaṭha* and *Muṇḍaka Upaniṣads*).

Purohit Swāmi, Shree and W.B. Yeats. 1937. *The Ten Principal Upanishads Put into English by Shree Purohit Swāmi and W. B. Yeats*. London: Faber and Faber Ltd.

Radhakrishnan, S. 1994. *The Principal Upaniṣads*. London: Allen and Unwin. Reprint, Delhi: HarperCollins (first published 1953).

Ranade, R.D. and S.K. Belvalkar. 1927. *History of Indian Philosophy, Volume 2: The Creative Period*. Poona: Bilvakunda Publishing House.

Roebuck, V.J. 2000. *The Upaniṣads*. Harmondsworth: Penguin Books.

Röer, E. (ed. and trans.). 1850–56. *The Brihad Aranyaka Upanishad*. Calcutta: Asiatic Society of Bengal. Bibliotheca Indica, 2 vols.

Shastri, J.L. (ed.). 1970. *Upaniṣatsaṃgraha Containing 188 Upaniṣads* [Collection of *Upaniṣads*]. Delhi: Motilal Banarsidass.

Varenne, Jean. 1960. *La Mahā Nārāyaṇa Upaniṣad: Edition critique, avec une traduction française, une Etude, des notes, et, en annexe, La Prāṇāgnihotra Upaniṣad* [The Mahanarayana Upanisad: critical edition, with a French translation, notes, and, in addition, the Pranagnihotra Upanisad], 2 vols. Paris: Editions E. de Boccard.

von Buitenen, J.A.B. 1962. *The Maitrāyaīya Upaniṣad: A Critical Essay*. The Hague: Mouton.

Whitney, W.D. 1984. *Atharva-Veda-Saṃhitā*, 2 vols. Revised and edited by C.R. Lanman (1905). Reprint, Delhi: Motilal Banarsidass.

UPAVEDAS

A number of supplementary texts to the Veda that deal with essentially non-religious knowledge such as statecraft (Arthaveda), music, dancing and the arts (Gandharvaveda), the art of archery and warfare (Dhanurveda), the science of medicine (Āyurveda) and the science of architecture (Sthāpatyaveda).

The art of archery is praised in the *Ṛgveda* in a hymn to war weapons and was regarded as the correct weapon of the kṣatriya. Usually, warrior-deities such as Rāma are depicted carrying bows, which are usually named. Śiva's bow, for example was Ājagava.

The *Gāndharvaveda*, attributed to the sage Bhārata Muni, was an appendix to the *Sāmaveda*, which deals with melodies appropriate to the recitation of the *Ṛgveda*.

Definitely the best-known is Āyurveda which remains to the present day a rival to allopathic medicine in India. Similar to mediaeval European medicine, Āyurvedic diagnosis is based on identifying an imbalance of the humours wind, gall, mucus and blood. The treatments are essentially based on the use of herbs, minerals, water and formic acid, although today yoga and massage can be used to supplement medicines. While some of the remedies appear to have a scientific basis, others rely on religious or magical techniques. However, the most important of the Āyurvedic texts written in the first and second centuries CE, the *Caraka* and the *Suśruta Saṃhitā*, make an attempt to classify medicines that belong to magico-religious treatments and those which belong to observed reactions to treatment. The Āyurveda was regarded as of divine origin in both its forms and was believed to have been revealed by Indra to Bharadvāja, who taught it to his disciples, and thus it has been passed on down through the ages. In the eighteenth century, European medical practice was combined with traditional Āyurveda, usually of the more pragmatic type, involving herbs, rather than that of sympathetic magic. This remains the medical system of India today.

See also: **Arthaśāstra; Āyurveda; Dhanurveda; Gandharvaveda; Indra; Rāma; Saṃhitā; Śiva; Sthāpatyaveda; Veda; Yoga**

RON GEAVES

Further reading

Stutley, Margaret and James Stutley (eds). 1985. *A Dictionary of Hinduism*. London: Routledge and Kegan Paul, 312–13.

UṢAS

'Dawn'. Vedic personification of daybreak. Uṣas is the most prominent female deity of the *Ṛgveda*, and her hymns contain some of the collection's most exalted poetry. Like her Greek counterpart Eos, Uṣas is a promiscuous figure. Under the name Aśvinī, she is the joint consort of her brothers, the divine twins or Aśvins. She is also the pre-Vedic firstborn of the primordial union of earth and heaven and, consequently, the recipient of her father's incestuous desires (*Ṛgveda* 1.161.5; 4.51.6). Uṣas is not only the harbinger of the day, the joy of humanity, but also embodies the abode of the soul after death. Another name for Uṣas is presumably Sūryā, the feminisation or daughter of Sūrya the sun. Under this indigitation, she is the wife first of Soma; second, the Gandharvas; third, Agni; and, finally, of mortal man (*Ṛgveda* 10.85.40).

See also: **Agni; Aśvins; Gandharvas; Soma; Sūrya; Vedic Pantheon; Vedism**

MICHAEL YORK

Further reading

Chattopadhya, Debprasad. 1973. *Lokāyata: A Study in Ancient Indian Materialism*, 3rd edn. New Delhi: People's Publishing House/ Tarun Sengupta. First published 1959.

Macdonell, A.A. 1974. *Vedic Mythology*. Reprint. Strasburg and Delhi: Motilal Banarsidass.
York, Michael. 1995. *The Divine Versus the Asurian: An Interpretation of Indo-European Cult and Myth*. Bethesda, MD: International Scholars Press.

UTPALĀCĀRYA

A student of Somānanda and the author of the *Īṣvarapratyabhijñākārikās* and two commentaries on the same text, in which he refuted the Buddhist oppositions to the teachings of monistic Śaivism. Also known as Utpalādeva (900–950 CE), he is in addition the author of a text of devotional poems in praise of Śiva entitled the *Śivavastotrāvali*. Utpalācārya was the founder of the Pratyabhijña school of Kashmiri Śaivism, and is known in the tradition as a siddha (perfected being). The recitation of his stotras (songs) from the *Śivavastotrāvali* remains a vital part of Śaiva worship in Kashmir and it is in these that the experiences of Utpalācārya can be encountered, which are then developed into philosophical expositions in his more well-known work, the *Īṣvarapratyabhijñākārikās*. Utpalācārya expounds a spiritual path that is open to the householder and not restricted by gender or caste. His work is known for the exposition of upāyas (ways, means), in which he develops a number of paths of realisation suited to the psychological or individual characteristics of the adherent.

See also: **Buddhism, relationship with Hinduism; Caste; Gārhasthya; Kashmiri Śaivism; Śaivism; Siddha**

RON GEAVES

Further reading

Bailly, Constantina Rhodes. 1987. *Shaiva Devotional Songs of Kashmir: A Translation and Study of Utpaladeva's Shivastotravali*. Albany, NY: SUNY.

UTSAVA

Introduction

Hindu practice is marked by a proliferation of festivals that enliven the cultural landscapes of India and, increasingly, of diasporic South Asian communities throughout the world. Globally and historically, festivals (L. festum, feast) provide occasions not only for feasting and socialising, but also for participation in various forms of entertainment. Festivals take place in both public and domestic spaces, offering venues for cultural performance, religious expression, social negotiation and economic exchange. Many festivals also function as spectacles, punctuating seasonal and calendrical routine. Spectacular aspects of festivals feature grand celebrations of the prevailing myths and unifying rituals of a given culture. Such myths and rites together underwrite dominant modes of production and consumption.

While many Hindus engage in the religious practices that underlie popular festivals, the festivals themselves are not reducible to any set of rituals or devotional observances. Festivals are experienced as holidays – some minor, some major. As such, without necessarily explicit reference to religion, festivals such as Dīvālī and Durgā Pūjā are widely viewed as occasions for homecomings, travel, shopping or relaxation from ordinary routines. Whether scheduled or spontaneous, Hindu festivals integrate the vast and diverse panoply of beliefs, images, values and observances that comprise Hindu practice.

Festical as pūjā and melā: an overview

'For every twelve months, celebrate thirteen festivals.' This proverbial refrain acknowledges the frequency and visibility of festivals throughout the Indian subcontinent. Most Hindu festivals feature multifaceted events extending through four or more days and nights. In a sequence of festival events, whereas most activities are observed with an air of casual compliance, the main days of culminating festivities are celebrated with more elaborate excitement.

At the centre of most Hindu festivals is the celebration of a pūjā (devotional service; literally, 'offerings'). However, pūjā rites are frequently overshadowed by a proliferation of less structured activities surrounding formal priestly observances. While providing for alternative modes of religious expressivity, informal events simultaneously serve many social and economic functions as well. In a typical festival scenario, rousing renditions by storytellers and puppeteers preserve traditional lore from the *Purāṇas* (myths of deities) while updating, localising and reinscribing the narratives. Singers, dancers and acrobats stage performances at multiple sites within a given location. For attending crowds, the attractions vie for attention. Lively processions of devotees ceremonially link sites of performance. These enacted networks serve to articulate – and, for believers, to achieve – periodic reintegrations of community.

A festival is a mood. Visiting pilgrims and tourists mingle with local participants and spectators. Festival organisers envision large crowds and invite vendors to attract trade in local crafts and produce. Whether the turnout exceeds expectations or proves more desultory, diverse activities heighten the festivities. Itinerant sādhus or 'holy men' come to town to perform stunts and provide consultations; hawkers mill about touting clay images, pinwheels and snacks.

Multisensory displays lend colour to the hullabaloo: drum cadences sound; bazaar posters hang from stalls where fragrant garlands are woven. Clouds of incense emanate through the festival grounds. Specialists adorn women's hands with mehndi (henna patterns); ice-candy men meander pushing their wagons of treats. Such entertainments amidst commercial commotion characterise the idealised milieu for what is known throughout South Asia as a melā (a fair, gathering; literally, 'mixing').

In the case of a titular pūjā, where the full festival is designated, for example, as a 'Śiva Pūjā' or 'Durgā Pūjā', there is no distinction to be made between 'pūjā' and 'festival'. Core pūjā events held in temples and homes are in metonymic relation to the festival as a whole; the pūjā-as-festival is more comprehensive than the pūjā-as-ritual. Just as the Christmas festival encompasses the figure of Santa Claus and trappings of commercialism along with the figure of Jesus and performance of the Mass, a grand pūjā encompasses economic activity along with religious ritual.

The Sanskrit term that translates the concept of festival most directly is utsava (celebration; observance), etymologically derived from ud- ('over'; 'upon') and su, sava ('pressing' of the soma sacrifice; 'oblation'; 'consecration'; 'setting in motion'). The term carries connotations of auspicious acquisition; correspondingly, of bestowal. It further denotes a public launching and, simultaneously, binding and loosing. Festivals reflect and bring to life each nuance suggested by these terms.

More broadly, in the lexicon of Hindu cultural performance, utsava ultimately combines salient features of melā (fair) and pūjā (devotional service). To the extent that a brahmanic pūjā reaffirms caste boundaries while a melā accommodates social mixing, the utsava or festival, in its hybridity, performs a calibrating function. Festivals mediate these important arenas of Hindu practice.

Locations of festival culture

Geographically, many festivals are linked to pilgrimage centres throughout the mythologised South Asian terrain. While the full range of festivals is pan-Indian, each region is apt to identify the annual festival of its favourite or titular deity as a high holiday to be celebrated with special fervour in an elaborate fashion. For this reason certain festivals, such as the Gaṇeśa Pūjā (Gaṇeśacaturthī) among Maharashtrians and the Durgā Pūjā among Bengalis, have become emblematic of regional identities.

Historically, although core pūjā rites often pre-date any festival context that may surround them, such historical precedence cannot be assumed. There are numerous instances of extant popular festivals, such as the spring festival Holī, to which pūjā ceremonies subsequently have been attached. The history of brahmanic appropriations is widely acknowledged. Genealogies of Hindu gods and goddesses are evident in iconographic representations. The transfer of cultic apparatus from one generation of deities to the next forms part of any pūjā legacy, and many layers of these histories survive in contemporary festivals.

Although linked to the myths of purāṇic and local deities, Hindu festivals are not sectarian. Participation in them is eclectic and inclusive. Vaiṣṇavas, Śaivites, Jains, Buddhists, Muslims, Sikhs and others mutually celebrate festivals of the diverse communities found in their localities. Festival greetings, food and gift exchanges, and gestures of hospitality routinely extend beyond communal boundaries.

Temples

Most Hindu festivals are centred in temple complexes. Core rites take place inside the temple, where brāhmaṇa priests officiate in presenting offerings to the presiding deity. Wide-ranging events and performances take place at various sites in and near a temple compound, including its main structures, open pavilion and bathing tank. Some pūjās are held near special trees in the vicinity and in outlying areas representing 'raw' nature in contrast to the 'cooked' culture of the temple. Rites at the temple are considered higher in importance or rank, and sometimes gendered as masculine, whereas rites outside are ancillary, presided over by non-brāhmaṇa officiants, and are often gendered as feminine. Processions intermittently move crowds away from the temple to publicise the festival while creating spiritual connections with, and energising, pathways to ancillary locations. Some processional rites portray wedding processions for gods and goddesses of neighbouring temples, replicating Hindu versions of organic cosmic unification through divine marriage (hieros gamos).

Homes

Festival events are held in domestic spaces as well as in temples and other public arenas. Observant Hindus often maintain small shrines in the kitchens of their homes. Daily, fortnightly and monthly pūjās are celebrated among the routines of domestic life. Life-cycle sacraments (saṃskāras, 'markings') such as the sacred thread ceremony (upanayana) form the primary domestic practices. The sixteen traditional sacraments are observed in homes with special ceremonies, dinners, visiting and gift exchange. Because they are private and invitational, saṃskāras are not usually viewed as festivals. Nevertheless the practices can overlap, and it is worth noting that saṃskāras and festivals alike represent a convergence of initiatory and sacrificial rites.

Workplaces

Festival events are sometimes observed in commercial zones as well. An example of such practices is seen in the annual Viśvakarman Pūjā, during which the tools of one's trade are revered as deities. (The god Viśvakarman – literally, 'All works' – serves as the Vulcan or Prometheus of the Hindu pantheon.) In this festival the tools do not represent deities mimetically, but are considered intrinsically to be the deities stripped of any anthropomorphic trappings of conventional clay images. During this festival, teachers make gestural offerings to pens and books, doctors to stethoscopes, musicians to sitars and tablas. Even in the busiest retail and industrial areas of Calcutta, festal garlands and painted coconuts adorn sources of livelihood that range from jewellers' scales to hydraulic lifts, and from carpenters' tools to cement mixers.

The festival calendar

Festivals serve to structure calendars of religious observance. Their frequent recurrence in the brahmanic ritual calendar reflects the generative theology of the *Purāṇas*. These mythological texts posit 330,000 metonymically linked gods and goddesses. Any of the numerous deities might be honoured in cycles of regional and/or pan-Hindu festivals.

Whether addressed to Kṛṣṇa or Śiva, Lakṣmī or Kālī, Gaṇeśa or Durgā, most Hindu festivals occur at astrologically determined moments of the lunisolar pūjā calendar. Most annual and seasonal festivals occur according to lunar cycles within the twelve-month solar calendar. Dates for observances are usually reckoned with reference to the pūrṇimā, or full moon. Festival schedules are published annually in a number of almanacs known as *Purohit Dārpāṇs* (priestly manuals) and *Pūjā Paddhatis* (liturgies).

Many festivals are designated for a certain day of the waxing moon of a given month, for example as the saptamī (seventh), aṣṭamī (eighth), ekādaśī (eleventh) or caturdaśī (fourteenth) day. The names of many festivals follow accordingly; for example, Durgāṣṭamī as 'Durgā's eighth' in the month of Āśvina (September–October) for the autumnal Durgā Pūjā. Widely circulated pamphlets contain astrological calculations prescribing the exact minutes appropriate for the pivotal rites of each pūjā.

Among festivals not linked to the religious calendar, occasional exigencies such as drought or famine give rise to large pūjās wherein the melā element is subdued and the tone less jubilant than in other circumstances. Numerous festivals are prompted by historical events. The lives and exploits of heroic figures are celebrated; major political upheavals are commemorated; and survival from disasters of the past is heralded. These events range from grassroots observances to nationally recognised holidays. For most such occasions, the programmatic surround of a generic pūjā festival provides a template.

Feasting

In accord with the etymology of festival as feast, elaborate dining constitutes not merely a nominal but a central aspect of festival life. Celebratory meals signify in two ways: through what one eats and with whom one eats. Communal dining entails the sharing of sustenance, of substance. Communal dining also represents the merging of experience and, accordingly, creates and renews communal identity. Festival feasts are scheduled in contrapuntal relation to cycles of fasting, and this alternation serves to intensify contrasting extremes of gustatory exuberance and renunciation. Given brahmanic preoccupations with caste purity and pollution, such feasting can become somewhat complicated, with rules of incorporation and exclusion, but such complexities need not be exaggerated as so often has occurred in neo-Orientalist accounts.

Traditionally, certain classes of food are believed to carry more pollution than others. Impurity generally correlates with porosity because surfaces with porous properties demonstrably retain odours and may be more absorbent than hard surfaces are. Therefore dry foods are favoured as snacks in the setting of a melā (fair), where less attention is paid to the caste (varṇa, class or caste category – literally, 'colour'; and jāti, caste group – literally, 'genus') of those who have prepared or handled the food. When cooked food is served in caste-observant situations, prevailing codes are often followed in terms of who may eat alongside whom. While concern with moral contagion can seem remarkable to those outside the culture, despite the fact that similar processes of stigmatisation are found elsewhere, this concern seems quite unremarkable to most privileged persons living within the culture. It is important, though, to note that change in such exclusionary customs is on the reform agenda not only for those disenfranchised by these practices, but for many contemporary progressive Hindus more generally.

A communion feast, whether in elaborate or token form, spreads the bounty of blessings – the grace of auspicious energy – that has been generated in the pūjā observances. Just as in Roman Catholicism the Eucharist is emblematic of shared partaking and of bonding of community among communicants, in pūjā settings what prevails is the rite of taking prasāda (a deity's leftovers; blessed residue). Although frequent and routinised, the distribution of prasāda becomes a highlight of festival events. After the image of a deity has been bathed, mixed substances used in the ritual are placed in the cupped hands of devotees. To ingest prasāda is to take on certain qualities, if not all potentials or properties, of the deity. It is also to share those qualities with others assembled and bonded in the festival community. Here, festival practice encompasses widely held notions of sacramental fragmentation and consumption that, for many religious traditions, reside at the heart of sacrifice.

Sacrifice and the study of festivals

A vast literature on Hindu festivals can be found in works by historians of religions, anthropologists and scholars from other disciplines in the humanities and social sciences, notably including cultural studies, folklore, popular aesthetics, visual culture, performing arts and political psychology. Approaches to widely varied festival practices often centre on transactional analyses that take into comprehensive account disparate elements of ideologies, cultural performances, social hierarchies, economic exchange and political processes.

A major example of transactional interpretation can be found in scholarship dedicated specifically to sacrifice. Sacrifice, encompassed within the institution of pūjā, is situated at the centre of most Hindu festival cycles. Brahmanic sacrifice (yajña) has been used as a paradigm for interpreting sacrifice in various religious traditions not only because it shares salient aspects with practices elsewhere, but also because Hindu traditions represent perhaps the fullest, most continuously preserved array of ceremonial detail available anywhere.

Functionalist approaches

From the Enlightenment through the twentieth century, festival rites were interpreted in light of various social and psychological functions thought to be served by selected practices. Viewing rites as instrumental 'keys of power', scholars isolated functional domains and then sought to locate practices cross-culturally within those domains. Such functions included jubilation (most festivals are indeed festive), invigoration, renewal, petition, increase, thanksgiving, propitiation (of angry 'primitive' gods), expiation, mortifications of the flesh (a Calvinist rendering of asceticism), purgation, catharsis, deflection of violence, ludic expression in play or sport, and the channelling of anxiety. Notwithstanding that some of these claims might well apply in certain instances, the use of these functions as ideal types proved reductive, and by the 1970s the method had been widely rejected.

Many studies of festivals failed to distinguish objectives from strategies, conflating ascribed goals with the ritual techniques that were used to achieve those goals. Here, throughout the halls of the academy, a teleological fallacy joined with functionalism in a festive dance of positivism. That gavotte begat serious misreadings of non-European practices. The legacy was inscribed in scholarly discourse, remaining largely unquestioned until the rise of postcolonial criticism.

Communication models

In another theoretical approach, the meanings, functions and structures of festivals have been widely studied in the light of communication theory. Sacrifice has been interpreted as a communication between devotee and deity, with the devotee as sender, the deity as receiver and the offering or scapegoat/victim as message. The message offering is necessarily marked and set aside from the economy – that is, consecrated. It is delivered through the ritual as medium, and the transaction is conducted by the priest as agent.

Sacrifice entails the offering of tangible goods (dāna) and/or intangible service (sevā) from devotee to deity. Following the communication model, offerings are usually mediated through the agency of an officiating priest. Śaivite and Śākta rites include both blood offerings and vegetarian offerings, whereas Vaiṣṇava rites involve only the latter. Blood offerings are presented only to female deities; male deities must receive them through the mediation of their female consorts. Goats are most commonly used in blood offerings. Ancillary ceremonies attend the marking and binding of the offering as it is consecrated and dedicated in the name of the devotee as host and sponsor.

Offerings of service (sevā) importantly include acts of austerity and renunciation. While gestural, such acts in their most extreme form dramatise putatively life-threatening gestures – fasting, observing vigils by foregoing sleep, rolling on thorns, etc. Sacrificial offerings are usefully seen not as acts of gift giving, which might transpire between equals, but as acts of 'giving up' as in 'giving up(ward)' in that, positionally, the devotee dramatises his or her subordination to the deity, and at the same time 'giving up' in terms of renunciation – renouncing ordinary comforts and entitlements while risking bodily harm in service to the deity.

A reciprocal element is implied in sacrificial offerings. In exchange for offerings tangible and intangible, devotees anticipate a communicative reply from the deity. The cycle of blessings in return, accordingly, may take the form of tangible goods in kind (ample crops in fields, full cupboards in homes and fulfilment through other signs of prosperity) or of intangible kinds of blessings, such as healing of disease or passing of school exams. The absence of blessings following a festival pūjā is usually rationalised as a failure of performance, either on the part of the priest's liturgical exactitude or on the part of the devotee's intention.

Structural aspects of festivals have claimed a place of privilege in recent scholarship. Threading through such work are interpretations drawn from linguistics, including social semiotics and related structuralist and poststructuralist modes of analysis. Current trends highlight postcolonial exigencies, such as cultural hybridity and alienation, that are found to be reflected in, and addressed by, contemporary festival practices.

Ritual formats

Within the purview of Hindu festivals, the formal agenda of a conventional pūjā incorporates five basic groups of ceremonies. First are consecrations, in which the objects and persons involved are set aside, dedicated and purified. (When rites are condensed for abbreviated festival formats, consecrations may be substituted metonymically for the entire proceedings.) Second are invocations, in which the gods are called to attend the ceremonies. Rites of invocation may be believed to have automatic efficacy to compel the deity's presence; alternatively, the invocations may be designed to persuade the deity to attend the festivities. More uncertainty attaches to persuasive rites, yielding a measure of anxiety, for which reason ancillary or secondary practices often proliferate.

The third pūjā phase consists of offerings, ritual prestations in which offerings are dedicated and proffered to the deity. Presentations then obligate or persuade the deity to respond to the fourth phase, namely entreaties soliciting divine gifts in return for offerings presented. Such entreaties often take the form of prayers, and may be individual or collective. The fifth and concluding phase of formal events is dismissals, which serve to relinquish the favour of the god's presence, thereby concluding an auspicious, risk-laden and consequential encounter with forces of power.

In the play of most festivals, episodes of singing and dancing recur intermittently. Lighter moments are intrinsic to the events and serve to aerate ceremonies that might otherwise prove dense and intense. The rhetoric of ritual encompasses many ludic elements. In Hindu traditions these elements have been fully theologised as līlā (play; divine sport). Kṛṣṇa is the deity most often seen to represent the ludic principle of līlā. During festival proceedings moments of līlā may coincide or alternate with the more sober strain of ceremonies.

Changing practices

Festival traditions seem always to have expanded and contracted with changing times. An example of a contemporary abbreviated form is seen in the Jaṭ-paṭ Pūjā, derived from jaldi ('quick'), which offers working housewives a chance to expedite offerings on the way home from work. A plate of pre-prepared offerings is available as she approaches a temple, and without waiting she is attended by a priest willing to recite abbreviated mantras with dispatch yet for maximum effect. Like Curry-in-a-Hurry fast food, the Jaṭ-paṭ Pūjā may be thought of as pūjā-on-the-run. This recent practice represents a consolidation of more elaborate past forms, now abridged in the interest of efficiency.

Perhaps a growing indifference to, or unwillingness to perform, festival labour corresponds to shifts from the rigours of ancient pilgrimage to the conveniences of modern tourism. Perhaps such indifference mirrors, in a cross-cultural instance, the transition from the figure of the warm and responsive boulevardier who tipped his hat to greet people in face-to-face encounters. His unworthy heir is the self-involved, postmodern flaneur or stroller of today who prefers to eye his own reflection in the shopping-mall window that separates him from the commodities he desires. The Jaṭ-paṭ Pūjā arguably waxes flaneuresque: there is no time to linger on the temple verandah and engage the blessed sight of Lakṣmī's image.

Festival economy

Hindu festivals celebrate cycles of expenditure and consumption. They also link the material realm of goods to the intangible realm of services. Terms popularly used for these categories of offering are dāna and sevā. Like religious 'services' in other religious traditions, ceremonies and rites accrue around central presentations of offerings. 'Service' consists in the act of devotion, but that devotional energy is often made manifest through a tangible offering. Tangible and intangible offerings converge; for example, food offerings entail service in their preparation. Offerings are diverse in kind: what is offered may be organic or inorganic, animal or vegetarian. It may be harvested from nature or crafted as emblematic artefact; it may be conventional or idiosyncratic in form.

For any material offering that is ceremonially presented during a festival, special significance is attached to the item. Offered objects are, as a consequence of their consecration in the pūjā cycle, removed from the market economy in order to circulate ceremonially in the gift economy of the festival.

Offered objects are believed to represent spiritual energy – specifically emotional and/or material 'expenditure' – of those sponsoring the offering. As noted regarding ritual formats, offerings are necessarily marked, often tagged with the names of those who paid for them. As such, the offered objects are surrogates and serve as substitutes for their sponsors.

An example of festival integration of goods and services is found in the Dharma Pūjā as it is popularly celebrated in rural south-western districts of West Bengal. In culminating rites, devotees swing from posts in dramatic acts suggesting life-threatening austerity. The devotees are fastened to hooks, or in sublimated ceremonies to harnesses, at the ends of ropes extending from the top of the posts. While 'hook swinging', devotees toss flower offerings into sacrificial fires below. The flowers represent a convergence of organic matter and devotional energy. In addition, since in this tradition the devotees are recruited from scheduled caste communities, whereas the sacred fire is attended by officiating brahmana priests, the offered flowers mediate the critical social distance created by caste practice. Similar displays of the presentation of offerings using modes of austerity occur in cognate festivals including the 'hook-swinging' ceremonies (widely chronicled during the Raj but now sublimated and rarely seen) and the Māriammā festival that still prevails in parts of South India.

Tangible offerings represent the desires of devotees. A festival economy, therefore, encompasses not only market and gift economies but also economies of desire. Transactional dynamics of conditionality and quid pro quo underlie events. Prayers, wishes and desires are at the heart of devotional religion generally, as reflected in the shared etymology of 'votive' offerings and 'vows'.

Many participate in Hindu festivals in order to fulfil vows (vrata) made to the presiding deity. The vows are promissory notes pledged to persuade the deity to grant a boon. Such vows are made formulaically: 'Oh Śiva, if my son passes his law exams I'll offer first fruits in your utsava (festival).' Whether fulfilled in advance, as insurance premiums, or after such wishes have been granted, as thanksgiving or closings, transactional aspects of the festival economy prove pivotal.

What is expended as offering is believed to be consumed by the deity. Brahmanic teachings hold that deities consume the scent of the offerings. Given the logical inevitability that the remains of offerings are in view following a pūjā, Hindu festival economy provides for the efficient practice of the taking of prasāda (blessed leavings; the god's leftovers). As noted above, in the distribution of prasāda devotees consume, as communion, a share of the auspicious remains. The ingestion of prasāda signifies 'respect pollution', a willingness to feel graced by what would normally pollute. Such a gesture dramatises devotees' ritual subordination to the deity.

Most importantly, with respect to the festival economy, whatever has been offered as expenditure during the festival pūjā is later, toward the end of the ceremonies, recycled in sacramental acts of consumption. Tangible offerings of things become the substance of prasāda; intangible offerings of service (seva) become intangible blessings (maṅgala). Dāna and sevā represent the devotees' communication to the deity mingling tangible and intangible forms, respectively; prasāda and maṅgala represent the deity's reciprocal reply to devotees in corresponding forms of matter and spirit conjoined. The alchemical economy of these transactions would seem to be markedly consistent with the concept of 'coded substance' found to underlie foundational brāhmaṇic concepts of caste (varṇa and jāti) and dharma (codes for conduct).

Festival rhetoric

Festivals entail performance and expressivity. Many interpretive tools applicable to theatre, identity, subjectivity and language can be used in interpreting festival events. Linguistically, the semantics of festival activities highlight any meanings that might be ascribed to what transpires, while festival syntax can be traced in the ordering and patterning of events. Much can be found in these areas of rhetoric and syntactics. Rhetoric, as persuasive speech, is at the very centre of the devotional expressions wherein offerings are extended to a deity for the fulfilment of desires.

Corresponding to each part of speech, festival rites express 'statements'. The nominative function is served by cult insignia or images (mūrti) representing deities; the genitive function by those devotees who hold, carry or manipulate the insignia. The dative function points to the interests of the sponsors who donate the offerings. The accusative or object is the gift, sacrificial victim or object offered. Ablative aspects of the festival are found in rites establishing agents, instruments and sites associated with events. If the festival is a sentence, its grand ritual processions are conjunctions, its abbreviated rites are contractions and drum cadences are punctuation marks. Worlds of interpretation can be opened in attributing prepositions to the proceedings. Grand public phases of a festival are performed in the indicative mood, whereas subtler or sometimes secret ancillary proceedings may instead reflect the more tentative qualities of the subjunctive. Finally, festival statements are expressive at times through hyperbole and at times through euphemism. The former are notably more prevalent in colourful Hindu practice.

Conclusion

Whereas multiple modes of analysis can be applied to Hindu festivals, it is important to acknowledge that the religious, aesthetic, social and economic momentum of festival life invites synthesis rather than analysis. Festivals spectacularly draw together disparate elements of Hindu belief and practice, integrating each element in dynamic recombinant configurations of renewal. The ceremonial heritages of popular festivals continue to be observed, while their ludic and less earnest significances are simultaneously celebrated.

See also: **Altars, domestic; Bhakti (as path); Blood sacrifice; Brāhmaṇa; Buddhism, relationship with Hinduism; Calendar; Caste; Dalits; Dāna; Dance; Deities; Diaspora; Dīvālī; Durgā; Durgā Pūjā; Fasting; Food; Gaṇeśa; Gaṇeśacatūrthi; Hinduism, history of scholarship; Holī; Iconography, modern; Image worship; Images and iconography; Jainism, Relationship with Hinduism; Jāti; Jyotiṣa; Kālī and Caṇḍī; Kṛṣṇa; Lakṣmī, Śrī; Līlā; Mandir; Mantra; Māriammā; Myth; Orientalism;**

Prasāda; Purāṇas; Purity and pollution, ritual; Pūjā; Purohita; Sādhu; Śāktism; Śaivism; Saṃskāras; Sevā; Sikhism, relationship with Hinduism; Śiva; Soma; Tapas; Tīrthayātrā (Pilgrimage); Upanayana; Vaiṣṇavism; Varṇa; Viśvakarman; Vrata; Yajña

SANDRA ROBINSON

Further reading

Abbott, J. 1932. *The Keys of Power: A Study of Indian Ritual and Belief.* New York: E.P. Dutton.

Freed, S.A. and R.S. Freed. 1998. *Hindu Festivals in a North Indian Village.* New York: American Museum of Natural History.

Hanchett, S. 1988. *Coloured Rice: Symbolic Structure in Hindu Family Festivals.* Delhi: Hindustan Publishing Corporation.

Hubert, H. and M. Mauss. 1964. *Sacrifice: Its Nature and Function.* Chicago, IL: University of Chicago Press.

Singh, S.B. 1989. *Fairs and Festivals in Rural India: A Geospatial Study of Belief Systems.* Varanasi: Tara Book Agency.

Sivananda. 1947. *Hindu Fasts and Festivals and Their Philosophy.* Rishikesh: Sivananda Publication League.

Underhill, M.M. 1921. *The Hindu Religious Year.* Calcutta: Oxford University Press.

Welbon, G.R. and G.E. Yocum (eds). 1982. *Religious Festivals in South India and Sri Lanka.* New Delhi: Manohar.

UTTARA MĪMĀṂSĀ

See: **Vedānta**

V

VĀCASPATI MIŚRA

Vācaspati Miśra (ninth century CE) was an important post-Śaṅkara philosopher. Vācaspati's work on Advaita Vedānta resulted in the foundation of the Bhāmatī school. He lived in Mithila (Bihar) but virtually nothing is known about his life.

Vācaspati was the author of a commentary on Śaṅkara's *Brahmasūtra Bhāsya* (Commentary on the *Brahmasūtras*), the *Bhāmatī* ('The Lustrous'). A vital basis for Vācaspati's thought was the *Brahma Siddhi* (Establishment of Brahman) of Mandana Miśra (a contemporary of Śaṅkara), an independent work of Advaita Vedānta. Renowned for his scholarship and objectivity, Vācaspati also wrote authoritative works on Nyāya and other orthodox schools.

Post-Śaṅkara Advaitins became concerned with problems about the relations between Brahman, māyā (illusion; God's creative power) and avidyā (ignorance or nescience). For Vācaspati, the only reality is the non-dual Brahman; the world of multiplicity (the result of ignorance) is appearance only. He explains how the locus of avidyā is the jīva (the finite, empirical individual) and the object of avidyā is Brahman. Ignorance is destroyed by knowledge (immediate intuition of Brahman).

See also: **Advaita; Brahman; Brahmasūtras; Jīva; Māyā; Nyāya; Śaṅkara; Vedānta**

MARTIN OVENS

Further reading

Hasurkar, S.S. 1958. *Vācaspati Miśra and Advaita Vedānta*. Darbhanga: Mithila Institute.

Ranganath, S. 1999. *Contribution of Vācaspati Miśra to Indian Philosophy*. Delhi: Pratibha Prakashan.

VĀHANAS

Vāhana is a term meaning 'vehicle' which refers to the attribution of an animal as a steed or mode of transportation to most of the major gods. Common vāhanas are Garuḍa, the half-eagle, half-human king of the birds associated with Viṣṇu; Nandi, the bull of Śiva; the tiger usually depicted with Durgā; the peacock of Skanda or

Murukan̲; the rat who is ridden by Gaṇeśa; the elephant of Indra; the owl of Śrī-Lakṣmī; and the swan that belongs to Brahmā.

The origin of vāhanas is obscure but they do not appear until the Purāṇic period, when they figure prominently in the myths associated with each god but they do not accompany the older Vedic gods. Walker suggests that they were introduced as part of the Vrātya rituals, originating from the obscure non-Vedic peoples who are variously described as precursors of yogis and non-Aryan travellers from outside India. They were associated with the gavāmayana sacrifice in which a cart drawn by a horse functioned as the place of worship in which the sacrifice was performed. The idea of a mobile temple or the association with a nomadic people is linked to the adoption of carriers for the gods, and in the *Aitareya Brāhmaṇa* the term simply refers to a cart or a beast of burden. The Stutleys support the idea of their origin being from outside India and note that most Mesopotamian gods are also depicted with vāhanas earlier than 1500 BCE. They suggest that they were transported to India by traders.

In post-Vedic mythology the vāhana becomes associated with the energy and character of the god and forms part of the mythology and cosmological representation. Metaphysical explanations abound; for example, the paradox of Gaṇeśa, an elephant, riding upon a rat is explained as an analogy of macrocosm and microcosm, the infinite present within the finite. Such symbolic meanings are associated with all the creatures that function as vāhanas, but it should also be kept in mind that the attribution of distinctive animals to the multiplicity of deities was an efficient method of distinguishing them from each other.

See also: **Brahmā; Brāhmaṇas; Deities; Durgā; Gaṇeśa; Garuḍa; Indra; Lakṣmī, Śrī; Murukan̲; Nandi; Purāṇas; Sacred animals; Śiva; Skanda; Vedic pantheon; Viṣṇu; Yogi**

RON GEAVES

Further reading

Stutley, Margaret and James Stutley (eds). 1977. *A Dictionary of Hinduism: Its Mythology, Folklore and Development 1500 BC–AD 1500*. London: Routledge and Kegan Paul.

Walker, Benjamin. 1968. *Hindu World*, vol. 2. London: George Allen & Unwin.

VAIKHĀNASAS

The Vaikhānasa texts have had a great influence on Vaiṣṇavism but their influence on currently surviving Vaiṣṇava schools is debatable. Even so, as a tradition it seems to have quite prominent in medieval times and perhaps until the late seventeenth century. The influence of the Vaikhānasa school might have been felt in Bengal. One scholarly view is that some of the Viṣṇu images that were discovered in the Bengal region (e.g. abhicārika-sthānika type) may have been based on the Vaikhānasa tradition.

See also: **Vaiṣṇavism; Viṣṇu**

PRATAP KUMAR

Further reading

Flood, Gavin. 1996. *An Introduction to Hinduism*. Cambridge: Cambridge University Press.

VAIRĀGYA

Occurring mostly in texts dealing with yoga and asceticism, this word conveys both an attitude and a state of mind. Derived from vi/rāga, a word implying 'dispassion' and 'indifference to emotion', it may best be translated as 'disenchantment' towards the psycho-physical world, accepting that re-enchantment is never a possibility. Vairāgya may be regarded as one of the motivations for leaving the social world to adopt an ascetic lifestyle. On any of the paths to enlightenment, the assiduous cultivation of vairāgya is essential if advancement is to be made. Equally, it arises automatically as the end result of following such paths. The word has been made famous as the name of the fourth book of Patañjali's foundational *Yogasūtras* and its flavour is brilliantly developed in the *Śatakatrayam* of the much-esteemed poet Bhartṛhari.

See also: **Bhartṛhari; Patañjali; Tapas; Yoga; Yogasūtras**

GREG BAILEY

Further reading

Whicher, Ian. 1998. *Integrity of the Yoga Darśāna. A Reconsideration of Classical Yoga.* Albany, NY: State University of New York Press.

VAIŚĀKHI

A major North Indian Hindu harvest festival celebrated in mid-April. In the Punjab it marks the new year, beginning on 13 April. It is fixed based on the solar calendar and falls in the month of Salgrand. Traditionally Hindus would offer grain and barley to brāhmaṇa priests from the harvest, but the festival took on a unique character for Sikhs. Initially the third Guru, Amar Das, who was spiritual leader of the Sikhs from 1552 to 1574, began to use Vaiśākhi as a time for his followers to gather in his company and worship God. It has been suggested that this was undertaken to wean them away from Hinduism but it is also likely that it was for convenience, as people would be already absent from their daily activities. However, Vaiśākhi was to take on even greater significance for Sikhs when Guru Gobind Singh, the last of the human Gurus, used the festival in 1699 for the creation of the Khalsa.

See also: **Brāhmaṇa; Calendar; Sikhism, relationship with Hinduism**

RON GEAVES

Further reading

Jackson, R. 1986. 'Hindu Festivals'. In *Festivals in World Religions*, Alan Brown, ed., on behalf of SHAP Working Party. London: Longman, 104–39.

VAIŚEṢIKA

One of the six systems of Hindu philosophy (Ṣaḍdarśana), the origins of the Vaiśeṣika tradition are obscure, pre-dating the Christian era. The *Vaiśeṣikasūtras* (date unknown) are attributed to the legendary founder of the system, Kaṇāda. Candramati's *Daśapadārtha-śāstra* (*c.*500 CE), preserved in Chinese and translated into English by H. Ui, is another important early text. Praśastapāda's *Bhāṣya* (Commentary) or *Padārthadharmasamgraha* (*c.*575 CE), a standard work of the school, represents a significant development.

Vaiśeṣika teaches pluralism, diversity and difference. The word 'vaiśeṣika' derives from 'viśeṣa', signifying particularity, uniqueness, distinction or distinguishing feature. The system is preoccupied with problems of ontology and metaphysics: how do we describe the many different sorts of things that we identify in the universe? It reduces the world to six (and later seven) padārthas or categories. All existents or objects of our knowledge come under padārtha. Vaiśeṣika classifies, lists or catalogues all knowable objects.

The categories

The categories are substance (dravya), quality or attribute (guṇa), action (karma), generality (sāmānya), particularity (viśeṣa), inherence or combination (samavāya) and non-being or abhāva (added later).

Substance signifies absoluteness and independence. Both material and spiritual substances are admitted. They include the ultimate elements or bhūtas: earth (pṛthivī), water (āpas), fire (tejas), air (vāyu) and ether (ākāśa). Time (kāla), space (dik), ātman (soul, self or spirit) and mind or internal organ (manas) are also regarded as substances.

Vaiśeṣika teaches atomism: the material substances are atomic in nature. An atom (paramāṇu) is without parts, eternal, indivisible, imperceptible, unique; it is the smallest particle of matter. Physical things are produced or created by atoms combining in different proportions. Thus destruction is merely the decomposition or dissolution of these combinations.

Each element has a peculiar quality which distinguishes it from the others. The quality of earth is smell; the peculiar qualities of water, fire, air and ether are taste, colour, touch and sound, respectively. The elements are the substrata of these qualities, but substances are distinct from the qualities they possess. Vaiśeṣika teaches four kinds of atom: earth, water, fire and air. Ether is infinite and eternal, an insensible, inactive medium: it is not atomic.

Space and time are imperceptible, indivisible substances, without parts, infinite and eternal (nitya): each is one great whole (eka). Souls (as well as atoms and minds) are many or infinite in number. Each soul is a spiritual substance, independent, eternal and all pervading. Mind is atomic but does not combine or produce compound things. Each soul has a mind, an eternal, imperceptible instrument or organ of knowledge.

In the *Vaiśeṣikasūtras*, we find that quality (the second category) is that which inheres in a substance – it does not possess action or quality, it does not produce any composite object. Kaṇāda lists the qualities as colour, taste, smell, touch, numbers, measures, separateness, conjunction and disjunction, priority and posteriority, understanding, pleasure and pain, desire and aversion, and volition. Qualities do not exist apart from substances. There are five kinds of activity (the third category): throwing up or down, contraction, expansion and motion. Action inheres in, and cannot exist apart from, substance. However, unlike quality (a permanent feature of a substance), actions are transient.

The fourth category, sāmānya, is one, eternal and resides in many. The common characteristic, the universal (e.g. cowness), and the individual, the particular (e.g. cow), are objective, separate realities. The one, eternal cowness inheres in many (transient) cows.

By noting the differences in their parts, we distinguish one composite thing from another. But one air-atom, for example, is similar to another air-atom. Vaiśeṣika proposes the fifth category, viśeṣa (peculiarity, particularity): each ultimate substance has a uniqueness or peculiarity of its own. Viśeṣas are many and eternal. According to Praśastapāda, samavāya (inherence), the sixth category, is the relationship among things that are inseparable, as in the relation of the container and the contained. Samavāya is eternal, inseparable connection or relationship. The relation between quality and substance is an example of samavāya. The viśeṣa inheres in its (eternal) substance; the action inheres in its substance and so on.

Vaiśeṣika teaches four kinds of abhāva (non-existence), the seventh category. A book, for example, does not exist before it is produced (prāgabhāva); it does not exist after it is destroyed (pradhvaṃsābhāva); it does not exist as a table (anyonyābhāva); and a gaseous book is absolutely non-existent (atyantābhāva).

God and liberation

Vaiśeṣika accepts the authority of the Veda and the law of karma. Kaṇāda does not consider God but later thinkers in the Vaiśeṣika and closely related Nyāya schools developed theism. Udayana, for example, attempted proofs of God's existence. An ordered universe, it was thought, could not be due to the eternal atoms alone, so God (eternal, perfect, omniscient) becomes the efficient cause of the universe (and atoms the material cause). God co-exists with the eternal atoms and souls (he does not create them): he is the 'prime mover', providing the original push or motion to the atoms.

The importance in India of notions of rebirth and release from painful saṃsāra (the wheel of birth and death) led Vaiśeṣika to add a doctrine of liberation to a system originally inspired by naturalism (i.e. protoscientific enquiry, the desire to provide an account of the physical world). By using the concept of adṛṣṭa (hidden or unseen potency, occult force), Vaiśeṣika explained how past actions lead to good or bad effects or results in future births. A person's deeds lead to merits (dharma) and demerits (adharma) which make up the individual's adṛṣṭa – and unintelligent adṛṣṭa requires God to supply motion to the atoms. Liberation is conceived as the cessation of pain, achieved when actions stop. A liberated soul retains its uniqueness or peculiar individuality – as pure substance, it is disconnected from mind and body, qualityless.

Importance and influence

Although ancient (and criticised by influential rival schools such as Vedānta), Vaiśeṣika, in association with the Nyāya or Logic school, survived as a vital, creative tradition for many centuries. In the modern era, Vaiśeṣika has attracted philosophers and scholars such as W. Halbfass and B. K. Matilal.

See also: **Ātman; Bhūtas (Elements); Halbfass, Wilhelm; Guṇas; Kaṇāda; Karma (Law of Action); Manas; Nyāya; Padārthadharmasaṃgraha; Padārthas; Ṣaḍdarśana; Saṃsāra; Udayana; Vaiśeṣikasūtras; Veda; Vedānta**

MARTIN OVENS

Further reading

Gough, A.E. (ed. and trans.). 1873. *The Vaiśeṣika Sūtras of Kaṇāda*. Benares: E.J. Lazarus & Co.

Halbfass, W. 1992. *On Being and on What There Is: Classical Vaiśeṣika and the History of Indian Ontology*. Albany, NY: SUNY Press.

VAIŚEṢIKASŪTRAS

The *Vaiśeṣikasūtras* (Aphorisms on Vaiśeṣika) form the basic text of the Vaiśeṣika school of Hindu philosophy. This text is attributed to Kaṇāda, the legendary founder of the system.

The date of the *Vaiśeṣikasūtras*, as well as their original arrangement and content, is uncertain. The text has been placed in the first few centuries CE. Scholars relied upon the text of Śaṅkara Miśra's fifteenth-century commentary, the *Vaiśeṣikasūtra Upaskāra* (The Ornament of the *Vaiśeṣikasūtras*), until the publication in 1961 of Candrānanda's commentary (possibly ninth century). Candrānanda's work is regarded as containing a more genuine version of the *Vaiśeṣikasūtras*.

The *Vaiśeṣikasūtras* begin by explaining 'dharma': it is defined as that which confers the supreme or ultimate good and exaltation. Knowledge (jñāna) of reality (tattva) through similarity and difference among the categories (padārtha) results in the supreme good. The *Vaiśeṣikasūtras* teach epistemological doctrines and a philosophy of nature.

See also: **Jñāna; Kaṇāda; Padārthas; Vaiśeṣika**

MARTIN OVENS

Further reading

Nozawa, M. (trans.). 1992. 'The Vaiśeṣikasūtra with Candrānanda's Commentary (1)'.

Numazu College of Technology Research Annual 27: 97–116.

VAIṢṆAVA

See: **Vaiṣṇavism**

VAIṢṆAVISM

Vaiṣṇava bhakti had its biggest impetus in the southern part of India. However, its beginnings, like those of the other schools, are traced to the oldest known text, the *Ṛgveda*. However, in the Āgama tradition and in the oral tradition Viṣṇu himself taught this bhakti to Śrī-Lakṣmī, who in turn taught it to Viśvaksena, the angel/messenger of the gods. Viṣṇu figures as one of the deities in the *Ṛgveda* and other Vedic texts. It is in the myths of the *Brāhmaṇa* (ritual) texts that Viṣṇu begins to occupy a considerable place. Scholars are divided in their opinion as to whether Viṣṇu was originally a non-Āryan god or exclusively a Vedic god. To what extent the non-Āryan and the Vedic elements have been assimilated is also a moot point. However, traditional Vaiṣṇava scholars believe that the *Ṛgveda* from the beginning represented a monotheistic religion and Viṣṇu is indeed the Supreme Deity mentioned in the same ancient text. Other scholars have suggested that Vaiṣṇavism was not based on the 'mythical fancy of the poets' but rather on the 'personal history of Vāsudeva Kṛṣṇa'. Emphasising the need to utilise the Buddhist and Jaina sources for a fuller understanding of the historical development of Vaiṣṇavism, scholars generally point out that Bhāgavatism in its initial development arose as a natural reaction to Brahmanism. According to the scholarly view, what eventually became known as Vaiṣṇavism was in fact the result of a coalescence of three important doctrines within Brahmanical religion. These are identified as: (1) Vyūha (emanation) theory, (2) the theory of Avatāra and (3) the Puruṣa-Prakṛti theory. It is this last theory that provided the place for the cult of Śrī.

Viṣṇu is associated with various aspects – he is represented as the god of fertility and a beneficent god. He is associated with the Sun, Indra, Varuṇa and other Vedic gods. One of the most important aspects that contributed to his pre-eminence among the gods is the myth about his three strides. He is described as encompassing the whole universe with his three steps. In the *Śatapatha Brāhmaṇa* (1.9.3.8) these steps acquire a special place as part of the Vedic ritual. One ascends the three worlds by taking the three Viṣṇu-steps in the context of the Vedic ritual. Viṣṇu is also associated with mountains. He is identified with the Vedic sacrifice, the Soma juice and the sacrificial post. Viṣṇu's navel has significant symbolism in that Brahmā, the creator, emerges from the lotus which springs from the navel of Viṣṇu. Viṣṇu's sleep is also significant – at the end of every age of the world Viṣṇu goes to sleep, and when he awakes the creative process begins. The thumb of Viṣṇu also has special significance both in mythology and ritual. Viṣṇu is described as going to the battlefield as big as a thumb to defeat the demons. In the context of the śrāddha ceremony performed for the deceased, the priest's thumb is pushed into the food offered to the deity while repeating the Viṣṇu mantra which recalls his three strides. Viṣṇu is also described as the door-keeper of the gods, which indicates the beginning of his prominence. He is thus seen as the protector of the gods. The black stone known as śālagrāma stone is particularly significant in relation to Viṣṇu. It is often represented in nine colours signifying the nine incarnations of Viṣṇu. In many classical texts (e.g. *Mahābhārata*) Viṣṇu's emblems and attributes are described elaborately. He is associated with his śudarśana wheel, the breast jewel (Kaustubha), conch-shell (śaṇka) and his vehicle known as Garuḍa. He is also described with innumerable names and epithets. In later Vaiṣṇava tradition all of these various aspects of Viṣṇu acquire special theological significance.

Classical sources for Vaiṣṇavism

Without having to take a theological point of view on whether or not Viṣṇu was already depicted as the supreme deity in these classical sources, it is useful to take a cursory look at these sources. They are generally made use of by both those who see Viṣṇu gradually evolving as the supreme deity as well as those who see him being already present in those materials as the supreme deity. These sources are the following:

- Vedic materials: the *Ṛgveda Saṃhitā* (special reference to 'Puruṣa-Sūkta' and 'Śrī-Sūkta'), *Taittirīya Saṃhitā*, *Śatapatha Brāhmaṇa*, *Taittirīya Āraṇyaka*.
- Upaniṣadic materials: *Iśa*, *Kena*, *Praśna*, *Muṇḍaka*, *Taittirīya*, *Bṛhadāraṇyaka*, *Chāndogya*, *Mahānārāyaṇāya* texts are more prominently used among other minor ones.
- Itihāsa materials: the entire *Rāmāyaṇa* text and some sections of the *Mahābhārata* ('Śāntiparva'/'Nārāyāṇīya' section and 'Mokṣadharma', 'Bhīṣmaparva/*Bhagavadgītā*' section, 'Anuśāsanaparva'/'Viṣṇusahasranāma' section, 'Āśvamedhikaparva/Anugītā' section).
- Vaiṣṇava *Purāṇas*: *Viṣṇu-*, *Nārada-*, *Viṣṇudharmottara-*, *Padma-*, *Varāha-*, *Garuḍa-* and *Bhāgavata Purāṇa.*
- Āgama materials:
  - *Vaikhānasa Saṃhitās*: *Ānanda-*, *Marīci-*, *Atri-*, *Kaśyapa-* and *Bhṛgu Saṃhitā.*
  - *Pāñcarātra Saṃhitās*: *Sāttvata-*, *Pauṣkara-*, *Jayśkhya-*, *Pārameśvara-*, *Pādma-*, *Īśvara-*, *Parama-*, *Ahirbudhnya-*, *Viśvaksena-*, *Nāradīya Saṃhitā* and *Lakṣmī Tantra.*

General philosophy

Viṣṇu as the ultimate reality/being

Vaiṣṇavism, like Śaivism and Śākta religion, has appropriated for its philosophical basis the Vedānta materials, such as the *Brahmasūtras* of Bādarāyaṇa, and for its devotional basis the *Bhagavadgītā*. Vaiṣṇava teachers of all branches have extensively commented on these two most important texts. Together with other upaniṣadic materials they provided the understanding of the nature of the ultimate reality which for the Vaiṣṇava teachers is none other than the Viṣṇu-Nārāyaṇa. Thus the idea of Brahman which appears in the *Brahmasūtras* and the upaniṣadic texts as an abstract notion is personified in the form of Viṣṇu. The abstract characteristics that are associated with the nature of Brahman, such as bṛhatva and brahmaṇatva (greatness), svarūpa, nirviśeṣa, nirguṇa and saguṇa natures, are attributed to Viṣṇu as Puruṣottama (Supreme Person) and the one who is the embodiment of infinite auspicious qualities and free from all imperfections.

Once Viṣṇu is associated with all the nature of Brahman, the abstract notions of Brahman are then interpreted in the light of what is known as Tattvatraya: Īśvara (Lord/God), cit (soul) and acit (matter). In integrating this three-natured reality of Viṣṇu, Sāṃkhya philosophy has provided the basis. In other words, the twenty-four tattvas that are described in the Sāṃkhya philosophy are recast in the context of Vaiṣṇava philosophy, especially in describing the relationship between the soul and matter (puruṣa and prakṛti). Thus the abstract notion of Brahman is understood as the personal God Viṣṇu, whom the devotees worship. The meaning of terms such as Sat, Brahman, Ātman are equated with the term Nārāyaṇa.

Being the ultimate reality, Viṣṇu is therefore described as the source of the universe, both the jīva (living) and prakṛti (matter). Viṣṇu is also the cause of the universe as there is no other being higher than him. He is the inner controller of all beings (antarātma), and is all pervasive (antaryāmin). Vaiṣṇava theologians derive the etymological meaning of Nārāyaṇa as follows: Nārā (universe of sentient and non-sentient beings) and Āyana (the ground of all being). They even suggest that the term Viṣṇu also connotes the same meaning. The term Viṣṇu denotes all-pervasiveness, the one who enters into all beings and non-beings, one who possesses all the auspicious attributes, such as knowledge, power and so on, and the one who is desired by all souls. Similarly Viṣṇu's other name, Vāsudeva, also denotes the one who abides everywhere. As such, the Vaiṣṇava theology brings together all three names – Viṣṇu, Nārāyaṇa and Vāsudeva – and identifies them with Brahman as the ultimate reality.

The nature of Viṣṇu

The fundamental qualities of Brahman viz. satyam (reality), jñānam (knowledge) and anantam (infinity), are attributed to Viṣṇu. Vaiṣṇava theology affirms simultaneously the two natures of Viṣṇu – his paratva (transcendence) and sulabhatva (immanence). As the supreme deity he is above all other gods and yet as personal God he is accessible to his devotees. The idea of avatāra is a distinctive feature of Vaiṣṇava theology. On the one hand it emphasises the transcendence of Viṣṇu and at the same time it emphasises his immanent nature in that he descends to the world of humans in his various manifestations in order to protect the righteous and punish the wicked. The *Bhagavadgītā* is the most valuable source material for the affirmation of the theory of avatāra and the doctrine of the divine incarnation.

As the supreme deity, Viṣṇu has three primary functions – creation, sustenance and destruction. In later Hindu theology, these three functions are divided between Brahmā as the creator, Viṣṇu as the preserver and Śiva as the destroyer. But in Vaiṣṇavism Viṣṇu himself represents all three primary functions. In other words, Viṣṇu creates Brahmā and entrusts to him the creation of the universe, he creates Rudra/Śiva and entrusts to him the destruction of the universe while he himself looks after the preservation of the universe.

Viṣṇu and his divine consort (Śrī-Lakṣmī)

One of the titles for Viṣṇu most often used by Vaiṣṇava theologians is the Lord of Śrī (śriyaṣ-pati). The question of the divine consort and her relationship to Viṣṇu is at the same time one of the most thorny issues that contributed to the split in the South Indian Vaiṣṇava tradition. While Vaiṣṇava tradition generally uses the name Lakṣmī to refer to the consort of Viṣṇu, the term Śrī is particularly significant in South Indian Vaiṣṇavism (also known as the Śrī Vaiṣṇava tradition). The name Śrī, according to Vaiṣṇava theologians, signifies various meanings depending on the root verb from which it is derived: it signifies 'the one who causes the Lord to listen' (ḍrāvayati) and hence the notion of accessibility associated with it; 'one who is sought by devotees' (śrīyate); 'one who approaches the Lord on behalf of the devotees' (śrāyate) and hence the idea of mediator (puruṣakāra); 'one who removes the sins of the devotees' (śṛṇāti); and 'one who promotes good' (śrīṇāti). The name Lakṣmī has various theological imports as well. The goddess is known as Lakṣmī because Viṣṇu acquired her (lābhāt); signifies the symbol of Viṣṇu (lakṣaṇāt); bestows material prosperity (lapsyanāt); is seated on the chest of Viṣṇu (lanchanāt); is full of lustre (laṣate); has a permanent association with Viṣṇu (lagyate); and is very modest (lajjate).

Different branches of Vaiṣṇavism accord her different ontological status in relation to Viṣṇu. While most branches treat her as a consort of Viṣṇu and hence secondary to him, within the Śrī Vaiṣṇava tradition, the northern school of Vedānta Deśika treats her as equal to Viṣṇu. The underlying question of the ontological status of the Goddess is the issue of whether her role in the scheme of the salvation of the devotee is on a par with that of Viṣṇu or a subordinate role as a mediator.

Viṣṇu and his divine attributes

One of the most important aspects of Vaiṣṇavism, especially in the South, is the idea that Viṣṇu is characterised by various essential, or primary, and non-essential, or secondary, attributes. In fact, central to the debate about whether Viṣṇu's consort Śrī-Lakṣmī is on a par with him or occupies a secondary role in the scheme of salvation is the issue of divine attributes. Of the two schools within Śrī Vaiṣṇavism, the southern school tended to deny Śrī-Lakṣmī the essential attributes that characterise Viṣṇu, whereas the northern school tended to favour the position that the goddess indeed shares in his essential qualities and hence has a pivotal role in the scheme of salvation.

These divine attributes of Viṣṇu are identified as the essential attributes of Viṣṇu. Within the upaniṣadic texts Brahman is described with five qualities – reality (satya), knowledge (jñāna), infinity (ananta), bliss (ānanda) and purity (amala). Vaiṣṇava theology attributes these five qualities to Viṣṇu and adds one more, viz. 'being the beloved of the goddess, Śrī' (śriyahpatitva). In addition to these, the Pāñcarātra ritual texts and the *Viṣṇu Purāṇa* ascribe six essential qualities to Viṣṇu. He is characterised by knowledge (jñāna), power (śakti), strength (bala), lordship (aiśvarya), energy (vīrya) and splendour (tejas).

The secondary attributes are, according to some Vaiṣṇava theologians, included in the six. However, some theologians distinguish them from the primary ones for the purposes of religious practice, within which they have some special significance. According to Rāmānuja, there are nineteen of these qualities: (1) intimate communion with devotees (sauśīlya); (2) tender affection (vātsalya); (3) soft-heartedness (mārdava); (4) straightforwardness (ārjava); (5) friendly disposition (sauhārda); (6) equal treatment (sāmya); (7) compassion (kāruṇya); (8) charm (mādurya); (9) incomprehensibility (gāmbīrya); (10) generosity (audārya); (11) skilfulness (cāturya); (12) steadfastness (sthairya); (13) courage (dhairya); (14) fortitude (śaurya); (15) valour (parākrama); (16) always desired (satyakāma); (17) firm resolve (satyasaṃkalpa); (18) fulfilment of obligation (kṛtitva); and (19) gratitude (kṛtajñatā). This last quality of Viṣṇu is an interesting one in that it provides an insight into the theological understanding of Viṣṇu. Unlike in many monotheistic understandings of God, the Vaiṣṇava theology understands God in the sense that he is indeed grateful to his devotees for the little things they do for him, such as pūjā, offering of flowers and so on. This is precisely why he is also understood as one who feels relieved after fulfilling his obligation (kṛtitva) to the devotees. In addition to these qualities, God in Vaiṣṇava theology takes a concrete shape and form and as such his divine body, which is described with a thousand heads and so on, has special meaning within the theology and religious practice of Vaiṣṇavism.

Viṣṇu and his incarnations

In Vaiṣṇavism God is understood as having several incarnations, a doctrine enunciated in the *Bhagavadgītā*. Vaiṣṇava theologians trace the idea to the Vedic texts, especially the 'Puruṣa Sūkta' in the *Ṛgveda*. In understanding the notion of incarnation, it is important to note that the Hindu notion does not simply suggest that God incarnates in some historical form – human or animal – but rather in a more complex one. The Vaiṣṇava notion makes a hierarchical distinction between five different types of incarnation. The first one is called the transcendental form (Para). Even though in his transcendental form God is not visible to the human eye, it is the manifested form of the unmanifest Brahman.

The second is the manifestation of Viṣṇu in the four forms (Vyūhas) that he takes in his various creative functions such as creation, sustenance and dissolution. This doctrine owes its origins to the Āgama ritual tradition, which is integral to the development of Vaiṣṇava theology. The doctrine suggests that there are six fundamental qualities that characterise the divine and these take different formations in the various forms (Vyūhas). The first is Vāsudeva, who appears with all his six qualities, viz. knowledge (jñāna), power (śakti), strength (bala), lordship (aiśvarya), energy (vīrya) and splendour (tejas), in equal measure. In this form he is considered equal to the transcendental form of Viṣṇu. The next one is Saṃkarṣaṇa, in whom knowledge and strength dominate. The third is Pradyumna, in whom the qualities of lordship and energy predominate. The fourth is Aniruddha, in whom power and splendour predominate. The entire creative process is undertaken by Viṣṇu in these various forms.

The third incarnation (Vibhavas) refers to the various physical forms that Viṣṇu takes – either as a human being or other forms of living beings. Both the epic texts (the *Rāmāyaṇa* and the *Mahābhārata*) and the various mythological texts (*Purāṇas*) deal with these in more detail. Each *Purāṇa* gives different descriptions of these incarnations. There are at least thirty-nine incarnations listed in a ritual text called *Ahirbhudhnya Saṃhitā*. The more commonly mentioned incarnations are numbered at ten and the most popular of these are the two, Rāmā and Kṛṣṇa, who are mentioned in the two epic texts (the *Rāmāyaṇa* and the *Mahābhārata*). The Kalkin incarnation is supposed to be the last one that would occur at the end of the Kali age. These manifestations are classified into two categories – primary (Sākṣāt) and secondary (Āveṣa). The primary ones are direct incarnations of Viṣṇu and the secondary ones have to do with the individuals into whom the divine power enters.

The fourth incarnation is called the image (arcā) avatāra. These are made in various metals or stone and consecrated according to the rites prescribed in the Āgama ritual texts. In temples there are two types of these images – those that are permanently fixed in one place, i.e. in the innermost chamber of the temple (garbhagṛha) and those that are placed outside the inner chamber for the purposes of carrying them in the processions and are hence known as movable images. The justification for the worship of the divine in his iconic form is found in the Āgama ritual texts and the purāṇic texts. According to the Vaiṣṇava belief, it is one of four ways to worship the divine: recitation of mantras (japa), offering of oblations (huta), offering worship to an image (arcana) and meditation (dhyāna). The Vaiṣṇava theologians place enormous emphasis on image worship because the transcendental form of the divine is unapproachable.

The fifth manifestation is called the indwelling spirit (Antaryāmin). According to Vaiṣṇava belief, even though Viṣṇu is transcendent he dwells in human beings in his immanent form (spirit). The divine dwells in both living and non-living beings. The idea of the divine as the indwelling spirit is supported in many of the upaniṣadic texts. The idea of the Supreme Self (Paramātma) and the individual self (Jīvātma) is at the basis of the idea of God as the indwelling spirit.

Viṣṇu and his relationship to the Jīva (soul)

As discussed earlier, Viṣṇu, according to the Vaiṣṇava theologians, is the Supreme Being, i.e. Brahman itself. The Jīva is the individual who is part of the divine being. The relationship between the Supreme Being and the Jīva depends on the philosophical position that one takes. Within Vaiṣṇava theology there can be different philosophical positions and three are most popularly known: the qualified non-dualist (Viśiṣṭādvaita) position of Rāmānuja, the dualist position of Madhva and the pure non-dualism of Vallabha. Nimbārka maintained both dualism and non-dualism simultaneously (Bhedābheda). According to Rāmānuja's position, the individual soul (jīva) is part of the reality of Brahman. He follows the logic of whole and part. As such, both the whole and the part are real, but they are one as a whole. In this sense, the individual soul is real and is intrinsic to the reality of the Supreme Being. According to Madhva, the individual is a separate entity which is created by the Supreme Being and as such it is different from the essential nature of the Supreme Being. Vallabha believes on the one hand that Viṣṇu is the only Supreme Being and at the same time affirms that the individual soul does exist and is a dependent reality. According to Nimbārka, the individual is both different and non-different from the Supreme Being.

Generally Vaiṣṇava theology affirms that there are different types of jīvas, viz. bound souls (baddha jīvas), liberated souls (mukta jīvas) and eternal jīvas (nitya jīvas). The bound souls continually go through the cycle of birth and death (saṃsāra) because of their bondage to their actions (karma) and can finally be liberated through spiritual discipline. The liberated ones are those which become free of bondage and attain final liberation to enjoy the eternal bliss of the Supreme Being. The eternal souls are those that are never in bondage and exist in the realm of the Supreme Being eternally. Their purpose is to engage in the service of the Supreme Being.

The scheme of salvation in Vaiṣṇavism

In Vaiṣṇava theology, the individual soul has the innate capacity to experience the eternal bliss of the Supreme and engage in his service. However, due to its ignorance (avidyā) about its true nature it remains bound. The origins of ignorance are considered inexplicable in Vaiṣṇava theology. It is said to be beginningless and therefore the individual soul does not acquire it at a certain point in time. Using analogical reasoning, Vaiṣṇava theology explains that it is mere separation from the Supreme Being, as in the case of a young prince who goes hunting with his father and gets separated in the forest. When, through the intervention of an able teacher, he acquires right knowledge of his true identity, he develops the desire for liberation and through discipline he attains final liberation.

Vaiṣṇavism and its spread throughout India

Vaiṣṇavism in the North

Worship of Viṣṇu in the North can be traced back as far as the Vedic period. In order to understand the historical development of Vaiṣṇavism, it would be necessary to look at the documented historical records. For instance, the Besnagar Inscription, which is dated to around the second century BCE, refers to a flagstaff erected in honour of Vāsudeva by the

Greek ambassador, while the Ghasundi Inscription mentions worship of Saṃkarṣaṇa and Vāsudeva. Another inscription at Nanaghat, which is dated to the first century BCE, also refers to worship of Saṃkarṣaṇa and Vāsudeva. While the earlier texts of the Hindus, such as the *Saṃhitās, Brāhmaṇas* and the *Upaniṣads*, do not give any evidence as to whether Vāsudeva and Viṣṇu are one and the same, it is in the *Bhagavadgītā* that we find the two names being associated with the same person. Thus, according to scholarly opinion it may be right to suggest that the *Bhagavadgītā* is the oldest text that clearly speaks about Vaiṣṇavism. The general scholarly view is that Kṛṣṇa was a popular deity who was subsequently identified with the Vedic god Viṣṇu.

According to historical records, worship of Vāsudeva flourished in the region of Mathura around the fourth century BCE. Some historians suggest that during the reign of Emperor Aśoka the religion of the Bhāgavatas was relegated to the background due to his open support for Buddhism, but by the time of the grammarian Pāṇini both literary and epigraphic records begin to mention the Bhāgavatas again. By the second century BCE the Bhāgavata religion began to spread beyond the Magadha region.

As the Bhāgavata religion spread beyond the Yamunā Valley into the non-Brahmanical regions of India, scholars believe that it came in contact with three non-Brahmanical religions, viz. Ājīvakas (materialist philosophers), Jainas and Buddhists. While some historians considered Bhāgavatism a subsect of the Ājīvakas, Jaina texts have represented Vāsudeva as an Arhat and Buddhist *Jātaka* texts have identified Vāsudeva as Sāriputta. It is suggested that in the third century CE it also came into contact with Christianity, which had been introduced to India by then. Historians generally believe that during the first three centuries of the Common Era, i.e. during the time of the Śākas and the Kushanas, the religion of the Bhāgavatas did not seem to enjoy much support even in its birth place, Mathura, due to the fact those two dynasties were worshippers of Śiva. It is only again in the Gupta period that Bhāgavatism receives much support. By this time the identification of Bhāgavatism with Vaiṣṇavism is clear. With the fall of the Gupta dynasty, the religion of the Bhāgavatas, or Vaiṣṇavism, ceased to be a force in the North and began to spread quite rapidly in the South.

Vaiṣṇavism in Maharashtra State

Although Vaiṣṇavism existed in this part of India for a long time, it was in the thirteenth century that a distinct Marāṭha Bhakti tradition developed. This is perhaps the result of many traditions coming together (e.g. Mādhvas, Nāthas, Sants and Vārkāris). The hymns of Haridas, who was inspired by Madhva's teachings, spread beyond Karnataka into Maharashtra. In Pandharpur in Maharashtra, the traditional deity was Viṭhoba/Viṭṭhal. It may have originally been a Śaiva cult but in the course of time it became identified with the Kṛṣṇa-Rāma cult. The hymns of Haridas became part of this Viṭṭhal cult. In the thirteenth century, another sect emerged, the Mahānubhāva (Manbhau) sect founded by Cakradhāra. And at the end of the thirteenth century Jñāneśvara founded another sect known as the Vārkāri sect. This sect is perhaps better propagated by Nāmdev (1270–1350 CE). He discouraged rituals, pilgrimage (tīrthayātrā), and asceticism (tapas). Inner quest and inner purity were emphasised more strongly than image worship. This tendency may be attributed to the growing influence of Islam. However, the later Marāṭha Vaiṣṇava saints (Ekanāth, 1548–98; Tukārām, 1608–49) did not advocate the removal of rituals and image worship.

Gauḍīya (Bengal) Vaiṣṇavism

The northern part of India caught up with the Bhakti movement around the fourteenth century and up until the seventeenth century there was a fervent devotional trend that gave rise to many devotional poets and mystics who spread Vaiṣṇava Bhakti throughout the northern part of India. In Bengal, the movement was spread by Caitanya, who lived in the fifteenth to sixteenth century. At an early age he became a mystic, even though he was initially trained as a scholar. The *Bhagavata Purāṇa* became the central text on which he based most of his teachings. The central theme of his teaching is the love of God represented by the Rādhā–Kṛṣṇa or Gopī–Kṛṣṇa love. The teachings of Caitanya were further elaborated and spread by the six Gosvāmis: Rūpa Gosvāmi, Sanātana Gosvāmi, Jīva Gosvāmi, Gopāla Bhaṭṭa, Raghunātha Dās and Raghunātha Bhaṭṭa.

Apart from these major devotional movements, Vaiṣṇava Bhakti gave rise to many devotional poets and saints in the North who sang hymns and songs in praise of Viṣṇu, mainly in his incarnational forms as Rāma and Kṛṣṇa. Rāmdās, Tukārām, Tulsīdās and many women poets such as Mīrābāī were instrumental in spreading the Vaiṣṇava devotional movement. One well-known group responsible for popularising Vaiṣṇavism in the North was the Bāuls of Bengal. Essentially bards, they sang in praise of Viṣṇu throughout rural areas.

Vaiṣṇavism in the South

In the South, the Vaiṣṇava Bhakti was spread mainly by the Tamil singer-poets known as Āḻvārs (those who are immersed). The Āḻvārs are twelve in number who lived at various periods between the fifth and the ninth centuries. The hymns that they sang in the temples of Viṣṇu were collected by an orthodox brāhmaṇa who settled in the South. He was Nāthamuni and the collection of the hymns came to be known as *Nālāyira Divyaprabandham* (Four Thousand Divine Hymns). The most famous of the Āḻvār singers was Nammāḻvār, who composed 1,102 verses known as *Tiruvāymoḻi*. These hymns are regarded very highly in Tamil Vaiṣṇavism and they have acquired the status of *Draviḍa Upaniṣad* or *Tamil Veda* (*Tamiḻ-marai*).

After the period of the Āḻvārs, the Vaiṣṇava tradition became gradually systematised in the hands of Sanskritic paṇḍits, beginning with Nāthamuni (ninth century CE) and then Yāmuna (tenth century), and took its final shape as the Viśiṣṭādvaita (Qualified Non-dual) philosophy in the hands of the great teacher Rāmānuja (eleventh century).

The Vaiṣṇava tradition of the South accepted the Veda (mainly the *Upaniṣads*), the *Āgamas* (ritual manuals) and the Tamil hymns of the Āḻvārs as the authoritative texts for the systematic understanding and exposition of the tradition. This tradition is popularly known by the term Śrī Vaiṣṇavas. In the hands of the Vaiṣṇava teachers, the tradition has come to occupy a prominent place in Vedānta. Rāmānuja taught a philosophy which included both the abstract notion of Brahman and the personal God, Viṣṇu. For him Brahman is none other than Viṣṇu-Nārāyaṇa worshipped with devotion. Thus he combined in his philosophy the devotional aspect of the Āḻvārs and the philosophical aspect of the *Upaniṣads*. In the thirteenth century Tamil Vaiṣṇavism witnessed a powerful theological debate between two scholars, Vedānta Deśika and Piḷḷai Lokācārya. Between the thirteenth and the eighteenth centuries the Tamil Vaiṣṇava tradition went through a period of further diversification and became divided into two major sects known as the Northern School (Vaḍakalai) and the Southern School (Tenkalai), otherwise known as the Monkey and Cat

Schools, respectively. These names derive from the different ways in which these animals carry their young, with baby monkeys needing to cling onto their mothers, while kittens are held in their mothers' mouths. The Northern School was represented by Vedānta Deśika and the Southern School was represented by Piḷḷai Lokācārya. Furthermore, two famous Vaiṣṇava temples also became involved in the formation of the two sects. The Kāñcīpura Viṣṇu temple became the seat of the Northern School and the Śrīraṇgam temple became the seat of the Southern School. Among other things, the two schools disagreed on whether or not human beings have any role to play in the scheme of their salvation. The Northern School emphasised the role of human effort, whereas the Southern School emphasised the total surrender of the devotee to Viṣṇu as Lord. While the Northern School spoke of Viṣṇu as both the goal and the means to salvation, the Southern School saw the divine consort, Śrī-Lakṣmī, as the means to the Lord and thus one could approach her in order to reach the Lord. At the present time, the two schools are not as polarised as they were in the past, and there is greater integration and mutual dialogue between the two on many theological points.

Kṛṣṇa Bhakti of Karnataka State

As a result of the South Indian Bhakti orientation, there was another significant development that took place in the form of Kṛṣṇa Bhakti. This school mainly spread in the state of Karnataka. It is principally represented by the philosopher-theologian Madhvā. He developed a philosophy called Dvaita Vedānta (Dualistic philosophy of Vedānta). Integrating Kṛṣṇa Bhakti, he saw Kṛṣṇa as the Supreme Lord, and the soul constantly longs for association with the Lord. The devotee, upon attaining salvation, does not become either identical with the Lord (as in the Advaita philosophy) or merged into the existence of God like a part and the whole (as in the philosophy of Rāmānuja), but rather remains separate and enjoys eternal communion with the Lord.

The Vaiṣṇava Āgama ritual tradition

The Āgama ritual tradition has generally claimed a parallel lineage to the Vedic ritual tradition. Most of the medieval temples and the subsequent temple ritual traditions have followed the Āgama tradition rather than the Vedic ritual tradition. The reason for this is that the Vedic ritual was not conceived as a temple-based tradition but, rather, is different both in its concept of deity and in the rituals associated with them. As Vedic ritual became a highly specialised activity and as the temple gradually became the locus of worship for the Hindu tradition, mainly since the medieval period in India, alternative ritual traditions were developed. The Āgama tradition became the dominant mode of temple ritual performance. Different sectarian traditions, such as Śaiva, Śākta and Vaiṣṇava, have their own Āgama texts that inform the ritual procedures and theologies that pertain to those different sects. Here we are only concerned with the Vaiṣṇava Āgama rituals texts. There are two rival schools of Āgama rituals – Pāñcarātra and the Vaikhānasa. The Pāñcarātra ritual tradition generally claims its origin from none other than Viṣṇu himself, who through Nārada declared to the world the significance of Vaiṣṇava worship through the Pāñcarātra ritual traditions.

Unlike the Pāñcarātra tradition, the Vaikhānasas have claimed a Vedic lineage through some of the Vedic sages. It is in this sense that it claims to be a Vaidika branch. Other than lineage, the theology of Vaiṣṇavism is the basis of both traditions and in that sense they are not theologically different, but differ in ritual procedures. The two schools – the Pāñcarātra and the Vaikhānasas – seem to have had a long history of struggle to control the various prominent Vaiṣṇava temples. For instance, the *Ānanda Saṃhitā*, a Vaikhānasa text, alludes to the conflict regarding ritual procedures in Vaiṣṇava temples.

See also: **Advaita; Avatāras; Āḻvārs; Āraṇyakas; Ātman; Bādarāyaṇa; Bāuls; Bhagavadgītā; Bhāgavatas; Bhakti; Bhedābheda; Brahmā; Brahman; Brāhmaṇa; Brāhmaṇas; Brahmanism; Brahmasūtras; Buddhism, relationship with Hinduism; Caitanya; Deities; Garuḍa; Gopī(s); Guṇas; Guru; Indra; Īśvara; Itihāsa; Jainism, relationship with Hinduism; Jīva; Kāñcīpura; Karma; Kṛṣṇa; Lakṣmī, Śrī; Madhva; Mahābhārata; Mandir; Mantra; Mathura; Māyā; Meditation; Mīrābāī; Mokṣa; Nammāḻvār; Nimbārka; Pāñcarātras; Pāṇini; Piḷḷai Lokācārya; Prakṛti; Pūja; Purāṇas; Puruṣa; Rādhā; Rāmā; Rāmānuja; Rāmāyaṇa; Rudra; Sacred texts; Śaivism; Śāktism; Saṃhitā; Sāṃkhya; Saṃsāra; Śaṅkara; Sant; Soma; Śrāddha; Śrī Vaiṣṇavas; Tapas; Tīrthayātrā; Tulsīdās(a); Upaniṣads; Vaikhānasas; Vallabha; Varuṇa; Vedānta; Vedism; Viśiṣṭādvaita; Viṣṇu; Yāmuna (Vedāntic theologian); Yuga**

PRATAP KUMAR

Further reading

Carman, J.B. 1974. *The Theology of Rāmānuja: An Essay in Interreligious Understanding*. New Haven, CT and London: Yale University Press.

Chakravarti, S.C. 1969. *Philosophical Foundation of Bengal Vaiṣṇavism – A Critical Exposition.* Calcutta: Academic Publishers.

Chari, Srinivasa, S.M. 1994. *Vaiṣṇavism: Its Philosophy, Theology, and Religious Discipline.* Delhi: Motilal Banarsidass.

Dasgupta, Shashibusan. 1976. *Obscure Religious Cults.* Calcutta: Firma KLM Pvt, Ltd.

Datta, C.K. 1973. *The Tattvatraya of Lokacarya, a Treatise of Visistadvaita Vedanta.* English and Hindi trans. B.M. Awasthi and C.K. Datta. New Delhi: Munshiram Manoharlal.

De, Sushil Kumar. 1961. *Early History of the Vaiṣṇava Faith and Movement in Begal from Sanskrit and Bengali Sources.* Calcutta: Firma K.L. Mukhopadhyaya.

Dutt, Lal Kanai. 1963. *The Bengal Vaishnavism and Modern Life.* Calcutta: Sribhumi Publsihing Co.

Gonda, J. 1954. *Aspects of Early Vaiṣṇavism.* Utrecht: Oostoek.

Gonda, J. 1993. *Aspects of Early Viṣṇuism.* Delhi: Motilal Banarsidass.

Goswami, B.K. 1965. *The Bhakti Cult in Ancient India.* Varanasi: Chowkamba Sanskrit Series Office.

Jagadeesan, N. 1977. *History of Śrīvaiṣṇavism in the Tamil Country: Post Rāmānuja.* Madurai: Kodal Publishers.

Kumar, P. Pratap. 1997. *The Goddess Lakṣmī: The Divine Consort in South Indian Vaiṣṇava Tradition.* Atlanta, GA: Scholars Press.

Majumdar, A.K. 1969. *Caitanya: His Life and Doctrine.* Bombay: Bharatiya Vidya Bhavan.

Mukhopadhyaya, Durgadas. 1990. *Religion, Philosophy, and Literature of Bengal Vaiṣṇavism.* Delhi: BR Publishing Corporation.

Narayanan, Vasudha. 1987. *The Way and the Goal: Expressions of Devotion in the Early Śrīvaiṣṇava Tradition.* Washington, DC: Institute for Vaishnava Studies & Centre for the Study of World Religions, Harvard University.

Ranade, R.D. 1988. *Mysticism in Maharashtra: Indian Mysticism.* Delhi: Motilal Banarsidass.

Ray, Manas. 1994. *The Bauls of Birbhumi: A Study in Persistence and Change in Communication in Cultural Context.* Calcutta: Firma KLM.

Raychaudhuri, Hemachandra. 1975. *Materials for the Study of the Early History of Vaishnava Sect.* Delhi: Oriental Books.

Schrader, Otto. 1916. *Introduction to the Pāñcarātra and the Ahirbudhnya Saṃhitā.* Madras: Adyar Library and Research Centre.

Sinha, Jadunath. 1973. *The Philosophy of Nimbarka.* Calcutta: Sinha Publishing House.

Smith, H.D. 1980. *A Descriptive Bibliography of the Printed Texts of the Pāñcarātrāgamas,* vols 1 and 2. Baroda: Oriental Institute.

Varadachari, V. 1982. *Āgamas of South Indian Vaiṣṇavism.* Madras: Prof. M. Rangacharya Memoria Trust.

VAIṢṆO DEVĪ

Punjabi oral or local tradition claims that Satī's arms fell at the cave shrine of Vaiṣṇo Devī in north-west India (Jammu and Kashmir) and, in so doing, legitimised this as a place of pilgrimage. This particular shrine is considered special because it houses the three cosmic forms of Śakti – Mahākālī (Great Kālī), Mahālakṣmī (Great Lakṣmī) and Mahāsarasvatī (Great Sarasvatī) – present in the form of stone outcrops (piṇḍis), who together create a beautiful virgin who was originally called Trikuta. The name Vaiṣṇo is an indication that this goddess is allied with the Vaiṣṇava ideal, particularly with purity. Furthermore, she is said to be waiting for Viṣṇu's final avatāra, Kalkin, to come and make her his consort.

Poster art identifies Vaiṣṇo Devī as a Durgā-type figure, seated on a tiger, brandishing various weapons in her eight hands. Mark Rohe has come to the conclusion that Vaiṣṇo Devī can be many things to many people. The Vaiṣṇava devotee might see her as an incarnation of Lakṣmī, the Śaiva may see her as a form of Durgā and the Śākta may simply see Vaiṣṇo Devī as the Mahādevī (Great Goddess), personified in many forms.

Vaiṣṇo Devī's shrine is arguably the fastest-growing pilgrimage site in India. This, it seems, is a pilgrimage site for the modern age, with plentiful accommodation and food, all the facilities a pilgrim might need and, in the days of e-commerce, even an internet site (http://www.maavaishnodevi.org) where those who are unable to make the journey to her cave shrine at the top of the mountain can satisfy themselves with virtual darśana.

See also: **Avatāra; Darśana; Durgā; Kālī and Caṇḍī; Lakṣmi, Śrī; Mahādevī; Śaivism; Śakti; Śāktism; Satī; Sarasvatī; Tīrthayātra; Vaiṣṇavism; Viṣṇu**

LYNN FOULSTON

Further reading

Erndl, K.M. 1993. *Victory to the Mother: The Hindu Goddess of Northwest India in Myth, Ritual, and Symbol.* New York: Oxford University Press.

Rohe, Mark 2001. 'Ambiguous and Definitive: The Greatness of the Goddess Vaiṣṇo Devī'. In T. Pintchman, ed., *Seeking Mahādevī: Constructing the Identities of the Hindu Great Goddess.* Albany, NY: State University of New York Press, 55–76.

Tewari, N. 1988. *The Mother Goddess Vaishno Devi.* New Delhi: Lancer International.

VAIŚYA

See: **Varṇa**

VALLABHA (VAIṢṆAVA THEOLOGIAN) (1479–1531)

A Telegu brāhmaṇa, Vallabha was a Vedāntic philosopher who founded a Vaiṣṇava bhakti sect. His school flourished in Mathurā, North India. Vallabha taught 'śuddhādvaita', or pure non-dualism 'undefiled by' māyā. His sect is known as Rudra-saṃpradāya and Puṣṭi Mārga (path of nourishment or fulfilment).

Vallabha was born in central India and was a precocious child, mastering the Veda and the *Purāṇas* at an early age. He identified an image of Kṛṣṇa on Govardhan Hill in Braj. Later, according to hagiography, the direct relationship with the Supreme Being was revealed to Vallabha by Kṛṣṇa.

Vallabha regarded the soul's connection to God as obscured by impurities. Rejecting asceticism as a means of liberation, cleansing of the soul is achieved via initiation into the saṃpradāya and taking the brahmasambandha mantra 'śrīkṛṣṇaḥśaraṇam mama', 'Radiant Kṛṣṇa is my refuge'.

Service (seva) to Kṛṣṇa may place the devotee in a position to receive His grace.

Vallabha was the author of *Anubhāṣya* (The Brief Commentary), a commentary on the *Brahmasūtras*. Puruṣottama commented on *Anubhāṣya* to produce the *Bhāṣya-prakāśa* (Lights on the Commentary). Vallabha also wrote a commentary on the *Bhāgavata Purāṇa*, the *Śrīsubodhinī* (Giving a Good Explanation).

For Vallabha, Śaṅkara's Advaita teaching was defective because it depended on the principle of māyā (illusion) to account for multiplicity and the apparent separation of God and the individual soul. According to Vallabha, the essence of the sole, independent reality Brahman (identified with Śrī Kṛṣṇa), is being (sat), consciousness or knowledge (cit) and bliss (ānanda). Souls and matter are real parts, subtle manifestations, of Brahman. God manifests Himself as many by His will (via his power of māyā).

Vallabha's saṃpradāya flourished after his death under the leadership of his second son, Vitthalanātha (1516–86). It exists today (with a mostly mercantile membership) and is particularly strong in, for example, Bombay, Rajasthan, Gujarat and western Uttar Pradesh.

See also: **Advaita; Bhāgavatas; Bhakti; Brahman; Brāhmana; Brahmasūtras; Dīkṣa; Kṛṣṇa; Mathurā; Māyā; Purāṇas; Puṣṭi Mārga; Saccidānanda; Saṃpradāya; Śaṅkara; Seva; Tapas; Vaiṣṇavism; Veda**

MARTIN OVENS

Further reading

Barz, R. 1976. *The Bhakti Sect of Vallabhācārya.* Faridabad: Thomson Press.

VALLABHA (VAIŚESIKA AUTHOR)

See: **Nyāyalīlāvatī**

VĀLMĪKI

Vālmīki as an individual plays a marginal role in the *Rāmāyaṇa* that bears his name and the major myths about him develop in much later texts. However, by the period when its first and last books were added around the core of the *Rāmāyaṇa*, he had become a character within the story. The *Bālakāṇḍa,* 'Childhood Book', opens with Vālmīki asking Nārada whether there exists in the world a truly exemplary individual and receiving the unequivocal answer, Rāma. Use of the śloka metre had by then become such a hallmark of the *Rāmāyaṇa* that there follows a story of how Vālmīki invented it (the śloka actually derives from an older, Vedic metre and is used also in the *Mahābhārata*, but most of the poem is in this simple narrative metre). After Vālmīki invents the śloka in sorrow at seeing a hunter kill a mating crane, Brahmā commissions him to compose the story of Rāma. This he does mentally, then teaches the poem to Kuśa and Lava, who sing before Rāma what purports to be the rest of the text; this is not explained until the *Uttarakāṇḍa* 'Further Book', when Vālmīki gives the exiled Śītā sanctuary at his hermitage, she gives birth to her sons Kuśa and Lava, and their subsequent singing of his story leads Rāma to recognise and acknowledge them as his sons.

Later legend makes Vālmīki an untouchable dacoit who realises the error of his ways after an encounter with the Seven Sages. He meditates on the mantra they give him (marā – the syllables of Rāma in reverse) so long that a termite mound (valmīka) grows over him. Much later the sages return and summon forth the now reformed individual, and he composes the *Rāmāyaṇa* (as above). Vālmīki is worshipped by the modern Valmik community (who reject this legend).

See also: **Brahmā; Mahābhārata; Mantra; Nārada; Rāma; Rāmāyaṇa; Śītā; Vedism**

JOHN BROCKINGTON

Further reading

Bloch, Alfred. 1963–64. 'Vālmīki und die Ikṣvākuiden' [Vālmīki and the Ikṣvāku dynasty]. *Indo-Iranian Journal* 7: 81–123.
Goldman, Robert P. 1976. 'Vālmīki and the Bhṛgu Connection'. *Journal of the American Oriental Society* 96: 97–101.
Leslie, Julia. 2003. *Authority and Meaning in Indian Religions: Hinduism and the Case of Vālmīki*. Aldershot: Ashgate.

VAMA DEVA SHASTRI, SWAMI

David Frawley, born in 1950, is one of the few Westerners recognised in India for his Vedic knowledge. He was given the name Vama Deva Shastri by Avadhuta Shastri in 1991. In 1995 the title Paṇḍit was conferred on him and he was awarded the Brahmachari Vishwanathji prize in Mumbai for his knowledge of Vedic teaching. In addition to his studies of the Vedic traditions, he is also a practitioner of Āyurvedic medicine and Indian astrology. Through his books, *Gods, Sages and Kings* (1991), *Myth of the Aryan Invasion* (1994), *In Search of the Cradle of Civilisation* (1995), *The Rig Veda and the History of India*, he has challenged earlier models of the ancient history of India. His work in the USA is achieved through the medium of the American Institute of Vedic Studies.

Vama Deva Shastri's influences are Ramana Maharshi, Sri Aurobindo and Paramhansa Yogananda, studying under their successors at various periods since his first contact with Indian spirituality in 1970. In many ways, he can be defined as a Western disciple of the nineteenth- and early twentieth-century Hindu renaissance which focused on Advaita Vedānta and Yoga as the 'true' Hinduism redefined as Sanātana Dharma.

See also: **Advaita; Āyurveda; Ghose, Aurobindo; Hinduism, modern and contemporary; Paṇḍit; Ramana Maharshi; Sanātana Dharma; Yoga; Yogananda, Paramhansa**

RON GEAVES

Further reading

Frawley, David. 1994. *Myth of the Aryan Invasion*. New Delhi: Voice of India.
www.vedanet.com (accessed 29 October 2005).

VĀMANA

See: **Avatāra**

VĀMANA PURĀṆA

See: **Purāṇas**

VĀNAPRASTHYA

The word vānaprastha (or vanaprastha), for which vaikhānasa seems to have been an ancient name, means one who pre-eminently dwells in a forest, and this stage of life in the abstract is described as vānaprasthya. The arrival of the time for adopting such a mode of life is variously or collectively said to be indicated by the sight of one's wrinkles, grey hair or one's grandchildren, suggesting 50 as the likely age of its adoption. The *Mahābhārata* contains numerous account of kṣatriyas adopting this stage of life, who also sometimes terminated their life in heroic fashion, of which the Great Journey undertaken by the Pāṇḍavas towards the end of their reign is an example. It was more usual to live out this period of life in an ascetic manner. Mahatma Gandhi (1869–1948) autobiographically described himself as practising this mode of his life after he gave up marital relations.

See also: **Gandhi, Mohandas Karamchand; Mahābhārata; Pāṇḍavas; Varṇa**

ARVIND SHARMA

Further reading

Kane, P.V. 1974. *History of Dharmaśāstra*, vol. 2, pt 2, 2nd edn. Poona: Bhandarkar Oriental Research Institute.

VARĀHA

See: **Avatāra**

VARĀHAMIHIRA

Sixth-century astronomer, mathematician and philosopher born near Ujjain, possibly of Persian background, and regarded as one of the Nine Gems of the court of King Vikramaditya. His writings include the *Bṛhatsaṃhitā*, a vast work that deals with omens and places great importance in astrology. He also wrote treatises on auspicious times for weddings and the right time for kings to venture out to war. He wrote a further two works on creating horoscopes, the *Bṛhad-jātaka*, also known as the *Horā śāstra* and the *Laghu jātaka*, well known and studied up to the present time. He is also known for the *Pañca-siddhāntikā*, or 'five treatises', in which he summarised the Indian astronomical knowledge of his time. These were: the *Paitāmaha*, a discussion of ancient or 'grandfather' traditions known as *Vedāṅga*; *Vāsiṣtha*, named after the sage, which is a transitional system between the old Indian systems and Western systems; *Sūrya*, believed to have been revealed by the Sun-god to Asura Magha, in which Indian astronomy first appears in its fully developed classical form; *Romaka*, Roman or Alexandrian astronomy derived from Ptolemy but acknowledging the Indian yuga system; and *Paulīśa*, based on the works of Paulus of Alexandria (d. 378 CE). The *Pañca-siddhāntikā* was translated in 1889 by G. Thibaut and S. Dvivedi.

See also: **Jyotiṣa; Sūrya; Vasiṣṭha; Vedāṅgas; Yuga**

RON GEAVES

Further reading

Kapoor, Subodh. (ed.). 2000. *The Hindus: Encyclopaedia of Hinduism*, vol. 4. New Delhi: Cosmo Publications.

Thibaut, G. and S. Dvivedi. 1889. *The Pañcha-siddhāntikā of Varāhamihira*. Banaras: Medical Hall Press.

VĀRĀṆASĪ

Vārāṇasī, more popularly known as Banāras, in official discourse, is an important pilgrimage-urban-sacred complex bordering the river Gaṅgā in the eastern part of the state of Uttar Pradesh. For Hindus, it is the centre of Śiva's universe, as well as the beginning and end point of human civilisation. Hindu mythology has it that Kāśī, the ancient name for Banāras, contains the whole world and everything on earth that is powerful and auspicious. Today Banāras is the site of the largest combined pilgrim/tourist trade in India.

The curing and purifying powers of the shrines, akhaṛās, liṅgas, tanks and other sacred places in Banāras have been referenced in Sanskrit and vernacular literature and in popular discourse for over a millennium. Of its three names, Kāśī is the most ancient, denoting an erstwhile kingdom or region of religious, political and commercial importance. The name Vārāṇasī may derive from the Varaṇā river (whose ancient name was Vārāṇasī), which meets the Gaṅgā to the north and downstream of the current city centre. Archaeological evidence suggests that Kāśī originally grew out from the confluence of the Varaṇā and the Gaṅgā. At some point after the first century CE, Kāśī and Vārāṇasī were used interchangeably to name the sacred-city complex. The name Banāras first appeared in Buddhist literature as Bārāṇasi, and then later evolved into Banāras under Muslim and colonial rule. Even though the ancient name Vārāṇasī was restored in official discourse in 1956 and Kāśī survives today as a name denoting the sacred complex, residents continue to prefer the name Banāras.

At the beginning of the first century CE, the sacred texts were extolling the beauty and protectedness of Kāśī and its importance as a place for spiritual salvation and philosophical learning. Its temples, shrines, wells and the sacred River Gaṅgā possess the capacity to cure, protect and assuage human suffering. More importantly, Banāras is pervaded by Śiva, whose historical prominence can be assumed from such ancient place names as Śaṅkarapurī, Mahādevapurī and Rudrapurī. Śiva's presence is apparent in every liṅga and in numerous shrines and temples. With Śiva's power this congested urban centre, once a forest of bliss (ānandavana), continues as avimukta because all the bonds of sin (avi) are forever severed (mukta) there. The ancient sacred zone of avimukta, much smaller than the contemporary city, was geographically situated within a cosmogonic maṇḍala. The sacred pathways devotees followed to gain merit and purification were layered and symbolised as kośas or sheaths. Today, surviving at the sacred centre of this maṇḍala is the shrine of Viśveśvara or Viśvanātha (a form of Śiva as patron deity).

Banāras is considered the Mahāśmaśāna, the 'great cremation ground' that will survive the dissolution of the universe. Today, cremations take place on two different ghāṭs along the river Gaṅgā, Maṇikarṇikā and Hariścandra, which is now complemented by an electric crematorium. This tīrtha, or pilgrimage place, and the cremation grounds in it draw meaning from their role as a crossing place, a way to the divine. Pilgrims continue to refer to ancient texts and *mahātmyas* that spell out the merits of performing rituals within the sacred maṇḍala. For example, the *Kāśī Khaṇḍa*, a text describing Banāras between the eighth and thirteenth centuries, contains mythologies of Kāśī's origins and powerful deities and liṅgas, stories of Śiva's wanderings and a delineation of the merits gained from pilgrimage, worship and bathing.

Today, Banāras is a vibrant city of close to 2.5 million residents. On any given day, it also welcomes a floating pilgrim population of around 50,000. On very auspicious days, the pilgrim population may exceed 2 million. The oldest part of the city is situated on the western bank of the sacred River Gaṅgā and is mediated by flights of steps (ghāṭs) that give residents and pilgrims access to the river's purifying waters. The Gaṅgā assists those who come to her for spiritual purification or passage to the next world.

The number of ghāṭs along the Gaṅgā has increased over time and today stands at about 125. They are set in stone along the crescent-shaped river front between the Asi and Varaṇā rivers. On the ghāṭs, visitors from across India and from other nation-states gather, perform worship rituals and interact as a community of devotees. Tīrtha purohits, the religious specialists who sit along the ghāṭs, officiate over pilgrims' offerings and guide their ritual interactions with the Gaṅgā and other deities. Daśāśvamedha, an ancient, sacred place (tīrtha and ghāṭ) and a neighbourhood of the City District of Vārāṇasī, is one of many gateways to the sacred Gaṅgā and one of the most merit-bestowing ghāṭs (others are Asi, Maṇikarṇikā, Adi Keśava and Pañcgaṅgā). Daśāśvamedha is the ancient site where Lord Brahmā performed a ten-horse sacrifice (daśa-aśva-medha) to gain the power to rule over King Divodāsa. Sacred texts mentioning important liṅga and shrines indicate that the southern section of the ghāṭ was the authentic site of ancient pilgrimage. The Śītalā temple contains the ancient liṅga of Daśāśvamedheśvara Mahādev, Śiva as Lord of Daśāśvamedha. Behind this temple, the shrine of Prayāgeśvara lies underneath the house of a pilgrim priest (paṇḍā). The power Lord Brahmā generated and the power provided by Gaṅgā are also manifested in the temples of Rāma and Sītā, Śulataṅkeśvara, Brahmeśvara, the Gaṅgā Devī and Bandī Devī, all located on the southern side of Daśāśvamedha ghāṭ and on the contiguous space of Prayāg ghāṭ. At these and other ghāṭs, pilgrims access the divine power of gods and goddesses through elaborate ritual practices, some guided and taught by local specialists. Yet Banāras is also a place where Hindus acknowledge and complain about the greed of pilgrim priests and other service providers in the midst of this sacredness, as they endeavour to reach divine power.

Apart from their sacred value and importance, the ghāṭs are also public spaces where all that is degenerate about the modern world resides. The city's domestic wastewater flows over and between the ghāṭs and into the Gaṅgā at multiple junctures, often very close to the places where pilgrims bathe. Wastewater also oozes out of the cracks in the ancient urban infrastructure and threatens human health during monsoon floods. All kinds of trades and occupational activities occur on the ghāṭ spaces, along with the washing of clothes for homes and businesses, the bathing of water buffalo and even human defecation. Indeed, Banāras residents acknowledge that dirtiness surrounds the sacred ghāṭ spaces and the pure waters of the Gaṅgā. But they also explain that Gaṅgā takes away all this dirtiness with her flow, especially during the monsoon,when she washes over the ghāṭs and coats them with a thick layer of silt. During torrential downpours, the beds of ancient tributaries fill with fastlowing streams of storm water and wastewater, all making their way past the ghāṭs and into the Gaṅgā.

The core of the economy of Banāras is formed by merchants and service providers catering to the needs of pilgrims and tourists – priests, boatmen, merchants selling ritual implements and offerings, and transport and accommodation agents. Banāras is also home to the Banāras-Hindu University, the largest university in Asia, and to a small-scale textile industry. Among the key players in the pilgrimage trade, paṇḍās claim rights to serve specific pilgrim groups on the ghāṭs they purport to own and on their adjacent properties. Mahants and pujārīs claim control of temples and shrines while maintaining them for pilgrims. Paṇḍās, tīrth purohits, mahants and pujārīs earn their livelihood through donations (dakṣiṇā or dāna) made by pilgrims for access to sacred sites, ritual services, blessings, shelter and the use of water and bathroom facilities. Their earnings are supplemented by commissions from other service providers who take care of pilgrims and assist them in rituals and shopping. All ritual transactions between priest and pilgrim are based upon the fundamental assumption that rights are inalienable because they are inherited through divine grace. But this assumption belies the fact that all priests have a persistent fear of losing these rights in contests for power and prestige to other members within and outside their caste group.

Boatmen are also important service providers in the local economy. They row wooden boats (and now steer motorised ones) for pilgrims and tourists who wish to move along the waterway or enjoy the aesthetic beauty of the landscape. Boatmen also compete with paṇḍās and tīrth purohits for control of ghāṭ spaces and rights to perform specific ritual services. As the sins of humans increase in the degenerate period of the kali yuga, residents argue that purification by an eternally pure Gaṅgā in Śiva's abode will be even more desirable. Therefore, it is likely that the combined pilgrim/tourist trade will thrive in Banāras in the future. With this, ritual specialists and pilgrim providers will continue to provide needed services and maintain the foundation of the local economy.

See also: **Brahmā; Gaṅgā; Kośa; Purohit; Rāma; Religious specialists; Sītā; Śītalā; Śiva; Tīrthayātra; Yuga**

KELLY D. ALLEY

Further reading

Alley, K.D. 2002. *On the Banks of the Ganga: When Wastewater Meets a Sacred River*. Ann Arbor, MI: University of Michigan Press.

Eck, D. 1980. 'A Survey of Sanskrit Sources for the Study of Varanasi'. *Purana* 22(1): 81–101.

Eck, D. 1982. *Banaras: City of Light*. New York: Alfred Knopf.

Freitag, S. (ed.). 1989. *Culture and Power in Banaras*. Berkeley, CA: University of California Press.

Kumar, N. 1992. *Friends, Brothers and Informants: Fieldwork Memoirs of Banaras*. Berkeley, CA: University of California Press.

Moti Chandra, D. 1985. *Kashi Ka Itihas*. Varanasi : Visvavidyālaya Prakāsana .

Pandey, R. 1979. *Kasi Through the Ages*. Delhi: Sundeep Prakashan.

Parry, J.P. 1994. *Death in Banaras*. Cambridge: Cambridge University Press.

Saraswati, B. 1975. *Kashi: Myth and Reality of a Classical Tradition*. Simla: Indian Institute of Advanced Study.

Singh, R.P.B. 1993. *Banaras (Varanasi): Cosmic Order, Sacred City, Hindu Traditions*. Varanasi: Tara Book Agency.

Vidyarthi, L.P., M. Jha and B.N. Saraswati. 1979. *The Sacred Complex of Kashi*. Delhi: Concept Publishing.

VARṆA

Varṇa is a Sanskrit term with a wide range of meaning. In some of the earliest works in Sanskrit, varṇa appears to have meant colour. In later years, however, varṇa came to signify the unchangeable social grouping into which a particular individual was born. There were said to be four varṇas, namely the brāhmaṇas, the kṣatriyas, the vaiśyas and the śūdras, whose positions in the social hierarchy were famously laid out in hymn 10.90 of the *Ṛgveda*, the oldest extant work in Sanskrit. There, the brāhmaṇas were said to be derived from the head of the Primal Man, the rajanyas (an equivalent of kṣatriyas) from his arms, the vaiśyas from his thighs and the śūdras from his feet. Such a hymn provided strong support for the theory codified in the *Dharmasūtra*s that the brāhmaṇas should be associated with the priesthood and sacred knowledge, the kṣatriyas with bearing arms and ruling, the vaiśyas with agriculture and trade, and the śūdras with service and menial labour. Further distinction between the varṇas was established owing to the classification of the brāhmaṇas, kṣatriyas and vaiśyas as dvijas, the twice-born, owing to their receipt of a second birth upon the inception of their study of the Veda. The śūdras, by contrast, were considered to have only a single birth, since they were barred from acquiring knowledge of the Veda. Members of the three twice-born varṇas were thus allowed to participate in Vedic sacrifices, while the śūdras were necessarily excluded. The division of both sacred and secular society into the three twice-born varṇas and the śūdras was particularly important for dharmaśāstra, an appendage of the Veda designed to aid the men and women of the Vedic community in understanding their rights and obligations. Unsurprisingly, the brāhmaṇa varṇa received the greatest attention from dharmaśāstra, since the brāhmaṇas' role in performing Vedic sacrifices and perpetuating Vedic knowledge placed them at the centre of the Vedic universe. Members of the śūdra varṇa, however, found themselves either neglected or disparaged by dharmaśāstra. In recent years, the notion of varṇa has proved itself a topic of contention, provoking radically different reactions from such luminaries as Mahatma Gandhi and B.R. Ambedkar.

See also: **Ambedkar, Bhimrao Ram; Dharmaśāstras; Dharmasūtras; Dvija; Gandhi, Mohandas Karamchand; Saṃhitā; Veda**

ETHAN KROLL

Further reading

Dumont, Louis. 1970. *Homo Hierarchicus: An Essay on the Caste System*. Trans. Mark Sainsbury. Chicago, IL: University of Chicago Press.

Ghurye, G.S. 1932. *Caste and Race in India*. London: Kegan Paul, Trench, Trubner & Co., Ltd.

Kane, Pandurang Vaman. 1941. *History of Dharmasastra*, vol. 2. Poona: Bhandarkar Oriental Research Institute.

Smith, Brian K. 1994. *Classifying the Universe*. Oxford: Oxford University Press.

Srinivas, M.N. 1962. *Caste in Modern India and Other Essays*. Bombay: Asia Publishing House.

VARUṆA

'Binder', 'encompasser'. The god most cited as an asura in the *Ṛgveda*; also the āditya *par excellence*. The wrathful, fetter-wielding Varuṇa is the punisher of ethical (chiefly ritual) infractions. From a transcendental bias in the understanding of spirituality, nineteenth- and twentieth-century writers invariably hailed Varuṇa as the highest achievement of Vedic thought. He is almost exclusively linked to the quasi-solar Mitra in a dvandvic formulation throughout the *Ṛgveda*. Varuṇa's link to nature would appear to be with the starless nocturnal expanse of the heavens (especially in the late Vedic *Brāhmaṇas*), but as with all āditya-asura expressions, whatever natural function, if any, is detectable, it is eventually superseded by conformity to an abstract personification – in Varuṇa's case, the moral order of the cosmos. Nevertheless, the remnants of Varuṇa's atmospheric connections led subsequently to his association with the celestial rivers and his post-Vedic transformation into a god of the ocean. As such, he becomes the Lokapāla of the west.

Originally, however, as the punisher of wrongdoing, Varuṇa's infliction is dropsy. His attribute/weapon is the noose. He is an 'all-seeing', spying and omniscient god (e.g. *Atharvaveda* 4.16.2–5), and his māyām or crafty magic (e.g. *Ṛgveda* 3.61.7, 5.85.5f., 7.28.4) becomes in time the power of the Hindu Brahman. But in the *Ṛgveda* we witness the gradual ascendancy of Indra over Varuṇa, and, considering Indra's opposition to Varuṇa as well as the fact that both Varuṇa's and Vṛtra's names are cognate (from vṛ- 'to cover'), whilst the mother of Varuṇa is Aditi/Diti and that of Vṛtra is Danu – both from the verbal root dā-, 'to bind' – Varuṇa-Vṛtra may be seen as developments from a single asuric hypostasis.

See also: **Asura; Brahman; Brāhmaṇas; Indra; Mitra; Vedic pantheon; Vedism**

MICHAEL YORK

VASIṢṬHA

One of the seven Vedic sages (ṛṣi), who were born from Brahmā, he is represented in the *Purāṇas* and the epics as the great rival of Viśvāmitra. Vasiṣṭha's name means 'wealth' and he was recorded as the owner of Kāmadhenu, the cow of plenty who fulfilled all wishes and arose from the churning of the ocean of milk at the beginning of creation. In the *Rāmayaṇa*, he is associated with the four sons of Daśaratha, whom he names and whose divinity he announces, although it is his rival Viśvāmitra who takes them to defeat the demons and introduces them to the court of Rāja Janaka, the father of Sītā. Vasiṣṭha's connection with Rāma leads to the belief that he was the guru of the young prince and avatāra, and the sacred text, the *Yoga Vasiṣṭha*, an advaitic reinterpretation of the *Rāmayaṇa*, uses the same device of questions and answers between sage and avatāra (as master and disciple) as is found in the *Bhagavadgītā*.

See also: **Advaita; Avatāra; Bhagavadgītā; Brahmā; Daśaratha; Janaka; Kāmadhenu; Purāṇas; Rāma; Rāmayaṇa; Ṛṣi; Sītā; Viśvāmitra**

RON GEAVES

Further reading

Stutley, Margaret and James Stutley (eds). 1985. *A Dictionary of Hinduism*. London: Routledge and Kegan Paul.

VĀSTOṢPATI

Vāstoṣpati is also Vāstu Puruṣa, Lord of the Site in the Vedic sacrifice and Guardian of the Dwelling Place, whether of the gods (the temple) or the home of the householder (gṛhastha). Vāstu ('dwelling' or 'site') is also the cosmos and cosmic order, and in this context Vāstoṣpati is a form of Rudra-Śiva. In temple architecture the Vāstu Puruṣa is integral to the ground plan. He is conceived as a prostrate male figure with his limbs stretched out in the cardinal directions, and is worshipped before work on the site commences. Similarly, in the home he is conceived of as lying sleeping with his trunk in the centre of the house, his head in the north-east corner, his feet in the south-west and his arms stretched out in the other directions. Offerings are made to him when moving into a new home. He protects the household and drives away diseases.

See also: **Gārhasthya; Mandir; Rudra; Śiva; Sthāpatyaveda; Yajña**

KATHLEEN TAYLOR

Further reading

Michell, George. 1977. *The Hindu Temple*. London: Elek.

Sinclair-Stevenson, M. 1971. *The Rites of the Twice-Born*. New Delhi: Oriental Books Reprint Corporation, 357–60.

VASUGUPTA (875–925)

Vasugupta was an exponent of Kashmiri Śaivism, regarded by practitioners as one of the five great philosopher-sages of the tradition, believed to have attained the highest states of consciousness through the practice of Trika Yoga, the development of Tantric cremation-ground asceticism into a householder religion akin to Śaiva Siddhānta. The Trika is a monistic system in which the nature of the Lord, the individual soul and the creation are all emanations of consciousness, forming a single reality which in its purest form is Maheśvara, the supreme Śiva.

The goal of the initiate is to merge the individual consciousness into pure or undifferentiated consciousness, expressed as Śiva or Kālī. At the same time as this monistic system attracted brāhmaṇa householders to Trika, Vasugupta, responding to a dream in which Śiva appeared to him, departed for the Mahādeva mountain in Kashmir. While at the mountain, the sage is believed to have had revealed to him the text of the *Śiva Sūtras* by Śiva himself, although some accounts state that he discovered the text inscribed upon a rock. The *Śiva Sūtras* provide an outline of the key teachings of Śaivite monism and remain one of the most important textual authorities of the tradition, supported by the doctrine of divine revelation.

One of the most significant principles developed by Vasugupta and first mentioned in the *Śiva Sūtras* was the concept of spanda, which in turn was to be further elaborated by other significant figures of the Kashmiri Śaivite tradition. Spanda can be described as a kind of 'vibration' or double-edged movement of pure consciousness inwardly to identity with the

Self and outwardly to identity with the object world. The essence of spanda pervades and controls matter and has some directive relationship with the vibrations of mind. Vasugupta taught the principle of spanda to his disciple, Bhaṭṭa Kallaṭa, who went on to develop the ideas in his *Spandakārikās* and its commentary, both written in the middle of the ninth century.

See also: **Kālī and Caṇḍī; Kashmiri Śaivism; Śaiva Siddhānta; Śiva; Tantrism**

RON GEAVES

Further reading

Flood, Gavin. 1997. *An Introduction to Hinduism.* Cambridge: Cambridge University Press, 167.

Pandit, B.N. 1997. *Specific Principles of Kashmir Śaivism.* New Delhi: Munshiram Manoharlal, 62ff.

VĀSUKI

The king of the serpents (nāgas) and lord of Pātāla (the lowermost region). Vāsuki is described as an enormous snake with hundreds of hoods on whose top the Universe rests. Vāsuki was born of the ṛsi Kaśyapa and Kadrū, daughter of Dakṣa (*Viṣṇu Purāṇa* 1. 15). Kadrū became the mother of the serpents, while her sister Vinatā, also married to Kaśyapa, had only two sons: the deformed Aruṇā and Garuḍa, the killer of serpents (nāgāntaka). The hostility between the latter and snakes is mentioned in many myths as a result of the rivalry between Vāsuki's mother and Vinatā. Serpents are closely connected with myths of the creation of the Universe. Vāsuki's brother Śeṣa eradicated the mount Mandāra (the axis mundi), and Vāsuki himself was employed by both devas and asuras as a rope in the churning of the ocean to get the amṛta (*Mahābhārata* 1. 17–19; *Viṣṇu Purāṇa* 1. 9).

See also: **Asuras; Dakṣa; Deities; Garuḍa; Nāgas; Purāṇas; Ṛṣi; Śeṣa**

FABRIZIO M. FERRARI

Further reading

Vogel, J.P. 1995. *Indian Serpent Lore or the Nagas in Hindu Legend and Art*. Reprint of the 1926 edition. Delhi: Asian Educational Services.

VĀTSYĀYANA, MALLANĀGA

Author of the *Kāmasūtra*, Mallanāga is his personal name, but, like Pakṣilasvāmin Vātsyāyana, he is more often known by his gotra (clan) name Vātsyāyana. He is sometimes referred to as a muni or a mahari (great ṛṣi), and a verse near the end of the book (*Kāmasūtra* 7.2.57) says that he composed it while in a state of chastity (brahmacarya) and concentration (samādhi). It is not clear what we should deduce from this about his lifestyle, nor how much personal experience underlies his detailed knowledge of his subject; like most ancient Indian writers he says next to nothing about himself. His style is only partly typical of sūtras, since he includes verses and discursive passages; it is thus similar to that of Kauṭilya's *Arthaśāstra.* Like Kauṭilya, he gives instructions on how to perform unscrupulous acts while disclaiming any advocacy of them. Unlike Kauṭilya, who places artha first, he declares dharma to be supreme among the four human aims.

He states that he is consolidating the work of predecessors; he mentions Śvetaketu Auddālaka (that is, son of Uddālaka; apparently this is the Śvetaketu who appears in the *Chāndogya Upaniṣad* and elsewhere) and Bābhravya. He also mentions seven other authorities who expanded on Bābhravya's work. These acknowledgements show that there was an extensive literature on kāmaśāstra, or the science of pleasure, before Vātsyāyana; consequently, references to aspects of this subject in the works of Kālidāsa and other poets do not necessarily mean that Vātsyāyana pre-dated them. However, there is an explicit mention of the *Kāmasūtra* 'composed by Mallanāga' in Subandhu's Sanskrit romance *Vāsavadattā* (Gray 1913: 69), so Vātsyāyana's work must have existed at the time of Subandhu, about the seventh century CE (Winternitz 1967: 622–24). The abovementioned similarities to the *Arthaśāstra* suggest that both works may belong to the same period, but this is by no means necessary.

See also: **Artha; Arthaśāstra; Brahmacarya; Dharma; Kālidāsa; Kāmasūtra; Kauṭilya; Gotra; Muni; Ṛṣi; Sūtra; Uddālaka Āruṇi; Upaniṣads; Vātsyāyana, Pakṣilavāmin**

DERMOT KILLINGLEY

Further reading

Gray, Louis H. 1913. *Vāsavadattā: A Sanskrit Romance by Subandhu*. New York: Columbia University Press. Reprinted Delhi: Motilal Banarsidass, 1962.

Śāstrī, D. 1964. *The Kāmasūtram of Śrī Vātsyāyana Muni with the Jayamaṅgalā Sanskrit Commentary of Śrī Yaśodhara. Edited with Hindi Commentary by Śrī Devduṭṭa [sic]-Śāstrī.* Varanasi: Chowkhamba Sanskrit Series Office.

Winternitz, M. 1967. *History of Indian Literature*, vol. 3, pt 2: Scientific Literature. Trans. Subhadra Jhā. Delhi: Motilal Banarsidass.

VĀTSYĀYANA, PAKṢILASVĀMIN

The earliest commentator on the *Nyāyasūtras*, Pakṣilasvāmin is his personal name, but he is more often known by his gotra (clan) name Vātsyāyana, meaning 'descendant of Vatsa'. His *Nyāyasūtrabhāṣya* (commentary on the *Nyāyasūtras*) consists of brief sentences which expand and supplement the sūtras, defining terms and setting agendas for later developments in this school. The style is similar to that of the grammarian Patañjali (second century BCE); however, he is usually dated in the fourth century CE. In any case he must have preceded the great Buddhist logician Dignāga, who severely criticised his work around 500 CE (Dasgupta 1922: 120, 306f.; Keith 1928: 483; Ganeri 2003: 414–19).

See also: **Buddhism, relationship with Hinduism; Gotra; Nyāyasūtras; Patañjali; Sūtra**

DERMOT KILLINGLEY

Further reading

Dasgupta, Surendranath. 1922. *A History of Indian Philosophy*. Cambridge: Cambridge University Press.

Ganeri, Jonardon. 2003. 'Hinduism and the Proper Work of Reason'. In Gavin Flood, ed., *The Blackwell Companion to Hinduism*. Oxford: Blackwell, 411–46.

Keith, Arthur Berriedale. 1928. *A History of Sanskrit Literature*. London: Oxford University Press.

VĀYU

'Wind'. The Vedic wind-god – originally signifying more the tempest, cyclone or dust-storm, in contrast to Indra as the breeze or rain-bearing storm. Vāyu's asuric qualities are not immediately apparent in the *Ṛgveda*. His rivalry with Indra is nevertheless detectable. He receives Varuṇa's epithet 'thousand-eyed', is identified as Varuṇa's breath (*Ṛgveda* 7.87.2) and, along with Mitra and Varuṇa, is capable of anger (7.62.4). He is also named as Tvaṣṭṛ's son-in-law (8.26.21f.). The chief metaphors for the asura concept were the volcano, drought and destructive wind 'invisible but for [its] sweep' (1.164.44, cf. 10.168.4). Eventually, Vāyu becomes the ruler of the north-west.

See also: **Asura; Indra; Mitra; Varuṇa; Vedic pantheon; Vedism**

MICHAEL YORK

VEDA

The Sanskrit word 'veda' means 'knowledge'. 'The Veda', or 'the Vedas', are a body of sacred texts. However, the boundaries of this body are uncertain, and sometimes the word refers to all sacred knowledge. Sometimes 'the Veda' is spoken of in the singular, but sometimes it is called 'the three Vedas' or 'the four Vedas', and some texts are called 'the fifth Veda'. The Veda have always been transmitted and preserved orally, by generations of pupils repeating them exactly as they have heard them from their teachers, without the use of writing. Many Hindus believe the Veda is eternal, but historians usually date the origin of the texts to around the last two millennia BCE (Witzel 2003: 68).

The term 'Vedic', meaning 'belonging to the Veda', was formed by Western scholars; the Sanskrit word is vaidika (often contrasted with laukika, 'worldly', demarcating two spheres of knowledge). 'Vedic Sanskrit' means the language of the Veda, which differs in vocabulary and grammar from the language of most Sanskrit texts; from the point of view of historical linguistics, it is an older form of Sanskrit. 'Vedic ritual' means the yajñas and other rituals referred to or described in the Veda, which differ greatly from most of the rituals practised by Hindus today. In history, the 'Vedic period' is roughly from 1500 BCE to 500 BCE.

To speak of sacred texts implies that there is a group of people for whom those texts are sacred (W.C. Smith 1993: 17f.). Since any attempt to define or identify Hindus as a group presents problems, it is not surprising that it is difficult to define or identify the Veda as a body of texts; different texts can be called Veda by different Hindus.

The word Veda

While the word veda etymologically means 'knowledge', it usually refers to knowledge that transcends the ordinary and gives power to the knower. It also belongs to a culture in which knowledge is contained in the individual's memory, often received from those who already possess it – typically elders – rather than being constantly accumulated by observation, experiment and computation, and deposited in books or databases, as in modern culture.

Besides what is usually referred to as the Veda, there are subsidiary Vedas such as Āyur-veda (medicine), Dhanur-veda (archery), Gāndharva-veda (music) and Sthāpatya-veda (architecture). Those who learn these sciences are equipped to practise their professions, in the same way as those who learn the Veda in the more usual sense are equipped to perform rituals. But knowledge of the Veda is not merely performative; it is a supranormal power in itself. The recitation of the Veda from memory, outside the ritual context, yields not only wisdom, brāhmaṇa status, proper behaviour, fame and prestige, but health and peaceful sleep; it can even confer the benefits of the ritual, without performing it (*Śatapatha Brāhmaṇa* 11.5.7.1–3; Eggeling 1882–1900, 5: 99f.).

The Vedic texts are often called śruti, literally 'hearing; what is heard'. This recalls the fact that they are received orally from a teacher, by the teacher from his teacher and so on. While to many modern literary theorists (and to users of mobile phones) the word text implies the use of writing, in this context it refers to a spoken sequence of words recorded in human memories. But how did this process of repeated speaking and hearing begin, or is it beginningless? The Vedic hymns themselves mention poets, called kavis or ṛṣis, who originated the hymns, describing them as endowed with supranormal insight, dhī (Gonda 1963). On the other hand, a well-known verse describes the hymns as having sprung from the primordial sacrifice performed by the gods (*Ṛgveda* 10.90.9). In later literature the

Veda is considered to be eternal and without any personal author; it was breathed out by the original being (*Bṛhad āraṇyaka Upaniṣad* 4.5.11; Roebuck 2003: 78). According to this view, the ṛṣis did not compose the hymns but saw or heard them by supranormal perception and passed them on to their pupils. Pūrva Mīmāmsā and Vedānta hold that the Vedas are without a personal author. Nyāya, however, holds that Īśvara is their author.

The word brahman, among its many senses, can also mean the Veda. The Veda is a manifestation in sound of the eternal Brahman, and it is knowledge of the Veda which makes a brāhmaṇa a true brāhmaṇā, since without such knowledge he would lack the power called brahman.

The concept of Veda is inextricably linked with Hindu notions of hierarchy. In the hierarchy of textual authorities, the Veda or śruti ranks above texts such as the *Mahābhārata*, the *Purāṇas* and the *Dharmaśāstras*; these are to be consulted in cases where the Veda does not give an answer. These texts are not śruti but smṛti, meaning 'memory'; they are not considered eternal, but derive their authority from their authors' knowledge of the eternal and authorless Veda. Rituals based on the Veda are called śrauta, meaning 'belonging to śruti'. They are more elaborate than those based on smṛti texts, which are called smārta; they require three fires and a team of specialist priests, whereas smārta rituals can performed by one brāhmaṇa at a single fire. In the hierarchy of varṇa, the brāhmaṇa ranks highest because he embodies and speaks the Veda.

Because it ranks high, the Veda is also rare. It is only accessible to those who have learnt it, it can only be learnt by members of the three upper varṇas who have been initiated with the sacred thread (upanayana) and it can only be taught by brāhmaṇas. In practice it is restricted to male brāhmaṇas, although the Veda itself indicates that in ancient times women could learn it. Even those who are entitled to learn it rarely do so. Although manuscripts have existed for centuries, and Vedic texts are now available in printed editions and even on the Web, the writing of the Veda is traditionally condemned. 'Those who sell the Veda, those who harm the Veda, and those who write the Veda, go to hell' (*Mahābhārata* 13, 24, 70). Similarly, the Vedic rituals are rarely performed, though they are used as a standard by which other rituals can be valued. The Veda is like gold bullion, which is too precious to circulate but serves as a measure and guarantee of the worth of what is current.

The structure of Vedic literature

Considered as a body of texts, the Veda is organised in a two-dimensional structure, as shown in Table 4. The structure reflects the Veda's ancient function of enabling each of the specialist priests who performed the Vedic ritual to learn his role. Each of the first three main columns in Table 4, separated by double lines, represents a particular kind of priest and the Veda that he learnt. The hotṛ, who recited hymns to the gods and also poured the offerings in the fire, had to know the hymns of the *Ṛgveda*. (The word 'hymn', the conventional translation of Sanskrit sūkta, may misleadingly suggest congregational singing; but these 'hymns' are recited by a single priest.) The udgātṛ was a singer; his repertory, the *Sāmaveda*, consists of hymns with tunes (sāman). The third type of priest, the adhvaryu, laid out the sacrificial ground and directed the ritual movements and operations such as preparing offerings. He had a speaking role as well, mainly short sentences in prose, but including some verses. Each of these short utterances is called a yajuṣ, so his repertory is the *Yajurveda*.

The *Ṛgveda*, the *Sāmaveda* and the *Yajurveda* are together known as the three

Table 4 The Structure of Vedic literature

Type of literature	**Ṛgveda** role of hotṛ (who invokes gods and pours offerings)	**Sāmaveda** role of udgātṛ (singer)	**Yajurveda** role of adhvaryu (director of movements)		**Atharvaveda** role of atharvans and aṅgirases (performing rituals for personal ends)
			Black Yajurveda	**White Yajurveda**	
Saṃhitā, containing *mantras* (material spoken or sung in the ritual) 1500–1000 BCE?	*Ṛgveda Saṃhitā*	*Sāmaveda Saṃhitā* (hymns, 95% from *Ṛgveda*, with tunes)	*Taittiīrya Saṃhitā*, *Kāhaka Saṃhitā*, *Maitrāyaṇīya Saṃhitā* (hymns and prose sentences, interspersed with *brāhmaṇa* material)	*Vājasaneyī Saṃhitā* (hymns and prose sentences) in Mādhyadina and Kāva recensions	*Atharvaveda Saṃhitā* (20% from *Ṛgveda*; some prose)
Brāhmaṇa (prose commentary on ritual) 1000–1700 BCE?	*Aitareya Brāhmaṇa* *Kauṣītaki Brāhmaṇa*	*Jaiminīya Brāhmaṇa* or *Talavakāra Brāhmaṇa* *Pañcaviṃṣa Brāhmaṇa*	*Brāhmaṇa* material included in *saṃhitā*; also *Taittirīya Brāhmaṇa*	*Śatapatha* ('100 paths') *Brāhmaṇa*	*Gopatha Brāhmaṇa*
Āraṇyaka ('of the forest') 800–600 BCE?	*Aitareya Araṇyaka* *Śākhāyana Āraṇyaka*		*Taittirīya Āraṇyaka*	*Bṛhad-Āraṇyaka* (= *Śatapatha Br* 14, 1–3)	
early prose *Upaniṣads* 600–500 BCE?	*Aitareya Upaniṣad* *Kauṣītaki Upaniṣad*	*Chāndogya Upaniṣad* *Jaiminīya Upaniṣad Brāhmaṇa* *Kena Upaniṣad* or *Talavakāra Upaniṣad* (part prose, part verse)	*Taittirīya Upaniṣad* Parts of *Maitri Upaniṣad*	*Bṛhad-Āraṇyaka Upaniṣad* (= *Śatapatha Br* 14, 4–6)	
verse *Upaniṣads* 500–300 BCE?			*Kaṭha Upaniṣad* (beginning in prose, but mostly verse) *Mahā-nārāyaa Upaniṣad Śvetāśvatara Upaniṣad*	*Iśā Upaniṣad*	*Muṇḍaka Upaniṣad*
later prose *Upaniṣads* 200 BCE–100 CE?			Parts of *Maitri Upaniṣad*		*Praśna Upaniṣad* *Māṇḍūkya Upaniṣad*

Note: The vertical axis gives a very rough representation of time, and the dates are only impressions. Texts listed highest in the table are those likely to be earliest; thus the *Saṃhitās* of the *Sāmaveda* were probably compiled later than the *Ṛgveda Saṃhitā*. But this should not be taken to mean that every *Brāhmaṇa*, for instance, was composed before any *Āraṇyaka* or *Upaniṣad*; the horizontal lines are structural rather than chronological.

Vedas or triple Veda. The last column, separated by a heavy line, represents a fourth Veda, the *Atharvaveda*, which is the repertory of a class of priests known as the atharvans and aṅgirases. They specialised in rituals for personal ends such as cures, curses, love-charms or acquisition of specific powers, which were separate from the ritual performed by the other three classes of priest. However, they sometimes claimed superiority over the other three, and joined them as an overseer and trouble-shooter (known as a brahman), who did not have a specific role but supervised the whole ritual, silently performing expiations to remove the potentially disastrous effects of any error or accident (Gonda 1975: 269). The general term for a verse or prose sentence uttered in the ritual is mantra; it can also refer to a non-Vedic ritual utterance. Each of the four collections of mantras is called a *saṃhitā.* They are traditionally named in the order *Ṛgveda Saṃhitā*, *Yajurveda Saṃhitā*, *Sāmaveda Saṃhitā*, *Atharvaveda Saṃhitā*. They can also be referred to simply as the *Ṛgveda*, *Yajurveda*, *Sāmaveda* and *Atharvaveda*.

The Veda is sometimes said to consist of three Vedas and sometimes four, excluding or including the *Atharvaveda*. But it is also spoken of in the singular. According to the *Bhāgavata Purāṇa* (1.4.14–24; Sanyal 1973, 1: 13f.), it was just before the beginning of the third yuga that the sage Vyāsa divided the original single Veda into four, entrusting each of the four Vedas to a ṛṣi and organising the system of transmission from teacher to pupil, to protect it in the approaching age of confusion and ignorance. This myth, like many others, sees a decline from a primordial perfect unity to the imperfect plurality found in our world (Killingley 2004: 270–73; 276).

Besides the mantras, the Vedas include further material, mainly in prose, which is not uttered as part of the ritual, but discusses it. This material is contained in the *Brāhmaṇas*, *Āraṇyakas* and *Upaniṣads.* The boundaries between these three are not hard and fast: the titles of the *Bṛhad* ('great') *Āraṇyaka Upaniṣad* (which is part of the *Śatapatha Brāhmaṇa*) and the *Jaiminīya Upaniṣad Brāhmaṇa* (which includes the *Kena Upaniṣad*) place them in two categories. The *Īśā Upaniṣad* is included among the mantras, in the *Vājasaneyi Saṃhitā*.

Turning Table 4 upside down, we can think of the *saṃhitās* and the mantras they contain as the bottom layer of the structure. The *Brāhmaṇas* were built on them, since they represent teaching given to those who already knew the mantras, and therefore must have been composed later (as indicated also by their language). The *Āraṇyakas*, where they exist as a separate category, are built on the *Brāhmaṇas* in the sense that they represent a further development in the history of ideas. The *Upaniṣads* are yet another layer; or rather they are several layers, since their language, literary form and ideas, particularly in relation to ritual, provide some clues as to their chronological order. In the table they are divided into three layers, though this division leaves many uncertainties, and some passages in the same *Upaniṣad* may belong to different layers. We should also allow for overlap between the layers, and remember that we have no way of dating them, though it is generally agreed that the early prose *Upaniṣads* were in existence before the time of the Buddha (itself uncertain, but around the fifth or fourth century BCE).

Besides the mantras, *Brāhmaṇas*, *Araṇyakas* and *Upaniṣads*, each of the four Vedas has its sūtras. These are instructions on how to perform the rituals, in the form of brief rules, often so brief that they make little sense without a commentary. They are divided into *Śrautasūtras*, dealing with the main Vedic ritual, performed by a team of priests with three (and sometimes more) fires, *Gṛhyasūtras* dealing with the domestic rituals which may be performed by the male householder with a single fire, and *Dharmasūtras*, which are the earliest systematic literature of dharma. The sūtras are sometimes counted as part of the Veda and sometimes not.

The open canon

We have called the Veda a body of texts, but we have also seen that it is not always certain which texts are comprised in this body. Frequent references to the 'three Vedas', both in the Veda itself and in other ancient literature, show that the *Atharvaveda* was not always included. The sūtras, as we have just seen, raise a similar question about the boundaries of the collection. Further, the list of *Upaniṣads* is not fixed; 108 is a traditional number, but lists of 108 *Upaniṣads* vary. *Upaniṣads* continued to be composed well into the second millennium BCE; many of the later *Upaniṣads* are ascribed to the *Atharvaveda*. Even among the *Saṃhitās*, there are or have been several *Saṃhitās* of each Veda, and there are collections of additional hymns outside the *Ṛgveda Saṃhitā* (Gonda 1975: 35–7). The notion of a canon, therefore, in the sense of a list or body of texts which includes all those considered sacred and authoritative and excludes those which are not, is hardly applicable to the Veda. Yet the term 'Vedic canon', and the notion of the Veda as a set of canonical texts, is fairly common in modern writing on Indian religion. If we are to use the term, we have to understand it in a special way (cf. Patton 1993).

The authority of the Veda is inextricably linked to the authority of the brāhmaṇas who preserve and recite it, and to the power of Vedic ritual. We can think of the Veda as the repertory of a class of performers. The validity of the performance depends on the correct utterance of the words, while the prestige and sanctity of the performers depend on their mastery of the words and also of the other parts of the performance; at the same time, the authority of the words depends on their use in the performance and on the authority of those who utter them.

While Vedic texts have been printed since the nineteenth century, there has never been a single edition of the whole, and such an edition appears unlikely; it is hard to see what texts would appear in it, and in what order. Although the Veda can be spoken of in the singular (in Sanskrit as well as in English), when we consider it as a body of texts we find that it is not one body but three, or four (or more if we count the different *Saṃhitās*), each containing mantras, *Brāhmaṇas*, *Araṇyakas*, *Upaniṣads* – of uncertain number – and perhaps also sūtras. This is because the Vedic texts were transmitted orally long before they were committed to print or even to writing, and their organisation reflects the numerous successions of reciters who transmitted them.

When post-Vedic writers cite Vedic texts as their authorities, they do not range over the whole Veda as described above. Pūrva Mīmāṃsa texts quote injunctions from the *Brāhmaṇas*; Vedānta texts quote the *Upaniṣads*. Though the *Dharmaśāstra* makes a general claim to the authority of the Veda, it is only the earliest texts, the *Dharmasūtras*, that actually quote it (Renou 1965: 8). When post-Vedic writers do use quotations, they may introduce them with expressions such as 'the Vājasaneyins recite in their saṃhitā', or 'the Atharvans recite', indicating a text that exists within a specific oral tradition, rather than in a book. Other forms of citation are 'it is heard in the Vājasaneya [i.e. the White Yajurveda]', or more simply 'it is said' or 'it is heard' (śrūyate), or the related term śruti.

But often the Veda is mentioned as an authority without any attempt at a specific citation. Thus Manu asserts that the Veda is the ultimate source of dharma

(*Manusmṛti* 2. 6–15; Olivelle 2005: 95). Even when he concludes this passage with an example, he does not cite chapter and verse, or give any indication that he has any particular Vedic text in mind. When the Veda is said to be the source of dharma the word can refer to all knowledge, rather than to specific texts (Lingat 1973: 8). This rests on the belief that the Veda contains all knowledge, even if a specific point cannot be traced in the texts we now have. For it is traditionally believed that the Veda that exists today is only a fraction of the eternal Veda. This idea is expressed mythologically in a *Brāhmaṇa*. Indra showed three mountainous heaps to the ṛṣi Bharadvāja, and from each he gave him a handful, saying that these were the Vedas (Deshpande 1993: 53, citing *Taittirīya Brāhmaṇa* 3. 10. 11. 4). Thus a practice may have Vedic authority even if it is not mentioned in the available texts. Acceptance of the authority of the Veda is sometimes used as a criterion for defining Hinduism (B.K. Smith 1989: 13f.). But this does not mean that the Vedic texts are necessarily used as authorities; rather, to claim that something is stated in the Veda is a way of asserting that it is true. For instance, Sir William Jones was told by paṇḍits that the practice of throwing an image of Durgā in the river 'was prescribed by the *Veda*, they knew not why' (Marshall 1970: 226). Paradoxically, the Veda is a canon, but it is an open canon.

The word veda is not unique in referring both to a more or less clearly bounded body of texts and to the truth which those texts are believed to contain; the same is true of the Jewish term Torah and the Christian term Gospel. But sometimes particular texts can be called Vedic on the grounds that they contain truth. Thus the International Society for Krishna Consciousness publication *Readings in Vedic Literature* contains only one text that is listed above as part of the Veda, the *Īśā Upaniṣad*; the other two texts are the *Bhagavadgītā* and an abridgment of the *Bhāgavata Purāṇa*. The editor explains that a text may be accepted as Vedic if it contains the doctrine of the Veda, 'even if the work is not one of the original scriptures' (Goswami 1977: 1). The word veda is used in the titles of some Christian texts, especially in South India (Halbfass 1988: 340). One example reached eighteenth-century Europe before the Veda itself, in a French version under the title *Ezourvedam*, probably meaning 'Veda of Jesus' (Rocher 1984).

The fifth veda

Another way in which the meaning of the word veda is extended beyond the texts described above is to call a particular text the fifth veda. This term is often applied to the *Mahābhārata* or the *Purāṇas*, or to both. It is also applied to the tradition of domestic rituals transmitted by women (Stevenson 1920: xiii), reinforcing the idea that the four Vedas are the preserve of men. Similarly, the collection of Tamil Vaiṣṇava bhakti poems, the *Divya-prabandha*, is called the Tamil Veda, especially the *Tiruvāymoḻi*, the collection of Nammāḻvār. However, the phrase 'fifth Veda' implies that there are only four Vedas in the usual sense of the term, in the same way that the phrase 'sixth sense' gains its meaning from the existence of a standard list of five senses. The currency of the phrase serves to preserve the idea of four Vedas, just as the currency of the *Mahābhārata* itself is said to preserve those four Vedas from profanation.

Oral transmission

Even when the Veda came to be written, this was considered greatly inferior to oral transmission. The Vedic texts speak of recitation, not reading; the practice of reading the Veda is first mentioned in texts which condemn it. Unlike many oral traditions, however, the oral transmission of the Veda ensured that text remained unchanged through centuries, as is shown in the exact correspondence between different reciters, the manuscripts of the Veda and the Vedic quotations which occur in post-Vedic literature.

Not only are the *Saṃhitās* themselves recited, but a version called the padapāṭha ('word recitation') was composed, in which each word was pronounced separately to clarify its grammatical form. A sequence of words a b c would be pronounced a, b, c. Since the normal pronunciation of Sanskrit involves variations in the ends and sometimes the beginnings of words, depending on the following or preceding sound (a phenomenon found in other languages, notably French, and known to linguists by the Sanskrit word sandhi), this separation provided a starting-point for grammatical analysis and exegesis. Step-wise recitation (krama-pāṭha) combines the two modes so that the beginning and end of each word are pronounced both separately and in combination: a b, b c, c d, d e, ... Further elaborations of recitation involve turning the sequences backwards as well as forwards, as in the spiral recitation (jaṭā-pāṭha): a b, b a, a b, b c, c b, b c, c d, d c, c d, . . . (Gonda 1975: 17; Deshpande 2004: 512f). These methods provide a check on the stability of the text.

That a text should be preserved unchanged without the use of writing conflicts with the findings of literary historians and anthropologists about the nature of oral literature. A typical orally transmitted text such as a ballad or an epic exists as a multitude of performances, each of which is partly improvised and not an exact repetition of any previous performance. This accounts for the many recensions and countless variations of the *Mahābhārata*, for instance. Some theorists have doubted that the Veda could have been transmitted unchanged without the aid of writing, or at least without a written text on which oral recitation could be modelled. An anthropologist has argued that it is only in a literate society that the idea of a stable text can exist (Goody 1987).

The transmission of the Veda without the use of writing, like the building of the pyramids without machinery, appears incredible because it requires an outlay in human resources which is difficult to imagine. It also requires the task of memorising to be separated from the use of the texts in ritual. This is achieved by what is called self-study (svādhyāya), where the text is recited outside the ritual context, reinforcing as well as demonstrating the reciter's knowledge. This practice became a ritual itself, which like other rituals brought benefits to the performer: not only prestige but health, and other benefits that result from performing sacrifices (*Śatapatha Brāhmaṇa* 11.5.7; Eggeling 1882–1900: 5.99–101). However, the existence of variant versions of the same mantras in different Vedic schools (Bloomfield and Edgerton 1930–34) suggests that, at a time when these texts were not yet decontextualised and fixed, they were transmitted orally from one performer to another, and changed in subsequent performances, in a manner typical of oral literature. There is also a practice called ūha, adapting a mantra to a context by changing 'I' to 'we', 'he' to 'she' and so on.

Vedic ritual

The ritual for which the Veda was learnt is very different from what is practised by Hindus today, except where Vedic rituals have been kept up in attenuated forms by certain families of brāhmaṇas, or where they have been revived in recent times. There is no mention of images or of temples. The Vedic yajña (often translated 'sacrifice', but this should not be understood as necessarily involving the killing of animals) was performed on a piece of ground prepared for the occasion, centred on the vedi, not in a permanent sacred place.

Most of the deities worshipped are of little importance today: Indra, the twin Aśvins or Nāsatyas, Varuṇa. Goddesses, such as Uṣas, are few. Śiva is known by his older name Rudra, but only three hymns in the *Ṛgveda* address him alone. Viṣṇu has only five hymns in the *Ṛgveda*; his importance is far more apparent in the *Brāhmaṇas*, where he is identified with the yajña. Two deities are identified with essential elements of the ritual: Agni, fire, and Vāc, speech. A third ritual deity is Soma, the drink offered and consumed in certain more elaborate yajñas.

An important figure in the yajña is the yajamāna, normally a married twice-born man, who engages the specialists to perform it and receives most of its benefits. This term (known in English in its Hindi form jajmān) is still used for the clients of ritual specialists.

With the growth of image worship and pūjā, perhaps around the last century BCE, the elaboration of the mythology of Viṣṇu and Śiva, and the decline of interest in Indra and other Vedic deities, Vedic ritual and mythology became increasingly irrelevant and obscure, while the language, especially of the mantras, became increasingly archaic. The need for methods of interpretation is seen already in the *Brāhmaṇas* and sūtras, and in Yāska's *Nirukta* (Gopal 1983). Pūrva Mīmāṃsā and Vedānta developed their own hermeneutics. As we have seen, a concept of the Veda arose which was independent of the Vedic texts. The decline in Vedic knowledge and practice was understood in terms of the yugas: in earlier ages people were capable of understanding and following the Veda, but not in the Kali age. Various texts are said to restate the essence of the Veda for the Kali age, such as the *Bhāgavata Purūṇa* or the *Tantras*. The Vīraśāivas explicitly reject the Veda, and bhakti saints such as Tukārām and Kabīr despise reliance on it. The Veda as a textual source has declined (Renou 1965).

The Veda and modern thought

Renewed interest in the Veda from the nineteenth century onwards is closely bound up with Western scholarship (Gopal 1983: 141–67). During the eighteenth century the Veda was discussed in Europe without being known (Figueira 1993). Jones translated some selections, but Anquetil-Duperron's Latin version of the *Upaniṣads* (1801–02) was the first large sample of the Veda to become accessible. In 1805 Colebrooke published a detailed description of the Veda, but concluded that further research would be difficult and unrewarding. Rammohan Roy's English translations of four *Upaniṣads* (1816–19) awoke new interest by finding rational theism in the Veda (Killingley 1993); but in the Brahmo Samaj which he founded, Debendranath Tagore reluctantly abandoned the idea of Vedic authority, and Keshab Chandra Sen largely ignored it.

Müller's edition of the *Ṛgveda Saṃhitā* (1849–74) and his subsequent use of it in his other works, established it as the principal Vedic text for European scholars, not only because its antiquity made it especially valuable for the comparative study of the history of languages, but also because he and other German Romantics saw it as an ancestral document of their own people, and as relatively free from the priestly influence which in their view marred other Vedic texts. Among Hindus this changed the perspective in which the Veda was seen, by focusing on the oldest texts and drawing attention away from those which were more clearly ritual in character; the *Brāhmaṇas* were often regarded as degenerate and unspiritual. Historical and comparative methods of study and Protestant emphasis on textual authority and primitive authenticity combined to corroborate this perspective. Its effects are seen most clearly in Dayananda Saraswati, who made the mantras his authority, subordinating the *Brāhmaṇas* and *Upaniṣads* to them.

As part of the change in perspective, the Veda came to be seen as a historical source – a use expressly rejected by Pūrva Mīmāṃsā The historical perspective undermined the traditional idea of Vedic authority, but it returned in a new form. The *Ṛgveda Saṃhitā* in particular became a record of the religious experience of the ancient Āryans, for writers as diverse as R.G. Bhandarkar, Vivekananda, Rabindranath Tagore and Nirad C. Chaudhuri. B.G. Tilak used astronomical evidence to date it to 4000 BCE or even earlier. Esoteric interpretations of the Vedic hymns were made by Coomaraswamy, Aurobindo Ghose and V.S. Agrawala (Gopal 1983: 164f.). Raimundo Panikkar (1977) translated and interpreted a wide range of Vedic texts from a Christian existentialist viewpoint.

See also: **Agni; Anquetil-Duperron, Abraham-Hyacinthe; Aśvins; Āyurveda; Bhagavadgītā; Bhakti; Bhandarkar, Ramkrishna Gopal; Brahman; Brāhmaṇa; Brāhmaṇas; Brahmo Samaj; Buddhism, relationship with Hinduism; Chaudhuri, Nirad C.; Colebrooke, Henry Thomas; Coomaraswamy, Ananda Kentish; Dayananda Saraswati, Swami; Dhanurveda; Dharma; Dharmaśāstras; Dharmasūtras; Durgā; Dvija; Gāndharvaveda; Ghose, Sri Aurobindo; Gṛhyasūtras; Hindu; Hinduism, history of scholarship; Image worship; Indra; International Society for Krishna Consciousness; Īśvara; Jones, Sir William; Kabīr; Languages; Mahābhārata; Mantra; Manu; Müller, Friedrich Max; Nammāḻvār; Nyāya; Paṇḍit; Pūjā; Purāṇas; Pūrva Mīmāmsā; Roy, Rammohan; Ṛṣi; Rudra; Sacred texts; Saṃhitā; Sen, Keshab Chandra; Śiva; Smārta; Soma; Śrautasūtras; Sthāpatyaveda; Tagore, Debendranath; Tagore, Rabindranath; Tamil Veda; Tantras; Tilak, Bal Gangadhar; Uṣas; Upanayana; Upaniṣads; Vaiṣṇavism; Varṇa; Varuṇa; Vedānta; Vedi; Vīraśāivas; Viṣṇu; Vivekananda, Swami; Vyāsa; Yāska; Yajña; Yuga**

DERMOT KILLINGLEY

Further reading

Bloomfield, M. and F. Edgerton. 1930–34. *Vedic Variants*, 3 vols. Philadephia, PA: Linguistic Society of America.

Deshpande, Madhav M. 1993. *Sanskrit and Prakrit: Sociolinguistic Issues.* Delhi: Motilal Banarsidass.

Eggeling, Julius. 1882–1900. *The Çatapatha-Brâhmana According to the Text of the Mâdhyandina* School, 5 vols. Oxford: Clarendon Press. Reprinted Delhi: Motilal Banarsidass, 1963.

Figueira, Dorothy M. 1993. 'The Authority of an Absent Text: The Veda, Upangas, Upavedas and Upnekhata in European Thought'. In Laurie L. Patton, ed., *Authority, Anxiety and Canon: Essays in Vedic Interpretation.* Albany, NY: State University of New York Press, 201–33.

Gonda, Jan. 1963. *The Vision of the Vedic Poets.* The Hague: Mouton.

Gonda, Jan. 1975. *Vedic Literature.* Wiesbaden: Otto Harrassowitz.

Goody, Jack. 1987. *The Interface between the Written and the Oral.* Cambridge: Cambridge University Press.

Gopal, Ram. 1983. *The History and Principles of Vedic Interpretation.* Delhi: Concept Publishing Company.

Goswami, Satswarupadasa. 1977. *Readings in Vedic Literature: The Tradition Speaks for Itself.* Los Angeles, CA: Bhaktivedanta Book Trust.

Halbfass, W. 1988. *India and Europe.* Albany, NY: State University of New York Press.

Howard, Wayne. 1977. *Sāmavedic Chant.* New Haven, CT: Yale University Press.

Killingley, Dermot. 1993. *Rammohun Roy in Hindu and Christian Tradition.* Newcastle upon Tyne: Grevatt & Grevatt.

Killingley, Dermot. 2004. 'Kāma'. In Sushil Mittal and Gene Thursby, eds, *The Hindu World.* New York: Routledge, 264–87.

Lingat, Robert. 1973. *The Classical Law of India*. Trans. J. Duncan M. Derrett. Berkeley, CA: University of California Press.
Marshall, P.J. 1970. *The British Discovery of Hinduism in the Eighteenth Century.* Cambridge: Cambridge University Press.
Olivelle, Patrick. 2005. *Manu's Code of Law: A Critical Edition and Translation of the Mānavadharmaśāstra*. New York: Oxford University Press.
Panikkar, Raimundo. 1977. *The Vedic Experience: Mantrāmañjarī: An Anthology of the Vedas for Modern Man and Contemporary Celebration.* London: Darton, Longman and Todd.
Patton, Laurie L. (ed.). 1993. *Authority, Anxiety and Canon: Essays in Vedic Interpretation.* Albany, NY: State University of New York Press.
Renou, Louis. 1965. *The Destiny of the Veda in India.* Delhi: Motilal Banarsidass. (Trans. of *Le Destin du Véda dans l'Inde*, Paris: E. de Boccard, 1960.)
Rocher, Ludo. 1984. *Ezourvedam. A French Veda of the Eighteenth Century. Edited with an Introduction.* Amsterdam and Philadelphia: John Benjamins.
Roebuck, Valerie. 2003. *The Upanisads.* London: Penguin.
Sanyal, J.M. 1973. *The Srimad Bhagvatam of Krishna-Dwaipayana Vyasa*, 2nd edn, 2 vols. Delhi: Munshiram Manoharlal.
Smith, Brian K. 1989. *Reflections on Resemblance, Ritual and Religion.* New York: Oxford University Press.
Smith, W. Cantwell. 1993. *What Is Scripture?* Minneapolis, MN: Fortress Press.
Stevenson, Mrs [Margaret] Sinclair. 1920. *The Rites of the Twice-Born.* London: Oxford University Press.
Witzel, Michael. 2003. 'Vedas and Upaniṣads'. In G. Flood, ed., *The Blackwell Companion to Hinduism*. Oxford: Blackwell, 68–101.

VEDA SAMAJ

The organisation started by Keshab Chandra Sen in Madras after his visit in 1864 to promote the teachings of the Brahmo Samaj. The aims of the Veda Samaj were to gradually abandon caste distinctions, abstain from child marriage and polygamy, campaign for widow remarriage and to encourage the usage of vernacular languages whilst ensuring the study of Sanskrit in a manner that would be conducive to the eradication of superstition. However, the radical rejection of image worship upheld by the Brahmo Samaj was a step too far for the Hindus of Tamil Nadu, but they agreed that the Veda Samaj should promote the theistic ideals of the Brahmo Samaj as long as they remained securely within the boundaries of classical Hindu beliefs.

Around 1870, the South Indian brāhmaṇa Sridharalu Naidu arrived in Madras after studying with the Brahmo Samaj in Calcutta. He took over the leadership of the movement and established it throughout South India. However, Sridharalu Naidu had imbibed a more thorough version of the Brahmo Samaj ideals and was not prepared to compromise with South Indian Hindu sensibilities. Brahmo Samaj literature was translated into Tamil and Telagu, including the works of Debendranath Tagore and Keshab Chandra Sen. Along with the erudite and charismatic Tamil brāhmaṇa Doraiswami Iyengar, who travelled widely throughout Bangalore, Mangalore, Trichinopoly and Tanjore, Sridharalu Naidu established the Brahmo Samaj-style reform of Hinduism in South India. However, his uncompromising stance lost original followers of the movement, although new sympathisers were gained.

After the deaths of these two pioneers in 1874, the Veda Samaj went into decline until revived by Pandit Basanta Ram in 1879. The original movement begun by Keshab Chandra Sen, with its diluted version of the Brahmo Samaj ideals, continued in several cities of South India until it disappeared in 1868. It was revived in 1871 by S.P. Narasimalu, who changed the name to the Brahmo Samaj of South India.

See also: **Brahmo Samaj; Naidu, Sridharalu; Sen, Keshab Chandra; Tagore, Debendranath**

RON GEAVES

Further reading

Jones, Kenneth. 1989. *Socio-Religious Reform Movements in British India. The New Cambridge History of India*, vol. 3. Cambridge: Cambridge University Press.

VEDĀṄGAS

Literally, 'limbs of the Veda', the Vedāṅgas are the ancillary disciplines for the study and interpretation of the Veda. They are six in number and are remembered by a traditional verse: *Śikśā kalpo vyākaraṇaṃ niruktaṃ chando jyotiṣaṃ*. They represent the earliest Hindu systems of knowledge, emerging as they do out of Veda, which itself means, in essence, 'knowledge', and are as follows:

1 Śikśā: literally, 'instruction', but best defined here as 'phonology', it aids the correct pronunciation and singing of Vedic chants. It examines the pitch of the Vedic accents and their relationship to notions of scalar organisation. Each of the four Vedas had its śikśā, 'textbook', called *prātiśākhya*; perhaps the best-known śikśā text is *Nāradīyaśikśā*, dated to around the fifth century CE.
2 Kalpa: 'rule', pertains to the rituals and rubrics for Vedic ceremonies. Many of these are given in the *Brāhmaṇas*, the rubric-filled texts associated with each of the four Vedas.
3 Vyākaraṇa: grammar, according to the traditional Indian system. The most famous grammarian was Pāṇini, but by his time (around the sixth century BCE) Vedic Sanskrit had already given place to classical.
4 Nirukta: 'etymology', explanations of words through their traditional derivations, set out in what are known as nighantus ('dictionaries'). The best known is Yāska's *Nirukta*.
5 Chandas: 'metrics', the study of prosody and verse forms. There are five basic Vedic metres, composed of pādas ('feet') and syllables (see, e.g., *Gāyatrī Mantra*).
6 Jyotiṣa: astrology, the traditional Indian study of the stars and planets (navagrahas) and their influences, including the twenty-eight lunar mansions called nakṣatra. Vedic rituals need to be performed at the right astrological moment for both individual and societal purposes. (This is especially important for weddings.)

The Vedāṅgas were traditionally studied by vaidika brāhmaṇas – 'brahmans versed in the Veda' – brought up from a very early age to memorise the Vedic texts for ritual purposes. This enormous oral repertoire is underpinned by study of the Vedāṅgas, whose purpose is to ensure the perfectly correct recitation of the Veda, at the correct times, without which ritual would be flawed.

See also: **Brāhmaṇas; Chandas; Gāyatrī Mantra; Jyotiṣa; Kalpa; Languages; Music; Navagrahas; Nirukta; Pāṇini; Śikśā; Veda; Vivāha; Vyākaraṇa; Yāska**

JOHN R. MARR AND KATHLEEN TAYLOR

Further reading

Basham, A.L. 1985. *The Wonder that Was India*. London: Sidgwick & Jackson.
Keith, A.B. 1966. *A History of Sanskrit Literature*. London: Oxford University Press.

VEDĀNTA

The term Vedānta refers to the last portion of the Veda (Veda plus anta = end) that is the *Upaniṣads*. Uttara Mīmāṃsā means 'exegesis of the latter [part]' of the Vedas, latter to the Pūrva Mīmāṃsā, the primary exegesis of the Vedas. The terms Vedānta and Uttara Mīmāṃsā are used to designate several philosophical and theological developments over many centuries.

The best known among these is Advaita Vedānta (absolute monism) of Śaṅkara (eighth century CE). According to Śaṅkara there is nothing either real or non-real apart from Brahman. Thus the individual self (ātman) must be understood as identical with Brahman. Because of not knowing the truth we superimpose (adhyāsa) this busy world on the lucid Brahman. Our superimposition is an act of mistaking an unreal object for a real one: we superimpose silver on a piece of a glittering shard. Removing false objects projected onto the real can only be experienced in an altered state of consciousness. Such an experience grants freedom from the repeated cycle of lives.

Śaṅkara's Advaita was austere. Subsequent Vedānta thinkers added a theistic aspect. Bhāskara reinterpreted the *Brahmasūtra*: the individual self (ātman) is both different and non-different from God (Brahman). This view was called the doctrine of difference with no difference (bhedābhedavāda).

The *Brahmasūtra* became conflated with Vaiṣṇava theology. Rāmānuja (twelfth century AD) commented on the *Brahmasūtra* in his work *Śrībhāṣya*: everything is Brahman or God. The individual selves and the material world are also real. Rāmānuja's doctrine is called 'qualified monism' (viśiṣṭādvaitavāda), because Brahman was qualified by knowledge and was described as merciful, all powerful and all pervading. This Brahman is God Viṣṇu and should be venerated through constant devotion.

Other interpreters of the *Brahmasūtra* also presupposed devotion to God. They found absolute monism problematic; their response was modified monism. Nimbārka combined both dualism and non-dualism (dvaitādvaitavāda).

The extreme position against monism was taken by Madhva (not Mādhava), who propagated difference between Brahman and the individual selves (dvaitavāda). An opposite view was expressed by Vallabha in his doctrine of pure non-dualism (śudhādvaitavāda). Others, like Caitanya, focused mainly on devotion to God.

See also: **Advaita; Ātman; Bhedābheda; Brahman; Brahmasūtras; Dvaita; Madhva; Pūrva Mīmāṃsā; Rāmānuja; Śaṅkara; Upaniṣads; Veda; Vedānta; Viśiṣṭādvaita**

EDELTRAUD HARZER

Further reading

Deutsch, Eliot. 1973. *Advaita Vedānta*. Honolulu, HI: University Press of Hawaii.

Lipner, Julius. 1986. *The Face of Truth: A Study of Meaning and Metaphysics in the Vedantic Theology of Ramanuja*. New York: SUNY.

Mahadevan, T.M.P. 1977. *The Philosophy of Advaita*. Wiltshire: Compton Russell.

Nakamura, Hajime. 1985. *A History of Early Vedanta Philosophy*. Delhi: Motilal Banarsidass.

VEDANTA SOCIETIES

See: **Ramakrishna Math and Mission**

VEDĀNTASŪTRAS

See: **Brahmasūtras**

VEDĀRAMBHA

This education saṃskāra, or rite of passage – literally, 'commencement of Vedic study' – did not appear in the ritual literature until well into the first millennium CE. Its absence in the ancient sūtras and other Vedic prescriptive literature has limited its currency. According to the *Vyāsa-Smṛti* (second to fifth century CE), the vedārambha should be performed some time after the upanayana and before the samāvartana. The rite is quite simple: after determining an auspicious day, rites to goddesses and deceased ancestors (mātṛpūjā and ābhyudāyika-śrāddha) are performed. The teacher establishes a domestic fire altar, then sits with the student on the western side of the fire. Two offerings of ghee are made to the Earth (Pṛthivī) and Agni if the student proposes to learn the *Ṛgveda*, to the mid-region (antarikṣa) and Vāyu in the case of the *Yajurveda*, to the Heavens (Dyaus) and Sūrya in the case of the *Sāmaveda*, and to the four directions and the Moon in the case of the *Atharvaveda*. Fire offerings are then made to Brahman, Chandas and Prajāpati. Finally the teacher gives the sacrificial fee (dakṣiṇā) to the officiating priest, after which the teaching of the Veda may begin.

See also: **Agni; Brahman; Guru; Prajāpati; Pṛthivī; Samāvartana; Saṃhitā; Saṃskāra; Śrāddha; Sūrya; Sūtra; Upanayana; Vāyu; Veda**

FREDERICK M. SMITH

Further reading

Kane, P.V. 1974. *History of Dharmaśāstra*, 2nd edn, vol. 1, pt 1, 529–35 (on the *Vyāsa-Smṛti*). Poona: Bhandarkar Oriental Research Institute.

Pandey, R.J. 1969. *Hindu Saṃskāras*. Delhi: Motilal Banarsidass, 141–42.

VEDI

Sometimes mistranslated as 'altar', the vedi is the sunken area between the fires in the consecration ground of a Vedic ritual. The area, strewn with grass, was where the gods were invited to sit as guests, while priests sang hymns and made offerings in their honour. Additionally, implements and offering ingredients were placed on the vedi before they were used. The word 'vedi' is feminine and is often homologised with masculine words in the Brahmanical ritual literature. The feminine dimension of the vedi is further highlighted by the fact that its hourglass shape is often compared to a woman with a slender waist. The vedi, plus the householder's fire (gārhapatya) and the offering fire (āhavanīya), comprised the central axis of the sacrificial ground, with the southern fire (dakṣiṇāgni) below. Each fire had its own altar, each with a unique shape: the gārhapatya round; the āhavanīya square; and the dakiṣināgni half-mooned shaped.

See also: **Yajña**

BRIAN BLACK

Further reading

Jamison, Stephanie. 1996. *Sacrificed Wife: Sacrificer's Wife*. New York: Oxford University Press.

Jamison, Stephanie. 1991. *The Ravenous Hyenas and the Wounded Sun: Myth and Ritual in Ancient India*. Ithaca, NY: Cornell University Press.

Staal, Fritz. 1983. *Agni: The Vedic Ritual of the Fire Altar*. Berkeley, CA: Asian Humanities Press.

VEDIC PANTHEON

The gods of the Vedic peoples of India whose sacred writings (the *Ṛgveda*, *Yajurveda*, *Samaveda* and *Atharvaveda*) constitute the oldest texts of Hinduism. The Vedic pantheon itself is primarily an expression of nature worship: its chief deities embody various natural phenomena, and the religion involving them is essentially this-worldly – responding to the worshippers' needs and desires for protection, health, wealth, progeny, victory and success. The most archaic stratum of the Vedic tradition reveals a materialistic, non-otherworldly bias that stems from and reflects the mundane spirituality of the Indo-European peoples among whom the Vedic tribes, along with the Iranians, Greeks, Italics (Romans), Celts, Germanics, Balts, Slavs and others, are numbered. Whilst the Indo-European spiritual understanding, as it can be recovered or reconstructed, comprehends a dynamic otherworld of enchantment, it is centred on this-worldly desires as the *summum bonum* of life – both desire in general and the specific ideals of material wealth (artha) and sexual pleasure (kāma). Consequently, the gods of the derivative Vedic pantheon are essentially the embodiments of values or basic desires already fulfilled. In this context, magical ritual that was focused on them primarily concerned the viability and security of the production techniques of the community itself.

The Vedic hymns tended to personify everything: both the immanent sacred forces of the natural world (the devas) and the operative counter-forces of chaos, sterility and annihilation (the asuras). The former were worshipped as gods (Dyaus, 'brightness'; Pṛthivī, 'earth'; Uṣas, 'dawn'; Indra, the rain-god; Agni, 'fire'; Sūrya, 'sun'; and Soma, 'moon' or the food of the gods); the feared latter were placated and treated *as if* they were gods and given apotropaic euphemisms (e.g. Mitra, 'friend'; Aryaman, 'comrade'; Bhaga, 'fortune'; Dakṣa, 'cleverness'; Amṣa, 'apportioner'). The asurian nature is chiefly understood in Vedic thought in the figures of the ādityas (of whom Varuṇa is chief), the drought-dragon Vṛtra, the demiurge Tvaṣṭṛ and the (destructive) 'wind' Vāyu. However, because the divine–asurian dichotomy was either incipient or not fully developed in either Indo-European or Vedic consciousness, and because of the Vedic use of placatory ritual, an inevitable conflation and confusion of divine and asurian prototypes occurs throughout the Vedic pantheon as it is found in the *Ṛgveda* and subsequent Sanskrit literature. But as Indra continues to ascend over Varuṇa in the *Ṛg*, the asuras become increasingly explicitly recognised as the enemies of the devas in the last period of Ṛgvedic hymns, in the *Atharvaveda* and eventually in historic Hinduism. But even in the Vedic period itself, unlike the devas, who express features and forces of nature, in general the metonymies used for the Asuras-ādityas are abstractions – without viable bases in natural phenomena and representing personifications of the cosmic void.

If the confusing ambiguity in distinguishing between gods and anti-gods represents a loss to the original awareness of materialistic and earth-oriented spirituality among Vedic peoples, another counter-trend that had seminal consequences is the idealistic speculations of Indian philosophy that begin to emerge in the late portions of the *Ṛgveda* and in subsequent Brahmanic thought. It could be argued that the development of a new breed of abstract and pantheistic deities (Prajāpati, Viśvakarman, Hiraṇyagarbha, Kāla ('time'), Skambha ('support'), Prāṇa ('breath') and Kāma ('desire')) reflect a thought-shift away from the material that might parallel a renunciatory ascetic ethic. Along with these creator-gods and/or identities of the eternal power of the universe, the personification of the divine brāhmaṇa priest, Bṛhaspati/Brāhmaṇaspati, is the prototype of Brahmā, the chief of the Hindu triad. By contrast, the neuter form of the same word, developed into the Absolute of Vedānta philosophy (Brahman). Whilst Brahman and the other speculative deities were never gods of the people, the Brāhmaṇic and Vedāntic developments reflect the growing hegemony of priestly thought (with its corollary of elaborate ritualisation) and the eventual eclipse of the original Vedic pantheon as an expression of life-affirmation, this-worldly orientation and naturalistic spirituality.

See also: **Agni; Artha; Aryaman; Asuras; Brahmā; Brahman; Bṛhaspati; Deities; Dyaus Pitṛ; Hiraṇyagarbha; Kāma; Mitra; Prajāpati; Pṛthivī; Soma; Sūrya; Tvaṣṭṛ; Uṣas; Varuṇa; Vāyu; Vedānta; Viśvakarman**

MICHAEL YORK

Further reading

Chattopadhya, Debprasad. 1973. *Lokāyata: A Study in Ancient Indian Materialism*, 3rd edn. New Delhi: People's Publishing House/ Tarun Sengupta. First published 1959.
Macdonell, A.A. 1974. *Vedic Mythology*. Reprint. Strasburg and Delhi: Motilal Banarsidass.
York, Michael. 1995. *The Divine Versus the Asurian: An Interpretation of Indo-European Cult and Myth*. Bethesda, MD: International Scholars Press.

VEDIC SCIENCES

See: **Vedāṅgas**

VEDISM

Vedism is a term used by scholars of religion to describe the beliefs and practices represented in the Vedas. Similar to Brahmanism, Vedism is a scholarly construct, useful in describing the main ideas articulated by particular ancient Indian texts, yet not to be taken as representing a distinct religion in the social reality of ancient India. Despite the prevalence of the term in secondary literature, various scholars have tended to define 'Vedism' differently. Monier Williams (1883), for example, used the term to refer specifically to those religious beliefs and practices represented by the hymns or *Saṃhitās*, the first strand of Vedic literature. More recently, Brian Smith (1989) has argued for a rethinking of 'Vedism' in terms of the principles of hierarchical resemblances that feature prominently in the Brāhmaṇas. The following entry follows Smith's construction of the term, thus differentiating Vedism, as that which is closely associated to the ritualism of the Vedas, from Brahmanism, which accepts the authority of the Vedas but finds its unique expression in non-Vedic texts like the *Dharmasūtras*, *Dharmaśāstras*, *Rāmāyaṇa* and *Mahābhārata*.

There are four Vedas (Ṛg, Sāma, Yajur and Atharva), each of which consists of four strands of literature: the *Saṃhitās*, *Brāhmaṇas*, *Āraṇyakas* and *Upaniṣads*. Most scholars agree that these texts probably were composed over a period of about one thousand years, roughly from 1200 to 300 BCE (Flood 1996). They contain a vast selection of material, including hymns, myths, legends, ritual instructions and philosophical speculations. It is important to keep in mind that there is not a single, unified theological or ideological perspective. Nevertheless, there are a number of recurring, interrelated ideas that are central to what we may consider the main tenets of Vedism, the most fundamental of which is ritual (yajña). Featuring mantras to be chanted during the ritual, myths explaining the origin of ritual, detailed instructions for how to perform all the major large-scale rituals and dialogues that criticise ritual, almost all Vedic texts assume a ritual context in one way or another.

The most prevailing mythological explanation of the Vedic ritual centres around the figure of Puruṣa, the cosmic man. According to this myth, which appears for the first time in the Puruṣa Sukta hymn in the *Ṛgveda* (10.90), the universe began with a sacrifice in which the body of Puruṣa was dissected and the elements of his body were reassembled to create an ordered universe. These themes of creation, dismemberment and re-creation continue throughout the *Brāhmaṇas*, where the mythology of Puruṣa becomes extended to Prajāpati.

Similar to Puruṣa, Prajāpati, whose name literally means lord of creatures, creates the world from his own corporality. Despite being the creator god, Prajāpati's creation is considered imperfect. The creatures that he creates are incomplete in one way or another: they lack breath, do not have enough food, do not have a name or are without shape. Furthermore, Prajāpati himself expends all his creative energy during the process of creation and is left completely exhausted. Similar to creation in the Puruṣa Sūkta, Prajāpati's creation is imagined in terms of restoring and reordering rather than making something from nothing. Within this mythological context, the Vedic sacrifice has its particular function, which is to complete the creation process and to restore energy to Prajāpati. Throughout this mythology not only is the universe made from a primordial male body, but it also shares with both Puruṣa and Prajāpati the same fundamental structure, thus pointing to a correspondence between microcosm and macrocosm. In this mythological scheme, what is natural is flawed and incomplete, but cultural practices like the Vedic ritual complete creation by giving things meaning by classifying and ordering all the distinct entities that comprise the cosmos.

The ritual texts claim to establish order by means of identifying the underlying connections that exist among different orders of reality. Often these connections were made among three spheres of reality: the cosmos, the body of the sponsor of the ritual (yajamāna) and the ritual sphere; in other words, between the macrocosm, the microcosm and the ritual. 'Bandhu', which literally means to be 'bonded' or 'related', is the word used throughout the ritual texts for these connections. Bandhus link up entities that exist within the cosmos, as well as connect individual entities to the transcendent. According to the Vedic literature, to be connected means that either one thing is a counterpart of the other or that two things are equated with each other. In other words, bandhus operate both vertically and horizontally.

The vertical scheme of bandhus is first articulated in the Puruṣa Sukta hymn where the four social classes (varṇa) are listed in relation to the body of Puruṣa. The hymn associates the head with the brāhmaṇas, the arms with the kṣatriyas, the thighs with the vaiśya and the feet with the śūdras. In this hymn the varṇa hierarchy is specifically associated with the social classes; however, throughout the sacrificial texts the same classification scheme can be used to order the entire universe. Accordingly, as Brian Smith (1994) has demonstrated, the varṇa system organises under one basic structure the realms of the gods, space, time, flora and fauna, etc. All of these different orders of the cosmos can be arranged hierarchically in groups that correspond to the social classes. Thus, there are brāhmaṇa, kṣatriya, vaiśya and śūdra gods, times of day, Vedas, trees, etc. The ritual texts consider the top of the hierarchy as ontologically more complete than the bottom. In this way, horizontal relations are between prototypes and counterparts. For example, the brāhmaṇa man is considered the most complete manifestation of a human being.

Horizontally, bandhus link entities of different orders, but with the same rank within their order. For example, the brāhmaṇa among humans was linked to Agni among the gods and the goat among animals; the kṣatriyas were linked to Indra and the horse; the vaiśyas to Viśvadevas and the cow; the śūdras had no corresponding deity, but were often linked to sheep among animals. The ritual texts are not always entirely consistent as to the horizontal correspondences. For example, sometimes kṣatriyas and not śūdras are linked with sheep. However, generally the ritual texts operate according to the same logic of correspondence and resemblance. Theoretically, as Brian Smith has observed, bandhus function as a connecting principle that can link together everything in the universe (Smith 1994: 12).

In post-Vedic literature Vedism developed in a number of ways: the *Śrautasūtras* systematised the details of ritual action; the Mīmāṃsā school of philosophy looked to the authority of the Vedas for its investigations into dharma; the smṛti texts extended Vedism beyond the ritual to the entire range of human activities.

See also: **Agni; Āraṇyakas; Brāhmaṇas; Brahmanism; Dharmaśāstras; Dharmasūtras; Mahābhārata; Prajāpati; Puruṣa; Pūrva Mīmāṃsā; Rāmāyaṇa; Śrautasūtras; Upaniṣads; Varṇa; Yajña**

BRIAN BLACK

Further reading

Flood, G. 1996. *An Introduction to Hinduism*. Cambridge and New York: Cambridge University Press.

Gonda, J. 1965. '*Bandhu* in the Brāhmaṇas'. *Adyar Library Bulletin* 29: 1–29.

O'Flaherty, Wendy Doniger. 1981. *The Rig Veda*. Harmondsworth: Penguin.

Smith, Brian. 1989. *Reflections on Resemblance, Ritual and Religion*. New York: Oxford University Press.

Smith, Brian. 1994. *Classifying the Universe: The Ancient Indian Varṇa System and the Origin of Caste*. New York: Oxford University Press.

Williams, Monier. 1883. *Religious Thought and Life in India, Part One: Vedism, Brāhmanism, and Hinduism*. London: John Murray.

VIBHŪTI

Vibhūti is typically associated with the sacred ash used by worshippers of the god Śiva, although the term itself can also refer to the miraculous powers described in the *Yogasūtras*.

When the sacred ash is placed on the forehead of devotees, it symbolises the spiritual third eye, which helps one develop self-realisation. It also acts as a reminder of an individual's mortality, since ash is all that is left after a body has been cremated: the body is only a temporary vessel, so worshippers should try to rid themselves of all worldly desires and māyā (illusion).

Sathya Sai Baba (b. 1926), a charismatic leader with millions of followers in India, uses an ash-like substance called vibhūti (that was formed on pictures of his predecessor Sai Baba) as a miraculous cure from various ailments.

See also: **Māyā; Sai Baba, Sathya; Sai Baba, Shirdi; Śiva; Yogasūtras**

ANGELA QUARTERMAINE

Further reading

Flood, G. 2005. 'The Saiva Tradition'. In G. Flood, ed., *The Blackwell Companion to Hinduism*. Oxford: Blackwell Publishing, 200–28.

Swallow, D.A. 1982. 'Ashes and Powers: Myth Rite and Miracle in an Indian-man's Cult'. *Modern Asian Studies* 16: 123–58.

VIDHI

According to Pūrva Mīmāṃsā, vidhi denotes a Vedic injunction or command to act. These commands to conduct rituals are to be followed exactly because the Veda is revealed truth and constitutes the ultimate authority. The prescribed acts fall into three categories: acts that are obligatory (nityakarma), which, while their performance produces no merit (puṇya), attract demerit (pāpa) if they are neglected; acts that are to be performed occasionally (naimittikakarma) and similarly earn no fruit, though non-observance entails negative consequences; and acts that are optional (kāmyakarma), which are enjoined for the attainment of certain goals. Not all Vedic statements are considered to be injunctions of this kind; other statements are classed as arthavāda.

See also: **Arthavāda; Pāpa; Puṇya; Pūrva Mīmāṃsā; Veda**

DENISE CUSH AND CATHERINE ROBINSON

Further reading

Grimes, John. 1996. *A Concise Dictionary of Indian Philosophy: Sanskrit Terms Defined in English*, new and rev. edn. Albany, NY: State University of New York Press.

Hiriyanna, M. 1985. *Essentials of Indian Philosophy*. London: George Allen & Unwin.

VIDYĀRAMBHA

One of the Hindu childhood saṃskāras, or rites of passage, the vidyārambha, or commencement of study, was a relatively late addition to the corpus of saṃskāras. It is not present in the older strata of prescriptive ritual, but is mentioned only in the early centuries of the first millennium CE. The rite is variously prescribed for boys aged 5 or 7. It is to take place on a day auspicious for learning, such as the tenth lunar day of the bright half of the month of Aśvina (Dassarā). The main deities invoked are Gaṇeśa (the lord of overcoming obstacles), Sarasvatī (the goddess of knowledge), Bṛhaspati (the Vedic divinity of mantra) and the child's family deities. The child then worships the teacher, who makes the child recite three times the words the teacher writes down. The child then presents clothes and ornaments to the teacher and circumambulates the images of the deities.

See also: **Calendar; Gaṇeśa; Guru; Mantra; Pradakṣina; Saṃskāra; Sarasvatī**

FREDERICK M. SMITH

Further reading

Kane, P.V. 1974. *History of Dharmaśāstra*, 2nd edn, vol. 2, pt 1. Poona: Bhandarkar Oriental Research Institute, 265–67.

Pandey, R.J. 1969. *Hindu Saṃskāras.* Delhi: Motilal Banarsidass, 106–110.

VIDYĀRAṆYA (d. 1386)

Vidyāraṇya is thought to have been a unique blend of religious renouncer and secular politician active in guiding the founders of the Vijayanagara kingdom in the early and middle parts of the fourteenth century. His cultural, intellectual and political contributions mark the beginning of what many believe went on to become the last great Hindu empire in South India. However, later historians believe the evidence on which these characterisations were based to be spurious and doubt Vidyāraṇya's connection to the founding of Vijayanagara. It is certain through the internal evidence of his works that he was Mādhava, the brother of Sāyaṇa, the commentator on the Veda. Before renouncing and taking the name Vidyāraṇya, he contributed widely to the separate branches of Sanskrit literature. The best known of these earlier works are the legal digest the *Parāśara-Mādhavīya* and the *Sarvadarśanasaṃgraha*, a broad assessment of the different schools of medieval Indian philosophy culminating in the Advaita Vedānta view.

In 1374, Vidyāraṇya became the pontiff of the Śṛṅgeri maṭha, or monastic institution, in south-west Karṇāṭaka. During this decade, he composed his most important work on Advaita, the *Pañcadaśī*, which became a standard work of the Vivaraṇa school of post-Śaṅkaran Advaita. Later, in about 1380, he composed his *Jīvanmuktiviveka* on the possibility of liberation while still living in the body. In this text, Vidyāraṇya made a distinction between the renouncer seeking knowledge and one who is a knower. The Advaitic insight of the knower of the Self as Brahman is considered insufficient to root out operative karma which causes future births. Liberation while in the body comes only to the knower through lifelong Yogic practices that safeguard knowledge and completely quiet the mind.

See also: **Advaita; Brahman; Jīvanmukta; Karma; Maṭha; Mokṣa; Śaṅkara; Sāyaṇa; Veda; Yoga**

ROBERT GOODDING

Further reading

Mahadevan, T.M.P. 1957. *The Philosophy of Advaita with special Reference to Bhāratītīrtha-Vidyāraṇya.* Madras: Ganesh and Co. Pvt Ltd.

VIDYASAGAR, ISHWARA CHANDRA (1820–91)

Prominent nineteenth-century Bengali educationalist and social reformer. Born Ishvarachandra Bandyopadhyay, he received a classical Sanskrit education in his youth at the Calcutta Sanskrit College (earning in 1839 the honorary title Vidyasagar, 'ocean of knowledge'). He then entered government employ as head paṇḍit of the College of Fort William in 1841, and rose to the rank of Principal of the Calcutta Sanskrit College a decade later. In 1855 he also took on the post of Special Inspector of Schools in several districts of Bengal, and then became a fellow of Calcutta University in 1857. He resigned from government service in 1858. Vidyasagar is considered a great promoter of Sanskrit in Bengal, and in some sense an advocate of an amalgamation of Eastern and Western learning. In private correspondence, however, he often showed a clear preference for the knowledge of Europe, as well as education in the vernacular among the masses of India. In this regard, among Vidyasagar's principal social concerns was the promotion of female education in Bengal. For example, he became associated in the early 1850s with the Bethune School, the first women's school in Calcutta. Vidyasagar also campaigned for the acceptance of widow remarriage. He published on this subject in the Brahmo journal *Tattvabodhini Patrika*. His involvement is considered to have been instrumental in the eventual passing of Act XV of 1856, which legalised widow remarriage. Finally, Vidyasagar is often characterised as a pioneer in the elaboration of Bengali prose, together with Rammohan Roy and Akshay Kumar Datta. While much of his written work was didactic, Vidyasagar also translated into Bengali the elements of several standard Sanskrit works. Vidyasagar became an honorary member of the Royal Asiatic Society in 1864, and later received the CIE (Companion of the Order of the Indian Empire).

See also: **Brahmo Samaj; Languages; Paṇḍit; Roy, Rammohan; Widow remarriage; Women's education**

MICHAEL S. DODSON

Further reading

Hatcher, B.A. 1996. *Idioms of Improvement: Vidyasagar and Cultural Encounter in Bengal*. Calcutta: Oxford University Press.

VIGRAHA

See: **Image worship**

VIJÑĀNABHIKṢU

Vijñānabhikṣu, who flourished in the sixteenth century CE, is renowned as a synthesiser of the teachings of different Hindu schools, especially Vedānta, Sāṃkhya and Yoga. He was the author of a commentary on the *Brahmasūtras* called the *Vijñānāmritabhāṣya* (The Nectar of Knowledge Commentary). Other works include a commentary on the *Bhagavadgītā* (*Īśvaragītābhāṣya*), the *Yogasārasaṃgraha* (Compendium on the Essence of Yoga) and the *Sāṃkhyasāra* (Essence of Sāṃkhya).

Vijñānabhikṣu's synthesis of the truths of the orthodox Hindu schools is called 'avibhāgādvaita' (indistinguishable non-dualism). It was produced against a background of Vedāntic authority and the development of bhakti (devotionalism) movements. Vijñānabhikṣu was a fierce critic of Śaṅkara's strict non-dualism. He regarded Śaṅkara's tradition as crypto-Buddhist and set out to interpret the *Brahmasūtras* as containing the truth of the Sāṃkhya school. Thus, for Vijñānabhikṣu, Bādarāyaṇa taught metaphysical dualism, the principles of prakṛti (nature or matter) and puruṣa (spirits). Vijñānabhikṣu combines Sāṃkhya with the Vedāntic truth of Brahman – the ultimate truth or reality is Brahman or Īśvara

(God), so he explains how prakṛti and puruṣa are different but exist on the ground of the non-dual Brahman as inherent powers.

Vijñānabhikṣu taught that Brahman (which is of the nature of pure consciousness) is the Inner Ruler (antaryāmin) of prakṛti and puruṣa. He does not identify the multiple puruṣa (spirits are many) with Brahman but they are conscious alone in essence. Puruṣa and Brahman are one, related as sparks to a fire. He also explains the creation of the universe via a concept of māyā as an evolute of the eternally real prakṛti (the world is not illusory). For Vijñānabhikṣu, Yogic practices provide the means by which spirits are liberated from their confusion with the evolutes of prakṛti. Experience of pain ceases for the individual puruṣa in the ultimate, perfect state of contentless consciousness, kaivalya ('isolation').

See also: **Bādarāyaṇa; Bhagavadgītā; Bhakti; Brahman; Brahmasūtras; Īśvara; Kaivalya; Māyā; Prakṛti; Puruṣa; Sāṃkhya; Śaṅkara; Vedānta; Yoga**

MARTIN OVENS

Further reading

Rukmani, T.S. 1981. *Yogavārttika of Vijñānabhikṣu*, vol. I. Samādhipada. New Delhi: Munshiram Manoharlal.

VINI YOGA

See: **Desikachar, T.K.V. and Vini Yoga**

VĪRAŚĀIVAS

Vīraśāivas are sometimes referred to as Liṅgāyats because they wear a small liṅga (phallic symbol of Śiva) on their bodies. The reputed founder of the school is one Basava, who lived in the twelfth century CE. This is challenged by K.C. Pandey (1954/1986), who calls attention to the writings of Rajasekhara (tenth century CE), where we are told that the yoga school is often called Śaiva, and that the Śaiva yogins display many of the characteristics of the Vīraśāivas, including the consecrated liṅga on the arm. For this reason, Pandey is inclined to regard Basava as a reformer rather than a founder.

In their teachings, the Vīraśāivas exhibit some orthodox (smārta) views, some typically Śaiva views and some distinctive ones. Ontologically, the system is monistic, the world and souls ultimately resolving themselves into Śiva. The essence of Śiva is often called Brahman and is characterised by Sat (being), Cit (consciousness) and Ānanda (bliss), just as in Advaita Vedānta. Through the movement of Śiva's śakti (power), a duality is set up between Śiva in himself, called Liṅgasthala, and the creation (= souls plus world), called Angasthala. The Liṅgasthala exists on three levels:

1. bhāvaliṅga: pure, simple, nondual existence;
2. prāṇaliṅga: a kind of subtle manifestation only perceivable by the mind (a kind of Śaivite equivalent of the Buddhist Sambhogakāya);
3. iṣṭaliṅga: the physical liṅga that is worn on the arm or set into a base.

The categories of existence are those of the Sāṃkhya plus eleven higher ones. In this system, a devotee of Śiva is called a bhakta, and liberation is understood as a realisation of blissful union (samarasya) with Śiva.

In many ways, the Vīraśāivas can be regarded as operating a rival system to that developed by smārta brāhmaṇas. Like the orthodox, they abstain from meat and alcoholic drink. They also employ orthodox-style rituals, though they substitute their own content for the brahmanical material. For example, their initiation ceremony (dīkṣa) substitutes a liṅga for the sacred thread; and the orthodox Gāyatrī mantra is exchanged for 'Oṃ nāma Śivaya'. Unlike the orthodox, they allow widows to remarry and menstruating women are not regarded as polluting.

See also: **Advaita; Bhakti; Brahman; Dīkṣa; Gāyatrī mantra; Mantra; Śaivism; Śakti; Sāṃkhya; Śiva; Upanayana; Widow remarriage**

PETER CONNOLLY

Further reading

Pandey, K.C. 1954/1986. *An Outline History of Saiva Philosophy.* Delhi: Motilal Banarsidass.

VIRGINITY

From the time of the *Brāhmaṇas*, some authors associated the importance of virginity with the religious idiom of purity (śauca). This made virginity a criterion for marriage in elite circles, encouraged parents to protect their daughters' virginity, created a symbolic view of daughters as asexual and led to arranged marriages at ever younger ages. Virgin daughters had such high status because of their categorical purity that some people worshipped them as virgin goddesses during Durgā Pūjā and believed them capable of transferring power via blessings to their brothers. Today, virginity still is important in many elite circles as a criterion for marriage, although it is not as rigidly enforced in cities as it once was.

See also: **Brāhmaṇas; Child marriage; Durgā Pūjā; Women's rites**

KATHERINE K. YOUNG

Further reading

Bennett, L. 1983. *Dangerous Wives and Sacred Sisters: Social and Symbolic Roles of High-Caste Women in Nepal.* New York: Columbia University Press.

Denton, L.T. 1992. 'Varieties of Hindu Female Asceticism'. In J. Leslie, ed., *Roles and Rituals for Hindu Women.* Delhi: Motilal Banarsidass, 211–31.

Fruzzetti, L.M. 1982. *The Gift of a Virgin: Women, Marriage and Ritual in a Bengali Society.* New Brunswick, NJ: Rutgers University Press.

Khandelwal, M. 2001. 'Sexual Fluids, Emotions, Morality: Notes on the Gendering of Brahmacharya'. In E.J. Sobo and S. Bell, eds, *Celibacy, Culture, and Society: The Anthropology of Sexual Abstinence.* Madison, WI: University of Wisconsin Press, 157–80.

VISHNUDEVANANDA (1927–93) AND SIVANANDA YOGA

Born in 1927 in Kerala. After school, he joined the Indian army, where he came across a pamphlet of '20 Spiritual Instructions' by Swami Sivananda. Inspired, he travelled to Rishikesh, and was initiated into saṃnyāsa (and given the name Vishnudevananda) by his guru in 1949. Already quite proficient in āsana and prāṇāyāma (posture and breath), he was appointed Professor of haṭha yoga at Sivananda's Ashram. In 1957 he was invited to teach abroad and travelled to Malaysia, Hong Kong, Japan and America, before settling in Montreal, Canada, and opening the first Sivananda Yoga Vedanta centre there in 1959. Today there are nineteen such centres in eleven countries, with numerous affiliated centres and teachers.

Vishnudevananda devised five fundamental principles of yoga – Proper Exercises, Proper Breathing, Proper Relaxation, Proper Diet and Positive Thinking and Meditation – as the basis of his teaching. Reflecting Vishnudevananda's own proclivity towards the physical aspect of yoga, there is a strong emphasis in Sivananda Vedanta centres on the practice of āsana. Suryanamaskar ('sun salutations') plus a standardised framework of twelve basic āsana (to which more elaborate postures can be added) are practised, along with prāṇāyāma and meditation. Although sessions can be physically intense, there is far less attention to alignment in the postures than, for example, in Iyengar yoga. There is also a strong devotional element in these centres, with prayers and kīrtana (devotional chanting) playing a significant role.

Vishnudevananda gained notoriety as 'the flying swami' for his practice of piloting a small plane over the trouble spots of the world (such as the Suez Canal and the Berlin Wall) while strewing flowers and chanting peace mantras. His influential *Complete Illustrated Book of Yoga* (Vishnudevananda 1960) became the standard Modern Yoga primer. He died in 1993.

See also: **Āsana; Iyengar, B.K.S. and Iyengar Yoga; Guru; Haṭha Yoga; Kīrtaṇ(a); Meditation; Saṃnyāsa; Shivananda, Swami; Yoga, modern**

MARK SINGLETON

Further reading

Vishnudevananda, Sw. 1960. *The Complete Illustrated Book of Yoga*. London: Souvenir Press.

VISHWA HINDU PARISHAD

The 'World Hindu Congress'. A chauvinist, Hindu fundamentalist cultural organisation which promotes an idealised vision of Hindu cultural and religious identity and which has close links to the Rashtriya Svayamsevak Sangh (RSS) and the Bharatiya Janata Party (BJP). The Vishwa Hindu Parishad (VHP) was founded in 1964 at a meeting presided over by Swami Chinmayanand, and at the urging of the RSS. The aim of the VHP was ostensibly to coordinate the strengthening and 'unification' of a Hindu religious identity. In this regard, it has been a central tenet of VHP doctrine that Hinduism has been 'weakened' by its essentially syncretic and diffuse character. In essence, however, the VHP has been closely allied to the extremist RSS agenda to 'Hinduise' India. In the early 1980s the VHP became active in a campaign to forcibly, if necessary, reclaim a series of Hindu temple sites currently 'occupied' by mosques at Ayodhyā, Mathurā and Vārāṇasī. L.K. Advani, India's deputy prime minister at the time of writing, utilised the resultant Rāmjanmabhūmi (the 'site of the birth of Rāma') movement to revitalise the political fortunes of the Hindu right. In this regard, the promotion of the god Rāma as the ideal Hindu ruler and the reclamation of his reputed birth place in Ayodhyā held particular political resonance. Since that time the VHP has played a key role in the destruction of the Babri Masjid at Ayodhyā, in 1992, the programme to construct a temple to Rāma in its place and the concomitant promotion of communalist sentiment and violence. The VHP is active outside India in fundraising and other related 'cultural activities'. Moreover, through its website (www.vhp.org), the manipulation of historical scholarship and the publication of 'educational' textbooks on Hindu civilisation, the VHP has effectively promoted a vision of Hindu entitlement which has proven to be politically volatile.

See also: **Ayodhyā; Bharatiya Janata Party; Mathurā; Nationalism; Rāma; Rashtriya Svayamsevak Sangh; Vārāṇasī**

MICHAEL S. DODSON

Further reading

Bhatt, C. 2001. *Hindu Nationalism: Origins, Ideologies, and Modern Myths*. Oxford: Berg.

Katju, M. 2003. *Vishva Hindu Parishad and Indian Politics*. Hyderabad: Orient Longman.

Ludden, D. (ed.). 1996. *Making India Hindu: Religion, Community and the Politics of Democracy in India*. Delhi: Oxford University Press.

VIŚIṢṬĀDVAITA

Viśiṣṭādvaita is a philosophical school of thought in the Vedānta tradition that attempted to merge the personal theism of Vaiṣṇava bhakti represented by the Tamil Āḻvār poets of the sixth to eighth centuries with a systematic philosophical treatment of the absolutist doctrines of the early *Upaniṣads*. It also arose as an attempt to counteract the monistic metaphysics of the Advaita Vedānta school, which did not accommodate the theistic bhakti devotionalism that had become very popular in medieval South India.

The chief figure and proponent of this school was the theologian Rāmānuja (d. *c.*1137 CE). The other significant thinker after Rāmānuja was Vedānta Deśika (*c.*1268–1369 CE), also called Veṅkaṭanātha, who, in addition to his other scholarly and literary works, became a polemicist for the Viśiṣṭādvaita against the Advaita Vedānta, and was founder of Vaḍagalais school within Viśiṣṭādvaita. Rāmānuja inherited the school's early doctrines that were formulated by Nāthamuni (tenth century CE) and Yāmunācārya (*c.*918–1038 CE), and he grounded the school in notions derived from his interpretation of the *Upaniṣads*, thus also giving school's practical side of bhakti worship a sound basis in a metaphysics explaining the relation of Brahman and the devotee. Rāmānuja's main works are the independent treatise the *Vedārthasaṃgraha*, which explains his philosophy in terms of his interpretation of Upaniṣadic texts, and his *Śrībhāṣya*, a commentary on the *Brahmasūtras* of Bādarāyaṇa. In addition to the Tamil prabandham literature preserving the works of the Āḻvār poet-saints, other foundational texts for Viśiṣṭādvaita and Śrī Vaiṣṇavism were the *Bhagavadgītā*, the *Viṣṇu Purāṇa*, and the *Pañcaratra Saṃhitā*. The influence of Rāmānuja's philosophic teachings deeply impacted the temple worship current in his time at places such as Śrīraṅgam and furthered the Śrī Vaiṣṇava religion in South India, which endures to the present time.

The term 'Viśiṣṭādvaita' was not current in Rāmānuja's time, but was coined about four centuries later, and expresses the principle concept that distinguishes Rāmānuja's school from the other schools of Vedānta. The main difficulty interpreters faced in commenting on the *Upaniṣads* was how to resolve the passages that state the equivalence of Brahman and the individual jīva, or soul, and the inanimate world, with those other passages that state that Brahman is different from the soul and the world. Rāmānuja's solution to this difficulty provided both the philosophic basis for the devotion to God characterising the Śrī Vaiṣṇava religion and the refutation of Advaita doctrines such as the illusory nature of the world. For Rāmānuja, Brahman is a unity or non-dual (advaita), yet is also qualified (viśiṣṭa) by its attributes, which include all souls and everything else in the inanimate world. The way that a soul possesses a body and at the same time is not identical with it is the same way that Brahman exists independently while at the same time possessing its attributes. In the same way that a body cannot live separately from a soul and is dependent on the soul for its existence, all individual souls and the inanimate world are dependent on Brahman for their existence and at the same time are essentially different from each other. Brahman, souls and the inanimate world are thus said to be in a relation called apṛthak-siddhi, or 'inseparability'. Thus Rāmānuja could account for the upaniṣadic statements expressing the unity of souls with Brahman and the statements about the plurality of objects that is perceived reality. The experience of conscious souls and the perceived world of inanimate objects are real, therefore, and not illusory, as Śaṅkara said. This doctrine of Viśiṣṭādvaita is called the śarīr-aśarīribhāva, or 'body–soul doctrine'. It also explains the unity and plurality of substances (dravya), which assume different forms as their attributes (adravya) in the inanimate, physical world and in the animate, metaphysical reality.

Souls move in this real world towards liberation through their inseparable relation with Brahman as its dependent attributes. According to the body–soul doctrine, individual souls, along with other different attributes in subtle form, form the dependent body of Brahman. In this way, Rāmānuja interprets the teaching on the ātman or self as the inner controller of all things in the *Bṛhadāranyaka Upaniṣad* (3.7), saying that Brahman is the inner controller all things, while itself still independent and unchanging. Brahman and the plurality of souls both possess a certain attribute which is itself also a substance called dharmabhūtajñāna, or 'attributive intelligence'. It is a substance because it can assume different forms, but also an attribute because it is dependent on Brahman and individual souls for its existence. As a substance, dharmabhūtajñāna is self-luminous and illuminates objects, thus permitting them to be known, but not knowing the objects itself. It is all pervasive in the case of Brahman, giving Brahman its omniscience, and it is the same in individual souls. But the sentience given by dharmabhūtajñāna is constricted by the soul's embodiment in mundane existence, relying on the sense organs. Therefore the expansion of a soul's attributive intelligence characterises the degree to which a soul is liberated.

Brahman in Viśiṣṭādvaita is a personal God who has descended in the form of the avatāras of Viṣṇu. The favoured term for the personal divinity in Viśiṣṭādvaita is Nārāyaṇa, and salvation after death for individual souls consists in living with Nārāyaṇa in the subtle realm of Vaikuṇṭha. For Rāmānuja the soul's liberation is granted by the grace of Nārāyaṇa, yet one must make efforts dedicated to the personal God that are intensely devoted to him. Rāmānuja endorsed the means of bhaktiyoga, which is more a way of knowledge than an emotion. In the Vaiṣṇava religion after Rāmānuja, the emotional and passionate way of prapatti, or 'surrender', became the more favoured means of receiving God's grace and release.

See also: **Advaita; Āḻvārs; Ātman; Avatāras; Bādarāyaṇa; Bhagavadgītā; Bhakti (as path); Bhakti movement; Brahman; Brahmasūtras; Jīva; Pāñcarātra; Purāṇas; Rāmānuja; Śaṅkara; Śrī Vaiṣṇavas; Temple worship; Upaniṣads; Vaiṣṇavism; Vedānta; Viṣṇu**

ROBERT GOODDING

Further reading

Chari, S.M.S. 1976. *Advaita and Viśiṣṭādvaita: A Study Based on Vedānta Deśika's Śatuduṣan*. Delhi: Motilal Banarsidass.

Lott, E.J. 1976. *God and the Universe in the Vedāntic Theology of Rāmānuja*. Madras: Rāmānuja Research Society.

van Buitenen, J.A.B. 1956. *Rāmānuja's Vedārthasaṃgraha: Introduction, Critical Edition and Annotated Translation*. Pune: Deccan College Postgraduate and Research Institute.

VIṢṆU

> The world originated from Vishnu; it is in Him that the world exists as a harmonious system; he is the sole sustainer and controller of the world, and in truth, the world is He.
>
> (*Viṣṇu Purāṇa* 1.1.35)

Portrayed as humanity's friend and protector, Viṣṇu is celebrated as the object of sacrifice during Vedic times. He is seen as the god who upholds the threefold universe, the brother of Indra and his close friend, and the *Ṛgveda* describes Viṣṇu as a solar deity associated with life and light. Viṣṇu, often identified with the sun, took three giant strides that encompassed the entire universe, perhaps a reference to the rise, culmination and setting of the sun. Extolled as 'the swift moving luminary', Viṣṇu is also celebrated as the god who, along with Indra, vanquished the demons who disturbed their peace. The root word 'Viṣṇu' in Sanskrit signifies entrance and may also connote the 'abode or resting place of all men', and one of the *Upaniṣads* professes that the goal of all beings is to become one with Viṣṇu. Known for his pervasive nature and his cohesive tendency, he is endowed with the ability to bring the world together, and eventually in people's minds Viṣṇu became known as the Supreme God, and it is believed that he placed himself in the world and that all beings in turn were placed in him.

The *Viṣṇu Purāṇa*, one of the three texts attributed to the first millennium CE (the other two being the *Harivaṃśa* and the *Bhāgavata Purāṇa*), describes the creation of the world and, while it acknowledges and attributes the origin of the universe to Brahmā as prajāpati (the creator), identifies Viṣṇu as the ultimate origin of all beings. Attributed to Parāśara, the father of Veda Vyāsa, the author of the *Bhagavadgītā*, the *Mahābhārata* and other *Purāṇa* texts, *Viṣṇu Purāṇa* states, 'From Vishnu was the universe produced and in him it exists; he brings about the preservation and the destruction of this universe, and he is the universe' (1.1.31). Addressing the cosmography of the universe, *Viṣṇu Purāṇa* places Viṣṇu as the centre or object of all sacrifices who reaches the lowest depths as Śeṣa (the snake) and the utmost heights as the Sun. The book also delineates the geographic entity of India by narrating the story of Bhārata, who through his devotion to Viṣṇu attained mokṣa, and it is after him that the region got the name Bhārata.

The *Viṣṇu Purāṇa* also names Viṣṇu as Nārāyaṇa (the mover of waters) and attributes his pervasiveness as encompassing not only the earth and upper air but also the world of water. Endowed with the power to protect his devotees from Yama (the god of death), Viṣṇu is credited with dominion over time as well. Later, the *Mahābhārata* venerates Viṣṇu as Nara Nārāyaṇa (the protector of waters), being that Viṣṇu is credited with naming waters as 'nara', as he identified water as his eternal abode. Viṣṇu is perceived as the cosmic god Nārāyaṇa, 'moving in the waters', pervading the whole universe. He is often shown in iconography seated or reclining on a seven-headed snake called Ananta Śeṣa, or Ananta (the endless), floating in the middle of the cosmic ocean, signifying a state of complete absorption before creation begins. In this representation he is also known as Anantaśayana (he who sleeps on the serpent Ananta), and is seen with his consort Śrī-Lakṣmī devotedly massaging his feet and Brahmā seated in a lotus nearby. Tradition attributes the suspension of all sacrificial ceremonies during the monsoon season to Viṣṇu's being asleep at this time of year. The cosmic nature of Viṣṇu is further alluded to in the belief that all that is seen and heard in the universe both inside and outside is attributable to Nārāyaṇa. Transcending physical phenomena, Viṣṇu is extolled as the son of Dharma, thereby launching him beyond the cosmic parameter into the ethical domain.

The transition from cosmic reality to an accessible deity who is an integral part of the temporal world is made possible through the concept of avatāras (incarnations). *Viṣṇu Purāṇa* elaborately describes how Lord Mahāviṣṇu (mahā refers to greatness) incarnates himself in the form of Vyāsa and classifies the Veda for the good of the people, for as such the Veda seemed to be an incomprehensible body of superior knowledge inaccessible to humanity. Thus the compilation, classification and consolidation of the Veda is essentially attributed to Viṣṇu, who divided Vedic lore into *Saṃhitās*, *Brāhmaṇas*, *Āraṇyakas* and *Upaniṣads*, each to be mastered by priests belonging to different classes like Ṛgs, Yajurs, Sāmas and Atharvans, and each branch codified appropriately. While the initial division of the Veda was established by Viṣṇu, the sub-branches evolved over a period of time.

Modern Hinduism credits Viṣṇu as the central god of the Trinity (Trimūrti) with Brahmā as the creator, Viṣṇu as the preserver and Śiva as the destroyer of the world and its beings. The Vedic cult of Viṣṇu-Nārāyaṇa was eventually absorbed into the worship of Bhagavān ('the one worthy of being worshipped') or Kṛṣṇa as extolled in *Bhagavadgītā*, the most well known religious text of modern India. Vaiṣṇavism represented Kṛṣṇa and Rāma as incarnations of God who appeared in the world at different points of time to preserve justice, establish order and protect the world from all evil forces. While the worship of Kṛṣṇa and Rāma was prevalent in both north and south India, the specific form and mode of worship varied.

In south India, Āḻvārs, literally meaning 'believers immersed in God', who were also revered as the incarnations of Lord Viṣṇu, sang his praise and established pilgrimage sites in various parts of south India during the sixth and seventh century, thereby spreading Vaiṣṇavism. Twelve Āḻvārs drawn from various castes, including a female, Āṇṭāḷ, sang divinely inspired songs that were later collected in the tenth century CE by Nāthamuni, a devotee of Lord Viṣṇu, and were later compiled as *Nālāyira Divyaprabhandam* (Four Thousand Divine Compositions). Nammāḻvār, the most celebrated of the Āḻvārs, composed the *Tiruvāymoḻi*, the utterance of the divine, consisting of 1000 distinctive songs in praise of Lord Viṣṇu. Considered equal to the Veda, widely known as the Tamil Veda, this literary text embodied devotion through overt emotion, expressing the longing of the devotee to become one with the divine Lord Viṣṇu. Conforming to the then Tamil poetic tradition, the poems address the inner 'akam', or the matters of the self and home, and the outer or 'puram', dealing with concerns of the outside world, politics and diplomacy, and use the metaphor of romantic love among humans to signify the devotion of the devotee to God and the pursuit of attaining oneness with the divine. The cosmic God thus enters the personal world of the devotee and situates himself within the context of home and hearth, and thus achieves temporal existence in several shrines all over Tamil Nadu. Śrīraṇgam temple near Tiruchirapalli in south India is a renowned Viṣṇu shrine which houses Lord Raṅganātha, and is visited by thousands of pilgrims from all over India and abroad.

During the medieval period, Vaiṣṇavism saw the emergence of four distinct traditions – the theism of Rāmānuja (Viśiṣṭādvaita), the dualism of Madhva (Dvaita), the non-dualist philosophy of Vallabha and the unconditional surrender to the guru proposed by Nimbārka (Bhedābeda). With absolute devotion for God as the central theme, Vaiṣṇavism expressed love in various ways – lover to beloved, friend to friend, servant to master and child to parent – using the body as the vehicle for the embodied soul that is yearning to seek union with the divine. Intensely emotional, Vaiṣṇavism encouraged an intimate, personal relationship with God characterised by weeping, singing and dancing. This emotional outpouring of devotion, bhakti, for Lord Viṣṇu spread throughout the country beyond southern India, with Lord Kṛṣṇa, an avatāra of Viṣṇu, as the object of worship, especially in the south and in Bengal, where Vaiṣṇavism branched off into Gauḍīya Vaiṣṇavism. In Maharashtra the Viṭṭhala cult gained popularity.

In Tamil Nadu the Śri Vaiṣṇava tradition forged together the Sanskrit tradition of worshipping Viṣṇu as the creator of the universe, as a transcendental being whose power sustains the cosmos with personal devotion to God manifested in the form of a lover pining for his beloved. In temple towns like Śrīrangam or Śrīvilliputhur, the deity partakes in all the temporal events associated with the temple and the shrine, and local legends weave the divine into the fabric of the town's social life. The aesthetic and emotional inspiration drawn from the poetry of the Āḻvārs fitted well within the philosophical framework developed in the *Bhagavadgītā* and the *Viṣṇu Purāṇa* of Sanskrit tradition. Devotees gained assurance that total liberation from the cycle of birth and death (mokṣa) was possible by observing one of two diverse paths: the first a path of unwavering devotion, faithful observance of rituals and sincere service to the Lord that would enable the soul to discard the temporal trappings and transcend the cycle of karma to gain direct entry into Vaikuṇṭha, the abode of Lord Viṣṇu; the second a path of surrender of self, soul and body whereby through divine grace the Lord would save the devotee. The Vaiṣṇava tradition forked into two sects: vaḍakalai, those who relied upon Sanskrit scriptures and sought salvation through bhakti (devotion); and tenkalai, those who adhered to the Tamil tradition of total surrender to the grace of God, who in turn would grant eternal salvation to the deserving. While in Bengal the ecstatic bhakti tradition flourished under Gauḍīya Vaiṣṇavism, popularising devotion to Lord Kṛṣṇa, in Southern India Śri Vaiṣṇavism was nurtured through Sanskrit scriptural and theological traditions within a deep-rooted local temple cultural tradition.

Although iconographic representations of Viṣṇu vary, two versions predominate. One has Viṣṇu in the reclining posture, accompanied by his consort Śrī-Lakṣmi, resting on the seven headed snake in complete absorption before creation, and is known as the Anantaśayana. The other has Viṣṇu in standing posture with his four hands each carrying a symbol to signify the God's pervasive and protective nature, cosmic consciousness and omnipotent power. One hand carries the conch shell, which connotes his creative powers by symbolising the primordial sound of creation and conquest over the asuras; the wheel signifies his sustaining powers by representing the cycle of time, the mace symbolises his power and authority and the lotus flower indicates his perfection in form and spirit, innate purity and the gradual unfolding of forms. Followers of Viṣṇu sport three vertical lines on the centre of their forehead, signifying his threefold manifestation of control and harmony over the world. His vehicle is Garuḍa, an enormous mythical bird, part human and part eagle, who is believed to be a manifestation of Lord Viṣṇu. According to legend, Viṣṇu presented himself in the form of Śālāgrāma, the ammonite fossil found in rivers, when Goddess Gaṅgā (the river personified as a goddess) desired that Viṣṇu be conceived as her offspring, and thereby Śālāgrāma became another common representation of Viṣṇu and is worshipped as his natural form.

While some Vaiṣṇavites believe that Viṣṇu is beyond attributes (nirguṇa) but expresses himself as a world full of colour, sound, texture and myriad sensory feelings, Viṣṇu's innumerable attributes are enumerated in *Viṣṇu Sahasranāma* (one thousand names of Viṣṇu), a garland strung by the legendary poet Veda Vyāsa, in his composition the *Mahābhārata*. 'Sahasra' (a thousand) is a euphemism for 'anantam' (innumerable), as the traits of the God are innumerable. After the War of Kurukṣetra was over and Yudhiṣṭhira was crowned king, Bhīṣma delivered the entire text of *Viṣṇu Sahasranāma Stotra* to Yudhiṣṭhira as a discourse on various aspects of life and dharma. The individual laudatory names of Viṣṇu in the song combine to describe the forms, functions and qualities of Lord Viṣṇu, and the song is chanted early in the morning and at dusk in temples; for example, the Raṅganātha (another name for Viṣṇu) temple at Srīraṇgam plays the song every day during the months of December and January even today. His association with water is signified through the name Nārāyaṇa, Hari, his protective persona, Padmanābha (lotus navel), his ability to create, Nīlameghaśyāma (the blue sky), his all-pervasive nature. Along with his attributes, the *Viṣṇu Sahasranāma Stotra* (celebratory verses) extols the qualities of Viṣṇu, his glorious actions and the benefits devotees and the universe will enjoy when these verses are chanted. Chanting these hymns is known to cure diseases, can be used for crossing several hurdles in normal life and as a ticket out of the cycle of birth, rebirth and death (saṃsāra). Scholars like Śaṅkara have provided commentaries for this stotra that have aided generations of laymen to understand and interpret the verses.

Viṣṇu's love and compassion encompass the human, animal and the semi-human worlds and establishes peace, justice and prosperity wherever his avatār (incarnation) appears. According to the *Bhagavata Purāṇa*, a literary text attributed to the first millennium CE, Viṣṇu's avatāras are twenty-nine; however, the most popular ones are ten. Given the cyclical cosmology of the Hindu theological vision of the universe, the universe is bound to dissolve, and Śiva, the destroyer god, will preside over this. However, when disturbances to world peace and harmony emerge every now and then, Viṣṇu as the preserver assumes different forms and establishes peace on earth by vanquishing the beings causing the disturbance. Viṣṇu's ten avatāras mirror the evolutionary pattern of the universe, beginning with an aquatic emergence of life represented by fish (Matsya avatāra) to save Manu, the first ancestor to be saved after the flood. The next incarnation was that of a reptile (tortoise-Kūrma avatāra) to support the mountain Maṇḍara on his back, so the gods could use it as a churn and, using a serpent for a rope, churn the ocean to retrieve the lost nectar of immortality. Next came Varāha (the boar), who saved the earth goddess from drowning in the cosmic ocean. Viṣṇu makes the transition from animal to human in his next avatāra – Narasiṃha or the man-lion – to destroy the demon king Hiraṇyakaśipu as he piled untold miseries on his son Prahlāda, who was a staunch devotee of Lord Viṣṇu. Acccording to legend, Hiraṇyakaśipu had obtained a boon from the gods by virtue of his staunch penance that he could not be killed by man or beast on land or water. Hence, Viṣṇu emerged in the form of Narasiṃha (man-lion) from a pillar, perched himself on Hiraṇyakaśipu's lap and ripped his heart out, so he would not inflict any more sufferings on Prahlāda for his unwavering devotion to lord Viṣṇu. In his next avatāra Viṣṇu takes the form of a dwarf (Vāmana) to restore harmony on earth and end the atrocious regime of the demon-king Bali. Lord Viṣṇu appeares in dwarf form and tricks Bali into granting him the space that three of his steps will cover. Upon being granted the request, Viṣṇu takes a gigantic form and takes two steps covering the earth; the third he places on Bali, thus ending his tyranny.

In his next avatāra as Paraśurāma, (Rāma with an axe) Viṣṇu takes the form of a militant brāhmaṇa who destroys all kṣatriya (varṇa) descendants of King Kārtavīrya. According to legend, Viṣṇu appeared as Paraśurāma, the son of Jamadagri, and killed Kārtavīrya, who oppressed his father. Kārtavīrya's enraged sons killed Jamadagri, a brāhmaṇa, in retaliation. Thereupon, Paraśurāma killed the entire male members of the kṣatriya clan, whose women replenished the clan with male progeny by copulating with brāhmaṇas. The next avatāra of Viṣṇu is Rāmacandra (Rāma with a bow), where Viṣṇu enters the world as Rāma, the son of Daśaratha, and vanquishes the demon Rāvaṇa, the abductor of his wife Sītā. Not only does Viṣṇu rid the world of the demon Rāvaṇa but he epitomises the virtuous son, model husband, exemplary king and a highly revered god. Dated to around the fourth millennium BCE, Viṣṇu's avatāra as Kṛṣṇa is at least as popular as his avatāra as Rāma, and he succeeds in saving the world from the oppressive rule of King Kaṃsa. The most celebrated philosophical treatise on the purpose of human existence occurs in the text *Bhagavadgītā* where Kṛṣṇa finally reveals his magnificent, infinite form with innumerable heads and limbs to Arjuna and the world. It is this avatāra of Viṣṇu that is most highly celebrated and appeals to humanity in multifarious ways. Viṣṇu's next avatāra is believed to be as Buddha, with the intent to promote non-violence and abolish needless slaughter of animals. Kalki is the final avatāra, which Viṣṇu is yet to assume, who will appear when the dark age comes to an end and whose birth will herald the dawn of a new era.

The ten avatāras bring out the tendency of Viṣṇu to absorb other deities and show his pervasive presence embracing the animal and the human world and his generosity and compassion shining through the various forms assumed. Viṣṇu's Daśāvatāras (ten avatāras) occupy a central role in dance repertoire and are included in almost all Bhārata Nāṭyam (south Indian dance form) performances as it offers a fertile ground for the expression of every known emotion. While every avatāra has a symbolic significance, the Kṛṣṇa avatāra in its entirety is the most meaningful avatār as it appeals to a wide array of beings. As a child, Kṛṣṇa's divine miracles entice the lay populace to come to him uninhibited and with childlike abandon. Kṛṣṇa as the young cowherd in a pastoral setting captures the hearts of the young maidens by playing ravishing music, which symbolises the divine love of God (Viṣṇu) which draws penitent souls to himself through his grace and compassion. This typifies the Bhakti movement, which used love between man and woman as a metaphoric expression of the divine love between humanity and God and the constant pull of the universal soul that draws the individual souls to its fold. The gopīs (cowherd girls) yearn for union with Kṛṣṇa and this yearning symbolically represents the desire of the jīvātma (individual soul) for final communion with the paramātma (universal soul). The cosmic dance Kṛṣṇa performs on the snake Kāliya after he has subdued the snake, as it has poisoned the waters of the river Yamunā, the only water source for the entire folk, displays his compassion, courage and generosity. Another popular image of Kṛṣṇa's generosity is his holding the mountain Govardhana in his hand and sheltering the villagers under it to protect them from the thunder and rain unleashed by god Indra. All these images have inspired artistic expressions in myriad forms – painting, sculpture, drawings and all conceivable art forms – and have been cherished for generations and remain popular in modern Indian society. The passionate love he showed his chief consort Rādhā was celebrated by various poets of the Bhakti movement and used to disseminate the divine love that Kṛṣṇa was capable of showing to each one of his believers and release them from their shackles that were holding them to the earth so as to enable them to achieve eternal salvation.

Kṛṣṇa further captivates generations of people through his magnificent role as teacher (guru) when he appears as Arjuna's charioteer in the Kurukṣetra War in the *Bhagavadgītā*. The long sermon he preaches to Arjuna encourages him to fight the war and if necessary kill his own kinsmen so as to establish virtue and righteousness in the world. The visual image of Kṛṣṇa as a charioteer in the battlefield of Kurukṣetra giving his divine advice to Arjuna has found expression in all conceivable artistic forms and adorns most Indian households even today. Mahatma Gandhi used some of the concepts idealised in the *Bhagavadgītā* – selfless commitment to the cause of Indian independence, active engagement in society in a spirit of detachment, non-violent action, action for the sake of action alone and undistracted devotion to one's occupation – all ideals drawn from Kṛṣṇa's inspiring speech to Arjuna urging him to selflessly engage in war without worrying about the consequences or the possibility of killing his own kith and kin in the war. Kṛṣṇa also draws pilgrims from around the country to Puri, Orissa, where he is celebrated as Jagannātha, the protector of the universe, at the temple there. The image of the god on a chariot is taken out in procession on the festival of Ratha Yātrā every year. The healing powers of Kṛṣṇa are the cause for the huge pilgrim influx into Guruvayur, Kerala, where the image of Kṛṣṇa with four hands holding a conch, a club and a lotus unequivocally establishes him as Viṣṇu.

While the most celebrated avatārs of Viṣṇu, Rāma and Kṛṣṇa are the subjects of the epics the *Rāmāyaṇa* and the *Mahābhārata* that have enthralled the populace for several centuries and have been recreated by various saints and schools of philosophy, in several different languages and versions, they have also inspired various spiritual and theological movements and cults in India. Hari Kathās (stories about the Lord) rendered by gifted speakers, musicians, storytellers, dancers and dramatists are sponsored by various cultural and spiritual organisations aspiring to keep ancient religious and social traditions alive in a constantly changing India. These events serve as a viable source of year-round entertainment and education to the multitudes in urban and rural areas. The advent of television further increased the accessibility of Viṣṇu in Indian households when the *Rāmāyaṇa* was broadcast on national television in seventy-eight episodes spread a little over a year, in 1987 and 1988. Watching the *Rāmāyaṇa* on television was considered a religious obligation and was done faithfully by about 95 per cent of the television-owning population, some of whom went to the extent of offering special prayers (pūjās) before the television set. In modern Indian society, Rāma is revered as a household god, shining as the exemplary son, modelling filial devotion, as loving husband to his wife Sītā, sworn to a monogamous relationship when kings were allowed to support a household full of women, as a sincere and loyal friend, loving brother, concerned environmentalist, just ruler, righteous citizen and a perfect role model for the modern Indian citizen to emulate.

Viṣṇu also assumes the avatāra of Kṛṣṇa who, in the *Mahābhārata*, is a heroic figures, a worldly-wise counsellor and politician who acts as a friend, advisor and ally of the Pāṇḍavas. Most famously, however, it is in the *Bhagavadgītā*, now, if perhaps not originally, part of the great epic, that Kṛṣṇa provides the most famous statement of the avatāra ideal as divine descent to uphold righteousness and combat evil (4.6–8). This is one of the reasons why many commentators have interpreted the *Bhagavadgītā* as a declaration of Kṛṣṇa's supremacy.

Indeed the International Society of Krishna Consciousness (ISKCON), a movement conceived by A.C. Bhaktivedanta Swami Prabhupada, which gives extraordinary prominence to the *Bhagavadgītā,* regards Kṛṣṇa as the supreme deity. This movement has spread the love of Kṛṣṇa throughout the world, inspired by Swami Rama Tirtha, who carried the message of Lord Viṣṇu to the West.

See also: **Āḻvārs; Āṇṭāḷ; Āraṇyakas; Arjuna; Asuras; Avatāras; Bali; Bhagavadgītā; Bhakti; Bhakti movement; Bhedābheda; Bhīṣma; Brahmā; Brāhmaṇa; Brāhmaṇas; Buddhism, relationship with Hinduism; Caste; Cosmogony; Dance; Daśaratha; Dharma; Drama; Dvaita; Gandhi, Mohandas Karamchand; Gaṅgā; Garuḍa; Gopī(s); Govardhana; Hiraṇyakaśipu; Images and iconography;**

Indra; International Society of Krishna Consciousness; Jagannātha; Kaṃsa; Karma (Law of Action); Karma (as path); Kṛṣṇa; Kurukṣetra; Lakṣmī, Śrī; Madhva; Mahābhārata; Mandir; Manu; Mokṣa; Music; Nāmmāḻvār; Nimbārka; Pāṇḍavas; Parāśara; Poetry; Prabhupada, A.C. Bhaktivedanta Swami; Prahlāda; Pūjā; Purāṇas; Rādhā; Rāma; Rāmānuja; Rāmāyaṇa; Ratha Yātrā; Rāvaṇa; Saṃhitā; Saṃsāra; Śaṅkara; Śeṣa; Sītā; Śiva; Tamil Veda; Television and radio; Tīrthayātrā; Trimūrti; Upaniṣads; Vaiṣṇavas, Śri; Vaiṣṇavism; Vallabha; Varṇa; Veda; Vedism; Viśiṣṭādvaita; Vyāsa; Yama; Yamunā (River); Yudhiṣṭhira

KOKILA RAVI

Further reading

Bhagawadpurana. 1980. Gorakhpur: Gita Press.

Bowen, Paul. (ed.). 1998. *Themes and Issues in Hinduism*. London and Washington, DC: Cassell.

Flood, Gavin. 1996. *An Introduction to Hinduism*. Cambridge: Cambridge University Press.

Hiryanna, M. 1932. *Outlines of Indian Philosophy.* London: George Allen and Unwin.

Jaffrelot, Christopher. 1996. *The Hindu Nationalist Movement in India.* New York: Columbia University Press.

Matchett, Freda. 2001. *Krishna: Lord or Avatara?* Richmond: Curzon.

Müller, Max F. 1983. *Vedic Hymns.* Delhi: Motilal Banarsidass.

O'Flaherty, W.D. (trans.). 1981. *The Rig Veda, an Anthology.* Harmondsworth: Penguin.

Olivelle, P (trans.). 1996. *The Upanishads.* Oxford: Oxford University Press.

Sharma, Arvind. 2003. *The Study of Hinduism.* Columbia, SC: South Carolina University Press.

Vishnupurana with Vishnuchitha's Commentary and Sridhara Swami's Atmaprakasa. 1910. 2 vols.

VIṢṆU PURĀṆA

See: **Purāṇas**

VIŚVADEVAS

The 'all-gods'. An ambiguous term used in the *Ṛgveda* to designate either all the gods or a generic and otherwise unidentified group of benevolent deities. As the latter, the Viśvadevas are ten in number, entitled to daily offerings and worshipped especially during funerary rites.

See also: **Saṃhitā; Vedic pantheon; Vedism**

MICHAEL YORK

VIŚVAKARMAN

'All-maker'. An original epithet of Indra's (*Ṛgveda* 8.87.2) and Sūrya's (10.170.4) that, in later Vedic times, emerged as an independent creator-god and eventually identified with Tvaṣṭṛ. Viśvakarman is the subject of two hymns in the *Ṛgveda*, where he is described as father and artificer of all things. These hymns may indicate a movement towards more impersonal conceptions of deity.

See also: **Indra; Sūrya; Tvaṣṭṛ; Vedism**

MICHAEL YORK

VIŚVĀMITRA

One of the most important of the Vedic seers and mentioned in the *Purāṇas* as a parogon of virtue, especially in the famous tale of his testing of Rāja Hariścandra. However, Viśvāmitra is prone to anger and this may be to do with his suspect lineage, as he was born a kṣatriya and not a brāhmāṇa, but rose to the latter rank through his particularly austere tapas. Thus Viśvāmitra challenges the common belief in hereditary brāhmaṇa status and may reflect tensions between the two highest castes competing for supremacy or the alternative ideal of brāhmaṇa membership through virtue. This competition of caste and birth versus achievement may also be the cause of the great rivalry that occurs in the epics and the *Purāṇas* between Viśvāmitra and Vasiṣṭha, even though both are counted amongst the seven sages regarded as 'mind-born' sons of Brahmā, and were according to the *Ṛgveda* both family priests to King Sudās.

See also: **Brahmā; Brāhmaṇa; Caste; Hariścandra; Itihāsa; Purāṇas; Ṛṣi; Saṃhita; Tapas; Varṇa; Vasiṣṭha**

RON GEAVES

Further reading

Stutley, Margaret and James Stutley (eds). 1985. *A Dictionary of Hinduism*. London: Routledge and Kegan Paul.

VIVĀHA

The *Laws of Manu* (*Mānava-Dharmaśāstra* 3.27–34), in agreement with other dharma texts and the *Mahābhārata* (1.96.8–11, 13.44.3–9), classifies marriage into eight types: Brāhma, Daiva, Ārṣa, Prājāpatya, Āsura, Gāndharva, Rākṣasa and Paiśāca. Not all of these are legal; rather, they indicate typologies of liaison, based on certain exchange relations. Jamison notes that '[w]hat distinguishes these types from each other are the occasion and circumstances under which the bride comes into the groom's possession' (Jamison 1996: 210–11). The Brāhma marriage is the most exalted of all. The father adorns and honours his daughter and gives her away to a man of Vedic learning and good character. The Daiva marriage is the gift of an ornamented daughter to a priest who observes proper ritual. The Ārṣa marriage is the legal gift of a daughter to a bridegroom in exchange for a bull and a cow, or for two pairs of them. The Prājāpatya marriage is one in which the bride's father gives her to a man with the stated expectation that they will both practise proper dharma. The first three of these types, and usually the fourth, are praised by the authorities on dharma. These same authorities are ambivalent about the next three, though most texts declare them to be illegal. The Āsura marriage is one in which the bride is given to a man in exchange for wealth. This appears to be the type most commonly practised in recent historical times; it is, in other words, the dowry system. The Gāndharva marriage is a union arising strictly from sexual intercourse and lust. The Rākṣasa marriage is forced abduction 'of a maiden, weeping and wailing, from her house, after smashing and cleaving and breaking (her relatives and household)' (Jamison 1996: 211). This marriage has an ambivalent status because in certain cases abductions were accorded a degree of legality. The last type is the Paiśāca, which is rape of a girl who is asleep, intoxicated or mentally unsound. This is invariably declared illegal.

See also: **Dharma; Dharmaśāstras; Mahābhārata; Manu**

FREDERICK M. SMITH

Further reading

Jamison, Stephanie. 1996. *Sacrificed Wife/Sacrificer's Wife: Women, Ritual and Hospitality in Ancient India*. Oxford: Oxford University Press, 210–35.

Kane, P.V. 1974. *History of Dharmaśāstra*, 2nd edn, vol. 2, pt. 1. Poona: Bhandarkar Oriental Research Institute, 516–23.

Olivelle, Patrick. 2005. *Manu's Code of Law: A Critical Edition and Translation of the Mānava-Dharmaśāstra*. Oxford: Oxford University Press, 109–10.

Pandey, R.J. 1969. *Hindu Saṃskāras*. Delhi: Motilal Banarsidass, 158–70.

VIVEKANANDA, SWAMI (1863–1902)

Swami Vivekananda, born Narendranath Datta, was raised largely in Calcutta (Kolkata). Having met Sri Ramakrishna Paramahamsa in 1881, by the time of

Ramakrishna's death in 1886 he had emerged as Ramakrishna's closest disciple. Narendranath subsequently led several of Ramakrishna's young disciples through a ceremony in which they initiated themselves into saṃnyāsa, thus forming the embryonic community from which the Ramakrishna Math and Mission developed.

From 1889, Narendranath undertook pilgrimages around India. By the end of 1892 he had become convinced of the need to use saṃnyāsis to raise India both materially and spiritually through service to humanity (sevā). In 1893 he attended the World's Parliament of Religions in Chicago, having adopted the title and name Swami Vivekananda. The resultant publicity enabled him to advance his project in India, and through lectures and classes to found Vedanta Societies in the United States and London. During this period he developed his characteristic theories concerning Advaita Vedānta and the ideal of a universal religion, Practical Vedānta, and Raja Yoga. On his return to India in 1897, Vivekananda established the Ramakrishna Mission and the Ramakrishna Math with its centre at Belur Math. He returned to the West in 1899/1900 and died at Belur in 1902.

Apart from the movement he created, Vivekananda influenced the development of modern yoga and other forms of alternative spirituality in the West, and his ideas have been taken up selectively by Hindutva thinkers. Considerable debate has taken place about Vivekananda's achievements as the foremost representative of 'Neo-Hinduism' – in particular about the continuity between his ideas and those of Ramakrishna and between his Neo-Vedāntic philosophy and earlier Advaita Vedānta, and the degree of his indebtedness to Western influences.

See also: **Advaita; Hindutva; Rāja Yoga; Ramakrishna, Sri; Ramakrishna Math and Mission; Saṃnyāsa; Sevā; Yoga, modern; Western popular culture, Hindu influence on**

GWILYM BECKERLEGGE

Further reading

Sen, A.P. 2000. *Swami Vivekananda.* New Delhi: Oxford University Press.

Sil, N.P. 1997. *Swami Vivekananda: A Reassessment.* Selinsgrove: Susquehanna University Press.

VRATA

A vow, generally undertaken by women, for a particular end, often involving abstinence, particularly from food. Vratas are generally thought to be part of an ancient indigenous tradition: although the word does occur in ancient texts, such as the *Ṛgveda* and the *Upaniṣads*, its meaning is fluid. In the *Ṛgveda* and the *Upaniṣads* it has a broader meaning related to dharma and maintaining the cosmic order. The Puraṇas link vrata with the energy generated by tapas, a connection based on the concept of the power of the śakti of the woman performing the vrata, the vratanī. *The Laws of Manu* identify vratas as part of penitential ritual. The current meaning is first found in the *Mahābhāratā*, where individuals, including women, take vows to restrict their behaviour.

The practice of a vrata entails ritual, listening to the origin myth, or koṭhā, of the vrata, reciting mantras and making decorative ālpanās (also known as kolam or raṅgolī) to ward off danger. A commitment to fasting, such as abstaining from certain foods, is made for a fixed period of time. Tuesdays and Saturdays are popular days for fasting as they are days special to the Goddess, to whom the vrata is offered. Vratas are performed mostly at home, without the presence of a priest, and there is also a social aspect as women gather together to hear the vratakothā. Stories and rituals are passed from mother to daughter, but when a woman marries she often adopts the practices of her mother-in-law, in whose house she now lives. Although the urban brāhmaṇa women hire a priest for the rituals, the availability of cheap vrata pamphlets and increasing literacy mean that women can keep vratas as their own domain.

One view of vratas is that they reinforce traditional values by socialising girls into accepting their role as good wife and guardian of the spiritual welfare of the family (and hence the nation) as most vratas are performed for the welfare (or acquisition) of husband and family. There is evidence that for married women the main function of vratas is the maintenance of an ordered life as part of their wifely duties, rather than desire for a specific end. However, there is an increasing tendency for women of all social groups to consider their own general well-being and not just that of their family. Vratanīs say they feel better for the discipline of vratas, and feel uneasy if they fail to observe them. Vratas can be seen as providing an area of ritual autonomy otherwise denied women in the Brahmanical tradition, and an important status within the family.

Vratas are still widely practised by all social groups of women, with new ones emerging, such as the Saṇtoṣī mātā vrata to the goddess popularised in a 1975 film. Under the influence of Rabrindranath Tagore they are also seen as part of folk culture, with ālpanās separated from their ritual meaning and studied as folk art.

See also: **Dharma; Dharmaśāstras; Fasting; Mahābhāratā; Mantra; Puraṇas; Śakti; Saṃhitas; Saṇtoṣī Mātā; Tagore, Rabrindranath; Tapas; Varṇa**

CYNTHIA BRADLEY

Further reading

McDaniel, J. 2003. *Making Virtuous Daughters and Wives: An Introduction to Women's* Vrata *Rituals in Bengali Folk Religion.* Albany, NY: SUNY Press.

McGee, M. 1987. *Feasting and Fasting: The Vrata Tradition and Its Significance for Hindu Women.* Ann Arbor, MI: University of Michigan Dissertation Services.

Pearson, A.M. 1996. *'Because It Gives Me Peace of Mind': Ritual Fasts in the Religious Lives of Hindu Women.* Albany, NY: SUNY Press.

VṚNDĀVANA

Vṛndāvana is a pilgrimage city in Northern India associated with the exploits of Kṛṣṇa and regarded by Vaiṣṇavas as the pivot of the world. The area known as Brājbhūmi, in the district of Mathurā, which includes Vṛndāvana, Govardhana and Gokula, has been a centre of Kṛṣṇa worship for centuries, dated to several hundreds of years BCE. Millions of pilgrims visit these places annually to join in the festivities that re-enact events from Kṛṣṇa's life as a human avatāra of Viṣṇu.

Vṛndāvana is most closely linked to the period of exile in Kṛṣṇa's childhood and youth where he was fostered out to Gokula, a settlement of cowherds residing on the banks of the river Yamunā. It is suggested that Kṛṣṇa-Gopāla, the cowherd deity, was assimilated into the Bhāgavata tradition which depicts Kṛṣṇa as a royal character in the *Mahābhārata*, somewhere around the fourth century BCE. This pastoral deity, an amorous young man, wanders through the forests of Vṛndāvana accompanied by his brother, destroying demons, dancing and making love with the gopīs, the maidens who attend the cows. Foremost amongst these is Rādhā, the divine mistress or consort of Kṛṣṇa. The love between the two becomes the symbol of ecstatic union between devotee and Lord, and their separation represents the longing of the devotee.

This intensely devotional tradition is best represented by Caitanya (1486–1533) and the cult of Bengali or Gauḍīya Vaiṣṇavism. Although Caitanya began his devotional life to Kṛṣṇa in Bengal, in

1510 he moved to Puri in Orissa with his six closest disciples, the Gosvāmins, and from here they set out on a pilgrimage journey in 1515 to rediscover the ancient locations associated with Kṛṣṇa's myths. It is believed that he was able to locate by spiritual power the places of Kṛṣṇa's pastimes in and around Vṛndāvana. However, the city owes much of its present fame as a renowned all-India pilgrimage site to the activities of the Gosvāmins who remained in the area after Caitanya returned to Puri, and the foremost of the city's temples claim to have been founded by them. As a consequence of the connection to Gauḍīya Vaiṣṇavism, the city is visited by thousands of Bengalis to this day.

Vṛnda refers to the Tulasī plant sacred to Viṣṇu and which grows in the local forests, and Vāna means forest. One of the most sacred sites in the city is the small area of Tulasī plants believed to be the rasa maṇḍala, the place where Kṛṣṇa danced with the gopīs, miraculously manifesting himself in a form for each one of them. It is customary for pilgrims to walk around the city with bare feet visiting the sites associated with Kṛṣṇa and the historic temples. This parikrama (circumambulation) is approximately 10 km and takes around three hours to complete. It is traditionally carried out on Ekādaśī, the eleventh day of the waxing and waning moon.

See also: **Avatāra; Bhāgavatas; Bhakti (as path); Caitanya; Gauḍīyas; Gopī(s); Govardhana; Kṛṣṇa; Mahābhārata; Mathurā; Rādhā; Tīrthayātrā; Tulasī; Viṣṇu; Yamunā (river)**

RON GEAVES

Further reading

Klostermaier, Klaus. 1969. *Hindu and Christian in Vrindaban*. London: SCM Press.

Morinis, E. Alan. 1984. *Pilgrimage in the Hindu Tradition*. Delhi: Oxford University Press, 33–35, 125–28.

VṚTRA

The 'holder', the 'restrainer'. Vṛtra is the antagonist of Indra and is often identified with the Vedic Chaos. Also called Ahi (*Ṛgveda* 2.11.5), he is a primordial being who abides on top of a mountain, where he retains celestial and terrestrial rivers. Vṛtra symbolises winter, coldness and drought. He is one of the sons of Tvaṣṭṛ and is depicted as a serpent who holds the waters and/or the sky between his coils. The terrible fight between Indra and Vṛtra – which is described as a cosmogonic myth – is told in *Ṛgveda* (1.32; 1.80) and ends with the killing of the latter and the liberation of the waters. In post-Vedic literature, Vṛtra is described as an all-pervading being (*Taittiriya Saṃhitā* 2.5.2.2; *Śatapatha Brāhmaṇa* 1.1.3.4–5), while in Purāṇic myths, he is said to be a brāhmaṇa whose killing (brahmahatyā) is expiated by Indra through an aśvamedha (horse-sacrifice).

See also: **Indra; Purāṇas; Saṃhitā; Tvaṣṭṛ; Yajña**

FABRIZIO M. FERRARI

Further reading

Lahiri, A.K. 1984. *Vedic Vrtra*. Delhi: Motilal Banarsidass.

VYĀKARAṆA

'Analysis', i.e. grammar, is one, and arguably the most important, of the six 'limbs of the Veda' (Vedāṅgas), alongside pronunciation (Śikṣā), metre (Chandas), etymology (Nirukta), astronomy (Jyotiṣa) and the art of rituals (Kalpa), disciplines auxiliary to the corpus of revealed texts (śruti) and devoted to helping their accurate transmission as well as the correct performance of rituals.

The subject of grammar is śabda, word, language or linguistic utterance. In turn, language is a special source of valid cognition (pramāṇa) that supplements and in some views transcends perception and inference, granted that the locutor is trustworthy. In other words, language generates knowledge. Grammar is an analysis of language, which is words, sentences and their components, but also how word and meaning relate and hence how words may correspond to ontological categories, as well as what psychological and logical conditions govern the grasp of an utterance's meaning. Thus, grammar is not solely descriptive, explaining the forms of correct usage and the rules that command it, but the discipline is also concerned, at least implicitly, with epistemology, logic and indeed metaphysics. The science of language is therefore also philosophy of language as well as linguistic philosophy.

Although there had obviously been many authorities, as cited in later literature, to antedate it, the earliest extant and uniquely influential treatise on grammar is Pāṇini's *Astādhyayī* (Eight Lessons) composed presumably in the fourth century BCE. A work of surpassing genius, the document is a thorough description of both the language of late Vedic texts and that of the educated classes (śistācarā) of its time, what is called 'worldly' (laukika) Sanskrit, now known as 'classical' Sanskrit. Pāṇini's grammar was accepted by all as normative, thus establishing the unchallenged inalterable form of the language that has endured to this day, an 'eternal' language far removed from the ever changing vernaculars (Prākrit).

Monumental, the *Astādhyāyī* consists of some 4,000 extremely concise rules in the shorthand sūtra style. So forbidding is the quasi-algebraic phraseology that no study of this text would be possible without strenuous training and the help of a commentary, of which there have been many, starting with the *Vārttika* (Elements of Interpretation) of Kātyāyana, grafted directly on Pāṇini's sūtras, followed closely and more exhaustively by the *Mahābhāsya* (Great Commentary) of Patañjali (second century BCE), who was the first to combine explicitly Pāṇinian grammatical analysis with psycholinguistic and philosophical speculations.

Apart from the great philosophers of language who have followed in the steps of Patañjali, Bhartrhari, Maṇḍana Miśra and Abhinavagupta, to name but three, grammarians subsequent to Pāṇini have found in his work the full scope of the grammar of a language he had come to define and, having few new observations to add, have mainly devoted their efforts to stretching Pāṇini's rules so as to account for later usages.

It has been claimed, justifiably, that grammar has played in India a role parallel to that of the natural sciences in Western civilisation.

See also: **Abhinavagupta; Bhartṛhari; Chandas; Jyotiṣa; Kalpa; Languages; Nirukta; Pāṇini; Patañjali; Sacred texts; Śikṣā; Sūtra; Veda; Vedāṅgas**

DANIEL MARIAU

Further reading

Cardona, G. 1994. 'Indian Linguistics'. In G. Lepschy, ed., *History of Linguistics*, vol. 1: Eastern Traditions of Linguistics. London: Longman.

Coward, H.G. and K. Kunjuni Raja. 1990. *Encyclopedia of Indian Philosophies*, vol. V: *The Philosophy of the Grammarians.* Delhi: Motilal Banarsidass.

VYĀSA

A legendary sage, also known as Kṛṣṇavaipayana, who is attributed with the authorship of the Mahābhārata and the eighteen major Purāṇas. However, the same ṛṣi is also believed to be the compiler of the Veda, a work that was obviously put together by a number of contributors over a period of centuries, and it may be that the name was used as a generic title for a post-Vedic compiler or arranger of sacred texts and applied to a number of eminent sages. In the Purāṇas, there are twenty-eight Vyāsas, considered to be incarnations of either Brahmā or Viṣṇu, who have compiled the Vedas in different ages. The attribution of the generic name to the compilers of the *Mahābhārata* and the major *Purāṇas* may have been a device to establish the authority of the new popular texts by connecting them to smṛti texts or from the arrangers themselves taking on a common assumed identity.

The mythology of Vyāsa declares him to be the illegitimate son of the sage Parāsara and Satyavatī. His dark complexion and birthplace on an island in the middle of the Yamunā river give him the alternative name Kṛṣṇavaipayana, although he is also known as Kānīna, the 'illegitimate'. He appears in the *Mahābhārata* as the father of Dhṛtarāṣṭra and Pāṇḍu, whose respective children began the war. It is recounted that his mother married King Sāntanu and gave birth to two sons. The elder died in battle, but the younger one died childless. Although Kṛṣṇavaipayana preferred a life of celibate solitude, he married the two widows of the younger son at the bequest of his mother, thus becoming the progenitor of the legendary conflict that is the central theme of the epic.

See also: **Brahmā; Dhṛtarāṣṭra; Mahābhārata; Pāṇḍu; Purāṇas; Veda; Viṣṇu**

RON GEAVES

Further reading

Dasgupta, Madhusraba. 1999. *Samsad Companion to the Mahābhārata.* Calcutta: Sahitya Samsad.

W

WAR AND PEACE

Because of its long history, spanning some four millennia and moving from small-scale societies into states and empires, the Indian subcontinent has seen its fair share of wars – but not religious wars, thanks to a common rule that kings must support all the religions within their realm, and not wars of expansion beyond the subcontinent. So important was the recognition of warfare (both offensive and defensive), including the existence of sheer power captured in the maxim that 'big fish eat little fish', that the problem of war was discussed in many genres. The *Veda Saṃhitās* celebrate warfare, with the chief warrior deity Indra, whereas the *Upaniṣads* promote asceticism, non-violence and peace, even though many ascetics came from warrior circles. The *Arthaśāstra*, the *Dharmaśāstras* and *Itihāsas* (the epics and *Purāṇas*) reflect on the moral dilemmas of warfare. Because warfare had religious dimensions, such as battle being ritualised and ethicised and death in battle guaranteeing heaven, the topic of warfare was called Dhanurveda, the Veda of Warfare (Veda being the category of scripture *par excellence*).

Hinduism accepts the premise that peace (śanti) is good, both political peace and spiritual peace. Hinduism has two positions on how to attain political peace: by non-violence or by just war. Two great statements (mahāvākyas) in the *Mahābhārata* capture the ethical dilemma: that supreme righteousness is ahiṃsā (ahiṃsā paramo dharmaḥ) and so is righteous violence (dhārmya hiṃsā tathaiva). The authors on dharma (ethics) proposed a conceptual solution to the apparent conflict between the call for non-violence and righteous violence. Dharma is of two basic types: sāmānya and viśeṣa. The ascetic/non-violent values were broadened in the classical period to apply to everyone (with ahiṃsā generally beginning the list); these are called sāmānya (common). By contrast, the virtues/principles according to caste, stage of life, sex, region and so forth constitute viśeṣa-dharma. According to this concept, the class duty of the kṣatriyas (warriors) is to protect society, using violence if necessary. A corollary of this is that artha (which includes the theory and practice of war) is considered one of the four legitimate goals of life (puruṣārtha). Conflict between non-violence and violence was avoided by arguing that non-violence was the universal value and that violence in the context of righteous war by kṣatriyas was a legitimate exception.

The *Mahābhārata* – especially the dialogue between Lord Kṛṣna and the warrior Arjuna in its most famous section, the *Bhagavadgītā* – explores the topic of righteous war (dharma-yuddha) in contrast to unrighteous war (kūṭa-yuddha), which has an unjust cause and uses secretive, unregulated means. Just cause here is rightful succession to the throne and the honouring of promises, more generally stated in the literature as maintaining or establishing justice according to public standards and the rules of just warfare. Just means would include upholding society by doing one's duty for the sake of duty as a kind of renunciation in action (nais-kāmya-karma-yoga). This is defined as using violence if need be but with a new yogic perspective, an equilibrium or mental peace in the midst of battle based on action without personal desire, a spirituality beyond greed that works for the ideal society (rāmrājaya) based on moral values and justice.

This epic and the *Rāmāyaṇa* give the following principles of just war: (1) clarity (an open fight with procedures agreed upon by both sides before battle); (2) discrimination and containment (war only in restricted places and times – which must be announced – and between restricted people, kṣatriyas, the corollary being that brāhmaṇas, the aged, women, children, peaceful citizens walking along the road, the mentally ill and the support staff for battle must be protected); (3) prudence (acknowledgement of the commonality of warfare and the need for an ethics of warfare grounded in realism, such as keeping Hinduism allied with the sources of political power to prevent abrogation of rights); (4) fairness and equality (battles between equals in physique, armour and psychology, stopped if warriors become panic-stricken, scatter, hide, become tired, sleepy, thirsty, disabled, have broken weapons or give the sign of unconditional surrender); (5) reciprocity (the Hindu version of the golden rule: 'One should not do unto others that which is unpleasant to oneself'); (6) self-defence (warfare to defend the community as an exception to the general rule of ahiṃsā); and (7) reconciliation after victory (reinstatement of a defeated king or his substitute and permission to maintain his own customs and laws as long as he accepted the victor's suzerainty).

In modern times, Gandhi interpreted the battle context of the *Gītā* allegorically – the eternal duel between the 'forces of darkness and of light' – because Hinduism has always evolved as a living religion. Gandhi's basic values were closely allied to the *sāmānya* principles. He extended the ethics of ahiṃsā to everyone as well as politicising and modernising them as the just means to a just end (Indian independence). By contrast, since independence the government has universalised conscription for men and has developed weapons of mass destruction for deterrence, arguing that these are just means and necessary for self-defence.

See also: **Ahiṃsā; Arjuna; Artha; Arthaśāstra; Bhagavadgītā; Dhanurveda; Dharma; Dharmaśāstras; Gandhi, Mohandas Karamchand; Indra; Itihāsa; Karma (as path); Kṛṣna; Mahābhārata; Purāṇas; Puruṣārthas; Rāmāyaṇa; Rāmarājya; Upaniṣads; Varṇa; Veda**

KATHERINE K. YOUNG

Further reading

Desai, M. 1946. *The Gita According to Gandhi*. Ahmedabad: Navajivan.

Dikshitar, V.R.R. 1944. *War in Ancient India*. Delhi: Motilal Banarsidass (2nd edn 1948).

Matilal, B.K. (ed.). 1989. *Moral Dilemmas in the Mahābhārata*. Delhi: Motilal Banarsidass.
Mehendale, M.A. 1995. *Reflections on the Mahābhārata War*. Shimla: Indian Institute of Advanced Study.
Kangle, R.P. 1988. (ed. and trans.). *The Kauṭilīya Arthaśāstra*. Delhi: Motilal Banarsidass.
Pyarelal, N. 1956. *Mahatma Gandhi: The Last Phase*. Ahmedabad: Navajivan.
Rosen, S.P. 1996. *Societies and Military Power: India and Its Armies*. Ithaca, NY: Cornell University Press.
Sarasvatisvami, P.C. 2000. *Hindu Dharma: The Universal Way of Life*. Mumbai: Bharatiya Vidya Bhavan.
Sharma, A. 1993. 'Gandhi or Godse? Power, Force and Non-violence'. In N. Smart and S. Thakur, eds, *Ethical and Political Dilemmas of Modern India*. New York: St Martin's Press.
Young, K.K. 2004. 'Hinduism and the Ethics of Weapons of Mass Destruction'. In S.H. Hashmi, and S.P. Lee, eds, *Ethics and Weapons of Mass Destruction: Religious and Secular Perspectives*. New York: Cambridge University Press.

WEBER, MAX (1864–1920)

German sociologist. Weber's work on Indian religions, translated as *The Religion of India* (1916–17; translated 1958; but see Kantowsky 1982 for a critical assessment of this translation), appeared during the First World War in an influential journal edited by Weber himself, the *Archiv für Sozialwissenschaft und Sozialpolitik*, as part of a series of articles concerned with the economic ethics of the major world religions. The first of these articles was 'The Protestant Ethic and the Spirit of Capitalism' (1905; translated 1930), an enormously influential attempt by Weber to supplement Marx's materialist account of modern capitalism by identifying the role of Protestant innerworldly asceticism in its emergence. Weber's articles on Indian religions, as well as those on Chinese religions and Judaism, were conceived as parts of this larger work, which, due to the circumstances in which Weber found himself in the last decade of his life, never achieved its intended form. The work was intended to explain the emergence of modern rationality, and the consequent disenchantment and secularisation of the world. For Weber the roots of this rationality lay in the problem of theodicy, to which the Judaeo-Christian and Indian traditions provided different solutions, each rationally consistent. The Indian theodicy was based on the doctrine of karma, which Weber regarded as the most coherent theory of this type (Weber 1958: 121) and which lies at the root of the caste system. By holding out the prospect of a better rebirth, to which one should rationally devote all one's effort, the caste system in turn hindered the development of capitalism in India. Weber's Protestant ethic thesis has been and remains the subject of extensive debate; by contrast, while the consequences of his work on India are also discussed (Gellner 2001), the starting point for his analysis, that the 'spirit of capitalism' is absent there, has been undercut by the work of more recent economic theorists who have denied the uniqueness of Western capitalism and pointed to the importance of India in a world economy prior to the eighteenth century (Frank 1998).

See also: **Hinduism, history of scholarship; Karma (Law of Action)**

WILL SWEETMAN

Further reading

Frank, A.G. 1998. *Re-Orient: Global Economy in the Asian Age*. Berkeley, CA: University of California Press.
Gellner, D.N. 2001. *The Anthropology of Buddhism and Hinduism: Weberian Themes*. Oxford: Oxford University Press.
Kantowsky, D. 1982. 'Max Weber on India and Indian Interpretations of Max Weber'. *Contributions to Indian Sociology* 16: 141–74.
Weber, M. 1958. *The Religion of India: The Sociology of Hinduism and Buddhism*.

Translated and edited by Hans H. Gerth and Don Martindale. Glencoe, IL: Free Press.

WESTERN CULTURE, HINDU INFLUENCE ON

From the English Romantic poets to the German philosopher Schopenhauer, a variety of significant Hindu influences on Western literature and philosophy are traceable, and instances of receptivity to aspects of Hindu thought are evident. Although complex, such influences illuminate aspects of European and North American intellectual history. It is possible to explore how, and to what extent, Hindu texts and learning were transmitted to and received in the West.

The relations between Hinduism and Western high culture have been interpreted, documented and discussed by scholars. Wilhelm Halbfass explored the intellectual encounter of India and the West from pre-Alexandrian antiquity until the present. Before Halbfass, Raymond Schwab (1884–1956) surveyed the 'Oriental Renaissance' in Europe. Recently scholars such as Fred Dallmayr, J.J. Clarke and Richard King have produced work which explores themes and debates relating to Orientalism, postcolonialism, comparative philosophy, Western perceptions and images of India and so on.

Some recent studies have concentrated on the relation between India and Ancient Greece. For example, M.L. West (1971) used historical and philological approaches in an attempt to determine possible 'Oriental' influences on Greek thought. He considered Ionian thought (550–480 BCE), Pherecydes, the Milesians and Heraclitus, as well as figures such as Parmenides, Pythagoras, Empedocles and Anaxagoras. Halbfass' concern, expressed in the first chapter of *India and Europe*, was the question of the role of India in the philosophical awareness of the Greeks (rather than actual or possible influences). Substantial works, including philosophical explorations and analyses, have been contributed by Thomas McEvilley, Vassiliades, Sedlar and others.

Inevitably selective and brief, this essay is restricted to consideration of some key periods, themes, texts, scholars, poets and philosophers. For example, we shall survey the Romantic movement, the influence of the *Upaniṣads* and *Bhagavadgītā*, Schopenhauer and Emerson.

We begin by illustrating the importance and influence of the work of Sir William Jones (1746–94).

From early Western Indology to the British Romantic poets

As early as 1651, Abraham Roger, a Dutch missionary who had lived near Madras, published in Amsterdam a translation of poems of Bhartṛhari, *Open Door to the Hidden Heathendom* (this work included an account of Hindu customs and religion).

However, pioneering scholars who concentrated on original Sanskrit texts emerged in the late eighteenth century. In 1785 an English translation of the *Bhagavadgītā* was published by Charles Wilkins (1749–1836), an event of key importance according to Jones. Authors such as E.J. Sharpe and K.G. Srivastava have traced the impact of Wilkins' translation on European culture, including the Romantic movement. Wilkins also translated the Śakuntalā episode from the *Mahābhārata* (1795) and the *Hitopadeśa Pañcatantra* (The Heetopades of Veeshnoo-Sarma) (1787).

Several recent studies by authors such as M.J. Franklin have explored and interpreted the nature and extent of William Jones' contribution and influence. A linguist and jurist, Jones founded the Asiatic Society of Bengal in 1784. His enthusiastic embrace of Sanskrit and Indian learning led to the legitimisation of Indian literature, comparative philology and

Indian philosophy as branches of academic enquiry. He perceived historical and structural relations between Indian languages and Greek and Latin, declaring that Sanskrit is more 'refined' and 'perfect' than Greek and more 'copious' than Latin. Noting 'affinities' in the grammatical forms and roots of verbs in Sanskrit and the European classical languages, Jones suggested a 'common source' from which Greek, Latin and Sanskrit 'sprang'.

In an era of British domination in India (both political and economic), how could Indian culture and learning be extolled? Jones' employer was the East India Company; Indian people were providing cheap or free labour; India was British property. Jones emphasised comparison: rather than study India as an alien, unrelated culture, scholars were motivated by the idea that Europe could learn about itself from India. Halbfass and others have pointed to Warren Hastings' calculation concerning the benefits of study of Indian thought and culture for British political rule in India.

Among Jones' publications was *Sacontala, or the Fatal Ring: an Indian Drama* (1789), an English translation of Kālidāsa's romantic verse drama *Śakuntalā*. Within two decades this popular work went into five English editions.

Jones' talents were recognised by literary London and he was elected a member of 'The Club' of Samuel Johnson (1709–84); among his friends were eminent men of letters such as Edmund Burke (1729–97) and Edward Gibbon (1737–94). The work of Jones (including his original hymns to Indian deities), of Wilkins and other early pioneering Indologists exercised a powerful influence on a variety of Western poets and intellectuals, including the Romantics. Halbfass considers such influential factors as Jones' 'deism' and the view of Indian traditions as especially ancient and pristine.

Jones influenced the 'Oriental' interests and themes of Lord Byron (1788–1824), Robert Southey (1774–1843) and Thomas Moore (1779–1852).

Southey composed a long narrative poem, *The Curse of Kehama* (1810), which involved Hindu mythology. It is a tale concerning the characters Kehama (the Raja of the world), Arvalan (his son), Ladurlad (a peasant) and Ladurlad's daughter (Kailyal). Ladurlad is cursed for attempting to protect his daughter from Arvalan. In his correspondence and the preface to the first edition of the poem, Southey expresses uneasiness and anxiety about his work, dismissing Hinduism as effectively 'fatal' and its 'fables' as 'monstrous'. In a recent study, B. Rajan attempts to interpret Southey's views and the nature of Southey's attitude to his own work.

Thomas Moore, a poet and musician born in Dublin, was the author of *Lalla Rookh* (1817), a work that became very popular. It involves a story in prose, connecting four tales in verse. Lalla Rookh, the emperor's daughter, is travelling from Delhi to Kashmir to marry a king. A young poet relates four tales during the journey. Lalla Rookh falls in love with the poet, who is revealed as the King (of Bucharia) she set out to marry. The four tales (in verse) are 'The Veiled Prophet of Khorassan', 'Paradise and the Peri', 'The Fire-Worshippers' and 'The Light of the Haram'. In 'The Fire-Worshippers', the Ghebers are resisting the conquering Muslims. It tells of Hafed (a Gheber) falling in love with the daughter of the Emir al Hassan (Hinda). J. Lennon (2004) considers *Lalla Rookh* in relation to Irish nationalism and Moore's use of allegory (the Ghebers representing the rebellious Irish).

The *Curse of Kehama* and *Lalla Rookh* are more complex examples of a particular class of literature, the 'Eastern' or 'Oriental' tale (or 'novel'), which became especially popular in the latter half of the eighteenth and early nineteenth centuries. As well as the work of Jones, influences on the genre included the *Arabian Nights Entertainments* (tales written in Arabic, an English translation appearing in 1705–08), which contained stories of Hindu (as well as Persian and Arabic) origin, and *The Generall Historie of the Turkes* (1603) by Richard Knolles. This latter work influenced Byron and Johnson.

Involving elements of the supernatural (and exotic settings), many Oriental tales concerned the adventures of heroes and villains. An example is *Tales ... of Inatulla of Delhi* (1768) by Alexander Dow, who also published *The History of Hindostan* (1768). Another example is Frances Sheridan's Oriental novel *The History of Nourjahad* (1767), a highly regarded work.

There has been recent scholarly interest in Byron's Orientalism (i.e. his attraction to 'Eastern' culture), including a study by N.B. Oueijan (1999) exploring his knowledge of Islamic culture. Relevant poems include *The Giaour* (1813), *The Bride of Abydos* (1813) and *The Corsair* (1814).

In *The Giaour*, Leila (a slave), in love with the Giaour (a Byronic hero), is dumped into the sea by Hassan (her Turkish lord). After killing Hassan, the Giaour is overcome with grief and remorse. Reading allegorically, Leila (from Circassia) has been interpreted as representing Greece, caught between European civilisation on the one hand and the Ottoman Empire on the other.

Other works of Byron, including parts of *Childe Harold* (begun in 1809) and *Don Juan* (1819–24), contain 'Eastern' settings and themes. The Romantic artist Delacroix (1798–1863) was inspired by Byron's Orientalism.

An attraction to Hinduism in the cases of Samuel Taylor Coleridge (1772–1834) and Percy Bysshe Shelley (1792–1822) has been documented and discussed. An important and interesting figure in intellectual history, Coleridge was active or influential in a variety of spheres – social theory, politics, religious thought and philosophy, as well as literature. He was interested in the idealist philosophy of George Berkeley (1685–1753) before he studied German philosophy. For Coleridge, British empiricism was inadequate to explain artistic creation. He was attracted to, and much influenced by, Kant (1724–1804) and Schelling's *System des transcendentalen Idealismus* (System of Transcendental Idealism; 1800). He preferred the idea of mind as active (not passive), and organic (not mechanical) metaphors to describe mind's workings. German philosophy was also fruitful in relation to his support for Christian doctrines. Schelling's thought was transmitted to English Romantics such as Shelley and Wordsworth (1770–1850) via Coleridge. In his *Biographia Literaria* (1817), we find accounts of Coleridge's own intellectual development (philosophical autobiography) as well as literary criticism. John Drew explores the history of Coleridge's encounter with Indian thought from the depiction of himself as the god 'Vishna' in 1797 (and his authorship of the famous opium-fuelled poem *Kubla Khan: a Vision in a Dream* (1816)) to his defence of Christianity. Coleridge's writings contain many references to India. At first in awe of Indian culture and learning, his initial Indophilia was later replaced by scepticism; Coleridge became concerned to undermine an idealised view of India (as the ultimate source of wisdom).

Shelley was described as 'completely Indian' (by Edgar Quinet). Among the poems discussed by commentators in relation to India and Hinduism are *Prometheus Unbound* (1820), *Ode to the West Wind* (1820) and *Adonais* (1821). He owned William Robertson's *Historical Disquisition Concerning the Knowledge the Ancients Had of India* (1791), the *Works* (1807) of William Jones and Edward Moor's *Hindu Pantheon* (1810); he studied Southey's *Curse of Kehama* and Sydney Owenson's novel *The Missionary – An Indian Tale* (1811). For S.R. Swaminathan,

Prometheus Unbound fuses Hindu and Greek mythology, and Platonism and Vedānta. Drew explores Shelley's image of India and the texts with which he was acquainted, offering an examination of the background and content of *Prometheus Unbound*.

The work of William Blake (1757–1827) presents a complex and intriguing case of possible Hindu influence. Scholars such as N. Frye and Foster Damon have pointed to Blake's awareness of Wilkins' translation of the *Bhagavadgītā*. He was initially considered 'mad', but the twentieth century witnessed an explosion of interest in Blake and his work. A variety of analyses and interpretations of his work have been produced, ranging from Jungian, Freudian and Marxist readings to studies relating Blake to Neo-Platonism and Swedenborgian teaching. In a recent absorbing study, David Weir (2003) considers the significance of the influence of the British 'discovery' of Hindu literature (the 'Oriental Renaissance') on the myths and ideals of Blake's poetry. He examines Blake in relation to the mythographic tradition of the eighteenth century, arguing that his mythic system emerges from the same historical context that gave rise to the Oriental Renaissance (a context including dissenting theology and republican politics). Weir seeks to show how Hindu mythology exercised a profound influence on the development of Blake's work.

Few major writers of the Romantic period have escaped consideration in relation to India and Indian thought. For example, scholars have discussed John Keats (1795–1821) and Wordsworth as well as Blake, Shelley and Coleridge. In general it is apparent that we find place names, costume, architecture, culture, thought, religion, art, etc. of the 'East' or 'Orient' (specifically Asia, North Africa or Eastern Europe) in the writings of the British Romantics. Readers of Romantic poetry might easily discern the possible presence of Hindu ideas and imagery: echoes of Hindu teaching on cosmic cycles and māyā in Shelley's *Ode to the West Wind* and *Adonais*, or reflections of Vedānta in Wordsworth and so on. And we might speculate on possible harmonies between Hindu thinking and Romantic sensibilities, themes and preoccupations, including Neo-Platonism and the sense of the transcendental and infinite.

Against a background of wars of independence and the French Revolution, Romanticism is generally characterised as a reaction against Enlightenment rationalism and empiricism, emphasising the importance of the 'imagination' and celebrating the self. The Romantic poets were receptive to the new English translations of Hindu literature, forming images of India and Indian thought via the writings of Jones and others.

The publication of Edward Said's *Orientalism* in 1978 led to a preoccupation with the relations between literary discourse and colonial politics. Thus Blake, Byron, Shelley and others have been examined in a context of viewing the Romantic period as a time of colonial expansion and world travel and exploration; issues and problems concerning 'colonial anxiety' and 'imperial guilt' in Britain, cultural differences, national identity and many other relevant topics have been debated by scholars such as T. Fulford and Leask (1992). Allen and Trivedi (2000) stress the importance of examining specific texts before deciding on 'macro-issues' of identity, colonialism, etc. Within British Romanticism as a whole, it is instructive to explore and appreciate the complexity of individual cases, for example the nature, context and development of Coleridge's perception of India as distinct from Byron's Orientalism. In any event a critical appreciation of the works, views and influence of William Jones is essential for the task of assessing Hindu influences in the Romantic period.

German Romanticism

Although the infatuation with India and Indian thought ('Indomania') shared by many German Romantics is well known and well documented, it is instructive and rewarding to explore and evaluate the diverse perceptions of and rich responses to India among a large number of writers.

The thought of J.G. Herder (1744–1803) was a key influence on the development of Romanticism and German Idealism. Herder was a poet, a critic of Kant and the Enlightenment and a philosopher of culture and history. He was attracted to, and participated in, the new discipline of Indology. His awareness of India and Indian thought was shaped by such materials as travellers' accounts and the German translations of the new English and French translations of Indian texts. He expressed great admiration for the *Śakuntalā* after encountering George Förster's 1791 German translation of Jones' English version. Herder contributed the foreword to the second edition of Förster's work.

Herder is associated with positive, idealistic and glorifying views of India. For him India was the 'cradle' of humanity, the source of civilisation. Although a Christian, he exhibited empathy for the people of India and Hindu thought. For him the Hindus were gentle, moderate and calm. He interpreted the essence of Hindu teaching as the idea of the absolute unity of all things; there is one Being as the basis of (in and behind) all things. Herder was also critical of aspects of Hinduism, including the caste system and the doctrine of the transmigration of souls.

Goethe (1749–1832) was another admirer of the *Śakuntalā*, but the nature of his encounter with and responses to India differs in various respects from that of his friend Herder. Singhal considered how Goethe was impressed by Indian poetry but was not attracted to the art, sculpture and mythology of India. Major Romantic poets who were attracted to and developed images of India included Novalis (1772–1801) and Heinrich Heine (1797–1856). A.L. Willson produced a study of these, together with writers such as Richter (1763–1825).

F. Schlegel was a key figure in the German Romantic movement; among his contributions was the theory of 'romantic irony'. He was attracted to the study of Sanskrit and ancient Indian texts. In 1808 he published his *Über die Sprache und Weisheit der Indier* (On the Language and Wisdom of the Indians), an important and influential work of European Indology. The work of his brother August Wilhelm Schlegel (1767–1845) was also a key influence on the development of Europe's awareness of Hindu thought and learning.

Halbfass considered how the German Romantic passion for an idealised India was linked to a critique of the European present. Thus a return to Indian origins and wisdom was proposed in order to restore a sense of wholeness and unity, and to counter or correct a preoccupation with rationalism and pragmatism. However, in the work of the Schlegel brothers and others, the Romantic enthusiasm for India transformed into academic Indology, a programme of critical, historical, philological, 'objective' research.

India and German philosophy: *Oupnek'hat*, Schopenhauer and Deussen

The French philologist Anquetil-Duperron (1731–1805) published a Latin translation of a collection of Persian translations of fifty *Upaniṣads* (1801–02). The title of this work was *Oupnek'hat* (a corruption of the word *Upaniṣad*). It is of key importance in the context of the development of European philosophical awareness of Indian thought. The *Oupnek'hat* awakened an interest in, and generated great enthusiasm for, India and Hindu thought.

Anquetil-Duperron articulated what he saw as similarities between Indian thought and various Western philosophers and traditions, including Plotinus (205–70 CE), Spinoza (1632–77) and Gnosticism. He discussed Kant in relation to Vedāntic thought in the appendix, 'De Kantismo'.

Oupnek'hat is renowned for its association with Schopenhauer. In the preface to his *Die Welt als Wille und Vorstellung* (The World as Will and Representation; 1818), Schopenhauer acknowledges that his own work was inspired by *Oupnek'hat*; he says that readers who have already received ancient Indian wisdom will be best prepared to hear his philosophy. Schopenhauer claims that the 'individual' and 'disconnected' utterances of the *Upaniṣads* could be deduced from his thought but he does not accept that his philosophy can be found in the *Upaniṣads.*

For Schopenhauer the writers of ancient Indian texts were concerned to answer the same questions which preoccupied Kant and himself. He equated the Upaniṣadic 'Brahman' (ultimate reality) with the Kantian 'Ding an sich' ('Thing-in-itself') and saw the Upaniṣadic teaching 'Tat tvam asi' ('That art thou') as an expression of Kantian transcendental idealism. Schopenhauer could equate concepts of different historical periods and perceive ideas at the same level as his own thought because he did not view the history of philosophy in terms of growth and progress. So fundamental truths which he claimed to have discovered were present, on his view, in Indian thought. Andrew P. Tuck and other scholars have regarded Schopenhauer as appropriating the *Upaniṣads* for his own purposes. On this view Schopenhauer could rediscover his philosophical achievements in another (foreign and exotic) context, the realm of Buddhist and Vedāntic thought. Study of Indian thought could also facilitate what Schopenhauer regarded as an independent critique of the Judeo-Christian tradition.

Indian philosophical studies emerged under the influence of eighteenth- and nineteenth-century German Idealism. In the late nineteenth century pioneering works on Indian philosophy by Paul Deussen, Max Müller and others used Kantian and Hegelian terminology and concepts. Following Schopenhauer, Deussen rediscovered one universal or basic truth in different traditions and historical periods. He claimed that the basis of religion and philosophy is the truth that the external world is mere appearance and not reality ('Ding an sich'), so the entire physical universe reflects how things are constituted for us, not how things really are. Deussen refers to the *Upaniṣads*, Greek philosophy (especially Plato and Parmenides) and German Idealism (in particular Kant and Schopenhauer) as representing the occasions on which philosophy understood its task and the solution demanded. For Deussen, philosophy was the study of the disjunction between appearance and reality. He referred to the great religious teachers as 'unconsciously' followers of Kant; that is, they regarded empirical reality, the space–time–cause world, as appearance only. Thus Deussen provided Kantian readings of the *Upaniṣads* and Vedāntic thought, portraying Indian philosophy as a tradition concerned to uncover the 'noumenal' reality behind 'phenomena'. He states that the external world of ordinary experience is mere 'māyā'; it is not, in Kantian terms, a disposition of things-in-themselves; it is not, in *Upaniṣadic* terms, the 'self' (ātman) of things. For Deussen, all religions depend on Kantian philosophy (which was expressed in a 'less definite' form in the *Upaniṣads*). So the same basic truth (concerning the phenomenal nature of the physical universe) is found, according to Deussen, in Plato, Śaṅkara and Kant. In other words, the most recent 'discoveries' of the major European philosophers were reflected in ancient Hindu texts.

Max Müller concentrated mainly on the Veda, *Upaniṣads* and Vedānta. His work was influential in both Europe and India. He was concerned with projects of the 'comparative science of religion', 'comparative theology' and 'comparative mythology' (but he never spoke of 'comparative philosophy'). For him only the Vedānta thinkers were engaged in a 'search after truth'. He referred to Vedānta philosophy as a system in which human speculation has reached its 'very acme'. India–Europe comparisons became irresistible in such an atmosphere of enthusiasm and receptivity. For example, Idealists could perceive parallels between Śaṅkara's concept of 'nirguṇa Brahman' ('Brahman without qualities' or ultimate reality) and such concepts as the 'Absolute' of the English philosopher F.H. Bradley (1846–1924), who published his *Appearance and Reality* in 1893.

From Anquetil-Duperron to Deussen and neo-Vedāntin philosophers there has been a tradition of associating Kantian idealism with Hindu (especially Vedāntic) thought. The relations between Indian thought, Kant and the post-Kantian German Idealists have been examined by scholars. For example, Halbfass considered Hegel and Schelling (1775–1854) as well as Schopenhauer. Kant himself was not acquainted with Sanskrit texts but scholars such as D.P. Singhal have speculated upon the nature and extent of his knowledge of India and Indian thought. Alleged parallels between Kant's views (on the nature of reality, knowledge, morality, aesthetics and God) and Indian (especially Hindu and Buddhist) teachings have led many to assume that he was familiar with Indian philosophy. He described the Hindus as 'tolerant', free of dogma and 'gentle'; his lectures on physical geography involved India, and he spoke on the customs and manners of the people of India. Kant developed his philosophy and taught in the latter half of the eighteenth century; his masterpiece the *Kritik der reinen Vernunft* (Critique of Pure Reason) was published in 1781. In this period it appears unlikely that Kant was in a position to receive direct knowledge of Indian philosophy, but Singhal points to the possibility that he was acquainted with materials such as travel accounts (Kant himself did not travel and did not leave his home town of Königsberg).

The post-Kantian Idealist J.G. Fichte (1762–1814) was not familiar with Sanskrit texts but his philosophy has been compared to Hindu thought. His *Anweisung zu einem seligen Leben* (The Way to the Blessed Life; 1806) has been related to the Advaita Vedānta of Śaṅkara. Fichte's thought influenced the German Romantics.

The work of Schelling represents an interesting and important case of European philosophical affinity with Hindu thought. His early work and letters reflected an interest in Indian studies. Later he recognised Vedānta philosophy as the most exalted 'spiritualism' or 'idealism' and was attracted to the doctrine of 'māyā'.

Whereas Schopenhauer is a celebrated instance of European receptivity to Indian thought, Hegel is portrayed negatively as contrasting with Schopenhauer. For Hegel, the procedure of merging or identifying the meaning of Western and Eastern philosophies is ahistorical. He regarded Indian thought as 'aufgehoben' or 'cancelled' and preserved in Western thought. For Hegel the 'Orient' represents a preliminary stage of the 'Occident'. There is one 'world spirit' (Weltgeist) and one world-historical process, so for Hegel the way of development (or the way of the Weltgeist) leads from the East to the West. Thus it is not possible to equate Indian with European thought; they are on different levels (European thought cannot return to Oriental thought). However, Hegel recognised the importance and usefulness of Indian studies and may be viewed as one of the very few major

European philosophers who was deeply interested in Indian thought.

New England Transcendentalism

Another significant encounter with Hinduism (especially Vedāntic thought) occurred in North America in the nineteenth century. Between 1830 and 1860, a religious, social and an intellectual movement, 'Transcendentalism', flourished in Massachusetts. Central figures in this movement were Ralph Waldo Emerson (1803–82) and Henry David Thoreau (1817–62). Both thinkers were attracted to Hindu texts.

The Transcendentalists were influenced by Platonism, German Idealism and European Romanticism. They rejected Calvinistic Christianity and materialism and affirmed the natural goodness of humanity, the unity and spiritual nature of the universe and the superiority of intuition over logical reasoning. They perceived in Hinduism philosophical and spiritual teachings allied to, and supportive of, their idealistic inclinations and goals.

Emerson read works of William Jones and was deeply impressed by the *Bhagavadgītā* after acquiring a copy of Wilkins' translation in 1845. His reading of Eastern literature expanded after 1837 and he was influenced by Rammohan Roy. Emerson's journals and essays (such as *Over-Soul*, *Plato*, *Fate* and *Illusions*) reflect a familiarity and an affinity with, and an assimilation of, Hindu concepts. He also wrote the poems *Brahma* and *Hamatreya.* Thoreau's encounter with Hinduism has been characterised as less intellectual than Emerson's. He was the author of the essay *Civil Disobedience* (1849) and of *Walden* (1854) and scholars have debated his attraction to yoga and Hindu teachings on detachment. Other Transcendentalists who were attracted to Hinduism and non-Western traditions included J.F. Clarke (1810–88), author of *Ten Great Religions* (1871), and S. Johnson (1822–82), author of *Oriental Religions and Their Relation to Universal Religions* (1873).

Concluding remarks: the vast scope of Hindu–West Studies

We have sketched some key cases of influence and receptivity but instances of Hindu–West encounters in the spheres of literature and philosophy in the nineteenth and twentieth centuries are numerous. Walt Whitman (1819–92), Herman Melville (1819–91), T.S. Eliot (1888–1965), Aldous Huxley (1894–1963), Christopher Isherwood (1904–86) and W.B. Yeats (1865–1939) are examples of major writers influenced by or attracted to aspects of Hinduism. In the philosophical sphere many comparative studies have emerged, together with reflections on methodology and the problematics of Hindu–West comparison. Thus investigation of Hindu–West literary and philosophical encounters offers opportunities for rich and rewarding study.

We have concentrated on philosophy and literature but a full, comprehensive grasp of the relation between Hinduism and Western high culture might include consideration of art, mathematics, music, Jungian psychology and even modern physics. For example, Partha Mitter (1992) has surveyed European reactions to Hindu sculpture, painting and architecture from the earliest explorers to modern twentieth-century appreciations. And J.J. Clarke has considered ways in which physicists such as E. Schrödinger (1887–1961) were attracted to Vedāntic thought. Among composers interested in Hinduism were Beethoven (1770–1827) and G. Holst (1874–1934). Holst studied Sanskrit and composed works on Indian subjects.

On the whole it is apparent that the question of Hindu influences on Western culture challenges us to review and assess familiar and well-researched cases (e.g.

Schopenhauer) but also offers exciting, diverse and multidisciplinary avenues of exploration as well as opportunities for hermeneutic reflection.

See also: **Advaita; Anquetil-Duperron, Abraham-Hyacinthe; Asiatic Societies; Ātman; Bhagavadgītā; Bhartṛhari; Brahman; Buddhism, relationship with Hinduism; Caste; Deussen, Paul Jakob; Dow, Alexander; Emerson, Ralph Waldo; Guṇas; Halbfass, Wilhelm; Hegel, Georg Wilhelm Friedrich; Jones, Sir William; Kālidāsa; Mahābhārata; Māyā; Müller, Friedrich Max; Orientalism; Pañcatantra; Roy, Rammohan; Śaṅkara; Schlegel, (Karl Wilhelm) Friedrich von; Schopenhauer, Arthur; Upaniṣads; Veda; Vedānta; Wilkins, Sir Charles**

MARTIN OVENS

Further reading

Allen, R. and H. Trivedi (eds). 2000. *Literature and Nation: Britain and India 1800–1990*. London: Routledge.

Barfoot, C.C. (ed.). 2001. *Aldous Huxley Between East and West*. Amsterdam: Rodopi.

Berg, J.J. and C. Freeman (eds). 2000. *The Isherwood Century: Essays on the Life and Work of Christopher Isherwood*. Madison, WI: University of Wisconsin Press.

Berger, D.L. 2004. *The Veil of Māyā: Schopenhauer's System and Early Indian Thought*. Binghamton, NY: Global Academic Publications.

Cannon, G. and K.R. Brine (eds). 1995. *Objects of Enquiry: The Life, Contributions and Influences of Sir William Jones, 1746–1794*. New York: New York University Press.

Chandra, S. 1989. *Albert Camus and Indian Thought*. New Delhi: National Pub. House.

Christensen, J. 1989. 'Perversion, Parody and Cultural Hegemony: Lord Byron's Oriental Tales'. *The South Atlantic Quarterly* 88: 569–603.

Clarke, J.J. 1994. *Jung and Eastern Thought*. New York: Routledge.

Clarke, J.J. 1997. *Oriental Enlightenment: The Encounter between Asian and Western Thought*. London: Routledge.

Dallmayr, F. 1996. *Beyond Orientalism: Essays on Cross-Cultural Encounters*. Albany, NY: SUNY Press.

Damon, S. Foster 1969. *William Blake: His Philosophy and Symbols*. London: Dawsons of Pall Mall.

Das, S.K. 2001. *Indian Ode to the West Wind: Studies in Literary Encounters*. Delhi: Pencraft International.

Dhawan, R.K. 1985. *Henry David Thoreau: A Study in Indian Influence*. New Delhi: Classical Publishing Company.

Drabble, M. (ed.). 1996. *The Oxford Companion to English Literature*. Oxford: Oxford University Press.

Drew, J. 1998. *India and the Romantic Imagination*. Delhi: Oxford University Press.

Eaves, M. (ed.). 2003. *The Cambridge Companion to William Blake*. Cambridge: Cambridge University Press.

Figueira, D.M. 1991. *Translating the Orient: The Reception of Śakuntalā in Nineteenth Century Europe*. Albany, NY: SUNY Press.

Flew, A. (ed.). 1979. *A Dictionary of Philosophy*. London: Pan Books Ltd.

Francis, E.V. 1972. *Emerson and Hindu Scriptures*. Cochin: Academic Publications.

Franklin, M.J. 1995. *Sir William Jones*. Cardiff: University of Wales Press.

Franklin, M.J. (ed.). 2001. *The European Discovery of India: Key Indological Sources of Romanticism*, 6 vols. London: Ganesha Publishing/Edition Synapse.

Frye, N. 1969. *Fearful Symmetry: A Study of William Blake*. Princeton, NJ: Princeton University Press.

Fulford, T. and P.J. Kitson (eds). 1998. *Romanticism and Colonialism: Writing and Empire 1780–1830*. Cambridge: Cambridge University Press.

Garland, H. and M. Garland. 1976. *The Oxford Companion to German Literature*. Oxford: Clarendon Press.

Gokhale, B.G. 1992. *India and the American Mind*. Bombay: Popular Prakashan.

Goodman, R.B. 1990. 'East–West Philosophy in Nineteenth Century America: Emerson and Hinduism'. *Journal of the History of Ideas* 51: 625–45.

Goren, L. 1977. *Elements of Brahmanism in the Transcendentalism of Emerson*. Hartford, CT: Transcendental Books.

Halbfass, W. 1988. *India and Europe: An Essay in Understanding.* Albany, NY: SUNY Press.

Honderich, T. (ed.). 1995. *The Oxford Companion to Philosophy.* Oxford: Oxford University Press.

Inden, R. 1992. *Imagining India.* Oxford: Blackwell.

Isherwood, C. (ed.). 1945. *Vedānta for the Western World.* New York: American Book–Stratford Press, Inc.

Jackson, C.T. 1981. *The Oriental Religions and American Thought: Nineteenth Century Explorations.* Westport, CT: Greenwood Press.

Kaul, R.K. 1995. *Studies in William Jones: An Interpreter of Oriental Literature.* Shimla: Indian Institute of Advanced Study.

Kearns, C.M. 1987. *T.S. Eliot and Indic Traditions: A Study in Poetry and Belief.* Cambridge: Cambridge University Press.

King, R. 1999. *Orientalism and Religion: Postcolonial Theory, India and 'the Mystic East'.* London: Routledge.

Krishna Sastry, L.S.R. 1998. *Sir William Jones: Interpreter of India to the West.* Hyderabad: Distributors, Booklinks Corp.

Kulkarni, H.B. 1970. *A Hindu Avatar: A Study of Hindu Myth and Thought in Moby Dick.* Logan, UT: Utah State University Monographs.

Leask, N. 1992. *British Romantic Writers and the East: Anxieties of Empire.* Cambridge: Cambridge University Press.

Lennon, J. 2004. *Irish Orientalism: A Literary and Intellectual History.* New York: Syracuse University Press.

McEvilley, T. 2002. *The Shape of Ancient Thought: Comparative Studies in Greek and Indian Philosophies.* New York: Allworth Press.

Makdisi, S. 1998. *Romantic Imperialism: Universal Empire and the Culture of Modernity.* Cambridge: Cambridge University Press.

Miller, B.S. 1986. 'Why Did Henry Thoreau Take the Bhagavadgītā to Walden Pond?' *Parabola* 12: 58–63.

Mitter, P. 1992. *Much Maligned Monsters: A History of European Reactions to Indian Art.* Chicago, IL: University of Chicago Press.

Moore, W.J. 1992. *Schrödinger: Life and Thought.* Cambridge: Cambridge University Press.

Myerson, J. (ed.). 1995. *The Cambridge Companion to Henry David Thoreau.* Cambridge: Cambridge University Press.

Nicholls, M. 1999. 'The Influences of Eastern Thought on Schopenhauer's Doctrine of the Thing in Itself'. In C. Janaway, ed., *The Cambridge Companion to Schopenhauer.* Cambridge: Cambridge University Press.

Oueijan, N.B. 1999. *A Compendium of Easter Elements in Byron's Oriental Tales.* New York: P. Lang.

Peltre, C. 2005. *Orientalism in Art.* New York & London: Abbeville Press.

Perl, J.M. and A.P. Tuck. 1985. 'The Hidden Advantage of Tradition: On the Significance of T.S. Eliot's Indic Studies'. *Philosophy East and West* 35: 115–33.

Prochazka, M. (ed.). 2000. *Byron East and West.* Prague: Charles University.

Rajan, B. 1999. *Under Western Eyes: India from Milton to Macaulay.* Durham, North Carolina, and London: Duke University Press.

Rayapati, J.P.R. 1973. *Early American Interest in Vedānta: Pre-Emersonian Interest in Vedic Literature and Vedāntic Philosophy.* London: Asia Publishing House.

Richardson, A. (ed.). 2002. *Three Oriental Tales.* Boston: Houghton Mifflin.

Richardson, A. and S. Hofkash (eds). 1996. *Romanticism, Race and Imperial Culture 1780–1834.* Bloomington, IN: Indiana University Press.

Said, E. 1978. *Orientalism.* London: Routledge and Kegan Paul.

Schwab, R. 1984. *The Oriental Renaissance: Europe's Rediscovery of India and the East 1680–1880.* New York: Columbia University Press.

Sedlar, J.W. 1980. *India and the Greek World: A Study in the Transmission of Culture.* Totowa, NJ: Rowman & Littlefield.

Sedlar, J.W. 1982. *India in the Mind of Germany: Schelling, Schopenhauer and Their Times.* Washington, DC: University Press of America.

Sharpe, E.J. 1985. *The Universal Gītā: Western Images of the Bhagavadgītā.* London: Duckworth.

Sikka, S. 2002. *W.B. Yeats and the Upanisads.* New York: P. Lang.

Singh, C.S. 1981. *The Chariot of Fire: A Study of William Blake in the Light of Hindu Thought.* Salzburg: University of Salzburg.

Singhal, D.P. 1972. *India and World Civilization*, 2 vols. London: Sidgwick and Jackson.
Smith, D. 2003. 'Orientalism and Hinduism'. In G. Flood, ed., *The Blackwell Companion to Hinduism*. Oxford: Blackwell Publishing Ltd, 45–63.
Spiegelman, J.M. 1987. *Hinduism and Jungian Psychology*. Scottsdale, AZ: Falcon Press.
Sri, P.S. 1985. *T.S. Eliot, Vedānta and Buddhism*. Vancouver: University of British Columbia Press.
Srivastava, K.G. 2002. *The Bhagavadgītā and the English Romantic Movement: A Study in Influence*. Delhi: Macmillan India Ltd.
Stunkel, K.R. 1979. *Relations of Indian, Greek and Christian Thought in Antiquity*. Washington, DC: University Press of America.
Swaminathan, S.R. 1997. *Vedānta and Shelley*. Salzburg: University of Salzburg
Swaminathan, S.R. 1998. 'Hindu Myths in Shelley's Prometheus Unbound'. *Vishvabharati Quarterly* 7.1.
Topping, M. (ed.). 2004. *Eastern Voyages, Western Visions: French Writing and Painting of the Orient*. Oxford: P. Lang.
Tuck, A.P. 1990. *Comparative Philosophy and the Philosophy of Scholarship: On the Western Interpretation of Nāgārjuna*. Oxford: Oxford University Press.
Vassiliades, D.Th. 2000. *The Greeks in India: A Survey in Philosophical Understanding*. New Delhi: Munshiram Manorharlal.
Versluis, A. 1993. *American Transcendentalism and Asian Religions*. Oxford: Oxford University Press.
Viswanathan, G. 2003. 'Colonialism and the Construction of Hinduism'. In G. Flood, ed., *The Blackwell Companion to Hinduism*. Oxford: Blackwell Publishing Ltd, 23–44.
Wall, W. 2001. 'William Blake and the Bhagavadgītā'. *Journal of Vaishnava Studies* 9.2: 97–117.
Wassil, G. 2000. 'Keats's Orientalism'. *Studies in Romanticism* 39: 419–47.
Weir, D. 2003. *Brahma in the West: William Blake and the Oriental Renaissance*. Albany, NY: SUNY Press.
West, M.L. 1971. *Early Greek Philosophy and the Orient*. Oxford: Clarendon Press.
Willson, A.L. 1964. *A Mythical Image: The Ideal of India in German Romanticism*. Durham, NC: Duke University Press.

WESTERN POPULAR CULTURE, HINDU INFLUENCE ON

Hinduism has played a significant role in the formation of Western popular culture over the last century and a half. Western popular culture has also played a significant role in the formation of Hinduism over the same time period. Hence Sanskrit words like karma, yoga (though not yet karma-yoga), mantra, guru and Tantra are used in common English parlance now. The word Hinduism, on the other hand, which is not Sanskrit but a Persian–English syncretism, denotes a category arguably derived as much from Western scholarship and transcultural fascinations as Indian historical and social realities. Clearly, Asian religions like Hinduism have come to inform and transform Western culture, even as they have also conformed and reformed themselves in the mirror of the West. The creative, highly syncretistic results have been dramatic for both the Western cultures and, just as significantly, the Asian religions themselves.

There is an interesting comparative observation to make here, and that is that Buddhism has played a far more significant role in Western popular culture in the last fifty years than has Hinduism. There are two simple markers of this fact to note. One is that nirvana has entered the common vocabulary (indeed, it even became a popular American rock band) but mokṣa has not. Second, one need only walk into any number of mega-book stores and proceed to the 'Eastern Religions' section. Inevitably, what one finds there is five to ten shelves given to Buddhism for every one given to Hinduism. The multiple reasons for this discrepancy – from the social inequalities of the caste system and the cultural foreignness of a perceived polytheism, through the successful Westernisation of Zen and the cultural attractions of Tantric Buddhism, to a very charismatic Dalai Lama – lie well outside the scope of so brief an essay as this. Nevertheless, they are worth noting.

As I have explored in detail elsewhere and Robert C. Gordon earlier argued with different materials and models but with similar results, we might fruitfully trace the pathways of Hinduism through Western culture over the last few centuries through two overlapping typologies, here capitalised to signal their strictly categorical or heuristic nature: one philosophical (Vedānta/Tantra), the other devotional (Guru/God/Goddess). The first typology develops through two Indian philosophical modes or meta-visions (darśana), that is, Vedānta, by which is generally meant the Advaita or non-dual school, and Tantra, in both its 'left-handed' or transgressive and 'right-handed' or conservative traditions. These two respective popularities, it turns out, correspond roughly with two modal historical eras, that is, the colonial period (pre–1950) and the postcolonial period (post–1950), with the countercultural and psychedelically catalysed 1960s representing the real shift or 'turning point' from Vedānta to Tantra as the preferred modal Western Hindu worldview. The second triple typology can only very roughly be construed in a similar historical or linear mode, although it is generally true that the rich bhakti or devotional strands and accompanying theological traditions of Hinduism entered Western culture in roughly this order: Guru, God and finally Goddess.

For the sake of discussion, we might define the Vedānta popularly received in the West as that philosophical school that reads the *Upaniṣads* through the lens of the non-dual unity of the Self (ātman) and the cosmic principle (Brahman) and tends to relegate the phenomenal world to the status of an epistemological error (avidyā), a psychological imposition (adhyāya) or a metaphysical illusion (māyā). The classical Indian philosopher Śaṅkara has usually been taken as the normative representative here, and some type of renunciation (saṃnyāsa) in the form of a monastic or ascetic lifestyle is implied as a logical correlate of the system's rejection of the phenomenal world of everyday experience and its biological round of birth and death (saṃsāra).

The Tantra generally implies some form of that Sāṃkhya division between the immortal witness Consciousness or male Person (puruṣa) and material female Nature (prakṛti). Unlike both classical Sāṃkhya and Advaita Vedānta, however, Tantric traditions generally insist on a deeper unity of these male and female metaphysical principles and tend, moreover, to sexualise this bi-unity both iconographically and ritually in explicitly erotic and often highly transgressive ways. The procreative sexuality and family life of the householder (gārhasthya) is the usual, but by no means exclusive, social context for this path. Much too simply but nevertheless instructively put, then, we might say that whereas Advaita Vedānta rejects the material world and the body as impermanent illusions for the sake of an eternal and totally transcendent release or liberation of consciousness (mokṣa), Tantra affirms both the transcendent and immanent orders within a paradoxical and fundamentally erotic unity of consciousness and energy, spirit and sex, soul and body. Or, if one prefers more traditional terms, one might summarise Tantra through the bi-unity of a single rhyming Sanskrit compound, bhukti-mukti, that is, the bi-unity of 'sensual delight and spiritual flight'.

Still in this definitional mode, we might briefly define a guru as any Indian teacher, often of a charismatic or missionary type, who has sought to communicate a particular tradition, here to a Western audience. The category of divinity in Hinduism, as is well known, is extremely fluid and basically polytheistic, even potentially humanistic (to the extent that human beings can manifest divinity, even be gods), although major reforming attempts in the last century and a half have tried to transform this stunning pantheon into an expression of an allegedly deeper monotheism or monism. Here, though, it is necessary simply to point out that of those Hindu deities who have successfully migrated into Western popular culture, Kṛṣṇa and Kālī (the God and the Goddess) have more or less dominated the stage, with Śiva, Gaṇeśa, Rāma, Hanumān and the Devī or Great Goddess (Mahādevī) playing more minor supporting roles.

How does the history of Hinduism and Western popular culture appear when it is viewed through the lenses of these two overlapping typologies?

As it turns out, Tantra and Vedānta had very different receptions in the West during the colonial and postcolonial periods. Advaita Vedānta was the first Indian philosophical school to attract real attention from real Western intellectuals, particularly in Germany in the early nineteenth century among Idealist and Romantic thinkers (Hegel, Schopenhauer and Deussen come to mind) and in America among the Boston Transcendentalists (Emerson and Thoreau) and more independent figures, like the poet Walt Whitman, whose obvious pan-eroticism, well-known bisexuality and stunning 'Song of Myself' and 'body electric' can be read in either Vedāntic or Tantric ways. The scholarly consensus, however, is that when Western thinkers turned East for inspiration, it was mostly to find evidence and inspiration for their own Western thought, not to adopt uncritically the systems of another culture. Moreover, they often imported their own Western ideas, such as the themes of historical progress and expressive individualism, into the traditional Hindu systems, where they did not previously exist in these forms.

Also of significant historical importance here is the Theosophical Society, established in 1875 in New York City by Helena Blavatsky, William Q. Judge and Henry Steel Olcott. Dedicated to the triple goals of nurturing a universal brotherhood, advancing the study of comparative religion, philosophy and science, and exploring the unexplained powers of nature and the latent psychical powers of man, the Theosophical Society would play a major role in how both Buddhism and Hinduism were received by Westerners for the next fifty years, until it was eventually eclipsed by other missionary efforts led by such men as Swami Vivekananda (Vedāntic Hinduism), D.T. Suzuki (Zen Buddhism) and Swami Paramhansa Yogananda (Self-Realisation Fellowship).

In terms of textual reception, special mention must be made of the *Upaniṣads*, a collection of authoritative scriptural texts closely aligned with the Advaita Vedānta school which received an early Latin translation in Europe, and the *Bhagavadgītā*, the first major Hindu scripture to receive an English translation, by the British colonial administrator Sir Charles Wilkins in 1785 as *The Bhagavat-geeta, or, Dialogues of Kreeshna and Arjoon*. Significantly, it is Kṛṣṇa not Kālī, the God not the Goddess, who speaks to the West in English first.

This intellectual labour prepared the cultural ground for later specifically Indian efforts, such as Swami Vivekananda's famous speeches at the 1893 Parliament of World Religions in Chicago. The latter are justly taken as the definitive entry point of 'Hinduism' into Western, and particularly American, popular consciousness, and here 'Vedānta' and 'Hinduism' were more or less (mostly more) conflated. Vivekananda's Vedāntic Hinduism had already passed through over half a century of profound Westernisation via various missionary, syncretistic and reform movements in Bengal (such as the Brahmo Samaj) before it arrived in the West. In some sense, then, what became popular did so precisely because its underlying logic and philosophy 'fitted' the cultural receptors that had helped form them in the previous decades in colonial India. In any case, Vivekananda's successful missionary efforts to the West in the subsequent decade set the tone and provided a kind of cultural paradigm for other Indian gurus to imitate and expand. He founded the influential New York Vedanta Society in 1894, for example, and his San Francisco Vedanta Society would build the first Hindu temple in North America in 1906. Hence dozens, indeed hundreds, of charismatic gurus would follow his example in the twentieth century, acting as the most effective and certainly the most dramatic transmitters of Hindu ideas and practices into Western culture.

Tantra got no such warm reception until the counterculture of the 1960s. Indeed, in the nineteenth century it was consistently vilified by Christian missionaries, colonial administrators and, after them, Indian reformers in India as representing the very worst forms of decadence and superstition that India had to offer. Nevertheless, Tantra remained a popular subject of nineteenth-century British novels. It also actually preceded Vivekananda to the USA in the person of Sylvais Hamati, a Syrian-Indian Tantric guru who claimed to hail from Calcutta (among other Indian cities) and taught a teenage Iowan boy (who later went by the name of Pierre Bernard) the secrets of the vīra-sādhana or 'discipline of the hero', first in Lincoln, Nebraska, around 1879, then in San Francisco and indeed across the entire country in the 1880s and 1890s (the two men finally split up, amiably through a financial exchange, in 1907 in Seattle).

As Robert Love has pointed out, Sylvais Hamati is probably the first real guru who had an impact on American culture. Before him, Americans such as Thoreau and Emerson read the *Bhagavadgītā* and created their own syntheses, but all of them lacked a human teacher from India. Hamati established a new pattern. And Bernard would go on to teach his master's heroic methods to great popular and financial effect (members of the Vanderbilt and Goodrich families were among his most devoted students) and to great scandal (Bernard was hounded by the police and a kind of tabloid journalism for much of his life). On a related note, it is important to point out that a term like yoga (by which was generally meant Haṭha-yoga) carried overwhelmingly negative and quasi-sexual connotations in American English in the early part of the twentieth century. It would take decades for the term to be sanitised and cleaned up; that is, it would take decades for Vedānta to safely subsume Tantra within American culture, before the latter answered back through the counterculture.

In any case, it was a much more ascetic Vedānta and more reputable Sanskrit words like ātman, Brahman and māyā that claimed the cultural ground in the first, colonial half of the twentieth century, partly through systematic missionary efforts and charismatic Hindu teachers like Paramhansa Yogananda and Swami Prabhavananda, but also through the writings of their most famous Western disciples. The British–American trio of Aldous Huxley, Christopher Isherwood and Gerald Heard, all connected to Prabhavananda in some way, is of special note here (as is the fact that Isherwood and Heard were both confessedly homosexual).

This Vedāntic first half of the century gradually gave way to a Tantric second half with the rise of the Beatniks, who, with the exception of Allen Ginsberg (another homoerotic American mystic attuned to Asia), turned mostly to Zen Buddhism, not Hinduism, for their inspiration. Jack Kerouac's 1958 *Dharma Bums* is paradigmatic in this regard. Here too we might place the slightly earlier but now influential Asian interests of C.G. Jung, who saw Tantric yoga as an analogue of his own archetypal psychology and gave an entire seminar on Kuṇḍalinī Yoga; the brilliant British-American trickster figure of Alan Watts, who defended free love (as an Anglican priest no less) and wrote about Tantra and sex almost as much as he wrote about Zen and meditation; and the rise of a shared American–British counterculture in the mid-1960s, with its 'sex, drugs and rock 'n' roll' revolution. All of this was decidedly postcolonial both in terms of timing and to the extent that the purpose of such efforts was certainly not to colonise Asia but to deconstruct and 'counter' the religious, political and sexual orthodoxies of the West. For the latter project, 'Eastern' ideas, symbols, practices and teachers were especially attractive and powerful.

The wide availability of psychedelic substances such as LSD (first discovered, really synthesised, by Albert Hofmann on 16 April 1943, a day the subculture playfully but seriously calls 'Better Friday') and mescaline (made wildly popular by Carlos Casteneda and his shamanic figure of Don Juan) played a key role in such mystical counterings. Rather ironically, it was the Vedānta student and high cultural figure Aldous Huxley who did more than anyone to prepare the cultural ground here. It was Huxley, after all, who wrote *the* psychedelic bible of the era (*The Doors of Perception*, 1954) and even helped coined the term psychedelic ('mind-manifesting') with his psychiatrist friend Humphrey Osmond. Even more curiously, it was Huxley again who introduced a young Timothy Leary to something called 'Tantra' in the early months of 1962 (mostly by suggesting he read scholars like Sir John Woodroffe, Heinrich Zimmer, Edward Conze and Mircea Eliade) and published his final novel, *Island*, at the same time, about a Tantric-psychedelic paradise island called Pala. The Palanians used Tantric sexual techniques to increase their pleasure and moderate their birth rates and ingested a mystical mushroom called Moksha to free them from the illusions of their own egos and ritually initiate them, at puberty, into a type of cosmic consciousness before a temple icon of Śiva Naṭarāja and a sensual statue of Śiva-Pārvatī (Ardhanārīśvara). Through such means, Huxley, once a proponent of Vedānta, now more or less guaranteed that much of the psychedelic subculture would be painted in bright Tantric colours. In a very similar vein, Leary's Harvard colleague Richard Alpert would become 'Ram Dass' after being turned on by two ontological inspirations: Hofmann's LSD and his Hindu guru, Neem Karoli Baba.

It was not just psychedelics that rendered Asian religions like Hinduism, Buddhism and Taoism so popular in the counterculture and made symbols like the yin–yang Tao symbol and the Hindu Oṃ instantly recognisable; it was also literature and music and, more particularly, experimental literature and rock music, both heavily influenced by the psychedelic subculture. As Christopher Partridge has noted, from bands like the Grateful Dead (who were actually more drawn to Sufism than Hinduism), the Velvet Underground, Pink Floyd, the Doors (named after Huxley's Bible) and Led Zeppelin, to writers like William Burroughs, Jack Kerouac, Hunter S. Thompson and Allen Ginsberg, the impact of hallucinogens and the influence of Eastern-inspired religious thought were omnipresent. Hence the album cover of the Beatles' *Sergeant Pepper's Lonely Hearts Club Band* features Mahatma Gandhi, Sri Yukteswar, Sri Lahiri Mahasaya, Sri Paramhansa Yogananda, the sexual magician Aleister Crowley and that literary patron saint of all of this – Aldous Huxley.

Sometimes this rock 'n' roll Hinduism was mostly iconic and had little apparent effect on the broader culture. Here we might mention the Jimi Hendrix Experience, whose second album cover, *Axis: Bold as Love* (released in December of 1967), featured a traditional image of the various manifestations of Viṣṇu, symbolic of the entire Hindu pantheon, with the band members' three heads replacing those of the Great God himself (the same image, by the way, this time minus the band members, would much later appear on a lunchbox in 1998; Kālī as the Goddess would get her own lunchbox too at the same time, as if to balance out the God).

Much more influential, indeed archetypal for the counterculture, was the conversion-like experience of George Harrison of the Beatles. After the filming of the 1965 Beatle film *Help!* (which opens with an attempted human sacrifice to an eight-armed Kālī-like goddess and involves the goddess' cult-like worshippers chasing the band around London to steal Ringo's ring, necessary for the original sacrifice), Harrison became interested in Hinduism. Soon after this, he would meet Maharishi Mahesh Yogi back in England through the ministrations of his wife (the Beach Boys also sat at this guru's feet). In 1968 the Beatles travelled to India, where they met with Maharishi Mahesh Yogi in Rishikesh in a widely reported and famously photographed visit. No doubt partly because of this iconic pilgrimage, *Life* magazine decided that 1968 was the 'Year of the Guru'. In 1969 Harrison met with A.C. Bhaktivedanta Swami Prabhupada (who in 1966 had founded the International Society for Krishna Consciousness (ISKCON)) at John Lennon's estate in Tittenhurst Park and performed the chart-topping 'Hare Krishna Mantra' with the devotees of the London Radha-Krishna Temple. In January of 1971 Harrison released his album *All Things Must Pass*, which included his hit single 'My Sweet Lord', a moving ballad whose refrain morphs from a very Western 'hallelujah' to a very Eastern 'Hare Krishna', in order to signal either the identity of the two theologies or a conversion from the former to the latter (it is not entirely clear). Whatever one makes of the Beatles' temporary encounter with Hindu gurus and Harrison's more lasting devotion to Kṛṣṇa as God, one thing is certain: the broad cultural impact of such events was very significant indeed.

The late 1960s and 1970s saw a development of these same patterns, with the God (Kṛṣṇa) gradually being overtaken by the Goddess (usually Kālī) in popularity. No doubt this was partly a reflection of the feminist revolution of the same time period and the gradual but dramatic entrance of women into the professional study of religion. It also, however, had something to do with the sexual revolution and the psychedelic, erotic and transgressive energies of rock music: Tantra and rock, at least in the West, share a common history. Nik Douglas, for example, working with Rolling Stones lead singer Mick Jagger, produced a devotional documentary entitled *Tantra: Indian Rites of Ecstasy*. The film featured beautiful shots of the Goddess as Durgā and Kālī, the ritual night-feeding of jackals and a symbolic re-enactment of the Five Ms of left-handed Tantra. The film is remarkable for its real-life, unromantic portrayals of Indian Tantrikas (Bāuls perhaps), for its haunting music and for its total absence of oral commentary. Douglas, working closely with artist Penny Slinger, would later go on to produce an elaborate volume on *Sexual Secrets: The Alchemy of Ecstasy* (1979), an illustrated manual on the philosophy, iconography and subtle physiology of Tantric sexual practice. In many ways, this was the height of what we might call the Western Tantric transmission, just after the feminist and sexual revolutions and just before the terrifying arrival of AIDS and the rise of the Religious Right in the States, the latter in perfect synchronisation with a growing and increasingly violent worldwide fundamentalism.

The Goddess as Kālī also made numerous appearances in Hollywood films, including *The Golden Voyage of Sinbad* (1974) and *Indiana Jones and the Temple of Doom* (1984), few of them particularly flattering. *The Deceivers* (1988), starring Pierce Brosnan as Captain Savage, who ends up converting to a particularly violent and erotic form of the Goddess as Queen of the Thugees, is probably the only real exception here. It is also worth noting that it was during this same time that Kālī became a veritable archetype for Jungian, some feminist and innumerable New Age writers. Her popularity among Western devotees is impressive indeed, more so for the fact that those features of Kālī that the Western devotees embrace and celebrate are often precisely those transgressive, sexual or violent aspects that the orthodox Hindu tradition has wanted to tone down, domesticate or even actively censor.

Also worth mentioning in this context is Arthur Avalon's *The Serpent's Power*, a translation, commentary and collection of line-drawings on the Sanskrit *Satcakranirupana*, literally 'A Description of the Six Cakras'. This highly technical text is worth highlighting here because there are probably few visual images that have had a greater impact on the popular religious imagination with respect to Hinduism than the cakra system, and it was Avalon's text that probably did more than anything else to introduce this system to the West, here in what would become its most widely accepted (Tantric) form. Interestingly, 'Arthur Avalon', as Kathleen Taylor has demonstrated, was almost certainly a bi-cultural fusion of two friends, Sir John Woodroffe, the Calcutta high court judge and practitioner of Śākta Tantra, and Atul Behari Ghosh, Woodroffe's Bengali friend who secretly did all the Sanskrit translations for his books (Taylor 2001).

The 1960s and 1970s saw any number of highly influential Indian gurus coming to the West and teaching a wide range of traditional (and not so traditional) philosophical systems. Here we have again the travelling missionary guru as one of the most effective and charismatic, if also often the most controversial, means of transmission of Hindu ideas and practices into Western culture. The arrival of these gurus reproduces, very roughly, the Vedānta-to-Tantra model proposed above. Hence the two 'earliest', most successful and most famous gurus of the 1960s were A.C. Bhaktivedanta Swami Prabhupada and Maharishi Mahesh Yogi, who taught a highly ascetic form of Kṛṣṇa devotionalism (ISKCON) and a very abstract form of yogic meditation (Transcendental Meditation), respectively. This ascetic pattern quickly gave way to a more erotic one as the decades progressed. Hence, predictably, many of the most popular gurus who followed them in the 1970s were either explicitly Tantric or Tantric in philosophical orientation. These ranged from the wildly eclectic and often left-handed teachings of Bhagwan Shree Rajneesh (later Osho), who moved his headquarters from Poona to Oregon in 1981, to the more philosophical and systematised Kashmiri Śaivism of Swami Muktananda, whose followers established the Siddha Yoga Dham Associates (SYDA) Foundation in 1974.

There were also, of course, popular Hindu gurus who did not come to the West and/or who do not quite fit into this general pattern. Among these mention must be made of Sathya Sai Baba, who, among other things, provided the logo for the Hard Rock Café chain ('Love All, Serve All'), founded by Isaac Tigrett, a disciple of Sai Baba, and Peter Morton in London in 1971.

The 1980s and early 1990s represent something of a crisis point for these guru traditions, as these years witnessed a whole series of widely advertised guru scandals within Hindu, Buddhist and Jain communities, inevitably involving some form of illicit sexual behaviour. Bernard Faure thus opens his multi-volume study of Buddhist sexuality by pointing out that the 1980s and 1990s witnessed a whole series of scandals that morally shattered Buddhist communities in both North America and Europe. As demographic evidence of this truth, he cites Jack Cornfield's study of fifty-four Buddhist, Hindu and Jain teachers in North America. The study revealed that thirty-four of them had had sexual relationships with their students.

Such patterns were especially obvious among Buddhist teachers, partly, Faure suggests, because of the erotic-transgressive logics of these Mahāyāna, Vajrayāna and Zen traditions (all basically Tantric in orientation). But such patterns were also more than evident among the popular Hindu mega-gurus, who were equally indebted to Tantra, this time in its many Indian forms. Rajneesh, for example, with his Oregon community embroiled in charges of phone-tapping, food-poisoning, fraud, arson, even attempted murder, was deported back to India. Shortly after the death of Muktananda, his community found itself involved in a series of scandals involving charges that the guru had had sexual contact with a number of women in the months leading up to his death, some of them disturbingly young (significantly, these reported events were often explained and defended in the Tantric terms of Śakti, kuṇḍalinī, etc.). Sai Baba's reputation among Western devotees has similarly suffered a tremendous blow after serious allegations of pederastic sexual abuse were widely and convincingly reported on the internet. And so on. A culture of denial, censorship and eventual disillusionment set in and, in many ways, is still present today.

In the meantime, and in a very different spirit, Hindu families and communities have settled in the West in great numbers, particularly since 1965, when America finally lifted the Asian Exclusion Act (1924). Significantly, just as the Western reception of Hinduism was taking a very dramatic countercultural turn from a colonially generated Vedānta to a post-colonially generated Tantra, Indian families began migrating to America in large numbers. Scholars such as Vijay Prashad have described the prehistory of these post-1965 migrations and have analysed some of the racist responses which these new American families have had to deal with, as well as the fantastically creative ways peoples of Asian and African descent have influenced one another in their shared struggle for social justice and equality in the New World (Prashad 2000, 2002). Iconic here with respect to the present topic are the dreadlocks of the Rastafarians, made so famous by the singer Bob Marley. The Rastafarians, it turns out, borrowed the dreadlocks from Afro-Jamaicans, who got them – along with the ganja (marijuana) – from Caribbean Śaiva Hindus.

Rastafarians and dreadlocks aside for a moment, the new Hindu families, very much unlike the mega-gurus whose broad appeal was built largely on their exotic teachings and charismatic presence, brought with them much more traditional, and hence much more conservative, forms of practice and belief (often of a theistic or bhakti nature). Their primary concerns, moreover, no doubt reflected the interests of every previous immigrant community: financial stability, education, acculturation and the preservation of their traditions in some form. Part of this process has involved efforts to challenge and correct what they perceive to be the inaccuracies, exaggerations and accents of American popular culture with respect to Hinduism. Hence the censorship campaigns mounted in 1999 when *Xena: Warrior Princess* (1995–2001) aired its 'The Way' episode, in February, with appearances by both

Kṛṣṇa and Kālī (the God and the Goddess again). The complaints were many, from the lesbian subtext of the show, to the apparently incredible notion that a television programme could portray a Hindu deity as fictional. The episode was pulled, revised and then reissued within six months, this time with a public announcement, ostensibly to appease those who had been offended.

What we might be seeing in such events (of which there are many) is a kind of pendulum effect, with the pendulum swinging back not so much to a conservative and ascetic Vedānta now, but to an ultra-conservative form of Hindu monotheism. We may be witnessing, in other words, a third general cultural pattern, from a philosophical colonial-generated Vedānta, through a transgressive countercultural-catalysed Tantra, to a much more conservative and devotional theistic God, the latter often taken as a literally real person, as if mythology were indeed history.

The latter move, of course, is not a popular cultural move at all. How this will impact Western popular culture remains to be seen. It seems doubtful, though, that Hinduism's recent turn to literalising monotheistic language and fundamentalist forms will carry much weight, at least here. Hence the vigorous and partially successful anti-censorship campaigns waged against the Hindu protestors with the *Xena* episode. Western intellectuals and devotees, after all, have tended to turn to Hinduism for theological systems, charismatic figures and psychophysical practices that they cannot find in their own Western traditions, and there is plenty of God and fundamentalism in the Western traditions.

Significantly and finally, then, yoga and Tantra are now popular cultural terms (not to mention that endlessly cited but seldom read text, the *Kāmasūtra*), whereas Vedānta is not. Moreover, there are plenty of Hindu gods to be found in Western popular culture (Kālī, Kṛṣṇa, Śiva, Gaṇeśa, and so on), but little, if any, Hindu monotheism as such. The knowledgeable reader can also easily detect Tantric themes in the erotic mysticism and esoteric Jesus of a contemporary blockbuster novel like *The Da Vinci Code* (perhaps that is one reason why it was a blockbuster). Moreover, in 2004 an American vīra or hero like Spider-Man began swinging in Indian cities, as his stories were reimagined by Indian writers and artists in the context of Hindu mythology, much of it Tantric in accent. Hence the alliterative Peter Parker became Pavitr Prabhakar, the radioactive spider-bite became a kind of śakti-pāt received in a dream initiation (svapna-siddha) from a Guru-god's siddhi or 'super power' (without any of these Sanskrit words begin invoked), the Green Goblin became a traditional Indian demon and so on.

Much of the latter reimagining, it turns out, sits on four decades of transcultural influence from America to India and back again. The eminently American genre of the comic book, after all, has been adopted and adapted by Indian writers and artists since 1967, when *Amar Chitra Katha* – a series of Indian comics based on Indian mythology, history and folklore – was created by an Indian editor, Anant 'Uncle' Pai, and a publishing house, India Book House. Much like the Western reception of Hinduism, the series began with a title on Kṛṣṇa, that is, the God, but soon expanded into stories from the *Rāmāyaṇa* and the *Mahābhārata* and then on to much of the full sweep of the Hindu pantheon and Indian history. We thus come full circle: from Hinduism to Western popular culture and back to Hinduism, now as Indian popular culture.

There is, I think, a certain hidden wisdom in all of this. It is, after all, not too difficult to detect in these innumerable colonial and postcolonial circuits and in these multiple fused figures a certain transcultural gnosis. Negatively put, such a wisdom refuses to honour the illusions of political identity, cultural essentialism or ethnic racism, however construed: Bob Marley's Śaiva dreadlocks are emblematic here (Prashad 2002). Positively rendered, such a gnosis delights in celebrating a common, mystically inflected humanity in one of the few places that this remains genuinely possible – the place of popular culture. The man beneath the mask, after all, can be named Pavitr as well as Peter. It makes no difference at all, not any important one anyway.

See also: **Advaita; Americas, Hindus in; Ardhanārīśvara; Ātman; Bāuls; Bhagavadgītā; Bhakti; Blavatsky, Helena; Brahman; Brahmo Samaj; Buddhism, relationship with Hinduism; Caste; Deities; Deussen, Paul Jakob; Diaspora; Durgā; Eliade, Mircea; Emerson, Ralph Waldo; Gandhi, Mohandas Karamchand; Gaṇeśa; Gārhasthya; Guru; Hanumān; Haṭha Yoga; Hegel, Georg Wilhelm Friedrich; Hinduism; Hinduism, history of scholarship; Hinduism, modern and contemporary; International Society for Krishna Consciousness; Jainism, relationship with Hinduism; Jung, Carl Gustav; Kālī and Caṇḍī; Kāmasūtra; Karma; Kashmiri Śaivism; Kṛṣṇa; Kuṇḍalinī Yoga; Mahābhārata; Mahādevī; Maharishi Mahesh Yogi; Mantra; Māyā; Mokṣa; Muktananda, Swami; New Religious Movements, Hindu influence on; Olcott, Henry Steel; Oṃ; Orientalism; Pañcamakāra; Pārvatī; Prabhupada, A.C. Bhaktivedanta Swami; Prakṛti; Puruṣa; Rajneesh, Bhagwan Shree; Ram Dass; Rāma; Ramakrishna Math and Mission; Rāmāyaṇa; Ṣaḍdarśana; Sai Baba, Sathya; Śakti; Sāṃkhya; Saṃnyāsa; Saṃsāra; Śaṅkara; Schopenhauer, Arthur; Tantras; Tapas; Theosophy and the Theosophical Society; Transcendental meditation; Upaniṣads; Vedānta; Viṣṇu; Vivekananda, Swami; Western culture, Hindu influence on; Wilkins, Sir Charles; Woodroffe, John; Yoga; Yogananda, Paramhansa; Zimmer, Heinrich Robert**

JEFF KRIPALS

Further reading

Bernard, F. 1998. *The Red Thread: Buddhist Approaches to Sexuality.* Princeton, NJ: Princeton University Press.

Gordon, R. 2001. *Gospel of the Open Road: According to Emerson, Whitman, and Thoreau.* Lincoln: Universe Press.

Humes, C.A. and Thomas Forsthoefel (eds). 2005. *Gurus in America.* Albany, NY: SUNY Press.

Kripal, J.J. 2007. *Esalen: America and the Religion of No Religion.* Chicago, IL: University of Chicago Press.

Kripal, J.J. 2007. 'Remembering Ourselves: Some Notes on the Counter Culture of Tantric Studies'. *Journal of South Asian Religions* 1(1) (June).

Love, R. Forthcoming. *The Great Oom.* New York: Viking Press.

McDermott, R. and Jeffrey J. Kripal (eds). 2003. *Encountering Kali: In the Margins, at the Center, in the West.* Berkeley, CA: University of California Press.

Partridge, C. 2004. *The Re-Enchantment of the West: Volume 1, Alternative Spiritualities, Sacralization, Popular Culture, Occulture.* London: T. & T. Clark.

Prashad, V. 2000. *The Karma of Brown Folk.* Minneapolis, MN: University of Minnesota Press.

Prashad, V. 2002. *Everybody Was Kung Fu Fighting: Afro-Asian Connections and the Myth of Cultural Purity.* Boston, MA: Beacon Press.

Taylor, K. 2001. *Sir John Woodroffe, Tantra and Bengal: 'An Indian Soul in a European Body'?* Richmond: Curzon.

Tweed, T.A. and Stephen Prothero (eds). 1999. *Asian Religions in America: A Documentary History.* New York: Oxford University Press.

Urban, H. 2003. *Tantra: Sex, Secrecy, Politics, and Power in the Study of Religion.* Berkeley, CA: University of California Press.

Versluis, A. 1993. *American Transcendentalism & Asian Religions.* New York: Oxford University Press.

WHITNEY, WILLIAM DWIGHT (1827–94)

The first important American Sanskritist, Whitney began the study of Sanskrit with a copy, borrowed from his brother, of Franz Bopp's *Sanskrit Grammar*. After a year of study at Yale and three further years in Europe with, among others, Rudolf von Roth (1821–95), Whitney was appointed Professor of Sanskrit at Yale in 1854. Two years later Roth and Whitney published a critical edition of the *Atharvaveda Saṃhitā*. A long-running and bitter public feud with F. Max Müller over Sanskrit and broader questions of linguistics began with Müller's criticisms of Roth and Böthlingk's Sanskrit–German dictionary, to which Whitney had contributed the vocabulary for the *Atharvaveda*. Whitney was critical of Müller's reliance on Sāyaṇa's commentary, and the delay its inclusion caused in the publication of his edition of the *Ṛgveda Saṃhitā*. Whitney's *Sanskrit Grammar* has been a standard text since its first publication in 1879.

See also: **Hinduism, history of scholarship; Müller, Friedrich Max; Veda**

WILL SWEETMAN

Further reading

Tull, H.W. 1991. 'F. Max Müller and A.B. Keith: "Twaddle", the "Stupid" Myth, and the Disease of Indology'. *Numen* XXXVIII: 27–58.

Whitney, W.D. and R. Roth (eds). 1856. *Atharva Veda Sanhita*. Berlin: Ferd. Dümmler.

Whitney, W.D. 1879. *A Sanskrit Grammar: Including Both the Classical Language, and the Older Dialects, of Veda and Brahmana*. Leipzig: Breitkopf and Härtel.

Whitney, W.D. 1892. *Max Müller and the Science of Language: A Criticism*. New York: D. Appleton.

WIDOW REMARRIAGE

In pre-modern Hinduism, local caste customs either did or did not allow widows to remarry. Many lawgivers did not allow elite women to do so. Because marriage (vivāha) was a sacrament and would continue in future lives, women had to remain faithful to their husbands (pativratā). Remarriage was difficult, moreover, because elite families wanted virgin brides. Some classical scriptures allowed women one exception: niyoga, which meant having a child, or even two, with their husband's younger brother (or sometimes another male family member). But Parāśara, in a controversial verse (IV.30), says that women can remarry when the husband has disappeared, is dead, becomes a saṃnyāsa, is impotent or is fallen. Most lower castes allowed remarriage, which they defined as a permanent relationship (although it often lacked ritual markers). But whether women actually remarried depended also on age, earning power and the decision of their sons or other male kin. Poor widows generally preferred remarriage, because it offered better survival opportunities for them and their children. Efforts to improve the status of widows by providing more options for them led to the Hindu Widows' Remarriage Act, 1856. But even after the law was passed and 'widow remarriage association homes' were developed (the first in Calcutta and another in Poona) to teach widows about independence, the problem of widowhood diminished only gradually over the next century.

See also: **Caste; Child marriage; Niyoga; Parāśara; Pativratā and Patiparameśvara; Saraswati, Pandita Ramabai; Virginity; Vivāha; Widowhood**

KATHERINE K. YOUNG

Further reading

Gill, C. and P. Gill (eds). 2001. *Shadow Lives: Writings on Widowhood*. New Delhi: Kali for Women.

Giri, V.M. (ed.). 2002. *Living Death: Trauma and Widowhood in India*. New Delhi: Gyan Publishing House.

Harlan, L. and P.B. Courtright (eds). 1995. *From the Margins of Hindu Marriage: Essays on Gender, Religion, and Culture.* Oxford: Oxford University Press.

Kane, P.V. 1968–77 [1930–62]. *History of Dharmaśāstra*, 5 vols, 2nd edn. Poona: Bhandarkar Oriental Research Institute.

Kitchlu, T.N. 1993. *Widows in India.* New Delhi: Ashish Publishing House.

Lamb, S. 2000. *White Saris and Sweet Mangoes: Aging, Gender, and Body in North India.* Berkeley, CA: University of California Press.

Leslie, J. 1989. *The Perfect Wife: The Orthodox Hindu Woman According to the Stridharmapaddhati of Tryambakayajvan.* New York: Oxford University Press.

Menski, W. 2003. *Hindu Law: Beyond Tradition and Modernity.* New Delhi: Oxford University Press.

Owen, M. 1996. *A World of Widows.* New Jersey: Zed Books.

WIDOWHOOD

The word vidhavā (widow) denotes 'one whose husband is gone' – that is, dead. It sometimes connotes a witch or ogress. In pre-modern Hinduism, a widow's plight in elite circles was defined by some authors as her inability to keep her husband alive and well – the sine qua non of her wifely role (pativratā) – and her lack of fidelity by choosing to save her own life instead of performing the auspicious act of burning herself on her husband's funeral pyre (satī). From this perspective, the widow represented death and inauspiciousness; she 'ate' her husband with her karmic jaw.

Underlying this negativity was the positive idea that elite families owed widows maintenance for life. But this might have led some to minimise widows' needs (thus avoiding heavy investments in non-reproductive women). Families wanted to control their sexuality, too (thus maintaining the family's internal harmony and external reputation). One solution was culturally endorsed support for widows at a subsistence level. This, in turn, amounted to a kind of imposed asceticism – chastity (brahmacarya), elimination of possessions (aparigraha) and fasting (upavāsa) – yet without the ascetic's prestige. The effect was to marginalise elite widows (or those who imitated elite lifestyles) in both family and public life. For some elite women, widowhood was a life of hardship and shame.

Hindus ritualised the transition to widowhood. In South Indian brahmanical circles, for instance, a widow dressed in her finery, passionately embraced her husband's corpse and tried to revive him. Failing at the latter, she asked people to rectify this injustice to her faithfulness, chastity, devotion, service and motherhood. Failing at that, too, she rolled on the ground in a frenzy. In some families, a widow repeated all these things on the tenth or twelfth day after her husband had been cremated, a time when his soul received a new spiritual body and ascended to heaven. She went to the side of a temple tank. Standing in front of a mound topped with a ball of mud, which represented her husband, she removed her jewels and auspicious symbols (including the auspicious mark on her forehead, her wedding chain and her bangles). After promising future fidelity to her dead husband, she received tonsure and donned a plain white sari (Dubois 1959: 350–54).

The absence of auspicious feminine symbols and the presence of culturally coded inauspicious ones marked her as a widow. No wonder curses directed at women included expressions such as 'May you have a bald head' or 'May your tāli (marriage necklace) be cut'. Even variants of this ritual added up to a dramatic rite of passage for the elite widow and reminded all women of their potential fate. According to the logic of karma, the sins (pāpa) that caused this unfortunate transformation from auspiciousness to inauspiciousness might have occurred in a former life and only now came to fruition.

This view was by no means the only pre-modern Hindu response to widowhood. Parāśara says, for instance, that women can remarry when the husband has disappeared, is dead, becomes a saṃnyāsa, is impotent or is fallen. Remarriage was common, moreover, in the lower castes, although some women found themselves alone, impoverished and struggling to care for young children. Negative traditions of widowhood changed dramatically, moreover, thanks to reforms in the modern period.

See also: **Brahmacarya; Divorce; Dubois, Jean Antoine; Karma; Pāpa; Parāśara; Pativratā; Sati; Widow remarriage**

KATHERINE K. YOUNG

Further reading

Dubois, Abbé. 1959. *Hindu Manners, Customs and Ceremonies*, 4th edn. Oxford: Oxford University Press.

Gill, C. and P. Gill (eds). 2001. *Shadow Lives: Writings on Widowhood*. New Delhi: Kali for Women.

Giri, V.M. (ed.). 2002. *Living Death: Trauma and Widowhood in India*. New Delhi: Gyan Publishing House.

Harlan, L. and P.B. Courtright (eds). 1995. *From the Margins of Hindu Marriage: Essays on Gender, Religion, and Culture.* Oxford: Oxford University Press.

Leslie, J. 1989. *The Perfect Wife: The Orthodox Hindu Woman According to the Stridharmapaddhati of Tryambakayajvan*. New York: Oxford University Press.

Kane, P.V. 1968–77 [1930–62]. *History of Dharmaśāstra*, 5 vols, 2nd edn. Poona: Bhandarkar Oriental Research Institute.

Kitchlu, T.N. 1993. *Widows in India*. New Delhi: Ashish Publishing House.

Lamb, S. 2000. *White Saris and Sweet Mangoes: Aging, Gender, and Body in North India.* Berkeley, CA: University of California Press.

Mazumdar, S. and S. Mazumdar. 2002. 'Silent Resistance: A Hindu Child Widow's Lived Experience'. *Annual Review of Women in World Religions*, vol. 6, eds. A. Sharma and K.K. Young. Albany, NY: State University of New York Press, 93–121.

Menski, W. 2003. *Hindu Law: Beyond Tradition and Modernity.* New Delhi: Oxford University Press.

Nagesh, H.V., P.S. Nair and A.P. Katti (eds). 1987. *Widowhood in India*. Ujire: Sri Dharmasthala Manjunatheshawara Educational Trust.

O'Hanlon, R. 1991. 'Issues of Widowhood: Gender and Resistance in Colonial Western India'. In D. Haynes and G. Prakash, eds, *Contesting Power: Resistance and Everyday Social Relations in South Asia*. Berkeley, CA: University of California Press, 62–108.

Olivelle, P. 2004. *The Law Code of Manu*. Oxford: Oxford University Press.

Owen, M. 1996. *A World of Widows*. New Jersey: Zed Books.

Patil, G.D. 2000. *Hindu Widows: A Study in Deprivation*. New Delhi: Gyan Publishing House.

Upadhyay, R.K. 1996. *Widowed and Deserted Women in Indian Society.* New Delhi: Harnam Publications.

Wadley, S.S. 1995. 'No Longer a Wife: Widows in Rural North India'. In L. Hanlan and P.B. Courtright, eds, *From the Margins of Hindu Marriage: Essays on Gender, Religion and Culture.* New York: Oxford University Press, 92–118.

WILKINS, SIR CHARLES (1749–1836)

British civil servant who began his career as a 'writer' (clerk) with the East India Company in Bengal in 1770. In a period when the Company emphasised the study of Indian vernaculars, Wilkins was one of the few among its members to take up Sanskrit. In 1783 Wilkins entered semi-retirement at Banaras, with the support of the Company and the objective of translating the *Mahābhārata*. Although he completed a third of the work, only his translation of the *Bhagavadgītā* (1785) was ever published. In his short preface, Wilkins interpreted the *Bhagavadgītā* as a monotheistic work, declaring that its aim was 'by setting up the doctrine of the unity of the Godhead ... to undermine the tenets inculcated by the Vedas'. For many years the only translation published in English, Wilkins' work, which was also quickly retranslated into French and Russian (both 1787) and from the French partially into German (1791), was influential in shaping European views of the *Bhagavadgītā* and those of the American transcendentalists, including Emerson. After returning to England in 1786, Wilkins published further translations, including the *Hitopadeśa* (1787), and a Sanskrit grammar (1808).

See also: **Bhagavadgītā; Emerson, Ralph Waldo; Hinduism, history of scholarship; Mahābhārata**

WILL SWEETMAN

Further reading

Lloyd, M. 1979. 'Sir Charles Wilkins, 1749–1836'. In *India Office Library and Records: Report for the year 1978*, 9–39. London: HMSO.

Wilkins, C. 1785. *The Bhăgvăt-Gēētā, or Dialogues of Krēēshnă and Ărjŏŏn.* London: Printed for C. Nourse.

WILSON, HAROLD HAYMAN (1786–1860)

English Indologist. Wilson went to India in 1808 as an assistant surgeon, but from 1816 was Assay Master at the mint at Calcutta. He was secretary of the Asiatic Society of Bengal from 1811 until his return to England in 1833, where he was the first holder of the Boden chair of Sanskrit at Oxford and, from 1837, director of the Royal Asiatic Society. His edition and translation of Kālidāsa's *Meghadūta* (1813) was followed by a Sanskrit dictionary (1819) prepared with the help of Indian scholars at the Sanskrit College in Calcutta, of which he was superintendent. His 1840 translation of the *Viṣṇu Purāṇa* inaugurated the Western study of purāṇic literature and thus the serious study of Hindu mythology, although the lasting influence of his rather narrow prescription of the content of an authentic *Purāṇa* has been regretted by later scholars. Among many other works Wilson published a translation of the *Ṛgveda Saṃhitā*, and several important essays on the religious practices and sects of contemporary Hindus, in which he stressed the heterogeneity of the beliefs and practices designated by the term 'Hinduism'. Wilson was among the last to defend the use of Indian languages rather than English in Indian schools; he advised the East India Company against banning sati and was president when Indians first became members of the Asiatic Society of Bengal in 1829.

See also: **Asiatic Societies; Hinduism, history of scholarship; Kālidāsa; Purāṇas; Saṃhitā**

WILL SWEETMAN

Further reading

Kopf, D. 1985. 'The Wonder that Was Orientalism: In Defense of H.H. Wilson's Defense of Hinduism'. In J.R. O'Connell, ed., *Bengal Vaiṣṇavism, Orientalism, Society and the Arts.* East Lansing, MI: Asian Studies Center, Michigan State University, 75–90.

Wilson, H.H. 1813. *The Mégha Dúta; Or, Cloud Messenger: a Poem, in the Sanscrit Language.* Calcutta: Printed by P. Pereira, at the Hindoostanee Press.

Wilson, H.H. 1819. *A Dictionary: Sanscrit and English.* Calcutta: Printed by P. Pereira, at the Hindoostanee Press.

Wilson, H.H. 1840. *The Vishṇu Puráṇa, a System of Hindu Mythology and Tradition.* London: Oriental Translation Fund Committee.

Wilson, H.H. 1840. *Two Lectures on the Religious Practices and Opinions of the Hindus.* Oxford: Combe.

Wilson, H.H. 1846. *Sketch of the Religious Sects of the Hindus.* Calcutta: Bishop's College Press.

Wilson, H.H. 1850–88. *Ṛg-Veda Sanhitā: A Collection of Ancient Hindu Hymns*, 6 vols. London: W.H. Allen.

WOMAN QUESTION

Because Hindus and others often consider Hinduism more a cultural continuum or a 'way of life' than a religion per se, it is viewed as being integral to all aspects of society. For this reason, Hinduism has been blamed for negative attitudes to women over the millennia. Some commentators on women's problems have argued, for instance, that the problems of women are universally caused by men's selfish and immoral power over women – the thesis of patriarchy. The matter is surely more complex, as some of these are common problems faced by women in many cultures and others are specific to particular strata, regions or times in India.

Some problems are, ironically, related to 'correctives' that are found in many cultures. One is the use of culture to counter men's sense of inferiority, because women give birth to them and rear them as children; men claim superiority to women or make them inferior to men by making them inferior in other ways – such as limiting their education. This can foster misogyny. Some classical and medieval Hindu works, for instance, say that women's own nature (svabhāva) is sinful, promiscuous, fickle, impure or dangerous.

Another corrective tries to solve the problem of men not knowing who their offspring are (which means that they must depend on either visual resemblance or the honesty of their wives) by directly or indirectly controlling women. In the past some elite Hindus tried to do so in three ways: guarding women's virginity before marriage (or eliminating the threat to their virginity by arranging child marriages), physically segregating and veiling them (purdah) or socialising them to absolute marital fidelity (strīdharma). In connection with the latter, wives were to treat their husbands as gods and serve them with utmost dedication no matter what their behaviour. The corollary of this insistence on control and fidelity was a social structure that lacked divorce and remarriage for most elite women. Moreover, widowhood became a life of shame and suffering partly because widows were blamed for their husbands' deaths and partly because they had to live ascetic-like lives to avoid being economic burdens on their in-laws. This made their self-immolation the sine qua non of being a good wife (satī). Because there was no other 'legitimate' possibility, such as an ascetic order, many elite women were resigned to this paradigm. But the matter is far more complicated than this. Despite rhetorical praise (arthavāda) of the pativratā ideal and dire warnings to those who might not follow it, even Manu, in his code of law, recognised a higher accountability: the happiness of women in the household (*Manusmṛti* 3.56–58). Some widows became ascetics anyway, moreover; others became tāntrikās who rejected the paradigm altogether; and still others became gaṇikās (courtesans), devadāsīs (temple women) or vīrāṅgaṇās (heroic women).

Another corrective compensates for the comparatively higher death rate for males at birth – 105 boys to 100 girls – by giving boys more food and access to medicine than girls in the first years of life. This happens in Hinduism, too. But the corrective for boys creates terrible problems for girls: they get sick or even die, which, along with abortion and infanticide, skews the sex ratio in favour of boys.

Social structures such as patrilocality/patrilineality (which are the most common) and hierarchy have contributed to serious problems for women the world over. Patrilocality/patrilineality places a premium on sons and allows for male bonding at the expense of women's bonding with natal kin or even of conjugal bonding (a mother's relation to her son sometimes remaining primary even after marriage). In Hinduism, this has contributed to son preference (female infanticide and poor health or death by neglect), sex selection (abortion of female foetuses after learning the sex by amniocentesis), dowry appropriation (voluntary gifts to a bride for her future security transformed into demands for particular gifts that the husband's family sometimes makes) and bride burning (punishment of brides who do not comply or to clear the way for new brides from whom to extort gifts). Hinduism has been implicated in these problems, because it has endorsed the original social structure, which it inherited from Vedic culture (even though some regions or groups, such as tribals, have had other social structures).

Cross-cultural studies show that hierarchy becomes prominent in chiefdoms and early kingdoms. It reflects a consolidation of economic and political power in men's hands – based partly on the selection of men for tasks that require comparative advantages of spatial orientation, size, strength and mobility and partly on the development of martial cultures and new technologies such as plough agriculture. The development of hierarchy affected women, albeit in different ways. One symbol of high status among women was their segregation; women were confined to the home. In elite Hinduism this made them economically dependent on men and reduced the possibility of specialised education in boarding schools. Although education was one domain that women could easily have entered, because men had no comparative advantage, urban men, already threatened because their male bodies no longer had functional importance for society, took extra measures to eliminate any possible competition from women. One symbol of low female status was working in the public realm (often in low-paying jobs).

Hierarchy affected women in additional ways. Because elite status for women was defined by marriage and having sons, being infertile or having only daughters (which was blamed on bad karma) lowered their status and could even lead to religious and social marginalisation if their husbands abandoned them or took new wives. If her husband was infertile, a woman could have intercourse for the sake of having a son with his brother (niyoga), although that custom was gradually abandoned. And here is another problem that some lower-caste women faced: being raped as a sign of upper-caste male authority.

The convergence of all these 'correctives' and social structures created a particularly strong male-oriented (androcentric) worldview. This not only had religious endorsement in some circles but also became the raison d'être of feminine identity and religious practice. Some texts told elite men that sons are necessary for their funerals, which helped to define their destiny as men. And other texts told elite women that total support of their husbands would give them a better rebirth or even help them attain heaven.

Times of historical stress made this androcentric worldview particularly oppressive for women, because the norms for their behaviour became rigid; men projected their own stress – caused by loss of power in the public world due to foreign invasions or competition from other religions – onto women. The texts of these periods are more rigid or misogynistic than others. Manu, for instance, who lived at a time of foreign invasions and social upheavals, emphasised the need to control women. At a personal level, too, stress among men can be a factor in social evils. Some texts by ascetics who were struggling to control their sexuality, for instance, were misogynistic.

These problems have been addressed over the past two centuries by several Hindu reform movements, the women's movement and the feminist movement. This has resulted in new laws and educational programmes by governments, non-governmental organisations and religious groups to improve the status of women. Although some problems have largely disappeared (sati, for instance, and child marriage), others continue, but less severely due to reforms in education and marriage law. However, others have become more severe – sex selection, for instance. Religion is not always the most important variable. Sometimes the most important one is social structure or degree of stress; sometimes it is poverty.

See also: **Abortion; Child marriage; Courtesans; Devadāsī; Dharmaśāstras; Divorce; Dowry; Feminism; Infanticide; Karma; Manu; Niyoga; Pativratā and Patiparameśvara; Sati; Strīdharma; Tantrism; Vedism; Virginity; Widow remarriage; Widowhood; Women, status of; Women's education; Women's movement**

KATHERINE K. YOUNG

Further reading

Das, M. 1984. 'Women Against Dowry'. In M. Kishwar and R. Vanita, eds, *In Search of Answers: Indian Women's Voices from Manushi*. London: Zed Books, 222–27.

Falk, N.E. 1998. '*Shakti* Ascending: Hindu Women, Politics, and Religious Leadership During the Nineteenth and Twentieth Centuries'. In R.D. Baird, ed., *Religion in Modern India*. New Delhi: Manohar, 298–334.

Gupta, C. 1998. 'Social Reform in Nineteenth Century Bengal and the Woman Question'. In K. Sengupta and T. Bandyopadhyay, eds, *Nineteenth Century Thought in Bengal*. New Delhi: Allied Publishers, 185–224.

Harlan, L. and P.B. Courtright (eds). 1995. *From the Margins of Hindu Marriage: Essays on Gender, Religion, and Culture*. Oxford: Oxford University Press.

Mathew, A. 1990. 'Dowry and Its Various Dimensions'. In L. Devasia and V.V. Devasia, eds, *Women in India: Equality, Social Justice and Devleopment*. New Delhi: Indian Social Institute, 79–88.

Menski, W. (ed.). 1998. *South Asians and the Dowry Problem*. GEMS No. 6. Staffordshire: Trentham Books.

Menski, W. 2003. *Hindu Law: Beyond Tradition and Modernity*. New Delhi: Oxford University Press.

Olivelle, P. 2004. *The Law Code of Manu*. Oxford: Oxford University Press.

Paul, M.S. 1986. *Dowry and Position of Women in India: A Study of Delhi Metropolis*. New Delhi: Inter-India Publications.

Ray, A.K. 1985. *Widows Are Not for Burning: Actions and Attitudes of the Christian Missionaries, the Native Hindus and Lord William Bentinck*. New Delhi: ABC Publishing House.

Sadasivan, D. 1979. 'Social Reform Movements in Tamilnadu with Particular Reference to Women'. In S.P. Sen, ed., *Social and Religious Reform Movements in the Nineteenth and Twentieth Centuries*. Calcutta: Institute of Historical Studies, 345–54.

Saxena, R.K. 1975. *Social Reforms: Infanticide and Sati*. New Delhi: Trimurti Publishers.

Sen, M. 2002. *Death by Fire: Sati, Dowry Death and Female Infanticide in Modern India*. New Brunswick, NJ: Rutgers University Press.

Sen, S. 2002. 'Towards a Feminist Politics? The Indian Women's Movement in Historical Perspective'. In K. Kapadia, ed., *The Violence of Development: The Politics of Identity, Gender and Social Inequalities in India*. New York: Zed Books, 459–524.

WOMEN, STATUS OF

The 'status of women' refers to the relative positions of either women and men or groups of women. But exactly what defines 'status' is vague. It might refer to one or more of the following: demography (a skewed sex ratio, say, due to infant or maternal mortality); religious norms for women's proper behaviour; literacy and education; decision-making; control of resources within the family; or level of participation in the public realm, including access to economic resources and political or religious authority. What might represent high status to insiders in one culture or particular circles of that culture, however, might represent low status to others. This problem is even more complicated because of controversy over what people mean by the word 'Hinduism', which is an English word derived from Indus (river or a region) and can refer to Indian culture in general or religious orientations (which are similar or different depending on one's perspective) in particular. Assuming that a 'family of shared resemblances' makes Hinduism a category of analysis, any discussion must account for its long history, complex caste system, regional differences (linguistic, ethnic, social), urban and rural distinctions and tolerance of local customs. Perhaps the most daunting problem – a common problem for anyone who wants to understand women's history – is that we must rely mainly on pre-modern works written by elite men, although we can read between the lines and supplement these, for some periods, with inscriptional and art-historical information. In addition, we can turn to ethnographic accounts for modern Hinduism, which in orthodox or marginal communities may have considerable continuity from the past.

According to the *Ṛgveda*, the earliest Hindu scripture (*c.*1700–800 BCE), women's status was 'high' compared with that of later periods. This tribal society was economically based mainly on pastoralism, socially on patrilineality, and religiously on a mostly male pantheon. These features are cross-culturally correlated with some male dominance. Nonetheless, it valued women as the complements of men. This is symbolised by the word dampati. Dam means 'she of the house' and pati means 'husband'. Combined, they mean 'couple'. The wedding hymn (*Ṛgveda* 10.85.44–47) says, 'May we be calm and united! May we be peaceful and unite together like the rivers mingling [in the ocean] and losing their separate entities. May we be like breaths united with the body. May we be united like the Lord and his creation. May we be united like the teacher and his disciple. May we love each other and be loyal to each other through our lives!' (Narayanan 2003: 35). The core values of this life-affirming society were progeny, prosperity and longevity. Because ritual was originally home-based, women were the ritual counterparts of their husbands. They had special roles and took over when their husbands went away. Approximately twenty women, such as Lopāmudrā (see *Ṛgveda* 1.179; 5.28; 8.91 and 10.39–40), were visionary poetesses (ṛṣikās). Others chanted the *Sāmaveda*. And a few women were warriors (Shah 1995: 153). Affirming women were images of goddesses such as the dawn (Uṣas), river (Sarasvatī), (mother) earth who protects the dead (Pṛthivī) and the embodiments or bestowers of elegant speech, prosperity and progeny (Vāk, Aditi, Rākā and Sinīvālī).

But this culture's spread to the Gangetic Valley, accompanied by state formation and urbanisation, led to a decline in the status of women. This was the kind of change that often occurs during the transition from small-scale to large-scale societies; men get more power not only because of their duties in warfare, plough agriculture and trade but also because of their control of centralised royal power and specialised knowledge. In ancient India, specialised religious knowledge, in particular, had a profound influence on elite women's status. When education moved from homes to 'boarding' schools, girls lost out unless their fathers taught there. Some girls had fathers who did. These probably included Gārgī, who publicly and smartly debated with Yājñāvalkya, and Maitreyī, who was called a brahmavādinī (*Bṛhadāraṇyaka Upaniṣad* 4.5.15). The authors of later texts occasionally referred to learned women. Pāṇini, a grammarian of the fifth century BCE, distinguished between ācāryā (a female teacher) and ācāryaṇī (a teacher's wife) or upādhyāyā (a female preceptor) and upādhyāyinī (a preceptor's wife). So did Hārita, who referred to brahmavādinīs who remain unmarried and devote their lives to Vedic study and ritual. When priests began to specialise in public rituals (śrauta), however, the ritual function of wives declined. Even so, women were still associated with the domestic ones (gṛhya) and were still necessary to make the public ones alive, powerful and effective.

After purity and impurity became key ritual concepts in the *Brāhmaṇas*, priests applied them to women. Menstruation and childbirth were impure, so they segregated women at these times. As a sign of attitudes to come, the *Śatapatha Brāhmaṇa* says that women, śūdras, dogs and crows embody untruth, sin and darkness (14.1.1.31). Women's purity meant marital fidelity, too, and impurity meant either premarital sex or adultery. To ensure the purity of their daughters for marriage, for instance, parents had to protect their virginity. Most parents, of course, wanted to shorten the time of this responsibility. Without initiation (upanayana) (*Śatapatha Brāhmaṇa* 11.3.3.1–7) and education, for instance, even young girls were available for marriage. As one result, they married boys who were considerably older; this practice gradually developed into child marriage. Another result was to confine elite women to domestic space. They were subordinate even there and ate after their husbands.

Elite women's status declined even more steeply early in the classical period (*c.*400 BCE–400 CE). This was a time of enormous stress for brahmaṇas, because foreign invasions by Bactrians and Kuśāṇas had led to foreign rule in the heartland and threatened the old brahmanical political alliance with the aristocratic warriors (kṣatriyas), as well as brahmanical religion itself, because many foreign rulers preferred Buddhism. The brāhmaṇas remembered, moreover, their loss of power during the Mauryan dynasty, especially under the Buddhist Aśoka (268–233), who had prohibited animal sacrifice, including the royal aśvamedha or horse sacrifice – an act that threatened not only the ritualistic core of the brahmanical worldview but also their livelihood and identity. They considered the Mauryans, Bactrians, and Kuśāṇas to be śūdras, observed that these śūdras favoured Buddhism and Jainism and found fellow brāhmaṇas either marrying into these communities or joining Buddhist and Jain monastic orders. Therefore they used their analytical and rhetorical skills to promote the twice-born (especially brāhmaṇas and kṣatriyas) and demote the śūdras. Fear that their women would be wooed by these 'śūdras' into either marriages or monasteries led some brāhmaṇa authors to think of women even more negatively than they already had and to circumscribe their behaviour accordingly. They described women and śūdras in similar ways or even grouped them together. It is possible that anxiety caused these men to project the negativity that they felt about their loss of public power onto women.

Manu (or the text attributed to him) *c.*200 BCE–200 CE exemplifies the ambiguity and, at times, misogyny (noted by modern feminists) that had developed. He speaks, for instance, of how wives are to serve their husbands, as śūdras their masters (1.91), and how they cannot undergo initiation into sacred learning (upanayana) and so are without knowledge of the Veda (2.67), like śūdras (4.108). Manu encourages women, moreover, to exercise self-control (5.165) or, if that is not forthcoming, to be controlled by their husbands. According to some passages, women's independence is severely curtailed, even in religious activities (5.155). Manu (or the men of his time) might have been keen to guard women (9.2–3), because he feared not only women's adultery but also their romantic love with śūdras and the possibility that they might join Buddhist and Jaina monasteries before or after marriage.

But a careful reading of Manu reveals that there are passages that offer other perspectives. If one passage says, for instance, that adultery can be a mere conversation or touch (8.356–58) or that a woman who has actually had sex with someone who is not her husband is to be 'devoured by dogs in a public square' (the male offender was to be burnt to death) (8.371–72), another passage says that she will be purified by her menses or that she is to be punished by being confined for a while to her house. In addition, there are some passages that offer a positive view of women: 'Where women are revered, there the gods rejoice; but where they are not, no rite bears any fruit. Where female relatives grieve, that family soon comes to ruin, but where they do not grieve, it always prospers. When female relatives, not receiving due reverence, curse any house, it comes to total ruin, as if struck down by witchcraft' (*Manusmṛti* 3.56–58; trans. Olivelle 2004). Because Manu has been labelled as the Hindu misogynist par excellence, it is important to remember the difficulties of his times, the ambiguities found in his work, the fact that he is by no means representative of Hindu law (there are many differing views from other historical periods and he gained high status as representative of the tradition only during the colonial period), that in any case local customs usually trump these texts and, finally, that women have had their own interpretations of all this and have often found ways of working around the limitations of negative scriptural passages.

The *Rāmāyaṇa*, also redacted during the early classical period, upholds the woman's vow of absolute fidelity to her husband (pativratā), even as it exposes a tragic dimension: Rāma's faith in Sītā's chastity, even though she had been held against her will by the demonic Rāvaṇa, but also his mandate as king to set examples of dharma for others to follow and his need to take seriously his citizens' concern that his wife is no longer chaste. Although Rāma personally never doubts Sītā's chastity, he treats her harshly. In Sītā's eyes, though, there are limits to the model of pativratā and the duty of a king. As an example of her own sense of will, integrity and justice, she finally refuses to obey her husband. When he orders one more ordeal to assuage public doubt, she asks mother earth to take her back to the furrows (which is where Sītā, which denotes furrow, had been born according to her origin myth).

Some passages in the *Mahābhārata* continue Manu's and the *Rāmāyaṇa*'s negative comments. Interestingly, the epic itself is aware that women's status has changed over history (1.113.4–8). Whereas at least some women in the Vedic age had knowledge of scriptures, now they are without this (13.40.11), and their intellect is dull (12.347.4). Their education, therefore, is devoted to household management (3.222.48–54) and the fine arts, which enhance their feminine charms. But the epics, too, have other passages that praise women and appreciate their roles.

These developments in the classical age resulted in a paradigm of four stages of life for an elite (twice-born) man. These included (Vedic) studentship (brahmacarya), householdership (gārhasthya), forest-dwelling (vānaprasthya) and renunciaton (saṃnyāsa). But the paradigm was different for elite women – maidenhood (kaumārya), wifehood (patnitva) and sometimes either widowhood (vaidhavya) or, optionally, self-immolation (sati). These were all related to the *one* goal of women's life: being a wife in this lifetime and the next, when wives would rejoin their husbands. (This rebirth orientation for women would later be challenged by bhakti and Tantrism, which viewed women as capable of liberation.)

Every wife wore auspicious symbols such as the mark on her forehead (boṭṭu/bindi/tilaka), bangles, a wedding chain (maṅgalasūtra) and so forth. Very few women chose sati. But some Hindus believed that this act was very auspicious, because it meant that these women attached more importance to rejoining their husbands than to their own lives. Widowhood was inauspicious, on the other hand, because some believed that the bad karma of these wives had killed their husbands. Elite widows, not surprisingly, removed all auspicious symbols. Brāhmaṇa widows, in addition, shaved their heads, wore plain white saris and followed an ascetic-like regimen (but without receiving the prestige attached to asceticism).

Female asceticism per se received no official endorsement, although it never completely disappeared. The classical worldview was structured by the opposition between desire (kāma), after all, and control of desire (yoga). Some men associated women with the former and themselves with the latter.

During the classical period's second half, life improved in the Gangetic plain. Kingdoms stabilised, the economy became robust, foreigners integrated and brāhmaṇas found ways of competing successfully against Buddhists and Jains. (Many scholars call this dramatic transformation of Vedic sacrificial religion into temple-oriented religion Hinduism.) These changes led to improvements in the status of śūdras, who became more demanding, and also women. 'Even women, vaiśyas, and śūdras', says *Bhagavadgītā* 9.32, 'shall attain the supreme goal'. The expansion of Gangetic culture and its religions (Vedic-brahmanical, Hindu bhakti, Jain and Buddhist) into the central and then southern regions required Hindus to integrate new peoples and compete for converts (these 'śūdras', after all, were often the holders of local political power and wealth).

By the early mediaeval period, bhakti sects were wooing śūdras and women by making the criterion for salvation humble service, loyalty and devotion to God – the very roles that had once defined their low status when done for men. Personal devotion, not priestly ritual, was at the centre of bhakti religion. Bhakti sects made the path to salvation possible within the householder stage of life, moreover, which provided śūdras and women with opportunities for salvation. Women became the paradigmatic devotees, in fact, because the two greatest gods were male – Śiva and Viṣṇu had risen in the pantheon as old Vedic gods had fallen – and love for these deities was the raison d'être of the religion. To be good devotees, men had to imagine being women in love; women could do the same thing, of course, much more easily. This proved so inspiring for many women that some took literally the call to love only God, bypassing marriage or even abandoning earthly husbands to marry the divine one. Although this was norm-defying, women of many regions and castes – Kāraikkāl Aammaiyār, Āṇṭāḷ, Mahādevī, Janābāī, Bahiṇābāī and Mīrābāī – overcame enormous obstacles to pursue their love for God, which made them into saints. Their vernacular inspirational poetry about love sometimes developed the status of scripture. This helped women and śūdras, because they no longer needed knowledge of Sanskrit and the Veda.

With the development of the *Purāṇas*, which popularised Hinduism, and the growing importance of agriculture and fertility symbolism, goddess worship, which had some antecedents that went back to the Indus Valley civilisation and Vedic religion, became popular. Some goddesses represented the good wife or consort (Pārvatī, wife of Śiva, for instance, Śrī Lakṣmī, wife of Viṣṇu, Sītā, wife of Rāma, or Rādhā, consort of Kṛṣṇa). Other goddesses, though, were supreme and independent deities. The *Purāṇa*s drew on Vedic hymns such as the *Devī-sūkta* (*Ṛgveda* 10. 125.3.4.5). The *Devibhāgavata Purāṇa*, speaks of goddesses as channels of grace and women as preferred gurus. The female-oriented form of bhakti, called Śāktism, was especially popular in eastern India. The importance of goddesses, moreover, influenced philosophy. When not supreme, the feminine principle was often prakṛti, the material or illusory principle. Depending on the system, this was a co-principle (in the dualistic Sāṃkhya), a principle of superimposition (in the non-dualistic Advaita Vedānta), or the supreme (male) deity's power or instrument to create (in some bhakti theologies).

Tantrism was even more radical in its reversal of norms, especially 'left-handed' Tantra. These tāntrikas worshipped Mahādevī, a goddess, and pursued an esoteric spiritual path. This path celebrated low-caste status and involved five forbidden things: consuming wine, meat, fish and parched grain, and having sexual intercourse outside marriage (pañcamakāra). The latter transformed the sexual act into a religious experience by postponing orgasm and then releasing the energy up through seven mystical centres (cakras). 'Right-handed' tāntrikas, on the other hand, either used a more symbolic approach or did their spiritual practices with their wives. Because of their identification with the feminine principle, some tantric texts argued against dowry, sati, rudeness to women, and the use of female animals in sacrifice. They argued, too, for the punishment of rape by death.

Some orthodox brahmanical thinkers supported salvation for women. We see this in several commentaries by Vedāntins on *Bhagavadgītā* 9.32. Śaṅkara (*c.* eighth century) indirectly said that women could attain salvation in this life, although he glossed the word paṇḍitā (a learned woman) in his commentary on the *Bṛhadāraṇyaka Upaniṣad* as one who knows about domestic things (gṛhatantraviṣayam) (Young 1994). And Rāmānuja (*c.* twelfth century) also accepted salvation for women but did not dwell on the topic – his successors, however, claimed that women were the pre-eminent devotees. (Other orthodox commentators such as the tenth-century Bhāskara rejected salvation for women. Some *Tantra*s, too, were transformed by brāhmaṇas, who argued that women and śūdras were ineligible to utter sacred symbols such as Oṃ or follow higher stages of the path to enlightenment.)

Sometimes orthodoxy itself took very different approaches. In Kerala, for instance, the Nambudiri brāhmaṇas had an unusual relationship with the matrilineal Nayar community. Younger sons had liaisons with the Nayar women; their children belonged to the Nayar community. This served both communities. Nayar men were warriors and often away from home for long periods of time; and because of primogeniture only the eldest Nambudiri man could marry within the community and inherit, which left younger Nambudiris without marriage.

So far, I have discussed representations of Hindu women in texts by brāhmaṇa men. But inscriptions reveal another class of women: temple women (devadāsīs). They formed their own female-headed groups outside the marital norms of brahmanically oriented society and had long-term sexual liaisons with elite men. Their activities ranged from singing and dancing in temple rituals and carrying lamps and waving flywhisks in temple processions to more mundane tasks such as making food offerings, plaiting garlands and preparing ritual substances and implements. Though of ambiguous sexual status – they were not pativratās – they nevertheless had high status because of their artistic fame, wealth, donations to temples, marriages to gods (in some regions) or close ties with kings and their courts. Similar in lifestyle to devadāsīs were courtesans (gaṇikās), who performed at court. Though much lower in status than either temple women or courtesans, ordinary prostitutes (veśyās), too, were outside the pativratā model.

From the thirteenth century, Hindu martial groups fought Muslim invaders. Some of their women, called 'manly or heroic women' (vīrāṇgaṇās), participated as warriors in these campaigns. And some queens, whose husbands had died in battle, became regents until their sons came of age. Many of these women – Kūrma Devī, Tārābāī, Ahalyābāī Holkar and Lakshmībāī, the Rānī of Jhansi – ignored the norms of strīdharma, found inspiration in warrior goddesses (symbols of independence such as Durgā) and assumed the role of men. And they were supported by their Hindu subjects. The explanation is a rule of dharma: exceptions are allowed in times of crisis.

Muslim rulers allowed each religion to follow its own system of family law. Even when Islamic law differed considerably from Hindu law, for instance, Muslims rarely interfered. Sometimes, though, Hindus imitated Muslim traditions. Given the growing defensiveness of Hindu culture as a way of coping with foreign rulers, some Hindus borrowed the traditions of purdah. This introduced even more restrictions for Hindu women. Although Hindu women might have benefited from some Islamic positions on women – the possibility of divorce or inheritance, say, and opposition to sati – they seldom did, because many Hindus reacted to Muslim invasions by withdrawing as completely as possible from interaction with them. Once again, some Hindu men might have tried to counter the stress created by loss of political power by viewing themselves as superior at least to their own women – and in control of them.

The advent of European rule was another time of stress for the brahmanical leadership. A particularly misogynistic view of women appeared in the eighteenth century *Strīdharmapaddhati*, an exposition for the daily routines of orthodox women (Leslie 1989). It was written by Tryambaka, a paṇḍita (traditional teacher), who belonged to the Maratha court in Tamil Nadu. The competition and stress caused by the presence of both Muslim and Christian missionaries might explain Tryambaka's especially negative views of women. In addition, bhaktas and ordinary Tamil women might have threatened brahmanical orthodoxy. Because of cross-cousin marriage, they had never experienced the negative effects of patrilineal social structure and pativratā norms.

At first the British did not want to interfere with Hinduism, fearing that they would alienate the population. But after listening to missionary and other critiques of Hinduism, they gradually became involved with social problems such as female infanticide, sati, child marriage, mistreatment of widows, women's lack of education and so forth. They were joined by Hindu groups such as the Brahmo Samaj, the Prarthana Samaj, the Arya Samaj and the Ramakrishna Mission. Brahmo Samaji Rammohan Roy (1772–1833), for instance, wanted to reform Hinduism by returning to the *Upaniṣads* and by eliminating sati, a practice that was particularly disturbing to him because a favourite sister-in-law had died in this way. He convinced British officials that it was not authorised by the original dharma. This led to Regulation XVII of 1829, which made sati illegal. Lal Devraj, who led the Arya Samaj, taught girls how to recite the Veda and perform Vedic rituals. This revival of Vedic learning for women appealed to groups such as the Sarada Devi Mission (named after Sarada Devi, wife of the Bengali saint Ramakrishna). With the help of Sister Nivedita, Gauri Ma, Sudhira Basu and Sarala Mukhopadhyaya, it restored to women brahmacāriṇī traditions. This way of thinking became increasingly popular in groups such as the Brahma Vidya Mandir, Kanya Kumari Sthan and Udyan Mangal Kanyalaya. Brāhmaṇa leaders – M.G. Ranade, Mrtyunjaya Vidyalankar, Ishwar Chandra Vidyasagar, Debendranath Tagore, Dayananda Saraswati, Keshab Chandra Sen, Behramji Malabari – were not the only ones to consider the problems of women. So did non-brāhmaṇa leaders – such as Jotirao

Phule, Subramaniya Bharati and E.V. Ranaswami – who compared the problems of women to those of outcastes. Hindu women themselves took up the cause, one of the first being the brahmaṇa Pandita Ramabai (1858–1822). She learned Sanskrit from her father, going on to challenge scriptural stereotypes of women and to instigate reforms, especially for widows, especially after her conversion to Christianity.

The Raj found itself between a rock and a hard place. On the one hand, it needed to bring Hindus under a common law in order to rule effectively. On the other hand, it also did not want to offend Hindu religious sensitivities, which might have led to political unrest. The British tried to resolve this dilemma by consulting with traditional religious authorities (paṇḍitas) on which Hindu laws to apply. With the adoption of the *Manusmṛti* on paṇḍita advice, they not only instituted the most problematic law code for women – less restrictive ones, such as that of Nārada or Parāśara allowed for divorce and other practices that benefited women – but also universalised it to all castes, thereby bringing many more women under its jurisdiction. Even many elite women's lives had been governed more by local custom than by any *Dharmaśāstra* text.

Although many Westerners – administrators, Orientalists and missionaries – were nobly motivated to improve the lives of Hindu women, others were more interested in rationalising the Raj's existence by saying that it was the 'white man's burden' to do so. Some women, such as Katherine Mayo, rationalised imperialism in this way. After travelling around the country in the 1920s, she wrote *Mother India*. This book severely criticised the treatment of women, animals, nationalist politicians and lack of sanitation. And it blamed these problems on the rampant sexuality of Indian men! Hindu women preferred to link reform with Indian nationalism. Many joined Mahatma Gandhi's non-violence movement as satyāgrahiṇīs, a word that denotes those who grasp/insist on that which is real and true and connotes those who use 'soul-force'. Realising that women had been 'caged' in their homes and subjected to too much tradition, Gandhi connected their liberation with national liberation. But as modern Indian feminists would later point out, Gandhi still clung to the idea of woman as wife and mother in the home.

Hindu women, in solidarity with other women, were taking liberation into their own hands. The Women's Indian Association lobbied governments and political parties for the right to vote (with support from the British suffragette movement) and more legal reforms. Together with the All India Women's Conference and the National Council of Women, they drafted an Indian Women's Charter of Rights and Duties to make sure that women would receive a fair deal in the new constitution. After Independence in 1947, the constitution prohibited discrimination on the basis of sex, legalised affirmative action and gave the secular government power to reform Hinduism. But it was the controversial Hindu Marriage Act of 1955 (with later amendments) and the Hindu Succession Act of 1956 that really changed Hindu family law for women. These measures made polygamy illegal, allowed separation and divorce, raised (again) the age of marriage and so forth.

Although legal progress was dramatic, social progress was slow. In the 1970s and 1980s women joined Marxist and Maoist labour movements, trade union protests, student agitations and the worldwide feminist movement. They saw links between black liberation, dalit (outcaste) liberation and women's liberation. They addressed social problems such as dowry and bride-burning, a uniform common law (highlighted by the Shah Bano case in 1985 about alimony for a Muslim woman), sex selection (after the introduction of amniocentesis technology), rape, domestic violence and sati (after the case of Roop Kanwar in 1987).

Women have had a hard time solving their social problems because of their ties with patrilineal social structures, which have been exacerbated by some aspects of colonisation and modernity. But women have had a far easier time with religious ones. In many circles, for instance, they have regained access to Vedic knowledge, Vedic ritual and asceticism. Female students now attend religious schools (kanyāgurukulas) in the holy city of Vārāṇasī. Widows have become respected saṃnyāsinīs there, too, as have female tāntrikās. Women have even become religious leaders of traditional (male) lineages and aśramas, a change that occurred in the late nineteenth and twentieth centuries (Sarada Devi took over from Ramakrishna, Mirra Alfassa, 'the Mother', took over from Aurobindo, Daya Mata from Yogananda, Godavari Mataaji from Upasani Bab, Gayatri Devi from Paramananda, Mathru Srisarada from Lakshmana, Asha Ma from Madhusudandas, Gurumayi Chidvilasananda from Muktananda, Mate Mahādevi from Lingananda and so forth). Other Hindu groups are divided on this development. Some Śaṅkarācāryas do initiate women and recognise them as gurus (one Śaṅkarācārya of Kanci, for instance, initiated Jñānānanda as a saṃnyāsinī in the 1970s and recognised her as a guru – but others do not). Some women bypass human male authority by suggesting that they do not need initiation because they are an incarnation of a supreme deity, as did the modern Bengali saint Anandamayi Ma.

The study of Hindu women has involved major changes in historiography. I will discuss four kinds of historiographic change. Each is a logical category and a chronological development (Sharma 1985).

The first is insider to insider during the pre-modern period. These insiders were brāhmaṇa men, who belonged to different philosophical schools or religious lineages. On the topic of women, they debated questions such as women's eligibility for Vedic ritual or asceticism, whether sati was permissible or not and so forth.

The second is outsider to outsider (missionaries such as Abbé Dubois, activists such as Katherine Mayo and Orientalists such as William Jones who wrote for other outsiders (Western audiences back home)). This was common during the colonial period.

The third is outsider (Western men and women) to insider (Indian men and women). The works of the former were published in India and used to teach Hindus about their religion. By the 1970s, as more Western women became academics and feminists, they joined the ranks of outsider Western men writing about Hinduism but looked more specifically at Hindu women. Inspired by feminism, with its central assumption that all women are oppressed by men, Mary Daly and her colleagues wrote extreme reports about the effects of religious customs – especially sati – on women. Textualists, on the other hand, tried to learn more about Hindu women's lives and goddess traditions and thus restore women's history. Sometimes, they used feminist analysis. Vedic scholars questioned whether the Vedic age was indeed a golden age, for instance, as A.S. Altekar had claimed. Anthropologists documented women's religion by interviewing women. Their descriptions were often unlike those of textualists. Although anthropological accounts cannot replace historical accounts for the simple reason that they are situated in the modern period, they have made major contributions to the field by recording what women themselves have to say about their religious lives and how they differ from those of men. In addition, descriptions of real lives make scholars more sensitive to the fact that there was likely a big gulf between texts and contexts in the past. And these new studies highlight the regional, caste, class and stage of life differences among Hindu women.

The fourth is insider to outsider. There are some precedents for this. Pandita Ramabai and Vivekananda spoke to British and American scholars in the nineteenth century about Hindu women and criticised misrepresentations. P.V. Kane wrote his five-volume *History of Dharmaśāstra* in 1930–62, which included challenges to Western stereotypes about Hindu women. He used Hindu texts but also comparative data. Indian anthropologists and sociologists have documented the insiders' perspective, too. The insider to outsider approach developed mainly in the last quarter of the twentieth century as Indian women (including those in the diaspora) began to stake out their own interpretations of women in the history of Hinduism (sometimes criticising Western scholarship in the process). Drawing on the (Western) intellectual fashions of critical theory, feminism, postmodernism and postcolonialism, some women criticised previous scholarship for focusing on texts rather than 'praxis', elite people rather than 'subalterns', and Western feminist bias rather than third-world feminist insights. Because of the growing tension between secularists (including many feminists) and Hindu fundamentalists, few 'insiders' searched for a distinctively Hindu viewpoint – although they were quick to defend Hinduism if Western feminists stereotyped Hindu women as mere pativratās, Hindu law as only that of Manu and so forth. Appealing to Hindu pluralism and Hindu nuance is now de rigueur in the changing power relations of insiders and outsiders.

Insider to insider – this takes us full circle. Insider female scholars supportive of a secular state and opportunities for women beyond their household roles criticise fundamentalist women by pointing out the dangers of maintaining old models of strīdharma as a way of protecting Hindu identity, which has become the rallying cry of Hindu fundamentalists. Female academics in India have yet to write from a Hindu fundamentalist perspective (unlike some Muslim women in the Middle East). But if they do they will change historiography once again – this time another version of insiders to insiders or insiders to outsiders, albeit with very different inside views.

See also: **Ācārya; Aditi; Anandamayi Ma; Āṇṭāḷ; Arya Samaj; Āśramas (stages of life); Bhagavadgītā; Bhakti; Brahmacarya; Brāhmaṇas; Brahmo Samaj; Buddhism, relationship with Hinduism; Caste; Child marriage; Courtesans; Dalits; Daya Mata, Sri; Dayananda Saraswati, Swami; Devadāsīs; Dharma; Dharmaśāstras; Diaspora; Divorce; Dubois, Jean Antoine; Durgā; Feminism; Gandhi, Mohandas Karamchand; Gārgī; Gārhasthya; Ghose, Aurobindo; Guru; Hinduism; Hindutva; Indus Valley Civilisation; Infanticide; Jainism, relationship with Hinduism; Jones, Sir William; Kāma; Kane, Pandurang Vaman; Kanyākumārī; Kāraikkāl Ammaiyār; Karma; Kṛṣṇa; Lakṣmi, Śrī; Lopāmudrā; Mahābhārata; Maitreyī; Manu; Mīrābāī; Mother, The; Muktananda, Swami; Nārada; Nivedita, Sister; Oṃ; Orientalism; Pāṇini; Pañcamakāra; Paṇḍit; Parāśara; Pārvatī; Pativratā and Patiparameśvara; Phule, Jotirao; Prakṛti; Prarthana Samaj; Pṛthivī; Purāṇas; Rādhā; Rāma; Ramakrishna Math and Mission; Rāmānuja; Rāmāyaṇa; Ranade, Mahadev Govind; Rāvaṇa; Religious specialists; Roy, Rammohan; Ṛṣi; Śakti; Śaktism; Saṃhitā; Sāṃkhya; Saṃnyāsa; Śaṅkara; Śaṅkarācāryas; Sarada Devi; Sarasvatī; Saraswati, Pandita Ramabai; Sati; Tagore, Debendranath; Tantras; Tantrism; Upanayana; Upaniṣads; Uṣas; Vānaprasthya; Vārāṇasī; Varṇa; Veda; Vedānta; Vidyasagar, Ishwar Chandra; Virginity; Viṣṇu; Vivekananda, Swami; Widowhood; Woman question; Women's education; Women's**

movement; Women's rites; Yajña; Yājñavalkya; Yoga; Yogananda, Paramhansa

KATHERINE K. YOUNG

Further reading

Altekar, A.S. 1959 [1938]. *The Position of Women in Hindu Civilization*, 3rd edn. Delhi: Motilal Banarsidass.

Bhose, M. (ed.). 2000. *Faces of the Feminine in Ancient, Medieval, and Modern India*. New Delhi: Oxford University Press.

Chakravarti, U. 1999. 'Beyond the Altekarian Paradigm: Towards a New Understanding of Gender Relations in Early Indian History'. In K. Roy, ed., *Women in Early Indian Societies*. New Delhi: Manohar, 72–81.

Jacobson, D. and S.S. Wadley. 1992. *Women in India: Two Perspectives*. Columbia, SC: South Asia Publications.

Jamison, S.W. 1996. *Sacrificed Wife/Sacrificer's Wife: Women, Ritual, and Hospitality in Ancient India*. New York: Oxford University Press.

Kane, P.V. 1968–77 [1930–62]. *History of Dharmaśāstra*, 5 vols, 2nd edn. Poona: Bhandarkar Oriental Research Institute.

Leslie, J. 1989. *The Perfect Wife: The Orthodox Hindu Woman According to the Stridharmapaddhati of Tryambakayajvan*. New York: Oxford University Press.

Narayanan, V. 1999. 'Brimming with Bhakti, Embodiments of Shakti: Devotees, Deities, Performers, Reformers, and Other Women of Power in the Hindu Tradition'. In A. Sharma and K.K. Young, eds, *Feminism in World Religions*. Albany, NY: State University of New York Press, 22–77.

Narayanan, V. 2003. 'Hinduism'. In A. Sharma and K.K. Young, eds, *Her Voice Her Faith*. Boulder, CO: Westview, 11–57.

Olivelle, P. 2004. *The Law Code of Manu*. Oxford: Oxford University Press.

Patton, L. 2002. *Jewels of Authority: Women and Text in the Hindu Tradition*. Oxford: Oxford University Press.

Roy, K. 1999. *Women in Early Indian Societies*. New Delhi: Manohar.

Sastri, S.R. 1952. *Women in the Vedic Age*. Bombay: Bharatiya Vidya Bhavan.

Shah, S. 1995. *The Making of Womanhood: Gender Relations in the Mahabharata*. Delhi: Manohar.

Sharma, A. 1985. 'The Insider and the Outsider in the Study of Religion'. *Eastern Anthropologist* 38: 331–33.

Sharma, A. (ed.). 2005. *Goddesses and Women in the Indic Religious Tradition*. Leiden: Brill.

Sugirtharajah, S. 1994. 'Hinduism'. In *Women in Religion*, eds J. Holm and J.W. Bowker. London: Pinter, 59–83.

Young, K.K. 1994. 'Women in Hinduism'. In A. Sharma, ed., *Today's Women in World Religions*. Albany, NY: State University of New York Press, 77–135.

Young, K.K. 2002. 'Women and Hinduism'. In A. Sharma, ed., *Women in Indian Religions*. New Delhi: Oxford University Press, 1–37.

WOMEN'S EDUCATION

In Vedic times, some elite women were initiated into Vedic learning, learned Sanskrit and studied Vedic rituals and lore. As initiates (yajñopavītinīs) and advanced students of scripture (brahmavādinīs), some even became teachers (paṇḍitās). But women gradually lost access to Vedic education, because brahmanical specialisation took it out of the home and into 'boarding schools' – which caused parents to worry about maintaining the virginity of their daughters. Gradually, marriage replaced upanayana as a rite of passage for girls. Many scriptures forbade women even to chant Vedic mantras. This made them like śudras (see *Manusmṛti* 9.18; *Baudhāyana* 1.11.7; *Mahābhārata* 13.40.11–12), who were without Vedic learning (avaidika). As with most things Hindu, this was not universally true. Sects such as the tāntrikas and Śrī Vaiṣṇavas continued to educate girls; Tirukkōnēri Dāsyai, for instance, wrote a commentary, on the *Tiruvāymoḻi*, which demonstrates her knowledge of the *Veda Saṃhitā*, *Upaniṣads* and other scriptures. Courtesans and devadāsīs, moreover, had training in temple and court performance traditions. Under the British, reforms led to education for some elite girls (often in missionary schools). Central and state governments since Independence have tried to increase female school attendance at all levels and women's literacy, but the statistics for women still lag behind those for men. Today, young women often study Sanskrit and the Veda in universities and women are being taught Vedic rituals and scriptures in religious organisations.

See also: **Courtesans; Devadāsī; Dharmaśāstras; Languages; Mahābhārata; Paṇḍit; Saṃhitā; Śrī Vaiṣṇavas; Upanayana; Upaniṣads; Virginity; Woman question; Women, status of**

KATHERINE K. YOUNG

Further reading

Basu, A. 1999. 'Women's Education in India: Achievements and Challenges'. In B. Ray and A. Basu, eds, *From Independence Towards Freedom: Indian Women Since 1947*. New York: Oxford University Press, 135–57.

Hooja, G.B.K. 1990. 'New Education Policy and Women's Development'. In L. Devasia and V.V. Devasia, eds, *Women in India: Equality, Social Justice and Development*. New Delhi: Indian Social Institute, 89–111.

Jeffrey, P. and R. Jeffrey. 1994. 'Killing My Heart's Desire: Education and Female Autonomy in Rural India'. In N. Kumar, ed., *Women as Subjects: South Asian Histories*. Charlottesville, VI: University Press of Virginia, 125–71.

Mookerji, Radha Kumud. 1989 [1947]. *Ancient Indian Education: Brahmanical and Buddhist*. Delhi: Motilal Banarsidass.

Olivelle, P. 2004. *The Law Code of Manu*. Oxford: Oxford University Press.

Shah, S. 1995. *The Making of Womanhood: Gender Relations in the Mahābhārata*. Delhi: Manohar.

WOMEN'S MOVEMENT

In the nineteenth century the British had tried to improve women's lot in connection with education, child marriage, divorce and remarriage, widowhood, and sati. Some had done so because of deep sympathy for Hindus. Others had done so, paternalistically, because of assumptions about the 'white man's burden'. And still others had done so because of assumptions developed by missionaries, who accused Hinduism of subjugating women. Brāhmaṇa men (M.G. Ranade, Mrtyunjaya Vidyalankar, Raja Rammohan Roy, Ishwar Chandra Vidyasagar, Debendranath Tagore, Dayananda Saraswati, Keshab Chandra Sen, Behramji Malabari and others) took up the challenge of reform to improve the lives of Hindu women. These Hindu reformers argued that Hinduism could be compatible with equality and modernity. Non-brāhmaṇa men such as Jotirao Phule, Subramaniya Bharati and E.V. Ranaswami linked the condition of women to that of the outcastes, blaming both problems on brahmanical Hinduism. And brāhmaṇa women such as Pandita Ramabai Saraswati (1858–1922) – whose father had educated her in Sanskrit learning, which had been forbidden to women in most circles – blamed brahmanical Hinduism for its mistreatment of women, especially child widows. Although this led to several liberalising laws, progress was slow. The British were afraid to inflame the sensitivities of Hindus after the revolt of 1857.

During the rise of India's independence movement, however, the Women's Indian Association began to consolidate legal reforms and introduce new legislation by lobbying both the government and political parties for changes. They educated women about the need for these, commented on bills and demanded the right to vote (with support from the British suffragette movement). They won the vote first at the regional level. In 1927, the All India Women's Conference (AIWC) was founded to further goals of the women's movement such as attaining national female suffrage, reforming personal law and securing guarantees of sexual equality in any future constitution. Many women, including Hindu women, joined

Mahatma Gandhi's struggle for national liberation. Approximately 17,000 of the 80,000 who were arrested during the salt march in 1930, for instance were women. They picketed and demonstrated. Women of many religious communities worked together on common problems such as the right to inheritance, fair divorce and remarriage. Women's organisations such as the AIWC, the Women's Indian Association, and the National Council of Women prepared for independence by drafting an Indian Women's Charter of Rights and Duties. This document included calls for sexual equality before the law in connection with voting, access to education, health services, pay, social insurance and so forth. As Independence approached, solidarity between Hindu and Muslim women became more difficult; tensions between the two communities in general led to violence at the time of partition.

Since independence in 1947, the Constitution has enshrined several rights for women. It prohibits discrimination on the basis of sex, for instance, with reference to social, political and economic acts (III:15; IV:39). It allows the government to use affirmative action as a way of improving their status. And it provides directions to ensure that women can earn adequate livelihoods with 'equal pay for equal work'. The Hindu Marriage Act 1955 and the Hindu Succession Act 1956 have made polygamy illegal, raised the age of marriage once more and allowed women to petition for restitution of conjugal rights, judicial separation and divorce. Women's studies scholars have recently exposed the links of this women's movement with imperialism, women's subordination and Gandhi's traditional views on women (that they should maintain the roles of wife and mother), but they acknowledge the enormous changes that have occurred since the British Rāj. In its next phase, this movement turned into second-wave feminism.

See also: **Brāhmaṇa; Child marriage; Dalits; Dayananda Saraswati, Swami; Divorce; Feminism; Phule, Jotirao; Ranade, Mahadev Govind; Roy, Rammohan; Saraswati, Pandita Ramabai; Sati; Sen, Keshab Chandra; Tagore, Debendranath; Vidyasagar, Ishwar Chandra; Woman question; Women's education; Women, status of; Widowhood**

KATHERINE K. YOUNG

Further reading

Bhasin, K. 1986. *Some Questions on Feminism and Its Relevance in South Asia*. New Delhi: Kali for Women.

Brouwer, J. 1999. 'Feminism and the Indigenous Knowledge System in India: An Exploration'. In R. Indira and D.K. Behera, eds, *Gender and Society in India*, vol. 1. New Delhi: Manak Publications, 14–30.

Butalia, U. 2002. 'Confrontation and Negotiation: The Women's Movement's Responses to Violence Against Women'. In K. Kapadia, ed., *The Violence of Development: The Politics of Identity, Gender and Social Inequalities in India*. New York: Zed Books, 207–34.

Dietrich, G. 1988. *Women's Movement in India: Conceptual and Religious Reflections*. Bangalore: Breakthrough Publications.

Dietrich, G. 1992. *Reflections on the Women's Movement in India: Religion, Ecology and Development*. New Delhi: Horizon India Books.

Dietrich, G. 1998. 'Dalit Feminism and Environment'. *Religion and Society* 45.4: 89–98.

Erndl, K.M. 1993. *Victory to the Mother: The Hindu Goddess of Northwest India in Myth, Ritual, and Symbol*. New York: Oxford University Press.

Falk, N.E. 1998. '*Shakti* Ascending: Hindu Women, Politics, and Religious Leadership During the Nineteenth and Twentieth Centuries'. In R.D. Baird, ed., *Religion in Modern India*. New Delhi: Manohar, 298–334.

Forbes, G. 'Reading and Writing Indian Women: The 50 Years Since Independence, 1947–97'. *Teaching South Asia: An Internet Journal of Pedagogy* 2:1 (2003).

Garb, Y. 1997. 'Lost in Translation: Toward a Feminist Account of Chipko'. In J.W. Scott,

C. Kaplan and D. Keates, eds, *Transitions, Environments, Translations: Feminisms in International Politics.* New York: Routledge, 273–84.
George, I. 1996. 'Shakti and Sati: Women, Religion and Development'. In A. Carr and M.S. van Leeuwen, eds, *Religion, Feminism and the Family.* Louisville, KY: Westminister/John Know Press, 358–76.
Gupta, C. 1998. 'Social Reforms in Nineteenth Century Bengal and the Woman Question'. In K. Sengupta and T. Bandyopadhyay, eds, *Nineteenth Century Thought in Bengal.* New Delhi: Allied Publishers, 185–224.
Kumar, R. 1993. *The History of Doing: An Illustrated Account of Movements for Women's Rights and Feminism in India, 1800–1990.* New York: Verso.
Kumar, R. 1994. 'Identity Politics and the Contemporary Indian Feminist Movement'. In *Identity Politics and Women: Cultural Reassertions and Feminisms in International Perspective*, ed. V.M. Moghadam. Boulder, CO: Westview Press, 274–92.
Kumar, R. 1995. 'From Chipko to Sati: The Contemporary Indian Women's Movement'. In A. Basu, ed., *The Challenge of Local Feminisms: Women's Movements in Global Perspective.* Boulder, CO: Westview Press, 58–86.
Kunjakkan, K.A. 2002. *Feminism and Indian Realities.* New Delhi: Mittal Publishers.
Mazumdar, V. and I. Agnihotri. 1999. 'The Women's Movement in India: Emergence of a New Perspective'. In B. Ray and A. Basu, eds, *From Independence Towards Freedom: Indian Women Since 1947.* New York: Oxford University Press, 221–38.
Narayanan, A. *Women and Indian Society: Options and Constraints.* New Delhi: Rawat Publications.
Ratté, L. 1985. 'Goddesses, Mothers, and Heroines: Hindu Women and the Feminine in the Early Nationalist Movement'. In Y.Y. Haddad and E.B. Findly, eds, *Women, Religion and Social Change.* Albany, NY: State University of New York Press, 351–76.
Ray, B. 2002. *Early Feminists of Colonial India: Sarala Den Chaudhurani and Rokeya Sakhawat Hossain.* Toronto: Oxford University Press.
Sen, I. 1997. 'Fundamentalist Politics and Women in India'. In J. Brink and J. Mencher, eds, *Mixed Blessings: Gender and Religious Fundamentalism Cross Culturally.* London: Routledge, 209–20.
Sugirtharajah, S. 2002. 'Hinduism and Feminism: Some Concerns'. *Journal of Feminist Studies in Religion* 18.2: 97–104.

WOMEN'S RITES

Some women's ritual roles are based on descriptions in Sanskrit scriptures such as the *Saṃhitas, Gṛhyasūtras, Dharmasūtras, Dharmaśāstras* and interpretations by schools such as Mīmāṃsā and Vedānta. Others are based on the Sanskrit *Āgāmas*, which are especially important for temple worship. But caste, local customs and oral traditions, too, inform women's rituals. Rituals are marked by gender in various ways. Men and women might have completely different rituals; they might perform the same ritual differently; or they might perform it in the same way but understand it differently.

Vedic ritual has been particularly important for the elite, especially brāhmaṇa men. Although women had a ritual role complementary to that of their husbands in the Vedic period (1200–800 BCE), their role was gradually marginalised due to the specialisation of ritual knowledge. This led to brāhmaṇa male priests as officiants rather than male and female householders, the bifurcation of ritual venues into home and public altars (with men dominating the latter). It led also to the distinction between gṛhya and śrauta rituals and the development of 'boarding schools' for Sanskrit-based education (including Vedic rituals) for elite boys, which left elite girls speaking vernaculars and performing mainly domestic rituals, which required only rudimentary Vedic knowledge.

Despite these historic changes, women were still required to give rituals power and efficacy – even the great, public (śrauta) rituals that many brāhmaṇa priests performed. Women were involved, moreover, in many of the Vedic rituals called saṃskāras, rituals that mark the stages of life through purification and by defining the goals to be achieved. Because most women lost Vedic knowledge and ritual expertise, many authorities said that they were not eligible for the rite of passage that initiated them into Vedic learning (upanayana) and the stage of student life (brahmacarya) (*Manusmṛti* 2.67). That said, there were exceptions.

The most important saṃskāra for women was the wedding, which began both marriage (vivāha) and the householder stage of life (gārhasthya). Common elements of the ritual included going round the sacred fire (pariṇayaṇa), also described as taking seven steps around the fire (saptapadī), and the groom taking his wife's hand (paṇigrāhaṇa). Other important samskāras for women included ones to promote conception, to have a son and to mark key stages in the development of both foetus and child.

Some authors referred to women's continuing performance of Vedic domestic rituals. Part of strīdharma was for a wife to help her husband in rituals, which is why some authors called wives sahadharmācarī, dharmacāriṇi, dharmaghāgninī or pativratabhāginī. Other authors referred to women performing domestic rites if their husbands or other male elders were away. Or they described precisely how women performed the vaiśvadeva ritual. These references challenge the theory of women's marginalisation in Vedic rituals. The Mīmāṃsika school, which specialised in Vedic ritual, made this refutation a cause célèbre. Jaimini (*c.* second century CE) and Śabara (*c.* fifth or sixth century CE) refuted two conservative arguments: only men were eligible to perform the rites, because masculine forms were in the injunctions; and only men were eligible, because only they owned property and could therefore finance rites. (See *Jaiminiyasūtras* 6.1.6–8; 6.1.13; 6.1.16 and Śabara's commentary.) Orthodox brahmanical communities such as the Śrī Vaiṣṇavas continued to support women's participation in Vedic rituals and Vedic learning, although the participation of women probably remained rare. Other communities marginalised the importance of Vedic rituals altogether except for the important saṃskāras.

Vratas (vows), a class of ritual in the Sanskrit religious tradition, became the domain of married women (although the *Dharmaśāstras* describe them as a class of ritual for men, too) partly because women could perform them at home and without priests or expensive items. The core of a woman's vrata consisted of an act of self-denial (for instance the denial of food) which would create good karma. That would enable her to have a son, cure an ill husband and so forth. Alternatively, the deity would graciously bless her by fulfilling the request. Performing these vows made someone an ideal wife (pativratā). Because vratas created power, women were supposed to have the permission of their husbands to perform them (*Manusmṛti* 5.155), although anthropological accounts say that mothers-in-law often gave permission, but were not supposed to use this power for personal desires. Texts classify vratas as kāmya-karma (action for the fulfilment of desire), but ethnographies show that women often understood them as the higher status nitya-karmas (constant and necessary acts), which they performed for their own confidence, well-being and spiritual welfare as well.

As modern anthropological accounts document, there are many other women's rituals (strī-ācāra) a subdivision of lokācāra. They may be performed alongside scriptural ones or in other contexts altogether. In Bengal, for instance, women gather for a feast to tell jokes and stories on the final day of a woman's unmarried life. In Gujarat, women celebrate a ritual that begins in the seventh month of pregnancy to avoid the danger of miscarriage. They set up a domestic shrine to the goddess and invite unmarried girls, or married women who have had children, to pray and sing. During the Navarātri festival, women invite the goddess into their homes to request protection and help (often through a possessed female devotee); they accompany the ritual with song. Rituals that celebrate a girl's onset of menstruation are common in some communities. In Tamil Nadu women isolate the girl, give her a ritual bath accompanied by songs to call forth Lakṣmī or some other goddess-wife and offer auspicious substances; in pre-modern times, child marriage then occurred. Women have special roles in death rituals as well. In Rajasthan, for example, they sing throughout the night to welcome the spirits who protect the household. These rituals express women's confidence in their womanhood, contribute to their perception of women's power and create solidarity among female members of the family.

Some women's rituals pertain to the change in a woman's status after the death of her husband. In the past, she might have chosen self-immolation (sati). According to the admittedly idealised description in the *Satidāha*, she calmly ordered the preliminaries, donned her bridal sari, benevolently blessed her relatives (even though they passionately tried to dissuade her), prostrated herself before her elders, requested their blessings (which they gave and prostrated themselves before her), led a procession to the cremation ground, did añjali to the crowd, climbed the ladder, sat on the pyre, tenderly placed her husband's head on her lap (or reclined with him) and maintained composure as she burnt. But she might have chosen widowhood instead of self-immolation. The rituals of widowhood were performed mainly by women, not brāhmaṇa priests. Before a symbol of her husband, a woman removed her auspicious symbols such as her bangles, wedding chains, other jewels, the mark on her forehead (bindi, boṭṭu) and all her hair. Then they made her wear a plain white sari.

See also: **Brahmacarya; Dharmaśāstras; Gārhasthya; Gṛhyasūtras; Jaimini; Manu; Pativratā and Patiparameśvara; Religious specialists; Sati; Śrī Vaiṣṇavas; Upanayana; Vedānta; Vrata; Widowhood**

KATHERINE K. YOUNG

Further reading

Freeman, J.M. 2001. 'The Ladies of Lord Krishna: Rituals of Middle Aged Women in Eastern India'. In N.A. Falk and R.M. Gross, eds, *Unspoken Worlds: Women's Religious Lives*. Toronto: Nelson Thomson Learning, 114–24.

Gaston, A.-M. 1991. 'Dance and the Hindu Woman: Bharatanatyam Re-Ritualized'. In J. Leslie, ed., *Roles and Rituals for Hindu Women*. London: Pinter, 149–71.

Gombrich, S.G. 1990. 'Divine Mother or Cosmic Destroyer: The Paradox at the Heart of the Ritual Life of Hindu Women'. In A. Joseph, ed., *Through the Devil's Gateway: Women, Religion and Taboo*. London: SPCK, 50–59.

Gupta, L. 1997. 'Hindu Women and Ritual Empowerment'. In K.L. King, ed., *Women and Goddess Traditions in Antiquity and Today*. Minneapolis, MN: Fortress Press, 85–110.

Hancock, M. 1999. *Womanhood in the Making: Domestic Ritual and Public Culture in Urban South India*. Boulder: Westview Press.

Harlan, L. 1995. 'Women's Songs for Auspicious Occasions'. In D.S. Lopez, Jr., ed., *Religions of India in Practice*. Princeton, NJ: Princeton University Press, 269–80.

Humes, C.A. 1997. 'Glorifying the Great Goddess or Great Woman? Hindu Women's Experience in Ritual Recitation of the *Devi-Mahatmya*'. In K.L. King, ed., *Women and Goddess Traditions in Antiquity and Today*. Minneapolis, MN: Fortress Press, 39–63.

Jacobson, D. 2001. 'Golden Handprints and Red-Painted Feet: Hindu Childbirth Rituals in Central India'. In N.A. Falk and R.M. Gross, eds, *Unspoken Worlds: Women's Religious Lives*. Toronto: Nelson Thomson Learning, 83–102.

Jamison, S.W. 1996. *Sacrificed Wife/Sacrificer's Wife: Women, Ritual, and Hospitality in Ancient India*. New York: Oxford University Press.

McDonald, Merryle. 'Rituals of Motherhood among Gujarati Women in East London'. In A. Joseph, ed., *Through the Devil's Gateway: Women, Religion, and Taboo*. London: SPCK.

McGee, M. 1991. 'Desired Fruits: Motive and Intention in the Votive Rites of Hindu Women'. In J. Leslie, ed., *Roles and Rituals for Hindu Women*. London: Pinter, 71–88.

Marglin, F.A. 1994. 'The Sacred Groves'. *Manushi* 82: 22–32.

Menski, W. 1991. 'Marital Expectations as Dramatized in Hindu Marriage Rituals'. In J. Leslie, ed., *Roles and Rituals for Hindu Women*. London: Pinter, 47–67.

Nagarajan, V.R. 2000. 'Rituals of Embedded Ecologies: Drawing *Kolams*, Marrying Trees and Generating Auspiciousness'. In C.K. Chapple and M.E. Tucker, eds, *Hinduism and Ecology: The Intersection of Earth, Sky, and Water*. Cambridge, MA: Harvard University Press for the Center for the Study of World Religions, 453–68.

Nagarajan, V.R. 2001. 'Soil as the Goddess Bhudevi in a Tamil Women's Ritual: The *Kolam* in India'. In A. Low and S. Tremayne, eds, *Sacred Custodians of the Earth?: Women, Spirituality and the Environment*. New York: Berghahn Books, 159–74.

Narayanan, V. 1994. *The Vernacular Veda: Revelation, Recitation and Ritual*. Columbia, SC: University of South Carolina Press.

Orr, L.C. 1994. 'Women of Medieval South India in Hindu Temple Ritual: Text and Practice'. In A. Sharma and K.K. Young, eds, *Annual Review of Women in World Religions*, vol. 3. Albany, NY: State University of New York Press, 107–41.

Thompson, C. 1983. 'Women, Fertility and the Worship of Gods in a Hindu Village'. In P. Holden, ed., *Women's Religious Experience*. Totowa, NJ: Barnes and Noble Books, 113–31.

Wadley, S.S. 2001. 'Hindu Women's Family and Household Rites in a North Indian Village'. In N.A. Falk and R.M. Gross, eds, *Unspoken worlds: Women's Religious Lives*. Toronto: Nelson Thomson Learning, 103–13.

WOODROFFE, JOHN (1865–1936)

British judge and gentleman scholar. Born in Calcutta, Woodroffe was educated in Britain at a Catholic public school and Oxford. He joined the Calcutta bar in 1890 and was appointed to the bench in 1904. Knighted in 1915, after retirement from the High Court in 1922 he taught Indian Law at Oxford from 1923 until 1930. Around 1906 Woodroffe took initiation from a brāhmaṇa tantric guru and śākta, Sivacandra Vidyarnava, and he may also have subsequently have taken initiation from a bhairavī (female tantric), Jayakali Devi. Sometime before 1912 Woodroffe began to study Tantric texts with a fellow disciple of Sivacandra, Atal Bihari Ghose (1864–1936), continuing to study with Ghose and others after the guru's death in 1914. From 1915 he began to lecture and to publish on Tantra, and to defend Hinduism and, in particular, Tantra against the attacks of both Western and Indian critics. Woodroffe sponsored the publication of a series of Sanskrit editions and English translations of Tantric texts, many of which appeared, together with other works on Tantra, under the name of Arthur Avalon. The first to appear, under the title *The Great Liberation*, was a translation of a modern Tantric work, the *Mahānirvāṇatantra*, which like other works of Woodroffe/Avalon presented a sanitised form of Tantra, in which the elements of Tantric ritual most objectionable to both non-tantric Hindus and European scholars were interpreted in an idealised or purely symbolic manner. Despite the use of the pseudonym, from the time of their publication Woodroffe was known to be associated with the Avalon works, and they have often been attributed to him and, after his death, republished under his name. Woodroffe's biographer, Kathleen Taylor (2001), has shown that the knowledge of Tantra in the Avalon works is substantially that of Atal Bihari Ghose and concludes that the figure of

Avalon is best understood as a symbiosis of Ghose's learning and Woodroffe's capacity to present it to a European public. Other works presenting a similar view of Tantra, such as *Shakti and Shākta* (1918) and *The World as Power* (1922–23), are less ambiguously Woodroffe's own, although still reliant on the (acknowledged) scholarship of Ghose and other Indian collaborators.

See also: **Brāhmaṇa; Guru; Hinduism, history of scholarship; Śāktism; Tantras; Tantrism**

WILL SWEETMAN

Further reading

Avalon, A. (trans.). 1913. *The Great Liberation*. London: Luzacs.

Taylor, K. 2001. *Sir John Woodroffe, Tantra and Bengal: 'An Indian Soul in a European Body'?* Richmond: Curzon Press.

Woodroffe, J. 1918. *Shakti and Shākta.* London: Luzacs.

Woodroffe, J. with P.N. Mukhopadhyay. 1922–23. *The World as Power.* Madras: Ganesh.

Y

YAJÑA

Yajña, sacrifice, has been understood as pre-eminent in the maintenance of cosmic order (ṛta) by many Hindus. Within Vedic religion, yajña was understood as an act with inherent power rather than an act of devotion, power over both the devas (deities), and the natural phenomena that they represent. The yajña requires four key elements: sacrificial matter (dravya), the act of giving the sacrificed object (tyāga), the target of the sacrifice (devāta) and an effective word that enables success (mantra). The cosmic significance of the act of sacrifice is clearly seen in the *Puruṣa Sūkta* of the *Ṛgveda*, where the devas create the physical universe and, more importantly, the social order of Hinduism (the varṇa system) from the body of the sacrificed Primal Man (puruṣa).

Early Vedic understanding of the sacrifice was primarily as a way of harnessing the power of natural phenomena, for the benefit of the sacrificer or to mark the passing of time, and rites of passage (saṃskāras). Devas of special concern to the worshipper were invited to attend the rite (and may indeed have been seen as present by the participants intoxicated with soma) and offerings were placed in the fire and conveyed to the other gods by Agni. These divine guests were honoured with food, gifts and hymns of praise recited by a poet priest. A typical sacrificial hymn contains an invocation in a tone of friendliness, fear or reverence (depending on the nature of the deva), praise of the great qualities or actions of the god and a request, either implicit or direct, that the god do something for the benefit of the sacrificer.

As only the gods could bring prosperity, long life, health, etc., priests were the agents whose skill induced the gods to part with these gifts. The sacrifice itself was carried out by the priests placing the correct gifts (those identified as containing 'sacrificial substance', medha) into the fire. The actual articles sacrificed could often be extremely expensive; in the earliest Vedic times human sacrifice (puruṣamedha) might be performed, or the sacrifice of a horse (aśvamedha) or, as stated in the *Aitareya Brāhmaṇa* (2.18), a goat. This section of the text refers to the 'movement' of medha from one creature to another, from man to horse, to ox, to goat, concluding with the instruction that the goat is the most suitable sacrificial victim.

However, by the end of the Vedic period the gifts offered in sacrifice had been standardised as grains, fruit, ghee and milk, which were seen as containing sufficient medha. The idea of substitution has always existed, so that monetary equivalents of cows and horses, or in later bhakti cults, the recitation of nāma japa (repeating the divine name) or a pūjā directed to a mūrti could be offered instead.

Eventually the sacrifice began to be viewed as a power in its own right. Centuries of brahmanical concentration on the sacrificial ritual brought about a changing view of reality, where the sacrifice was understood not merely as a way of getting favours from the devas, but as the primary support of the cosmic order and the universe itself. This led to a substantial shift in the social importance of the brāhmaṇas, as those individuals who possessed the mantras which empowered the sacrifice were effectively viewed as being essential to the support of the cosmos. Such a view is clearly developed in the *Manusmṛti* (1.98–101).

As more attention was put on the sacrificial ritual, particularly the divinised elements of the fire sacrifice, Agni, fire itself and the god of fire, Bṛhaspati, lord of prayer and the divine cultic priest, and Soma, the libation, attracted greater attention. The role of Agni in particular changed a great deal. As the recipient of all the gifts offered to the devas, Agni had long been identified with them. Such a view is made clear in the *Ṛgveda* (2.1.3,4,6; 5.3.11). Agni was also understood as having three characters, for his existence in heaven, on earth and in the waters. These three natures were reflected in the three fire pits used in the performance of yajña: the Gārhapatya fire was used to prepare food for the sacrifice, the Āhavaniya was the fire used to actually place the offerings, and the Dakṣina was used for both warding off hostile spirits and receiving offerings for departed ancestors (pitṛs). As the food prepared on the fire of earth is offered on the fire of heaven, Agni thus links humanity, not only with heaven, but with the departed ancestors. Agni is thus the unifying power of the cosmos.

The Vedic hymns came to be understood as formulations of the truth in sound. Such ritual formulations are called mantras. Great importance was given to speech and mantras, as this was the means by which the basic correspondences and identities of the sacrifice were set out. Thus, when saying, 'You, O Agni, are Indra,' the brāhmaṇa is identifying the subject of the sacrificial rite in a way that confirms that identity.

This understanding of Vedic sacrifice underwent a substantial alteration in the philosophy of the *Upaniṣads*, which understood the sacrifice as being internalised within the individual practitioner. This begins through a development that encouraged the understanding of the devas as being identified with aspects of the human body (such as the *Bṛhadāraṇyaka Upaniṣad* 3.1.3–6), which explicitly connects the mouth with Agni. The emphasis in many of the *Upaniṣads* upon building up tapas (spiritual heat) within the practitioner is frequently seen as an internalisation of the fire of the yajña that maintains the cosmos. This is further developed, particularly, in the *Gārbha Upaniṣad*, which lists in detail the correspondences between the inner and outer rite.

Another significant understanding of sacrifice is that the dharmic actions that are required of a gṛhastha (householder) are referred to as 'yajñas', although only two retain the explicit sacrificial aspects associated with the Yajña.

Sacrifices involving animals do still continue in some Hindu traditions, though more large-scale animal sacrifices are encountering a great deal of criticism from animal rights protestors. The sacrifice of goats to Kālī continues at the Kalighat Temple in Calcutta and at particular Nepalese festivals. Numerous village traditions, particularly amongst lower-caste Hindus, emphasise the importance of blood sacrifices to local goddesses, such as Māriammā or Śītāla. This is not to say that animal sacrifice is normative, as in fact the vast majority of pūjās involve the offering of other things (ghee, grains, curd, flowers), but it is certainly still a part of vernacular Hindu practice.

See also: **Agni; Bhakti (as path); Bhakti Movement; Blood sacrifice; Brāhmaṇa; Brahmanism; Bṛhaspati; Dharma; Dharmaśāstras; Deities; Gārhasthya; Image worship; Kālī and Caṇḍī; Mantra; Nepal, Hindus in; Popular and vernacular traditions; Pitṛs; Puruṣa; Pūjā; Sacred animals; Saṃhitā; Saṃskāra; Soma; Tapas; Upaniṣads; Utsava; Varṇa; Vedic Pantheon; Vedism**

IAN JAMISON

Further reading

Fuller, C.J. 1992. *The Camphor Flame. Popular Hinduism and Society in India*. Princeton, NJ: Princeton University Press.

Klostermaier, K. 1994. *A Survey of Hinduism*. Albany, NY: State University of New York Press.

Sharma, R. Shriday. 1989. 'The Spirituality of the Vedic Sacrifice'. In Sivararaman Krisna, ed., *Hindu Spirituality* 1: 29–40.

YĀJÑAVALKYA

A major figure in the *Bṛhadāraṇyaka Upaniṣad*, the sage Yājñavalkya is the disciple of Sanatkumara. Gārgī, the first female Indian philosopher that we know of, is found in dispute with him over the nature of reality. Yājñavalkya is engaged in dialogues concerning the relationship between ātman, brahman and the world.

It is Yājñavalkya who is asked how many gods exist. He reduces his original answer, straight from the Vedic text, in which there are 333 million, by stages down to one, the unutterable and nameless Brahman. Yājñavalkya is perceived as supporting a non-dualistic philosophy in regard to reality and being, and is drawn upon for inspiration by the followers of *Advaita Vedānta*.

See also: **Ātman; Brahman; Gārgī; Upaniṣads; Vedānta**

RON GEAVES

Further reading

Mani, Vettam. 1993. *Puranic Encyclopaedia*. Delhi: Motilal Banarsidass.

YAJÑOPAVĪTA

See: **Upanayana**

YAJURVEDA

See: **Saṃhitā**

YAKṢAS

A term of indeterminate derivation, yakṣa is used in the Veda as an adjective or epithet for such high gods as Varuṇa and Agni; a numinous divinity; and the indwelling spirit or soul. Most later sources identify Yakṣas as devas or devatās, not in the sense of the 'high gods' of Hinduism, but rather as the multiple tutelary deities of the Hindu, Buddhist and Jain South Asian landscape. Closely identified with trees in their iconography and mythology, Yakṣas and Yakṣiṇīs have often been identified as the 'Dryads' of South Asian traditions. Sculpted images of Yakṣas and Yakṣiṇīs abound in South Asian iconography, covering the walls of medieval Hindu and Jain temples and ancient Buddhist stūpa complexes.

With the rise of the gods of classical Hinduism in the epic and Purāṇic literature, the Yakṣas became increasingly reduced to mere tree or fertility spirits. However, many of the features of Hindu devotionalism have their origins in the Yakṣa cults, and many of the cults of the local deities of present-day popular/vernacular traditions conform to the ancient Yakṣa-type. The standard Yakṣa worship shrine (caitya), a slab surmounted by a stone or phallic emblem, placed beneath a tree and enclosed with a surrounding wall, is the prototype of the Hindu temple as well as of the early iconography of the Śiva liṅga. The iconography of male Yakṣas, with their animal heads, great bellies and massive bodies, anticipates that of Gaṇeśa; while that of the lithe, seductive Yakṣiṇīs flows directly into the imagery of the Yoginīs of Hindu Tantra. Veneration of the Yakṣas, which traditionally included blood sacrifice but also offerings of flowers, was the precursor of the bhakti-style worship of the high gods of classical Hinduism, which it pre-dated by several centuries.

See also: **Agni; Bhakti; Blood sacrifice; Buddhism, relationship with Hinduism; Gaṇeśa; Itihāsa; Jainism, relationship with Hinduism; Mahābhārata; Popular and vernacular traditions; Purāṇas; Ramāyaṇa; Śiva; Tantras; Varuṇa; Veda**

DAVID GORDON WHITE

Further reading

Coomaraswamy, A.K. 1993 [1928–31]. *Yakṣas: Essays in the Water Cosmology*, ed. Paul Schroeder. Delhi: Oxford University Press.

Misra, R.N. 1981. *Yakṣa Cult and Iconography.* New Delhi: Munshiram.

YAMA

'Twin'. The first mortal to die; the Vedic ruler of the dead and judge of the departed. Yama and Manu ('man', 'mind') are sons of the solar figure Vivasvat and the enigmatic Saraṇyū. In the Asya Vāmīya hymn (*Ṛgveda* 1.164.46), Yama is identified as both Agni and Mātariśvan. Yama and his twin sister Yamī are considered the parents of humanity, but in their dialogue in the *Ṛgveda* (10.10), Yama rejects his sister's amorous advances. Yama's original twin is Manu, the two together being an instance of the Aśvins – with Manu/Indra embodying living humanity; Yama/Agni, the chthonian expression of humankind. In Epic and later times, Yama has become the ruler/protector of the south.

See also: **Agni; Aśvins; Indra; Vedic Pantheon; Vedism**

MICHAEL YORK

YAMUNĀ (GODDESS)

Clothed in blue and riding her vehicle the tortoise, Yamunā is the goddess associated with the river of the same name, also pronounced 'Jumnā'. From its source in the Himālayas at Yamunotrī, the Yamunā runs through Delhi to the Braj country of Mathurā and Vṛndāvanā, where it is the setting of many events in the childhood and adolescence of the deity Kṛṣṇa, as narrated in the *Bhāgavata Purāṇa*. According to the *Ṛgveda*, the goddess Yamunā is also known as Yamī, whose incestuous overture was rejected by her twin brother Yama, master of the netherworld. The sibling relationship of Yamī and Yama is celebrated on the occasion of Bhāī Dūj, or Yama Dvitīya, the last day of the Dīvālī celebrations (Kārttika, śukla pakṣa 2), when brothers may be served food and venerated by their sisters, who in turn receive a fraternally bestowed gift.

See also: **Dīvālī; Himālayas; Mathurā; Purāṇas; Saṃhitā; Vṛndāvana; Yama**

ANDREA MARION PINKNEY

Further reading

Hawley, J.S. and D.M. Wulff. 1996. *Devi: Goddesses of India*. Berkeley, CA: University of California Press.

YAMUNĀ (RIVER)

The river Yamunā is one of the three holiest rivers of India, along with the Ganges and Sarasvatī. The Yamunā rises in the Himālayas and joins the Ganges at Allahabad. The river runs through Mathurā and Vṛndāvana and has many associations with Kṛṣṇa and his brother Balarāma. The river is also deified as the goddess Yamunā, alternatively known as Yamī. Praise for the Yamunā as both river and goddess is found in the *Yamunāṣṭakam* of the Vaiṣṇava theologian Vallabha, but in the present era the actual river is very polluted. Consequently, the Yamunā is the focus of campaigns by environmentalists and devotees, many of whom find a precedent for ecological action in the story of Kṛṣṇa subduing the poisonous water serpent Kāliya who was fouling the Yamunā.

See also: **Balarāma; Gaṅgā; Himālayas; Kṛṣṇa; Mathurā; Sacred geography; Vaiṣṇavism; Vallabha; Vṛndāvana; Yamunā**

DENISE CUSH AND CATHERINE ROBINSON

Further reading

Chapple, C.K. and M.E. Tucker (eds). 2000. *Hinduism and Ecology: The Intersection of Earth, Sky and Water*. Cambridge, MA: Harvard University Press.

Nelson, L.E. (ed.). 1998. *Purifying the Earthly Body of God: Religion and Ecology in Hindu India*. Albany, NY: State University of New York Press.

Prime, R. 1992. *Hinduism and Ecology: Seeds of Truth*. London: Cassell.

YĀMUNA (VEDĀNTIC THEOLOGIAN)

Yāmuna (Yāmunācārya) is traditionally regarded as the grandson and successor of Nāthamuni, reputedly the first in the line of Śrī Vaiṣṇava teachers, who is credited with editing the hymns of the Āḻvārs. Yāmuna championed bhakti as a path to the divine, and sought to reconcile Vaiṣṇava and Vedāntic thought. In many respects, Yāmuna's theology anticipates that of Rāmānuja, whom tradition has seen as his disciple. For example, Yāmuna's understanding of the world as the body of the divine is the basis of Rāmānuja's soul–body analogy for the relationship between God and creation.

See also: **Āḻvārs; Bhakti (as path); Rāmānuja; Vaiṣṇavas, Śrī; Vaiṣṇavism; Vedānta; Viśiṣṭādvaita**

DENISE CUSH AND CATHERINE ROBINSON

Further reading

Brockington, J.L. 1981. *The Sacred Thread: Hinduism in its Continuity and Diversity*. Edinburgh: Edinburgh University Press.

Radhakrishnan, S. 1929. *Indian Philosophy*, vol. 2. London and New York: George Allen & Unwin/Humanities Press.

YANTRA

Yantra is a Sanskrit term meaning a device or instrument, especially a harness or other support mechanism, being derived from the verbal root √yam, meaning 'to control or harness'. In its technical sense, yantra refers to a geometric diagram which is used to 'harness' power, either as an aid to meditation or as a focus for ritual activity, or, alternatively, is worn on the body as a charm or talisman, used for protection and/or the acquisition of particular powers.

The use of yantras is associated with the practice of Tantra. Theoretically, each yantra is uniquely associated with a particular power or ritual aim and also possesses a corresponding mantra that may be recited in ritual or meditative contexts. Often a yantra is further associated or identified with a particular deity. Most philosophical elaborations of Tantra describe the cosmos as comprising an infinite array of sentient powers or energies (śakti), to be mastered by the adept through ritual subjugation or worshipful propitiation. Each of these energies has three aspects: its visual form (yantra), its sound form (mantra) and its 'personality' or god-form (devatā). Yantra is thus thought to be an essential component in the mastery of cosmic energies that comprises Tantric praxis.

The medium on which a yantra is drawn is either paper or metal, and the medium used is sometimes said to determine the relative effectiveness of the yantra – in this, the rarer, precious metals such as gold and silver are generally considered to be more effective, but for some yantras (often with the purpose of mastering the baser powers of black magic such as killing or invoking ruin on an enemy) a baser medium such as iron is prescribed. Less permanent materials are also used in some ritual contexts, such as the inscribing of a yantra in sand or with certain powders – these are most often formally dispersed at the conclusion of the ritual.

Certain geometric yantras, usually those which are circular in form and symmetrical, are also known as maṇḍalas, and, further, are considered to be representations of the cosmos in its entirety, as well as of the cosmogonic process. Perhaps the paradigmatic yantra of this kind is the well-known Śrīyantra (also known as the Śrīcakra). Popularised by the lineages of the Śrīvidyā school of Tantra, the Śrīyantra is considered to represent the cosmic form of the goddess Tripurasundarī, whom the Śrīvidyā holds to be supreme.

There also exist numerological yantras, and these might be thought to comprise a separate category. These generally are inscribed in the form of 'magic squares'; that is, numbers arranged in grid form (3 × 3, 4 × 4 or larger), wherein the sum of each row and column is a constant. This type of yantra emerges from the traditions of jyotiṣa (astrology), wherein the numbers are associated with planetary energies. The use of these numerological yantras is almost exclusively talismanic – that is, they are worn on the body for protection and health – as opposed to being used for ritual worship or meditation.

See also: **Jyotiṣa; Mantra; Śakti; Tantrism**

TRAVIS L. SMITH

Further reading

Khanna, M. 1981. *Yantra: The Tantric Symbol of Cosmic Unity*. London: Thames and Hudson.

Subramanian, V.K. 2001. *Saundaryalaharī of Śaṅkarācārya*. Delhi: Motilal Banarsidass.

YĀSKA

A reputable grammarian and sage, a predecessor of Pāṇini, who is mentioned in the *Mahābhārata*. Yāska's dates are uncertain, ranging from 700 to 500 BCE, but he remains the oldest known author of the *Nirukta*, commentaries that consist of explanations or etymological interpretations of difficult words in the Vedic hymns. It is believed that Yāska and Sāyaṇa saved the Indian people from the plight of losing the ability to read the Vedas as they had become unintelligible due to transformations in language and grammar, even to scholars. The *Nirukta* is in three parts: *Naighaṇṭuka*, a collection of synonymous words; the *Naigama*, a collection of words peculiar to the Vedas, and the *Daivata*, words relating to deities and sacrifices; all of these are followed by Yāska's commentary, in which he explains the meanings of words and provides Vedic passages as illustration.

See also: ***Mahābhārata*; Pānini; Saṃhitā; Sāyaṇa**

RON GEAVES

Further reading

Mani, Vettam. 1993. *Puranic Encyclopaedia*. Delhi: Motilal Banarsidass.

YAŚODĀ

According to the *Harivaṃśa*, Yaśodā becomes the foster mother of Kṛṣṇa due to a secret exchange of babies shortly after Kṛṣṇa is born. Unaware of the exchange, Yaśodā regards Kṛṣṇa as her biological son without knowing he is God, and therefore feels intense maternal love that holds profound theological significance: through attachment to the mischievous and adorable Kṛṣṇa, Yaśodā is liberated from saṃsāra and enjoys an extremely intimate relationship with God. Though she occasionally suspects that Kṛṣṇa may be Viṣṇu in disguise, Kṛṣṇa gracefully deludes her with his divine māyā and thereby enables her to adore him as her human son. Due to such intimacy and its soteriological value as elaborated in the Tenth Book of the *Bhāgavata Purāṇa*, Yaśodā is considered a paradigmatic devotee by Vaiṣṇava theologians and poets, whose devotional practices involve assuming her maternal role in order to cultivate a similar salvific affection for Lord Kṛṣṇa.

See also: **Harivaṃśa; Kṛṣṇa; Māyā; Purāṇas; Saṃsāra; Vaiṣṇavism; Viṣṇu**

TRACY COLEMAN

Further reading

Bryant, Edwin F. (trans.). 2003. *Krishna: The Beautiful Legend of God. Śrīmad Bhāgavata Purāṇa. Book X*. London: Penguin Books.

YELLAMĀ

South Indian mythology connects the goddess Yellamā with Māriammā and Reṇukā. Although Reṇukā appears as the wife of a sage, Jamadagni, in the *Purāṇas*, local goddess mythology reinterprets the story. Reṇukā is beheaded by her son Paraśurāma (an avatarā of Viṣṇu) at the behest of his father because he suspects his wife's infidelity. As Reṇukā runs from her son she falls into the arms of an untouchable woman. Unfortunately, Paraśurāma beheads both women. In the confusion, as the two women are resurrected the untouchable woman's head ends up on the pure body of the brāhmaṇa woman. This then becomes the goddess Yellamā, while the pure head on the untouchable body becomes Māriammā. There are many variations of this myth.

Yellamā's most important temple, a popular place of pilgrimage is near the town of Saundatti in northern Karnataka, where her mythology ties her to this location. Here, Yellamā is loosely identified with Pārvatī, the wife of Śiva. Although she may have connections with pan-Indian deities, her worship is local in character as devotees approach her for her help with various problems

See also: **Avatarā; Dalits; Mandir; Māriammā; Pārvatī; Purāṇas; Tīrthayātrā; Varṇa; Viṣṇu**

LYNN FOULSTON

Further reading

Bradford, Nicholas J. 1983. 'Transgenderism and the Cult of Yellamma: Heat, Sex and Sickness in South Indian Ritual'. *Journal of Anthropological Research* 39.3: 307–22.
Foulston, Lynn. 2002. *At the Feet of the Goddess: The Divine Feminine in Local Hindu Religion*. Brighton and Portland, OR: Sussex Academic Press.

YOGA

Familiar worldwide for its gentle physical exercises to promote comfortable, stable posture, Yoga is a comprehensive system of purifying consciousness in order to attain clear experience of one's self and nature. While the term yoga (yuj, 'yoke') refers generally to a pan-Indian corpus of spiritual techniques, it is the opposite of ecstasy (Eliade 1954: 359, 361); rather, it aims to establish the self firmly in its own nature of silent pure consciousness. The wide variety of methods counted as types of Yoga include Bhakti, Karma, Jñāna, Mantra, Kuṇḍalinī, Kriyā, Laya, Rāja and Haṭha, to name a few. Its early history is speculatively traced to Central Asian shamanism, the postures depicted on Harrapan seals and the Vedic hymns (Feuerstein 1989: 95–114), and more convincingly to doctrines in ancient *Upaniṣads.* The earliest known references to Yoga as a means of self-realisation, however, are in *Kaṭha Upaniṣad* 2.12 and *Śvetāśvatara Upaniṣad* 6.13 (400–200 BCE), the latter of which mentions Yoga along with Sāṃkhya as a means to liberation. *Carakasaṃhitā*, the *Mokṣadharma Parvan* (12.168–320) and *Bhagavadgītā* in the *Mahābhārata*, and Aśvaghoṣa's *Buddhacarita* present early and less systematised versions of Sāṃkhya and Yoga doctrines. The classical systematic formulation of Yoga occurs in Patañjali's *Yogasūtra*, which borrows significantly from Buddhist and Jain sources and primarily shares the dualist ontology of Prakṛti and Puruṣa with classical Sāṃkhya as presented in Īśvarakṛṣṇa's *Sāṃkhyakārikās.*

Classical Yoga

A discriminating person recognises that all experience is suffering (*Yogasūtra* 2.15). Future suffering, however, is avoidable (*Yogasūtra* 2.16). Its cause is the conjunction between the silent witnessing self (Puruṣa) and the object of experience, nature (Prakṛti) (*Yogasūtra* 2.17), through which the self assumes ownership of the components of nature that make up the individual personality and body (*Yogasūtra* 2.23) because of ignorance (*Yogasūtra* 2.24). In the absence of ignorance, the conjunction is destroyed and the self becomes isolated in Kaivalya (*Yogasūtra* 2.25). The direct means to the destruction of ignorance is unwavering knowledge of the distinction between the self and nature (*Yogasūtra* 2.26). Practice of the eight limbs of yoga (Aṣṭāṅga Yoga) brings about the destruction of impurity and the radiance of knowledge (*Yogasūtra* 2.28).

The state of ignorance

The self reflects ('re-sees', anu-paśya) all the cognitions that occur as fluctuations in consciousness (*Yogasūtras* 1.4, 2.20), including feeling, sense experience, correct knowledge, error, verbal conception, imagination, sleep and memory (*Yogasūtra* 1.5–11). The afflictions – ignorance (the fundamental affliction that promotes the others), erroneous identification of the self with aspects of nature, attachment, aversion and the desire to continue to exist (*Yogasūtras* 2.3–9) – predispose one to act in certain ways, like dispositions in Sāṃkhya. Under their influence, one performs good and bad actions (karma) which deposit corresponding impressions that bear results in subsequent experience of joy and misery, and in determining the length of one's life and one's next birth (*Yogasūtras* 2.12–14). Experience in turn deposits impressions that reinforce or weaken the afflictions, colour one's memory, shape one's future habits and determine future acts in a continuous cycle of action and impression.

The means of Yoga

Yogic practices have the two-fold effect of weakening afflictions and settling consciousness (*Yogasūtra* 2.2). Meditation (*Yogasūtra* 3.2) weakens active afflictions (*Yogasūtra* 2.11). The fluctuations of consciousness are quieted through long, uninterrupted, respectful practice and through dispassion for objects experienced or learnt about (*Yogasūtras* 1.12–16). Many techniques to clarify consciousness and remove the obstacles to it are enumerated, ranging from cultivating friendliness towards the happy, compassion towards the sad, joy towards virtue and disregard towards vice (*Yogasūtra* 1.33) to meditation on a desired object

(*Yogasūtra* 1.39) and surrender to the omniscient lord who is free of afflictions and karma by reciting oṃ (*Yogasūtras* 1.23–29, 2.45). Obstacles that agitate awareness include illness, lethargy, doubt, carelessness, apathy, incontinence, erroneous views, impatience with progress and instability (*Yogasūtra* 1.30), and these generate other side effects (*Yogasūtra* 1.31). Focusing on a single object of attention also counteracts these obstacles (*Yogasūtra* 1.32).

Focusing on an object may involve the admixture of verbal and conceptual cognitions (*Yogasūtras* 1.41–42). When, due to purification of the memory, it is free of admixture, the object alone fills the awareness without any sense of its distinction from the observing consciousness in what is called saṃprajñāta samādhi, 'focused settled awareness' (*Yogasūtras* 1.43, 3.3). Practising settling the awareness on ever subtler objects of attention leads to a second type of samādhi, 'settled collected awareness', called asaṃprajñāta samādhi, 'non-cognitive collected awareness', in which all fluctuations of consciousness cease and only residual memory traces interrupt it (*Yogasūtras* 1.46, 1.18). This experience of the pure self in turn cultures dispassion for the activity of the three Guṇas (*Yogasūtra* 1.16). When one becomes skilled in asaṃprajñāta samādhi on a subtle object, clarity of inner consciousness arises that bears only true knowledge and concerns individual objects rather than the generalities derived from inference and verbal knowledge (*Yogasūtras* 1.47–49). Its memory traces displace those of incorrect knowledge (*Yogasūtra* 1.50) and the other afflictions (*Yogasūtra* 2.10). Focused settled awareness on various objects produces many special abilities, such as knowing the past and future, understanding the speech of all beings, etc. (*Yogasūtras* 3.16–52, 4.1). Finally, when one becomes filled solely with the knowledge of the distinction between the self and nature, one becomes omnipotent and omniscient (*Yogasūtra* 3.49).

The goal of Yoga

Yet even the knowledge of the distinction between the self and nature is a fluctuation of consciousness that does not belong to the silent witnessing self. When it is also quieted, the seed of all faults is destroyed, completely silent awareness free of any seeds of interruption (nirbīja samādhi) is achieved in the state of absolute isolation of the self (*Yogasūtras* 1.51, 3.50). Nature, which no longer serves any purpose in providing experience to the self, recedes into its unmanifest state so that a pure equilibrium is reached between Prakṛti and Puruṣa (*Yogasūtras* 3.55, 4.34) in the state of Kaivalya. All fluctuations of consciousness cease (*Yogasūtra* 1.2) and the self is established in its own nature, silent pure consciousness (*Yogasūtra* 1.3, 4.34).

See also: **Aṣṭāṅga Yoga; Bhagavadgītā; Bhakti; Guṇas; Haṭha Yoga; Indus Valley Civilisation; Īśvarakṛṣṇa; Jñāna (as path); Kaivalya; Karma; Kriyā Yoga; Kuṇḍalinī Yoga; Laya Yoga; Mahābhārata; Mantra; Oṃ; Patañjali; Prakṛti; Puruṣa; Rāja; Saṃhitā; Sāṃkhya; Sāṃkhyakārikās; Upaniṣads; Yogasūtras**

PETER M. SCHARF

Further reading

Banerji, Sures Chandra. 2000. *A Companion to Yoga: With Glossarial Index and Bibliography.* Calcutta: R.N. Bhattacharya, 111–66 (bibliography).

Bronkhorst, Johannes. 1993. *The Two Traditions of Meditation in Ancient India.* Delhi: Motilal Banarsidass.

Campbell, Roy. 1997. *Yoga: A Bibliography of British Publications Since 1950: Extracted from the British National Bibliography.* Glasgow: Pillar Publications.

Crangle, Edward Fitzpatrick. 1994. *The Origin and Development of Early Indian Contemplative*

Practices. Studies in Oriental Religions 29. Wiesbaden: Otto Harrassowitz.
Dasgupta, Surendranath. 1922. 'Sāṃkhya-Yoga'. In *A History of Indian Philosophy*, vol. I. Cambridge. Reprint: Delhi: Motilal Banarsidass, 1975, 208–73.
Dasgupta, Surendranath. 1924. *Yoga as Philosophy and Religion.* [1st edn London.] Delhi: Motilal Banarsidass, 1987.
Dasgupta, Surendranath. 1930. *Yoga Philosophy in Relation to Other Systems of Indian Thought.* Calcutta. Reprint: Delhi: Motilal Banarsidass, 1974.
De Michelis, Elizabeth. 2004. *A History of Modern Yoga: Patañjali and Western Esotericism.* London; New York: Continuum.
Eliade, Mircea. 1954. *Yoga: Immortality and Freedom.* Trans. from the French [*Le Yoga: Immortalité et Liberté.* Paris: Librairie Payot] by Willard R. Trask. Bollingen Series 56. 2d Princeton, NJ: Princeton University Press, 1969 [1st edn 1958].
Feuerstein, Georg. 1989. *Yoga: The Technology of Ecstasy.* Los Angeles, CA: Jeremy P. Tarcher.
Feuerstein, Georg. 2003. *The Deeper Dimension of Yoga: Theory and Practice.* Boston, MA: Shambhala.
Frauwallner, Erich. 1973. *History of Indian* Philosophy, vol. I. Trans. V.M. Bedekar. Delhi: Motilal Banarsidass, 76–116, 'The Philosophy of the Epic: The Yoga'; 217–353, 'The Sāṃkhya and the Classical Yoga System'; 321–53, 'The Yoga System'.
Jarrell, Howard R. 1981. *International Yoga Bibliography, 1950 to 1980.* Metuchen, NJ: Scarecrow Press.
Monro, Robin, A.K. Ghosh and Daniel Kalish. 1989. *Yoga Research Bibliography: Scientific Studies on Yoga and Meditation.* Cambridge: Yoga Biomedical Trust.
Mukerji, P.N. (trans.). 1977. *Yoga Philosophy of Patañjali: Containing His Yoga Aphorisms with Vyāsa's Commentary with Annotations by Hariharānanda Āraṇya.* Calcutta: Calcutta University Press. [Reprint: Albany, NY: SUNY Press, 1983.]
Prasāda, Rāma (trans.). 1912. *Patañjali's Yoga Sūtras with the Commentary of Vyāsa and the Gloss of Vāchaspati Miśra: With an Introduction from Rai Bahadur Śrīśa Chandra Vasu.* Delhi: Oriental Books Reprint Corporation, 1982. [1st edn Allahabad: Pāṇini Office.]
Thakar, Manik and Vashishtha Narayan Jha. 1995. *Bibliography of Yoga.* CASS Bibliography Series, Class H 8. Pune: Centre for Advanced Study in Sanskrit.
Varenne, Jean. 1976. *Yoga and the Hindu Tradition.* Chicago, IL: University of Chicago Press.
Vasu, Śrīśa Chandra. 1914–15. *An Introduction to the Yoga Philosophy.* New Delhi: Oriental Books Reprint Corporation, 1975. [1st edn Allahabad: Pāṇini Office.]
Weiman, Mark. 1980. *Yoga, a Bibliography.* Berkeley: Movable Foundation Workshop Press; Darby, PA: Norwood Editions.
Whicher, Ian. 1998. *The Integrity of the Yoga Darśana: A Reconsideration of Classical Yoga.* Albany, NY: SUNY Press.
Whicher, Ian and David Carpenter. 2003. *Yoga: The Indian Tradition.* London and New York: RoutledgeCurzon.
Woods, James Haughten (trans.). 1914. *The Yoga System of Patañjali: [. . . with the Yogabhāṣya of Vyāsa and Tattvavaiśāradī of Vācaspatimiśra].* Delhi: Motilal Banarsidass, 1966. [1st edn Harvard University Press.]

YOGA INSTITUTE, THE SANTA CRUZ

See: **Yogendra, Shri and the Yoga Institute, Santa Cruz**

YOGA, MODERN

Introduction

Yoga in the contemporary world is commonly presented by its exponents as the continuation of an unbroken tradition dating back several thousand years. However, in the light of recent scholarship, it is clear that many of the forms of belief and practice referred to today as 'yoga' represent historically specific phenomena which cannot be straightforwardly identified with yoga's pre-modern manifestations. 'Modern Yoga' refers to the body of theory and practice that began to develop in the mid- to late nineteenth century through the contact of largely English-educated urban Indians with Western modes of thought and expression. Their distinctly modern synthesis of Western esoteric philosophy, popular psychology, physical training and science with indigenous Indian religion represents a crucial moment of self-definition in the religious, social and intellectual history of India. One term chosen to designate this new and composite credo was 'yoga'. Since then, with the increasing commerce of ideas between India and the West, Modern Yoga has become an important, yet paradoxical, ideological export: a symbol of the pristine spiritual legacy of India, but one which often seeks validation and expression though modern Western paradigms. Throughout its short history, Modern Yoga has had a close relationship with Western esoteric thought, and in its more recent stages should be understood against the background of New Age religion (Hanegraaff 1998).

The genesis of Modern Yoga

Possibly the first textual expression of Modern Yoga is Swami Vivekananda's *Rāja Yoga* of 1896. In his youth Vivekananda (1863–1902) was greatly influenced by the Brahmo Samaj leader Keshab Chandra Sen (1838–84) and was an active member of his organisation. Sen himself had formulated a proto-Modern Yoga that incorporated significant elements of esotericism and 'spiritual' Christianity. For a time, Sen was an advocate of Unitarianism, a liberal Protestant denomination which insists on the common foundation of all religions and encourages its members in spiritual experimentalism. He was also greatly influenced by American Transcendentalism and sometimes used Ralph Waldo Emerson's writing as inspiration for his lectures. The Transcendentalists, like the Unitarians, favoured Romantic introspection in the religious life over mediated forms of worship, and Sen made this kind of personal, experiential revelation (which on occasion he called 'the yoga faculty') a central component of his thinking.

An account of the genesis of Modern Yoga must take into account Vivekananda's early involvement with Sen, as well as his receptivity to the ideas of the esoteric avant-garde of East Coast America. Following his dramatic debut at the Chicago Parliament of Religion in 1893, Vivekananda had become the darling of the adherents of such esotericism. *Rāja Yoga*, written for this religiously liberal American audience thirsty for the wisdom of the East, is in part a translation of and commentary on the *Yogasūtras* of Patañjali (with special emphasis on the 'aṣṭāṅga yoga' section, 2.28–3.9) and in part a practical manual of yoga techniques. The book, which has had a formative influence on most subsequent expressions of Modern Yoga, constantly reiterates the proposition that authentic spiritual knowledge must rely on practical, empirical experience and a cultivated receptivity to the influx of divine power. Religious faith based on received dogma, Vivekananda argues, is unscientific and therefore worthless. This kind of conviction was being lent validity at the time by the emergent discipline of empirical psychology, and Vivekananada himself seems to have incorporated many of the ideas of William James, the father of humanistic psychology, directly into his own yoga philosophy. Psychology and Modern Yoga were born at the same time, and have continued to influence each other throughout their histories.

Vivekananda's work is seminal for most subsequent representations of Modern Yoga. Those who followed directly in his wake tended to emulate his selective interpretation of Patañjali's canonical text, as well as his enthusiasm for Western esoteric thought (such as Mesmerism) and humanistic psychology. Swami Rama Tirtha (1873–1906), who visited America in 1903, and Paramhansa Yogananda

(1893–1952), who lived in America from 1920 to 1935, are particularly clear examples. Even today, many exponents of Modern Yoga demonstrate a clear debt to the innovations of Vivekananda, and his synthesis laid the foundation for the contemporary association of yoga with the New Age movement.

The Theosophical Society and Modern Yoga

The Theosophical Society, founded by Blavatsky and Olcott in 1875, was also instrumental in establishing the tone and terminology of what would become Modern Yoga. The Society generated significant popular interest in 'Eastern' mystical and occult practices, which helped to create a receptive environment for ambassadors of Indian wisdom and yoga such as Vivekananda. Over and above this, however, Blavatsky was wont to credit herself and her Society with the single-handed revival of what she saw as the moribund yoga tradition of India. She also on occasion claimed to be the first to have introduced it to Europe and America. While it is true that the Theosophists' influence on Modern Yoga is pervasive, they were in actual fact contributing to the creation of a syncretic corpus of beliefs culled from freemasonry, European esotericism and Indian and Egyptian arcana, which they sometimes designated by the term 'yoga'.

Typology of Modern Yoga

The twentieth century saw a steady rise in the popularity of yoga in the West, and a radical diversification of the practices and beliefs associated with it. Although yoga, in its modern sense, has become something of a portmanteau term encompassing many variegated and often disparate methods of 'self-realisation', psychotherapy and physical fitness, some clear patterns can nonetheless be discerned in its growth and development. Figure 2 gives an interpretation of the main varieties of Modern Yoga found in English-speaking milieus worldwide:

According to De Michelis, after Vivekananda's initial formulation of 1896s Modern Yoga developed into various schools, each concerned with the holistic development of the mind, body and spirit of the individual ('Modern Psychosomatic Yoga', or MPsY). In the decades following the publication of *Rāja Yoga*, some MPsY schools began to lay a marked emphasis on the physical aspect of practice (i.e. the practice of āsana, or posture, and prāṇāyāma, or the control of the breath) while others focused mainly on the mental (i.e. concentration and meditation). As a result two further branches emerged: Modern Postural Yoga (MPY) and Modern Meditational Yoga (MMY). Both valorise practical performance and downplay the theoretical component, with intellectual scrutiny of doctrinal foundations rarely featuring prominently. For these branches of Modern Yoga, as for Vivekananda, it is expected that understanding will come through direct experience rather than reflection, reasoning or dogma. Practitioners are left to make sense of the relationship of the practices to their own lives, and to this end often call upon the prevailing interpretive frameworks of New Age religion. MPY and MMY are generally considered to be not only compatible but complementary, and it is common for Modern Yoga practitioners to engage in both. Modern Denominational Yoga (MDY), by contrast, became more widespread in the 1960s with the appearance of various ideologically sectarian movements incorporating elements of Modern Yoga practice. These groups tend to be more exclusivist and insular than MPsY schools, and to have stable and dogmatic belief structures to which members are expected to adhere. The authority and persona of the guru are likely to be

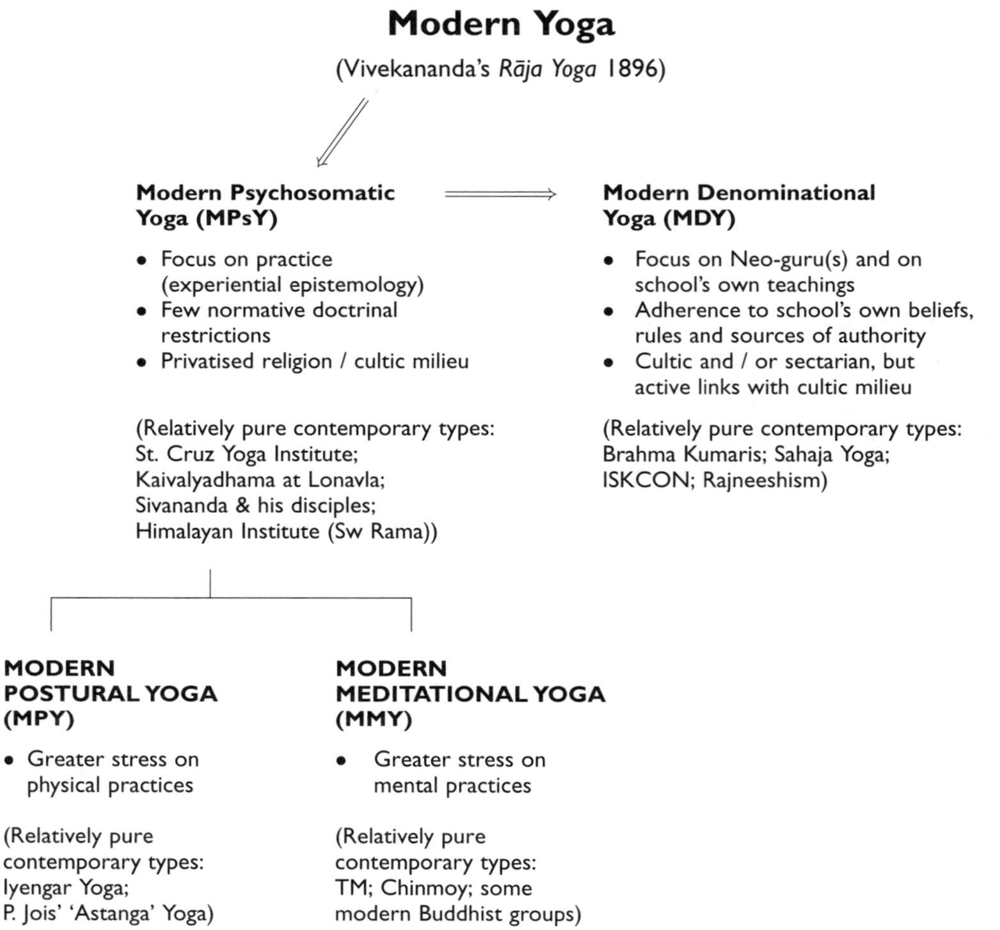

Figure 2 Typology of Modern Yoga (Vivekananda's *Rāja Yoga* 1896)

Source: De Michelis, Elizabeth. 2004. *A History of Modern Yoga: Patañjali and Western Esotericism*. London: Continuum.

paramount. Such groups have not exerted a great influence on the development of mainstream Modern Yoga and are not as significant in this context as MPY and MMY.

The West, 1900–50

In the first decades of the twentieth century, gurus and teachers capitalising on the impact of Vivekananda expanded the range of connotations of the word 'yoga' to incorporate an eclectic bundle of Western esotericism and occult practices. One such import was New Thought, which enjoyed an enormous vogue in early decades of the century and traces of which can already be found in Vivekananda's work. A direct descendant of European Mesmerism and a forerunner of certain strands of contemporary New Age religion, the New Thought movement promoted the power of positive thinking, through which one accesses the divinity that dwells immanently in the human unconscious. Once attuned to this personal stream of indwelling, cosmic energy, one is said to acquire full control of one's material and spiritual destiny. New Thought's most successful exponent in the context of yoga was 'Ramacharaka', in all likelihood the pen name of Chicago lawyer and editor of the *New Thought* journal, William Walker Atkinson. The series of practically-oriented manuals and courses that he authored between 1903 and about 1917 helped to create a popular impression of yoga as an Eastern form of New Thought combined with naturopathy and Romantic nature religion. Another figure who drew heavily on New Thought was Paramhansa Yogananda, who arrived in America in 1920, just before the enforcement of the draconian Asian Exclusion Act, which was to bar the entry of Indian immigrants to the US until 1965. For the next fifteen years, Yogananda enjoyed an almost unique position as spokesman for yoga in America, and his message, radically adapted to his enthusiastic Western audience, consolidated the position of Modern Yoga as a melting pot of Indic lore, esoteric miscellanea and popular psychology.

India, 1900–50

In the early part of the century, yoga was mainly associated with mental procedures ('Modern Meditational Yoga' in the above typology). Although this trend continues to this day, from the 1920s onwards there was a surge in popularity in India of the physical practices of yoga, in particular āsana ('Modern Postural Yoga'). Figures like Kuvalayananda and Yogendra brought biomedical standards to bear on haṭha yogic techniques, blurring the line between science and metaphysics and contributing to the creation of a therapeutics of yoga. T. Krishnamacharya and his now world-famous students also played a significant role in the development of an international, intensely physical neo-haṭha yoga. If yoga today is virtually synonymous with the practice of posture, it is largely due to their influence (for example Indra Devi, B.K.S. Iyengar, Pattabhi Jois and T.K.V. Desikachar). Mention must be made of Swami Shivananda and his enormous contribution to the promotion and propagation of Modern Yoga. The style and content of his numerous books have been consistently emulated by other Modern Yoga authors, and his many influential disciples (such as Vishnudevananda, Satchidananda and Satyananda) have exerted a major influence on the theory and practice of yoga in India and the West today. The rise of postural yoga in India during this period is also intimately linked to the struggle for independence, which was finally won in 1947. In the discourse of Indian nationalism (such as that espoused in later life by Vivekananda), yoga is conceived of as a tool for the spiritual and physical regeneration of the people. Training programmes would often combine yogāsana practice with other physical and martial disciplines, such as wrestling exercises and jiu-jitsu.

From 1950 to the present

The post-Second World War years saw a growth of popular interest in yoga in the West and the rise to prominence of several posture-oriented systems. During the 1950s a proliferation of practical manuals, such as those of Indra Devi, promised unassailable health through a radically secularised and medicalised version of yoga. American physical culturists (like former Mr America Walt Baptiste) also helped to align yoga with Western notions of sport and exercise. Mention should be made here of the influential work of Theos Bernard, whose participant/observer account of a haṭha yoga sādhana (1950) was an important forerunner of the encyclopedic guides of Vishnudevananda and Iyengar. In the 1960s the rise of 'flower power' brought yoga to the attention of a generation of young Americans and Europeans. The wholesale embrace of Indian metaphysics and yoga by countercultural icons (such as the Beatles' spiritual romance with the Maharishi Mahesh Yogi) reinforced the position of yoga in the popular psyche and inspired many to join the 'hippy trail' to India in pursuit of alternative philosophies and lifestyles. Paul Brunton's *A Search in Secret India* (1934) and Yogananda's *Autobiography of a Yogi* (1946) are among the books that have helped to generate a myth of mystical India and a fascination with the practices of yoga.

Increased media attention brought yoga closer to the mainstream, and printed primers and television series throughout the 1960s and 1970s, such as Richard Hittleman's *Yoga for Health* (first broadcast in 1961), encouraged many to take up yoga in the comfort of their own home. The 1970s and 1980s were a period of consolidation for Modern Yoga in the West, with the establishment and expansion of a significant number of dedicated schools and institutes. The period also saw an enduring rapprochement of yoga with the burgeoning New Age movement, which in many ways represents a new manifestation of Modern Yoga's century-old association with currents of esotericism. By the mid-1990s yoga had become thoroughly acculturated in many urban centres in the West. Statistics concerning practitioner numbers are infrequent and often unreliable, but they all indicate an exponential growth in the popularity of yoga from the mid-1970s to the present day. The 1990s 'boom' made yoga into an important commercial enterprise, with increasing levels of merchandising and commodification. The franchising of the Bikram system in 2003 and similar developments have further reinforced the role of big business in yoga (Carrette and King 2005).

See also: **Aṣṭāṅga Yoga; Blavatsky, Helena; Brahmo Samaj; Desikachar, T.K.V. and Viniyoga; Guru; Haṭha Yoga; Indra Devi; Iyengar, B.K.S. and Iyengar Yoga; Jois, K. Pattabhi and Ashtanga Vinyasa Yoga; Krishnamacharya, T.; Kuvalayananda, Swami and Kaivalyadhama; Maharishi Mahesh Yogi; Nationalism; New Religious Movement, Hindu role in; Olcott, Henry Steel; Patañjali; Satchidananda, Swami and Integral Yoga; Satyananda, Swami and the Bihar school of Yoga; Sen, Keshab Chandra; Shivananda, Swami; Theosophy and the Theosophical Society; Vishnudevananda and Sivananda Yoga; Vivekananda, Swami; Western Culture, Hindu influence on; Western Popular Culture, Hindu Influence on; Yoga; Yogananda, Paramhansa; Yogasūtras**

MARK SINGLETON

Further reading

Alter, J. 2004. *Yoga in Modern India, Between Science and Philosophy*. Princeton, NJ: Princeton University Press.

Baier, K. 1998. *Yoga auf dem Weg nach Westen* [oga on its Way to the West]. Wurzburg: Konigshausen and Neumann.

Bernard, T. 1950. *Hatha Yoga*. London: Rider.

Carrette, J. and R. King. 2005. *Selling Spirituality: The Silent Takeover of Religion*. London and New York: Routledge.

Ceccomori, S. 2001. *Cent Ans de Yoga en France* [One Hundred Years of Yoga in France]. Paris: Edidit.

De Michelis, E. 2004. *A History of Modern Yoga: Patañjali and Western Esotericism*. London: Continuum.

Fuchs, C. 1990. *Yoga im Deutschland: Rezeption-Organisation-Typologie* [Yoga in Germany: Reception, Organisation, Typology]. Stuttgart: Kohlhammer Verlag.

Hanegraaff, W. 1998. *New Age Religion and Western Culture, Esotericism in the Mirror of Secular Thought*. New York: State University of New York Press.

McKean, L. 1996. *Divine Enterprise, Gurus and the Hindu Nationalist Movement*. Chicago, IL: University of Chicago Press.

Strauss, S. 2004. *Positioning Yoga, Balancing Acts Across Cultures*. Oxford and New York: Berg.

YOGANANDA, PARAMHANSA (1893–1952)

Yogananda was born in 1893 into a wealthy family in Bengal, India. His original name was Mukunda Lal Ghosh. He died in 1952 in Los Angeles, and is seen as one of the earliest and most effective disseminators of yoga in the West. Famous modern followers include George Harrison, Deepak Chopra and Ravi Shankar.

In 1910 he became a disciple of Swami Sri Yuteswar Giri, a Yoga master, and in 1915 took the traditional vows (dīkṣā) to become a svāmi (monk) with the name of Paramhansa Yogananda. Two years later he founded a school for boys combining modern educational methods with yoga and spiritual values. The school was praised by Mahatma Gandhi. In 1920 Yogananda was chosen to be India's representative to the Boston International Congress of religious leaders. From then on he travelled widely in the United States and elsewhere, lecturing to large audiences, and was even received by President Coolidge at the White House. After 1935, Yogananda concentrated on his writing, producing various books, including the bestselling *Autobiography of a Yogi*.

Yogananda founded his main organisation, the Self-Realisation Fellowship (SRF), in 1920. Its current headquarters is in Los Angeles, with a core community of monks and nuns, and a global network of meditation centres and prayer groups. The main objectives are to promote Kriyā Yoga and Yogananda's own writings. His teachings can be seen as a hybrid of Hindu and Christian beliefs. In 1955, Sri Daya Mata (Faye Wright) became the director of the worldwide organisation, one of the first women leaders of an international religious movement.

However, there is a rival organisation, the Ananda Church of Self-Realisation, founded by a disciple of Yogananda, and they claim to be the valid heirs. As a result of a failure to renew copyright by the SRF, the Ananda Church now publishes the *Autobiography of a Yogi*. The result has been a long and often acrimonious dispute.

See also: **Dīkṣā; Gandhi, Mohandas Karamchand; Kriyā Yoga; Self-Realisation Fellowship; Svāmi; Yoga**

ELIZABETH PUTTICK

Further reading

Yogananda, Paramhansa. 1996. *Autobiography of a Yogi*. London: Rider.

YOGASŪTRAS

The *Yogasūtras*, the founding text of the systematic study of Yoga, although traditionally attributed to the grammatical commentator Patañjali, were probably composed between the third and fifth centuries CE in the form in which they are received. Several sūtras, for example *Yogasūtras* 3.14–15, 4.15–21, employ the specific terminology of Buddhist idealism, and *Yogasūtra* 4.16 disputes the doctrine that an object depends for its existence upon a single cognition, a doctrine articulated in the Vijñānavāda of Asaṅga and Vasubandhu (270–350 CE). It is therefore unlikely that the *Yogasūtras* (Eliade 1969: 370–72; Woods 1914: xiii–xvii), or at least the fourth chapter (pāda) (Dasgupta 1975: 230), were composed before the end of the third century CE. The text consists of 195 sūtras, 'brief aphorisms', divided into four pādas, 'chapters', on samādhi 'settled awareness', sādhana 'means', vibhūti 'powers', and kaivalya 'self-sufficiency'. Vyāsa composed the commentary *Yogasūtrabhāṣya* (*c.*600–840 CE) on the text.

See also: **Buddhism, relationship with Hinduism; Kaivalya; Patañjali; Yoga**

PETER M. SCHARF

Further reading

Dasgupta, Surendranath. 1975. *A History of Indian Philosophy*, vol. I. Delhi: Motilal Banarsidass [1st edn Cambridge, 1922].

Eliade, Mircea. 1969. *Yoga: Immortality and Freedom*, translated from the French [*Le Yoga: Immortalité et liberté*. Paris: Librairie Payot, 1954] by Willard R. Trask. Bollingen Series 56. 2nd edn Princeton, NJ: Princeton University Press [1st edn 1958].

Hartranft, Chip. 2003. *The Yoga-Sūtra of Patañjali: A New Translation with Commentary.* Boston, MA and London: Shambhala Classics.

Mukerji, P.N. (trans.). 1983. *Yoga Philosophy of Patañjali: Containing His Yoga Aphorisms with Vyāsa's Commentary ...with Annotations ...by ...Hariharānanda Āraṇya.* Albany, NY: State University of New York Press [1st edn 1977 Calcutta University Press].

Prasāda, Rāma (trans.). 1982. *Patañjali's Yoga Sūtras with the Commentary of Vyāsa and the Gloss of Vāchaspati Miśra: With an Introduction from Rai Bahadur Śrīśa Chandra Vasu.* Delhi: Oriental Books Reprint Corporation [1st edn Allahabad: Pāṇini Office, 1912].

Rukmani, T.S. 1981. *Yogavārttika of Vijñānabhikṣu: Text, with English Translation and Critical Notes, along with the Text and Translation of the Pātañjala Yogasāras and Vyāsabhāṣya.* New Delhi: Munshiram Manoharlal.

Rukmani, T.S. 2001. *Yogasūtrabhāṣyavivaraṇa of Śaṅkara: Vivaraṇa Text with English Translation, and Critical Notes along with Text and English Translation of Patañjali's Yogasūtras and Vyīsabhīṣya.* New Delhi: Munshiram Manoharlal.

Woods, James Haughten (trans.). 1914. *The Yoga System of Patañjali: [...with the Yogabhāṣya of Vyāsa and Tattvavaiśāradī of Vācaspatimiśra].* Delhi: Motilal Banarsidass, 1966 [1st edn Harvard University Press].

YOGAVĀSIṢṬHA

The *Yogavāsiṣṭha* includes over 32,000 Sanskrit verses that narrate an extended dialogue between the teenage prince Rāma and his spiritual advisor, the Vedic sage Vasiṣṭha. The encounter begins when the sage Viśvāmitra enters Daśaratha's court, asking the king to send his robust son Rāma to battle demons and protect the sages who are being harassed in their āśrama retreat. Rāma baulks at the idea of warfare and, just as Kṛṣṇa counsels Arjuna to take heart and fight in the *Bhagavadgītā*, Vasiṣṭha, after days of discourse and storytelling, convinces Rāma to quell the demons.

In the process of instructing Rāma about the nature of truth, Vasiṣṭha tells more than fifty tales, several of which are nested within one another. A patchwork of narrative and philosophy emerges that has captured the imagination of Hindus and others for hundreds of years. Summary versions of the *Yogavāsiṣṭha*, translated into Persian, provided Muslims with a sympathetic introduction to Indian philosophy, and the stories of the *Yogavāsiṣṭha* continue to enthral their hearers.

The history of this text entails several hundred years of accretions, resulting in increasingly larger versions as well as many abridgements. According to several scholars, most notably Mainkar and Slaje, the core ideas of the text can be traced to the *Mahābhārata.* According to Mainkar, a lost proto-text in the form and philosophy of the *Upaniṣads* was expanded into the *Lāghu-Yogavāsiṣṭha*, at which time several ideas of the Buddhist Yogācāra school were incorporated. This text, which Slaje refers to as the *Mokṣopāya*, was probably composed in the eighth or ninth century. Over the course of about four hundred years, it grew to its present form, which Mainkar has designated as the 'Mahā-Rāmāyaṇa Kasmirian synthesis'. This version includes significant ideas from the Śaivite Trika school.

The *Yogavāsiṣṭha* consists of six sections that document Rāma's process of spiritual inquiry. It begins with his despair (Vairāgya), followed with a book on the nature of desire for liberation (Mumukṣu). The middle two sections discuss the nature of creation (Utpatti) and existence (Sthiti). The final books set forth the process of pacifying the mind and overcoming the allure of the world (Upaśama), resulting in liberation or enlightenment (Nirvāṇa).

The later versions of the *Yogavāsiṣṭha* build upon three key notions: mind-only, or citta-mātra (of Buddhist origin); the power of creative will, or pauruṣa (found both in Buddhism and in the *Mahābhārata*); and living liberation, or jīvanmukta, for which the *Yogavāsiṣṭha* is cited extensively in later Hindu literature. The *Yogavāsiṣṭha* emphasises the nature of worldly creation as dependent upon structures of the mind and expands the Vedic centrality of desire into a sanctified process of emergence or spanda.

One of the most memorable stories includes the tale of how Queen Cudala achieves liberation before her husband and disguises herself as a brāhmaṇa sage in order to bring her husband into an understanding and experience of liberation. Goddesses play an important role within the text, which combines key ideas and practices of Yoga, Vedānta, Sāṃkhya, Yogācāra Buddhism and Kashmiri Śaivism.

See also: **Arjuna; Āśram(a) (religious community); Bhagavadgītā; Brāhmaṇa; Daśaratha; Jīvanmukta; Kashmiri Śaivism; Kṛṣṇa; Mahābhārata; Rāma; Rāmāyaṇa; Ṛṣi; Sāṃkhya; Upaniṣads; Vasiṣṭha; Vedānta; Yoga**

CHRISTOPHER CHAPPLE

Further reading

Chapple, C. 1986. *Karma and Creativity*. Albany, NY: State University of New York Press.

Hanneder, J. 2000. 'The *Yogavasistha* and Its Kashmirian Recension, the *Moksopaya*: Notes on their Textual Quality'. *Vienna Journal of South Asian Studies* 44: 183–210.

Mainkar, T.G. 1977. *The Vasistha Ramayana: A Study*. New Delhi: Meharchand Lachhmandas.

Mitra, V.L. (trans.). 1998. *The Yogavasistha of Valmiki: Sanskrit Text and English Translation*, 4 vols. Ed. and rev. Ravi Prakash Arya. Delhi: Parimal Publications.

Pansikar, W.L.S. (ed.). 1911. *The Yogavasistha of Valmiki with the Commentary Vāsiṣṭhamahārāmayanatātparyaprakāsha*. Bombay: Nirnaya Sagar Press. Reprint: New Delhi: Munshiram Manoharlal, 1981.

Sivananda, S. 1941. *Stories from the Yogavasistha*. Shivanandanagar: The Divine Life Society.

Slaje, W. 1993. 'Sarvasiddhantasiddhanta: On "Tolerance" and "Syncretism" in the *Yogavasistha*'. *Vienna Journal of South Asian Studies* 36: 307–22.

Slaje, W. 1994. *Vom Moksopaya-Sastra zum Yogavasistha-Maharamayana. Philologische Untersuchungen zur Entwicklungs- und Uberlieferungsgeschichte seines indischen Lehrwerks mit Anspruch auf Heilrelevanz*. Vienna: Osterreichischen Akademie der Wissenschaften.

Slaje, W. 1998. 'On Changing Others' Ideas: The Case of Vidyaranya and the *Yogavasistha*'. *Indo-Iranian Journal* 41(2) (April): 103–24.

Slaje, W. 2001. 'Observations on the Making of the *Yogavasistha*'. *Le Parole e i Marmi: Studi in Onore di Raniero Gnoli nel suo 70esimo Compleanno*, ed. Raffaele Torella. Roma: Istituto Italiano per l'Africa e l'Oriente, 771–96.

Venkatesananda, S. (trans.). 1984. *The Concise Yogavasistha*. Albany, NY: State University of New York Press.

Venkatesananda, S. 1993. *Vasistha's Yoga*. Albany, NY: State University of New York Press.

YOGENDRA, SHRI (1897–1989) AND THE YOGA INSTITUTE, SANTA CRUZ

Born in 1897 at Degam, Gujarat. Like Swami Kuvalayananda, he was a student of Paramahansa Madhvadasji. His Yoga Institute at Santa Cruz (near Mumbai) was set up in 1918 for research into the health benefits of yoga. Today it advertises itself as 'the oldest organised centre for Yoga in the world'. In 1919, he travelled to America, where he established the Yoga Institute of America on Bear Mountain, outside New York. He stayed for four years, working with a number of avant-garde Western doctors, such as Benedict Lust and John Harvey Kellogg, and giving what were perhaps the first ever āsana demonstrations in America. During this period, X-ray was used for the first time to understand the processes of yoga (vastra dhauti). It is in large measure due to Yogendra's efforts that yoga began to be integrated in the field of alternative and complementary medicine.

Prevented from returning to the US in 1924 by new immigration laws, he turned his attention to the Indian institute, initially financing the project with a protective polish he had invented. His research dealt mainly with the physiological effects of yoga. Like Kuvalayananda, he was concerned to provide scientific corroboration for the health benefits of yoga and to put yoga techniques into the service of healing. He and his institute published a large body of material on the practical benefits of yoga, such as *Hatha Yoga Simplified* and *Yoga Personal Hygiene* (both 1931). The institute continues to publish and to run courses on practical yoga. Although his work is not very widely known in the West today, Yogendra is a key figure in the creation of Modern Yoga. He died in 1989.

See also: **Āsana; Kuvalayananda, Swami and Kaivalyadhama; Yoga; Yoga, modern**

MARK SINGLETON

Further reading

Rodrigues, S. 1982. *The Householder Yogi: Life of Shri Yogendra*. Bombay: Santa Cruz.

YOGI

The modern mainstream understanding of the term yogi ('practitioner of yoga') identifies these as persons practising a combination of meditative and physical exercises, in accordance with the teachings of the *Yogasūtras* of Patañjali, and the techniques of haṭha yoga developed by Gorakhnātha and others. Purāṇic mythology portrays Śiva as a mahāyogi, a 'great yogi', whose yogic practice both emits and reabsorbs the phenomenal universe. Human yogis are, however, portrayed in a very different light in the *Mahābhārata*, in which warriors leave their dying bodies and ascend to heaven by 'yoking themselves to yoga'. In the *Tantras* and popular medieval literature, yogis are generally depicted as sinister magicians who practice their 'yoga' to take over other people's bodies, seduce women and amass supernatural powers for themselves. This negative characterisation of yogis continues to the present day in India, where some 'yogis' are both feared and despised as wanton criminals.

See also: **Haṭha Yoga; Gorakhnāth; Mahābhārata; Patañjali; Purāṇas; Siddha; Śiva; Tantras; Yogasūtras**

DAVID GORDON WHITE

Further reading

White, D.G. 1996. *The Alchemical Body: Siddha Traditions in Medieval India*. Chicago, IL: University of Chicago Press.

YUDHIṢṬHIRA

Hero of the *Mahābhārata* and wise leader of the Pāṇḍavaṣ. He exercises a restraining influence over his impulsive, more belligerent brothers, which overshadows his own martial skills and can be misinterpreted as undue passivity. Steadfast fidelity to dharma earns him the title 'Dharmarāja' and leads to his siring being attributed to a personified divine Dharma, an allegorical figure who blesses him towards the end of his forest exile and who eventually escorts him to heaven in the guise of a dog. Even in the earlier stages of the narrative his character is not static: he journeys from complacency to disillusion. The crisis is precipitated by his glorying in military and material might, trapping him – for reasons not entirely clear – in the disastrous dicing game that culminates in dethronement and exile. Cheated by his opponents, his virility outraged by his inability to come to the aid of his wife, he nevertheless maintains the integrity and purity of himself and his brothers, counselling patience despite the distress and guilt he feels at their suffering. At Virāṭa's court he assumes the name Kaṅka, evoking ideas of a bird characterised by its ability to wait patiently and silently for its prey, but an active quality with a brooding, menacing aspect. Nevertheless, his desire for peace almost outweighs his thirst for justice, but it is his tragedy to realise that justice can be achieved only by the subordination of his personal integrity: trading on his reputation for truthfulness, he utters a lie that earns him a stinging rebuke from Arjuna – just one of the many tactics that dishonour the climactic battle. Victory, entailing the death of the Pāṇḍavas' sons and of many of his allies and the annihilation of his Kaurava cousins, brings him no satisfaction, and it is with distaste and reluctance that he is persuaded to resume the responsibilities of kingship.

See also: **Arjuna; Dharma; Kauravas; Mahābhārata; Pāṇḍavaṣ; Rāja**

MARY BROCKINGTON

Further reading

Brockington, M. 2001. 'Husband or King? Yudhiṣṭhira's Dilemma in the *Mahābhārata*'. *Indo-Iranian Journal* 44: 253–63.

Brockington, M. 2003. 'Husband or Slave? Interpreting the Hero of the *Mahābhārata*'. *Proceedings of the 12th World Sanskrit Conference*, Helsinki. Delhi: Motilal Banarsidass.

YUGA

The term yuga (literally, 'yoke') has many meanings. It is sometimes used for the number 4 and as a designation of various periods of time. In early Indian astronomy it designated a five-year cycle (beginning with the conjunction of sun and moon in the Dhaniṣṭa nakṣatra on the first tithi of śuklapakṣa of Magha, the autumnal equinox). In that period of five years the solar year of 366 days and the lunar year of 360 days were 'yoked' together by adding two intercalary months at the end of the third and the fifth year when the cycle of 62 full moons and 62 new moons was completed.

The more popular use of the term yuga, however, occurs in connection with the later 'world-ages' (kalpas) made up of four yugas. Traditional accounts do not agree on their length. According to the *Manusmṛti*, each kalpa begins with a Kṛta-yuga, lasting 4,000 years, followed by a Tretā-yuga, lasting 3,000 years, a Dvāpara-yuga of 2,000 years and finally a Kali-yuga, lasting 1,000 years. Each of these yugas is preceded and followed by a sandhya (twilight-period) lasting 400, 300, 200 and 100 years, respectively. The four (human) yugas together comprise 12,000 human years: this span of time is called a yuga of the devas (divya-yuga). One thousand of these divya-yugas constitute one Day of Brahmā – the same duration is allotted to one night of Brahmā. Seventy-one divya-yugas constitute one manvantara.

In the *Purāṇas* we find variant accounts of yugas – all connected with huge numbers. According to the *Viṣṇu Purāṇa*, each Mahāyuga (Day of Brahmā) consists of a Kṛta- or Satya-yuga lasting 1,728,000 human years, a Treta-yuga lasting 1,296,000 years, a Dvāpara-yuga lasting 864,000 years and a Kali-yuga lasting 432,000 years. According to the *Purāṇa* the condition of the world is constantly deteriorating and living conditions for humans worsen from the Kṛta-yuga (also called the Golden Age) down to the Kali-yuga (also called the Iron Age):

> Morals and piety will decrease day by day, until the world will be wholly depraved. Property alone will confer rank, wealth will be the only source of devotion, passion will be the only bond of union between the sexes, falsehood will be the only mean of success in courts, and women will only be the object of sense gratification. Earth will only be treasured for her mineral resources, dishonesty will be a universal means of subsistence, and arrogance will take the place of learning. Thus in the Kali age decay will constantly proceed, until the human race approaches annihilation. (4.24.73–93)

In the Kṛta yuga dharma was four-footed and complete – and so was truth – and no gain accrued to humans by unrighteousness. In the other three yugas, dharma was successively deprived of one foot and through theft, falsehood and fraud merit was diminished by one-fourth. People were free from disease in the Kṛta age; they accomplished all their aims and lived 400 years. In the succeeding ages life was lessened by one-quarter each. In the Kṛta yuga austerity was the chief virtue, in the Treta yuga wisdom, in the Dvapāra yuga the performance of rituals and in the Kali yuga dana ('giving', charity) is the means to find salvation. The *Purāṇas* describe the present age as close to universal chaos and final destruction. According to the *Viṣṇu Purāṇa* the Kali-yuga will end with the apparition of Viṣṇu's Kalki-avatāra, who will defeat the wicked and liberate the virtuous and initiate a new Kṛta-yuga.

See also: **Avatāra; Brahmā; Deities; Dharma; Dharmaśastras; Manvantara; Purāṇas; Viṣṇu**

KLAUS K. KLOSTERMAIER

Further reading

Bühler, G. (trans.). 1886. *The Laws of Manu, SBE vol. 25.* Oxford: Oxford University Press.

Doniger, W. and B.K. Smith (trans.). 1991. *The Laws of Manu.* Harmondsworth: Penguin.

Kak. S. 2000. *The Astronomical Code of the Ṛgveda*, 2nd edn. Delhi: Manoharlal Munshi Ram.

Kane. P.V. 1958. *History of Dharmaśāstra*, vol. 5, pt 1. Pune: BORI.

Wilson, H.H. (trans.). 1961. *The Viṣṇu Purāṇa: A System of Hindu Mythology and Tradition.* Calcutta: Punthi Pustak (first published 1840).

Z

ZIMMER, HEINRICH ROBERT (1890–1943)

German Indologist, son of Heinrich Friedrich Zimmer (1850–1910), also a Sanskritist and the author of an important early work on Vedic civilisation. The younger Zimmer was professor at Heidelberg from 1922 until 1938, when his opposition to the Nazis caused his dismissal. He afterward lectured at Oxford and at Johns Hopkins and Columbia Universities. Zimmer did much to popularise Indian art in the West; in particular, his work on maṇḍalas (1926) contributed to the growing interest in Tantra initiated by the work of Sir John Woodroffe. It was this work which brought Zimmer to the attention of C.G. Jung; the two became friends and Zimmer significantly influenced Jung's understanding of India. After Zimmer's death Jung published his last work, on the life and teachings of Ramana Maharsi (Zimmer 1944). Other works on Indian myths and symbols (1946), philosophies (1951) and art (1955) were edited and published after his death by the comparative mythologist Joseph Campbell (1904–87).

See also: **Hinduism, history of scholarship; Jung, Carl Gustav; Ramana Maharshi; Tantras; Woodroffe, John**

WILL SWEETMAN

Further reading

Zimmer, H. 1944. *Der Weg zum Selbst* ['The Way to the Self']. Zürich: Rascher.

Zimmer, H. 1946. *Myths and Symbols in Indian Art and Civilization*. New York: Pantheon.

Zimmer, H. 1951. *Philosophies of India*. New York: Pantheon.

Zimmer, H. 1955. *The Art of Indian Asia: Its Mythology and Transformation*. New York: Pantheon.

Zimmer, H. 1984. *Artistic Form and Yoga in the Sacred Images of India*, trans. G. Chapple and J.B. Lawson. Princeton, NJ: Princeton University Press. (First published in German, *Kunstform und Yoga im indischen Kultbild*. Berlin: Frankfurter Verlags-Anst, 1926).

Index